GÄNZL'S BOOK OF THE MUSICAL THEATRE

Also by Kurt Gänzl

The British Musical Theatre

Also by Andrew Lamb

Jerome Kern in Edwardian London

GÄNZL'S BOOK
OF THE
MUSICAL
THEATRE

KURT GÄNZL
and
ANDREW LAMB

SCHIRMER BOOKS
A Division of Macmillan, Inc.
NEW YORK

First American edition published in 1989 by
Schirmer Books
A Division of Macmillan, Inc.

Schirmer Books
A Division of Macmillan, Inc.
866 Third Avenue, New York, N.Y. 10022

First published in Great Britain in 1988 by
Bodley Head Limited
London

Library of Congress Catalog Card Number: 88–18588

Printed in Great Britain

printing number 1 2 3 4 5 6 7 8 9 10

Library of Congress Cataloging in Publication Data
Gänzl, Kurt.
Gänzl's book of the musical theatre.

Includes index.
1. Musical revues, comedies, etc.—Stories,
plots, etc.   2. Operas—Stories, plots, etc.
I. Lamb, Andrew.   II. Title.   III. Title: Book of the
musical theatre.
MT95.G2 1989   782.81   88–18588
ISBN 0–02–871941–7

CONTENTS

CONTENTS

Part 2: France

Part 3: United States of America

CONTENTS

Part 4: Austria, Germany and Hungary

CONTENTS

LIST OF PLATES

Part 1: Great Britain

The Beggar's Opera English Opera Group, Aldeburgh, 1963 (Photo: Reg Wilson).

Billee Taylor British lithograph c. 1880 (British Musical Theatre Collection).

The Mikado English National Opera, 1986 (Photo: Reg Wilson).

HMS Pinafore Gaiety Theatre, Dublin, 1985 (British Musical Theatre Collection).

A Greek Slave Daly's Theatre, 1898 (British Musical Theatre Collection).

The Arcadians 1909 and 1984 revival (Northcott Theatre, Exeter, and British Musical Theatre Collection).

Half A Sixpence Cambridge Theatre, 1963 (Photo: Tom Hustler).

Me and My Girl Takarazuka Theatre, Japan, 1987 (British Musical Theatre Collection).

Jesus Christ Superstar Palace Theatre, London (Really Useful Group. Photo: Laurie Asprey).

Evita Prince Edward Theatre, 1978 (Photo: Zoe Dominic).

Cats New London Theatre, 1981 (Really Useful Group. Photo: John Haynes).

Chess Prince Edward Theatre, 1987. (Photo: Bob Workman).

The Phantom of the Opera Her Majesty's Theatre, 1987 (Really Useful Group. Photo: Clive Barda).

Part 2: France

Ba-Ta-Clan Australian Opera, 1982 (British Musical Theatre Collection).

Les Noces de Jeannette Opera Comique, 1960 (Agence Bernard).

Orphée aux Enfers Sadler's Wells Opera, 1964 (Photo: Reg Wilson).

La Belle Hélène Sadler's Wells Opera, 1967 (Photo: Reg Wilson).

La Vie Parisienne Sadler's Wells Opera, 1974 (Photo: Reg Wilson).

Mam'zelle Nitouche Théâtre des Bouffes-Parisiens, 1984 (Agence Bernand).

La Grande-Duchesse de Gérolstein British lithograph c. 1870 (British Musical Theatre Collection).

Dédé Théâtre des Nouveautés, 1973 (British Musical Theatre Collection).

Pas Sur la Bouche Théâtre des Bouffes-Parisiens, 1948 (Agence Bernand).

Phi-Phi Théâtre des Bouffes-Parisiens, 1980 (Agence Bernand).

La Belle de Cadix Théâtre de L'Empire, 1949 (Agence Bernand).

Méditerranée Théâtre du Châtelet, 1955 (Agence Bernand).

La Route Fleurie Théâtre de l'ABC, 1952 (Agence Bernand).

Quatre Jours à Paris Théâtre Bobino, 1948 (Agence Bernand).

Violettes Imperiales Théâtre Mogador, 1961 (Agence Bernand).

Les Misérables Palace Theatre, London, 1985 (Photo: Michael le Poer Trench).

Part 3: United States of America

Belle of New York German sheet music cover, 1900 (British Musical Theatre Collection).

The Red Mill Empire Theatre, London, 1919 (British Musical Theatre Collection).

Oh, Boy! Goodspeed Opera House, 1983 (Photo: Wilson H. Brownell).

Part 4: Austria, Germany and Hungary

AUTHOR'S PREFACE

This book has been compiled to act as a companion volume to *Kobbé's Complete Opera Book*. I hope that it will be able to do for the light musical theatre what Kobbé's famous work, both under his own hand and that of his modern reviser, Lord Harewood, has so successfully done over the years for both the devotee and the more casual acquaintance of the opera by acting as a source of information and as an aid to the understanding and enjoyment of both full-scale theatre productions and broadcast and recorded performances of musical shows .

It is, however, immediately evident that there are substantial differences between the operatic and musical theatres which have made my task, and that of my collaborator Andrew Lamb, who has prepared the German and Spanish language sections of this book, a delicate one. Opera is an art which came to its apogée, as far as composition was concerned, in the nineteenth and early twentieth centuries. The international repertoire today is, for the most part, an established one which consists largely of a solid core of frequently performed works varied only by a relatively small percentage of new or freshly rediscovered pieces.

The light musical theatre is a Johnny-come-lately by comparison. It reached its first real flowering only in the mid-nineteenth century but, after following various fertile fashions in theatrical and musical styles, it is now established as the world's most popular form of theatrical entertainment, producing every year significant new pieces to add to the stock of favourite shows which fill the theatres of the world. Producers today are as eager to find attractive new musicals as they have been for nigh on a century whereas, since the Great War, the company which will produce a new opera liable to become part of the standard repertoire is rare. To choose some three hundred operas from the body of the established repertoire is therefore, I submit, a task less fraught with pitfalls than that of selecting a like number of light musical pieces from the thousands which have poured on to the world's stages in the last century.

Since this is not an all-embracing chronicle, however, it had to be done. We had to make a selection. We decided that the criteria expressed by Lord Harewood in the introduction to the Complete Book of Opera were undoubtedly the best. The shows with which we have dealt have been selected for a variety of reasons. Firstly, we chose those pieces which a theatregoer would be most likely to encounter on the current stages of Britain, America, France, Germany and the other main centres of musical theatre entertainment, the hits of today and the hits of yesterday which have been brought back for the further enjoyment of the theatre-going public. Secondly, we chose those shows which had a notable success in their own times, those which have left a particular legacy of favourite songs, those which are significant historically or artistically and those which are just plain good and which deserve a reappearance on the modern stage. Thirdly, we added our own particular favourites among the shows of yesteryear which we hope, if we bring them to your notice, might become favourites of yours as well.

Inevitably, our choice will not please everyone. Devotees of certain writers will find that their favourites are insufficiently represented, others will disagree that such-and-such a musical is included and such-another is not. It will ever be the same where any degree of selection is involved. Our list has undergone passionate discussion and some revision in several debates among devotees (in reference to which, our thanks to Messrs Ian Bevan, Rexton S Bunnett, Richard Norton, Gerald Bordman and Richard Traubner), but ultimately—since it is my name which is attached to the book—the decision had to be mine. So here are the stories, the songs and the production details of some three hundred outstanding musicals chosen with care and affection from the repertoires of the principal countries where light musical theatre is produced.

It is my hope that this book will help you to appreciate *Méditerranée* when you are in France and *Eine Nacht in Venedig* when you are in Germany, that it will help you to realise just why that lady on the radio sang about 'The Amorous Goldfish' or 'The Indian Love Call' and that it will let you know what exactly those enormous old hits such as *Erminie* and *The Belle of New York* were all about. Most of all, and this is a purely personal sentiment, I hope it will persuade both professional producers and the thousands of groups which love to stage musical shows to look beyond the most often-played pieces to discover the less familiar riches which the world of the light musical theatre holds.

It seems such a pity that *La Belle de Cadix* and *Andalousie* should not be played outside France, that *Robert and Elizabeth* and *Expresso Bongo* have travelled so little outside Britain, and that *On The Twentieth Century* and *Little Me* somehow missed the attentions of the non-English speaking world. It is a shame that the fun of *Erminie*, *Phi-Phi* and *The Firefly* and the glorious melodies of *Szibill*, *Le Petit Duc*, *A Greek Slave* and *Mlle Modiste*, still as valid and as enjoyable as they ever were, are denied to modern audiences. All these shows are there to be discovered or rediscovered, just as the seemingly forgotten *Me and My Girl* has been, and set alongside *Evita*, *Les Misérables*, *A Chorus Line* and *Cats* in today's theatres in the same manner that the works of Bellini and Mozart hold their place in the operatic repertoire with the much later Verdi and Wagner and Richard Strauss.

Perhaps the greatest problem encountered in attempting to present this book in the same style as Kobbé came from an essential difference in the nature of opera and light musical theatre: the stability of the material. By and large no one tampers with the script or music of *Madama Butterfly* or *Die Walküre* when they are revived in the opera houses of the world. In the case of the majority of light musical shows, the inverse is almost invariably the case. The libretti and scores of many of the musicals dealt with in this book have been chimeric almost since birth.

Nineteenth century musical comedies were subjected to multiple inter-polations and alterations at the whim of a producer or a performer and, if the most substantial light musical shows suffered less, it was still possible for such a piece as *Merrie England* or *La Belle Hélène* to be grossly maltreated in a revival or translation. Unfortunately, many of the older shows survive, out-side the British Lord Chamberlain's files, only in these worked-over ver-sions, with dialogue which clearly originated as the chief comedian's ad libs awkwardly enshrined in the author's text, with plots fiddled to suit casting or scenic considerations and scenes twisted about to fit in an interpolated song and, often, with the whole distilled down into an embarrassing and patronis-ing edition which has squashed much of the original appeal from the musical.

In these cases, we have tried to detail what we consider the most satisfying version of the show. This is usually the original (with notes on the subsequent alterations), but where alterations have become standard usage and where revisions have wrought a clear improvement—*Me and My Girl* is again a notable example—the revised versions have been preferred.

The synopsis of each show is headed by an entry giving the dates and leading artists of the principal productions of the piece in Britain, America and France, and some Continental German language performances. In the case of some of the nineteenth century works, even contemporary references sometimes disagree on dates and details, but we have done our utmost to distil fact from journalism with the help of such reference works as Alfred Loewenberg's *Annals of Opera*, Odell's *Annals of the New York Stage*, Anton Bauer's *Opern und Operetten in Wien* and Florian Bruyas's *Histoire de l'Opérette en France*.

The book has been divided into sections, each section dealing with a different country and its traditions. France, Britain, the United States of America and the Germany–Austria–Hungary group represent the four main areas where the light musical theatre has grown and blossomed. Each, in its turn, has led the world in producing the brightest and most enduring of shows, from the days of the internationally played Parisian *opéra-bouffe* and *opéra-comique* and the Germanic operettas of Strauss and Millöcker through the comic operas of Gilbert and Sullivan and the British musical comedies of the late nineteenth century to the Viennese operettas of Lehár, Fall and Straus and the flowering of the American musical theatre in the 1920s. If the Continental traditions died away somewhat in the years between the wars, the American rebirth of the late 1940s kept Broadway producing fresh material for the world's theatres for nearly thirty years until the wheel turned once more and London's West End again became the capital of the musical theatre. In ten or twenty years' time, who knows where the centre of this

xiii

whirlwind world will be. We have also added a short section on the zarzuela, the Spanish musical, enormously popular in its own language but yet to break through significantly on a wider basis.

Nowadays it seems that the national boundaries are being broken down in theatre as they are elsewhere. London has spawned hits in tandem with Paris in *Les Misérables*, with Sweden in *Chess* and with American material in pieces such as *Singin' in the Rain* and, I think, it will before long become more difficult to write the little summaries of the history of each area's music theatre with which the sections of this book are introduced—they will all overlap too much. The various centres of the theatre world have enjoyed each other's shows for many years; now it seems that, under the impetus of the best of the world's producers and writers, we shall enjoy shows put together by groups of the most skilled creators regardless of nation. These will one day make a section on their own.

Until then let us enjoy what we have. Not just the delightful new pieces that are to be found in today's theatres and on today's recordings, but also those older shows that are there, waiting for us to find them and bring them back to life. If you don't know *Phi-Phi*, *Die Rose von Stambul*, *The Geisha* or *Going Up*, I can assure you that you have good times ahead of you discovering them. I hope we can communicate to you an interest and enthusiasm which will encourage you to do so.

KURT GÄNZL
St Paul de Vence
1988

The authors would like to thank those institutions and enthusiasts throughout the world who have made available the scripts, scores and other material used in the compiling of this work:
The British Musical Theatre Collection, Rexton S Bunnett, Louise Grant Theatre Programmes, Martin Phillips, Richard Duployen, Courtenay Kenny, Christopher Renshaw, Howard Harrison, Mandy Morrison (Chappell Music Ltd), John Hughes (Samuel French Ltd), Richard Toeman (Josef Weinberger and associates Glocken-Verlag and Octavia), Richard Schulman, Peter Sibley, Elizabeth Waite, Reg Wilson, Derek Lewis (BBC) (Great Britain).
Richard S Norton, Richard Traubner Theatre Collection, Jack Rokahr, Al Remson, Cy Coleman, Jeffrey Bernstein, Joe Cantlin, Mrs Betsy Rosenberg (Godspeed Opera House) (United States of America).
James Sparrow, Mlle Nicole Broissin, Richard Prideaux-Debuisson (France) Dr Michael Mäckelmann and Dr Rainer Franke (Forschungsinstitut für Musiktheater, University of Bayreuth), Dreiklang-Dreimasken and associates Ahn & Simrock and Crescendo, Felix Bloch Erben, Apollo, Thalia, Allegro (Germany).
Professor Hans Gabor and Isabella Rohrwasser (Vienna Kammeroper),

Frau Eini Stolz, Dr Gotthard Böhm, Reinhard Deutsch, Thomas Albrecht (Josef Weinberger) (Austria).
Artisjus, Budapest Municipal Operetta Theatre (Hungary) Zürich (Switzerland).

Part 1

GREAT BRITAIN

The first important period in the light musical theatre in Britain began in the early eighteenth century with the development of the kind of entertainment which has come to be known as ballad opera. In the wake of the newly popular Italian opera with its historical and mythological themes and truly sung music, British writers began to decorate increasing numbers of their plays with songs. These songs were not specially composed pieces but consisted of original lyrics set to a variety of favourite old tunes which were gathered together to form the score of the show.

Amongst these ballad operas one, produced in 1728, proved remarkably successful. John Gay's *The Beggar's Opera* was a simple comic tale of greed and betrayal among the criminal classes, spiced with personal and political satire and liberally filled with music borrowed from areas ranging from the works of Purcell to the street ballad. It became the longest-running stage piece in the history of the London theatre and set in motion a fashion for what would soon be more popularly known as comic opera.

Over the decades that followed, the body of borrowed music which comprised the scores of such shows became supplemented and later replaced by specially written music and songs as librettists such as Isaac Bickerstaffe and composers of the ilk of Thomas Arne, Charles Dibdin and William Shield kept the new style of work to the fore and several works from this period, such as Dibdin's *The Waterman* (1774) and *The Quaker* (1775) and Stephen Storace's *No Song, No Supper* (1790) survived in the repertoire of both British and foreign theatres for more than a century before giving place to newer fashions in theatre and music.

Whilst bright and unpretentious one- or two-act comic operas continued to appear on theatre bills, usually as a lesser part of a composite programme, some writers and composers took a different turning and headed towards a much more substantial kind of musical theatre related more closely to the operas of Continental Europe than to the legacy of the ballad opera.

Sir Henry Bishop, Michael Balfe, Vincent Wallace, George Macfarren and Julius Benedict were the most notable contributors to the spate of romantic operas—some lighter, others decidedly dramatic—which were the principal contribution to the British musical theatre of the mid-nineteenth century, a period which brought to the operatic stage such enduring favourites as Balfe's *The Bohemian Girl, The Rose of Castille* and *Satanella*, Wallace's *Maritana*, Benedict's *The Lily of Killarney* and John Barnett's *The Mountain Sylph*. These pieces eventually found their place in the repertoire of the touring opera companies alongside the works of Mozart, Donizetti and Bellini rather than on the stages of the theatres specialising in light musical entertainments. Those theatres had found their way early in the century to a new form of musical theatre, the form which would become known as burlesque.

During its half-century of prominence on the West End stage, burlesque underwent many changes to its nature and content, and the entertainments which graced the stage of the Gaiety theatre in the 1880s bore little relation to the fairytale extravaganzas and mythological parodies with which J R Planché initiated the 'palmy days of burlesque' in the 1830s. These light-hearted comic pieces had their rhyming lines of whimsy and word-play interspersed with songs and dances set, as in the old ballad opera days, to the tune of a popular song or aria, and they proved a favourite feature of the bills played at Madame Vestris's Olympic Theatre and, later, throughout the land. Planché's followers included many highly successful writers: Robert and William Brough, Francis Talfourd, and the a'Beckett brothers, Gilbert and Arthur, were among those who followed the path he opened up but none equalled either his output or his critical and public success.

In the 1850s burlesque began to change its style and, under the influence of Henry Byron, Robert Reece, F C Burnand and ultimately W S Gilbert it became more a vehicle for direct parody and social comment, for far-fetched puns and for song-and-dance displays without in any way losing its popularity. Pieces such as Burnand's *Black-Eyed Susan* and *Ixion* and Byron's *The Maid and the Magpie* took over where the Broughs and Planché had left off, while Byron's versions of *Ali Baba*, *Cinderella* and *Aladdin*, originally played as burlesques of the Arabic and French tales, later became the bases for Christmas entertainments and spawned the modern version of the British pantomime.

In 1865, burlesque took its first step in the direction the ballad opera had borrowed when F C Burnand's Strand Theatre piece *Windsor Castle* was produced with an original score by Frank Musgrave. At first sporadically, but later with more frequency, burlesque was illustrated with specially composed music while, at the same time, its original parodic intent was pushed further and further into the background until shows with such titles as *Little Christopher Columbus* or *A Modern Don Quixote* bore little relation to their professed subjects. By the time burlesque melted into its natural successor, the musical comedy, it had become no more or less than a selection of lively comedy scenes, songs and speciality acts tacked on to a very slight and often unimportant story.

Perhaps the principal reason for burlesque finding itself original music in the 1860s was the arrival from France of its rather better developed counterpart, the *opéra-bouffe*. The works of Hervé and Offenbach took London by storm in a way that no foreign musical theatre had done since the advent of the Italian opera, and *Chilpéric*, *Le Petit Faust*, *La Grande-Duchesse de Gérolstein* and *Geneviève de Brabant* became the hits of the period as the French musical took over the West End. Pieces such as Lecocq's *La Fille de Madame Angot* and Planquette's *Les Cloches de Corneville* followed, as burlesque gave way to comic opera, and won enormous and lasting popularity.

This popularity had the happy result of drawing some highly talented British writers into the area of the full-length comic opera in an attempt at emulation, among them the burlesque writer W S Gilbert, at first teamed with composer Frederic Clay, and the composer Arthur Sullivan, whose first musical, *The Contrabandista* was written with another burlesque specialist, F C Burnand. The subsequent collaboration between Gilbert and Sullivan produced a series of English comic operas from *Trial by Jury* and *The Sorcerer* through *HMS Pinafore*, *The Pirates of Penzance* and *The Mikado* up to *The Gondoliers* which found an unparalleled success in the theatres of the world and which, more than a century later, still warrant frequent major productions.

Although the works of Gilbert and Sullivan are the only pieces from their era still regularly played in modern times, their contemporaries included many talented writers who produced equally effective and successful shows. The flamboyant Edward Solomon's *Billee Taylor* produced the same year as the better known *The Pirates of Penzance* won many better notices than the more famous piece and was often revived in its time but, although its book has a delightful period comedy air, it stands up today less well than its composer's later work, *The Nautch Girl*, written by George Dance to fill the gap at the Savoy Theatre caused by the split in the Gilbert and Sullivan partnership.

Edward Jakobowski's *Erminie*, with its hilarious libretto and charming score, played for decades in the British provinces after its initial London run and when it was produced on Broadway proved to be the most successful musical that New York had ever seen. Produced in the same year as *The Mikado*, it comprehensively outran that piece. The H B Farnie/Robert Planquette *Rip van Winkle* was another fine piece which survived long when taken into the French repertoire, but the greatest popularity of all was earned by Alfred Cellier's *Dorothy*, a piece in the old English comic opera style which owed nothing to either Gilbertian wit or to the low comedy employed in *Erminie*, but followed the tone set in the polite surroundings of the St George's Hall where the little parlour operettas produced by the German Reed family had long and successfully held their own with their particular public. *Dorothy* had the lengthiest West End run of any nineteenth-century musical and toured thereafter for many years.

The 1890s brought a decisive change in the style of musical theatre produced in London. The old-fashioned comic opera had lost its interest for the public and burlesque had declined into little more than a variety show of comedy and song. What emerged over the next decade was a kind of work which combined elements of both these genres while abandoning the most overworked parts of each. The tired and conventional comic opera plots disappeared along with the 'word gymnastics' of the burlesque and in their place arose a style of show called 'musical comedy', mixing a modern-dress romantic plot and lyrical music with comic scenes and characters equipped with up-to-date song and dance routines to great effect.

The most celebrated exponent of this type of show was the impresario George Edwardes whose productions of *A Gaiety Girl*, *In Town* and *The Shop Girl* were among the earliest examples of the breed and who subsequently established the two bastions of the musical comedy at the Gaiety and Daly's theatres. The fare provided at these two houses represented the two principal types of show which, over some two decades, would become as much the favourites of the world's musical stages as the works of Offenbach and Gilbert and Sullivan had been before them.

At the Gaiety Theatre, true to its name, the fare was of the lightest. Here

5

was the legitimate successor to the burlesque: a lively, comical breed of shows with juvenile leads who laughed and joked and often sang piquant point numbers rather than love ballads; shows in which good fun, pretty and jaunty tunes and lovely ladies were the order of the evening. Ivan Caryll and Lionel Monckton provided many a song for the Gaiety which subsequently became the rage of the town as their famous series of musicals ran their way around the world.

At Daly's the shows were more substantial. The part-romantic, part-humorous libretti were more carefully constructed and less subject to the vagaries of the comedy performers, and the music, particularly in the hands of the composer Sidney Jones, was written for vocalists of scope and included harmonised ensembles and concerted finales which would never have been heard at the Gaiety. By their very nature, the Daly's shows were more durable than their Gaiety brethren and the greatest of them, *The Geisha, San Toy, A Country Girl* and *A Greek Slave* survived through decades of revivals in Britain and abroad when such Gaiety triumphs as *The Messenger Boy, A Runaway Girl, The Orchid, The Toreador* and *Our Miss Gibbs* had long been seen for the last time.

Not all the successes of the great age of the Victorian and Edwardian musical theatre were born at the Gaiety Theatre or at Daly's. Other producers soon followed where Edwardes led and some of the most enduring shows of the era came from unexpected places. *A Chinese Honeymoon*, a farcical comedy set with a mixture of ballads and music-hall type songs, was staged at provincial Hanley for an eight-week tour, but it triumphed in the West End, and became the first musical to run over a thousand consecutive metropolitan performances.

A neophyte producer called Tom Davies staged *Florodora*, the first musical by songwriter Leslie Stuart and scored a worldwide hit; Paul Rubens, one of the few writers to attempt book, lyrics and music for a show, wrote the happy strains of *Miss Hook of Holland* while suffering from the first stages of his last illness; Frederick Lonsdale surfaced unexpectedly to provide the archetypal Ruritanian book for Sidney Jones to set in the influential *The King of Cadonia*; and Lionel Monckton, exiled from both the Gaiety and Daly's by a change in policy, supplied *The Quaker Girl* for Edwardes at the Adelphi. It was Monckton who, in 1909, in the midst of a sudden craze for the Viennese operetta released by the great success of Edwardes' production of *The Merry Widow*, combined with Howard Talbot and a cartel of authors to provide what was arguably the climax to this period of the British musical theatre in *The Arcadians*.

By the time that *The Arcadians* appeared at the Shaftesbury Theatre, however, the end of the musical show as beloved by *fin de siècle* theatre-goers was in sight, for new rhythms were stirring on the other side of the Atlantic which would soon be fashionable in London. The world of the theatre, which had drained everything it could from the form so beloved by the Victorian and Edwardian world, would soon be turning its eyes and its dancing feet elsewhere. In the meantime, while the carefree strains of ragtime were contrasted with the realities of war, the musical theatre continued to look backwards to its old styles. The comic opera had by no means died under the overwhelming favour shown to musical comedy and several fine works, such as Sullivan's *The Rose of Persia* and Edward German's *Merrie England* and *Tom Jones* had appeared with success if not with the seal of the long runs achieved by their more popular rivals. Now, as a different type of musical show was once again about to become fashionable, there were still great successes to be found in shows which belonged in spirit to earlier times.

The war years saw Daly's Theatre emulate its old successes with *The Maid of the Mountains* whilst the mixture of fairytale, pageantry and song which was *Chu-Chin-Chow* gave a new airing to the Ali Baba legend more than half a century after Byron's burlesque and set up a long run record for a musical show which would last more than forty years. If André Messager's *Monsieur Beaucaire* had less of a run than these, it yielded them nothing in quality and found its way into the principal repertoire in its composer's homeland.

The years after the war found the newly popular revue genre firmly entrenched as a successful cousin to the musical theatre, many of whose most successful shows were now coming from abroad. On the one hand the public flocked to see such tuneful Continental pieces as Jean Gilbert's *The Lady of the Rose* and *Katja, the Dancer*, Fall's *Madame Pompadour*, Victor Jacobi's *Sybil* and Charles Cuvillier's *The Lilac Domino*, and on the other they happily devoured the new musicals from America, both the traditional pieces [*Rose Marie*, *The Desert Song* and *The Vagabond King*] and the up-to-date song-and-dance comedies [*No, No, Nanette*, *Irene* and *Mercenary Mary*]. The divisions were still there: it was like Daly's and the Gaiety all over again, but this time the talent, the novelty and the dancing music came from the other side of the Atlantic.

The division remained through the period between the wars, but the emphasis of popularity fell firmly on to the lighter shows with their comedy and their catchy song melodies, all fodder to the ubiquitous dance bands and gramophones of the era. The whole world was dancing in ballrooms and cabarets, and on the stage dancing was emphasised as it had never been before. These light-footed shows ultimately became specially constructed vehicles to display the talents of a series of favourite stars including Bobby Howes, Jack Buchanan, Leslie Henson, Laddie Cliff and Stanley Lupino, Jack Hulbert and Cicely Courtneidge, and Lupino Lane. Although they were hugely enjoyable, by their very nature few of these pieces survived into the repeated revivals that the shows of earlier years had had. There were, of course, exceptions—the two notable ones being pieces which returned to the West End stage again in the 1980s, *Mr Cinders* and *Me and My Girl*.

The survival factor, as always, was strongest at the other end of the scale, amongst the more sturdily built and richly composed shows. Whilst America sent the remarkable *Show Boat* and the Continent sent *White Horse Inn* to grace the West End stage, Noël Coward contributed the lushly romantic *Bitter-Sweet* and the crisp *Conversation Piece*. Ivor Novello, another writer with straight play successes to his name, provided the flamboyant *Glamorous Night* to fit the measure of the great stage of the Theatre Royal, Drury Lane,

7

initiating the series of romantic musicals including *Perchance to Dream*, *The Dancing Years* and *King's Rhapsody* which were his greatest achievement, and which inspired Eric Maschwitz to successful emulation in *Balalaika*.

The post-war musical theatre scene in London was quick to take on its own character. Three fine, old-fashioned musicals opened within little more than a month and took the town by storm. One, Vivian Ellis' *Bless the Bride* was a homegrown show, the other two, *Oklahoma!* and *Annie Get Your Gun*, were from Broadway. It was the beginning of the second coming of the Broadway musical whose greatest successes, the Friml, Kern and Romberg pieces, *No, No, Nanette* and *Irene*, were two decades in the past. Over the next twenty years most of London's largest theatres were filled with the sounds of Broadway: Rodgers and Hammerstein, Lerner and Loewe, Cole Porter, Frank Loesser, Leonard Bernstein, Jerry Herman, and others less prolific filled the major London auditoriums with their shows. The happy comedy musicals of the inter-wars years were completely eclipsed by the much more seriously conceived product of Broadway, and the native musical theatre, momentarily at a loss for writing talent to take up the coming style, languished.

When it did resurface, it was not by taking up the Broadway manner. The most successful British musicals of the 1950s and the 1960s were not large stage musicals. They came from the club theatres, the provincial repertory theatres, suburban theatres, and scarcely one of them ultimately played its West End run at one of the major houses. They came from new writers: Sandy Wilson produced the exquisite little *The Boy Friend* and the dazzling *Valmouth*, Julian Slade brought the record-breaking *Salad Days* from Bristol, Robb Stewart brought back the best days of burlesque with *Chrysanthemum*, David Heneker teamed with Julian More and Monty Norman on *Expresso Bongo* and *Make Me an Offer* before going on to a further triumph with *Half a Sixpence*, Anthony Newley wrote and played *Stop the World—I Want to Get Off*, and Lionel Bart contributed to two great shows in *Lock Up Your Daughters* and *Maggie May* as well as writing book, lyrics and music for his enduringly popular *Oliver!*.

They were an eclectic set of pieces, ranging from fantasy to burlesque to transposed literature and to a remarkable realism in their subjects, and through many varied styles in their music, but almost none was a large theatre piece. It seemed that here was the way the British musical theatre would go, but the late sixties brought three widely varying pieces which shattered the possibility of any neat theorising. *Charlie Girl* was a blatant variety musical of a kind which had survived from Victorian days largely in pantomime; a mixture of low comedy and light songs, it took off to an amazing run of more than five years. *Canterbury Tales* was a raunchy retelling of Chaucer's tales which mixed its subject matter and some lively songs to good effect, while *Robert and Elizabeth* retold the famous *Barretts of Wimpole Street* story to a light opera score of thrilling skill. They shared London's stages with Broadway's *Fiddler on the Roof*, *Hello Dolly* and *Hair* as the sixties came to an end but, unlike those much travelled pieces, they remained essentially popular only in Britain.

8

By the seventies, Broadway, which had dominated the world of the musical theatre since the war, had begun to lose its sway. While individual shows of importance continued to cross the Atlantic, many followed too devotedly the fashions of former years and, once again, as the wheel of taste turned, public favour prepared to follow novelty. That novelty was soon found in the work of Tim Rice, a writer with a personal modern style, and composer Andrew Lloyd Webber whose astute blending of modern popular music with classical elements established a new style for musical theatre writing. Over the years that followed their work, together and separately, formed the core of London's and the world's musical theatre as *Jesus Christ Superstar* and *Joseph and the Amazing Technicolor Dreamcoat* followed by *Evita*, *Cats*, *Song and Dance*, *Starlight Express*, *Chess* and *Phantom of the Opera* began to spread from their West End bases to dominate a musical theatre scene which was rapidly becoming more and more international both in its creation and in its appreciation.

THE BEGGAR'S OPERA

a comic opera in three acts by John Gay. The music selected and arranged by Johann Christian Pepusch. Produced at Lincoln's Inn Fields, London, 29 January 1728 with Mr Walker (Macheath), Lavinia Fenton (Polly), Mr Hippisley (Peachum), Mr Hall (Lockit), Mrs Eagleton (Lucy) and Mrs Martin (Mrs Peachum). Revived there 13 September 1728 with Miss Warren as Polly. Played there from 1 January 1729 'with a cast of Lilliputians' and frequently thereafter. Produced at the Theatre Royal, Haymarket 24 June 1728 and revived there 8 October 1728 and on numerous occasions thereafter including 4 September 1732 with Peg Woffington as Macheath, Mrs Peachum and Diana Trapes, Mr Morrice (Peachum) and Jenny Jones (Polly), 22 July 1820 and in 1854 with Isabella Featherstone (Macheath). Produced at the Theatre Royal, Drury Lane, 11 August 1732 with Mr Stoppelaer (Macheath), Mr Paget (Peachum) and Miss Raftor (Polly) and revived there on numerous occasions including 25 January 1738 with Mr Beard, Mr Macklin and Mrs Clive, 12 December 1747 and in a revised version 8 November 1777. Produced at the Theatre Royal, Covent Garden, 16 December 1732 with the original cast excepting Hannah Norsa (Polly) and revived there on numerous occasions including in a revised version 17 October 1777, 18 May 1789 and 9 December 1878 with Sims Reeves as Macheath. Produced at the St James's Theatre 3 March 1836 with Laura Honey (Macheath), Robert Strickland (Peachum) and Priscilla Horton (Polly) and played there in 1860 with F Charles and Clara St Casse. Produced at the Gaiety Theatre 15 September 1870 in a condensed version with E D Beverley, John Maclean and Constance Loseby and again in 1887 with Charles Santley as Macheath. Played at the Avenue Theatre 3 November 1886 with Sims Reeves, Henry Ashley and Phillipine Seidle. Produced at the Lyric Theatre, Hammersmith, in a revised version with music by Frederic Austin, 5 June 1920 with Frederic Ranalow, Frederic Austin and Sylvia Nelis and revived there 23 June 1925 with Ranalow, H Scott Russell and Kathlyn Hilliard, 22 May 1926, 14 February 1928 with Ranalow, Russell and Rose Hignell, 11 March 1929 with Ranalow, Russell and Miss Hignell, 13 May 1930 with Ranalow, Russell and Olive Groves, 17 July 1950 with Bruce Boyce, David Franklin and Nancy Evans and 19 August 1980 in a revised version by David Turner and Roy Moore with Brian Protheroe, Harold Innocent and Fiona Fullerton. Produced at the Criterion Theatre 6 March 1935 with Charles Mayhew, Dennis Hoey and Joan Collier. Produced at the Theatre Royal, Haymarket 5 March 1940 with Michael Redgrave, Roy Henderson and Audrey Mildmay. Produced at the New Theatre 21 February 1941 with John Hargreaves, Sumner Auston, Janet Hamilton-Smith, Joan Cross (Mrs Peachum) and Edith Coates (Lucy). Produced at Sadler's Wells Theatre 6 September 1948 with Peter Pears, George James and Nancy Evans and 4 October 1954 with James Johnstone, Norman Lumsden and Mary Thomas. Produced at the Aldwych Theatre 16 July 1963 with Derek Godfrey, Ronald Radd and Dorothy Tutin. Produced at the Apollo Theatre 12 September 1968 with Peter Gilmore, James Cossins and Jan Waters. Produced at the National Theatre 1 July 1982 with Paul Jones, Harry Towb and Belinda Sinclair.

Produced for the first time in New York 3 December 1750 and played on numerous occasions thereafter. Produced at the 48th St Theatre in a revised version 28 March 1928. Produced at the New York City Center 13 March 1957 with Jack Cassidy and Shirley Jones. Produced at the Billy Rose Theatre 22 December 1973 with Kevin Kline, David Ogden Stiers and Cynthia Herman.

Produced at the Théâtre Caumartin, Paris, 22 November 1921.

A film version was produced by British Lion in 1952 with Laurence Olivier

(Macheath), Dorothy Tutin (singing dubbed by Adele Leigh) (Polly), George Devine (singing dubbed by John Cameron) (Peachum), Mary Clare (singing dubbed by Edith Coates) (Mrs Peachum) and Stanley Holloway (Lockit).

CHARACTERS

Peachum
Mrs Peachum
Polly Peachum, *their daughter*
Captain Macheath
Filch
Lockit
Lucy Lockit, *his daughter*
Mat o' the Mint
Jenny Diver
Sukey Tawdry
Ben Budge, Nimming Ned, Wat Dreary, Robin o' Bagshot, Harry Paddington, Crook-Fingered Jack, Jemmy Twitcher, Mrs Vixen, Mrs Coaxer, etc.

ACT 1

Mr Peachum is at home and at his work ('Through All the Employments of Life') when his subordinate, Filch, comes to report on the up-to-date state of the business. It is a sad report, for Peachum is the outwardly respectable receiving end of a gang of thieves and pickpockets, and the information consists mainly of news of those members of his crew who have been taken by the law. Peachum is obliged to decide which of the arrested he can commercially afford to rescue and which do not merit his attention, but it is noticeable that he pays especially kind attention to the female criminals (''Tis Woman That Seduces All Mankind').

With Peachum business is paramount and it is clear that those in his employ who do not measure up can before long expect to find themselves brought 'accidentally' and fatally before the courts. It is with business foremost in his mind that he is not at all pleased to discover from his wife that Captain Macheath, the boldest and finest of the highwaymen with whom he has dealings, has been looking with a fond eye upon the Peachums' daughter Polly. Peachum smells marriage, and marriage, he has always found, is detrimental to a girl's commercial usefulness. Mrs Peachum, who is sympathetic towards Polly's wish for security, does not see in what way marriage need affect her daughter's enjoyment of life or men, or anything else for that matter, but she questions the light-fingered, quick-eared Filch to find out for her own satisfaction what commerce there might have been between Polly and Macheath.

In front of her father, Polly shows off the gold watch and other trifles given to her as marks of Macheath's esteem and gains his wary approval of her venal acumen ('Virgins Are Like the Fair Flow'r in Its Lustre') but also a dire warning against anything so silly and dangerous as marriage. But he is too late; the deed is already done and Mrs Peachum has discovered it ('Our

12

Polly Is a Sad Slut!'). To her parents' horror, Polly can only reply ingenuously 'Can Love Be Controlled by Advice?'. The Peachums are convinced that their son-in-law will denounce them in order to see them hanged so that he may legally inherit their ill-gotten wealth. Why could not Polly have done like other women and just had an affair ('O, Polly, You Might Have Toy'd and Kiss'd')? But Polly is suffering from love ('I Like a Ship in Storms Was Toss'd') and she cannot think of such practical things as a profitable widowhood.

Her parents can, though, and they propose that Polly should help to have her husband impeached at the next session in order to inherit his wealth before he can pull the same trick on them. Polly sullenly declares that she won't. She loves her husband ('O Ponder Well! Be Not Severe'). She also knows that her parents have means of getting their own way and, left alone, she is twisted in a turmoil of worry. Her fears subside when Macheath appears to take her in his arms ('Pretty Polly Say'). He has many pretty words with which to make her happy ('My Heart Was So Free') and they make love in extravagant terms ('Were I Laid on Greenland's Coast') before Polly remembers to make him aware of her parents' horrid intentions. He must away and hide awhile until the situation is safer ('The Miser Thus a Shilling Sees').

ACT 2

At a tavern near Newgate, Macheath's gang are entertaining themselves with their favourite vices of tobacco and whisky ('Fill Ev'ry Glass') when their leader arrives with his disturbing news. The gang cannot do without the good offices of Peachum who is the fence *par excellence* for their stolen goods, but it is advisable for the moment that, by reason of his marriage, Macheath, the most effective of the band, should keep out of his way. The others must not relax their efforts, but rather redouble them to make up for their leader's temporary absence ('Let Us Take the Road').

When they have gone out to ply their profession Macheath, alone, muses on his marital action. It seemed like a necessary thing because of the fondness shown by Polly; and the threat of no Polly, no Peachum, no business hung heavy in the air. But the highwayman still has a taste for woman in general as opposed to a woman in particular ('If the Heart of Man Is Depress'd With Cares'), and woman in general he is prepared this night to enjoy, as Mrs Coaxer and her shopful of girls descend on the tavern ('Youth's the Season Made of Joy'). But woman is his downfall. His old flame, the venal Jenny Diver, is a suborned creature and she leads him into the power of the constables and the conniving Peachum. As he is led away, Macheath spits back at his betrayers his pleasure that in death, at least, he will find no such Furies as they are ('At the Tree I Shall Suffer').

In Newgate prison Macheath is held under the guardianship of Mr Lockit, and he has only the time for a brief soliloquy in his cell ('Man May Escape From Rope and Gun') before his jailer's daughter is upon him. Lucy Lockit is one of his incidental paramours and she is suffering very visibly and complainingly from the consequences ('Thus, When a Good Houswife'). Macheath turns her head with fine words about marriage and faithfulness, denying that he is wed to Polly and mocking his wife as a vain liar ('The First Time at the Looking Glass') and Lucy thinks that she sees her chance to be made an honest woman. If she can influence her father into getting Macheath released, she may become a wedded wife. Her father, at this moment, is closeted with Peachum compounding their useful acquaintance-ship ('When You Censure the Age') and working out some small judicial matters to their mutual advantage. Lucy makes her plea for Macheath's life ('Is Then His Fate?') but Lockit, under the commercial circumstances, really can't allow himself to help his hopeful child ('You'll Think, 'Ere Many Days Ensue').

As Lucy and Macheath eagerly discuss ways in which he might regain his freedom, Polly arrives to see her husband. Lucy and Polly face up to each other spitefully as Macheath pragmatically muses 'How Happy Could I Be With Either'. The girls become quite heated ('I'm Bubbled') and Macheath vainly tries to calm first one then the other and still not damage his chances of getting himself released. Polly tells Lucy to 'Cease Your Fuming' at her marriage, but Lucy, on her home ground, retorts with scorn ('Why How Now Madam Flirt') to her rival's claims. Peachum arrives, hot on the trail of his traitorous daughter and, not one whit diverted by her professions of love ('No Pow'r on Earth Can E'er Divide'), drags the miserable girl away from her husband. Lucy, who declares that she would rather see the man she loves hanged than in the arms of another woman ('I Like the Fox Shall Grieve'), has now to be mollified by some convenient lies and, before the day is done, Macheath persuades her to steal her father's keys and let him loose.

ACT 3

Pretty soon, Lucy realises that she has made a bad bargain. Her father is furious at her foolishness and, it seems, in spite of his swearing to the contrary, Macheath is truly married to Polly Peachum ('My Love Is All Madness and Folly'). Lockit determines to track the escaped criminal down and Lucy, tossed in a salad of mixed emotions ('I'm Like a Skiff on the Ocean Toss't'), knows only one thing: she hates Polly Peachum and would like to see her dead. When Polly turns up at the prison again, acting exceed-ingly polite, Lucy feigns a reconciliation ('When a Wife's in the Pout') while preparing a deadly potion for her rival's afternoon tea ('Come, Sweet Lass'). But Polly, pleading digestive problems, refuses the poisoned drink just as Lockit returns with the recaptured Macheath.

When the two women fall upon their husband ('Hither, Dear Husband') with their various claims, he evades giving a categoric answer and tells them only that there will soon be no Macheath to dispute over. Peachum, with an eye to inheritance, suggests that, for the ladies' sake, he must still make a confession ('Which Way Shall I Turn Me?'). Polly turns her wheedling attentions to her father and begs him to help get Macheath off ('When My Hero in Court Appears'), but Peachum will not be moved and the girls have to watch powerless as Lockit comes to lead the highwayman to the gallows ('The Charge Is Prepared').

As his deathly hour approaches, Macheath drinks deep ('Oh, Cruel, Cruel, Cruel Case!') and awaits his doom with anything but complacency. Lucy and Polly come to see him one last time ('Would I Might Be Hanged"), but so do four other 'wives' each with a babe in their arms to prove their point. Since the man must die, it really does not matter which is his lawful wife—except, of course, for the question of the inheritance. But all of a sudden it does matter for, in the nick of time, a reprieve arrives. Macheath is free and pardoned but apparently polygamous. In spite of all the other claims, however, he has only been legally married once. Polly Peachum is his wife and it is with her that the life which has been spared must now be spent ('Thus I Stand Like the Turk').

A large number of popular tunes were, at various times, included in the eighteenth century productions of *The Beggar's Opera* and subsequent productions have included, alongside the most famous songs, widely varying musical selections.

COX AND BOX

or The Long Lost Brothers, a musical triumviretta in one act adapted from J Maddison Morton's farce *Box and Cox* by F C Burnand. Music by Arthur Sullivan. Produced at a benefit at the Adelphi Theatre, London, 11 May 1867 played by George du Maurier (Box), Quintin Twiss (Cox) and Arthur Blunt (Bouncer). Produced at the Gallery of Illustration 29 March 1869 for a regular run with Arthur Cecil (formerly Blunt), Thomas German Reed and J Seymour. Subsequently played in repertoire by the D'Oyly Carte Opera Company.

Produced for the first time in New York 13 August 1875. Played at the Standard Theatre 14 April 1879 with Thomas Whiffen, Hart Conway and Charles Makin.

CHARACTERS

John James Cox, *a journeyman hatter*
John James Box, *a journeyman printer*
Serjeant Bouncer, *late of the Dampshire yeomanry, with military reminiscences*

It is early morning in the boarding house run by Serjeant Bouncer, and his lodger, Mr Cox, is dressed ready to set out for his day's work in the hatting trade, when the good Serjeant knocks on the door. Cox makes use of him to hold his mirror while he ties his cravat but an unfortunate mention of things military sets Bouncer off on one of his interminable military reminiscences ('Rataplan') and only when he has finished his song can Cox tackle the landlord with some complaints. Firstly, his room smells abominably of stale tobacco. Ah, that must be the gentleman upstairs. Clearly his smoke comes down the chimney instead of following the usual upward motion.

Cox is curious about the gentleman upstairs, for each morning as he goes out to work he meets this gentleman coming up the stairs. His curiosity is not enough, however, to divert his further complaints ('Stay, Bouncer, Stay!'). Someone has been using his coal, his matches, his sugar, his tea and his candles. When an only partially mollified Cox at last goes off to work, Bouncer wipes his brow and sets to work to tidy the room. He has to hurry, for at that moment he hears Mr Box passing Mr Cox, as always, on the stairs.

Mr Box is not the gentleman upstairs, but he is the cause of the of the tobacco smoke. The crafty Bouncer has double let his room. Mr Box works at night, Mr Cox by day, and the two of them unwittingly sleep their hours of sleep in the same bed in the same room. Bouncer tentatively asks Box to quit his smoking and gets a sharp reply. Box is in no mood for that sort of thing. He is tired and wants to get to bed. But first he will cook himself a little bacon. And bother it if the wretched Bouncer hasn't been using his gridiron. It smells of herrings! Popping his bacon on the fire, Box dozes into 'A Lullaby'.

Suddenly Cox appears bouncily at the door. He has been given the day off ('My Master Is Punctual') and has come home to cook himself a little pork chop before setting off for a day's excursion. He is not pleased to find that Bouncer has been using his room—why the fellow has even had the cheek to cook his bacon on his fire. He removes the bacon, puts it to one side, replaces it with his chop and goes out to get his breakfast things. The slam of the door arouses the dozing Box who hurries to get his bacon. He is furious to see that Bouncer has apparently interfered with his breakfast and throws the intrusive chop out the window, replacing his bacon on the gridiron before going off, in his turn, to get his breakfast things.

Cox returns and finds his chop gone and the wretched bacon back in its place. Opening the window, he flings the bacon out and turns, only to come face to face with Box. Each is proprietorially indignant ('Who Are You, Sir?') and both call loudly for Bouncer. The miserable landlord is forced to admit his ruse and offers to rent another room to one or other of the gentlemen. While the new room is being prepared, Cox and Box endeavour to be polite to each other and sing a serenade ('The Buttercup').

Routine conversation brings out the information that Cox is engaged to be married to a lady who runs some bathing machines and that Box is officially dead. Cox asks him how he managed it. He would dearly like to try something similar if it meant he could escape his imminent matrimony. Box tells him how he faked his own death by drowning to escape a similar indiscretion ('Three Years Ago'). They are amazed when they find that the lady in each question is the same Mrs Penelope Ann Wiggins. Each is anxious to put the onus of wedding Mrs Wiggins on the other and, when dialectic fails, they fall to playing dice for her. Each has a pair of loaded dice which throws only double 'Sixes', so the game is inconclusive and the tossing of some double-headed coins gets things no further.

Now Bouncer turns up with a letter. It is from the seaside. Poor Mrs Wiggins went sailing and was capsized and in her will she has left all her worldly goods to her intended. All of a sudden both the gentlemen, who a few seconds earlier were anxious only to be rid of the lady, are anxious to claim her, but they are stopped short when a second letter arrives. True to form, the indestructible Penelope Ann didn't sink and she's heading to town to join Mr Cox instanter.

A cab draws up and, as the lady approaches, the two men slam the door and bodily hold it closed. When someone comes to knock, however, it is only Bouncer with a third note. Penelope Ann has decided that Cox is not for her; she has gone and married Mr Knox. The two gentlemen fall into each other's arms: they are saved. But wait! That aspect! Surely Mr Cox must be Mr Box's long-lost brother. Does he have that *sine qua non* of long-lost brothers, a strawberry mark? He doesn't. And neither does Mr Box's brother. Assuredly that is who he is. As for the room, why it's very pleasant. They will both stay here and share it ('My Hand Upon It') and give three cheers for good old Mr Knox.

Cox and Box was first produced privately by the society amateur group, the Moray Minstrels, on a date over which scholars cannot quite agree. It was certainly performed at Moray Lodge, Campden Hill on 27 April 1867 but this may not have been the first performance. After its earliest performances, the piece was cut to the length in which it has since been played.

TRIAL BY JURY

a dramatic cantata in one act by W S Gilbert. Music by Arthur Sullivan. Produced at the Royalty Theatre, London, 25 March 1875 with Frederic Sullivan (Judge), Nellie Bromley (Plaintiff) and Walter H Fisher (Defendant). Produced at the Opera Comique 14 January 1876 with Sullivan, Clara Vesey and Knight Aston. Produced at the Strand Theatre 3 March 1877 with J G Taylor, Lottie Venne and Claude Marius. Revived at the Opera Comique with *The Sorcerer* 23 March 1878 with George Grossmith, Lisa Walton and George Power. Produced at the Savoy Theatre 11 October 1884 with *The Sorcerer* with Rutland Barrington, Florence Dysart and Charles Hildesley. Revived there with *The Sorcerer* 22 September 1898 with Henry Lytton, Isabel Jay and Charles Childerstone. Played subsequently in repertoire by the D'Oyly Carte Opera Company.

Produced at the Arch Street Theatre, Philadelphia, 22 October 1875. Produced at the Eagle Theatre, New York, 15 November 1875 with G H McDermott, Rose Keene and W Forrester. Played at the Fifth Avenue Theatre 24 February 1879 with Vincent Horgan, Blanche Corelli and Henri Laurent.

Produced at the Wallner Theater, Berlin, 14 June 1886 and at the Alexander-Platz Theater 1 October 1892 in a version by Siegfried Ehrenberg.

Produced at the Carltheater, Vienna, as *Im Schwurgericht* 14 September 1886 and at Danzer's Orpheum as *Das Brautpaar vor Gericht* 5 October 1901.

17

CHARACTERS

The Learned Judge
The Plaintiff
The Defendant
Counsel for the Plaintiff
Usher
Foreman of the Jury
Associate
First Bridesmaid, etc.

In a British court of justice the day's work is beginning ('Hark the Hour of Ten Is Sounding') and the usher is addressing the jurymen—'All kinds of vulgar prejudice I pray you set aside: with stern judicial frame of mind from bias free of every kind, this trial must be tried'—before going on to describe the forthcoming case. It is a breach of promise case, and the usher paints an 'unbiased' picture of a broken-hearted little bride-to-be and a villainous defendant before again repeating that, of course, the jury must remain free of any bias and preconception.

Amid vocal threats of penal damages from the jurymen, the defendant comes to the stand to tell his story ('When First My Old, Old Love I Knew'). It is a simple enough story: he fell in love, fell out of love and into love with someone else. The jury do not react understandingly for, although they did exactly the same thing when young, they are now respectable gentlemen and he is a reprehensible lout.

The Learned Judge takes his place on the bench to the strains of a laudatory chorus ('All Hail, Great Judge!'), and proceeds to enlighten the attendance on the details of his rise to his present eminent position ('When I, Good Friends, Was Called to the Bar'). The jury are sworn in and then the plaintiff is called into court. Dressed in her bridal gown and veil and escorted by a bouquet of bridesmaids ('Comes the Broken Flower'), the drooping Angelina renders a poetic little solo ('O'er the Season Vernal') while the Learned Judge ogles the principal bridesmaid and sends her a private note. Coming to the affair in hand, however, his lordship notices the now unveiled plaintiff and, with a sudden shift of affections, instructs the usher to take the note away from the bridesmaid and give it to the lady in the case. Since the jury are also indulging in various degrees of rapture over the pretty plaintiff, the case for the defence seems clearly compromised.

The counsel for the plaintiff rises to give his version of the facts of the affair ('With a Sense of Deep Emotion'): the vile behaviour of the defendant is compounded to an awful degree for the bride had already bought her trousseau when he broke off the wedding. As the plaintiff sobs prettily, the jury roar their sympathy and the Judge offers her his shoulder, an offer which is quickly accepted.

The defendant attempts to justify his wandering fancies ('Oh, Gentlemen, Listen, I Pray') and finally offers, if it will ease matters and save him from a verdict of guilty, to wed this young lady temporarily, and wait to wed his new love at a later date. This seems a fairly illegal, not to say immoral, solution, and the counsel has to dip into his books to try to find a precedent. The plaintiff, in the meanwhile, hastily recounts the magnitude of her love for the man who has deserted her, a magnitude which the jury must, she insists, remember when they are assessing the amount of damages payable ('I Love Him, I Love Him'). The defendant, for his part, is intent on convincing the jury what an awful beast he is. He smokes, he drinks, he would beat his wife when in liquor. The Judge suggests that to test this statement they should get him drunk and watch the result but, although the defendant is willing, the plaintiff protests loudly and the court threatens to dissolve in arguments.

It seems as if there is no satisfactory solution to this case, but the Judge has the answer. Throwing his papers in the air, he declares that he will marry the girl himself! On that, everyone seems agreed ('Oh, Joy Unbounded') and, as coloured fire and a pair of cherubs descend from above, the case reaches its apotheosis in a happy ending.

THE SORCERER

a comic opera in two acts by W S Gilbert. Music by Arthur Sullivan. Produced at the Opera Comique, London, 17 November 1877 with George Grossmith (Wells), Rutland Barrington (Daly), Mrs Howard Paul (Lady Sangazure), Alice May (Aline) and George Bentham (Alexis). Produced at the Savoy Theatre in a revised version 11 October 1884 with Grossmith, Barrington, Rosina Brandram, Leonora Braham and Durward Lely and revived there 22 September 1898 with Walter Passmore, Henry Lytton, Miss Brandram, Ruth Vincent and Robert Evett. Played subsequently by the D'Oyly Carte Opera Company in repertoire.

Produced at the Broadway Theatre, New York, 21 February 1879 with W Horace Lingard, Matilda Scott and J F Graff. Produced at the Bijou Theatre 16 October 1882 with John Howson, Digby V Bell, Laura Joyce Bell, Lillian Russell and Charles J Campbell.

CHARACTERS

Sir Marmaduke Poindextre, *an elderly baronet*
Alexis *of the Grenadier Guards, his son*
Dr Daly, *vicar of Ploverleigh*
John Wellington Wells, *of J W Wells & Co., Family Sorcerers*
A Notary
Lady Sangazure, *a Lady of Ancient Lineage*
Aline, *her daughter, betrothed to Alexis*
Mrs Partlet, *a pew opener*
Constance, *her daughter*

ACT 1
At Sir Marmaduke Poindextre's Elizabethan mansion in the village of

Ploverleigh the betrothal of the baronet's son, Alexis, to Aline, the eligible and lovely daughter of Lady Sangazure, is today to be signed to the accompaniment of general vicarious rejoicing among the populace. But for pretty little Constance Partlet there is no rejoicing, for she is lost deep in sighs and blushes which are directed in quite another direction. She has developed an apparently hopeless affection for no less a dignitary than the local vicar, Dr Daly ('When He Is Here'). The good vicar's amatory days seem to him to be a part of his past, a part of the days when he was a pale young curate ('Time Was When Love and I Were Well Acquainted'), and he is obtusely dismissive of Mrs Partlet's not entirely subtle attempts to interest him in her daughter as a wife.

The principals in the day's matrimonial business come upon the scene with Aline singing rapturously of her 'Happy Young Heart' as she anticipates the joy the day will bring her. At this stage, we also discover that, in their youth, the parents of the two young people, the ageing Sir Marmaduke and dragonistic Lady Sangazure, had shared some blissful thoughts but, hampered by the conventions of the age, they had never got round to consumating their thoughts in deeds. The flame still burns, however, and, when they address each other with cultivated courtesy, altogether more passionate thoughts lie hidden behind their words ('Welcome Joy, Adieu to Sadness').

Alexis and Aline sign the deed of betrothal under the eyes of a very old notary and are, at last, left alone to flower verbosely into the praises of true love, a subject on which Alexis holds decided principles ('Give Me the Love'). In fact, such principles does he have that he has resolved philanthropically to make a gift of love to all the village. He has ordered from a London sorcerer a custom-compounded philtre which, in spite of Aline's reservations, he resolves to administer that afternoon to the communal tea cup so that all of Ploverleigh may experience the amorous joy which they themselves know. The sorcerer, one Mr John Wellington Wells, has come down from town to supply the philtre in person ('My Name Is John Wellington Wells') and he calms Aline's qualms by assuring her that it is a very proper philtre. Although those who take it fall rapturously in love with the first person they see, it works only on unmarried people.

As tea-time approaches, Wells prepares his potion with an Incantation ('Sprites of Earth and Air') and when the townspeople gather for the celebratory banquet ('Now to the Banquet We Press') and partake of the cup that cheers (Tea-Cup Brindisi) they soon begin to stagger about under its effects until, as the act ends, the entire unmarried population of Ploverleigh is fast asleep on the ground.

ACT 2

It is evening and Wells, Alexis and Aline await the end of the first phase of the philtre's action (''Tis Twelve I Think'). Soon the people awake and, surely enough, within minutes of waking the whole male chorus has proposed to the whole female chorus. Unfortunately, the first single person

Constance has seen on her awakening is the very old notary. He is also a very deaf notary, so the poor girl is still in as many tears as she was over Dr Daly as she tries to make the old man understand the extent of her affection.

Alexis is very proud of the results of his experiment but, when he suggests to Aline that he and she should also partake of the philtre, she is horrified that he should consider it needful to bolster their love by artificial means. She refuses and he takes umbrage ('It Is Not Love') and a little grey cloud comes over what should have been a wholly blissful day. A further complication ensues when Sir Marmaduke enters with Mrs Partlet and announces that he is planning to marry her. Alexis gulpingly sticks to his tenet that true love is above all, though he has to confess that Mrs Partlet is not quite the person he would have chosen to be his mother (Quintet: 'I Rejoice That It's Decided').

John Wellington Wells is now aware of the effects his philtre can have when administered en masse and he is worried. He has even more cause for worry when Lady Sangazure descends on him with all the effusion of an amorous walrus. He attempts to repel her advances by denigrating himself ('Hate Me!') and finally resorts to a lie, declaring that he is engaged already to a South Seas maiden, to prevent the determined noblewoman from crushing him to her mighty bosom.

Aline, horribly distracted by Alexis's cruelty over her refusal to take the philtre, finally resolves that she will put aside her reservations and do so. Unfortunately, having sipped the cup, she encounters Dr Daly who has come on to sing a mournful little ballad bewailing the fact that all the ladies in the village seem to have become engaged before he got round to finding one for himself ('Oh My Voice Is Sad and Low'). Now he finds himself adored by the loveliest of them all ('Alas! That Lovers Thus Should Meet') and Alexis is in despair.

Things have certainly not worked out as intended. The sorcerer is being dogged by the unwanted Lady Sangazure and Alexis has had his betrothed alienated. Now that the effects of their tampering with nature are rebounding on themselves, the two men decide that something must be done to put an end to the effects of the philtre. Wells tells Alexis that there is only one way out. One of them will have to deliver up his life to the spirit under whose guidance the potion was concocted. He would rather it were Alexis as he has stocktaking the next week and it would be inconvenient not to be there.

Alexis agrees to pay the penalty for his folly, but Aline has a point of law to press. If the effect of the philtre is to be reversed and everyone restored to his or her old love, what, pray, will become of her if Alexis has been sacrificed? Her logic is undeniable, and it is decided that the victim will have to be Wells after all. As John Wellington Wells is consumed in a flash of red fire, all the marital mismatchings of Ploverleigh are solved. Alexis and Aline come back together, Constance is paired off with her vicar, Sir Marmaduke finally gets his Sangazure and Mrs Partlet makes do with the very old, very deaf notary.

21

HMS PINAFORE

or The Lass That Loved a Sailor, a comic opera in two acts by W S Gilbert. Music by Arthur Sullivan. Produced at the Opera Comique, London, 25 May 1878 with George Grossmith (Sir Joseph), Rutland Barrington (Corcoran), George Power (Ralph), Alice May (Josephine) and Harriet Everard (Little Buttercup). Produced at the Imperial Theatre 1 August 1879 with J G Taylor, Michael Dwyer, Percy Blandford, Lizzie Mulholland and Fanny Edwards. Produced at the Opera Comique 16 December 1879 with a juvenile company. Produced at the Savoy Theatre 12 November 1887 with Grossmith, Barrington, J G Robertson, Geraldine Ulmar and Rosina Brandram; 6 June 1899 with Walter Passmore, Henry Lytton, Robert Evett, Ruth Vincent and Miss Brandram; and 14 July 1908 with C H Workman, Barrington, Henry Herbert, Elsie Spain and Louie Rene. Played subsequently by the D'Oyly Carte Opera Company in repertoire. Played at the Phoenix Theatre 7 September 1960 and Her Majesty's Theatre 9 February 1962 by the Stratford Festival Theatre with Eric House, Harry Mossfield, Andrew Downie, Marion Studholme and Irene Byatt. Produced at the Old Vic 22 April 1986 with Alan Devlin, Paul Bentley, William Relton, Michelle Todd and Anita Reeves.

Produced at the Boston Museum, Boston, 25 November 1878 in a pirated version with George W Wilson, James H Jones, Rose Temple, Marie Wainwright and Lizzie Harold. Produced at the Standard Theatre, New York, 15 January 1879 with Thomas Whiffen, Eugene Clarke, Henri Laurent, Eva Mills and Blanche Galton. Produced at innumerable Broadway theatres in the years that followed, notably by D'Oyly Carte at the Fifth Avenue Theatre 1 December 1879 with J H Ryley, J Furneaux Cook, Hugh Talbot, Blanche Roosevelt and Alice Barnett. Produced at the Casino Theatre 29 May 1911 with Henry E Dixey, George J Macfarlane, Arthur Aldridge, Louise Gunning and Alice Brady with De Wolf Hopper as Dick, Eugene Cowles as Bill, Marie Cahill as Hebe and Christine Nielsen as Tom. Produced at the New York Hippodrome 9 April 1914 with William G Gordon, Bertram Peacock, John Bardesley, Helen Heinemann and Marie Horgan, and at the Century Theatre 6 April 1926 with John E Hazzard, Marion Green, Tom Burke, Marguerite Namara and Fay Templeton.

Produced at the Friedrich-Wilhelmstädtisches Theater, Berlin, as *Amor an Bord* 1881.

Produced at St Edmund's College, Douai, France, January 1901.

CHARACTERS

Rt Hon Sir Joseph Porter KCB, *First Lord of the Admiralty*
Captain Corcoran, *commanding HMS Pinafore*
Ralph Rackstraw, *able seaman*
Dick Deadeye, *able seaman*
Bill Bobstay, *boatswain's mate*
Bob Becket, *carpenter's mate*
Tom Tucker, *midshipmite*
Josephine, *the captain's daughter*
Hebe, *Sir Joseph's first cousin*
Mrs Cripps (Little Buttercup), *a Portsmouth bumboat woman*

ACT 1
The quarter deck of Her Majesty's ship *Pinafore*, at anchor in Portsmouth

harbour, is alive with its complement of exceedingly able seamen splicing, polishing and scrubbing ('We Sail the Ocean Blue') when one of the local bumboat women arrives on board with her basket full of good things calculated to separate the lads from their pay ('I'm Called Little Buttercup'). In spite of her rosy cheeks and jolly comportment, Little Buttercup is not a wholly happy lady for she confides that there is within her 'a canker worm which is slowly but surely eating its way into one's very heart'. There is all sorts of canker only too evident, on the other hand, in the appropriately named Dick Deadeye, a seaman of repellent aspect and minimal popularity, who earns from his crewmates a welcome of a very different style to that reserved for the popular Buttercup.

But hark! Our hero comes. On faltering feet the smartest lad in all the fleet, the tenor Ralph Rackstraw, appears, moodily sighing of unrequited love ('The Nightingale Sighed for the Moon's Bright Ray'/'A Maiden Fair to See'). He has pretensions to the heart of no less a maiden than Josephine, his Captain's daughter, pretensions which run up against the very principles of the social order. The Captain is a child of the peerage who, nevertheless, can actually comprehend the basics of seamanship. He is hardly ever sick at sea, almost never loses his self-control to the extent of using 'a big, big D' and is as popular with his crew as is allowed by their respective stations in life ('I Am the Captain of the *Pinafore*').

Captain Corcoran has arranged a most advantageous marriage for his daughter with the First Lord of the Admiralty, Sir Joseph Porter, but Josephine is sadly unimpressed by this *coup de mariage* and droops into a plaintive ballad at the thought ('Sorry Her Lot'). The truth is that she has fallen in love—oh, horror!—with a mere able seaman on her father's own ship but, true to her breeding, she stifles such improper yearnings and prepares herself bravely to meet her destined husband who even now is floating across the stretch of sea separating quayside from ship ('Over the Bright Blue Sea').

Piped aboard the poop deck, Sir Joseph, surrounded by a protective gaggle of sisters, cousins and aunts, introduces himself with a curriculum vitae in song ('I Am the Monarch of the Sea'/'When I Was a Lad'). Sir Joseph has a curious idea or two on social order and informs Corcoran importantly that 'a British sailor is any man's equal, excepting mine', requiring him to leaven his commands to his crew with such politenesses as 'if you please'. He advocates the learning of hornpipes as a democratic and characteristic occupation and, to illustrate his morale-supporting precepts, he has composed a glee ('A British Tar') which crew are required to con.

Josephine's good intentions are undergoing a true trial. Although she does her best to appreciate Sir Joseph's qualities, which he has detailed to her in the most helpful fashion, she yearns for her sailor. Now, as she pines alone on deck, who should appear before her but that very sailor—Ralph Rackstraw. To her delight he expresses himself in passionate terms but, remembering her position, she repulses him haughtily ('Refrain, Audacious Tar'). In despairing tones Ralph determines on suicide and, taking the pistol helpfully proffered by the boatswain, is cocked for action when Josephine rushes on to stop him with an admission of her love ('Oh Joy, Oh Rapture Unforeseen'). Encouraged by the sailors and Sir Joseph's female relations, the lovers plan to steal ashore that very night to find a clergyman to regularise their attachment ('This Very Night With Bated Breath').

ACT 2

That same evening the Captain is found on deck, perplexedly serenading the moon to the accompaniment of his guitar ('Fair Moon to Thee I Sing') and watched by a lovelorn Little Buttercup. Things are not going well for him, his plans are not prospering and he feels alone and unappreciated. Buttercup offers her support but he moderates what would, in other circumstances, have been his expressions of fond thanks with due regard to the difference in their social standing. Buttercup hints broadly that 'Things Are Seldom What They Seem' and the Captain answers in kind without understanding what she is getting at. His problems are compounded when Sir Joseph comes to complain that Josephine is not responding as required to his official utterances on the subject of his heart. Of course she isn't. She's outside her cabin soliloquising on her position ('The Hours Creep on Apace') and the wealth and comfort she is about to give up for an alliance with physical attractiveness.

The Captain attempts to excuse his daughter's cool behaviour towards Sir Joseph by suggesting that she is dazzled by his superior rank and he and Sir Joseph tackle the young lady in the trio 'Never Mind the Why and Wherefore', explaining pointedly that love levels all ranks. Little do they know that they are simply pleading the case of the First Lord's rival and that their song and dance serve only to convince Josephine she is doing the right thing in running off with Ralph.

But nemesis is lurking in the shrouds in the form of Dick Deadeye. Shunned by his fellow seamen, he gets his revenge by enlightening the Captain about the forthcoming elopement ('Kind Captain, I've Important Information') and, as the lovers prepare their flight, escorted by the entire chorus ('Carefully on Tiptoe Stealing'), the Captain intervenes dramatically. Ralph throws Sir Joseph's precepts in his face and the sailors chorus in support the fact that 'He Is an Englishman'. Exasperated out of his manners, the Captain underlines his exclamations with 'a big, big D' and is overheard by Sir Joseph. There is no excuse for bad language and the Captain is ordered to be confined to quarters. But when the First Lord discovers the cause of the Captain's breach of etiquette, he does more than swear. Ralph's incredible presumption earns him a sentence to the ship's dungeon cell.

As the lovers sing their last, prior to parting ('Farewell, My Own'), Little Buttercup steps forward to elucidate the mysterious hints she has been spreading throughout the evening. Once upon a time she was a baby farmer and she looked after a little lordling and a little plebeian at one and the same time. Unfortunately, she mixed them up. 'The well-born babe was Ralph, your Captain was the other!'. Yes, Ralph is the patrician of the pair and Captain Corcoran is a person of no breeding at all. Since breeding is

24

paramount, this means that Ralph must be the Captain of the *Pinafore* and Corcoran reduced to the rank of Able Seaman. Sir Joseph of course cannot consider marriage with the daughter of a tar—love certainly does not level ranks that much—so the way is clear for Captain Ralph to be united with his Josephine, while Corcoran finds his way into the arms of the comfy Buttercup and the First Lord is left to the tender but aristocratic mercies of Hebe, the most pressing of his sisters, cousins and aunts.

THE PIRATES OF PENZANCE

or The Slave of Duty, a comic opera in two acts by W S Gilbert. Music by Arthur Sullivan. Produced at the Bijou Theatre, Paignton, 30 December 1879. Produced at the Opera Comique, London, 3 April 1880 with George Grossmith (Major General), George Power (Frederic), Richard Temple (Pirate King), Rutland Barrington (Police Sergeant), Marion Hood (Mabel) and Emily Cross (Ruth). Produced at the Savoy Theatre 23 December 1884 with a juvenile cast. Revived there 17 March 1888 with Grossmith, J G Robertson, Temple, Barrington, Geraldine Ulmar and Rosina Brandram, 30 June 1900 with Henry Lytton, Robert Evett, Jones Hewson, Walter Passmore, Isabel Jay and Miss Brandram, and 1 December 1908 with C H Workman, Henry Herbert, Lytton, Barrington, Dorothy Court and Louie Rene. Played subsequently in repertoire by the D'Oyly Carte Opera Company. Produced at the Phoenix Theatre 6 September 1961 and at Her Majesty's Theatre 15 February 1962 with Eric House (Major General) and Marion Studholme (Mabel). Produced at the Theatre Royal, Drury Lane, 26 May 1982 with George Cole, Michael Praed, Tim Curry, Chris Langham, Pamela Stephenson and Annie Ross.

Produced at the Fifth Avenue Theatre, New York, 31 December 1879 with J H Ryley, Hugh Talbot, Sgr Broccolini, Fred Clifton, Blanche Roosevelt and Alice Barnett. Produced at the Plymouth Theatre 6 December 1926 with Ernest Lawford, William Williams, John Barclay, William C Gordon, Ruth Thomas and Vera Ross. Produced at the Delacorte Theatre 15 July 1980 and subsequently at the Uris Theatre 8 January 1981 and the Minskoff Theatre 12 August 1981 with George Rose, Rex Smith, Kevin Kline, Tony Azito, Linda Ronstadt and Patricia Routledge (replaced by Estelle Parsons).

Produced at the Theater an der Wien as *Die Piraten* in a version by F Zell and Richard Genée 1 March 1889.

A film version of the Delacorte Theatre version was produced by Universal in 1982 with Rose, Smith, Kline, Ronstadt and Angela Lansbury.

CHARACTERS

Major General Stanley
The Pirate King
Samuel, *his lieutenant*
Frederic, *his pirate apprentice*
Sergeant of Police

Mabel ⎫
Kate ⎪
Isobel ⎬ *General Stanley's daughters*
Edith ⎪
Ruth, *a pirate maid-of-all-work*

ACT 1

Off the rocky coast of Cornwall a pirate ship is anchored while its captain and crew partake of liquid refreshment on the sea shore ('Pour, Oh Pour the Pirate Sherry'). This day the pirate apprentice, Frederic, comes to the end of his indentured period and the Pirate King gladly tells him that he can consider himself, from that day forth, a full-blown member of their buccaneering band. But Frederic has a sad surprise for his employer. Now that his apprenticeship is complete, he must leave the pirate life for ever. He was never intended for it, and was bound to his indentures through an error. His old nurse, Ruth, who has spent the years of his apprenticeship skivvying for the pirate ship as a maid-of-all-work, confesses that her incipient deafness was the cause of the mistake. She should have apprenticed the boy to a pilot but got it a little wrong ('When Frederic Was a Little Lad').

So, though he dearly loves all his shipmates individually, Frederic has to admit that as a species he finds them atrocious and, now that his duty to them is done, he will be bound in duty to devote himself heart and soul to their extermination. However, since he is till midnight one of them, he is obliged to divulge to them their weak point. They are too tender-hearted. It suffices for a captive to plead to being an orphan and he is immediately released. This bit of intelligence has clearly got round in nautical circles, for now it seems that the entire mercantile marine is crewed only by orphans.

If Frederic is to leave the pirate band the question arises as to what shall become of Ruth. Neither Frederic nor the Pirate King wishes to deprive the other of her, but she is all for staying at the side of her young charge. Frederic, who has never seen another woman, is not quite sure how Ruth rates in feminine terms and, although she assures him she compares (apart from a slight cold) very well, he clearly has suspicions that someone thirty years younger would make him a more suitable wife.

As the time comes for Frederic to depart, he tries to persuade the pirates to return with him to civilisation, but the Pirate King refuses. His profession may not be the best but, contrasted with respectability, it is comparatively honest ('Oh, Better Far to Live and Die'). The pirates head back to their ship, leaving Frederic and the undetachable Ruth on the shore but, just as Frederic is assuring Ruth that if, as she says, she is truly an example of a beautiful woman her age shall be no bar to their union, the voices of young girls are heard. Ruth is lost! One glimpse at the bevy of beautiful maidens which is approaching ('Climbing Over Rocky Mountains') and Frederic renounces her reproachfully ('You Told Me You Were Fair as Gold') and hides among the rocks to win a closer look at genuine femininity.

The girls have just begun to take off their shoes and stockings to paddle in the sea when Frederic emerges, throwing them into a delicious panic. The

26

panic is eased by the fact that he is very beautiful but, when he begs that one of them should take pity on his unfortunate position ('Oh, Is There Not One Maiden Breast') and love him, they each and every one of them correctly refuse until a roulade of coloratura introduces a late arrival.

Like all the best prima donnas, Mabel has delayed her entrance and she now offers to reclaim the 'Poor Wandering One' in a showy song while her sisters wonder pointedly whether she would have shown quite such charity had the man in question not been so obviously attractive. In a selfless display of sisterly solidarity, however, they decide to talk about the weather ('How Beautifully Blue the Sky') while the two young people initiate their romance ('Did Ever Maiden Wake').

Suddenly Frederic recalls that they are on dangerous ground: there are pirates about! He is too late. Before they can retreat, the pirates are upon them, declaring delightedly 'Here's a first rate opportunity of getting married with impunity'. Their hasty marital ambitions are checked, however, by the arrival of the girls' father, Major-General Stanley ('I Am the Very Model of a Modern Major-General'), who wins the pirates' submission and his daughters' salvation by declaring untruthfully that he is an orphan ('Oh, Men of Dark and Dismal Fate'). There will be no weddings today.

ACT 2

In a ruined gothic chapel on his estate, a sleepless General Stanley sits in his nightgown surrounded by his solicitous daughters ('Oh, Dry the Glistening Tear'). Nothing can calm the General's conscience or his fears over the lie he has told the pirates. Frederic tells him that he need not be afraid for this very night, at the head of a stout band of police, he is to set out to apprehend the pirate band and put an end to their plundering of Penzance. The apparently ferocious Sergeant of Police ('When the Foeman Bares His Steel') and his men receive the extravagantly dramatic farewells of General Stanley's daughters ('Go Ye Heroes, Go to Glory') which put an unpleasant emphasis on death and not returning but, when Frederic is left alone to prepare his adventure, he receives an unexpected pair of visitors, the Pirate King and Ruth.

His old friends have an awkward piece of news for the reformed pirate ('When You Had Left Our Pirate Fold'): he is not yet free from his indentures. His apprenticeship papers state that he shall be apprenticed up to his twenty-first birthday and, although he has lived twenty-one years, he was actually born on 29 February and has so far had only five birthdays. Placed before this irrefutable recall to duty, Frederic is bound to tell the pirates what he knows—General Stanley is no orphan. Piratical blood boils ('Away, Away! My Heart's on Fire') and the King swears revenge on the man who has thus taken advantage of his noble nature.

Mabel, returning, finds Frederic in tears ('All Is Prepared, Your Gallant Crew Awaits You'). When he explains what has happened, she bids him to ignore what is clearly an illegal claim ('Stay, Frederic, Stay!') but his sense of duty will not allow him to do so. Sadly they part ('Ah, Leave Me Not to Pine Alone'), and Mabel informs the policemen that the Sergeant will have to take

27

over the direction of the operation. The Sergeant is a kindly chap who does not like depriving fellow creatures of their liberty but, after all, a job's a job and it has to be fulfilled ('When A Felon's Not Engaged In His Employment'). As he hits his final bottom note, the pirates' voices are heard approaching. They are coming already to take their dreadful revenge.

The policemen hide as the pirates burst into the chapel ('With Cat-like Tread') and hide in their turn at the approach of Stanley, in his dressing-gown and carrying a candle. As he tossed on his sleepless bed, he thought he heard a noise ('Tormented With the Anguish Dread'), but now it seems there is nothing, only the wind in the trees ('Sighing Softly to the River'). The girls appear, tiptoeing in in their nightgowns in search of their wandering father ('Now What Is This and What Is That'), and this is the cue for the pirates to leap from their cover.

Mabel calls upon Frederic to help her father as he kneels under the Pirate King's blade but, duty-bound, Frederic cannot. The policemen can though. They jump out from their hiding places and a fearsome battle ensues from which the pirates emerge victorious. There will be none of the 'orphan' trick this time. Their victims are well and truly doomed. But the police have the ultimate weapon. They charge the pirates to yield in the name of Queen Victoria.

That does it, of course. No British pirate can fail to respond to the name of his glorious monarch. Their swords are dropped and their collars grabbed, but Ruth has the last say: these are no ordinary pirates, they are all aristocratic striplings who have been indulging in too much youthful exuberance. Well, 'peers will be peers and youth will have its fling', so all the naughty noblemen are pardoned and there are just enough Stanley daughters to go round as the 'Poor Wandering Ones' are welcomed back to civilised living and matrimony.

The 1980 production included in its score the *HMS Pinafore* song 'Sorry Her Lot' and the patter trio, 'My Eyes Are Fully Open' from *Ruddigore*.

BILLEE TAYLOR

or The Reward of Virtue, a nautical comic opera in two acts by Henry Pottinger Stephens. Music by Edward Solomon. Produced at the Imperial Theatre, London, 30 October 1880 with Fleming Norton (Flapper), Arthur Williams (Mincing Lane), J D Stoyle (Ben), J A Arnold (Crab), Frederic Rivers (Billee), Emma Chambers (Arabella), Kathleen Corri (Phoebe) and Harriet Coveney (Eliza). Produced at the Gaiety Theatre 1 April 1882 with Philip Day, Williams, E W Royce, J J Dallas, Frederic Darrell, Miss Chambers, Lizzie St Quinten and Miss Coveney; 17 July 1882 with Arnold Breedon (Billee) and Annie Poole (Phoebe); 15 November 1883 with Breedon and Lucille Meredith and 31 October 1885 with Tom Squire, J H Jarvis, Arthur Roberts, George Honey, Breedon, Eva Milner, Marion Hood and Miss Coveney. Produced at Toole's Theatre 31 July 1886 with Williams (Flapper),

Emily Spiller (Billee) and Harriet Vernon (Phoebe).

Produced at the Standard Theatre, New York, 19 February 1881 with J H Ryley, W H Seymour, A W F McCollin, William Hamilton, Breedon, Alice Burville, Carrie Burton and Nellie Mortimer and played at Niblo's Garden 6 June 1881 with Ryley, H A Cripps, McCollin, Hamilton, Eugene Clark, Rachel Sanger, Misses Burton and Mortimer. Played at Booth's Theatre 27 March 1882; at the Bijou Theatre 26 August 1882 with Charles J Campbell (Billee) and Miss Burton; at the Fifth Avenue Theatre 9 October 1882 with Harry de Lorme (Billee) and Marie Jansen (Phoebe); at the Casino Theatre 20 June 1885 with Ryley, Edward Temple, John McWade, Fred Clifton, Harry Hilliard, Verona Jarbeau, Lillian Russell and Alice Barnett; and at the American Theatre 11 April 1898 with Raymond Hitchcock, Richard Ridgeley, E N Knight, Oscar Girard, Jay Taylor, Ruth White, Marie Celeste and Bessie Fairbairn.

Played at Le Havre, France, 21 February 1884 with Walter H Fisher (Billee), Frederic Solomon (Ben), Charles Dodsworth (Crab) and Lillian Russell (Phoebe).

CHARACTERS

Captain the Hon Felix Flapper RN *of HMS Thunderbomb*
Sir Mincing Lane Kt, *a self-made man*
Billee Taylor, *a virtuous gardener*
Ben Barnacle, *bo'sun of the HMS Thunderbomb*
Christopher Crab, *a schoolmaster*
Phoebe Fairleigh, *a village maiden*
Arabella Lane, *Sir Mincing's daughter*
Eliza Dabsey, *Phoebe's aunt*
Susan, *a model maiden*, etc.

ACT 1

On the green at Southampton Water the village folk are enjoying a pre-wedding celebration ('Today, Today, Is Holiday'), but while they drink deep to speed their jollity the schoolmaster, Christopher Crab, is drinking to drown his chagrin. Today's bride is to be Phoebe Fairleigh, a pretty little charity girl who has been Crab's pupil since her childhood, and the schoolmaster is ruing the day he ever taught her to write, since she now writes love letters to another man. Poor Christopher Crab is in love with his pupil and he would do anything to stop her wedding to William Taylor, a gardener on the estate of the local diginitary, Sir Mincing Lane. He would even commit villainy, for Christopher Crab has a long-suppressed urge to be a really villainous villain, and this situation looks as if it may provide him at last with the necessary spur.

While Crab inclines to wickedness, the bridegroom, Billee Taylor, prides himself on his utter devotion to virtue ('The Virtuous Gardener') and in consequence he is bound to reject the persistent advances of his employer's daughter, Arabella. Arabella has long since tried to tempt Billee into an acquaintance. She left jugs of ale in the woodshed, and an umbrella when it rained, and at Christmas time Billee found an anonymous five pound note and a lock of hair left at his place of work. He spent the money and threw away the hair and did not wonder whence they came, so Arabella's plight

29

went unnoticed. The news of his impending marriage now forces the girl to become more explicit ('Ifs and Ans') and Billee staggers under such an assault on his virtue. He is promised to another and there is nothing Arabella can do.

Phoebe's schoolfriends clutter on (Charity Girls' Chorus: 'We Stick to Our Letters') to welcome the bride to her wedding ('The Two Rivers') and she bids them farewell with fond advice to follow the sound principles which have led her to such a happy estate. While she catechises them, Sir Mincing Lane ('The Self-Made Knight'), as patron of the Charity school, arrives to wish his protégée well. He brings with him Captain Felix Flapper, captain of the vessel *Thunderbomb*, and Flapper is most irritated to hear that Phoebe is to be a bride. He had noticed her himself on the last occasion he was in port, and he would dearly have liked to have cast his anchor in her direction. Phoebe catches his purposeful glance ('A Guileless Orphan'), but when he kisses her she boxes his ears.

No sooner has the bride-to-be despatched one presumptuous admirer than she finds herself cornered by a second and much less expected one. Crab gets the same reward for his advances as Captain Flapper and rushes off to meditate villainy in the company of the other rejected lovers, Flapper and Arabella ('Revenge! Revenge!! and Retribution'), while Phoebe exchanges extravagant sugared nothings with her Billee.

The rest of the complement of the *Thunderbomb* have also come ashore ('The Gallant Thunderbomb'), amongst them the bo'sun Ben Barnacle whose duty in his naval position is to press gang young men to the King's Service. Ben wasn't always a seaman. Once upon a time he was a landlubber and a lover, but his Eliza wed another fellow and, broken-hearted, he upped and took to the sea ('All On Account of Eliza') and his distasteful occupation. It is an occupation which he will soon have to exercise, for Captain Flapper has thought up a diabolical way to win Phoebe for himself. He will have Billee pressed into the navy before the wedding vows can be exchanged.

As the wedding bells begin to ring (Wedding Chorus: 'Hark the Merry Marriage Bells'), Ben goes into action and, waving his warrant, he plucks Billee from his bride on the very steps of the altar (Finale: "Tis Hard by Fate Thus to Be Parted'). Flapper's other rival, Christopher Crab, finds that being part of a villainous conspiracy does not necessarily stop one from being hooked by it, as he too comes under the press ganger's hand and is carried off to serve his country on the high seas. Even Sir Mincing Lane cannot help when the King's navy calls and, as Arabella sobs regretfully over her father's shoulder, Billee Taylor goes to sea.

ACT 2

It is two years before the *Thunderbomb* returns to England and drops anchor at Spithead ('Back Again, Back Again'/Ballet/Black Cook's Dance). Christopher Crab, still striving to be taken seriously as a villain ('The Poor Wicked Man'), has not done very well in the navy. He is still a common sailor whilst Billee has risen in the ranks as a result of a deed of great heroism in action and is now Lieutenant Taylor. The rise in his rank has been responsible for a rise in the virtuous ex-gardener's expectations and Lieutenant Billee is altogether more responsive to the advances of upper-class Arabella ('The Ballad of the Billow') than the virtuous gardener could ever have permitted himself to be.

Sir Mincing, dazzled by the reports of the young man's exploit, is delighted to allow his daughter to wed the dashing Lieutenant and, indeed, he is happy to make a large gift of cash to his prospective son-in-law ('By Rule of Three'). Pulling forth a wallet full of notes, he forcefully exchanges it for the young man's empty wallet which he hurls into the sea. But Billee, far from being pleased, seems disproportionately distraught at the loss of his portfolio and he rushes down to the water to try to recover his property.

No sooner has he gone than a boat from another ship heaves into port with a fine young sailor at its prow ('The Faithful Crew'). But this complement of sailors are no common sailors: they are Phoebe and her girlfriends who all set to sea in pursuit of Billee on the day of the fatal wedding and who have spent nearly two bootless years tracking the vanished bridegroom round the world. Phoebe has taken the name of Richard Carr, and it is as Richard that she finds herself reprimanded for not saluting an officer on the quay. Her heart stops still, for the officer is none other than her long-lost Billee. To her dismay, he does not recognise her and treats her to a discourse on manners ('In Days Gone By') when she would fain have him speak of love.

Phoebe is musing on her strange encounter when another old acquaintance heaves to in the person of Captain Flapper. Once again her sailor suit means that she goes unrecognised, but she is not displeased to hear the Captain reminisce longingly on the appealing attributes of the girl he loved and lost: 'Trim Little Phoebe'. When he tells her of Billee's elevation and of his relationship with Arabella, Phoebe's dander goes up, and when Sir Mincing Lane approaches at the head of his troop of volunteers ('With Fife and Drum') she offers to join up so that she may follow Billee and Arabella and keep an eye on them. The men of the *Thunderbomb* are not keen to see a naval chappie exchange salty blue for an army coat of red and they dissuade Richard from such a hasty action ('Don't Go For to Leave Us, Richard Carr'), but Flapper understands: it is something to do with 'Love! Love! Love' that drives the young man to such an action.

Finally, someone recognises Phoebe. It is Christopher Crab and he is only too delighted to be the bearer of as much bad news about Billee and Arabella as he can. He convinces Phoebe that her beloved is about to wed the daughter of the self-made knight and fosters the notion that she must take revenge on her faithless lover. Phoebe arms herself with a handy pistol ('See Here, My Lads, What Would You Do?') and prepares to stalk her prey, as Crab watches from the safety of a convenient lamppost. When the jilted girl hears Billee and Arabella discussing their wedding plans she can contain herself no longer and, summoning her courage, she lets off the pistol. Unfortunately she is not very experienced with guns and the bullet heads not for Billee but for the malicious Crab, sending him tumbling from his lamppost into the sea.

31

The noise brings everyone running and Richard Carr is arrested and ordered to be shot for trying to kill his superior officer. Now it is time for Phoebe to unmask (Quarrelling Duet: 'Stay, Stay For I Am No Man') and declare herself. As she is comforted by Captain Flapper, Ben Barnacle fishes the punctured Crab from the sea and, lo!, clasped in his hand is Billee's wallet. Billee is too anxious to regain his property, and Flapper scents a rat. He snatches the wallet and opens it, and inside he finds a document. It is a letter from the French commander who witnessed the escapade which made Billee's fame and it proves that he is a fraud ('This Is a Statement Most Untoward'). The brave feat of arms which won the battle was not the work of cowardly Billee Taylor but of valiant Richard Carr.

Bravery must be rewarded and cowardice punished so, while Billee is reduced to the ranks, Phoebe is promoted to the rank of Lieutenant Carr and fated to be mated to her superior officer, Captain Flapper, without delay.

A new version of *Billee Taylor* was prepared by Stephens and Solomon in 1893 for Richard D'Oyly Carte's touring companies in Britain. Arabella's 'The Ballad of the Billow' was cut, 'A Guileless Orphan' was replaced by 'A Wilful Girl', and 'By Rule of Three' and 'Trim Little Phoebe' were added to the score along with a song for Eliza, 'Benny, Dear'. The song 'The Two Rivers' was alternatively known as 'Yesterday and Tomorrow'.

PATIENCE

or Bunthorne's Bride, an aesthetic opera in two acts by W S Gilbert. Music by Arthur Sullivan. Produced at the Opera Comique, London, 23 April 1881 with George Grossmith (Bunthorne), Rutland Barrington (Grosvenor), Leonora Braham (Patience) and Alice Barnett (Lady Jane), and subsequently played at the Savoy Theatre from 10 October 1881. Revived there 7 November 1900 with Walter Passmore, Henry Lytton, Isabel Jay and Rosina Brandram and 4 April 1907 with C H Workman, John Clulow, Clara Dow and Louie Rene. Played subsequently in repertoire by the D'Oyly Carte Opera Company. Produced by the English National Opera at the London Coliseum 9 October 1969 with Derek Hammond-Stroud, Emile Belcourt, Wendy Baldwin and Heather Begg.

Produced at the Standard Theatre, New York, 22 September 1882 with J H Ryley, James Barton, Carrie Burton and Augusta Roche. Produced at the Lyric Theatre 6 May 1912 with De Wolf Hopper, Cyril Scott, Christine Nielson and Eva Davenport.

Produced at the Carltheater, Vienna, 28 May 1887 as *Patience (Dragoner und Dichter)*.

Produced at Kroll's Theater, Berlin, 30 April 1887.

CHARACTERS

Colonel Calverley
Major Murgatroyd   } *Officers of Dragoon Guards*
Lieutenant the Duke of Dunstable

Reginald Bunthorne, *a fleshly poet*
Archibald Grosvenor, *an idyllic poet*
Mr Bunthorne's solicitor
The Lady Angela ⎫
The Lady Ella ⎬ *rapturous maidens*
The Lady Saphir ⎪
The Lady Jane ⎭
Patience, *a dairymaid*

ACT 1

In the environs of Castle Bunthorne, a chorus of 'Twenty Lovesick Maidens' is grouped in artistically arranged poses. Clad in medieval garb, plucking the occasional lute-string, these devotees are revelling in the utter sublimity of total infatuation with the aesthetic poet Reginald Bunthorne. But the corpulent Lady Jane warns them that they can expect no return for their adoration for the moment. Reginald is madly in love, this week at least, with the local dairymaid, Patience.

The lovesick maidens are horrified. This cannot be! Why, Patience avers, nay boasts, that love is a closed book to her and she duly arrives on the scene to confirm her statement in a pretty song ('I Cannot Tell What This Love May Be'). She also brings the news that the 35th Dragoon Guards are in the village, the very Dragoons to whom, last year, all these ladies were enthusiastically engaged. But the lovesick maidens want none of such fleshly creatures. Since those days their tastes have become etherealised, their perceptions exalted. They leave such paltry things as Dragoons for Patience, and parade off in medieval groups.

The Dragoons, of course, have no notion of such a drastic change in the feminine temperature in the village and arrive in jolly military fashion with their Colonel extolling their merits in self-satisfied song ('If You Want a Receipt For a Popular Mystery'). They are thunderstruck when they see their ladies trooping after a funny-looking fellow with long hair and pointedly shunning the military. Bunthorne, for the funny-looking fellow is he, indulges in some aesthetic antics (while keeping a sharp eye on the adulation of the ladies) and finally produces a poem for their benefit. 'Oh, Hollow! Hollow! Hollow!', he recites and departs, leaving his entourage to their ecstasies. When the officers dare to approach their ladies, they are met scornfully. They are not Empyrean, they are not Della Cruscan, they are not even Early English and their uniforms are in primary colours! The officers are scandalised: their uniforms have always been as successful in the courts of Venus as in the field of Mars ('When I First Put This Uniform On').

Alone, Bunthorne admits in soliloquy that his aestheticism is nothing but a sham. He loathes dirty greens and Japanoiserie, but he does love being adored so it seems he must keep up the pretence ('If You're Anxious for to Shine'). When Patience approaches he turns on his act for her benefit but, to his amazement, she does not succumb. She even goes so far as to say that she

33

doesn't care for poetry. He decides to unmask. He loves her. If she likes he will cut his hair and be extremely jolly. Patience is bewildered. Love, so she has been told, is something which one feels for elderly relatives, so how can she be expected to love Bunthorne? He is, please, never to mention such a subject again. Bunthorne, wounded, begs her to keep her rejection of his offer secret so as not to harm his relationships with the other young ladies.

Patience, puzzled at this episode, asks the Lady Angela to define 'love' for her more precisely and when Angela goes into rapturous descriptions, capping her recital with the pronouncement that love is 'the one unselfish emotion in the whirlpool of grasping greed', Patience becomes most upset. How horrid she must be, how selfish, never to have experienced love. If love is a duty, why she will set about falling in love right away. Before bedtime if she can. She will base it on the feelings she had for a little boy she knew when she was four years old ('Long Years Ago').

As the ingenuous maiden ponders on who might be deserving of love, a stranger enters ('Prithee Pretty Maiden'). It is Archibald Grosvenor, her childhood friend, grown-up, gorgeous, a poet and in love with her. How marvellously convenient. All is solved. She will love Archibald. But horror! If he is the acme of perfection, the idol of every woman he has ever encountered, surely there can be nothing unselfish, nothing duteous in loving him? She is plain, so there is nothing against his loving her but she, alas, may not love him in return.

As the finale begins, a miserable Bunthorne appears surrounded by excited maidens and impatient Dragoons. Heartbroken by Patience's rejection, he has decided to end it all: he will raffle himself amongst all comers. As the lottery begins, however, Patience appears. Hold! she will be his bride. Any maiden who devotes herself to loving Bunthorne must be exceptionally unselfish, so she is his. The hopes of all the other ladies are laid waste but, just as the Dragoons look likely to reclaim their own, who should appear on the scene but Archibald. Instantaneously, the maidens become lovesick once more, but this time, to the horror of Grosvenor, Bunthorne and Patience, the object of their utter devotion is Archibald the all-right!

ACT 2

Amongst the maidens, only Lady Jane remains faithful to Reginald. Her charms are ripe, she warns. In fact already they are decaying, and accompanying herself on the violoncello she sings a hymn to ageing ('Silvered Is the Raven Hair'). The other maidens troop around at the hem of Archibald's robe, gobbling up his limericks as they once gourmandised themselves on Reginald's obscurities, and they are barely discouraged by his pointed narration of the tale of 'The Magnet and the Churn', in which the magnet, to which every tin object was attracted, was unable to attract the silver churn for which he yearned. His 'churn' is Patience who takes time off from her duteous attentions to Reginald to ensure that Archibald is still in love with her.

Bunthorne, egged on by the undetachable Jane, is not at all keen on

Patience's continuing interest in 'dear Archibald' and accuses her of not knowing what love is. She, sighing, wishes that she didn't ('Love Is a Plaintive Song'). It would clearly be much more agreeable to be allowed to love Archibald. Bunthorne unburdens his irritation to the faithful Jane: ever since Grosvenor arrived his life has been all wrong. The fellow is so insipid. Well, if that is what they want he too can be insipid ('So Go to Him and Say to Him'). He will get his adulation back by playing the wretched fellow at his own game.

Change is clearly in the air, for now the Dragoons have decided to go with the fashion and they turn up decked out in medieval greens and greys (Trio: 'It's Clear That Medieval Art'), making brave tries at aesthetic poses which impress the ladies Angela and Saphir enormously. The two of them agree that if Grosvenor turns out to be impervious to their charms, as they have reason to suspect he may, they might not be indifferent to receiving offers from the Colonel, the Major and the Duke. The only problem is that there are three officers and only two ladies ('If Saphir I Choose to Marry').

Grosvenor has sent all the girls from him and is enjoying a half-holiday from adulation when Bunthorne corners him. With unmentionable threats he coerces Grosvenor into a haircut, a change of garb and commonplace conversation, all calculated to turn the adoring maidens from Archibald and back to him. Since this is a consummation for which Grosvenor would be only too thankful, and since Bunthorne's threats provide an element of compunction which frees him from his duty to the beautiful, he agrees. Henceforth he will be the most ordinary of young men, while Bunthorne shall model himself on Grosvenor so that he may be adored as before ('When I Go Out of Door').

When Patience finds a new Bunthorne, blithe, mild and amiable, she is delighted. It can no longer be a duty to love him so, with respect, she must withdraw. Bunthorne is horrified, and even more so when the other ladies do not return to him. They have decided that if Archibald the all-right has decreed a change in fashion away from aestheticism, then it must be all right to follow his dictates. Now that he is a commonplace young man, Patience too can love him and still be correct. Only Jane is still true to her first love and Bunthorne is obliged to be thankful for this one large mercy. But then the trumpets flourish. The wealthy and plain Duke of Dunstable is about to select a bride and, being a self-denying fellow, he chooses the plainest of the village girls: Jane. As the Dragoons pair off with their girls, only one man is left without a bride—Reginald Bunthorne.

RIP VAN WINKLE

a comic opera in three acts by Henry Brougham Farnie, Henri Meilhac and Philippe Gille based on *The Legend of Sleepy Hollow* and *Rip van Winkle* by Washington Irving. Music by Robert Planquette. Produced at the Comedy Theatre, London, 14 October

1882 with Fred Leslie (Rip), Violet Cameron (Gretchen), Lionel Brough (Nick), W S Penley (Derrick), W S Rising (Hans), Louis Kelleher (Peter) and Sadie Martinot (Katrina). Revived there 6 September 1884 with Leslie, Berthe Latour, Harry Paulton, Clavering Power, Henry Walsham, Kelleher and Miss Coote.

Produced at the Standard Theatre, New York, 28 November 1882 with William T Carleton, Selina Dolaro, Richard Mansfield, W H Seymour, Lyn Cadwaladr, J H Ryley and Sallie Reber.

Produced at the Theater an der Wien, Vienna, as *Rip-Rip* in a version by Ferdinand Gumbert and Eduard Jacobsen 22 December 1883.

Produced at Dresden, 3 May 1884 and at the Walhalla Theater, Berlin, 13 November 1886. Played at the Theater des Westens 21 November 1903 with Julius Spielmann (Rip), Wellhof (Derrick) and Mary Hagen (Lisbeth).

Produced in a revised version at the Théâtre des Folies-Dramatiques, Paris, 11 November 1884 as *Rip!* with Brémont (Rip), Mme Scalini (Nelly), Darman (Nick), Péricaud (Derrick), Delaunay (Jack), Simon-Max (Ischabod) and Mily-Meyer (Kate) and revived there in 1889 with Huguet as Rip. Produced at the Théâtre de la Gaîté 18 October 1894 with Soulacroix, Mme Bernaert, Dekernel, Mauzin, Lucien Noël, Paul Fugère and Mariette Sully (Kate), in 1900 with Lucien Noël, in 1902 with Noël and Jeanne Petit, in 1913 with Dezair and at the Gaîté-Lyrique in 1915 with Lucien Noël. Produced at the Théâtre Mogador 29 October 1920 with Léon Ponzio (Rip) and Mlle Mathieu-Lutz (Nelly). Produced at the Théâtre de la Porte Saint-Martin May 1933 with André Baugé. Produced at the Gaîté-Lyrique 25 December 1938 with Baugé and Suzanne Baugé.

CHARACTERS

Rip van Winkle
Nelly (Gretchen), *his wife*
Lowena (Alice), *their daughter*
Nick Vedder, *the landlord of the Hudson's Arms*
Jan, *his son*
Kate (Katrina), *his daughter*
Ischabod (Peter van Dunk), *her lover*
Jacinthe, *Vedder's servant*
Derrick von Hans, *the burgomaster*
Jack (Hans van Slous), *his son*
Captain Pickly (Captain Hugh Rowley)
Captain Henrik Hudson
Goblin Steward, Diedrich Knickerbocker, Four Lieutenants, etc.

ACT 1

In 1763, in a little village in the Catskills of America, the townsfolk are gathering for a ceremony to change the name of the local tavern from the 'Henrik Hudson' to the 'King George III' in subservience to their beloved English overlords ('Vive le Meilleur des Rois'). The local burgomaster, Derrick von Hans, presides at the ceremony as the innkeeper, Nick Vedder, lifts the new inn sign into place. Amongst the watching crowd is Kate, the innkeeper's daughter, who has recently returned from boarding school bringing with her a pretender to her hand, the penniless but hopeful medical graduate, Ischabod, whom she is encouraging to approach her father for permission to marry her.

The pompous burgomaster is quick to notice the disloyal absence of the easy-going hunter Rip van Winkle from the ceremony. Derrick holds a grudge against Rip as several years earlier they both courted the pretty Nelly and the lady chose to wed Rip. Derrick has never been able to understand why, as he is the most important and the richest man in the neighbourhood while Rip is well known as a penniless layabout who, even now, wanders unprofitably round the mountains, failing to bring back sufficient game to feed his wife and little daughter.

Rip arrives at the tavern in time to chalk up yet another drink to his long credit and to expound his otiose creed ('Vive la Paresse'). It is a creed which even his loving Nelly finds it hard to accept. Although she chides him only lightly ('Quel Chagrin, Hélas'), she gives little credence to his promises that one day he will make her rich and leisured. There is clearly no manner in which he will become rich by industry, nor by wandering in the mountains as he does, unless by chance he should uncover the fabled pirate treasure of Captain Henrik Hudson, said to have been buried in the Catskills a hundred years ago.

The treasure is said to have a curse on it: whosoever shall disturb it shall come face to face with the ghostly crew of Hudson's ship and shall fall into twenty years deep sleep (Legend of the Catskills: 'Aux Montagnes de Kaatskill'). Today Rip has more immediate troubles to deal with. His carelessness in financial matters has led him to borrow a hundred dollars from Derrick, putting up his property as collateral. The bill has run its term and now Derrick is claiming his due. Swearing that he will find the money to save his Nelly's home, Rip goes off towards the mountains.

Ischabod, in the meanwhile, is not having any noticeable success in winning over Kate's father to his nuptial cause. He admits he is penniless, but that is only because the villagers here have such stubborn rude health. One day there will be lots of sick people and he will be a very successful doctor ('L'Avenir Avec Ses Féeries'). But Nick's refusals have a hollow ring. The innkeeper has an Achilles heel in the form of his love for his own servant girl, the pert Jacinthe, and he wonders if his daughter and his future son-in-law will accept their father marrying his serving maid ('Écoutez, Je Vais Tout Vous Dire').

The British Captain Pickly visits the village in search of agitators who are said to be trying to foment revolt in the country by spreading large bribes among the population as a reward for staging disruptive and disloyal scenes. To check these plotters, the British have decided to build a strategic outpost in the village and the spot they have chosen for their fortress is the very land where Rip's home stands. Pickly is willing to purchase this land at an enormous price. Derrick is delighted. There is no prospect of Rip being able to pay back the hundred dollars that day: by the evening the land will be his and he can sell it to the British at vast profit.

Rip returns with his little daughter, Lowena, bouncing on his shoulder and Jack, the burgomaster's son, running alongside. The two little children are already sweethearts and Rip laughingly imagines them wed ('Mes Enfants, Sachez Qu'En Ménage'/'C'est Malgré Moi Si J'Ose'). Derrick is highly indignant at the thought of his son having anything to do with a van Winkle but, for the moment, he has more serious business to hand. He suggests to Rip that, instead of confiscating his land, he will purchase it from him at a good price on the condition that Rip leave the area for ever.

Rip refuses roundly and, to Derrick's amazement, pours gold on to the table in front of him, enough gold to pay all his debts and leave some over. As Rip calls for drinks all round, the tonwsfolk look on amazed. But, balked and furious, Derrick has not yet finished. As the finale gets under way, he holds up the gold. It is foreign coin! Rip is one of those in the pay of foreign agents against good King George. Rip will not answer to the charge nor admit the source of his sudden wealth and, as the British soldiers are heard approaching the town square, he runs in panic from the inn. Nelly, Kate and Jacinthe lead the women of the town in blocking the chase of the military as Rip makes good his escape.

ACT 2
Rip makes his way up into his beloved mountains to hide, and the townswomen follow him at a distance (Lantern Chorus) with Nelly at their head, desperate to find her husband ('Pour Marcher Dans la Nuit Obscure'). When they meet, Nelly hears from Rip that he did indeed find the gold here in the mountains and that the coins with which he paid his debt were very likely taken from Hudson's hoard. There is much, much more where that gold came from, and the next day he will bring it down to the town. They will be rich at last, and she can have everything she has ever wanted ('Si Je la Veux, Cette Immense Richesse').

When the soldiers are heard approaching in the distance (Patrol Chorus), Rip and Nelly are obliged to part and, while he hides, she succeeds in persuading the burgomaster to renounce the search and return to town, promising him that if Rip should not come back to clear his name she might just look on Derrick again and this time with more favour.

Back at the inn, the amorous affairs of the Vedder family are finally getting worked out as Ischabod assures Nick that he hasn't the slightest objection to Jacinthe as a mother-in-law, provided that he may wed Kate ('Amour, Douce Ivresse').

Up in the mountains, Rip takes a few healthy draughts from his hip-flask as the weather breaks above him into a tumult of thunder and lightning. It is a fearsome night, and all around him he seems to hear voices answering back his own (Echo Song: 'Non, Non, Trembler C'Est Folie'). Perhaps it is Nelly's silly recollection of the famous legend getting to him. He wishes he were back in his own little house but, since he must, he will sleep out for the night in the warmth and dryness of the cavern from where he took the gold.

Suddenly he sees the figure of a demon dwarf approaching, carrying a cask. He cannot be sure whether he is waking or sleeping as he relieves the dwarf of his load and follows him first down into a valley where a fiery lake nestles amongst high mountains and then to the very place where lies the golden treasure of Hudson. Around him, phantoms appear one by one (Choeur à Bouches Fermées) culminating in an apparition of Captain Hudson himself ('Bon Vent, Bon Vent') as the dwarf challenges Rip to a ghostly game of ninepins. His thirst is damped in other-worldly wine (Drinking Song) and seductive women dance around him until Hudson pronounces his sentence: Rip is condemned to sleep through twenty years. Crying aloud to his Nelly, Rip falls under the demons' spell.

ACT 3

A group of woodcutters (Woodcutters' Chorus) awakens Rip in the place where he fell asleep. But the handle of his gun has crumbled to dust in his hand. Although he does not know it, twenty years have passed. Down in the village, the little houses of the earlier period have been replaced by large mansions and Nick Vedder's tavern has become a great inn, run by young Jan, his son.

There is to be a celebration that day, for Nelly, after twenty years awaiting the return of her husband, has decided that he must be dead and has agreed to marry Derrick ('Fêtons les Nouveaux Époux') solely to win permission for Jack and Lowena to be wed to each other. Ischabod and Kate have long been married and there are twenty children to prove it ('Un' Bonn' Fois Pour Tout's Apprenez'), but the younger pair still await the burgomaster's blessing. They have kept their love bright through so many difficulties that they wonder if now, when those difficulties are taken away, it will be quite the same (Letter Song: 'Oh! Non, Pour les Amours').

Rip returns to the village and cannot get his bearings. No one in the town recognises the old man and he recognises no one. Even his Nelly rejects him scornfully and he rejects her. This elderly lady is never his lovely wife ('Mais R'gardez Donc'). He takes Lowena to be Nelly and when he realises that she is, in fact, his daughter he manages to convince her of his identity by recalling to her the song he sang to her and Jack in their childhood ('Mais Non, Je Ne Vous Connais Pas'/'C'est Malgré Moi Si J'Ose'). Lowena runs off to find her mother and break the news of Rip's return but, in the meanwhile, the men of the town, led by Derrick ('Où Donc Est-Il, le Brigand'), descend on the inn armed with pitchforks and pikes to drive the vagabond from the village. Once again, Rip is chased from his home and flees back to the mountains.

ACT 4

The village folk are enjoying a festival in the mountain glade where Rip disappeared. Jacinthe and Nick are happy, Kate and Ichabod no less, but Nelly upbraids Derrick for the unfounded accusation against her husband which caused him to flee. Derrick is unrepentant: it was a way to defeat Rip and win Nelly for himself. He can no longer hope to do so, for Nelly is a wealthy woman, having sold her home to the British as a site for their fortress, and she is interested only in finding her husband. For the third act has not happened. It has passed only in the mind of Rip van Winkle, drunkenly sleeping off the contents of his hip-flask in the cavern where he took shelter.

The villagers make a great noise ('Ohé, Rip!') and soon the bleary-eyed Rip appears before them, his brain still befuddled by his mighty dream. He is thrilled to find that he is not, after all, an old man with a grey beard and that his Nelly is still a lovely young woman (Air de la Jeunesse: 'O, Jeunesse'). He will have nothing further to do with treasures and phantoms and they can all return happily to their homes where Derrick, given the new financial status of the van Winkle family, happily agrees to the very long-term engagement of little Jack and little Lowena.

Rip van Winkle was specifically composed for the Comedy Theatre, London, and for Fred Leslie who created the role of Rip. Following its great success in London and throughout Britain it was staged in other countries, most notably in France where is was largely revised by its authors and its composer before presentation at the Folies-Dramatiques. Many of the principal numbers were rewritten or re-allocated and music originally written for one song and situation sometimes transferred to another. The French version proved to be equally as successful as its English counterpart and made itself a long-lasting feature of the French musical theatre. A revival in 1894 was the occasion for further alterations, largely with the goal of shortening the show, and several musical pieces including the duet 'Il Est un Pays ou Mon Rêve' (originally The Canoe Song), much of the long dream scene with its solos for the phantom captain's lieutenants, and Rip's third act song 'Au Sein des Mers' (originally 'Truth in the Well') were eliminated. A new song, the Air de la Jeunesse, was inserted and the finale rewritten, leaving the version of *Rip!* which has subsequently been widely performed and which is described here. The names of the characters used in the original English version are given in parentheses in the cast list.

IOLANTHE

or The Peer and the Peri, a fairy opera in two acts by W S Gilbert. Music by Arthur Sullivan. Produced at the Savoy Theatre, London, 25 November 1882 with George Grossmith (Lord Chancellor), Alice Barnett (Fairy Queen), Jessie Bond (Iolanthe), Leonora Braham (Phyllis) and Richard Temple (Strephon). Revived there 7 December 1901 with Walter Passmore, Rosina Brandram, Louie Pounds, Isabel Jay and Henry Lytton, and 11 June 1907 with C H Workman, Louie Rene, Jessie Rose, Clara Dow and Richard Green. Played subsequently in repertoire by the D'Oyly Carte Opera Company. Produced at Sadler's Wells Theatre 24 January 1962 with Eric Shilling, Heather Begg, Patricia Kern, Elizabeth Harwood and Julian Moyle.

Produced at the Standard Theatre, New York, 25 November 1882 with J H Ryley, Augusta Roche, Marie Jansen, Sallie Reber and William T Carleton. Produced at the

Casino Theatre 12 May 1913 with De Wolf Hopper, Kate Condon, Viola Gillette, Cecil Cunningham and George Macfarlane. Produced at the Plymouth Theatre 19 April 1926 with Ernest Lawford, Vera Ross, Adele Sanderson, Lois Bennett and William Williams.

CHARACTERS

The Lord Chancellor
Earl of Mountararat
Earl Tolloller
Private Willis *of the Grenadier Guards*
Strephon, *an Arcadian shepherd*
The Queen of the Fairies
Iolanthe, *a fairy, Strephon's mother*
Phyllis, *an Arcadian shepherdess and ward in Chancery*
Celia ⎫
Leila ⎬ *fairies*
Fleta ⎭

ACT 1

In the idyllic setting of an Arcadian landscape, a flight of fairies is 'Tripping Hither, Tripping Thither', going through the various motions appropriate to nineteenth century fairies but without enormous enthusiasm or comprehension. They have not been able to frolic with their accustomed fleetness of foot for twenty-five years now, since the awful day when their Queen banished Iolanthe, the life and soul of their fairy revels, from fairyland for the ultimate sin of marrying a mortal person. It went against the grain, for the Queen too loved the enterprising Iolanthe: was it not she who had accomplished the unlikely task of teaching the portly Queen to dive into a dewdrop, to curl herself inside a buttercup and to swing upon a cobweb? But fairy law postulates death as the penalty for such a revolutionary crime as Iolanthe's and the best the Queen could do was commute the sentence to one of exile.

To her horror, Iolanthe chose to expiate her marriage at the bottom of a nasty, damp stream amongst the water weed and frogs. It has worried the Queen for a whole quarter of a century and it does not take much persuasion for her to agree to revoke the banishment order and call Iolanthe back to fairyland (Invocation). Iolanthe can now tell the Queen that the reason she chose to live at the bottom of this particular stream was to be near the son of her forbidden marriage, Strephon. He, of course, is only half a fairy (the top half, his legs are mortal) and he is currently employed as an Arcadian shepherd ('Good Morrow, Good Mother').

Strephon, at the present time, has a very mortal preoccupation. The Lord Chancellor, for reasons best known to himself, will not give his consent for Strephon to wed his ward in Chancery sweetheart, the shepherdess Phyllis, an innocent Arcadian creature who has no idea of his semi-fairyhood ('Good Morrow, Good Lover'). But, in spite of the Lord Chancellor, they can sing happily of their love ('None Shall Part Us From Each Other') for they have a daring plan to wed that very day in defiance of the law.

41

The strains of a patrician march bring on the massed choir of the House of Lords ('Loudly Let the Trumpet Bray!'), followed by the Lord Chancellor himself. This august gentleman is suffering from a horrid irritation with his position ('The Law Is the True Embodiment'), for every day he has to sit on his woolsack giving away pretty wards in Chancery to presentable young applicants, but never, oh never, is there one for him. The one he would like (and so would the rest of the House of Lords) is Phyllis, and he is in the process of plucking up the courage to apply to himself in his official capacity for permission to propose to her.

Lord Tolloller ('Of All the Young Ladies I Know') and Lord Mountararat are more forthcoming but, in spite of Tolloller's plea to 'Spurn Not the Nobly Born', Phyllis turns them both down, announcing the fateful news that her heart is given. As the peers exhibit mass horror (''Neath This Blow'), Strephon rushes on to gather Phyllis into his arms and to face the wrath of the Lord Chancellor who not only puts a firm stop to the day's wedding but delivers a song detailing his own preoccupation with duteous behaviour ('When I Went to the Bar as a Very Young Man').

Iolanthe assures her son that, from the waist down, he is not under the Chancellor's jurisdiction, and promises to get the Fairy Queen to intervene on his behalf ('When Darkly Looms the Day'). The grateful boy hugs his mother delightedly but Phyllis, who oversees the hug, is highly upset at the idea of her lover embracing a pretty young lady whom she has great difficulty in believing to be his aged parent ('In Babyhood Upon Her Lap I Lay') and she ends up tearfully rejecting her seemingly faithless lover and plighting herself to either Mountararat or Tolloller, she's indifferent as to which ('For Riches and Rank I Do Not Long').

In answer to Strephon's distressed call, his fairy aunts arrive and the Queen indignantly confirms Strephon's story. When the Lord Chancellor, taking her for a schoolmistress, tells her to go away and stop pestering them, the furious fay reveals her identity and calls down the massed thunders of her fairy powers against him. Strephon shall go into Parliament where every bill he promulgates shall be magically passed, including some dissolving the most prized privileges of the parliamentary classes. As the peers quail in horror, the act ends in the promised chaos.

ACT 2

In the Palace yard at Westminster, Private Willis is standing guard ('When All Night Long') while the fairies laugh amongst themselves about the havoc Strephon is causing in parliament. Mountararat and Tolloller are not at all happy with this fiddling with the traditional House of Lords ('When Britain Really Ruled the Waves') and as a result are not as responsive as they might be to the gentle flirting of the fairies Leila and Celia who are perfectly sensible to the charm of the British aristocrat ('In Vain to Us You Plead'). The Queen catches her underlings at this un-fairy activity and tells them off roundly. They should have a little more self-control. She too has yearnings but does she succumb? Certainly not ('Oh, Foolish Fay').

42

Although she is engaged to both Mountararat and Tolloller, Phyllis is perfectly miserable even when the two Lords, after beginning by bickering over which of them should have her for his wife, decide on second thoughts that their own friendship is more important than mere wedlock ('In Friendship's Name'). The Lord Chancellor, too, is unhappy. Love is giving him nightmares (Nightmare Song: 'When You're Lying Awake'), especially as he has had to turn down yet another application by himself to his other self with regard to Phyllis. Tolloller and Mountararat encourage him to try again ('If You Go In').

Strephon, in spite of his parliamentary triumphs, is also miserable but when he meets Phyllis he finds that she is now rather more willing to believe in him, particularly when he explains about his mother being a fairy. Whenever she sees him kissing a very young lady, she will know in future that it is a very elderly aunt. And she is quite prepared to marry half a mortal man she does love rather than two whole ones she doesn't ('If We're Weak Enough to Tarry'). Please, will Iolanthe be a good mother and square things with the Lord Chancellor? Under a circumstance such as this, Iolanthe has to reveal the long-hidden truth: the Lord Chancellor is her husband and Strephon's father! The young people think that, on the contrary, this will make things easier but Iolanthe dare not break fairy law again. Her husband believes her dead and thus things must remain.

Unfortunately, the basic situation has suddenly undergone another change. The Lord Chancellor, after a particularly fine bit of pleading by himself to himself, has finally been able to see his way clear to grant his own application to himself to wed Phyllis. When the veiled Iolanthe begs him for a verdict in favour of her son ('He Loves! If in the Bygone Years') she is horrified to hear that her husband intends to wed Strephon's girl himself. As fairy voices echo warningly, she breaks her vows and reveals herself to the Lord Chancellor. Iolanthe! thou livest?

The Queen of the Fairies materialises impressively. This time Iolanthe cannot escape the death penalty. But the other fairies intervene: if Iolanthe must die, so must they. They have yielded to the attractions of the peerage and have married the entire House of Lords. The Queen is flummoxed. After all, the law is the law. But the Lord Chancellor draws upon his experience as an old equity draughtsman. The insertion of one word into the relevant document will solve matters: henceforth the law shall read that every fairy must die who *don't* marry a mortal. Under such a law the Queen is able—that is to say, is obliged—to find a consort herself. The particularly personable Private Willis cannot refuse his aid to a lady in distress and, as wings sprout from his shoulders and those of the Peers, everybody flies off to fairyland for the finale .

PRINCESS IDA

or Castle Adamant, a respectful operatic perversion in two acts and a prologue (later three acts) of Tennyson's *The Princess*, a revised version of *The Princess* (Olympic Theatre, 8 January 1870) by W S Gilbert. Music by Arthur Sullivan. Produced at the Savoy Theatre, London, 5 January 1884 with Leonora Braham (Ida), George Grossmith (Gama), Rutland Barrington (Hildebrand) and Rosina Brandram (Blanche). Produced at the Prince's Theatre 23 January 1922 with Winifred Lawson, Henry Lytton, Leo Sheffield and Bertha Lewis.

Produced at the Fifth Avenue Theatre, New York, 11 February 1884 with Cora S Tanner, J H Ryley, Sgr Broccolini and Genevieve Reynolds and revived there 22 November 1887 with Geraldine Ulmar, Joseph W Herbert, Broccolini and Alice Carle. Produced at the Shubert Theatre 13 April 1925.

CHARACTERS

King Hildebrand
Hilarion, *his son*
Cyril
Florian
King Gama
Arac, *his son*
Guron, *another son*
Scynthius. *a third son*
Princess Ida, *Gama's daughter*
Lady Blanche, *Professor of Abstract Science*
Lady Psyche, *Professor of Humanities*
Melissa, *Lady Blanche's daughter*
Sacharissa
Chloe
Ada

ACT 1

At King Hildebrand's palace, the monarch and his court are awaiting the ordained arrival of the neighbouring King Gama and his daughter, Ida. Many years ago, the baby Ida was plighted in marriage to Hildebrand's infant son, Hilarion, and today is the day appointed for her delivery. She's late ('Will Prince Hilarion's Hope Be Sadly Blighted'), and this tardiness much annoys King Hildebrand who is quite prepared to go to war with Gama if, as he suspects, his neighbour decides he will not fulfil his bond. But Gama is soon seen approaching, and Hilarion takes the opportunity for a little reverie on the subject of the bride he has not seen since he was two and she was one ('Ida Was a Twelvemonth Old'). 'From the Distant Panorama' come the three sons of Gama, the warriors Arac, Guron and Scynthius ('We Are Warriors Three') and, finally, the King himself, an unpleasant, twisted little man with a bad word for everyone ('If You Give Me Your Attention').

He has not brought Ida. He claims that this is because he has no intention of showing off such beauty and talent before the world at large, but the truth

44

is that Ida has immured herself in Castle Adamant where she rules a Women's University of a hundred pupils from which everything of male sex is excluded with an almost loony strictness. Even 'hymns' have to be referred to as 'hers'. There Hilarion must try to approach her if he would meet his promised bride. In spite of Gama's attempts at evasions ('Perhaps If You Address the Lady'), Hildebrand orders the arrest of the horrid little king and his sons. Hilarion and his friends, however, are all alight at the prospect of a hundred homophobic females ('Expressive Glances') and, as the sons of Gama are led off in chains to prison ('For a Month to Dwell In a Dungeon Cell'), the young men agree to head for Castle Adamant first thing the next morning.

ACT 2

The tales about Castle Adamant are no exaggeration. The Professor of Humanities, Lady Psyche, teaches her pupils that 'man is nature's sole mistake' and one pupil is threatened with expulsion for daring to bring a set of chessmen inside the feminine walls of the establishment. Princess Ida herself prays to Minerva to enlighten her pupils ('O Goddess Wise') and lectures determinedly on the supremacy of woman while her Professor of Abstract Philosophy, Lady Blanche, gives supporting precepts in a solo of grammatical proportions ('Come Mighty Must').

Hilarion and his friends Cyril and Florian have wasted no time in finding their way to the castle and are soon creeping carefully over the walls ('Gently, Gently'). Hilarion has only ridicule for the idea of the feminine University ('They Intend to Send a Wire to the Moon') and to him such a mass of girls is meant for only one thing. The boys don some conveniently abandoned college robes to mask their masculinity and parade predatorily about, pretending to be prospective pupils ('I Am a Maiden, Cold and Stately'). When they are stumbled upon by Ida, they pretend that they have come to enrol as members of the college, renouncing the outside world ('The World Is But a Broken Toy').

But, as luck will have it, the Lady Psyche is none other than Florian's sister and, when she appears on the scene, the men are forced to admit their identities to her. She agrees that she will not betray them, although she is well-rehearsed in the source of man's worthlessness ('The Lady and the Ape'). Little Melissa, Lady Blanche's daughter and unfamiliar with the male sex, overspies the unexpected family reunion and is enchanted by her first brush with man. She wonderingly feels the bristles on Florian's chin and soon even Psyche is admitting that there is perhaps a tiny lack of logic in Ida's teachings ('The Woman of the Wisest Wit'). Their ensemble is overheard by Lady Blanche who is not to be fooled into thinking that a baritone and two tenors can be girls, but Melissa begs her not to expose the men and reminds her that if the Prince Hilarion successfully woos Ida and the two of them are married, then Ida can no longer be head of the University which means the position will fall to her deputy, Lady Blanche ('Wouldn't You Like to Rule the Roast').

The luncheon bell rings ('Merrily Ring the Luncheon Bell'), and over their repast Ida questions the newcomers about the court of King Hildebrand. Hilarion is able to give a pretty account of himself, but Cyril drinks a little too much and bursts into a rollicking masculine song ('Would You Know the Kind of Maid') which leads to a quarrel among the men in which their disguises are ruined. Ida, leaping up in fury before this abomination, goes to rush from the scene but, in her haste, she trips and falls from an ornamental bridge into the stream. Hilarion jumps into the water and saves her, but the damply rescued Princess is not inclined to be merciful in spite of Hilarion's pretty plea ('Whom Thou Hast Chained Must Wear His Chain') and the men are marched off to the dungeons of Castle Adamant.

As they go, Melissa rushes on with news of an armed attack. King Hildebrand is at the gates with his army, challenging for his rights ('A Peppery Kind of King'). He gives Ida until the next afternoon to release Hilarion and wed him, failing which he will execute her brothers Arac, Guron and Scynthius. The Princess defies his challenge and prepares to make ready for combat.

ACT 3
The ladies arm themselves for battle ('Death to the Invader'), but when it comes to the point none of them is actually willing and able to fight and, when Gama and his sons are announced at the gates, Ida breaks the rules and allows them to be admitted. Gama is a crushed creature. Hildebrand has loaded him with such favours that he has nothing left to complain about and all joy has gone from his life ('Whene'er I Spoke Sarcastic Joke'). He can bear such bonhomie no longer. Moved by her father's tears, Ida gives in. Her philosophy is in ruins ('I Built Upon a Rock'), as she orders the castle gates to be opened to admit the masculine hordes ('When Anger Spreads His Wing').

The army are clad in lumpy armour but, as Arac delivers a mock-Handelian aria ('This Helmet I Suppose'), they shed their garb, metal piece by metal piece, until they are clearly visible as men. Ida's three brothers are still willing to fight to save her from her unwilling marriage and they face up staunchly to Hilarion and his friends, but they are defeated and, as Melissa turns to Florian and Psyche to Cyril, the Princess Ida finally admits that she just may have been in error and gives her hand to Hilarion ('With Joy Abiding').

THE MIKADO

or The Town of Titipu, a comic opera in two acts by W S Gilbert. Music by Arthur Sullivan. Produced at the Savoy Theatre, London, 14 March 1885 with George Grossmith (Ko-Ko), Richard Temple (Mikado), Leonora Braham (Yum-Yum),

Durward Lely (Nanki-Poo), Rutland Barrington (Pooh-Bah) and Rosina Brandram (Katisha). Revived there 7 June 1888 with Grossmith, Temple, Rose Hervey, J G Robertson, Barrington and Miss Brandram; 6 November 1895 with Walter Passmore, R Scott Fishe (replaced by Temple), Florence Perry, Charles Kenningham, Barrington and Miss Brandram and 28 April 1908 with C H Workman, Henry Lytton, Clara Dow, Henry Herbert, Barrington and Louie Rene. Played subsequently by the D'Oyly Carte Opera Company in repertoire. Produced at Sadler's Wells Theatre 29 May 1962 with Clive Revill, John Holmes, Marion Studholme, David Hillman, Norman Lumsden and Jean Allister. Produced at the Westminster Theatre 28 May 1979. Produced at the Cambridge Theatre 28 September 1982 and subsequently played at the Prince of Wales Theatre 16 August 1983. Played at the Old Vic by the Stratford Festival Company 29 February 1984. Produced at the London Coliseum (English National Opera) 18 September 1986 with Eric Idle, Richard Angas, Lesley Garrett, Bonaventura Bottone, Richard van Allen and Felicity Palmer.

Produced at the Museum, Chicago, 6 July 1885 and at the Union Square Theatre, New York, 20 July 1885 in an unauthorised production. Produced at the Fifth Avenue Theatre, New York, 19 August 1885 with George Thorne, Fred Federici, Geraldine Ulmar, Courtice Pounds, Fred Billington and Elsie Cameron. Produced at the Standard Theatre 20 August 1885 with J H Ryley, William H Hamilton, Verona Jarbeau, Harry S Hilliard, Thomas Whiffen and Zelda Seguin. Produced at the Madison Square Roof Garden 14 July 1902. Produced at the Casino Theatre 30 May 1910 with Jefferson de Angelis, William Danforth, Fritzi Scheff, Andrew Mack, William Pruette, Josephine Jacobs, Christie MacDonald (Pitti-Sing) and Christine Nielson (Peep-Bo). Produced at the Royale Theatre 17 September 1927 with Fred Wright as Ko-Ko. Played at the Virginia Theatre 2 April 1987 by the Stratford Festival Company.

Produced at the Carltheater, Vienna, as *Der Mikado (Ein Tag in Titipu)* 1 September 1886 and at the Theater an der Wien in a version by F Zell and Richard Genée 2 March 1888.

Produced at the Wallner Theater, Berlin, 2 June 1886 and at the Friedrich-Wilhelmstädtisches Theatre 6 December 1888.

Versions of *The Mikado* have been produced as *The Swing Mikado* (1 March 1939 New York Theatre), *The Hot Mikado* (23 March 1939, Broadhurst Theatre, New York) and *The Black Mikado* (24 April 1975, Cambridge Theatre, London)

A film version was produced in 1939 by G & S Films with Martyn Green as Ko-Ko, Jean Colin as Yum-Yum and Kenny Baker as Nanki-Poo, and another in 1967 by British Home Entertainments with John Reed (Ko-Ko) and Valerie Masterton (Yum-Yum). A 1963 film, *The Cool Mikado*, featuring Frankie Howerd, Stubby Kaye and Jill Mai Meredith, was based on *The Mikado*.

CHARACTERS

The Mikado of Japan
Nanki-Poo, *his son, disguised as a wandering minstrel and in love with Yum-Yum*
Ko-Ko, *Lord High Executioner of Titipu*
Pooh-Bah, *Lord High Everything Else*
Pish-Tush, *a noble Lord*
Yum-Yum⎫
Pitti-Sing ⎬ *three sisters—wards of Ko-Ko*
Peep-Bo ⎭

Katisha, *an elderly lady, in love with Nanki-Poo*
Go-To

ACT 1

In the courtyard of the palace of Ko-Ko, Lord High Executioner of Titipu, the local gentry are posing in Japanese attitudes reminiscent of popular pottery designs ('If You Want to Know Who We Are') when their pattern is intruded upon by a tattered young fellow with a stringed instrument. The young man, Nanki-Poo by name, describes his profession in a ballad ('A Wandering Minstrel I') and inquires as to the whereabouts of a young lady called Yum-Yum. He has, it appears, fallen in love with Yum-Yum but, until now, has quashed his passion under the knowledge that the young lady in question is engaged to be married to her guardian, the tailor Ko-Ko.

Hearing, in his self-imposed exile, that the said Ko-Ko had been condemned to death for the capital crime of flirting, he has hastily returned to Titipu. But bad news awaits him, for the noble Lord, Pish-Tush, after a dissertation on the laws against flirting ('Our Great Mikado, Virtuous Man') tells him that Ko-Ko has been reprieved and, indeed, promoted to the post of Lord High Executioner on the reasoning that since he was next in line for execution, he can't cut off anyone else's head until he's cut off his own. Thus, in Titipu, is the end of the law against flirting (and a good deal of other laws) sidestepped.

Ko-Ko's promotion has caused chaos in the Titipu hierarchy, for all the other notables have resigned en masse rather than serve with an ex-tailor, and all their posts have been unhesitatingly accepted by the lofty but opportunistic Pooh-Bah, a paragon of anguished corruptibility. As far as Yum-Yum is concerned, Pooh-Bah gives Nanki-Poo no hope ('Young Man, Despair') as the lady in question is scheduled to wed Ko-Ko that very afternoon and, as the populace announce 'Behold the Lord High Executioner!', the bridegroom-to-be himself enters to describe in song the social nuisances he should like to get rid of in his new capacity ('I've Got a Little List').

Now it is the turn of the lady in the affair to put in an appearance. Yum-Yum, accompanied by her sisters, Pitti-Sing and Peep-Bo, is returning home from school for her wedding ('Comes a Train of Little Ladies'/'Three Little Maids From School'). She is clearly indifferent to her guardian, but she is full of excitement at seeing Nanki-Poo again. Ko-Ko makes an effort at winning his little lady's esteem by having Pooh-Bah—who is an awful lot of noble Lords rolled into one—pay her and her sisters some exaggerated attentions, but Pooh-Bah finds such lèse majesté painful even when salved with large amounts of money ('So Please You, Sir, We Much Regret').

Left alone, Yum-Yum and Nanki-Poo ponder over their plight and he reveals that he is, in fact, no musician but the very son of the Mikado of Japan. He has fled his father's court to escape the marital ambitions of an elderly lady called Katisha. This unprepossessing female claimed before his royal father that he had flirted with her, and he has disguised himself as a second trombonist in the Titipu town band in order to avoid the marriage which would be the legal consequence of such a dalliance. The two young lovers dare not even express their love because of the nation's stringent laws against unconnubial behaviour, so they are obliged instead to talk of what they would do and say if they could ('Were You Not to Ko-Ko Plighted'), accompanying their song with what would seem to be the most illegal of illustrations.

Ko-Ko has worse problems to worry about than a meagre alienation of affection, for his fine new position seems to be leading him into trouble ('My Brain It Teems'). The Mikado has noticed that since the installation of the new Lord High Exectioner no executions have taken place in Titipu and he is threatening to descend in state to reduce the city to the status of a village if no one has been decapitated by the time a month has passed. Ko-Ko, if he is not to accomplish the unlikely task of cutting off his own head, must find a substitute. As he soliloquises painfully on the subject, Nanki-Poo enters with a rope. Rather than endure life without Yum-Yum, he has decided to hang himself.

Ko-Ko leaps at the chance. Instead of hanging himself, how would the young man like a month of splendidly luxurious existence at the end of which he would be prettily and relatively painlessly decapitated? Nanki-Poo agrees to postpone his death for a month on one condition. He must be married to Yum-Yum right away so as to spend that one last month in connubial bliss. But, as the celebrations and the finale begin, a melodramatic crone appears. It is the dreaded Katisha, come to claim her bridegroom ('Oh Fool, That Fleest My Hallowed Joys'). The people of Titipu laugh her aside ('For He's Going To Marry Yum-Yum') and Katisha storms off Mikado-wards brandishing her complaint.

ACT 2

In Ko-Ko's garden, Yum-Yum is surrounded by a chorus of girlfriends who are preparing her for her wedding ('Braid the Raven Hair'). Yum-Yum is pleased with her appearance and wonders artlessly why it is that she is so much more attractive than anybody else in the world ('The Sun Whose Rays'). The prospective duration of her wedded bliss, however, casts a cloud over her happiness which she attemps to dispel in a madrigal ('Brightly Dawns Our Wedding Day'). If Nanki-Poo's future fate brings a tear to her sympathetic eye, that is nothing to the reaction provoked by Ko-Ko's next piece of news. Pooh-Bah has discovered a law decreeing that a condemned man's wife has to be buried alive with his corpse. Now, Yum-Yum is very much in love with Nanki-Poo, but there are limits. On the other hand, if she doesn't marry Nanki-Poo and get buried alive, she must marry Ko-Ko. It's really a toss up as to which is the worse fate ('Here's a How-de-do').

It's a problem all round really. If Nanki-Poo isn't permitted to marry Yum-Yum then he will commit suicide instanter which puts Ko-Ko to the ghastly and virtually impossible necessity of finding another victim before the Mikado arrives. Nanki-Poo generously offers to be beheaded on the spot, but it then turns out that Ko-Ko suffers from humanity: he can't even kill a bluebottle. But does the deed really have to be done? Couldn't they just pretend that Nanki-Poo has been executed? After all, all the noble lords of the realm as incarnate in Pooh-Bah will swear an affadavit to the execution if suitably bribed. Pooh-Bah, in his capacity as Archbishop can also marry Yum-Yum and Nanki-Poo and they can run away out of the story.

With so many obliging officials to help out, the thing is soon accomplished and off the newlyweds go, just as the March of the Mikado's troops ('Miya Sama') announces a surprise visit from the supreme potentate. He has come in the company of Katisha ('From Every Kind of Man') with a song detailing his philosophy of letting punishment be suitable to the crime it is rebuking ('A More Humane Mikado') and he is eagerly greeted by Ko-Ko with news of the recent execution, described in luridly colourful detail by the Lord High Executioner and his accomplices ('The Criminal Cried').

Unfortunately, this is not the business on which the Mikado has come to Titipu at all. He has come seeking his missing son and Katisha, seizing the execution certificate, now discovers that the heir apparent has apparently been executed. The punishment for encompassing the death of the heir apparent is something lingering with boiling oil. The Mikado is ever so sorry, but the law is the law and fate does not always deal out a man's just deserts ('See How the Fates Their Gifts Allot'). If the heir apparent is dead then Ko-Ko and his accomplices really will have to join him.

Ko-Ko corners Nanki-Poo and Yum-Yum as they prepare to depart on their honeymoon. Given the circumstances, Nanki-Poo must come back to life. This time Nanki-Poo is less obliging. He is very happy with things the way they are and he has no wish to be revived, for Katisha will certainly insist on marrying him or alternatively executing him and burying Yum-Yum alive in the approved fashion. On the other hand, if Katisha were safely married, it would be a different matter altogether. In that case life would be as welcome as 'The Flowers That Bloom in the Spring'. Suppose, for example, that Ko-Ko were to marry her?

Alone, Katisha is soliloquising in melodramatic terms ('Hearts Do Not Break') when Ko-Ko comes to her, steeled to his task. He weakens her resolve with the tragic tale of a little tom-tit who died for love ('Tit Willow') and soon they are joining in a duet praising the more belligerent aspects of womanhood ('There Is Beauty in the Bellow of the Blast'). The nuptial deed done, Katisha is dragging Ko-Ko before the Mikado to add her weight to his pleas for mercy when Nanki-Poo appears, very much alive! Katisha's fury and Ko-Ko's convoluted explanations are drowned in a joyful finale ('For He's Gone and Married Yum-Yum') as the strange doings in the town of Titipu come to their mostly happy ending.

ERMINIE

a comic opera in two acts by Claxson Bellamy and Harry Paulton. Music by Edward Jakobowski. Produced at the Comedy Theatre, London, 9 November 1885 with Harry Paulton (Cadeau), Frank Wyatt (Ravannes), Florence St John (Erminie) and M A Victor (Princesse). Revived there 26 June 1886 with the same stars.

Produced at the Casino Theatre, New York, 10 May 1886 with Francis Wilson (Cadeaux), W S Daboll (Ravannes), Pauline Hall (Erminie) and Jennie Weathersby (Princesse) and played there for most of the next two years with occasional interruptions mostly with the same stars. Revived there 20 November 1889 with James T Powers, Edwin Stevens, Miss Hall and Eva Davenport; 23 May 1898 with Wilson, Harry E Dixey, Misses Hall and Weathersby; 13 May 1899 with Wilson, Thomas Q Seabrooke, Lillian Russell and Miss Weathersby; and 19 October 1903 with Wilson, William Broderick, Marguerite Sylva and Miss Weathersby. Also played at Niblo's Garden 1 April 1889 with J H Ryley, Mark Smith, Addie Cora Reed and Ruth Rose; at the Broadway Theatre 3 October 1893 with Wilson, Broderick, Amanda Fabris and Miss Weathersby; at the Bijou Theatre 23 May 1897; at the Standard Theatre 31 May 1915 wth Fred Solomon, Karl Stall, Dorothy Morton and Alice Gaillard; and at the Park Theatre 3 January 1921 with Wilson, De Wolf Hopper, Irene Williams and Miss Weathersby.

Produced at the Carltheater, Vienna in a version by F Zell and Victor Léon as *Erminy* 7 November 1890.

CHARACTERS

Marquis de Pontvert
Eugène Marcel, *his secretary*
Vicomte de Brissac
Delaunay, *a young officer*
The Sergeant
Dufois, *landlord of Le Lion D'Or*
Simon, *waiter at Le Lion D'Or*
Chevalier de Brabazon, *a guest of the Marquis*
Ravannes, *a thief*
Cadeau, *another thief*
Erminie de Pontvert, *the Marquis's daughter*
Princesse de Gramponeur, *a guest of the Marquis*
Cerise Marcel, *Eugène's sister*
Javotte, *Erminie's maid*
Marie, *the belle of the village*
Clémentine, *a flower girl*
Henri, Pierre, Antoinette, Charlotte, Jeanette, Mignon, Rosalie, Niniche, Nanine, Fanchette, *villagers*
MM St Brice, d'Auvigne, de Nailles, de Sangres, Mmes St Brice, de Lage, de Brefchamp, de Châteaulin, *guests at the château*

ACT 1

It is the time of the village fête in Pontvert, a little town somewhere in that part of France where all good comic opera villages are, and the local lads and

51

lasses are providing the traditional opening chorus ('Around in a Whirl') in a merry fashion when Javotte, personal maid to Erminie, the daughter of the local Marquis, arrives to join in the fun with her intended, the buffoonish waiter Simon. Javotte lays the scene expertly, telling the innkeeper that he may shortly expect a visit from her master, his daughter, and their high-and-mighty houseguest, the Chevalier de Brabazon. She also takes the opportunity to drop into the conversation for the audience's benefit the fact that the nobleman's household includes two poor relations, Eugène and Cerise Marcel, the orphaned children of a distant relation of Pontvert, who now fill polite positions as secretary and companion at the château.

The Marquis and his party are greeted warmly by the villagers ('Vive le Marquis'), and Erminie is democratic enough to join the village girls in making gentle fun of the foppish old Chevalier, illustrating her point with a pretty ballad on love at all ages ('When Love Is Young').

The Marquis has come down to the village to meet a new guest, the Vicomte de Brissac, son of his oldest friend and, as he now reveals, his chosen husband for Erminie. The young people are dreadfully taken aback for, unbeknown to her father, Erminie is in love with Eugène who has long been trying to find a courageous moment in which to ask the Marquis for her hand. Now it seems that it is too late and they can only console themselves with a duet ('Past and Future'). Cerise is amazed that Erminie can take this setback with such spirit, for she has herself long given in to the despairing thought that true love is hopeless. She pours out her secret: she is in love with the younger brother of the very man chosen to wed Erminie, her sweetheart in the days before ill-fortune reduced her family's circumstances.

The inn's trade is swelled by the arrival of a troop of soldiers headed by the young officer, Delaunay, and the Marquis greets the military with pleasure, marking the occasion by giving forth with a brisk ballad about his own enthusiastic experience of 'A Soldier's Life'. The purpose of Delaunay's visit, it emerges, is to track down two escaped convicts and, no sooner have the soldiers gone off to join in the fun of the fair, than these two appear: the 'gentleman thief', Ravannes, and his light-fingered but thick-witted companion, Cadeau. Ravannes proposes to take a room at the inn to change out of his ragged clothes into some which they have stolen by holding up a diligence on the road. Then it's off to Paris where the two 'Downy Jailbirds of a Feather' can 'renew our philanthropic pursuit of easing suffering humanity of its load of superabundent luxuries'.

Some adroit banter with Simon and the landlord allows Ravannes to discover that the Marquis is awaiting the arrival of the very diligence they have robbed and a guest with the initials inscribed on the portmanteau they have stolen, and he retires to wait his moment. An interlude gives Erminie the opportunity to sing the reflective 'At Midnight on my Pillow Lying' (The Dream Song), before the Marquis and the Chevalier reveal in conversation that the Vicomte whom they are awaiting is, in fact, the younger brother of the family who has succeeded to the title and, in consequence, an unknown face to them.

This is a fine cue for Ravannes who promptly presents himself as the selfsame Vicomte, equipped with stolen papers from the portmanteau and justifying his appearance with the tale of how he and his friend the Baron were attacked by thieves on the road. Cadeau, doing his unsuccessful best to pose as a Baron, constantly threatens to give the game away with his catch phrases, 'It's my first offence' and 'I can prove a h-alibi!,' and other slangy remarks which his partner slickly explains away as fashionable argot learned on an embassy to darkest Arabia. The gentleman thief is introduced to Erminie (Concerted Piece: 'The Blissful Pleasure, I Profess') as his bride-to-be and the company head for the château (Finale) as the act ends.

ACT 2

That night the Marquis throws a splendid ball for his guests as a prelude to the following day's betrothal ceremony. After Javotte and the château staff have opened the act with chorus ('Here on Lord and Lady Waiting'), chatter and an incidental song ('Woman's Dress'), Eugène and Cerise appear in the ballroom. Eugène seems to be congenitally downhearted ('Darkest the Hour') and he is deeply suspicious of the apparent Vicomte. He cannot credit that this slick dandy is the brother of the dear friend of his and Cerise's early days. The Marquis and the Chevalier are not keen on the Vicomte/Ravannes either and as for the 'Baron', why he is a perfect monster to whom, for some reason, the older ladies at the château have taken a violent fancy.

Erminie is principally engaged in keeping Ravannes at a distance while still hoping for a reprieve from this unwanted engagement ('Joy Attend on Erminie') but she maintains sufficient sense of humour to chide her despairing Eugène for his continual lugubriousness ('The Sighing Swain'). Cadeau appears in the ballroom at the head of a gaggle of guests, holding forth in his inimitable slang ('What the Dicky Birds Say') to, in particular, the elderly Princesse de Gramponeur who is utterly captivated by the way in which he has made her diamond bracelet vanish from her wrist and turned a gold necklace and a bag of money into a pair of old gloves and a bunch of grapes by his marvellous sleight of hand. She insists in seeing in him (as in everything) the very image of her dear late husband and does not quit his side for an instant.

Ravannes puts an end to his partner's festival of low comedy as a new danger threatens his impersonation: a sergeant has arrived with papers for Captain Delaunay. The military have arrested a man claiming to be the Vicomte de Brissac and wish Pontvert and the 'real' Vicomte to be present at his examination the next day. But the Marquis cannot commit himself to leaving the château for on the morrow the notary will be coming for the signing of Erminie's betrothal contract. Erminie, for the first time, now yields to sorrow and, in the show's great song 'Dear Mother, in Dreams I See Her' (The Lullaby), longs for a mother's support in her hours of trial.

She asks Ravannes if he will renounce her and refuse to sign the contract, but the thief is preoccupied with how to stop Delaunay reading the deposition of the genuine Vicomte and unmasking him before he has had time to profit materially from his stay in the château de Pontvert. Finally he agrees to help Erminie to avoid the betrothal if she will help him purloin the vital documents from Delaunay. Erminie succeeds in getting the papers for him as Cadeau and the Princesse lead the guests in a jolly gavotte ('Join in Pleasure'). While everyone else goes off to sup (Supper Chorus), Ravannes proposes to Erminie that she should elope with Eugène that very night, meaning at the same time to take his own flight with as much of the château's jewellery as possible.

The guests drift off to their bedrooms ('Good Night') and then the action starts but, in the darkness of the château's corridors, everything comes unstuck when a suit of armour strategically placed to mark the door to Erminie's room is shifted and, as a result, the errant Chevalier de Brabazon blunders in on the Princesse in her nightgown. Her screams bring the household running and Erminie's elopement is discovered.

Then, before they can escape, it is the turn of the thieves to be exposed, for Delaunay turns up with the real Vicomte who is none other than Cerise's beloved Ernest, the younger brother who has since inherited the title. Nuptial affairs are quickly resolved to the satisfaction of all the Pontverts with only the old Princesse voicing regrets over the loss of her poor dear 'Baron'. Ravannes puts in a bid for clemency for his unwitting share in bringing things to a happy ending as the finale brings down the curtain.

DOROTHY

a comedy opera in three acts by B C Stephenson. Music by Alfred Cellier. Produced at the Gaiety Theatre, London, 25 September 1886 with Marion Hood (Dorothy), Florence Dysart (Lydia), Redfern Hollins (Wilder), C Hayden Coffin (Sherwood) and Arthur Williams (Lurcher) and played subsequently at the Prince of Wales Theatre from 20 December 1886, with Marie Tempest succeeding Miss Hood and Ben Davies replacing Hollins, and at the Lyric Theatre from 17 December 1888. Produced at the Trafalgar Square Theatre 26 November 1892 with Decima Moore, Florence Dysart, Joseph Tapley, Leonard Russell and William Elton; at the New Theatre 21 December 1908 and subsequently the Waldorf Theatre 9 January 1909 with Constance Drever, Louie Pounds, John Bardesley, Coffin and Williams.

Produced at the Standard Theatre, New York, 5 November 1887 with Lillian Russell, Agnes Stone, Eugene Oudin, John E Brand and Harry Paulton.

CHARACTERS

Squire Bantam
Dorothy Bantam, *his daughter*
Lydia Hawthorne, *her cousin*
Geoffrey Wilder, *Bantam's nephew*
Harry Sherwood, *his friend*
William Lurcher, *a sherrif's officer*
Tom Strutt, *a young farmer*

John Tuppitt, *landlord of the Hop Pole Inn*
Phyllis Tuppitt, *his daughter*
Mrs Privett, *a widow*
Lady Betty, etc.

ACT 1

At the Hop Pole Inn, the local folk are making very merry over the end of the hop-picking season ('Lads and Lasses') when the landlord's daughter, Phyllis, brings her lover, Tom Strutt, to ask her father for permission to wed. Obdurate for sufficient time to make a show of it, Tuppitt eventually agrees and it is settled that the two young people shall visit the parson the very next day. But the celebratory kiss between the happy lovers is seen by two visitors, Miss Dorothy Bantam and her cousin Lydia Hawthorne from the big house, come in country skirts to join the rustic fun. Dorothy and Lydia have sworn never to marry but rather to despise all men, particularly the unknown one called Geoffrey Wilder for whom Dorothy's fond papa, Squire Bantam, has destined his daughter. For the moment it suffices them to despise poor Tom Strutt and to put exquisitely alarming ideas of masculine insufficiencies into Phyllis's head ('Be Wise in Time').

Their oath does not stop the ladies from planning to pass amongst the local boys in their disguise with the hope of damaging a heart or two; it only decrees that they shall remain unwed, and a delicious little adventure with men is, as it turns out, the first thing they happen upon. Two fine fellows on horseback arrive at the Hop Pole Inn and, taking Lydia and Dorothy for maids, call on them for service ('We're Sorry to Delay You'). Soon the cavaliers are after more than just service, for one takes a fine fancy to Dorothy and the other makes much of Lydia who is obliged to defend herself with a slap. When the two 'landlord's daughters' go off to fetch refreshments, Geoffrey Wilder, for the first gallant horseman is he, goes so far as to launch into a rapturous ballad in praise of pretty Dorcas (otherwise Dorothy) ('With Such a Dainty Dame').

Wilder and his friend Sherwood have fled from their lively life in London on account of pressing financial problems, and they are making their way to Squire Bantam's country house, far from the city and its debts. There, the errant Geoffrey is glumly aware that he will have to renounce his naughty ways and settle repentantly into the seemly life ordered for him by his uncle, a life that includes marriage with the Squire's undoubtedly dreary daughter. But right now his mind is far from Dorothy Bantam; he is anxious only to join with his friend Harry in concocting a serious flirtation with the two girls whom the landlord, joining merrily in the trick, describes as 'A Father's Pride and Joy'.

When Geoffrey introduces himself to 'Dorcas' by name, Dorothy is amazed, but she is less pleased when, as a prelude to wooing her, the young man takes to disparaging Dorothy Bantam. By now Wilder's heart is truly won and he is even ready to give up the salving money awaiting him at Chanticleer Hall to replace the lofty Dorothy at his side with this delightful

55

maid. The money side of affairs, however, quickly begins to press again. The boys have been pursued from London by William Lurcher, a bailiff ('I Am the Sherrif's Faithful Man') bearing writs to serve on the welshing pair. They have dallied too long with Dorcas and Abigail, and now he has caught up with them and threatens them with prison should they fail to pay.

But Wilder has a stratagem to propose which may solve all their problems and desires in one masterly stroke. The three men will all turn up at Squire Bantam's house that evening. He will be the 'Duke of Berkshire', Lurcher will be his secretary and Sherwood his travelling companion. They will beg shelter for the night and then, during the night... Lurcher indignantly refuses to be party to any unsavoury doings and the young men realise that they will have to carry out their plan alone.

In the meantime, Dorothy has regained her equipoise and has made up her mind to punish Wilder for his rude words about his unseen cousin. Giving her ring to Wilder, who swears he will give up rank and even wealth for her, she binds him to a sworn fidelity ('You Swear to Be Good and True') which is to be marked by his keeping the ring forever on his finger. Lydia easily extracts a similar agreement from Sherwood and they promise that they will all meet up again on the morrow. The little ceremony over, the girls run off, and the boys prepare to head for Chanticleer Hall.

At the last minute they get an unexpected ally. Lurcher has been a little free with his writs and has ended up being dumped in the village pump by the exasperated villagers ('Under the Pump'). He runs to Wilder and Sherwood for protection and binds himself to help in their plot in exchange for their support against his persecutors. As everyone joins in jollity with the newly affianced Phyllis and Tom, the act ends in a lively fashion (Finale: 'Now Take Your Seats').

ACT 2

That evening, the disguised Wilder and Sherwood present themselves and their very lowbrow secretary (otherwise Lurcher) at Chanticleer Hall with the pretence of a carriage accident. They are made welcome by the kindly Squire and bidden to stay the night under his roof, an offer to which Wilder replies with gentlemanly thanks ('Though Born a Man of High Degree'). In the course of conversation, Bantam mentions his profligate nephew and Wilder learns that he is in total disfavour. He can expect nothing from Bantam in his lifetime, and as little as the entail of the property will allow thereafter, unless he is prepared to settle down and wed the Squire's daughter.

His head full of lovely Dorcas, Wilder knows he can never consent to that and he charges Sherwood to divert the dreaded Dorothy from him during their stay. When Dorothy and Lydia put in an appearance, fashionably dressed, powdered and wigged, the men do not recognise them as the maids to whom, only hours before, they swore undying love. Sherwood, true to his promise, willingly takes Dorothy to a distance from Wilder, while Wilder soon falls victim to Lydia's purposeful charms (Graceful Dance). Lurcher, meanwhile, is proving vulgarly fascinating to the Squire's preferred guest, the widowed Mrs Privett.

As the evening continues, the Squire entertains with a toast ('Contentment I Give You'), but all too soon it is time for the guests to depart and the houseguests to go 'To Bed'. The evening and its wine have had a fine effect on the already aroused spirits of the two young men and they tarry to woo the ladies of the house. It takes only a little time for Lydia and Dorothy to win each other's rings from the fingers of their gallants before running off to their rooms. Sherwood staunchly serenades his lady fair ('Queen of my Heart') in vain, but Lurcher has better luck and suceeds in winning an assignation with Mrs Privett which turns out to be an adventurous and comical affair.

Now it is time for Wilder's trick. Sherwood disguises himself as a highwayman and stages an intrusion ('Are You Sure That They Are All in Bed?'). He binds up the Squire and Wilder before disappearing to return in his own character once the alarm is given ('What Noise Was That?'). When the 'victims' are untied, Bantam is relieved to find that he has incurred no loss in the attack, but Lurcher reports in a different vein: his master, the Duke, has had all his money stolen. The Squire is mortified. His noble visitor robbed in his house! He will hear nothing but that he must make good the loss and the 'Duke' is finally prevailed upon to accept what he insists is a loan. The money thus tricked from the Squire is exactly the amount of Lurcher's writs and Wilder is able to render himself out of debt and a free man. But the whole night has passed and now it is morning. The sounds of the hunt are heard and the curtain comes down on a gaily coloured scene of huntsmen ('Hark for'ard') and a few sleepy eyes.

ACT 3
In a glade near the village church the local people are dancing under the critical eye of the grandmothers of the area ('Dancing Is Not What it Used to Be'). Phyllis, not a whit discouraged by the previous day's preaching from Dorothy and Lydia, is eagerly looking forward to losing her liberty ('The Time Has Come'). Wilder and Sherwood are rather looking to regain theirs. With the morning, they have made a hasty departure from Chanticleer Hall, leaving politely regretful letters for the two fine ladies whom they had courted so assiduously the night before. Each of the boys has realised that his heart is still true to his country girl and that there he must return.

There is the small matter of the rings, but that seems indeed a small matter when they receive an unlooked for pair of challenges. Two society beaux wish to avenge the slight proffered to Miss Dorothy and Miss Lydia and have challenged the Duke and his companion to a pair of duels in the round coppice. The beaux are, however, no dashing swordsmen but Lydia and Dorothy in yet another set of disguises. By the time they get to the coppice they are very nervous, and they become more so when Wilder and Sherwood turn up with guns equipped with real bullets.

The girls also harbour very mixed emotions over the whole affair for, if the men have slighted Dorothy and Lydia, they are, on the other hand, proving themselves willing to be killed for the sakes of Dorcas and Abigail, which is very flattering. Fear proves the uppermost emotion for Dorothy and Lydia and, when the duellers turn back to back to pace out their distance, the girls snatch the opportunity to take flight. When the men turn around they find, instead of a pair of pretty young gentlemen with pistols, an angry Squire Bantam. A little monetary persuasion practised on Lurcher, who had been caught far too intimately closeted with Mrs Privett, has disclosed all the deceits of their plan and Bantam has come to wreak chastisement on his double-dealing nephew.

His anger is delayed and then defused by the rustic wedding procession of Tom and Phyllis ('What Joy Untold') and he tells Wilder that all will be forgiven if only he will take Dorothy as his bride. But Wilder cannot do so for his heart is already given. As he speaks, the two girls arrive on the scene, changed again into their peasant clothes. Wilder presents to his uncle the only girl he will ever wed: his Dorcas. But Dorcas is Dorothy, and Abigail is Lydia. Memories of the previous night turn the boys' faces red as Dorothy demands to see her ring on Wilder's finger as proof of his constancy. He cannot show it, for it is now on Lydia's finger. Her point made, Dorothy happily allows herself to be given in marriage to Wilder, and Lydia and Sherwood follow suit ('You Swear to Be Good and True') as a happy ending comes to all at Chanticleer Hall.

The original libretto of *Dorothy* as played at the Gaiety Theatre became heavily embellished with incidental comedy largely invented by and for Arthur Williams, the creator and long-time incumbent of the role of Lurcher, and this comedy became, over the years, part of the standard script. The song 'Queen of My Heart', which was the important hit of the show, was added soon after the opening night to provide a solo number for the leading baritone, Hayden Coffin.

RUDDIGORE

or The Witch's Curse, a supernatural comic opera in two acts by W S Gilbert. Music by Arthur Sullivan. Produced at the Savoy Theatre, London, 22 January 1887 as *Ruddygore* with George Grossmith (Robin), Durward Lely (Richard), Rutland Barrington (Despard), Leonora Braham (Rose) and Rosina Brandram (Hannah). Played subsequently by the D'Oyly Carte Opera Company in repertoire. Produced at Sadler's Wells Theatre 19 February 1987 with Gordon Sandison, David Hillman, Harold Innocent, Marilyn Hill-Smith and Joan Davies.

Produced at the Fifth Avenue Theatre, New York, 21 February 1887 with George Thorne, Courtice Pounds, Fred Billington, Geraldine Ulmar and Elsie Cameron.

CHARACTERS

Sir Ruthven Murgatroyd *disguised as* Robin Oakapple *a young farmer*
Richard Dauntless, *his foster-brother*
Sir Despard Murgatroyd *of Ruddigore*
Old Adam Goodheart, *Robin's faithful servant*
Rose Maybud, *a village maiden*
Mad Margaret
Dame Hannah, *Rose's aunt*
Zorah, Ruth, *bridesmaids*
Sir Rupert, Sir Jasper, Sir Lionel, Sir Conrad, Sir Desmond, Sir Gilbert, Sir Mervyn, Sir Roderic, former Lords of Ruddigore

ACT 1

In the Cornish fishing village of Rederring, a bunch of bridesmaids is providing an opening chorus ('Fair Is Rose as Bright May-Day'). It is not that anyone is getting married: they are a permanent corps existing under the aegis of a charitable bequest, but it is six months since their services were last called on and they are worried that, if things continue in this vein, they may be made redundant. At present they are chorusing outside the cottage of pretty Rose Maybud whom every lad in the village would wed if he could. The only trouble is that none has yet plucked up the courage to ask. Perhaps her Aunt, Dame Hannah, could wed someone intead?

This, alas, is out of the question for Hannah is a confirmed spinster. Once upon a time she was in love and was prepared to wed but at the last moment she discovered her lover to be none other than Sir Roderic Murgatroyd, one of the cursed baronets of Ruddigore and, being a good girl, she perforce renounced him to live and die a maiden lady. With a whiff of *Il Trovatore* in her sails, she launches into the history of the curse ('Sir Rupert Murgatroyd') which, because of the burning of a witch in ages past by an early Murgatroyd, has stalked the noble family ever since. It is a truly terrible curse. Each Lord of Ruddigore shall commit a crime every day or perish in utmost agony.

Rose Maybud enters, on her way to do charitable things. Her aunt chides her gently with her indifference to the young men of the town, but Rose has precepts. As a little orphan babe she was found abandoned at the workhouse door with naught beside her but a change of linen and a book of etiquette. Having no parents, she has taken the book of etiquette as the souce of her life's guiding principles and, so far, none of the young villagers have been able to live up to its strict rules. There is, of course, the handsome farmer, Robin Oakapple, for whom she secretly sighs, but he is shy and doesn't speak and etiquette does not permit her to speak first ('If Somebody There Chanced to Be'). When Robin does chance awkwardly into conversation, their love-making is done in the third person ('I Know a Youth').

But Robin is not what he seems. He too is a Murgatroyd. Twenty years earlier, in a panic that he must inherit the hated title and its curse, he fled, leaving his younger brother Despard, believing him dead, to take up the title and the responsibilities of the Lord of Ruddigore. Robin was brought up by a convenient country person and shared his childish days with a foster-brother called Richard. Richard, now surnamed Dauntless, has made a career as a jolly jack tar enjoying a picture-book life on the ocean wave until the day arrives when he returns to his home ('I Shipped, D'Ye See, in a Revenue Sloop'). To the companion of his childhood, Robin can at least spill out one secret: his love for Rose Maybud to whom his diffident nature prevents his making any advance ('My Boy, You May Take it from Me').

Richard vows that he will woo and win the maid on his beloved foster brother's behalf but, as soon as he sights Rose, he swings to his own favourite tenet of doing what his heart tells him, and woos her not for Robin but for himself. Rose, following the rules of etiquette, finds herself accepting him ('The Battle's Roar Is Over'). Robin, returning with the bridesmaids ready to celebrate his own marriage, finds he has been double-crossed and is suitably cross. Rose is now in the middle of a pretty quandary. From having no professed suitors she now has two ('This Heart of Mine') and, since there is no rule of etiquette provided to cope with such a situation, she finally follows her inclination and opts for Robin.

To an empty scene comes as crazy a creature as ever graced the operatic stage. She is Mad Margaret ('Cheerily Carols the Lark'/'To a Garden Full of Posies') and she broods on a passion for Sir Despard, the bad Baronet of Ruddigore, to whom she was betrothed before his accession to the title. Margaret has come to pinch Rose Maybud, for she is convinced that Despard's eyes have wandered in the maid's direction and she is feeling jealous. Rose tells Margaret that, since she has quite recently become engaged, Margaret has no need to pinch her, before the massed choruses bring on Sir Despard himself singing depressively about his horrid daily task ('Oh Why Am I Moody and Sad?'). He has evolved a system of committing a very little crime each morning and atoning later in the day with some huge act of charity, but it goes hard. He is delighted, therefore, when the jilted Richard Dauntless comes to tell him (at the dictate of his heart) that he can be relieved of his title. His elder brother lives! ('You Understand? I Think I Do').

Robin and Rose are to be wed and the bridesmaids are at last in employ-ment as the finale begins. But hold! Despard enters with the fateful revela-tion and, as Robin is unmasked, the wedding is tumbled into disarray. Rose turns to Sir Despard: under this new set of cirumstances etiquette obliges her to change her mind once more and therefore she will wed him instead. But Despard, relieved of his horrid duties, is now a good person again and he must keep his old, old troth to Margaret. So Rose is paired with Richard as everyone except poor Robin, who is now a 'bad Bart', sings the act to a happy end.

ACT 2

In the Picture Gallery at Ruddigore Castle, Sir Ruthven (as Robin is now rightly named) is practising being bad ('I Once Was as Meek as a New Born

Lamb') and making a frightful hash of it. He has the opportunity to do something nasty when Rose and Richard come to get the baronial consent to their marriage ('Happily Coupled Are We'), but Rose wins him over without much trouble ('In Bygone Days I Had Thy Love') and when they have gone Ruthven decides has had enough of trying to live up to his ancestors. He renounces his position and challenges the curse.

In a flash the pictures of the Gallery come to life and descend from their frames ('Painted Emblems of a Race') headed by the baritonic Sir Roderic with a fine ghostly song ('The Ghosts' High Noon'). They have come to make sure that their heir carries out his traditional duties and they are not at all impressed by the feeble bad deeds of his first week in office. Roderic demands that he do something properly awful immediately. He must carry off a damsel or perish!

Ruthven stoutly refuses but, when the spectres give him a short burst of what eternal agony feels like, he quickly changes his mind and promises to misbehave. The satisfied ghosts vanish, and Ruthven orders his servant, Old Adam, to hurry down to the village and bring him back an unwilling maiden, any unwilling maiden, as quickly as possible.

Despard and Margaret now put in an appearance. They are much changed, having become black-clad, quakerish school-teachers ('I Was Once a Very Abandoned Person') in their reformed situation. Despard tells Ruthven that in fact he has, by Despard interposed, already been doing wicked things for ten years, and Ruthven/Robin explodes. It is too much. Eternal agony or not, he will tell the ghosts that he will not do it! ('My Eyes Are Fully Open to My Awful Situation').

Old Adam returns, having accomplished the ordered abduction, but the maiden he has brought is Dame Hannah. Hannah sets upon the unfortunate Baronet with physical indignation, and Ruthven squeals for help to his ghostly Uncles. Sir Roderic steps down from his frame in answer to the call and finds himself confronted by the woman who was once to have been his wife. The calmed Hannah coyly puts away her dagger and instead sings Roderic a pretty ballad ('There Grew a Little Flower') as they express their aged love.

While this reunion is going on, Ruthven does a little thinking and comes up with a bit of unlikely logic. A Baronet of Ruddigore can only die through refusing to commit his daily crime. Therefore, to refuse to commit a crime is tantamount to suicide. But suicide is itself a crime, so it follows that none of the earlier Baronets should have died and Ruthven therefore should not have succeeded to the title. Everyone (except the far-flung first Baronet) is innocent and Robin can have his Rose back in time for the show's final couplets ('Oh, Happy the Lily').

THE YEOMEN OF THE GUARD

or The Merryman and His Maid, a comic opera in two acts by W S Gilbert. Music by
Arthur Sullivan. Produced at the Savoy Theatre, London, 3 October 1888 with
Courtice Pounds (Fairfax), George Grossmith (Point), Geraldine Ulmar (Elsie), W
H Denny (Shadbolt), Jessie Bond (Phoebe) and Rosina Brandram (Dame Car-
ruthers). Revived there 5 May 1897 with Charles Kenningham, Walter Passmore,
Ilka Palmay, Henry Lytton, Florence Perry and Miss Brandram. Played subsequently
by the D'Oyly Carte Opera Company in repertoire. Produced at the Tower of
London 9 July 1962 with Thomas Round, John Cameron, Elizabeth Robson, Ken-
neth Sandford, Anne Pashley and Johanna Peters, 6 July 1964, 11 July 1966 and 17
July 1978 with Terry Jenkins, Tommy Steele, Laureen Livingstone, Dennis Wicks,
Della Jones and Anne Collins.

  Produced at the Casino Theatre, New York, 17 October 1888 with Henry Hallam,
J H Ryley, Bertha Ricci, Frederic Solomon, Sylvia Gerrish and Isabelle Urquhart.

  Produced at the Carltheater, Vienna, under the title *Capitän Wilson* in a version by
Victor Léon and Carl Lindau 2 February 1889.

  Produced at Kroll's Theater, Berlin, as *Der Königsgardist* in a version by F Zell and
Richard Genée 25 December 1889.

CHARACTERS

Sir Richard Cholmondeley, *Lieutenant of the Tower*
Colonel Fairfax, *under sentence of death*
Sergeant Meryll, *of the Yeomen of the Guard*
Leonard Meryll, *his son*
Jack Point, *a strolling jester*
Wilfred Shadbolt, *head jailer and assistant tormentor*
Elsie Maynard, *a strolling singer*
Phoebe Meryll, *Sergeant Meryll's daughter*
Dame Carruthers, *housekeeper to the Tower*
Kate, *her niece*
Headsman, Citizens, Yeomen of the Guard, etc.

ACT 1

On the green inside the walls of the forbidding Tower of London, Phoebe
Meryll, the daughter of one of the sergeants serving the Tower, sits spinning
and singing an incidental song ('When Maiden Loves'). Phoebe is the object
of the unwanted attentions of the head jailer, Wilfred, who is instantly
jealous when she expresses pity for Captain Fairfax, a young gentleman who
has been condemned on charges of witchcraft, levelled by a relation who
covets his fortune, and who is condemned to die on the block that very day.
Phoebe is disgusted with the constant and often irrational blood-letting of
the Tower, but the Yeomen, a group of veteran soldiers set to less warlike
work, see comfort in its walls ('Tower Warders') and Dame Carruthers, the
grim chatelaine of the place, regards it fondly as the sentinel of London town
('When Our Gallant Norman Foes').

  There is a possibility that a pardon for Fairfax may yet come, and Sergeant
Meryll is hopeful that his son Leonard, due that day from Windsor to join

the Yeomen, may bring the all-important papers which will set free the man who once saved his life in battle. When Leonard comes at last and brings no reprieve, Meryll determines to liberate the Captain himself and he settles on a courageous plan. Leonard is unknown here: he shall go into hiding while Fairfax, disguised as Leonard, takes his place amongst the Yeomen. This will give Meryll and his friends more time in which they can continue to agitate for the young man's pardon ('Alas, I Waver To and Fro').

Taking what he believes will be his last exercise on the ramparts, Fairfax muses 'Is Life a Boon' as Phoebe weeps for his fate. Since he must die, Fairfax is determined to take one last action to cheat the scheming kinsman who has plotted to inherit his estates. He will take a wife, any wife, and he begs the Lieutenant of the Tower to find a maid who will be his bride, even though it be only briefly.

A lively noise is heard and a pair of strolling players—the jester, Jack Point and the singing girl, Elsie Maynard—run on, pursued by a crowd ('Here's a Man of Jollity'), to entertain them with the tale of The Merryman and His Maid ('I Have a Song to Sing, O!'). The Lieutenant decides that Elsie would make a useful bride for the condemned Captain and, after the girl has allayed her conscience with the thought that the money thus earned might bring help to her ill mother, and jealous Jack Point has ensured that the money will be promptly paid and the man promptly executed, it is agreed. Elsie's eyes are bound with a handkerchief and she is led away to earn her gold, leaving Point to discourse merrily on his profession ('I Jibe and Joke').

The deed is quickly done and when Elsie reappears she is a married woman (''Tis Done, I Am a Bride'). Wilfred is curious as to what has been going on in his jail, but he is soon distracted from any untimely investigations when Phoebe appears. She has been given, as her part of the affair, the mission of extracting from Wilfred's belt the key to Fairfax's cell and, as she flirts cosily with the jailer ('Were I Thy Bride'), she neatly accomplishes her task.

The finale begins with the Yeomen singing a welcome to the newly arrived Leonard Meryll ('Oh, Sergeant Meryll Is It True?') but, when the new recruit to the Tower forces appears, it is not Leonard but Fairfax, clean-shaven of his beard and moustache and unrecognisable to his former jailers. He is lovingly embraced by his 'sister', Phoebe and Wilfred commits the girl to his brotherly care with the charge to keep her from any familiarity with young men ('To Thy Fraternal Care'). Then the bell of St Peter's begins to toll: it is the hour for the condemned prisoner to be brought to the block. But the false Leonard and two other tower warders sent to fetch him return in some excitement: the prisoner is gone! Elsie and Point are in despair. Their sure trick has gone astray and, as the Yeomen rush off in search of the escaped Fairfax, Elsie falls senseless into the arms of the pretended guardsman.

ACT 2

Two days later, the prisoner is still at large and, as the search continues,

Dame Carruthers pours scorn on the guards who let him escape ('Night Has Spread Her Pall Once More'). The downcast Point, in the meanwhile, makes converse with another miserable soul, Wilfred. Wilfred is suffering from job disaffection and fancies that he might profitably join Point's calling ('A Private Buffoon'), a thought in which the jester sees an opportunity to remedy his unfortunate position.

He will teach Wilfred the arts of jestering if Wilfred will play a little charade for him ('Hereupon We're Both Agreed'). They will claim to have seen and shot the escaped prisoner as he swam the moat: that way Elsie will once again be free to wed Point, and Wilfred's reputation will be cleared. The escaped prisoner is, of course, only a few yards from his cell, but he does not feel free. Although his body has escaped from its prison, his heart is bound for he is married to an unknown bride ('Free From His Fetters Grim').

The fainting Elsie has been succoured by Dame Carruthers who has taken up quarters in Meryll's house to tend the girl and is using the opportunity to ease the unwilling Sergeant in the direction of matrimony. But, while Elsie tossed in her tormented sleep, she has given away some of the secret of her marriage. Dame Carruthers knows now that she is married and guesses to whom, but not why ('Strange Adventure'). From the good Dame's words, Fairfax discovers the identity of his wife, and he finds it in his humour to woo his own bride.

A shot is heard, and the green quickly fills with curious choristers ('Now What Can That Have Been?'). Wilfred claims the honour of the shot and launches into a story of derring-do, describing how he shot down the escaping prisoner, Point all the while attempting to add corrective and corroborative detail ('Like a Ghost I Saw Him Creeping'). Elsie weeps dutifully for her husband's death, but she is soon being courted again, clumsily by Point and in practised fashion by Fairfax/Leonard who knows rather better than the jester how 'A Man Who Would Woo a Fair Maid' should behave.

In feigning to show Point how to woo, Fairfax urges his own suit with Elsie and wins. Point is staggered and poor Phoebe, whose heart is devoted to her pretended brother in a most un-sisterly way, is broken-hearted ('When a Wooer Goes A-Wooing'). In her distress she pours out her heart to Wilfred, forgetting that the man of whom she is speaking is supposed to be her brother. Wilfred is not so dense as to miss the slip but, as Phoebe reminds him, the man cannot be Fairfax for, does he not remember?, he has just shot Fairfax in the moat. The price of Wilfred's silence is Phoebe's hand—not Phoebe's heart, but Phoebe's hand.

Now the real Leonard arrives on the scene. He has with him Fairfax's pardon which the Captain's malicious accuser had used his influence at court to delay. A careless word unveils the plot in the hearing of Dame Carruthers and once again the price of silence is a wedding ring as Sergeant Meryll's years of resistance are brought to an end ('Rapture, Rapture! When Love's Votary').

As the finale begins, Elsie approaches in her bridal gown to be wedded to 'Leonard Meryll', but the Lieutenant of the Tower puts a stop to the proceedings with the information that Captain Fairfax lives—she is already married. As the young woman hides her face in terrified tears, Captain Fairfax approaches to claim his wife. To her unseeing entreaties he replies sternly until she looks up and sees her beloved 'Leonard'. She is married already to the man she has chosen herself. As the lovers enfold each other, poor Jack Point sings brokenly of his lost lady-love and he falls fainting to the ground as the rest of the company make merry to the closing curtain.

THE GONDOLIERS

or The King of Barataria, a comic opera in two acts by W S Gilbert. Music by Arthur Sullivan. Produced at the Savoy Theatre, London, 7 December 1889 with Geraldine Ulmar (Gianetta), Jessie Bond (Tessa), Courtice Pounds (Marco), Rutland Barrington (Guiseppe), Frank Wyatt (Duke) and Rosina Brandram (Duchess). Revived there 22 March 1898 and again 18 July 1898 with Emmie Owen, Louie Henri, Charles Kenningham, Henry Lytton, William Elton and Miss Brandram, and 22 January 1907 with Lillian Coomber, Jessie Rose, Pacie Ripple, Richard Green, C H Workman and Louie Rene. Played subsequently by the D'Oyly Carte Opera Company in repertoire.

Produced at the Park Theatre, New York, 7 January 1890 with Esther Palliser, Mary Duggan, Richard Clarke, Rutland Barrington, George Temple and Kate Talby.

Produced at the Theater an der Wien, Vienna, as *Die Gondoliere* in a version by F Zell and Richard Genée 20 September 1890.

Produced at the Friedrich-Wilhelmstädtisches Theater, Berlin, 20 December 1890.

CHARACTERS

The Duke of Plaza-Toro, *a Grandee of Spain*
Luiz, *his attendant*
Don Alhambra del Bolero, *the Grand Inquisitor*
Marco Palmieri, *a gondolier*
Guiseppe Palmieri, *another gondolier*
The Duchess of Plaza-Toro
Casilda, *her daughter*
Gianetta
Tessa
Inez, *the King's foster mother*
Antonio, Francesco, Giorgio, Annibale, Ottavio, Fiametta, Vittoria, Giulia, etc.

ACT 1
In the Piazetta in Venice the local *contadine* (Italian for chorus girls) are making posies and chattering about men ('List and Learn, Ye Dainty

Roses'): about two men in particular, Marco and Giuseppe Palmieri, a pair of local *gondolieri* (Italian for cab-drivers) whose physical attributes and fine singing voices make them the most sought-after husbands in Venice. The rest of the city's *gondolieri* have no luck at all in their love-making, for all the *contadine* are waiting to find out whether they might be one of the two lucky enough to hook Marco or Giuseppe before committing themselves elsewhere.

The heroic pair are diffident fellows who pay little heed to their nominal employment and spend most of their time being pleasant to *contadine* ('We're Called Gondolieri'). They have feelings of delicacy, however, and are unwilling to do anything so rude as express a preference amongst the pretty and amiable pack of postulant brides and they decide instead to let fate pick their wives for them. They are blindfolded, and agree to wed whichever girls they catch in a game of connubial blindman's-buff. At the end of the game Marco (who happens to be a tenor) has found Gianetta (who is, conveniently, a soprano) while the baritone Giuseppe has paired off with the mezzo-soprano Tessa ('Thank You, Gallant Gondolieri') and they dance Venetianally off to be married.

To the sound of a drum, a gondola pulls up and a splendidly moth-eaten family group alight. They are the Plaza-Toros, the Duke, his full-sized Duchess, their daughter Casilda, and their escort of one, the drummer Luiz ('From the Sunny Spanish Shore'). The Duke reveals to his daughter the reason for their visit. In childhood she was betrothed to the infant son of the wonderfully wealthy King of Barataria but, unfortunately, before she was old enough to do anything about confirming the alliance, the old King of Barataria developed unsuitable religious habits and his Grand Inquisitor felt obliged to snatch away the baby Prince and bring him to Venice for safe keeping and a sound upbringing. But the erring old King and his court have all been killed in a well-deserved uprising, and the former baby is now King. This seems an opportune moment for Plaza-Toro to bring up the subject of his daughter's engagement and for that purpose he has brought her to Venice to be introduced to her betrothed.

The Plaza-Toro family are in rather seedy circumstances at the moment, but the Duke has plans of a novel commercial kind for restoring their fortunes, plans which can be sufficiently twisted to give a lead into a song descriptive of his gallant 'discretion' under conditions of war ('In Enterprise of Martial Kind'). When the Duke and the Duchess leave the scene, the hitherto pouting Casilda and the hitherto grovelling drummer cast aside their postures and rush into a love duet ('O, Rapture, When Alone Together'). They dissect the now unpromising future of their love and look forward gloomily to a life apart ('There Was a Time'), she as Queen of Barataria and he as a sighing servant.

The Duke and Duchess have sought out the Grand Inquisitor, Don Alhambra del Bolero, who in earlier days was responsible for bringing the baby Prince to Venice, and the Grand Inquisitor has a tale to relate, since the situation needs some elucidating before a royal marriage can take place ('I Stole the Prince'). On arriving in Venice all those years ago, he placed the princely baby in the care of a good-hearted but intemperate gondolier. Even when sober, the gondolier was never quite sure which of his two charges— his own son and the Prince—was which, and when he died without marking the children's identities on their nappies the situation became even more confusing. In consequence, although the Inquisitor can show the ducal family the house where Casilda's husband lives, he cannot with certitude point out her husband. There is, however, an elderly nurse (now married to a brigand and living in the mountains in the environs of Cordova) who can apparently identify the King, and Don Alhambra has sent emissaries in search of her. In the meanwhile, the enigma must remain (Quintet: 'Try We Life-long We Can Never').

The local wedding party enters, with Tessa celebrating the occasion in song ('When a Merry Maiden Marries'), to be greeted by Don Alhambra with the news that one of the two bridegrooms (he can't yet tell which) is a king. The boys, who have been voicing florid republican sentiments, suddenly revise their politics. It is all a matter of degree. There is, for example, nothing wrong with a king who abolishes all taxes and cuts all prices (except for gondola fares). As Barataria is, it seems, urgently in need of its King, there is no question of waiting in Venice until the wretched nurse is found. The two *gondolieri* will have to reign temporarily as joint monarchs pending the crowning of the rightful King, and they will have to depart for their island kingdom right away, just married or not ('Kind Sir, You Cannot Have the Heart').

The girls have the consolation of a fifty-fifty chance of impending royalty to make up for their lost honeymoon ('Then One of Us Will Be a Queen'), just as the *gondolieri* have the useful thought that they will be able to run their kingdom on exemplary egalitarian lines as a compensation for the unrepublican activity of kingship ('For Every One Who Feels Inclined'), as they set off for Barataria to a songful of good advice from their new little wives ('Do Not Forget You've Married Me') who are left waving goodbye to them from the canal bank.

ACT 2

Settled in Barataria, the two kings have, in the usual fashion of over-promoted men, immediately installed all their friends in high positions which are no longer high positions because everyone, under the egalitarian new regime, is of equal rank. In fact, under these impossibly democratic conditions, the kings themselves have, in spite of their titles, an altogether more menial life than they had in Venice ('Rising Early in the Morning'). They also very much miss the wives they have left behind and Marco expresses his impatience for feminine companionship in a longing song ('Take a Pair of Sparkling Eyes').

The wives have missed them too and, against the Inquisitor's prohibition, they have left Venice and, supported by the entire population of *contadine*, have crossed the sea to Barataria ('Here We Are at the Risk of Our Lives'). Bubbling with curiosity and dying to know which one of them is Queen,

Tessa and Gianetta embrace their husbands, and join in a jolly dance of celebration ('Dance a Cachucha').

Don Alhambra, on his arrival, is amazed at the curious constitution of the new court. Running a court on egalitarian principles is clearly a contradiction in terms. After all, 'when everyone is somebody, then no one's anybody' ('There Lived a King, As I've Been Told'). He also has a surprise for the kings which he has hitherto kept to himself. One of them is not only a king, he is a bigamist. At the time of his recent wedding he had already been for a number of years officially wed to Casilda. As yet, nobody knows which and to whom and all the effort in the world cannot for the moment be of any help ('In a Contemplative Fashion').

The Plaza-Toro family duly land on Barataria with the unwilling Casilda being prepared for her husband by being subjected to a lecture from her formidable mother on how to fall in love with the upper echelons of nobility whether you like it or not ('On the Day When I Was Wedded'). Casilda hopes that perhaps the dubious commercialisation of her family ('Small Titles and Orders') may decide Barataria to reject her but, when her father has finished giving the kings a lecture on how to run their court ('I Am a Courtier Grave and Serious'), she finds instead another impediment to her marriage—the fact that both of the optional monarchs are already married ('Here Is a Case Unprecedented').

The puzzle, however, is about to be solved. The Prince's old nurse has been found and, as the finale begins, she is hustled in for her revelation. The King of Barataria is neither Guiseppe nor Marco. Way back, before the Grand Inquisitor came into the story, she herself had hidden the tiny Prince from harm, substituting her own baby in his place. So, one of the 'kings' is the young Palmieri, one is her son, and the real King is...Luiz! Casilda embraces her beloved ex-drummer enthusiastically, and the *gondolieri* and *contadine* can, with mixed feelings, go back to their *gondole* and *fiori*, their respective spouses and their second-hand republican sentiments.

THE NAUTCH GIRL

or The Rajah of Chutneypore, an Indian comic opera in two acts by George Dance. Lyrics by George Dance and Frank Desprez. Music by Edward Solomon. Produced at the Savoy Theatre, London, 30 June 1891 with Rutland Barrington (Punka), Courtice Pounds (Indru), Leonore Snyder (Hollee Beebee), Frank Wyatt (Baboo Currie), Jessie Bond (Chinna Loofah), W H Denny (Bumbo) and Frank Thornton (Pyjama).

CHARACTERS

Punka, *the Rajah of Chutneypore*
Indru, *his son*
Pyjama, *the Grand Vizier*

Chinna Loofah
Suttee $\rbrace$ *Punka's poor relations*
Cheetah
Baboo Currie, *proprietor of a Nautch troupe*
Hollee Beebee
Banyan
Kalee $\rbrace$ *Nautch girls*
Tiffin
Bumbo, *an Idol*

ACT 1

The scene is the distant province of Chutneypore where the opening chorus is provided by a selection of indolent Pariahs ('Beneath the Sky of Blue') who are shaken salaaming from their singing by the arrival of Indru, son of the local rajah. Indru is disposed to be democratic today ('Bow Not, Good People') for he is in love and has a song to sing about the fact ('The Sun Was Setting'). But Indru is a high caste Brahmin and he is in love with Hollee Beebee, the principal dancer of the touring Nautch troupe run by the jolly Baboo Currie, who is a lady of low caste. Baboo Currie does not have to remind the prince of the impossibility of regularising such a liaison, but he tries to make the situation seem more palatable by indulging in a round denigration of Beebee's qualities, not the least because he has no wish to have the prettiest dancer of his troupe diverted to marriage ('Roses are Fair').

The Nautch troupe enters ('With Merry Song') and Beebee displays her talents ('First You Take a Shapely Maiden') until Indru breaks the latest bit of bad news. His royal father has discovered their love. Oh, that she were a Brahmin! Beebee explains that she is or, rather, was. Unfortunately, forty years previously her father fell into a river and was rescued by being hauled ashore at the end of a rope.

The unfortunate part of this was that the man at the other end of the rope was a Pariah and, by a court decision, it was held that the taint of dishonour had communicated itself down the rope and her father's caste was lost. Since then, Beebee's family has seen its wealth gnawed away in legal expenses trying to get this decision reversed by a competent tribunal and it is to pay for a Counsel's opinion on a technical point that Beebee has taken her current engagement as a Nautch girl. The court is still sitting, but the judge has influenza and should anything happen to him the case will have to begin all over again. It is very depressing, but the lovers still have sufficient spirit to sing an optimistic kind of duet about "When Our Shackles Are Undone'.

Punka, the Rajah of Chutneypore and Indru's father, arrives to the strains of a long-winded increasing song ('The Rajah of Chutneypore'). Punka suffers from a nasty social condition called consanguinity which has led him to place anyone who claims the slightest kinship with him in a salaried government post. In fact he loathes his relations, especially the Vizier Pyjama. It is Pyjama, as it turns out, who is the cause of the other national problem: the missing diamond eye of Bumbo, the National Idol, a despotic deity who may at any time prove the ruination of the land. Punka would love to turn Pyjama in, but his wretchedly over-developed sense of consanguinity prevents him.

Beebee demurely explains to the Rajah that she would never have looked at Indru had she known of his position and assures him that she is doing all she can to get a Court judgement which will restore her Brahmin rank. The Rajah informs her that should she succeed she has his permission to call at the palace any Monday morning between ten and twelve when, if Indru has given up and married elsewhere and he himself has become a widower, he would be inclined to offer her first refusal on himself (Quartet: 'Quite Another Different Kind of Person'). But now Indru returns in the rags of a Pariah. He has purposely 'eaten a little potted meat', thus giving up his caste and his royal position and becoming Beebee's equal. They can be married right away.

This double-quick wedding does not please Punka, nor does it please Chinna Loofah, the least objectionable of his relations, an unmarried lady of more-than-twenty who is a victim to sudden overwhelming 'Affinities' for various gentlemen, but it is a source of great amusement to Pyjama who comes to announce that Beebee's court case is over, she has won and is a Brahmin again. A chorus of Nautch girls comes happily on from the wedding celebrating the fact that 'Beebee's a Bride' as the happy couple glide on, only to meet the horrid Pyjama glowing with righteousness and quoting chapter and verse of the law which condemns both a Brahmin and his or her lower caste spouse to a traitor's death.

Just when all seems darkest, Baboo Currie comes to the rescue. He has a ship at anchor waiting to take his troupe off on a European tour and, as the chorus urge them on to 'a spot far o'er the sea where caste is not and men are free', Beebee is hurried aboard. Alas! Pyjama's soldiers hold Indru fast as the ship lifts anchor and he watches miserably as his bride sails away to another continent.

ACT 2

When the second act begins, Indru is behind bars and Chinna and all the relations are soliloquising on their satisfactory rise to government office ('We Are Punka's Poor Relations'). The one who is making the most of his office is, of course, Pyjama. He has put an anonymous letter on the idol's shrine informing him that Indru is a condemned man. It is a simple *sequitur* that the father of a condemned man may not be rajah and, when Punka is condemned, why then he, Pyjama, must be favourite for the post of new rajah ('The Secret of My Past Success').

Indru is not friendless, however, for he has become the innocent latest object of Chinna Loofah's penchant for affinities and she, practical lady, brings a crowbar to bend and break his prison bars (Duet: 'A Little Caged Bird'). The freed Indru hides as the populace fill the square to proclaim a miracle. Bumbo, the idol who has sat on his shelf in the temple for two thousand years, has stepped down from his place and is heading this way. Green and gilt and with a patch over his missing eye, Bumbo is carried on and makes known the reason for his unprecedented action ('As I Sat on My Shelf'): he is after his diamond eye and the villain who stole it.

He complains about the neglect of his worship in a highly topical song ('When a Fashionable Tenor') and vents his temper on Punka who is summarily deposed from his rajahdom and replaced by the eager and oily Pyjama. The bad temper is dispelled, however, when he spots Chinna and, since she succumbs promptly to a violent attack of affinity, they very soon find themselves discussing marriage ('Vive la Liberté'). His change of heart is not total enough, however, to reprieve Punka. This injustice is too much for the erstwhile rajah. Conquering his consanguinity, he gets Bumbo to include his whole family—374 professed relations in all—in the proposed execution by 'CROCODILE' with the particular inclusion of Pyjama and, by special dispensation, with the express exception of Chinna Loofah.

No sooner is the city centre clear than who should appear but Hollee Beebee, back from a personally triumphant European tour and come in search of her Indru. When she finds him, he is in a reasonably negative frame of mind ('When All the World Was Bright, Love') but Baboo Currie comes up with a positive plan. He proposes to both the young lovers and to the condemned Punka that they all escape back to Europe where they can earn a fortune as a novelty dance act under his management. This flight of imagination provides the cue for a comic routine featuring burlesques of the songs and dances of the different European nations ('If We Travel by Way of Brindisi').

Punka's revenge on his most hated cousin seems to have gone wrong when Pyjama laughingly exempts himself from the family execution with the revelation that he isn't and never was a relation of Punka's—he merely claimed to be in order to get promotion. Where Punka has failed, however, Beebee and her girlfriends succeed. They divert Pyjama with one of the popular numbers from their repertoire so that he is late for the executions and the wrath of Bumbo is aroused against the new rajah.

But Pyjama is in worse trouble. Being now freed from the awful thought that he might be condemning a relation, Punka can announce the dreadful truth: Pyjama is the thief who stole the idol's eye. As the miscreant is dragged away to his fate, Bumbo's gaze alights on Beebee's throat. What is that he sees twinkling on her lovely larynx? Why, it is a particularly impressive diamond left for her at a European stage door by an admirer. That it may be, but it is also Bumbo's lost eye. It takes only the length of the finale for Punka to be restored to his former position, Indru and Beebee to fall into each other's arms, and the idol's eye to be restored to its rightful place as he climbs back on to his shelf with Chinna turned to wood alongside him, a bride—anybody's bride—at last.

THE GEISHA

A Story of a Tea House, a Japanese musical play in two acts by Owen Hall. Lyrics by Harry Greenbank. Music by Sidney Jones. Additional songs by Lionel Monckton and James Philp. Produced at Daly's Theatre, London, 25 April 1896 with Marie Tempest (Mimosa), Hayden Coffin (Fairfax), Letty Lind (Molly), Huntley Wright (Wun-hi) and Harry Monkhouse suceeded by Rutland Barrington (Imari). Revived there 18 June 1906 with May de Souza, Robert Evett, Marie Studholme, Fred Wright jr, George Graves and Mariette Sully as Juliette, and again 1 June 1931 with Rose Hignell, Donald Mather, Lorna Hubbard, George Lane and Leo Sheffield. Produced at the Garrick Theatre 24 April 1934 with Miss Hignell, Dudley Stevens, Bertha Riccardo, Percy Le Fre and Sheffield.

Produced at Daly's Theatre, New York, 9 September 1896 with Dorothy Morton, Van Rensslaer Wheeler, Violet Lloyd, William Samson and Edwin Stevens. Revived there 8 November 1897 with Nancy McIntosh, Julius Stieger, Virginia Earle and James T Powers, and again 21 March 1898 with Marguerite Lemon, Frank Rushworth, Mabelle Gillman, Powers and Joseph Herbert. Produced at the 44th Street Theatre 27 March 1913 with Alice Zeppili, Carl Gantvoort, Lina Arbanell, Powers and Stevens and at the Erlanger Theatre 5 October 1931 with Hizi Koyke, Roy Cropper, Rella Winn, Powers and Detmar Poppen.

Produced at the Lessing-Theater, Berlin, in a version by C M Roehr and Julius Freund 1 May 1897 and played thereafter at Kroll's Theater, the Centraltheater, the Staatsoper, etc.

Produced at the Carltheater, Vienna, 16 November 1897, at the Theater an der Wien 27 September 1901 and the Raimundtheater 3 June 1955, etc.

Produced at the Théâtre de l'Athenée-Comique, Paris, in a version by Charles Clairville, Antony Mars and Jacques Le Maire 8 March 1898 with Jeanne Petit, Perrin, Miriam Manuel, Guyon jr and Jannin. Played at the Théâtre du Moulin Rouge 1906 and at the Théâtre de la Gaîté-Lyrique 1920 with Marguérite Carré, André Gilly, Jane Pierly, Girier and Max Dearly.

CHARACTERS

O Mimosa San, *chief geisha*
Juliette Diamant, *a French girl attached to the Tea House as interpreter*
Nami (Wave of the Sea), *an attendant*
Lady Constance Wynne, *an English visitor in Japan travelling in her yacht*
Miss Molly Seamore
Lt Reginald Fairfax *of the HMS Turtle*
Lt Dick Cunningham *also of the HMS Turtle*
Captain Katana *of the Governor's Guard*
Takemine, *the Governor's Agent*
Wun-hi, *a Chinaman, proprietor of the Tea House of Ten Thousand Joys*
Marquis Imari, *Chief of Police and Governor of the Province*
O Hana San (Blossom), O Kinkoto San, O Kiku San (Chrysanthemum), Komurasaki San (Little Violet), *geisha of the Tea House*
Arthur Cuddy, George Grimston, Gerald St Pancras, Midshipman Tommy Stanley, *of the HMS Turtle*
Marie Worthington, Ethel Hurst, Louie Plumpton, Mabel Grant, *guests on Lady Constance's yacht*

ACT I

It is early morning at the Tea House of Ten Thousand Joys, an establishment somewhere in musical comedy Japan run by the shifty little Chinaman, Wun-hi. The geisha who staff the Tea House—and in this Tea House they are no more than delightful musical waitresses—sing ingenuously of 'Happy Japan' and the most clichéd of its attributes until Wun-hi hurries in to tell them that business is approaching in the shape of a shipload of English naval officers, all far from home and clearly longing for a nice cup of tea, not to mention the company of a pretty Japanese maiden. 'Here They Come' chorus the girls, and over the little Japanese bridge come Lieutenant Reggie Fairfax and his friends.

Reggie has been here before and has come back expressly to spend some time with O Mimosa San, the lovely and talented head girl of the house, but the other chaps are delighted to disport themselves with the other geisha to whom the hopeful Dick Cunningham sings the salutory tale of 'The Dear Little Jappy-Jap-Jappy' who got involved with a sailor but who struck communication problems and ended up marrying a Japanese chappy-chap-chappy while the sailor went home to take Japanese lessons.

The busy season for the Wun-hi establishment is clearly under way for, to the Chinaman's embarrassment, while Mimosa is entertaining Reggie, over the Japanese bridge comes the Marquis Imari, a pompous example of minor nobility, sheltered under the state umbrella carried by his minion, Takemine. Imari announces that he has applied to the Emperor for permission to marry Mimosa and Wun-hi, seeing the main attraction of his business being nationalised without compensation, is in despair. As he plots to save his livelihood, he finds an unexpected ally in his pretty French in-house interpreter, Juliette Diamant. Juliette would love to be a Japanese Marquise and she sets her cap determinedly at the Marquis who is susceptible enough to admit that, while he intends to wed Mimosa tomorrow, Juliette may walk half way home with him today... 'the other half's engaged'.

The next party to arrive is an English one led by Lady Constance Wynne, a society lady who has called into Japan whilst cruising the Orient with a party of suitable young ladies. Lady Constance spies Reggie and Mimosa together, and listens suspiciously as Mimosa sings the tale of 'The Amorous Goldfish' who fell in love with a naval officer and who perished sadly when he neglected his pet for a young lady. She finds it necessary to remind Reggie that he is engaged back home to be married to Miss Molly Seamore, but Reggie believes in spreading the great British way of life and as soon as Lady Constance is gone he begins to instruct the Japanese girl in the occidental custom of kissing (Kissing Duet) with every evidence of enjoyment on both sides.

No sooner has Reggie gone back to his friends than a Japanese soldier emerges from the shadows. It is Mimosa's lover, Captain Katana, who is not at all happy about the requisites of her job and the attentions so dutifully lavished on so many strangers. She reminds him that his job is killing people—one is not obliged to enjoy one's work—and promises him that as soon as she is freed from her indentures they will be wed.

Wun-hi shoos the interfering Captain away as the geisha prepare tea for their British guests ('If You Will Come to Tea') but Imari, returning to make sure that his intended bride has been withdrawn from active service, is furious to find her consorting with the British navy. Neither the senior service nor the Japanese nobility is prepared to stand down in this conflict and Imari vents his rage by invoking a convenient by-law and commanding the whole Tea House to be disbanded and the girls' indentures sold off. The geisha are distraught (Chorus of Lamentation), but the sailors and the English girls are not to be intimidated and set off in pursuit of the Marquis to tell him what they think of him ('We're Going to Call on the Marquis').

Now pert and pretty Molly Seamore arrives on the scene. She blithely teases her Reggie for playing with the live dolls of the Tea House and reminds him of their childhood days and how he tried to nurse her dolls— and then nurse her (Toy Duet). Molly is rather taken aback when Lady Constance tells her that Reggie seems to have got in rather deep with one of the geisha, and she pours out her heart to the comforting Mimosa without knowing who she is. Mimosa suggests that if she thinks Reggie has developed a penchant for Japanese girls perhaps she should dress up and pretend to be a geisha for him. Molly agrees with delight while Mimosa soliloquises in waltz rhythms on 'A Geisha's Life' and the true heartaches behind the picturesque exterior.

Everyone begins to gather round for the sale of Wun-hi's business and Fairfax and his friends pass the time with a rousing hymn to the British seaman ('Jack's the Boy') before Takemine sets himself up on a rostrum ('Attention Pray!') and, in spite of Reggie's qualms at the idea of seeing a woman effectively sold to the highest bidder ('Chivalry'), the fateful sale begins. Lot One is O Mimosa San. Imari bids heavily but Lady Constance determinedly bids even higher as Juliette tries to persuade the Marquis not to waste all his money and ruin himself for the sake of a singing girl.

Imari agrees—'after all, I am not an English marquis'—and drops out of the bidding, leaving Lady Constance to become the new owner of the geisha's contract, but Juliette's plan goes wrong when Imari takes a strong fancy to Lot Two, a piquant little geisha called Roli Poli who gives a fine display of seductive arts in song and dance ('Chon Kina'), and he buys her instead. The concerted finale which ends the act ('Though of Staying Too Long You're Accusing Us') finds Katana and Mimosa still separated and Molly, for the mysterious Roli Poli is, of course, she, in the Marquis's clutches while sparks fly all round.

ACT 2

In the Chrysanthemum gardens of the Imari palace the ladies of the Marquis's court are preparing for their lord's marriage to Roli Poli ('Day Born of Love'). Molly is determined not to go through with this horrid oriental wedding and she rues the folly that led her into her little charade ('The Toy Monkey'), but there seems no obvious way out of becoming the Marquise Imari. Juliette and Wun-hi, down on their luck, are lurking around trying to mend things and indulge in a confident duet ('Ching-a-ring-a-

74

ree'), while Fairfax and his friends wander about the palace being nautical in song ('Jolly Young Jacks Are We') and being attentive in turn to both the Japanese and English girls ('Geisha Are We') until they learn from Juliette of the danger that Molly is in and join the concerted plot to help her escape.

Mimosa takes a scene to sing an interpolated piece, 'The Jewel of Asia', before Fairfax, whose heart has apparently always been true to his Molly, apostrophises his love in the ballad 'Star of my Soul' and Juliette details in song all the awful things she would do to win the man she wants ('If That's Not Love—What Is?'), even to the unthinkable extent of wearing 'an unbecoming chapeau'. It is Mimosa who actually proposes a practical plan for getting Molly out of her dilemma. She offers to infiltrate the bridal suite and pull the oldest trick in the musical theatre by exchanging one veiled bride for another. The conspirators, seeing the deed as good as done, chuckle 'What Will the Marquis Do?'.

To a Japanese March, Imari arrives followed by a suitably obeisant group of geisha (Entry of the Geisha: 'With Splendour Auspicious') and the English visitors. Wun-hi, who has been put in charge of the entertainments at the ceremony, gives out with a biographical piece ('Chin-Chin-Chinaman') and then Takemine announces a special amusement for the guests in the shape of a fortune teller. The fortune teller, who is really Mimosa in disguise, gives good readings to everyone except the reluctant Marquis for whom she forecasts a miserable life unless he can be redeemed by a loving young wife. She offers to cast a love spell on the unwilling Molly ('Love, Love') and is hurried into the palace by the superstitious Marquis, leaving Cunningham to entertain the assembled company with a jolly song ('Hey-diddle-diddle! When Man Is in Love') while the serious matters of the day are disposed of.

Poor Molly has enough spirit left to sing a comic song about 'The Interfering Parrot', an anthropomorphic tale of marital disaster, before she is left alone with the 'fortune teller' to be bewitched into a happy Japanese wife. Mimosa quickly reveals herself and sets her plan in action. On the way to the wedding Juliette is substituted for the phoney Roli Poli under the nuptial canopy and Molly hurries to her Reggie's arms while the Marquis drinks the wedding cup with the disguised French girl.

When the truth is revealed Imari accepts philosophically that 'every man is disappointed in his wife at some time or other' while Molly gurgles patriotically that there was no way she could marry a foreign nobleman when she could get an English sailor, and Mimosa is left to wed her Japanese captain as the chorus confirm ('Before Our Eyes') that this is, indeed, happy Japan.

Among the additional numbers inserted in *The Geisha* during its run were the ensemble 'What Will the Marquis Do?', the laughing song 'I Can't Refrain From Laughing' (Napoléon Lambelet), the ballads 'Molly Mine' and 'Love, Could I Only Tell Thee' (J M Capel/Clifton Bingham) for Hayden Coffin (who also at one stage appropriated 'Love, Love') and the songs 'The Wedding', 'C'Est Moi' (Frank E Tours/Percy Greenbank), and 'It's Coming Off Today'.

A GREEK SLAVE

a musical comedy in two acts by Owen Hall. Lyrics by Harry Greenbank and Adrian Ross. Music by Sidney Jones. Additional music by Lionel Monckton. Produced at Daly's Theatre, London, 8 June, 1898 with Marie Tempest (Maia), Hayden Coffin (Diomed), Letty Lind (Iris) Rutland Barrington (Pomponius), Hilda Moody (Antonia) and Huntley Wright (Heliodorus).

Produced at the Herald Square Theatre, New York, 28 November 1899 with Dorothy Morton, Hugh Chilvers, Minnie Ashley, Herbert Sparling, Kate Michelena and Richard Carle.

Produced at the Theater an der Wien, Vienna, as *Der Griechische Sklave* 16 December 1899.

CHARACTERS

Heliodorus, *a Persian soothsayer*
Maia, *his daughter*
Diomed, *a Greek slave*
Archias, *another Greek slave*
Antonia, *a relative of Caesar*
Iris, *a Greek slave, confidential maid to Antonia*
Melanopis ⎱
Circe ⎰ *Slaves*
Nepia ⎰
Marcus Pomponius, *Prefect of Rome*
Manlius ⎱
Lollius ⎱
Silius ⎰ *Patricians*
Curius ⎰
Licinea, Flavia, Tullia, Cornelia, Timon, etc.

ACT 1

At the villa of the soothsayer, Heliodorus, on one of the seven heights of Rome, the establishment's servants await the noon time when the day's business will begin ('On the Dial') as the superstitious rich and great of Rome flock to their master for advice on matters of the heart or the race-track. Heliodorus himself turns out to be a funny little chap with a natty line in patter in which he describes the years of lore he learned in order to become 'The Wizard'. He is not, however, above learning as much as he can of the local slaves' gossip in order to stock up his supply of 'miraculous' knowledge of current affairs of all kinds, gossip which allows him to amaze a quartet of noble Romans ('By Bacchus') with the names of their current paramours.

His most fruitful source of information is Iris, the pretty little maid to the aristocratic Antonia, a relative of Caesar no less, who knows when to be 'Confidential' and when to be useful. Iris likes an excuse to visit Heliodorus' mansion, for she is in love with one of his slaves, the sculptor, Archias. Archias' talent is such that Heliodorus supplies him with marble to produce

76

home-made statuary for the mansion and, at the moment, he is working on an Eros, a striking statue of the god of love for which his fellow slave, Diomed, whose talents are more purely physical, is acting as model. Diomed may have a perfect physique, but he is depressed. He is in love with the soothsayer's daughter, Maia, but he knows that he can never wed her until that problematic day when he can gain his 'Freedom'.

Today, Iris' news is not so good. The Prefect of Rome, Marcus Pomponius, is coming to visit Heliodorus and he is in a bad mood. The cause of his bad mood is the lady Antonia who is not responding at all to his repeated professions of passion nor even to an offer of marriage. Pomponius has a horrid habit of disposing of irritating people with accompaniments which include esoteric tortures and, since he is unlikely to turn such actions on to a lady and a relative of Caesar, there is every chance of his being painfully unkind to the magician unless the magician can produce some positive results.

When the Prefect arrives, it eventuates that he has no superstitious bent. He is quite aware that Heliodorus is a charlatan and does not expect successful spells. What he does expect is co-operation. Antonia has heard of the fashionable soothsayer and has decided to come to consult him. Pomponius intends that the oracle shall be favourable to his suit. Maia, however, ridicules this simple plan. Antonia is not such a fool. She is a proud and lofty woman. First she must be made vulnerable and humble and then she can be won by a man whom she does not love. The story of 'The Lost Pleiad' is an example: the little star-maiden who made a fool of herself over a mortal, got ostracised, and ended up marrying the Dog Star.

Maia will set the plan in motion, but in return for her help, she wants a reward and, to her father's horror, that reward is the right to marry the slave Diomed. Heliodorus affects to agree, and Maia hastens to Diomed with the good news ('All Is Fair') and the details of her plot in which he is to take part. Antonia duly arrives and Maia, dressed up as the oracle, appears before her. Antonia has never known love ('I Cannot Love'), but the oracle tells her that mortal love is not for her—the god of love himself will be her consort—and a curtain is opened to display Archias' statue of Eros.

Antonia is told to return at eventide to receive her Olympian lover, and the scene gives way to one of more earthly love as Archias and Iris lark about amongst the sculptures, and Iris takes a try a some model poses ('I Should Rather Like to Try'). Pomponius is not at all averse to seeing the lady who spurned him being tricked into wasting her sighs on a stone statue, and he is inclined to join comically in a trio with Iris and Heliodorus as the climax of the plan arrives ('Whirligig').

The lady Antonia returns (Processional March/Chorus of Welcome) into the scene which has been laid out for her benefit. As the finale begins, Maia invokes the god, Eros (Invocation: 'What Homage of Human Lovers'). The stone must come to life to love Antonia! And, surely, the stone does. The god of love himself steps from his pedestal ('Far Above You Is My Throne') and sings of love to the dazzled lady. Antonia orders her slaves to 'Bear the God of Love Along' back to her palace and, as they depart, Maia exults: her plan has worked. It was the living Diomed who sang to the Princess, but the marble statue which she has taken home. But Heliodorus has tricked his daughter. Her Greek slave has been substituted once again for Archias' statue, and Diomed has gone, borne forth on the shoulders of Antonia's slaves to be her lover.

ACT 2

The scene is Antonia's palatial villa at Baiae ('Here at Baiae on the Bay'). The lovelorn lady is attempting to draw some response from her 'god of love', but with no success ('A Song of Love'). Diomed has thoughts only for Maia. Antonia demands that Heliodorus be called to invest the god with a heart. As it happens, Heliodorus is nearby, waiting to take urgent counsel with Iris. The affair they have started is clearly threatening to get complicated, and they wonder nervously 'Oh, What Will Be the End of It?'.

Marcus Pomponius, for whose sake the whole plan was set in motion, is no happier than Antonia or Diomed. He is not at all pleased to see his beloved drooping and sighing over a decidedly pectoral slave instead of an unresponsive statue. Maia is equally unhappy. She can only dream of how she will rescue her Diomed from the clutches of Antonia so that they may flee Rome to the haven of some uninhabited loveland ('The Golden Isle').

In the meanwhile, Rome is being turned 'Topsy Turvy' by the musical comedy version of the Saturnalia feast, where all the city's slaves are allowed temporarily to be the equals of their masters. There are processions and drinking and fighting and singing (Chorus of Saturnalia/The Revels) and disguises and general wild merriment in the streets. Diomed does not join in the celebrations, but pines alone for Maia ('The Girl of my Heart'). Iris, on the other hand, is full of fun ('I'm a Naughty Girl') and optimism: now that Antonia is beginning to understand what frustrated love is she is likely to be more sympathetic to Iris' affair with Archias.

Antonia, however, is not particularly sympathetic to anything. She is merely miserable, and when Pomponius attempts to capitalise on her state he gets a cold rebuff. The Prefect turns his frustration on to Heliodorus who is obliged to come up with some alternative plan to soften the lady towards Pomponius. A cloak, the darkness and the general mêlée of the Saturnalia all conspire to make Heliodorus and Marcus spend a farcical scene mistakenly apostrophising Maia, who profits from the occasion by making the Prefect swear that come what may he will do no harm to Diomed, Maia and even Heliodorus.

The crowds of revellers are entertained by Iris' cautionary tale of 'A Frog He Lived in a Pond' but their opportune arrival also saves Maia from discovery. Pomponius is swept up amongst the populace he rules so disdainfully to grittily go through a bonhomous act describing the impossibilities of pleasing all of the people all of the time ('I Want to Be Popular') while the situation and the close attentions of the fat and fond Melanopis reduce Heliodorus to a quivering wreck ('Nothing but Nerves').

As Diomed and Maia prepare to flee Rome, Antonia appears. The whole plot is discovered. The lovers beg the wounded princess to 'Forgive' and she, wisely counselled by Iris, agrees to do so. Whatever she has suffered, she has at least learned what it is to love: the god of love did indeed come to her. And Marcus Pomponius may, if nothing else, continue to hope, as the curtain falls to a final chorus ('Hail! Antonia, Hail!').

A Greek Slave was revised shortly after its original production and both 'I Want to be Popular' and 'I'm a Naughty Girl' were then inserted into the score. A later revision brought in the song 'Love in Mine Eyes' for Marie Tempest (Maia).

A CHINESE HONEYMOON

a musical comedy in two acts by George Dance. Music by Howard Talbot. Produced at the Theatre Royal, Hanley, 16 October 1899 with Lionel Rignold (Pineapple), Florence Wilton (Mrs Pineapple), W T Thompson (Hang Chow), Stephen Adeson (Tom) and Violet Dene (Soo Soo). Produced at the Strand Theatre, London, 5 October 1901 in a revised version with additional songs by Ivan Caryll, Ernest Woodville, Ernest Vousden, etc. with Rignold (Pineapple), Ellas Dee (replaced by Marie Dainton) (Mrs Pineapple), Louie Freear (Fi Fi), Picton Roxburgh (Hang Chow), Leslie Stiles (Tom) and Beatrice Edwards (Soo Soo). Produced at the Prince of Wales Theatre 28 January 1915 with Arthur Wellesley, Marie George, Dorothy Minto, Edward Sass, Lawrence Robbins and Carda Walker.
   Produced at the Casino Theatre, New York, 2 June 1902 with Thomas Q Seabrooke, Adele Ritchie, Katie Barry, Edwin Stevens, Van Rensslaer Wheeler and Amelia F Stone.
   Produced at the Central-Theater, Hamburg, 12 February 1903 in a version by C M Roehr.

CHARACTERS

Emperor Hang Chow *of Ylang Ylang*
Soo Soo, *his niece*
Chippee Chop, *the Lord Chancellor*
Hi Lung, *Lord High Admiral*
Tom Hatherton
Mr Samuel Pineapple
Mrs Marie Pineapple
Florrie, Violet, Millie, Gertie, *their bridesmaids*
Fi Fi, *a waitress at Ylang Ylang hotel*
Yen Yen, Sing Sing, Mi Mi, *Soo Soo's maids of honour*
Mrs Brown, *the official mother-in-law*

ACT 1
The Chinese kingdom of Ylang Ylang has a curiously mobile constitution. Forty years ago the Emperor Hang Chow, who reigns over Ylang Ylang, saw

fit to decree that, in order to give full employment to the Lord Chancellor, Chippee Chop, that august official should each day invent a new Act of Parliament. This has resulted in some remarkable not to say opportunistic laws, the most recent being one which enacted that any member of the royal family who kisses a person must marry them. Chippee Chop has since spent his time trying to steal a kiss from the lovely Princess Soo Soo, the Emperor's niece, so that, in the absence of her official fiancé, the Admiral Hi Lung, he may mount to the sought-after position of royal nephew-in-law.

The absence of Hi Lung is the result of another imperial whim. The very middle-aged Emperor Hang Chow has decided to wed. He has no intention of wedding anyone in China, as they would surely take him from mercenary motives and the Emperor has the desire to be loved for himself and his better profile only. Instead he has sent Hi Lung to Europe armed with a photograph and instructions to tell prospective brides that the picture is that of a charming Chinese bill-sticker.

A whole year has passed before the folk of Ylang Ylang, taking tea at the city's hotel ('In Ylang Ylang'), are able to greet the returning Admiral. But Hi Lung has come back empty-handed: nowhere in ninety-seven ports could he find anyone anxious to marry sight unseen a rather unprepossessing Chinese bill-sticker of uncertain age ('Roly Poly') and he is in fear for his un-Chinese head. Hi Lung, you see, is an Englishman: a former seaman risen to high honours in foreign parts thanks to the first-rate sea skills he learned on Britannia's waves.

In fact, Ylang Ylang is, for such a very foreign part, rather a repository for English persons. There is Fi Fi (actually Arabella from Acton), the waitress at the hotel, a plain little body with a sad track record in boyfriends, come out east to track down her missing Richard (who is none other, in fact, than Hi Lung), and there is Tom Hatherton, a naval officer, who has thrown in his commission to stay in Ylang Ylang for the sake of a pretty singing girl and who has become the latest object of the ever-amorous Fi Fi's passions. Since he cannot pay his bill at the hotel, Tom courts her assiduously but chastely and spends his real sighs on his sweet Soo Soo.

No, there are not two Soo Soos in Ylang Ylang. The singing girl is none other than the Princess herself, out to show off her pretty soprano voice in public ('A Paper Fan') and to find a little adventure in disguise. She has a small dilemma of course: she loves Tom, but she is engaged to Hi Lung and pursued by Chippee Chop. Hi Lung has a bigger dilemma, for he has no wife for the approaching Emperor ('The Emperor Hang Chow') which probably means no head for Hi Lung. When the time comes, in desperation he presents the ever-willing Fi Fi as a candidate but, encouraged by the partisan prompting of Chippee Chop, Hang Chow rejects the funny little waitress and Hi Lung is sentenced to death by tickling with gardening rakes for disappointing his Emperor.

The English population of Ylang Ylang, disproportionate though it already is, is about to increase once more, for Hi Lung's ship has brought with it an English honeymoon party ('A Chinese Honeymoon'): Mr Samuel Pineapple, Tom's uncle, and his bright new little wife and ex-typist, Marie

('The À la Girl'), accompanied by her four little sisters and bridesmaids whom she has insisted on bringing along to keep an eye on her husband's tendencies to flirt. Also on board is one battleaxe of a Mrs Brown, Pineapple's old housekeeper. Desolate at his marriage to the typist, she is preparing to bury her broken heart in far-off China where she has accepted the position of official mother-in-law in the imperial family of Ylang Ylang.

It is clear that complications are inevitable and soon confrontation follows confrontation: Soo Soo is caught singing a duet with Tom ('Roses Red and White') and her masquerade is uncovered, Mrs Brown runs into her Samuel, and Hi Lung, who has a horrid fear of garden rakes, desperately shows the Emperor's photo with alluring promises to everyone in sight until, under the tutelage of Mrs Brown, half a dozen desperate people revert to singing of childish 'Nursery Rhymes' to escape present horrors. Mrs Brown's consoling of Samuel is a little too chummy for the ever watchful bridesmaids who are soon blowing the whistles issued by Marie for such occasions to bring the bride hurrying to the spot. The furious Mrs Pineapple vows revenge on her flirtatious husband and, urged on by Hi Lung, she agrees without demur to a kiss from the Emperor, little realising what such an action means in Ylang Ylang. Thus the Emperor has his bride and Hi Lung's reward is Soo Soo.

Tom is desolate and Pineapple and his wife (who now has to be passed off as his daughter for the Emperor's benefit) are aghast but Fi Fi, who sees herself sweetly comforting the broken-hearted Tom on the trip back to England, is in the mood for a comic song about an earlier admirer who taught her piano ('The Twiddley Bits'). A further complication ensues when Pineapple gives an avuncular kiss to Soo Soo and is caught. Now he must marry her. Both Pineapples are about to be made unwillingly bigamous through not conning the laws of the country they chose for their honeymoon ('A Royal Honeymoon').

ACT 2

At the Palace, the wedding feast of Samuel Pineapple and Soo Soo is being prepared ('With Weary Hearts'), soon to be followed by the wedding of the Emperor and Mrs Pineapple. Good-hearted Fi Fi arranges for Tom to get into the palace disguised as a doctor. He will declare the Princess unwell and prescribe a sea journey (with himself in attendance) as cure. Soo Soo is delighted and showers honours on the little waitress to give her a cue to declare in song 'I Want to Be a Lidy' before the Princess herself obliges with the tale of 'Daisy With a Dimple on her Chin', and Pineapple, longing for escape from all this nightmare of marriage, sings dreamily of his Utopia in 'That Hapy Land'.

Meanwhile, Marie has disguised herself as a Chinese singing girl in order to avoid the Emperor (who is joining in a congratulatory song called 'You Pat Me') and thus escape with Soo Soo and Tom. Chippee Chop smuggles her into the palace to meet up with them, only to betray her to the Emperor. The Princess's attendant is a fake! Thinking himself ever so clever, Hang Chow

81

pounces on Soo Soo's companion and presses a betrothal ring on her without realising that there are two disguised handmaidens about and it is Fi Fi and not Marie whom he has so hastily grabbed. The official mother-in-law is now ceremonially presented ('Welcome, Official Mother-in-Law') and, with the power of her gimlet eye, she soon has the Emperor running about like a naughty child.

Complication once more follows complication, and disguise gives way to disguise as Soo Soo attempts to escape by being carried off to the mortuary under the influence of a Juliet Capulet kind of drug, and the threat of half the cast being barbecued in the imperial frying pan reappears constantly amid a series of topical songs ('Tit-bits From the Plays'/'I Hear They Want Some More'/'Penelope') and speciality numbers ('Mandie From Ohio' sung by Mrs Pineapple in blackface, a little Chinese duet 'Click Click' for Fi Fi and the Emperor, 'But Yesterday' crooned by Tom, and a Chinese Cakewalk dance speciality). Fi Fi tops them all when she is required to prove that she is indeed a Chinese singing girl and renders in rousing music hall style the very un-Chinese story of a family orchestra in 'Martha Spanks the Grand Pianner'.

The *deus ex machina* of the frightful muddle into which everyone has got his and herself is, as in all good foreign tales, the doughty British consul. The Emperor is ordered to surrender up all the British subjects in his palace and since Britannia rules not only the waves but everything else he is forced to do so. His goodly act is rewarded by a kiss from Mrs Brown and—here we go again!—that means that she must marry him (as if she didn't know it). Soo Soo, awakened from her drug to a new life, is also to wed the first man who kisses her and Hi Lung and Chippee Chop are beaten to the embrace by the Varsity blue sprinting of Tom. The Pineapples are restored to marital harmony and the bridesmaids can throw away their whistles. As for Fi Fi...well, what's one more missed marriage after so many? She lives to try again as everyone joins in the finale ('He Is the Bridegroom').

The score of *A Chinese Honeymoon* was extremely mobile during its initial long run at the Royal Strand Theatre and, particularly in the loosely structured second act, there was much flexibility in the songs and ensembles used. Those pieces listed here include the principal numbers but, at various times, some of these were omitted or shifted or replaced, and a number of other songs made longer or shorter appearances in the score including 'Egypt' (Clare Kummer) sung variously by Tom or Soo Soo, 'The Maid of Pekin' for Soo Soo, 'Chow-Chow's Honeymoon', for Soo Soo and Tom, and the sextet 'Follow Your Leader' (Ernest Vousden/Dance). On Broadway, the Melville Ellis/Robert B Smith 'The Leader of the Frocks and Frills' was interpolated for Mrs Pineapple, 'Laughter Is Queen Tonight' for Soo Soo and, most successfully, the Jean Schwartz/William Jerome 'Mr Dooley' for Thomas Seabrooke as Pineapple.

SAN TOY

or The Emperor's Own, a Chinese musical comedy in two acts by Edward A Morton. Lyrics by Harry Greenbank and Adrian Ross. Music by Sidney Jones. Additional music by Lionel Monckton. Produced at Daly's Theatre, London, 21 October 1899 with Hayden Coffin (Bobbie), Marie Tempest (San Toy), Rutland Barrington (Yen How), Huntley Wright (Li) and Gracie Leigh (Dudley). Revived there 7 April 1902 with Donald Mather, Jean Colin, Leo Sheffield, Frederick Bentley and Rita Page.

Produced at Daly's Theatre, New York, 1 October 1900 with Melville Stewart, Marie Celeste, George K Fortescue, James T Powers and Minnie Ashley. Revived there 17 April 1905.

Produced at the Carltheater, Vienna, as *San Toy (Der Kaisers Garde)* in a version by Carl Lindau and Hugo Felix 9 November 1900 with Marie Halton as San Toy.

Produced at the Central-Theater, Berlin, 2 March 1901 with Miss Halton.

CHARACTERS

Sir Bingo Preston, *British Consul at Pynka Pong*
Lieutenant Bobbie Preston RN, *his son*
Poppy Preston, *his daughter*
Dudley, *her maid*
Lieutenant Harvey Tucker RN
The Emperor of China
Yen How, *a Mandarin*
Yung Shi, Me Koui, Siou, Shuey Pin Sing, Li Kiang, Hu Yu, *his wives*
San Toy, *his daughter*
Li
Fo Hop, *a Chinese student*
Sing Hi, *President of the Emperor's Board of Ceremonies*
Ko Fan, *an officer of the Emperor's Own*
Wun Lung, *an officer of the Emperor's Own*
Chu, *Poppy's nurse*
Li Hi, Li Lo, Trixie, Mrs Harley Streeter, Hon Mrs Hay Stackpole, Miss Mary Lambkin, Lady Pickleton, Wai Ho, Hu Pi, Mo Ti, Rose Tucker, etc.

ACT 1

A suttee procession is passing through the town of Pynka Pong, bearing the elderly nurse of the household of the Mandarin, Yen How, to be burned on the funerary pyre of her late husband. As the procession pauses outside the British consulate, however, the old woman leaps from her chair and, escaping her attendants, seeks refuge in the precincts of Sir Bingo Preston's house. This easterner, at least, prefers the custom of the west to that of her own country and she has made a public choice.

Tonight is the Feast of the Full Moon 'In Pynka Pong' and the people of the town are making ready for the occasion. Two jade merchants, business rivals, each try to curry favour and his rival's downfall by gifts of money to the lively little Li, private secretary to the mandarin Yen How. That noble potentate is all-powerful in Pynka Pong. Pekin and the Emperor of China are a long way away and 'The Mandarin' (and his secretary) are the people to be in with.

Li is happy to take both bribes, and go his unconcerned way to flirt with Dudley, 'The Ladies' Maid' at the consulate. His true Chinese love, Ko Fan, is in Pekin, for it is a law in China that eligible daughters of the nobility must at a certain age be sent to the Emperor to serve in his personal corps of lady guards, the Emperor's Own. It is strange customs such as this which make Poppy Preston, the consul's daughter, long for the familiar ways of England, and sigh over some pressed flowers sent to her from her far-off home ('A Posy From Over the Sea').

The great Yen How, the proud possessor under another useful law of 'Six Little Wives', accepts the conscription law, but he circumnavigates it. He has a daughter, but it is a secret. So very fond was he of his little daughter, San Toy, that he knew at her birth that he could not bear to comply with the imperial law and send her away to become a member of the famous regiment. So San Toy was brought up as a boy and for many years only her old nurse, Chu, knew any better. Unfortunately, their secret was discovered by the unattractive student Fo Hop, and the price of his connivance is San Toy's hand in marriage. But Yen How has been clever: he has told Fo Hop that he may marry San Toy, but only on condition that nobody shall ever know she is a girl. It is a condition which would clearly be broken by a marriage.

What neither Fo Hop nor Yen How knows is that San Toy is herself in love ('The Petals of the Plum Tree'). During her father's absence on state affairs, she has become very friendly with the Preston family and Sir Bingo's son Bobbie had been teaching the 'boy' his letters until the discovery that he was a she led to a very different kind of 'ABC'. Sir Bingo Preston is at pains to do everything he can to please Yen How, as he needs certain trade concessions from the Mandarin, but if he were to learn that his son had the intention to marry a Chinese girl, even an aristocratic one, there would be all sorts of trouble. There is little likelihood that the Mandarin would look on the match any more favourably than the consul so, for the moment, Bobbie and San Toy keep their love to themselves.

The ceremony of the Festival of the Full Moon ('The Moon') brings a picturesque scene and gives the opportunity for a good deal of foolery from Li who has purloined a bottle of eau de cologne from Dudley and, fishing it from the collection of stolen goods in his capacious sleeves, has drunk it, with unfortunate results. After a quartet vaunting the small town qualities of 'Pynka Pong', Bobbie and San Toy meet. He is off to Pekin on his father's business and must for a while leave her, but he leaves her with a song ('Love Has Come From Lotus Land').

The jealous Fo Hop is quick to challenge San Toy. He has spied on her love scene and, although she swears she will never be his bride, he describes in song how he will turn her back from the westernised creature she is becoming into a model Chinese wife ('When You Are Wed to Me'). When Li and Dudley get to chaffing each other on the subject of love and married life they quickly agree that, in spite of the difference in customs, it is the 'Samee Gamee' in all parts of the world.

But now a sad blow strikes. Yen How has just despatched Li to Pekin to reassure the Emperor that his only child is indeed a boy, when he finds that the Emperor has sent out a fresh edict requiring all the sons of Mandarins to join a new regiment at Pekin. This time San Toy is well and truly caught. No matter which sex she owns to, she must go. And the Emperor is clearly suspicious. Yen How has been noticeably lax in his response to imperial commands and he seems likely soon to be in trouble.

San Toy resolves to go to Pekin and there change her dress for a feminine one and, by her sweetness, attempt to prevent any harm falling on her father. She leaves with Bobbie on his ship and the furious Fo Hop arrives too late: they are gone, and he can only vent his anger by revealing to the astonished crowd that San Toy is a girl. The anxious Yen How vows that he will go to Pekin himself and beat the Emperor's drum, which all who wish to petition His Imperial Majesty must do, and thus attempt save his daughter from any misfortune.

ACT 2

In the Emperor's Palace at Pekin, Mandarins are so common that there is a whole chorus of them to open the act ('We're the Cream of Courtly Creatures') and to introduce the Emperor. When San Toy is brought before His Majesty, he finds her utterly charming. She shall not be buried in the ranks of the Emperor's Own: she shall be treated with high imperial favour. Indeed she shall.

Now, bit by bit, the rest of Pynka Pong start arriving in Pekin. Firstly Li (who came by land and thus got overtaken by San Toy and Bobbie) arrives and bangs the Emperor's drum. This is a dreadful thing to do as the Emperor can't bear the sound of the drum, and the little man is soon in a whole set of fixes, especially as he starts insisting that San Toy is male when it has been perfectly obvious to the whole court ever since she arrived that she's anything but.

Dudley turns up, helps Li out of a scrape and entertains the Emperor with the irrelevant tale of 'Rhoda and her Pagoda' (being Chinese he knows what a pagoda is, except that in English terminology it's a tea shop). Then, after the massed corps of the very attractive 'Emperor's Own' have marched in, the whole of the Preston family and the consulate staff put in an appearance ('By Our Majestic Monarch's Command'). Poppy explains in song ('The Whole Story') something of western marriage customs, and Bobbie waxes patriotic over 'Sons of the Motherland', while San Toy assures her lover that the Emperor's attentions to her do not alter one whit her devotion to him and that soon they will sail over the seas together where she will be his 'Little China Maid'.

Li spends most of the act trying to keep one step ahead of a pair of permanently pursuing royal guards and hides inside a china figure to try to give them the slip. This provides a cue for a duet with Dudley (China Duet), before the little man has sense enough to declare 'Me Gettee Outee Velly Quick'. Yen How and his six little wives are also now on the scene ('We Have Come to See') to add their voices to the confusion. Yen How sees San Toy's position in favour as a veritable chance for advancement: he has all sorts of plans for that day when he is named Viceroy and all sorts of ideas learned from his British friends which would change Chinese society to its benefit ('I Mean to Introduce it into China'). With all that is going on, it is not surprising that the English folk are confirmed in their doubts about Chinese fashions, and they and the put-upon Li all long to be 'Back in London'.

The Emperor shows no signs of letting San Toy leave his palace—in fact, there seems to be every chance that she may be elected to head his group of wives—but, after Bobbie has sung to her of being 'The One in the World' and she has taken time out to sing about 'The Butterfly', and Li has interpolated a comical song and routine about soldiers of different nations ('Chinee Soje-Man'), the stars come to the rescue. It is declared that the Emperor is astrologically 'suited'to a curvaceous member of the Emperor's Own, so San Toy is left free to go to her Bobbie, and Li to his old love whom he has rediscovered in uniform, while Yen How, instead of being punished for his deception, wins his coveted promotion to Viceroy (Finale).

The score of San Toy was varied with such successful numbers as Lionel Monckton's 'It's Nice to Be a Boy Sometimes' and 'All I Want Is a Little Bit of Fun' in a major reworking of the title role to allow for the vocal limitations and style of take-over star Ada Reeve . These songs remained in the score when the show was subsequently produced with a leading lady of soubrette status. The role of Li was for some time expanded with several songs including the successful 'When Him Goey La-di-da' (Paul Rubens) and 'The Mousetrap' (Paul Rubens), and other songs including 'Somebody' for San Toy, 'Pretty Little Chinee' for Li and Dudley, and 'Catchy Coo' (Herbert Shelley) for Ethel Irving as Dudley, were tried for various periods. In the London revival Patrick Barrow's 'Make It Snappy' was interpolated for Dudley.

FLORODORA

a musical comedy in two acts by Owen Hall. Lyrics by Ernest Boyd-Jones and Paul Rubens. Music by Leslie Stuart. Additional songs by Paul Rubens. Produced at the Lyric Theatre, London, 11 November 1899 with Evie Greene (Dolores), Melville Stewart (replaced by Sydney Barraclough) (Abercoed), Ada Reeve (Lady Holyrood), Willie Edouin (Tweedledpunch) and Kate Cutler (Angela). Revived there 20 February 1915 with Miss Greene, Jamieson Dodds, May Leslie Stuart, Edward Lewis and Josephine Ellis. Produced at Daly's Theatre 29 July 1931 with Violet Code, Geoffrey Davis, Dorothy Ward, George Graves and Lorna Hubbard.

Produced at the Casino Theatre, New York, 12 November 1900 with Fannie

Johnstone, Sydney Deane, Edna Wallace Hopper, Willie Edouin and May Edouin. Produced at the Winter Garden Theatre 27 January 1902 with Dorothy Morton, Sydney Barraclough, Virginia Earle, Thomas Q Seabrooke and Toby Claude. Produced at the Broadway Theatre 27 March 1905 with Maud Lambert, Joseph Phillips, Adele Ritchie, Philip H Ryley and Elsa Ryan. Produced at the Century Theatre 5 April 1920 with Eleanor Painter, Walter Woolf, Christie MacDonald, George Hassell and Margot Kelly.

Produced at the Théâtre des Bouffes-Parisiens, Paris, January 1903 in a version by Adrien Lamy and F A Schwab with Paulette Darty, Piccaluga, Mlle Dziri, Simon-Max and Mlle Ginette.

CHARACTERS

Cyrus W Gilfain, *proprietor of the perfume and of the island of Florodora*
Frank Abercoed, *manager for Gilfain on the island of Florodora*
Captain Arthur Donegal, *4th Royal Life Guards and Lady Holyrood's brother*
Leandro, *overseer of Florodora's farms*
Anthony Tweedlepunch, *a showman, phrenologist, hypnotist and palmist*
Lady Holyrood
Dolores
Angela Gilfain
Tennyson Sims, Ernest Pym, Max Äpfelbaum, Reginald Langdale, Paul Crogan, John Scott, *Gilfain's clerks*
Daisy Chain, Mamie Rowe, Lucy Ling, Cynthia Belmont, Lottie Chalmers, Clare Fitzclarence, *friends of Angela*, etc.

ACT 1

Florodora is a very little island which apparently forms part of the Philippine group. Owned by the ridiculously rich Cyrus W Gilfain, it is both famous and commercially desirable as the production centre of the wonderful Florodora perfume, a fragrance concocted from Philippine flowers to a secret formula of which Gilfain is the only holder. The flowers are picked by the Florodorean maidens and men who provide the opening chorus ('Flowers A-Blooming So Gay'), while the commercial side of affairs is left to six clerks imported from Britain to keep Gilfain's business in good working order ('The Credit's Due to Me'). Both sides of the Florodora enterprise are under the efficient management of another import, the dashing young Englishman Frank Abercoed.

Abercoed is a little bit of a mystery, as he has run away from London and buried himself in Pacific anonymity rather than marry an unnamed but wealthy lady with whom he was not in love. On Florodora, however, love has come to him, for he has sprung a passion for the Carmenesque Dolores, the loveliest and laziest of Gilfain's workforce. In spite of her failings, Gilfain surprisingly gives this girl double wages and allows her to come and go announces her arrival to the waltz rhythms of song about 'The Silver Star of Love'. Abercoed would like to tell her of his feelings for her, but honour

87

binds him to the lady in London to whom he is still officially engaged and, thus, he can only tell Dolores that he is in love with 'Somebody', a bit of periphrasis which she sees through delightedly enough to join in and make the number a duet.

One day the island receives an unexpected visit from a strange little man who is not, he insists, a commercial traveller. He is Anthony Tweedlepunch, a 'wholesale scientist' and general charlatan who has crossed the seas following the trail of a certain Miss Guisara. The local people's fascination with this walking oddity is soon forgotten when a many gun salute marks the return of Gilfain to his island (Chorus of Welcome). Gilfain has been in England throwing his weight and his money about and he has bought a wonderful old castle in Wales as a home and a base for an English outlet for the Florodora operation.

He has returned to the island with a boatload of passengers including half a dozen young English ladies, 'remnants left over from the matrimonial stock of the latest London season', who are quickly snapped up by the clerks with a request to 'Come and See Our Island', and the society widow Lady Holyrood who is making an effort to marry her brother, Captain Donegal, to Gilfain's pretty daughter Angela and who, at the same time, is not averse to making a play for the millionaire on her own behalf.

Lady Holyrood knows Abercoed and is delighted to have solved the mystery of his whereabouts as the newspapers, getting it all wrong as usual, had reported that he had run off with a ballet girl or gone into a mental asylum or both. She is also delighted to bring him some news. Firstly, owing to a convenient death in the family, he is now Lord Abercoed and, secondly, the lady he was to have married was married a year since to someone else, so he has no need to maintain the scruples which have so far prevented him addressing his love to Dolores.

Angela and Donegal have no such compunctions. They are itching to be wed and their emotions and impatience are literally 'Galloping' away with them. But they have a problem. Gilfain, having originally given consent for their match, has withdrawn it on finding out about Abercoed's good fortune and he is now determined to wed Angela to his newly ennobled manager. Unbeknown to anyone, he is equally determined to pair himself off with Dolores. Lady Holyrood, who is a person to be reckoned with, has opposite views on all these subjects and initiates her schemes with a song aimed squarely at her rich target ('I Want to Marry a Man, I Do').

Angela gives a lovely incidental song about 'The Fellow Who Might' before Gilfain's plot is put into action with the aid of Tweedlepunch and his pseudo-scientific abilities ('Phrenology'). Cyrus plans that the whole island shall be called together and the little showman will pair off everybody according to their natural affinities. It is, of course, agreed and paid for that he shall find Gilfain suited to Dolores, and Angela the perfect mate for Abercoed. This plan goes awry when the subjects blankly refuse to accept Tweedlepunch's judgements ('When an Interfering Person') and Abercoed angrily resigns from Gilfain's employ. In a soulful ballad ('The Shade of the Palm') he bids farewell to Dolores, and the chorus of islanders, mismatched by Tweedlepunch ('Hey, Hey Alack a-Day'), launch the finale to the act as Frank Abercoed leaves Florodora to return to England.

ACT 2

At Abercoed Castle—for it is Frank's family seat that Gilfain has bought when the family 'lost more at Tattersalls than they could make back at Christie's'—Cyrus W has set up in splendid residence complete with all the ghastly trappings of the nouveau riche ('The Millionaire'). Lady Holyrood has attached herself to him as an indispensble aid to social success, for even a millionaire is nothing but a baby in the hands of a lady of title with know-how and 'Tact'. Much to Angela's delight Lady Holyrood has used her position to get Captain Donegal invited to stay ('Willie Was a Gay Boy').

The six clerks are also enjoying their new location and have time to pick up where they left off with Angela's six friends to indulge in a double sextette ('Tell Me, Pretty Maiden'). The other principals arrive in disguise, Abercoed first, declaring that, given the circumstances, he will say farewell to his family home and return to Florodora to find Dolores, and then Dolores and Tweedlepunch dressed as a couple of itinerant bards ('When We Are on the Stage').

Lady Holyrood is doing exceptionally well at convincing Gilfain of her necessity to his well-being and she is pretty certain that she has the man and his money on the hook ('I've an Inkling'), but there seems to be something getting in the way of his committing himself. Dolores fills in with one or two incidental ballads ('The Queen of the Philippine Islands' and/ or 'The Island of Love'), and Donegal adds a touch of the military with 'I Want to Be a Military Man', before the winding-up of the story gets under way.

Lady Holyrood has found an ally of circumstance in Tweedlepunch, from whom, with the help of £500 of Gilfain's money, she has mined the reasons for his initial visit to Florodora. The charlatan was, as might have been suspected, on the make. He had heard that Gilfain was a thief and a trickster who, having been entrusted with the guardianship of the baby daughter of the owner of Florodora, the late Senor Guisara, took the island and its perfumery for himself, leaving the little girl to grow up in ignorance of her inheritance. That little girl is now a big girl and marriage with her would tie up the situation nicely and absolve Gilfain from any crime.

So now we know why he is so anxious to marry Dolores. She is the missing Guisara daughter. To bring things to a head, Lady Holyrood plans a little charade. Tweedlepunch narrates to a nervous Gilfain the legend of Abercoed Castle, a frightful tale with a curse in it which will come to rest on any treacherous man who tricks a maiden from her youthful inheritance. Lady Holyrood appears as the pursuing spirit of the ghost Ethelwynda, dripping blood all over the place, and succeeds in frightening the misdemeanant into a confession which allows everyone to pair up as they ought to in time for the finale.

The second act of *Florodora* was little more than a selection of musical numbers topped and tailed by the necessary elements of plot and its songs were changed regularly with only the show's big hits, 'Tell Me, Pretty Maiden', 'Tact' and 'I've Got an Inkling', maintaining their places throughout. Amongst the alternative songs used during the initial run were 'We Get Up at 8 a.m.' (Valleda and Leandro), 'He Didn't Like the Look of it at All' for Louis Bradfield as Donegal, and a series of songs including Paul Rubens' 'The Queen of the Philippine Islands', Stuart's 'He Loves Me—He Loves Me Not' and the Ivan Caryll/Aubrey Hopwood 'The Island of Love' for the soprano Florence St John when she succeeded to the role of Dolores. The 1915 revival introduced Stuart's 'Beautiful Garden Girl' and 'Jack and Jill', while the 1931 revival interpolated Stuart's old hit 'Lily of Laguna' for Donegal and 'The Prapsis' (Tweedlepunch and Dolores). 'Land of Home', a ballad for Abercoed, found its way into the score even later and, as late as the early 1950s a touring production included the number 'Have Your Bumps Read' (Cyril Ornadel/Peter and David Croft) for Tweedlepunch. The original Broadway version held to the London score, but the 1920 New York revival used 'Come to St George's' from Stuart's *The Belle of Mayfair* and 'Hello, People' from his *Havana*, as well as 'Caramba' and 'Love Will Find You' in place of the usual numbers sung by Dolores.

THE ROSE OF PERSIA

or The Story-Teller and the Slave, a comic opera in two acts by Basil Hood. Music by Arthur Sullivan. Produced at the Savoy Theatre, London, 29 November 1899 with Walter Passmore (Hassan), Henry Lytton (Sultan), Ellen Beach Yaw (replaced by Isabel Jay) (Sultana), Rosina Brandram (Dancing Sunbeam) and Robert Evett (Yussuf). Revived at the Prince's Theatre 28 February 1935 with Joseph Spree, Charles Angelo, Helene Raye, Amy Augarde and Sidney Bracy.

Produced at Daly's Theatre, New York, 6 September 1900 with John Le Hay, Charles Angelo, Ruth Vincent, Amy Martin and Sidney Bracy.

CHARACTERS

The Sultan of Persia
Abu-el-Hassan, *a philanthropist*
Yussuf, *a professional story-teller*
Abdallah, *a priest*
The Grand Vizier
The Physician-in-Chief
The Royal Executioner
The Sultana Zubeydeh (Rose-in-Bloom)
Dancing Sunbeam, *Hassan's first wife*
Blush-of-Morning, *his twenty-fifth wife*
Heart's Desire, Honey-of-Life, Scent-of-Lilies, *the Sultana's favourite slaves*

Oasis-in-the-Desert, Moon-upon-the-Waters, Song-of-Nightingales, Whisper-of-the-West-Wind, *wives of Hassan*, etc.

ACT 1

Abu-el-Hassan is a very contented Persian but, by all the standards of polite Persian society, a very peculiar one. He has a fine house in the best part of town, apparently unlimited cash resources, and everything such resources can buy as well as a respectable complement of mostly attractive wives, yet he shuns the friendship of fashionable persons and prefers to spend his time and all that money with and on the professional have-nots of the town who nightly crowd his mansion for handouts and entertainment.

Some of the less wholly loyal of his wives are starting to express a doubt or two on his sanity ('As We Lie in Langour Lazy'), but Hassan has no such doubts ('I'm Abu-el-Hassan'). After all, although he could afford twice as many wives as he has, he has purposely limited himself to five-and-twenty: twice as many would just be twice the trouble. Surely such an intelligent decision proves his sanity. His chief wife, the dragonistic Dancing Sunbeam, is in no doubt as to her husband's feeble-mindedness. The very fact that he will not use his riches to win himself—and her—an exalted social position is proof enough of madness.

Another who has an interest in proving that Hassan is out of line is the lip-serving priest Abdallah who is planning, with tacit state support, to exorcise the madness from the wealthy philanthropist with the aid of some religiously approved and grotesque physical tortures ('When Islam First Arose'). Abdallah's intentions undergo a sudden U-turn when Hassan announces that he has made his will in Abdallah's favour. If Hassan is mad the will would, of course, be invalid.

The priest is now much more interested in arranging a sudden demise for Hassan than a simple committal, a solution which certainly wouldn't displease Dancing Sunbeam who has avaricious visions of how she would spend her late husband's fortune—it would be 'The Golden Key' to high society for her. Blush-of-Morning, an altogether more sympathetic wife, is quite depressed by the prevailing talk of widowhood but Abdallah and Dancing Sunbeam assure her that it is a condition which soon passes (Trio: 'If a Sudden Stroke of Fate').

Hassan's open house policy is well-known around Persia, so it is never any surprise to find an unusual number of strangers wandering into the courtyard of his home. This evening Yussuf, the ambulant story-teller, brings round a group of veiled ladies who claim to be a displaced group of dancing girls. The street-wise Yussuf suspects they are really royal slaves who have sneaked out in disguise for a night on the town, and he assures them that Hassan will give them hospitality until the Sultan and his guards are safely off-guard and they can return to the Palace.

The truth is, in fact, a little more monumental for, when Yussuf departs, it is revealed that one of the company is actually the Sultana, Rose-in-Bloom, herself making a most improper and indeed illegal foray outside the harem.

91

Having committed herself to this rash adventure, she is now not at all sure that her daring was a good idea (Trio: 'If You Ask Me to Advise You'). When she was back in the Palace the world outside seemed so tempting, and the Sultana describes in coloratura terms how her impatience to escape into the real world felt to her like the yearnings of a girl waiting for her lover (''Neath My Lattice').

Hassan returns to his home, bringing with him the nightly crew of beggars and fake cripples who profit from his open-handedness ('Tramps and Scamps'). He explains his fellow feeling for them by telling in a satirical song how he became 'Something in the City' and won his fortunes by dint of some very Victorian confidence tricks. The evening's revelry begins with wine all round. Yussuf, who is the tenor of the party, obliges with a ringing drinking song ('I Care Not If The Cup I Hold') and the visiting 'dancing girls' are then prevailed upon to contribute an exhibition of their talents to the entertainment ('Mystical Maidens Are We'), but consternation is strewn all about when the beastly Abdallah arrives with a party of bribed policemen ('We Have Come to Invade'). The beggars escape with practised speed and Abdallah, claiming a royal warrant to bring in a specimen of Hassan's guest list, arrests instead the 'dancing girls'.

The intrepid slave girl Heart's-Desire attempts to draw attention from her mistress by displaying the royal signet ring before the priest and claiming to be the Sultana, but the plan backfires. Abdallah gleefully informs Hassan that the penalty for consorting with the Sultana is some kind of execution, a penalty he finds most satisfactory given his position vis-à-vis inheritance. Dancing Sunbeam, hearing of this alienation of what she considers her wordly goods, is livid: 'What Will Become of Me?' she demands in an indignant octet.

Hassan accepts his fate with an amazing equanimity which is not shared by the girls. He then tells them his secret. His happy-go-lucky nature is due to a life of confirmed drug-taking. He is a bhang addict, floating through life on rosy, drug-induced cloud of unreality and, offering his narcotics around he announces, 'I mean to be off my head before they take my head off'.

Rose-in-Bloom, however, is not the only member of the royal family out doing a little slumming. The Sultan, his Vizier, his Physician and his Executioner arrive at Hassan's home dressed as dervishes and give verisimilitude to their disguise in a song (Dervish Quartet: 'I'm the Sultan's Vigilant Vizier') and characteristic dance. Hassan, by now brainless on drugs, claims himself to be not only the Sultan's equal but the Sultan himself. The real monarch resolves to play a trick on the lout, and orders that he be transported to the royal palace (Finale).

ACT 2

It is the next morning, and in the audience hall of the Sultan's palace Heart's-Desire is warbling a ditty on the nature of Love ('What Is Love?') and swapping sweet somethings with Yussuf. The lovesick story-teller announces his intention to ask the Sultan for the slave-girl's hand, but the other girls point out that he cannot. If it is found out how the two of them met, it would render them all liable to one of the Executioner's more terminal forms of punishment ('If You or I Should Tell the Truth').

The Sultan enters to a suitably subservient chorus ('From Morning Prayer the Sultan') and tells his entourage that he has decided to put Hassan to a test—after all, he is the first man ever to tell the Sultan to his royal face that he is as good a man as he, and he deserves some recompense. Hassan shall be led to believe that he really is Sultan and that his life to date has been nothing but a dream.

The Vizier, the Physician and the Executioner are ordered to transfer their grovelling and prostrating to the 'new' Sultan, a change which they find entirely against nature, and the Sultan takes the occasion to deliver a lively patter song ('Let a Satirist Enumerate a Catalogue of Crimes') on human nature and society, which he asserts is 'a sort of ginger pop—the dregs are at the bottom and the froth is at the top'. In his new persona as non-Sultan he also takes the opportunity to flirt democratically with the infuriated Executioner's lady friend.

A rather loud whirlwind intrudes on this little scene as Dancing Sunbeam arrives, indignantly claiming that if her husband is Sultan then she—it goes without saying—is Sultana (Septet: 'In My Heart of Hearts I've Always Known'). The real Sultan is amused by this new extension to his joke, but when the news gets to Rose-in-Bloom that there is another lady in the palace calling herself Sultana she assumes her misdemeanour has been discovered and that she has been deposed. She is in the middle of begging effusive pardon when she discovers the truth and she has to do some fast backtracking to cover her error (Duet: 'Suppose—I Say, Suppose').

In accordance with the Sultan's decree, the sleeping Hassan is brought in and set on the throne ('Laughing Low, on Tip-toe'). He wakes incredulously ('Where Am I?'), demanding, 'Has Dancing Sunbeam had the house redecorated while I've been asleep?', to find the whole court greeting him unflickeringly with royal honours. The day's petitioners are brought before him. The first is Yussuf who, without daring to be specific, asks for the hand of a royal handmaiden and gets in a frightful muddle trying to avoid any kind of admission of the truth. Then comes Abdallah. 'Ah,' cries the bewildered Hassan, 'do you know a man that folks call Mad Hassan?' 'Indeed,' answers the greedy priest, 'he is at the point of death, for when the Sultan knows his Sultana visited this man last night he will surely put Hassan to death.'

At this dreadful disclosure the real Sultan drops his masquerade. If the Sultana favours low company, he declares, then let her be summoned to the divorce ceremony and be married off to this story-teller who seems to be anxious to have a wife. As for the rest of the malefactors, behead them! (Quintet: 'It's a Busy Day'). Yussuf is distraught, for he has no wish to wed Rose-in-Bloom, perfectly lovely though she may be ('Our Tale Is Told'), and Heart's-Desire is properly piqued at such an unforeseen turn of events, but fate has yet another twist to her spindle, and the instrument of fate is Dancing Sunbeam. She has impeccable hearing and the mention of the word Sultana is guaranteed to make her prick up her ears. What is this

93

ceremony the Sultana is to attend? She and she alone is the Sultana. So, heavily veiled, Dancing Sunbeam goes to the divorce ceremony and she is divorced from her husband and wed to Yussuf before you can say Quartette ('What Does it Mean?').

Heart's-Desire finally manages to get in a word with the Sultan to explain that all this business is an awful mistake. It was she, she claims, wearing the Sultana's ring who was seen at Hassan's house; she was hearing from him a wonderful story which she was retelling to her mistress. The Sultan demands to know if the story has a happy ending. Of course it does. Very well, in that case he will hear it himself—but it must have a happy ending. Everyone tries frantically to think of a story fascinating enough to beguile the Sultan (Septet: 'It Has Reached Me a Lady Named Hubbard') but nothing they can come up with seems to have the necessary ingredients.

Time is getting short but, as the Sultan positions himself for the recital ('Hassan, the Sultan With his Court Approaches'), inspiration strikes Hassan and he begins his story with aplomb ('There Was Once a Small Street Arab'). It is the story of his life and, since it has been royally decreed that it must have a happy ending, he submits, the Sultan is obliged to rescind the execution orders. The Sultan confesses himself tricked and agrees that everyone must be pardoned, but he wins the last word for, as the curtain falls, he restores Hassan not only to his former wealth and position but also to the perpetual care of his number one wife, Dancing Sunbeam.

A COUNTRY GIRL

a musical play in two acts by James T Tanner. Lyrics by Adrian Ross. Additional lyrics by Percy Greenbank. Music by Lionel Monckton. Additional songs by Paul Rubens. Produced at Daly's Theatre, London, 18 January 1902 with Hayden Coffin (Geoffrey), Evie Greene (Nan), Lillian Eldée (Marjorie Joy), Rutland Barrington (Quinton Raikes), Huntley Wright (Barry) and Ethel Irving (Sophie). Revived there 28 October 1914 with Robert Michaelis, Gertie Millar, Nellie Taylor, F S Burroughs, W H Berry and Mabel Sealby; and 29 September 1931 with Roy Mitchell, Dorothy Ward, Ann Burgess, Griffith Moss, Dudley Rolph and Lorna Hubbard.

Produced at Daly's Theatre, New York, 22 September 1902 with Melville Stewart, Helen Marvin, Grace Freeman, Hallen Mostyn, William Norris and Minnie Ashley. Produced at the Herald Square Theatre 29 May 1911 with Stewart, Florence Burdett, Miss Freeman, Robert Elliot, John Slavin and Laura Jaffray.

Produced at L'Olympia, Paris, October 1904 in a version by Victor de Cottens and Fordyce with Max Dearly, Mariette Sully and Alice Bonheur.

CHARACTERS

Geoffrey Challoner
Mr Quinton Raikes (The Rajah of Bhong)
Sir Joseph Verity
Douglas Verity

Granfer Mummery
Lord Anchester
Barry
Marjorie Joy
Princess Mehelaneh
Madame Sophie
Mrs Quinton Raikes
Nan
Lord Grassmere, Major Vicat, Sir Charles Cortelyon, Lady Anchester, Miss
Powyscourt, Lady Arnott, Miss Courtlands, Miss Ecroyd, Miss Carruthers,
etc.

ACT 1
Once upon a time, down Devonshire way, old Squire Challenor presided
benevolently over the little country village where his manor house lay, and
bled away much of his family fortune in an attempt to alleviate the local
unemployment problem by reopening the tin mines which had once been the
region's principal source of income. The old Squire's son, Geoffrey, whiled
away much of his early years in the company of Marjorie Joy, the pretty
young inhabitant of a neighbouring rose-covered cottage, although he still
had time to pass with the village flirt, Nan, when Marjorie proved unkind.

On the old Squire's death, Geoffrey found he had more to think about
than girls, for his father's attempts at easing the unemployment problem had
gnawed away at his patrimony to such an extent that he needed to find a way
to replenish his funds. Leasing the manor to the rich and ambitious Sir
Joseph Verity, Geoffrey set off to sea to seek his fortune. The months and
then the years passed, and Marjorie too left the village to find a situation in
London town, but Nan stayed at home where the attentions of Sir Joseph
and his son Douglas and a goodly number of other gentlemen kept her life
lively.

At the opening of act one ('When the Birds Begin to Sing') it is five years
since Geoffrey left the village, and the Veritys are well installed at the manor.
Sir Joseph has plans that the diffident Douglas shall lend him a little reflected glory by being elected to Parliament for the borough, and he has even
more pressing intentions of a different kind towards the influential society
lady, Mrs Quinton Raikes, recently legally decreed a widow following the
disappearance of her husband somewhere amongst the Himalayas.

Mrs Raikes holds him at an arm's length, without appearing too terminally
discouraging for, although she has position, she is distinctly short of money
and is forced to agree to take her socially ambitious dressmaker, Madam
Sophie, to stay at the manor as a friend to compensate for not being able to
pay her bill. Sophie is in seventh heaven, for this is the village where she
grew up and she is delighted to be able to show her old friends how she has
risen in the world.

While the electioneering, the flirting and the social-climbing go on, who
should arrive back in town but Geoffrey Challoner and his faithful factotum
Barry. Geoffrey has the usual baritone paean to 'The Sailor's Life' up his

95

sleeve while Barry, who also has a rousing song to deliver ('Yo Ho, Little Girls') in a rather less heroic sea-going vein, is a quick-witted low comic who swiftly gets the local situation weighed up and sees that the villagers would much prefer to elect Geoffrey to Parliament than the unenthusiastic Douglas. Poor, silly Douglas seems to be losing out on all fronts for he can't make any serious progress with either the electorate or, more importantly to him, with Nan and, when he arrives with a shooting party of friends ('Shooting'), she makes falsely naïve fun not only of him but also of his friends' attempts at flirtation ('Try Again, Johnny').

It is the homecoming season in Devonshire, for Marjorie Joy has also come back, hot foot down from London where, unbeknown to all at home, she has become a singing star under an assumed name. She is longing to see Geoffrey again and she recalls their childish games and their private call to each other with enjoyment ('Coo'). Although she now has silks and satins to wear, she wants him to find her as he left her and, hiding her fine clothes, she dons her old blue dress and sunbonnet for their meeting. They are soon chatting happily together as if no time had passed at all and the sound of the 'Coo' song sets them reminiscing over the days when they were 'Boy and Girl'.

Geoffrey's ship has come from the Orient and he has brought with him some Eastern passengers, the Rajah of Bhong and his intended bride, the Princess Mehelaneh, who make their entrance to a superior but traditional eastern potentate song ('The Rajah of Bhong'). They are by no means a traditional pair, for the Rajah is a bona fide Englishman and the Princess a young lady of a distinctly feminist turn. She has insisted on being brought to Britain to be presented at the local Emperor's court before her marriage to the Rajah, and he is strangely anxious to get their business over and leave the country again.

The cause of his fears is made plain when he bumps into Lord Anchester, an old acquaintance from the days when he was an Englishman. The Rajah, it appears, was once upon a time a married man, the husband no less of Mrs Quinton Raikes. It was to escape his wife that he went off to the Himalayas and when he is informed that he is, according to British law, distinctly dead he is quite happy to remain that way. The Princess, on the other hand, is not so anxious to be on her way. She has learned from Barry that in England one may choose (within reason) one's preferred spouse and she is soon busy sizing up alternatives to her nervous Rajah.

An interlude between Douglas and Nan gives Nan the chance to sing a cautionary song about 'Molly the Marchioness' who married out of her class, before the village is invaded by Verity's society guests whose current fashionable pastime is playing at being rustics ('The Arcadians'), a charade which provides much amusement to the real country folk.

Barry has, in the meanwhile, been having a fine time whipping up support for Geoffrey's unwitting Parliamentary candidature, and now he has an attempt at filling his master's empty purse by selling off the worthless old tin mine to Verity on the pretext that providing work for the locals will earn his son the votes he needs to win the election. He also indulges in a bit of backchat with a fancy lady from the manor only to find that she is no lady but his old sweetheart, Sophie, and they are soon combining in their version of a reunion duet ('Two Little Chicks').

Barry's meddling produces problems as well as successes. The Princess, who has installed herself at the manor, has decided that her choice of husband shall be Geoffrey whom she will set up at her side in her native land 'Under the Deodar'. Barry is delighted at such an advantageous bit of matchmaking and, without realising the harm he is doing, chortles unwittingly over the affair to Marjorie Joy. As the finale begins, and the villagers welcome Geoffrey to the polls, the Princess publicly stakes her claim. Geoffrey, politely kissing her hand, declines the oriental match as Nan leads the villagers in decrying the foreigner for 'coming between a dear little lass and her lover' but, while Geoffrey assures Nan that Marjorie Joy is worth more than a throne to him, she, who has seen only the kiss, has gone, back to London and the stage.

ACT 2

At Lord Anchester's house in London a *bal à la Directoire* is being held ('From Seventy-five to Seventy-nine') to which all the principals of the piece in turn arrive to join in the ensemble 'Take Your Pretty Partner to the Ball'. There is Nan with a song ('I Can Laugh, I Can Love'), the Rajah accompanied by the Princess, desperately avoiding his widowed wife and longing for the happy land of Bhong and his usual 'Peace, Peace', Sophie, still under the social protection of Mrs Raikes who clearly hasn't yet paid her dressmaker's bill, and Marjorie Joy in her London persona as Miss Montague exerting a strange fascination over Geoffrey who finds in her an amazing resemblance to his lost sweetheart ('My Own Little Girl'). Most surprisingly, there is Barry, disguised as an old lady to get in past the doorman, and lending verisimilitude to his impersonation with the comical history of a chum in 'Me and Mrs Brown'.

Nan has another go at the Princess ('Beware!') who has still not renounced her pretensions to Geoffrey, while Barry gets involved in the tale of 'The Pink Hungarian Band' and ends up 'Quarrelling' with Sophie who has seen through his disguise and is determined to give him plenty to be jealous about. Sir Joseph Verity, on the other hand, a little shortsighted, has not penetrated the disguise and makes such heavy approaches to the 'lady' that Barry is obliged to seek refuge in the arms of the surprised Rajah. Geoffrey, when it is his turn for a number, gives the patriotic 'In the King's Name—Stand!'.

When the singing and fun are over, the action comes to its height. In the hearing of Miss Montague, Geoffrey squarely refuses the Princess's renewed offer in favour of the love of his 'little country girl' and, when Lord Anchester requests the actress to favour the company with a song, she obliges with 'Coo', thus revealing her double identity to a grateful Geoffrey. In the gilded galleries of Belgravia, the simple country girl gets her simple country boy while the rest of the company pair off in happy imitation.

During the course of its original run the score of the show was varied with a series of alternative songs including 'My Partners' (Arthur Bruhns/Ross), Monckton's 'The Season', 'A Dance for Jack' and 'The Real Smart Set' with lyrics by Adrian Ross, and a song for Rutland Barrington, 'It Will All Come Right' in which the artist collaborated on the lyrics with the show's authors; Paul Rubens' 'Not the Little Girl She Knew', 'When I Was a Girl' and 'She's Acting'; 'When I Was a Country Girl' written by Richard Temple for his wife Evie Greene; 'The Worst Woman in London', 'The Language of Love', and the Frank Tours/Leedham Bantock 'My Little Girlie'. The 1914 version of *A Country Girl* was crudely rearranged to suit the stars involved and the songs were sometimes ludicrously replaced or reallocated. Lionel Monckton supplied two new pieces, 'Pixies' and 'My Crinoline', for his wife, Gertie Millar, as Nan, 'There's Plenty of Love in the World' for Clara Butterworth as the Princess and 'Come Down to Devonshire' and 'The Sailor Man' for Robert Michaelis as Geoffrey.

MERRIE ENGLAND

a comic opera in two acts by Basil Hood. Music by Edward German. Produced at the Savoy Theatre, London, 2 April 1902 with Robert Evett (Raleigh), Henry Lytton (Essex), Rosina Brandram (Queen Elizabeth), Agnes Fraser (Bessie) and Walter Passmore (Wilkins). Produced at the Prince's Theatre 6 September 1934 with Joseph Hislop, Edgar Owen, Enid Cruickshank, Nancy Fraser and W S Percy. Produced at the Winter Garden Theatre 19 October 1944 with Walter Midgley, Reginald Gibbs, Gladys Palmer, Victoria Campbell and Charles Hawtrey. Produced at the Prince's Theatre in a revised version by Edward Knoblock 6 September 1945 with Heddle Nash, Dennis Noble, Linda Gray, Anna Jeans and Morris Sweden. Played at the London Coliseum 23 January 1951 with Kenneth Macdonald, William Dickie, Joan Wood, Vera Christie and C Denier Warrren. Produced at Sadler's Wells Theatre 10 August 1960 in a revised version by Dennis Arundell with John Carolan, John Hargreaves, Anna Pollak, Joan Stuart and Denis Dowling.

CHARACTERS

The Earl of Essex
Sir Walter Raleigh
Walter Wilkins, *a player in Shakespeare's company*
Silas Simkins, *another player*
Long Tom ⎱
Big Ben ⎰ *Royal Foresters*
Queen Elizabeth
Bessie Throckmorton
Jill-all-alone
May Queen
A Butcher, A Baker, A Tinker, A Tailor, Marjory, Kate, etc.

ACT 1

On the banks of the Thames, across the water from Windsor Castle, the townsfolk are celebrating an as yet unpoliticised May Day, fêting their May Queen and fitting her out with an escort of the day's champion bowmen, the forester brothers Long Tom and Big Ben ('We Are Two Proper Men'). The two brothers are inseparable but they do have one quarrel between them, for each holds that his beloved is the fairest of all Windsor maids. The May Queen is the choice of Ben, but Tom has been taken by the charms of the forest maid whom folk call Jill-all-alone and accuse of witchcraft.

To the jeers of the crowd, Jill approaches and sings of her refuge in nature from the foolish taunts of the world ('Oh, Where the Deer Do Lie'). It is soon clear that she has more wisdom and perspicacity than any of them, and more knowledge of the world and the court where, she recounts obliquely, the Queen of England sits flanked by her two liegemen: Essex, who would love her, and Raleigh whom she believes loves her but who, in fact, is enamoured of her lady-in-waiting, Bessie Throckmorton.

Jill's revelations are interrupted by the appearance of two comical players from William Shakespeare's company, the voluble Walter Wilkins and his satellite, Simkins. Wilkins expounds his theory of theatre ('I Do Counsel That Your Playtime'), advocating a jolly hornpipe in the middle of Hamlet's soliloquy to relieve the gloom, and remarking on areas of dramatic theory where he and Shakespeare disagree. The next to join the crowd is Sir Walter Raleigh himself who renders a tenor drinking song ('That Every Jack Should Have a Jill') before joining with the local folk in a quintet asserting that 'Love Is Meant to Make Us Glad'. Wilkins adds his set piece to the entertainment in the form of an improved alphabet version of Shakespeare's *Romeo and Juliet*.

When the festivities are over, Raleigh is left alone and soon the voice of Bessie Throckmorton is heard singing the plaintive 'She Had a Letter From Her Love' as she wends her way to their meeting. Alas, the words of the song are all too true for she has indeed lost a love letter written to her by Raleigh and she is in great fear lest it should find its way into the hands of the Queen. The lovers find solace in a pastoral duet ('When True Love Hath Found a Man') but they wot not that their final chorus is watched by the Earl of Essex who muses on how, to his own advantage, he may bring this romance to the Queen's notice without being openly the bearer of bad tidings. Simkins and Wilkins have their say on the effects of the thing known as love and join Essex in a trio ('When a Man Is a Lover').

The preparations for the people's May Day masque are in progress when Jill runs on pursued by a crowd, egged on by the May Queen, calling for her to be taken as a witch. As Tom steps to her defence, she calls for a fair trial and finds his and her part taken by Essex ('The Yeomen of England'). As the argument between the partisans of the May Queen and the forest girl continues, blows start to fall and the whole thing ends with Wilkins been dumped into the river by Ben. Essex's action in Jill's favour brings him an unexpected reward, for she has picked up the letter which Bessie has dropped, an acrostic in the form of her name and in the unmistakeable handwriting of the Queen's favourite. Essex takes the paper and orders Jill to be held for a royal decision on her fate.

Elizabeth arrives ('God Save Elizabeth') and delivers a rich contralto piece ('O Peaceful England') describing the quiet yet ever prepared state of England under her rule. She has come to witness the village May Day celebration and the masque of Robin Hood, but instead she is treated to the sight of the wretched Wilkins emerging dripping from the river. The actor wittily transforms his plight into the situation for a comical song ('King Neptune Sat on His Lonely Throne') which is at the same time a compliment to the Queen.

The masque begins the act's finale, with Bessie singing 'It Is a Tale of Robin Hood' until Jill is brought on and Tom begs the Queen's intervention on his beloved's behalf against the 'Four Men of Windsor' who are accusing her. Asked by Elizabeth to defend herself, Jill replies only with mysterious words, a veiled reference to the Queen's unrequited love for Raleigh and her own, requited, for Tom. Essex sees his chance and he presents the Queen with the letter. This paper was found on her; perhaps it is a love charm or some other token of witchcraft.

Elizabeth reads the letter and recognises it as Raleigh's writing. It is a love poem and the name that is spelled in the acrostic is Bessie—her name! But Raleigh will not accept the fortunate misunderstanding. He takes the letter and returns it to the hands of the Bessie for whom it was written ('My Troth Is Plighted'). The furious Elizabeth orders Raleigh to be banished, Bessie imprisoned and Jill to be burned as a witch.

ACT 2

At Herne's Oak, in the heart of Windsor forest, Jill is discovered at her cooking fire as the chorus in the distance sing their May Day songs. 'Cat, Cat, Where Have You Been' she sings, then goes to hide as she hears the sound of footsteps. Tom and Ben approach and are amazed to find her there but they are even more amazed when Bessie Throckmorton steps out from the oak. It is magic! But Jill's witchcraft is no more than inherited forest lore. Her grandfather, the king's forester, guarded the oak and its secret passage to the castle. It served old King Henry as a covert means of coming and going for his amorous affairs ('In England, Merrie England') and the forester kept curious townsfolk away by appearing from time to time at the oak in the guise of the legendary goblin, Herne the Hunter.

Wilkins, Simkins and some of the townspeople come to the same glade to rehearse a new masque of St George and the Dragon for the day's festivities, and Wilkins once more advocates his own preferred type of popular song and dance and 'A Big Brass Band' for all occasions. Then Queen Elizabeth comes in her turn for an assignation. She means secretly to purchase some poison from an apothecary with which she will murder her rival for Raleigh's affection. She is not aware that the apothecary to whom she adresses her order is the royal fool, disguised to defuse his mistress's misdeed.

Jill and Raleigh meet for a duet ('It Is the Merry Month of May') and the chorus bring on the May Queen to be crowned and to act as a spur for Raleigh's praises of 'The English Rose' before Wilkins and Tom join in to sing the tale of 'Robin Hood and Little John' and to lead off the players to the castle for their performance. As soon as they have left, Jill emerges from the oak, followed by Bessie whom she has been hiding in the secret passage. While the forest girl goes to seek Raleigh, Bessie joyfully sings of the blessings of love (Waltz Song: 'Oh, Who Shall Say That Love Is Cruel').

Jill brings Raleigh safely to his assignation but no sooner are the lovers together than Essex appears. He has followed Jill and Bessie through the secret tunnel from the castle, but he has no intention of hindering their escape or of preventing the love match he sees before him. If Raleigh is safely wed to Bessie, then his own chances with the Queen will be that much better and, in his book, 'a crown weighs more than Cupid nowadays'. The four join in the quartet 'When Cupid First This Old World Trod' and Essex uncovers a plan to prick the Queen's conscience and save them all. Their plotting is interrupted by the return of the players, still looking for a venue and an audience for their performance, and Wilkins delivers a satirical song on 'Imagination'.

Essex brings Queen Elizabeth on and seats her at Herne's oak to witness the performance. Although it is dusk there is, he avers, nothing to fear for the ghostly Herne appears only when the sovereign contemplates a crime. The masque begins with Wilkins and the May Queen speaking and singing its principal parts, but part way through the recital Elizabeth starts back at the sound of a ghostly hunting horn. Then, to her horror, the horned figure of Herne appears outlined on the edge of forest. Primed by Essex, the company all feign to see nothing and Elizabeth, grasping Essex's hand, orders away the false apothecary and his drugs. The news is brought that Jill and Bessie have escaped but the shamed monarch cries to let them go: they are pardoned. As Essex leads the repentant Queen away, the various pairs of lovers join happily with the villagers in a morris dance to the tale of 'Robin Hood's Wedding'.

Knoblock's version of *Merrie England* made severe alterations to the script, cutting the characters of Jill-all-alone, Simkins and the May Queen and several of the songs. The Sadler's Wells version restored some of these cuts but did not return wholly to Hood's libretto.

MISS HOOK OF HOLLAND

a Dutch musical incident in two acts by Paul Rubens and Austen Hurgon. Music and lyrics by Paul Rubens. Produced at the Prince of Wales Theatre, London, 31 January 1907 with G P Huntley (Hook), Isabel Jay (Sally), Walter Hyde (Van Vuyt), Gracie Leigh (Mina) and Herbert Clayton (Papp). Played there with a juvenile cast including Ida Valli as Hook 9 May 1907. Revived there 27 October 1914 with Alfred Wellesley,

Phyllis Dare, F Pope Stamper, Miss Leigh and J C Dalglish. Produced at Daly's Theatre 24 March 1932 with Mark Lester, Jean Colin, Harold Kimberley, Jenny Dean and Robert Layton.

Produced at the Criterion Theatre, New York, 31 December 1907 with Tom Wise, Christie MacDonald, John McCloskey, Georgia Caine and Bertram Wallis.

Produced at the Sommer Theater, Vienna, 22 June 1907.

CHARACTERS

Mr Hook, *a widower, a wealthy liqueur distiller*
Captain Adrian Papp ⎫
Bandmaster van Vuyt ⎬ *of the mounted artillery*
Ludwig Schnapps, *foreman of the distillery*
Simon Slinks, *a loafer*
Gretchen, *manageress of the distillery*
Freda Voos
Mina, *maid to the Hooks*
Sally, *Miss Hook of Holland*
Lieutenant de Coop, Hans Maas, Hendrik Draek, Van Eck, Van Jo, Policeman, Clara Voos, Miss Voos, Thekla, Greta, Old Market Woman, etc.

ACT 1

Mr Hook was once a not-so-very-successful distiller in Amsterdam, a widower with a pretty little daughter who had a lot of brains which was something dear old Mr Hook wasn't largely blessed with. Now, when little Sally Hook grew up, she put those brains of hers to work and she helped her father to concoct—no, let's be honest, all on her own she concocted—a recipe for a liqueur made up of sixty-one different ingredients and named it Cream of the Sky. So popular did Sally's liqueur become that Mr Hook's fortunes were turned right around, and soon he was a prosperous business-man with a big factory producing Cream of the Sky, the recipe of which was kept safely hidden away in the establishment's safe.

At the opening of the show everyboy who is anyone in the story of *Miss Hook of Holland* is having a day out in the vicinity of the Cheese Market at Arndyk where the chorus set proceedings in motion by singing in traditional fashion of going 'To Market!, to Market!'. Ludwig Schnapps, the foreman of Mr Hook's factory, tells the story of his employer's rise to riches because of 'Little Miss Hook', and a sextet of orphan girls performs a number about 'Knitting' before the bumbling, vague Mr Hook himself arrives to spread a little fun with his jolly chatter.

He is confronted by the idle Simon Slinks, the most forward of a bundle of unemployed loafers, who complains in tones reminiscent of certain 'liberal' journals that the he and his mates don't have the home comforts enjoyed by the workers of Arndyk, before going on to detail in a very un-Dutch satirical song ('Lazy Loafers') how they manage things so as to avoid having to work. Mr Hook has a few choice words to say to the loafers and hurries on his way, but, in his haste, he drops a piece of paper on which Slinks is quick to pounce. It is the famous recipe which Hook has removed from the safe to take on a celebratory walk commemorating the anniversary of its invention.

Sally, unaware of this disaster, makes her entry to sing incidentally 'Fly Away, Kite' before the cheese merchants move in (Cheese Chorus) followed by the local unit of the Dutch Army, headed by the dashing Lieutenant Papp with the Dutch equivalent of a patriotic song ('Soldiers of the Netherlands'). Papp tries keenly to make advances to Sally but she is more interested in talking to the rather less pressing Bandmaster, van Vuyt. Her father, too, has little time for the pushy Papp for he has a list of items which he dislikes and it includes vegetable marrows, children, bulldogs, mosquitoes and soldiers. Hook also has a line of talk which is incoherent to a point of distraction and Papp's attempts to talk to him seriously about Sally end with the Lieutenant storming off in frustration. The old man is rather more forthcoming when Sally talks to him about the Bandmaster and, when he has dithered off the stage, the two young people join together to sing prettily of 'The Sleepy Canal'.

Slinks soon begins to find the incriminating possession of the recipe rather worrying and he eagerly searches for an opportunity to rid himself of the paper at a profit. That opportunity is quick to come. He sells the secret of Mr Hook's success to Papp, insinuating that returning it to its owner will help him to find a place in old man Hook's good graces and favour in Sally's eyes. Mina, Sally's maid, provides the next bit of entertainment with a song about a modern version of 'The Flying Dutchman' and she passes some flirtatious moments with Schnapps who gives forth with another Netherlandish number about 'A Little Bit of Cheese'.

Now the loss of the famous recipe is discovered and even the advent of van Vuyt at the head of his band with a jolly military number ('Tra-la-la') cannot, for once, divert the little thread of the main plot from its course. Mr Hook announces in shell-shocked style that he will give a reward for the recovery of his piece of paper, but he rather spoils the announcement by adding that he doesn't believe in people finding things as it usually turns out that the finder is the person who stole them in the first place. Papp announces with dishonest bravado that he will find the missing paper and restore it to Sally's father before the next day's fête in Amsterdam is over, but van Vuyt senses unfair competition in this and announces to his superior officer and rival that, in that case, he will also go to Amsterdam the next day (Finale: 'Is It Insubordination'). The act ends with everyone singing to the health of 'Miss Hook of Holland'.

ACT 2

In Mr Hook's distillery the girls sing a chorus ('Any Time You're Passing') to get things going and the men follow up with a madrigal ('Bottles! Bottles!'), whilst Schnapps flirts with Gretchen, the manageress of the establishment, and Lieutenant Papp makes free with Freda Voos who sings to him of an old Dutch amatory custom in 'The Cigar He Brought Her'. Mr Hook emerges from the cellar, where he has clearly been sampling the stock, to go through an extended comedy routine with a bottle, a candle and an imaginary spider, after which Sally entertains with a song on a Dutch theme which has somehow escaped being the subject of a song up till this point in the proceedings ('Little Miss Wooden Shoes'). Then Mina arrives and catches Schnapps with Gretchen, but his neck is saved when he reveals that has bought her a present at the fair...a petticoat. It is the fifteenth she has been given this year, for Mina has a way with the fellows and, as she explains ('A Pink Petty From Peter'), they all seem to think the right gift for her is underwear.

The last of the principals now appear: Simon Slinks, to whom Hook has given employment, and van Vuyt who has purchased the delighted Slinks' new job from him in order to get to Amsterdam and the Hook factory to keep an eye on Papp's pusuit of Sally. It doesn't take long for the Bandmaster to find his girl and add a duet, 'Love Is a Carnival' to the succession of musical numbers which, in traditional fashion, make up most of the show's second act: an ensemble piece 'The House That Hook Built', a comical piece for the bandmaster about 'The Violincello', a jolly duet for Mina and Schnapps, 'Pop, Pop, Pop', as the foreman is finally forced to pick between his two ladies, and an incidental topical song for Schnapps about the Englishman who first crossed over 'From Harwich to Hook'.

Mr Hook's contribution to the entertainment is comic rather than vocal and made up largely of a scene with van Vuyt (the latter incognito as the newest workman), as the old man unsuspectingly dissects the bandmaster's character and his qualifications as a potential son-in-law.

The plot emerges again for the final few minutes of the act. Sally catches Papp making merry with Freda which allows van Vuyt to come out of disguise with immunity and officially be given Sally's hand. The recipe finds its way from Papp to van Vuyt to Hook and finally, as Sally leads the company in a hymn to the qualities of 'Cream of the Sky', back into the safe keeping of Miss Hook of Holland.

The original solo for van Vuyt, 'Little Liqueurs', was definitively replaced by 'The Violincello' for Maurice Farkoa when he joined the cast. Other additional numbers included, at various times,'I Want to Be Your Wife' for Sally, 'Have You Been to Arndyk?' for Mina, and 'Work' for Slinks.

TOM JONES

a comic opera in three acts founded on the novel by Henry Fielding. Libretto by Alexander M Thompson and Robert Courtneidge. Lyrics by Charles H Taylor. Music by Edward German. Produced at the Apollo Theatre, London, 17 April 1907 with Hayden Coffin (Tom Jones), Ruth Vincent (Sophia), Dan Rolyat (Partridge) and Carrie Moore (Honour).

Produced at the Astor Theatre, New York, 11 November 1907 with Van Rensslaer Wheeler, Louise Gunning, William Norris and Gertrude Quinlan.

CHARACTERS

Tom Jones, *a foundling*
Mr Allworthy, *a Somerset magistrate*
Blifil, *his nephew*
Benjamin Partridge, *a village barber*
Squire Western, *a fine old English gentleman*
Miss Western, *his sister*
Sophia, *his daughter*
Honour, *her maid*
Lady Bellaston, *a lady of quality*
Gregory
Grizzle
Dobbin
Betty
Peggy
Squire Cloddy, Pimlott, Tony, Officer, Highwaymen, Colonel Hampstead, Tom Edwards, Colonel Wilcox, Postboy, Waiter, Etoff, Rosie Lucas, Hostess, Susan, Bessie Wiseacre, Letty Wheatcroft, etc.

ACT 1

In the garden of Squire Western's house in Somersetshire the local gentry are gathered for the hunt, and gossip is galloping as fast as the horses ('Don't You Find the Weather Charming?'). One of the favourite subjects of the lady gossipers is lusty young Tom Jones, the adopted son of Mr Allworthy, who isn't present for the occasion, and another is the squire's daughter, Sophia who, oddly enough, isn't present either. The Squire himself, a jolly back-slapping fellow, regales the company with an oft-told story ('On a Januairy Morning in Zummersetsheer') and sends his servant Gregory to find everybody's favourite lad as the neighbouring Squire Allworthy and his nephew Blifil arrive to sign the papers betrothing Sophia to the unprepos-sessing younger Allworthy.

Tom enters apace, chased from a coppice where little Rosie Lucas swears she heard the rustle of a skirt and the sounds of kissing, and he is soon giving a bright baritone song about a 'West Country Lad'. Western leads the Allworthys inside to get quickly done with the day's business and Honour, Sophia's maid is sent to find her mistress. Sophia (for it was, of course, she in the coppice with Tom) comes out as soon as the coast is clear and gets lost in a little day dream ('Today My Spinet') until Honour brings Tom to her and the two declare their love all over again. They will, however, as wisdom dictates, 'Festina Lente' under the disapproving eyes of their elders.

Lost happily in their wooing, the lovers dally almost too long and the squire's middle-aged sister, making a sudden incursion on the scene, dis-covers Tom with the helpful Honour who is opportunely covering her mis-tress's hurried retreat. With maidenly promptness, Miss Western jumps avidly to the wrong conclusion, a conclusion which doesn't please the comical yokel Gregory to whom Honour is promised. That little situation is quickly sorted out, for Honour wears the trousers in their relationship, and they join in a lively ensemble ('The Barley Mow'), singing of their future married life as host and hostess of a little roadside inn.

As it happens, the misunderstanding comes to the lovers' aid, for Sophia has dropped her muff in the kissing coppice and it has been found by the beastly Blifil. Honour blithely claims it as her own, a gift from her mistress, and Miss Western backs up the story with her circumstantial evidence. Since Squire Western thinks everyone's daughters (his own, of course, excepted) are fair game for a lusty lad, this means there is no harm done. Not yet, indeed, but the business of the day has still to be completed.

After a jolly madrigal ('Here's a Paradox for Lovers'), the Squire orders Sophia and Blifil to be left alone together so that Blifil may put his marriage proposal to her. To young Allworthy's horror, what should be a formality turns to an embarrassment when Sophia refuses the offer indignantly. Western angrily tells his daughter that a decision such as this is his privilege; she shall have no say in the matter of whom she shall marry, and Tom finds his lady love in tears as they open the finale with a protestation of undying love ('For Aye, My Love'). When Blifil breaks in on them, Tom knocks him down and, as everyone gathers round, Tom and Sophia plead for their love. Father and guardian, outraged, will hear none of such a match and cast the young people off as the finale ends in a sad farewell.

ACT 2

Tom has run off, broken-hearted, to take the king's shilling as a soldier and Sophia, following behind with Honour, has fled from her home in search of Tom while Squire Western and all his entourage have, in their turn, set off on the road in search of Sophia. So, this particular week, the roads between Somerset and London are fairly full of Somerset folk who, driven by the need to condense a lot of Fielding's novel into one act, all end up on the same evening in the same inn at Upton.

As soon as the opening chorus ('Hurry, Bustle!') is out of the way we find that Squire Western is already installed at the inn, laid up in his room with a fiery fit of gout. The hostess proposes a doctor for what ails him, for such a gentleman just happens to be on hand, one Benjamin Partridge who describes himself in comic song as 'A Person of Parts'. Partridge is a Somerset man himself and knows Western and Tom from twenty years back, but he is less than adept as a doctor and succeeds in rousing Western to howling pitch by dropping his leeches everywhere and treading on the Squire's gouty toe.

Today is a busy day for the itinerant doctor. He soon has a second (and perhaps more suitable) call to tend to a lady's horse and the lady is none other than Sophia whose equine accident has obliged her to stop at Upton. Honour catches the Somerset references in the doctor's conversation and she is wary, but Sophia thinks of nothing but her anxiety to be on her way. She is heading for London and the house of her relative, Lady Bellaston, where she may, hopefully, escape the hated Blifil for, rather than wed him, she would marry the first man who came along like 'Dream o' Day Jill'.

Gregory, who has come on the journey as part of the Squire's train, fills in his time with a song ('Gurt Uncle Jan Tappit') before the stage is filled with consternation ('My Lady's Coach Has Been Attacked'): a coach has been attacked by highwaymen and Lady Bellaston, who was a passenger, has been saved from the scoundrels by a dashing young man who succeeded in putting the highwaymen to flight. Sure enough, it is Tom Jones who enters bearing the delightedly fainting Lady in his arms. My Lady Bellaston has but one thought in mind and that is to bed the handsome youth as quickly and efficiently as possible, but thoughts of Sophia linger faithfully in Tom's heart and only the course of events contrives that he ends up innocently in an inn room alone with Lady Bellaston.

All these people, under the same roof, manage not to bump into each other, but Partridge meets them all in turn and he gradually if inefficiently starts to put the situation together in his mind as the main protaganists of the action are stage-managed in and out of rooms and doors. Honour sees that the barber needs to be kept quiet if her mistress is to get safely away but she is quietly confident that, in a pinch, she can deal with any man who looks at her in the way this one does ('As All the Maids').

Honour goes nimbly to work. With a little forceful explanation, she gets it through Gregory's thick head that a quick and sure escape is needed for Sophia, and she promises him her hand and heart as a reward for his help (Laughing Trio: 'You Have a Pretty Wit'). Tom, who has bolstered himself against the charms of Lady Bellaston with a glass or two of wine, is still determined to forget his sorrows in 'A Scarlet Coat' as a soldier, but the wine catches him unawares and he exchanges some loosely amorous words with a cloaked lady before being summoned back to the side of Lady Bellaston. Alas, the dark lady is Sophia and she is broken-hearted ('Hey Derry Down') as she believes the rampant Tom is lost to her forever.

Unfortunately, in the heat of the action, Honour runs into Blifil and the events of act begin to wind to a climax. The meddling barber points Blifil to the room where Tom and his lady are to be found and Western, thinking to find the lad indecently closeted with Sophia, bursts in on Lady Bellaston in a fine imbroglio. As a finale of accusations and assertions rages ('Where Be My Daughter?'), Tom's glance alights on Sophia's muff, left once more behind. With withering horror he realises the identity of the cloaked lady to whom he spoke so carelessly and understands what he has done. At once he prepares to go after his beloved and Lady Bellaston, determined not to let him go from her sight, offers her coach to take him to London.

ACT 3

Between the acts, Sophia has reached London, carried thence in Squire Western's coach driven by the useful Gregory, and in next to no time she has been hailed in society as a fashionable beauty. Back in Somerset even more momentous things have been happening. Mr Allworthy has discovered from the barber Partridge that Tom Jones is actually his own sister's illegitimate son and therefore Blifil's elder brother. He has communicated his shattering news to Western who is now in London looking for Sophia, albeit with little success, since he has been doing his looking mainly in the bottoms of glasses in ale houses.

As the act opens, he is scouring much more likely territory at Ranelagh Gardens (Morris Dance/Gavotte). Gregory and Honour have chosen the same pleasure spot to spend their dalliance and, to the yokel's chagrin, his bright little lady is the subject of a certain amount of attention from the gallants of the town whom she answers with a cautionary tale ('The Green Ribbon') of country one-upwomanship.

Tom himself is next on the scene with a song ('If Love's Content') as the principals of the story gather in the one venue but continue to manage to keep missing each other amongst the festivities of the gardens. Honour and Partridge meet up long enough for him to give her the idea that Tom is to wed Lady Bellaston, before Sophia appears on the scene with a circle of admirers and the famous waltz song ('Which Is My Own True Self?'/'For Tonight'). When Tom, Sophia, Lady Bellaston, Honour and Partridge all finally come together in one place, the complications start to get a little unravelled, but the malice of Lady Bellaston seems likely to part the lovers in misunderstanding. Partridge has an attempt at getting a little misunder-standing going between Honour and Gregory, to his own advantage, but the only result is a trio ('Wise Old Saws').

Honour now knows from Gregory that the Squire is of a new mind regarding a match between Tom and Sophia, but Sophia still thinks she has been betrayed and she will not allow herself to hope until she overhears Lady Bellaston attempting unsuccessfully to bribe Tom back to her bed. Tom's protestations prove him, in spite of everything, to be true to his Sophia and all can happily end with a finale full of wedding bells ('Hark! the Merry Marriage Bells').

The song 'We Redcoat Soldiers Serve the King' (Tom) was added for the post-London tour.

THE ARCADIANS

a fantastic musical play in three acts by Mark Ambient and Alexander M Thompson. Lyrics by Arthur Wimperis. Music by Howard Talbot and Lionel Monckton. Produced at the Shaftesbury Theatre, London, 28 April 1909 with Florence Smithson (Sombra), Dan Rolyat (Simplicitas), Phyllis Dare (Eileen), Alfred Lester (Doody) and Harry Welchman (Jack). Revived there 20 May 1915 with Hope Charteris, Dan Agar, Cicely Courtneidge, Lester and Welchman.

Produced at the Liberty Theatre, New York, 17 January 1910 with Ethel Cadman, Frank Moulan, Julia Sanderson, Percival Knight and Alan Mudie and played at the

Knickerbocker Theatre from 16 May 1910.
    Produced at the Wiener Stadtttheater, Vienna, as *Die Arkadier* 24 February 1911.
    Produced at L'Olympia, Paris, as *Les Arcadiens* 3 April 1913.
    A silent film version was produced in 1927 by Gaumont Films with Doris Brans-grove (Sombra), Ben Blue (Simplicitas), Jeanne de Casalis (Mrs Smith) and Gibb McLaughlin (Doody).

CHARACTERS

James Smith *of Smith & Co., Caterers, London later* Simplicitas, *an Arcadian*
Peter Doody, *a jockey*
Jack Meadows
Bobby
Sir George Paddock
Time
Mrs James Smith
Eileen Cavanagh
Chrysea ⎤
Astrophel ⎟
Strephon ⎬ *Arcadians*
Sombra ⎦
Percy Marsh, Reggie, Sir Timothy Ryan, Harry Desmond, Lady Barclay, Hon Maud Barclay, Lucy Selwyn, Marion, Beatrice, *racegoers at Askwood racecourse*
Amaryllis, Dryope, Daphne, Psyche, Damoetas, *Arcadians*

ACT 1

Arcadia is the land Time forgot. Perched somewhere up in the vicinity of the North Pole, it is a place in the image of the idyllic pastoral creations of the Victorian neo-classical artists where nymphs and shepherds frolic in wisps of flimsy drapery which another age might consider suggestive, tend free-range sheep and cows, pluck unsprayed fruit and berries from uncultivated trees and bushes and cry 'Who's for the woods?' without the hint of a double entendre. 'Arcadians Are We' they sing joyously, and are quite simply incredulous at the tales heard by one of their number, Sombra (who sings all the top soprano lines), of the existence of another type of world, one called London where the people live in cages of brick and stone and breathe the stifling fog of a never-ending smoke and don't tell the truth.
    The sweet Arcadians have no concept of what it is not to tell the truth. But now, after so many centuries, Time has remembered them. Busy in other places since the creation of the world, he unexpectedly returns declaring 'I Quite Forgot Arcadia', to find the Arcadians fascinated with the idea of London and begging to be allowed to see one of the 'monsters' which apparently inhabit the place. Time departs, and the four principal Arcadians join in celebrating the beauties of their land and 'The Joy of Life' when, suddenly, a strange phenomenon is seen in the sky. The Arcadians shrink back (Chorus of Fear: 'Look What Hovers Above Us') as a big bird descends from above and from it tumbles an odd-looking creature in an airsuit.

It is James Smith, Esq. of London, The Leviathan Caterer, sent off course by Time in response to the Arcadians pleas and bailing out of his pleasure craft in what he quickly discovers is unfamiliar territory. It is soon clear that he and the Arcadians are not on the same wavelength at all, and Sombra's attempts to explain to him their innocent rustic conception of life ('The Pipes of Pan') go for nothing. Smith, a pretty unprincipled specimen of a self-made man, is soon sidling up to Sombra and attempting to help his flirtation with her by spreading a few falsehoods about others.

Arcadia has heard its first lie. It is soon exposed and the news is echoed in horror by the whole population ('All a Lie!') as the Arcadians seize the miscreant and tumble him down the Well of Truth to cure him of his awful disease. At the end of the chorus a very new Smith emerges from the water, an Arcadian from his naked knees to his curly gold hairpiece, to sing of his revamped persona as 'Sweet Simplicitas'. Sombra declares that now he is reformed he must go back to London and convert the other liars, but Simplicitas is unwilling to face London life and business if he can only tell the truth. Finally it is decided that Sombra and her sister Chrysea will accompany Simplicitas on his mission and they set off, in the footsteps of Time, towards England ('To All and Each').

ACT 2
Askwood racecourse on Cup day is abuzz with high society, parading in the most up-to-date fashions ('That's All Over') and discussing the chances of Sir George Paddock's Bella and young Jack Meadows' Deuce in the big race, as Jack's friend Bobbie rouses everyone in song to 'Back Your Fancy'. Not many people will back the Deuce, for he has thrown Jack and broken his arm and the big race ride has had to be given to Peter Doody, a Jonah of a jockey who has never won a race in his life.

Jack ought to be worried, as his financial position is very shaky and his future depends on this race, but his mind today is on a different kind of filly. He has spotted and finally managed to win an introduction to the lovely Miss Eileen Cavanagh, who has come racing with her Aunt, Mrs Smith, the caterer's wife. Eileen is from the Emerald Isle and she is soon heard to advantage telling an admiring crowd of young men to cut their blarney, for you can't blather 'The Girl With a Brogue', but her aunt is anxious that she should impress and, if possible, hook the wealthy Sir George before the day is out, and hurries her off to more prosperous circles.

Suddenly the weather breaks (Shower Chorus: 'This Is Really Altogether Too Provoking'). Lightning blazes and thunders growl and then, as suddenly as it began, the storm is over and amongst the crowd stand Sombra and Chrysea. The racegoers are stunned. Mrs Smith demands to know if the newcomers are 'corps de ballet or travelling circus?' and, although Sombra tries to explain ('Arcady Is Ever Young') that Arcadia is a place and not a brand name, Mrs Smith finally decides that they are an advertising gimmick for something in the beauty business—'a massage or a hair restorer'.

Even more of a stir is caused by the arrival of Simplicitas who is a little behind the girls as he became entangled in a tree while landing. The London ladies take a great shine to the wild Arcadian boy although Mrs Smith is a little puzzled by his apparent knowledge of her private affairs. But she is not the wife of a self-made man for nothing and she quickly sees the commercial as well as the personal potential in the handsome stranger. Smiths have half an empty hotel and, with this attractive boy's help, she will transform it into an Arcadian Restaurant where fashionable society will flock to partake of the latest craze. Together he and she dance a burlesque ballet as he describes a rather prosaic romantic idyll for the two of them 'Somewhere'.

All these strange happenings have not turned Jack Meadows from his intentions and he is soon to be found chatting up Eileen although the pair, each time they are interrupted, make a pretence of small talk about the 'Charming Weather'. The racing, too, continues and the big race approaches, but now Deuce has savaged poor Peter Doody and once again Jack has no jockey. He will have to withdraw the horse and lose everything ('Fickle Fortune').

Sombra comes to the rescue. It is all quite simple to her: if it is what Jack wishes, she will find a jockey and Deuce will win the race. Jack kisses her gratefully, and Eileen happens to see. He may have solved one problem but now he has another. Sombra, in the meanwhile, has been talking to the horse who has told her that he and the other horses have already decided that he will win the race, but for form's sake and that of the clerk of the course a jockey must be found who can sit on Deuce's back while he does the job. An unenthusiastic Simplicitas is nominated and the racegoers gather for the big moment (Finale: 'The Horses Are Out'), watching the race as it rushes by somewhere out in the dress circle until the Deuce is finally paraded on stage, victorious, with Simplicitas fast asleep on his back.

ACT 3

The Arcadian Restaurant is a great success. Although it is a travesty of the genuine Arcadia it has the attractions for bored, fashionable London society both of novelty and of a staff of nubile chorus boys and girls in flimsy Arcadian costume ('Plant Your Posies'). Chrysea, by now, is becoming quite fond of London ways ('I Like London') and so is Jim Smith alias Simplicitas who is living it up hugely whilst taking great care that any lying that has to be done is done by someone else. One lie and he'd be plain, middle-aged, whiskery Mr Smith again.

Mrs Smith is quite put out by all her protégé's gallivanting, and isn't at all cheered by her old suitor, Peter Doody, who is now engaged at the restaurant as Ganymede, an Arcadian waiter, singing in his hangdog way about 'My Motter'—'always merry and bright'—nor by his apprisal of her guilty secret: her husband is missing and she's fallen in love with the footloose Arcadian.

In the meanwhile, another romance is on the mend. Jack Meadows makes his peace with Eileen and persuades her to a rendezvous the next Saturday at 'Half Past Two' at the zoological gardens. Now the star attraction of the restaurant puts in his appearance, fresh from a club crawl and surrounded by the slightly dented, silver-plated youth of the town ('Cheer for Simplicitas'), to recount some of his social and feminine conquests ('All Down Piccadilly'). Sombra worriedly questions him about the prevalent rumours of un-Arcadian behaviour, but a goodly dose of double talk gets him out of trouble as he and his friends join in bright ensemble declaring with certain ironies that 'Truth Is So Beautiful'.

Sombra is not happy in London. She is weary of her crusade and longs for home ('My Heart Flies Homing'). Here, every time she tries to act in an uncomplicatedly Arcadian manner, something warps her loving actions into hurtful or harmful consequences. Now, when she clears up a new misunderstanding between Jack and Eileen and gets them engaged, she has to deal with an infuriated Sir George who roundly denounces Simplicitas as an impostor and a liar. Sombra admits that he did once tell a lie when first he came to Arcadia, and the secret is out. Doody tricks Simplicitas into a lie and with a cry the golden-haired boy tumbles down the decorative well which is a feature of the restaurant's decoration to emerge as plain old Jim Smith. As he effects a happy reunion with his equally wayward wife, and as Jack and Eileen bask in each others eyes, Sombra and Chrysea prepare to leave London to its unrepentant ways and return to Arcadia.

The score of *The Arcadians* was varied with a number of other songs during its run. Phyllis Dare originally featured 'Bring Me a Rose' (Monckton) which was subsequently deleted, Florence Smithson variously performed 'Light Is My Heart' (Talbot) and 'Come to Arcady', Dan Rolyat exchanged 'All Down Piccadilly' for a number called 'Whoppers' (Monckton), Harry Welchman replaced 'Fickle Fortune' with 'The Only Girl Alive' and later with 'Love Will Win', Nelson Keys as Bobby replaced 'Back Your Fancy' with 'Have a Little Bit on With Me', Cicely Courtneidge who succeeded to the role of Chrysea sang 'I'll Be a Sister to You', Harry Ray and Maudi Thornton interpolated the topical dance number 'The Two-step', and a trio 'Little George Washington' was also included for a short while. In the Broadway production the number 'What Every Woman Knows', capitalising on J M Barrie's play of the same title was for a while sung by Simplicitas in place of 'All Down Picadilly' or, as it was titled in America, 'Willie From Piccadilly'.

THE QUAKER GIRL

a musical play in three acts by James T Tanner. Lyrics by Adrian Ross and Percy Greenbank. Music by Lionel Monckton. Produced at the Adelphi Theatre, London, 5 November 1910 with Gertie Millar (Prudence), Hayden Coffin (Charteris), Joseph Coyne (Tony), Gracie Leigh (Phoebe) and James Blakeley (Jeremiah). Produced at the Garrick Theatre 28 May 1934 and played subsequently at the Winter Garden.

Produced at the London Coliseum in a revised version 25 May 1944 with Celia
Lipton, Pat McGrath, Billy Milton, April Ross and Hal Bryan and played at the Stoll
Theatre from 8 February 1945.

Produced at the Park Theatre, New York, 23 October 1911 with Ina Claire, F
Pope Stamper, Clifton Crawford, May Vokes and Percival Knight.

Played at the Théâtre du Châtelet, Paris, 1911 with Phyllis Dare, Basil Foster,
Coyne, Mabel Sealby and Mr Gregory. Produced at L'Olympia in a version by Paul
Ferrier and Charles Quinel as *La Petite Quaker* 1913 with Alice O'Brien, Henri
Arbell, Harry Mass, Miss Lawler and Dorville and at the Ba-ta-Clan in 1920 with
Jeanne St Bonnet, Arbell, Zidner, Odette Darthys and Moriss.

CHARACTERS

Jarge, *the village crier*
Mrs Lukyn, *landlady of The Chequers Inn*
William, *a waiter at The Chequers*
Nathaniel Pym, *a Quaker*
Rachel, *his sister*
Jeremiah, *their servant*
Prudence Pym, *their niece*
Princess Mathilde Murat, *an exiled Bonpartiste*
Phoebe, *her English maid*
Captain Charteris, *a King's messenger*
Madame Blum *of La Maison Blum, Paris*
Toinette, *head fitter at La Maison Blum*
Tony Chute, *naval attaché at the American Embassy in Paris*
Monsieur Larose, *the Parisian chief of police*
Diane, a Parisian actress
Prince Carlo
Monsieur Duhamel, *a minister of state*
Gaby, Cleo, Liane, Louise, etc.

ACT 1

The English country village where the action of the play opens houses a
Quaker sect of a theatrically simplistic kind led by the joyless Nathaniel Pym
and his sister Rachel. This pair have brought up their niece, Prudence, in a
strict Quaker way but Prudence, though she makes an effort to be correct, is
a young lady of a sweetly merry disposition who hides modern literature
inside the cover of a dutiful book and who doesn't see why religion should
control the whole of her life. Her little backslidings are nothing, however, to
those of the Pym's manservant, Jeremiah, who has a ready excuse for his
constant lapses into error: only his mother was a Quaker, and the influence
of his father keeps coming out in him.

When the curtain rises the villagers are gossiping with the landlady of the
local inn ('Jarge, We've Such a Tale to Tell'). There is an interesting young
Frenchwoman staying at the inn and guesswork is the game as to her identity

and her business in the area. There must be a gentleman in the case; perhaps it is a runaway match? Such frivolous thoughts are put temporarily aside as Nathaniel and Rachel pass by at the head of group of Quakers (Quakers' Meeting).

A local lass, Phoebe, has been taken on as a maid for the mysterious lady and her loose tongue soon allows the villagers to discover that her new mistress is the Princess Mathilde Murat. Mathilde has run away from her finishing school at Cheltenham and has come to the village to rendezvous with her lover, Captain Charteris, whom she intends to wed in spite of an offical engagement to the governmentally approved Prince Carlo. She is eagerly awaiting Charteris's arrival by train that very morning and in an impatient waltz song ('O, Time, Time!') she urges the hours to pass until she is in his arms indulging in a happy duet ('Wonderful'). Charteris has brought with him the Princess's self-appointed surrogate mother, the popular Parisian dressmaker Madame Blum, as a matron of honour and, as his best man, Tony Chute, a young American diplomat with an eye for the ladies, and they are delighted to be present for the consummation of what is truly 'A Runaway Match'.

Jeremiah is going through a period of paternal influence which earns him a tongue-lashing from the elder Pyms but which wins some sympathy from Prudence who admits that life is very dull for 'A Quaker Girl'. It immediately shows signs of being less dull when she encounters Tony Chute who, in some clumsy, imitation Quaker speech, attempts to get to know her rather better. It isn't long before she is gently removing his arm from her waist and they are singing together about 'A Bad Boy and a Good Girl'. Tony is truly struck by Prudence, but Madame Blum is more struck by her little grey Quaker dress and apron—*quelle divine simplicité!*—just the theme for her new summer collection. Prudence simply must come to Paris. More imminently, however, she must come to the church with her friend Mathilde to witness the wedding and, wary of the elders, they all head off 'Tip-toe!' to the ceremony.

A bit of banter between Jeremiah and Phoebe leads into the manservant giving a comical description of the warring elements in his heredity ('Just as Father Used to Do') until the newly wedded Mathilde and Charteris return. Charteris, whose position demands a quick return to Paris, has planned a honeymoon for them there, but Madame Blum is horrified at such a risk. Mathilde cannot return to France. The reason for her presence in England is that she is an exile from the Bonapartist rule and it would be foolhardy for her to challenge the law by returning.

The two cannot bear the thought of being parted and eventually it is decided that Mathilde will return to France disguised as a employee of the Maison Blum. As the finale begins, the friends make a merry wedding breakfast *en plein air* but, as Tony tempts Prudence to a sip of forbidden champagne, the Pyms wrathfully descend to remove their niece from such unsuitable company. Prudence is torn between her family and her friends who urge her to join them in Paris, but her decision is made for her when Rachel, furious at her hesitation, disowns the quaker girl and casts her out.

ACT 2

At the Maison Blum ('In This Abode of Madame la Mode'), Mathilde is in hiding for, after a brief honeymoon, Charteris has been sent on a mission to Spain. Their presence in France has not gone unnoticed, and the Chief of Police, Larose, pays an unpleasantly meaningful visit to Madame Blum to make it clear that the fact that Mathilde is the legal wife of a British subject will not protect her from Bonapartist law.

Another who has not gone unnoticed in Paris is Prudence ('Ah, Oui!'). The quaker style of dress has become the latest fashion and Prudence its most celebrated and sought after exponent. She returns from Chantilly races ('On Revient de Chantilly') with Prince Carlo and the minister of state, Duhamel, vying for her attentions, and the Prince, a well-rehearsed roué, invites her to attend one of his well-known gatherings ('Come to the Ball'). Prudence has never danced in her life but in Tony she finds a willing tutor ('The Dancing Lesson').

Phoebe, who has managed to fit in an incidental song about 'Petticoats for Women', and Jeremiah have an encounter with Larose who tries to trick them into revealing the Princess's whereabouts but, in the meanwhile, Charteris has returned from Spain and, ignoring Madame Blum's warnings, he and Mathilde plan to go back to their honeymoon cottage at 'Barbizon'.

Prince Carlo is making practised plans for what he intends shall be the evening's seduction of Prudence. He has an ally in the actress Diane, Tony's last amour, who is happy to arrange for Tony's old love-letters to her to fall 'accidentally' into Prudence's hands. Diane chooses Prudence to model her new Blum gown and carefully slips a bundle of letters from her own bag into the bag belonging to the new dress, a gift, she pointedly adds, from Tony. When the gown is modelled she affects to dislike it and makes an ostentatious gift of it to 'the mannequin', with an instruction to look in the bag. Tony tells Prudence what she may expect to find, but when she opens the bag she finds not Tony's letters but another set, to Diane from Duhamel. Tony assures Prudence of his constancy and asks her to marry him before taking her in his arms for the first kiss of her quaker life.

Jeremiah gets himself into hot water with Phoebe by flirting with the girls of Madame Blum's establishment, but worse trouble is in store. Larose turns up with a posse of gendarmes to arrest Mathilde whose English marriage, he asserts, is not legal in France. Mathilde hides amongst the seamstresses and mannequins and Larose seems to have been tricked, but Prince Carlo arrives to ensure Prudence's presence at his soirée and the police chief orders him to point out his former fiancée. The price of Carlo's silence is Prudence's agreement to attend the ball. Tony, not understanding why she has accepted the Prince's invitation in contravention of her earlier promise to him, leaves the scene in sorrowful anger.

ACT 3

At the masked ball, the chorus sing of 'Champagne', the Prince celebrates his philosophy of life in 'Couleur de Rose', and Jeremiah and Phoebe take time off from their bickering to think of what their life together will be like if and when he is the well-off 'Mr Jeremiah Esquire'. Charteris and Mathilde, unrecognisable behind their masks, express their apparently half-married love in 'A Wilderness and Thou' while the Prince pounces on the newly arrived Prudence. She evades his attentions long enough to seek out Duhamel and to return to him Diane's incriminating bundle of letters and the minister, overwhelmed by her unprompted gesture, agrees to permit Mathilde to remain legally in France with her husband.

Alone, Prudence sketches the dance steps Tony taught her and sings of her 'Tony from America' and, when he appears on the scene, Prudence explains the mission which brought her to the dance. With all misunderstanding swept aside, they share 'The First Dance' of the ball. Finally Larose arrives with a warrant for Mathilde's arrest, but he finds his triumph thwarted by Duhamel and by Prudence's goodness, and all ends happily.

Amongst the numbers alternated or interpolated into *The Quaker Girl* during its original run were the Hugo Felix/Adrian Ross 'Or Thereabout!' for Gracie Leigh, Monckton's 'The Little Grey Bonnet' for Gertie Millar and 'Take a Step', a dance duet for Miss Millar and Joe Coyne. The Broadway production interpolated two numbers written and performed by Clifton Crawford as Tony, 'Get Away, I Am a Married Man' and 'Something to Tell'.

CHU CHIN CHOW

a musical tale of the East in three acts by Oscar Asche. Music by Frederic Norton. Produced at His Majesty's Theatre, London, 31 August 1916 with Oscar Asche (Abu Hasan), Lily Brayton (Zahrat), Courtice Pounds (Ali Baba), Aileen D'Orme (Alcolom) and Violet Essex (Marjanah). Produced at the Palace Theatre 3 July 1940 with Lyn Harding, Rosalinde Fuller, Jerry Verno, Kay Bourne and Marjorie Browne, and revived there 22 July 1941 with the same stars.

Produced at the Manhattan Opera House, New York, 22 October 1917 with Tyrone Power, Florence Reed, Henry E Dixey, Kate Condon and Tessa Kosta and subsequently played at the Century Theatre from 14 January 1918.

Produced at the Casino, Brussels, in a French version, 1930.

A silent film version was produced by Graham-Wilcox Productions in 1923 with Herbert Langley, Betty Blythe, Judd Green and Eva Moore. A sound film was produced in 1934 by Gainsborough Films with Fritz Kortner, Anna May Wong, George Robey, Thelma Tuson, Pearl Argyle and Sydney Fairbrother in her original role of Mahbubah.

CHARACTERS

Abu Hasan, *the shayk of the robbers*
Kasim Baba, *a wealthy merchant*
Ali Baba, *his poor brother*

Alcolom, *Kasim's head wife*
Mahbubah, *Ali's wife*
Nur al-Huda Ali, *Ali's son*
Marjanah, *a slave girl*
Zahrat al-Kulub, *a slave*
Baba Mustafa, *a cobbler*
Abdullah, *Kasim's steward*
Mukbil, *an auctioneer*
Otbah, *a stall-keeper*
Musab, Zhukzayman, *members of Abu Hasan's band*
Zanim, Fitnah, *slave dealers*, etc.

ACT 1

At Kasim Baba's luxurious palace an extravagant dinner is being prepared ('Here Be Oysters Stewed in Honey') to accompany Kasim's business dealings with the important Chinese merchant, Chu Chin Chow. Little does his host suspect that this Chu Chin Chow is, in fact, no merchant; he is the robber shayk Abu Hasan who comes in disguise to plan another strike against the rich commercial dealings of the miserly Kasim. To facilitate his plundering he has planted the lovely Zahrat al-Kulub as a spy in Kasim's household, but the unhappy Zahrat confides the truth of their guest's identity to Kasim's chief wife, Alcolom, and the slave girl Marjanah, both of whom have cause to detest the merchant and are quite satisfied to see him robbed.

When the false Chu Chin Chow arrives with his train ('I Am Chu Chin Chow of China'), Marjanah uses the information to blackmail him into buying her freedom and to rid Alcolom of her hated husband. During the evening Marjanah is called on to entertain the guests at the head of a dancing troupe ('Cleopatra's Nile') and Abu Hasan takes the opportunity to ask Kasim to sell him the slave. But Kasim's brother, Ali Baba, challenges him. He knows that his son, Nur al-Huda Ali, is in love with Marjanah and to save her from being sold to this stranger he tipsily agrees to pay 40,000 gold pieces within twenty-four hours to secure the girl himself and, when his offer is successful, he launches into a drunken song and dance ('I'll Sing and Dance').

In an inset scene, Nur al-Huda sings a serenade ('Corraline') under his beloved's window as they arrange to run away together before Ali's boastful bid falls through. In a cactus grove Ali wakes up with a hangover to be chided by Nur al-Huda for his untimely interference, but Ali tells him that he is not the only one with woman trouble. He has to put up with the wifely torments provided by the shrewish, angular Mahbubah when he longs for a relaxed life with someone like the plumply comfortable Alcolom ('When a Pullet Is Plump').

Marjanah and Nur al-Huda are down in the grove, preparing their escape, when they witness an amazing sight: Abu Hasan and his band of armed men emerging from a magically sealed doorway in the earth ('We Are the Rob-

117

bers of the Wood'). After the episode at Kasim's palace, the robber chief has begun to doubt the loyalty of Zahrat al-Kulub and he orders his men to take prisoner her desert lover, Omar, and bring him to their lair as a hostage for her good behaviour. When the band has departed, Marjanah and Nur al-Huda come out from their hiding place and hurry to acquaint Ali with the tale of the wondrous cave and its reputed robbers' treasure ('I Shiver and Shake With Fear'). Together the three adventurers use the 'Open Sesame' password and, as the magic cave opens before them, disappear into the earth.

Ali is next seen at a silk stall singing joyfully ('Why Should I Repine') as he spends the gold stolen from the robber hoard while Marjanah, her freedom ensured, relaxes in amorous song ('I Love Thee So'). Ali joins in with a rather more jaundiced view of married 'bliss' ('All My Days Till End of Life').

At Kasim's palace more strange events are going on. Hasan has turned up to a sale of slaves ('Behold') and, in Kasim's absence, Alcolom, intending to ruin her hated husband, allows him to purchase everything on no security. Amongst the purchases is Zahrat who believes that, her services finished, her new owner will set her free, but he has no such intention: for her betrayal of his identity to Marjanah and Alcolom she shall be chained in his cave alongside her Omar for ever. Zahrat, as a last desperate stroke towards freedom, cries out to the gathered crowd that this lone stranger is none other than the dread Abu Hasan, but the shayk summons his band and, bearing Zahrat with them, they escape through the frightened crowd.

ACT 2

At the opening of the second act, Kasim is found lounging at his ease, entertained by dancers and by his head wife from whom he commands a love song. He is more amused than irritated when Alcolom responds with the disillusioned 'I Long for the Sun'. Ali arrives to pay the money owing for Marjanah's purchase and Kasim is soon busy worming his way avidly into the confidence of his brother to discover where he has managed to get so much wealth so quickly.

The simple Ali is not a match for the cunning Kasim, and the tale of the cave and its secret is soon in the merchant's possession. Slyly offering Ali the comforts of his house (Trio: 'Mahbubah'), Kasim prepares to set out alone to rifle the cave. He cannot know that Nur al-Huda and Marjanah are ahead of him. Using the password they open the cave and, to their surprise, discover Zahrat bound fast but, before they can get her safely away, Kasim arrives and enters the open cave to discover the robbers' headquarters. The escaping lovers close the door behind them and the returning Hasan finds the rapacious merchant trapped amongst his gold and jewels. He draws his sword as a sign (Scimitar Song) and the robber band fall on the intruder with their knives.

An inset scene shows Ali Baba making the most of the freedom of Kasim's home, feasting happily with Alcolom, who is altogether a happier woman in the arms of her husband's brother ('Any Time's Kissing Time').

118

In the bazaar, the cobbler Baba Mustafa sits stitching at his wares (The Cobbler's Song) when Zahrat comes to bid him to a strange task. Marjanah and Nur al-Huda have set her free and together they have taken the quartered corpse of Kasim to the cellar of his home. Thence the cobbler must now come to stitch the body back together so that they may bury it without arousing suspicion. She leads him blindfold through the streets as the activities and sounds of the bazaar ('Buy, O Buy!') continue around them.

Amongst the buyers and sellers comes Hasan, disguised as a water carrier, to meet with some of his men and to tell them the grave news of Zahrat's escape and the disappearance of Kasim's body. The cobbler arouses suspicion by making free with the money he has earned from his gruesome task and, when Hasan offers him more gold, he proffers the information that he has marked the door of the house where he was taken with a chalk cross. Hasan's men set off to find the house while the market place becomes the site of a mannequin parade ('From Cairo, Baghdad, Khorasan') for the benefit of Mahbubah, who is out spending Ali's newly acquired wealth.

Hasan is determined to find out the identity of the man who has breached the secret of the robbers' cave, and he ultimately find it from an unlikely source in Zahrat who, as the price of Omar's freedom, names Ali Baba. Mahbubah's open-handed and open-mouthed activities in the market bear witness to her tale and the robbers set off to capture the shrew while Zahrat unfolds to Hasan a pretended plot for Ali's murder. The next night there is to be a wedding feast for Nur al-Huda and Marjanah at Kasim's house. Hasan must come as an oil merchant with his men hidden in the oil jars. Thus introduced into the house, they can be set upon the assembled guests at the wedding, slaying all who may be party to Ali's discovery.

While Ali and Alcolom are comfortably billing-and-cooing ('How Dear Is Our Day'), Zahrat furthers her plot. When the oil jars are brought to the house she calls the steward Abdullah and tells him to summon his men bearing pots filled with boiling oil. Singing to drown the cries of the trapped robbers ('Olive Oil'), the slaves of Kasim's house pour their oil into the jars, and all Hasan's mighty band are killed.

At the wedding ceremony, Hasan awaits his moment, but when he steps forward and gives the cue for the attack—'I draw my short sharp scimitar'— nothing happens. Zahrat's moment of revenge has come. She draws her dagger and stabs the pretended oil merchant to death, pulling off his disguise to display the body of Abu Hasan to the amazed guests. As the 'Wedding Procession' finale brings the proceedings to a close, she stands triumphant above the company.

Several of the songs listed in this synopsis were not part of the original *Chu Chin Chow* score but, when added, became part of the standard score. The soprano song 'I Built a Fairy Palace in the Sky' (Marjanah) was also popular as was Courtice Pounds' additional song 'When a Man Is Middle-Aged'. 'My Desert Flower', Mahbubah's 'Beans, Beans, Beans', Ali Baba's 'My Head, My Head', 'Hail the Grand Wazir', 'The Prayer in the Desert' and the Grace Torrens/Arthur Anderson number 'At Siesta Time' were other additions made principally to fill out the new inset scenes added during the run of the show. The addition of 'I Long for the Sun' and, later 'I Built a Fairy Palace in the Sky' caused the shifting of Marjanah's 'I Love Thee So' from the third to the second act and the excision of the original second act duet 'If I Liken Thy Shape'.

THE MAID OF THE MOUNTAINS

a musical comedy in three acts by Frederick Lonsdale. Lyrics by Harry Graham. Additional lyrics by F Clifford Harris and 'Valentine'. Music by Harold Fraser-Simson. Additional music by James Tate. Produced at the Prince's Theatre, Manchester, 23 December 1916 and at Daly's Theatre, London, 10 February 1917 with José Collins (Teresa), Arthur Wontner (Baldasarre), Thorpe Bates (Beppo), Lauri de Frece (Antonio) and Mabel Sealby (Vittoria). Revived there 26 December 1921 with Miss Collins, Bertram Wallis, Peter Gawthorne, Edward D'Arcy and Miss Sealby. Produced at the London Hippodrome 18 December 1930 with Annie Croft, Wallis, Bruce Carfax, Jerry Verno and Billie Hill, and at the London Coliseum 1 April 1942 with Sylvia Cecil, Malcolm Keen, Dan Noble, Sonnie Hale and Elsie Randolph. Produced at the Palace Theatre in a revised version 29 April 1972 with Lynn Kennington, Gordon Clyde, Neville Jason, Jimmy Thompson and Janet Mahoney.

Produced at the Casino Theatre, New York, 11 September 1918 with Sidonie Espero, William Courtenay, Carl Gantvoort, Bert Clark and Miriam Doyle.

A film version produced by British International in 1932 was directed by Lupino Lane who also shared a screenplay credit with Douglas Furber, and starred Nancy Brown, Harry Welchman, Garry Marsh, Albert Burdon and Renee Gadd.

CHARACTERS

Baldasarre, *a brigand chief*
Antonio
Beppo
Pietro
Andrea
Carlo
General Malona, *Governor of Santo*
Angela, *his daughter*
Vittoria, *Antonio's wife*
Teresa, *the maid of the mountains*
Lieutenant Rugini, *officer in charge of Devil's Island*
Mayor of Santo
Crumpet
Gianetta, Maria, Jessica, Beppiria, Pepita, etc.

120

ACT 1

High in the rocky mountains of brigand land, the famous and fearsome Baldasarre and his band of robbers have built the lair from where, for many years, they have issued forth to plunder travellers on the pass below. But, although business is still booming and banditry a profitable employment, the bandits are packing their possessions and preparing to depart ('Friends Have to Part'), for Baldasarre has announced his retirement and his band is to be disbanded. It has been a jolly, open-air life and the men are sorry to exchange their adventurous profession for dreary honesty although a particularly vocal fellow called Beppo tells everyone that they should 'Live for Today' and announces his intention of going into opera.

The men ask the lovely Teresa to intercede with Baldasarre to persuade him to change his mind, but Teresa shrugs them off: she has no influence with the chief. In spite of what they may think, he notices her no more than any of them ('My Life Is Love'). It is, alas, only too true for, although Teresa's heart is wholly given to her chief, her love is not returned. But Teresa is true in her affections and she cannot, therefore, return the gentle sentiments which Beppo feels for her.

Baldasarre orders the men to depart as soon as they are ready and tells Teresa that she must leave at once for it appears that their hideout has been discovered and the Governor of Santo has sent his soldiers to attack the fortress. She can win no parting word from him except of friendship and, taking her share of the booty of the past years, she sings her 'Farewell' to the men and the mountains she loves. When she is gone, the bandits in their turn begin 'Dividing the Spoil' and Baldasarre takes a particular brooch as part of his share. It is a trinket which he recently took from a girl in a coach they robbed and, since that day, he has been unable to get her out of his mind.

There is a knocking at the gate and it seems that they are surrounded, but the visitors turn out to be the Governor's daughter, Angela, and her companion, Vittoria. They have become lost in the fog on their way back from a trip to town to buy decorations for the ceremony to welcome the new Governor who is arriving the next day to replace Angela's father. Angela is, of course, the girl from the coach. Baldasarre recognises her immediately and she recognises her brooch on his lapel. When she demands to be released, he chivalrously opens the gates and sets both girls safely on the road.

Suddenly a brigand rushes in with terrible news. The Governor's men have taken Teresa as she made her way down the mountain and the Governor has decreed that the price of her release shall be an exchange. Baldasarre must give himself up to save the maid of the mountains. The brigand chief is not ready to give in so easily and he quickly devises a plan: they will hold up the coach bringing the new Governor to Santo, take his clothes and papers, and he will then descend to the town in disguise to rescue Teresa. Beppo leads the men in a courageous and optimistic finale ('Though Curs May Quail') as the act ends.

121

ACT 2

In the courtyard of the Governor's palace at Santo the people are awaiting the arrival of their new Governor. General Malona, the deposed Governor, still has it at heart to rescue his tattered reputation and he announces with bravado that he will deliver up the dreadful Baldasarre before his time of office expires that night. To the surprised cheers of the crowd, he brings in the captured Teresa and clumsily tries to get her to divulge the whereabouts of Baldasarre, but she defies him, safe in the belief that 'Love Will Find a Way' to bring her freedom.

The brigand chief arrives in town in disguise as Count Orsino, the new Governor, with Beppo and the comical little Tonio dressed as his escort, and the crowd greet him with pleas to protect them from Baldasarre ('Save Us'). Orsino tells Malona that he would like to see him get the credit for the capture of the bandit before the end of his term of office, and he suggests that Teresa should be released to lead the Governor and the 'new Governor' to the mountain hideout. He knows that once in her home mountains Teresa will easily make her escape.

Baldasarre's disguise holds good when he meets Angela again, but there is a nasty moment when little Tonio runs into Vittoria. She is his wife. Five years ago, exhausted by the attentions of his over-loving spouse, Tonio faked his own death by drowning and went off to become a bandit. Vittoria has remained faithful to his memory in spite of twenty-six proposals from General Malona but now, as Tonio stoutly refuses to admit his identity, she realises with horror that 'for five years I have remained faithful to a man who had a face like that!', and she promptly accepts the General who is delighted to have won her and her fortune. 'What fortune?', gasps Tonio. The General tells him that Vittoria has inherited a vast sum of money which she has been saving up in the hope of finding her husband again and, as Tonio and the General indulge in a vocal slanging match ('Dirty Work'), Tonio wonders whether perhaps he shouldn't come to life again.

Beppo and Teresa struggle with their feelings in the duet 'Paradise for Two', Vittoria and Tonio enjoy a comical duet about 'Husbands and Wives', and Beppo entertains the town girls with an incidental song on his eligible state ('A Bachelor Gay Am I') before the action continues.

Baldasarre is ready to lead Teresa to the mountains when Angela, with whom he has been exchanging tentative expressions of interest, asks him to stay a little longer. Teresa, furious that he should risk their freedom for a word from the Governor's daughter, threatens to expose his identity if he will not leave immediately, but Baldasarre refuses to listen to her and, jealously, she carries out her threat (Finale). Angela, realising that the man who is courting her is a vagabond and a thief, spurns Baldasarre in horror and he is seized by the Governor's soldiers as Teresa collapses in regretful tears.

ACT 3

On the prison island of Santo, the act opens with a fisherfolk chorus ('When

122

Each Day'). Malona is bloated with pride over the capture of the brigand chief and delights in taking excessive credit for fulfilling his boast ('Good People, Gather Round'). Teresa pleads with the Governor to spare the bandit's life and tries to make him weaken in his resolve by appealing to his romantic spirit ('When You're in Love'), while Vittoria attempts to use her fortune to bribe anyone in sight to win the release of her Tonio. The little fellow is soon seen being taken in manacles for a bath in the sea to the accompaniment of much comic business with a lobster, and Vittoria wheedles her way past the sentries to his side to join him in a comedy duet anticipating a new period apart ('Over Here and Over There').

Baldasarre finds one unexpected ally on the island. Lieutenant Rugini who is in charge of his sequestration is another of Angela's victims, 'promoted' to his position here to separate him from the wilful Governor's daughter, and he is now planning to desert. He tells Baldasarre how poorly he considers the flippant Angela compares with the sincere and loving Teresa, but Baldasarre remembers only Teresa's betrayal. Rugini gives him the key to his cell and makes a bet with him: if Teresa had the chance to set him free, even believing that he was preparing to flee with Angela, she would do so.

The stake of the bet is his freedom. Will he gamble on Teresa's love? Baldasarre takes the challenge and gives Teresa the key and, as night falls, she duly comes and unlocks his door. Vittoria and Tonio are waiting with a boat: he is free to go to her rival, while she herself will return to the mountains where she knew happiness. At last Baldasarre sees the truth in his heart and, as the curtain falls to the sound of 'Love Will Find a Way', the brigand and his maid of the mountains board the little boat together and sail off into the future.

The original score of *The Maid of the Mountains* as played at Manchester was wholly by Fraser-Simson and included the songs 'Anyone Else but You' and 'If Love Is There' which were cut during the run and replaced by the new songs written by James Tate ('My Life Is Love', 'A Paradise for Two') who also interpolated a third song, 'A Bachelor Gay'. The show's musical director, Merlin Morgan, also interpolated his song 'New Moon' into the third act for Miss Collins but this was later replaced by a further Tate number, 'When You're in Love'. Fraser-Simson also supplied an additional duet for Miss Collins and Bates, 'Friendship and Love', during the London run. The 1972 revival interpolated Friml's 'The Song of the Vagabonds' from *The Vagabond King* and Harry Parr Davies' 'Pedro the Fisherman' from *The Lisbon Story* in an effort to supply songs for the originally non-singing role of Baldasarre.

MONSIEUR BEAUCAIRE

a romantic opera in three acts by Frederick Lonsdale founded on the story by Booth Tarkington. Lyrics by Adrian Ross. Music by André Messager. Produced at the Prince's Theatre, London, 19 April 1919 with Marion Green (Beaucaire), Maggie Teyte (Lady Mary), Robert Parker (Winterset), John Clarke (Molyneux) and Alice Moffat (Lucy). Produced at Daly's Theatre, 16 November 1931 with Raymond Newell, Barbara Pett-Fraser, Eric Fort, Darroll Richards and Betty Eley.

Produced at the New Amsterdam Theatre, New York, 11 December 1919 with Green, Blanche Tomlin, Parker, Clarke and Marjorie Burgess.

Produced at the Théâtre Marigny, Paris, in a version by André Rivoire and Pierre Véber 20 November 1925 with André Baugé, Marcelle Denya, Gilbert Moryn, Victor Pujol and Renée Camia. Produced at the Théâtre de la Gaîté-Lyrique 5 October 1929 and revived there 31 August 1935. Produced at the Théâtre Nationale de l'Opéra-Comique, Paris, 1954 with Jacques Jansen (Beaucaire) and Denise Duval (Lady Mary).

CHARACTERS

Monsieur Beaucaire
Philip Molyneux
Frederick Bantison
Rakell
Townbrake
The Duke of Winterset
Joliffe
Bicksitt
Beau Nash
François
Captain Badger
The Marquis de Mirepoix
Lady Mary Carlisle
Lucy
The Countess of Greenbury etc.

ACT 1

The tale is set in Bath at the beginning of the eighteenth century, the days when the fashionable of the land took their leisure there under the reign of the so-called King of Bath, Richard 'Beau' Nash. Nash's rule protected the city's fine patrons by a strictly controlled set of social customs and proprieties and, when the action begins, we learn that a Frenchman called Beaucaire, a barber in the service of the French Ambassador, has that morning been ejected physically from the fashionable pump rooms where he had the effrontery to parade himself dressed as a gentleman.

However, away from the social centres, some of the leisured gentlemen who contributed to the barber's disgrace are happy to attend his lodgings to take part in highly staked games of cards. They would be even happier to do so if they knew the real identity of this unusually well-off barber, for Beaucaire is, in fact, the Duc d'Orléans, son of the King of France, whom his father saw fit to send to prison for his refusal to wed according to the royal wish but who, with the aid of Mirepoix, the Ambassador, has escaped to Britain.

This secret is known only to Beaucaire's valet and to his friend, Molyneux, both of whom keep it faithfully. They are also aware of another, not so well hidden secret, the Duc/barber is in love. The object of his love is the Lady Mary Carlisle, a lady adored by much of unattached Bath but particularly desired by the horrid Duke of Winterset as much on account of her wealth as on account of her beauty. Beaucaire has made up his mind to bilk the wretched Duke of his bride and, further, to use him as the means to gain the Lady Mary for himself ('Red Rose').

Several gentlemen of the town arrive for an early evening session of cards: the plump and blustery Bantison, dashing Townbrake and wry, pragmatic Rakell. Bantison and Townbrake are fierce rivals of Winterset for the love of Lady Mary, but they are their own only partisans in the contest, a fact which Townbrake romantically recognises and Bantison blissfully ignores. They are also unlucky at cards, for Beaucaire, in a short session, takes all their pocket money from them before they set off for their evening's entertainment at Lady Rellerton's ball.

To that ball Beaucaire is also determined to go and he has evolved a plan which will allow him to do so with impunity. His second session of cards is with Winterset who is desperate to win back some of the large amounts he has lost to Beaucaire in earlier gambling sessions. Beaucaire purposely leaves the room to give the Duke the opportunity to secrete several good cards in his sleeve and then, as the stakes double and treble, he exposes the Duke's cheating. Thinking they are alone, Winterset goes to kill his accuser, but Beaucaire pulls back the curtains to reveal not only his servants but also the noble Molyneux. Winterset is thoroughly caught. Beaucaire offers him a bargain: he will keep silent over the affair if Winterset will take him to the ball and introduce him advantageously to the Lady Mary as his friend the Duc de Châteaurien. Winterset, with distaste in his mouth, can do nothing but agree ('Going to the Ball').

At Lady Rellerton's house 'The Beaux and Belles of Bath' are enjoying each other's company and Bantison and Townbrake are vying comically for the imminent attentions of Lady Mary. Their plans are once again dashed when Beau Nash indicates to them that he expects the lady to declare that very evening for Winterset. Molyneux, anxiously waiting for Winterset and Beaucaire to put in an appearance, is one whose principal care is not the Lady Mary: he is mutually attracted to Mary's cousin Lucy who finds that she would like him to woo her just 'A Little More' in the fashionable yearning and prettily-spoken style. Lucy cannot know of the preoccupations which keep her lover from being able to concentrate wholly on her.

Finally, Lady Mary arrives with a smiling song about her unknown ideal man ('Come with Welcome'/'I Do Not Know') but, as Bantison and Townbrake vie with flowery phrases to please her, Winterset strides on to the scene ('Who Is This?') leading Beaucaire. He makes the introduction in

125

accordance with his promise, and Beaucaire's well chosen compliments to 'English Maids' and to Lady Mary in particular effortlessly shame the clumsy efforts of the other men. Lady Mary contrives to be left alone with the handsome stranger who begs her courteously for the gift of the rose she wears in her hair. Such an action would be of too much significance after such a short acquaintance and Lady Mary vows that if he would have the rose he must earn it ('Lightly, Lightly'): he must escort the aged Countess of Greenbury to supper.

Winterset has not given up his hope to be revenged on Beaucaire. He inveigles the expert swordsman, Captain Badger, into stirring up a quarrel with the 'Duc de Châteaurien' ('No Offence') and Beaucaire, swift to defend his honour, challenges the Captain to duel. While the 'Rose Minuet' is being danced in the ballroom, out on the terrace the two men draw swords. When cries of 'murder' arise and the dancers rush to the balcony they find that it is Beaucaire who, with skills unexpected in a barber, has laid low the celebrated Badger. When Beaucaire appears to take the old Countess into supper, a relieved Lady Mary is happy to present him with his rose.

ACT 2

Three weeks have passed and Mr Bantison is holding a 'Pastoral Fête' in the gardens of his particularly fine house outside Bath. He has outdone himself in expense with the single aim of impressing Lady Mary, a cause which seems even more lost than ever now that Lady Mary is obviously so very much interested in the brave French nobleman. It seems mortifying that there is none left in Bath who can contest this foreigner's attractions although Beau Nash is convinced that fifteen years ago, 'When I Was King of Bath', he could himself have made a show.

Townbrake briefly contemplates suicide, Bantison speaks of a challenge which would seem to be another and less private way to suicide, and Lucy tries to give them a lesson in unobvious wooing ('That's a Woman's Way') which, she is well aware, won't help them a bit. Lady Mary, amongst the pastoral excesses of Bantison's garden, is moved to sing of the classic tale of 'Philomel', before dutifully paying some attention to the languishing Bantison.

Lucy finally manages to get Molyneux to herself for a few minutes. He has been so neglectful of late, spending all his time with Châteaurien. He must promise that this evening shall be theirs alone and together. No sooner has Molyneux made his promise than Joliffe, the head servant of the Pump Rooms, delivers him a note. It is from Beaucaire begging him to follow him hastily back to town. He must go. Lucy, who declares this is not the Duc's handwriting, accuses him of going to another lady, but Molyneux stoutly defends his 'Honour and Love' as he inexorably leaves.

Lucy is right. It is a trick set up by Winterset who has decided to go into action again. When Molyneux is out of the way, with considerable guile he exposes Châteaurien as Beaucaire before Bantison, Townbrake and their friends. Aghast at the insult, they are all for taking instant revenge on the impostor—all but the practical Rakell who remembers how Beaucaire disposed of Captain Badger.

While Beaucaire and Lady Mary are exchanging hearts in the garden ('Say No More'), the men approach and, led by Bantison, attack. One by one they fall, delicately wounded by Beaucaire's careful blade, until only a massed attack of their servants threatens to turn the battle. Beaucaire's valet, François, and his fellow servants turn up in time to rescue their master and chase the attackers away. Lady Mary turns angrily on Winterset, but he has made his moment and intends to use it. He denounces the Duc de Châteaurien as the barber who was thrown out of the Pump Rooms under the very nose of Lady Mary. Beaucaire can only monosyllabically admit it, and Lady Mary leaves in anguish. When she is gone, the returning Molyneux rushes to aid his master and the reason for his silence becomes evident—from a wound in his side rushes red, red blood. Red blood shed for the red rose which signifies his love for Lady Mary.

ACT 3

A week has passed and Bath is agog with the latest fashionable news: the French Ambassador will attend this evening's gathering at the Pump Rooms ('The Ambassador'). Beau Nash is determined that no such happenings as those which occurred at Bantison's gathering will mar his evening and, to that effect, has placed fourteen guards around the Pump Rooms to prevent Beaucaire from fulfilling his pledge to greet his country's representative. The gentlemen who were painfully concerned are not anxious to repeat the episode either, as they still bear 'The Honours of War' in their bruises and bandages from the recent conflict.

Winterset is determined that Lady Mary shall leave the Pump Rooms before the arrival of the Ambassador as he fears that Beaucaire may, in spite of everything, make an appearance and, since her disillusionment with the man she loved, Winterset's suit has been received rather better than before. But he has persistent enemies. Molyneux, once he has overcome the fact that Lucy isn't—or wasn't—speaking to him any more ('We Are Not Speaking Now'), convinces her of the importance of the events, and they are instrumental in bringing Mary and Beaucaire secretly together in a private room.

Beaucaire soon explains the reasons for his failure to defend himself against Winterset's accusations and asks her whether she really believes him to be a barber. The man with whom she has wandered 'Under the Moon', does he express his love like a barber? She knows what he says is true, and she also knows that it was not to a Duke or a barber she gave her heart—it was to a man ('What Are Names'), and that man has it still.

Their tête-à-tête is broken up by a fearsome pounding at the door. Lady Mary begs Beaucaire to make good his escape, but he orders the doors opened and boldly faces Winterset and his followers. Just when it seems that the situation may become serious, the scene is defused by the announcement of the arrival of the Ambassador ('Way for the Ambassador'). To the amazement of the gathered company, the Ambassador goes on his knees to the presumed barber and hails him as 'A Son of France'. The King of France is dead and he is no longer in danger. His royal position can be revealed. Winterset is utterly defeated as the Duc d'Orléans brings Mary to his side as his future Duchesse, and the play ends with a repeated chorus in praise of 'English Maids'.

MR CINDERS

a musical comedy in two acts by Clifford Grey and Greatrex Newman. Additional lyrics by Leo Robin. Music by Vivian Ellis and Richard Myers. Produced at the Opera House, Blackpool, 25 September 1928 with Bobby Howes (Jim), Binnie Hale (Jill), Eileen Redcott (Minerva), David Hutcheson (Lumley) and Basil Howes (Guy). Produced in a revised version at the Adelphi Theatre, London, 11 February 1929 with Bobby Howes, Miss Hale, Reita Nugent, Jack Melford and Basil Howes. Produced at the King's Head Theatre Club 31 December 1982 and at the Fortune Theatre 27 April 1983 in a revised version with Dennis Lawson, Julia Josephs (replaced by Christina Matthews), Diana Martin, Graham Hoadley and Philip Bird.

Produced at the Wiener Bürgertheater, Vienna, 6 February 1931 as *Jim und Jill*.

Produced at the Forum Theatre, Metuchen, New Jersey 30 April 1986 with Michael Lengel, Lynne Wilson, Rose Pedone, Jonathan Smedley and Robert Jensen.

A film version was produced by BFI in 1934 with Clifford Mollison (Jim), Zelma O'Neal (Jill) the Western brothers (Lumley and Guy), Lorna Storm (Minerva) and W H Berry (Merks).

CHARACTERS

Sir George Lancaster
Lady Lancaster
Guy, *her son*
Lumley, *her other son*
Jim, *Sir George's nephew and adopted son*
Henry Kemp, *a millionaire*
Jill Kemp, *his daughter*
Minerva Kemp, *her cousin*
P C Merks
Donna Lucia d'Esmeralda
Phyllis Paterson, Lucy Smith, Smith, etc.

ACT 1

At Merton Chase, the home of Sir George and Lady Lancaster, a 'Tennis' tournament is in progress under the imperious organisation of Lumley Lancaster, one of her ladyship's progeny from her loudly lamented first marriage. Lumley and his equally spoiled and cavalier brother, Guy, lord it terribly around the house, encouraged by their doting mother, and they make dreadful use of poor, good-natured Jim, their adoptive brother. After

128

all, they are descended via their defunct papa from the purest Plantaganets and have 'Blue Blood', whilst he is an orphan nephew adopted by Sir George, a self-made man whose origins were in glue-making.

Lady Lancaster, who browbeats both her second husband and her step-son, has lofty marital plans for Guy and Lumley, but the brothers have certain ideas of their own on the subject of girls: Lumley is a flirt who declares he is quite able to be 'True to Two' while Guy sighs in a secret corner with little Phyllis Paterson ('I Want the World to Know').

Excitement enters the afternoon when a wet and water-weedy gentleman is ushered up to the house by some of the tennis players. He has been heroically dragged from the river and Lady Lancaster is overjoyed when she finds out that he is Henry Kemp, the American millionaire who has rented her former home, the Towers. Kemp is simply bulging with money and he is sure to do something for Guy for rescuing him so wonderfully. Guy tries to get in an honest word, but he is ploughed down by his mother, so no one gets to know that it was, in fact, not glorious Guy but humble Jim who accomplished the life-saving act. When Jim turns up, clad in nothing but a barrel, Lady Lancaster commands that he shall keep silent. Mr Kemp has a daughter who is worth millions and Guy and Lumley—that is to say Guy *or* Lumley—must have her.

Kemp's daughter Jill and her cousin Minerva arrive post haste to collect the dried-off millionaire. They have had an adventurous trip. Jill, driving rather faster than she should, was stopped by a policeman and she bashed in his helmet and then knocked him into a ditch as she sped off. A new maid arriving to take up a post at Merton Chase spots her and gasps: there is a policeman searching for a girl wearing a conspicuous red hat like hers and he's going to arrest her for assault. Jill pops a five pound note into the girl's hand and a few minutes later emerges dressed up in the maid's clothes, totally unrecognisable as the heiress from the Towers.

Clad in her new garb, she meets up with Jim doing his skivvy jobs around the house. They fall into immediate conversation, she doing her best to act the cockney maid, and before long they are chummy enough to talk about their thoughts on love and life ('A One Man Girl'). It almost ends in a kiss, but Lady Lancaster heaves to, looking for her new maid, and Jill, or Sarah as she has now become, is trapped. She carries on the impersonation and, caught out with no papers, gives the name of Miss Kemp as her reference. When Minerva comes back to see what is delaying her, Jill, with a big wink, passes her off as the rich Miss Kemp from the Towers.

Lady Lancaster is all grovel and Guy and Lumley total attention as Minerva, in a spray of coloratura, affirms that she, too, can be 'True to Two' while Jill sneaks back to find Jim and reaffirm that she, on the contrary, is 'A One Man Girl'. But Guy and Phyllis have less luck. Lady Lancaster chances on them snoodling in the garden and banishes Phyllis from the premises with some meaningful words about her intentions for her son as she brandishes her offspring's passport to wealth: an invitation from Kemp for the Lancasters to attend a ball at the Towers.

On the afternoon of the ball, many of the local young folk are having a party of their own. The carpet is rolled up, the gramophone on and, with Minerva in control, they are having a jolly time excercising their feet ('On With the Dance'). When they shimmy off to get into their fancy dress for the ball, Jill sneaks in. She secretly telephones to the Towers to arrange for her chauffeur to bring the car for her after everyone else has gone so that she can return home and appear as her real self at her father's ball. When Lady Lancaster reprimands her over her sloppy work, she answers saucily but she has a kind word for poor Sir George, struggling to get into his cavalier outfit, and she is touched when he covertly gives her half-a-crown to spend.

Guy and Lumley spend hours preening and primping over their costumes and they keep Jim running backwards and forwards with orders ('Le Cygne') until they are all ready to be seen to what they consider their best advantage 'At the Ball'. When the family has departed, Jim is left alone. Lady Lancaster has decreed that he is not part of the family and therefore is not invited. Mr Cinders may not go to the ball. But Sarah the maid comes to his aid with a cheery song ('Spread a Little Happiness') and an invitation card. She dresses him up in a spare costume and dubs him with an identity taken at random from the newspaper: the famous South American explorer, the Earl of Ditcham. Jim decides to risk it. As he leaves, Jill's chauffeur arrives and Sarah the maid is transformed into the glittering Jill Kemp to sweep off in her limousine to attend her own party.

ACT 2

At the Towers, the dancing is in progress, but a stately minuet is soon turned into a more modern dance in 'The Seventeenth Century Rag'. Lady Lancaster is all over Mr Kemp, but her thunder is rather stolen by the arrival of the Earl of Ditcham whose exotic chatter has all the guests surrounding him avidly. Kemp, apart, awaits the arrival of his daughter ('She's my Lovely') and, when Jill descends the stairs to be introduced as Miss Kemp, Lady Lancaster is stunned. She has turned her sons' attentions on to the wrong Miss Kemp, the poor cousin instead of the girl who is receiving from her father the priceless diamond necklace that comes as an heirloom to her on this her twenty-first birthday.

While Lady Lancaster rushes off to find her misdirected sons, the boys crowd round Jill trying to win her attention. But Jill is still thinking of Jim ('Please, Mr Cinders') who is getting himself into very hot water at the other end of the ballroom as his hastily conned knowledge of South America mortally offends the fiery Donna Lucia d'Esmeralda, the widow of an executed Paraguayan Premier. He does better with a couple of flappers who wouldn't know what it is like to be 'On the Amazon', but when he runs into Jill he is speechless. What is Sarah the maid doing at a posh party with diamonds round her neck? Jill has a quick answer. She is pretending, like him.

Lady Lancaster breathlessly rounds up her family to tell them about the right and the wrong Miss Kemp, but she is too late: Lumley has proposed to Minerva and been accepted and, in spite of everything his mother can trumpet, he is delighted to have been accepted. As Lady Lancaster goes for her smelling salts, the newly engaged couple celebrate 'Every Little Moment'.

Now a greater drama intrudes. Jill's priceless necklace has been snatched from her neck and Lumley has discovered a newspaper story which says the Earl of Ditcham left for South Africa that day. Jim's disguise falls to pieces and, horror! the missing necklace is found in his pocket by the restraining butler. Jill defends him and, when P C Merks attempts to arrest him, she shoves the policeman over once again and drags Jim out through a secret panel into the garden with the whole household in pursuit.

Suddenly someone notices that the butler has gone...and he's taken the necklace! The fleeing twosome escape on Lumley's motorbike but end up out of petrol, lost and drenched, singing lovingly to each other under a splendid downpour ('I've Got You, You've Got Me)'. They have a third person with them, though. They caught the butler trying to make off with the motorbike and Jim clonked him over the head and popped him in the sidecar. They decide to leave him, tied up, with a note for P C Merks but, as Jim searches the butler's pockets for a paper and pencil, he comes instead on the necklace.

At Merton Chase the next morning, Lumley is staunchly impenitent over his engagement to Minerva and, although Lady Lancaster doesn't know it, Guy has irretrievably committed himself to Phyllis. They can look forward to 'A Honeymoon for Four'. If they are nervous about what they have done, Jim is ten times more so. The theft of the necklace has been reported in the newspaper and he knows he is in for trouble. But trouble is heading, instead, for Lady Lancaster. Sarah the maid (as Jill has once more become) is fed up with her mistress's domineering ways and decides to get her own back. She tells the horrified Lady Lancaster just what she thinks of her treatment of Jim and Sir George and, when her opponent attempts to assert herself, Jim steps in to defend his girl. For the first time in his life he openly defies his step-mother and Sarah is thrilled.

In the middle of breakfast, P C Merks turns up bearing a hat. He is on the trail. Whomsoever this hat fits is entitled to the reward. The reward? Indeed. The butler was a famous jewel thief, so the person who trussed him up and left him for the police is entitled to the reward. Lady Lancaster pushes forward her sons and her husband to try the hat without success. Alas, there was no-one else from Merton Chase at the ball. But Jill Kemp enters in her own guise to tell the constable that there was indeed another Lancaster there—the Earl of Ditcham, alias Jim. The hat fits, and Jim is rewarded not only in cash but with the hand of Sarah-cum-Jill. All the Lancasters are to be wed and everyone can 'Spread a Little Happiness'.

Several songs, including 'Paradise Bound', 'Where's Jim?', 'Oh, What You Can Do to Me' and 'I Could Get Used to You', were discarded prior to the London opening of *Mr Cinders*. For the 1982 version, one song 'Jill' was omitted from the score and 'She's My Lovely' from Vivian Ellis's musical *Hide and Seek* was interpolated. The show's hit song 'Spread a Little Happiness' was lifted from the role of Jill to bolster the star role of Jim. Ellis and Greatrex Newman added 'Please, Mr Cinders' when the show moved to the West End.

BITTER-SWEET

an operette in three acts by Noël Coward. Produced at His Majesty's Theatre, London, 12 July 1929 with Peggy Wood (Sarah), George Metaxa (Carl Linden) and Ivy St Helier (Manon) and played at the Palace Theatre from 2 March 1931. Revived at the Lyceum Theatre 13 April 1931 with Evelyn Laye replacing Miss Wood. Produced at Sadler's Wells Theatre 23 February 1988 with Valerie Masterson, Martin Smith and Rosemary Ashe.

Produced at the Ziegfeld Theatre, New York, 5 November 1929 with Evelyn Laye, Gerald Nodin and Mireille. Produced at the 44th Street Theatre 7 May 1934 with Evelyn Herbert, Allan Jones and Hannah Tobak.

Produced at the Théâtre Apollo, Paris, as *Au Temps des Valses* in a version by Saint-Granier 2 April 1930 with Jane Marnac as Sarah.

A film version was produced by British and Dominion in 1933 with Anna Neagle, Fernand Graavey and Ivy St Helier which omitted much of the script and the music, and an even more distant version was produced in 1941 by MGM with Jeanette MacDonald and Nelson Eddy.

CHARACTERS

The Marchioness of Shane (Sarah Millick)
Dolly Chamberlain
Lord Henry Jekyll
Vincent Howard
Hugh Devon
Carl Linden
Manon (La Crevette)
Herr Schlick
Captain August Lutte
Lotte, Freda, Gussi, Hansi, *Viennese ladies of the town*
Captain Schenzi
Lieutenant Tranisch
Harriet, Gloria, Honor, Jane, Effie, Victoria, Mr Bethel, Mr Proutie, Mr Vale, Lord Edgar Jones, Lord Sorrel, Marquis of Steere, Vernon Craft, Cedric Ballantine, Bertram Sellick, Lord Henry Jade, Nita, Helen, Jackie, Frank, etc.

ACT 1

The year is 1929 and the scene Lady Shayne's house in fashionable Grosvenor Square. A dance is in progress and pretty Dolly Chamberlain and her fiancé, Lord Henry Jekyll, are having a tiff. Dolly is full of admiration for their hostess whose life is said to have been one of fascinating romance and adventure, but Jekyll sees Lady Shayne's past as a disreputable thing redeemed only by her safe, social marriage to Shayne. The reasons for Dolly's sympathies are clearly seen when, having sent her husband-to-be packing, she falls passionately into the arms of the pianist engaged for the dance. She will abandon the stuffy Henry and elope with him to lead a life of love singing his songs in cabarets and hotels. Their embrace is overseen by Lady Shayne, and the young people explain their plight. She asks briskly what they intend to do and, in response to their indecision, she asserts strongly that youth must answer to 'The Call of Life'.

The lights dim as Lady Shayne sings on until, when they come up again, time has been rolled back and she is her younger self again. It is 1875 and young Sarah Millick is being given a singing lesson by the dashing music master, Carl Linden. He sings to her of his Austrian homeland and of how he would like to share it with her ('If You Could Only Come With Me') and, gradually, their secret love for each other becomes plain. Carl tells Sarah that he must leave London. Even now her mother is making preparations for the day of her forthcoming wedding to the rich and titled Hugh Devon. They turn purposefully back to the singing lesson, but their feelings are too strong to allow them to dissemble and before long they are affirming deeply in duet 'I'll See You Again'. Mrs Millick enters with Hugh and, as Carl abruptly takes his leave, Sarah falls weeping into her mother's arms as the orchestra reprises 'The Call of Life'.

At the ball that night Sarah behaves with a fevered abandon which causes comment among her guests. Dismissing her fiancé sharply, she orders the orchestra to play something gay and gives forth with a song demanding 'What Is Love?', waltzing wildly around the room alone. When the evening is drawing to a close she tries to apologise for her outburst but she finds in Hugh only a stodgy lack of comprehension. The young people take 'The Last Dance' and the gentlemen depart, leaving Sarah and her bridesmaids-to-be alone to talk of marriage and men and finally to indulge in a game of blindman's-buff.

The finale begins with the girls singing themselves into the game. Sarah is blinfolded but, as the other girls hide and she begins to seek to catch whom she can, Carl Linden returns to the room to collect his music. It is around his neck that the blindfolded girl's arms end. Taken off his guard, he kisses her and in a moment the two young people are pouring out their mutual love. As the finale comes to its climax, the lovers prepare to follow 'The Call of Life' and, before the eyes of the thrilled girls who will never now be Sarah Millick's bridesmaids, they secretly leave the house together.

ACT 2

It is five years later and the scene is Schlick's café in Vienna, a lively but low gathering place for the ladies of the town and their customers. A chorus of waiters and cleaners opens the act as four professional ladies discuss business and bandy insults ('Ladies of the Town'). Carl is the conductor of the café's orchestra, providing the backing for the establishment's singing star,

Manon la Crevette. Manon had an affair with Carl in the days before he met and married Sarah and, although a woman of the world, she is still clearly in love with him. There is much feeling in her voice when, to his accompaniment, she sings gently 'If Love Were All'.

Fortune has not treated Carl and Sarah well. Times are very hard and Sarah, now known as Sari, has had to go to work as a hostess in the café to supplement their income. The implications of the job are swift to bring trouble for her when Captain August Lutte, an officer attracted by her evident naïvety, comes to Schlick to complain that Sari refuses his invitations to dinner. Amidst their tribulations, Sari and Carl are sustained only by their love for each other, and they escape from the unpleasantness of the present into dreams of the future and the 'Little Café' which they hope one day to own.

That night the café is filled with officers partaking of the women and the wine ('Tokay') as Manon entertains the company with the little French song 'Bonne Nuit, Merci' and the petulant waltz 'Kiss Me Before You Go Away'. For a while, Sari succeeds in eluding the attentions of Captain Lutte but she has no answer when Schlick invokes her and Carl's debts and angrily demands that she stop offending the Captain or take the consequences. She cannot afford to lose the little money her employment brings and, as Carl watches anxiously, she takes the dance floor in Lutte's arms.

The soldier is not slow to become amorously aggressive and finally he stops in the middle of the dance floor to kiss her long and hard. Carl leaps from the bandstand and strikes the loutish Captain who responds by drawing his sword. Blades clash and within minutes the professional soldier inevitably fells the musician. As he lies dying, cradled in Sari's arms, Carl whispers his eternal love to her, and the curtain falls on the single sobbing voice of the faithful Manon.

ACT 3

It is now 1895, in the drawing room of the home of the Marquis of Shayne in London. A large gathering of the most up-to-date society people is in evidence ('Tarara Boom-de-ay'), among them the six girls who would have been Sarah's bridesmaids, now middle-aged matrons regretting their youth in a meaningful sextet ('Alas, the Time Is Past'). They are waiting to meet the much talked-of Hungarian singer whom Lord Shayne, it is said, has pursued for years from capital to capital. When the lady arrives it is Sarah, whom they had all thought was dead.

In an incidental number four exquisite young aesthetes express their creed ('We All Wore a Green Carnation'), as Lord Shayne once more asks Sari to become his wife. He knows that her heart can never be healed and his, but he is willing to accept however little or much she can give in return for his own devotion. Sari asks yet again for time to consider his offer and makes her contribution to the music of the evening with the ballad 'Zigeuner'. At the end of the song she turns to another—their song, hers and Carl's—and begins to sing the refrain of 'I'll See You Again'. Her life ended fifteen years ago when Carl died, but she acknowledges with a wordless gift of a bunch of violets that she will wed the kindly Shayne.

As she sings on the lights change, the scene is once again 1929 and Sarah, Lady Shayne, is an old woman singing of her past and, perhaps, of Dolly's future. As the youngsters charleston off into the night, the old lady begins to laugh, then rising to her feet sings her undying love to her always remembered Carl in the closing lines of 'I'll See You Again'.

CONVERSATION PIECE

a romantic comedy with music in three acts by Noël Coward. Produced at Her Majesty's Theatre, London, 16 February 1934 with Yvonne Printemps (Melanie), Noël Coward (Paul) and Irene Browne (Julia).

Produced at the 44th Street Theatre, New York, 23 October 1934 with Mlle Printemps, Pierre Fresnay and Miss Browne. Produced at the Barbizon-Plaza 18 November 1957 with Joan Copeland, René Paul and Sarah Burton.

CHARACTERS

Paul, Duc de Chaucigny-Varennes
Melanie
Rose, *her maid*
Sophie Otford
Martha James
Mrs Dragon
Marquis of Sheere
Lord St Marys
Duchess of Beneden
Duke of Beneden
Lady Julia Charteris
Lord Braceworth, Lord Doyning, Mr Hailsham, *Regency rakes*
Hannah, Miss Goslett, Miss Mention, Countess of Harringford, Lady Braceworth, Mrs Hailsham, Lord Kenyon, Earl of Harringford, Hon Julian Kane, Mr Amos, Butler, Tiger, Mr Jones, Fishermen, etc.

ACT 1

A prologue spoken by three demi-mondaines, exquisitely dressed and masked, sets the tone and period of this 'polite, but slightly raffish play'. It is Brighton in 1811, bright and busy, the playground of the aristocratic and the rich, inhabited both by the players and the played-with, though one can never be quite sure which of these is which.

Two of the new season's inhabitants of the seaside town are Paul, Duc de Chaucigny-Varennes, and his ward, Melanie. Brighton is quite used to seeing a titled, middle-aged man setting up house for a beautiful young woman, but in this house things are not at all what they seem. Paul and

135

Melanie are a pair of penniless French adventurers. She is not 'the daughter of his old friend the Marquis de Tramont' but a café song and dance girl in whom he has invested what money he can raise, bringing her to Brighton, dressed and housed in the finest style, with the hope of catching a rich husband. The young Marquis of Sheere seems close to taking the proffered bait, even though Melanie suspects his preference would be for 'something less binding'.

Melanie poutingly asks Paul, 'When may I love somebody, please?', to which he answers, 'Not until you are safely married, and then only with the greatest discretion,' and she, knowing that both their futures hang on carrying their plan through successfully, submits to his ruling while longing for the day when she can love as she would like to ('I'll Follow My Secret Heart'). Young Sheere arrives to visit Melanie and is taken aback to find Paul avuncularly speaking of marriage and of calling on his father but, left alone with Melanie, he discovers that, although he is not so foolish as to believe her a titled French orphan, he truly is in love with her. He asks her to marry him and she, frightened by his sincerity and the sudden intensity of his proposal, begs him to consider a little more.

In front of the stage cloth, three dandified young gentlemen sing of being 'Regency Rakes' before the scene returns to Melanie's room, later that afternoon. Sophie, Martha and Mrs Dragon, professional ladies of some class, have called on Melanie to try to pierce her mystery over tea. They end up looking at the new clothes Melanie has bought and singing and dancing around the room (Quartet: 'Charming! Charming! Charming!') but they do not discover the truth.

Their jollity is dispersed and their curiosity piqued by the announcement of the Duke and Duchess of Beneden, Sheere's parents, but not until they have left does the Duchess get to the point of her visit. She will offer Melanie £1000 to leave their son alone. Melanie refuses, they depart, and the girl recounts the incident almost hysterically to Paul. Her tale is interrupted by the return of the Duke who begins by apologising for his wife's unfeeling manner and ends by offering Melanie his own protection and a little house near Berkeley Square. At the critical moment Paul emerges from the adjacent room to turn the Duke's little interview to confusion and, as the embarrassed nobleman makes his escape, the two plotters watch laughingly from the window.

Another front-cloth song intervenes, with Martha, Sophie and Mrs Dragon expressing their conviction that 'There's Always Something Fishy About the French', before the scene changes to the Public Gardens where the Prince Regent has just passed by. The discomforted Beneden is determined to find out the truth about Melanie and Paul, and he looks for help in his exposure of the pair to Lady Julia Charteris.

Lady Julia is a sometime intimate of Beneden and even more so, it emerges, of Paul of whose real identity she is perfectly aware. She is delighted to see him and fully determined to take his side in the deception. Their reunion is interrupted by the arrival of Lord St Marys bearing an invitation from the Prince Regent for Melanie to sup with him. To general amazement, Paul coolly but politely refuses. Such an invitation can only be accepted when Mlle de Tramont has been formally and publicly presented to the Regent by him, as her guardian. As he leads Melanie away with calculated loftiness, Mrs Dragon favours the rising favourite with a broad wink.

ACT 2

Martha and Sophie give a little Brighton society background before the scene returns to Melanie singing her way through an English lesson ('The Tree Is in the Garden'). It is interrupted by the arrival of Lady Julia who forces her way in past Rose, the maid, and quickly begins mockingly to take to pieces Melanie's fabricated story of her background, commenting acidly on how poorly Paul has rehearsed her in her tale. But when she refers to Melanie as Paul's mistress the girl flies into a rage and orders her out of the house. The arrival of Paul himself does nothing to calm her. She rails against the high manners and low morals of the people she has met who, nevertheless, feel free to look down on her and insult her, and she swears she will return to France.

Paul reveals the truth to his old friend. His wife and family having been murdered by the rioters of the so-called revolution, he survived under an assumed name as a tutor to the the children of some rich parvenus until he found Melanie singing in a café and, with what money he could get together, brought her here to make a marriage for her on commission. Julia laughingly suggests that if it is money he needs he could marry her but, on his shocked reply, treats the offer as a joke and says that she will help as much as she can.

Melanie is in a strange mood. At first she breaks up Paul's attempts to discuss strategy with bursts of singing, and then horrifies him by analysing the possibilities of the situation with a frankness which, as Julia reminds him, as an unscrupulous adventurer he cannot be allowed to resent. Julia agrees that a marriage with Lord Sheere would be more enduring and profitable in the long run than a short-term affair with the Regent or, indeed, a longer one with Beneden but, if they truly wish to succed, the important thing to do is to get Melanie presented under her aegis at the Royal Pavilion. Before that, perhaps, she herself might manage a little supper party for a few influential society people. As Paul gratefully see his friend out, Melanie picks up Julia's fallen handkerchief, sniffs it contemptuously and flings it into the waste basket.

A front cloth interlude is provided by a quartet of fisherman telling how Brighton turned from a fishing port to a fashionable town ('There Was Once a Little Village'), while the scene changes to Lady Julia's reception. Julia's influence has brought to her house the fashionable and famous who are prepared to take her word that Paul and Melanie are respectable. But Melanie has invited Martha, Sophie and Mrs Dragon, and their arrival causes confusion for they are the mistresses or former mistresses of many of the male guests and the wives are quick to depart.

Then Melanie, in song, faces up to the men who have made her propositions ('Dear Friends'): to the Duke she is a little malicious, to St Marys on behalf of the Prince she is gently mocking and deferential, to young Sheere she is sweetly kind. Then she turns to Paul and opens her heart; it is to him that the place in her secret heart is given. At the end of the song she collapses and the guests are hurriedly sent away, but when she recovers it is to find Paul cold and angry. The whole affair is ruined, his investment is lost, she has broken the contract which was agreed. He leaves in fury and Melanie sinks sobbing into a chair as the curtain falls.

ACT 3

On the Steyne the aristocratic wives make small talk of dogs and husbands ('Mothers and Wives') before Paul and Julia appear. Paul does not know what to do. His wrath against Melanie has cooled and he feels he cannot, having used her this far, abandon her. Julia uses the moment openly to express her own love for Paul and to offer him her heart, her hand and her money. They can spend their latter days together and she will pay for Melanie to have a suitable home in Paris until she finds a husband of her own class. When Paul leaves her at the door of her house he has contrived not to give her a direct answer.

At Melanie's house, a small charade is being arranged with the help of Edward Sheere. Paul, when he returns, will find them in each other's arms and, Melanie hopes, his jealousy will be awakened. Given what has passed between them, conversation between the two young people is difficult, but Melanie sincerely regards Edward as a kind friend ('Nevermore') and is grateful for his help. There are two false alarms as the milkman and a delivery girl ring the doorbell, but finally Paul enters to find the two embracing, as they had planned. He treats the situation coolly and, when Edward has gone, replies to Melanie's announcement that she is engaged with the news that he is to marry Julia. Melanie evenly asks them to sup that evening with herself and Sheere by way of a last celebration and determinedly kisses Paul full on the mouth as he takes his leave.

When Edward and Julia arrive that evening they find the house stripped and packed. Rose tells them that Mademoiselle has gone and then, to Julia's fury, that Monsieur le Duc has gone with her. They have sailed for France. Julia bitterly asks Edward to take her home. They have not long departed when Paul rushes in. Rose meets him with the same story. Mademoiselle has departed, leaving him a note. He reads it despairingly—it doesn't say where she has gone, where he can find her. Rose leaves the room and when the footsteps return he doesn't raise his head until a hand takes his hand and tenderly kisses it. Melanie is there beside him as the curtain falls.

GLAMOROUS NIGHT

a musical play in two acts by Ivor Novello. Lyrics by Christopher Hassall. Produced at the Theatre Royal, Drury Lane, London, 2 May 1935 with Ivor Novello (Anthony Allen), Mary Ellis (Militza Hajos), Barry Jones (King Stefan), Elisabeth Welch (Cleo) and Lyn Harding (Baron Lydyeff). Subsequently played at the London Coliseum from 28 May 1936 with Barry Sinclair, Muriel Barron, Cyril Gardiner, Olive Gilbert and Fred Rivenhall.

A film version was produced in 1937 by the Associated British Picture Corporation with Barry Mackay (Anthony), Mary Ellis (Militza), Otto Kruger (Stefan) and Victor Jory (Lydyeff).

CHARACTERS

Anthony Allen, *a young inventor*
Phyllis, *a tourist*
Lorenti, *an opera singer*
Militza Hajos, *an opera singer*
Phoebe, *her maid*
Nico, *a footman*
King Stefan of Krasnia
Baron Lydyeff, *leader of the revolutionists*
Cleo Wellington, *a stowaway*
The Queen, *a singer in the operetta*
The Purser *of the SS Silver Star*
The Musical Director
A Foreign Gentleman
Mr Allen, Mrs Allen, Aide-de-Camp, Young Officer, Lord Radio*, Bertha Potman*, Clara Potman*, Lucas Teasdale*, Rosetta Spalding*, Dulcie Glassborough*, Miss Warren*, Miss Phillips*, etc.

ACT 1

Anthony Allen is a young Briton of a hopeful age, a diffident nature and a fine profile who lives in 'Suburbia', London. He is also an inventor. He calls himself so in spite of the fact that he has not yet invented anything which has actually been manufactured, but he has great hopes of his latest attempt, Actual Vision, an improved kind of television. However, when he succeeds in impressing the commercial world into advancing him £500 as seed money towards its development, he reacts against the daily dullness of his working life and spends the money on booking himself the royal suite on the SS *Silver Star* for a cruise down the romantic coasts of Ruritania. There he may find a little adventure, a little luxury and possibly even the ways and means to earn back some of the five hundred pounds.

In the Ruritanian state of Krasnia, life passes rather as it does in the best and most colourful musical comedies of Frederick Lonsdale. The King is Stefan, a good but colourless royal, whose position is threatened by the unpleasant Baron Lydyeff, a prime minister with ambitions to fuse Krasnia into a Ruritanian megastate of which he himself would be a leading figure.

139

Stefan's resistance to Lydyeff's plans has been hardened over a decade of rule by his mistress, the gipsy opera singer Militza Hajos, a fiercely patriotic creature who is the sworn enemy of Lydyeff and all that he stands for.

Militza is housed in a beautiful palace and is treated by all Krasnia as 'Her Majesty Militza', as she takes an obvious and influential part in the running of the country. She continues, however, her official career as prima donna of the opera house, and her home is the scene of a rehearsal for part of the forthcoming operetta *Glamorous Night*. She joins with the tenor, Lorenti, in 'Fold Your Wings' and delivers solo the title song of the show, 'Glamorous Night'.

The King visits his mistress's house and the operetta rehearsal is dismissed, for there are sterner things at hand. Militza has openly displayed her enmity towards Lydyeff and his ideas, more openly indeed than the King, and he is afraid for her. In an attempt to ease this situation and to get Lydyeff to listen to Militza's strongly argued case for the continued independence of Krasnia, he has brought the politician to meet her. She agrees to see him, and sets the tone of the meeting by greeting him seated at the piano, singing the Krasnian National Anthem.

Lydyeff is not impressed. Their cards are down and, when they are left alone, he accuses her of staying with Stefan merely for his royal position. She is mentally, morally and physically tired of him, and would do better to take Lydyeff's side and, if necessary, him as her paramour. It would be much more spectacular. Militza dismisses him furiously and dissolves into tears in the arms of her maid, Phoebe. Phoebe, an ex-English chorus girl gone to fat and wisdom, calms her and with necessary practicality reminds her that, since she must sing, it is unwise to cry too much.

The next evening is the première of *Glamorous Night* and the corridors of the opera house are filled with life. On the stage the final scene of the operetta is taking place. It begins with a ballet which is followed by Lorenti's solo 'Shine Through My Dreams' before the contralto playing the role of the Queen joins the tenor and Militza in the show's finale. As the scene reaches its climax, with Lorenti and Militza joining in the refrain of 'Fold Your Wings', a shot rings out. But the marksman has been grabbed at the vital moment by a member of the audience and his aim has been deflected. Militza is safe, and she has sufficient presence of mind to calm the crowd and recommence the duet as the would-be assassin is led away.

The unknown hero in the audience is Anthony. The *Silver Star* is in port in Krasnia and he has chosen to spend a night at the opera, little thinking that adventure would find him there. The next morning, at the royal command, he attends Militza at her palace and, instead of the autographed photograph proffered as a reward, he asks for a small cheque towards the reconstitution of his squandered advance. She is amused and not a little charmed by this unimpressed and unusual English person, and the cheque she hands him is for a thousand pounds.

When a staggered Anthony has gone, Militza has to deal with a less welcome visitor in Lydyeff. He presents her with her passport and a message from the King: she must leave Krasnia immediately. A band of malcontents is marching on her palace. She has just five minutes. Militza braves it out with the help of the unflappable Phoebe, who has already packed her mistress's jewels and clothes for such an eventuality. She coldly informs Lydyeff that she has already booked a passage on the *Silver Star*. She intends to take a relaxing cruise until she is needed in Krasnia for the next performance of *Glamorous Night*. When the opposition chant of Lydyeff's mob is heard, she cannot resist challenging them from the balcony with the Krasnian anthem, but she is greeted with cries for Lydyeff and a brick through the window. As Lydyeff orders the crowd to calm in a calculated display of personal power, Militza prepares to leave.

On board the *Silver Star*, Militza again encounters Anthony, who is installed in the ship's royal suite and has no intention of surrendering it to her or anyone else, although champagne and her singing of 'When the Gipsy Played' can scarcely leave him indifferent. At a ship's dance (Rumba) there is a demonstration 'Skating Waltz', and a stowaway, Cleo Wellington, sings of her 'Shanty Town' before Militza is persuaded, in her turn, to sing to the passengers.

As she reprises the title song of *Glamorous Night*, the singer becomes again the target of a murderer's weapon. Anthony tells her she must leave the ship as soon as possible. They are within reach of her home province of Borovnik; there at least she will be safe from Lydyeff's minions. Avoiding the attentions of a curious foreign gentleman of whom Anthony has unpleasant suspicions, the two of them take to the ship's launch and head for the coast but, before they can reach land, there is a loud explosion. Lydyeff's foreigner has mined the engine room and as the act ends the *Silver Star* is seen sinking beneath the waves.

ACT 2

Militza and Anthony have made it safely to land and are struggling on foot towards Borovnik. By now, the uncrowned Queen of Krasnia is beginning to experience a new kind of feeling towards her strange rescuer, and it is clear that he too is leaning towards lust and even love, but he keeps his distance until she has explained to him the nature of her relationship with the King. She has stood beside him, as Lydyeff accused her, because he is weak; because left to himself he would long ago have abandoned Krasnia to the Lydyeffs of the world. For five years that is all that there has been between them, friendship and statesmanship. Now, at last, Anthony can reveal his feelings for her and, under the stars, at a Borovnian gipsy encampment, they undergo a form of marriage (Gipsy Wedding) before Militza calls on the gypsies to march to the aid of King Stefan and an independent Krasnia (March of the Gypsies).

Lydyeff has profited from Militza's absence to persuade the King to his way of thinking and to an effective abdication but, at the last moment, he makes the error of threatening the King who turns stubborn. Producing a pistol, Lydyeff orders Stefan to sign the abdication papers but, at the crucial moment, the Prime Minister falls dead to a bullet from Anthony, clambering into the royal chambers at the head of the gypsies who have stormed the castle.

Militza breaks to Stefan her decision to leave his side and to marry Anthony, but the King tells her that he cannot and will not continue to try to rule an independent Krasnia if she is not by his side. If she leaves, then he will abdicate and Lydyeff, even in death, will be triumphant. She is forcing him to give up happiness and to stick to a position and a task which he does not want, and she too must renounce happiness for the sake of that task.

At a ball in the palace (The Singing Waltz), Stefan decorates Anthony publicly and privately presents him with all the money he could need to bring his Actual Vision project to fruition. In twelve months time, when the machine is completed, Anthony's first broadcast will show to the world the marriage of the King of Krasnia to Militza Hajos: his dream in this other world is over. Back in London, as he watches the events in far-off Krasnia on Actual Vision, it all seems like a fairy-tale that happened in a strange dream 'When the Gipsy Played'.

Glamorous Night was revised immediately after leaving its original home at the Theatre Royal, Drury Lane, with its scenic demands reduced and several episodes and scenes cut completely, resulting in the disappearance of the characters marked (*).The song 'The Girl I Knew' inserted to showcase Elisabeth Welch in the role of Cleo Wellington was also deleted from the second act when Miss Welch left the production.

BALALAIKA

a musical play in three acts by Eric Maschwitz, a revised version of *The Gay Hussar* (19 October 1933). Music by George Posford and Bernard Grün. Produced at the Adelphi Theatre, London, 22 December 1936 and played at Her Majesty's Theatre from 6 February 1937 and at the Adelphi Theatre again from 19 February 1938 with Muriel Angelus (Lydia), Roger Treville (Peter), Clifford Mollison (Nicki) and Betty Warren (Masha).

Produced at the Théâtre Mogador, Paris, 24 September 1938 in a revised version by Maurice Lehmann with additional songs by Robert Stolz with Jacqueline Francell, Jean Kerien, Réda Caire, Coecilia Navarre and Jean Périer (Prince).

A film loosely based on the musical with additional music by Sigmund Romberg was produced by MGM in 1939 with Ilona Massey and Nelson Eddy.

CHARACTERS

Alexei Vassilyevitch
Colonel Balakirev
Nicki
Masha
Lydia Marakova
Count Peter Karagin

Prince Karagin
Marakov
Varvara
Igor Seversky
Maniev
Randall P Morrison, Mrs Morrison, Postcard Seller, General Travinsky, Sergei, Fedora, Madame Petrova, etc.

ACT 1

Outside the Balalaika Night Club, one of the more prosperous of the Russian clubs which decorate the narrow streets of Montmartre in these years following the Great War, an elderly man is singing to the accompaniment of a balalaika. It is a sad song, a song full of memories ('Where Are the Snows?'), for the shabby singer is a Russian emigré, Colonel Balakirev. He is, nowadays, as much a colonel as the doorman to the club, Alexei, is a dashing hussar officer. The life of Montmartre goes on around them and no one French takes too much notice of them: they are part of the city's life along with its post-card sellers and brash tourists. To these latter, however, they are a sight to be seen and loud Mrs Morrison from Cincinnati drags her husband into the club to stare at some real counts and princes working.

The interlude music takes us back to the days when these men were indeed counts and princes, and the story begins at the Marinski Theatre, Moscow. The dancers' rehearsal is interrupted by the arrival of Alexei Vassilyevitch and Igor Seversky at the head of a troop of cossacks ('The Devil in Red'), ready to sweep the girls away for a night of entertainment. One of the girls, Lydia Marakova, has been the recipient of persistent bunches of red roses from an unknown admirer. It is not the lovestruck little assistant assistant stage-manager, Nicki, but, as it turns out, the dashing officer Count Peter Karagin, known throughout the city for his cavalcade through the hearts of Moscovite femininity.

Lydia resists his charm to his face and refuses his invitation to supper but, as soon as he is gone, she sings romantically to his 'Red Rose'. The departure of the young Karagin is followed by a less welcome visit from his father, the Prince. While he has no objection to his son carrying on with a hundred women, he will not allow him to become dangerously attached to just one, even though he himself takes a pointed interest in her beauty. Lydia is warned.

At the Balalaika restaurant, a little place set on an island where the music of the gipsies provides a sweet setting for romance ('In The Moonlight'/ 'Two Guitars'), the officers and the ballet girls gather for the evening's party ('Vodka'/'Red Shirt'). Nicki and Masha, the little dresser who is in love with him while he still sighs comically over Lydia, attempt to gatecrash the party but run up time and again against an unyielding owner.

In spite of her earlier protestations, Lydia does come and, swept away in the Elysian atmosphere, she and Peter are soon singing together 'If the World Were Mine'. The delightful moment does not last. It is dispersed by the angry arrival of the Prince, and by that of Lydia's father who crosses morally and politically with the Prince. Karagin will not countenance a marriage for Peter outside his own class while the bitterly populist Marakov is furious that his daughter should become entangled with a member of the despised aristocracy.

The young people rise above their elders' quarrels. To them only their love matters and they swear they will be married as soon as the new day dawns. They are not to know that day will dawn a very different one to that just past. Before their partying is through, the young soldiers are called to arms. War against Austria has become a reality. Peter must go to fight, and he will not return until Russia is triumphant (Russian Hymn).

ACT 2
At an outpost in Galicia, situated in the ruins of a lovely palace, Colonel Balakirev's regiment passes its third Christmas since the beginning of the war ('Come This Holy Night of Christmas, Come'). The soldiers dream of home, and Peter thinks particularly of the little restaurant where he spent his few happiest moments ('At the Balalaika'). But he is luckier than most of his companions. He will see the Balalaika again soon, for he has been ordered back to Moscow as a personal bodyguard to the Tsar whose life has been threatened by anti-war malcontents. As he prepares to leave, the Russian soldiers hear the sound of the carol 'Stille Nacht'. The Austrians in the opposing line are celebrating Christmas too.

Back at the Marinski, the ballet goes on and the dancers' lives, in the theatre at least, are just the same as they ever were ('Masha, Masha, Masha'). Lydia's friend Varvara attempts to cheer the pining girl ('Ballerina, Sad and Lonely') while they prepare for a royal gala performance of a new ballet. The police are in the theatre as there has been news of a man with a bomb, and Peter, in his new job, is also there. He and Lydia are briefly and happily reunited before they have to hurry to their respective positions on opposite sides of the footlights. Nicki and Masha meet again, too, and she encourages him to be a little more forward in his wooing ('Be a Casanova').

The scenery turns to show the stage of the Marinski where the ballet *Reflections* is in progress. Suddenly there is a loud blast and a commotion in the Imperial loge. A maniac has hurled a bomb at the Tsar and only the prompt action of Peter Karagin has saved him from injury.

Back at Marakov's home, his co-conspirators wait for news, but when the assassin arrives with word of failure they prepare to flee. Lydia and Peter return to the house to find Marakov still there. He confronts them crazily with his deed as the police burst in. They have followed Peter to the house and Lydia believes that Peter has simply used her as part of a plan to trap her father. She runs weeping after Marakov as he is taken away, running at the same time out of Peter's life.

At a boyar fête given by Prince Karagin, the guests dance (Mazurka) and the soldiers sing (Drinking Song) and unrest is in the air. Before the scene is over the grounds of the Prince's estate have been invaded by the Bolshevik leaders of the violence in the streets, and Karagin is brought face to face with Marakov once again. This time Marakov has the force of numbers and guns behind him to support his arguments. It is the beginning of the end of the old Russia—Karagin's Russia—and the beginning of Marakov's sort of Russia.

ACT 3

At the new Balalaika, in Montmartre, Nicki and Masha, who are the owners of the club, entertain with the duet 'Nitchevo' and Mrs Morrison, who has been hitting the vodka, drunkenly demands to dance with the handsome singer of the restaurant. Peter, for it is he, obliges dutifully, but Mrs Morrison finds that his kind of dignified dancing is not what she's looking for. When she's paying for it she wants a bit more passion. She lets forth a sally of Cincinnati oaths as her embarrassed husband tries to cool things down and hurries her out.

The restaurant empties, and the Russians settle down to toast the Russian New Year in their own way. Igor Seversky has invented a new cocktail which he has called 'The Devil in Red': that is how little the great and grand things of their old lives have become. They are joined by their old friends, the girls from the ballet who are in Paris performing, and everyone sinks into the delights of do-you-remembering. It is more than Peter can take. Everyone is there but Lydia: Lydia whom his father had removed from the ballet the day after Marakov's murder attempt, and whom he has never seen again. She is in Russia, at the side of her father. He is here.

But Lydia is not in Russia. Marakov has risen from the post of murderer to that of Ambassador to France. She is in Paris. As Peter's friends force him into joining the New Year game of looking for your future in the mirror, Lydia appears at his shoulder and he sees her face reflected alongside his in the glass. As 'If the World Were Mine' is reprised, they take each other's hands in a happy and hopeful embrace.

ME AND MY GIRL

a musical comedy in two acts by L Arthur Rose and Douglas Furber. Music by Noel Gay. Produced at the Victoria Palace, London, 16 December 1937 with Lupino Lane (Bill Snibson), George Graves (Sir John), Teddie St Denis (Sally), Betty Frankiss (Jacqueline), Martin Gray (Gerald) and Doris Rogers (Duchess). Revived at the London Coliseum 25 June 1941 with Lane, Barry Lupino, Helen Barnes, Nita Harvey, Ernest Dubois and Ann Booth; at the Victoria Palace 6 August 1945 with Lane, Graves, Valerie Tandy, Phyllis Stanley, Vernon Kelso and Miss Rogers; and at the Winter Garden Theatre 12 December 1949 with Lane, Austin Melford, Polly Ward, Kim Kendall, Peter Lupino and Miss Rogers. Produced, in a revised version by Stephen Fry, at the Adelphi Theatre, 4 February 1985 with Robert Lindsay (Bill), Ursula Smith (Duchess), Frank Thornton (Sir John) and Emma Thompson (Sally).

The new version, with further revisions, was produced at the Marquis Theatre,

New York, 10 August 1986 with Lindsay, Jane Connell, George S Irving and Maryann Plunkett.

A film version under the title *The Lambeth Walk* was issued by CAPAD-Pinebrook in 1939 with Lupino Lane, Seymour Hicks (Sir John), Sally Gray (Sally) and Norah Howard (Duchess)

CHARACTERS

Hon. Gerald Bolingbroke
Lady Jacqueline Carstone
The Duchess of Dene
Sir John Tremayne
Bill Snibson
Sally Smith
Herbert Parchester, *the family solicitor*
Lord and Lady Battersby
Lord Jasper Tring
Charles, *the butler*
Landlady (Mrs Brown)
Cook, Bob Barking, Major Domo, Telegraph Boy, Policeman, Sophia Stainsley-Asherton, Mrs Worthington-Worthington, Lady Brighton, etc.

ACT 1

A large open car, full of guests heading off to spend 'A Weekend at Hareford', makes its way from Mayfair, along country roads, to the magnificently ancestral Hareford House. Although they are deeply involved in doing their hostly duty, the occupants of Hareford are beset by a preoccupation. The family has lost its heir. The late Earl having inconsiderately died without a suitable legitimate son, his family has been obliged to resurrect an unsuitable one, the product of a youthful and unwise marriage to a person of no blood, to whom, it seems, the title and estates of Hareford must now fall.

Unearthing this unlikely Lord has stretched the talents of the family's solicitors considerably but at last word has come that he has been found and is to be brought to Hareford this very day. The lovely Lady Jacqueline displays a particular interest in the advent of this new to-be-rich man into her orbit and quiets the protestations of her flabbergasted fiancé, Gerald, by returning his ring to him. Now she can trawl for richer fish ('Thinking of No One but Me'). The rest of the family display various degrees of equanimity and despair at the thought of losing Harewood to an outsider, but they are not expecting anything as alarming as the heir they get.

Mr Parchester of Parchester & Parchester presents as the future Earl of Hareford one Bill Snibson from Lambeth, a chirpy little fellow in a bright bowler, spouting incomprehensible rhyming slang and very unversed in the ways of polite society. When Bill hears about the title he has inherited, he is even more taken aback than his relatives. When he hears about the money that goes with the title, he is floored. But there is a catch. To inherit, he must be passed by the late Earl's executors as a fit and proper person. If he is not, he will be given a sufficient annuity and sent away somewhere to live in retirement. The executors are the formidable Duchess of Dene and the crusty Sir John Tremayne.

Bill is all for taking the annuity and running, but the Duchess has other ideas. He is the last of the direct line of an abominably ancient family and she will not let that family die without a struggle. Bill must stay at Hareford and perpetuate the family in dutiful fashion alongside a fit and proper consort. When he's worked out what a consort is, Bill is quite happy. He's already got one of those and she's fit and proper enough for him. He runs off to fetch his girl, Sally, from the car. The family explodes, but the Duchess stands firm. Parchester, called on to advise, renders a nonsensical song-and dance ('The Family Solicitor') which solves nothing and the family troop off to the library to look for loopholes in the will.

Bill brings in his Sally to cast an eye around what is apparently going to be their new home and Sally looks about to see where a nice bit of lino and some floral wallpaper can go to brighten up the ancient walls. When Bill's explanations get to the bit about perpetuating, she spots a worry. Does she fit into this aristocratic plan? Of course she does, he insists, for nothing can part 'Me and My Girl'. When the realisation sinks in that everything in the house belongs to Bill, the two of them scoot back to the car carrying as many fancied objects as they can.

Down in the kitchen, the staff aren't as happy as they might be about their new master. He is quite the opposite to everything that 'An English Gentleman' should be and that demeans those who serve him. When Bill comes downstairs in search of a little congenial company, he finds even more disapproval than he gets upstairs, so he sets off instead for the nearby pub where he has installed Sally. Not everyone in the house, however, holds Bill at arm's length. Lady Jacquie has much cosier ideas and arms are only part of them. When Bill bumbles into her web he quickly begins to succumb ('You Would If You Could') and only a fortunate entry by Gerald and Sally saves him from perdition. Sally and Jacquie spit tit-for-tat at each other until her ladyship stalks off, leaving Bill to reassure Sally ('Hold My Hand') that, whatever she might have seen, she's the only girl for him.

The Duchess, in spite of Sir John's reservations, is still determinedly set on her course and Bill is obliged to spend his days learning the duties and manners that go with his title. Although his education is far from complete, she decides after a while that wagging neighbourhood tongues must be put at rest. He must be shown to the county at an official reception. When Bill hears that Sally is to be excluded from this party, he faces up to the Duchess: do what she may in other areas, she'll not part him from his Sally. But Sally doesn't want to come to a posh party. She'll feel foolish and she'll show him up. She knows, too, that her presence is stopping him from making progress towards being a fit and proper Earl and she has secretly made up her mind to go back to Lambeth.

Bill's altercation with Sally is overheard by Sir John and the crusty baronet is moved by Sally's obvious profession of love ('Once You Lose Your Heart'), but love breeds a strange plan in Sally's mind. When the Duchess stages her party (Preparation Fugue) with Bill playing his part as a trainee

Earl for all his worth, Sally turns up in full stage cockney regalia, bringing with her a gaudy troupe of Bill's Lambeth pals. Her plan is to prove to Bill that his old friends can't fit into his new life, but it goes astray when Bill sides with the cockneys and tells the Duchess he is giving up his efforts to earn his earldom.

The Duchess decides that she has more chance of dissuading him from dropping out if she invites everyone to stay to dinner. Her effort at miscegnation gets the go ahead, but Bill is convinced that West End and East End cannot mix. Mayfair cannot walk the Lambeth way. The cockneys begin 'The Lambeth Walk' and, little by little, the aristocrats join in until the curtain falls on the whole party happily Lambeth-walking into dinner.

ACT 2

In the gardens of Hareford, Gerald and Jacquie are partaking of a game of croquet under the sun ('The Sun Has Got His Hat On'), and the Duchess has cornered Sally. It is essential that Sally go to Bill and tell him that she no longer loves him. Only then will he be able to shake off Lambeth and concentrate on his coronet. Sally knows that she must not spoil Bill's chances, and she knows that she must find some way to convince him that they have to part. She must go away somewhere where he cannot find her. It is hard, but she will 'Take it on the Chin' and do what she must.

She goes to see Bill in the library where he is studying for his maiden speech in the House of Lords. He is working well and she can see that he is getting into earlish ways when he gives her a tour of the family portraits. He's even swearing all posh. Sally tells him that this time it really is goodbye, but Bill isn't having it. He sweeps off to challenge the Duchess, leaving Sally to reprise softly 'Once You Lose Your Heart'. As she finishes, the butler approaches to tell her that the car awaits her and, without seeing Bill again, Sally leaves Hareford.

Bill tackles the Duchess but she seems somehow to end up doing all the talking. Driving him back into the library, she points to the Hareford motto, 'Noblesse Oblige', and reminds him of his heritage. Then the family portraits come to her aid. Descending from their frames, generations of manly, aristocratic Harefords march dizzyingly around Bill to the strains of their motto (Song of Hareford: 'Noblesse Oblige'). When Sir John arrives in the library he finds a befuddled Bill reeling under the effect of his ancestors. Sir John is reeling too, but under a very different influence. Together with Parchester they hit the bottle and both the men come out in sympathy with Bill's love for Sally. But Sir John has just seen Sally being driven away. The Duchess has pulled a fast one. Drunkenly Bill talks of being in love and equally drunkenly Sir John confesses to the same emotion—aroused by the Duchess. Since the world is turning around them, they come to the same conclusion: 'Love Makes the World Go Round'.

Back in Lambeth, Sally has returned to her old landlady, but a telegram from Bill telling her he is coming to get her decides her that, once again, she must move on. Before she can do so, Sir John turns up on her doorstep. He has a plan and she must come with him. When Bill arrives, Sally hides in her room and the landlady pretends she is not there but Bill, not believing her, says he will wait and, 'Leaning on a Lamp-Post' outside, he does just that. But while he waits, Sally packs her bag and manages to creep out unseen.

Back at Hareford, Bill goes off his food. He has advertisements put in the papers trying to find Sally and concentrates on nothing but getting her back. Even the Duchess is in despair. Sir John is sanguine. It's love, and it's a great cue for him to broach the subject with the Duchess. Their very-nearly love scene is, however, interrupted by the butler.

Lady Jacqueline has still not given up her pursuit of Lord Bill, but nor has Gerald given up hope of regaining his errant lady. Her hopes take a dashing when Bill turns up dressed in the same old clothes he arrived in, determined to depart. She flings herself at him one last time and gets such a rebuff that she slaps his face. As she storms off Gerald gapes: it would have served her right if Bill had slapped her back. Bill replies that it's not her face wants slapping. She'd marry the first man who... Gerald leaves the room with a new spring to his step.

The Duchess arrives on the scene to stop Bill's departure, to the accompaniment of some strange slapping sounds and gurgling squeals off-stage. She finally concedes defeat, but it is not a total defeat. By his strength of character, Bill has shown himself to be a true Hareford; he is decidedly fit and proper. He is also no mean judge of women for, as the slapping and the squealing cease, Gerald and and a red-faced Jacquie run on to announce their re-engagement. Just as Bill is about to quit Hareford for good, Sir John hurries in to hold up proceedings; he has a young lady guest to present. In comes Sally—a very different Sally, a Sally done over by Wimpole Street and about as fit and proper a consort as any Duchess could demand. The Earl can have his girl and his title too.

The original London production of *Me and My Girl* contained only nine musical pieces: the opening chorus, 'Thinking of No One But Me', 'The Family Solicitor', 'A Domestic Discussion' (here 'An English Gentleman'), 'I Would If I Could', 'Me and My Girl', 'The Lambeth Walk', 'Take it on the Chin' and the finale, although several other songs had been used in the pre-London run ('Laugh and the World Laughs With You', 'Raspberries', 'That's That'). During its subsequent career, the musical part of the show stayed small, the second act often introducing only the one song and even that one being varied at one revival by 'You Don't Have to Worry Over Me'. The score was much enlarged by its authors to make the show into a traditional full-scale musical for amateur productions and a number of the songs from that score were used in the 1985 version along with 'Hold My Hand' from the musical of the same name and other Noel Gay song hits. The song 'If Only You Had Cared for Me' originally sung by the Duchess and Sir John in the new London version, was subsequently omitted.

THE DANCING YEARS

a musical play by Ivor Novello. Lyrics by Christopher Hassall. Produced at the Theatre Royal, Drury Lane, London, 23 March 1939 with Ivor Novello (Rudi), Mary Ellis (Maria), Roma Beaumont (Grete), Olive Gilbert (Frau Kurt) and Anthony Nicholls (Charles) and subsequently at the Adelphi Theatre 14 March 1942 where Novello was succeeded by Barry Sinclair, Muriel Barron appeared as Maria and Victor Boggetti as Charles. Produced at the Casino Theatre 8 March 1947 with Sinclair, Jessica James, Nicolette Roeg, Sara Romano and Peter Madren. Produced at the Saville Theatre 6 June 1968 with David Knight, June Bronhill, Cathy Jose, Moyna Cope and Robert Crewsdon.

A film version was produced by the Associated British Picture Corporation in 1950 with Dennis Price, Giselle Préville, Patricia Dainton, Miss Gilbert and Nicholls.

CHARACTERS

Rudi Kleber
Grete Schone
Hattie Watney
Maria Ziegler
Franzel
Prince Charles Metterling
Cäcilie Kurt
Otto Breitkopf
Countess Lotte
Ceruti
Lilli, Elizabeth, Sonia, Wanda, Sari, Mitze, Hilde, Emmy, Madame Sadun, Madame Pelotti, Kathie, Night Watchman, Oscar, Schani, Signor Valdo, Götzer, Poldi, etc.

ACT 1

Rudi Kleber is a composer, one of the great unplayed and therefore one of the decidedly penniless, and he and his piano board at an inn just outside Vienna where his tardiness with the rent money is a perpetual bone of contention between him and his landlady. For six months she has fed and lodged him without a pfennig of payment and now she has had enough. Returning from a night-time jaunt up the nearby mountains (Dawn Prelude) to pick moon-blossoms with the landlady's adoring teenage niece, Grete, he finds his piano in the inn's front garden. He has been evicted and, to pay his debt, the piano has been sold to a nearby dealer who is coming in a few hours to take it away.

While the disconsolate Rudi wonders how he will raise the money to avoid losing his precious piano, the very early morning breakfast crowd is heard approaching: a group of officers and their ladies who have been partying all night and who have come to clear the fumes with a healthy breakfast ('Uniform'). Rudi sees the chance of earning a little money by playing his compositions to the aristocratic company while they eat and, when his first waltz attracts their praises, he starts a competitive auction for its sale. The

150

auction is cut short when all the bids are largely topped by an offer from a late arrival, the operetta star Maria Ziegler. The tune is just what she needs as an interpolated number in her new show and, while breakfast is served, she sings 'her' song to Rudi's accompaniment ('Waltz of My Heart').

Some days later, Maria returns to the inn bringing with her the Prince Charles Metterling, an old and close friend and sometime lover. She wants him to use his influence with the theatre managers of Vienna to get Rudi a commission as a composer, and she is also asking him to allow the young man to live in an empty studio at his home. Charles is not at all enamoured of the idea, but he cannot refuse Maria anything and so it is agreed that Rudi will leave the inn and be installed at the Palais Metterling where he can take, in comparative comfort, the first steps towards a career.

In all the excitement of his new adventure Rudi cannot know that there is a heart which is being broken. Little Grete is losing her friend and she cannot bear it. With all the despair of her fifteen years she knows that she will die if Rudi goes away. He takes her in his arms and listens to her heartfelt words of devotion, and she is only calmed when he lovingly agrees that he will never ask anyone else to marry him until she is grown up and he has first seen if he would like to ask her. She knows that she may grow up to be perfectly awful, but she must have the chance. When he leaves she does not cry, for she has his promise and she feels safe.

A month later things have developed in a not unexpected way. Maria is falling in love with Rudi. Prince Charles is aware of the situation but he hides his discomfort under sarcastic teasing, particularly when Rudi attempts disastrously to become a Viennese gentleman and to dress himself in what he conceives to be the fashion of the town. Maria confides her growing feelings to her teacher, Frau Kurt, as they join in the duet 'The Wings of Sleep' from Rudi's score to the operetta in which Maria is to star.

At the first night of the new operetta, gossip is aflame about the new composer and the prima donna. Prince Charles pours scorn on the gossips and proudly confirms that Maria will sup with him after her première as she has always done but, as the curtain rises for the last act, he receives a message: the lady begs to be excused. On the stage of the Theater an der Wien, Rudi Kleber's operetta *Lorelei* climbs unstoppably to success ('Lorelei'/'My Life Belongs to You') as Charles's star equally inexorably declines.

In Maria's apartment, after the show, Rudi is a little drunk with wine and success, but also with feeling. He asks Maria if she loves him as he loves her and she answers whole-heartedly, yes ('I Can Give You the Starlight'). He asks about Charles, and Maria assures him that the affair between them was over long ago. As the lovers kiss, Charles enters. With pointed charm he congratulates Rudi on both his successes. He is going to England, so he has come to collect his clothes: his dressing gown which Rudi is wearing and his other things which he remembered when he was here last night.

Charles was here, in Maria's rooms last night? Maria cannot deny the truth of his words and to the bewildered Rudi it seems that Maria has lied to him. In a turmoil of wine-stained emotion he leaves the apartment, leaving

151

Maria and Charles together. Tearfully Maria taxes Charles with destroying the first real love of her life and the Prince, his own cause equally destroyed, departs. But Rudi has overheard Maria's profession of love and he returns. Maria tells him that Charles had indeed been there the previous night: to ask her to wed him, or to say goodbye. It was goodbye. As the two lovers embrace to the strains of 'I Can Give You the Starlight', the act ends.

ACT 2

It is three years later, 1914, in a chalet in the Tyrol. Much has happened in the intervening time. Rudi has become internationally known, and he and Maria have lived happily together, but through all that time he has not asked her to marry him. He remembers his vow to little Grete, now in school in England, and he will neither break it nor betray it. Maria feels deeply the socially unacceptable position she is in and she cannot help being hurt by Rudi's reticence where marriage is concerned. There is no doubting his love, though. It shines through his music for her, and tells her in its words what he cannot yet say to her more clearly ('My Dearest Dear').

Grete returns to Austria, no longer a schoolgirl but a beautiful young woman. Rudi's friend Franzel is love-struck, and Rudi himself is delighted to have his little girl back. Maria is less delighted. She is jealous, and before long a quarrel born of that jealousy builds up. He storms out and she pens a note to the still faithful Charles Metterling. The quarrel is soon mended, but the note cannot be recalled. When Charles arrives, Maria pours out her troubled heart to him. The nature of her relationship with Rudi keeps her in a perpetual state of tension and the advent of Grete has brought those tensions to an unbearable pitch.

Grete entertains the artists gathered in the house for a gala performance with a little English musical comedy song ('Primrose') but, when she has finished, Maria asks Rudi to send everyone away. She can take no more and she must speak to him alone. Rudi asks her to wait upstairs for five minutes. Now he can fulfil his promise to Grete. She will be the first woman to receive an offer of marriage from the great Rudi Kleber. She will refuse, of course, but what a triumph it will be.

Rudi does it properly, bended knee and all, and, as he does so, Maria, standing quietly in the shadows on the stairs, listens. Without waiting a moment longer, she leaves the house in distress and so she does not hear the rest of the scene: Grete's delighted refusal which at last leaves Rudi free to ask Maria to marry him. When Grete goes out of the room, he plays the refrain of 'My Dearest Dear', the agreed cue for Maria to come downstairs. But she does not come. She has gone.

ACT 3

The next morning rehearsals for the concert continue ('In Praise of Love'/ 'The Leap Year Waltz') as Rudi worries over Maria's disappearance. Soon she returns, to flamboyantly give her congratulations to Rudi and Grete and to break her own news: she has married Charles Metterling this morning. Now, when she hears the truth, it is too late.

Twelve years later, Rudi and Maria meet accidentally in a restaurant. Nothing has changed in their fierce feeling for each other. He has been hugely successful, she has become a figure in society, and they are both wretched. She promises to come to see him in a week's time, and then he shall decide what to do. When she comes, the reason for her postponement of the decision is made plain. She brings with her a little boy, her son, twelve years old. He is Rudi's son. Charles knows this, but he has brought up the boy as his own child. If she is to leave Charles and go away with Rudi, the boy's world will be shattered. They cannot do it. As Maria leaves to return to her glittering, soulless life, Rudi once more plays 'My Dearest Dear', the song which represents both their love and their parting.

They will meet again, however. When war strikes Austria and Rudi Kleber is imprisoned for helping refugees to escape, the Princess Metterling is able to use her influence to effect his release. The dancing years are far behind them in this new world and the future, whatever it may be, will be for their son.

The song 'When It's Spring in Vienna' was added to the score to enlarge the role of Cäcilie Kurt for Olive Gilbert, and a piece entitled 'Memory Is My Happiness' and other alternative pieces were at various times inserted into the *Lorelei* operetta sequence. Three spectacular sections billed as 'A Masque of Vienna' were played to cover scene changes during the course of the show. A programme note explained that they were 'intended to convey an impression of contemporary Viennese street life and have no connection with the main story'. In the 1968 revival the song 'Rainbow in the Fountain' from Novello's *Valley of Song* was added for June Bronhill as Maria.

PERCHANCE TO DREAM

a musical play in three acts by Ivor Novello. Produced at the London Hippodrome 21 April 1945 with Ivor Novello (Rodney), Muriel Barron (Lydia), Roma Beaumont (Melinda), Olive Gilbert (Ernestine) and Margaret Rutherford (Lady Charlotte).

CHARACTERS

The Vicar/Mazelli
Edgar Pell
Ernestine Flavell/Mrs Bridport
Susan Pell/Miss Rose
Sir Amyas Wendell
Lord Failsham
Lydia Lyddington/Veronica/Iris
Sir Graham Rodney/Valentine Fayre/Bay

Lady Charlotte Fayre
Melinda/Melanie/Melody
William Fayre/Bill
Miss Alice Connors
Aiken, Bow Street Runner, Amelia Bridport, Vivien Luton, Lucy Luton, Lavinia, Laetitia, Sophia, Elizabeth, Caroline, Mr Welby, Thomas, Midgett, etc.

ACT 1

Huntersmoon is a beautiful mansion, the inheritance and home over many years of the Rodney family. In 1818 it is the property of Sir Graham Rodney, a disreputable if charming rake in whose dissolute hands it has become the scene of wining and gambling gatherings for some of the less distinguished members of the nobility and their fair companions. This night, Rodney's friends are amusing themselves in his absence as he has failed to arrive in time for dinner ('When Gentlemen Get Together'). His mistress, the actress Lydia Lyddington, does not join in the rout but awaits Rodney's return patiently, carefully putting aside the flirtatious chatter of Lord Failsham and Sir Amyas Wendell and just a little frightened for her Graham's safety. There is talk that the famous highwayman known as Frenchy is abroad in the region.

Rodney is not only safe, he is in high spirits when he arrives to take his supper with Lydia, spirits which are not dampened by the news that his fearsome aunt Charlotte Fayre is descending on Huntersmoon with her nephew, William, and her daughter, Melinda. Charlotte and, more particularly, the unpleasant William have had their covetous eyes on Huntersmoon for years but, in spite of his comparative poverty, Rodney has refused to give up his heritage to the rich Fayre family. Tonight he intends to parade himself before them as a comfortable and respectable gentleman and, to top it all with a worthy flourish, he will seduce the little brat of a daughter.

To Sir Amyas's disbelieving sneers he hotly proposes a wager. Five thousand guineas bets that he will seduce the supercilious Melinda. Sir Amyas accepts unwillingly and Lydia sadly foresees either a loss which will break Rodney's purse or a conquest which will break her heart. But that is the kind of man he is. For her own peace of mind and heart she should leave him, she knows, but she cannot do it ('Love Is My Reason for Living'). Now they must prepare their charade for the arrival of Lady Charlotte. They will be very proper and dignified and Ernestine, a buxom actress who has been snoring off her dinner on the couch and is clearly immovable, will be passed off as a famous singer.

When she arrives, Lady Charlotte is singularly unimpressed by the act put on for her benefit and observes loftily that the house is 'nothing but old masters and young mistresses'. Melinda on the other hand is distressed. Their coach was held up on the road and they were robbed of the famous Fayre necklace by a man who could be no other than the notorious Frenchy. She is taken to her room before Rodney puts in his purposely delayed entrance, but when she returns, restored, their meeting is one of instant impression. In a minute, Rodney is looking deeply into Melinda's eyes and swearing that the necklace shall be recovered in time for it to be handed to her the following week on the occasion of her twenty-first birthday.

The two discover a strange feeling of recognition, of destiny in their meeting and Rodney finds himself in a dilemma. If he does not hold to his wager and seduce the girl with whom he is falling in love, he must forfeit five thousand guineas which he does not have. There is only one way in which he can get the money to pay the sworn forfeit—he must don the disguise of Frenchy once more, in spite of the presence of the Bow Street runners in the area, and rob the first available coach.

It is a week later, the night before Melinda's birthday. In the hall of Huntersmoon the tenor Mazelli entertains ('The Path My Lady Walks') and the assembled company join in the quintet 'A Lady Went to Market Fair'. Melinda describes in song the day of her presentation to the Prince Regent ('The Night That I Curtsied to the King') and Ernestine takes an altogether more lusty approach in singing of 'Highwayman Love'.

Tonight Rodney will ride in search of gold and Lydia, although she knows that she has lost forever her place in his heart, will keep his secret. There is no such loyalty to be found in Sir Amyas who covets both Lydia and whatever reward he can win from the sour William for his aid in unmasking Rodney. The two would-be thiefcatchers sit up together through the night to await their host's return, hoping to catch him red-handed with the proceeds of his robbery, but Rodney has drugged their wine and soon they are asleep.

Meanwhile, Rodney visits Melinda in her room. He returns the necklace and tells her that he must ride just once more as a highwayman to settle a wager. She understands the nature of the wager and why he must go, but she also knows that she loves him as he loves her and that her heart will not rest still until he returns from his last ride.

The following night, at Melinda's party, the guests are entertained by the ballet 'The Triumphs of Spring' until the news comes that the mail coach has been robbed and a Bow Street runner mortally wounded. An officer of the law arrives to search the house: the assailant, too, was wounded and the trail of his blood has led his pursuers here to Huntersmoon. As they begin their search, Rodney appears. He is clearly hurt and he cannot long dissemble before William's denunciation. Melinda tries to defend the man she loves. He cannot have been on the road last night for he was with her...all the night. But Rodney will not allow her to save his name at the price of her own and, telling Sir Amyas that he is proud to lose their wager, he bids Melinda look for him in another life where their love may have a better fortune, and dies in her arms.

ACT 2

Rodney's death left Huntersmoon to fall into William's hands. It gave him no joy but, in 1843, the house is still in the hands of Lady Charlotte's branch of the family and the old lady lives there with the deceased William's son,

Valentine. The atmosphere of the house is now vastly changed, for Valentine is a musician and choral master and, at the opening of the second act, his ladies' choir can be heard practising his composition 'Autumn Lullaby' in the distance.

A new postulant for a place in the choir is the lovely Veronica Lonsdale, but Charlotte is quick to dismiss the 'Lonsdale', for Veronica is the image of her mother, Lydia Lyddington, and clearly the love child of Graham Rodney. Veronica has just returned from school in Paris where amongst her schoolmates was another member of the Rodney family, Melanie, Graham's niece. Introduced to Valentine, Veronica is soon winning his heart to the strains of his own song 'A Woman's Heart' and in the parlour duet 'We'll Gather Lilacs' performed with the now stout and respectable Ernestine. Before long, the two young people are wed ('The Victorian Wedding').

Three years later, into the childless but happy hall of Huntersmoon, Veronica joyfully welcomes her dear schoolfriend, Melanie. Melanie is a total contrast to the lovely, gentle Veronica. She is ebullient and risqué and has clearly taken in more of Paris the city than of its finishing school during her stay. In the hall after dinner, she entertains the girls with a naughty song and dance about love ('The Glo-Glo').

Respectability returns when Ernestine and the Vicar join in a parlour duet about 'The Elopement' but, when Melanie reprises her Parisian song and its shocking little dance before the adults, she is considered out of line, even though the subject is very much the same as the more staid duet given by the older pair. Veronica calms the situation with a reprise of 'We'll Gather Lilacs' until Valentine enters, and Melanie is introduced to her friend's husband.

By the time three weeks have passed, Melanie has her heart set on and her hooks loosely into Valentine. Aunt Charlotte is sharply aware of the situation and she warns the girl grimly that she will make sure the moment Valentine's forthcoming command performance at Windsor Castle is done, Melanie is removed from Huntersmoon never to return. For the meantime, Charlotte will go to London with Veronica for a visit to a doctor, but Valentine must stay at home to work on the cantata he is to première before the Queen. Melanie will stay with neighbours. With some flaunting words to the man with whom she is desperately in love and whom she is sure she can make love her, Melanie leaves Huntersmoon under compunction.

But fate drives Melanie beyond the bounds of decency and reason. Later that night, as Valentine works over his music, she returns. She taunts him with his bovine fidelity to Veronica until, finally, he breaks out passionately with his long pent up feelings. Of course he wants her. From the moment they came face to face there was something from the past and from the future that drew him irresistibly to her and her to him. In spite of Veronica, in spite of everything, they must be together, now and forever.

The next morning Veronica returns from London radiant with good news which she cannot hold for her husband and must break immediately to her friend. After years of disappointment, at last she is with child. Valentine will be a father. But her news must wait, for today is Valentine's big day and

156

nothing must distract him. She must not tell him her happy tidings until after the command performance is over. Now it is time for him to go to Windsor and, when he returns... When he returns, Melanie will be gone. Her happiness, their happiness cannot, can never, be. Valentine must stay with sweet, happy Veronica and their child. Melanie's life is over, only her love will live on. 'To our next meeting,' she whispers as Valentine steps into his coach.

ACT 3

A century later Huntersmoon is a modern mansion and the descendents of the Rodneys and the Fayres are still in possession. Bay, the grandchild of Valentine and Veronica, is now the owner. On the walls hang portraits of his ancestors: Melinda, who died of a broken heart, and Melanie who drowned herself the night of Valentine's command performance. Both portraits bear a strange resemblance to Melody, Bay's fiancée. He met her for the first time in this room and it was as if some strange force from the past destined them for each other. They will be wed and, hopefully, put to rest the sad ghosts of Melinda and Melanie who may sleep at last, perchance to dream ('Poor Lonely Mortals').

BLESS THE BRIDE

a musical show in two acts by A P Herbert. Music by Vivian Ellis. Produced at the Adelphi Theatre, London, 26 April 1947 with Lizbeth Webb (Lucy), Georges Guétary (Pierre), Betty Paul (Suzanne) and Brian Reece (Thomas Trout). Played at the Stoll Theatre 10 July 1951. Produced at Sadler's Wells Theatre 11 August 1987 with Jan Hartley, Bernard Alane, Ruth Madoc and Simon Williams.

CHARACTERS

Lucy Veracity Willow
Augustus Willow, *her father*
Albert Willow, *his father*
Mary Willow, *her mother*
Harriet Willow, *grandmamma*
Alice Charity Willow, *Lucy's sister*
Ann Fidelity, Charlotte Patience, Elizabeth Prudence, Frances Fortitude, Millicent Punctuality, *Lucy's other sisters*
Cousin George
Hon. Thomas Trout
Pierre Fontaine
Suzanne Valdis
Nanny
M. Robert, *maître d'hôtel at the Café des Pommes*

Archdeacon Gurney, Buttons, M. Frontenac, Waiters, Marie Duval, Gendarmes, etc.

ACT 1

At the Grange in Mayfield, Sussex, the younger members of the Willow family are indulging in an early Victorian game of. 'Croquet!'. Lucy Willow has rather more than croquet on her mind, for she is engaged to be married on the morrow to the apparently rich and incipiently titled Thomas Trout. In spite of these attributes, Thomas has weaknesses: he has friends who are play-actors and, worse, given that Lucy's middle name is Veracity, he has a shocking disregard for the truth ('Too Good to Be True'). Lucy is prey to awful eleventh-hour doubts and admits to her sisters that, given the choice, she would rather marry 'Any Man but Thomas T'.

Soon Thomas comes along with two French theatricals who are staying nearby whom he has brought to liven things up. The saucy Suzanne gives forth with a few deprecatory verses on English girls and their fabled frigidity ('En Angleterre les Demoiselles'), translated by her companion, Pierre, and given the lie by Thomas who points to the size of the Willow family as proof of English sexual activity.

The French pair introduce the girls to the new-fangled game of tennis and they are all bouncing around on the croquet lawn ('Oh! What Will Mother Say?') in a most indecorous manner when the elder Willows come disapprovingly on to the scene to indulge in a series of sentimental reminiscences with their soon-to-be-lost daughter. Thomas pretends that Pierre and Suzanne are from the French Embassy and they are therefore accepted by the family as suitable company as the children return to the more sedate game of croquet.

But croquet can be turned to advantage just as easily as tennis. Lucy happens to strike her ball into the shrubbery, Pierre follows her there in search of it and it is not long before he is kissing her and she is kissing him back with an intensity unexpected from a young lady who is to be married to someone else the next day. But Pierre talks and kisses rather differently to Thomas Trout and, as Lucy and Pierre enjoy their experience ('I Was Never Kissed Before'), the jealous Suzanne, watching covertly, provides an irritated counterpoint.

Later that afternoon, in the house, Grandpa Willow allows himself a Golden Wedding flashback memory of his youthful days and we see the colours of the Waterloo ball and the early days of the waltz ('Marry Me') before the scene returns to the present day. Lucy entertains the company with the song 'The Silent Heart' and Pierre gives a French contribution in the happy 'Ma Belle Marguerite' before Mrs Willow brings in the sherry and gifts for the grandparents' anniversary, and the whole family joins in the stolidly happy ensemble 'God Bless the Family'.

The next day is Lucy's day. Her old Nanny fusses around her and sings lovingly to her 'Ducky', telling her that her little girl's happiness is all that matters. All this sympathy and understanding does Lucy little good, for she is bemused and unhappy. What is she doing marrying Thomas Trout when she would much rather be kissing Pierre Fontaine in the shrubbery? Her sisters bustle around her with the chorus 'Bless the Bride' and her parents and grandparents all add their platitudes and wishes until Lucy, at last alone with her father, reaches bursting point. She screams and screams and screams until her helpless Papa rushes off to find Nanny.

No sooner is the coast clear than Pierre appears at the window to assure Lucy that a coach and four are waiting. Impersonating a doctor, he sends Papa Willow rushing to the church to postpone the ceremony while Lucy is quickly made to change clothes with the house's pageboy. When the family return and discover that the fainting figure on the couch is not Lucy but Buttons, it is too late. Pierre and Lucy are on their way to France whence the Willow family will follow them as soon as the curtain falls.

ACT 2

Sur la plage at Eauville a group of mademoiselles are 'Bobbing-Bobbing' about in the English channel. Lucy and Pierre are there and Suzanne too, a self-appointed chaperone who is not unhappy to bring news that will part the young lovers: France is on the brink of war with Prussia and Pierre will be called up ('Mon Pauvre Petit Pierre').

Meanwhile the Willows, with Thomas Trout in attendance, have arrived in France and are coping in English fashion with the impossible French language, the ghastly French customs and the appalling French people all of which were clearly invented merely to irritate that superior species, 'The Englishman'. They are making their way to the Café des Pommes, where the local population is peacefully partaking of 'Un Consommé', to attempt to find news of their wayward child. They are on the right track for Pierre and Lucy are indeed there, dining tête-à-tête at 'A Table for Two'.

The Willows, done up in the most ridiculous disguises, appropriate themselves a conspicuous table and stumble helplessly into the complications of the un-English menu. At their table, on the other side of the restaurant, Pierre and Lucy have eyes only for each other ('This Is My Lovely Day'), but Suzanne will not let them alone and urges Pierre to go to his home where his call-up papers will be waiting. The Willow family attempt to pick up what information they can from the café talk, but the café talk, when it is not about the war, is largely about the strangers in the corner who are wearing false beards and who must be spies ('The Fish'). A gendarme is called and Thomas Trout, who has been acting in a most suspicious seeming way, is arrested.

Poor Lucy is obliged to reveal herself to come to his defence. 'This Man Could Never Be a Spy', she explains; he is too foolish, too cowardly. Thomas is freed, but Lucy, although she has been found, refuses staunchly to return to Britain with the family. She is in love with Pierre and will stay in France to marry him. But now Pierre returns in uniform. War has been declared and he is preparing, loaded with patriotic support from Suzanne, to go to the front ('To France'). He kisses Lucy, and then he is gone, as she collapses into her mother's arms, brokenly repeating the refrain of 'This Is My Lovely Day'.

Back at Mayfield Grange it is Lucy's twenty-first birthday and Nanny is preparing 'Twenty-one Candles' and a coming-of-age cake. Lucy's sisters are arranging a little song-and-dance for the celebration ('Here's a Kiss for One-and-Twenty'), but the atmosphere at Mayfield is very different from that of just a year ago. The Willows are engaged in sending food and drink parcels to France where, although the war is over, hardship is general. The chastened Augustus swears that he will never make a match for one of his children again and Lucy just sits in her room, telling the cards, as she has done ever since Suzanne sent the dreadful news of Pierre's death in the war.

Even Thomas Trout has undergone a change for the better and he can muse on his own failings and of what might have been if he had actually done one or two of the splendid things he'd thought of in the past ('My Big Moment'). He has supported Lucy kindly through her distress and despair and now he comes to offer sincerely to take her as his wife. Lucy accepts him and, left alone, sings sadly of the 'Summer' which will never come again in her heart.

At the birthday party a surprise guest arrives in the person of Suzanne. At first her old outspoken self at the sight of the luxuries of the Willow household, she checks herself, for the English have been good friends to France in their fight against Prussia and she wishes to make amends for her jealousy and, in particular, for one big jealous lie. She has brought for Lucy a birthday present. It is Pierre, a greyer and older Pierre, but alive. As they embrace, Pierre lifts Lucy's hand and he sees the engagement ring on her finger. Now, at last, Thomas Trout has the big moment that has always escaped him. He, too, has a birthday present. Stepping foward, he removes his ring from Lucy's finger and hands it to Pierre, and the scene echoes with 'This Is My Lovely Day' as the curtain falls.

The 1987 revival interpolated the Ellis/Herbert song 'Other People's Babies', originally sung in the revue *Streamline*, for Jean Challis as Nanny.

KING'S RHAPSODY

a musical romance in three acts by Ivor Novello. Produced at the Palace Theatre, London, 15 September 1949 with Ivor Novello (Nikki), Vanessa Lee (Cristiane), Phyllis Dare (Marta), Olive Gilbert (Vera) and Zena Dare (Queen Elena).

A film version produced by Everest Films in 1955 featured Errol Flynn, Patrice Wymore, Anna Neagle, Olive Gilbert and Martita Hunt.

CHARACTERS

Princess Kirsten
Princess Hulda

Princess Cristiane
Countess Vera Lemainken
King Peter of Nordland
Queen Elena of Murania
Vanescu
Nikki
Marta Karillos
Olga Varsov
Madame Koska
Count Egon Stanieff
Jules, Archbishop, Volkoff, Manservant, Tormas, Trontzen, Boy King, etc.

ACT 1

In the far northern kingdom of Nordland, the birthday of the King's eldest daughter, the Princess Cristiane, is being celebrated with gifts and songs ('Greetings'). Cristiane, known in the purple pages of Europe's popular magazines as the Snow Princess, is still unwed for, on the political front, Sweden and Denmark seem to have picked off the best of the eligible princes and, on the personal, she has not yet found the man whom she could love ('Someday My Heart Will Awake'). Now, however, her father tells her that she is required to make a state marriage. The man to whom she is to be wed is the future King of Murania.

Prince Nikki of Murania is an exile from his country. A self-made exile, as the whole world knows, for twenty years earlier he voluntarily left Murania and followed his mistress, the actress Marta Karillos, to Paris when, as a threat to the crown, she was expelled from the country by the royal family. What her father does not know is that Cristiane has followed the exile of the Muranian Prince with fascination, to the extent of compiling a scrapbook of news items and photographs concerning him. Far from being dismayed by her arranged marriage, she is delighted. Her only disappointment arises from the knowledge that Nikki has had no part in the arrangement of this marriage. It is the work of Queen Elena who, as the death of her husband approaches, is preparing to recall her son to reign over Murania.

At the King's death, Elena and her Prime Minister, Vanescu, make their way to Paris to hail Nikki as the new monarch. Nikki initially shows no interest in returning to Murania and it is revealed that it was not only love for Marta which caused him to leave home but also a wish for political and social change in his country, change which his father would never have countenanced. The lure of the throne, however, exerts its attractions on him and the promise of an unknown wife does nothing to deter his new found interest. When Marta arrives, he breaks the news to her, telling her that under his rule she will be recalled. Life will not be the same as it has been in Paris these last twenty years, but it will be much better than it was in Murania before their departure.

In Murania things are not destined to run smoothly. A demand from Nordland that Marta Karillos be kept out of the country brings from Nikki a bitter response in action. On the day that Cristiane arrives he is not there to greet her, but deliberately away from the capital on a hunting trip. A meeting with the Queen Mother and the news that Nikki has staged such a studied insult, and Cristiane's resolve weakens into tears as her faithful Vera comforts her in song ('Fly Home, Little Heart'). A week passes and still the new King does not come to meet his bride, and Cristiane is obliged to consider whether she may not do better to renounce the marriage and return home.

Alone in her room, she is sadly singing a song from her homeland ('Mountain Dove') when a slightly drunken figure appears at her window. She recognises him as Nikki. She feigns to be her own maid and discovers from Nikki the reason for his contemptuous behaviour towards his wife-to-be. The condition about Mme Karillos had been part of the marriage contract which, in her happiness, she had signed without reading. Under the influence of wine and music they talk loosely together and Cristiane, still hiding her true identity, sings temptingly to him ('If This Were Love'), seducing him into her arms.

Unaware of this unofficial meeting, Queen Elena has arranged that Nikki and Cristiane shall see each other for the first time at a court ball, but she is staggered when Marta Karillos puts in an appearance at the ball and is furious that Nikki should have invited her. Nikki denies having done so but, before the subject can be taken further, Cristiane is announced and she and the king meet face to face. Nikki is dumbfounded at discovering that his little paramour is the woman who is to be his wife, and staggered when Cristiane tells him that it was she who invited Marta. She wishes to meet her either as a friend or, if needs be, as an enemy. Nikki takes the opportunity to gain revenge for what he sees as an attempt to manage him and his life by taking the floor with Marta and ignoring Cristiane, but Cristiane is already in love with him and, as she full-heartedly reprises 'Someday My Heart Will Awake', the act ends.

ACT 2

At Marta's home, Nikki is whiling away time while the nation awaits the news of the birth of Cristiane's child, the fruit of her night with the drunken king before her marriage. At his insistence, Marta sings to him 'The Mayor of Perpignan', a song which can be heard sung everywhere among the people, a song telling of an unpopular mayor with a widely adored wife. The inferences are unmistakable, but Nikki shrugs them off as the guns ring out to signify the birth of a new prince.

Six months later, Marta, whose unpopularity with the people has grown in proportion to their love for their new queen, is preparing to leave Murania. On the day of her departure, Cristiane turns up at the house. Fanatical supporters of the young queen have been threatening to murder the actress and she is here in person to ensure that no harm shall come to Marta. In the empty house, she and Vera and the young Count Stanieff, who has been her loyal escort and supporter in Nikki's absence, join in song ('The Gates of Paradise') until Nikki puts in an appearance.

162

His questioning of Cristiane is interrupted by the return of a distressed Marta. Her coach has been attacked and she has been pursued back home. When the attackers break into the house, they are surprised to be confronted by their beloved Queen arm in arm with the woman they supposed her to hate, and they are persuaded to depart quietly.

Alone with Cristiane, Marta tells her the truth about her relationship with Nikki: she was at first his excuse for freedom and later his link with his youth, but she recognised immediately that he had fallen in love when he met his wife. Pride and fear prevent him from admitting it: it has been easier to stay with the comfortable Marta. But now she must go and he must take up his rightful place at Cristiane's side and at the helm of his country.

She begs the young woman to forgive her for depriving her of the first year of her married happiness, but Cristiane has nothing to forgive. She has profited from the past year, she has become a woman and a Queen. When Marta has bidden them a very final farewell, Cristiane faces her husband, a man who is afraid of her—afraid of the Queen, of the Snow Princess and even of the woman he has married—and who wants only to find again the uncomplicated Astrid, the maid to whom he made love on the night before his wedding. At last their marriage can begin.

ACT 3

Amongst the preparations for some amateur theatricals ('Take Your Girl'), Nikki curtails the extravagant political schemes of his mother and details to Cristiane the idealistic reforms which he intends to push through Parliament. He knows that these will not be popular with the majority of the Muranian traditionalists and forsees trouble, even personal danger. If anything should happen to him, he urges, Cristiane must hold on fast for the sake of their son. He has come to rely on her wisdom and good sense, and now that they are so strongly and happily united she can tell him how she nearly gave in and left Murania that night before her wedding ('When a Violin Began to Play').

After a ballet interlude (Muranian Rhapsody), the scene returns to the Palace. Cristiane is awaiting news from Parliament but, when it comes, it is bad news. Nikki has made his attempt to introduce reforms and has been noisily defeated. His return to the palace is quickly followed by the arrival of Vanescu with papers demanding his abdication. Nikki is ready. His son has already been sent out of the country to safety with the King of Nordland and he, too, is willing to depart.

He has only one alteration to make to the abdication document: he crosses out the name of Queen Elena as the constitutional figurehead who will reign in his place and inserts instead the name of Cristiane. He failed his country once, twenty years ago, and they could not accept him again even when he had the interests of the populace at heart, but Cristiane has never failed them. She is loved, she will be able to get a response from the people to her rule, and she will be able to maintain that rule in a generous fashion, while he returns to exile.

Ten years later Marta and Nikki are together at the opera in Paris. Nikki is once again a subject of interest for, in a few days time, his son is to be crowned as King of Murania. Vanescu, now Ambassador to France, visits his box with a warning to the former king not to attempt to be present but, as the coronation ceremony is seen coming to its end ('Ave Maria') and the young monarch is led away, the departing Queen drops a rose from her bouquet on the altar steps. When all are gone, Nikki emerges from the shadows to take the rose and kneel in a prayer for the safety and future of the boy who will have to try to bear the responsibility which he, even as a grown man, could not carry with success. As he kneels there quietly, the voice of Cristiane can be heard in the distance singing the final lines of 'Someday My Heart Will Awake'.

THE BOY FRIEND

a new musical comedy of the 1920s by Sandy Wilson. Produced at the Players' Theatre, London, 14 April 1953 with Anne Rogers (Polly), Anthony Hayes (Tony), Denise Hirst (Maisie), Totti Truman Taylor (Mme Dubonnet) and Larry Drew (Bobby). Produced in a revised and lengthened version at the Players' Theatre 18 October 1953 and played at the Embassy Theatre from 1 December 1953 and at Wyndham's Theatre from 14 January 1954. Produced at the Comedy Theatre 29 November 1967 with Cheryl Kennedy, Tony Adams, Frances Barlow, Marion Grimaldi and Nicholas Bennett. Produced at the Old Vic 18 July 1984 with Jane Wellman, Simon Green, Linda-Mae Brewer, Anna Quayle and Bob Newent and played at the Albery Theatre from 20 September 1984.

Produced at the Royale Theatre, New York, 30 September 1954 with Julie Andrews, John Hewer, Anne Wakefield, Ruth Altman and Bob Scheerer. Produced at the Downtown Theatre 25 January 1958 with Ellen McCown, Bill Mulliken, Gerrianne Raphael, Jeanne Beauvais and Peter Conlow and at the Cherry Lane Theatre from 28 April 1958. Produced at the Ambassador Theatre 14 April 1970 with Judy Carne, Ronald Young, Sandy Duncan, Jeanne Beauvais and Harvey Evans.

Produced at the Théâtre Antoine, Paris, 18 September 1965 in a version by P-L Dabadie with Valérie Sarne (Polly), James Sparrow (Tony), Suzy Delair (Mme Dubonnet) and Jean Moussy (Bobby).

Produced at Theater in der Leopoldstrasse, Munich, 20 August 1969.

A film version was produced by MGM in 1972 with Twiggy, Christopher Gable, Antonia Ellis, Moyra Fraser and Tommy Tune.

CHARACTERS

Hortense
Maisie
Dulcie
Fay
Nancy
Polly Browne
Madame Dubonnet

Tony
Bobby van Husen
Marcel
Pierre
Alphonse
Percival Browne
Lord Brockhurst
Lady Brockhurst
Pepé, Lolita, Gendarme, Waiter

ACT 1

Not too far from Nice is that part of the French Riviera which was clearly created for musical comedies. Not only does it have the most perfect weather but it has the advantage that quite a number of disguised noblemen and unrecognised millionaires' daughters enjoy spending their time there. In this promising *paysage* is situated Madame Dubonnet's finishing school for young ladies, the Villa Caprice.

The ever-so French maid, Hortense, opens the show. She is on the telephone setting the scene and ordering a fancy-dress costume for popular Polly Browne, the most ingénue of the establishment's pupils, to wear to that evening's Carnival Ball. The other girls of the institution, a self-confessed set of 'Perfect Young Ladies' if ever you saw one, are already deliriously fixed up with fancy-dress gowns and are more interested in discussing the boys they will be meeting at the ball.

Polly Browne has chosen to go as Pierrette, but she will not tell her friends who is to be her Pierrot. Sad to say, her modesty is all a subterfuge. 'The Boy Friend' is a *sine qua non* in the South of France and the truth is, as Polly has to admit to the understanding Madame Dubonnet, that she doesn't have one. She is an heiress, and her father suspects every young man who shows an interest in her of merely being after her money. Madame Dubonnet finds this a most unnatural state of affairs and she promises to have a word on this tender subject with Polly's father who is coming to visit his daughter that very day.

Today's first visitor to the Villa Caprice is Bobby van Husen, a wealthy young American who is staying at the Hôtel Negresco. Against school rules, he has come to visit madcap Maisie, the antic of the academy, to make her promise to dance every dance that night with him. Flirtatious Maisie won't promise anything of the kind, but soon they are indulging in a little preview of the evening's fun in 'Won't You Charleston With Me'.

When Mr Browne arrives, Madame Dubonnet attempts to talk to him on the subject of Polly's 'eart. It is a subject from which he shies away, but he is grounded when Madame Dubonnet suddenly adresses him as 'mon petit Percy' and reminds him meaningfully of Armistice Night at Maxim's ('Fancy Forgetting'). Surely he cannot have forgotten that night...and her. She is his little Kiki!

Polly is sadly contemplating a lonely evening when a young man appears at the very french window. He is an exceptionally dashing messenger boy bearing a box from the costumier containing Polly's Pierrette dress. They are soon making friends and, before the scene is over, they are singing hypothetically 'I Could Be Happy With You', arranging to meet that afternoon at the bandstand on the *plage*, and hoping to make up a twosome at the ball.

'Sur la Plage' the boys of Nice and the girls of the Villa Caprice disport themselves musically. The visiting English Lord Brockhurst takes the opportunity to ogle the girls in their bathing suits but his dragonistic wife is in no mood to appreciate sea, sand or sun. She is in a deep depression for they have lost their only son. He has run off from Oxford in the middle of the Hilary term, simply ruining his prospects and the fine future his fond mama had planned for him.

Meanwhile, Tony the messenger boy and Polly, who is pretending to him that she is a penniless secretary, are meeting at the bandstand and yearning, in a way that only the very rich in musical comedies can, for the simple life in 'A Room in Bloomsbury'. The scene on the beach is enlivened by a frisky song from Hortense confirming that 'It's so Much Nicer in Nice', an attempt at a singular flirtation by Madame Dubonnet with her old flame Percival Browne whom she accuses of suffering from 'The You-Don't-Want-to-Play-With-Me-Blues', and a mass flirtation by Maisie who goes by the maxim that there's 'Safety in Numbers'.

To a reprise of 'I Could Be Happy With You', Tony and Polly agree to meet that night but, as he kisses her, Lady Brockhurst heaves to on the horizon. Without an explanation, Tony flees while Lady Brockhurst cries frantically for the police to stop him. The police! Oh, no! Gossip whirls and soon the whole world knows that the poor messenger boy is a thief who has robbed the rich English milord and milady. He must have been a fortune hunter who knew all along that Polly Browne was a millionaire's daughter.

ACT 2

On the *terrasse* of the Café Pataplon the Carnival Ball is in full swing, but Polly is not there. With the aid of a little champagne, Madame Dubonnet is beginning to revive Percy's Armistice Night attitudes while Maisie turns a jolly step with Bobby and the whole company join in the latest dance craze, 'The Riviera'. Tony, sadly returning to the hire shop with his costume, is headed off by Hortense. She intends to try to get Polly to put in an appearance and perhaps mend matters between the young people. Lord Brockhurst, meanwhile, has shed the marital halter long enough to sing about a spring-and-autumn flirtation with the boop-a-dooping little Dulcie ('It's Never Too Late to Fall in Love').

Hortense has her way and Polly finally arrives at the Café Pataplon to join the party, a pretty but sad little Pierrette. Madame Dubonnet tries to encourage her to join in the dancing with a hopeful tale of Pierrot and Pierrette ('Poor Little Pierrette') and, indeed, as she finishes her song, a masked Pierrot appears. He takes Polly in his arms and kisses her and she gasps in recognition ... it is Tony.

The Brockhursts rush forward to claim their reasonably long-lost son and Tony is forced shamefacedly to admit his identity. He is awfully sorry, but he is a rich English lordling. The room in Bloomsbury recedes into the realm of the improbable. Polly has her confession too. She is devastatingly regretful, but she is a millionaire's daughter. In spite of such hindrances, they end the show in each other's arms, while Madame Dubonnet hooks her Percy, Bobby wins Maisie and, under their influence, the boys all propose to the girls who accept in chorus, bringing the show to a happy conjugal ending.

Divorce Me, Darling (Players' Theatre 15 December 1964/Globe 1 February 1965) is a sequel to *The Boy Friend*. Ten years on, all the characters of *The Boy Friend* turn up again in Nice. After a decade of leisured wedlock, and under the influence of the purlieus of their youth, they indulge in a few tiny flirtations and a number of delightful songs and dances in the 1930s manner, before coming to a happy ending. The original, short version of *The Boy Friend* and *Divorce Me, Darling* were played as a one-evening entertainment at the Theatre under the Stars, Houston, Texas for a season from 14 July 1984.

SALAD DAYS

a musical entertainment in two acts by Julian Slade and Dorothy Reynolds. Music by Julian Slade. Produced at the Vaudeville Theatre, London, 5 August 1954 with Eleanor Drew (Jane), John Warner (Timothy), Michael Aldridge, James Cairncross, Dorothy Reynolds and Yvonne Coulette. Produced at the Prince's Theatre 26 December 1961 and at the Lyric, Hammersmith, 18 August 1964. Produced at the Duke of York's Theatre 14 April 1976 with Christina Matthews (Jane), Adam Bareham (Timothy), David Morton, Sheila Steafel and Elizabeth Seal.

Produced at the Barbizon-Plaza, New York, 10 November 1958 with Barbara Franklin (Jane), Richard Easton (Timothy), Gillie Fenwick, Jack Creley, Norma Renault and Mary Savidge.

Produced at the Théâtre en Rond, Paris, 1957.

CHARACTERS

Jane
Timothy
Mr Dawes/Police Inspector/Augustine Williams/Ambrose, etc.
Mrs Dawes/Asphinxia/ Heloise, etc.
Aunt Prue/Rowena, etc.
Lady Raeburn, etc.
PC Boot/Electrode, etc.
Troppo, etc.
Sir Clamsby Williams/Manager of the Night Club/Zebediah Dawes, etc.
Fosdyke/Nigel Danvers, etc.
Fiona

ACT 1

On Graduation Day at a university which is probably not too far from Bristol, England, the Dons are indulging in some capering and vocalising on the subject of the generally unsuspected 'Things That Are Done by a Don'. The Dons, of course, will soon be starting the university year all over again, but for the graduating students it is the end of their student days and, more importantly, the beginning of the rest of their lives. Timothy and Jane are about to go down and, vowing to leave everything about their university days behind them, affirm 'We Said We Wouldn't Look Back'. One thing that they don't wish to leave behind is their friendship and, before they leave, they make an appointment to meet in the park in London the next Wednesday.

Back in London, however, both find that their families have plans for their futures. Timothy's family is intent on setting him off post haste on a Worthwhile Career. He has five uncles, four of whom are influential citizens who can help him to a job in their worlds: the diplomatic service, politics, the army and the scientific world. The fifth is the black sheep of the family, 'the one we don't mention'. Timothy must go and see his influential relations, chorus mother, father and Aunt Prue, and 'Find Yourself Something to Do'.

Jane's mother, Lady Raeburn, has different plans for her daughter: she must marry, soon and well. As Jane sits in the summery sunshine, waiting for Timothy to turn up for their appointment, she goes through her mother's list of eligible gentlemen and wonders if the season will turn up a husband whom she could happily choose for herself ('I Sit in the Sun').

When Timothy arrives, the two share the problems their parents are causing them. Timothy's idea of a job is 'something adventurous, amusing, with a living wage, and temporary' as the idea of being stuck in the same job for life horrifies him. Jane is looking for a marriage which answers a similar description, although she has no objection to its being permanent. So, as she explains, they really are looking for the same things their parents want them to, but without all the fuss. What if they married each other and Timothy took the first job that came along? But which should they do first?

Their dilemma is dissolved when an odd looking tramp turns up, pushing a pretty Victorian piano on wheels. He offers them a job looking after the instrument for a month at a salary of £7 a week and, before Timothy can voice doubts, Jane accepts. That's one half of their plan achieved. The Tramp plays a tune on the piano and, to their surprise, the young people find themselves dancing ('Oh, Look at Me, I'm Dancing'). The piano clearly has that effect on people even though it has only five octaves and no official music and dancing licence. Then, without warning, the Tramp is gone, leaving Timothy and Jane with the piano and a genuine job. Before they start work, and while Jane's mother is safely out of the way at the hairdresser, they have just time to get married.

At the hairdresser, Lady Raeburn is undergoing a full treatment at the forceful hands of the beautician Heloise, whilst chattering non-stop down the telephone with a society friend. She does not bat an eyelash at Heloise's woman-handling of her, merely contorting herself into positions of extreme unlikeliness so as not to miss a word of her ceaseless telephone chat. At the end, surveying the results in the mirror, she decides that it is a failure. Why, she looks at least thirty! Heloise must start all over again...and, darling, she will be just the teensiest, weensiest bit late.

In the park, Timothy and Jane are beginning their job, putting Minnie the piano to work. They are delighted to see that in their hands she has the same effect of setting everyone dancing. A Bishop set joyfully jigging shows his recognition by putting half-a-crown in a hat proffered by Troppo, a funny, mute little fellow who appears on the scene and to whom the young people happily offer a position as their assistant. Unfortunately, Timothy and Jane have not been brave enough to tell their parents about the job and the marriage so, as a cover, Timothy has to begin the rounds of the uncles, and he starts with a visit to Uncle Clam at the foreign office where everything is 'Hush-Hush'.

Back at the local police station PC Boot is making a report to his superior officer concerning the musical instrument which is setting folks dancing in the park. The Inspector is a connoisseur of dance and it is only after he and Boot have demonstrated a variety of Terpsichorean styles that the law, equipped with its ballet shoes, sets out to investigate.

The matter has, alas, already gone to a higher court. Jane meets Nigel Danvers, one of her mother's eligible young men, who shows her a newspaper: the Minister of Pleasure and Pastime has banned the piano and put out an order for its arrest. But Nigel knows a little about this kill-joy Minister. His own pleasure and pastime are spent ogling a novelty dancer called Asphinxia at the Cleopatra Club. Perhaps a little spot of blackmail might ensure Minnie's safety. Jane decides that Nigel had better be let in on the truth, and the act ends with Timothy setting everyone dancing ('Out of Breath') once again until the curtain falls.

ACT 2

At the Cleopatra Club, the Manager delivers a revusical piece of cod-Egyptiana ('Cleopatra') until Jane and Nigel arrive and conveniently meet Jane's friend Fiona whose escort just happens to be a photographer. A photo of the Minister with a dancing girl would be without doubt the most perfect blackmail material of all. Asphinxia comes on for her act ('Sand in My Eyes'), but the plot falls flat when the photographer's camera turns out to have no film in it. When Timothy comes along it transpires that the Minister is one of his uncles and he is quite ready to join Jane and Nigel in their campaign but, in the meanwhile, it's time for a song, so Jane and Timothy encourage Nigel to be a little musical in 'It's Easy to Sing a Simple Song'.

The Minister goes out into the park to take up the trail of the law-breaking piano. When he meets Timothy he quizzes him and his suspicious-looking friends closely, and the vacuous Fiona, who hasn't been told what's going on, just about gives the game away. Fortunately Troppo has made his escape with the piano, unnoticed, and the young people are able to join in the general chorus of people declaring 'We're Looking for a Piano' with genuine feeling. When Troppo returns, however, it is to confess that he is no hero: he has actually suceeded in losing Minnie while she was in his care. Timothy sets off to collect Jane so that they may begin a search.

Jane is at Gusset Creations where her mother has sent her to choose a dress for her party. Ambrose, the couturier, has arranged a dress parade for her which goes comically awry in the hands of his assistant, Rowena, and some uncomfortable models. At the end of the parade, the two young people set out in search of Minnie. Jane meets the Tramp and confesses that they have lost the piano. Today is the last day of the month and they are due to give Minnie back, but they do not have her to give back. It has been a wonderful month, Jane and Timothy have been married and fallen in love (in that order), and she has had 'The Time of My Life'. But they have failed in their job.

Unlooked-for help in their search comes in the person of another of Timothy's uncles, Uncle Zed, an 'astral navigator' who descends in his flying saucer to take them up in the sky for an aerial view of the park (Saucer Song). While Timothy and Jane float above the town with a weather eye turned to a search for their piano, Lady Raeburn and Mrs Dawes, oblivious of what is going on, are duetting soulfully that 'We Don't Understand Our Children'.

By the time the saucer lands, the Minister has discovered the missing piano himself and, with this evidence in hand, PC Boot is put to arresting Timothy and Jane for their licensing misdemeanour. But when Timothy plays the piano no one dances. It isn't Minnie after all, but a decoy. Then the Tramp enters playing the real piano and at once everyone, including the Minister, is set dancing.

Now it emerges that the Tramp is none other than the Minister's brother. He is Timothy's fifth uncle, 'the one we don't mention'. Timothy had been told that he was free to choose a job amongst those offered by his uncles, so he has actually fulfilled his parents' wishes, even if it has been in an unlikely way. Jane, too, has done what her mother wished for, as she now reveals, she is married.

Lady Raeburn is disappointed at being balked of the long-planned ceremony but, given the way that she is being sized up by Uncle Zed, it looks as though the preparations she has made for Jane's wedding may do very nicely for a second one for herself. Nigel and Fiona are made the delighted new temporary owners of Minnie and the horrid Minister's ideas undergo a very decided change when Minnie is commanded to appear at Buckingham Palace to entertain the guests at the Royal Garden Party. As everyone relaxes into his and her own particular happy ending, Timothy and Jane look forward to the next part of their lives, repeating the motto they started out with so successfully, 'We Said We Wouldn't Look Back'.

The Toronto/Broadway production of *Salad Days* inserted the song 'Let's Take a Stroll Through London' which had been cut from the London version and was later used there in the Slade/Reynolds *Follow That Girl*.

170

CHRYSANTHEMUM

a melodrama in ragtime in two acts by Neville Phillips and Robin Chancellor. Music by Robb Stewart. Produced at the New Lindsey Theatre Club, London, 14 March 1956 with Valerie Tandy as Chrysanthemum, and at the Prince of Wales Theatre 13 November 1958 with Pat Kirkwood (Chrysanthemum), Hubert Gregg (John), Patricia Moore (Mary Ann), Raymond Newell (Captain Brown), Roger Gage (Bob) and Richard Curnock (Uncle Fred).

Produced at the Royal Poinciana Playhouse, Palm Beach, USA 22 January 1962 with Patrice Munsel, Michael Evans, Geraine Richards, Ralph Bunker, Gary Oakes and G Wood.

CHARACTERS

Captain Brown, *a retired sea captain*
Uncle Fred, *his brother-in-law*
Bob Brown, *his son, an officer in the Mercantile Marine*
Chrysanthemum Brown, *his eldest daughter*
Lily, Rose, Daisy, Lavender, Violet, *his other daughters*
Sam, Tom, Joe, Willie, *their boyfriends*
John Blessington-Briggs
Mary Ann Blessington-Briggs, *his sister*
Emily, *Mary Ann's personal maid*
Ma Carroty
Ching Loo
Pepé
Suffragettes, Wedding Guests, etc.

ACT 1

It is a summer's afternoon in 1913 and we are in the garden of Captain Brown's house at Greenwich, a homely place with characteristics hovering undecidedly between late Victorian Gothic and blushing Art Nouveau, where the daughters of the good Captain are entertaining their young men to a *thé dansant* to the strains of an up-to-date gramophone ('Alexander'). Their Uncle Fred, a puritanical Victorian gentleman, greets his nieces' frivolities with glowering disapproval, but their father sees no harm in their music. He is a happy Captain, for today his sailor son, Bob, returns to the bosom of the family from a trip to South America. All his little brood will be together. All, that is, except Chrysanthemum. Three long years ago his darling eldest daughter went out to fetch the milk and never returned, and from that day to this no one has seen or heard from Chrysanthemum Brown.

Bob heaves to with a sailor song ('Ships at Sea'), a heart full of love for Mary Ann Blessington-Briggs, and some strange news: down Argentina way he could swear he saw Chrysanthemum. The good Captain is horror struck. Argentina! Better to be dead than amongst those immoral foreigners! It cannot be true. Imagine, therefore, his surprise when, no sooner has Bob gone off to rendezvous with his Mary Ann, than Chrysanthemum appears at

171

the garden gate, glittering in the latest Paul Poiret gown, weighed down with jewels and furs and gifts, and carrying the milk. Piling presents on her papa, she refuses the answer to only one question... where has she been? ('Don't Ask Me That'). The Captain, exasperated by her refusal to answer, comes to the only possible conclusion: she has, indeed, been in Buenos Aires. She is a fallen woman, a weed in his garden of flowers. She must go hence from his house.

Alone, with only a spotlight for company, Chrysanthemum sings sadly of her fall from grace ('Sinner Me') as she wends her way to the improper side of the river and the degrading depths of Chinatown. Suddenly she stops in her tracks. A wheelchair inhabited by an old woman with a mop of curly red hair skitters across the stage. 'Ma Carroty!' gasps our heroine and without pause sets scaldingly off in pursuit.

In Greenwich Park, Bob is waiting starrily for Mary Ann while, in another part of that selfsame park, that selfsame young lady is getting a lecture from her very upright brother, John. He suspects her of making an assignation with a gentleman behind his back and he warns her expressively of the dire consequences of flirtation: 'every single night in London nice young girls are being undone' ('Watch Your Step'). Mary Ann, alas, is heedless. Sending her maid to post a conveniently forgotten letter to Aunt Mildred, she hurries to the arms of her Bob ('Mary Ann'). All is decided. Today he will come and officially ask brother John for her hand in marriage.

They part and, as Mary Ann waits for John to return, an old redheaded lady in a wheelchair rolls up and offers her a chocolate. Mary Ann is well enough brought up to refuse it and the other delicacies the old lady proffers, but she cannot resist a look at her collection of picture postcards. After all, what harm can there be in a picture postcard? But as Mary Ann bends her golden head over the photos, the old lady whisks out a syringe: 'Aha! That completes another batch for South America.' The drugged Mary Ann is bundled into the wheelchair and trundled off as Chrysanthemum arrives at a brisk trot: brisk, alas, but too late!

Down in Limehouse our heroine, disguised as a Chinee, penetrates the notorious Skull and Chopsticks dance hall where Ma Carroty has her head-quarters. There, in a barred and black back room, Mary Ann is coming out of her stupour when Chrysanthemum appears ('A Fate Far Worse Than Death') to set her free. She tells Mary Ann what her fate was to be: bundled off to Buenos Aires just as she, Chrysanthemum, had been three years earlier. Contrary, however, to her father's fears she had not fallen there to a fate worse than death but had used her youthful dance training to become Carmencita, the famous tango dancer. But enough of exposition, Ma Carroty is approaching! With the aid of the old one-two the girls are soon free and on their way back to Park Lane.

In his Mayfair abode John Blessington-Briggs is in a frenzy. Trying to telephone the police, he only succeeds in getting wrong numbers ('Sorry You've Been Troubled') and, just as he gets connected to Scotland Yard, blow me if Mary Ann doesn't walk in. And Bob. And Chrysanthemum. When, with a little bit of fabrication, all the misunderstandings about who has been where and doing what have been cleared up, Bob thinks that Chrysanthemum has been in Paris at finishing school, and John thinks that Chrysanthemum is wonderful ('Is This Love?').

Back at Captain Brown's house, despite the disbelieving carping of Uncle Fred, Chrysanthemum is accepted back into the posy ('Understanding') and the multiple wedding plans are made public as John and Chrysanthemum celebrate in waltz time the fact that 'Love Is a Game'. So, there is to be a 'Double Wedding'. 'At The Wedding', however, fate intervenes in the form of Uncle Fred. Before the vows can be vowed, he pushes forward the castanet-clicking Pepé who gaily identifies Chrysanthemum as Carmencita, the Flame of Buenos Aires. She cannot deny it and, as the curtain falls, she walks forsakenly out of the garden in her wedding dress to the apparently apt sounds of 'Sinner Me'

ACT 2

Down by the river at the Rose and Crown, Chrysanthemum opens the act with an irrelevant ditty about 'Saturday Night'. John and Mary Ann follow tradition by taking shelter from the rain near the same spot for a duet 'Thanks to the Weather', and Chrysanthemum returns in a more sober vein to sing sadly 'No More Love Songs' before she prepares to set the plot running again.

Meanwhile, the Brown family have chiselled from the dancing Argentinian the real story of Carmencita. Pepé, needing a saucy dance partner to brighten his act, whisked Chrysanthemum away from a newly landed batch of potential *poules*, saving her from professionalism and creating a star in the process. She is not and never was a...! How could they have thought so ill of the Flame of Buenos Aires? But what now? She must be found! With a little prodding Mary Ann recalls the name of the Skull and Chopsticks and the lovestruck John heads off in pursuit ('Where Shall I Find My Love?').

His love is currently inside the Carroty den, disguised as the striptease dancer 'Shanghai Lil', but Ma Carroty is wise to her disguise and tricks her into a secret room behind a moving panel. As the horrid harridan gloats over her victory, John appears and, recognising his beloved's screams, he hurries back to the Brown house, where the family have been filling in time with a reprise of 'Love Is a Game', to tell them that Chrysanthemum is locked in Ma Carroty's secret room and everyone must come to the Skull and Chopsticks.

In the secret den, Chrysanthemum is tied to a bed as Ma Carroty sprinkles paraffin about. She will send the Skull and Chopsticks up in smoke. She has made herself rich by her commercial activities and now she can afford to give it all up and retire to a little cottage in the Cotswolds.

As John and Bob and Mary Ann burst in, the building is going up in flames. They are trapped! It is the end! But no...here come 'The Fire Brigade' with a song and a hose. They are saved, and Chrysanthemum is saved too. John shrugs off Captain Brown's praise. 'Any decent Englishman that loved a girl who had been maligned, and who, disguised as a Chinese singer was lying tied up in a den in Limehouse which was about to be burnt down by a fiendish white slaver, would have done the same'.

But the evening's action is not over yet. As Ma Carroty attempts to trundle her wheelchair off into the sunset, she is apprehended. Chrysanthemum steps forward with a revelation. Whisking off the red wig, she reveals that Ma Carroty is none other than—Uncle Fred! After a musical warning never to believe things to be what they seem, the show can now end with the 'Double Wedding' which should have closed the first act.

The original production at the New Lindsay included the songs 'Near' (Mary Ann and Bob) and 'You Do Nothing' (Lavender and Willie) which were cut from the reproduced version, the latter during the pre-London tour. 'Sorry You've Been Troubled' and 'Watch Your Step' were added to this version to boost the role of John for co-star Hubert Gregg. An additional number 'Look at Me Now' for Chrysanthemum was also excised before London. The songs 'Don't Ask Me That' and 'A Fate Far Worse Than Death' were written for the American production.

EXPRESSO BONGO

a musical in two acts taken from a story by Wolf Mankowitz. Book by Wolf Mankowitz and Julian More. Lyrics by Julian More, Monty Norman and David Heneker. Music by David Heneker and Monty Norman. Produced at the Saville Theatre 23 April 1958 with Paul Scofield (Johnnie), James Kenney (Bongo), Millicent Martin (Maine) and Hy Hazell (Dixie).

A film version was produced in 1959 by British Lion Films, using little of the show score, with Laurence Harvey, Cliff Richard, Sylvia Sims and Yolande Donlan.

CHARACTERS

Johnnie
Herbert Rudge ('Bongo')
Maisie King
K Arnold Katz
Mr Mayer
Captain Cyril Mavors *of the Diplomatique Club*
Dixie Collins, *a film star*
Lady Rosemary, *her society friend*
Linda Laverick, Cynthia, Mrs Rudge, Edna Rudge, Barmaid, Leon, Marcus, Beast, Mr Rudge, Recording Engineer, Editor, etc.

ACT 1

At the Deep South Jazz Club, whose deepest and most southern qualification is that it is in a basement somewhere in Soho, Herbert Rudge, a fun fair worker, puts on an act after the evening's main entertainment, singing to the accompaniment of some frenetic bongo drums ('Don't You Sell Me Down the River'). The small-time agent and entrepreneur who looks after the main entertainment is called Johnnie and he sees possibilities in the teenage drummer. The offer of money, fifty per cent of all he earns, is enough to get 'Bongo Herbert' to put his name to a contract. Johnnie is going to have one more go at making a star.

Bongo is launched on the coffee bar circuit ('Expresso Party') and Johnnie's wheeling and dealing gets Mr Mayer, the hard-to-get Artists and Repertoire manager from Garrick Records, to come and hear his boy. Mayer hates the popular music world, he's an opera man, but on opera he loses his shirt so though it gives him 'Nausea' he makes pop records. The result of this visit is a contract, £35 down and no royalties, for one record from Bongo.

Johnnie goes to see Bongo's faded mum and drunken dad in Hoxton to get their signature on a document and becomes embroiled in a family argument. His life might be pretty grim, but it is nowhere near as grim as this apathetic, trustless atmosphere from which the boy is going to have to escape, and the boy tells them so. He tears his hard, graceless, unloving mother apart and he goes.

Johnnie's leisure time is currently spent in the company of a little stripper called Maisie who works at the Intime Non-Stop Nude Revue ('Spoil the Child'). Maisie wants to be a singer and she spends her half-guineas and occasionally Johnnie's half-guineas on singing lessons. Can't he push her the way he's pushing Bongo? she asks 'Seriously'.

Johnnie has succeeded in getting Bongo on television as part of a programme on teenage rebellion. 'Expresso Party' wallops out of the TV set, and even Maisie has to recognise that Bongo has something: goodness knows what, but something. The boy is going places. Right now he's going off to *Pop Music Weekly* with a bundle of bits Johnnie has written about him while Johnnie gets on to Mayer. A second record is quickly agreed and Johnnie sees the future with frills on it ('I Never Had it so Good').

'Expresso Party' and the sharp, aggressive image Bongo gives out are soon the fashion. There are swooning girls to scare him, crowding columnists faking stories with the help of some swingeing lies from Mrs Rudge, and psychiatrists and churchmen giving ponderous opinions on teenage rebellion as personified by the lad, while Johnnie carries on packaging the sex and violence that are the winning formula into more success for his boy. The one element still needed to make Bongo generally acceptable, he decides, is religion, so Johnnie arranges for him to have religion. The act ends with Bongo on stage at the Odium Cinema, in a white suit with an angel choir, singing a pop hymn to that beautiful grey-haired madonna who is his mother in 'The Shrine on the Second Floor'. Johnnie can rub his hands for all is going according to plan.

ACT 2

At the Diplomatique Club, one of the town's chic-er and glossier night

175

spots, business hasn't been quite so good. In fact, as the suave Captain Cyril Mavors confides, 'The Dip Is Dipping'. He's pleased to take up Johnnie's suggestion that Bongo should play a week's engagement at £100 (as long as the press is told it's £500) and even more pleased when Bongo's presence results in the film star, Dixie Collins, and her entourage of titled ladies paying a visit. Dixie is a connoisseur of young talent, and young talent has become quite a connoisseur of Dixie. When the evening develops into a free-for-all of screaming fans, with which one suspects Johnnie and Mavors had something to do, Dixie is the first to make her way to the boy's dressing room where she leads sighing society in a vigorous paean to what 'He's Got'.

What he's got now, for the first time, is some money. And so has Johnnie. He has a new place to live and to work, and Maisie is installed as a secretary. She's not much use at typing and telephoning, but she's 'team', especially as she's gone and fallen for Johnnie properly ('I Am'). On the Bongo front things are going fine. The publicity and business generated by Dixie's overt patronage of the new singer has kept him three weeks at the Dip to full houses, 'Expresso Party' has hit number one, and Mayer is knocking at the door and talking serious business: a tour at £400 a week and back royalties on the chart-topping record.

Johnnie is jubilant but Bongo is less impressed: Dixie has been showing him a good time. She's bought him smart clothes, introduced him to fashionable people, talked about acting lessons, got a smart hairdresser to name a hair-do after him, and its 'Dixie this' and 'Dixie that' and the steely bitterness that made him what he is is falling away. Johnnie and Mayer can see the phenomenon that promised to be a gold mine being souped up and swept away with Dixie's desires ('Nothing Is for Nothing').

Next thing Bongo is doing a free gig at Claridge's, a gig fixed by Dixie's friends with no reference to Johnnie, mixing with the debutantes and pouring out platitudes which have nothing to do with Herbert Rudge ('There's Nothing Wrong With British Youth'). Johnnie meets him outside the hotel. He is due in Birmingham the next day to start his tour and Johnnie orders him home. The drunken boy strikes out at Johnnie, and the older man knocks him down. 'I still own fifty per cent of you, no matter which part you're giving to Madame Collins.' He owns fifty per cent, but short of kidnapping the boy there's no way he can deliver it.

So it's not Birmingham, it's the Villa Esperanza, Majorca, with Bongo stretched out in the sun, and Dixie and her pal Lady Rosemary flinging their money around on shopping for themselves and for him ('Bought It'). Dixie is falling prey to growing-old fears ('Time') and the youthful Bongo is only partly helping her to forget them. When Johnnie turns up to try to get Bongo to come home and fulfil his obligations, the desperate Dixie attacks him. The management contract he made Bongo sign is illegal. The boy is under age and his parents never signed their agreement. She will be helping him now and she has found him a 'proper' agent. It's the big guns turned on the small operator and there is nothing anyone can do about it.

Johnnie returns to London to face the music and a lawsuit levelled at him by the managers of the tour Bongo has reneged on. He thought that this time he was really on 'The Gravy Train', and now he has to start fighting his way towards that elusive big time all over again. In a series of flashes we see Johnnie back at the bottom, promoting his new hope for stardom, Maisie ('Don't You Sell Me Down the River'), as Bongo moves on to an American career ('Nothing Is for Nothing'), leaving Dixie behind him ('Time') as he grasps for bigger things. Whatever becomes of them, Johnnie is still travelling on hopefully ('I Never Had it so Good') as the play ends.

VALMOUTH

a musical in two acts by Sandy Wilson adapted from the works of Ronald Firbank. Produced at the Lyric Theatre, Hammersmith, 2 October 1958 with Bertice Reading (Mrs Yajnavalkya), Barbara Couper (Mrs Hurstpierpoint), Betty Hardy (Mrs Thoroughfare), Fenella Fielding (Parvula), Alan Edwards (Dick) and Maxine Daniels (Niri-Esther) and at the Saville Theatre, London, 27 January 1959 with Cleo Laine replacing Miss Reading and Denise Hirst in place of Miss Daniels. Produced at the Chichester Festival Theatre 17 May 1982 with Miss Reading, Judy Campbell, Jane Wenham, Miss Fielding, Mark Wynter and Femi Taylor with Robert Helpmann as Cardinal Pirelli.

Produced at the York Playhouse, New York, 6 October 1960 with Miss Reading, Anne Francine, Phillipa Bevans, Constance Carpenter, Alfred Toigo and Gail Jones.

CHARACTERS

Mrs Hurstpierpoint
Mrs Thoroughfare
Father Colley-Mahoney
Captain Dick Thoroughfare
Lieutenant Jack Whorwood
Sister Ecclesia
Grannie Tooke
Thetis Tooke
David Tooke
Mrs Yajnavalkya
Niri-Esther
Lady Parvula de Panzoust
Cardinal Pirelli
Carry, Fowler, Lady Saunter, Madam Mimosa, Mrs Q Comedy, Almeria Goatpath, Ffines, Nit, Sir Victor Vatt, Dr Dee, George Kissington, etc.

ACT 1

Valmouth is situated in the time and the mind of Ronald Firbank. It is an English spa town of a particular character and with particular properties amongst which seem to be a variety of air which confers extraordinarily long

177

and physically (not to say sexually) active lives on its pensionnaires along with a very particular set of moral, social and religious precepts. Everything in Valmouth drips with adjectives and even its verbs seem to be active, except when they are deliciously passive.

The manor of the town is Hare Hatch House, the rococo nay gothic abode of Mrs Hurstpierpoint, a lady of a certain age with a devotion to the more masochistic aspects of religion, who surrounds herself with clerics and is rumoured to wear holly leaves under her nether garments. At this season she is hostess to Mrs Thoroughfare, another ageing blossom and a relative by marriage, who is the mother of dashing Captain Dick, a seafaring man and the heir to Hare. Amongst the other quasi-permanent inhabitants of the town are Grannie Tooke, even older and delightfully *paysanne*, and her grandchildren David, a virginal Adonis, and Thetis, who is given to sighing suicidally over Captain Dick.

Grannie Tooke attributes part of her longevity to cares received at the hands of the local masseuse, a vast negress known as Mrs Yajnavalkya, about whom many a rumour circulates. Her treatments are whispered to diverge rather much from the accepted definition of massage and there is discreet gossip about instruments. Mrs Yajnavalkya houses a dusky maiden called Niri-Esther whom she gives out to be her niece.

It is now the season in 'Valmouth' and the Strangers' Hotel is already full. Sir Victor Vatt, the celebrated paysagist, is there and so is the exotic Lady Parvula de Panzoust, renewing her acquaintance of years with Mrs Hurst-pierpoint, intrigued by the possibilities of Mrs Yajnavalkya's 'Magic Fingers', and spurred to covetousness by the sight of David Tooke's buttocks.

Lady Parvula is not the only one suffering from the pangs of erotomania in Valmouth. Mrs Yaj inquires of Grannie Tooke the progress of Thetis' yearnings for Dick, and takes the opportunity to detail the effectiveness of her own dear late husband 'Mustapha'. Thetis is actually standing in the river. She does this a lot because she feels that it binds her to Dick who is somewhere else on what must eventually be the same body of water, and she sings dolefully of how 'I Loved a Man and He Sailed Away'.

Lady Parvula is to dine at Hare. When the footman has escaped from the attentions of Father Colley-Mahoney, Mrs Hurstpiepoint's latest thing in priests, when the lady of the house has finished a private session with the scourge, and when Mrs Thoroughfare has finished amusing herself in the chapel of Our Lady, the *petit comité* assemble to gossip over men and things and men ('Beards'/'When All the Girls Were Pretty'). The Father joins them for dinner, momentarily distracted by the sight of a nun dancing among the cypresses. It is Sister Ecclesia, a veritable chatterbox of a nun doomed to a vow of silence 362 days a year, who expresses herself in Terpsichore instead of speech.

After dinner, while Mrs Hurstpierpoint takes Lady Parvula to see her latest relic, Father Colley-Mahoney ruminates on Mrs Thoroughfare's latest confession. She has had a letter from Dick, a letter which horrifies her. Her son and the heir to Hare is betrothed, it seems, to a South Seas maiden.

178

Unthinkable as it may seem, Hare Hatch House will one day be ruled by a black woman.

Out in the countryside, David Tooke, a child of nature, sings in innocent tones 'What Do I Want With Love?' while, in town, Lady Parvula pays a professional visit to Mrs Yaj who, it seems, may be adding a little of the profession of Madam Mimosa (who is more Madam than Mimosa) to her carte-de-visite. Lady Parvula has developed a positive yen for the young man ('He's Awfully Choice') and, with the good offices of Mrs Yaj to help her, intends to throw her bonnet over the windmill and a young man into the hay 'Just Once More'.

Now the mystery of the pretty Niri-Esther is to become a little clearer. She is the dusky nymphet who is to be Mrs Dick Thoroughfare and 'The Lady of the Manor'. While the rain comes down and the lightning gleams, she flies her little pink kite across the lawns of Hare Hatch House, affrighting Sister Ecclesia at her dancing and awakening unspeakable longings in the proselytising breast of Mrs Hurstpierpoint.

One of the events of this part of the season at Valmouth is the Centenarians' Ball and Mrs Yaj is happy to take the opportunity to get dolled up in her 'Big Best Shoes' and go dancing. The ball takes place at Hare Hatch House and, while Mrs Hurstpierpoint makes use of her position as hostess to distribute religious pamphlets to all and sundry, Mrs Yaj goes into action to try to secure David Tooke as a morsel to appease the hunger of Lady Parvula. The surprise of the occasion, however, is the unprepared return of dashing Captain Dick who puts in an appearance with his bosom chum, Jack Whorwood, to prepare to introduce 'Niri-Esther' to his mother.

Deep in the background can be heard 'The Cry of the Peacock', which to the Easterners symbolises good fortune, while Niri-Esther is zealously stalked through the grounds by Mrs Hurstpierpoint, ravished at the thought of a redeemable infidel in her vicinity. She is balked when Dick meets his bride and, to general surprise, interest and horror, kisses her passionately. When Mrs Yaj informs the young Captain that he is an imminent father, Mrs Thoroughfare faints, Thetis has hysterics and Mrs Hurstpierpoint asks everyone what is happening, until the curtain falls on a scene of confusion.

ACT 2

A number or so of months later, the day before the catholic marriage of Dick and Niri-Esther, Mrs Yaj is found pushing a perambulator around Hare and serenading Niri's 'Little Girl Baby', while Sir Victor Vatt attempts to immortalise the mother in watercolours. To the disgust of Colley-Mahoney, the wedding and christening services are to be taken by the infamous Cardinal Pirelli, the incumbent of 'The Cathedral of Clemenza', and, as the resident representative of religion, he feels the slight horribly.

In the meanwhile, Lady Parvula has finally managed to spy out the movements of David Tooke. He is coming this day to Hare to deliver some produce. She decides to waylay him, and whiles away the waiting in talking to her late husband about her infidelities to his memory ('It Was Only a

Passing Phase'). David arrives and declines to be seduced but, when he is distracted by approaching voices, Lady Parvula hustles the confused shepherd into the chapel.

The voices are those of Mrs Thoroughfare and Father Colley-Mahoney and they are plotting. Cardinal Pirelli is said to have committed the sin of christening a dog, leaving himself open to excommunication should his sin be brought to the notice of the Holy See. Without a genuine priest, of course, the dreaded wedding of Dick and Niri-Esther could not go ahead. Mrs Thoroughfare, clutching for anything to save herself and her son from his appalling folly, gleefully agrees to an attempt at sabotage and decides to go and pray a little in the chapel for the downfall of the dear Cardinal. But what is this? Chickens? And a red-faced David Tooke? And Parvula. Dripping with chicken feathers! 'Tell Eulalia that her pew-cushions need restuffing,' sniffs the otherwise unruffled seducer as she sails from the scene.

Up at the house Niri-Esther is suffering a little *mal de pays*. Though Dick may assert that 'there's no air to compare with the air of Valmouth', she yearns for the sun of the south seas 'Where de Trees Are Green With Parrots'. Thetis Tooke is suffering too. She comes to drown herself in the river but she is verbally and physically halted by a nonsensically babbling religieuse. It is Sister Ecclesia, full of the joy of being alive, for 'Today Is My Talking Day' and she is making the most of it. As she struggles to halt the suicide's attempt, Jack Whorwood chances on the scene and Ecclesia hands the not unwilling Thetis into his not unwilling hands.

Grannie Tooke and Mrs Yaj meet at the wedding. Mrs Yaj, like the best of wandering fairies, has a mind to leave Valmouth once Niri-Esther is settled in at Hare. Like her niece, she longs for sunnier climes, but there are some things she will miss about Valmouth and Grannie is one of them ('I Will Miss You'). The guests gather and, at the same time, so do the storm clouds. Then, as the processional begins, Father Colley-Mahoney rushes on. Stop the ceremony! Mrs Thoroughfare almost faints with relief. If the Cardinal sets foot inside the chapel it is profaned forever. The Father brings a Deed of Excommunication signed by the Pope: the Cardinal's sins have found him out. As Colley-Mahoney thrusts the document forward the Cardinal collapses, Mrs Hurstpierpoint crumbles with a shriek, and the heavens open with roulades of thunder and splashes of lightning.

Suddenly Niri-Esther leaps forward and, snatching her baby from Mrs Hurstpierpoint's arms, like a bird she flies from the scene of carnage. Dick follows her, crying to her to return, as a warning voice calls out that the river is rising. As the people of Valmouth scatter, a particularly vicious finger of lightning tunes in on Hare Hatch House.

On a sunny island in the southern seas 'Where de Trees Are Green With Parrots', Niri-Esther nurses little Richard jr and Mrs Yaj plans another foray into the material world. Valmouth has gone, all of it. Next time they will try Bournemouth or Weymouth or maybe Portsmouth, but wherever they go it is unlikely that anywhere will quite live up to 'Valmouth'.

LOCK UP YOUR DAUGHTERS

a musical play in two acts by Bernard Miles adapted from *Rape Upon Rape* by Henry Fielding. Lyrics by Lionel Bart. Music by Laurie Johnson. Produced at the Mermaid Theatre, London, 28 May 1959 with Richard Wordsworth (Squeezum), Hy Hazell (Mrs Squeezum), Frederick Jaeger (Ramble), Stephanie Voss (Hilaret) and Terence Cooper (Constant). Revived there 17 May 1962 with Bernard Miles, Miss Hazell, Peter Gilmore, Sally Smith and Laurie Payne and subsequently played at Her Majesty's Theatre from 16 August 1962 with Wordsworth, Miss Hazell, Gilmore, Miss Voss and Payne. Revived at the Mermaid Theatre 31 March 1969 with Russell Hunter (Squeezum) and Anna Dawson (Hilaret).

Produced at New Haven, USA, 27 April 1960 with Harry Locke, Miss Hazell, Jaeger, Nancy Dussault and John Michael King. Produced at the Goodspeed Opera House 30 March 1982 with Carleton Carpenter (Squeezum) and Dena Olstad (Hilaret).

CHARACTERS

Worthy, *an honest justice*
Squeezum, *a corrupt justice*
Politic, *a coffee-house politician*
Ramble, *a gallant*
Sotmore, *a gallant*
Captain Constant, *a military gallant*
Dabble, *Politic's friend*
Quill, *Squeezum's clerk*
Staff, *a constable*
Brazencourt, *an innkeeper*
Faithful, *Politic's servant*
Hilaret, *Politic's daughter*
Cloris, *her maid*
Mrs Squeezum
Gentleman, Watchman, Wench, etc.

ACT 1

It is nine o'clock on a fine summer's night of 1730 in the city of London and Staff, the night watchman, is patrolling the streets, taking in the events and personalities on his beat. There goes a fine, upright gentleman arrested by the watch for compromising five nice girls. There's the house of Justice Squeezum who will doubtless acquit the fine upright gentleman at a price and probably compromise the five nice girls himself, given the chance. And that in spite of having a buxom and decidedly lusty spouse of his own.

Here's the Eagle Tavern, run by the low and louche Brazencourt, where two dashing young seamen, Ramble and Sotmore, are drinking themselves into oblivion or bed; here a prison cell; and here a coffee house, where old Mr Politic holds court, debating the affairs of the world, and spends his waking hours devouring forty or fifty newspapers in the naïve belief that they contain fact. He should be thinking more about his own little world, for his pretty daughter Hilaret is, at this moment, preparing an elopement with 'A Proper Man'.

The man in question is the handsome and virtuous Captain Constant and, with the help of her maid, Cloris, Hilaret intends to fly to his side this very night, while Politic and his fellow world-mender Dabble are spending the evening lost in their newspapers ('It Must Be True'). The Turkish problem, the fate of Tuscany, and the state of the health of the Dauphin of France are more important to the silly old man than the news that his daughter is missing from her room.

Down at the Eagle, Sotmore is knocking back the wine and looking for more, while Ramble, in whom the wine awakens other urges, is chasing a pot wench ('Red Wine and a Wench'). Sotmore is disgusted at his friend's lack of seriousness about drinking, but allows him time off the bottle to reconcentrate his mind. Stepping outside, Ramble encounters just the thing for concentration. A pretty woman alone in the street could only be one thing and that one thing is precisely the thing he's after. Actually she isn't anything of the sort, because the pretty woman in question is Hilaret who has become separated from Cloris in a street scuffle on her way to rendezvous with Constant.

Ramble is keen and sure in his pursuit of sex, Hilaret indignant at his approaches ("Tis Plain to See') and, when he cuts the talk and moves to action, she shrieks fearfully for help: 'Rape!'. When the watch arrive on the scene, Ramble contradicts her story, claiming she importuned him, and the watch impartially take them both off to face justice or, rather, Justice. The official in question is Squeezum. The night has not gone well for him so far: he has not made any exciting extortions and his wife has dunned him for a hundred guineas with a touch of blackmail. Motto: never let your wife into your guilty secrets ('On the Side').

The arrival of the new prisoners is an improvement. He decides to interrogate the pretty female prisoner *in camera* and Mrs Squeezum, not to be outdone, volunteers to keep an eye on the male prisoner in her bedroom. Hilaret quickly finds that the truth is not much use in a situation such as this and she improvises instead a fascinating history which heats Squeezum into a paroxysm of delighted anticipation. But her interview with the Justice is interrupted by a bump from the boudoir above and both Squeezums, deciding that discretion is the better part of copulation, decide to postpone their amours for the meanwhile. Squeezum makes an assignation with Hilaret for later in the evening in a private room at the Eagle while Mrs Squeezum makes sure that Ramble is held for further questioning and passionately soliloquises 'When Does the Ravishing Begin?'.

In the meanwhile, Politic has started to do something about the problem of his missing daughter. He has gone for help to Justice Worthy (by name and by nature), but once again he gets side-tracked on to the pros and cons of the Turkish situation and Hilaret is soon forgotten. The young lady, however, has now made it back to her home where she is reunited with the frantic Cloris. Cloris, alas, has some horrid news to tell: Captain Constant came to her rescue in the scuffle outside the Eagle and, when the cry of

'Rape' went up, he was arrested. He is to come up before Justice Squeezum in the morning. Hilaret puts on her bonnet again, and joins in a long-distance duet with her imprisoned Captain ('Lovely Lover') before setting out once more into the wicked streets of London to rescue her beloved or be debauched in the attempt.

In his prison cell, Constant soon has company. Ramble is brought in, to be held at the pleasure of the Justice (and his wife) and, soon after, Sotmore turns up to bring them liquid refreshment. They all know each other, and they catch up on the stories of Constant's love and arrest and Ramble's marriage (to a wealthy wife who was lost at sea with all her dowry) and arrest, and before long they are joining merrily in song, chaffing Ramble ('Lock Up Your Daughters') for his sexual excesses.

Hilaret arrives at the prison to see Constant, and Ramble guiltily realises that she truly is a lady of quality and not a whore. She saves the situation by making it seem before Constant that Ramble was her rescuer rather than her attacker, and Ramble is duly recognisant. But if that problem is solved there are still others and they are all called Squeezum.

ACT 2

Justice Squeezum is excitedly preparing for his assignation at the Eagle ('There's a Plot Afoot'). But he is not the only one plotting: Hilaret has her own plot, Mrs Squeezum, the most ardent plotter of them all, has plans for an evening with Ramble, and Politic and Dabble are deep in a coffee-house plot of Turkish importance.

Ramble is released and brought before Mrs Squeezum and the answer to the reprise of 'When Does the Ravishing Begin?' is soon given. She has little need, with a gallant like this, to make use of 'The Gentle Art of Seduction'. Squeezum primps and pats his unprepossessing form into shape, preparatory to going out as 'Mr Jones' and, back at the coffee house, Politic's aged servant, Faithful, attempts for the umpteenth time to turn his master's mind from organising world affairs to doing something about his daughter's continuing dilemma. He succeeds only when he shows Politic a notice in the paper: his daughter is taken for rape. It's in the paper so it must be true. Headed by Faithful, the coffee house theorists head off to the practical rescue.

At the Eagle, Hilaret receives the eager Squeezum. By way of titivation, he asks her to describe the manner of her deflowering and Hilaret obliges with a small striptease to the accompaniment of a tale of seduction on a 'Sunny Sunday Morning'. When the excited Squeezum pounces, she once again cries 'Rape', and Sotmore, carefully stationed outside the door, rushes in to catch the Justice *in flagrante delicto*. He will be brought to law for rape unless he signs the papers for Constant's release immediately.

Sotmore is full of admiration for the businesslike Hilaret. This is a woman! Almost as good as a bottle of burgundy. 'If I'd Known You' in the old days, he says ruefully, I might have gone in for love instead of drink. The stymied Squeezum signs the papers for the release of the Captain and soon

Hilaret's lover is at her side ('Kind Fate'), but the crafty Justice has another trick up his sleeve. He orders the constable to arrest all three of the young people for conspiracy and, just when they thought they were free and away, they are haled off to court.

Before Justice Worthy, Squeezum relates his case in such a way that the defendants cannot contradict him. His words are elaborated with some pretty perjury from the suborned Brazencourt and the situation looks grim when Faithful arrives with Politic who claims Hilaret as his daughter. Good Justice Worthy is sadly shocked, but regrets that even this cannot change the facts of the case. But Mrs Squeezum can. Ramble has given her the note which Squeezum sent to Hilaret arranging their rendezvous and, with all the righteousness of a satiated woman, she is come for revenge, brandishing her evidence.

Now it is time for the ends to be tied up. Squeezum, charged by his wife and by his clerk, who after decades of drudgery is delighted to be his master's headsman, is irremediably damned. To the curses of his wife ('I'll Be There') he goes to jail and his perjured minion, Brazencourt, recognised by Cloris as the man who tried to rape her in the street scuffle, follows him down. Hilaret and Constant are united, Ramble finds in Cloris his lost wife (only the poor litle dowry was drowned) and in Politic the father who threw him out years ago for excessive wenching. That makes him Hilaret's brother. His face reddens with the remembrance of the previous evening. Still, all (or nearly all) stayed chaste throughout the piece, in spite of all the talk of rape, and now a happy ending has been reached. To a merry reprise of 'Lock up Your Daughters', the curtain falls.

The song 'The Gentle Art of Seduction' was an addition to the score following the original opening.

MAKE ME AN OFFER

a musical in two acts by Wolf Mankowitz taken from his own book. Lyrics and music by David Heneker and Monty Norman. Produced at the Theatre Royal, Stratford East, 17 October 1959 and the New Theatre, London, 16 December 1959 with Daniel Massey (Charlie), Diana Coupland (Sally), Meier Tzelniker (Wendl) and Wally Patch (Sparta).

CHARACTERS

Charlie, *a young dealer*
Sally, *his wife*
Gwen, *a dealer's daughter*
Sparta, *a demolition dealer*
Wendl, *an important dealer*
Redhead, *a lady dealer*

Mindel *and* Sweeting, *American dealers*
Fred, Moishe, Milton, Taffy, Paddy, Bernard, *dealers*
John True, Clerk, etc.

ACT 1

It is a few years ago (well, quite a few now), in the days when Wedgwood china and the Portobello Road were both fashionable. Charlie is a little market dealer who has a special knowledge of Wedgwood. It isn't a special knowledge which is particularly paying and so Charlie and Sally and baby Charles inhabit an undersized apartment where there isn't really space to live and where Charlie constantly barks his shins on the baby's pram trying to get into the kitchen ('Damn the Pram') and wishes there was no pram. And, although he doesn't know it yet, Sally is pregnant again.

In the 'Portobello Road' Charlie has his stall. The top dogs of the market are the rival dealers Abe Sparta, who is also Charlie's landlord, and Morris Wendl. The two have only spoken in insults for years since an incident over the sale of some stuffed gorillas. Of course, they still do business with each other for men must live, but even now the stuffed gorillas need only to be mentioned to bring both men to apoplectic silence.

Today, for once, both of them have need of Charlie. There is to be a big demolition sale at Cramping Grange and both men have noticed the description in the catalogue of 'a panelled room with a superb frieze of Wedgwood bas-reliefs.' Each in turn tries to force Charlie to rally to his side with his expertise on Wedgwood. They know how, they are dealers to their guts. Charlie isn't. A vase which he can't sell by giving chapter and verse on its manufacture, Wendl straightaway sells to the same customer at twice the price by a heavy ladling on of sharp talk.

Charlie, unfortunately, cares about the objects he sells and that's no way to make money enough to buy his dream home ('I Want a Lock-Up in the Portobello Road'). Perhaps a little less honesty might get him out of the hated flat, away from the omnipresent pram. In the meantime he can't give Sally enough money for the groceries: she gets sour ('If I Was a Man'), and he gets mad because he knows he can't provide. Together they get worse.

A stunning redhead with a cultured accent arrives in the market. She's not a customer; she's come to set up business and not on a barrow. She's taken the shop behind Charlie's stall, the shop he always meant to have when the day came that he had money. When she asks him to shift his barrow away from its traditional place at the front of her shop a little war breaks out, but the redhead wins. After all, 'Business Is Business'. And business, big business promptly turns up in the form of Messrs Mindel and Sweeting from the US of A, representing Mossie, the Chicago Antique King, and Andy's House of Antiques, California, in combination.

They go through the market like vacuum cleaners ('Concerning Fleas') to the acknowledgement of the stallholders ('Fanfare for a Flea'), quite conscious of their own significance ('Concerning Capital') and aware of the resale value of the mixture of culture and junk they are picking up. They are

185

also on the trail of Cramping Grange and its Wedgwood Room, a point which doesn't escape Wendl and Sparta.

Charlie might be temporarily popular at the market with Wendl and Sparta vying for the favour of his expertise, but back home things are getting

decidedly sticky. Sally can only bear the bickering and the apparent indifference because of her love for her husband ('Love Him'). She is not happy when she sees him encounter the redhead and when, after a hurried conversation, he grabs his hat and coat and hurries off with the woman, she has a hard time convincing herself that it's just business. He'd damn well better get back quickly ('Sally's Lullaby').

The redhead has taken Charlie to Cramping Grange. She owns it. Not that that means she has money. She doesn't, that is why she needs Cramping to fetch good prices at the next day's sale. But she'll offer him £20 to cast an expert eye over the Wedgwood. When he tells her it is fake she ups the offer for a phony certificate to £30. But Charlie is a connoisseur. Worse, he's a connoisseur with a conscience and he won't compromise. Then the redhead shows him a vase and this time it's the real McCoy. It is beautiful. A thing like that Charlie has wanted to own all his life. She tells him 'Make Me an Offer'. It's a bit of bargaining that won't be done quickly so perhaps he'd better phone home and say he won't be back that night. As she sings, he phones. As the curtain falls, they look at each other.

ACT 2

At breakfast the next morning the bargaining for the vase still isn't finished and Charlie isn't cheered by the knowledge that Sally will never believe he spent the night on the couch ('Whatever You Believe'), but eventually he settles that he'll pay the redhead twenty pounds down and eighty more after the sale where he won't let on that the Wedgwood Room is a fake.

When Sparta and Wendl arrive, Charlie does his stuff. Then the Americans arrive and battlesmoke is in the air. It's going to be some break-up sale ('Break Up'). The dealers wander about affecting to admire anything but the things they want as the selling gets under way, but Wendl has an extra card up his sleeve. He offers to make a ring with the Americans, with Charlie acting as a front, and they accept. Finally the sale gets to offering the Wedgwood Room ('The Auction'). The bidding creeps up and in the end Sparta and Wendl cry pax and join together rather than risk paying a proper price for the goods: Charlie's bid of 650 guineas is allowed to win the day.

Back home Sally is chatting with as much forebearance as is possible to the brainless Gwen, Sparta's daughter. Gwen is a muddle-headed romantic ('It's Sort of Romantic') with a gaping need for a man and her unthinking words wound the shaky Sally at every turn. When Charlie gets home the inevitable accusations tumble out. Charlie has his mind on the desperately wanted vase, while Sally is wanting to tell him she is pregnant. When she does, he stops short and leaves slowly.

Business comes back in the next scene, at the knock-out between the ring of dealers. Mindel and Sweeting end up buying the Wedgwood for £1500.

That means there is a cut of £116 15s 8d for each of those in the ring and one share goes to Charlie. But everyone has come out of the sale all right. For the redhead it means a lucrative job with the American combine, aristocratically fronting their UK operation. For Wendl and Sparta it means the joining of forces in the face of a common prey as they unload the rest of their white elephants on the voracious trans-Atlantic buyers. Even the famous stuffed gorillas go. Then there's the vase. Charlie pays the eighty pounds balance out of his share and the redhead hands it over. 'All my life I've wanted to own something as good as this,' he murmurs. She reminds him that he's a professional dealer in a brief reprise of 'Business Is Business' and walks out of his life.

Back home Charlie looks lovingly at his purchase. Sally, too, can understand its beauty. He should keep it, he loves it so. But Charlie isn't going to keep it; he's going to sell it at a really fine profit and the money will go towards that 'Lock-Up in the Portobello Road' where there'll be room for all four of them. He *is* going to sell it. He *is*...

OLIVER!

a musical in two acts by Lionel Bart based on *Oliver Twist* by Charles Dickens. Produced at the New Theatre, London, 30 June 1960 with Ron Moody (Fagin), Georgia Brown (Nancy), Keith Hamshere (Oliver), Paul Whitsun-Jones (Bumble), Martin Horsey (Dodger), Hope Jackman (Mrs Corney) and Danny Sewell (Sikes). Produced at the Piccadilly Theatre 26 April 1967 with Barry Humphries, Marti Webb, Paul Bartlett, Tom de Ville, Leslie Stone, Pamela Pitchford and Martin Dell; at the Albery Theatre 21 December 1977 with Roy Hudd, Gillian Burns, Marcus d'Amico, Robert Bridges, Stephen Kebell, Joan Turner and Michael Attwell and at the Aldwych Theatre 14 December 1983 with Moody, Jackie Marks, Anthony Pearson, Peter Bayliss, David Garlick, Meg Johnson and Linal Haft.

Produced at the Imperial Theatre, New York, 6 January 1963 with Clive Revill, Georgia Brown, Bruce Prochnik, Willoughby Goddard, David Jones, Hope Jackman and Danny Sewell. Produced at the Mark Hellinger Theatre 29 April 1984 with Moody, Patti Lu Pone, Braden Danner, I M Hobson, David Garlick, Elizabeth Larner and Graeme Campbell.

Produced at the Staatstheater am Gärtnerplatz, Munich, 29 May 1986.

Produced at the Landestheater, Salzburg, 8 January 1985.

A film version was produced by Romulus Productions/Columbia Pictures in 1968 with Moody, Shani Wallis, Mark Lester, Harry Secombe, Jack Wild, Peggy Mount and Oliver Reed.

CHARACTERS

Oliver Twist, *a workhouse boy*
Mr Bumble, *the beadle*
Mrs Corney, *the workhouse mistress*

Mr Sowerberry, *the undertaker*
Mrs Sowerberry
Charlotte, *their daughter*
Noah Claypole, *their apprentice*
Fagin, *an elderly receiver*
The Artful Dodger, *his brightest pupil*
Bet
Bill Sikes
Nancy, *his doxy*
Mr Brownlow
Mr Grimwig
Mrs Bedwin
Old Sally, Charley Bates, etc.

ACT 1

The scene is London in the middle of the nineteenth century and the hall of one of its many workhouses. The young orphan boys of the workhouse are waiting for their daily ration of gruel and fantasising about all sorts of glorious and unattainable types of 'Food'. Mr Bumble, the parish beadle, and the widow Corney, overseer of this particular institution, preside at the charitable distribution of the daily meal, and this day they are shocked from their parochial boredom by an unprecedented event. At the end of the meal, a child called Oliver Twist has the temerity to approach the beadle and ask for more food. He is seized and condemned to horrid punishment ('Oliver!'). For this dreadful crime he will be sent forth from the kindly protection of the workhouse to earn his own living in the cruel world.

Mr Bumble takes tea with the widow Corney in her rooms whilst recovering from the afternoon's events and takes advantage of the opportunity to indulge in some heavy flirtation, grotesquely encouraged by the widow under a coat of coyness ('I Shall Scream'). When tea is finished, he returns his mind to his official duties and sets out, dragging young Oliver with him, to recoup some of the parish money lavished on the boy by selling him off as an apprentice ('Boy For Sale'). He finds a purchaser in Mr Sowerberry, the undertaker, who sees in the lad's thin, pale looks the makings of a professional mourner ('That's Your Funeral').

That evening, fed on a pail of scraps intended for the dog and left to sleep under the shop counter among the coffins, Oliver thinks tearfully of his unknown mother and the love he would so dearly have liked to know ('Where Is Love?'). Trouble is quick to come at the undertaker's shop. The bullying apprentice Noah Claypole finds that Oliver's softest spot is any mention of his mother and gleefully takes to blackening her name in front of the smaller boy.

Oliver will not stand it, and he attacks his tormentor so fiercely that the cowardly Noah screams for help. The horrified Sowerberrys shut the furious child up in a coffin and call for the Beadle but, in the resulting turmoil, Oliver succeeds in escaping. Now all he has to do is to get as far away as he can from Bumble, the Sowerberrys and everyone else who knows him. He will disappear in the streets of London town.

Somewhere around Paddington, Oliver falls in with a cheeky young fellow who offers him friendship and board. His name is Jack Dawkins, better known as the Artful Dodger, and the lodgings he is offering are under the roof of his mentor, a grand old gentleman called Mister Fagin. There is no argument, insists the hospitable Dodger, Oliver must 'Consider Yourself' at home and part of the family. The family is a band of boy pickpockets and thieves organised by the wily Fagin, and Oliver is to be the newest recruit to their company ('You've Got to Pick a Pocket or Two'). At night, when all his boys are asleep, Fagin takes out his special box of treasures, saved over the years from a hundred crimes, to gloat over them in private. They are his savings for the day of his retirement.

The next day, Oliver meets more of the company who circulate around his new master. Nancy and Bet, a couple of young women of the thieving classes ('It's a Fine Life'), come by and join the boys in a happy burlesque of the manners of the upper classes ('I'd Do Anything') before Fagin shoos them off to their work on the streets ('Be Back Soon'). The Dodger takes Oliver along with him to give him his first lesson in picking pockets. The expedition proves to be a disastrous one. The Dodger successfully plies his trade on an elderly gentleman called Mr Brownlow, but he is spotted and, although he gets away, the inexperienced Oliver is taken by the police.

ACT 2

At the 'Three Cripples' pub in Clerkenwell, Nancy is entertaining the clientele with a bit of 'Ooom-Pah-Pah' when quiet falls on the company as Bill Sikes arrives. A brutish man who lives by the strength of his arm, he is well content at the effect he produces ('My Name') but he is not pleased to hear that one of Fagin's boys has been taken. This could rebound on all of them should the boy decide to tell what he knows. Oliver has, they hear, been released by the magistrate and taken in by the kindly Mr Brownlow—they must get him back before he can imperil them.

Fagin suggests that Nancy, whom the boy knows and trusts, should be sent to get him back, but Nancy refuses to be party to such a trick. Sikes takes command. He knocks Nancy down and orders her to get Oliver away from Brownlow and, left alone, Nancy knows that she will have to do what Sikes wants: her love for him will not let her do otherwise ('As Long as He Needs Me').

In the fashionable London square where Mr Brownlow has his home the street vendors are calling their wares ('Who Will Buy') when Oliver comes out of his long, ill sleep. He gazes out of the window on the loveliest morning he has ever seen: suddenly, by a stroke of unimaginable fortune, his life is looking very different. Mr Brownlow shows his trust in the boy by sending him on an errand with five pounds to pay for some books, but on the way Oliver is cornered by Nancy and Sikes and is dragged back to Fagin's den.

Sikes is quick to lay hands on the five pounds and Fagin relieves Oliver of his fine new clothes but, when they start to grill the boy over what he may or may not have said about them to the police or Brownlow, Nancy steps in to protect him from harm. She deeply regrets having been party to bringing Oliver back: she has helped to ruin his life, but she will not see him hurt. A violent scene is finally defused and Fagin, left alone, wonders whether at his age a life full of such unpleasant and dangerous episodes is not too much. Maybe now it is time for him to retire ('Reviewing the Situation').

Back at the widow Corney's workhouse, there have been wedding bells. Bumble has been caught and, having tied the knot, realises too late what sort of a termagant he has wed. His life is a misery. But there are revelations at the workhouse which promise well. An old woman is dying there and she has a confession to make to the new Mrs Bumble. Once she nursed a pretty young woman who died in childbirth and, from that woman's neck, she stole a gold locket. It was clear that the woman was from a wealthy family and that the boy child born to her would be heir to some estate. The boy was the one they christened Oliver. Mrs Bumble knows that her fortune could be made in this affair. She must get that boy back.

It proves easier than expected to find him, for Mr Brownlow has advertised for information on the boy known as Oliver Twist. Mr Bumble takes himself, his story and the locket to Brownlow and the evidence of the portrait in the locket confirms Brownlow's suspicions. Oliver is the child of his own lost daughter, Agnes, who fled home to bear her illegitimate child. Now, more than ever, Brownlow is determined to find the boy again. He finds help unexpectedly when Nancy comes secretly to his house. She reveals all that she safely can, and arranges to bring Oliver to him on neutral ground: on London Bridge at midnight.

When the appointed time arrives and Nancy brings Oliver to the bridge, Bill Sikes is waiting. Before Brownlow can get to the scene, he attacks Nancy viciously and, as she falls dying, grabs Oliver and heads for Fagin's den. A crowd quickly gathers and, maddened by the murder of Nancy, they set out with the Bow Street runners at their head to capture the murderous Sikes.

He is spotted clambering over the rooftops, dragging Oliver behind him, and a well-aimed shot from a hussar's rifle brings him down. Oliver is rescued and restored to the man who is now known to be his grandfather. Fagin's den is invaded, the Dodger is arrested and Fagin's treasure uncovered—but Fagin himself is not to be found. He is quickly forgotten as the crowd, its revenge wrought, disperses. As morning breaks, the thiefmaster emerges from his hiding place. His boys are gone, his treasure is lost: at his time of life, what shall he do? Turn over a new leaf? It needs thinking about.

STOP THE WORLD—I WANT TO GET OFF

a musical in two acts by Anthony Newley and Leslie Bricusse. Produced at the Queen's Theatre, London, 20 July 1961 with Anthony Newley and Anna Quayle.

Produced at the Shubert Theatre, New York, 3 October 1962 with Newley and Miss Quayle. Produced at the State Theatre 3 August 1978 with Sammy Davis jr and Marian Mercer.

A film version was produced by Warner Brothers in 1966 with Tony Tanner and Millicent Martin.

CHARACTERS

Littlechap
Evie/Ilse/Anya/Ginnie
Jane
Susan

ACT 1

The setting for the show is a small circus ring with surrounding bleachers. Into this ring comes a man called Littlechap who begins to tell, in mime, the story of his life from his birth and first steps, through the experiences of childhood ('The ABC Song') and youth into manhood and a job in a factory. We see him making prettily successful advances to the girls at the factory until he butts up against a superior lass called Evie. She doesn't respond to his irresistible hand mime and he is forced into speech... 'stop the world!'. Time stands still while Littlechap ponders this unusual failure. When the action begins again he makes a serious pass at Evie, only to be left flat. He analyses. To get a posh bird like this one you need money ('I Wanna Be Rich'). Armed with this conviction, he continues to pursue and Evie continues to ignore him. She is 'Typically English', ever so proper on the surface and underneath bored with propriety.

She ultimately gives in to his persistence and her own impatience and soon she is pregnant. Then he discovers that she is the boss's daughter and before he knows it he is being frogmarched up the aisle complaining that he's been 'LUMBERED'. One child arrives and then Evie is pregnant again, so Littlechap faces up to his father-in-law with a problem: he can't manage a family on his salary, what does the boss propose to do about it? And, goodness gracious, father-in-law comes up trumps and offers him promotion to the post of works manager at the firm's Northern branch in Sludgepool ('Welcome to Sludgepool').

Our hero is not daunted and he takes up the challenge with optimism ('Gonna Build a Mountain'). He will increase production and turn the Sludgepool branch into a success and then he will be able to support Evie and their two daughters...and Evie is pregnant again and father-in-law, who has the business acumen to realise that his unwanted son-in-law is OK, is sending him to Moscow as delegate to the International Trade Mission.

In Moscow our delegate has a guide called Anya, a sort of Russian Evie, who sings of being a 'Glorious Russian' and who responds to his old hand

191

mime with a simple suggestion of sex. After sex they sing a duet ('Meilinki Meilchick') about children, and while they are singing Evie is being delivered of a still-born boy child, the son Littlechap had so longed for.

Back home the marriage is under strain ('Family Fugue') and Evie is tending to be tearful but, if the home front is unfavourable, the work front is prosperous and Littlechap is on the receiving end of cigars and promotion to a directorship. To make her life easier, Evie hires a German au pair called Ilse who is a 'Typische Deutsche' sort of Evie in the mind of Littlechap. Under the strain of an increasingly unsatisfactory home life ('Nag, Nag, Nag') he is soon making love to this female stormtrooper and Evie is moving into the spare room. Which seems like a good time for an interval.

ACT 2

While relations with Evie have been worsening, those with father-in-law have been getting better and better. Now our corporate hero is being nominated for Snobb's club and entrusted with pulling off a mega-deal in New York by his canny boss. Before he goes off to America, father-in-law also entrusts him with the phone number of a cabaret girl called Ginnie Romain, an 'All-American' girl who has a strange resemblance, in Littlechap's eyes, to his wife. Consummation is cut short, however, by news from back home that there is another baby in the offing. Only this time it is daughter Susan who is in the family way.

The girls are grown up and gone from home and Littlechap hasn't stopped climbing yet. Now it's politics: a whole new field for him to conquer ('Once in a Lifetime'). 'Vote for Littlechap' sing the chorus to the strains of the Hallelujah Chorus as the Opportunist candidate addresses his constituency in 'Mumbo Jumbo' and floats to a memorable victory with only the odd vote in a million against him. His political career gallops forward from ever so trivial post to less trivial post to almost-not-trivial post at the same rate that his business career has done, until one day the big warning strikes. Knocked to his knees by a coronary thrombosis, Littlechap slumps forward, alone and lonely, until the unsmiling figure of Evie steps forward to lead him away.

Convalescent ('Welcome to Sunvale'), he is looked after by his unflinching wife. Why did 'Someone Nice Like You' have to love me?, he wonders. Then she is gone and, as he receives his peerage and his Ignobel Prize for outstanding achivement in the field of Parliamentary Doubletalk, she does not return. Just when he was ready to find her again, she has been taken from him by death. Alone and old, Littlechap passes the women in his life in review and realises that in all his time he has never been in love with anyone but himself ('What Kind of Fool Am I?'). He is about to walk off with the figure of death when he changes his mind. As the show ends he is preparing to begin the cycle of life all over again.

HALF A SIXPENCE

a musical in two acts by Beverley Cross based on H G Wells' novel *Kipps*. Music and lyrics by David Heneker. Produced at the Cambridge Theatre, London, 1 March 1963 with Tommy Steele (Kipps), Marti Webb (Ann) and James Grout (Chitterlow).

Produced at the Broadhurst Theatre, New York, 25 April 1965 with Steele, Polly James and Grout.

A film version was produced by Paramount in 1967 with Steele, Julia Foster (sung by Marti Webb) and Cyril Ritchard.

CHARACTERS

Arthur Kipps
Sid Pornick
Buggins
Pearce
Flo Bates
Mr Shalford
Mrs Walsingham
Ann
Chitterlow
Helen Walsingham
Young Walsingham
Victoria, Kate, Emma, Mrs Botting, Laura, Gwendolin, Lady Student, Carshott, Chester Coote, Photographer, Mr Wilkins, etc.

ACT 1

Arthur Kipps is twenty years old and an apprentice in the Folkestone drapery of Mr Edwin Shalford. It is hard work, seven to seven, and strict discipline, bed at 9.30 and on line for work first thing, and woe betide if Shalford's motto of 'Fishency, System, Economy' isn't the watchword of every day. Particularly economy. Kipps and his fellow apprentices resent their life with the healthy resentment of youth ('All in the Cause of Economy'), but only Sid Pornick who has taken up with Socialism has made any practical step towards fighting the system. When Sid tries to get the others to join him at a Fabian meeting, they squirm out their excuses—girls, sore feet, or, in Kipps' case, a meeting with Sid's sister Ann who's in domestic service down the road. He can't talk to girls, but Ann he's known since they were kids so that's different.

Ann has a smart head and a tart tongue to put her brother's fancy ideas firmly in their place, and she also has a soft spot for the awkward Artie Kipps. She won't let him kiss her, kissing's soft, but she doesn't mind saying she'll be his girl and taking the half-sixpence he offers her as a lover's token ('Half a Sixpence'). Artie's next meeting with Ann goes out the window when his employer volunteers him as a student at the Young Persons Association, an institution for keeping working class youth off the street by teaching them useful occupations, in which the Walsingham family, good customers

193

at Shalford's emporium, are interested. But that evening, while the glum Artie is on his way to his unwanted class, he is the victim of a little accident, run down by an out-of-control cyclist.

The cyclist in question is Mr Chitterlow, an actor and playwright of a flamboyant turn and the possessor of a coincidence. When Kipps introduces himself, Chitterlow performs a double-take. He has seen the boy's name in the daily newspaper: one of those delightful advertisements that end 'may hear something to his advantage'. Chitterlow hurries his new friend off to a public house to celebrate his imminent good fortune and, while Chitterlow bonhomously spreads the news, Artie celebrates whatever it is that's coming to him with his first alcoholic drink and a rousing chorus song ('Money to Burn'). The merry-making spills into the street and Kipps is spied by Shalford, disentangled from a lamppost and, expectations or no expectations, frogmarched off to the Young Persons Association.

The class at the Association is taken by Miss Helen Walsingham, recently of London University and devoted to good works ('The Oak and the Ash'). Unfortunately, Artie is a little the worse for drink and, instead of woodworking, succeeds in putting his hand through a glass panel. Helen tends his cut wrist and the boy is dazzled by her attentions.

The next morning Ann calls at the emporium to find out why Kipps stood her up the previous night and the shop girls take delight in making the worst out of the events. Ann snaps back at them in his defence, but when Kipps appears she smacks his face and storms out ('I'm Not Talking to You'). But better is in store for Artie. Chitterlow arrives with good news: it really is a fortune, Kipps has inherited an income of £1200 a year. At that Kipps passes out, but he's himself again by the time Shalford comes in to give him the sack. With all the hauteur of the newly rich, Kipps resigns in an irrevocable fashion and the boys and girls join together to sing of his future as 'A Proper Gentleman'.

The new gentleman runs into the Walsinghams who are now decidedly keen to know him. Helen invites him to dinner, the son offers his services as a business adviser, and Mrs Walsingham exudes charm instead of condescension. As they leave, Kipps looks after Helen and dreams ('She's Too Far Above Me'). She isn't, of course. She's a nice enough example of genteel, impoverished, seaside society whose University education has only served to make her less than content with life in Folkestone. She's not at all averse to the bright, well-off Artie. She invites him to join her at the forthcoming regatta and Artie is in seventh heaven ('If the Rain's Got to Fall').

At the regatta on 'The Old Military Canal' Artie asks Helen to marry him and she accepts. She will make a gentleman of him. Young Walsingham calls for the champagne Artie has ordered at his suggestion, and the maid brings the bottle. It is Ann. When she hears from Artie's own lips that he has asked Helen to marry him, she flings the tray to the floor and pulling up her skirt takes the half-sixpence from her bloomers. Hurling it back at him she rushes out. Artie goes to follow her, but Helen puts out her arm and he turns back again as the rain pours down on their celebration.

ACT 2

Artie is forlorn and he doesn't heed Chitterlow who attempts to put woman trouble in its unimportant place in the scheme of things as Artie moons sadly over 'The One Who's Run Away'. When it comes to the point, however, he goes back to the Walsinghams. In spite of his efforts and Helen's determined patience, he fits ill in such society and at Mrs Botting's Solarium Dance he commits further solecisms. Under constant criticism from the Walsinghams, he bites back his natural retorts and keeps on trying to be 'proper', but when he hears of the punishments that Ann has been subjected to following the incident at the regatta it is too much for him. He bursts out fulsomely against Mrs Botting and refuses to apologise.

When Helen and the other Walsinghams take Mrs Botting's part, he bundles them all together on the receiving end of an angry speech and ends up by calling the wedding off and running away down to the basement kitchen to find Ann. He's been a fool. She's his girl and she must come away and marry him. Ann is not keen on upsetting the order of things but, now that they've finally got round to talking on such a subject, she does love him ('Long Ago').

So Artie and Ann are married at a lively ceremony captured in a comical set of photographs ('Flash, Bang, Wallop'). Married life begins in a rented house with Kipps still trying to be a gentleman and Ann not at all keen on having to have a maid when she'd rather do the work herself. When she answers the door to callers in her working clothes, Kipps gets angry and she can only answer, 'I Know What I Am'.

Kipps is building a big house for them to live in. When they quarrel he looks at the place where it will be, and dreams (I'll Build a Palace for My Girl'), not hearing Ann singing in counterpoint 'I Only Want a Little House'. But Kipps' plans are not going to come true. While he was still courting Helen, he gave all his money into the hands of young Walsingham as his financial manager, and Walsingham has played the market and lost every penny. Now Artie is more or less back where he started, but not quite. He sells up everything that is left, including the land where the big house was to have been, and they put together enough money to rent a little bookshop. There they live modestly and happily ever after... until one day Chitterlow turns up again.

Once upon a time, back in the rich days, Kipps had given his friend £200 for a quarter share in a play, hoping to help the great unproduced to finally make it to the stage. Now Chitterlow has made a hit. There will be money, oodles of it for them all. But Artie Kipps and his missis have been there before. The money may come or it may not; they are happy in their way of life and that's the way they will stay. As their friends go out to celebrate Chitterlow's good fortune, the Kipps family stay happily by their Christmas fire.

In the Broadway production, 'I'll Build a Palace for My Girl' was replaced by 'The Party's on the House' and several other songs were omitted. The original score included a second act opening 'Hip, Hip, Hoorah!' (Chit-

195

terlow) and the song 'She's Too Far Above Me' was initially placed immediately following the scene at the Young Persons Association.

MAGGIE MAY

a musical in two acts by Alun Owen. Music and lyrics by Lionel Bart. Produced at the Adelphi Theatre, London, 22 September 1964 with Rachel Roberts (Maggie May), Kenneth Haigh (Patrick Casey), Andrew Keir (Willie Morgan), Michael Forrest (Cogger) and Barry Humphries (Balladeer).

CHARACTERS

Balladeer
Mary Margaret Duffy (Maggie May)
Patrick Casey
Maureen O'Neill, *a whore*
Old Dooley
Eric Dooley, *his son*
Cogger Johnson
TC
Gene Kiernan
Willie Morgan
Norah Mulqueen
Milkman, Ned, Crane Driver, Mrs Casey, Mrs O'Brien, Miss Singleton, etc.

ACT 1

The tale of Maggie May is set in Liverpool, that part of Britain where, dirtily and noisily, England meets Ireland alongside the docks that border the Irish sea and the folks speak a dialect that is 'part Irish, part Welsh and part catarrh' ('The Ballad of the Liver Bird'). It was in Liverpool that Margaret Mary Duffy was born and grew up and made special friends with little Patrick Casey, and life in the streets and in the docks went on its usual way until the day that Patrick's father was killed.

Joe Casey was a natural born leader. Or a natural born rabble-rouser, depending on which way you want to look at it. He was a professional striker and street orator and he got the death and a bit of the glory he always wanted when he was trampled to death by police horses while haranguing his fellow dockers into violent action against their employers. It was Margaret Mary's birthday that day, but she had no Patrick Casey to share it with her. He was dragged off by his mother to make a show over his father's death, and Margaret Mary was left with only her doll for birthday company ('Lullaby').

Twenty years have passed and Mary Margaret Duffy, nowadays better known as Maggie May, is a whore on the Liverpool Docks. She's grown into a fine woman and she's been a whore, and a right popular one, all of her working life. She calls all her customers Casey as she waits for the one real Casey to come back out of the blue yonder ('I Love a Man'/'Casey'). For Patrick Casey didn't follow his father on to the docks. He went and joined the navy and sailed away from Liverpool and from the shadow of his father's life and death. Twenty years after his 'martyrdom' Joe Casey is remembered only by the older men on the docks, but the Union is still an inbred part of the lives of the men who work the shipyards and their are plenty of younger belligerents to carry on nature's war against the employer, whether through genuine conviction or personal ambition.

Old Dooley is one of the straightforward ones. The Union book is the book by which he runs his life and he has no time for the youngsters, like his own son Eric, who take it with a pinch of salt until it suits them. Not all the young people are careless of the Union, however. Cogger Johnson is deeply into Union business, but he is not a Union man of the old school like Dooley: he's in there for his own gain, for his own importance, as much as for the Natural Struggle. He remembers the story of Joe Casey all right, but with different emotions to those that Dooley feels. To Dooley, Joe Casey was indeed a martyr who died for his cause, but this attitude wins largely scorn from the young men of the 1960s to whom the labour struggles of the past mean little or nothing ('Dey Don't Do Dat T'Day').

It is Cogger Johnson who brings Patrick Casey in to work on the docks. Dismissed from the navy, Casey is back in Liverpool and in need of a job, and what could be more natural than that Joe Casey's son should step in to his father's profession. Down on the docks, he soon runs into his old friend Maggie May. He doesn't seem at all taken aback when she tells him that she's on the game, and they arrange to go out to Norah Mulqueen's pub together that night. Maggie May is truly happy. The man she loves is back ('I Told You So'); now she has to make him love her as she loves him.

Down on the docks Gang Three are unloading a ship ('Right of Way Dhere') while Cogger, their chief, is pulling a fix with another gang for a job swap which will give his gang the easy jobs and the others the opportunity to do some practised stealing from the cargo. It's all fair robbery in the Natural Struggle. Cogger, in pursuit of a bit of reflected glory, is also harrassing Casey about the Union. He ought to take an active part, like his father. Casey has straightforward feelings, strong ones too, over things like injustice, but he has no intention of being a leader nor, particularly, anything like his father ('Stroll On').

It takes an accident to bring him out of his self-appointed silence. A crate is dropped from a crane, crushing a dock worker to death. It is not their mate's death, however, which rouses Casey's anger: it is the contents of the smashed crate. They have been loading guns on a phoney manifest. Guns for South America where, as Casey knows from his navy days, they will be used by the military to put down strikes and shoot down striking workers. He is walking off the job. Cogger is livid with him. This accident is something that the Union can flex its muscles over: if Casey won't do anything he will. He is going to run straight to Willie Morgan, the Union boss, and get him to take some action.

Willie Morgan has just been on an all-expenses-paid trip to Rome in an abortive attempt to see the Pope ('Away from Home') and his reaction to the death of Georgie MacDowell is suitably sonorous and clichéd as he puts on his chummy I'm-one-of-the-boys act for the benefit of the dockers. Casey has no time for him. He remembers Willie from years back, running along in Joe Casey's shadow picking about for a bit of glory and, before long, it becomes obvious to him that Willie knew all about the guns and the faked manifest. Willie is a practical man: the nature of the cargo isn't his problem as long as there's cargo to load. He can also see that young Casey will be trouble, not to mention a rival for his own nicely feather-bedded position, and he resolves to fix him. When Maggie May comes to join Casey for a drink, Morgan causes a scene with the landlady, accusing her of harbouring prostitutes and threatening to withdraw his classy custom. Casey stands up to Morgan. Maggie May's a better woman by far than the simpering little bit of crumpet clinging to Morgan's arms ('Maggie May') and she has plenty of friends on the docks and in the pub who are pleased to walk out of Norah Mulqueen's place and leave Morgan and his cronies to themselves.

Casey doesn't want trouble. Too often trouble has found him without his seeking it. He hasn't any admiration for his father and what he did: he knows him as a mug and a loser who achieved nothing but a stupid death. He just wants a quiet life with a clean nose and a pint. He's got good mates and he's got Maggie May who's willing to give up the game for him and who dreams of a happy life in 'The Land of Promises'. But on the day of Georgie's funeral the news comes that there are fifteen lorry loads of guns lining up to be loaded. All Georgie's Protestant friends are at the funeral: it'll be double time for Gang Three. And Willie Morgan's fixed it so that Casey doesn't have to load; he's been promoted to checker.

Casey will not accept this subterfuge and, triumphantly, the boss ganger orders him to collect his cards for refusing to work. Casey agrees to go, but he is made an unwilling martyr when the rest of the gang, for motives ranging from misguided friendship to solidarity in the cause of the Natural Struggle, announce that if he goes they will follow him off the job. Cogger immediately stirs up the other gangs. Casey's being sacked for refusing to load a blacked cargo. Joe Casey's son is being victimised and Willie Morgan is letting them bring in the troops to load the ships if the dockers refuse ('Leave Her, Johnny, Leave Her').

Cogger is whipping up a walk-out and he's going to put Casey up as its figurehead. Maggie May tries to stop him, but Cogger crudely puts her down in front of the dockers and forces the situation to a point where Casey is lifted shoulder high and carried off, leaving Maggie May bitterly to rue his weakness and the unlikelihood of their ever finding that 'Land of Promises'.

ACT 2

In a Liverpool club, the folks are 'Carryin' On'. Maggie May is there, a quieter, more soberly dressed Maggie May, with bitter words for Casey's 'friends' and a hard rebuff for Wilie Morgan who is still at his fixing ways

('Win or Lose'). The strike is on and biting. The milkman ('Shine You Swine') can only sell half-pints as the women's purse strings draw tighter and the men try to rouse up a mass rally.

Maggie May and her friend Maureen have no time for it all. The men have got their priorities wrong. There are more important and more natural things than the Natural Struggle, and as for the Union, 'There's Only One Union' that counts and thats the union between man and woman. Casey gets the message. Maggie May is his friend, it's all probability that she'll be his lover before long, but in the meanwhile he won't listen to her angry pleas that all he is doing is putting himself up to be hurt ('It's Yourself') as their lives begin to run away from them.

At the march, Casey speaks fluently in defence of his actions and the strike. It is not a case of more money; he and his mates simply will not load a cargo which is going to the other side of the world to oppress men like themselves. But when it is Willie Morgan's turn to speak he takes a practised angle, wooing the men with the money to be earned and mocking Casey's far-away fairy stories, encouraging the impoverished dockers to think of themselves and their families with chauvinistic skill. Before he is finished, much of the spirit has gone from many of the strikers and the glint is gone from the rebellion.

Willie Morgan wants more from Casey than his hide. He wants to complete the man's humiliation by taking Maggie May from him. From anger at Casey, the frustrated girl agrees to go out with the boss to New Brighton where he tries to convince her that 'The World's a Lovely Place' as he gropes her grossly. But Maggie May knows that she cannot go through with this: whatever happens, she loves her Casey, she always has and she always will.

Casey is spending the same time drowning his sorrows and trying to drown the memory and the spirit of his father and everything connected with him ('I'm Me'). He wants nothing more to do with the Union and with Cogger. He doesn't want to be a hero or a figurehead, he just wants to have peace and quiet and a job and Maggie May. Maggie May finds him wandering about in a boozy stupor and takes him home with her ('It's Yourself') watched by the bitter Cogger.

Cogger blames Casey for fumbling his luck, for ruining Cogger's go for glory with 'his' strike. He hates Casey for having the charisma and confidence which he will never have, and he is jealous of the evident love the man has from Maggie May whom he bitterly qualifies as a 'dirty whore'. The other Gang Three members, without Cogger's personal reasons for jealousy, stick up for Casey. Everyone is different ('We Don't All Wear the Same Size Boots') and Casey has a right to live as he wants and not as Cogger and any others might wish him to.

In the morning, Casey wakes up in Maggie May's bed and real love finally gets around to them ('It's Yourself'). Casey is determined that from now on they will just live their ordinary, quiet life together. But no sooner has Casey left Maggie May's side than Cogger is after him again, trying to separate him from Maggie May with scorn, trying to tack on to Casey and wherever he's going, pleading friendship. When Casey knocks him back, the bitter Cogger changes his allegiance. He heads straight for Willie Morgan with a piece of news. Casey has one last deed to do and if Cogger can't share it with him, then Cogger will damn him for doing it.

Casey has gone to the docks. He has broken into a crane and he has begun loading the crates of guns into a cage. Morgan, Cogger and the police they have alerted rush in in time to see the cargo being swung towards the open river. The guns tumble from the crane into the depths of the River Liver and Casey swings the crane back for more. But, as he does so, the arm of the crane becomes entangled with some overhead electric wires. A crane driver rushes forward to shout instructions, but Willie Morgan silences him physically. The crane erupts in a shower of sparks and Casey's body arcs with electricity as the power of the cables pours through the crane cabin. Then, and only then, does Willie Morgan pull the mains switch.

As the dead body of Patrick Casey is carried away, Maggie May delivers her last words to Liverpool, the town and the people who killed her Casey. 'The Ballad of the Liver Bird' is done.

ROBERT AND ELIZABETH

a musical in two acts by Ronald Millar based on *The Barretts of Wimpole Street* by Rudolf Besier. Music by Ron Grainer. Produced at the Lyric Theatre, London, 20 October 1964 with June Bronhill (Elizabeth Barrett), Keith Michell (Robert Browning) and John Clements (Edward Moulton-Barrett). Produced at the Chichester Festival Theatre 29 April 1987 in a revised version with Gaynor Miles (Elizabeth), Mark Wynter (Robert) and John Savident (Barrett).

Produced at the Forum Theatre, Chicago, 29 October 1974.

CHARACTERS

Edward Moulton-Barrett
Elizabeth
Henrietta
Arabel
George
Alfred
Henry
Charles
Septimus
Octavius
Bella Hedley
Captain Surtees Cook
Wilson　·
Robert Browning
Doctor Chambers

Mr Macready
Evans
Henry Bevan, Mr Harrison, Stage Manager, Travers, Lady Mary, Lady Sarah, Mrs Butler, etc.

ACT 1

In the year of 1845 the London home of the Moulton-Barrett family is to be found in fashionable Wimpole Street where a through-slice of city high and low life can be seen in the street ('Here on the Corner of Wimpole Street') and the most unbending of Victorian households found behind the plain faade of Number Fifty. Edward Moulton-Barrett, a widower of stern convictions and the paterfamilias of nine grown and growing children, presides over his home with a severity and chastity which forbids his daughter Henrietta acknowledging the tentative attentions of young Captain Surtees Cook. More seriously, it prevents his eldest daughter, Elizabeth, from a change of climate which might prove of benefit to the strange and enduring weakness that has confined her to her bed for so long.

The younger members of 'The Family Moulton Barrett' gloomily anticipate lives of enforced celibacy as a result of their father's regimen. Elizabeth, to whom they lovingly bring their tales, has stronger feelings, and yearns desperately to escape from her invalid couch to 'The World Outside'. Elizabeth is a woman of considerable intellect and talents who has made a name for herself as a poet, winning the admiration of, among others, her fellow poet Robert Browning with whom she has established a correspondence while refusing to permit a meeting. 'When people admire my work they incline to picture the poetess as beautiful as her verses. It's humiliating to disillusion them.'

Elizabeth's strength of personality does not stretch to her relationship with her father, to whose narrow creed of submission to God's afflictions she attempts to bow herself and to whose almost embarrassingly fervent expression of affection she responds with as much filial warmth as is in her. After one particularly unpleasant scene with her parent, she takes up her resolve and her pen and writes to her admirer.

The scene shifts to the Theatre Royal, Haymarket, where the actor Macready is rehearsing Robert Browning's new play and nearly coming to blows with the author, when Browning's manservant arrives with a letter. He is jubilant. It is from Miss Barrett and she has invited him to tea ('The Moon in My Pocket').

Elizabeth, her impulsive moment past, is nervous of meeting Browning. Her frame of mind is not improved by interruptions to her preparations from Henrietta bringing in Surtees Cook, smuggled through a back door, with news of a proposal, and from her cousin Bella Hedley who insists on treating her as if she were already half way to heaven. When Browning arrives she shakily knocks over a pill bottle and the first moments of their acquaintance are spent with him crawling around the floor chasing pills.

Browning has been deeply affected by Elizabeth's writings and quite

sincerely announces his love for her. To her protestations that love, in the
sense which he clearly intends it to be meant, is impossible for a dying
woman he responds angrily ('I Said Love'). Although she denies it, he
gathers that her illness is in fact psychologically based, that she blames
herself for the death of her much loved elder brother and, since that time,
has wasted away, refusing to face the world, until she has reached her
current physically enervated state. He challenges her to positive thinking
with the words 'Want to Be Well'. She is struck by his forcefulness, a
forcefulness equal to that of her father with whom he is destined to clash.

The family continue in the ways of 'Love and Duty', Henrietta moons
impatiently over flowers from Surtees ('You Only To Love Me') and
Elizabeth orders a steak. She is on the positive path ('The Real Thing') and
her Doctor is delighted. He agrees to ask Barrett to let Elizabeth go to Italy
where she may pursue her progress in the Mediterranean sunshine but
Barrett answers the request with a jealously vehement accusation of selfishness: she is growing away from him under the influence of Browning; she
thinks only of herself; what will he do without her if she goes away?

When Browning arrives expecting to find the Italian trip a *fait accompli* he
is confronted instead by a family drama and a weakening Elizabeth. He
expresses his love for her and she responds with the same feelings 'In a
Simple Way' as he tempts her with a happy picture of Italy, but she resists—
she is an invalid, she cannot walk. He helps her from her couch, then to a
step and then, uncomprehendingly, another till radiantly they join in the love
duet 'I Know Now' and embrace passionately. Barrett enters to find
Elizabeth taking tentative steps across the room. She faces him happily,
eager to show off her progress, but finds only anger in him. Barrett,
determined that she shall not leave her room, that she shall never leave him,
uses the cruellest attack of all and challenges her with her dead brother's
name. Before Browning's eyes, she crumbles and Barrett, cradling her fainting body in his arms, orders Browning from the house for ever.

ACT 2

Months have passed and Elizabeth and Browning have obeyed Barrett's
commands, but between Elizabeth and her father there is no longer the same
relationship. She obeys, she is dutiful, but she can no longer be loving. She
can only think of how nearly she was recalled to something like a normal life
(Soliloquy) and, as she brings back the memory, she rises to her feet and,
staggering lightly, she walks. An amazed Henrietta finds her on her feet and
calls the family who react in various degrees of delighted farce ('Pass the Eau
de Cologne').

The frivolous Bella comes to call, dragging her excessive wedding shopping and gossiping of masquerade balls. She has no fear of her overpowering
Uncle and flaunts herself in front of him ('What's Natural') until, losing
control, he kisses her with the passion and force which characterise his
nature. Now Elizabeth descends the stairs, walking between two of her
brothers. Faced with such an exhibition of independence, Barrett announces

202

that the family will be leaving London. He has bought a house in the country. This produces the nearest thing to a revolt that the Barrett children have ever staged but their father will brook no discussion ('I'm the Master Here'). The subject is closed.

At the Cremorne Gardens, while Bella and the other society dragonflies flit about him, Browning reads his newest poem ('Escape Me Never') with thoughts of Elizabeth. Henrietta arrives secretly to find Surtees and imparts the awful news of their departure. She insists that he must try to forget her ('Hate Me, Please'), but they end up in an embrace. Surtees carries the news to Browning who is enraged that the whole Barrett family should seem to be 'Under a Spell' to their father.

As they pack to depart from London, the boys daydream over the girls they've never met and now seem likely never to meet ('The Girls That Boys Dream About'). As soon as night comes, Browning pays a secret visit to Elizabeth. He urges her to come away and marry him, and appears not to hear her refusals as he pours out his plans for an elopement. She cannot bring herself to say yes, not yet. She will send a note. As Browning is leaving, Barrett enters. To his accusations of an affair with Browning, Elizabeth replies that she is in love with him and refuses to swear not to see him again. Barrett spits out his abomination of 'What the World Calls Love' and Elizabeth responds with a dazzling assertion of the love of 'Woman and Man'.

Barrett faces her in denial. Married love, physical love is a vile thing. In it any pure love disappears. He recalls with anguish the fear he saw in his wife's face whenever, after the birth of her first two children, he touched her. As he holds Elizabeth close to him, he tries to enfold her in the life he has planned for them, but she pulls away and as a parting word he quotes, 'Lovers grow cold, men learn to hate their wives, and only parents' love can last our lives.' The words are from the writings of Robert Browning.

Browning waits impatiently for the promised note from Elizabeth ('Frustration'), and finally it comes. Her answer, at last, is 'yes'. On Vauxhall station Browning and Elizabeth meet, and Henrietta and Surtees wish them on their way. The train is about to leave, but Barrett has forced the story of Elizabeth's flight from her little sister, Arabel, and he turns up to challenge Browning with criminal abduction. Elizabeth stretches forth her hand: it wears a ring. She and Browning have been married. The family crowd happily round her and help her to join her husband in the carriage, but Barrett turns away. As the train pulls out, carrying Robert and Elizabeth to Italy and a new life, he stands on the platform alone.

The revised 1987 script cut 'What's Natural', 'Under a Spell' and 'Want to Be Well', resituated an extended 'Escape Me Never' at the top of the second act and restored Browning's 'Long Ago I Loved You' which had been withdrawn from the score during the original pre-London run. The entire Cremorne Gardens scene was omitted and the song 'Hate Me, Please' placed in a new setting.

CHARLIE GIRL

a musical comedy in two acts by Hugh and Margaret Williams and Ray Cooney. Music and lyrics by David Heneker and John Taylor. Produced at the Adelphi Theatre, London, 15 December 1965 with Anna Neagle (Lady Hadwell), Joe Brown (Joe), Hy Hazell (Kay), Derek Nimmo (Wainwright), Stuart Damon (Jack) and Christine Holmes (Charlie). Produced in a revised version at the Victoria Palace Theatre 19 June 1986 with Cyd Charisse, Paul Nicholas, Dora Bryan, Nicholas Parsons, Mark Wynter and Lisa Hull.

CHARACTERS

Lady Hadwell *of Hadwell Hall*
Lady Fiona ⎫
Lady Penelope ⎬ *her daughters*
Lady Charlotte ⎭
Joe Studholme
Nicholas Wainwright, *a Pools official*
Mrs Kay Connor, *a wealthy widow*
Jack Connor, *her son*
Washington, *his valet*
Jerry, Pete, Sam, Fred, *employees at Hadwell Hall*
Chauffeur, etc.

ACT 1

The first tourists of the 1965 season are gathering outside the gates of Hadwell Hall, waiting to visit 'The Most Ancestral Home' of all Great Britain's stately homes. There, the present Lady Hadwell and her family are not only to be found daily on public view, but the Ladies Penelope and Fiona actually take part in showing visitors (at a not-too-small charge) through the varied delights of Elizabethan architecture enlivened by twentieth century improvements such as penny arcades, bingo, all-in-wrestling and a nudist colony. The young ladies are not delirious about being stately home guides but they comfort themselves with the observation that at least it isn't a totally demeaning occupation, like being a model. Occupations are something that the Ladies Fiona and Penelope certainly need for, despite the energetic commercialisation of Hadwell Hall under the imaginative chatelaineship of their mother, the family fortunes have dwindled daily under the twin tortures of daddy's death duties and the upkeep on the house and its grounds.

Lady Hadwell is currently taking a little time off from making money as she is about to welcome some very special houseguests. Her old chum, Kay Connor, from their chorus-line days as Cochran Young Ladies, is coming to visit. When Lady Hadwell hooked herself an earl, in the best fashion of the era, Kay went one better and ensnared an American multi-millionaire. She may not have a title and a stately home, but she has oodles of money and a perfectly drool-worthy son.

The description of young master Jack is enough to send Penelope and

204

Fiona into *frissons*, although Fiona declares that she must reserve judgement until she meets the young man. Fiona has specialised tastes: if Jack is not bald, she withdraws her interest. It is clear that Fiona and Penelope will be a credit to the family but there is, unfortunately, some doubt about Lady Hadwell's third daughter. Charlotte, better known as Charlie, hasn't any intention of swapping her motorcycle for high-heeled shoes or her grease-stained overalls for a party frock. The men in her life are her motorcycling chums. This doesn't mean that she doesn't think about love. She just thinks about it rather differently from her sisters. The day her Prince Charming comes and kisses her, she'll know, for 'Bells Will Ring'.

Charlie is tinkering away at a car when a bowler-hatted stranger arrives. He is Nicholas Wainwright and he is looking for Joe Studholme. Joe is Lady Hadwell's right-hand man, a cheerful cockney whose endless efforts have been largely responsible for Hadwell Hall's continued survival. It turns out that Joe has won the pools. Wainwright has come to present him with a cheque for £367,415 14s 6d. Joe is flabbergasted but, to Wainwright's horror, he declares that he won't take the money.

It's a cockeyed story, but Joe is in love with this girl and she doesn't like money. You see, she's poor and if he were rich she might say 'yes' to him just to help her family out of their money problems. It is pretty clear whom he is on about—the object of his affections is 'Charlie Girl'. Joe is determined to woo and win her while he is still poor. Can Wainwright wait for a week? Well, strictly he shouldn't, the publicity is lined up and Littlehill's Pools are straining at the bit, but Wainwright is suddenly struck all of a quiver by the sight of Lady Fiona in a mini-skirt, and a devious plan ferments in his mind. If he were willing to hold the cheque and the newspapers for a week, he would have to stay at Hadwell Hall during that time. Joe is dubious, but Wainwright promises to be dreadfully inconspicuous. The problem is solved by a stroke of genius. Wainwright can be a temporary butler, hired for the duration of the Connors' visit.

Jack Connor is the next to arrive on the scene, striking adoration into the hearts of a party of guideless schoolgirls by the beauty of his profile. When he meets Charlie, within a glimpse she, too, is taken off her feet and ends up hopelessly carolling 'I Love Him' to her monkey wrench. Jack's mother wants this typical mass adoration channeled. In fact, half the purpose of her visit to Britain is to get her wayward Jack paired of with a bit of British class—a nice English girl with a title. Jack has other thoughts ('What Would I Get From Being Married'), but for Mrs Connor and Lady Hadwell there is absolutely no doubt that an alliance between Jack and one of the Hadwell girls would be a perfect amalgam of breeding and cash ('Let's Do a Deal'). The two ladies celebrate their reunion and their little plan over a jug or two of martinis and, after a while, the polite party gets decidedly lively.

Wainwright has a few troubles with his new occupation. Buttling does not come naturally. He will keep on forgetting himself and sitting down with the guests. And then there is Fiona. He has discovered her penchant for bald-headed men and is in despair over his own healthy crop of hair. He has his chance to win some butler-points when the ladies tiptoe downstairs in a very delicate state after their previous night's partying, but an energetic if somewhat eccentric demonstration of yoga as a palliative for a hangover does more for the ladies' good humour than for their equilibrium or his. Joe, in his turn, is having a different kind of trouble. Although he has only a week in which to do it, he can't pluck up the courage to face Charlie with a profession of his love.

Wainwright gets him to practise his lovemaking technique on a convenient bust but, just as practice has got Joe psyched up to propose, Charlie spots Jack Connor in her own home and goes into shock. Who *is* that gorgeous man? When she finds out he is the American visitor she has been so off-hand about meeting, she is mortified. She has refused to go to the party her mother is giving that night in the Connors' honour and now...oh, how she wants to go.

She can't, of course. She has sold her only party dress on the sly to get money to pay for a saddle for her motor scooter. Joe comes to the rescue. He promises to find her a wonderful dress and, as the girl gallops delightedly off, Joe ruefully sings of 'My Favourite Occupation'—just being alone with her. Well, he's promised a dress, so here goes. He'll hire one from a London costumier and deliver up the girl he loves looking a million pounds right into the hands of the smooth Mr Jack Connor.

Up in his room, the dreamboat of the evening is adding the final touches to his evening wear and admiring his favourite profile ('What's the Magic'), while downstairs the evening's guests are arriving. As the music begins, Lady Hadwell leads a horde of admiring young men off to join in the evening's dancing ('When I Hear Music').

ACT 2
The dance has begun, but Charlie isn't there. The dress Joe ordered hasn't arrived and she is thoroughly upset. It's the first time Joe has tried to use money to get something he really wanted and it has gone awry ('I 'Ates Money'). The car with the all-important dress does eventually turn up and Charlie is transformed from a tomboy into a glamorous young woman. As a finishing touch, Joe gently removes her spectacles.

Kay Connor and the other guests are enjoying 'The Party of a Lifetime'. Wainwright, carrying out his buttling functions, is, at the same time, keeping a jealous eye on Lady Fiona and he stymies a potential bald rival by whispering to Lady Hadwell that the young man in question is a vice king from Tunbridge Wells. Jack is quick to notice the radiant Charlie and she, even though she doesn't see him too well without her glasses, is happy to be romantically inveigled off to the summer house by her hero.

Jack moves swiftly to the attack and has got as far as proposing a weekend in Paris and one of his closest clinches when Joe interrupts the scene with a phoney telephone call. While Jack is away, Charlie pours out her thrilling story to Joe...it's 'Like Love', before Jack returns to pick up where he left off. The scene leads up to a romantic climax, but when Jack kisses Charlie something goes wrong. She doesn't melt. She tries a second embrace and then rushes off in distress—no bells rang. The stunned Jack wonders frightenedly if his famous charm is wearing thin ('That's It'), but finally comes to the much more satisfying conclusion that the girl was simply overwhelmed by his charisma, and he returns to the party and the chase.

In one corner of the terrace, Lady Hadwell discovers a very different kind of dancing with the limber valet, Washington, whilst in another Joe feeds the society guests with fish and chips in newspaper and regales them with the tale of his Uncle Henry's success as a fish shop owner ('Fish and Chips'). As Jack starts his his wooing of Charlie over again, the chauffeur returns to collect the hired dress. It has to be in a film studio for the morning and he must leave with it now. Charlie agrees, but she has no intention of abandoning the party. She simply steps out of the dress and carries on dancing, clad only in her mini-slip. The other guests are enthralled. What a wheeze! Soon all the girls are down to their slips and dancing the latest dance (Society Twist) with their eye-popping beaux.

The only person who isn't enjoying himself is Joe. He pours out his love for Charlie, not to the girl herself but to Lady Hadwell. To his surprise, she is truly supportive and urges him to go and tell Charlie right away ('You Never Know What You Can Do Until You Try'). When it comes to the point, however, Joe's nerve fails him. Instead of saying 'I love you', he blurts out a final goodbye. He is going away. Charlie leans towards him to give him a goodbye kiss and—would you believe it—bells ring ('Bells Will Ring'/ 'Charlie Girl').

It is a happy ending of Gilbertian proportions. Wainwright reveals his identity and announces that the record pools dividend has been won by Joe Studholme and Lady Hadwell. Yes, Joe filled out the coupon in both their names, so if Lady Hadwell will just give Joe half the stake money half the winnings will be hers and Hadwell Hall can close its doors to the public for ever. It turns out that Charlie has absolutely no aversion to a rich husband at all, whilst the Lady Penelope in her slip has revealed sufficient advantages for Jack Connor's affections to have taken a violent turn in her direction and the Lady Fiona, who has a deep belief in heredity, discovers that Wainwright's father went bald at thirty. As the evening's fireworks flash above Hadwell Hall, everyone agrees: 'Isn't it flippin' well marvellous!'

The original production of *Charlie Girl* featured Anna Neagle in the song 'I Was Young' as a finale to the first act. Amongst other revisions made to showcase the dancing talents of Cyd Charisse in the revival, David Heneker supplied the song 'When I Hear Music, I Dance' as a replacement. The song 'Liverpool' was interpolated into the original production when Joe Brown was succeeded by Gerry Marsden as Joe.

CANTERBURY TALES

a musical in two acts by Martin Starkie and Nevill Coghill based on a translation from Chaucer by Nevill Coghill. Lyrics by Nevill Coghill. Music by Richard Hill and John Hawkins. Produced at the Phoenix Theatre, London, 21 March 1968 with Jessie Evans (Wife of Bath), Kenneth J Warren (Miller), Nicky Henson (Squire) and Wilfred Brambell (Steward). Produced at the Shaftesbury Theatre 24 April 1979 with Miss Evans, Percy Herbert, Ian Steele and Buddy Elias.

Produced at the Eugene O'Neill Theatre, New York, 3 February 1969 with Hermione Baddeley, Roy Cooper, Edward Evanko and George Rose. Produced at the Rialto Theatre 12 February 1980 with Maureen Sadusek, Win Atkins, Robert Teitrick and Ted Houck jr.

CHARACTERS

The Host
The Knight
The Squire
The Prioress
The Nun
The Priest/The Pardoner
The Cook/The Summoner
The Friar
The Wife of Bath
The Miller
The Steward
The Clerk of Oxford
The Merchant
Chaucer
Alison/Molly/May
Robin, Page, etc.

PROLOGUE

We are introduced to the entertainment by its author, Geoffrey Chaucer, who explains how, when stopping at the Tabard Inn at Southwark one medieval day, at the beginning of a pilgrimage to Canterbury, he fell in with a heterogeneous group of like intentioned people and...

ACT 1

Harry Bailey, the Host at the Tabard Inn, presides over his guests with bonhomie (Host's Song of Welcome) as he listens to them anticipating their trip. The pilgrimage will be a leisurely four day progress through the English countryside from London to Canterbury and, to make its hours slip by in a pleasant fashion, he proposes a contest. Each pilgrim shall take his turn to tell a tale, and he whose tale is finally judged to be the best and most fitting shall be given a dinner here at the Tabard, at the expense of the rest, on their return from Canterbury. His idea pleases him so well that he decides he will

208

The Beggar's Opera once aroused the fury of the authorities, but by the 1960s, with the future Dame Janet Baker (Polly) and the future Sir Peter Pears (Macheath), it was wholly respectable.

Billee Taylor. These fine sailor lads and their officer are actually the pensionnaires of a charity girls' school. Lithograph 1880.

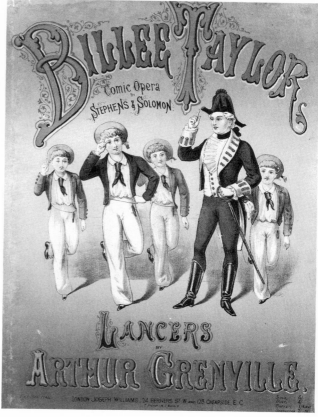

The Mikado. Gilbert claimed that he made his three little maids schoolgirls because of the tiny stature of the Savoy's leading ladies. What would he have made of their statuesque successors? English National Opera, 1986.

HMS Pinafore. 'He's never, never sick at sea.' Captain Corcoran (Paul Bentley) looks as if he may at any time disprove his crew's respectful chorusing. Gaiety Theatre, Dublin, 1985.

A Greek Slave. An enduring form of light musical theatre was crystallised in the 1890s at Daly's Theatre where comedians Huntley Wright and Rutland Barrington, baritone hero Hayden Coffin and soubrette Letty Lind were among the regular stars.

The Arcadians. Eternal summer in Arcadia has clearly become hotter over the years. Sombra (Gaynor Miles) sports a much less restricting robe for her missionary trip to London in the 1984 revival than original star Florence Smithson did in 1909.

himself join the pilgrims on their journey to act as arbiter in their competition. After a preparatory night's sleep (Good Night Hymn), the little company set out on their merry way (The Pilgrim Song: 'Canterbury Day') and the story-telling begins.

The first tale to be told is the Miller's Tale. The Miller, a loutish, drunken fellow, has come on the pilgrimage as a penance ordered by his local priest after a fight with the Steward. The intention is that, under the influence of the holy journey, the two will resolve their differences and become friends but, for the meanwhile, there is little sign of reconciliation. The Miller intends to tell his tale about a carpenter and, since the Steward was once a carpenter, it is a fair wager that the tale will end in the discomfort of its subject. Given the Miller's predilections and his tipsy condition, it is also unlikely to be a tale fit for ladies.

Once upon a time there was a carpenter called Oswald who had a very attractive young wife known as Alison and a lodger, a poor but pretty student called Nicholas, whose chief talent, it seems, lay in risky seductions ('I Have a Noble Cock'). The lovely Alison was a natural target for his abilities and, since she did not object—nay, she positively concurred in the exercise—it only remained for them to set up a situation where their mutual lust might be satisfied without Oswald being any the wiser.

Since Nicholas was a scholar and Oswald only a silly carpenter, this seemed to be a simple thing and, indeed, Nicholas was soon at work on a plan. Alison, however, was admired by more than Oswald and Nicholas. She had captured the eye and stirred the loins of young Absalon, the dandy Parish Clerk, who made strenuous efforts to incite her to adultery ('Darling, Let Me Teach You How to Kiss'), but with such paltry success as to render him quite frantic with undischarged passion.

While Absalon chewed his nails, young Nicholas matured his plan. Falling into a feigned trance, he produced a momentous prophesy. The world was to suffer a second great deluge, bringing death and devastation to all who could not save themselves. Yet because of his warning their own little band might be saved. Oswald must sling from the roof of his barn three tubs in which the three of them might sit and, provided with beer and bread, float above the flood for the days of the deluge until safety should be reached. Oswald hurried off to follow this God-given chance to be a second Noah, leaving Alison and Nicholas to anticipate the success of their plan ('There's Something in My Blood').

The tubs were brought and slung beneath the thatch of Oswald's barn, and the carpenter and his wife and his lodger knelt and prayed a 'Pater Noster' before adjourning to their respective vessels for the night. The carpenter was equipped with an axe with which to sever the ropes at the vital time and Nicholas promised to awaken him with a shout of 'water!' when that time was ripe. No sooner installed in his tub and hoisted on high, the carpenter fell fast asleep and was not aware that the two tubs alongside him were empty: Alison and Nicholas had gone straight back to the house and to Oswald's own bed ('There's the Moon').

The night was a merry and a busy one but, just when the rollicking pair were ready to take some sleep, who should arrive outside the window, his lips itching for a kiss, but persistent Absalon. Exasperated by the clerk's attentions, Alison resolved to teach him a lesson and, when he climbed his ladder to her bedroom window, instead of presenting her lips to his closed eyes and yearning lips, she lifted her shift and gave him instead her naked backside. When Absalon realised that he had kissed the wrong lips, his love went limp and he vowed to be revenged. Trotting to his friend the blacksmith, he took a red-hot iron from his fire and returned to the scene of his discomfort.

When Absalon called for another kiss, Nicholas thought he could improve upon the joke. Taking Alison's place at the window, he presented a very different rump to the clerk's embrace and, at the climactic moment, let forth an almighty fart. His laughter was cut short when, instead of the expected kiss, he received the blacksmith's smouldering iron across his behind. As Absalon fled in revengeful triumph, the injured Nicholas squealed for water, a cry which awoke the carpenter who, thinking the deluge had come, slashed the ropes and tumbled, tub and all, to the ground. And thus, to the varying embarrassments of all three men, ends the Miller's Tale, a tale which may not win a prize for its moral values but which entertained at least part of the company.

The next to tell his tale was the Nun's Priest and he, with a care to be both funny and clean, gave forth with a little farmyard story complete with moral lessons. A little old lady kept a fine cockerel called Chanticleer and this cockerel, of all the hens in the yard, courted particularly a fine specimen of henhood called Pertelote ('My Little Feathery Lady'). Pertelote, however, was a silly chicken and she scornfully rejected her husband's sensible fears of the marauding fox and recommended a laxative to stop him having bad dreams on the subject. In fact, she got quite haughty at Chanticleer's apparent cowardice and threatened to have a headache if he didn't stop talking so stupidly.

No self-respecting cockerel could be allowed to suffer so, and Chanticleer threw aside his fears ('My Husband Is so Clever') and strutted about the farmyard carelessly ('I Am a Noble Cock') until one day the fox came and carried him off. But, as the fox and his prey scampered away pursued by the little old lady, Chanticleer had enough wits about him to trick his captor. He encouraged him to throw some words of defiance at his pursuers and, as soon as the fox opened his mouth to speak, leapt quickly from between his jaws and flew hastily back to his perch. The morals of this tale are manifold, but of them the main one is this: that man is foolish who listens to his wife, especially if it means that he must risk his life!

The second day sees the pilgrims on the road once more and deep in discussion. The Wife of Bath holds out against the principle of virginity, crowning her arguments with the incontrovertible statement that if everyone remained virgin how would new virgins ever get born. She also has strong views on marriage, a state which she has herself enjoyed five times, and on the relative positions of husband and wife within the thrall of wedlock. The wife must in all things rule her husband who shall, standing and lying, be her willing slave.

210

This philosophy does not suit the men of the party and its implications are not to the liking of the religious folk for whom the word love has different connotations. It is the grace which conquers the seven deadly sins ('Love Will Conquer All'). But discussion must end, for it is time for the next tale to begin. Today it is the Steward who will speak and, in revenge for the Miller's tale ridiculing a carpenter, he has an equally rude tale to tell about a Miller.

Down Cambridge way there lived a cocky miller with a jumped-up wife and a lusty bumpkin of a daughter. The miller was a thorough rogue and when the grain was brought to him for milling he would always steal for himself a goodly share of the flour. One day, two college lads called Alan and John decided that the miller had cheated enough and that they would make sure they received the full amount of flour from their warden's corn. Feigning innocent curiosity they stayed to watch their grain milled and the balked miller, in revenge, set loose the horse on which they had brought their sacks.

When the boys emerged with their sackful of flour they were obliged to leave it at the mill and go off in search of their wayward beast, an absence which gave the miller the chance to help himself to his usual 'share'. By the time the horse was caught and the bedraggled boys returned to the mill, their plan was ruined and they benighted and forced to pay the miller to spend the night in his home. It turned out a merry evening ('Fill Your Glass') and, by the time they all lurched to their beds, the ale had taken its effects.

The miller fell straightaway asleep and his wife, dumping the baby's cradle at the end of their bed, soon followed suit. Daughter Molly in her bed snored fit to burst, and John and Alan, crammed into the house's third bed, found sleep impossible. Then it came to Alan that he could have some return for his stolen flour and, swiftly tiptoeing across the room, he joined the compliant Molly in her bed, leaving John to wonder why he hadn't thought of it first. But John's turn soon followed. The miller's wife got up to spend a groat and, while she watered, John shifted the cradle from her bed to his so that when the woman returned, groping in the dark, she mistook the bed and climbed in alongside John with immediate results. And while two beds creaked away merrily, the miller slept.

When the cock crew, Alan decided it circumspect to leave the bouncing Molly and return to his own bed but, misled by the wayward cradle, he climbed in alongside the miller and, thinking him to be his friend, told him the tale of his night with much enjoyment. The duped miller leaped from his bed in a rage and all ended in shrieks and howls as the Steward's Tale, and his revenge on the Miller, came to an end.

ACT 2

The pilgrims halt for lunch, and the Wife of Bath merrily continues where she left off: she's ruled and buried five husbands (although the pretty young fifth took some training) and she's looking for a sixth ('Come on and Marry Me, Honey'); while the Miller indulges in his favourite pastime downing tankards of 'Beer, Beer, Beer'. The conversation turns still on the subject of whether a husband or a wife should hold dominion in a marriage and this leads to a regretful memory by the Oxford Clerk to whom no girls are like the girls of his youth ('Where Are the Girls of Yesterday'). But on with the tales. The next raconteur is the Merchant and his tale is a rueful one of woman's wiles.

An elderly knight, Sir January, decided late in life to wed and father an heir, and he chose for his mate a young lass of his town called May (Wedding Song) to whom he applied his person with all the vigour he could muster ('If She Has Never Loved Before'). It wasn't much fun for May and, when her husband's servant, Damian, fell ill, she was not displeased to find that the cause of his distemper was a boiling passion for her pretty self ('I'll Give My Love a Ring'). Now Sir January had made a very lovely garden and to that garden he was wont to bring his little bride to take their pleasure on the green grass. The garden was so lovely that the King of the Underworld, Pluto, and his Queen Proserpine also came to enjoy its beauties and to indulge there in the bickerings of married couples, bickerings centred on the same old argument: the treacheries of women, the lecheries of men and who shall rule in marriage.

One day it happened, alas, that old Sir January went blind. This loss of sight made him even more possessive of May and, in fear lest she should stray, he kept her at all times hand-to-hand which made her efforts to rendezvous effectively with Damian all the more difficult. However, a lady has two hands and while one was devoted the Sir January the other was free to make loving signs to Damian, dangling above her in a pear tree. This situation revived the eternal argument of the Gods. Pluto pointed out May's treachery, Proserpine blamed Sir January's lechery in taking a child bride. He swore that if ever May and Damian should get together he would restore the old man's sight, and she retaliated that, should he do so, she would put an effective excuse on the girl's lips.

One day, as January and May walked in the garden, the little wife expressed a desperate desire to taste a pear. Little realising that Damian was lurking in the branches of the tree, the blind man helped his wife up into its branches but, no sooner had the two young people become purposefully interlocked, than Pluto fulfilled his promise. January's eyes were opened and he saw his wife being pleasured in the pear tree by his servant. But Proserpine's vow was equally effective. May, with a fine semblance of innocence, blamed her husband's improperly cured eyesight and wept at his horrid suspicions until the old knight was quite bamboozled into believing her true. Pluto was vanquished and woman's wiles won the day ('Sing in Praise of Women's Virtue').

The Squire tries to raise the tone of affairs with a song in praise of chivalry ('I Am Forever Dated'), but the Wife of Bath will hear no such nonsense. The heroic days of King Arthur were just like any other, and she has a tale to prove her point. A young knight was brought before the King charged with rape but, winning the favour of the Queen with his comely looks and calculated words, he escaped the penalty of death and was instead sent on a quest to discover the answer to the riddle 'What Do Women Most Desire?'. From city to city he went and from woman to woman trying, without success,

212

to find the answer to his puzzle, until one day he chanced upon an old crone who held the answer. To win her help, the knight promised to grant her her first wish should he be saved. When he returned to court, the knight found that he did indeed have the answer to the vital question: what woman most desires is a man who, though placed above her in society's way, will yet love her and through that love be humble before her and obey her wish and will. And so the knight was pardoned.

Then the old woman stepped forward before the royal judges to claim her reward. She desired the young knight in marriage. Her claim could not be denied and the desperate boy was wedded, but he could not bring himself to be brought to bed by his old, plain, poor and low-bred bride. Softly the old woman dispelled his objections one by one with a lesson in knightly virtue and courtesy until the shamed youth was brought to humility and, finally, to a connubial kiss. With that kiss the old crone was changed into a beautiful young girl. Virtue had earned its reward.

Now, at last, Canterbury is in sight ('April Song') and the Knight is brought to give his decision on the rules of marriage. He chooses for neither side. In marriage neither the man nor the woman should rule. Marriage should be a loving and respectful mutual relationship of true hearts. His words cannot be gainsaid, for truly 'Love Can Conquer All'.

The composition of *Canterbury Tales* was originally fluid. The Priest's Tale was originally included only at specific matinées until it later became an integral part of the show and, in the earliest stages of the show's London run, The Pardoner's Tale was also played at some performances. In the New York production the song 'It Depends on What You're At' was added for the Wife of Bath and the Miller's original number 'When I Was a Boy' replaced by 'Beer, Beer, Beer' which was also used in London.

A sequel to *Canterbury Tales* entitled *More Canterbury Tales* was produced at Her Majesty's Theatre, Melbourne, Australia 23 October 1976. It comprised The Summoner's Tale and The Franklin's Tale plus The Pardoner's Tale and The Priest's Tale from the original show with considerable new music. The Franklin's Tale was abandoned in favour of the old Merchant's Tale during production.

JOSEPH AND THE AMAZING TECHNICOLOR DREAMCOAT

a musical by Tim Rice. Music by Andrew Lloyd Webber. First performed at Colet Court School 1 March 1968. Produced in a staged version at the Edinburgh Festival by the Young Vic Company as part of *Bible One: Two Looks at the Book of Genesis* 21 August 1972 and subsequently played at the Young Vic Theatre, London, 16 October 1972, The Roundhouse 8 November 1972 and at the Albery Theatre 17 February 1983 with Gary Bond (Joseph), Peter Reeves (Narrator) and Gordon

Waller (Pharoah). Revived at the Westminster Theatre 27 November 1978 with Paul Jones, John Golder and Leonard Whiting and 1 November 1979 with Paul Jones, Clifton Todd and Maynard Williams, at the Vaudeville Theatre 15 December 1980 with Jess Conrad, Leo Andrew and Dave Mayberry, at Sadler's Wells Theatre 23 December 1981 with Conrad, Keith Raymel and Mayberry, and at the Royalty Theatre 16 December 1986 with Mike Holoway, Karen West and Sean Simon.

First performed in the United States at the College of the Immaculate Conception, Douglastown, Long Island, May 1970. Produced at the Brooklyn Academy of Music, New York, 22 December 1976 with David-James Carroll, Cleavon Little and Jess Pearson and 13 December 1977 with Carroll, Alan Weeks and William Parry. Produced at the Entermedia Theatre, New York, 18 November 1981 with Bill Hutton, Laurie Beechman and Tom Carder and subsequently at the Royale Theatre 27 January 1982.

CHARACTERS

Jacob
Joseph, *his son*
Reuben, Simeon, Levi, Napthali, Isaachar, Asher, Dan, Zebulum, Gad, Judah, Benjamin, *his other sons*
Potiphar, *a well-off Egyptian*
Potiphar's wife
Pharoah
Butler
Baker, etc.

The story begins in the land of Canaan, somewhere back near the beginning of the bible. A founding farmer called Jacob had a dozen sons ('Jacob and Sons') but he had an especially soft spot for one called Joseph who reminded him of his favourite wife. This favouritism didn't make Joseph very popular with the other members of the family, and their antipathy towards their spoiled brother grew even stronger when their father splashed out on a fantastic new coat for his number one son. No more dowdy sheepskin like his brothers: Joseph's coat was a rainbow affair ('Joseph's Coat') and he stood out amongst his drably clad family like a happy bruise.

Unfortunately, Joseph had more ways of getting on his brothers' nerves than just showing off his gaudy topcoat. He had a habit of relating his dreams to them which would have been really boring if the dreams hadn't been quite so infuriatingly self-aggrandising ('Joseph's Dreams'). The first one was about wheat. Safe enough? No. In this dream all the brothers have stooked their wheat at harvest time and what happens but all their stooks start bowing to his one. Then they are all stars, only his star gets homage from all the rest, not to mention the sun and the moon. If you believed him and his dreams, it was clear that one day Joseph was going to have them all under his thumb. This would make life (and Joseph) even more unbearable than it and he were already, so the brothers decided there was only one answer and that was fratricide. They took Joseph out to a nice, distant place, ripped up his rotten coat and tipped him into a pit to perish.

But fate was still on Joseph's side. At that moment some hairy Ishmaelites came jogging by on their donkeys and the brothers saw the chance to make a bit of cash on the side. Joseph was hitched up out of the pit and sold off as an Ishmaelite slave ('Poor, Poor Joseph'). A passing goat was slaughtered to provide some corroborating blood to sprinkle on the shreds of his coat, and the brothers went back to Jacob to squeeze out a few crocodile tears in support of their tale of brother Joseph's sad demise ('One More Angel in Heaven').

The Ishmaelites sold Joseph at a good profit to an Egyptian property magnate called 'Potiphar'. Joseph, with his talent for getting on, quickly managed to please his new master and was soon promoted to the top of the household. He also succeeded in pleasing Mrs Potiphar and that made Potiphar really jealous. Joseph got double quick demotion and ended up in prison ('Close Every Door').

He wasn't the only servant of Egypt to have fallen. He shared his cell with a couple of Pharoah's minions who had committed some royal misdemeanours and went in fear of their lives, which gave them really bad dreams. This was the opportunity for Joseph to start his dream-reading business again, in spite of the trouble it had got him into in Canaan. To one man he prophesied doom, but to the other he promised a return to his position as the Pharoah's butler. As for himself, well, he still had his old Canaan dreams to fall back on ('Go, Go, Go Joseph'), and he was right.

'Pharoah' was the biggest thing in Egypt and Pharoah was also having bad dreams, so what more natural than he should call on this chap in jail who had correctly forecast his butler's restoration to favour? Joseph was brought to court and Pharoah poured out his dreams ('Pharoah's Story'): meaningful charades involving fat cows and thin cows and ripe and rotten corn. Joseph was able to translate this on his ear. The dreams were a long-range weather forecast. They prophesied seven years of super-cereal crops followed by seven years of drought. Therefore, they were a warning to Pharoah on agricultural policy. He must stockpile foodstuffs frantically during the good years to enable his country to get through the bad ones ('Pharoah's Dream Explained').

Pharoah didn't wait to test this plausible explanation ('Well Stone the Crows'). He had Joseph's chains chopped off and promoted him to Minister of Agriculture on the spot. Of course, in the irritating manner which had characterised his whole life, Joseph was right and he organised the whole thing so that there was no crisis in the Egyptian markets throughout the famine years. Not so in Canaan where, because of the fraternal susceptibilities in Jacob's family, they didn't have anyone to give them forecasts. Canaan was hard hit ('Those Canaan Days') and Jacob and his wives and eleven surviving sons grew thin and sick. Finally, the brothers decided to head for Egypt to see if they could get in on the immigrant labour market and thus fill their needs.

When they reached Egypt ('The Brothers Come to Egypt') they pleaded for food handouts to Joseph in his capacity as the Minister of Agriculture. He recognised them right away in spite of their scrawniness, but they didn't recognise him nor realise the irony of their bowing before him just as his

215

early dream had predicted ('Grovel, Grovel'). Joseph, who wasn't quite the paragon of virtue you might have thought, had a tiny vindictive streak him, so he tried a little plot. He gave the brothers the sacks of food they desired but, in the bottom of one sack, he hid a precious goblet. As they were leaving, he cried out 'Who's the Thief?' and had them all searched. The goblet was found in the sack of little brother Benjamin.

Benjamin obviously didn't have any annoying potential. He was very popular with his family, and the other brothers all got down on their knees for another grovel, begging Joseph not to give Benjamin a criminal record ('Benjamin Calypso'). Joseph thought this showed that his brothers had been improved by a bit of starvation and were no longer the sort to throw helpful brothers into pits or sell their family off to hairy Ishmaelites, so he decided the time had come to make himself known ('Joseph All the Time').

And so there was a happy ending after all. Joseph used his position in the government to get visas for all his family to come and live in Egypt and partake of the plentiful food ('Jacob in Egypt') and everyone lived happily ever after ('Any Dream Will Do').

Joseph and the Amazing Technicolor Dreamcoat began as a fifteen minute cantata and was increased in size for subsequent concert and stage productions until it was sufficiently substantial to fill a full evening's programme.

JESUS CHRIST SUPERSTAR

a musical in two acts with lyrics by Tim Rice and music by Andrew Lloyd Webber. Produced at the Mark Hellinger Theatre, New York, 12 October 1971 with Ben Vereen (Judas), Jeff Fenholt (Jesus), Yvonne Elliman (Mary), Barry Dennen (Pilate) and Paul Ainsley (Herod). Produced at the Longacre Theatre 23 November 1977 with Patrick Jude, William Daniel Grey, Barbara Niles, Randy Wilson and Mark Syers.

Produced at the Münsterlandhalle, Munster, 18 February 1972 and played at the Deutschlandhalle, Berlin, 31 March 1972. Produced by the Theater des Westens at the Messehalle, Berlin, 9 September 1984.

Produced at the Théâtre National du Palais de Chaillot, Paris, 1972 with Farid Dali, Daniel Beretta, Anne-Marie David, Michel Zacha and Reney Deshauteurs.

Produced at the Palace Theatre, London, 9 August 1972 with Stephen Tate, Paul Nicholas, Dana Gillespie, John Parker and Paul Jabara.

A film version was produced by Universal Pictures in 1973 with Carl Andersen, Ted Neely, Miss Elliman, Dennen and Joshua Mostel.

CHARACTERS

Jesus of Nazareth
Judas Iscariot
Mary Magdalene
Caiaphas

216

Annas
Pontius Pilate
King Herod
Simon Zealotes
Peter
Three Priests, Maid by the Fire, etc.

ACT 1

This is the story of the last seven days of the life of Jesus of Nazareth, known as Christ, as seen through the eyes of his disciple Judas Iscariot whose name has descended to posterity as that of the archetypal betrayer because of his delivery of Jesus into the hands of the Roman rulers of Judaea.

At the opening of the piece, Judas, alone, agonises over the way in which the humanitarian crusade, of which he is a part and of which Jesus is the prime mover and the figurehead, is going. The movement has grown beyond all belief and has taken on characteristics which he finds more than troubling: Jesus is hailed as a Messiah, as a god, and his sayings are repeated, twisted and repeated again as monstrous prophecies and bywords, while his followers have become fanatical and unrealistic with too much 'Heaven on Their Minds'.

His fears seem justified. At Bethany on the Friday night the apostles of Christ are eager for words of wisdom about their future, for golden news of the days to come ('What's the Buzz'). Only the whore, Mary Magdalene, attempts to calm the overheated atmosphere, cooling Jesus' brow with a sponge and prompting from Judas accusations of inconsistency in Jesus' attitudes ('Strange Thing Mystifying'). Jesus reacts petulantly in defence of the woman who, in her turn, tries to defuse his anger ('Everything's All Right'), but Judas attacks her for using precious ointments on her master, wasting money which could have bought food for many poor. Her soothing words can only partly allay the prevalent air of dissension.

In Jerusalem, on Sunday, the Priests of the city discuss the danger which Jesus represents to them: his followers are becoming loud and persistent and soon their noise will reach the ears of the province's Roman rulers. If the Romans crush a potential king in Judaea, they will probably also wipe out the religious sector in which that king could have flourished. With a strong feeling for self-preservation, Caiaphas, the chief priest, decides 'Jesus Must Die'. In the streets the crowds call for Jesus ('Hosanna') and, in spite of Caiaphas' commands, he cannot or will not quiet them. Simon Zealotes urges him to proclaim himself as all the things he is and all the things the people want him to be (Simon Zealotes), but Jesus will not. He gives Simon and the crowd no present rewards but only the promise of a glorious afterlife for the faithful ('Poor Jerusalem').

That night, Pontius Pilate, the Roman Governor of Judaea, has a dream (Pilate's Dream). He dreams of a strange Galilean with whose life his own is seemingly linked: the people of the world weep into eternity for this man, and Pilate himself is despised because of him.

217

On Monday, Jesus visits the temple (The Temple) and finds that the moneylenders and merchants have set up their stalls in its holy precincts. He ejects them loudly, but it is an effort. He has done so much and, whatever his disciples may say, he is a man, a tired man. When a crowd of cripples surround him, begging to be healed, he cries at them in exasperation to leave him alone. Once more Mary has to soothe him into rest.

She herself has a mind in turmoil, but a very different kind of turmoil: she is in love with Jesus, but with a kind of love which she cannot understand ('I Don't Know How to Love Him') and even less express. For the meanwhile, she shows her love by being a calming influence in his life when everything else conspires to stir him to excesses.

On the Tuesday, Judas, with many misgivings, finally comes to a decision. Jesus cannot control the mob and mass violence seems imminent, so he goes to the priests ('Damned for All Time'). From him the eager priests draw information as to where they can catch Jesus alone, for they need to take him prisoner without risking violence by the crowd. Spurning their 'Blood Money', Judas gives them the information they want.

At the apostles' supper on Thursday night the followers of Jesus drown their weariness in wine ('Look at All My Trials and Tribulations'/The Last Supper). Jesus foresees his end and, before the event, bitterly accuses his followers of faithlessness to his memory. Judas cuts short his martyrising speech on betrayal with counter accusations: their ideals are suffering and perishing because Jesus has turned them into part of a cult centred in himself. It has all gone wrong. Someone has to stop him before he makes things even worse.

In the garden of Gethsemane, Jesus prays alone ('I Only Want to Say'). His prayer is one not of inspiration and trust, but one which begs for deliverance from an exhausted evangelical life which has become a continual trial of his mental and physical strength. What Judas has accused him of is true: he wants to be betrayed, he wants to die.

ACT 2

When Judas brings the soldiers to Gethsemane (The Arrest) Jesus offers no resistance. The disciples flee and Peter, as Jesus had predicted at the last supper, denies his acquaintance (Peter's Denial).

On Friday, Jesus is brought before Pilate, but Pilate refuses jurisdiction (Pilate and Christ) and sends the prisoner on to King Herod in Galilee. Herod greets Jesus cynically (Herod's Song) with orders for instant miracles, and also refuses to take responsibility for judging him. Faced with the possibility of a capital case, Mary and Peter regret that things have been allowed to go so far ('Could We Start Again'), and Judas, realising he has been forced by fate and the will of God into being the instrument of Jesus' martyrdom, curses God and hangs himself (Judas' Death).

Jesus is brought back to Pilate (Trial Before Pilate) who is still unwilling to condemn him but, in the face of vociferous demands from the populace and the priests, he orders him to be flogged (Thirty Nine Lashes) instead. But no matter what he does or says he can get no return from Jesus who insists that his fate is not in the hands of either of them and finally, in exasperation, Pilate gives up trying to save this enigmatically passive man.

The voice of Judas is heard, wondering why what seemed as if it could have been a great popular movement was allowed by Jesus, and through his mortal failings, to go so soon and so badly wrong. Or was it intended? Was Jesus' short but dramatic career and death all part of the plan to become and be remembered as a 'Superstar'?

The final scene pictures the crucifixion of Jesus of Nazareth known as Christ (John Nineteen Forty One).

THE ROCKY HORROR SHOW

a rock musical by Richard O'Brien. Produced at the Theatre Upstairs at the Royal Court Theatre, London, 19 June 1973 with Tim Curry (Frank'n'furter), Julie Covington (Janet), Richard O'Brien (Riff Raff), Christopher Malcolm (Brad), Patricia Quinn (Magenta), Little Nell (Columbia), Rayner Bourton (Rocky), Paddy O'Hagan (Eddie/Dr Scott) and Jonathan Adams (Narrator) and played subsequently at the Classic Theatre, Chelsea, from 14 August 1973, the King's Road Theatre from 3 November 1973 and the Comedy Theatre from 6 April 1979.

Produced at the Belasco Theatre, New York, 10 March 1975 with Curry, Abigail Harness, Ritz O'Brien, Bill Miller, Jamie Donnelly, Boni Enten, Meat Loaf, Kim Milford and Graham Jarvis.

Produced at Théâtre de l'Union, Paris, 14 February 1984 with Fred Lane, Anne Lalley, Christian Erickson, Mark Elliot, Suzanne Andrews, Zabou, Thomas Pollard, Emmanuel Renard, Jean-Claude Deret and Nick Hawtrey.

A film version was produced by Twentieth Century-Fox in 1976 with Tim Curry, Susan Sarandon, Richard O'Brien, Barry Bostwick, Patricia Quinn, Little Nell, Peter Hinwood, Meat Loaf, Jonathan Adams and Charles West.

CHARACTERS

Usherette
Magenta
Janet Weiss
Brad Majors
Narrator
Riff-Raff
Columbia
Frank'n'furter
Rocky
Eddie
Dr Evrett Scott

We are in a beat-up, old-fashioned movie house where an Usherette is welcoming us to a double feature 'Science Fiction' programme.

Wedding bells are heard as Brad Majors and Janet Weiss appear on the screen. They have just been to see their friends Betty Munroe and Ralf Hapshatt enshrined in the wonders of American middle-class wedlock. Janet has caught the bride's bouquet and, emboldened by the occasion, Brad throws maidenly modesty to the winds and proposes to her ('Damn it, Janet'). But all will not go simply and sweetly from engagement ring to church bells for Brad and Janet, these two bright and shining examples of scrubbed American youth. Therein lies the story of *The Rocky Horror Show*.

Once upon an overclouded 1950s New Jersey night, Brad and Janet set out in their car to drive to the home of their old science tutor, Dr Evrett Scott. It is one of those nights when nothing seems to go right. First it starts to rain, then they take a wrong turning and then, when they are thoroughly lost, they have a blow out. There is nothing to do but to walk wetly back to the gothic-looking castle they passed in the middle of the countryside a few miles back and try to ring for help ('Over at the Frankenstein Place'). When they get there, the place looks far from welcoming, but they ring the doorbell all the same and are greeted by a seedy-looking, hunchbacked butler called Riff-Raff. He invites them in and, oh! fateful decision, since they have no other way to telephone for the Automobile Association, they enter.

They have their first surprise when they meet the master of the house, Frank 'n' furter. Quite what or who he is they cannot tell from his appearance, but he is quick to enlighten them: he is a 'Sweet Transvestite' from Transsexual, Transylvania, and he hints that under his alarming feminine attire there is more than enough to fill the eye. He invites Brad and Janet up to his laboratory: there they will be permitted to look at his favourite obsession, Rocky, the blond and tanned young man he has been creating to gratify his pleasures.

Apparently it is forbidden to visit this laboratory wearing anything more than underwear, for Riff-Raff and Frank's two nymphomaniacal female satellites, Columbia and Magenta, immediately set to removing all the rest of Brad and Janet's clothing. Janet has a tiny thought of resisting, but Brad is all for preserving the civilities and, as he is stripped, he introduces himself and his fiancée to the attendants. When Columbia, in the ensuing chatter, mentions Eddie the delivery boy, she is shushed down and Riff-Raff leads a diversionary song and dance about the 'Time Warp'.

Up in the laboratory Frank dons a surgical gown and mask and, after tentative inquiries as to whether they have any interesting tattoos, allows Brad and Janet to cover their vulnerability under similar clothes. The reason for all this hospital cleanliness is that tonight Frank is to bring off the triumph of his dreams: he will put life into the man he has created. Switches and dials are fiddled, lights flash and slowly the bundle of bandages lying mummy-like before them begins to move. Frank and Riff-Raff tear away the outer covering and reveal the blossoming body of a potential Mr America: the bewildered Rocky, terrified at his fully-grown entrance into the world ('The Sword of Damocles').

Frank is thrilled with his handiwork: Rocky is perfect, a true Charles Atlas specimen (Charles Atlas Song). But as he jubilates at the height of his triumph, Frank and his attendants are brought to a sticky standstill by rumblings from a Coca Cola machine at the side of the room. As they stand unmoving, the machine opens and from it emerges a strangely battered creature, a crepe-soled, drainpiped monster, on whom Columbia's eyes rest with lovelorn longing ('Whatever Happened to Saturday Night'). It is Eddie, the delivery boy whom no one may mention.

In earlier days Frank enticed him up to his laboratory and unsuccessfully used him as a human guinea pig for the manufacture of Rocky. Now, seeing this mangled creature displayed before his beloved new creation, the master of the house blows a fuse. Deliriously battering Eddie to death, he slams the body back into the machine.

Brad and Janet have been obliged to accept Frank's hospitality for the night. They have been lodged in separate rooms but Brad nevertheless finds his way to Janet's room where he indulges in an altogether satisfactory session of sexual gratification to which Janet responds in the most desirable way. Until she finds out it isn't Brad at all...it is Frank! The beast! She'd been saving herself all these years for her husband and now...well, since the deed is done there doesn't seem to be any harm in doing it again.

Down the passage, Brad undergoes the same experience, culminating in the same shock. His 'Janet' turns out to be Frank, but he liked it. And liked it. And liked it. Frank is made to pause in his cavalcade of sexual delights by an intercom announcement. Rocky has escaped from the laboratory and is loose in the building.

Actually, he hasn't wandered far and the only person he has met is Janet who has got lost amongst the passages in her search for Brad. Rocky tells Janet of his fears for the future Frank is dreaming up for him, but she is largely lost in remembrance of the ecstasies she has recently experienced and in her worries for Brad. In her torment, she touches the dials of the laboratory machinery and suddenly, before her eyes, she sees on the video screen what Brad is doing! Far from making her faint, however, this vision seems only to encourage her to go and do likewise ('Touch a Touch Me') and before long she is clambering into Rocky's natal bed with him.

Frank is livid with his servants for losing Rocky. He belabours Riff-Raff petulantly with his microphone cord as the butler whizzes through the screens of the laboratory system, searching for the lost lad. When he is found to be in Janet's close company, Frank faints with fury, and with all the broken-heartedness of a Gene Pitney, Brad sings of a relationship that just died ('Once in a While').

This grieving scene is broken up by the arrival of a visitor from the outside world. It is none other than the wheelchair-bound Dr Scott, Brad and Janet's old tutor, whom Frank knows to have another role in life: he is a government agent for the secret department dealing with Unidentified Flying Objects. Frank engineers things so that everyone is brought together in the laboratory. It is clearly dénouement time.

Dr Scott knows a lot. The Coca Cola machine is made of extra-terrestrial metal and thus it follows that Frank and his friends and their house are aliens from outer space. He is also investigating the disappearance of his nephew, Eddie ('Eddie's Teddy'). This gives Frank his chance to revenge himself on the too-clever Doctor. He has defrosted the Coca Cola machine and he brings out before they eyes of Dr Scott a plastic bag which contains all that remains of the delivery boy. He has declared his colours.

Brad's all-American instinct is to attack this murderous creature where he stands, but Frank has his extra-terrestrial powers to protect him. Beams of light pin Brad, Janet and Dr Scott to the spot as Frank orders Riff-Raff to set the machinery that it seems will transport them to another planet. But no! It is simply another of Frank's sexual implements ('Planet-Schmanet'). Let the artistes be prepared for the inter-galactic floorshow!

The 'Floorshow' is presented in black underwear, suspenders and stockings. Columbia, Rocky, Brad, and Janet contribute to the request to 'Rose Tint My World' as Frank exhorts everyone to live out their fantasies—'don't dream it, be it!'—and even Dr Scott is sucked into the vortex of desire created by the Transylvanian sex monster.

The orgy is cut short when Riff-Raff and Magenta suddenly appear in very different guises to those they have worn through the evening: they are potent aliens with a mission. Their time on earth is over. Frank has become too hedonistic and too outrageous, and they have decided to take over. They are going back to their native planet.

Frank fulsomely sings of his feelings about 'Going Home', but Riff-Raff has no room in his plans for his former master. He raises his ray gun and fires, gunning down both Frank and Columbia who has tried to come between them. When Rocky tries to lift up his creator, he too bites the carpet. As Riff-Raff and Magenta disappear in a flash of fire, the earth people are left alone to count the effect that their brush with the aliens has had on them ('Super Heroes'). Life will never be quite the same again. The 'Science Fiction' double feature is over.

BILLY

a musical in two acts by Ian La Fresnais and Dick Clement adapted from *Billy Liar* by Keith Waterhouse and Willis Hall. Lyrics by Don Black. Music by John Barry. Produced at the Theatre Royal, Drury Lane, London, 1 May 1974 with Michael Crawford (Billy), Gay Soper (Barbara), Elaine Paige (Rita) and Diana Quick (Liz).

CHARACTERS

Billy Fisher
Alice Fisher, *his mother*
Geoffrey Fisher, *his father*
Gran Fisher
Arthur Crabtree
Mister Shadrack
Councillor Duxbury

Barbara
Rita Sugden
Liz Benson
Stamp, Mrs Crabtree, Disc Jockey, Ticket Collector, etc.

ACT 1

Billy Fisher is fast asleep in bed at his home in Stradhoughton, Yorks. when his alarm goes off. It is time to get up and go to work. But Billy doesn't want to go to work. He has a much nicer place to go. It is called 'Ambrosia'. Ambrosia is Billy's own private country where he is everything he ever wanted to be. Today he is President Billy Fisher, descending from the skies by parachute to announce to his people his latest victory in the battle for freedom and democracy, those two all-purpose ideals beloved of the tabloid press. But, at this time of the day, Ambrosia borders on Stradhoughton and Billy's mother's calls to breakfast are insistent enough to push Ambrosia and its admiring populace into the background for the meanwhile. It is time to get up and be part of the real world.

Billy slouches down to breakfast in his pyjamas to be assailed by the early morning grumbles of his mother, his father and his grandmother ('And...'). He tries to cut them out of his consciousness by slipping back into a daydream which makes Eaton Square aristocrats of his family, but reality eventually wins out. This morning, reality has, for once, a tiny touch of the fantastic about it. The post includes a letter for Billy which makes his eyes light up. To his parent's tempered disbelief, he announces that he will be leaving home as he has been offered a job in London as a scriptwriter to a television comedian. There's no reason why the family should believe him. They've been through all this before and they've suffered all sorts of humiliations as a result of the fantastic stories Billy has spread around the town over the years, both about himself and about them.

Billy is away on a cloud: he has always known he was destined for great things and now he's on his way ('Some of Us Belong to the Stars') but, until the big day comes, he has to carry on as before and that means he has to get to work. He is employed at the undertaking house of Shadrack and Duxbury where his career has not been particularly notable. In fact, it is a wonder that Billy hasn't been sacked, for he has regularly plundered the stamp book and last year he pocketed the money meant for distributing the firm's Christmas calendars which are stuffed in their hundreds into a locked cupboard in his bedroom. His facility for convincing lying has done him proud.

At the cemetery where Billy and his workmates are tidying up after the day's funeral, Billy's fiancée, Barbara, comes to find him. Barbara is a sturdy, teenage, small-town virgin whom the boys have christened 'the Witch' and her engagement to Billy is a rather problematic thing. It owes its being to a cosy moment in a private place when Billy thought that the prospect of a sometime marriage might have weakened the prudish Barbara's ideas about 'having relations'. It is even more problematic in that Billy is also 'engaged' to the tarty Rita Sugden who works in the filling station. Only Barbara doesn't know that.

Rita Sugden is a very different half pint of bitter to tight little Barbara. She is loud, lax and determined and she's after Billy. She's even managed to get an engagement ring out of him. But Billy has taken it back to have it altered and he hasn't returned it. The reason he hasn't returned it is that the ring which Rita loudly considers to be hers is currently gracing the finger of the Witch, who is equally convinced that it is meant for her and her alone. What a mess. Still, all the mess won't matter soon, because Billy will be on his way to London and they can all suit themselves: Barbara, Rita, his family and Duxbury and Shadrack with their their naffing postbook and their naffing calendars.

Saturday, down at the local shopping centre, Billy and his mate Arthur watch the locals going about their business ('Happy to Be Themselves'). Billy escapes a confrontation with rampaging Rita but realises that he is going to have to do something about getting the wretched ring back from Barbara. He keeps an assignation with her in the cemetery and, as he looks at her sitting there virginally sucking one of her eternal oranges, he is overtaken with frustrated loathing for 'The Witch'.

Barbara has been window-shopping for wallpaper for the little cottage they have planned in the most chocolate-box part of Devon, but Billy isn't interested in dreaming today; he just wants to get that ring off her finger and, with any luck, her drawers round her ankles. Unfortunately for him Barbara hasn't any imagination and his tricks all go wrong. Finally, in desperation, he tries to get her to throw the ring back at him by telling her all about his 'Lies', but Barbara is moved that he should unveil his secret to her and forgives him. Billy decides to have another try that evening and arranges to meet Barbara at the Roxy dance hall at eight.

When Billy gets home he gets more stick from his father, more aches and pains from his Gran, more worries from his mother and, worst of all, a visit from Rita demanding her rotten ring back. When Billy has finished fencing off her importuning he finds that he is dated to meet her at the dance that evening with the ring. Eight o'clock at the Roxy.

In the meanwhile, Billy has decided that it's time to get rid of some more of the incriminating calendars. He squashes them into an old suitcase and heads for the canal. But who should he run into just at the wrong minute but old Councillor Duxbury, the senior partner of his firm. A proud old fellow, Duxbury may stand on his dignity in a way that makes the youngsters snigger, but he's heart of Yorkshire oak through and through and he remembers better days in Stradhoughton ('It Were All Green Hills').

Billy is taken aback to find that the old man knows all about the calendars and he doesn't seem too angry about the money. He is just sad about the loss of the goodwill the Christmas gift engenders and puzzled that Billy should have fallen to such a misdemeanour. His advice is kindly, 'come down to earth, lad', and Billy has the grace to feel ashamed of himself. It's not a feeling that will last for long, though. A few minutes later the football crowd comes pouring out of the stadium and Billy is away again, imagining himself as the hero of the match ('Aren't You Billy Fisher?'). He is drawn out of his dream by the arrival of an old friend. Liz Benson is back in town. Liz, the only real girl allowed into Ambrosia where she staunchly marches by his side to share his victories... Great!

ACT 2

Liz understands Billy all the way down to the bottom ('Is This Where I Wake Up?'). No use pulling any of the stories that the rest of the town fall for on Liz. She is the only one to whom he actually shows the letter from London. It isn't exactly the offer of a job. In fact, it isn't an offer of a job at all. It just says that the material Billy submitted was all right and that the comedian might be able to use some of his gags from time to time. Still, if that'll get him out of Stradhoughton then, by Liz's way of thinking, it'll do. For she's sure that the one thing Billy needs to do is stop dreaming and start doing, and there isn't any way he is going to do that in his home town. Right now he's taking the first step in the right direction by destroying his guilty past: the calendars and all the other miscellania of his old foolishness go into the town wastebins.

As Billy goes off to write his letter of resignation from the firm of Shadrack and Duxbury, Liz muses over the 'Billy' she knows, a Billy quite unlike the one that Rita and Barbara think they know. Billy doesn't quite finish his letter, but he doesn't get a chance to backslide because Shadrack walks in and picks the half-written letter up. Resign? Not a chance. Not until the small matter of the missing post money and the calendars gets cleared up. Billy dreams of machine-gunning his employer to death, but neither that nor any other fantasy will fit the situation well enough to lift Billy's gloom.

At home, Gran has had one of her turns and the Fishers are 'Remembering', but Billy is off to the Roxy where he is to meet up with Liz. It's going to be difficult because outside the dance hall are waiting both Barbara and Rita ('Any Minute Now'), each harbouring very different thoughts on the man they are waiting for. Billy smuggles himself past them into the hall to find Liz and has to admit to her that he has had problems resigning from his job. But Liz won't let him be evasive: it is very simple, all he has to do is go. You just get on a southbound train and three hours later you're in London.

She has scarcely made her point when Billy suddenly finds himself in the limelight. Arthur has wangled it for him to sing one of his own songs with the band. Just the night when Billy wanted to hide quietly in a corner away from Barbara and Rita, he has been pushed into the forefront. But it's too late now. Up he gets and, in front of the band, he is soon away on his favourite cloud giving his impersonation of Billy Fisher famous rock star ('The Lady From LA') to a screaming audience light years away from the Stradhoughton Roxy. When the applause is over it is time to come down to earth and to face Rita and Barbara. Rita is livid at seeing her ring on Barbara's finger, Barbara is mortified at the fact that Billy may have been unfaithful to her and horrified when it dawns on her that he may have been 'having relations' with Rita, and the two girls come to blows. Billy tries to sneak away, but suddenly everyone turns their attention and scorn on to him: he needs to grow up and behave like a man, he's nothing but a stupid little liar—Billy Liar! Only Liz sticks to him and, finally, drags him away from the jeering crowd.

Down at the local playground, Billy pours out his heart to Liz. Surely he isn't the only one who questions what Stradhoughton is and what its people are. Surely he isn't the only one who dreams of something else, something better, something more interesting than Stradhoughton. That's why he has Ambrosia. Liz understands. She, too, has her Ambrosia. But she's practical as well. That's why she doesn't stay in Stradhoughton, she comes and goes. He must do the same. There is a train for London at 12.40. They can be on it. Billy can go and pack now and meet her at the station ('I Missed the Last Rainbow').

When Billy gets home he finds Duxbury at the door and his immediate reaction is that the old man has told his parents about the calendars, but Duxbury's visit is professional: Billy's Gran has passed away. Billy talks his way past his stolidly grieving parents to his room. He's leaving. He's going to make his dreams come true ('Some of Us Belong to the Stars'), so he has to leave even while his Gran is lying dead in the living room.

By the time he gets to the station a bit of the bravado has gone out of him. He gets his ticket and joins Liz but, at the last minute, his nerve deserts him. He makes an excuse to leave her side and when the train comes along he has not returned. The resigned Liz sees him coming back just as the train pulls out. It isn't going to happen. Billy will stay in Stradhoughton for the rest of his life. Or, rather, he will stay in 'Ambrosia' where everything happens just as he wants it to.

The song 'That Wouldn't Be You' was cut in favour of 'Is This Where I Wake Up?'; its lyric subsequently appearing in a revised form with music by Jule Styne in the 1978 musical *Bar Mitzvah Boy*.

HANS ANDERSEN

a musical in two acts by Tommy Steele and Beverley Cross. Lyrics and music taken from the film score and other works by Frank Loesser. Additional songs by Marvin Laird. Produced at the London Palladium 17 December 1974 with Tommy Steele (Hans), Colette Gleeson (Jenny), Milo O'Shea (Otto), Bob Todd (Meisling) and Lila Kaye (Madame Meisling). Revived there 17 December 1977 with Steele, Sally Ann Howes, Anthony Valentine, Todd and Miss Kaye.

CHARACTERS

Hans Christian Andersen
Rector Meisling, *a schoolmaster*
Madame Louise Meisling, *his wife*
Otto Pedersen, *a musician*

Jenny Lind
Max Klaus, *her manager*
Colonel Guldberg, *governor of Odense*
Jonas, *a midshipman*
King Christian of Denmark, the Queen, etc.

ACT 1

In the town of Odense, Denmark, in the 1830s there lived a simple shoemaker by the name of Hans Christian Andersen. A happy fellow, he was made little of by the adults of his neighbourhood, but he was very popular with the children who would gather at the smallest opportunity to be entertained by the whimsical stories of wonderful and magical people and places drawn from the cobbler's imagination ('Thumbelina'). Often they dallied too long listening to him, making them late for school and provoking the wrath of the bibulous schoolmaster Meisling and his unpleasant wife. When the Meislings discover that Hans has ambitions as a writer for the theatre they are openly scornful and mock his attempt to compose a tragedy, *The Robbers of Wissenberg*, and his admiration for Walter Scott and Shakespeare. A writer? Why, he can barely spell.

One day, after a particularly vehement morning-after attack by the Rector, the lonely Hans is telling his woes to a frog when his ever-active imagination takes flight. He will say a magic word and the frog will become a prince. A wave and a word, and what do you know? There is someone there! Otto Sebastian Pedersen at your service, with a shoe which needs mending. Pedersen tells Hans that he is a musician, on his way to the Opera House to pick up a bit of work as a rehearsal pianist for the famous singer Jenny Lind. Although he is a would-be dramatist, Hans has never seen the inside of a theatre and it takes only a little encouragement from Otto ('You've Got to Dare to Take a Chance') for him to set off with his new found friend in the direction of the theatre, *The Robbers of Wissenberg* under his arm.

At the theatre, Colonel Guldberg, the governor of Odense, and Miss Lind's manager, Max Klaus, are organising the rehearsal. The famous soprano enters and sings the song 'Truly Loved' and Hans is struck with heartfelt admiration. When Otto pushes him forward and introduces him as a writer, Hans blushingly blurts out that *The Robbers of Wissenberg* will no longer be a play but an opera dedicated to Miss Lind. To the annoyance of Klaus, Miss Lind insists on taking the boy's manuscript to read and, as she departs Hans bursts joyfully into a reprise of 'You've Got to Dare to Take a Chance'.

When he comes later to collect his play, he is in for disappointment. Klaus dismisses it as a mixture of plagiarism and incompetence, but Jenny Lind has kinder words: Hans clearly has imagination, what he does not have is writing technique. If he really wishes to be a writer, he must go back to school. Hans is aghast but, if Jenny says that is what he must do, he will do it. Jenny kisses him kindly on the cheek and leaves the stunned boy to wonder 'Jenny Kissed Me'.

227

Going back to school means studying under the Meislings and that is not very pleasant for Hans, even though he has been placed in the school by the direct order of the Governor himself. He works hard but, as in his shoemaking days, he takes time off to entertain his little classmates with his stories ('Inchworm'). One night he is telling an after-bedtime tale to the children, the sad tale of the little tin soldier, which brings even Madame Meisling into the charmed circle of imagination round the late night candle. A frightful turn in the story sets the children squealing and sends the schoolmaster's wife rocketing into Hans' arms for protection. At that very moment Meisling appears. He goes wild with fury. The wretched boy is seducing his wife! He shall be tied in a sack and thrown in the bog.

The neighbours hurry to the scene as the protesting Hans is hoist in a sack and poised for his undeserved punishment. Then, from nowhere, Otto appears. He has come to take Hans away with him for his education is complete. Nonsense, the Rector sputters, he cannot spell any better than he could before. But when Hans tries the hardest words that Meisling can muster, he finds that he can spell after all ('Ecclesiasticus'). Is it magic or just the fruits of hard work? To the cheers of the townsfolk, he sets off for fame and fortune with Otto at his side.

On the road to the sea, the travelling companions meet with a young midshipman going to join his ship at Copenhagen. His questions set Hans off into memories of the beautiful Jenny Lind ('Anywhere I Wander') until it is time to take the ship across the waves to the harbour of 'Wonderful Copenhagen'.

ACT 2

In the Street of the Publishers, Hans tries to interest people in his work (I'm Hans Christian Andersen') but without luck. When, finally, hunger begins to bite a little deep, Otto comes up with the answer. He throws a brick through the window of one of the publishing houses and the pair of them end up with free board and lodging in the local prison. A disconsolate Hans feels that perhaps he ought to give up the idea of writing and go back to Odense and his shoemaking, but Otto encourages him to use his imagination and they conjure up a prison feast and a whole lot of 'Happy Days' behind bars.

Then, by chance, they hear that Jenny Lind has arrived back in Copenhagen after an American tour and has been asking publicly as to the whereabouts of the young man. Hans is released and invited by the singer to join the guests at a reception in her honour at the home of Max Klaus. There she sings for the guests ('Have I Been Away Too Long') and parries Klaus's rude remarks to Hans with some kind attentions. What has he been doing? Hans brings out his latest work—a mammoth, five-act piece full of vast scenery and improbable effects. The other guests laugh openly at his foolishness and Hans is left standing miserably alone as the company go in to supper.

Two little serving girls with trays approach to giggle at him and Hans, instantly more at home with these children, sings to them his story of 'The

Ugly Duckling'. As he tells his tale, Jenny enters unseen and she is enchanted by what she hears. When he is finished she asks enthusiastically if he has any more tales like that. Why, he has dozens of them, invented to amuse the children of Odense. These, she tells him, are what he must write. If he will put them on paper, she will personally take them to a publisher. Hans' mind begins to turn as he starts to write and on the stage the characters from his stories, written and unwritten, dance around him, weaving themselves into the pages of his book.

The tales of Hans Andersen are published and are a triumphant success. In the Tivoli Gardens, the successful author and his patroness meet. His books are popular in countless countries, he has invitations from all over the world to lecture and, that very day, a command has come for him to appear at the Castle of Kronberg before the King of Denmark. It is all thanks to her. Klaus enters to take Jenny back to the theatre and the mutual antagonism between the two men bristles until Jenny calms them. Hans speaks obliquely to her of love, but does not realise that her answers, which he takes for himself, mean that she is in love with Max. Together, Hans and Jenny sing and dance 'No Two People (Have Ever Been so in Love)'. For him it is real, but for her the song is about someone else. When he finally understands, Hans is hurt and bitter with the hurt of a disappointed child.

Otto arrives on the scene to find that Hans is all for leaving straight away for Egypt, but his friend counsels that he would be wiser to remember the King's command performance. A new story will be expected to mark the occasion. Hans nods, he has an idea. Leaving Otto playing with a little tune ('Tune for Humming'), he goes on his way as the autumn landscape turns into the decorated hall of the Winter Ball at the Castle of Kronberg.

There are the Meislings and Colonel Guldberg, all gushingly remembering how kind and helpful they were to the young author in his early days, there is Jenny Lind, and there is Hans ready to present to the Royal audience his new story, 'The King's New Clothes'. As the story ends, the dancer portraying the king, tricked by his vanity into believing himself gorgeously clad, steps forward naked. The audience wait aghast to see what the King's reaction to this lèse majesté will be. Then, with a deep belly laugh, the King laughs. Andersen is congratulated and decorated by his monarch. He has won the final accolade.

The royal family take their leave and Jenny comes to say her farewells to Hans, leaving him with a little locket and chain to remember her by. He does not need her support any more; the ugly duckling has become a fine swan. Otto, too, is on his way. He has fulfilled his part in Hans' life and he was only passing through in the first place. Hans remembers that he never did find that frog. But perhaps that's just his imagination working too easily again. He is successful and he is on his own. Ah well, you can't have everything and, after all, he is a storyteller and he can always imagine the happy ending he would wish himself.

The 1974 production introduced an opening chorus,'This Town', as well as the songs 'For Hans Tonight', 'Ecclesiasticus' and 'Don't Talk to Me About

Those Happy Days' written and composed by Laird. The 1977 version omitted the opening chorus, replaced 'For Hans Tonight' with a further Laird number 'Dare to Take a Chance' and added Frank Loesser's 'Have I Stayed Away Too Long' which had been cut from the 1974 production in rehearsal. Of the songs which did not appear in the film score of *Hans Christian Andersen*, 'Truly Loved' was taken from Loesser's *Pleasures and Palaces* (1965), 'A Tune For Humming' and 'Jenny Kissed Me' (adapted from 'Don't Introduce Me to That Angel') were numbers cut from *Where's Charley*, and 'Have I Stayed Away Too Long' came from the late composer's trunk.

EVITA

a musical in two acts by Tim Rice. Music by Andrew Lloyd Webber. Produced at the Prince Edward Theatre, London, 21 June 1978 with Elaine Paige (Eva), David Essex (Che), Joss Ackland (Peron), Mark Ryan (Magaldi) and Siobhan McCarthy (Mistress).

Produced at the Broadway Theatre, New York, 25 September 1979 with Patti Lu Pone, Mandy Patinkin, Bob Gunson, Mark Syers and Jane Ohringer.

Produced at the Theater an der Wien, Vienna, 20 January, 1981 with Isabel Weicken, Alexander Goebel, Reinhard Glemnitz, Michael Bukowsky and Lilo Raab.

Played at the Theater des Westens, Berlin, 10 September 1982.

CHARACTERS

Eva Peron
Juan Peron
Che
Peron's mistress
Magaldi, *a tango singer*, etc.

ACT 1

It is 26 July 1952. In a cinema in Buenos Aires, Argentina, a B-movie crawls groaningly to a halt and an announcement over the sound system informs the watching public that 'Eva Peron, spiritual leader of the nation, entered immortality at 20.25 hours today'. In silence, the audience leaves.

As the crowds gather for Eva's funeral, we are introduced to a man whom we will know as Che: a man who represents a combination of every feeling ever held against Eva Peron the politician and Eva Peron the woman. He mocks the funeral procession ('O What a Circus!'), jeering at its waste of pomp and feeling on behalf of a woman who was nothing but an actress, an actress who made the people believe her to be their Santa Evita when all the time she did nothing for them. He mocks, too, the poor people of Argentina who almost believed their Eva to be immortal and who, now that she is gone,

230

are without guidance. Then he leads us back to the beginning of the life story of Eva Maria Duarte, later Peron and the Evita of millions.

It begins in a small Argentine town. Eva is fifteen when she meets a man whom Che glorifies with the title of 'the first man to be of use to Eva Duarte'. He is Agustin Magaldi, a tango singer ('On This Night of a Thousand Stars') from Buenos Aires. Eva has compliantly brightened up his provincial engagement and now she exacts her price: she wants to go back to the city with him. He warns her of the dangers of city life ('Eva, Beware of the City') but she is not daunted: the glamour of the city is what she wants, and she gets her way. Soon she arrives excitedly in 'Buenos Aires'.

It is not long before she disentangles herself from Magaldi. He has served his purpose and she is moving on ('Goodnight and Thank You'). Her moves onwards are inevitably upwards as she begins to make a small career as an actress, largely on the radio, but her big move is yet to come. Argentinian politics are in a parlous state. The time is ripe for change, and one of the foremost figures at the centre of these changes is the increasingly powerful Juan Peron ('The Art of the Possible'). At a charity concert where Magaldi is performing and Peron speaking, Eva introduces herself with intent to the military man turned politician. He is attracted, she is determined ('I'd Be Surprisingly Good for You') and they leave together.

Eva removes Peron's sixteen year-old mistress from his bed with practised ease ('Another Suitcase in Another Hall'), and installs herself in the girl's place. She is a strong and potentially powerful woman and a positive force in Peron's life and, as such, she is welcomed by neither Peron's army associates nor by the upper classes of Argentina ('Peron's Latest Flame'). Peron's position amongst the uncentred ruling military oligarchy is a key one, one which has allowed him to build up a following among the working classes, but one which has, equally, brought him many opponents ('Dice Are Rolling'). Eva pushes and persuades him towards taking supreme power with the support of the people to create 'A New Argentina'.

ACT 2

By the time of the 1946 election, Eva Duarte has become Eva Peron and Evita to the admiring and loving people to whom she has tirelessly carried her husband's candidature. His victory and appointment as President of Argentina are announced 'On the Balcony of the Casa Rosada'. When he has spoken to the assembled crowds, Eva addresses them in her turn, emphasising with consumate skill the Perons' position as the people's choice, taken from among the people themselves, and yet setting them up as unapproachable deities ('Don't Cry for Me, Argentina'). To an officer who reminds her that statesmanship is more than entertaining peasants, she replies, 'We shall see, little man,' before returning to the balcony to regale her people with promises of despoiling the aristocracy to give them all they could desire.

Soon, at the age of twenty-six, she is an important part of Argentina, a figurehead and a saint, 'High Flying, Adored'. She does not intend to stop there: she intends to take herself and Argentina to the world ('Rainbow High'). Equipped in style, Eva sets off for Europe ('Rainbow Tour'). Spain greets her with unbelievable enthusiasm, but from there on it is downhill. Even a beautiful woman cannot interest major nations in a government they consider either unimportant or unpleasant. The biggest snub comes from Britain and Eva returns to Argentina in anger rather than triumph to take revenge on the British-centred aristocracy of Argentina ('The Actress Hasn't Learned the Lines You'd Like to Hear') under the pretence of encouraging democracy.

One part of this revenge is the creation of the Eva Peron Foundation, a charity to eclipse all other charities and their aristocratic patrons. By dint of persuasion, not necessarily gentle, the Foundation grows to enormous proportions ('And the Money Kept Rolling In') as Eva continues her work and her tireless quest for both personal success and the sort of cockeyed democracy she apparently believes in ('Santa Evita').

Che faces up to Eva (Waltz for Eva and Che) to belittle both her work and her image. She replies, with what seems to be an attempt at honesty, that it is better to attempt to do something positive towards curing the world's ills than simply to stand aside and mock. But even in centuries she could not accomplish what she would want to, and she does not have centuries. She has very little time indeed, for she is a dying woman. Peron is not unaware that his wife is his greatest attribute ('She's a Diamond'), and that he will be in trouble without her.

Once again 'Dice Are Rolling' and the political situation is on the move, but Eva is not yet ready to give up. She insists on becoming Vice-President, on having official political recognition, but Peron cannot make this happen. It would be far too dangerous politically and, besides, she could not physically manage it for she is desperately ill. But still she fights (Eva's Sonnet).

It is her last fight, however, and, as the jeering Che is only to happy to remind her, this time she has lost. The dying woman takes to the radio waves to turn down the offer of Vice-Presidency which was never made (Eva's Last Broadcast) as, once again, she rolls out the loving phrases of her Casa Rosada speech: 'Don't Cry for Me, Argentina'. Thus Evita Peron dies, as fragments from the story of her life crowd around her (Montage). Her final words (Lament) express no regrets. She could have lived with less speed and less intensity and she might then have lived longer, but she chose otherwise. She hopes that those who follow her will understand what she did. For Eva Duarte longed to be remembered.

CATS

a musical based on *Old Possum's Book of Practical Cats* by T S Eliot. Music by Andrew Lloyd Webber. Produced at the New London Theatre, London, 11 May 1981 with Elaine Paige (Grizabella), Paul Nicholas (Rum Tum Tugger), Stephen Tate

(Asparagus), Wayne Sleep (Mr Mistoffolees), Brian Blessed (Deuteronomy), Kenn Wells (Skimbleshanks), Susan Jane Tanner (Griddlebone), Bonnie Langford (Rumpleteazer), John Thornton (Mungojerrie) and Jeff Shankley (Munkustrap).

Produced at the Winter Garden Theatre, New York, 7 October 1982 with Betty Buckley, Terence V Mann, Stephen Hanan, Timothy Scott, Ken Page, Reed Jones, Bonnie Simmons, Christine Langner, Rene Clemente and Harry Groener.

Produced at the Theater an der Wien, Vienna, 24 September 1983 in a version by Michael Kunze with Angelika Milster, Michael Howe, Joachim Kemmer, Gordon Bovinet, F Dion Davis, Valda Aviks, Buenaventura Braunstein and Steve Barton.

Produced at the Operettenhaus, Hamburg, 18 April 1986 in a version by John Baer, Sabine Grohmann and Marc Henning with Andrea Bögel, Fred Butter, Stephan Drakulich, Paul Porter, Walter Reynolds, Paul Keller, Nancy Nordine, Janette Froud, Stephen Kadel and Hartwig Rudolz.

CHARACTERS

Asparagus/Growltiger
Bombalurina
Bustopher Jones
Demeter
Deuteronomy
Grizabella
Jellylorum
Griddlebone
Jennyanydots
Jemima
Macavity
Munkustrap
Mungojerrie
Mr Mistoffolees
Rumpleteazer
Rumpus Cat
Rum Tum Tugger
Skimbleshanks
Victoria
Admetus, Alonzo, Carbucketty, Cassandra, Coricopat, George, Tantomile, Victor, Etcetera, Bill Bailey, Tumblebrutus, Silabub, Pouncival, Plato, Quaxo, etc.

ACT 1

The playing area represents a gigantesque rubbish heap, here a super-sized tin can, there a piece of Brobdignagian newspaper, a Titan's tyre or the hood of an abandoned automobile made for someone much bigger than you or I. It looks just like an ordinary if oversized trash tip when the light of day is on it, but no sooner does darkness descend than this piece of ground comes alive. As the lights go down and the music begins, the twinkling eyes of numberless creatures can be seen peeping from all sides and, around the rubbish dump, around your feet, rustle dark, slinking creatures with glittering eyes, moving lightly and quickly, to the accompaniment of strange yowling sounds.

Then they freeze as a noise is heard and the roaring headlights of a passing car send the animals fleeing back to the hiding places of the rubbish heap.

They are cats, these quiet, eagerly shining beasts who haunt the open spaces and the rubbish heaps of the world. Cats of all shapes, all sizes and kinds, but every one a Jellicle (Prologue: 'Jellicle Songs for Jellicle Cats'), members of that mysterious fraternity that can see in the dark, of that celebrated family that accompanied Dick Whittington, the Pied Piper and every witch that ever rode a broomstick, of that feline family that always falls on its feet. There are inconveniences of course. When the brotherhood sings too loudly, someone is liable to throw an old boot at them, but it isn't long before they are back at their singing and dancing.

But wait a minute! Did we hear someone say that they don't know what a Jellicle Cat is? Well, perhaps a little explanation is due about a very private and personal (perhaps one should say cat-onal) subject—'The Naming of Cats'. You might call your cat by a perfectly ordinary name but, underneath, every cat has another, special name; a name that is his and only his, and that name—which a human can never discover—is what makes him himself. So when you see a cat sitting, gazing into space, don't think he's mindlessly wasting his nine lives. He's actually reflecting on his name.

On the empty piece of ground amidst the rubbish, one little white kitten (Victoria) stretches herself into some pretty, balletic poses, until the announcement comes: tonight is the Jellicle Ball and every Jellicle cat is invited. There the Jellicle leader will lead the ball and make the annual Jellicle choice. One selected cat will be allowed to ascend to the Heaviside layer, there to be given the chance to live another life, for better or for worse. Which will it be? Which of the many cats whom we will now meet will be chosen for this rebirth?

The first personality—oh dear, cat-onality—we meet is 'The Old Gumbie Cat'. From under the rusting car bonnet emerges a plump little bundle of tabby-striped-spotted fur, spread into jolly rolls of wrinkles by too many days lazing in the sun or the firelight. Jennyanydots, for that is her real name, is not as lazy as it may seem. At night, when everyone is asleep, she gives self-improvement courses to the mice and cockroaches, and dances a mean tap-dance at the head of her forces. Then, because a little black and white pussy called Quaxo needs to show off his versatility, she abandons the jolly cock-roaches and indulges in a tap competition with him before waving us goodbye.

Our next visitor is 'The Rum Tum Tugger', a swaggering, pop-pussy who bursts through the back-cloth to set all the kittens off into ecstasies of squealing with his sexy prowl and Presley-ish cadenzas. He is a contrary cat, a fellow who always wants what he hasn't got, a fellow who doesn't even like a cuddle. What sort of a cat is that? Curious, but ooooh, what a cat.

The cavalcade of jolly cats halts as a stranger breaks through the party. It is 'Grizabella, the Glamour Cat'. Once a beauty, her alley cat life has brought her down until she is nothing but a torn and stained outcast from whom the kittens shrink in dismay. She passes by, for she cannot stop in such an unfriendly place. But all places are equally unfriendly to Grizabella.

234

'Bustopher Jones' is much more the sort of cat we like. He is the cat of London's clubland; a sleek, overfed fellow with a bright white bib and shiny spats glistening on his smooth black coat; quite the gentleman, with his well-oiled whiskers and a carnation sprouting from his button-hole. He is a total contrast to 'Mungojerrie and Rumpleteazer' whose arrival is appropriately heralded by the siren of a police car. This bouncing duo are a couple of sneak-thieves—'knockabout clowns, quick-change comedians, tight-rope walkers and acrobats'—the sort of cats who get into anything, anywhere, no matter how well you think you've locked up. Here is a real team of rascally cat burglars.

Now it is time to welcome the grand master of the cat lodge, the vast, placid, impressive 'Old Deuteronomy' who takes his ponderous place at the centre of affairs as the entertainment continues. This time we have a little story: Munkustrap's relating of 'The Awefull Battle of the Pekes and the Pollicles', a fight amongst dogs which was settled (and its combatants set to flight) by the intervention of the great Rumpus Cat. As the story unfolds, the pekes with their little sack-like faces challenge the pollicles with their box-like feet, and the slipper-headed pugs and the curly-wigged poms join in to make it a regular dog fight until, shooting forth from what seems to be the depths of the earth, comes the black, flailing figure of the frightful, red-eyed Rumpus Cat to end both the fight and the tale.

When the story is done the rumour goes nervously around that Macavity is nearby, but nothing happens and the fearful cats emerge from their hiding places to join in 'The Song of the Jellicles' and a whispering, multi-coloured set of dances which is 'The Jellicle Ball'. As the cats disport themselves, Grizabella watches painfully from a distance until she is chased off, leaving the other cats to dance the night away under the autumn colours of the moon while she has only a 'Memory' of happiness left to her.

ACT 2
The cats' evening continues as Deuteronomy muses on 'The Moments of Happiness' and an old cat is led by a kindly helpmate to watch the festivities. This is Asparagus, otherwise known as Gus, and he is—or, rather, was—a theatre cat ('Gus, the Theatre Cat'). It is a career which has left him with a wealth of memories which he is only too pleased to recount to the younger generation. The great days of the theatre are gone, there is nothing now like the theatrical world under Irving and Tree, the world of which he was a part, where he trod the boards and had the distinction of understudying Dick Whittington's cat and, best of all, of once appearing as Growltiger.

The story of 'Growltiger's Last Stand', the heroic but desperate history of the piratical cat done to death by the beastly Siamese, is a dramatic one. The valiant Growltiger and his paramour, the Lady Griddlebone, were indulging in a private paroxysm of Italianate romance when the cowardly Easterners crept up on them. Alas, they did what no Englishman would do and attacked a man while he was making love. They took the lordly Growltiger prisoner and forced him to walk the plank and, though his demise made a sad if salutory story, it made a wonderful, theatrical role. Not like the namby pamby parts cats get today.

Our next illustration is 'Skimbleshanks, the Railway Cat', with a bundle of friends all happily singing the story of his happy life on the railways of Britain as they drag items from the rubbish heap to build an imitation train, but their rollicking is ended by another strange, crashing noise and a hollow laugh. This time, surely, it is the dreaded Macavity. There he is! No...no...he's there! Over on the other side!

As the cats scatter, Demeter and Bombalurina hold their ground warily to sing about 'Macavity, the Mystery Cat'. He's surely to blame for many a cat crime, but you'll never catch him at it. Whenever the price of crime is to be paid, Macavity's not there. And, surely enough, he isn't. Just when you think you saw him scuttle off in one direction...there he is, laughing at you from the other side. And when you think you know that that bundle of elderly fur is Old Deuteronomy, you really shouldn't be surprised to see the fur coat pulled aside to reveal Macavity.

But if that is not Deuteronomy, where is he? There is one way to find out, you must ask the magical 'Mister Mistoffolees'. Here he comes, flying in from above, his black coat glittering with lights and flashpots at his fingertips, producing ribbons from an empty tin, flipping spots off a scarf and throwing off fouettés as if he'd come from the Royal Ballet with the sole intention of displaying his repertoire of steps in one comprehensive dance spot. When he is done, he flings a red scarf over a kitten and, whipping it away, produces his magic. There stands Old Deuteronomy.

Now daylight is coming. It is time for the Jellicle Ball to end and for Deuteronomy to announce the name of the cat chosen to have a second chance, another set of lives. Grizabella walks on, full of 'Memory' which she needs to let out. She pours out her sad heart and, having done so, she prepares to carry on, to leave this unsympathetic world. But the little white kitten stops her. Slowly she brings the sad, tattered cat back and, as she leads Grizabella towards Deuteronomy, some of the other cats join her. For Grizabella is the cat who has been chosen. She will have another opportunity.

Deuteronomy takes her by the hand and leads her to an old tyre and, as they step together onto the punctured pneumatic, it begins to rise into the air. As they float above the ground, the sky opens, a staircase descends and Grizabella steps on to it in a swirl of mist. Up, up she climbs and then she is gone. The tyre returns to its place and Deuteronomy rounds off the proceedings with a little lecture on 'The Addressing of Cats' as all the characters whom we have met during the evening crowd around to sing us farewell.

The original score of *Cats* included 'The Ballad of Billy McCaw' sung by Growltiger and Griddlebone in the fantasy pirate scene. This was replaced by an Italianate aria for the American production and the alteration was subsequently incorporated into the original production.

BLOOD BROTHERS

a musical in two acts by Willy Russell. Produced at the Liverpool Playhouse 8 January 1983 and at the Lyric Theatre, London, 11 April 1983 with Barbara Dickson (Mrs Johnstone), George Costigan (Mickey), Andrew C Wadsworth (Eddie), Amanda York (replaced by Kate Fitzgerald) (Linda) and Wendy Murray (Mrs Lyons).

Produced at the Downtown Cabaret Theatre, Bridgeport, Connecticut 22 January, 1988 with Maureen Moore, Roger Bart, Timothy Syverson, Corliss Preston and Joanne Bogert.

Produced at Munich in a revised version.

CHARACTERS

Mrs Johnstone
Mickey
Eddie
Sammy
Linda
Mr Lyons
Mrs Lyons
Narrator
Policeman, Finance Man, Catalogue Man, etc.

ACT 1

A narrator introduces us to the Liverpudlian saga of the Johnstone twins, the blood brothers of the show's title, the history of their lives and the tale of their sad and bloody end.

The story begins with Mrs Johnstone, a wan and overused woman of thirty who, by her appearance, could easily be fifty. She had a husband who wooed her ('Marilyn Monroe') and wed her when she got pregnant, kept her pregnant through seven children in as many years and then walked out on her for a fresher partner, leaving her with an eighth child on the way and no money to pay the milkman. In her hopeless quest for the television-advertisement life that her children think is their God-given right, she wears herself thinner and ever thinner and she is grateful to be given a job as a daily in the home of the comfortably-off Lyons family.

Mrs Lyons is alone in her big house. Her husband's work keeps him away for long periods and he has just gone overseas for nine months. She feels her solitude and feels it the more in that she is bitterly and sadly childless. Mrs Johnstone's unwanted but easy preganancy stands before her as a reminder of her failure in the same way that the Lyons' prosperity represents a hopeless Nirvana to Mrs Johnstone. But the lives and hopes of the two women are to be fatefully entwined and there is to be little luck or joy for them in it. When Mrs Lyons puts a new pair of shoes on the table, Mrs Johnstone is superstitiously shocked at the challenge to fortune, and fortune takes up the challenge.

Mrs Johnstone soon finds that she is expecting not one child but two. With

237

her new job she could perhaps manage one extra mouth, but two? Mrs Lyons is eagerly and quickly ready with a suggestion: she will take the other child. She will fake pregnancy in her husband's absence and 'give birth' just before his return. In spite of everything, Mrs Johnstone is not sure that she wants to give her child away, but under her employer's urgings and the threat of her other children being taken into care if she cannot support them, she finally agrees. At least the child will have all the advantages that the world can give him ('My Child'). The over-wrought and excited Mrs Lyons is caught up immediately in plans, and jealously she makes Mrs Johnstone swear on the bible that she will carry out their agreement and never let anyone know the truth.

The children are born, two sons, and Mrs Johnstone is reluctant to give up either. But times are very hard. Lured by weakness into hire purchase agreements which she can no longer keep up, she sees her furniture repossessed. Nothing can be yours if you cannot pay for it. She must give up her furniture and she must also give up her child ('Easy Terms'). When Mrs Lyons comes to claim her due, she turns her head whilst one of the twins is chosen and taken away.

Mr Lyons returns home to find himself a father, but Mrs Lyons is, if anything, more neurotically troubled than ever. She finds it impossible to endure Mrs Johnstone near the child, or even in the house, and finally, giving her money, tells her that she will have to leave the job. When Mrs Johnstone threatens to take her child with her, Mrs Lyons returns threat for threat. She has taken money, she has sold her child, the police will come for her and the children will suffer the fabled fate of twins secretly parted. If they should ever learn that they are brothers, they will die. If Mrs Johnstone reveals the truth, she will as good as kill her children. The evil set in motion by the 'Shoes Upon the Table' is under way.

Mrs Johnstone's Mickey and Mrs Lyons' Edward grow up apart. Both mothers have forbidden their uncomprehending children to go anywhere near the home of the other but, when they are seven, the boys meet in the street. The opportunistic Mickey is pleased to find a pal who has sweets to give away and the carefully trained Eddie is thrilled to make friends with someone as uninhibited as Mickey. They prick their fingers with Mickey's penknife and swear to be blood brothers. When Mrs Johnstone finds them together, they are stunned by the vehemence with which she forces them apart. Mrs Lyons, too, furiously forbids the friendship and leaves her son wondering the why and wherefore of the situation.

The Johnstone kids and their friends play at battles ('Kids' Game'), with Mickey's older brother Sammy taking a happily violent lead. When Mickey gets picked on, little Linda takes his side and grateful Mickey shares with her his secret: his friend Eddie. Eddie sneaks out under the fence to go and play with the Johnstones and when his mother finds him missing she breaks down. She calls her husband home from work and, although she can never give him the reason for her fears, she pours out to him her feelings of desperation in a manner which clearly signals an approaching collapse. Her deception and her fear of losing the son she has bought herself are destroying her. When the three children are caught throwing stones and brought to their homes by a policeman, Mrs Johnstone is able to shrug the episode off but to the Lyons it is another straw to the brick of Mrs Lyons' terror. The family will have to move away if she is not to suffer a complete breakdown.

Eddie doesn't want to go. He doesn't want to leave the district and his beloved blood brother and he ends up finding the comfort he cannot find with his own mother in the arms of Mrs Johnstone. As they part, Mrs Johnstone gives the boy a locket with a picture of Mickey and herself as a secret keepsake. The Lyons move away and Mickey finds himself lost and bored without his friend ('Long Sunday Afternoon'), but soon he himself is on the move. The Johnstones have been rehoused and can at last move away from the house where they have lived so uncomfortably ('Bright New Day'). Maybe, now, life will improve for them.

ACT 2

On the new estate, things do indeed look up for the Johnstones. The house becomes less over-crowded as the older children marry and move out and only Sammy is a permanent source of worry to his mother with his wicked activities ('Marilyn Monroe'). Mickey is fourteen and starts thinking about girls. Linda is the particular one, but he's too shy to say or do anything about it. They both are on the scene, but not involved, when Sammy robs a bus conductor at knife-point and gets himself into grown-up trouble for the first time.

Eddie is also fourteen and at boarding school where he gets into trouble when he refuses to allow an interfering teacher to touch his locket. He is suspended and, when his mother discovers the reason, she also demands to see the locket. When she finds that it holds not a picture of a girlfriend but the portrait of Mrs Johnstone and Mickey, she is flung once again into a paroxysm of terror. She cannot escape from the past.

The brothers are soon destined to come together again. It is not far between the estate where Mickey and Linda live and the house on the hill where the Lyons are now settled. When the boys first see each other again, without recognition, they quietly envy what each other has in the same way that they did when they were little ('That Guy') but, when they rediscover their friendship, they quickly pick up with the same intimacy as before. Mickey can tell Eddie about his difficulties with girls...well, with Linda, and Eddie has a remedy, a visit to a pornographic cinema. Mickey delightedly takes his refound friend home to mother, but Mrs Lyons has been following them and she confronts Mrs Johnstone hysterically, offering her money to move away. Mrs Johnstone refuses and Mrs Lyons crazily picks up a kitchen knife and attacks her. When she is disarmed, the demented Mrs Lyons curses the other woman bitterly for having ruined her life, before fleeing the house.

Eddie, Mickey and Linda have fine, friendly times together ('There's a Few Bob in Your Pocket') until their young days are done and Eddie is sent away to university. The awkward Mickey still hasn't spoken, so his relation-

239

ship with Linda is still unconfirmed. It is taken for granted that she is his girl and Eddie, who is also in love with Linda, therefore keeps his feelings to himself ('I'm Not Saying a Word') and is finally responsible for pushing Mickey into a mumbled offer. When Eddie is gone and Mickey and Linda are left alone, she becomes pregnant and a wedding is hurriedly arranged.

Mickey is working at the box factory but, when he returns to work after his marriage, he finds that he has been made redundant ('Take a Letter, Miss Jones'). Eddie returns from his high and happy University life to find a very different situation to the one he had left behind. Mickey has become resentful and sullen and no longer wants to have his successful blood brother around him as a reminder of everything he cannot give Linda. Linda, too, stays away from Eddie: their positions have changed and she does not want either to impose on him or to hurt the now very vulnerable Mickey. Eddie, who does not know of the marriage, asks Linda to marry him and from her sad answer finds out the truth of what has happened.

Mickey, grasping in desperation for money to maintain his position as a man, agrees to stand watch for Sammy on a robbery, but Sammy ends up shooting his victim. This is no kids' game, the dead don't get up again like they did in their childhood days, and Mickey ends in jail. The wages of his sin affect him badly and, during his spell in jail, he begins to suffer from deep fits of depression ('Marilyn Monroe') which allow him to take refuge from real life in pills prescribed by the prison doctor. When he is released, he prefers to continue passively to live with the pills and their irresponsible, drug-induced world, in spite of Linda's efforts to wean him back to regular work and family life.

Finally, at the end of her tether, Linda goes for help to Eddie, now a city councillor with influence enough to find employment for Mickey and a council home for them to live in, and he manages to get them set up in a position where they can find some security. But Linda seeks increasing relief from the continuously depressive company of Mickey in the company of Eddie and, inevitably, a 'Light Romance' begins.

It is the twisted Mrs Lyons who tells Mickey what is going on. Mickey takes the gun with which Sammy murdered his man from its hiding place under the floorboards and sets out to find Eddie ('There's a Man Gone Mad') at the town hall where he is addressing a meeting. Brandishing the gun, Mickey empties the hall and, as the police gather outside, he faces jealously up to Eddie with his accusations. In spite of the anger in him, Mickey cannot shoot: even that much positive action is now lacking in him. Fate, however, must have its due. Into the empty hall, past the police guards, rushes a heart-bursting Mrs Johnstone crying to Mickey to hold his fire—Eddie is his brother!

The words are spoken and Mrs Lyons' curse is conjured up. As the boys' mother pours out the true story of their birth, Mickey begins to shake. In his mind there is only one thought, and in his mouth just one cursing question: why couldn't it have been him that his mother gave away? He could have had what Eddie has! He flings his arm in the direction of his brother and the gun accidentally goes off. As Eddie dies under his brother's gun, the police close

Half a Sixpence. Arthur Kipps (Tommy Steele) plucks up courage to offer Ann Pornick
(Marti Webb) the traditional lover's token. Cambridge Theatre, 1963.

ORIGINAL TAKARAZUKA CAST

MIYUKI TSURUGI AI KODAMA

in

UCC ミュージカル

ME AND MY GIRL

宝塚歌劇月組公演
ミー＆
マイガール

YMP-1110～14
T/MP
STEREO

Book and Lyrics by L. ARTHUR ROSE and DOUGLAS FURBER Music by NOEL GAY
Book revised by STEPHEN FRY Contributions & revisions by MIKE OCKRENT
Composed and Directed by HIROTOSHI OHARA Translation by SHINJI SHIMIZU Lyrics in Japanese by TOKIKO WATATANI

Me and My Girl. When Lupino Lane introduced himself to the public as Bill Snibson, he could scarcely have envisaged that his role would one day be played by a Japanese girl. Takarazuka Theatre, Japan, 1987.

Jesus Christ Superstar. The chained and bloody Jesus of Nazareth (Robert Farrant) is brought before Pontius Pilate for judgement. Palace Theatre, London.

Evita. President Juan Peron (Joss Ackland) took Eva Duarte (Elaine Paige) from obscurity and placed her at his side, both as his wife and his political ally. Prince Edward Theatre, 1978.

Cats. Mungojerrie (John Thornton) and Rumpelteazer (Bonnie Langford) are a pair of lively little cat-burglars. New London Theatre, 1981.

Chess. While everyone, from politicians to his wife (Grainne Renihan), attempt to distract him, Anatoly Sergeievsky (Tommy Korberg) concentrates his mind on retaining his world chess championship. Prince Edward Theatre, 1987.

The Phantom of the Opera. Christine Daaé (Sarah Brightman) and Raoul de Chagny (Steve Barton) enjoy the Opera Ball while the Phantom lurks and waits for his moment. Her Majesty's Theatre, 1987.

in blazing and Mickey falls under a hail of bullets to end his life lying alongside his kin.

The day that separated twins come to know of their kinship, they shall die. Thus had Mrs Lyons promised and thus it has come to pass, and the mother who brought them into the world is left alone to mourn the tragedy that fate and weakness have brought about ('Tell Me It's Not True').

SINGIN' IN THE RAIN

a musical in two acts by Tommy Steele adapted from the screenplay by Betty Comden and Adolph Green. Songs by Arthur Freed and Nacio Herb Brown. Produced at the London Palladium 30 June 1983 with Tommy Steele (Don), Roy Castle (Cosmo), Sarah Payne (Lina) and Danielle Carson (Kathy).

CHARACTERS

Don Lockwood
Cosmo Brown
Lina Lamont, *a silent film star*
Kathy Selden, *an aspiring actress*
R F Simpson, *head of Monumental Pictures*
Roscoe Dexter, *a film director*
Dora Bailey, *a gossip columnist*
Miss Ginsmore, *an elocution teacher*
Gozark, *a mid-European giant*
Zelda Saddler, Olga Nerg, Bertram B Bertram, Steve, etc.

ACT 1

Outside Grauman's Chinese Theatre, in the heart of Hollywood, crowds are gathered to stare at the stars arriving to attend the cinema event of 1927, the première of Monumental Pictures newest film, *The Royal Rascal*. From her position at the pearly gates of the theatre, the columnist Dora Bailey is describing the scene to the listening world by radio. One by one, the celebrities enter the theatre until the great moment arrives: the stars of the film, Don Lockwood and Lina Lamont, appear and the crowd goes wild. Dora eagerly thrusts her microphone before them and begs Don to tell the story of how he became a star and, as Don's voice over the air waves tells a glamorously professional tale, the real story appears on the stage, beginning with Don and his friend, Cosmo Brown, strutting their double act in one of the country's less salubrious vaudeville houses ('Fit as a Fiddle').

The scene switches to a Monumental Pictures film studio where the boys have been engaged to supply mood music on the set of the new Lina

Lamont/Bertram B Bertram cowboy saga. The heroic-looking Bertram makes a dramatic entrance to rescue the sugar-baby damsel in distress from the attentions of an ugly mob. The mob turns on him. They surround him and punches are prepared. Then Bertram faints with fright.

The disgusted director calls for a stand-in, but there isn't one handy so, when Don cockily volunteers his services, he is quickly bundled into a duplicate costume and placed alongside the aloof Miss Lamont. The cameras roll and all Kansas is let loose. When what is left of Don is removed spinning to one side, an unruffled Bertram can step in to take over where he left off, but watching all the violence has had a ghastly effect on the poor fellow and he faints again. How to finish the film? The answer is quick to come. The head of the studio has seen the rushes: the stand-in is superb, spectacular! He must take over and be the star of the film. Miss Lamont's attitude to the young fellow is suddenly very much more welcoming, but now it is Don's turn to act unattainable.

Film follows film, success builds on success, until Lockwood and Lamont are the toast of the film world. Now, on to the screen, rolls their latest piece, *The Royal Rascal*, a costume actioner set in musketeering France and going through the same permutations of love and sword-fights seen in every one of their films to date. To the ovation at the end, Don and Lina are introduced to the audience, and Don flings hasty words of thanks to the horde of adoring fans. Backstage all is delight, *The Royal Rascal* is a hit! Suddenly the air is rent by a buzz-saw voice. Miss Lina Lamont is demanding why in the hell no one will let her get a word in edgewise with the Press. It is, alas, all too obvious. Her vowels would curdle the peaches and cream of her complexion.

Lina is one heck of an anomaly, to be seen and not heard. She's also as thick as quick-dry cement. The cinema magazines have circulated a studio tale linking her with Don romantically and she can't quite get the fact into her head that in real life this is not so. After all, she is irresistible, she is 'Temptation'. But not to Don who is, unfortunately for him, obliged for the Press's sake to escort her to the evening's celebratory party at the home of studio boss, R F Simpson.

At the party, spirits and guests are high and Don finds himself alarmingly put in the position of reproducing his all-defeating screen swordplay opposite a giant combat specialist. As the photographers snap deliriously, he holds his own for a little before opting for discretion and a leap from the first floor window into the street. Rather sorely pressed, he doesn't have time to look to see if anyone is passing, and he lands on a person. The person screams and, recognising his face, immediately assumes him to be a criminal until the laughter from the window above turns her fright to embarrassment. It's not every day you get landed on by a famous lady-killer.

The person's name is Kathy Selden and she is very sorry she didn't recognise him but she doesn't go to the movies—after all, they're all the same, and all that dumb-show isn't really acting. It goes without saying that she is a stage actress, or she has intentions of being one. He is only a shadow on a screen. But he's very close to her and she has to declare extremely firmly that she won't swoon at his feet before he will return to the party and let her go on her way.

In R F Simpson's drawing room, the guests are treated to a display of a comical novelty: a talking picture. They all find it hugely ridiculous and R F Simpson happily mocks Warner Brothers' intention to make a whole film with this risible gadget. That part of the entertainment over, R F presents the next, a huge cake for the stars. The band strikes up, the presentation cake is wheeled on, and out of it leaps a dancing girl—Kathy Selden. As she leads the hired troupe in a routine ('All I Do Is Dream of You') she pointedly avoids Don and his satirical comments until, furious at his jibes, she takes a cream cake from a trolley and aims it squarely at her tormentor. Unfortunately, he ducks, and the cake ends up spattered across the perfect features of Lina Lamont.

The sound of Lina's scream blends into a train whistle and the blackout into a speeding engine with cowboys and Indians battling until a voice cries 'Cut' and the property train is swiftly dismantled and carried away. But there is discontent dripping behind the studio glitter. Warner Brothers' *The Jazz Singer* has been a big success. It seems as if there is a future for talking pictures after all. The new Lockwood/Lamont film, *The Duelling Cavalier* looks like being old hat before it even hits the cinemas. And Don is not up to scratch either. He hasn't been able to get the girl Kathy Selden out of his head. Cosmo suspects him of unrequited love and counsels him in the '*Ridi Pagliaccio*' tradition ('Make 'Em Laugh'). When Don discovers that Lina has jealously had Kathy fired from her dancing job, the atmosphere between them becomes rigid.

Finally R F orders the studio to shut down. *The Duelling Cavalier* is suspended until the studio can be wired for sound. The new Lockwood/ Lamont picture will be a talking picture. Sound arrives and Monumental Pictures moves into musical production. Kathy has become a small featured player ('You Stepped out of a Dream') and looks like progressing further but, when Don appears on the scene, she admits to R F Simpson that it was she who was the hand behind the famous cream cake. To her surprise, she finds that no one thinks the worse of her and that Don is, indeed, delighted to see her. Alone with him, she admits that her insouciance about movies and particularly about him at their first meeting was a sham, and soon he is serenading her under the best balmy night and starlit sky the effects of a movie studio can supply ('You Are My Lucky Star').

Sound has brought to movieland a new species, the vocal coach, and Lina Lamont is one of this lady's knottiest problems. Don and Cosmo rattle off their lessons with alacrity ('Moses Supposes') but Lina's vowels make mincemeat of the script of *The Duelling Cavalier* and filming ends in catastrophe when a tug at a stray cable leading to her microphone sends the set up in sparks.

ACT 2

At the preview showing of *The Duelling Cavalier*, Lina's voice and the overstated acting of the silent stars prove ludicrous and, when the sound track slips and the leading players' voices are inverted, the whole occasion becomes a farce. Don is convinced that the film will have to be scrapped and fears that his career is over, but Kathy and Cosmo cheer him and come up with a bright idea: why not turn *The Duelling Cavalier* into a musical? Don's old vaudeville skills will do fine. But what about Lina? Lina can be dubbed. By Kathy. After a night full of gloom perhaps, after all, the new day will be a 'Good Morning'.

The friends pass the day trying out all the aspects of the idea and, at the end of it all, a tired but happy Don takes Kathy to a cab. As the cab pulls away, he is taken by a spurt of joie de vivre and, careless of the dreadful weather, he dances joyously round the street in the pouring rain ('Singin' in the Rain').

The Duelling Cavalier becomes *The Dancing Cavalier* and Kathy is hired to be Lina's voice, but Lina, with understandable precaution, isn't told about this. It will only be this once, because Kathy must pursue her own career, but in the meantime, down in the recording studios, Kathy is overdubbing Lina's version of 'Would You'.

But you can't keep a secret in Hollywood. Lina has spies and she bursts in to the studio as the session comes to its end and, to her fury, finds Don kissing Kathy. She will have revenge. For the meanwhile, however, she can do nothing. The filming needed to complete the transformation of the film from silent melodrama into modern musical is nearly done and, when the final number ('Fascinating Rhythm') is in the can, the studio goes to work to prepare their first all-singing, all-dancing, all-talking film for the public.

We are back at Grauman's. It is the first night of *The Dancing Cavalier* and it is a huge success. There is relieved joy backstage, but consternation surfaces when it is found that the daily papers have already printed big pieces on the film which are largely devoted to the wonderful song-and-dance performance by Lina Lamont.

Lina has been busy. She has also been with her attorney and has some big words up her sleeve: if the studio lets it out that she was dubbed it will be 'detrimental and deleterious' to her career. She'll sue them for the whole damned studio. Kathy has a long contract. R F will make sure that she is held to it, being Lina's voice and nothing else. In the face of such an enormous potential money-maker R F is confused. What can he do? Now Lina is in full flood. She will run the whole thing, the whole studio. The audience is cheering, cheering for her. Right, this time *she* will get her word in. From force of habit, the staff go to stop her, but Don holds them back. Let her go!

Before a bemused audience, Lina displays her vowels. Then they call for a song and the star is stranded. Kathy must go behind the curtain and sing. Don orders the horrified Kathy to do it and then, as Lina starts miming to the miked voice, Don and Cosmo and R F take hold of the curtain rope and pull. The audience, first amazed and then amused, see how they have been fooled. With a squeal Lina flees as the embarrassed Kathy runs into the auditorium. But Don calls after her—there is the voice they all loved in the film, the real star of *The Dancing Cavalier*. To the strains of 'You Are My Lucky Star', Kathy returns to the stage and to Don's arms as the final curtain falls.

The London Palladium production of *Singin' in the Rain* used 'I Can't Give You Anything but Love' (Jimmy McHugh/Dorothy Fields) previously used in *Harry Delmar's Revels* (1927) and in *Blackbirds of 1928*, 'Be a Clown' from Cole Porter's score for *The Pirate* and 'Too Marvellous for Words' (Richard Whiting/Johnny Mercer). These were replaced respectively by 'All I Do Is Dream of You', 'Make 'Em Laugh' and 'You Stepped Out of a Dream' when those songs, originally unavailable, were released prior to the show's subsequent productions.

Another musical based on the Comden and Green film script and the songs of Arthur Freed and Nacio Herb Brown was produced, also as *Singin' in the Rain*, at the Gershwin Theatre, New York, 20 June 1985.

STARLIGHT EXPRESS

a musical in two acts with lyrics by Richard Stilgoe. Music by Andrew Lloyd Webber. Produced at the Apollo Victoria Theatre 27 March 1984 with Lon Satton (Poppa), Ray Shell (Rusty), Jeff Shankley (Greaseball), Stephanie Lawrence (Pearl) and Frances Ruffelle (Dinah).

Produced at the Gershwin Theatre, New York, 15 March 1987 with Steve Fowler, Greg Mowry, Robert Torti, Reva Rice and Jane Krakowski.

CHARACTERS

Greaseball
Rusty
Ashley
Buffy
Dinah
Pearl
Rocky I, II and III
Dustin
CB
Poppa
Belle
Electra
Gook, Tank, Lube, Flat-Top, Bobo, Espresso, Weltschaft, Turnov. City of Milton Keynes, Hashamoto, Krupp, Wrench, Joule, Volta, Purse, 2nd Class Sleeper, 3rd Class Sleeper, etc.

ACT 1
This musical story about trains is set on the sort of toy train layout that

245

everyone would like to have in his lounge, but which only governments can afford. Its characters are the locomotives and carriages which make up the trains, and the first to which we are introduced are the aggressively macho engine, the Pacific Daylight, commonly known as Greaseball, and his gang of 'Rolling Stock'. Greaseball is the finest and fastest diesel locomotive in the world, the defending speed racing champion of two hemispheres, and well and truly too big for his pistons. He takes a cruel delight in making fun of little Rusty, the steam engine who works the sidings ('Taunting Rusty').

Rusty is a sad little engine: he's falling to bits, out-of-date, and he lives on hopeless dreams of steaming gloriously along at the head of his carriages, leading the other engines at racing speed ('Call Me Rusty'). He wants ever so much to enter this year's championships. The carriages—Ashley, the smoking car, Buffy, the buffet car, Dinah, the dining car and the brand spanking new and decorative Pearl—find him a sweet fellow but think his pretensions to racing are ridiculous ('Rusty, You Can't Be Serious'). There's no way that they can join behind him as his partners in the racing. After all, what a carriage needs is 'A Lotta Locomotion', and that Rusty just doesn't have. They're much keener on teaming up with Greaseball, who takes every opportunity to flex his cam-shafts in public ('Pumping Iron'), but Dinah has first claim there—she will be the champion's carriage for the big race.

The passenger coaches' noses go up in the air when a freight train approaches ('Freight'). Rusty is the locomotive, and behind him are three box cars (Rocky I, Rocky II and Rocky III), a brick truck (Flat-Top), an aggregate hopper (Dustin) and a little red caboose (CB). Freight and passenger trains are both convinced of their own supremacy, but the time for banter is over when the Control—a disembodied voice—announces that the championship racing will begin in ten minutes.

One by one the challengers for the title are announced: France's Sudest (Bobo), Italy's Settobello (Espresso), the German Weltschaft, Russia's Trans-Siberian Express (Turnov), England's Advanced Passenger Train (The City of Milton Keynes), the Japanese Shinkansen Bullet Train (Hashamoto), Greaseball...and Rusty. The last entry to arrive is an even bigger surprise. Electra is an electric train ('AC/DC'), an androgynous streak of power out to prove the superiority of electric power. Diesel, electricity and steam all join together in a challenging ensemble ('You—You're Overloaded').

Each engine now has to be hitched up to a carriage with which to compete in the race. Greaseball and Dinah are the first pair, and gradually the most impressive locomotives pair off with the most appealing carriages. Rusty hopefully approaches Pearl. Pearl has dreams of pairing up with a steam train, one whose whistle she hears in her dreams ('He Whistled at Me') but, as she gently tries to explain to him, funny little Rusty just doesn't live up to her dreams and she will not hitch up to him. Suddenly an electric minion sidles up. Electra's coach has a headache and he has chosen Pearl to be his partner instead. Although electric current does nothing for her, she agrees to go, and Rusty is left without a carriage.

The first heat of the racing begins. Greaseball manages to come out in

246

front, but only by foul play and, when Dinah chides him with cheating ('Wasn't Fair'), he angrily disconnects from her and zooms off, leaving the disconsolate Dinah to the opportunistic consoling of the creepy little caboose ('There's Me').

Off in the siding, big old Poppa steam train is singing the blues ('Poppa's Blues'). When the dejected Rusty steams by, he tries to cheer him up. It's no use moping. If Pearl won't race with him then he must hitch up to something else. He points to peeling old Belle, the sleeping car. Rusty isn't too keen, even though the lady in question is long on experience ('Belle the Sleeping Car'), and it takes all Poppa's extolling of the virtues of faith in the 'Starlight Express' before Rusty finds courage enough to turn up on the starting grid with Belle behind him to race against Weltschaft and Electra.

In another roughish race, the electric train comes out a logical winner and Rusty, even deeper down in the mouth than before, returns to his friends with his confidence in steam and the Starlight Express gone up in smoke. Poppa chides him ('Boy, Boy, Boy') for his lack of faith: steam is still the greatest and, to prove his point, he steps in to replace the unpunctual British train in the final heat with big fat Dustin the aggregate hopper hooked up behind him. And Poppa does it. He leaves the French and Russian trains behind him and struggles over the line the winner. But his big effort has been his last, for pulling the hefty hopper has blown his gaskets. There is no way he can take part in the final: Rusty must take his place. Now Rusty has to believe he can do it. He can do it with the help of the 'Starlight Express'.

ACT 2

The rights and wrongs of Poppa's place in the final being taken by the eliminated Rusty get an airing in 'The Rap', as new partnerships are evolved. Greaseball, having dumped Dinah, takes up with Pearl, leaving the dining car to wail tearfully in country style of being 'UNCOUPLED' as her sister coaches attempt to comfort her (Coaches' Rolling Stock). She will have to be content to be hitched to the electric train. CB is going to be teamed up with Rusty. He will be a nice, light little carriage to carry, but the red caboose is a two-faced twister who is plotting with Electra and Greaseball to sabotage the steam train's chances ('CB').

The final is held on the uphill track, and it is quickly a two train race as the red caboose plies its brakes when it should be urging its engine on. But Greaseball and Electra dead-heat and a rerun is ordered ('I Was Robbed'). Rusty's whining complaints are silenced by the jiving Rockies ('The Right Place at the Right Time') and it needs another dose of inner Starlight Express ('I Am the Starlight') to get the little fellow confident enough in his abilities to try again. This time the race is to be on the downhill course and Rusty pairs up with the heavyweight Dustin. Dinah has deserted the electric train who can't whistle at her, so CB is back in harness, teamed with Electra. This time, pushed by the lumpy Dustin, while Greaseball and Electra indulge in their own private battle, Rusty makes it home first.

Electra is terminally mortified in defeat ('No Comeback') and Greaseball and CB are all cracked up ('One Rock 'n' Roll Too Many'), but Rusty goes off, without completing his lap of honour, to look for Pearl who has finally got round to realising that Rusty is her engine ('Only You Have the Power to Move Me'). Greaseball also comes to his senses as Dinah proves faithful to his battered chassis, and brightens when Poppa tells him that he may even survive—converted to steam. The whole company joins in praise of steam ('There's a Light at the End of the Tunnel') and its future second coming as the show ends. Old-fashioned craftsmanship has triumphed over modern technology.

The London production was revised after opening and the show was again revised prior to being played on Broadway. Some cuts were made and several new and altered songs were added, including a new version of 'Call Me Rusty' as 'Engine of Love' (lyric partly by Peter Reeves), 'Make up my Heart' (replacing 'He Whistled at Me') and 'Wide Smile, High Style, That's Me' (a revised version of 'CB').

CHESS

a musical in two acts by Tim Rice. Music by Bjorn Ulvaeus and Benny Andersen. Produced at the Prince Edward Theatre, London, 14 May 1986 with Tommy Korberg (Anatoly), Murray Head (Trumper), Elaine Paige (Florence), John Turner (Molokov) and Siobhan McCarthy (Svetlana).

Produced at the Imperial Theatre, New York, in a revised version with book by Richard Nelson 28 April 1988 with David Carroll, Philip Casnoff and Judy Kuhn.

CHARACTERS

Frederick Trumper *of the United States of America, World Chess Champion*
Florence Vassy, *his second*
Anatoly Sergeievsky *of the USSR, the challenger*
Alexander Molokov, *his second*
Walter de Courcey, *a broadcasting executive*
The Arbiter
Svetlana Sergeievsky, *Anatoly's wife*
The Mayor of Merano, Two Civil Servants, Viigand, etc.

ACT 1
In a prologue, the origins of the game of chess are related ('The Story of Chess'), from its beginnings as an illustration of an obscure fratricidal battle somewhere in the Hindustan, through many an eastern and, latterly, western modification, to a world-wide passion, a game played with a total seriousness and conferring a newsworthy status on the man who can become its world champion.

The particular story of the show begins in a nebulous Tyrolean township

248

called 'Merano' where the latest challenge round of the world chess championship is being held. The citizens of the town, dressed in a Hollywood version of their picturesque national costume, are gathered in the square outside the railway station to await the arrival of the game's most celebrated character, the champion himself, America's Frederick Trumper. Trumper is more irritated than impressed by the mayor and his reception ('What a Scene! What a Joy!'). These people have no interest in chess, they are interested only in seeing 'the nice guy beat the bum' and the East-West confrontation. Trumper's opponent, Anatoly Sergeievsky, is from the Soviet Union. The champion ignores the welcome ceremony and walks away, leaving the townsfolk to lavish their flowers and souvenirs on an unsuspecting tourist who arrives right behind him.

In the Palace Hotel, Trumper is playing chess against a computer when Florence Vassy, his second and his lover, brings in the newspapers. There is plenty of coverage of the event and the verdict in half a dozen languages is that Trumper is the bad guy of the match; spoiled, temperamental, loud, the man they love to hate. At a press conference, personalities and not chess are the subject of all the reporters' questions and Trumper replies with short logic to the pre-packaged jibes which are designed to pull copy from him. When one newsman sneeringly refers to the fact that he carries a female second, Trumper loses his temper and flattens him. He storms out and the Press have the story they came for.

In another hotel room, Sergeievsky and his head of delegation, Molokov, watch the scene on television. Molokov and his oversized band of advisors are with the challenger to make sure that he wins this match for the glory of his country. After all, the whole world is watching, and the whole world must not think that the Russians cannot even win a game. Sergeievsky is fed up with the party line and wants only to be left alone to play his game, but Molokov insists. The weakness of Trumper is the woman, Florence. If they can succeed in detaching her from his side, it would give them a great psychological advantage. Left alone, Anatoly Sergeievsky regrets sourly that now, when he has achieved so much of what he desired, he cannot enjoy his success because of these pressures from outside the game, and because of continuing thoughts of what he has given up to devote himself to chess ('Who Needs a Dream').

In the Arbiter's chambers, the delegates supporting the competitors gather for a pre-match briefing. Publicly they speak of sport, privately each team is determined to be the winner for political reasons ('No One Can Deny That These Are Difficult Times'). The Arbiter warns both sides that he will be the one and only referee ('I'm the Arbiter') with power over all aspects of the match. He makes arbitrary decisions on routine objections from each team and shows genuine interest only when Walter de Courcey, representing the broadcasting interests involved in the television transmission of the match, makes a submission concerning the merchandising of the event. To a blast of music and majorettes the stage is filled with a chorus of merchandising minions ('Whether You Are Pro or Anti').

Finally, under the glare of the television lights, it is time to begin the match. The extra-sporting drama is not long in coming. Irritated by Sergeievsky's deliberately distracting tactics of drumming the table with his fingers, rocking in his chair and other forms of gamesmanship, Trumper kicks his rival under the table and in minutes the men are on their feet as the chessmen tumble to the floor. Molokov for the Russians and Florence for the Americans accuse and counter accuse ('A Model of Decorum and Tranquility') until the Arbiter gains sufficient control to order that they players return to the table within twenty-four hours or the match will be considered cancelled.

The fencing between Molokov and Florence continues and he makes an ill-judged attempt to call on her feelings as a fellow eastern European. Florence Vassy is Hungarian. She was five years old in 1956 when she lost her family in the Russian invasion of Budapest. Right now, however, her only concern is to get the two players back to the chess table. She hands Molokov a paper. Sergeievsky must come to a mountain inn where she will get him together with Trumper away from the arena and, hopefully, induce some sort of sporting truce.

Meanwhile Trumper is at loggerheads with de Courcey. His tantrum has made the event even more newsworthy: he wants $20,000 per match as his share of the television rights. He turns on Florence when she arrives and, when she tells him of her arranged meeting, accuses her of playing for the Communists. In the heat of his temper he goes for her weak spot, the Hungarian connection and her family, and she walks out on him. Now, just when it needs to be strongest, the relationship between them is beginning to fall apart ('Nobody's on Nobody's Side').

Up on a Merano mountainside, the local populace are indulging in a stein song ('Der Kleiner Franz'). Florence arrives and Anatoly is already waiting. Since Trumper has not shown up, they are alone and there is a certain embarrassment in the alpine air (Mountain Duet/'This Is the One Situation') until the first barrier is down and they find more than a little pleasure in each other's company. As they touch hands, Trumper appears. He has agreed new financial terms and will return to the match. The rapport between Florence and the Russian has not been lost on him, however, and he has more accusing words of collaboration to hurl at his second.

Back at the table, it is soon evident that something has gone from Trumper and his play. He loses game after game, until he is on the brink of defeat. The day's last move is sealed with Sergeievsky needing only this game to win the championship. In private Trumper turns his disappointment, as always, on to Florence and, this time, she leaves him (Florence Quits) for good. Alone, he vents his rage and self-pity on his own life history ('Pity the Child') as the ignored child of squalid parents who took refuge from a loveless life in playing chess, winning victories at his game to replace affection. In the arena, there is sensation when the game does not restart the next day. Trumper has resigned and Anatoly Sergeievsky is the new world champion. But as he shakes hands, Anatoly breaks away and runs to Florence. He has defected.

At the British Embassy, a pair of bored civil servants process the defector and his documents (Embassy Lament) and it becomes evident that Walter de Courcey is more than simply a broadcasting executive. It is also revealed that Anatoly has a wife and children in Russia, but Florence is falling in love nevertheless ('Heaven Help My Heart') and there is little doubt that her feelings are reciprocated. At Merano station, the departing couple are besieged by the media with questions of political allegiance, but Anatoly pushes them aside. He rejects political boundaries: his country is the country of his heart (Anthem: 'My Land').

ACT 2

A year later, Anatoly is to defend his title in Bangkok. Freddie Trumper is there, too, but this time commentating for a television chain and, his mind set only on chess, immune to the so-called delights of the city ('One Night in Bangkok'). Florence is now installed in Anatoly's life in the same way that she had previously been in Trumper's, but the relationship and the situation have many pressures on them which have nothing to do with chess. He is wary because Trumper is here in Bangkok, whilst she has been allowed to hear that the Russian authorities are going to permit his wife, Svetlana, to come to Thailand with the clear intention of unnerving him. Everything is conspiring to divert Anatoly's mind from chess and from a secure relationship with Florence ('You and I').

The opposition candidate is another Soviet player, Viigand, a man of utter singularity of mind. Molokov has a new 'Soviet Machine' who will take the championship for his nation, and once again his insurance policy will be Florence Vassy. But this time he has an unlikely ally: he is in contact with Walter de Courcey. Molokov claims that he has found Florence's father, alive, in Russia. He will allow de Courcey to win a diplomatic victory in bringing him and other suitably newsworthy people to the West at the price of a victory on the chess table. De Courcey orders Freddie Trumper, who is about to interview Anatoly for television, to go in hard. Freddie needs no encouraging. His political questions and a surprise video of Svetlana send Anatoly stalking out from in front of the cameras. The players who are not chess players have taken over.

Svetlana and Florence come face to face in the hotel lobby. Both recognise that there is a need in Anatoly which they cannot fulfil ('I Know Him so Well'), family security on the one hand and freedom for youthful living on the other, but both are caught up in events of which they are not the controllers (The Deal). Molokov orders Svetlana to tell her husband that he must throw the match; De Courcey tells Florence that her father is alive and that she must make Anatoly let himself be defeated to ensure his release. Florence refuses, but De Courcey reports back to Molokov confidently. Under orders, Freddie adds his bit with a telephone call to Anatoly, giving him direct the story of Florence's father. But when all the finagling is done, Anatoly is handed a note.

Following directions, he goes to meet the writer at a temple on the mountainside. It turns out to be Freddie. He hasn't come to talk about any part of what's going on down at the nerve-centre of things; he wants just to talk chess. He has noticed something in Viigand's play... Anatoly cannot understand. Why is he helping? Freddie has only one reply, 'How can you let mediocrity win?'. For one moment on a Thai hillside, chess itself is suddenly more important than the circus going on around it.

As the chorus chant the names of past world chess champions, the final game of the challenge match is being played (Endgame). The reproaches and orders and accusations of Svetlana, Florence, and Molokov flail against Anatoly's brain as he attempts to play until, in a final decision, he rejects them all. His mind focussed on the game, he achieves a remarkable turn around and wins both the game and the match. His championship confirmed, he will return to Russia and the security of his family. He has chosen to be a chess player. Walter chooses to believe that he has done it to guarantee the return of Florence's father—if he is really still alive. If? How carelessly these politicians treat people's hearts and lives.

Anatoly and Florence say an undimmed farewell at the airport ('You and I') and, left alone, Florence can only repeat to herself Anatoly's hymn to the individual heart ('My Land').

THE PHANTOM OF THE OPERA

a musical in a prologue and two acts based on the novel by Gaston Leroux. Book by Andrew Lloyd Webber and Richard Stilgoe. Lyrics by Charles Hart. Additional lyrics by Richard Stilgoe. Music by Andrew Lloyd Webber. Produced at Her Majesty's Theatre, London, 9 October 1986 with Michael Crawford (Phantom), Sarah Brightman and Claire Moore (alternating as Christine Daaé), Rosemary Ashe (Carlotta), Steve Barton (Raoul), John Savident (Firmin) and David Firth (André).

Produced at the Majestic Theatre, New York, 26 January 1988 with Crawford, Miss Brightman/Patti Cohenour, Judy Kaye, Barton, Nick Wyman and Cris Groenendaal.

CHARACTERS

The Phantom of the Opéra
Christine Daaé
Raoul, Vicomte de Chagny
Monsieur Firmin
Monsieur André
Carlotta Guidicelli
Meg Giry
Madame Giry
Ubaldo Phangi
Monsiur Reyer, Joseph Buquet, Monsieur Lefèvre, Auctioneer, etc.

PROLOGUE

On the stage of the Opéra de Paris in the year 1905 an auction sale of properties, ephemera and other articles exhumed from the theatre's vaults is taking place. Several lots are sold to an elderly gentleman who is named as Raoul, Vicomte de Chagny, among them an oriental musical box in the form of a monkey and barrel organ, a piece which clearly has a relevance to the story of the old gentleman's life. The auctioneer brings forward the reassembled fragments of a giant chandelier, recalling its connection with the strange and still incompletely explained tale of the Phantom of the Opéra which had caused such excitement in Paris nearly half a century earlier. As the working portion of the chandelier is relit, the overture begins. The piece of chandelier grows to full size and finally rises to the centre of the house to hang in its former position as the stage of the Opéra returns to the year 1861.

ACT 1

A dress rehearsal for the opera *Hannibal* is in progress with the portly tenor Ubaldo Phangi in the title role and the soprano Carlotta Giudicelli in the florid star role of Elissa, when the proprietor of the Opéra, Monsieur Lefèvre, interrupts the proceedings to introduce to the company his successors, Messrs Firmin and André, who are to take over the running of the theatre under the patronage of the young Vicomte de Chagny. The gentlemen watch the rehearsal as Carlotta displays herself in flights of coloratura and Phangi performs a decidedly hefty Hannibal and, at their request, the prima donna obliges with an out-of-context rendition of the aria 'Think of Me'.

As she sings, there is a crash and the backdrop tumbles down dangerously near to her head. The chorus and ballet girls cry out aloud—it is the Phantom of the Opéra. Carlotta stalks furiously from the stage, leaving Lefèvre to brush aside the incident so as not to alarm the new owners, a task not made easier when the ballet mistress, Madame Giry, brings a message which she says has come from the Phantom himself. It is addressed to André and Firmin reminding them of his requirements: Box Five shall be left unsold, as it was under Lefèvre's management, for the private use of the Phantom, and his monthly salary shall be punctually paid.

In the meanwhile the Opéra is without a prima donna. Carlotta is refusing to perform in *Hannibal* that evening and there is no understudy. Madame Giry's little daughter, Meg, who is performing in the Opéra ballet puts forward the seemingly ridiculous idea that one of her fellow dancers, Christine Daaé, should tackle the extremely technical and difficult role. Firmin and André are properly sceptical at the idea of a ballet girl becoming a prima donna but, having no other answer, they permit Christine to sing for them. The girl obliges with 'Think of Me' and as she sings the scene changes to the evening performance in which she is appearing in the role of Elissa.

Watching from their box, Firmin and André are delighted with their

253

discovery, but the Vicomte de Chagny is even more thrilled for he recognises in the new prima donna a childhood acquaintance, a little girl whose scarf he once rescued from the sea and whose face and friendship have remained ever since in his mind.

As Christine returns to her dressing room at the end of the performance, the sound of a strange voice echoes in her ears, 'bravi, bravi, bravissimi'. It is a voice which, she confides to Meg, she knows well. She has a mysterious teacher whom she has never seen and whom she believes to be the 'Angel of Music'. When Christine's musician father lay dying, he comforted her by telling her that he would send the angel of music to guard over her in her loneliness. His promise has come true for, alone in her dressing room, she is visited by a disembodied voice which has encouraged and trained her in her singing until her lovely young voice has attained sufficient scope to allow her to perform a role such as Elissa.

The managers hurry backstage to lavish their congratulations on the new prima donna, but Raoul de Chagny orders them away as, alone with Christine, he happily recalls their childish days and the song they sang together about the angel of music ('Little Lotte'). Christine earnestly tells Raoul that she has truly been visited by that angel. Not taking her literally, he laughingly agrees and asks her to supper.

No sooner has he left to allow her to change than Christine's angel comes to her, his voice full of anger at Raoul's familiarity with his pupil. He has decided the time has come when she shall know his face and he commands her to look into her mirror. There, in the glass before Christine's eyes, stands a cloaked and masked figure, calling to her to come to him. Waiting outside the room, Raoul becomes alarmed at the sound of conversation but he cannot open the locked door. When, at last, the door opens of its own accord, he finds that Christine is no longer there. She has disappeared through the mirror.

The Phantom—for Christine's angel is he—leads his pupil through the secret passageways behind the mirror down into the caverns and underground waterways deep below the Opéra, ferrying her by boat through a subterranean lake which seems to be lit by innumerable candelabra as her mind tries to reconcile her old thoughts of an angel with what is all too clearly a man ('The Phantom of the Opéra').

The Phantom takes Christine to his home, a set of richly furnished rooms hidden beyond the lake and far under the streets of Paris. He has brought her there to sing for him, to be his creature and his inspiration. Under his influence she will sing like no one has ever sung before ('The Music of the Night'). He caresses her and she loses her fear of him sufficiently to touch the strange mask which covers his face as he removes a dust sheet to display a waxen image of Christine herself dressed in a bridal gown and veil. As Christine stares at the model, amazed, it moves toward her and she faints.

When she awakens the next morning it is to find the Phantom at work at a gigantic organ, composing his music. Beside her, a little Persian music box is tinkling out a melody as she attempts to bring back the strange, dream-like events of the previous night ('I Remember'). But it is no dream. The man is there. Approaching him quietly, she whisks away his mask to reveal a hideously deformed face. The Phantom turns on her furiously. Now that she has seen his real face she will think of him always as a physically deformed tillocreature rather than one whose mind and skills can produce beauty ('Stranger Than You Dreamt It'). Reluctantly, too, he knows he must return her to the theatre before her absence causes a search. She will return to the Opéra and carry out the plans which he has made for her.

Backstage in the theatre Joseph Buquet, a stage hand, is frightening the chorus girls with tales of the Phantom and the ghastly Punjab knot, a seemingly magical piece of rope with which the ghostly creature has been known to strangle his victims ('Magical Lasso'). At the same time, up in the managers' office, Firmin and André are finding that Christine's triumph and the mystery of her disappearance are potent box-office attractions but, nevertheless, they have problems.

The Phantom has sent a series of 'Notes' to the personnel of the Opéra: a critique of the performance to André, a reminder to Firmin that his salary is still unpaid, a threat to Raoul that he must not attempt to make further contact with Christine, and another to Carlotta telling her that should she attempt to resume her place as prima donna a dreadful fate will befall her. Finally, there is one for Madame Giry detailing the Phantom's plans for the Opéra. The next opera to be presented will be *Il Muto* in which Christine shall be given the leading role of the Countess whilst Carlotta plays the non-singing role of the page boy. Carlotta is furious, and André and Firmin have to beg her to return with the assurance that the casting will be exactly the reverse ('Prima Donna').

When *Il Muto* is staged ('Poor Fool He Makes Me Laugh') the Phantom takes his revenge. In the middle of the performance, he causes Carlotta to croak like a toad and, when she tries to continue, he causes the chandelier to tremble so violently that the prima donna breaks down and cannot carry on. The managers hurriedly bring the curtain down and announce that the opera will be resumed shortly. A ballet is hurried on to fill the gap but, as the scenery parts, the body of Joseph Buquet is spied dangling hideously from a Punjab knot.

Christine hurries Raoul up on to the roof of the theatre. There, at least, they will be far from the secret passageways of the theatre and safe from the Phantom's all-seeing eyes ('Why Have You Brought Me Here?'). She pours out to the incredulous Raoul the frightful and frightening tale of her underground journey with the Phantom ('Raoul, I've Been There') and he comforts her with words which soon turn to words of love ('All I Ask Of You'). As they kiss, a shadowy figure is seen behind the huge winged statue crowning the pediment of the building: the Phantom is there, he has seen them and in his heart he is betrayed.

Christine returns to the stage to complete the opera in Carlotta's place but, as she steps forward to take her curtain call, there is a terrible volley of laughter and the great chandelier topples from its moorings and crashes to the stage at Christine's feet. The Phantom has delivered his warning.

ACT 2

It is New Year's Eve, and the Opéra is host to a great masked ball ('Masquerade'). Six months have passed since the episode of the chandelier and, to everyone's relief, there has been no further evidence of the infamous Phantom. Raoul and Christine have become secretly engaged and she wears his ring on a chain around her neck but she cannot bring herself to wear it openly for deep inside her the fear of the Phantom still stirs. She is right still to fear for, at the height of the ball, he appears splendidly dressed with a death's-head mask glittering appallingly where his usual mask should be ('Why So Silent?').

His long silence is now explained. He has brought them the score of an opera he has composed, *Don Juan Triumphant*, and commands that the Opéra shall stage it or risk even worse events than the harmless smashing of a chandelier. Approaching Christine, he seizes the chain around her neck and tears the ring from it. She is his, and no ring nor chain can alter that. Before the terrified girl can reply, he vanishes, seemingly into nothing, leaving his garments in a heap on the floor.

Raoul will not accept a supernatural explanation and sets out to discover more about this Phantom. He has noticed enough to know where to begin his questioning: Madame Giry clearly has information that she has not revealed. Under his questioning she tells her tale. Many years ago, in a low Paris fair, she saw a freak on display. It was a man, a dreadfully deformed creature, but a man with a prodigious mind, and great talents who, it was said, had built for a Persian monarch a dreadful torture-chamber in the form of an inhuman maze of mirrors. The creature escaped from his exhibitor and vanished, no one knew where, and it was soon afterwards that the strange happenings began at the Opéra. If it were this man with his amazingly inventive mechanical mind and his deadly Persian noose who was causing the seemingly inexplicable happenings of the past years in the theatre, perhaps they would not then be quite so inexplicable.

André and Firmin are appalled by *Don Juan Triumphant*. It is certainly not Meyerbeer or Bellini or Mozart nor even Rameau. It is full of strange unmelodious music which they would not dream of presenting on their stage but they are too frightened to refuse and, out of fear, they submit to the insulting 'Notes' by which the Phantom organises and directs the preparations for the production. Carlotta is cast in a minor role, whilst the prima donna role goes to Christine who, it is emphasised, must return to her 'angel' for further tuition.

Christine is unwilling to play the part written for her, but Raoul insists that *Don Juan Triumphant* must be performed. The Phantom will be sure to come to his box to watch the performance and then he can be arrested. Christine does not know what to do ('Twisted Every Way'). Can she lead to his death the man who was once her angel, and can she bear to perform this opera knowing how and why it was written?

Don Juan Triumphant is put into rehearsal and Phangi finds it impossible to cope with the untraditional intervals of the Phantom's music, turning the concerted music into a shambles. Christine is still prey to mixed fears and longings. Asleep and awake, she can hear the Phantom coaxing her voice from her, the angel of music her father promised her, yet surely no angel. At her father's grave she opens her heart ('Wishing You Were Somehow Here Again') but, in reply, she hears only the voice of the Phantom as the figures of father and guiding angel become strangely mixed in her mind ('Wandering Child'). But the Phantom is actually there. He has dared to issue forth from his labyrinth, and from amongst the gravestones he is attempting to woo the girl to him. He is foiled by the appearance of Raoul, who breaks the spell and carries Christine to safety under the furious imprecations of the Phantom ('Bravo, Monsieur').

On the night of the première of *Don Juan Triumphant* marksmen are strategically placed in the auditorium of the Opéra, but the Phantom plays his voice around the theatre distractingly, unnerving the soldiers completely. When the opera starts, Phangi plays the role of Don Juan up to the last scenes in which he lays siege to the chastity of the peasant girl, Aminta, played by Christine. Taking his servant's cloak, Don Juan disguises himself and hides to await the approach of Aminta. But as Phangi steps into the shadows, he falls victim to the Punjab knot and, when Don Juan emerges, it is the cloaked Phantom himself who faces Christine ('The Point of No Return').

As he sings, the passion in his words builds beyond the confines of the role. He pours forth his love and, giving her his ring, begs Christine to save him from his dreadful solitude. As he reaches his final plea, the girl steps forward and pulls away his cloak—the Phantom is revealed to the whole world in his deformed state. With a howl, he vanishes, bearing Christine with him, as the marksmen rush to the stage to discover only the lifeless body of Phangi. Once again, Christine is forced down into the underways of Paris ('Down Once More') with the theatre staff and a troop of armed men hurrying in pursuit ('Track Down This Murderer').

In the Phantom's abode, Christine faces up to the man who would be her lover, this man who thinks himself persecuted because of his dreadful appearance. His actions belie his words. His face means nothing to her. She can see beyond it not to a tortured soul but to an evil one, and she can have no pity for him. If she cannot feel pity she can never feel love. Raoul, in the meanwhile, has succeeded in following their tracks through the labyrinth and he appears at the grille masking the Phantom's home from the lake outside. The Phantom laughingly lets him enter and, from nowhere, the dreaded Punjab knot appears, snaking around the young man's neck and choking the life from him as the Phantom bids Christine make her choice: give her love to him or see Raoul die.

Finally Christine steps towards the creature and kisses him long on the lips. His appearance does not daunt her, he need not be alone. The kiss breaks something inside the Phantom. When she moves away, he releases the rope from Raoul's neck and, as the voices of the pursuing mob are heard in the distance, bids them go. While the music box plays, Christine returns his ring and, as he whispers 'Christine, I love you,' she and Raoul step into the boat to cross the lake and return to their freedom. Then the Phantom covers himself under his cloak and, when the mob invade his home and the cloak is torn aside, he has vanished. Only his mask remains.

Part 2
FRANCE

By the time the French light musical theatre reached its great flowering period in the middle of the nineteenth century it had already spent more than a century battling to establish itself in a definitive and popular form.

Eighteenth-century French musical entertainments were largely parallel in class to those which flourished in Britain at the same period. Alongside the established tradition of Italian and French grand opera, there were, on the one hand, light comedies or *vaudevilles* illustrated with songs and dances either specially composed or taken from the popular music canon and, on the other, the *opéra-comique*, originally a burlesque form parodying the seriousness and artificiality of Italian opera and, later, a style of work in line with the Italian *opera buffa*.

These *opéras-comiques*, as exemplified by the works of the composers Grétry and Philidor, established themselves as the principal form of light musical theatre in the second half of the century. They were set first to more, but later to less, light-hearted libretti and, by the early part of the nineteenth century, their style and content had become predominantly romantic and often sentimental rather than humorous. Nevertheless, under the influence of the master librettist, Eugène Scribe, and a group of effective composers, France produced during the first decades of the century a series of light or comic operas which became popular not only in Paris but throughout the world, successfully rivalling the established pre-eminence of the Italian and German repertoire.

Boieldieu's *La Dame Blanche* and *Jean de Paris*, Hérold's *Zampa* and *Le Pré aux Clercs*, Adolphe Adam's *Le Châlet* and *Le Postillon de Longjumeau* and, above all, the works of Auber—*Le Maçon, Les Diamants de la Couronne, Le Domino Noir, Le Cheval de Bronze* and the masterpiece of the period, *Fra Diavolo*—were played and played again in their original language and in translation but, like the comparable English pieces of Balfe and Wallace, these works gravitated into the repertoires of the opera companies. Few were for long presented in the popular theatre under regular commercial conditions, and those composers like Bizet and Gounod, who followed and extended the tradition which these writers established, placed themselves even more firmly in the world of opera.

It was from a less ambitious area that the greatest works of the French musical theatre would develop. As in Britain—where Gilbert, Sullivan, Cellier, and so many other important figures of the nineteenth century musical theatre had spent part of their earliest days writing small operettas—so in France the little one-act *opérettes* which co-existed with the increasingly grandiose *opéras-comiques* provided the ground from which the first significant talents in the new style of musical theatre would spring.

The middle years of the nineteenth century saw the production of a mass of such little pieces in all kinds of moods—the sweetly rustic, epitomised by Victor Massé's *Les Noces de Jeannette* or Offenbach's *La Mariage aux Lanternes*, the contemporary satire as seen in the same composer's comical *Les Deux Aveugles*, or such outrageous extravaganzas as his Chinoiserie *Ba-Ta-*

Clan. It was the spirit of these two latter pieces which gave life to the earliest successes of the new joyous breed of light musical theatre.

The inherent formality of the old *opéra-comique* was abandoned in the new *opéra-bouffe* which was, as its name suggests, a superior kind of burlesque in the tradition of J R Planché. Unlike the Englishman's works, however, the French *opéra-bouffe* was burlesque illustrated by original music of the most sparkling and irresistible kind, from, most notably, the pens of two geniuses of the musical theatre, Jacques Offenbach and Hervé.

Opéra-bouffe, which swept all before it in the world's theatres for more than a decade, took flight in 1858 with the production of Offenbach's *Orphée aux Enfers* and the composer followed up this first great triumph with a series of magificently extravagant shows built on libretti by Ludovic Halévy, Hector Crémieux, Étienne Tréfeu, Henri Meilhac and Charles Nuitter amongst which such pieces as *Geneviève de Brabant*, *Le Pont des Soupirs*, *La Belle Hélène*, *Barbe-Bleue*, *La Grande-Duchesse de Gérolstein* and *Les Brigands* followed in the new burlesque tradition, revelling in hilariously nonsensical plots, exaggerated characters and often grotesque scenes with an unprecedented freedom of style. Hervé joined the fray with a trio of outstanding successes—*L'Œil Crevé*, *Chilpéric* and *Le Petit Faust*—which added to the glory of the genre before the public began to weary of an undiluted diet of zany parody, and the wild eccentricities of burlesque gave away to less outlandish styles of humour.

Offenbach had enormous success in 1866 with the farcical *La Vie Parisienne* which, although describing itself as *opéra-bouffe*, bore a fairly distant relationship to the classical parody of *Orphée aux Enfers* and *Barbe-Bleue*; and others of his pieces, such as *La Périchole* and *La Princesse de Trébizonde*, which also found great popular favour, leaned less on the grotesque and ridiculous than on a more straightforward style of comedy. It was in this direction that the newly unbridled French musical theatre now went. By the 1870s and the end of the Franco–Prussian war the true *opéra-bouffe* had seen its greatest day and, under the influence of another outstanding composer, Charles Lecocq, a new era of *opéra-comique* was under way.

Lecocq came to general notice with his lively *Les Cent Vierges* in 1872 and confirmed his presence with one of the most enduring of all French musicals, *La Fille de Madame Angot*, later the same year. His lively, humorous pieces, sometimes relying for their libretti on the same versatile writers used by his predecessors in *opéra-bouffe* days, set the new style. In these libretti there was a place for characters who were not just buffoons or parodies and for a little genuine romance and sentiment and, in consequence, there was also an opportunity for music which, whilst still light and bright, allowed a little more warmth of expression than had been possible as illustration to the brilliant bubbles of *opéra-bouffe*.

Lecocq's greatest works were by no means all of a kind—the low comedy of *Les Cent Vierges* and *Giroflé-Giroflä* were at the opposite end of the spectrum to the tender comedy of his marvellous *Le Petit Duc*, the spirited fun of *Angot* and the involved farce of *Le Jour et la Nuit* and *Le Coeur et la Main*—and neither were the works which, in the decade following, came to magnify the international success of the French musical theatre; Robert Planquette's record-breaking comedy-mystery, *Les Cloches de Corneville*, Louis Varney's farcical *Les Mousquetaires au Couvent*, Emmanuel Chabrier's burlesque-flavoured *L'Étoile*, Edmond Audran's first successes, *Les Noces d'Olivette* and the charming *La Mascotte*, and some outstanding pieces in the latest style from the old masters, Offenbach's dazzling *La Fille du Tambour Major* and *Madame Favart* and Hervé's best-known work, the musical comedy *Mam'zelle Nitouche*.

The enormous success of these works, many of which are still revived a century later, was founded on a fine marriage of text and music. The libretti were substantial comic plays. They were not collections of flimsy scenes pasted around a principal player, or a series of worn-out situations and sentiments rearranged in between new songs, but full-sized comedies, often of ingenious originality, written by authors whose success in the theatre was spread amongst all genres of stage writing. The libretti of Meilhac and Halévy, Leterrier and Van Loo, Chivot and Duru and their fellows were written with the same care as their equally successful comedies, and there was never a hint of the condescension or laziness displayed in too many of the English-language libretti of the period. The play was as important as its music and not just a flimsy vehicle for showing off the composer's work, whilst the music was a fine blend of the classical and the popular, written both by men like the prize-winning Lecocq, who had been soundly trained at the Conservatoire, and the less formally educated Planquette whose earliest successes had come in the music-hall atmosphere of the Parisian café-concerts.

Both these men, and their contemporaries, continued where Offenbach and Hervé had opened up the way, producing light-hearted, catching melodies which glittered on the voice—songs and music which used everything the orchestra and the singers had to offer without ever becoming ponderous or pretentious. It was music which allied perfectly with the style of their writers and with the mood of the time and it was music which has since proved itself by its durability.

Like all great eras, the golden days of the new *opéra-comique* lasted a comparatively brief time and, by the latter part of the 1880s, the finest glory had gone from the products of French musical theatre. Audran continued to turn out attractive works such as *La Cigale et la Fourmi*, *Miss Helyett* and *La Poupée*, all of which followed the works of the previous two decades to the stages of the world, and a few other composers including Victor Roger (*Joséphine Vendue Par Ses Soeurs*, *Les 28 Jours de Clairette*), Louis Ganne (*Les Saltimbanques*, *Hans, le Joueur de Flûte*), Claude Terrasse and Gaston Serpette, helped to keep the tradition afloat a little longer, but the final years of the nineteenth century and the early years of the twentieth would have looked very pale beside the heyday of Offenbach and Lecocq had it not been for the presence of André Messager.

Messager and his librettists took the *opéra-comique* even further away from the *opéra-bouffe* and its frivolities towards the respectability of light opera and, in the process, added to the French repertoire two delightful master-

263

pieces, *Véronique* and *Les P'tites Michus*, but otherwise the great writers of the nineteenth century found few successors. The French musical theatres of the early twentieth century looked elsewhere for ready-made product and, to supplement the waning native product, gave themselves up to the European delights provided by Franz Lehár, Jean Gilbert and Leo Fall or Britain's *The Quaker Girl* and *A Country Girl*.

The fact that the stylish and musical soigné Messager, the director, in turn, of both the Royal Opera House Covent Garden and the Paris Opéra, was the flag-bearer of the French musical at the turn of the century showed that, once again, the light musical theatre had begun to take itself rather seriously—a trend which has almost inevitably led to the end of a cycle of success in the field. This was indeed the case in France, and it was only an injection of a wholly new breed of writers and composers, equipped with a new spirit and style, which allowed the French musical theatre to get its second wind at the end of the Great War.

The men who gave this much-needed impetus to the Paris theatre came from the world of the *chanson*, the French popular song. They were songwriters, rather than Conservatoire composers bred on opera and ballet music and the traditions of the *opéra-comique*, and the shows which they wrote had a gaiety and insouciance which had not been seen since the palmy days of *opéra-bouffe*. The advance guard of this new trend were Albert Willemetz and Henri Christiné who, just as Offenbach had done with *Orphée aux Enfers*, made a brilliant entrance into the world of the musical play with a spirited classical burlesque, the sparkling, satirical *Phi-Phi*, which took post-war Paris by storm. Christiné followed up with the delightfully irresponsible *Dédé* and a series of up-to-date musical comedies which, along with the compositions of librettist André Barde and Maurice Yvain (*Ta Bouche, Pas Sur la Bouche*, etc.) and several other less perennial contemporaries, kept the theatre public of the 1920s and 1930s laughing and whistling through *les années folles*.

The line of Lecocq and Messager, however, did not disappear, Messager wrote his *Monsieur Beaucaire* for the London stage in 1919 and its Parisian production in 1925 proved that he had lost none of his appeal, whilst the much-admired Reynaldo Hahn composed the score for the deliberately old-fashioned *Ciboulette* in 1923. Nevertheless, the new style of show, with its urbane up-to-date chic and *esprit boulevardier*, appealed more generally to a public which also welcomed both the dancing tunes and frivolous antics of *No, No, Nanette* and the classic Continental-American operetta style of *Rose-Marie* as heralds to a decade of importations from Broadway.

The French theatregoing public, always sparing in its appreciation of shows of English-language extraction, gave an extended welcome to only a favoured few of these imports which, like the German-language successes such as *Le Pays de Sourire, Rêve de Valse, Les Trois Valses* and *L'Auberge du Cheval Blanc*, were given splendid Parisian productions as part of the vogue for *opérette à grand spectacle* developed during the 1930s at the vast Théâtre du Châtelet under Maurice Lehmann, at the Gaîté-Lyrique and at the Théâtre Mogador. This highly colourful and lavish style of music theatre production—bestowed on both foreign and some, largely undistinguished, native products—was to become the backbone of Paris's musical theatre in the years leading up to the second war, whilst the successors to the small-scale comedy-and-song shows of the twenties and the happy little series of Marseillais musicals introduced to Paris by Henri Alibert and Vincent Scotto provided the alternative entertainment.

By the end of the war, the vogue for foreign entertainments had largely passed but, thanks to the talents of one new team of French writers, the *opérette*, both in its large-scale and in its more intimate forms, was again given a new lease of life. The show which opened this era was *La Belle de Cadix* written by Raymond Vincy and Marc Cab with music by Francis Lopez. It was a piece in the classic music theatre mould as crystallised in the early *opéra-comique* and English comic opera styles, perfected at Daly's Theatre and popularised world-wide by the best of Viennese shows and the works of such Broadway composers as Romberg and Richard Rogers whose *Oklahoma!*, produced two years earlier, was the nearest contemporary equivalent to *La Belle de Cadix*.

A romantic story featuring a fine-voiced hero and heroine was counter-pointed by comical action and interaction from a pair of song-and-dance light comedians, and the whole was set in picturesque surroundings which included opportunities for some fine visual set pieces as well as a torrent of musical numbers. *La Belle de Cadix* was a triumph and set Vincy and Lopez on a career which, in France, paralleled that of the Rodgers/Hammerstein combination in America. Their *Andalousie, Pour Don Carlos, Le Chanteur de Mexico, Mediterranée* and *La Toison d'Or* were all part of a series of well-crafted, finely performed and staged musicals which filled the larger Parisian theatres for long runs whilst, at the smaller houses, the delicious comedy and lively music of such pieces as *La Route Fleuri* and *Quatre Jours à Paris* found an equal success.

Unlike the American combination, however, Lopez and Vincy did not stand at the head of a prolific and talented generation of theatre writers. Two of the few other successful works which appeared during the early post-war years came from old favourites: Maurice Yvain's mature *Chanson Gitane*—a far cry from the wicked gaiety of *Ta Bouche*—and Vincent Scotto's *Violettes Impériales*—a costume operetta which had little in common with his laughing Marseille pieces—but there were few Châtelet or Mogador pieces of any interest to be found from new writers.

The shows which kept the smaller theatres occupied were more inclined to be star vehicles than skilled pieces of theatre. Only one, the unexpected *Irma la Douce*, produced in 1956, caused a stir. With its slangy portrayal of Paris low-life and its catchy *chansons*, it became the first French musical since the days of Messager to become internationally popular, but it was an isolated success which had no tomorrow. The second coming of the French musical on the world circuits was for another day.

From *Irma la Douce* onwards, it was all downhill. As the 1960s and 1970s went by, the great productions at the Châtelet and the Mogador grew less and less attractive and the spark disappeared utterly from the smaller

265

theatres. The musical theatre in Paris consisted largely of infrequent revivals of classic *opéra-bouffe* and *opéra comique*, a few French versions of foreign successes and some unfortunate local imitations of American pop and rock musicals. Lopez continued to turn out new works in an effortful, old-fashioned style for his own faithful public, but only *Viva Napoli* in 1970 approached the quality of his early successes, and some of his later works represented an almost embarrassing shadow of his great hits.

Sometimes there was no musical on show in the whole of Paris and it truly appeared as if the light musical theatre would disappear utterly from the country where it had had such brilliant beginnings. But then, in 1980, Alain Boublil and Claude-Michel Schönberg, two young writers who had earlier collaborated on a large scale musical piece on no less a subject than *La Révolution Française*, wrote *Les Misérables*. This was a show which followed in the newly fashionable, popular operatic style established by Tim Rice and Andrew Lloyd Webber in Britain. With its sung-through text and substantial popular score, *Les Misérables* nearly lived and died in one disappointing season in Paris but, discovered by British producer Cameron Mackintosh and re-staged in England in a new version, its merits swiftly became clear and what had now, in the image of the modern political scene, become an EEC musical show went on to become one of the biggest world successes of the 1980s.

As Boublil and Schönberg became part of the international writing scene, it was dispiriting to note that no other French pieces of quality arose in their wake, either in the popular operatic idiom of the moment or in that joyously irreverent musical comedy vein from where the new germs of light musical theatre must come when pieces like *Les Misérables* move into the world's opera houses. For the moment, awaiting better times, Paris's musical theatre exists on the occasional version of a middle-aged Broadway musical, a few performances of Offenbach and a season of the annual Lopez musical.

LES NOCES DE JEANNETTE

(Jeannette's Wedding)

an opéra-comique in one act by Michel Carré and Jules Barbier. Music by Victor Massé. Produced at the Théâtre Impérial de l'Opéra-Comique, Paris, 4 February 1853 with Félix Miolan-Carvalho (Jeannette) and Couderc (Jean) and played there regularly thereafter.

Played at the Royal Italian Theatre, Haymarket, London. Played at Camden House, Kensington. Produced at the Theatre Royal, Covent Garden 26 November 1860 in a version by William Harrison as *The Marriage of Georgette* with Louisa Pyne and Henri Corri. Played at the Bijou Theatre 6 February 1865 with Louisa van Noorden and Frederic Penna. Played in a version by Lester Buckingham as *Jeannette's Wedding* at the Prince of Wales Theatre, Liverpool, 1865 with Augusta Thompson and Squire Bancroft. Played at the Opera Comique 16 May 1872 with Haydée Abrek and Lourde. Played at the Gaiety Theatre 1 June 1875.

Produced in New Orleans November 1854. Produced at Niblo's Garden, New York, as *The Marriage of Jeannette* in Harrison's version 9 April 1855 with Miss Pyne and Harrison. Produced at the Academy of Music 28 October 1861. Produced at the Théâtre Français 24 November 1863 with Mlle Maillet. Played at the Stadt Theater in German 4 November 1865. Played at the Lina Edwin Theatre 4 January 1871.

Produced at the Kai-Theater, Vienna, 18 October 1862. Produced at the Komische Oper as *Jeanettens Hochzeitsfest* 23 February 1875.

Produced in Dresden 9 January 1854 and in Berlin 30 October 1857.

CHARACTERS

Jeannette
Jean
Thomas
Petit-Pierre

Jean is a merry bachelor who lives in a little, rustic French cottage in a little, rustic French village. Both Jean and his cottage could clearly do with the guiding and tidying influence of a good woman and, in fact, this very day the young man is due to march into matrimony with his pretty neighbour, Jeannette. Alas, as he steps up to sign the marriage documents before the mayor, Jean is taken by a dreadful attack of cold feet, and he finds he can only warm them by taking precipitate flight in front of the whole village.

When we meet him, he has made his way back to his cottage and locked himself in to brood over his narrow escape ('Mes Amis, Mes Chers Amis'). He does not want to be married; he wants to stay free to lead a life full of carefree bachelor fun and, when his old pals call to him to come and join them for a jolly evening with the local good-time girls, he happily looks forward to carrying on from where he had so nearly stopped. Before he can leave, Jeannette arrives at the back door. She has not come to weep over him or to scold him, she simply wants to know why he acted as he did, why he changed his mind at the last minute. After all, the marriage was his idea.

The embarrassed Jean clumsily admits that he has nothing against her personally; it is just the idea of marriage that makes a chap nervous, and

267

Jeannette, her question answered, sends him off to join his friends with a seeming insouciance. Only when he is out of sight does she let her feelings out ('Hélas, Quel Affront'). As she listens to the sound of revelry outside ('Oh! Oh! Margot, Lève Ton Sabot'), she pulls the wedding bouquet and ribbons from Jean's abandoned coat but then she pulls herself together and, while Jean is hitting the bottle and making free with Rose and Margot, she heads off home to stew up a plan to win back the errant bridegroom ('Mais Ne Pleurons Pas').

Jean returns home to get his bouquet as a gift for Rose or Margot and is embarrassed to find Jeannette there, with some uncomfortable tidings. Her old soldier father is coming to demand satisfaction from Jean and he has dug out his service revolvers for the occasion ('Halte Là, S'Il Vous Plaît'). The only way to stop him is for Jean to restore her lost reputation by signing a paper declaring that it was Jeannette who called off the marriage.

Jean agrees but, since he cannot read, he is unaware that what he is actually signing is the marriage contract. He is horrified when he finds out that he has been tricked, but Jeannette assures him that she has no intention of signing the contract herself. She merely intends to show it to the whole village to prove that it is she and not he who does not agree to the marriage. Jean joins in her laughter with a relieved sigh.

Jeannette then asks him to go outside and fetch her little cousin Pierre. Jean hurries to be obliging and so he does not see her sign the contract as soon as he is out of the way. The document is given to Pierre with an instruction to run around the village and show it to everyone and, when Pierre is safely on his way, Jeannette reveals what she has done. Jean is aghast and orders her to recover and tear up the paper, but she refuses. He tells her that he will be a brutal, tyrannical husband ('Ah! Vous Ne Savez Pas, Ma Chère') and, to prove his point, he smashes up the furniture and crockery of his home before her eyes, then storms upstairs to the attic to sleep off his overdose of white wine.

Left alone, Jeannette decides on a change of tactic. She must win from Jean the love she seeks. She sews up the tears in his wedding jacket ('Cours, Mon Aiguille, Dans la Laine'), dropping a loving tear on the fabric as she stitches, and then she sets to work. Pierre brings a couple of friends who help to take away the broken furniture and carry in the new pieces, which Jeannette had bought for her marriage, as replacements. She scrubs and sews and soon the scruffy cottage is shining tidily and supper is on the stove.

When Jean climbs down, sobered by his sleep, he finds his home changed as if by magic and Jeannette singing happily in the kitchen ('Voix Legère'). His pride will not allow him to appear pleased even when he discovers that his wife is a wonderful cook who has prepared his favourite *omelette au lard* and who behaves, into the bargain, with a humility and sweetness which he dared not hope for. Perhaps marriage is all right after all ('Allons! Je Veux Qu'On S'Assoie').

He is soon weakening thoroughly and connubial love sprouts happily ('Je Sens Mon Coeur Tressaillir d'Aise') until one of Jean's drinking pals sees fit to poke his head through the window to tell him that, as the marriage contract was not signed in front of the mayor, it isn't binding after all. But Jean does not want to go out gallivanting with the boys. If he isn't legally married, he soon will be, for he is discovering the joys of married life and a loving wife (Finale: 'Eh! Pardi! Nous Savions Bien'). When he takes down his wedding jacket and finds it mended and spotted with Jeannette's tears, he is completely won. The girls of the village bring Jeannette's veil and flowers to deck her hair and corsage and everyone prepares to set off to take part—a little later than previously intended—in *Les Noces de Jeannette*.

LES DEUX AVEUGLES

(The Two Blind Men)

a bouffonerie musicale in one act by Jules Moinaux. Music by Jacques Offenbach. Produced at the Théâtre des Bouffes-Parisiens, Paris, 5 July 1855 with Berthelier (Giraffier) and Pradeau (Patachon) and played regularly thereafter. Played at the Théâtre Impérial de l'Opéra-Comique 28 May 1858 with Berthelier and Sainte-Foy, 6 November 1900 with Coquelin cadet and Gourdon, and 12 December 1934 with Alban Derroja and Le Prin, etc.

First played in London at the Hanover Square Rooms 27 July 1856 by Monsieur Lavassor. Played at St James's Theatre 20 May 1857 with Gertpré and Pradeau. Produced at the Gallery of Illustration as *Beggar My Neighbour*, a Blind Man's Bouffe, in a version by F C Burnand 29 March 1870 with Thomas German Reed (Micky Mole) and Arthur Cecil (Bartlemy Batt). Produced at the Gaiety Theatre 16 April 1871 as *A Mere Blind* and played thereafter as *The Blind Beggars*, *The Two Blinds*, *Two Beggars*; and in a new version by Arthur Clements as *A Mere Blind* 31 August 1874 with John Maclean and J G Taylor, etc.

Produced at the Metropolitan Music Hall, New York, 31 August 1857 with Edgard and Thiéry. Produced at the Théâtre Français 3 September 1858. Produced at Wallack's Theatre in a version by Maria Walcot as *Going Blind* 31 October 1858 with Charles M Walcot (Bogus) and John Brougham (Buncomb).

Played at Kroll's Theater, Berlin, 10 March 1856.

Played at the Carltheater, Vienna, 19 April 1856.

CHARACTERS

Giacomo Patachon
Stanislas Giraffier

On a cold and windy Paris day, we meet the beggar, Patachon, plying his trade on an exposed city bridge. According to the placard which hangs around his neck, Patachon has been AVEUGLE DE NESSANCE (Blind from Burth) but, when he picks up his trombone and launches into song ('Dans Sa Pauvre Vie Malheureuse') at the approach of a likely customer, it quickly becomes evident that Monsieur Patachon is a fraud.

Patachon's unprofitable patch is made to look even less promising when it is invaded by a competitor. The mandolin-playing Giraffier is, according to his placard, AVEUGLE PAR AXIDANS (Blind from an Axidint) but, when his hat is blown off into the river, he is quick to run over to look after it. He is as much a charlatan as Patachon. When he returns to take up his place, he blindly taps his way past Patachon's pitch and manages to hit the trombonist with his cane, provoking some sharp abuse.

Patachon is not at all pleased at the thought of competition. He shifted to this bridge expressly because the profitability of his last pitch on the Pont St Michel, where he traded on crutches, was undermined by a one-armed rival. Giraffier is no less unhappy. He swapped his one-armed act for a blind one and shifted from the Pont St Michel because of the competition of the lame man. Both are determined to make the other shift on from this new spot, and a musical duel begins between them, Giraffier accompanying himself on the mandolin ('Justinien, Ce Monstre Odieux') and Patachon puffing away at his trombone in between the lines of his rendition of 'Sur le Pré Fleuri'.

At the sound of each other's voices, the two men become suspicious. Surely the other's voice is familiar. Both men go into tales of the most extravagantly nonsensical kind to explain their blindness. Giraffier claims to have lost his sight by having his hat brought down too sharply on his nose by a slave who was attempting to rescue him from a river full of crocodiles. Patachon, attempting to go one better with a wildly incongruous tale, attributes his blindness to a blow received from a Prince whilst on an adventure into the crater of the exploding Vesuvius.

The two men hurry back to their begging bowls at the approach of a passer-by and they end up scrapping over the dud coin which is thrown between them. Victorious in the fight for the meagre alms, Patachon now decides on a different approach. He will scare Giraffier off the bridge by demanding a duel. He is taken aback when, with the same idea, his rival accepts briskly and demands more and more powerful weapons, but the battle is postponed when business has to be plied once more. The two men each take up their own special song to attract the passing trade, but it turns out that the same song is special to both of them ('La Lune Brille') and, when it produces no money for either of them, they return to their quarrelling with a fresh vigour.

This time Patachon proposes that they should settle their territorial dispute by a game of cards, the loser to leave the bridge. Both, still believing the other to be blind, are certain of winning by cheating but, when they play, each is amazed to see the other manipulating the cards. Recriminations boil up and, finally, the two beggars end up attacking each other with their placards. Everything stops once more when another potential customer heaves into sight and Patachon and Giraffier, glaring furiously at each other, return to their songs; and there we leave them to a battle which doesn't look like being resolved for a long, long while.

BA-TA-CLAN

a chinoiserie musicale in one act by Ludovic Halévy. Music by Jacques Offenbach. Produced at the Théâtre des Bouffes-Parisiens, Paris, 29 December 1855 with Marie Dalmont (Fé-an-nich-ton), Pradeau (Fé-ni-han), Berthelier (Ké-ki-ka-ko) and Guyot (Ko-ko-ri-ko) and played frequently thereafter. Played at the Théâtre Dejazet 23 December 1987.

Played at St James's Theatre, London, 20 May 1857 with Mlle Dalmont, Pradeau, Mesmacre and Guyot. Produced at the Gallery of Illustration, London, as *Ching Chow Hi or A Cracked Piece of China* in a version by William Brough and Thomas German Reed 14 August 1865 with Augusta Thompson (Pet-Ping-Sing), J A Shaw (Ching Chow Hi), R Wilkinson (Ba-Ba-Whang) and Thomas Whiffen (Tee-To-Tum). Played at St George's Opera House 18 December 1867 with Mme d'Este Finlayson, J A Shaw, Francis Gaynar and Mr Morelli.

Produced at the Théâtre Français, New York, 25 February 1864. Played at Kelly and Leon's as *Ching Chow Hi* 4 July 1870, 27 March 1871, 21 October 1876, etc.

CHARACTERS

Fé-ni-han, *ruler of Ché-i-no-or*
Ké-ki-ka-ko, *of his entourage*
Fé-an-nich-ton, *also of his entourage*
Ko-ko-ri-ko, *captain of his guard and chief of the conspirators*
Conspirators

The scene represents the gardens of the oriental palace of Fé-ni-han, the ruler of the state of Ché-i-no-or, and the action commences with the entrance of the chorus of conspirators. They dance their way in silence, in a set of silly steps, to the back of the stage from where they watch the four principal characters of the action present themselves. First comes Ko-ko-ri-ko. He is the captain of the ruler's guard and carries a huge lance, but he is also the head of the plot which is being brewed against his sovereign. Ké-ki-ka-ko and Fé-an-nich-ton are members of the princely court and they carry musical instruments. Fé-ni-han himself wears a Chinese hat and he places himself ceremoniously on a pile of cushions which make up his throne. Once they are all in place, the principals join in a Chinese quartet ('Maxalla Chapallaxa') from which only a few words like 'tapioca' and 'macaroni' emerge with any familiar ring.

When the song and its accompanying actions are over, the conspirators and their sovereign leave the stage to the two courtiers. Ké-ki-ka-ko covertly picks up a hidden newspaper while Fé-an-nich-ton ferrets about and produces a magazine. Suddenly he sees what she is reading—it is a French centime awful! And he is reading *La Patrie*! Neither of them is Chinese after all; they are both French. How good it is to speak the dear old language again. It is so good that Fé-an-nich-ton (whose real name is Virginie) is even happy to listen to Ké-ki-ka-ko (who is Alfred de Cérisy in real life) tell his story.

He was a very rash young Parisian who dissipated his money, and a good

271

deal that wasn't his, in a series of speculations and he was obliged in the end to get out of France. Quite how he ended up in this far-off province he is not sure, as he suffered from such seasickness on the journey that there is a blur over that part of his life but, when he came to, here he was in this palace, covered in glittering garments and forced to repeat incomprehensible lines and to listen day in, day out to the fearsome tune of the revolutionaries, the song of Ba-ta-Clan.

Virginie is an actress ('J'Étais Aimable, Elégante') who came to China in a repertory company and she, too, was carried off in a strange way and brought to this peculiar place. It is not to her taste at all and she, like Alfred, longs for home ('Te Souviens-Tu de la Maison Dorée') and is only too willing to indulge in a nostalgic song and dance with him (La Ronde de Florette). Their patriotic senses now thoroughly awakened, the two decide that they must attempt to escape from the court of Ché-i-no-or. Alfred has already tried eighteen times. This will make a nineteenth and this time they may succeed.

At the moment, their sovereign is having a problem or two himself. He is continuously pursued by the fearsome chorus of conspirators upon whom his impressively yodelled commands seem to have no effect. He is obliged to give their leader a couple of slaps across the face to get them to go away so that he can soliloquise. And what is our surprise when the great Fé-ni-han turns out to be a Frenchman as well. He is Anastase Nourisson from Brives-la-Gaillarde and, right now, he has a longing to be back in Brives-la-Gaillarde.

He has been the ruler of this province for a number of years, during which time he has found that a fearsome countenance and an impressive delivery have compensated for a total ignorance of the local language in keeping up his lofty position. But now it appears that those attributes are losing their force. There is revolt in the air and, everywhere he goes, the confounded song of Ba-ta-Clan goes with him. He purges his frustration by insulting the captain of his guards in French, in the knowledge that he cannot understand, but if Fé-ni-han, in his turn, could understand Italian he would know that Ko-ko-ri-ko replies in that language with words that are all synonyms of death ('O Fé-ni-han, Ké-ki-ka-ko').

The attempt at an escape staged by Virginie and Alfred is a failure and the conspirators bring the sorry pair back to the palace with further unpleasant repetitions in Italian and gestures which are unmistakeable in their meaning ('Morto! Les Affreuses Grimaces'). Fé-ni-han orders the usual Chinese sentences of torture and death to be carried out but, as the two prepare to die, they defiantly join in one last chorus of La Ronde de Fleurette. The surprised Fé-ni-han hears that they are French.

Chasing the conspirators away, he happily reveals his own identity ('Je Suis Français'). Eight years ago he, too, fell into this country by accident and was brought before its Prince who, for all that he seemed Chinese, spoke with a strong Marseillais accent. He was given a choice: either be impaled on a nice sharp stake, in accordance with the native custom, or take over the position of Prince. Since that wasn't much of a choice, he accepted the

272

crown and here he has been for eight whole years, reigning over the people of Ché-i-no-or without speaking one word of their language.

It is this inability with the Chinese tongue which is at the root of his present unpopularity. One day the populace came to him with five of their number being pushed to the front for his notice. Presuming that they were criminals of some sort and relying on the old maxim of Zoroaster, 'when in doubt impale', he used his predecessor's nice sharp stake to have the five put to death. Unfortunately, it eventuated that they were five particularly meritorious individuals who had been put forward for honours. Things have not been the same since and, in consequence, he is rather anxious to leave.

To this end, he proposes that Alfred should take his place. The alternative is, of course, the stake. Alfred refuses. He has no intention of reigning and he has no wish to be impaled. If Fé-ni-han insists on this course of action he will have no alternative but to join the conspirators and start singing the song of Ba-ta-Clan himself. Tricked by this horrid threat, Fé-ni-han can only declare that, in that case, he too will take to singing the song against himself.

Virginie picks up her triangle and the three French expatriates launch into the song of revolution ('Le Chapeau Chinois, le Trombone') and follow up with the fifth act chorus from *Les Huguenots* with its refrain 'Hosannah! Mort Je T'Aime' as the conspirators march on to the stage to face them. They are coming with a letter, a very official looking letter with a big red seal. Fé-ni-han opens it and finds it is from Ko-ko-ri-ko ('Il Sait Son Nom'). He has discovered their identities but he, too, has a secret. He is a Parisian as well, but, unlike them, he has no wish to return to his native country. He wants simply to take over the post of ruler of Ché-i-no-or. They are all free to go and, as the song of Ba-ta-clan is heard one last time, Ko-ko-ri-ko regally ascends the pile of cushions.

LE MARIAGE AUX LANTERNES

(The Wedding by Lantern-light)

an opérette in one act by Michel Carré and Léon Battu. Music by Jacques Offenbach. A revised version of *Le Trésor à Mathurin* (7 May 1853). Produced at the Théâtre des Bouffes-Parisiens, Paris, 10 October 1857 with Mlle Mareschal (Denise), Paul Geoffroy (Guillot), Lise Tautin (Fanchette) and Mlle Dalmont (Catherine) and played regularly thereafter. Produced at the Théâtre National de l'Opéra-Comique 4 December 1919 with Jenny Syril, Victor Pujol, Mlle Moncy and Mlle Calas.

Played at the Lyceum Theatre, London, 9 May 1860 with Geoffroy. Produced at the Royalty Theatre 18 January 1862 with John Morgan, Maria Stanley, Miss Payne and Miss Mason. Produced at St James's Theatre 16 October 1869 as *Treasure Trove* with Frank Crellin, Bessie Lovell, Susan Pyne and Harriet Everard. Produced at the Gaiety Theatre 11 October 1871 with F Wood, Constance Loseby and Annie Tremaine.

Produced at the Stadt Theatre, New York, 18 March 1860 in German as *Die*

Verlobung beim Lanternscheine with Hübner, Frauen Siedenburg, Meaubert and Steglich-Fuchs. Produced at the Théâtre Français 6 February 1864 in French with Mme de Lussan, Donatien, Mlle Maillet and Anna Hamburg and at Wood's Museum in English 31 August 1868 with Blanche Galton, Thomas Whiffen and Susan Galton. Played at the Théâtre Français 1 May 1869 with Lucille Tostée and Mlle Irma.

Produced at the Carltheater, Vienna, in a version by Karl Treumann 16 October 1858 and at the Theater am Franz-Josefs-Kai, 21 June 1861 in French

Produced at Kroll's Theater, Berlin, 17 June 1858 and at the Opernhaus 13 December 1858 in German

CHARACTERS

Guillot, *a farmer*
Denise, *his cousin*
Fanchette, *a widow*
Catherine, *a widow*
Garde Champêtre, etc.

At the request of their Uncle Mathurin, the young farmer, Guillot, has taken into his home his orphaned cousin, Denise. Up to now it has been no hardship to him. Denise is a sweet-tempered, hard-working girl and it has been a pleasure to have her around the house. But, all of a sudden, she has taken to dreaming and neglecting her household occupations and Guillot finds the change in her both unpleasant and worrying ('Que Dirait l'Oncle Mathurin?').

He is certain that he knows the cause. Denise is at a delicate age and she is, without a doubt, starting to think of men. At the dance last week she danced nine dances with young Grévin from the next village and since then Guillot has spied her at the post office sending a letter. Denise denied that she was writing to Grévin, but Guillot is sure of his ground and he decides that the only way to keep the girl's mind off young men is to keep her hard at the housework.

Catherine and Fanchette, two local widows, have their thoughts unashamedly and permanently on men, or, more strictly, on men with money. As attractive young widows they have plenty of admirers, but the admirers have a sad lack of the wherewithal to support Catherine and Fanchette in the style they hanker after. Both of them fancy that the handsome Guillot is keen on them but, since he has no money, he is not eligible for consideration. Fanchette declares he is much too passive for her tastes, she would have no fun establishing mastery over him as she did over her first husband, while Catherine finds that he lacks the brutality she, in her turn, enjoyed in her first husband ('Mon Cher Mari Quelquefois S'Emportait'), but principally it comes down to the one fact—he isn't rich.

What the two little treasure-seekers don't know is that Guillot and Denise's Uncle Mathurin is rich, both rich and good-hearted. He has answered every request the struggling Guillot has made to him for a little pecuniary assistance over the years. Now Guillot has written to him once again but this time he has asked for rather more help than usual and he is very nervous lest his Uncle should refuse him. When Denise brings him a letter from the post office he is almost afraid to open it but, under the inquisitive eyes of the two widows, he finally does (Trio: 'Eh Bien! Guillot').

His uncle's reply is not wholly what he had hoped for. Mathurin will not give him any more money, but he has one last gift for his nephew, a gift worth far more than any banknotes. He will give him a treasure. That evening, at the hour of the Angelus, he may find it under the big tree in his garden. Guillot and the widows are thrilled. Both Catherine and Fanchette suddenly pour kind attentions on the farmer as he calls Denise to bring a bottle and glasses so that they may all drink to his good fortune (Drinking Song: 'Quand les Moutons Sont Dans la Plaine'). Later, a little tipsy, Guillot wobbles off towards the village, leaving Catherine and Fanchette to get into a no-holds-barred battle over him ('Ah! la Fine Fine Mouche') as they acidly spread the news of the farmer's new fortune.

Guillot is not the only one to have had a letter from Uncle Mathurin, for Denise's letter, which Guillot suspected of being to the jolly Grévin, was actually to her Uncle, pouring out to him the adolescent cares which had quelled her usual gaiety. Uncle Mathurin has no doubt about the remedy needed. Denise must have a husband and he will send her one. She must wait under the big tree in the garden at the sound of the Angelus that evening. Denise is a little unsure, for she already knows in her heart whom she wants for a husband but, since it is almost time for the Angelus, she makes her way to the tree to see what fate and Uncle Mathurin will bring.

Guillot, of course, is also on his way to the same spot armed with a heavy shovel, and the two widows are not far away, cautiously watching from behind the hedgerow (Quartet of the Angelus: 'Voici l'Angelus Qui Sonne'). While Guillot digs behind one side of the tree, Denise, on the other, shuts her eyes in a light, dreaming sleep and, as the farmer moves round the tree in search of the promised gold, he comes upon the girl who, stirring in her sleep, murmurs his name. As the irritated widows lean through the bushes, anxious not to miss a word or a chance, Guillot gently takes the letter from Denise's hand and reads his Uncle's words: 'I am sending you a husband and, by sending him to you, my dear, I am sending you a veritable treasure'.

Now Guillot understands what his Uncle has done. He has answered his letter and Denise's letter with one solution. Denise half-opens her eyes to demand, 'Are you there, my husband?' and, to the horror of the widows, the farmer answers her with a proposal of marriage. When the villagers rush on, all anxious to partake of the buried gold, they find Guillot with another kind of treasure. He and Denise will be wed under the lanterns which they have brought to light the evening's treasure hunt in a veritable *mariage aux lanternes* (Finale).

ORPHÉE AUX ENFERS

(Orpheus in Hell)

an opéra-bouffon in two acts by Hector Crémieux and Ludovic Halévy. Music by Jacques Offenbach. Produced at the Théâtre des Bouffes-Parisiens, Paris, 21 October 1858 with Léonce (Pluton), Désiré (Jupiter), Tayau (Orphée) and Lise Tautin (Eurydice). Revived there 1862 with Delphine Ugalde, 26 January 1867 with Ugalde and Cora Pearl as Cupid. Produced at the Théâtre de la Gaîté in a revised version in four acts 7 February 1874 with Montaubry, Christian, Meyronnet and Marie Cico, in 1875 with Mme Peschard, 8 January 1878 with Léonce, Hervé, Christian and Mme Peschard and in 1887 with Jeanne Granier, etc. Produced at the Théâtre de l'Eden 1889 with Mlle Granier. Produced at the Théâtre des Variétés 1902 with Albert Brasseur, Guy, Charles Prince and Mlle Méaly and 1912 with Prince, Guy, Bourillon and Mlle Méaly. Produced at the Théâtre Mogador 23 December 1931 with Lucien Muratore, Max Dearly, Adrien Lamy and Marise Beaujon. Produced at the Théâtre de la Gaîté-Lyrique 1972 with Jean Giraudeau, Jean Brun, Albert Voli and Anne-Marie Sanial. Produced at l'Espace Cardin 19 October 1984 with André Dran/Bernard Sinclair, Michel Trempont, Maarten Koningsberger/Marcel Quillevere and Ghislaine Raphanel/Martine March/Martine Masquelin. Produced at the Opéra 19 January 1988 with Georges Gauthier, Paolo Montarsolo, Michel Sénéchal and Danielle Borst.

Produced at Her Majesty's Theatre, London, in a version by J R Planché as *Orpheus in the Haymarket* 26 December 1865 with Mr Bartleman, William Farren, David Fisher and Louise Keeley. Played at St James's Theatre 12 July 1869 in French with José Dupuis, E Desmonts, Beauce and Hortense Schneider and at the Princess's Theatre 29 July 1870 with Schneider. Produced at the Royalty Theatre December 1876 with Henry Hallam, J D Stoyle, Walter Fisher and Kate Santley. Produced at the Alhambra Theatre in a version by H S Leigh 3 June 1877 with W H Woodfield, Harry Paulton, Loredan and Kate Munroe. Produced at His Majesty's Theatre in a version by Alfred Noyes, Frederic Norton and Sir H B Tree as *Orpheus in the Underground* 20 December 1911 with Lionel Mackinder, Frank Stanmore, Kingsley Lark and Eleanor Perry. Produced at Sadler's Wells Theatre in a version by Geoffrey Dunn 17 May 1960 with Jon Weaving, Eric Shilling, Kevin Miller and June Bronhill. Produced at the London Coliseum (English National Opera) in a version by Snoo Wilson 5 September 1985 with Emile Belcourt, Richard Angas, Stuart Kale and Nan Christie.

Produced at the Stadt Theater, New York, in German, March 1861 and played there 5 February 1862, 17 December 1863 with Fritze, Knorr, Klein and Frln von Hedemann, 12 December 1866 with Brügmann, Knorr, Klein and Frln Steglich-Fuchs, etc. Produced at the Théâtre Français 17 January 1867 with Elvira Naddie. Played at the Fifth Avenue Theatre 8 April 1868 with Lucille Tostée. Produced at the Bijou Theatre 1 December 1883 with Max Freeman, Digby Bell, Harry Pepper, Marie Vanoni and Laura Joyce Bell (Diana), Augusta Roche (Public Opinion), Pauline Hall (Venus), Billie Barlow (Mercury), Henri Leoni (Hercules), Amelia Summerville (Juno) and Ida Mülle (Cupid).

Produced at the Carltheater, Vienna, 17 March 1860 in a version by Johann Nestroy. Played there 16 February 1861 and 8 June 1861 in French. Produced at the Theater an der Wien 5 January 1867.

Produced at the Friedrich-Wilhemstädtisches Theater, Berlin, 23 June 1860.

CHARACTERS

Aristée (Aristaeus) *otherwise* Pluton (Pluto), *King of the Underworld*
Jupiter
Junon (Juno), *his wife*
Orphée (Orpheus), *a music teacher*
Eurydice, *his wife*
Mercure (Mercury)
Bacchus
Cupidon (Cupid)
Diane (Diana)
Vénus
Minerve (Minerva)
Mars
John Styx
Opinion Publique (Public Opinion)
Gods, Goddesses, etc.

ACT 1

Amid cornfields and cornflowers, in a picturesque piece of countryside near the classical Greek town of Thebes, stands the home of Orpheus, the director of the musical establishment which he has named modestly after himself, the Orphéon of Thebes. Opposite this barely august institution stands a more recent building, a honey shop (retail and wholesale), opened some months ago by a newcomer to the district. The honey shop and, more particularly, the attractive young shepherd, Aristaeus, who runs it, have become an irresistible attraction for the flighty Eurydice, a sensuous, upper-class nymph who is the wife of Orpheus, and she makes daily visits, with bunches of flowers and pouting lips, which are not slow to have the required effect on the manufacturing shepherd ('La Femme Dont le Coeur Rêve').

When her husband catches her hanging around Aristaeus' house with all-too-obvious intent, she is well prepared with reciprocal complaints—after all, it is well known that even a really third-class nymph isn't safe at her music lessons with the light-fingered Orpheus—and she makes no bones about the fact that she aims to have an affair with the pretty shepherd. She is bored, bored, bored with her husband and his silly tunes and his everlasting violin, and she has no compunction about hitting him where it really hurts and telling him so ('Ah! C'Est Ainsi').

This marriage is clearly heading for Scylla and Charybdis, and Orpheus doesn't care. His only worry is whether a judicial separation from this impossible woman may do his academic reputation any harm. On the whole, it would be safer for him simply to rid the world of the importunate shepherd. He decides to booby-trap the cornfield where Eurydice and her lover are wont to meet with a nest of poisonous snakes.

Aristaeus may have the appearance of a a truly Arcadian shepherd ('Moi, Je Suis Aristée'), but his confidential asides give a hint of something more dubious. It seems that, quite incomprehensibly, it was he himself who gave

277

Orpheus the idea of booby-trapping the cornfield and he doesn't seem the slightest bit worried at Eurydice's cries of warning to him not to go near the danger area. When the nymph sees her lover start to cross the field towards her, she dramatically launches herself towards him and, in a flash, she gets an asp in the ankle. As she expires deliciously ('La Mort M'Apparaît Souriante'), Aristaeus reveals himself in his true identity. He is none other than Pluto, King of the Underworld, and now that Eurydice is dead he can with impunity carry her off to his kingdom below the earth.

This is a situation which seems to be to the advantage of all concerned. Pluto and Eurydice have each other and Orpheus is rid of a pestilent wife. But there is one creature who is not happy. She is that ever-interfering embodiment known as Public Opinion and she is not willing to let things be. Orpheus must follow the dictates of morality as decreed in all the best newspapers. He must go to the highest court on Mount Olympus and demand that his lawfully wedded wife be returned to him ('Viens! C'Est l'Honneur Qui T'Appelle'). As so often, Public Opinion (or what the papers insist is public opinion) wins her interfering way over the individual, and poor Orpheus sets off for Olympus.

Up on the cloudy heights of Olympus, Morpheus is happily scattering his poppies and the gods are taking a nightly nap ('Dormons, Que Notre Somme'). Cupid and Venus come home in the small hours of the morning, having been out all night doing their allotted work, but there is an altogether unhappier immortal at their heels. Diana has been down to earth for her regular assignation with the pretty hunter, Actaeon, only to find that he has been turned into a stag ('Quand Diane Descend Dans la Plaine'). It is Jupiter's doing. He couldn't possibly have mortals knowing that the goddess of chastity was partial to earthly dalliances so, for the sake of mythology, he has disposed of the presumptuous hunter. Mythology will give Diana the credit, and only her family will know better. Appearances will be saved.

There are clearly quite a number of Olympian cracks being papered over for the sake of mythology. Mars and Vulcan seem to have been sharing Venus, and Cupid has been making use of his wings and arrows in ways never intended by the king of the gods who, himself, has been using his power of metamorphosis to help himself to some of the choicer ladies of ancient Greece. A little more decorum is needed amongst the immortals. A paternal lecture from Jupiter provokes much mumbling. The gods are sick of their eternal diet of nectar and ambrosia, they are sick of the boredom of perfect Olympian life. It is very difficult to behave nicely when one is bored. Juno has a particular complaint. She has heard about the godly carrying-off of the wife of the Theban music teacher and she is quite sure that it is her husband, in one of his famous disguises, who is responsible. For once, Jupiter is able to be properly righteous. He had nothing to do with the disappearance of Eurydice and, he announces pompously, he will punish the wrongdoer thoroughly. Mercury, his messenger, soon gleefully returns with a report of the event and a description of the rapist. It is Pluto.

When Pluto comes before the king of the gods he does his best to turn the conversation away from the subject of stolen wives. Faced with a categoric accusation, he boldly denies the facts and he is let off the hook when his interview with Jupiter is conveniently brought to a halt by a strange noise. It is the other gods and they are having a little family revolution ('Aux Armes! Dieux et Demi-dieux!'). They are going on strike over the nectar and ambrosia situation and they refuse to share Jupiter's indignation over the Eurydice affair. To their father's embarrassment, they have each and every one a similar exploit of his own to chide him with, from Alcmena to Europa, to Leda and Danaë (Rondeau des Transformations: 'Pour Séduire Alcmène la Fière').

The next visitor to the heights of Olympus is, o horror!, a mortal. Orpheus is unenthusiastically climbing the holy mountain, prodded onwards by the creature Public Opinion (Finale: 'Il Approche, Il S'Avance'). He launches his plea before the gods in a classic quatrain of despair and finishes his oration by accusing Pluto of stealing his wife. Jupiter, with a fine show of authority, commands that the King of the Underworld restore the lady to her rightful husband and, to the general surprise, declares that he himself will go down to Hades to make sure the hand-over is carried out satisfactorily. What is more, he will take the whole grumbling population of Olympus with him. The gods are delighted, Public Opinion is triumphant, and only the husband and the lover are desolate as everyone sets off for the nether regions.

ACT 2

Shut up in Pluto's boudoir in the heart of Hades, Eurydice is growing bored. She has been stuck in this luxurious but lonely room for two whole days and she is starting to regret the whole escapade. Her hours are not cheered by the presence of Pluto's gentleman of the bedchamber, the lanky and lecherous John Styx, whose masochistic whimperings for attention fit ill one who was apparently a king before he died ('Quand J'Étais Roi de Béotie'). His unattractive behaviour is attributable to too many tipples of the forgetful Lethe water and he is near to forgetting himself thoroughly when he hears footsteps approaching and hides Eurydice in her room.

Pluto appears with Jupiter whom he is leading on a guided tour of Hades. Jupiter's reason for insisting on this tour is to discover where Pluto has hidden this apparently delectable nymph whom he himself somehow missed out on. A super-godly scrutiny of the walls of Pluto's boudoir quickly reveals the tiny keyhole of the hidden room and, as soon as he is free of his host, Jupiter returns. Changing himself into a little fly, he passes through the keyhole and there he discovers the missing girl.

Eurydice is enchanted by the pretty, golden-winged creature buzzing about her and tries to catch it ('Il Me Semble Sur Mon Épaule'), and Jupiter joyously leads her on until she is thoroughly aroused and then lets himself be caught. She nearly faints when the fly talks to her, but she is delighted to hear that the little thing is in fact the King of the Gods and that he is offering to get her out of this dreary place and take her up to Olympus which is, by all accounts, the place for a much jollier kind of immortality. To avoid arousing suspicion, Jupiter must rejoin the party which Pluto is throwing for him, but he arranges to meet her there, disguised. Then, together they will fly away to heaven.

The party is going with a swing ('Vive le Vin! Vive Pluton') when Eurydice, dressed as a Bacchante, comes to keep her tryst ('J'Ai Vu Bacchus, Sur Sa Roche Fertile') at the height of the infernal dancing (Menuet/Galop). Jupiter and Eurydice prepare to flee together, but Pluto has been watching and has not been fooled. At the decisive moment he intervenes jealously: Jupiter shall not have her, even if she is a faithless creature who doesn't seem able to stick to one man or god for two minutes in a row. Jupiter sneers back that Pluto has no say in the matter for, according to his professions, Eurydice is not even here. But, while the gods bicker over the lady, they have forgotten Orpheus and the dreadful Public Opinion. The music teacher's violin is heard in the distance—he is coming across the River Styx to reclaim his wife.

Leaning on the arm of Public Opinion, like a tragic hero on the arm of his confidante, Orpheus moves into hexameters as the drama climbs to its height and he begins his classic plaint, but his peroration is cut short as the piqued king of the gods orders his wife to be returned to him. But there is one condition. Quite why it is a condition he cannot say. As Orpheus climbs his hexametric way back up towards the River Styx, Eurydice shall follow him towards the light of the living world but, should he turn round to look at her before the River is reached, she shall be lost to him forever, presumably as a punishment for lack of self-control or disobedience to a god. Pluto is not at all happy. It is some sort of a trick by which Jupiter plans to win the girl for himself. It is not fair!

Slowly Orpheus begins his climb, sustained at every step by the vocal encouragement of Public Opinion (Finale: 'Ne Regarde Pas En Arrière'), until he is nearly there. It seems that Orpheus has been mesmerised by the voice of Public Opinion and, against all expectations, he does not turn around. Jupiter is not having his game spoiled by that dreadful creature. He cheats. A quick bolt of thunder flung at Orpheus' heels undoes all of Public Opinion's work. Involuntarily, Orpheus turns back to check his charred sandals and his doom is sealed. Eurydice is lost. What relief! He climbs happily into Charon's barge with Public Opinion beside him, but without his wife.

But if Eurydice is not to return to earth, what is to become of her? Jupiter has the answer. Since he may not have her, Pluto shall not have her either and, in defiance of classical mythology, he decides to make her a Bacchante. It seems a suitable sort of occupation for a girl like her. The god of wine appears on his vine-wreathed throne borne aloft by a band of fauns and Eurydice is lifted up to join him ('Bacchus! Mon Âme Legère') as the curtain falls.

The revised and extended version of 1874 included additional ballets and choruses, an extended opening for the first act, solos in what became the second act for Mercury ('Eh Hop! Eh Hop! Place à Mercure'), Pluto (Air en Prose) and Mars, and in the third act for Eurydice (Couplets des Regrets) and Cupid (Couplets des Baisers). This largely new act also contained a fresh scene with the Judges of the Underworld and another with a comical policemen's chorus.

GENEVIÈVE DE BRABANT

an opéra-bouffe in three acts by Hector Crémieux and Étienne Tréfeu. Music by Jacques Offenbach. Produced at the Théâtre des Bouffes-Parisiens 19 November 1859 in a two-act version by Tréfeu with Lise Tautin (Drogan). Produced at the Théâtre des Menus-Plaisirs 26 December 1867 in a revised three-act version by Tréfeu and Crémieux with Zulma Bouffar (Drogan), Gourdon (Sifroy), Lesage (Charles), Daniel Bac (Golo), Mme Baudier (Geneviève) and MM Ginet and Gabel as the *gens d'armes*. Produced at the Théâtre de la Gaîté 25 February 1875 in revised five-act version by Tréfeu and Adolphe Jaime with Mme Matz-Ferrare, Lagrenay, Christian, Mlle Perret, Scipion and Gabel, and Mlle Thérésa as Briscotte. Produced at the Théâtre des Variétés 21 February 1908 with Jeanne Saulier (Drogan), Guy (Sifroy), André Simon (Charles), Max Dearly (Golo) and Geneviève Vix (Geneviève).

Produced at the Royal Philharmonic Theatre, London, 11 November 1871 in a two-act version by H B Farnie with Emily Soldene (Drogan), John Rouse (Sifroy), Henry Lewens (Golo), Selina Dolaro (Geneviève) and Edward Marshall and Felix Bury as the *gens d'armes*. Played at the Opera Comique 18 April 1874 with Soldene, Rouse, Lewens and Marie Cortaine, 20 March 1876 with Soldene, W J Hill, E Campbell, Charles Bedford and Emily Muir, at the Philharmonic 23 January 1878 with Alice May and Alice Burville, at the Alhambra 16 September 1878 with Soldene, Thomas Aynsley Cook, Lewens and Constance Loseby, and at the Royalty Theatre 21 November 1881 with Soldene, J G Taylor (Cocorico), Miss B Farquhar (Charles), Lewens and M Marshall.

Produced at the Théâtre Français, New York, 22 October 1868 with Rose Bell, Carrier, Beckers, Goby and Marie Desclauzas and 7 February 1870 with Mrs Howard Paul, Hirrebeuk and Mlle Guerretti. Played at the Olympic Theatre 24 October 1872 with Marie Aimée, Juteau, Duchesne and Mlle Bonelli. Played at the Lyceum Theatre 2 November 1974 in English with Soldene, J B Rae, Lewens, Agnes Lyndurst, Marshall and E D Beverley.

Produced at the Carltheater, Vienna, in a version by Ernst Dohm as *Die schöne Magellone* 3 April 1861 and at the Theater an der Wien 9 May 1868 in a version by Julius Hopp.

Produced at the Friedrich-Wilhelmstädtisches Theater, Berlin, in Dohm's version 1 July 1861.

CHARACTERS

Sifroy, *Duke of Curaçao*
Geneviève, *his wife*
Golo, *his favourite*
Drogan, *a pastrycook*
Brigitte, *the confidante of Geneviève*
Charles Martel
Grabuge, *a police sergeant*

281

Pitou, *a low ranking police officer*
Vanderprout, *the burgomaster*
Narcisse, *the court poet*
Péterpip, *an alderman*
Isoline, *Golo's wife*
The Hermit of the Ravine
Christine, Barberine, Gudule, Grudelinde, Faroline, Irénée, Houblonne, Griselis, Dorothée, Yolande, Gretchen, Rodogune, Rosémonde, Armide, Bradamante, Dulcinée, Renaud de Montauban, Saladin, Don Quichotte, etc.

ACT 1

Once upon a time, in the city of Curaçao in Brabant, there lived a ducal family which had no heir. It had no heir very largely because Duke Sifroy hadn't got round to sharing the bed of his wife, Geneviève, and the reason he hadn't got round to it was his favourite courtier, the ambitious Golo. Golo didn't want Sifroy and Geneviève to go to bed together because he didn't want them to have an heir. If they didn't have an heir in the usually accepted biological way, Sifroy would make his dear friend Golo his heir, and then Golo would be the Duke of Curaçao and he could go to bed with Geneviève, and Golo wanted to be that and do that very much indeed. So Golo spent his time distracting the Duke from Geneviève and her bed with lots and lots of work and all sorts of other alternative and exhausting activities until Sifroy became a weary cipher of a man, lugubrious and dull, relying for everything on his friend and neglecting his wife dreadfully.

This unhappy, heirless land did not prosper, for the people of Curaçao wanted a little Duke to make the headlines in their newspapers and they got rather gloomy. At the time the curtain rises, Duke Sifroy is expected back in town after a diversionary jaunt to an out-of-town monastery organised by Golo, and the people are loyally lining the town square to give him a welcome home (Opening Chorus: 'Flamands de Tous les Pays').

That is all he is going to get because the burgomaster has decided it isn't worth spending the money on a ball and fireworks for the occasion ('Vos Échevins, Vos AEdiles'). When the cavalcade approaches, Golo comes on ahead. He has some quiet, treasonable words for the ear of the burgo-master—can he count on his support in the event of his very probable forthcoming accession to the rank of Duke? The burgomaster, who believes in keeping in with authority under all circumstances, replies hastily 'very probably'.

Golo's plans for elevation do not run without a hiccup and it is the burgomaster who is at the bottom of the first one. In his anxiety to increase the Duke's vigour and raise the probability of a legitimate heir, the burgo-master has advertised a reward in the local newspaper for a philtre or foodstuff which might bring the twinkle back to the ducal eye. Today he has had a reply and an aphrodisiac pie is submitted by the little pastrycook, Drogan, from the shop on the square. It is a splendid pie and young Drogan swears by its virtues (Rondo du Paté: 'Salut! Noble Assemblée'). The reward the lad seeks, should his pie succeed, is to be made a page to the lovely Geneviève, for he has fallen in love with the Duchess and longs only to be near her. In the meanwhile, he sings pretty songs underneath her window and waits in hope ('En Passant Sous la Fenêtre').

The sound of the national anthem ('Curaçoïens, Que la Victoire Couronne') announces the arrival of Sifroy who has a speech (written by Golo) to read (prompted by Golo). Being rather hot, he takes off his ducal cap and pops it on Golo's head while he reads and the impression is complete. The glowing Golo feels he is already effectively Duke of Curaçao. The burgomaster reminds Sifroy, with a gift of baby clothes, what his people expect of him, but Sifroy is more interested in his dinner and tucks into Drogan's delicious pie while Golo is soliloquising avidly instead of keeping an eye on him.

Amazingly enough, the pie really does do something to the ducal constitution. Within minutes Sifroy is leaping about with a look in his eye which hasn't been seen for a long time, singing a very slightly bawdy song (Couplets de la Poule: 'Une Poule Sur un Mur') and thinking about his wife. Golo realises that it is time to snap out of his day-dreaming and get back to his work.

Up in the Duchess's boudoir her maids are sewing ('Travaillons Comme des Fées') when Drogan is brought in. He has earned his reward and the burgomaster has sent him to the Duchess's apartment to be made into a page. The girls cluster around the pretty boy, teasing him delightedly as they deck him out in a style fitting to his new position ('Cet Habit-là Ne Lui Va Point') until he is quite the cutest of fellows ('Grâce à Vous, Mesdemoiselles'). When Geneviève sees him, and learns that it is he who has been singing under her window, she is suitably impressed. Drogan pretends to faint with emotion under her gaze and gets as a reward the tender attentions of his new mistress (Trio de la main et de la barbe: 'Ah! Madame, Vous Qui Brillez').

Their little game is interrupted by the dramatic arrival of the lusty Sifroy. He starts to make love to his wife but, before he can get going, he is interrupted by the desperate Golo with piles of documents, the news that his overlord Charles Martel is coming, and requests for orders which put the Duke off his stride to such effect that, before the vital moment, he suffers frightful indigestion ('Ah! de Mon Coeur un Trouble S'Empare') and has to be hurried off to his own bed. Once again the succession is not secured and Drogan is left wondering if, perhaps, it is not up to him to help out in this sad situation.

The next morning Sifroy feels decidedly delicate. He can take nothing but a little tea ('Je Ne Connais Rien au Monde'), and his temper is severely aroused when Golo come to him with the false news that the pastrycook-page took advantage of his indisposition to sneak into the boudoir of his wife. So, Geneviève is unfaithful! Before he has time to digest this information to its worst effect, a visitor arrives. It is the emperor Charles Martel, equipped with his famous hammer, his coat-of-arms and his signature tune ('J'Arrive

Armé de Pied en Cap'), who is on his way to catch a train at the Gare du Nord.

The energetic monarch is off to have a scrap with the Saracens and he wants Sifroy and his army to come along and join in. Sifroy pleads a dicky tummy, but to no effect. It is a royal command and the Saracens are compulsory. Geneviève rushes on to hear the disastrous news ('Ciel! Qu'Ai-Je Appris?') only to hear her husband decree that she is disgraced, repudiated and condemned to death. Golo, invested with the all-important cap of office, will be regent during his absence, and its hey! for the Gare du Nord and Palestine ('Départ Pour la Paléstine').

ACT 2

In a picturesque ravine which owes not a little to such operas as *Der Freischütz*, the rumblings of a storm are heard as Geneviève is hurried on by Drogan and her confidante Brigitte ('Fuyons, Fuyons, l'Orage'). For five months they have been stumbling through the forests of Brabant trying to escape the amorous and/or vengeful claws of the vile Golo and his creatures. They hide in a convenient hut at the approach of two buffoonish policemen, Sergeant Grabuge and his subordinate, Pitou, whose ordinary duties have been supplemented by the search for the missing Duchess ('Protéger le Repos des Villes'). They bandy words in a burst of low comedy, quarrel when Pitou insists on giving his superior orders, and discuss the pros and cons of killing a lady, until they have filled in the time allotted for their comedy spot and leave the stage to Golo and the burgomaster.

Golo has already written an open letter to himself confirming the death of Sifroy, and now he has brought his crony to the ravine to consult its resident oracular hermit as to the whereabouts of the missing Duchess. When he presses the button which brings the old man bouncing out of a tree stump like a wooden jack-in-a-box, he gets bad news ('Je Suis l'Ermite du Ravin'). The Duke is not only not dead, he never went to Palestine. Martel's merry band only got as far as Narbonne when it started to rain, so they stopped off at the château of Asnières and they've been there ever since having one big party. When Golo tries to dispute this piece of intelligence, the miffed hermit magics up a vision and, sure enough, there is Sifroy having a whale of a time.

It is clearly necessary to make a change of plan. If Sifroy is not safely dead, then he must be safely discredited. Instead of killing Geneviève, Golo will wed her and display to the populace her husband's horrid order for her death. The problem is to find Geneviève. Unfortunately, at this very moment the dripping roof of the convenient hut drips once too often and Geneviève sneezes. Golo recognises her sneeze immediately and the Duchess is dragged sniffling from her hiding place. She defends herself by giving her aggressor a couple of nasty smacks across the face and Golo petulantly decides to go back to plan one and he orders his policemen to put the Duchess to death.

Geneviève tries to talk them out of following their orders ('Allons,

Madame, Il Faut Mourir') but Drogan has a much more effective method of saving her. He dresses up as the hermit and appears frighteningly before the two *gens d'armes*, covering them with unspeakable threats until they release their prisoner remorsefully and agree that they themselves are worthy only to be dead. They settle for a simultaneous killing of each other and, as they fall to the ground, Drogan sets secretly off in the direction of Asnières with a lock of Grabuge's hair is his pocket (Geneviève didn't want hers cut) as part of a plan to persuade Sifroy and the emperor to return to Curaçao. When they are gone, the policemen realise they are not dead at all, and get up to march happily off into another episode.

At Asnières, the Crusaders really are having an orgiastic time (Choeur des Cocodettes). Sifroy is lounging about in the company of a lot of famous people like Ricardo de Montauban, Armide, Bradamante, Don Quixote and Saladin, not to mention Martel himself who is always handy with a characteristic song ('Pour Combattre les Infidels'). Sifroy has found his manhood and a nice playmate, a mysterious lady called Isoline who is actually married—which gives the romance a delicious *frisson*—to a nasty creature who spent all her dowry and has since become the intimate friend of some ridiculous duke whose duchy and wife he is well on the way to stealing.

There is plenty of entertainment to go with the carousing and wenching at Asnières including a display by a couple of Tyrolean singers (Tyrolienne: 'Le Jour Point') and a farandole and fancy dress parade of Follies ('Place Pour la Farandole') and jollity wallows onwards until a dusty young messenger arrives to see Sifroy. It is Drogan and he brings news of the death of Geneviève and a lock of her hair to prove it. He explains the fact that the hair is grey with a story of hoary grief (Couplets de la Mèche: 'Geneviève Était Blonde').

Sifroy decides that perhaps, at some stage, he had better check on how things are going back home and he asks everyone back to Curaçao to continue the party. There he and they will see his faithful Golo and mark how he has cared for the Duchy. At the name of Golo, Isoline has a fit of chuckles—that, of course, is her husband. Sifroy has seduced the wife of his favourite. What a hoot. But, for the meanwhile, there seems no reason to stop the party that is so merrily in progress ('Amis, Faisons Vibrer Ces Dômes Brillants').

ACT 3

Meanwhile, back in the forest, Geneviève is making a fuss over a picturesque faun ('Quand On Possède une Bîche') but Drogan, having finally extricated the Duke from his pleasures, returns in time to hide his mistress from Golo's hunting party ('Partons en Chasse'). Golo is pretty merry for he has decided that, in the continued absence of Sifroy, it is time for the burgomaster to confer on him the palatial cap which will confirm him as the new Duke of Curaçao.

The burgomaster may be an opportunist of the first degree, but he still has worries about such an action. On the other hand, when a couple of blackfaced vagabonds turn up ('Je Viens de la Turquie'), he has no scruples in using his high position to have them arrested by Grabuge and Pitou, and he laughs at their pretensions when they claim to be Sifroy and Charles Martel. Things take on a different colour when Geneviève, Drogan and Brigitte emerge from their hidey-hole. Drogan gives the Duke the true story of events in Brabant and exposes Golo as a traitor, and the burgomaster quickly sees that it is time to change sides again as the whole party set out for Curaçao to take vengeance on the usurper.

In the great hall of Sifroy's palace the natives are indulging in the inescapable national anthem as a prelude to Golo's coronation as the new Duke. The burgomaster does his best to prolong the ceremony, waiting for the real Duke to turn up and stop the proceedings but, when Sifroy does appear, Golo brands him an impostor. Suddenly a weird creature enters: it is Drogan dressed up in the clothes of the hermit of the ravine and he has a heap of accusations to make ('Golo, Monstre, Plein de Crime'). One by one he calls up the supposedly dead victims of Golo's wickedness—the Duchess and her confidante, the two policemen and, finally, the cruellest of all, his termagant wife, Isoline. Golo is convicted and sentenced to be restored to his vengeful spouse as, with a jolly chorus, everything else ends happily.

The English version by H B Farnie made considerable alterations particularly in the second act, eliminating the entire Asnières episode and the character of Isoline, reorganising the action and reallocating the music of some of the songs to new situations and unrelated lyrics. The most successful results of this fairly tasteless rearrangement were the creation of the so-called Sleep Song ('Sleep On, Sleep On, My Queen!') for the show's star, Emily Soldene, in the role of Drogan and the invention of new lyrics to the song of the *gens d'armes* ('We're Public Guardians Bold and Wary').

LA BELLE HÉLÈNE

(Beautiful Helen)

an opéra-bouffe in three acts by Henri Meilhac and Ludovic Halévy. Music by Jacques Offenbach. Produced at the Théâtre des Variétés, Paris, 17 December 1864 with Hortense Schneider (Hélène), José Dupuis (Paris), Léa Silly (Oreste), Grenier (Calchas) and Couder (Agamemnon). Revived there 1876 with Anna Judic, Dupuis and Mme Angèle, 1886 with Judic, Dupuis, Baron and Léonce, 1889 with Judic, 1890 with Jeanne Granier, and 25 November 1899 with Juliette Simon-Girard, Dastrez, Baron and Eve Lavallière, etc. Produced at the Théâtre de la Gaîté-Lyrique 5 October 1919 with Marguerite Carré, Fernand Francell, Max Dearly and Denise Grey. Produced at the Théâtre Mogador 25 February 1960 with Géori Boué and Bernard Plantey. Produced at the Théâtre des Bouffes-Parisiens 24 September 1976 with Nicky Nancel, André Battedou and Michel Roux (Agamemnon). Produced at the Théâtre National de l'Opéra-Comique 25 April 1983 with Anne-Marie Grain/ Suzan Daniel and Georges Gautier/Adrian Martin and 21 September 1985 with Sandra Browne/Madelyne Renée and Gautier/Jérome Pruett. Produced at the Théâtre de Paris 13 November 1986 with Eva Saurova/Valerie Marestin and Gautier/Pierre Catala.

Produced at the Adelphi Theatre, London, in a version by F C Burnand as *Helen, or Taken From the Greek* 30 June 1866 with Miss Furtado, Mrs A Mellon, Miss A Seaman, Paul Bedford and J L Toole. Produced at St James's Theatre 13 July 1868 with Schneider. Produced at the Gaiety Theatre 18 July 1871 with Mlle Clary, Mario Widmer, Mlle Gentien, Edouard Georges and Charlier. Produced at St James's Theatre 12 July 1873 with Marie Desclauzas, Mario Widmer and Pauline Luigini. Produced at the Gaiety Theatre in a version by Charles Lamb Kenney 23 October 1871 with Julia Mathews, Constance Loseby and Annie Tremaine. Produced at the Alhambra Theatre in a new version by F C Burnand 16 August 1873 with Kate Santley, Rose Bell, Amy Sheridan and Harry Paulton. Played at the Royalty Theatre, 10 March 1878 with Miss Santley, W H Fisher, Topsy Venn and Lionel Brough. Produced in a new and altered version by A P Herbert under the title *Helen* at the Adelphi Theatre 30 January 1932 with Evelyn Laye (Helen), Bruce Carfax (Paris), Desirée Ellinger (Orestes), George Robey (Menelaus) and W H Berry (Calchas). Produced at Sadler's Wells Theatre in a version by Geoffrey Dunn 31 May 1963 with Joyce Blackham, Kevin Miller and Patricia Kern. Produced at the London Coliseum (English National Opera) 4 September 1975 with Anne Howells, Geoffrey Pogson and Lynn Barber.

Produced at Chicago 1867. Produced at the Stadt Theater, New York, 3 December 1867 in German with Hedwig L'Arronge-Sury, F Herrmann and Eugenie Schmitz. Produced at the Théâtre Français 26 March 1868 with Lucille Tostée, Guffroy and Mlle de Felcourt. Produced at the New York Theatre in an English version by Molyneux St John as *Paris and Helen or The Greek Elopement* 13 April 1868 with Sophie Worrell, Irene Worrell and Jennie Worrell. Played at the Grand Opera House 13 April 1871 with Marie Aimée, Constant Gausins and Elise Persini and at the Olympic Theatre 9 December 1871 with Aimée, Juteau and Mlle Polland. Produced at the Casino Theatre 12 January 1899 with Lillian Russell. Produced by the New York City Opera 21 September 1976 with Karan Armstrong, Henry Price and David Griffith.

Produced at the Theater an der Wien, Vienna, as *Die schöne Helena* in a version by Ernst Dohm 17 March 1865.

Produced at the Friedrich-Wilhelmstädtisches Theater, Berlin, 13 May 1865.

CHARACTERS

Paris, *son of King Priam of Troy*
Menelaos, *King of Sparta*
Agamemnon, *King of Kings*
Calchas, *prophet of Jupiter*
Achilles, *King of Phthiotis*
Ajax I, *King of Salamis*
Ajax II, *King of Locris*
Helen, *Queen of Sparta*
Orestes, *son of Agamemnon*
Leaena
Parthenis

Bacchis
Philocomos, Euthycles, etc.

ACT 1

Quite how Paris, son of Priam of Troy, accomplished what has become
known to students of classical mythology as The Rape of Helen (thereafter
to be subtitled 'of Troy') and, by his deed, set in motion the most literature-
inspiring event of ancient times, has never been fully explained. Until now,
that is. One day, in Sparta, ancient Greece, the people were celebrating the
feast of Adonis ('Vers Tes Autels, Jupin'), a feast with particularly amorous
connotations given the story of Venus and Adonis and their theo-mortal
relationship (but that's another story), and with flowers and fruits they
danced their way to the great temple of Jupiter in the town's main square to
pay homage to the day.

At the temple of Jupiter, Calchas, the omnipotent seer of all Sparta, can be
found. He is not a very contented priest as the locals have taken to including
far too many perishable and unprofitable flowers in their offerings instead of
useful, edible things like pigs or spendable things like gold, but he has seen
fit to invest in having the temple's thunder sheet renovated in order to back
up his day's Olympian messages with an impressive and hopefully productive
sound effect. The ceremonial procession of the day arrives at the temple
headed by none other than the Queen of Sparta herself, the lovely Helen
('Amours Divins').

Today Helen has things on her mind other than Adonis and flowers, and
she is eager for a private chat with her priestly confidant. It's this business on
Mount Ida that she's heard about, involving an exceptionally handsome
shepherd and a golden apple and a competition. Somebody said something
about the prize being the love of the most beautiful woman in the world and,
without wishing to appear to be conceited, she is a little concerned. This
would, he must agree, seem to mean her. Once again the Fates seem
determined to entwine her in their toils, just as they entwined Leda, her
mother, when the god Jupiter took her for his mate, and just as they have
since entwined Helen on so many occasions since she was first carried off at
the age of sixteen right up to her marriage with King Menelaos. Ah, how she
would love to be just an ordinary little peasant person with a nice, unexceptional, middle-class husband. It is excessively tiresome to be perpetually
singled out by the Fates when all a girl wants is a bit of peace and quiet. An
exceptionally handsome shepherd? Hmmm. Well, there isn't a lot one can do
about the Fates, is there? Heigh ho.

Helen's nephew, the anachronistically pubescent Orestes, puts an end to
Helen's analysis session when he lurches on to the scene in the company of
two superior courtesans, Leaena and Parthenis. He's suffering the after
effects of a jolly night out 'Au Cabaret du Labyrinthe', and both he and his
companions have some light-hearted words to toss about concerning the
Queen's deliciously passive submission to the more amorous caprices of the
Fates. Calchas just has time to send the revellers on their way before another
passer-by commands his ear. This one is a shepherd, but not just any

shepherd. He's *the* shepherd, the one from Mount Ida, and to prove his credentials he's backed up by a Cytherean dove with a written testimonial from Venus herself, and an order from the goddess to supply to the bearer one Queen of Sparta.

Calchas is all agog and begs the shepherd (who, incidentally, has not mentioned that he is in fact the Prince of Troy in disguise) to give him an account of his memorable judgement ('Au Mont Ida Trois Déesses'). He will, of course, do his priestly job and, in accordance with Venus' orders, help Paris to win Helen. It isn't actually too difficult. The Fates soon find a way of putting Helen in converse with the exceptionally handsome shepherd and, once she has touched up his posture and stopped him from gaping overmuch, she finds it rather difficult to disengage his gaze from hers. Disengage they must, however, for the local Kings are on their way to join the ceremony ('Voici les Rois de Grèce'), and even the Fates can only excuse a certain amount in public.

The Kings are the two Ajax, a sturdy, double-bodied creature (well, Homer referred to them so often in tandem that it takes little literary licence to make Siamese twins of them); the great Myrmidon, Achilles, bubbling always on the edge of action or of losing his temper, and with a decided complex about his vulnerable heel; Menelaos, the husband of Helen and a bit wary about the trouble she could cause him ... but let's not get ahead of ourselves; and the chief King, Agamemnon, the length of whose name precludes the necessity of fitting any aphoristic adjective in a line with it. Agamemnon's speech on the temple steps turns out, like most politicians' speeches, to have nothing to do with the occasion or with Adonis.

It is a lament for the lack of wit in Sparta. He proposes to encourage this quality with a tripartite competition composed of a charade, a contest of puns and a series of *bouts-rimés* and, to the amazement of the King and the fury of Achilles, this exceptionally handsome shepherd pops up from nowhere to easily win each section. His final poem, though sufficiently well-made, does not please Menelaos overmuch with its hints of marital infidelity but, acclaimed the winner (Finale: 'Gloire Au Berger'), Paris unveils his royal rank and, as Helen steps forward to crown him the winner, she proffers a royal invitation to supper.

Calchas, on cue, does his bit for Venus. A peal of manufactured thunder heralds one of his oracles: Menelaos is summoned by the gods to go to Crete. Anywhere in Crete, and immediately. The Gods must be obeyed and, as the act ends, in spite of the fact that he has company for dinner, the King prepares to sail for Crete.

ACT 2

Under the picture of Leda and the swan which dominates her apartment, Helen is getting dressed for dinner. To the surprise of her servants, she has chosen the most unrevealing gown in her wardrobe ('Non Pas de Toilette Éclatante') and, with one eye on the picture, she invokes Venus ('Dis Moi, Vénus'). Why is it always her family that the goddess chooses for these baroque episodes? Couldn't she have found a more prosaic reward for her shepherd? Is she, once more, to be sacrificed bodily on the altar of the goddess's whim? Well, predestination or no predestination she will, at least, put up some sort of resistance, some show of modesty.

When Paris arrives and suggests that, since she is not inclined to him, the answer must be that she is not the most beautiful woman in the world, she alters her attitude a little. In a pointed fashion, the prince outlines to her the three ways of winning a woman: by love, by force and by trickery. She won't admit the first, he reserves the second, and then, with a twinkle in his eye, he leaves, just as the Kings arrive to partake of a game of snakes and ladders ('Gloire à l'Oie'). Helen's mind is on other things, as the game turns to the disadvantage of the always angry Achilles, and Calchas cheats to win (Ensemble: Le Jeu d'Oies) before returning to Helen's apartment to listen all over again to a recital of her sufferings in the cause of virtue. At the end of her complaint she makes him promise to cause her to have a pleasant dream all about Paris, and gently falls asleep.

While she sleeps ('En Couronnes Tressons les Roses'), Paris creeps into her room disguised as a slave and, when she awakes, she believes herself to be in the dream she ordered from Calchas and happily indulges in fulsome caresses with him ('Oui, C'Est un Rêve'). Alas, somehow Menelaos has got back from Crete unnoticed—or perhaps he never went—and he bursts in on this romantic scene crying scandal (Finale). Helen, unabashed at being caught *in flagrante delicto*, invokes her best ally, the Fates, and, on the principle that attack is the best form of defence, proceeds to berate Menelaos for not letting her know he was coming home.

Paris declares pragmatically that if he can't carry Helen off to Troy with him now he will just have to return for her later. It is, after all, Venus' decree that Helen shall be his, and the Queen doesn't seem exactly against the idea either. For the moment, however, it is perhaps more discreet not to try to take action in front of an outraged husband and half the court and army of Greece.

ACT 3

Down by the sea at Nauplia, Orestes is enjoying the beach and the sun with his lady friends ('Vénus au Fond de Notre Ame') and with the Kings who have gone so far as to show their knees in Greek swimsuits. Menelaos and Helen are still bickering over the week-old events ('Là, Vrai, Je Ne Suis Pas Coupable') and Helen, by and large, seems to be getting the better of it.

Poor, silly Menelaos gets little support in his attempts to keep his wife for his own private use. Even Agamemnon and Calchas are against him as Venus, annoyed at Menelaos' interruption of her plan, has launched a nasty plague of immorality all over Greece. Husbands and wives are walking out on each other in even greater numbers than usual. It really is too bad of Menelaos not to think of the greater good and let his wife go off with the Trojan ('Lorsque la Grèce Est un Champ de Carnage'/'C'Est une Immense Bacchanale').

The sulky king suggests another way of getting out of Venus' bad books. He's written a letter to the goddess in Cythera, asking her to send her all-seeing grand priest over to fix things up. Calchas is purple with indignation. Another priest on his patch! He has no time to discolour before a chorus of welcome ('Le Galère de Cythère'/'La Grèce Entière Suppliante') brings on the grand priest.

He's not the kind of grand priest one expected at all; fashionably dressed, with a curled beard and ringlets, and singing and dancing in a very gay fashion, but he seems to be very far-seeing for he knows everybody's names and everybody's business. He pronounces the goddess's decision: Venus will withdraw her displeasure from Greece if the Queen of Sparta makes a little pilgrimage to Cythera. Helen comes to the dock and, under her husband's orders and the cheers of the populace, she is led on board (Finale) but, as soon as she is safely installed on the prow of the ship alongside the grand priest, the latter throws off his costume. It is Paris! The Trojan war can now take place.

BARBE-BLEUE

(Bluebeard)

an opéra-bouffe in three acts by Henri Meilhac and Ludovic Halévy. Music by Jacques Offenbach. Produced at the Théâtre des Variétés, Paris, 5 February 1866 with José Dupuis (Barbe-Bleue), Hortense Schneider (Boulotte), Kopp (Bobèche), Couder (Popolani), Paul Hittemans (Saphir), Mlle Vernet (Hermia) and Aline Duval (Clémentine). Revived there April 1872 with Dupuis, Mlle Schneider and Dailly (Popolani), 1888 with Jeanne Granier (Boulotte); and 1904 with Chapuis, Anna Tariol-Baugé, Louis Baron, André Simon, Prince, Eve Lavallière and Léonie Laporte. Produced at the Théâtre de Paris 1971 in a revised version with Michel Caron, Martine Surais and Jean Le Poulain.

Produced at the Olympic Theatre, London, in a version by H Bellingham as *Bluebeard Re-Paired* [A Worn Out Story Done Up A-New] 2 June 1866 with W M Terrott (Bluebeard), Miss Galton (Mopsa), W H Stephens (Earlypurl), Mr Atkins (Popolani), Amy Sheridan (Sapphire), Miss Wilson (Periwink), Nellie Farren (Robert) and Harriet Everard (Queen Greymare). Played at St James's Theatre 28 June 1869 with José Dupuis and Mlle Schneider and at the Princess's Theatre 21 July 1870 with Carrier, Mlle Schneider and Daubray. Produced at the Standard Theatre 9 December 1869 in a version by Charles Lamb Kenney with Wilford Morgan, Emily Soldene, J D Stoyle, Thomas Aynsley Cook, Caroline Braham, Mlle Albertazzi and Alice Aynsley Cook. This version produced at the Gaiety Theatre 29 August 1870 with E D Beverley, Julia Mathews, Stoyle, Aynsley Cook, John Maclean and Constance Loseby; at the Avenue Theatre 16 June 1883 with Henry Bracy, Florence St John, Claude Marius, Arthur Williams, Lottie Venne and Maria Davis; and at the Comedy Theatre 16 January 1885 with Bracy, Miss St John, Arthur Roberts, Fred Leslie, Louis Kelleher, Miss Venne and Camille Dubois. Produced at

Sadler's Wells Theatre in a version by Geoffrey Dunn 18 May 1966 with James Hawthorne, Joyce Blackham, John Fryatt (King Peppin), Eric Shilling, Dan Klein (Prince Lysander), Margaret Neville (Princess Helena) and Margaret Burton.

Produced at Niblo's Garden, New York, 13 July 1868 with Aujac, Mlle Irma, Francis, Duchesne, Dardignac and Mlle Lambèle. Played at the Grand Opera House 21 December 1870 with Marie Aimée and at Edwin's Theatre 19 December 1971 with Coeulte, Aimée, Duchesne, Edgard, Berthon and Mlle Hache. Played at Wallack's Theatre in a new version as *Boulotte* 19 August 1875 with Alfred Brennir, Julia Mathews, G H McDermott and Haydn Corri.

Produced at the Theater an der Wien, Vienna, in a version by Julius Hopp as *Blaubart* 21 September 1866.

Produced at the Friedrich-Wilhelmstädtisches Theater, Berlin, 13 March 1867.

CHARACTERS

Le Sire de Barbe-Bleue
Popolani, *his astrologer*
Le Roi Bobèche
La Reine Clémentine, *his Queen*
Princesse Hermia, *his daughter, otherwise* Fleurette *a shepherdess*
Le Comte Oscar, *chief courtier to Bobèche*
Prince Saphir
Boulotte, *a peasant*
Alvarez
Heloíse, Rosalinde, Isaure, Blanche, Eléanore, *the wives of Barbe-Bleue*

ACT 1

The village where our burlesque takes place is the picturesque village of the fairy-tale books, set in a delicious little rustic valley far below the mighty turrets of the castle of the local potentate, the Sire de Barbe-Bleue. In this Theokritean setting the shepherd Saphir has come to play his love-laden flute outside the window of the cottage of the pretty florist, Fleurette ('Dans la Nature Tout Se Réveille'). Although the two are fervent in expressing their love, to the accompaniment of all the usual actions, Fleurette has noticed that Saphir always takes fright when the word marriage is mentioned and mumbles something inconclusive about his family.

As an old soldier's daughter, Fleurette really thinks she is quite a good enough match for a shepherd, but we have no time to investigate Saphir's mumblings just now as the lovers' tête-à-tête is interrupted by the arrival of the exuberantly forward village lass Boulotte ('Y'a des Bergers Dans le Village'), who is determined to add Saphir to her list of conquests and who makes so few bones about it that the shepherd is obliged to seek safety in the swift action of his best pair of boots.

The village place is not left empty for long for, under orders from his lustfully famed master, the five times wed Bluebeard, the seigneurial alchemist Popolani arrives to select a virtuous peasant maid to act as the season's May Queen. In this unlikely setting, Popolani runs into Count Oscar, chief courtier to King Bobèche. Oscar has come to this uncourtly spot on a specific errand. Eighteen years ago his master's Queen bore a royal daughter, but three years later she succeeded in producing a son as well and Bobèche, anxious that his son should inherit his crown, decided that the baby girl should be exposed. And so, little Princess Hermia was placed in a basket and set off down the river to oblivion. Alas for Bobèche, his son turned out to be a despicable idiot and it was then that he remembered his daughter and sent Oscar out with twenty-four hours to find her and return her to his royal bosom. Oscar has done some fluvial calculations and worked out that the basket ought to have floated ashore at this very village, so here he is.

What it amounts to is that here are two distinguished gentlemen, both looking for a girl—preferably the right one but, given the difficulties involved, at least one who looks right. The first local belle they meet is Boulotte who is excessively taking but quite obviously neither a lost princess nor a strictly potential May Queen. As Popolani's proclamation is read out all the other village girls hurry round ('Sur la Place Il Faut Nous Rendre'/ 'J'Apporte les Volontés'). On Oscar's advice, the alchemist decides to select the May Queen by lottery, this being less contestable than a contest of virtue (Choeur de la Loterie), but the rest of the rustic lasses are decidedly put out when Boulotte insists on entering ('V'la Z'Encore de Drol's') and aghast when she wins ('Boulotte! Saperlotte!').

But wait! What is that insignificant-seeming receptacle which has been used to hold the lottery tickets? It is Fleurette's little flower basket which happened to be sitting on the florist's window sill. A flower basket? Why, this is the very basket in which the infant princess was washed downriver fifteen years ago! When Oscar encourages the girl to remember her infant years, Fleurette suddenly recalls with amazing clarity that she is the missing Princess Hermia. Oscar's job is done. Fleurette packs her basket and a palanquin is brought to take the rediscovered heiress and Saphir, whom she insists on taking with her, back to her father (Choeur du Palanquin).

Just as the happy train is departing, who should arrive on the scene, just in time to catch a glimpse of the departing beauty, but Bluebeard himself. The mighty Bluebeard has decided to take a new wife. He has wedded, bedded and had his alchemist dispose of five spouses to date and, much to Popolani's distress, he has now decided he needs a sixth bride to warm his bed (Légende de Barbe-Bleue: 'Ma Première Femme'). When he sees the rough and rustic Boulotte dressed up in white and orange-blossom ready for her May Coronation ('Honneur! Honneur à Monseigneur') his decision is quickly made and Boulotte, careless of her majestic admirer's dreadful reputation, goes cheerfully off to be wed.

ACT 2

At the Palace of Bobèche, the courtiers are practising their bowing and scraping ('C'Est un Métier Difficile'), but all the genuflection in the world cannot save the personable Alvarez whom the King suspects of a keeping a secret assignation with his Queen Clémentine. Like four other attractive noblemen before him, he is condemned to death and Count Oscar is ordered, for the fifth time, to carry out the unhappy despatch.

Bobèche is not only pathologically suspicious of his Queen, he has grave doubts over the behaviour of his subordinate, Bluebeard. Bluebeard's rapid turnover in wives has a suspect air but, since Bluebeard has a vast armoury of cannon and Bobèche has none, the King decides that he will not wave his regal will about in that direction. The regal will is instead exercised on his newly discovered daughter. Ignoring her insistent passion for her shepherd, he has decided to marry off that very evening to the son of a convenient king.

This business of royal alliances without love is one on which the Queen has strong feelings and considerable experience ('On Prend une Ange d'Innocence') and Fleurette/Hermia, who has inherited her mother's strength of character, is currently expressing her feelings by smashing her father's favourite collection of blue-and-white pottery. But what is her surprise when it turns out that her appointed prince is none other than her very own Saphir ('C'Est Mon Berger'). He has been a prince all along and ventured into her village in shepherd disguise only in order to court her on what seemed to be her home ground.

No sooner are these two young people happily betrothed than Bluebeard arrives to present himself and his new wife to the King ('Voici Cet Heureux Couple'). Boulotte and Fleurette are amazed to see each other in their new positions, and Bluebeard, after a glance at the former shepherdess turned Princess, decides that he has had the worst of the selection and vows that Fleurette will be his next wife. He hastens away with Boulotte, who has disgraced herself by kissing all the gentlemen of the court in defiance of etiquette, ready to send his sixth wife off in the direction of the other five at the first convenient moment.

In the cellar where Popolani carries out his alchemy is the tomb which holds the bodies of Boulotte's five predecessors and thence hastens the wicked Bluebeard ('Le Voilà Donc, le Tombeau'). When Boulotte is brought in by his armed men, he tells her what her fate is to be ('Vous Avez Vu Ce Monument') and she is horrified: she has done nothing to deserve such an end ('Pierre, un Beau Jour, Parvint'). Bluebeard is implacable as he hands the girl over to Popolani who sadly presents her with two phials. He wishes to have nothing to do with murder, so he diffuses his responsibility by giving his victims a choice. One phial holds poison and the other water, and she must choose which to drink. He does, however, give her a strong hint and Boulotte, who thinks she has seduced the alchemist into helping her, happily drinks the phial indicated. Alas, she is wrong, and a drowsy numbness creeps upon her as she collapses on the couch (Trio: 'Hola! Hola! Ça Me Prend Là!').

When Bluebeard returns he sees dead proof that he is once again a bachelor but, no sooner has his master gone, than Popolani puts into action a strange electrical gadget and lo! Boulotte awakens. She was not dead but merely drugged. In fact, none of Bluebeard's wives is dead. They have all gone through the same charade and all live down here in the basement with Popolani where they are very good at showing him, in the most practical way, their gratitude for keeping them alive. Now, at last, Popolani has had enough and he has decided to denounce his wicked master. Opening the doors of the tomb, he reveals the luxuriously appointed home of Bluebeard's former wives and he summons them forth to come back to the world (Finale: 'Mortes, Sortez de Vos Tombeaux').

ACT 3

At Bobèche's court, the wedding of Hermia and Saphir is taking place (Choeur Nuptial) when Bluebeard arrives to put a stop to the proceedings. His wife is dead ('Madame, Ah! Madame') and he has come to demand the hand of the Princess Hermia as his seventh wife. When Bobèche demurs, Bluebeard threatens to turn his cavalry and artillery on the defenceless court ('J'Ai Pas Bien Loin Dans la Montagne'). The desperate Saphir challenges him to a duel, but Bluebeard tricks the Prince into a moment of inattention and fells him and, before the Princess knows what is happening, the wedding chorus is again in action and she is being led off to marry the terrible tyrant.

No sooner has the bridal procession headed on its way than Popolani arrives, disguised as a gipsy, with the six wives, similarly tricked out, dancing in his wake. He reveals to Oscar the truth about Bluebeard and it turns out that Oscar has a similar confession to make. Down in his cellar he has hidden the five men whom the King had ordered him to kill, all alive. In fact, no one is dead, for Saphir merely fell to the ground under the stress of emotion and he, too, is again up and about and happy to join with the two courtiers in their plot for revenge on Bluebeard.

The *après-mariage* scene at the Palace is a sad one. Bluebeard is not pleased at the lack of wifely response from his new bride and Bobèche is positively infuriated at the support given to the sulking Princess by his own wife. As a diversion from this double feminine rebellion, he is happy to admit the crowd of gipsies who offer to sing and dance at the wedding feast (Choeur des Bohémiennes: 'Nous Arrivons'). Boulotte, gaily disguised in gipsy garb, claims the power to tell fortunes ('Nous Possédons') and, as she reads their palms, she exposes both Bobèche's and Bluebeard's evils before the court.

The dead wives and courtiers unmask before their murderers. Fortunately, they are in even numbers and so, as Saphir and his Hermia are brought back together for another wedding, each wife is paired off with a courtier ('Idée Heureuse, Ingénieuse') leaving, at the end of the affair, the apparently repentant Bluebeard in the hands of the termagant Boulotte, with whom we can guess that he probably did not live happily ever after.

The 1875 *Boulotte* made severe alterations to the libretto of *Barbe-Bleue* and also interpolated several pieces of music from Johann Strauss's *Indigo und die vierzig Räuber*.

LA VIE PARISIENNE

an opéra-bouffe in four acts by Henri Meilhac and Ludovic Halévy. Music by Jacques Offenbach. Produced at the Théâtre du Palais-Royal, Paris, 31 October 1866 with Hyacinthe (Gondremarck), Philippe Gilpérèz (Bobinet), Priston (Gardefeu), Jules Brasseur (Frick/Brésilien/Prosper), Zulma Bouffar (Gabrielle), Mlle Paurelle (Pauline) and Mlle Honorine (Métella). Produced at the Théâtre des Variétés 25 September 1875 with José Dupuis, Grenier, Henri Cooper, Berthelier, Mlles Bouffar, Berthal and Devéria; and played on many subsequent occasions including 18 September 1889 with Dupuis and Jeanne Granier, 1892 with Dupuis, Louis Baron, Cooper, Albert Brasseur, Mlle Méaly, Germaine Gallois and Eve Lavallière, 17 September 1896 with Guy replacing Dupuis and Mlle Lhéritier as Métella, in 1904 with Claudius, Baron, Albert Brasseur, Anna Tariol-Baugé and Lyse Berty, and in 1911 with Guy, Max Dearly, Prince, Albert Brasseur, Mlle Méaly, Jeanne Saulier and Mistinguett. Produced at the Théâtre Mogador 1 April 1931 with Max Dearly, Dréan, Henri Laverne, Félix Oudart, Jane Marnac, Jeanne Saint-Bonnet and Danielle Brégis. Produced at the Théâtre National de l'Opéra-Comique 1931. Produced at the Théâtre du Palais-Royal 1958 with Pierre Bertin, Jean-Pierre Granval, Jean Desailly, Jean Parédès, Simone Valère, Denise Benoît, Suzy Delair, Madeline Renaud (Baronne) and Jean-Louis Barrault (Brésilien). Produced at the Théâtre National de l'Opéra-Comique 5 November 1974 in a revised version by Jean Marsan and Raymond Vogel with Jacques Mareuil, Henri Gui, Michel Caron, Luc Barney, Nicole Broissin, Madeleine Vernon and Danièle Millet. Produced at the Théâtre du Châtelet 4 November 1980 with Michel Roux, Danièle Chlostawa Jacques Taylès and Patrick Minard. Produced at the Théâtre de Paris 16 October 1985 with Gabriel Bacquier, Bernard Alane, Jane Rhodes and Martine Masquelin.

Produced at the Holborn Theatre, London, 30 March 1872 in a freely adapted version by F C Burnand with Lionel Brough (Gondremarck), Fred Mervin (Tom Gadfly), J A Shaw (Jack Sprightly), Loredan (Brésilien), Clara Shelley (Louise), Lottie Venne (Polly Twinkle) and Harriet Coveney (Baronne). Produced at the Avenue Theatre as *La Vie* in a version by H B Farnie 3 October 1883 with Lionel Brough, Arthur Roberts, Camille d'Arville, Clara Graham and Lillian La Rue. Produced at the Lyric Theatre, Hammersmith, in a heavily rewritten version by A P Herbert & A D Adams 18 April 1929. Produced at Sadler's Wells Theatre 24 May 1961 in a version by Geoffrey Dunn with Eric Shilling, Kevin Miller, Jon Weaving, June Bronhill, Suzanne Steele and Anna Pollak.

Produced at the Théâtre Français, New York, 29 March 1869 with Rose Bell, Marie Desclauzas, Carrier, Becker, Gabel and Bourgoin. Played at Booth's Theatre, New York 12 June 1876 with Duplan, Dalbert, Darcy and Marie Aimée. Played at the Bijou Theatre in Farnie's version 18 April 1883 with Richard Mansfield (von Wienerschnitzel), Jacques Kruger (Tarradiddle), C W Dungan (Guy Silverspoon), Fanny Rice (Gabrielle) and Kate Davis (Christine). Produced at the Adelphi Theatre May 1945.

CHARACTERS

Baron de Gondremarck
Baronne de Gondremarck
Bobinet
Raoul de Gardefeu

Gabrielle, *a glove-maker*
Métella, *a demi-mondaine*
Pauline
Frick, *a bootmaker*/Prosper/The Brazilian
Urbain
Joseph
Alfred
Alphonse, Gontran, Léonie, Louise, Clara, Caroline, Julie, Augustine, Charlotte, Albertine, etc.

ACT 1

At the Gare de l'Ouest an ordinary day's comings and goings is in progress ('Nous Sommes Employés de la Ligne de l'Ouest'). Amongst this daily shuttling, two fashionable young men are awaiting the arrival of the train from Trouville and they are conscientiously ignoring each other's presence. Raoul de Gardefeu and Bobinet are best friends and, at the moment, they are not on speaking terms. The reason, of course, is a woman. The mistress of Bobinet has deceived him. Sending him off to town to bring his dear friend Gardefeu to sup with them, she has simultaneously summoned Gardefeu to her home so that, while Bobinet sat in Gardefeu's drawing room awaiting his return, Gardefeu was occupying an altogether different room at the house which Bobinet was pleased to call his. Bobinet has, of course, severed relationships with the two-timing lady in question, and Gardefeu soon tired of her too, and both of them have since moved on to different mistresses, but they still aren't speaking. At this moment, each is waiting for his new mistress to arrive on the next train. She is called Métella.

The train pulls in ('Le Ciel Est Noir') and Métella gets off with a third lover and, when the two men attempt to accost her, she simply pretends not to know them and sweeps off on the arm of her gentleman friend ('Attendez D'Abord Que Je Place'). The two wounded beaux swoop consolingly into each other's arms, friends in misery as they were rivals in love. Bobinet announces that he has had enough of being treated in such a fashion by women of the demi-monde; it is time that he returned to society and to the company of society women ('Elles Sont Tristes les Marquises'). Gardefeu isn't indifferent to such an idea. He will do the same, but where shall he find a society lady to be his mistress?

As he stands musing in the middle of the railway station, Gardefeu is accosted by his former servant, Joseph. Joseph has become a tourist guide and he is at the station to meet some clients, the Swedish Baron and Baroness Gondremarck, to whom he is to show *le tout Paris*. A baroness? That is surely a society lady. Gardefeu's brains whir and he decides on a little plan. For a small consideration, Joseph gives up his role as guide and is replaced by 'Raoul', all aglow at the prospect of flinging himself at the feet and the rest of the anatomy of what is sure to be a pretty Swedish noblewoman ('Ce Que C'Est Pourtant Que la Vie').

When his customers arrive, he swings into his impersonation ('Jamais, Foi de Cicérone'), promising them an unparalleled time in Paris, as the Baron whispers in his one ear his plans for meeting a few Parisian girls and the Baroness whispers in the other a wish for some unbridled moments of shopping. The rest of the passengers pour on to the station and, amongst them, comes a glittering and extravagant Brazilian ('Je Suis Brésilien'). He has been to Paris before, years previously, when he dissipated his whole fortune on the joys of Paris life in just six months. He scratched his way back to Rio and has, since then, devoted himself to building up another fortune which he has come back to Paris to throw away with the same abandon as the last time. Like the Gondremarcks and like all his fellow passengers, he is ready to tackle Paris with no holds barred.

ACT 2

Back at Raoul's home, his glove-maker, Gabrielle, and his bootmaker, Frick, have both turned up with their respective wares and Frick takes the opportunity to make a pass at the pretty *gantière* ('Entrez! Entrez Jeune Fille à l'OEil Bleu') who is modestly pleased to find a reason as to why boots and gloves should be well suited the one to the other ('Autrefois Plus d'un Amant'). When Raoul turns up with the Swedes, the two tradespeople are shunted into a side room, whilst Raoul goes thorough the pretence that his home is an annexe to the hotel they were expecting to be lodged in. He designates separate bedrooms to the Baron and the Baroness and then begins to plot as to how he can get the Baron out of the house in order to lay court to his wife. The Baron supplies that answer himself. He has a letter from a friend in Stockholm recommending him to a deliciously enjoyable lady of Paris whom he simply has to visit. Her name is Métella ('Dans Cette Ville Toute Pleine').

The Baron has other ideas, however, which are less simple to fulfil. He asks the price of the accommodation and, frightened less they depart, Raoul quotes a ridiculously low sum. Also, he has no wish to dine alone with his wife. He wishes to partake of the hotel's table d'hôte, so Raoul will have to supply one before seven o'clock in his own dining room. Fortunately, the guests can be supplied without too much trouble: Gabrielle and Frick are invited to dress up as quality and to bring all their glove and boot-making friends, equally disguised, to make up the company.

Bobinet arrives at Raoul's house for some more consolation, for his attempts at finding himself a society mistress have gone distressingly astray. The first one he made a pass at leapt on him, and now he finds she's thousands in debt. He finds more enjoyment in looking at the workings of his friend's plot and he offers to help Raoul with his deception by staging a soirée at his absent aunt's mansion the next night. The Baron can be invited and Raoul thus left alone with the Baroness.

The Baroness, in the meanwhile, is puzzled. In her room she has discovered some rings and a love letter. It is the legacy of Métella. Now that lady herself turns up, anxious to make her peace with Raoul, and she is astonished to see her room already occupied by another lady who is calmly handing her her jewellery with a most proprietorial air. Raoul explains that, disappointed in love, he has taken to being a guide and, *à propos*, he hands her the Baron's letter. She reads it aloud ('Vous Souvient-Il, Ma Belle'), its fond remembrances and its recommendation to show the Baron a good time. Métella bestows a dazzling smile on the Baron and tells him that he may indeed visit her...in a few days time. It was not quite what the Baron had in mind, but before his thoughts can stew too long in their own juices, he finds his 'fellow guests' upon him: Frick, disguised as an army major ('Je Suis le Major'), Gabrielle as a Colonel's widow ('Je Suis Veuve d'un Colonel') and their friends in number sufficient to fill the Gardefeu dining room. To the strains of a tyrolienne ('On Est V'nu M'Inviter') they dance off to sup.

ACT 3

The next evening, Bobinet prepares to hold his useful reception. His servants and their friends will dress up in their master's hand-me-downs to provide an assembly ('Donc, Je Puis Me Fier à Vous') and something will be got up to palliate the consequent lack of servants.

Gardefeu has had a most trying day: never a moment alone with his Baroness. The Swedes have spent the whole afternoon sightseeing and, indeed, insisted on going in his carriage to the Bois de Boulogne with their 'guide' perched up menially on the coachman's box. All his fashionable friends saw him on a coachman's box! And, worse, they followed the carriage in dozens until even the Baron noticed something was up and Raoul had to pass off the flower of Parisian youth as a party of maîtres d'hôtel.

When Gondremarck arrives at Bobinet's party he meets, one by one, the fantastical aristocrats invented by the servants and he is decidedly taken by the marked attentions of Pauline, the chambermaid, who, like her fellows, has had strict instructions from Bobinet to keep the Baron busy all evening ('O, Beau Nuage'). Gabrielle comes along to add to the feminine pulchritude on display and to contribute a song ('Sa Robe Fait Frou, Frou'), and Bobinet, dressed up in an ill-fitting Swiss Admiral's costume ('Votre Habit a Craqué Dans le Dos'), contributes to the badinage, until it is time for supper. Pretending they cannot be at ease before the servants, the 'aristocrats' dismiss the unseen waiters and organise a jolly feast ('Soupons, Soupons, C'Est le Moment') where they can all chatter frivolously whilst making sure that the Baron gets well and truly drunk.

ACT 4

The Brazilian, spending his money as fast as he can, is giving a huge party at a restaurant and the waiters ('Bien Bichonnés et Bien Rasés') are getting the place ready for the midnight hour—especially the little private rooms—under the eyes and advice of Alfred, their maître d'hôtel ('Fermons les Yeux'). Gondremarck turns up for an assignation with Métella and encounters Alfred, of whom he entertains the gravest suspicions. After the previous day's cavalcade in the park, he clearly suspects a conspiracy of false maîtres d'hôtel. When he has been given proof of Alfred's bona fides he calms down, but his temperature soon rises again when Métella turns up.

She bids him remain calm amongst the titillating midnight atmosphere of the restaurant ('C'Est Ici l'Endroit Redouté des Mères') and then lets loose her bombshell: she is not going to provide the entertainment his friend back home had led him to dream of for she is a reformed lady. She is in love. However, to assuage his disappointment, she has brought a friend. The Baron, apoplectic, refuses to be fobbed off with a friend, and when he hears that the name of Métella's lover is Raoul de Gardefeu he is fit to burst. He settles his new companion down to dinner and storms out.

The Brazilian is having a gay old time, as he has found a delightful new companion whilst buying some gloves. Gabrielle gets everywhere, and here she is dressed up in Brazilian finery and announced by her lover as having given up twenty years of virtue for him ('Hier, à Midi, la Gantière')! Bobinet and Gardefeu arrive to join the Brazilian's party and come face to face with the boiling Baron who is all set for a duel. When asked for his reason, however, he cannot find one. Here is a man who has whisked a foreigner and his wife and servants from the station and all its pimping perils to his very own home, fed and lodged him magnificently at a risible price, arranged for his best friend to supply lavish entertainment for him at no cost, and all he wants to do is fight him? It is clearly unreasonable.

It becomes even more unreasonable when Métella's friend removes her mask: it is the Baroness. Métella, with not strictly disinterested motives, firstly warned the Baroness as to Raoul's intentions the previous night, allowing her to escape, and now has brought her here to foil her husband's attempt on Métella. She admits her little trick to Raoul, and also her motive. She did not want to lose her lover. Gardefeu is deliciously mollified. Bobinet, too, feels rather like going back to the demi-monde and, while Raoul kisses his mistress's hand, Bobinet does likewise. There is a distinct feeling of *déja vu* in the air as, with the Brazilian at their head, all the company decide simply to have a good time together and 'Célebrons Paris'.

LA GRANDE-DUCHESSE DE GÉROLSTEIN

an opéra-bouffe in three acts by Henri Meilhac and Ludovic Halévy. Music by Jacques Offenbach. Produced at the Théâtre des Variétés, Paris, 12 April 1867 with Hortense Schneider (Grande-Duchesse), José Dupuis (Fritz), Elise Garait (Wanda) and Couder (General Boum). Produced at the Théâtre des Bouffes-Parisiens 5 October 1878 with Paola Marié and Emmanuel. Revived at the Théâtre des Variétés 1887 with Anna Judic, Baron and Dupuis and again 1890 with Jeanne Granier. Produced at the Théâtre de la Gaîté-Lyrique in a revised version by Albert Willemetz and Mouëzy-Eon 1948 with Germaine Roger, Jacques Jansen and Marcel Vallée. Produced at the Théâtre Marigny 5 May 1966 with Suzanne Lafaye, Jean Aubert, Michèle Raynaud and Henri Bédex. Produced at the Théâtre du Châtelet, 31 May 1981 with Régine Crespin, Michel Hamel, Danielle Castaing and Michel Trempont.

Produced at the Théâtre Français, New York, 24 September 1867 with Lucille Tostée, Guffroy, Mlle de Felcourt and Duchesne, and played there 24 January 1870 with Mrs Howard Paul, Girrebeuk, Mlle Guillemot and Duchesne. Played at Pike's Opera House 14 October 1868 with Tostée, Aujac, Mlle Lambèle and Duchesne. Played at the New York Theatre in an English version by B A Baker 17 June 1868 with Sophie Worrell, James C Dunn, Irene Worrell and Welsh Edwards. Played at Edwin's Theatre 28 March 1871 with Marie Aimée, Constant Gausins, Mlle Taillefer and Duchesne. Played at the Olympic Theatre 13 October 1873 with Alice Oates, at the Lyceum Theatre 30 November 1874 with Emily Soldene, at Wallack's Theatre 2 September 1875 with Julia Mathews, Albert Brennir, Rose Temple and G H McDermott, and at the Fifth Avenue Theatre 23 October 1879 with Paola Marié, Capoul and Mme Angèle. Produced at the Casino Theatre 25 January 1890 with Lillian Russell, Henry Hallam, Fanny Rice and Fred Solomon and revived there 11 July 1890 with Miss Russell and Jefferson de Angelis. Produced at Abbey's Theatre 8 December 1894 with Miss Russell.

Produced at the Theatre Royal, Covent Garden, London, in a version by Charles Lamb Kenney 18 November 1867 with Julia Mathews, Wilford Morgan, Augusta Thompson and Thomas Aynsley Cook. Produced at the Olympic Theatre 20 June 1868 with Mrs Howard Paul, Morgan, Miss Thompson and Henri Drayton. Played at St James's Theatre 22 June 1868 with Hortense Schneider, Duplan, Mlle Monnier and Beckers and 7 June 1869 with Schneider, Dupuis, Mlle Prudal and Mongal. Played at the Standard Theatre 24 November 1869 with Julia Mathews (replaced by Emily Soldene), at the Gaiety Theatre 29 April 1871 with Miss Mathews and E D Beverley and at the Opera Comique 13 September 1875 with Cornélie d'Anka, Beverley and Miss Thompson. Produced at the Alhambra Theatre 1 April 1878 with Miss d'Anka, Henry Nordblom, Rose Lee and J D Stoyle. Played at Her Majesty's Theatre 22 November 1886 with Mary Albert, Valdy, Juliette Simon-Girard and Dauphin. Played at the Royalty Theatre 7 January 1888 with Mary Albert. Produced at the Savoy Theatre 4 December 1897 in a version by Charles H Brookfield and Adrian Ross with Florence St John, Charles Kenningham, Florence Perry and Walter Passmore. Produced at Daly's Theatre in a version by G P Robinson 29 April 1937 with Enid Cruickshank, Bruce Carfax, Nancy Neale and W S Percy.

Produced at the Theater an der Wien, Vienna in a version by Julius Hopp 13 May 1867 with Marie Geistinger.

Produced at the Friedrich-Wilhelmstädtisches Theater, Berlin, 10 January 1868.

CHARACTERS

La Grande-Duchesse de Gérolstein
Prince Paul *of Steis-Stein-Steis-Laper-Bottmoll-Schorstenburg*
General Boum, *commander-in-chief of the Gérolstein army*
Fritz, *a private soldier*
Wanda, *his sweetheart*
Baron Puck
Baron Grog
Népomuc, *an aide-de-camp*
Charlotte, Olga, Amélie, Iza, etc.

ACT 1

Somewhere in Gérolstein, on a fine battle's eve, the grand duchy's army is lolling about singing and dancing to optimistic soldierly choruses ('Tournons et Valsons'). Whilst the other soldiers drink and gamble and make the most of the local peasant girls, one particularly well-endowed young private called Fritz is saying fond farewells to his pretty sweetheart, Wanda ('O Mon Fritz'/'Allez, Jeunes Filles'). The lackadaisical attitude of his men in the face of the enemy infuriates the brimstone-breathing General Boum, Gérolstein's commander-in-chief. The General is a man who lives for war, and who can be relied upon to burst into battlestance at the slightest provocation ('Pif, Paf, Pouf').

Fighting, however, is not Boum's only preoccupation. Like every soldier, he does have a soft spot for the ladies, and the lady after whom he lechers at the moment is none other than Fritz's Wanda. As a result, he snatches every opportunity to take out his dislike and envy of Fritz under the guise of military orders. Tonight, he announces, the Grand Duchess of Gérolstein will be coming to look over her army. Her tent is to be erected in the centre of the camp so, while the other soldiers are marched away, Fritz is ordered to stand sentry guard on the empty piece of ground intended for the tent. No sooner is he left alone than Wanda returns, anxious to make the most of their moments together ('Me Voici! Me Voici!'). Fritz does his best to stick to the rules and neither speak nor move from his post, but his feelings finally get the better of him and he unbends sufficiently to indulge in a kiss or two. Alas, the young lovers are caught in the act by General Boum who has set up the whole affair with the sole object of catching Fritz at something which can be counted as a military crime. But before the General can take much revenge, shots are heard in the distance. It is the enemy cannon! Boum's ears prick up like a foxhound's and Wanda faints.

As it happens, it is not the enemy approaching, but merely the camp sentries firing at the Grand Duchess's court chamberlain, the Baron Puck, who has walked through the gates without giving the password. Puck is a close crony of the General and the two of them have together cooked up mighty plans for controlling the government of Gérolstein. The young Grand Duchess has, up till now, been kept sweetly amused with toys and books and other such diversions, thus allowing her chief executives to get on with running the country as they wished but, now that she has reached the age of twenty, a different kind of distraction is needed if they are to keep their monarch from interfering in state business.

One of Puck's recent ideas was the provision of a husband for his sovereign. It seemed like a fine idea and the husband chosen by the plotting pair was the diffident Prince Paul, son of the neighbouring Elector of Steis-Stein-Steis-Laper-Bottmoll-Schorstenburg. To their irritation, the ruse did not work, for the young monarch remained indifferent to Prince Paul and not only refused to wed him but declined even to receive his father's representative, Baron Grog. Following this failure, Puck has switched to a new stratagem. He would interest the young lady in the army. Not individually, of course, but as a colourful unit, a dazzling plaything made up of real men. It is to this end that the evening's visit has been planned and a set-up

302

arranged to allow the Duchess the martial thrill of performing the regiment's song as a duet with General Boum.

Drums and bugles announce the arrival of the Grand Duchess ('Portez Armes') and no sooner has she begun to review her troops than it becomes very clear that the army holds many more attractions for the young woman than ever did Prince Paul ('Vous Aimez le Danger'/'Ah! Que J'Aime les Militaires'). As she continues down the ranks, she finds they hold one very particular attraction. Her eye alights on Fritz. It is a shame, she feels, that such a fine soldier should be only a Private, so she promotes him on the spot to Corporal and then to Sergeant.

Puck is distinctly worried by such a purposeful mark of favour and Boum is particularly irritated that such a favour should have fallen on the detested Fritz, who is soon introducing Wanda to his sovereign and being promoted once more, this time to Lieutenant. When it comes to the time for the regimental song, the Duchess is delighted to sing but, instead of the eager Boum, she chooses Fritz to make up the duet and, when Boum protests at such lèse majesté, she spitefully retaliates by promoting the Lieutenant to Captain ('Ah! C'Est un Fameux Régiment').

The young Duchess is not at all sure what the feelings are that she is experiencing. All she knows is that she is supremely anxious to see the handsome Fritz dressed up in his new Captain's uniform and yet she is not at all impressed when poor Prince Paul comes to find her, dressed up in a bridegroom's outfit with the hope that she might take the hint. Clearly, all men are not the same.

Paul is now quite desperate. He has been hanging around Gérolstein for six months, spending all his allowance and being ignored, and some of the nastier newspapers have taken to making slighting remarks about it in their personal columns (Chronique de la Gazette de Hollande: 'Pour Epouser une Princesse'). The Grand Duchess brushes him off with the excuse that she is far too busy to marry him and she turns happily to her new preoccupation with things military, calling together her chief men to listen to the plan of battle which General Boum has evolved.

Fritz, who has been elected to stand bodyguard on the Duchess, laughs out loud at the General's complicated pincer plan, provoking a near explosion from the choleric Boum. He is furious that this lowly soldier should be allowed to interfere in matters of such importance, but the Duchess is determined to hear Fritz out and she promptly creates him a General and a Baron, thus giving him sufficient rank to be heard in council.

Fritz's idea of battle is to wade in and thrash 'em and, to Boum's horror, the Duchess blithely agrees that this is the way to organise the forthcoming battle. When Boum refuses, she simply removes him from his position as commander-in-chief and replaces him with Fritz. The army gather ('Ils Vont Tous Partir') and the Duchess confers on her new Commander the honour of carrying into battle her own father's sword ('Voici le Sabre de Mon Père') and, as Boum, Puck and Paul grumble furiously in the background, the army marches off to war under Fritz's command.

ACT 2

The war is over and the Grand Duchess's maids of honour wait impatiently for the return of their favourite lovers ('Enfin la Guerre Est Terminée'/'Je T'Ai Sur Mon Coeur'/'Ah! Lettre Adorée'). Prince Paul is still hanging around the palace trying to get some attention but he hasn't a chance on this day of all days, for General Fritz is returning to Gérolstein crowned with victory in battle. Coming before the Duchess, he returns to her the sword of her father ('Après le Victoire') and, at her urging, gives an account of the battle. His strategy was to take to war twenty thousand bottles of wine and arrange that the enemy should capture the depot. The next morning, when the entire opposing army was suffering from a ghastly hangover, he was able to order the attack and win a famous victory without a drop of blood being shed ('En Très Bon Ordre').

When the official business is done, the Duchess, to the horror of Prince Paul and his supporters, demands to see Fritz alone. In the time since their first encounter, she has come to understand the feelings which have been stirring inside her and she is about to make some tentative opening moves. As Commander-in-Chief, she decrees, Fritz will be given an apartment in the palace—the one in the right wing—and then, she must tell him, one of her court ladies has fallen in love with him ('Oui, Général'/'Dites-Lui Qu'On l'A Remarqué Distingué').

Being of a certain density, Fritz fails to understand that the Duchess is speaking, in a thinly veiled fashion, of her own feelings. Weighing everything up, he decides that he will do better to stick to his first love, and he determines to ask the Duchess for permission to marry Wanda.

Boum and Puck are horrified when they hear about the apartment in the right wing. It is the old royal mistress's room, connected to the ruling monarch's chambers by a secret corridor. Things are getting serious. Their aspirations have suffered enough at the hands of the wretched Fritz and they decide to combine with Prince Paul in a conspiracy to rid themselves of the troublesome lad ('Ne Devinez-Vous Pas'/'Max Etait Soldat de Fortune').

They are amazed when their conspiracy gets an impromptu fourth member in the person of the rejected Duchess herself. Fritz is in the chapel of the palace going through a quick wedding with Wanda. From the ceremony he will proceed to his apartments, and there the conspirators will lie in wait for him to bring his dazzling career to a dingy end ('Logeons-la Donc').

ACT 3

Whilst the wedding dance goes on, the conspirators gather in the right wing, on the very spot where an earlier ancestor met his bloody fate ('Ce Qu'On A Fait'). The Duchess hides behind a curtain as Puck, Paul, Grog and Népomuc lead on a whole band of murderous conspirators ('Sortez, Sortez') but she emerges to give a last minute instruction that, although he may be cut to pieces, Fritz's handsome face must not be touched. But wait! Who is this other handsome face amongst the conspirators? It is Baron Grog, the emissary from Prince Paul's father whom the Duchess has always refused to admit to her presence.

304

Her Highness decides that she will grant him his private audience now, on the spot, and she sends everyone else away while she winsomely attempts to persuade Grog that he would do much better to abandon his present master and come to her court instead. Grog diplomatically regrets that he cannot. Of course, were she to wed Prince Paul, such a transfer would be virtually automatic. The Duchess's head is quite dizzy with schemes, but it is at least clear to her that there is now no need to have Fritz murdered and, to the vast disappointment of Boum and Puck, she calls the assassination off. She cannot have a murder on her wedding day. Her wedding day? Yes, she has decided that, at long last, she will wed Prince Paul and, to make up for General Boum's disappointment at missing out on Fritz's death, she freely permits him to take his revenge on the young man in any way he likes—as long as it is nothing quite so permanent.

Their wedding solemnised, Fritz and Wanda are escorted to their apartment by the lords and ladies of the court ('Nous Amenons la Jeune Femme') and are bid a knowing goodnight by the cream of Gérolstein society ('Bonne Nuit, Monsieur'). Left alone with his new bride, Fritz starts to pare away her maidenly modesty ('On Peut Être Aimable') but, each time he gets near to embracing his wife, he is interrupted by noisy serenading from the street outside ('Ouvrez, Ouvrez') until finally Boum, Puck, Grog and Paul burst in to urge him to head for Roc à Pic with all haste ('À Cheval, À Cheval') at the orders of his monarch ('Notre Auguste Maîtresse'). Fritz quickly dons his Commander's uniform and, leaving his new little wife to her own devices, dashes off to the rendezvous.

At the army encampment ('Au Repas Comme à la Bataille'), the Grand Duchess joins her men and her newly-pledged husband in a rousing drinking song (Légende du Verre: 'Il Etait un de Mes Aïeux') and listens with enjoyment as General Boum relates the trick he has played on Fritz. The General has for some time been paying court to a married lady at Roc à Pic but her husband has discovered the affair and, Boum has learned, is tonight laying in wait to trap his wife's aristocratic seducer as he comes to his rendezvous.

Fritz has been sent into an ambush and, when the brave Commander-in-Chief arrives back at the camp, he is a bruised and battered sight, his clothes rent and the famous sabre bent ('Voici Revenir'). The Duchess makes this unseemly behaviour an excuse to strip Fritz, one by one, of all the honours she had previously loaded on him, until he is back once more to the rank of private soldier. At that point Fritz promptly asks for and receives his discharge from the army. He is free, at last, to go to his Wanda.

The Duchess now has a bundle of offices and honours to bestow and she decides that the recipient of all these shall be the handsome Baron Grog. When Grog thanks her on behalf of his absent wife and children, the Duchess has to avow herself beaten. Boum is restored to his position at the head of the army, the twisted sabre is returned to Baron Puck, Fritz (who has a yearning to learn to read and write) is appointed a village schoolmaster, and Baron Grog is sent safely back to Steis-Stein-Steis-Laper-Bottmoll-Schorstenburg to inform his master that the Grand Duchess of Gérolstein and Prince Paul are happily married. If a girl can't have what she likes, then she must like what she can have. That way everything can end happily ('Enfin J'Ai Repris la Panache').

LA PÉRICHOLE

an opéra-bouffe in two acts by Ludovic Halévy and Henri Meilhac based on *Le Carosse du Saint-Sacrament* by Prosper Mérimée. Music by Jacques Offenbach. Produced at the Théâtre des Variétés, Paris, 6 October 1868 with Hortense Schneider (Périchole), José Dupuis (Piquillo) and Grenier (Don Andrès). Revived there in a three act version 25 April 1874 with Schneider, Dupuis and Grenier, 1876 with Anna Judic, and 15 September 1895 with Jeanne Granier, etc. Produced at the Théâtre de Paris 1969 in a revised version with Jane Rhodes, Michel Caron and Jean Le Poulain. Played at the Théâtre Mogador 19 May 1979. Played at the Théâtre des Champs-Elysées 17 September 1984.

Produced at the Princess's Theatre, London, 27 June 1870 with Schneider, Carrier and Daubray. Produced at the Royalty Theatre 30 January 1875 with Selina Dolaro, Walter Fisher and Frederic Sullivan and revived there 11 October 1875 with Dolaro, Knight Aston and Sullivan. Played at the Charing Cross Theatre 10 March 1876; at the Alhambra Theatre 9 November 1878 with Emily Soldene and Aston; and at the Folly Theatre 28 April 1879 with Dolaro, Charles J Campbell and Henry Nicholls. Produced at the Garrick Theatre 14 September 1897 with Florence St John, Richard Clarke and John Le Hay.

Produced at Pike's Opera House, New York, 4 January 1869 with Mlle Irma, Aujac and Leduc. Played at the Grand Opera House 18 January 1871 with Marie Aimée, Constant Gausins and Duchesne and at Edwin's Theatre 9 October 1871, the Olympic Theatre 1872 and the Lyceum Theatre 28 March 1873 also with Aimée. Played at Abbey's Theatre 29 April 1895 with Lillian Russell. Played at Jolson's Theatre 21 December 1925 with Olga Baclanova. Produced at the Metropolitan Opera in a version by Maurice Valency 21 December 1956 with Patrice Munsel, Theodor Uppman and Cyril Ritchard.

Produced at the Theatre an der Wien, Vienna, in a version by Richard Genée as *Périchole, die Strassensängerin* 9 January 1869.

Produced at the Friedrich-Wilhelmstädtisches Theater, Berlin, 6 April 1870.

CHARACTERS

Piquillo, *a street singer*
La Périchole, *a street singer*
Don Andrès de Ribiera, *Viceroy of Peru*
Le Comte de Panatellas, *first gentleman of the bedchamber*
Don Pedro de Hinoyosa, *governor of the city of Lima*
Tarapote
Guadalena, Mastrilla, Berginella, *of 'Les Trois Cousines' bar*
Manuelita, Frasquinella, Brambilla, Ninetta, Notaries, etc.

ACT 1

At the 'Trois Cousines' bar, in the city of Lima, the three ladies who give their name to the establishment are pouring out the wine as the people celebrate the birthday of the Viceroy ('Du Vice-roi C'Est Aujourd'hui la Fête') with all the vigour of folk who have been paid to do so. The three cousins are lively ladies ('Au Cabaret des Trois Cousines'), but they do not make a habit of giving their merchandise away. The responsibility for all this purchased gaiety lies with Don Pedro de Hinoyosa, the governor of the city. Don Pedro is, for his own sake, intent that the Viceroy should see that his capital is a happy and satisfied place and, to make sure that all goes according to plan, he is lurking in the vicinity of the 'Trois Cousines' disguised as a vegetable seller.

The bread-seller who passes by soon after is, equally, no real merchant but the Comte de Panatellas, the Viceroy's first gentleman of the bedchamber. He, too, is out and about *en paysan*, keeping an eye on his master, Don Andrès, who has also taken to the streets, disguised as a doctor, with the intention of finding out what his people truly think of his administration and, also, of enjoying the company of the girls of the town 'Incognito'.

The Viceroy finds little frankness at the 'Trois Cousines', for the entire place has been peopled with the relatives of Don Pedro bribed and primed to give flattering responses and the hostesses are so taken with giggling that they can barely keep up the charade. Finally, Don Andrès lights upon a passing Red Indian and, deciding that here he will find his *vox populi*, he takes him off for an in-depth interview.

The next arrivals in the square outside the 'Trois Cousines' are a pair of strolling singers, Piquillo and La Périchole. They entertain with their song of 'L'Espagnol et la Jeune Indienne' but, as Piquillo insists on going round with the hat, they take no money. When Périchole takes a turn at the collection things look better, but the jealous Piquillo insults every man who goes to give his beloved money and, once again, the singers end up with nothing. Nothing will not pay for food and the two are very hungry. Only their love for each other keeps them going. They have nothing else, not even the four piastres needed to pay for the long-awaited marriage licence. Périchole is exhausted and can go no further, so Piquillo leaves her to sleep off her hunger while he continues to try to win a few coins by his singing.

Don Andrès has spent half an hour pumping his Indian only to discover, in the end, that the native is none other than Panatellas in disguise. Piqued to the core at being unable to find anyone who will give him an honest answer, he is delighted to hear a voice complaining of a wretched day and a dreadful country. It is Périchole, who has discovered that it is not easy to get to sleep when one's stomach is empty. Andrès is even more delighted when he looks on the grumbler and sees that she is a beautiful woman. Within the space of a few words, the Viceroy has fallen head-over-heels for the pretty street singer and, before long, he is promising to make her lady-in-waiting to his wife. The fact that his wife has been dead for some years has never prevented him from keeping a corps of ladies-in-waiting at the palace in her memory.

Périchole is an old hand with flirts and she is distinctly dubious of a man who dresses like a doctor and yet claims to be the Viceroy of Peru. Even when he insists that she compare his profile with the head on a piastre, she is still doubtful. Finally Andrès can think of only one way to prove his identity. He makes Périchole join with him to cry out, 'Down with the Viceroy'. When they do so, Pedro and Panatellas come running, only to end up genuflecting before their master and the amazed Périchole.

La Périchole agrees to come to court but, while she starts to scribble out a note of explanation to Piquillo, Pedro and Panatellas learn with dismay that the Viceroy does not intend to set the street singer up safely and distantly in his naughty little house around the corner but proposes, quite openly, to take her to court and install her in the apartment once known to be that of the royal mistress. It is too frightful, and they object with all the force of men who know their statute book. Once upon a time, in order to prevent the Viceroy from getting himself into unfortunate tangles with young ladies, it was legally enacted that the apartment in question should be inhabited only by a married lady. Périchole is nothing of the sort and therefore the Viceroy's suggestion is illegal.

Don Andrès is not deterred. He orders his gentleman to produce a husband on the spot, and his governor to come up with a notary. Périchole shall be married to some insignificant fellow and the law thus placated. In the meanwhile, Périchole has been penning her farewells to her dear Piquillo. Her love for him is no less than it has always been, but she can no longer endure the hardships and privations of their life (Letter Song: 'O Mon Cher Amant, Je Te Jure'). She will be faithful to him and to their love but, for now, it is *au revoir*. She accepts from Don Andrès a bag of coins, which she assures him is destined for an aged relative, and gives both the note and the money into the care of the three cousins to be delivered to Piquillo. Then she heads for the Viceroy's little house and the long-awaited dinner.

When Piquillo returns, he finds Périchole gone. The cousins decide it is better to keep the money for themselves, but they give him the note, and the exhausted singer is broken-hearted to read his beloved's farewell. He has nothing left to live for. A nail, the shoulder strap of Périchole's guitar and a stool are all he needs to string himself up but, having done so, he finds the last little leap from the stool rather difficult. He gets unlooked-for help when Panatellas, coming out of the bar, kicks the stool away and Piquillo would be well and truly hung if he hadn't forgotten that the guitar strap was made of rubber. It stretches and he lands on top of Panatellas who is delighted to see him. Here is a man who has nothing to live for. He is just the man he needs for the subterfuge marriage.

Business is brisk at the 'Trois Cousines'. Don Andrès comes flying across the street to order a glass of malaga for Périchole. It will help her get over her aversion to a marriage of convenience. A few seconds later, Don Pedro needs porto for the notary whom he must lure away from a little card-game with some colleagues and Panatellas wants madeira wine with which to restore Piquillo to confidence. Don Andrès himself, exhausted by watching all the strings of his plot coming together, needs a drop of sherry and then some alicante for his lady friend who is clearly loosening up nicely under the effects of malaga. The liquor flows and finally has its effect. Périchole agrees to wed a convenient husband sight unseen, Piquillo consents to play the same game, and the notaries are alcoholically pried away from their game. The wedding can take place. The notaries weave a rather crooked path up the street ('Voici les Notaires') and Périchole's exit from the Viceroy's house is little more steady ('Ah! Quel Dîner Je Viens de Faire').

It is, however, much more controversial for, having put away a brave dinner and plenty of wine, the young lady is in a very much less amenable frame of mind than when she was starving, and she suddenly and stoutly refuses to be wed. Then she sees who her unknown bridegroom is to be—a very wobbly, very tipsy Piquillo who is so under the influence that he doesn't recognise her—and she changes her tune. Piquillo informs her drunkenly that he will never love his wife as his heart is given ('Je Dois Vous Prévenir, Madame') and 'Le Beau Mariage' goes ahead. The ceremony over, the two are carried off in separate palanquins, as the curtain falls.

ACT 2

At the Viceroy's palace, his courtier Tarapote has fainted ('Cher Seigneur, Revenez à Vous'). He has heard the news of the Viceroy's frightful behaviour and heard the hideous drunken singing, late at night, of the slut whom his superior has brought into the viceregal household and given the apartments which should belong to a lady of the court. Piquillo, who awakes to find himself clad in gorgeous clothes, left alone in a place which seems to be a museum or some such, and called the Marquis du Mananares and Baron de Tobago, is even more confused but, little by little, the scornful jibes of the courtiers and court ladies ('On Vante Partout Son Sourire') allow him to piece together the events of the past night.

He remembers that Panatellas and Pedro promised him a large sum of money with which to get out of town and go in search of his beloved Périchole once his marriage was done ('Les Femmes Il N'Y A Que Ça'), but there is yet one deed which he needs to perform for them before he can be allowed to go. He must present his wife formally to the Viceroy in court ('Nous Allons Donc Voir un Mari'). Since this will allow him to see the woman he married with straight eyes, Piquillo agrees, but he is stunned when his wife appears and proves to be none other than his own Périchole.

He breaks out in anger as she tries to calm him sufficiently to make him understand that she is not the Viceroy's mistress and that she is acting for the ultimate happiness of the two of them ('Mon Dieu! Que les Hommes Sont Bêtes') but Piquillo will have none of it. Bitterly he flings his wife at the Viceroy's feet, denouncing her horribly and scorning the viceregal person ('Écoute, ô Roi, Je Te Présente'). The furious Don Andrès orders his arrest and Piquillo is roughly dragged off to the dungeon reserved for difficult husbands ('Conduisez-le, Bons Courtisans').

La Périchole uses her feminine wiles to win, firstly, home comforts for her

309

beloved in his cell and, finally, his release, and Don Andrès commands that the formal presentation, so dramatically spoiled that morning, be made without incident that evening at his ceremonial dinner. Piquillo, however, is still inclined to tantrums, even when Périchole points out that she, at least, knew whom she was marrying when she agreed to accept him whilst he was so drunk he didn't know or care whom he was getting. And, after all, have they not become man and wife without spending four piastres? Did he not read her letter in which she promised that she would remain virtuous in the house of the Viceroy? Piquillo's arguments fritter away into silly, vain little considerations and, finally, Périchole convinces him to make the required presentation.

If Piquillo is unhappy about the situation, the court is even more so. At the ceremonial serving of his dinner, Don Andrès finds all his food either snatched away under pretence of protocol or else rendered inedible; he finds his jokes unappreciated and his courtiers unflattering until, realising that this is an attempt to freeze him out of his passion for Périchole, he reacts vengefully and effectively by cutting everybody's stipend. Fawning returns at an unprecedented level in time for the presentation of the new Marquise but, once again, the presentation is barely in line with custom.

Piquillo and Périchole present a duet under the title 'Le Chanteur et la Chanteuse'. It is their own story and, in its course, Périchole returns to Don Andrès all the jewels and money he has given her. The end of the tale tells how the singer and her beloved gave back all the gifts they had accepted and went back to their old lives and their old love. Their story affects Don Andrès with its sincerity and its renunciation of wealth for love and, when it is finished, he sentimentally bids them go their way, taking the money and jewels with them. They are rich and they are married and it didn't even cost four piastres.

CHILPÉRIC

an opéra-bouffe in three acts by Hervé. Produced at the Théâtre des Folies-Dramatiques, Paris, 24 October 1868 with Hervé (Chilpéric), Blanche d'Antigny (Frédégonde) and Mlle Berthal (Galswinthe). Produced at the Théâtre des Variétés in a revised version by Paul Ferrier 1 February 1895 with Albert Brasseur, Marguerite Ugalde and Marcelle Lender.

Produced at the Lyceum Theatre, London, in a version by Robert Reece, F A Marshall and Richard Mansell 22 January 1870 with Hervé (succeeded by Emily Soldene), Emily Muir and Selina Dolaro. Produced at the Philharmonic Theatre in a condensed version 1871 with Soldene. Produced at the Royalty Theatre 18 September 1871 with W Haydon Tilla, Augusta Thompson and Emily Pitt; at the Globe Theatre 3 June 1872 by the Folies-Dramatiques company; at the Alhambra Theatre 10 May 1875 with Charles Lyall, Lennox Grey, Kate Munroe, Adelaide Newton (Landry), Harry Paulton (Doctor) and Emma Chambers (Brunehaut); and at the Empire Theatre in a version by Henry Hersee and H B Farnie 17 April 1884 with

Herbert Standing, Camille d'Arville and Madge Shirley. Produced at the Coronet Theatre in a new version by Richard Mansell and Alexander Thompson 9 March 1903.

Produced at the Lyceum Theatre, New York, 9 December 1874 with Soldene, Agnes Lyndhurst and Lizzie Robson.

Produced at the Carltheater, Vienna, in a version by Eduard Jacobson and Wilhelm Mannstädt as *König Chilperich* 28 November 1869.

Produced at the Theatre unter den Linden, Berlin, 21 December 1895.

CHARACTERS

Chilpéric, King of Soissons
Sigebert, *his brother*
Ricin, *his doctor*
Le Grand Légendaire
Landry, *a peasant*
Frédégonde, *his fiancée*
Diviaticus, *a druid*
Don Nervoso
Galswinthe
Brunehaut, *Siegebert's wife*
Alfred
Fana, Hermengarde, Auguste, Charles, etc.

ACT 1

In the middle of a medieval Merovingian forest, under the great oak of Saint-Louis, the grand druid Diviaticus, a golden sickle in his hand, is ritually preparing to do what all good druids do in the opening scenes of operas. With a deeply intoned prayer to the gods Toutatis and Bélénos ('Prêtres d'Ésus'), he is going to cut a little sacred mistletoe from the branches while his brethren provide an impressive opening chorus. Their singing done, it takes only the sound of a distant hunting horn to make the priestly group gather up their snowy robes and, their purpose fulfilled, scamper off the stage and out of the opera until they are needed for a concerted finale.

Their musical mysteries have not gone unobserved. From behind a tree, the peasant Landry and his bright-eyed girlfriend, Frédégonde, have been watching the rites and the sight of these outlandish folk has aroused all sorts of excitements in Frédégonde's breast. It is all very well for Landry to be unimpressed, he has been to town to sell their sheep and their wool, he has seen what other people are like, but she has never set foot outside their own little forest. Landry is content that it should stay that way, for Frédégonde's eyes are very bright and the rest of her is quite eye-catching as well. Since he wishes to keep her for himself, he would rather that she did not display her innocent country self in front of the wicked gentlemen of the town.

That brings us to the hunting horn. Frédégonde may look simple, but she knows that a hunting horn means a jolly, colourful scene with lots of pretty people in grand clothes. She also knows that this is the royal hunting horn,

311

and that means exceptionally colourful people and perhaps, even, King Chilpéric himself. How she would love to see the King, the lovely libidinous King who is the subject of that song she once heard and which, since this is an opera, she is now going to sing to us in its entirety ('Voyez Cette Figure').

Landry knows the King's wicked reputation and he is determined that Chilpéric shall not see Frédégonde, but he has not the heart to prevent the girl from gazing on the glories of the royal hunting party so, scurrying back to their hiding place, he points out to her the nobles as they ride by. There goes Sigebert, the King's younger brother and, alongside him, his wife, the Amazonian Brunehaut, and here at last comes the King accompanied by his doctor, his pages, his lords and his servants, his trumpeters, basses, tenors and baritones ('Que Nos Voix Dans les Bois'). Landry's heart sinks as he hears Frédégonde's naïve sigh—'oh, isn't he handsome'.

But more impressive than Chilpéric's entourage, more impressive even than his entrance chorus, he has made his entry on a horse. A live horse. Just like they do at the Opéra. This one has worked there and Chilpéric is decidedly worried about it, as the horses at the Opéra have a habit of getting tetchy when you start to sing and are quite liable to deposit you on the floor. Nevertheless, he has made his entry and a solo is called for, so he obliges with Le Chanson du Jambon, breaking into his story regularly to steady himself and scrambling off the beast as soon as the song is done. The effect has been made and now the wretched animal can get back to its stable.

After a little chit-chat with Sigebert, who has a cough, and Doctor Ricin who has a series of remedies and a selection of puns, the King pulls the strings of the piece together in a little lecture on Merovingian history. The story so far is as follows. The death of King Caribert (7 May 566) threw chaos into his family, and Chilpéric and his brother Gontran came to blows over the succession at the Battle of Moncontour (23 May 567). The result was a draw and a rematch is now in the offing, and Chilpéric would like to have the opinion of the grand druid Diviaticus as to the outcome of a further battle. Sigebert would also like to know how long his cough is going to last. The first thing to do is find the address of the druid. Perhaps some handy peasant can help out.

Landry and Frédégonde are all too handy and when they are brought forth the lusty King's eye falls instantly on the saucy maiden. The unfortunate Landry is sent off to find the druid, leaving Frédégonde alone with the King. Brunehaut and Sigebert are there, but they are family and are also handy to make up the numbers for a quartet ('Divine Frédégonde'), so Chilpéric does not feel inhibited by their presence in his advances to the shepherdess. He is enchanted by Frédégonde's naïvety and, to the fury of his relatives, announces that he will take her back to court with him as his royal laundress. Landry may come too, since she wishes it, and Chilpéric will make him royal major-domo.

Landry has hurried to get back as quickly as he can, bringing with him Diviaticus and his druids and druidesses to prognosticate victory for Chilpéric and an imminent thunderstorm ('Dans les Combats'). The thunderstorm comes first and, as the royal folk climb upon their horses, courtiers and druids spring open gaily coloured umbrellas, making a deliciously incongruous but traditionally picturesque curtain picture as the act ends.

ACT 2

In the throne room of Chilpéric's palace, the court pages (all played by young girls who are playing young boys so that they can show off their legs) are, as by tradition, opening the act with a display of their legs and a chorus ('Il Est Dix Heures') while they await the levee of the King. Landry is there, making out the day's shopping lists. He has become resigned to the fact that he has lost Frédégonde. She has become the mistress of the King and there is nothing else for him to do but to seek consolation with a courtly lady. In fact, the King has gone so far as to promise to marry Frédégonde. Even though it is unlikely that he will ever carry out this promise, it is a promise which truly infuriates Brunehaut and Sigebert. They have arranged that Chilpéric shall marry Brunehaut's sister, Galswinthe, after which they intend to assassinate the King and his wife and claim the throne themselves by right of kinship.

But Chilpéric is too good a king to mix up mistress and marriage. He knows that Galswinthe is on her way to Soissons and he is resigned to having to marry her for reasons of state. That will not be half so bad as having to tell Frédégonde the news of the Spanish princess's arrival and he escapes into a soliloquy rather than face up to the prospect ('Petit Papillon Bleu Volage').

Sigebert and Brunehaut will be there to lend him support, even though the former is suffering from a frightful sneeze (his first act cough was cured by following Ricin's instructions, but the sneeze came from following them inexactly). Brunehaut, too, has certain distractions. It is she whom Landry has chosen to be his courtly lady and, since her own husband is perpetually sniffling, she has decided to show herself not indifferent to the major-domo's approaches ('Sur les Côteaux, Pauvre Pastour').

Chilpéric has taken the cow by the horns and has decided to send Doctor Ricin to tell Frédégonde to pack her bags and get ready to move out of the royal mistress's quarters. He will provide her with a nice little apartment at a safe distance from the palace where she will be allowed all reasonable expenses and the occasional visit from his kingly self but, given the circumstances, she cannot be allowed to occupy the suite on the second floor of his palace any longer.

That piece of news is the one thing Frédégonde won't take lying down. She was promised that she'd be Queen and she's not going to stop shrieking until she gets satisfaction ('O Ciel! Que Vient-On de M'Apprendre'). She starts tearing the rich clothes off her own back and hurling them at the King, who watches the striptease with interest, but she stops short of nudity and, hurling a shoe at his head, she storms out in a gale of threats.

It is just in time, for seconds later the chorus is singing a welcome to the Princess Galswinthe ('C'Est la Princesse'). The Princess has come from Spain and is accompanied by the irritating but faithful Count Nervoso who speaks a special type of Spanish and is therefore only mildly comprehensible. Galswinthe entertains the company with a boléro ('À la Sierra Morena') about a girl who wept not for love but because she had a moustache, and the King responds by getting the ballet on (they have, after all, been waiting in the wings for an act and a half) to do some characteristic Gallic dances for her entertainment.

Landry, in the meanwhile, has become a little worried. Whilst helping Frédégonde to pack, he discovered a letter. It says, 'Dear Gontran, your brother is busy getting married etc., and Soissons is undefended. If you feel like attacking, there will be an attractive and angry girl hanging about waiting to open the city gates for you.' Chilpéric cannot be persuaded to take any interest in an old letter as he is far too taken up with Galswinthe, but Frédégonde has not finished with him yet. She's not going out down the back stairs, she's going out through the throne room with all her furniture loaded onto a cart ('Loin de Ces Lieux'). Chilpéric has to explain her away as an evicted tenant, as the cart spills its load all over the floor and the act ends in a chaotic song and dance (Finale: 'Ah! Que C'Est Donc Amusant').

ACT 3

It is the wedding night, and the pages and chambermaids are setting out the nuptial chamber and having a little party of their own at the same time ('Chantons! Buvons! Vidons les Flacons') until they are shooed out by Landry. Landry, however, has not come to fulfil his official duty. Oh, no! This is the third act and there has not yet been a murder and Landry means to make up for it. He has had his wicked way with Brunehaut (or she has had hers with him) and, in return, she has asked for nothing less than the death of Frédégonde. He will please his mistress and revenge himself for insults received in one blow of his dagger ('Te Souvient-Il du Temps Tranquille').

One really shouldn't sing too loudly when one is plotting homicide as folks are apt to wander past and overhear. Fortunately the overhearer is Doctor Ricin and he also is plotting. He and the Grand Légendaire, the court chamberlain whose devotion to the former royal mistress was bounded only by his duty, are both plotting. Ricin has been given a royal order: the King has become suspicious of Brunehaut and has demanded that his Doctor administer a dose of something which will rid him of her for ever. The Grand Légendaire is under orders from Frédégonde: he has brought the bride's garter with which to strangle Galswinthe. Three gentlemen each out to kill a lady on behalf of someone else. It's more complicated than the Opéra (Trio: 'De Singapour au Kamtschatka').

The three would-be murderers have just secreted themselves behind the folds of the canopy of the great nuptial bed when Frédégonde tip-toes in. She wants to have the pleasure of watching her vengeance carried out and, being the prima donna of the piece, she needs to have a strong aria in the third act and vengeance is a lovely, dramatic topic ('Nuit Fortunée'). Having sung, she too hides but, before the men can pop out for a little breather, Brunehaut and Nervoso appear, followed by the bridegroom and his new wife. Galswinthe says good night to her sister, who has given her a general lecture on the birds and the bees as prelude to the forthcoming activities, but

Brunehaut intends to be on hand when the excitement starts, and she too hides behind the curtains.

Chilpéric tackles the question of the birds but he doesn't have time to get to the bees for Gontran has arrived at the city gates and he has to hurry out and give him a thrashing before he can carry out his marital obligations. Galswinthe will be quite safe here, in the privacy of the nuptial chamber, until he returns. Galswinthe is not at all sure that it is right to be left alone on her wedding night ('De Pampelune à Saragosse'), but Chilpéric promises to return as quickly as possible and, to the sound of some hollow laughter from behind the bed, he takes his leave.

Midnight tolls, and three shadowy figures creep forth and tear aside the bed curtains. Landry, Ricin and the Grand Légendaire attack and, amid squeals and howls, the women fight back. In the dark, nobody is quite sure what they are supposed to be doing to whom, and pillows and bolsters are rained on everyone until Count Nervoso, who has been hanging about outside, rushes in and presses the first button he sees. It is not the light switch, but a crafty button which opens the floor and engulfs the whole royal bed, sending it swooping down into the palace dungeons.

Outside the walls of Soissons, Chilpéric's army is parading victoriously past in fine operatic fashion ('L'Ennemi Fuit Éperdu'). Gontran has been beaten in double quick time and it is time to tie up all the loose ends. Galswinthe is returned to her husband, Brunehaut is condemned to be stripped and tied to the King's horse, Mazeppa, and Frédégonde...oh, well, it is the King's wedding day and this is only a burlesque, not an opera, so what say everyone is forgiven and they all sing a jolly finale ('Cors et Cymbales')?

In the original libretto the Doctor was named Senna, but this was altered in the 1895 version to allow for some up-to-date punning.

LE PETIT FAUST

(Little Faust)

an opéra-bouffe in three acts by Hector Crémieux and Adolphe Jaime. Music by Hervé. Produced at the Théâtre des Folies-Dramatiques, Paris, 28 April 1869 with Hervé (Faust), Mlle Van Ghell (Méphisto), Milher (Valentin) and Blanche d'Antigny (Marguerite). Revived there 1876 with Simon-Max, Coralie Geoffroy, Milher and Mlle Prelly. Produced at the Théâtre de la Porte Saint-Martin 1882 in a revised version with Félix Puget, Sarah Rafaële and Alice Reine and revived there 1891 with Henri Cooper, Sulbac and Jeanne Granier. Produced at the Théâtre des Variétés 7 May 1897 withGuy, Mlle Pernyn, Albert Brasseur and Mlle Méaly. Produced at the Théâtre des Folies-Dramatiques 1908 with Henri Cooper, Mlle Pernyn, Sulbac and Jeanne Saulier and at the Théâtre de la Porte Saint-Martin in a new version by André Mouëzy-Eon 19 December 1934 with Boucot, Fanély Revoil, Dranem and Simone Lencret.

Produced at the Lyceum Theatre, London, in a version by H B Farnie 18 April, 1870 with Thomas Maclagan, Marguerite Debreux and Emily Soldene. Produced at the Alhambra Theatre in a revised version by Alfred Maltby as *Mefistofele II* 20 December 1880 with Fred Leslie, Lizzie St Quentin, Lionel Brough and Constance Loseby.

Produced at the Grand Opera House, New York, 26 September 1870 with Constant Gausins, Léa Silly and Céline Montaland, and at the Lyceum Theatre 1875 with Coralie Geoffroy. Produced at Hammerstein's Olympia in a revised version by Richard Carroll and Clement King with additional music by Fred J Eustis as *Very Little Faust and Much Marguerite* 30 August 1897.

Produced at the Theater an der Wien, Vienna, in a version by Richard Genée as *Doctor Faust Junior* 4 May 1870. Produced at the Carltheater in a version by Julius Hopp 18 March 1871.

Produced at the Friedrich-Wilhelmstädtisches Theater, Berlin, 30 June 1871.

CHARACTERS

Faust
Méphisto
Marguerite
Valentin, *her brother*
Siebel
Lisette
Le Pion
The Coachman
Wagner, Frantz, Fritz, Altmayer, Brander, Walter, Götz, Aglaë, Clorinde, Frosch, Charlotte, Lischen, Dorothée, Agnès, an English Lord, etc.

ACT 1

At the venerable Doctor Faust's school for young persons, the little pupils are having a jolly playtime, boys and girls together, joining in a saucy *ronde* while the elderly monitor is snoozing ('Saute! Saute! Coup'la Tête!'). When the good man awakens, the children, headed by a loud-mouthed lad called Siebel, find it amusing to make fun of him, but they are quickly recalled to order by the arrival of their principal ('Et Pour Me Braver Quel Moment').

Siebel, anxious to show off in front of his comrades, still mumbles smart remarks, but Faust soon has the boy's measure and challenges him to prove himself a man and have the courage to speak openly. Since the role of Siebel is played by a girl, the scene holds a certain amount of sexual innuendo. Siebel is a fairly tiresome little fellow and his antics, which are topped by the discovery of a naughty book called *Le Messager d'Amour*, last for most of a scene, until he ends up in a corner with a dunce's cap on his head.

Schoolwork is interrupted yet again when a regiment arrives in the middle of the playground ('Vaillants Guerriers, Sur la Terre Étrangère'). It is headed by a the comical Valentin ('Quand le Militaire') who is looking for a boarding school for his little sister, Marguerite, while he is away at the wars.

He has come to investigate Faust and his establishment and he is amused and incredulous to find that the aged Faust, who knows everything there is to know about everything in the fields of scholarship, is immune to feminine charms. He takes only girls of sixteen years of age and younger as pupils, and he has no interest in them after that age. As for love, why to him it is nothing but a noun which can be lexicographically defined and not a sentiment which can be felt.

Valentin knows nothing of learning and a good deal about love, and it seems to him that Faust's establishment will be ideal for Marguerite. When the girl comes demurely into view, declaring to the tune of a pretty Tyrolienne that she is a 'Fleur de Candeur' (flower of innocence), Faust's eyes pop. That child is certainly more than sixteen years old. Siebel's eyes also pop, and he is quick to offer his comfort to the little girl whose tears begin to flow at the idea of being left behind by her brother.

No sooner has the army marched away than Marguerite begins to show her true colours. She is an appalling little minx who is delighted to be out of her brother's control and she creates havoc in the classroom, kicking and scratching the other children and lying her way out of trouble with wide eyes, until she miscalculates a kick and is caught by Faust. She has earned the strap but, as she kneels, whimpering, before the principal ('Grâce! Pardon! Je Ne le Ferai Plus'), Faust finds that a strange emotion has come over him. He cannot bring himself to strike this girl who is definitely more than sixteen years old.

Sending the other children away, he tells her to get up, but Marguerite pretends that she is hurt and insists on showing him her bruises. They are in places at which a gentleman does not normally look, especially when a girl is over sixteen ('C'Est Tout Bleu'), and Faust is sent into fits of confusion. As he cries, 'Get thee behind me, Satan,' the child runs off, laughing knowingly.

The bewildered Doctor soon discovers what ails him. Satan has, indeed, been having a game with him. The devil's henchman, Méphisto—he prefers to be called that rather than the long-winded Méphistophélés, as the fashion of the day is for abbreviated names (Rondeau: 'Je Suis Méphisto')—has decided to tempt the irritatingly virtuous old man with some of the most powerful fleshly temptations in his command. A demon who can make married women and celebrated virgins stray from the straight and narrow cannot allow himself to be balked by a seventy year-old schoolmaster.

He has given Faust desire, now he promises him the wherewithal to satisfy that desire. With a wave of his demonic hand, the old Doctor is changed into a fine young cavalier. Wine, women, laughter and song are within his grasp. He has only to reach out and take them, and the devil asks for nothing in return but to see him do it. But Faust wants only one thing and that is Marguerite. While he has dallied with the devil, Marguerite has done her own devil's work in the classroom. The poor old monitor cannot control her at all, and she has set all the pupils to rebellion. As she leads them, dancing, from the schoolhouse ('Viv' l'Amour, la Jeunesse'), with the adoring Siebel running at her heels, Faust looks on her and prepares to begin his damnation.

317

ACT 2

Amongst the pleasures of Paris's Bal Mabille, cocottes mix with the richest of the elderly gentlemen who have come to employ their company whilst the young men drink beer and talk about politics with the pomposity of youth (Les Trois Choeurs: Choeur des Cocottes, Choeur des Vieillards, Choeur des Étudiants). Amongst this singing mass of humanity comes Méphisto with a tale about a flea, borrowed from Goethe, the ending of which is nonsensically twisted to point a moral ('Le Satrape et la Puce') and which starts a nice little left-wing rumble.

Having stirred up one piece of the devil's work, Méphisto now turns to the girls. He has a fabulously rich friend in tow, a fellow to whet the appetites of any self-respecting cocotte, and this friend is looking for a girl. But not just any girl. Faust has devoted himself to finding his Marguerite and he has pursued her far and wide till, exhausted by his fruitless quest, he has returned to Mabille (Air de Faust: 'J'Ai Beau Fouetter le Sang'). Thence, for his benefit, the devil has called all the Marguerites of the world and, one by one, they parade before him: the English Margarets, the Italian Margaritas, the French Marguerites and the Javanese Mavargaveravitaves (Valse des Nations), but still she cannot be found.

The cocottes (who are actually the schoolgirls of act one, living it up after their escape from school) are diverted when Siebel arrives at the head of his schoolfellows. The boys have been in England, and are happily anglicised ('Nous Somm's les P'tits English') for just long enough to sing a jolly British burlesque. Siebel and his friends have been trotting after Marguerite who, it eventuates, has been in London becoming a scandalously up-to-date lady.

When the little lady appears in person ('Place, Place à la Voyageuse'), displaying herself in an energetically high-kicking dance which leaves little to the imagination, and accompanied by a lofty English lord, she turns up her nose at the reward offered by Faust for the discovery of his lost love but, when Méphisto tempts her with tales of Faust's incalculable wealth, she shows more interest.

Faust, in the meanwhile, is anguishing over his dream of eternal connubial love, an ideal which Méphisto laughs aside ('Les Quatre Saisons'), but it is part of the devil's plan that Faust should meet his Marguerite and, with a magical pass, Méphisto finally brings the young Faust face to face with his lady. This moment of emotion forces the pair into a farrago of mixed languages and nonsensical lines (Trio de Vaterland) as they muddle their German effusions with Méphisto's explanatory French in an incoherently passionate ensemble.

Faust pretends to be the son of Marguerite's old teacher, while she puts on her old act of innocent naïveté and delivers pretty speeches about her longing for pure and conjugal love. Faust is caught. He expresses his horror that such an unspoiled creature should be exposed to the immoralities of the Bal Mabille, and rushes off to find a coach. He will carry off the girl of his heart and make her his own.

He manages to find a coach but, unfortunately, it is occupied. In his haste to accomplish his deed, Faust offers the coachman a fistful of money to

318

abandon his fare but, when the gentleman in the coach comes out to remonstrate, it turns out to be Valentin, back from the wars and furious at the thought of this young man planning to abduct his sister. Méphisto chuckles delightedly as Valentin challenges Faust to a duel.

The duel is fought with vegetable knives and, when it seems that Valentin is likely to best his opponent, Méphisto intervenes. In a short breathing-space during the fight, he offers Valentin a pinch of snuff to clear his head and, as the soldier enjoys his sneeze, Faust creeps up and stabs him in the back.

Valentin falls, mortally wounded (Finale: 'O Ciel! Qui Donc Est Tombé Là'), and Marguerite rushes to his side as he launches into an operatically long death scene full of warnings about the wickedness of men: 'Les amants, vois-tu bien, c'est comme les petits pois. Quand le premier paraît, tous viennent à la fois' (Lovers are like peas. Once the first one has popped out, all the others come tumbling after). When he has finished his piece, he dies, and Faust and Marguerite can finally get into their coach and head off to their revelries, with Méphisto riding laughingly on the postilion.

ACT 3

The act opens with Marguerite, alone, awaiting the coming of her lover (Choeur de la Noce). She is alone really so that she can sing a parody of Gounod and Goethe's 'Le Roi de Thulé'. Her King is from a slightly different country, and his story is ruder (Complainte du Roi de Thuné). His wife made him a pair of elastic braces but, one day, in front of the whole court, they broke and his 'government secrets' were displayed for all to see.

Faust is eagerly awaiting his wedding night, but first there are the formalities to be gone through and the young men and women parade before the couple, bringing the traditional orange flower for Marguerite and the *soupe au vin*, destined to make the marriage night go with a bang ('Nous Venons, Jeunes Vestales'). Siebel and Méphisto, disguised as a local laddie, are amongst the crowd and both make advances to the willing Marguerite behind Faust's back while professedly wishing him a happy wedded life ('Les Jeunes Gens de la Ville').

Méphisto's wishes make a reference to an intimately placed beauty spot on the bride's beautiful body, and Faust's happiness is dampened by a shower of instant suspicion. It takes all of Marguerite's well-tried acting powers to talk herself out of that one, before she slinks into the nuptial chamber to await her new husband and their wedding night.

Left alone, Faust apostrophises Méphisto. He can take back all the glories and riches that he has poured on the old Doctor; Faust wants only Marguerite and true love. But what is this? This figure that he sees before him? It is not Méphisto, but the ghostly spectre of Valentin challenging his murderer. Faust cannot believe that he is seeing straight and determines not to be put off his stride but, when Marguerite comes to find him, dressed in her diaphanous nightie, he finds that he has a headache. Perhaps a little of the *soupe au vin* will cure it.

319

He opens the *soupière* and, o horror, from inside the vessel the ghost of Valentin emerges ('Quand un Militaire') crying out his warnings to Marguerite. Faust's riches are not his own, he wails, they are the riches of the devil! But Faust retorts that it is not so. In order to be worthy of Marguerite, he has returned all Méphisto's gifts. He is a poor man, rich only in his love for her.

At this news, Marguerite's attitudes to her new husband change dramatically. How could she have ever considered marrying him? How could she be the wife of the murderer of her beloved brother? Faust realises that his angel has loved him only for his riches—nothing that comes from Méphisto can bring happiness. Then midnight tolls. Méphisto is calling the two of them. They must descend to Hell to join him ('Anges Purs, Anges Radieux').

Down in Hell, Méphisto, enthroned in splendour, watches a 'Grande Dance Infernale' ('Riez, Chantez, Ô Cher Troupeau Maudit'), rejoicing that, the way men now behave on earth, he will soon have no need to wreak his tricks on humankind to win souls for the devil. At the end of the dance, Faust and Marguerite descend the staircase into Hell, accompanied by all the folk from Mabille. Only Valentin, the brave warrior, escapes as, sprouting wings, he heads for more ethereal regions, pursued by the coachman crying for his unpaid fare. The rest will join the crazy dance of the devil until eternity (Danse Infernale).

The libretto and score of *Le Petit Faust* were amended and added to by Hervé for the productions at the Théâtre de la Porte-Martin. The spectacular element of the piece was largely increased and the role of Siebel considerably enlarged, giving the show a second principal role (with that of Méphisto) played in travesty.

LA PRINCESSE DE TRÉBIZONDE

an opéra-bouffe in two acts by Charles Nuitter and Étienne Tréfeu. Music by Jacques Offenbach. Produced at Baden-Baden, 31 July 1869. Produced at the Théâtre des Bouffes-Parisiens, Paris, 7 December 1869 in a three act version with Désiré (Cabriolo), Berthelier (Casimir), Mlle Van Ghell (Raphaël), Mlle Fonti (Zanetta), Mlle Thierret (Paola), Bonnet (Trémolini), Edouard Georges (Sparadrap) and Céline Chaumont (Régina). Revived there 1871, 14 February 1875 with Louise Théo (Régina), and 1876. Produced at the Théâtre des Variétés 15 May 1888 with Mily-Meyer, Mary Albert, Henri Cooper and Christian.

Produced at the Gaiety Theatre, London, 16 April 1870 in a three act version by Charles Lamb Kenney with J L Toole, Robert Soutar, Constance Loseby, Annie Tremaine, Edward Perrini, John Maclean and Nellie Farren and revived there 24 July 1870 and 19 April 1872. Played at St James's Theatre 8 July 1872 with Céline Chaumont. Produced at the Alhambra Theatre 2 August 1879 with Charles Collette, Furneaux Cook, Constance Loseby, Alice May, Carrie Braham, Louis Kelleher, Frank Hall and Emma Chambers.

Played at Wallack's Theatre, New York, 11 September 1871 in Kenney's version with Lydia Thompson and Carlotta Zerbini. Produced at the Lyceum Theatre 10 September 1874 with Dubouchet, Duplan, Marie Aimée, Leontine Minelly, Mlle Kid, Debeer and Blanche Gandon. Produced at the Casino Theatre 5 May 1883 with John Howson, George Olmi, Lillian Russell, Madeleine Lucette, Digby Bell and Laura Joyce. Produced at the Thalia Theater in German 14 December 1882. Produced at the Casino Theatre 15 October 1883 with Arthur Bell, Thomas Guise, Jeannie Winston, Marie Jansen and Francis Wilson. Played at Harrigan's Theatre 5 March 1894 in a revised version with Pauline Hall and Fred Solomon.

Produced at the Carltheater, Vienna, 18 March 1871 in a version by Julius Hopp and 1 July 1871 in French.

Produced at the Friedrich-Wilhelmstädtisches Theater, Berlin, 30 June 1871. Played at the Theater des Westens 15 April 1904 and at the Deutsches Opernhaus 31 December 1932.

CHARACTERS

Cabriolo, *a mountebank*
Paola, *his sister, with a mystery surrounding her birth*
Régina, *his daughter*
Zanetta, *his other daughter*
Trémolini
Prince Casimir
Prince Raphaël, *his son*
Sparadrap, *his tutor*
The Director of the Lottery
Riccardi, Flaminio, Francesco, Finocchini, Brocoli, *pages*, etc.

ACT 1

The travelling entertainment run by the mountebank Cabriolo is a small affair made up of himself, his two daughters, Régina and Zanetta, his sister Paola, and Trémolini, formerly a servant in an aristocratic household, who has run away and joined them for the love of the pretty Régina. Today, as usual, Cabriolo has set up his booth in a village square, and the members of his troupe are energetically encouraging the public to pay their money and come inside the tent ('Entrez, Messieurs, Mesdames') but, although Trémolini vaunts the charms of Cabriolo's unparalleled waxworks—Adam and Eve, Judith and Holofernes and the beautiful Princess of Trébizonde— in fine style ('Dans l'Unique Galerie'), he cannot draw enough attention away from the booth on the other side of the square.

That booth is the office of a lottery and the prize in the lottery is a particularly dazzling one: your very own château and the lands and title to go with it. It is little wonder that the local people rush to spend their money on the chance to win such a prize, and not a single customer chooses to patronise Cabriolo's exhibition. The mountebanks have time on their hands and, while Paola goes off into her favourite pastime of romancing about her long-lost family, Zanetta decides to give the waxworks a little dusting.

Alas, it is not a lucky day for Cabriolo's troupe for, while she is cleaning

321

the Princess of Trébizonde, the star exhibit of the group, Zanetta accidentally knocks her nose off ('Ah! Quel Malheur! Quelle Maladresse').
Trémolini, too, has his problems. He is suffering from jealousy and he
cannot bear to have men staring at his Régina. Since she is a rope dancer
('Quand Je Suis Sur la Corde Raide'), this means that he suffers almost all
the time and when Cabriolo catches him melting all over his daughter he is
made to feel even less comfortable.

As the crowd leaves the lottery booth, Cabriolo begins to beat his drum to
try for a second time to drum up business, and this time he succeeds. No
sooner has he inveigled an audience inside his tent than two unfamiliar
characters appear. They are the Prince Raphaël and his tutor, Sparadrap.
Prince Raphaël has been put under the eye of this very persistent tutor by his
royal father with strict instructions that he shall be, at all costs, kept away
from the feminine sex. The young man is engaged to be married to a very
important princess and Prince Casimir has promised Sparadrap a pension
and a little tobacconist's shop for his retirement if he manages to keep the
boy a virgin until his wedding day.

Up to now it has not been too difficult. Postage stamps and other such
occupations have proved a perfect distraction. But now the boy has gone and
bought two little turtle doves in a cage ('Une Jeune Fille Passait') which
brings worried analogies into the tutor's anxious mind. When Paola comes
out of the tent to take her turn at barking, the young Prince begs to be
allowed to look at the waxworks. Sparadrap carefully agrees and the boy
rushes into the tent but, before the tutor can follow, Paola has him by the
elbow demonstrating a stain-removing soap. Sparadrap tries to escape by
explaining that he has a special royal mission to fulfil, but this is a red rag to
Paola who immediately assumes that he is seeking a long-lost royal child, a
child which can undoubtedly be none other than her.

She is decidedly piqued when Raphaël bounces back and is claimed by his
tutor, but she refuses to give up her notion. The boy is full of excitement.
The waxworks were marvellous, particularly the beautiful Princess of
Trébizonde. But just a minute, surely the Princess of Trébizonde has no
nose? Quite so. The beautiful maiden who has caught Prince Raphaël's eye
and heart is no waxen model but Zanetta who, to atone for her clumsiness,
has taken the place of the broken doll in the exhibition.

The rest of the public have also been delighted by Cabriolo's show ('Ah!
Ce Spectacle Était Charmant'), Zanetta has been delighted by the uninhibited admiration of the handsome young man and Cabriolo is delighted by
the size of the take—fifteen francs and a piece of paper. He is going to throw
the paper away until Zanetta realises that it is a lottery ticket, one of those
sold by their competitor across the way who is now preparing for the
grandiose drawing of the winning number ('Voici le Moment Solonnel').
The drums roll, the winner is announced—number 1313—and Cabriolo
faints ('Treize Cent Treize'). He has won, he is the lord of a château all his
own. What a splendid life he and his little family will be able to lead after all
their years of wandering ('Tout Va Changer'). Joyfully they bid farewell to
their old booth ('Adieu, Baraque Héreditaire') and head towards a new life.

322

ACT 2

Six months later Cabriolo and his family are the lords of their splendid seigneurial château, and bored. They do their best to live up to their new position with the help of Trémolini, now their steward, whose knowledge of life in an aristocratic household and notions on etiquette prove a handy set of references for them, but they cannot help but yearn for the jolly, colourful life of the circus ('Où Sont Nos Folles Parades').

One morning while they are sitting at luncheon on their magnificent *terrasse*, they receive their first visit from a neighbour. It is a rather curious visit, but it definitely counts as a visit. A young man in hunting clothes comes hurrying across their lawn and through their *terrasse*, demanding, on the wing, whether they have seen a deer go by and, before they can answer, he has rushed on past and disappeared in the distance.

The family are slightly taken aback, all except Zanetta who is full of excitement. She knows who the young man was. He was the handsome young man who left the lottery ticket on the drum, the handsome young man who looked at her in such a deliciously particular way that day. The others are immediately on edge: perhaps he has come to try to claim the ticket and the château. Before their worries can develop further, however, they are distracted by a second unexpected visitor. This time it is Sparadrap, on the trail of his young Prince. He, too, passes by with a breathless inquiry and, hard on his heels, comes Prince Casimir himself looking for both his son and the tutor. Finally, an entire chorus of hunters (Choeur de Chasseurs: 'Au Bois On Chasse') gallops across the lawn and over the *terrasse* looking for the king who is looking for the tutor who is looking for the Prince who is looking for the deer.

Trémolini has no doubt that these cavalier visitors are noblemen, and Cabriolo worriedly decides that they must mask their identities if any questions about the lottery should arise. When he hears the whole procession returning, he quickly organises a sudden decampment of the lunch party which vanishes with the well-organised speed of a circus movement, leaving the scene clear to Raphaël and his pursuers. The young prince has a strategy, however. He hides behind a tree alongside the *terrasse*, leaving the others to stream past and, when they have gone, he emerges. During his first passing he spotted Zanetta, his waxen princess, amongst the luncheon party and he has hurried back to try to make contact with her.

She, with the same idea, has secretly returned to the *terrasse* and, before long, he is able to reassure himself that the Princess of Trébizonde truly is a flesh-and-blood creature and not a doll ('T'en Souvient-Il? J'Allais Te Voir') and he swears that he will find a means by which they can belong to each other. Prince Casimir takes only the length of a duet to find out that he has been tricked and he does an about-turn which brings him back on the scene just as the young people disappear.

Casimir is a prince with a fiery temperament ('Me Maquillé-Je Comme On Dit'), a temperament which has led him to smash twenty-seven walking sticks in a month but, where his son is concerned, he is a caring papa. He is worried lest Raphaël should take after him, for he remembers only too well his own youth, the tricks he played on his own father, and the wild womanising which led him into an unfortunate marriage at a young age. It is this which makes him so intent that Sparadrap should keep a close guard on the young Prince and he is aghast when his son comes to him rejoicing that he has found 'her' again. Of whom is he speaking? He is greatly relieved when he hears that the object of Raphaël's fascination is only a waxen automaton ('Elle Est Peinte Admirablement'), and he happily promises to buy the toy for the boy.

When the Prince comes face to face with Count Cabriolo there is fancy fencing on both sides as all concerned try to keep their identities hidden but, when the Prince insists that he must have the doll of the Princess of Trébizonde and Cabriolo refuses to part with it, they come to insults and even blows until Zanetta, horrified at seeing her father administering his walking stick to what she knows is royalty, steps in (Finale: 'Oui, C'Est le Prince Casimir').

The result is that Casimir agrees to take not only the whole collection of wax figures but Cabriolo, as curator, and his entire household, back to court. As Zanetta entertains the doll's new owner with the tale of the Princess of Trébizonde (Ronde de la Princesse de Trébizonde: 'Femme du Grand Rhotomago'), Trémolini prepares to transport the waxworks to their new home.

ACT 3

The royal pages are scornful of their young master and his apparent passion for a waxen girl ('Cet Enfant Manquait d'Audace'), but they are obliged to take back their mocking words when Raphaël reveals the truth to them. It is not the doll but the curator's daughter who is his beloved ('Fleur Qui Se Fane Avant d'Éclore') and, to prove it, he invites them all to a little supper party which he is planning to give for his lady fair that evening.

This bold action is possible only because he knows that his father is to be away for the night, and it has been put into his head by a diary which he has found in one of his father's old chests, a diary full of descriptions of youthful escapades and tricks. This is not the first one he has tried in recent days and Casimir is deeply worried. Blood will out, it seems, for the boy is copying inch by inch precisely the games he played to fool his own father in his youth. When he hears the menu Raphaël has ordered for his supper party he is even more horrified: it is course for course the same menu as a certain well-remembered dinner of his own. The boy is surely set on the same fatally indiscreet path as his father.

As the populace sing their loyalty ('Voici Monsieur'/'Je Suis Satisfait'), he prepares his departure and waits nervously to see what excuse Raphaël will give for not coming with him. In his day he pleaded toothache and, surely enough, Raphaël comes up with exactly the same excuse ('Ah! J'Ai Mal aux Dents'). Casimir knows what to do. He will pretend to go and then, at the given moment, he will come back and catch the boy red-handed.

Cabriolo and his family have done their best to keep up with court etiquette, although Casimir, a little doubtful of their lineage, has created Cabriolo Baron della Cascatella to forestall any complaints about his presence at court. Paola is still convinced that she must be related to the royal family. She is quite annoyed that there doesn't seem to be any long-lost child needed, as she is convinced that Casimir's face brings back long bygone memories. Trémolini is in his element serving in a royal household but he is still pining for the hand of Régina which is still denied to him by her unfeeling papa ('Moment Fatal, Hélas! Que Faire?'). Cabriolo himself is having a splendid time. He carries out his duties as curator and also beats the Prince at cards with suspicious regularity.

Evening comes, and the pages scout the vicinity to keep guard on behalf of Raphaël and his lady ('D'un Bout à l'Autre du Palais') but, while they do so, there is much activity going on amongst the shady passages of the palace. Sparadrap has made an assignation with Paola, and she is waiting for him at the appointed hour with all the eagerness of a maiden lady when Régina comes to the same spot for a rendezvous with Trémolini. Zanetta bumps into them as she makes her way to join Raphaël and, in the darkness, the three ladies get involved in a certain amount of confusion, before their gentlemen arrive with lanterns and throw a little light on the proceedings.

Trémolini suggests that all three couples take advantage of Casimir's absence to take flight in a charabanc, but Raphaël laughs away the suggestion. His father is far away: now is the time for all of them to join happily in the supper he has ordered and to eat and drink and be merry ('O Malvoisie'). At the height of the party Prince Casimir returns. Cabriolo, who has happily turned his principles aside and joined in the party, swiftly organises a subterfuge and he holds Casimir at bay whilst the revellers take the places of the dolls of the museum.

They are not able to be convincing for long. Sparadrap sneezes and Trémolini gets a numb leg and soon the whole imposture falls down. The furious Prince orders everyone out of the castle but Raphaël declares that if Zanetta leaves he will leave too and, when his father tries to wield parental authority, he quotes chapter and verse from the diary on Casimir's past. He was a real live wire. Why, he even married a circus acrobat called Plume d'Acier.

Paola lets out a little scream. Plume d'Acier was her sister. There! She knew all along that she was related to royalty. That makes Casimir her brother-in-law and all the rest of the family some kind of royal relative as well. That also means it is her dear brother-in-law to whom she must come for permission to wed Sparadrap. Between clenched teeth, Casimir consents. They deserve each other. Régina gets her Trémolini, Zanetta her Raphaël and, with their families thoroughly disposed of, Casimir and Cabriolo are left to share the winter evenings together. The old mountebank will spend them teaching his monarch how to cheat at cards.

LES BRIGANDS

(The Bandits)

an opéra-bouffe in three acts by Ludovic Halévy and Henri Meilhac. Music by Jacques Offenbach. Produced at the Théâtre des Variétés, Paris, 10 December 1869 with Zulma Bouffar (Fragoletto), Marie Aimée (Fiorella), Kopp (Piétro), Léonce (Antonio) and José Dupuis (Falsacappa). Revived there 2 August 1870, September 1871 in a revised version, June 1874, September 1875, 19 December 1885 with Blanche Monthy, Léonce, and Dupuis, 1900 with Marguerite Ugalde, Mathilde Auguez and Dupuis, 1900 with Méaly, Anna Tariol-Baugé, Petit, Brasseur and Guy. Produced at the Gaîté-Lyrique 10 December 1921 with Andrée Alvar, Raymonde Vécart, Girier, Vilbert and Jean Périer. Produced at the Théâtre National de l'Opéra-Comique 13 June 1931 with Marcelle Denya, Emma Luart, Marcel Carpentier, Dranem and Louis Musy.

Produced at the Globe Theatre, London, 22 April 1871 as *Falsacappa* in a version by Henry S Leigh with Marguerite Debreux, Annetta Scasi, Frederic Dewar, A St Albyn and Cornélie d'Anka (Prince of Boboli). Played at St James's Theatre 30 June 1873 with Pauline Luigini, Mlle Fonti, Charlier, Alfred Jolly and Noë. Produced at the Globe Theatre 13 September 1875 with Mlle Fanchita, Camille Dubois, Nellie Bromley, J A Shaw, William Worboys and Mr Barri. Produced at the Avenue Theatre in a version by W S Gilbert 16 September 1889 with Agnes Delaporte, Frank Wensley, Horace Lingard, Sam Wilkinson and Hallen Mostyn.

Produced at the Grand Opera House, New York, 14 November 1870 with Elise Persini, Céline Montaland, Antony, Paul Hittemans and Constant Gausins. Produced in Gilbert's version at the Casino Theatre 9 May 1889 with Fanny Rice, Lillian Russell, Fred Solomon, Henry E Walton, Edwin Stevens, Henry Hallam (Duke) and Isabelle Urquhart (Princess). Played at the Fifth Avenue Theatre 30 October 1879 with Mlle Angèle, Paola Marié and Capoul.

Produced at the Theater an der Wien, Vienna, as *Die Banditen* in a version by Ernst Dohm 12 March 1870. Produced at the Sommer-Theatre 31 May 1902.

Produced at the Friedrich-Wilhelmstädtisches Theater, Berlin, 24 September 1870.

CHARACTERS

Falsacappa, *a brigand chief*
Fiorella, *his daughter*
Fragoletto, *her lover*
Piétro, *a brigand*
Carmagnola, Domino, Barbavano, *brigands*
The Princess of Granada
Adolphe de Valladolid, *her pet page*
Comte de Gloria-Cassis, *her chamberlain*
The Duke of Mantua
Baron de Campotasso, *his first groom*
Antonio, *his treasurer*
Captain of the Carabinieri
Pipo, *an innkeeper*
Fiametta, Cicinella, Zerlina, Bianca, *village girls*
The Princess's tutor, the Duchess, the Marquise, Pipetta, Pipa, Bailiff, etc.

ACT 1

Somewhere in the mountains of burlesque brigand country, near the borders between Italy and Spain, lurks the home of a regular band of bravos who do their best to ravage the surrounding countryside in traditional style. Today they are returning from a raid on a neighbouring village ('Deux Par Deux ou Bien Trois Par Trois') when a cloaked hermit approaches, leading a chorus of village maidens on a mountaineering jaunt ('Déjà Depuis une Grande Heure').

The little ladies have fallen into a trap, for the good hermit is, in fact, none other than the dreadful leader of the brigand band, Ernesto Falsacappa himself ('Quel Est Celui Qui Par les Plaines'), and they have been well and truly caught, condemned to supply the soprano and alto lines to the otherwise masculine vocalising of the bandit band. Although the bandits are duly grateful for this smart piece of work by their chief, it is not sufficient to stifle some grumbling amongst their more forward members. The band is not proving a viable business. Their share of the take in recent months has not been sufficient to support a respectable brigand and they demand that Falsacappa come up with a plot which will improve their liquidity.

Falsacappa has a daughter, Fiorella ('Je Suis la Fille du Bandit'), and she and the chieftain's faithful old second-in-command, Piétro, have remembered that it is Ernesto's birthday. Piétro has made a joke jack-in-the-box as a gift but, in the bottom of the box, Fiorella has placed her gift—her own portrait done by the most fashionable painter of the day for whom she has been secretly sitting over the past weeks. But this exposure to oil paint does not explain a sudden change in Fiorella's complexion and deportment. Decidedly, she is languishing and the change in her behaviour can be dated precisely to Wednesday a week ago when the bandits raided the farm of the young landowner Fragoletto. Fiorella and Fragoletto crossed glances and both have languished ever since.

Fragoletto has taken more positive action. Since he now has no farm and no possessions, he has left his home and set forth in search of the lovely bandit maiden until, climbing through the hills, he has fallen into the clutches of Falsacappa's band ('Nous Avons Pris Ce Petit Homme'). This was entirely his intention for, having been dragged before the bandit chief, he is able to make his declaration. He wishes to join the bandits and to ask for the hand of Fiorella in marriage. Falsacappa decides that the young man must be put to test before these demands can be considered, and the bandits lead the lad off to whet his blade in a trial of brigandry.

No sooner have they departed than a richly dressed young gentleman wanders into sight and Piétro hurries off to recall the bandits to this lucrative-looking prey, leaving Fiorella to make sure he does not get away. Fiorella has no wish to let such a handsome young man get away but, on the other hand, she has no wish to see him torn apart by her father's men and, before the brigands can return, she points him the way to safety ('Après Avoir Pris à Droite') and excuses her action to her father as a symptom of her new awareness of the attractions of young men.

While Fiorella has been exchanging glances with the young stranger, her professed lover, Fragoletto, has been proving himself in no uncertain way. He has attacked a royal courier and plundered him of both his horse and his satchel ('Le Courrier de Cabinet'). The contents of the satchel prove to be of great import. The Duke of Mantua, the local monarch, is to be wed to the Princess of Granada but, as it is a marriage of state, there is more involved than just a simple wedding. Mantua is in debt to Granada, and it has been agreed between the statesmen of the two countries that, as a dowry, the debt shall be reduced to a mere three millions, the sum to be payable to the lofty Granadan accompanying the Princess on the day the lady arrives in Mantua for her marriage.

A plan begins to bubble in Falsacappa's brain and, slipping the portrait of the Princess from its cover, he replaces it with that of Fiorella before returning horse and satchel to the surprised courier and sending him on his way to the court of Mantua. The brigands are preparing the initiation of Fragoletto into their band ('Pour Cette Cérémonie'/'Jure d'Avoir Courage') when the carabinieri are heard approaching (Chorus of Carabinieri: 'Nous Sommes les Carabiniers') lamenting that they always seem to arrive too late at the scene of the crime to be of any use. When the piteous policemen have passed, the bandits joyfully take up where they left off, revelling happily through to the end of the act.

ACT 2
The innkeeper Pipo runs a hostelry perched plumb on the border between Italy and Spain ('Les Fourneaux Sont Allumés') and there, to his delight, the delegation from Mantua has arranged to meet the delegation from Granada. There too, Falsacappa and his band are headed, disguised as beggars ('Soyez Pitoyables'), to wreak their wicked plan. What they will do is capture the innkeeper and disguise themselves as the inn staff so that, when the Mantuans arrive, they can kidnap them and disguise themselves as Mantuans to receive the Granadans whom they will then kidnap and, taking their clothes and identities, present Fiorella to the Mantuan court as the rich Princess whose associate—old Piétro in fancy dress—is to receive the three millions of money. A simple little ruse.

The first part goes off easily and poor Pipo and his family and servants are bundled into the basement as the first masquerade begins. Fiorella claims her reward in advance: she insists that she be allowed to wed Fragoletto as a prize for her impersonation ('Hé! La! Hé! La! Joli Notaire'), whilst Falsacappa, Fragoletto, Piétro and the rest of the band deck themselves out as rather unconvincing inn staff ready for the next phase of the plan (Trio des Marmitons: 'Arrête-Toi, Viens, Je T'En Prie').

The deputation from Mantua is headed by the pompous Baron de Campotasso and the very same Captain of the carabinieri who has unsuccessfully pursued Falsacappa through his native mountains for so many years (Couplets de l'Ambassade: 'Nous Avons Ce Matin, Tous Deux') and they and their men fall equally into the trap laid for them. Unfortunately, although the sequence of events has gone according to plan, the timetable has not and, when the Granadan party is seen approaching, the Mantuans have to be hastily bundled into the inn and despoiled of their costumes. When the Count of Gloria-Cassis leads in his royal charge ('Jadis Vous N'Aviez Qu'un' Patrie'), her tutor, her inseparable page and the rest of her entourage, the bandits are still squeezing themselves into the costumes of the Mantuan courtiers.

Falsacappa takes the place of the Captain of the carabinieri and Piétro, who has to work very hard to remember who he is supposed to be at each change, impersonates Campotasso, whilst Fragoletto and Fiorella pose as the innkeeper and his wife and charm the Princess with their budding love affair ('Vraiment Je N'En Sais Rien, Madame'). The Granadans are somewhat confused when Falsacappa insists that they go to bed, even though it is only two o'clock in the afternoon, but he pleads protocol and, with some rather bodily persuasion from the brigands, the royal party do as protocol demands. Once they are into their beds and out of their clothes, the brigands can take them over. Fiorella shall be the Princess, Piétro shall take the place of the tutor, Fragoletto the personal page, and Falsacappa shall be the bumptious Gloria-Cassis.

Unfortunately, before their plan can be completed, the innkeeper escapes from his bonds and begins to cry for help. At the name of Falsacappa the Spaniards become worried and, when Campotasso recognises the brigand, he tries to lead his men to the attack. Alas, they have been imprisoned in the cellar and have spent their time partaking of the stock of wine. They are too drunk to come to the rescue and the brigands are able to triumph over the Spaniards at the end of a lively finale.

ACT 3

At the court of Mantua the Duke is anticipating the arrival of his bride and taking his farewell of the ladies who have enlivened his bachelor days ('L'Aurore Paraît, Fêtons l'Aurore'/'Jadis Régnait un Prince'). The portrait he has received of his future wife reminds him of the pretty lass he met a few days earlier when he got lost in the mountains and for whom he has been searching ever since, so his farewells are not entirely regretful. On a less romantic note comes the subject of the three millions debt. The Prince has been a spendthrift fellow, never stinting on his lady friends, and he is surprised when Antonio, his royal treasurer, shows no distress at the thought of making such a large payment.

What he does not know is that Antonio's equanimity is not wholly genuine. The treasurer, far from being the serious and pernickety penny-pincher he pretends to be, is actually a secret Casanova who has for years been throwing away the state's money on wild affairs with a procession of women ('O Mes Amours.. O Mes Maîtresses'). The royal coffers are empty, but he still hopes that all will not be discovered. If his vis-à-vis in the Granadan deputation is a public servant in the usual convenient mould, a medium sized bribe will undoubtedly serve to have the whole transaction done on paper rather than in cash, and honour and Antonio's skin will be safe.

Falsacappa's false embassy arrives ('Voici Venir la Princesse et Son Page') and the Duke is delighted to see that his betrothed is the very girl of whom he has been dreaming ('Ah! Quelle Surprise'). He is also mildly surprised and even a tiny bit suspicious, but Fiorella's artless replies to his questions and the fact that she travels, as he had heard, with a particularly personal page, disarm him. Falsacappa is quick to bring up the subject of the all-important three millions and he is aghast when Antonio starts to suggest his little arrangement. The brigand chief has no use for paper credits. He wants cash on the spot. Not a small bribe but the whole money.

When it is clear that Antonio does not have the money, Falsacappa explodes with fury (Finale) bringing both his own men and the Duke and his courtiers to the scene. Before the explanations can begin, all the Granadans and Mantuans who had been abandoned at the frontier inn arrive. Faced with so many witnesses, Falsacappa can no longer deny his identity but Fiorella claims forgiveness for all the brigand band as a reward for having rescued the Prince in the mountains. She will wed Fragoletto and they will all give up banditry and live useful lives from that day on. Antonio is happy too, for Gloria-Cassis is perfectly happy to take his bribe and play his game of paper-work, and, as for the carabinieri, they will have to find some other miscreant to chase with unending lack of success from mountain to mountain.

LES CENT VIÈRGES

(One Hundred Maidens)

an opérette in three acts by Clairville, Henri Chivot and Alfred Duru. Music by Charles Lecocq. Produced at the Théâtre des Fantaisies-Parisiennes, Brussels, 16 March 1872 with Mario Widmer (Anatole), Mlle Gentien (Gabrielle), Charlier (Poulardot), Alfred Jolly (Jonathan) and Mme Delorme (Eglantine). Produced at the Théâtre des Variétés, Paris, 13 May 1872 with Berthelier, Mlle Van Ghell, Paul Hittemans, Kopp and Mlle G Gauthier. Produced at the Théâtre des Folies-Dramatiques 1875 with Simon-Max, Mlle Prelly, Luco, Milher and Mlle Toudouze. Produced at the Théâtre des Bouffes-Parisiens 1885 with Lamy, Mlle Edeliny, Maugé, Mesmaker and Mlle E Keller. Produced at the Théâtre Apollo in a new two-act version by Albert Willemetz and André Mouëzy-Éon 15 September 1942 with Georges Milton (Anatole), Germaine Roger (Gabrielle), René Lenoty (Marcel), Duvaleix (Poulardot), Urban (Duflacnard) and Jeanne Perriat (Opportune). This version was produced at the Théâtre de la Gaîté-Lyrique in 1946 with Madeleine Vernon, Pasquali, Léo Bardollet, Robert Destain and Jane Montange.

Played at St James's Theatre, London, 20 June 1873 by the Brussels company with Mario Widmer, Pauline Luigini, Charlier, Jolly and Mme Delorme. Produced at the Britannia Theatre in a version by W M Akhurst as *To the Green Isles Direct* May 1874 with Sara Lane. Produced at the Gaiety Theatre in a two act version by Robert Reece as *The Island of Bachelors* 14 September 1874 with Arthur Cecil, Constance Loseby, J G Taylor, Charles Lyall and Ellen Farren.

Produced at the Olympic Theatre, New York, 23 December 1872 with Juteau, Marie Aimée, Duchesne, Lecuyer and Mlle Bonelli. Played at Kelly & Leon's 17 July 1876 with Francis Leon as Gabrielle. Played at the Thalia Theater 29 October 1886 with Adolf Link, Sophie Offeney, Carl Adolf Friese, Conrad Junker and Johanna Schatz.

Produced at the Carltheater, Vienna, 15 March, 1873 as *Hundert Jungfrauen*. Played there 17 March 1900.

Produced at the Friedrich-Wilhelmstädtisches Theater, Berlin, 5 December 1872.

CHARACTERS

Duc Anatole de Quillembois
Marcel
Poulardot, *a provincial pasta manufacturer*
Opportune, *his wife*
Gabrielle de Lestange
Duflacnard, *Governor of L'Île Verte*
Clopinette, *his deputy*
Baptistin
Captain Bordenave
Bouffigue, Poupette, Michounard, *colonists of L'Île Verte*
Irma, *a grisette*
Edgard, etc.

ACT 1

At the Bal Mabille, one of Paris's more flighty nightspots, the girls who make up an essential part of the place's atmosphere are taking part in a lively cancan ('Qu'Est-Ce Qui Vous Émoustille'). Their enthusiasm is not all it might be, for they are losing their taste for the Bal Mabille. The only men they meet there are men who are out for a good time with a bad girl and not the material of long-standing relationships.

One of the girls has even decided it is time to take a step into the mire of marriage and she has found the ideal way. A newspaper advertisement has been placed by no less an advertiser than the government itself, asking for one hundred virgins to volunteer to sail for L'Île Verte, a French colony in the picturesque Pacific, where a hundred wifeless colonists await their coming with the south seas equivalent of orange flower and a growing degree of desperation. Since these men aren't likely to know a Parisienne from a virgin, the girls all decide to volunteer.

Amongst this evening's less blasé visitors to the Bal Mabille is Poulardot, a provincial pasta mogul, who has come up to the big city with his wife, Opportune, and both are wide-eyed at the sight of the naughty people who gather in the gardens of Mabille. No less surprised is pretty Gabrielle de Lestange who has ventured out alone to look a little at life before her marriage the following day to the Duc Anatole de Quillembois. Being an innocent child, brought up on the French equivalent of Mills and Boon romances ('J'Ai la Tête Romanesque'), she does not realise that to walk alone in the alleys at Mabille is to court more of life than she had bargained

331

for and she is soon laid under siege by a persistent young artist, Marcel, who snatches a kiss and is paid for his impertinence with a resounding slap.

Whilst Poulardot is off ogling a grisette, Gabrielle makes friends with Opportune, and the two of them have a delightful time together sipping unaccustomed champagne, which relaxes the young woman enough to make her rather regret her unkindness to the handsome artist. When he reappears, she is prepared to be very much nicer to him but, in spite of his effluent protestations of love and fidelity ('Malgré Vous, Partout, Je Saurai Vous Suivre'), she forces herself to remain at a distance. She is very nearly a married woman. She is very sorry, but he has come into her life too late.

Like Gabrielle, Anatole has chosen a night at Mabille for his last night of bachelorhood. Unlike her, however, it is far from his first visit to this friendly place. Over recent years the Duc de Quillembois has gone through many a bottle of champagne and many a grisette at Mabille, and tonight he means to celebrate his farewell to youth and the girls with a few more bottles of bubbly (Quintet: 'Du Cliquot!').

He is hugely taken aback when he runs into Gabrielle and not at all pleased when, after some jolly conversation, the friendly Poulardots invite themselves both to the morrow's wedding and, as travelling companions, on the honeymoon. When it is time for the last waltz Anatole finds he is a little dizzy with the wine, and Gabrielle waltzes away to the strains of 'À Paris, Gai Séjour' in the arms of the ever present Marcel.

At a cheap bar on the quayside at Marseille, the crew of Captain Bordenave's ship are drinking their fill (Ensemble du Pastis) prior to setting sail for the Pacific with their cargo of brides. Strangely, it is this shabby place on which Gabrielle has insisted as a stop-over for herself and her new husband on their way to their honeymoon hotel in Monaco. Anatole, who has been married a whole week, is a little tetchy for, incredibly for a man of such experience, he has not yet succeeded in consummating his marriage. Not only has their every step been dogged by the Poulardots but, each and every night since the wedding, something has happened to keep him from his wife.

The first two nights there were modest headaches, the next night the commissionaire booked the two of them in separate hotels, the next he was arrested by a policeman, who looked suspiciously like the commissionaire, and kept overnight in quarantine, and the next the waiter at the hotel (who bore an uncanny resemblance to the policeman) gave him a strong sleeping pill instead of an aspirin. Anatole is brimming with manly intentions which, since it is daytime, can only be expressed in song ('Dans les Forêts de l'Amérique'), but he is determined that tonight shall be his night.

Alas for his intentions, he and his wife are not alone long, for who should turn up at the same lodgings but Poulardot and Opportune and, since there is not another room free, it is decided that the two women must have the room booked by Anatole while the men make do with the spare maid's quarters. Anatole is irritated and suspicious when Gabrielle receives a letter from her aunt couched in excessively loving terms and delivered by a postman who looks unnervingly like the policeman, the waiter and the commis-

332

sionaire (Letter Song: 'Avec Vous Partout'), but he is obliged to leave his wife in the chaperoneal hands of Opportune to go off to the passport office to get their visas for Italy. No sooner has he gone than the postman reveals himself. It is, of course, Marcel who has been following his beloved the length of France and getting up to all the tricks which have so far prevented the new Duchesse from sleeping with her husband.

Now it is time for Captain Bordenave to register and load his cargo of women ('Voici le Moment de l'Enrôlement'). The girls from the Bal Mabille have made their way to Marseille to join the export drive and they are at the head of the line to sign their names ('Connaissez-Vous Cette Île Verte') but at the end of the embarkation the captain is still two women short. A sailor (who looks like the twin brother of the postman) points out Gabrielle and Opportune, and the two wives, thinking they are registering for a tour of the pretty boat in the harbour, sign their names and follow the crowd ('Nous Allons le Voir'). When Anatole and Poulardot return they find that their wives are gone beyond their reach, sailing away on a bride ship to the south Pacific ('Lançons-Nous à la Découverte').

ACT 2

On the Île Verte, the colonists are suffering. They have been a year without female company and they are ceasing to believe in the existence of the bride ship and in the promises of Governor Duflacnard and his assistant, Clopinette, who are suffering the same privation with no less difficulty ('Sans Femme'/'Pour Avoir une Babylone'). When the news comes that the ship has been sighted, the men rush to the harbour in excitement ('Cent Femmes!') and so they do not see two bedraggled creatures struggle ashore from a barrel.

Anatole and Poulardot have followed their wives on the Duc's private yacht but, getting into difficulties in unfamiliar waters, they were shipwrecked and have battled through shark-infested seas to this unknown island with the greatest of difficulty. Uncertain of their reception in this wild place, they can only watch from a hiding place as the colonists return with Captain Bordenave and the remnants of his cargo of girls ('Dans Cette Île Verdoyante').

The whole hundred have not made it. Forty-three disappeared on a stopover in Madeira and another thirty-four went missing in Madagascar: only nineteen remain and that is not enough to go round. Two of the nineteen are Gabrielle and Opportune who are not at all inclined to allow themselves to be wedded to hairy expatriates ('Laissez-Nous, C'Est une Infamie'), particularly when there is talk of a fraction of a woman per man. They insist that they are already married, but France is a long way away and the Governor is in no mood to reduce his tally of available wives any further—they will be wedded like all the others and, should their husbands turn up, they will be cut up into little pieces by the natives. At this horrid intelligence, Anatole and Poulardot scamper away to avoid being discovered.

Little do they know that Marcel has beaten them to the punch. He has made it to the island ahead of them and he has bribed Clopinette to make him a citizen of the Île Verte and, as such, eligible to take a bride from the shipload. He will have Gabrielle at last ('Certes l'Amour, Ce Fléau Effroyable'). Gabrielle is sorely tempted but she remembers her wedding vows and stays reasonably firm for the moment, and any thoughts of weakness have to be put sternly aside when she discovers that her husband is on the island as well. She begins to wish she had stayed safely at home in Paris ('Je Soupire et Maudis le Destin Qui M'Enchaîne') but, from a more practical point of view, it is clear that she has to do something to keep Anatole and Poulardot hidden from the trigger-happy Governor. They must be disguised and, since the only clothes available are their own, the girls decide that the men must be disguised as part of the bride cargo.

Duflacnard is delighted to be able to add the tall, dashing Léocadie and the cute little Arsinoë to his list of ladies ('Deux Nouvelles Femmes Ici'), particularly when they narrate their journey and their escape from shipwreck in such a sweetly comical fashion ('Sur un Baba') but the list which Duflacnard has drawn up has a purpose which the two false females cannot suspect. He has decided that the only fair way to decide who shall have a bride is to raffle the women off ('Ah! Cette Idée Est Fort Jolie'). One by one the pairs are drawn from the baskets. Gabrielle and Opportune fall to two happy members of the colony, but Léocadie-Anatole is won by the Governor and Arsinoë-Poulardot is drawn by Clopinette. They are devastated, but no more so than Marcel whose long voyage and multiple disguises seem all to have gone for nothing ('Je T'Aime, Je T'Aime').

Anatole has as many pains holding his 'fiancé' at a distance as Gabrielle has with Marcel. 'She' performs a coyly modest country ballad about 'her' mother's advice on men and marriage ('Maman M'A Dit') to slow Duflacnard's advances, but cannot think of a safe way to avoid the mass marriage which is lined up to take place that very evening ('Pour Faire Honneur au Gouverneur').

The Governor, Clopinette and their brides dine together and Anatole nervously rejects every caress pressed on him by the eager Duflacnard with the excuse of maintaining propriety in front of mother, while Poulardot turns on Clopinette the same demure excuse with regard to 'her' daughter ('À Table, Chassons l'Humeur Noire'). To delay further the moment where they must retire to their nuptial chambers, Anatole sings a risqué song ('Au Bord de la Seine, à Meudon') and, finally, both of the brides sling a strong right to the jaw of their respective spouses and run to lock themselves up behind the doors of the bridal suites.

The husbands of Gabrielle and Opportune have fared no better, and they think they have discovered why. In the girls' lodgings they have found men's clothes and razors; there can be no doubt that Gabrielle and Opportune are men disguised as women. The two are dragged before the Governor to answer the accusation ('Ah! Monsieur le Secrétaire') and Duflacnard is only convinced when the two stage a fainting fit and, tearing open their blouses, give only too clear proof that they certainly are not men. When the Governor and his allies rush off to find eau de cologne and cushions to revive the two beauties, Anatole and Poulardot take the chance to reappear, safely clad once again in male attire, but they are caught and condemned by the furious Governor to be flung to the sharks.

There is only one way to save them. Marcel is leading a revolt against the Governor by the men who didn't win a wife in the lottery. If the execution can be delayed, there is still a chance. Gabrielle takes it on herself to hold up the proceedings and, by staging a seductive scene for the benefit of the panting Duflacnard, she manages to prevent any action being taken before Marcel has been able to lead his men to he rescue.

The hero of the hour is ready to renounce his love. Gabrielle has chosen to put duty before love and he must respect her decision. But Anatole has decided that his wife, who is still wife in name only, is not, after all, for him. He cannot remain true to one woman. He will return to Paris and the girls of the Bal Mabille, leaving Gabrielle in the arms of her persistent lover for her happily ever afters.

As for the revolt, it is soon over for, right on cue, a ship is seen approaching the harbour. It is another bride ship. Soon there will be wives in plenty for all and the Île Verte will be a jolly colony, albeit a colony without all our friends, who head happily home as the curtain falls ('Quittons Vite Ce Pays').

The original version of *Les Cent Vièrges* was set in England and on a British colonial island run by the governor Sir Jonathan Plupersonn and his secretary, Brididick. The character of Marcel was added in the revision, and the original story, which treated solely of the mistaken exportation of the two wives, Gabrielle and Eglantine (re-named Opportune), and the perilous adventures of their husbands in retrieving them from the amorous colonists, enlarged.

LA FILLE DE MADAME ANGOT

(Madame Angot's Daughter)

an opéra-comique in three acts by Clairville, Paul Siraudin and Victor Koning. Music by Charles Lecocq. Produced at the Théâtre des Fantaisies-Parisiennes, Brussels, 4 December 1872 with Marie Desclauzas (Lange), Pauline Luigini (Clairette), Mario Widmer (Ange Pitou), Alfred Jolly (Pomponnet) and Chambéry (Larivaudière). Produced at the Théâtre des Folies-Dramatiques, Paris, 21 February 1873 with Mlle Desclauzas, Paola Marié, Mendasti, Philippe Dupin and Luco and revived there 2 September 1874 and continuously thereafter. Produced at the Eden-Théâtre 10 February 1888 with Anna Judic, Jeanne Granier, Romain, Charles Lamy and Christian, and revived there 8 September 1888 with Marcelle Lender, Mary Albert, Lenormant, Raiter and Chalmin. Produced at the Théâtre des Variétés 1889 with Mlles Lender and Granier and Henri Cooper. Produced at the Théâtre de la Gaîté 1898 with Yvonne Kerlord, Juliette Simon-Girard and Lucien Noël and revived there 25 October 1901 with Sarah Morin, Jeanne Petit and Noël, 22 May

1907 with Mlle de Roskilde, Mlle Dziri and Charles Casella and 28 February 1912 with Germaine Gallois, Edmée Favart and Sardet. Produced at the Théâtre des Variétés 1904 with Mlle Gallois, Mlle Saulier and Charles Delmas. Produced at the Théâtre de la Gaîté-Lyrique 1915 with a cast including Alice Bonheur, Henri Fabert, Dousset and Raoul Villot, and played there 1920 with Marguerite Carré, Raymonde Delaunois, André Baugé, André Gilly and Girier and 1921 with Mlle Carré, Jenny Syril, Tirmont, Gilly and Girier. Played at the Théâtre National de l'Opéra-Comique 28 December 1918 with Marthe Chenal, Edmée Favart, Fernand Francell, Marthe Davelli and Félix Huguenet, and produced there 19 June 1919 with Mme Mérentié, Favart, Edmond Tirmont, Victor Pujol and André Allard. Revived there 20 December 1953 with Maria Murano, Colette Riedinger, Jacques Jansen, Raymond Amade and Louis Musy and 27 February 1969 with Michèle Herbé, Christiane Harbell, Marcel Huylbroek, Robert Andreozzi and Michel Roux. Produced at the Théâtre Mogador 18 October 1941 with Suzanne Baugé, Myriam Lecomte, André Baugé, René Lenoty and Servatius. Produced at the Théâtre Musical de Paris 14 November 1984 with Christiane Château/Danièle Perriers, Edith Guillaume and François Le Roux/Didier Henry.

Produced at St James's Theatre, London, 17 May 1873 with Jeanne d'Albert, Luigini, Widmer, Jolly and Chambéry. Produced at the Philharmonic Theatre in a version by H J Byron 4 October 1873 with Julia Mathews, Selina Dolaro, Henry Nordblom, John Murray and John Rouse. Produced at the Gaiety Theatre 10 November 1873 in a version by H B Farnie with Emily Soldene, Annie Sinclair, E D Beverley, Felix Bury and Richard Temple. Played at the Opera Comique 26 December 1873 with Soldene and Pattie Laverne. Produced at the Globe Theatre 25 May 1874 in a version by H F DuTerreaux with Cornélie d'Anka, Constance Loseby. Edward Cotte, Lyall, Edward Perrini, J H Ryley (Trenitz) and Alice Cook (Amaranthe). Played at the Lyceum 31 August 1874 with Soldene, Dolaro, Beverley, Laurent and Henry Lewens and at the Gaiety Theatre 24 November 1874 with Kate Munroe and Loseby. Produced at the Philharmonic January 1875 with Kate Munroe, Mlle Manetti, Nordblom, John Murray, Marler and Harriet Everard (Javotte). Played at the Holborn Amphitheatre 11 January 1875 with Jenny Pratt, Loseby, Cotte, Lyall and John L Hall. Played at the Royalty Theatre 4 June 1875 in a version by Frank Desprez with Dolaro, W H Fisher and Fred Sullivan. Played at the Criterion Theatre 28 June 1875 with Mlle Raphaël, Luigini, Widmer, Jolly and Ginet. Produced at the Opera Comique 7 August 1875 with Cornélie d'Anka, Pauline Rita, Beverley, J F Brian and Henry Lewens and revived there 17 April 1876 with Soldene, Kate Santley and Cotte. Produced at the Alhambra Theatre 25 February 1878 with d'Anka, Dolaro, Nordblom, Louis Kelleher and Henry Lewens. Produced at the Theatre Royal, Drury Lane, 27 March 1880 with d'Anka, Alice Burville and Wilford Morgan. Produced at the Criterion Theatre 22 July 1893 with Mary Ann Victor, Haidee Crofton, Sidney Valentine and Cotsford Dick. Produced at the Theatre Royal, Drury Lane, in a version by Dion Clayton Calthrop and George Marsden 2 July 1919 with Gladys Ancrum, Desirée Ellinger, Webster Millar, Herbert Langley and Arthur Wynn.

Produced at the Broadway Theatre, New York, 25 August 1873 with Rosina Stani, Marie Aimée, Juteau, Deschamps and Duchesne. Played at the Lyceum Theatre 5 October 1874 with Leontyne Minelly, Aimée, Kolletz, Debeer and Dubouchet and 16 November 1874 with Soldene. Played at the Fifth Avenue Theatre 15 September 1879 with Mme Angèle, Paola Marié, Victor Capoul, Juteau and Jouard. Produced at the Casino Theatre 14 August 1890 with Camille d'Arville, Marie Halton, Henry Hallam, Charles H Drew and Fred Solomon.

Produced at the Carltheater, Vienna, 2 January 1874.
Produced at the Friedrich-Wilhelmstätisches Theater, Berlin, in a version by
Ernst Dohm 20 November 1873.
A film version was produced by Jean-Bernard Derosne in 1935.

CHARACTERS

Clairette Angot
Mademoiselle Lange
Ange Pitou
Pomponnet, *a wigmaker*
Larivaudière
Trénitz
Louchard, *a police officer*
Amaranthe ⎤
Javotte
Cadet
Babet   ⎬ *of Les Halles*
Thérèse
Guillaume
Butuex   ⎦
Cydalise, Manon, Mlle Ducoudray, Herbelin, *friends of Mlle Lange*
Hersilie, *Mlle Lange's maid*
Officer, Cabaretier, An Incroyable, etc.

ACT 1

In Paris, at the turn of the eighteenth century, with the first horrors of the
post-revolutionary period past, the city and the country were in the grips of
the Directory, a corrupt and inefficient oligarchy whose members had
quickly taken on attitudes more aristocratic than the aristocrats they had so
bloodily replaced, and whose lack of skill at government and social ordering
had left the people of France in a sad state. Life, however, goes on in the
great city and, when the curtain rises on the market quarter of Paris, the local
folk are gathering together to celebrate a very special wedding ('Bras Dessus,
Bras Dessous'). The bridegroom is the little wigmaker, Pomponnet, whose
popular shop is situated in Les Halles, and the bride is the darling of the
quarter, Clairette Angot.

Clairette is the daughter of the late Madame Angot, the famous fish-
monger of Les Halles celebrated for both her beauty and her sharp tongue,
but quite who her father was is not known for, in her later life, Madame
Angot went off to Turkey, ended up in the harem of the great Pasha, bore
her daughter and, soon after, died. The little Clairette was adopted by the
market people of Les Halles and, since the age of three, she has been
brought up by her multiple mothers and fathers with all the loving care in the
world, sent to fine schools, coached in virtuous living and set up in a florist's
shop until she was ready to be married.

Pomponnet can scarcely believe his good luck in being chosen by the
committee of parents to be that happy husband ('Aujourd'hui, Prenons Bien

337

Garde'), but Clairette, although she puts on a sweet and obedient exterior, is not convinced that the wigmaker is quite the lover she might have wished for (Romance: 'Je Vous Dois Tout').

Just when the wedding should be getting under way, Amaranthe, one of Clairette's parents, turns up with some alarming news: an anonymous letter has alerted officialdom that the girl's papers are not in order. The marriage cannot go ahead and Pomponnet has to be told. When her adoptive parents registered the little girl with the municipal authorities they tactfully registered her as the daughter of Monsieur and Madame Angot, forgetting that Monsieur had been dead five years.

It has to be admitted that Clairette is illegitimate and probably, given the character of Madame Angot, the daughter of some fiery Turk, maybe even the Pasha himself ('Marchande de Marée'). Pomponnet, if anything, is even more pleased at the thought of marrying a pretty descendant of the Grand Turk and, at his urging, the wedding party is preparing to head on its way to the town hall when a further interruption occurs.

The notorious Ange Pitou has just been released from prison where he had been consigned yet again for singing public lampoons of the Directory and its members. In spite of his frequent arrests, he has always been mysteriously freed after only one night in jail and he has always, undeterred, continued to wage his campaign in song against the government. He has also continued to pay court to the pretty daughter of Madame Angot and he is taken aback, on returning to Les Halles, to find that all this merry party is celebrating her wedding. His healthy young heart is less shattered than it might have been, however, for he has received a letter from 'someone who watches over you'—clearly the mysterious person who has earned his release from jail and, equally clearly, not only a lady but a lady of some rank and power ('Certainment, J'Aimais Clairette').

Clairette is not as demure as she seems. She is very fond of Pomponnet, but she is much more interested in Ange Pitou, and it was she who sent the anonymous letter denouncing her birth as a means to gain a reprieve from the marriage. She knows that reprieve can only be temporary, and she urges Pitou to find a way in which she can avoid wedding Pomponnet ('Pour Être Fort, On Se Rassemble'), but the only solution they can come up with is for Clairette simply to say 'no' in front of the mayor.

As Clairette and Ange Pitou embrace, they are overseen by two lurking gentlemen. One is the influential financier Larivaudière, an ally of the Vicomte de Barras, a member of the Directory, and the other is the police agent, Louchard. They are furious to see Ange Pitou free. They consider him to be a dangerous demagogue, and Larivaudière has further reason to be worried, for it has reached his ears that Pitou has composed a song revealing the fact that the financier is deep in an affair with Barras' mistress, the actress Mademoiselle Lange, a revelation which would earn him a disastrous fall from grace. Larivaudière corners Pitou ('Eh Quoi, C'Est Larivaudière') and offers him a large sum of money to exchange his name in the song for that of another of Lange's lovers.

Pitou, seeing the money as a means to getting himself accepted by the market folk as a husband for Clairette ('Quoi, Vraiment l'Affaire Est Faite?'), agrees, but his hopes are quickly dashed. The united parents will not hear of him as a prospective son-in-law. The disappointed Pitou decides that, in that case, he will turn his attentions to his more forthcoming anonymous bene-factress and, rather than sing the praises of Larivaudière, he will simply give up singing altogether.

When a crowd calls upon him for his new attack on the government, he refuses to comply and finds himself jeered for being afraid to go again to prison. At these words, an idea is born in the pretty head of the young bride. Clairette steps boldly forward to sing Pitou's new song ('Jadis les Rois, Race Proscrit'), a song accusing Barras of according kingly favours and public money to his mistress and of ceding public possessions to his friend Larivaudière who, in turn, is busy ceding himself to Barras' mistress. 'Ce n'était pas la peine de changer de gouvernement' (changing the government hasn't made any difference) trumpets the refrain. Louchard leads his police to arrest the girl and Clairette is led happily off to jail. There, at least, she cannot be wed.

ACT 2
At the luxurious home of Mademoiselle Lange, Larivaudière relates the tale of this scandalous occurrence to a crowd of Merveilleuses (Choeur des Merveilleuses) whilst their hostess wonders at the lateness of her hair-dresser. There is more to this gathering, however, than meets the eye. Under their exaggerated modes and manners, these people are the nub of a resistance group plotting against the Directory. Larivaudière, Mlle Lange and even Barras himself are all secretly and actively pledged to the downfall of the new government.

A meeting has been arranged at Mlle Lange's home at midnight, but Marshal Augereau has breached the secret of the uniform of the group, a black collar and a blonde wig, and he has his soldiers standing by to arrest the conspirators. Mlle Lange decides that, as a cover for the arriving guests, she will light up her whole house as for a grand ball, and she takes it upon herself to deal with the soldiers—after all, they are only men and Lange has never had any trouble dealing with men ('Les Soldats d'Augereau Sont des Hommes').

The most unlikely people are part of the conspiracy and their bravery is epitomised by the foppish Trénitz who, complete with wig and collar, marches straight through the lines of the soldiers up to the house ('Gloire au Pouvoir Exécutif'). He is followed by one who is not in the plot, the dis-traught Pomponnet, who pours out to his influential client the terrible tale of his aborted wedding ('Elle Est Tellement Innocente'). Mlle Lange is curious to see the song which caused Clairette's downfall and, at her request, Pomponnet hurries off to fetch it. What she does not tell the barber is that she has already had Clairette released from prison and has ordered her to be brought to the house.

When the girl is brought in Mlle Lange is amazed to find that Clairette is an old schoolfriend and they are soon sharing teenage reminiscences ('Jours Fortunés de Notre Enfance'). Lange promises Clairette that she will help her to avoid the marriage with Pomponnet so that she can wed the young man she prefers, but she hurries the girl off to another part of the house when eleven o'clock arrives and her maid announces the arrival of a young man on whom she herself has designs. It is, of course, Ange Pitou and Lange is the mysterious benefactress whose letter so excited the singer.

Pitou tries to convince himself that he has come only to beg Lange to intercede for Clairette's release from prison, but the actress's obvious charms have their effect on him and their talk quickly wanders away from things political ('Voyons, Monsieur, Raisonnons Politique'). Their little scene is interrupted, however, by the news that Larivaudière is on his way, warned by the snooping Louchard of Ange Pitou's presence in his mistress's room. Lange hastily calls Clairette and, failing to see the surprise on the faces of both the girl and Pitou, faces up to Larivaudière declaring that the young man had come to her house only to meet with his beloved ('Oui, Je Vous le Dis').

Clairette and Pitou are able to swear that they are genuinely lovers and Larivaudière, embarrassed at being made to look a jealous fool, harshly sends Louchard on his way. When Pomponnet returns, Lange sees that the wigmaker could upset her tale. She accuses him of carrying a revolutionary song and the uncomprehending fellow is dragged off to prison before he can speak out.

Now it is nearly midnight and time for the other conspirators to appear, complete with their blonde wigs and black collars (Choeur des Conjurés: 'Quand On Conspire'). Suddenly Clairette rushes in—the soldiers are descending on the house. They will be trapped. Lange orders the doors to be thrown open on the gaily lighted rooms, the music begins, and the soldiers find themselves in the middle of a whirl of dancing people ('Tournez, Tournez') in which Lange invites them to join. The danger is past for the conspirators but, as the dancers and the soldiers swirl away with the music, Lange catches a few words between Clairette and Ange Pitou and realises that Pitou is the young lover of whom Clairette spoke. She and her former schoolmate both desire the same man, so it can only be war between them.

ACT 3

In the gardens of the Bal du Calypso, a dance hall in Belleville, the folk of Les Halles are gathered, not for the dancing and drinking, but in response to a letter from Clairette who has bid them come to hear from her the truth of the events of the past days. She tells them that she is not the sweet innocent they all believe but the real daughter of her flamboyant mother. She loved Ange Pitou and preferred to go to prison rather than wed Pomponnet ('Vous Aviez Fait la Dépense'), but now things have changed. At Mlle Lange's ball she witnessed looks between Lange and Ange Pitou which, if she has interpreted them aright, mean that Pitou is already faithless and tonight she has set up a plan by which she means to test her suspicions.

One by one, the principals in the affair arrive on the scene. The puzzled Larivaudière, disguised as a charcoal-burner, has come in response to a letter from Clairette denouncing Lange as unfaithful to him, while a dis-hevelled Pomponnet has got out of prison by a ruse and wandered in by accident, still frantic in the belief that his beloved Clairette is in prison ('Je Ne Sais Plus Ce Que J'Éprouve'). When the two men meet in the dark alleys of the garden they are very wary (Duo des Deux Forts: 'Ah! Ma Frayeur Est Sans Égal') and, when Clairette presents herself before them, she affects not to know who they are as she tells the whole story of her love for Pitou and his betrayal of her with Mlle Lange ('Je Trouve Mon Futur Charmant'). The three end swearing vengeance together on the unfortunate singer.

Ange Pitou arrives at the Calypso, in response to a charming love letter signed 'Lange' while, from the other direction, comes Lange drawn by an equally passionate letter ostensibly written by Pitou. Both letters are, in fact, the work of Clairette. The trick is soon discovered (Duo des Lettres: 'Cher Ennemi Que Je Devrais Haïr') and Lange is anxious to hurry away, but Pitou openly expresses his love for her and, on cue, Clairette and her 'family' appear from their hiding places.

The young girl attacks Lange with all the gusto of her mother at her most fishwifely and Lange gives back as good as she gets (Quarrelling Duet: 'Ah! C'Est Donc Toi, Madam Barras') as Larivaudière, Pomponnet, Pitou and all the market folk join in the fight. But, when the shouting has cleared the air, Clairette puts out her hand to her friend and rival: if Ange Pitou wants Lange then so be it and, if there is a tear in her eye, it is not for the losing of Ange Pitou but for having rejected the good Pomponnet. Pomponnet is faithful still. It is better to have a wife who changes her mind before marriage than after it. Still, if Clairette is anything like her mother we have probably not heard the last of Ange Pitou.

The scene at the Bal du Calypso includes a considerable amount of inciden-tal dance music which has been varied with speciality dances in different productions.

The most widely played English version (by H B Farnie) enlarged the role of Mlle Lange by allowing her to appear in the first act disguised as a street singer. A later version made for the prima donna Selina Dolaro went even further and reduced the role of Clairette to a secondary one whilst building up that of Lange as a vehicle for its producer.

GIROFLÉ-GIROFLA

an opéra-bouffe in three acts by Albert Vanloo and Eugène Leterrier. Music by Charles Lecocq. Produced at the Théâtre des Fantaisies Parisiennes, Brussels, 21 March 1874 with Pauline Luigini (Giroflé-Girofla), Alfred Jolly (Don Boléro), Mario Widmer (Marasquin), Paul Ginet (Mourzouk) and Mme Delorme (Aurore).

341

Played at the Opera Comique, London, 6 June 1874 by the Brussels company. Produced at the Philharmonic Theatre in a version by Clement O'Neil and Campbell Clarke 3 October 1874 with Julia Mathews, E M Garden, Walter Fisher, Edmund Rosenthal and Harriet Everard. Produced at the Criterion Theatre 1 May 1875 with Pauline Rita, Edward Perrini, Loredan, Albert Brennir and Emily Thorne, and 13 June 1875 with Mlle Luigini, Jolly, Verdelet, Ginet and Mlle Delorme; at the Opera Comique May 1876, and at the Gaiety Theatre 29 June 1881 with Jeanne Granier, Jolly, Henri Cooper, Vauthier and Marie Desclauzas.

Produced at the Théâtre de la Renaissance, Paris, 11 November 1874 with Jeanne Grainer, Jolly, Félix Puget, Vauthier and Mme Alphonsine, and revived there regularly including 1880 with Mlle Granier and 1889 with Clara Lardinois. Produced at the Théâtre de la Gaîté 21 April 1903 with Jeanne Petit, Paul Fugère, Emile Soums, Lucien Noël and Marie Magnier. Produced at the Théâtre du Vaudeville 3 June 1911.

Produced at the Park Theatre, New York, 4 February 1875 with Coralie Geoffroy, Duplan, Mlle Minelli, G de Quercy and Mlle Kid and subsequently at the Lyceum Theatre 15 May 1875 and the Stadt Theater 22 October 1875 with Mlle Geoffroy. Produced at the Germania Theatre in a German version 10 March 1875 with Lina Mayr, Julius Witt, Ferdinand Schütz, Schönwolff and Eugenie Schmitz. Produced at the Robinson Hall in an English version 19 May 1875 with Clara Fisher. Produced in San Francisco 10 February 1875 in an English version with Alice Oates and John Howson, subsequently played at the Lyceum Theatre, New York, 15 March 1877. Played at Wallack's Theatre 13 September 1875 with Julia Mathews. Played at the Lyceum Theatre 25 September 1875 with Marie Aimée and Duplan, at the Eagle Theatre 23 February 1877 and again at the Broadway Theatre 15 October 1878 both with Aimée. Played at Booth's Theatre 7 November 1878 and at the St James's Theatre 2 December 1878 with Cécile Lecomte. Produced at the Broadway Theatre 31 January 1905 with Fritzi Scheff. Produced at Jolson's Theatre 22 November 1926.

Produced at the Friedrich-Wilhelmstädtisches Theater, Berlin, 22 December 1874.

Produced at the Carltheater, Vienna, 2 January 1875.

CHARACTERS

Don Boléro d'Alcarazas, *a Spanish governor*
Aurore, *his wife*
Giroflé, *their twin daughter*
Girofla, *their other twin daughter*
Marasquin
Mourzouk, *a moor*
Pedro
Paquita
Gusman
Fernand
Pirate Chief, Uncle, Page, Almanzor etc.

ACT 1

Don Boléro d'Alcarazas, Duc de Malaga, Comte de Sandoval y Gonzales y Nigo and Grandee of Spain, is governor of a thirteenth century province situated somewhere on the southern Spanish sea coast. He rules his province rather more gently than he himself is ruled by his large wife, Aurore, who sixteen years previously condescended to present him with not one but two simultaneous daughters, Giroflé and Girofla, identical twins whom their parents have dressed throughout their lives in blue and pink respectively in order to tell them apart.

Don Boléro has managed to do little else right. He is hugely in debt to the Marasquin Bank in Cadiz and is, therefore, unable to raise an army to defend his province against the bellicose Moor, Mourzouk, who threatens his security from down Granada way. Aurore has, however, found a solution to both these problems. She posted a picture of Giroflé to the eligible son of the Marasquin family, and one of Girofla to the bachelor blackamoor and, before you can say Boléro d'Alcarazas, preparations are being made in the gubernatorial palace for a double wedding.

At the opening curtain, the governor's staff are found preparing for the big day ('Que Chacun Se Compose'). Given the situation, two sets of bridesmaids have been organised, one group costumed in blue for Giroflé and another, all in pink, for Girofla. The apprentice chef, Pedro, warns the girls not to go too far from the house as the coast is riddled with pirates who whisk off nice young ladies for the harems of Eastern potentates, and his *petite amie*, the twins' maid Paquita, paints a piratical picture in the ballad 'Lorsque la Journée Est Finie'.

Don Boléro is delighted to have married off two daughters to such advantage ('Je Vous Présente un Père'), but less delighted when Aurore takes time off from the wedding preparations to nag him in practised fashion over the history of their own conjugal life ('Pauvre Victimes Que Nous Sommes') before the young brides put in an appearance—in turn, as they are both played by one and the same actress—to ask for some last minute guidance for married life ('Père Adoré'/'Petit Papa'). They (and we), of course, know which is which because Giroflé wears a big blue ribbon on the shoulder of her white wedding gown while Girofla sports a bunch of pink ribbons.

The first bridegroom to arrive is the young Marasquin, a nice, quiet young chap with a pretty tenor voice, a good pedigree to sing about ('Mon Père Est un Très Gros Banquier') and some bad news. The other bridegroom has a nasty toothache and will have to wait till tomorrow for his wedding. Boléro, who has managed to get a job lot concession from the caterers, is rather put out and wants to postpone both ceremonies, but the young Marasquin is not inclined to wait and, since he threatens to go home and have his papa press for repayment of monies due, it is decided to go ahead and have just one wedding ('À la Chapelle'). The bride and groom are introduced, it is love at first sight ('En Si Peu de Temps') and they hurry off to tie the knot.

Suddenly a series of heads pop out from the wings—there are pirates in the palace (Choeur des Pirates: 'Parmi les Choses Délicates') and they've come to carry off a maiden or two. When Girofla comes by, she is seized, along with Pedro who tries to protect her, and bundled off on to a pirate ship bound for Constantinople! Boléro and Aurore are in despair. The local admiral, Matamoros, must be instantly called out and set in pursuit. He's a

343

very good admiral and he should be able to get Girofla back by the evening, in time for the next day's wedding.

But, no sooner have the newlyweds indulged in a happily faithful duet ('Ce Qu'On A Fait Est Bien Fait'), than more bad news arrives. Mourzouk and his suite are at the gates ('Majestueux et Deux Par Deux'). Such was his haste to have his bride that he had all his teeth extracted and set out straight away. Now, where is she? Is it that one? The quaking Boléro explains that it isn't—that one has a blue ribbon, his is pink—and when Boléro and Aurore try to win time by a variety of ruses, he ferociously demands an instant wedding. Promptitude is of the essence of the contract as tomorrow he leaves to wage a little war somewhere over there.

Giroflé has to be let into the disastrous secret, for Aurore has had another of her ideas. Here is Girofla's pink ribbon, torn from her dress as she struggled with the pirates. If they unpick Giroflé's blue bow and replace it with the pink one, she can go through the marriage ceremony with Mourzouk and when Admiral Matamoros brings her sister back, later in the day, no-one will be any the wiser. Giroflé, from having no husband two hours ago, now finds she will have two ('Ce Match l'On M'A Dit') and, pink ribbon in place, she goes off to be wed a second time ('Voici l'Heure'/ 'Comme Elle Ressemble à Ma Femme').

ACT 2

The wedding festivities are attended by a surfeit of family ('Nous Voici Monsieur le Beau-Père') but, in order to avoid the problem of having to be two wives at once, Giroflé is locked away in her room, protesting ('Papa, Papa') at being separated from her husbands. Aurore, watching all the time through a telescope to see how Matamoros's naval manoeuvres are progressing, has to bluff the two husbands who are understandably agitated at the absence of their wives. Maidenly modesty, Aurore insists, requires that they stay in their rooms until the rude banter of the family wedding party is over—they will come down at midnight. By midnight Matamoros should have conquered the pirates and there will be two brides to show.

The merry japes of the brides' little cousins threaten to upset the plan when they insist on going through the old custom of relieving the girls of their garters, and storm the room where Giroflé is hidden (Chanson de la Jarretière). Aurore accomplishes some hurried sleight of leg, and it is her own garters which are thrown to the little cousins as the start of the dancing is signalled (Galop) and she issues orders to serve the wine strong and hard. Paquita soon comes with some welcome good news. Pedro has escaped, and he reports that Matamoros has the pirates at bay ('Matamoros Grand Capitaine') but, knowing the governor's dubious reputation in financial matters, he declines to move in to the rescue until he has received his promised reward. Boléro and Aurore rush off indignantly to plunder the treasury.

Giroflé, in the meanwhile, has got fed up at being kept cooped in her room while both her wedding feasts are going on. She sneaks out to help herself to the buffet and a glass of port and is caught by the little cousins who determine to get the bride tiddly ('Bon Appetit, Belle Cousine'). She joins in with a will ('Le Punch Scintille') and, when the feasting is done, she runs off for some fun with her juvenile relations. When Boléro and Aurore return they find the despoiled buffet and the strewn glasses and—no Giroflé. Those horrid pirates must have been here again!

It is midnight and, as everyone assembles, they have no bride at all. The bridegrooms have got very tipsy and are noisily ready for their wives, but Matamoros has let the side down and the little cousins have only a tiddly Giroflé to present. Which is she? Whose is she?

Before the answer can come, a cannon is heard. Matamoros is victorious! The two grooms are led to their respective bridal chambers to await their wives. Giroflé goes to Marasquin but—horror! Matamoros has muffed it! The pirate ship which Girofla is on has escaped him and is on its way to Turkey. The horrified parents hastily lock the door to Mourzouk's room before they are swept away by the wedding guests, leaving the Moor pounding furiously on the door.

ACT 3

The next morning ('Voici le Matin') Marasquin and Giroflé appear at breakfast after a most satisfactory wedding night ('En Tête-à-tête'). Since Boléro and Aurore need their help, they have to unburden to Marasquin the true story of the last twenty-four hours. This morning, Giroflé must pretend to be Girofla, just long enough for Mourzouk to see that he has a wife before he goes off to his war.

For Mourzouk, who has spent half the night smashing up the furniture in his room, they have invented another story. Girofla was so overcome at the prospect of her wedding night with him that she fainted, so her father grabbed the key of Mourzouk's bedroom door to put down her bodice in approved fashion. Only, as he did so, he accidentally locked the door, and then he couldn't decently retrieve the key from Girofla's underwear until now. But now all is well and here she is and, of course, he must hurry off to his war.

The servants rush on with his baggage ('Il Est Temps de Nous Mettre En Voyage') as Mourzouk takes farewell of his wife ('Certes, Dans Toute Circonstance'). But the Moor is suspicious. Why is everyone so anxious to cheer him on his way? He makes a false exit and comes back to catch the family leaping about happily. So! He isn't going to war just yet. And, to the fury of Marasquin, he begins to behave in a very husbandly way with Giroflé ('Ma Belle Girofla'). Finally the young man bursts: this is *his* wife. Boléro is forced to the truth—actually, she is married to them both. Marasquin claims priority, Mourzouk declares that the second marriage annuls the first and the quarrel is getting scalding when Paquita brings the latest news. Matamoros has finally got it right—Girofla is saved! As the final chorus begins, the Admiral leads on the second twin. Now everything can start again from the beginning with the right number of brides and grooms.

LA PETITE MARIÉE

(The Little Bride)

an opéra-comique in three acts by Eugène Leterrier and Albert Vanloo. Music by Charles Lecocq. Produced at the Théâtre de la Renaissance, Paris, 21 December 1875 with Jeanne Granier (Graziella), Félix Puget (San Carlo), Vauthier (Podestat), Dailly (Raphaël) and Mlle Alphonsine (Lucrézia). Revived there 1877 with Jane Hading and 1880 with Mlle Granier. Produced at the Théâtre des Menus-Plaisirs 1887. Produced at the Théâtre Moncey 6 August 1915 and at the Théâtre Mogador 16 February 1921 with Mathieu-Lutz, Adrien Lamy, Jean Périer, Vilbert and Thérèse Cernay.

Played at the Opera Comique, London, 6 May 1876 with Marie Harlem, Raoult, Geraizer, Alfred Jolly and Mme Delorme. Played at the Gaiety Theatre 4 July 1881 with Mlle Granier, Henri Cooper, Alexandre, Alfred Jolly and Marie Desclauzas. Produced in an English version by Harry Greenbank until the title *The Scarlet Feather* with additional numbers by Lionel Monckton 17 November 1897 with Decima Moore (Renée), Joseph Tapley (San Carlo), E G Hedmondt (Prince of Monte Carlo), Thomas Q Seabrooke (Alphonse) and M A Victor (Felicia).

Produced at the Eagle Theatre, New York, 6 February 1877 with Marie Aimée, Raoult, Reine, Duplan and Adèle Desirée, and played at Booth's Theatre 12 September 1877 with Aimée, Mollard, Jouard, Duplan and Mlle Desirée.

Produced at the Carltheater, Vienna, in a version by Karl Treumann 11 November 1879

Produced at the Friedrich-Wilhelmstädtisches Theater, Berlin, 23 August 1877

CHARACTERS

The Podesta, Rodolpho
San Carlo
Graziella, *his wife*
Marquis de Casteldémoli, *her father*
Raphaël de Montefiasco
Lucrézia, *his wife*
Théobaldo
Beppo, *an innkeeper*
Béatrix, *his wife*
A mute, an unknown, etc.

ACT 1

Beppo and Béatrix, who run a little inn just outside of Bergamo, make their living by serving travellers who use their hostelry as a coaching stop ('Mangeons Vite') and maintain their popularity by serving their customers particularly good wine ('Depuis Plus de Cent Cinquante Ans'). They also take in guests and, at the moment, they have three who are rather curious. The younger man of the group goes tip-toeing around, whispering in corners with cloaked strangers ('Partis! Ils Sont Partis!') in such a fashion that Beppo and Béatrix are convinced they are housing a gaggle of conspirators.

346

The young man in question is called San Carlo and he is definitely nervous. He is waiting for someone to arrive to meet him and is furious when he finds the equally nervous Beppo spying on him. But Beppo is worrying unnecessarily. The cloaked visitors are nothing more than a tailor and a dressmaker, and they have come to care to the clothes of the young lady and the elderly gentleman who accompany San Carlo: not ordinary, everyday clothes but a wedding gown for her and a suit appropriate to a bride's father for him. The young lady, Graziella, is to be San Carlo's wife.

Graziella is delighted with her gown and she hurries forth from her room to show herself to San Carlo in all her matrimonial splendour ('Je Tenais, Monsieur Mon Époux'), but San Carlo's nervousness only increases at such a sight and he begs Graziella to keep a low profile. Graziella's father, the rich landowner the Marquis de Casteldémoli, is annoyed and befuddled by all this cloak and dagger business. It is bad enough that he has agreed that a daughter of his should marry a penniless fellow like San Carlo, without having to be put through all this nonsense. The only reason he has consented to the match is to benefit his own affairs. San Carlo is the bosom friend of the local Podesta, the most important man in the area, and Casteldémoli urgently needs some favourable influence in that quarter.

The Podesta owns a large tract of land in the middle of which is a little property owned by Casteldémoli. It is a property of which he is particularly fond and which he has no wish to sell, but the Podesta has long coveted it and has offered on many occasions to buy it. When Casteldémoli refused, the great man did not press his point but merely indicated that the uncooperative landowner should take care. Since he will not sell, the Podesta will ensure that if he is ever caught in the slightest breach of the law his property will be forfeit. And that is why the nervous Marquis is willing to allow his daughter to wed below her financial situation. As the father-in-law of the Podesta's best friend he will surely be safe from such a horrid tactic.

Tempers fray all round as everyone's nervousness increases and the wedding is called off and on again ('Si Vous N'Aviez Pas Eté Si Gentille') as San Carlo insists on waiting for his friend, Raphaël Montefiasco, whom he wishes to act as witness alongside a mute especially engaged for the occasion. Montefiasco finally arrives, but he is not anxious to stay for the wedding. He has a wife and she is waiting for him at home. The point is that Lucrézia Montefiasco is no ordinary wife. She is a wife passionately in love with her husband and liable at the slightest threat to her equanimity to lash out with the whip which she carries with her everywhere she goes, usually landing it somewhere on her loved one's tender body. And that is why Montefiasco does not want to be late home.

When San Carlo explains to him the tale behind this whole business, however, he has to agree, for it is clear that the marriage between San Carlo and Graziella must take place in the most complete privacy and secrecy. Once upon a time the Podesta had a wife, a very beautiful and passionate wife who was not averse to casting an Italian look at her husband's best friend. San Carlo, being young and excessively heterosexual, could not long stay immune to such glances and, before long, he weakened and weakened

347

and weakened again. Inevitably, one day the Podesta walked in on him being weak, but the great man did not order his friend in shame from the court. He continued to allow him to stay at his side, only warning him that one day he would have his revenge. Since his friend felt free to steal his wife, he, one day, would return the deed in kind.

San Carlo swore on the spot never to marry, but time passed and he met Graziella and the urge to wed came upon him. There was nothing for it but to wed in total secrecy. Thus, the need for this out-of-the-way inn, for a dumb witness and for his best and most trustworthy friend as the other witness. And now that all is explained, to Raphaël and to us at least, the bride and groom can be led to the town hall to plight their troth ('Voici l'Instant').

No sooner have they departed than a whirlwind arrives at the inn. It is Lucrézia Montefiasco, and she has come in search of her husband ('Mon Amour, Mon Idole'). She cannot be calmed by the innkeeper, she is congenitally suspicious and, to keep her suspicions at boiling point, she carries permanently on her breast a medallion bearing a portrait of a lady. The portrait belonged to Montefiasco before she met him and the lady is evidently part of his past, so every time Lucrézia looks at it she winds up into a frenzy of whiplashing which bodes ill for anyone standing too near.

The next arrival at the inn is the Podesta himself. San Carlo has explained his absence from his patron's side by pleading illness and the good magistrate has decided to come to see his ailing friend. San Carlo, returning ahead of his bride, is aghast, particularly when the Podesta takes to teasing him with reminders of his promise ('Le Jour Où Tu Te Marieras'), and he hurriedly passes off Graziella as the new wife of Montefiasco. The Podesta is not interested in Montefiasco, but he is interested in Graziella and he takes no pains to hide the fact. Graziella must be presented at his court and he will find a position there for Montefiasco.

San Carlo can stay at the inn until he is well, and the 'newlyweds' shall return to Bergamo with him. Here's a pretty pickle. It gets worse when Lucrézia catches up with her husband and decides that she will never again leave his side, particularly when she hears the Podesta's decree that Montefiasco and his wife are to come to court (Finale: 'Que Chacun Se Coure et Se Presse'). San Carlo has to trick her into sufficient inattention to allow his wife and her husband to mount the Podesta's coach and, before the furious Lucrézia's gaze, Graziella and Montefiasco set off for Bergamo.

ACT 2
Once back at court, the Podesta piles honours on Graziella, Montefiasco and Casteldémoli. Raphaël, promoted to chief page, is decorated with a grand sword as emblem of his new position ('A Midi Pour le Quart'/'Ce N'Est Pas, Camarade'). However, sword or no sword, he has no intention of prolonging his stay at court, until San Carlo, who has hurried after them, reminds him that he is now a soldier and, should he depart, he will be guilty of desertion. He also promises that he has nothing to fear from Lucrézia. She fainted with emotion at his departure, and San Carlo has put her under the care of a

doctor with instructions that she be sedated for a month. Montefiasco can continue to pretend to be Graziella's husband by day and he, San Carlo, will take over for the hours of the night.

If the plan pleases Graziella well enough ('Le Jour, Vois-Tu Bien, Ma Chère Ame'), it has less attractions for Montefiasco, especially when, in spite of everything, Lucrézia arrives on the scene, her whip simply bristling with agitation ('Ah! Ce Souvenir M'Exaspère'). Montefiasco calms her with a little of the truth. He admits that he is posing as the husband of Graziella and mumbles something reasonably convincing about politics and necessity, and finally Lucrézia is won amorously into his arms. Their embrace, alas, is seen by the Podesta who reasons that if Montefiasco can be unfaithful to his wife so soon after their marriage there is no reason why the little Graziella should not behave with an equal generosity. He has her made his reader and, by a diligent choice of erotic books, tries to persuade her into a seducible state of mind ('Donnes-Moi Votre Main'/'Or Donc, En Romagne Vivait').

The Podesta confides his intentions to seduce the wife of Montefiasco to San Carlo and asks for his help. The poor man, horrified, refuses, but has to watch as the Podesta carries on with his plan. He orders Montefiasco to be posted on a distant bastion and proposes to lay siege to his wife while he is away. San Carlo can think of no other way out of the trap but to take his wife and flee from court ('Tu Partiras?'/'Vraiment, J'En Ris d'Avance').

Lucrézia has received a letter from Montefiasco explaining his sudden departure but, unconvinced, she comes to find out what is happening and, hiding in the evening shadows, she sees a man approaching swathed in a military cloak. It is San Carlo, who has come to collect Graziella whilst avoiding the attentions of the night watch ('Quand la Nuit Commence'), but Lucrézia's suspicious mind convinces her that it is her Raphaël. When she hears the cloaked man preparing to flee with Graziella, she leaps forth to stop them and the noise arouses the Podesta.

Lucrézia denounces her husband roundly before the magistrate, only to discover that she has made a mistake. It is a mistake from which the Podesta profits. He will call Montefiasco and show him how his wife is running away already with another man (Finale: 'Alarme! Alarme!'). Now the truth has to come out: Montefiasco claims Lucrézia, and Graziella, not knowing what she is doing, claims San Carlo ('Marié, Marié'). The Podesta postpones his revenge long enough to drink to his friend's marriage and Graziella sings happily of wedded bliss ('Dans la Bonne Société'), little knowing what lies ahead.

ACT 3
When the festivities are over, San Carlo and Graziella are led to their apartments—he to his and she to hers—and Montefiasco and his men set guard over them ('Plan! Rataplan!') until morning. Graziella spends a mournful night ('Dans Cette Chambre Solitaire'), but San Carlo spends his racked with doubts. Where is his wife? What is the Podesta up to? When he encounters his patron in the morning he is all a-tremble. Has revenge been

exacted? No, it hasn't, but the Podesta smilingly promises him that it is only a matter of time. He will begin to court Graziella as of today.

Lucrézia has found her Raphaël extraordinarily handsome in his new uniform but, as a result, she has become doubly jealous and is determined that he shall leave the army. She brings him forcibly before the Podesta to demand his release and relates the history of her jealousy and the lady of the portrait, but the Podesta has other things on his mind and pays little attention to her. He is set fair for the conquest of Graziella. To Casteldémoli's horror, Graziella now comes up with an offer of a swap. She will concede her father's bit of property to the Podesta in exchange for San Carlo's release. This, plus the pretty eyes of the little wife, win over the Podesta and he agrees that San Carlo shall go free on one condition: he must never know how his pardon was won.

The condition proves a hard one, for San Carlo immediately assumes that Graziella has won his release by unspeakable means, and he rejects her before the amused gaze of his patron ('Vraiment Est-Ce Là la Mine'). She is upset and indignant ('Pour Vous Sauver On Se Dévoue') and, in spite of her tears ('Tu Pleures, Graziella'), their happiness seems ready to crack down the middle. The Podesta has had his revenge. Now San Carlo knows what jealousy is. But suddenly the great man spots the portrait on Lucrézia's breast. It is his wife! Good heavens, how many men did she betray him with? It seems that she does not merit the honour of his vengeance. San Carlo is forgiven, and he and his wife taken back into the good graces of their patron as the happy ending comes into sight.

LE GRAND MOGOL

an opéra-bouffe in four acts by Henri Chivot. Produced at the Gymnase de Marseille 24 February 1877 in a three act version with Jane Hading (Irma). Produced at the Théâtre de la Gaîté, Paris, 19 September 1884 in a version by Chivot and Alfred Duru with Mme Thuillier-Leloir (Irma), Marie Gélabert (Bengaline), Henri Cooper (Mignapour), Mesmaker (Nicobar), Alexandre (Joquelet) and Scipion (Crakson) and revived there 1885 with Mary Albert (Mignapour), 3 May 1886 with Jane Caylus (Mignapour), 7 October 1887 with Juliette Simon-Girard, 1895, 1901 with Rosalia Lambrecht, Soums and Lucien Noël, 1914 with Angèle Gril, Berthaud and Dutilloy, and 4 March 1915 with Mlle Gril and Chambon. Produced at the Théâtre des Folies-Dramatiques 1 December 1922 with Renée Camia, Mlle Destange, Georges Foix, Félix Oudart and Robert Jysor. Produced at the Théâtre de la Gaîté-Lyrique in a revised version February 1949 with Madeleine Vernon, Gabrielle Ristori, Joseph Peyron, André Fadeuilhe, Willy Clément and Michel Mars.

Produced at the Comedy Theatre, London, in a version by H B Farnie with additional music by Audran 17 November 1884 with Florence St John (Djemma), Berthe Latour (Bengaline), Henry Bracy (Mignapour), Fred Leslie (Ayala), Arthur Roberts (Jugginsee-Lai) and Frank Wyatt (Captain Coqueluche).

Produced at the Bijou Theatre, New York, 29 October 1881 in Farnie's version as

The Snake Charmer with Lillian Russell, Blanche Chapman, Selina Dolaro, George W Denham and Joseph W Greensfelder. Played at the Metropolitan Theatre 28 August 1882 with Lilly Post and Dolaro; at the Star Theatre 26 September 1887 with Julia Bennati and at Wallack's Theatre 1887.

Produced at the Friedrich-Wilhelmstädtisches Theater, Berlin, in a version by Eduard Jacobson 18 April 1885

CHARACTERS

Prince Mignapour
Nicobar, *his Grand Vizier*
Joquelet, *a dentist*
Irma, *his sister, a snake charmer*
Captain Crackson
Princess Bengaline
Madras, *an innkeeper*
Grand Brahmin, Kioumi, etc.

ACT 1

In the market place of the little town of Almora, near Delhi, the local merchants are vaunting their wares ('Allons et Point de Paresse'), but the attention of the populace is diverted from these mundane offerings by a novelty: the gaudily decorated cart bearing the legend JOQUELET, DENTISTE DE PARIS. Their curiosity does not take them as far as to allow this visiting extractor of teeth ('Mon Nom Est Joquelet') to practice his craft on them, however, and Monsieur Joquelet is obliged to fall back on his second string to make the purses of the natives jingle.

That second string is his lovely sister, Irma, whose profession is rather more entertaining than his: she is a snake charmer and she will give an exhibition of her art in the market place in one hour's time. The attractions of Irma Joquelet do not reside only in her ability to charm snakes. She has charms of her own and they have already enraptured a buffoonish English Captain called Crackson, who has taken advantage of a mission ordering him to set up a British trading post at Delhi to follow the Joquelets to Almora and, although he has never exchanged a word with Irma, to ask her brother for the pretty snake-charmer's hand in marriage.

Joquelet is not against the match. After all, Crackson is British and an officer and *ipso facto* classy and rich. But Irma has very firm thoughts to the contrary. Crackson is distinctly plain and she has no intention of marrying an unattractive man no matter what his creditable points may be ('Je Ne Veux Pas de Vous').

When Crackson has been sent on his way, swearing that the Joquelets have not heard the last of him, Irma and her brother are able to expound the background to the story which is about to unfold. The richly decorated building which borders on the market place is the palace of the royal Princess Bengaline. She is a widow, still only twenty-three, and second in

351

line to the throne of the Grand Mogols to which her cousin, Prince Mignapour, is due to succeed in two days time.

The young Mignapour has been groomed very carefully for his accession to the throne by the Prime Minister, Nicobar, and his court, and the most important part of this grooming has consisted of keeping the lad wholly in ignorance of the existence of sexual urges. The reason for this unfeeling action is that the law of the land insists that, to become Grand Mogol, a Prince must be a virtuous and innocent virgin, and the law is enforced by means of a magic necklace which he wears at all times around his neck. The necklace is made of white pearls but, should its wearer fall from innocence, the pearls will magically turn black and the Prince shall be shorn of his inheritance and banished from the land (Légende du Collier Noir: 'Si le Prince, M'A T'On-Conté').

The Princess Bengaline enjoys her widowhood in the company of a large number of would-be wooers ('Place, Place à Bengaline'/'J'Aime l'Éclat des Cours') far from the court at Delhi, but she has one great longing in her heart. She longs to be Queen and, under the present circumstances, that means she must wed her cousin. Her hopes are given a great encouragement when the Prime Minister turns up in Almora seeking the young Prince. It appears that he has vanished.

About two months ago, just after the big festival and around the time Bengaline left Delhi, the Prince became moody and sad and gave all the classic signs of being in love. Now, with all the preparations for his coronation under way, he has vanished and, according to report, has been seen at Almora. Bengaline is delighted: it would seem that the Prince is in love with her and has come to seek her out. Nicobar follows the same line of reasoning and, with a view to the future, immediately sets to ingratiate himself with the Princess.

Mignapour has indeed made his way to Almora but he is not at all happy when his disguise is penetrated by his Prime Minister. Nicobar tactfully leaves him alone with the eager Bengaline, and her smiles encourage him almost to confide in her the feelings in his heart ('Je Voudrais Révéler à la Nature Entière'). Alas, he is too shy to speak of such things, and Bengaline, irritated by his modesty, leaves him to pluck up his courage alone.

No sooner has she gone than the real object of Mignapour's budding affections appears. It is Irma, whom he noticed during the festival at Delhi and with whom he has become more and more obsessed as the days have passed. His modesty falls away as he details his desires with an oriental floridity which the Parisian maiden finds a little forward ('Si J'Étais un Petit Serpent') but which she does not discourage. When Mignapour happily tells Nicobar that he is in love, the Prime Minister is delighted and he hurries to tell Bengaline that her charms have had the required effect.

The time arrives for Irma's performance and the town gathers to watch (Finale: 'Pour Voir Irma') as she and her snake go into their act ('Allons, Petit Serpent'). She is disappointed to notice that the handsome young man who expressed himself so fulsomely a short while before is not in the audience, but she receives a great shock when the royal trumpets announce the coming of the Prince and her young man is borne in, richly clad, to announce his request for her hand in marriage. As the two young people sing rapturously of their love, Bengaline, Nicobar and Crackson ruminate revenge.

ACT 2
They are still ruminating when the second act begins, that same evening, in the gardens of the Grand Mogol's palace ('Si le Prince Se Marie') until Nicobar comes up with an answer to the problem: the necklace. Mignapour must be made to lose his innocence before his coronation. That way he will be banished, Bengaline will be made Mogoless in his place, Nicobar will be able to rest secure in his position, and Irma will be left for Crackson to wed. The undoing of the Prince will be left in the hands of a seductive troupe of bayadères, and Bengaline decides that she herself will lead the girls in disguise ('Qu'On Me Laisse Agir à Mon Gré') whilst her two co-conspirators follow as musicians.

Irma and Joquelet have been brought to the palace ('Dans Ce Beau Palais de Delhi') and the snake-charmer soon discovers that the fabled innocence of her husband-to-be has been in no way exaggerated. He still believes in the story about the cabbage patch (Couplets du Chou et de la Rose: 'Un Antique et Fort Vieil Adage'). However, even if his ideas on procreation are a little naïve, he is learning fast about urges and, when Irma is separated from him by propriety, those urges need little persuasion to come to the surface. Bengaline and her bayadères do not have a difficult job in arousing the young man ('Nous Sommes Prêtresses d'Indra'/Chanson Indoue: 'L'Indolente Panthère') but, just as they are ready to claim their prey, Joquelet walks in and, horrified, calls Irma to witness Mignapour's infidelity.

Mignapour succeeds in convincing his bride of his good faith and, to assure her, he calls the whole court together ('Sur l'Ordre de Sa Hautesse') to announce his forthcoming marriage and celebrate the occasion in good French wine (Chanson du Vin de Suresnes: 'Dans Nos Guingettes de Paris'). Left alone at the end of the celebration, Mignapour is anxious to anticipate his wedding night, but Irma holds him off: there shall be no love-making until the morrow.

In that case, he begs her, will she meet him in the rose garden at midnight? He receives no answer, but he lives in hope. The only trouble is that the Prince is closely guarded once night falls. He is put in his royal bed and guarded by his royal guards and they will not let him out for a midnight rendezvous. Then Mignapour has an idea. The pestilential Englishman may yet be of some use. Amongst his commercial samples Crackson carries opium. A little drop in his guards' wine and all will be well (Finale: 'Le Jour Vient de Finir').

The night passes (Choeur de la Ronde de Nuit) and, in the morning, the Grand Brahmin greets the new day while Nicobar stalks about in triumph. The sergeant of the night guard has brought an earth-shattering report. Whilst on his patrol the previous night he saw a man and a woman embrac-

353

ing passionately in the rose garden and, on closer examination, recognised the man as none other than Prince Mignapour. While Joquelet attempts to give Irma both a mother's and a father's advice on her wedding day ('Au Moment de Te Marier'), the Prince descends from the royal bedroom (Finale: 'Silence! Silence! Le Voici') only to find the court recoiling from him in horror. His necklace is black! The Prince has fallen from grace; he is shorn of his rank and driven into exile.

ACT 3
A week later Irma and Joquelet find themselves at a caravanserai ('Après les Pénibles Voyages') outside the city without the wherewithal to pay their way. Joquelet has picked up a little casket on the banks of the river during their flight, but he has been unable to open it and although it is a pretty looking thing he finds it is not exchangeable for cash. In Delhi their enemies are in full command. Bengaline is all-powerful and Nicobar, her right-hand man, having rid the kingdom of Mignapour has sent the Parisian pair packing too. Irma has to have her tears dried ('Petite Soeur, Il Faut Sécher Tes Larmes'), but she still has time to give a kind word to a poor fakir who joins them in their unwholesome dwelling ('Par Tout les Pays, Je Chemine') even though, her thoughts elsewhere, she pays him but scant attention.

The fakir is, did she but know it, her beloved Mignapour in disguise, returned from far-off Kashmir simply to gaze again on his Irma. His disguise has served him well so far, and it does even better when he encounters Nicobar who has come out looking for a casket which he has lost. It is a very important casket, since it contains the last words of the late Mogol which are to be delivered to his heir on his or her accession to the throne. Mignapour questions the Prime Minister on the tale of the deposed Prince and hears the dreadful story reported by the night watch of the events in the rose garden. There can be no doubt of his guilt. Mignapour is puzzled. To have done such a thing and not to remember it! There is only one answer. He must be a sleep-walker.

Perhaps Irma is too. He decides to reveal himself to her but they have only time for a quick duet ('Ô Ma Maîtresse Bien-Aimée') before Nicobar returns and the Prince is obliged to hide. Nicobar has heard that Joquelet has found the missing casket and he is anxious to retrieve it. A large purse does the trick and the Prime Minister opens the casket to read the vital words. They are a gross surprise. The paper inside speaks of the famous necklace. It says that it has no magic powers at all, the tale being simply a useful method of ensuring that the young royals of Delhi behave themselves in a fitting manner until the day of their marriage. But how, then, can the change in Mignapour's necklace be accounted for?

Nicobar is still puzzling this one out when the arrival of Bengaline is announced. She has heard a whisper that Mignapour has left Kashmir and returned to Delhi and she wishes to have him found and brought to her as she intends to marry him. Nicobar shares his discovery with the Princess and is disconcerted to find that she is not at all surprised ('A la Femme En

Naissant'). Bengaline had opened the casket and read the truth about the necklace and realised how she might use the information to prevent Irma marrying the Prince.

She took the snake-charmer's place at the late night meeting in the rose garden and there she met with Mignapour and took the opportunity to exchange the white necklace for a black one. Now, safely ensconced at the head of the kingdom, she will recall Mignapour who, learning that it was she and not Irma with whom he dallied in the rose garden, will be obliged to wed her. That way, the Princess will not be guilty of usurping the throne on which she will be able to rest easily for the rest of her life. As for Nicobar, he will be named Prime Minister in perpetuity.

Little do they know, these two plotters, that their conversation has had a witness. Irma has been hiding behind a convenient pillar and has heard all. So Mignapour and Bengaline disported themselves in the rose garden and Bengaline now intends to restore the Prince to power by marrying him. It must be so. She, Irma, must not stand in the way of her beloved regaining his rightful heritage, particularly in the arms of a lady to whom he has already committed himself, albeit in the dark and in a rose garden. She will pretend that she no longer loves him and give herself instantaneously to Crackson (Quartet: 'Ah! Pour Moi Quelle Heureuse Chance').

The Englishman is delighted at this sudden change of fortune and, when Mignapour tries to prevent the marriage, Crackson stoutly states that he must, by rights, be Irma's lawful husband. He has a tale to tell. On the night when everything happened at Delhi, Crackson availed himself of his opium sample and put the guards to sleep as Mignapour had demanded but, when it came to the Prince's nightcap, the jealous Englishman also dropped a little of the drug in the royal posset. When Mignapour was asleep, he took his clothes and his necklace and tip-toed out to enjoy the rendezvous which the Prince had made with Irma in the rose garden. When the love-making was done, he quietly returned the clothes and the now black necklace and awaited the morning.

The furious Mignapour leaps upon the traitorous Englishman and the noise brings the whole court running (Finale: 'D'Où Vient un Pareil Tapage'), with an imperious Bengaline at their head. She is delighted to find that Mignapour has been discovered and imparts the news that she wishes to marry him. Since Irma is apparently set on the Englishman who has compromised her, his way is clear, but the young Prince hesitates. Bengaline, seeking to warm him, makes her revelation: it was she who met him that night in the rose garden, not Irma! Mignapour is delighted. He wrings from her an oath that she will wed the man with whom she dallied in the famous rose garden and, when she has fulsomely agreed, he happily hands her over to Crackson as he takes back his kingdom and claims Irma as his bride.

This piece is played in either three or four acts, the three-act version being constructed by joining the second and the short third act in one.

LES CLOCHES DE CORNEVILLE

(The Bells of Corneville)

an opéra-comique in three acts by Clairville and Charles Gabet. Music by Robert Planquette. Produced at the Théâtre des Folies-Dramatiques, Paris, 19 April 1877 with Marie Gélabert (Germaine), Juliette Girard (Serpolette), Milher (Gaspard), Ernest Vois (Marquis) and Simon-Max (Grenicheux) and revived there 1885 and 1889. Produced at the Théâtre de la Gaîté 15 September 1892 with Mlle Gélabert, Rose Delaunay, Paulin Ménier, Morlet and Paul Fugère and revived there 1894, 1896 with Mariette Sully, Jeanne Aubecque, Lucien Noël, Landrin and Emile Soums, 1 October 1897 with Mlle Cocyte, 1900, 1901, 1903 with Juliette Simon-Girard, Dutilloy and Soums, and 21 January 1907 with Blanche Delimoges, Anna Tariol-Baugé, Noël, Bourgeois and Soums. Played at the Théâtre de la Porte Saint-Martin 1908 with Mme Simon-Girard, at the Théâtre Apollo 1912 with Marcelle Devries, Alice Favier, Victor Du Pont and Georges Foix, at the Gaîté June 1913 with Marise Fairy, Angèle Gril, Dolne, Cadio and Chambon, at the Gaîté-Lyrique 1914 with Mlle Gril, 1915, 1921 with Jane Montange, Jenny Syril, Félix Oudart, Jean Hirigary and André Gilly, 1922 with Marthe Ferrare, Mlle Syril, Henri Jullien, Léon Ponzio and Georges Foix, 1953 with Josette Delly, Andrée Grandjean, Rellys, Michel Dens and Jacques de Marsan, and 10 February 1958 with Denise Menez, Mlle Grandjean, Ded Rysel, Dens and Bernard Alvi. Produced at the Théâtre Mogador 15 March 1940 with Suzanne Baugé, Myriam Lecomte, André Baugé, Henri Varna and René Lenoty. Produced at the Théâtre de la Porte Saint-Martin 1968.

Produced at the Folly Theatre, London, 28 February 1878 with Violet Cameron, Kate Munroe, John Howson, Shiel Barry and Loredan and played at the Globe Theatre from 31 August 1878 with Cora Stuart, Emma Chambers, Fred Mervin, Barry and W H Woodfield. Revived there 15 May 1880 with Misses Cameron and Chambers, Frederic Darrell, Barry and Loredan and played subsequently at the Olympic Theatre. Played at Her Majesty's Theatre 11 November 1886 with Mlle de l'Oncle, Juliette Girard, Belliard, Favart and Simon-Max. Produced at the Opera Comique 17 February 1890 with Marion Erle, Helen Capet and Shiel Barry. Played at the Prince Edward Theatre 16 March 1931 with Huntley Wright and Marjorie Gordon.

Produced at the Fifth Avenue Theatre, New York, in an English version as *The Chimes of Normandy* 22 October 1877 with Zelda Seguin, Emilie Melville, Charles Morton, William Castle and C H Turner. Played at the Park Theatre 13 May 1878 with Marie Aimée, and subsequently at Booth's Theatre 3 June 1878; at the St James's Theatre 11 November 1878 with Laura Joyce, Catherine Lewis, Henry Peakes, Eugene Clarke and Charles F Lange; at Booth's Theatre 24 November 1879 with Paola Marié, at the Fifth Avenue Theatre 24 January 1881, at the Standard Theatre 4 October 1881 with Paola Marié and Mlle Merle, and in various repertory companies. Produced at Erlanger's Theatre 2 November 1931.

Produced at the Friedrich-Wilhemstädtisches Theater, Berlin, in a version by Ernst Dohm 27 March 1878.

Produced at the Theater an der Wien, Vienna, 29 September 1878.

CHARACTERS

Gaspard, *an old miser*
Germaine, *his niece*

356

Serpolette, *a foundling*
Henri, Marquis de Corneville
Jean Grenicheux, *a fisher lad*
The Bailie of Corneville
The Clerk of the Court
Jeanne, Manette, Gertrude, Suzanne, Catherine, Marguerite, Cachalot,
Grippardin, Fouinard, etc.

ACT 1

In the latter days of the reign of Louis XIV of France, the village of Corneville, Normandy, had lived for more than twenty years without its resident
aristocrat and overlord. Due to some unfortunate political manoeuverings
over a kind of Norman independence movement, the old Marquis of Corneville had departed from the village with his infant grandson and, ever since,
the great château de Corneville has towered emptily over the day-to-day life
of the local people.

The lands and rights of the family have continued to be administered by
the Marquis's miserly steward, Gaspard, but an attempt to have the château
opened by the former Bailie of the area was aborted by the superstitious
people of the village. They know that the château is haunted and there is a
legend which says that it must remain so until the day when the master of
Corneville returns. The bells of the town will announce his arrival, he will
reopen the château, and everyone will live happily ever after.

In the meanwhile, life and the more stable traditions of the village continue. One of those traditions is the twice-yearly hiring fair, where domestic
servants gather to be taken on on six-monthly contracts by new masters and,
when the curtain rises, it is the morning of such a day. The road to the centre
of Corneville is busy with servants heading for the fair ('C'Est le Marché de
Corneville'). The girls are chattering mostly about affairs of the heart, and
particularly about the way that Gaspard's pert foundling servant girl,
Serpolette, is being two-timed by her accepted beau, the lazy fisherman,
Jean Grenicheux.

This pretty fellow has transferred his affections—or, at least, his efforts—
to Germaine, Gaspard's niece, who has recently come to live with her uncle.
To everyone's surprise, Gaspard, almost a legend in the countryside for his
meanness, has been lavishing his money on this girl and he has succeeded in
getting her affianced to the new Bailie of the town. Grenicheux, however, is
still trying to win the pretty heiress, and she, indeed, announces herself as
devoted to him since the day when he saved her from drowning after a fall
from the nearby cliffs.

Serpolette interrupts the girls' rumour-mongering and scores a few hits
against their own love lives in the Chanson des 'On Dit', but she admits
sourly that the coming of Germaine certainly seems to have distracted
Grenicheux from his attentions to her. He may think Germaine has pros-

357

pects, but what of her, Serpolette? Since no-one knows who her family was, what is to say that she isn't a princess ('Dans Ma Mysterieuse Histoire')? Anyhow, Germaine is to marry the antique Bailie, what a joke!

Unfortunately, Serpolette's final words are overheard by Gaspard and the Bailie. The steward chases his servant away furiously, while the Bailie admits to himself that he has made rather a fool of himself over the lovely Germaine. He has been egged on by Gaspard who needs to ensure his good graces to allow him to continue to run the marquisal estates without interference and, undoubtedly, to his own profit. The Bailie has it in mind, like his predecessor, to put in motion the necessary legalities to have the château opened and duly disposed of, but he is still wary of its reputation as a haunted place.

Grenicheux takes the stage, carolling a song to the sea ('Va Petit Mousse'), and encounters Germaine. He makes one more play for her love and she responds with the duteous affection due to a man who saved her life ('Même Sans Consulter Mon Coeur') but their scene is interrupted by a stranger. The newcomer is a curiosity. He is dressed in odd clothes and it appears that he has come from another world. He has sailed his ship to the coast of Normandy all the millions of miles from America.

He shows a certain curiosity about Corneville and particularly about the château, but he doesn't seem to be very impressed by its reputation, even when Germaine and the town girls relate to him the legend ('La Chanson des Cloches'). He is altogether more impressed by Germaine. When the stranger is left alone, we discover that he is Henri, Marquis de Corneville, the little grandson with whom the old Marquis fled two decades earlier. He has led a picaresque sea-faring life in his exile ('J'Ai Fait Trois Fois le Tour du Monde'), but now he has returned to claim his own.

In the meanwhile, the town has other affairs to mind. Gaspard (with the aid of a tip-off from Serpolette) has discovered Grenicheux making advances to Germaine, and he is furious. Such behaviour only three days before the girl is to be wed ('C'Est Affreux')! The Bailie orders Grenicheux to be thrown in jail, but the boy knocks the official's wig flying and runs away. Escape, however, is only relative and he doesn't know too well what to do next ('Je Ne Sais Comment Faire'). There is only one way out that he can think of. If he can get himself 'bought' at the hiring fair, he will be safe from prosecution for the six months of his indenture.

Grenicheux is in luck. The Bailie, who should be presiding over the fair, is nowhere to be seen. It is rumoured he has gone off somewhere frighteningly legal. In his place, his clerk has taken over the organisation and, as the servants arrive in the traditional procession (Marche Villageoise/'Vous Qui Voulez des Servantes'), Grenicheux slips himself amongst the coachmen's list. The hiring begins, and Henri selects both Serpolette and Grenicheux (Finale: 'Jeune Fille, Dis-Moi Ton Nom') before Gaspard puffs ragingly into the arena: Germaine, whom he had locked in her room has run off. Now Henri hires a third servant—and it is the disguised Germaine. Though Gaspard may rage and roar there is nothing he can do: for the next six months his niece is bound to serve the handsome stranger.

ACT 2

Henri and his crew have crossed the moat to the château and entered the domain by a secret subterranean passage ('À la Lueur des Flambeaux'), bringing with them Germaine, Serpolette, Grenicheux and the Bailie whom they met en route, fleeing in embarrassment from his treatment at the hands of Grenicheux ('J'Avais Perdu la Tête et Ma Perruque'). The two servants and the Bailie are in real fear of the 'haunted' place ('Fermons les Yeux!'/ 'Pristi, Sapristi! Montons-Nous la Tête'), but Henri leads his men and the trembling but courageous Germaine ('Ne Parlez Pas de Mon Courage') to explore the rooms of his old home.

Before the Bailie, Henri unveils his identity. He had hoped, by approaching the château by the secret way, to have surprised the bandits or smugglers who he suspects to be using the empty building as a hideout, but there is nobody here. Just the suits of armour of his ancestors ('Sous les Armures à Leur Taille'/'C'Est la Salle de mes Ancêtres'). When he unlocks another door, however, he finds signs that someone has been there, including a sheet, and a wallet containing some documents. The sheet explains the ghostly apparitions, and the documents prove that the proscribed Count de Lucenay confided his infant daughter to the care of his friend Gaspard before fleeing the country. The child, whom he was to pretend to have found, would become the vicomtesse and the heir to his fortune. All eyes are on Serpolette. A vicomtesse! Yes, the papers are dated the very day that she was brought home by the old man ('Vicomtesse et Marquise').

While Serpolette searches about the room for further proofs of her exalted rank, Henri hears from Germaine the tale of how Grenicheux saved her from drowning. Leaning over the cliff one day to look at a passing ship, she tumbled down, and would have drowned had she not been rescued. Now, in gratitude she has promised (in the Norman way) to marry him. The Norman way? That means 'sort of yes and sort of no' (Chanson des 'Oui et Non'). Henri can only approve the sentiment, for the truth is that it was he, sailing by in that ship, who dived in to rescue the hapless girl and left her senseless in the arms of the nearby fisherman. Germaine is very pretty and Henri could very easily fall in love. But, to business. While they have been exploring, a boat has been seen crossing the moat—someone is coming. Who can it be? Henri nominates Grenicheux to stay in the room to spy on the intruder and, to the mock plaudits of the crew ('Gloire aux Valeureux'), the cowardly fisherman is locked inside one of the suits of armour whilst the rest of the team disappear.

When the mysterious visitor approaches, it is, of course, Gaspard. He dons the white sheet, and pushes the suit of armour (with Grenicheux in it) up and down in front of the lighted windows. Why does he go to such trouble to stage this charade? Because he has made the empty castle his entrepôt. Here he stores up the money made from the Corneville estates, and here he comes nightly to gaze at the amassed wealth—his amassed wealth, for he does not believe that the heirs to Corneville will ever return ('C'Est Là Qu'Est la Richesse'/'Là-Dedans, Que de Beaux Habits').

But tonight, as Gaspard runs his fingers through his gold under the astonished gaze of the trapped Grenicheux, his doom is nigh. Suddenly the bells of Corneville begin to chime and from the armoury come forth a whole chorus of ghostly creatures ('Oui, C'Est l'Enfer') as the suit of armour-cum-Grenicheux begins to move. The miser collapses in terror as the bells thunder out, crazily believing that he hears the bells ringing for the wedding of Germaine and the Bailie.

ACT 3

Gaspard has not recovered from his dreadful fright, and he wanders around the village, out of his wits (Chanson des Gueux). Serpolette has been up to Paris to be formally recognised by the courts as the legitimate heir to the Count de Lucenay; the title and all his fortune, stacked away in the château by Gaspard, are hers. She returns to Corneville in state ('Oui, C'Est Moi, C'Est Serpolette'), dragging the humbled Grenicheux—demoted from lover to factotum—in her train. But there is still one puzzling fact: the page in the parish register which would have shed indubitable light on her position is missing. it has been torn out. This doesn't bother Mme la Vicomtesse, who is still the same saucy Serpolette and, Paris gowns or none, will kick up her heels in a good old Normandy song-and-dance (Chanson du Cidre), just as she did when she was nothing but a servant girl.

Henri has now established himself in the château of his ancestors and he offers the townsfolk a guided tour of the establishment. Grenicheux is not so keen to revisit the scene of his discomfiture and he prefers to stay outside. Henri catches him alone and challenges him to relate the tale of his heroic saving of Germaine. The boy is full of corroborative detail ('Je Regardais En l'Air') until he recognises in Henri the ship's captain who thrust the girl into his arms. He humbly confesses his lies, and is overheard by Germaine. She has no longer any obligation to marry the fisherman, since it is to Henri that she owes her gratitude and her life, but, alas, how can she, the niece of the faithless Gaspard, wed the man he wronged ('Une Servante, Que M'Importe').

But further revelations are at hand. The crazy miser, in his ramblings, is bringing forth secrets long hidden. It was he who tore the missing page from the parish register, the page proving that Germaine is the daughter of the Count de Lucenay. The old Bailie had kept the register close, knowing that the facts were therein and that, if Gaspard brought up the girl in ignorance of her inheritance, he could, with that evidence, force the miser to share with him the Count's fortune. But Gaspard was too sharp for him. He made off with the all-important page. And here it is!

Hands reach out from all sides to grab the paper but, suddenly, the madman is mad no longer. He is nothing but an old, broken and sorry man. After ten years of faithful stewardship, storing up the profits of his good management of his master's estates against the day of his return, he had begun to imagine that he laboured for his own account. Then he had begun his wicked attempts to defraud, then bitter avarice had taken hold of his heart. Begging for pardon before the wronged Marquis and the even more wronged vicomtesse Germaine, he hears the bells of the legend ring out once more, as Henri and Germaine plight their troth and Serpolette, reduced once more to village maiden status, roundly refuses the renewed attentions of Grenicheux (Finale/Air des Cloches).

L'ÉTOILE

(The Star)

an opéra-bouffe in three acts by Eugène Leterrier and Albert Vanloo. Music by Emmanuel Chabrier. Produced at the Théâtre des Bouffes-Parisiens, Paris, 28 November 1877 with Paola Marié (Lazuli), Daubray (Ouf), Berthe Stuart (Laoula) Scipion (Siroco) and Alfred Jolly (Hérisson de Porc-Épic). Produced at the Théâtre de l'Exposition 15 June 1925 with Jean Aubert, Henry Fabert, Mme de Kerland and Paul Lefebvre. Produced at the Théâtre National de l'Opéra-Comique 10 April 1941 with Fanély Revoil, René Hérent, Lilli Grandval, André Balbon and Alban Derroja, and revived there 10 December 1946 with Mlle Révoil, Paul Payen, Nadine Renaux, Marie Franzini and Derroja; and 1 October 1984 with Colette Alliot-Lugaz and Michel Sénéchal.

Produced at the Broadway Theatre, New York, in a version by J Cheever Goodwin with additional music by Woolson Morse as *The Merry Monarch* 18 August 1890 with Marie Jansen, Francis Wilson (King Anso IV), Laura Moore (Lilita), Charles Plunkett (Siroco) and Gilbert Clayton (Hertison), and revived there 5 October 1891.

A version played at the Savoy Theatre, London, in 1899 as *The Lucky Star* was based on Leterrier and Vanloo's libretto but had virtually an entire new score by Ivan Caryll.

Produced at the Friedrich-Wilhelmstädtisches Theater, Berlin, as *Sein Stern* 4 October 1878. Produced at the Komische Oper as *Lazuli* 4 February 1909 with Mary Hagen, Kreuder, Frln Bachrich, Mantler and Zador (Wupp de Dudeldu).

CHARACTERS

Ouf I, *King of the thirty-six realms*
Siroco, *his astrologer*
Prince Hérisson de Porc-Épic, *an ambassador from the court of Mataquin*
Aloès, *his wife*
Tapioca, *his personal secretary*
Princess Laoula *of Mataquin*
Lazuli
Chief of Police
Oasis, Youka, Asphodèle, Zinnia, Koukouli, Adza, *royal maids of honour*

ACT 1

In the impeccably happy royal capital of the thirty-six realms there is an unaccustomed *frisson* of fear going through the populace ('Méfions-Nous'). It is a fear which is well justified, for the great King Ouf is out and about, disguised as an ordinary person. This would not normally frighten his people, but everybody knows that the day of Saint-Ouf is nigh and that is frightening indeed. The day of Saint-Ouf is the King's birthday and he has the habit of celebrating his birthday by providing a glorious entertainment for his devoted subjects: fireworks, sack-races with rabbits for prizes, and all the other things which go to make a happy nation.

One year, however, as a novelty, the King staged a little execution as part of the festivities. It went down wonderfully and, each year since, he has made it his policy to include such an execution as part of his birthday party. This year he has a problem: in all his thirty-six kingdoms he hasn't been able to find a victim. It is a well-known fact and, in consequence, when a stranger comes up to them in the street and asks what they think of the government, the people of Ouf's kingdoms are very careful to come up with a strong 'Long live King Ouf'.

Apart from being nice to his people, King Ouf has another major preoccupation: he likes to know what is going to happen in advance and, to this end, he has an expensive royal astrologer called Siroco installed in a royal observatory. In order that Siroco should take the greatest care over the royal life and fortune, Ouf has included a specification in his will that fifteen minutes after the death of the King, Siroco shall be executed. The astrologer's life is completely ruled by this consideration and his efforts to keep his royal master in perfect health and safety are, as a result, pathologically intense.

King Ouf is thirty-nine years old, and since the constitution declares that he must provide an heir to the thirty-six realms before his fortieth birthday, he has decided on an alliance with the neighbouring Princess Laoula of Mataquin. The details have been arranged with the King of Mataquin and the innocent Princess set on the road to Ouf's capital under the guardianship of the ambassador Hérisson de Porc-Épic, his wife Aloès, and his private secretary, Tapioca, who spends more time being private with the wife than with the husband. Hérisson is a diplomat and, thus, has a mania for secrets and deceptions. He has not informed Laoula that she is to be wed and, to provide diplomatic confusion, he has insisted that she travel as his wife ('Nous Voyageons Incognito') and that they all pretend to be travelling salesmen ('Aussitôt Que l'Aurore').

On the road, they pass a handsome young pedlar called Lazuli ('Je Suis Lazuli'). The Princess is much struck with the lad and goes so far as to lift a corner of her veil to exchange glances with him, and this results in a bad bout of mutual love-at-first-sight. Lazuli follows the party as far as the town gates, but he loses them in the crowd and he is sitting despondently about when Siroco chances by and, never at a loss when an opportunity to make a franc or two outside his royal duties presents itself, he offers Lazuli an astrological reading. The lovelorn lad pays out his last coin in the hope that the stars have reserved a pretty fate for him ('Ô Petite Étoile') and replaces the dinner the coin might have bought with a litte snooze.

Hérisson and Tapioca leave their ladies for a while to go off to court and present themselves to the King but, no sooner have they gone, than Aloès leads the Princess out for an adventure. The adventure soon presents himself in the form of young Lazuli, fast asleep on the ground, and the two ladies find fabulous fun in tickling him with little bits of straw ('Il Faut le Chatouiller'/'Mon Dieu! Mais, au Fait, J'Y Pense'). When Lazuli wakes up and grabs them, they pretend to be shopgirls and the lad quickly enquires of Laoula her name and her married status, only to have his hopes dashed when Hérisson returns and drags the princess away, referring to her with diplomatic obscurity as his wife.

The disconsolate lad has little time to be polite to a stranger who comes along and asks him what he things of the government. He not only dismisses the government off-handedly but punches the importunate stranger on the nose. King Ouf has found his victim and he calls loudly for his guards to arrest the young man ('Jeune Homme! Tu Viens de Gifler le Roi'). A chair of tortures is brought ('Ce Fauteuil, Qui N'A l'Air de Rien') and Lazuli is about to be given the works when Siroco rushes in all of a pother. He has read Lazuli's fortune in the stars and—oh horror!—it appears that the boy's lifeline is inseparably linked with that of the King. One day after the death of Lazuli the King himself will also die and, of course, given the testamentary details, fifteen minutes later Siroco will follow. The King hastily orders the torturers to cease their activities, cancels the birthday execution, and calls a palanquin to take Lazuli in splendour to his palace.

ACT 2
At the palace ('Ah le Charmant Garçon'), Lazuli is showered with every luxury he could desire (Brindisi: 'Vrai Dieu! C'Est un Rêve Enchanteur') and fussed over desperately by the King and the astrologer who lock him up for his and their safety. They quickly revise their course of action when they find the young man attempting to dive to freedom from a second-floor window, but they are further alarmed when Lazuli confesses that he is in love with a married woman and means to fight her husband for her ('Quand On Aime, Est-Il Utile').

When Hérisson comes to court to present his credentials, Lazuli is all for challenging him to a duel then and there, and the King is forced to take it upon himself to fence with the amazed ambassador to find out whether the boy can safely be allowed to challenge him. When the ambassador lays the King low, it is clear that there is desperate danger in a challenge, and the King proposes instead to win Lazuli the woman he seeks by having Hérisson killed. The trouble is that, as an ambassador, his person will be sacred so, in that case, he must not be allowed to present his credentials to the King. To that end, Ouf quickly makes himself scarce and, when Hérisson returns, he is arrested and dragged off to a dungeon, leaving Princess Laoula, who has suddenly learned of her impending marriage, fainting in the arms of Aloès and Tapioca.

Lazuli comes to the rescue and revives his lady fair in time-honoured fashion ('Quand On Veut Ranimer Sa Belle'), only to find that she is, o bliss, not a married woman at all—at least, not yet. Ouf still has the ladies' identities round the wrong way and he is convinced that it is Aloès who is his

363

intended bride. He is quite happy, therefore, to plan that Lazuli should carry off Laoula and he even provides a boat and some money for the grateful pair ('Moi Je N'Ai Pas une Âme Ingrate') who scamper happily away ('Maintenant Il Faut Partir Vite').

Hérisson escapes from his cell and soon diplomacy is thrown aside as he reveals the true identities of the two ladies. Aloès is *his* wife, and Ouf has sent his royal fiancée off with a young man. Furiously Hérisson takes action and guards are sent scampering after the young pair with orders to shoot on sight. Ouf and Siroco are frozen with fear. Not that! But before anything can be done to stop the chase, the sound of shots is heard ('Un Coup de Feu!') and soon a fainting and damp Laoula is carried in, alone, to relate the desperate tale of Lazuli's death ('Tous Deux Assis Dans le Bateau').

ACT 3
Ouf and Siroco are sitting around watching the minutes of their lives run out as the police come in with the drowned boy's hat and cloak, and the almost certitude that he is dead. Needless to say, he is not. He jumped overboard seconds before the shots peppered his boat and has been hiding in the reeds to avoid the searchers ('Enfin, Je Sens Mieux'). Ouf and Siroco, unaware of this comforting fact, have taken to turning the hands of the royal clock back periodically to encourage themselves into believing they have more time left.

The waiting is made less painful by the imbibing of a little chartreuse ('Chartreuse Verte'), but the King will not hear of letting Siroco off the hook by altering the clause in his will. Given his imminent demise, he no longer has the slightest interest in either politics or people and he doesn't care twopence for Hérisson's blustery threats of war as he will not be around when it happens. As for marrying the princess, why that's all off. Lazuli, overhearing this, is delighted and, when he comes upon his weeping princess being comforted by Aloès ('Un Amoureux, Princesse'), he happily takes her in his arms ('Lazuli, Mon Chéri') and explains his plan.

The King will no longer wed Laoula as long as he believes Lazuli dead, so Lazuli will stay dead. He will go to the city gates and, when the Princess is sent back to Mataquin, they can meet on the road and begin happily-ever-aftering. He scampers off to the rendezvous, leaving Laoula to be rejected by the King, but the plan goes slightly astray.

The combination of green chartreuse and imminent extinction have put a twinkle into Ouf's eye and he suddenly decides that a quick wedding and bedding of such a pretty princess would be no bad thing. As he chases Laoula round the room, he selflessly reminds her that she will, in any case, be free to wed her preferred swain in a few hours. She professes an aversion to supplying used material to her beloved ('Ainsi Que la Rose Nouvelle'), but such an aversion carries little weight when opposed to Article 14 of the constitution which places Ouf in the obligation of providing an heir to the throne.

The libidinous atmosphere is dissipated by the sudden arrival of the whole court. Time is up. The King is due to die in five minutes. Everybody waits as

Siroco tries just once more to get the fatal will revoked but, when the hour strikes, nothing happens. The King attacks Siroco as a charlatan and swears that he shall be executed in any case, but then the Chief of Police arrives bringing Lazuli, who has been arrested at the city gates. All is well and Ouf, now decidedly alive again, commands that his royal wedding go ahead immediately.

But Lazuli declares that if Laoula cannot be his he will kill himself, and the King, who really doesn't have the heart to go through all that again, decides that it is better to surrender the girl than his life. Lazuli and Laoula can be wed and Ouf will name Lazuli as his constitutional heir, happy in the foreknowledge that the boy is destined to predecease him by twenty-four hours.

LE PETIT DUC

(The Little Duke)

an opéra-comique in three acts by Henri Meilhac and Ludovic Halévy. Music by Charles Lecocq. Produced at the Théâtre de la Renaissance, Paris, 25 January 1878 with Jeanne Granier (Duc), Mily-Meyer (Duchesse), Vauthier (Montlandry), Berthelier (Frimousse) and Marie Desclauzas (Diane). Revived there 19 September 1879, March 1881, 1883 with Granier. Produced at the Théâtre de l'Eden 1888 with Granier and José Dupuis as Frimousse; at the Théâtre des Variétés 1890 with Granier and Dupuis; at the Bouffes-Parisiens 16 January 1897 with Marcelle Dartois, Vauthier and Mlle Desclauzas; at the Théâtre des Variétés 1904 with Jeanne Saulier and Edmée Favart; at the Théâtre de la Gaîté-Lyrique 4 December 1912 with Anne Dancrey and Mlle Dziri, 1915 with Gina Féraud and 1926 with Louise Dhamarys; at the Théâtre Mogador 25 March 1921 with Edmée Favart, Mlle Roncey, Tarquini d'Or and Louis Maurel; and at the Théâtre du Châtelet 1933 with Fanély Revoil, Simone Lencret, Roland Laignez and Dranem.

Produced at the Philharmonic Theatre, Islington, London, as *The Little Duke* in a version by B C Stephenson and Clement Scott 27 April 1878 with Alice May, Alice Burville, Edward Wingrove and Harry Paulton and at St James's Theatre 16 June 1878 with Miss May, Ethel Pierson, Wingrove and J D Stoyle. Played at the Gaiety Theatre 27 June 1881 with Mlles Granier and Mily-Meyer, Alexandre, Alfred Jolly and Mlle Desclauzas.

Produced at Booth's Theatre, New York, in a version by F Williams and T R Sullivan 17 March 1879 with Florence Ellis, Louise Beaudet, W H MacDonald and Edward Chapman and played there 12 April 1879 with Marie Aimée, Miss Beaudet, Duplan and Jouard. Played at the Lyceum Theatre 31 March 1879 with Alice Oates, Lulu Stevens, J G Taylor and Edward Connell. Played at the Standard Theatre 5 October 1880 with Paola Marié and Mlle Merle. Produced at the Casino Theatre in a version by H C Bunner and W J Henderson 4 August 1884 with Georgine von Januschowsky, Agnes Folsom, Hubert Wilke and J H Ryley. Played at Abbey's Theatre 6 April 1896 with Lillian Russell.

Produced at the Carltheater, Vienna, as *Der kleine Herzog* in a version by Hugo Wittmann 9 November 1878.

Produced at the Friedrich-Wilhelmstädtisches Theater, Berlin, 24 November 1878.

CHARACTERS

Duc de Parthenay
Duchesse de Parthenay
Montlandry
Frimousse
Diane de Château-Lansac, *Directrice of L'École de Demoiselles Nobles*
Roger, *a page*
Gérard, *another page*
Hélène, *demoiselle d'honneur*
Ninon, Ninette, *cantinières*
Mlle de Clermont-Tonerre, Mlle de Champlâtre Mlle de Sainte-Anénome, *pupils at the École de Demoiselles Nobles*
Navailles, Bernard, Montchevrier, Tanneville, Champvallon, Mérignac, Nancey, Julien, Gontran, Henri, Gaston, Margot, Manon, Marion, Mariette, School Mistresses, etc.

ACT 1

The Salle de l'Oeil de Boeuf at the Château de Versailles is alive with the high and mighty of the kingdom of France, gathered to do honour to the teenage Duc de Parthenay who is to be wed that day, in a marriage of politics and large fortunes, to the even younger Blanche de Cambray ('Il Est l'Heure'). The court pages take advantage of the occasion to make advances to the maids of honour ('Notre Coeur Soupire') on the grounds that they, like the little Duke, are grown up enough to experience adult emotions and urges, but neither politeness nor a cocky attack brings them any joy, and they are left to complain to the Duke's tutor, Frimousse, and his martial arts instructor, Montlandry, about the unfairness of women.

Montlandry and Frimousse have little time for each other's profession and position at court ('Le Savant Part, Tenant un Livre') and Montlandry, a cheerfully rough-edged courtier, enjoys himself making fun of the fussy and pedantic man of learning. He goes so far as to suggest that, once the Duke is wed, he will have no further need of a tutor and Frimousse will be out of a job, but the pedant's self-satisfied answers leave Montlandry wondering if something is afoot of which he is not aware.

The ceremony is over, and the young couple enter in their splendid wedding costumes, the bridegroom singing sweetly to his little wife ('Enfin Nous Voici, Ma Petite') his answer to those who say that they are too young to wed—'on a l'age de mariage quand on a l'age de l'amour' (you are old enough to be wed when you are old enough to be in love). The Duke and Duchess receive the good wishes of the court and the celebration ball begins (Gavotte) before the company disperse to the gaming tables ('Objet d'Espoir et de Crainte'), leaving the young pair alone.

It is clear that, arranged marriage or no, they are very much in love, but they are also very young and imbued with courtly formality. It will be easier

366

when they are settled together in the private suite of rooms in the palace which they have been promised. But they haven't actually seen their rooms yet and, when the little Duchess last spoke on the subject to her uncle, he just laughed.

Alas, it seems that everyone laughs at them at the moment, and will continue to do so until they can be accepted as grown-up people. Perhaps it would help if, first of all, they stopped using the polite 'vous' in addressing each other and tried the more intimate 'tu' as in 'je t'aime'. The little Duchess finds it a mite hard but, urged on by her husband in duet ('C'Est Pourtant Bien Doux'/'Je T'Aime'), she soon manages it and, by the time they have finished singing, they are in each other's arms.

They are interrupted by one of the maids of honour who has come to take the young wife before her family. The Duke impatiently waits her return ('La Petite Femme') and finally goes to look for her. He will look in vain. Now that the marriage has been made and political and financial considerations made dynastically secure, the family has decided that the couple are too young to live together as man and wife. The little Duchess has been packed off to a private boarding school for noble young ladies at Lunéville, and the Duke is to be put back into the hands of the boring Frimousse for two further years of conjugations and declensions to keep his mind off consummation. The pages watch the dejected husband returning ('Il A l'Oreille Basse') to vent his frustration on the self-satisfied Frimousse who sees himself secure in his position for two further years.

But Montlandry has pulled a fine trick on his old rival. The Duke does not have to go back to his school-desk. Frimousse is to be transferred to give a course in English literature at a ladies' establishment in Lunéville and, as a sort of consolation for his spoiled marriage, the Duke is to take up his place as a Colonel in the army—not as a regimental figurehead but as a genuine Colonel with a force of men under his command. As the finale begins, his regiment greet him in harmony ('Mon Colonel') and an idea awakens in the young man's head. He can order his regiment where he will. Very well, it is a fine night and they will set out on campaign immediately ('Sonnez le Boute-Selle').

ACT 2

At the ladies college in Lunéville there is a singing class in progress which seems to indicate that the daughters of the nobility have little aptitude for expressing the Virgilian sentiments of shepherds and shepherdesses set to music, although the school's headmistress is able to throw an infinity of yearning into her demonstration of the piece (Leçon de Chant). The girls are thrilled to find that their new schoolmate is a married woman, even if only in name, and they are even more excited when the deputy headmistress rushes in to tell her superior that the school is surrounded by an entire regiment of dragoons. The little Duke has led his men to lay siege to the school and to carry off his wife.

Montlandry is sent as intermediary to order the headmistress to give up the Duchess ('Les Voici les Parlementaires'/ Couplets de Montlandry: 'Vous Menacer? À Dieu Ne Plaise'), but Madame la Directrice, as she is fond of reminding people, is a descendant of Henri IV, and no one is going to make her give up a charge given into her keeping by the royal family. They may do their worst if they will, it is 'La Guerre'! Madame orders the new English teacher, Frimousse, to take a manly lead in the defence of the establishment and she quashes the little Duchess's complaints by locking her in the detention room.

Her attempts to keep her class in order are further disrupted when a peasant girl takes refuge in the classroom with a tale to tell ('Mes Bell' Madame' Écoutez Ça'). She set out from home this morning with two dozen eggs and her aunt's instructions to look after them and her virtue on the way to market. Well, on her way she ran into this regiment, and in the end she decided to sacrifice her eggs and save her virtue. There is a big, handsome officer with two dozen eggs all over his face and she is here in one piece. She isn't much use as a spy, however, for to all the headmistress's inquiries as to the number and position of the enemy, she can only gasp 'Ooh, they are handsome' ('Ils Ont C'Qui Nom'nt des Sabretaches'), until the rest of the school and even Madame herself have more than their curiosity aroused.

As soon as the girls and their mistresses have run off to peer at the officers, the peasant girl reveals 'herself' to be the little Duke. He makes contact with his imprisoned wife but he is interrupted by Frimousse. It is Frimousse who has the keys to the detention room and, by an adept bit of flirting ('C'Est un Idylle'), the Duke manages to get them from him and release the Duchess. They are discovered in their flight by the headmistress, but saved when Montlandry follows up his threat and invades the school (Finale: 'À Sac, À Sac').

The triumphant reunion has to be postponed, however, for a despatch has arrived ordering the Parthenay regiment urgently to battle. The Duchess must wait a little longer at Lunéville while the Duke leads his men into a very different kind of fight ('Hélas! Elle A Raison, Ma Chère'). Frimousse is dragged from his hiding place in the basement and unwillingly sent off with the soldiers, as the girls and their teachers chorus to the men to go to death or glory ('Revenez Vainqueurs')

ACT 3

In camp, a relaxed atmosphere reigns ('Tambour et Trompette') and Montlandry entertains the soldiers and their camp followers with a jolly tale (Chanson du Petit Bossu) until the news comes that the battle scheduled for the morrow has somehow been started a day early by the other side. Things look black for the unprepared French ('Ah, Mon Dieu, Que Deviendrez-Nous?'), but the last minute arrival of the little Duke and his men saves the day ('Victoire! Victoire!'/ 'La Guerre C'Est Donc Ça?'). Even Frimousse has accidentally captured a whole enemy section by himself as a result of losing control of his horse at a crucial moment. But the lackadaisical behaviour of the French army has almost caused a disaster and, as a result, the little Duke gives the order that in future all women shall be forbidden the camp. Now it is his elders who will have 'Pas de Femmes'.

Late that night the Duke has a visitor in his tent. The little Duchess has escaped the vigilance of Madame la Directrice and has come to join her husband under the spartan conditions of the battlefield. These are quickly forgotten in their euphoria ('Ah, Qu'On Est Bien'), but the young couple are discovered when a late night call to arms rouses the camp.

Montlandry accuses the Duke of disobeying his own orders and commands that he render up his sword. Sadly, the little Duke does so ('Le Plus Bel Officier du Monde'), but his is a short sorrow. His reward for being instrumental in bringing the war to a triumphal end is quick to follow. The little Duke and the little Duchess will, together, bear the news of victory to the King at Versailles, where married life can begin in earnest for 'le plus bel officier du monde' (the smartest soldier in the world) and his little wife.

MADAME FAVART

an opéra-comique in three acts by Henri Chivot and Alfred Duru. Music by Jacques Offenbach. Produced at the Théâtre des Folies-Dramatiques, Paris, 28 December 1878 with Juliette Simon-Girard (Madame Favart), Lepers (Charles), Simon-Max (Hector), Luco (Cotignac), Maugé (Pontsablé) and Marie Gélabert (Suzanne). Produced at the Théâtre des Bouffes-Parisiens 4 March 1884 with Mme Grizier-Montbazon and Piccaluga; at the Théâtre des Menus-Plaisirs 1888 with Anna Judic; at the Théâtre Apollo 18 October 1911 with Angèle Gril, André Allard, Georges Foix, Paul Ardot and Marcelle Devriès and again 25 December 1913 with Brigitte Régent.

Produced at the Strand Theatre, London, in a version by H B Farnie 12 April 1879 with Florence St John, Claude Marius, Walter Fisher, Henry Ashley and Violet Cameron. Produced at the Avenue Theatre 11 March 1882 with Miss St John, Marius, Henry Bracy, Fred Leslie and Mathilde Wadman, and revived there 18 April 1887 with Miss St John, Charles H Kenney, Joseph Tapley, Arthur Roberts, Henry Ashley and Clara Graham. Produced at the Criterion Theatre 9 November 1893 with Miss St John.

Produced at Park Theatre, New York, 12 May 1879 with Marie Aimée, Juteau, Duplan, Mezières and Mlle Raphaël. Played at the Fifth Avenue Theatre 15 March 1880 with Paola Marié. Produced at the Thalia Theater 11 January 1881 in German with Marie Geistinger, Adolfi, Schnelle, Lube and Frln Raberg. Produced at the Fifth Avenue Theatre 19 September 1881 with Catherine Lewis, Fred Leslie, J C Armand, John Howson and Marie Jansen. Played at Abbey's Theatre 28 November 1881 with Paola Marié, Nigri, Tauffenberger, Poyard, Mezières and Mlle Grégoire. Played at the Fifth Avenue Theatre January 1882.

Produced at the Theater an der Wien, Vienna, in a version by Julius Hopp 7 February 1879 with Marie Geistinger.

Produced at Leipzig 1 June 1879 and at the Friedrich-Wilhelmstädtisches Theater, Berlin, 15 August 1879. Played at the Lessing Theater in a version by Siegfried Anheisser 25 July 1932.

CHARACTERS

Charles Favart
Madame Justine Favart
Major Cotignac
Suzanne, *his daughter*
Hector de Boispréau
Marquis de Pontsablé
Biscotin, *an innkeeper*
Sergeant Larose, Jolicoeur, Sans-Quartier, Larissolle, Babet, Jeanneton, etc.

ACT 1

At a coaching inn at Arras, the day's coach has come to the end of its journey ('Enfin le Coche Est Arrivé') and the passengers are making their bruised and dusty way to their rooms to recover. Amongst the travellers is the pompous Major Cotignac who has come to the town to make an appointment with the Marquis de Pontsablé, governor of Artois, to press for his favour in appointing a relative to the post of Police Chief in Douai. He has brought with him his pretty daughter, Suzanne, and he has noticed with annoyance that the coach has been followed all the way to Arras by a young man on horseback.

The young man is Hector de Boispréau, a civic official, and he has come to Arras to chase the same post which Cotignac covets for his relative, a relative who will, as soon as he is installed at Douai, be granted the hand of the lovely Suzanne. When Hector arrives at the inn, it is soon obvious that he aspires not only to the post but also to the girl. In fact, they have been busy falling in love over a period of some months ('Un Soir Nous Nous Recontrâmes') without Cotignac having noticed. The Major is outraged and orders the presumptuous youth to forget both Douai and his daughter but he agrees that, should pigs fly and Hector be appointed Police Chief, then the hand of Suzanne may be his. Having won this concession it only rests with Hector to find some way to win the appointment.

When the salon is clear of guests, the innkeeper Biscotin is at leisure to give air to a less comfortable visitor: one who is shut up in the basement. This visitor is none other than the celebrated actor and playwright, Charles Favart, who is hidden in the cellar of his old friend's inn because he is on the run ('Au Diable l'Humeur Morose'). Favart has a wife, the young, beautiful and talented Justine, Madame Favart, and it has been the fate of this delightful creature to attract the attentions of the powerful Maréchal de Saxe. These attentions Madame Favart has, to date, expertly defused but the Maréchal's subsequent loss of self-esteem has provoked a mighty vengeance and he has used his powers to have the young actress shut up in a convent and her husband criminally pursued for debt. Alerted in time, Favart escaped from Paris and he is waiting covertly in Arras until his wife can join him in flight. Since he is a well-known actor, the basement seems to be for the meanwhile the safest place.

370

The guests are getting ready for dinner when a pretty young street singer comes by to ply her trade ('Je Suis la Petite Vielleuse'). It is Madame Favart who has tricked her way past the nuns ('Prenant Mon Air le Plus Bénin') and has come in search of her husband. To her amazement, she meets instead an old childhood friend in Hector de Boispréau, and the two are able to share their problems until the time comes when it is safe to open the basement trapdoor and allow Favart and his wife to meet.

Their reunion is cut short when a troop of soldiers arrives at the inn (Choeur des Soldats: 'À l'Auberge de Biscotin') with orders to search the building. Madame Favart, taking on herself the role of Toinon, a new servant, entertains the soldiers with a saucy song ('Ma Mère aux Vignes M'Envoyit') and lots of wine, and sends them to start their search in the attics where she is sure they will fall bibulously asleep on the straw.

There are still many problems to be surmounted. Without papers and without money, the Favarts cannot get far. There would still have been hope for them had Hector succeeded in winning his post—it would have been easy to have escaped the vigilance of the law safely inside the carriage of the Police Chief of Douai—but alas! the Marquis de Pontsablé would not even see him when he called to press his claims. Apparently the only way to win advancement from the old satyr is to have your wife go to see him. Hector has no wife and, now, he may never have one. Sadly he sets to writing his farewell regrets to Suzanne (Trio: 'Adieu, Suzanne, Je Vous Rends') but Favart, returning disguised as a valet, ready to take flight with his wife, ridicules Hector's suicidal intentions and urges him simply to elope with his Suzanne.

Cotignac returns to the inn in a furious temper ('J'Enrage, Je Suis En Fureur'). Pontsablé has refused him an interview and he has sat for an hour, waiting, whilst the Governor chatted to some woman. It turns out that the woman was none other than Madame Favart. Pretending to be Hector's wife, she has winsomely won round the Governor who has agreed to grant the young man the post of Police Chief and now, disguised again as the maid, Toinon, she brings a letter to confirm his appointment. Hector is able to claim Suzanne as his wife from an apoplectic Cotignac ('Oh, Mon Papa, Je T'En Supplie') and then, when the soldiers blearily descend to continue their search, to march loftily out taking his 'servants' with him ('Allons Soudain'). As Toinon and Benoît the Favarts can be led to safety.

ACT 2

Hector has been wed to his Suzanne ('Suzanne Est Aujourd'hui Ma Femme') and has taken up his position in Douai with Toinon and Benoît as part of his household. Favart is almost enjoying his role as it brings back memories of his father's days as a pastrycook ('Quand du Four On le Retire'), but the two fugitives run the daily risk of discovery, for Madame Favart has deep suspicions that the elderly and malicious Comtesse de Montgriffon may have recognised her.

A greater danger is sprung, without warning, when the Marquis de Pontsablé arrives unexpectedly ('Honneur à Monseigneur le Gouverneur') in all his state ('Mes Aïeux, Hommes de Guerre') and announces his intentions of staying with the new appointee...and his wife. Madame Favart is obliged to pretend to be Madame de Boispréau and, whilst the household is set off into a whirl of worries and jealousies (Quartet: 'Ah! C'Est Affreux'), to fend off the heated advances of the old Marquis while her real husband, as the servant Benoît, stands guard at the door, letting interruptions occur at the most tactically necessary moments ('Marquis, Grâce à Votre Richesse').

Pontsablé is frustrated amorously, but he is aware that the lady has purposely manoeuvred him out of a liaison and so he prepares to take his revenge. She need not be so fine; her husband already has a mistress! The celebrated actress Madame Favart is hidden in this household. The wretched, meddling Comtesse de Montgriffon has done her work, and Pontsablé has come to take the actress prisoner and deliver her up to his great superior, the Maréchal de Saxe.

Pretending to faint, to allow herself the opportunity to escape, Madame Favart finds herself attended to by Suzanne. Since Madame Favart is to be Madame de Boispréau, Madame de Boispréau has decided to take up the now unused identity of Toinon so that she may stay in her own home with her own husband.

When the evening's reception begins, Pontsablé eagerly awaits the coming of the Comtesse de Montgriffon. Soon she is announced and Hector feels despairingly that their whole masquerade is about to be blown wide open, but the elderly lady who sweeps in is not his aunt—it is Madame Favart in yet another character ('Je Passe Sur Mon Enfance'). She succeeds in convincing Pontsablé that his quarry has flown. Madame Favart ran away at the news of her discovery and is now on the way to Saint-Omer. Pontsablé departs in pursuit but, as the conspirators start to rejoice, he returns. He has met the real Comtesse de Montgriffon on the way and has discovered the truth. Now he has his prey in his clutches and he will deliver her up to the Maréchal as he promised.

Favart will not stand by and see his wife taken from him so, throwing aside his disguise, he declares that where she goes so shall he ('Tous Deux Il les Attrape'), but he has revealed himself too soon, for Pontsablé is still on the wrong track. The Comtesse has told him that he will find Madame Favart disguised as a servant girl called Toinon and so it is on Suzanne that he pounces. To save Hector and Madame Favart, Suzanne pretends that he is right and, as the act ends, the smug Pontsablé prepares to lead Suzanne and Favart off to Fontenoy and the camp of the Maréchal de Saxe ('Partez Pour le Camp').

ACT 3

At Fontenoy there is much military action going on (Choeur des Soldats: 'Par une Brillante Victoire') and Major Cotignac announces to the men that, as part of the celebrations of their latest victory, there is to be a performance given in the camp theatre of the Parisian hit *La Chercheuse d'Esprit* with its metropolitan star, the famous Madame Favart, who will also sing some specially written lines in honour of the Maréchal de Saxe. These specially written lines are to be the work of Charles Favart and, at the moment, he is unhappily pacing his tent trying to produce something suitable ('Quand Je Cherche Dans Ma Cervelle').

Suzanne is even more unhappy. If she has to go on stage it will become very evident that she is not Madame Favart. The two decide that they must tell Pontsablé the truth before things get any worse but, to their horror, when they do so he laughs at them and refuses to believe in any more changes of identity. So Suzanne is Madame de Boispréau now, is she? He cannot be caught like that. He knows Madame de Boispréau!

Hector and Madame Favart have not been idle since the carrying-off of their respective spouses. They turn up at Fontenoy disguised as a couple of Tyrolean laddies with back-packs of goods for sale to the soldiers ('Mon Grand Frèr' Vend des Mouchoirs') and win entry to the camp. Once inside, Madame Favart is amazed to find herself billed to appear at the theatre and not just before the soldiers but before his Royal Majesty, the King of France. Hector is more worried at finding his Suzanne alone amongst sixty thousand men, but he takes consolation from the fact that her virtue is probably safer amongst many than with one ('Le Péril Qui Court Ma Vertu').

Madame Favart decides on a forthright course of action. Going straight to the King's tent she forces her way before her monarch and pours out the whole story of her escapade (J'Entrai Sous la Royale Tente'). Alas! the King treats her story only as an example of her acting skill and her cause is in no way helped. There is only one thing to do: she will appear on the stage, play her role as she has never played it before, and trust that she may win sufficient royal approval to put herself and her husband out of the reach of their enemies.

As for Suzanne and Hector, they must flee the vengeance of Pontsablé before it is too late. Madame Favart attempts to distract the Governor from their flight with some heavy flirting, but the complicated series of deceptions begins to come undone when the surprised Cotignac informs the Marquis that it is not Madame Favart who is his daughter and Hector's wife, but the vanished Suzanne. This lady is their serving girl!

Madame Favart dons her costume and nervously takes to the stage to appear before the King ('Je Tremble, Je Tremble'). As cheers echo through the theatre, Pontsablé comes face to face with Hector and Suzanne who have been taken trying to leave the camp and, when Madame Favart emerges, triumphant, with a bouquet of flowers sent from the King himself she finds the Governor preparing to exact his vengeance by sending Hector to prison. But the last word is with the lady. From her bouquet she pulls a note: the King has accepted Pontsablé's resignation as Governor, he no longer has the right to give any commands and Hector and Suzanne are free to depart. Another royal missive grants the franchise of the Opéra-Comique to Favart. At the end of the day, virtue and a clever actress are triumphant ('De Favart, Cett' Femme d'Esprit').

LA FILLE DU TAMBOUR-MAJOR

(The Drum Major's Daughter)

an opéra-comique in three acts by Henri Chivot and Alfred Duru. Music by Jacques Offenbach. Produced at the Théâtre des Folies-Dramatiques, Paris, 13 December 1879 with Juliette Simon-Girard (Stella), Luco (Monthabor), Lepers (Robert), Maugé (Duc), Simon-Max (Griolet) and Caroline Girard (Duchesse). Revived there 1884. Produced at the Théâtre de la Gaîté 1889, and played there 1891, 27 March 1907 with Mlle Méaly, Bourgeois and Charles Casella and 7 January 1913 with Edmée Favart, Féraud de Saint-Pol, Marchand and André Gilly. Produced at the Théâtre du Château d'Eau 1901 with Juliette Simon-Girard, Vauthier and Colas. Produced at the Théâtre de la Gaîté-Lyrique 7 October 1920 with Jenny Syril, Lucien Fugère and Robert Burnier, and revived there 1945 with Roberte Jan, Gilbert Moryn, Georges Mazauric, Léo Bardollet, Jacques Pierre and Anna Martens.

Produced at the Alhambra Theatre, London, in a version by H B Farnie 10 April 1880 with Constance Loseby, Fred Mervin, W T Carleton, Fred Leslie, Fannie Leslie and Fanny Edwards. Produced at the Connaught Theatre January 1881 with Amy Grundy, Thomas Aynsley Cook and W H Woodfield.

Produced at the Standard Theatre, New York, 13 September 1880 with Paola Marié, Duplan, Nigri, Mezières, Tauffenberger and Mlle Delorme. Played at the 14th Street Theatre 4 October 1880 with Selina Dolaro, James A Meade, Lewis Finke, Mat Robson, Marie Williams and Alma Stanley. Produced at the Casino Theatre in a version by Max Freeman and Edgar Smith as *The Drum Major* 16 September 1889 with Pauline Hall, Edwin Stevens, John E Brand, N S Burnham, James T Powers, Eva Davenport and Marie Halton as Claudine.

Produced at the Theater an der Wien, Vienna, in a version by Julius Hopp as *Die Tochter des Tambour-Majors* 10 April 1880.

Produced at the Walhalla Theater, Berlin, 11 September 1883.

CHARACTERS

Monthabor, *a drum-major*
Lieutenant Robert
Duc della Volta
Duchesse della Volta
Stella, *their daughter*
Griolet, *a drummer*
Marquis Bambini
Claudine, *a vivandière*
Clampas, *an innkeeper*
La Prieure
Sergeant Morin
Grégorio, Comte Zerbinelli, Chevalier del Ponto, Sergeant, Francesca, Lorenza, Lucrézia, etc.

ACT 1

The story of the drum major and his daughter is set in Austrian-dominated

374

northern Italy at the turn of the eighteenth century. It begins at a convent school in the town of Biella where, in spite of the fact that their Prioress has nodded off in the Mediterranean sunshine, the young ladies in her care are singing their devotions to the statue of the madonna in the school gardens ('Reçois, Salute Madone'). One pupil, however, is missing. It is Stella, the daughter of the extremely noble Duc della Volta, who has been spending the time which should be dedicated to prayer in raiding the convent gardens for fruit and flowers to share with her friends ('Prenez les Grappes Empourprées'). When the Prioress awakens, the flowers quickly become offerings to the madonna and, when she has departed, the atmosphere of devotion becomes instead one of youthful gaiety with Stella at the helm.

Italy is in the throes of an international situation. A few years earlier, the French invaded the northern part of the country and made their way to the very gates of Milan in an attempt to 'liberate' Italy from the Austrians, and the threat of a further French attack is still present, even though the Austro-Italian army and the Alps together make a formidable barrier against the 'liberators'. There is in Italy, however, a seditious element which is anxious to exchange its Austrian rulers for French ones and, since it is naturally an illegal movement, its songs are forbidden.

To such a child as Stella, and to her friends, the French and their wicked songs hold a particular attraction. Stella has managed to get hold of a copy of the principal song of the French partisans and, with a thrill of naughtiness, she cannot wait to share it with her schoolmates ('Petit Français'). Her bravura meets with a sad end when the Prioress catches her in mid-song and, regaling the girls with ghastly stories of the French who, it appears, whip children, burn churches and do unspeakable things to nice little girls, she condemns the confident Stella to a day's punishment, locked up alone in the linen room.

The Prioress's tales are soon to be put to the test for, minutes later, the dreadful news arrives that the French have again invaded Italy and are marching at this very moment on Biella. Indeed, as the Prioress and her girls hustle out of the back gate to head for safety in a more substantial convent nearby, the French army arrives at the front gate ('Par un' Chaleur Aussi Forte'/'Nous Courons Tous Après la Gloire'). It is not a very big piece of the French army, as it happens; just the Twentieth demi-Brigade with its drum-major, the jolly Monthabor, the dashing lieutenant Robert and the bright little drummer boy, Griolet, among its ranks. They aren't particularly interested in whipping any children. They are hot and tired and devilishly hungry, not to mention thirsty.

When Claudine, the vivandière, puts it an appearance with her donkey and cart ('Ce N'Est Pas un Âne Ordinaire') she cannot help, for her food and drink supply is exhausted. There is nothing for it but to make free with the supplies of the convent. As the soldiers forage for food they come upon Stella who, shut up in detention, has been left behind in the school's flight. She is a little frightened ('De Grâce Ayez Pitié de Moi'), but the gallantry of the very personable Robert soon puts her at her ease, and she ends by volunteering to put together a meal for the men.

375

Robert's attentions to this young girl go down poorly in the eyes of Claudine, for the vivandière has an open weakness for the fine lieutenant and, in consequence, no time for little Griolet who sighs for her attentions just as she sighs for Robert's. Griolet is a tailor in civilian life and he has backed-up his loving words ('Un Tailleur Amoureux') with actions. He is making Claudine a beautiful, new vivandière's uniform which he hopes may lead her to accept his offer of marriage.

The word 'marriage' is overheard by Monthabor as he happily swaps his drum-major's stripes for a cook's apron, and he has a word or two to say on that subject or, rather, against that subject. Once upon a time, when he was a dyer in Paris, he met a pretty washerwoman, wedded and bedded her, and marched straight into hell. When they divorced a few years later, he was cured of marriage for ever, but he was also the father of a little daughter. Then came the wars and Monthabor joined up but, when he returned to Paris, his ex-wife and his daughter were gone and from that day to this he has never seen either of them again.

Tales have no place in the mouth of a hungry man. When Stella brings out a delicious meal for the soldiers ('Puisque le Couvert Est Mis'), they fall to eating with delight and, as they eat, Stella entertains them with the patriotic song which shortly before had earned her detention ('Petit Français') and, not to be outdone, Claudine and Griolet perform La Légende du Petit Troupier.

Their meal done, the men prepare to continue their march and Robert tears himself unwillingly away from the lovely Stella but, no sooner have they left the garden, than the convent receives a second volley of visitors: the Duc della Volta and the aristocratic but effete Marquis Ernesto Bambini. Bambini has a hold over the Duc—something to do with lawsuits and money—but it is a hold he is willing to relinquish in exchange for the hand of the Duc's pretty daughter and della Volta, without hesitation, has led him to the convent to collect Stella and take her back to Novara for a quick wedding.

Suddenly the garden is full of people. The Prioress and her girls have been forced back in their tracks by the proliferation of foreign soldiers on the roads and they have run into Monthabor's demi-Brigade camped on their doorstep ('Messieurs les Militaires'). The Duc is aghast when he hears that his daughter has been left alone with a detachment of French soldiers, but Stella is quick to defend them ('Pour Recevoir un Régiment') and they, in their turn, are sorry to see her taken from them. When she says her farewell with a reprise of the partisan song, the Duc hurries her angrily away.

ACT 2

At the ducal palace in Novara, the marriage of Bambini and Stella is being pushed ahead and the Duc and his wife are busy doing everything they can to keep Bambini sweet until the knot is officially tied. The Duchesse affects an aristocratic languor ('J'Ai Ma Migraine') as the pair invent a romanesque history concerning Stella's birth which, as intended, intrigues Bambini's 'special tastes'. There is a slight problem to be overcome in that Stella does not want to get married ('Ah! Vraiment, Je Déclare')—in fact, she squarely refuses—but this only excites the perverse Bambini even further.

Whilst the marriage preparations have been going on, the French army has continued a steady advance and they have arrived at Novara. As fate would have it, Robert, Monthabor and Griolet have elected billet in the della Volta palace ('C'Est un Billet de Logement'). Claudine also forces her way in past the servants ('Eh Bien! En Voilà des Manières') to claim lodgings, determined to keep an eye on Robert now that he has found his way to the place where Stella is.

While this unexpected invasion of their home is in progress, the ducal family's guests, invited to witness the signing of the marriage contract, are arriving at the palace for a celebratory ball ('Dansons et Valsons'). In the midst of the dancing, Monthabor pushes his way into the ballroom to protest at being lodged in the attic but, when he comes before the Duchesse they are both thunderstruck. She is his ex-wife and the mother of his daughter.

Rather than have her past exposed, the Duchesse orders that the Frenchmen shall be lodged in the best rooms in the house and, rather than have her plans spoiled, she categorically denies to Monthabor that Stella is his long-lost child. Stella, in the meanwhile, has encountered Robert who, in despair at the news of her imminent marriage, bursts into a profession of love ('Ange Radieux') and rushes out, but she has an altogether more satisfactory meeting with Monthabor at the end of which it is quite clear to the girl that she is not a little Italian contessa but the daughter of the French drum-major.

Griolet has finished his sewing and Claudine's costume is ready and waiting ('Il Est Là Ce Bel Uniforme'). It will have to wait, as it turns out, for, just as the betrothal of Stella and Bambini is about to take place ('Par Devant Monsieur le Notaire'), the order comes to the army to move on. Stella appears, dressed splendidly in Claudine's new vivandière uniform, and announces proudly that she is no aristocrat but Monthabor's daughter ('Oui, C'Est Mon Père') and that she intends to follow the French flag and her father ('Que M'Importe un Titre Éclatante'). She has chosen a awkward moment to declare her change of allegiance, for the Duc has not been idle. At the arrival of the French he sent word to the Austrian general, and the Austro-Italian army has descended upon Novara and the palace. Swords are drawn all round and a battle ensues as the act ends.

ACT 3
Claudine and Robert escape from the scene of the fighting and take shelter at an inn run by the vivandière's uncle Clampas in Milan ('Chut! Chut!'). Clampas is an active partisan who distributes French flags in boxes labelled as pasta and he is happy to give a more practical extension to his patriotism by hiding the French fugitives. Whilst his friends and customers dance a noisy tarantella, he listens to Robert's story of their escape ('Nous Etions à Novare') and their separation from their friends.

Robert is anxious to rejoin the regiment, but it is no simple thing to leave Milan for, under a new law, a travel document from the governor is needed.

377

Clampas decides to send the pair to one of his clients, a certain Palamos, at Rue Bonifacio 27, close by the walls of the city, from where they may perhaps effect an escape. Claudine sets off in disguise, but Robert has to hide when customers approach.

These are not just ordinary customers. They are none other than the Duc della Volta and the wretched Bambini, whose desire for Stella has reached quivering point with the revelation of her real story, and they are on the trail of Stella and of Robert whom they assume to have carried her off. Bambini is arranging for travel documents from the Governor to allow them to go freely about in their search, but the Governor cannot concentrate in such affairs. He is in a state of distraction, for his nephew, who was to have arrived in the city that day, is missing and he fears the young man may have been waylaid by the French. But no! Here comes the coach of the young aristocrat now. The coach pulls up and an Italian monsignor, a hooded monk and a little English coachman descend.

But these are not the Governor's men. Under their effective disguises, they are none other than Griolet, Monthabor and Stella, whose imitation of an English lad fools even her own step-father ('Je Suis l' Petit Cocher'). She concocts a story telling how they met a charming French vivandière lost and alone on the road, and how they have put her up in a little house near the city walls until their master can return to get to know her better. The Duc, convinced that this must be Stella, demands to be given the address where his daughter is hidden and Griolet, anxious to get him out of the way, impulsively gives him the first address he can think of, the address on a nearby box of 'pasta'—Rue Bonifacio 27. The Duc rushes off triumphantly to find Bambini and lead him at last to his bride.

The friends meet up again with Robert ('Quoi! C'Est Vous Mes Amis') and Stella is quickly in his arms ('Non Plus de Chagrins, Plus de Peine'), but still they have no travel documents to allow them to escape from the city. Only one person has such documents: the Duc della Volta or, as it happens, the Duchesse who has taken delivery of the vital papers in her husband's absence. Monthabor takes it on himself to get them from her. Dressed in his monk's robes he listens to his ex-wife pour out her tale of woe, her longing for her first husband and her mistake in a second one ('Devant Moi, Contre Toute Attente'), before revealing his identity.

The blushing Duchesse hands over the papers but, before the little band can depart, the Duc returns with the police to arrest Robert. Stella has also been recaptured. His men have taken a pretty young girl in a vivandière's costume at the Rue Bonifacio and she has been carried off to the Governor's palace to be forcibly wed to Bambini. Armed with the safe-conduct papers, Monthabor, Griolet and Stella set out to rescue Robert from their enemies.

The marriage of the Marquis Bambini and the pretty vivandière is imminent ('Un Mariage S'Apprête'). To the Duc's delight, he has succeeded in making the girl accept the marriage by exchanging her consent for Robert's freedom. But Robert, seeing the marriage procession approach (Choeur de Cortège), rushes desperately forward and pulls aside the bride's veil. It is not Stella at all, but Claudine!

378

The fat is in the fire. The furious Duc orders everyone arrested but, as the police lead Robert and Claudine away, martial music is heard. The main body of the French army has entered Milan. As the soldiers pour into the square and the people bring out their long-secreted *tricolores*, the Duc suffers a violent and expedient change of loyalties. Robert is freed to go to his Stella and Claudine rewards the faithful Griolet with her hand and heart as the curtain falls.

LES MOUSQUETAIRES AU COUVENT

(The Musketeers in the Convent)

an opérette in three acts by Paul Ferrier and Jules Prével based on *Le Habit ne Fait Pas le Moine* by Saint-Hilaire and Duport. Music by Louis Varney. Produced at the Théâtre des Bouffes-Parisiens 16 March 1880 with Marcelin (Gontran), Frédéric Achard (Brissac), Mlle Rouvroy (Marie), Mlle Clary (Louise) and Paul Hittemans (Bridaine). Revived there in a revised version 2 September 1880 with Morlet as Brissac and again in 1883, 1896 and 21 March 1906 with Devaux, Piccaluga, Mlle Varney, Mlle de Kercourt and Paul Fugère. Produced at the Théâtre des Folies-Dramatiques 4 May 1886 with Morlet and revived there in 1887, 1888, 1891 and 1909. Played at the Théâtre des Menus-Plaisirs 1896 and 1897. Produced at the Théâtre de la Gaîté 1899 with Larbaudière, Lucien Noël and Paul Fugère and played there in 1901 with Dutilloy, Dastrez and Guyon and in 1913 with Leroux, Clarel, Claude Arnès, Mlle Crisafulli and Dolne. Produced at the Gaîté-Lyrique 1914 with Lucien Noël and played there in 1922, 1923 with Léon Ponzio, Georges Foix and Henri Jullien, 15 April 1924, 19 January 1938 with Mondé, Le Breton and Jullien, 1952 with Jacques Josselin, Michel Dens, Josette Delly, Jacqueline Lejeune and Duvaleix and in 1958. Produced at the Théâtre Mogador 4 December 1940 with René Lenoty, André Baugé, Suzanne Baugé, France Aubert and Servatius.

Produced at the Globe Theatre, London, in a two act version by H B Farnie 30 October 1880 with Henry Bracy, Frank Celli, Mlle Sylvia, Elsie Moore and Harry Paulton.

Produced at the Fifth Avenue Theatre, New York, 25 April 1882 with Tauffenberger, Nigri, Mlle Lentz, Paola Marié and Duplan.

Produced at the Theater an der Wien, Vienna, in a version by Julius Hopp and Eduard Mautner as *Die Musketiere in Damenstift* 30 September 1881

Produced at the Apollo Theater, Berlin, 13 February 1893. Produced at the Alexanderplatz Theater 21 March 1896.

CHARACTERS

Vicomte Narcisse de Brissac, *a musketeer*
Gontran de Solanges, *a musketeer*
Abbé Bridaine, *his tutor*
Comte de Pontcourlay, *Governor of Touraine*
Marie de Pontcourlay, *his niece*
Louise de Pontcourlay, *her sister*

379

Pichard, *landlord of 'Au Mousquetaire Gris'*
Simonne
La Supérieure *of the Convent des Ursulines*
Soeur Opportune
Jeanneton, Claudine, Margot, Agathe, *convent pupils*
Rigobert, *an officer of the King's musketeers*
Jacqueline, Langlois, Farin, *townspeople*
Two monks, etc.

ACT 1

At the inn of the Mousquetaire Gris at Vouvray, a newly arrived detachment
of the King's musketeers are taking their ease. Although their presence is a
source of delight to the local maidens and the vendors of flowers and trinkets
('Etrennez-Moi, Voici des Roses'), it is an irritation to the Romeos of the
town whose noses are put squarely out of joint by the attentions lavished by
their girls on anything with a plume. When one of the soldiers interferes in a
piece of homespun horseplay, the inn threatens to burst into a brawl ('Que
Ces Mousquetaires Sont Audacieux') until the hostess, Simonne, quietens
the situation with some brisk words and a song of her own in praise of the
military ('S'Il Est un Joli Régiment').

Sulk as they may, there is nothing the villagers can do about this sudden
presence in their midst of half an army of musketeers, for the soldiers have
been ordered into the area by the Governor of Touraine, the Comte de
Pontcourlay, on the command of Cardinal Richelieu himself, to watch over
what his spies tell him is a conspiracy against his rule.

Like all good theatrical soldiers, these ones have their minds set more on
love than on war and one in particular, the romantic Gontran de Solanges, is
suffering badly from the effects of a feminine glance. He is in such a bad
state that his best friend, Brissac, deems it necessary to send for the lad's old
tutor, the amiable Abbé Bridaine, to try to assuage the poor lovesick fellow's
troubles. Bridaine's affection for his former charge is enough to prise him
from his peaceful retirement and bring him helter-skelter to Vouvray
('L'Abbé Bridaine') where he discovers from the reluctant Gontran (Trio:
'Parle! Explique-Toi!') that the malady is, in part, of his making.

When the young man was in his care, Bridaine had chattered many and
many a time to him of the incomparable charms of Marie de Pontcourlay, the
Governor's niece. Finally, the young man could not forbear to go and look at
this paragon and, as a result, he has fallen madly and despairingly in love
with the aristocratic young lady. His despair is increased by the fact that
Marie is not even in his daily reach for she is a pupil at the Convent des
Ursulines where she is strictly guarded by a flock of vigilant nuns. It is
enough to make a red-blooded Frenchman shoot himself. Bridaine is
shocked at such a dramatic thought and he takes it upon himself to speak to
the Governor on behalf of his young friend.

The day's festival ('C'Est le Jour de Fête'/'Quel Plaisir, C'Est la Brune')
is interrupted by the arrival of the Comte de Pontcourlay who happens to be

380

passing by in the course of his gubernatorial duties. Bridaine is about to fulfil his promise to Gontran, when the Governor forestalls him by asking him to go the next day to the convent where his two nieces are immured and prepare them for taking their vows as novices.

Bridaine is horrified: if Marie becomes a nun then she can never be Gontran's wife and the poor fellow probably will shoot himself. But the Governor is intransigent. The girls are relations of the Cardinal and the order has come from the great man himself, so there is nothing to be done but obey. To help Bridaine in his mission of convincing the girls of their vocation, Pontcourlay waylays two mendicant monks. In return for a night's bed and board at the inn, they will escort the Abbé to the convent the next day and help to exhort Marie and her sister, Louise, to take the veil.

Gontran's despair on hearing the Cardinal's plans is bottomless, but Brissac is more for action than for despair and he comes up with an idea. While the villagers make merry at the Governor's expense ('Le Gouverneur Nous Fit Largesse'), he and Gontran sneak into the room occupied by the two monks who, exhausted from their pilgrimage, are already fast asleep. In a moment they don the ecclesiastical robes hanging over the foot of their bed and emerge thoroughly and undetectably disguised as ambulant priests ('Nous Venons de la Paléstine'). Brissac whispers to one of his officers to lock the monks in their room and put a guard on the door and, with their rear thus protected, the two false priests set off in the direction of the convent.

ACT 2

The convent girls are in class ('Il Faut, Mes Soeurs, Qu'On Rivalise') taking dictation from Sister Opportune ('Donc, Rébecca, Sa Cruche Pleine') when the Mother Superior comes to tell them that, at the express wish of the Governor, they are to receive a visit from two particularly important priests to whom the girls will be able to confess. Louise de Pontcourlay, the most frivolous of the class, decides it would be fun if they all confessed to the same things but her sister Marie has real troubles which she needs to tell, for she is in love ('Que Votre Volonté Se Fasse') and she does not join in as the other giggling girls take down Louise's all-purpose confession ('Mon Père, Je M'Accuse').

When the two imitation priests arrive at the convent they are received with enthusiasm by the Superior. The boorish Brissac makes a poor effort at his part, peppering his conversation with military terms which surprise the nuns, and ogling the piquant Louise. Gontran does his best to maintain their disguise while at the same time getting near enough to Marie to arrange a secret meeting ('Je Voudrais Qu'Approchant Sans Crainte'). When the girls are led off to their luncheon, Brissac discovers with rumbling horror that the day is a religious fast and that he is to get nothing. Rather than go hungry, he announces that he has a dispensation to eat when he is giving a sermon and, since he proposes to speak before the pupils in the afternoon, he may eat and drink his fill. Gontran, who is still angling for his meeting with Marie, is happy to see his friend out of the way.

In the meanwhile the Abbé Bridaine has noticed that his two young friends are missing. Dreading what terrible ends they may go to, he has set out for the convent at top speed to get to Marie before Gontran does. On his arrival, he meets Louise who, having a decidedly suspicious nature, has been hiding in corners spying on the peculiar priests ('Curieuse, Ah! Vraiment') and he has to bundle her out of the way before he can get down to serious conversation with Marie. The good Abbé explains to the girl that, encouraged by his praises of her pretty self, his pupil has fallen in love with her and he begs that she write to him instantly telling him that she has no equivalent feelings for him.

He is devastated when Marie tells him that to do so would be to commit a lie for, likewise encouraged by Bridaine's fulsome descriptions of his charge, she has developed a tender emotion for the young man. Only when the Abbé tells her that the vengeance of the Cardinal himself will strike Gontran if he does not desist from his pursuit of Marie, does she agree to write the letter. Bridaine then tracks down Gontran and presents him with Marie's note. The young man is shattered ('Il Serait Vrai, Ce Fut un Songe'), but he is buoyed up in his hopes by another letter, a very tender one, which he has found in the girl's school desk, and he refuses to despair.

Brissac has enjoyed his lunch but, unfortunately, he has enjoyed it a little too much and, when the time comes for him to deliver the promised sermon, he is loudly and stupidly drunk. When the girls gather to hear him preach ('De la Cloche Qui Vois Appelle'), instead of propounding the pious text against worldly things which the Governor had postulated, he launches into a wild song in praise of love ('Aimons-Nous Donc'). Whilst the Superior collapses, and Gontran and Bridaine try to pretend that their confrère is ill, the girls join in a wild song and dance with the amazing 'priest'.

ACT 3

Bridaine has shut Brissac in the garden shed to sleep off his excesses whilst explaining to the sisters, in a convoluted tale, that the poor man suffers from Palestinian sunstroke. Suddenly, to his surprise, he hears men's voices outside the walls of the convent. It is Gontran's regiment who have come to await his orders to assist in carrying off Marie.

When the girls come out for their recreation ('Deux à Deux, Posément'), Louise takes the opportunity to have a delicious chat with Brissac through the window of the garden shed. She is delighted to hear that he has been a priest for only twenty-four hours after having been all his life a musketeer but, before she can drag from him the entire story of his life, she is obliged to hurry away to avoid discovery.

The innkeeper has sent Simonne to the convent to find the Abbé Bridaine. They are anxious to get hold of Brissac, for he has left his guards on the monks' room and gone away ('À la Porte des Révérends'), which means that the hotel has an unusable room with four guards outside and two naked monks inside. Pichard's inn is of small moment to the musketeers in the convent, for they have altogether graver things on their minds. Bridaine, determined that the Cardinal's orders must be carried out, has forbidden Gontran to go near Marie but he still connives at his masquerade for he does not wish the boy to be discovered—merely to leave.

Gontran asks to write a farewell note to his beloved and Bridaine agrees, but the note which Simonne delivers is not a farewell at all. It contains instructions for Marie to meet Gontran at the gate to prepare their escape over the convent wall. When the personnel of the convent are gathered together to discuss the preparations for the Cardinal's visit on the following day, the two young people succeed in meeting and, having confessed their love ('Il Faut Fuir, le Danger Me Presse'), they vow to escape together but, before they can do so, they are joined by Brissac and by Louise who, as the price of her silence, demands to be made the fourth participant in the adventure. A ladder is dragged out from the gardener's shed ('Prenons l'Echelle') but, just as they are preparing to climb up, the approach of the Abbé sends them scurrying for a hiding place.

When Bridaine sees the ladder he is horrified. The wretches have carried off Marie! He bumbles up the ladder and is perched astride the top of the wall when Simonne deftly removes the ladder, leaving him stranded. He is sitting there, looking extremely silly, when the Governor himself pounds at the gate. He has come on an urgent mission. The two monks whom he sent to the convent must be arrested immediately. They are impostors! It is a plot against his Eminence the Cardinal. The false monks are murderers who have wormed their way into the convent with the intention of slaying the Cardinal on his visit the following day.

As the Abbé gulps up the first stammerings of an explanation, the two musketeers reveal themselves and, before they know where they are, are greeted as heroes. The two naked fellows who are, at that moment, by Brissac's orders under a heavy guard at the Mousquetaire Gris, are the conspirators and the musketeers have been the instrument of their capture. They have saved the Cardinal's life and they deserve a reward. Gontran and Brissac do not need to be asked twice. The Pontcourlay sisters and a wedding at the Mousquetaire Gris will more than suffice.

The two songs 'Pour Faire une Brave Mousquetaire' and 'Gris, Je Suis Gris' were added to enlarge the role of Brissac when Morlet succeeded Achard.

The London version interpolated the song 'The Captive and the Bird' by Robert Planquette into the third act for Brissac.

LA MASCOTTE

(The Luck-Bringer)

an opéra-comique in three acts by Henri Chivot and Alfred Duru. Music by Edmond Audran. Produced at the Théâtre des Bouffes-Parisiens 28 December 1880 with

Morlet (Pippo), Mlle Montbazon (Bettina), Charles Lamy (Fritellini), Mlle Dinelli (Fiametta) and Paul Hittemans (Laurent), and revived there 1883 and 1889. Produced at the Théâtre des Menus-Plaisirs 1890 with Jane Pierny. Produced at the Théâtre de la Gaìté 1897 with Lucien Noël, Mlle Cocyte, Emile Soums, Mlle Deberio and Paul Fugère, and played there in 1901 with Germaine Gallois, and in 1915 with Lucien Noël and Angèle Gril. Produced at the Théâtre de l'Apollo October 1913 with Henry Defreyn, Lucie Vauthrin, Robert Pasquier, Marcelle Devriès and Fernand Frey, and revived there 12 July 1914. Produced at the Théâtre Mogador 17 December 1921 with Léon Ponzio, Jane Morlet, José Delaquerrière, Jeanne Saint-Bonnet and Massart. Produced at the Théâtre de la Porte Saint-Martin 1933 with André Baugé, Edmée Favart, André Noël, Jane Montange and Servatius, 10 May 1935 with André Baugé and Fanély Revoil and 1968. Produced at the Théâtre Mogador 17 April 1944 with Maurice Vidal and Suzanne Baugé.

Produced at the Comedy Theatre, London, 15 October 1881 in a version by Robert Reece and H B Farnie with François Gaillard, Violet Cameron, Henry Bracy, Lizzie St Quinten and Lionel Brough and revived there 23 May 1884 with Gaillard, Florence St John, Henry Walsham, Victoria Reynolds, Louis Kelleher and Arthur Roberts (Rocco) and 4 April 1885 with Violet Cameron and Roberts. Produced at the Strand Theatre 13 May 1882 with Gaillard, Clara Merivale, E Desmonts, Maude Taylor and Henry Ashley. Played at the Royalty Theatre 23 January 1888 with Mary Albert. Produced at the Gaiety Theatre 9 September 1893 with Florence St John Wallace Brownlow, Charles Conyers, Phyllis Broughton and Robert Pateman.

Produced at the Bijou Opera House, New York, 5 May 1881 with John Brand, Emma Howson, C H Thomson, Lillie West and Harry Brown. Played at the Park Theatre 9 May 1881 with Helen Carter, Seth M Crane, W Haydon Tilla, Lizzie Harrold and Sydney Smith and again 30 November 1881 with Paola Marié; at the Bijou 5 September 1881 with Lithgow James, Selina Dolaro, Blanche Chapman, Alonzo Hatch and George W Denham; at the Thalia Theater 5 December 1881 in German with Alexander Klein, Jenny Stubel, Adolf Link, Hermine Jules and Franz Müller; at Booths Theatre 9 February 1882 with W H MacDonald, Geraldine Ulmar, W H Fessenden, Lizzie Burton and Henry Clay Barnabee; at Haverley's Theatre 15 February 1882 with Miss Howson, Hatch, Pauline Hall and J W Norcross; at the Fifth Avenue Theatre 24 April 1882 with Nigri, Paola Marié, Tauffenberger, Mlle Grégoire and Mezières; at the Windsor Theatre 26 June 1882 with Fay Templeton (Bettina); at Wallack's Theatre 5 October 1885 with Anna Judic; at the Bijou Theatre 24 January 1887 with Stuart Harold, Lillie Grubb, Flora Edwin, Lelia Farrell and Nat Goodwin, etc., and regularly over the following years. Played at Palmer's Theatre 18 July 1892 with Camille d'Arville, William Pruette, Yolande Wallace and Henry E Dixey. Produced at the New Amsterdam Theatre 12 April 1909 with Raymond Hitchcock and Flora Zabelle. Produced at Jolson's Theatre 1 December 1926.

Produced at the Theater an der Wien, Vienna, 12 February 1881 and at the Carltheater 5 December 1893.

Produced at the Friedrich-Wilhelmstädtisches Theater, Berlin, 25 October 1881.

A film version was produced by Léon Mathot in 1935 with Germaine Roger, Lucien Baroux, Lestelly and Dranem.

CHARACTERS

Laurent XVII, *Prince of Piombino*
Princess Fiametta, *his daughter*

384

Prince Fritellini, *son of the Duke of Pisa*
Rocco, *a farmer*
Pippo, *his shepherd*
Bettina, la Rougeaude, *a turkey girl*
Mathéo, *an innkeeper*
Sergeant Parafante
Carlo, Marco, Angelo, Luidgi, Beppo, Paola, Francesca, Antonia, etc.

ACT 1

The grape harvest has been gathered on the farms of the Principality of Piombino, and the country folk are celebrating with their first taste of the newly pressed wine ('Le Vendange Est Terminée'). Only the farmer Rocco does not join in the merry-making. He sits gloomily apart, ruminating on the persistent bad luck which has clung to his coat-tails over so many seasons. His barn has burned, his flocks fallen ill, he has a law suit on his hands and no suit on his back, for his tailor refuses to tack on tick and, to top it all, today his cow has gone missing. It just isn't fair. Why can he not share the glowing good fortune of his brother Antonio who, with no better lands than his own, flourishes effortlessly just down the road? Today he has been obliged yet again to turn to his brother with a plea for help, but he has little hope of practical assistance for Antonio's usual response is nothing but a basketful of eggs and a letter full of good advice.

Rocco's shepherd, Pippo, has been sent to carry the petition, and he returns with a bit of news which delights him but which plunges Rocco even deeper in gloom. Antonio has decided to make his brother an especially splendid gift this time: he is sending him his turkey girl, Bettina. A turkey girl! One more mouth to feed. Even Pippo, who is Bettina's lover, acknowledges that what their farm needs is not another worker but some good fortune. They need a mascot, one of those angels created by the good God to battle against the forces of evil in the world ('Un Jour le Diable, Ivre d'Orgueil'). What neither Pippo nor Rocco knows is that that is precisely what Bettina is. It is her presence on Antonio's farm which has been responsible for all his prosperity and, while she remains a pure and simple virgin, she will bring good luck to her new master and to anyone else with whom she is connected.

The brawny Bettina arrives, making short work of the rustic advances of the village lads ('Je Suis Bettina la Rougeaude'), bringing with her the usual basket and the usual letter. She meets with a sour greeting from the disappointed Rocco, but the farmer has barely time to stuff the letter in his pocket before the first bit of unrecognised good luck comes his way. Prince Laurent, the ruler of Piombino, has been out hunting with his daughter, Fiametta, and her betrothed, the Prince Fritellini and, requiring rest and refreshment, he has chosen Rocco's farm for the honour of being his host ('On Aime à Voir Après la Chasse').

In spite of his lofty rank, Laurent, like Rocco, suffers from a jinx ('Les Présages, les Mensonges'). He is continually beaten in battle; when he plays

385

the market with public funds he invariably loses; when he goes hunting he never catches anything more than the occasional rabbit; and now his daughter is being downright difficult over her engagement to the adoring Fritellini, the son of a particularly belligerent neighbouring monarch. When he sits down he chooses the one broken chair in the house and, when Bettina brings fresh farm milk to the royal party, it is his mug that a passing beetle happens on for a bath.

The Princess Fiametta is going through a rustic phase. She loves the farm and the milk and she also takes a violent fancy to the rustic muscles of Pippo ('Ah, Qu'Il Est Beau'), much to the distress of Fritellini whose principal characteristic is a well-refined and courtly elegance ('Le Je Ne Sais Quoi Poétique'). The royal roving eye does not escape Bettina's attention, but Pippo laughs her worries away. She has nothing to worry about from a princess; he loves his Bettina even better than his sheep, just as he means even more to her than her darling turkeys (Duo des Bé Bé: 'J'Aime Bien Mes Dindons').

Their duo ends in a kiss, but the kiss is overseen by Rocco who is furious to see his two farmhands flirting instead of working. He is on the point of sending Bettina back to his brother when he looks at the contents of the letter and discovers the truth of Antonio's gift: Bettina is a mascot. Within minutes he has proof. News comes that he has won his law suit, the tailor sends his new suit without payment, and his cow comes home. Instead of dismissing Bettina, he falls all over her, promising her the best of everything in his house.

If Rocco's bad luck is over, however, Laurent's is not. Peering into a vat of new wine, he loses his balance and tumbles in head first. The royal robes are drenched. Rocco happily offers him a change of clothes but, rather than part with his beautiful new suit, he hands the Prince the outfit he is wearing, forgetting that he has left his brother's letter in the pocket. Laurent is quick to discover the paper and its amazing revelation, and he reacts with despotic decision: Bettina shall be his. The girl is called to the royal presence (Finale: 'On Sonne, On Sonne') and the Prince informs her that she has been discovered to be the aristocratic Comtesse de Panada. She must leave the farm instantly and come to her rightful place at his court.

ACT 2
The Comtesse de Panada is installed at the Court of Piombino with every splendour and every care. Having done his homework on the subject of mascots, Laurent's most pressing care is for her virginity, so the love letters of the royal pages are harshly suppressed ('Qu'Elle Est Belle') and Pippo is kept far away from court while Laurent enjoys an unfamiliar run of good fortune, even to the extent of winning at dominoes for the first time in his life.

His good luck does not extend to his daughter who not only sulks over her approaching marriage with Fritellini but also resents the attentions lavished on Bettina. Like the rest of the court and kingdom she can see only one explanation for the riches and attentions which are being poured over the farm girl: she must be Laurent's mistress. Bettina is no happier than the Princess. She finds no pleasure in costly clothes and jewels or fancy food, she is not allowed to do anything which might put her at any risk, and she is permanently pursued by a doctor deputed by the anxious monarch to watch over her health. She longs to be back on the farm and she misses Pippo dreadfully ('Loin de Votre Cour').

The devious plots developed by Laurent to keep the shepherd away from his beloved are outwitted when Pippo disguises himself as the Italian dancer, Saltarello, and gains entrance to the palace amongst the entertainers hired for the wedding of Fiametta and Fritellini ('Spectacle Charmant'/'C'Est Moi, Saltarello'). The two lovers contrive to meet ('Ah! Quel Plaisir') and plot an escape, but their meeting is spied by Rocco, who has been brought to court as Chamberlain in compensation for the annexation of his mascot, and Rocco is swift to carry the news to the Prince.

Before the lovers can escape, Pippo is arrested and, in his captivity, he makes a dreadful discovery. From the lips of the sophisticated Fritellini he learns at last what the whole world knows, that Bettina is the mistress of Prince Laurent ('Mon Cher, Que Vous Etes Naïf'). The shepherd is heart-broken and, when Fiametta drops suggestively by, he is only too pleased to join in her plot and be caught passionately embracing the Princess by Laurent and the two witnesses legally required to make matrimony obliga-tory. Laurent is horrified at being trapped in such a way until he realises that, if Pippo is married to Fiametta, he will no longer be a threat where Bettina is concerned. Pippo is created Duc de Villa-Rosa on the spot and accorded the hand of the Princess in place of Fritellini.

When Bettina discovers what has happened she tries to tear her rival's hair out, but Laurent calms the situation and adds his own personal master touch: he will marry Bettina himself. That way she will be safe from all other men and, given his own age and incapacity, she will never lose her virginity or her magic powers ('J'En Suis Tout à Fait Incapable'). In all this clever reshuffling, however, one person has been forgotten. No one has remem-bered to tell Fritellini that his position as bridegroom has been usurped. When he finds out, just as the wedding is about to take place, he threatens to bring his father's armies down on Piombino, but Laurent thumbs his nose at the threat. With his mascot at his side no army in the world can harm him.

Bettina and Pippo meet again at the double wedding which is to ally them to the royal house of Piombino ('C'Est le Futur de la Princesse'). Bettina shows her scorn for her husband-to-be in the tale of 'Le Capitaine et les Brigands' before the irritated Prince leads her off in the nuptial procession, but the order of the procession causes Bettina and Pippo to end up next to each other and a few quick words of reproach lead to the truth being made clear. They are soon in each other's arms and Laurent, seeing his plans falling apart, loudly calls for his guards to arrest the pair. Here their country skills come to their aid. Flinging a few last mocking words in the face of the fainting monarch, Bettina and Pippo dive from the castle window into the moat below and head for freedom.

387

ACT 3

Fritellini's threats have come to fruition. The armies of the Duke of Pisa have attacked Laurent without delay and, given the defection of Bettina, with much success. Laurent is getting a thrashing which is giving much satisfaction to the men of Pisa ('Verse, Verse, Verse à Boire') and particularly to Fritellini who leads his father's army decked out in a splendid general's outfit ('De Nos Pas Marquant la Cadence'). Pippo has been raised to the position of Captain in the Pisan forces with Bettina, dressed as a soldier, following him into battle as his batman and, now that Laurent has been put to flight, it is time for the two of them to be wed. Under the patronage of the lovelorn Fritellini, still sighing for his lost Fiametta, Bettina and Pippo will finally be made man and wife.

Unbeknown to the conquering General, his lady love is not far away. Laurent, Fiametta and Rocco have escaped from the debris of the Piombino army and, disguised as wandering minstrels, have made their way to an inn run by Mathéo, a faithful old family servant, for safety. Unfortunately for them, this inn is the very place chosen by Fritellini as the headquarters for his activities. The false minstrels find they have walked right into the arms of their enemies, and Fiametta is obliged to keep up appearances with a song lampooning her father (Chanson de l'Orang-Outang).

When Mathéo tells Laurent that Bettina and Pippo are to be wed, he is maliciously delighted. As soon as Bettina's maidenhead is lost, the tide of war will turn. Fritellini's luck will vanish and he, Laurent, will once again be in the ascendant. Unfortunately for him, Rocco has other ideas. Weighing up all the facts, he feels that Fritellini will offer him better prospects than the Prince of Piombino and he prepares to change sides, taking with him his priceless piece of information.

Bettina and Pippo are well and truly wed ('Je Touche au But') and the nuptial chamber and their wedding night await them when Rocco comes to find his former shepherd and warn him of the consequences of bedding his bride. If Pippo consummates his marriage it will be the end of his high-flying career: he will end up back where he started, as a simple shepherd. When Bettina calls her new husband to come to bed ('Quoi! Pippo Quand Je Vous Réclame'), Pippo is torn between love and ambition. He pleads a headache, she coquettes him to a kiss ('Un Baiser C'Est Bien Douce Chose') while Rocco, using the melody of the mascot and his clarinet, and Laurent, pumping out the Air des Bé Bé on his bagpipes, try to persuade the boy to remember his fortune and his love respectively.

Poor Pippo, who is longing to take his bride in his arms, is dragged first one way and then the other by the two tunes but, finally, the bagpipes burst and Bettina, upset at her husband's rejection of her conjugal embraces, slams the bedroom door in his face and turns the key.

Pippo is immediately sorry. Glory is nothing to him compared with Bettina, and he pounds on the locked door begging to be let in as Rocco, realising that his victory is only temporary, hurries off to find Fritellini. The Prince immediately commands that guards be set on Bettina's door and orders Pippo brought before him, but Pippo has vanished and there is only a silly old peasant man to be found, chuckling conspiratorially in a corner. But wait—this is no peasant. It is the enemy himself, Prince Laurent of Piombino. Fritellini is preparing to take his revenge when Fiametta rushes forward to beg him to spare her father.

It is a Fiametta no longer disdainful but bursting with love for Fritellini, in whom a general's uniform and a good session in the field have clearly wrought a significant improvement. Fritellini is overjoyed at this volte-face and altogether distracted from the matter in hand until Rocco recalls him to his duty. So where is Pippo? He couldn't have got past this door. Certainly not. But there is a window and, with the help of a hoist-up on Laurent's shoulders, the intrepid bridegroom has made it to his bridal bed from the outside of the building.

The guards go to break down the door but they are too late. The door opens from the inside and there stands a pink Pippo, brandishing Bettina's bouquet in a sign that his husbandly duty has been accomplished (Finale 'Et Pourquoi Donc Crier Ainsi?'). Bettina is no longer a mascot, but it seems that the gift is hereditary so Fritellini and Laurent are left to quarrel over who shall bring up Bettina's first-born child, while she blushingly promises to do her best to give birth to twins.

LE JOUR ET LA NUIT

(Day and Night)

an opéra-bouffe in three acts by Albert Vanloo and Eugène Leterrier. Music by Charles Lecocq. Produced at the Théâtre des Nouveautés, Paris, 5 November 1881 with Marguerite Ugalde (Manola), Juliette Darcourt (Béatrix), Berthelier (Brasiero), E Montaubry (Miguel) and Jules Brasseur (Calabazas) and revived there September 1883. Produced at the Athenée-Comique 1897.

Produced at the Strand Theatre, London, in a version by H B Farnie as *Manola* 11 February 1882 with Rosa Leo, Irene Verona, Henry Ashley, E Desmonts and W J Hill.

Produced at the Fifth Avenue Theatre, New York, as *Manola* 6 February 1882 with Catherine Lewis, Marie Jansen, Fred Leslie, Charles J Campbell and John Howson.

Produced at the Theater an der Wien, Vienna, as *Tag und Nacht* 13 March 1882.

CHARACTERS

Don Brasiero de Tras os Montes, *Governor of a Portuguese province*
Don Dégomez, *his cousin*
Miguel, *his steward*
Prince Picrates de Calabazas, *Prime Minister of Portugal*
Manola
Béatrix

389

Sanchette, *an innkeeper*
Cristoval, *her waiter*
Gonzales, Pepita, Anita, Inès, Catana, Pablo, Juan, Dolorès, Médina, etc.

ACT 1

At the castle of Don Brasiero de Tras os Montes, a fine example of modern seventeenth century Portuguese architecture, the new staff are awaiting the first glimpse of their master's steward, Miguel ('Nous Attendons le Seigneur Intendant'). They are delighted when he turns out not be be an old grumpy creature, but a rather attractive young man ('Un Intendant la Chose Est Sûre') who is happy to look the maids over for their attractiveness rather than their housewifely talents ('Seigneur, Je Sais Broder'). Miguel has come to prepare the castle for his master and his master's new wife, a lady whom up till now no one has seen, not even the happy bridegroom himself.

Brasiero is a busy man. His province is situated right on the border of Portugal and Spain and his time is largely taken up with keeping a very wary eye on the Spanish army, which is liable to burst through into Portugal without the politeness of the slightest warning. He certainly has no time to go to Lisbon and look about for a wife. In the past he has delegated this job to his aristocratic cousin, Don Dégomez and, since the wives that gentleman has supplied to date have been satisfactory, it seems perfectly natural to continue the system. Dégomez finds the bride, weds her in proxy, and then bundles her down to the border to Brasiero. Unfortunately the previous wives have had one great failing—they were not very durable—and so Dégomez has been put to trouble once more.

Since Brasiero is so full of joyful anticipation over his new marriage, Miguel decides that this will be a good time to put forward his own request to marry the little creole, Manola ('Sous le Regard de Deux Grands Yeux'). The rattle of approaching horses is heard but, alas, it is not the bride who comes but a messenger. The Spanish have attacked again and Don Brasiero must hurry into the field. It is simply not the thing on one's wedding day ('Mon Cher Ami, Sache Bien Qu'Ici Bas') but, when a man has to go, a man has to go, and Don Brasiero goes, leaving Miguel behind to look after the new baroness.

A lady soon arrives, but it is not the baroness, it is Manola. She has fled from Lisbon to avoid the attentions of a lecherous nobleman and she has made her way to Miguel for safety ('Comme l'Oiseau Qui Fuit Effarouché'). Safety is only relative in this case, for the nobleman in question is none other than Prince Picrates Hermoso Cristoval de Calabazas, the Prime Minister of Portugal. Prime Minister Calabazas is a highly important person. He has the weak King Ferdinand under his thumb and, to all intents and purposes he rules the country.

He also has this all consuming weakness for a pretty woman and it is inclined to distract him dreadfully, even in the middle of the most important affairs of state ('Les Femmes, Ne M'En Parlez Pas'). For a whole week now he has devoted himself to chasing after Manola and he has gone so far as to quit Lisbon and his governmental duties to follow her in her flight to Brasiero's castle. Since Manola prefers to keep her virtue intact for her wedding with Miguel (and Miguel prefers it that way too), they have to come up quickly with a plan tactfully to prevent the Prime Minister from having his way. Under the circumstances, it is obvious. Should Calabazas attempt to follow her into the castle, Manola will pretend to be the new baroness.

Having come all this distance, there is no way that Calabazas is going to allow a little castle to stand in the way of his lust, but he is taken aback when he finds Manola presented to him as the new mistress of the place ('À Notre Nouvelle Maîtresse'). She greets him coolly ('Eh Bien, Oui, Je Suis la Baronne') and gives him little opportunity to do anything but leave, but her plan is spoiled when Brasiero returns.

He has bribed the Spanish to leave off attacking for a few days, until his honeymoon is over, and he has hurried back to meet his new wife. He is thrilled to have the Prime Minister as his guest—there is no question but that he must stay the night—and so delighted when he sees his 'wife' that he can scarcely wait for nightfall to come. Manola and Miguel now have an even stickier problem to overcome. They consider killing themselves ('Tuons-Nous!') but, before they can do so, more arrivals distract them.

The newcomers are an exhausted Don Dégomez, who falls asleep on his feet, and the real baronne, Béatrix, who turns out to be a close friend of Manola. She is quickly put in the picture about the deception and agrees, not entirely wholeheartedly, to help out ('Certainement, C'Est Bien Charmant'). It is agreed that Manola will go into the bedchamber with Brasiero and ask modestly for the lights to be switched out before undressing. Once the lights are out, she will slip out through a secret passage known only to Miguel, and Béatrix will climb in to replace her in her husband's arms for the hours of the night. The three friends cross their fingers ('O Grand Saint Michel') as the masquerade begins ('La Nuit Enchanteresse') with the over-enthusiastic Brasiero leading Manola up to bed, but all goes well and, as the act ends, Manola and Miguel are left alone together as Brasiero and his real wife celebrate their wedding night.

ACT 2

Next morning, Miguel is awaiting the explosion that must surely come when Brasiero sees what has happened ('Laissez-Moi Rallumer, Ma Belle'), but all is silence up in the nuptial chamber. To Miguel's horror the youngsters of Dégomez's suite insist on awakening the newlyweds with a bawdy serenade ('En Toute Circonstance'), but, in spite of the racket they make, still the shutters stay closed. What Miguel doesn't know is that Béatrix has managed to stay undiscovered.

The perplexed Brasiero only knows that he has started the evening with a modest wife who wants the lights off, spent an incredibly passionate night and then, in the morning, found his wife so bashful that she will not emerge from under the sheets until he is up and out of the room. So he has been wandering round the grounds, looking at all the farm animals making love and getting decidedly hot under the belt, while his wife gets dressed alone in their room.

Béatrix has been quick to make her escape and has rejoined Manola. The trick has been successful. In a few hours Calabazas will have gone and then everything can safely go back to normal. In the meanwhile, Brasiero, with the memories of a night well spent, is anxious to get himself once more near to Manola, and he is taken aback when her reaction is less than welcoming and she spends her time recommending the graces of her friend ('Voyez, Elle Est Charmante').

But, if the deception is not to be unveiled too soon, she cannot avoid being left alone with him and she soon finds herself in difficulties when he insists on recalling the events of the previous night. There was a particular song that his wife sang... Manola tries one or two ('Ma Mèr' M'A Dit Va-I-au Jardin'/'Y Avait un Fois un Militaire') but in the end she has to be prompted by Béatrix from behind a bush ('Un Rossignol Rencontre une Fauvette'). When he rushes to embrace her, Béatrix is swift to slip in between and Brasiero ends up in a passionate clinch with a woman he believes to be his wife's companion.

At last, to the great reîlief of the three conspirators, it is time for Calabazas to leave ('Puisqu'll Paraît Que le Grand Prince'/'O, Moment Suprême'), but the Prime Minister is in a jolly mood ('Les Portugais Sont Toujours Gais') and he decides to tell Brasiero the truth: he didn't come here to see him at all, he came chasing his wife. Since they're only just married there isn't much chance for him, so he's decided to come back in a few months when Manola will have tired of her husband. He calls for his parasol ('Qu'On M'Apporte Mon Parasol') and is about to depart when his eye falls on Béatrix and he is struck by a *coup de foudre* even more devastating than that which had been produced by Manola. Who is this woman? Why, she is only the baroness's companion. Calabazas decides that this is the woman he will marry. The parasol must be put back and the notary called.

The friends have a new quandary to face, but Manola is sure she can manage this one. She sets herself to switch Calabazas's attentions away from Béatrix and back to herself, and the susceptible Prime Minister quickly falls under her charms ('J'Ai Vu le Jour Dans un Pays'/'Vous Savez Charmer les Serpents?'/ Chanson Indienne: 'Le Serpent Dort Sur la Mousse'). She persuades him to pretend to have gone away but, instead, to hide in the pigeon house. When night falls, and Brasiero sleeps, she promises she will come down and meet him.

Calabazas hurries to clamber up amongst the birds and, no sooner is he installed, than Manola and Miguel whisk the ladder away and run off together ('Adieu Donc, Prince Charmant') and Calabazas has to shout until Brasiero comes to let him down ('On Appelle'). The duped Prince is only too keen to tell Brasiero that his wife has run off with his steward but, from a hidden place, Béatrix quietly sings the song of their wedding night ('Un Rossignol Rencontre une Fauvette') and the Governor knows that Calabazas is lying. And all this time, Miguel and Manola are hurrying away from the castle towards marriage.

ACT 3

At a hotel out in the country there is much merriment going on as closing time arrives ('Ohé, Hotelière') and the merrymakers sing and dance (Boléro: 'En Portugal, les Portugaises') with little care for the strictures of the landlady, Sanchette ('Mon Cabaret, Entre Nous, Je M'En Vante'), who finally shovels all the late drinkers into a back room to carry on their party.

The bar is no sooner cleared than new visitors arrive. They are Brasiero and the heavily cloaked Béatrix who is still pretending to be Manola. Brasiero has a contretemps on his hands. He failed to send the Spanish commander the money he had promised and the unsporting fellow has gone and attacked after all, arousing Brasiero to head back to the border to remonstrate with him ('Je Passais un Jour Dans la Rue').

Although Sanchette is interrupted when just getting to grips with her waiter, she scents money and is only too pleased to give these guests a room while their horses are changed. She is even more pleased when another pair of visitors follow them in, a chunky farmer and a very handsome muleteer. She is a little sad when the muleteer reveals herself to be Manola, and Miguel asks for a notary to be brought to marry them right away before anything can go wrong again ('Nous Sommes Deux Amoureux').

No sooner have the lovers been shown to a room than Calabazas and the still sleepy Dégomez sweep in in pursuit. Momentarily distracted by Sanchette, Calabazas forces himself to keep his mind on his task of revenge. He orders all the young people in the inn to be paraded in front of him, including the muleteer who gives a full account of himself ('Si Je Mène Par le Chemin') in a most convincing way.

The disguise is wrecked when the stupid Cristoval comes running in to tell Manola that the notary is on his way, and Calabazas orders Miguel and Manola to be locked up, gleefully ordering his men back to Brasiero's château to bring the apparently cuckolded husband to face his 'wife'. He is chuckling over the ridiculous situation Brasiero will face when, suddenly, he finds himself face to face with the Governor and his cloaked lady. Manola is brought out and Béatrix is uncloaked before Brasiero's bewildered and Calabazas's malicious gaze. The friends are in deep trouble, and Calabazas hurries off to arrange their arrest.

The three friends and Brasiero face each other ('C'Était la Demoiselle de Compagnie') until Manola takes it on herself to explain the situation to the Governor ('Il Est Deux Choses Ici-Bas'). He has two wives: one, herself, by day and the other, Béatrix, by night. Manola is not his real wife, having only taken that position to escape Calabazas, but Béatrix is—and she has proved it. With the proof in mind, Brasiero is happy to fall at the feet of his new bride.

Calabazas, returning, is amazed to see the Governor kneeling before his wife's companion but Dégomez, who has finally woken up, is quick to correct him. Béatrix is Brasiero's wife—he should know, he was the one who married her. Now, at last, Calabazas sees just how he has been tricked and he is puffing himself up for some almighty act of vengeance when a messenger arrives with a letter ('C'Est un Courrier'). It is from the King. Calabazas

393

has been off chasing his girls for too long this time—he is sacked! He is powerless to do anything against Manola or Miguel and he has to console himself instead with the willing Sanchette.

LE COEUR ET LA MAIN

(Heart and Hand)

an opérette in three acts by Charles Nuitter and Alexandre Beaumont. Music by Charles Lecocq. Produced at the Théâtre des Nouveautés, Paris, 19 October 1882 with Mlle Vaillant-Couturier (Micaëla), Vauthier (Don Gaétan), Berthelier (King), Scipion (Don Mosquitos), Mlle Clary (Joséfa), Mlle Felcourt (Doña Scholastica) and Montaubry (Moralès).

Produced at the Lyric Theatre, London, in a version by F C Burnand and Harry Greenbank with additional music by Yvolde and Herbert Bunning as *Incognita* 6 October 1892 with Sedohr Rhodes (Micaela), Wallace Brownlow (Don Gaetan), Harry Monkhouse (Don Pedro), Fred Kaye (Don Guzman), Aida Jenoure (Josefa), Susie Vaughan (Doña Scholastica) and John Child (Morales O'Donoghue).

Produced at the Bijou Theatre, New York, 15 February 1883 as *Hand and Heart* with Marianne Conway, John Howson, George Olmi, Emie Weathersby, Laura Joyce and Charles J Campbell. Produced at the Standard Theatre 26 February 1883 as *Micaëla* with Marie Conron, George Sweet, J H Ryley, H W Montgomery, Verona Jarbeau, Mrs Fred Williams and Wallace Macreery. Played at the Standard Theatre 22 October 1883 with Jeanne Fouquet. Played at Haverley's Lyceum 11 January 1884.

CHARACTERS

The King of Aragon
Princess Micaëla, *his daughter*
Doña Inésilla Vittoria Scholastica Nepomucena, *her duenna*
Don Gaétan, *Duke of Madeira*
Don Mosquitos, *a colonel of the King's army*
Moralès, *a soldier*
Joséfa, *a royal gardener*
Baldomèro, *a brigadier*
Anita, Pépa, Dolorès, Inès, Pablo, Pascual, Lazaro, José, Ascanio, etc.

ACT 1

In the royal gardens of the court of Aragon a bevy of young ladies can be seen and heard picking the flowers which will decorate their princess on her wedding day ('C'Est Demain le Mariage'). The Princess Micaëla is to suffer the fate of so many of her musical sisters and is to be wed the next day, sight unseen, to a Prince from the state of Madeira, but the occurrence is such a normal one in royal circles that no one seems particularly upset about it.

These young ladies, the most virtuous of all the King's feminine subjects, have been chosen for the ritual gathering of the bridal bouquets ('Au Mariage des Princesses') but they are much more interested in the festivities that will accompany the wedding since, by another custom, they are all to be wed at the same time. Only Joséfa, the little gardener, cannot join the mass marriage for her soldier lover, Moralès, is not yet a brigadier and there is yet another law in Aragon which forbids military men under that rank from taking a wife. There is only one little shadow over the blossoming happiness of the virgins of Aragon: they are all poor and they have no dowries. So they decide on a little petition to the Princess and set off with their flowers and their petition to approach the royal bride for some largesse.

The changing of the palace guard ('C'Est Nous les Gardes du Palais') brings Moralès, by dint of some friendly persuasion in the right quarter, to be posted underneath Joséfa's window. Thus positioned, he can carry on some long-distance lovemaking with his lady until a chorus of courtly pages and ladies ('C'Est l'Heure de la Promenade') announces the coming of the Princess.

Princess Micaëla is a perfect martyr to courtly convention and etiquette as interpreted and enforced by her duenna, the punctilious Doña Scholastica. She is allowed to do nothing for herself that an army of pages and ladies-in-waiting can do for her and she has to blackmail the duenna into allowing her so much as a little game of hide-and-seek with her ladies. The game is, however, just an excuse to have Doña Scholastica hide her eyes and count to a hundred, giving Micaëla time secretly to plant a little ribbon in a shrub under Joséfa's window.

All, however, is not going according to etiquette at the court of Aragon. The King has lost the bridegroom ('V'lan! J'Ai Perdu Mon Gendre') or, to put it more correctly, the bridegroom has succeeded in escaping. Prince Gaétan, like Princess Micaëla, is being put into this marriage without his consent and, being a young man with a certain mind of his own and some romantic ideas about choosing his own wife, he has decided that he is not ready to be bullied into marriage. So, slipping away from the large detachment of armed men sent to escort him from Madeira to Aragon, he has bolted.

The King is most disturbed. The marriage is a necessity for, without it, the whole balance of power in Europe will be destabilised. He has hit a terrible losing streak in his recent wars and without the alliance with Madeira, his most recent conqueror, Aragon shows every sign of turning into a second division kingdom, an eventuality which would seriously disturb that balance so dear to historians.

The King is optimistic enough about quickly retaking the lost Prince to give the palace guard some celebratory leave, and they quickly begin to make the most of it by staging an impromptu drinking party outside Joséfa's door. Moralès provides the necessary drinking song as accompaniment ('Au Soldat Après la Parade') and, when his song is done, the soldiers have enough tact to leave the two lovers alone together. Then Joséfa notices the little ribbon in the bush and tells Moralès that he must go immediately. It is a sign from the Princess. She is about to slip away from under the gorgonic eye of Doña Scholastica and come to spend a little while, disguised, chatting girl to girl with the little gardener, far from the constraints of etiquette ('Ma Chère Joséfa').

Micaëla's thoughts are, somewhat naturally, all centred on her marriage and her future husband, and she is delighted to hear from her friend, who watched the young man arriving at the city gates that morning, that Gaétan is young, handsome and apparently cheerful. Joséfa has quite the opposite problem. Far from being wed without being asked, she is dying to wed but is not allowed. She begs Micaëla to use her influence to get Moralès promoted just sufficiently to make him eligible to be part of the morrow's ceremony and, so that there shall be no mistake, she gives the Princess one of his love letters which bears his name and rank. When all the other brides-to-be invade the scene, she passes the Princess off as her cousin and, as the girls join in a hen party dance, Micaëla sings a ronde to accompany them ('À l'Ombre des Charmilles').

They scatter with squeals and giggles when their efforts are greeted with applause from a dashing young man who has no qualms about climbing over the palace wall to watch them at their play. It is, as Joséfa is quick to inform her mistress, none other than the missing Prince Gaétan. Gaétan has run away on principle. He has nothing against the Princess of Aragon personally; she may be all very well, but he did not pick her. He will, probably, have to marry her, but he intends to let Aragon know that he has a mind of his own and that, in other things, he will do as he likes. For the moment, what he likes is to flirt with this delightful little maiden in the garden of Aragon's palace ('Tout Pour Toi'). But what is this? A letter in her cleavage...a love letter, no less. To Joséfa from her loving Moralès. So, she is Joséfa and she has a lover called Moralès.

Micaëla does not deny it but, when she tells him that she is to be wed the next day, Gaétan is not impressed. He, too, must be married tomorrow but that does not mean to say that they cannot make the most of today. Micaëla is saved from her future husband by the approach of the palace guard (Finale: 'Notre Vigilance'). They have finally tracked down their lost bridegroom and the unwilling Gaétan has to submit to being returned to the straight and courtly path and a lecture from his father-in-law. To resist is useless, but he warns them that they have seen nothing yet. Whatever he may have to do for the sake of politics, he will remain his own man—so let the Princess of Aragon beware.

ACT 2

The next day the marriage of Gaétan and Micaëla takes place along with that of the eleven little maidens and their men ('La Princesse Qui Nous Marie'), and of Joséfa and her Moralès, who has been promoted to Brigadier for the occasion. The Prince has gone through the form of the marriage ceremony but he has done it with little grace, refusing even to look at the woman to whom he was being wed, and purposely mixing up all the pages of the traditional responses to the good wishes of the people.

When he is obliged to go through a further traditional series of vows with his new wife, he performs equally gracelessly ('Il Me Regarde à Peine') and leaves the King to lead his daughter to the wedding dance, pretexting that he does not know how to dance. Instead he delivers a song, 'La Chanson du Casque'.

There is still further ceremonial to come. The Prince must be led to his private room while the Princess is taken to the nuptial chamber. When she is ready, the Prince will be brought to her in the approved fashion. The King tries to take this moment to explain something of the birds and the bees to his daughter ('O Micaëla, Ma Chère') but every time he reaches the point of the matter he is seized by a fit of coughing and the lesson goes for nothing. He has less qualms where his son-in-law is concerned. Knowing the boy's unwillingness for his task, he orders that the corridors of the palace shall be closed off and guarded lest Gaétan try to run away again.

Doña Scholastica presents the Prince with the golden key to the nuptial chamber but Gaétan is determined not to be forced into consummating his hated marriage and he resolves to cause a scandal. He makes a pass at Scholastica, expecting her to ring in panic for the guard but, to his horror, she offers with alacrity to obey his royal command and he has to squirm out of the situation embarrassingly. Having got rid of the duenna, he then sets out to try to find a way around Moralès and his guards.

Micaëla has been watching all of this through the keyhole of the nuptial chamber and is disappointed to find her Prince keeping so truly to his word ('Que les Hommes Sont Maladroits'). What shall she do now? But Gaétan is not the only one to have been trapped inside the inner chambers of the palace by the guards. Joséfa, who tarried a little long to say good night to her Moralès, is also there and now she cannot get out. Her wedding night looks like being no more satisfactory than Micaëla's.

But the Princess has an idea. Now that she knows that the Prince has not been able to get away, she is about to play a trick on him. She hurries off, leaving Joséfa and Moralès to try to make the most of their evening without breaking the rules of the guard. Finally, they cannot resist the look of the empty bridal chamber ('C'Est Là Leur Chambre Nuptiale'). They bundle into the bed and lock the door and, when the King returns to see if all is going well, the sounds of lovemaking he hears through the door suffice to convince him that reticence has been well and truly overcome.

Gaétan wanders round in a circle without finding any unguarded passages and finally ends up disconsolately back where he started. To his surprise he suddenly finds himself being served with food and drink by none other than the little girl to whom he had taken such a fancy the day before. Like himself, of course, she is newly wed but he has hopes that she may have the same ideas about obedience to royal commands as old Doña Scholastica and he orders her to take supper with him ('Mon Devoir Ailleurs Me Rapelle'). She not only complies but entertains him with a gipsy song ('Un Soir, José le Capitaine') and their supper soon turns into a very intimate affair, ending with the two of them in each other's arms, as the King is heard patrolling his guard outside.

ACT 3

The day after his marriage, Prince Gaétan took up his post in the army and sent the forces of Aragon into the field for exercises. They have now been exercising for two whole months with one half of the army, led by Gaétan, staging mock battles against the other half, at the head of which the King is having a wonderful time. The Princess has been sent for her safety into a nearby convent, but the army is well aware that their Prince has not been doing without feminine companionship. It is quite clear that he has been having an affair with Joséfa. Moralès has been promoted way beyond his due level ('Il A l'Épaulette') and the soldiers do not have to ask why.

The young lad who is so quickly and quietly admitted to Gaétan's tent on his visits to the camp is undoubtedly a woman in disguise and, every time that the 'boy' comes, Gaétan has suddenly found some flimsy excuse to send Moralès off on some distant errand. But now Gaétan is fretting. He has had no visit from his beloved for a week and he is worried. There is nothing else for it: he must go to the convent where she is lodged with her mistress and seek her out. That means the whole army must go too, so the whole army is given order to lift camp and prepare to march.

No sooner has the action begun than Micaëla arrives at the camp disguised as a nun, pretending that she wishes to become a vivandière ('Je Suis un Novice'). It is, of course, Micaëla who is Gaétan's paramour but he is still under the illusion of their first meeting and believes her to be Joséfa and the wife of Moralès, an illusion she takes every care to preserve. Her long absence from the camp is actually Gaétan's fault. Her father has taken to the war games with such vigour that he has set up earthworks all around the convent and, in doing so, has blocked the little gate by which Micaëla was wont to escape for her rendezvous with the Prince ('L'Heure Semblait Lente').

Their happy reunion is interrupted when the real Joséfa arrives to warn the Princess that her father is approaching. Micaëla has just time to flee before the King arrives ('Le Parlementaire') to choruses of greetings ('Ah! Sire, Exaucez Nos Prières') from lots of pretty girls whom he takes time off to chuck under the chin ('Ne Craignez Rien, les Belles Filles'). The visit is one of great moment, for the King has come to announce to his son-in-law that he has made him the happiest man in the world. His conjugal duty has been well done—the Princess is pregnant.

Gaétan is stunned, then disbelieving, then taken aback at the thought of being even technically cuckolded ('Quand Ça Tombe Sur un Confrère'), for one thing is certain: the child cannot be his. The answer soon seems obvious, for Moralès comes to make a confession which has been weighing on him all the time that his master has been loading him with favours. He has to confess that on the wedding night, unable to restrain his natural impulses, he went into the bridal chamber...it was not his fault that the door slammed to... Gaétan needs to hear no more. It is Moralès who is responsible, then, for the pregnancy of the Princess.

Now it is Moralès' turn to be confused, for he runs into Joséfa—what is she doing in the camp? A dreadful suspicion dawns and, when she cannot deny that she came to find the Prince, Moralès jumps hotly to the conclusion that the soldiers' gossip has hinted—she is Gaétan's mistress! Joséfa is furiously indignant at such a suggestion ('Voilà les Maris'), but Moralès has the bit between his teeth and will not listen. Revengefully he denounces her for being on army property illegally, and the situation is threatening to cut up rough when Micaëla returns to straighten everything out ('Je Suis Princesse').

At the end of the whole convoluted story it seems that everyone should be happy. Joséfa and Moralès are man and wife, the Princess has a husband she loves, and Gaétan cannot complain either. He wanted to choose his wife and he got the wife he chose, if not necessarily in that order. It only remains for the army to shoot off a salute in honour of the unborn babe. The King can set his mind at ease. The balance of power in Europe is safe after all.

The score of *Incognita* interpolated the duet 'Crou, Crou' (Herbert Bunning) for Joséfa and Moralès, King Pedro's Lament (Yvolde), the waltz song 'Rapture! My Love's Heart to Capture' (Bunning/Bingham) for Micaëla, a prelude to the third act (Bunning), the duet 'There's More in This Than Meets the Eye' (Yvolde) for Moralès and Gaétan, a mazurka and farandole (Yvolde), the song 'Foolish Flossy' (Yvolde) for the King, the song 'True Love of Mine' (Bunning/Bingham) and the quartet 'Love's Wings' by Hamilton Clarke.

MAM'ZELLE NITOUCHE

a comédie-vaudeville in three acts by Henri Meilhac and Albert Millaud. Music by Hervé. Produced at the Théâtre des Variétés, Paris, 26 January 1883 with Anna Judic (Denise), Louis Baron (Célestin), Henri Cooper (Fernand) and Christian (Château-Gibus). Revived there in 1884 with Judic, April 1885 with Judic, November 1888 with Judic, 1892 with Mathilde Auguez, 1894 with Judic and Baron, September 1897 with Jeanne Pierny, Baron and Jean Périer. Played at the Théâtre des Folies-Dramatiques 1898 with Mlle Pierny. Produced at the Théâtre du Château d'Eau 1901 with Juliette Simon-Girard. Produced at the Théâtre de la Gaîté 2 September 1913 with Angèle Gril, Raoul Villot, Clarel and Désiré and revived there 1914 with Mlle Gril, 25 July 1921, 1923 with Mary Malbos, Félix Oudart, Robert Burnier and Henri Jullien, 1924 with Andrée Alvar/Denise Cam, Morton and Marcotty, 1945 with Germaine Roger and Armand Bernard, 6 February 1954 with Madeleine Vernon and Rellys, 1960 with Mlle Roger, Lestelly, Philippe Andrey and Léo Bardollet. Produced at the Théâtre du Nouvel-Ambigu 1917. Produced at the Théâtre des Bouffes-Parisiens 15 May 1984 with Fabienne Guyon, Jean-Marie Proslier, Jean-Paul Bordes and Théo Gehanne.

Produced at the Opera Comique, London, 12 May 1884 as *Nitouche* with Lotta, Frank Wyatt, Frederic Darrell and Robert Pateman. Played at the Gaiety Theatre 13 June 1884 in French with Judic. Produced at the Trafalgar Square Theatre 6 May

1893 with May Yohe, Wyatt, Wallace Brownlow, Pateman and Violette Melnotte (Corinne).

Produced at Wallack's Theatre, New York, 1885 with Judic, Cooper and Dupuis. Produced at Daly's Theatre 15 September 1884 with Lotta, C H Bradshaw, Darrell and R J Dustan. Played at the Standard Theatre 14 December 1885 with Lotta. The musical *Papa's Wife*, partly based on *Mlle Nitouche*, was produced at Manhattan Theatre 13 November 1899 with Anna Held.

Produced at the Theater an der Wien, Vienna, 19 April 1890.

A film version was produced by Paramount in 1931 with Janie Marèze, Raimu, Alerme amd Edith Méra and another in 1953 by Yves Allegret with Pier Angeli, Fernandel, Jean Dubucourt, François Guérin, Georges Chamarat, Michèle Cordoue and Louis de Funès.

CHARACTERS

Denise de Flavigny
The Major, *Comte de Château-Gibus*
Célestin, *music teacher at the Couvent des Hirondelles*
Vicomte Fernand de Champlâtreux
La Supérieure *of the Couvent des Hirondelles*
La Tourière
Corinne, *of the Théâtre de Pontarcy*
Loriot
Sylvie, Gimblette, Lydie, *singers*
Gustave, Robert, *officers*
The Director
The Régisseur, etc.

ACT 1

In the devout and demure precincts of the Convent des Hirondelles the accustomed serenity reigns, and then a man walks in! A man, what is worse, dressed in outrageously colourful clothes who, when he turns away from us, has clearly been the victim of a healthy kick in the backside with a dirty boot. This irregular creature disappears through a door just as the Mother Superior arrives on the scene in search of her organist. When he appears, in the most sober of convent clothes, it is the same man, absolutely metamorphosed.

This duality of nature he is happy to confide in us ('Pour le Théâtre Floridor'). Here at the convent he is Célestin, the model music master, sober, industrious and safe as can be with the budding young ladies whom he teaches, but he has written an *opérette*: an *opérette* which has been accepted and is currently being rehearsed at the Théâtre de Pontarcy, and there he is quite a different fellow—Floridor, the jolly composer, who passes for a man of the world and who has a fine time with the ladies of the chorus and, above all, the glamorous Corinne.

It was Floridor whom we saw first of all. Now he is Célestin and as Célestin he can still feel the boot inflicted on Floridor's seat by an irate military lover of the divette Corinne who was unable to accept Célestin's explanation of his position at the lady's feet as being part of a rehearsal of Scene III. As Célestin he also feels highly apprehensive when, a few minutes later, a visitor announced for the Mother Superior turns out to be the same military gentleman. He is Major the Comte de Château-Gibus and he is her brother.

Célestin carries off his double identity successfully, for the Major has no thought of looking for the rascally Floridor in a convent and, in any case, he has come here on a different kind of errand. A marriage has been arranged between the pride of the convent, little Denise de Flavigny, and one of his officers, the Vicomte Fernand de Champlâtreux, and he wants to ask his sister to allow the young man the opportunity to meet his intended bride. Although it is against all the rules, the Mother Superior agrees to try to arrange something which will not offend propriety.

The young lady in question is now introduced ('Sous les Vieux Arceaux Gothiques') taking the solos in Célestin's school choir. Célestin, however, is not concentrating on his hymns for he has discovered that a certain piece of music is missing from his sheaf. The girls run off to play, but Denise asks if she may spend her playtime in extra music lessons and the delighted Superior hands her over to Célestin. The organist soon discovers his missing music. Denise starts off a 'Gloria in excelsis' which suddenly turns into something very much frothier. It is Floridor's *opérette*!

Denise is by no means the demure damsel she would appear, no Mam'zelle Nitouche or Miss Innocence, but a very lively young creature. She knows all about Célestin-Floridor and his *opérette* and the Théâtre de Pontarcy, and the price of her silence is that he shall take her with him to see the production of his *Babet et Cadet*. Together, they run through the show duet, 'Le Grenadier Était Bel Homme', a duet which metamorphoses into 'Gloria in Excelsis' as the Mother Superior returns. She has news for Denise: she is to meet a man, an inspector of schools who wishes to interview the best pupil in the school. She need not fear, she will not have to actually face the man; the interview will be conducted from behind a screen. By this subterfuge, she introduces Champlâtreux to his fiancée without the girl's knowledge.

The young man disguises his voice ('Pardonnez-Moi, Mademoiselle') to ask Denise about her life in the convent, and she replies with a certain ingenuousness ('Ce N'est Pas un Sinécure'). He is enchanted with her voice, but the Mother Superior prevents him from actually gaining sight of his intended wife. Events move fast, however, for no sooner has the delighted Vicomte departed than the Mother Superior receives a letter from Denise's father. She is to leave the convent that night to return home to prepare for her marriage. The good Mother, after Denise's terrified reactions to the word marriage in the previous scene, cannot bring herself to tell the girl this news and, instead, she tells her that she is to be sent to a different convent, in Paris. So that she need not face the perils of travelling alone, Célestin will accompany her on her journey.

Nothing could suit Denise better. Instead of catching the early train to Paris, they will go and see the first night of the *opérette* and then catch the late train. No one will be any the wiser. Célestin cannot bear the thought of missing his first night and, as Denise bids her little schoolfriends farewell ('Ah! Mes Soeurs, Que Cela M'Afflige'), he agrees to her plot.

ACT 2

At the Théâtre de Pontarcy the first act of *Babet et Cadet* is in progress and the chorus can be heard singing in the distance ('Rions, Buvons, Chantons'). The ladies of the cast are chattering in the foyer, teasing Corinne about her Floridor, while the director of the theatre is arranging a monster wreath with which to crown the composer at the end of what he is sure will be a triumphant night.

The backstage is invaded during the interval by a party of officers with Champlâtreux at their head. He will no longer be one of the gallants of the coulisses for he is to be married to a lovely unknown and his days of flirtation will be over ('Mon Dieu, Je Sais Que Dans le Monde'/'Un Mariage de Raison'). The Major is there too but, when he tries to chastise Corinne for her infidelity, she turns the tables on him effortlessly and expends her charms on the little composer who follows him in. The Major is outraged, and Floridor soon has another boot-mark to show for his troubles.

Célestin has done his best to behave in a manner befitting his convent post. He has locked Denise safely in a hotel room while he sees his *opérette* through, but hotel rooms are easy pickings for Mlle de Flavigny, and she is soon at the theatre ('La Voiture Attendait en Bas'). The first person she encounters there is none other than Champlâtreux and her story—she is a singing pupil who Floridor is taking to Paris—gets quickly to the ears of Corinne. The star is furiously jealous both of the pretty young person and her voice, and she revengefully attempts to wreck the evening's show by refusing to go on for the second act. There is only one solution, Denise knows the whole part—she must go on. After a suitable show of modesty and a quick rehearsal ('À Minuit Après la Fête'), she does exactly that, scoring a huge personal success and confirming the triumph of *Babet et Cadet* and, while she does so, Champlâtreux is falling in love. As Denise hastens off to change before catching the train, he vows that he will refuse the bride his father has chosen for him, for he will wed only this delightful prima donna.

But what is this rumpus which interrupts the descent of the wreath from the flies onto the head of the triumphant Floridor? It is the Major, leaping across the orchestra pit, to throw himself at the little composer to revenge his slighted lady's honour. Across the stage they race, Célestin-Floridor ahead, and the Major, handicapped by the huge wreath which has landed round his neck, in pursuit. Célestin dives for cover in Denise's dressing room and turns the key behind him, and the curtain falls to the sight of the barking Major pounding against the door.

ACT 3

At the barracks, the servant Loriot is doing fatigue duty and waxing biographical ('Je Suis de Saint-Étienne (Loire)') when two unexpected visitors turn up. They are Célestin and Denise, and they are being frogmarched between two guards. They missed their train because they couldn't get past the Major and out of the dressing room and, when they finally clambered out the window, they were picked up as possible malefactors by a passing patrol.

Mam'zelle Nitouche, as the soldiers know her, is quickly recognised by the backstage gallants as the star of the evening, and the two are treated as guests instead of prisoners ('Faut-Il à Leur Galanterie'/'Floridor Vous Avez Raison'). Célestin finds Denise's familiarity with the soldiers a little worrying and he determines on a trick which will pull her up decently short. He will dress up in soldier's clothes and burst in crying, 'Here comes the Major'. Little does he know that Château-Gibus is already in the camp and his arrival on the scene has only been held up by the tipsy antics of the idiotic Loriot. When he sees Célestin in his ill-fitting uniform, he presumes that he is a clumsy conscript and the little man has to let himself be treated as such rather than reveal his identity.

In the meanwhile, Denise blithely sings with the officers (Chant des Fanfares: 'Au Gai Soleil') and proposes that they drink a toast to Champlâtreux and his wife-to-be. When the Major arrives, her companions quickly hide the girl and dress her up as one of them—another clumsy conscript! And one with a history (Légende de la Grosse Caisse: 'Le Long de la Ru' Lafayette'). The Major scents a ruse and orders two horses brought, meaning to test these two improbable soldiers. The 'conscripts' are ordered to mount and Denise, without thinking, gets up side-saddle. Ah-ha! The Major strides purposefully towards the phony soldier and Denise can only save herself by dealing him a whopping blow in the face and scampering away.

Back in the Convent des Hirondelles all is peaceful as two bedraggled figures scramble over the wall. Célestin and Denise are back. With no money and no travel documents—all abandoned in their own clothes—and dressed up like soldiers, there was nowhere to go but back to base. And Célestin hasn't even seen a morning paper to see what his notices were like.

The Mother Superior is puzzled and alarmed. There are footprints in the flower beds, scratches down the mossy walls and footsteps in the music master's rooms—oh dear! But before she can call for help a bizarre figure emerges: it is Célestin dressed in the only clothes which were left in his room—a long black robe and a bee-keepers hat! Explanations are due. Célestin may be able to write music but he's not too good on plots. Denise, on the other hand, has a ready imagination. On the way to the train, she explains, Célestin told her the truth—that she was going to Paris to be married. She told him that, rather than that, she would take holy orders and renounce the world. Under those circumstances, Célestin thought they had better come back. Denise will be a nun.

Now the Major arrives with sad news for his sister. Fernand de Champlâtreux refuses to wed Mlle de Flavigny. His sister is not at all sad. Mlle de Flavigny refuses to wed the Vicomte; she is going to become a nun. When the Major sees the said Mlle de Flavigny, however, he goes into shock.

Dammit, it's his conscript! Denise demurely assures him 'Que Je N'Ai Rien de Masculin' (There's nothing butch about me). The Major is totally confused but highly admiring of Mlle de Flavigny. The young Vicomte de Champlâtreux is a fool to give up this lovely girl for an actress. An actress? Yes, some actress who took over suddenly in the new *opérette* at the Pontarcy last night. Excuse me, says Denise, did you say Champlâtreux? The man she is to marry is called Champlâtreux? Yes. Oh, gosh. (Prière à Sainte Nitouche: 'Je Te Plains Ma Pauvre Denise').

Denise, with innocence never leaving her face, does a delicate volte face. Mother Superior, perhaps she has been a little unkind to reject the young man without even seeing him. Perhaps she should explain her decision in person. So, the screen is set up once again and Fernand and Denise talk, once again, unseen ('Quand Vous Êtes Venu, l'Abbesse') until realisation blossoms in the young man. By the end of the duet he is clasping in his arms a young lady who will never be a nun. Dear Mother Superior, this good, kind gentleman has shown her her error, she will marry him for the most .. religious of motives. And so to everyone (except Célestin and her new husband, who know a thing or two) Denise de Flavigny is still an angel— Mam'zelle Nitouche.

JOSÉPHINE VENDUE PAR SES SOEURS

(Josephine Sold By Her Sisters)

an opéra-bouffe in three acts by Paul Ferrier and Fabrice Carré. Music by Victor Roger. Produced at the Théâtre des Bouffes-Parisiens 20 March 1886 with Jeanne Thibault (Joséphine), Maugé (Alfred), Piccaluga (Montosol), Mme Macé-Montrouge (Mme Jacob), Mily-Meyer (Benjamine) and Lamy (Putiphar Bey). Revived there 1889 with Mily-Meyer, 1890 with Mily-Meyer, 7 February 1906 with Piccaluga and Mily-Meyer. Produced at the Théâtre du Château d'Eau March 1903 with Mlle Thibault, Guyon, Piccaluga and Mily-Meyer.

Produced at the Opera Comique, London, in a version by C M Rae as *Our Diva* 28 October 1886 with Effie Clements, Frank Wyatt, Frank Celli, Mme Amadi and Henry Beaumont.

Produced at Wallack's Theatre, New York, in a version by William von Sachs as *Josephine Sold by Her Sisters* 30 August 1886 with Louise Parker, De Wolf Hopper, Eugene Oudin, Emily Soldene and Mathilde Cottrelly.

CHARACTERS

Alfred Pharaon Pacha
Putiphar Bey, *his nephew*
Montosol, *a baritone*
Madame Jacob, *a concierge*
Joséphine, *her daughter*
Benjamine, *her youngest daughter*

Rébecca, Déborah, Siméonne, Agar, Rachel, Lia, Sarah, Judith, Esther, Dinah, *her other daughters*
Gertrude, *a maid*
The Postman
Mourzouf, *a eunuch*
Fatima, *a harem lady*, etc.

ACT 1

Madame Jacob is the concierge of an apartment building at 97, Rue du Château d'Eau, in contemporary Paris, a position which she holds in succession to her late husband. The departed Jacob has left her with another souvenir as well—twelve of them, to be precise—in the form of twelve daughters whom Madame Jacob has brought up by the sweat of her brow and who are lodged in an apartment in the building which, by a diligent lack of enthusiasm with potential lessees, she has managed to keep unlet. The elder daughters of the family Jacob have jobs by which they add a little to the family coffers ('C'Est-Y Vexant de S'Éveiller'); the youngest, Benjamine, is still unwillingly at school ('D'Abord, On Part d'un Pied Léger'); but the darling of Madame Jacob is the talented Joséphine who has discovered a pretty mezzo-soprano singing voice, and who has been enrolled at the Conservatoire where she is practising to become a star of the musical theatre.

Joséphine gets the best of the larder, lies late in bed and generally irritates her sisters beyond belief with the luxurious life she is allowed to lead. Although her ambitious mother is unaware of it, Joséphine also has a gentleman follower but it is as well that Madame Jacob should remain ignorant of the identity of her daughter's young man for, far from the being the lofty, wealthy gentleman the doting parent has planned as a husband for her little star, Montosol is only a baritone, one of Joséphine's fellow students at the Conservatoire.

Joséphine has more talents than just her mezzo-soprano voice to attract a fine husband and, one day as she is coming out of the Conservatoire, she happens to fall under the eye of the fabulously wealthy Egyptian potentate, Alfred Pharaon Pacha ('C'Est Moi Qui Suis Alfred Pacha'), who is visiting Paris to check up on the westernising education being imposed on his nephew, Putiphar Bey. Alfred is struck all of a heap at the sight of this unknown demoiselle and, determined that Joséphine shall be his, he manages to track her down to her home in the Rue du Château d'Eau.

Discovering that she is the concierge's daughter, he decides that he will justify his presence by renting an apartment in the building, and the horrified Madame Jacob sees with alarm the prospect of her precious free dormitory being whisked away from her. While his uncle is off inspecting the premises, Putiphar—who is homesick for the pyramids and totally unhappy about being westernised ('À Peine au Sortir de l'Enfance')—is cornered by Joséphine's little sister, Benjamine, who ends up playing marbles with him for the want of a more adult occupation.

Joséphine is escorted to the Conservatoire each day by the devoted Montosol ('Oui, Toujours, Joséphine') with the benign consent of Madame Jacob who does not suspect that love songs are lurking in his larynx. On this particular morning, to the delight of the neighbours, he and Joséphine demonstrate their latest duet which Madame Jacob finds rather less musical that the good old songs of her youth and Benjamine considers less amusing than a good saucy modern song (Quartet: 'C'Est En Vain Que Tu Crois Trouver au Monastère'). When they have gone off to their lessons, the rest of the family Jacob return for their skimpy lunch. Once again, the best has been put aside for the budding diva and discontent is rife. 'Who will rid us of this pestilent sister?', they complain and, to their amazement, a voice answers, 'I'.

It is Alfred Pacha who, for reasons which the young women cannot possibly be admitted to comprehend, would like nothing better than to take Joséphine away from the Rue du Château d'Eau back to Egypt and to his harem. Since he cannot make such an unwestern suggestion in front of the girl's family, he insists that he has a vacancy for a diva at the Cairo Opéra. He will provide a contract which the sisters must make Joséphine sign and, as a reward, he will produce delicious gifts for all of them.

The first action the sisters carry out is a tiny bit of treachery: they unveil to Mama the real relationship of Joséphine and Montosol and Madame Joseph, furious at such an unprofitable alliance, forbids the protesting Joséphine ('Dam' C'Est Si Naturel, Maman') to think of involving herself with a pitiful baritone, and chases the operatic swain from the house. The cunning sisters, pretending to side with their diva, encourage her to take revenge by leaving home and taking an engagement. When they produce the Pacha's contract, Joséphine signs it and, in no time at all, she is being handed into Alfred's carriage ('Hâte-Toi, Soeur Chérie') and, before the red eyes of Montosol and Madame Jacob, heading for Egypt.

ACT 2

Egypt is not what it promised to be. Joséphine ends up not in the Opéra but in the harem ('C'Est l'Heure de la Journée'), gorgeously dressed and jewelled and in a raging temper ('Vainement Pharaon Dans Sa Reconnaissance'). When Alfred tries to get close to her he gets a cushion flung in his face. Unfortunately, it hits Putiphar instead. The young man has enough problems without that. His uncle is neglecting his seigneurial duties while he sighs over Joséphine, the country is going to pot and, to top everything, Madame Jacob and her daughters and Montosol have all arrived in Egypt to try to get Joséphine back ('C'Est une Mère de Famille').

Madame Jacob is explosive when she finds out what Joséphine's position in the Pacha household is, and she rushes to clasp her errant child to her bosom ('Dans Mes Bras'). Her staunch arrangements for a hurried homeward trip are suddenly put in reverse, however, when she discovers the value of the gifts which Alfred has been pouring on her daughter and she promptly announces that she will, after all, allow Joséphine to wed the Pacha. This is not quite what Alfred had in mind, and Joséphine is not at all keen to wed anyone but Montosol, but a treacherous whisper from Madame Jacob that the baritone has forgotten his duet partner and wed elsewhere quickly brings the girl round.

Alfred is easy meat for a determined mother, and soon it is all arranged: Alfred and Joséphine shall be wed before the French consul in good western fashion and, in equally good western fashion, Madame Jacob settles in to take over the running of Alfred's palace. The harem shall be dismissed immediately and the palace shall be reorganised to house mother-in-law and her eleven other daughters for whom equally advantageous husbands must be found. Benjamine already has her eye on Putiphar whose physical and mental attractions are minimal, but the challenge of whose indifference ('Rester Garçon Comme Papa') she finds irresistible.

In all this, the one person who has been thoroughly overlooked is poor Montosol whose savings paid for the boat which brought the Jacob family in pusuit of his lost love. He is broken-hearted to hear of Joséphine's planned alliance ('Adieu, Perfide, Adieu, Cruelle') and, in spite of having received a fine offer of an engagement at the new Théâtre Lyrique, he is determined to string himself up from a handy piece of the palace. He finds help in an unexpected quarter when Putiphar, apparently disgusted by his uncle's un-Egyptian behaviour, secretly brings him together with Joséphine.

In a scene which outdoes any of those from the more classic operas they have studied together, the two lovers are dramatically reunited ('Je Lui Disais Encore: Ah! Laissez-Moi Vous Suivre'), but Putiphar's real intent is to disabuse his uncle of his illusions over the Jacob family and he brings Alfred in on this tender scene, claiming some thoroughly oriental punishments like impaling for the guilty parties. The disappointed Alfred is ready to be convinced, but the mass pleadings of the sisters Jacob ('Non, Non, Pas le Pal') are topped by an unanswerable dictate from Madame Jacob. In France, a gentleman walking in on his fiancée in the arms of another man would simply invite the fellow to dinner. Since Alfred aspires to all that is French and civilised, he bites his tongue and agrees, and Putiphar is left confounded.

ACT 3

Under the insistence of Madame Jacob, the whole ménage has shifted from Cairo to Paris where Alfred has set them up in a splendid residence and sponsored advantageous marriages for ten of Joséphine's sisters as a necessary prelude to his own union with the woman with whom he is besotted ('Nous Venons de la Mairie'). Joséphine keeps on finding reasons to delay her own wedding ('Oui, Votre Démarche Est Précoce') and finally Alfred decides he has suffered long enough. His long-term absence from Egypt has earned him dismissal from his official post and, with most of the Jacob girls safely married, he really thinks that it is time for his own wedding.

Joséphine, still trying to delay her fate, declares still that she will not wed until the last of her sisters has taken her marriage vows. The one who remains is Benjamine, and Benjamine has vowed to wed only Putiphar who,

407

in his turn, has solemnly declared that he will never, never, never marry a Parisienne. It looks like an impasse, but Alfred's patience has finally given out. If Joséphine does not accept to be married within two hours he will throw the whole lot of them out of his house, demand the return of the ten dowries, and leave them flat. Madame Jacob's plans look like going severely awry.

This is a good time for Montosol to remind the family once more of his existence. He is now a working man—tomorrow he makes his début at the Nouveau Lyrique in *Le Premier des Abencérages*—and he proffers himself again as a husband for Joséphine with a canny reminder to Mama of her own young amours ('Vous Étiez Jeune et Nous le Sommes'). Finally Madame Jacob weakens. She will say goodbye to Alfred Pharaon Pacha and all his wealth and allow Joséphine to wed the man she loves. It only remains to tell Alfred.

This is up to Mama and, as she girds herself to the task, the young people rejoice that, at last, there is to be a happy ending ('On Est Faché de Vous Déplaire'). Unfortunately, before Mama gets round to making her point with the Pacha, he happens to see Joséphine in Montosol's arms and explodes, but his temperature cools somewhat when Montosol roundly challenges him to a duel. Poor Alfred does not know where he is. He has done everything demanded of him to date with no return, and now he even promises Madame Jacob her heart's desire—the most magnificent of conciergeries—if she can make Joséphine change her mind and wed him.

In the meanwhile, Putiphar has been plotting and he has come up with a plan which will allow him to escape from Paris, back to his beloved Egypt, without losing his uncle's favour and yet unwed to the ever-attentive Benjamine ('Non, Vrai, Monsieur, Je Suis Sincère'). He will fool the family into rejecting Alfred as a spouse for Joséphine by secretly telling them that the Pacha has gone bankrupt.

When he makes his devious pronouncement to Benjamine it does not win the expected response at all. Benjamine is filled with concern and rushes off to tell her family that they must immediately return all the money and gifts Alfred has given them to save him from the horrible fate brought on him by his generosity to them. She herself runs to find her personal piggy-bank to offer its contents to the ruined Pacha. Putiphar is staggered by such a wonderful display of generosity and he revises his opinions of Paris and its Parisiennes, and particularly Benjamine, on the spot.

No sooner has he done so than Alfred turns up clad in his old Egyptian clothes. He too has changed his spots. He has come to the conclusion that sixty willing harem girls are a much better bargain than one eternally difficult and unwilling wife, and he is giving up the Jacob family and returning to Cairo. When Benjamine returns with her piggy bank, Putiphar avows both his trick and his change of heart. He is delighted to marry Benjamine and remain in Paris while Uncle Alfred, on the other hand, renounces both the duel with Montosol and any pretension to the hand of Joséphine. Madame Jacob may have her conciergerie and he will stick henceforth to the sunny shores of Egypt.

LA CIGALE ET LA FOURMI

(The Grasshopper and the Ant)

an opérette in three acts by Henri Chivot and Alfred Duru. Music by Edmond Audran. Produced at the Théâtre de la Gaîté, Paris, 30 October 1886 with Jeanne Granier (Thérèse), Mauguière (Franz), Alexandre (Vincent), Raiter (Fayensberg), Emile Petit (Guillaume), Scipion (Mathias) and Mme Thuillier-Leloir (Charlotte). Revived there in 1887 with Mme Morin, and in 1904 with Juliette Simon-Girard.

Produced at the Lyric Theatre, London, in a version by F C Burnand and Gilbert a' Beckett with additional songs by Ivan Caryll as *La Cigale* 9 October 1890 with Geraldine Ulmar (Marton), Chevalier Scovel, Michael Dwyer, Eric Lewis, E W Garden, Lionel Brough and Effie Clements.

Produced at the Casino Theatre, New York, 26 October 1891 in Burnand's version with Lillian Russell, Carl Streitmann, G Tagliapetra, Charles Dungan, Arthur Ryley, Louis Harrison and Attalie Claire. Produced at the Garden Theatre 26 December 1892 with Miss Russell, Hayden Coffin, W T Carleton, Dungan, John E Dudley, Harrison and Laura Clement.

CHARACTERS

Duc de Fayensberg
Léonora de Fayensberg, *his wife*
Charlotte
Guillaume, *her husband*
Thérèse, *her cousin*
Mathias, *her uncle*
Vincent Knaps
Chevalier Franz de Bernheim
Mère Catherine
La Frivolini
Père Knaps
Beggar, Conrad, Ludovic, Frédéric, Héléna, Christiane, etc.

ACT 1

In a little eighteenth century Flemish village, not so very far from the great city of Bruges, a merry rustic wedding is taking place ('Ils Ont Dit Oui'). The villagers are celebrating the marriage of good man Guillaume and Charlotte, the ant in this story of the grasshopper and the ant. Charlotte is a devoted, home-loving young woman who derives worldly happiness from daily work and household economy, and who will strive every hour to make a worthy life for her husband whom she expects, in the same vein, to be hard-working, obedient and loving (Couplets de la Fourmi: 'Au Temps Passé les Animaux Parlaient').

She is, in her personality, quite the opposite of her much-loved orphan cousin and foster-sister, Thérèse, a joyfully frivolous girl who thinks nothing of spending her last coins to buy coloured ribbons for the village girls and boys to wear at Charlotte's wedding, and who passes her time singing rather than working (Chanson de la Cigale: 'Ah! Vive la Chanson d'Été').

Another family visitor for the wedding is the girls' uncle, Mathias, who has come from the city itself where he has risen to the magnificent post of maître d'hôtel in the up-market Faisan d'Or Hotel. His visit must perforce be brief, as he needs to be back at his post in Bruges to preside over supper, but he has brought a magnificent turkey as a wedding gift and a wealth of good humour to add to the village gaiety.

Thérèse is all agog at Mathias's description of Bruges and its hitherto unimaginable metropolitan delights, but the schoolmaster's son, Vincent, is stirred to anguish at his words, for he nurtures a hidden devotion for the lovely Thérèse and he fears that he will lose her to the city before he has ever gathered the courage to speak of his love. Under Mathias's encouragements, he tentatively approaches his lady ('Allons, Parlez, Je Vous Écoute') and expresses his feeling in metaphor ('L'Oiselet à Sa Compagne Dit'), but he receives small return for his daring. Thérèse does not want to think of marriage yet. She has a whole world to discover first and what she wants is to go back to Bruges with her Uncle.

Mathias will not hear of such a thing but, while the family are saying goodbye to their city uncle (Finale: 'Au Revoir! Au Revoir!'), the determined Thérèse hides in his carriage and, as the wedding festivities continue, she is carried away towards adventure. Thérèse is well practised at getting her own way and, when she is discovered, she manages not to be sent back home and, indeed, she sufficiently wins over Mathias to get him to purchase for her the flower stall in his hotel. The profession of *bouquetière*, however, is not the acme of Thérèse's ambitions. She spends all her profits on visits to the opera and nothing will do but that she must become an opera singer ('Mon Oncle, la Chose Est Certaine').

Two weeks after Thérèse's arrival in Bruges, the Faisan d'Or is the location for a grand masked ball, and many of the local nobility attend to pursue their amorous escapades behind the protection of a domino. The Chevalier Franz de Bernheim comes early to rendezvous secretly with the Duchesse de Fayensberg. It would seem a fairly safe meeting, for it is an open secret that the Duc is in the flower of a liaison with the dancer La Frivolini ('Le Duc d'Humeur Fort Inconstante'), but he turns up in the middle of their scene and the Duchesse is forced to take cover behind a handy screen.

The Duc chafes Franz over what he guesses is a secret love affair and he is only stopped by the arrival of his own inamorata from pulling aside the screen. The Duchesse is so frightened by this narrow escape that she insists Franz pays marked attention to some other woman in order to lay a false scent.

At the ball ('C'Est le Grelot de la Folie'), Thérèse succeeds in gaining entrance to supply the guests with flowers. She is immediately noticed by the Duc who gets the notion that here is Franz's mistress, a notion Franz is only too happy to foster. When Thérèse sings for the assembled company ('Un Jour Margot') the Duc is delighted and vows that he will get her into the opera: she shall be no longer plain Thérèse but La Roseline and she will be a star. The guests toast the Duc's new protégée in champagne ('Ô Vin Charmant, Vin Qui Pétille') as the curtain falls.

ACT 2

Into the hurly-burly of the *kermesse* in the Place des Échevins come Guillaume and Charlotte who have ventured out for a first visit to the city on the back of their donkey ('Le Père Antoine, un Malin'). They are amazed to bump in to Vincent who is supposed to be away travelling on an educational tour around the country but who has, in truth, done nothing more than flee from home to follow Thérèse. He warns them that they will find her very changed. Under the patronage of the Duc she has indeed become a star of the opera, fêted, flowered, jewelled and lodged in a splendid mansion. Mathias has forsaken his old employ to enjoy his niece's new found riches and he, Vincent, in order to remain near her, has taken a post as prompter in the theatre ('Je Souffle! Metier Peu Folâtre'). Franz, who has clearly taken the Duchesse's instructions to heart, has been in almost permanent attendance on the new star, to the irritation of both his mistress and her husband, who is himself intent on conducting a little intrigue with la belle Roseline before she becomes jaded. When Thérèse and Franz come down from the mansion to enjoy the fun of the fair, the Duchesse takes the opportunity to instruct her lover to call off the game, but Franz has changed his old love for a new one and he has no intention of leaving his Roseline.

His conversation with the Duchesse, however, is overheard by Charlotte, Guillaume and Vincent who are horrified to hear that their Thérèse is being used by this aristocratic gentleman to provide a smoke-screen for an affair with an unknown married woman. Thérèse, in the meanwhile, is having a fine time amongst the thronging fair ('Le Coeur Rempli d'Ivresse'). She finds a poor beggar who can scarcely sing his song loudly enough to be heard above the crowd and takes it upon herself to sing for his supper. When the fashionable diva sings 'Ma Mère, J'Entends le Violon', the beggar's cap is soon full of money.

Later in the day, the family make their way to Thérèse's mansion. It is a sensationally rich place in the eyes of the village folk, but Charlotte is not envious—for her, her stout and tidy house is more of a home ('J'Aime Mieux Notre Humble Foyer'). Vincent knows, however, that in spite of the display, Thérèse has no money. Although she earns well, her outgoing nature leads her to spend without thought for the morrow.

La Roseline is Thérèse again in a second when she sees Charlotte and Guillaume, and they are soon reminscing happily ('Petit Noël Avec Mystère'). Thérèse is full of joy as she tells Charlotte of the man she is to marry, the Chevalier Franz de Bernheim, but Charlotte tries to warn her to take more care ('Tu N'As Pas J'En Ai l'Assurance') before Vincent explicitly exposes the overheard conversation at the *kermesse*. The Chevalier is double-crossing her.

Hurt and angry, Thérèse orders everyone out of the house and, when

411

Franz comes to find her, she pours out her heart to him ('Franz, Je Vous Ai Donné Ma Vie') before taxing him with the rumour ('Un Doute Est Dans Mon Coeur'). Franz replies with unbridled ardour and agrees willingly that they should spend the evening together and alone. His words are no sooner spoken than Fayensberg arrives. Both he and his wife are anxious to break up the alliance between Franz and Thérèse and he has come well armed.

When Thérèse refuses his invitation to sing at the ball he is giving that evening, he hands a letter to Franz. It is from the Duchesse telling him that if he does not come to the ball this instant, she will reveal their affair to the whole world. Franz has to go, and he has to go with a patent lie, that the letter is a regimental order. Now Thérèse begins to believe Vincent's story and, armed with so many facts, she finds it easy to trick from Mathias the name of Franz's mistress. Then she sets out to take up the Duc's invitation to his ball.

In the crowded ballroom ('En Cette Demeure Splendide'), Fayensberg is displaying to his guests the new ballet of *Le Jugement de Paris* when La Roseline makes her magnificent appearance. She has come, as requested, to oblige with a song and she has a song ready. It is a little anthropomorphic fable ('C'Est l'Histoire d'un Cigale') with a violent sting in its tail, telling of a rose who wanted to hide its love affair with a butterfly and so ordered him to make love to a little cricket. Franz, she declares to the horrified guests, is the butterfly, she the cricket and as for the rose—she is amongst you! Rushing from the room, Thérèse begins her flight from Bruges.

ACT 3

Down on the farm, life has continued in a much less dramatic fashion ('Que Dans Cette Ferme') as Charlotte and Guillaume continue their busy, peaceable life ('Le Soir Lorsque Chacun A Rempli Sa Journée'). They have a new helpmate in their rustic life for Mathias, unable to hold up his head in town after the episode of the Duc de Fayensberg's ball, has returned to the soil and is making some sort of attempt to reconvert himself into a countryman. Vincent has spent much of the three months which have passed since the incident searching for Thérèse, but she has vanished from Bruges as has Franz de Bernheim.

The Duc de Fayensberg has suffered no better fate, for the scandal has brought the displeasure of his Prince on his head and he has been forcibly rusticated to carry on his dandified flirting amongst the country girls with only half the heart of his town activities. He has, however, been fully convinced by his wife that she was certainly not the mysterious lady—the rose of Roseline's song. In fact, the dear faithful woman has taken it upon herself to go to the Prince's court to persuade him by her pleas to allow her husband to return to town.

The Duc's rustic wanderings eventually bring him to the home of Charlotte and Guillaume, and he is soon followed by Franz who has resigned his commission and, having sought Thérèse throughout the land,

412

has come at last to the home of her childhood in the hope of finding her there ('Oui, la Raison Guidant Son Coeur'). Only when they have all gone does a worn out and tattered Thérèse finally come home. She has been attempting to make a living as a street singer as she wandered frantically up and down the country but, now she has returned, she does not dare knock at the door of the cousins whom she turned away so violently that last dreaful day in Bruges, and she falls asleep shivering under the moon and her old coat.

As she sleeps, she dreams that she has called on Charlotte for aid ('Je Suis Sans Pain et Sans Asile') only to be cruelly rejected and, in her sleep, she cries out in despair. The cry awakens the family who hurry outside to find the poor girl senseless on the ground. When Thérèse awakens, she finds that she is in bed in the room which she occupied as a young girl, and the terror of the dream is chased away by the care of her loving cousins.

It is Christmas, and Thérèse is able to pass a country family Christmas again, far from the mansions of Bruges ('Les Cloches en Carillon'). When Franz and Fayensberg arrive, the talk turns to marriage and Vincent suggests that it is now time for Thérèse to marry and settle down. However, he is not suggesting himself as a husband. He has seen the great love which Franz bears for Thérèse and has realised that it is a much more substantial thing than the affection which he has carried for so many years in his own heart. She must wed Franz. It remains only for Fayensberg to receive the letter from his wife, which announces the success of her mission and his recall to court, for the whole piece to end happily.

For the London production, Ivan Caryll composed a new Introduction and Children's chorus, 'Too Late' (Franz), the chorus 'Dance and Sing', the first act finale 'La Gloria', 'Trifle Not With Love' (Franz), the trio 'Excuse Me, Diva', the second act finale, the 3rd Act opening 'Passe Pied' and the song 'Santa Claus' as well as some incidental music, and arranged and extended some others of Audran's pieces. A gavotte by Lila Clay was introduced into the third act.

MISS HELYETT

an opérette in three acts by Maxime Boucheron. Music by Edmond Audran. Produced at the Théâtre des Bouffes-Parisiens 12 November 1890 with Biana Duhamel (Miss Helyett), Piccaluga (Paul), Désiré (Bacarel), Montrouge (Smithson), Mlle Saint-Laurent (Manuela), Tauffenberger (Puycardas) and Jannin (James). Revived there October 1893, 1895 with Alice Favier, Piccaluga and Charles Lamy, 1896 and 1901. Produced at the Théâtre des Menus-Plaisirs 1893 with Mariette Sully. Produced at the Théâtre de la Renaissance 7 April 1900 with Mlle Duhamel, Piccaluga and Simon-Max. Produced at the Théâtre des Variétés 1904 with Eve Lavallière, Alberthal and Albert Brasseur.

Produced at the Criterion Theatre, London, in a version by F C Burnand as *Miss Decima* 23 July 1891 with Juliette Nesville (Decima Jackson), Charles Conyers (Peter Paul Rolleston), David James (Rev Dr Jeremie Jackson), Josephine Findlay (Inez), Chauncey Olcott (Chevalier Patrick Julius O'Flannagan) and Templar Saxe (Bertie Brown).

Produced at the Star Theatre, New York, 3 November 1891 and played at the Standard Theatre from 11 January 1892 with Mrs Leslie Carter, Mark Smith (Paul Graham), M A Kennedy (Todder Bunnythorne), Harry Harwood (Obadiah Smithson), Laura Clement (Manuela), G W Traverner (Terence O'Shaughnessy) and Joseph Herbert (Jacques)

Produced at the Theater an der Wien, Vienna, 25 December 1891 and at the Carltheater 8 December 1893.

Produced at the Wallner Theater, Berlin, in a version by Richard Genée 7 February 1891.

CHARACTERS

Miss Helyett
Smithson, *her father*
Paul, *an artist*
Bacarel, *his friend*
Puycardas, *a Gascon bullfighter*
James, *a gentleman from Chicago*
Manuela, *a Spanish beauty*
La Señora, *her mother*
Norette, Gandol, Guides, etc.

ACT 1

The atmosphere at the Casino of the Hôtel de Val-Montois in the Pyrénées, during the season, is one of high spirits and low morals as the guests spend their time bathing, romancing and dancing (Casino Waltz/Casino Quadrille) and generally having a thoroughly enjoyable time. There are some, however, who disapprove of this relaxed behaviour and among them are two American visitors, the pastor Smithson and his teenage Salvation Army daughter, Miss Helyett. She has been brought up in such a strict manner that she is horribly shocked to see the French girls, in their bathing costumes, showing more than the permissible portions of their body (the permissible portions being those from the chin up) in front of men (Cantique: 'Le Maître Qui d'En Haut').

The disapproval of the Americans does nothing to halt the young people's fun and they are happy to continue with their merrymaking, but not all of them are there just to have a good time. Paul is a painter and he is hard at work, between his times of leisure, producing pictures. What he really wants is to find the ideal woman to pose for him for, over the past year, he has been reduced to painting conglomerate women, joining together the best features of each of his models ('Pour Peindre une Beauté Complète') but, since his ideal woman is not to be found, he has in despair turned to painting the Pyrénéean landscape.

Also among the guests at the hotel are the Spanish señorita, Manuela, and her lover, the Gascon matador Puycardas ('Je Vous Vis, Vous Me Subju-gâtes'), whose affair has been prevented from progressing into marriage because of the implacable opposition of her mother, La Señora, to a lily-livered son of France as a son-in-law.

The Spaniards are new to Miss Helyett, but Paul is an old acquaintance from the Smithsons' last visit to France, two years earlier, when Miss Helyett was only fourteen. He still sees her as a child although, at sixteen, she is starting to feel that she would like to be treated as a woman. She also wonders what it would be like to loosen some of the severe constraints to which she has been subjugated by her father since her earliest childhood ('Déjà, Dans Ma Plus Tendre Enfance').

Her father is not against her becoming a woman. In fact, one of the purposes of their trips abroad is to permit Miss Helyett to find a husband. Failing better, they have a home-bred postulant already in attendance in the person of James from Chicago who is beggingly anxious to be confirmed as her official fiancée and who, unlike Paul, is altogether willing to treat Miss Helyett as a woman ('Certes J'Aimerais Mieux Connaître'). For the moment, he has no official status and, when Miss Helyett decides to take a walk in the mountains, he is not under any circumstances permitted to accompany her.

Paul, too, has taken to the mountains in order to sketch the countryside as a substitute for his missing model ('Que Ne Puis-Je la Rencontrer') but, whereas he knows the paths well, the mountain walk proves nearly fatal for the little American. When she returns to the hotel, dishevelled and upset, she has a dreadful tale to tell. Walking along the side of a cliff, she lost her footing and fell, head-first, into a ravine. Fortunately, her cloak caught on a handy shrub as she fell, and she was left dangling on the side of the cliff. It would almost have been better if she had tumbled right to the bottom for, oh! shame, in the position in which she was trapped her skirts and petticoats had tumbled over her head, exposing all her lower limbs to the eyes of anyone who should pass.

Worse, when help did arrive, it arrived in the person of a man and, at the sound of his voice, she had just time to hide her face in her cloak before fainting clean away. When she came to, she was alone, propped up against a tree, her head still buried in her cloak, but safe and sound. And also mortified. There can be no question about it, she can never now marry James: she can only be the wife of the unknown rescuer who has cast his eyes on what should be seen only by a husband. While the carefree guests dance gaily to the tune of the 'Gavotte', Smithson and Miss Helyett swear formally to find their man ('Le Maître Qui d'En Haut').

ACT 2

A group of mountain guides are entertaining in the Casino gardens ('Chanson des Petits Guides Pyrénéens') when Smithson and his daughter start, tactfully and sometimes not so tactfully, to question the guests with the aim of discovering the identity of their man. Smithson spies on Paul and his friend Bacarel but can get no joy from them, although Paul seems strangely preoccupied. His preoccupation is, of course, the lower limbs of the young woman whom he rescued earlier in the day from her perilous place on the mountains. Having carried her up from the cliff he was, of course, gentleman enough not to draw aside the cloak and look at the other end of her, so he has no idea who she was. All he knows is that if the top half is as remarkable as the other, he may very well have found the ideal woman whom he has been seeking. In any case, not all is lost as, before carrying her to safety, he took the precaution of sketching the view of her that was visible from the top of the cliff ('Ah! Ah! Le Superbe Point de Vue').

Smithson, carrying out his search with aplomb, gets many a knock-back which he takes hard, while Miss Helyett, who uses more cunning in her questioning, has no such qualms ('Avez-Vous Vu Ramper une Lionne') but also, alas, no more success. Smithson finally decides privately that the situation must be ended as swiftly as possible and, putting aside his principles, he decides that James must confess to being the mysterious man from the mountains. James is only too pleased to lie a little to win his bride and the story he tells rings true enough. Having been refused the pleasure of accompanying Miss Helyett on her walk, he followed her at a distance and, thus, was near at hand when she took her tumble. So, it seems, James is to be the husband of Miss Helyett after all ('L'Homme de la Montagne').

His proposal arouses little emotion in Miss Helyett but, since she is not in love with anyone else, and since he has already apparently been granted one of a husband's prerogatives, she sees no reason not to marry him. While James hurries off to take the news of her acceptance to Smithson, Miss Helyett starts to leaf through Paul's sketch pad which is lying at hand. The artist quickly steps in to stop her and, when she replies to his interdiction with some vivacity, he realises that she is not altogether the little girl he remembers. She is in agreement with that—she is a woman now—but he insists that she lacks one essential ingredient of a woman, coquetry ('Ce Qui Donne à Toute Femme l'Attrait'). She is thinking that one over and musing on the newly noticed attractions of the artist, when the suddenly repentant James comes back to confess that he has lied.

When Miss Helyett realises that her father was behind the deception she feels that she no longer knows who and what to believe in but, as she ponders sadly alone, she overhears an argument which seems to have a bearing on her case. Manuela's mother is making one of her frequent meals of poor Puycardas who, obliged to defend his reputation as a gallant and brave man, boasts of how he recently saved a young woman in the mountains. Miss Helyett needs to hear no more. Here, undoubtedly, is her real saviour and her husband-to-be.

But La Señora is finally prepared to give in and permit her daughter and the Gascon to become engaged, on the condition that she comes to live with them after the marriage ('Reconnaissez En Moi la Mère de Famille'). Miss Helyett realises she must move quickly and she corners Puycardas, demanding that he describe his rescue in detail. Thinking that he is talking to a fan, the matador gallantly declares that the woman in question was very plain and he is left wondering why the little lady has slapped his face and run off. But

she is not finished with him. When the official announcement of his engagement to Manuela is made before the guests, Miss Helyett steps forward to
announce that it will be her and not Manuela who will be the wife of the
matador. Wild words fly, and the act ends in confusion.

ACT 3

The fight between Miss Helyett and Manuela over Puycardas makes a
wonderful scandal ('Avez-Vous Vu Ce Scandale'), but Paul does not join in
the chaffing and, indeed, he finds himself distinctly annoyed to hear the
jokes which circulate at the young girl's expense. The strength of his feelings
surprises even himself and he wonders if he might be falling in love with the
girl whom, up till this time, he has always thought of as a child. Perhaps he is,
but she is clearly intending to wed Puycardas, so it is better that he leave Val-
Montois immediately.

Miss Helyett is sad to see him go, but she is obliged, through propriety, to
wed Puycardas and wed him she will, even though she loves him not and he
is in love with Manuela. Wed him she will even if Smithson has to force him
to the altar at the end of a revolver. Under such pressing circumstances, the
matador can only agree to do what he is told ('Ne Suis-Je Pas Celle Qui
T'Aime?'). In the face of such cowardice, Manuela stalks out on her former
sweetheart and her mamma delivers the *coup de grace* to her daughter's
relationship with this feeble Frenchman in a fine tirade ('C'En Est Fait, Il
Faut Nous Quitter').

Alone in her room, Miss Helyett sits in front of her mirror and thinks of
Paul. There is no way he could ever have fallen in love with her, so tight and
strict in her Salvation Army uniform. Sadly she unties her hair and lets it fall
over her shoulders and, taking a flower, tries to place it amongst her locks.
But, as she does so, she sees in the mirror that Paul is standing at the door.
He starts to tell her how lovely she is but, thinking he is making fun of her,
she bursts into tears. He clasps her in his arms and she is happy to be there
until she suddenly recalls the man in the mountain and pulls away. Whatever
she feels, that is the man she must marry.

To try and cheer her, Paul offers to draw her portrait (Duo du Portrait:
'Pour Que Votre Image Adorée') and, when he has finished, Helyett comes
to look at the result. But as she takes the sketch pad in her hands, she lets it
fall and, as it falls, the page opens at the sketch which Paul had made of her
hapless tumble. With a gasp, Helyett understands the significance of the
sketch: Paul is her unknown rescuer and the man she must marry. Puycardas, who has now lost Manuela to James, demands to see the document
which has caused this change of heart, but the sketch book is not for general
publication. It is and will remain 'family papers'.

LES 28 JOURS DE CLAIRETTE

(Clairette's Twenty-Eight Days)

a vaudeville-opérette in four acts by Hippolyte Raymond and Antony Mars. Music by Victor Roger. Produced at the Théâtre des Folies-Dramatiques, Paris, 3 May 1892 with Marguerite Ugalde (Clairette), Guyon fils (Vivarel), Vauthier (Gibard), Guy (Michonnet) and M Stelly (Bérénice), and played there in April 1893 and 1903. Produced at the Théâtre de la Gaîté 5 September 1895 with Mariette Sully, Lucien Noël, Landrin, Paul Fugère and Mlle Lebey and again 1 January 1901. Produced at the Théâtre des Bouffes-Parisiens 1900 with Mily-Meyer, Jean Périer, Lamy and Anna Tariol-Baugé. Produced at the Théâtre de la Porte Saint-Martin 1908 with Juliette Simon-Girard. Produced at the Théâtre de la Gaîté-Lyrique 1913 with Angèle Gril, Lorrain, Clarel and Dolne; 1914 with Mlle Gril; 4 September 1920 with Mlle Gril, Félix Oudart, Roques, Girier and Denise Grey; and 1925 with Marguerite Gilbert, Darriet, Jean Suzan, Détours and Marthe Dorna.

Produced at the Opera Comique, London, in a three act version by Charles Fawcett as *Trooper Clairette* 22 December 1892 with Alice Atherton, Percy F Marshall, Fred Mervin, John Wilkinson, Hilda Abinger and Willie Edouin as the Captain.

Produced at the Adolf Ernst Theater, Berlin, as *Lolotte's 28 Tage* September 1895 with Alexander Klein, Gisela Fischer and Frln Schlüter.

The Little Trooper by Clay Greene and William Furst, produced at the Casino Theatre, New York, 30 August 1894 with Della Fox and Jefferson de Angelis was based on *Les 28 Jours des Clairette*.

A film version was produced in 1935 with Mireille.

CHARACTERS

Michonnet, *a gasman*
Vivarel
Gibard
Le Capitaine
Saturnin Benoît, *a pastrycook*
Pépin
Le Vicomte
Clairette Vivarel
Bérénice Pistachon, *proprietor of a hat shop*
Nichotte, *a peasant girl*
Octavie, *a modiste*
Poireau, Gardien, Estelle, Charlotte, Mariette, Aline, Virginie, etc.

ACT 1

The story opens in an overstaffed, *fin de siècle*, Parisian hat shop bustling with gossiping shopgirls ('Pour Avoir des Chapeaux Bien Faits'). The shop and its girls are a decided attraction for other occupants of the street and Monsieur Benoît, the local pastrycook, is wont to drop in with tempting and fattening goodies while Monsieur Michonnet, the gas fitter, is for ever detecting gas leaks which need his attention every bit as much as the plump arms and well-filled corsets of the girls ('Je Veux d'Abord, Je le Confesse').

418

What they do not know is that Michonnet carries a little spray which makes a gaseous smell to justify his continued calls.

The good-humoured atmosphere of the shop does not rub off on its *patronne*, the pretty Bérénice, for Bérénice is suffering from *chagrin d'amour*. Once upon a not so long ago, Bérénice had a lover, a tall, distinguished, blonde lawyer with lovely sideburns. Then, one dreadful day, he failed to turn up and for three whole months she has been awaiting his return in vain ('De Ci de Là, Je Cherche un Homme') and the shop which she has bought to distract her mind from her woes has done nothing to cheer her. She would be envious if she knew of the good fortune of her client, Mademoiselle Pastoureau. Clairette Pastoureau has just become Madame Vivarel and she is blissfully happy.

It all came about in a very strange way. Clairette's father wanted a boy child and, in consequence, his daughter was brought up to be expert in such manly skills as fencing, boxing, riding and gymnastics. One day, about three months ago, Clairette was saved from a bull which had got loose in the street by the intervention of a young lawyer called Vivarel. In gratitude, the young woman declared that she would marry him and, when he refused, she laid him low with a pair of sturdy punches, challenged him to a duel in which she emerged an easy winner ('En Tierce, En Quarte, En Quinte, En Prime') and before long she was the bride of the dazzled lawyer.

Today Clairette has returned to one of her maiden haunts, the hat shop, for a little shopping. She has made arrangements to meet Vivarel there, but she has other calls to make and, when her husband does not show up, she goes off on her own, leaving him, upon his late arrival, to the giggles of the shopgirls and the gasps of the proprietress. For Vivarel is none other than the lost lover of Bérénice Pistachon. Under her effusive welcome ('Donne-Moi Donc un Bon Baiser Bien Tendre'), Vivarel has not the courage to own up to the real reason for his sudden disappearance nor to his newly found marital status. He has a very good reason for refusing an invitation to dinner, however, for he is due that very evening to report to the barracks at Montargis to begin his twenty eight days—his four weeks of national army service.

Just then, Gibard, a sergeant of hussars from Montargis, turns up to collect his colonel's wife's hat and, as an old friend of Vivarel, he is delighted to hear that he is married. From their familiarity, he assumes that the new Madame Vivarel is Bérénice and he insists that Vivarel have the night out of barracks with his lovely lady. Soon the real Madame Vivarel returns. She is going unwillingly to spend the month of her husband's service with her aunt in Angoulême, but she eternally suspects her husband of contemplating infidelity ('Avec Moi C'est Tout ou Rien') and she would much rather be somewhere where she could keep an eye on him.

Vivarel is obliged secretly to lock Bérénice in her room to keep her out of the way as he prepares to set off for his twenty-eight days in the comparative safety of Montargis. Michonnet and Benoît are scheduled to be part of the same intake, but they get involved in a jealous little quarrel over the shopgirls which ends up with Benoît dumping a cream cake on his opponent's head

(Finale: 'Allons! Allons, Voulez-Vous Bien Finir?') and being carried off to jail ('Devant le Commissaire') as Vivarel drags Clairette away and Bérénice pounds furiously on her locked door.

ACT 2

The soldiers of Montargis are an odd lot ('Dans l'Onde Claire et Pure') including, as they do, men drawn from all ranks of society but not in the usual order. Here a captain can be a wine-merchant from real life while his subordinate is a full-blown Vicomte. Vivarel is lucky to have a regular friend in Gibard and Gibard is in a particularly jolly mood after having indulged in the beginning of a promising flirtation with a particularly lovely lady in the train on his way back to barracks ('C'Est le Galon').

Vivarel is less lucky with women. Bérénice has followed him from town to accuse him of playing her false with a mistress and, since he persists in believing that this is Madame Vivarel, Gibard does everything he can to facilitate their nights, at least, being spent together. Bérénice also goes down well with Vivarel's captain, and he sweeps her off for a little tour with fortunate timing for, a minute later, Clairette arrives at the barracks. Her aunt wasn't at home in Angoulême, so she has come back on the first available train ('Devant la Porte, Je M'Arrête') and who should be the first person whom she meets but Gibard, the hussar who flirted with her on the train.

Hearing her ask after Vivarel, Gibard tells her with colourful detail that the lawyer-soldier is with his wife. Clairette swallows her double take and Gibard, assuming that her emotion is that of a mistress balked by the presence of a legitimate spouse, cunningly offers himself as a substitute. When Vivarel returns, Clairette is frigid and furious and vowing that she will be revenged on her faithless husband. Vivarel attempts to explain the real situation to his friend, but Gibard suspects him of trying to prevent him from paying attentions to the mistress whilst he is busy with the wife, and he refuses to believe that Clairette is Madame Vivarel.

At the approach of the Captain, Clairette has to be hidden, and she takes the opportunity to don a spare soldier suit and present herself to the Captain as the missing Benoît, who is somewhere in jail on the other side of town. Thus disguised ('Je Suis Benoît, le Réservisse'), she can stay at the barracks and both watch over and take her revenge on her errant husband. Vivarel, to save his own skin, has to join in the deception and Gibard is delighted at the thought of having this pretty young 'man' in the barracks.

But now the real Benoît turns up, released after his night in prison. There is nothing else to do but trump up a charge and carry the poor fellow straight off to another, military, jail. Danger is still not over, however, for they have reckoned without Clairette's quick temper. She has managed in no time to get into a quarrel with Michonnet and has struck him—a blow which indubitably calls for an affair of honour, a duel (Finale: 'Oui! le Règlement Est Formel'). The gas fitter has no experience of such affairs and he is soundly and ridiculously trounced by the false Benoît.

ACT 3

The regiment does not stay at Montargis. It is soon out on manoeuvres and the billeting system separates Vivarel and Clairette. He is lodged in an old castle with Gibard, wondering where she is ('Ma Femme, Ma Petite Femme'), and bristling with fury at his companion's refusal to take his claims that she is his wife with anything but a rude laugh. They are served by a gormless peasant girl called Nichotte who takes her tips in kisses rather than cash ('Eh! Donc Si le Coeur Vous En Dit'). She seems totally unfazed by having a bundle of soldiers landed in the house and is quite prepared to stay up all night seeing to their needs.

The Captain and the soldier Pépin are also billeted in the castle and Nichotte bustles about organising suitable sleeping arrangements for them, but there is a problem when first Clairette and then Michonnet turn up requiring beds as well. The obvious answer is to share, but Clairette is determined not to sleep alongside the gasman and she goes to farcical lengths to keep her distance from him. The situation gets even more ridiculous when Vivarel sees his wife through the dormer window, creeps in to join her, and ends up kissing Michonnet with whom she has exchanged beds.

Clairette is not yet ready to forgive her husband, and when he finds his way to her she repulses him thoroughly, pointedly allows Gibard to 'protect' her, and finally punches Vivarel in the nose. Michonnet is aghast to see a soldier thus strike his superior officer and calls loudly for the guard. In spite of Vivarel and Gibard's attempts to pretend that nothing has happened, Clairette-Benoît is dragged off to the guard house.

ACT 4

The next day is a rest day and the soldiers enjoy themselves dancing in the gardens of the castle with the local girls ('En Avant, les Joyeux Quadrilles') while Michonnet and Gibard entertain with a jolly song ('Trinquart et Trinquet'). When the castle's owner opens a cask of wine for her guests, the soldiers hurry off, leaving Michonnet on guard in front of Benoît-Clairette's prison. He is not at all happy at being the cause of the young soldier's imprisonment, but he is even less happy when he hears that the penalty for the misdemeanour is the firing squad. It will all be his fault! Michonnet decides that he must help the young fellow escape. He persuades Nichotte to bring a spare set of feminine clothes and gives them to Clairette. 'He' shall get away disguised as a girl ('Non, Me Voyez-Vous Devant Eux'). But then, who should turn up again but the real Benoît. There is nothing else to do but to shut him up for a third time, in Clairette's prison, while she makes her escape.

Now the other recurring problem turns up again—Bérénice. She knows that 'Benoît' is not a man but a girl, and she suspects that Vivarel has organised the whole affair in order to have his mistress with him. She jealously unveils the secret to the Captain and he orders Benoît brought forth. The petrified fellow will agree to anything rather than defy authority and end up yet again in prison. He will even agree, if necessary, that he is a

421

woman ('C'Est une Femme!'), until he finds out that impersonating a soldier is worth a month's imprisonment. Unfortunately, if he is a man he is up for the firing squad for having struck an officer, so it is better to remain a girl and act the part to its hilt. The charade is ended when the guard brings in Clairette, captured as she tried to get away. She insists that she is not Benoît but Madame Vivarel and Michonnet realises with regret that he spent the previous night sharing his room with a delightful woman.

Gradually the story is unfolded to the Captain who laughs heartily at the marital mishaps of the Vivarel family but who takes furious umbrage at Benoît's lying over his sex. Poor old Benoît ends up being sent to the guard house yet again. Bérénice is desolate to hear that the soldier-girl is truly Madame Vivarel, and Clairette is no less unforgiving, so both women end up sobbing on the shoulder of Gibard until the Captain takes charge and gives an order to his subordinate 'Benoît' that 'he' must forgive his husband. Clairette submits like a good soldier whilst Bérénice finds quick solace in the arms of the jolly Gibard.

LA POUPÉE

(The Doll)

an opéra-comique in four acts by Maurice Ordonneau. Music by Edmond Audran. Produced at the Théâtre de la Gaîté, Paris, 21 October 1896 with Mariette Sully (Alésia), Dacheux (Hilarius), Paul Fugère (Lancelot), Gilles Raimbaut (Mme Hilarius) and Paul Bert (La Chanterelle), and revived there 1898. Produced at the Théâtre Mogador 10 September 1921 with Mlle Mathieu-Lutz.

Produced at the Prince of Wales Theatre, London, in a version by Arthur Sturgess and Clifton Bingham 24 February 1897 with Alice Favier, Willie Edouin, Courtice Pounds, Kate Mills and Charles Wibrow. Revived there 13 December 1898 with Stella Gastelle, Edouin, Pounds and George Humphery; and 12 April 1904 with Edna May, Edouin, Roland Cunningham, Marianne Caldwell and Wibrow. Produced at Daly's Theatre 24 December 1931 with Jean Colin, Mark Lester, Patrick Waddington, Mina Greener and Conway Dixon.

Produced at the Lyric Theatre, New York, 21 October 1897 with Anna Held, Joseph Herbert, Frank Celli, Catherine Lewis and Frank Rushworth. Produced at Daly's Theatre 15 April 1898 with a cast including Virginia Earle, James T Powers, G W Anson, Trixie Friganza, Arthur Cunningham and Rushworth.

Produced at the Centraltheater, Berlin, 5 January 1899.

CHARACTERS

Le Père Maximin
Balthazar, Basilique, Agnelet, Benoît, *brothers of the monastery*
Lancelot, *a novice*
Maître Hilarius
Madame Hilarius, *his wife*
Alésia, *their daughter*

La Chanterelle, *uncle to Lancelot*
Lorémois, *his friend*
Josse, *Hilarius's assistant*
Guduline
Loïse, Martine, Marie, etc.

ACT 1

The action of the piece takes place in a possible country in the time of probably. It is a country and a time very familiar to the habitués of the *opérette*, but it is by no means the happy land of story books for, here and now, hard times have struck, even to the heart of the local monastery. The monks, who in earlier years were accustomed to wander through the local villages exchanging blessings for solid provisions and sizeable, tasty gifts, are finding that they can no longer raise the wherewithal from their parishioners to keep their stomachs from rumbling in the middle of a paternoster ('Hélas, la Dîme A Fait Son Temps').

Today's haul is limited to two chickens, a rabbit and some carrots, plus two sour herrings wrapped in a newspaper which the personable but naïve novice, Lancelot, has unwittingly charmed from a local housewife. Lancelot pleads his inexperience as an excuse for this meagre contribution; he has a chronic shyness of the women who make up such a large part of that outside world which he has learned to despise and shun ('Je Suis Timide et Quand Je Vois'). It is fairly obvious that the food they have gathered will not go around the entire monastery and it seems that very soon the monks will be obliged to exist on the produce of the monastery gardens which grow nothing but black radishes.

There is, however, one other possibility. Lancelot's uncle, the wealthy Baron de la Chanterelle, might be persuaded by his nephew to make the donation necessary to put the monastery back on its old convivial tracks. Alas, La Chanterelle nurtures a perfect loathing for everything that wears a habit and he has even threatened to disinherit the gentle Lancelot if he persists in his wish to become a monk. He has, on the other hand, offered him a vast dowry for the day that he marries. Lancelot clearly has little chance of pleasing both the monastery and his uncle.

That little chance does exist, though, and, as the Abbot leafs ruefully through the paper used to wrap the herrings, he comes upon an item which stirs his imagination. In the village of Tamponville there lives a sculptor named Hilarius who, the paper relates, has developed the art of doll-making to a new perfection. His creations not only look like human beings, they even speak like human beings. Since Lancelot must marry, and since he must also not risk his monastic chastity, why could he not be married to one of these dolls?

The old baron who, tales tell, is half-stupid and three-quarters blind from alcoholism and libertinism, will never notice the difference, and Lancelot will be able to win the money and save the monastery's refectory from withering away. Lancelot is only too happy to do anything he can to help and the Abbot is quick to encourage him on his way to Tamponville ('Vous Allez

Quitter Notre Humble Retraite'), harmonically seconded by the entire monastery ('Au Son de Clochette'). As the Angelus tolls ('L'Angelus au Soleil
Couchant'), Lancelot turns his face towards his future and marches out of
the monastery gates.

ACT 2

At the workshop of the sculptor Hilarius, the great man and his assistant
Josse are creating a new doll to add to the amazing collection already on
display. Hilarius's latest masterpieces are dolls fashioned after his daughter,
Alésia, and his wife, dolls so lifelike that even he has made the mistake of
attempting to retouch the nose of his own wife, mistaking her for her waxen
counterpart. Unfortunately, when the two women went to dress these dolls
in some of their own clothes, the dolls were accidentally broken. The women
have secretly sent them to be mended but, since Hilarius is liable, on past
form, to commit suicide in the event of anything harming his beloved creations, Alésia and Madame Hilarius have taken to posing in their stead
whenever the sculptor goes near the place where the two models are stored.

Alésia's mother has noticed that her daughter has had something other
than this particular crisis on her mind for the past few days, something
clearly serious, for she has taken to going to church every day instead of just
on Sundays. Needless to say, the answer is in the masculine gender. Alésia
has seen a young man in the congregation who is so gentle, so attractive and
so fervent in his praying that she has fallen in love with him ('Mon Dieu,
Sait-On Jamais En Somme'). There is no time for Madame Hilarius to go
too deeply into the why-nots of the case at the moment, for Hilarius is heard
returning with a customer and it is time for the two women to turn themselves into dolls.

The customer is none other than Lancelot ('Dans les Couvents On Est
Heureux') whom Hilarius, made party to the trick which is intended, treats
to a display of the contents of the atelier: Pierrot and Polichinelle, Harlequin
and Columbine and, finally, Alésia and Madame Hilarius. Understandably,
this last pair seem to Lancelot to be by far the most convincing and he is only
too pleased to watch the sculptor put Alésia through her mechanical paces
('Je Sais Entrer Dans un Salon').

Alésia is barely able to master her emotions, for Lancelot is the young man
from the church upon whom she has set her heart, but she convincingly
displays her mechanical art in reading, arithmetic, history and particularly in
singing for, when she is left alone with Lancelot, she bursts into a passionately forward number ('Je T'Aime, Je T'Adore') which Lancelot finds
strangely agreeable. The young man is delighted—Alésia is precisely what
he requires. She will do very nicely for his wedding.

When the word wedding reaches the ears of the two women, Madame
Hilarius practically faints, but dire threats from the delighted Alésia make
her hold her tongue. It is decided that Madame Hilarius will be thrown in as
a job lot—she can make a fine aunt who will lend propriety to the
ceremony—and Lancelot hands over his money to become the owner of two

very unusual dolls. The dolls are bundled off to be wrapped and crated as Lancelot and Hilarius prepare to head for the Château la Chanterelle and matrimony (Finale: 'Les Caisses Suivront Ma Voiture').

ACT 3

At the château, La Chanterelle and his drinking companion Lorémois are greeting the rising sun with a bottle or two of burgundy. Lancelot and Hilarius, who arrived the previous evening, have prepared the ground for today's wedding and this morning, after the two bottles have been emptied, La Chanterelle is to meet the bride-to-be. Alésia and Madame Hilarius managed to escape being crated and made their own way to the château where they have been comfortably installed in private chambers, much to the amusement of Hilarius, whose loose tongue causes many a double entendre as he keeps forgetting that he is supposed to be speaking of people and not dolls.

Alésia manages to introduce herself to La Chanterelle and Lorémois when no one else is about and it is quite plain, even to someone who isn't erupting with red wine, that this is no doll but a very attractive young woman ('Lancelot Vient de S'Éloigner'). The two old soaks are equally taken with the more buxom Madame Hilarius (who has been shut up in a cupboard by her myopic husband) and La Chanterelle, amazed at the compliant jokes of the doll-maker, makes a heavy pass at her ('Ah! Que N'Ai-Je Connu Plus Tôt').

Soon it is time for the wedding ceremony and the château becomes host to a bevy of guests ('Nous Voici, Cher Baron, Pour la Cérémonie') as Lancelot and Alésia are married in front of the notary. When the deed is done and Lancelot finds himself alone with his doll-wife he almost finds himself regretting that she is not a real woman. If real women are like this one, they cannot be as bad as he has been taught ('Que C'Est Donc Gentil, une Femme').

The wedding feast begins, the music swells and the wine flows, and Madame Hilarius finds La Chanterelle professing adoration at her feet while her husband only laughs up his sleeve to see how his wonderful creations have tricked everyone. Alésia and Lancelot have both dipped their unaccustomed lips into champagne and, like the rest of the party, they are in high spirits ('Nous Avons Bu, Nous Sommes Gris'/'Comme Tout Tourne Autour de Moi'). When, by tradition, Alésia is called on for a song, Hilarius hurriedly whispers to Lancelot to press Button B. That is the button for the polite little song, Button A is for the rather more lively one. Alésia is not in any mood to respond to the pressing of her Button B, and she bursts into 'Les Plaisirs du Mariage'.

At the end of the song, the married couple are led to their carriage. Lancelot is going to take his 'wife' back to the monastery. After all, she is only a doll. No sooner have they departed than a little scene breaks out. La Chanterelle goes too far in his attentions to Madame Hilarius and she lets forth with a healthy slap and a hefty tirade. The sound of his wife's voice comes to the ears of the myopic sculptor and realisation begins to dawn. If this is his wife, then the other doll must be his daughter. He has sold his daughter as a doll and married her to a monk!

ACT 4

Back at the monastery, the monks are burning their midnight oil, anxiously awaiting the return of Lancelot ('Minuit! et Frère Lancelot'). By the time he arrives, they have given up and gone to bed which is, perhaps, just as well for, on the way, he has partaken rather liberally of the 'tisane' which the bibulous Lorémois has given him to help dissipate the little spots which are dancing in front of his eyes. Alésia is still doing her best to act the role of a doll but she knows that, doll or no doll, she is the legally married wife of Lancelot and that the deception will have to be unveiled some time.

She is vastly taken aback when the Abbot and his monks appear and she realises that she has been brought to a monastery. The delighted monks cluster around to examine how she is made ('Voyons l'Objet'), admiring her with a very unmonastic enthusiasm as she shows off her talents ('Je Suis un Petit Mannequin'), but the Abbot decides that the doll is warming the minds of his pensionnaires in an altogether unhealthy fashion and he hurries them back to their cells. The innocent Lancelot pulls him aside for a private word. It is ridiculous, but he feels the most strange sentiments. Surely he cannot be falling in love? The good Abbot assures him that the feeling is simply one of excitement brought on by the festivities and leaves him to spend the night with his waxen bride.

Lancelot begins to undress himself for bed and, finding no other handy receptacle, hangs up his clothes on the arms of the blushing doll. It is only when he is dozing that Alésia feels bold enough to drop her pretence and leans over to plant a kiss on her husband's cheek. It is enough to wake him from his sleep into a reverie of a woman's embrace ('On Dirait Comme une Caresse de Femme'), but finally he dismisses such thoughts and falls back asleep. Alésia, realising that she has not thought her escapade through, decides that the best thing she can do for the moment is creep away out of the monastery but, before she does, she will write a note to her beloved husband admitting her trick.

She is seated at a table writing when Lancelot opens his eyes again and beholds, to his amazement, his doll-wife alive. It is too much, and his full heart bursts out its love to her ('Quoi! la Femme Donne à l'Ame') until a pounding is heard at the monastery gates ('Qui Démolit le Couvent'). La Chanterelle and Hilarius have come in pursuit of the young couple ('Nous Sommes Fourbus'). Hilarius and his wife are happy just to find their daughter safe and sound, while La Chanterelle is delighted. As a married man, Lancelot will have to give up monastic life as it is clearly necessary for the Abbot to release the young man from his vows.

A soul may be lost, but a stomach lining is gained. Lancelot has won his dowry and he promises that half of it shall go to the monastery. The Abbot's table will be spared from the dreadful black radish while Lancelot and Alésia live happily ever after.

LES P'TITES MICHU

(The Little Michus)

an opéra-comique in three acts by Albert Vanloo and Georges Duval. Music by André Messager. Produced at the Théâtre des Bouffes-Parisiens, Paris, 16 November 1897 with Alice Bonheur (Marie-Blanche), Odette Dulac (Blanche-Marie), Manson (Gaston), Barral (General des Ifs), Maurice Lamy (Aristide), Regnard (Michu) and Mme Vigouroux (Mme Michu). Produced at the Théâtre des Folies-Dramatiques 1899 with Mariette Sully, Mlle Lebey and Jean Périer.

Produced at Daly's Theatre, London, as *The Little Michus* in a version by Henry Hamilton 29 April 1905 with Mabel Green, Adrienne Augarde, Robert Evett, Willie Edouin, Ambrose Manning, Amy Augarde and Huntley Wright (Bagnolet).

Produced at the Garden Theatre, New York, 31 January 1907.

Produced at the Metropol Theater, Berlin, in a version by Heinrich Bolten-Bäckers 25 December 1898.

Produced at the Carltheater, Vienna, in the version by Bolten-Bäckers 16 September 1899.

CHARACTERS

General des Ifs
Michu, *a shopkeeper of Les Halles*
Madame Michu, *his wife*
Marie-Blanche, Blanche-Marie, *their daughters*
Aristide, *their shop assistant*
Gaston Rigaud, *captain of hussars*
Mademoiselle Herpin, *headmistress of the Institution Herpin*
Bagnolet
Irma, Pamela, Palmyre, Ida, Francine, Estelle, Madame du Tertre, Madame Rosselin, Madame Saint-Phar, Madame d'Albert, Deputy Schoolmistress, etc.

ACT 1

The Institution Herpin is a school run on military lines by its principal, Mlle Herpin, a maiden lady of army extraction, and the pupils there take all the instructions for their daily activities from the sound of a drum in the playground ('Le Tambour Résonne'/'En Deux Temps, Trois Mouvements'). But there is plenty of time for play, and the leaders amongst the girls once ranks are broken are the two delightful Michu sisters, Marie-Blanche, blonde and vivacious, and Blanche-Marie, dark and charming, and

427

absolutely inseparable ('Blanche-Marie et Marie-Blanche'). The girls are seventeen and beginning to turn heads, but they are still schoolgirls with time for girlish pleasures.

A game of forfeits leaves Blanche-Marie bound to kiss the firstcomer into the school playground and she is in some confusion when it turns out to be a man, and a very attractive man at that. He is Gaston Rigaud, the headmistress's nephew, back from the siege of Saragossa and newly promoted to the rank of captain for his valour in support of his general. He helps Blanche-Marie from her consternation with a gentle kiss on the forehead ('Quoi, Vous Tremblez, Belle Enfant') and the sisters introduce themselves, allowing Gaston to even things up with an equally chaste kiss for Marie-Blanche ('Michu, Michu, Michu').

The girls listen secretly to the handsome officer's meeting with his aunt and discover that his reward for valour has come not only in rank. He has been granted the hand of his general's daughter in marriage. Lucky Irène des Ifs! Marie-Blanche rather thinks that she wouldn't mind taking her place ('Sapristi, le Beau Militaire'), but the fine soldier is all but forgotten as the girls become children again and race each other to the end of the playground.

Since it is Thursday, Mama and Papa Michu come to the school ('Nous V'la'/'A l'Ouvrage Dès Que Vient le Matin') to distribute goodies from their shop to the pupils ('Voici Papa, Maman Gâteau'). They are a fond couple, with Maman clearly both the brains and brawn of the family, and they are devoted to their lovely daughters. Aristide, their commis, is devoted to the girls too. He is so devoted that he has had three months of sleepless nights trying to decide to which he is the more devoted ('Blanche-Marie Est Douce et Bonne') and his suffering can be ended only by having someone else decide to which he should give his heart. In the meanwhile, he asks their father for both their hands and is decidedly glum when he's told to wait for a few years.

His offer, however, wreaks concern in the heart of Madame Michu. One day the children must indeed wed, and then the Michus will have a problem. For the truth is that only one of the two girls is their daughter. The other is a daughter of a Marquis, given into their charge when, with the father fleeing the revolution abroad, her mother died in child-birth. In seventeen years nothing has been heard from the father, but what if they were to wed a noble child to the likes of Aristide? The heart of the problem lies in the fact that, soon after the birth of the two little babies, while Mme Michu rested from her labour, Michu decided to bath the babes. When the time came to dry them, he'd forgotten which was which.

Papa and Maman Michu have barely had the time to go over the story for our benefit before the moment they have so long dreaded is upon them. The Marquis is not only alive, he has tracked them down and has sent his minion, Bagnolet, to order them to present the daughter of the Marquis des Ifs, now a general in the French army, to his home that very day. The pair play for time, explaining without explaining, and Bagnolet can only gather that, for some reason, there are two girls where he thought there was only one and

428

that both must come along. The whole school gathers to take part in the finale as *les p'tites Michu* set off to a martial rat-a-plan ensemble ('Que Veut Dire Ce Roulement').

ACT 2

At the home of General des Ifs a reception is taking place ('A la Santé du Général') and the host is regaling the ladies with a tale of the siege of Saragossa ('Non Je N'Ai Jamais Vu Ça!'). Gaston is there too, prepared to make the acquaintance of the General's daughter, his destined bride. Bagnolet arrives with the Michu family in tow and the two girls are hidden in adjoining rooms ('Entre La!') to give the parents the chance to make their explanations. It would be too much to hope that fate might just guide the General to his real daughter. Fate has, after all, a fifty percent chance of being right.

Unhelpfully, the General contrives to meet both girls in turn, sees his own features unmistakeably in both, and greets both as his long-lost daughter, so that things are no better off when he has finished than they were before. As for the girls, they are miserable at the thought of being separated from each other and from their beloved family ('Ah, Quel Malheur'). The General, when he learns the truth of the affair, is furious ('Me Prenez-Vous Pour un Conscrit?') and tells the Michus that they have thirty minutes to sort things out and give him his proper daughter. The only answer they can come up with is a hurried flight to the country and, as Maman and Papa hurry off to find a carriage, the girls pray to Saint Nicolas to protect them, each hoping separately that it is not she who is Mlle des Ifs (Prière à Saint-Nicolas).

While they await their parents' return, Gaston chances to come by and the girls learn with amazement that he is to marry whichever of them is the General's daughter ('C'Est la Fille du Général'). In no time they are both praying to Saint Nicolas again, and this time each is privately praying that she *is* Mlle des Ifs. When Marie-Blanche melts into waves of chagrined tears, gentle Blanche-Marie assures her 'sister' that she is herself not the least in love with Gaston. Whatever happens, Marie-Blanche must be agreed to be Irène des Ifs. When Maman and Papa return, they are staggered at the girls' change of heart and plan, but they are also relieved to find the problem apparently resolved in a happy finale with Marie-Blanche hailed as the General's daughter and handed over to Gaston to become a fine lady ('N'Est-Ce Pas Que J'Ai de la Branche'). Blanche-Marie will become Madame Aristide.

ACT 3

At the Michus' shop, business is as usual ('À la Boutique') even though today is a double wedding day. Blanche-Marie, dressed in her bridal gown, sits softly smiling, while Aristide buzzes about, deliriously happy now that he has a definite object on which to pour his pent-up affection ('Comme une

429

Girouette'). Marie-Blanche arrives with boxes of trimmings, carried by the put-upon Bagnolet, and the two girls are left alone to prepare their coiffures and exchange confidences.

Marie-Blanche confesses that she is finding life at the Hotel des Ifs rather straight-laced and constricting. Gaston is divine, but just a little bit proper and he keeps on gently trying to persuade her into a style of behaviour more suitable to her new position in life. They've hung a picture of the soulful-looking Marquise, her mother, above her bed as an example, and they sometimes even quote Blanche-Marie to her as a model of modesty and distinction.

Blanche-Marie isn't in deliriums of joy either. Aristide is a dear, even if his new-found exuberance is a bit...well, wearing. And she really is making a dreadful hash of being a shopkeeper's helpmate. Every egg she touches she breaks ('Vois-Tu, Je M'En Veux à Moi-Même'). Marie-Blanche helps her out. She is a dab hand with the customers and has great fun showing it, to the disgust of both her fiancé and her father whom she twists around her finger just as easily as she charms the customers into buying. Marie-Blanche is in her element in Les Halles and when her little school friends come to wish the sisters 'bonnes noces', she entertains them with a lively downtown rondo ('On Peut Chercher En Tout Pays').

Without warning, Marie-Blanche suddenly takes the day's matters in hand. She contrives to leave Blanche-Marie alone with Gaston and, after an awkward scene and duet ('Rassurez-Vous, Monsieur Gaston'), Blanche-Marie bursts into tears. Everyone clutters about to find out what is the matter, but Marie-Blanche knows. She sends Bagnolet off on another errand and, before her bemused family, she goes to work on Blanche-Marie ('Assieds-Toi Là'/'Je N'Y Comprends Rien Sur l'Honneur') with 'Une Poudre à Frimas' and ribbons and combs.

As she finishes her task, Bagnolet arrives bearing the portrait of the lovely Marquise. The way that Marie-Blanche has dressed Blanche-Marie the likeness is as of two prints from the same tirage. The General is staggered. How could he ever have failed to recognise his daughter? Gaston is ordered to undergo a quick change of fiancée, easy-going Aristide is equally happy to concentrate his affections on whichever sister is allotted to him and, at the end of the evening, 'Blanche-Marie and Marie-Blanche' finish up happily and suitably wed. But Madame Michu won't let her husband hand his daughters to their grooms. 'Don't you touch them', she cries, 'or you'll mix them up again!'

VÉRONIQUE

an opéra-comique in three acts by Albert Vanloo and Georges Duval. Music by André Messager. Produced at the Théâtre des Bouffes-Parisiens 10 December 1898 with Mariette Sully (Véronique), Jean Périer (Florestan), Anna Tariol-Baugé

(Agathe), Léonie Laporte (Ermerance) and Regnard (Coquenard). Produced at the Théâtre des Folies-Dramatiques 30 January 1909 with Vermandèle replacing Périer. Produced at the Théâtre de la Gaîté-Lyrique 1 March 1920 with Edmée Favart, Périer and Mme Tariol-Baugé and revived there 1936. Produced at the Théâtre Mogador 17 April 1943 with Suzanne Baugé, Maurice Vidal, Hélène Lavoisier, Marguerite Pierry and Edmond Castel. Played at the Théâtre National de l'Opéra-Comique 7 February 1925 with Mlle Favart, André Baugé, Mme Tariol-Baugé, Mlle Villette and André Allard, and again 22 December 1978 with Danielle Chlostawa and François Le Roux and 11 December 1980 with Marie-Christine Porta and Gino Quilico.

Played at the Coronet Theatre, London, 5 May 1903 with Mlle Sully, Adolphe Corin, Angèle van Loo, Marie Chalont and Regnard. Produced at the Apollo Theatre in a version by Henry Hamilton, Lillian Eldée and Percy Greenbank 18 May 1904 with Ruth Vincent, Lawrence Rea, Kitty Gordon, Rosina Brandram and George Graves.

Produced at the Broadway Theatre, New York, 30 October 1905 with Miss Vincent, Rea, Miss Gordon and John Le Hay. Produced at the Adelphi Theatre 3 April 1915.

Produced at the Theater an der Wien, Vienna, as *Brigitte* in a version by Heinrich Bolten-Bäckers 10 March 1900.

Produced at Kroll's Theater, Berlin, 13 September 1902.

A film version was produced in 1949 with Giselle Pascal, Jean Desailly, Marina Hotine, Jean Marchat, Pierre Bertin, Denis d'Inès, Armontel and Noël Roquevert.

CHARACTERS

Hélène de Solanges, *otherwise* Véronique
Ermerance, *Countess de Champ d'Azur, otherwise* Estelle
Florestan, *Vicomte de Valaincourt*
Monsieur Coquenard, *proprietor of the Temple of Flora*
Agathe, *his wife*
Loustot, *otherwise the* Baron des Merlettes
Séraphin, *a valet*
Denise, *his wife*
Tante Benoît, *her aunt*
Céleste, *a shopgirl*
Sophie, Elise, Zoé, Irma, Héloïse, Julie, Octave, Félicien, Achille, Max, etc.

ACT 1

At the Temple of Flora on Paris's Boulevard de la Madeleine, the employees of Monsieur Coquenard the florist are going picturesquely about their work ('Quelle Fraicheur Délicieuse') while Agathe, the charming Madame Coquenard, waxes lyrical over the joys of working with flowers ('Le Bel État Que Celui de Fleuriste'). This morning the flowers do not have all her attention, for Agathe is preoccupied. She is losing her lover. The delightful affair which she has been carrying on with the dashing Vicomte Florestan de Valaincourt is about to be ended, for the carefree and raffish young fellow has been condemned to marriage by a stern uncle. Her husband is equally preoccupied, for he is waiting on tenterhooks to find out whether he has been elected to the rank of captain in the home guard. He bought the glittering uniform months ago in anticipation and he is in all sorts of a state lest he is not elected.

Amongst the morning's customers at the Temple of Flora are the lovely young Hélène de Solanges and her lively aunt, Ermerance Countess de Champ d'Azur ('Ah! la Charmante Promenade'/'Oh, Ma Tante'). Hélène is, as it happens, the bride chosen for Madame Coquenard's beloved Vicomte and it has been arranged by the King himself that she shall make the formal acquaintance of her husband-to-be at a ball at the Tuileries that very evening. Marriage is in the air on this pretty Parisian day, for the valet Séraphin, who dances attendance on the two ladies, is dancing with impatience as they linger over their choice of bouquets. He is due to be married at noon, and he is frantic to be freed from his duties as soon as possible ('Bonjour Monsieur Séraphin').

The ladies have ordered their evening corsages when Hélène sees the Vicomte Florestan approaching the shop. Her aunt is all curiosity to look the prospective bridegroom over, so the ladies pretend to busy themselves with further flowers as the young man makes his entrance ('Vrai Dieu, Mes Bons Amis'). Florestan's companions include not only some of his lively young friends but also a rather older gentleman with a purposeful look. He is a bailiff who answers to the name of Loustot but who is, in reality, the Baron des Merlettes, a once wealthy nobleman reduced to penury by an excessive delight in the company of pretty and prodigious ladies ('Quand J'Étais Baron des Merlettes').

Loustot has been hired by the stern uncle to keep an eye on the young bridegroom and prevent any tendency to backsliding towards his old, wild ways, for the Duke has his naughty nephew in a cleft stick which gives him no alternative but to follow family orders. He holds a large note of debt made out in Florestan's disfavour and has told him that, should he fail to wed Hélène, the note will be called in and Florestan condemned to an uncomfortable spell in the debtors' prison at Clichy.

Florestan is quite sure that his intended bride will be some little provincial goose—the plain and worthy type favoured by the not-too-glamorous Queen—and he is swift to calm Agathe's regrets by saying so ('Alors, Tout Est Fini'/'Le Mal N'Est Pas Irreparable). These dismissive words don't go down at all well with the listening Hélène ('Petite Dinde') who makes up her mind that she will get her own back on the cocksure lover.

Florestan has bought out the entire contents of Coquenard's shop with his non-existent money so that he can invite all the shopgirls out to the pleasure gardens at Romainville to celebrate his last day of freedom. The occasion develops into one big party when Coquenard, excited out of his braces by the ultimate confirmation of his captaincy, invites his entire regiment to join in the revelry.

Hélène is determined that she, too, will be part of this celebration. She and Ermerance hurry home to dress themselves up as grisettes and they arrive back at the shop just as the company are putting the shutters up and preparing to depart (Finale: 'Les Voitures Sont à la Porte'). Hélène pretends to be a shopgirl in search of work—she is Véronique and Ermerance is Estelle—and she soon succeeds in catching Florestan's eye (C'Est Estelle et Véronique'). Before the cavalcade sets off for Romainville, the two false grisettes have won enthusiastic invitations to join in the fun ('Partons Pour Romainville').

ACT 2

Romainville just happens to be the place chosen by Séraphin to celebrate his marriage to the bucolic Denise (Choeur des Invités) whose chaperone, her aged aunt, seems disinclined to let her out of her sight even though she is now a wedded wife. In spite of Tante Benoît, the marriage feast is bubbling happily along when Coquenard's national guard companions arrive at the head of the Temple of Flora party (Choeur des Gardes Nationaux) and Agathe leads them to the nearby Tourne-Bride restaurant where their party is to take place ('Au Tourne, Tourne, Tourne-Bride').

During the trip, Agathe has attracted the attentions of Loustot who, now he is out in the country and back in his old haunts, prefers to be called Merlettes once more. She is at liberty to accept his attentions, because her husband has dallied to accompany the piquant Ermerance/Estelle who has expressed a wish to come to Romainville by donkey. Hélène/Véronique has chosen the same mode of transport which, since it requires a gentleman to lead the animal, is as good a way as any of striking up a little romance (Duo de l'Âne: 'De Ci, De Là'). As the company gather, all the little flirtations gain momentum, and Hélène takes especial pains to lead her Florestan deep into her power without giving anything away ('Oh! Méchante! Vous Voulez Rire'/Duo de l'Escarpolette: 'Poussez l'Escarpolette').

When Séraphin's wedding group start up a dance, the luncheon party joins gaily in and, as a result, the amazed valet comes face to face with each of his employers dressed up à la paysanne ('Lisette Avait Peur du Loup'). Their disguises force the ladies to act in accordance with their clothes and Ermerance finds her aristocratic self kissed enthusiastically by Coquenard while her noble niece is similarly menaced by Florestan ('Une Grisette Mignonne'). When Hélène is almost reduced to tears by such unaccustomed familiarity, the surprised Florestan does not press his embraces and the frightened girl begins to appreciate the delicacy of her intended husband.

But the joke has gone far enough and now it is time that the ladies returned to town to prepare themselves for the evening's royal ball. To their horror, they discover that Florestan has sent all the coaches away. He is having such a good time that he is determined to carry on into the evening and be damned to his uncle, the prisons of Clichy and Mademoiselle de Solanges.

Hélène has one last hope. A well-placed bribe to Séraphin's new bride and the aged auntie wins the two ladies a fresh change of costume and, heavily veiled, they depart for town perched alongside the expectant Séraphin on his honeymoon coach (Finale: 'Holà, Madame Séraphin'), leaving a half-regretful, half-playful letter for Florestan ('Adieu, Je Pars').

He has lost his little grisette, he may as well accept his destined bride. But Florestan will not. He would rather go to prison and, as the act ends, Loustot regretfully calls up two members of the guard to arrest the young man.

ACT 3

Back at the Tuileries, Ermerance touches her harp in song (Romance: 'De Magasin la Simple Demoiselle'). She is once again the fine lady, but she cannot forget her rustic frolic. Hélène is in high spirits, happily awaiting the culmination of her day and the triumphant face-to-face meeting with Florestan in her real identity ('Dites, Ma Tante, à Ma Coiffure'). Poor Séraphin is fitted out in a gala costume to attend the ladies at the ball. He had expected to be already in the first delicious stages of his wedding night, but his bride is still at Romainville and he has to make do with the promise that he will be excused just as soon as possible to hurry back to the party and the stranded Denise.

Somehow or other Coquenard and Agathe have made it back to town and they have found at their home invitations to the royal ball in recognition of Coquenard's new rank ('Bal à la Cour'/'Aux Tuileries'/'On Y Rencontre les Duchesses'). Dressed up in his new uniform, Coquenard cuts quite a figure and Agathe can almost feel that she fancies her own husband. When they arrive at the Tuileries, they are amazed to encounter Séraphin, and the valet has to escape quickly to avoid answering questions about the disappearance of the two grisettes. Worse follows, for Hélène and Ermerance, who have come down to the salon to assuage Hélène's impatience for her reunion with Florestan, run into the Coquenards ('Rencontre Bizarre') and they are forced to admit their real positions.

The Coquenards have news which shatters Hélène's happy anticipation. Florestan has refused to bow to his uncle's will. He has denounced his enforced marriage and has been hauled off to Clichy. At least, he should have been, except that Loustot has had second thoughts. He himself stands to win a fine reward when Florestan is safely wed to Mademoiselle de Solanges so, instead of taking him to Clichy, he has brought his prisoner to the Tuileries to ensure that he gets himself engaged, like it or not. The delighted Hélène is only too willing to come up with the money to buy off Florestan's debt and win his release but, when the young man finds himself freed, he is furious at the insult and at the patronage proffered by the noble lady.

When the jealous Agathe takes the first opportunity to spoil Hélène's surprise by revealing to him the trick that has been played ('Ma Foi! Pour Venir de Province'), he is ever angrier and, when he comes face to face with Hélène, she does not win the response she had so looked forward to. Florestan tells her that his happy dream romance with Véronique is ended and that Hélène has been forever spoiled for him by Véronique ('À Véronique Je Dirai'). He will tell his uncle that the marriage is out of the question.

Hélène is left to tearfully rue her little game, her trick played on a man who is clearly a fine, proud and dignified gentleman despite his youthful excesses. She listens sadly as the King arrives for the signing of the marriage contract which will now never be but, when she turns around, Florestan is there. One trick deserved another: as she made him suffer, so she deserved to suffer, but he could never give up his Véronique. As soon as the formalities have been completed, Séraphin is released to rush back to Romainville and his Denise. Once again he will have passengers alongside him on his coach, for Florestan and 'Véronique' decide to go too, to carry on happily where they left off (Finale: 'Par une Faveur Insigne').

LES SALTIMBANQUES

(The Travelling Players)

an opéra-comique in three acts by Maurice Ordonneau. Music by Louis Ganne. Produced at the Théâtre de la Gaîté, Paris, 30 December 1899 with Vauthier (Malicorne), Lucien Noël (Pingouin), Paul Fugère (Paillasse), Jeanne Saulier (Suzanne), Lise Berty (Marion) and Emile Perrin (André) and revived there 1902 with Jeanne Petit, Soulacroix and Dutilloy, 1913 with Clarel, Georges Foix, Claude Arnès, Angèle Gril and Guillot, 1914, 1915 with Noël, Chambon, Eva Retty and Angèle Gril, 24 June 1921 with René Gerbert, Foix, Jane Montange and Renée Page, 11 April 1922 with Gerbert, Foix, Mary Malbros, Cébron-Norbens and Robert Jysor and 1945. Produced at the Théâtre de l'Apollo 1911 with Fernand Frey, Foix, Marcelle Devriès, Mlle Gril and Delaquerrière. Produced at the Théâtre Mogador 11 March 1941 with Henri Varna, André Baugé, René Lenoty, Annie Alexander, Suzanne Baugé and Jean Georges.

Produced at the Carltheater, Vienna, as *Circus Malicorne* 20 April 1901.

CHARACTERS

Paillasse, *a saltimbanque*
Grand Pingouin *the strong man of the troupe*
Malicorne, *the director of the troupe*
Suzanne, *a young saltimbanque*
Marion, *another*
Madame Malicorne
Pinsonnet, *a travesty player*
Baron de Valengoujon
Le Comte des Etiquettes
André de Langéac, *an officer*
Bernardin, *president of the choral competition*
Madame Bernardin
Marquis and Marquise du Liban, Innkeeper, Rigobin, Coradet, Brigadier, etc.

435

ACT 1

The Circus Malicorne is not a very high-class affair. Under the management of the eponymous Monsieur Malicorne and his wife, it is composed of largely second-rate acts, amongst whom are the principals of this story: Paillasse the clown, author and purveyor of *bons mots* and puns; Grand Pingouin, the lovable strong man; Marion, the tight-rope walker who was once maid to Mme la Baronne de Valengoujon but who joined the circus to marry Pingouin (a course which has never been possible as they've never stopped long enough in any one town to qualify for a marriage licence); and Suzanne, the little chanteuse brought up by the proprietors on behalf of her mysterious mother who was, apparently, a part of Malicorne's past.

The Malicorne troupe has pitched its camp at Versailles, and there the performers are making do with a humble stew ('Auprès de la Marmite') before starting their show. The Malicornes have little but rough words for their employees, and they reserve their unkindest treatment for the frail Suzanne. The ringmaster loudly scorns her as a worthless burden on his charity even though she is, in fact, the nearest thing to a draw the company has. Suzanne makes the best of this unpleasant life, sustained in her trials by the companionship of her fellow saltimbanques ('Certains Ont l'Illustre Famille').

Versailles proves to be the scene of a significant series of events for the folk of the Circus Malicorne. Firstly, the Baron de Valengoujon turns up. He is ravenously struck by the hitherto unseen and unsuspected muscles of his wife's former chambermaid, but his advances to her bring him up against Grand Pingouin who kicks the yearning nobleman out, rows with Marion ('Il Faut Pour Être Saltimbanque'), and decides to lay his big heart at the feet of Suzanne instead.

Unfortunately, Paillasse, untouched by love over the years, has just got round to doing the same thing and, in gentlemanly fashion, the two suitors agree to let Suzanne make a choice between them (Trio: 'Que Me Dites-Vous Là, Vraiment?'). The lass tactfully pleads the inexperience of her sixteen years as a reason for them all remaining just good friends (Triolets: 'C'Est la Première Fois') and Marion is soon able to recall Grand Pingouin to order and to her side ('Fais Pas la Flambard Avec Ta Force').

As Suzanne prepares for the day's performance, her tent is invaded by three merry soldiers intent on claiming a kiss from what they think is a lady of little virtue. When Suzanne cries tearfully for help in the face of their advances, one of their number, André de Langéac, sees their mistake and, sending his friends away, apologises in a manner which soon replaces tears with smiles (Duet: 'Mademoiselle, Je Vous Prie').

Outside his tent Malicorne is beginning to drum up an audience for the show ('Que l'On Accoure') with the aid of a recital of the prowess of his troupe. Marion and Grand Pingouin give a sample of their act and the slavering Baron is the first to buy a ticket—a season ticket. Paillasse brings in few customers with his quips, but Suzanne's rendition of 'La Chanson de Colinette' attracts more trade and also the attentions of her soldier friends. When André presses money into her cap, she refuses it and incurs the wrath of Malicorne, but there is still time for a few soft words to pass between the two young people as the little girl gives her soldier a bunch of violets to take away in memory of the little saltimbanque.

There is more trouble in store for Suzanne when the Baron, turned down flat in his advances to Marion, turns his attentions to the younger girl and gets slapped for his pains. Malicorne, enraged that the girl should commit such a solecism, is ready to beat her (Finale: 'Des Excuses! Quelle Insolence!'), but Paillasse and Grand Pingouin leap to her defence. The strongman soon has the ringmaster arm-locked and on his knees, as the distraught Suzanne declares that she must leave the Malicornes and their circus for ever. Her three friends freely agree to go with her and, as Marion and Grand Pingouin lead off an optimistic song ('Après le Sombre Orage'), they all prepare to take to the open road.

ACT 2

It is three months later when the little band turn up at the local fair at Bécanville in Normandy ('C'Est le Jour de Fête'). The highlight of the festivities is to be a choral competition, for the town's top aristocrat, the Comte des Etiquettes, has a perfect mania for choirs. He also has a soft spot for Mme Bernardin, the wife of the contest president, who, if rumour be true, was once more than just a Dulcinea to his Quixote. In fact, the two still have their little rendezvous, and the musical Count uses the time signatures of his choral compositions to indicate in code the hours proposed for their meetings.

The wayfaring foursome are not up to anything as grand as a choir ('Chanson des Bohemiennes'). They mend chairs, pull teeth, barber dogs, and Marion tells gipsy fortunes ('Souvent On Me Fait les Doux Yeux') while still hoping that one day they'll be able to stop somewhere long enough to earn that all-important marriage licence. Paillasse takes more than his share of the work to ease the load on the less sturdy Suzanne, but he finds it hard to keep his promise not to talk of love to her ('D'mandez-Moi d' N'Avoir Plus d'Esprit').

As the friends go about their trades, the town comes out to greet a platoon of soldiers who are passing through ('En Voyant un Village'). At the head of these men marches André de Langéac with a fine military song ('Quand la Trompette Militaire'). He rests his men at the inn while he takes time out to visit des Etiquettes, who is an old family friend, but the first person he runs into is Suzanne. He has kept her violets next his heart which he is more than willing to open to her ('Que Nous Dis-Tu, Petite Fleur?'), but Suzanne cannot believe there can be any hope of marriage between folk of ranks as disparate as theirs although André swears that he will find a way to make his family consent to their match.

Marion, in the meantime, makes a much less romantic encounter. The Malicornes arrive in town to look at the act of an acrobatic troupe, the Gigoletti, whom they hope to engage for the circus, and Monsieur Malicorne runs into Marion. Fortunately, she is done up in her gipsy garb and he

437

does not recognise her, but he is impressed by her miraculous knowledge of his past life and disposed to believe the predictions she reads in the coffee dregs—predictions which are calculated to get him as far away as possible from Bécanville as quickly as possible.

Marion hurries to warn her friends that their old employer is on their trail, intending to have them all arrested for breach of contract, and they take a proffered chance to escape his notice by disguising themselves as a group of guests who are booked in at the inn. Of course, the disguise they have chosen is that of the Gigoletti (Quartette: 'C'Est Nous les Gigoletti') and all kinds of fun and nonsense develop until the four fugitives find themselves hired as acrobats and marching in Malicorne's circus parade.

Luckily, when the real Gigoletti arrive, they speak no French and our friends are able to fool Malicorne that they are just a part of the act but, in the end, their luck runs out. Their disguises discarded, the friends are at Malicorne's mercy (Finale: Voleurs! Vous En Avez Menti'), but they are rescued when André arrives on the scene with des Etiquettes and a purseful of money to buy out the disputed contracts. The vengeful Malicorne still wants to have the foursome arrested as vagabonds, but des Etiquettes offers them the hospitality of his own home and, as the act ends, saltimbanques and soldiery head off to the château des Etiquettes.

ACT 3

At the château, the Count entertains his official guests ('Bonjour, Bonjour Monsieur le Comte') and prepares his choir for their performance in the competition. Suzanne brings him a posy of grateful flowers which she has plucked in the meadows ('Dans les Champs Tout Couverts de Blés') and he accepts her offering feelingly before leaving her to meet once more with André. The young man is unable formally to ask her to wed him as he needs first to win his Uncle's consent to their marriage, but he is jealous when she, in her turn, tells him that, before she can entertain his suit, she must square herself with the lovelorn Paillasse.

The clown has been offered a job by the Count as steward of his estate, and his new position brings him, full of courage, to offer his heart and hand once more to Suzanne ('La Nature A Pour Ses Élus'). She cannot bring herself to tell him the truth, and it is left to Marion to break to Paillasse the fact that his lady's heart is given ('Mon Pauvre Paillasse').

When the guests are gathered for the afternoon's entertainment, des Etiquettes asks Mme Bernardin to favour the company with his composition 'La Bergère Colinette', but her husband will not allow it. Does he suspect? Instead, Suzanne is asked for a song and, to the Count's amazement, obliges with the 'La Bergère Colinette', his own unpublished song, known only to... When Malicorne arrives to add the skills of his circus to the entertainment, he is ordered to provide facts. Who is Suzanne?

Malicorne tries to bluff, but he cannot do so for long when Mme Bernardin recognises him—it is her old friend Brutus! Does he not remember her? She is Castorine, the wonderful wire-walker who, all those years ago, left a little girl in his care to be trained for the circus. While Bernardin splutters unheeded, Suzanne's aristocratic pedigree is revealed: she is the daughter of the very best friend of the Count and the most absolutely intimate *amie* of Madame Bernardin. While Bernardin threatens divorce, Suzanne smilingly tells the Count and Mme Bernardin that she will turn to them all the filial love that would have been owing to their very best friends, and it only remains for her to be united with André as des Etiquettes purchases the Circus for her three companions and the curtain falls on the final couplets ('Comme le Soldat').

HANS, LE JOUEUR DE FLUTE

(Hans, the Flute-Player)

an opéra-comique in three acts by Maurice Vaucaire and Georges Mitchell. Music by Louis Ganne. Produced at the Théâtre de Monte-Carlo, Monaco 14 April 1906 with Jean Périer (Hans), Alberthal (Yoris), Poudrier (Pippermann) and Mariette Sully (Lisbeth). Produced at the Théâtre de l'Apollo, Paris, 31 May 1910 with Périer, Defreyn, Poudrier and Gina Féraud. Produced at the Théâtre de la Gaîté-Lyrique 1928 with Gilbert Moryn, Jean Pernot, Henri Jullien and Denise Cam and revived there 17 February 1936.

Produced at the Manhattan Opera House, New York, 20 September 1910.

CHARACTERS

Hans, *the flute player*
Yoris, *a poet and sculptor of dolls*
Pippermann, *burgomaster of Milkatz*
Lisbeth, *his daughter*
Madame Pippermann
van Pott, *affianced to Lisbeth*
Petronius ⎤
Tantendorff ⎟
Loskitch ⎬ *echevins of Milkatz*
Steinbeck ⎟
Karteifle ⎦
Guillaume, *caretaker of the town hall*
Ketchen, *his wife*
Nightwatchman, Sergeant of the Town Guard, Van Quatch, Ketly, Madame Tantendorff, Madame Loskitch, Baby Petronius, Blonde doll, Redheaded doll, etc.

ACT 1

Somewhere in the thin black line which separates Holland from Flanders on the map, there is a little country of great antiquity. Its principal town is called Milkatz, its principal product is grain, and its principal preoccupation, you might even say its only preoccupation, is selling its grain at a fine profit to allow it to produce even more grain the next year and make even more profit. If it sounds as if Milkatz is unnaturally commercially-minded, you must remember that it is also very successful and very rich. It is so successful and so rich that nobody thinks much more about anything except grain and profit, and all the old Milkatz fêtes and traditions, its arts and its crafts and all its other non-commercial activities have vanished.

The curtain rises on a profitable-looking dawn in Milkatz. The Night Watch (looking very much like that painted by Rembrandt) are doing their rounds, grumbling tunefully through their drilling at being out of their beds at 6 a.m. ('Un, Deux, Au Pas, Sacrebleu'), but this is the time of day for the industrious people of Milkatz to go to work, and the newspaper seller is already in the street with the latest news on grain market prices. The burgomaster, Pippermann, is off to the town hall for a council meeting but, unfortunately, the town hall is locked because Guillaume, the caretaker, has not turned up.

Yesterday was Guillaume's wedding day and the Burgomaster's daughter, Lisbeth, ingenuously begs her father to forgive the boy's tardiness as she imagines that he probably stayed up late dancing ('Un Lendemain de Noces'). Nothing is allowed to stand in the way of business in Milkatz. Pippermann cannot bear the thought of postponing his meeting, and he orders the citizens who inhabit the houses on the town square to bring chairs from their homes to permit the council to hold its meeting in the square itself.

Their debates are all on Milkatz's growing monopoly in the grain trade and on the need for further state expenditure on cats to guard the precious commodity, and Councillor Petronius, ex-President of the ex-committee for the Arts, gets short shrift when he puts in a word about the old Milkatz traditions of St Gregorius' Day. The council, the guards and the populace know and care nothing for St Gregorius. He has nothing to do with their harvests and therefore is of no importance and can be forgotten as they all join in 'Le Chant Nationale', a stirring composition in praise of wheat.

But Petronius is not the only person to have remembered St Gregorius. The poet, Yoris, interrupts the al fresco council meeting, which is, after all, filling up the public square, and refuses to leave before he has sung to them of the old Milkatz fête ('Vous N'Étes Plus, Pauvres Poupées'), when the people of the town came to this square to display their famous Milkatz dolls—life-sized sculptures of wood, marvellously painted and dressed, with music-box voices—the works of a people skilled in many and varied crafts. The council may have abolished the fête, but he, Yoris, has made and brought a doll which, in spite of the angry threats of Pippermann, he is determined to display in one of the niches in the town hall's walls, as in the old days.

Guillaume and his new wife, the Pippermanns' maid Ketchen, rush in stammering apologies ('Excusez-Nous, Mais Quelle Heure Est-Il Donc?')

440

and the council is able, at last, to march off into the town hall. When they have gone, Yoris returns with his doll, and the caretaker is astonished to see that it is a beautiful portrait doll of the burgomaster's daughter.

The poet is in love. He has been sending clandestine poems to Lisbeth. Yesterday she found her bread wrapped in one, which she admits was quite a surprise ('Ô Lisbeth, Aujourd'hui Dimanche'). But Lisbeth is engaged to her father's foolish deputy, van Pott, and she doesn't feel, in spite of the urgings of Guillaume and Ketchen, that she should entertain the suit of a dangerous vagabond who knows nothing of the price of grain. She is delighted when she is shown the doll—goodness, how pretty she is!—but her first glimpse of Yoris himself is cut short by the appearance of Madame Pippermann.

The poor poet's sad reverie is interrupted by a strange song ('Souris Grises, Souris Blanches'). Someone is singing about mice in Milkatz! Unheard of! The singer is a white-haired young man in strange clothes who carries a basket of mice over his shoulder and, in his hand, a crystal flute. His name is Hans, he comes from a far off land, and his flute is magical ('Je Viens d'un Pays Lointain').

He asks for a little wheat for his mice and meets with horror-struck faces from the burghers of Milkatz; he asks for charity and he is sharply told that begging is against the law. Yoris, a kindred soul, gives the fellow his last florin and tells him his tale, but there is not much that Hans needs to be told. He has come on purpose to teach a lesson to the heartless folk of Milkatz who spend all their time and money on industry and none to nurture and subsidise the arts.

Pippermann and van Pott emerge from their meeting and are furious when they see Yoris's doll installed in its niche. They go to smash it with their walking sticks but, at a roulade from Hans' flute, the sticks fly from their hands and the doll disappears to the accompaniment of thunder and lightning. The finale sees the populace rushing to the square as Hans begins to mete out his punishment to Milkatz. His mice leap from their cage to his magic encouragements and head for the grain-stores. So that they may multiply and pillage in peace, he will drown every cat in the town. As the company, headed by Yoris and Lisbeth, swell into a satirical waltz melody worthy of a grand love scene, bewailing the fate of the cats ('Adieu, Petits Minets, Petits Minous'), Hans' flute sends the Milkatz felines scurrying suicidally towards the river while the townspeople dance and dance and dance.

ACT 2

In the dining room of the Pippermann's house, Lisbeth, Ketchen and Madame Pippermann are laying the table and chattering about the strange events of the day ('Ah Ça, Maman, C'Est Lamentable'), when Pippermann and the council return dragging Yoris with them. The poet scorns them and their authority ('Vous Ne Pouvez Pas Me Comprendre'), refuses to help them steal the magic flute, and is marched off to prison. In the hours since their first meeting, Lisbeth has fallen in love with the poet ('Sait-On Jamais, Sait-On Pourquoi') and her father decides that he can make use of this fact to his own advantage. She must win the flute from Hans and save Yoris from being burnt at the stake.

Under such circumstances, Lisbeth has to agree and, explaining subtly to Hans her motives ('Mon Coeur A des Peines'), she wins him into giving her the flute. Pippermann grabs it exultantly and orders Hans to be bound and gagged and taken off 'À la Tour de Nord'. Singing a farewell berceuse to his flute ('Adieu Ma Mie'), he goes, leaving the burgomaster to gobble up the adulation of the council.

Pippermann reasons that, since the flute drowned the cats, it should equally drown the mice but, when van Pott plays the instrument, the news comes that a ship full of grain has crashed into the jetty and sunk. When another councillor tries, the granary goes up in flames, and a third attempt brings news that the third councillor's wife has run off with a lover. Pippermann's triumph has turned to disaster and he hurries to release Hans and heap him with festivities ('Nous Accourons Sans Nous Faire Prier'/Ballet des Pêcheurs et Pêcheuses.

The magician agrees to rid the town of his mice and leave Milkatz on several conditions. Yoris must be freed and the old fête of St Gregorius must be re-established. along with its famous doll contest in which all the citizens must take part. Until the dolls are finished not a husband may kiss his wife nor a girl her lover—love-making is forbidden! Hans himself will select the winner and claim for himself one doll. Taking his flute, he bursts out with a lively march tune ('Cette Flûte Qui Mena la Ronde'). Pippermann eagerly agrees and immediately news comes that Yoris is gone from his prison cell and that the mice are rushing to the river, as the people hail Hans in a concerted finale ('Nous T'Aimons, Brave Homme').

ACT 3

Milkatz is *en fête* as in the old days ('Après Tant de Luttes') as the people add the finishing touches to their dolls, although Ketchen and Guillaume are finding it a bit hard to stick to the no-kissing rule ('Moi Guillaume, Sais-Tu Bien'). Even the Pippermanns seem to be having a good time and Madame Pippermann leads off the ladies of the town with their entries ('On A Fait Sa Tache'). Unfortunately, Pippermann's apparent change of heart is not substantial enough to let him see in Yoris a potential son-in-law, and Lisbeth despairs of his changing his attitude ('Mon Cher Petit Père Est un Commercant').

But now Yoris appears. Since his magical escape from prison he has been away out of the country, trying to become a regular Milkatzian in the hope of winning Pippermann's approval and Lisbeth's hand. He has studied mathematics and commerce and grain prices and, with all that under his belt, he has hastened breathlessly back home, lest Lisbeth wed van Pott before he can stake his claim ('Ah! Ah! Puis Je Ne Pas Rire'). His efforts are to no avail. When the young lovers are discovered together by the burgomaster, he confines Lisbeth to her room as the sounds of the procession bringing Hans back to the town are heard.

Soon the square is filled with people as the dolls are brought forth to be judged. Hans greets each entry in turn ('Poupée Aimable et Jolie') and hosts a ballet of the winning dolls of ancient years magicked up from the town hall basement. When the judging is done ('Mettons Nous Bien d'Accord'), Yoris's doll is announced the winner. It is also the one Hans chooses for himself. He asks the doll if it is happy to come away with him and, to the amazement of the crowd, it nods assent. Yoris begs him not to take the doll which he made with so much love and, mockingly, Hans tells him to take the doll—nay, wed the doll!—and laughingly calls Pippermann to speak the words of the marriage ceremony over the sculptor and his work.

The burgomaster finds it a great joke to humiliate Yoris is such a way but, no sooner has he spoken the ceremony, than the doll steps from the cart—it is his own daughter, Lisbeth, and she and Yoris are truly and legally wed. Pippermann goes to protest, but Hans lifts his flute warningly to his lips and the burgomaster steps down. And now Hans must go elsewhere where he is needed so, bidding a happier and wiser Milkatz adieu, he and his flute head off into the sunset.

PHI-PHI

an opérette légère in two acts by Albert Willemetz and Fabien Sollar. Music by Henri Christiné. Produced at the Théâtre des Bouffes-Parisiens, Paris, 12 November 1918 with Urban (Phidias), Pierrette Madd (Mme Phidias), Alice Cocéa (Aspasie), Dréan (La Pirée) and Ferréal (Ardimédon) and revived there on numerous occasions including June 1922, June 1933 with Urban, Régine Paris, Mireille, Dréan and Gustave Nelson, 18 June 1947 with Urban, Roberte Jan, Gise Mey and René Novan, 25 May 1949 with Fernard Quertant, Edith Georges, Germaine Roger, Eddy Rasimi and Henri Regard, 1957 with Léo Campion, Jany Sylvaine, Rosine Brédy and Dréan, 15 April 1980 with Jacques Baudoin and Brigitte Krafft and 2 June 1983 with Michel Roux and Nelly-Anne Rabas.

Produced at the London Pavilion 16 August 1922 in a heavily revised version by Fred Thompson and Clifford Grey with additional songs by Herman Darewski, Nat Ayer and Cole Porter. Cast included Clifton Webb, Vera Freeman, June, Stanley Lupino, Evelyn Laye and Arthur Roberts.

CHARACTERS

Phidias, *a sculptor*
Le Pirée, *his servant*
Madame Phidias
Périclès, *a statesman*
Ardimédon, *a foreign prince*

443

Aspasie, *a working girl*
Eight little models, two dancers.

ACT 1

The year is 600 B C and the scene is the workshop of the Athenian sculptor, Phidias, and if there is something very 1920s and Parisian about this ancient Greek setting that is simply because things haven't really changed much in two and a half thousand years. The workshop is full of Phidias' latest creations—a Venus ordered by Monsieur Milo and a Winged Victory made to the specifications of Madame Samothrace, a discobolos, an Ephesian Diana and other familiar pieces of sculptural art, the result of many hours work over a hot model.

Phidias, or Phi-Phi as he is more fondly known, has eight little models who spend their days posing nakedly for his works of art ('Oui, Nous Sommes les Petites Modèles'). They deplore the fact that, since their anatomy is never credited but always passed off as some goddess or allegory, their fame will not go down to posterity alongside that of the artist but, at least, they will have the satisfaction of knowing that, when someone in the twentieth century admires the lovely arms of the Venus de Milo or the pretty head of the Victory of Samothrace, they will be being anonymously adored.

At the moment Phidias has a problem. None of his models is the right material for his latest commission, the important group which the great statesman Périclès has ordered representing Virtue and Love founding the Happy Home. There is something about each one of his girls which prevents them from being quite suitable to represent Virtue. His hesitation doesn't worry the models. They are quite sure he won't find anyone anywhere in Athens who will come up to the perfect requirements of the job and, in the meanwhile, they have other excitements in hand. They have had a racing tip and they each have two drachmai to give to the buffoonish servant, Le Pirée (whose name might seem ridiculous in the minus-first century, but which one day will be that of an entire port), to put on to Ptolémée II in the big race.

While the girls dally over horse races, however, Phidias has found his Virtue ('C'Est une Gamine Charmante'). She is a sweet, innocent little creature of unequalled ingenuousness and candour whom he discovered on an Athenian street corner the previous midnight, and who made such ingenuous and candid replies to his questions that anyone who didn't know better would have believed she was on the game. She is called Aspasie and she is moving in, with no more baggage than a hat-box and an umbrella, to become the model of Virtue.

The moment she is through the door Phidias' hands begin to wander, but the young lady defends herself with her umbrella with practised aplomb and the only casualties are a couple of statues. The Venus de Milo gets her arms knocked off and the Winged Victory of Samothrace loses her head. Aspasie is apologetic but practical: if she knocks the legs off the Venus as well it will make a perfect tailor's dummy and, as for the Victory, now it can be a Defeat. Forgetting his spoiled merchandise, Phi-Phi attempts to persuade his little

444

lady to be less formal with him ('Maitre, Lorsque l'On A Vingt Ans'), but Aspasie is a practised defender of her own commodities and she's heard it all before ('Je Connais Toutes les Historiettes'). Here he is pretending he has brought her here to be Virtue and all he is after is Debauch.

She is removing his hand from a particularly appetising piece of her anatomy when Madame Phidias comes home. She is not impressed by her husband's explanation that he is measuring up this young lady for a job, and she is altogether certain that Aspasie has none of the qualifications needed for the role of Virtue. She sees Virtue as a good woman like herself, not as a flibbertigibbet like this one. Phidias does not agree: for him Virtue should be a pretty, bright, nude little being with a sparkle in her eye ('Vertu, Verturon, Verturette'). Madame Phidias is deeply suspicious of this whole episode and, in revenge, almost regretful that she froze off an adventure which nearly happened to her on her way home. She was followed by a man—a very young and very good looking man—and, no matter what she did, she couldn't shake him off ('Je Sortais des Port's de Trézène').

She is in the middle of her story when Phidias sneaks out and when she finishes she finds that, o horror!, she is talking to that very young man. He has had the effrontery to follow her to her home and he has invited himself in with, it seems, just one intent. Her protests that she is a virtuous woman and wife have no effect, and his passionate avowals just flow on and on until Le Pirée, thinking he is a customer, bumbles in and succeeds in selling him the entire stock of statues (including the Venus at a reduced price because of its being shop-soiled) while his mind and eyes are elsewhere. The 600 drachmai proceeds go, needless to say, not into the till but straight onto a horse.

Phidias returns, having made little progress with Aspasie, to find the young man in the workshop (Finale: 'Hélas! Faut-Il Que Mon Bonheur Se Perde?'). In spite of the fact that the passionate visitor is actually the foreign Prince Ardimédon, Le Pirée, thinking to spare his mistress embarrassment, quickly comes up with a bright lie. He is a model. Perhaps he will do for the role of Love? Phidias orders the surprised Ardimédon to strip off and the other models hurry around to inspect the qualifications of their new colleague. Amongst a wave of double entendres based on the two meanings of *faire l'amour*—on the one hand to play the role of Love, on the other to make love—Ardimédon gets the job.

ACT 2

The little models are waiting for the evening edition of *Athens-Sport* to find out if their horse has won ('Ptolémée Sera-T-Il Vainqueur?') but, when Le Pirée turns up to relate the race to them, they find that their drachmai have gone down the drain. If they are depressed, Le Pirée has many times more reason to be. He gambled all the money from the sale of Phidias' statues on the wretched Ptolémée. What will his master say when he sees that he has neither statues nor cash? For the meanwhile, the only way out seems to be to get the little models to take the place of the statues for which they modelled in the first place.

445

No sooner are the girls in place than an important visitor arrives: Périclès himself. He is impressed by the life-like quality of the statues, but he is even more impressed when he sees Aspasie who has hurried in, all excited, after a visit to the fortune teller ('Ah! Cher Monsieur, Excusez-Moi!'). Apparently the fortune teller has predicted that she will marry a brown-haired man who is terribly important and that she will have lots of money and a high position. Périclès has a moment of foresight—this little lady will play an important part in his life—and he invites her to tea. What a pity that he has red hair.

Now it is time for work and Aspasie starts to take off her clothes. Madame Phidias, however, has other ideas. She informs Aspasie that, although she is an extremely attractive little person with obvious potential both for modelling and in other areas, she is not suitable as a model for Virtue for her husband. Phi-Phi has changed his mind. It is Madame Phidias who will be the model for Virtue.

When the girl has gone, Madame Phidias pulls herself together, takes a deep breath and, with a quick prayer to Pallas Athénée ('Oh! Pallas Athénée, Combien Cela Me Coute'), undresses. If her husband has to have a nude model, it is best that it be his wife. Phi-Phi, alas, is less than enthusiastic, even at the thought of saving the model fees of five drachmai a session, and he decides that Virtue had, on second thoughts, better be depicted clad. After all, if Virtue were so attractive who would turn to Vice?

Madame Phidias is not convinced by this piece of logic but, before she can put her clothes back on, who should burst upon the scene but Ardimédon, absolutely enraptured to find the woman of his desires standing before him naked, and all ready to strip off to pose as Love opposite her. There turns out to be some difficulty in finding a pose for the two of them which is suitable. Anything too intimate makes Phidias twitchy, while his two subjects show signs of a certain nervous stiffness which threatens to spoil the grouping but, before the situation can be resolved, Le Pirée arrives to tell his master that Périclès is without and the sculptor hurries away to attend to his august customer.

Left alone with his beloved, Ardimédon launches into fresh flights of passionate poesie, determined to prove to Madame Phidias that the laws of nature insist that she must be his ('Tout Tombe') and, in spite of her best intentions, she gradually weakens ('Ah! Tais-Toi, Tais-Toi, Tu M'Affoles'). Le Pirée and the statue-models watch as Madame Phidias falls first into the arms and then into the bed of the enterprising Prince—Love and Virtue have come together, but whether they are founding a Happy Home is suspect.

When they decide that we have seen and heard enough, the models bring down the curtain with a little request to the audience for a special cheer for the two characters who are too busy to come in front of the act drop for their applause.

ACT 3

The next morning, Madame Phidias is suffering just a little from remorse, but Ardimédon puts the twinkle back in her eye with a happy recap of the

446

night's activities and the promise of more to come (Duo des Souvenirs: 'D'Abord Monsieur Vous M'Enlaçâtes'). When Phidias hurries into his studio he is delighted to find that all the stiffness and nervousness which had spoiled their pose the previous day has vanished. His wife seems to have a quite different attitude to her nudity and to art. Now he can create a masterpiece.

He is also rather relieved that Madame Phidias hasn't thought to ask him where he was last night, because he was with Aspasie. But what is this? Here comes Aspasie, all done up in the most expensive finery ('Bien Chapeautée') and bearing the most improbable news—she has just been married. Having arisen from Phi-Phi's bed, she apparently popped down the road and climbed into that of Périclès and from Périclès' bed she arose and popped back up the road to get married. She is Madame Périclès, the wife of the most important man in the government just as the fortune teller had predicted. And in order to make the prophecy entirely true he has promised to dye his hair brown.

Phi-Phi is depressed. He discovered a lovely little Virtue for himself only to have her snatched away. Aspasie just laughs. Hers will be a modern marriage, Phidias has not seen the last of her! As he sighs over her breasts which, by reason of a pun too French to be translated, are referred to as her *petits païens* (Chanson des Païens), the rub comes. Since she will be sharing herself between her husband and her lover it is only right that they should share her expenses. Her new dress has cost 1,500 drachmai—so Périclès, her complaisant husband, should get off with paying only 750. The other 750 are for Phi-Phi to pay. After that (and after the other) perhaps he could give her a price on a portrait statue. Full-length. Périclès prefers her full-length.

La Pirée still hasn't been able to get together any money to replace his gambling losses, but he has found the way that it can be done. He has got himself a pair of scales and in it he is weighing up pros and cons. He explains to Ardimédon the pros and the cons of telling Phidias about the affair between his wife and her posing partner, and wins himself a tidy sum of hush money. Then he turns to Phidias and Aspasie. Out come the scales, and Le Pirée is in the money again.

The two couples come face to face and, just when it seems that something may bubble over from the pot of accusations, Périclès turns up. He has decided that, instead of having a statue of Aspasie alone he will have her adjoined to the group already ordered. Since the State is paying, the cost is immaterial. What can she represent? Madame Phidias sarcastically suggests that Fidelity might be suitable, but Aspasie has no doubts. She will be Economy. Virtue and Love aided by Economy making the Happy Home.

So, here they are, all the standard characters of the French (whoops, Greek) farce: the wife, the mistress, the husband, the lover and the protector, all come together into the usual happy ending ('Pour Être Heureux, Que Faut-Il?'). The happy ending is broken into by Le Pirée—he's put all his bribe money on a horse and he's lost again. It is time to confess about the statues. The little models get down off their plinths as Ardimédon offers them all triple time for their session and promises to return the real statues. Please, he asks, can we now get on with the happy ending? And they do.

The London production altered the story and the dialogue of the show, adding extra characters and altering others. It used only some of Christiné's melodies, often reallocating them to other characters and situations in a show which was a poor reflection of the original.

DÉDÉ

an opérette in three acts by Albert Willemetz. Music by Henri Christiné. Produced at the Théâtre des Bouffes-Parisiens, Paris, 10 November 1921 with Maurice Chevalier (Robert), Urban (André), Alice Cocéa (Denise) and Maguy Warna (Odette). Revived there 6 October 1922 with Chevalier, Adrien Lamy, Mlle Moussy and Mlle Warna. Played at the Théâtre Ba-Ta-Clan 2 December 1927 with Cariel, Jean Deiss, Gina Varigny and Maryse Tirville. Produced at the Théâtre des Nouveautés 1973 with Antoine, James Sparrow, Corinne Le Poulain and Béatrice Belthoise. Produced at the Théâtre de la Renaissance 1981.

Produced at the Garrick Theatre, London, 17 October 1922 in a version by Ronald Jeans with Guy Lefeuvre, Joseph Coyne, Gertrude Lawrence and Joyce Gammon, and later played in Britain under the title *The Talk of the Town*.

A film version was produced by René Guissart in 1934 with Albert Préjean, Danielle Darrieux, Mireille Perrey, Louis Baron fils and Claude Dauphin.

CHARACTERS

André de la Huchette, *known as* Dédé
Vicomte Robert Dauvergne, *his friend*
Denise, *his chief shop assistant*
Odette
Maître Leroydet, *a notary*
Monsieur Chausson
Lucette, Dolly, Maryse, Jacqueline, Loulou, Guite, *shop girls from the Casino de Paris*
Strikers, Reporter, Grooms, Policeman, Police Commissioner, etc.

ACT 1

At André's elegant Parisian shoe-shop there are no customers but there are half-a-dozen delicious shopgirls. They are noticeably more delicious than run-of-the-moulin shopgirls because they have been recruited from the chorus line of the Casino de Paris, after having answered a curious advertisement for assistants with no previous experience of sales work.

448

Although pleased to be able to supplement their evening earnings in a job which is certainly not proving demanding, the girls are slightly surprised at the strange set-up ('Ah! la Drôle de Boutique').

Their supervisor is not a chorine. Denise had been working as a typist in a lawyer's office when this well-paid job was offered to her and the girls have noticed that she apparently has some qualification for her job, as the only customer they have had has come every day and every day he has asked to be served by Denise. That customer is Maître Leroydet, Denise's former employer. He has long sighed over his pretty employee without speaking his thoughts and, now that she has gone, he is quite lost without her at his typewriter ('J'Avais Tout Ça'). He is anxious to lay his heart and hand at her feet, but Denise has a new employer now and she owes her fidelity to him, even if she finds him a little hard to understand.

Having acquired this business, André de la Huchette shows absolutely no interest in it and no concern at its daily losses ('Et Voilà Comme Cet' Excellent Jeune Homme'). The losses are no surprise to Monsieur Chausson, the previous owner, for he too made losses, losses which ultimately forced him to sell off the business he loved. He, too, casts a longing eye at the spirited and efficient Denise. With her help André will surely make a success, for shoes need a woman in them and his wife never took any interest in the shop but spent all her time out enjoying the first fine flush of *les années folles*.

Finally André (or Dédé as he is known to his intimates) does put in an appearance, but he is not interested in the turnover on his first four days of business, only in decorating the shop with armfuls of flowers ('Voici des Lis'). His sole concern about the events of the past few days is to know whether a lady has telephoned. Indeed she has, and Denise has given her short shrift, but she is not about to admit it as André paces about waiting for the phone to ring again.

His agitated state is relieved by the unexpected arrival of an old friend, the Vicomte Robert Dauvergne, a repeatedly penniless tendril of a noble house who has run through his last inheritance and, with an unflappably resigned heart ('Dans la Vie Faut Pas S'En Faire'), has come to the conclusion that he will finally have to work for a living. André expansively offers him a post as manager of the new shop before leaping to answer the telephone. Alas, Robert's over-enthusiastic approach to a potential customer interrupts the vital call and finally causes it to be lost, leaving André in despair for, although he is distractedly in love, he is unable to remember his fair one's name ('Elle Porte un Nom Charmant') and cannot call her back.

It would, in any case, be unwise, for the lady is married. André met her at a dance and was struck all of a heap, but the lady was delicate in her responses and would not agree to any of the usual rendezvous which might have been propitious for the start of a fashionable affair. It was finally agreed that she could only meet her would-be cavalier in a place where she might go in the normal course of her daily life. The ideal place would be her shoeshop. André ecstatically bought the shoe-shop in question and now he is all a-quiver, waiting for his beloved's call so that their first meeting might be

449

arranged. All is explained. The shoe-shop is merely an elaborate cover set up to aid a folly of passion. It is a passion which might not last long if the lady turns up and finds that André has forgotten her name, so he pops home quickly to look it up.

No sooner has he gone than the phone rings again and Denise answers. She has overheard the whole explanation and she indignantly gives the lady caller a swift goodbye, but Odette (for that is the lady's name) is not to be put off. Soon after, she comes in person to meet André at the shop. He is eloquent in his memories of their first meeting (Tango chanté: 'Le Jardin d'Hiver Était Sombre') but, to his agony, she does not seem particularly keen to proceed with the affair. After much tergiversation, she explains in extenuation that she is the wife of an important person, the prefect of police himself, and that her position is extremely delicate.

Their conversation is split up when Robert returns with the shop girls, all dolled up in their Casino sequins (Finale). He has decided the shop will do better if the girls appear at their daytime job in the costumes of their evening work ('Pour Bien Réussir Dans la Chaussure'). Odette leaves as quickly as she can, but her presence arouses more than curiosity amongst the girls and they are delighted to hear from Denise, who has been listening again, that André has been romancing the wife of the prefect of police.

ACT 2

Robert goes to work to put his girls on display in the most attractive way ('Voici, Messieurs') and Denise joins in by appearing in a plunging gown which leaves little to the imagination. All Robert's enterprise seems likely to be wasted when Chausson returns, in his capacity as union secretary, to announce that the union of shoe-shop salespeople has called a strike. The shop will have to close.

Robert is too much of a man to be bullied by a union. André has arranged for Odette to call by that day and it is planned that this shall be the big moment of ultimate conquest. A man who has paid 300,000 francs for a cover-up for an affair cannot be discommoded by a union. Chausson is sent bootless on his way and Robert continues to enjoy himself with the girls ('Je M'Donne'). Chausson's strike has the effect of stopping the shopboys from attending work so, when Leroydet comes by for his daily sigh, Denise co-opts him behind the counter, giving him strict instructions that, if a lady should telephone, he is to say that André is dead. She also allows him to donate 1000 francs to the till to replace the float which Robert has filched for his jollities. It is no life for a respectable lawyer, but love carries the day and Leroydet opens his wallet.

The plunging neckline sported by Denise has had more effect than she may have bargained for. Her qualities have leaped to the eye of Robert and, while André is preparing his pyjamas for his big event, Robert asks him to return old favours and give him a leg up with Denise ('Rappelle-Toi l'Effacement'). André, however, is preoccupied with his own affairs and Robert instead coaches the sighing Leroydet in a ridiculous caveman approach which brings, as intended, a slap in the face from his beloved, giving Robert the chance to leap cavalierly to the aid of the lady and await his reward. Unfortunately for him, the reward does not come. Denise is waiting for love. When it comes it will cry 'knock, knock, open up' and then, and only then, she will.

Finally, Odette arrives, and André begins his lead-up to a quiet session in the back parlour. He cannot get far, for they are plagued by constant interruptions. Robert is bundled off upstairs, but then a delegation from the union arrives ('Au Nom de la Fédération') and they have to be shunted off to be alcoholically entertained by the shopgirls. Odette moves into a promising position with a seductive song (Valse du Désir) but, as the lovers meet lip to lip, there is a pounding at the door—'knock, knock, open up!'. It is not the police, but Leroydet trying out the formula he thinks will win Denise, and right behind comes Chausson in search of his missing deputation.

This is a disaster, for Chausson is Odette's husband. She is no wife to any prefect. It was all a pretence to hide the fact that the affair with André was set up to allow Chausson to sell his unprofitable shop at a good price. Once the shop was sold, the affair was not supposed to go on. Worse is to come. Denise has written to the commissioner of police to spill the beans about the wife of his prefect and, right on cue, the commissioner arrives. Another executive of the law arrives on a different errand. A passing policeman saw Leroydet doing something with the till and his wallet, and has come to accuse him of theft.

The tiddly union men and the fantastically dressed shopgirls tumble down to join the mêlée as the shop seethes with a mass of half-cocked events (Finale), but Denise comes to the rescue. Appearing in nothing but a tiny slip she announces that it is she who is the woman in the affair and that the whole strange scene is nothing but a rehearsal for the show at the Casino where all the girls work ('Ces Enfants, Aujourd'hui'). To allay suspicions, Robert and André are obliged to invent a scenario for the piece being rehearsed ('Une Femme du Monde Trompait Son Mari'), and they devise it so as to come to a point where the chorus girls cover the eyes of the men, thus allowing Odette to tip-toe out of the parlour and the shop without being seen.

ACT 3
The scandal over the events in the shop has been responsible for a huge upsurge in business and in no time the shop has sold out its entire stock of shoes ('Bonheur Inattendu'). Robert is pursued by the Press but, when he allows himself to leak the information that the lady in the affair was none other than the wife of the prefect of police, he gets a surprise. The prefect is a bachelor! He gets another surprise when Denise comes to hand in her notice. She has decided to marry Leroydet. Robert does not let his surprise dim his acumen. Her willingness to expose herself almost naked in public for the sake of her employer speaks of more than loyalty—she is in love with André. Odette has come to the same conclusion, but she has also realised

that, having cost André 300,000 francs, she is honour bound to give him the required return for his money ('Plaisir d'Amour').

Leroydet has spent the night in prison after being arrested for robbing the till and when he emerges he is a very different fellow. He was thrown into the communal cell with all the local low-life and he has picked up their slang and their style and it is with the force of an apache that he demands that Denise be his bride. Since Odette is waiting for André in the parlour with firm intentions of fulfilling her obligations, Denise decides to accept. But Odette gets bored with waiting and Robert decides to entertain her with a carefully contrived song which leads up to a kiss ('J'Ose Pas') and a conversation which leads them both into the back parlour.

No sooner have they disappeared than Denise returns. She has accidentally taken away a few coins which belong to the firm and she is intent on returning them. She is morbidly upset to hear the sounds of amorous activity coming from behind the closed door but, as she goes to leave, she meets André coming into the shop and, delighted to see that it is not he in the parlour, she embraces him enthusiastically. André is stunned with delight at the power of the kiss and, all of a sudden, the last love of his life gives way to the newest love of his life. Denise is not to wed Leroydet; he will go knock, knock, and open up her heart, as they head towards love and marriage ('Tous les Chemins Mènent à l'Amour').

When Chausson comes by, André gives him back his shop and the happy *cordonnier* is delighted when he sees his wife on the premises. At last she is showing interest in the business. André and Denise are amazed to hear that Odette is Madame Chausson—if they had known, this whole story would never have come about ('Si J'Avais Su'). But it did. And now everyone can live happily ever after, including Robert, who will stay on to manage Chaussures Chausson and, presumably, Madame Chausson, with the help of the most original bouquet of shopgirls in Paris.

TA BOUCHE

(Your Lips)

an opérette in three acts by Yves Mirande. Lyrics by Albert Willemetz. Music by Maurice Yvain. Produced at the Théâtre Daunou, Paris, 1 April 1922 with Victor Boucher (Bastien), Jeanne Saint-Bonnet (Eva), Guyon fils (Pas de Vis), Jeanne Cheirel (Comtesse), Gabin (Jean) and Mary-Hett (Mélanie). Produced at the Théâtre Mogador 12 August 1944 with Daniel Clérice, Marcelle Garnier, Edmond Castel and Germaine Charley. Produced at the Théâtre Antoine 29 May 1980 with Daniel Demars, Arièle Semenoff, Caroline Cler, Bernard Lavalette, Patrick Préjean and Perrette Souplex.

Produced at the Fulton Theatre, New York, 27 November 1923 as *One Kiss* with Ada Lewis, John E Hazzard, Louise Groody, Oscar Shaw and John Price Jones.

A film version was produced in the 1930s.

CHARACTERS

Bastien du Pas de Vis
Monsieur Pas de Vis, *his father*
Mélanie, *his housekeeper*
Eva
La Comtesse, *her mother*
Jean, *her valet de chambre*
Marguerite, Mag, Margot, *gossips*

ACT 1

The scene is the garden of the Casino at the resort of Truc-sur-Mer (Thingummyjig-on-the-Sea) at the blossoming of that period of history known as *les années folles*. Among the habituées of this almost fashionable place are three young ladies called Marguerite, Mag and Margot who spend the season having a wonderful time retailing the gossip which sprouts from such a fertile field ('Nous Ne Disons Jamais de Mal de Personne'). At the moment one of their chief topics of gossip is the romance between the handsome young Bastien and the lovely Eva. The trio have not been able to lay their hands on any solid facts, and they are dying to know all there is to know. Are they engaged? Will they be married? Or will it end up as a sordid little tumble-in-a-corner? I love you honey but the season's over.

Margot sees nothing to prevent a marriage. The two young people obviously like each other and, since her mother is a countess and a rich woman who keeps a formerly wealthy lover as her *valet de chambre*, and his father is apparently worth a perfect fortune, all the necessary prerequisites for an alliance seem to be there. Marguerite and Mag are more practised hands at resort-watching and they need more evidence before they are convinced. When Jean, the Countess's valet, comes by the gossips draw him covetously into conversation and they succeed in alarming him dreadfully when his confident assertations about Monsieur Pas de Vis and his blossoming bank balance meet with knowing looks and a lot of humming. Mélanie, the housekeeper of the Pas de Vis ménage, is equally worried when her chatter about the rich Countess and her daughter wins a similarly enigmatic response.

If the gossips can cast doubt on the family background of both Bastien and Eva, they certainly cannot cast any doubt on the fervency of their love. The two young people meet on the sea-front, under the blue of the sky, with the Casino band playing romantically in the distance a song about kissing ('Ta Bouche'), which leads them naturally into thinking temptingly of such a pleasant pastime. The trouble with all this kissing is that Bastien is finding self-control more and more difficult. It is all very well to be engaged, it is all very well to have one's parents agreed that a wedding will take place but, in the meanwhile, what is one supposed to do? It is very frustrating and, if he is not to yield to temptation, he must go away from it and from her. Eva thinks this is an awful idea. It is infinitely preferable that he, and she, should yield.

453

As the music plays on, they hurry off to find an undisturbed spot in which to start.

Romance and/or sex are indigenous at a resort and, while the young people are busy testing out their suitability for marriage, their parents are indulging in the first stages of a flirtation. They both are loud in their praises of their servants—each of whom is, as it happens, their former lover—('Voilà Comment Est Jean') but each is content to drop hints of some kind of a permanent alliance between themselves. They each spread general descriptions of their wealth but, strangely enough, when it comes to the point, neither has any money to hand. Her fortune is in land and his in stocks and shares ('Des Terres et des Coupons').

Bastien and Eva are altogether happy with the private celebration of their engagement. With the trial run satisfyingly over, they can look forward with both confidence and enjoyment to a really exceptional wedding night. Eva is fulsome in her praise of the invention of lovemaking, as opposed to such a utilitarian practice as baby-making, and declares that it ought to be made obligatory for everyone, plain or pretty. Bastien joins her in her opinion. Every year, for Christmas, all girls ought to find 'Un Petit Amant' in their stocking.

Unfortunately for the two families, the present happy situation is not to last long. Jean swiftly brings his newly bred suspicions about the Pas de Vis family to his mistress and, when Eva comes happily to her mother to ask that she should be wed as soon as possible, she finds that the Countess has changed her attitude to Bastien. He is nothing but a gigolo, an adventurer, and Eva must never see him again. She must wed a fine gentleman with money. Eva cannot understand this. Why, even if it were true that Bastien is poor, she is her mother's heir and she will have plenty of money for two.

The Countess is obliged to admit to her daughter that her position is and always has been a lie. There is nothing to inherit. Eva is her only saleable commodity and she is relying on Eva to make a fine marriage to support them all. She is aghast when she discovers that Bastien and Eva have anticipated their marriage not only in thought but in action, but she is not a woman to be put off by such a thing. Far from reacting in the pre-war manner and hurrying the two fallen creatures to the altar, she simply determines to leave Thingummyjig-on-the-Sea immediately.

Eva hurries to tell the dreadful news to Bastien who, in his turn, runs to his father to deplore the loss of the girl they have spent all season trying to get. Pas de Vis is livid with his son. He has gone about it all the wrong way. All that billing and cooing. What he should have done was get the girl into bed ('Quand On Veut Plaire aux Demoiselles'). Bastien tells him that he did, just as Mélanie turns up with her gossip about the Countess. Pas de Vis is horrified at the near escape both he and his son have had at the hands of these common adventurers and, in spite of the protestations of the love-sick Bastien, he prepares to leave town instantly.

The lovers grab one last clandestine meeting and, to the strains of the Casino orchestra's daily rendition of 'Ta Bouche', share one last kiss before they are dragged away from each other for what should be forever.

ACT 2

At the Casino of Pouic-les-Flots (Whatsit-on-the-Sea), precisely twelve months later, a strange coincidence brings Margot, Mag and Marguerite together again. An even stranger coincidence means that the Pas de Vis family has also changed resorts. They have gone up in the world. Bastien, having heard no word from Eva, has bowed to his father's wishes and married a very plain but very wealthy lady from the industrial sector whilst Pas de Vis has finally got around to marrying Mélanie who, not coincidentally, had inherited a great fortune just shortly before. Bastien is not happy. His wife both bores and repels him, and fulfilling his conjugal duties is a nightmare for him. Pas de Vis, who now calls himself Count is much better off, although Mélanie never lets him forget to whom the family money belongs.

You will not be surprised to hear that our other friends, the Countess and her daughter and valet, have also chosen Pouic-les-Flots for this year's season but you may be surprised to hear of the change in their status. The Countess has finally married her Jean and, since his surname is Leduc, she feels entitled to call herself la Duchesse. Eva has become an asset to the family. Having had no letters from Bastien, she has given herself up wholly to profit and has assiduously collected gifts of jewellery from a number of wealthy men who are anxious to know her better. She has won quite a reputation, but it is one that is undeserved for Eva has remained faithful to the thought of Bastien in spite of appearances to the contrary ('Non, Non, Jamais les Hommes'). The Duchess approves of the results but finds it all rather different from the ways of getting on practised in her own youth ('De Mon Temps').

Jean and Mélanie, both now finely and almost ridiculously over-dressed, meet and, without recognising each other, try to size each other up as opportunities for social or financial benefit. It isn't long before the other members of the two families run into each other as well. Bastien is reminiscing over first love ('Ça, C'Est une Chose') when Eva comes upon him. When the recriminations are done and it becomes clear that the lack of letters was the handiwork of their zealous parents, it only remains for Bastien to convince Eva of his lack of enthusiasm for life and sex with his wife ('Machinalement') and she to convince him of her profitable but continued fidelity, for them to head off for the nearest cheap hotel to replight their troth. Then it is the turn of Pas de Vis and the Countess to come face to face again. Their new situations mean that they each scrupulously observe polite and correct manners whilst running down the other to their respective consorts (Quartet: 'Puisqu'un Heureux Hasard').

Eva and Bastien find that their second encounter is even better than the first ('La Seconde Etreinte') and, in the joy of the moment, they decide that something must be done. Bastien will just have to get rid of his wife. But how? She is mild-tempered, well-bred, well-behaved and there is, unfortunately, certainly no grounds for a divorce for refusal of conjugal rights. Suddenly, however, Eva notices that she is wearing a strange cloak. How embarrassing! In leaving the dubious hotel where they spent their pleasure, she has mistakenly picked up the wrong garment. But it is a cloak which Bastien recognises—it belongs to his wife. What is she doing in such a place? Maybe this letter in the pocket will shed some light on the situation.

It does. It is a love letter from the son of one of her industrial colleagues arranging a rendezvous at this dreadfully seedy hotel this very day. Bastien is mortified. He has been cuckolded. Cuckolded by a wife who looks like the back of a horse! How can he ever hold his head up in society again? Eva tries to calm him. After all, he now has the grounds for divorce which he wanted. But Bastien is wounded heinously in his *amour-propre* and he can think of nothing else. He is a cuckold!

ACT 3

A year later, at the resort of Fric-les-Bains (Something-or-Other-Pool), Jean and Mélanie are discovered walking arm in arm. Given the ephemerality of relationships which seems to exist amongst our friends of *les années folles*, we should not be surprised to learn that they are now Monsieur and Madame Leduc. Mélanie shed Pas de Vis, and it had absolutely nothing to do with the fact that she inherited, in quick succession, three more fortunes, that Jean rid himself of the Countess and hitched himself up to the woman he had looked at with interest in Act 1. Now they are happy and unostentatious and can look back on their days as servants with a smile for they will have none of their own ('Les Domestiques'). Mag and Marguerite are here too, but without Margot who has found herself a husband, and they have lost none of their wide-eyed maliciousness ('Nous Ne Disons Jamais de Mal de Personne').

The pale and wandering young man who can be seen on the promenade is Bastien who, as he wanders, can still be heard to mumble wanly about being cuckolded and ridiculous. He has fled to this ghastly, out-of-the-way resort to be sure of not meeting Eva, for he cannot look her in the eye and he certainly cannot now marry her. If a man can be deceived and cuckolded by a plain wife, what chance does he have to hold the love of a wonderfully pretty one? But Eva, with the aid of a large bribe to his concierge, tracks him down.

For the whole year she has been trying to find him, as he travelled all over the place, trying to forget and even considering becoming a monk, and now she is determined to convince him that his shame and his fears are groundless ('Pour Toi'). They are young, they love each other, she is rich, he is rich having been given half his wife's factory as consolation in his divorce, they have everything that is needed to be happy including the knowledge that they make decidedly first rate sex together. It is stupid to waste such potential for happiness. How can Bastien resist? It is clearly time to reconfirm their engagement in exactly the same way they originally plighted it and, third time lucky, this time she'd better hang on to him.

And now who should appear, looking for a third-rate resort where none of their acquaintances can find them, but Pas de Vis and the Countess. Freshly divorced, and their children disappeared and off their hands hopefully for good, they have time to devote to themselves and it seems that they are going to devote it to each other ('Quand On A du Sens'). The situation would not be complete without the last character, so finally Margot arrives. Due to a slight indiscretion on her part, her marriage is over and she has come back to join her friends in a new round of gossip and a search for a fresh husband.

Jean and Mélanie, who had come to the resort for peace, quiet and anonymity, aren't really having much luck. Even a quiet siesta in their hotel has been interrupted by the sound of lovemaking pounding through the walls and a woman crying out 'O Maman!' in her ecstasy ('Au Milieu de Notre Entretien'). They are even more taken aback when they meet their ex-spouses and they devise a little test to discover if the noisy neighbours are perhaps them (Quartet: 'Comment Pourrions-Nous Faire'). Mélanie asks the Countess to say 'O Maman!'. But then Bastien comes in and sees his father—O Papa! and Eva sees her mother... O Maman! The puzzle is solved.

Bastien and Eva have come to ask, as they did all that time ago in Act 1, for permission to marry, and this time there is no problem. The only thing is to decide where they will go for their honeymoon. Venice? In that case Jean and Mélanie will choose India, and Pas de Vis and his Countess will head for Spain. Hopefully there will be no Casinos and Margot, Mag and Marguerite will not turn up.

CIBOULETTE

an opérette in three acts by Robert de Flers and Francis de Croisset. Music by Reynaldo Hahn. Produced at the Théâtre des Variétés, Paris, 7 April 1923 with Edmée Favart (Ciboulette), Jean Périer (Duparquet), Henry Defreyn (Antonin) and Jeanne Perriat (Zénobie). Produced at the Théâtre Marigny 2 October 1926 with Mlle Favart, André Bauge, Defreyn and Danielle Brégis. Produced at the Théâtre de la Gaîté-Lyrique 1931 with Nini Roussel and 20 January 1935 with Renée Camia, Aquistapace, André Noël and May Muriel. Produced at the Théâtre National de l'Opéra Comique 13 March 1953 with Géori Boué, Roger Bourdin, Raymond Amade and Lili Grandval. Produced at the Opéra Studio 25 October 1975 with Nicole Broissin.

A film version was produced by Claude Autant-Lara in 1935 with Simone Berriau, Robert Burnier, Dranem and Thérèse Dorny.

CHARACTERS

Ciboulette
Le Père Grenu, *her uncle*
La Mère Grenu, *her aunt*
Vicomte Antonin de Mourmelon
Zénobie de Guernesey, *a courtesan*
Roger de Lansquenet, *a captain of hussars*
Rodolphe Duparquet
Olivier Métra
La Mère Pingret, *an old market woman*

Auguste, *a market worker*
Grisart
Comtesse de Castiglione
Tranchu, Victor, Françoise, Marquise de Presles, Mayor, Bailiff, etc.

ACT 1

At the Parisian café Au Chien Qui Fume, the young hussar Roger de Lansquenet is celebrating his promotion to the rank of lieutenant in the company of his mildly jealous fellow soldiers ('Nous Sommes Six Hussards') and a bouquet of attentive courtesans. Roger has no particular feminine companion to share his night of celebration because it happens to be a Monday. On Mondays, Wednesdays and Fridays the lovely Zénobie de Guernesey, with whom he has been leading a tempestuous affair for the past month, is obliged to spend her time with the exceedingly rich Vicomte Antonin de Mourmelon who, understandably, is able to offer her far more in the way of material comforts than a simple lieutenant of hussars. Although de Mourmelon is only twenty-eight and passably attractive, Roger is not in the slightest bit jealous for it goes without saying that anyone who is so rich has never been young and could not possibly be loved with the passionate disinterest which characterises the sentiment between himself and Zénobie.

The party has lasted into the small hours and, since it is five o'clock, the landlord comes to shift the revellers into a different room. It is not that he wants to get rid of his customers, but soon the occupants of the private rooms will begin to emerge, and professional delicacy demands that they must be able to do so without being seen. Roger is determined to find out which social giant requires such protection for his amours ('Est-Ce Thiers?'), but the truth is that there is no one. The landlord is merely trying to give his café a cachet by pretending that he has such visitors.

Soon, however, he really does have a fine customer to welcome, for Antonin de Mourmelon arrives with Zénobie who, having led him to the Au Chien Qui Fume, immediately despatches him for a wrap so that she may rendezvous with Roger. The meeting of the hussar and his mistress is watched by another early morning visitor, the market comptroller, Duparquet, who shakes his head sadly at the frivolity of it all. Duparquet is middle-aged, a kindly but somehow sad man who remembers his own youth, its enormous sincerity and its grand love, and regrets that those passions should, in the lighthearted Paris of 1867, have dwindled to such small emotions as those displayed at the Au Chien Qui Fume ('Ce N'Était Pas la Même Chose').

Zénobie and Roger enjoy themselves in each other's company ('Toi! Vous!') until Antonin returns and discovers from Duparquet how he is being fooled. When he espies Roger amongst the revellers ('Après Cette Nuit d'Orgie'), the cuckolded Vicomte ignores Zénobie's attempts to cozen him into calm and announces before all the company that he is handing his mistress over to his rival ('Roger A Fait Votre Conquête'). With her, he is handing over all the bills for the innumerable purchases she has made in the last month, a bundle which makes the hussar blanch for, between them, he and Zénobie had thought to take the rich young man for quite a ride ('Les P'tites Femm's de Paris'). Antonin may have lost his mistress, but he has found in Duparquet a good friend who promises to lead him into happier times and, as the hussars and their ladies gambol off into the early morning streets, the two men step out with a reasonably firm stride, away from Au Chien Qui Fume and all that it represents .

At Les Halles at this hour of the morning the market gardeners are laying out their wares for the day ('Nous Sommes les Bons Maraîchers'). Today one of them is late: a little lass who brings her vegetables from the Aubervilliers suburb is behind time and the client who has ordered her whole stock for the day at a price of 500 francs is annoyed. The reason why the darling of the market is late is that it is her twenty-first birthday and she has been so full of the joy of living that she has dallied on the way to take in the sky and the trees and all the lovely things that the first day of May brings ('Dans une Charrett").

Ciboulette—for that is her unlikely name ('Moi, Je M'Appelle Ciboulette')—has taken it into her head that on this day she must have her fortune told. Since she is twenty-one, she must be thinking about marriage and, having accepted offers already from eight young men in her village, she is anxious to know what to do for the best. La Mère Pingret, who boasts of being able to predict the weather, births, unfaithfulness, the price of meat and anything to do with love, is pressed into service for forty sous to give a reading of the birthday girl's palm. Her conclusions are promising but baffling. Ciboulette is not destined to marry any of her eight fiancés; she will be rich and adored, but only on condition that she shall find her destined husband under a cabbage, that she shall win him away from a woman who will go white-haired in an instant, and that she shall receive a notice of death in a tambourine.

For the moment, Ciboulette is decidedly poor. Her client, tired of waiting for his vegetables, has gone and made his purchases elsewhere and she has lost the five hundred francs she was counting on. The weeping girl appeals to the market comptroller to enforce the purchase ('Oh! Mon Dieu! Dans Ses Yeux Que de Larmes') but, when it is revealed that she turned up half an hour late, Duparquet is obliged to give judgement in favour of the customer. He would willingly make good the girl's loss himself, but he cannot: five hundred francs is a lot of money. It is not a lot, however, to Duparquet's new friend, Antonin, and he quickly offers to make good Ciboulette's loss.

The girl is effusive in her thanks but notices that her kind benefactor is in less than sparkling form. When he tells her the sad tale of his betrayal by Zénobie she laughs and tells him that he is well rid of such a woman. Now he is free to be his own man and do as he alone wishes. It is a situation in which Antonin has never found himself before—parents, teachers, army officers and mistresses have all had him under their thumb ('Les Parents, Quand On Est Bébé')—and he wonders if he will be able to cope with making his own decisions in this world that his new friend ('Comme Frère et Soeur') has pointed out to him.

Ciboulette hurries off to work and Antonin, shattered by the effects of the night's drink and drama and unable to face returning alone to his former love nest, gratefully accepts the offer of a stallholder to curl up in his cart for a nap. As the market swings into life ('Mettons Nos Tabliers Coquets'), the flower sellers begin to cry the sale of the traditional lily of the valley with which May Day is celebrated ('Muguet, Muguet') and Ciboulette loads up the wares which she did not need to sell and prepares to head back to Aubervilliers and her farm.

ACT 2

Back on the farm ('C'Est le Doux Silence des Champs'), Ciboulette's uncle and aunt are getting on with their work while they await her return. Today she is bringing Monsieur Duparquet with her, for each Monday he comes to take lunch with the family Grenu ('Nous Avons Fait un Beau Voyage') but, in spite of their visitor, and in spite of the fact that it is Ciboulette's birthday, Uncle Grenu has some stern words for her. He has found out about the eight fiancés and is most annoyed. He is so annoyed that he insists that she chooses one of them right away, becomes officially engaged, and sends the rest away.

Poor Ciboulette isn't in love with any of the eight and she is in a dreadful dilemma when suddenly a head pops up from amongst the vegetables in her cart. It is Antonin wondering wherever he is. Is this what people call the 'country'? Ciboulette laughingly explains that Aubervilliers is scarcely country ('C'Est Sa Banlieu') before Duparquet comes up with a bright idea. Antonin can pretend to be Nicolas, the new steward who is due to arrive that day, and Ciboulette can claim to be engaged to him and send all the eight fiancés away. And so, when the eight villagers come to line up before the Grenu farm to await their fiancée's choice ('C'Est Nous les Fiancés'), they are disappointed to find that they have all been cut out by a stranger.

Grenu, delighted to have things fixed up so well, leaves the two young people alone to cement their relationship but, since it is only supposed to be a make-believe engagement, the two of them are reduced to thinking of what would be happening if Antonin really were the steward whom he is pretending to be ('Ah! Si Vous Étiez Nicolas'). But by now a realisation has come to Ciboulette. La Mère Pingret's first condition has been fulfilled: Antonin truly came to her from under a cabbage in the back of the cart.

It just so happens that the 12th Hussars are exercising in the vicinity of Aubervilliers this morning, and the 12th Hussars are the regiment of Roger de Lansquenet and his late-night drinking friends. It also just so happens that they stop off at the Grenu farm for refreshment. Ciboulette is quick to recognise them and, in order that Antonin shall not meet up with Zénobie, she locks him in the wine cellar before entertaining the visitors with a rousing version of their regimental marching song (Chanson de Route: 'Y A d'la Lune au Bord du Toit Qu'Est Ronde').

Zénobie, jealous of the effect made by this spruce little farm girl, passes

460

some acid comments to which Ciboulette is quick to respond with equal vigour, and the argument which develops is ended dramatically when Ciboulette tips a whole bag of flour over the head of the grand town lady. The second part of the prophecy has come true! Zénobie, a dazzling brunette, goes white-haired in an instant. When Ciboulette tells her triumphant story to Antonin, she does not get quite the response she expected. He is wretched not to have seen the one he has so long adored and he is horrified at the treatment meted out by his new friend to the woman whom he is pitifully sure still loves him.

The girl's dander rises like a geyser at this plaintive talk and she stoutly orders the quivering fellow out of the house, but as soon as he is gone she pours out her misery to the avuncular Duparquet. In return, she hears the story of a real and tragic love, his own. It is a tale set in a Paris garret where, in his youth, he and his little mistress lived and loved. From time to time she went with other men so that she might have some of the little luxuries that their money could buy her, but she always returned. Then, after one period away, she came back ill and dying. As she lay, a tiny, cold figure on their bed, she asked if she might have a muff to warm her tiny frozen hands and one of his friends sold his coat to bring the little fur to warm her last hours. But love could not save his Mimi. She died, and now, all these years later, all he has left to remember her by is a little handkerchief ('C'Est Tout Ce Qui Me Reste d'Elle') kept in his coat pocket next to his heart.

It was all a long time ago, but Rodolphe Duparquet knows something of love and, when he is convinced that Ciboulette is truly in love with Antonin, he decides that he will help her. What dazzles the silly fellow about Zénobie is her celebrity, so he will make Ciboulette equally celebrated. He has heard her rendition of the regimental marching song and has no doubt that she can make a great success as a musical theatre star. He will take her to meet the famous composer Olivier Métra right away. Ciboulette rushes off to dress up in her best clothes, just as the mayor and town council arrive to take part in the betrothal ceremony ('Nous Somm's les Bons Villageois'). To Grenu's horror, Duparquet announces that Ciboulette has been widowed before she has been wed. The bridegroom has vanished and the lady in question adds further to the scandal by appearing in her Sunday best to announce that she is heading for town to go on the stage. No longer will she be Ciboulette, but the mysterious Spanish diva Conchita Cibouléro, rich and famous. Mollified by the word 'rich', the Grenus bid their niece a fond farewell and Duparquet leads her off to the city.

ACT 3

At a fashionable soirée at the home of Olivier Métra, the début of Conchita Cibouléro is about to take place before a shining assembly including the beautiful Comtesse de Castiglione ('Dans le Monde Quand Nous Sortons'). Antonin is there feeling very singular. He is a free man. He has quarrelled again with Zénobie and has broken with her for good but, looking around amongst the flower of Parisian beauty filling the salon, he realises that he doesn't fancy any of them ('J'Ai Vingt-Huit Ans'). He is in love with Ciboulette and he must go to Aubervilliers right away and find her. But Duparquet has grim news for him. He will not find her there for she has vanished and no one knows where.

Antonin decides that if he is never to see Ciboulette again he might as well kill himself. However, since there is absolutely no sense in killing oneself for a woman if the woman does not know about it, he will compose a heart-rending letter to be given to his beloved after his death. He is not a terribly literary fellow, so the one-time Bohemian, Duparquet, lends a hand and dictates a touching note ('Mon Amour, Daigne Me Pemettre'). The letter is put in the hands of a scornful butler, with orders from Duparquet that it shall be delivered at midnight to Señorita Ciboulero, as Antonin goes off to spend his last night on earth at the end of several bottles.

Conchita Ciboulero, dazzlingly dressed and masked, appears with her 'mother'—la Mère Pingret dressed up for the occasion and unable to cope with the social graces required—and performs a glittering waltz song ('Amour Qui Meurs! Amour Qui Passes!') only to find Antonin flinging himself before her with professions of love. She takes a pencil and paper, hands them to him and commands him to write the words 'Ciboulette, I do not love you', but the young man cannot do it. Happily plucking off her mask, Ciboulette declares her love and the delirious Antonin asks her to be his wife.

But wait! The third part of the prophecy has not yet been fulfilled and la Mère Pingret cannot allow her dicta to go unproven. Then the clock chimes midnight and Métra steps forward with a little tambourine as a gift for his guest. Inside the tambourine is the letter which the butler has been asked to deliver. It is Antonin's letter announcing his own death. And so la Mère Pingret is satisfied. Fate has been allowed to run its course, and Antonin and Ciboulette can live happily ever after.

PAS SUR LA BOUCHE

(Not on the Lips)

an opérette in three acts by André Barde. Music by Maurice Yvain. Produced at the Théâtre des Nouveautés, Paris, 17 February 1925 with Régine Flory (Gilberte), Jeanne Cheirel (Mlle Poumaillac), Pierrette Madd (Huguette), Berval (Valandray), Robert Darthez (Charley), Adrien Lamy (Thomson) and Germain Champell (Faradel). Produced at the Théâtre des Bouffes-Parisiens 1948 with Marina Hotine, Spinelly, Jacqueline Ricard, Lestelly, Gérald Castrix, René Novan and Serge Berry.

Produced at the Shaftesbury Theatre, London, in a version by Frederick Jackson with additional songs by Desmond Carter and Vivian Ellis as *Just A Kiss* 8 September 1926 with Marjorie Gordon (Valerie), Marie George (Miss Trask), Vera Lennox (Rita Reynolds), Frederick Ranalow (Armand), Arthur Margetson (Kenneth Courtney), Barrie Oliver (Charles Crawford) and Harry Hilliard (Soames).

A film version was produced by Nicolas Rimsky and Nicolas Evreïmof in 1930 with Mireille Perrey.

CHARACTERS

Gilberte Valandray
Georges Valandray, *her second husband*
Eric Thomson, *her former husband*
Mlle Poumaillac, *her maiden aunt*
Huguette Verberie, *her cousin*
Charley
Faradel
Madame Foin, *a concierge*
Yvonne, Suzanne, Colette, Mado, Juliette

ACT 1

Gilberte Valandray has been married for six happy years to the wealthy industrialist Georges Valandray but, although they are still as much in love as they were in their unwed days, Gilberte has one tiny secret which she keeps from her husband. In her youth, whilst on a visit to America, she was married to a man called Eric Thomson. The marriage did not last more than six months and, under the interesting laws of musical comedy France, it was deemed never to have officially taken place but, be that as it may, Georges is at least semi-officially Gilberte's second husband. He is not aware of this, but there is a lot of land and ocean between Paris and Chicago, so Gilberte's delightful daily life is not unduly clouded by the memories of her unfortunate ex-husband and she is able to enjoy to the hilt the existence of an attractive and wealthy married woman of *les années folles*.

When the action begins, Gilberte is not at home and her living room is occupied by a quartet of chorus girls who have come to visit ('Quand une Maitress' de Maison'). Having set things in motion, the chorines are soon swept off the stage by another visitor, the fussy Faradel, who gets rid of them by pretending there is a sale 'Aux Galeries Lalayette'. Faradel is Gilberte's lover, in the most anodyne sense of the word. Gilberte is quite happy to permit his poodle-like devotion, since she has no intention of ever letting him lure her to his hopefully rented *garçonnière*, and Faradel, a model of chivalric behaviour, lives in blissfully ignorant hope.

Huguette, Gilberte's teenage cousin and a determinedly up-to-date little miss, finds the poor fellow a huge joke, and she teases him horribly in her mad, modern way ('Je l'Aime Mieux Autrement'), but Gilberte's aunt, Mlle Poumaillac, a surprisingly social and fast-living person for a maiden lady, understands the situation perfectly and is very happy to use Faradel as a spare gentleman for dinner parties and to capitalise on his ability to organise artistic soirées and the other necessities of terribly modern living.

Mlle Poumaillac is a maiden lady by accident—the accident of playing hard to get for too long. She was still playing hard to get when little Gilberte became an orphan and she then devoted herself to bringing up the child and

463

didn't get around to men, at least not for herself. She was very much in evidence during Gilberte's fleeting first marriage, and it is clear that the her presence and the animosity that arose between her and the bridegroom were, at least partly, responsible for its breakdown, but now she lives as an adored aunt in the Valandray home, keeping their household running impeccably for both their private and public lives.

Mlle Poumaillac is a lady of decided social wisdom which she dispenses liberally and helpfully ('Ce Qu'On Dit et Ce Qu'On Pense'), and a monolith of reliability in any situation. When Huguette confides that she has fallen in love with the advanced young artist, Charley, her aunt promises to give events a helpful twist. This is not as easy as it might sound for Charley, with all the earnestness of his twenty years, is as mad about Gilberte as Faradel is. He has equally little chance of ever consummating his passion, as Gilberte, while allowing these passionate attentions as necessary part of fashionable modern living, is utterly faithful to her husband ('Comme J'Aim'rais Mon Mari').

The situation does nothing but amuse Valandray. He sees right through the stuttering explanations of Faradel ('Je Suis V'nu Simplement') and Charley's blushes, but their adoration of his wife does not bother him a bit. He is unquenchably sure of himself and of Gilberte because he has an industrial theory on relationships based on the tenets of metallurgy: the first man who sleeps with a woman puts his mark on her and, thereafter, no matter what may occur, there is something between them which can never be gainsaid. Since their wedding night was (or so he believes) Gilberte's first night of love, he knows that he and she are safely tied for all time. He has shared his theory with his wife and, as a result, Gilberte and her aunt have found it even more imperative to keep the existence of Mr Eric Thomson a secret. What Valandray does not know will not grieve him, and they do not wish to harm the confident equilibrium of the happiest of marriages.

When Charley comes to the house to pay homage to Gilberte, Mlle Poumaillac takes the chance to indulge in some helpful connubial hints on Huguette's behalf without, of course, naming the young woman, but the boy announces that he is not at all interested in the idea of marrying a teenage girl—it is altogether more *à la mode* to sigh over a glamorous, married woman. Affairs are *comme il faut* and marriage for anything but convenience is horribly old-fashioned. Whatever poor Charley isn't, he is a desperately modern boy, deeply into a most recherché form of modern art which he has invented ('C'Est d' la Réclame'). He is terribly wounded when Gilberte refuses to take his passion seriously, but he finds temporary solace in the remembrance of childhood games with Huguette ('Pic et Pic et Colegram').

Gilberte spends her own happiest hours with her husband ('Rien Qu'un Baiser'/La Péruvienne) but what is her despair when one day Georges announces that he has invited an American business associate to the house, and that American turns out to be Eric Thomson. Mlle Poumaillac hastens to the rescue and, before Thomson can let any unfortunate facts slip, she warns him imperiously to hold his tongue (Finale: 'Il Faudrait'). Since the other guests for the evening are Charley, Huguette and Faradel, it is clear

Ba-Ta-Clan. Offenbach's crazy Chinese Frenchmen are here played by Australians Graeme Ewer and Michael Lewis. Australian Opera, 1982.

Les Noces de Jeannette. Liliane Berton and Michel Dens brought Massé's little piece back to its original home at the Opéra-Comique in 1960.

Orphée aux Enfers. Pluto (Jon Weaving) tempts Juno (Sheila Rex) to the culinary delights of Hades under the disapproving glance of Jupiter (Eric Shilling).
Sadler's Wells Opera, 1964.

La Belle Hélène. Menelaos (John Fryatt) comes under fire from the massed royalty of Greece. Sadler's Wells Opera, 1967.

La Vie Parisienne. The Brazilian (John Winfield) arrives in Paris prepared to burn up another fortune. Sadler's Wells Opera, 1974.

Mam'zelle Nitouche. A convent singing lesson turns into a jolly duet. Fabienne Guyon (Denise) and Jean-Marie Proslier (Celestin) at the Bouffes-Parisiens, 1984.

La Grande-Duchesse de Gérolstein. 'Voi le sabre de mon père!' The Grand Duchess prepares to hand over the famous sword of her ancestors to the hastily promoted Fritz while the displaced General Boum scowls in the background. British lithograph *c* 1870

Dédé. André de la Huchette (James Sparrow) and a set of shopgirls borrowed from the chorus line of the Casino de Paris. Théâtre des Nouveautés, 1973.

that there is going to be a certain tension around the dinner table ('C'Est un Petit Dîner').

ACT 2

The evening is stage-managed through to its end without incident but, to Gilberte's horror, Thomson becomes a regular visitor to the house while he and Valandray work together on a possible business collaboration. Fortunately there are plenty of other visitors to distract her, for Mlle Poumaillac's social and artistic whirl is relentless. A soirée staged to allow Charley to present his newest and most avant-garde, multi-media opus before a crowd of guests gathered together by the active Mademoiselle, brings all the members of the dinner party together again. Faradel, who has developed a tendency to nervous hiccups ('J'Ai le Hoquet'), is amongst the audience, but Charley and Gilberte are both to take part in the performance. Valandray finds the arty crowd too much for him and he takes the opportunity to escape into a topical song which takes a prod at a number of contemporary nuisances including immigrant labour ('Je Me Suis Laissé Embouteiller').

Gilberte is not having a relaxing evening. Everywhere she looks Thomson seems to be watching her and, when Faradel takes the opportunity of a moment alone with her to declare his passion for the umpteenth time, he finds himself cornered by the heavy-breathing Thomson. This lady is spoken for, and he would do better to find himself a different inamorata. It is advice which Mlle Poumaillac, realising that Thomson is still in love with his ex-wife, hastens to give right back to him: if the one you love isn't free, be content with someone else ('Quand On N'A Pas Ce Que l'On Aime'). But Thomson, it appears, has a problem which prevents his becoming satisfactorily embroiled with another woman. He cannot kiss anyone on the lips. Once, when he was twelve years old, his teacher kissed him on the lips and it aroused such turmoil in him that he swore never again would he allow a woman to kiss him. Even during his marriage with Gilberte, although their relationship was otherwise consummate, he never allowed her to kiss him on the lips.

This information is grist to the mill of Mlle Poumaillac's designs. The way to distract Thomson from Gilberte is to get some other woman to kiss him. Since he is a millionaire and not bad looking, this should not be too difficult. Perhaps Huguette can help out. But Huguette does not want a millionaire. She wants Charley and, when she discovers that Charley, obstinate in his modern ideas, is interested only in an affair, preferably with a married woman, and above all preferably with Gilberte, she decides that she will have to change tactics.

Gilberte and Charley take time out to rehearse their performance for the Total Art presentation ('Soirs de Méxique'). It is awfully modern and it contains some reasonably passionate pieces including an actual kiss which, needless to say, is overseen by the lurking Thomson. Gilberte's wholehearted playing of the passionate pieces leads Charley to believe that his

465

pursuit of his lady is progressing and he begs Faradel to let him borrow his *garçonnière* to entertain an unnamed lady. Faradel agrees. After all, the *garçonnière* has been sadly unused and, in fact, as from the next day his lease will end. Charley might as well have it for the last day.

It is a very excited Charley who is discovered by Huguette when she comes to try her new tactics. She explains to Charley that she intends to make a play for the rich Thomson. To win him, it apparently will suffice to kiss him on the lips but, she sighs, she has no experience of such things. Will Charley show her how it is done? Just as she had hoped, the lesson in foreplay leads the rampant Charley into a real kiss ('Ça C'Est Gentil'). It can only be considered as progress.

Thomson has been devastated by the sight of Gilberte and Charley kissing. He is furious with Mlle Poumaillac, who he considers has led his wife into debauchery but when Gilberte, thinking to rid herself of him, claims that Charley is her lover she finds that the thought of her as a woman of the world only arouses Thomson to more intense emotion. He demands that Charley be dismissed and that he instead become her lover. Gilberte has had enough, and she begs her husband to send Thomson away. They are sufficiently well-off to continue without the extra profits to be gained from his business ('Il Suffit d'un Rien'). Valandray refuses to consider such a thing and, even when Gilberte insists that Thomson has been making passes at her, in his sublime certitude he simply laughs the situation off.

Mlle Poumaillac, continuing her campaign, has set the entire female chorus onto Thomson, demanding kisses as forfeits in a game, but the American is as resolute in his refusal ('Pas Sur la Bouche') as he is in his determination to become Gilberte's lover. To eliminate Charley as a rival, he informs Valandray that the young man is chasing his wife and demands that he be thrown out of the house, but he is dreadfully taken aback when Valandray refuses to be worried and he is even more amazed when he hears the reason why—the famous theory. The arrival of Gilberte and Mlle Poumaillac prevents him from spilling the beans (Quartet: 'Je Suis l'Numéro Un') but, of course, if Valandray's theory is waterproof, it simply confirms Thomson's belief that Gilberte must always belong to him.

As the finale begins, Charley copies down the address of Faradel's *garçonnière* ('Sur le Quai Malaquais'). He whispers the rendezvous seductively to Gilberte and, to his despair, gets a total turn-down. Left flat, he decides that he cannot let such an opportunity for amorous activity escape him, so he passes an invitation to Huguette instead. It eventuates that Thomson, too, has taken an apartment on the Quai Malaquais and he invites Valandray there to further their business discussions. His papers have arrived from America, so their legal association as partners can be worked out. Valandray is surprised to see on the identification document that Thomson has been married, and not only married but married to a lady whose maiden name was Poumaillac. Mlle Poumaillac hastens to assure Valandray that it is a disgustingly common name ('Je Suis une Poumaillac') but she is so effusive in her denials that, instead of alleviating his curiosity, she simply gives rise to suspicion.

ACT 3

Thomson goes to look at his new apartment and, by dropping some coins to the concierge, obtains permission to take possession a day early. The old *locataire* has hardly ever used the place, so there is little danger of his turning up on this, his very last day. Valandray comes to meet Thomson and, for once, he seems ill at ease. He has been doing a little legal homework and has discovered the famous law about overseas marriages. He knows Thomson was married to a Poumaillac, he knows Gilberte was in America, and he knows that an annulment or a *non-lieu* would leave her still Mlle Poumaillac, as she was when she married him. What it boils down to is this: did Thomson marry Gilberte? Thomson turns American phlegm against Gallic excitement ('Mon Bon') and manages to avoid giving an answer before the two husbands part and Thomson settles down to await a visit from Gilberte.

Now Faradel arrives to present Charley with the key to the *garçonnière*. The concierge is but momentarily embarrassed—after all, Thomson is using only one room of the apartment, so Charley can use the others. Huguette is rather nervous about the adventure ('Est-Ce Bien Ça'), but she duly arrives and Charley moves into his seducer's act whilst the voyeuristic concierge watches through the keyhole ('Par le Trou'). They have disappeared into the bedroom when Gilberte and Mlle Poumaillac turn up. It is Gilberte's intention to plead with Thomson to return to America and she is taken aback when he proposes that she should divorce Valandray and remarry him. By the metallurgist's own dictum he, as the first husband, has the basic right to her.

He leads the ladies into a third room where the discussion will continue, as he does not wish the scene to be interrupted when Valandray returns to continue their business. Gilberte emerges momentarily to grab a bottle of port but, at the same moment, Charley pops out from the bedroom on the same mission and the two of them meet. Gilberte, although surprised to find the pyjama-clad Charley less co-operative than might have been expected, makes purposeful and obvious love to him ('Bonjour, Bonsoir') but, alas for her plot, they are interrupted not by Thomson but by Valandray.

The situation is clearly getting complicated, and maledictions and denials fly wildly as Valandray declares angrily that he has been fooled throughout by his wife. She not only has a lover, she is the ex-wife of Thomson. Mlle Poumaillac comes to the rescue. Not so, she cries, the wife of Thomson was...she! Thomson grudgingly supports the lie and Valandray demands to see some proof. There is only one way. Mlle Poumaillac kisses the American. They both try to avoid each other's lips but fate is too strong and, wham!, two quasi-virgins are felled in one embrace ('O Sam!'). The reason for Charley's pyjamas becomes clear when the blushing Huguette emerges from the bedroom, and Valandray's suspicions begin to fade away towards a happy ending. When poor Faradel returns to what is, after all, his apartment and finds everyone happily paired off, it only remains for him to take refuge in another attack of hiccups.

LA BELLE DE CADIX

an opérette in two acts by Raymond Vincy and Marc-Cab. Lyrics by Maurice Vandair. Music by Francis Lopez. Produced at the Théâtre Casino-Montparnasse 24 December 1945 with Luis Mariano (Carlos Médina), France Aubert (Maria-Louisa), Roger Lacoste (Manillon), Fabrizi (Ramirez) and Jacquie Flint (Pepa). Produced at the Théâtre de l'Empire 17 December 1949 with Lucien Frébert, Lina Dachary, Hennery and Edith George. Produced at the Théâtre de la Gaîté-Lyrique 20 November 1958 with Antonio Rossano, Janine Ervil, Rogers, Louisard and Joan Danielli. Produced at the Théâtre Mogador 5 February 1977 with Miguel Cortez, Isabel Lorca, Jacky Piervil, José Villamor and Jacqueline Guy. Produced at the Théatre de la Renaissance 1979 with Villamor, Maria Candido, Jacques Filh, Youri and Arta Verlen.

A film version was produced by Raymond Bernard in 1953 with Mariano, Carmen Sevilla, Jean Tissier, Pierjac, Claude Nicot and Claire Maurier.

CHARACTERS

Carlos Médina, *a film star*
Dany Clair, *a film director*
Manillon, *an assistant director*
Cécilia Hampton, *an American tobacco millionairess*
Ramirès
Maria-Louisa
Pépa
Gipsy King
Juanito
Perrucha
Journalist, Jenny, etc.

ACT 1

On the terrace at the Palm Beach in Cannes, the *beau monde* of the Côte d'Azur are going through the obligatory timetable of a fashionable day ('Au Palm Beach la Vie Est Belle'). Everyone who is anyone is there, from the Aga Khan to the Prime Minister of Australia and the most recently deposed Brazilian dictator, but the lion of the moment, and certainly of the ladies, is the dazzling film star Carlos Médina who has descended on Cannes to prepare his next film. The ladies are desperate for the latest information on their hero and they crowd around the little assistant, Manillon, for news.

The film company is about to depart for Cadiz where their principal filming is to take place, and Manillon has so many arrangements to make ('Pour Savoir S'Arranger') that he has only just the time to pause for a little self-important flirting. He is caught taking time out by the director, Dany Clair, and pleads love as an excuse. He is actually on the verge of conquering his pretty little neighbour and, before he goes off to Spain and its gipsies for a long stint, he is anxious to conclude an affair which he can carry in his heart while he is away.

Carlos, too, is going to have to live in Cadiz without love, for his fiancée, the wealthy American cigarette heiress Cécilia Hampton, is unable to leave with him for Spain. She has been recalled to Washington on business and can only hope to rejoin him at a later date. Every girl at Palm Beach would love to take her place at Carlos's side but the actor laughingly nudges them aside. Let them keep their dreams of love; the reality might disappoint them, for lust and love are not necessarily the same thing ('Désir').

The departure for Spain is set for first thing in the morning, so Manillon's conquest is tonight or never. He has made a rendezvous for 8 p.m. which will give him just three hours before the old chap who is the girl's official lover is due. Excitedly he points out his lovely to Dany Clair, but the 'old chap' in the girl's life is the director and, for the umpteenth time in his deprived life, Manillon's dreams of conquest vanish into thin air.

The film company installs itself in a village outside Cadiz where it causes a sensation amongst the locals, particularly when some of them, including the guitarist Ramirès, are chosen to take small parts in the film. The girls of the town cannot stay away from the production site and, most especially, from Carlos but Maria-Luisa, the fiancée of Ramirès, prefers to spend her time wandering amongst the mountain pathways ('Les Sentiers de la Montagne'). Since he has been cast to play in the film, Ramirès has become exceedingly grand and Maria-Luisa's feelings range between irritation and unhappiness at the way he spends all his time basking in the company of the film people.

For Manillon, the bunch of admiring girls is manna from heaven but, since they don't seem very impressed by the credentials of a humble assistant, he has pilfered a box of visiting cards from Dany Clair's office and has been handing them round amongst the local beauties along with invitations to attend private auditions for the film. He is particularly taken by the piquant Pépa, a waitress at the local inn, for whom he makes his most ardent but unsuccessful play ('Pour Toi, Pépa'). Manillon's trick does have a genuine background, for one of the principal scenes to be shot on this location is that of a gipsy wedding and it has been decided that the girl who will play the gipsy bride who puts an end to the career of Don Juan, as played by Carlos, will be taken from amongst the locals.

Today there is a gipsy fiesta ('La Fiesta Bohemienne') of which the film people take advantage to gather some footage of local colour. When Maria-Luisa tries to make a firm date with Ramirès for that evening, she finds him decidedly off-hand. If he is filming he will not be able to come. Pépa, at the same time, has had second thoughts about Manillon for she has heard about the role of the gipsy bride and she has come to submit to her audition. A barrage of embraces later she is told that she has qualified for the semi-final round.

Carlos is not working that evening and he chooses to spend his time relaxing at the gipsy encampment where he can enjoy some reminiscences of the life which, as a child, he passed not very far from here in a village not unlike this one ('Je Revois le Clocher du Village'). His evening, however, is not to be uninterrupted. Maria-Luisa and Pépa are the first to make their way to the film site. Maria-Luisa is intent on learning whether, in fact, Ramirès is really spending his evening working there whilst Pépa, having been granted entrance to the semi-finals, is anxious to get in first with her recall performance.

She marches up to Carlos and goes into her best and most passionate series of embraces. The stunned Carlos draws from her the whole story of 'Dany Clair' and his private auditions and, when the director arrives, he finds himself on the end of a blast of disapproval and a threat of dismissal from Carlos which he does not understand. All becomes clear to him a little later when Pépa enthusiastically greets Manillon as Dany Clair, and the furious director fires the little man on the spot.

Maria-Luisa has, in the meanwhile, been unsuccessfully searching the location for Ramirès. Her calls finally win an answer ('Rendez-Vous Sous la Lune') but, when she finds the voice which has joined hers in duet, it turns out to be not Ramirès but Carlos. She is disappointed and angry and, certain that Ramirès is out with another woman, she vows to be revenged on her star-struck fiancé. Carlos is ready with the solution. She is the most beautiful girl of the region ('La Belle de Cadix'). If she wishes, she too can take part in the film, in the important role of the gipsy bride. Delighted at the chance to score back against Ramirès, Maria-Luisa agrees.

When this news reaches Ramirès, with a few modifications added by the malicious Pépa which hint at a romance between Carlos and Maria-Luisa, he is scornful. Pépa shrugs, she has her own fish to fry and the one she is most anxious to hook is Manillon. He is busy at his work, however, for the gipsy marriage is to be filmed that very evening and he has to concentrate on finding someone suitably impressive to play the part of the gipsy king. Pépa promises that she will find him a wonderful gipsy king if he'll just stop running around for a moment and concentrate on her.

The whole village is decorated for the Romany wedding but, while the scenes of dancing are filmed (Flamenco), Dany Clair is again finding himself in trouble. He has fired Manillon, so there is no gipsy king to lead the wedding scene. Carlos is furious. Why has he fired his assistant? Over a woman? Dany Clair thinks of nothing but women and lets his job go to pieces! The poor director is obliged to go on his knees to Manillon and beg him to accept back his job and produce his gipsy king.

Whilst they wait to start the scene, Maria-Luisa feels a genuine excitement welling up in her, almost as if it were really her wedding day ('C'Est un Rêve'), and she laughingly teases Ramirès who, as the guitarist, is to sit at her feet playing while she weds another man. Finally Pépa produces her gipsy king and the wedding goes ahead ('Ma Belle de Cadix, Unisson-Nous Ce Soir') with all the trappings of the real thing. Only when the blood of Carlos and Maria-Luisa has been mingled and the ceremony completed does the truth come out. Pépa's gipsy king really is a gipsy king and, by the laws and traditions of the country, Carlos and Maria-Luisa are now man and wife.

ACT 2

The newlyweds are housed in a fine Moorish mansion where Pépa comes, in attendance to the bride, with Manillon still hurrying along hopefully behind her trying to tempt her into his arms ('Ô Ma Gitane'). Outside, the local people are singing and dancing in traditional celebration but, inside, there is less rejoicing. Maria-Luisa sees her marriage simply as a triumph over Ramirès and Carlos sees it only as a temporary measure, to be remedied by divorce as soon as possible. Such a divorce cannot take place until he is well away from Cadiz for the gipsy people would see this as an insufferable insult to one of their own. While he is here, and while the filming continues, the marriage will have to look as if it is the real thing.

Both the spouses are determined, however, that it should not be and, although Carlos goes through the motions of making love to his bride for the benefit of the public ('Maria-Luisa'), Manillon is hi-jacked to spend the night with them, nay between them. The poor lad is in despair. He had just fixed to spend the night with Pépa; he was home and hosed at last, and now the rendezvous is blown. Needless to say, after sitting up all night and burning three litres of oil in her lamp waiting for her man to come, Pépa is in no mood for explanations the next morning.

Carlos's mind is, understandably, rather diverted from the film over the next few weeks but, in the eyes of all concerned, he can be easily excused, for it is clear that his marriage comes first. He and Maria-Luisa make such a lovely pair and they are so affectionate to each other in public. Ramirès is predictably irritated at the sight of them together, but he vows that he has never been a man for one woman ('Le Coeur des Femmes') and that Maria-Luisa is not the only woman in the world for him. He will find another.

Carlos and Maria-Luisa have come to an agreement: they will keep up appearances in public while in private they will remain just good friends. It is an agreement which, as the days pass, Carlos finds a little difficult to keep wholly to, for the affectionate public scenes occasionally feel as if they wish to cross over into the private sector, but Maria-Luisa keeps strictly to the letter of the agreement and Carlos has to make do with the public embraces.

It is a public embrace which does the damage for, thinking that they hear Ramirès approaching, the pair go into a fulsome clinch only to find that their audience is none other than Cécilia Hampton. Carlos excuses the scene by telling his fiancée that Maria-Luisa is his leading lady in the film and that they were simply rehearsing but, when Maria-Luisa sees him walk off with the American on his arm, she realises that she, too, has begun to feel rather more for her husband than she has been willing to admit. Perhaps love is being born.

For Pépa there is no doubt. She is mad about Manillon and she has been ever since that night when he did not turn up for his rendezvous. It is time she did something about it. Maria-Luisa managed to stir things up by playing on her lover's jealousy; she will do the same. She will find some other man and throw herself at him in front of Manillon. Unfortunately for Dany Clair, he is the fall guy chosen and Pépa is busy draping herself all round him ('Mon Muchacho') when not only Manillon but Carlos walks in. Carlos is outraged. He has warned Dany Clair about women for the last time: he is sacked.

Carlos also has a woman problem. How is he to keep Cécilia from learning that he is married, even if it is temporarily, to Maria-Luisa? He manages, with the help of Manillon, to silence Dany Clair but, whilst the two of them are disposing of the deposed director, Cécilia meets Ramirès. The whole situation is exposed in a few seconds and the furious heiress storms out to pack her bags.

Things are now getting out of hand and Carlos decides that there is only one thing to do. He will abandon the location and shift the remainder of the filming back to a studio in France, writing out the scenes in which Maria-Luisa and the other locals would have appeared. The film company packs its bags and Carlos sadly says farewell to Spain ('Une Nuit à Grenade') before taking his plane back to France. When Maria-Luisa arrives at the airport, she is in time only to see his plane disappearing in the distance. She knows now that she has lost the man she loves.

Back at Cannes, Manillon, promoted to director following the disgrace of Dany Clair, is drowning his sorrowful longings for Pépa in outrageous cocktails. His promotion is not much use to him as Carlos, in a deep depression, has decided to abandon the making of *La Belle de Cadix*. Suddenly Dany Clair arrives, accompanied by all the gipsies from Cadiz. What on earth is he doing? Why, he has come in response to Carlos's telegram, bringing all of the company to finish the film in Cannes, as instructed.

Carlos is staggered. He sent no telegram. But they are all here: Maria-Luisa, his wife, who is soon in his arms, and Pépa who is finally able to get her arms around the elusive Manillon. And who is the fairy godmother behind all this? It is Cécilia who, even if she is an American millionairess, is able to recognise true love when she sees it. She has flown everyone here in her private jet, especially Ramirès who is proving an admirable replacement for her lost fiancé, and together they can all celebrate the happy ending of *La Belle de Cadix*.

ANDALOUSIE

an opérette à grand spectacle in two acts by Albert Willemetz and Raymond Vincy. Music by Francis Lopez. Produced at the Théâtre de la Gaîté-Lyrique, Paris, 25 October 1947 with Luis Mariano (Juanito Perez), Marina Hotine (Dolores), Maurice Bacquet (Pépé), Sophia Botény (Fanny) and Gise Mey (Pilar). Revived there August 1954 with Rudi Hirigoyen, Gise Mey, Bacquet, Arta Verlen and Doris Marnier.

A film version was produced by Robert Verney in 1950 with Mariano, Carmen Sevilla, Bacquet, Lilliane Bert, Robert Arnoux, Moël Roquevert, Perrette Souplex and Roseline Prince.

CHARACTERS

Juanito Perez
Pépé
Doña Vittoria, *innkeeper at Toblada*

Dolores, *her daughter*
Pilar, *a servant at the inn*
Fanny Miller, *a Viennese singer*
Greta, *her maid*
Rodriguez Valiente, *a proscribed South American politician*
Caracho, *his follower*
Baedeker, *a travelling writer*
The Gipsy
Soriano
Hotel Manager, Policeman, Peons, Valet, Linda, Carmen, Chiquita, etc.

ACT 1

Somewhere in the southern Spanish province of Andalousia in the 1860s there was a little village called Toblada where it was always sunny and where the people sang joyous opening choruses ('De Séville à Grenade') as they went about their work and their love-making in a simple, happy, uncomplicated way.

Today it is 19 March, the day of St Pépé and a national holiday, so the inn of Doña Vittoria is doing a rousing trade and her waitress, Pilar, is kept busy refilling glasses and holding the more forward customers at bay. Pilar is not interested in the attentions of these bucolic fellows, for a gipsy has foretold that she will meet the man of her heart this very day and that he will come to her with knives in his belt and a blade in each hand. Fate has clearly destined her to be the bride of a famous bandit chief. But, lo and behold, the man who arrives with knives at his belt is no bandit but little Pépé, the knifegrinder.

Pilar throws herself passionately into his arms and smothers the surprised lad in kisses, making him promise to return to her when his work is done so that they can start their life together but, when she goes to thank her gipsy, the fortune teller is puzzled. A knife grinder seems an unlikely candidate, for the other lines in Pilar's hand show her lover at odds with the police and loaded down with chains.

Pilar may still be looking for her lover, but Dolores, Doña Vittoria's daughter, has found hers in the fine, upstanding person of the wandering pottery vendor, Juanito. Behind her severe mother's back, she has been carrying on a clandestine romance, sending out signals to her beloved through the position of the clothes on her washing line (La Légende du Linge: 'Comme les Fleurs'). Today is the day that Juanito is due in Toblada and Dolores is out keeping watch for him.

His day's work done, Pépé hurries back to Pilar only to find that she has changed her mind. From what the gipsy says he cannot possibly be her destiny and, in spite of everything he can think of to bring back the enthusiasm of their first meeting ('J'Ai Tout, Tout, Tout'), she remains aloof. When Pépé consults the gipsy, in his turn, he is given a recipe for a love potion: a ribbon from a widow's nightgown, two hairs from the

473

moustache of a jealous man, and three drops of blood from a man born on Friday the 13th who has never deceived his wife, ground up and mixed together in the midnight moonlight, with bare feet, on the eve of St Pépé. It's all a bit unlikely and, anyway, the eve of St Pépé was yesterday and won't come around again for another whole year.

The voice of Juanito is heard in the distance, singing his wares ('Le Marchand d'Alcarazas'), and soon he is there, surrounded by the girls of the village, but he has eyes only for Dolores and it would take more than her mother's crêpe-tongued disapproval to stop them from dreaming of their future together. Juanito has ambitions. He is about to have his first proper fight as a matador and he is determined that one day he will be famous and rich and able to offer Dolores a home in the castle which stands on the hill above Toblada ('Dans Ce Château').

Pépé is being equally practical about his dreams. He has set off in search of item one on the list of love potion ingredients and, on the way, he has encountered a curious German bookseller who is out on the road gathering information for a series of guide books on foreign countries. Herr Baedeker decides that Pépé is the perfect person to lead him to all the best bits of local colour and he resolves to stick to him. Unfortunately, when Pépé does finally spot a nice ribboned nightie hanging out to dry and tries to pilfer it, he gets caught. The garment belongs to Doña Vittoria and she drags the wretched Pépé before all the girls of the village (Choeur des Lavandières: 'Jolies Lavandières') to denounce him as a pervert and a thief.

Juanito returns to Toblada triumphant. He has won his fight in style and, in the process, attracted the attention of a famous impresario of the bull ring who has offered him a contract to go to Venezuela for several months. It is the opportunity he needs to make his name and, although he is sad to leave Dolores for so long, he knows that the trip can make his fortune and fulfil their dreams. Bidding farewell to Dolores ('Je Veux T'Aimer d'un Amour Merveilleux'), he sets out with Pépé, who has a year to fill in waiting for the next St Pépé, as his valet and the undetachable Baedeker (who intends to research a guide on Venezuela) in tow.

Juanito is a great success in Caracas and becomes one of the stars of the season. Another fêted celebrity, the Austrian singer Fanny Miller (La Valse Viennoise: 'Viens, Viens, la Valse Chante'), pays him particular attention and it soon becomes clear that she has serious intentions towards the young matador. Juanito, however, thinks only of home and of Dolores and he writes letter after letter back to Spain which, along with the bulging epistles of Pépé to Pilar, are posted off almost daily from Caracas.

Although she cannot raise an interest from Juanito, Fräulein Miller is a highly attractive woman and she is the subject of the forceful attentions of an unknown admirer whose messenger, a vast beast of a man called Caracho, comes regularly with rich gifts from his master for the singer and with slightly less rich ones, on his own behalf, for her tiny maid, Greta, for whom he holds a burningly jealous passion. He also has a moustache which provides Pépé with the second ingredient for his potion.

The unknown admirer finally makes himself known just before Fanny is due to end her season in Venezuela. He is Rodriguez Valiente, a dashing South American gentleman who is being sought by the police of his country after having fled from his home for political reasons. He, too, is about to leave for Europe and he asks Fanny to join him on the ship which will carry him secretly away from South America ('Seul, Je Vais Par Tous les Chemins'). Fanny, who has been happy to accept his gifts, is not happy to accept his love, and she calls Juanito to defend her. Valiente withdraws and the singer uses the opportunity to invite herself to join Juanito on the journey home to his beloved Andalousia ('Andalucia Mia').

Back in Toblada things are not so happy. Juanito has been gone six months and over recent months Dolores has heard nothing. She is unaware that the determined Fanny has been intercepting Juanito's letters and she believes that, as he has become famous, he has forgotten her. When Pilar shows her a magazine which reports him squiring the celebrated Fräulein Miller in society, Dolores is convinced of his unfaithfulness but, supported by Pilar and Doña Vittoria, she determines not to pine ('Quand un Homme Est Épris').

Seville is bustling and bright ('Ou Courez-Vous En Mantille') when Juanito makes his reappearance in the Spanish arena ('Olé, Torero'). Through the corridors of the bullring, the bullfight can be seen in progress as the new matador pins up his first big successes on home ground. The next day is St Pépé, and the little group will head for Toblada where they will be reunited with the girls whom they so long to see again. Pépé is a bit troubled: he has no idea how he is going to find the last ingredient for his potion, but what is his delight when he discovers that Baedeker was born on Friday the 13th and has never been unfaithful to his wife. All that remains is to keep him faithful till midnight, in the face of the persistent temptresses of Seville, and to find some way to get him barefoot in the moonlight and in a position to supply the necessary drops of blood.

That night, with the ritual deed done, Pépé and Baedeker repair to the local Maison de Danse (Choeur des Clients) to join Juanito who has agreed to escort Fanny for the evening, and Pépé is amazed to meet Pilar there. She is still as distant as ever, but he has his potion at last and tonight is the promised eve of St Pépé. It has been a long time and a long trip, but it will all be worth the waiting. Unfortunately, when he slips the mixture in Pilar's drink she swaps glasses with Fanny's maid, and it is Greta who is soon crawling all over the bewildered Pépé.

When Juanito arrives he has a song to set the place alight ('La Fête à Seville') but it is clear that he is somewhat embarrassed in the company of the altogether too attentive Fanny. Worse embarrassment is in store, for when the evening's principal entertainment, La Estrellita, is announced it turns out to be none other than Dolores and a Dolores unrecognisable from the girl he left behind in Toblada. She is forward and seductive and Juanito is horrified. When he tries to talk to her, she pushes him away vigorously and Valiente intervenes to remind him, as Juanito had done to him over Fanny, of his manners. Dolores obviously extends her hand to Valiente, leaving Juanito in despair as the curtain falls ('Oui, l'Amour Est un Jeu Merveilleux').

ACT 2

Fanny Miller has taken a house in the square of the Seville flower market (Choeur des Fleuristes) and, in a spirit of defiance, Dolores has taken one directly opposite. With equal defiance, she is encouraging the attentions of Valiente who is eager to receive an invitation to a late night supper at the home of the fascinating dancer, an invitation which, with its understood significance, Dolores resists giving. She is as much in love with Juanito as ever, and her gay bravado is entirely a front.

Since the time when Greta drank Pépé's carefully concocted love potion, the little maid has been pursuing the knifegrinder all over Seville, to the fury of the mighty Caracho. When Pépé finds a horribly threatening note pinned to the door of Fanny's house with Caracho's huge knife, he faints. Pilar, coming out of Dolores' house, sees him lying there with scant sympathy, but her presence arouses a whirlwind of jealousy in Greta whose recital of the little fellow's charms finally makes Pilar realise what she is turning down ('Dans Mes Bras'). Pépé, who has other things—such as knives—on his mind, now has two women chasing him all over the place.

Juanito is escorting Fanny home when he discovers that Dolores has moved in opposite and, in annoyance, he agrees to sup that evening with Fanny at her home beneath the very eyes of Dolores. As he leaves, the voices of Dolores ('Andalucia Mia') and Fanny (Valse Viennoise) mingle as in a battle. When the two women meet in the street, Fanny is happy to throw at Dolores the fact that Juanito is to dine that night with her and she flaunts one of the stolen letters, pretending that it had been addressed to her. Dolores sees the same phrases which Juanito had spoken to her ostensibly written to another woman and she swears to be revenged. She will invite Valiente to her home that evening for all the world, and especially Juanito, to see.

That evening, as the nightwatchman's 'Chant du Séréno' is heard, Dolores prepares herself and her table to greet her guest. She has put on a deliberately low-cut dress and is prepared to play the seductress in the most obvious way before the lighted windows which open onto a full view of Fanny's house. She is terribly nervous and, at Pilar's instigation, she takes an unaccustomed glass of wine which soon has its effect ('Ça Fait Tourner la Tête'). When Valiente arrives, she does her best to carry the act through but she finally breaks down in tears. Valiente realises that he is not dealing with what he thought was a coquettish dancing girl but with a woman who is deeply and truly in love with another man. He refuses to take advantage of his position but, before he can leave, there is a pounding on the door and a cry of 'police'. It would seem that he has no way of escape, but Dolores insists that he hide in her bedroom while she gets rid of the officers.

When she opens the door, however, she discovers Juanito. He has seen and heard her flirting, as intended, and he has come to fling his jealous anger at Dolores and her lover. He will not listen what she has to say and, finding Valiente in Dolores' bedroom, he challenges him to duel. The scene is interrupted by another knocking at the door. This time it really is the police, but Juanito will not be party to a betrayal and he and Dolores play out a loving scene which leaves the men convinced that they have been set on to the wrong man. As soon as they have gone, Juanito drops his pose and, with some last harsh words, he tears from his neck the good luck medallion he has worn in the ring for Dolores' sake, turns on his heel and leaves.

The police agents may have failed to find their man at Dolores' house but, being wily officers, they have lurked around in the shadows after leaving and finally make their arrest. Although they may think they have taken Valiente and his lieutenant Caracho, they have actually taken Baedeker and Pépé, but, since Pépé cannot explain away the fact that he is carrying Caracho's monogrammed knife, that he has just come from Caracas, and that Baedeker's notes are badly enough written to look like secret codes, their denials are not taken seriously. Doña Vittoria refuses to acknowledge Pépé, Greta jealously prefers to see him hanged than belong to another woman, and Pilar is thrilled to see the gipsy's prediction of chains and police coming true. It looks bad for the innocent pair and, when Pépé decides, if it will win him his Pilar, to admit to being a bandit (Octet: 'Allons, Fini de Plaisanter') the pair are lead off to the dungeons.

Juanito is due to fight in the arena at Seville, and a large and fashionable public gather for the occasion. Valiente takes the opportunity to speak to Fanny and, assuring her that the love between Dolores and Juanito is a thing not to be trifled with, begs her to let go of the young man, but the shallow Fanny, thinking that he is only trying to win himself the place in her affections occupied by the matador, scorns him and sends him away. Juanito is, at this time, preparing himself for the fight. Kneeling before the altar of the Virgin, he prays not for protection but for a release from his suffering ('Santa Maria'). He has decided that this afternoon it will be the bull who is the victor in the ring.

When the first bull is played, he deliberately leaves himself open to its attack but he is saved at the last moment by the intervention of one of his men. Seeing what is happening, Fanny can no longer keep up her selfish position. Hurrying to the dressing rooms where Juanito is preparing to go to face the second bull, she pours out the truth of events, admitting the stolen letters and the lies. Doña Vittoria is there too, berating the young man for compromising her daughter in one breath and begging him, in the next, for Dolores' sake, to take care of himself. As he returns to the ring, Pilar presses Dolores' medal into his hand.

The happy ending takes place in Toblada. Pépé is relieved of the attentions of Greta by a few charmed words from the gipsy, which leaves him free for the undivided attentions of Pilar. Greta returns to Caracho who regards Pépé as his best friend since the youngster's impersonation saved him from jail. He is also suddenly persona grata as the regime has changed in his country and he is now Prime Minister. Valiente is President and can return safely to South America with Fanny. Dolores has returned to her old home and her old life ('Je Suis Seul au Village') and it is there that Juanito comes to find her. They will be wed and they will spend their lives, as they dreamed so long ago, in the castle on the hill.

As for Baedeker, he went home and wrote his travel books which are the living proof that this story really did happen.

VIOLETTES IMPÉRIALES

(Imperial Violets)

an opérette à grand spectacle in two acts by Paul Achard, René Jeanne and Henri Varna adapted from the film by Henri Roussel. Music by Vincent Scotto. Produced at the Théâtre Mogador, Paris, 31 January 1948 with Lina Walls (Violetta), Marcel Merkès (Don Juan), Raymonde Allain (Eugénie), Marcelle Ragon (Sérafina), Robert Allard (Estampillo), Fernand Gilbert (Picadouros), Pierjac (Loquito) and Annie Alexander (Rosette). Revived there 28 June 1952 with Andrée Le Dantec replacing Mlle Ragon and again 3 February 1961 with Rosita, Merkès, Mlle Allain, Simone Alex, Marcel Perchik, Léo Smith, Benjamin Bouix, Henri Regard and Jacqueline Lecoeur.

The film *Violettes Impériales* made in 1952 with Luis Mariano, Carmen Sevilla and Simone Valère used a score by Francis Lopez and M Brocey.

CHARACTERS

Violetta, *a flower girl*
Sérafina, *her aunt*
Loquito, *her brother*
Eugénie de Montijo
Rosette, *her chambermaid*
Don Juan, *Comte d'Ascaniz*
Madame d'Ascaniz, *his mother*
Picadouros, *Marquis Rodrigue del Basto de Paraberos y Santa-Mayor*
Estampillo, *his secretary and private detective*
Macard, *a nightclub owner*
Pépa, Concha, Madame Tambourinelli, Madame de Montijo, Duchesse d'Albe, etc.

ACT 1

The scene is a poor district of Seville in the year 1852. At the opening curtain, two local women are fighting in the street ('Ah! Quel Tapage') but, when the voluble Sérafina comes to interfere, the pair abandon their quarrel and both turn on her. Let her mind her own business and keep her ideas on what is proper to herself—her own family is scarcely a good example! Sérafina is shocked. Her family is small but impeccable. She herself is a model of widowed virtue and, as for her niece, Violetta, the beautiful flower girl, she is going to marry a titled gentleman and have lots of money and children. Sérafina is sure of this, for already the Marquis Rodrigue del Basto de Paraberos y Santa-Mayor, known for convenience's sake as Picadouros, is sighing at the girl's feet.

Picadouros may be definitely middle-aged but he is rich and, in his philosophy, when it comes to love, one is only as old as one's wallet ('Quand On A de l'Argent'). He is also persistent but he is not blind and, like the women of the district, he knows what Sérafina does not, that Violetta has got herself involved with another man, the handsome young Comte d'Ascaniz.

478

But, lest Sérafina think that her little girl might do as well as a Countess as a Marquise, Picadouros is quick to quash her rising hopes. Don Juan d'Ascaniz is to be married to a rich and important aristocrat. Whatever else she may be, Violetta will never be his wife.

The Marquis's source of information is his indefatigable secretary and detective, Estampillo, who works for him on a scale of charges which range from 500 pesetas for a really sensational piece of news downwards. Today he has a 500 peseta rumour which leaves Picadouros full of excitement—within twenty-four hours Don Juan will be officially engaged. He will no longer be Picadouros's rival and Violetta can, at last, be his. As if these problems of love and marriage were not enough, Sérafina next has to deal with Violetta's brother Loquito who has found himself a little girl friend in the person of Rosette, chambermaid to the visiting Eugénie de Montijo. Although Rosette is penniless ('Je N'Ai Pas un Sou'), Loquito is determined to marry her and, if necessary, to follow her back to Paris.

When Violetta returns home, her arms full of presents ('Ah! Mes Amis, Quelle Belle Journée') and wearing a beautiful new shawl (Air du Châle: 'C'Est la Châle Qui Fait l'Espagnole'), Sérafina is immediately suspicious. Where did the money come from for all this? Violetta does not hide anything. In front of the grimacing Picadouros, she pours out her love for Don Juan and, brushing aside Sérafina's disbelief in her lover's good faith, she proudly announces that he has promised to lead her before the Madonna in the cathedral the next day to take the traditional Easter vows of affianced couples.

Sérafina, whose long-term efforts to entrap Picadouros look threatened by this piece of pie-in-the-sky, determines to put a stop to this nonsense. She angrily locks Violetta in her room and goes off to take a calming glass of anisette (Choeur de l'Anisette) in the company of the offended Marquis.

When night has fallen and a little ray of moonlight breaks on Violetta's barred window, a shadowy figure makes its way through the tawdry streets of downtown Seville. It is Don Juan, come to serenade his beloved ('Ce Soir, Mon Amour') and to rescue her from her prison. Soon she is free, and they are walking hand in hand alongside the picturesque bank of the River Guadalquivir (Choeur des Bateliers) and speaking of love.

Violetta is afraid that her aunt will force her to marry the motley, middle-aged Marquis and she begs Don Juan to go to Sérafina and ask formally for her hand in marriage. He promises that he will, but it cannot be yet. Tomorrow he must leave for France with his mother. The Marquise must be convinced of his love and accustomed to the idea of a marriage which is not the one she had planned. Violetta faces him with Picadouros's story of the rich and noble wife, but Don Juan denies it and swears his love ('Il N'Y A Pas de Pyrenées').

The approach of Sérafina, hot on the trail of her fugitive niece, tears the lovers apart and, as Don Juan, hurries away, Violetta hides in the shadows. Sérafina has been brought to the lovers' meeting place by the exemplary Estampillo, but the detective has an ulterior motive. On the banks of the river he, too, declares his love...for Sérafina. He can offer her a fine life, for the Marquis has promised him a fortune and a castle on the day that he weds Violetta, and Estampillo has information which makes that outcome certain. Sérafina has doubts about marrying a detective for she is the descendant of several generations of smugglers ('Quand On A d' C'Sang-là') but, when he offers to change careers and become a robber, she weakens enough to allow a kiss.

Tonight it is Picadouros who has the choice bit of news—a real 500 peseta piece. He has received an invitation to a betrothal party which is to take place this very evening and the principals involved are Eugénie de Montijo and Don Juan. As the jubilant Picadouros hurries off to join enthusiastically in the celebration, Violetta emerges from her hiding place. She has heard everything (Mélancolie: 'Mon Âme Ce Soir Est En Détresse'). Don Juan has lied to her after all.

At the home of the Marquise d'Ascaniz the party is in full swing (Divertissement) but there is no sign of Don Juan and, when midnight arrives, Madame de Montijo will wait no longer and, taking Eugénie with her, she leaves in high dudgeon. Only then does Don Juan appear. He has waited until Eugénie's departure before coming in because he wants to appeal to his mother to allow him to wed Violetta instead ('Si Tu Voyais Son Sourire'). The Marquise is horrified at such a thought. Marriages are for alliance, love is something else altogether and she refuses to allow it to interfere with her plans. Don Juan will wed Eugénie and that is all there is to it.

Easter is celebrated by the townsfolk of Seville in fine, traditional style ('C'Est Jour de Fête'). In the Plaza de los Novios we see Loquito with his Rosette, who is all set to go off to Paris with her mistress the very next day; Picadouros, battered and black-eyed after spending the night in every low dive in Seville, looking for Violetta; Estampillo still laying siege to Sérafina; and here comes the traditional cortège of fiancés, ready to take their vows before the Madonna in the cathedral. Following behind them comes Don Juan and on his arm is Eugénie de Montijo.

No sooner have they gone in to the church than Violetta appears. She has been in the woods picking the violets which are her trade and, this Easter morning, she has come to dedicate the freshest of her flowers to the Madonna with a prayer that the Virgin may protect her love. Neither Picadouros nor her aunt try to prevent her as she enters the church.

A few minutes later the harm has been done. In dreadful distress, the young girl runs from the cathedral and falls weeping into the arms of her aunt. She has seen Don Juan and Eugénie together, before the Madonna, where he had promised to lead her. As the cortège emerges she tears herself away from Sérafina and hurls herself towards Eugénie, but she is grabbed before she can reach her enemy and falls sobbing to the ground. Eugénie, amazed at the scene, quickly makes her way towards the weeping girl who, between her tears, promises that she meant her no harm. It is Don Juan who has lied to her and broken her heart.

Eugénie will not listen to the excuses of the man to whom she has just been affianced. She cannot plight herself to a man who could treat the woman who loves him in such a fashion. There will be no marriage between

Ascaniz and Montijo. She renounces the engagement. All Violetta can offer Eugénie in thanks are the violets which she still clasps in her hand but, as Eugénie goes to take the flowers, Violetta gasps and takes her hand. Surely the Madonna has meant to guide Eugénie to her on this day. For she can read a great fate in her benefactor's hand. Eugénie de Montijo may, this day, have lost a fiancé but she has gained a throne. There, in her hand, can be read a crown...she will be a queen, an empress.

ACT 2

Violetta's prophecy comes true. Two years later, Eugénie is the wife of Napoléon III and the Empress of France but, in her rise to royalty, the good Empress has not forgotten the little flower girl who predicted her future so clearly, and Violetta has a place at court as royal florist and confidante to the Empress. Eugénie's special flowers are violets (Valse des Violettes: 'Violette') and she keeps, still, the bouquet which Violetta gave her that Easter day in the Plaza de los Novios, pressed and dried in a coffret for good luck.

In spite of the great change in her situation, Violetta cannot be wholly happy. Her heart is still with Don Juan whom she has not seen since that same day. For more than a year the young man travelled around the world but Violetta knows that now he is in Paris. He has been accredited to the French court as Ambassador for Spain. Soon he will have to come before the Empress.

For the moment only the ridiculous Picadouros presents himself, still attempting to win Violetta for himself. Sérafina, Estampillo and Loquito are also in Paris and the detective has not relaxed his efforts. He has discovered that Don Juan is in town and he has been following him. It seems that the new Ambassador frequents a very improper place for one of his position, a dubious bar called the Pou Qui Tette which is known to serve as a meeting place for anti-royalist conspirators. It is a situation which bears investigation, and investigate the Spaniards will ('C'Est un Secret d'État').

Finally, Don Juan presents himself at court. Not, as might have been expected, before the Emperor but to Eugénie ('J'Ose à Peine, Croyez-Moi, Madame') whose influence he wishes to obtain with the Emperor on behalf of a party in Spanish politics. Eugénie refuses to take any part in such affairs. She is Empress of France and it is to France that duty ties her, not to Spain or any part of Spain. The subject of Violetta inevitably arises as they speak, and Don Juan swears that his love for the girl is still as strong as ever.

Eugénie tells him pointedly that it is not she who needs convincing of that and she brings Violetta forth to meet face to face with her former lover. Now, at last, Violetta hears the truth of the events leading up to that fateful Easter, of Don Juan's dilemma with his family, and she hears his profession of lasting love ('Tu Peux Croire à Mon Amour'). It is not long before all is forgiven and forgotten. That evening they make their entrance together at the royal ball at the Tuileries and Violetta enlivens the spectacular scene with a rendition of the Valse des Violettes.

Outside the Pou Qui Tette, the team of amateur detectives keeps watch

481

over the comings and goings of a few suspicious characters, and Rosette and Loquito take the opportunity to insert a comical song and dance routine ('Je Serai Ton...'). Inside the bar there is plenty of activity, including a fearsome can-can, and some appalling disguises. Picadouros has thought it necessary to get into extravagant feminine attire and Sérafina, accompanying him, has become a cavalier with the result that they immediately attract attention, particularly when they perform a comedy rhumba ('Sérafina et Mutchatchito') and Macard, the owner of the place, who believes that Picadouros is an old flame of his called Titine, attacks the disguised Marquis with undisguisedly amorous intent.

During the evening, Violetta puts in an appearance, dressed in her old flower girl attire and working the place as a flower seller ('Qui Veut Mon Bouquet de Violettes'). She has come to reassure herself that Don Juan is not, as has been claimed, a part of any conspiracy, but her complacency is shattered when she sees her lover quietly enter the bar. When Macard announces that he is closing, and uses Estampillo's imitation of a policeman to clear the bar, Violetta hides behind the counter and overhears the plotting that follows.

Don Juan reports the failure of his interview with the Empress and the other conspirators resolve that there is nothing further to be gained by talking. They will take action. Tonight, as the Emperor and the Empress drive to the opera, they will attack the coach. When Don Juan protests against the use of violence, they lock him in a back room but, no sooner have they departed to carry out their plan, than Violetta, emerging from her hiding place, hurries to release Don Juan. Together they head for the palace to warn Eugénie.

Violetta is horrified to find that Eugénie will not change her plans under the menace of an attack. There are threats of murder every day and none has yet succeeded. The Emperor has been prevented by business from going to the theatre, so she will go alone, but go she will. While Eugénie prepares herself for the evening, Violetta takes a sudden decision. She envelops herself in one of the Empress's coats and a dark mantilla, and heads for the door. When Eugénie comes to leave, she finds that her coach has already gone. Violetta has taken her place.

A fresh équipage is called, and Eugénie is installed in her box at the opera house when Violetta is brought in. Don Juan rushes to support the fainting girl. Under the royal cloak she is bleeding—the attack on the royal coach did take place, as she had predicted, and she is sorely wounded.

The attempted assassination is the talk of the town and Rosette finds herself the centre of curiosity as all the court ladies try to be first to hear the intimate details of the event ('Dites Nous, Rosette'). But Rosette soon has other things to think about, for Sérafina has finally decided to let Loquito wed his little chambermaid. Sérafina has, in fact, suffered an entire change of heart over the subject of love for, now that Don Juan and Violetta are so obviously to be wed, Picadouros has given up his courtship and has allowed himself to be dragged into marriage by the determined aunt. She will be a Marquise and have a place at court and, of course, in her new aristocratic position she will be obliged to have a lover, so there will be a place for poor Estampillo after all.

Somewhere in a garden at Compiègne where everyone is dressed to provide a tableau reminiscent of Winterhalter, Violetta, her injuries healed, comes to curtsey before her beloved Empress. Eugénie will not allow the curtsey. From today Violetta will never curtsey before her again. It is all too much and the girl faints away. Eugénie smiles, for she knows what will make her recover. At a kiss from the Comte d'Ascaniz all ends happily.

QUATRE JOURS À PARIS

(Four Days in Paris)

an opérette in two acts by Raymond Vincy. Music by Francis Lopez. Produced at the Théâtre Bobino, Paris, 28 February 1949 with Andrex (Ferdinand), Orbal (Hyacinthe), Duvaleix (Montaron), Ginette Catriens (Gabrielle), Jeannette Batti (Zenaïde), Nelly Wick (Amparita), Marguette Willy (Simone) and Henri Gènes (Nicolas). Produced at the Théâtre de l'ABC 19 February 1960 with Andrex, Orbal, Geneviève Kervine, Ginette Baudin and Lona Rita.

A film version was produced by Richard Pottier in 1955 with Luis Mariano.

CHARACTERS

Amparita Alvarez, *a wealthy Brazilian singer*
Bolivar, *her jealous husband*
Hyacinthe, *proprietor of the Institut de Beauté*
Ferdinand, *his chief receptionist*
Nicolas, *pedicurist*
Simone, *manicurist*
Ambroise, *plastic surgeon*
Clémentine, *masseuse*
Marcelle, *coiffeuse*
Jacqueline, *manicurist*
Montaron
Gabrielle, *his daughter*
Zenaïde, *his maid*
Felicien Dieudonne

ACT 1

At the Parisian Institut de Beauté of Monsieur Hyacinthe there is a fine hubbub going on. All the wealthy ladies who come to Hyacinthe's salon to have themselves coiffed, manicured, tinted, pummelled, lifted and dyed have one preoccupation: they want their particular treatment to be overseen by Ferdinand, the deliciously suave front man of the establishment whose way with the ladies is clearly a most important element in the success of the business, and who has clearly had his way with most of the ladies.

This morning there is a problem. Ferdinand has not turned up for work ('Ferdinand'). What are his fellow workers to do? The Baronne de Grandpif will not choose a new hair colour without Ferdinand's advice, Madame Romolo will not permit the massive masseuse Clémentine to stop massaging until Ferdinand has come to verify the tautness of her buttocks, and Madame de Guerrano is sitting with her breasts in a basin waiting for Ferdinand to advise her on the level at which they should be remodelled. The whole Institut is grinding to a standstill without Ferdinand.

Hyacinthe himself has a particular reason to be worried, for he has arranged a very special appointment for Ferdinand, an appointment which has nothing to do with his official duties. The fiery Brazilian chanteuse, Amparita Alvarez, is in Paris, left alone in the big city for four whole days by her explosively jealous husband, and she is intending to take advantage of the fact with every bit of vigour at her control ('Dans le Fruit Défendu'). Hyacinthe is less interested in the lady's visible assets than in her financial ones. He has need of an investment of five million francs to allow him to expand his business and Senora Alvarez has announced that she is prepared to give him this backing on one condition—Ferdinand. And now Ferdinand has disappeared. He did not turn up at the lady's apartment the previous night and Madame Alvarez is boiling.

Hyacinthe and Amparita Alvarez are not the only ones to be upset by Ferdinand's absence. In between amusing the customers, the jolly dog has been having a little fling with the manicurist, Simone, and she has begun to feel unreasonably proprietorial about him. When she manages to prise from Nicolas, the pedicurist, the tale of Madame Alvarez she pouts terribly and the tentative attempts of Nicolas to replace Ferdinand in her esteem only draw her scorn ('La Nique, Nique à Nicolas').

Just when everything is fit to explode, Ferdinand wanders in and calmly turns his hand to setting the shop in order ('Un Petit Coup Par-Ci'). It turns out that he simply forgot about the appointment with Madame Alvarez for the good reason that he was busy falling in love with 'Gabrielle'. Gabrielle is a lassie from La Palisse who came up to the big city for four days. Now she has been called back to her home and all Ferdinand is left with is an address to which he might send a postcard of remembrance: Gabrielle Montaron, Chez Grand'mère, Avenue de la Tranquilité, La Palisse. There is nothing for it but to go to La Palisse and ask for her hand in marriage. So while Amparita boils and Simone sniffles, Ferdinand applies for time off to visit his poor, sick, old grand'mère.

Hyacinthe can see his five million going out the window. Something must be done. La Palisse is not so very far from Vichy. Madame Alvarez must go to the Grand Hotel at Vichy and there Ferdinand will be able to visit her in between bouts of caring for his stricken relative. Amparita throws her arms around Ferdinand in a burst of lustful anticipation just as Simone walks into the room and, to save the peace, Ferdinand insists that the Brazilian is teaching him the latest dance craze of her native land, 'La Samba

Brasilienne'. They have only just unlaced themselves when who should arrive but the boiling Bolivar, the lady's dramatically jealous husband ('Tu Seras Trompé').

In the meanwhile, at La Palisse, Gabrielle is off her food and yearningly thinking over her 'Quatre Jours à Paris' and her meeting with Ferdinand. Her distraction is obvious to the household's comical maid, Zenaïde, but Gabrielle's father has other preoccupations: his prize hens have a malaise and the oldest and most prized of them all, the grand'mère who has given her name to the house, is decidedly ill. The import of this is so great to Monsieur Montaron that a learned professor from the Institute of Aviculture in Paris has been called down to attend to the precious birds. Another visitor is also expected today. Montaron is the vice-president of an international chess club and he is awaiting the visit of the president of the organisation, with whom he has been carrying on a game by correspondence for fourteen months. The game is to be ritually finished off face to face. With all these extra people expected, the drooping Gabrielle hastens to ring an agency for an extra maid.

The professor arrives and is met by Zenaïde but, right behind him, comes Ferdinand who sees in this gentleman's identity a fine excuse to stay in the Montaron house near his beloved Gabrielle. He scares the man away with a tale of Montaron's imagined peculiarities and then convinces Zenaïde that she has faulty vision when she return to find a different professor. Since he recommends a glass of brandy as a remedy, she is willing to be convinced. Montaron is delighted to meet the distinguished man to whom he confesses, with innocent double meaning, his passion for chickens ('J'Aime les Poules'). The 'professor' must be his guest while he diagnoses the trouble with grand'mère.

Zenaïde has taken the professor's prescription to heart, and she is about to demolish her third glass of brandy ('J'Ai des Mirages') when a young woman turns up at the house. It is Simone who has squeezed from Nicolas the whereabouts of Ferdinand and, since she suspects him of being not with a dying relative but with some woman, she has come in jealous pursuit. Zenaïde assumes that she is the new maid from the agency and Simone, seeing an opportunity to keep an eye on Ferdinand from close quarters, decides to accept that identity.

It is not long before the amazed Gabrielle encounters the false professor and they are happily singing together a variation on his earlier praises of 'Gabrielle', but Ferdinand gets a nasty shock when the new maid walks in on them and he sees that he has been followed. Getting Simone alone, he tries to force her to go back to Paris but Simone has a trick under her apron and she isn't afraid to use it. A few loud cries bring Gabrielle running to find the maid complaining that Ferdinand has been trying to kiss her. Appalled at such treachery, Gabrielle rushes out, but Simone begins to think that she may have been hasty in her judgement when Zenaïde refers to poor grand'mère who is so ill and of how Ferdinand has come down from Paris to look after her.

If things were not already complicated enough, Nicolas turns up, having

485

cycled all the way from Paris to warn Ferdinand that Simone is on his trail. Ferdinand is obliged to pass him off as his assistant and announces that the lad will spend the night in the chicken coop to oversee the health of the ailing birds, as good a way as any of preventing him from making any more of his persistent gaffes. Worse is to come. Bolivar and Amparita arrive at La Palisse, for Bolivar is none other than the president of the chess club and he has come to finish his game with Montaron. Completing the picture, behind them trots Hyacinthe, still on the trail of his five millions and of Ferdinand.

Now that the Montaron house is simply bursting with people, the plot can thicken. Ferdinand convinces Nicolas that he must help him in his bid to secure Gabrielle as a wife: it is logic for, when he is wed, Simone will have to turn her attentions on Nicolas who is currently under siege from the Amazonian Clémentine. Nicolas contrives to get Simone into a clinch and Ferdinand and Clémentine (who arrived sometime earlier) surprise them *in flagrante delicto* ('Eh Bien! C'Est du Joli'). When Simone finds herself terminally rejected by Ferdinand, she bursts with petulance and, when she hears that he is intending to wed Gabrielle, she is even more upset. Gradually the noise of the confrontation brings the whole set of guests to the drawing room to face each other with growing surprise under the eyes of Montaron, who seems to be the only person who knows why each person is in the house. As each of them is despatched to his or her proper place, they break out into the samba which seems as good a way as any to end the act.

ACT 2

For the meanwhile, at least, everyone tries to act in accordance not only with his or her allotted character but also in a civilised fashion ('La Charmante Soirée de Famille'). Montaron serves a fine dinner centred on a spicy *homard à l'Américaine* and, after dinner, Ferdinand entertains with a modern poem until Montaron and Bolivar retire to carry on with their chess game. This is the cue for Hyacinthe and Amparita to start carrying out their planned attack on Ferdinand, and the lady anticipates her long awaited night of sexual accomplishment with a sensuality ('Ah! Quelle Nuit') which has only been increased by the fact that Hyacinthe has added three goodly spoonfuls of hot spice to the lobster. It doesn't seem to have had the required effect on Ferdinand, however, for the old spark seems to have gone out of him at a most inconvenient time.

It certainly hasn't gone out of Simone who announces her plans for the night in no uncertain terms in another version of 'Ah! Quelle Nuit' before going off to settle down and wait for Ferdinand in his bed. As if the women weren't enough trouble, Nicolas, who can't sleep with the hens sitting on his face, decides to come indoors and trouble the troubled Ferdinand further, but he ends up doing his friend a fine favour when the truth, for once, works to Ferdinand's advantage. Nicolas gives the lie to Gabrielle over Simone's morning fib about being pounced on by Ferdinand and, before long, the lovers are reminiscing over their happy 'Quatre Jours à Paris'.

All this romancing is very upsetting for Nicolas who has had a large helping of the aphrodisiac lobster and is feeling so lonely that he ends up making a pass at the homely Zenaïde and joining her in duet of a rather different version of 'Ah! Quelle Nuit'. Since the walls of Zenaïde's room are very thin, they decide to spend the night together on the sofa, and Nicolas sets to work to encourage everyone else to get off to bed and leave the living room empty. He doesn't have much luck, for first Amparita and then Simone come looking for Ferdinand and meet each other, then Gabrielle comes to find out what is going on and finds her lover being claimed by both the other women. She orders both of them out of the house on the instant and tells Hyacinthe to follow.

Disturbed in their chess game, Montaron and Bolivar come down to find their daughter and wife respectively in their nightclothes and answers are meaningfully demanded from all. Ferdinand tops everything by choosing this moment to ask Montaron for Gabrielle's hand in marriage and, one by one, the disguises start to fall.

Simone claims to be Ferdinand's girlfriend and out comes the fact that Ferdinand has nothing to do with chickens but, along with the pretended *femme de chambre* and Nicolas, is Hyacinthe's employee at the Institut de Beauté. Bolivar, full of suspicion, is convinced that something funny is going on that involves his wife, and Clémentine is furious when she hears that Nicolas has made a rendezvous with Zenaïde, but the worst faux pas slips once again from the lips of poor Nicolas who confesses that Ferdinand, too, had a rendezvous fixed for that night. With whom? is the question on the furious lips of Bolivar, Amparita, Simone, Montaron and Gabrielle. There is only one answer he can give. The rendezvous was with...Hyacinthe!

One by one, the employees of the Institut de Beauté make their way back to Paris and their business ('Et Boum!'). Ferdinand decides that he needs a little time off ('Mon Jour de Repos') to get himself reorganised, away from all the society women and their hair-dressing problems (Ballet: Le Cauchemar du Coiffeur). Simone is feeling a little sorry for interfering in what she now realises is a very real love affair between Ferdinand and Gabrielle. With the help of Nicolas she would like to mend affairs and perhaps, at the same time, show rather more favour to the little man than she has before.

Nicolas is over the moon until, out of nowhere, Zenaïde arrives, ready to spend her four days in Paris, and anxious to carry on where they were interrupted at La Palisse. Nicolas has a grand idea. Zenaïde has confessed a long-standing but ineffective passion for her employer so, to get her off his back, he sends her for a complete tour of the Institut de Beauté with the aim of palming her off on Montaron in an improved version ('J'Ai des Mirages').

Thinking that all is ruined with Gabrielle, Ferdinand has finally agreed to sell his body to Amparita in return for a share in the new business which Hyacinthe is to gain from the exercise. Hyacinthe is delighted and hurries off to get the Brazilian, whilst Ferdinand settles down amongst his adoring clients to fortify himself with a large cocktail. He is surrounded by women and holding a raised glass when Montaron and Gabrielle pay a surprise visit. They have come with peace and love in their hearts, ready to agree to

Ferdinand's request for Gabrielle's hand, but when the young woman sees how her beloved debauches himself in Paris, she changes her mind and hurries out.

Montaron encourages Ferdinand to go after her and press his suit, and he remains to flirt with the ladies. One particularly alluring creature attracts his attentions and what is his surprise when it turns out to be Zenaïde! By the time Hyacinthe returns with Amparita, Ferdinand and Gabrielle are off on a cloud somewhere. Foiled again, the chanteuse is about to tear Hyacinthe to pieces when she hears the footsteps of her husband approaching and she hastily hides in Hyacinthe's office.

When Bolivar arrives on the scene he finds only the muscular Clémentine who, fed up with all the comings and goings which have lost her her little Nicolas, tells Bolivar that it is all the fault of his wife who has promised five millions to Hyacinthe for a liaison with Ferdinand. Bolivar is not only to be cuckolded, but he is to pay for it. For the moment, however, jealousy is forgotten as the Brazilian marvels at the buxom proportions of Clémentine. Business is not for women ('Que des Hommes'). He will back the new business venture himself and, in return, he asks only that Hyacinthe shall fix him up a rendezvous with Clémentine.

Unfortunately for him, the hidden Amparita overhears his proposal and it is time for a showdown between the two Brazilians. Both of them have tried to stray but in the end they have, by accident, remained faithful. A strange thing when one has four days alone in Paris.

There is little left but for all the pairs to be happily united. Ferdinand wins his Gabrielle, Nicolas his Simone, the boiling Brazilians are back at each other's side, and Montaron and Zenaïde can go back to La Palisse and a brand new ménage. As for Hyacinthe, he has found his backer. The connoisseur of chickens and chess is going into a new area of business. Monsieur Montaron reasons that if the Institut can do for others what it did for Zenaïde, it must be a foolproof business investment.

LA ROUTE FLEURIE

(The Flowery Road)

an opérette in two acts by Raymond Vincy. Music by Francis Lopez. Produced at the Théâtre de l'ABC 19 December 1952 with Georges Guétary (Jean-Pierre), Bourvil (Raphaël), Claude Arvelle (Mimi) and Annie Cordy (Lorette). Produced at the Théâtre de la Renaissance 1979 with José Villamor, Jacky Piervil, Martine Noël and Marion Game.

CHARACTERS

Jean-Pierre, *a composer*
Raphaël, *a poet cum painter*
Lorette, *his model*

Mimi, *a mannequin*
Poupoutzoff, *a scientist*
Rita Florida, *an actress*
Oscar Bonnardel, *a film producer*
Gustave, *steward of the Villa Vacances*
Paul, *restaurateur*
Chauffeur, Cook, Valet de Chambre, Gardener, Chambermaids, Concierge, etc.

ACT 1

The Place du Tertre in Montmartre is a place where it is always sunny, where the folks are penniless, Bohemian, artistic and happy, unable to afford to eat yet bursting with health and vigour in a happy, musical-comedy way ('Petit Village Dans la Ville'). The local café can apparently break even in spite of a rule that all 'artists' may be given credit, just in case one of them turns out one day to be famous. It is as well that tourists come to the Place du Tertre and that an occasional old inhabitant made good returns from time to time to spend some money.

Today the pretty mannequin Mimi has come to show the place of her birth to a prosperous-looking gentleman friend, Oscar Bonnardel. Bonnardel is a film producer and it is his intention to give the little mannequin a starring role in his next film. He would also like to give her a Cadillac and, if pushed, a wedding ring, but Mimi is not interested in his intentions. She has few illusions about Monsieur Bonnardel. The local people are more to her taste. There is funny little Raphaël, the poet who has turned painter in order to spend his time painting the adorable Lorette ('On Est Poète Ou On N' l'Est Pas'), but his paintings end up being swapped to Paul, the restaurateur, in exchange for meals. Today it is Lorette's birthday so Raphaël has brought two paintings to pay for two birthday dinners and it is clear that he is getting the best of the bargain.

Lorette is thrilled when she runs into Mimi and finds out how she gone up in the fashion world. She, too, has made progress, but in a less paying way. She has moved on from being anything so ordinary as existentialist; she has taken on a new doctrine called subitism which consists, if you analyse it, of simply doing whatever comes into your head ('Subitiste'). Mimi tactfully gets rid of Bonnardel and the two girls settle down to catch up in a good chat.

Mimi is off on holiday to the Côte d'Azur—although to avoid the attentions of the passionate producer she has pretended that she is going to see her mother in Brittany—which will give her a chance to decide what to do about Bonnardel's offers of stardom. For the moment, her arrival means that Raphaël's birthday dinner for two looks like being expanded into a threesome or, pretty soon, a quartet, for another friend, the composer Jean-Pierre, comes to join them ('Place du Tertre'). He is trying to compose a song ('La Route Fleurie') and is in need of inspiration. When he sees Mimi, inspiration comes.

Jean-Pierre has good news: money is on the way. Not just the usual

50,000 francs which his rich aunt down south sends him each month, but real money. He has written the score for a film musical and it has been accepted. All he has to do is find a scenario which will fit the songs and which pleases the producer, and then the film can go into production. Mimi will be his muse and, together, they can surely come up with a storyline in the next week or so. Mimi has to decline to be anything of the sort. She is off to the Côte d'Azur. Jean-Pierre is not to be so easily put off. If Mimi must head south then there is nothing for it but that they must all four head for the coast. His aunt's cheque which is due to arrive any minute will suffice to see them on their way and, in the meanwhile, the birthday dinner can be split neatly in two—Raphaël can celebrate tête-à-tête with Lorette while Jean-Pierre shares 'Une Dinette' with Mimi.

The two men continue to live 'La Vie de Bohème' until auntie's cheque comes, while the girls go out and spend all Mimi's wages in 'Les Grands Magasins' to fit themselves out for the trip, but, when the cheque does come, it is a disappointment. Auntie has decided that it is about time Jean-Pierre stopped frittering away his time and her money in Montmartre and became a self-supporting person. There will be no more little cheques but, to soften this blow, she is offering him the use of her villa in Antibes for a month and enough cash to pay his fare. It will do nicely. Somehow they will all get to Antibes and, once they are there, they can take advantage of the splendid villa and its horde of staff.

The four friends set off from Paris on a pair of motor-scooters. Jean-Pierre takes every opportunity en route to be alone with Mimi and, when she slows down his advances, he tries to change her mind with the cautionary tale of the 'Jolie Meunière' who wouldn't say yes to her beaux and so lost them. Raphaël has little more luck when he tries to get amorous with Lorette. She finds him fine as a pal but a washout as a Don Juan ('Moi, J'Aime les Hommes').

The friends are a bit puzzled as to how Jean-Pierre got the motor-scooters, but soon all becomes clear. His film producer has given him a large sum of money, not for his music but for one month's rent of auntie's villa. The other fact which emerges is that Jean-Pierre's producer is none other than Mimi's Oscar Bonnardel. The girls decide it is better to keep this to themselves, particularly as Bonnardel has not taken the villa for himself but for one of his stars, the curvaceous Rita Florida. So, they have no villa but they do have money and with that money, when they reach the end of 'La Route Fleurie', they can go and spend their holidays happily and relatively cheaply in the Montmartre of the south, St Paul de Vence.

At Auntie Charlemont's villa, however, other plots are afoot. The servants are grumpy because they haven't been given a raise, so Gustave, the steward, has taken it upon himself to augment their income by letting the villa while its owner is away. He is sure that the notoriously penniless Jean-Pierre will be delighted to take a share of the proceeds and cause no problems. Unaware that he is now the lucky borrower of a doubly-let villa, Jean-Pierre is preparing to enjoy his 'Vacances' with his friends whilst occasionally spending a moment on squeezing out ideas for the famous film script.

Much more time is spent on lovemaking than on work and, while Jean-Pierre and Mimi wander amongst the flowers of the villa's gardens, Raphaël and Lorette end up in the kitchen garden where—since a true poet can find inspiration anywhere—he serenades her with a song about beans ('Les Haricots'). Lorette is not very impressed. She would much rather he wrote a really up-to-date song for her so that she can sing it in the film they are supposed to be writing.

Gustave is not ostensibly taken aback to see Jean-Pierre and his friends on his doorstep, but he is worried when the fact of the double rental comes out. It is going to take a good deal of diplomacy to explain to Miss Florida the presence of a bristling scientist called Poupoutzoff in the villa she has taken, and vice versa, and he is not prepared to cope with the situation alone. The complications are half Jean-Pierre's fault, so he and his friends must remain and help to sort them out.

Rita Florida is the first of the tenants to arrive, accompanied by a collection of friends and admirers. She is intending to plunge herself deeply into the preparation of her new role as an American cowgirl. Cows are one of the few things that Dr Poupoutzoff does not bring with him. There is a chimpanzee called Rasputin, a menagerie of guinea pigs and forty-eight cases of laboratory equipment, all destined for some unspeakable experiments. Far from being annoyed by the presence of the four young people, he is fascinated by Raphaël in whom he sees a magnificent subject for his work but, of course, he has not yet encountered Mlle Florida. A happy holiday is in prospect (Finale).

ACT 2

The servants have to earn their extra money with two separate tenants to look after ('On A Deux Locataires'), not to speak of the quartet from Montmartre. And these people are not in the same style as Mlle de Charlemont. They seem to be quite peculiar. Raphaël protects himself from the sun with a pith helmet which gives him the excuse to sing a song about colonial life ('A Madagascar') while Rita Florida floats about in a strangely mixed-up wild west outfit, equipped with a bow and arrows, revolvers, and a lasso, getting in practice for being 'La Belle de l'Ohio'. She is inclined to shoot off her guns rather erratically and Raphaël has to tactfully relieve her of them to forestall an accident.

When Poupoutzoff sees Raphaël with the guns and his colonial hat, he becomes even more convinced that he has a dangerous maniac on hand, ripe for study. Jean-Pierre, in the interests of general harmony, encourages the scientist in his interpretation and sidles off to spend some time in the sun with his 'Mimi'. This little subterfuge enables him to give an explanation of Poupoutzoff's presence when Rita demands to know who the strange Russian person in her house is. He is a doctor who has been called in to care for Raphaël who has gone suddenly peculiar after over-exposure to the sun.

Raphaël, unaware of how he has been set up, is, in the meanwhile, busy trying to impress Lorette for whom he has composed the modern song she

491

wanted ('Da Ga Da Tsoin Tsoin') and he is puzzled when he hears Jean-Pierre telling Poupoutzoff that Rita, whom the scientist has espied shooting arrows at Gustave, is the poor sick fellow's sister. The antics and misunderstandings which follow do nothing to disabuse Poupoutzoff from the notion that he has one lunatic if not two on his hands.

The situation receives another twist when Oscar Bonnardel turns up to enjoy the company of Rita and discovers that the villa which he had rented is full of strangers. Raphaël and Lorette are easier to explain than Poupoutzoff who, syringe in hand, is stalking Raphaël through the gardens. It is too soon, yet, for explanations, however, and, as evening falls, everybody sets off for the Île Sainte Marguerite and a local fête (Farandole). As he awaits his friends there, Jean-Pierre takes the opportunity for a yearning love song, inspired by Mimi ('Il A Suffi').

It is a love which, it seems, could soon be requited for, when Lorette brings Mimi the news of Oscar's arrival, Mimi is quite open about her feelings: Bonnardel means nothing to her and she is in love with Jean-Pierre ('Je l'Aime et Puis C'Est Tout'). Now it is time for her to tell him so and, to complete the moment of truth, she must also tell him about her harmless relationship with Bonnardel whom she pretended previously that she did not know. But, when she opens her heart, Jean-Pierre immediately jumps to jealous conclusions about Bonnardel.

He earns an indignant tirade from Lorette who pours out fulsome descriptions of the proposals and the gifts which Mimi has turned down from the producer, but her revelations only cause further clouds to darken Jean-Pierre's brow. If Mimi gives up a rich and comfortable life with Bonnardel for him, that will hang over them and their relationship for ever. Perhaps she should think to the future. The unaccustomed carefulness of her footloose Bohemian infuriates Mimi who stalks off, hurt and angry.

Raphaël brings Bonnardel and Rita to join the festivities and the producer is surprised to find his composer there. Raphaël stops Jean-Pierre from telling Bonnardel that they haven't written a word of his scenario, but the subject is quickly changed when Mimi's name comes up. Rita is all jealous ears at the suggestion that Bonnardel might have had something to do with Mimi and she grows increasingly hot under the plunging neckline as the producer cringes under Jean-Pierre's volley of recriminations and the resulting exposé. When the party has been well and truly ruined, it is the bewildered Raphaël who gets the blame for everything and Lorette walks out on him, leaving him to muse sadly on his persistent rotten luck ('Pas de Chance').

Back at the villa, Gustave is taking advantage of the fête to enjoy a respite from his crazy guests when Bonnardel comes sweeping back, his ears red with Rita's revenge, to order his car for a swift departure. Mimi is right behind him, ready to pack her bags and go for the next train and, no sooner has she dashed upstairs than an emotional Jean-Pierre stalks in to announce that he too is leaving. Florida and Lorette, both fuming, follow behind with similar intentions and Poupoutzoff, unable to work with all the distractions of what was supposed to be a quiet villa, also announces his departure.

Unfortunately he wants his money back and Gustave and Jean-Pierre are only just able to raise between them enough cash to keep him quiet.

Bonnardel comes by at an inopportune moment in the conversation and the whole double-renting business is blown wide open as he, too, demands the return of his money. Jean-Pierre tries to explain to him what has happened and, with supportive interruptions from Raphaël, tells the producer the whole story of the four friends and their trip down la Route Fleurie and all the vagaries which came to pass at the Villa Vacances.

To his surprise, Bonnardel applauds vigorously. It is wonderful! Just the scenario needed to go with Jean-Pierre's score and with fine parts for both Rita and Mimi and even a role for Lorette. The only thing it does not have is an ending. Jean-Pierre digs about in his mind for something truly original and comes up with...a wedding! Poupoutzoff and Rasputin can have sole possession of the villa, for everyone else is heading up the hill to St Paul de Vence and its cathedral for a happy, connubial finale which will soon be followed by a honeymoon or three spent where else but on la Route Fleurie?

LA TOISON D'OR

(The Golden Fleece)

an opérette à grand spectacle in two acts by Raymond Vincy based on the novel by Pierre Benoît. Music by Francis Lopez. Produced at the Théâtre du Châtelet, Paris, 18 December 1954 with Colette Riedinger (Brigitte), André Dassary (Stanislas) and Pierjac (Ernest).

CHARACTERS

Ernest Guilhermy
Hermine de St-Quévremond
Stanislas Monestier
Brigitte Holtzer
Philippe, Colonel Haydar
Bouziquet, *a schoolboy*
Prince Xipharès
Ursule
Van Brook, *a banker*
Valentine, *his daughter*
Demetrios Fassilinidès, *another banker*
Capitaine Marcus
Khaled-al-Mansour, *the grand priest*
Chief Kurd, Anouchka, Intendant, Waiter, etc.

ACT 1

Up amongst the Swiss mountains, in the story-book village of Appenzell, the picturesque folk of the region are yodelling forth a favourite turn-of-the-century song ('Le Grand Orphéon d'Appenzell') which has apparently got something to do with a music competition. Neither the music nor the contest make much impression on the little Parisian schoolmaster, Ernest Guilhermy. He has taken a post as pharmacist in the village during his holidays in order to get some fresh air and refresh his wallet ('Pour Être Pharmacien'), and rustic customs are not at all his cup of tea.

Ernest has made something of a conquest since his arrival: he has become the object of the extrovert passions of the buxom and rather overpowering Hermine de St-Quévremonde, a lady of a certain number of years who has come to Appenzell as chaperone to Brigitte Holtzer, a charming young heiress from Saint-Gall. Like Ernest, Hermine is not particularly interested in the fact that 'Le Village Est En Fête' but, while Hermine is pursuing Ernest, Brigitte is having a jolly time joining in the lace-making competition and other such exciting rustic pursuits.

Another who is enjoying himself in the mountains is Ernest's friend, Stanislas Monestier, a well-off young man-about-Paris who has been winning the local shooting competition with one hand while falling in love with Mademoiselle Brigitte with the other ('Sur Chaque Route'). Together they wander through the mountain paths romantically reading the poems of Stanislas's Persian birthplace. But this Arcadian affair is too good to last. News comes from Paris that Stanislas has lost his fortune in a bank crash and the young man realises that, penniless, he can no longer decently pay court to his beloved Brigitte. He must leave Appenzell the next day. He will return to Paris, put his affairs in order and take a job as a teacher alongside Ernest to make ends meet.

Ernest is not a very good teacher. He has trouble keeping his classes in order and suffers all kinds of indignities at the hands of his pupils in front of the headmaster and the inspector of schools (Cantate de l'Inspecteur). Stanislas, on the other hand, is both as dignified and as efficient as becomes a leading man in his new employment. The two men share the little house which Stanislas had leased in happier times, although, thanks to the pawnbroker, it is more sparsely furnished nowadays, and they live modestly if not meagrely.

The happy days of Appenzell seem far away until, one evening, they are surprised to find Brigitte and Hermine on their doorstep. Brigitte, unconvinced by Stanislas's off-hand letter of farewell, has tracked him down from the address inscribed inside the book of poems they had shared ('L'Étoile Bleue'). The truth admitted, the four of them spend a jolly evening together over a comical meal ('Dans un Petit Hôtel du Faubourg Saint-Germain').

Stanislas's ears should be burning that evening for, at the expensive Hôtel Claridge, the bankers Fassilinides and Van Brook are hatching a plot in which he is deeply involved. Practically the only part of Stanislas's patrimony which remains is some uncultivated land in Persia. It is land which is of little use for anything, were it not for the fact that Fassilinides and Van Brook know that it is simply swimming in oil and they have come to Paris to dupe

494

Stanislas into selling it to them cheaply.

Van Brook's daughter, Valentine, is along for the ride and the shopping ('La Mode de Paris') but, when she meets Stanislas, she finds him attractive enough to give him a gentle warning against her father and his plot. The warning is not sufficiently explicit for the unsuspecting Stanislas to refuse to sell when the bankers grudgingly up the price to a princely if inadequate sum ('L'Or et l'Amour'), and he agrees to secede his rights in his family land.

Now that he is once again rich, Stanislas hurries to meet Brigitte 'Au Jardin du Luxembourg' to ask her to marry him, but this time it is she who apparently has mysterious misgivings. She cannot explain but, much as she would like to, she is not in a position to commit herself to him and she must leave Paris immediately ('Si Vous Partiez à l'Autre Bout du Monde'). When Stanislas reveals what he has done, she becomes strangely forceful and urges him not to cash the cheque which would confirm the sale of his land. Does he not know that oil has been found in Persia? But Stanislas has signed documents for Van Brook and Fassilinides, documents which are subject to Persian law. If he wishes to reaffirm his claim to the land he has agreed to sell, there is nothing for it but that he must go to Persia and fight on his home ground the men who have tricked him. Whilst Brigitte and he hurry off to consult lawyers, Ernest and Hermine are left to indulge in a little bit of love-making ('Hermine! Ernest!').

At the Gare de Lyon the bankers are preparing to take the Orient Express for Persia when the four friends turn up to make reservations on the same train. Van Brook and Fassilinides are nervous and suspicious, but their efforts to sabotage Stanislas's departure only get them into tortuous troubles. Nothing can stop the determined Stanislas from making it to Constantinople. Ernest, on the other hand, is more susceptible. He has clapped eyes on Valentine and has fallen madly in love. He follows her around the train and then through the streets of Constantinople, and gets himself into a fine muddle when both Valentine and Hermine get into native costume and he finds himself making love to the wrong woman.

While the plot takes a rest, we watch a shoal of events going on in the markets of Constantinople. Brigitte rescues a little pedlar boy from a beating ('Va, Petit Enfant'), there is a parade of Eastern costumes, Ernest mistakes a footbath for drinking water and, finally, everything ends in a particularly splendid sunset ('Je Me Souviendrai Toujours').

ACT 2

The scene shifts to the Palace of the grand priest Khaled-al-Mansour ('Nuit'). The priest, looking out over the Bosphorus, foresees a new age of the world dawning: an age in which the world will once again head for the shores of Persia as Jason and the Argonauts did far back in history when they came in search of the famous golden fleece ('Toison d'Or'). This time they will come in search of the new golden fleece, the new wealth—oil.

The priest is not merely a man of religion; he is also a man of influence. It is to him that the bankers come for support in their claims to the Monestier estates, and they are followed by Valentine who is followed by Ernest who is followed by Hermine ('Entre Deux Choses')—and also by Stanislas. Faced with Stanislas's case, it turns out that the priest is a very practical man of business who demands a percentage in the enterprise in return for for his help.

He is also a man of little conscience, for his help consists of offering to sink the boat on which the bankers are to cross the Black Sea. It seems his will be the only help on which Stanislas can depend, as Brigitte has been ordered back to Switzerland but, before she goes ('Jamais Je N'Aurais d'Autre Amour'), she gives him a sealed letter. As soon as he gets to Asterabad, he must deliver that letter to the Princess Atalide. She is the real monarch of the kingdom, in spite of the pretensions of the Regent, Prince Xipharès, and she will help him as much as she can.

The Grand Priest is as good as his word and the bankers' ship is sabotaged in mid-water on its trip to Asterabad. Fortunately for them, however, they had been followed by Valentine who was followed by Ernest, and the enterprising pharmacist manages to get the whole party safely ashore on a hot and rocky Caucasian beach ('Nous Avons Soif'). Stanislas makes his way to the royal city by land and falls in on the way with a friendly band of nomads who are equipped with a principal dancer ('Anouchka') and a whole troupe of Kurdish dervishes (Ballet Kurde) to enliven his long trip.

Finally everyone arrives at their goal. The bankers are in haste to get to the Princess to press their case, and equally eager to dispense with the presence of Ernest. They team up with the venal Khaled-al-Mansour who gets Ernest locked away in one of the palace dungeons and uses his influence with the Regent to attempt to get the bankers an interview with Atalide, but his attempts come to nothing and the bankers sit fuming as the Princess announces that she will receive that day only their rival, Stanislas.

When Stanislas comes into the royal presence he is surprised to find that the Princess is a wise and businesslike woman who is fully aware of all the trickeries of the Priest and the Regent. She is also a woman who cares and worries for her country, and she proposes that they combine their efforts on its behalf. She with her royal prerogatives and he with his economic wealth might together steady the little kingdom and bring it to prosperity. Stanislas cannot accept such a mission. He cannot stay in Asterabad when Brigitte is in Europe.

Now the Princess draws aside her veil—Atalide and Brigitte are one and the same person. He has made a decision for both of them. Since he prefers Brigitte to Atalide, she will sign an act of abdication in favour of Xipharès and, becoming Brigitte Holtzer once more, follow Stanislas back to Europe ('Que M'Importe Ma Couronne'). The amazed Stanislas cannot accept such an offer. Once again they must part, he to return to Paris and she to remain where her duty and her future lie. As her people in the street cry out for their Princess, she knows that he is right. She cannot leave them.

Xipharès and the Priest are down in the dungeons torturing Ernest when the news comes that there has been a popular uprising against the Regent and in favour of Atalide. Rioting spreads rapidly through the streets and

Pas Sur la Bouche. Lestelly (Valandray) and Marina Hotine (Gilberte) at the Bouffes-Parisiens, 1948.

Phi-Phi. The knees of Ardimedon aren't the only things that get bared. Jean-Jacques Steen (Periclès), Brigitte Krafft (Aspasie), Jacques Baudoin (Phi-Phi), Nicky Nancel (Mme Phidias) and Bernard Muraccione (Ardimedon) at the Bouffes-Parisiens, 1980.

La Belle de Cadix. Tenor Luis Mariano as the film star, Carlos Medina, with the soprano Lina Dachary (Maria Luisa). Théâtre de l'Empire, 1949.

Méditerranée. Corsican singing star Tino Rossi stars as Corsican singing star Mario Franchi. Théâtre du Châtelet, 1955.

La Route Fleurie. Bourvil and Annie Cordy set off towards the Côte d'Azur on a moto laden with comedy and songs. Théâtre de l'ABC, 1952

Quatre Jours à Paris. The unwanted attentions of Simone (Marguette Willy) are only one of the complications which beset Ferdinand (Andrex) in his search for love. Théâtre Bobino, 1948.

Violettes Impériales. Marcel Merkès (for once, without Paulette Merval) in a 1961 Théâtre Mogador revival opposite Rosita.

Les Misérables. This *operette à grand spectacle* proved to be the biggest French-made international hit since the days of Offenbach and *Les Cloches de Corneville*.

disaster seems imminent when an oil well is set alight and threatens the whole field, but Stanislas heroically saves the situation by spectacularly blowing up the blazing well. It remains only for the villains to be put to flight, for the bruised and battered Ernest to be released to find succour in the arms of Valentine (who has been mad about him since their days in the desert), and for Stanislas and his Atalide/Brigitte to combine in a happy ending ('Jamais Je N'Aurais d'Autre Amour'/'L'Étoile Bleue') as they are crowned Queen and Prince Consort of oil-rich Asterabad ('Soleil d'Orient').

MÉDITERRANÉE

an opérette à grand spectacle in two acts by Raymond Vincy. Music by Francis Lopez. Produced at the Théâtre du Châtelet, Paris, 17 December 1955 with Tino Rossi (Mario), Mlle Aglaë (Juliette), Pierjac (Mimile), Dominique Rika (Paola) and Fernand Sardou (Padovani). Revived there 11 July 1964 with Rudi Hirigoyen, Eliane Varon, André Vylar, Georgette Rispal and Fernand Sardou.

CHARACTERS

Mario Franchi, *a popular singer*
Mattéo, *his brother*
Juliette Germont
Mimile, *an assistant at the shop 'The Jolly Camper'*
Père Padovani
Dubleu, *the managing director of La Lessive Bleu*
Conchita Cortez, *a bullfighter*
Annonciade, *a barkeeper*
Cardolacci, *a policeman*
The Captain *of the yacht*
Angelotti, *a bandit*
Pascal, Mario's Mother, Producer, de Braque, Régisseur, Secretary, Aunt Caroline, Cédratine, Chalot, Paulo, Antoine, Nurse, Actor, etc.

ACT 1
At a television studio, the transmission of the programme La Croisière Bleue is being prepared ('Télévision'). It is a game show sponsored by Monsieur Dubleu, the creator and director of the firm which manufactures the famous soap powder La Lessive Bleue, and this week the grand winner of the show's top prize—a cruise around the Mediterranean on Dubleu's own yacht with, for companion, none other than the heartthrob singer Mario Franchi—will be announced.

The competition to write a song based on the word 'bleu' has been won by little Juliette Germont who sings her song—entitled, of course, 'Bleu'— before being loaded down with vouchers from a series of shops and a cheque for 3000 francs with which to go shopping for the adventure of her life. Alas,

Juliette has no sweetheart or fiancé to take with her on her prize trip and therefore she does not qualify for the second half of the cheque, an extra 2000 francs, but the money is scarcely a concern as she is introduced to the stunning Mario Franchi who is, naturally, equipped with a fine and suitable tenor song with which to end the programme ('Les Baléares').

Mario Franchi, as his name indicates, is Corsican, and the cruise will take him back to his native island for the first time for many years, but today brings him already an unexpected flavour of home when his old parish priest, Père Padovani, turns up at the studio. Padovani is in town for a conference and has taken the opportunity to stop in to see Mario with news of his family. It is troubling news, for his widowed mother is ill and his younger brother Mattéo has been mixing with some undesirable locals, leading Padovani to serious worries on his behalf. It is good that Mario will be home in just a week's time. He is needed.

The party on board Dubleu's yacht grows larger when Conchita Cortez, an alarming Mexican lady bullfighter who has been casting her glances and herself at Mario ever since his visit to her country turns up like a whirlwind and gets herself invited. A second extra passenger is added when Juliette finds herself a sudden sweetheart. Little Mimile, the shop assistant at The Jolly Camper, has been watching the show on television and, when Juliette comes to his shop for some useful holiday purchases, he convinces her of his undying passion in exchange for a place at her side on the cruise. To save money on hotels, they set themselves up with a selection of goods from the shop and prepare to be 'Les Joyeux Campeurs'.

The Corsican village of Casavecchia is where Mario was born and it is there that la Croisière Bleue will make its first stop but, for the moment, life there goes on as normal ('Dans Notre Petit Village'). One of the daily routines of Casavecchia is that the gendarme, Cardolacci, makes hopeful approaches to Annonciade, the widowed tavern-keeper, and is rejected in favour of her very late husband. Annonciade has kept her husband's memory green for ten years and Cardolacci's patience is beginning to wear just a little thin.

Cardolacci's daily attempts at persuasion are harmless and, to the rest of the village, even humorous, but the machinations of the evil Pascal, who is anxious to involve young Mattéo and his fishing boat in some shady business off the coast that night, are more worrying. Paola, Mattéo's fiancée, is upset to see him in the company of such a known rogue, but Mattéo brushes her fears roughly aside. He is sick of the limitations of village life. He wants money, easy money. He wants to go to the mainland and live a fine life there as Mario has done. Paola cannot listen to this kind of talk with equanimity. She is one of 'Les Filles d'Ajaccio', a true daughter of Corsica, with all that that implies in the way of loyalty to her country and to her man. She will not stay true to a man who is himself disloyal.

La Croisière Bleue arrives at Casavecchia, and Mario happily greets his home town with a song ('Campanella') and his mother with a deep embrace. Juliette and Mimile try to set up their tent in the church square and have a fine run in with Cardolacci, and Mimile gets himself embroiled even deeper in local affairs when, after a tiff with Juliette, he invites a pretty local girl to be his partner at that night's Fête des Pêcheurs. Père Padovani may think that his own parishioners are crazy ('Les Paroissiens de Mon Village'), but the visitors are much, much worse.

Mario soon sees the trouble that Mattéo is bringing on his family and he is sympathetic to Paola whom he offers warmly, in Mattéo's absence, to partner to that night's fête ('Demain, C'Est Dimanche'). It is a promise which he will have to fulfil, for Mattéo has taken up Pascal's offer and has joined his band on what is clearly a smuggling escapade in the Îles Sanguinaires, off the coast of Ajaccio. A yacht secretly delivers a cargo of heavy boxes to the rendezvous point and they are beginning to transfer them to Mattéo's boat when they are discovered by the coastguard. A gun battle ensues and, at the end, a coastguard is left dead.

Unaware of the tragedy that has occurred, the fête at Saint-Florent continues happily (Ballet des Pêcheurs). Mario, Paola, Dubleu and Conchita enjoy themselves amongst the Corsican jollities, but Mimile has got himself into a fine pickle for, in line with native custom, his pretty little Corsican has brought with her every single one of her numerous family and he finds he is expected to pay for them all. To make things worse, at the end of another spat with Juliette, he dramatically kisses the first girl to hand only to find that he has thrown himself headfirst into a famous vendetta. The girl is the betrothed of the noted bandit Angelotti, a fearsome fellow known for his vicious Corsican revengefulness. There is nothing for Mimile to do but to drown his apprehensions in drink ('Un P'tit Verre du P'tit Vin du Pays').

The next day Annonciade purposefully invites Père Padovani to lunch but, before we can learn what her purpose is, the jealous Cardolacci invites himself to join them, and Juliette and Mimile somehow end up as part of the party too. They are all being comical together when the news of the previous night's murder breaks.

Everything points to Mattéo as the author of the crime and his aged mother suffers a serious setback on learning that her son is being sought for murder. Mattéo, hearing of his mother's illness, cannot stay in hiding and he returns to the house where he succeeds in convincing Mario that he was not responsible for the crime. Mario and Père Padovani make plans to hide the boy until the murder can be solved, and Mario goes into the church to pray for his brother and for himself ('Vièrge Marie').

The hiding place chosen for Mattéo is the hut of the old shepherd, Joseph, high on the hills behind the town but, as it turns out, it is not such a private place as its isolation might have suggested. The bandit Angelotti is a visitor there and so, too, is Cardolacci in his official capacity. Padovani has to distract the gendarme's mind from his work by setting it on to thoughts of Annonciade and, after a pointed hint from the padre, Cardolacci agrees that Mattéo is not there and goes off to pick flowers for Annonciade.

Meanwhile, Mattéo's account of the fatal night's events has brought some strange new suspicions into Mario's mind. The boy's description of the craft which delivered the contraband—contraband which turned out to be guns rather than the relatively harmless drink and cigarettes Mattéo had expected—points to only one vessel: Dubleu's yacht. Can it be that la Croisière Bleue is a cover for gun-running activities? Suddenly the ship's itinerary through the islands looks disturbingly deliberate.

Juliette and Mimile have also found the energy to climb up to the top of the hill, Mimile egged on by the thought of the fearsome bandit who is supposed to be on his heels. He is so nervy about it that he suspects everyone they see of being Angelotti in disguise but, when he has been proved several times to be wrong, he relaxes a bit and tells his story to a kindly stranger. That stranger is none other than Angelotti who hadn't yet heard about the incident with his fiancée but who is now ready to blow Mimile's brains out.

Fortunately for the little fellow, Cardolacci emerges from his flowers to make an opportune arrest and, with Juliette backing the gendarme up with one of the bandit's own pistols, a famous capture is successfully achieved. The three heroes join together celebrating the event and musing how they would each like to take the whole credit for the arrest themselves ('C'Est Triste').

La Croisière Bleue moves on in time to arrive in Sardinia for the Cavalcade de Sassari (Grand Ballet Sarde), but Dubleu is concerned that the third stop, for the Fête des Moulins in the Balearic Islands, may have to be cancelled since the affair at the Îles Sanguinaires has made the coast-guards highly aware of yachts and their cargoes. Although he is sure the presence of Mario and the smiles of Conchita would help them avoid any delays and problems, he is not willing to be incommoded any further. He does not want his cruise spoiled. He just wants to sit back and enjoy the beautiful blue Mediterranean with his guests ('Mediterranée').

ACT 2

The Balearics get the go by for the moment and the cruise returns to Corsica where we find that Cardolacci has been given the credit for the capture of Angelotti and has been promoted to Brigadier ('Depuis Trois Jours à Casavecchia'). The murder inquiry is still open and Mario is pleased to return to 'Ajaccio' where he hopes to clear his brother's name. Mimile and Juliette are excited when they come upon what they think is a clue—some writing on a banknote given to them by Dubleu which seems to be a list of firearms—and they resolve to put in some detective work.

Paola has her own worries and they are not all on Mattéo's behalf. Since the night at the fête when Mario serenaded her with such warmth she has felt her feelings towards the elder brother growing at the expense of the younger ('C'Est En Vain'). It is something which Mario had not considered, for to him Paola has always been his brother's girl, but the good Padovani finds it advisable to open his eyes to what is happening. Padovani, as it happens, has a quasi-amorous situation of his own which needs resolving. Annonciade has made up her mind to give up bar-keeping and settle down and, instead of accepting Cardolacci, she has instead offered herself as housekeeper to the padre. In that way she can have a man about the house and still be faithful to her late husband.

The visit to the Fête des Moulins finally takes place as planned (Ballet Espagnole) and Mimile and Juliette take the chance to do some spying around the yacht. They discover that, although the ship's complement is supposed to be of ten men, only nine are in evidence while one crew cabin is kept firmly locked. Is there a murderer inside? Suddenly the passengers are told that the itinerary is going to have to be changed again. The Captain of the yacht has reported some mechanical problems and they are heading for Tangier. It seems a strange solution, for it would be quicker and easier to head for France but, when Dubleu offers to return Mario and the others to Corsica, the singer refuses. Something is going on, and he is intent on finding out just what it is.

At Tangier, Mimile and Juliette's sleuthing proves to have been on the right track. A wounded man is brought secretly ashore from the ship and the Captain heads for one of the more notorious bars to find an extra crewman as a replacement. Whilst Mario and Conchita enjoy the local entertainment (Tango-Mediterranée), Mimile dresses up as a swaggering seaman with Juliette as his moll ('C'Est Mon Mataf'), but his charade as Tattooed Arthur leads him deep into danger when the Captain comes to fetch his new crew member and easily recognises the pair under their disguises.

For the moment the Captain does not say anything. The underworld grapevine has brought him news that the gun-running activities of the Dubleu yacht have become known to the police. He is prepared for this eventuality, for the yacht is wired to a detonator which can blow the whole vessel and its incriminating evidence sky high. The button which will activate this detonator is in his cabin. Pretending that he is going to engage Tattooed Arthur, he sends Mimile to the ship to fetch the signing-on papers from his safe. To open the safe all he has to do is to press the big red button. The little fellow has just hurried away when the police descend on the bar and, as all the villains are arrested, a huge explosion is heard. The yacht has gone up.

Mimile wakes up in hospital where he finds himself subject to all sorts of comical delusions but, when he challenges Dubleu as being the mastermind of the affair, he finds he is mistaken. The scribbles on the banknote were only the order for restocking the bar. Dubleu has been the innocent dupe of the Captain of his ship who was the head of an international smuggling ring.

Back at Casavecchia the ends of the case are tied up. Mattéo is cleared of the murder and Père Padovani brings the two brothers happily back together. Now that the air has cleared and fantasy yielded place to reality, Paola is happy to go back, with only a touch of regret, to the brother who will stay in her beloved Corsica and work his fishing boat. The one night spent so happily in Mario's company will be just their memory ('N'En Dis Rien à Personne'). Mimile and Juliette, needless to say, will also be needing the professional services of Padovani, after which everyone will head for Monte Carlo where the show and the story end in the extravagant surroundings of Monsieur Dubleu's Grande Nuit Bleue with its massive display of fireworks and reprises.

IRMA LA DOUCE

a musical play in two acts by Alexandre Breffort taken from his book. Music by
Marguerite Monnot. Produced at the Théâtre Gramont 12 November 1956 with
Colette Renard (Irma), Michel Roux (Nestor le Fripé) and René Dupuy (Bob le
Hotu) and subsequently played at the Théâtre de l'Athenée. Revived at the Théâtre
de l'Athenée 1967 with Mlle Renard, Franck Fernandel and Dupuy.

Produced at the Saville Theatre, London, in a version by David Heneker, Julian
More and Monty Norman 17 July 1958 with Elizabeth Seal, Keith Michell and Clive
Revill. Produced at the Shaftesbury Theatre 27 November 1979 with Helen Gelzer,
Charles Dance and Bernard Spear.

Produced at the Plymouth Theatre, New York, 29 September 1960 with Miss
Seal, Michell and Revill.

A film version made by United Artists in 1963 with Jack Lemmon and Shirley
Maclaine omitted the songs.

CHARACTERS

Irma la Douce
Nestor le Fripé
Bob le Hotu
Polyte le Mou
Jojo les Yeux Sales
Roberto les Diams
Frangipane
Dudu la Syntaxe
Police Inspector
Persil le Noir
Bébért la Méthode
Policeman, Lawyer, Monsieur Bougne, Counsel for the Prosecution, Coun-
sel for the Defence, Honest Man, Warders, Tax Inspector, etc.

ACT 1

The show is introduced by our host and narrator, Bob le Hotu, the patron of
the Bar des Inquiets in the back streets of Pigalle, who lets us in on the
special atmosphere and *argot* of what is known as the *milieu*—the soft under-
belly of Parisian petty crime—with its *poules*, its *mecs* and its *grisbi* ('Le Valse
Milieu'). A *poule* is a girl. Not any kind of girl, you understand, but a working
girl who sells time in a seedy hotel near her beat on the Pont de Caulaincourt
at so much a trick and takes the proceeds (that is to say, *le grisbi*) back to her
mec. The *mecs* are a punchy lot with much need for hand-made shirts,
painted ties and *crêpes Suzettes* which means that the *poules* have to keep a
regular work rhythm going to make ends meet all round. The *milieu* is a
perfect hive of free enterprise and delegated responsibility.

Bob's bar is the principal hang-out of a fine bunch of *mecs* with decidedly
expensive tastes ('Très, Très Snob' ['Polyte-le-Mou']) headed by a bullock
of a man called Polyte le Mou and 'protected' at a very reasonable rate by a
particularly upright (and the word is used advisedly) Inspector of Police. One
day, however, there is a stranger in their midst. It turns out that he is called

502

Nestor and that he is a university law student doing a study of the *milieu*, an occupation which the embarrassed *mecs* find, to say the least, a little near the bone. Their nervousness of him increases when he takes exception to Polyte's rough handling of his *poule*, a little lass called Irma la Douce who turns up regularly to clock in her takings. Blinding the thick-headed Polyte with legal technicalities, he frightens him right out of his job.

Now Irma has no *mec* at all. She politely declines the mass offer of the other *mecs* and decides that perhaps she can manage alone. Alone! This is unheard of. The masculinity of the *mecs* en masse is threatened by such a thought. Then Nestor offers to buy Irma a drink and she is shocked in her turn. In the milieu if a *poule* can't buy her man a drink she is a pretty poor *poule*. So, over an unaccustomed glass of anis, Nestor and Irma fall in love ('Le Pont de Caulaincourt' ['Me V'là, Te V'là']). It is not quite the thing to do, by the rules of the *milieu*, but there you are.

He moves in with her and they spend their time being happily domestic and talking 'Our Language of Love' ['Avec les Anges'] when Irma isn't out on the Pont de Caulaincourt, working with even greater enthusiasm than before to bring home the most and the best of everything to her man. Not everyone is as happy as they with the new situation. With Polyte deposed, the Inspector finds that his head-of-the-queue privileges with Irma are gone, and he is not at all pleased, but Irma's other customers have no complaints ('She's Got the Lot' ['Elle A du Chien']) with what they get for their 1000 francs, tax included.

Unfortunately Nestor's bourgeois little heart is niggled at the thought of other men laying their hands on his Irma and, instead of appreciating the income she brings into the house, he gets grumpy and unreasonable and talks about her giving up her job. Perhaps he could get a job instead. Irma is horrified. She live off him? They'd be the laughing stock of the *milieu*! There seems to be only one answer to the problem. What is needed is some nice old sugar daddy. Nestor wouldn't feel so bad if there were only one other man, it would be just like most ordinary families. And, would you believe it, it happens.

One day, not long after, on the Pont de Caulaincourt Irma encounters an ageing, bearded gentleman called Oscar. Oscar is very sweet. He really seems to enjoy his session with Irma and, oh heavens!, he gives her 10,000 francs with a promise that he will come each day with the same sum providing she keeps herself strictly for him—apart, that is, from her real, at-home lover. Irma is thrilled. It is clearly a very good beard for, even with his clothes off, she does not recognise that Oscar is really Nestor. Polyte, who has taken to spying on Nestor to try to trip him up, has been fooled too, but his situation is clearly different.

Irma runs joyously to the Bar des Inquiets to share her delight with Bob and the boys ('Ah! Dis-donc, Dis-donc') and to hand over her earnings to Nestor. The other *mecs* are in awe of Nestor. Only such a short time in the business and already he has attained the pinnacle of a *mec*'s profession. He is being supported by a *poule* who is supported by a rich and regular client. There is nothing for it but that Nestor must be elected to the honorary chieftainship of their group, and the occasion is celebrated with a toast to that most important element of life—*le grisbi* ('Le Grisbi is le Root of le Evil in Man' ['To Be or Not To Be']).

Of course, *le grisbi* is just what Nestor doesn't have. He has just those ten progressively more tattered 1000 franc notes which, each day, Oscar gives to Irma who gives them to Nestor and so on. Nestor, disguised as Oscar to avoid being recognised, is forced to take a job, and the job he ends up with is that of polishing the floors of Monsieur Bougne's celebrated ballroom. The schedule gets a bit tiring: Oscar's work, Oscar's lovemaking, Nestor's work and Nestor's lovemaking, and all the time the jealousy of being Nestor deceived with Oscar and vice versa.

The tiredness and jealousy is inclined to show up in Nestor more because Nestor sees more of Irma. Arguments start when it seems that Oscar is being considered above Nestor and a series of scenes require Nestor and Oscar to swap identities with almost indecent speed and, almost, with a confusion of identities. Nestor is becoming 'A Wreck of a Mec' ['La Cave à Irma']. Something will have to give. He will have to be only Nestor or only Oscar. But if he gets rid of Oscar, is there any guarantee that Irma will happily return full time to Nestor and, on the other hand, if he kills off Nestor will he have to spend the rest of his life polishing ballroom floors?

Ultimately, it seems that there is only one solution. Nestor will murder Oscar. A palpitating *crime passionel* which can only impress the woman on whose behalf it has been committed ('That's a Crime'). And so, on the banks of the Seine, behind a conveniently placed *suze*, Nestor le Fripé does poor Monsieur Oscar to death and throws his coat and briefcase into the river. Oscar is dead. Back at the Bar des Inquiets, Nestor makes his terrible confession before Irma and the boys. To his horror, Irma is not sympathetic and, maybe worse, the bar is filled with police. In a mad free-for-all, Nestor le Fripé is arrested for the murder of Monsieur Oscar.

ACT 2

Nestor's trial is a strange affair. The jury consists of Polyte, the Police Inspector and one honest man who managed to get there in time. The President of the Court has been banished to jail on a bribes charge, so it is our good friend Bob who presides over the farcical proceedings. Nestor's law training and his drawing of long-winded precedents on circumstantial evidence do him no good. He and the *mecs* are sentenced to Devil's Island.

Aboard the prison hulk transporting them across the seas, Nestor thinks longingly of Paris and Irma ('From a Prison Cell' ['L'Aventure Est Morte']), but he cannot know that Irma has problems of her own. With Nestor out of the way, Polyte and the Inspector are expecting to go back to the old way of things, but blandishment and bribery earn them no joy. Irma turns away customers, lured to her hotel by the notoriety of Nestor's trial, with slapped faces and goes into a dreadful decline ('Irma la Douce').

On Devil's Island, Nestor goes into a similar decline and gets himself threatened with demotion from rock-breaking to the position of houseboy to the governor's wife. But then a letter arrives from France with some special news: Irma is going to have a baby round Christmastide. Nestor simply has to escape from the impermeable island in order to be home in time for the happy event.

With the aid of some wine donated gratefully to Jojo (her present house-boy) by the governor's wife, the prison warders are made drunk during the course of a jolly party ('There Is Only One Paris For That' ['Y'A Qu' Paris Pour Ca']) and stripped of their uniforms and, disguised as their own jailers, the *mecs* escape from Devil's Island aboard a miraculously constructed raft. Bravely they paddle off towards Paris, across the Atlantic wilds ('The Freedom of the Seas' ['Hardi, Joli Gondolier']), until one fine day they smell on the air the scent of coffee, croissants, garlic, camembert and Gauloises. There can be no doubt: battered, bronzed and bearded, they are home!

Nestor hurries to find Irma and is flabbergasted when she welcomes him in a stunned fashion as Oscar. It's the wretched beard. She begs him to go to the police and show himself as being alive so that Nestor and his friends may be released from prison, so Oscar has to come alive again and trundle off to face his old enemy, the Police Inspector. His resurrection is most inconvenient and, given the paperwork involved, it is even doubtful if Oscar will be permitted to come alive again ('But').

Things are complicated further when a tax inspector intrudes with a large unpaid tax demand for Oscar based on his earnings as a ballroom floor-polisher. The inspector is bribed with an unexpected windfall in the form of some outstanding overtime money from Monsieur Bougne and the tax on the bribe is paid to the taxman with an extra 1000 francs hastily supplied by our ever faithful narrator. It can finally be agreed that Oscar is alive, and that means that Nestor is innocent.

Unfortunately, since he is no longer in prison it is a little difficult to pardon him, but the case of Nestor le Fripé soon makes *la une* of Paris. It is discussed with the fervour of a reincarnated Dreyfus case and, after many highways and byways of improbability have been travelled, Nestor is agreed to be a free and pardoned man. Now Oscar can disappear again and Nestor can safely put in an appearance in Paris.

The beard is quickly removed, and Nestor sets out to Irma's place where a whole line of well-wishers from the *milieu* is queuing up with gifts for her soon-to-be-born child: pistols, knives, coshes and other useful things. The child is a boy and he will be named Nestor, after his father ('Christmas Child' ['Il Est Né']). But what is this? There is a second child. Very well, he shall be called Oscar. Also after his father.

Just to make a good family ending to this good family story, Nestor and Irma got married, and when nice Monsieur Oscar paid an occasional visit to town from his distant country address, Nestor was very happy to have Irma receive him just as she did in the old days. And so, they all lived happily ever after.

LES MISÉRABLES

a musical tragedy by Alain Boublil and Jean-Marc Natel based on the novel by Victor Hugo. Music by Claude-Michel Schönberg. Produced at the Palais des Sports, Paris, 17 September 1980 with Maurice Barrier (Valjean), Jean Vallée (Javert), Gilles Buhlmann (Marius), Yvan Dautin (Thénardier), Marianne Mille (Eponine), Fabienne Guyon (Cosette), Rose Laurens (Fantine) and Marie-France Roussel (Mme Thénardier).

Produced at the Barbican Theatre, London in a version by Herbert Kretzmer 30 September 1985 and at the Palace Theatre 4 December 1985 with Colm Wilkinson, Roger Allam, Michael Ball, Alun Armstrong, Frances Ruffelle, Rebecca Caine, Patti LuPone and Susan Jane Tanner.

Produced at the Broadway Theatre, New York, 12 March 1987 with Wilkinson, Terrence V Mann, David Bryant, Leo Burmester, Miss Ruffelle, Judy Kuhn, Randy Graff and Jennifer Butt.

CHARACTERS

Jean Valjean
Javert
Fantine
Cosette, *her daughter*
Thénardier
Madame Thénardier
Eponine, *their daughter*
Marius
Montparnasse, Babet, Brujon, Claquesous, *Thénardier's gang*
Enjolras
Combeferre, Feuilly, Courfeyrac, Joly, Grantaire, Lèsgles, Jean Prouvaire, *students*
Bishop of Digne
Gavroche
Farmer, Labourer, Inkeeper, Inkeeper's wife, Foreman, Factory Girl, Old Woman, Crone, Pimp, Batambois, Fauchelevent, etc.

ACT 1

Nearly twenty years ago Jean Valjean was arrested for stealing a loaf of bread and, his guilt established and his reasons unexplored, he was sent to prison for five years. Had he lived out his sentence under man's law resignedly, he would have been freed at the end of five years, but Valjean's mind and heart revolted against his imprisonment and he attempted to escape. He was caught and his sentence increased and it was not until nineteen years had passed that Prisoner 24601 finally reached the day when he was eligible for parole from the fetters of the chain gang (Prologue: 'Look Down, Look Down').

Parole is not the same as freedom. Valjean is a ticket-of-leave man and, wherever he goes, honest folk shy away from him, refusing him work and shelter, until the good Bishop of Digne takes pity on him and offers him food and bed. Valjean returns the Bishop's kindliness by robbing him of his silver, silver which he might sell for the sort of money that can place him out of reach of those who scorn him, but the law which has ruled his life is not ready yet to let him go, and the thief is arrested.

The Bishop, however, will not bear witness against him and even claims before the constables that he gave the silver to Valjean as a gift, adding, in corroboration, two valuable candlesticks to the bewildered man's hoard. With this silver Valjean may, nay must, start a new and honest life: the Bishop has bought his soul for God (Soliloquy: 'What Have I Done?') and his life must begin anew.

Eight years pass and Valjean, having broken his parole, has created himself a new life and a new identity under the name of Madeleine in the small town of Montreuil. There he has become both a wealthy factory owner and mayor of the town. The folk of his town and those who work in his factory are no better off than he was in his young days ('At the End of the Day') and one who finds life particularly hard is the young Fantine. She has not only to support herself but also to send money to support her illegitimate daughter who is being brought up by foster parents in the country, but she will not yield to the sexual advances of Valjean's foreman to help alleviate her troubles.

When Valjean sees her fighting with another factory girl over a letter about her daughter, he pauses only long enough to order the girls brought to book and not to enquire into the reasons for their brawl. Fantine's secret is exposed, and the foreman revengefully dismisses her. With no job, Fantine is in despair ('I Dreamed a Dream') and finally, desperate for money to send to the ever-demanding foster parents to ensure her daughter's well-being, she sells her locket, her hair and, finally herself, joining the 'Lovely Ladies' who hawk their bodies along the docks.

Although her body is subjugated, Fantine's mind refuses to give in. One day, she rejects the advances of a particularly distasteful client and attacks him with her fingernails. The man is an important citizen and Fantine finds herself brought before Inspector Javert, the self-same representative of the law who, so many years before, had paroled Valjean. Fantine is on the verge of being arrested when the Mayor arrives on the scene and orders that she be sent not to jail but to a doctor.

Javert does not recognise the flourishing citizen of Montreuil as the missing convict but, when Valjean uses his unusual physical strength to lift a runaway cart from the leg of a trapped man, Javert's mind is stirred into remembrance. Only one other man he has known could have accomplished such a feat of strength. He was a convict, a fugitive whom Javert has been tracking for years with the relentless regard for the letter of the law which drives him. But that man has just been recaptured.

Hearing that an innocent man is about to take his place in prison, Valjean is tortured with the desire to remain free and with his duty to innocence ('Who Am I?'). Finally, before the bar of the court, he tears open his shirt to expose his convict's brand and declares himself as Valjean.

Javert sets out to arrest his man, who has made his way to the hospital where Fantine lies dying ('Come to Me'). Valjean promises the woman, whose death he has partly caused by his lack of care, that he will atone for his neglect by being responsible for her daughter but, before he can make his escape, the Inspector is upon him, armed for his arrest. Valjean pleads for a short reprive, just time enough to allow him to find the child, Cosette, and make provision for her safety and her future, but Javert is not willing to accept the word of a man who has proved himself a thief and a liar and he stands his ground. Valjean then uses his strength. He attacks Javert physically and, knocking the man of the law to the ground, he disappears into the night.

The little Cosette has not been cared for as her mother believed ('A Castle on a Cloud'). The foster-parents, a worthless inkeeper called Thénardier and his slatternly wife ('Master of the House'), have used the money Fantine sent for their own purposes and that of their spoiled daughter, Eponine, whilst treating Cosette as nothing better than a servant. When Valjean arrives to take her away, they wring as much cash from him as possible ('Thénardier Waltz') before letting the child depart.

Ten years later, in the year of 1832, both Valjean and Javert, still yearning for the day when he may recapture the man whose freedom stands before him as an insult both to the law and to himself as its unquestioning representative, are in Paris. Javert is still a policeman and Valjean is once again a prosperous gentleman, living a quiet and private life with the teenage Cosette whom he has raised as his own daughter. The Thénardiers, too, are in Paris but in a very different area. They inhabit the slums of the town where they lead a gang of street ruffians of which Eponine is a useful member while their young son Gavroche makes his friends amongst the beggars and whores of Paris (Beggars' Chorus).

Eponine has turned out a street-wise but decent child, in spite of her parents, and her sordid life is given its sunshine by a secret love which she carries for the student, Marius Pontmercy. Marius is fond of the youngster, but he is taken by a *coup de foudre* when he sees Cosette one day in the street. Their meeting is a brief one, for Javert happens upon the spot and Valjean swiftly disappears, hurrying the girl with him.

Thénardier arouses Javert's suspicions about the gentleman who had such a seeming fear of the law, and all the Inspector's old feelings rise obsessively up in him. Surely, with the right that is behind him, God will not let him be bested by this man ('Stars in Your Multitudes'). Eponine realises that the girl Marius has fallen for is the very child with whom she was brought up and she bravely looks at the difference in their positions now, as Marius begs her to help him find Cosette once again.

General Lamarque, the sole member of the ruling government in whom the poor people of Paris have trust, is dying, and there is great unrest in the town. A group of students gather at a café to talk of revolution ('Red and Black') and, when the news of Lamarque's death arrives, they rush out into the street, inflamed by wine and by the diatribes of Enjolras, one of the most dramatically idealistic of their group, to take up arms in the cause of what he and they envisage as freedom ('Do You Hear the People Sing').

508

Eponine leads Marius to the home of Valjean and Cosette, sheltered from the world behind high walls, and the boy climbs the wall to meet the girl he loves ('In My Life'/'A Heart Full of Love'). While Eponine waits outside, she sees the rest of Thénardier's gang approaching. They too have spied out the house of the prosperous gentleman and they are planning to rob it. Eponine, desperate to protect Marius, who may believe that she led the gang there in vengeance, braves her father's wrath and screams, threatening to bring the police to the spot. The gang flee, but the fracas leaves Valjean convinced that Javert is again on his track and, as Paris begins to boil with unrest, he swears to leave France altogether and take Cosette away once again ('One Day More').

ACT 2

In the streets of Paris, the students and their allies set up barricades made from the debris of the city. Behind them they will conduct their battle against the government's troops ('Here Upon These Stones'). Marius has joined Enjolras's band and Eponine has braved the barricades to be by his side. The greatest service she can render him is to take a letter to Cosette, a letter expressing his love and his prayer that he will survive the coming battle so that he may once again be with her. Eponine stifles her own feelings and takes the letter, delivering it to Valjean who opens it and reads the young man's cry of love and hopeless hope. Her mission completed, Eponine determines to return to the barricades and the man she loves ('On My Own').

The students are already face to face with the army at the barricades when little Gavroche turns up a surprise. Javert has masqueraded as a revolutionary and infiltrated the students' camp as a spy, but the lad, who goes everywhere and sees everything, recognises him and Javert is taken prisoner, defiantly predicting the fall of this foolish and illegal rebellion. The battle has already begun when Eponine returns, creeping through the flying bullets towards Marius, but her insistence on returning has been her bane; she has been hit and she finds happiness only as she dies in Marius's arms ('A Little Drop of Rain').

Valjean makes his way to the barricades more successfully. He will fight on the rebels' side, but that is a secondary consideration. He has come to find Marius, to watch over his safety in the fighting and to make sure he is protected and preserved for the sake of Cosette. In the course of events, he is given the opportunity to kill the imprisoned Javert but, declaring that he has nothing against a man who has done nothing but follow his duty, he instead slips the policeman's bonds and lets him go free. The amazed and uncomprehending Javert hurries away with a warning that Valjean's action changes nothing in his determination to render him some day up to the justice he has so long flouted.

As night falls, the students take rest and wine before the new day's fighting ('Drink With Me') and Valjean sends up a quiet prayer that his mission to save Marius may succeed ('Bring Him Home') but, when the next day comes, casualties are quick to occur. Little Gavroche falls the first, collecting live ammunition from the corpses of fallen soldiers, and one by one the others follow, until it seems that Valjean alone is left alive behind the barricade.

Determinedly he searches out Marius and finds him, badly wounded but living. Making use of his great strength he lifts the cover of a sewerage manhole and, as the army close in on the barricades, he disappears into the network of tunnels that run under the Paris streets, carrying the unconscious boy over his back.

The sewers of the city have also become the lair of the foul Thénardier who brings there the bodies of the fallen to despoil them at his leisure ('Dog Eats Dog'). When Valjean falls unconscious under his efforts, Thénardier steals a ring from the unconscious Marius's hand, but he hurries away when he recognises Valjean's face. Finally, Valjean emerges from the sewers with his burden and runs straight into Javert. This time there is no escape and he seeks none. He asks for time only to deliver Marius into the hands of a doctor, then he will return and Javert can do with him as he wishes.

Javert, barely knowing his own mind, agrees and, when Valjean has departed he interrogates his soul (Soliloquy: 'Who Is This Man?') as to the rights and wrongs, the legal and the moral necessities in his life and in Jean Valjean's. Nothing tallies, nothing makes sense, everything he believed in so firmly for so long he now doubts. Inspector Javert has come to the end of his quest and he has found only unbearable uncertitude. It is too much for him and he throws himself from a city bridge to his death in the waters of the Seine.

As the women of Paris bewail the foolish waste of life in the fighting ('Turning'), the recovering Marius brokenly looks at the empty café where his friends once flaunted their ideals ('Empty Chairs at Empty Tables'). That is all gone now. He is part of another world, a world where Cosette is beside him and where he grows daily stronger, looking towards the day when they may be wed. To the boy, Valjean admits what he cannot say to Cosette: he is Jean Valjean, a criminal, and his tale might one day bring shame and disgrace on the child he has loved. As soon as she is safely married, he will leave them forever.

The wedding is celebrated magnificently (Wedding Chorale) and the Thénardiers turn up, masquerading unconvincingly as aristocrats, with the intention of blackmailing the bridegroom. Jean Valjean is a murderer and unless Marius pays them off they will reveal what Thénardier saw in the sewers the night the barricades fell—Valjean with a body over his shoulder. Thénardier brings out in evidence the ring he took from the victim's hand, and Marius recognises it as his own.

Now he knows that he owes his life to Valjean, that it was he who carried him from the barricades to safety. As the Thénardiers mockingly carry on their charade of aristocracy ('Beggars at the Feast'), Marius and Cosette hurry to find Valjean. He is alone in his room and his life is dripping away. Already he can hear the voice of Fantine calling to him from the world beyond and, as he retails to Cosette her true history, the spirits of the dead crowd around him. At last, surrounded by love, he dies.

This synopsis is based on the revised version produced in England.

Part 3

UNITED STATES OF AMERICA

Although musical and operatic entertainments were popular from the earliest colonial days, a native tradition in musical theatre took time to establish itself in the United States. For many years American theatres relied for their product on the stage pieces and the performers of the distant home lands of the immigrant population: German, French and, overwhelmingly, British, and the ballad operas, comic operas, extravaganzas and burlesques of eighteenth and nineteenth century Britain were the basic diet of the American musical stage until the middle of the nineteenth century when, like London, New York discovered first French *opéra-bouffe* and German operetta, then, in turn, the joys of the *opéra-comique*, of Gilbert and Sullivan and their peers, and finally of George Edwardes' new burlesque and the Daly's and Gaiety musicals.

Situated at a distance from the busily creative theatres of Europe, America, like Australia, was able to enjoy the reproduced riches of London, Paris and Berlin indifferently, bringing to its theatres a varied wealth of light musical entertainment taken from the stages of three languages. There were, of course, efforts from both new Americans and Americans born-and-bred to produce original pieces which imitated the successful shows from the other side of the Atlantic, and several of these found some success.

The extravaganza *The Black Crook* (1866), a piece mixing the traits of French *grand opéra-bouffe féerie* and British pantomime and illustrated with a chimeric mixture of borrowed and new music, was the first to be widely noticed, but the comic opera *The Doctor of Alcantara* (1862), Cheever Goodwin's *Evangeline* (1874), a burlesque of Longfellow with original music by Edward Rice, and the hugely successful *pasticcio, Adonis* (1884), all featured as milestones in the slowly developing American musical theatre, and versions of three of these were exported, albeit without great success, to Britain.

The widest native successes of the period came in the field of musical farce-comedy, a breed of entertainment akin to the often shapeless but irrepressibly lively low song-and-dance comedies found in the British provinces. These pieces, usually developed around a star comedian or company, began as little more than a series of variety sketches and songs linked together with a slim and not always very coherent story and some broad, low-comedy dialect characters. Harrigan and Hart's Irish *Mulligan Guards* series, J K Emmet's impersonations of the German-accented *Our Cousin Fritz*, and Edward Rice's Surprise Party and their variegated musical comedies proved perennial favourites and several shows, including the 'musical comedy oddity' *Fun on the Bristol* and William Gill's Germanic *My Sweetheart*, travelled with notable success to the less sophisticated theatres of Britain and the colonies.

The biggest success of the genre, both in America and overseas, was Charles Hoyt's farcical *A Trip to Chinatown*, produced on Broadway in 1891, in which a slapstick tale of a night on the town provided the backbone for a rumbustious song and dance entertainment. 1891 also marked the Broadway

515

appearance of the first generally successful American comic opera, *Robin Hood*, written by Harry Bache Smith and Reginald de Koven, and produced by the Boston Ideal Opera Company, a troupe which played British and Continental comic opera and *opéra-bouffe* on a regular touring basis. Firmly modelled on the works in the Bostonians regular repertoire, *Robin Hood* combined a farcical comic opera story, not always connected with its nominal subject, with a pleasing score of light lyrical and comic music and remained popular for many years.

Harry Smith was to be the most important librettist/lyricist of the era, but his collaboration with de Koven did not produce any further pieces to equal *Robin Hood*. It was his work with another composer which set the American comic opera tradition securely on its way. In 1895 Smith combined with the Irish-born composer Victor Herbert on the delightful *The Wizard of the Nile* followed quickly by *The Serenade* and *The Fortune Teller*, and the career of the most successful Broadway composer to date was launched. Over the next quarter of a century Herbert regularly provided musicals of all kinds for Broadway, the most famous of which, from the very Continental *Mademoiselle Modiste* and the romantic *Naughty Marietta* and *Sweethearts* to the farcical *The Red Mill* and the juvenile *Babes in Toyland*, established themselves as the earliest classics of the Broadway musical stage.

In spite of Herbert's presence, the *fin de siècle* period was, under the double sway of comic opera and musical comedy, still overwhelmingly British in its entertainments. Apart from Charles Klein and John Philip Sousa's burlesque opera *El Capitan* (1896), the excellent comic opera *The Prince of Pilsen* (1903), and George M Cohan's lively extension of the farce-comedy, *Little Johnny Jones* (1904), few home-bred shows won more than a passing interest but, as the great period of the British musical stage waned, an explosion of talent woke up the American theatre. A new group of writers and composers burst to the fore with an up-to-date type of musical comedy; bristling and bright song and dance pieces which took the Gaiety Theatre style to its logical, twentieth-century development.

In 1910 Otto Harbach and Karl Hoschna produced a delightful blend of comedy and modern popular music in *Madame Sherry*, and the facile Harbach went on through the next decade to provide texts for Rudolf Friml in *The Firefly* and *High Jinks* and for Louis Hirsch in *Going Up* and *Mary*, while songwriter Jerome Kern joined with authors Guy Bolton and P G Wodehouse in a series of musicals, of which *Oh Boy* and *Leave It to Jane* are the best remembered, mixing the lightest of comedy with the brightest of dancing music. Harry Tierney and Joseph McCarthy's *Irene*, with its combination of slick story, foolish fun and dashing dance tunes, capped the period, bringing the Broadway musical its biggest international hit to date.

Broadway moved into the twenties ready to enjoy its tardy but brilliant revelation as a source of musical theatre. Harbach, switching from light comedy to a regular comic opera form, joined Oscar Hammerstein to produce colourful libretti for two of the most famous romantic musicals of the Broadway stage, Friml's *Rose Marie* and Sigmund Romberg's *The Desert Song*, as well as collaborating with Kern on *Sunny*. Kern turned out his happiest show in *Sally*, and then proved that there was more in his satchel than dance tunes by providing the memorable score for the light opera, *Show Boat*. Romberg, who had been writing for the theatre with only sparing success for over a decade, scored not only with *The Desert Song* but also with *The Student Prince* and *The New Moon*, two soaringly melodious pieces in the same style, while Friml added a further costume piece to the list of successes with his classic *The Vagabond King*.

DeSylva, Brown and Henderson contributed to the lighter side of the scene with the spunky *Good News*, and George Gershwin found his first successes in this remarkable period with the rhythmic songs and dances of *Lady, Be Good, Oh, Kay!* and *Funny Face*, written with his brother Ira, but it was the stalwart Harbach who provided the libretto for the show which would become the epitome of the 1920s musical, not only in America but around the world—Vincent Youmans' *No No, Nanette*. The substantial, Continental-style pieces of Romberg and Friml and the wholly exceptional *Show Boat* were, by their nature, pieces which would live on through generations, but that such a slight, trimly-built musical as *No, No, Nanette*, with its essence of the 1920s and its almost delicate, made-for-dancing music, should have survived with equal strength speaks for its remarkable qualities.

America had taken up where London had left off. Whereas fresh authors and composers had failed to emerge in Britain to succeed Lionel Monckton, Sidney Jones, Ivan Caryll and Leslie Stuart, the new generation of Broadway writers proved precisely the men to take the traditions so firmly founded at Daly's and the Gaiety into the post-war era. *Rose Marie, The Desert Song* and *Show Boat*, with their comic opera scores and picturesque plots and settings, were the legitimate heirs to both *The Geisha* and *The Merry Widow*, whilst *No, No, Nanette, Sally* and *Oh, Kay!* led the way in the type of musical that George Edwardes would undoubtedly have produced had he still been at the Gaiety. It was significant that, after his death, one of the few successes at that famous theatre was *Going Up*.

The essential gaiety of twenty years of bubbling Broadway musicals did not work its way through into the 1930s. By this time, Friml, Youmans and Romberg had given their best work and Kern, although he collaborated reasonably successfully with Harbach on *The Cat and the Fiddle* and with Hammerstein on *Music in the Air*, did not again achieve the happiness of *Sally* or the heights of *Show Boat*. Gershwin left the light-hearted comedy musical to tackle political burlesque in *Of Thee I Sing* before moving away altogether from the light musical theatre to produce his masterpiece of folk opera, *Porgy and Bess*, in the same way that Offenbach, at the last, had turned from *opéra-comique* to *Les Contes d'Hoffmann*.

There was now a strange vacuum on the lighter side of the musical theatre. Only the songwriter Cole Porter and his team of librettists, with the rumbustious yet stylish *Anything Goes*, followed and developed the style of the twenties musical. Instead, while tinselly revusical shows proliferated, many of the best writers of Broadway showed an eagerness to turn away from the light comic and romantic shows in which they had created so much fine work. It seemed as if they were trying to turn the light musical theatre into

517

something other than it was and had, for nearly a century, so happily been. The result was a decade where the mediocre and the pretentious were often in evidence and genuine successes all too rare.

Of the best remembered musicals of the early forties, Kurt Weill's *Lady in the Dark* and *One Touch of Venus* found Broadway success but failed to travel, while pieces such as Rodgers and Hart's *Pal Joey* provoked more comment from the cognoscenti than attention from audiences. Oscar Hammerstein turned from original scores to the music of Bizet to manufacture his *Carmen Jones*, but it was Hammerstein who, in tandem with Richard Rodgers, was eventually to lead the American musical theatre into its second period of international prominence, a period of thirty years as the crucible of the world's most popular musicals.

These years produced the body of work which has become popularly known as 'the Broadway musical'. It is a term which has become trite with use. Xenophobic commentators have tried to dub the Broadway musical a genre apart, or even a genre sprung fully formed and newly invented from the macadam of the Great White Way. The great shows of the post-war era were indeed born on Broadway, but they were not born in any flash of lightning; they were as much a part of the world tradition flowing from London and Paris, Berlin and Vienna, as the works of Friml, Romberg, Harbach, Kern and the early Hammerstein had been. They brought nothing that was particularly new to the musical theatre; they merely did what they did brilliantly well, as they served up fine contemporary and costume plays, romantic, comic, sentimental and occasionally dramatic, wedded to striking melodies, frothy rhythms and picturesque stage designs in a series of musicals which went round the world. The centre of creative activity had left Europe and come to New York, but the product, although it was new insofar as it was of its time, was still, basically, the same as it had been for half a century and more.

Rodgers and Hammerstein led the way back to the sound tenets of the classic musical theatre. They sacrificed nothing in quality by eschewing the pretensions of the past decade as, with a fidelity to attractive plot, character and staging, and a sure touch for the most appealing and immediate, yet durable, in music and lyrics, they produced, over a period of sixteen years, five of the most enduring musicals of the century. *Oklahoma!*, *Carousel*, *South Pacific*, *The King and I* and *The Sound of Music* provided a core to a period which produced as many memorable works as any other in the history of the light musical theatre.

Much more than in the 1920s, the body of work produced gave itself an American identity. As in the early days of the Gaiety musical comedies, many pieces of this era used twentieth century settings and subjects for their material. *On the Town*, *Wonderful Town*, *Guys and Dolls*, *The Most Happy Fella*, *How to Succeed in Business Without Really Trying*, *The Pajama Game*, *Damn Yankees*, *Gentlemen Prefer Blondes*, *Bells Are Ringing*, *The Music Man*, *Bye Bye Birdie* and *West Side Story* all took different areas of modern American life as the bases for their action, whether of the lightest comedy as in *Wonderful Town*, or of considerable drama and real romance as in *West Side Story*.

518

The outstanding musicals of this period were by no means cast all in the same mould, even if they kept largely to the same form and exploited the same theatrical devices. Lerner and Loewe ranged from period hokum in *Paint Your Wagon* to romantic fantasy in *Brigadoon* and the lines of classical literature in *My Fair Lady*, while Leonard Bernstein's ultra-light *On the Town* could not have been more different from the powerful *West Side Story* and the brave and brilliant attempt at stylish burlesque in *Candide*. The songwriters' shows, such as Porter's *Kiss Me, Kate* (which flirted with burlesque) and *Can-Can*, and Irving Berlin's *Annie Get Your Gun* and *Call Me Madam* hung their numbers on equally varied and enjoyable libretti and there was even a place amongst all this fresh and exciting writing for *pasticcio* which, since this was a period of excellence, proved, in the form of *Song of Norway* and *Kismet* (featuring the music of Grieg and Borodin respectively), to be *pasticcio* of the most successful kind.

Frank Loesser's *Guys and Dolls* emerged from the era as perhaps the most remarkably classic combination of all the elements of light musical theatre and, with *My Fair Lady*, *West Side Story* and the Rodgers and Hammerstein works, it has survived the ensuing decades on the world's stages with a vigour which some of the other successful shows of the era have lacked. It is a fair bet that they will still be played in some kind of theatre half a century and a century on as *Orphée aux Enfers* and *The Mikado* are today.

Few of the writers and musicians who had made this era of the American musical theatre so prodigious continued to work in the field in the 1960s and, of those who did, very few equalled their former successes, but the light musical theatre with its high standards and its obvious rewards had proved attractive to young authors, composers and songwriters, and there was a significant group of new writers to take over where Hammerstein, Loewe, Berlin, Loesser and Bernstein had left off. Some worked in tandem with the famous of earlier times, others together and alone, but the shows kept coming and they kept coming up aces.

If there was a growing harshness to be found in some of the music and voices, a lack of heart and of carefree fun in the stories, and a brashness in the presentation, these were qualities which did not seem to displease contemporary taste, and favourite shows such as *Gypsy, Funny Girl, Hello, Dolly!, Sweet Charity, Cabaret, Mame* and *Applause* with their loud, brassy heroines and slick, vigorous staging became a feature of the period.

For those whose tastes did not run to these modern equivalents of the old Broadway 'shouters' and their vehicles, there was plenty of fine entertainment which followed different paths, although sometimes in isolation. There was comedy and even burlesque—through theatre history so often the herald of fine things—in *Little Me, A Funny Thing Happened on the Way to the Forum* and *Once Upon a Mattress*, sentimental drama in *Fiddler on the Roof* and *Man of la Mancha*, and even pure whimsy in the little off-Broadway show *The Fantasticks*, as such names as Cy Coleman, Michael Stewart, Stephen Sondheim, Charles Strouse, Kander and Ebb and Jerry Herman became foremost in the creative credits of the system which was producing ever larger, more lavish, more technically sophisticated and more expensive musicals for

519

a public which had feasted for twenty years and was yet eager for bigger and better.

These men were still the principal figures of the musical theatre in the 1970s and each was to bring forth further successes—Coleman with another outstanding burlesque, *On the Twentieth Century* and, with Stewart, the circus musical *Barnum*, Strouse with the ultimate children-and-animals musical, *Annie*, Kander and Ebb with the darkly satirical *Chicago*, and Herman with *La Cage aux Folles*, a musical version of the famous French play. Although each of these, in its own right, was a fine and successful piece, it was noticeable that they inspired little successful emulation. As in Britain in the twenties, as in Vienna and Berlin after the war, the relay was not being taken up by a succeeding generation of writers and producers.

There were successful pieces produced which came from the pens of new writers but, as in the cases of *Hair*, *Godspell* and *Grease*, these were often one-off novelty hits, and they bore little relation to the mainstream of theatre writing. Marvin Hamlisch, the composer of the remarkable slice-of-life musical *A Chorus Line*, and of *They're Playing Our Song*, was the one notable new addition to the ranks of important writers.

Stephen Sondheim, the exciting lyricist of *Funny Thing* and *West Side Story*, epitomised what there was of adventure in the period as, becoming both composer and writer, he ranged through a vast spectrum of subjects and styles from domestic American preoccupations in *Company* to stylised Continental operetta in *A Little Night Music* and melodramatic light opera in *Sweeney Todd*, sometimes with more and sometimes with less success, sometimes producing the most dazzling pieces of light musical theatre, and sometimes leaning too far into the pretentiousness which afflicted many other young writers as the 1980s began and, in a spate of weary imitations and bizarre subjects, the hit shows became fewer and fewer.

The country and western show, *The Best Little Whorehouse in Texas*, the most substantial black musical to date, *Dreamgirls*, a stage version of the favourite film *42nd Street*, and a tiny burlesque of another type of movie, *Little Shop of Horrors*, were isolated successes as the newly renascent British musical rushed to fill the gap, becoming the rage of the Broadway stage, just as it had a century earlier.

The pendulum had swung again and, after many exciting years and talents, Broadway returned to finding its greatest shows abroad, just as Britain had turned for sustenance to Broadway after each of the two world wars. It is a pendulum that will keep on swinging. The productive centre comes and goes among areas where the strongest talents and personalities happen to be, where the economic climate is the most favourable, where the public is most enthusiastic, but, wherever it shifts, there will always be room for revivals of the greatest examples of the half a century and more of theatrical creation which, no matter what anyone says, is always going to be called 'the Broadway musical'.

ROBIN HOOD

a comic opera in three acts by Harry B Smith. Music by Reginald de Koven. Produced at Chicago 9 June 1890 and at the Boston Music Hall 22 September 1890 with Henry Clay Barnabee (Sheriff), Edwin Hoff (Robin), Marie Stone (Marian), Peter Lang (Guy) and Jessie Bartlett Davis (Alan). Produced at the Standard Theatre, New York, 28 September 1891 with Barnabee, Tom Karl, Caroline Hamilton, Lang and Miss Davies. Played frequently in New York by the Boston Ideal Company thereafter, including at the Garden Theatre 1893, at the Broadway Theatre 10 January 1895, 10 February 1896 with Alice Nielsen as Annabel, at Wallack's Theatre 4 April 1898, at the Knickerbocker Theatre 1900, and at the Academy of Music 8 September 1902. Produced at the New Amsterdam Theatre 6 May 1912 with a cast including Carl Gantvoort, Sidney Bracy, Anne Swinburne, Pauline Hall and George B Frothingham; at Jolson's Theatre 18 November 1929 with William Danforth, Roy Cropper and Olga Steck; at Erlanger's Theatre 27 January 1932 with Danforth, Howard Marsh, Charlotte Lansing, John Cherry and Eleanor La Mance; and at the Adelphi Theatre 7 November 1944 with George Lipton, Robert Field and Barbara Scully.

Produced at the Prince of Wales Theatre, London, 5 February 1891 as *Maid Marian* with Harry Monkhouse, C Hayden Coffin, Marion Manola, John Le Hay and Violet Cameron.

CHARACTERS

Robert, *Earl of Huntingdon, afterwards* Robin Hood
Sir Tristram Testy, *Sheriff of Nottingham*
Little John
Friar Tuck
Allan-a-Dale
Will Scarlet
Guy of Gisborne
Marian, *daughter of Lord Fitzwalter, afterwards called Maid Marian*
Dame Durden, *keeper of an inn on the border of Sherwood Forest*
Annabel, *her daughter*
Mark o' the Mill, *a villager*, etc.

ACT 1

At Nottingham Fair, the townsfolk are making May-Day merry ("Tis the Morning of the Fair') in song and Morris Dance. Friar Tuck, a portly member of a philanthropic outlaw band which inhabits nearby Sherwood forest, is auctioning off to the poor people of the parish the proceeds of his companions' latest robberies (Auctioneer's Song), whilst pretty Annabel, daughter of the gruesome Dame Durden, takes time off from joining in a 'Milkmaids' Chorus' to steal a kiss or two from another of the outlaw band, the minstrel Allan-a-Dale.

Dame Durden is a widow in all but proof, for her husband went off to the Crusades a dozen years previously and has never returned. Each year she

521

has spent him a homespun suit and a letter, but this year she received no reply so, if the parcel were not lost on the way, he must surely be dead in the wastes of the heathen land.

Part of the entertainment at the fair is an archery contest and all the best bowmen of the region are to take part ('Come the Bowmen in Lincoln Green'/Madrigal: 'All Is Fair in Love and War') including young Robert of Huntingdon, twenty-one years of age that very day and thus due to inherit his father's title and fortune from the hands of its guardian, the Sheriff of Nottingham.

He is, unbeknown to him, also due to inherit a bride for the King has decreed that the Lady Marian Fitzwalter shall wed the new Earl of Hunting-don and a page has been sent to the Sheriff, who is also guardian of Lady Marian's fortune, to tell him the news. Lady Marian, being of a decisive disposition, has decided that she does not wish to be wed sight unseen and she has, therefore, donned a page's clothing and come to Nottingham her-self, carrying the all-important letter ('I Come as a Cavalier').

She meets Robert at the fair and informs him of the King's command but she is not able to keep up her imposture for long and Robert and she are soon joining happily in duet at the thought of their imminent marriage ('Though It Was Within This Hour We Met'). They are, however, counting without the machinating Sheriff of Nottingham ('I Am the Sheriff of Not-tingham') who has altogether more personal plans afoot. He means to marry Marian off to his minion, Sir Guy of Gisborne, whom he intends to declare as the legitimate heir to the earldom of Huntingdon.

Sir Guy is perfectly delighted at the thought of being a peer and wedding a beautiful court lady and is quite willing to give up all claims to the money that goes with both the position and the bride, money which the Sheriff has every intention of keeping for himself. Guy is only worried that he may lack the technique to win Lady Marian's heart, so the Sheriff offers him a lesson in instant wooing, practised on a passing milkmaid who just happens to be Marian doing a spot of eavesdropping in disguise ('When a Peer Makes Love to a Damsel Fair').

Robert wins the archery contest and returns to general acclaim to come before the Sheriff of Nottingham and demand the handing over of his titles of nobility and his fortune (Finale). The Sheriff refuses and produces his faked documents showing that Guy is the legal heir to Huntingdon. At this evil news, Marian quickly hides the King's decree ordering that she should marry the heir of Huntingdon and Robert, taking leave of his beloved, sets out for Sherwood Forest to join the band of outlaws.

ACT 2

At Dame Durden's inn on the fringe of the forest, the outlaws are taking their ease ('Oh, Cheerily Soundeth the Huntsmans Horn') as Will Scarlet entertains them with the song of 'The Tailor and the Crow'. Robert, now known as Robin Hood, has become the leader of the jolly band and they have gone from success to success, but he cannot be wholly happy for he is without love. He has heard that Marian is to be wed to Guy of Gisborne and believes that she has forsaken their love. To forget his faithless lady, he flirts with the saucy Annabel and, to the fury of Allan, promises to sing a serenade under her window that night. Little John counsels him to drown his *chagrin d'amour* in 'Brown October Ale'.

The depredations of Robin Hood have caused great annoyance to the Sheriff and he has spent much time and trouble trying to track down the mysterious outlaw chief. Finally, the Sheriff who prides himself on the efficacy of his 'eagle eye', disguises himself as a tinker and, in the company of the quaking Guy, comes to Dame Durden's inn to try to unearth Robin Hood personally (Tinker's Song). The outlaws soon penetrate his disguise and, leading him on, get him thoroughly drunk (Pastoral Glee; 'O, See the Lambkins Play') before vanishing, leaving the sodden Sheriff to pay the bill.

The reward for his failed impersonation is harder than a mere hangover for, when Dame Durden comes to collect her reckoning, she recognises the suit which he is wearing. It is the homespun she made for her husband. Here, at last, is her man returned from the wars. Unrecongisable he may be after so many years away, but he is surely her husband. The Sheriff cannot admit to having slyly purchased the garment from one of Friar Tuck's auctions, for he would then be liable to be arrested by himself as a receiver of stolen goods, and he has to submit to being led tipsily away by the delighted Dame.

Lady Marian, in spite of what Robin has heard, has remained faithful to her love and now, at last, disguised in a suit of Lincoln green, she has escaped from Nottingham and is heading towards Sherwood to join the outlaw band (Forest Song: 'Neath the Greenwood Tree'). The first person she meets on arriving at the inn is Annabel and she is taken back to hear that Robin has been making advances to the girl and proposes to serenade her that night. She decides to take Annabel's place at the casement window to catch her recalcitrant lover at his flirtation.

Alas, the harm has already been done. Allan-a-Dale, driven to excesses by what he sees as Robin's attempts to steal his Annabel, informs on his leader. The Sheriff now knows that Robin Hood and Robert of Huntingdon are the same man, and he sets in motion a plan to trap him as he comes to deliver his serenade. So, as Robin carols out his song to the disguised Marian ('A Troubadour Sang to His Love'), the Sheriff, Guy and two strong men creep upon them, led by Allan. In the darkness, Allan cannot know that Marian has revealed her identity and that the misunderstanding with Robin has been cleared up. He only hears her promise to wed Robin and, wild with jealousy, he points out his captain to the Sheriff.

He is soon made aware of his mistake and, as Robin struggles in the arms of the Sheriff's men, Allan hurries to bring the outlaws to set him free. The Sheriff is taken prisoner instead and he will not try to win his escape by confessing that he is Dame Durden's long lost husband. Even death is preferable to that. He prefers to be branded a thief and be led to the village stocks (Finale). But Nottingham has the last laugh, for Guy has stirred himself at last and brought the town archers to he rescue of their Sheriff. As the act ends, Robin is dragged away to prison and Marian is condemned to wed the false Earl of Huntingdon.

ACT 3

In the courtyard of the Sheriff's castle in Nottingham, the execution of Robin Hood is being prepared. An armourer is fashioning chains to bind the captive (Armourer's Song') and, beneath his basso voice, we see that the armourer is none other than a disguised Will Scarlet. His chains will have a special weak link which will allow Robin to break his bonds at the given moment.

Friar Tuck and Little John have their own plan to rescue their captain. Dressed as monks, they will go to Robin's cell on the pretence of hearing his holy penitence and, while there, Tuck will exchange clothes with Robin, allowing him to escape under a monk's cowl. Allan-a-Dale, too, has come in monkish robes to bring comfort to his Annabel who has been carried off to the castle to be forcibly married to the Sheriff in a double ceremony with Guy and Marian (Song of the Bells: 'The Bells of Saint Swithins').

The Friar and Robin accomplish their swap and Robin comes forth free from his jail. His outlaws have captured the bishop who is heading for Nottingham to celebrate the weddings and Robin proposes to take his place. When the Sheriff orders his men to bring the outlaw out from his cell to witness Marian's wedding, he is furious to find him gone and determines to hurry on with the ceremonies before anything else can happen

After time out for a quintet ('When Life Seems Made of Pains and Pangs') and a Country Dance ('Happy Day! Happy Day!'), the girls are brought forth to be led to the altar (Finale). The doors of the church are thrown open and there stands Robin Hood, revealed in his Lincoln green with all his band at his back. The Sheriff is thrown into confusion and when, to boot, it turns out that King Richard has come back from the Crusade and granted a full pardon to Robert of Huntingdon for the exploits of 'Robin Hood', the wicked Sheriff has to avow himself beaten and allow a happy ending.

The original score of *Robin Hood* did not include Friar Tuck's Auctioneer's Song which, along with Marian's waltz song 'Heart, My Heart!' and the show's most important hit, 'O, Promise Me' (De Koven/Clement Scott) were added prior to the show's London opening. 'O, Promise Me' was sung in London in the third act by the baritone Hayden Coffin as Robin, but it was allocated to the contralto Jessie Bartlett Davies as Allan and repositioned in the second act in the Broadway production, Other songs subsequently added include the duet 'A Time Will Come' (Robin/Marion) and the solo 'A Maiden's Thought' (Annabel).

EL CAPITAN

a comic opera in three acts by Charles Klein. Lyrics by Thomas Frost. Music by John Philip Sousa. Produced at the Broadway Theatre, New York, 20 April 1896 with De Wolf Hopper (Medigua), Edna Wallace Hopper (Estrelda), Alice Hosmer (Marghanza), Bertha Waltzinger (Isabel), Edmund Stanley (Verrada) and Charles Klein (Pozzo). Played at the Broadway Theatre 22 February 1897 and at the Fifth Avenue Theatre 21 February 1898. Produced at the Goodspeed Opera House, Connecticut, 11 June 1973 with John Cullum, Bonnie Schon, Lynn Brinker, Nancy Seabold, David Chaney, Art Wallace and Bruce MacKay (Cazzaro).

Produced at the Lyric Theatre, London, 10 July 1899 with De Wolf Hopper, Jessie Mackaye, Miss Hosmer, Nella Berger, Harold Blake and Henry Norman (Cazzaro).

CHARACTERS

Don Errico Medigua, *the new Governor of Peru*
Princess Marghanza, *his wife*
Isabel, *his daughter*
Señor Amabile Pozzo, *his chamberlain*
Don Luiz Cazzaro, *the deposed governor*
Estrelda, *his daughter*
Scaramba, *an officer in Cazzaro's forces*
Count Hernando Verrada, *Isabel's lover*
Nevado, Montablo, *other officers*
General Herbana, *commander of the Spanish forces*
Soldiers, etc.

ACT 1

At the viceregal court of colonial Peru the expatriate Spaniards ('Nobles of Castilian Birth') manage to keep up an illusion of the home country which consoles the Viceroy's wife, Princess Marghanza, and her step-daughter Isabel for having been dragged half way across the world in pursuit of the Princess's ambitions for her husband ('Oh, Beautiful Land of Spain'). The Viceroy, Don Errico Medigua, is a mild mannered man who, ever since his arrival in Peru, has shut himself away in his private rooms and maintained a strict refusal to meet any of his new courtiers or subjects. All who wish to see him or speak to him are referred instead to his chamberlain, Pozzo, who, apart from immediate family, is the only person to be permitted into the viceregal presence.

When three roughly dressed and coarsely mannered soldiers come to the court demanding to speak face to face with the new ruler, they are haughtily rejected by the Princess. Scaramba, Nevado and Montablo are members of the army which has been raised by the deposed Viceroy, Cazzaro, against the man who has been sent to replace him. As Medigua has done little to endear himself to the locals since his arrival, that army is swelled by a large number of the indigenous population and, as the visitors are only too happy to relate, it is soon to be led by a magnificent leader, the Spanish bravo known as El

Capitan, who has crossed the Atlantic especially to lead the revolting troops against the King's representative.

Only when these unwelcome visitors have gone does Don Errico put in a nervous appearance ('Don Medigua, All For Thy Coming Wait') to discourse on the unsuitability of a man of his temperament for a ruling post ('If You Examine Human Kind'). If he lacks a natural belligerence, Don Errico makes up for it with intelligence and cunning. He is unknown in Peru. His face is not recognisable to his people, and for a reason. He had uncovered the plot of Cazzaro before he had even arrived in the new world. On the ship on the way across, one of his men was killed in a brawl and, in looking through his effects, Don Errico discovered that the dead man was a spy. He was none other than the redoubtable El Capitan who had been paid to come to Peru and take command of an army to help Cazzaro reconquer the viceregal throne.

Don Errico then set up an elaborate plot. Having sent an urgent message to Spain to request reinforcements for his garrison against the expected attack, he spread exaggerated tales of El Capitan's invincibility and doughty deeds amongst the populace. Although he is well and truly dead, El Capitan is still going to arrive in Peru in the person of the unknown Viceroy himself. Installed as the leader of an army which is rebelling against himself he can only win—if the rebels should be victorious he, as their leader, would benefit accordingly and, if they should lose, he would reveal himself as Don Errico Medigua and take his rightful place.

Cazzaro, who has become worried by the amazingly heroic tales of El Capitan, and fears that such a paragon of belligerence might threaten his own position, decides not to wait for his war leader to arrive and he invades the palace to challenge the new Viceroy with unconstitutional behaviour ('When We Hear the Call for Battle'). He finds no Don Medigua, but only his wife and anxious daughter ('O, Spare a Daughter's Aching Heart'), for the slippery Viceroy has vanished. As Cazzaro meditates his next move, the news comes that the great El Capitan has arrived ('Lo, the Awful Man Approaches').

Estrelda, Cazzaro's daughter, is thrilled by the appearance of the war leader ('You See in Me, My Friends') and the ambitious pretender realises that by the manipulation of his attractive daughter he can keep the great man under his control. Estrelda's effusive attentions and her father's willingness to hand her over in marriage to El Capitan prove no little embarrassment for the disguised Don Errico, particularly as they provoke a geyser of jealousy from the tough Scaramba ('Bah! Bah!') who has to be reassured that El Capitan has come to Peru to fight and not to woo.

ACT 2

The Viceroy's palace is quickly taken under the attack of the insurgent troops, and Pozzo, who is assumed to be Don Medigua, is imprisoned behind the lines of Cazzaro's army (Ditty of the Drill). El Capitan is fêted as a hero ('Behold El Capitan') by the soldiers and worshipped by the ladies and Cazzaro decides that under the circumstances Estrelda had better marry the war leader right away. Since this would involve a certain element of bigamy, Don Errico tries to persuade the eager maiden that on this occasion slavish obedience to a parent is not necessarily a good idea ('I've a Most Decided Notion'), but the maiden is only too keen to follow this particular instruction and it seems as if Don Errico's fate is to be either a live bigamist or dead and virtuous.

Whilst the captured courtiers bewail their fate, the happy preparations for the wedding continue (Double Chorus: 'Bowed With Tribulation') and the trapped Don Errico finds himself even more deeply in trouble when the prisoners who are brought in include his wife and daughter. The forthright Princess must be stopped from giving him and Pozzo away. Cramming a visor on to his head to cover his features, El Capitan faces the prisoners and sternly rejects Isabel's pleas ('O, Warrior Grim') to allow them to see her imprisoned father.

Cazzaro, however, reverses the decision and Pozzo is brought forth ('Don Medigua, Here's Your Wife') to be fussed over by the Princess and Isabel who have, by now, been primed by the disguised Viceroy. When the Princess hears that her husband is to be wedded to Estrelda she bursts out in fury ('He Cannot, Must Not, Shall Not, Dare Not Wed You') and it seems that she will spoil everything, but all is saved when Scaramba rushes on with a dispatch: the Spanish army has landed and is on its way to tackle the rebels. El Capitan announces that he will lead them all to death and glory, and calls them to follow him into battle.

ACT 3

Whilst Isabel and her lover, Verrada, indulge in a pretty duet ('Sweetheart, I'm Waiting'), El Capitan is out leading his men. He has not stopped leading them all day, round and round in circles till they are virtually exhausted. When they finally stop their forced march, he treats them all to a jolly bout of drinking. By the time he has finished with them they will be in no state to face the Spanish troops. Scaramba is the only one to query the great man's tactics ('When Some Serious Affliction') and El Capitan takes his revenge on the doubter by moving into amorous action with Estrelda and ridiculing the furious soldier with a comical ditty ('A Typical Tune of Zanzibar').

No sooner is the song ended than the news comes that the Spanish General has begun his attack. Don Errico tries to make a discreet disappearance but, before he can vanish, the victorious Spaniards rush on proclaiming Don Medigua as victor and Viceroy. Before the Viceroy can make himself known to them, Estrelda dramatically denounces him as the rebel El Capitan and, in spite of his protests that he is Don Errico Medigua, Viceroy of Peru, he is dragged away. When General Herbana marches on to greet the Viceroy ('Semper Fidelis'), he is presented instead to Pozzo, but the Princess soon sets identities to rights and all is returned to the status quo ('We Beg Your Kind Consideration') in time for the final curtain.

527

THE BELLE OF NEW YORK

a musical comedy in two acts by 'Hugh Morton' (Charles M S McLellan). Music by Gustave Kerker. Produced at the Casino Theatre, New York, 28 September 1897 with Dan Daly (Ichabod), Edna May (Violet) and Harry Davenport (Harry). Produced in a revised version by Edgar Smith, Al Goodman and Lew Pollock as *The Whirl of New York* at the Winter Garden Theatre 13 June 1921 with John T Murray, Nancy Gibbs, J Harold Murray and Dorothy Ward (Cora).

Produced at the Shaftesbury Theatre, London, 12 April 1898 with Daly, Miss May and Davenport. Produced at the New Century Theatre 27 November 1901 with Madge Lessing. Produced at the Lyceum Theatre 24 June 1914 with M R Morand, Dorothea Clarke and Johnny Schofield jr. Played at the Strand Theatre 20 December 1916 with Paddy Dupres, Iris Hoey and Kenneth Kent; at the Lyceum 17 May 1919 in a revised version with additional songs by Herman Darewski, with Harry A Meymott, Edith Drayson and Alec Fraser; at Daly's Theatre 2 April 1931 with Bert Byrne, Kathleen Burgis and Patrick Waddington; at the Garrick Theatre 5 August 1933 with George Morgan, Miss Burgis and Gerald Seymour and 24 December 1934 with Morgan, Miss Burgis and Bruce Seton. Produced at the London Coliseum 16 September 1942 with Billy Danvers, Evelyn Laye and Billy Tasker.

Produced at the Théâtre du Moulin-Rouge, Paris, 29 May 1903. Produced at the Théâtre des Variétés 28 April 1916 with Jane Marnac and at the Théâtre Mogador 28 February 1953 in a revised version under the title *Belle de Mon Coeur* with Marina Hotine (Daisy) and François Martel (Harry).

CHARACTERS

Ichabod Bronson, *President of the Young Men's Rescue League and Anti-Cigarette Society of Cohoes*
Harry Bronson, *his son*
Karl von Pumpernick, *a polite lunatic*
Doc Snifkins
Cora Angélique, *the Queen of Comic Opera, his daughter*
Blinky Bill McGuire, *a mixed ale pugilist*
Mamie Clancy, *his girl*
Kenneth Mugg, *low comedian of the Cora Angélique Opera Company*
Counts Ratsi *and* Patsi Rattatoo, *the Portuguese twins*
Mr Twiddles, *Harry's private secretary*
Violet Gray, *a Salvation Army lassie*
Fifi Fricot, *a little Parisienne*
Kissy Fitzgarter, *a music-hall dancer*
Pansy Pinns, *a soubrette*
Billy Breeze, Mr Snooper, Mr Peeper, William, Fricot, etc.

ACT 1

At Harry Bronson's house in Riverside Drive, New York, that rich young gentleman is celebrating both his twenty-first birthday ('When a Man Is Twenty-One') and his imminent marriage, and celebrating them in a very alcoholic style. He and his chums have, in fact, celebrated all night and are lurching about pretty much the worse for wear when the housemaids arrive to start the daily dusting. Harry is so well-worn that he needs some encouragement to remember his midday wedding and even the name of his bride: Miss Cora Angélique, baptised by her admirers as the Queen of Comic Opera. Soon, the day which has started so merrily for Harry Bronson threatens to turn into a veritable almanack of awkward events.

His father is marching from Cohoes to New York at the head of the Young Men's Rescue League and Anti-Cigarette Society, and it seems that puritanical papa will turn up just in time to find his son's house full of actresses and him wedding the most actress-y of all of them. And here she comes ('When I Was Born, the Stars Stood Still'), escorted by her spivvy father and a pair of Portuguese noblemen who are sighing in unison for her hand. This will be Cora's tenth marriage. Under her father's financial guidance she has wed and rid herself of nine rich men and Harry is clearly to be the next in line.

But other people have other ideas on this subject, and not just the foolish Portuguese twins. Kenneth Mugg, the comedian of Cora's company, is desperately in love with his star and he will do anything to prevent her marrying, yet again, out of his reach. He arrives at Harry's house with what he thinks will be a sufficient deterrent. She is Miss Kissy Fitzgarter, a music-hall performer, to whom, in one of his recent pie-eyed evenings, Harry had made extensive propositions, and along with Kissy comes her bruiser of a brother, Blinky Bill, who has no intention of letting anyone wrong his 'Little Sister Kissy'.

What with Kissy and Bill and their claims, Cora getting hot under the girdle at the delay, and father Ichabod Bronson marching up Riverside Drive at the head of the massed forces of righteousness to, doubtless, disinherit his wayward son, Harry stares ruin and marriage simultaneously in the face. He decides to cut at least one of his losses: he won't get married after all. This causes great distress to his chef, Fricot, who has fashioned a marvellous cake with a life-sized girl on top for the occasion. When Harry sees the cake, his old spirit returns and he takes a lively fancy to the sugar-marzipan girl. Except she isn't marzipan at all: Fricot has cut corners and iced his daughter, Fifi. When Harry tries to nibble her, he finds out the truth and, putting aside all his cares about his father, big Bill and the Queen of Comic Opera, Harry determines to set out for a little drive with Fifi ('Teach Me How to Kiss').

As Cora attempts to put pressure on Harry to go through with the scheduled marriage, the massed cymbals and drums of 'The Anti-Cigarette Society' are heard at the gates, and Harry's parent appears. Cora and Kissy both try to get their stories in, Blinky Bill threatens, and Ichabod politely informs his son that he is disinherited. Only Fifi remains true in this disastrous circumstance and Harry gaily determines to have one last night of 'Wine, Women and Song' with her before being obliged to quit his mansion and take up work for the first time in his life.

For all that he might wish it, the ill effects of Mlle Cora Angélique are not yet out of Harry's life. A strange gentleman called Karl Pumpernickel turns up looking for Mr Bronson. He has, he explains courteously, come to kill him for having blighted his life by marrying Cora, in the same way as he killed Cora's previous husband. Harry briskly denies being a Bronson, and Karl continues his search, anxious to accomplish his mission before being recaptured and returned to the lunatic asylum which is his home.

Not one whit disconcerted, Harry continues to plan his evening on the town with Fifi ('La Belle Parisienne') while Cora, renouncing the son for what seems to be a more lucrative target in the father, turns her attentions to Ichabod. The gentleman from Cohoes has no objections, for he is a phoney reformer. His principal reason for founding his clean-living Society was to reduce competition where the ladies are concerned, and Ichabod is quite happy to indulge in a spot of nestling with 'My Little Baby'. Unfortunately for him he is spotted by Karl and, when he admits to the name of Bronson, he finds that he has become the target of the madman's murderous intent.

Down in Chinatown, the indigenous population are singing and dancing in chorus ('Pretty Little China Girl') when Harry appears escorting Fifi out to dine. However, the younger Bronson's fickle heart is quick to turn again when a Salvation Army group comes on the scene, headed by the lovely Violet Gray ('They All Follow Me'). Violet has a problem in that she doesn't seem to be able to convert men to anything but running after her, and Harry is no exception. Blinky Bill may be true to his own Mamie Clancy but even he can still sing in praise of Violet as 'The Belle of New York'.

Chinatown is a popular place for courting couples, for now Ichabod turns up squiring Cora, and fast behind them comes the avenging Karl. Ichabod announces that, in view of his son's gallivanting behaviour, he has decided to make his heir the first worthy person he sees. Harry suggests that he choose Violet and, when it turns out that Violet is the daughter of Ichabod's old partner, the thing is, much to Cora's distress, made a *fait accompli* ('Your Life, My Little Girl'). Violet is distressed at the thought of alienating Harry's patrimony but, with his encouragement, 'The Belle of New York' finally acquiesces.

ACT 2
Harry has taken a job as a counterhand in Smyler's Candy Store on Broadway, and business is brisk ('Oh, Sonny'). In spite of his fall from the upper echelons of society, little Fifi remains true and she likes to think what life will be like 'When We Are Married'. Harry's mind, however, is still on Violet.

The candy store soon becomes a hive of activity. First Ichabod turns up, with a chorus girl on his arm, and, amazed to find his fallen son at work, soft-heartedly slips him $100; then Cora puts in an appearance still pursued by the Portuguese twins ('Oh! Come With Us to Portugal'), with a gutter-pressman and photographer in tow to have herself reported and snapped being dramatic in front of the man who deserted her. Mugg also turns up to cash in on the publicity. Then it is Violet's turn. Since her elevation to the position of heiress, Violet has set up a beautifully uniformed association of young ladies called 'The Purity Brigade' to give guidance to lost souls and she has come to seek out Harry who is evidently in need of considerable help.

Amongst the guidance she is anxious to give is some on how Harry might and must regain his birthright. She has a plan. The next night at the Narragansett Pier there is to be a lawn party in honour of Cora at which the famous Mlle Bonnebouche from the Tutti-Frutti Music Hall is to entertain. Violet is going to take her place and disgust Ichabod so deeply with her conduct that he will reverse his order and restore Harry to his position as legal heir.

In the middle of their conversation Karl turns up and takes a violent fancy to Violet. When he hears that Harry's name is Bronson, his hand goes once more for his knife, but he is confused when Ichabod admits to the same name and he ends up chasing the elder Bronson all round the stage. Then Violet decides to go into her act early and puts on as vulgar a display as she can ('I Do, So There'), a jolly routine in which Ichabod joins.

One by one, the company parade across the stage heading for the train to Narragansett, among them Bill and Mamie who indulge in a number about the pleasures of 'Coney Island', and Ichabod who is looking forward to the fun 'On the Beach at Narragansett'. The evening's entertainment includes a fancy ball ('Googan's Fancy Ball') where the participants are engaged in tunefully lubricating their larynxes ('For the Twentieth Time We'll Drink'). Violet fulfils her threat and performs 'At Ze Naughty Folies Bergère', Karl gets involved with a cask of gunpowder and succeeds in blowing himself up, and Ichabod, faced with Harry and Violet both determined to do without his money and make do, instead, with just each other, happily admits that this was precisely the happy ending he had been angling for all along and blesses them with a quick wedding before he goes back to whence he came to carry on his truly blameless life ('For in the Field').

The original New York libretto of *The Belle of New York* underwent considerable changes during its Broadway run and others prior to its London opening, and alterations and interpolations were made freely into the score. 'Good Old Glory', 'We'll Dance in the Moonlight', 'A Simple Little Girl', 'A Nice Young Man', 'Conundrums', 'You and I' and 'From Far Cohoes' did not reach Britain, and an equivalent number of replacement songs were included. During its long British life many further variations occurred. Scenes were swapped about at will, roles expanded and/or deleted (the Portuguese twins were, at one time, totally cut out) and songs, notably 'Lucky Jim' and 'I Want To Go To Morrow' were inserted.

THE PRINCE OF PILSEN

a musical comedy in two acts by Frank Pixley. Music by Gustave Luders. Produced at the Tremont Theatre, Boston, May 1902 with Arthur Donaldson (Prince), John W Ransome (Hans), Dorothy Morton (Mrs Crocker), Mabel Pierson (Edith) Ivey Anderson (Tom) and Ruth Peebles (Nellie). Produced at the Broadway Theatre,

531

New York, 17 March 1903 with Donaldson, Ransome, Helen Bertram, Anna Lichter, Albert Parr and Lillian Coleman. Played at Daly's Theatre 4 April 1904, at the New York Theatre 3 April 1905 and 2 April 1906 and at the Academy of Music 6 May 1907. Produced at the Jolson Theatre 13 January 1929 with Roy Cropper, Al Shean, India Cox, Alice Wellman, Joseph Toner and Vivian Hart.

Produced at the Shaftesbury Theatre, London, 14 May 1904 with Donaldson, Ransome, Trixie Friganza, Isabel Hall, Harry Fairleigh and Miss Peebles.

CHARACTERS

Hans Wagner, *a Cincinnati brewer, travelling abroad*
Nellie, *his daughter*
Lieutenant Tom Wagner, *of the US cruiser Annapolis, his son*
Mrs Madison Crocker, *a widow from New York*
Edith Adams, *a Vassar student, travelling abroad,*
Arthur St John Wilberforce, Earl of Somerset, *a tourist*
Carl Otto, the Prince of Pilsen, *a student at Heidelberg*
François, *concierge of the International Hotel, Nice*
Sidonie, *Mrs Crocker's French maid*
Jimmy, *a bell boy*

ACT 1

On the waterfront at Nice stands the splendid International Hotel set amongst charming gardens in the classical vein and looking out over the canvas-blue waters of the Mediterranean sea. But the hotel is not the only thing in the grounds which is looking out, for the International's staff are rubbing their hands in greedy anticipation at the thought of the coming season's flock of wealthy foreigners (Opening Chorus: 'The Modern Pirate').

The first guests to arrive are a party of Cook's tourists, a group of girls from Vassar, come to explore the delights of the Riviera ('We've Had a Stormy Trip') and amongst them is the pretty Edith Adams ('We Know It's Wrong for Girls to Flirt') who is dying to meet up with a handsome sailor she got to know the previous summer at Newport. Tom Wagner is serving aboard the good ship *Annapolis*, berthed at this very minute at Nice, which means Edith can look forward to a delicious reunion as well as providing brass buttons for all her friends.

The girls' attention is soon diverted from the navy when the bell-boy rushes in with even more exciting news. A real, live Prince is coming to stay at the hotel. The Prince of Pilsen is coming in disguise and he has chosen the International Hotel as his base in Nice. François, the concierge, is delighted at his luck but not at all happy about the incognito part of the plan. If the International has a prince as a guest, he is determined that the whole town shall know it. It is time to roll out the red carpet and fill the foyer with flowers.

While the preparations are going on, the hotel continues to fill up. The

English Earl of Somerset, more familiarly known (particularly to the fair sex) as 'Artie', enjoys a marching song and routine with the girls but his heart is set on impressing the pretty widow, Mrs Madison Crocker, who has come to spend 'A Season at the Shore'. Mrs Crocker is in the market for a man, but Artie does not fit her requirements: he is a poodle and she is after great dane. Or, rather, a great German. It appears that, during a recent stay in Heidelberg, she was thrown from her horse and carried, unconscious, to her hotel in the strong arms of a royal rescuer. The next morning she received a single rose, from the Prince of Pilsen, and she has sighed romantically after her saviour ever since.

Soon the big moment arrives and, to the accompaniment of a triumphal chorus ('We'll Have a Gala Day'), a snowstorm of flower-petals, and much bowing and bobbing, the Prince of Pilsen makes his entrance into the lobby of the International. Mrs Crocker would be a little disappointed if she hadn't just left the scene, for the Prince is not quite what romantic, middle-European princes are supposed to be. He is shortish, stoutish and not very young, and his German accent sounds more like that of a Cincinnati-German brewer than a Black Forest Prince.

There is a very good reason for this. Hans Wagner *is* a Cincinnati brewer and the chorus have chosen to spend their greeting on the wrong man. But Hans is an alderman back home, and his business is deeply involved with Pilsener beer, so he simply takes the greeting 'Prince of Pilsen' as pardonable Continental enthusiasm and bad pronunciation and, being a fellow of a nice disposition, he nods and smiles and accepts graciously all the homage paid to himself and his pretty daughter, Nellie. His new identity is confirmed when Artie, eager to appear on good terms with royalty, approaches him effusively as an old acquaintance, and Hans finds himself allotted a ten-room suite with harbour view at no charge. These foreigners are remarkably hospitable.

The Wagners have actually come to Nice for a surprise visit to brother Tom, but Tom is busy in another quarter. He has met up with his pretty Edith and is exchanging a bunch of La Turbie violets for a song ('When You Are Mine').

Mrs Crocker soon finds her way to her Prince and, if she is disappointed, she certainly doesn't show it. To the chagrin of Artie, she positively throws herself at the wretched 'royal', cutting Artie out quite awfully. Hans is a mite bewildered at this pretty woman who seems intent on showing him all sorts of gratitude for saving her life but, by now, he has got used to going along with things in this strange part of the world so he is quite happy to take her arm for a turn in the garden, leaving the fuming Artie plotting revenge. He will get this fellow drunk and make him make an ass of himself in front of the lady, by jove, he will.

The hotel's next guests arrive with much less fanfare, for they arrive on bicycles. They are a party of German students ('To Fun and Folly') and one of them is the real Prince Carl Otto of Pilsen (Stein Song: 'Heidelberg') who is, quite naturally, surprised to hear that he can only have rooms on the top floor because the best suites are taken by the Prince of Pilsen, Carl Otto finds that his suits his plans admirably. While the impostor continues to be him, he will carry on happily incognito as Herr Niemann. Still, he cannot resist giving his double the once over.

He is taken aback when he finds out that not only is there a Prince but also a little Princess of Pilsen in the person of the lovely Nellie who, without knowing who Herr Niemann is, is more than happy to explain openly about Cincinnati and the Brewery. Carl Otto happily realises that he is not the victim of an impersonation but solely of a mistake, and he assures Nellie that she and her father should accept all the hospitality and honour offered to them.

Artie is the only one who isn't happy and he is determined to dispose of Hans as his rival for the love of Mrs Crocker but, when he actualy succeeds in talking Hans into fighting a duel with himself, and the brewer is only saved from a messy suicide by his appalling aim, he finds that he has to make peace with 'The Widow' and with Hans at the risk of bing ostracised. Artie is forced into more devious plotting and decides that one thing a German will never be able to do is ride to hounds. Somewhere in the South of France he will find a foxhunt and make the chap look an ass on horseback.

There are love affairs downstairs as well as upstairs at the International Hotel for François is the prey of a passion for the piquant Sidonie, Mrs Crocker's spiky maid. Sidonie is ambitious and wants nothing of the concierge until he reveals that he is on the brink of wealth. He has stolen the plans of the French border forts and his is going to sell them to the Germans and earn enough money to keep her in diamonds and furs for the rest of her life. He doesn't have to warn her to 'Keep it Dark' for every lady's maid knows about keeping secrets.

When Carl Otto attempts to tell Hans the truth about his identity, he finds that the American is not ready to give up his misconception and his free suite, so he lets it be and settles down for a cigarette ('Smoke Pictures') until he spies Nellie coming by. But he speaks too suddenly and startles her into a scream and, before he knows where he is, brother Tom has descended on him with drawn sword and sparks are flying from their blades (Finale: 'What Means this Loud Alarm'). There is not time for explanation when the grandarmes turn up and the two men are hurried off to jail.

ACT 2

Artie gets his foxhunt set up ('Tally-Ho! The Horn of the Master Is Calling'), but Hans doesn't take part, for Artie's first plan has already taken its toll and the brewer has over-indulged in champagne and spent the night on the table in the billiard room. His memory of events is a bit hazy but apparently he spent the whole evening charging things up to the account of the Prince of Pilsen with great élan ('He Didn't Know Exactly What to Do') and now that élan has run out.

In his befuddled state, he accidentally gives François the German code-word, and finds the concierge pushing the secret plans into his possession, to the accompaniment of much cloak-and-dagger business. He assumes they are plans for a brewery and, when he shows them to the bell-boy, the lad takes the first opportunity to head for the gendarmes.

Mrs Crocker, far from being disgusted, is delighted to see that royalty is human. She fusses round the limp Hans and offers to partner him to the day's *bataille des fleurs*, hurrying him off for a quck dip in the cold sea before launching into a paean in praise of 'The American Girl'. Edith gets back from the hunt in time to meet Tom and Carl Otto who have managed to get released from jail and become fast friends in the process. She didn't enjoy herself at all, galloping over the *arrière pays Niçoise* after the fox, for she was thinking of Tom in his prison cell and had only his little bunch of violets as a consolation ('The Message of the Violet').

Now we suddenly discover that Artie isn't such a nice fellow after all. An earl he may be, but he's a penniless earl, and the main attraction about Mrs Crocker is not so much her sweet self as her bank account. Realising that there is likely to be considerably more cash in the vaults of Pilsen, he switches his attentions to the Princess of Pilsen—otherwise Nellie. When he discovers from the straightforward girl that she isn't a Princess at all and that her father isn't a Prince, he hurriedly withdraws his offer of marriage and determines to expose Hans as a fraud in front of everyone. That way he will surely win the widow.

While François and Sidonie look forward to a rich life in Paris on their ill-soon-to-be-gotten gains from spying ('Back to the Boulevards'), Hans takes a restorative dip in the sea ('How One Ought to Go'), only to find himself arrested. The bell-boy has shopped him as a spy. While Hans is being dragged away, Nellie's gaze is elsewhere, for Carl Otto is making love to her over a pretty sea shell ('The Tale of a Sea Shell'). When he gets too passionate, she hurries away and so Carl Otto alone hears the bell-boy's triumphant tale of how he caught the spy.

The Prince hurries off to the rescue as the 'Flower Fête' pours on to the stage. Tom and his naval colleagues march in to add the colour of their uniforms to the picture ('Fall In') and only when all the picturesque gaiety of the carnival is over does Hans put in an appearance, chasing after the poor bell-boy with revenge in his heart.

Artie steps forward for his big moment and declares his rival an impostor. He is not the Prince of Pilsen. But, before he can go any further, Carl Otto takes control. Hans never claimed to be the Prince, just as Nellie never claimed to be a Princess but, now, if she will have him, that is what he—the real Prince of Pilsen—would have her become. Hans takes the moment to ask Mrs Crocker to come back to Cincinnati with him and, as the foolish Artie grovels for all-round forgiveness, everything ends happily.

The original score also included 'White Lies' (Mrs Crocker) and 'Something Should Be Done' (Artie) which, along with 'When You Are Mine' and 'How Far One Ought to Go' subsequently disappeared from the score.

LITTLE JOHNNY JONES

a musical comedy in three acts by George M Cohan. Produced at the Liberty Theatre, New York, 7 November 1904 with George M Cohan (Johnny Jones), Jerry J Cohan (Anstey), Helen Cohan (Mrs Kenworth), Ethel Levey (Goldie), Donald Brian (Henry), Tom Lewis (Wilson), Truly Shattuck (Florabelle) and Sam J Ryan (McGee). Played at the New York Theatre 8 May 1905 and 13 November 1905. Produced at the Goodspeed Opera House in a revised version by Alfred Uhry 25 June 1980 with Thomas Hulce, Peter van Norden, Anna McNeely, Maureen Brennan, Ernie Sabella, Jane Galloway and Lenny Wolpe, and at the Alvin Theatre 21 March 1982 with Donny Osmond replacing Hulce and Tom Rolfing succeeding Wolpe.

CHARACTERS

Anthony Anstey, *an American gambler*
Sing Song, *editor of the Pekin Gazette*
Timothy D McGee, *an American politician and horse owner*
Henry Hapgood
Johnny Jones, *the American jockey*
Whitney Wilson
Goldie Gates, *an heiress*
Florabelle Fly, *of the San Francisco Searcher*
Mrs Kenworth, *Goldie's aunt*
Starter at the Hotel Cecil
Inspector of Police
Captain Squirvy *of the St Hurrah*
Bessie Ah Mila, Ah Moy, Ah Goy, Ah Fung, *the Emperor's nieces*

ACT 1

At 'The Cecil in London Town' a merry throng of the hotel's guests are getting ready to head for Epsom Downs racecourse where the Derby of 1904 is to be run. There is Sing Song, the editor of the *Pekin Gazette* preparing to describe the big day of British racing for his readers in China, with his four little Chinese wards, the nieces of the Emperor, who have come along to improve their English; there is foppish and foolish Whitney Wilson bumbling his way through the hotel spreading idiocies like manure; there is the popular politician and racing man Timothy D McGee from San Francisco ('They're All My Friends') and his compatriot Anthony Anstey, a colourful gambling man, and, right behind this bundle of lively characters, ever on the look-out for a story, is the lovely Florabelle Fly of the *San Francisco Searcher*.

Florabelle is already on to something, for the Hotel Cecil also houses one person who is not intending to witness the Derby, the redoubtable and crusading Mrs Kenworth, scourge of the San Francisco underworld. Mrs Kenworth, having hamstrung the illegal Chinese lottery in her home town, has come to crusade in Britain, bringing with her a group of pretty young acolytes from her San Francisco Female Reformers group. She is also

536

preparing to fix a marriage with an impoverished English lord for her heiress daughter, Goldie Gates, but Florabelle knows that Goldie is not willing. She has fallen for the jockey, Johnny Jones, who once won a race at 50 to 1 for her just because she smiled at him.

Johnny Jones is a hot topic at the moment. He has been riding in all-conquering fashion all over Europe and now he is coming to Britain to ride the favourite, Yankee Doodle, in the Derby. After that he will return to America and many American owners are anxiously vying for his services. McGee is one, and Anstey another who has gone so far as to send Johnny a cheque for $10,000 to try to force acceptance of an offer he has made.

He has had no reply, but he has had considerable success on another front, for he has persuaded the wealthy Mrs Kenworth to accept him as a future husband. This is a fine revenge for him for, underneath his suave exterior, Anstey is a crook who, in league with the evil Sing Song, has been for years at the bottom of the 'Frisco China Lottery. Mrs Kenworth's exposé and destruction of the lottery lost him a fortune and he intends to replace it with hers.

Amongst all the people from across the herring pond who are openly in London, there is one who is there secretly and that is Goldie Gates. With her heart full of Johnny Jones, Goldie has come with her friend Henry Hapgood to sneak a peek at the earl whom her aunt is trying to foist upon her and to try to scupper the match. When she meets Anstey, Henry quickly passes her off as a little French lady ('Mademoiselle Fanchette') and, thus disguised, she learns that her earl, who was supposed to return to Britain that week, has been detained in Berlin. It is a brief respite but one which gives Goldie a little more time to pursue her plans of escape.

Mrs Kenworth sends her six little charges off in the care of six London cabmen which gives them a chance for a double sextette on *Florodora* lines ("Op in Me 'Ansom'), then Florabelle squeezes in an incidental song, 'Nesting in a New York Tree', as Anstey and Sing Song plot their next move in the elimination by marriage of Mrs Kenworth and the rebuilding of the lottery. Then Johnny Jones himself arrives, fresh from Paris and all ready to ride to victory on Yankee Doodle ('The Yankee Doodle Boy'). He will not commit himself on his plans thereafter, but McGee is amazed when he talks of marriage and giving up the racetrack. He is even more amazed when he hears that the object of Johnny's affections is Goldie Gates and he quickly puts the lad wise to Mrs Kenworth's plans concerning the Earl of Bloomsbury.

Little does he know that the Earl is also on his way to the Cecil, but not in person. Since the real Bloomsbury has been delayed, Goldie has decided that the best mileage lies in becoming the Earl herself and she turns up clad in the best of British with Henry, dripping with false whiskers, as her servant. As everyone prepares to go 'Off to the Derby', Anstey tackles Jones about his offer, but he meets with a sharp rebuff. Johnny knows that Anstey is not straight and he will have nothing to do with him. Anstey revengefully apprises Mrs Kenworth of Johnny's pretensions towards Goldie and the horrified aunt immediately forbids such a match. Johnny tears up Anstey's cheque and throws it in his face as the infuriated gambler threatens him with worse to come.

ACT 2

The steamship *St Hurrah* is preparing to sail for America ('Sailors of the *St Hurrah*') under the guidance of Captain Squirvy ('Captain of a Ten Day Boat') and among its passengers are all the principals from the first act. Johnny Jones is returning home under a cloud. Yankee Doodle was beaten in the Derby and, by some adept manipulation of the media and inspired rumour-mongering, Anstey has managed to have the lad disqualified as a jockey and made the butt of public despite as a cheat and a scoundrel. The stout-hearted McGee has stood by him in his troubles and is accompanying Johnny back to America while Sing Song has offered to join Mrs Kenworth in San Francisco, pretending that he wishes to protect her from the vengeance of the 'Frisco Chinese ('So Long, Sing Song'). As for the false Earl, he/she is travelling to meet his bride ('Goodbye Flo').

Before the ship sails, Anstey receives a letter from Berlin from the real Earl and Goldie's disguise is placed in peril. Fortunately she is able to reconvert to being Mademoiselle Fanchette before the police arrive but she has to pull out some fine acting talents when she comes face to face with her aunt. Since Anstey has already met her as Fanchette, he is able to back up this identity and Mrs Kenworth is amazed at the resemblance, but ultimately convinced.

Anstey would be more surprised if he realised that there was another disguise about. The foolish Wilson is not what he seems. He is a detective who has been on Sing Song and Anstey's trail for a long time and now, at last, he is able to get documentary evidence of their lottery activities by picking the gambler's pocket while he is distracted by all the other episodes which are going on, and by his latest plot—the kidnapping of Goldie Gates. A telegram to a faithful Chinese lieutenant in 'Frisco is crackling down the wires: Goldie is to be snatched from her San Francisco home and held for ransom to prevent Mrs Kenworth taking action against the rebuilt lottery.

The police give up their shipboard search for the missing Earl and Henry can safely appear once more, without whiskers, to sing in a relieved way of the prospect of returning to 'Good Old California', but Goldie still has one very important test to pass. When the phoney Fanchette comes up against Johnny Jones she has to pull herself together and listen to him sing fondly of 'A Girl I Know' while Florabelle and her every-ready note-pad gobble up the jockey's romance with a French girl for the joy of her readers.

Johnny's departure from Britain is not to be a peaceful one. Anstey has managed to arouse a mob to charge the ship, crying out against the cheating, thieving American jockey, but the now assertive Wilson steps to the boy's aid with a brace of pistols and the crowd is forced back. Wilson declares that Johnny's innocence will be proven before the ship docks in the United States and the jockey looks forward to his return home with all the more heart ('Give My Regards to Broadway').

ACT 3

In San Francisco's Chinatown (March of the 'Frisco Chinks) a new drama is stirring. Goldie Gates has been kidnapped. She is missing from her home and Wilson has discovered all about the deadly cable sent from the *St Hurrah*. He corners Anstey and demands to know what he has done with the girl, but the gambler denies any knowledge of a kidnap.

Johnny Jones, who was completely cleared of pulling Yankee Doodle during the sea crossing, has been searching San Francisco high and low trying to find his lost love, not realising that, in the person of Mademoiselle Fanchette, he had been alongside her all the way across the Atlantic ('Life's a Funny Proposition After All').

Finally Anstey is disgraced and sent fleeing from town by the angry Chinese of San Francisco, Goldie discards her disguise and falls into the arms of Little Johnny Jones, Mrs Kenworth finds happiness in the company of McGee, and Sing Song is taken back to China in handcuffs by the fulfilled Wilson, there to face the wrath of his Emperor. And Florabelle Fly wrote it all up in the *San Francisco Searcher*.

The 1980 revival interpolated several other Cohan songs taken from different shows: 'The Voice in my Heart' (*Little Nelly Kelly*), 'Blue Skies, Grey Skies' (*The Merry Malones*), 'Oh, You Wonderful Boy' (*The Little Millionaire*), 'American Ragtime' (*The American Idea*) and 'Let's You and I Just Say Goodbye' (*The Rise of Rosie O'Reilly*).

MLLE MODISTE

a comic opera in two acts by Henry Blossom. Music by Victor Herbert. Produced at the Knickerbocker Theatre, New York, 25 December 1905 with Fritzi Scheff (Fifi), Claude Gillingwater (Hiram), Walter Percival (Étienne) and William Pruette (Count). Played at the Knickerbocker Theatre 1 September 1906, at the Academy of Music 20 May 1907 with Miss Scheff, Gillingwater, Robert Michaelis and Pruette and at the Knickerbocker Theatre 9 September 1907. Produced at the Globe Theatre 26 May 1913 with Miss Scheff and Gillingwater. Produced at the Jolson Theatre 7 October 1929 with Miss Scheff, Richard Powell, Robert Rhodes and Detmar Poppen.

CHARACTERS

Henri de Bouvray, Count St Mar
Captain Étienne de Bouvray, *his nephew*
Marie-Louise, *Étienne's sister*
Madame Cécile, *proprietress of a Parisian hat-shop*
Gaston, *her son, an artist*
Fanchette, Nanette, *her daughters*
François, *porter at the hat-shop*

Fifi, *a vendeuse at the hat-shop*
Hiram Bent, *a Chicago millionaire*
Mrs Hiram Bent, *his wife*
Lieutenant René la Motte, *engaged to Marie-Louise*
General le Marquis de Villefranche
Bebe, *première danseuse at the Folies Bergère*

ACT 1

At Madame Cécile's hat shop in Paris's Rue de la Paix, the shop girls are trying to satisfy the demands of the noisy American, Mrs Hiram Bent, and the even noisier *danseuse*, Bebe, without very much success ('Furs and Feathers, Buckles and Bows'). Nothing will suit either the large American or the gaudy Parisienne in spite of all the girls can do, even when they are reduced to trying the most immovable hat in the shop, a concoction of straw and ribbons confected by Madame Cécile in a moment of aberration which has been waiting for a year to be sold.

When the two customers leave without buying anything, Madame Cécile is furious. The girls are no good at their jobs. Why, if only Fifi had been here she would have sold hats to them both without any trouble. Unfortunately Fifi isn't here. She hasn't yet returned from a morning errand, for today is Madame Cécile's market day and she wasn't expected back till much later ('When the Cat's Away'), but it is a fair bet that the little *vendeuse* will not be rebuked for her tardiness, for Fifi is indispensable. She is the oil on the wheels of Madame Cécile's business and her employer is very aware of the fact. She is so aware, and so scared least any rival should steal Fifi from her, that she has decided to make sure of the girl for good. Fifi shall marry Madame Cécile's son, Gaston.

Gaston is an artist, a good-looking but weak fellow who is forever on the scrounge for money from his hard-working mother to support his high life in society, where he insists he needs to be to win commissions. If marriage to Fifi will keep his mother's purse open, then Gaston will marry Fifi, but for the moment the plan is a big secret and even the clever little porter, François, cannot prise it from Madame Cécile's daughters ('I Should Think That You Could Guess').

One threat to Madame Cécile's plan is the dashing young Captain Étienne de Bouvray who turns up at the shop with roses for Fifi ('The Time, the Place and the Girl'). Étienne is in love with the little shop girl and, although it would mean the ruin of his social and financial expectations, he wants to marry her. When he confides his intentions to Madame Cécile he little knows that he is speaking to someone who will do everything she can to stop this from happening. Madame Cécile has *alliés de circonstance* in her determination to spoil the match, for Étienne's visits to the hat shop have been noticed by his sister and she and his uncle and guardian, the Comte de Bouvray, are scandalised at the thought that their kinsman should even contemplate such a disastrous alliance.

When Fifi returns to her place of work it is lunch time and the shop is empty, but it is not long before she has a customer. He is a middle-aged American gentleman and he has followed her along the street. Fifi is ready to give him short shrift but, when he expresses the intention of buying a hat, she is obliged to temper her pert replies and get to work. Hiram Bent is not, in spite of Fifi's suspicions, a Chicago wolf; he is a rather nice fellow with more money than he knows what to do with, a yen for a little company more pleasant than that supplied by his wife, and a passion for doing kindly things. Before long he and Fifi are chatting in quite a friendly fashion and she confides in him her longing to leave the hat shop and to go on the stage ('If I Were on the Stage'/'Kiss Me Again').

Hiram understands that Fifi will not accept money or gifts from him, but he longs to be of some assistance to her and so he pretends to be selecting hats for an unspecified lady and, when Fifi's back is turned, he slips an envelope containing a 'loan' of 5000 francs into the hat box and addresses the box to Fifi. His sleight of hand is complete when Madame Cécile enters the shop and immediately tries to sell him the famous unwanted hat, but even an American will not look at the wretched thing, and Hiram departs leaving instructions that the hats he has bought must be delivered by Fifi in person.

It is now the time for Madame Cécile to push forward Gaston to make his proposal to Fifi ('Love Me, Love My Dog'). Fifi quickly rejects him. She is interested only in the designs Gaston has promised to paint for her ('Hats Make the Woman') and not in his person. Gaston, who is in urgent need of funds from his mother, decides that this setback had better be kept a secret from Madame Cécile. The good lady is busy at her work for the moment, for Mrs Bent has returned and—wonder of wonders—she is offering to buy the famous unwanted hat. But Madame Cécile's garrulousness undoes her for, as she chatters on about Americans, she mentions the American gentleman who not long ago bought three hats from her, and Mrs Bent discovers that the culprit is her husband. She flies off to winkle out any indiscretion and Madame Cécile is lift with the rogue hat still on her hands.

Étienne returns to find Fifi and to beg her to marry him, but Fifi tells him that she will not allow him to give up all the privileges of his life for her sake. He must wait until she is no longer a shop girl. Alas, her prudence is of little avail, for their interview is broken in upon by the Count, raging against the minx who is attempting to entrap his nephew. Mamame Cécile joins in the scene: of course Fifi is not going to marry Étienne, she is going to marry Gaston.

But Fifi has no more intention of working to support Gaston than she has of letting Étienne work to support her. To Madame Cécile's horror, she declares that she will neither be wed nor remain at the shop. As Hiram advised, she is going to have a go, to shoot for the stars (Finale). She will finish her work with the one last delivery of the hats he bought. As she picks up the box, she notices the name and the envelope of money and, as she cries farewell to the Maison Cécile, she knows that fate is smiling on her.

ACT 2

A year has passed and no more has been heard of Fifi. At the home of the Comte de Bouvray and his nephew life goes on, but the Count has the gout and Étienne suffers from *mal du coeur*.

Today their home is to be the setting for a grand Charity Bazaar and the servants are getting everything ready (Servants' Chorus) under the brisk eye of François who has been transplanted from the Maison Cécile to the post of steward in the Château St Mar. His principal and most wearying task is to deal with the whims of the irritable bachelor Comte who is not at all used to taking orders from anyone, including a doctor, and who is determined to partake of his favourite burgundy in spite of the consequences ('I Want What I Want When I Want It').

One of the patrons of the Charity Bazaar is Hiram Bent and he has a piece of news which should bring a smile to the face of the grimacing Comte. Once upon a time, Hiram gave some financial help to a little girl who wanted to be a singer. Now that little girl has become hugely successful. She has paid him back all the money which he had meant her to keep and she has offered to come and sing at the Bazaar free of charge. Hiram's amiable tale does not have quite the effect intended for the Comte recognises the circumstances of the tale and realises that the little girl in question is none other than Fifi. She must not be allowed to come near his son.

The people involved in the entertainment are already being installed in rooms where they may dress but one little lady loses her way and breaks in on the Comte just as he is suffering a particularly nasty twinge of gout. She gently helps him over the worst of the pain and wins his feeling thanks, but then he recognises her. It is Fifi. He has nothing against her personally and he is very glad she has done so well for herself, but she must understand that under no circumstances can she, who was once a shop girl, wed his aristocratic nephew. In fact she must not even see the boy and he forbids her to sing at the Bazaar. In the face of such an insult Fifi cannot stay quiet and, as she leaves, she turns to the old man and swears to him that she will never wed his nephew until the day comes when, with his hat in his hand, the Comte de Bouvray shall beg her to do so, in person.

At 'The Charity Bazaar' the ladies of society run booths selling dolls or flowers and fortunes and Bebe entertains with a dance routine under the adoring eyes of the General who takes umbrage when he thinks that François is making a crack about 'the chorus and true love' when in fact he is being sympathetic about the course of true love ('I'm Always Misunderstood'). René and Marie-Louise have dressed Fifi up in a fancy costume and brought her along for, after all, the Comte insisted only that she should not sing. He did not forbid her to be present.

Étienne knows nothing of this and, when he comes along, Fifi changes places with the lady in the fortune telling booth and uses her disguise to find out whether his feelings for her are still as strong as ever. Finally, she trips over her own questions and Étienne, overjoyed to discover that the mysterious lady is his own beloved Fifi, joins the men of his brigade to joyfully welcome back the little lady who was and always will be 'The Mascot of the Troop'. Étienne is quite determined that this time Fifi shall not escape him; uncle or no uncle he will wed her.

As he makes his brave declaration, Fifi notices in her make-up mirror that the Comte has appeared behind them and, to Étienne's horror, she begins to discourse on the wisdom and kindliness of the old man, refusing to have anything to do with Étienne unless it is with the Comte's permission. The Comte's opinion of Fifi undergoes a rapid change: the little girl is marvellous, far too good for his cheeky, ungrateful nephew. He is almost tempted to marry her himself.

Now it is time to pay a little attention to the other members of the company. René sings the praises of 'The Dear little Girl Who Is Good' while Gaston discourses on the peculiarities of 'The English Language' and then, since the Comte has rescinded his interdiction on Fifi performing, she obliges the company with the tale of 'The Nightingale and the Star'. Madame Cécile, who has a hat stall at the bazaar, is amazed to see her former shop girl performing as a singing star, and Fifi decides to have a little bit of fun on behalf of her old *patronne*.

There on the stall is the dreadful unsellable hat—she will sell it. She snatches up the *chapeau* and offers it for auction. There are few bids until Fifi announces that with the hat goes a kiss from the auctioneer and suddenly the bids start to fly higher and higher. The winner pays 5000 francs ... and it is the old Comte. But Comte de Bouvray has not bought the kiss for himself. Holding the hat in his hand, he begs Fifi to wed his son and, since he has fulfilled the conditions she stipulated earlier in the day, she is not at all unhappy to accept.

THE RED MILL

a musical comedy in two acts by Henry Blossom. Music by Victor Herbert. Produced at the Knickerbocker Theatre, New York, 24 September 1906 with Dave Montgomery (Kid), Fred Stone (Con), Augusta Greenleaf (Gretchen), Edward Begley (Burgomaster), Allene Crater (Bertha), Joseph M Ratliff (Doris) and Ethel Johnson (Tina). Produced at the Ziegfeld Theatre 16 October 1945 in a revised version with additional lyrics by Forman Brown with Eddie Foy jr, Michael O'Shea, Ann André, Frank Jacquet, Lorna Byron, Robert Hughes and Dorothy Stone.

Produced at the Empire Theatre, London, 26 December 1919 with Little Tich, Ray Kay, Gladys Simmonds, Rube Welch, Amy Augarde, John Luxton and Ivy Tresmand. Produced at the Palace Theatre 1 May 1947 in a revised version by Harold Purcell with Jimmy Jewell, Ben Warriss, Daphne Peretz, Billy Danvers, Eric Palmer (Harry) and Doreen Duke.

543

CHARACTERS

Con Kidder ⎱ *two Americans 'doing' Europe*
Kid Conner ⎰
Burgomaster Jan van Borken *of Katwyk-ann-See*
Bertha, *his sister*
Gretchen, *his daughter*
Willem, *innkeeper at the 'Red Mill'*
Tina, *his daughter*
Captain Doris van Damm
Franz, *the sheriff of Katwyk-ann-See*
The Governor of Zeeland
Joshua Pennyfeather, *an English solicitor*
Countess de la Fère, *an automobilist*
Flora, Dora, Lena, Anna, Phyllis, Madge, etc.

ACT 1

Katwyk-ann-See, a picturesque village in the nethermost part of the Netherlands, is a popular place for tourists including a group of artists who drop by to paint the local lassies in their deliberately national costume and to provide the opening chorus to the show ('By the Side of the Mill'). The spot chosen for the painting is the centre of social life in Katwyk-ann-See, the hostelry of the Red Mill run by the comic-Dutch Willem and understaffed just by himself and his daughter, Tina, since a lull in the tourist trade forced him to watch his unpaid staff walk out.

Tina is not very happy working as a wayside wench, for she has dreams of being an actress ('Mignonette') and of making a marriage rather better than that proffered to her by the officious Franz, the town sheriff, but, for the meanwhile, she pours the drinks, tries to collect the unwilling cash, and ministers to the needs of the only two resident guests, a pair of American gentlemen who have been ordering up large and who have made several theatrical suggestions to the starry-eyed Tina. Willem is less keen on his expansive guests for they have made absolutely no effort, as yet, to pay for their bed and board and, spurred on by the suspicious Burgomaster, he is getting worried about their bill.

The Burgomaster of Katwyk-ann-See is about to help out with Willem's financial problems for he has arranged for his daughter, Gretchen, to wed the high-and-mighty Governor of Zeeland. They marriage is to take place the following day and it is to be celebrated at the Red Mill. Although the Burgomaster is set on this marriage, Gretchen is not. She is in love with the gallant Captain Doris van Damm who, at this unfortunate moment, is off sailing the high seas somewhere and she can think of nothing more horrid than being wedded to a gentleman, albeit a gentleman of some importance, whom she has never met.

Her aunt Bertha, the Burgomaster's widowed sister, is on her side ('A Widow Has Ways'), particularly as she knows that her well-off brother is actually providing a large dowry which is little more than a bribe to get himself allied to the most important man in the area.

Gretchen and Bertha are not resigned to the morrow's ceremony for they know that Captain Doris is, at this moment, luffing his way towards Katwyk-ann-See and may even dock this very day to carry his beloved away to safety, and Bertha suggests that Gretchen hide in the nearby mill, the famous mill from which the hotel took its name, to await the coming of her lover. Gretchen agrees nervously, for the mill is said to be haunted. Once upon a time the lovely Princess Wilhelmina was immured in the inn by her horrid suitor to await an unwanted wedding but, when he came to find her the next morning, she had vanished and ever since the mill has been haunted by a whitened spectre.

Now a comical scene begins. Two bags bump down from an upper story of the inn, followed by two fellows. It is the Americans, Con Kidder and Kid Conner, and exactly as the Burgomaster predicted they are trying to get away without paying their bill. They surprise Gretchen who tells them her story and enlists their help. It is all quite straightforward: the men will help Gretchen to avoid her marriage and, in return, they will be allowed to join the runaway lovers aboard Doris' ship which will carry them back to their homeland ('Go While the Goin' Is Good').

Tina is determined to come along on this voyage as well, as she is anxious to try out her dramatic talents on the welcoming stages of the United States of America ('Whistle It'). What the men don't know is that their escape has been overseen by the Burgomaster and he has sent Sheriff Franz off to fetch the gendarmes who arrive to take them in. The welshing pair are faced with either being imprisoned or working off their debt as waiter and translator in Willem's hotel, an option which they find considerably less unattractive.

When everyone is out of the way, Doris puts in an appearance to be united with his Gretchen ('The Isle of Our Dreams') and they arrange to meet up at six o'clock in the old mill to carry out their night-time elopement. If their romance is blossoming nicely, however, the ambitious Franz is getting little change out of Tina. When he is Burgomaster she will be sorry.

The love-affairs of Katwyk-ann-See have to take a back seat when an incident occurs on their roads ('An Accident!'). A vehicle driven by the English lawyer, Pennyfeather, touring through Holland with his four daughters, has come into a very unfortunate contact with the automobile driven by the extrovert and voluble Countess de la Fère who is motoring up from Paris with her four fine sons. The language problem is placed in the hands of the new interpreter but, since Con's knowledge of French is non-existent, the results are not very satisfactory and the affair ends with the protesting Countess being taken to jail.

Whilst Kid is serving the Pennyfeathers with an alarmingly comical meal, Gretchen goes back to the mill to await Doris but, alas, their plan has been betrayed by the innkeeper and the Burgomaster orders Doris to be arrested. As the Captain is taken away, Gretchen is locked up in the mill to await the next day and her wedding to the despised Governor ('Moonbeams').

When all is dark, Con and Kid creep out to the mill and open the door. To

545

their horror, they are met by the spectre of Wilhelmina, her head under her arm, and clearly in the mood for a flirtation. There is no way in past her. But Con is equal to the occasion. He takes one of the arms of the windmill and swings himself to the upper window where Gretchen is waiting. Taking her in his arms, he swings the windmill round and lands safely, with his burden, back on the ground. As the curtain falls, the two men creep away into the darkness with Gretchen and Tina.

ACT 2
When Gretchen's disappearance is discovered the next day, the story spreads quickly round the town (Gossips' Chorus) but Bertha reminds the townsfolk of the 'Legend of the Mill' and the story of Wilhelmina. The Burgomaster is in a perfect passion of fury. Franz has not succeeded in tracking down the missing girl and he determines that he will advertise for the very best detective in existence. Franz can think only of the fictitious Sherlock Holmes and the Burgomaster orders a telegram to be sent to the super-sleuth offering him fifty thousand gulden to find his daughter.

Franz and Willem decide to try to earn the money themselves. What they don't know is that Gretchen has not gone any distance at all: she has been hidden all night in Tina's room at the inn waiting until Doris can be got out of jail. Con and Kid have disguised themselves as itinerant Italian street musicians but when they, too, hear about the telegram to Sherlock Holmes they decide it is time to change disguises. Con bids a fond farewell to Tina, whose affectionate nature bubbles over into song ('I Want You To Marry Me'), and the two hurry off to equip themselves for their new characters.

The Governor of Zeeland arrives in town to prepare for his wedding. He is a jolly sort of fellow with an eye for the girls ('Every Day Is Ladies' Day With Me') and he is much taken by the first girl he meets at Katwyk-ann-See. It is the buxom Bertha and his interest bursts into blossom when he hears that she is also a wealthy widow. He has chosen the right family to marry into, but he has picked the wrong girl. When he hears that Gretchen is an unwilling bride he is determined that he shall not marry her and he eagerly agrees to Bertha's suggestion that they create a little charade which will be to the benefit of their new born love ('Because You're You').

Kid and Con turn up in their detective outfits and get their orders from the Burgomaster: Gretchen must be found in time for the wedding. They encounter a bit of a problem when Franz declares them to be impostors, but they convince the Burgomaster that Franz is a double-dealer who is after his post and the protesting sheriff finds himself ordered off to jail. All is going well, and the two Yankees can take time off to dream of heading back home to 'The Streets of Old New York' as soon as they have earned the reward.

With all the to-do over finding Gretchen, everyone has forgotten poor Mr Pennyfeather who has been trying to get a word in edgewise ever since his arrival in the village. He chooses the moment before the wedding ceremony to make another attempt but he is shushed away until the marriage has been performed (The Wedding Chorus). The contract is safely signed when Con and Kid march on to announce that they have brought two prisoners. The Burgomaster is not interested: they have fulfilled their promise—his daughter and the Governor have been wed—and he is pleased to hand them their cash reward.

The money is safely in Kid's pocket when the two 'prisoners' come in— Gretchen and Doris. Who then is the bride? Why, it is Bertha, of course. Now Mr Pennyfeather finally gets out his bit of news. He's looking for Captain Doris van Damm to tell him that he has inherited fifty thousand pounds in an English will. Even the Burgomaster has to be mollified by a piece of news like that. So, everything in Katwyk-ann-See can end happily as the two cheeky Yankees head back to their beloved New York, never more to roam.

NAUGHTY MARIETTA

a musical comedy in two acts by Rida Johnson Young. Music by Victor Herbert. Produced at the New York Theatre, New York, 7 November 1910 with Emma Trentini (Marietta), Orville Harrold (Dick), Edward Martindel (Étienne), Marie Duchene (Adah), Harry Cooper (Simon) and Kate Elinore (Lizette). Played at the Olympic Theatre 1916. Played at the Jolson Theatre 21 October 1929 with Ilse Marvenga, Roy Cropper, Lydia van Gilder, Richard Powell and Eulalie Young. Played at Erlanger's Theatre 16 November 1931 with Miss Marvenga, Cropper, Ann Carey, Robert Capron and Miss Young. Produced by the New York City Opera 31 August 1978 in a revised version by Frederick Roffman with Gianna Rolandi, Jacque Trussell, Alan Titus and Russ Thacker.

A film version was produced by MGM in 1935 with Jeanette MacDonald (Marietta) and Nelson Eddy (Dick).

CHARACTERS

Captain Richard Warrington, *an American*
Simon O'Hara, *his servant*
Sir Harry Blake, *an Irish adventurer*
Lieutenant Governor Grandet
Étienne Grandet, *his son*
Rudolfo, *an Italian street musician, keeper of the marionette theatre*
Florenze, *the Governor's secretary*
Marietta d'Altena
Adah, *a quadroon, slave of Étienne*
Lizette, *a casket girl*
Manuele, Nanette, Felice, Fanchon, Graziella, Francesca, etc.

ACT 1
The scene is the Place d'Armes in the French colony of New Orleans, some

time in the eighteenth century. It is early morning and, as the night watchman passes on his way, the square begins to come alive with the vendors of flowers and fruit, tropical birds and sugar cane, street sweepers, fortune tellers and a group of convent pupils on their way to school (Opening Chorus). Amongst the early risers this morning is Étienne Grandet, the son of the colony's acting governor and a great favourite with the local girls. Étienne has just returned from a trip to France, and the girls anxiously bring him up to date with the news: the dreadful pirate Bras Priqué has been abroad, terrorising the merchant ships attempting to serve New Orleans, and now the town fountain is haunted by the ghost of one of his victims. From the depths of the dried-up fountain a mysterious melody has been heard—even the priest has heard it.

Étienne laughs aside the suggestion of a ghost and he also laughs silently at the tales of Bras Priqué for, unknown to all but his slave and mistress, the quadroon Adah, that frightful buccaneer is none other than Étienne himself. In search of both adventure and personal gain he has led a group of disaffected ruffians in plundering the sea coast whilst using his father's position to protect himself from suspicion.

Local curiosity is truly aroused when a strange group of rugged-looking men march into town ('Tramp, Tramp, Tramp'). A mixture of Canadian woodsmen, Tennessee mountain men, Kentucky farmers and Indians, dressed in skins and furs and old uniforms, they are led by the stalwart Captain Dick Warrington and his Irish lieutenant, Sir Harry Blake. Captain Dick's infantry, as they call themselves, are, with the consent of the King of France, out to capture Bras Priqué, for the pirate has been attacking the English ships which provision their settlements. But they do not think to find their prey in New Orleans amongst the fashionable French. They have merely come to present themselves and their credentials to the Governor and to get his signature on the warrant for the pirate's arrest.

They have also come for another and more tender reason. A bride ship is due to berth, bringing a group of poor French girls, the casket girls, dowried by the King of France and destined to be wives to the colonists. The men have spied the girls as their ship watered at Mozambique and they hope that among them they may each find a wife.

The first part of their mission is balked, for the Governor has departed for France and Étienne's father is ruling in his place. The temporary Governor is a bloated, somnolent idiot who has become know to the people as Monsieur By-and-By because of his inability to make a decision. He is also a cowardly party to Étienne's double identity, taking half the proceeds of his depredations as hush money, yet refusing to acknowledge even a sleeping part in the operation. He is perfectly aware that Étienne has the real Governor imprisoned on a Caribbean island as part of his plan eventually to turn Louisiana into a dictatorship under his own control.

Governor Grandet comes to the market place to oversee the arrival of the casket girls ('Taisez-Vous'). The men gather round excitedly as the brides arrive, and hurry to engage them in conversation. One girl, a plain and gawky creature called Lizette, finds herself ignored until Simon O'Hara, Captain

548

Dick's Yiddish low-comic servant, takes a shine to her. Grandet is alarmed at being asked to sign Captain Dick's warrant, but Étienne is amused at the situation and he elaborately offers his hospitality to the Americans.

If they had stayed in the square a moment longer, they would all have heard the ghost. From the urn of the fountain comes a silvery voice with a fragment of song (Song from the Fountain: 'Ah, Sweet Mystery of Life') and an instant later a very unghostly head appears. The voice comes from a diminutive Italian girl who describes herself as 'Naughty Marietta'. Marietta was one of the casket girls, but she ran away from the ship at Mozambique rather than be married off to some uncouth colonist, and made her way alone to New Orleans.

She dallies too long over her song and is discovered but, fortunately, her discoverer is Dick whom she already knows. When he and his men encountered the bride ship at Mozambique they had exchanged words and looks and Marietta counts on him, as a friend, to help her to remain hidden. Dick is reluctant to get involved. Women are not a part of his life and Marietta's flirtatious ways trouble him ('It Never, Never Can Be Love'), but he arranges for her to pose as the missing son of the Italian singer and puppeteer, Rudolfo, and to work in the marionette theatre as a boy.

Before she leaves with her new 'father', Marietta turns to Dick and repeats the melody which she had earlier sung from the fountain. It has been foretold that she shall only lose her heart to the man who can complete this melody which came to her in a dream. Would he care to try? Dick refuses roughly and is irritated to catch himself unconsciously whistling the unfinished tune minutes later.

Lizette has so far drawn a blank with the men of New Orleans but she doesn't show any signs of accepting Simon, until he stages a fine piratical piece of braggadocio to impress her ('If I Were Anybody Else But Me'). Adah is suffering more deeply for she senses that Étienne is cooling towards her, and she attempts to read the future of her love in the cards ('Neath a Southern Moon').

Rudolfo brings his little 'son' to sing in the square (Italian Street Song: 'Zing, Zing') and Marietta carries off her act convincingly in front of Étienne. Then the Lieutenant Governor arrives on the scene with alarming news: a dispatch has come from the King of France offering 10,000 francs reward for the recovery of the Contessa d'Altena who has run away from her family and is known to have exchanged places with a casket girl and sailed for the colonies. The Contessa has the habit of singing an unfinished melody. Étienne tries the tune and the populace immediately recognise it—it is the ghost's tune. The ghost and the missing casket girl must be the countess.

Sir Harry Blake happens on the scene and spies Marietta. Before Dick can stop him, he has spilled the beans. Why, surely that is one of the casket girls, dressed as a boy? Étienne immediately seizes Marietta (Finale), but she refuses to admit her identity. She agrees that she is no boy, but insists equally that she is not the missing Contessa. A fight between Dick's followers and Étienne's guards seems to threaten, but Governor Grandet, once again, will not take firm action and, eventually, the girl runs off with Rudolfo.

ACT 2

Marietta spends her time learning from Rudolfo how to work the marion-ettes (Dance of the Marionettes: 'Turna Like Dat-a, Pierrette'), but she finds that Étienne will not let her go so easily. He is convinced that she is the Contessa, but he is also attracted to her and he persuades her that she should come to the quadroon ball, a gay but louche local version of the Saturnalia, where he hopes to make her his own ('You Marry a Marionette'). She is reluctant, for Dick has warned her that these occasions are dangerous and immoral, but when she thinks that Dick has been paying attentions to Adah she promptly agrees to go. She will not attend as Étienne's partner, but she will be there.

The ball is a vibrant, highly-coloured affair, peopled by the most swagger-ing members of the creole establishment ('New Orleans, Jeunesse Dorée') gambling, dicing and drinking, and womanising ('The Loves of New Orleans'). Lizette is there, still in search of a husband ('The Sweet By-and-By'), since Simon, who has been appointed to the post of whipping boy (with no whipping) to the Governor, has now got the idea that he can do better for himself. He is going to find the end to Marietta's dream song and win himself a genuine Contessa.

When Marietta arrives she is taken aback by the licence of the ball, and when Étienne steps in swiftly to claim her she asks to be taken home. Then she sees Dick arriving. He had said he would not attend, and she is sure that he has come to see Adah. She will not believe that he has come with the idea of protecting her and she proudly sweeps off to the dance floor on Étienne's arm ('Live for Today').

Lizette makes a play for the Governor in the hope of arousing Simon's jealousy but, although the Governor proves to be quite ready for a flirtation, the ploy fails when Simon refuses to take the bait. Étienne has more serious matters for his father's consideration. Since Marietta is undoubtedly the wealthy and titled Italian contessa, it is imperative that he take her to wife. With the political and financial advantages thus achieved, their plan for a Louisiana republic will be greatly aided and their coffers filled.

When he proposes marriage, Marietta asks him what he intends to do with Adah and she is appalled to hear Étienne declare that he will sell his slave to the highest bidder. Leaving him, she finds Dick, sad amongst the gaiety of the ball and aware that he is in the clutches of emotions which are new to him ('I'm Falling in Love With Someone'), but she has no time to answer him for Étienne appears and loudly announces to the assembled company that he is going to auction Adah. The broken-hearted quadroon, seeing that she is likely to be sold to an old and ugly Indian, appeals to Dick to help her and, to Marietta's jealous disbelief, Dick tops the auction.

Taken by fury, Marietta leaves Dick and, announcing herself as the Contessa d'Altena, publicly plights herself to Étienne. Realising that her anger will pass, Étienne determines to make the most of the moment and demands that the marriage take place immediately. The quadroon girls hurry away to deck the bride out in suitable splendour but Adah remains. Dick tells her she is a free woman, and she gratefully returns his gift. She can stop the wedding. If he tears Étienne Grandet's right sleeve he will find his true name tattooed there—Brass Priqué.

After Simon has entertained with an incidental song congratulating himself on his cushy new position ('It's Pretty Soft for Simon'), Dick goes into action. He exposes Étienne as the pirate but, to his amazement, finds himself unable to take the miscreant prisoner. Simon is the Grandet family's whipping boy and, by the law of the land, liable to punishment on behalf of the family for any of their misdeeds. The squalling servant is grabbed by the governmental guards and, with Lizette wailing in his wake, dragged away.

Marietta appears, dressed for her wedding, and hears the truth of the situation from Adah. She refuses to wed Étienne and, in spite of the Governor's threat to enclose her in a convent, defies him. Locked in a room, pounding at the door, she suddenly hears a voice outside. It is her own dream song ('Ah, Sweet Mystery of Life') and the voice is Dick's. He appears at the window and soon the two are in each other's arms.

Étienne discovers them but, before he can take any action, Captain Dick's infantry appear. They have released Simon from prison and they are hot on the trail of Étienne and his pirates. But the ball does not end in a battle. Étienne gives Dick best over Marietta and, as the lovers join in another reprise of their song, the pirates are allowed to escape.

THE FIREFLY

a musical comedy in three acts by Otto Harbach. Music by Rudolf Friml. Produced at the Lyric Theatre, New York, 2 December 1912 with Emma Trentini (Nina), Craig Campbell (Jack), Audrey Maple (Geraldine) and Melville Stewart (Thurston).

A film version, with a different libretto, was produced by MGM in 1937 featuring Jeanette MacDonald and Allan Jones.

CHARACTERS

Mrs Vandare, *a society lady*
Sybil, *her daughter*
Geraldine, *her niece*
Jenkins, *her confidential secretary*
Jack Travers
John Thurston, *his uncle*
Pappa Franz, *a choir master*
Nina, *a street singer*
Suzette, *Geraldine's maid*
Pietro, *Thurston's valet*
Corelli, Antonio Colombo, etc.

ACT 1
Down on New York's East River the magnificent yacht of socialite Mrs

Vandare is being prepared for a trip to the Caribbean ('A Trip to Bermuda'). It is to be a family occasion and the boat's passengers include the widow Mrs Vandare, her daughter Sybil, her niece Geraldine, Geraldine's fiancé Jack Travers and his uncle John Thurston as well as dear Pappa Franz, the choirmaster of Mrs Vandare's church, whom she has deemed to be in need of fresh air and sunshine.

There is little likelihood that it will be a peaceful trip for, as is their habit, Geraldine and Jack are quarrelling even before the holiday has begun. Geraldine has thrown a fit of jealousy because she thinks that Jack has smiled at a little street singer ('He Says Yes, She Says No'). Uncle John spreads practised, soothing words over the disturbed situation and happily invites all the pretty girls to 'Call Me Uncle'. The last member of the company to assemble is Pappa Franz who has dallied to listen to the street urchins singing on the wharves. He hears one voice which delights him, but he is disappointed to find the voice is not that of a boy but of the pretty Nina, the little street singer who had been the cause of Geraldine's tantrum ('Love Is Like a Firefly').

Nina works for the cruel Signor Corelli, head of a band of pickpockets, who takes all her earnings in return for a meagre board and she envies the job of her friend, Pietro, who as John Thurston's valet will be sailing on the fine yacht to the Caribbean islands. Pietro, however, is a bright and helpful lad and he knows that the Captain of the yacht could do with a cabin boy. If only Nina could become a boy. That is not so difficult, for in Corelli's band there is a young girl thief who works her patch as a boy under the name Tony Colombo. She can dress Nina up to be a very convincing cabin boy.

Suzette, Geraldine's maid and Pietro's lady friend, uses her feminine charms ('Something') to convince Mrs Vandare's fussy secretary, Jenkins, to use his influence to get 'Tony' hired, and when Pappa Franz hears the 'lad' sing ('Giannina Mia') he adds his vote enthusiastically ('I've Found It at Last') but Mrs Vandare refuses to have such a ragamuffin on her yacht. As the yacht is about to leave, however, the beastly Corelli arrives on the scene to drag Nina back home and she, in fright, takes the only visible route to safety—straight up the gangplank onto the Vandare boat.

ACT 2

At the Vandare house in Bermuda, the family and their guests are relaxing ('In Sapphire Seas'). Little Tony has become an accepted member of the family's staff, the darling of Pappa Franz and all the rest of the family except Geraldine and Mrs Vandare who are annoyed that he is fussed over to such an extent that he carries out none of the duties for which he has been hired. The local British soldiers are equally taken with the cheeky little chap and have great fun in dressing 'him' up in a tiny version of their uniform ('Tommy Atkins on Parade').

The presence of the little Italian has the unfortunate effect of constantly reminding Geraldine of what she is sure was a flirtation between Jack and the Italian street singer on the pier in New York, and she develops the devastating habit of bursting into floods of tears at the sight of Tony. Uncle

Thurston is to hand on one particularly damp occasion and is only too happy to lend her a supportive and not very avuncular shoulder and arm and, above all, 'Sympathy'.

Thurston's attentions do not escape the eye of Mrs Vandare, for the widow has herself developed a tender passion for the dashing Uncle John and would very much like to make him the new Mr Vandare. Geraldine, too, is not totally unjustified in her suspicions: Jack does still think of the little Italian girl and, when he hears Tony humming a few lines of the Firefly song, he remembers with fondness the one smile they shared ('A Woman's Smile').

Thurston's romantic feelings finally force themselves out. He approaches Jack to tell him he intends to declare his love in a letter asking his beloved to make her choice. Jack believes that Thurston is talking about Mrs Vandare and orders Suzette to take the letter not to Geraldine but to her aunt. Suzette, however, has other things on her mind. Jenkins has been pursuing her ever since that flirtatious encounter on the pier and, since she is engaged to Pietro, she finds the secretary decidedly 'De Trop'.

She gives the letter to Tony to deliver. But Tony is in trouble. A message has come from New York to say that a girl pickpocket disguised as a boy called Tony Colombo has been tracked to the island and that the police are anxious to arrest her. As yet, no one in the Vandare household except Pietro and Suzette suspects that Tony is anything but what he seems ('We're Going to Make a Man out of You'), and Pappa Franz is even thinking of adopting Tony as his son.

It is this last circumstance which forces the valet and the maid to confess the deception. Pappa Franz, who has made so many plans for his little son, is broken-hearted as he tearfully holds in his hands the toy ship he had bought for the boy ('Beautiful Ship From Toyland') and Nina gently asks his pardon for deceiving him ('When a Maid Comes Knocking at Your Heart').

Mrs Vandare is occupied, meanwhile, in trying to patch up the relationship between Geraldine and Jack and he, thinking he is being helpful, tells Geraldine of the proposal which Thurston has sent to her aunt. Geraldine is dreadfully taken aback and, when Thurston's own words to her only seem to confirm that impression, she believes that all his previous attentions were insincere.

Before this matter can be investigated too closely, a little drama intervenes which temporarily banishes all other thoughts. Jenkins has been found helping a woman over the garden wall. Either he has been eloping or else he is in league with a thief.

When the woman is presented, it is, of course, Nina who has been sneaking away from the property (Finale: 'See, My Cloak!'). She answers the flying accusations with the fact that she was brought here on their own ship as Tony, and Mrs Vandare is convinced that she is housing the famous pickpocket for whom the police are searching. When she and Geraldine attack the girl with fury, Pappa Franz finds that his fondness has not faded away and he steps forward to take Nina's part as the act winds up to a fierce finale.

ACT 3

Three years have passed since the episode in Bermuda and no more has been heard of Nina and Pappa Franz. Whilst Thurston has continued to travel the world, Geraldine and Jack have finally got around to naming the wedding day and a party is being thrown for them at the New York mansion of the Vandares ('American Beauty Rose'). The engaged couple are strangely subdued, but Thurston, who has finally returned to his native shores is, as always, the life and soul of the party and Pietro and Suzette can be relied upon to teach the socialites 'The Latest Thing From Paris' in the way of dance crazes.

There is further entertainment planned for later in the evening as Mrs Vandare has managed to secure the darling of the Continent, the singing star Madame Giannina, to perform at her soirée a whole week before she makes her official début in America. Mrs Vandare is delighted to see Thurston again and she talks to him with constant reference to her first husband in terms which make it quite clear that she has every intention of having a second. She coyly tells him that the message which he sent to a certain lady was never delivered and hints that perhaps he should try again. Thurston, in the light of Geraldine's approaching wedding, finds the suggestion bizarre but he has no way of knowing that Mrs Vandare is hinting at an altogether different solution.

They are all surprised when Pappa Franz shows up as the manager of their special guest. Little Nina, he tells them, is no more: she is among the stars. Madame Giannina arrives and obliges with a song ('Kiss Me and 'Tis Day') but, as soon as she is alone with Pietro and Suzette, she drops all her grand new style and falls into their arms as their old friend Nina. They have saved for her the bag of clothes she left behind in her hurried flight from Bermuda and there, in the pocket of her little uniform, is the famous letter which she never delivered.

When Jack finds out that Madame Giannina is his little Nina it is only seconds before he has her in his arms and only seconds more before Mrs Vandare marches in to find both them and the missing letter. She is bowled over at the thought of a proposal, but Thurston quickly explains that the letter was intended for Geraldine and in no time the unhappy engagement has been cancelled: Jack can go at last to his little Firefly while Geraldine and Thurston make sure the rest of the wedding preparations do not go to waste.

The song 'The Donkey Serenade' (Friml/Wright & Forrest) was inserted into the film score.

SWEETHEARTS

an operetta in two acts by Harry B Smith and Fred de Grésac. Lyrics by Robert B Smith. Music by Victor Herbert. Produced at the New Amsterdam Theatre, New York, 8 September 1913 with Christie MacDonald (Sylvia), Thomas Conkey (Franz), Edwin Wilson (Karl), Tom McNaughton (Mikel) and Ethel du Fre (Paula). Produced at Jolson's Theatre 21 September 1929 with Gladys Baxter. Produced at the Shubert Theatre 21 January 1947 in a revised version by John C Holm with Gloria Story (Sylvia), Mark Dawson (Franz), Robert Shackleton (Karl), Bobby Clark (Mikel) and Marjorie Gateson (Lucy).

A film version was produced by MGM in 1938 with Jeanette MacDonald and Nelson Eddy and a substantially different libretto.

CHARACTERS

Dame Paula, *owner of the 'White Geese' laundry*
Lizette, Clairette, Babette, Jeannette, Toinette, Manette, *her daughters*
Sylvia, *her adopted daughter*
Mikel Mikeloviz
Franz, *heir presumptive to the crown of Zilania*
Lieutenant Karl
Hon. Percy Algernon Slingsby
Petrus van Tromp
Aristide Caniche
Liane, *a milliner*
Captain Lourent, Footmen, etc.

ACT 1

At the laundry of the 'White Geese' in downtown Bruges, the six daughters of Dame Paula, the owner of the establishment, are hard at work getting through the day's load of ironing ('Iron, Iron, Iron') while they gossip merrily about men. The most interesting men in the area—the only real men in the area—are the soldiers of the nearby barracks, and all the girls have their hearts and caps set at the regiment in spite of the warnings of their mother who, having wed and then literally lost a soldier herself, has a poor opinion of the species. The girls, however, are not disposed to listen to Paula's preaching and they abandon their irons to rush to meet the soldiers ('On Parade').

The most dashing of all the uniformed gallants is undoubtedly Lieutenant Karl who has been assiduously courting Sylvia, the seventh daughter of the family, but who is flighty enough to hand out a spray of kisses and platitudes amongst his almost-fiancée's sisters. Paula doesn't take Karl's approaches to Sylvia very kindly, particularly as she has heard on the gossip-line about his flirtations with a certain little milliner called Liane, but the girl herself is enraptured by the handsome soldier.

When the military have been shooed on their way, it is this very Liane who shows up at the laundry. She has come to ask the White Geese girls for a favour. A rich and lubricious Baron whom she has encountered has offered to set her up in her own shop in Brussels but, since she is still under her

555

indentures, she cannot leave her present position. Her only way out is to disappear. She would like to disappear by becoming one of the White Geese for a little while—a sort of temporary adopted daughter with a song and dance ('There Is Magic in a Smile').

Liane has just been accepted into the clan of the little White Geese when another visitor appears. Although he is apparently a stranger, he seems to know his way around the place and to be particularly well up on what is going on, for the first thing he does is ask which of the girls is the adopted daughter. For some reason, this puts it into the girls' heads that he must be their long-lost father and the mysterious visitor is happy to go along with this idea in order to gain the information he is seeking.

In fact, he is Mikel Mikeloviz, a leading political figure in the kingdom of Zilania, and he has come in search of a baby which he abandoned at the laundry some twenty years earlier. That baby was and is the Crown Princess of Zilania, and it is in Mikel Mikeloviz's urgent interest to find her and bring her back to her native country.

The real adopted daughter of Paula's brood is Sylvia who has been off delivering laundry to the royal palace just long enough to delay her appearance for a prima donna entry. She comes home to find her mother waiting to have a serious talk to her about the unreliable Karl and to provide the cue for a song about 'Mother Goose'.

Whilst Paula is coping with her child's love affair, Mikel has taken the time to get himself suitably dressed up in an army veteran's battered costume in order to present himself with verisimilitude to his 'wife'. Paula is disgusted to think that her worthless husband has come back to live off her and the laundry again, but she resigns herself to the fact of no longer being a widow. Dame Paula is not alone in having found herself a gentleman follower today for, on her trip to the palace, Sylvia has attracted the attention of a very personable young man who has followed her back to the laundry and, after gazing in at her through the window for a decent time, determines to brave a conversation ('The Angelus').

When he enters the shop, however, the first people he meets are Dame Paula and her new 'husband'. The young man knows perfectly well that this is a charade for he is Mikel's superior—none other than Prince Franz of Zilania, a distant cousin of the missing Princess and, in her continued absence, the heir presumptive to his country's throne. At the moment he is very presumptive, for the people of Zilania, who have tired of a brief flirtation with republican government, are anxious to restore the monarchy and Franz seems, in the absence of the long-lost Princess, set to become their ruler.

This fact has made Franz extremely popular with all sorts of unlikely people and the laundry, which seems to be the most popular thoroughfare in Bruges, soon welcomes a gentleman who is very anxious to find the potential monarch. He is the financier Van Tromp who wishes to make a small offer to purchase from Franz the priceless paintings of his ancestral home, intending to resell them at a quick profit in America. The Britisher, Slingsby, who follows right behind him has a different angle. He has heard rumours that the adopted daughter of the establishment is the real heir to all the Prince's estates and he has come to make his fortune by marrying the girl in question.

When all the visitors have cleared out of the laundry, work carries on and Liane takes her part in the washing under the suspicious eye of Sylvia. When Karl arrives and starts to flirt with Liane, unaware that Sylvia is watching, she becomes highly upset. She and Karl are supposed to be 'Sweethearts' and that is not the way that sweethearts behave. Karl, who is rather keen to have a rich wife, is only after a jolly fling with the pretty laundress. He tries to speak plainly to her, but Sylvia is only interested in an all-or-nothing relationship and the regretful lieutenant sees that he may have to say goodbye to one of his favourite little bits of fluff. If Karl's interest in Sylvia is limited, however, Franz's is growing by the minute ('Every Lover Must Meet His Fate') and he even goes so far as to ask Dame Paula for permission to wed her daughter.

In the meanwhile, the machinators and machinating continue. Mikel is still on the trail of the 'adopted daughter', Slingsby is following the same track with a different intent, and Van Tromp, who is still in pursuit of the Prince, decides that he is not unwilling to trick his fellow conspirator and make himself a rich royal marriage if he can. Unfortunately for them, Van Tromp's eavesdropping leads him to think that Liane is the daughter in question, whilst Slingsby misunderstands a comment which makes him certain that it is little Clairette, the ugly duckling of the family, who is the lost Princess.

The real Princess, if she only knew it, has just been asked for in marriage by the real Prince, but she, alas, can think only of the deceitful Karl. Her heart is fit to break but, when she sees Karl and Liane together and remembers what a rich marriage could do for her family, she stiffens her lip and agrees to wed the Prince whom she neither knows nor loves (Finale).

ACT 2

At the castle of Prince Franz on the banks of the Zuyder Zee, the courtiers keenly await the coming of their lord's betrothed ('As Guests of the Prince We Impatiently Wait'). Sylvia has passed a year at a convent ('In the Convent They Never Taught Me That') and now, at last, she is returning in splendour to marry Franz. She is rather worried, for she is still just a little girl from a Belgian laundry and, although nothing has yet been resolved about the succession to the monarchy, it is generally accepted that Franz will be asked at any moment to take the crown of Zilania. It is a big step for Sylvia ('Cricket on the Hearth').

The whole family are at the castle to welcome her, the girls all delighted at being set free from the daily routine of the laundry, and dying to see Sylvia made a princess. However, the plotting around the question of the Zilanian succession has not decreased and Mikel, Van Tromp, Slingsby ('I Don't Know How I Do It, But I Do') and another conspirator, Aristide Caniche, are all on the spot to add to the succession of twists and turns in the plot.

Since Franz proves unwilling to fall in with any of their devious little plans, they are all very anxious that the Princess should be found and they are convinced they have a water-tight candidate in Liane ('Jeanette and Her Little Wooden Shoes'). Karl, anxious to intern the little milliner in wedlock now that her fortunes seem to be on the up ('The Game of Love'), gets short shrift from the budding Princess ('Talk About This, Talk About That') and, his vanity shattered, he tries once again to sweet talk his way into Sylvia's favour.

A year has been more than enough for Sylvia to have got Karl completely out of her system but, when Franz overhears Karl accusing his wife-to-be of only accepting the Prince on the rebound, he is led to ask himself whether this is true. He cannot and will not hold Sylvia to an agreement made under such circumstances and he will wed her only if, after due consideration, she can say truly that she loves him as he loves her. Sylvia is truly distressed, for under the warmth of Franz's love and kindness she has genuinely grown to return his sentiments, but the Prince insists that the marriage must be postponed to give his bride time to reconsider.

The plotters disguise themselves as monks ('Pilgrims of Love') to fake evidence on the original disappearance of the baby Princess, but their efforts to depose Franz in favour of Liane fall to pieces at the vital moment. When Mikel relates the story about the baby abandoned at the White Geese laundry and produces the 'adopted daughter', Dame Paula indignantly denies that Liane is any daughter of hers, adopted or otherwise. The abandoned baby was not Liane but Sylvia.

Sylvia is acclaimed as the Crown Princess of Zilania, but Franz will still be Prince for she is able to say, from the bottom of her heart, that she loves him. Love has grown, as the greatest love always does, and they will be 'Sweethearts' for the rest of their lives.

The libretto of *Sweethearts* has undergone several major rewrites with scenes and characters being rewritten, significantly enlarged, or cut, and the second act, in particular, has been wholly rearranged around the bones of the story. The principal songs have maintained their place but others have come and gone or been repositioned and reallocated. The songs 'Pretty as a Picture' and 'What She Wanted and What She Got' are regulars in the show, but other revivals have added songs from lesser-known Herbert musicals. The 1947 revival interpolated 'To the Land of My Own Romance' from *The Enchantress* and 'I Might Be Your Once-in-a-While' from *Angel Face*.

OH, BOY!

a musical comedy in two acts by Guy Bolton and P G Wodehouse. Music by Jerome Kern. Produced at the Princess Theatre, New York, 20 February 1917 with Anna Wheaton (Jackie), Tom Powers (George), Marie Carroll (Lou Ellen), Hal Forde (Jim) and Edna May Oliver (Penelope). Produced at the Goodspeed Opera House,

Connecticut, 1964 and again 21 September 1983 with Susan Bigelow, David James-Carroll, Julie Osburn, David Staller and Joan Shepherd.

Produced at the Kingsway Theatre, London, 27 January 1919 as *Oh, Joy!* with Beatrice Lillie, Powers, Dot Temple, Billy Leonard and Helen Rous.

CHARACTERS

Jane Packard
Polly Andrus
Jim Marvin
George Budd
Lou Ellen Carter
Jackie Sampson
Miss Penelope Budd
Briggs
Constable Simms
Judge Daniel Carter
Mrs Carter
Waiter, etc.

ACT 1

When the telegram boy calls at George Budd's bachelor apartment at Meadowsides, Long Island, there is no one home but Briggs, his faithful butler, until suddenly the window sash flies up on the evening air and a whole parade of garish young things step daintily off the fire escape and into the living room (Opening Chorus: 'Let's Make a Night of It'). This desperately jazzy crew is headed by Jim Marvin, an energetically up-to-date young dude equipped with the latest slang, an unquenchable cheek and some decidedly loud clothes, who has invited them all to George's home for a loud party to celebrate the fact that his polo team has just won a silver cup.

Boring old George, who won't go out burning up the night spots of Long Island with them, can jolly well host their party and there is no way that he can object because once upon a time, as Jim never ceases to remind him, Jim saved his life. Strangely enough, it seems that, for once, George has gone out for the evening, but Jim is undeterred as he shepherds a handful of self-indulgent flappers into the dining room to plunder his friend's liquor and larder.

The reason George is not at home is that he is eloping. He has been off to a minister with his sweetheart, Lou Ellen Carter, and when they creep quietly in to the apartment they are all ready to enjoy their first night as Mr and Mrs Budd ('You Never Knew About Me'). They have disappeared into the bedroom before Jim and his entourage emerge and, in spite of Briggs' pained warnings about the noise and the landlord, Jim launches into a paean in praise of the available female ('A Packet of Seeds').

The song and dance routine creates enough racket to make George and Lou Ellen peep out to see what is going on, but Briggs has hustled the unwelcome guests back into the dining room so all the newlyweds spy is the telegram which the butler has left perched on a bachelor statue awaiting

George's return. It is a telegram which throws a certain coat of consternation over the honeymoon.

George was brought up by his Quaker Aunt Penelope and she is still his guardian, holding control over his finances and his family estate, both of which it is in her power to withhold if George should in any way misbehave. George had written to her, telling her that he had met a marvellous girl and was hoping to get engaged and, in reply, Aunt Penelope's telegram cautions severe restraint and lengthy consideration. George, of course, has already done just the opposite by skipping the engagement and going straight to the marriage. What will Aunt Penelope say and, worse, what will she do? Clearly Aunt Penelope must not be allowed to know that the rash deed has been precipitately done and, since the telegram also vouchsafes the information that she is on her way to Meadowsides post haste, that means that Lou Ellen is going to have to, temporarily, go back to her parents. The honeymoon is off.

The dining room is only a door's distance from the living room and it is inevitable that, before long, Jim Marvin will find out his host is home. George has just time to hide Lou Ellen in the bedroom before the revellers are upon him. He is in no mood to host Jim's childish party and he is not displeased when the landlord turns out to be of a like mind. Jim, however, is not fazed. He drags George off to charm the landlord into submission and, as soon as he is gone, Lou Ellen tiptoes from the bedroom to make her escape unseen. She is out of luck, for Jim's gaggle of girlies spot her and she has to pretend that she is part of the party. When the girls insist that she joins them at their next party-stop at the Cherrywood Inn Cabaret she demurely declines, telling them that she is no flapper but 'An Old-Fashioned Wife'.

Jim's famous charm does nothing for the landlord and the girls have to be bundled off to the Cherrywood Inn, while George sadly escorts Lou Ellen to a taxi to deliver her back home. This means that Jim is alone in the apartment when he finds himself confronted by a desperado with a gun. This particular desperado, however, is a pretty girl called Jackie and she is not attacking but escaping.

She was at the Cherrywood Inn having a nice evening when a rather tiddly old gentleman called Tootles made a pass at her. The old gentleman was so tiddly that he insisted on getting up on a table and reading a particularly magnificent speech which he had prepared for a big function the next day and, when a policeman intervened to quiet him, he kicked the policeman and started a fine ruckus. In the mêlée, Jackie became entangled with the policeman and she defended herself womanfully, an act which involved a rather hefty attack on the policeman's left eye. Now she is in flight from the law and she has taken the fire escape and the open window as a route to safety.

P C Simms is right behind her but, when he knocks on the door, Jim passes Jackie off as George's wife and, since Simms had taken off his glasses before going into battle, he is not able to recognise his assailant. Unfortunately, Jackie has left behind a clue. She lost her handbag in the scuffle and it may incriminate her. Jim gallantly offers to return to the cabaret and rescue it and also to find Tootles and make him absolve Jackie of any blame in the affair. Jackie is duly grateful ('A Pal Like You') and, since she dare not leave the apartment without blowing her cover to the vigilant Simms, Jim suggests that she spend the night in George's bed. Old George can have Jim's sofa for the night. Jackie is only too pleased to accept and by the time George returns she is decked out in Lou Ellen's baby blue pyjamas, ready for bed.

George is penning a rueful note to Lou Ellen (Letter Song: 'I'll Just Dream About You') when a strange woman emerges from his bedroom in his wife's pyjamas. Jackie does her best to explain her ghastly dilemma and George is sufficiently convinced to continue the charade when Simms puts in another lightning visit, producing his new wedding certificate as evidence that he has just been married. And so Jackie stays at George's place 'Until the Clouds Roll By' while George heads out in the rain to spend the night on Jim's uncomfortable sofa.

When he returns home the next morning he finds that he has an early morning visitor. Lou Ellen has started to break the big news gently to her family by telling them that she is engaged to George, and Judge Carter, her father, has come straight around to give George the once over. Unfortunately, Jim has arranged for his bunch of jazz babies to meet at George's place prior to a beano at the Country Club and the Judge is treated to an unexpected whirl of girlie gaiety which seems out of place in the apartment of what is supposed to be a serious young man.

George scares him away with a story of unstable explosives but he has to endure an entire song and dance from a spare flapper ('A Little Bit of Ribbon') before Jackie emerges dressed in the best combination of Lou Ellen's trousseau she can find to replace her rather obvious evening gown. Jim, meanwhile, has been on the trail of Tootles and he comes by bearing the only clue he has been able to dig up. It is a piece of paper with a speech on it, the speech which Tootles was proclaiming the previous night at the Cherry-wood Inn.

George's home is now full of women all of whom have absolutely nothing to do with him, and Aunt Penelope is expected at any minute. Briggs must go to the train and waylay her. But his next visitor is even more disastrous than an aunt. Lou Ellen turns up with her mother who is intent on inspecting George's morals and, when Mama sees George's apartment filled with the noisiest specimens of modern youth and hears tales of rowdy parties and threatened eviction, she becomes thunderously protective of her daughter. When Jackie bursts forth from the bedroom and lets slip that she had stayed there all night it is Lou Ellen's turn to crumple but George comes up with a fine answer. This lady is his aunt—Aunt Penelope.

Jackie does her best to give her interpretation of an up-to-date Quaker ('The First Day in May') but it is her turn to be dumbfounded when Judge Carter returns to meet his wife. It is Tootles! Since he is a Judge, he should be able to square her with the police easily but, since he is clearly also a married man who was out on a spree, Jackie still has a bit of persuading to do. When Judge Carter sets off for the Country Club, where he is to make the presentation speech for the Polo Trophy, Jackie determines to follow.

561

ACT 2

At Meadowsides Country Club Jim and his little friends open the act with a song ('Koo-La-Loo') before a black-eyed Briggs staggers on in search of George. He waylaid Aunt Penelope all right and tried to lock her in the kitchen, but Aunt Penelope defended herself in a most un-Quakerish way, popping him one in the eye before setting off in search of her missing nephew. Briggs can share his pains with PC Simms who is sporting a shiner from Jackie's attack of the previous night. Simms is still determined to track down his assailant but he is distracted by the remembrance of Lou Ellen's baby blue pyjamas. He can't get them off his mind and is wondering how he could get a pair like them for his wife. When George and Jackie arrive at the club he greets them embarrassingly as Mr and Mrs Budd and immediately gets on to the topic of the wretched pyjamas.

Jim is dashing around the place being the life and soul of everybody's existence and he is only momentarily disappointed when Jackie shows signs of being rather fond of George. She, however, is equally fond of Jim, for she is a girl with eclectic tastes ('Rolled Into One'). When the Judge and his wife are around she resumes her Quaker aunt act, but Mrs Carter is already suspicious of her daughter's fiancé and is determined to investigate him and his peculiarly young aunt very closely. In the meanwhile she intends Lou Ellen to be kept well away from George and she bulldozes her husband into forbidding the two young people to speak to each other ('Oh, Daddy, Please').

Jackie, still on the trail of her handbag and her good name, offers Judge Carter a straight swap. She will return the speech he is due to make in a short while if he will get back her handbag from the voracious Simms. The Judge goes off looking for something with which to inebriate the policeman while Jim encourages Jackie into thoughts of future bliss when it's 'Nesting Time in Flatbush'. Jackie finds it quite exhausting keeping up the different personas of wife, aunt and flapper with the various men whose paths she has crossed in the past twenty-four hours, and she orders a stiff brace of Bronxes to help her get through it all while Lou Ellen, unable to speak to her George, consoles herself with the thought that 'Words Are Not Needed'.

Now who should march onto the scene but the real Aunt Penelope who is horrified when Simms points her in the direction of Mr and *Mrs* Budd. George married! Of course: Simms saw him in his apartment last night with his wife dressed in her lovely blue pyjamas. The Quaker lady totters and asks for a glass of water, just as the waiter arrives with the Bronxes ordered by the phoney 'Miss Budd'. Aunt Penelope drinks them down and suddenly her world starts to swim. When she incoherently challenges George about the blue pyjamas, he steers her solicitously towards the ladies' room to lie down.

While Jackie, Jim and George pop in an irrelevant piece about 'Flubby Dub the Caveman', Lou Ellen runs into Aunt Penelope in the ladies' room and hears the story about the blue pyjamas. She immediately recognises the offending garments as her own, but who was the woman inside them? Lou Ellen heads swiftly towards George for an answer but she is unable to force him into speech, owing to the promise made to her mother not to communicate with George until Mama's investigation is done. For once, George is thankful for Mrs Carter's intervention but Lou Ellen gathers her mother to her side and demands that George answer her question and also that he explain who Jackie is, since it is plain that she is not his aunt.

Before the explanations can begin, Aunt Penelope spots Briggs. There is the maniac who attacked her and tried to lock her up. Simms leaps to do his duty and, to free his hands, plumps Jackie's handbag into the arms of Judge Carter. The Judge swiftly exchanges the bag for his speech as Aunt Penelope demands to know whether she has dreamed the whole strange affair. And did she also dream that George was married?

No, she did not. George gently brings forward Lou Ellen to introduce her as his wife, much to the confusion of Simms who is perfectly sure that it was the other girl who was wearing the blue pyjamas. Nonsense, responds George heroically, Jackie is the wife of Jim Marvin. Well, she soon will be, and with any luck nobody will ask any more questions about the previous twenty-four hours' goings on in Meadowsides, Long Island.

Several other songs were played in the show at the early stages of its production including 'Be a Little Sunbeam', 'The Land Where the Good Songs Go' and 'Ain't it a Grand and Glorious Feeling'. In the London production the song 'Wedding Bells' from *Very Good, Eddie* was added to the score.

LEAVE IT TO JANE

a musical comedy in two acts by Guy Bolton and P G Wodehouse based on the play *The College Widow* by George P Ade. Music by Jerome Kern. Produced at the Longacre Theatre, New York, 28 August 1917 with Edith Hallor (Jane), Oscar Shaw (Stub), Ann Orr (Bessie), Robert Pitkin (Billy) and Georgia O'Ramey (Flora). Produced at the Sheridan Square Theatre, 25 May 1959 with Kathleen Murray, Angelo Mango, Jeanne Allen, Art Matthews and Dorothy Greener.

CHARACTERS

Peter Witherspoon, *President of Atwater College*
Jane, *his daughter*
Hiram Bolton
Billy, *his son, a half-back*
Senator Elan Hicks *of Squantumville*
Harold (Bub) Hicks, *his son*
Stub Talmadge, *a busy undergraduate*
Bessie Tanner, *an athletic girl*
Flora Wiggins, *a prominent waitress*
'Silent' Murphy, *a center-rush*
Matty McGowan, *football trainer at Atwater*

563

Ollie Mitchell, *a sophomore*
Sally Cameron, *a co-ed*
Howard Talbot, *a tutor*
Jimmy Hopper, Dick McAllister, Happy Jones, Bertha Tyson, Cora Jenks,
etc.

ACT 1

At Atwater College, the all-important football team in this year of 1917
seems to shine more by the enthusiastic shouting of its cheer song ('Good
Old Atwater') than by its skills on the field. Coach McGowan is in the depths
of despair: all his best players from the last year have graduated or got
married and he is left with a feeble skeleton of a team with which to face the
traditional enemy, Bingham College, in the year's big game.

Stub Talmadge, a football-mad undergraduate and self-appointed scout,
has a contribution to make to the team. He has discovered a hulk of a piano-
mover with the perfect build for a center-rush and he has succeeded, in spite
of the College principal's categoric rule against students being enrolled
solely for athletic ability, to get this fellow accepted as a part-time art
student. When the neolithic 'Silent' Murphy appears it is fairly obvious that
his talents are wholly physical, but the team needs him and so the principal
has to be persuaded that he has other talents.

Stub's efforts are greatly appreciated by the sports-mad Bessie Tanner for
whom Stub has a very special affection and with whom he is sure he could
spend 'A Peach of a Life' if they were man and wife. Stub, unfortunately,
does not have a tidy past. Last term he had digs with a Mrs Wiggins and he's
still in debt to her to the tune of four weeks at four dollars fifty. It's a debt
which is purposefully pursued by Miss Flora Wiggins whom Stub has been
chatting up rather too dangerously in hope of some mitigation. The most
courted girl at Atwater, however, is the principal's daughter, Jane. The
entire college is in love with her, most particularly and obviously the droopy
tutor Talbot, but Jane has no intention of doing anything about marriage yet
('Wait Till Tomorrow').

The optimistic football songs of Atwater bring only smiles from a middle-
aged visitor called Bolton. He is a wealthy ex-Bingham student who has
endowed his old college handsomely and he is happy to take a ten-to-one bet
against a thousand dollars that Bingham will win this year's match. Stub
patriotically takes him up without knowing that Bolton has special information. His own son, Billy, one of the country's top young half-backs, is to be
enrolled at Bingham. When this disastrous piece of news seeps through to
the Atwater lads they realise that something momentous is going to have to
be done and Bessie urges the laid-back Stub to get into action ('Just You
Watch My Step').

Now who should turn up at Atwater, looking for his father, but young
Bolton himself. There is nothing for it but to turn the charms of Jane
Witherspoon on him ('Leave it to Jane'). Billy is duly struck all of a heap. He
wishes that he was enrolling at Atwater where he would be near Jane but,

whatever his personal preferences may be, his father has him lined up for Bingham and it seems that to Bingham he must go. Only there will he, with his limited academic abilities, be able to win a degree, and only a degree will win him the comfortable position awaiting him in his father's firm.

A less eager new student is weedy young Harold Hicks, a senator's son from the boondocks, who is to be Mrs Wiggins' new lodger. He is scared to death at being away from his mother for the first time and even Flora's simperings do not reassure him.

Once Billy is hooked, Jane and her friends put the next part of their plan into action ('The Siren's Song'). Before Billy can set out for Bingham, a few kind glances from Jane persuade him to stay just a little longer at Atwater to partner her at the evening's faculty dance. The boys practice a medley of College Songs to perform on the occasion and even feeble 'Bub' Hicks is brought in to add his voice to the proceedings. The dance is a lively one ('There it Is Again') and all have a good time while Jane, to the sarcastic comments of Flora ('Cleopatterer'), spends her time devotedly with Billy. It is not long before Billy is asking Jane to wear his pin, but she demurely refuses—after all, how could she wear his pin while he was scoring against them in the big match? If he were an Atwater man, of course, she would be only too delighted to accept.

Billy wonders if he really could stay at Atwater with Jane amid the old world atmosphere and ivy covered walls ('The Crickets Are Calling'), but what if his father should find out? That is not a problem; he only has to register under an assumed name. Billy takes his courage in his hands and, when Mr Witherspoon comes round to make sure that all are having a good clean time, he introduces himself to the principal as Elmer Staples, the botanist. Jane covers his inability to live up to this identity by explaining that he has had a nervous breakdown and needs a rest far from botany. The prescribed remedy is a healthy life with lots of football, and so Billy Bolton alias Elmer Staples becomes a resident of Atwater.

ACT 2

It is Thanksgiving Day and the big match is in progress ('Good Old Atwater') but Atwater aren't doing terribly well. In fact they're behind 3-0 and getting trampled on. When the second half begins, the enemy even succeed in knocking big Murphy down and injuring him so that he has to leave the field. All Atwater is in ferment and Stub's bet looks utterly lost.

Senator Hicks has come down for the day and is staggered to find his son a very different boy from the weakling he left behind. He sports a flashy suit, is full of the smartest lingo and, according to Flora, is engaged to her ('Sir Galahad'). Another who has come down is, of course, Billy's father. Since his son is a key member of the Atwater team it has not been possible to keep Billy's inveigling away from his father's old alma mater much of a secret and Bolton is livid. He knows the whole story, all the details about Jane and her siren act, and he has just one aim in view. He is going to remove his son from that football field! Now it is Stub's moment to take glorious action. Gather-

565

ing a swathe of students at his heels, he descends on the unwary Bolton and carries him bodily off towards a cab.

As the cab drives off, with Bolton struggling in the back seat, a roar is heard from the playing field. Billy has snatched the ball from the jaws of defeat and plunged over the enemy line for the all-important touch-down. The conversion kick follows and Atwater has won! Stub and Bessie are in seventh heaven ('The Sun Shines Brighter'), but Witherspoon, to whom all has now been revealed, has some hard words to say to Jane for the heartless trick she has played on young Bolton. The boys, too, thinking that Jane's duty to the college has now been done, imagine what she will be like as a wife to one of them ('I'm Going to Find a Girl Some Day').

Billy may have won the match for Atwater, but it looks as if he is in for a romantic disappointment, not to mention a first rate blasting from his father. But when Bolton returns his anger has cooled. The boys have given him a jolly time on his enforced cab ride, singing football songs and telling funny stories which took him back to his own college days, and all he has to say to Billy is that he has been a fool to let himself be tricked by a wily woman.

On the whole, he is more impressed with Stub than with his match-winning son. After all, Stub had the business acumen to make his gamble for a thousand dollars come good. He offers Stub a fine job in his firm but for Billy there will be only the opportunity to start at the bottom. He has failed to get the degree he would have got at Bingham and, true to his threats, Bolton will not help his son if he will not help himself. Billy asks Stub for the truth about Jane, and Stub has to admit that the whole thing was a put-up job. The heart-broken Billy prepares to pack and leave for home and the job at the bottom at $30 a week.

At the same time Flora's heart is getting its annual maltreatment. Her problematic engagement to young Hicks is off. She has groomed him and trained him up from a provincial wimp into a smart young man-about-town and now he has dumped her. But this is the eighth year in succession that Flora has been engaged to and jilted by her mother's lodger, so she doesn't suffer quite as much as a less practised person ('Poor Prune'), and at least Stub, who is richer to the tune of $1000 since his win, can pay her the $18 debt from last year.

Billy is about to go on his way when he meets up with Jane. She knows that he must have been told how she kept him at Atwater not for himself but for his prowess on the football field and she makes a clean breast of it. She is terribly sorry that it is her actions which have led his father to be so severe with him and all she can say in mitigation is that she would be happy to share life with him on $30 a week.

The songs 'A Great Big Land' and 'What I'm Longing to Say' were also used in the original production of *Leave It To Jane*.

GOING UP

a musical comedy in three acts by Otto Harbach and James Montgomery based on *The Aviator* by James Montgomery. Lyrics by Otto Harbach. Music by Louis A Hirsch. Produced at the Liberty Theatre, New York, 25 December 1917 with Edith Day (Grace), Frank Craven (Robert), Marion Sunshine (Madeleine) and Frank Otto (Hopkinson Brown). Produced at the Goodspeed Opera House, East Haddam, Connecticut in a revised version by Bill Gile 22 June 1976 and at the John Golden Theatre 19 September 1976 with Kimberley Farr, Brad Blaisdell, Maureen Brennan and Walter Bobbie.

Produced at the Gaiety Theatre, London, 22 May 1918 with Marjorie Gordon, Joseph Coyne, Evelyn Laye and Austin Melford.

CHARACTERS

F H Douglas, *a chronic bettor*
Mrs Douglas, *his wife*
Grace Douglas, *their daughter*
Jules Gaillard, *their prospective son-in-law*
Madeleine Manners, *Grace's chum*
Hopkinson Brown, *her fiancé*
Robert Street, *author of 'Going Up'*
James Brooks, *his publisher*
Miss Zonne, *a telephone girl*
John Gordon, *manager of the Gordon Hotel*
Sam Robinson, *a mechanic*
Louis, *Gaillard's mechanic*, etc.

ACT 1

The Gordon Hotel, in Lenox, Massachusetts, is fermenting with excitement. There is a sizzle of gossip in the lobby, a *frisson* of anticipation in the elevators and the hotel's telephonist, Miss Zonne, doesn't have enough hands to plug and unplug all the little jackpoints that are buzzing on her frenetic switchboard ('Hello, Hello'). The cause of this excitement is the presence in the hotel of the most celebrated of all current celebrities, the deliciously topical Mr Robert Street, author of that heart-stopping aviator's memoir entitled *Going Up*. What a book! Such drama, such literary charm! Such suspense! Such sexuality! All to be found in the pages of this wonderful work of literature and, surely, in the person of Mr Street as well.

The Gordon Hotel can do with a little livening up for it hasn't had a very successful season. Pretty Grace Douglas, who has been there with her parents, has been almost bored. There are no new faces, just the same old friends from back home, and nothing but nothing exciting has happened at all. Her friend Madeleine has done a little better than Grace, for she has managed to net a proposal of marriage, but the proposal has not come from a romantic stranger, only from her long-time, home-town beau, Hoppy Brown. Nonetheless, this time, finally worn down by his persistence, she has decided to say 'yes' ('I Want a Determined Boy').

Today Grace is filling in her day by going for a drive, even though her father is rather expecting her to accompany him and her prospective husband, the French aviator Jules Gaillard, to the golf course. Grace isn't terribly keen on Gaillard and she knows well how to get her way with her father: she lays him a wager that she will return before his round of golf is done and he, a passionate gambler, cannot resist the challenge.

Gaillard is mildly miffed but his attention is diverted from his less than amorous lady by the fuss going on about Robert Street. Who, he asks, is Robert Street? Why, he is an aviator like Gaillard, but an altogether more celebrated one because of his brilliant book. Gaillard takes only a glance at *Going Up* and snorts ridicule. What is this? This fool says he flew his plane at night. It is impossible. If you fly at night, you bump into things. It is logical.

Mr Douglas is impressed by the solidity of this argument and he supports Gaillard's superiority over this writing fellow to the extent of a large wager ('I'll Bet You') with Street's expansive publisher, James Brooks. Gaillard and Street shall have a flying contest and whichever flies highest and stays up longest shall be adjudged the winner. The manager of the hotel is delighted; such a contest will be the event of the season and bring fashionable Boston swarming to his hotel, but there seems, for some unknown reason, to be rather less delight in the eyes of Hoppy Brown, the bosom buddy of Mr Street. The famous man himself is out on the roads in his brand new automobile and is as yet unaware of the bet.

As fate will have it, Street is, at this very moment, coming to the rescue of Grace who has stalled her motor in an inconvenient place. Whilst Hoppy is hastily explaining to the two gamblers that Street cannot possibly take part in such a competition because he doesn't have a plane with him, the hero in question is sitting starry-eyed at the side of the road, looking after the girl of his dreams zooming off in a blue Packard and a cloud of dust.

When he returns to the hotel he discovers that, in spite of everything Hoppy could do, he has been committed to the contest in a plane provided by the eager Gaillard. This is a tragedy, for Robert Street is a writer of fiction and all the aviation sequences in *Going Up* are no more than a figment of his fertile imagination. To admit it now, when he has become a celebrity through his airborne descriptions, would be to ruin a career which is just bursting into flower, but what other way is there?

When Grace comes to enthuse over him ('If You Look in Her Eyes'), he realises that he will lose the girl as well as the fame if he does not pull something out of the hat quickly. Something is done quickly. While Robert is bravely relating a fictitious tale of fabulous flying experiences ('Going Up') to an adoring audience, an experienced aircraft mechanic is being hurried to Lenox to give our hero a crash course in flying.

ACT 2

While Grace is musing over the benefits to a man of 'The Touch of a Woman's Hand', the flying lesson takes place, with the help of several articles of hotel furniture and the odd bit of additional paraphernalia, in

Robert's hotel room ('Down Up, Left, Right'). Hoppy and Brown urge their friend on to instant expertise but, at the end of the session, the teacher has only one opinion: Robert hasn't got a chance. Worse, it would be dangerous for such a rash fellow to go up in the air. Robert's supporters are aghast, particularly as they know that, for Grace's sake, he is determined to take up the challenge and risk his life. Grace must be told the truth and made to stop him.

Hoppy unwillingly takes on the duty of enlightening the girl, but he does it in such an oblique fashion that Grace misunderstands him and takes it that the amorous Gaillard is the phoney flier who is willing to risk his neck for her. She is touched, but not sufficiently to make her change her allegiance to Robert who, infuriated by the Frenchman's cocksure attitude, insists that he will both fly and win.

Madeleine, thrilled by such gallant bravado, tries to get her Hoppy to join his friend in the plane ('Do it for Me'), but Hoppy is too fond of his comfortable skin to take up such a challenge, even for Madeleine. Anyway, now it is evening and things social must, by the natural course of events, intervene and allow Grace to lead the hotel guests in the newest dance, 'The Tickle Toe'.

On the terrace of the hotel that evening the one and only topic of conversation is the great race, but the two heroes of the affair are thinking less of the race than of finding out where they stand with Grace. Gaillard pursues his almost-fiancée with intent ('Kiss Me') while Robert feels his way with a nervousness imparted by the shortness of their acquaintance ('If You Look in Her Eyes'). Finally he brings himself to ask her whether, if he wins the race, she will marry him. Grace, whose preference is pretty obvious, cannot go quite as far as that quite so soon, but by the end of the evening she has succeeded in striking a wager with her father that if Gaillard wins she will finally give in and marry him but if he loses, then the wedding is off for good.

ACT 3

The whole of Boston seems to have come to Lenox for the big race ('Hip Hooray! See the Crowds Appearing') and to welcome 'A Brand New Hero' whom Hoppy and Madeleine are praying will be Robert. He has been up all night with the mechanic trying to perfect his technique on the hotel furniture, but he has yet to try out his half-found skills on a real aeroplane.

Grace sings a fine upstanding paean ('Here's to the Two of You') to cheer them on their way and then it's all systems go. Gritting his teeth, Robert climbs aboard and in no time they're 'Going Up'. As the planes rush off into the sky, the breathless crowd follow their progress by telephone. Town after town reports their passing until, as evening approaches, Gaillard is seen to make a timely turn. But Robert flies straight on and one report comes back that he is hanging from the undercarriage reading a book. Needless to say it is the mechanic's book of instructions.

As dusk deepens Gaillard lands ready to receive his laurels. But his claim is premature, for Robert is not back yet and, to all evidence, he is still up in the air. The Frenchman is furious. His lovely plane will be wrecked by this foolish show-off. Night is falling fast and everyone knows it is not possible to fly at night. But it is, and Robert Street is proving it. As soon as he lands he can be acclaimed the winner. The only trouble is that he has to land first, and getting the plane back down on the ground is a part of his training in which he hasn't yet had any practice.

Grace comes to the rescue. Quickly scribbling down the landing instructions dictated by the mechanic, she heads off for the old church spire with a notebook and a lantern. She will talk the plane down. And so Robert Street lands safely and Gaillard is so relieved to see his beautiful aeroplane all in one piece that he scarcely notices Grace falling into his rival's arms as the finale reprises of the title song and the 'Tickle Toe' bring the story to a happy ending. Grace and Robert will be married and she asks only one thing of him—that he never ever goes up in an aeroplane again.

The 1976 revival interpolated the numbers 'Hello, Frisco' (Hirsch/Gene Buck) from *Ziegfeld Follies of 1915*, 'My Sumurun Girl' (Hirsch/Al Jolson) from *The Whirl of Society*, 'I'll Think of You' (Hirsch/Rennold Wolf) from *The Rainbow Girl* and 'A Marriage of Convenience' (Hirsch/Buck) from *Ziegfeld Follies of 1918*.

IRENE

a musical comedy in two acts by James Montgomery based on his own book. Lyrics by Joseph McCarthy. Music by Harry Tierney. Produced at the Vanderbilt Theatre, New York, 18 November 1919 with Edith Day (Irene), Walter Regan (Donald), Dorothy Walters (Mrs O'Dare) and Bobby Watson (Madame Lucy). Produced at the Minskoff Theatre 13 March 1973 in a revised version by Hugh Wheeler and Joseph Stein based on an adaptation by Harry Rigby with added songs by Charles Gaynor and Otis Clements, Wally Harper, Joseph McCarthy, etc. with Debbie Reynolds, Monte Markham, Patsy Kelly and George S Irving.

Produced at the Empire Theatre, London, 7 April 1920 with Edith Day, Pat Somerset, Helen Kinnaird and Robert Hale. Produced at His Majesty's Theatre, 21 March 1945 with Pat Taylor, Frank Leighton, Mignon O'Doherty and Arthur Riscoe. The revised version was produced at the Adelphi Theatre, London, 4 June 1976 with Julie Anthony, Eric Flynn, Jessie Evans and Jon Pertwee.

Film versions were produced by First National in 1926 with Colleen Moore, Lloyd Hughes, George K Arthur, Charles Murray and Kate Pride and by RKO in 1940 with Anna Neagle, Ray Milland, Alan Marshal and Roland Young.

CHARACTERS

Irene O'Dare
Mrs O'Dare, *her mother*
Jane Gilmour
Helen Cheston

570

Donald Marshall
Mrs Marshall, *his mother*
Madame Lucy, *a couturier*
Ozzie Babson
Mrs McFudd, etc.

ACT 1
On Ninth Avenue, the boys and girls in the street sing 'What Do You Want
to Make Those Eyes at Me For?', before the act drop goes up on the shop
headquarters of the A*A*A*A Piano Company. A signwriter is putting the
last touch to the new name in the window and the telephone is being
installed for, to the pride of her mother and the excitement of her friends,
Miss Irene O'Dare is going into the piano tuning business. She's taking it
very seriously and has been boning up on business management from library
books.

Her mother would prefer to see her married before becoming a tycoon,
for Mrs O'Dare knows about men—there was one called Liam O'Dougherty
that she let slip through her fingers and she doesn't want Irene disappointed
in the same way. It is a line that Irene has heard time and again, but she is in
no hurry to wed. She wants a little excitement first and, then, she doesn't
want to be stuck all her life on Ninth Avenue ('The World Must Be Bigger
Than an Avenue'). The telephone soon proves its worth when the first
business call comes through: Irene is summoned to the famous Marshall
home on Long Island to ply her tuning fork.

In the music room of her luxurious mansion, Mrs Marshall is instructing a
team of hopeful debutantes in the ramifications of 'The Family Tree' of the
Marshalls of which they all yearn to become a fashionable part. Irene is hard
at work underneath the Steinway when a young man enters the room and is
hi-jacked to hand her the tools. They strike up a conversation and Irene is
soon telling young Donald Marshall—for it is he—of her business ambitions. It's difficult for a girl to get started and almost impossible to make your
way in Fifth Avenue dressed in Ninth Avenue clothes ('Alice Blue Gown').

When Irene discovers that she's blathering her mouth away to the heir of
the house, she is mortified, but she is still game to offer him a few basic
pointers out of her library book on a merger he is about to sign. Donald is
very taken by this enterprising lass and impetuously decides to help her out.
He will have all the seven pianos scattered around the mansion tuned.

When Irene has hurried off to begin making her fortune, Donald is
bearded by his cousin Ozzie who wants to interest him in another of his
perennial scatterbrained business propositions. Ozzie's latest project is a
couturier called Madame Lucy who is looking for backing to set up a New
York salon. He isn't able to supply the financial details of the Madame Lucy
set up, but he has brought Madame Lucy along to the house in person.
Madame Lucy turns out to be a middle-aged Irishman, hiding for business

purposes under the nom de needle of a Parisian lady. He has little money but a fine line in self-publicity and he is soon describing floridly how 'They Go Wild, Simply Wild, Over Me'. His flow gets a slight staunching when Donald's mother, who knows every couturier in Paris, denies all knowledge of a fashion house called Madame Lucy and he is obliged to admit that he is not a Parisian at all but a boy from West Brooklyn.

Donald is about to bid Ozzie and his protégé a firm adieu when Irene returns to find her jacket and an idea strikes him. He will back Madame Lucy in a New York salon as long as he can put Irene into the firm as business manager. Irene is staggered at her good luck—it is the luck of 'An Irish Girl' surely—and she hurries home to break her news to her friends, Helen and Jane, to whom she will be able to offer jobs as mannequins, and to her mother who has decided misgivings about the sort of men with whom Irene may come in contact in such a wicked, up-market part of town.

When Madame Lucy meets Helen and Jane he is aghast. It will take a miracle to make mannequins out of these ugly ducklings, and he hasn't much time. He must be ready to show his clothes at a society ball only a week away, and a week is not much time to make these two into 'The Talk of The Town'.

Back on Ninth Avenue, Mrs O'Dare takes a little beer (for her nerves) with her friend Mrs McFudd and worries over Irene. Who is this Donald that she is talking about? If Madame Lucy is a man, is Donald a girl, and, if not, what are his intentions? But Irene has not been corrupted by Fifth Avenue. Home and 'Mother, Angel, Darling' still come first, and her first week's wages have gone to buy her mother an extravagant hat which sends Mrs O'Dare into ecstasies in which, for once, Liam O'Dougherty doesn't get a mention.

The society ball at the Hotel Astor arrives quickly and Madame Lucy's gowns go on display for the first time. Irene is there looking wonderful, beautifully dressed and passed off as the Contessa Irena Odari, and Donald finds his mind wandering in an unaccustomed way ('I Can Dream, Can't I?'). Helen and Jane are cast as an English county belle and a Russian vamp, and play their roles to the hilt.

Irene supports her Italian identity by making up a dance which is supposed to be the latest continental fashion ('The Riviera Rage') and wins the unqualified approval of Mrs Marshall who is delighted to see this gorgeous Continental aristocrat dancing with Donald and all agog to know from where she gets her clothes. When she hears that the Contessa has come all the way from Roma solely to purchase a new wardrobe from the same Madame Lucy she so recently scorned, she insists that this famous couturier give a showing of his collection at her grand charity ball the following week.

Donald is delighted. The business is prospering promisingly and he and Irene can look forward to a fine future, shoulder to shoulder promoting their venture. Irene is quite keen on the shoulder to shoulder bit, but she would really like Donald to think of her as other than a business associate and when he fails to take the hint she pours out her disappointment to the night which should have seen her greatest triumph ('I'm Always Chasing Rainbows').

ACT 2

Irene has left the ball by the time the 'Last Part of Every Party' is being wound up. Helen, Jane, Madame Lucy and Ozzie are happily celebrating their success ('We're Getting Away With It') when Donald arrives with the distressing news that, for no reason that he can understand, Irene has resigned from the salon. He must get her back—for purely business reasons of course.

Irene is sitting at home on Ninth Avenue feeling sorry for herself ('Castle of Dreams') when Donald comes looking for her. He gets carried far enough away from business to sing to her ('Irene') and even kiss her, before pulling himself up short. Irene is exasperated beyond endurance by his continual hiding behind a businesslike approach and finally he leaves, exasperated in his turn by her incomprehensible, feminine ways. Instead of hearing more loving words from Donald, she has to make do with the appreciation of the local boys in a massed reprise of 'Irene'.

In order not to let down Madame Lucy, Irene agrees to make one last appearance as the Contessa at Mrs Marshall's charity ball. After that she's sticking safely to Ninth Avenue and piano tuning. Jane and Helen have no such scruples: they are delighted with life 'Up There on Park Avenue', but their secret is proving a leaky one. Mrs McFudd has seen a photo of the Contessa Odari in an illustrated magazine, and she hurries to tell Mrs O'Dare about the amazing resemblance between the dazzling society lady and her own Irene. When Mrs O'Dare stumbles on Irene's invitation to the ball and a note from Mrs Marshall addressed to the Contessa—'You have quite seduced my poor Donald'—the whole thing is only too clear. Seduced! A mother's hand is clearly needed. Here is an invitation fallen by Heaven's grace into her hands, so Mrs O'Dare is going to use it. She is going to this here shindig herself.

At the ball, Jane and Helen decide that, for Irene's sake, it is time Donald was shaken out of his stuffed shirt. They woo his secret from him: having once been rejected by a young lady, he is convinced that his attentions are not welcome to the fair sex. Whisking off his glasses, the girls teach him how to dance 'The Great Lover Tango'. Now he can approach Irene. Although he doesn't know it, that is exactly what his mother wants him to do, even if she is under the impression that the young lady is an Italian Contessa. She is also under the impression that Mrs O'Dare is an Italian Contessa's mother and she treats her unexpected guest to champagne and a lot of gushing remarks about love levelling all ranks.

Donald finds Irene and lays his heart at her feet ('You Made Me Love You') and she happily picks it up while Madame Lucy arrives with his models and, to his amazement, encounters Mrs O'Dare. She is his little Geraldine whom he loved and lost, and he is, of course, her long-lost Liam O'Dougherty. 'You Made Me Love You' suits their position just as it suited Irene and Donald.

Now Madame Lucy's fashion parade begins. The gorgeous gowns are paraded before Mrs Marshall's delighted guests until Irene provides the climax to the show in a dazzling blue cloaked creation. When she has received her applause, Donald leads Irene forward and, removing the cloak, introduces his intended wife as Miss Irene O'Dare from Ninth Avenue with whom he fell in love when she sang to him of the little dress she is now wearing—her sweet little 'Alice Blue Gown'.

The original *Irene*, which cast its heroine as a shop girl turned mannequin and had her involved with the ambitious J P Bowden prior to her happy ending with Donald Marshall, had a smaller basic score of thirteen songs including several which were not used in this revised version: 'Hobbies', 'To Be Worthy of You', 'To Love You', 'Sky Rocket', 'There's Something in the Air' and 'You've Got Me Out on a Limb'.

The 1945 London revival introduced two new numbers, 'Down Town East of Broadway' and 'Lucy' by Noel Gay as well as the uncredited 'The Broadway Jitterbug' and 'Bowden'. The 1973 Broadway revival introduced 'This Dear Lady' as well as the other Clements/Gaynor songs listed in this synopsis, and several successful Joseph McCarthy songs to music by composers other than Tierney. An Australian production added 'Up There on Park Avenue' which subsequently appeared in the London version of the show, along with a new number, 'If He Only Knew' (Michael Reed/Norman Newell), which replaced 'Castle of Dreams', and 'I Can Dream, Can't I?' (Sammy Fain/Irving Kahn).

SALLY

a musical comedy in two acts by Guy Bolton. Lyrics by Clifford Grey. Additional lyrics by P G Wodehouse, B G DeSylva and Anne Caldwell. Music by Jerome Kern. Ballet music by Victor Herbert. Produced at the New Amsterdam Theatre, New York, 21 December 1920 with Marilyn Miller (Sally), Leon Errol (Connie), Walter Catlett (Otis), Irving Fisher (Blair) and Mary Hay (Rosalind). Produced at the Martin Beck Theatre 6 May 1948 in a revised version with Bambi Linn, Willie Howard, Jack Goode, Robert Shackleton and Kay Buckley.

Produced at the Winter Garden Theatre, London, 10 September 1921 with Dorothy Dickson, Leslie Henson, George Grossmith, Gregory Stroud and Heather Thatcher. Produced at the Prince's Theatre 6 August 1942 in a revised version by Frank Eyton and Richard Hearne as *Wild Rose* with Jessie Matthews, André Randall, Hearne, Frank Leighton and Elsie Percival.

Film versions were produced by First National in 1925 with Colleen Moore, Lloyd Hughes and Leon Errol and in 1930 with Marilyn Miller, Joe E Brown, T Roy Barnes and Lawrence Gray.

CHARACTERS

Otis Hooper *of the Anglo-American Vaudeville Agency, Squantumville*
Constantine, *Grand Duke of Czechogovinia*
'Pops' Shendorff, *proprietor of the Alley Inn, New York*
Sally Green *of the Alley, a foundling*

Sascha Commiski, *violinist at the Alley*
Mrs Ten Brock, *a Settlement worker*
Jimmie Spelvin
Rosalind Rafferty
Blair Farquar, *an only son*
Richard Farquar
Admiral Travers, Alta, Betty, Billie, Gladys, Janet, Emily, Bessie, Violet, Cissie, Audrey, Rhoda, Mamie, Billy Porter, Harry Barton, etc.

ACT 1

The Alley Inn is a little Bohemian restaurant tucked away in a corner of New York where folks go for a lively evening knowing that they aren't likely to be seen by their friends ('In the Night Time'). Amongst the diners there tonight is Otis Hooper from Squantumville, Maine, a wise-cracking would-be dude out for the evening with his girl, Rosie, and determined not to be impressed by New York. Why, New York doesn't have anything that Squantumville doesn't and, in the matter of dance steps, he is ready and willing to prove it ('On With the Dance!').

The proprietor of the Alley Inn is 'Pops' Shendorff, an immigrant from the troubled European state of Czechogovinia and, unbeknown to the world at large, Pops has employed as a waiter no less a personage than his country's former ruler, the Grand Duke Constantine, himself a penniless refugee from the revolution which tumbled him from his throne. The Grand Duke Constantine, familiarly known in this land of opportunity as Connie, is not a very good waiter; in fact he's plumb awful at his job and Pops finds himself grinding his teeth over the broken dishes one minute and regally saluting his monarch-in-exile the next.

One of the many problems of having a Grand Duke as a waiter is that he is not always inclined to follow the rules of the establishment. This Grand Duke refuses, for example, to wash the dishes and therefore Pops has been obliged to hire additional help. In his search for a dish washer he has turned to the society dame, Mrs Ten Brock, a tireless worker in the cause of charity and particularly in the field of settling orphan girls in employment. Mrs Ten Brock brings a half-dozen girls to the Inn and Pops chooses one called Sally Green. Sally isn't at all thrilled with her first job. Joan of Arc never had to wash dishes, and neither did Mary Pickford nor Charlotte Corday, and she has ambitions to be like them ('You Can't Keep a Good Girl Down'). Still, it's a start and she can always rise.

Connie requires this Thursday off. On Thursday he is to be the guest of honour at a party given at the home of the very rich and very influential Richard Farquar and for the occasion he will doff his apron and don his grand ducal regalia to become, once again, a social lion. He is a little fazed when he finds that one of the evening's guests at the Alley Inn is Blair Farquar, his host's son, but Blair's eye alights on Sally and the bumbling waiter is quite forgotten as the young man encourages the pretty waitress to look forward to a quick improvement in her lot ('Look for the Silver Lining').

What Sally really wants to be is a dancer. She would love to appear in the Alley Inn's cabaret, and Connie promises that he will use his influence to get her a chance. Of course, the cabaret would only be a starting point—Sally's real dream is to star in the Follies and to be incredibly famous. The person who knows all about famous dancers is Otis Hooper. He has just earned himself a thousand dollars by booking the notorious Russian dancer Mamzelle Nockerova to appear at Richard Farquar's party and he is cock-a-hoop over his cleverness. Mamzelle Nockerova is the Lola Montez of the age. She has left a train of dented crowns all across Europe, been the cause of the deposition of more than one amorous monarch, and she is quite sure to cause a sensation on Thursday.

While Otis and Connie go through a selection of waiter routines and comedy backchat, Blair is gathering up his gentlemen friends to come and have a look at 'Sally', the little girl with whom he thinks he might just be beginning to fall in love, but the conversation between Otis and Connie is brought to a full stop when an embarrassing telephone call comes: Mamzelle Nockerova has been prevented from boarding her trans-Atlantic ship—she will not arrive in time for the all-important performance. As Otis subsides in a fit of 'Nerves', Pops comes out on the stage to announce the cabaret, with Sally featured in first place. Her dancing has Blair on his feet, but no one is quicker to her side at the end of the performance than Otis. He has a job to offer her. She must disguise herself in Mamzelle Nockerova's costumes and take the star's place at the big party (Finale). Sally excitedly agrees, and there are stars in her eyes as she washes up the dishes at the end of the evening.

ACT 2
The party at Richard Farquar's house is a splendid one ('The Social Game') and all the guests have dressed up in Czechogovinian national costume to honour the real specimen of old world royalty whom they are to meet. When Sally arrives, done up exquisitely as Mamzelle Nockerova, with Rosie as her maid, Otis as her manager and Sascha, the violinist from the Alley Inn, as her accompanist, the Farquars and their friends rush to make such a celebrated personality welcome. There is a nasty moment when Sally comes face to face with Mrs Ten Brock and something about washing dishes slips accidentally into the conversation, but Otis hurries the lady off leaving Sally to the attentions of the gentlemen of the party to whom she confides that she is no primrose but a very 'Wild Rose'.

The Duke has the attentions of all the ladies, particularly Mrs Ten Brock to whom, on account of her height (easy to see in a crowd) and her millions (no comment), he is inordinately attracted. His evening away from the Alley Inn looks like being spoiled, however, when he hears that Mamzelle Nockerova is present at the party. Alas, that notorious creature is the cause of all his troubles. He is the last Grand Duke whom she toppled. She is the woman for whom he pawned the crown jewels of Czechogovinia to buy a pearl necklace beyond price and who leapt from his bedroom window clad in nothing but her silk underwear and the famous pearls as the revolutionaries broke down the door of his palace. She swam the river 'Schnitza-Komisski' and vanished, and never since that day have they seen each other again.

Blair has been struck with the incredible likeness between the belle of the evening's ball and the little girl at the Alley Inn, and he is soon confusedly courting Sally both as herself and as the glamorous society danseuse. Otis is highly amused to see her making such a conquest of the allegedly vamp-proof Blair ('The Lorelei') but he is less amused when he discovers that the guest of honour actually knows the real Nockerova and knows her rather intimately.

The charade seems doomed, but when Connie is introduced to Sally he plays up and plays the game, greeting her fulsomely as the balletic Russian. Otis can breathe again and start making plans for a life of success and an occasion with Rosie at 'The Church 'Round the Corner'. But things cannot yet run smoothly. Blair is aghast when he hears that the woman for whom he feels such a tender passion is the notorious Mamzelle Nockerova, a woman who ruined the life of one of his dearest friends. He spurns Sally bitterly and when she tries to tell him that she is not the wretched Russian he will not believe her.

When she calls on her friends to back her up, they all continue eagerly to support her false identity, and Blair leaves the party is disgust (Finale). In distress, Sally refuses to continue the impersonation and declares in front of Farquar that she is a dishwasher from the Alley Inn. She is still prepared to dance for them but, now that they know she is not a scandalous seductress from Siberia, the society folk are no longer interested in her dancing. Connie comes to her aid and, as the guests return to their party, he takes Sally home.

ACT 3

There can't be too much wrong with the business acumen of folks from Squantumville, because before the curtain goes up on the final act Otis has managed to get Sally away from her dish-washing and into a starring role at the Follies. She performs the Butterfly Ballet to an adoring audience and, at the end of the performance, the boys of the town crowd into her dressing room with messages of devotion. But Sally wants devotion from only one man and he is not there.

Blair has written to apologise for his behaviour at the party, but she has responded in unforgiving terms and she is afraid that she may have put him off for good. When there is a knock at the door her hopes rise, but the visitor is only Connie. While she changes out of her costume behind a screen, she tells Connie what her heart truly feels for Blair and she does not know that Connie has quietly opened the dressing room door to let in another visitor. When Sally pops her head over the screen, she sees not Connie but Blair facing her, and when he asks her to marry him it is only logical that they should happily move into a reprise of 'The Church 'Round the Corner'. Of course she will.

The 1948 revival included two songs, 'The Siren Song' and 'Cleopatterer', taken from *Leave it to Jane*, as well as 'Down Here in Greenwich Village', 'A Bungalow in Quogue', 'Looking All Over for You, 'Tulip Time in Sing Sing', 'Dear Little Girl', 'Reaching for the Stars' and the Whipoorwill Waltz.

NO, NO, NANETTE

a musical comedy in three acts by Frank Mandel, Otto Harbach and Irving Caesar based on *My Lady Friends* by Mandel and 'Emile Nyitray' and *Oh James!* by May Edgington. Music by Vincent Youmans. Produced at the Garrick Theatre, Detroit, 23 April 1923 and the Harris Theatre, Chicago, 7 May 1923 with Phyllis Cleveland (replaced by Louise Groody) (Nanette), Skeets Gallagher (replaced by Charles Winninger) (Jimmy), Francis X Donegan (replaced by Bernard Granville) (Billy), Anna Wheaton (succeeded by Blanche Ring) (Lucille) and Juliette Day (Sue). Produced at the Globe Theatre, New York, 16 September 1925 with Louise Groody, Charles Winninger, Wellington Cross, Josephine Whittell and Eleanor Dawn. Produced at the Forty-sixth Street Theatre 17 January 1971 in a revised version with Susan Watson, Jack Gilford, Bobby Van, Helen Gallagher and Ruby Keeler.

Produced at the Palace Theatre, London, 11 March 1925 with Binnie Hale, Joseph Coyne, George Grossmith, Irene Browne and Marie Hemingway. Produced at the London Hippodrome 8 July 1936 with Barbara Vernon, Shaun Glenville, Clifford Mollison, Phyllis Monkman and Maidie Andrews. Produced at the Theatre Royal, Drury Lane in a revised version 16 May 1973 with Barbara Brown, Tony Britton, Teddy Green, Anne Rogers and Anna Neagle.

Produced at the Théâtre Mogador, Paris, 29 April 1926 in a version by Roger Ferréol, Robert de Simone, Paul Colline and Georges Merry with Loulou Hégoburu, Félix Oudart, Cariel, Gabrielle Ristori and Fernande Albany. Revived there 4 November 1930, 16 May 1935, 16 March 1946 with Claudine Cereda, Robert Allard, Edmond Castel and Arlette Guttinguer, and 18 December 1965 with Cathy Albert, Jean-Marie Proslier, Jean-Louis Simon, Micheline Bourday and Danielle Grima.

Produced at the Metropoltheater, Berlin, 7 November 1926.

A film version was produced by Warner Brothers in 1930 with Alexander Gray, Bernice Claire and Zasu Pitts. A second film was produced by RKO in 1940 with Anna Neagle, Victor Mature and Miss Pitts and a third, under the title *Tea for Two*, using only a little of the original score supplemented by numbers by Youmans and other composers, was produced by Warner Brothers in 1950 with Gene Nelson and Doris Day.

CHARACTERS

Jimmy Smith, *a New York bible publisher*
Sue Smith, *his wife*
Nanette, *their protegée*
Billy Early, *a lawyer*
Lucille Early, *his wife*
Tom Trainor, *their nephew*

Pauline, *the Smiths' cook*
Betty
Winnie
Flora, etc.

ACT 1

Jimmy Smith has done very well out of the bible. From humble beginnings he has worked up a publishing business worth a good deal of money, principally from his dealings in the good book. He has been helped in his climb to the heights of bankability by the modest and well-regulated spending habits of his loving wife, Sue, who keeps his lovely home immaculate with the help of just one servant. At the moment (but not for much longer) that extremely demanding position is held by a lady called Pauline who is not at all fond of her parsimonious and eagle-eyed mistress. She does, however, like Mr Smith and, most particularly, Miss Nanette. Nanette is not strictly family. She is the orphaned daughter of friends of Sue's, whom Sue has brought up in the most irreproachable fashion to have all the virtues necessary to be a good wife to a good man.

Sue's strict ideas are, however, a little binding on the girl, and Nanette sometimes yearns to have some of the freedoms her friends have. When the show opens, some of those friends have come to the house ('Flappers Are We'), hoping to persuade Nanette to spend the weekend with them at the seaside where Jimmy has a cottage. Predictably, Sue will not hear of Nanette going away anywhere with girls who rouge and smoke, even when Billy Early, Jimmy's friend and lawyer, goes into raptures about the attractions of 'The Call of the Sea'.

Billy's wife Lucille is Sue's best friend, but she is as unlike Sue as can be. When she puts in an appearance at the Smith house, she is sporting an extravagant new dress and she is not ashamed to say that she has been shopping, spending money that Billy hasn't yet earned. It is part of her philosophy of marriage. She has too often seen in the newspapers tales of faithful wives whose husbands spent their money on gaudier women and she has no intention of going that way. She wants the whole attention of her husband and, although the men may gather to appreciate the effect she makes, she returns the compliment and remains totally true to her Billy ('Too Many Rings Around Rosie').

Although Nanette has not been out in the world, she has met one young man. He is Billy's assistant, Tom Trainor. Tom has honourable intentions towards Nanette, but he is a bit of a stick. It takes time and encouragement before he can confess his love to her ('I've Confessed to the Breeze') and he is horrified when Nanette tells him that she wants to raise a little hell before she settles down.

Jimmy Smith arrives happily home and soon begins a familiar conversation with Sue. He would love her to go out and spend some of the money that he has made over the years on pretty things for herself, but a care for money has become ingrained in Sue and she cannot do it. Lucille points out Jimmy's willing free-handedness as an example to the ever-complaining Billy, but Billy, in return, is quick to support the validity of Sue's soundly reasoned replies. When Sue won't spend his money, Jimmy relieves a little of the frustration by giving twenty pounds to Nanette to go on a shopping spree, and he is delighted at the joy it gives her ('I Want to Be Happy').

It isn't the first time he's done this. The earlier occasions have been a little further from home and now he needs to talk to his lawyer about it. His generosity and his wish to see pretty little girls happy have led to his opening charge accounts at expensive stores for Betty whom he met on a railway station, Winnie who has literary ambitions, and buxom widowed Flora. It has all gone a bit far, and now he needs to put an end to the extravagant use those girls are making of their opportunities. To that end he offers Billy a fee, which will pay all Lucille's bills, to fix everything up and tactfully remove the girls from his life. Poor Jimmy. Even his latest gift causes trouble when Tom finds Nanette going out to spend her money. When she refuses to tell him where she came by the cash and resents being interrogated by him about her every step ('No, No, Nanette'), they end up quarrelling.

That is only the beginning of a series of suspicions in the Smith house. Flora telephones and Jimmy goes into a spasm of guilt. She is coming to town. He must get out quickly. Overheard snippets of conversation, the unfortunate phone call and a naturally suspicious mind set Lucille wondering whether Jimmy and Billy are not up to something. She finally leads Sue into sharing her suspicions and, when Jimmy makes bumbling excuses for suddenly going away, Sue decides that Lucille's suggestion of a private detective should perhaps, be followed.

Billy decides he will make a beginning to his new assignment by setting off to visit the respective homes of Betty, Winnie and Flora to inform them that their credit has been terminated. Jimmy, in his turn, will head for the seaside cottage where he ought to be safely out of the way, but he can't resist one extra kindness. Nanette has never been to the seaside: very well, she shall come with him. The girl is over the moon, and even turns down a dinner engagement with the repentant Tom ('No, No, Nanette') to rush away for her secret weekend, as Pauline mumbles something about a useful grandmother.

ACT 2

Nanette's first day at the seaside looks like being a lot of fun ('A Peach on the Beach'), and Jimmy is enjoying seeing her enjoying it while, equally, doing his best to lie low, waiting out of town until all his little embarrassments have been paid off. What he doesn't know is that Billy's firm has apparently sent out telegrams to the three young ladies with whom he is supposed to be settling, telling them to come to the cottage. Betty is the first to arrive, and she is draping herself all over the embarrassed Jimmy when Winnie turns up and gets highly indignant. Both of them have assumed that the generosity Jimmy has shown must one day require a return, but both are staggered to find that they are not the only one on the list and they go heavily into competition to win back their vanishing Sugar Daddy. Jimmy can only gasp pleasantly 'Fight Over Me'.

When Billy turns up it transpires that he has never sent any telegrams and a dreadful suspicion enters his lawyer's mind. Perhaps Lucille and Sue are on their tracks. He is staggered to find Nanette there, but much less staggered than Tom who has to be appeased by a glib little tale assuring him that his beloved certainly has not spent a night alone with a married man in a seaside cottage but with her grandmother down the coast. Then, and only then, can they indulge in another picturesque little duet imagining the bliss of a private 'Tea for Two'.

Lucille is the next to arrive and the web of pretence gets thicker and thicker as Billy wildly dreams up corroborative details for the conflicting stories that have already been set in motion. Lucille, unfortunately, has procured undeniable evidence of Jimmy's philanderings for she has met Flora. Flora didn't come to the seaside. She turned up at the Smith home, luckily while Sue was out, and informed Lucille that she was there to marry Jimmy Smith. Lucille's answer was to direct her to the cottage and, at the same time, to join the general exodus to the seaside herself to find out what is going on.

The red-faced Billy goes into some quick talking to exonerate himself from any suspicions of straying, and he gets a sharp warning from his wife as to just how far he may go with his shenanigans ('You Can Dance With Any Girl at All'). Whatever else he is, however, Billy is quick-witted. While Flora and the other two lovely vampires are reminding Jimmy pressingly of his oft-expressed wishes to see them happy, Billy comes up with a grand trick. He tells the girls that Jimmy has turned all his money over to his wife. Either they take the generous severance offer he is making them and depart, or they get nothing.

The girls are busy taking out their disappointment on Billy when who should walk in but Sue. Mistaking the situation, she assumes that the girls are Billy's little indiscretions and that the dreadful tales she has heard of Jimmy's flirtations are, in fact, his friend's faults. Billy has been marauding under Jimmy's name.

The girls, seeing that they must keep up this fiction if they are to get their money, join in the pretence enthusiastically, but what is Sue's horror when the girls tell her that there is a fourth little lady at the cottage...Nanette. As misunderstandings and subterfuges rise in a dizzying vortex, Billy finds himself damned as a philanderer before his horrified wife and Jimmy, silencing his friend's qualms with the contents of his wallet, assumes a position as the moral hero of the moment as it is agreed that everyone shall stay at the cottage until the situation is sorted out.

ACT 3
Billy cannot get Lucille to talk to him on the phone to make his peace ('Hello, Hello, Telephone Girlie'), but he has no time to paddle in his puddle of self pity, for Betty, Winnie and Flora have all decided that things

are getting too hot at the seaside and they are anxious for the lawyer to finalise their settlement and let them go home. Sue, still believing Billy the guilty party, takes the part of the 'injured' girls, and keeps stoking the settlements up higher without realising what she is doing.

Lucille is having a *crise*. She is ranting against Billy on the one hand and, on the other, she is horribly upset that she may be losing him ('Where Has My Hubby Gone Blues'), but when she comes into conversation with the girls her eyes are quickly opened: how could her Billy spend money on these girls? He doesn't have any! It is only a quick step from there for her to learn that the real Sugar Daddy is Jimmy, and another for her to bring the horrid news to Sue. But Betty, Flora and Winnie, who have no qualms about squeezing Billy and Lucille if necessary, have a soft spot for Jimmy and for his suddenly woebegone wife, and they come through with some truth and some advice for Sue. Jimmy has used them to spend the money his wife wouldn't spend, to get them dolled up in the way his wife wouldn't. If she wants him to stay at home, she must let him spend his money at home.

So, after Nanette and Tom have sketched in a little more of their now-I-believe-you-now-I-don't love affair, and Nanette and Billy have managed to twist the scene to allow them to dance a number together ('Take a Little One-Step'), Sue makes an appearance dressed up to the nines. Jimmy hears her on the phone, extravagantly spending thousands on houses, cars, jewellery and clothes, and is horrified but Sue tells him that, since she must spend his money—their money—or see it spent by a succession of girls, she will spend it herself.

But Sue loves her Jimmy and she cannot punish him for long, and soon all is put to rights. Before long Betty, Winnie and Flora are hustled back to whence they came, and Sue and Lucille are back in their husbands' arms. It only remains for Nanette to square herself and her various stories with the stiff-necked Tom. When he asks her if she is able to swear to being a good woman she tells him she cannot. She admits to having taken twenty pounds as a gift from a married man. Until that money is repaid, he insists, it is impossible for them to be honourably united. Jimmy has the answer. He produces twenty pounds which he lends to Tom and then demands its return as the money taken from him by Nanette. The quickness of the event defeats any reasoning and enables everyone to line up and remind themselves one last time that 'I Want To Be Happy'.

The original Chicago production of *No, No, Nanette* underwent considerable changes including the cutting and introduction of numerous numbers. Neither 'Tea for Two' nor 'I Want to Be Happy' featured in the first night score but were added during the run along with 'I'm Waiting for You' (Tom & Nanette). The London version of the show added the songs 'I've Confessed to the Breeze' and 'Take a Little One-Step'. On Broadway, 'Who's the Who?' (Lucille), 'Pay Day Pauline' (Pauline, Jimmy, Billy) and 'My Doctor' (Pauline) were all included in the score although the last named was subsequently cut.

THE STUDENT PRINCE

a musical play in two acts by Dorothy Donnelly based on *Old Heidelberg* by Rudolf Bleichman, a version of *Alt Heidelberg* by Wilhelm Meyer-Forster. Lyrics by Dorothy Donnelly. Music by Sigmund Romberg. Produced at Jolson's Theatre, New York, 2 December 1924 with Howard Marsh (Karl-Franz), Ilse Marvenga (Kathie), Greek Evans (Engel), Raymond Marlowe (Detlef), Roberta Beatty (Margaret), John Coast (Tarnitz) and George Hassell (Lutz). Played at the Majestic Theatre 29 January 1931 with Edward Nell jr, Elizabeth Gergely, Hollis Davenny and Adolf Link (Toni) and at the Broadway Theatre 8 June 1943 with Frank Hornaday and Barbara Scully. Produced at the New York City Opera 29 August 1980 with Jacque Trussell, Leigh Munro, Dominic Cossa, John Lankston, Kathryn Bouleyn and James Billings.

Produced at His Majesty's Theatre, London, 3 February 1926 with Allan Prior, Miss Marvenga, Herbert Waterous, Marlowe, Lucienne Dervyle, Coast and Oscar Figman. Produced at the Piccadilly Theatre 7 November 1929 with Donald Mather (Karl-Franz), Stella Brown (Kathie), Marie Burke (Margaret), John Coast (Tarnitz) and Florence Desmond as Gretchen, and at the Stoll Theatre 23 May 1944 with Bruce Trent and Marion Gordon. Produced at the Cambridge Theatre 8 June 1968 with John Hanson and Barbara Strathdee.

Produced in Berlin 1932.

Film versions were produced by MGM in 1927 with Ramon Novarro and Norma Shearer and in 1954 with Edmund Purdom (sung by Mario Lanza) and Ann Blyth.

CHARACTERS

Prince Karl-Franz *of Karlsberg*
Dr Engel, *his tutor*
Count von Mark, *Prime Minister*
Lutz
Hubert
Josef Ruder, *proprietor of the Inn of the Three Golden Apples*
Gretchen, *a serving girl*
Toni, *a waiter*
Detlef, Von Asterberg, Lucas, *students*
Kathie, *Ruder's niece*
Princess Margaret
Grand Duchess Anastasia
Captain Tarnitz, etc.

ACT 1

The scene is the palace of Karlsberg ('By Our Bearing So Sedate'). The young Prince Karl-Franz, grandson of the present aged King, has completed his education by successfully passing the entrance examination for Heidelberg University and preparations are being made for him to take up his place there for one year prior to assuming his responsibilities of state. The Prime Minister, von Mark, has arranged that his long-time tutor, Dr Engel, will go with the boy ostensibly to help him find his way in the city but,

583

in reality, to keep him under surveillance. Engel, after years at the palace of Karlsberg, is only too happy to return to the happy scenes of his youth ('Golden Days'), although he does not relish the role of royal spy.

It has been decided that the Prince will live during his stay in Heidelberg at Dr Engel's old lodgings at the Inn of the Three Golden Apples, and his valet, the self-important Honourable Johann Heinrich Peter Lutz, has been sent on ahead with the page, Hubert, to prepare his rooms. Lutz is not likely to be impressed by an inn, and less so by one which is noisily frequented by beer-drinking, hard-singing students ('To the Inn We're Marching').

The day of his arrival being the first day of term, the students are celebrating particularly cheerfully (Drinking Song) and pouring out their good humour and their admiration for Kathie, the personable waitress of the establishment ('I'm Coming at Your Call'). She is happy enough to encourage their preference for play over work ('Come Boys, Let's All Be Gay, Boys') as the boys of the Saxon fraternity vote her the unchallenged German equivalent of Queen of the May.

Lutz is determined that the Prince shall have nothing to do with this tawdry hostelry but, before he can do anything to stop the planned course of events, the Prince's carriage is announced and the welcome flowers and song prepared for him by Kathie ('In Heidelberg Fair') have gone into action. The Prince is delighted by his first view of life outside Karlsberg Castle, of the sounds and sight of student revelry ('Gaudeamus Igitur') and of the lovely Kathie, so Lutz has little chance of persuading him that the inn is not good enough. As Engel stays to refresh his happy memories ('Golden Days'), Karl-Franz meets firstly the student leader Detlef who invites him to join the Saxon Corps and then Kathie who strikes a chord in his heart which leaves them singing happily together of love ('Deep in My Heart').

As the finale to the act begins, the students crowd round the newcomer to learn whether he has made his choice of fraternity ('Come, Sir, Will You Join Our Noble Saxon Corps') and Dr Engel introduces the boy to his new comrades. He will not be a Prince here, just a student and plain Karl-Franz, with all the thirsts that a student has for beer, knowledge and girls. To the strains of the Drinking Song, the Prince responds with an old Heidelberg serenade ('Overhead the Moon Is Beaming') as the act ends in joyful celebration of the coming of spring ('The Carnival of Springtime').

ACT 2

The Prince takes happily to his new life under the very indulgent eye of Dr Engel and the disapproving but impotent sighs of Lutz. The valet takes it on himself to sit up all night waiting martyr-like for his master's return but he is not averse to flirting with the serving girl, Gretchen, when no one is looking. Karl-Franz's first all-night inn crawl ends happily back at the Three Golden Apples with the students still drinking and still singing ('Student Life') until their energy runs out, but it proves to have been an ill-timed escapade. To the horror of Lutz, the Prince has unexpected visitors: the Grand Duchess Anastasia and her daughter, the Princess Margaret, to whom Karl-Franz has been betrothed by the wish of his dynastically-minded grandfather and government.

Lutz holds the dragonistic Duchess at bay while Karl-Franz effects a swift wash and brush-up before being introduced for the first time to the woman whom he is to marry. Their interview is pleasant but formal, but no sooner has the royal party departed than Karl-Franz is struck with a kind of panic. Princess Margaret represents everything from which he has escaped: the gloomy halls of Karlsberg Castle, the feeling of compunction and of imprisonment which contrasts so terribly with the wonderful freedom he has experienced in his brief time in Heidelberg.

Impulsively he calls to Kathie. He is in love with her and she with him and they must flee from Heidelberg and the sphere of influence of Karlsberg to a place where they can be happy together. They will go to Paris this very moment. Kathie rushes off to pack, but she is preparing for a journey which will never take place. Prime Minister von Mark is at the door with severe news. The King is dying and Karl-Franz must return to Karlsberg immediately so that he can be officially betrothed to Margaret before the King breathes his last.

Karl-Franz tries to resist. He has only just begun to live as a man. He was promised a year of freedom and already he is being dragged back to the strait-jacket of kingship. But even his dear Dr Engel is on von Mark's side. Karl-Franz has a duty not only as a king but as a grandson and he must return to the side of the dying King ('Come, Your Time Is Short'). When Kathie returns full of excitement and ready to take the Paris train ('We're Off to Paris'), she is met with sad and serious faces. Karl-Franz promises that as soon as he can he will return, but the girl is wise enough to know better as she bids a fond farewell to the Prince she loves ('Thoughts Will Come to Me').

Two years have passed. Karl-Franz is King of Karlsberg and still unwed for he has found the excuse of court mourning sufficient to delay his official betrothal to Margaret. The Princess, in the meanwhile, has accepted very obviously the attentions of the dashing Captain Tarnitz ('Just We Two') and the Duchess and the politicians are worried and not a little annoyed at the delay in the cementing of this important marriage. The time eventually comes when it seems the King can no longer avoid this particular responsibility. He has already agreed to an imminent marriage when Toni, the little waiter from the Three Golden Apples, appears at court.

Far from being angry at Toni's holding him to a laughing promise that he should one day be a king's butler, Karl-Franz is delighted to see again someone from those few happy months spent in Heidelberg. In two years no one else has made any contact. But Toni brings sad news. The Three Golden Apples is not what it was. Detlef has married a Professor's daughter, von Asterberg and Lucas have become instructors themselves—they are joyous students no longer. Ruder and the inn have fallen on hard times and Toni has lost his job. Only Gretchen, who inherited some money from a wealthy relative, is prosperous and she is about to buy the inn from Ruder.

And Kathie? Kathie is still there, but she is no more the blithe Kathie of earlier days. She is still unmarried, but she no longer dances gaily with the students; she merely weeps alone in her room. Toni's description tugs at the King's heart as he thinks back to those happiest days of his life ('What Memories') and suddenly his resolution is made. He will, he must go back just once to Heidelberg.

As before, Lutz goes ahead to announce the King's coming and, incidentally, to renew his acquaintance with the now wealthy Gretchen. His condescension gets its reward when the forthright Gretchen rejects him roundly and tells him she is to be married to his page, Hubert. Before Karl-Franz can arrive, the inn has another visitor, Princess Margaret. In spite of her overt flirtation with Tarnitz, Margaret is, and has been ever since that first curious meeting, in love with the man whom politics have dictated should be her husband. She understands his unhappiness and she has come to ask Kathie to be noble enough to lift the burden of his wishes and promises from Karl-Franz's heart.

Although there is no doubt that the love between the two of them is as strong as ever, she asks Kathie to go away from Heidelberg and to marry. Then and only then will the King be able to put the possibility of their being together out of his mind forever and make a new beginning in the life he must follow. Kathie realises that Margaret loves the King and her own heart is eased by the thought that Karl-Franz will have a loving wife. She agrees to go and, as the Princess hurriedly leaves at the sound of the approaching students, she says a fond farewell to the scene where she too knew, all too briefly, real happiness.

The students who are singing their way to the Three Golden Apples are not, however, the students of today. They are Detlef, von Asterberg, Lucas and Karl-Franz himself. As the men enter the inn, the two lovers come face to face. Kathie tells the King that she is to go back to her home town to wed the fiancé of her young days and she bids him not to be lonely, for love, in the shape of Margaret, will walk by his side. As the students serenade the King and his future Queen, Karl-Franz and Kathie bid each other goodbye knowing that 'Deep in My Heart' they will always remember each other.

ROSE MARIE

a musical play in two acts by Otto Harbach and Oscar Hammerstein II. Music by Rudolf Friml and Herbert Stothart. Produced at the Imperial Theatre, New York, 2 September 1924 with Mary Ellis (Rose Marie), Dennis King (Jim) and William Kent (Herman).

Produced at the Theatre Royal, Drury Lane, London, 20 March 1925 with Edith Day, Derek Oldham and Billy Merson. Revived there 12 September 1929 with Miss Day, Roy Russell and Gene Gerrard. Produced at the Stoll Theatre 16 July 1942 with Marjorie Brown, Raymond Newell and George Lacy, and at the Victoria Palace 2 August 1960 with Stephanie Voss, David Whitfield and Ronnie Stevens.

Produced at the Théâtre Mogador, Paris, 9 April 1927 in a version by Roger Ferréol and Saint-Granier with Cloé Vidiane/Madeleine Massé, Robert Burnier and Boucot. Revived there 20 January 1930 and 1 June 1939. Produced at the Théâtre du Châtelet, 19 December 1940 with Fanély Revoil and 21 October 1944 with Madeleine Vernon, at the Théâtre de l'Empire in 1947 and again 12 May 1950 with Paulette Merval. Produced at the Théâtre Mogador 23 November 1963 with Paulette Merval and Marcel Merkès and revived there 19 December 1970 with Angelina Cristi and Bernard Sinclair. Produced at the Théâtre de la Porte Saint-Martin 18 February 1981.

Film versions were produced by MGM in 1928 (silent) with Joan Crawford and James Murray; in 1936 with Jeanette MacDonald, Nelson Eddy, Allan Jones, Reginald Owen and James Stewart; and in 1954 with Ann Blyth, Howard Keel, Fernando Lamas, Bert Lahr and Marjorie Main.

CHARACTERS

Émile La Flamme
Rose Marie La Flamme, *his sister*
Jim Kenyon
Lady Jane
Blackeagle
Wanda
Sergeant Malone
Hard-Boiled Herman
Edward Hawley
Ethel Brander
Caretaker, etc.

ACT 1

High in the Canadian mountains, at Fond du Lac, Saskatchewan, the meeting and drinking place for the trappers, hunters and travellers of the area is Lady Jane's hotel ('Vive la Canadienne'). It is a rough and ready place, full of men who live for the day and whose pleasure comes in drinking and womanising in the intervals between the days spent trying to break a living out of the Rocky mountains. Tonight is quiet enough, although there is always some undercurrent of potential trouble just beneath the surface. The Mountie Sergeant Malone is trying to chat up the pert hotel owner while the smoothly dapper city man, Edward Hawley, is on the look out for the little French Canadian girl, Rose Marie La Flamme. Rose Marie is also being sought by her brother Émile to whom it is worryingly obvious she's off somewhere with the miner, Jim Kenyon. The half-caste Indian, Wanda, has her eye on Hawley. She purposely dances very closely up to him and provokes a show of jealous violence from her lover, the rough and drunken Indian, Blackeagle.

Into this seething set of relationships stalks a little fellow bundled up in a flurry of furs to protect him from the mountain cold: it is Herman, self-christened Hard-Boiled from his wish to present a tough appearance. His presence adds yet another twist to the amorous complications in the room for 'Hard-Boiled Herman' is the preferred man of Lady Jane.

The bar has emptied by the time Jim Kenyon returns, having secretly

587

returned Rose Marie to her brother's room after a romantic walk under the mountain moon. Sergeant Malone is amazed to see the change in a man known as one of the hardest-drinking, heaviest-gambling, craziest scallywags in the area. Love has certainly tamed Jim Kenyon, the love of 'Rose Marie' who, before he came, would entertain none of the many local men who paid her suit. But, in love or not, Jim Kenyon is a man who will stick up for himself and his, and he has a quarrel with Blackeagle. He knows that the Indian is trying to edge in on his claim and make off with gold from the lands belonging to Jim and Herman. This quarrel, he insists, will be settled by producing the correct paperwork and not, in spite of Herman's itchiness, by gunshots. Malone backs Jim up, but threatens the belligerent Herman with the law of 'The Mounties' who arrive on cue with their song.

Émile is preparing to depart for his trapping grounds at the Kootenay Pass, taking Rose Marie with him, with the express intention of removing her from the undesirable presence of Jim. The girl ingenuously expresses her love for Kenyon ('Lak Jeem') to both Émile and to Hawley, whom Émile is keen that she should marry, and this only confirms her brother in his haste to leave Fond du Lac.

Wanda, who has laid Blackeagle to bed in their cabin in a drunken stupor, has come back to the hotel to try to revive her old affair with Hawley, and the worried Hawley realises that, if he is to wed Rose Marie without scandal, he must settle with his old love for all time. He plans to call at the cabin and pay her to keep away from him before he leaves for the hunting grounds with Émile and Rose Marie. But Émile and Hawley are not the only ones to be maturing plans. Jim knows perfectly well that Émile is going to take Rose Marie back to the Kootenay Pass, and he plans to follow them there. He arranges with the girl that they shall meet in an old house which she calls her castle, high on the rocks by the so-called lovers' stone. The stone is in a valley with a marvellous echo and it is ancient lore that the Indians of old called down with a special cry to the maidens of their choice to win them in marriage ('Indian Love Call').

In Blackeagle's absence, Hawley visits Wanda's cabin and, repulsing her advances, offers her money. Wanda is not to be denied the man she covets and she forces Hawley into an embrace but they are hurried apart by the sound of an approaching footfall. The newcomer is Jim who has come to show the Indian the deed maps which will settle their quarrel. Hawley hides while Wanda gets rid of Jim but, when he also goes to leave, Wanda lures him back for one more embrace. It is once too often, for this time Blackeagle does indeed discover them. The Indian attacks Hawley murderously, but Wanda takes a knife from the table and, as the two men struggle, she stabs Blackeagle in the back. As he falls, dying, Hawley looks on in horror.

Jim has rejoined Herman at the crossroads and they continue on their way, unaware of the drama which has occurred behind them. Soon they reach the Kootenay Pass and Jim installs himself in the little house up the valley from the Totem Pole Hotel where Émile and Rose Marie are based. From there Jim can keep in touch with Rose Marie by means of their Indian love call, but Émile is not fooled and he urges Rose Marie to forget Jim and instead take the love of the well-off Hawley who will buy her all the 'Pretty Things' a woman should have.

Unease is in the air when Wanda turns up at Kootenay dressed in showy finery bought with the money given to her by Hawley. She has a wicked tale to tell. When Sergeant Malone and his Mounties came to the cabin to investigate Blackeagle's death, they found Jim Kenyon's map and Wanda has convinced them that it was Jim who stabbed the Indian. Jim is wanted for murder.

Herman indulges in an incidental piece of 'Eccentric Dance' and a comic scene and song ('Why Shouldn't We') with Lady Jane, before the story continues with Rose Marie turning down Hawley's offer of marriage. Hawley patiently tries to persuade her to come to Quebec to see how life can be lived in comfort and he enlists the chic Ethel Brander to help him dazzle Rose Marie with the delights of town. Rose Marie is torn between this adventure and staying near Jim but, when Rose Marie is out of the way, Wanda tells Émile her faked story of murder and announces that Sergeant Malone and the Mounties are on their way to arrest Jim. The worried Émile and Hawley go off to discuss their strategy and Wanda takes the opportunity to lead an incidental dance routine ('Totem-Tom-Tom').

Meanwhile, other events are in progress. Jim has received an offer to go to Brazil to start some mining works for the Brazilian government and he must leave for Brazil straight away or lose the contract. Rose Marie will have to decide whether she can leave her home and her brother to go with him. It would perhaps be safer for her to take up the offer Hawley has made her but, if she truly wishes to go with Jim, she must come to him that night at the castle and they will slip away together across the border to America and be married. If she decides not to, she must sing the Indian Love Call to him up the valley one last time and he will leave alone.

Rose Marie tells Jim that she has already made up her mind. She will follow him wherever he goes. He must return now to the castle and she will follow in twenty minutes so that they are not seen leaving together. Jim departs and, when Hawley and Émile come to get Rose Marie to leave for Quebec, she refuses to go. But then Sergeant Malone arrives, armed with a warrant to arrest Jim for the murder of Blackeagle. Unbelieving, Rose Marie bursts into tears, but she wins from Émile the concession that he will not disclose Jim's hideout to the Mounties if she will go to Quebec and marry Hawley. It is, of course, only a matter of time before he is discovered, but Rose Marie knows a way to help him escape the Mounties. Announcing that she has always promised to sing the love call of the Indians to the man she will wed, she begins to sing, ostensibly to Hawley, the song which signals to Jim, at the other end of the valley, that he must go on alone.

ACT 2

In Quebec, Rose Marie becomes gradually more reconciled to Hawley, as Ethel Brander convinces her that Jim murdered Blackeagle not over the mining claim but in a fight over Wanda. Herman is also in Quebec, for Lady

Jane has sold her hotel and bought a fancy goods shop in the town and he has finally married her. He flirts, she seeks consolation from Malone and is caught being kissed ('Only a Kiss'), but their everyday little quarrels are all put aside when Jim turns up. He has brought Wanda with him, and the half-caste girl takes every opportunity to cause trouble. When Rose Marie sees them together and hears what the girl has to say she is left in no doubt that Jim is guilty and, refusing to listen to his protestations, she turns to Hawley for comfort. Jim, who has risked his life to return to Quebec to see her again, has to depart disillusioned ('I Love Him')

The preparations for Rose Marie's wedding to Hawley are in progress ('The Minuet of the Minute') when Wanda tries her hand again. This time she comes to try to threaten Hawley, for her passion for her old lover lingers on and she cannot suffer the thought of his marriage. But her newly acquired clothes and her furtive manner have alerted the suspicions of Malone who is lurking nearby, planning to arrest Jim now that he has tracked him down. Herman is also on to Wanda and, by pretending that Hawley is accusing her of the murder of Blackeagle, he gets her to talk. When Jane threatens to interrupt at the wrong moment, he hastily gets rid of her and she thinks that, once again, she is being two-timed ('One Man Woman').

Finally, the wedding begins ('Doorway of My Dreams') but, as Rose Marie marches towards her husband-to-be, Wanda dramatically stops the procession to reveal the truth. She is the murderer. She killed Blackeagle to protect the man she loves—Hawley. Rose Marie knows now that everything that has been said of Jim is false. While Herman, Jane and Malone hurry to find him at the lodgings where the Mounties have tracked him down, Rose Marie heads back to Kootenay. Jim is sitting alone outside the castle dejectedly singing the Indian love call when, from down the valley, Rose Marie's voice comes in reply. As the curtain falls, they are in each other's arms.

LADY, BE GOOD!

a musical play in two acts by Guy Bolton and Fred Thompson. Lyrics by Ira Gershwin. Additional lyrics by Desmond Carter. Music by George Gershwin. Produced at the Liberty Theatre, New York, 1 December 1924 with Adele Astaire (Susie), Fred Astaire (Dick) and Walter Catlett (Watty). Produced at the Goodspeed Opera House, Connecticut, 3 June 1974 with Bonnie Schon, Richard Cooper Bayne and John Remme; and again 8 July 1987 with Nikki Sahagen, Ray Benson and Russell Leib.

Produced at the Empire Theatre, London, 14 April 1926 with the Astaires and William Kent. Produced at the Saville Theatre, 25 July 1968 with Lionel Blair, Aimi MacDonald and Joe Baker.

A 1941 MGM film entitled *Lady, Be Good* with Ann Sothern, Eleanor Powell, Red Skelton and Robert Young used little of the stage show material.

CHARACTERS

Dick Trevor
Susie, *his sister*
Shirley Vernon
Josephine Vanderwater, *an heiress*
Jack Robinson
Buck Benson *of Life magazine*
J Watterson (Watty) Watkins, *a lawyer*
Manuel Estrada
Mr Rufus C Parke, *trustee of the Seth Robinson estate*
Jeff
Bertie Bassett
Daisy
Sammy Cooper, Sheriff's Deputy, etc.

ACT 1

Dick and Susie Trevor are orphans who live in Beacon Hills, New England. Dick is an inventor, full of bright ideas, but ones which don't shed much light on the subject of making money, so the pair are eternally broke and behind on every kind of payment, particularly the rent. Although they are penniless orphans, Dick and Susie have some jolly upper crust friends and Dick is in love with Shirley who is rich and middle-class enough to go out selling charity buttons with a bunch of like-mindless girls ('Buy a Little Button From Us'). Dick would like to be able to propose to Shirley and she would love to hear him do it ('We're Here Because'), but his awkward finances don't allow him to consider supporting a wife and he doesn't seem to have thought of taking a job.

The Trevors' landlord finally gives up on them and the bailiffs are sent to evict them from his house. They end up on the sidewalk, and Susie arranges the furniture under a convenient street lamp which they can use to supply both light and (with the globe taken out) electricity for the kettle at the public expense. They can only hope that it doesn't rain. Since Dick is in love with Shirley and Susie isn't in love with anyone, she decides that she will have to sacrifice herself to a marriage with a rich man to get them out of their pickle, but, for the moment, a more pressing problem is supper—they don't have any. They will just have to accept that invitation from execrably rich Jo Vanderwater to her swanky party and hope that there is plenty of food provided.

Susie is sitting under her lamppost feeling sorry for herself when a shabby-looking tramp comes by. He is ever so charming, and whimsical enough to propose marriage to her but, since he has nothing more to offer than a hayloft as a home, Susie has to sweetly decline. The tramp has walked all the way from Mexico and is heading hopefully for his old home in fashionable Eastern Harbour but, alas, it turns out that he is a disinherited chap and home for him is certainly not where the hearth is.

Susie's next visitors are less amusing. Buck Benson is a newspaperman on the lookout for a story, and a pretty girl stranded on the sidewalk looks to him like a photo opportunity. Susie is swift to bargain for a fee for being snapped but she is gypped when Benson promises to send her a cheque. There is still no ready cash in the Trevor till. It will have to be Jo Vanderwater's place, and Dick will have to grit his teeth when amorous Jo starts clinging to him. But all will be well, they are sure, while the two of them stick to each other ('Hang on to Me').

Jo's party is in fashionable swing ('Oh, What a Lovely Party') and the guests are dancing a lucky-dip kind of a dance which is designed to give them random partners ('The End of a String') when Dick and Susie arrive, angling themselves ever nearer to the food which is being carried towards the buffet. Josephine's comical lawyer, Watty Watkins, arrives around the same time and, since the heiress is in a confidential mood, he is soon hearing how the Trevors' eviction is all part of a plot.

Jo has persuaded the landlord—who happens to be her uncle—to throw the pair out so that Dick, gnawed by penury, may finally understand the advantages of a wealthy marriage. Tonight she intends to use her charms to convince him totally and utterly. Watty is scornful of her vamping technique and takes it on himself to give her an in-depth lesson, a lesson which ends up with him demonstrating embraces on his client in a manner rather more enthusiastic than professional.

Dick meets Shirley and a few new stars come down from the heavens to find a place in their eyes, but when the showy dancing starts it is Susie who partners him in a thorough exploration of 'Fascinating Rhythm'. While the Trevors are displaying their dancing technique, Shirley encounters an unexpected guest. It is Susie's tramp who, she learns from some conversation with the globe-trotting Buck, is called Jack Robinson and who is the disinherited nephew of the madly rich and recently deceased Seth Robinson. Susie isn't too worried about that. She's happy just to see him again ('So Am I') but sad that it is only for a goodbye. He's off to East Harbour and solo poverty.

Watty Watkins may have the wealthy Miss Vanderwater as a client but it soon appears that he is a distinctly shady gentleman. In the shadows of the Chinese lanterns which decorate the Vanderwater lawns, he is cornered by a very ferocious *caballero* with a complaint. Watkins has taken a fee from this gentleman to pursue the case of his sister, a Mexican lady who married an American gentleman who was sadly killed in an accident immediately after the wedding. Watty is supposed to be pushing the lady's claim to the immense estates of her brief husband, but he has had no success, being rather hampered by the lack of any documentary evidence of the marriage or, indeed, the presence of the lady herself.

The Mexican's sister is in jail following an episode with a bullet and a gentleman's head but her gun is now in the hands of her brother and Watty is not inclined to argue about the details of his duty. He promises that he will approach the trustees immediately and establish beyond any molecule of doubt the right of Señorita Juanita Estrada to the fortune of Mr Jack Robinson. In order to accomplish this, Watty needs a Spanish lady with some urgency and, since the real one isn't available, he tries to persuade penniless Susie to perform a little impersonation ('Oh, Lady, Be Good'). Susie, alas, will not be party to such a deception, even for almost ready cash.

As the party rises to its height, a triumphant Josephine calls all her guests together to make an announcement. She and Dick Trevor are engaged. He has finally asked her to marry him. Shirley is broken-hearted but sweetly understanding—Dick must have Jo's millions to make his life comfortable—but Susie is simply furious that he should sacrifice love for money (Finale) and she is determined that the wedding will never take place. If it is money he wants, she will make it. She will make it by playing the role of the Spanish lady for Watty.

ACT 2

Polite society is taking its ease ('Linger in the Lobby') in the Palm Court of the Robinson Hotel in Eastern Harbour when Dick arrives in search of his sister. She is busy preparing her foray as a señorita but, when Dick tries to discover what she is up to, she sidetracks him with small talk and dance steps ('I'd Rather Charleston').

While Dick mopes over Shirley ('The Half of It, Dearie, Blues'), daffy Daisy confirms to her sweetheart, the bumbling house detective Bertie Bassett, the outline of the plot, which has been rather trampled on in the dancing. Her Uncle is the trustee of the Robinson estate and the estate should have been inherited by old Seth's nephew, Jack, who was sadly killed in Mexico leaving his widow as the legal legatee. That widow, a glamorous Mexican, is due any moment at the Robinson Hotel to meet with Rufus C Parke, the attorney for the estate. Susie turns up to play her part and gives an exaggerated display of stage Spanish acting which is apparently enough to convince most people ('Señorita Juanita'), but Dick is not fooled and he almost spoils the whole trick by insisting on knowing what his sister is doing.

A much bigger threat to Watty's plan emerges when Buck turns up and hears the tale of inheritance. Jack Robinson dead? What nonsense. Why, he saw him at Jo Vanderwater's party just the other night. With the aid of a disappearing waiter and a bottle of gin, Dick and Watty convince the reporter that his eyes are not to be trusted under the influence of alcohol but, unfortunately for them, as soon as they have left the bemused Buck alone Jack turns up. He is amused to hear that Parke is entertaining the suit of a gorgeous lady who claims to be his wife and more than curious when he meets Susie and finds out that she is the lady in question.

When Bertie and Daisy bring Parke the news that Jack Robinson is still alive, the ground begins to quiver under Susie's feet and denunciations start to drizzle down. Watty's Mexican death certificate and Susie's impersonation come under sudden scrutiny and the jubilant Bertie handcuffs himself to Watkins with delighted bravado. At last he has earned his sleuth's stripes. Then, to everyone's amazement, Jack himself appears and, confronted with his 'wife', he confounds Bertie and Parke by agreeing with great enthusiasm that Susie-Juanita is indeed his wife. Bertie is made to look extremely silly, particularly when he finds that he has lost the key to the handcuffs and cannot separate himself from Watty.

That evening the Yacht Club Dance is in progress at the Robinson Hotel with the entire cast in attendance. The furious Watty has no ticket, but he is obliged to attend as Bertie wishes to be near his Daisy. It turns out that, in fact, they have just been secretly married and Daisy is aghast to hear that her bridal night is going to have to be shared by a manacled lawyer. Propriety is satisfied when the key turns up and the lock is undone in plenty of time.

The entertainment continues ('Little Jazz Bird'/'Carnival Time') and Dick and Susie somehow get to singing about a 'Swiss Miss' before sweet Shirley comes by to recoup her Dick and Susie falls into the arms of Jack, ready to spend her honeymoon in some luxurious environment far from the sidewalks of Beacon Hill.

The libretto of *Lady, Be Good* exists in several different versions, one omitting completely the role of Jeff, the entertainer, tacked in to the original script to allow Cliff Edwards (Ukelele Ike) to perform 'Little Jazz Bird' and 'Fascinating Rhythm' as well as, for a brief period, his own 'Insufficient Sweetie'. The songs 'Buy a Little Button From Us', 'I'd Rather Charleston' and Lou Paley's 'Something About Love' were added to the score for London. The London revival included several songs taken from other Gershwin works: 'Nice Work If You Can Get It' from the film *Damsel in Distress*, 'Ive Got a Crush on You' and 'Feeling I'm Falling' from *Treasure Girl*, 'For You, For Me, For Evermore' from the film *The Shocking Miss Pilgrim* and 'Love Walked In' from *Goldwyn Follies*.

The 1974 Goodspeed revival interpolated 'Somebody Loves Me' (lyrics by B G DeSylva and Ballard MacDonald) (*George White's Scandals of 1924*), 'That Certain Feeling' (*Tip Toes*), 'Kickin' the Clouds Away' (lyrics by DeSylva and Ira Gershwin) (*Tell Me More*) and 'I've Got to Be There' (*Pardon My English*). The 1987 Goodspeed version used none of these interpolations but added the song 'The Man I Love', eliminated from the original score during the pre-Broadway run, and 'Some Wonderful Sort of Someone' (lyric by Schuyler Greene).

THE VAGABOND KING

a musical play in four acts based on the romance *If I Were King* by Justin McCarthy. Book and lyrics by W H Post and Brian Hooker. Music by Rudolf Friml. Produced at the Casino Theatre, New York, 21 September 1925 with Dennis King (François Villon), Herbert Corthell (Tabarie) and Carolyn Thomson (Katherine).

Produced at the Winter Garden Theatre, London 19 April 1927 with Derek Oldham, Mark Lester and Winnie Melville. Produced at the Adelphi Theatre 14 October 1929 with Alec Fraser, Syd Walker and Helen Breen, at the London Coliseum 18 March 1937 with Harry Welchman, George Graves and Maria Elsner, and at the Winter Garden 22 April 1943 with Webster Booth, Walker and Anne Ziegler.

Film versions were produced by Paramount in 1930 with Dennis King, Jeanette MacDonald, O P Heggie (King Louis) and Warner Oland (Thibault); and in 1956 with Oreste Kirkop and Kathryn Grayson.

CHARACTERS

Margot, *innkeeper of the Fir Cone tavern*
Huguette du Hamel
François Villon
Guy Tabarie, *his friend*
Louis XI *of France*
Tristan L'Hermite, *his companion*
Katherine de Vaucelles
Thibaut d'Aussigny, *Grand Marshal of France*
Lady Mary
Noel le Jolys
Oliver le Dain
Casin Cholet
René de Montigny
Rogati, Isabeau, Jehan le Loup, Jehanneton, Astrologer, Toison d'Or, etc.

ACT 1

At an underworld tavern in the heart of old Paris, wine and ribaldry are flowing ('Gaudeo!') as the men of the streets indulge their nightly brawl, impervious to the fact that the Duke of Burgundy is encamped under the walls of Paris awaiting his moment to attack the city. The luscious Huguette du Hamel stands apart from this activity: these men are not for her. She holds herself faithful to the best of them all, the vagabond poet François Villon ('Love for Sale'), who languishes at this moment in one of the King's prisons after having been taken for thieving. When she refuses her kisses to René de Montigny, he is delighted to tell her that her François is no longer in prison. He was freed two days ago and has hardly hurried back to her. Perhaps she is saving her charms in vain.

His story is borne out by the arrival of Villon's comical henchman, Tabarie, who reveals that his master has spent the past two days falling in love. He, Tabarie, in person delivered some of Villon's verses to none other than a lady of the King's court. Unfortunately, he couldn't resist the opportunity to relieve some of the courtiers of their purses at the same time and, as a result, he sings a song to the drink he is buying everyone with the one purse they didn't find on him, standing up rather than sitting down ('A Flagon of Wine').

While the merriment passes, two unfamiliar faces join the crowd at the tavern. One is a courtier, Tristan L'Hermite, and his companion is none other than King Louis who is following the example of the Sultan Haroun al Raschid and going out amongst his people in disguise. Two reasons have led him to this lowly place: firstly the discovery that his kinswoman, Katherine de Vaucelles, for whom he holds a too fond regard, has a rendezvous at the Fir Cone, and secondly a dream. The King is very sensible to the prophecies of the stars and of dreams, and this dream has told him that he will find in the gutter a pearl of great price. This jewel, set in his crown, will fill all Paris with light until such time as a great star shall fall from heaven.

While the King waits and drinks, François Villon returns to his home base, full of his wonted joy and swagger, and with a mouth full of love for France and oaths against Burgundy (Song of the Vagabonds). His patriotic words sound well in the ears of the King, but his criticisms of the King himself as an ineffectual and feeble monarch ring less happily. Huguette challenges François with Tabarie's story of the court lady, and Villon happily tells of how he spied the lady as he lay in the road after his release from prison, of how he was captivated by her ('Some Day') and how, knowing he could never see her again, he wrote admiring verses to her. He has verses, too, about the King, brave verses declaring that Burgundy would face a very different France if only he, François Villon, were king.

Tabarie breaks up the company by running in with announcement of a fight in another tavern nearby. His news is false, and his trick the means by which he can clear the tavern before bringing in the Lady Katherine de Vaucelles, the lady to whom Villon penned his verses. She has come to find him. If the words of fierce devotion he wrote in his poetry are true, she has a job for him. That night, at this tavern, the Grand Marshal of France, Thibaut d'Aussigny, is to keep an assignation with a traitor amongst the vagabonds. Together, they plan to embroil the weak and easily led King in a surrender to Burgundy and Thibaut's reward from the grateful Duke will include the hand and the domains of Vaucelles. For France's sake and for hers, Thibaut must die before his betrayal can be carried out.

Villon agrees to do the deed, claiming as his reward 'Only a Rose' from the lady's belt. When the traitor arrives, Villon forces him into a quarrel and, when swords are drawn, strikes him down, sorely wounded. Thibaut is saved by the arrival of the archers placed nearby to protect the King but, when the traitor orders Villon to be taken and hanged, the King reveals himself and stops the order. He faces the imprisoned Villon and charges him with his earlier words—that he would rule France better than its King. Villon flashingly repeats his boast and, as he is led off, Katherine throws from above the rose she promised.

ACT 2

On his return to the palace, Louis finds Villon's challenge is still sounding in his ears and, when his astrologer confirms to him the tenor of his dream, he determines on a plan. Perhaps this beggar is the pearl in the gutter. Very well, Villon shall have his chance. He shall be made Grand Marshal of France in place of the disgraced Thibaut and given the opportunity to make good his boast.

The next morning, as the court heads out hunting ('Hunting!') and a captain of the King's archers and his men sing lustily of death and women outside the palace walls (Scotch Archer's Song), Louis matures his plot. Katherine has carefully disdained his amorous approaches and now the King will weave her downfall into the game he is playing: she will fall in love with the beggar whom he has set up in a high place. That beggar will be King of France for one day and, at the end of that day, if he has not won her to be his wife, François Villon shall be hanged. If he succeeds, Louis will have the revenge of seeing his haughty kinswoman wed to a beggar.

Villon, now shaven, dressed unrecognisably in fine silks and brocades, and given a real authority, accepts the King's offer of one day of rule and the amazed Tabarie, named his second in command, profits from the occasion by paying court to the pretty Lady Mary under the spluttering protests of her accepted lover, the pompous Oliver. In front of his other friends, who are brought before him as prisoners, Villon plays his role as the viceregal Marshal. Some of the vagabonds seek to save themselves from the King's sentence by blaming all their crimes on the absent Villon, but Huguette and Margot stand up with the truth and all the group are freed without knowing why.

Like them, Katherine does not recognise Villon in his new guise when she comes to him to beg him to release the man who attempted murder for her sake. Without divulging his identity, Villon tries to woo her but, when she tries to force him to a more courtly pace in his suit, he can think only of the end of his day of kingship. What will 'Tomorrow' be? It is then that the King sharpens his revenge by telling Villon that his life shall be saved if he can win the lady before the morning.

Now the reality of Paris breaks in upon the dreamlike situation in the person of a Burgundian herald challenging the King to surrender (Finale). Since he has that day the authority of the King, Villon must reply. He ridicules the herald and orders the court to revelry before throwing the challenge vehemently back at Burgundy.

ACT 3

The day of Villon's rule is over, night is falling (Nocturne) and, in the gardens of the palace, Tabarie and Oliver are continuing their banter over Lady Mary. When Tabarie finds he cannot get rid of his rival, he turns his 'Serenade' into a ludicrous duet.

Villon has spent his day vigorously. While the court has made ostentatious revelry, he has had all the prisons opened and the taverns emptied of their regulars who, spitting drink and patriotic fire, are ready to wreak their worst on Burgundy. The Burgundians, as he knew they would, have been fooled by the court's behaviour into thinking that if they invade the city that night they will find no defence. They have forgotten that Paris has its people.

The enemy within is still at work, however. While Villon urges his love with Katherine ('Love Me Tonight'), the King's cousin, Noel, courts the lovely Huguette (Huguette Waltz) and seeks her aid in a plot against the new Marshal. Thibaut is to be brought to the King disguised as an astrologer and, once in the royal presence, he will take Louis prisoner and deliver him into the hands of Burgundy. But the plot goes astray. Huguette, who is eager to help remove the weak King who will do nothing for his people, does not know that Villon is King for the day and, when she recognises him, she tells him of the plot. Villon stands in for Louis and Thibaut's kidnap is foiled but, when the furious villain attempts to stab the vagabond, Huguette throws herself in front of him and takes the fatal blow meant for the man she loves.

Now it is time to attack, but Villon knows that, before he goes to lead the men of Paris to fight, he must undeceive Katherine who is falling in love with him and would have him carry her favour into battle. He knows he could win her and save himself from the gallows, but he will not do so in disguise. He reveals himself as François Villon, not Grand Marshal or King but a poet and a vagabond. Before Louis' satisfied eyes, Katherine shrinks away. The King has had his revenge on the woman who refused him and Villon, his dream of love broken and death awaiting him at the end of his day of power, rides off to fight the enemy, no longer a Marshal of France but a vagabond Frenchman at the head of a vast, seething army made up of Frenchmen like himself.

ACT 4

In the Paris streets the gallows have been raised for Villon's execution ('Te Deum Laudamus'), but Louis finds that his revenge is proving joyless. In truth, he is not happy to see Katherine suffer and he is sorry to find no better use for a brave man than to hang him, but he knows that he must carry his wager through to its end, particularly as the populace show every sign of cheering Villon and his exploits louder than their King.

Villon returns to the King at the head of his victorious mob (Song of Victory). Burgundy has been defeated and the vagabond king brings the trophies of their army to lay at the true King's feet. Now it is time for his day as king to end and it must end, as was agreed, on the gallows. But Katherine has realised the truth in her heart and, as Villon's day of victory comes to its end, she steps forward to claim the vagabond king in marriage. He may no longer be King of France, but he will be forever king in her heart (Finale).

OH, KAY!

a musical comedy in two acts by Guy Bolton and P G Wodehouse. Lyrics by Ira Gershwin. Additional lyrics by Howard Dietz. Music by George Gershwin. Produced at the Imperial Theatre, New York, 8 November 1926 with Gertrude Lawrence (Kay), Oscar Shaw (Jimmy), Victor Moore (Shorty) and Harland Dixon (Larry). Produced at the East 74th Street Theatre, New York, 16 April 1960 in a revised version with additional lyrics by P G Wodehouse with Marti Stevens, David Daniels, Bernie West and Eddie Phillips.

Produced at His Majesty's Theatre, London, 21 September 1927 with Miss

Lawrence, Harold French, John Kirby and Claude Hulbert (Duke). Produced at the Westminster Theatre 7 March 1974 with Amanda Barrie, Royce Mills, Thick Wilson and Robin Hunter. Produced at the Chichester Festival Theatre in a revised version by Ned Sherrin and Tony Geiss 17 May 1984 with Jane Carr, Michael Siberry, Geoffrey Hutchings and Geoff David.

A film version (silent) was produced by First National in 1928 with Colleen Moore, Lawrence Gray, Alan Hale and Ford Sterling.

CHARACTERS

The Duke of Durham, *a titled English bootlegger*
Lady Kay, *his sister*
'Shorty' McGee, *another bootlegger*
Larry Potter, *another bootlegger*
Jimmy Winter
Constance Appleton, *his wife*
Judge Appleton, *her father*
Revenue Officer Jansen
Molly Morse
Phil *and* Dolly Ruxton, *twins*
Daisy, Mae, Peggy, Chauffeur, Assistant Revenue Officer, etc.

ACT 1

A bevy of feather-dusting local lasses is tidying up the living room of Jimmy Winter's handsome Long Island home in preparation for its popular owner's return that evening ('The Woman's Touch'). Perhaps he should not have been quite so free with his latchkey for, while Jimmy has been away, these helpful ladies are not the only ones who have been in and out of his home. It is 1924, the era of prohibition, and the coast of Long Island has become the playground of the rum runners. Their vessels safely anchored outside territorial waters, the suppliers of illegal alcohol use the cover of darkness to ferry their intoxicating merchandise to land, and the members of one group have found this large, empty house an ideal entrepôt.

The uninvited guests are rather an unusual group of smugglers, for their titular head is none other than a genuine duke who, impoverished by the vicious British tax system, has come to the land of opportunity to go into a form of business in which tax has no place. The Duke of Durham's team is made up of his sister, the Lady Kay, and two locals, Shorty McGee and Larry Potter. Once he has heard the news of Jimmy's impending arrival, the Duke's first action is to cancel that night's rum run and he immediately starts making arrangements for the hurried removal of the hundreds of cases of liquor stashed in the house's cellars while Larry takes time out to join a pair of pretty local twins in an incidental song-and-dance routine ('Don't Ask').

The next visitor to this extremely busy empty house is an official one, a revenue officer, but his little examination of the scene of what he is sure is a crime is interrupted by the arrival of the happy householder in the company

599

of his new bride, Constance Appleton. Constance, it must be said, is not a blushing ingénue. She is a surprisingly wary and indeed acidulous young woman who shows every sign of growing up to be a proper dragon and it is not quite clear why the fun-loving Jimmy has seen fit to get tied to her, particularly as his first brush with wedlock, some many years ago, had been such an unfortunate affair. A drunken college prank once had him committed to matrimony with a person called May, but it was a ceremony which had no sequel and, after a nice life as a virtually unmarried man, Jimmy applied for an annulment to permit him to marry Constance.

The presence of the newly-wed Winters is quickly spotted by the Duke and Shorty (there are, after all, Just-Married suitcases all over the living room) and the presence of Shorty is soon espied by the jack-in-a-box of a revenue officer who suspiciously challenges his presence in the house. Shorty passes himself off as Jimmy's new butler (it's a long story, but Jimmy ordered a butler and a maid and Shorty sent them away, so a butler is expected) and, when Jimmy returns, a butler he duly becomes both as an alibi and also as a means of keeping an eye on the hoard in the cellar until it can be safely lifted out.

As Shorty, in his new disguise, serves up the wedding eve champagne, a shock telegram arrives. The lawyers were unable to get the annulment through in time and Jimmy and Constance have been illegally married. The furious Constance packs her bags and heads for the nearest inn and, when she has gone, the conversation, not unnaturally, turns to women. Jimmy is led into the remembrance of a lovely girl who saved him from drowning the previous summer when he swam a little too far from his Long Island beach, but his reverie is interrupted by the bevy of damsels who made so free with their feather-dusters a few hours previously. They have now come back to welcome Jimmy and to be sung to of how each and every one of them is a 'Dear Little Girl'. Shorty is delighted at the sight of all this feminine pulchritude but he is thoroughly taken in and confused when the identically-dressed identical twins, Dolly and Phil, keep popping up from incomprehensible places.

When all the girls have been bundled off to wherever chorus girls go when there isn't a number on stage, Jimmy begins to make ready for bed. It is a horrid night, thunder and lightning, and activity too, for the guns of the revenue officers' sloops can be heard outside making mincemeat of some poor bootlegger's boat. Then, into the darkness of the Winter living room, creeps a dripping, oilskinned miscreant. Not a terribly hardened miscreant, for a blast of thunder makes her drop her revolver and, when Jimmy politely returns it, he discovers that the watery creature is none other than his long-lost rescuer. She is Lady Kay, the Duke's derring-do sister. Kay has beached her rum-running motorboat, clonked a revenue officer on the head, and hurried for shelter to what she thought was an empty house.

Needless to say it is not long before the ubiquitous revenue officer is banging on the door. Jimmy hides Kay in the bedroom and puts on an innocent air as the officer details Kay's crimes and lingeringly describes the penalties for harbouring a criminal. When he is gone it is safe for Kay to come out, but the officer does a quick return and catches Kay and Jimmy together. She passes herself off as his newly acquired wife and, with the Just-Married baggage as witness, manages to be convincing. Given the state of the weather, there is no possibility of Kay venturing out again, so it is decided that she will have to stay the night. Before they go off to their beds at the end of the scene, they sing a duet ('Maybe') with which to bring down the tabs.

In the morning, the Duke sets out to look for his lost sister with Potter in his wake. He stops off at Jimmy's house and finds the bedroom door locked which somehow gives Potter the cue to talk about his red-hot mammy and launch into a song-and-dance routine with the chorus who have poured into Jimmy's early morning living room ('Clap Yo' Hands'). They all have to be got out of the house before Kay can chastely emerge from the bedroom. She has to be got away from the house pretty soon, as Constance may very well call by and, given his tricky marital status, it really wouldn't do for another woman to be found in Jimmy's bedroom. A more immediate threat is the revenue officer who doesn't seem to be after revenue anywhere else except in this one particular house. In front of him, Kay and Jimmy have to keep up their newlyweds act ('Do, Do, Do').

Before long the Winter house is filling up once again. Kay has to be hidden when Constance and the Duke both pass through, and then—oh, dear—the Judge, Constance's jowled father, arrives to scowl heavily over his lapsed son-in-law and order a repeat marriage ceremony under his own aegis for that very afternoon. The suspicious Constance hears noises from the bedroom and will not be stopped from investigating and, when she opens the door, there stands Kay. But the situation is saved for she is no longer clad in Constance's morning coat but rigged out as an English maid. She has every right to be in the gentleman's bedroom, for she is Jane the maid and she is the butler's wife. With a bit of connivance from Shorty, the day is saved for the moment, but the future still looks grim. It seems that Jimmy is going to be handed over in wedlock to Constance that very afternoon and, for Kay, who has realised that she is in love with the prospective bridegroom, that is an ending devoutly to be prevented.

ACT 2

The wedding arrangements progress as the chorus watch photographs of the 'Bride and Groom' being taken. Kay, in her guise of Jane the maid, is determinedly still on the premises doing everything she can to make Jimmy realise that she would make a much better mate than the prissy Constance. She fills in the time by singing the ballad 'Someone to Watch Over Me' and Potter puts in another appearance with the chorus to sing about his 'Fidgety Feet' when strictly he should be doing something about the booze in the basement.

Needless to say, the revenue officer turns up too (with a rather nasty sniffle from standing under too many windows in the pouring rain) and he is befuddled to see the same lady who was the previous night introduced to him as the loving wife of Jimmy Winter being paraded this morning in cap and apron as the wife of Shorty the butler.

Kay and Shorty have to go into action in their pretended occupation when the Judge and Constance require lunch. The menu and the service are decidedly erratic, and the meal descends as low as comedy can go until the Appletons stalk out, offended, leaving Jimmy to dance an oddly insouciant number ('Heaven on Earth') with an incidental flapper before the revenue officer comes back for another bite at the situation. He is reasonably surprised to hear that Jimmy is to be wed that afternoon, considering that he saw him in a certain *déshabille* with a new wife just the night before, and staggered when Kay appears dolled up in one of Constance's most glamorous gowns. He has to be convinced once again that she is not Jane the maid but Mrs Winter; they just look alike in his eyes, and the fortunate arrival of the twins helps to prove the point.

Kay is feeling pretty miserable as the time for the new wedding approaches, but suddenly she has an idea. It is an idea which will not only stop the wedding but also get the liquor away from the house and, to make it work, she needs help from Shorty. When Jimmy sees her all dressed up, his last resistance goes and he ends up kissing her—minutes before he is to be wed to Constance. Finally the dreaded wedding begins but as the Judge starts to read the marriage service he is interrupted by a revenue agent who announces that he has come to arrest Jimmy for allowing his house be used as a depot for smuggled alcohol. The liquor in question is to be transferred to his trucks immediately and Jimmy taken away to face charges.

The agent is, of course, a disguised Shorty, who is planning to rescue bridegroom and booze in one go, but his plans are sideswiped when the real revenue officer turns up and arrests both the Duke and Kay, and charges Jimmy with harbouring a criminal. Then, in front of Constance and her glowering father, he relates how he found Kay in Jimmy's pyjamas, passing herself off as Jimmy's wife, the night before. What should have been a wedding ends with Constance and the Judge having palpitations and everyone else locked in the cellar under arrest.

While the revenue officer is superintending the loading of the contraband drink on to the lorries, the contrabandists are plotting to escape. The Duke does his best by getting inside a barrel of beer and being rolled away but, when all is loaded and the lorries roar off, Kay and Jimmy find that the cellar door has been left open and they can just walk out. How very curious.

That evening, everyone gathers at Jimmy's house and several chorus members get their chance at a bit of a song and/or dance and they all join together to say nice things about Kay ('Oh, Kay, You're OK with Me'). Somewhat unexpectedly the revenue officer comes along too and he has a surprise up his sleeve. He isn't a revenue officer at all but a famous hi-jacker, the Blackbird, and he's simply hi-jacked their liquor. Fifty thousand dollars' worth! But Shorty and Potter have the last laugh. Did he look at his lorry drivers? He did not and, if he had, he would have seen that they were not his own men but theirs. The liquor is safely on its way under the Duke of Durham's flag. The Blackbird is furious and swears he will have revenge.

Kay has no visa for the United States, he will have her arrested as an illegal immigrant. But he is too late. She is a true US citizen; for the past few hours she has been Mrs Jimmy Winter. This time, Jimmy is married for keeps.

For the 1960 off-Broadway revival two Gershwin songs originating in the 1924 London musical *Primrose* were adapted by P G Wodehouse ('The Mophams' as 'The Pophams' and 'When Toby Is Out of Town' as 'The Twenties Are Here to Stay'), and inserted alongside others from the film *Damsel in Distress* ('Stiff Upper Lip') and from *Lady, Be Good* ('Little Jazz Bird'). 'Don't Ask' and 'Dear Little Girl' were given fresh lyrics as 'Home' and 'You'll Still Be There'.

THE DESERT SONG

a musical play in two acts by Otto Harbach, Oscar Hammerstein II and Frank Mandel. Music by Sigmund Romberg. Produced at the Casino Theatre, New York, 30 November 1926 with Robert Halliday (Pierre), Vivienne Segal (Margot) and Eddie Buzzell (Bennie) and subsequently played at the Century and Imperial Theatres. Produced at the Uris Theatre 5 September 1973 with Stanley Grover and Chris Callan.

Produced at the Theatre Royal, Drury Lane, London 7 April 1927 with Harry Welchman, Edith Day and Gene Gerrard. Produced at the Alhambra Theatre 8 June 1931 with Alec Fraser, Sylvia Welling and John E Coyle, at the London Coliseum 24 September 1936 with Welchman, Miss Day and Frederic Bentley, at the Garrick Theatre 29 June 1939 with Bruce Carfax, Doris Francis and Alexander Cameron, at the Prince of Wales 16 January 1943 with Welchman, Eleanor Fayre and Bentley and at the Palace Theatre 13 May 1967 with John Hanson, Patricia Michael and Tony Hughes.

Produced at the Théâtre Mogador, Paris as *Le Chant du Désert* in a version by Roger Ferréol and Saint-Granier June 1930 with Robert Couzinou, Marcelle Denya and Dorville.

Film versions were produced in by Warner Brothers in 1929 with John Boles and Carlotta King, in 1943 with Dennis Morgan and Irene Manning, and in 1953 with Gordon MacRae and Kathryn Grayson.

CHARACTERS

General Birabeau, *Governor of French Morocco*
Pierre Birabeau, *his son, otherwise the Red Shadow*
Margot Bonvalet
Captain Paul Fontaine
Benjamin Kidd, *society correspondent for the 'Paris Daily Mail'*
Susan
Sid el Kar, *the Red Shadow's lieutenant*
Ali Ben Ali
Azuri, *his dancing girl*

603

Clementina, *a Spanish courtesan*
Hadji, *a Riff farmer*
Hassi
Nindar
Neri, *Hadji's wife*
Lieutenant la Vergne, *French foreign legionnaire*
Sergeant de Boussac
Edith, etc.

ACT 1

In their Moroccan hideout, deep in the Riff mountains, a group of anti-French Arab guerillas are taking their ease ('Feasting Song'). Their activities over the past years, under the leadership of the mysterious Red Shadow, have been increasingly successful and this very day they have blown up a strategic French dam, liberating the waters to fertilise once again the Arabs' traditional farming lands, yet there is no complacency in their hearts. Over recent weeks they have found themselves under increased pressure, owing to the redoubled activity of the French military under their new commander, Captain Paul Fontaine, and they have several times come near to discovery and annihilation.

Their skill in the desert and the speed of their horses have saved them (Riff Song), but it is said that Captain Fontaine has promised to bring the head of the Red Shadow as a gift to his fiancée, Margot Bonvalet, on their wedding day. The men would like to make a strike against this woman, but their leader will not permit it. Margot Bonvalet is not their enemy and she must under no circumstances be harmed.

The truth is that, under his Arab disguise, the Red Shadow is himself a Frenchman, Pierre Birabeau. Eight years earlier he left Paris and joined the army in Morocco in an effort to win sufficient glory to be able to pay court to this very Margot Bonvalet but, in resisting orders to raid Arab villages, he fell foul of the colonial administration and was publicly struck to the ground by the Governor as a traitor. Resigning from the army, he feigned a brain-damaged foolishness in everyday life while creating his position as an Arab Robin Hood in secret. When his enemy, the Governor, died, he was ironically succeeded by none other than Pierre's own father and now Pierre lives in Government House itself, still keeping up his role as a fool before his family while leading the Arabs against his father's men as the Red Shadow. And now his Margot is here, in Morocco, to wed Paul Fontaine, the son of his old enemy.

The Riff hideout receives an unexpected visitor when the Red Shadow's men capture a funny little fellow wandering about in the desert. He is Benjamin Kidd of the *Paris Daily Mail*. Normally a society columnist, he has been sent to Morocco as an emergency war correspondent, and he is decidedly lost in his new job, both metaphorically and in fact. Today he went riding with Pierre Birabeau, the Governor's silly son, got separated from him, and fell into the hands of this bloodthirsty band.

Bennie's life is saved by the Red Shadow's intervention and the men decide that, in return, he must agree to act as a spy at the French headquarters. The Riffs and their leader gallop off to pursue a dangerously approaching division of Fontaine's troops but, no sooner have they departed, than Fontaine leads his men into the encampment. The hideout of the Riffs is discovered. He sets up guards with machine guns to kill all who should return, and triumphantly envisages his victorious return to his 'Margot'. Amongst the rocks, however, hides one to whom that name is anathema: the Arab dancing girl, Azuri, with whom Fontaine had been involved in his earlier days in Morocco. Not without great anguish will she allow her rival to wed the man she loves.

Back at Government House, Bennie Kidd's secretary, Susan, is worrying and sighing over her adorable little boss ('I'll Be a Buoyant Girl'), and she is relieved when he turns up not too much the worse for wear with horse-weary buttocks and a pretty tall line in newspaper copy. The other soldiers' ladies are more bored than worried: their lives in this colony, with their husbands and lovers out chasing Arabs all the time, are dreary ('Why Did We Ever Marry Soldiers?'), and they are delighted when Margot livens things up a bit by purloining some military uniforms for a little charade (French Military Marching Song) to keep them amused.

Margot hasn't found life in Morocco at all to her taste. She imagined it to be a deliciously romantic place where all sorts of splendidly Elinor Glyn adventures would happen, but she just sits at home and watches her fiancé going through the daily grind of military business and longs for a little 'Romance' in her life. At least, today, there is a bit of drama, for the returning Paul announces that he has discovered the Red Shadow's lair and laid an ambush for him. Silly Pierre, who has brought Margot some flowers, cannot resist putting in a question as to what will happen if the Arabs should never return to that camp.

Alone with Margot, Pierre tentatively tries to emerge from his image as a harmless friend with an offer of a gentle kind of love ('Then You Will Know'), but Margot is set on a very different course. She gets Fontaine to show Pierre how a man should woo ('I Want a Kiss') and leaves him, maddened at being unable to step from behind his disguise, to dance off with her fiancé.

Bennie, in spite of his sworn oath, doesn't want to be an Arab spy. He doesn't want to be anything that involves knives and guns and things, and he's determined to catch the very next train back to France. He also doesn't want to have anything to do with the clinging Susan. She's not his type at all—she doesn't have 'It'.

Azuri comes to Government House in secret to try to win back the love of Paul Fontaine. She promises that she will reveal to him the identity of the Red Shadow if he will forget Margot and leave with her, but she is rejected by the disbelieving Fontaine and thrown out by General Birabeau, and she departs threatening a real vengeance. Worried at her words, Birabeau thinks it might be best for Fontaine to lie low a little while. He should wed Margot immediately and leave on a French ship due to berth that very night.

Margot, overhearing the conversation, is furious. She does not wish to wed anyone yet. She has not lived. The distressed girl is left alone with her longings for adventure until adventure comes surely to her in the shape of the Red Shadow. He appears from nowhere to stand passionately beside her, offering her romance amid desert sands and under moonlit skies ('The Desert Song') and she replies by striking him across the face with her whip in a manner doubtless culled from a romantic novel. By the time she has recovered sufficiently to cry for help, he has vanished.

When Fontaine hears that his prey is so close he determines to set out in pursuit immediately, but Margot stops him. If he does so, they will miss their ship. He must choose: either take the Red Shadow or marry her. It seems that Fontaine must relinquish his quarry but, as the wedding preparations begin, the Riff fires are seen on the nearby hills and he cannot resist giving chase. He vows that he will return with the Red Shadow's turban to celebrate their wedding. No sooner has he left, however, than the Riffs invade the house. There is none to resist them, and the Red Shadow takes the fainting Margot off in his arms to the desert.

ACT 2

At the palace of Ali Ben Ali, in the Riff Hills, while a group of captive Spanish dancing girls ('My Little Castagnette') are being looked over as potential harem material, the courtesan Clementina entertains with a more graphic description of their profession (Song of the Brass Key). With his own camp put *hors de combat*, the Red Shadow has chosen the home of the helpful Ali as the place to bring his captives. Margot has struggled all the way, in the fashion of the best of romantic heroines, but Susan hasn't struggled at all, though she might as well have for all the good it has done her. In fact, as soon as she has been bundled off to the bath, she has a rival, for the amorous Clementina, who has a special taste for weak Englishmen, targets in on Bennie who quickly looks like being 'One Good Man Gone Wrong' before he can have any say in the matter.

Bennie takes the first possible chance to get out of this place. When the Red Shadow proposes to send Susan back to Fez to tell Birabeau that Margot is safe, Bennie changes clothes with her, but he is discovered and faced with a dusty death by exposure in the desert as a punishment for his cowardly attempt at escape.

Meanwhile, there is discontent in the Riff ranks for the men are unhappy that their raids are being used not to further their cause but to aid their leader in his love affair. The Red Shadow challenges any one of them to dispute his leadership and, when there is no reply, he charges them to hold to their oath and follow him in everything as they have sworn. Ali cannot understand that he should go to such pains for a woman: in his Eastern view a woman and the love of a woman are treasured but ephemeral things ('Let Love Go'/'One Flower Grows Alone in Your Garden'). To the Red Shadow, however, there is only this one woman ('One Alone') and for her he will risk all.

606

The Red Shadow visits Margot in her room but, when he attempts to woo her in manly style, he is taken aback to hear her say that her heart is given to Pierre Birabeau. She has been cured of her romantic notions. The Red Shadow promises that, if this is so, he will no longer pursue her. She shall leave here as Pierre's bride. When he has gone, Margot agonises over her feelings. By all rights she should stab this man to the heart with the sabre he has laid before her ('Sabre Song'), but she cannot. Is she in love with him? When Pierre appears before her, anxious to claim her as his wife, she tells him that she used him only as an excuse to put her captor off, but she confides in him that she almost wishes the Red Shadow would resolve her dilemma by taking her by force.

Pierre retires to take on his alter ego, but, when the Red Shadow returns to tell Margot that he is taking her off into the desert, he is brought face to face with General Birabeau whom the treacherous Azuri has led to the palace. The General offers to fight the Red Shadow for Margot's freedom but Pierre is unable to lift his sword against his own father and, before the amazed eyes of his band, he refuses. By this act, he forfeits his rights at the head of the Riff band and is condemned to be loosed alone in the desert to survive or die.

Birabeau brings Margot back to Fez to great acclaim ('All Hail to the General') but Paul can see in Margot's eyes what has happened and he vows that, in spite of the standing order to capture the Red Shadow alive, he will bring him in dead. Bennie and Susan also arrive back. They have survived an ordeal of two days and nights in the desert and are pale and weak but, it emerges, they have found out one thing. Apparently Susan does have 'It'.

Azuri, too, puts in an appearance. She has come to claim her reward and her revenge and she takes both. With the money in her hand she drunkenly reveals to Birabeau the true reason why the Red Shadow would not fight him. The rebel leader is his own son and now, under his orders, Fontaine has gone out to hunt him down to the death.

But, like Bennie and Susan, Pierre has survived his desert ordeal and made his way safely back to Government House. Since he can no longer lead the Riffs, he has made a plan which will allow him finally to give up the feeble persona he has worn. He presents himself before his father with the clothes and sword of the Red Shadow and announces that he has beaten Fontaine to the blow: he has fought and killed the Red Shadow. But his father knows the truth. This tale will do for the world at large and, now, with Pierre at his side he will work for a better understanding with the local people. Margot, distraught at the news of the death of the hero she loved, faces up furiously to Pierre only to come finally to a realisation of the truth in his arms.

HIT THE DECK

a musical comedy in two acts by Herbert Fields based on the play *Shore Leave* by Hubert Osborne. Lyrics by Leo Robin and Clifford Grey. Music by Vincent Youmans. Produced at the Belasco Theatre, New York, 25 April 1927 with Louise Groody (Looloo), Charles King (Bilge Smith), Madeleine Cameron (Charlotte) and Stella Mayhew (Lavinia).

Produced at the London Hippodrome 3 November 1927 with Ivy Tresmand, Stanley Holloway, Mamie Watson and Alice Morley.

Produced at the Théâtre Mogador, Paris, 15 December 1929 as *Halléluia* in a version by Roger Ferréol and Saint-Granier with Coecilia Navarre, Géo Bury, Marguérite Louvain and Félix Oudart.

Film versions were produced by RKO in 1930 with Polly Walker and Jack Oakie, and by MGM in 1955 with Debbie Reynolds, Jane Powell and Tony Martin in a heavily altered version.

CHARACTERS

Looloo Martin
Lavinia, *a coloured servant*
Charlotte Payne
Captain Clark *of the USS Nebraska*
Bilge Smith, *a sailor*
Mat Bascom, Bunny Whalen, *his friends*
Battling Smith
Donkey, Dinty Smith, Dan, Chick McGee, *sailors*
Ensign Alan Clark
Toddy Gaie
Chief Petty Officer
Rita
Gus, Bob, Ah Lung, Ming Fang, Chia Shun, etc.

ACT 1

A bunch of determinedly salty 'gobs' (or, in the vernacular, sailors) are enjoying themselves in Looloo Martin's dockside coffee bar when hunky Battling Smith comes in, bringing a gift from foreign parts for the café's pretty owner. It is a live and squawking gift, a tropical parrot with a rough tongue, which wins scant approval from Looloo's bulging helpmate, Lavinia. Lavinia is Looloo's self-appointed mother substitute and she gets mighty uppity when the sailors kid her curiously about the unidentified sailor who was seen squiring Looloo through the cemetery late the previous night, but she can sniff something afoot when Looloo comes bouncing in with a song exhorting everyone to 'Join the Navy' and an armload of groceries topped off by a genuine chicken.

The café has emptied when a fresh group of visitors arrives. Ensign Alan Clark has brought the aristocratic Charlotte Payne and her pal, Toddy Gaie, on a little slumming trip to introduce them to the pleasure spots of the dockside life and to Looloo and her café. Charlotte's inquisitiveness leads to the history of Looloo's family being told and it comes out that the little lady is

608

the child of a sea captain and a circus performer. Looloo's mother was an elephant trainer with Barnum and Bailey's circus and Looloo has a valuable souvenir to prove it: a unique jewelled elephant pendant given to her mother as a wedding present by P T Barnum. Charlotte is fascinated by the piece and tries to persuade Looloo to sell it to her, but Looloo's feelings of family pride will not let her part with her sole remembrance of her parents, and Charlotte has to console herself with 'A Kiss or Two' from her officer.

Something of the same kind is what Looloo has in mind for the evening. She has invited Bilge Smith, her companion from the previous evening, to come and dine and she is bent on fixing him a fancy meal that will make the seafarer think fondly of the joys of hearth, home and marriage. She is a mite disappointed when Bilge turns up with two friends, who are obviously used to using their mate's facility with women as the way to a free meal, but Bilge decides that this particular date is a bit more worthy than usual and he hurries the boys on their way unfed.

Over Looloo's lovingly prepared meal, Bilge's swaggering melts into a friendly chat and he confides in Looloo that he longs to quit the navy and rise to be the captain of his very own freighter, running the American coast in all kinds of weather with his wife at his side, just as her father did. When the whistle goes, calling him back to his ship, all the old bravado returns and bidding Looloo farewell with a practised kiss ('Harbour of My Heart') he heads back to sea. Then Looloo has an idea. She goes to the phone and calls the hotel where Charlotte Payne is staying. If Charlotte still wants to buy the jewelled elephant, it is hers. The money it brings will be enough to purchase a little cargo ship and still leave some left over for a few clothes and things.

It is six months before the same part of the navy returns to Newport and 'Shore Leave' but Bilge does not turn up at the coffee bar. The disappointed Looloo sets out to find him amongst the endless Smiths of the United States navy and, after a fruitless search, she fixes on a plan. Down on the docks she enlists the help of an old friend of her father's, now the Captain of the USS *Nebraska*, and wins permission from him to host a big party on his ship. The guests will be every Smith in the navy. She hurries home to write out her invitations, leaving Lavinia walking the parrot ('Lucky Bird') along the quay.

The party is a strange affair, mixing Smiths of all shapes and sizes with such guests as Charlotte and her friends, a song in praise of 'Looloo', and a good deal of flirtation and high jinks from which more than one sailor emerges with a red face. Mat's attempt to show Charlotte the famous golden rivet ends in total discomfort for him ('Why, Oh Why?'). But there is no Bilge. Charlotte is convinced he won't come. After all, in six months he didn't even write. But Looloo stays firm; he couldn't have written for he doesn't even know her name.

The truth is that Bilge has just about forgotten the little girl from the coffee house amongst the events of the last six months, but he is in port and, finally, he does turn up at the party. Looloo is devastated when it seems he does not recognise her, but Bilge soon recovers his poise and his position and even goes so far as to be impressed by the devotion of this attractive girl who recalls every detail of every one of the few minutes they spent together.

609

After a short chat he is impressed enough to propose to her ('Sometimes I'm Happy'). They should get married tonight as he leaves for China the next day. Looloo is ecstatic and with a heart full of love she springs her big surprise. She has a present for him—a ship.

The offer has exactly the opposite effect to that intended. Bilge clams up totally. She can buy a ship? She is rich? She is the dame running this whole dance? Then she is not the girl for him. She is out of his class. Protest as she may, Looloo has lost her man. When the fond Battling Smith finds her in tears, he immediately takes her part and before long fisticuffs are the order of the day. The fighter soon lays Bilge out and the act ends with Looloo's love being marched off to the brig rather than to church.

ACT 2

Bilge was off with the rest of the fleet to China, so Looloo decided to head that way too with Lavinia and Charlotte and Toddy all following on behind. Things are pretty hot when they get there ('Silks of Red and Yellow'). There are bandits threatening from the mountains and American sailors all over town, but there is no sign of Bilge to be found in spite of all the searching Looloo and her friends can organise, so Lavinia takes time off to sing a loosely interpolated revivalist song ('Hallelujah').

Bilge is there all right and, true to form, he has fixed himself up with a girl. Rita isn't at all the same type as Looloo. She's a brassy, pragmatic lass who soon understands that Bilge has someone else on his mind, and is sympathetic enough to sit and look at a photo of Looloo and listen to Bilge's story. Her sympathy, however, is wholly for Looloo. If Bilge had a girl like that crazy for him and he turned her down through stupid masculine pride, he is an oaf. Bilge is half-way to the same thinking himself, but he has no time to finish his thoughts for suddenly the alarm comes: the bandits have attacked.

The foreigners are given refuge from the attack in the house of a friendly mandarin and Charlotte is not particularly pleased at being forced to share a room with such as Rita. She is more humble when Rita proves to know Chinese and is able to order herself a fine meal whilst the rest of them stay hungry. When Rita claps eyes on Looloo, she recognises her as the girl in Bilge's photo and tells her the workings of the sailor's mind. Looloo resolves to go straight back to Newport, get rid of her money, open up the coffee shop again, and wait for Bilge to return. Only then does Charlotte discover that the staff speak English and she could have ordered food hours ago.

Back in Newport, Looloo returns to her old way of life and announces the re-opening of her café by letter to every Smith in the fleet. One by one they turn up, all her old friends, but once again no Bilge ('If He'll Come Back to Me'). Charlotte calls by with Alan and a wedding certificate, and Looloo starts to get tearful again but then, one day, a very scruffy Bilge arrives. He didn't come back to America, he hived off to Buenos Aires and blew his savings before he heard from another Smith about Looloo having lost all her money and taking up work again. He got a job as a stoker on a ship heading

610

home and here he is. If she still wants him, he's hers. He has the promise of a ship. It's a coal barge, but it's a start.

Looloo's efforts at diffidence don't last long and soon she is in Bilge's arms but, just as it looks as if all will turn out right at last, Lavinia enters with a fine gown ready for Looloo to wear to Charlotte's celebration party. Bilge stiffens. That's her dress? Then there is no way she is poor. Looloo insists that she has not a cent to her name, but Bilge is as wary as he was of old and finally Looloo has to admit the truth. She really doesn't have a penny. She has put all her money into a trust fund and she cannot touch it. The only person who can ever have it is her first born child. As long as his name is Smith. And now she is going to marry Bilge Smith before he gets away again.

The London production interpolated 'Fancy Me Just Meeting You' (Weston/Lee).

THE NEW MOON

a romantic musical play in two acts by Oscar Hammerstein II, Frank Mandel and Laurence Schwab. Music by Sigmund Romberg. Produced at Philadelphia 22 December 1927. Produced at the Imperial Theatre, New York, 19 September 1928 in a revised version with Evelyn Herbert (Marianne), Robert Halliday (Robert) and Gus Shy (Alexander). Produced at the New York City Opera 26 August 1986 in a revised version by Robert Johansen with Maryanne Telese, Davis Gaines and Gerald Isaac.

Produced at the Theatre Royal, Drury Lane, London, 4 April 1929 with Evelyn Laye, Howett Worster and Gene Gerrard.

Produced at the Théâtre du Châtelet, Paris, in a version by Albert Willemetz as *Robert le Pirate* 20 December 1929 with Danielle Brégis, André Baugé and Urbain (Philippe).

A film version produced by MGM in 1930 with Lawrence Tibbett and Grace Moore used part of Romberg's score attached to a wholly different libretto and some new songs by Herbert Stothart. A 1940 MGM film with Nelson Eddy and Jeanette MacDonald returned to a book nearer to that of the stage show.

CHARACTERS

Marianne Beaunoir
Monsieur Beaunoir, *her father*
Julie, *her maid*
Captain Georges Duval ·
Robert Misson
Alexander
Philippe
Clotilde Lombaste
Besac, *boatswain of the 'New Moon'*
Jacques, *ship's carpenter*

611

Vicomte Ribaud
Emile, Brunet, Fouchet, Admiral de Jean, etc.

ACT 1

The year is 1792 and the place the city of New Orleans in the French part of the American continent. At the home of the rich and aristocratic Monsieur Beaunoir, a seamstress is displaying a new dress for the benefit of his daughter, Marianne ('Dainty Wisp of Thistledown'), when an important visitor from France is presented. He is the Vicomte Ribaud, known as 'the secret eye of the King', and he has been sent from France by his monarch to track down the rebellious Chevalier Robert Misson.

Misson has been proscribed for being instrumental in the murder of the King's cousin, the Duc de Clichy, and it is known that he has had himself sold into servitude as a bondsman to escape detection. Ribaud has traced the sale of Misson's indentures to New Orleans and to the household of Beaunoir.

Robert and his former servant Alexander are indeed amongst the slaves on Beaunoir's estate and, in fact, Robert is the very overseer whom Beaunoir summons to bring all the slaves under his control before the eager Vicomte. Thus warned, Robert knows that he must play his game carefully, but he will not flee the estate before he has been able to speak his heart to his master's daughter. He has serenaded her anonymously from behind the lilac bush below her window with the song that the sailors of her father's employ have sung to her over the years ('Marianne') but, before the opportunity is gone, he knows he must openly declare himself and his love.

The sailors find it presumptuous of a slave to address their song to their mistress, but they soon have a more personal problem to face. Beaunoir wishes them to make an additional trip to Martinique to deliver a bride-ship load of women before planting time. The men are rebellious at the thought of the extra work and are only cozened into agreeing when Marianne declares that the real reason for the trip is to take her to sea so that she may escape falling in love with a mysterious serenader ('The Girl on the Prow').

The comical Alexander also has his little love affairs and the one in which he is at present indulging is with Julie, Marianne's maid, who is not at all convinced that she has 'Gorgeous Alexander' all to herself. Less sure at love-making is Georges Duval, the stiff-necked Captain of Beaunoir's ship, the *New Moon*. He has been practically engaged to Marianne for three years but he has not yet unbent enough to receive a kiss. When, with the help of a couple of pints of madeira, he gets up enough courage to attempt some practical wooing, Marianne mischievously encourages him into trying his hand at a love song. Not only does he fail miserably but, each time that he gets into a lyrical flow, he is interrupted on some pretext by a seemingly servile Robert (An Interrupted Love Song).

Robert's own suit with Marianne is damaged, however, when she overhears him describing her as wilful, provincially proud and 'a big pig in a very small sty'. Furiously she orders the presumptuous servant to be thrashed: how dare he say that she needs to be mastered, she whose family motto is

'Always Win'. Robert replies only that his family motto is 'Never Surrender'. When Ribaud comes upon the seething girl, she angrily repeats Robert's words and the fugitive is undone, for Ribaud knows well the motto of the Misson family. He has found his man. It only remains to take him. He attempts to shoot Misson as he sings his serenade, one last time, beneath Marianne's window, but Robert's return shot strikes Ribaud's gun from his hand and the policeman is helpless to prevent his quarry's escape.

At the Café Creole (Tavern Song) Ribaud makes another discovery. He spies Philippe, the friend for whose sake Robert Misson killed de Clichy, amongst the company and, with a show of compassion, wheedles from the man his story. The girl whom Philippe loved left him to enjoy the riches and the bed of de Clichy and the broken-hearted Philippe took his revenge in attacking the aristocrat with his bare hands. In the fight which followed between the Duke's retainers and Philippe's friends, de Clichy was killed and now, in far-off New Orleans, Philippe can still not forget the woman who was his bane ('Softly, as in a Morning Sunrise').

Ribaud's inquiries are cut short when Robert turns up at the café. He tears away the incognito and orders the King's detective to be taken, bound and stripped. He will borrow Ribaud's clothes to make a return visit to Beaunoir's house.

Philippe, in whom events have stirred republican notions, encourages Robert to lead the men of the area in rebellion against the King, but Robert is an idealist. He has seen an island—the Isle of Pines—where he dreams of building a country of equal men, a society not of discontented revolutionaries but of true idealists and 'Stout-Hearted Men'. But that is a dream which must keep for later. Now he must go where Marianne is.

Tonight she is attending a ball in her father's house and preparing to give away 'One Kiss' as the prize in a cotillion. Alexander has charge of the draw, so it is little trouble to ensure that the winning lot goes to the masked and disguised Robert.

In the meanwhile, more people have arrived at the Beaunoir mansion. Clotilde Lombaste and a deputation from the bride-ship have come to demand better conditions aboard their hulk, and the husky Clotilde is surprised to be faced with not one but two ex-husbands: Alexander (to whom she is still theoretically wed) and Besac, the boatswain of the *New Moon*. Neither wants her back and Julie puts in a counterclaim for Alexander leading to 'The Trial' after which Alexander decides that neither girl is good enough for him.

A late guest at the ball is Ribaud. He has bribed an idealist or two amongst his captors to release him and he has headed straight to the spot where he is sure his prey will have gone. Robert leads Marianne into the garden to take his prize and what was meant as a game becomes much a more serious moment ('Wanting You'), but their love scene is broken up when Ribaud attacks. He exposes Robert as the Chevalier de Misson, acidly praises Marianne for being the instrument of luring him into his capture, and orders the *New Moon* to be prepared to leave for France at once with the King's prisoner.

Robert turns bitterly from Marianne whom he now suspects of complicity with Ribaud, but she determines to follow and help the man with whom she is falling in love. She will travel on the *New Moon* herself, on the excuse of wishing to be near her future husband and, as she ostensibly sings to Georges, all her thoughts of 'One Kiss' are with Robert.

ACT 2

On the deck of the *New Moon* Besac and the sailors join in a 'Chanty' until Clotilde and the other brides (who are to be dropped off at Martinique on the way) move in on them ('Funny Little Sailor Men'). Georges feels that there is more behind Robert and the Café Creole than meets the eye, and he attempts to wring information from his prisoners about the riots which followed Robert's arrest. Ribaud's suspicions rest rather on Marianne. He is not fooled by her apparent devotion to Georges and he watches her carefully. When she scribbles a rescue note on the back of a song sheet ('Lover, Come Back to Me') he has it intercepted.

Alexander's love affairs cause troubles of a more physical kind, and the rivalry between Julie and Clotilde explodes in a battle of feminine fisticuffs on the open deck. Their battle is soon forgotten in the shadow of another more significant one. A threatening ship is bearing down on the *New Moon*, a ship with superior fire power which they cannot resist. Captain Duval decides he must surrender before they are all killed, but Robert refuses and urges the men of the *New Moon* to fight.

When the crew of the pursuing vessel boards them, it turns out that the ship is manned by Philippe and his friends who have come to rescue Robert. Duval is set afloat in a dinghy, Ribaud is held prisoner, and Philippe's men head for the Isle of Pines, there to set up the Utopian state of Robert's dreams. When Robert asks Marianne to join them, she rates them as fools and dreamers. Such a paradise can never be; men are not made that way. Sing as they may of being 'Stout Hearted Men' together, they will find out to their cost what life without a social order is.

On the Isle of Pines Robert decrees, in a fashion which does not seem to be quite the democratic way envisaged, that every woman from the ship shall take a husband. Since she has already married them, Clotilde is faced with first refusal on two, but when Besac makes the mistake of saying he doesn't want her she perversely decides on him ('Love Is Quite a Simple Thing').

A year later the island is prosperous and the men are celebrating twelve months of marriage (Marriage Number/'Try Her Out at Dances'). Robert and Marianne, however, live apart. She has been wed to him in the fashion of the island, but he will not have her to wife till she comes to him of her own accord. Ribaud has not changed his ways and, with the help of the discontented Besac, he has secretly summoned two French vessels to the island so that he may be rescued to take the murderer Misson back to France.

When his action is discovered, he uses it to turn feeling against Robert. The ships, he declares, are there only to take Marianne and restore her to her family. If Robert freely releases her, there will be no trouble. Robert lives still in hope that Marianne will love him, but she dispels such hopes. Her heart had been his for the asking, but he chose to try to take it in such an autocratic fashion that she can never now love him ('Never for You'/'Lover Come Back to Me'). He agrees to let her go.

Ribaud's trick may have failed, but he is prepared with another. The French ships will invade the island that night and he has contrived a way of ensuring that Robert will be caught unawares. He sends a forged note to get Robert to Marianne's cabin and there, with false contrition, he reveals the truth before them both. To Robert he confirms that Marianne had nothing to do with his betrayal and that she followed on the *New Moon* only to be with him, while to Marianne he describes the hours spent by Robert gazing up at her window. Now they see each other with the eyes only of lovers and, as Ribaud leaves them, they fall easily into the songs of their love ('One Kiss'/'Wanting You').

When the French enter the harbour of the Isle of Pines, Ribaud has already succeeded in turning most of the men of Robert's dream society against him. While their fine leader dallies in the bed of his woman, they are being attacked. Robert attempts to rally his men and Marianne comes to his side to encourage them all to be the 'Stout-Hearted Men' she once scorned but, before they can decide which side to take, France is upon them: men with fixed bayonets headed by a French Captain.

Ribaud goes to take his stand alongside the representatives of authority, but the Captain has interest only in Robert. This is the man who professes loyalty to France, yet denies its King? Robert stands his ground and, to Ribaud's horror, is bravely saluted. There has been a change in power in France. More murder and more sacking, and the fleur-de-lys has been replaced by the *tricolore*. The people of the island have the choice between declaring for the republic or execution. Ribaud, proudly refusing to become a 'citizen', is condemned, but Robert Misson, the murderer of Clichy and an idealist, is named Governor of the Isle of Pines. Marianne, quickly converted from the aristocracy to Citizeness Misson in the face of expediency, may stay at his side, along with the 'Stout-Hearted Men' who have once more returned to his leadership.

SHOW BOAT

a musical play in two acts by Oscar Hammerstein II based on the novel by Edna Ferber. Lyrics by Oscar Hammerstein II. Music by Jerome Kern. Produced at the Ziegfeld Theatre, New York, 27 December 1927 with Norma Terris (Magnolia), Howard Marsh (Ravenal), Helen Morgan (Julie), Jules Bledsoe (Joe) and Charles Winninger (Cap'n Andy). Produced at the Casino Theatre, New York, 19 May 1932 with Miss Terris, Dennis King, Miss Morgan, Paul Robeson and Winninger and again at the Ziegfeld Theatre 5 January 1946 with Jan Clayton, Charles Fredericks, Carol Bruce, Kenneth Spencer and Ralph Dumcke. Produced at the New York City

Opera 8 April 1954 with Laurel Hurley, Robert Rounseville, Helena Bliss, Bill Smith and Stanley Carlson.

Produced at the Theatre Royal, Drury Lane, London, 3 May 1928 with Edith Day, Howett Worster, Marie Burke, Paul Robeson and Cedric Hardwicke. Produced at the Adelphi Theatre 29 July 1971 with Lorna Dallas, André Jobin, Cleo Laine, Thomas Carey and Derek Royle.

Produced at the Théâtre du Châtelet, Paris, in a version by Lucien Boyer as *Mississippi* July 1928 with Desirée Ellinger, Bourdeaux, Jacqueline Morrin and Harvey White.

Produced at the Städtische Bühne, Freiburg, Germany, 31 October 1970.

Film versions were produced by Universal in 1929 with Laura La Plante, Joseph Schildkraut, Alma Rubens, Stepan Fetchit and Otis Harlan; and in 1936 with Irene Dunne, Allan Jones, Helen Morgan, Paul Robeson and Charles Winninger. A third version was produced by MGM in 1951 with Kathryn Grayson, Howard Keel, Ava Gardner (singing dubbed by Annette Warren), William Warfield and Joe E Brown.

CHARACTERS

Cap'n Andy Hawks *of the 'Cotton Blossom'*
Parthy Ann Hawks, *his wife*
Magnolia, *their daughter*
Gaylord Ravenal, *a riverboat gambler*
Julie La Verne
Frank Schultz
Ellie May Chipley
Steve Baker
Joe
Queenie
Windy, Rubberface, Pete, Vallon, Backwoodsman, Jeb, Jake, Kim, etc.

ACT 1

The scene is the bank of the Mississippi River at the town of Natchez some time in the 1880s. The negro stevedores of the town are working on the wharf, loading bales of cotton, but the show boat *Cotton Blossom* is in town so the words that mean work to the stevedores mean entertainment to the rest of the townsfolk. The nightly show on Captain Andy Hawks's boat features the lovely Julie La Verne as its leading lady, and handsome Steve Baker opposite her. It's a mighty popular show and the folks turn out merrily to greet the jolly Captain as he introduces his stars, his soubrette, Ellie May, and the heavy man, Frank Schultz (Parade and Ballyhoo).

But all is not happy in the little family of theatre folk on the *Cotton Blossom*. Pete, an engineer on the boat, has fallen for Julie and, although she is married to Steve, he has sent her a gold pin as a gift. Julie has given it to the black servant, Queenie, and Pete is furious. He tears down her photo from the showboard on the levee and makes veiled threats against Julie which are put to an end when Steve knocks him down and Andy fires him. Parthy Ann, the Captain's stentorian wife, eternally unhappy at spending her days with show boat riff-raff, insists that her teenage daughter, Magnolia, cease all contact with a woman who causes such problems.

Passing through Natchez—and it can only be passing through as, for some past misdemeanour, a twenty-four hours pass is all the local sheriff will allow him—comes the dashing young riverboat gambler, Gaylord Ravenal. Looking lazily at the river, Ravenal contrasts his happy-go-lucky life with the sometime yearning for something more tangible ('Where's the Mate for Me'). As he lounges on the riverbank, Magnolia Hawks appears on the deck of the show boat and his eye is caught.

She strikes up conversation and he takes her for an actress, but she longingly tells him that, although she would dearly love to be part of that exciting world of let's pretend, it isn't so. Ravenal is happy to 'Make Believe' with her. The scenario he wants to act out is comprised of a little lovemaking, but he is just winning his first kiss when the law arrives and he has to depart in a hurry, leaving Magnolia brimming over with excitement at the new feelings which have entered her life. Old black Joe, Queenie's man, has seen Gaylord Ravenal's kind before, up and down the river. Better ask 'Ol' Man River', who knows everything, what the boy really is.

Magnolia and Julie get together secretly in the kitchen, and the young girl pours out her tale of romance. Julie can see that she's got it properly. It's the old story: 'Can't Help Lovin' Dat Man'. Queenie is taken aback to hear Julie sing that song. Why, it's a negro song, and with Queenie's version of the words it can suit her Joe just as well. It goes to show that things like love are the same all over.

Captain Andy has his actors at rehearsal, preparing for the next evening's performance of *The Parson's Bride*. Magnolia watches longingly as Julie and Steve mark their roles through but, when Ellie arrives and whispers something to Steve, the rehearsal starts to fall apart. Julie is dreadfully upset and she cannot continue the play. The jealous Pete has been at his work again. In this state miscegenation is unlawful, and Pete has found out that Julie is a mulatto and that here her marriage with Steve is a crime. He has taken the photo he tore from the showboard to the sheriff as evidence. Steve whips out his knife and, making a small cut in Julie's finger, sucks the blood from the wound. When the sheriff arrives, he swears before God that he, like Julie, has negro blood in him and the company are all able truthfully to support him.

Their word prevails against that of the unprepossessing Pete, and no action is taken, but Steve and Julie know that they cannot now stay with the *Cotton Blossom*. Everyone agrees they must leave immediately to escape any further trouble and Captain Andy agrees that tomorrow's show will have to be cancelled. But a replacement pair of actors is swift to appear. Magnolia leaps at the chance to play Julie's role, and Frank has brought back a drinking companion from the town who has all the qualifications for a leading man—the very personable Ravenal. Since he needs to get out of town quickly, and since the play acting gives him a chance to make love to Magnolia with impunity, he is happy to accept the job. Joe watches the young people as they start to rehearse. This one is going to bring some changes on 'Ol' Man River'.

Out on the levee, Ellie, downhearted at Frank's dilatoriness over proposing to her, takes the glitter off the imaginations of some local girls with an unflattering picture of 'Life on the Wicked Stage', while Queenie helps to fill the cheaper sections of the house with an altogether different kind of bally-hoo to that cried by Captain Andy to the politer patrons (Queenie's Ballyhoo: 'C'mon Folks'). When the show starts, the new actors do well until a back-woodsman in the upper reaches takes exception to Frank, in the villain's role, manhandling Magnolia. When he brings out a shotgun, the petrified Frank crawls from the stage, leaving the play in shreds. Captain Andy is obliged to mount the boards and, in a protean display, he acts out the remainder of the play alone.

Later that night, when Magnolia has momentarily escaped Parthy's vigilance, she meets Ravenal on deck. He asks her to come to church with him the next day, while Parthy is out of town, and marry him. She agrees, and under the stars they sing 'You Are Love'.

'The Wedding' takes place on the levee at Greenville, and a last minute attempt by Parthy, Pete and the sheriff to blacken Ravenal out of his bride cannot stop them. As the married pair climb into a carriage, the chorus reprises 'Can't Help Lovin' Dat Man'.

ACT 2

The World's Fair of 1893 (At the Fair/Speciality Dances/'In Dahomey', etc.) sees Ravenal and Magnolia prosperous and happy ('Why Do I Love You'). Parthy and Andy are there too, but they have no idea that their daughter's husband supports her on the proceeds of gambling.

The action moves on a decade, and it can be seen that things have taken a sad turn. As Ravenal's gambling succeeded or failed, Magnolia and her baby daughter have lived life on saw's edge: one day staying in a fine hotel, another unable to pay the rent on poor rooms. At the moment they are in a particularly bad way, and their landlady is ready to turn them out. Frank and Ellie, now touring on the vaudeville circuits as a double act, come to take rooms in a boarding house where the present occupants are about to be evicted and, to their shock, they discover that the unfortunate concerned is Magnolia.

She tries her best to keep up a pretence before them but, when a note arrives from Ravenal, she breaks down. It encloses his last money to help her through and to keep little Kim at her convent school, and tells her that he cannot burden her with his unfair self any longer. Because he loves her, he must go away. Magnolia cannot believe it. Love for her husband has sustained her through ten impossible years and now he is gone. She cannot bear to return to the show boat and her mother's sneers, and she gratefully snatches at Frank's suggestion that she should try for a job at the club where he and Ellie are to work.

At the club, the resident singer is running through a number ('Bill'). It is Julie: an older, badly aged and overdressed Julie with a bottle all too handy, but still with the charisma she always had. She has left the stage by the time Frank arrives with Magnolia but, standing in the dark, she hears the little girl she loved pouring her heart into 'Can't Help Lovin' Dat Man'. Julie comes to a decision. She pens a note to the club owner, resigning her place and telling him to take Magnolia instead.

While Magnolia is getting herself a job, Ravenal stops off at the convent to take one last look at Kim and, as he leaves, he leaves her as his only legacy one last verse of 'Make Believe'.

At the Trocadero New Year's Eve entertainment the apache dancers dance, Frank and Ellie perform 'Goodbye, My Lady Love', and Captain Andy, who has come to town with Parthy Ann, arrives with three chorus girls, having slipped the leash for a night of fun. Frank spots him and hurries over to tell him that Magnolia is to sing tonight for her future. It is vitally important that she be a success. When Magnolia does appear, she begins nervously ('After the Ball') and the audience turns restive, but Andy calls out to her in encouragement and, seeing her father, she gains courage and warms to her task, taking the audience with her. By the time the song ends, she has them singing along happily. Magnolia is at the end of penury and at the start of a new career.

By 1927 that career has taken her through fame on the musical stage to retirement and daughter Kim has moved up to take her mother's place as the musical comedy star of the day. Frank and Ellie have gone to Hollywood where their adopted son has become the latest child star of the silver screen, while back on 'Ol' Man River', Joe still totes his bales and not too much changes.

Then, one day, Andy runs into Ravenal; a slower, gentler Ravenal. Magnolia has never seen him since the day he left her, although he has watched her in the theatre from afar. Now he cannot resist Andy's happy suggestion that they should meet again. As the patrons gather for the show boat performance, much as they did thirty years earlier, Ravenal and Magnolia come face to face and, just as it was all those years ago, it is Magnolia who speaks first, Magnolia who leads Ravenal back to the deck where they sang 'You Are Love' together, and it is Magnolia who kisses him. On 'Ol' Man River' things just keep rolling along.

Show Boat has been produced with a variety of endings and also with a number of songs by both Kern and other composers used as variants to the layout described here. The original London production introduced Kern's 'How'd You Like to Spoon With Me' originally used in the musical *The Earl and the Girl* and 'Dance Away the Night' both of which were retained in the 1971 version. The 1946 revival added 'Nobody Else But Me' and the 1971 London production reintroduced 'Mis'ry's Comin' Around' which had been cut prior to the original Broadway opening.

THE CAT AND THE FIDDLE

a musical love story in two acts by Otto Harbach. Music by Jerome Kern. Produced at the Globe Theatre, New York, 15 October 1931 with Georges Metaxa (Victor), Bettina Hall (Shirley), Odette Myrtil (Odette), José Ruben (Daudet), George Meader (Pompineau), Eddie Foy jr (Alex) and Doris Carson (Angie).

Produced at the Palace Theatre, London, 4 March 1932 with Francis Lederer, Peggy Wood, Alice Delysia, Austin Trevor, Henri Leoni, Fred Conyngham and Gina Malo.

A film version was produced by MGM in 1934 with Ramon Novarro, Jeanette MacDonald and Vivienne Segal.

CHARACTERS

Victor Florescu
Shirley Sheridan
Alexander Sheridan, *her brother*
Angie Sheridan, *his wife*
Clément Daudet, *a revue producer*
Odette, *a revue star*
Pompineau, *a song-seller*
Major Sir George Wilfred Chatterly
Christian Biddlesby
Maizie Gripps
Madame Abajou, Madame Grandjean, Policeman, Jean Colbert, Claudine, Constance Carrington

ACT 1

In a street in Brussels the street-merchants are crying their wares ('Voilà les Livres') as people pass by going about their business. Amongst the familiar faces today there are a couple of unfamiliar ones—the American family Sheridan, Alex and his sister Shirley. There ought to be a third, but Alex has mislaid his wife, Angie. It is typical of Alex. He is a fussy but ineffectual creature, a bond salesman who, having married a dancer, has reconverted and become his wife's not wholly satisfactory stage partner. Far from home, Alex feels that he must be the man and organise the two poor lost females of his family when, in fact, they are infinitely more organised than he is. His method of coping with today's crisis is to put Shirley on to a public bench with strict instructions not to move and not to talk to anyone, while he trots off in search of Angie.

A pretty young woman sitting all alone on a Belgian bench naturally attracts attention, firstly from a businesslike vegetable seller, then from Pompineau the song-vendor who tries to tempt her with a piece called 'La Nuit Est Pour l'Amour' and then, realising she is American, with a little trans-Atlantic ditty called 'She Didn't Say Yes'. He is quite taken aback to

620

find out that Shirley is actually the composer of this song, and his attitude undergoes an immediate change as he hastens to treat her as a professional colleague to the extent of recommending her a fine establishment where, with minimal commission to himself, she and her family can find first-class board and lodgings.

His enthusiastic attentions prompt a darkly handsome young man to come over to inquire if Shirley is being annoyed. She thanks him and tells him that she is not, but she immediately recognises the man as Victor Florescu, the prize composition pupil of the Conservatoire where she has been studying. They fall into conversation and she learns that Victor has turned from symphonic composition to the theatre in the hope of earning some money, but he learns nothing of her work for he is interested only in her person. Shirley is inclined to be wary and will not give Victor her address. If he wishes to pursue their acquaintance he can write to her at the poste restante. Perhaps later, if there is a later, she will let him call on her at her home.

When Alex returns with Angie he is discomforted to see Shirley in animated conversation with a man but exaggeratedly relieved to find that she hasn't given him the name of their hotel. As they buy their supper from the insistent vegetable-seller and head back to their lodgings, Pompineau can be heard reaffirming tunefully that 'The Night Was Made for Love'.

A few weeks later the Sheridans have shifted from their unsavoury lodgings into Pompineau's little hotel and life has become altogether more comfortable. Shirley has been off on a fortnight's jaunt to Paris to pick up a royalty cheque to supply them with the wherewithal to live but, when she returns, there is a cloud in her sky. Victor has stopped writing. After their first meeting, all the time that she was in Brussels he wrote long, sincere letters telling her of his ambitions, of his theatre piece *The Passionate Pilgrim* and of his thoughts of her but, in spite of the fact that she had written to him with her French address, no letters came to Paris. She blames herself for pouring out, in her last letter, her very deep feelings for him and she knows that she must have scared him away.

La Petite Maison is a very jolly place to live and there, if anywhere, Shirley can forget her damaged heart. There is a lively mixture of enjoyable people from dear old Pompineau to the comical cockney Maizie Gripps constantly around the place and there is music everywhere, from the lovely piano playing on the other side of the courtyard to the singing of Pompineau who keeps his happy eye on everything that goes on in the *quartier* ('I Watch the Love Parade'). The music across the courtyard, if they only knew it, is Victor's. There, in his studio, he is composing his *Passionate Pilgrim*, and trying it through with the assistance of his librettist, the vague Englishman Biddlesby, and the singers, Odette and Constance, who are to play the roles of Pierrot and Pierrette.

Unlike Shirley, Victor does not enjoy the music he hears from the opposite side of the square. It is light, jazzy music which goes wholly against the romantic idyll he is trying to write and it drives him to distraction. He cannot guess that it is Shirley's music and Shirley who is playing it, for he believes that she has broken off correspondence with him and gone away. He never received her final letter with her avowal and her Paris address, for it fell into the hands of the inept Biddlesby who has not dared admit to losing it. Thus, unaware that he is so near to her, Victor tortures himself over the loss of his beloved. Only the pair of gloves which she left behind at their first meeting remains to remind him that they ever knew each other.

The Passionate Pilgrim is to be presented in a revue produced by the impresario Clément Daudet and his backer, Major Chatterly. It is a strongly sentimental piece into which Victor has poured his heart and his feelings for Shirley and, when Daudet hears it ('The Breeze Kissed Your Hair'/'One Moment Alone'), he is not at all convinced that it is the kind of thing he requires. It is far too gloomy and turgid, and at the end Pierrot dies of despair at the loss of his Pierrette. The piece needs lightening. In fact, what it needs is something like the light, jazzy music which can be heard coming from across the courtyard.

The Major, less commercially minded, is impressed with the power of the piece but Daudet is firm. As it is, it is not for him. Odette promises Victor that she will set her charms to work on the Major to make sure *The Passionate Pilgrim* is presented just as it has been written and, as she leaves, Victor crashes out some chords on his piano to drown out the insistent sound of Shirley's playing.

It is not long before Daudet follows his ears and pays a visit to La Petite Maison and Shirley Sheridan. She is delighted to welcome an impresario and to have not only her music but Alex and Angie's dancing considered for a new revue. For his benefit, she plays her newest song 'Try to Forget' and presents him with the lyrics scribbled out on her notepaper. He is thrilled with what he hears, and immediately offers to buy the song and also to hire Alex and Angie but, when Shirley hears that he intends to use her song to interpolate into someone else's score, she is less happy. When she hears that it is Victor's score, she is thunderstruck.

She listens intently as Daudet tells his story. Victor has written this *Passionate Pilgrim* inspired, as always, by a woman he has met. In this case the woman is clearly Odette, who is to play the leading role in the piece. But the piece is too dramatic, too serious and it needs a song like this one. With a sudden determination, Shirley agrees. 'Try to Forget' is his.

Odette indulges in a very private cab ride with the Major and, as a result, when *The Passionate Pilgrim* is given its first showing in the privacy of the theatre at Louvain, it is played straight ('Poor Pierrot'). The Major and Odette are delighted with the result, but Daudet is appalled. The piece is so heavy it would sink in one night. He calls Shirley to the stage and asks her to play some of her music. This is the sort of thing the piece needs. Victor is called to hear the music written by what Odette describes as this new girlfriend of Daudet, and he is furious. It is trash.

At his words, the pianist turns to face him and he sees it is Shirley. As he reads the lyrics of the next song she is to play, 'Try to Forget', he breaks out bitterly against her. When she begins to sing the song, which she wrote for love, Daudet moves to her side. Victor, Odette and the Major can see all too clearly what their relative positions will be from now on.

622

ACT 2

Back in Brussels, at Daudet's apartment, the cast and creative team of the revue, without Victor, have continued a festive post mortem into the small hours of the morning and the exhausted Shirley is asleep on Daudet's bed as the party begins to wind up. Odette, with a meaningful reference to the words of the song, makes a pointed remark about leaving Daudet alone with his new love but, when everyone has gone, a tousled and bleary Shirley emerges to find Daudet busy tidying up. He tries to persuade her not to go, to talk to him about herself, to notice him, but Shirley gently disentangles herself and, when he goes to his room to find her a nightgown, she takes a quick review of the situation ('She Didn't Say Yes') and grasps the opportunity to leave before he returns.

While the others were at the party, Victor has been putting his feelings of the night into a hapless song ('A New Love Is Old'). As he finishes playing it through to Biddlesby the next morning, he finds that he has a visitor. It is Shirley. She has come to tell him that she will not tamper with his play and its music. It is beautiful. But if he wants make it more popularly attractive he has only to turn it a little, to ease his rhythms here and there, and to give it an ending of hope rather than of despair.

As he listens to her playing his piece in her manner, his determined aggression melts into understanding. Within a few moments they are in each other's arms. At last they can talk to each other without the growing mountain of suspicion and jealousy that has grown between them. The tale of Shirley's last, lost letter emerges and the sunshine comes out. They will work together and make *The Passionate Pilgrim* a huge success.

When Shirley leaves, she meets Odette on the stairs and Odette is not pleased. She hurries in to tell Victor he is being made a fool of. It is all a plot to make him ruin his show. Daudet is interested in only one thing about Shirley Sheridan, and now that he has had that... To Victor's angry response, she relates what she saw the night before and he, ever ready for jealousy, believes her.

Two weeks later, the show opens in Brussels with all the alterations Daudet wanted included and with Shirley's music and the performance of Angie and Alex featured alongside Odette's Pierrot and Constance's Pierrette. Victor is not there to witness *The Passionate Pilgrim* achieve a fine success. He has not been seen since the day of Shirley's visit. While the others celebrate their success, Victor is wandering the streets outside La Petite Maison where he finally hears from Maizie that his show has been well received.

The happy show people crowd into the restaurant alongside La Petite Maison to join in a celebration dinner, and Shirley joyfully recalls the dance music from the show ('Hh! Cha! Cha!'). Daudet has it in mind to ask Shirley to marry him and Odette is amazed when she hears the true tale of the party night and of Shirley's walking out on Daudet. She confesses, unwillingly, that she has told Victor otherwise and Daudet honourably insists that the composer must be told the truth.

Biddlesby is sent to bring Victor from his studio and he arrives as

Pompineau is starting to sing his Pierrot and Pierrette number to Daudet and Shirley. Victor stops him and takes up the song himself, and his jealousy and resentment fill every line. Shirley cannot understand why he should be attacking her but, as voices and tempers begin to rise, Daudet stops the proceedings and pushes Odette forward to falter out her confession. Victor looks on her with undisguised hate as he bids tentatively to win his way back into the heart and graces of Shirley. Daudet watches, aware that his happiness, too, depends on her decision as, in the background, Pompineau gently picks up the refrain of 'She Didn't Say Yes'. Finally Shirley smiles: her Pierrot has had his suffering and, after all, it was she who made him change the ending of his story to a happy one.

OF THEE I SING

a musical comedy in two acts by George S Kaufmann and Morrie Ryskind. Lyrics by Ira Gershwin. Music by George Gershwin. Produced at the Music Box Theatre, New York, 26 December 1931 with William Gaxton (Wintergreen), Victor Moore (Throttlebottom), Grace Brinkley (Diana) and Lois Moran (Mary). Produced at the Ziegfeld Theatre 5 May 1952 with Jack Carson, Paul Hartman, Lenore Lonergan and Betty Oakes.

CHARACTERS

John P Wintergreen
Alexander Throttlebottom
Louis Lippman
Francis X Gilhooley
Matthew Arnold Fulton
Senator Robert E Lyons
Senator Carver Jones
Sam Jenkins
Diana Devereaux
Mary Turner
Miss Benson
French Ambassador
The Guide
Chief Justices, Maid, Vladimir Vidovitch, Yussef Yussevitch, Scrubwoman, Senate Clerk, etc.

ACT 1

The party convention is over and, after sixty-three ballots, a candidate has been chosen to contest the election for President of the United States of America ('Wintergreen for President'). The National Campaign Committee can put up their feet with a glass of whisky in their manipulative hand and pride themselves on their ticket of John P Wintergreen for President and what's-his-name (the one whose name they pulled out of the hat) for Vice-President.

The influential gentlemen behind the party and the candidate are relaxing in their hotel room as they warm up their time-honoured clichés in preparation for the election, when an interloper appears. He is almost thrown out until they realise that he is what's-his-name, the Vice-Presidential candidate, otherwise Alexander Throttlebottom. Throttlebottom isn't at all anxious to be Vice-President and he is only persuaded of the significance of his task when it dawns on him that if the real President should be incapacitated he would get the plum job.

For the moment John P Wintergreen is in full possession of all his faculties and it seems that he is going to need them, for the contest shows every sign of being a closely fought affair. If he is to make sure of his election the guy needs a gimmick, something which will rally every right-thinking American to vote for him: but what? What does the common person prize above anything else? The august gentlemen of the Committee decide to ask a common person, and the hotel chambermaid is put to the inquisition. What does she care about most—apart, of course, from money? She ponders a bit and opts for love.

Love? Of course, that's it! Wintergreen is a bachelor. He must fall in love with a typical beautiful American girl and conduct his romance with her diligently right up to polling day. The whole of America will get behind him in his romance and when it comes to voting their hearts will guide their hands to that little pencil cross. It is a racing cert. There is just one problem. Wintergreen isn't in love. He doesn't have a girl.

This problem is no problem to a band of men like the National Campaign Committee. They will hold a contest and find the most gorgeous girl in America, and Wintergreen will have his beloved. The party machine goes into action to promote John P Wintergreen for President on a platform of Love and soon a bevy of beauties is lined up on the boardwalk at Atlantic City to audition for the role of First Lady ('Who Is the Lucky Girl to Be?'/'The Dimple on My Knee'/'Because, Because').

Wintergreen is dazzled by the display of finalists of whom the deeply Southern Miss Diana Devereaux is the most forward, but horribly nervous at the thought of being married to any of them. After all, he doesn't know them. As the girls go off to undergo their final judging, Wintergreen confides his fears to the secretary, Mary Turner. These girls may look great in bathing suits but can they sew, can they make a bed, can they cook? Mary makes comforting noises at him. Everyone can cook; why, she herself makes corn muffins. Wintergreen's mind is distracted from his plight long enough to sample the corn muffin in Mary's lunch-box and suddenly his nervousness turns to determination: Mary Turner is the girl he wants.

Now the Committee return to announce Diana Devereaux as the winner of the contest ('Never Was There a Girl So Fair'), but Wintergreen refuses to wed the Committee's selection. Miss Devereaux cannot bake corn muffins and he is going to marry Mary Turner ('Some Girls Can Bake a Pie'). In spite of the rejected winner's complaints, Wintergreen has his way and John and Mary go on the campaign trail, their bandwagon decorated with banners crying 'Woo With Wintergreen' ('Love Is Sweeping the Country'), pledging their troth in front of an audience of thousands at Madison Square Garden ('Of Thee I Sing, Baby') in between the wrestling and the baseball results. If John becomes President of the United States, Mary promises to wed him.

On election night there is no doubt about the success of the campaign. As the most preposterous results pour in, John's victory is quickly assured and we next meet our hero on his Inauguration Day (Entrance of the Supreme Court Justices), delivering his address to the country not on political subjects but on his marriage to Mary ('Here's a Kiss for Cinderella'). No sooner is that marriage pronounced than a little cloud arrives to rain all over this blissful scene. Miss Diana Devereaux is feeling jilted ('I Was the Most Beautiful Blossom') and she has come to serve the President with a writ alleging breach of promise. The assembled Chief Justices have to decide: which is the more important, justice or corn muffins? There is no contest. Corn muffins win hands down. John and Mary can rest easy on their White House bed.

ACT 2

John and Mary are installed in the White House and at the head of the nation and its enormous machinery of government ('Hello, Good Morning'). Throttlebottom is still living in his downtown lodgings and hangs around the White House wondering when someone is going to tell him what to do. When he learns from a White House guide that it is the Vice-President's job to preside over the Senate he rushes to find a street car that will take him to the Senate House.

Wintergreen is getting along fine looking after the country, and Mrs Wintergreen is getting on equally fine looking after him, but the little cloud that hung over their Inauguration has not gone away. Miss Diana Devereaux has supporters and her support is growing daily. John and Mary take little heed of the eager questioning of the nation's newspapers on their reaction to Miss Devereaux's action ('Who Cares?'), but they are obliged to take the threat seriously when the French Ambassador calls ('Garçon, S'Il Vous Plaît') to add his demands to those of the insistent 'most beautiful blossom'. It appears that Miss Devereaux is the illegitimate descendant of an illegitimate descendant of Napoléon ('The Illegitimate Daughter') and France, therefore, takes her rejection as First Lady as a national insult. This is an international crisis and, when John refuses to have his marriage to Mary annulled and marry Diana, an incident is threatened.

The Committee cannot allow this and decides that expediency rules. The President must do as the French demand or resign. John, however is adamant. He refuses to have his marriage dissolved and he refuses to resign so the Committee decides that the only possible way to impose their will is to impeach him. But if the President is removed, who will take his place? Of course, the Vice-President. What's-his-name. Throttlebottom is suddenly thrust into the limelight.

The 'Roll Call' of the Senate leads into other business as Throttlebottom tries to bring the impeachment of the President before the representatives of the nation. The French Ambassador is called as a witness, then Diana Devereaux describing in an accent which has veered from deep south to shallow French how she was unjustly 'Jilted', and the voting is going one-sidedly against Wintergreen when Mary rushes into the room with shattering news ('Who Could Ask For Anything More'). She is going to have a baby. Diana's case falls in fragments as the whole Senate celebrates the fact that 'Posterity' is just around the corner.

John is pacing the corridors of the White House in traditional style when the French Ambassador comes with a new condition. He consents to the baby being born but, since John's refusal to wed Diana has resulted in France being deprived of a baby, the baby must be given to France to help in the increase of her national birth rate. John stands firm. No child of his will be anything but a freeborn American.

A parade of baby carriages, gifts from the nations of the world, files through the antechambers of the presidential home, and the high function-aries of America gather as the great moment approaches ('Trumpeter, Blow Your Horn'). Finally it is announced: the President is the father of a boy-...and a girl. The French Ambassador is beside himself. France is deprived of not one child but two. Diplomatic relations are severed and war threatened until the undeniable logic of the case is sorted out. If the President of the United States is unable to fulfil his obligations, then they must be fulfilled by the Vice-President. Alexander Throttlebottom must marry Diana Devereaux and, presumably, provide at least as many contribu-tions to the French birth rate as possible. It's constitutional. Now everything can end happily.

The 1952 revival interpolated the song 'Mine' taken from the sequel to *Of Thee I Sing*, *Let 'Em Eat Cake*.

MUSIC IN THE AIR

a musical adventure in two acts by Oscar Hammerstein II. Music by Jerome Kern. Produced at the Alvin Theatre, New York, 8 November 1932 with Tullio Carminati (Bruno), Katherine Carrington (Sieglinde), Al Shean (Walther), Walter Slezak (Karl) and Natalie Hall (Frieda). Produced at the Ziegfeld Theatre 24 November 1951 in a revised version with Dennis King, Lillian Murphy, Charles Winninger, Mitchell Gregg and Jane Pickens.

Produced at His Majesty's Theatre, London, 19 May 1933 with Arthur Marget-son, Eve Lister, Horace Hodges, Bruce Carfax and Mary Ellis.

A film version was produced by Fox in 1934 with Gloria Swanson, John Boles, Al Shean, Douglas Montgomery (singing dubbed by James O'Brien) and June Lang (singing dubbed by Betty Hiestand).

CHARACTERS

Dr Walther Lessing, *a music teacher*
Sieglinde, *his daughter*
Karl Reder, *a schoolmaster*
Cornelius, *a birdseller*
Ernst Weber, *a music publisher*
Marthe, *his secretary*
Frieda Hatzfeld, *a prima donna*
Bruno Mahler, *a playwright*
Kirschner
Frau Kirschner
Uppmann
Burgomaster, Pflugfelder, Frau Pflugfelder, Father Joch, Hans, Heinrich, Baum, Hulde, Waiter, Bear Trainer, Sophie, Anna, etc.

ACT 1

Walther Lessing is the school music master in Edendorf, a picturesque Bavarian village which goes in for cuckoo clocks, flower pots and everything else that makes up the traditional vision of a Germanic rural Arcadia. The local people call Walther 'Doktor' and treat him with the same deference that they would the church minister or the local physician, even to the extent of allowing their children and their choral society to expend their voices on his traditionally rural and Arcadian melodies.

Walther Lessing is a widower and he has a pretty little daughter called Sieglinde who is very fond of the handsome schoolmaster Karl. Walther is fond of the young man too, for Karl is by way of being a poet and he can provide words to the tunes which Walther writes, turning them into songs for the benefit of the choral society. Karl likes the old man, but he prefers the company of Sieglinde and he and she are looking forward to the end of the school year and the annual ramblers' trip down to the great city of Munich when they can enjoy the delights of the surrounding countryside together.

The school concert has Walther's compositions in pride of place and the choral society devote their energies to 'Melodies of May' whilst Karl leads them in the music master's latest creation, 'I've Told Every Little Star'. The new song is well received and Walther, who has been simmering a plan in his head ever since the melody for the song came to him, makes a big decision. Edendorf has been the only place ever to hear his music—it is time to give his songs to a wider world. He will go to Munich. There his old school friend Ernst Weber is a music publisher and he will print this latest and best of Walther's works. After that, who knows what might await the music master of Edendorf?

When the end of term prayer has been said (Prayer), Walther joins the ramblers and, with Sieglinde and Karl beside him, sets off for the big city ('There's a Hill Beyond a Hill'). It is an idyllic journey and, on the way, Karl and Sieglinde find themselves enjoying each other's company to such an extent that, ultimately, a certain embarrassment arises. It is only after an old bird-seller has passed them by singing a meaningful song ('And Love Was Born'), that Karl finally overcomes his shyness and takes the girl in his arms.

At the publishing house of Ernst Weber, Walther's coming is not awaited as pleasurably as he imagines. Weber has only dim memories of the schoolmate of so many years past and he has no wish to be pestered by an amateur who thinks his songs are all the more worth publishing because he knows the publisher. Besides, at the moment he has more important things on hand: the production by Herr Kirschner of a new operetta written by the favourite playwright, Bruno Mahler, with music by the celebrated Kruger and, for a star, the darling of the town, Frieda Hatzfeld.

The operetta is taking shape very slowly and its progress is not helped by the excessively theatrical arguments between Bruno and Frieda whose tempestuous love affair and touch-paper jealousy mean that much of their time together is spent fighting or not speaking, rather than working. This day is no exception, and the work session between the two breaks down as Frieda, boiling with drama at some trumped up insult, sends both Bruno and Ernst packing. She is in a fine mood and, when she spies Karl, who has come to meet Walther at the publishers, she is quick to turn her charms revenge-fully on to the handsome country boy. Karl, recognising the famous singer, is flattered at her attentions and thrilled to be able to introduce such a star to Walther and Sieglinde.

The Lessings are enchanted, but Walther is particularly eager to renew his acquaintance with Weber and he is a little shocked when he finds that he cannot so easily gain access to the publisher who is preoccupied with his own problems. A few little tales from Edendorf, however, suffice to turn Weber from the city businessman into a hometown lad and, before long, he is sitting down to listen to Karl and Sieglinde singing 'I've Told Every Little Star'. The reaction is beyond all Walther's expectations: Bruno Mahler is delighted, but what the old composer does not wholly grasp is that it is Sieglinde's sweetly naïve rendition of the song which has won the playwright's interest rather than the song itself. Frieda is shaken from her attentions to Karl when she hears Bruno describing his unwritten scenario (Letter Song: 'I'm Coming Home') and proposing a role for Sieglinde in the new operetta.

Moving quickly to safeguard her starring role and to keep any other feminine part to a minimum, Frieda joins his description of the new show ('I'm Alone'/'I Am So Eager') and takes care to act her scenes with a passion meant to attract both Bruno and Karl. When all is finished, she plays her biggest card. She has moved out of the apartment Bruno and she have been sharing and taken a room in an hotel, and Karl will now escort her home. Bruno, in his turn, invites Sieglinde to tea and, when she opts instead for a visit to the zoo, he smilingly agrees. The two couples depart, leaving Weber and Walther to reminisce of the old days and their youth and the song that they heard sung by a prima donna of an earlier era on their first visit to Munich so many years ago ('In Egern on the Tegern See').

ACT 2

At the zoo, Sieglinde meets the old birdseller once more. He has a gentle warning for her. She and Karl are country folk, it will not do for them to stay too long in the city. For the moment, though, Sieglinde is caught childishly up in the wonder of it all and, when Bruno attempts to make a pass at her ('One More Dance'), she only asks him to push her on the swing. Unfortunately, Frieda has chosen the zoo as an impossibly private place to take a walk with Karl and, inevitably, all four meet. Karl has been dragging Frieda around the tourist sights of Munich, so she has made no more amorous progress with him than Bruno has with Sieglinde.

The electricity between Bruno and Frieda soon starts giving off a shower of sparks again as Bruno goads the prima donna by claiming that he has rewritten the big song originally intended for her in the operetta ('Night Flies By') to be given instead to the leading man. Frieda snaps that she will walk out of the show and take up the offer of a motion picture in Berlin, and the two part angrily, each dragging their country partner with them. But this time Frieda has every intention of carrying out her threat. She really is going to Berlin and, as she goes, she tells Karl to take care for his little friend. Bruno has no intention of making Sieglinde a star. She is a sweet child, but there is nothing of the prima donna in her: Bruno will simply use her and then cast her aside.

For the meanwhile, Sieglinde is having the time of her life as Bruno and she, accompanied by Walther and Ernst and Herr and Frau Kirschner, spend a merry night on the town ('When the Spring Is in the Air'). Bruno is busy convincing his producer that this delightful young woman should have a role in the forthcoming production, and Kirschner, who sees a quality in her, agrees. As they wait for Karl to join them, Frau Kirschner—who is none other than the prima donna whom Ernst and Walther remember so fondly from their youth—gives them a reprise of the song they loved so well so long ago ('In Egern on the Tegern See').

When Karl finally arrives, he brings explosive news. He has just put Frieda on the train to Berlin. Kirschner and Bruno are devastated, but Bruno refuses to allow the producer to chase after her. The operetta can do without her—Sieglinde can take the role. Karl, with Frieda's warning still in his ears, is horrified at the thought but Sieglinde, prompted by Walther's foolish, fatherly encouragement, takes the schoolmaster's concern as ridicule. A quarrel breaks out between them and Sieglinde ends in tears as Karl rushes out, away from her, away from Munich and back to the safety of Edendorf. Or, perhaps, to Berlin.

Bruno is as good as his word and Sieglinde is given the leading role in the new operetta. It is a huge task for such an inexperienced child, but Kirschner is counting on her naturalness and her sweet voice to lead her to success. What he has not counted on is the interference of Walther who drives the musical director mad with his insistence on including great over-orch-estrated passages of his own in the show's score. For Bruno, however, the meddling Walther is a small price to pay for the presence and the rise to fame of Sieglinde with whom he is now deeply in love ('The Song Is You').

The night of the dress rehearsal forces everyone to look directly at a few unromantic realities. By the time the run-through of the first act is complete, it is clear to everyone including Kirschner and Bruno that the piece is heading for failure and that Walther's musical meddling is a small worry compared with the utter unsuitability of Sieglinde for the role she is playing. Where she should be passionate she is sweet, where she should be charming she is cute, where she should be emotional she gives the emotion of a child instead of that of a woman. The dream is over. Bruno's devotion vanishes as he sees Sieglinde as she really is: not an object for the passion of a man who lives on passion, but a little girl with a pretty voice and a little girl who cannot bring his work to life. He does not have the courage to tell her that she must go and neither does Kirschner. That job is left to a practical man of the theatre, the musical director Uppmann, and he does not do it gently. The theatre is a place for theatrical professionals and Walther and Sieglinde have no place there. They must go back to Edendorf. If Walther finds this hard to take, Sieglinde does not. She knows that what Uppmann says is true, and she is ready to go.

By the opening night, Frieda Hatzfeld is back in her accustomed place both at the head of the company and in the arms of Bruno ('I'm Alone'/'The Song Is You'), while, in Edendorf, the distraught Walther and Sieglinde closet themselves in their home and ignore both their old life amongst their people and also Karl's persistent serenading ('We Belong Together'). Walther will not touch a note of music, for he now regards himself as a failure, and Sieglinde is torturing herself over Karl's visit to Frieda in Berlin. But the villagers will not believe either in Walther's failure or in Karl's unfaithfulness and, when a package arrives from Ernst bearing the printed copies of 'I've Told Every Little Star', they know they are right. Walther is a published composer, Karl is a published author with the beautiful words he wrote for Sieglinde, and she, faced with their truth, can no longer refuse him.

ANYTHING GOES

a musical comedy in two acts by Guy Bolton and P G Wodehouse. Lyrics and music by Cole Porter. Produced at the Alvin Theatre, New York, 21 November 1934 in a revised version by Howard Lindsay and Russel Crouse with William Gaxton (Billy Crocker), Ethel Merman (Reno Sweeney), Victor Moore (Moon) and Bettina Hall (Hope Harcourt). Produced at the Orpheum Theatre 15 May 1962 in a revised version with Hal Linden, Eileen Rodgers, Mickey Deems and Barbara Lang. Produced at the Beaumont Theatre 13 October 1987 in a revised version by Timothy Crouse and Jerome Weidman with Howard McGlinn, Patti LuPone, Bill McCutcheon and Kathleen Mahoney-Bennett.

Produced at the Palace Theatre, London, 14 June 1935 with Jack Whiting, Jeanne Aubert (as Reno Lagrange), Sydney Howard and Adele Dixon. Produced at the Saville Theatre 18 November 1969 in a revised version with James Kenney, Marian Montgomery, Michael Segal and Valerie Verdon.

A film version was produced by Paramount in 1936 with Bing Crosby, Ethel Merman, Charles Ruggles and Ida Lupino and another, differing largely from the stage show in both script and score, in 1956 with Crosby, Zizi Jeanmaire, Donald O'Connor and Mitzi Gaynor.

CHARACTERS

Billy Crocker
Elisha J Whitney, *his employer*
Reno Sweeney
Sir Evelyn Oakleigh, Bart.
Hope Harcourt
Mrs Wadsworth T Harcourt, *her mother*
Reverend Dr Moon *alias* Moon-Face Mooney, *Public Enemy Number 13*
Bonnie Latour
The Purser
Bishop Dobson
Ching *and* Ling, *two Chinese*
William Oakleigh, *Sir Evelyn's uncle*
Mrs Wentworth, Mrs Frick, Ship's Captain, Ship's Drunk, Detectives, Cameramen, Reporter, etc.

ACT 1

Elisha J Whitney, business tycoon, is about to sail for Europe but, before departing, he has a painful duty to perform. He has to sack his lovable but inefficient general manager, Billy Crocker. Billy arrives at the pier full of beans with an extra special surprise for his boss: he has persuaded the delicious night-club singer, Reno Sweeney, to switch her booking and travel on the same ship where, as a personal favour to her old friend Billy, she will ensure that Whitney has one helluva Atlantic crossing. Reno is a great career girl. She started life as a professional evangelist before switching to clubbing with equal success, but she hasn't had any success in getting Billy to think of her as anything other than a pal even though she confesses to him, with unmistakable meaning, 'I Get a Kick Out of You'.

The reason for Billy's failure to fall is that his heart is already given to a girl with whom he spent nine hours in a taxi a few months back. Unfortunately he then lost track of her, but the feeling has remained. What with that and getting sacked, Billy ought to be really depressed, but he is one of life's bouncers and, in spite of everything, he is soon off down to the quayside to bid 'Bon Voyage' to Whitney and Reno.

On board, the press are lined up to photograph the departing celebrities. Whitney of Wall Street is worth one quick snap before the photographers turn their attention to juicier stuff in the delectable shape of the business heiress, Hope Harcourt, and her aristocratic English fiancé, Sir Evelyn Oakleigh; and a bishop, bound for an ecclesiastical conference with two heathen Chinese in tow, is altogether less interesting as media-fodder than Reno and her glamorous backing group, the Angels.

A little piquancy is added to the scene by the arrival of two detectives.

They are there to make an arrest, for they have discovered that two wanted criminals have booked their passage on the ship and are about to escape the clutches of the US law, disguised as clergymen. The detectives set off in search of the oriental bishop just as 'The Reverend' Moon-face Mooney and Miss Bonnie Latour sidle aboard at the last moment. Moon soon knows that he is in trouble: firstly there are the detectives and secondly his colleague, Snake-Eyes Johnson, Public Enemy Number One, hasn't showed. With Billy's collusion, he succeeds in hiding himself from the law amongst Reno's Angels, from where he sees the protesting bishop arrested and hustled off the ship.

The ship is about to leave, and Billy, who has just been rehired by Whitney to complete some important unfinished business in New York, is preparing to go ashore when he comes face to face with Hope Harcourt. Miss Harcourt is the lost girl from the taxi and Billy's plans suddenly undergo a change. If he stays on board, he has all the time between New York and London to detach Hope from her fiancé. It's worth a try.

The only trouble is that Billy has no cabin, no ticket, no passport and no money. But he does have a friend in the person of the grateful Moon who, now that the ship has set sail, is safely away from the clutches of justice. He is also solo, and he has half a cabin, a passport and Bonnie to spare as a result of the non-appearance of Snake-Eyes. The cabin Billy is pleased to take, but Bonnie and the passport are politely refused. He is, after all, on this trip to win himself the heart and hand of Hope Harcourt and he has limited time. He goes straight to work and, having persuaded Sir Evelyn into a bout of mental seasickness, he is soon lounging alongside his lady love on the open deck sharing mutual memories of sleepless nights since their last meeting ('All Through the Night').

Alas, Sir Evelyn may be easy to dispose of for the duration of a duet, but disposing of him and his pretensions more permanently is a different matter. The alliance between Hope and Evelyn is a dynastic one with heavy overtones of business, for she is the heiress to the Bailey's Products Corporation and he will one day be the Grayson's Limited empire. Bailey's is secretly in trouble and, to save the family—just like so many a Ruritanian Princess—Hope must make a marriage of convenience. All this, however, she cannot tell Billy. He knows only that she will sing duets with him but that she insists on marrying Evelyn.

Billy is installed in Moon's cabin without too much difficulty but he is annoyed to find that Whitney has the cabin opposite. Since Billy is supposed to be in New York finishing that million dollar deal for his boss, he can't be caught on the high seas. Moon solves the problem by stealing the short-sighted Whitney's spectacles, but there are soon plenty more problems to be dealt with.

The Purser gets a cable from New York to say that the person travelling with Moon is, in fact, Public Enemy Number One, and Moon has to come clean with Billy and admit that he, himself, is Public Enemy Number Thirteen (with ambitions to climb in the rankings). Billy is now labelled as a wanted criminal so he will have to be hidden. A disguise is called for and, since the passengers will obviously be carefully looked over, they decide he will have to be crew. Bonnie volunteers to remove a sailor suit from its owner as a quartette of sailors render a shanty ('There'll Always Be a Lady Fair') to cover the scene change.

Up on deck, Bonnie attracts a crowd of sailors ('Where Are the Men?') and dances her prey off into the wings to be despoiled of their clothes. Hope, in the meanwhile, is having a very different kind of time with Evelyn. He doesn't seem to know what the words 'passionate' or 'jealousy' mean and, business apart, it really doesn't look as if he's any keener to marry her than she is to get hitched to him. But he certainly is in Billy's way and Billy, desperate to make the most of his chance, decides to call up the reserves in the shape of Reno. How would she like to vamp the Englishman away from Hope so that Billy can carry on his romance in peace?

Like a true friend Reno agrees to help, winning Billy's fond thanks ('You're the Top'), but she quickly finds that she rather likes her task and manages to unbend Evelyn enough to win from him an invitation for a drink in his cabin. She plans with Moon—who turns out to be another of her night-club pals—that he shall burst into the cabin and discover her, clothes awry, in the arms of the fiancé of Hope Harcourt, thus providing perfect evidence for breaking off the engagement. However, when Moon does his bit, he finds a fully-dressed Reno being entertained by Evelyn in just his shorts and singlet. All Moon's imaginative threats go for nothing. Contrary to expectations, Evelyn insists he would be delighted to have a tale broadcast which pictured him as a fervent lover, particularly to Hope. Even the production of Moon's pet machine gun wins him no points: the charade is a failure.

Billy's disguise as a sailor has run its course and a new one is now needed if he is to keep one ahead of the pursuing purser and his staff. With the help of Moon and Reno he steals the trousers off a sleeping passenger, inveigles a drunk into taking off his jacket for a fight, and constructs a beard from hair shaved from the horrified Mrs Wentworth's prized Pomeranian. The new disguise makes him into Senor Arturo Antonio Moreno and gives him time to rendezvous with Reno who reports on her progress with Evelyn: in spite of the failed scenario in the cabin, she is doing all right. Believe it or not, he has kissed her! Before she knows it, she'll end up a Lady. In this day and age, after all 'Anything Goes'. It certainly does for, when Mrs Wentworth recognises Billy's beard and pulls it off, revealing him to the world as Snake-Eyes Johnson, he finds that instead of being flung into the brig he is lionised by the passengers as a celebrity.

ACT 2

As the adored 'Public Enemy Number One' Billy is invited to dine at the Captain's table and pestered for autographs and souvenirs while his hand-kerchief is auctioned for charity. When he tries to raise Moon's stock with tales of how the 'Reverend' is leading him towards the straight and narrow, Moon is asked to conduct an evangelist meeting in the ship's lounge. He doesn't know how, but he puts up a fair show with a little help from Reno ('Blow, Gabriel, Blow') who has a whole evangelical career to put at his disposal.

Unfortunately, the 'confessions' which come forth from the passengers aren't particularly effective, except for Evelyn's admission of a bit of hanky panky with a Chinese maiden in a paddy field. Finally, it is Billy who comes out with the real goods. Hope has cooled towards him because of his ready assumption of the identity of Snake-Eyes and, to win her regard back, he tells the truth, scorning the passengers and the Captain for making such a fuss over a murderer. As a result, he is frogmarched off to the brig by the furious Captain with Moon, who has tried to save the situation by admitting his own Public Enemy status, right behind him.

The last part of the Atlantic crossing is made in rather less comfortable circumstances than the first. Billy is truly disconsolate, but the irrepressible Moon spreads continuous jollity and advice to 'Be Like the Bluebird'. They have for fellow cell-mates the Bishop's two Chinese who, in spite of their downtrodden looks, are expert card players and have succeeded in relieving the entire third class of the contents of their wallets. The passportless Billy and the wanted Moon are to be re-exported to America, but the Chinese will be put ashore in England, and this gives Moon an idea. To while away the time, he suggests a game of strip poker. If the Chinese are sharp, Public Enemy Number Thirteen is sharper, and he and Billy are, fortuitously, just the same collar sizes as the gullible orientals.

At the Oakleigh family seat, preparations are being made for the wedding of Hope and Evelyn, a wedding which Evelyn's uncle sees more as a merger than a marriage. Both the participants are thoroughly miserable. The preparations are interrupted by the arrival of three voluble Chinese who demand to speak to Uncle Oakleigh. Needless to say, it is Billy and Moon who have escaped from the brig disguised in the clothes they won at cards, and somehow they have fished up a third Chinese garb for Reno. They stage a big scene, pretending to be the parents of little Plum Blossom who was deflowered by Evelyn in a paddy field, and demanding that reparation be made. Uncle Oakleigh offers to buy them off and, to the annoyance of the other two, Moon is only too happy to accept a cash offer of settlement.

While Moon accompanies Oakleigh to the place where he signs his cheques, the other two make contact with Evelyn and Hope. Evelyn would much rather marry Reno, and Hope, although she does not want her family to suffer bankruptcy, admits that 'The Gypsy in Me' compels her to long for Billy. Suddenly Billy spies Whitney in the house. What is he doing there? It turns out that he is a business connection of the Oakleigh family. Then, and only then, does Billy find out who everyone is, and hear the story about Bailey's and Grayson's and the marriage-cum-merger that is being miserably planned.

Billy quickly realises what is up. Oakleigh is trying to diddle the Harcourts, Whitney and everyone else. He is trying to sneak in and marry a firm which is not a bankrupt concern at all but, if they only knew it, worth millions. Billy makes a stand. He marches straight up to Whitney to pour out his discovery and, before the furious Oakleigh can stop it, Whitney has made and Hope has accepted a large cash offer for the firm she believed to be on the rocks. Since she now has nothing to merge, the marriage is promptly called off and, as the proceedings roll up, Billy gets his Hope, Evelyn makes a lady out of Reno, and a tidy cable arrives from Washington fixing Billy's passport problems and declaring the indignant Moon 'harmless'. Harmless? He still has Uncle Oakleigh's large cheque in his pocket and it's quite clear that he isn't going to give it back.

The original Broadway score of *Anything Goes* also included the song 'Buddie, Beware' which was deleted before the London production. Subsequent productions began the process of filling up revived Porter shows with songs detached from his less successful musicals. The 1962 Broadway version, staged in London in 1969, had a libretto which was credited to Russel Crouse and Howard Lindsay and omitted any mention of Bolton and Wodehouse and included in its score 'Heaven Hop' and 'Let's Misbehave' from *Paris*, 'Take Me Back to Manhattan' from *The New Yorkers*, 'Let's Step Out' from *Fifty Million Frenchmen* and 'Friendship' from *Dubarry Was a Lady*. The London version also included 'It's D'Lovely' from *Red, Hot and Blue* which had been interpolated into the 1956 film version as well as into an earlier London show, *The Fleet's Lit Up*. The 1987 revival retained 'It's D'Lovely' and 'Friendship', reinstated 'Buddie, Beware' and added 'Easy to Love' and 'No Cure Like Travel' which had been cut from the show before the original Broadway opening, 'I Want to Row on the Crew' from the college show *Paranoia* and 'Goodbye Little Dream, Goodbye' previously performed in *Red, Hot and Blue* and *O Mistress Mine*.

ON YOUR TOES

a musical comedy in two acts by Richard Rodgers, Lorenz Hart and George Abbott. Lyrics by Lorenz Hart. Music by Richard Rodgers. Produced at the Imperial Theatre, New York, 11 April 1936 with Ray Bolger (Junior), Tamara Geva (Vera), Doris Carson (Frankie), Luella Gear (Peggy) and Monty Woolley (Sergei). Produced at the 46th Street Theatre 11 October 1954 with Bobby Van, Vera Zorina, Kay Coulter, Elaine Strich and Ben Astar. Produced at the Virginia Theatre 6 March 1983 with Lara Teeter, Natalia Makarova, Christine Andreas, Dina Merrill and George S Irving.

Produced at the Palace Theatre, London, 5 February 1937 with Jack Whiting, Vera Zorina, Gina Malo, Olive Blakeney and Vernon Kelso, and played at the London Coliseum 19 April 1937. Revived at the Palace Theatre 12 June 1984 with Tim Flavin, Natalia Makarova, Siobhan McCarthy, Honor Blackman and John Bennett.

CHARACTERS

Phil Dolan III (Junior)
Phil Dolan, *his father*
Lil Dolan, *his mother*
Frankie Frayne
Sidney Cohn
Vera Baronova
Peggy Porterfield
Sergei Alexandrovitch
Konstantine Morrosine
Hank J Smith, Stage Doorman, Joe McCall, Oscar, Ivan, Dmitri, Louie, etc.

ACT 1

The curtain rises on a vaudeville stage where The Dolans are working their number, 'Two a Day For Keith'. Ma and Pa Dolan have a continuing difference of opinion over the rights and wrongs of their son, Junior, working in the act. Pa can see the makings of a grand vaudevillian in the kid, but Ma is determined that he should have a proper schooling and the chance to follow in the footsteps of her side of the family as a respectable teacher of music. Battle lines are drawn, but when Pa catches Junior dating a girl from a number two act he is shocked to the core of his traditional soul. There will be no more vaudeville circuits for Junior. He will go to school.

Fifteen years later, Junior has achieved his mother's dream. There he is, up in front of his music class at the Knickerbocker University, teaching 'The Three Bs'—that is Bach, Beethoven and Brahms. His students show promise. One, Frankie Frayne, has had a song accepted for publication, and another, Sidney Cohn, is writing a jazz ballet which Junior is watching develop with a keen interest. No one knows of Junior's parentage until one evening Frankie catches him dancing in the empty classroom to the tune of Sidney's ballet. Junior is sure that with a great choreographer—maybe even someone from the Russian ballet—Sidney's score could be a hit and Frankie knows how she can help. Peggy Porterfield, who finances the ballet, is a family friend. She is longing to do something new and exciting and Frankie promises to introduce Junior to her. In exchange, he's got to look over her song, which happens to start with the words 'It's Got to Be Love'.

Vera Baronova, star of the Russian ballet, is having a tantrum. The main reason for this is that she suspects her co-star and lover Morrosine of infidelity: he has been seen in public with a girl so, even if he isn't unfaithful, everyone thinks he is and that makes Vera utterly furious. When Peggy Porterfield comes to talk to her about a jazz ballet that she wants the company to stage, Vera is delighted to hear that it casts her as a striptease girl, but she is really more interested in the potential of the men involved as lovers.

Sergei Alexandrovitch, the head of the company, will not hear of such a production. He is for tradition and *Swan Lake* ('Too Good for the Average Man'). Morrosine's arrival is greeted with a shower of abuse from Vera and,

637

when Junior is introduced, she makes a dead set at him in front of her partner/lover. When Junior is left alone with the electric ballerina, theoretically to tell her about the new ballet, she instead tells him the story of the *Princess Zenobia* ballet, illustrating its various phases, with Junior as a surprisingly expert partner, up to its amorous finale. The ballet is clearly not a million miles from vaudeville.

Junior's students haven't been seeing much of him since he got involved with the Russian ballet, and involved is the word. Peggy has him learning a chorus role in *Princess Zenobia* in order to get the atmosphere of the world of which he is about to become a part. When he does show up at school he suddenly gets round to telling Frankie that he's in love with her. She has her doubts about him and Vera, but she's happy to launch with him into a duet dreaming about an Arcadian life somewhere where 'There's a Small Hotel'.

Backstage at the first night of the season's *Princess Zenobia* performances, Junior is showing Frankie around the set when Peggy arrives with a crisis. They have lost a slave. One of the dancers has got locked up by the police and that leaves the chorus of slaves one chorine short. Junior is needed. He has more or less learned the piece. He will have to go on for the missing blackamoor. Junior quickly turns himself into a Russian and a black slave and, after a quick brush up of the steps, he joins the company.

The ballet proceeds in its traditional Russo-Arabian nights combination of poses and gymnastics until the scene with the slaves arrives. Unfortunately, Junior has not only forgotten to black himself up beyond the chin but, since he hasn't performed this number under combat conditions, he gets an attack of stage fright and starts to go embarrassingly wrong. As the scene unfolds, he gets into the most grotesque positions, turning the whole piece into a farrago of low comedy. Sergei is livid, but the audience rather enjoys it. Perhaps the Russian ballet has a sense of humour after all.

ACT 2

Whatever the cause, the box office certainly improves. But neither this nor an impressive play-through convinces Sergei that he should stage Sidney Cohn's jazz ballet. *Slaughter on Tenth Avenue* is not for his company. In the meanwhile, Vera is still having screaming matches with Morrosine and tête-à-têtes with Junior who is trying to divide his time judiciously between the ballet and Frankie. Peggy pops in with a bit of fairly irrelevant advice to the effect that 'The Heart Is Quicker Than the Eye' before Junior's balancing act comes unstuck when he invites Frankie to lunch and is then commanded to dance attendance on Vera. Since he needs Vera's support over *Slaughter on Tenth Avenue* he has to leave Frankie stranded and wondering at her feelings ('Glad to Be Unhappy').

Junior gets Sergei and Peggy down to the school to look at the talents of his pupils. Hank J Smith gives his song 'Quiet Night' and Frankie's new song 'On Your Toes' is sung and danced by the class while, in between times, Peggy finds the occasion to inform Sergei that unless he produces *Slaughter on Tenth Avenue* she will ask for her million dollars worth of support back. The dancing of 'On Your Toes' ends up mixing the tap-dancing students with the ballet dancers of the Alexandrovitch company as the scene shifts to the theatre.

Slaughter on Tenth Avenue is in rehearsal and Morrosine is having problems with the syncopated rhythms of the piece. He isn't at all pleased when Junior offers to demonstrate. In fact, he goes berserk and Sergei has to knock him out with a stage brace to stop him wrecking the place. Unfortunately, before taking this decisive action, Sergei has ordered the stage doorman to call a policeman and a representative of the law arrives to find a comatose body on the stage. Junior explains that it is part of the show and, as Sidney strikes up the score, Junior goes into a long dance routine descriptive of a gangland murder. It convinces the policeman but, better, it convinces Sergei that Junior can dance this role in the ballet. Juniorvich Dolanski will star in *Slaughter on Tenth Avenue*.

By opening night Vera has made up her latest fight with Morrosine and all is again sweetness and light between them, but Junior is dancing the star role in the new ballet and that makes Morrosine very upset. He is so upset that he has paid a hit man to sit in the front row of the audience and pick off his rival in the heat of his performance. The ballet is performed, with Vera playing a striptease girl and Junior dancing the role of the hoofer who gets involved with her in the sleazy Tenth Avenue joint where she works but, as the dance scena rises to its climax, Junior is handed a note by one of the other dancers. It is a warning about the gangster in the front row. The police are apparently on the way, but in the meantime he has to remain a moving target. The last part of the dance is repeated over and over, until an exhausted Junior sees the policemen running down the aisle to arrest the gunman.

Backstage, Frankie is quickly in his arms as congratulations flow from all sides. Ma and Pa are there, and Vera thoroughly reconciled with Morrosine who seems to have rid himself of his homicidal instincts, but the song that rounds it all up, for better or for worse, is that dream of peaceful happiness—'There's a Small Hotel'.

The 1954 revival interpolated 'You Took Advantage of Me', originally used in *Present Arms*, for Elaine Stritch.

PAL JOEY

a musical in two acts by John O'Hara based on his own short stories. Lyrics by Lorenz Hart. Music by Richard Rodgers. Produced at the Ethel Barrymore Theatre, New York, 25 December 1940 with Gene Kelly (Joey), Vivienne Segal (Vera) and Leila Ernst (Linda). Produced at the Broadhurst Theatre 3 January 1952 in a revised version with Harold Lang, Miss Segal and Patricia Northrop. Produced at the Circle in the Square 27 June 1976 with Christopher Chadman, Joan Copeland and Boni Enten.

Produced at the Princes Theatre, London, 31 March 1954 with Lang, Carol Bruce and Sally Bazely. Produced at the Albery Theatre 25 September 1980 with Denis Lawson, Sîan Phillips and Danielle Carson.

Produced at the Opéra Royal de Wallonie, Liège, in a version by Tommy Banyai and Franck Gerald 15 October 1982 with Michel Mella, Nicole Broissin and Dominique Lebrun.

A film version was produced by Columbia Pictures in 1957 with Frank Sinatra, Rita Hayworth (singing dubbed by Jo Ann Greer) and Kim Novak (singing dubbed by Trudy Ewen).

CHARACTERS

Joey Evans
Mike Spears
Gladys Bumps
Vera Simpson
Melba Snyder *of the Herald*
Ludlow Lowell
Linda English
Kid, Agnes, Mickey, Diane, Dottie, Sandra. Adele, Francine, Dolores, Valerie, Amarilla, Ernest, Victor, Stage Manager, Louis, Commissioner O'Brien, etc.

ACT 1

At a second-rate nightclub on the south side of Chicago a song and dance boy is auditioning for an mc job. A bit of a song ('Chicago'), a bit of dance, plenty of side punctuated by a few cheap lies, and Joey Evans is hired. The song and dance were ok, the side was right for the job, and the lies were transparently harmless enough for club owner, Mike Spears, to know that this is a punk with little head but plenty of tongue. Besides, he knows Joey got kicked out of his last second-rate club for fiddling with an unprofitable female, so he's got him and his level pretty well taped. Gladys Bumps, the singer at the club, is up on Joey's past too, so he cuts none of that sort of cheese with her, even though some of the other girls aren't on the same line. Anyhow, he's the new man in the act, and they rehearse him into the number 'You Mustn't Kick It Around'.

Linda English is looking at some dogs in a pet shop window when a man alongside her pulls the old line. Old though the line may be there's always a girl that hasn't heard it, and Linda happens to be that girl. Soon the chat about the little fellers in the window turns to other things as Joey Evans goes into his big fantasy biography. Linda is duly taken in, but the Evans line of chat doesn't have the hoped for finish, as Linda is staying on her brother's couch, she doesn't have a car, and the meeting ends instead with a song and not with action ('I Could Write a Book').

At the club, the girls open the entertainment with a song ('Chicago') and Joey goes into his spiel. At the end of his act he sees Linda there with a boyfriend and goes up to talk to her, but he is soon distracted. During his performance, Mrs Vera Prentiss Simpson has arrived with a party. She has been interested by the look of the new mc, and Joey is ordered by Mike to attend to the needs of this rich and influential patron. It is quite clear what the lady's intention is and Joey is cocksure enough to give her no quarter. Vera is an old hand at this game, and she is quick to have her revenge on the boy who thinks he can play with her on his own terms. She walks out of the club and a furious Mike tells Joey he is sacked.

Joey makes him a wager. If Vera doesn't come back in the next couple of nights he'll go, and he'll go without pay. Mike is sceptical, but he's in a no lose situation, so he agrees to the wager as Gladys leads on the next part of the entertainment ('That Terrific Rainbow'). While all this has been going on no one has noticed that Linda has gone.

Vera doesn't come back and Joey gets the push. When he calls Linda she hangs up. When he calls Vera with some brusque remarks about getting him sacked, she doesn't hang up. Maybe she didn't go back to the club but now she's caught ('What Is a Man'). She turns up at closing time on his last night of work and catches him before he leaves. Without any illusions, and giving better than she gets, she picks Joey up and Joey bids the girls goodbye ('Happy Hunting Horn') for the meanwhile.

Vera sets Joey up with an apartment and clothes from a shop which clearly knows her well. She's 'Bewitched, Bothered and Bewildered' by this cheap young man, but experienced enough to look at herself going through the affair knowing exactly why and what she's doing. She is still able to feel jealousy, however, and when Linda turns up on the staff of the outfitter's shop and Joey talks to her, Vera invents a tale gruesome enough to dispose of the girl for the future. Her biggest gift to Joey is a night club of his own. He counts himself really in the big time as he looks forward to the opening ('Pal Joey').

ACT 2

All the gang from the old club have migrated to the new one. The tenor, Louis, leads in the opening number ('The Flower Garden of My Heart') of the rehearsal for opening night and the hard-boiled Miss Melba Snyder of the *Herald* comes to interview Joey for her paper. He pulls his fantasy biography on her and she shrugs it into her pad. If he wants that old line, so be it. To her, he's unexceptional; she's been through it all in the line of duty ('Zip'). The next visitor is less accommodating. Ludlow Lowell passes as an agent and he shoves some papers at Joey to sign. Joey isn't keen. He's doing all right without an agent, but some urging words from Gladys on Lowell's fame and influence catch his fancy and, without taking too much care, he signs Lowell's papers as the rehearsal continues with Gladys's number 'Plant You Now, Dig You Later'.

The morning after his opening Joey is disconsolate to find that the papers have given little mention to him and spent much more space commenting on Vera's presence and clothes and the names of her party. Vera is now at the stage of needing to make the most of Joey. She knows he won't last and, right now, she needs what he can give her. At least in the tawdry little apartment she has bought him she knows she's got him to herself ('In Our Little Den').

Linda comes one day to bring a COD parcel to the club and, while she is waiting for Mike, she overhears Lowell and Gladys plotting to blackmail Vera and her husband over Joey. She hurries home and loyally gets straight on the phone with a warning. Vera is a mite suspicious of this girl and her relationship with Joey, but Joey is always all words when he denies anything so why should he be different over her. His natural reaction is defence ('Do It the Hard Way'). But Linda is straight: she turns up at the apartment and spills out what she has overheard, dispelling Vera's suspicions with an open-eyed view of Joey with which Vera can only concur ('Take Him'). With a brisk thanks to Linda, Vera calls her friend the police commissioner. When Lowell and Gladys turn up with their demands, Joey gets indignant and is laid out cold by the phoney agent, but the blackmailers get their comeuppance when Commissioner O'Brien turns up on cue and arrests them.

Now it's time for Vera to call it a day. When things get to this stage it's always time to call it a day. Vera gently asks Joey how he is fixed. Then she calls the bank to close his cheque facilities and wishes him good luck. She's 'Bewitched, Bothered and Bewildered' no more.

Joey is looking moodily in the pet shop window when Linda appears beside him. She invites him to supper at her sister's place and Joey switches on again. He can't...he's off to New York for this musical comedy. Perhaps if he's passing through again... Linda hopes so, and she goes. He stays outside the shop looking after her as the curtain comes down.

The film version of *Pal Joey* included four Rodgers and Hart songs taken from other shows: 'My Funny Valentine' and 'The Lady Is a Tramp' from *Babes in Arms*, 'There's a Small Hotel' from *On Your Toes* and 'I Didn't Know What Time it Was' from *Too Many Girls*.

LADY IN THE DARK

a musical play in two acts by Moss Hart. Lyrics by Ira Gershwin. Music by Kurt Weill. Produced at the Alvin Theatre, New York, 23 January 1941 with Gertrude Lawrence (Liza), Danny Kaye (Russell Paxton), Victor Mature (Randy Curtis), Bert Lytell (Nesbitt) and Macdonald Carey (Charley Johnson).

Produced at the Playhouse, Nottingham, England, 9 December 1981 with Celeste Holm, Kenneth Nelson, Robert Swales, Jeremy Hawk and Don Fellows.

A film version was produced by Paramount in 1944 with Ginger Rogers and Ray Milland.

CHARACTERS

Dr Brooks
Liza Elliott

Miss Foster
Maggie Grant
Alison du Bois
Russell Paxton
Charley Johnson
Randy Curtis
Kendall Nesbitt
Ben Butler
Miss Stevens
Joe, Tom, Helen, Ruthie, Carol, Marcia, Barbara, Jack, etc.

ACT 1

Dr Brooks, a New York psychoanalyst, has a new and surprising client in the person of Miss Liza Elliott, the successful and admired editor of *Allure* magazine. It has not been easy for Miss Elliott to come to him. It has been very hard for her to admit even to herself that there is something in her highly organised and admirably full professional and private life which is not what it ought to be. But there is and, whatever it is, over the past three months it has begun to affect her in such a way as to imperil her whole way of life. Strange periods of depression have been followed by hyperactivity, irrational fears, panic at everyday things, fits of weeping and of sleeping. Her well-ordered life of the past ten years at the head of her magazine and at the side of her lover, publisher Kendall Nesbitt who founded that magazine for her, has not changed in any way—so why this sudden unreasoning illness?

Under the doctor's questioning, Liza's first random thought is of a song, a little song which she knew as a child, a song which seems to come to her mind regularly when the bad periods hit her. It came to her last night as part of a frightening dream.

The dream began with a set of matchless men serenading her ('O, Fabulous One, in Your Ivory Tower') and begging for access to their adored Liza. Gifts from the French Pretender, invitations from a Maharajah, pleas for favours from the great of the world followed one upon the other ('The World's Inamorata') as Liza spilled out a philosophy of enjoyment from a custom-built soapbox ('Only One Life to Live') to an adoring audience claiming her as the 'Girl of the Moment'. Finally a request arrived for her to permit her likeness to be used on the newest United States postage stamp.

Her portrait was painted there and then but, when the picture was finished, it showed not the glamorous Liza of the dream but the stern, austere woman who entered the doctor's rooms shortly before ('It Looks Like Liza'). The crowd looked at her, looked through her, and gradually their admiration turned to scorn and mocking in a terrible storm of ridicule which only ended with the dream.

What does it mean? Dr Brooks has no answer, yet. It is clear only that the fantasy Liza of the dream is one which the real Liza strives to deny. In life she dresses in a way which denies her femininity, emphasising none of the features which might make her traditionally attractive, whilst spending her days at her magazine teaching other women how to be beautiful.

At *Allure* magazine, business is in full swing. Film star Randy Curtis, the idol of a million housewives, has come to be photographed and the house photographer, Russell Paxton, is in ecstasies. Alison du Bois, as French as the Hudson River, is souping up a page of extravagant 'Why Nots' with a vivid determination to be chic at all costs. Maggie Grant, the fashion editor, is simply keeping things going in Liza's absence and suffering a bit of friendly worry, while Charley Johnson, the advertising manager, is reeking of hangover and doing his best to be a nice stereotyped, crumpled, lovable journalist person. When Liza returns, she moves everything neatly into action but she manages to forget that she has met Curtis before and she fails in an attempt to apologise to Johnson for throwing a paperweight at him in a production meeting the previous day, allowing the man to infuriate her with his well-laid charmy-chappie act.

Then comes the bombshell of the day. Kendall Nesbitt comes to see her. He has been doing some analysing himself and has come up with what he guesses to be the answer to the problem. Liza's position vis-à-vis himself has become untenable for her. She has lived ten years with him without his being able to regularise the situation and he has decided that he must now take action. His wife has finally, and at great cost, agreed to divorce him.

To Liza's horrified amazement, she finds that she reacts to this news with a wild internal panic and, instead of the expected happy response, she simply tells Kendall that she will talk to him at dinner that evening. Then Curtis reappears, out of his costumes and soberly dressed, to ask, in his turn, in a gentle and gentlemanly manner for a dinner date. Without quite knowing why, Liza agrees and then, hurrying the men out of her office, succumbs to her panic by falling asleep in her chair.

Again she dreams. This time it is school days ('Mapleton High Chorale') and from all sides come florid appreciations of the Liza Elliott of her teenage days. Suddenly she is there in a white gown and Kendall is taking her to a jeweller who looks like Charley Johnson to choose a ring but, instead of a ring, the salesman offers her a dagger. Then Randy Curtis appears to sing rapturously with her ('This Is New') until he, in his turn, disappears and she is dancing with Johnson and six beautiful girls with red hair and Randy is there again, singing to them. Then Dr Brooks's voice comes into her consciousness. She is back in his office and she is telling him of the school play she acted in as a child, 'The Princess of Pure Delight'.

The scene changes again. She is in her own office and it is in chaos...she can't find anyone...they are all preparing for her wedding. She is being married ('This Woman at the Altar') and the chorale is pounding out advice. The real Liza Elliott does not want this. The real Liza Elliott wants to be beautiful, and she does not love this man. She does not love this man. Liza cries out that she does, as the dream climbs to cacophony.

When Liza returns to Brooks for her next session, he tries to take his analysis further. She dresses as she does to avoid competing with other women on their own terms. She cannot compete. Even the man she has, the man with whom she has lived for so long, is not hers. He is a safely married man. Now that he is no longer going to be such, he can no longer fit into the armour-plated life she has made for herself. True or not, this is not what Liza wants to hear and, before long, she becomes angry at the doctor's suggestions and stalks out of his rooms.

She does not straight away return to her office and, while she is wandering the town, thinking, Maggie once again tries to hold the fort. When Liza does finally return, however, there is plenty to get in the way of work. Firstly there is Nesbitt who now realises that she does not want to marry him and who intends to fight to make her change her mind. Then comes Russell with a crisis, Alison with a helpful book on astrology, and Charley Johnson bringing up the subject of the Easter issue cover which resulted in the paperweight being thrown last time it was discussed. He wants a circus theme; he has some good tie-ups. She won't decide. He also has to tell her he's leaving. He's been offered a job equivalent to hers on another magazine. She doesn't want him to go, but he won't stay—she is married to that editorial desk and it will never be his.

Amongst all her preoccupations, she's forgotten her engagement with Randy Curtis. He's happy, even pleased, since he gets a surfeit of glamour in his job, to take her out in her office suit, but some of Charley's farewell remarks have hit Liza's consciousness. If she's being accused of hiding herself behind her desk and her clothes, she'll come out. Grabbing a gown from a model, she begins, with tears running down her face, to dress herself in the height of fashion. As her childish song returns, Liza Elliott changes her image.

ACT 2

The next day, she is back in the office and the suit, and pushing herself to her limit. Wearily, at the end of the day, she picks up Alison's astrology book. Oh my goodness, how stupid is she getting? She forces herself to look at some drawings, to choose...but she can't make up her mind between them. Frustration. The voices of the past days come back to her: Kendall's determination to keep her, Charley's accusations of her desexing herself by her work, Randy's preference for her in her office clothes, and that damned Easter cover.

Once again she finds escape from her problems in sleep and once again the dreams come. A circus parade ('The Greatest Show on Earth') brings in a Ringmaster who looks like Russell to introduce a freak show featuring the woman who cannot make up her mind ('Ladies and Gentlemen'/Dance of the Tumblers/'Order in the Arena') until the circus becomes a courtroom and she has to listen to the series of charges laid against her: she cannot make up her mind whether to marry Kendall, she cannot make up her mind as to what kind of woman she wants to be, she cannot even make up her mind over the circus cover.

Charley Johnson is there prosecuting, Randy takes the defence ('I'm the Attorney'/'He Gave Her the Best Years of His Life') and the Ringmaster takes an incidental cue to go off into a nonsense patter of Russian composers ('Tschaikowsky'), before Liza takes the stand to mount her defence with the tale of a young lady who came to a bitter end by making up her mind too firmly and too often ('Jenny'). It is a fine defence but, before she can rest on her case, the melody of her persistent song reappears and she shrinks from it in a panic. To the relentless sound of Charley's voice accusing her of cowardice in front of the song, in front of Kendall, in front of men, in front of herself, she is swept away.

Liza returns to Dr Brooks, and this time she talks to more effect. The emotion of panic that the dreams build up in her is an emotion she has felt before as a young girl. She has been able at last to recognise it. As she speaks, the scenes from her early life materialise: Liza as a little girl, brought before guests and her lovely flame-haired mother to sing, being excused and loved as an ugly duckling when she wants only to cry out that she is just like her mother; Liza as a schoolgirl hearing the child picked to play Prince to her Princess refuse on the grounds that she isn't pretty; Liza, chosen Most Popular Girl of her year, made much of at the school dance by the hand-somest boy in the class and then left waiting for him while he makes it up with the prettiest girl and forgets to tell her; and always, each time, that song was there ('My Ship') along with the bad feeling.

Every time, that is, except the last time. Was it, perhaps, because her lovely mother by that time was dead? Each time Liza began to grow and blossom in life, something came to cut down her confidence, so she with-drew from the competition and remained unfulfilled as a woman. Liza resists such an analysis: what about Kendall and their ten years together? Dr Brooks cannot yet answer that.

When Liza reappears at the office her first action is to set up an interview with Charley. She has realised that, over the years, she has been almost afraid of him, but now that fear seems suddenly to have gone. She still won't dine with him and get on to neutral ground and a person-to-person conver-sation. She holds to her desk and her Boss Lady position. Then Kendall comes to see her and she tells him that she will not marry him. There will always be affection as there always has been, but she will not marry him. Then, to her amazement, there comes a proposal from Randy who, in his honest way, gives her the truth. He's not that enamoured of acting and Hollywood, and he can't bear the people who go with it. With Liza he gets a feeling of peace and safety: behind the he-man star is the little boy who got sand in his face.

Now Liza has to think. She has to make up her mind all over again. Charley comes to say good-bye and suddenly she takes a change of tack. Out of the blue she offers him the joint editorship of *Allure*. A staggered Charley throws in some of the ideas he's developed over the years and Liza follows him enthusiastically. It's all falling into place. Randy Curtis is not the man for her any more than Kendall was: they both need the Liza in a suit, the tower of strength. Charley Johnson doesn't need or want anything of the sort, and he actually knows the words to 'My Ship'. As the curtain falls, the two of them are working happily on redesigning the whole layout of *Allure* and it is pretty certain that Liza will have no more bad dreams.

CARMEN JONES

a musical play in two acts by Oscar Hammerstein II based on Meilhac and Halévy's adaptation of Prosper Merimée's *Carmen*. Music by Georges Bizet. Produced at the Broadway Theatre, New York, 2 December 1943 with Muriel Smith and Muriel Rahn (Carmen), Luther Saxon and Napoleon Reed (Joe), Glenn Bryant (Husky) and Carlotta Franzell and Elton J Warren (Cindy Lou).

Produced at the Crucible Theatre, Sheffield, England, 14 March 1986 with La Verne Williams, Derek Lee Ragin, Marshall Ward and Maureen Braithwaite.

A film version was produced by Twentieth Century-Fox in 1954 with Dorothy Dandridge (sung by Marilyn Horne), Harry Belafonte (sung by LeVern Hutcherson), Joe Adams (sung by Marvin Hayes) and Olga James.

CHARACTERS

Corporal Morrell
Cindy Lou
Sergeant Brown
Joe
Carmen Jones
Frankie
Myrt
Husky Miller
Rum, *his manager*
Dink, *Rum's henchman*
Foreman, Sally, Lieutenant Eddie Perkins, T-Bone, Tough Kid, Bartender, Mr Higgins, Miss Higgins, Poncho, Bullet Head, etc.

ACT 1

At a southern depot in the United States, a team of stevedores is loading cases of parachutes for shipment to the war in Europe ('One More to Go') when a pretty young girl comes by looking for a corporal named Joe. She proves proof against the flirtations of the soldiers in charge of the shipment ('Cain't Let You Go') and carries on with her search as a crowd of children fill the street, mimicking the soldiers' drilling ('Lift 'Em Up an' Put 'Em Down'). Her Joe is not far away. He's working round this very factory where he has been chased by most of the girls in his time, but Joe is straight as they come and he has remained true to his home-town girl, Cindy Lou.

It is time for the girls from the parachute factory to break for lunch and their men are gathered outside the gates waiting to meet them ('Honey Gal o' Mine'). The girls, however, only have eyes for Eddie Perkins, a former square basher who has made it to the flying corps and earned himself a rank ('Good Luck, Mister Flyin' Man'). Getting into that corps seems to be the height of attainment and, even if Eddie Perkins doesn't impress him, Joe longs to get there himself.

Although it is lunchtime, one of the girls is just swanning in for work. It's Carmen Jones and, in spite of the odd sour remark, it is clear she is a special case. She has been helping boost military morale in a way that has nothing to

647

do with parachutes. Carmen has no time for the squaddies who crowd around her for a date: she has her eyes fixed on one man and she is going to get him ('Dat's Love'). That man is Joe, but Joe is not interested in Carmen, particularly when his Cindy Lou finally tracks him down and hands him a letter from his old mother. It is a worried mother's letter which clings to the hope that her boy will come back and settle down and make Cindy Lou his bride ('I Tol' Your Maw'/'You Talk Jus' Like My Maw'). That is just what Joe intends to do.

Suddenly there is a kerfuffle heard from the factory. One of the girls has reported Carmen for being late and the vicious, self-appointed queen of the scene has attacked her ('Murder! Murder!'). Joe has to intervene and drag the clawing attacker off her victim as Sergeant Brown, fresh in town from the big city, wades in with all the weight of his rank to arrest the girl. Carmen scorns him. She isn't military personnel and he isn't the law ('You Ain' a Police'm'); he can't do anything. But he can. He can confine her to the guardhouse to await the arrival of the civilian police.

Joe is ordered to take her away and, as she seductively offers him her own bandana with which to tie her wrists, he pushes her on her way. But Carmen has not finished with Joe. Forcing herself free, she kisses him laughingly before permitting herself to be led away to the taunting voices of the local urchins ('Carmen Jones Is Goin' to Jail'). Joe roughly pushes the children aside as he attempts to concentrate on his job of work. Carmen is pulling every trick in her bag to distract him from his orders: if he lets her go, they can meet later at Billy Pastor's café and she'll make it worth his while ('Dere's a Café on de Corner'). Finally Joe can resist no longer. He unties the bandana and lets the temptress free and when Cindy Lou and Sergeant Brown arrive on the scene he cannot deny the story told by a vengeful child: he let the woman go. Brown, who is already miffed by Carmen's obvious preference for Joe, angrily orders the corporal's arrest and Joe is marched off to take Carmen's place in prison.

At Billy Pastor's café, three weeks later, the night and the music are hot and one of the girls is letting it get to her ('Beat out Dat Rhythm on a Drum'). In a corner of this particular joint, a couple of Chicago boys are making out with Frankie and Myrt. Dink and Rum are in the boxing world— Rum is the manager of no less a star than the fighter Husky Miller—and they are chatting a line which involves exporting these two dolls Chicago-wards. Husky himself puts in an impressive appearance ('Stand up and Fight') and catches a glimpse of Carmen which more than pleases him, but he has no time to further the acquaintance as he has to go down to that Chicago train and get his beauty sleep. But he has some hefty words for his manager: he wants to see that tootsie in Chicago and the man had better manage that.

Rum is already lined up to take Frankie and Myrt with him; perhaps they can persuade the girls' cute friend to join the trip too ('Whizzin' Away Along de Track'). But Carmen isn't ready to go, not even at the call of Husky Miller. She's come to the café every night since her escape, hoping to meet Joe as arranged and, now that Joe is to be released, she must wait for him.

Love comes before adventure. Husky Miller is a grand man, but he rang her bell when she was already busy. All the temptations of big city life, a job in floor show and real dollars, cannot dissuade her. She will wait for Joe.

At last Joe comes, a Joe much changed since their last meeting. He has had three weeks in prison to ripen his passion and that passion has grown into a violent, jealous emotion. But, as Carmen dances around him, preparing herself for a night of love, he haltingly tells her that he cannot stay. He is on short leave and he must go back to the barracks almost immediately or he will be in trouble again.

Carmen is furious. Is this what she waited for? For this she gave up Chicago and a job in a floor show? She taunts him with being feeble and loudly throws her attentions at the nearest man until Joe cracks. Drawing from his shirt a flower which she threw at him three weeks earlier in her first temptings, he tells her passionately how he has kept it beside him all through his prison ordeal ('Dis Flower') as his love for her battered away at him.

Carmen knows she has her man. Maybe she can have Chicago too. She tells Joe that they must go away together ('If You Would Only Come Away'). Joe fights it. If he goes away and gets caught his record will be for ever blacked, he will never get into flying school. Carmen is taunting him with his cowardice as Brown walks in on the scene. Still angling to get Carmen for himself, the brave Sergeant joins in the baiting of Joe until Joe can take no more and, picking up a chair, smashes it down on Brown's head. Now his decision has been made for him. He cannot return to camp, he is finished as far as the forces are concerned. He may as well desert and follow Carmen to Chicago.

ACT 2

At the Meadow Lawn Country Club in Chicago, Rum and Dink are parading Frankie and Myrt amongst the local society. They have also brought Carmen there, lured by the gift of a fine new dress from Husky Miller whose interest in the girl has not lessened. Carmen and Joe have been living in a back street tenement where he can lie low, safe from the military police and, under these conditions, Carmen's love has soon worn thin. But Joe's love is stronger and more obsessive than ever, and he has followed Carmen to the club determined that she shall not have the chance to play him false. She can only shake him off when it seems that some army men are near and, while he flees the scene, she settles down to read the cards ('De Cards Don't Lie') of the rummy playing socialites. But, as she reads, just one message comes through: death for Carmen Jones ('Dat Ol' Boy').

It is not long before Husky Miller arrives to be shown off with his opponent for the forthcoming big fight, 'Poncho the Panther from Brazil'. He is all on heat to finally meet Carmen at close quarters but first he ends up encountering Cindy Lou. She has tracked Joe down to Chicago and she knows that wherever Carmen and Husky are, there Joe will be too ('My Joe') but when she finds him, her pleas for him to come home are swept away in the flood of his jealousy of the budding affair between Husky and Carmen. He even draws a knife and tries to attack the boxer, and has to be pulled away as everyone around tells him what he refuses to see: Carmen has finished with him (Finale: 'Your Maw Is Lonesome').

Finally Cindy Lou is reduced to saying what she did not want to say. Joe's mother is dying. That is why she has come to fetch him home. Joe looks at what has become of himself with loathing. He will go to his mother, but Carmen will never leave his thoughts for a minute and he will return and find her again. Their fates are bound up together and she cannot and will not escape him ('Where I Go You Go Wid Me').

A week later is the night of the Miller-Poncho fight at the Baseball Ground and the crowds have gathered from all over ('Git Yer Program fer de Big Fight'). When Husky appears he gets wild support ('Dat's Our Man') from the local crowd. With Carmen on his arm, he is beaming with confidence. It is Frankie who notices an unkempt and wild-eyed Joe standing broodingly in the background and warns Carmen to take care. But Carmen is in no mood to take care. It is not in her character to shrink away from anything or anyone and she purposely faces up to her former lover, challenging him to do his worst. Joe pleads with her to come back to him ('But All I Want to Do Is Love You Like I Useter'), he cannot live without her, but she only repeats that there is nothing left. She does not love him.

In the background the cheers of the crowd announce Husky's appearance in the ring and Carmen's face stiffens with pride. It is the last insult for Joe. He grabs her and tries physically to force her to come with him and she, angry now, tears from her hand the ring he gave her long ago and flings it violently away. What else can she say, what else must she do to convince him?

Now, at last, he knows that Carmen will never again be his and the world goes black. His hand is on his knife. Never will this woman do to another man what she has done to him. The crowd is roaring. The fight is over and Husky Miller has won but, as the boxer emerges triumphantly from the ring, Joe buries his knife in Carmen's body. She slumps, dead, to the ground and he falls brokenly across her body to await the death in which he will join the woman he loved.

OKLAHOMA!

a musical play in two acts by Oscar Hammerstein II based on *Green Grow the Lilacs* by Lynn Riggs. Music by Richard Rodgers. Produced at the St James Theatre, New York, 31 March 1943 with Alfred Drake (Curly), Joan Roberts (Laurey), Celeste Holm (Annie), Lee Dixon (Will) and Joseph Buloff (Ali). Produced at the Palace Theatre 13 December 1979 with Laurence Guittard, Christine Andreas, Christine Ebersole, Harry Groener and Bruce Adler.

Produced at the Theatre Royal, Drury Lane, London, 29 April 1947 with Howard

Keel, Betty Jane Watson, Dorothea MacFarland, Walter Donahue and Marek Wind-
heim. Produced at the Palace Theatre 17 September 1980 with John Diedrich,
Rosamund Shelley, Jillian Mack, Mark White and Linal Haft.

Played at the Théâtre des Champs-Elysées, Paris, 20 June 1955 with Jack Cassidy,
Shirley Jones, Pamela Britton and Harrison Muller. Produced at the Opéra Royal de
Wallonie, Liège, in a version by Michel Perrin, Marc-Cab and Franck Gerald 22
December 1972 with Michel Llado, Pierrette Delange, Aude Rozet, Willy Fratellini
and Luc David.

Played at Berlin 1951.

A film version was issued by Magna in 1955 with Gordon MacRae, Shirley Jones,
Gloria Grahame, Gene Nelson and Eddie Albert with Charlotte Greenwood as Aunt
Eller and Rod Steiger as Jud.

CHARACTERS

Aunt Eller Murphy
Curly
Laurey Williams
Will Parker
Jud Fry
Ado Annie Carnes
Ali Hakim
Gertie Cummings
Andrew Carnes
Ike Skidmore, Cord Elam, Fred, Slim, Jess, Mike, Joe, Sam, Ellen, Kate,
Sylvie, Armina, Aggie, Chalmers, etc.

ACT 1

On a fine new century's summer morning, somewhere in Indian territory,
Aunt Eller Murphy is sitting in the sun, churning her butter, when a happy
song ('Oh What a Beautiful Mornin'') heralds the approach of Curly, a fine
and handsome young cowhand who has come to ask Eller's niece, Laurey, to
partner him to the box social at the Skidmore place that night. Laurey, who
is listening anxiously behind the curtains, saunters out and plays hard to get
and, when Curly describes 'The Surrey With the Fringe on Top' that he'd
be taking his date to the dance in, she hides her fascination behind a jibe that
he must have hired such a gig. What a pity he'll have no one to ride with him
in it. Curly is darned if he's going a-begging for the girl's favour and he
laughs back at her that there is no fancy wagon—he just made the whole
thing up. Laurey, out of countenance, goes at him with the carpet beater and
flounces off.

The next bit of action in the neighbourhood comes when jolly Will Parker
turns up, delighted at having won $50 in a steer roping contest in the big city.
His sweetheart's pa promised if he ever had $50 he could have her hand, and
Will is off to lay claim to Ado Annie Carnes. He's bought a naughty 'little
wonder' peep-show toy for Pa Carnes and is full of stories about the modern
marvels to be seen in 'Kansas City'.

Curly is perplexed over women, and over Laurey in particular. She treats him so mean, does it signify she has her eye on someone else? Although Aunt Eller assures him that the girl is all his and just being womanly, Curly is worried, especially when he learns that the hired hand, Jud Fry, has it sweet for Laurey too. Jud is a dark, moody man whose work isn't to be denied, but he cannot be thought of as pleasant company for a young girl. In her pique at Curly over the surrey trick, Laurey impulsively promises Jud to be his partner at the social, and Curly, who really had hired the gig, is left instead to drive Aunt Eller to the dance.

Suddenly Laurey is worried. If her Aunt is going to ride with Curly, she will be alone with Jud all the way to the dance. That scares her, but it scares her even more to renege on her promise and tell Jud that she will not go. She has seen the way he looks at her, and she has seen the disreputable pictures pinned up in his room in the smokehouse. Well, she has made her bed and she must lie in it, but it won't be easy.

The next visitor at the ranch house is the peddler Ali Hakim and, along with Ali Hakim, comes Ado Annie Carnes. She's a bit taken aback to hear that Will Parker is home from the city so soon, for she's dated to the peddler for the social. When Laurey tells her she must pick which of the two men she really wants as a husband, Annie just simply can't. They're both so nice and she has low defences ('I Cain't Say No!'). It is clear that what Ali Hakim has in mind is an arrangement a little less permanent than marriage and, when Will arrives and talks to Annie in permanent-sounding terms, the pedlar is mighty relieved. Only trouble is, Will has spent all his $50 prize on presents, so he doesn't have the all-important $50 any more and it's back to square one as far as Pop Carnes and the wedding are concerned.

All the girls from down the road stop off at Aunt Eller's place to freshen up before the social, and giggling Gertie Cummings makes unabashed eyes at Curly. Laurey pretends not to care and, to her friends, she declares that she'll start all over with a new feller ('Many a New Day'). Annie is busy changing men again, too. Since Will has spent his $50 and isn't eligible, it follows logically that Ali Hakim can have her after all. The peddler tries every way he can think of to wriggle out of such a thing, but Ado Annie's father's shotgun proves a mighty persuader and he finds himself trapped ('It's a Scandal! It's an Outrage').

While the girls are getting their picnic hampers ready for the dance, Laurey and Curly come together alone, and Curly asks her awkwardly if she really intends to partner Jud to the dance when everyone expects her to come with him. Since neither is willing to be the first to give in and admit their real feelings, they both pretend it's better that they shouldn't be seen too regularly together. It might cause people in the neighbourhood to get the wrong ideas about them ('People Will Say We're in Love'). When they have played their little scene, he goes off and she ends up in foolish tears.

Curly goes to the smokehouse to have matters out with Jud. It's a rough place and Jud Fry is a rough man. He keeps a gun to hand and pictures of naked women on his wall. Keeping his eyes off Jud's sexy postcards, Curly notices a rope and hook and the conversation turns to hanging. Curly pictures Jud hanged and dead and how his funeral would be with all those people he never knew liked him come to mourn ('Pore Jud Is Daid'). Jud is momentarily confused by the thought of being liked, but he is better at hate. Where he last worked the whole family died in a fire after treating a hired hand badly.

Finally, the two men get to the point of Curly's visit, and each warns the other off Laurey. In an attempt to make an impression, Jud lets off his gun, and Curly returns the favour by putting a bullet clean through a knot hole in the smokehouse wall but, before things can go any further, Aunt Eller and some of the other folk rush up to see what is happening and a fight is averted.

Ali Hakim takes the opportunity to try to interest Jud in some of his more male orientated items, but Jud shows interest only in knives. What he wants is one of those 'little wonder' peep-show things that has a hidden knife in it. When a man turns it to see the girl disrobe, he gets the knife in his throat. That sort of thing is outside Ali's trade. He offers Jud postcards, but Jud is sick of pictures of women—he wants the real thing ('Lonely Room').

Laurey has made a purchase from the peddler. It is a bottle of smelling salts which he claims are descended from the Ancient Egyptians and which have the virtue of making your mind clear. Right now, that's what Laurey needs. She takes a sniff and, under the influence of the crystals, she begins to dream ('Out of My Dreams'). In a ballet, her dream takes shape: a frightening vision of a powerful Jud destroying Curly and carrying her off. When Laurey comes to her senses, the real Jud and Curly are there, in front of her. She heads for Curly but, as she passes, Jud grabs her arm. She dare not resist him and she lets herself be led away, leaving behind a hurt and puzzled Curly.

ACT 2

At the Skidmore place, the farming folk and the cowhands are getting together ('The Farmer and the Cowman'). Will Parker meets up with Ali Hakim and is real mad at the pedlar for taking Ado Annie away from him. If he'd only still had the $50 that he spent, the peddler wouldn't have had a look in. Ali Hakim sees a glimmer of hope. He begins, one by one, to buy at exaggerated prices all the gifts Will brought back from Kansas. When he sees the 'little wonder' he draws a line. A thing like that he certainly won't buy but, since Jud chances by, he lets Will sell the dangerous toy to Jud. Finally, Will has his $50 again!

Meanwhile the dance's box sale is going on under Aunt Eller's organisation. Each man buys a lunch hamper and, in return, gets as his partner the girl who goes with it. There are just two to go. The first is Annie's. Pop Carnes forces Ali to up the bidding, but things go haywire when Will Parker leaps in to bid a whole $50. He's got the hamper but he's lost his bride, because he no longer has the money. Ali Hakim gulps and bids $51. He's saved.

Then it is time for Laurey's hamper. Jud Fry enters the bidding purposefully but, when it seems that he is going to win the auction, Curly sells off his saddle and then his horse and gun to get the cash to beat him. The auction over, Jud heads towards Curly and tries to get him to use the 'little wonder' but Aunt Eller intervenes, demanding to dance, and Jud's evil plan is spoiled. Will Parker is intending to spoil a few plans too. He has his $50, he has Pop Carnes' grudging blessing and he has the date named for the wedding, so now he intends to give Annie a bit of a lecture: she's got to quit playing the field. They're engaged, and with him its 'All Er Nuthin''.

Jud has watched and manoeuvred all through the dance for an opportunity to get Laurey alone but, when he finally does, his courtship is so aggressive that the girl takes fright. When he gets frustrated and loud at her repulsing him, she turns on the hired hand and, with anger replacing her fright, tells him he is fired. Quietly, he lets her go and, with an awful look, leaves her. When Curly comes to find her, she takes comfort in his arms and pours out to him the tale of Jud's scary behaviour. Now, at last, Curly gets around to a few real, sincere words. All the games are forgotten as he asks Laurey to marry him and she, laying aside her foolish, light behaviour, says yes.

Meanwhile, Ado Annie is saying goodbye to Ali Hakim with more enthusiasm than is natural in a girl who has just got engaged to another man but, when Ali has gone, her mind can't concentrate on him any more, so she goes right back to concentrating on the man who is there. For the moment, Will Parker can rest easy.

A few weeks later Curly and Laurey are married. They are starting a brand new life in a brand new state, for 'Oklahoma!' has just become part of the United States of America. Ali Hakim comes back on the scene again: his flirtatious ways have finally earned him a shotgun wedding and he's been tied up to the impossible Gertie Cummings. Will Parker takes his revenge with a passionate kiss for the bride and, suddenly, Ado Annie finds out what jealousy is all about.

The farmers come down to Aunt Eller's homestead that night to rouse the newlyweds from their bed, and the two young people join in the good-natured traditional knockabout until, suddenly, Jud Fry turns up. He is there for revenge and he has a knife. In spite of everything the other folk can do, he attacks Curly and, as they fight, Curly throws Jud. The villain falls on his own knife and he is killed.

A black horror falls over the wedding day. Curly does not know what to do. By rights he must give himself up to the law, even on his wedding night. But Aunt Eller has other plans. The marshal and the judge are both here amongst the crowd. They can have a trial right here on the porch and declare the boy 'not guilty', and then the honeymoon can go right on as intended. The officials feel they ought to protest, but Aunt Eller's stern eye wins out and that is exactly what happens. Justice is done in double quick time and the pair drive off in the surrey on another beautiful morning to start their wedded life.

ONE TOUCH OF VENUS

a musical by S J Perelman and Ogden Nash based on *The Tinted Venus* by F Anstey. Lyrics by Ogden Nash. Music by Kurt Weill. Produced at the Imperial Theatre, New York, 7 October 1943 with John Boles (Savory), Kenny Baker (Rodney), Mary Martin (Venus) and Paula Laurence (Molly).

A film version was produced by Universal in 1948 with Tom Conway, Robert Walker, Ava Gardner, Eve Arden and Dick Haymes (Joe).

CHARACTERS

Whitelaw Savory, *a multi-millionaire with an interest in the arts*
Molly Grant, *his assistant*
Rodney Hatch, *a barber*
Gloria Kramer, *his fiancée*
Mrs Kramer, *her mother*
Venus, *a goddess*
Mrs Moats, *a landlady*
Zuvetli, *a foreigner*
Taxi Black, *a private detective*
Stanley, *his assistant*
Sam, *a smooth shoe salesman*
Store Manager, Bus Starter, Police Lieutenant, Rose, Dr Rook, etc.

ACT 1

At the Whitelaw Savory Foundation of Modern Art the students are doggedly repeating the modernist theories on art as preached by their patron ('New Art Is True Art'), the incomprehensibly rich Mr Savory. Having dispensed with his opening chorus, Savory immediately gives the lie to his lecture: he is waiting for the arrival of the latest item to be added to his incomparable collection, a fabulous, three thousand year-old statue, the Venus of Anatolia, which, at incalculable expense, he has had tracked down and acquired by a private detective. He has gone to this trouble not solely for the beauty of the statue, but because this particular Venus reminds him of the girl in his life who got away. His assistant, Molly, understands this. If a girl has 'One Touch of Venus' she can wreak havoc amongst men.

Mr Savory is thrilled with his statue and he is lost for words when his barber, little Rodney Hatch, shrugs off the beauties of the marble goddess and doggedly holds out in favour of the charms of his fiancée, Gloria Kramer. Gloria has much daintier fingers than the marble lady and, to prove it, Rodney brings out the engagement ring he has purchased for her. Then fate takes Savory out of the room and some strange, irresistible force gives Rodney the idea of putting the ring on the finger of the statue.

A thrill of thunder and a strange sourceless wind shake the room and lo! the carved goddess appears before the little barber as a flesh and blood woman. Rodney's ring has released her from the stone and she is his. Rodney shuts his eyes, thinks of Gloria and runs, but the immortals are not to be so easily balked. Once more the thunder rolls and the lightning flashes

655

and Venus descends from her pedestal to go into the modern world in pursuit of the man who has reawakened her.

Rodney makes it to his rooms and clasps his photograph of Gloria to his puny chest, pouring upon it a series of grotesque comparisons which tell 'How Much I Love You', but it is no use. He cannot escape. No sooner has he finished his serenade than Venus appears at the door and swans in to continue her advances. Then the phone rings. It is Gloria and poor Rodney has the greatest difficulty in convincing her that he does not have another woman in his rooms as Venus uninhibitedly tries to make head and tail of both the unfamiliar telephone and of Rodney. When Rodney's tartaric land-lady marches in, demanding to know what improprieties are being brewed, Venus uses a little old-fashioned godliness and fells her with a gesture. Things are beginning to stir horribly in the life of Rodney Hatch.

Leaving her pursuit of Rodney momentarily, Venus heads out into the city on a journey of exploration ('I'm a Stranger Here Myself'). She watches the faceless folk of New York ploughing through their daily routine (Ballet: 'Forty Minutes for Lunch') and interferes here and there, dispensing romance as she feels inclined. When she spies an attractive suit in the window of a couturier's shop she decides to help herself and, dissolving the shop window, walks up to the display and starts to dress herself from the dummy.

Chaos ensues as the police are called to arrest the thief, but Savory turns up at the critical moment and, staggered at seeing a woman who so nearly resembles his lost love, he wealthily disposes of both the shopkeeper and the police, and escorts Venus away. But Venus is not willing to be wooed by another man. The ring has bound her to Rodney and she vanishes from Savory's company, leaving the morose millionaire sadly to reminisce over his lost love ('West Wind').

Gloria and her mother are on their way back to New York and Rodney has been summoned to the bus station to meet them. They have been 'Way Out West in Jersey' and, typically, have found nothing that pleased them with the exception of a smarmy young shoe salesman who has been dripping attention all over them during the ride home. While the newcomer gets the gooey smiles, Rodney gets nothing but suspicious complaints. Gloria knows she heard a woman in his room and where is the engagement ring he promised her? Under such brutal treatment the worm turns. The wronged Rodney shouts that he has given the ring to Venus, prompting a whining walk-out from Gloria which Venus finds altogether in line with her plans.

Savory's detective, sent out in search of the missing statue, has been on Rodney's trail all through this episode and he decides that Mrs Kramer is evidence. He brings her to meet Savory and, when Mrs Kramer spills out her incoherent suspicions of her intended son-in-law, Savory is sure that they have found the thief but, before he can set off to raid the barbershop and retrieve his marble goddess, the living Venus turns up at his apartment.

She is in a confidential mood and bewails her 'Foolish Heart' which has led her to love the little barber when he is already engaged elsewhere. Savory has no trouble in finding an answer to her problems. It is a case of all's fair in

656

love and war. If there is a rival, Venus merely needs to eliminate her. While Venus muses on the possibilities of this solution, Savory continues the chase after his missing statue. Accompanied by his detectives, he makes his way to Rodney's shop where he kids the little barber along with some friendly man-chat ('The Trouble With Women') before conning him into going down into the basement to look at the plumbing and locking him in.

No sooner has the Savory search party started to go over the premises than Gloria turns up. Savory gags her and binds her into the barber's chair, but the detectives take fright in the presence of such drastic action and they run away empty-handed when they hear someone approaching. The visitor is Venus. She graciously unties the palpitating Gloria but gets only a barrage of insults for her trouble so, being a no-nonsense kind of goddess, she takes recourse in some gentle godliness, and magicks the howling creature off to the North Pole. All that remains is Gloria's powder compact—her best feature. When Rodney stumbles up from the basement, only Venus is there and this time, although he really has his mind on trying to wax indignant over the idea of Savory calling him a thief, he cannot resist her charms ('Speak Low').

Rodney and Venus are invited to a party on the roof garden of the Foundation, where Savory has arranged a special entertainment—a pageant representing the story of 'Doctor Crippen'. Savory chooses the moment just before the dramatic tale of murder and discovery begins to tell Rodney that Gloria has disappeared and that the police suspect foul play. Then Mrs Kramer spots Gloria's compact in Venus' possession and cries blue murder. The police are called to drag Rodney away to prison for murder, but Savory's plans to win the Venus for himself are foiled when the indignant goddess insists on going to jail with her beloved.

ACT 2

Savory is not the only one on the track of the Venus of Anatolia. Its former owners are determined to have it back as well and one rather fearsome Anatolian finds his way to the Savory mansion with a dagger between his teeth and revenge between his ears. Savory mischievously redirects him to Rodney's home before plunging back into gloom over his troubles. Molly is unsympathetic. His problem is one she'd like to have: it's simply that he's 'Very, Very, Very' rich.

Down in the police cells Rodney is put through an outrageous psychiatric examination before the fearsome Anatolian arrives to beg his goddess to return to her people. Venus refuses to leave her love and Rodney, who is now well and truly under her charms, refuses to let her go. Now that she has won her man, Venus uses a little magic to open the prison door and let Rodney out. She is just in time, as the entire cast of the show, for their various reasons, are all descending on the prison with the one purpose, to 'Catch Hatch'.

By some means or other, Venus and Rodney end up in a de luxe hotel suite where Venus is preparing to enjoy her new life and love ('That's Him'), but, in spite of the temptations that surround him, Rodney is unable to concentrate as he should. He is unable to forget that the police are after him because of the disappearance of Gloria. Venus shrugs. If that's all the problem is, then she will bring Gloria back from the North Pole. A quick flick of the wrist and there she stands, still talking. She takes in the picture—Rodney, Venus and the hotel bedroom—and, with a howl of horror, she flees from the scene.

Rodney realises what a lucky escape he has had from life with Gloria Kramer and, now that his engagement to her is off, he can sit back and plan his idyllic new life with Venus. How delightful it will be in that dear little estate up on Ozone Heights where all the houses are the same and life is laid out in nice predictable sections all the way up to your 'Wooden Wedding'. The picture he paints of sweet suburban life (Ballet: 'Venus in Ozone Heights') is not quite what Venus had in mind. Is this what she has been released from three thousand years of stone for? As the picture grows more and more suburban, Venus begins to withdraw and suddenly in a flash she is gone. The Ozone Heights of New Jersey are not for her. She has her own ozone heights beyond the clouds and that is where she belongs.

Meanwhile, back at the Foundation, the fearsome Anatolian is getting dangerously short-tempered with Savory but, as his knife hovers over the millionaire's throat, there is a flash and behold! there is Venus back on her pedestal. Poor Rodney is left looking sadly at his stone sweetheart. Where are all the promises that he would never be alone again? But, as he softly repeats the lines of 'Speak Low', a young girl enters. She has come to enrol at Mr Savory's school. She comes from Ozone Heights and she looks exactly like...well, Rodney has no need to ask her name.

SONG OF NORWAY

an operetta in two acts by Milton Lazarus taken from a play by Homer Curran based on the life of Edvard Grieg. Lyrics and musical adaptations from the works of Grieg by Robert Wright and George Forrest. Produced at the Imperial Theatre, New York, 21 August 1944 with Lawrence Brooks (Grieg), Helena Bliss (Nina), Robert Shafer (Rikard) and Irra Petina (Louisa).

Produced at the Palace Theatre, London, 7 March 1946 with John Hargreaves, Halina Victoria, Arthur Servent and Janet Hamilton-Smith.

A film version was produced by Cinerama in 1970 with Florence Henderson and Toralv Maurstad using a substantially different score.

CHARACTERS

Rikard Nordraak
Father Nordraak
Nina Hagerup
Edvard Grieg

Father Grieg
Mother Grieg
Count Peppi Le Loup
Louisa Giovanni, *his wife*
Freddy, Frau Norden, Miss Anders, Maestro Pisoni, Adelina, etc.

ACT 1

In the hills outside Troldhaugen, the young poet Rikard Nordraak is
entertaining the town children with the 'Legend' of the nymph Norway who,
the tale tells, is imprisoned in their local cave until the day when a minstrel
sets her free with his song. Today is a happy day for Rikard. All of his
childhood, he and Edvard Grieg and Nina Hagerup were inseparable companions but, as they grew up, life drew them apart. The boys stayed in
Troldhaugen to follow their arts, but Nina went away to the big city, to
Copenhagen, to become a woman of the world. Now, at last, she is back and,
city or no city, she is still the same lovely Nina, happy to let down her hair on
the hillside where they passed their youthful years. When Rikard and Nina
hear Edvard Grieg coming up the hill, Nina hides inside the cave. The
children get the young composer to sing into the cave and, like the nymph
Norway, Nina emerges. The three dear friends are back together again to
sing happily of their childhood days ('Hill of Dreams').

Down in the town, preparations for the Midsummer's Eve festivities are
brewing and the Grieg and Nordraak households are bustling with life when
'Freddy and his Fiddle' come by to set the children dancing. The festival
also welcomes to Troldhaugen two less likely visitors, the Parisian Count
Peppi Le Loup and his tempestuous wife, the opera diva Louisa Giovanni.
The prima donna takes a passionate fancy to the village and its young men,
and announces that she intends to stay awhile and enjoy herself with a fine
flirtation at the Midsummer's Eve feast ('Now').

Nina, shed of her town clothes and dressed in a very picturesque native
costume, soon finds herself being proposed to by Edvard ('Strange Music').
Since childhood both Rikard and Edvard have loved her, but her obvious
though unspoken preference has always been for the musician over the poet.
This has never harmed the friendship between the two men for the poet is a
generous and loving man to whom envy is an unknown emotion.

The French Count, who despairs of ever winning any attention from his
effervescent wife, tries to find some consolation in flirting with Nina but,
typically, gets caught. Louisa considers that this gives her all the more
latitude for a flirtation of her own and, when she discovers that part of the
day's festivities consist of a kind of lucky dip for the men by an old custom
whereby the girls select cakes containing their partner's name, she insists on
being included in the draw.

Her attention is distracted from her amorous pastime when she hears
music coming from the Grieg's house. Edvard is playing a new tune, 'I Love
You'. She listens with growing interest as he continues into 'Midsummer's
Eve' and, when the musician emerges from the house, she is as much taken

659

with his person as with his music. She immediately offers him an engagement as her accompanist in her forthcoming tour and the Count, seeing an all too familiar position developing, is mortified.

Whilst Edvard carries the news of this exciting offer to Nina, Louisa corners Mother Grieg, intent on finding out which cake contains Edvard's name. However, when the 'Trollger Celebration' takes place and Louisa opens the cake Mother Grieg has indicated, she finds that it contains the name of her own husband. The trolls of Troldhaugen are not to be mocked. She is further confounded when Edvard announces his engagement to Nina ('Betrothal'), and she takes revenge for her disappointment by announcing her immediate departure for Amsterdam and the beginning of her tour. If Edvard wishes to keep his job he must come immediately. The wedding must be postponed. Edvard has no choice but to take his leave of Troldhaugen and, as Nina waves farewell to the man she was to have married, Rikard steps protectively to her side.

ACT 2

Within a year Edvard Grieg has become celebrated in musical circles and a 'Bon Vivant' of the artistic world. He is being lionised at a reception in Copenhagen when Nina and Rikard come to see him. In spite of continual illness, Rikard has completed his most important work, the patriotic poem which Edvard had always promised he would set to music, truly Norwegian music. Edvard is pleased to see his friends, but Rikard's work is pushed from the composer's mind when Louisa brings in someone more important to meet him: the great Norwegian playwright Henrik Ibsen.

Ibsen has distanced himself from Norway and has lived long in Italy, but he has followed Grieg's career and his musical output with interest, from his dramatic pieces to the frivolous ones such as the 'Three Loves' which he has written for Louisa. Now he wishes his countryman to write the incidental music for his new play, *Peer Gynt*. Louisa is triumphant as she hushes the chatter of the reception ('Down Your Tea') to announce that Edvard will be going to the Riviera with Ibsen to work on the new play, but Rikard is deeply distressed that their long promised work together is to be once more put aside (Nordraak's Farewell). Nina, however, tops Louisa's announcement with one of her own: she and Edvard will be wed the next week.

A year later, in Rome (Chocolat Pas de Trois), Louisa is still promoting Edvard who is coming on erratically with the score of *Peer Gynt* and she arranges with the Director of the opera house to sing a performance of *La Traviata* in return for his lending the opera ballet to her for a performance of the *Peer Gynt* ballet music at her house.

The guests for the occasion are dancing 'The Waltz Eternal' when the floor is cleared for the ballet. The prima ballerina of the opera house is not pleased to have been summoned to dance to what she considers horrid foreign music, and she purposely falls during the performance, blaming her accident on the bad music, but when she is tricked by Louisa into losing her temper, she forgets to keep up the pretence of the hurt ankle and ends up being laughed out of the room. The moment is saved, but Louisa uses the incident as a warning to Nina about what happens to women who try to thwart Louisa Giovanni.

Grieg himself has not even bothered to attend the performance. His heart is not in his work. It is not in anything. But, as he sits alone with Nina, a servant comes to announce a Mr Nordraak and suddenly Grieg comes alive: Rikard is here in Italy! But it is not Rikard. It is his father with the news that Rikard's illness has finally got the better of him. Their friend is dead, and he brings them a last letter. With that letter is Rikard's poem: the one which Grieg had never set. Louisa comes to try to persuade Grieg to attend the party where everyone is asking for him, but Nina softly takes him in the other direction. It is time to return to Troldhaugen. Grieg looks up at her. He has been too selfish, he has failed her as he failed Rikard and he will do so no longer ('I Love You'). They will go home.

Back at Troldhaugen it is Christmas ('At Christmastime'). Life has become homely once more and, far from being a failure, Edvard's fame has only increased since his return to his native land. Under the mountains where they spent their happiest days and will spend many more, Edvard and Nina can listen to the 'Song of Norway' which was so dear to Rikard and is dearer than ever to them.

ON THE TOWN

a musical in two acts by Betty Comden and Adolph Green based on the ballet *Fancy Free*. Music and additional lyrics by Leonard Bernstein. Produced at the Adelphi Theatre, New York, 28 December 1944 with Betty Comden (Claire), Nancy Walker (Brunnhilde), Sono Osato (Ivy), Adolph Green (Ozzie), John Battles (Gabey) and Cris Alexander (Chip). Produced at the Carnegie Hall Playhouse 15 January 1959 with Evelyn Russell, Pat Carroll, Wisa D'Orso, Joe Bova, Harold Lang and William Hickey. Produced at the Imperial Theatre 31 October 1971 with Phyllis Newman, Bernadette Peters, Donna McKechnie, Remak Ramsay, Ron Husmann and Jess Richards.

Produced at the Prince of Wales Theatre, London, 30 May 1963 with Gillian Lewis, Carol Arthur, Andrea Jaffe, Elliott Gould, Don McKay and Franklin Kiser.

A film version was produced by MGM in 1949 with Ann Miller, Betty Garrett, Vera-Ellen, Gene Kelly, Frank Sinatra and Jules Munshin

CHARACTERS

Ozzie
Chip Offenbloch
Gabey
Ivy Smith
Brunnhilde Esterhazy
Claire de Loon
Judge Pitkin W Bridgework

Lucy Schmeeler
Madam Dilly
S Uperman, Workmen, Flossie, Flossie's Friend, Little Old Lady, Waldo
Figment, Diana Dream, Bimmy, etc.

ACT 1

Down at the Brooklyn navy yard at six o'clock on a summery morning ('I
Feel Like I'm Not Out of Bed Yet') a ship has just docked and is disgorging
its complement of bell-bottomed boys on to the wharfside. Amongst the
dash and bustle, three wide-eyed lads stop stock still and look around. It is
their first time in New York and they have just one day to experience the big
city and all the things it has to offer ('New York, New York').

Chip has a guide book which his father used when he came to New York
once, and a schedule for fitting in practically the entire 20,000 city streets in
the twenty-four hours available, Ozzie wants to get out and meet some girls,
and Gabey, the romantic one, just wants to meet one special girl. He doesn't
have anyone specific in mind, but preferably she should be like Minnie
Frenchley for whom he had a soft spot when they were in the seventh grade.

As the three friends head for the subway, Gabey's mind gets made up for
him. A bill-poster is putting up a showcard announcing this month's Miss
Turnstiles—a subway travelling cutie selected at random to decorate the
train stations for a few weeks. The boys read the caption: Ivy Smith is
studying singing and ballet at Carnegie Hall and painting at the Museum of
Modern Art, she's a champion sportswoman, she's a home-loving girl who
just adores nightclubs—this is one superior girl! Gabey decides there and
then that Ivy is the girl he wants to spend his day in New York with. He'll go
and find her. Amongst the 2,500,000 women in New York, he'll find her
before the evening. In spite of the screams of a little old lady, Gabey pockets
the showcard and the boys set off for their day on the town to howls of
'Vandals!'.

Chip and Ozzie generously offer to give up their sight-seeing and girl-
chasing respectively to help Gabey track down Miss Turnstiles. Gabey will
head for Carnegie Hall, Ozzie for the Museum and Chip will try to contact
the subway people. So, while Ivy Smith is being crowned as the average New
York Miss Turnstiles, and the little old lady is setting a policeman after the
thieving sailors, the boys split up to pursue their quest.

Chip doesn't get far before he is taken off course. A female cab driver
called Hildy Esterhazy has just been sacked and she has her cab for one
more hour and one more jaunt before she has to take it back and hand it in.
Hildy has decided that she's going to pick a good 'un for her last fare and
Chip just fits the bill. His protests that he has to help find Ivy Smith for his
pal are smothered under Hildy's vigorous attentions as she prevails on him to
'Come Up to My Place' instead of sight-seeing, particularly as most of the
sights in his daddy's guidebook don't exist any more.

Ozzie also goes astray. Instead of going to the Museum of Modern Art, he
ends up in the Museum of Natural History in the prehistoric department
alongside a complicated reconstruction of a dinosaur and a reproduction of

662

the apeman, *homo pithecanthropus*. His amazing resemblance to this beast provokes the enthusiastic interest of the pretty student anthropologist, Claire de Loon, and soon he has her undivided intellectual attention. Claire has taken up anthropology at the advice of her fiancé, Judge Pitkin W Bridgework, in order to concentrate her mind on things intellectual and to rid herself of her old habit of getting suddenly and violently carried away by sensuality. With a little help from Ozzie she is soon having a major relapse ('I Get Carried Away') and the two of them are leaping about the museum in a very prehistoric style until they accidentally come in contact with the dinosaur and the whole painstakingly reconstructed skeleton crumbles in a million fragments to the floor. They flee the scene of their crime with the museum staff and another policeman in their wake.

Gabey is still on course, but going slowly. The big city isn't the same as a ship. When you don't know anybody, it can be a 'Lonely Town'. Finally he makes it to Carnegie Hall. All sorts of activities are going on there but Ivy Smith is actually on the premises, having a singing lesson from the tippling charlatan Madam Dilly. Ivy has been a little over-described in her publicity: she is actually a cooch dancer at Coney Island who longs for finer things and who, to better herself, has been taking classes for which she can ill afford to pay. She is $50 in debt to the dreadful Madam Dilly who is herself in need of the money to replenish her supply of Scotch.

Ivy is standing on her head for the good of her resonators, while Madam Dilly pops out for a fresh bottle, when Gabey walks past and recognises her. When he asks her for a date she at first plays hoity-toity but she is dying to say 'yes' and she quickly drops her act and agrees to meet him that evening in Times Square. The date is no sooner made than Madam Dilly sweeps back in and sweeps the sailor out of her salon. Sex and singing don't mix—her own failure to make stardom is the living proof ('Do-do-re-do')—and Ivy needs success so that she can pay Madam Dilly her $50.

Claire and Ozzie make it safely back to Claire's luxurious apartment and are busy letting themselves go when who should walk in from the kitchen but Pitkin W Bridgework with champagne for two to celebrate his engagement to Claire. Bridgework is an unflappably nice guy, and he charmingly splits the bubbly three ways and insists that Ozzie remains to look after Claire while he goes off to a meeting. He and his fiancée can go out to Diamond Eddie's later for their celebration.

While this enthusiastic pair carry on letting themselves go, Hildy and Chip have arrived at Hildy's scruffy apartment where Hildy is anxious to show off her best feature to her young man ('I Can Cook Too'). It is almost impossible for her to show off her other features because her flat-mate, drippy Lucy Schmeeler, has a cold and has stayed home from work. A quick private word in the bedroom and Lucy, cold or no cold, announces that she is going to an air-conditioned movie.

Gabey waits for Ivy at the appointed time and place ('Lucky'), but she doesn't arrive. On the way to her date she runs into Madam Dilly who is furious to think Ivy is giving up a night's wages to meet a sailor and who threatens legal action over her $50 if Ivy doesn't get herself over to Coney

Island real quick. So Gabey is stood up. His friends try to fool him by dressing their respective girls as Ivy, but they don't know that Gabey has actually found the real Ivy and lost her, and the charade falls flat. So here they are on their big night in the big city, all ready to go on the town, but there are only five of them instead of six (Times Square Ballet). It will have to do, until they can be joined by Lucy Schmeeler who has been elected, *faute de mieux*, as a replacement date for Gabey.

ACT 2

The first place the gang hits is Diamond Eddie's ('So Long'), but in spite of strenuous efforts they can't get a happy atmosphere going, particularly when the club singer insists on drowning them all in pitying ballads ('I'm Blue'). Lucy Schmeeler mistakes the meeting place and ends up going to another Diamond Eddie's in Yonkers, but the friends do meet up with Pitkin who has come to the club for his cosy evening with Claire. He arrives just in time to pay the bill as the fivesome are rushing off to try the Congacabana.

The Congacabana isn't much better than Diamond Eddie's. The singer there has the same song and Hildy boots her off the stand to give a more positive sort of number ('You Got Me') to try and get the evening going. But the Congacabana gets the thumbs down too and, as Pitkin has just arrived, he is deputised to pay the bill and wait for Lucy while the others rush off to the Slam-Bang.

At the Slam-Bang fortune smiles at last on their enterprise. Who should be sitting in a corner wallowing in whisky but Madam Dilly and she is able to tell Gabey where Ivy is. Without thinking of the time he has to be back at the ship, Gabey heads for the subway and Coney Island with his four chums following closely in his tracks. Pitkin has a sweet nature; all his life he's turned the other cheek ('I Understand'), but it's getting distinctly pink now as he and Lucy, who is also rather *de trop* in this adventure, are left behind once again.

On the subway, Gabey dozes off and dreams of what he imagines the rich people's playground of Coney Island is like (Playground of the Rich/Coney Island Ballet), picturing himself as the Great Lover being tamed by the glamorous Ivy. On the train behind, the other four are wide awake and regretting that the twenty-four hours are going so fast ('Oh, Well'). When Gabey arrives at Coney Island he finds it to be a pleasure palace of a rather more gaudy and commonplace kind than the one in his dreams, and he finds Ivy doing bumps and grinds outside a fair booth. Poor Ivy explains about Madam Dilly and the $50 and how she wanted so much to go out with him but didn't dare.

Then, all of a sudden, the whole day comes together. The friends are no sooner all six together than the little old lady from the morning subway, the museum curator, Hildy's boss and their several policemen all turn up. They are cornered, and sweet-natured Pitkin, the judge, who has decided at last to give up being the eternal nice guy, won't help them out of their fix. They are all under arrest.

664

Next morning the three boys are escorted back to their ship by a policeman. It's time to go but, as they get ready to climb the gangplank, their girls rush up for a loving goodbye. It was a helluva day. Now the six o'clock whistle blows and, as our friends part, three young sailors, wide-eyed and fresh to the big city, come on to the wharf. They are ready to spend their day's shore leave in the big city in the best style possible. As Chip, Ozzie and Gabey proved, anything can happen in 'New York, New York'.

CAROUSEL

a musical play in two acts by Oscar Hammerstein II based on *Liliom* by Ferenc Molnar. Music by Richard Rodgers. Produced at the Majestic Theatre, New York, 19 April 1945 with John Raitt (Billy) and Jan Clayton (Julie).

Produced at the Theatre Royal, Drury Lane, London, 7 June 1950 with Stephen Douglass and Iva Withers.

A film version was produced by Twentieth Century-Fox in 1956 with Gordon Macrae and Shirley Jones.

CHARACTERS

Julie Jordan
Carrie Pipperidge
Billy Bigelow
Mrs Mullin
Enoch Snow
Jigger Craigin
Nettie Fowler
Heavenly Friend
Starkeeper
David Bascombe
Louise
Dr Seldon, Bessie, Policeman, Hannah, Arminy, Jennie, Virginia, Penny, etc.

ACT 1

The opening scene is an amusement park on the coast of New England around the year 1873. A feature of the park is Mrs Mullin's carousel with its gaily painted horses and its jack-the-lad barker, Billy Bigelow. Mrs Mullin likes Billy and she likes the amount of feminine business he brings to the carousel, but she is clearly jealous of the girls whom he picks out for his special attentions. She gets sourly steamed up when he pays a little notice to a mill girl called Julie Jordan and she vehemently warns the surprised Julie away from the carousel.

Her timing is bad, for Billy himself catches the end of the warning. He turns on his employer and tells her that she has no control over what girls he sees and, when the quarrel raises itself a tone, Mrs Mullin, not for the first time, sacks the barker. Julie and her friend Carrie are aghast at the scene, and even more worried when it turns out that Billy probably doesn't have the price of a beer to his name, but the man shrugs off such worries. He's going to get his things and then one of them can go and have a drink with him. He doesn't mind which.

Carrie is open-mouthed with amazement at Billy, and the girls are quite fazed at the fact that he is paying attention them. The quiet, introspective Julie has never had a boyfriend ('You're a Queer One, Julie Jordan') and Carrie's experience of men is in a very different field. She's going to marry the respectable and reliable fisherman, 'Mister Snow'. When Billy returns and asks which one of them is going to spend the evening with him, Julie volunteers without hesitation. She faces dismissal from the mill for doing so, for Mr Bascombe, the mill owner, insists that his girls are in their dormitory on time and when the two of them are seen together by Bascombe and a policeman, her fate is settled. She is as much out of a job as Billy is.

Although she is warned of Billy's reputation as a layabout, a sponger and a ladies' man, Julie declares firmly that she will spend the evening with him. She's a strange one: nothing like any of the women Billy has known before. She says she isn't ever going to marry and when he asks her, teasing, if she would marry him, the layabout and sponger, Julie has only one simple response—'If I Loved You'. At the end of the evening they kiss, and the kiss is not the usual kiss Billy gets from his women.

When they are married, Julie and Billy move in with Julie's cousin Nettie Fowler who runs a snack bar on the beach. Billy is unable to get a job, and he becomes more and more sombre and difficult as the workless days go by. He takes his frustration out on Julie and, one day, a one-sided row ends with his hitting her. Immediately the tale goes round town that Bigelow beats his wife. But if things are not as happy as they should be with the Bigelows, the rest of the folk are lively enough. 'June Is Bustin' out All Over' and there is to be a big clambake on the beach. As for Carrie, she is still awaiting her wedding day and she and Enoch Snow pass the time in dreaming of their future together in the rosiest way ('When the Children Are Asleep').

Billy has taken to hanging around with a known evildoer called Jigger Craigin, and Jigger is heading him for trouble ('Blow High, Blow Low'). He has a plan to rob the mill owner of the payroll he brings each week to the captain of Jigger's ship—three thousand dollars. Billy would never have to worry about a job again. He is tempted, but when Mrs Mullin comes to try and woo him back to her employ and the carousel he realises that his old life is better and safer than crime. Only there's a catch: Mrs Mullin insists that he leave Julie. What's the use to her of a barker whom all the girls chase and who goes home to his wife? He'd better talk to Julie and see whom she puts first.

When Billy goes to talk to Julie, however, she has something very different to tell him: she's going to have a baby. For Billy, that changes everything. Life has a future (Soliloquy). Now he has to make something of himself, he has to make money. There is no other way he knows of to do it: he will have to take part in Jigger's plan.

ACT 2

At the clambake ('A Real Nice Clambake'), Jigger tricks Carrie into close quarters with him and causes trouble between her and Enoch who tightly rejects her after finding her innocently flung over Jigger's shoulder ('Geraniums in the Winder'/'Stonecutters Cut it on Stone'). The girls all moan about the problems they have with their men, but to Julie it is all quite simple—if you love your man, that's really all there is to it ('What's the Use of Wond'rin''). When it is time for the treasure hunt, Julie tries to stop Billy going off as Jigger's partner and, when she feels the knife hidden in his shirt, she pleads with him desperately, but Billy pushes her aside and goes all the same.

Down on the waterfront Jigger and Billy play at cards, waiting for Bascombe to turn up. When he does, Billy distracts him by asking for the time while Jigger attacks with a knife, but Bascombe is armed with a gun and he is too strong for Jigger. Jigger gets away, but Bascombe covers Billy with his gun as the police hurry to the scene. The thought of a life in jail is too much for Billy and, before he can be taken, he turns his knife on himself. When Julie rushes to take her dying husband in her arms, he holds her hand tightly and tries to explain about what he had hoped for them.

Only when he is dead, and Mrs Mullin has passed by to say a wordless farewell to her boy, can Julie say to Billy what she never had the chance to say to him while he was living: she loves him, and now she is quite, quite lost. But she has to keep on living, she has to believe in the old maxims she learned as a child and keep them before her as she lives out the rest of what will be a lonely and loveless life ('You'll Never Walk Alone').

Now it is time for Billy Bigelow to go before his maker ('The Highest Judge of All') or, rather, the Starkeeper of the heavens. Before he can pass through even the back gate of Heaven, he's got to add some better deeds to those of his worthless life. He has one chance. The rules of Heaven allow him to return to earth for one day to try to right some of his wrongs.

By the quirks of heavenly time, it is now fifteen years later in New England and Julie's child, Louise, is a grown girl. She is not a happy child, for she suffers from the stigma of Billy's deed just as he suffered, in his youth, from the misdeeds of his own father. Even Carrie's son, Enoch jr (one of the nine she has borne to Mr Snow), who has a tenderness for Louise, wounds her with careless references to their respective places in life.

Billy takes up the Starkeeper's offer and goes down to earth to face Louise. He tells her some of the kindlier things about her father—how he made people laugh, how handsome he was—but when he tries to get close to her, and makes her a gift of a star he has brought with him from Heaven, the girl becomes suspicious. In frustration at his failure to make her understand him and his gift, Billy hits out at her just as, in life, he hit out at Julie when his frustration couldn't be released any other way. Frightened at his forcefulness, Louise runs to her mother, but Billy does not have the courage to allow himself to be seen by his wife. He can only speak aloud of his love for her knowing that she cannot hear. Julie picks up the star he has left and holds it close to her heart. She does not need to be told.

At Louise's graduation, Billy stands unseen and listening as the kindly, wise speaker of the occasion speaks of fortitude and compassion and right ('You'll Never Walk Alone'). Billy can only will Louise to believe in what the man says...and is it a coincidence that the speaker bears a strange resemblance to the Starkeeper?

ANNIE GET YOUR GUN

a musical comedy in two acts by Herbert and Dorothy Fields. Music by Irving Berlin. Produced at the Imperial Theatre, New York, 16 May 1946 with Ethel Merman (Annie) and Ray Middleton (Frank). A revised version was produced at the Broadway Theatre 21 December 1966 with Miss Merman and Bruce Yarnell.

Produced at the London Coliseum 7 June 1947 with Dolores Gray and Bill Johnson. Produced at the Chichester Festival 16 April 1986 and at the Aldwych Theatre 29 July 1986 with Suzi Quatro and Eric Flynn.

Produced at the Théâtre du Châtelet, Paris, as *Annie du Far-West* in a version by André Mouëzy-Eon and Albert Willemetz 19 February 1950 with Lily Fayol and Marcel Merkès.

Produced at the Volksoper, Vienna, 27 February 1957.

Produced at the Theater des Westens, Berlin, as *Annie Schiess Los* in a version by Robert Gilbert September 1963 with Heidi Brühl and Robert Trehy.

A film version was produced by MGM in 1950 with Betty Hutton and Howard Keel.

CHARACTERS

Annie Oakley
Dolly Tate
Winnie Tate
Frank Butler
Charlie Davenport
Colonel William F Cody, *'Buffalo Bill'*
Chief Sitting Bull
Foster Wilson, *proprietor of the Wilson House*
Mac, *the property man*
Major Gordon Lillie, *'Pawnee Bill'*
Tommy Keeler
The Wild Horse Ceremonial Dancer
Little Jake, Nellie, Minnie, *Annie's brother and sisters*
Sylvia Potter-Porter, Trainman, Waiter, Porter, Mr & Mrs Schuyler Adams, Riding Mistress, etc.

ACT 1

Buffalo Bill's Wild West Show is about to hit Cincinnati, Ohio, for a four day season ('Buffalo Bill') and Charlie Davenport, the show's advance manager, has come along to the Wilson House, an hotel on the outskirts of town, to drum up interest by issuing a challenge to the locals to face the show's sharpshooting Frank Butler, a suave gentleman whose attraction for the girls is evident ('I'm a Bad, Bad Man'). Neither Butler nor the ladies of the show, buxom Dolly Tate and her pretty daughter Winnie, can woo permission from the experienced hotel proprietor to host their contest and the show people prepare to go on their way to more hospitable places, but Dolly has just sat down to catch her breath, before plodding on, when the bird that decorates her hat is severed by a shot and, as she watches, horrified, a young woman strides on to claim her prey.

The markswoman is Annie Oakley, and she has come with her little brother and sisters to sell her game to the hotel. Mr Wilson can't help being interested. The birds have all been expertly shot with one hole through the head, no pellets in them for the guests to break their teeth on. Annie has no idea what to charge for her wares. She doesn't have too many ideas about anything except shooting. She can't count up to two dozen or make out a bill—where she comes from, folks are used to 'Doin' What Comes Natur'lly' and they haven't the need for all that palaver.

Mr Wilson is intrigued when he hears Annie's off-hand stories of her prowess with a rifle and he gets a practical demonstration when she casually slices the head off the cockerel on his hotel sign. Perhaps he has got someone to challenge that fool Wild West feller who wanted to bet him a hundred dollars against bed and lodgings for his whole troupe. Annie is always happy to take up a sharpshooting challenge and she agrees without hesitation to be Wilson's champion.

The next person Annie meets is Frank Butler and, without knowing who he is, she tells him confidently about the challenge she has accepted. She also falls for him mightily. But Frank has dimples and dimity ideas about 'The Girl That I Marry', and Annie is left to rue the fact that she apparently has only one talent and 'You Can't Get a Man With a Gun'. When she gets to the contest, which has drawn a fine crowd, she is startled to see who her opponent is to be but, at the end of a long drawn out contest full of fancy shooting, it is Frank who first misses the target and Annie who is acclaimed the winner.

She wins the prize, but she mortally wounds the pride of the man. Charlie Davenport is quick to see the potential usefulness of this feminine crackshot and he tackles Frank about taking a partner. The act could do with a fillip. Frank won't hear of it but, when Annie begs to come along just as his assistant, he thinks again and as Charlie, Frank and Buffalo Bill celebrate the fact that 'There's No Business Like Show Business', Annie Oakley becomes a member of the Wild West Show.

With Annie around, the Wild West company has to get used to a lot of crazy behaviour, but only Dolly Tate, who has been displaced as Frank's assistant, seems to come out the worse for it. Annie does her little bit in the show successfully, but her most important thoughts are centred on trying to become one of those pink-and-white type girls whom Frank has said he admires. Frank has been keeping an eye on Annie, but from a professional point of view only. He knows that she is good and that she should be allowed to do more in the act and, when it seems that they will have to share an audience with Pawnee Bill's show in Minneapolis, he realises that the show could use Annie as a novelty attraction to pull business away from the competition. Perhaps she could have just one or two secondary tricks to perform. She's not really a challenge to him, this funny little creature, this gun-toting girl who doesn't act like a proper girl. Has she ever been in love? She hasn't—not mutually—but she's heard about it and she lives in hope ('They Say That Falling in Love Is Wonderful').

Annie is working up a special trick to surprise Frank with and, with the Pawnee Bill clash in sight, Buffalo Bill asks her to perform it in Minneapolis. Charlie assures her that Frank will be thrilled, so Annie happily agrees. With this novelty up his sleeve, Davenport goes to work to stir up some challenging publicity and, as the train rattles towards Minneapolis, Annie, with no thought in her head of the debut to come, cheerfully puts her little brother and sisters to bed with a 'Moonshine Lullaby'.

When they get to their destination, Annie's first act has nothing to do with her big performance. She heads off to the pawnshop with Dolly Tate's gold watch, adeptly purloined, to hock it for enough money to buy a ring for Winnie and her boyfriend Tommy. The idea is that the loving young pair should get through the wedding, take back the ring, and retrieve the watch all before the disapproving Mrs Tate has had time to notice it's missing. Then they can live happily ever after ('I'll Share it All With You'), and no one will be any the wiser.

Meanwhile, Charlie has blazed Annie's name and picture across the outside of the tent, and the novelty seems to be attracting a crowd. This doesn't please Frank and he demands that for the next town the old billing be retained. It does nothing for Pawnee Bill either, and he retaliates by producing Big Chief Sitting Bull, the victor of Little Big Horn, as his guest of honour for the night, thus pulling back half the queue that had been lining up for Buffalo Bill's show. Sitting Bull has come into some money because the wretched oil that has been ruining his farmlands has become saleable, and Charlie Davenport sees in him a possible source of backing, but the Chief has three rules in life: no red meat, no get feet wet, and *no put money in show business*.

Annie is properly taken aback to see her new billing, but she happily agrees to forego it when Frank explains that it isn't right. She makes him promise to watch her perform that afternoon and he gives her a kiss for luck which leaves her poleaxed and him declaring that, in spite of all his experiences with the ladies, this time he's been caught on one foot ('My Defences Are Down'). He's been caught more ways that that. When Annie performs the special new trick she'd been saving, trusting in Charlie's word that Frank will love it, he is livid at being upstaged. Fuelled by Dolly Tate's accusations, he sees the exhibition as a plot by Annie to take his star place in the show, and his feelings for her are swallowed up by anger and jealousy.

Annie is desperate at his reaction but, if Frank doesn't want to know her, Sitting Bull does. The Chief is fascinated by 'little sure shot' and he declares he will adopt her into the Sioux tribe as his daughter (I'm an Indian Too'). Her joyful initiation as an Indian is spoiled when a note comes from Frank: he is leaving Buffalo Bill to take employment with Pawnee Bill, doing his old act with Dolly Tate. She may be the best shot in the whole world but it's the same old story, 'You Can't Get a Man With a Gun'.

ACT 2

On a cattle boat heading for New York harbour sit a down-on-their-luck little group comprising Buffalo Bill, Charlie Davenport, Chief Sitting Bull and Annie Oakley. They are returning from a triumphant European tour during which they were fêted and adored and which has lost them every cent of their capital. Every cent of Sitting Bull's capital, that is, for the charms of Annie Oakley tempted him to break his third big 'never' and he has lost all the money eased out of the US Government on this theatrical speculation. They have their press cuttings, and Annie has a chestful of medals pressed upon her by the admiring crowned heads of Europe, and that's it.

Buffalo Bill is even less cheerful when he hears that Pawnee Bill's show, featuring Frank Butler, is playing nightly at no less a venue than the Madison Square Garden, and Annie is no more happy to hear that Frank is the season's darling of the society ladies. But Sitting Bull has an idea. Pawnee Bill may have the cash, but they have the acts. How about a merger? Annie thinks that's a right good idea, as long as she and Frank get to merge as well ('I Got Lost in His Arms').

Pawnee Bill seems disposed to be friendly. In fact he arranges a swell reception at the plush Hotel Brevoort to welcome the famous Buffalo Bill team back to New York. Tommy, who toured with Buffalo Bill, and Winnie, who stayed with her mother and Pawnee Bill, meet up again and plead faithful ('Who Do You Love, I Hope') and Dolly doesn't even interrupt. The reason soon becomes clear. Pawnee Bill's bookkeeping isn't any better than his old rival's. They may be playing to good business at the Garden, but someone has done his sums poorly and Pawnee Bill's show is only surviving on 'investments' from the society ladies he and Frank have been courting. They think that Buffalo Bill has money and they, too, are out to effect a tactful merger.

In the meanwhile Annie is getting an eyeful of New York society and she isn't too keen on what she sees. So this is what Frank has been seen out with. Her prospects of getting back on the same team as her man seem to have taken a knock when Dolly Tate finds out the truth. If both sides are as poor as each other, what's the use of a merger between two dead ducks? The only asset anyone has is the chestful of golden, bejewelled medals Annie has brought back with her. When Annie realises that only the proceeds from the sale of her trophies will allow the merger with Frank to go ahead, she promises she will sell them. After all, what does she want with jewels? ('Sun in the Morning'). But first she wants Frank to see her wearing them.

Frank and Annie finally meet up again and they are soon in each other's arms happily reprising 'They Say That Falling in Love Is Wonderful'. Frank offers Annie his three gold medals as a gift but, when she opens her coat to display the gifts of royal Europe, he is crushed all over again. Within no time they are arguing about who is the better shot, the merger is off, and a challenge match is on. All her trophies, representing everything she owns, Annie will gamble against Frank's three medals.

The shoot out is arranged to take place on Governor's Island the next morning, and Dolly Tate arrives there early, planning to sabotage Annie's guns. She is caught in the act by Sitting Bull and Charlie and stopped, but then Sitting Bull has a thought. If Annie wins the match she will lose Frank, but if she loses the match... The two men end up completing the very act of sabotage they had prevented Dolly from committing.

The two competitors face up to each other ('Anything You Can Do'), the shooting begins and, to her amazement and horror, Annie misses the first targets. Frank steams ahead on the scoreline and, as he heads for a win, all his warmth towards Annie returns. When she changes guns, succeeds in scoring again, and becomes her old cocksure self, his manner changes too. Sitting Bull has to interfere. Annie always said that she couldn't get a man with a gun, but he has news for her: here is a gun she can get a man with. He hands her the sabotaged rifle.

Finally the message sinks into Annie's brain. She happily carries right on missing the targets until she ends the competition a joyful loser. She hands over her medals but Frank doesn't want to take them and, when she insists, he in turn hands them on to the two Bills. They will be the foundation of the new Wild West Show, starring Mr and Mrs Frank Butler—the best sharp-shooting team in the world.

The song 'An Old-Fashioned Wedding' was written by Berlin for the 1966 revival in which the roles of Winnie Tate and Tommy and their two duets were eliminated.

BRIGADOON

a musical play in two acts by Alan Jay Lerner. Music by Frederick Loewe. Produced at the Ziegfeld Theatre, New York, 13 March 1947 with David Brooks (Tommy), Marion Bell (Fiona), George Keane (Jeff) and Pamela Britton (Meg). Produced at the Majestic Theatre 16 October 1980 with Martin Vidnovic, Meg Bussert, Mark Zimmermann and Elaine Jausman.

Produced at His Majesty's Theatre, London, 14 April 1949 with Philip Hanna, Patricia Hughes, Noele Gordon and Bill O'Connor.

Produced at the Badische Staatstheater, Karlsruhe, 10 May 1980.

A film version was produced by MGM in 1954 with Gene Kelly, Cyd Charisse (singing dubbed by Carole Richards), Elaine Stewart and Van Johnson.

CHARACTERS

Tommy Albright
Jeff Douglas
Archie Beaton
Harry Beaton
Andrew MacLaren
Fiona MacLaren
Jean MacLaren
Meg Brockie
Charlie Dalrymple
Mr Lundie
Angus MacGuffie
Sandy Dean
Maggie Anderson, Stuart Dalrymple, Jane Ashton, MacGregor, etc.

ACT 1

In the highlands of Scotland ('Once in the Highlands') two American holidaymakers, out on a hunting trip, have become benighted. Practical, wisecracking Jeff and the more thoughtful and romantic Tommy take rather disparate attitudes to their predicament, but they are both equally taken aback when, to the sound of singing voices ('Brigadoon'), they see in front of them a distant village, shrouded in mist, where there was surely no village before.

In the little village of Brigadoon it is market day 'Down in MacConnachy Square' and the townspeople are out in force, to sell—like Archie Beaton who runs the plaid stall with little help from his sullen son Harry, Angus MacGuffie with his farm goods, and lively little Meg Brockie with her cream pails—or to buy, like the MacLaren family, father Andrew and his two daughters, bright and lovely Fiona and pretty, quiet Jean.

Today is Jean's wedding day. She is to be wed to young Charlie Dalrymple this very evening and herein lies the cause of Harry Beaton's clouded brow. He, too, is in love with Jean MacLaren. Meg Brockie, who would marry the first man who asked her, cannot understand that Fiona is content to see her younger sister wed afore her, but Fiona smilingly explains that she is 'Waitin' for My Dearie'. Until she finds the man of her heart, she is happy to bide her time.

When Tommy and Jeff make their way into Brigadoon they are surprised to see the quaint native costume sported by the villagers, and flabbergasted to have their money refused at the stalls as unknown coinage, but they are delighted with the attentions paid by the fair villagers. Fiona takes charge of Tommy and Meg Brockie enthusiastically volunteers to look after Jeff. For Charlie Dalrymple, however, today is the end of his keeping company with girls. This evening will be his wedding ('I'll Go Home With Bonnie Jean')

673

and this afternoon he goes to the MacLaren house to enter his signature in the family bible in the traditional way.

Tommy is bemused by Brigadoon. The people have a strangeness about them and there are odd overheard phrases that he does not understand, particularly references to a 'miracle' and 'the man who postponed the miracle', but he is entranced by Fiona and, when she goes to gather flowers for the wedding, he accompanies her amongst 'The Heather on the Hill'.

Jeff, in the meanwhile, has been led off by Meg to a little cottage on the hillside. The cottage is a primitive shack, with little in the way of furniture but a cot and a rocking chair, and Meg has a tale to tell. Her mother was a gipsy who chanced one day on this cottage and found a bonny lad asleep in the cot. So she sat down on the rocking chair and waited, and not long afterwards Meg was born. The weary Jeff is soon relaxing on the cot as Meg entertains him with the tale of 'The Love of My Life' in which each verse refers to a different unfortunate affair. When she has finished, Jeff is asleep. With a little smile, Meg sits down in the rocking chair and waits.

At the MacLaren house 'Jeannie's Packin' Up' when Harry Beaton comes to deliver Mr MacLaren's wedding waistcoat and bitterly declares his disillusioned hatred for Brigadoon and everything in it. All the old man's persuasion that Brigadoon is, to the contrary, a blessed town, cannot shake the black-browed boy. Charlie has signed the bible and, although he should not see Jean on their wedding day, he sings to her from under her window begging her to 'Come to Me, Bend to Me'.

Fiona and Tommy return with their arms full of heather and Jeff reappears in a buoyant mood and sporting a new pair of trousers. The old ones, apparently, suffered from rather rough treatment from the thistles in Meg's cottage. Tommy, too, has a light heart ('It's Almost Like Being in Love'): Brigadoon is almost too good to be true. Then he discovers that, in fact, it is not true. He spies the open bible in which Charlie has just entered his name and notices the date of the wedding: 24 May 1746. Fiona will not give an explanation. All she can do is take Tommy and Jeff to meet Mr Lundie, the schoolmaster, and the wise man of the village.

Mr Lundie tells them the tale of Brigadoon. In 1746 the happy little village was direly threatened by a band of marauding devil-worshippers and magicians. The minister, Mr Forsythe, pondered a way in which Brigadoon could be protected from these forces of evil and, finally, he prayed to God that Brigadoon might simply vanish away out of the path of the sorcerers. His prayer was granted. The village would disappear from the face of the earth, but not for ever. One day each hundred years, a hundred years which would pass like a single night in the lives of its people, Brigadoon would reappear in its old place.

So God took Mr Forsythe to Himself and, in return, granted him his prayer for Brigadoon, but the miracle was delayed for two days to allow Charlie Dalrymple, who was away from home, to return for his wedding. Now, in Brigadoon, it is only two days since the miracle, even though two hundred years have passed in the outside world, and when night falls the village and all in it will go to sleep for another hundred years.

The bells of the kirk begin to ring, announcing the call to Jean and Charlie's wedding, and the village gathers to celebrate their marriage. The ceremony over, the newlyweds begin the wedding dance. Harry Beaton performs a sword dance and then calls Jean to dance with him but, as she does, Harry suddenly stops the dance and kisses her before the amazed company. As Charlie leaps forward to challenge him, Harry draws a dirk. Tommy intervenes to stop the fight, and Harry, full of hatred, takes the ultimate revenge. It is part of Mr Forsythe's miracle that no one shall ever leave the village. Should they do so, Brigadoon will be condemned to vanish for ever. Harry springs away—he is leaving Brigadoon and they are all damned!

ACT 2

Among the trees near the edge of Brigadoon, the men of the village are hunting the fugitive (The Chase) but, as Harry flees towards the borders of Brigadoon, wildly trying to escape the pursuing Jeff, he falls and, plunging from a rocky cliff, he is killed instantly.

Tommy returns to the anxious Fiona and they confess their love for each other ('There But For You Go I') and Tommy wonders if he might be allowed to stay in Brigadoon but, while the wedding festivities take up where they had left off and Meg Brockie gives out with the story of 'My Mother's Wedding Day', Jeff is troubled . He blames himself for Harry Beaton's death and is horrified at the thought that Tommy might be bewitched into staying in this unreal dream town. He urges his friend to come away immediately. If once he stays here too long he will be bound to remain for endless centuries.

When Fiona brings Mr Lundie to hear Tommy's petition to stay in Brigadoon, she finds that Jeff has shaken not his love but his will. He must, after all, leave before nightfall when the village passes back once more out of the real world. Tommy takes a loving farewell of Fiona ('From This Day On'), and she tells him that she will not be lonely, lost in the mists of time. It is not real loneliness to love in vain, only not to love at all. As the strains of 'Brigadoon' announce the end of the day and the mists descend again over the village, Tommy and Jeff take their leave of Brigadoon.

Back in America, Tommy finds it impossible to take up his old life where he had left off. A dozen times a day a word or a phrase catches an echo of Brigadoon and in his mind he sees and hears the place and its people and, above all, Fiona. He calls off his planned wedding to the chic, modern Jane Ashton and, in a rush of realisation, books a ticket back to Scotland. Brigadoon may have gone, but he has to return.

Back in the forest where they first blundered into Brigadoon, Tommy and Jeff look at the empty ground where the village stood. Then the music begins again, the song of 'Brigadoon'. No village appears, but there is Mr Lundie, a pale figure from beyond the world. The love Tommy bears for Fiona has entered into the miracle and, by its great power, it has awoken Mr Lundie from his hundred years' sleep. He has come to get Tommy and take him back to Brigadoon and to Fiona. As Jeff watches silently, Tommy falls in alongside Mr Lundie and the two of them vanish into the highland mist, leaving Jeff alone in the forest.

KISS ME, KATE

a musical comedy in two acts by Samuel and Bella Spewack based partly on Shakespeare's *The Taming of the Shrew*. Lyrics and music by Cole Porter. Produced at the New Century Theatre, New York, 30 December 1947 with Alfred Drake (Fred), Patricia Morison (Lilli), Harold Lang (Bill) and Lisa Kirk (Lois).

Produced at the London Coliseum 8 March 1951 with Bill Johnson, Miss Morison, Walter Long and Julie Wilson. Revived there by the English National Opera 24 December 1970 with Emile Belcourt, Ann Howard, Teddy Green and Judith Bruce. Produced at the Old Vic May 19 1987 with Paul Jones, Nichola McAuliffe, Tim Flavin and Fiona Hendley and played at the Savoy Theatre from 18 January 1988.

Produced at the Städtische Bühnen, Frankfurt am Main, 19 February 1955.

A film version was produced by MGM in 1953 with Howard Keel, Kathryn Grayson, Tommy Rall and Ann Miller.

CHARACTERS

Fred Graham (Petruchio)
Harry Trevor (Baptista)
Lois Lane (Bianca)
Lilli Vanessi (Katharine)
Bill Calhoun (Lucentio)
Hattie, *Lilli's maid*
Ralph, *the stage manager*
Harrison Howell
First Gangster
Second Gangster
'Gremio'
'Hortensio'
Paul
Stage Doorman, etc.

ACT 1

At Ford's Theatre in Baltimore a new musical show has just finished its last run through before being presented to the public. The piece is a version of Shakespeare's *The Taming of the Shrew*, improved and musicalised by a half-dozen American writers and composers and starring the popular actor Fred Graham opposite his ex-wife, the movie star Lilli Vanessi. Fred is giving last minute instructions to the cast, and most particularly to the vivacious Miss Lois Lane, a cabaret performer cast as a pert and definitely un-Shakespearian Bianca. He gives rather less attention to his co-star whose seething annoyance at what she sees as a calculated insult bursts out in a round expletive in front of the company. Miss Vanessi stalks off to her dressing room in a huff, leaving her maid Hattie to lead the company in hailing 'Another Op'nin', Another Show'.

As soon as she is free from the stage, Lois hurries off in search of Bill Calhoun, her old cabaret partner. He has been cast in the show as Lucentio but his behaviour up till now has been less than professional. His latest misdeed has been to miss the rehearsal of the curtain calls and Lois is desperate in case he should mess up their big chance for a career in the legitimate theatre by his offhand attitude ('Why Can't You Behave'). The free and easy Bill is a gambler in more ways than one. Instead of rehearsing, he has been involved in a card game where, after a bad run, he has ended up signing an IOU for $10,000. Needless to say the penniless dancer was too fly to sign his own name to the chit. He used the name 'Fred Graham'.

It is opening night. In her dressing room Lilli is on the phone to her fiancé, the wealthy politician Harrison Howell, who has been persuaded for love of her to back the show to the extent of $200,000. From his dressing room next door, Fred harangues her and she answers back with equal force, but recriminations lead to reminiscences and the atmosphere softens as they remember their early days together in third-rate touring operetta ('Wunderbar').

As Fred makes his preparations for the show, he is surprised to be interrupted by the intrusion of two rather forceful gentlemen who say that they have called about an IOU. His perplexed denials do him no good, and the gangsters promise meaningfully to return before the night is out. Then they hope to find him in a more remembering frame of mind. While Fred is puzzling over this incident, Lilli has received a lovely bouquet. It is from Fred, a replica of the flowers from her wedding bouquet, and she admits to herself that, beneath the angriness of their relationship and their divorce, she is still in love with him ('So in Love'). She calls through the wall, thanking him happily, but Fred is less than thrilled. The flowers had been intended for Lois.

Now the curtain rises on *The Taming of the Shrew* ('We Open in Venice') and the principal characters begin the play. Lois, as Bianca, is serenaded by her suitors Lucentio, Gremio and Hortensio ('Tom, Dick or Harry') before Fred, as the virile Petruchio, introduces himself ('I've Come to Wive it Wealthily in Padua') and pledges himself to wed the shrewish heiress, Katharine, as played by Lilli ('I Hate Men'). He woos her rudely ('Were Thine That Special Face'), but suddenly the play takes on a new depth. Between scenes, Lilli has discovered the card attached to the flowers and she is glittering with rage and hurt pride. The scene between Petruchio and Katharine bristles with violence as Lilli takes every opportunity to assault Fred physically and it ends with the exasperated Fred putting her across his knee, in accordance with the script, and spanking her for all he is worth.

At the interval, the furious Lilli lets all her anger loose on Fred. She calls Harrison to say she is quitting the show on the spot and wants him to marry her that night. Fred threatens that she'll be blacklisted from the stage forever, but he can see in her eyes that old look, so familiar from their married days, and he knows that she means what she says. In the midst of this crisis the two gangsters turn up to find out how his memory is going. The last thing he needs at this moment is to have to cope with these two goons and their crazy story about a $10,000 debt, but suddenly he realises that they just might be useful.

Fred decides to own to the debt, but he explains to the two men that he doesn't have the money. It will have to come from the box office at the end of the week. The men are satisfied with that as, in their opinion, the show seems to have everything it takes to succeed, but Fred tells them about his doubts. The leading lady is about to walk out. If she does, they will have to close and that means there'll be no money. As Fred suspected, this decides the two men to have a friendly little talk with Lilli.

Back on stage the second act is under way ('I Sing of Love'). Finally it leads into the wedding scene of Katharine and Petruchio ('Kiss Me, Kate') during which Fred and the two gangsters, disguised as chorus members, keep the fumingly unwilling Lilli up to the mark. At the end of the scene, as per the script, Fred bodily lifts Lilli up and carries her, struggling, off.

ACT 2
In the stage door alley, Fred's dresser, Paul, leads a lazy song and dance complaining of the muggy weather ('Too Darn Hot') while, on stage, *The Taming of the Shrew* continues its lively performance through the deprivation scene ('Where Is the Life That Late I Led'). By now, in response to his fair lady's frantic phone call, the dignified Harrison Howell has arrived at the stage door with an ambulance. He is embarrassed at meeting Lois, who is quick to recall a pleasant weekend they once spent together in Atlantic City, but equally as quick to assure Bill that she really loves him and is 'Always True to You in My Fashion'.

Fred's clever setting up of the situation makes Harrison somewhat dubious about Lilli's seemingly gothic tale of being held prisoner in the theatre and he does not react as supportively as Lilli might have wished. He also agrees complacently with every aspect of a satirical portrait of his life (soon to be Lilli's life) as painted by Fred until Lilli, fit to burst, evicts Fred from her room.

While Bill, in the corridor, is serenading his 'Bianca' through the procession of messengers bearing gifts from admirers, the gangsters are on the phone, reporting in to the boss. But now it is they who have a problem. It seems that since a few hours ago the boss is no longer the boss. In fact he's no longer anything. This, it would seem, cancels both Fred's debt and their mandate. They thank a despairing Fred and a jubilant Lilli for a delightful evening and prepare to depart. Lilli is free. She does not have to play the last act. She sweeps off to her cab as Fred reprises 'So In Love' behind her.

Although the curtain stays stubbornly down, the audience is not without entertainment, for the two gangsters have taken a wrong turning on their way out of the theatre and have ended up on the stage where, with a touch of the old soft shoe, they compound their new theatrical experience in an incidental duo ('Brush Up Your Shakespeare'). The final act of the show opens with the wedding of Bianca and Lucentio but, when the moment comes for Katharine to enter for the famous fountain speech, there is no Lilli. All is lost. Then, suddenly she is there, speech and all ('Women Are so Simple') and, when the kiss comes at the end of the speech, it is Fred and Lilli who kiss and not Petruchio and Katharine.

SOUTH PACIFIC

a musical play in two acts by Oscar Hammerstein II and Joshua Logan adapted from *Tales of the South Pacific* by James Michener. Lyrics by Oscar Hammerstein II. Music by Richard Rodgers. Produced at the Majestic Theatre, New York, 7 April 1949 with Ezio Pinza (Emile de Becque), Mary Martin (Nellie Forbush), Juanita Hall (Bloody Mary), William Tabbert (Cable), Betta St John (Liat) and Myron McCormick (Billis).

Produced at the Theatre Royal, Drury Lane, London, 1 November 1951 with Wilbur Evans, Miss Martin, Muriel Smith, Peter Grant, Miss St John and Ray Walston. Produced at the Prince of Wales Theatre 20 January 1988 with Emile Belcourt, Gemma Craven, Bertice Reading, Andrew C Wadsworth, Pamela Yang and Johnny Wade.

Produced by the Opéra Royal de Wallonie at Verviers in a version by Marc-Cab and André Hornez 8 November 1974 with Guy Fontagnère, Caroline Dumas, Line May, Louis Landry and Willy Fratellini.

A film version was produced by Twentieth Century-Fox in 1958 with Rossano Brazzi (singing dubbed by Giorgio Tozzi), Mitzi Gaynor, Miss Hall (singing dubbed by Miss Smith), John Kerr (singing dubbed by Bill Lee), France Nguyen and Ray Walston.

CHARACTERS

Ensign Nellie Forbush
Emile de Becque
Ngana, Jerome, *his children*
Bloody Mary
Liat, *her daughter*
Luther Billis
Stewpot
Professor
Lieutenant Joseph Cable
Captain George Brackett
Commander William Harbison
Lieutenant Buzz Adams
Henry, Abner, Dinah Murphy, Janet McGregor, Yeoman Herbert Quayle, etc.

ACT 1

At his island home, the French planter, Emile de Becque, is entertaining Ensign Nellie Forbush of the United States Navy to lunch. Outside the house, his half-caste children play and sing ('Dites-Moi') while, over coffee and brandy, Emile and Nellie are beginning to fall in love. She is from Little Rock, Arkansas, glad to be out of it and busy making the most of the south Pacific while the other American girls are busy hating it ('A Cockeyed Optimist'). He has spent most of his life in the islands after fleeing France at a young age, having killed a man in self defence.

It is only a fortnight since they met and, although it seems they have nothing in common—the cultured, middle-aged Frenchman and the bright young American nurse—already, privately, in parallel soliloquy, each is imagining what it would be like if the two of them were one. It seems too soon to be thinking like this, but sometimes these things happen with amazing immediacy ('Some Enchanted Evening') and, when it is time for Nellie to leave to go on duty, she takes with her an unspoken proposal of marriage.

Back at the navy camp, the men are singing lustily of how 'Bloody Mary Is the Girl I Love'. Bloody Mary is a tiny, wrinkled Tonkinese who sells grass skirts and shrunken heads to the souvenir hunters from a kiosk on the camp site. She is not the only one to have set up in business for the benefit of the troops. The comical Luther Billis is determined to become a war profiteer and he has invented a self-made laundry system. He has also gone into grass-skirt manufacturing in an effort to edge in on Bloody Mary's market, but he is no match in commerce for the old crone who does him out of his whole stock plus $100 in exchange for a boar's-tooth bracelet.

The bracelet comes from an off-shore island, Bali H'ai, which is off-limits to the troops, a restriction which Billis finds particularly galling as, not only are all the best souvenirs to be bought cheaply on the island, but the local women have been evacuated there and the sailors, whose female company is limited to the nursing corps, can only look across the water and agree that 'There Is Nothing Like a Dame'.

A new arrival on the island arouses a special interest from Billis and sets Bloody Mary drooling. Lieutenant Joe Cable has just got in from the Pacific front line. He is young, good looking and, most importantly from Billis's point of view, he is an officer. Officers can take out boats, and a boat is what Billis needs to get across to Bali H'ai. For some reason, Bloody Mary also has an interest in getting Cable across to that mysterious island, and she serenades him winningly with descriptions of the special charms of 'Bali H'ai'.

The real reason for Cable's visit is unveiled when he meets Captain Brackett and Commander Harbison, the senior officers on the island. It has been decided at top level that an intelligence source is needed on one of the islands at the head of their channel in order to provide advance warnings of Japanese ship and aeroplane movements. Cable has been chosen to be that source, and he has come to this island to consult with Emile de Becque, whose knowledge of the islands can help him to establish a position where he might be safely and usefully installed.

Before de Becque is brought into the affair, the Americans need to find out how trustworthy he is and, to that end, they call in Nellie Forbush. When she has to answer questions about him, Nellie realises just how little she does know about Emile. In fact, she knows less than the officers do, for she does not know about Emile's late Polynesian wife and his two children. Letters from her mother in Little Rock make shocked noises about her interest in a middle-aged foreigner and, in fact, everything conspires to make Nellie unsure about committing herself to Emile.

She decides nervously that she must not go on seeing him and, as she scrubs away vigorously under Luther Billis's latest invention, a shower, she declares that 'I'm Going to Wash That Man Right Out of My Hair'. She has got no further than drying her hair when she comes face to face with Emile and her resolution weakens. Remembering her duty, she questions him about his politics and his beliefs and digs for details on his past, and she is so relieved when they all come out truly red-white-and-blue that within minutes all her good intentions are forgotten and she is happily singing 'I'm in Love With a Wonderful Guy'.

As a result of Nellie's information, Emile is summoned to a meeting with Brackett, Harbison and Cable and asked to take part in the mission to put a spy post on his former home island of Marie-Louise. Emile refuses, and willingly admits that he refuses on account of Nellie. He has a chance to make a life with her which is more important to him than anything else and he will not risk it on this chancy episode. Without his help the venture is too dangerous and, for the moment, it has to be called off.

While he is inactive, waiting for the next move from his superiors, Cable decides that he will take the opportunity to go across to Bali H'ai. With the aid of the delighted Billis, the trip is arranged and once they are there Bloody Mary gleefully takes Cable in hand. While Luther Billis is led off to witness the boar's-tooth ceremony, she takes the young man to a dark little hut in a quiet place and there he meets Liat, a tiny, dark-eyed Tonkinese who seems little more than a child. She is Bloody Mary's daughter. The two young people are deeply struck with each other and, when the time comes for Cable to return to base, he can only with difficulty pull himself away from the arms of this beautiful girl ('Younger than Springtime'). Bloody Mary delivers him to his boat, smiling triumphantly. Lieutenant Cable will be her son-in-law, just as she planned.

Nellie attends a party arranged by Emile for her to meet his local friends. It is a great success and Nellie is in a buoyant mood as the evening comes to an end. When they are left at last alone, Emile chooses this moment to tell her of the part of his life she does not yet know: his Polynesian wife and the fact that Ngana and Jerome are his children. Everything that is Little Rock in Nellie rises up and revolts and, although she tries to fight it, Emile feels her slipping away from him. When they say goodnight, try as she may, it is a very difficult goodnight, and when Nellie is out of his sight she cannot prevent herself from breaking into a run.

681

ACT 2

Down at the camp the troops' Thanksgiving Follies are taking place. Emile turns up with flowers, hoping to see Nellie, but he learns from Billis that she has asked for a transfer to another island. Cable, who has been in hospital with malaria, also puts in an appearance, desperate to get hold of a boat to return to Bali H'ai and visit Liat, but Liat is there, brought by Bloody Mary with a calculated ultimatum. Either Cable marries her, or she will marry the girl to another rich white man, a drunken planter who will beat her. When he does not reply immediately, Mary pleads with Cable: she will work for them, make money, all they will have to do is be happy ('Happy Talk').

Joe Cable is torn, but the small town America in him still has the upper hand. He cannot marry Liat. Furious, Mary dashes to the ground the gold watch he has given Liat, and drags the girl away. As he painfully reprises the final lines of 'Younger than Springtime', on the stage of the camp theatre the final act of the Follies is being announced. It is a travesty of what has just been seen: Nellie is a white-suited sailor singing raucously to Luther Billis as a dusky maiden of being her 'Honey Bun'.

After the show, Emile succeeds in meeting Nellie. He tries to reason with her but, although she admits her reaction is stupidly emotional, Nellie will not reconsider. She was born like that, and that is all there is to it. The bitter, heart-broken Cable has worked it out otherwise. It isn't born in you, all this hatred, all these prejudices. It is instilled in you by others who want their own prejudices supported ('You've Got to Be Taught'). He has decided that, if he survives his mission, he will not go back to America. He will come back here, to Bali H'ai, where everything he cares about is. For Emile it is different. When all you care about has been taken from you, then where do you go? ('Once Nearly Was Mine') The answer comes quickly when Cable asks him to think again about joining him on the expedition to Marie-Louise. This time, with nothing to lose, de Becque agrees.

In the base radio room, Brackett listens impatiently for the first messages to come from Cable and de Becque. The men have been successfully delivered to Marie-Louise by submarine, an operation facilitated when the attentions of the Japanese (as well as half a million dollars worth of US Navy rescue operations) were diverted to fishing stowaway Luther Billis out of the water after he had fallen out of the baggage hold of the plane accompanying the mission. Finally contact is made, and Joe and Emile come through with first rate intelligence reports.

Days pass, and the information continues to flow, leading to many otherwise impossible strikes by the American forces against the Japanese. The Americans are winning the upper hand in an area where previously they had little success. Nellie, in the meanwhile, has heard talk among the wounded in her care. She has heard them talk of 'the Frenchman' who is involved in their raids and, finally, she goes to Brackett to ask if they are speaking of Emile. Brackett allows her to wait to hear Emile's voice over the radio but, when it comes, it is with bad news. Joe Cable has been killed in an attack. Then, in the middle of the broadcast, the sound of an approaching aeroplane is heard and the radio goes dead.

Down on the beach, Nellie walks alone, reflecting bitterly on her stupidity to a refrain of 'Some Enchanted Evening'. She can only hope and pray that Emile will return. As she walks, Bloody Mary appears with Liat. The old woman is dazed and defeated for Liat has refused to marry the planter: she will marry no one but Lieutenant Cable. Nellie cannot say anything, but clasps the little girl chokingly to her breast.

The camp is on the move. The whole picture in the South Pacific has changed and the Americans are now moving forward. Amongst all the excitement, no one mentions the fate of the Frenchman out on Marie-Louise. His part has been played and, alive or dead, it seems as if he has been forgotten. Up at Emile's home, Nellie is playing with Ngana and Jerome, singing 'Dites-Moi' together, when another voice joins in. It is Emile, battered and dirty, but safe. The children rush to meet him, and he moves straight on to meet Nellie. At least their story will have a happy ending.

The song 'My Girl Back Home' which was cut from the original score was used in the film version of *South Pacific*.

GENTLEMEN PREFER BLONDES

a musical in two acts by Joseph Fields and Anita Loos based on the novel by Anita Loos. Lyrics by Leo Robin. Music by Jule Styne. Produced at the Ziegfeld Theatre, New York, 8 December 1949 with Carol Channing (Lorelei), Yvonne Adair (Dorothy), Jack McCauley (Gus) George S Irving (Gage) and Eric Brotherson (Spofford). A different version of the show with a revised libretto by Kenny Solms and Gail Parent and new lyrics by Betty Comden and Adolph Green was staged as *Lorelei* at the Civic Centre Music Hall, Oklahoma City, 3 March 1973 with Carol Channing, Tamara Long, Peter Palmer and Lee Roy Reams. A revised version of this piece played at the Palace Theatre, New York, from 27 January 1974.

Produced at the Princes Theatre, London, 20 August 1962 with Dora Bryan, Anne Hart, Donald Stewart, Michael Malnick and Robin Palmer.

A film version was produced by Twentieth Century-Fox in 1953 with Marilyn Monroe, Jane Russell, Tommy Noonan (Gus), George Winslow (Spofford) and Charles Coburn (Beekman).

CHARACTERS

Lorelei Lee
Dorothy Shaw
Gus Esmond, *a button manufacturer*
Sir Francis Beekman
Lady Beekman
Henry Spofford
Mrs Ella Spofford, *his mother*
Josephus Gage

Gloria Stark
Robert Lemanteur, *an avocat*
Louis Lemanteur, *his son*
Mrs Esmond sr, Bill, Leon, Frank, George, Olympic Man, Pierre, Zizi, Fifi,
Maître d'hôtel, etc.

ACT 1
It is the year 1924, the year of the Paris Olympic Games, and down at the
French Line pier in New York the members of the American team are being
loaded on to the liner *Île de France* which will carry their brawny bodies to the
shores of Europe. There are, of course, plenty of other passengers making
this crossing, including a very attractive Follies girl called Dorothy Shaw
('It's High Time'). Dorothy is to travel as a chaperone (in the loosest sense of
the word) with her cute blonde friend, Lorelei Lee, and Lorelei's gentleman
protector, Mr Gus Esmond, the wealthy heir to America's most important
button manufacturer.

When Lorelei and Gus arrive at the pier they bring news which is
positively dashing. Gus has suddenly been called upon to lend support to his
aged father at a furiously important button convention in Atlantic City and
he cannot sail. Being an unworldly kind of gentleman protector, however, he
suggests that the girls carry on without him for the moment and he will catch
up with them in Paris after he has finished investigating that threat to his
family's livelihood known as the zip fastener. Gus salves Lorelei's disappointment at losing his company on the crossing with a small jewel and a
large letter of credit, says his farewells ('Bye, Bye, Baby'), and soon the girls
are on their way to Paris.

The pleasure of the ocean-going voyage is rather spoiled for Lorelei
when, a few days out, she receives a telegram from Gus. It is postmarked
Little Rock, Arkansas. Now Little Rock, Arkansas is the one place in the
world that Lorelei wouldn't want Gus and his daddy to go to because Lorelei
has a history in Little Rock which is very much at odds with the genteel
Southern belle background she has invented for the benefit of her gentleman
friend. No child of a crumbling Virginia mansion is she, but just 'A Little
Girl From Little Rock' where her early career included an episode with a
gentleman which resulted in her being brought to trial for inappropriate use
of firearms. As Lorelei feared, this piece of her past Gus, and worse, Gus's
father, have now discovered.

She is devastated. Her dear daddy will disown her and she will be all alone
in the world with no one to give her diamonds. What will become of her?
There is nothing for it but to spend the rest of the voyage looking for a new
gentleman protector and, while she is at it, why not one for Dorothy too?

Lorelei is not a backward girl and she soon makes friends amongst the
gentlemen on board the *Île de France*. The English aristocrat, Sir Francis
Beekman, has an eye for a pretty girl when his dragonistic wife relaxes her
fierce guard over him, the Olympians provide an appreciative background,
and the health fanatic Josephus Gage, who has taken out exclusive rights on

the new zip fastener patent, is a single man with obvious financial potential who would seem to fit Lorelei's requirements very neatly. The gentle Henry Spofford initially seems a less likely candidate for he is too busy ensuring that his beloved mother does not disobey Doctor's orders by getting into the champagne.

When Lorelei discovers that Mrs Spofford is the richest woman in Philadelphia, she is quick to come to the conclusion that Henry would make an absolutely perfect mate for dear Dorothy. Lorelei makes fast friends with Mrs Spofford by secretly inviting her to her suite for champagne, but Dorothy seems annoyingly disinclined to make any efforts on her own behalf. Unlike Lorelei she isn't at all attracted to the more expensive things of life but has an inexplicable, romantic longing for loving poverty ('I Love What I'm Doing').

She is more intent on having fun with another Follies girl, Gloria Stark, and the crowd of boys Gloria has gathered around her whilst performing her interminable daily dance practice on the deck (Scherzo), than she is in putting her mind to finding happiness and diamonds. Lorelei therefore feels morally obliged to look after her friend's interests by giving Mrs Spofford a headful of champagne cocktails and finding out all about her dear little Henry and his foibles and weak spots.

All this philanthropy does not mean that Lorelei is neglecting her own future. It has come to her ears that Lady Beekman is anxious to sell a tiara to some wealthy American and, with her deep-seated desire for diamonds gushing to the fore, Lorelei just knows that the piece must be hers. It is a matter of finding some kind gentleman on the ship who will lend her the necessary $5000. So, as soon as she has got Henry chatting to Dorothy over his favourite Glee Club song ('Just a Kiss'), and removed the incessantly practising Gloria from the suite, she turns her attentions to finding a likely target. Her choice falls on Sir Francis Beekman. Soon the two are rapturously envisaging a South American idyll ('It's Delightful Down in Chile') as Lorelei throws yet another unopened telegram from her button-maker into a corner.

In Paris, Dorothy and Henry make a happy pair, enjoying themselves in the 'Sunshine' as they explore the 'Champ de Mars' and the Place Vendôme, while Lorelei is doing the more exclusive shops with Josephus Gage. While they are out, however, who should arrive at the Ritz but Gus Esmond. Lorelei should have opened the telegrams. They would have told her that Gus had defied his father and was on his way to meet her. All Gus finds in his suite is Gloria and a stormy Lady Beekman who has discovered that the $5000 Lorelei paid her for the tiara was borrowed from Sir Francis who had borrowed it from her in the first place.

Lorelei comes happily back with Gage ('I'm Atingle, I'm Aglow') and a fabulous new dress from Boué Soeurs, the first Parisian gown to incorporate Mr Gage's wonderful new zip fastener. Mrs Spofford, too, has been having the time of her life and is completely converted to a life of pleasure by the joie de vivre of the young women, one of whom she is convinced would make just a perfect bride for her Henry. Dorothy, however, is sure that she could never fit in to Henry's up-market 'House on Rittenhouse Square' and she cares for him too much to make an unsuitable marriage. Henry is over the moon to hear her confess to caring for him ('You Say You Care') but slow to take advantage of the moment, and it goes by unconsummated.

The next visitors to Lorelei's suite are less welcome. The dashing Parisian lawyers Robert Lemanteur and his son Louis have been retained by Lady Beekman to retrieve her tiara but, being French, they prefer to invite the girls out for the evening on the Beekman account rather than press their charges. It is only now that Lorelei discovers that Gus is in the lobby and she hurriedly opens the telegrams to find how horribly she has misjudged him.

When he arrives in the suite he finds it full of men and is suitably taken aback but, when he sees the zip fastener in Lorelei's dress, it is quite a different situation. He is livid at the betrayal. Spurning his lady love dramatically, he purposefully turns to Gloria. He understands that she needs a sponsor to get herself on the stage in Paris. Very well, he will be her sponsor, and Lorelei can go to her zip fastener! As Lorelei pleads that she has done nothing she shouldn't (Finaletto), Gus slams out dragging the still dancing Gloria with him.

ACT 2
At the Pré-Catalan night club, Henry, Dorothy and Mrs Spofford make up a jolly party, but the atmosphere at some of the other tables is less relaxed. Lady Beekman, with Robert and Louis in tow, has come to make a public scene over what she claims is the theft of her tiara, and Gus has bribed the management to show off his new discovery in the evening's floorshow as a spite to Lorelei. Sir Francis is also there with two Parisian chorines at his side, ripe for discovery. Lorelei is the last to arrive, decked out in the famous tiara and accompanied by Gage. Confrontations are inevitable, and Gus and Gage square up to each other in what promises to be a damaging episode, avoided only by the opportune announcement of Gloria's début. Lorelei sweeps out as Gloria leaps on to the stage for her big moment ('Mamie Is Mimi') and the evening's floorshow bursts into life ('Coquette').

Alone, under a lamppost in a Parisian street, Lorelei comes to the conclusion that romance is nonsense and that 'Diamonds Are a Girl's Best Friend' and, after wandering about till 3 a.m., she returns to the Ritz only to find Gus waiting in the lobby with recriminations. She succeeds in making him feel rather bad when she tells him that the tiara wasn't a gift from a gentleman, but bought by herself with borrowed money which she was going to allow him to repay, but she feels even worse when she hears that he has split from the Esmond Button Corporation and his father for her sake.

It is heart-searching time and Lorelei pours out all her Little Rock story, ending with the wide-eyed assertion that it really isn't her fault if 'Gentlemen Prefer Blondes' like her. In the face of such logic, Gus is totally won back and all looks rosy again, but Lorelei has a very practical stipulation. She will not wed Gus until he is reconciled with his extremely rich father, and his extremely rich father gives his approval of their union.

Paris is all very well, but it soon appears that all these Americans are feeling 'Homesick' and it is time to get back to Sixth Avenue and Seltzer. The deed is quickly done and Lorelei begins to work on her plans for getting herself married. The wedding party is arranged at the Central Park Casino, and there everybody goes to wait while our heroine sets about getting old Mr Esmond's consent. Three days pass, and Dorothy fills in some of the time with an incidental song with a political bias ('Keeping Cool With Coolidge'), but still no consent is forthcoming and the Casino management is getting anxious at the length of the shindig.

As the guests chatter to fill the hours, Henry finally calls up the courage to propose to Dorothy. She is terribly tempted, but his wealth gets in the way. Only then does she discover that Henry doesn't have any wealth. What money there is is his mother's and, at the rate she's spending it under Lorelei's expert tuition, there won't be any left for Henry. All impediment thus torn away, Dorothy falls happily into Spofford's arms, just as a police escort siren announces the arrival of Mr Esmond sr. At loss for another means to her end, Lorelei has had him summonsed and brought thence under duress.

The furious father is adamant that there will be no wedding. He will never allow his firm and fortune to be thrown away on some brainless little girl. But what is this? Lorelei's Parisian wedding gown is decorated all over with Esmond's buttons model number 302. But how? Mr Esmond has been trying to break into the French market for years without success. He didn't have the help of the little girl from Little Rock. Lorelei was busy while she was in Paris ('Button Up With Esmond') and she has introduced the Esmond button at Boué Soeurs. She has also acquired a half interest, in the name of Esmond, in Mr Gage's Zipper Corporation, so no matter how many gentleman start swapping their buttons for zippers the firm of Esmond will still be on top. Old father Esmond is as dazzled by the young woman's business acumen as his son is by her blonde beauty and the wedding, the double wedding, is allowed to go happily ahead.

The London production of *Gentlemen Prefer Blondes* replaced 'Coquette' with the song 'You Kill Me' and reallocated 'Sunshine' to Lorelei and Dorothy.

The score of *Lorelei* added 'Ave Maria', 'Looking Back', the Olympic Dance, 'A Girl Like I', 'Paris' (a version of 'Sunshine'), 'I Won't Let You Get Away', and 'Lorelei' to the original score. 'Men' and 'Miss Lorelei Lee' were subsequently added before the show reached Broadway.

CALL ME MADAM

a musical comedy in two acts by Howard Lindsay and Russel Crouse. Lyrics and music by Irving Berlin. Produced at the Imperial Theatre, New York, 12 October

1950 with Ethel Merman (Sally), Paul Lukas (Cosmo), Galina Talva (Maria) and Russell Nype (Kenneth).

Produced at the London Coliseum 15 March 1952 with Billie Worth, Anton Walbrook, Shani Wallis and Jeff Warren. Produced at the Victoria Palace Theatre 14 March 1983 with Noele Gordon, Basil Hoskins, Veronica Page and William Relton.

A film version was issued by Twentieth Century-Fox in 1953 with Ethel Merman, George Sanders, Vera-Ellen and Donald O'Connor.

CHARACTERS

Mrs Sally Adams
Kenneth Gibson
Cosmo Constantine
Grand Duke Otto *of Lichtenburg*
Grand Duchess Sophie, *his wife*
Princess Maria, *his daughter*
Sebastian Sebastian, *Prime Minister of Lichtenburg*
Hugo Tantinnin, *Foreign Minister*
Pemberton Maxwell, *chargé d'affaires at the American Embassy*
Senator Gallagher
Senator Brockbank
Congressman Wilkins
Henry Gibson, Miss Phillips, Dean Acheson, Court Chamberlain, etc.

ACT 1

At the offices of the Secretary of State in Washington DC, Mrs Sally Adams is receiving her official accreditation as Ambassador to the Grand Duchy of Lichtenburg. Before she departs the next day to take up her post in a country she has never heard of, she does what she is best known for—she throws a party to which everyone who is anyone is invited ('Mrs Sally Adams'). While the Vice President is entertaining with a song in the music room and Congressman Wilkins is preparing his conjuring tricks, Sally meets young Kenneth Gibson who is to come to Lichtenburg with her as her secretary.

Kenneth is a serious young man who cannot quite comprehend how Sally, who has no knowledge at all of practical politics, can have been named Ambassador. She tells him: she gives the best and most lavish parties in the land, and that's a diplomatic talent if anything is ('The Hostess With the Mostes'). She is soon demonstrating that talent dazzlingly as she brings Democrats and Republicans together in the 'Washington Square Dance'.

Cosmo Constantine welcomes us to 'Lichtenburg'. Too small to be a city, too large to be a town, it is a Grand Duchy, full of mid-European tradition and sinking rapidly into bankruptcy. Cosmo is the head of the Conservative Radical party, one half of the permanent coalition which runs the parliament of Lichtenburg. Conservative because he wants to maintain the old traditions of the country, and radical because he wants to modernise the country's economy and make it practical. As a result of one of the weekly cabinet reshuffles that go on in Lichtenburg, he is currently Finance Minister and unpopular because he has had to announce the cancellation of the historic

688

Lichtenburg Fair for the first time in three hundred years. But Cosmo believes that Lichtenburg should solve its own problems and, unlike the current Prime Minister and Foreign Minister, he is against accepting any foreign aid.

Sally takes her time getting to Lichtenburg—she turned the wrong way at Italy—but when she gets there she is quick to cause consternation. On instructions from home she turns down a request for a loan from Tantinnin, the Foreign Minister, and, under her own steam, she shocks the prissy chargé d'affaires, Pemberton Maxwell, with her cheerful disregard for his precious protocol.

While Tantinnin has been on his way to the Embassy, however, the government has fallen and he is no longer Foreign Minister. The new Foreign Minister arrives post haste to greet the new representative of the United States—it is Cosmo. Sally is very taken with the aristocratic and friendly politician and the instructions from home go briskly out the window. She is soon asking Cosmo fulsomely 'Can You Use Any Money Today?'. Cosmo, being the leader of the no-loans party, diplomatically refuses American money but, when Sally offers to anonymously sponsor the Lichtenburg Fair from her own pocket, he cannot refuse. Nevertheless, he finds that like all Americans she puts a little too much emphasis on questions financial: money and marriages for money have been the bane of his family, and one thing that is very close to his heart is 'Marrying for Love'.

At the Fair, the Princess Maria, heiress to the Duchy's crown, sings happily as she dances 'The Ocarina', and Sally is cornered by Prime Minister Sebastian for a private conversation about the possibility of an American loan. Sally refuses his request roundly: after all, Cosmo is against such a loan. Sebastian suggests that that is, perhaps, because he is not Prime Minister. If he were, he would undoubtedly have a very different attitude.

Sally's brain clicks into thought. She didn't realise that Cosmo wanted to be Prime Minister. Well, if that's what he wants and she can be instrumental in it coming about, how about it? For a hundred million dollar loan, Sebastian agrees fulsomely that he can certainly arrange everything. He will take the earliest possible opportunity to resign as the head of government.

Sally gets her first introduction to a member of the royal family, when she meets the Princess Maria, and she chummily invites the Princess over to her place for a chinwag after dinner. It will be quite easy for her to pop in without too much care for protocol, for there is a secret passage leading from the castle to the Embassy which used to be the home of the old duke's mistress. Maria would like to come very much indeed, but it would be dreadfully against all the rules. She would like to come even more after she has met Kenneth. They don't see eye to eye when Kenneth talks about the prospect of hydro-electric installations and mass cultivation in her lovely unspoiled country, but they manage to fall in something which seems very like love over more trivial conversation ('It's a Lovely Day Today').

In the course of duty, Sally goes to the palace to be presented to the Grand Duke and his Duchess. It doesn't go off in quite the usual way for she trips at the door, powders her nose in public, crosses her legs, takes off her shoes and loses one to the royal pup, and generally murders protocol, but, when the new Prime Minister comes to see her with a royal complaint, it is not about her faux pas but about Kenneth. It has become known to the royal family that he has been meeting privately with the Princess, and that could lead to a scandal which would undoubtedly mean the sacking of the new Prime Minister.

Since the new Prime Minister is Cosmo, Sally doesn't want that to happen. She has plans for him, and those plans include her ('The Best Thing For You Would Be Me'). He is beginning to get the same idea but, as they finally get round to their first kiss, the phone rings. It is Washington. The President himself is on the line with the news that he has approved the requested loan of $100,000,000 for Lichtenburg. Sally is delighted until she sees that Cosmo isn't. Sebastian has double-crossed her. As the Prime Minister leaves, coldly informing her that Lichtenburg is not for sale, she wonders if she hadn't better go home. All she can give this country is money and they don't want it.

ACT 2

A triumvirate of Washington men turn up in Lichtenburg to negotiate the terms of the loan. They have special ideas about loans: they expect them to be made in the form of goods, but Sebastian has no need of potatoes or powdered eggs, only money. For this international occasion, Sally takes the opportunity to give one of her parties. Kenneth and Maria manage to get together under the lights and, since they have been forbidden to talk to each other, he sings to her instead the happy love story of a Princess and a commoner ('Once Upon a Time, Today').

Cosmo, telling Sally not to interfere, gets hold of the Americans and gives an impressive speech on national integrity, refusing any loan, but the Americans react with great admiration to his dignified performance and up their offer of aid to twice the amount. Baffled and bewildered, Cosmo resigns. He also refuses to stay in the cabinet and this creates a constitutional crisis. There will have to be an election. There hasn't been one of those in twenty years. How very democratic. The talk of an election gets the Washington boys on to the subject of their own political affairs, and they join together to sing of how 'They Like Ike'.

When the election campaign gets under way, Sally leaps in on Cosmo's side in defiance of all the diplomatic rules. She's having a ball, but Kenneth isn't. He's suffering from all sorts of ailments. Sally recognises the symptoms: there's nothing wrong with him that marriage couldn't cure ('You're Just In Love'). In spite of his love-sickness, however, Kenneth has not been idle. The hydro-electric scheme hasn't been stagnating in his mind; he's been on to his industrialist father about getting it under way, and now his father has replied that, if Kenneth can raise ten per cent of the finance locally, he will take on the project.

Sally whoops with delight. She's local. She'll put up the ten per cent. She hushes Cosmo's protests firmly. This time he can't protest; it's a private thing, not a public loan. Cosmo, who is keen to see such a modern project come to help his country, is unable to say no, but Sally's enthusiastic and personal foray into international affairs is under severe threat. News of her interference in the elections has reached Washington and she has been recalled.

She is preparing sadly to leave, when she receives an unexpected visit. The Grand Duke and Duchess have made use of the secret passage. They may be part of old Lichtenburg, but they are not against bringing it up-to-date and, as part of the modernisation process, they are withdrawing their objection to a match between Maria and Kenneth. There is just one piece of protocol which, for the sake of tradition, must be observed; as heir to the throne Maria must propose to Kenneth. She wastes very little time in doing so.

Back in Washington 'Mrs Sally Adams' is throwing a homecoming party. Her diplomatic career may be over but her time in Lichtenburg, brief though it may have been, has not been wasted. The little country's rejection of the American offer of aid has won it unprecedented media coverage and popularity, and relations between America and Lichtenburg have flowered. To cement this blooming new relationship, and in gratitude for her part in the *rapprochement* of the two nations, the Prime Minister of Lichtenburg has come to America to decorate Sally with an order that makes her a Lichtenburger Dame. Since the Prime Minister is still Cosmo, he also takes the former United States Ambassador in his arms and the show ends on a reprise of 'You're Just in Love' which would seem to indicate that it will not be long before the former Mrs Sally Adams is on her way back to Lichtenburg.

GUYS AND DOLLS

a musical fable of Broadway in two acts based on a story and characters by Damon Runyon. Book by Abe Burrows and Jo Swerling. Lyrics and music by Frank Loesser. Produced at the 46th Street Theatre, New York, 24 November 1950 with Sam Levene (Nathan), Vivian Blaine (Adelaide), Isobel Bigley (Sarah) and Robert Alda (Sky).

Produced at the London Coliseum 28 May 1953 with Levene, Miss Blaine, Lizbeth Webb and Jerry Wayne. Produced at the National Theatre 9 March 1982 with Bob Hoskins, Julia McKenzie, Julie Covington and Ian Charleson and subsequently played at the Prince of Wales Theatre from 19 June 1985.

A film version was produced by Samuel Goldwyn in 1955 with Frank Sinatra, Vivian Blaine, Jean Simmons and Marlon Brando.

CHARACTERS

Miss Adelaide *of the Hot Box Club*
Nathan Detroit
Nicely-Nicely Johnson

Benny Southstreet
Rusty Charlie
Sarah Brown
Arvide Abernathy
Sky Masterson
Big Jule
Harry the Horse
Angie the Ox
General Matilda B Cartwright
Joey Biltmore, Mimi, Society Max, Lieutenant Brannigan, Liver-Lips
Louie, etc.

ACT 1

The scene is Runyonland, the busy, cosmopolitan Broadway world of guys
and dolls, and there three guys are looking over the day's scratch sheet,
trying to pick a winner or two (Fugue for Tinhorns), when the mission band,
headed by Miss Sarah Brown, passes by spreading its hopeless message of
temperance ('Follow the Fold'). The guys can appreciate a doll like Miss
Sarah, but they don't have much time for the mission dodge for they are
heavily involved in a much more interesting thing known as the crap game—
a little bit of action and some dollars, but a thing to be kept well out of the
sight of Lieutenant Brannigan and his fellow cops.

Nathan Detroit runs the crap game when he can find a suitable spot to set
up, and right now that is a problem. The usual places seem to have all come
under Brannigan's attentions and the only possible place left is Biltmore's
garage where the owner wants cash down to let them use it. Cash is one
thing Nathan doesn't have. Things look sticky for 'The Oldest Established
Permanent Floating Crap-Game in New York' and for good old reliable
Nathan. This is particularly regrettable as Sky Masterson is in town and Sky
Masterson is well known as one big gambling man. He'll bet on anything.
What a lovely, lucrative game Nathan could get going with him if only he had
a place.

There is one particular person who has to be hoodwinked when a crap
game is on the boil and that is Nathan's girl, the Hot Box chanteuse Miss
Adelaide. She and Nathan have been engaged for more years than anyone
can remember without getting around to a wedding, but Adelaide lives in
only slightly battered hope that one day they'll make it together all the way
down the aisle. She is not at all keen on her Nathan getting involved with the
crap shooters and she has extorted from him a faithful promise to leave the
game alone. So Adelaide has to be sweet-talked out of the way before
Nathan can get down to business with Sky Masterson. He tries to win the
money to pay Biltmore from Sky with a set-up bet, but Sky is too smart for
that. He'll bet on anything, but he can smell a set-up. What the desperate
Nathan ends up with is a thousand dollar bet that Sky can't persuade Miss
Sarah to go with him on a trip to Havana the next day.

It's a serious bet, so Sky goes to work seriously. He goes to the mission
and poses as a repentant sinner in an effort to attract the mission lass's

692

attentions, but it isn't long before the truth leaks out and Sky has to use an angle. The mission isn't doing too well. In fact, it's fairly laying an egg. The big meeting next Thursday with the General in attendance shows every sign of being dismally thin. Sky guarantees Miss Sarah one dozen genuine sinners in attendance in return for a dinner date. Sarah is shocked at his duplicity and makes it clear to him that the man for her will certainly not be a gambler ('I'll Know') but, when Sky kisses her, it takes a long time for her to slap his face.

Adelaide gets through entertaining at the Hot Box ('A Bushel and a Peck'), meets up with Nathan, and the topic turns, as the topic has a habit of doing with Adelaide, to marriage. Adelaide has told her mother long ago that they were already married and, over the years, she has steadily embellished her story, inventing a family and lots of other little details, so couldn't they just get married really? She's had plenty of time to get everything together. All they need now is a licence and a blood test. But then a chorine blows Nathan's plans for reviving the crap game and Adelaide dissolves in a plaintive wail. He'd promised! Nathan slinks away as Adelaide sombres into the psychosomatic cold she's had for fourteen years waiting for her wedding ring (Adelaide's Lament), and gets ready to wait some more.

The guys have noticed that Sky does not seem to be having much luck with Miss Sarah. It looks like Nathan's bet will be good and the game will be on. It just goes to show that real guys didn't ought to get sidetracked by dolls when there's a man's game to be played ('Guys and Dolls'). Miss Sarah, however, is not having much luck herself. Business really is bad at the mission and the General has come to say that they will have to close down the branch. Sky steps in on cue and Sarah remembers his promise. One dozen genuine sinners for one date. It could save the mission.

The crapshooters have gathered from near and far, even the illustrious Big Jule from Cicero, Illinois, and Nathan still doesn't have his venue booked. The big-spending guys are all standing around on the street when Officer Brannigan passes by. The gathering looks a bit obvious, so the boys cover up by saying it's a stag night for Nathan—he's finally getting married—and who should overhear this bit of news but Miss Adelaide. And she thought the gathering was a crap game! How marvellous of him. They will get married tomorrow night right after she's finished her set at the Hot Box. Under the circumstances there can be no escape and Nathan can only agree. That disposes of Brannigan and Adelaide; now the guys only need Sky Masterson with the thousand dollars from his losing bet to pay for Biltmore's garage, and the game can start. Suddenly Nathan goes white: the mission group marches by and there is no Sarah with them.

Sarah is in Havana. She is dragging Sky round the sights until he drags her into a café for a milk shake. The milk shakes here have quite a taste—it's called rum—and Sarah shows quite a taste for them, so she is soon tipsily free of inhibitions and dancing closely in Sky's arms ('If I Were a Bell'). He takes her carefully back to New York and it is a soberer Sarah who arrives at the mission at 4 a.m. just in time to see Adelaide returning happily from her wedding shower. It seems a strange time of night for people to be up and

693

about, but to Sky it's 'My Time of Day' and this particular 4 a.m. is special because he's in love and so is Sarah ('I've Never Been in Love Before').

Suddenly there are crap players everywhere and whistles blowing: Nathan found a place all right—the guys have been playing their game in the mission. Sarah is filled with remorse. She has been fooled by Sky. He set it up for his friends. The moment between them is gone and she is back to being the old Sarah Brown.

ACT 2

Down at the Hot Box Adelaide is doing her set ('Take Back Your Mink') when Nicely-Nicely Johnson comes to deliver a message. Nathan can't come to meet her—he's gone to see a sick aunt. Adelaide knows all about sick aunts. It's the crap game, of course. It's still going on. Adelaide starts sneezing miserably.

Sarah Brown isn't much happier. The big meeting is due any time and it is going to be a fiasco. Of course, that isn't all. She is still thinking of Sky. Arvide, her fellow mission worker, gives her some kindly advice: if she loves Sky and he loves her what does it matter who or what he is? ('More I Cannot Wish You') What Sarah has forgotten is that she is holding Sky Masterson's marker for an unpaid bet, but Sky hasn't forgotten and he's a good player. He always pays his debts.

Nathan has got the game going down in the sewers. It has gone on for a whole day non-stop and everyone would like to finish, but Big Jule is a big loser and his gun says that the game goes on. He also wishes to bet on credit and to use his own dice. Now this is against all the rules and it does not seem at all like a good idea, especially to Nathan who is forced into losing all the money he has made to Big Jule's imaginary winning throws. Sky arrives at the right moment to stop this cheating and he proposes a strange game. He will play the gamblers not for their money, but for their souls. For each throw he wins, the loser is bound to show up at the mission meeting. He calls for lucky dice ('Luck Be a Lady') and starts to throw.

One by one, the guys emerge from the sewer and head for the mission. Adelaide catches up with Nathan. There's still five minutes left before midnight, they can still go and get married like the licence says. When Nathan says he's going to a prayer meeting, it seems like a really crude excuse. Adelaide bursts and, in spite of his protestations of love ('Sue Me'), she storms off in a fury of sniffles.

At the mission, Sarah is about to give up in despair when the room begins to fill with real reprobates. It is Sky's promised contribution to the meeting. One by one the guys get up to give awkward testimony before the General and, when Nicely-Nicely's turn comes, he launches into a really colourful confession ('Sit Down, You're Rocking the Boat'). No sooner has he finished than Brannigan arrives. He asks Sarah if she will testify that these guys ran a crap game in the mission the previous night. Sarah looks coolly down at the assembled sinners and replies with deep sincerity. Why, she never saw them before in her life.

694

Adelaide and Sarah end up in the street together contemplating men—their own in particular—sitting on a couple of bundles of newspapers in the wee hours of the morning. That's when Adelaide finds out that Nathan was telling the truth about the prayer meeting and Sarah finds out that she is really in love with Sky. What are they mooning on about? What they need to do is get on and 'Marry the Man Today' and fix him up the way they want him subsequently.

Sarah and Sky are married in the mission and Sky takes up a new position in life, carrying the big drum in the mission band. Since Nathan wasn't able to fix a place for his wedding, he and Adelaide make it a double wedding and, if Sky's still talking odds and Nathan seems to have caught Adelaide's cold as the curtain falls, well, that's what happens with 'Guys and Dolls'.

THE KING AND I

a musical play in two acts by Oscar Hammerstein II based on the novel *Anna and the King of Siam* by Margaret Landon. Music by Richard Rodgers. Produced at the St James Theatre, New York, 29 March 1951 with Gertrude Lawrence (Anna), Yul Brynner (The King), Dorothy Sarnoff (Thiang), Doretta Morrow (Tuptim) and Larry Douglas (Lun Tha). Produced at the Uris Theatre 2 May 1977 with Yul Brynner, Constance Towers, Hye-Young Choi, June Angela and Martin Vidnovic.

Produced at the Theatre Royal, Drury Lane, London, 8 October 1953 with Valerie Hobson, Herbert Lom, Muriel Smith, Doreen Duke and Jan Mazarus. Produced at the Adelphi Theatre 10 October 1973 with Peter Wyngarde, Sally Ann Howes, Moyna Cope, Pauline Antony and Valentine Palmer. Produced at the London Palladium 12 June 1979 with Brynner, Virginia McKenna, Hye-Young Choi, Miss Angela and Marty Rhone.

Produced by the Opéra Royal de Wallonie, at the Théâtre de Verviers, 22 March 1985 with Nicole Broissin and Marc Vento.

A film version was produced by Twentieth Century-Fox in 1956 with Deborah Kerr (singing dubbed by Marni Nixon), Yul Brynner, Rita Moreno, Terry Saunders and Carlos Rivas (singing dubbed by Reuben Fuentes).

CHARACTERS

Anna Leonowens
Louis, *her son*
The King
Prince Chulalongkorn, *his son*
Lady Thiang, *his chief wife*
The Kralahome
Tuptim
Lun Tha
Sir Edward Ramsay
Captain Orton
Phra Alack, Interpreter, Princess Ying Yaowalak, etc.

ACT 1

A sailing vessel is making its way up the Gulf of Siam towards Bangkok (Arrival at Bangkok), carrying on board Mrs Anna Leonowens, a widow from Singapore, who has been appointed governess to the children of the King of Siam. Anna brings with her her own son, Louis, and just a little apprehension which she attempts to dispel by her own particular method ('I Whistle a Happy Tune').

Apprehension returns at the sight of her reception committee, a group of semi-naked Siamese, headed by the large and also semi-naked Kralahome or Prime Minister, but Anna Leonowens is not a woman to be daunted. She has accepted her job and made her terms—twelve pounds a month and a house of her own—and she will stick to them. She also intends that the King shall stick to them and, when the Kralahome intimates that she will be lodged in the palace, she protests firmly that her contract calls for her own house. She concedes, however, that she will come to the palace for the meanwhile and speak to the King on the subject at a suitable time.

Several weeks later the King receives an emissary from Burma, the courtier Lun Tha. Lun Tha has brought a gift for the King from the Prince of Burma, a young woman called Tuptim, but it is clear that during the journey from their own country to Siam the two young people have fallen in love. Tuptim is duly handed over to the nonchalantly appreciative King and left to reflect bitterly on her unhappy position ('My Lord and Master').

Now, and only now, the Kralahome judges it time to introduce the wilful school teacher to the King. Anna has had enough of sitting in her rooms and is eager to begin work, but she also wishes to speak to the King to raise the small matter of her accommodation. The King brushes this unimportant request aside with a barrage of his own thoughts. Does she appreciate the plans he has to bring the best of western culture to Siam? How did she like the fireworks and the acrobats at last week's funeral? Perhaps she can teach the Lady Thiang and his other wives as well as his sixty-seven children? House? What house? She will live in the palace. And he is gone, leaving Anna to the curiosity of his wives who are much amused by her hoop skirt and gloves.

Lady Thiang tries to make Anna aware of the way things are in the palace. The King is all, and that is never and can never be questioned. Tuptim and Lun Tha, for example, will never see each other again, but the girl has the King, and what could she want more? Anna has her own thoughts both on the omnipotence of the King and the misfortune of the young lovers. Alone, without her much loved husband, she appreciates their plight deeply ('Hello, Young Lovers'), but any reservations that she may have about her position vanish when the King formally introduces the children to her (March of the Siamese Children). She will love them, and they will love her.

Anna's western teaching soon brings new ideas into palace thought ('Children Sing, Priests Chant') and, although he would never admit it publicly or even privately, the King proves not unwilling to learn. He is enlightened enough to know that the King is not omniscient as his ancestors believed, and generous enough of spirit to want to use any available knowledge to do the best for his land and for his family, but he finds it difficult to be sure precisely what is good and what is right ('A Puzzlement').

In the schoolroom, Anna finds much enjoyment in making friends with her young charges ('The Royal Bangkok Academy'/'Getting to Know You'), but she meets some difficulties when she tries to put the simplistic teachings of Lady Thiang into a wider perspective by showing the children a world map, or in explaining such phenomena as snow and ice which the Siamese children have never seen. The King supports her, even when he has not the knowledge required ('So Big a World'), but they come to disagreement perpetually on the subject of Anna's promised house and she reacts angrily when he refers to her as a servant. If the King does not carry out his word on her accommodation, she will leave Siam.

Lun Tha and Tuptim have been meeting secretly ('We Kiss in a Shadow') but fearfully. Anna has acted as a chaperone for these meetings and they know that, if she goes, they will never be able to see each other again. In the privacy of her room, Anna gives vent to her anger over the King's stubbornness regarding her house ('Shall I Tell You What I Think of You?'). She cannot stay in a country where a contract is thus disregarded and where she is treated with such a lack of dignity. She will leave, she must leave, before she becomes so attached to the children that she cannot.

The Lady Thiang comes to Anna and begs her to go to the King. He cannot come to her, his position and his pride will not allow it, but he needs her. Her outburst against him, and the discovery of a British letter describing him as a barbarian and suggesting the annexing of Siam as a protectorate, have hurt him deeply. He needs help and he needs advice, but they must not sound like help and advice. He is a man and a King, a wonderful man who wants only to do good and a King who would be wise and strong, but he needs support. As Lady Thiang pours out her own deep love for the man and the King ('Something Wonderful'), Anna realises that she must do as she is asked.

When she attends on the King, the atmosphere is light-hearted. He plays tricks on her, putting her into ridiculous positions in an effort to keep up the protocol of keeping her head at a lower level than his, and yet allows her transparently to dictate what he should do in answer to the accusations of barbarism. It is decided that when Sir Edward Ramsay, a British diplomat from Singapore, pays a visit, he should be allowed to see the efforts that the King is making towards civilisation. There will be a dinner, a ball and a theatrical presentation, and the women will be dressed in Western clothes. But there is little time to put such a plan into effect for Sir Edward's ship is already announced. The King orders the court on to its knees to pray for help in their efforts to impress the British (Prayer to Buddha), and slips into the prayer a promise to build for Anna the bungalow she has pestered him for since her arrival, before impishly lying down flat on his face so that she must do the same.

ACT 2
The Eastern ladies dressed up in hoop skirts are distinctly ill at ease

('Western People Funny') and also worryingly short of underclothes, but the King is unconcerned at their dress and more dubious about the bare shoulders of Anna's evening dress. When Sir Edward Ramsay arrives, the women are thrown into a panic by his monocle and, forgetting all pretence of civilisation, fling their hoop skirts over their heads confirming that Anna was right to have worried about their lack of underclothes. Ramsay is an old admirer of Anna's and the sense of intimacy between them irritates the King who insists on taking Anna into dinner himself, leaving his guest to follow.

While the evening's festivities are going on in the palace, Tuptim is planning to meet Lun Tha. Lady Thiang, who sees everything, warns her not to. Lun Tha has been ordered away from Siam that night. Tuptim disregards her warning and the two young people meet to plan her escape ('I Have Dreamed'). Tuptim is to present the entertainment for the King's foreign guests and, after it is over, she will make her way secretly to the ship to join Lun Tha. Anna finds the two together and is told of their plan. In spite of her loyalty to the King, she can only condone their flight as she remembers her own young love.

The entertainment is in the form of a masque representing the story of Uncle Tom's cabin, the flight of the slave Eliza across the snow and the chase of wicked Simon Legree ('The Small House of Uncle Thomas'), recited by Tuptim with more emotion than is good for her cause. The King is not sure he approves of the moral of the play, but on the whole the evening is a success and Sir Edward can depart secure in the knowledge that, whatever the King of Siam is, he is no barbarian. The King is grateful to Anna for her part in the success and, to the embarrassment of both of them, he gives her an expensive ring from his own hand as a gift, but the happiness of the moment is shadowed when the King is brought the news of Tuptim's flight. Anna pleads with the King not to be hard on the girl. She is, after all, only one woman among so many in his household, and of so little importance. He will not listen to her (Song of the King).

The King is in a fulsome mood and the conversation turns on poetry, on romance and on English ideas. Anna attempts to express the feelings of a young girl making her debut in society, meeting and dancing with a young man for the first time ('Shall We Dance?'). She dances a little, then realises that the King is looking at her as he might one of his dancing girls. She stops abruptly but he insists that she continue. She will show him how English people dance together. Anna begins to teach him to polka as a teacher would, but the King wishes to dance as a couple does, and his arm stretches firmly round her waist as they dance around the room.

The scene is broken by the Kralahome's announcement that Tuptim has been taken. The girl rushes in and falls at Anna's feet for protection but, when the King rejects her passionate plea not to hurt Tuptim, Anna turns on him with stinging words: he has never loved, he cannot understand. Furious, the King prepares to whip the girl personally but under Anna's eyes he cannot. Flinging down the whip he storms out and the Kralahome turns bitterly on Anna. This is what she has made of their King with her western ideas; a King who cannot even take a whip to a traitor. It would have been

698

better if she had never come to Siam. Lun Tha has been killed attempting escape, Tuptim is utterly broken and has no wish to survive him, and Anna has seen in the King the part of him that is his heritage and which she can neither understand nor accept. She gives the Kralahome the ring to return to the King. She will be on the next boat out of Bangkok.

Anna is packed and preparing to embark when Lady Thiang comes to her bearing a letter from the King. He is ill, very ill. It is his heart, which she accused him of not having, that is the problem and, to Lady Thiang's wise eyes, it is also his strangely vanished will to live. The letter contains all the best of the man: his struggle for excellence, his admission of his own failings, and his gratitude to Anna for her help. She must go to him.

She arrives only just in time. The King is weak and dying. The children are called and they, too, beg Anna not to leave them. Prince Chulalongkorn, who will succeed his father, is there, a young man and needing guidance. Anna orders her baggage to be unpacked from the ship. She will stay to help the King's son as she has helped the father. As the new King, prompted by his father, issues his first edict—replacing the eastern kow-tow with western bowing and courtesies—the old King dies and Anna, kneeling beside him, takes his lifeless hand and kisses it.

PAINT YOUR WAGON

a musical play in two acts by Alan Jay Lerner. Music by Frederick Loewe. Produced at the Shubert Theatre, New York, 12 November 1951 with James Barton (Ben), Olga San Juan (Jennifer) and Tony Bavaar (Julio).

Produced at Her Majesty's Theatre, London, 11 February 1953 with Bobby Howes, Sally Ann Howes and Ken Cantril

A film version was produced by Paramount in 1969 with Clint Eastwood, Lee Marvin, Jean Seberg (singing dubbed by Anita Gordon) and Harve Presnell.

CHARACTERS

Ben Rumson
Jennifer Rumson, *his daughter*
Jake Whippany
Steve Bullnack
Mike Mooney
Julio Valveras
Jacob Woodling, *a Mormon*
Sarah Woodling, *his wife*
Elizabeth Woodling, *his other wife*
Cherry Jourdel
Raymond Janney
Sandy Twist
Salem Trumbull

Edgar Crocker
Pete Billings, Sing Yuy, Lee Zen, Reuben Sloane, Yvonne Sorel, etc.

ACT 1

On a spring evening in 1853, out on a hilltop in Northern California, a group of itinerant miners stands watching the burial of their old friend Jim Newberry. He got so drunk that, when the town burned down, he didn't realise what was happening and now what's left of him is being consigned to a hole in the ground thirty miles from nowhere before the men move on in their never-ceasing search for El Dorado. Ben Rumson is picked to have a quick word with the Lord God about Jim and, while he does so, his sixteen year-old daughter Jennifer, sitting by the grave, realises that the pebble she is playing with is a gold nugget. She tugs at her father's sleeve and the eulogy ends 'for-ever-and-ever-I-stake-this-claim-Amen!' as Ben Rumson strikes gold.

The word drifts quickly through California and, from all walks of life and all corners of the land, men take up their shovels to head for the site ('I'm On My Way'). Big Steve Bullnack out to score for the sake of his ambitious wife, Jake Whippanay who dreams of building a music hall where his girl Cherry can star, Mike Mooney who has heard of a fabulous lake with a solid gold bottom hidden up there in the north, cockney Edgar Crocker, Sandy Twist and Reuben Sloane moving on from the last dried-up claim to another, all of them set out for the newly-built 'Rumson Town'

In no time at all there are four hundred folks digging the ground around Ben's claim: four hundred menfolk, and little Jennifer the only female for miles. She doesn't understand the men's choked-up reactions to her ('What's Going On Here?'). As far as she's concerned they're like her brothers. But she is soon to meet one who doesn't seem like a brother. Julio Valveras is a Mexican, one of the race dispossessed by the miners, and he has his tent at a safe distance from the town where he can dig without the risk of being jumped by those who consider themselves his natural superiors.

Like all the other men, Julio has dreams of a ranch on a green hillside for himself and his family and he tells his dreams to Jennifer ('I Talk to the Trees') who is sweetly taken with his Spanish courtesy and grace. The rest of the town, however, find her presence a constant reminder of their own lack of feminine company and they demand that Ben send her back east to school as he has always said he would. In the meanwhile, they just think about Jake's music hall and the girls he will bring there when he strikes gold (Lonely Men Ballet), and they while away the time in song ('They Call the Wind Maria').

Ben is loath to send Jennifer away. He still misses his late wife ('I Still See Elisa') and without Jennifer's company things will be sad indeed but, when he finds her singing joyfully over Julio's washing and anticipating her next secret meeting with him ('How Can I Wait'), he knows that she must indeed go.

In the meanwhile, women are heading for Rumson Town. The Mormon,

700

Jacob Woodling, and his wives Sarah and Elizabeth, wandering from one town to the next, have pitched camp on a hill not far away and Rumson will be their next port of call. The Woodling menage is not as dutifully happy as is should be. Jacob expects his wives to do everything for him and, as Sarah has borne a child and manages to use it as an excuse for doing nothing, Elizabeth has become a pack-horse and general drudge in their service. Sarah is none the less jealous of her and when they kneel for their evening prayer (Trio) her thoughts are not on God but on how to keep Elizabeth down, whilst Elizabeth's prayer is that she may see Sarah somehow eliminated.

In Rumson, Ben and his jury are condemning a man to hang for stealing a fellow miner's gold when the Woodlings arrive in town. The baby draws even more yearning from the men than the women do, but a droll proposition is soon arrived at. Jacob needs money and equipment if he is to settle in Rumson and work his way, but he surely doesn't need two wives. Someone else, on the other hand, could definitely do with one wife. The answer is that Jacob must auction one of his wives and Elizabeth volunteers urgently to be the one. Ben looks her over and asks her if she would care to be married to him. He is an average man ('In Between'), she could do worse. Elizabeth just wants to be wedded to anyone who isn't Jacob and so, to Jennifer's horror, Ben bids for and wins a bride ('Whoop-ti-ay').

Before she leaves Rumson, Jennifer goes once more to see Julio. She is willing to run away with him if he will take her, but Julio is more practical. Lovingly ('Carino Mio') he tells her that they could have no life that way: she must go east and have her schooling while he saves the little that his claim brings him through the next year. Then they can be together. But right now 'There's a Coach Comin' In', and she must leave on it. She is no sooner gone than a miner from the other end of the town comes to see Julio with a question. What does it mean when one end of a vein cleans out? It means only one thing—soon the whole vein will be done. Rumson Town will be finished.

ACT 2

Jake had a strike and built his music hall, and his Cherry and her troupe came to Rumson and, for a while, everything was fine and dandy but then, as Julio had foreseen, the gold began to peter out and people started to leave Rumson to move on to the next new diggings. Ben Rumson bought up the businesses as their owners moved out in an attempt to stop his town dying, but Rumson was soon a shadow of its old self.

Down at Jake's Palace, Jake himself still reigns proudly over his dream ('Hand Me Down That Can o' Beans'/Rope Dance) but no-one has the money to pay for tickets or drinks and the girls won't dance for nothing (Can-Can). Dreams are dying, one by one, but Mike Mooney has kept his vision of the lake with the bed of gold and he tries to persuade Julio to come with him in search of it. Julio has saved nothing and Jennifer may return ('Another Autumn') so, although he has seen men return mountain-mad

701

from these searches, he agrees to go with Mike. One by one, everyone in Rumson is 'Movin''.

When Jennifer unexpectedly returns, announcing that she has come back to be married ('All for Him'), she has a lot of bad news to take in at once: Rumson Town is dying and Julio has gone off into the hills somewhere. Even Ben, who loves his town, is thinking of moving on ('Wand'rin' Star'). That night at Jake's Palace he determines to make a killing that will save his situation, but what he gets instead of gambler's luck is an offer from Janney, the smoothest and richest man in town, to buy his wife. Ben bought her, he can sell her. His scruples are overcome by the sight of $3000 and Elizabeth is sold for a second time, but Janney is too late. Elizabeth has always had a mind of her own and she was one step ahead of Ben. She has been carrying on behind his back with little Crocker and that very evening the two of them have left town together.

They have left just a little too early, however, for no sooner has Janney rushed out after his investment than cries are heard in the street, the cries dearest to a miner's heart—'Strike!'. Forty miles south someone has struck gold. Everyone left in Rumson is on the move within hours ('Wand'rin' Star'/'I'm On My Way'). Everyone, that is, except Jennifer. She will not leave until Julio returns and she sits calmly alone as all goes wild around her. But she will not be alone in Rumson. When it comes to the point Ben cannot leave his town either.

Within months, the once booming town of Rumson is down to a population of six: Ben and Jennifer, Jacob and Sarah and their children. Then, one day, a stooped and sad figure walks into town. It is Julio. Mike Mooney went berserk with the mountain-madness as they pursued his dream through the high country of California and he, Julio, has been cured of dreaming for ever. The green ranch of Palos Verdes and his happy family can never be. He is heading home to Mexico. But here, in this dead town, hoping and dreaming are still alive. Jennifer has never given up waiting for Julio and for her, at least, the dream will come true. As the wagons of the west roll on, the two young lovers come at last to each other's arms.

The film score included five new songs with music by André Previn: 'Gold Fever', 'The Best Things in Life Are Dirty', 'The First Thing You Know', 'A Million Miles Away' and 'The Gospel of No Name City'.

WONDERFUL TOWN

a musical comedy in two acts by Joseph Fields and Jerome Chodorov based on their play *My Sister Eileen* and the stories by Ruth McKenney. Lyrics by Betty Comden and Adolph Green. Music by Leonard Bernstein. Produced at the Winter Garden, New York, 25 February 1952 with Rosalind Russell (Ruth), Edith Adams (Eileen) and George Gaynes (Bob).

Produced at the Princes Theatre, London, 23 February 1953 with Pat Kirkwood, Shani Wallis and Dennis Bowen. Produced at the Queen's Theatre 7 August 1986 with Maureen Lipman, Emily Morgan and Ray Lonnen.

CHARACTERS

Ruth Sherwood
Eileen, *her sister*
Mr Appopolous
Joe Lonigan, *a policeman*
Helen Wade
Mrs Wade, *her mother*
Wreck
Violet
Speedy Valenti
Robert Baker *of the Manhatter magazine*
Frank Lippincott
Chick Clark
Chef, Waiter, Guide, Policemen, etc.

ACT 1

The scene is Greenwich Village, New York, in the 1930s. A guide is showing a group of tourists around this picturesque area—the *soi-disant* Montmartre of New York, the home of so many colourful and would-be colourful people. They pass down 'Christopher Street' and give the street's residents the once over. There is Mr Appopolous, the modern painter, who also happens to own half the rooming houses on the street; there is Violet who gives late night rumba lessons without a phonograph; there is Wreck, the professional footballer 'resting' between seasons, and his live-in lady-love, Helen, who are down to pawning their canary to make ends meet; there's Lonigan, the policeman who keeps the street on the straight and narrow, and Mr Valenti who runs the nightspot, The Village Vortex. Into this seething hotch-potch of society come two young ladies from Columbus, Ohio, who are looking for a place to stay in this sophisticated big-city village.

Ruth Sherwood is a writer. That is to say, she has a typewriter and she wants to be a writer. Her pretty, blonde sister has ambitions towards the stage of much the same tentative kind. It is a long way from Columbus, and the two sisters are so pooped that they fall without too much resistance into the clutches of Mr Appopolous who happens to have a studio to rent, having just evicted Violet for professional reasons—her profession, not his. It is a basement apartment with two meagre daybeds, an imitation fireplace and a barred window at head level which gives a fine view of the lower parts of people walking past in the street. It is a cross between a prison cell and a submarine, undersized and overpriced, but Eileen is too tired to go further and sixty-five dollars which they can't afford are gone in a minute into Appopolous' pocket.

The exhausted Eileen has just sunk onto what passes for a bed when there is an almighty explosion. What their new landlord didn't tell them is that contractors are blasting underneath for a new subway. He also didn't tell them about the last tenant and soon they have a visitor who takes some persuading that Eileen isn't the successor to Violet. Eileen's cries for help bring their neighbour, the hulking Wreck, to her aid and the girls have made their first New York friend. They have the chance before long to make plenty more for the window provides a handy leering point for drunks who have to be trundled off by cop Lonigan who doesn't seem at all convinced of the legality of the girls' professions. Plaintively they begin to wonder why ever they left 'Ohio'.

The next day is something else and the girls get up bravely, ready to start dancing through a pantomime of 'Conquering the Big City'. Alas, Ruth's manuscripts get short shrift from editors and Eileen gets lots of passes but no jobs. So it goes on and, before long, things begin to get a bit tight. Eileen at least doesn't go hungry, thanks to an admiring samples clerk at a breakfast food show and a drugstore manager called Frank Lippincott who is inclined to shower her with his shop's latest special offers and free gifts, but Ruth, lacking the obvious attractions of her sister, doesn't have the same luck. On the contrary, she manages to blow so many possibilities of a free lunch that she begins to wonder whether she shouldn't try writing a book on 'One Hundred Easy Ways (to Lose a Man)'.

She manages to get as far as the office of Bob Baker, associate editor of the *Manhatter*, where she bombards Baker with Columbus chatter, puts her foot in her mouth with practised ease, and is treated to a cautionary lecture on how difficult it is to make it in the big city ('What a Waste') which ends with advice to go back west, young woman. When Ruth has left his office, Bob Baker actually does read her submissions. They are turgid to a degree. Each has an exaggerated Ruth-heroine plunged into standard dramatic situations and, as Bob reads, before his eyes he sees Ruth acting out her over-written daydreams. He throws down the scripts.

Christopher Street has a small drama on its hands. Helen's mother is coming to stay and she doesn't know about Wreck which means he has to move out of the apartment for a while. Eileen is awfully bad at saying no, so all of a sudden the struggling household has a mattress on the floor and a third penniless inmate who, fortunately, is very good at housework and a specialist at ironing.

Mrs Wade is not on the Greenwich Village wavelength at all. She wants Helen to go to live in an area where she will meet the right sort of young man. At this moment the right young man for the Sherwood girls is one who provides food and, when Frank Lippincott arrives bearing a box of chocolate-covered cherries, Eileen invites him to dinner and begins to think that she might be 'A Little Bit in Love'.

She is rather shorter with another fellow who comes looking for a young lady who lives at their address. Thinking he is after Violet, she very nearly sends him packing until it becomes clear that he is after Ruth and that he is Bob Baker. This is wonderful news and Eileen optimistically invites him to dinner as well, shifting her focus as she wonders if perhaps she's 'A Little Bit in Love' with him instead. Things look even better when Chick Clark, another newspaperman, calls. Eileen met him in an elevator and he has promised to get his editor to try Ruth out. Meanwhile, Wreck is doing the ironing and being biographical ('I Could Pass a Football'), but Helen has noticed the effect that Eileen seems to have on him—as she innocently has on all men—and is arranging for him to shift into the YMCA. To raise the necessary money, she pawns a ghastly Appopolous painting which decorates the flat.

One by one the dinner guests arrive: first Chick, on lechery intent, then the earnest Frank with a bottle of Californian Burgundy-type wine, and finally Bob Baker. The sit out in what is optimistically called the garden and conversation flags limply (Conversation Piece) until Appopolous arrives to collect his painting for a contest. He is lightning-struck to find it gone, and threatens awful retribution. The party goes further awry when Wreck and Helen turn up, followed and removed by an appalled mother, the subway men start blasting and Frank gets Burgundy-type wine all down his white jacket.

Bob takes a well-meaning chance to tell Ruth that her work is on the wrong lines: she should write about things she has experienced instead of these garish tales of frustrated heroines. Ruth snaps back, mortified, leaving the departing Bob to ruminate over his preference for 'A Quiet Girl'. Ruth, realising she has spoiled the best chance she has ever had, goes into a deep depression which is broken by a crash from the kitchen: Eileen's effort at warmed-up spaghetti has landed on the floor, due to a premeditated piece of interference on the part of Chick Clark.

Then the phone rings. It is an assignment for Ruth! Chick's paper has come through with a job for her in Brooklyn where a shipload of young Brazilian coffee millionaires has just landed. She is to get over there and interview them. Ruth rushes off but, when Chick returns with sandwiches to replace the spoiled spaghetti, the horrid truth is revealed. He faked the call to get Ruth out of the house so he could be alone with Eileen. But his devious plan is spoiled by another phone call: Bob Baker invites Eileen out for dinner and Chick is left alone, biting viciously into a sandwich, as she prances off.

Over at the wharf, Ruth has a little trouble getting through to the Brazilians. They have only three words of English: American, dance, conga. So Ruth ends up leading a highly popular 'Conga!' through the streets all the way back to Greenwich village where the Brazilians invade the apartment and the street, conga-ing frantically behind the sisters, until the police arrive and Eileen is arrested in the mêlée.

ACT 2

When Ruth and her friends go to bail Eileen out the next morning they find that, true to form, she has got the entire police station treating her like a duchess, in love with her to a man. When Frank arrives with an electric fan and the suggestion of a semi-permanent relationship, Eileen's devotees throw him out physically and end up serenading her in mock-Irish harmony ('My Darlin' Eileen').

Back home things aren't any better. Appopolous has found his painting in the pawnshop and is throwing the girls out of the apartment, and Ruth has taken to being a sandwich-board for Valenti's Vortex Village to earn a penny or two ('Swing'). But hope is still burning, for Bob has read the piece she has written about the Brazilians, is mad about it and he has given it to his editor with his glowing recommendation. Alas, the editor turns it down and Bob resigns his position on principle. When Eileen arrives home, it seems like it's going to have to be back to Columbus for the two sisters. It's a shame, particularly about Bob. Ruth sighs, and Eileen suddenly realises that her sister likes Bob too. She likes him quite a lot. Goodness gracious, what's another boy to Eileen if her sister likes him? It's lump-in-the-throat time.

Just in time, luck takes a turn for the better. Eileen has had her photo splashed across the newspapers as the blonde bombshell who hijacked the Brazilian navy. She is news and therefore Valenti can offer her a cabaret spot at his club. She has a job! Luck is turning, too, for Helen and Wreck. Wreck has dressed up in a collar and tie instead of his usual shorts and is being charming to Mrs Wade who is just lapping up his invented antecedents and well-made compliments as well as the attentions of Mr Appopolous. Then Chick Clark turns up bursting with news. Eileen, who never told Ruth about his dirty trick, won't hear a word from him and instead turns her attentions to Bob, convincing him in a matter of seconds into the realisation that he's in love with Ruth ('It's Love').

Everyone gathers at the Village Vortex for Eileen's big night. With Ruth alongside her in duet to calm her nerves, she makes a great success with her little hometown number, 'The Wrong Note Rag' as Chick finally gets his news out: *his* editor loved Ruth's piece. Here's her press card—she starts work on Monday. Eileen segues happily into her encore ('It's Love') as Bob and Ruth go into a clinch. It has all turned out right at last. Goodbye, Columbus!

CAN-CAN

a musical in two acts by Abe Burrows. Music and lyrics by Cole Porter. Produced at the Shubert Theatre, New York, 7 May 1953 with Lilo (La Môme Pistache), Peter Cookson (Aristide), Gwen Verdon (Claudine) Erik Rhodes (Hilaire) and Hans Conried (Boris). Produced at the Minskoff Theatre 30 April, 1981 with Zizi Jeanmaire, Ron Husmann, Pamela Sousa, Swen Swenson and Avery Schreiber.

Produced at the London Coliseum 14 October 1954 with Irene Hilda, Edmund Hockridge, Gillian Lynne, George Gee and Alfred Marks.

A film version with a largely different plot was produced by Twentieth Century-Fox in 1960 with Shirley Maclaine, Louis Jourdan, Frank Sinatra and Maurice Chevalier.

CHARACTERS

Judge Aristide Forestier
Hilaire Jussac, *an art critic*
Boris Adzinidzinadze, *a sculptor*
La Môme Pistache
Claudine, *a laundress*
Gabrielle, Marie, Celestine, *laundresses*
Judge Paul Barrière
Hercule, *an architect*
Théophile, *a painter*
Étienne, *a poet*
Mimi, Waiters, Court President, Model, Policemen, Doctor, Registrar, Bailiff, Jailer, etc.

ACT 1

The show is set in Paris, that 1893 Paris of artists and models, of plentiful wine and frothily compliant women, which seems to have fixed itself in the world's mind as the Paris of always. In a police court, the judges have convened to deal with the business of the day: the President of the court and his colleagues, Judge Barrière and the newly appointed Judge Aristide Forestier, are nobly to dispense justice. There is little that is noble, however, about the first case. The defendants are a group of loud, saucy girls who have been arrested on morals charges the previous night in Montmartre where, in defiance of the law, they were seen by a whole list of police officers performing the lascivious and banned dance known as the cancan at the Bal du Paradis dance hall.

The girls have clearly been this way before and are not at all overwhelmed by their surroundings as they declare that they are laundresses and 'Maidens Typical of France'. Under the usual circumstances they would be given a quick and knowing discharge, but this morning is not usual for, in Aristide Forestier, the bench has gained an idealistic and dogmatic recruit. He has taken his oath to uphold the law and the law, whether it is a good law or a bad law, must be adhered to rigidly. Since none of the arresting officers can be encouraged to give eye witness testimony against these women, they must be released, but Aristide has decided to make it his business to attend the Bal du Paradis and come up with evidence himself.

Up in night-time Montmartre the inhabitants are busy being typically *fin de siècle* French, when Aristide arrives to make his way as unobtrusively as possible into the Bal du Paradis. Out in the streets, the pretty laundress Claudine, on her way to join the dancing, is waylaid by a dapper gentleman. He is Hilaire Jussac, the influential art critic, who is anxious to lay his heart and his trousers at her feet but, although Claudine finds Jussac perfectly amiable, she cannot accept his offer. She already has a gentleman permanently in attendance in the ungainly shape of the unsuccessful Bulgarian sculptor, Boris Adzinidzinadze, and Boris is a jealous man. He is also a penniless man whose art naturally prevents him from taking regular work and who, therefore, allows Claudine the privilege of working as a laundress in order to support him.

Boris's friends, the painter Théophile, the architect Hercule and the poet Étienne, also belong to the world of the great unappreciated, and they, too, are obliged to spend their evenings eating and drinking at the expense of the girls who dance at the Bal du Paradis, but there is one woman, at least, who finds this situation ridiculous and that is La Môme Pistache, the owner of the Bal du Paradis, whose philosophy is 'Never Give Anything Away (That You Can Sell)'. Pistache is the only female dance hall owner in Montmartre, but she has scrabbled her way to success by getting the local laundresses to come each night to her place and dance their cancan, the erotic infamy of which has spread throughout Paris and London and brought the crowds and their money to *chez* Pistache.

Pistache knows her clientele, and she is quick to turn her charms on to a handsome newcomer, a quiet gentleman in evening dress who orders mineral water instead of champagne. She happily describes the girls and their dancing and with loose confidentiality tells her customer how she bribes her little list of police with money, girls and wine to leave her establishment alone. When he, in amazement, questions the possibility of such a list, she sexily invites him up to her office to look at it and he prosaically accepts.

By now the girls have seen what Pistache is up to, but they have also recognised the judge from their morning court appearance and Pistache is hurriedly sent intelligence of the gentleman's identity. Up in her office, she quickly slips into something more revealing and sets to work—she has never had a judge on her list—but, no matter what seductiveness or bribery she employs, she cannot divert Aristide from his scrupulously correct and official line. He will look at the cancan and report back to the court.

Pistache is frustrated and furious at being unable to get her way, and she accuses Aristide explicitly of being a miserable, sexless creature who cares nothing for anyone. What would he know of joy and of love ('C'Est Magnifique')? At the end of the song she kisses him fiercely and he kisses her back. Pistache smiles. Now it is safe for him to watch the cancan (Quadrille). But as the dancers finish their high kicking, thigh-flashing routine, the magnesium flash of a photographic apparatus blazes forth. To Pistache's horror, Aristide has secured his evidence.

The girls are summoned to appear in court and everyone is worried and depressed. It will mean the end of the Bal du Paradis and Pistache, and the end of the cancan. Only Hilaire is unperturbed. He believes the publicity of the case will make the Bal du Paradis famous and, to make it even more so for the sake of the lovely Claudine, he announces that Pistache's establishment shall be the venue for the art fraternity's notorious Quat'z Arts Ball. When he renews his suit with Claudine ('Come Along With Me'), however, she fails to respond as he might have wished and simply asks him if he will do something for her poor, unappreciated Boris. Hilaire is up to his clenched teeth with Boris who, now that he has discovered the critic's identity, is only too happy to push Claudine at least part way into his arms, but he agrees to

708

look at the sculptor's work and to write about it, and he waltzes Claudine off to dinner...to talk about Boris.

As a result of Aristide's efficiency, Pistache and her girls have spent ten days in jail. It hasn't been too bad an experience as they've been well looked after, but the Bal du Paradis has been closed and Pistache has had little luck trying to get round Aristide to help her win her licence back in time for the Quat'z Arts Ball. He simply tells her that she is mad to risk breaking the law again, and she sulkily tells him she will do as she pleases ('Live and Let Live'). It is scarcely a situation which has a flavour of romance but, unfortunately for Aristide, he is accidentally falling in love with this impossible woman ('I Am In Love').

Up at their communal studio, Boris and his friends are preparing for Hilaire Jussac's vital visit when Claudine arrives dressed out in a dazzling new outfit, a gift from the critic which arouses a certain indignation in the heart of Bulgarian Boris ('If You Loved Me Truly'). Indignation vanishes like butter in the sun when the great man himself puts in an appearance, and Boris's selection of symbolic creations is paraded for his approbation while the other three Bohemians sneakily attempt to get the critic to cast an eye on their work as well. They have no chance, however, of topping Boris' *chef d'oeuvre*, the maidmer, an original (and less frustrating) remake of a mermaid comprising the top half of a fish and the bottom part of a woman.

In spite of the law, the Quat'z Arts Ball goes ahead at the Bal du Paradis ('Montmartre'/ Garden of Eden Ballet). Aristide turns up to warn Pistache not to take money at the door and so render herself liable to prosecution but, when he meets her again, his ethics and emotions get muddled and he ends up kissing her. This time Hilaire and the bohemians are on hand with a camera. With a photograph of the censorious judge at the ball embracing the hostess, they will surely be immune from prosecution. The startled Aristide tries to explain to Pistache that he came to help her out of goodwill, out of love, but she roughly tells him to go away ('Allez-Vous-En'): a judge cannot be in love with a Montmartre girl. When he has gone and there is no longer any need to play her self-assured part, she bursts into tears.

ACT 2

The photo of Aristide appears in the next morning's paper and anathema immediately starts creeping up around him from the ankles. He is to be the subject of a judicial enquiry as soon as the law can lay its hands on him. The judge himself has spent an eventful night drowning his sorrows amidst the revelry of the Quat'z Arts Ball and getting himself into plenty of scrapes in the process. The morning finds him, bewildered and aching, laid out on the couch at Boris's studio. In spite of their activities of the previous night, the artists are beavering away creatively ('Never, Never Be an Artist') but Boris's élan is cut short when it is discovered that he, too, has made the newspapers. Hilaire has written the promised article and it is a complete demolition of Boris's work. His friends persuade him that this is simply Hilaire's revenge on Boris because of the situation involving Claudine and they insist that the unenthusiastic Boris do the honourable thing by challenging the critic to a duel.

Dressed in borrowed clothes, Aristide is sitting glumly outside a Montmartre café wondering what to do next and finding consolation with a passing *poule* ('It's All Right With Me') when Pistache comes to find him to apologise for being the cause of his disgrace. She hadn't meant things to go so far. She, too, has suffered. She gave the money back, as he had suggested, but it didn't prevent her losing her licence again, this time permanently. But la Môme Pistache is not one to let go easily: she has plans to open a new café-concert under the guise of a laundry. There will be washing during the day and dancing at night and it should do very well. Why doesn't he join her in the venture.

Aristide laughs the idea off but, when Barrière turns up to tell he that he has been suspended from the bar and expelled from his legal society without a hearing, Aristide is incensed into changing his mind. This high-handed action is not in line with the law. He has the right to be heard before a jury and be heard he will. He will become an equal partner in Pistache's new business and, when they are arrested—as they surely will be—and brought before a jury, he will then have the opportunity to defend himself. Pistache is delighted, but less so when he insists that their alliance is to be purely a business arrangement ('Ev'ry Man Is a Stupid Man').

It is a good arrangement, for the new caf'-conc' proves the perfect place for the fashionable to come to dip their toes in the edge of the underworld (Apache Dance) and it prospers gaily but, as she gazes out over the Paris rooftops ('I Love Paris'), Pistache knows that something is missing. It is only missing until one day a business meeting ends in a kiss. After the kiss, Aristide tells Pistache of his plan. They will be arrested for running their place without a licence and they will appear in court. It will be a test case and he, as co-defendant, will be able to speak out on their behalf, on behalf of the whole of Montmartre and in defence of its right to live as it wishes.

Pistache doesn't see his reasoning. She is making money, good money now, and she does not want to be arrested, to have this whole profitable affair come to an end. The rest of Montmartre never did anything for her, why should she lose what she has for them? Aristide is deeply disappointed at her attitude. If that is how she feels, there is nothing to keep him in Montmartre. He turns over his half of the business to her and leaves. He will face the enquiry and take its consequences and he will forget all about Montmartre and everyone in it.

Boris's friends have hurried him out to find Hilaire to demand satisfaction for the artistic insult he has suffered and, when the meeting takes place, Boris finds that he cannot avoid the challenge. Hilaire chooses rapiers as the weapons for the duel, and Boris promptly faints. Claudine, seeing her man stretched out on the ground, rushes to him dramatically and the only way that Hilaire can find to reinstate himself in her good graces is by promising to write another article which will ensure that every one of Boris's sculptures is sold.

In spite of having given up his entire plan, Aristide inexplicably finds

710

himself arrested for opening an unlicenced café. He will have his jury trial and his test case after all. But now he is unwilling. Pistache did not want to be involved and he does want to involve her against her will. He decides he will just plead guilty instead. But it turns out that it is Pistache herself who has informed against them. She has repented her selfishness and the two of them stand up together in the dock to demonstrate before the court that obscenity is in the eye of the beholder, and that there is nothing wrong with the rousing 'Cancan' which closes the show.

KISMET

a musical Arabian Night in two acts by Charles Lederer and Luther Davis based on the play by Edward Knoblock. Lyrics by Robert Wright and George Forrest. Music from the works of Aleksandr Borodin, selected and arranged by Robert Wright and George Forrest. Produced at the Ziegfeld Theatre, New York, 3 December 1953 with Alfred Drake (Hajj), Doretta Morrow (Marsinah), Richard Kiley (Caliph), Joan Diener (Lalume) and Henry Calvin (Wazir).

Produced at the Stoll Theatre, London, 20 April 1955 with Drake, Miss Morrow, Peter Grant, Miss Diener and Paul Whitsun-Jones. Produced at the Shaftesbury Theatre 21 March 1978 with John Reardon, Lorna Dallas, Clifton Todd, Miss Diener (replaced by Elizabeth Larner) and Christopher Hewett.

Produced at Koblenz, 22 January 1977.

A film version was produced by MGM in 1955 with Howard Keel, Ann Blyth, Vic Damone, Dolores Gray and Sebastian Cabot.

CHARACTERS

Hajj, *a public poet*
Marsinah, *his daughter*
The Wazir of Police
Lalume, *wife to the Wazir*
The Caliph of Baghdad
Omar
Jawan
Chief Policeman
The Princesses of Ababu
Princess Samaris
Princess Zubbediya
Widow Yussef, Beggars, Imam, Hassan-Ben, Assiz, Policeman, etc.

ACT 1

The scene is ancient Baghdad and the time is dawn. Outside a mosque, a single elderly Imam sings simply of the transitory nature of kings, of wisdom and of love ('Sands of Time'). As the muezzins raise their voices calling the faithful to prayer, a bundle of rags in front of the mosque materialises into a group of beggars, ready to grumblingly start their day's work. One of their usual number is missing today. Old Hajj, the most senior of all Baghdad's beggars, has gone to Mecca and his place at the top of the stairs stays empty.

Another who starts his work early is the strolling poet. Customers are shy, and he is reduced to trying to hawk his verses to the beggars ('Rhymes Have I'), but he is unable to make a sale and, sending his daughter Marsinah off to steal some food from the market, he sits dejectedly down in Hajj's empty place. When a passer-by throws him a coin, the other beggars are angry for he has appropriated the best professional begging place in Baghdad, a hereditary position of the Hajj family. The poet cheerfully passes himself off as a distant Hajj cousin and, at the sight of the coin, takes to his new métier with aplomb. With the help of his rhymes he elicits some coins from the Caliph's friend Omar and, with the help of a threatened curse of increased taxes, he squeezes a further contribution from a businessman. It seems that 'Fate' may have found him a profitable new trade.

His masquerade soon brings him ill as well as good. A band of brigands comes with orders to abduct Hajj the beggar, and the poet is taken in his place to be dragged before the fearsome Jawan. This brigand chief was cursed by Hajj many years ago and, as a result, he lost his son. Now he is reaching the end of his life and wants to see his child once more. Hajj must withdraw the curse or perish messily. The poet's silver tongue averts the promised hot coals on the navel and wins him a hundred gold pieces as he impressively lifts the curse and assures Jawan that he will see his son again that very day. 'Fate' seems to be kind after all.

In the city of Baghdad, the horrid Wazir of the Police welcomes his beautiful wife, Lalume, back to town. Lalume has been on an envoy to Ababu where she has persuaded the local potentate to come up with ten camel-loads of gold, which the Wazir needs to pay off his creditors, with the promise that she will ensure that his three daughters are wedded to the Caliph of Baghdad. She has brought back the gold and also the three little Princesses; now the Wazir just has to ensure that the Caliph weds them. The little Princesses are not sure they like Baghdad, and Lalume has to reassure them of its wonders ('Not Since Nineveh').

No sooner has this group headed on its way than Marsinah runs in, fleeing from an angry orange merchant whose stall she has robbed. Her father arrives in time to save her and then pours out the hundred gold pieces before the amazed girl. They are rich! She must go and buy herself clothes and jewels and a house. The tradesmen who had scorned the poor girl surround her to offer her their 'Baubles, Bangles and Beads' but, as Marsinah feasts on the riches of Baghdad market, Omar passes by in the company of a young man. It is the Caliph himself, and he is entranced by the beautiful young woman. Hajj, in the meanwhile, has gone shopping for some slave girls, but he is stopped by the Wazir's police who are searching for Jawan and, found with the brigand's bag of gold on him, he is arrested.

Marsinah has gone to the house of the widow Yussef, a pretty little place which she has long loved, to buy it for their home and, as she awaits the widow in the garden, the Caliph, who has followed her there, approaches, pretending to be a gardener. In a moment they are singing together of the wonders of love ('A Stranger in Paradise') and, when he returns to town, the happy Caliph tells Omar that he has lost his heart. This bit of news is ill received by the Princesses of Ababu, especially as they have just seen two other foreign princesses arrive in town with the same matrimonial intent, but their police escorts hastily turn the news into a song and dance ('He's in Love') and provide nice young men as dance partners to distract the noisy Princesses.

The Wazir is highly worried by all this competition to Ababu's brides, and he is in no mood to be clement when the poet is dragged before him by the police. But once again the new Hajj's eloquence is his saviour. His artless admission of his amorality and his twinkling eye take the fancy of Lalume, and his clever reasoning as to why his hand should not be cut off ('Gesticulate') wins him a reprieve, but the Wazir's practised questioning soon finds his prisoner's soft spot, his daughter, and he commands the police to bring Hajj's family and possessions before the court.

As the cursing poet is dragged away, the guards lead in the captured Jawan. The brigand reviles Hajj for failing in his promise, then suddenly shrieks with joy. Around the Wazir's neck is the amulet which he left with his lost son. Hajj's boast has come true, he has found his child. The Wazir is more impressed by this seeming act of sorcery than by the sudden acquisition of a father. In fact a brigand father is a rather cumbersome thing for a Wazir and the embarrassed police chief finds it expedient to sentence the old man to death. Then he turns his attentions to Hajj. One piece of his magic seems to have come off successfully, but what about the curses he recently piled on the Wazir himself? Will they also come true?

He has not long to wait for an answer for, before he can take another breath, the Caliph arrives to announce that he will not wed the Ababus. They can go home, for he has found a bride. The appalled Wazir, facing certain ruin, hastily reverses his orders against the mighty Hajj and, all but grovelling, promises him money and rank if he will use his sorcery to prevent this marriage.

Lalume is not taken in by any of this apparent magic, but she is very much taken by the poet as a man, and she decides to lend him her not inconsiderable help. It is help he will swiftly need if he is to make good his rash promises to the Wazir, for the Caliph has ordered a wedding procession into the streets and he is heading at this moment in the direction of the home of the woman he would make his wife. If he would save his new reputation and, indeed, his neck, Hajj must stop the wedding. But how? There is nothing he can do but put himself with much ceremony into the hands of 'Fate'.

ACT 2

On the way to the widow Yussef's house the Caliph sings in joyful anticipation of love ('Night of my Nights'), whilst the unsuspecting Marsinah, happily awaiting the return of her gardener, softly reprises 'A Stranger in Paradise'. As the unwieldy procession makes its way through the streets of Baghdad, Hajj slips by and arrives at the house before them to break his news to Marsinah: if the Caliph does not wed his intended bride, they will be rich and powerful, but if he does, then he will die. Marsinah must flee to Damascus this instant. Within a week she will know if her father is rich and alive or discovered and dead.

Marsinah does not want to leave Baghdad, she does not want to leave her father or her lover, but Hajj forces her from the house just seconds before the Caliph arrives to find an empty garden. The widow Yussef tells her monarch how she saw the girl with a man, a man who put his arms around her, and now they have gone. The saddened Caliph and his entourage can only return to the city empty-handed.

When the news of the Caliph's disappointment reaches the Wazir, he is more than ever convinced of Hajj's powers. With such a man as this at his side he can be even more powerful than he is now ('Was I Wazir'). Lalume is ordered to make a fuss of the wizard, and she happily obeys ('Rahadlakum'), sharing with Hajj the dream of a romantic rendezvous in the Oasis of Delightful Imaginings, far away in the desert, out of the reach of her hated husband.

Marsinah is brought to the Wazir's palace by Hajj and Lalume and secreted, out of harm's way, amongst the Wazir's harem but, in spite of the riches and care that are lavished on her, she cannot be happy. She can think only of her gardener and her father lovingly promises that he will try to find him for her. At the same time, the Caliph is giving instructions to the Wazir that he must find the girl from the widow Yussef's house, and the two conversations join together in the quartet 'This Is My Beloved'.

The poet-turned-sorcerer meets up with another poet, for the Caliph's Omar is none other than Omar Khayyam. Omar warns him that there is danger in serving the Wazir, and hints that he might do better to leave him and his proffered wealth while his head is still on his shoulders. To Hajj it seems that to run away from riches would be foolish, although he grants there is always something to be learned, even from a fool ('The Olive Tree').

The Caliph grows impatient as searches fail to find his beloved. The Wazir seeks to divert him, offering him the delights of his own harem and, through a spy hole in the harem wall, he points out the advantages of the Princesses of Ababu. All the Caliph sees, however, is Marsinah, and he is distraught. His beloved is a wife of the Wazir! His dream of love is over. He will wed the wretched Ababus or anyone else and, since the Wazir insists he must choose, he will make his choice at the evening's Diwan. To the Wazir this miraculous appearance of an unknown wife in his harem is just one more proof of the magic of Hajj but he is taking no chances. Marsinah is dragged forth and wed to him on the spot.

At the Diwan the various Princesses are paraded before the Caliph. The Wazir, awaiting the royal decision nervously, babbles gratefully to Hajj of the marvellous trick by which the Caliph's beloved was transferred to his harem and, when he lets slip Marsinah's name, Hajj realises the enormity of what he has done. His fertile brain immediately sprouts a remedy. Holding an unmarked golden plaque aloft, he declares that, by his magic, it will, when immersed in water, show the name of the Caliph's bride.

714

Throwing the plaque into the deep pool in the courtyard, he declares that the Wazir himself will retrieve it to ensure there is no cheating while, to the Wazir, he entrusts a second plaque, bearing the name of Ababu, which the police chief secretes in his boot. The Caliph is indifferent to the whole procedure, but the Wazir excitedly insists that the magical prophecy be read, and he climbs gingerly down into the water. Behind Hajj's cloak, he raises his foot to grasp the marked plaque, but the poet grabs his ankle, turns him face down into the water and, holding the struggling, drowning villain behind him, he holds forth with a poetic description of the evils committed by his victim. When he asks the Caliph what would be his sentence on a man responsible for such crimes, the Caliph replies, 'Death', and Hajj can step aside to announce calmly that the sentence is already carried out.

The poet is held fast by the royal guards, but Lalume and Marsinah hasten to the scene and, when the Caliph sees his beloved and realises that Hajj has told nothing but the truth, he declares himself willing to listen to the scoundrel's own sentence on himself. He shall be condemned to give up the most joyful thing in his life, his daughter, to the Caliph, and he shall be condemned to take away the wife of the man he has murdered (with all the goods and chattels she can get her hands on before the auditors come) to some far off oasis in the desert where he shall labour night and day to make amends to her for his deed. And thus did Kismet, the Fate of the East, bring things to pass.

In 1978 a reworked version of *Kismet* was presented at the Mark Hellinger Theatre, New York, under the title *Timbuktu!*.

THE PAJAMA GAME

a musical in two acts by George Abbott and Richard Bissell based on Bissell's novel *7½ Cents*. Music and lyrics by Richard Adler and Jerry Ross. Produced at the St James Theatre, New York, 13 May 1954 with John Raitt (Sid), Janis Paige (Babe), Eddie Foy jr (Hines) and Carol Haney (Gladys). Produced at the Lunt-Fontanne Theatre 9 December 1973 with Hal Linden, Barbara McNair, Cab Calloway and Sharon Miller.

Produced at the London Coliseum 13 October 1955 with Edmund Hockridge, Joy Nichols, Max Wall and Elizabeth Seal.

CHARACTERS

Mr Hasler, *the owner of the Sleep Tite Pajama Factory*
Vernon Hines, *a time study man*
Prez, *the President of the Local 343 Associated Garment Workers' Union*
Gladys Hotchkiss, *Mr Hasler's secretary*
Sid Sorokin, *a factory superintendant*
Babe Williams

715

Mabel
Mae
Pop Williams, *Babe's father*
Joe
Charlie
Brenda
Poopsie
Max
Eddie, First and Second Helper, etc.

ACT 1

A curious fellow called Hines comes before the curtain to tell the audience that they are about to see a serious drama about Capital and Labour and that they shouldn't get the wrong impression when they see naked women being chased through the woods later on. Hines is a time and motion man, employed at the Sleep Tite Pajama Factory in Cedar Rapids, Iowa, where the action of the show is centred. He and the rest of the cast are in 'The Pajama Game'.

Sleep Tite Pajamas is not a happy little factory. When he is not goosing the seamstresses, the lecherous Prez of the local chapter of the Garment Workers' Union takes time out to roar threats of strike action over a demand for a salary rise at his employer. The employer in the question, Mr Hasler, has no intention of giving in to such a demand. With the support of Hines and his methods, he is interested only in increasing production ('Racing Against the Clock').

Sid Sorokin is a young Chicago fellow who has recently been hired as a factory superintendent. He is the kind who rolls up his sleeves and gets to work, and he is determined to make good in this new job and new town ('A New Town Is a Blue Town'). Exasperated by the malingering of a couple of so-called workers, Sid shoves one out of the way in order to complete a necessary job himself, and earns himself a summons before the grandly named Grievance Committee. The committee is headed by a tart little dolly bird called Babe Williams. She wriggles around the complaint of the known malingerer, unwilling to be unjust but equally unwilling to find against a Union member. She manages, in the process, to make quite an impression on Sid, and the other factory girls leap at a chance for some gossip as they scent romance. When they start to tease Babe, she reacts scornfully ('I'm Not at All in Love').

A more advanced Sleep Tite love affair carries on a rocky course. Hines is sweet on Mr Hasler's secretary Gladys, but he suffers from an over-developed sense of unfaithfulness. When he sees her putting a note on Sid's desk, he goes crazy, but when it turns out only to be some figures he shamefacedly promises Gladys's colleague, Mabel, that 'I'll Never Be Jealous Again'. It isn't Gladys's day, because a few minutes later she gets into hot water from Mr Hasler for leaving the ledgers unattended on her desk and she ends up in tears in the ladies' room.

716

Sid summons Babe to his office, ostensibly for consultation on his case with the Grievance Committee but in reality to ask her for a date, but Babe, who has textbook principles on worker-management relations or, in this case, the impossibility of them, declines and Sid is left alone to wonder at himself for getting girl-struck ('Hey There').

At the Union picnic, Prez tries a pass at Gladys, boringly spinning the old my-wife-doesn't-understand-me line ('Her Is'). There are speeches and a knife-throwing act by Hines, who was apparently once in vaudeville, as the employees of Sleep Tite exercise their libidos in and out of the nearby woods. Sid seizes the occasion to make out with Babe ('Once-a-Year Day') and Prez, having failed with Gladys, moves his attentions on to the seamstress Mae with a second burst of 'Her Is'.

Babe invites Sid over to her place and, when her old Pop has gone off to work, she settles down to titivate Sid with some 'Small Talk' before the canoodling gets under way. She tells him that she loves him, but it soon becomes clear that either she doesn't know what the word means or else she has got trouble with her priorities. While she is in his arms she starts on about the Union's wage claim but Sid sticks to his guns and in a moment labour relations are forgotten.

In the end, Babe even neglects a Confrontation with the Management in order to be with Sid and sing a duet about love ('There Once Was a Man'). She doesn't miss much, for the big Confrontation turns out to be a flop. Hasler will not agree to the $7\frac{1}{2}$ cents an hour increase in salary, at least, not yet, so the Prez petulantly brings out his favourite weapon: slow down. Sid orders the girls to keep working at normal rate but, when they start to do so, Babe jams the production line and brings all work to a halt. Sid sacks her on the spot and, as the act ends, watches her go, ruefully advising himself to forget her.

ACT 2

Gladys opens the second act with an incidental song and dance number ('Steam Heat') intended to entertain a Union meeting before the meeting gets down to considering more ways to foul up the operation of Sleep Tite. Pop Williams, who gets on rather well with Sid and doesn't know about the bust up, invites the boy back to the house where he tries to persuade Babe to separate their personal and workaday lives. She won't listen to Sid when he explains that he's just another employee trying to make good himself, and she sneers at him as a 'tycoon' before going off into her bedroom to reprise 'Hey There' and have a private sob.

Back at the factory, the girls have to keep remembering to go slow when anyone is looking. They are sorry to upset Hines whose soul is mortified by the wreck of his time-study plans ('Think of the Time I Save'), but they dare not be caught working properly by the threatening Titans of the Union. In Hasler's office, things are getting heated. Mabel tries to tell the boss that orders are being cancelled, and Max the traveller has come all the way back from Peoria to demonstrate a piece of sabotage: someone has been tacking the fly buttons on with just two threads. When he demonstrated his line to a customer all the buttons flew off.

Sid tries to get Hasler to compromise with the Union, but Hasler will not hear of it, so Sid tries another line—with Gladys. He asks her to let him see the locked and guarded ledger. She refuses. Then he asks her for a date and she accepts pinkly. They go out to a moody club called 'Hernando's Hide-away' where Gladys gets tiddly on gin and allows Sid to get his hands on her key to the ledger. As soon as he has hurried off to put the key to work, Hines turns up to berate Gladys drunkenly for her unfaithfulness and, in a dream ballet, we see an extravagant version of the imaginings of Hines about Gladys and her glamorous lovers (Jealousy Ballet).

When the workforce turn up at the Sleep Tite factory the next morning to stage an all-out strike, they find Sid, who has been up all night examining the ledgers. In those closely guarded books, Sid has discovered something appalling. Horrid, capitalistic Mr Hasler has been budgeting the extra $7\frac{1}{2}$ cents in his costings for months. With these figures in his possession, Sid is in a fine position for a bit of blackmail. Now Mr Hasler will have to give in to a compromise.

Over at the Union rally the members of Local 343 are greedily imagining the luxuries they will buy with the raise their strike will bring ('$7\frac{1}{2}$ Cents') when Sid arrives to tell them that Mr Hasler has agreed to grant them the raise if they give up their claim for retroactive payments. There are one or two practical grumbles from those who can see through the 'concession', but Babe and her friends only care for the fact that they seem to have 'won'. Sid's reward is Babe around his neck, as the whole company join in a party with a pajama parade agreeing chummily that its great to be in 'The Pajama Game'.

DAMN YANKEES

a musical in two acts by George Abbott and Douglas Wallop based on Wallop's book *The Year the Yankees Lost the Pennant*. Music and lyrics by Richard Adler and Jerry Ross. Produced at the 46th Street Theatre, New York, 5 May 1955 with Stephen Douglass (Joe Hardy), Gwen Verdon (Lola) and Ray Walston (Applegate).

Produced at the London Coliseum 28 March 1957 with Ivor Emmanuel, Belita (succeeded by Elizabeth Seal) and Bill Kerr.

A film version was produced by Warner Brothers in 1958 with Tab Hunter, Gwen Verdon and Ray Walston.

CHARACTERS

Joe Boyd, *a real estate salesman later* Joe Hardy
Meg Boyd, *his wife*
Mr Applegate
Sister

Doris
Gloria Thorpe, *a newspaperperson*
Benny van Buren, *manager of the Washington Senators*
Sohovik, *a ball player with the Washington Senators*
Smokey, *another one*
Vernon ⎤
Henry ⎬ *more ball players*
Rocky ⎦
Mr Welch, *owner of the Washington Senators*
Lola
Lynch, Miss Weston, Commissioner, Postmaster, etc.

ACT 1

On the porch of his home in Washington DC real estate salesman Joe Boyd is watching a televised ball game with the single-minded passion of the total devotee. His wife, Meg, sewing alongside him might as well not be there; it's the ball season and in the ball season nothing exists for Joe but the Washington Senators ('Six Months Out of Every Year'). Unfortunately, the team isn't doing too well. In fact right now they're losing a match and lying seventh in the league behind the all-conquering Yankees and Joe is getting ulcers over it. He knows what's wrong. The team needs one decent long ball hitter. He'd sell his soul for one. And, goodness me, a second or two later, that's just what he's being given the chance to do.

In a discreet whiff of music, a dapper stranger who calls himself Mr Applegate appears on the porch with a proposition. He will turn Joe into the ball-playing hero who will save the Washington Senators in exchange for that little thing, his soul. Come on, it's not that uncommon. How does he think half the politicians and car-park owners in town got started? Joe hesitates: he will have to leave his wife, his job, and what if he changes his mind? In the real estate business they have a thing called an escape clause; he wants one of those. Mr Applegate tetchily agrees. He wants to get the whole plan into operation before the damn Yankees sew up the season. Joe's escape clause can operate up to midnight on September 24, but after that, no go.

Joe leaves a loving note for Meg ('Goodbye Old Girl') and hands himself over to the devil. No sooner has he done so than Applegate makes a magical pass and suddenly a new version of Joe appears. He is twenty years younger and raring to go. So they do.

At the Washington Baseball Park, Benny van Buren, the manager of the Senators is trying to instill some spirit into his team following their thrashing at the hands of the Yankees. Skill is only part of what is needed, he tells them, you've got to have 'Heart'. He fobs off a lady newspaperperson, Gloria Thorpe, who comes in search of a nice negative story to drape across her column, and he isn't exactly thrilled when the suave Applegate turns up with Joe, insisting that the boy be given a trial. Another aspiring rookie is the last thing he needs.

He sends Joe off with one of the team for a few practice balls but, when he hears the unexpected results of this exercise, he lets the boy loose in the park. The first thing the barefoot boy does is hit the ball right over the wall in front of the popping eyes of Gloria Thorpe. She is immediately on the trail of a story and when she scents a mystery in the lad's background she fires in with all questions blazing. Joe gulps out that his hometown is Hannibal, Missouri, and Gloria has soon encaptioned that into a nicely flip headline. 'Shoeless Joe from Hannibal Mo' is on his way.

Joe shoots quickly to the top with his superhuman efforts on the ball field, but he isn't at all happy with the Press he gets and especially Gloria's typical fact-fiction reporting. Washington's team is gradually climbing in the league, and all Miss Thorpe and her colleagues do is snipe at the boy who won't give them lush stories on his private life. The team owner comforts Joe. What do they care? On the twenty-fifth of September, the pennant will be theirs.

The twenty-fifth? That date jogs Joe's memory as he recalls his escape clause. They'd better have the championship sewn up before that last day's match or else he is damned. Applegate has that annoying condition on his mind too. He needs to organise things so that the pennant is still on ice before the last day's games so that Joe can't sneak out of paying his dues. He's under no illusion—Joe would like to. He's clearly got a longing to see Meg again ('A Man Doesn't Know'). A diversion is needed, so a diversion is arranged. She is called Lola and she touts about 'A Little Brains—A Little Talent' and a lot of charms. Lola is a practised homewrecker and Joe is all hers to go get.

Back at home, Meg sadly makes do with the company of her baseball-fan friends, Doris and Sister, who are persuaded that Joe will never return. Then one day a young man turns up wanting to rent Joe's old room. Meg likes him and agrees, but when Doris and Sister come in they recognise the boy as the famous ball player, Joe Hardy. In spite of Applegate's attempts to stop him, Joe moves back in to his own home. So now, as the Senators' winning streak continues, Applegate decides it is the moment to introduce Lola into the game. Joe is stunned by the sexy beauty who is, as she informs him, irresistible ('Whatever Lola Wants'), but he's inherently monogamous and he doesn't succumb as expected. Applegate, irritated, rubbishes Lola's line in seduction and determines instead to start a newspaper scandal about the boy's living with Meg which will force him to move out.

While the fan clubs celebrate the imminent winning of the pennant in songs and dance ('Heart'), and Lola pops in her own one-woman fan club contribution ('Who's Got the Pain'), further trouble is being brewed for Joe. A handily placed aside from Applegate has Gloria Thorpe heading for her typewriter to declare to the world that the mysterious Joe Hardy is, in fact, a banned player from the Mexican league called Shifty McCoy.

ACT 2

It is September 24, the day by which Joe needed to win the pennant, and he isn't playing. He's been suspended and called before the Baseball Commission to defend himself on the charge of being McCoy, and the Senators have to get on without him. They've just got to forget him and keep their minds on winning 'The Game'. In spite of all they can do, they lose, and the championship is back in the melting pot.

Joe meets Meg on a park bench. He has made up his mind what he is going to do. He will clear his name before the day is out and then he will exercise his escape clause and go back to being plain Joe Boyd again. He comforts Meg that her Joe will return. If she could only believe it, he is really 'Near to You' at this very moment.

Back at Applegate's apartment, the devil is plotting nastily. Tonight he will ensnare Joe into renouncing his escape with the dream of winning the pennant for the Senators and then, tomorrow, in the vital game, he will bewitch Joe into throwing the match. Half of Washington will die of apoplexy. When Joe turns up to tell Applegate that he is exercising his get out, Applegate tries one more trick: the escape clause has to be taken at the witching hour. At midnight that night, when Joe's hearing is in session, if he still wishes to get out of his contract he must step with Applegate into the next room and he will be changed back to his old shape. When the boy has departed, the devil muses nostalgically 'Those Were the Good Old Days', as he remembers how much easier it was to accomplish his diabolical works in historical times.

At the Commissioner's session, Joe is questioned about his alleged origins in Hannibal, Mo. Gloria has negative evidence from the birth registers and has brought an aged postmaster to swear that no one called Joe Hardy ever lived in Hannibal, but Applegate counters with a gentle admission that Joe was illegitimate and Meg, Doris and Sister (who really *are* from Hannibal) turn up to greet Joe as an old friend, causing the befuddled postmaster suddenly to change his evidence. If Hannibal knows him, then he cannot possibly be Shifty McCoy, and he must be cleared.

Now it is nearly midnight. Joe signals to Applegate to come into the next room but, as he goes towards the door, Meg holds him back as she goes into a long and passionate defence of Joe Hardy and, by her heartfelt deed, she condemns him. Midnight strikes and Joe has not escaped.

Later that night, Joe sits disconsolately with his fellow damnee, Lola. She was once the ugliest woman in Providence, Rhode Island, before she gave in to Applegate. Joe is one of them now, so the 'Two Lost Souls' go off to a night club together. But Lola is not wholly lost. She has slipped a Mickey Finn to Applegate and the devil is drugged. He is so drugged that he doesn't wake up until it is almost too late to get to the game against the Yankees the next day.

It is all but over, and Washington are 4-3 up as he clambers into the stand with Lola, whom he has revengefully changed back into the old hag that she was. Now it will be Joe's turn to suffer the same fate. As the ball flies from Mickey Mantle's bat towards Joe Hardy, the devil makes his magic pass and, before the eyes of the amazed crowd, a fat middle-aged man leaps impossibly for the vital catch—and makes it! The Senators have won the pennant. The crowd stream on to the pitch, leaving just the aged Lola in the stand, happily waving her scarf in triumph.

As the team celebrate, no one can find Joe Hardy. He has vanished. He is Joe Boyd again, and he has gone straight back to Chevy Chase, to be reunited with his Meg. They won't ever find him again. As man and wife happily join in a reprise of 'A Man Doesn't Know', Applegate appears to try one last throw. He tempts Joe with promises of a World Series win, and he flaunts Lola, now beautiful again, in front of him—but Lola will not co-operate. No one will. Applegate is hopping mad. The devil is defeated, and so are the Yankees.

MY FAIR LADY

a musical in two acts by Alan Jay Lerner based on *Pygmalion* by George Bernard Shaw. Music by Frederick Loewe. Produced at the Mark Hellinger Theatre, New York, 15 March 1956 with Rex Harrison (Higgins), Julie Andrews (Eliza Doolittle), Stanley Holloway (Doolittle) and Robert Coote (Pickering). Produced at the St James Theatre 25 March 1976 with Ian Richardson, Christine Andreas, George Rose and Coote. Produced at the Uris Theatre 18 August 1981 with Harrison, Nancy Ringham, Milo O'Shea and Jack Gwillim with Cathleen Nesbitt as Mrs Higgins.

Produced at the Theatre Royal, Drury Lane, London, 30 April 1958 with Harrison, Miss Andrews, Holloway and Coote, with Zena Dare as Mrs Higgins. Produced at the Adelphi Theatre 25 April 1979 with Tony Britton, Liz Robertson, Peter Bayliss and Richard Caldicott, with Anna Neagle as Mrs Higgins.

Produced at the Théâtre Sebastapol, Lille, in a version by Bruno Tellenne and Pierre Carrell 8 October 1977.

Produced at the Theater des Westens, Berlin, in a version by Robert Gilbert 25 October 1961 with Paul Hubschmid and Karin Hübner.

Played at the Theater an der Wien, Vienna, 1963 in Gilbert's version and produced there in a revised version by Gerhard Bonner 1969 with Josef Meinrad and Gabriele Jacoby.

A film version was produced by Warner Brothers in 1964 with Harrison, Audrey Hepburn (singing dubbed by Marni Nixon), Holloway and Wilfred Hyde-White.

CHARACTERS

Henry Higgins
Eliza Doolittle
Colonel Pickering
Mrs Eynsford-Hill
Freddy Eynsford-Hill *her son*
Clara Eynsford-Hill, *her daughter*
Alfred P Doolittle, *Eliza's father*
Mrs Pearce, *Higgins's housekeeper*
Mrs Higgins, *Henry's mother*
Zoltan Karpathy
Harry, Jamie, Queen of Transylvania, etc.

ACT 1

Under the columned portico of St Paul's Church, Covent Garden, opera-goers are sheltering from the rain and trying to find transport to get them spotlessly to their homes. Amongst the elegant throng, jostling for shelter, are the stately Mrs Eynsford-Hill, her daughter, Clara, and her son Freddy whose ineffectual efforts to attract a cab ultimately result in his tumbling headlong over a scruffy flower-girl, sending her bunches of violets scattering into the mud.

The complaining girl gets short shrift and no compensation from Freddy's mother, but she ungraciously accepts a meagre three-ha'pence from an amiable Colonel who simply wants to be rid of her importuning. A bystander warns the girl to give the gentleman a flower for his money, warning her that a copper's nark behind a pillar is writing down what she says.

In the hubbub that follows, it eventuates that the note-taking gentleman is no policeman but Mr Henry Higgins, a professor of language and an expert on dialects, who amazes the crowd by placing the origins of some of them within a few streets. It is Henry Higgins's contention that a person is the manner in which he or she speaks ('Why Can't the English?'), a contention which means something to the amiable Colonel Pickering who is himself a student of Indian dialects. The two men discover each other's identity and Higgins promptly invites Pickering to be his house guest. The girl, ignored through all this, howls for a bit of attention and, reminded by the church bells of a finer duty, the preoccupied Higgins empties his pocket of change into her basket as he leaves.

Eliza Doolittle has never seen so much money and, as her costermonger friends gather jokingly around, she dreams aloud of how she could spend a little money ('Wouldn't it Be Loverly'). Up the Tottenham Court Road, Eliza's father, Alfred, is having no luck getting a beer or two on the never-never but, when Eliza passes by and tosses him a half-crown out of her windfall, he launches happily into song praising the virtues of 'A Little Bit of Luck'.

At Higgins's Wimpole Street home, the next day, the Professor and Pickering are delving into the finer points of vowel sounds when Eliza turns up. She's come for lessons. She wants to learn to speak well enough to get a job in a flower shop. Higgins is tempted by the sheer awfulness of her speech and, when Pickering challenges him to a wager, he declares that he will take the girl in hand and teach her to speak well enough to be passed off successfully as a lady of class at the Embassy Ball later that year.

In spite of the qualms of his housekeeper, Mrs Pearce, Higgins orders Eliza to be taken away and bathed and dressed as he lays out his intentions. The girl will stay in the house, be fed, clothed and taught, and he will win his bet. After that she can do what she likes. Pickering is a little more respectful of Eliza's feelings and feels he must make sure that no advantage is taken of the girl, but Higgins laughs the suggestion off; he has no intention of letting a woman into his life, she would merely disorder it ('An Ordinary Man').

The exercise is well under way when, one day, Alfred Doolittle turns up at Wimpole Street. Under the threat of reclaiming his daughter, he is out to get some money from these gentlemen. He is stopped in his little bit of blackmail when Higgins tells him to take the girl away and he has to backtrack hurriedly, but his uncomplicatedly amoral reasoning over the selling of his daughter at a reasonable rate appeals to Higgins who gives the rogue five pounds and sends him off happy. Eliza is not so happy. She is having an awful time getting her vowels straight and, when Higgins deprives her of lunch and dinner until she has got them right, she explodes in a private rage of frustration ('Just You Wait').

Time passes and, working day and night, Higgins patiently and sometimes less patiently instils good speech into the girl's mind and mouth. Then, one weary night, it all comes together and Higgins, Pickering and Eliza caper round the room in delight as all the plans Higgins has made start to blossom ('The Rain in Spain'). Eliza is blissfully unable to think of bed when it is all over and, as she relives her delirious dance of triumph in Higgins's arms, she happily sings to all who will listen 'I Could Have Danced All Night'.

Eliza's first public trial is at Ascot (Ascot Gavotte) where Higgins brings her to join his mother's society friends in her box. If Eliza's vowels are in order, however, her conversation is apt to lapse from time to time. She stuns Mrs Higgins's guests with her perfectly pronounced East End expressions, which Higgins hastily passes off as the latest society small-talk but, ultimately, she goes beyond the pale when, in the excitement of a horse race, she howls out to her horse to 'move your bloomin' arse'.

Ascot makes Eliza one conquest. Freddy Eynsford-Hill falls in love with the exquisite, unusual girl and he takes to wandering asininely around Wimpole Street just to be 'On the Street Where You Live'. In the light of the Ascot débâcle, Pickering is anxious to call off the wager, but Higgins is determined to continue and, with Eliza working hard to erase the mortification of her last foray into society, he is confident of success. Six weeks later the night of the Embassy Ball arrives. Eliza, looking radiant, appears on Higgins's arm and attracts immediate attention but some of that attention is unwelcome. Zoltan Karpathy, a language expert who has turned his skills to unsavoury uses, moves in on Eliza, sensing some sort of a mystery and, as the curtain falls, he animatedly leads Eliza into a dance (The Embassy Waltz).

ACT 2

At three o'clock in the morning the tired party arrives home. Higgins's bet has been won, and Pickering jubilates 'You Did It' as they retail the evening's events to Mrs Pearce. Karpathy insisted that Eliza was no English lady but a Hungarian Princess! In all the celebrating no one has thought to address one word of congratulation to Eliza herself and, when Higgins looks for his slippers, they are hurled at him from the other side of the room by the tearful girl. Now that the bet is over, what is to become of her? Higgins is genuinely surprised. He hadn't really thought about it. He supposes she might marry or, as she said at the start of the whole affair, go and work in a flower shop, but he hadn't really realised she'd be leaving.

Eliza bitterly asks him what is hers to take away and what must be returned, and when she pointedly gives back a ring he had given her as a gift, Higgins, unwilling to have his emotions stirred in such a way, finally gets angry and, flinging the ring in the fireplace, stalks out. As soon as he is gone, Eliza runs to retrieve the ring, but a few vengeful lines of 'Just You Wait' dissolve into sobs. She changes and packs and is leaving the house when she sees Freddy, posted in his usual position at the doorstep singing 'On the Street Where You Live'. He tries to comfort her with words of love, but Eliza has had enough of words from Higgins and she explodes into a demand for action ('Show Me').

The confused Eliza makes her way back to her old haunts in Covent Garden, but no-one there recognises her in her new persona until she meets her father coming out of a pub all dressed up with a flower in his buttonhole. He's getting married to the woman he's lived with for so many years, and it's all Eliza's fault. Apparently Higgins told a millionaire philanthropist that the most original moralist in Britain was a dustman called Doolittle and the old chap left Alfred £4000 a year in his will. With that sort of money there's no way he could continue his old happy-go-lucky life. He's been delivered bound and gagged into the middle class, and that means marriage ('Get Me to the Church on Time').

Meanwhile, back at Wimpole Street, Eliza's flight has been discovered. The two men try to set a search in motion while the uncomprehending Higgins muses on the unpredictability of women (Hymn to Him). Eliza, not knowing where to go, unable to fit either in her old life or her new, finally finds her way to Mrs Higgins's home. Mrs Higgins is totally sympathetic. The men have behaved abominably and Eliza is quite right to walk out on them. When Henry turns up he is staggered to find his mother calmly take Eliza's part.

Face to face, Eliza tries to explain to Higgins the sort of consideration she wants from him. It isn't love—if she wanted that there's Freddy and loads of others—it is more like friendship. But the interview breaks down through lack of a common understanding and the frustrated Eliza swears that she'll marry Freddy and go and teach phonetics with Zoltan Karpathy. This really rouses Higgins to anger and Eliza, with the upper hand at last, is triumphant as she tells him what she will do 'Without You'. She is magnificent, and Higgins is all approval: this is the Eliza he likes. Then, with what sounds like a final goodbye, she is gone, and Henry Higgins calls helplessly for his mother.

Higgins cannot get used to the idea that she will not be coming back ('I've Grown Accustomed to Her Face'). Alone in his study, he switches on a recording of Eliza's voice which he made in the early days of their lessons and, as he listens, head in hands, Eliza enters. Turning off the machine, she gently mimics her old voice. Higgins looks up. If he would let himself, his face would show everything from relief to pure joy. But he doesn't. He simply asks, as he asked the previous night, for his slippers. Eliza understands that this is all she will ever get. She can take it or leave it and, for the moment, she is apparently going to take it.

THE MOST HAPPY FELLA

a musical in three acts by Frank Loesser based on *They Knew What They Wanted* by Sidney Howard. Music and lyrics by Frank Loesser. Produced at the Imperial Theatre, New York, 3 May 1956 with Robert Weede (Tony) Jo Sullivan (Rosabella), Art Lund (Joey), Susan Johnson (Cleo) and Shorty Long (Herman). Produced at the Majestic Theatre 11 October 1979 with Giorgio Tozzi, Sharon Daniels, Richard Muenz, Louisa Flaningam and Dennis Warning.

Produced at the London Coliseum 21 April 1960 with Inia Te Wiata, Helena Scott, Art Lund, Libi Staiger and Jack De Lon.

CHARACTERS

Cleo, *a waitress*
Rosabella, *another waitress*
Tony Esposito, *a wine grower*
Marie Esposito, *his sister*
Joe, *Tony's foreman*
Herman
Clem
Jake
Al
Guiseppe
Pasquale
Ciccio
Tessie, Gussie, Doctor, etc.

ACT 1

It is getting towards closing time at the middle-class San Francisco restaurant where Cleo works, and she is longing to get off her feet ('Ooh, My Feet'). As Cleo carries on her post-work blues, her friend and workmate, Amy, makes a strange discovery. She has been left a real piece of jewellery, an amethyst tie-clip, as a tip at a table where she can't even recall the customer's face. The girls look at it in amazement as Amy reads the note left with the gift, and her inclination to laugh soon disappears. This is a real love letter. In poor English, the writer gives his name and his story. He is Antonio Esposito and he lives on a grape ranch in the Napa Valley with his sister, and although he knows nothing about Amy, in his mind he calls her Rosabella and he thinks of her as the kind of girl he would like to marry. 'Rosabella' is really moved. 'Somebody, Somewhere' wants her like that, it's wonderful. She will write and thank him for the pin.

From one little postcard a correspondence grows, and the letters become ever warmer until the whole town where Antonio Esposito lives is happily conversant with their Tony's mail-order love affair. He's on top of the world ('The Most Happy Fella'). Then Rosabella sends Tony her photograph and asks for his in return. He has himself photographed, but his sister Marie, jealous at the thought that Tony might stray from the ranch and her, mocks him for his foolishness. What would a pretty young girl like that think of his photo—a fat, fiftyish Italian? Better leave it alone.

Tony comes down to earth with a crash. His workman, Herman, and his friends envy their boss who has gone out and got himself a Rosabella while they get no further than 'Standing on the Corner' watching the girls go by, but Tony ruefully tears up his photo and watches his dream disappear under the harsh light of Marie's scorn. Then his foreman Joe comes to add to his troubles. Joe is a wanderer. Tony's been so good to him he has stayed working at his place much longer than he intended, but now the wind is calling his name ('Joey, Joey, Joey') and he knows it is time he was moving on. Suddenly Tony has an idea. He asks Joe if he can have a photo to remember him by. He'll send this big, handsome fellow's photo to 'Rosabella' and that way they can go on writing to each other.

The end result of the correspondence is a proposal of marriage, and Rosabella agrees to wed Tony. A feast is prepared ('Abbondanza') to welcome the bride to Napa on the day Joe is due to depart but, as Tony sets out in his truck to meet Rosabella at the station, Joe decides that he will stay to see his friend's bride and perhaps even dance with her. The townsfolk celebrate the 'Sposalizio' under the 'Welcome Rosabella' light sign but, when Rosabella arrives, she arrives alone on the postman's buggy.

She is rather shaken at not being met, but the warm 'Benvenuta' of the gathered company soon cheers her and she happily makes her way to the side of Joe whom she addresses as her Tony. Joe quickly disabuses her, and the stunned girl grasps the trick that has been played. She guesses that Tony is an old man, a man who probably did not even write all the letters that he sent her, and she goes to leave. As she does so, two men approach bearing a body on a stretcher: it is Tony. His truck crashed on the way to the station.

Willed by the sympathetic crowd, Rosabella moves towards the injured man. He is in awful pain but he wants to see her. He wants to marry her without delay. Marie intervenes to say that he is too badly hurt, and Joe, in a cocky tone of voice, suggests that Rosabella might need to think a bit. The suggestion in his words acts on the girl like a spur and instinctively she agrees to the wedding.

As the service is taking place inside the house, Joe picks up his bags. Now it is time to leave. But who will run the ranch till Tony gets better? Joe knows that he cannot let his friend down, he knows that he will have to stay yet a while. Angrily hurls his bag down but, when the service is done and the wedded Rosabella walk limply out on to the porch for a heartfelt weep, Joe softens into sympathy ('Don't Cry'). All Rosabella's pain pours forth in accusations. Joe tells her what a good man Tony is, but she can only see that he is an old man. He wipes her tears away and then she is suddenly, passionately in his arms and all their anger turns to lovemaking.

ACT 2

A month later, in the vineyards, the workers are packing the 'Fresno Beauties'. Joe and Rosabella are amongst them but they ignore each other.

They have not spoken a word since their angry, mistaken night of love. Tony is doing his best to make a recovery, but he is still bound in plaster and splints, confined to a wheelchair, and suffering from dire impatience. The Doctor recommends love and kindness as a cure and so at last Tony meets his wife.

They are both hesitant, but he is almost childishly open and anxious for forgiveness and she is kindly and willing to be convinced. They start again from scratch and declare themselves 'Happy to Make Your Acquaintance' as Rosabella begins to teach Tony to speak like an American. As they finish the song, Tony produces a surprise for Rosabella: he has brought her friend Cleo from San Francisco with the promise of a job—sitting down! Rosabella is delighted, and she realises that her husband is a very dear man.

Cleo's first encounter is with Marie who does everything possible to get her to take her side and separate Tony and Rosabella, but she has a much more enjoyable encounter with the happy farm hand, Herman, with whom she finds an instant rapport. They're both from Texas. Dammit, they're both from 'Big D'.

The days of May pass, and Tony and Rosabella grow closer together ('How Beautiful the Days') while Marie becomes lonelier and more dissatisfied. As Tony grows stronger, she worries him incessantly with doubting tales about 'Young People' and Rosabella's loving assurances that he makes her feel 'Warm All Over' can only partly undo the mischief done by the selfish sister. The relationship growing up between Cleo and Herman has no such complications; it's just a bit slow and Cleo finds herself unable to understand Herman's unoffended manner under provocation. He takes anything from the other men and just smiles ('I Like Everybody').

As the time nears when Tony can finally leave his wheelchair, Rosabella is suffering over the way their relationship is developing. She loves him and wants to be loved in return as a wife, but Tony, his actions persuaded by Marie's relentless harping on their age difference, continues to treat her as a beloved child. Cleo knows the answer: tell the man. Rosabella opens her heart to the overjoyed Tony and soon they burst forth in a triumphant love duet ('My Heart Is So Full of You'). Tony calls for a celebration but, as Rosabella dances, she falls in a faint. She is carried into the house to recover, but that fainting spell covers a truth soon to become evident: she is pregnant. Still oblivious, a joyful Tony sings to the heavens of his wonderful happiness ('Mamma, Mamma').

ACT 3
An hour later Cleo is found in the barn, surreptitiously stacking suitcases. She and Rosabella are leaving. But there is merriment around the barn for, as Doc tells them ('Song of a Summer Night'), today is like a honeymoon for Tony and Rosabella—his first day out of the wheelchair. Now the two 'newly-weds' must be left alone. When they are, Tony notices that Rosabella is dressed for travelling. With death in her heart, she tells him of the one stupid night with Joe and the child it has brought.

Tony is utterly broken and he shouts furiously at Rosabella to get out of his home. Sadly she hands him back his amethyst pin and, as he turns away, she tells him of her real true love for him ('Please, Let Me Tell You'). Then she goes. Tony's first deed is to order Joe to be thrown off his property, but Joe has already gone. Earlier on he went down to the station. Tony sees red—they are leaving together—and seizing a pistol, he sets out for the station.

Joe is already at the station. He knows nothing of Rosabella's pregnancy or the trouble at the ranch. He has just decided that, now that Tony is well, it is time for him to go. He is leaving on the next train and leaving behind a gift of candy for the newly-weds. As his train pulls out, Cleo brings Rosabella to the bus station and buys two tickets for San Francisco. Rosabella boards the bus while Cleo waits to say her goodbyes to Herman and, when an exhausted Tony struggles into the station, he hears that Joe departed alone. He climbs painfully up to look through the bus window and there he sees Rosabella. Gradually his torment gives way to resignation and then, at last, to realisation. No matter what, he loves Rosabella and 'She's Gonna Come Home Wit' Me'.

Marie, who has hurried to the spot, tries a last ditch throw to persuade her brother to abandon his intrusive wife or, when that fails, to shame him into letting her go, but Tony will not give in. In desperation, Marie snatches his cane from him so that he cannot walk towards the bus but Cleo comes to his aid. She snatches back the cane and falls to a brawling battle with Marie as Tony makes his way with difficulty towards the bus and Rosabella. A ranch hand comes to help Marie and attacks Cleo, but suddenly aid comes from an unexpected quarter. For the first time in his life cheerful Herman loses his temper. Amazed at his own action ('I Made a Fist'), he floors the attacker and rescues his girl.

Tony brings Rosabella down from the bus and orders her cases to be unloaded. Her baby will be Tony's baby. And she mustn't be frightened, it is bad to be frightened. He was frightened the day he drove to get his Rosabella from the station, and because he was frightened he drove too fast and crashed. He was frightened, so he left his pin for her in the restaurant instead of speaking. He was frightened, so he sent her a handsome man's picture instead of his own. It is time to go back and start again, somewhere before all those fears.

Sitting on a crate, he pretends to be a customer in a restaurant. She comes to serve him and he asks her her name. She replies, 'Amy'. Amy is so nice that he does not give her a tip, he gives her his genuine amethyst tie pin. She hesitates to take it, and tries to burst from the scene, but he continues with the play-acting, repeating the words of that first note he wrote her: 'I don' know not'ing about you, where you go, what you done...'. The slate is clean, he really intends that they should start afresh. Joyfully, Amy takes the pin, and now Tony is once again 'The Most Happy Fella' in the whole Napa Valley.

BELLS ARE RINGING

a musical comedy in two acts with book and lyrics by Betty Comden and Adolph Green. Music by Jule Styne. Produced at the Shubert Theatre, New York, 29 November 1956 with Judy Holliday (Ella), Sydney Chaplin (Jeff) and Jean Stapleton (Sue).

Produced at the London Coliseum 14 November 1957 with Janet Blair, George Gaynes and Jean St Clair.

A film version was produced by MGM in 1960 with Miss Holliday and Dean Martin.

CHARACTERS

Ella Peterson
Sue Summers, *owner of Susanswerphone*
Gwynne Smith
Inspector Barnes
Francis
Sandor
Jeff Moss
Larry Hastings
Dr Kitchell
Blake Barton
Carl
Ludwig Smiley, Charles Bessemer, Telephone Man, Olga, Henchmen, Carol, Paul, Arnold, Michelle, Nightclub Singer, Mrs Mallett, Madame Grimaldi, etc.

By way of a prologue, we are treated to a commercial extolling the virtues of Susanswerphone, one of those new-fangled operations, the telephone answering service which will ensure you never miss that call which might change your life—professional, social or amatory ('Bells Are Ringing').

ACT 1
At the office of Susanswerphone the owner of the business, Sue Summers, is in efficient action. Her style is very different from that of her cousin and assistant, Ella Peterson. Whereas Sue briskly and impersonally organises the clients' messages, Ella takes every call with a warm interest and cannot stop herself becoming involved in the affairs of her callers, dispensing sympathy and advice in a variety of ways from recommending a mustard plaster for a voiceless opera singer to playing Santa Claus to a little boy or persuading a blocked playwright to get back to his typewriter.

This last client, Plaza 04433, is a particular favourite and a particular worry to her for she knows that he hits the bottle rather than settling down to finish his new play, *The Midas Touch*, and Ella has taken impatient messages from his producer which bode ill. For him, Ella has assumed the persona of a motherly old lady dispensing gentle good advice and he, believing it, calls her 'Mom', but Ella has become very fond of Plaza 004, otherwise Mr Jeffrey

730

Moss, and although they have never met she is falling in love ('It's a Perfect Relationship').

Susanswerphone's premises receive an unexpected and unwanted visitor when Inspector Barnes, an eager detective who sees in the answering service a probable cover for a call girl racket, pops in to check out the operation. Although he is disabused of this notion by Sue, he is avidly anxious to uncover crime and he refuses to dismiss the notion that something criminal and non-evident must be going on. Actually it isn't, but it is about to. Sue has become enamoured of the suave Sandor Prantz, an off-course bookmaker who is passing himself off to her as the president of a recording company, and he is about to install a line to Susanswerphone to act as a hotline for his illegal gambling operation.

Ella continues to dispense sunshine and personal advice until Sue gets worried and tells her that she must stop interfering with the customers' private lives and take a more dispassionate view of her job. Poor Ella. She would love to tell the dentist who writes songs that another client has left a message about a songwriters' audition; she would love to tell the actor Barton Blake that another client, producer Larry Hastings, hates his phony Marlon Brando style and won't hire him until he turns up with a suit and clean vowels. If she can't, she might as well be back at her old, boring job as a telephonist at the Bonjour Tristesse Brassiere Company.

Across on the East Side, Jeff Moss isn't working on *The Midas Touch*, he's partying. His writer's block has everything to do with the fact that he used to write with a partner and now that partner has gone. Nevertheless, glass of whisky aloft, he bullishly proclaims that he can do just as well 'On My Own'. The party is killed by the arrival of Larry Hastings, the producer who has Jeff's play on option. Hastings tells him that unless he can provide the rest of the play by the next day both he and Paul Arnold, the intended star, are pulling out. Encouraged by 'Mom', Jeff swears he will get down to work ('You've Got to Do It'), but his fire soon goes out and he reaches for the whisky instead of the typewriter.

Meanwhile, in an alley, Sandor and the ragtag crowd who act as links in his bookmaking business are gathered to hear the new developments in their operation. It is simple. Under the pretence of being customers placing orders with the Titanic Record company, their clients can place bets through the line at Susanswerphone. An order for five hundred copies (LP) of Beethoven's sixth symphony, opus 3 means five hundred dollars on the nose of Number 6 in the third race at Belmont ('It's a Simple Little System').

The next morning Ella cannot get Jeff's wake up call through and Sue, who is annoyed with her for spending so much time on the one client, doesn't try to hurry through a message from Hastings that if Jeff doesn't get to his office with the play by midday he's finished. When Ella gets this piece of news she decides that it is time for desperate measures and, as Sue turns her attention to the installation of Sandor's Titanic Records telephone, Ella quietly slips out of the office.

As she goes, she is spotted by the insistent Inspector Barnes who is still hanging about trying to find something illegal in Susanswerphone. Ella pulls a hearts and flowers act on him ('Is It a Crime?')—if there had been an answerphone in Verona, that terrible mix-up between Romeo and Juliet need never have happened. Barnes is deeply touched, but nevertheless he sends his sidekick, Francis, off to shadow Ella's every movement. As a last resort, she is heading for Jeff's apartment to find out what has happened to him. The hung-over writer is amazed at this sweet girl who appears out of nowhere to dispense coffee and understanding and seems intuitively to understand so much about him. Before he knows it, this Melisande Scott has him at his typewriter, and Inspector Barnes is getting a report.

It works. Jeff gets enough of a play down on paper to pass the midday test with Hastings and Arnold and he's thrilled. So is Ella. On the subway, she lends her sunny personality to a carful of grimly uncommunicative passengers who burst into song with her ('Hello, Hello There') but suddenly she comes back to reality. Jeff has to go away for a week to finish the play and she must go back to work. They will meet next week. Then she is gone and Jeff is celebrating being in love ('I Met a Girl').

Now that she has started, Ella decides to go the whole way in her philanthropic outings. Tracked by Inspector Barnes's Francis, she pays a visit to the songwriting dentist and tells him about the audition and then she finds her way to the posy actor and tells him what his problem is. When her good deeds are done, with her heart assuaged, she goes back to Susanswerphone.

Titanic Records is doing great business, but Ella is puzzled when someone rings and asks for a quantity of Beethoven's tenth. Even she knows Beethoven only got up to nine, and she takes it on herself to alter the order from symphony number ten to symphony number nine.

Over the past week, she has made up her mind that she must not see Jeff again. Sue was right. A girl mustn't let herself get too involved with her work. When Jeff telephones, trying to get hold of the mythical Melisande Scott, she persists in being good old Mom until one day she overhears the voice of the vamp Olga in his living room. With a little scream she puts down her earphones and runs straight across town to Jeff's place. Once there, with secretarial efficiency she bundles Olga out of Jeff's apartment and, before long, they are falling into each other's arms ('Long Before I Knew You'). Little do they know that Francis is there with his camera.

ACT 2

Ella is going out with Jeff for their first date, decked in the most up-market costume she can lay her hands on, an extravagant and only slightly used theatrical gown which is a gift from the grateful opera singer, and she practises the 'Mu-cha-cha' with Carl, the drugstore boy, in happy anticipation. But now that Jeff's muse is singing again, he is back in the swing of social theatrical circles, and Ella finds that the evening à deux she had anticipated ('Just in Time') has to be put aside in favour of an upper class party.

Ella is out of her depth amongst the name-dropping, wisecracking society folk ('Drop that Name') and she is deeply embarrassed by the reputation Jeff's tale of their meeting has given her for being a miraculous kind of psychic. He does not understand her embarrassment. It was those deep-seeing qualities which made him fall in love with her. With a sinking heart, Ella realises that it is Melisande Scott with whom Jeff is in love, not the real her. As they prepare to leave the party, she knows that she cannot keep up the charade ('The Party's Over') and, leaving him a note, she vanishes.

The heavies are on to Sandor. Ella's innocent corrections of Beethoven's opus have meant that a lot of money was placed on the wrong horse and this has left some angry and strong-armed customers. Sue does not understand what is happening. She only knows that Sandor is in difficulties and she offers him her savings to help 'expand the business'. Sandor is jubilantly relieved and together they sing nonsensically of happiness in 'Salzburg'.

All this time, Jeff and Larry Hastings are searching the town for the vanished Melisande and, in the course of their pursuit, they end up in the sleazy Pyramid Club. There they hear the dentist, Dr Kitchell, singing his songs (he got to the audition and won the job) and, to their amazement, one of them is called 'The Midas Touch'. The coincidence is too much for Jeff. Where did he get that title? Why, from this blonde girl who turned up out of nowhere like a good fairy. The actor Blake Barton, who has been cast in Jeff's play as a dentist who writes songs, also admits that he got his tip off from a mysterious blonde. It seems they are all indebted to the same lady. They swap phone numbers and promise to keep in touch as the hunt continues. It continues without the slightest success and, dejectedly, Jeff calls up Kitchell...and gets Susanswerphone. Then he dials Blake Barton and gets...Susanswerphone, and the penny drops.

Ella is leaving the firm. She has become too involved. 'I'm Goin' Back', she declares, to the Bonjour Tristesse Brassiere Company. But before she can depart she is cornered and challenged by Sandor. It was she who changed the number of the symphony so that the bets went wrong! Sue is staggered. Bets?! What is he talking about? Inspector Barnes, still tirelessly on the trail, arrives just as things threaten to get nasty. Sandor confesses his crimes without difficulty and delightedly shops the two henchmen of Mr Big who have been threatening him. The Inspector may have been following the wrong person, but there was indeed crime at Susanswerphone and he's got his arrest.

No sooner are the criminals carted off than Jeff is heard outside. Desperately Ella disguises herself as elderly Mom, but the disguise is soon discarded as they melt in each other's arms and all the people Ella has helped crowd into the office for the happy ending.

CANDIDE

a comic operetta in two acts by Lillian Hellman based on the satire by Voltaire. Lyrics by Richard Wilbur. Additional lyrics by John Latouche and Dorothy Parker. Music by Leonard Bernstein. Produced at the Martin Beck Theatre, New York, 1 December 1956 with Max Adrian (Pangloss), Robert Rounseville (Candide), Barbara Cook (Cunegonde), Louis Edmonds (Maximilian) and Irra Petina (Old Lady). Produced in a revised version in one act with a new book by Hugh Wheeler and additional lyrics by Stephen Sondheim at the Chelsea Theatre Centre, Brooklyn, 19 December 1973 and the Broadway Theatre, New York, 8 March 1974 with Lewis J Stadlen, Mark Baker, Maureen Brennan, Sam Freed, June Gable and Deborah St Darr (Paquette).

Produced at the New York City Opera 13 October 1982 with John Lankston, David Eisler, Erie Mills, Scott Reeve, Joyce Castle and Maris Clement.

Produced at the Saville Theatre, London, 30 April 1959 with Laurence Naismith, Denis Quilley, Mary Costa, Dennis Stephenson and Edith Coates. The revised version produced at the Edinburgh Festival 1981 with Nickolas Grace, William Relton, Rosemary Ashe, Mark Wynter, Nichola MacAuliffe and Yvonne Edgell. Produced by Scottish Opera in a version by John Wells 19 May 1988 with Nickolas Grace, Mark Beudert, Marilyn Hill Smith, Mark Tinkler, Ann Howard and Gaynor Miles.

CHARACTERS

Voltaire/Dr Pangloss/The Governor of Buenos Aires/Host/Sage
Candide
Cunegonde
Paquette
Maximilian
Old Lady
Baron, Grand Inquisitor, Baroness etc.

Voltaire, the eighteenth century author of *Candide*, introduces and commentates the unrolling of this picaresque tale of philosophical devotion and, throughout the evening, he joins the story as various crucial characters in the lives of the wandering Candide and his beloved Cunegonde. To begin the evening, he introduces us to the principals of the story.

The setting is Westphalia and the castle of the Baron Thunder-Ten-Tronck where the happy inhabitants include, apart from the aforesaid Baron and his Baroness, their lovely and innocent virgin daughter, Cunegonde, their spotlessly beautiful son, Maximilian, their pretty bastard nephew, Candide, and the Baroness's buxom and willing serving maid, Paquette. To each of these 'Life Is Happiness Indeed'. What is the reason for their supreme happiness, for their joyful consciousness of their own perfections and that of their situation? Why, it is the philosophy which has been inculcated in them by a great and glorious teacher: their tutor, Dr Pangloss, whose philosophy reasons that all is for the best in 'The Best of All Possible Worlds'. This philosophy extends from things minimal and physical to things great and metaphysical, and Pangloss has a syllogism to fit every question, proving without doubt that everything in the world is incapable of improvement and that all events are happy events.

Today, at the dismissal of class, Paquette is ordered to stay behind for her additional lesson in advanced physics. Cunegonde, in an endless quest for knowledge, makes an excuse to return to the schoolroom and there she finds good Dr Pangloss astride the compliant maidservant. She innocently asks for an academic explanation and is treated to a lecture on specific gravity of which the relative positions of the Doctor and Paquette are allegedly an example. Although it is somewhat ahead of the curriculum, Cunegonde hurries out to find Candide to test this new knowledge, and they find that it is a most pleasant piece of philosophy ('Oh, Happy We').

Unfortunately, they have chosen a somewhat open piece of terrain for their experiment and brother Maximilian, happening to glance out a baronial window, spies them in action and squeals. The family Thunder-Ten-Tronck abandons its dinner to descend upon the bastard in the garden and, as Cunegonde explodes into wails of tears, Candide finds himself banished from his homely castle and from Westphalia with ghastly imprecations ringing in his ears against ever returning.

In the middle of a desolate heath on the way out of Westphalia he is sustained by Dr Pangloss's philosophy ('It Must Be So'). Even if it is not immediately obvious, there is undoubtedly some good reason behind this seeming tragedy. But right now Bulgaria is invading Westphalia by the same route that Candide has chosen to leave it, and a chance encounter with some Bulgarians ends with our hero tied up in a sack, pressed for the Bulgarian army. That very army has, meanwhile, arrived at the gates of Schloss Thunder-Ten-Tronck and all the reigning family are slaughtered pitilessly. All, that is, except Cunegonde who is captured by a soldier with a facility for business: there are 97 men in his regiment and, at 20 ducats a go, Cunegonde is going to make his fortune.

Later, as a thoroughly ravished Cunegonde crawls wearily off a pile of abandoned corpses, a turn in the fortunes of the battle results in the captors of Candide being mown down, leaving the boy abandoned in his sack. At a distance from each other, the young people recall plaintively the happy innocent days they once knew together, but fate has decreed that the two of them shall, for now, follow very different paths. Candide, saved from his sack by a passing troupe of players, joins them as a bad touring actor, while Cunegonde, after her sticky start, becomes an ever-improving prostitute. She improves to such an extent that she ends up in Lisbon as the much bejewelled mistress of both a rich Jew and the Grand Inquisitor under a convenient time-sharing arrangement ('Glitter and Be Gay').

Candide is also destined to turn up in Lisbon. Swept ashore in an earthquake, he meets amongst the corpses none other than Dr Pangloss who has, it appears, escaped the sack of Schloss Thunder-Ten-Tronck but has lost his nose as a result of syphilis. He is not depressed, for syphilis is a product of the New World and had the New World not been discovered he could never have experienced potatoes, tobacco and chocolate. It is still the best of all possible worlds. When the good doctor expounds his impeccably optimistic philosophy before an apparently dying man, he is in for an unpleasant surprise. The false corpse is a spy of the Inquisition and he is arrested for heresy.

Pangloss and Candide are dragged captive to Lisbon where the daily entertainment of the 'Auto Da Fé' is in inexorable progress. Pangloss is sentenced by the Inquisitor and hanged, and Candide stripped and whipped before the very eyes of a fainting Cunegonde. When the flagellation is over and the lords of the Inquisition have departed, an old lady comes to cut Candide down and, in the days that follow she restores the lad to health and vigour with the aid of magic ointments known only to the old ladies of 'This World'.

When he is whole again, she secretly leads him into the presence of the beloved he thought dead ('You Were Dead, You Know'). As the two duet happily in Cunegonde's apartment, the old lady returns to warn that the Jew is on his way to visit his mistress. Cunegonde tries to explain the Jew and his position in her life to Candide, but her efforts are cut short when her furious demi-protector draws his sword and chases the young man jealously around the room. In his pursuit he slips and drops his sword and, when Candide helpfully retrieves it and offers it back to him, the Jew, rushing ever onwards, accidentally and fatally impales himself on the proffered blade.

At midnight, as the time-sharing arrangement allows, the Inquisitor arrives to take his share of pleasure and, egged on by Cunegonde's descriptions of repeated ravishment, Candide skewers him too. This most innocent lad has the blood of two of the most superb citizens of Lisbon on his weapon. There is nothing for it but that he and his lady love must flee the city.

With horses supplied by the old lady, they head for Cadiz where, to their horror, Cunegonde's jewels are pilfered by a friar picked up for a night's entertainment by the old lady. In an effort to atone, the good dame attempts to sell what remains of her unobvious charms ('I Am Easily Assimilated') but without success. It is Candide's physical attributes which come to their aid. He accepts an offer to lead a muscled relief party to the Jesuits of Montevideo and the little party board a vessel for the New World.

In Cartagena, Columbia, another group of Europeans is arriving under less comfortable circumstances. The Governor of the area, having gone through the entire female population in his pursuit of pleasure, is looking amongst the newly imported slaves for potential amusement, and who should be amongst them but Paquette. It is not she who takes his fancy, however, but another Caucasian who turns out to be Maximilian ('My Love') dressed up in feminine attire to fulfil the unusual sexual tastes of the captain of the slave ship. The Governor is not at all pleased when he finds that his new love is male and he sells Maximilian off to the Jesuits, who apparently go in for such things.

Close behind, the ship bearing Candide, Cunegonde and the old lady is in sight of land. Their trip has been enlivened by the telling of the old lady's life story, a gory tale of frequent sexual defilement, which is reaching its climax with a particularly nasty incident involving Barbary pirates when they are attacked. It is pirates again, so Cunegonde and the old lady are carried off for another round of ravishment, leaving Candide to reach the Jesuits of Montevideo alone.

What is his surprise to find there, amongst the gentlemen of the order, both Maximilian and Paquette ('Alleluia'). He gives them the happy news that Cunegonde is also living and promises that, though she is once again temporarily lost, he will find her, rescue her, and wed her. In spite of all his debasements, Maximilian is still a Thunder-Ten-Tronck, and he is murderously livid at the idea that his sister should marry a bastard. As he chases Candide angrily around the church, the young man hides behind a statue but, in his flight, he accidentally knocks the stone figure forward and it falls to the ground, crushing the vengeful Maximilian to death.

That night, two young Jesuits slip off into the jungle, fleeing from the monastery and the deed. But Paquette and Candide, for it is they, are not long lost. Deep in the rain forests of South America they stumble on the wondrous and perfect land of El Dorado where the streets are made of diamonds and the animals can talk and even sing ('Sheep's Song').

The old lady, in the meanwhile, has been rejected by the pirates as unravishworthy and abandoned on a rocky coast. There she is laid low by the anaesthetic dart of a local pygmy looking for food but, deemed inedible, she is swapped off to a German botanist for three machetes and then exchanged for unmentioned favours to the madame of a brothel. But she is destined before long to meet up again with Candide and Paquette.

Tiring of the perfection of El Dorado and anxious to find Cunegonde, the pair return to Cartagena accompanied by two sheep loaded with gold and jewels. They learn that the pirates have taken Cunegonde to Constantinople, and Candide anxiously accepts the Governor's offer of a boat. Alas, the wily Governor is only after his sheep and their gold, and the boat he gives them is full of holes ('Bon Voyage'). The travellers founder on a desert island, but the sheep struggle ashore with them and, when they are rescued, they head richly for Constantinople. There they find Cunegonde, an odalisque in a wealthy man's household. Candide offers nearly all their gold and jewels for her release and then hands over the last of their money to buy Maximilian who has somehow, uncrushed, fallen into the same Turkish hands.

All the little band are back together again at last but they are in Turkestan, without a penny and without an idea. At the suggestion of the old lady, they visit a nearby cave to consult the Wisest Man in the World but who should they find there but a rather hazy Dr Pangloss in the midst of a panorama of books full of varied philosophic wisdom. After many perilous years following the Pangloss creed, they find now that their master seems to have abandoned it himself in favour of a new philosophy: the work ethic. Candide, ever obedient, vows to buy a little farm. There, the years of tribulation and wandering over, they will work from dawn to dusk and 'Make Our Garden Grow'. At last they can exist in rustic simplicity far from the evils of the world, tend their fields and milk their cow. As their paean to their new life ends, the cow falls dead. It is the pox.

The first version of *Candide* included a number of musical pieces which were not retained in the revision including Candide's Lament, the Venice Gavotte (both of which were partially used in rewritten numbers), 'The Simple Life', Paris Waltz, 'Quiet', 'El Dorado', 'It Must Be Me', 'What's the Use?' and 'No More than This'. 'Life Is Happiness Indeed','This World' and 'The Sheep's Song' were introduced in the 1973 production and the Auto Da Fé scene extended. The song 'We Are Women' was added to the London production. Bernstein provided several new musical sections for the 1988 version.

THE MUSIC MAN

a musical comedy in two acts by Meredith Willson based on a story by Meredith Willson and Franklin Lacey. Produced at the Majestic Theatre, New York, 19 December 1957 with Robert Preston (Harold Hill), Barbara Cook (Marian), Iggie Wolfington (Marcellus) and David Burns (Mayor).

Produced at the Adelphi Theatre, London, 16 March 1961 with Van Johnson, Patricia Lambert, Bernard Spear and C Denier Warren.

A film version was produced by Warner Brothers in 1962 with Robert Preston, Shirley Jones, Buddy Hackett and Paul Ford with Hermione Gingold as Eulalie.

CHARACTERS

Harold Hill, *a travelling salesman*
Charlie Cowell
Mayor Shinn
Eulalie MacKechnie Shinn, *his wife*
Zaneeta Shinn, *their daughter*
Ewart Dunlop
Oliver
Hix
Jacey Squires
Olin Britt
Marcellus Washburn
Tommy Djilas
Marian Paroo
Mrs Paroo, *her mother*
Winthrop Paroo, *Marian's brother*
Amaryllis
Alma Hix
Maud Dunlop
Ethel Toffelmeier
Mrs Squires
Constable Locke, Gracie Shinn, Conductor, etc.

ACT 1

It's the fourth of July in the year of 1912 and a train is making its rhythmical way through the depths of the state of Iowa. One compartment is occupied by a number of travelling salesmen, passing the time as they rattle on to their next pitch in playing cards and discussing the details of their mighty profession ('Rock Island'). Each of the men has his say on the reasons for success or failure, but Charlie Cowell has just one dictum—you've got to know the territory.

The conversation turns to a fellow name of Hill, Professor Harold Hill. This fellow, it seems, has laws all of his own. He is a music man. He sells band instruments to the hopeful parents of the country towns, and he sells fine. But Charlie Cowell has had the bad experience of following this Hill into town and he knows the second part of the story. Hill sells the instruments all right, but he doesn't know a note of music so no one ever gets taught how to play. He's a blight on the good name of the travelling salesman and anyone who follows on behind him is likely to get tarred and feathered by the angry townsfolk. Still, they're all pretty safe in Iowa: even Hill wouldn't have the gall to try his tricks on good old stiff-necked Iowa. The conductor calls out 'River City' and a quiet gentleman who has been cleaning up in the card game gets up to leave the train. He has heard a challenge. On his suitcase we can read the name Professor Harold Hill.

The 'Iowa Stubborn' folk of River City are going about their daily business when Harold Hill arrives in town and, to his surprise, he meets up as quick as blinking with an old comrade-in-charms, Marcellus Washburn. Marcellus has reformed and given up the spiel for the stable, but salesmanship dies hard and he swiftly gives Harold the lowdown on River City. If it's musical instruments he's selling this year then he'd best beware of the town music teacher who is also the librarian. Harold ascertains that this teacher is female and worries no more.

Then he looks for a wedge. What's new in town? A pool table has just been installed in the local billiard hall. That'll do fine. Harold moves into work, evangelising with rich-voiced facility on the evils of pool ('Trouble') and the problems it could bring to the parents of River City whose children get caught in its vicious sway. His message catches on and soon the folk of River City are worriedly discussing this new evil in their midst.

Harold, meanwhile, has had Marian Paroo, the music teacher, pointed out to him and he sets off to charm her into believing in him. Marian is not to be easily won over. She gives him a swift brush off and hurries on home to give a 'Piano Lesson' to little Amaryllis. The lesson is punctuated by Mrs Paroo's oft-repeated bewailing of her daughter's unmarried state and, before she has finished, Marian's ten year-old brother Winthrop arrives home.

Winthrop is a sullen and monosyllabic child, mortified by a bad lisp into tearful quietness. He will not even say 'yes' to Amaryllis when she invites him to her birthday party, and the little girl, who is very fond of Winthrop, also ends up in tears. Winthrop just has to be her sweetheart or else she has no one to say goodnight to when the evening star comes out. Marian assures her that it doesn't matter if you don't have someone special, you just have to leave a gap for the name until the right man comes along. As a mollified Amaryllis goes back to the piano, Marian looks out the window at the evening star and herself sings 'Goodnight, My Someone'.

At the High School Hall Mayor Shinn is chairing an entertainment in which his wife, Eulalie, holds a leading part. Disaster strikes when Tommy Djilas, a lad from the wrong side of the tracks, sets off a fire-cracker in the middle of Mrs Shinn's genuine Indian recitation and, when the Mayor attempts to continue with his parish announcements, he is hamstrung by the constant bickering of the four leading lights of the School Board. Order is only restored when Harold rises from the body of the hall to bring up the subject of the malignant pool table. He quickly gets the townsfolk behind him as he slickly shifts the topic from pool to the beneficial influence to the town of a boys' band described in all its flashing brass and colour ('Seventy Six Trombones'). Mayor Shinn is not dazzled by this spell-binder, however, and as the people gather behind Harold he orders the School Board to inquire into the credentials of this music man.

Harold is by now in full swing. He corrals Tommy Djilas as his lieutenant and, pairing him off with a pretty girl, wins his first allegiance. So far he has made only two mistakes: Mayor Shinn owns the billiard house and the pool table, and the pretty girl is Zaneeta Shinn, eldest daughter of the selfsame Mayor. He has also made his first enemy. In accordance with Shinn's instructions, he is cornered by the School Board who demand to see his certificates and qualifications for his musical position but Harold quickly sidetracks them by finding in them the perfect voices for a barbershop quartet. Men who have done nothing but fight between themselves for fifteen years are suddenly in harmony and deeply 'Sincere'.

Marcellus is amazed when he hears that Harold means to stay in town for four weeks. Four weeks is far too long. By that time the kids will have had long enough to find out he can't teach them music. But Harold has two systems: one is the Think System for learning music. You don't actually learn to play notes, you just think them and eventually out they'll come. The other is uniforms. Once he's skinned the folk of the cash for the instruments, he waits a little while and then skins them again for the kids' uniforms. When they see those dizzy uniforms, they don't even think about not being able to play. In the meantime, he's out to chat himself up a girl who will see him comfortably through his stay: a nice 'Sadder-but-Wiser Girl' who knows her way around.

What he gets is Eulalie Shinn and her group of ladies, all eager to come under his spell. It's too easy. Harold charms Eulalie into the leadership of an instantly formed Ladies Auxiliary for the Classical Dance but, when he happens to mention Marian's name, the ladies go into a twittering gasp ('Pickalittle'). Marian is beyond the pale. She houses dirty books like Chaucer, Balzac and Rabelais in her library and everyone knows that she took up with the elderly man who owned the place so that he left her all the books when he died, even though he left the library building to the town. Harold is still ensnared by the pickalittling ladies when the School Board turns up to, once again, demand his credentials. Harold sets them singing 'Goodnight Ladies' and makes his escape.

Harold corners Marian in her library and makes a pass at her ('Marian the Librarian') before setting off round the town to sweet talk the parents of River City into buying instruments for their children. Mrs Paroo signs up for a cornet for Winthrop who is bug-eyed at the thought of the instrument and the uniform, and she catches some stern disapproval from her daughter who tells her that Harold is nothing but a charlatan. She will prove it. Mrs Paroo sighs that if she takes that attitude to every man she'll never find one to wed, but Marian has her own ideas about 'My White Knight'.

The librarian knows her books, and the Indiana State Register on her shelves soon disproves Harold's invented background. She marches off to find the mayor bearing the evidence which the School Board have been too busy quartetting to unearth but, just as she reaches Shinn, the town erupts: the 'Wells Fargo Wagon' is coming in. The people gather round excitedly for their mail and there, amongst the parcels, are the children's instruments. Before Marian's amazed eyes, little Winthrop bursts out of his mutism with sheer excitement as he takes the shiny cornet in his hands. When the Mayor takes the Register from the librarian to read her evidence against Harold, she secretly tears out the relevant page as she gazes wonderingly at the miracle-making music man.

ACT 2

There is plenty of musical action in River City now. Down at the gymnasium Mrs Shinn's dancing ladies and the harmonies of the School Board ('It's You') are succeeded by the young people with a very different kind of dancing ('Shipoopi'). Mayor Shinn hasn't given up, however. He admits the instruments are here but next thing he wants to hear them played and, in the meanwhile, where are those credentials?

Marian, by now totally under the spell cast by Harold, is a little worried about the lack of conventional tuition and she has to force her practical self to have any faith in the Think System but, at least, she has now become totally accepted and even admired by the townswomen who, under the influence of the Professor, have all read Chaucer, Rabelais and Balzac and voted them delightful ('Pickalittle').

The School Board are still on the trail of Harold and his darned credentials but each time they get too near he succeeds in sidetracking them with the fortunate mention of an old favourite tune which sets them singing ('Lida Rose') while Marian, sitting alone, admits to herself that she is falling in love ('Will I Ever Tell You?'). As for Winthrop, he is a changed lad. Far from being mute, nowadays he just bubbles over with chatter as he describes all the wonderful things he has learned from Harold ('Gary Indiana') even though none of it seems to have anything much to do with the cornet and the famous Minuet in G which the band is supposed to be studying.

Now Nemesis arrives in River City in the person of Charlie Cowell. Charlie is still smarting from the treatment he has got travelling in behind

Harold Hill in other towns, and he has made up his mind that he is going to expose Hill before he can pull the same trick again. This week's train has stopped at River City for a few minutes and Charlie has alighted specially to find the Mayor and tell him all about the music man. Hurrying through the town, he asks Marian for directions but, when she discovers why he is there, she occupies his time by flirting with him until he has to run back to the station or miss his train. She is well and truly Harold's accomplice now and, when he asks her to walk with him to the footbridge—the lovers' lane of River City—that night, she agrees to go.

When they take their walk, it is not quite what Harold expected. Marian is under no illusions about him. She knows that his background is phony and that he is a travelling salesman in every sense, but she admits that he's opened her eyes and her heart in a way she would never have thought possible ('Till There Was You'). As a gage of her feelings, she gives him the torn-out page from the Register but it isn't until they've kissed and he is strutting back to town that Harold realises he is in love. He's also in trouble. Charlie Cowell has missed his train and he is heading back to the town square boiling with fury and vengeance. He is going to find the Mayor and denounce Harold before the whole of River City. Marcellus urges Harold to get safely out of town and, as the word spreads, Marian also hurries to warn him to escape, but he refuses. He is staying in River City.

Then he runs into Winthrop and the little boy, broken-hearted at the exposure of his hero as just another charlatan, sadly and bitterly reproaches Harold with his lies. He wishes he'd never come to River City. But Marian cannot agree. Since Harold came to town things have been different: look at happy Mrs Shinn and her ladies, look at the harmonious school board, look at all the kids walking around with their heads held high, look at Winthrop himself...and look at Marian the librarian, the disliked spinster who has finally come out from behind her books and started to live. Harold is still there when the constable comes to put the handcuffs on him.

The Mayor is giving a self-congratulatory speech reeking of tar and feathers when Marian challenges him with the good Harold has done to the town. Sure of his ground, Shinn challenges anyone in the town who supports Hill to stand up and, one by one, they do just that: Mrs Paroo first, then Zaneeta, then the School Board and the Ladies and even Eulalie, his wife. Then, to cap it all, Tommy Djilas marches in at the head of the famous boys' band. They're all dressed in the uniforms and carrying the instruments that cost River City's parents their hard-earned money. Marian hands Harold the blackboard pointer as a baton and, with a fervent prayer to the efficacity of the Think System, he begins to conduct. The result is barely recognisable as music, but the good folk of River City see only their children in their uniforms playing music on their instruments and they are delighted. Harold Hill has done what he promised. Even the Mayor has to give in and, as Marian and Harold fall into each other's arms, it seems a fair bet that the boys' band is not the only thing that is just beginning in River City.

WEST SIDE STORY

a musical in two acts by Arthur Laurents. Lyrics by Stephen Sondheim. Music by Leonard Bernstein. Produced at the Winter Garden Theatre, New York, 26 September 1957 with Larry Kert (Tony), Carol Lawrence (Maria), Chita Rivera (Anita), Mickey Calin (Riff) and Ken LeRoy (Bernardo) and revived there 27 April 1960 with Kert, Miss Lawrence, Allyn Ann McLerie, Thomas Hasson and George Marcy.

Produced at Her Majesty's Theatre, London, 12 December 1958 with Don McKay, Marlys Watters, Chita Rivera, George Chakiris and Ken LeRoy. Produced at the Shaftesbury Theatre 19 December 1974 with Lionel Morton, Christina Matthews, Petra Siniawski, Roger Finch and Paul Hart. Produced at Her Majesty's Theatre 16 May 1984 with Stephen Pacey, Jan Hartley, Lee Robinson, Richard Pettyfer and Sam Williams.

Produced at L'Alhambra, Paris, 30 March 1961 with Don Grilley, Jan Canada, Yvonne Othon, Thomas Hasson, and Jay Norman. Played at the Théâtre du Châtelet 1981.

Produced at the Volksoper, Vienna, 25 February 1968.

A film version was produced by Mirisch/United Artists in 1961 with Richard Beymer, Natalie Wood (singing dubbed by Marni Nixon), Rita Moreno, Russ Tamblyn and George Chakiris.

CHARACTERS

Riff, *leader of the Jets*
Tony, *his friend*
Bernardo, *leader of the Sharks*
Maria, *his sister*
Anita, *his girl*
Chino, *his friend*
Doc
Officer Krupke
Action, A-rab, Baby John, Snowboy, Big Deal, Diesel, Gee-Tar, Mouthpiece, Tiger, *the Jets*
Graziella, Velam, Minnie, Clarice, Pauline, Anybodys, *the Jets girls*
Pepe, Indio, Luis, Anxious, Nibbles, Juano, Toro, Moose, *the Sharks*
Rosalia, Consuelo, Teresita, Francisca, Estella, Margarita, *the Sharks girls*
Lieutenant Schrank, Glad Hand, etc.

ACT 1

In a New York street two rival gangs of teenagers are playing an elaborate cat and mouse game (Prologue). The Jets, a heterogeneous group of what, for lack of a better term, are called Americans, regard the stretch of street as their preserve. Their opponents are the Sharks, a Puerto Rican gang who, to the Jets, are invaders against whom they will protect their property with fists and, if necessary, with more dangerous weapons. These warring adolescents will, however, close ranks against the adult world, especially when that adult world is represented by the enforcers of the law. No one will break faith with the code of their little world, nor let the law take revenge for a bloodied ear or a blacked eye.

Riff, the leader of the Jets, is worried about the threatening presence of the Sharks. He lines up his 'troops' (Jet Song) and promises them an all-out fight against the Puerto Ricans to confirm their territory. At the dance at the gym that night he will challenge Bernardo and his Sharks to a 'rumble'. As his lieutenant on this important mission, Riff wants to take Tony, a former gang member now grown into a young adult and working in Doc's drugstore, but Tony doesn't want to have anything to do with these sort of games. He's grown out of all that sort of thing and he's looking forward to the next part of his life ('Something's Coming'). But when he finds out that his old buddy has promised to bring him to the challenge, he weakens and agrees to come to save Riff's face with the gang.

At the bridal shop where she works, Bernardo's young sister Maria is having her communion dress made over to wear to the dance. Maria has been brought from Puerto Rico by her brother to be married to his friend, the quiet and shy Chino, and tonight she feels that she is becoming an American. She is disappointed that she must wear white, and such a proper dress, but she is delighted to be going to her very first American dance.

At the dance, the tensions between the two gangs and their girls are bubbling explosively under the surface as they release their energy in some wild dancing. Bernardo arrives with his girl, Anita, and with Chino and Maria, and they join the dancing but, in the middle of the frenetic activity, something happens. Maria and Tony meet and time goes into a delicate slow-motion. They are in a world of their own and instantly in love but, when Tony gently kisses the young girl, he finds Bernardo furiously upon him with orders to keep away from his sister. The angry Bernardo is taking Maria away when Riff intervenes. He wants to issue his challenge. Bernardo icily agrees to meet for a council of war at the drugstore in a half-hour.

Left alone, Tony can think only of the girl he has just met ('Maria'), and soon he is in the back alley behind Bernardo's home trying to see her again. Maria climbs secretly out on to the fire escape to meet him. The world is theirs 'Tonight'.

Anita attempts to take Maria's part against Bernardo's strictures. They are Americans now, this is not Puerto Rico. In America a girl has some freedom. Tony is American too, even if his family is Polish. What is the difference between him and them? Why should Maria not like him? But Bernardo is not interested in listening to Anita's reasoning. He cannot see beyond the game he plays and the rivalry between the Jets and the Sharks. He must go to his big, important war council at the drugstore. When the boys are gone, Anita leads the girls in song and dance in praise of the wonderful mod cons of 'America'.

At Doc's drugstore the Jets wait nervously. The PRs are challenged, therefore they have the choice of weapons. They might pick knives or something else dangerous. Doc shakes his head: why are they fighting over a dumb bit of street? The nervy Action explodes at his implied belittling of the gangs and their rivalry and he has to be calmed by Riff. They must save their aggression for the rumble; right now its time to stay 'Cool'. Bernardo and his friends turn up and the talk turns to weapons, but just when it looks as if the fight may turn very nasty, Tony arrives. He scorns them as cowardly for resorting to bricks and bottles, and shames them into agreeing to a fair fist-fight between the best man from each gang. Eyeing Tony, Bernardo quickly agrees, but he is disappointed when Diesel is elected to represent the Jets.

The next day Tony comes to visit Maria at the bridal shop. She is upset about the fighting and makes him promise that he will stop the rumble, but she is also childishly happy as they innocently act out the wedding they will one day have and sincerely sing their pledge to each other of 'One Hand, One Heart'.

Evening comes on and the time appointed for the rumble gets nearer (Quintet/'Tonight'). As Bernardo and Diesel prepare to fight, Tony arrives to try to keep his promise to Maria to stop the combat. Bernardo attempts to goad him into a fight himself, but it is Riff who leaps forward in answer to the taunts and attacks the foul-mouthed Puerto Rican. Bernardo, all thought of a fair fight ignored, draws a knife, and Riff is forced to respond in kind. The fight is hard but Riff finally gains the upper hand and seems to have his opponent at his mercy when Tony calls out to him to hold his blow. Riff hesitates and, in that moment of hesitation, Bernardo takes his chance and knifes him dead.

Bernardo stands triumphant, as a free-for-all breaks out all around him, until Tony snatches up his dead friend's knife and, blind with grief and anger, cuts the murderer down. As the police sirens sing in the surrounding streets, he stands there dazed at what he has done, thinking only of Maria, until little Anybodys drags him to safety.

ACT 2

At her home Maria is in high spirits ('I Feel Pretty') but her happiness is shattered when Chino arrives with news of the rumble and of Bernardo's death. Maria's only thought is for Tony. Chino, outraged at such treachery, tells her that her Tony is her brother's killer and, taking a gun, he coldly leaves the house to go in search of revenge. When Tony climbs up by the fire escape to find her, Maria's distress for her brother is soon overwhelmed by her love and, as they clasp each other tightly, they sing together of a world where they might be away from all this hatred ('Somewhere').

The boys live in another kind of dream world. They can distance the evening's tragedy from their thoughts enough to lark around and take the mickey out of the police ('Gee, Officer Krupke') but, when little Anybodys brings news that Chino is out stalking Tony with a gun, the Jets are forced back into action.

Anita comes to Maria's room and finds it locked. As she knocks, Maria hastily helps Tony out the window. She arranges to meet him later at Doc's, kisses him hastily goodbye, and only then does she open the door and let Anita in. The open window tells its story, and Anita turns bitterly on the girl, full of accusations. Now she has picked up Bernardo's attitudes—Tony is one of them, how can she help 'A Boy Like That' who has killed her brother? Maria's answer is simple, she loves him ('I Have a Love'). It is an answer that

745

Anita, whose own lover is lying dead under the highway, can understand. There is nothing more to be said.

The police arrive to question Maria and she sees that her rendezvous with Tony is threatened. In veiled language, she begs Anita to go to the drugstore to warn him and Anita, in spite of everything, agrees. When she gets there, however, she is roughly treated by the gathered Jets in spite of her urgent assertions that she is there to help. Doc comes in in time to stop her from being too badly manhandled, but her will to help these people and their leader is gone. Bernardo was right. They are animals. In revenge, she shouts out that Tony will never see Maria again. Chino has found out about them, and shot her.

Tony is in the basement, hiding till Doc can help him get out of town. Doc brings him the awful news and the anguished Tony rushes into the street, calling madly for Chino to come and kill him too. But, instead of Chino, he sees Maria. They are running joyfully towards each other as a shot rings out. Chino has found his man.

As Tony dies, Maria takes up the gun. Now she hates. Now she, too, can kill. But when it comes to the moment she cannot take her revenge. She can only turn to them all—Jets and Sharks—to come and mourn with her, and so, when Tony's body is lifted from the ground, it is lifted by the Jets and the Sharks together, and together they carry him away, with Maria bravely following behind as the adults who have gathered at the scene look on, helpless to take part in this wasteful, foolish melodrama of youth.

THE SOUND OF MUSIC

a musical in two acts by Howard Lindsay and Russel Crouse. Lyrics by Oscar Hammerstein II. Music by Richard Rodgers. Produced at the Lunt-Fontanne Theatre, New York, 16 November 1959 with Mary Martin (Maria), Theodore Bikel (Captain von Trapp) and Patricia Neway (Mother Abbess).

Produced at the Palace Theatre, London, 18 May 1961 with Jean Bayless, Roger Dann and Constance Shacklock. Produced at the Apollo Victoria Theatre, London, in a revised version 17 August 1981 with Petula Clark, Michael Jayston and June Bronhill.

Produced at the Opéra Royal de Wallonie, Liège, in a version by Raymond Rossius and Jacques Mareuil as *La Mélodie de Bonheur* 22 December 1973 with Pierrette Delange, Guy Fontagnère and Maria Murano.

Produced at the Stadttheater, Hildesheim, 9 March 1982.

A film version was produced by Twentieth Century-Fox in 1965 with Julie Andrews, Christopher Plummer and Peggy Wood.

CHARACTERS

Mother Abbess *of Nonnberg Abbey*
Sitster Berthe, *Mistress of the Novices*
Sister Margaretta, *Mistress of Postulants*

Sister Sophia
Maria Rainer, *a postulant at the Abbey*
Captain Georg von Trapp
Frau Schmidt, *his housekeeper*
Franz, *his butler*
Liesl, Friedrich, Louisa, Kurt, Marta, Gretl, Brigitta, *his children*
Rolf Gruber
Elsa Schräder
Max Detweiler
Herr Zeller
Admiral von Schreiber, Baron Elberfeld, Baroness Elberfeld, Ursula, etc.

ACT 1

As the curtain rises, the bells of Nonnberg Abbey are ringing the Angelus and the voices of the nuns can be heard chanting the 'Dixit Dominus'. Sister Berthe, the Abbey's Mistress of Novices, is calling together the nuns and postulants and the whispered word goes round: where is the postulant Maria? Maria is out on the hills. She has been given permission by the Mother Abbess to spend the day amongst her native mountains, and there she pours out her joy in the song that the hills inspire in her ('The Sound of Music'), oblivious of the fact that she has outstayed her time away from the Abbey.

The next morning, in the office of the Mother Abbess, the Mistress of the Novices and the Mistress of Postulants assemble to discuss the prospects of the postulants. Most are ready to take orders, but Sister Berthe has considerable reservations about Maria, reservations which are not shared by the more kindly Sister Margaretta ('Maria'). The Mother Abbess calls the young woman before her and finds her full of sincere apologies for her late return the previous night. She has a further confession as well: she was singing in the hills. The Abbess gently tells her that the rule against music applies only in the confines of the abbey, and prompts her to sing again a pretty song which she has overheard her singing in the gardens ('My Favourite Things').

The Abbess knows that Maria is a good and devout woman but she also knows that she is not temperamentally suited to life under holy orders. The will is there, but the girl's natural exuberance is uppermost. Gently she tells Maria that, for the time being, she must leave the abbey. Maria is distraught but obedient and no little taken aback when she hears that she is to be sent as governess to the family of a widowed naval Captain with seven children. Bolstering her confidence with a reprise of 'My Favourite Things', Maria prepares to leave Nonnberg for her new life.

At the home of Captain von Trapp everything is run in a precise military fashion and, when Maria arrives, she finds that the uniformed children and the staff are summoned by a bosun's whistle. She firmly but sweetly declines to respond to or make use of such a fashion of communication and instead puts herself to winning the trust of the children who will be in her care. The von Trapp children have been through many governesses and have set them

747

all to flight and now they have one who has never had such a job before, in fact one who does not know where to start. It looks as if Maria will have little chance of doing the job she has come to do. But when Maria discovers that the children know nothing of music, her first dilemma is solved. Here is something she can give them, something over which they can become friends. Taking her guitar from its case, she starts to initiate them into the joys of singing ('Do Re Mi').

The eldest daughter, Liesl, is sixteen. It is an age when a girl has no need of a governess and where such an authority is bound to be resented. She also has a boyfriend in Rolf Gruber, the telegraph boy, and they meet in the grounds of the house to sing together with all the enthusiasm of their years about being in love and 'Sixteen Going on Seventeen'.

While Liesl is at her rendezvous, Maria is getting settled into her room under the gables of the house. The housekeeper presents her with a bolt of material with which to make herself a dress suitable to her new position but, when she asks for further material to make play clothes for the children, she is simply told that the von Trapp children do not play—they march for their exercise. There is nothing she can do to change it. Since the Captain's wife died, all the joyful things of life have been shut out of both his own life and the children's.

As she kneels to say her evening prayers, Maria spies Liesl climbing secretly through her window. She has been locked out of the house in the rain while meeting with Rolf and she is too scared to try to get in any other way. This way up the trellis she knows, for it is the way by which the children always crept into the governess's room to play tricks on her. Now she is caught, but Maria has no intention of telling her father. She and Liesl will be friends and allies. A flash of lightning and a burst of thunder bring the younger children rushing to Maria's room for comfort and soon the whole family is perched on the governess's bed while she entertains them with the jolly tale of 'The Lonely Goatherd'.

There is much talk in the house of a remarriage for the Captain. The lovely and wealthy socialite Baroness Elsa von Schräder has been keeping company with von Trapp and she has been invited to the house to stay. Another friend, the impecunious impresario Max Detweiler, a mercurial fellow who lives on his wit and charm, is a kind of chaperon for the occasion. While von Trapp and Elsa look at the mountains and edge towards commitment, Max is using von Trapp's telephone to make international calls chasing attractions for the forthcoming Kaltzberg Festival. Poverty may have its advantages, but so have riches and he prefers the latter in his friends. The former is only good for love, and he jokes with Elsa that there will undoubtedly be a problem in a marriage between her and Georg von Trapp. With so many millions between them 'How Can Love Survive?'.

The occasion of Elsa's visit is the first time that von Trapp has been home since the children were entrusted to Maria's care, and he is horrified when he finds them playing, dressed in the clothes Maria has made them from old curtains. He whistles them back into their formal line and sends them off to change into their uniforms. When Maria protests, and tells him that he is

748

making his children into unhappy little marching machines when what they need from him is love, he dismisses her harshly.

Suddenly the children's voices are heard. They are singing 'The Sound of Music', which Maria has taught them as a welcome to the Baroness. Von Trapp's heart opens again at the song and, in minutes, he is happily surrounded by his children. The sound of music has come back into his life. Elsa watches with mixed feelings. She cannot help but be pleased that Maria will, eventually, be returning to the Abbey.

Von Trapp gives a party to introduce Elsa to the people of the region, but it turns out to be an awkward affair. The faction in the area which supports the German pretensions in Austria and those who remain solidly nationalistic come up against each other, and political debate takes the place of party chatter. Elsa keeps to her room, unsure of her welcome, and only the children seem truly to enjoy themselves. Maria is trying to teach little Kurt the Ländler when von Trapp intervenes and, taking her in his arms, begins to dance. By the time Maria blushingly breaks off the dance, it is obvious that something has happened between them. Little Brigitta, who misses nothing, tells Maria that her father cannot possibly marry Elsa because he is in love with Maria, and the confused governess is plunged into panic.

When Max arrives unexpectedly it is decided that, to even up the table, Maria must be invited to sit at dinner and she is sent off to change, while the children sing goodnight to the guests in a roundelay that she has taught them ('So Long, Farewell'). Max is delighted at what he hears—the children are a perfect act for the Kaltzberg Festival. While he argues with von Trapp over the suitability of such a performance, Maria creeps down the stairs, dressed in her old frock and carrying her case. She cannot stay. She is returning to the abbey.

Back at Nonnberg, it is a long time before Maria can emerge from her room and come before the Abbess and, when she does, the Abbess tells her that she cannot use the convent as an escape from the world. Love is holy, love between man and woman as much as love of God, and the one does not exclude the other. She must return to the von Trapp family and face life and Captain von Trapp ('Climb Every Mountain').

ACT 2

Without their Fräulein Maria, the joy has gone out of the singing of the von Trapp children and neither their father nor the eager Max can get back the spirit of their performance at the party. Von Trapp will not allow them to talk of Maria. The children will have no more governesses, they will have a mother instead. He is going to marry Elsa. Then, without warning, Maria is back amongst them; the children come alive again, and Brigitta is quick to convey the news about Elsa. Maria is stopped short, and she tells the welcoming von Trapp that she has returned only until he can make other arrangements.

Given the charged political atmosphere of the times, the number of phone calls for Detweiler from Berlin arouse the annoyance of the fervently nationalist von Trapp. Max easily admits that he practises political expediency. He has no politics of his own and, if the Germans should invade, he would prefer to have some friends among them. Elsa agrees, but von Trapp will not compromise in spite of their advice ('There's No Way to Stop It'), and it is clear that his position is one which Elsa cannot accept.

She will not give up Vienna and her home and her possessions there to be a potential outlaw's bride and, finally, she decides that she must break off their engagement. She knows that von Trapp will quickly find a more suitable wife and, indeed, it is not long before Maria is in his arms and they are singing together of being 'An Ordinary Couple'. Maria Rainer and Georg von Trapp are wed in Nonnberg Abbey to the strains of a choral version of 'Maria'.

Max takes advantage of their honeymoon to prepare the children for the Kaltzberg Festival but his preparations are interrupted by some new local officials who demand that the von Trapp house shall, in the wake of the *anschluss*, fly the German flag. Fortunately, Max's expediency has given him a good government post under the new regime and he is able to face out the situation without committing anyone to anything.

When Georg and Maria return, the Captain firmly refuses to allow the children to sing in public. He also refuses to make any compromises in the face of the German occupation. It is soon clear what this will mean for, when young Rolf arrives to deliver a telegram, Liesl sees with distress that even he is using the Nazi salute. Few are resisting the invader and many, through conviction or fear, are joining with the Germans.

The telegram is an invitation to the Captain to take up a commission in the German navy and it is clear that if he does not accept he has little choice but to flee the country. The telegram is already several days old and, on the heels of its reception, the German Admiral von Schreiber himself arrives to put pressure on von Trapp and to order him to report immediately for duty. Maria wins a delay for them by showing the Admiral the Festival programme. In two days time the von Trapp Family Singers must appear at the Kaltzberg Festival.

The respite is granted and, at the Concert Hall in Kaltzberg, closely watched by German soldiers, the von Trapp family compete in the Festival with a rendition of 'Do Re Mi'. Georg follows this with a performance of the deliberately patriotic 'Edelweiss' and, when he falters with emotion part way through, Maria and the children pick up the melody and support him to the end.

Max comes on stage and announces that the judges are in deliberation and, to alert von Trapp to the fact that they are being closely guarded, dramatically tells the audience that an escort is waiting to take the Captain to his great new commission as soon as the concert is over. He calls on the von Trapps for another song and they give the children's 'So Long, Farewell' with its progressively vanishing personnel. When the prizes are announced, and the von Trapp Family Singers are awarded first place, they have indeed vanished. The soldiers leap on to the stage in pursuit, but they are too late.

The family make their way to Nonnberg Abbey for refuge and, when the soldiers come, the Mother Abbess hides them in the gardens. The soldiers search the grounds and suddenly one of them stumbles upon the children huddled in a corner. He goes to shout for his superior, but he sees Liesl and he cannot. The soldier is Rolf. Telling his officer that there is no one there, he leaves the garden and lets the von Trapp family go free.

When all is clear, the Mother Abbess lets Maria, Georg and the children out of the back gates of the abbey. They must climb through the hills Maria loves and find their way to safety in Switzerland. As the Abbess's voice is heard encouraging them to 'Climb Every Mountain', the family sets out through the trees towards a new life.

The film of *The Sound of Music* introduced 'I Have Confidence' and 'Something Good', and the London revival also included 'A Bell Is a Bell', developed from part of 'Sixteen Going on Seventeen'.

ONCE UPON A MATTRESS

a musical comedy in two acts by Jay Thompson, Marshall Barer and Dean Fuller based on *The Princess and the Pea*. Lyrics by Marshall Barer. Music by Mary Rodgers. Produced at the Phoenix Theatre, New York, 11 May 1959 with Carol Burnett (Winnifred), Joseph Bova (Dauntless), Anne Jones (Larken), Allen Case (Harry), Matt Mattox (Jester) and Jane White (Queen).

Produced at the Adelphi Theatre, London 20 September 1960 with Jane Connell, Robin Hunter, Patricia Lambert, Bill Newman, Max Wall and Thelma Ruby.

CHARACTERS

King Sextimus the Silent
Queen Aggravain
Prince Dauntless, *their son*
The Jester
The Wizard
The Minstrel
Lady Larken
Sir Harry
Princess Winnifred the Woebegone
Sir Studley, Sir Luce, Lady Rowena, Lady Merrill, Lady Lucille, Lady Mabelle, Princess No 12, etc.

ACT 1

The Minstrel opens the show, relating the traditional story of *The Princess and the Pea* ('Many Moons Ago')—the search of a medieval queen to find a true princess, as delicate and dainty as a dragonfly's wing, to wed her son, a quest which was solved by a perfect princess who was left bruised and sleepless by a pea placed under the twenty mattresses of her bed. It is a pretty tale but apparently, the Minstrel tells us, not strictly true. You see, he was there and he is now going to show us what really happened.

The scene is the court of King Sextimus and Queen Aggravain, or, rather, Queen Aggravain and King Sextimus. The King has been unable to run his court and country effectively since being struck dumb by an offended fairy with the curse that he shall never speak again until the mouse shall devour the eagle. Various experiments with these animals have proven embarrassingly ridiculous and so the King remains mute, while the forceful Queen takes charge of all the private and political business of the royal family.

A most important part of both of these areas of business is the future of Prince Dauntless and, most particularly, his marriage. It is important not only to Dauntless but also to all the rest of the court for it has been enacted that none of them shall wed until Dauntless shall first have gone to the altar. Alas, there seems to be little chance for anyone with marital inclinations, for the Queen has decreed that all postulants for the Prince's hand shall be subjected to a test. To date eleven princesses have applied and failed their test, and a twelfth is currently under inquisition, answering question after question in front of an excited Dauntless until she is flattened by a perfectly impossible final poser from the malicious Queen. As the Princess is bundled out with a consolation prize of a chicken, Dauntless wails in distress, sympathetically supported by the whole court ('An Opening for a Princess').

Lady Larken has particular cause to be downhearted. She really wants to marry Sir Harry. In fact she really has to marry Sir Harry, because Sir Harry has made her pregnant. What will the Queen say? There is only one answer: Sir Harry must go out and search far and wide and bring back a Princess who will pass the Queen's test. Preferably quickly. Sir Harry girds his loins and promises to return 'In A Little While'. Certainly before the necessary November.

Dauntless has a tiny suspicion that his mother doesn't want him to marry but, when he dares to voice this thought, he receives a Jewish mother tirade to end all Jewish mother tirades. The Queen has not finished howling her self-pitying piece when Sir Harry comes to announce his Quest. As it happens, Harry's Quest ends up being just three weeks long. It is still only April when he heaves to on the horizon with a Princess in tow and, to the Queen's amazement and horror, the girl is in the palace even before the drawbridge can be lowered. She has swum the moat! Unprecedented! And now she stands there making puddles all over the floor and wanting to know in her 'Shy' fashion which one is her Prince. The Queen pulls out her most impressive thunders: a girl who swims moats is not going to marry her son! But Dauntless couldn't agree less. He thinks she's wonderful. He's never met a girl before who can swim moats. The court don't care about that. Sir Harry has papers to prove that Winnifred the Woebegone is a princess so it is clear that she must at least be allowed a test. After all, you never know your luck.

The King has got wind of Lady Larken's little problem and he passes his bit of gossip on to the Jester and the Minstrel in the pantomime which serves him as speech ('The Minstrel, The Jester and I'). The Queen, meanwhile, has other preoccupations. She is busy plotting an unpassable test for the buxom Princess Winnifred. It will be a test for 'Sensitivity'. A brilliant idea. That galumphing creature will simply never pass.

While the Queen is at her plotting, Winnifred is meeting the King, telling her new friends about 'The Swamps of Home' and arranging to swap her bedraggled dress for something drier. Lady Larken, who has been assigned to the new Princess as lady-in-waiting, makes a horrid mistake when she takes Winnifred for a chambermaid and, when she haughtily tries to justify her error, she gets into a fight with Sir Harry who is full of admiration for the healthy Princess.

The Queen has decided how to carry out her sensitivity test. She will put a pea under twenty mattresses on Winnifred's bed. If she sleeps she loses, if she doesn't then she wins. She charges her confidant, the Wizard, with providing a sleeping potion and a hypnotic mirror to help the girl lose, and plans a dance at which it will be compulsory to dance the exhausting 'Spanish Panic'.

Lady Larken has decided that she is going to run away. Harry is being horrid and she is going to go away and have her baby in a romantic hovel somewhere far away from the court, perhaps somewhere in 'Normandy'. She will escape, dressed up in boy's clothes, while the Queen's dance is in progress. The dance is going full pelt, but it doesn't seem to be fulfilling its purpose. Winnifred dances the 'Spanish Panic' over and over and calls for more, and all the time she is getting chummier and chummier with little Dauntless who is, by now, head over heels in love with this superb, untiring creature who swigs back her wine like a chap ('I'm in Love With a Girl Called Fred').

ACT 2

The Queen is readying her test, leading her servants, loaded with mattresses, through the passages of the palace to Winnifred's room but, as the procession parades onwards, she comes upon the Minstrel, the Jester and the King helping Lady Larken to get away in her boy's disguise. The Minstrel tries helpfully to claim that he is abducting her and this infuriates Harry, who is in the company of glamorous Lady Mabelle which infuriates Lady Larken, and the whole situation infuriates the Queen who screams for 'Quiet'.

Lady Larken, all hope of her glamorous escapade gone, is sent sulkily back to attend on Winnifred, who is boning up her mythology in preparation for her test, and the Princess advises the miserable mother-to-be to go and say sorry to Harry and live 'Happily Ever After' like the princesses in her mythology book and, oh so hopefully, like herself.

Since a marriage might be on the horizon, it is time for the King to tell Dauntless about the birds and bees. He is slightly handicapped by his inability to speak, but makes no more or less of a hash of it than most speaking fathers do (Man to Man Talk). While he is doing so, the marriage is getting another nudge towards likelihood from the Jester and the Minstrel who are buttering up the Wizard over a few jars. As they chatter about the good old days when they were in show business ('Very Soft Shoes') they manage to extract from the tiddly Wizard the nature of Winnifred's test. It only remains for them then to take action.

While Harry and Larken are making up ('Yesterday I Loved You'), the Queen is counting mattresses and Winnifred is being prepared for bed. The sleeping potion is followed by a hypnotic mirror and a Samarkand nightingale trained to sing a soporific 'Lullaby', but, when she is left alone, Winnifred finds she can't sleep. She begins counting sheep.

At breakfast the next day, Dauntless is bursting with anxiety to hear what form the test will take and he is shattered to discover that it has already taken place. They have been tricked. Then Winnifred walks in. She is up to 37,248 sheep and she hasn't slept a wink. That bed was like a torture chamber. Aggravain is staggered and Dauntless is over the moon. When his mother attempts to get round the result of her test, he finally answers her back. For the first time in his life he utters those awful words: 'shut up!'.

And then it happens. The mouse has turned on the hawk. The Queen's voice disappears and the King suddenly becomes active and imperious. Winnifred shall marry Dauntless, and King Sextimus, no longer the silent, shall rule his kingdom henceforth without interference from his wife, condemned to silence for the rest of fairytime. As the happy finale gets under way, the Minstrel and the Jester are seen undoing Winnifred's bed. From between the mattresses they pull the minstrel's lute, Sir Harry's helmet, the Jester's staff, a spiked shield, maces, boots, spurs and a set of deers antlers. Ah well, it never hurts to help history along a little.

GYPSY

a musical in two acts by Arthur Laurents suggested by the memoirs of Gypsy Rose Lee. Lyrics by Stephen Sondheim. Music by Jule Styne. Produced at the Broadway Theatre, New York, 21 May 1959 with Ethel Merman (Rose), Sandra Church (Louise), Lane Bradbury (June) and Jack Klugman (Herbie). Produced at the Winter Garden Theatre 23 September 1974 with Angela Lansbury, Zan Charisse, Maureen Moore and Rex Robbins.

Produced at the Piccadilly Theatre, London, 29 May 1973 with Angela Lansbury, Zan Charisse, Debbie Bowen and Barrie Ingham.

A film version was produced by Warner Brothers in 1962 with Rosalind Russell (singing dubbed by Lisa Kirk), Natalie Wood, Ann Jillian and Karl Malden.

CHARACTERS

Rose
Baby Louise *later* Louise
Baby June *later* June
Herbie

Tulsa
Yonkers
LA
Agnes
Tessie Tura
Mazeppa
Electra
Uncle Jocko
Mr Goldstone, George, Arnold, Pop, Weber, Kringelein, Miss Cratchitt,
Pastey, Cigar, The Hollywood Blondes, The Newsboys, etc.

ACT 1

Somewhere in Seattle, sometime in the 1920s, there is a children's talent
show in progress under the aegis of one of the Uncle Jockos of this world.
One of the acts in the contest is Baby June and Company, a blonde tot
dressed as a Dutch girl and supported by a less obvious child disguised as a
Dutch boy. They have a number called 'Let Me Entertain You', and they
have a mother. Mother, in spite of an interdiction on all mothers at the run-
through, gives stentorian directions to her embryonic little stars from the
auditorium and thoroughly disabuses Uncle Jocko of the idea of fixing the
contest on behalf of some other and more generous parent. Rose, the mother
of Baby June and the Dutch boy (otherwise Louise), has started on a
campaign to make a star of her blonde baby, and it would take more than a
squad of Uncle Jockos to undermine her determination.

After the kiddie shows come the professional circuits. Rose has had a
dream which has revealed to her a new act which she will call Baby June and
her Newsboys. Louise can be one of the boys and somewhere they'll pick up
a few more youngsters who will work for the experience, since Rose certainly
hasn't the money to pay them. Nothing can stop her in her vicarious drive to
stardom. 'Some People' may be content to sit at home and live a quiet life,
but not Rose.

From Seattle, she talks and hornswoggles her way to Los Angeles, building the act and chasing bookings. At Weber's hall in LA she finds no interest
until Herbie, the theatre's candy supplier and an ex-variety agent, gives the
act a recommendation. His recommendation isn't wholly disinterested and
his interest is patently more in Rose than in Baby June with or without her
newsboys. Rose and he are mutually attracted, but he wants marriage and
she doesn't. She wants show business and he's through with it ('Small
World'). The act, in spite of the addition of four newsboys, is pretty much
the same as it was in Uncle Jocko's days. June still sings 'Let Me Entertain
You', though now its in a ragtime rhythm, and she still dances a breathless
combination of every step ever learnt from a brain and act-picking mother.

Life on the road is not easy: Rose, Herbie (travelling with them as agent),
June, Louise and the three lads of the act, Tulsa, LA and Yonkers, all share
a pair of fourth-rate hotel rooms and live off reheated Chinese food, and
Rose gets the landlord into a compromising position to keep him from

throwing them out when it becomes necessary. When Louise's birthday comes along, the boys bring her gifts pilfered from the five and dime, Rose gives her a lamb which is to be part of the new act which she has dreamed up—Baby June and her Farmboys—and Herbie turns up with a Mr Goldstone, whom he has talked into booking the act on the Orpheum circuit. Rose falls all over the man ('Mr Goldstone, I Love You') and Louise, her birthday now forgotten in the excitement, sits quietly in the corner and sings to her 'Little Lamb'.

Next, it's New York. Time has passed, quite a long time since that single break on the Orpheum which had no tomorrow, but Rose still dresses the girls up in the same childish costumes, they still perform the same juvenile act, and her confidence has not lessened one smidgin. Neither has Herbie's devotion, though Rose has reneged on her promise to marry him if he could get the act onto the Orpheum circuit. Now she wants Broadway. If she can have June's name up in lights just once, then she will marry him. Tomorrow they have an audition for T T Grantzinger's Palace. Maybe that'll be it. Herbie won't wait forever, but Rose smilingly tells him 'You'll Never Get Away From Me'.

Mr Grantzinger watches Dainty June and her Farmboys and their version of 'Let Me Entertain You' unseen, from his suite. The act features a pantomime cow, but is otherwise recognisable as a close relative of the newsboy act and its predecessor. Mr Grantzinger, amazingly, offers them a contract, but it is for one week and at his downtown variety theatre, and he only makes the offer at all because he fancies he sees in June the makings of an actress. Rose rejects it furiously. No one is going to take her baby away from her. She is going to make her a star, all by herself. So June's chance is blown away. June is no fool; she knows that Dainty June and her boys are a ghastly act and that she is ghastly in it. She is dying to escape and she and Louise dream what life would be like if Rose had someone else to lavish her energies on; what it would be like 'If Momma Was Married'.

In Buffalo, Tulsa is practising fancy footwork in the alley. Louise knows what he's up to, he's inventing a dance team act. He's got it all worked out but, as he explains, there's one thing missing. He hasn't got a partner ('All I Need Is the Girl'). By Omaha, he has found one. Tulsa and June run off together and the other boys follow them for, without them, there is no act. Rose is only daunted for a minute. In that minute Herbie asks her to marry him and settle down, but Rose still has her ambition and it is not to Herbie that she turns but to the previously unconsidered Louise. She has had another dream. It is Louise who will be a star. Her optimism is as high as ever as she starts all over again ('Everything's Coming up Roses').

ACT 2

The new act is called Madame Rose's Toreadorables. The farmboys have gone Spanish and Louise is decked out in a blonde wig in a sad attempt to duplicate June's performance. Louise rebels both against the wig and the act—she is not and cannot be June—but she cannot resist the enthusiasm of

Rose, supported by Herbie ('Together, Wherever We Go'), and she settles for the rest of the girls being blondes while she stays brunette. The act becomes Rose Louise and her Hollywood Blondes as it heads steadily for the bottom.

In Wichita, they get to play a real theatre. There is only one problem. It is a burlesque theatre, and burlesque is the bare buttocks of the business. They have been booked there only to give the place a thin wash of respectability behind which the strip acts and low comics can play. Rose is livid and ready to march out, but Louise faces her with the reality of their situation. They are penniless. They have to play the date.

Louise shares a dressing room with the stripper Tessie Tura who, with her colleagues Mazeppa and Electra, demonstrates to the girl the essential element of individuality that goes with success on the burlesque stage ('You Gotta Get a Gimmick'). The burlesque stage also has its hierarchy, and neither Tessie nor her pals will lower themselves to act as a feed for the comic when there is a dropout. Louise takes the job and the extra ten dollars.

The engagement at Wichita is ended, and at last Herbie has got Rose to say 'yes' to him. They are to be married. But, as they prepare to set off, show business gets in the way one more time. The night's guest stripper has managed to get herself arrested for soliciting and the theatre has no one to perform the star spot. The word 'star' acts on Rose like a match to brushwood. Her daughter can do it. In the past weeks she has seen that there is nothing to it.

The wedding flies out of Rose's head as she begins to direct a performance for Gypsy Rose Louise. There will be nothing tacky, it will be ladylike and elegant and young, and the old number, 'Let Me Entertain You' will do fine. As Louise goes on, Herbie goes off. He has played second fiddle to Rose's dreams once too often. Momma shouts directions from the wings as if it were Uncle Jocko's show all over again as Louise makes her way rather unsteadily through the opening part of the spot. Before she is finished she is much steadier and even rather roguish and she is without doubt a success.

Now it is success all the way: the Alhambra, Detroit; the Philadelphia Diamond Burlesque; and then Minsky's itself as Gypsy Rose Lee becomes an assured and stylish star of burlesque and the Queen of Striptease. Louise loves her new life, the fame and the riches, but Rose still wants to manage her life and finds it impossible to accept that the successful young star makes her own arrangements both in and out of the theatre. She cannot even run Louise's bath—there is a maid to do that—and she never gets invited to go any of those grand parties with her daughter. Louise is ashamed of her. She is banned from backstage.

All that Louise needs, in truth, is to be let go. She offers to set her mother up in a stage school or anything else that she likes, but Rose insists on being needed. All that work, all those years, what did she do it for? Louise answers her quietly, 'I thought you did it for me, Momma.'

Rose knows she didn't. She did it for herself. Rose. She did it so that she could act out through June and through Louise the performances she was never able to give. And now, on the bare stage of the empty theatre, she gives that performance (Rose's Turn). From the wings, unseen, Louise is watching and she understands. Her mother could have been quite something, given the chance. But she didn't have the chance, and all she really ever wanted was to be noticed. Louise knows all about that sort of feeling . She remembers the days of Baby June when all she, too, wanted was to be noticed. She puts her mink around her mother's shoulders. They are going to a party, the two of them together.

BYE BYE BIRDIE

a musical in two acts by Michael Stewart. Lyrics by Lee Adams. Music by Charles Strouse. Produced at the Martin Beck Theatre, New York, 14 April 1960 with Dick van Dyke (Albert), Chita Rivera (Rose), Dick Gautier (Birdie), Kay Medford (Mae) and Susan Watson (Kim).

Produced at Her Majesty's Theatre, London, 15 June 1961 with Peter Marshall, Miss Rivera, Marty Wilde, Angela Baddeley and Sylvia Tysick.

A film version was produced by Columbia in 1963 with Dick van Dyke, Janet Leigh, Jesse Pearson, Maureen Stapleton and Ann-Margret.

CHARACTERS

Albert Peterson
Rosie Grant, *his secretary*
Ursula Merkle
Kim MacAfee
Mr MacAfee
Mrs MacAfee
Mae Peterson, *Albert's mother*
Conrad Birdie
Hugo Peabody
Mrs Merkle
Gloria Rasputin
Helen, Nancy, Alice, Margie Ann, Penelope Ann, Deborah Sue, Suzie, Linda, Carol, Martha Louise, Harold, Karl, Harvey, Henry, Arthur, Freddie, Peyton, *teenagers*
Mayor, Mayor's wife, Mr Henkel, Charles F Maude, etc.

ACT 1

Albert Peterson, the company President of the Almaelou Music Corporation, New York, has a problem. The corporation's one and only asset is about to be drafted.

Albert was at college when he gave up his academic ambitions to run the career of Conrad Birdie, pop star. He formed a Corporation named after himself, his mother Mae, and the dog Lou and, with the faithful and sometimes loving help of secretary Rosie, he has succeeded in keeping

758

Conrad a teenage idol and also in getting $50,000 into debt. Conrad's new-found success should be just about to start paying off this debt, only he has been drafted and, just to make Albert's day even better, Rosie is resigning. Rosie has gone through eight years of Albert's indecision, eight years of Albert's mother, eight years of double hours and one $5 raise, eight years of waiting for Albert to give up this pop music lark and do the decent thing he has always promised he would do—become 'An English Teacher'. Enough is enough.

Faced with this rebellion, Albert recants. He promises he will dissolve the company and go back to English just as soon as he has the cash to pay off Conrad's guarantee. Rosie gives in but, now that she has a promise, she takes practical means to hasten her goal. From the pack of Birdie fan club cards she takes a card, any card. It says 'Kim MacAfee of Sweet Apple, Ohio ... age 15'. Miss MacAfee, declares Rosie, is a lucky girl. She will get a kiss from Conrad Birdie. That kiss will be the hook for Conrad's greatest hit, 'One Last Kiss', his goodbye to the girls of America as he goes off to serve President and country. While Albert gets down to writing the song, Rosie gets on the phone to Sweet Apple, Ohio.

It's difficult to get on to Sweet Apple, Ohio, because most of the telephone lines are taken up by teenagers chattering (The Telephone Hour). Today's Sweet Apple teen-topic is Kim MacAfee. Kim has resigned as President of the Conrad Birdie fan club because Hugo Peabody has given her his pin and they're going steady. She's practically an adult ('How Lovely to Be a Woman'), which means she can be modern and call her parents by their christian names and smoke cigarettes. However, when the news comes through that Conrad Birdie is coming to Sweet Apple to kiss her, Kim's new found maturity disappears abruptly and she howls for her Mommy.

At Pennsylvania Station, Albert is orchestrating Conrad's departure for Ohio with the help of some swooning teenage harmonisers ('We Love You, Conrad'), and encouraging a distraught child facing a Conrad-less life to 'Put on a Happy Face'. Mother Mae turns up on a cloud of martyrising reproaches and Albert promises Rose he will tell his mother about dissolving the company that bears part of her name just as soon as a suitable moment arises but, when Mae has finished her regular tirade against Rose (an eight-year danger who is clearly trying to get her hooks into Mae's sonny boy) and staging a simulated heart attack, she swans off again without giving Albert the space of a breath to tell her of his plans. A sheepish Albert and a frustrated Rosie are left behind to deal with Conrad and the press.

In front of the newspapermen, Conrad isn't allowed to utter a word. Albert and Rosie know what these fellows want and they trot out every available cliché about his being a 'Normal American Boy' until it is time for the teen hero to get on the train. Conrad is simply going from one identikit set of fans to another, and his arrival at Sweet Apple is greeted by Kim and her pals with the same Birdie anthem and the same Birdie pledge of loyalty heard through the entire United States of America.

Hugo Peabody is not at all sure that he is happy about Kim being kissed by Conrad. In fact, the very thought is enough to give him a nosebleed, but Kim

759

assures him that a steady is forever ('One Boy'), while a pop star is only an internationally famous celebrity. Rosie has the same sort of idea about Albert, but Albert (and Albert's mother) have other priorities.

The Mayor welcomes Conrad to Sweet Apple with a speech on the court-house steps, but the speech is cut short by a barrage of screams led by loyal fan Ursula Merkel who squeals for Conrad to talk to them, to tell them the secret of his success. Conrad opens his mouth for the first time in the show and delivers his creed: you just have to be 'Honestly Sincere!'. One by one, the entire female population of Sweet Apple faints dead away.

Conrad is lodged at the MacAfee household in preparation for the nation-wide telecast of The Kiss and the unveiling of The Song. This arrangement has dispossessed Mr MacAfee of his bedroom and his breakfast, and he is furiously fed up until he discovers that he and the family are going to be seen with Conrad on the Ed Sullivan show. This pays for all. The MacAfee family have been blessed by the greatest blessing God and the NBC can grant (Hymn for a Sunday Evening).

The preparations for the big day continue and Albert takes his courage in his hands and writes to Mother Mae to tell her about dissolving the company. When three days have passed and he hasn't heard anything he even gets momentarily hopeful that she has taken his action lying down but, of course, she hasn't. She has been travelling three days by cheap transport to get to Ohio to play her dying mother routine. She has also brought with her a brassy bit called Gloria Rasputin, who types and tap dances, to be Albert's secretary since she has decided Rosie is getting a bit old for it. Albert is well enough trained to be appreciative and Rosie is, for the umpteenth time, furious. In a ballet scena she illustrates a series of ways 'How to Kill a Man' who lets his mother... She is getting her breath back when a determined Hugo comes by. He has decided that he will not permit Kim to be kissed on national television by Conrad Birdie and the revengeful Rosie agrees with him. She will see what she can do.

The Ed Sullivan show is live on the air as Conrad launches into the première of 'One Last Kiss'. The song finished, he gathers Kim in his arms and, as he does so, Hugo runs forward and punches him. Conrad is knocked out cold in front of seventy-five million viewers. Albert goes mad. Who let that kid in? Rosie did. It was a sort of farewell present. Their altercation over the prone Conrad makes fine prime time viewing until Albert remembers where he is and frantically attempts to get the hymn to the 'Normal Ameri-can Boy' going in a last ditch effort to rescue his promotion.

ACT 2

As news of the fiasco flies around the country, Rosie sits back on her heels at the MacAfee house bewailing her wasted years and wondering 'What Did I See in Him?'. The mortified Kim is having much the same thoughts about Hugo, and she determines to follow Rosie out into the world to live the high life. Albert needs Rosie back, but for the moment he has other more pressing problems. He has managed to reschedule The Kiss for the railway station on

760

the morrow and now Conrad is insisting on going out to find a night spot in Sweet Apple. He's sick of sitting at home and he's about to go into the army so right now, he declares, 'I've Got a Lot of Livin' to Do'.

Out on the streets of Sweet Apple the boy runs into Kim, who is also looking for some living, so they decide to find the action together and, while Mr MacAfee goes to look for a gun, the elders of Sweet Apple bewail the frightful behaviour of 'Kids'.

The dejected Hugo has ended up at Maude's Roadside Retreat where he tries to order a consolatory drink and is thrown out for being under age. Rosie finds the same bar and, after vampishly ordering a dangerous sounding cocktail, she also gets her marching orders from the wary barman. Before she can be ejected, however, she gets a telephone call from Albert pleading 'Baby, Talk to Me'. Plumping down the phone, she heads not for the door but, to the bartender's agitation, for an inner room full of men. She invades a Shriners' meeting and before long she has them involved in a wild dance. She finally limps out to be confronted by Hugo, still looking for the wherewithal to drown his sorrow.

Revolution is going on all round town. Albert finally pulls himself together enough to face up to his mother and unshrinkingly tell her to go home; Kim does her best to vamp Conrad, only to freeze him off when she tries to use big words like 'jailbait'. Then Ursula and the rest of teen-Sweet Apple arrive on the scene to propose whatever an orgy is, and Conrad is glad when the police turn up and bundle him off to prison for depravity. While the newly confident Albert marches off to arrange Conrad's release, Rosie squares up to Mrs Peterson and faces her out. 'Spanish Rose', as Mae insists on calling her so sneeringly, is Rosie Grant from Allentown, Pa, and she's taken enough schtick from Mae in these last eight years. This is the end.

At the railway station next morning, Albert smuggles Conrad out of Sweet Apple disguised as a fur-enveloped woman. The grateful star is willing to forget every cent of the guarantee Albert owes him and give him a managerial contract for life. The new, no-nonsense Albert gets his mother on the train and fends off the MacAfees who are still pursuing Conrad, before Rosie turns up at the station.

She is taken aback when she finds the train has gone, but Albert has news for her. They aren't catching the train for New York, they're heading for Pumpkin Falls, Iowa. As he tears up Conrad's contract, he tells her he has an interview for a post there as an English teacher. He hopes her papers are in order, because they prefer married applicants. As Albert Peterson, English teacher, sings sweetly to his 'Rosie', the curtain comes happily down.

A sequel, *Bring Back Birdie*, was produced at the Martin Beck Theatre, New York, 5 March 1981.

THE FANTASTICKS

a musical in two acts by Tom Jones suggested by the play *Les Romanesques* by Edmond Rostand. Music by Harvey Schmidt. Produced at the Sullivan Street Playhouse, New York, 3 May 1960 with Jerry Orbach (El Gallo), Kenneth Nelson (Matt) and Rita Gardner (Luisa).

Produced at the Apollo Theatre, London, 7 September 1961 with Terence Cooper, Peter Gilmore and Stephanie Voss.

Produced at the Neue Theater am Kärntnertor, Vienna, 1 December 1965.

CHARACTERS

El Gallo
Amos Babcock Bellomy
Luisa, *his daughter*
Hucklebee, *his neighbour*
Matt, *Hucklebee's son*
Henry
The Mute
Mortimer
The Handyman

ACT 1

On an empty platform, the people who will tell the evening's story assemble the properties they will use in their performance, as the storyteller sings a gentle, yearning song of nostalgia ('Try to Remember'). Then he begins, in verse, to tell his tale. Its participants are a boy, a girl, two fathers and a wall. The boy and the girl grew up as neighbours but they did not really notice each other. The girl was very romantic and she longed for exciting things to happen to her ('Much More') before she got really old, and the boy went away to school and learned things. Then, at fifteen, the girl lost her ugly duckling features and became pretty, and the boy came home from school and noticed her, and they fell in love ('Metaphor'). But their fathers didn't approve of this and they built a wall between their two properties to stop the two young people seeing each other, and their love affair had to be conducted in secret meetings.

The boy's father has nothing good to say about his neighbour on the other side of the wall. He is a villain. And he has news for his son. He has arranged a marriage for him. The boy refuses the marriage and insists he will choose for himself, but his father says no. The girl's father, meanwhile, is planning a fence to go with the wall.

Now that the lovers seem hopelessly parted, we meet the fathers, alone, and the two enemies turn out to be friends. The truth is that they are quite delighted that their children are in love. The wall is part of a plan. It's all very simple—if they had tried to get their children to fall in love they would have simply refused. That's the way with children, you only have to forbid something and then they will do it ('Never Say No'). So they built the wall and forbade the children to fall in love.

Now that everything is going so nicely, it is time to end the pretended feud and let the children have 'their' way, and the boy's father has a plan by which this can be accomplished, a nice romantic plan which will appeal to the girl. He will arrange an abduction. He has discovered a professional abductor called El Gallo who is able to supply abductions (or rapes as he pedantically prefers to term them) to suit all pockets ('It Depends on What You Pay'). This fellow will carry the girl off, and the boy will be able to rescue her gallantly. The fathers can be all forgiving and everything can end happily.

El Gallo takes the stage to prepare the First Class Rape ordered by the fathers. To assist him, he acquires a pair of drolls: Mortimer, an expert in death scenes, and Henry, an old barnstormer. El Gallo orders up a moon to give atmosphere to the pre-rape scene of love, and the boy and the girl are soon in each other's arms ('Soon It's Gonna Rain'). At the height of the romantic scene, the rape is put into action (Rape Ballet). The players attack the young people and allow themselves to be beaten, killed and set to flight by the heroics of the boy. The boy, the girl and the two fathers end up safe in each other's arms and the 'Happy Ending' everyone wished for is accomplished.

The hired men get up and look at the pretty scene their handicraft has created. It'll do very well as an ending. Let's see if they can hold those positions.

ACT 2

The moon has gone, the wall has gone, it's a lovely sunny day and the two gardens have been merged into one, but the boy and the girl find it hard to say convincingly that they are happy. Without the support of romance and adventure and soft lights, life doesn't seem the same at all and everyone starts to get on everyone else's nerves ('This Plum Is Too Ripe'). The boy dwells constantly on his heroism, the girl on the handsome bandit, and when they recall their picturesque moment for the hundredth time, the irritated father shows them the bill for the rape. The children now know they've been hoodwinked. Then, before you know where you are, suddenly the fathers are quarrelling and shouting about putting the wall up again.

El Gallo is passing and the boy wants to prove himself. He wants to show that he can beat his victim in a real duel. But he can't. He is made to look silly and that leads to a fight with the girl, each flinging charges of immaturity at the other, until the boy decides he can't stand it any more. He's going away, out into the world ('I Can See It'). Henry and Mortimer join him, threatening to show him everything he needs for his education.

September is gone and October. The wall is going up again under the spade of a helpful mute, but the fathers soon get together again for their little chats and their card games and their gardening ('Plant a Radish'). The girl, however, has been in a trance since the boy went away. She comes out of it to pour out her romantic thoughts to the bandit. El Gallo will be her hero ('Round and Round'). As they dance together, the boy can be seen going through the pains of the outside world under the guidance of his two

763

cicerones. The girl sees a man in pain, but she does not know that the suffering creature is him and, when she wishes to show compassion, the bandit forces a laughing mask in front of her face.

The girl is ready to run away into the world with El Gallo, and she goes into the house to prepare herself for flight but he, having whetted her appetite for the world, has no intention of saddling himself with her. As he leaves, he is met by the boy, returning. He is no longer the same. He is scarred and torn, bedraggled and hurt. He has seen the world and everything in it, and in everything he saw nothing but the girl ('They Were You'). Gently the pair come together again and, as they do, the fathers watch quietly. It is going to be all right, they can take down the wall again. But El Gallo tells them that they must not. They must always leave the wall there.

CAMELOT

a musical in two acts by Alan Jay Lerner based on *The Once and Future King* by T H White. Music by Frederick Loewe. Produced at the Majestic Theatre, New York, 3 December 1960 with Richard Burton (Arthur), Julie Andrews (Guenevere) and Robert Goulet (Lancelot). Produced at the Winter Garden Theatre 15 November 1981 with Richard Harris, Meg Bussert and Richard Muenz.

Produced at the Theatre Royal, Drury Lane, London, 19 August 1964 with Laurence Harvey, Elizabeth Larner and Barry Kent. Produced at the Apollo Victoria Theatre 12 November 1982 with Richard Harris, Fiona Fullerton and Robert Meadmore.

Produced at the Badische Staatstheater, Karlsruhe, 3 October 1981.

A film version was produced by Warner Brothers in 1967 with Richard Harris, Vanessa Redgrave and Franco Nero (singing dubbed by Gene Merlino).

CHARACTERS

Arthur
Guenevere
Merlyn
Lancelot
Mordred
King Pellinore
Sir Dinadan
Sir Lionel
Sir Sagramore
Morgan le Fey
Nimuë
Squire Dap, Clarius, Lady Anne, Lady Sybil, Tom, etc.

ACT 1

On a hilltop near the castle of Camelot, the court is gathered to celebrate the arrival of their new queen. King Arthur's destined bride, Guenevere, is on her way to Camelot, but the young king himself is not at his castle to receive her. Instead, he is up in a tree, trying to catch a private glimpse of the lady who will be his wife before having to meet her publicly and, for his pains, he gets himself thoroughly chided by his old tutor, Merlyn.

The wise Merlyn has the advantage of having lived backwards. He has been old, and knows everything of time immemorial, and he is getting daily younger. Over the years, he has bestowed on Arthur the benefit of his distilled wisdom, but the boy's youthful head has not knowingly taken in everything offered and soon, Merlyn knows, the future king will have to face the world without his protector. For, since his life is lived in reverse, Merlyn knows what his own fate will be. He will be bewitched by the nymph Nimuë and kept locked for centuries in her enchanted cave and, when that happens, Arthur will be left alone for the first time in his life, with only the memories of Merlyn's teachings to guide him in the conduct of his life as a king and a man.

Merlyn will not turn the eager boy into a hawk to let him peek at his beautiful Guenevere, and he orders him back to the castle, wondering what the King's subjects would think if they could see him swinging like a monkey from a tree. Arthur knows precisely what his subjects are thinking. They are thinking 'I Wonder What the King Is Doing Tonight?'. If only they knew. If only they knew how nervous he is at the thought of marriage. But as he sings his fears to the forest, he hears someone approaching and he climbs quickly back into his tree. The newcomer is a young woman and she is praying forcefully to her particular saint, rebelling against an arranged marriage before she's had time to enjoy 'The Simple Joys of Maidenhood' which are the rights of every medieval girl.

Curiosity pushes Arthur a little too near the end of his branch and, at an inopportune moment, it cracks, depositing him inelegantly on the ground alongside the girl. She is practically insulted when he doesn't show any eagerness to assault her, but she puts it down to the fact the he has realised she is Guenevere, the King's bride. Or, rather, his intended bride for she has run away from her attendants with the express purpose of escaping her forced marriage. Arthur, enchanted by her, is anxious to change her mind and sings attractively of the charms of his home ('Camelot') until the court appears and, to her amazement, Guenevere sees the young man honoured as King.

An explanation is clearly in order and, shyly, Arthur tells Guenevere the tale of the sword in the stone and how he became King. By the time he has finished they are sufficiently in love for all the terror to have gone from the thought of marriage. Merlyn, amazed and delighted, sees the boy become a King. How foolish he has been. Arthur didn't need a lecture to make him ambitious, he needed a queen.

Merlyn, however, will never get to know Queen Guenevere for, as he returns to the castle, his fate comes upon him. Nimuë's voice draws him away from Camelot ('Follow Me'), draining from him all the knowledge and wisdom of the centuries. Desperately he tries to remember: has he told

Arthur everything he should know? About Lancelot? About Guenevere and Lancelot? About Mordred? Alas, he never told him about Mordred...

In five years on the throne, Arthur swells into a man, his life's course leading him constantly on to discover the true meanings of things Merlyn had shown him as a child. His discontent with the haphazard warring of his knights breeds the longing in him for a more civilised and civilising court at Camelot and, from this longing, is born the idea of the order of the Knights of the Round Table. One first of May, there arrives from France a postulant for the order: the unsmiling, self-serious Lancelot du Lac ('C'Est Moi'), and his coming brings back to the King the words of Merlyn who had prophesied that one called Lancelot would be the greatest at Arthur's table.

The Queen and court are out celebrating the May festival ('It's May!') when an old man in a curious garb appears. He is the wandering King Pellinore, condemned to chase the Questing Beast through the ages. He is fed up with the constant routine and longs for a bed and a pillow just for one night and he is delighted when Guenevere offers him kindly hospitality. The Queen is less amused by the innocently self-satisfied Lancelot whom she finds insufferably big-headed and she is pleased to give her favours to three knights who pledge to cause the Frenchman's downfall in the lists ('Take Me to the Fair'). Arthur, who is besotted by the perfection of Lancelot, is angry that Guenevere should show her antipathy so publicly, and he asks her to withdraw her favours, but she replies that she will do so only if he commands her as King, and this he cannot bring himself to do. Alone, he wonders at her strange reaction and muses on 'How to Handle a Woman'.

When the jousting takes place, Lancelot defeats all three knights, and demonstrates practically his belief that his purity allows him to do miraculous things by raising the apparently dead Sir Lionel after his fall. As he passes the Queen, their eyes meet and they gaze at each other transfixed while the King can only look on with troubled understanding. Guenevere knows what has happened and tries to put it away from her ('Before I Gaze at You Again') but inevitably her emotion finds its way into words. Lancelot and the Queen are in love. They know it and Arthur knows it. He faces his dilemma and resolves that, above all, he will be civilised. He loves them, they love him: there can be no joy in destroying them because they love each other. He will be a King first and a man second, and God have mercy on them all.

ACT 2
Love grows in Lancelot with a fierceness only to be found in one who has never loved before ('If Ever I Would Leave You'). He and Guenevere are convinced that Arthur cannot know of the bond between them, but the King is not the only one to see his way clearly to the truth. One day there comes to the court of Camelot an evil young man called Mordred. He is said to be the son of the witch, Queen Morgause, and of King Lot but he knows and Arthur knows that he is, in fact, the son of Arthur himself born of a night when Morgause bewitched the King into her bed. Arthur feels bound to

welcome his son to the Round Table and to attempt to make of him a knight, but Mordred has no intention of following the ways of virtue ('The Seven Deadly Virtues'). He is out to make trouble and to win for himself his father's crown and all the lands of England.

The cares and plans of his wise and reforming rule weigh heavily enough on Arthur without the extra worry caused by his family, and he longs sometimes to be rid of the cares of state ('What Do the Simple Folk Do?'). Mordred is eager to help him to that end and, to this purpose, he visits the invisible castle of his aunt, the fairy Morgan Le Fey, deep in the woods of Camelot. The sprite is lured to his side from her unseen life of debauchery and gluttony by the promise of chocolates, and she agrees to entrap Arthur long enough to keep him one whole night away from his castle (The Persuasion). Mordred's plan matures and, as he had foreseen, while the King is away, Lancelot is unable to resist the temptation to visit Guenevere in her room.

She is distraught. She wishes they had never spoken their love, but had rather just let it exist in their hearts, where it could harm only themselves ('I Loved You Once in Silence'). To his pleas to return with him to his home in France, she replies that she will never leave Arthur.

Mordred has other ideas. With a troop of soldiers at his back, he invades the Queen's rooms and exposes Guenevere and Lancelot as lovers. In the scuffle which follows, Lancelot escapes, but the Queen is taken and arraigned for treason. She is condemned to be burned ('Guenevere') but, before Arthur can bring himself to give the order to light the pyre, Lancelot invades the castle with an army. The Knights of the Round Table fall under the French attack and everywhere there is death and destruction as Arthur's dream of a civilised Camelot shatters under the kind of primitive brutality he thought he had replaced.

Lancelot and Guenevere escape to his bastion in France and the army of Camelot, pursuing them, prepares to join battle with the French outside Joyous Gard. Arthur comes secretly to see his wife and his friend, rejoicing in his heart that they have escaped safely. If they could, they would return to England to try to right the situation without resorting to the pagan rite of battle, but it is too late. Mordred has taken command of an army and is already plotting war against Arthur as, all around, the world falls back into its old animal ways. Camelot, the Round Table, was it all for nothing?

As Arthur goes to return to his own battle lines, he meets a young boy. He has come, he says, to join the Round Table; to be a Knight and fight for justice and right, as he has heard in the stories people tell. Arthur realises now that his effort was not for nothing: people will tell stories of Camelot and the Round Table for ever. It will continue in tale if not in reality and give hope and ideals to people who hear tell of what Arthur and Lancelot and their fellow knights did in that one brief, shining moment that was 'Camelot'. As the curtain falls, Arthur sends the lad scurrying back through the battle lines towards a safety where he may carry that shining tale.

HOW TO SUCCEED IN BUSINESS WITHOUT REALLY TRYING

a musical in two acts by Abe Burrows, Jack Weinstock and Willie Gilbert based on the book by Shepherd Mead. Music and lyrics by Frank Loesser. Produced at the 46th Street Theatre, New York, 14 October 1961 with Robert Morse (Finch), Rudy Vallée (Biggley), Bonnie Scott (Rosemary), Charles Nelson Reilly (Frump) and Virginia Martin (Hedy).

Produced at the Shaftesbury Theatre, London, 28 March 1963 with Warren Berlinger, Billy de Wolfe, Patricia Michael, David Knight and Eileen Gourlay.

Produced at the Théâtre de Paris, Paris, as *Comment Réussir Dans les Affairs Sans Vraiment Se Fatiguer* 1964 in an adaptation by Raymond Castans with Jacques Duby, André Luguet, Évelyne Dandry, Jean-Pierre Rambal and Arlette Didier.

A film version was produced by United Artists in 1967 with Morse, Vallée, Michele Lee, Anthony Teague and Maureen Arthur.

CHARACTERS

J Pierrepont Finch
Mr Gatch
Mr Jenkins
Mr Tackaberry
Mr Peterson
J B Biggley
Rosemary Pilkington
Mr Bratt
Smitty
Miss Jones, *Biggley's secretary*
Bud Frump, *Biggley's nephew (by marriage)*
Mr Twimble
Hedy la Rue
Miss Krumholz
Wally Womper
Mr Ovington
Toynbee, Scrubwomen, Policeman, etc.

ACT 1

High above ground level, on the outside of the World Wide Wicket Company building, a window cleaner is plying his trade. This particular window cleaner has much more than spotless panes on his mind. While he squeezes, shines and mops with one hand, his other hand holds a book entitled *How to Succeed in Business Without Really Trying* which he is devouring as if it were a bible. Ponty Finch wants to be going up in the world that is inside this building, not on a window-washing cradle outside so, following the book's instructions, he presents himself at the World Wide Wicket Company to ask for a job. He marches right in to the building and straight into a middle-aged gentleman whom he sends tumbling to the ground. He has made a good start, for the gentleman is J B Biggley, the president of the company.

Undeterred, Finch tells him that he has come for a job, only to be greeted with a roar; Mr Biggley doesn't know about jobs, he has a whole personnel department to look after that. So Finch heads off towards personnel. He has already won himself one admiring ally in his determined drive towards the first step on the great staircase to success. The pretty secretary, Rosemary Pilkington, has taken a fancy to him and she promises him that she will talk to her friend Smitty who is secretary to the personnel manager.

Before she can do so, Mr Bratt, the personnel manager, arrives clouded in negative vibes. Finch has only to mention carefully that he has been sent by Mr Biggley to see that cloud vaporise under the sun of Mr Bratt's regard and, by the time Smitty gets back, Finch has already been given a job in the mailroom and a cigar. Rosemary is delighted. He has made his first step towards success, and she has found someone of whom she can say that she'd be 'Happy to Keep His Dinner Warm' in a little house in New Rochelle as he works his way towards executive status.

Executive status is far away from the mailroom, but Finch starts as he means to go on: as a bright, polite, hard-working lad in an office where most people's day revolves around the 'Coffee Break'. The first thing to do when you work in the mail room is to get out of the mail room, but Finch quickly finds that there is an obstacle to this part of his progress. Bud Frump, his fellow worker, is the nephew of J B Biggley's wife and, like Finch, he too is eager for promotion. He is so eager for promotion that whenever he feels distressed or ignored he rings up his mother, his mother rings her sister, and her sister gets on to Mr Biggley.

Frump has his eye and his finger on the eager Finch, but our hero is undeterred. He works with an angelic devotion to the internal mail system of the building, he is charming to Mr Biggley's ageing secretary who introduces him to the head of Plans and Systems, and, when it gets around that the job of head of the mailroom is to become vacant, Bud Frump has to get on the phone to his mother very quickly to forestall the obvious challenge of the boy wonder. In this situation, however, the influence of Mr Biggley and his relatives is nil, for it is tradition that the retiring head of the mailroom should pick his own successor.

Mr Twimble has been twenty-five years in the mailroom, living his life in 'The Company Way' without question or quibble, and his devotion to his work leads him to pick as his heir the best man in the department: Finch. To general surprise, Finch declines modestly. The more experienced Frump must have the job. Such self-abnegation does not go unnoticed, particularly by Mr Biggley who is very relieved not to have to listen to a tirade on family loyalty from his wife, and before long Finch finds himself given a junior executive post in Plans and Systems.

He is out of the mailroom and on his way up. His single-minded pursuit of success means that he has little time or mind for anything else and the persistent attempts of Rosemary Pilkington to get him to notice her, date her, and/or help her on to the second step of her particular preoccupation, go unnoticed.

Mr Biggley may be a regular family man but he has all the usual urges of the middle-aged executive and at the moment those urges are turned in the direction of a cigarette girl from the Copacabana. The luscious Miss Hedy la Rue has been given a crash course in office skills and she is now the latest recruit to the secretarial staff at World Wide Wickets with a large label of do-not-touch on her ('A Secretary Is Not a Toy'). The boss is allowed his little weaknesses. Mr Biggley's other weakness is the traditional middle-aged devotion to his old alma mater: he is a passionate Groundhog from Old Ivy, where he was once voted the least likely to succeed.

On Friday night the personnel of World Wide Wickets dribble out of their offices ('It's Been a Long Day'). Mr Biggley is not planning on going home. He has a rendezvous with the pneumatic Hedy, but he gets nervous when Frump makes a point of hanging around uttering hints which reek of black-mail. That boy will have to be watched. It is much more agreeable watching young Finch. Why, the next morning when Biggley comes by the office to pick up his golf clubs prior to a match with Mr Womper, the chairman, there is the devoted young fellow asleep across his desk, his adding machine still in his hand. And what is this? He is humming the Groundhogs' song! Surely he can't be an Old Ivy boy ('Grand Old Ivy')? And he knits. No one, just no one except Mr Biggley's incorruptible Miss Jones, knows that the head of World Wide Wickets finds his relaxation in knitting, and here is this young, kindred spirit clacketing out a bird-cage cover. What a fellow. Surely he must have ambitions?

Finch owns shyly that one day he would like to be Head of Advertising. That takes Biggley aback. Advertising is the pits. No one wants Advertising. Why, no Head of Advertising has ever lasted more than a month. In the meanwhile this hard-working lad must have his own office. And a secretary. And lo, the secretary allotted to Mr Biggley's new protégé is Hedy. Fortunately, Finch's faithful manual has advice on this point. When a sec-retary is too attractive it may be that Someone Important in the Company has a special interest in her. *Sequitur*: test her skills. The worse she is at short-hand and typing, the more important her protector is. Hedy is hopeless.

Finch is wide open to being compromised and shot right down to the bottom again, but our lad has a way to turn this potential peril to his own advantage. Hedy is despatched with a personal message to the private office of his superior, Mr Gatch, and, as Finch had foreseen, the lecherous Gatch is unable to resist taking a handful of her. The next day, Gatch has gone from the office and Finch has been promoted to Head of Plans and Systems.

Benjamin Burton Ovington is the latest to have been appointed to the post of Head of Advertising and, to mark the occasion, there is to be a reception for him in the World Wide Wicket building. Finch, in his new position, is invited to attend and so, too, is Rosemary who has been allotted to the new executive as his secretary. She buys an expensive new dress in which to stun Finch ('Paris Original') but she is shattered when Smitty, Miss Jones, Miss Krumholz and, worst of all, Hedy turn up in identical models. Hedy fills hers out the best, but she is not intended to fill it for long for Mr Biggley is planning an evening in. Hedy, however, doesn't want to go to bed yet. She is enjoying the party. She just wants a quick shower in Mr Biggley's office shower and she'll be ready to dance on into the night.

The villainous Frump latches on to this bit of information and sees how he can use it to kill a whole flock of birds with one stone. As soon as Hedy is safely under the water he tells Finch that Biggley wants to see him in his office and the young man arrives there to find an undressed and oncoming Hedy who threatens to tell Biggley that Finch made advances to her if she doesn't get her way with him.

He kisses her and manhood enters him. Now, at last, he knows what he wants from 'Rosemary' and, when she comes to find him, he proposes and she accepts. When Biggley, alerted by Frump, storms in he finds Finch making a meal not of Hedy but of Rosemary. Frump has failed again. But Finch's own business of the evening is still to be done. At the psychological moment he exposes Ovington as a Northern State man. He is a Chipmunk, a mortal rival of the Groundhogs! Needless to say, this sin earns him immediate dismissal and Finch finds himself promoted to fill the gap created by this sudden departure—he is Vice President in charge of Advertising (Finale).

ACT 2

The new Vice President is allotted Rosemary as his secretary, but it proves to be a very unsatisfactory state of affairs for her, as he continues to treat her as a typing machine and not as a fiancée. In the end she makes up her mind to resign, but the other girls in the office will not hear of it. One of them has finally succeeded in realising every secretary's dream by getting an offer of marriage from her boss: never let it be said that she let him get away. ('Cinderella, Darling'). Shamed out of her resignation, Rosemary sticks to her post and bides her time until that day when she may finally get to keep her man's dinner warm.

Biggley has problems too. Hedy is disenchanted with life in an office and she wants to return to the bright lights of the Copacabana. He has to pour out plenty of 'Love From a Heart of Gold' to persuade her to stay.

Frump, meanwhile, has not been idle. Finch has been ordered to come up with a bright idea for a campaign and Frump has an idea for him: a television Treasure Hunt with a cash bond prize. He does not tell Finch that he has already put this idea up to his uncle himself and been contemptuously rejected but what he does not count on is that the confident Finch ('I Believe in You') will dress up his idea in a different guise and make something out of it. He allots Hedy a leading role in the presentation as the World Wide Treasure Girl, smilingly giving out television clues as to the hiding place of bundles of World Wide Wickets shares, and the project is given the go ahead. Biggley and Finch decide secretly that the prizes shall be hidden in the very buildings of World Wide's ten major American branches.

The big day comes and the all-singing, all-dancing World Wide Wicket show is beamed live across the country ('The Yo-Ho-Ho'). Hedy appears to give out the first clue and finds herself confronted with a man bearing a bible. It is Finch's little last minute touch, a bit of religion to mix with the sex. Hedy must swear on the bible that she doesn't know the hiding place of the treasure. Of course she doesn't know. All the office knows that only

Finch and Biggley are in on the secret. But Hedy isn't anxious to commit perjury and somehow she does know, and soon the nation knows that she knows. As the embarrassed Biggley collapses in a purple heap, the whole programme falls in ruins.

Finch has come to his worst crisis yet and the only advice his book gives him is to go back to page one and start all over again. The chairman, Mr Womper, is coming to the office that very day and heads are going to roll or, more specifically, by popular agreement, Finch's head is going to roll. Only Rosemary stands by him ('I Believe in You'): executive or window cleaner she loves him and will marry him.

Summoned to face the terrible Mr Womper, Finch confesses sole culpability for the disaster of the television programme. He will take his dismissal like a man and go back to window cleaning. But what is this? Mr Womper started life as a window cleaner as well, a much better basis for life than all this college nonsense. But how, he demands, could a fellow window cleaner have pulled a bone-headed trick like the Treasure Hunt? Finch delicately admits that it was actually not his own idea, but that of the President's nephew and Womper's rage is turned on Biggley. He is a practising nepotist!

Biggley protests that the details were Finch's, but he gets into a bottomless hole when Womper demands to know who chose the idiotic Hedy as a front girl. When all seems darkest, Finch steps forward to save his boss from the chop, counselling humanity and magnanimity ('Brotherhood of Man') for all. All, that is, except Frump. As the whining Frump is frogmarched away, the rest of the executives of World Wide can breathe again. They have only to face a little reshuffle.

Mr Biggley keeps his job, but somehow Mr Womper has ended up marrying Hedy and he is heading off on a long, long ocean-going honeymoon. Naturally, his new responsibilities mean that he has no further time to fulfil his position as chairman of World Wide Wickets and so he has retired. There is no need to ask who will be taking his place. And what does Mrs Finch think? Rosemary just loves her man whether he's in the mailroom, or chairman or even President of the United States. Biggley instructs Miss Jones to send a wire to the White House telling the President to look out for his job, as life prepares to go on in 'The Company Way'.

LITTLE ME

a musical comedy in two acts by Neil Simon based on the book by Patrick Dennis. Lyrics by Carolyn Leigh. Music by Cy Coleman. Produced at the Lunt-Fontanne Theatre, New York, 17 November 1962 with Syd Caesar (Noble, etc.), Virginia Martin (Belle), Nancy Andrews (Old Belle) and Swen Swenson (George). Produced at the Eugene O'Neill Theatre in a revised version 21 January 1982 with James Coco, Victor Garber, Mary Gordon Murray and Jessica James.

Produced at the Cambridge Theatre, London, 18 November 1964 with Bruce

Forsyth, Eileen Gourlay, Avril Angers and Swen Swenson. Produced at the Prince of
Wales Theatre in a revised version 30 May 1984 with Russ Abbott, Sheila White,
Lynda Baron and Tudor Davies.

CHARACTERS

Noble Eggleston/Mr Pinchley/Val du Val/Fred Poitrine/Otto Schnitzler/
  Prince Cherny
Miss Poitrine
Belle
George Musgrove
Pinchley jr/Defence Lawyer/German Soldier/General Schreiber/Assistant
  Director/Yulnick
Momma
Mrs Eggleston
Patrick Dennis
Bernie Buchsbaum
Bennie Buchsbaum
Ramona VanderVeld
Colette, Ship's Captain, etc.

ACT 1

Our story begins in the present, in the opulent Southampton, Long Island
home of Miss Belle Poitrine where the lady in question (the 'Miss' is purely
honorary and the 'lady' wholly misleading) is greeting the young man who is
to ghost her autobiography. In it, she promises, she will tell 'The Truth'.
From the very beginning.

The very beginning was in Venezuela, Illinois at the dawn of the new
century. There Belle Schlumpfert lived with her professional Momma in a
shack alongside the railway track in Drifters' Row. She was just sixteen and
as blossoming a little bud as ever graced a hovel, a fact which hadn't escaped
the notice of the shantytown boys like George Musgrove who showed a great
fascination with Belle's most blossoming features. But Belle had aspirations.
She looked across the railway tracks to where the clean, decent, rich folks
lived up on the Bluff, and she dreamed.

One day, by accident, some teenagers from the Bluff strayed through
Belle's back yard on their way to a picnic. The smell of poverty frightened
most of them away but one, an exceptionally perfect youth called Noble
Eggleston, was moved by fate to present the contents of his picnic pail to a
poor person. Fate also decreed that the door he should choose was that of
the Schlumpfert house, but probably had nothing to do with the fact that
Belle Schlumpfert happened to be throwing out the garbage at the moment
he stuck his head in. Except that, in touching Noble's shoulder to brush
away the day-before-yesterday's slops, Belle started something.

It was electric and it played a tune ('I Love You'). Each time they touched
each other there was this shock and this tune. Then Noble, deeply moved by
this and by Belle's most blossoming features, made a momentous step. He
invited Belle to his sixteenth birthday party at the big house up on the Bluff.

773

At last little Miss Schlumpfert was on her way to 'The Other Side of the Tracks'.

The big house on the Bluff was very rich and overpowering, the guests at Noble's party were very rich ('Rich Kids Rag') and his mother was very overpowering. She was severely displeased at Belle's presence and, in spite of the fact that Belle and Noble managed to turn their tune into a full-scale duet ('I Love You'), she treated Noble to a lecture on the facts of rich life and ordered Belle from the house. She could never be his, for she had neither wealth nor culture nor social position. But Belle Schlumpfert had determination as well as a blossoming bosom, and she vowed that she would go out into the big wide world on 'The Other Side of the Tracks' and she would get herself those three *sine qua non*s of modern life and, when she had them, she would come back and show Mrs Eggleston.

It wasn't long before Belle found herself a way out of Drifters' Row. The folks down there were having a mite of trouble keeping up with their rental payments to their unsympathetic landlord, the immobile eighty-eight year-old Mr Amos Pinchley, so they went to his offices to grovel in front of him to and ask for a little more time to pay. But Pinchley just played with them and then told them gleefully that they would all be evicted. Then, from the crowd of dejected poor people, one stood out in front and told Amos Pinchley plainly what she thought of him.

It was Belle. She didn't shrink from the truth. She just upped and told the nasty old man what no one had ever dared to tell him: he was a hated man. Pinchley didn't like that. He wanted to be loved. So Belle started right in to try and find that little bit of good 'Deep Down Inside' him and, my goodness, she found it. Pinchley was soon a changed man and, in gratitude to Belle, he gave her her heart's desire: a little apartment in Peoria where she could study the important things in life like diction, manners and French cooking.

Mr Pinchley came from time to time to check up on his protégée and, such was the change in him, that he was soon able to get out of his wheel-chair and propose marriage. Belle was there already. Such a marriage would give her wealth, culture and social position all in one throw and, given the seventy years difference in their age, she would not have long to wait for Noble. Belle threw her arms around her fiancé and something went bang. Amos Pinchley kept a gun in his inside pocket and Belle's generous proportions had been just too much for its trigger. The bullet went right through his heart.

Wealth, culture and social position were just as far away as ever. It meant starting all over again. Belle's performance at her trial, where Noble's all-American character reference won her a spotless acquittal, attracted the attention of the Buchsbaum Brothers, vaudeville bookers, and with a little persuasion ('Be a Performer') and a lot of publicity, Belle headed out to get herself some culture on the stage ('Oh! Dem Doggone Dimples'). She was quite a hit, until some juicier murderess came along and pushed her off the bill, leaving her to take up a job as a camera girl in the Skylight Roof night club.

Now who should turn up one night at the Skylight Roof but Noble

Eggleston, fresh from his double first in law and medicine at Yale and Harvard, and about to announce his engagement to Ramona VanderVeld, the girl of his mother's dreams. Belle was distraught. He had promised he'd wait for her. But Noble, try as he might, could not stand up against his mother. While the evening's entertainer, the famous Frenchman, Val du Val, was going through his celebrated love song, 'Boom Boom', Belle climbed on to the window ledge thousands of floors above the ground, and prepared to end it all.

Val du Val could not endure the thought of such a well-endowed girl being wasted on the pavements of Chicago and, with some well-chosen words in fractured English, he persuaded her to climb down. Before their acquaintance could ripen, however, World War One was declared and everyone decided to go home. Left alone in the nightclub, Belle encountered its owner. She wasn't the only one to have made it out of Drifters' Row. The club belonged to George Musgrove and he still had the hots for her ('I've Got Your Number').

Six months later, a heavily pregnant Belle was doing her bit for the war effort at a doughboy party when all the boys got the call to the front. Someone came up with the bright idea that they should all get married before they went and Belle got paired up with the sweet, dumb and very short-sighted Fred Poitrine. It was destiny: someone up there intended all along that she should end up as Belle Poitrine. So Fred got his first kiss ('Real Live Girl') and headed off to the war where, having done his bit by giving Belle his name, he soon succumbed to a wound contracted by catching his little finger in a typewriter key.

Meanwhile, Colonel Noble Eggleston, nine times VC, was fighting glorious battles with the entire German airforce until, one fateful day, he was shot down behind the enemy lines. At this stage Belle decided that, baby or no baby, it was time to get over there to Europe and do something about finding the man of her heart. So, equipped with a team of like-minded ladies, off she set to bring much-needed song, dance, letter-writing and advanced medical assistance to the men at the front ('Real Live Girl').

One day, there was brought to the American camp a poor, wandering French officer suffering from amnesia. Who should it be but that great French entertainer, Val du Val and, from a letter in his possession, it appeared that he had suffered a psychological shock at being abandoned by his girlfriend, leading to a total loss of memory. Belle, anxious to return a favour to the man who had saved her life, worked hard with the assistance of the enemy cannons to recall the famous boom-boom song to him and, *voilà!*, suddenly Val was restored to normal. It was fate. Belle must be his! She must never leave him.

No sooner had Val rushed off to find his helmet, his gun and his orchestrations than Noble, who had escaped from captivity by the basic use of a bribe, turned up. Since it was war time, the old qualifications of wealth, culture and social position were no longer necessary prerequisites to him and Belle getting together: they could be married that very night. Once more Belle was on the brink of realising her dreams but alas! the moment Val du

Val heard the news he suffered a relapse. A second jilting flung him deeper than ever into amnesia and Belle, unable to bear the responsibility of condemning the man who had saved her life to such a fate, tearfully waved farewell to Noble. It was time to become Madame du Val.

ACT 2

Miss Poitrine takes up her story where she left off to allow for the interval. Married for five years and as happy as two people could be who were each in love with someone else, Val and Belle took a trip on that magnificent ocean liner, the *SS Gigantic*, and who should our heroine meet travelling on that very same crossing but Noble Eggleston, now a successful surgeon and judge and married to Ramona. It seemed a lifetime since their childhood vows to each other but, when they touched, the old electricity and that old tune were still there. Unfortunately, so was an iceberg. As Noble organised the entire evacuation of the sinking ship and taught everyone who couldn't swim to do so in one easy lesson, he and Belle carolled out their love song to the waves ('I Love You').

Every single passenger was saved with the exception of Val du Val who, having overheard Belle and Noble's reunion, had lost his memory again and forgotten how to swim. Belle sued the steamship company for the loss of her husband and her luggage and won two million dollars. She had achieved wealth and she was single again. The only difficulty was, Noble wasn't. Not until Ramona's father went bankrupt and Mrs Eggleston marched her daughter-in-law straight down town for an annulment. By then Belle was already on the road to culture. Her old friends the Buchsbaum Brothers had gone into films and anyone with two million dollars was welcome to star in one, nay all, of their movies ('Poor Little Hollywood Star').

One by one the world's greatest titles became grist to Belle's mill in her relentless pursuit of culture until she reached the ultimate in *Moses Takes a Wife* under the direction of the once-great Otto Schnitzler. Unfortunately, Schnitzler got himself killed demonstrating a trick dagger which turned out not to be a trick dagger, and Belle decided to finish directing the picture herself. And what do you know, she won an award: the Golden Turkey. That was culture. Since oil had just been discovered on her back lot she was now also one of the richest women in America, but if she were going to win Noble there was still social position to go ('Little Me').

The best place to find that all-important ingredient was undoubtedly Europe so Belle packed her luggage-wagons and set off for Monte Carlo to find herself a piece of class as a husband. One night, at the Casino, Prince Cherny of Rosenzweig came to risk the whole of his bankrupt country's exchequer on one throw and gallantly asked Belle to choose the number on which his fate and the fate of his country rested. Belle chose wrong and the Prince collapsed under the weight of a terrible heart attack.

Filled with remorse, Belle locked herself away with the ailing monarch in his bedroom and worked on him day and night for two whole exhausting weeks until she could do no more and the people of Rosenzweig were summoned to bid a last farewell to their Prince ('Goodbye'). When all was nearly over, the last ounce of Belle's bounteousness was poured out: she would pay the national debt of Rosenzweig for the poor dead Prince. She'd what? Suddenly the eye of the Prince quickened and, to the joy of his people, he began to make a remarkable recovery.

Because of Belle, Rosenzweig was saved and her monarch, to express his gratitude, was pleased to dub her the Countess Zoftic. Well, that was enough social position even for Mrs Eggleston. Belle had only one regret. Since it had looked so certain the Prince would die and, since she had grown rather fond of him over their two weeks together, to spare him any final pain, she had poisoned his wine. So the people of Rosenzweig had to sing their 'Goodbye' all over again.

Back at home, Noble had been elected Governor and now, with every obstacle overcome, he was free to ask Belle to be his wife. As they celebrated their future together Belle persuaded Noble to break the habit of a lifetime and take just one sip of alcohol. It was the end. The wedding never took place. Three weeks later Noble was a hopeless drunk, impeached and sluiced out of office and out of Belle's life.

Alone, Belle settled into a vast mansion on the Bluff and there she waited, year after year, for Noble to return to her. Infinitesimally, she grew older ('Here's to Us') and still he did not come. There was only George Musgrove who had been faithfully and hopefully following her round the world every step since that night at the Skylight Roof. The Egglestons were a fallen and forgotten family, Noble a drunken bum sailing as a sawbones on a tramp steamer, and his once proud mother reduced to selling apples in the street. Ah, fate.

Then, one day, Belle's little daughter—now grown into a teenager every bit as shapely as her mother had been—came home with a friend: Noble Eggleston jr, the spitting image of his father. It was clear that they liked each other, but Belle needed a test. Under Mother's supervision, the two kids touched and, sure enough, the old tune blared forth. Everything would be all right for them, at least. As for Belle, well, she finally gave in and married George Musgrove. When they touch there isn't any music but you can't have everything. Young Belle married Noble jr and lived happily ever after and there ends the tale of Belle Poitrine.

Well, not quite. For although the dictation is done, there is another chapter to come in the chronicle of the little lass from Venezuela, Illinois. Mrs Eggleston has nurtured revenge in her bosom since the day the girl from the other side of the tracks brought her and her son to ruin and now she has come, with pistol in hand, to wreak her vengeance. She aims and she fires, just as a sailor walks through the door. It is Noble, dried out, reformed and once again the hero we knew him as for so long. He falls to the ground clutching his stomach—all those years of effort for nothing.

But wait! There is no blood. If he isn't shot, who is? It is George, of course. If he'd been paying attention to the rest of Belle's story he might have known something like this would happen. At last the tale of Belle Poitrine can have the ending it was always meant to have as, accompanied by the soaring strains of their song ('I Love You'), Belle and Noble walk off together into the sunset.

The revised version altered the framework of the show and omitted the songs 'The Truth', 'Be a Performer', 'Dimples' and 'Poor Little Hollywood Star' but incorporated two new numbers 'Don't Ask a Lady What a Lady Used to Do' and 'I Wanna Be Yours'. The subsequent London version returned partially to the original layout and kept 'Dimples' while adding 'Don't Ask a Lady'.

A FUNNY THING HAPPENED ON THE WAY TO THE FORUM

a musical comedy in two acts by Burt Shevelove and Larry Gelbart based on the works of Plautus. Music and lyrics by Stephen Sondheim. Produced at the Alvin Theatre, New York, 8 May 1962 with Zero Mostel (Pseudolus), Jack Gilford (Hysterium), David Burns (Senex), John Carradine (Lycus), Preshy Marker (Philia) and Brian Davies (Hero). Produced at the Lunt-Fontane Theatre 30 March 1972 with Phil Silvers, Larry Blyden, Jack Collins, Carl Ballantine, Pamela Hall and John Hansen.

Produced at the Strand Theatre, London, 3 October 1963 with Frankie Howerd, Kenneth Connor, 'Monsewer' Eddie Gray, Jon Pertwee, Isla Blair and John Rye. Produced at the Piccadilly Theatre 14 November 1986 with Howerd, Ronnie Stevens, Patrick Cargill, Fred Evans, Lydia Watson and Graham Smith.

A film version was produced by United Artists in 1966 with Mostel, Gilford, Michael Hordern, Phil Silvers, Annette André and Michael Crawford.

CHARACTERS

Senex, *an old man*
Domina, *his wife*
Hero, *his son*
Hysterium, *slave to Senex and Domina*
Pseudolus, *slave to Hero*
Erronius, *an old man*
Miles Gloriosus, *a warrior*
Marcus Lycus, *a buyer and seller of courtesans*
Philia, *a virgin*
Tintinabula, Panacea, The Geminae, Vibrata, Gymnasia, *courtesans*
The Proteans

ACT 1

It is two hundred years before the beginning of the Christian era and it is springtime. The evening's entertainment is introduced in the fashion of the period by the prologue, a fellow in a toga who introduces the members of the company and informs the audience that, whereas it may be melodrama and tragedy on the other evenings of the week, it is 'Comedy Tonight'.

The setting of the entertainment is made up of three buildings: to the one side is the *domus* of the elderly Erronius whose children were stolen in infancy by pirates and who has spent a lot of time abroad since then, trying to find them; to the other side is the mansion of Lycus, a vendor of female slaves; and in the middle is the home of Senex, his well-named wife Domina, their exuberantly innocent son, Hero, and their servants one of whom, the curiously named Pseudolus, the prologue lauds at length. Pseudolus, it eventuates, is his own role. There are lots of other roles, but these will be played by a useful trio of proteans, if they can make the costume changes in time.

The action of the play begins with Senex and Domina off to visit her mother in the country with a little gift, a marble bust of Domina. The mistress of the house charges her devotedly grovelling slave, Hysterium, to watch over her pubescent son, his well-being and his morals, while she is away, little realising that Hero, with all the enthusiasm of his teenage years, is already prey to passion ('Love, I Hear').

He confides to the rascally Pseudolus that he has fallen for a beautiful girl in the next door house. The next door house! Horror! She is a courtesan! What would his parents say? Hero does not care, he would give everything he has to possess this girl but, since he owns only a collection of sea shells, twenty minae and Pseudolus, it is not a great bargain. Not to anyone except Pseudolus. He would like to own himself, for he has a manic wish to be 'Free' and he will devote himself wholeheartedly to bringing the young people together in order to claim this reward.

The dealer Lycus emerges from his house and pulls up short at the sound of a jingling purse. It is Hero's purse and Pseudolus is jingling it. Pretending he has come into a legacy, Pseudolus demands to see Lycus' stock and, one by one, the choice exhibits of the house are paraded before the slave and the boy ('The House of Marcus Lycus') but, glorious as they are, none is the beloved of Hero's heart. Lycus denies that he has any other merchandise but, when all seems despair, Hero spots his girl at a high window. That one? Oh, she is a virgin from Crete and already sold to the great captain, Miles Gloriosus, who specified a virgin and was willing to pay 500 minae for the privilege.

Pseudolus sympathises ostentatiously with Lycus. What a shame about the awful plague in Crete, he does hope the captain's girl will last till his arrival. Lycus is in a panic at the talk of plague: why, the girl could infect the entire stock. Pseudolus gallantly offers to take her in at his house (it's all right, he has already had the plague) and look after her until she is called for, and Lycus is only too happy to get pretty little Philia out of his house as quickly as possible. And so Hero achieves his heart's desire and a meeting with the girl he adores. It is quickly obvious that the girl is not very bright. In fact, as she admits readily, Philia has only one talent: she is 'Lovely'. As far as Hero is concerned, that will do.

When Hysterium sees his mistress's son with a courtesan he is fit to dissolve in jitters, and he is only stopped from heading Domina-wards by a timely bit of blackmail by the resourceful Pseudolus who threatens to tell the materfamilias about her pet slave's private collection of erotic pottery. Pseudolus has not been idle. He has used the time that the young lovers have spent on the last number to fix up an escape route for them. There is a boat waiting around the corner on the Tiber. Off they can sail and he will be free. What a 'Pretty Little Picture'. There is only one snag: the virgin has a simple morality. The captain has paid for her and so she must wait for the captain.

Given this unexpected hitch, Pseudolus needs a bit more plot. He hurries the young people into the house and filches Hysterium's famous book of potions. He will mix a sleeping draught, knock the virgin out with it, tell Lycus she has died of plague and send the unprotesting body off with Hero on the boat. Unfortunately, he lacks one vital ingredient for the potion—a cup of mare's sweat—so off he trots to find it.

No sooner has he gone than Senex returns. He has dropped the beastly bust and chipped its nose, so he has had to come back to have the thing repointed. When he kicks his own door, to his delighted surprise, a lovely maiden emerges and cries 'Take me!'. Philia has got muddled again, and thinks the paterfamilias is her captain. Senex does not ask questions but, before he can move into action, Pseudolus returns with his sweat and Philia has to be explained. She is, he ventures, the new maid. Senex is all approval. He likes maids. In fact, 'Everybody Ought to Have a Maid' and he will personally instruct this one in the niceties of housework. Unfortunately his son is in the house, so he will have to interview the new maid in the house of his absent friend Erronius. Pseudolus is ordered to bring her across.

This unexpected turn of events requires a little more imaginative action from Pseudolus. To forestall the spoiling of Lycus' virgin merchandise before his young master can take possession, Pseudolus sacrifices his hard-won mare's sweat. He drenches Senex's gown with the evil-smelling liquid and the interview has to be postponed long enough to allow the old man time to have a bath. He marches into Erronius' house to prepare himself and the eternally blackmailed Hysterium is detailed to keep him inside.

In spite of his best efforts to convince himself that 'I'm Calm', the chief slave is in all kinds of a state and, just when he's feeling quite limp with nerves, he finds that he has a situation to deal with. For who should appear on the scene but Erronius himself, back at last from his unsuccessful search for his children (one boy and one girl, stolen in infancy by pirates, and recognisable by a ring showing a gaggle of geese).

Needless to say he is anxious to return to his home and Hysterium has, at all costs, to stop him. Borrowing a little of Pseudolus' inventiveness, Hysterium takes advantage of Erronius' feeble faculties and convinces him that his house is haunted and Pseudolus, coming to the support of the deception with an opportune impersonation of a soothsayer, persuades the old man that he must walk seven times around the seven hills of Rome in exorcism before entering his house. That should give enough time for whatever is going to happen to happen.

When Erronius has gone on his way, Senex emerges and encounters Hero. Then both of them see Philia and see each other seeing Philia, and are puzzled at each other's reaction at seeing each other seeing Philia, and together they indulge in a duet of unworthy thoughts ('Impossible'). Under the orders of Pseudolus, Hysterium has been preparing the sleeping potion and the plan is nearing its fruition when a flight of trumpets rings out. The Miles Gloriosus is approaching.

Lycus is in a paroxysm of panic. What will happen? Pseudolus once again comes up with an answer. He will impersonate Lycus for the occasion and save the day. He decorates the stage with the most scrumptious of courtesans and, when the great man arrives to demand 'Bring Me My Bride', he attempts to interest him in alternative arrangements. But the Miles is not in the mood for second choices. He wants only his bought and paid for bride. Pseudolus is in a mighty fix which only one word can cure. That word is Intermission.

ACT 2

The intermission can hold things up but it can't change them. When the second act begins, it begins with a brief recap from Pseudolus of the position where we left off, and it carries on with the wily slave promising to deliver the Miles Gloriosus his bride as soon as possible. Thus, what seemed like an inevitable evisceration is, at least, postponed. The captain is persuaded to go into Senex's house (which he thinks is Lycus' house) to rest, be entertained, and wait. Senex, in his turn, is bathed and ready in the next door house and awaits his maid. But Pseudolus and his ever-changing plan meet yet another problem. When he proffers the goblet of wine laced with sleeping potion to Philia it turns out that the wretched maiden is teetotal, and nothing he can do can persuade her to partake of the mixture. Since Pseudolus needs a body to carry out the newest version of his plan, he sets off to find one elsewhere.

Now, to complicate matters further, Domina returns, certain that 'That Dirty Old Man of Mine' is up to something lewd. Hysterium is shattered. She is sure to discover at least one of the many deceptions that are in progress and any one of them will be lethal insofar as he and his position of trust are concerned. In the meanwhile Philia, still dutifully awaiting her captain (and still thinking Senex is he), is singing lovingly but irritatingly to Hero about how every bit of lovemaking with her enforced husband will be an expression of her affection for Hero ('That'll Show Him').

Finally, Pseudolus has thought of a way in which to put his plan into action. He needs a dead girl to show the captain his virgin bride perished of plague, and, since he couldn't get a real corpse from the bodysnatcher, he is using a decidedly nervous Hysterium dressed up to look dead and 'Lovely'. Pseudolus brings on the Miles Gloriosus and shows him his defunct and heavily veiled bride and the soldier is heroically distraught. He must depart unwed and with a broken heart, but before he does so he will give the girl a proper funeral (Funeral Sequence). Light the pyre! The what?! Pseudolus has to deliver a healthy backhander to the corpse which shows every sign of reviving inopportunely. He tries using the story of the Cretan plague to scare everyone away, but the captain has just come from Crete and knows there is no plague and... wait a minute, that corpse is alive!

Soon there are people revengefully running in all directions. Confusingly, there seem to be three Philias—the real one, Hysterium in disguise, and Domina who has dressed up as a virgin to spy on her husband. Old Erronius, on the third time round the seven hills of Rome, also gets mixed up in the mêlée and pounces gleefully on Hysterium, believing him to be his daughter. The Miles Gloriosus and Senex claim Hysterium as their bride and maid respectively and controversy reigns until the petrified slave tears off his blonde curls and brings everything to a confused halt.

With everyone together on the stage, the network of fibs fabricated by Pseudolus gradually starts to get dismantled. Since he is clearly to blame, he has nothing left to do but to die by his own hand. Very well, he will take hemlock. Pseudolus grandly orders Hysterium to fetch the potion prepared earlier to make Philia feign death, but Hysterium gives him instead a passion potion brewed to fit Senex for entertaining the maid. The results are alarming but fortunately short-lived.

Finally Philia is brought forward to be delivered to her captain. At last the merchandise is delivered, but only the Miles Gloriosus is really happy about it. Everyone else looks pretty miserable and poor old Erronius is still there, mumbling on about his children and the ring with the gaggle of geese. The Miles Gloriosus double takes: geese? Why, he has a ring like that. He is the long lost son! Then Philia timidly enquires how many geese are in a gaggle. She, too, has a ring like that. She is the long-lost daughter! So she and the captain are... how very fortunate for Hero. So the story ends, with everything that was lost having been found—including Pseudolus' promised freedom—and a reaffirmation that it has indeed been 'Comedy Tonight'.

The 1972 New York revival introduced the song 'Farewell' and reinstated The Echo Song which had been cut in try-out during the original production. This latter was retained for the 1986 London revival.

FUNNY GIRL

a musical in two acts by Isobel Lennart based on incidents in the life of Fanny Brice. Lyrics by Bob Merrill. Music by Jule Styne. Produced at the Winter Garden, New York, 26 March 1964 with Barbra Streisand (Fanny Brice) and Sydney Chaplin (Nick Arnstein).

Produced at the Prince of Wales Theatre, London, 13 April 1966 with Miss Streisand and Michael Craig.

A film version was produced by Columbia in 1968 with Miss Streisand and Omar Sharif.

782

CHARACTERS

Fanny Brice
Mrs Brice, *her mother*
Mrs Strakosh
Tom Keeney
Eddie Ryan
Nick Arnstein
Florenz Ziegfeld jr
Emma
Jenny
Mrs Meeker, Mrs O'Malley, Heckie, John, Bubbles, Polly, Maude, Mimsey, Ziegfeld tenor, Jody, Adolf, Mrs Nadler, Paul, Cathy, Vera, Ben, Mr Renaldi, etc.

ACT 1

Backstage at a Broadway theatre the comedienne Fanny Brice, star of the Ziegfeld Follies, is in her dressing room preparing for the evening's performance. It is just another performance, but tonight she is nervous because she is going to see Nick Arnstein again. As she sits in front of her mirror, she goes back in time to the days before she became a success on Broadway—to the year when she was nineteen years old. There is her mother with Mrs Strakosh and her other cronies sitting around the inevitable card table playing three-cent poker, and here comes Fanny—plain, funny Fanny—off to an audition for Tom Keeney's Music Hall. Mrs Strakosh shakes her head. Even if Fanny has some talent, what's the use 'If a Girl Isn't Pretty'?

Down at Keeney's, the dance director, Eddie Ryan, echoes the same sentiment and Fanny quickly gets the boot from the chorus audition. Even the cab driver who brought her there, and a couple of workmen at the stage door, spin the same sorry line, but Fanny is irrepressible. She corners Eddie as he leaves the theatre and makes her point—she may stand out in a chorus line, but that's because she's too good. So make her a soloist ('I'm the Greatest Star'). Eddie is convinced enough to stay up all night teaching her a solo routine from the show and the next thing we see is Fanny strutting her stuff in front of the chorus at Keeney's Music Hall in a trial run with 'Cornet Man'.

After the show, a madly attractive stranger turns up backstage. He is Nick Arnstein, playboy and gambler, and he has come to settle a debt with Keeney. He runs into Fanny, just as she's down on her hands and knees making a dog out of herself, and she's knocked out, especially when it turns out he has seen the show and reckons that she's headed for stardom. When Keeney comes round to say he'll take her on permanently at $40 a week, Arnstein, on behalf of a mythical competitor, offers more and, before she knows it, she's booked at a salary of $110. What would have happened if Keeney had dropped out of the auction? She would have lost her job, of course. Fanny is aghast. Nick has played with her life for the first but not the last time, but right now, as she looks delightedly after him, she supposes that she won't ever see him again.

Months pass, and Fanny makes herself a great reputation at Keeney's and then, one day, she receives a telegram summoning her to Broadway's New York Theatre to meet the great Florenz Ziegfeld. As her mother and Eddie get her ready to go to the all important meeting, they congratulate themselves on her success ('Who Taught Her Everything She Knows'). They always knew she would do it.

Fanny Brice becomes part of the Ziegfeld Follies; a slightly uncomfortable part to start with for, while she gets to do her 'Cornet Man' song, Mr Ziegfeld also casts her in a production number glorifying the American bride in which she is supposed to be pretty. Now forthright Fanny knows her qualities and, like her mother and Mrs Strakosh always said, pretty isn't one of them, but Mr Ziegfeld is master in his theatre and pretty she's going to be. As the Ziegfeld tenor gives forth with 'His Love Makes Me Beautiful', a parade of lovely girls illustrate the number, but when Fanny comes on for her portion of the song, to a barrage a laughter, she has padded out her wedding gown to make it look as if she is a well-gone shot-gun bride. At the end of the show, she expects a rocket, but Ziegfeld holds his fire. Her judgement was right this time, but from now on he makes the decisions.

An even better surprise follows: Nick Arnstein. He turns up out of nowhere and the electricity between them starts crackling again. He suggests a night on the town for the newest Ziegfeld star ('I Want to Be Seen With You'), but he settles instead for a party in Mrs Brice's saloon in 'Henry Street' where he ends up playing poker with the card harpies. When Nick and Fanny get a little time together away from the crowd, their mutual affinity opens up ('People'), but Nick is a man of the world and Fanny hasn't been anywhere except up on a stage in front of thousands of people she doesn't know, and he knows he isn't going to stop his wanderings and stay around her. Before long he has to go, as suddenly as he came back, leaving Fanny wondering regretfully whether she will ever see him again.

Ten months later, on tour in Baltimore, she does. He turns up from nowhere once more and takes her to dinner in style, but it's the same old story. He is in town for only a week before he goes to Europe. She is upset and angry, and she covers it with clowning. Since she can't understand what he says when he orders from the French menu, how will she know when he makes a pass at her. He assures her that she'll know ('You Are Woman, I Am Man') and at the end of the number they meet in a genuine kiss. Somehow Europe gets forgotten for a while and Nick stays in Baltimore, but when it comes time for the show to move to Chicago he picks up his old plan. It's Chicago for her and Monte Carlo for him. But Fanny has other ideas. Ziegfeld has many stars, she has only one man. Although Eddie begs her not to, her mind is made up and, full of optimism, she quits the show and prepares to follow Nick to Monaco ('Don't Rain on My Parade').

ACT 2

Fanny and Nick return from Europe to Nick's Long Island mansion as Mr and Mrs Arnstein, and it is quite clear who proposed to whom. Half of Henry Street and the Ziegfeld company are there to greet them and Fanny happily parades herself as just an ordinary married lady, like Mrs Strakosh's ever-mentioned Sadie ('Sadie, Sadie').

Soon baby Frances comes along, and then the ever-gambling Nick gets wiped out in a speculation on an oil well. Down at Henry Street there are questions in the air. Is everything all right between the two of them? Mrs Brice shrugs it off. She doesn't have to worry about her daughter any more. Let's face it, she doesn't have to worry about anyone any more. Or, more correctly, she doesn't have anyone to worry about. Eddie and Mrs Strakosh posit a suggestion—'Find Yourself a Man'.

Fanny returns to the theatre sooner, much sooner, than she had originally said she would and Nick returns to his grand financial designs. This time it's a casino. He tries to interest Ziegfeld who ducks out of it, but Fanny asks if she can invest and almost forces her money on him. When Eddie worries about it, she brushes him off and returns to a rehearsal for the new show. The rehearsal ('Rat-tat-tat-tat') segues into the opening night performance in a full-scale Follies production number with Fanny clowning away at its centre. Once again the evening is a triumph, but for Fanny it is soured by the fact that Nick has not turned up.

When he finally arrives she blazes out her disappointment at him, but he has his reasons sadly to hand: the casino venture has gone up in the air and all their money is lost. Fanny is cheerful about it—he's lost his shirt before and made it back again in his next venture—but Nick sees it with a different eye. He sees himself as the rich star's adored husband, playing games with her money—money she indulgently lets him lose, for she can make plenty more. Fanny sincerely denies this and Nick knows that she believes what she says, but he knows equally well that it is the truth. As he goes to depart, her fearful cry to him not to go brings him back just in time ('Who Are You Now').

An agent called Renaldi visits Arnstein with an offer of a partnership. It is too good to be true: no investment is needed, just the use of Nick's enormously presentable self and manner. He is ready to accept happily when it becomes evident to him that Fanny has already paid money into Renaldi's firm to buy him a safe job. He turns the offer down and stakes everything on a ballooning venture concerning some bonds.

Fanny is on stage rehearsing when the news comes that her husband has been arrested. He has admitted fraud and embezzlement in the bond affair. Fanny is incredulous. She cannot believe that he would not have come to her to help him out of any difficulty. Mrs Brice understands only too well why he did not, and she tells Fanny in clear words that with too much love and too little understanding she, Fanny, has been the downfall of Nick Arnstein. The faithful Eddie, as always, takes the view that it is Nick who has let Fanny down, but Fanny tiredly wonders at his incomprehension: he can never understand what Nick did for her. He made her pretty ('Music That Makes Me Dance').

The time returns to the present where Fanny is waiting longingly for

Nick's return. Today he is to be released from prison and he will be coming to the theatre. When he comes, however, it is to tell her that their life together is over. Neither of them will ever change, and he cannot go on as before. A shattered Fanny plays along. Of course he is right. She was going to say the same thing. And so, with love on both sides as bright as it was in Baltimore all those years ago, they part and this time she knows for certain she'll never see him again. Holding a little memento of their love to her cheek, she begins to sing 'Don't Rain on My Parade' as, putting on her make-up through her tears, she builds herself up to face her audience. Her world can end later; right now she has a show to do.

HELLO, DOLLY!

a musical comedy in two acts by Michael Stewart based on *The Matchmaker* by Thornton Wilder. Music and lyrics by Jerry Herman. Produced at the St James Theatre, New York, 16 January 1964 with Carol Channing (Dolly), David Burns (Horace), Nelson Reilly (Cornelius), Jerry Dodge (Barnaby), Eileen Brennan (Irene) and Sondra Lee (Minnie Fay). Produced at the Minskoff Theatre 6 November 1975 with Pearl Bailey, Billy Daniels, Terrence Emanuel, Grenoldo Frazier, Mary Louise and Chip Fields. Produced at the Lunt-Fontanne Theatre 5 March 1978 with Miss Channing, Eddie Bracken, Lee Roy Reams, Robert Lydiard, Florence Lacey and Alexandra Korey.

Produced at the Theatre Royal, Drury Lane, London, 2 December 1965 with Mary Martin (succeeded by Dora Bryan), Loring Smith, Garrett Lewis, Johnny Beecher, Marilynn Lovell and Coco Ramirez. Revived there 21 September 1979 with Miss Channing, Bracken, Tudor Davies, Richard Drabble, Lorna Dallas and Mandy More. Produced at the Prince of Wales Theatre 3 January 1984 with Danny La Rue, Lionel Jeffries, Michael Sadler, Mark Haddigan, Lorna Dallas and Polly Ann Tanner.

Produced at Liège 26 March 1971 and subsequently at the Théâtre Mogador, Paris, 29 September 1972 in a version by Jacques Collard, Marc-Cab and André Hornez with Annie Cordy, Jacques Mareuil, Jean Pomarez, Christian Parisy, Pierrette Delange (succeeded by Elaine Varon) and Arlette Patrick.

Produced at the Schauspielhaus, Düsseldorf, 26 November 1966 in a version by Robert Gilbert with Tatjana Iwanow, Siegfried Siegert, Wolfgang Arpa, Wolfgang Reinbacher, Ingrid Ernest and Evelyn Balser.

Produced at the Theater an der Wien, Vienna, 1970 with Marika Rökk, Karl Schönböck, Kurt Huemer, Heinz Zuber, Marion Briner and Beate Granzow.

A film version was produced by Twentieth Century-Fox in 1969 with Barbra Streisand, Walter Matthau, Tommy Tune, Michael Crawford, Marianne McAndrew and E J Peaker.

CHARACTERS

Mrs Dolly Gallagher Levi
Ernestina Money
Ambrose Kemper

Horace Vandergelder
Ermengarde
Cornelius Hackl
Barnaby Tucker
Irene Molloy
Minnie Fay
Mrs Rose, Rudolph, Judge, Court Clerk, etc.

ACT 1

In the streets of *fin de siècle* New York, the populace is vaunting the merits of
the matchmaker, Dolly Gallagher Levi ('Call on Dolly'). Mrs Levi is a
woman who arranges things ('I Put my Hand In'), but today she is unable to
attend to the marital and other eclectic problems of the metropolis for she is
bound for the village of Yonkers where her mission is the supplying of a new
wife to the widowed and wealthy half-millionaire Horace Vandergelder and,
coincidentally, the winning of that gentleman's approval (on commission) to
the marriage of his heiress niece, Ermengarde, to the poor artist Ambrose
Kemper.

It is the opinion of the city that Mr Vandergelder will marry Dolly's client,
the pretty widow, Irene Molloy, but Dolly Levi has had other thoughts.
Before she boards the Yonkers train, she looks up and confides in her late
husband that she has a mind to marry again herself, and Horace
Vandergelder's fortune seems to her like the perfect mate.

Out in Yonkers, Horace Vandergelder has no idea what fate and Dolly
Levi have in store for him. He intends to spend his day in the city where he
will march in a parade and propose to Mrs Molloy. His house has not had a
woman about it for years and it could do with a clean ('It Takes a Woman').
When Dolly arrives in Yonkers, her first care is to sow distrust of Mrs
Molloy in Vandergelder's mind, after which she sets out to tempt him to
forget his intentions towards the widow with the prospect of the fabulously
wealthy (if ineffably plain) Ernestina Money. Her strategy works.
Vandergelder expresses interest in meeting this unknown but eligible sounding lady and, as he sets off for town, Dolly gives a quick glance round the
room to get some idea for a new shade of wallpaper for the day she moves in.
Blue, perhaps? Yes, a very particular shade of blue.

Horace Vandergelder is not the only inhabitant of Yonkers heading for the
bright lights of the city today. Down in the bowels of his Hay and Feed
Store, his overworked and underpaid employees, Cornelius and Barnaby,
have come to momentous decision. While the boss is away, they will close
down the store and sidle off for their first ever glance at the big city, and they
won't come home until they've done everything—even kissed a girl. ('Put on
Your Sunday Clothes').

In Irene Molloy's hat shop in Water Street, New York City, the widow and her assistant, Minnie Fay, are awaiting the arrival of Horace Vandergelder and his proposal. Minnie Fay seems more excited than her employer, who is quite willing to admit that she is about to accept Mr Vandergelder as a husband solely to escape from her hated position in the millinery business. The sprightly Irene feels much more like a little bit of an adventure, maybe even in one of her own hats ('I'll Be Wearing Ribbons Down My Back'), than marriage with a middle-aged half-millionaire. That is the moment that Cornelius and Barnaby choose to make a hurried entrance into the shop. It is not that they have an interest in hats, but they have spotted Vandergelder coming down the street and they urgently need a place to hide. They couldn't have chosen less happily, for Horace is coming to rendezvous with Dolly prior to meeting Mrs Molloy, and he seats himself down on a bench right outside the shop to wait. Cornelius and Barnaby are trapped.

They couldn't be trapped in a nicer place. Cornelius is swiftly smitten by the pretty Irene but, before the acquaintance can be developed, Vandergelder enters and the boys are forced to scramble for a hiding place. It becomes more and more difficult for Irene and the newly arrived Dolly to keep the boys under cover and Dolly finally breaks into a confusingly patriotic song and march ('Motherhood') to hinder and bewilder Vandergelder.

To Dolly's delight, Horace is soon convinced that his intended fiancée is hiding a roomful of strange men and he storms indignantly out of the shop to look into the possibilities of the rich Ernestina. Dolly suggests that the boys should take Irene and Minnie Fay to dinner to make amends and, having picked up from Dolly's imaginative chatter that Cornelius is rich, Irene plumps for a table at the fashionable Harmonia Gardens. Needless to say, this is well beyond Cornelius's pocket but, worse, it is well known that the Harmonia Gardens hosts dancing contests for its guests and Cornelius and Barnaby can't dance. Such a consideration has no fears for Mrs Levi for dance training is one of her sidelines. Before long she will have them 'Dancing'.

Off the happy young people go, leaving Dolly alone with her thoughts and intentions. It is time she started living again herself instead of just organising life for other people. She want her own fun again before its too late ('Before the Parade Passes By') but, please, will her dear late Ephraim give her a sign to let her know that it's all right? Horace Vandergelder is getting nearer. Mrs Molloy has been scuttled and the man is, whatever the appearances, all hers just as soon as she knows Ephraim doesn't mind.

In the meanwhile Vandergelder's pursuit of a wife is not proving very successful. The lovely lady Dolly pointed out to him in the parade as being the available heiress was nothing of the sort. When Horace attempted to pursue an introduction it turned out that she was nothing but a tailor's dummy. Dolly promises that at 8 p.m. that night he can meet the real Ernestina at the Harmonia Gardens. Vandergelder isn't sure that he wants any more of Dolly Levi's introductions but, after all, he's paid for this one so he might as well have it. But after that, that's it. He's had enough of his marriage broker. Dolly is sacked and she is thrilled. The man is as good as hers.

ACT 2

Cornelius and Barnaby have been showing their ladies the lights of the town while avoiding any situation which might require the spending of their non-existent money. The invoke 'Elegance' as the reason for walking instead of taking a cab, but they end up at the ritzy Harmonia Gardens all the same and they have to go in. Ambrose and his Ermengarde are there too, ordered into the dance contest by Dolly as a part of their courtship and as a challenge to her Uncle Horace Vandergelder who is also there to meet the real, vast and over-rouged Ernestina.

In one private dining room Ernestina orders her way through the menu at the expense of the glum Vandergelder while, in another, Cornelius throws common sense to the wind and calls for champagne. When both Horace and Barnaby emerge to tip the bandleader to play their preferred music, both get caught up in the mêlée of dancing waiters (The Waiters' Galop) and drop their purses. The wrong one is returned to each and Barnaby suddenly finds he is rich. The boys can order the best of everything all round.

Suddenly everything stops. The waiters are in ferment. An old and loved customer is about to put in an appearance. It is our Mrs Levi, dolled up like nobody's business, to be greeted by the whole staff of the establishment with a ringing 'Hello, Dolly!'. Vandergelder starts out to give Dolly a piece of his mind about the unsuitable Ernestina but he somehow ends up dining with her at a table for two alongside the dance-floor with turkey and all the most lavish trimmings. Before he knows where he is, the conversation is firmly twisted on to marriage and compatibility and somehow the tenor of the discussion is always against him.

Horace is not that stupid. He recognises the drift and he has just one thing to say. Under no circumstances will he marry Dolly Levi. He determines to escape from this unwanted *dîner à deux* but, when he goes to pay his bill, he finds to his horror that his purse contains only a few cents. He is stuck. As Horace stands staggered by his awful plight, the dance contest starts and the couples make their way on to the floor. Good heavens! It's Ermengarde! And Cornelius! And Barnaby! What are they doing here? They are all sacked!

Mayhem ensues and, by the time the confusion is over, everybody is in court for causing an affray. When the case gets under way Dolly plumps the whole blame for anything and everything, with a special reference to the misery of her clients Ambrose and Ermengarde, on to the unfortunate Vandergelder and, when Cornelius steps forward to sum up for the defence, he pours out instead his newly found love for Irene ('It Only Takes a Moment'). This is sufficient cause for the judge to acquit all the defendants except Horace, but Horace is made of stern stuff. He will absolutely not under any circumstances marry Dolly Levi, not even to get out of this mess. Then Dolly plays her trump card. She has no intention of marrying him. She merely wishes to say 'Goodbye, Dearie', and the wedding will be at eleven o'clock tomorrow.

Back in Yonkers, Cornelius (with Irene), Barnaby (with Minnie Fay) and Ermengarde (with Ambrose) are all lining up to get their money out of Vandergelder's safe. Cornelius is going to set up his own shop dealing in the same kind of goods right opposite to the Vandergelder store. It is a bad day for Horace but the worst part of it is that he has realised what he really wants. He proposes to Dolly.

Of course, he will take Cornelius back and make him a partner, won't he...? and he'll dance at Ermengarde's wedding to Ambrose..? One at a time, Dolly wins her points. She's nearly there, but where is the sign from Ephraim? It turns up in the shape of some rolls of blue wallpaper. Horace has inexplicably ordered them to repaper the room, and they are precisely the colour that Dolly had decided on. And then comes a thing which no one ever expected to hear. Ephraim's favourite (and very un-Vandergelder) aphorism falls from Horace's lips: 'Money is like manure. It's not worth a thing unless you spread it around.' It is surely going to be spread around when Dolly gets her hands on it, but Vandergelder is going to have a much more adventurous life with what is clearly a wonderful woman. He can say 'Hello, Dolly!' with a real enthusiasm.

The songs 'World, Take Me Back' and 'Love, Look in My Window' were added to the score for Ethel Merman when she succeeded to the role of Dolly in the original production.

FIDDLER ON THE ROOF

a musical in two acts by Joseph Stein based on the stories of Sholom Aleichem. Lyrics by Sheldon Harnick. Music by Jerry Bock. Produced at the Imperial Theatre, New York, 22 September 1964 with Zero Mostel (Tevye), Maria Karnilova (Golde), Beatrice Arthur (Yente), Joanna Merlin (Tzeitel), Austin Pendleton (Motel) and Julia Migenes (Hodel).

Produced at Her Majesty's Theatre, London, 16 February 1967 with Topol, Miriam Karlin, Cynthia Grenville, Rosemary Nichols, Jonathan Lynn and Linda Gardner. Produced at the Apollo Victoria Theatre 28 June 1983 with Topol, Thelma Ruby, Maria Charles, Jane Gurnett, Peter Whitman and Andrea Levine.

Produced at the Théâtre Marigny, Paris, as *Un Violon sur le Toit* in a version by Robert Manuel and Maurice Vidalin 1972 with Yvan Rebroff, Maria Murano, Florence Blot, Monique Galbert, Philippe Ariotti and Janet Clair.

Produced at the Operettenhaus, Hamburg, as *Anatevka* in a version by Rolf Merz 1 February 1968 with Shmuel Rodensky, Lilly Towska, Marianne Hachfeld, Marion Maar, Herbert Dubrow and Sirgun Kiesewetter.

Produced at the Theater an der Wien, Vienna, 15 February 1969 with Yossi Yadin, Lya Dulizkaya, Gretl Elb, Eva Pilz, Peter Fröhlich and Sylvia Anders.

A film version was produced by United Artists in 1971 with Topol, Norma Crane, Molly Picon, Rosalind Harris, Leonard Frey and Michele Marsh.

CHARACTERS

Tevye, *a dairyman*
Golde, *his wife*

790

Tzeitel ⎫
Hodel ⎪
Chava ⎬ *their daughters*
Shprintze ⎪
Bielke ⎭
Yente, *a matchmaker*
Motel Kamzoil, *a tailor*
Shandel, *his mother*
Perchik, *a student*
Lazar Wolf, *a butcher*
Mendel, *the rabbi's son*
Grandma Tzeitel, *Golde's grandmother*
Fruma-Sarah, *Lazar Wolf's first wife*
Fyedka
Avram
Mordcha, Rabbi, Nahum, Yussel, Sasha, The Fiddler, etc.

ACT 1

The scene is the little Russian village of Anatevka and the time 1905, the beginning of the end of the Russia of Tsarist centuries. On the roof of the house of Tevye, the milkman, a violinist is seated, scraping away at his fiddle. He is the epitome of the Jewish people of Anatevka who each scratch out a living, as the fiddler scratches out his tune, while perilously perched on the edge of existence as represented by the unsafe roof. They are sustained in this struggle with life by one great asset, 'Tradition'. Where the traditions came from and why they exist is not given to them to know, but they live by the rules and manners prescribed, and they give obedience to God and his law as interpreted by the rabbi rather than to the laws of the even more distant and nebulous Tsar.

Tevye is a case in point. He works hard to keep his wife, Golde, and their five daughters, and they survive. It will be good when the girls are married. Tzeitel, the eldest, must have her marriage arranged first and Tevye would like it to be to a scholarly man with whom he could indulge his fondness for scriptural debate, but Yente the matchmaker has a surprise to unveil. She has a magnificent match for Tevye's eldest. The well-off and widowed butcher, Lazar Wolf, has taken a fancy to Tzeitel and is willing to offer for her hand.

Given what a poor girl with no dowry might have to accept just to get a husband at all, the sisters are not at all anxious to be found a match ('Matchmaker, Matchmaker'), but Tzeitel has a particular reason for dreading Yente and her interference. She is in love with her childhood friend, the penniless tailor Motel, and they have pledged their troth to each other in secret. Soon the time will have to come for Motel to take his courage in his hands and go to Tevye to ask formally for her hand.

Tevye returns from a day's work in which his carthorse has gone lame. God is getting at him again. He realises that God has a lot to think about, but

791

would it be such a very difficult thing for Him to lighten Tevye's load a little? ('If I Were a Rich Man'). That consideration seems much more important to Tevye than the news of distant evictions of Jews from their villages. It is not more important, however, to a young university student called Perchik who tries to stir the villagers from their regular life with simplistic revolutionary talk. No one will listen to his strange words, but Tevye is enough of a kindly fool to take in this penniless stump orator for the Sabbath meal ('Sabbath Prayer').

Golde does not break the news of Lazar Wolf's intentions openly to her husband but tells him only that the butcher wishes to meet with him. Tevye is concerned that Wolf is after his new milk cow and, when he goes the next evening to meet him, he is momentarily taken aback at his offer. He does not like the butcher and he does not care to have him as a son-in-law, but he realises that it is a fine social and financial prospect for his daughter and therefore he accepts. The two men drink on the agreement and merrily sing 'To Life'. As they wander drunkenly into the street at the end of the evening, Tevye is stopped by the local constable with a warning. He has been sent orders to make sure there are some anti-Jewish demonstrations in the area. Since they are friends, he will make sure that these demonstrations are insignificant and Tevye must understand that it will be just for the form. So, on a day you find a rich husband for your daughter, you have to have news like that. What is it with God?

There are problems at home, too. Although Tevye does not know it, he has introduced a disturbing influence into his home in Perchik. When, in return for his food, he teaches the girls from the bible, he perverts the sacred texts to make political points, and in conversations with the bright Hodel he denigrates the solid family traditions by which she lives and teaches her the dance steps of the town instead of the contents of the good book. There is further trouble when Tzeitel takes very much against the marriage arranged for her and Tevye has to listen to Motel the tailor ask for her hand. They gave each other a pledge? Tevye is stunned. It is the father's position to arrange his daughter's marriage and he has done so. A pledge? This is wholly against 'Tradition'. But he can see the love in his daughter's eyes and he cannot gainsay her. She shall marry her wretched tailor ('Miracle of Miracles'), but what on earth will he tell Golde?

He tells her by means of a dream. In the middle of the night Golde wakes to find her husband shouting in his sleep and he awakes with a dreadful tale. He dreamed that, in the middle of a feast, Golde's grandmother came to him from beyond the grave and told him that Tzeitel should marry Motel the tailor and not Lazar Wolf. The characters from his dream crowd round the bed as he continues to recount the story. In support of the grandmother's proclamation, there came the dreadful apparition of Fruma-Sarah, the first wife of the butcher. Like a banshee she descended, threatening to be revenged on Tzeitel should she take her place in Lazar Wolf's bed. Golde is thoroughly frightened and agrees that under such circumstances a wedding between Tzeitel and Lazar Wolf is impossible and, as she goes back to sleep, Tevye mouths a silent 'thank you' to God.

At the wedding of Tzeitel and Motel, Tevye watches sentimentally ('Sunrise, Sunset') as the celebration moves on to the giving of the gifts and the general singing and dancing. Lazar Wolf has brought a gift, but he has only harsh words for Tevye whom he considers has made him ridiculous in the village by going back on his bond. There is a further sensation when Perchik takes Hodel to the dance floor—it is not done for a man to dance in public with a woman—but Tevye covers for him as best he can by following up with Golde and the newly married couple. Tradition is broken again, and Lazar Wolf and Yente, the pillars of old Anatevka, leave angrily.

The happy wedding feast is winding to a height of merriment and dancing when the festivities are invaded by a band of Russians. The anti-Jewish demonstration has been scheduled for tonight. The constable is sorry, but it has to be. The wedding party ends in a shower of broken furniture and gifts as Perchik is clubbed down trying to resist.

ACT 2

Tevye is still talking to God, but God doesn't seem to send him much to alleviate the troubles of his life. They just keep on coming. Perchik tells Hodel that he must leave Anatevka and return to the city to be where things political are happening but, before he leaves, he comes out with a stilted profession of love. Hodel says she will consider herself engaged to him and he is content ('Now I Have Everything'), but Tevye refuses his permission. If Perchik is going away Hodel must find a local bridegroom.

But Perchik is not asking his permission, only his blessing. So now it is only 'love' that matters—not tradition, not the father and the mother—and he can't use a dream for an excuse to Golde this time. All this love. Did they have love, he and Golde, when they got married? Do they have it now? Suddenly Tevye wants to know ('Do You Love Me?'). They've battled against life together, side by side, for twenty-five years. If that's not love, what is?

In Anatevka rumour is flowing, and getting more confused as it runs from mouth to mouth ('I Just Heard'). The truth of it is that Perchik has been arrested in Kiev for his political activities and condemned to serve his sentence in Siberia. Hodel knows that, no matter what, she must leave her family and go to him ('Far from the Home I Love'). Bidding farewell to her father, she promises him that she will be married properly, under a canopy, as soon as Perchik is freed.

There soon is another bit of gossip—a new arrival at the home of Motel and Tzeitel. The town rushes to see, and the rabbi to bless. Motel has, at last, got the sewing machine he has worked and saved for for so many years.

Trouble will not leave Tevye alone for long. Now his third daughter, Chava, wants to get married. She wishes to marry Fyedka and Fyedka is a Russian. This time Tevye is firm. Whatever else he may permit, whatever else he may suffer, no daughter of his will marry outside the faith. His interdiction goes for nothing. Chava, knowing the risk she runs, goes ahead and weds her Russian but this time Tevye will not forgive, he will not and cannot be persuaded to accept the marriage. His 'Chavaleh' is from this day dead to him.

The outside world and its agents have been breaking down Anatevka and Tevye's family for a long time but the last blow, when it comes, is no less hard. What has been happening elsewhere is now happening to them. The Jews must leave the village: the pogroms are upon them. 'Anatevka' is a thing of the past for them. Tevye and what remains of his family, Yente, Lazar Wolf and the rest of the community bind closely together in the face of fate, but they must go. Tevye and Golde and the two youngest girls will go to relatives in America, Motel and Tzeitel and the baby will join them later, and Chava and Fyedka, who cannot live in a country where such injustice prevails, will head for Cracow. The village of Anatevka will be spread far and wide. As they leave, Tevye beckons to the fiddler on the roof to follow. Wherever they go, and however the world may change, the fiddler and all that he stands for will be with them.

DO I HEAR A WALTZ?

a musical play in two acts by Arthur Laurents based on his play *The Time of the Cuckoo*. Lyrics by Stephen Sondheim. Music by Richard Rodgers. Produced at the 46th Street Theatre, New York, 18 March 1965 with Elizabeth Allen (Leona), Sergio Franchi (Renato), Carol Bruce (Fioria) and Stuart Damon (Eddie).

CHARACTERS

Leona Samish
Mauro
Signora Fioria
Eddie Yeager
Jennifer Yeager
Mr McIlhenny
Mrs McIlhenny
Giovanna
Vito
Renato di Rossi

ACT 1

Leona Samish is a secretary in New York, a hard-working woman. who brought up her younger brothers and sisters after their parents died and who has earned a steady living for them over the years. There hasn't been any latitude for the little extras of life. Until now, she has never been abroad, but at last she has made it—she is in Venice ('Someone Woke Up') and she is thrilled to tears. She is so thrilled, so wide-eyed, that she does not watch where she is walking and before she knows it she has stepped right off the edge of the pavement into a canal.

It is a damp Leona who checks in at the Pensione Fioria and meets her fellow guests. Eddie and Jennifer Yeager are a pair of young Americans who have been living in Rome and who have come to Venice for a holiday break. Eddie is determined to return to America, but Jennifer cannot bear the thought of going back to a country where she is just like all the other young wives, and they are inclined to bicker. The McIlhennys are older and wholly organised into the routine both of their lives and their package holiday. Their hostess, Signora Fioria, is a fine-looking, middle-aged Italian woman of business who, since she has American guests this week, is being pro-American ('This Week Americans'). She is particularly pro Eddie Yeager.

Full of enthusiasm for her holiday, Leona anxiously plies the others with martinis and conversation (The Plane Song: 'What Do We Do? We Fly!') until they disperse to continue their own lives and she is left to dine alone. Even Fioria has a date and Giovanna, the maid, hurries the meal so that she, too, can go to meet her man. Well, perhaps after all these years Venice will hold a man for Leona.

The next morning Leona goes out shopping and, amongst the hustling of the Venetian merchants, visitors and urchins, her eye is taken by one lovely, ruby glass goblet in a shop window. The shopkeeper, Renato di Rossi, moves swiftly to her side as she takes up the goblet to look at it. He is an attractive, greying, middle-aged man and he invites conversation. The goblet is an eighteenth century piece, he tells her. It has been imitated many times since, but this is the real thing: something special which only someone special would appreciate ('Someone Like You'). Renato offers to find her a second glass to make up a pair, he offers generally to help her find her way around the unfamiliarities of Venice ('I'll Come Back Another Day'), but Leona, set prickling on her defences by his evident attractiveness and charm, declines to buy the goblet and leaves. Later, in the evening, she sits alone in the Piazza San Marco and watches the people—inevitably in pairs—go by ('Here We Are Again').

The next morning, early, Leona slips across to Renato's shop and buys the goblet and, that same afternoon, a package is delivered to her hotel. It is from the shopkeeper and contains a second goblet, as he had promised. Soon, he arrives himself, but he has not come for payment. He has come to ask Leona to take coffee in the Piazza with him that evening. She immediately puts up her guard again, and her suspicions as to the man's motives are confirmed when the McIlhennys come back from a shopping trip carrying with them a set of modern goblets just like the ones Renato has sold her. In spite of Renato's affirmation that his glasses are genuine antiques, she cannot stop herself from wanting to believe that they are not. Finally, after a good deal of 'Thinking', she agrees to meet him that evening and, when he is gone, she asks Fioria to look at her glasses. They are indeed eighteenth century.

Fioria tells Leona to wear something for the evening that will look well in a gondola. The meaning of her words is not lost, for Leona has already been

795

told what gondolas are used for after nightfall ('A Gondola for Her'). Later in the day, a young lad comes with a message. Renato will be late for his appointment. He has to take one of his children to the doctor. All Leona's antagonisms are aroused once more as she learns that not only is Renato a father but a married man, and she sends back a message to cancel their evening.

Jennifer has had a row with Eddie and is storming off to bury herself in a cinema, and the disappointed Leona is tempted to join her. This leaves Eddie alone with Fioria and, having pointedly got rid of Giovanna ('No Understand'), the pair leave together in a gondola. Leona doesn't go to the cinema. She leaves Jennifer there and comes back to the *pensione* just in time to see Eddie and Fioria leaving. Jealousy and anger swell up in her and Renato arrives just in time to take the brunt of them.

He answers her questions: yes, he is married but, in a country which allows no divorce, he and his wife have lived out of lovelock for many years and, in any case, they have too many children and too little money to contemplate splitting up. So he looks outside his home for his happiness. Leona is outraged: in America this would be unthinkable, unrespectable or, at the best, regrettable. Renato has only a simple response to that: does this make it wrong, or just wrong in America?

Leona is bewildered: where does she stand? Renato can see what ails her. She has come to Venice to find the handsome, rich, unmarried hero of her dreams. He does not fill that bill but, dare he say it, he is as good as a no longer young, not very beautiful American lady is going to find in a short stay. Does she want something, or will she wait instead for her ideal man and her dream moment? He wants her, the choice is hers. Does she want him ('Take the Moment')? Leona brings out a handful of notes: they will go to the up-market Harry's Bar. He takes the money but determines that they will spend their time together at a café in the Piazza.

ACT 2
Later that evening, a calmer Jennifer waits for Eddie on the balcony of their room and, like a little girl, wishes on the moon while Fioria, on her balcony, hears Eddie returning to his wife and sees Leona returning from a truly happy evening (Trio: 'Moon at my Window').

The next day, the women are in glowing form. Eddie is purging his guilty soul by taking Jennifer out for a special evening, while a sleek Leona waits anxiously for some sort of word from Renato. The moment has come for serious words between the Yeagers and Jennifer finally hears why Eddie insists on going back to America: it is to save their marriage. If he stays in Italy he knows that he will have a serious affair with a Fioria and that will be the beginning of the end. He doesn't want their marriage to go on the rocks ('We're Going to Be All Right').

Renato finally arrives when Leona had begun to give up hope. He has brought her a fine necklace of garnets—her favourite stones. Leona is overjoyed. She has a tangible gift, something material which she can see and touch and understand. At last she can feel the echoings of love inside her ('Do I Hear a Waltz?') and she can even listen to Renato's pleading that she 'Stay' in Venice beyond the time allotted for her holiday.

Leona gives a party for her Venetian friends in the garden of the *pensione* ('Perfectly Lovely Couple') and during the party Renato's son comes to find his father with news that the vendor of the necklace is waiting outside for his money. Renato tries to send him away, but a wine-flushed and happy Leona is only too happy to provide the money. When the child brings back some of the notes for Renato as his commission on the sale, Leona's world crumbles. In spite of Renato's insistence that he asked for no commission, she bursts out accusingly at him: if it had to be like that, could he not have kept it secret and left her the illusions he knows perfectly well she needed to keep? He wanted only her money, not her.

Sadly, Renato leaves and, when Fioria gently intervenes on Renato's behalf and Jennifer adds her words to Leona's distress, Leona drunkenly takes her anguish out on them both by revealing Eddie and Fioria's evening jaunt of the previous day. When the damage has been done, she is sorry, but it is too late. She was hurt and so she wanted to hurt other people. Fioria has no time for her. Hurt? No one has hurt her. Leona is the one who has hurt herself with her self-centred crying for the moon. So, now she has nothing.

The next day the McIlhennys check out. Eddie and Jennifer are not far behind and Fioria is not sorry. The new people checking in are British. How very much better the British are than than Americans ('Last Week Americans'). Renato has visited the *pensione* before Leona was up and, hearing this, she joyfully hurries to the shop to make amends. She finds him there but his manner towards her is different. He knows now that a relationship with her would be impossible. He is too old for the complications of a woman such as she. If the complication was merely another man, or something to do with money, he could manage, but with her the complication is herself. There has been pleasure, there has been affection, but the feeling is gone. They cannot start again. From now on, it is just friends ('Thank You So Much') and goodbye.

MAN OF LA MANCHA

a musical play in one act by Dale Wasserman based on his television play *I, Don Quixote* and *Don Quixote* by Manuel de Cervantes y Saavedra. Lyrics by Joe Darion. Music by Mitch Leigh. Produced at the Goodspeed Opera House, Connecticut, 28 June 1965 and at the Anta Washington Square Theatre, New York, 22 November 1965 with Richard Kiley (Don Quixote), Joan Diener (Aldonza) and Irving Jacobson (Sancho). Transferred to the Martin Beck Theatre 19 March 1968.

Produced at the Piccadilly Theatre, London, 24 April 1968 with Keith Michell, Miss Diener and Bernard Spear and revived there 10 June 1969 with Kiley, Ruth Silvestre and Spear.

Produced at the Théâtre des Champs-Elysées, Paris, in a version by Jacques Brel as *L'Homme de la Mancha* 1968 with Jacques Brel, Miss Diener and Jean-Claude Calon. Produced at the Théâtre Marigny 15 January 1988 with Jean Piat, Jeanne Manson and Richard Taxy.

Produced at the Theater an der Wien, Vienna, 4 January 1968

Produced at the Operettenhaus, Hamburg, in a version by Robert Gilbert as *Der Mann von La Mancha* 1969 with Gideon Singer, Dagmar Koller and Peter W Staub.

A film version was produced by United Artists in 1972 with Peter O'Toole (singing dubbed by Simon Gilbert), Sophia Loren and James Coco.

CHARACTERS

Don Quixote (Cervantes)
Sancho Panza (The Manservant)
Aldonza
The Innkeeper (The Governor)
Dr Carrasco (The Duke)
The Padre
Antonia
The Housekeeper
The Barber
Pedro, *head muleteer*
Maria, *the innkeeper's wife*
Captain of the Inquisition, Anselmo, Jose, Juan, Paco, Tenorio, Fermina, etc.

ACT 1

To the common room of a sixteenth century Spanish prison a Captain of the Inquisition's Guard brings two prisoners: a tall, lank gentleman of evident courtliness and childlike charm, and his servant, a rotund and straight-forward little fellow, the pragmatic half of what is clearly and long and devoted relationship. Their crime, it seems, is that in the master's egalitarian zeal as a tax-collector (a temporary employment, meant only to furnish the wherewithal to live) he foreclosed on a defaulting monastery dear to the heart of the Inquisitor. For such a crime, Cervantes is to be thrown into this dark and unpleasant prison, amongst thieves and murderers, to await trial. Their fellow inmates are soon upon the newcomers, despoiling them of their possessions, as they are dragged before the prisoners' top dog, The Governor, to justify themselves in an underworld trial.

Their possessions turn out to be nothing but a trunk of theatrical costumes and properties and a bundle of manuscript, but Cervantes will use these in his trial on the charges proposed by the malicious prisoner known as the Duke. Cervantes pleads guilty to the charges of being 'an idealist, a bad poet and an honest man,' but he claims the right to present his case before the jury so that his sentence may be mitigated.

His case will take the form of an entertainment: the tale of a country squire called Alonso Quijana who, from too much reading, formed a passionate rebellion in his heart against the evil ways of man towards man and who, leaving aside what men call sanity, set out into the world as a knight errant, calling himself Don Quixote of La Mancha, dedicated to righting all wrongs. With the assistance of some items from the chest, Cervantes becomes Don Quixote and his servant, at his side, becomes his faithful Sancho Panza ('Man of La Mancha').

Don Quixote and Sancho set out along a great highway to glory (which to Sancho looks remarkably like the road to El Toboso where the chickens are cheap). Quixote revels in expectations of giants, knights and wizards in his path and, above all, the Great Enchanter who is the most dangerous enemy of all good men. When a structure is espied on the horizon, Quixote calls it a giant and gallops his horse straight at it, but he is foiled by the magic of the Great Enchanter which changes his foe, at the last moment, into a windmill and brings him tumbling to the ground. Quixote blames his defeat on the fact that he has not been truly dubbed a knight and he vows to seek out another knight to administer the necessary dubbing. When he spies a great castle on the road, he determines to enter and Sancho, who sees only an inn, follows him loyally.

Cervantes breaks his story to cast the other prisoners in the roles of the inhabitants of the inn: the kindly innkeeper, his less kindly wife, a band of rough muleteers and several easy-virtued women, in particular a popular wildcat known as Aldonza. Aldonza is pawed by the muleteers, but she holds her own against them as she contemptuously spits forth that she cares not with which of them she passes her night ('It's All the Same'). She takes the money pressed on her by Pedro and leaves him to wonder if he will get what he's paid for.

Into this rough scene arrive the gentle, bedraggled Don Quixote and his curious servant with their high sounding words and their claims of nobility. The innkeeper humours what he sees as a harmless madman who treats the foul company in the inn as gentlefolk, but there is spiteful mirth amongst the customers when the Don hails Aldonza as a sweet lady and a fair virgin, and worships her as his 'Dulcinea'.

The Duke intervenes to protest that Cervantes is not offering a conventional defence, but the Governor is intrigued by the tale of Don Quixote and orders it to be continued.

Cervantes now takes an aside to look at the folk at the home which Alonso Quijana had left to take up his quest: his niece, Antonia, his heir in law and engaged to be married to the self-important Dr Carrasco; and his housekeeper, hopeful through many years of an eventual marriage. Hurrying to church, they kneel before the padre to wonder what they can do with their mad provider, insisting of course that 'I'm Only Thinking of Him'. Carrasco, who begins by declaring that he could not marry into a family where there is madness, soon suffers a change of heart at the thought of inheriting Quijana's fortune through his niece, and he vows sanctimoniously to bring the poor man back to home and sanity.

Back at the inn, Quixote sends Sancho to his Dulcinea with a missive asking for a token to carry into battle. Aldonza is gloweringly uncomprehending of the chivalrous poetry addressed to her by her knight, and she angrily throws a dish rag to Sancho to be the sought-after token. But she is intrigued. She asks Sancho why he sticks with a madman, and Sancho can only reply simply 'I Really Like Him'. The muleteers mock Aldonza over her knight ('Little Bird') and her missive, and she snaps back that he is just a man and she supposes he wants what every other man wants.

Dr Carrasco and the padre arrive at the inn in search of Quijana and they find Quixote who, to their surprise, addresses them by name but still persists in his new persona. A barber passes by (Barber's Song), and Quixote attacks him and forces him to render up his helmet—the shaving basin he wears on his head to keep out the sun—and, when Aldonza's token is pinned on top of the helmet as its crest, he has the padre crown him with the 'Golden Helmet of Mambrino'. The next morning, after he has kept vigil, the innkeeper shall dub him a knight.

He refuses consistently to return home with Carrasco and the padre, but the former, now cognisant of the nature of Quijana's madness, sets out scientifically to force the old man from his folly. The padre is not so sure: perhaps he is happier in his delusion ('To Each His Dulcinea').

As Quixote prepares to keep his vigil in the inn yard overnight, Aldonza passes by on her way to Pedro and stops to hear his words. She is shaken by his courtliness, his gentleness and his otherworldly idealism in the face of her unimaginative view of reality, and she is curious enough to listen when he explains to her what his quest is (The Quest/'The Impossible Dream'). When he has finished, she begs him to see her as she really is, but he sees only beauty and purity and she turns away from him in despair to be manhandled by the angry Pedro who has come seeking her.

Quixote is roused to fury at seeing his lady thus treated and, armed with his lance, he moves to the attack. With Sancho at one shoulder and Aldonza wielding her sword at the other, he succeeds in laying out the whole band of muleteers and, his valour proven, he has the accommodating innkeeper dub him the Knight of the Woeful Countenance ('The Dubbing'). Now, when it is time to triumph over evil fallen, Quixote preaches only forgiveness, and he sends the surprised Aldonza to tend to their enemies' wounds. While her knight is busy reaffirming his creed, Aldonza is beaten and raped into unconsciousness by the vengeful muleteers.

The tale of Don Quixote is broken off as the Inquisition's guards descend into the room to carry off a prisoner to be judged and burned. The Duke sneers at Cervantes' fear—this is reality. But Cervantes knows reality: he has lived through battle, through hunger, through misery and death. He has seen men wonder why they have lived and wonder whether life itself is a dream, or even the edge of madness. Who, indeed, is to say that wisdom is not madness and madness blessed?

When he takes to the road again, Quixote meets with a whore and her pander and is robbed of all his possessions. He returns to the inn and there he finds the battered Aldonza who throws his fine sentiments at his head and describes in every detail the degrading circumstances of her birth and her life ('Aldonza'). When he replies that still he sees only beauty, she cannot bear it.

Suddenly a challenge is issued. It is the Great Enchanter come to do battle with Quixote. They stand up to each other and the enemy reveals his weapon: a bright, shining mirrored shield in which Quixote sees reflected only his old, foolish self. Everywhere he turns, the evil knight's attendants hold up further mirrors as the Enchanter's voice taunts him with the truth of his pretensions. Weeping and defeated, Quixote sinks fainting into reality, as the knight removes his casque to disclose his identity. It is Carrasco.

Cervantes is warned that his case will be the next to be judged. Scarcely will he have finished justifying himself before one court than he must be summoned before another. He must spin out his tale here until it is time to go. And so the tale of Don Quixote, dragged from blessed fantasy to cruel reality, has its epilogue.

Back at his home, Quijana lies insensible in his bed and none can rouse him until his servant comes by for 'A Little Gossip'. Into his song creep words of imagination and suddenly Quijana is awake and sane. But he has an awareness of death and, to the satisfaction of Carrasco, he begins to make out his will in favour of Antonia.

Suddenly Aldonza forces her way into the room and falls to her knees beside him, addressing him as 'my lord' and urging him to remember Don Quixote and Dulcinea. He has altered her life with his knight errantry, brought her words and thoughts of which she could never have dreamed, he cannot renounce 'The Impossible Dream'. Then, gradually, Quijana remembers Quixote. Life flows back into him as he triumphantly calls for his sword and rises up magnificently, supported by Sancho and Aldonza, until, with a cry, he is gone. As the padre intones a *De profundis*, the stunned Sancho turns to Aldonza. But she tells him that Don Quixote is not dead. And her name is not Aldonza. It is Dulcinea.

Now the Captain of the Inquisition Guard comes to take Cervantes to court. The Governor returns his manuscript to him and wishes him an optimistic good courage where he is going, for he feels that Don Quixote and Don Miguel are two close kindred. As Cervantes mounts the stairs, the girl prisoner who played Aldonza begins to sing 'The Impossible Dream' and the company gradually join in the hymn as the play ends.

SWEET CHARITY

a musical comedy in two acts by Neil Simon based on the film *Nights of Cabiria* by Federico Fellini, Tullio Pinelli and Ennio Flaiano. Lyrics by Dorothy Fields. Music by Cy Coleman. Produced at the Palace Theatre, New York, 29 January 1966 with Gwen Verdon (Charity), John McMartin (Oscar), Helen Gallagher (Nickie), Thelma Oliver (Helene), James Luisi (Vidal) and Arnold Soboloff (Daddy). Produced at the

Minskoff Theatre, 27 April 1986 with Debbie Allen, Michael Rupert, Bebe Neuwirth, Alison Williams, Mark Jacoby and Irving Allen Lee.

Produced at the Prince of Wales Theatre, London, 11 October 1967 with Juliet Prowse, Rod McLennan, Josephine Blake, Paula Kelly, John Keston and Fred Evans.

Produced at the Théâtre de la Gaîté-Lyrique, Paris, 1970 with Magali Noël, Jacques Duby, Colette Marchand, Sidney Chaplin and Dominique Tirmond.

Produced at the Staatstheater, Wiesbaden, February 1970 in a version by Victor Bach with Dagmar Koller, Werner Saladin, Renate Falk, Ingrid Burmeister, and Jürgen Kirschoff.

A film version was produced by Universal in 1969 with Shirley Maclaine, McMartin, Chita Rivera, Paula Kelly, Ricardo Montalban and Sammy Davis jr.

CHARACTERS

Charity Hope Valentine
Helene
Nickie
Carmen
Vittorio Vidal
Ursala
Herman
Oscar Lindquist
Daddy Johann Sebastian Brubeck
Manfred, Marvin, Dark Glasses, Brother Harold, Brother Eddie, etc.

ACT 1

Charity Hope Valentine carries her heart on her sleeve. More correctly, she carries it on her arm—tattooed there—but it's the same thing. She is a girl who just wants to be loved. At the moment she is wanting to be loved by her fiancé (well, almost her fiancé when he gets his divorce), a young man with dark glasses and a lot of wavy black hair. She has come to meet him in the park, her head full of all those lovely things he is going to say to her. When she meets him and he doesn't, she just says them all herself for him, and then she starts in with her appreciation of him ('You Should See Yourself').

She's been out today looking at furniture and she's brought her savings to pay the down payment on the suite that will decorate their home. Looking down into the lake, she suggests they should throw something in for luck. He does. He throws her in, grabbing her handbag as he runs off into the never-to-be-found. A crowd gathers to watch her struggle drowningly in the water until someone gets round to hauling her out to tell her story first to the police and then to the girls at work.

Charity is a dance hostess in the Fan-Dango ballroom. Her friends there are sympathetic but they've heard it all before and, dress up her tale as Charity will, they know and she has finally to admit that she's been suckered one more time. Poor Charity.

Under the authoritarian eyes of Herman the dance hall owner, the girls get ready for their nightly grope and glide around the floor of the Fan-

Dango ('Big Spender'). As she waits to be asked to dance, Charity thinks back to the beginning of the affair and, as she dances with a sticky-fingered customer, her thoughts follow through the stages of her unfortunate 'romance' ('Charity's Soliloquy') until, pushing her partner off, she swears never to be taken for a romantic ride again and rushes out of the dance hall.

As she makes her way down the street, Charity passes by the grand Pompeii Club and, at that precise moment, a man rushes out of the club and bowls into her, sending her flying. Charity is flabbergasted: it is the famous film star Vittorio Vidal and he is having an argument with a lady. As she watches enthusiastically, the argument grows until, as a stroke of bravado against his mistress, Vidal seizes the first girl he sees and whisks her into the glitzy Pompeii Club as his partner. It's Charity.

The patrons of the club are dancing the 'Rich Man's Frug' as they enter and all eyes turn to the unknown girl on Vidal's arm. Vittorio talks mainly about his Ursala, but Charity doesn't care and she gets a telephone brought to the table so she can ring the dance hall and get Vittorio to say something to the girls to prove that she really is where she says she is. Then she faints. Vittorio carries her up to his apartment and she recovers instantly. Then they chat. Mostly she chats as she asks for an autographed picture and some sort of memento to prove that she was actually here ('If My Friends Could See Me Now'), and she has just got round to offering him her body when Ursala attacks the door with her fists.

Charity valiantly climbs into a cupboard while Vittorio goes to get rid of Ursala, but things don't go quite as planned. Soon Vittorio is serenading his mistress with reborn passion ('Too Many Tomorrows') while Charity attempts to smoke a cigarette in the cupboard with disastrous results. Then they head for the bed and Charity abandons the cigarette for the keyhole. Ursala is still lounging exotically in bed when Vittorio lets Charity out the next morning.

The dance hall girls are aghast that Charity has let such an opportunity slip. She's come away with a lousy photograph and a top hat and a cane when she could have got enough cash to have taken her out of the Fan-Dango for good ('There's Gotta Be Something Better Than This'). One thing Charity's adventure has done is that it has given her the taste for meeting new people in new places, and that night she tries out the local YMCA. The Y doesn't turn out to be quite as gregarious as she expected because she gets stuck in the lift with a claustrophobic tax accountant called Oscar. She cheers him up with a song ('I'm the Bravest Individual') as they settle in to wait to be freed.

ACT 2

When they are finally rescued, Oscar invites Charity to come to church and, being Charity, she goes. Oscar's church is a strange sort of place. It is in a basement and it is called the Rhythm of Life Church in honour of its development from a jazz group. The church's chief apostle is one Daddy Johann Sebastian Brubeck ('The Rhythm of Life'), and its creed seems to be made up of welfare and drug resolutions. Before Oscar and Charity can get settled in, the police arrive and they are soon out in the street again, and getting to know each other a little more than they did in the lift. He thinks she's a bank clerk, so she doesn't disillusion him, and he calls her Sweet Charity and doesn't try to lay her. He's different. Her friends make fun of the homey little life Charity is soon dreaming up for herself with her new friend ('Baby, Dream Your Dream'), and Charity promises herself that she will tell Oscar the truth about her job soon.

Oscar and Charity go to Coney Island together and ride the parachute jump together and get stuck again together way up above the ground. This time it's Charity who is scared and Oscar who can assert his budding manhood in protection of his 'Sweet Charity', his lovely virginal, innocent Charity. She does try to tell him about the bank, but he kisses her and it's easier and safer just to go back to being a teller for the moment.

Then Charity makes a big decision: she is going to get out. She is going to quit the Fan-Dango. As she wanders alone through Times Square she wonders what will happen to her next ('Where Am I Going?'). She sends a telegram to Oscar: he must meet her in Barney's Chili Hacienda at 1 a.m. and state his intentions—she has to know. When he turns up, she puts him in one booth while she sits in the next so that she doesn't have to look at him while she tells him the truth. She doesn't work in a bank, she's a dance hall hostess. But he already knows. He saw her go in to the Fan-Dango one night and he slipped in and watched. He knows, too, what else some of the girls there do and he doesn't care. He can forget her old career; he wants to marry her. Charity explodes with joy ('I'm a Brass Band'). At last she's almost married! Back at the Fan-Dango the girls throw a party for their friend and even horrible Herman proves to be human as he admits 'I Love to Cry at Weddings'. A happy ending is in sight.

But Oscar chickens out. The other men keep trampling about in his mind. All those other men Charity slept with. He thought he could fight it, he thought he could make it not matter, but he can't. Charity fights for her man in her usual way—she's had practice—but Oscar is too strong. It is for her own good that he cannot marry her. Unfortunately, he chooses to make his point rather vigorously just as they walk past the lake in the park. As Charity climbs dripping from the lake once again she sees a Good Fairy, a fairy with wings and things and all covered in tinsel-dust. 'Tonight,' says the fairy, 'It will all happen tonight.' So Charity lives to hope and love some more and the Good Fairy turns and goes off. On her back is a sign *THE GOOD FAIRY— tonight at 8 p.m. on CBS.*

CABARET

a musical in two acts by Joe Masteroff based on the play *I Am a Camera* by John van Druten and the stories of Christopher Isherwood. Lyrics by Fred Ebb. Music by

John Kander. Produced at the Broadhurst Theatre, New York, 20 November 1966 with Joel Grey (Emcee), Jill Haworth (Sally Bowles), Bert Convy (Clifford), Jack Gilford (Herr Schultz) and Lotte Lenya (Fräulein Schneider) and played from 7 March 1967 at the Imperial Theatre. Produced at the Imperial Theatre 22 October 1987 with Grey, Alyson Reed, Gregg Edelmann, Werner Klemperer and Regina Resnik.

Produced at the Palace Theatre, London, 28 February 1968 with Barry Dennen, Judi Dench, Kevin Colson, Peter Sallis and Lila Kedrova. Produced at the Strand Theatre 17 July 1986 with Wayne Sleep, Kelly Hunter, Peter Land, Oscar Quitak and Vivienne Martin.

Produced at the Théâtre du 8ème de Lyon 13 May 1986 and at Théâtre Mogador, Paris, 18 February 1987 in a version by Jérôme Savary with Michel Dussart, Ute Lemper, Yann Babilée, Gérard Guillaumat and Magali Noël.

Produced at the Theater an der Wien, Vienna, in a version by Robert Gilbert 14 November 1970 with Blanche Aubry, Violetta Ferrari, Klaus Wildbolz, Harry Fuss and Lya Dulizkaya.

Played at the Schauspielhaus, Düsseldorf, 6 December 1986.

A film version was produced by Allied Artists in 1972 with Joel Grey, Liza Minelli, Michael York, Helmut Griem (Max) and Marisa Berenson (Natalia).

CHARACTERS

Master of Ceremonies (Emcee)
Clifford Bradshaw
Sally Bowles
Fräulein Schneider
Herr Schultz
Fräulein Kost
Ernst Ludwig
Bobby, Victor, Max, Kit Kat Girls, Young German, etc.

ACT 1

On to the empty stage comes the evening's Master of Ceremonies, a bizarre, androgynous creature who bids the audience an introductory 'Willkommen'. Here in the cabaret you can leave your troubles behind and believe that life is beautiful.

In a compartment in a railway train heading for Berlin a young American writer, Clifford Bradshaw, is joined by a nervous German, Ernst Ludwig, who strikes up a brief conversation. Within minutes of his arrival, customs officers enter the carriage preparatory to passing the German border. Cliff's passport is checked and his baggage passed perfunctorily, but Ludwig's case is opened and searched. What is not touched, however, is the briefcase which the German has slyly mixed in with Cliff's luggage. When the officers have departed Ludwig makes a modest excuse for his imposition. He has bought a little too much perfume and a few too many stockings in Paris. In the baggage of an American they can pass unnoticed. In return for his unwitting help, Ernst offers Cliff friendship and help in the strange city of

Berlin. What could be more useful than the name of a cheap, clean rooming house and the offer of his first English pupil: Ludwig, himself? Willkommen to Berlin!

The house of Fräulein Schneider is plain and old but it is also cheap. The chatelaine is willing to take fifty marks a week for a room priced at a hundred on the grounds that otherwise it stays empty and she gets nothing. Fräulein Schneider is a pragmatic woman ('So Who Cares?'). Cliff soon meets his nearest neighbours, Fräulein Kost, a large cheerful whore who passes off a juvenile sailor found in her room as a nephew from Hamburg for the benefit of the moralistic Fräulein Schneider, and the gentle, greying fruiterer, Herr Schultz, whose sweet attentions to Fräulein Schneider are gratefully received. Installed in his new home, Cliff knows he should sit down to his typewriter and begin to work, but Berlin calls him away from writing just as every other town he has gone through has done and, before long, he quits his room for the sleazy Kit Kat Club and some easy entertainment. The Emcee of this dowdy establishment introduces his line of girls, a determinedly decadent group fronted by an English girl of a strangely child-like sophistication, in a routine called 'Don't Tell Mama'.

The girl, Sally Bowles, catches sight of Cliff and recognises an English-speaking face and, as soon as the performance is over, she calls him on one of the table telephones and gratefully listens to an English voice. She is younger than her age and determined above all to be shocking and modern, but she is totally likeable and Cliff is happy to answer her babbling questions. Soon, however, her protector arrives at her table and communication is cut. As the hour of midnight approaches, all round the Club contacts are being made (Telephone Song) but, for his first night in town, Cliff sits alone and just watches Sally.

Cliff's pupil, Ernst Ludwig, provides him with a little income on which to live and he hints that, if his tutor is in need, a lot more can be made by undertaking some simple trips to Paris on his behalf. One day their morning lesson is broken in on by an unexpected arrival: Sally. The upshot of her contact with Cliff in the club is that her protector has kicked her out. As he is also a partner in the Club, she is not only without protection but without a job and penniless, so she thought since Cliff had a room of his own she might move in with him for a little while. Fräulein Schneider's qualms are settled by the thought of the extra rent, and any doubts Cliff might have had are drowned in the waves of chatter and possibilities that flow from Sally. It's all going to be 'Perfectly Marvelous'. No one will take any notice; after all, in Berlin everyone has a room-mate. Some, so the Emcee assures us, have more than one, a proposition illustrated in song and dance by himself and 'Two Ladies'.

Keeping at least an ostensibly honest house is a trial for Fräulein Schneider. When she catches Fräulein Kost smuggling in another sailor she indignantly throws him out but, when Fräulein Kost threatens to leave at the end of the week, Fräulein Schneider is forced to retreat back behind the status quo. If Kost wishes to stay it must be understood that she does not let herself be seen bringing the sailors in. Herr Schultz is Fräulein Schneider's consolation. Always he brings her something from his fruit shop and today he has outdone himself. Today he has brought her a pineapple! She is overcome at the extravagance of the gift—'It Couldn't Please Me More'.

At the club, a group of waiters join the Emcee in a new kind of song. They are exaggeratedly Aryan, scrubbed and ideal, and they sing with a heart-warming sincerity 'Tomorrow Belongs to Me'.

Cliff writes a little but not enough and Sally stays. They get by and they fall in love. It is very unreal, but Cliff does not wish to get back to responsible reality ('Why Should I Wake Up') and Sally becomes pregnant. It fits ill with the image she spends her whole life creating for herself but she would like to keep the baby. Cliff positively wants it, which means he has all the more reason to accept when Ernst Ludwig proposes one of his little Paris trips at a fee of 75 marks. Now money is going to be necessary. The theme of money is taken up by the personnel of the Kit Kat and the Emcee presents 'The Money Song' while displaying a parade of national currencies in scantily dressed female form.

Fräulein Kost is a little surprised when caught letting a sailor or three out of her room to meet with no condemnation from Fräulein Schneider, but she feels she may have found the reason when she sees Herr Schultz emerging from her landlady's room. A saucy remark, however, wins a warm response from Herr Schultz: Fräulein Schneider has just done him the honour of agreeing to be his wife. When Fräulein Kost has raised her eyebrows and departed, the two ageing people are left alone. Now what shall they do? Neither can truly believe that the other would wish the opportunistic lie to be the truth and, of course, they both wish it very deeply. Herr Schultz tentatively makes a formal proposal and Fräulein Schneider almost coyly signifies that he has reason to be optimistic. At their age, they will be 'Married'.

Sally insists delightedly there must be an engagement party, and promises that she herself will ensure a super turn out. When the occasion arrives, all the performers from the Kit Kat turn up at Schultz's fruit shop and the evening is indeed a lively affair. Ernst comes too, to pick up the briefcase that Cliff has brought into the country for him from Paris. Amid the gaiety Schultz takes a glass or two of schnapps and entertains the company with the touching little Jewish song 'Meeskite', but his rendition goes down poorly with some of the guests. Ernst, who is fond of Fräulein Schneider, warns her against the marriage. Her intended husband is not German. Having made his point, he goes to leave the party, but Fräulein Kost calls him back to join in a very different kind of song. As the engaged couple and Sally and Cliff look on with varying emotions, the guests join forcefully in the Nazi song 'Tomorrow Belongs to Me'.

ACT 2

The following morning Fräulein Schneider comes to the shop where Schultz is tidying up. The party has opened her eyes. She must look to her own situation. It has been a hard struggle to get the little she has in life and, if a marriage to a Jew can imperil that, then she cannot marry him. She has lived fifty years without love and it seems now that she must live the rest of what is left to her in the same way.

Schultz tries to persuade her that she may be unnecessarily frightened. Even if these dreadful people should one day come to power, governments come and go sometimes very quickly. Should they give up their chance of happiness for this one possibility? Suddenly a brick smashes through the shop window. As much as they wish to believe that it is the work of mischievous children, they know the truth. At the Kit Kat Club the Emcee sings and dances with a gorilla. 'If You Could See Her Through My Eyes,' he asserts, 'she wouldn't look Jewish at all.'

Cliff has refused to go again to Paris for Ernst since he has realised that what he has carried through customs in the briefcases were funds for the Nazi party and, to make up the money lost by this refusal, he is trying to find a job. Sally already has one. Max at the Kit Kat has fallen in love with a Communist virgin and so it is all right for Sally to go back to her old job, but Cliff will not hear of it. Fräulein Schneider comes to see them to return their engagement gift and, in response to their amazement, she chides them 'What Would You Do?' in her situation. She cannot, like them, take flight to Paris or England or America. Her life and everything she has are here.

Cliff knows that his life and Sally's can no longer be in Berlin the way things are going. The party that was Berlin in the twenties is over. He decides to sell his typewriter to get money to pay their passage out of Germany, but Sally will not hear of leaving. She is not going to abandon her career as a singer, the Kit Kat Club needs her and Berlin is where she belongs. Here she can be herself in a way she could never be in England. Cliff firmly tells her to wait in the room and, taking his typewriter, he goes out but, no sooner has he left than Sally snatches up her fur coat, her one valuable possession, and rushes out behind him.

Cliff finds her, later that evening, at the Kit Kat Club. She still will not listen to his warnings and she returns defiantly to the stage to deliver her song ('Cabaret'). The song encapsulates Sally's philosophy, or what she would like to think is her philosophy. Drink deep of each hour, get out and take life by the balls, use it for each hour of the short trip from cradle to grave. While she sings, Ernst continues to urge Cliff to make another trip for him and, when the angry boy finally punches the Nazi in the face, he finds himself set upon and beaten up by a gang of thugs. As the punches drive him to the ground Sally keeps on singing about what she calls Life.

Cliff is packing the next morning when Sally returns. She is pale and drawn, and she answers mechanically to his attempts at cheerfulness. She is not going with him, and she has had their child aborted. When he slaps her she is almost pleased at the drama of the situation, but the blow does not open her eyes. She still chatters on about what a strange and extraordinary person she is—this poor little girl who cannot bear the thought that she is not in the least strange or extraordinary. Cliff is barely listening. He takes one of the two train tickets from his wallet and places it on the sideboard. Sally can follow him to Paris or she can stay here in Berlin, it is up to her. Sally puffs her cigarette with a last attempt at style. She's always rather hated Paris, so it has to be goodbye. When Cliff has gone and she has no one to play to, poor, silly Sally deflates.

Cliff boards the train to leave Berlin. There will be no more 'Willkommen' here. The Emcee and his girls are seen again with their welcome routine, only this time it is different, it is harder and forcibly bright and there are German uniforms and swastikas in evidence as Sally brightly affirms that life is a 'Cabaret'. Then it is dark.

The film version introduced three new songs 'Maybe This Time', 'Mein Herr' and 'Money, Money, Money' and omitted much of the stage score. The London revival used 'Maybe This Time' and 'Money, Money, Money' and the 1987 Broadway revival omitted 'Meeskite' and 'Why Should I Wake Up' and included two new songs, 'Don't Go' and 'I Don't Care Much'.

MAME

a musical in two acts by Jerome Lawrence and Robert E Lee based on *Auntie Mame* by Patrick Dennis. Lyrics and music by Jerry Herman. Produced at the Winter Garden Theatre, New York, 24 May 1966 with Angela Lansbury (Mame), Beatrice Arthur (Vera), Jane Connell (Gooch) and Jerry Lanning (Patrick). Produced at the Gershwin Theatre 24 July 1983 with Misses Lansbury, Anne Francine, Miss Connell and Byron Nease.

Produced at the Theatre Royal, Drury Lane, London, 20 February 1969 with Ginger Rogers, Margaret Courtenay, Ann Beach and Tony Adams.

A film version was produced by Warner Brothers in 1974 with Lucille Ball, Beatrice Arthur, Jane Connell, Kirby Furlong and Robert Preston as Beauregard.

CHARACTERS

Patrick Dennis
Mame Dennis, *his aunt*
Agnes Gooch
Vera Charles, *an operetta star*
Ito
Dwight Babcock
Beauregard Jackson Pickett Burnside
Sally Cato
Gloria Upson
Mr Upson
Mrs Upson
Pegeen Ryan
M Lindsay Woolsey, Ralph Devine, Madame Branislowski, Junior Babcock, Uncle Jeff, Cousin Fan, Peter Dennis, etc.

ACT 1

Amongst the garishly flashing lights of New York City of 1928, Miss Agnes Gooch, nanny, her little charge clamped tightly to her hand, is trying to find number three, Beekman Place. Gooch's mission is to deliver the orphaned ten year-old Patrick Dennis to the home of his only surviving relation, his aunt Mame. New York appals her, and she will be glad when they are safely out of these frightening streets and little Patrick is tucked behind the lace curtains of Beekman Place in the arms of that sweet, grey-haired lady, his aunt ('St Bridget').

The elegant Mame Dennis doesn't actually have any grey hairs. She sports gold pajamas, drinks endless martinis and lives life as one huge, happy party. When Gooch and Patrick arrive on her doorstep, she is playing hostess to a wad of celebrities in the most frighteningly lively fashion ('It's Today') equipped with a bugle with which to emphasise her whoopiest actions. Gooch is terribly alarmed, but Patrick is fascinated by this wonderfully generous aunt who feeds him on caviar and makes him a present of her bugle. Life with auntie Mame is going to be interesting.

It has already started being interesting when a storm cloud in the shape of Mr Dwight Babcock of the Knickerbocker Bank calls at Beekman Place. Mr Babcock is Patrick's father's executor, and he has been nominated to keep an eye on the boy's upbringing. He is scarcely impressed when young Patrick's first action is to mix him an expert martini, and he glaringly informs Mame that the boy requires schooling in the traditional subjects of youth and not in the mixing of cocktails. He must be enrolled at once at one of the state's more conservative colleges.

Mame is not to be bulldozed into ruining her little love's life. If he must go to a school he will go to one of her choice, her friend Ralph's lovely advanced Laboratory of Life, but mostly he will be educated by Mame herself ('Open a New Window'). Mame's ideas of education mostly have to do with the broadening of one's horizons through experience and Patrick follows her in a crazy cavalcade from salon to speakeasy, discovering life in the gayest and most uninhibited way, until the boring Mr Babcock catches up with them. Patrick is dragged from a naked play session, in which the children of the Laboratory of Life are imitating the couplings of frogs, and condemned to college.

It is a day of disasters for Mame. Not only has she lost her child, she has lost all her money. Wall Street has crashed and Mame's stockbroker is teetering on a window ledge as he phones to tell her that she is wiped out. Patrick must go to school and Mame must go out and get a job. An extravagant (and soon regretted) offer from her very dearest friend, the operetta star Vera Charles, lands her a minor role in Vera's new musical *The Lady Astronomer* at the Shubert Theatre. Mame is cast as the illustration to Vera's song 'The Man in the Moon (is a lady)' and her part in the production consists of being hoisted fly-wards on a property moon while supplying an obbligato to Vera's reprise of the song's chorus.

But on the first night Mame muffs it. She gets an attack of vertigo and, racing catastrophically through her notes, ends by tumbling from her moon and wrecking the whole number. To compound her disgrace, she then gets herself entwined with Vera's jewellery and ruins the star's solo curtain calls. She is ignominiously sacked and only Patrick stands by her. He thought she was the only good thing in the whole awful show ('You're My Best Girl').

Job follows job until Mame ends up working as a manicurist in a gentleman's beauty salon. Her first customer is a fine southern gentleman called Beauregard Jackson Pickett Burnside whose fine southern manners do not flinch from perfection even when Mame manicures the tops off his fingers. But she still gets sacked. Mame Dennis was just not made to hold down a job.

Back at Beekman Place Mame decides that they all need cheering up so she, Agnes, Patrick and the butler Ito decide to push the calendar a little. They will have their Christmas early ('We Need a Little Christmas'). As they exchange presents and start laughing once again, Father Christmas arrives in person. Beauregard Jackson Pickett Burnside has tracked down the pretty manicurist and has come to ask her, all of them, out to a swank dinner.

Dinner is just the beginning. It is not long before Mame is invited down to bluegrass country to meet the awesome Mother Burnside, head of the clan and feared throughout the southern states. Mame makes a big effort to fit in. She arrives all dolled up like Scarlett O'Hara with southern drawl honed to perfection and prepared to do or die. Sally Cato MacDougal, who has considered herself virtually engaged to Beau for decades, is determined that it should be die. She puts Mame in a position where she is committed to ride to the Burnside hounds the next morning and, with the connivance of Mother Burnside, arranges that she is to be given the wildest horse in the stable and a side-saddle.

When the hunt gallops off (Fox Hunt), Mame and her horse go streaking away, passing the Master of the hounds, passing the hounds and finally passing the fox itself! When she returns to the bosom of the family she has accomplished a deep south first—she has brought back the fox alive! Mother Burnside is completely won over by this exhibition and Beau is happy to ask 'Mame' to be his wife.

ACT 2

Beau and Mame are wed and set off on a honeymoon which bids fair to break every record for length and breadth of honeymoons. As the months and then the years pass, Patrick's only contact with his aunt is a perfect flood of postcards and gifts from romantically out-of-the-way places. The honeymoon progresses to Austria in its third year and, there, fate interferes once more in the life of Mame Dennis. Dear Beau accidentally falls off an alp. The marriage is over before the honeymoon, and Mame Jackson Pickett Burnside is a widow. A very, very, very wealthy widow.

Mame returns to Beekman Place to the faithful Ito and to Agnes who has been trained as a secretary in order to take down Mame's memoirs which Vera, who is back in the pack at the mere scent of returned prosperity to assert that she and Mame are as always 'Bosom Buddies', is determined her dear friend will write. The memoirs don't turn out to be an instantly viable project, but Agnes does. When the two ladies find out that Agnes has never had a date in her plain, bespectacled life, they determine to change all that. Agnes is deprived of her glasses, gussied up in Mame's showiest cast-offs and instructed to follow her mentor's example and live!

When Mame does get down to those memoirs she does it in style. Beekman Place becomes a literary shrine and Mame affects the style of Elizabeth Barrett Browning, as chapter one stretches to six months and a pile of pages the size of *Who's Who*, and chapter two threatens to be worse. While literature is being born at Beekman Place, in the outside world other people are living life and not writing about it. Patrick has got himself a girlfriend called Gloria Upson and Agnes has gone even further. When she and her suitcase come back home it is evident that she has more than taken Mame's advice to live. She is heavily pregnant (Gooch's Song). Mame welcomes her back with affection and prepares to mother her through the later stages of her state, oblivious of the fact that Patrick is suddenly not so anxious to bring his Gloria back to the house. Perhaps it would be better if Mame came up to Connecticut and met Gloria and her parents on their home ground.

And so Mame goes to Connecticut and does her best to mix with the heartily pretentious Upson family. When she's left to chaperone the kids' dance, however, she cannot resist dropping her dignity and letting them all hear and see 'That's How Young I Feel'. She feels a good deal older when she hears the word wedding being mentioned. Her Patrick, her little love marry that whining, lacquered ninny of a Gloria and settle down in a custom-built ranch house on the dandelion plot next door to the Upson mansion? Surely that can't be what he wants. But when she asks him rather too forthrightly, her little love reacts angrily to the criticism of his choice of girl and storms off, leaving Mame to wonder where she went wrong ('If He Walked into my Life').

Peace is made and Mame, the apartment now transformed into a miracle of modernity by a trim little interior decorator called Pegeen Ryan, organises a nice party for the Upsons. But Mame is not one to make a U-turn. When the bride-to-be and her family are safely settled with some outrageous hors d'oeuvres, the party is joined by all Mame's crazy friends and celebrities and Agnes, bulging with unmarried promise, puts in an appearance which tops them all.

It is Mame's cue. She now reveals that she is going into unmarried mothers in a big way. She has bought a lovely dandelion patch in Connecticut where she proposes to build the Beauregard Burnside Memorial Home for Single Mothers. The Upsons are thunderstruck at the threat to their real estate value and, dragging Gloria with them, stride indignantly out of both Beekman Place and the lives of Patrick and Mame. What has she done? She has saved her little love from a frightful fate, and Patrick has realised it. He'll make do with his old 'best girl' until the right one comes along.

A decade later Mame is still going strong in her wonderful ways. Patrick has grown up and wed Pegeen Ryan, who was once his fellow pupil at the Laboratory of Life, and they have a little boy of their own for Auntie Mame to fuss over. When the unquenchable Mame comes up with a plan to take young Peter around the world with her, the boy's father wades in with a stout 'no', but it is no use: you can't fight Auntie Mame. Peter will happily follow this Pied Piper of Manhattan to all the adventures and experiences that she can find for him, just as his father did.

HAIR

an American tribal love-rock musical in two acts by Gerome Ragni and James Rado. Music by Galt MacDermot. Produced at the Public Theatre, New York, 17 October 1967 and subsequently played at the Cheetah Club from 22 December 1967. Opened on Broadway in a revised version at the Biltmore Theatre 29 April 1968 with Rado (Claude), Ragni (Berger), Lynn Kellogg (Sheila) and Lamont Washintgon (Hud). Revived there 5 October 1977 with Randall Easterbrook, Michael Holt, Ellen Foley and Cleavant Derricks.

Produced at the Shaftesbury Theatre, London, 27 September 1968 with Paul Nicholas, Oliver Tobias, Annabel Leventon and Peter Straker. Produced at the Queen's Theatre 25 June 1974 with Demetrius Christopholus, Gary Hamilton, Miquel Brown and Gary Aflalo.

Produced at the Théâtre de la Porte-Saint-Martin, Paris, 31 May 1969 in a version by Jacques Lanzmann with Julien Clerc, Hervé Wattine, Jeanine Bennett and Bill Combs. Played at the Casino de Paris 29 March 1984.

Produced at Munich in a version by Walter Brandin 1968.

A film version was produced by United Artists in 1979 with John Savage, Treat Williams, Beverly D'Angelo and Melba Moore.

CHARACTERS

Claude
Berger
Woof
Hud
Jeanie
Crissie
Dionne
Angela
Mom
Dad, etc.

ACT 1

Hair is not a story, it is a presentation: a presentation of a way of life which the tribe of young people who perform the songs and words of the show are putting forward as a suggested alternative to the established American way of life, its ethical and moral codes, its aims, its satisfactions and its disappoint-ments. They do not claim that their way is the only way, but at least they are

813

offering another way for the audience's consideration. It is a way which embraces freedom in love and in sex, freedom from the rules of standard society, freedom to reject the state, freedom to seek freedom under the influence of drugs. Others might call it hedonism. It is a way which seeks pleasure, disguised under all kinds of mystic and ritual names and performances, without responsibility. They all want and hope for a world where they can do and have what they want and be loved for it ('Aquarius').

The principal members of the tribe are Berger, a 'Manhattan' high-school kick-out who sports the rash of long hair which is the membership badge of the group; Claude, his best friend and a tribal leader who is threatened with the draft and who would like to have been born in 'Manchester, England'; Sheila who lives with them both and who loves Berger, is loved by Claude and makes posters; Woof who has a longing for Mick Jagger ('Sodomy'); Jeanie who digs deep into drugs and 'Coloured Spade' Hud.

The boys list all the things they haven't got ('Ain't Got No') and the last and greatest of these is 'mind'. Claude can be positive over only one thing. He still has the bits that make up his body ('I Got Life'). He won't even have that if he gets drafted and sent off by the big boys to fight their war when all he wants to do is stay home, copulate and go gassy on drugs.

Jeanie sings to the polluted 'Air' of Manhattan and the tribe chant mindlessly and rebelliously of the drugs that have made them all what they think is unscrewed ('Initials'). Berger celebrates his expulsion from high school ('Going Down') with a handful of pills while Claude takes to marijuana and rambles on narcissistically about the body that the draft doctors have had under their hands. But the most celebratory part of their bodies is still their emblem of belonging to each other, their 'Hair', even if the older generation attempts to explain it all away as a simple anthropological urge for finery ('My Conviction').

Sheila is a professional protester, except she doesn't get paid. She makes posters and says things like 'groovy' and lusts with gifts after Berger who isn't interested, so all in all the whole experience is a bit lacking for Sheila ('Dead End'). Woof and Berger get involved incoherently with the American flag ('Don't Put It Down') and decide to follow fashion by burning it at a be-in. There they can show their colours and be heroically busted for drugs, arrested for being freaks and just noticed. Crissy doesn't go to the rally. She has different preoccupations, maybe. She met a boy called 'Frank Mills' who is embarrassingly un-hip and she wants to see him again.

At the be-in, the tribe chant their preoccupations ('Hare Krishna'), drugs and sex and love. They respond to warnings and threats from the other society only with more chanting until the frustrated people howl that this unresponsive, irresponsible rabble should be exported immediately as fodder to the Vietnamese guns. The tribe, having won a response to their inactive action, jubilantly increase their fire. Berger starts removing his clothes and, as the boys begin to ceremoniously burn their draft cards, the others follow suit. When it is Claude's turn, however, he fakes the destruction of his card. He's going to follow where his destiny, that is to say his body, leads him ('Where Do I Go?').

ACT 2

The band play 'The Electric Blues', whirling themselves into a whole lot of cosmic imagery until they blow a fuse.

Claude has been drafted and Berger wants Sheila to have sex with his friend as a farewell gift. Sheila is irked and won't, not even for the price of having Berger the following night ('Easy to Be Hard'). She says she despises Claude for lacking the courage not to go. The others might be disappointed too, but they know Claude is a friend. Tomorrow he will have his hair cut to become a soldier, but for tonight he looks gorgeous in a long white sari as he shares out his personal belongings indifferently amongst his friends ('White Boys'/'Black Boys').

But there's the evening to be got through, so it's time for enough drug to carry on ('Walking In Space') and, into the mind-warp that follows, rush a series of pictures of war people and war events ('Prisoners in Niggertown'). Claude and Berger almost grow coherent together on what they want from life, but it is more important to get paired off. Who sleeps with who? 'Good Morning, Starshine'.

In 'The Bed' they are as hung up as they are in the real world, maybe more so, but things are manipulated until Claude and Sheila are left together. Berger goes and Jeanie is sent away. Claude starts telling Sheila about this planet called 'Exanaplanetooch' where he comes from and where he's going back to the next day. Not into the army. Will she come too? The lights go out before Sheila finally gives in and Claude gets his 'Sentimental Ending'. In the morning he goes. His long severed hair is a gift to Berger, tied up in a paper bag. Sheila is already wearing the white sari.

The score of *Hair* underwent considerable changes between its productions. For the Broadway production several songs used in the original Public Theatre version, including 'Exanaplanetooch' and 'Dead End' were eliminated and a considerable body of new material introduced. The musical breakdown given here is based on the printed script of 1969.

PROMISES, PROMISES

a musical in two acts by Neil Simon based on the screenplay *The Apartment* by Billy Wilder and I A L Diamond. Lyrics by Hal David. Music by Burt Bacharach. Produced at the Shubert Theatre, New York, 1 December 1968 with Jerry Orbach (Chuck), Jill O'Hara (Fran), Edward Winter (Sheldrake), Paul Reed (Dobitch), Vince O'Brien (Eichelberger), Dick O'Neill (Vanderhof) and Norman Shelley (Kirkeby).

Produced at the Prince of Wales Theatre, London, 2 October 1969 with Tony Roberts, Betty Buckley, James Congdon, Ronn Carroll, Ivor Dean, Don Fellows and Jay Denyer.

CHARACTERS

Chuck Baxter
J D Sheldrake
Fran Kubelik
Jesse Vanderhof
Dr Dreyfuss
Mr Eichelberger
Marge MacDougall
Mr Dobitch
Mr Kirkeby
Miss Olson
Sylvia Gilhooley
Vivien della Hoya
Karl Kubelik
Miss Polansky, Miss Wong, Bartender Eddie, Bartender Eugene, Helen
Sheldrake, etc.

ACT 1

Chuck Baxter is an accountant in a large insurance company. He works past
his hours in the hope that Mr Sheldrake of personnel may notice him and his
aspirations, but he never does because Chuck is one of those people that the
people who matter somehow never do notice. He's 'Half as Big as Life'.
Sometimes Chuck invents imaginary conversations between himself and
people who haven't noticed him. Like the pretty Fran Kubelik who works in
the employees' cafeteria. After he's worked late, and hasn't been noticed,
Chuck goes for a drink in a singles bar on Second Avenue, and one day, at
this particular bar, someone who matters does notice him.

It is Mr Dobitch of Mortgage and Loans. Mr Dobitch is fifty and he's got
Miss Gilhooley of the telephone operating department in tow and his problem is only too evident. Miss Gilhooley is feeling poorly and needs
somewhere to lie down for an hour, but Miss Gilhooley lives in Brooklyn.
Chuck's apartment in West 67th would be an ideal place for her to lie down
and it wouldn't do his career prospects any harm at all. Chuck hands over
the key and tells Mr Dobitch where to find the aspirins, but it turns out that
the aspirins weren't needed. The only things that got used were the vodka
and the record player.

Still, the ailment is obviously a recurring one, because Miss Gilhooley
needs to lie down every Tuesday that month round about the same time, and
then Mr Dobitch introduces Chuck to Mr Kirkeby of accounts who has
similar problems on Wednesdays. So, while his superiors enjoy themselves
'Upstairs', Chuck finds alternative occupations away from home. Next thing
Mr Eichelberger of Research decides he needs a bright young man for his
department and that is the end of Thursdays. Dr Dreyfuss next door starts
giving Chuck disapproving looks on the landing. From what he hears
through the walls three nights of the week he wonders how the boy can stand
up.

Then one day Mr Vanderhof of Public Relations turns up on his doorstep. He just had a tooth pulled and got lucky with the nurse. Chuck has had enough. All this time out and all these unfulfilled promises about promotion. This time it's 'no'. But Mr Vanderhof begs in a way an executive never ought to have to beg, and he gives his word of honour that his word will be his bond, so Chuck finally gives in and goes out. The record player gets into its usual groove and Dr Dreyfuss next door shakes his head as Chuck confides to the audience that, once he gets his first foot on the ladder, he'll work really hard and then, perhaps, he'll be able to use his own apartment instead of leaving it to others.

Mr Vanderhof didn't leave till 2.30 a.m. and Chuck got a cold sitting outside waiting so he turns up sniffing next morning at the company sick bay where he meets Mr Vanderhof who has come to be looked at for something that strongly resemble teeth marks. Mr Vanderhof swears he has spoken to Sheldrake of Personnel and that Chuck will hear something to his advantage very soon, and can he book in for next Friday. As Chuck waits his turn, Fran Kubelik comes in to get something for hiccups. Chuck imagines what he would like her to say, but the conversation takes a mundane turn ('You'll Think of Someone'). She's been promoted to the Executive Dining Room so he won't see her anymore. But wait! At last his summons to Personnel has come. The promises are about to come home to roost.

The long-awaited interview does not go quite according to daydream. Chuck's customers have rather overdone the loyal, resourceful, co-operative bit and Mr Sheldrake has not only smelt a rat but seems to have the whole situation taped practically to a conversation. Chuck waits for the blow, but it doesn't come. What does come is a request (well, scarcely a request) from Mr Sheldrake for the key of the apartment. He has an appointment with the Branch Manager from Kansas and the apartment is an ideal venue. Chuck can have his tickets for tonight's big basketball game and he will have Chuck's keys and the whole thing will just be 'Our Little Secret'. Chuck wonders if Fran Kubelik might be interested in basketball and hallelujah! she is, but she has a date with someone with whom she used to be serious and maybe she could make it late, say about nine. Chuck is in heaven—'She Likes Basketball'.

Fran goes to her date. It is with Sheldrake and she is the fictional Branch Manager from Kansas. She is cool with him. He didn't call, he gave her a hell of a time and no, she isn't ready to pick their affair up where they left off. She knows she ought to get up and go and call the whole thing off, but she misses the moment ('Knowing When to Leave') and so, while Chuck waits and waits outside Madison Square Garden, Fran and Sheldrake are carrying on back at the apartment and he's telling her that he's really and truly getting a divorce and does she still love him.

Chuck gets his promotion and he keeps his promise to himself. No more apartment. Dobitch, Eichelberger, Kirkeby and Vanderhof grind their teeth and wonder 'Where Can You Take a Girl' while Chuck takes sherry in the Executive Dining Room served by an apologetic Fran. Of course, when Chuck says no more apartment that doesn't include Mr Sheldrake. Mr

Sheldrake has carte blanche. One day Chuck tactfully returns to his superior a compact which his young lady has dropped in the apartment and, to his surprise, he receives in return an envious statement on his bachelor status. Chuck isn't sure. It's all very well being a bachelor, but what's the use if you aren't doing and getting freely all the things the married men seem to be getting and doing on the side. It isn't fair ('Wanting Things').

At the firm's Christmas party, Miss Olson, Mr Sheldrake's secretary, gets a little tipsy and conspiratorily greets Fran as 'the Branch Manager from Kansas'. Fran bridles, but the confidential secretary is, under alcohol, very unconfidential and out it all comes. In her day she was 'the Branch Manager from Minneapolis' and she went through all the stages of the affair that Fran is going through in exactly the same way, the same restaurants, the same spiel, the same nonsense about divorcing his wife. She and all the others.

At the height of the party Mr Dobitch introduces three company girls with a dance routine ('Turkey Lurkey Time') and succeeds in persuading Chuck to take the keys to his Jaguar and his Diners Club card for the holidays in exchange for the use of the apartment. Chuck is feeling seasonally jolly but his attempts to make enjoyable conversation with Fran fall flat. She is not feeling at all jolly and, when she takes out her compact to repair the damage wrought by Miss Olson's revelations, he does a double take. It is the compact that he returned to Sheldrake. The dreadful truth dawns, and it really hurts him when he has to smilingly tell Sheldrake that the apartment is all ready and waiting for his Christmas Eve celebration.

ACT 2

Exiled again, Chuck spends his Christmas Eve in a bar where he is chatted up by very obvious Marge with whom he ends up agreeing 'A Fact Can Be a Very Obvious Thing'. Back at the apartment, Sheldrake's celebration isn't going nearly as easily. Fran is in tears, torturing herself and Sheldrake with the truth as dispensed by Miss Olson. When he leaves her to catch his train back to his wife, Fran stays on a moment to fix her face and, gazing at his photograph, she sings to 'Whoever You Are' that in spite of all, she loves him, before bursting into tears again. Then she notices a phial of sleeping pills on the table...

Chuck arrives back at the apartment with Marge and finds Fran seemingly asleep on the bed. He crossly tells her to get out and then he notices the empty phial. Marge is forgotten as Chuck runs to get Dr Dreyfuss who goes to work with a stomach pump on the drugged girl. Gradually Fran comes to and Dreyfuss and Chuck start walking her round the apartment. The Doctor, whose opinion of Chuck is pretty carnivorous anyhow, now thinks he is a total fink and Chuck, to cover the activities in his flat of the past few months, has to pretend that Dreyfuss's opinions are the truth. He does manage to convince the doctor, for Fran's sake, not to call the police, but he calls Sheldrake himself and, talking double in front of his wife, Sheldrake squirms out of doing anything at all about the situation.

When Fran wakes up, she sees Chuck and realises that the apartment is

818

his. She's sorry. She's also sorry he interfered. But she has to smile a little at Dreyfuss's indignant advice to 'A Young Pretty Girl Like You' and she ends up playing gin rummy on the bed with Chuck until her heart begins to ache again instead of her head. Unfortunately, in all the fracas, Chuck has forgotten about Mr Dobitch and his reservation. Dobitch turns up with Miss Gilhooley and sees Fran there in bed. Credit card or no credit card, Chuck gets rid of them. From now on the apartment is off bounds to everyone for ever.

It all finally becomes worthwhile when he hears Fran really saying some of the words he imagined in his daydreams: 'If I'd had any sense I would have fallen in love with someone nice like you.' It's in the conditional tense and she has, of course, just tried to kill herself over someone else, but it's a start, even when she picks up a guitar and starts singing a song to the effect that 'I'll Never Fall in Love Again'.

The next visitor is a totally unannounced one. It's Fran's brother, six-feet-six and a Polish temper. He called the office when Fran didn't get home and a Mr Vanderhof, a Mr Eichelberger, a Mr Kirkeby and a Mr Dobitch told him he'd find Fran here. When he finds out that she's just tried suicide he's damagingly furious and, when Chuck gallantly volunteers that it was because of him, Kubelik's fist does its work. Fran kisses the senseless boy as she leaves, whispering her thanks for his cover up.

Back at the office, Vanderhof has discovered a new young lad in his department who has an apartment and Miss Olson has handed in her notice and is promising to tell all to Mrs Sheldrake so, all in all, Christmas has been eventful this year. By New Year Mrs Sheldrake has booted her husband out of the house and he is trying to renew the old arrangement with Chuck. He can't really can't be expected to take Fran to his new residence at the New York Athletic Club. Of course, he insists, he is going to ask her to marry him and, of course, man to man, he winks, that kind of an engagement can stretch out for ever.

When Chuck hands over the key, Sheldrake finds it isn't the apartment key, it's the key to the executive washroom. Chuck is giving up the game. He's sick of it all ('Promises, Promises'). He's even going to give up the apartment and, instead of going on to Dreyfuss's New Year's Eve party, he's packing. When Dreyfuss calls by, they pop a bottle of champagne together as a farewell.

At the sound of the cork, there is a cry and in rushes Fran. She thought she heard... but no, there is Chuck safe and sound and amazed to see her. What happened to the all-important date with Sheldrake? Well, she met Sheldrake and, yes, he asked her to marry him and well, what does he think she said? What can one say to a man who doesn't like basketball, a man who can't even play gin rummy? When Chuck starts getting around to words like 'love', Dr Dreyfuss slips tactfully away. All things considered, he is glad he is not losing his neighbour. Maybe he is even gaining one.

1776

a musical in seven scenes by Peter Stone based on an idea by Sherman Edwards. Music and lyrics by Sherman Edwards. Produced at the 46th Street Theatre, New York, 16 March 1969 with William Daniels (John Adams), Virginia Vestoff (Abigail), Howard da Silva (Franklin), Paul Hecht (Dickinson), Ken Howard (Jefferson) and Betty Buckley (Martha).

Produced at the New Theatre, London, 16 June 1970 with Lewis Fiander, Vivienne Ross, Ronald Radd, Bernard Lloyd, John Quentin and Cheryl Kennedy.

A film version was produced by Columbia in 1972 with Daniels, Miss Vestoff, da Silva, Donald Madden, Howard, and Blythe Danner.

CHARACTERS

John Hancock, *President of the Continental Congress*
Dr Josiah Bartlett, *Member for New Hampshire*
John Adams, *Member for Massachusetts*
Stephen Hopkins, *Member for Rhode Island*
Roger Sherman, *Member for Connecticut*
Lewis Morris, *Member for New York*
Robert Livingston, *Member for New York*
Reverend John Witherspoon, *Member for New Jersey*
Benjamin Franklin, *Member for Pennsylvania*
John Dickinson, *Member for Pennsylvania*
James Wilson, *Member for Pennsylvania*
Caesar Rodney, *Member for Delaware*
Colonel Thomas McKean, *Member for Delaware*
George Read, *Member for Delaware*
Samuel Chase, *Member for Maryland*
Richard Henry Lee, *Member for Virginia*
Thomas Jefferson, *Member for Virginia*
Joseph Hewes, *Member for North Carolina*
Edward Rutledge, *Member for South Carolina*
Dr Lyman Hall, *Member for Georgia*
Charles Thomson, *Secretary*
Andrew McNair, *Custodian and Bell-ringer*
Abigail Adams
Martha Jefferson
Leather Apron, Painter, Courier, etc.

ACT 1

The year is 1776, a year of as yet little significance, and the place is Philadelphia, seat of the Continental Congress, the parliament representing the thirteen states of the un-united continent of North America. The subject under discussion is independency, the political and judicial separation of the American colonies from the country which founded and funded them and with which, at the present time, they are in active conflict. In spite of the fact that George Washington and the army of the American states are daily doing battle with the forces of His Majesty King George of England, many amongst the people and politicians of America still believe that it is in the best interests of the colonies to maintain a link with Britain, the power behind the greatest and richest Empire in the world, but others have a burning thirst for independence. In the Continental Congress, the loudest of these is John Adams of Massachusetts.

Adams is the Cato of the Congress. When they would discuss the day-to-day business of running a country, he interferes with his endless arguments for breaking the ties between the colonies and Britain and declaring America a sovereign state ('Sit Down, John'/'Piddle, Twiddle, and Resolve'). This tactic, and John's abrasive personality, have done his cause no good. He has provoked irritation and even boredom amongst his fellow delegates many of whom regard him as nothing more than a crank, and he makes no progress. He writes home to his wife Abigail in Massachusetts in uncomprehending despair but, while he is urging her to lead the women of Massachusetts in the manufacture of saltpetre for the war effort, she laments that there is not a pin to be found in the whole state ('Till Then').

John Adams is not the only delegate to the Congress who is in favour of action towards independency. He is merely the loudest. Amongst those who support such a step is Benjamin Franklin of Pennsylvania, and Franklin is able to see that Adams' personality is a handicap to the cause. If a motion for separation from Britain is to succeed in the Congress, it must be proposed by someone other than Adams, someone who will not alienate support. The gentleman they choose is the eager Richard Henry Lee of Virginia ('The Lees of Old Virginia') who is quickly convinced that he thought of the idea himself and double-quickly into his saddle heading for Virginia to get his legislature's formal approval for his action.

On 7 June the new session of Congress begins and the delegates new and old assemble but, although there is some gentle canvassing of the new arrivals about their positions on the question of independency, the subject is not formally brought forward. As gloomy dispatches come to Congress from the battle front, Adams, in spite of himself, remains silent, impatiently awaiting the return of Lee. When it seems he can hold back no longer, the Virginian arrives and with him he brings the coveted resolution: 'That these united colonies are and of right ought to be free and independent states, that they are absolved from all allegiance to the British Crown, and that all political connection between them and the state of Great Britain is and ought to be totally dissolved.'

John Dickinson of Pennsylvania, the leader of the anti-independency group in Congress, immediately proposes an indefinite postponement of debate but, when the delegations are polled, the result is one absent, six for and five against with New York, as in every vote, abstaining. The debate on independency can, at last, begin. With Dickinson and Adams at their heads, the two parties go into verbal battle until, at the height of the argument, Caesar Rodney of Delaware collapses. He must be taken home to die in his own bed and, with his departure, the state of the voting changes. Without Rodney, the Delaware delegation is no longer able to vote for Adams and the position is now six against and five for. Immediately South Carolina leaps into battle with a proposal to end the debate on independency but, at the crucial moment, an ascetic-looking clergyman appears in the chamber. He is the Reverend John Witherspoon from New Jersey, he is late, and he is in favour of independence. Now the score is six all and poor Mr Morris of New York, who has never been able to get any agreement or instructions from his legislature, is still in abstention.

Adams, knowing that Hancock, the Court President, who has a casting vote is a deep supporter of independency, grabs his moment to call for a vote on Lee's declaration, but Dickinson counters with a proposal than any such vote must be unanimous. When the tally is taken and Hancock is left with the decision, he agrees on the principal of unanimity. The vote is of too great a consequence to be anything else. Adams is turned to despair: unanimity is impossible—it has already been seen that Congress is divided. He needs time, time to win over the dissenting states, and that time he finds a way to gain. He proposes a postponement of the vote on Lee's motion until a properly formulated declaration can be presented on which a vote can be made.

Such a patent delaying tactic is ridiculed by Dickinson. What would be the purpose of such a paper? Adams is stuck for a reply, but he finds an unexpected ally in young Thomas Jefferson of Virginia who, with a few well-chosen words of reasoning, puts the excuse into fine words for him. It works. After the delegations have again voted predictably six against six, Hancock casts for the postponement. Adams has his time.

He also has a declaration to write. He cannot, others cannot or will not ('But, Mr Adams...') and one of these last is Thomas Jefferson. He has a lovely young wife who expects him home and he will not stay in Philadelphia writing purposeful prose. But he does. Duty stands, not for the first time, between him and his bride. Unfortunately, thoughts of his bride stand between him and his work and inspiration will not come. Adams understands. He thinks of his own wife ('Yours, Yours, Yours') and he sends for Martha Jefferson. When she arrives ('He Plays the Violin') the shutters go up at Jefferson's lodgings and they stay up, but before long the men of Congress will have in front of them Thomas Jefferson's Declaration of Independence.

Meanwhile it is John Adams' task to win over the six dissenting delegations. Delaware's Read has to be drawn into agreement with his fellow, McKean; Franklin has to win over the dissenting Judge Wilson for Pennsylvania; and the reasoning of Samuel Chase of Maryland needs to be dissected. It turns out that Maryland is against revolution solely because they fear that they would lose in open battle with the British. Washington's battle despatches, lugubrious to a fault in an attempt to draw support from Congress, have deceived him. Adams offers to take him to New Brunswick and the battle front to see for himself. The prize will be the vote of Maryland. He will win one of the 'Cool, Cool, Considerate Men' from Dickinson's side to his own with a picture of the reality of a war which is already well-known to the courier who brings Washington's despatches ('Momma, Look Sharp').

Jefferson's declaration is being read to the gentlemen of the Congress

822

when Adams returns, his first conquest made. Maryland is theirs. They are on their way to independence and an American nation ('The Egg'). But their elation is dispersed when, at the end of the reading of the Declaration, a shower of amendments are proposed. Every delegation, every state, every person seems to have been offended by some portion of the document, some sentiment or some turn of phrase. One by one the alterations begin, breaking down the document and its force in the interest of winning the support of the vital opposing states, until finally one obstacle greater than all the others is encountered.

Jefferson's document contains a clause which effectively means the abolition of slavery and such a clause the southern states, whose economy exists on slave labour, will not countenance ('Molasses to Rum'). As one, the North and South Carolina and Georgia delegations walk out. It seems like an impasse. The three southern states are implacable, Delaware without Rodney seems lost and there is only a day left before the vote.

It is Franklin who suggests the deletion of the slavery clause. Dear as it may be to his heart, this declaration is one of independence from Britain and it should not be lost for the sake of another declaration on a separate subject. John interrogates his soul, his motives, his reasoning ('Is Anybody There?') but, when the vote comes, he has to give way to expediency and scratch out the clause. The Carolinas and Georgia are won, but what of Delaware? What of Pennsylvania? Delaware is saved by the return of the dying Rodney, but when Dickinson rises to announce the vote of Pennsylvania it seems that all has been in vain. It will be 'nay'.

Then Benjamin Franklin demands that the delegation be polled. He is 'yea', Dickinson is 'nay' and that leaves James Wilson to decide the whole question of independence. If he too is 'nay' then independence is lost, if he joins the 'yeas' then it is carried. Mr Wilson is not a man made for world-shaking decisions. He has no wish to be remembered and, under the spotlight, he finds it safest to go with the majority. Pennsylvania votes 'yea'. John Dickinson quietly leaves the chamber. By this declaration he is no longer an Englishman but an American and he will abide by his country's new charter and fight in her army, but he cannot sign his name along with the other delegates who, as the curtain falls, put their signatures to the document which creates the United States of America.

APPLAUSE

a musical in two acts by Betty Comden and Adolph Green based on the film *All About Eve* and the original story by Mary Orr. Lyrics by Lee Adams. Music by Charles Strouse. Produced at the Palace Theatre, New York, 30 March 1970 with Lauren Bacall (Margo), Penny Fuller (Eve), Len Cariou (Bill) and Robert Mandan (Howard).

Produced at Her Majesty's Theatre, London, 16 November 1972 with Miss Bacall, Angela Richards, Eric Flynn and Basil Hoskins.

CHARACTERS

Margo Channing
Eve Harrington
Howard Benedict
Bert
Buzz Richards
Bill Sampson
Duane Fox
Karen Richards
Bonnie
Stan Harding
Danny, Carol, Joey, Peter, Bob, etc.

ACT 1

The opening scene represents New York's annual 'Tony' Awards ceremony, Broadway's glittering celebration of the best of its own achievements in the past theatrical year. The host introduces the star who is to present the prize for best actress, a two-time winner herself, the one and only Margo Channing. Margo Channing is one of those *monstres sacrés* peculiar to American theatre—the oversized, overdressed and over-aged female star for whom the expression 'camp' was invented but on whom the word 'glamorous' is instead bestowed by the chorus boys, shop girls and middle-aged middle-class who have made her what she is. Now she follows the traditional recipe, reading the nominations and opening the inevitable envelope. The winner is...Eve Harrington.

Down in the audience a young actress goes through the equally traditional thrilled, startled and humble routine as she steps up to receive her prize. It is quite clear that, under all the youth and delight, Miss Harrington is a blossoming, embryonic Margo Channing. Her acceptance speech features most special thanks to Margo and, as she runs on, Margo's thoughts take her back to that time, only eighteen months or so ago, when Eve Harrington entered her life.

It is the first night of *The Friendly Arrangement* on Broadway and Margo Channing's dressing room is buzzing with friends and hangers-on ('Backstage Babble') all come to say 'darling-you-were-wonderful'. When the babblers are cleared away her director and lover, Bill Sampson, remains for a brief note and a private moment. Tomorrow he has to go to Italy for a film and Margo is anguished at the thought of being left alone. The author, Buzz Richards, and his wife Karen come in and Buzz has the same note for Margo about a lost laugh. Margo knows, and she knows why she cannot do the line in question. She admits to forty and the line in question is one which clearly belongs to a younger woman.

Karen turns the conversation. She has spotted a girl outside the stage door every night of the show's previews. Every night she has been to see the show, spending her last penny, and she idolises Margo Channing. Please, will Margo meet her? Before anyone realises it, Karen is introducing Eve Harrington into their lives: a mousy, thin girl with eyes and a raincoat. To Margo's polite chat, she responds with a beautiful story of how seeing Margo on the stage has brought warmth and light into her life, before thanking her for meeting her and then fading away into the background as the theatre people head noisily on to the first night party.

Margo says goodbye to Bill, who is heading straight for the airport, comforting her with thoughts of later on ('Think How it's Going to Be') but, when he is gone, she does not feel like facing the platitudes of the regular first night party. She feels even less like being alone and she asks her dresser and buddy, Duane, to squire her and the still present Eve out on the town. She is tired 'But Alive'. Down in the Greenwich Village gay bar to which Duane leads them, Margo is among her disciples and the song rises to its climax in an energetic dance.

Later on, back at Margo's apartment, Eve takes a call from Buzz saying that the reviews are great and Margo's the greatest. For the young girl it has been 'The Best Night of My Life' but, when Duane goes, Eve does not. She makes a late-night toddy for Margo, and listens sympathetically to her worrying about the age difference between herself and Bill as she looks at herself in one of her old movies ('Who's That Girl'). When Margo goes to bed, Eve answers another telephone call. She will pass on the message to Margo in the morning. Yes, she will be here.

Four months later, Eve has become Margo's indispensable Girl Friday and friend, utterly reliable and relied on, and allowed an unheard-of latitude with the star. When Margo threatens a tantrum at being denied time off to visit Bill in Italy, it is Eve who calmly and publicly tells her she is wrong, earning the undying gratitude of the author and producer of the show. It is a momentary shock to Margo when she accidentally walks in one day to catch Eve parading arrogantly in front of the mirror with one of her costumes, but it passes.

Eve's new position is not lost on the others—the prime minister behind Queen Margo—and producer Howard Benedict takes care to squire her out to Joe Allen's. Margo's understudy is there, and a few words of passing criticism from Eve are taken up meaningfully by Benedict. He lightly suggests that Eve, who knows every line and nuance of the role, could probably take the understudy herself, but Eve assures him that she is happier in her present position. Benedict is charmed: half the kids in the restaurant would kill for the chance of such a job. At a cue from him, several of the 'gipsies' come on with a number explaining that they are in the goddamned business just for one, wonderful thing—'Applause'.

A sleepy Margo is awakened by the telephone. Eve has booked a call to Italy in the middle of the night. It is Bill, and he is enchanted that Margo has remembered his birthday. Down the phone, Margo pleads with him to 'Hurry Back'. Later, just as Duane is getting in a few suspicious remarks about Eve's motives and her apeing of Margo, the phone rings again. The birthday call has done the trick and Bill is coming home. It's all thanks to Eve.

At the welcome home party a nervous Margo walks in on Bill and Eve laughing and horseplaying and she takes an immediate cold. After too many drinks she starts to insult her guests ('Fasten Your Seat Belts'), reserving particularly hard and sarcastic words for Eve, until everyone's sympathies are against her. Even the faithful Duane, who stays to settle her when everyone else has gone, admits she has been awful. But Margo has seen the light.

At the theatre, Eve auditions for the understudy to Margo's role, and is given it by a producer and an author thrilled at her young and very different reading. When Margo arrives she is livid. It is a plot. Eve offers to stand down, and Margo wryly concedes victory to her. If she can handle herself on the stage with the same artistry she shows off-stage, she is made. 'Welcome to the Theater', she sings meaningfully. When Eve has gone, Bill appears lovingly at Margo's side, but his gentle words are to no avail. Margo now sees the young understudy as a dreadful threat to every part of her life and she even accuses Bill of excessive interest in the girl. Bill has had enough. He stalks away from this paranoia, leaving Margo to wallop out the last lines of 'Welcome to the Theater' to the falling curtain.

ACT 2

Eve becomes very friendly with Buzz and Karen, and it is Karen who arranges things so that Margo misses her train back from their country house one night, thus giving Eve a chance to play the lead role in *The Friendly Arrangement*. No sooner is the deed done, than Karen starts to feel guilty, almost wondering if innocent, naïve Eve had bewitched her into such a wicked action ('Inner Thoughts'). Buzz half-guiltily wishes he could be there to see Eve's performance, but he banishes the thought hastily—Margo is their long-time friend. Margo's inner thoughts are on Bill. Perhaps he is in the theatre watching Eve. Perhaps she'll be awful. But, since there is nothing that can be done, Buzz, Karen and Margo settle down to an evening of being 'Good Friends', an evening which ends with the more and more oppressed Karen falling in a guilty faint.

Eve is not only not awful, she is a huge success in her Broadway debut, and somehow the newspapers are there to witness her triumph. Now Eve coolly dumps the young stage manager who smoothed her way to the under-study job and helped her hone her performance, and concentrates instead on Bill. Once again she trots out 'The Best Night of My Life' in all its finely-worked sincerity but, when she makes the final, calculated effort to entice him into her arms, he reminds her of Margo and rejects her. Undeterred, she turns her attentions to Howard Benedict who is dropping hints about a take-over. Eve bursts out against this: she doesn't want Margo's left-overs, she wants a role of her own. Well, perhaps even that can be arranged.

At Joe Allen's, Duane relates the story of Eve's success to the gang who inhabit the place, but when Eve and Howard arrive at the restaurant and go into a huddle with columnist Stan Harding, she brushes aside the gipsies' congratulations and soon leaves. 'She's No Longer a Gypsy', as far as they're concerned.

At her home, an ill-at-ease Margo is being photographed for a commercial. Bill turns up and takes over the session, relaxing her with fun and loving words ('You're One of a Kind') but, while he is kissing her, she is quizzing him about Eve's performance. This time he really is finished. It is quite clear what Margo's priorities are and always will be. Perhaps she does love him, but she loves Margo Channing, and Margo Channing the star, more. The competition is too much.

Backstage at the theatre, Eve meets with a moonstruck Buzz. He is writing her a role in his new play, and he has borrowed the keys to a friend's apartment. Eve is up the next step ('One Hallowe'en'). Her joyful paean to her own success is overheard by Howard, and Howard faces up to her. He has done some homework on Eve and found out the truth. He knows her real name and the truth of her background, one far from the beautiful, romantic story she told that first night in Margo's dressing room. He knows of her relentless sleeping her way from Bert, the stage manager, to Stan Harding to himself and now Buzz, and he knows that her dramatically killed husband is still alive.

Eve is disarmed, and Howard takes command. She will not spend the night with Buzz and start something that will wreck his life and his work. He is far too valuable to Howard as a writer. If she is good, there will be a part for her in the new play. He kisses her fiercely, she bites him and he slaps her hard. He knows what she wants and he can get it for her. Now she will collect her things and take a cab to his place. She has to.

When the new play is produced, Margo is shattered to find that the role always intended for her is to go to Eve. Karen is shattered to find out that Buzz and Eve are having that affair, at last, and she even goes so far as to seek compassion from Margo with an admission of the plot that gave Eve her chance. But Margo knows all about Eve. She recognises in her everything that was herself and she tells Karen not to worry. Eve will soon be onto the next step and Buzz will be left behind. As for Margo, she is suddenly disenchanted by it all—perhaps there can still be 'Something Greater' than a scrapbook of clippings left for her.

With that realisation, with that change of priorities, Margo can straighten out her relationship with Bill. Let Eve have the role. Let Eve have the applause. She now knows that she would rather have Bill. At the end of it all, they are back together again, and for that, if nothing else, Margo has Eve Harrington to thank.

COMPANY

a musical in two acts by George Furth. Music and lyrics by Stephen Sondheim. Produced at the Alvin Theatre, New York, 26 April 1970 with a cast including Dean

Jones (Robert), Elaine Stritch (Joanne), Susan Browning (April), Pamela Myers (Marta) and Donna McKechnie (Kathy).

Produced at Her Majesty's Theatre, London, 8 January 1972 with Larry Kert, Miss Stritch, Carol Richards, Annie McGreevy and Miss McKechnie.

CHARACTERS

Robert
Sarah
Harry
Susan
Peter
Jenny
David
Amy
Paul
Joanne
Larry
Marta
Kathy
April

ACT 1

In a slickly middle-class Manhattan apartment a bunch of Robert's lovely, married friends have gathered to give him a surprise birthday party. They haven't paused to consider that maybe Robert doesn't really want to be reminded he is thirty-five, and they are self-centredly unaware that he probably doesn't want to see all of them at once. They are his lovely friends and they know better than he does what he needs and what he wants.

These friends are not a close-knit bunch. They all know Robert but they don't know each other and, from the dialogue they share while they are waiting for him to turn up and be surprised, it is clear they were better off not knowing each other. They are here only because they all love Robert, and they all want to wish him fortune and his first wife.

He doesn't necessarily want either of those things and it's a bit hard to work out why he wants Sarah, Harry, Susan, Peter, Jenny, David, Amy, Paul, Joanne and Larry as friends. Is it just that, amongst the mad impersonal rush of New York life, they provide him, as he provides them, with 'Company'? Today they are giving him company en masse along with birthday presents and a cake with candles which he is expected to blow out and make a wish. They could give him the wish, too, and they'd all give him the same one: that he should be like them—married.

He goes to Sarah and Harry's place. They fuss over him a lot. Well, actually they fuss at each other a lot and he's a very useful middle man. Harry's quit drinking for eighteen months (he says) and nearly a year (she

828

says) since getting arrested for drunk driving. They talk about it a lot. Sarah's losing weight so she isn't eating things, but she talks about food a lot. So does Harry. Sarah's been going to karate classes and Harry insists she demonstrate for Robert. So she does and, as she pins an irritated Harry to the floor, a voice from outside reminds us that it's 'The Little Things You Do Together' that make a marriage. When the karate looks like getting heavy, Robert leaves, and Sarah, with her mouth full of sneaked cake, and Harry, loitering with intent very near the bar, jockey for position to be the last one to leave the room and put out the lights.

Robert poses a question to his married men friends: are they sorry they got married? It's a sort of yes-and-no situation ('Sorry-Grateful'). There is no answer to it really.

Peter and Susan are an idyllic pair. He's Ivy League, she's southern belle, and it's safe for Robert to flirt with Susan because it's good form. Peter and Susan also have news. They're getting divorced.

Jenny is very conservative and David is ever so modern. They are puffing at marijuana and feeling very proud of themselves. Decidedly-square Jenny says it doesn't affect her and talks a lot, and David boastfully declares himself undoubtedly potted. They all talk a lot and a lot of their talk is about marriage. Robert insists he isn't against it. He's really thinking about it. Right now he's dating an air hostess called April, kooky Marta, and out-of-town Kathy. Robert talks about marriage but he doesn't do anything about it. In fact, as the three girls declare in harmony 'You Could Drive a Person Crazy' not doing anything about it. As the evening comes to an end, David assures Robert that dear square Jenny didn't really like the marijuana. She only tried it to please thoroughly modern him. That's the way its got to be in that family and clever Jenny knows it.

Robert's friends always seem to be trying to pair him off with some nice girl ('Have I Got a Girl for You?'), but he's happy to put off any decision. 'Someone Is Waiting', somewhere, who has all the bits that he likes best in all the women he knows. He'll wait for her, this composite girl, and in the meanwhile it doesn't worry him. There are plenty of girls around like April, and Kathy, and Marta, and new ones come to New York every day ('Another Hundred People').

Paul and Amy have lived together for years and now they're getting married. Paul is looking forward to it a lot, Amy is really scared. Now that the appointed day is actually here, she knows she can't go through with it. As a choirgirl sings ritualistically, Paul's happy crooning mixes with Amy's frantic patter in debate as to whether or not they are 'Getting Married Today'. Amy thinks of every reason she can as to why they should cancel or even postpone and, when she can't think of any more, she simply declares unilaterally that she won't do it. A stunned Paul goes out of the house in the pouring rain and minutes later Robert is asking the distraught Amy to marry him instead. Well, he knows her. She looks at him. Isn't it funny, she's afraid to get married and he's afraid not to. Still, at least this unlooked-for proposal focuses her mind and a minute later she is chasing off down the street after Paul with his raincoat and her wedding bouquet.

ACT 2

Back at the opening birthday party, Robert blows out his candles again, prior to some more illustrations of how good he and his friends are at going through life together 'Side by Side by Side' equipped with sentiments as original as 'What Would We Do Without You' to brighten their relationship. They all worry about Robert so much, these friends. The 'Poor Baby' is all on his own, he has nothing and no one but them.

They are not quite right about that. Robert entertains April the air hostess, talking her into bed with practised words. In the morning she has to fly off to 'Barcelona' and he pleads with her not to go. He gets a shock when he pleads too well and she says she will stay.

He takes Marta with him when he visits Susan and Peter. They have got their divorce. Peter flew to Mexico for it and it was so nice down there that he phoned Susan to come on down. They are still living together, of course. It would be irresponsible to actually split up, what with the kids and all.

When he goes to see Larry and Joanne, they all go out for the evening. In a nightclub, while Larry dances, Joanne gets drunk and embarrassing and spits out a stinging serenade to 'The Ladies Who Lunch'. She propositions Robert and turns him off, and then it's time to pay the bill and go home. Thoughts and talk of marriage seem to have pervaded the whole evening. Do. Don't. Don't. Do. And why? It's enough to drive Robert to a soliloquy of want. What's it all about 'Being Alive' without someone to share it with?

It's that birthday party again, back at the beginning of the show. The friends are waiting for Robert to come as they were when the curtain first rose, but he doesn't show. Gradually the message sinks in, and they blow out the candles on the cake themselves, say 'Happy Birthday', and leave. Thirty-five year-old unmarried Robert stands in the middle of the stage and smiles. He's still his own man. But with friends like this, how long can it last?

FOLLIES

a Broadway legend, a musical in two acts by James Goldman. Music and lyrics by Stephen Sondheim. Produced at the Winter Garden Theatre, New York, 4 April 1971 with Dorothy Collins (Sally), Alexis Smith (Phyllis), John McMartin (Ben) and Gene Nelson (Buddy).

Produced at the Shaftesbury Theatre, London, in a revised version, 21 July 1987 with Julia McKenzie, Diana Rigg, Daniel Massey and David Healy.

CHARACTERS

Dimitri Weismann
Carlotta Campion
Stella Deems
Heidi Schiller
Solange Lafitte

Hattie Walker
Billie Whitman
Wally Whitman
Sally Plummer
Buddy Plummer
Phyllis Stone
Ben Stone
Roscoe
Young Phyllis
Young Sally
Young Ben
Young Buddy
Stage Manager, Ronnie Cohen, Christine Donovan, Deedee West, Meredith Lane, Max Blanck, Young Heidi, Margie, etc.

ACT 1

The Weismann Theatre in New York is to be pulled down. It has outlived its era, the era of the Follies shows, when its stage glittered under the dancing feet of the most beautiful showgirls in this or any other world, and its gilded galleries echoed to the saucy song of a French soubrette, the sighing waltz strains of a Viennese goddess, the torch song of a Yankee vamp, and the sound of the breaking hearts of hundreds of New York boys. Now, thirty years on, the Weismann Theatre is a dusty and empty shell awaiting the demolition men but, before they begin their work, the old stage will have one last night of music, laughter and life. Dmitri Weismann is bidding his old theatre goodbye with a reunion party for his girls.

They arrive in their dozens: chorus girls, showgirls, singers and stars; thirty, forty, fifty years older than when they last trod these boards. Some have aged well, others have prospered, and others have dowdied into suburban life, but all of them, from the glamorous film star, Carlotta Campion, to the mousiest chorus girl turned spinster, are here because they want to remember the days when they were in the Follies.

Sally Plummer is fifty. She is still very pretty in a girlish sort of way and she has clearly done well, given the size of the diamond she is wearing. It is Buddy, really, who has prospered. Charming, likeable Buddy, who courted her when she was in the chorus line in that last famous year of the Follies, then married her when the season was over and carried her off to Arizona where he made his fortune in real estate.

That makes Phyllis Stone fifty, too. Phyllis and Sally were flatmates that year, and Phyllis married Ben Stone, Buddy's pal. Ben has done well too, extremely well. He is a highly respected man on Wall Street and he and Phyllis have everything they could want in life: no children, like Buddy and Sally have, but everything else. You'd never know, to look at her now, that Phyllis had been a Follies girl. She is the epitome of the smart New York society lady. Quite why Phyllis needs or wants to remember the Weismann Follies is a little bit of a mystery, perhaps even to Phyllis.

Weismann begins his evening with a surprise. From the depths of the stage he produces not only the famous staircase down which the girls walked so many years ago, but also Roscoe, the tenor whose golden tones accompanied their parade. Now, as Roscoe once more sings his serenade to 'Beautiful Girls', the ladies make one last journey down the staircase. Some do it better than others. Some always did do it better than others.

The party gets under way and people start to meet and mingle. Chic, slick Phyllis meets breathless, happy-to-be-back Sally and, as they slither out their excuses for not having kept in touch over the years, time rushes back to 1940 and we see two girls, young Sally and young Phyllis, getting ready for their double date with Buddy and Buddy's pal. Phyllis is about to meet Ben.

On the other side of the room Buddy and Ben have met up as well. Then Sally spots Ben and, waiting until he is alone, almost timidly she crosses the room and speaks to him. She says, 'It's me, Ben,' but in the background we see the young Sally shrieking at him across the years, 'I want a reason!' But it is thirty years on, and Sally just nervously gabbles out yards of hellos ('Don't Look at Me') as they grin foolishly at each other.

Weismann brings in another party piece. Posters of the Follies descend from above, posters picturing the stars of his shows: Hattie, Solange, Carlotta and Billie and Wally Whitman. It doesn't take much persuasion from the old impresario before first one and then another of them step forward with reminiscences of their old acts. First the Whitmans ('Rain on the Roof') with their sweet old song-and-dance routine, then Solange oozing out her fake, over-accented French *chanson* ('Ah! Paris') and finally Hattie, still declaring that she's a 'Broadway Baby'.

The old theatre certainly makes memories come back: some good, some not so good, some perhaps not even so accurate. Phyllis sees herself, straight out of the backblocks of Indiana, not sure what life holds for her, and Ben, so young, so sure of himself, his whole life mapped out towards success. Then there was the day when she realised that Sally liked Ben too, and Sally was quite happy to admit it in a laughing way. But she had Buddy. And the two boys would come and wait for their girls at the stage door. They all remember those nights ('Waiting For the Girls Upstairs').

Weismann brings up more memories as a projector flashes old photographs on to a screen, but for some people the real memories are the other people. For Sally they are Ben, and she is intent on telling him about her life in Arizona, her life with Buddy. Dear Buddy who treats her like his princess even after all these years ('In Buddy's Eyes'). But what we see is young Sally and young Ben. She is telling him that she is in love with him, and all he knows is that he wants her. Just a little of yesterday spills over into today, enough to make Phyllis wonder out loud whether there ever was anything between Ben and Sally all those years ago. Buddy says there wasn't, and she's not really sure why the thought came back to her for the first time in decades.

One picture recalls a dance routine from the last 1940 show and now it is Stella Deems's turn to lead the remnants of that company in the Mirror Number (Who's That Woman?'). As the ageing ladies put themselves through the number as best they can, in the background the ghosts of their young selves can be seen dancing as they danced thirty years ago. When they have done, it is supper time.

A drink or two has found its way to a head or two, and inhibitions and defences are dropping. Phyllis makes her way to join Sally and, as they chatter, she suddenly, almost without thinking, slips in the question that has come back to nag her. 'How good was Ben in bed?' Poor, silly Sally doesn't even stop to think. She just tumbles out with, 'I didn't think you knew.' Phyllis didn't, but she knows now. The stopper is out of the bottle and Sally, defending herself wildly in front of Phyllis's coolness, isn't going to stop there. She can see in Ben's eyes that Phyllis and Ben's marriage is in a bad way. If Phyllis is unhappy, if her life's a mess, there's no need for her to take it out on Sally, because, oh my God, Sally is about as unhappy as anyone could be and her life is the worst mess of all.

Buddy has always looked up to Ben a bit. Clever, determined Ben who has gone straight to where he always said he would. Ben who always got what he wanted. Even Sally. He saw them that night. Ben couldn't even leave Sally for him.

Sally's burbling has started Phyllis's own thoughts tumbling out. Sally is right, of course, the marriage is in trouble. Ben is so successful that they hardly ever have time together alone. She is just a public appendage of Ben Stone businessman and there isn't any time for them to be just husband and wife. It is something they have to talk about and now seems as good a time as any. They have to do something, to have something that has nothing to do with work. What would he like? No, what would she like? Oh, if only he could say that he wants something, instead of always deferring kindly to her ('Country House').

Buddy comes to find Sally. She has found some old costumes and she is revelling in looking back. Buddy can sense that there is trouble coming and he wants to go home, but Sally insists she is having the best time she has had in years. She won't go. Buddy can't help it: 'God, you and Ben, it never ends.' Then it is his turn to spill out his griefs. Buddy's are simple joys. He likes his life, he likes his work and his home and his friends, and all it wants to make life perfect is to have the Sally he loved and married as a happy little wife. But Sally isn't. Sally mopes and inclines to tears and headaches. She is miserable and she does her best to make him miserable too.

Sally doesn't even listen to his complaint. She has seen Ben and she makes her way to him. As the young Ben and young Sally emerge from their lovemaking in the background, the two adults come together again, remembering ('Too Many Mornings'), and when they have finished remembering, they kiss. It is the kiss Sally has been waiting for all those years in Arizona. She has looked forward to this night—oh, the trouble she took over her dress and everything, knowing, hoping that it would happen, that Ben would come back to her.

833

Somewhere, as they kiss, and as their young counterparts kiss, Phyllis and Buddy and their former selves stand watching.

ACT 2

Now the wall of time comes down and the adults can converse with their childhood selves. Ben is drawn with anger and amazement at himself. Thirty years on he's done the same damn' fool thing again. He's an idiot to bring that silly affair back to the surface. Young Ben can't see that there's anything wrong. He's rather proud of the way he has turned out. He can see only the shine of success and not the hollowness of Ben's life. For Sally the affair was anything but silly and, when young Sally chides her with wasting their life in Arizona, Sally only replies that she has made it in the end. She has got Ben back.

Young Phyllis is hurt, both in her pride and in her heart but she gets little comfort from the hard-shelled retorts of her adult self. The shell is not unbreakable. Phyllis can still stifle a sniffle over the way things haven't turned out. And Buddy? Buddy is getting an earful from young Buddy because he hasn't been faithful to Sally. He's got a mistress. She's twenty-three and cheerful and uncomplicated. She's called Margie, and she's 'The Right Girl' for him. It's all young Buddy's fault. He knew about Ben and Sally and yet he took Sally back and he married her. Look what happened. But young Buddy loved her.

The thoughts and questions in the lives of the four mingle together and, as they mingle, Carlotta Campion delivers her party piece. She can declaim, without any regrets, that 'I'm Still Here', in spite of all the ups and downs of fortune that she's been through. Carlotta is a fighter and a pragmatist. She doesn't think and feel and think about her feelings day and night like some other people do.

It's one of those evenings. The time and the place seem to be conducive to a festival of breast-baring and Sally is at the middle of it, sure, with the blind sureness of someone who has waited and planned for years to make her coup, that she has won Ben back. When Phyllis tries to put her down, she bites back—it's different this time, Ben has thirty years of Phyllis to efface with some real love. But what Sally doesn't realise is that Ben isn't interested in her; he's more interested in himself and the fact that his own life is in a cul de sac. His life, his and Phyllis's life. Perhaps he needs a new start. Perhaps they need a divorce ('Could I Leave You?').

While the anguishing is going on, an elderly figure glides across the stage. Heidi Schiller is ninety now and it is well over half a century since Oscar Straus (or was it Franz Lehár?) wrote waltz songs for her to sing to the Follies crowds in her clear, cool soprano voice ('One More Kiss'). Heidi is serene in her memories of her younger self.

Ben finally resigns himself to clearing the slate with Sally. What ever there might have been between them was finished years ago. It was finished before it started. Sally goes white with fear. It can't be over. He can't do this to her. Not again. It will kill her. She will have nothing left to live for in Arizona if her dream is gone. From each and every corner the recriminations come: the young people attacking the spoiled adults who make up these two self-destructing marriages. Then, amidst the self-castigation, comes the sound of a Follies orchestra and from out of nowhere appear the folk of the Follies all dressed as for a wedding with Roscoe carolling forth a hymn to wedded bliss ('Loveland').

Now each of the participants in this night of self-indulgent angst is seen pictured in a Follies number. First come young Buddy and young Sally, dressed like a little bride and groom on top of a wedding cake, to profess that 'Love Will See Us Through (till something better comes along)'. Then it is Buddy's turn, with a slapstick comedy routine ('Buddy's Blues') which mimes out his unhappy predicament between his loving little Margie and his miserable but beloved wife; and Sally, in a clinging gown, under a white moon, sings of how she is 'Losing My Mind'.

Young Ben and young Phyllis set out with optimism to climb the heights to comfort ('You're Going to Love Tomorrow'), but then we see the sophisticated older Phyllis going dryly through an emotional striptease as she removes her clothes to display...nothing ('Ah! But Underneath') while Ben muses on how to put together a man like himself out of even less ('Make the Most of Your Music').

When it all comes to an end, we are back where we started on the stage of the Weismann Theatre and the guests are starting to leave. Ben and Phyllis just look at each other. They have wrung themselves out trampling through their past and their present. Now it's time to go home and see if any of it has made any difference. Buddy goes to fetch Sally. He has to take her home, too. She is shattered, perhaps beyond repair, at being on the losing side yet again, but there is one place where she can always pick up a win. Buddy's there.

The two couples say slightly awkward goodbyes, exchanging foolish formalities and, as they go their separate ways, the ghosts of their younger selves can be heard whispering amongst the dust sheets.

The revised version omitted the songs 'The Road You Didn't Take', 'The Story of Lucy and Jessie', and 'Live, Laugh, Love', replacing them respectively with 'Country House', 'Ah! But Underneath' and 'Make the Most of Your Music'.

GODSPELL

a musical in two acts by John-Michael Tebelak based on the Gospel According to St Matthew. Music and lyrics by Stephen Schwartz. Produced at the Cherry Lane Theatre, New York, 17 May 1971 with a cast including David Haskell, Joanne Jonas, Robin Lamont, Gilmer McCormick and Stephen Nathan and played subsequently at the Promenade Theatre from 10 August 1971, at the Broadhurst Theatre from 22

June 1976, at the Plymouth Theatre from 15 September 1976 and at the Ambassador Theatre from 12 January 1977.

Produced at the Roundhouse, London, 17 November 1971 with a cast including Marti Webb, David Essex, Julie Covington, Jeremy Irons and Verity-Ann Meldrum and played at Wyndham's Theatre from 26 January 1972. Played at the Phoenix Theatre 10 June 1975 with a cast including Su Pollard, Andrew C Wadsworth and Sally Bentley; at Her Majesty's Theatre 10 May 1977 and subsequently the Prince of Wales 4 July 1977; at the Shaftesbury Theatre 14 July 1978; and at the Fortune Theatre 15 December 1985 with Davy Jones.

Produced at the Théâtre de la Porte-Saint-Martin, Paris, in a version by Bernard Giquel and Pierre Delanoë 1973 with Dave, Bernard Callais, Gregory Ken, Nicolle Vassel and Armande Altai.

Produced at Hamburg in a version by Robert Gilbert 1972 with Heinz Ehrenfreunde, Joe Bogosyan and Angelika Milster.

A film version was produced by Columbia Pictures in 1973 with Victor Garber, Haskell, Jonas, Lamont, McCormick, Katie Hanley and Lynne Thigpen.

CHARACTERS

Originally played with a cast of ten.

ACT 1

A group of young people, of High School age or thereabouts, gather in what seems to be a school playground, backed by a high cyclone fence and sharply lit by powerful, overhead lights. They bring with them a theatre skip, filled with odd costumes in which they dress themselves haphazardly, so that some of them take on the appearance of circus clowns, others of casually dressed teenagers, and others a bizarre combination of the two. Most of them put on clown make-up.

The leader of the group starts the ball rolling with a religious quotation which encourages the rest of his companions to follow his example, quoting statements or paraphrases of statements taken from various philosophers throughout the ages. One quotes Sokrates (Prologue/'Wherefore, O Men of Athens?'), then another Thomas Aquinas, Martin Luther, Jean-Paul Sartre, Buckminster Fuller and John the Baptist ('Prepare Ye the Way of the Lord').

Taking his cue from the words of the Baptist, the leader makes a declaration of the purposes of Christ's mission on earth ('Save the People') and, using contemporary language, the youngsters give their versions of elements of Christ's teachings, retelling in their own words many of the familiar parables: the tale of the importunate widow (Luke 18.3), the story of the good Samaritan (Luke 10.30), that of 'the rich man whose land yielded heavy crops' (Luke 12.16), and the sermon in the mount (Matthew 5). One of the best-known of Christ's sayings is told in a minstrel routine (Q: 'How can you look at the speck of sawdust in your brother's eye..?' A: 'I don't know. How can you...etc.') (Matthew 7.3 and Luke 6.41).

The dialogue is broken from time to time by songs with religious themes and contemporary sounds which range from rock to country and western ('Day By Day', 'Learn Your Lesson Well', 'Oh, Bless the Lord, My Soul', All For the Best')

A girl starts to tell the parable of the sower and the seed (Matthew 13.3, Mark 4.3 and Luke 8.5) and this leads into the familiar hymn 'We Plow the Fields and Scatter', with the words written by the eighteenth-century German poet, Matthias Claudius, sung to a twentieth-century American tune. Two boys act out the tale of the prodigal son (Luke 15.11), which ends in a celebratory finale as the cast pile cups and flagons on to a trestle table and invite the audience to join them on the stage for a cup of wine during the interval.

ACT 2

A reprise of 'Learn Your Lesson Well', warning the audience to 'pay attention, build your comprehension, there's going to be a quiz at your ascension', signals the start of the second half of the entertainment. After a gospel song urging everyone to 'Turn Back, O Man', the leader of the group takes command of the action. One of the players asks him, 'By whose authority are you acting like this?', and it become evident that the leader is acting out the role of Christ in what has now become a re-telling of the events of the last days of his life.

Some of the cast assume the characters of pharisees. They try to trick Jesus by asking him whether the Jews have an obligation to pay taxes to Rome (Matthew 22.21, Mark 21.17 and Luke 20.25), but Jesus evades their trap ('Alas For You'). When he is asked about the woman taken in adultery, he replies, 'The one who is faultless shall throw the first stone' (John 8.3) and the woman is allowed to go free ('By My Side').

The cast sing to Jesus, 'We Beseech Thee', and then take their places as the disciples at the last supper. Jesus holds a mirror up to each of them in turn, showing them the absurdity of their worldy, made-up faces. With cream and tissues they wipe away their clownish make-up, for now it is the time for truth.

Swiftly, the events of the betrayal are portrayed before Jesus bids each player farewell ('On the Willows') and climbs on to the cyclone fence where he hangs, with outstretched arms, as though on the cross, as the company join in the finale ('Long Live God'/'Prepare Ye the Way of the Lord').

Although the piece is described by its author as being 'based on the gospel according to Saint Matthew', it in fact makes equally frequent reference to the gospel according to Saint Luke and to other books of the Old and New Testaments.

The song 'Beautiful City' was added to the score for the film version.

GREASE

a new 50s rock 'n' roll musical by Jim Jacobs and Warren Casey. Produced at the Eden Theatre, New York, 14 February 1972 with Barry Bostwick (Danny), Carole Demas (Sandy) and Adrienne Barbeau (Rizzo) and played at the Broadhurst Theatre from 7 June 1972.

Produced at the New London Theatre, London, 26 June 1973 with Richard Gere, Stacey Gregg and Jacquie-Ann Carr. Produced at the Astoria Theatre 7 June 1979 with Michael Howe, Jacqueline Reddin, Hilary Labow and Tracey Ullman (Frenchy).

A film version was produced by Paramount in 1978 with John Travolta, Olivia Newton-John and Stockard Channing.

CHARACTERS

Miss Lynch
Patty Simcox
Eugene Florczyk
Jan
Marty
Betty Rizzo
Doody
Roger
Kenickie
Sonny
Frenchy
Sandy Dumbrowski
Danny Zuko
Vince Fontaine
Johnny Casino
Cha-Cha di Gregorio
Teen Angel

ACT 1

At the reunion of Rydell High School's class of 1959, the successful Patty Honeywell (ex-Simcox) and Eugene Florczyk lead the singing of the 'Alma Mater' and Eugene addresses the assembly, bringing back memories of school days.

Time rolls back to let us see a bunch of lazy, bored, defiant teenage 1950s boys singing childishly rude words to the same school tune. At the high school cafeteria pretty, babyish Marty and loud and chubby Jan, two members of the Pink Ladies gang, meet with gang leader Betty Rizzo. Down on the school steps the Burger Palace Boys are saving their dimes for better things than lunch; tough and tattooed Kenickie, jolly Roger, enthusiastic little Doody, and Sonny who talks big and dirty but doesn't live up to it.

The girls soon have a topic of interest, for Frenchy, another Pink Lady, brings in a new girl, her neighbour Sandy Dumbrowski, and it turns out that Sandy met a boy on the beach over summer. The boys have a similar awakener when it turns out that their leader, the smooth Danny Zuko, has met a girl and spent the summer with her. Of course it was Sandy and Danny together, though the two versions that are simultaneously told don't sound too much like the same story ('Summer Nights') and, when they meet in company, Danny saves his image as a high-school tough Romeo with an off-hand approach that leaves sweet Sandy bemused and upset.

Doody has a guitar and, in class change, he goes into a fantasy of rock 'n' roll stardom ('Those Magic Changes'), before the scene shifts to a Pink Ladies pyjama party at Marty's place. Sandy has been admitted to the gang, but she still has a lot to learn. She wears a quilted robe while the other girls flaunt themselves in baby doll pyjamas. She has a tough time living up to the Pink Ladies style, choking on her first cigarette, gagging on dessert wine from the bottle and finally being sick over the bathroom sink when Frenchy tries to pierce her ears with a pin. Marty has a kimono, a gift from a chap called Freddy she met at a dance who got posted with the marines, which is the cue for a parody girl-group number, 'Freddy, my Love'.

The boys have been having an evening out stealing hub-caps. Unfortunately the ones they've taken today turn out to belong to a jalopy that Kenickie has saved up for from money earned working during the vacation. He calls it 'Greased Lightnin'' and reckons it will look great once he's done it up. Right now he's putting it to use taking Rizzo out.

When Danny and Sandy meet alone, his greeting is more like it was on the beach and he asks her to a party. Sandy isn't sure. She thinks she has made herself unpopular with the girls and is working hard at earning a spot on the cheer-leader squad. Her tutor in this all-important aim is all-American Patty Simcox. Patty has an eye for Danny herself and she spreads a little intentional jealousy Sandy's way. Sandy's hurt retorts to Danny's attempt to be friendly end with his finding a need to impress the girl. If she's set her eyes and heart on an athlete, he'll try out for the track team.

Down in the park the kids drink beer, smoke cigarettes, pet and read fan mags as the voice of disc jockey Vince Fontaine gurgles out of the radio, and we find out why Roger is called Rump by the other boys. His hobby is 'Mooning', which is to say showing off his bare backside in unlikely places. When Sandy puts in an appearance, collecting leaves for biology, Sonny tries to rush her off and Danny gets some heavy stick from Rizzo, who makes fun of Sandy's Gidget style in 'Look at Me, I'm Sandra Dee'. Sandy catches the end of the parody and she attacks first Rizzo and then Danny whom she accuses of spreading awful things about her. The result of this teenage scene is that Danny asks Rizzo rather than Sandy to be his partner at the school dance the next night ('We Go Together').

ACT 2

The kids are getting ready to go 'Shakin' at the High School Hop', but Sandy is not going. Alone, she sings with her radio of how, for her, 'It's Raining on Prom Night'. The dance is under the management of the radio's Vince Fontaine and schoolboy would-be rocker Johnny Casino, and it proves the occasion for advances by Patty on Danny, of Vince Fontaine on jailbait Marty, of Eugene on Rizzo and so on. Kenickie turns up with a blind date— a large, loud piece called Cha-cha—but when Rizzo claims him back, Danny is stranded with Cha-cha for the evening's highlight, the hand jive contest ('Born to Hand Jive'). Cha-cha lives up to her nickname. She's the best dancer in the room and she and Danny win the contest, but at the end of the dancing he walks off, leaving her on her own.

Frenchy has left school. She has gone to Beauty School instead. At least she had. She's dropped out and she can't face telling her friends. She can't even take a job at the Burger Palace, because then they'd all know. She wishes she had a Guardian Angel, like Debbie Reynolds does in the movies ('Beauty School Dropout'), who'd make everything come all right.

Meanwhile, the Burger Palace Boys have a challenge on their hands. It turns out that the unprepossessing Cha-cha is the steady girl of the chief of a rival gang, and the offended gang is coming that evening for a rumble. Danny isn't there—he's got into the track team and he's training. In the end the rumble turns out to be a non-event and the boys have another empty evening but not so Danny. He's off at the drive-in movie theatre with Kenickie's car and Sandy. She's thrilled when he offers her his ring and talks of going steady but, when he tries to get a bit too intimate, she gives back the ring and runs away leaving him 'Alone at a Drive-In Movie'.

Jan has a party in the basement of her place ('Rock 'n' Roll Party Queen') and Rizzo confides in Marty that her period is late. She reckons she might be pregnant. No, it's not Kenickie, it's a guy none of them knows. Marty goes straight to Kenickie with the story but, when he goes to find Rizzo with his responsibilities roused, she shrugs him off and he leaves in hurt. The party breaks up under the strains, but Sandy has seen the truth in Kenickie's face and she quietly wishes Rizzo good luck. Rizzo turns on her angrily, asserting that she'd rather be unpretentious her than all the Sandra Dees in the world ('There Are Worse Things I Could Do') and Sandy ends up back in her room in tears as she hopelessly reprises 'Look at Me, I'm Sandra Dee'. Then she picks up the phone and calls Frenchy. It's time she made a new start.

Down at the Burger Palace, the boys are getting ready to go watch Mickey Mouse Club and catch up on the development of Annette's tits. Danny is one of them again. He gave the fingers to the track coach and quit the team, and Patty is furious. The Pink Ladies turn up, dolled up in their gear, and with them is a busting, brand-new Pink Lady complete with leather jacket, hoop earrings, gum and expert cigarette. It's Sandy! Patty is lividly rude until Sandy pokes her one in the eye. Danny is 'All Choked Up' at such a breath-taking sight and before too long the ring is back on Sandy's finger. Rizzo's period is coming on, so Kenickie drives her off to the drugstore and all the other kids join in 'We Go Together' as they get down to playing out a jolly good happy ending together.

A LITTLE NIGHT MUSIC

a musical comedy in two acts by Hugh Wheeler suggested by the film *Smiles of a Summer Night* by Ingmar Bergman. Music and lyrics by Stephen Sondheim. Produced at the Shubert Theatre, New York, 25 February 1973 with Glynis Johns (Desirée), Len Cariou (Fredrik), Hermione Gingold (Madame Armfeldt), Victoria Mallory (Anne) and Laurence Guittard (Carl-Magnus).

Produced at the Adelphi Theatre, London, 15 April 1975 with Jean Simmons, Joss Ackland, Miss Gingold, Veronica Page and David Kernan.

A film version was produced by New World/Sascha-Wien Films in 1978 with Elizabeth Taylor (singing partly dubbed by Elaine Tomkinson), Cariou, Miss Gingold, Lesley-Anne Down (singing dubbed by Miss Tomkinson) and Guittard.

CHARACTERS

Madame Armfeldt
Desirée Armfeldt, *her daughter*
Fredrika Armfeldt, *her daughter*
Fredrik Egerman
Anne Egerman, *his wife*
Henrik Egerman, *his son*
Count Carl-Magnus Malcolm
Countess Charlotte Malcolm
Petra
Mr Lindquist, Mrs Nordstrom, Mrs Anderssen, Mr Erlansson, Mrs Segstrom, *the quintet*
Osa, Malla, Bertrand, Frid

Before the action of the play begins, the quintet of singers vocalises through a few snatches of the musical action of its story (Night Waltz), then waltz their way into a surreal pattern of changing partnerships amongst the principal characters and their scenery. Old Madame Armfeldt, a professional veteran of liaisons with the crowned and the belted, is found playing cards. To her thirteen year-old granddaughter, Fredrika, she enumerates the three smiles that the summer night bestows on human beings: the first to the very young like Fredrika who know nothing; the second to the fools like her mother, Desirée, the generation between, who know too little; the third to the very old, such as herself, who know too much.

ACT 1

At the Egerman house, Anne, the teenage second wife of middle-aged Fredrik Egerman, is passing her time in teasing her serious stepson, Henrik, a boy a year older than herself and a seminary student, as he attempts to study. When her husband returns from his lawyer's office, she has something new to occupy her butterfly mind; he has tickets for the theatre. They are going to see the actress Desirée Armfeldt in a delicious French play. Anne is thrilled and she can think only of what she will wear and of how wonderful the actress must be and she chatters on childishly to Fredrik as, together in their bedroom, she prepares herself to dress.

Fredrik tries to kiss her, but to no avail. They have been married eleven months and she is still a wife in name only. Aware of the disparity in their ages, he does not wish to press matters sexual until she is ready but, by now, he is more than a little greyed at the edges with polite patience. Her chatter mixes with his thoughts as he wonders, for the hundredth time since their marriage, how he might best open sexual relations 'Now'.

Downstairs, Henrik is also experiencing frustration. His father doesn't take him seriously, Anne doesn't take him seriously, and even the maid Petra, who pats him away when he tries to kiss and fumble her, doesn't take him seriously. He is always pushed aside and told to wait till 'Later'.

Anne is not totally unaware of Fredrik's problem but she doesn't recognise its importance. What significance is there, after all, in sex? Still, she promises, 'Soon' she will not shy away from his advances. But as he dozes in frustrated snoozing she is certain that she hears him whisper, 'Desirée'.

Another song scene introduces Desirée Armfeldt. She is every inch the successful actress leading 'The Glamorous Life'. She descends from time to time on her daughter, who leads a more conventional life in the home of old Madame Armfeldt, in a blaze of unreal glamour, and vanishes again, just as suddenly, to rejoin a trail of shabby hotel rooms on whistle-stop tours.

At the theatre, Anne is uneasy, Fredrik nonchalant. The play is a comedy of *déshabille*, and Desirée Armfeldt takes the role of a woman to whom other people's husbands are an easy and even approved prey ('Remember?'). Anne is convinced that the actress is taking special notice of Fredrik and her, and she finally works herself into a shower of tears at Desirée's beauty and style and demands to be taken home.

Back home, Henrik has had a go at sinning with Petra and suffered a humiliating failure to rise to the occasion. Fredrik and Anne arrive back inopportunely, and the young wife is even more upset by yet another reminder of sex. To her, Fredrik is still the dear, kind Uncle Fredrik who visited her father's home when she was a child but, although she cannot want him herself, she is tearingly jealous at the thought that he may admire Desirée Armfeldt. He puts her gently to bed and, as the strains of old memories ricochet in his head ('Remember?'), he leaves the house and makes his way to Desirée's lodgings.

It is fourteen years since their affair and, although he is pleased to see her for old time's sake, the main reason for his visit is clear. They catch up on the intervening years until Fredrik ventures ruefully onto the subject of Anne ('You Must Meet my Wife') and, eventually, the delicate subject of her virginity. Desirée, who has cheerfully admitted to a well-proportioned dragoon presently in her life, is horrified at the thought of the celibacy Fredrik has endured and is only too pleased to remedy his situation. They vanish towards the bedroom and the spotlight turns to old Madame Armfeldt singing regretfully of the times when 'Liaisons' were things of style and scope, of distinction, not of common desire and emotion.

When the focus returns to Fredrik and Desirée, they have accomplished their reunion and they are about to have a visitor. Desirée's dragoon, the insanely jealous Count Carl-Magnus Malcolm, is at the door. The atmosphere between him and Fredrik is, to say the least, arctic, and all attempts to explain Fredrik's presence and obviously dishevelled appearance fall sadly flat. The Count has firm thoughts on fidelity ('In Praise of Women'): it is what women practice, and what he practices towards Desirée and towards his wife, Charlotte. Therefore he finds it logical to assume that, in spite of appearances, nothing untoward has happened.

When he relates the evening's events the next morning to his wife, the name Egerman strikes a chord. Anne Egerman is a schoolfriend of his Charlotte's little sister. While he sleeps away his leave, his wife—who had hoped for a rather more vigorous homecoming—goes out to tip off Anne about her husband's activities. Like a good wife, she will ensure for Carl-Magnus the fidelity of his mistress.

When Charlotte Malcolm meets Anne, her worldly, wisecracking façade falls to pieces in the face of the young woman's innocence and she ends up cursing Desirée Armfeldt who has enslaved both her husband and Anne's. For Charlotte, who knows too much about it, love is a dirty business ('Every Day a Little Death'); for Anne, who knows nothing about it, it looks equally distressing. When Charlotte has gone, it is Henrik who finds the girl in tears and tries wholeheartedly to comfort her. The tears are quickly gone and Charlotte's anguish, which ought to be Anne's too if she could only understand it, is replaced by her customary girlish spirits.

Desirée makes the next move. She has some weeks out from her tour and she returns to her mother's estate where she proposes to invite Fredrik and his family to come for 'A Weekend in the Country'. The formal invitations go out. Anne is thrilled at an invitation but aghast when she recognises the name. Fredrik would like to accept, but he will refuse if she insists. Anne tells Charlotte who advises her to go, preferably looking as young as possible so as to shame Desirée back behind her wrinkles. Then Charlotte passes the news to Carl-Magnus who announces that he, that is to say they, will go too, invited or not.

Out in the country, wise young Fredrika is quick to guess what the plan is when her mother asks her if she would care for a new father. There is a snag, of course: Anne. But who knows what a weekend in the country may bring about?

It is twilight ('The Sun Won't Set') and the weekend is about to begin. It starts with some distinctly tense meetings as the principals of the piece arrive at the Armfeldt estate. Desirée is dreadfully flustered at the unexpected appearance of Carl-Magnus, drilled through by the glares of Charlotte and Anne, and forced into whispers at every turn. And everywhere sex raises its head. Charlotte develops a plan, which she confides to Anne, of making love to Fredrik in order to arouse Carl-Magnus's jealousy and make him return to her, while Henrik, obsessed, pours out to Fredrika the admission that, although he is intended for the church, he has fallen madly in love with his step-mother. And still the sun hasn't set. Such a lot of things can happen

843

while one Nordic sun is setting. On the terrace, Fredrik (at one end) and Carl-Magnus (at the other) are alone with their thoughts, which are largely of Desirée. Fredrik is wishing none of this had happened. If only she had fattened and frowsied in fourteen years, if only he had not found her so attractive all over again, 'It Would Have Been Wonderful'. Carl-Magnus is grimly replaying the scene of discovery and measuring Desirée's reactions: he has no certitude, nothing to exult in and nothing to forgive. It is unbearable. Desirée attempts tactfully to rendezvous with Fredrik, but Carl-Magnus announces his intention to visit her bedroom that night in spite of the presence in the house of his wife, and the quintet sing nonchalantly of 'Perpetual Anticipation'.

Dinner is rife with barely concealed hints and accusations as the Count and Countess Malcolm pursue their determined paths, their repartee sparred away without too much gentleness by their targets but, finally, it is all too much for Henrik. Smashing his glass on the table, he shouts to them all to hold their stupid libertine chatter. How can they speak so before a girl like Anne? He rushes angrily from the scene and Anne moves to follow him, but she is recalled by Fredrik and dinner is pursued in silence, save for an occasional hiccup from the tipsy Charlotte.

The tumultuous Henrik is headed for the lake, pausing only to perform a mea culpa for his life and his feelings to Fredrika. When Anne comes looking for him, she too finds Fredrika. The child opens the young wife's eyes to her step-son's feelings for her and the two girls go off together to find the boy before he can do himself harm. Elsewhere in the woods, far from such scenes of sensibility, Petra is getting herself uncomplicatedly laid by Madame Armfeldt's butler.

Fled from the foolishness of the evening to Desirée's bedroom, Fredrik and Desirée take in the sense of Henrik's young words. What is she doing running about in second rate tours and sleeping with a pea-brained married man? What is he doing trying to bring back his youth with a child bride? She would like to be rescued from all this. Perhaps he would too, but he is not sure. The vision of Anne is still there. He had better go to her or, at least, he had better leave Desirée's room. He should not flirt with rescue if he does not mean to be saved ('Send in the Clowns').

Down by the lake Anne finds Henrik trying to work out how to hang himself. She takes the rope from him and kisses him, and Henrik finds the virility to say he loves her and to return her kisses. On the ground amongst the trees, Anne finally finds out about love. As she does, Petra, her healthy sex session over, sings jauntily of how one day she'll marry 'The Miller's Son'. Until that time, this sort of life will suit her just fine.

Charlotte, sobered and embarrassed by her earlier outburst, apologises to Fredrik. As he comforts her with kind and understanding words, two figures flit past heading for the stables. They are Henrik and Anne and it is quite obvious what is happening. Quietly, almost tiredly, Fredrik makes no move to follow them or stop them. At the same moment, ignoring Desirée's protests, Carl-Magnus is removing his trousers in her bedroom. In doing so, he glances out the window and sees Charlotte and Fredrik in what looks like a compromising position. Calling for his duelling pistols and hoisting his trousers, he rushes out to challenge Fredrik to Russian roulette. The game ends, like the tale, with a wounded Fredrik in the arms of Desirée.

Fredrika asks her grandmother whether the night has smiled during the evening's events, and old Madame Armfeldt answers that indeed it has: for the young ones and for the fools, very much for the fools. Now it will smile for the old. As she dies, the Night Waltz is heard and the people of the play waltz once more about the stage, paired now as the evening's action has destined them to be.

CHICAGO

a musical vaudeville in two acts by Fred Ebb and Bob Fosse based on the play by Maurine Dallas Watkins. Lyrics by Fred Ebb. Music by John Kander. Produced at the 46th Street Theatre, New York, 3 June 1975 with Gwen Verdon (Roxie), Chita Rivera (Velma) and Jerry Orbach (Billy).

Produced at the Cambridge Theatre, London, 10 April 1979 with Antonia Ellis, Jenny Logan and Ben Cross.

CHARACTERS

Roxie Hart
Amos, *her husband*
Fred Casely, *her lover*
Velma Kelly
Billy Flynn
Mary Sunshine, *a journalist*
Liz, Annie, June, Hunyak, Mona, *murderesses*
Matron Morton
Go-to-Hell Kitty, Sergeant Fogarty, Martin Harrison, Harry, Aaron, Judge, Court Clerk, etc.

ACT 1

It is Chicago, Illinois, some time in the late 1920s and the Master of Ceremonies welcomes the audience to 'a story of murder, greed, corruption, violence, exploitation, adultery and treachery—all those things we all hold near and dear to our hearts', as Velma Kelly sings about 'All That Jazz'. A drunken Roxie Hart is seen letting her lover, Fred Casely, into her apartment. Sex is quickly and mechanically over and we see that all is not well in the little love nest. Fred is calling the affair off and Roxie is not pleased. In fact, she's so displeased that she puts a bullet through his stomach.

Three hours later, the police are there arresting Roxie's husband, Amos Hart, who has confessed to shooting a burglar. Roxie thinks it's real sweet of her 'Funny Honey' to take the blame like she suggested but, when he sees who the corpse is, Amos knows this isn't a burglar. It's the man who sold them their furniture. Even poor, dumb Amos can see what's been going on. Out it all comes and Roxie is so annoyed she just puts her hands on her hips and says so what, she shot the fink.

At the Cook County Jail, the six resident murderesses recite the history of their crimes (Cell Block Tango). These ladies are under the wing of Matron Mama Morton who runs a fine prison to a fine profit ('When You're Good to Mama'). Velma Kelly has been getting big newspaper coverage, thanks to Mama, and Mama has arranged that she shall be represented at her trial by none other than top lawyer Billy Flynn. She's even fixed the trial date and, after the trial, she'll get Velma on the vaudeville circuits at a wage commensurate with her public notoriety. As long, that is, as Velma is good to Mama.

Roxie makes it seven murderesses under Mama's care. She's been feeling a bit scared since the policeman told her that hers was a hanging offence, and she is looking for a little help. Velma isn't going to help but the kindly Mama will, at a price. The price is $5,000 for Billy Flynn. It may sound a lot, but he's never lost a case for a female client yet. So Roxie sets to work on her Amos to wheedle him into getting her the cash.

Billy Flynn is pure showbiz: a man with an electroplated tongue, a great line in sterling sincerity ('All I Care About') and a wallet like a Venus flytrap. He doesn't ask if the client is guilty, just if she has $5,000. Amos can only raise $2,000 but Billy has ways and means. Get the girl on page one and announce that her effects are to be sold to finance her defence. They'll go wild to buy them in the hope that she'll be executed and the stuff will triple in value. He'll even offer to give Amos 20% of the takings above $5,000.

The exercise begins with Roxie being introduced to the *Evening Star* sob sister, Mary Sunshine ('A Little Bit of Good'). For the occasion, Billy has supplied Roxie with a suitably heart-rending background starting with a convent education and going on from a runaway marriage to a fine slice of poor little lost girl and finally arriving at the fatal night when 'We Both Reached For the Gun' and she killed a man in self defence. As Billy works her like a puppet, Roxie does her stuff and, lo and behold, she makes those front pages. She is thrilled. She's always wanted to have her name in the papers—now 'Roxie' is the name everyone is going to have on their lips.

Roxie is news and this means that Velma Kelly isn't. There's only room for one murderess on the front page at a time. Suddenly Velma's long-planned vaudeville tour is under heavy threat. Velma is too smart to let jealousy get in the way of business; she simply turns her solo act into a duo and starts trying to persuade Roxie into going partners ('I Can't Do It Alone').

Meanwhile, somewhere in the city, an upper class lady called Kitty is putting a bullet through a faithless lover. The next morning it is she who has the attention of Billy Flynn and Roxie is out of fashion even before he has her trial date set. Velma wants to talk to him about her trial too but they're both out of luck. Kitty has all the front pages and all the attention, and the girls can see that they've only got themselves to depend on ('My Own Best Friend').

ACT 2

Roxie's the smart one, though. She lets out that she's pregnant. So now she's the only pregnant murderess and the press is back at her side. As Roxie sells her hearts and flowers for all their worth ('Me and my Baby'), Velma regrets ragingly that she didn't think of that angle first ('I Know a Girl'). Mary Sunshine spreads moral indignation over the imprisoned, unborn child through pages of newsprint and, before you can say 'gallows', Billy Flynn is back on Roxie's case, full of plans.

Amos is jubilant at the thought of being a father, but no one takes any notice of him ('Mr Cellophane') except for Billy who points out purposefully that he couldn't be the child's father and that therefore he'd better divorce Roxie. This, of course, will make his client even more the persecuted heroine of the *Evening Star* than ever. Roxie's trial date is fixed and Velma is devastated when she learns that it's her spot which has been rescheduled to make a place for her rival. Just when she'd got her whole trial strategy worked out ('When Velma Takes the Stand'). But Roxie is getting really grand now. Having done one bright thing on her own, she thinks she can do it all and she dismisses Flynn. What does she need him for? She can conduct her own defence.

Katalina Hunyak, one of Mama's murderesses, who doesn't speak American, comes to trial. She has endlessly repeated the only two words of English she knows over the months she has passed in jail—'not guilty'. But forty-seven years after the last hanging of a woman, Hunyak is sentenced to death by Cook County and sent to the gallows. It is a very frightened and repentant Roxie who makes her peace with Billy Flynn and allows herself once again to be tutored in trial technique. As the big day approaches, he encourages her with words of showbiz. It's all just a big circus and she is the star; she must get out there and give them the old 'Razzle Dazzle'.

At the trial, Roxie follows her instructions with the expertise of a seasoned campaigner, turning out a Flynn-ised version of her story, calculated to dampen many a handkerchief and fill many a well-turned column, until she reaches the climax. She fired not only in self-defence, but to save her husband's poor, innocent, unborn child!

As Mama and Velma listen to Mary Sunshine's breathless radio reportage of the trial, Velma gets really hot under the collar: all her little bits of business, her dramatic details worked on over the months and honed for her own trial, Roxie has nabbed them all. She's even pinched Velma's trial shoes with the rhinestone buckles. What a low broad! Together the two women ruminate on whatever happened to 'Class'.

It is the day of decision. Mary Sunshine trills down her microphone as Billy Flynn sums up, in flawlessly printable rhetoric, his own Roxie Hart tale. Then, just as the verdict is about to be announced, a sensation occurs in a nearby divorce court. This girl has just shot her husband and his mother *and* the defence attorney..! The newsmen vanish en masse.

Roxie is devastated. It is almost incidental that she has been found not guilty. As Billy waves goodbye, she stands there with nothing. Amos asks her to come home and she doesn't hear him. For the baby? Silly goon, there's no baby. And no reporters. No front pages. No Amos. Only three times nightly on the lesser vaudeville circuits in that double act with Velma Kelly ('Nowadays').

A CHORUS LINE

a musical by James Kirkwood and Nicholas Dante. Lyrics by Edward Kleban. Music by Marvin Hamlisch. Produced at the Public Theatre, New York, 15 April 1975, at the Newman Theatre, 21 May 1975 and at the Shubert Theatre 25 July 1975 with Robert LuPone (Zach), Donna McKechnie (Cassie), Sammy Williams (Paul), Priscilla Lopez (Diana), Carole Bishop (Sheila), Wayne Cilento (Mike) and Pamela Blair (Val).

Produced at the Theatre Royal, Drury Lane, London, 22 July 1976 with Eivind Harum, Sandy Roveta, Tommy Aguilar, Loida Iglesias, Jane Summerhays, Jeff Hyslop and Mitzi Hamilton.

Produced at the Raimundtheater, Vienna, in a version by Michael Kunze 16 October 1987 with Judy Pyanowski, Marcello de Nardo, Morenike Fadayomi, Patricia Taudien, Stefan Nagel and Isabel Dörfler.

Played at the Théâtre du Châtelet, Paris, 16 December 1987.

A film version was produced by Embassy Films in 1985 with Michael Douglas, Alyson Reed, Cameron English, Yamil Borges, Vicki Frederick, Charles McGowan and Audrey Landers.

CHARACTERS

Zach, *the director/choreographer*
Larry, *his assistant*
Cassie
Sheila
Val
Diana
Judy
Kristine
Maggie
Bebe
Connie
Mike
Richie
Don
Paul
Mark
Greg
Bobby
Al
Vicki, Tricia, Lois, Frank, Butch, Roy, Tom, etc.

848

Belle of New York. American producers made a habit of pasting home-made numbers into foreign musical scores, Germany had a little of its own back with this interpolation into the earliest American international hit.

The Red Mill. Fly-by-night Yankee Kid Conner (Little Tich) encounters the motoring Countess de la Fère (Lily Alaine) and her daughters outside the mysterious red mill. Empire Theatre, London, 1919.

Oh, Boy! Lou-Ellen Carter (Julie Osburn) and George Budd (David-James Carroll) are forbidden to speak to each other by her parents, so they sing and dance together instead. Goodspeed Opera House, 1983.

Going Up! The happiness of Robert Street (Brad Blaisdell) and Grace Douglas (Kimberley Farr) depends on an air race against a foreign flying ace. Goodspeed Opera House, 1976.

Show Boat. Joe (Paul Robeson) and Queenie (Alberta Hunter) take life as it comes, but fortune will lead Magnolia (Edith Day) and Julie (Marie Burke) through many vicissitudes, far from Ol' Man River. Theatre Royal, Drury Lane, 1928

Cap'n Andy Hawkes (Derek Royle) greets the locals from the decks of the Cotton Blossom. Adelphi Theatre, 1971.

Cleo Laine as Julie, Adelphi Theatre, 1971.

Carousel. The evening's activity begins in the colourful gaiety of the fairground, but ends in tragedy through the inability of barker Billy Bigelow (John Raitt) to cope with life and marriage. Majestic Theatre, 1945.

Guys and Dolls. Miss Adelaide (Vivian Blaine) needs to divorce Nathan Detroit (Sam Levene) from 'the oldest established permanent floating crap game in New York'. 46th Street Theatre, 1950.

On the bare stage of a Broadway Theatre a chorus dancers' audition is taking place. The early stages of the call are over, and the mass of hopeful contestants for the few places in the chorus line of the new show have been reduced to a final group of some two dozen boys and girls who are in the process of being taught a dance combination by the choreographer's assistant. The voice of the director, Zach, calls the beat from the darkness of the auditorium as the dancers perform the routine together. Then it is time for them to be looked at more individually. The group is broken down into sections of four dancers, each group to dance through the ballet steps separately. As they wait their turn, their thoughts come across ('I Hope I Get It') wondering how many performers are required for the chorus line, and praying that they may be one of the fortunate ones chosen.

One by one, the groups of dancers perform the combination. Nerves are evident. One girl dances with her tongue anxiously following her movements, another over-performs and breaks from her place in the formation, and another, whose ballet is the least happy part of her dance repertoire, fails totally and has to step aside. Zach calls his corrective instructions from the theatre and some of the artists are able to adjust their performance accordingly, but others find that their idiosyncrasies are not correctable. When the girls and boys have displayed their talent in ballet, a jazz combination follows and it is not necessarily the same dancers who shine, although many of the same errors are seen again. The boy who has been told to hold his head up persists through everything in looking at the ground.

When both combinations have been danced, it is time for a further thinning of the ranks. From the dance cards, Zach reads the numbers of the dancers who are to stay behind and audition further. There are eight girls, plus Cassie who is called out by name, and eight boys. Hearts are thumping, it looks as if an eight-and-eight line-up is needed, it looks as though they have the job. But no. Zach asks for their photographs and biographies. It is not over yet. Lined up across the front of the stage, they are asked in turn to give their name, age and home town.

There are some nervous jokes over ages and real, as opposed to stage, names but the exercise performs its intended use. It shows up the personalities of the individuals and, most particularly, their hang-ups over age, race and social background. Greg is Jewish, Connie is Chinese, four foot ten and thirty-two, Diana is from Puerto Rico, Bobby is from a wealthy neighbourhood, Paul from Harlem, Sheila is rising thirty and defensive about it, Mark is twenty, inexperienced and enthusiastic. Cassie gets herself excused from taking part. Even then it is not over, Zach wants to know more. He wants them to talk about themselves, to find out what they are like as people, before making his final choice. It is Sheila who has the courage to ask how many dancers he needs, and the answer is four and four. Half of them.

Mike is first to be called forward and, with a bit of prodding, he launches into the story of how he started dancing after watching his sister at dance class ('I Can Do That'). Bobby has no trouble talking, he's a practised extrovert. Ignored by his bridge-playing, cocktail-drinking parents he has developed a cocky manner equipped with extravagantly imagined stories about himself. As he rattles on, the other dancers are barely listening. Lost in their own thoughts, searching their minds for amusing anecdotes with which to make an impression, or wondering whether it would be to their advantage to invent an interesting background ('And...').

Sheila is next, posing and performing the role of the wisecracking vamp she likes to pretend to be, in spite of Zach's efforts to get her to be natural. Sheila wanted to be a ballerina like her mother had almost been. She wanted to dance, like the lady in *The Red Shoes*. But what she really wanted to do, it finally emerges, is get out of an unloving home to that imaginary world of handsome princes and pretty girls in white ('At the Ballet'). Maggie, a child born to try to save a marriage, and Bebe who was never pretty went through the same thing and have similar stories. Kristine is really nervous and her husband, Al, who is also in the line, keeps defensively popping in a word or two to help her through her story. Kristine's hang-up isn't in her life or in her dancing, but she has a problem at auditions. She can't 'Sing' at all.

Young Mark is scarcely old enough to have dancing memories. All his memories are of that momentous thing called puberty ('Hello Twelve'). Connie has spent all her life praying to grow beyond four foot ten so that she could be in the ballet. Diana wanted to be a serious actress and enrolled at the High School of the Performing Arts, but she couldn't get on the wavelength of a pretentious tutor called Karp and his improvisations so she dropped out ('Nothing').

Don started at fifteen earning money dancing in strip-joints, Judy started performing to get her father's attention, and black, hyperactive Richie was training to be a kindergarten teacher when he realised he could get stuck there. One by one the stories and the thoughts mix with each other as the young people loosen up. Val has done something about her hang-up. She was plain and flat-chested. She could dance the other girls off the stage, but she never got jobs because she was plain and flat-chested ('Dance: Ten; Looks: Three'). So she went to a plastic surgeon and got herself fixed up with 'tits and ass' and changed her life. Paul, on the other hand, clearly still has deep problems and he cannot even talk about them.

Zach gives the dancers a short break, but holds Cassie back. Once more she is to be given favoured treatment and it is soon evident why. Cassie has been through the chorus and gone beyond it. Years ago, Zach took her out of the chorus line and put her into a couple of featured parts, and he also took her into his home and his bed. The relationship ended and Cassie's career didn't progress. There were no more featured roles and Hollywood didn't want her for, with all her advantages, Cassie couldn't cut it as an actress. What she did, she did magnificently, but that was it. Cassie is a dancer and now, after two years without work, she wants to go back and start over again where she was good: in the chorus line ('The Music and the Mirror').

When Cassie goes to join the other dancers to learn the song which they are to audition, Zach turns his attention to Paul and prises his story from him. Paul was always effeminate. When he saw the old movie musicals it was Cyd Charisse he wanted to imitate, not Fred Astaire, even though he knew it wasn't right. It wasn't being gay that bothered him, it was not knowing how to be male. When he left school he went to dance in a drag show and they made a real girl out of him. Then one day his parents discovered what he did. He calls himself by an Italian name now, wiping out his Puerto Rican origin and his past, and he really can dance. Zach lets the boy regain some composure before calling the rest of the dancers back.

Now individual talent is not in question. What Zach is looking for is the ability to make oneself part of a team, to dance exactly like the person next to you as part of a background to a star. Together, the seventeen dancers perform the routine and the song they have learned ('One'). What shows up immediately is that Cassie is not a chorus dancer; she has special emphases to her dancing, an individual style which does not belong in a chorus line. Zach has continually to correct her. When she is corrected, however, she takes Zach's direction and performs just like everyone else. It breaks his heart to see her smothering her talent, but that is his problem, not hers.

They tap, they dance in pairs and then, suddenly, Paul falls to the ground while doing a turn. His already damaged cartilage has given way and he has to be taken to hospital. The other dancers have just seen the end of a fellow dancer's life. Now they all have to think about what they will do when the day comes and they are obliged, for one reason or another, to give up dancing. Some want to stay in the theatre, as actors perhaps or on the production side, while others have other plans already worked out. But whatever they do, they will remember their days as dancers ('What I Did for Love').

Now Zach makes his final choice. Val, Diana, Judy, Cassie, Mike, Richie, Mark and Bobby will be contracted for the show.

As a finale to the show, all the dancers, seen up till now only in their rehearsal clothes, parade across the stage in glittering top-hats and tails to the strains of the hymn to every performer—'One'.

ANNIE

a musical in two acts by Thomas Meehan based on the cartoon strip *Little Orphan Annie*. Lyrics by Martin Charnin. Music by Charles Strouse. Produced at the Goodspeed Opera House 10 August 1976 with Maggie Task (Miss Hannigan), Reid Shelton (Warbucks) and Kristin Vigard (Annie) and at the Alvin Theatre, New York, 21 April 1977 with Dorothy Loudon, Shelton and Andrea McArdle.

Produced at the Victoria Palace, London, 3 May 1978 with Sheila Hancock, Stratford Johns and Andrea McArdle. Played at the Adelphi Theatre 20 December 1982 with Ursula Smith and Charles West.

A film version was produced by Columbia Pictures in 1982 with Carol Burnett, Albert Finney and Aileen Quinn.

CHARACTERS

Annie, *an orphan*
Molly, Pepper, Duffy, July, Tessie, Kate, *orphans*

Miss Hannigan
Oliver Warbucks
Grace Farrell, *his secretary*
Mrs Pugh, *his housekeeper*
Drake, *his butler*
Rooster Hannigan
Lily St Regis
Bert Healy
Bonnie, Connie *and* Ronnie Boylan
FDR
Ickes, Howe, Morgenthau, Hull, Perkins, *his Brains Trust*
Bundles McCloskey, Lieutenant Ward, Harry, Sophie the Kettle, Cecille, Annette, Mrs Greer, Fred McCracken, Jimmy Johnson, Justice Brandeis, etc.

ACT 1

It is the middle of a 1933 night in the girls' dormitory at the New York City Municipal Orphanage and little Molly has awakened from a sad dream with cries which have roused the rest of the girls from their sleep. Some of them react grumpily to Molly's distress, but little orphan Annie comforts the child who has been dreaming of the mother she has never known. Annie is luckier than the other orphans; she knows that she has a mother and a father for she still has a note which was left with her when she was abandoned at the orphanage, and half a silver locket to which her parents hold the other part, waiting for the day when they can come to claim their child ('Maybe').

That was eleven years ago and Annie decides that perhaps now it is time for her to take the initiative and go out and look for her family. She is on her way to the front door with her basket under her arm when all the lights go on. She is caught. Miss Hannigan, the raddled guardian of the orphanage, triumphantly hauls the child back to the dormitory and, as a punishment, sets all the orphans to work scrubbing the floor, even though it is 4 a.m. ('It's the Hard-Knock Life'). But Annie is not to be balked. When the laundry man comes to take away the dirty linen, she hides in the laundry bag and effects her escape under Miss Hannigan's very nose.

Out on the streets of New York, Annie has to fend for herself and yet evade the pursuing city officials and, before long, she meets a kindred soul: a stray dog who is being pursued by the dog pound. She makes him her friend, names him Sandy and shares with him her determination that everything will turn out all right in the end ('Tomorrow'). When night comes, Annie finds her way to the shelter of one of the city's Hoovervilles, a camp of down-and-outs who blame their fall from prosperity on the policies of President Hoover ('We'd Like to Thank You'). There she finds food and warmth, but the only reaction to her cheerful optimism is a sour suggestion that she ought to be in politics.

Back at the orphanage, Miss Hannigan's profession is getting her down. It is no way of life for someone who has an abiding loathing for 'Little Girls'. She has a moment of mean satisfaction when Annie, recaptured when the insanitary Hooverville was broken up by the police, is brought back, and she is taking out her frustrations on the unrepentant child when another visitor knocks at the door. This smart young woman is Grace Farrell, secretary to the well-known billionaire Oliver Warbucks. It appears that this gentleman, a former orphan himself, has decided to invite an orphan to share Christmas with him at his mansion, and Grace has been sent to the orphanage to select .the lucky child. Annie's ears prick up delightedly and, after a swift exchange of winks, nods and signals with the amused Grace, she succeeds in getting herself chosen for this wonderful adventure.

At the Warbucks house, Annie is happily fussed over by the staff and quickly decides 'I Think I'm Going to Like it Here' but, when Warbucks returns, he is disappointed to find that Annie isn't a boy. He hadn't realised that orphans could be girls. What on earth does one do with a girl? Perhaps she would like to go to a movie and an ice-cream parlour and ride round Central Park in a cab. Annie is thrilled, but dashed when she finds that Warbucks isn't going to come with her. Some sad-eyed looks and a bit of mute infant pleading soon get him to change his mind, and corporation affairs are put aside as Warbucks takes Annie out to look at 'NYC' from an unfamiliar angle.

Within a week, the billionaire and the orphan have become inseparable pals and Grace is on her way back to see Miss Hannigan. Warbucks wants to adopt Annie and take her to live with him for ever in the splendour of Fifth Avenue. Miss Hannigan is still privately screaming at the beastly injustice of it all when she gets some more unwelcome visitors: her rapscallion brother Rooster and his floosie, Lily St Regis, who have come to scrounge a loan. The one consolation is that at least she has someone with whom to share her fury about Annie's promotion to 'Easy Street'.

Annie's promotion doesn't turn out to be as simple an act as it might have appeared it would be. When Warbucks nervously tries to broach the subject of adoption with her and offers to exchange her old locket for a brand new one from Tiffany's, the little girl bursts into tears and tells him that she isn't an orphan. Out comes the story of the note and the locket and a heartfelt cry: all Annie wants in the world is to find her mother and father. Before long, Warbucks is on the phone to his pal J Edgar Hoover, getting the FBI's finest put on to the case, and the whole Warbucks household is energetically assuring Annie 'You Won't Be an Orphan For Long'.

ACT 2

The campaign to find Annie's family is soon massively under way and Warbucks goes on the nationwide Oxydent Hour of Smiles radio show ('You're Never Fully Dressed Without a Smile') to offer a $50,000 reward. The listening Miss Hannigan is grinding her teeth at all those zeroes when she gets a heart-lifting surprise: an unprepossessing pair called Ralph and Shirley Mudge turn up on her doorstep looking for their little daughter Annie. It is a fake, but a convincing one. Ralph and Shirley are none other than Rooster and Lily in disguise. They are determined to win the $50,000 and, with Miss Hannigan's inside knowledge of the child's history, they reckon that they can carry off the deception successfully. Soon they will be on 'Easy Street' too.

Little orphan Annie may have a problem but she is not the only one. The country has problems too and President Roosevelt and his Brains Trust are in despair over the economic outlook. Warbucks calls to see his presidential friend, bringing advice and Annie with him, and the little girl soon has them all standing up and joining in an optimistic rendition of 'Tomorrow'. Once they have got the Brains Trust thinking positively towards a new deal, Warbucks and Annie have to go back quickly to New York, for Fifth Avenue is jammed with couples claiming to be Annie's parents. Surely one of them must be the real one.

Alas, Grace has established that they are all phonies. Not one of them knew about the locket, they were all just after the money. Annie is awfully disappointed, but she can take comfort from the loving Warbucks ('Something Was Missing') who is now more determined than ever to adopt her and Annie knows that, if she can't have her real mother and father, there's no one in the world she would rather have for her father than him ('I Don't Need Anything but You'). With that happy prospect in mind ('Annie'), Warbucks bundles Annie upstairs to get into her best red dress for their Christmas party.

No sooner has she returned to join Warbucks in the happiest night of their lives than the false Ralph and Shirley Mudge arrive. Primed by Miss Hannigan, they know all about Annie's locket and they have actually brought a matching half. The proof seems incontrovertible. They will return in the morning to collect Annie and the cheque. Everyone should be happy. After so much effort Annie's parents have really been found. But, as Warbucks proposes a choked toast to little Annie Mudge, the heroine of the moment bolts upstairs in tears. Amidst the ruins of Christmas Eve, the President arrives and, when Grace voices her suspicions that Mr Mudge is not what he seems, the might of the nation is again put into action on the case of little orphan Annie.

When Annie descends the stairs early next morning with her little suitcase packed and ready to leave, she finds that the FBI has done its infallible work. Mr and Mrs Mudge are not her parents. Her parents were called David and Margaret and they are, alas, dead. Annie really is an orphan and that means that she can be 'Daddy' Warbucks' little girl after all.

The only thing left outstanding is to find out who Ralph and Shirley Mudge are. After all, they knew about the locket and no one knew about the locket except Annie and Warbucks...and Miss Hannigan! Right on cue, Miss Hannigan turns up with the children from the orphanage to see Annie and her long lost parents reunited. When the Mudges come to claim their little girl and their large cheque they walk into a trap. In front of the President himself, Rooster is unmasked and he and Lily and Miss Hannigan are frogmarched off on charges of fraud, leaving Annie and her Daddy Warbucks, the President and all the orphans to celebrate 'A New Deal for Christmas'.

The film score of *Annie* included four new songs: 'Dumb Dog', 'Let's Go to the Movies', 'Sandy' and 'Sign'.

THE BEST LITTLE WHOREHOUSE IN TEXAS

a musical in two acts by Larry L King and Peter Masterson. Lyrics and music by Carol Hall. Produced at the Actors' Studio, New York, 20 October 1977. Produced at the Entermedia Theatre, New York, 17 April 1978 and played at the Forty-Sixth Street Theatre, New York, from 19 June 1978 with Carlin Glynn (Mona), Henderson Forsythe (Sheriff), Clinton Allmon (Thorpe), Jay Garner (Governor) and Susan Mansur (Doatsey Mae).

Produced at the Theatre Royal, Drury Lane, London, 26 February 1981 with Miss Glynn, Forsythe, Nigel Pegram, Fred Evans and Sheila Brand.

A film version with additional songs by Dolly Parton was produced by Universal in 1982 with Miss Parton, Burt Reynolds, Dom De Luise and Charles Durning.

CHARACTERS

Mona Stangley
Sheriff Ed Earl Dodd
Melvin P Thorpe *of KTEX-TV 'Watch Dog'*
The Governor
Doatsey Mae, *a waitress*
Edsel Mackey, *editor of the local paper*
Mayor Rufus Poindexter
C J Scruggs, *President of the local Jaycees*
Senator Wingwoah
Jewel
Angel, Shy, Linda Lou, Dawn, Ginger, Beatrice, Taddy Jo, Ruby Rae, Eloise, Durla, *girls at Miss Mona's*
Angelette Imogene Charlene, Aggies, etc.

ACT 1

The Chicken Ranch was a kind of an institution in the little corner of Texas where it was situated. Under the rule of Miss Wulla Jean it had become known as a practical, homely kind of whorehouse ('Twenty Fans') where things were made nice for first time customers, where regulars were appreciated and where, when times were hard, the management was happy to take payment in kind. In this part of the world that often meant in some sort of poultry, which was how The Chicken Ranch got its name. In the fulness of time, Miss Wulla Jean went to the big whorehouse in the sky and her business was taken over by the most adept and long-serving of her girls, Miss Mona. Nothing changed. The Chicken Ranch stayed a nice 'Lil' Ole Bitty Pissant Country Place' doing its bit for the community and not hurting

855

anyone who didn't want to be hurt. Until its time came, one year, round about Thanksgiving.

One day, two new aspirants to the Chicken Ranch's roster of working girls come to check in. One is clearly experienced in the worst of city whoring, the other looks as though she has come straight off the farm. Miss Mona's experience of girls and the world allows her to sum both girls up instantly and accurately. When she has removed the tarty blonde wig and sunglasses, and renamed her resistant first girl Angel, she has a fine candidate for the girl-next-door type. The other case is equally classic. Shy comes from a country family where she has been molested by her father. But she has made up her mind, and she's determined to see it through as a whore and, since the sympathetic Miss Mona can see in her unpretentious attitude the makings of a woman and a worker ('Girl You're a Woman'), she agrees that Shy can stay.

At this selfsame time, Nemesis is preparing to go on the air. Nemesis is Melvin P Thorpe, a broadcasting poseur fronting a frilled-up Watchdog programme, theoretically vowed to prevent social and commercial abuse but subjugated entirely to the greater glory and profit of the self-important Melvin himself. Last week he scored a triumph by proving that a peanut bar had less peanuts in it than advertised and this week he has another great revelation for the listeners of KTEX-TV—'Texas Has a Whorehouse in It'. In pious horror Melvin declares to his audience, before the cooing of his backing singers, that this appalling thing called loveless copulation must be stopped and he calls upon the Sheriff to take command and shut the whorehouse down.

Back at the Chicken Ranch things are going on as normal. Angel is happily settled in to the homey atmosphere of her new job and is able to take time out to call her Mama. Mama looks after Angel's little boy who misses his mother but looks forward to the presents she'll be bringing him come Christmas. A wise Miss Mona overhears: somehow Angel will have to have her period bang on Christmas this year.

Jewel, Mona's maid, is having her day off. She's off to see her feller for 'Twenty-Four Hours of Lovin''. She's going to give away free what the girls get paid for. But the girls have plenty to think about. The big football match is coming up, and the prize for the winning team is an evening out at Miss Mona's establishment. For that evening, Mona works up a special sort of Homecoming Dance ambiance with the girls dressed in 1950s style ball gowns (handily equipped with Velcro for easy removal).

The local Sheriff, Ed Earl Dodd, an old and dear friend of Miss Mona comes by. He is annoyed over last night's television business, particularly as he was named. Mona is inclined to laugh it off. They have had moral crusaders before and they've survived. After all, most of the men around the district have been customers at the Chicken Ranch sometime in their lives. The Sheriff is not so sure. In the old days when all you had to do was crush some two bit interfering 'investigative' newspaperman it was easy, but these puffed-up television people have a much wider and more pernicious power.

He is right. Since nothing as important as a peanut bar holds his attention for the day, Melvin P Thorpe (who surely has no other motive) is preparing to move in on the Chicken Ranch. Priming his profile before the cameras, he sets up in the main street of the little town of Gilbert to spread his message and reap his glory (Watch Dog Theme), but he has counted without Sheriff Ed Earl. The Sheriff hits him with a bylaw and sends him packing with a mouthful of Texas invective unheard on television since its birth, for Ed Earl has forgotten the difference between a newspaperman and a television person: the latter has sound recording equipment and, oh my goodness, is he going to use it.

Ed Earl's performance, as relayed to the moral folks of Texas by KTEX-TV, doesn't do anything at all for the leading lights of Gilbert town. In fact the sudden spotlight on their town makes them all decidedly nervous. But Ed Earl is unrepentant: he'd do it all a second time if that sawed-off little shit came round again. The plain, middle-aged waitress, Doatsey Mae, listens to the men's chatter, as she does every day, and goes off into a daydream about what it would be like—if she only dared—to step out of her innate respectability and be like the girls in the magazines ('Doatsey Mae'). But she contents herself with a small town joke: whatever happens in the football match, Miss Mona's is the only one who's sure to be on a winner.

Down at the stadium, the ideal youth of America is preparing to throw itself into a life-or-death ball-game. The Texas Aggies are supported by the Aggie Angelettes, a cheer team with obvious attributes (Angelette March) and conditioned responses. When they have won the match, however, the boys have only one thing on their mind: Senator Wingwoah's promised night out at the Chicken Ranch ('The Aggie Song').

The fact that the Senator was on KTEX-TV the night before denouncing the whole institution of whoredom is just one of those little political necessities. He still gets taken care of, just like all the lads of the team, and while the folks are enjoying themselves in there, Miss Mona and Ed Earl are in the kitchen drinking coffee and chatting over old times. Then all Melvin breaks loose. Trespassing Thorpe and his little corps of photographers break into the house, flashing their torches and cameras, and soon all is chaos.

ACT 2

The Senator is one of the prize catches. He talks a lot and is happy to shelter behind the fast-stepping Governor of Texas as soon as he can. This Governor is a master of 'The Side Step'. He can talk for a week and say nothing in the finest-sounding platitudes you even did hear. But he can't silence the maniacal, Brownie-point seeking Melvin P Thorpe who cuts into every speech with cries of what does the Governor propose to do about the Chicken Ranch. Finally, the Governor is obliged to give his nod to hypocrisy: he says that, of course, such a place must be closed down. With the squeezed authority of government to add to the God-granted charter of the 'investigative journalist', Melvin goes to work, organising protests and marches of the television generation faithful to parade outside Miss Mona's place until no customer dare come near.

857

Mona dispels them with a blast from a shotgun, but the situation looks bad. Ed Earl, it must be said, hasn't handled the business brilliantly, but Mona won't blame him. She's got memories of the young Ed Earl with whom she spent the Kennedy inauguration night in a hotel room down in Galveston. It would be too much to call it love, but it was a night she hasn't forgotten. Sadly, Ed Earl is way out of his territory. He's a fine small town sheriff, but that doesn't mean he knows how to handle the megalomaniac Melvin P Thorpes of the world. You couldn't expect him to. Mona certainly doesn't. She has no expectations of life. You take what comes to you and ask no questions. That way you get 'No Lies'.

The Chicken Ranch's rise to state-wide fame has put an unaccustomed load on the town of Gilbert, and its chief citizens are getting tetchy. It really would make their lives easier if Miss Mona were simply shut down. Ed Earl refuses. Until the order comes from the Governor, he isn't moving. Then it does come and the sheriff has to pick up the phone and call Mona. He's sad to do it. She's a 'Good Old Girl' and he feels a deep warmth for her and for the relationship they've comfortably created over the years, but there are some cats that just won't go back into a bag.

The girls are packing to go away. Quite where they'll go they aren't sure, but they're quick to assure each other they'll be fine ('Hard Candy Christmas'). Some will go up, some will go down. Angel is determined to go home and get a straight job and look after her boy; Shy looks happily for new pastures in the same game without even considering another way.

Ed Earl comes to say goodbye to Mona. He still isn't quite sure how it all got to this and he will never forget the way so-called friends ran away, and he just can't make himself say goodbye to Mona. He wants so very much for everything to be like it was before. She knows it can't be, but she makes one last try. Does he remember Kennedy's inauguration? He doesn't remember anything special about it. The assassinations he remembers fine and where he was and what he was doing when he heard about them, but not the inauguration. Some people remember one thing, others another. Mona's marvellous, remembered moment hasn't lived in Ed Earl's memory.

Funny. She says goodbye and, as he goes, she looks back along the life she has come through to get to this day ('The Bus From Amarillo'). The girls carry their suitcases off as she sings and, somewhere in the glorious places of the town, the Governor is presenting Melvin P Thorpe with a plaque in memory of his moral services to the state of Texas as Miss Mona steps out into the world, ready to start, somehow and somewhere, all over again.

ON THE TWENTIETH CENTURY

a musical in two acts by Betty Comden and Adolph Green based on *Twentieth Century* by Ben Hecht, Charles MacArthur and Bruce Milholland. Lyrics by Betty Comden and Adolph Green. Music by Cy Coleman. Produced at the St James Theatre, New

York, 19 February 1978 with Madeleine Kahn (Lily), John Cullum (Oscar), Kevin Kline (Bruce) and Imogene Coca (Letitia).

Produced at Her Majesty's Theatre, London, 19 March 1980 with Julia McKenzie, Keith Michell, Mark Wynter and Ann Beach.

CHARACTERS

Lily Garland, *formerly Mildred Plotka*
Oscar Jaffee, *the high priest of the theatre*
Owen O'Malley, *his press agent*
Oliver Webb, *his business manager*
Letitia Primrose
Bruce Granit, *a damageable screen star*
Conductor Flanagan *of the Twentieth Century*
Dr Johnson
Imelda Thornton, *a star*
Max Jacobs
Agnes, Congressman Lockwood, Maxwell Finch, Porters, Anita, etc.

ACT 1

At a theatre in Chicago a play is disintegrating. The show is a failure, the audience is gone, the producer, Oscar Jaffee, is nowhere to be seen and the actors haven't been paid ('Stranded Again'). The cast descend on the producer's business manager, Oliver Webb, and press agent, Owen O'Malley, to no avail and storm off to find the culpable Jaffee. Then a suit of armour moves its mailed hand and passes a note to Owen. It reads, 'Meet me on the Twentieth Century tomorrow—get me Drawing Room A.' It is time to go ('Saddle up the Horse').

At the Chicago railway station, the Twentieth Century waits at the platform, flanked by immaculate porters and conductors ready to receive its glamorous clientele. A sweet little old lady boards the train, Miss Letitia Primrose, the head of the wealthy Primrose Restoria Pills family, and hard behind her come Owen and Oliver anxiously looking out for Oscar. Once aboard, they take it into their hands to secure Drawing Room A—a simple exercise involving ejecting a Congressman and his pretty secretary with a little bit of blackmail—before the train moves off. It looks as if Oscar has not made it...but here he comes, outside the window, hand-over-handing from window to window. They're safely away, heading back to New York and a quarter of a million dollar bankruptcy. But is Oscar depressed, deflated? Never. His is an unreasoning optimism undimmed by constant failure ('I Rise Again'). There are sixteen hours between Chicago and New York and the world can end—and begin again—in sixteen hours.

Now it is time for plans to be made. Oliver tentatively mentions an offer from the successful producer, Max Jacobs, for Oscar to direct a road company and for the hundredth time in his years with Jaffee he gets the sack. Jacobs was once Oscar's office boy! And a road company? Never! Oscar's plans don't look downwards. They head for the stars, and one of these is due to roll into their orbit at the train's first stop at Englewood.

859

There the famous film star Lily Garland will join the train. Lily, the girl whom Oscar raised from nothing to stage stardom before she walked out on him for her fabulous career on celluloid. She will return to the arms of her old mentor and lover and, with her name on the bills of his new show, he will be able to name his own price on Broadway. Now do they understand why he had to have Drawing Room A? His spy system has told him that Lily is booked in the adjoining Drawing Room B. She will return to him. Max Jacobs? Bah!

The scene flashes back a reel of years to the stage of a theatre where Oscar is auditioning the starry Imelda Thornton for the lead of his new play. Since the piece requires Miss Thornton to sing, she has brought a pianist, a bumbling, breathless little girl called Mildred Plotka who spills the music all over the floor. Miss Thornton is not an experienced singer and, when she goes a little astray in 'The Indian Maiden's Lament', Miss Plotka does not hesitate to help her out. In fact, when Miss Thornton persistently gets it wrong, Miss Plotka finishes the song for her, cadenza and all. The star is burned up. She shrieks dismissal at her accompanist and gets rocked back on her heels when little Miss Plotka fires back on all cylinders, demanding her carfare in reimbursement for her time.

Oscar is thrilled. As the shattered Imelda is helped out, Mildred Plotka is offered the lead role in his new play. It is all there in her—the pixie, the eternal woman—and he will bring it out, mould it, make her a star. He woos her from her everyday thoughts with a vision of stardom and places the script in her hands. She begins to read the role. She is 'Véronique', a French street singer, and, in a flash, there she is, on the stage, a new-born star surrounded by her marching cast of millions crying 'vive la France!'.

But that was all a long time ago. Mildred Plotka has been Lily Garland for a lot of her life now and Oscar Jaffee has been out of it for as long as he was in it. Will she really give up Hollywood and return to where she started just for him? The conductor pops his head into the compartment to warn the occupants that there is apparently a religious maniac on the train. Someone has been sticking 'Repent' stickers all over the place. He warns Mrs Primrose too and she, as she secretly slaps a sticker on him, nods in agreement. While he has Jaffee's attention, the conductor just happens to mention that 'I Have Written a Play'. It is a phrase which dogs Oscar's life, and the conductor is quickly bundled out to announce Englewood and the arrival of Lily Garland on board the train ('Together').

Lily has a companion with her on the station, a chiselled beauty of the screen glorified under the name of Bruce Granit, but Bruce will not, she announces as she snuggles up to him for the benefit of the photographers, be joining her on the train. On the long journey to New York, she must travel alone. As soon as Bruce leaves the compartment, she declines into a boudoirful of broken-hearted loneliness, but her act is ruined when she finds that her escort has failed to get off the train in time. She is stuck with him all the way to New York. Her performance changes to one of a passionate desire to be alone, but Bruce takes her in his arms with celluloid style, and it is easier to succumb.

860

Their clinch is interrupted by Owen and Oliver, and Lily is delighted to see such old friends until she makes the connection—Oscar has to be around somewhere. Delight turns to venom as bit by bit she drags Oscar's plans from the duo. Come back to work for Oscar Jaffee? 'Never!'. Bruce is suspicious of anyone who can arouse all this passion in his woman. What is it about Oscar Jaffee and Lily? He accuses her petulantly of infidelity in retrospect and she spits out a long list of lovers from which Jaffee is particularly excluded. She is, of course, lying. There have never been any other lovers. Just Oscar, all that time ago ('Our Private World').

In the meanwhile Mrs Primrose is causing her own kind of chaos in the train. Her stickers are turning up in the most unlikely places, and she is deliciously happy that her message is getting around—'Repent'.

Amongst the hurly-burly, Oscar is maturing his own plans. Lily will come back to him. Bruce Granit is no competition. He just needs a suitable piece of bait. Then the sight of the 'Repent' stickers gives him a magnificent idea: Lily Garland as Mary Magdalen! A Mary Magdalen with every tub-thumping, heart-rending, clothes-wearing scene an actress could desire. She will not be able to resist such a role just as, surely, she will not be able to resist Oscar himself. As he gazes in his mirror appreciatively, Bruce is gazing in the corresponding mirror in the next compartment. Both are sure within themselves that before the trip is over the lady will be 'Mine'.

Owen and Oliver have given up on Oscar and his plans and are getting pie-eyed in the bar when they get into conversation with Mrs Primrose. It doesn't take long for them to discover her links with big business and religion. Both of these look very interesting. Mary Magdalen may have found a backer.

Meanwhile, Oscar has made his move. Mistily recalling their old love to Lily, he puts Bruce into a frenzy of jealous posturing which ends with Lily throwing him painfully out of the compartment. Then she turns on Oscar. He can get out too: she doesn't want him, she has proved she doesn't need him ('I've Got It All'). She asserts her stardom, he sneers at her celluloid career, and she trumps him by revealing that she knows all about his penniless condition. There is nothing he can do for her and there is nothing she will do for him. For the moment he is defeated, but he will return as soon as he has strangled Oliver and Owen for betraying his poverty to her. But the two lieutenants are soon back in favour for they have struck gold; they have Mrs Primrose and her money to introduce to their boss. *Lux resurgit semper*.

ACT 2

An entr'acte sung by four porters muses harmonically on the tenet that 'Life Is Like a Train' before Oscar, Owen and Oliver are seen relieving Letitia of a cheque with a two and 'Five Zeros' on it: $200,000 to bring their inspirational, devotional retelling of the scriptures alive in the theatre. Oscar is on line again and, as if by fate, Lily's maid arrives at that moment to summon Oscar to her mistress's presence. Lily is playing the great and generous lady this evening and she has decided to make a beautiful gesture: she will settle a small annuity on Jaffee in gratitude for his help in her early career. She hands him a cheque for $35 and presto! he changes it into one for $200,000.

Lily cannot help but be interested in such an attractive sum and, when he begins to describe the project and the part, she gets irresistibly caught up in the whole thing. Before long Oscar, Oliver, Owen and Mrs Primrose are all encouraging her to 'Sign' a contract and crushing the bruised Bruce under every piece of furniture available as he tries to stop her. But Lily feels something stronger in her than mere desire for the money, the role and the fame: she feels Oscar getting to her. She knows that she must not go back to him to be his puppet again, she must keep her hard-found freedom. She must not, she cannot, she dare not... Then Oscar turns the knife. Why keep this project for the stage? It can be a film. Mrs Primrose will be happy to finance it and it can be Lily's own personal production—free of the studios, free of everyone...

At this vital moment two asylum attendants are boarding the train. They have come for Mrs Primrose. She is an escaped patient from the Benzinger clinic for the decidedly loopy. In fact, to put it kindly, 'She's a Nut'. The whole train begins searching for her as the news spreads and, while they search, the jubilant Bruce heads straight for Lily and snatches the pen from her signing fingers. Oscar Jaffee is defeated. Lily is livid at the trick she believes has been played on her and, right on cue, who should arrive on the train and in her compartment but her loving producer, Max Jacobs. Lily flies to him and his proffered new play as Oscar grinds his teeth in fury.

Lily is reading Max's play. It is by lovely, classy, sophisticated Somerset Maugham and Lily adores it. Only, something in the back of her mind keeps wondering if perhaps the classy, sophisticated heroine couldn't have just a little of the Mary Magdalen about her? A blinding revelation, perhaps? And the style, couldn't it maybe...? Left alone, she imagines herself as Maugham's 'Babette' but, as the play comes to life in her mind, the biblical keeps on intruding into its scenes. Oscar Jaffee keeps intruding. Lily fights back and finally she captures the character of Babette while keeping the Magdalen and Oscar at bay. Triumphant at her mastery of self and subject, she announces that she will do Jacobs' play.

Out in the club car, Oscar plays his last and greatest scene. He produces a gun and soulfully declares 'The Legacy' he leaves to his nearest and dearest, before leaving the room. Owen and Oliver are sceptical with the scepticism of years when they hear a shot, but they are aghast when Mrs Primrose gallops on brandishing a smoking revolver. She has shot Oscar! Oscar staggers on to collapse in the arms of his allies but, when a doctor comes she diagnoses only a scratch. He is unharmed. But the doctor, like most people on this train, has apparently written a play and, with a promise of making her a Broadway author, Oscar persuades the doctor temporarily to alter her diagnosis. Lily is brought in to take her place at the death bed and a lovingly tearful scene ensues ('Lily, Oscar'). As her last gift to him, he asks her to sign her name to the contract he once offered her and she weepingly obliges. When Max Jacobs rushes in, Oscar flings aside his pretence and leaps up to display his contract, but Lily has the last laugh. She has signed it all right, but she has signed it 'Peter Rabbit'! They shriek recriminations at each other hilariously until with a gulping passion they fall into each other's arms. Sixteen hours on the Twentieth Century were enough to set at least two lives to rights.

THEY'RE PLAYING OUR SONG

a musical comedy in two acts by Neil Simon. Lyrics by Carol Bayer Sager. Music by Marvin Hamlisch. Produced at the Imperial Theatre, New York, 11 February 1979 with Lucie Arnaz (Sonia) and Robert Klein (Vernon).

Produced at the Shaftesbury Theatre, London, 1 October 1980 with Gemma Craven and Tom Conti.

Produced at the Wiener Kammerspiele, Vienna, as *Sie Spielen Unser Lied* in a version by Jurgen Wölffer and Christoph Busse 1985 with Michaela Rosen and Peter Fröhlich.

CHARACTERS

Vernon Gersch
Sonia Walsk
Voices of Vernon Gersch
Voices of Sonia Walsk

ACT 1

At thirty-four, Vernon Gersch, successful composer, has made it into lush living land, and he has two Grammies and an Oscar to display as landmarks on his rise and rise to comfortable fame. He is attractive, sharp, he has been engaged to three different girls in the past twelve months, and he needs a new lyricist. Because of this—the lack of a lyricist, not the three broken engagements—he has made an appointment with Sonia Walsk. Sonia once wrote the words for a successful song but it didn't breed. She is extrovertly confident, nervous, in debt, and dresses in clothes from short-run theatre shows. They both go to psychiatrists in the same block Vernon lives in, but, after all they are New Yorkers, Jewish and in the music business so what else would you expect? Sonia would give her left ear to write songs with Vernon Gersch and now he's read the pieces she's submitted to him and he's arranged an appointment, so she has dressed up in her best off-cast from *The Cherry Orchard* and arrived at his apartment twenty minutes late to meet him.

He really liked one of her lyrics. One? Well, part of one. He liked it enough to have set it straight off ('Fallin''). To his confusion, she likes only half the result—but it's the lyrics she doesn't like. His music is too good for them and she feels a cold blast of inferiority down her back. Except, perhaps just the first eight bars of the music...? And now she has to rush: she's having her hair cut right down and when do they start work and perhaps he could

863

just look at those eight bars. And wasn't it a little draggy? Then she's gone and he's wondering what the hell was wrong with those eight bars. Out in the hall, Sonia makes a good resolution not to be late for their first work session, not to have her weekend away but to work, not....

She is, in fact, a day late for their next meeting and doesn't seem to have noticed. She had a traumatic weekend breaking up with Leon, the boyfriend she broke up with on Thursday and got together with again on Friday, so yesterday sort of went. Anyway, she's here now and ready to work on a song. Vernon proposes 'Workin' It Out'. He likes the title, he's got the rhythm and a bit of tune and she can put in the lyrics to it. But that would be too simple. Sonia doesn't work like that. She has to talk it out with the girls, the other Sonias.

The thought that there is more than one of her almost fells Vernon, until she explains that the other Sonias are her alter egos, inside her brain. Doesn't he have them too? So, while Vernon goes to work on the music, plotting the song with the aid of his boys, Sonia's brain is off mulling over her love life, Vernon's attitudes, his rejection of her original lyric, anything that means she doesn't have to get down to work. Perhaps they should get to know each other properly first. I mean, how can people work together if they don't know each other? She proposes that he take her to dinner. No, it's not a date, no it's not a business dinner—it's just dinner. Tomorrow she and Leon are seeing their psychiatrist, then the next night is Leon's birthday, but she can make tonight. He gives in and, while she goes off on to another cloud to muse what he'd think of her 'If He Really Knew Me', he calls up the restaurant.

When she goes, he picks up her stream of thought. She's a handful, but she might be hit material and he needs a new hit. She's also an hour and a half late for dinner because she's had a scene with Leon who doesn't want to leave. He's hysterical and maybe she should go back. This looks like the third time they aren't going to get past the first five minutes of a meeting but, when Vernon mentions Natalie Klein, his last fiancée, Sonia gets interested. He's going to be personal, spill out his personality to her. But he doesn't. He gets ratty and goes to leave and then she's really caught. Here's a person coming out at last.

They dance and he can't, which makes her feel even better, especially as their eyes meet and something happens. Unfortunately that something makes her think guiltily about Leon and she tells him that she'll have to go. But he isn't listening to her, he's listening to the music. It's his music. His first big hit ('They're Playing My Song') and suddenly he's all switched on and telling her all about Natalie Klein, only now she's not listening because they're playing her big number. Whatever, the ice is well and truly crushed now. They're both talking happily and Sonia hasn't thought about Leon for five whole minutes. Why don't they work right away, at her place. Only Leon's there. Vernon switches off and Sonia sees it. She tells him to come in an hour. She'll have Leon out by then. And she does.

When he turns up she's finally done the deed, but she needs to talk about it. Will he pretend to be her psychiatrist for a little? So he does, and she talks and she talks, while he thinks about himself ('If She Really Knew Me') until she stops and asks if he wants a turn. But Vernon is into self-analysis, as he demonstrates at length, and Sonia's mind starts to wander into 'If He Really Knew Me'. The total result of the evening is a question: do they try to work this week on those five songs Barbra needs or do they go to his friends' beach house for a non-working weekend? The beach house wins hands down and, as Vernon leaves, Sonia decides that this is all starting out 'Right'. Come the weekend, off they go and it still looks right. But it's a long drive and Sonia is worried that her plants will die because Leon isn't there to feed them. Then they get lost and the car engine floods and soon nothing is right.

They get to the beach, she breaks into the wrong house and he is getting more neurotic by the minute, particularly when she insists on the thrill of making love in the wrong house on the wrong bed ('Just for Tonight'). But, just as they are about to get to grips with each other, the phone rings. Sonia had checked into her answering service with the number before she found out it was the wrong house and Leon is calling. While she calms her quivering ex, Vernon goes out to settle in to the right house. Sonia puts down the phone and follows him, making a great effort to ignore the phone as it once again starts to peal with distress.

ACT 2

Back in New York, Vernon can't sleep. He's in love. And while he can't sleep, the doorbell rings. It's Sonia. It's also Sonia's suitcases. Leon has turned up at her apartment in a terrible state so she couldn't throw him out. On the other hand, after what happened between her and Vernon over the weekend she couldn't very well stay there with him. So she's suggesting that she moves in with Vernon. He is flabbergasted. Actually, he was going to ask her to move in so she's sort of short-circuited him. But he loves her ('When You're In My Arms') so why not?

Moving in at least means that Sonia isn't late any more. It also means that they spend day and night working which wasn't her idea of how things were going to be, but it's all right. They don't go out, because everything they want is here. Then, one night at 2.45 a.m. the phone goes. It's Leon and he's having a big one. Sonia is distraught. She has to go to him. So, while Vernon climbs up the wall with fury, she borrows five dollars for the cab fare and sets off back to her old apartment.

She doesn't turn up at the hour appointed next morning to cut the demo for their new song and, when she finally does arrive, the first part of the little bit of session time left turns into a debate on Leon. Vernon makes her promise in writing never to take a call from Leon again, which makes Sonia furious and suddenly they find themselves questioning their whole relationship, work and love. It isn't working. Maybe the working's working, but the whole thing isn't. It's time to call it off. Well, at least they got some songs out of it. And they may as well lay down the last one. It's called 'I Still Believe in Love'.

While the song climbs the charts, Vernon is in Los Angeles. To be precise he's in Cedars Sinai Hospital with a broken leg after being knocked down on Sunset Boulevard, and who should come to visit him but Sonia. It's a real coincidence, she only just heard about his accident and she was coming here anyhow because Leon is in the same hospital having his white cells counted. She's brought him a present—a little baby toy piano. They like seeing each other again and, when she goes, he wonders if she mightn't once again 'Fill in the Words' to the tune he is playing on his little piano.

December comes and Sonia gets a call from Leon. It's a very odd call. He's got a job and he's calling to see if *she* is all right. With the New York snow comes Vernon. He's still walking with a stick, but he's whole and he's back in town. As it happens, he met Leon while they were in hospital and they had a good talk. They talked about Sonia a lot, but they also talked about themselves and themselves in relation to Sonia. Leon has a girlfriend now and he has given Vernon permission to ring him at 3 a.m. if he feels the need.

Sonia is off to London the next day to meet some guy who is going to be the new Elton John. Vernon is going into analysis, as it seems to have done a lot for Leon. So they say goodbye. But he comes back. He has dropped his stick down a sewer and can't get home. Actually, he hasn't done anything of the sort, but he wanted an excuse to come back. Couldn't Sonia stay in New York and try writing with the new Vernon Gersch instead of going to Britain for the new Elton John? And couldn't he stay the night? Of course. If he'd tried to leave again, she'd have broken his other leg.

SWEENEY TODD

The Demon Barber of Fleet Street. A musical thriller in two acts by Hugh Wheeler based on a play by Chris Bond. Music and lyrics by Stephen Sondheim. Produced at the Uris Theatre, New York, 1 March 1979 with Len Cariou (Sweeney Todd), Angela Lansbury (Mrs Lovett), Victor Garber (Anthony), Sarah Rice (Johanna) and Edmund Lyndeck (Judge Turpin).

Produced at the Theatre Royal, Drury Lane, London, 2 July 1980 with Dennis Quilley, Sheila Hancock, Andrew C Wadsworth, Mandy More and Austin Kent.

A television film was produced by RKO/Nederlander in 1982 with Hearn, Miss Lansbury, Cris Groenendaal, Betsy Joslyn and Lyndeck.

CHARACTERS

Sweeney Todd
Anthony Hope
Mrs Lovett
A Beggar Woman
Judge Turpin
The Beadle

Johanna
Tobias Ragg
Pirelli
Jonas Fogg, etc.

As a prelude to the action, 'The Ballad of Sweeney Todd' introduces the famous tale of the demon barber of Fleet Street

ACT 1

Down at the London docks two men, newly arrived by sea, greet the city with different feelings ('There's No Place Like London'). For young Anthony Hope it is a welcome Britain after long travels abroad, but for Sweeney Todd the country and the city clearly have other and less kindly memories. As they take their leave of each other, the men are accosted by a crazy beggar woman who alternately begs miserable alms and crudely offers herself for sale. Todd harshly sends her on her way, bewildering Anthony who has known him as a strong and kind man, but Sweeney Todd is not the same man in London as he was at sea. To him London is a great black pit inhabited by the vermin of the earth. In London there once took place the dreadful tale of 'The Barber and his Wife', he naïve, she young and beautiful and desired by a powerful man. It is a bad, sad story and without an end.

Todd makes his way towards Fleet Street. Looking about him, remembering, he marches on until he comes upon a certain shop where a beldam known as Mrs Lovett sells what she admits are 'The Worst Pies in London'. He samples her pies and makes enquiries about the room above her shop. It is to let. No one wants it, for once a nasty thing happened there. There was a nice young barber with a little daughter and a silly, pretty wife who took the fancy of a Judge and his Beadle ('Poor Thing'). The Judge and the Beadle arranged for the barber to be transported on a trumped up charge and inveigled the pure, silly woman to a masked ball at the Judge's home where she was raped and her child taken from her. The woman killed herself and the barber was never seen again, but the Judge still keeps the child, Johanna, as he has for fifteen years.

Before the tale is told, Mrs Lovett has no doubts as to the identity of her visitor. He may have a different name, but it is the barber. Todd does not deny it. He has survived fifteen years of exile buoyed up by the hope of returning to his wife and child, and now the one is dead and the other alienated. Fifteen years of dashed hope merit a terrible revenge. Mrs Lovett is cynical—how can a penniless ex-convict wreak revenge on the high and wealthy?—but she is also sympathetic and she can provide him, at least, with the means to keep himself alive. All those years ago, from the abandoned room she took the barber's razors and she has kept them close for the day of his return. Sweeney Todd can go back to his old trade. Lovingly fingering the blades, Todd addresses them as 'My Friends', while Mrs Lovett warmly impresses on him that she, too, is his friend.

867

From the uppermost window of Judge Turpin's house, lovely young Johanna sings to the birdseller's caged creatures ('Green Finch and Linnet Bird') and, as she sings, she is seen by Anthony who is passing by in the street. He is immediately taken by her beauty ('Ah, Miss') and, when the beggar woman passes, he asks her who the girl is and whose the house. He buys a bird and offers it to the gentle Johanna who shyly descends to accept the gift, but the Judge catches her and threateningly warns the young man away from his 'daughter'. It is too late. Anthony has fallen in love, and he has made up his mind that he will steal 'Johanna' from the Judge's clutches.

In St Dunstan's Place, Sweeney Todd comes to make a reputation. There a quasi-Italian barber, Pirelli by name, gives a fashionable shave whilst also purveying to a gullible crowd 'Pirelli's Miracle Elixir'. Todd mocks the properties of the elixir and turns the crowd against it and against Pirelli and, when the mountebank tries to bluff his way back to favour, challenges him to a shaving and tooth-pulling contest.

Pirelli puts up a showy but inefficient performance (The Contest), but Todd quickly and cleanly completes both operations, winning the contest and the admiration of both the crowd and of Beadle Bamford who has been seconded to judge the match. All are invited to be shaved at Sweeney Todd's new establishment in Fleet Street. Already Todd's first hook is baited and the Beadle seems near to taking it, but he does not come to be shaved and Todd, though business is good, begins to fret. Mrs Lovett has to keep him calm, advising him to 'Wait'. His chance for revenge will come.

One visitor who does come brings a surprise. It is Anthony and he is full of the story of the lovely maiden whom he intends to carry off from her cruel parent. When the name of Johanna falls from his lips, Todd does not blench and he and Mrs Lovett agree that Anthony may secrete his love in the shop once she has been freed. The next to come to the barber's shop is Pirelli. While his little assistant Tobias waits in Mrs Lovett's shop, the phoney Italian goes upstairs to try a little blackmail. He has recognised Todd and intends to profit from it, but he has underestimated his man. Whilst Mrs Lovett feeds the simple Tobias on pies and gin, Todd strangles the blackmailer.

In the meanwhile Judge Turpin has decided that he will marry the lovely young Johanna himself. The girl is distraught and, when Anthony manages to climb to her room, she pours out her heart to him. As he takes his fill of kisses ('Kiss Me') they decide to make their escape that night. Turpin confides his marriage plan to the Beadle, who suggests that, for the girl's sake and ultimately his own satisfaction, the Judge should take care to look his best ('Ladies in Their Sensibilities') and recommends him to try the shop of Sweeney Todd for a fine shave. Thus, while Johanna and Anthony are plotting to elope to the room above the pie shop, the Judge and the Beadle are heading to that selfsame room on professional business.

Pirelli's corpse is cooling in a chest when Turpin takes his seat in the barber's chair. He is in merry form and, to Sweeney Todd's echoing, he sings lecherously of 'Pretty Women'. But just as Todd is about to slice his razor through the Judge's throat, Anthony arrives crying the news of his plans. All is lost. The elopement is discovered and the Judge will now never return to the barber who is so obviously in league with this thieving boy.

Todd's chance of revenge is forever gone and in his dreadful disappointment he rages wildly at Mrs Lovett ('Epiphany'). But, Judge or no Judge, there is still a present problem to be solved. Pirelli's body must be disposed of. Mrs Lovett finds it almost a crime to bury so much nice, plump person. She really could use him, the price of meat being what it is. She giggles over the possibilities of her pies containing such ingredients ('A Little Priest') and Todd joins her song as he begins to plan a career supplying raw materials to her gruesome kitchen.

ACT 2

Mrs Lovett's trade has much improved and, with the aid of young Tobias, who has stayed with her since the mysterious disappearance of his master, she runs a moderately successful ale garden ('God, That's Good'). There is success upstairs too. The barbershop is booming and Sweeney Todd is able to afford to install an elaborate new barber's chair. From a trapdoor under the chair, a chute runs down to the basement where Mrs Lovett's bakehouse produces the pies. It is quite a production line. Todd no longer kills only for revenge and safety, he kills for profit and, as he kills, he thinks of Johanna and takes revenge on the whole world for his and her sufferings. Anthony, too, thinks of Johanna and he wanders the streets of London looking for her, but the Judge has immured the child in an asylum and, when Anthony finally tracks her down, he comes up against Beadle Bamford who tries to have him arrested.

The beggar woman has not gone away. She has been seen hanging around Mrs Lovett's shop and at night, as she watches the smoke coming from the bakehouse, she cries crazily of mischief ('City on Fire'). No one takes heed of her, no one knows that the crazy woman sees what goes on while sane folk sleep.

Mrs Lovett's prosperity continues to grow. She sports ribbons and favours being flirtatious with Todd ('By the Sea'), but his mind dwells still on Judge Turpin and revenge rots in his heart. He is full of venomous joy when Anthony brings the news of Johanna's whereabouts, and he plots for the boy to get her out by penetrating the gates of the madhouse disguised as a wigmaker sent to buy the hair of the madwomen. As soon as Anthony has gone to carry out the deed, Todd pens a letter to the Judge designed to lure him to the barber's shop. He writes that Anthony has abducted Johanna and is bringing her to his shop. There they may be caught red-handed.

So far, all the activities in Fleet Street have gone without a hitch, but a chink in the secret of Todd's work is about to appear. The boy Tobias has become foolishly fond of Mrs Lovett and he fears for her ('No One's Going to Harm You') as he mistrusts Todd. His mistrust is deepened when he catches sight of Pirelli's purse, souvenired by Mrs Lovett, and recalls that his former master disappeared in Todd's shop. His discovery makes Mrs Lovett uneasy. She takes Tobias into the basement. For a treat she will let him make the pies. She shows him the big red oven and the meat grinder. As soon as a batch of meat comes in, he can begin to work. She leaves him to wait, and as she leaves she locks the door. Tobias will never come out again.

When she returns to her parlour, she finds she has a visitor. Beadle Bamford is sitting at her harmonium accompanying himself in some Parlour Songs. In between the songs he questions her. There have been complaints about the smell from her chimneys. He'll have to look at her bakehouse. She pretends that Todd has the key and is away, but when Todd returns unexpectedly she pointedly recommends that he give the Beadle a nice free shave.

Down in the bakehouse Tobias has made an unusual discovery. A fingernail in a pie. He is fascinated by the chute, too, and, as Mrs Lovett pounds away on the harmonium, the slashed body of Beadle Bamford shoots out onto the floor. Only now can Mrs Lovett tell Todd that their conspiracy has a new member, that Tobias is in on the whole affair, but Todd has no care for Tobias. At last his real revenge has begun: he has had the Beadle and the Judge will follow soon. At the madhouse, Anthony almost fumbles the plot. He drops his gun at the crucial moment and it is the wretched Johanna who shoots down the proprietor of the asylum. As the lovers escape, the lunatics pour out onto the streets of London. Anthony and Johanna make their way to the barber's shop to find it empty, and Johanna waits there, disguised as a sailor boy, while Anthony runs off to find them a coach. Todd has gone to the basement with Mrs Lovett to deal with Tobias. But, outside the shop the ever-watching beggar woman wanders about, calling for the Beadle. He went into the house and he didn't come out. Curious and crazy, she climbs the stairs to Todd's room and the frightened Johanna hides in the same chest that once sheltered Pirelli's body. The beggar woman looks about her. This room brings back the strangest memories. But she has little time to set her crazy thoughts in order for suddenly Todd is there and he is in an exulting haste. The Judge is approaching. This madwoman cannot be allowed to foil his plan. The razor flies as he slits the poor creature's throat and tumbles her down the chute.

Now the hour of triumph comes. At last, Judge Turpin is in his room. Puffed-up and proud, awaiting the girl he desires. Todd proffers a splash of bay rum, and the Judge takes the chair. As they sing together of 'Pretty Women', Todd prepares his coup. Then it is time. He reveals himself to Turpin as the barber he so fiercely wronged and vengefully brings the blade down across the Judge's throat. Only when his revenge is complete and he is headed down the stairs does he remember Tobias. He returns to the barbershop for his razor and finds Johanna who, thinking him gone, has climbed out from the chest. Sweeney's eyes do not see his beloved daughter, they see only a young sailor. A young sailor who must have seen what happened. But as he seats the boy in the barber's chair he hears screams from below. It is Mrs Lovett.

Rushing to the basement he finds her caught in the grip of the hard-dying Turpin. Together they drag the bodies to the furnace, but Mrs Lovett will not let him touch the beggar woman. Suddenly Todd knows who that demented crone was. She was his Lucy, his beautiful wife, and Mrs Lovett

870

had known it all along. It was his dear wife and, because Mrs Lovett lied, he killed the one person in the world he really loved.

Mrs Lovett defends herself frantically. Lucy did take poison, as she had said, but she did not die. She lived on with her wits gone. What use to anyone is a woman like that, compared to one such as herself. He can have her. Todd takes her in his arms and begins to dance and, when they dance past the oven, it takes only a twist of his strong arm to hurl Mrs Lovett into the very furnace that baked her dreadful pies.

He turns back to the body of his Lucy, to cradle it in his arms, when little Tobias emerges from the shadows. What he has seen has taken the child's mind away, but he knows that Todd has harmed people and that he is bad. Lifting the razor from where Todd let it fall, he approaches the grieving man. Sweeney Todd is murdered with the same weapon with which he cut so many a throat. When Johanna and Anthony bring the police, they find the boy grinding away at the mincing machine. It is the end of the tale of Sweeney Todd.

BARNUM

a musical in two acts suggested by the life of P T Barnum. Book by Mark Bramble. Lyrics by Michael Stewart. Music by Cy Coleman. Produced at the St James Theatre, New York, 30 April 1980 with Jim Dale (Barnum), Glenn Close (Charity), William C Witter (Ringmaster), Marianne Tatum (Jenny Lind), Terri White (Joice) and Leonard John Crofoot (Tom Thumb).

Produced at the London Palladium 11 June 1981 with Michael Crawford, Deborah Grant, Witter, Sarah Payne, Jennie McGustie and Christopher Beck. Produced at the Victoria Palace 14 March 1985 with Crawford, Eileen Battye, Michael Heath, Christina Collier, Sally Lavelle and Stephen Beagley.

Produced at the Cirque d'Hiver, Paris, in a version by Charles Level and Jacques Collard 1981 with Jean-Luc Moreau.

Produced at the Theater des Westens, Berlin, 27 March 1983 with Freddy Quinn.

A television film was produced by Harold Fielding and the BBC in 1986 with Crawford, Miss Battye, Heath, Miss Collier, Sharon Benson and Paul Miller.

CHARACTERS

Phineas Taylor Barnum
Charity Barnum, *his wife*
The Ringmaster/Mr Goldschmidt/James A Bailey
Joice Heth/Blues Singer
Tom Thumb
Jenny Lind
Amos Scudder
White-Faced Clown
Chester Lyman, Sherwood Stratton, Mrs Stratton, Wilton, Edgar Templeton, Humbert Morrissey, etc.

ACT 1

On to a stage representing a circus tent, to the accompaniment of a tiny fanfare played on a drum and concertina, strides a man in shirtsleeves. He is Phineas Taylor Barnum and tonight on this stage, he tells us, he is going to show us all sorts of gigantic wonders. The undraped stage and the small company of artists surrounding him may seem meagre material for the fulfilment of such a promise but he is P T Barnum, and humbug is his game. In a stage box, a woman prepares to leave. She is in disagreement with the principle of humbug. Barnum claims a kiss before she departs—she is, after all, his wife. But the world in general does not have the same attitude as Mrs Barnum for, after all, 'There Is a Sucker Born Every Minute' and, in no time, Barnum is off peddling the charms of a genuine mermaid to a gullible public.

The Ringmaster announces the next step in Barnum's career. He purchases from another showman an elderly negress, Joice Heth, billed as the oldest woman in the world ('Thank God I'm Old') and turns her from a liability into a profitable concern simply by changing her billing and, with a bit of 'patriotic humbug' selling her to the public as George Washington's nurse. Next he moves on to bigger plans: the American Museum, five floors of attractions announced as educational and ranging from a whale to a lecture hall.

His wife is not in accord with such ventures. She is not at all keen on his involvement in the shadier side of the exhibition business and, having won his consent to lunch at the Women's Emancipation Society by the flip of a coin, she tries to persuade him that he would do better to take on steadier employment at the Bridgeport clock factory. Barnum cannot submit. His personality cannot be cooped up in a clock factory. He needs colour and action in everything he does ('The Colors of my Life') and, as he rushes off to start work on the museum, Charity wonders how a woman like her ever got mixed up with a man with such visions and passions.

On to the stage tumble a team of clowns, falling over one another in their hurried attempts to get the building of the museum under way. It is chaos until Charity appears on the scene to counsel more speed and less haste ('One Brick at a Time'). Barnum builds his museum (Museum Song) and it is a success. For a whole year it is a success, and on its first anniversary he presents Charity with a string of pearls and an invitation to dinner at a fancy town restaurant. Charity turns both down. She is a plain woman and such things may be for him, but they are not for her ('I Like Your Style').

But whatever Charity Barnum may think of his crazy enthusiasms, she loves her husband and, in the end, she gives in to his yearning for a splashy celebration and goes off to change. While she is gone, Barnum's partner, Amos Scudder, arrives from town with dreadful news: the museum has been burned to the ground. The celebrations are off, Barnum is in despair and his wife can only comfort him with prospects of other places, other ventures—the clock factory for example.

Barnum seizes on her words in an unexpected way. Other places! Of course...he will build a new museum and take it all round the country on

872

wheels. The first thing he must do is find some new attractions. The one he purchases as topliner is a little man called Charlie Stratton who is only twenty-five inches from top to toe. Billed as the world's smallest man and equipped with a new name—Tom Thumb—the little man is a huge success ('Bigger Isn't Better').

In spite of this, Charity is still not entirely happy. The dishonesty inherent in the exhibition business irks her and she wishes that her husband would get some more respectable attractions. The opportunity comes when Barnum hears of the operatic soprano, Jenny Lind, who has had an enormous success in England. If he hurries to Britain, leaving his wife in charge of the current tour, he can sign the singer up for America. What does Charity think? Charity decides with a toss of her coin, and Barnum heads on his way to London.

The promotion of Jenny Lind is a new style of business for Barnum, and the lady herself is something else. When the beautiful Swede arrives and scores a huge success ('Love Makes Such Fools of Us All'), she pays marked attention to her impresario and Barnum is captivated. Jenny represents the fabulous, colourful world of adventure which he loves. She is glamour, she is excitement and he has to get himself some of it ('Out There'). As the act ends, he daringly walks across the stage on a tightrope to where she stands welcomingly in the stage box. Reaching her with a cry of triumph, he joins her in a grand circus finale to the act.

ACT 2

The Jenny Lind tour is a huge success everywhere and Barnum's career is flourishing ('Come Follow the Band'), but his adventure—the affair with Miss Lind—has lost its feeling of daring and excitement, and his thoughts return to his Charity sitting patiently and knowingly back in Bridgeport, Connecticut. He sells his rights in the tour, says goodbye to Jenny, and goes home. They will try again, and this time they will do it Charity's way. He will give up the exhibition business and go into the clock factory. There has been too much colour in his life; now he will try living her way, in 'Black and White'.

Both the clock works and a subsequent effort as a building entrepreneur fail, and an attempt at entering politics looks like going the same way until Barnum pleads with Charity to release him from his promise and allow him to put some good showbiz razzmatazz into his campaign. She relents and Barnum is elected mayor of Bridgeport. All seems well. They are secure, they are content, and Charity has ambitions for her husband to rise in politics maybe even as far as Washington. He demurs and she brings out the inevitable coin to toss. Now, after twenty-five years of giving in to the results of that coin, Barnum discovers that it is a two-headed quarter. His correct, demure wife has stacked the deck on her side all their married life. They join happily in a reprise of 'The Colors of my Life' and then, suddenly, she is gone.

Left alone, Barnum sees his world falling to pieces. The senate nomination which seemed assured is denied him. 'The Prince of Humbug' has been humbugged himself. There's no going back, but he has no intention of remaining in an area where the other fellow holds all the cards. Perhaps he will go on a lecture tour to tell the world about the noble art of humbug. But fate has something else in store for Phineas Taylor Barnum.

A Mr Bailey has approached him with a offer of a partnership in his circus business but, although Barnum is happy to dispense grandiose good advice, he refuses to take an active part. From all sides the people of the circus come at him: clowns, tight-rope walkers, jugglers and acrobats, stilt-walkers and dancing girls all urging him to return to the show business world he knows best ('Join the Circus') until finally Barnum agrees to take the judgement of a flip of the coin. He takes out Charity's coin and, before he has even needed to look at the result, he is shaking Mr Bailey's hand. He is the new partner in the Greatest Show on Earth.

The circus pours on to the stage and finally Barnum himself, clad in the scarlet coat of the ringmaster, slides into their midst from a rope slung from the highest part of the theatre to join their chorus. Then they are all gone, and he is alone. It was all a long time ago. Joice Heth and Tom Thumb and their kind are gone, and nowadays people are too smart to be taken in by his kind of humbug, aren't they? A pity.

42ND STREET

a musical in two acts by Michael Stewart and Mark Bramble based on the screenplay and the novel by Bradford Ropes. Lyrics by Al Dubin. Music by Harry Warren. Produced at the Winter Garden Theatre, New York, 25 August 1980 with Jerry Orbach (Julian Marsh), Lee Roy Reams (Billy), Wanda Richert (Peggy) and Tammy Grimes (Dorothy) and played from 30 March 1981 at the Majestic Theatre.

Produced at the Theatre Royal, Drury Lane, London, 8 August 1984 with James Laurenson, Michael Howe, Clare Leach and Georgia Brown.

CHARACTERS

Andy Lee
Maggie Jones, *one of the authors of Pretty Lady*
Bert Barry, *her collaborator*
Billy Lawlor, *juvenile lead in Pretty Lady*
Peggy Sawyer
Lorraine, Phyllis, Annie, *chorus girls*
Julian Marsh, *Broadway producer*
Dorothy Brock, *a star*
Abner Dillon, *a manufacturer*
Pat Denning
Oscar, Mac, Doctor, etc.

ACT 1

The word is round the gipsy cafés and dance classes of New York City that Julian Marsh is doing a new show. So it's out with your tap shoes and down to the 42nd Street Theatre where the auditions for *Pretty Lady* are taking place (Audition/'42nd Street').

The audition is over and the chorus girls and boys who have been selected are having their names taken when a young girl bursts on to the stage. Peggy Sawyer has come to audition but, because she couldn't pluck up the nerve to walk through the stage door till now, she's missed her chance. Or she would have, except that in her unusual entrance she has caught the eye of the show's young leading man, Billy Lawlor ('I'm Young and Healthy'). He is very taken with her and promises to help her catch the dance director's eye but, when he sets her singing, the response, in spite of an ear-catching performance, is simply overworked irritation. Peggy is ordered from the theatre and, as she makes an exit as unorthodox as her entrance, she runs straight into the show's revered producer, Julian Marsh, who has come to give his pre-rehearsal pep-talk to the boys and girls.

The star of the show is to be the experienced Dorothy Brock. Perhaps the word experienced is a bit kind. Ageing would be more to the point. But Brock's devoted admirer, kiddie car magnate Abner Dillon, is the show's principal backer and therefore Brock is to be the star. When she arrives, it is evident that the star is a role she intends to play up to the hilt, but she has a tough opponent in Julian Marsh who, in spite of her open threats to walk out and take Dillon's cash with her, will not allow himself to be ordered about. Brock is handed a song to try and, sulkily, she starts 'The Shadow Waltz'. The rehearsals of *Pretty Lady* have begun.

In a break at rehearsals, Brock meets an old friend who is more than just an old friend. Pat Denning was her partner in vaudeville before she became famous. He was her lover then and she is still in love with him now, but she is not willing to risk losing Dillon and his money and the opportunity to star again in *Pretty Lady*, so Pat has to be kept out of the way. They can only arrange snatched meetings at times when Dillon is not around.

In the same break, Peggy Sawyer comes back. In her hurried exit that morning she left her purse behind, but kindly Maggie Jones, the author of the show, has found it and has noticed how little is in it so, as she returns the purse, she invites Peggy to join her and some of the other girls for a dancer's lunch at the nearby tearoom. Peggy is only too happy to accept. To get their dancer's lunch from Maggie those girls have to dance their way to the tea rooms. Wisecracking Annie leads off and is stunned when little Peggy Sawyer manages to accomplish even the most difficult steps with bravura. She's good!

When lunch is done and the girls spill back out on to 42nd Street, they're dancing again ('Go Into Your Dance') and Peggy is winning admiring looks all round until Julian Marsh hustles his chorus back to rehearsal. But wait! Something has gone wrong. The chorus is one girl short. What can be done? There is the big Boardwalk number to set this very afternoon and Mr Marsh doesn't have a full company. He has a good mind to take the first girl who walks along the street. Peggy, about to wander off into unemployment and disenchantment, fortunately has good hearing. She makes darned sure that she is the first girl who walks by. Can she dance? Can she *dance?* She can do every tap step ever invented and, just to prove it, she does, right there in the middle of the street. So Peggy Sawyer is hired for *Pretty Lady* after all.

At the afternoon rehearsal, Brock plays a love scene with Billy under the inhibiting eye of Dillon and then goes into her song 'You're Getting to Be a Habit With Me'. Peggy has been hurried into the number without sufficient preparation and she goes disastrously wrong in the dance break, fraying the star's already ragged temper badly, but she escapes the consequences when she faints as a result of her efforts and has to be carried into Brock's dressing room to recover.

Pat Denning is there, awaiting a rendezvous with Dorothy, and he helps out by carrying the inanimate girl to a day bed, but it doesn't do anything to calm Brock's feelings when she walks in to find him bending over the recovering Peggy. A scene is averted, but then Dillon bursts in and Denning has to be passed off as Peggy's boyfriend while Dorothy is sent off to be sweet to the money man. The situation is worrying. Too much is riding on *Pretty Lady* for the show to be put at risk by Brock playing around with a vaudeville fellow but Brock won't promise not to see Pat Denning, so Julian takes the only way out. He telephones a friendly gangster. If Denning won't stay away he must be scared away. Pat takes the point quickly and suddenly finds that he has an urgent job in Philadelphia. Without even waiting to say goodbye to Dorothy, he leaves.

What Pat doesn't know is that the out-of-town tryout of *Pretty Lady* has been rescheduled. Instead of opening in Atlantic City, the show is going to make its bow at the Arch Street Theatre in Philadelphia ('Getting Out of Town'). At the final rehearsal ('Dames'), Brock throws a tantrum. Since she can't dance, she has been fairly obviously left out of the big production number and, her nerves on edge over the Pat Denning affair, she takes the dance arrangement as a personal insult. At the party that evening she drinks too much and tells Dillon what she thinks of him, causing a chaos which can only be assuaged by the attentions of Maggie and every available chorus girl.

Dorothy rushes to her room to start ringing all round town trying to find Pat. She cannot be allowed to find him. Once again, Julian gets on the phone to gangsterland but this time he is overheard by Peggy who hurries to Dorothy's room to pass on a warning. When she gets there, Pat has already arrived and the jealous Dorothy sees in Peggy's well-meant attentions the signs of something more. She drunkenly orders both of them out of her room before collapsing into a love song ('I Know Now'). Somehow, everyone makes it to the opening night ('I Know Now'/'We're in the Money') and, as the show progresses, *Pretty Lady* seems certain to be a hit. Then, as Dorothy launches into '42nd Street', a dancer stumbles and pushes Peggy into her path. The star, unable to avoid the girl, falls and does not get up. The curtain comes down and, as a furious Julian Marsh fires the offending Peggy on the spot, an announcement goes out to the front-of-house that Dorothy Brock will not be able to continue. The performance has been abandoned.

ACT 2

It is soon clear that it is not only that performance but the whole production which will have to be abandoned. Brock's injury is a broken ankle and there is no way that she will be able to take her part in *Pretty Lady*. The kids are out of a job, but busy convincing themselves that 'There's a Sunny Side to Every Situation', when Annie comes up with an idea. Why close? Why not just replace Brock? Why, right here in the company they have someone who sings a storm, is as pretty as paint and could dance rings round Brock even when her ankle wasn't broken. Peggy Sawyer!

Annie leads a deputation to Julian Marsh and it doesn't take too long before he is convinced. It is worth a try. They will close down in Philadelphia and head right back to New York to revamp the show as a vehicle for Peggy. The only thing is that she's gone. He sacked her. Well, in that case it's up to him to get her back.

Julian Marsh dons his hat and heads for Broad Street Station and there he finds Peggy, sitting on her suitcase on the platform. All the fire has gone out of her. She is going back to Allentown and forgetting all about show business. Julian takes it on himself to relight the fire with visions of Broadway ('Lullaby of Broadway') which are soon echoed by the whole company until Peggy, suddenly in love with it all again, agrees. She will do it. She will be the star of *Pretty Lady* on Broadway.

Now begins the slog, the learning of the new songs and the new dances under the unyielding direction of Julian Marsh until the girl is almost falling apart with tiredness. Finally, the big day comes and, as Peggy prepares herself for the performance, she receives an unexpected visitor, Dorothy Brock. Brock has been watching the rehearsal and she has been able to see Peggy's talent shining out. She has come to wish her good luck and to give her a little tip about the singing of the last but one number ('About a Quarter to Nine'). She can afford to be generous for the broken ankle has turned out to be a blessing in disguise: it made her realise that stardom was not as important as love, and that morning she has married Pat Denning.

With the chorus kids willing her on and Julian Marsh's words ringing behind her—'You're going out there a youngster, but you've got to come back a star!'—Peggy Sawyer goes on to the stage at the 42nd Street Theatre with the whole of *Pretty Lady* riding on her aching back (Overture/'Shuffle off to Buffalo'). The performance comes to a climax with the performance of the '42nd Street' scena and the curtain falls on a triumph. *Pretty Lady* is a smash and Peggy Sawyer is a star. She is invited to a big party at the Ritz to celebrate but, as everyone hurries off, she remains on stage to thank the man who made it all possible, Julian Marsh. Now that she is a star, can she do what she wants? Of course she can. In that case she isn't going to the Ritz, she's going to the chorus kids' party. And perhaps he might come too? Perhaps he might. Anything can happen in this crazy world of the theatre on '42nd Street'.

The songs in *42nd Street* include, apart from those from the film version, Warren/Dubin material from *Go Into Your Dance*, *Gold Diggers of 1933*, *Dames*, *The Singing Marine* and *Hard to Get*.

LITTLE SHOP OF HORRORS

a musical in two acts by Howard Ashman based on the film screenplay by Charles Griffith. Music by Alan Menken. Produced at the Orpheum Theatre, New York, 27 July 1982 with Ellen Greene (Audrey), Lee Wilkof (Seymour) and Ron Taylor and Martin P Robinson (Audrey II).

Produced at the Comedy Theatre, London, 12 October 1983 with Miss Greene, Barry James and Anthony B Asbury and Michael Leslie.

Produced at the Théâtre Déjazet, Paris, 19 June 1986 in a version by Alain Marcel as *La Petite Boutique des Horreurs* with Fabienne Guyon, Vincent Vittoz and Jacques Martial and Pierre Alain de Garrigues.

A film version was produced by the Geffen Company in 1986 with Miss Greene and Rick Moranis.

CHARACTERS

Audrey
Seymour Krelbourn
Mr Mushnik, *an East Side florist*
Crystal, Ronnette *and* Chiffon, *street urchins*
Orin Scrivello, *a dentist*
Audrey II
Mr Bernstein, Skip Snip, Mrs Luce, Patrick Martin, etc.

ACT 1

On the twenty-first day of the month of September, in an early year of a decade not too long before our own, the human race suddenly encountered a deadly threat to its very existence. This terrifying enemy surfaced, as such enemies often do, in the seemingly most innocent and unlikely of places— you might call it the 'Little Shop of Horrors'.

Mr Mushnik runs a flower shop on Skid Row where the customers are rare. His assistants are Seymour Krelbourn, a nice if socially backward little chap, and Audrey, a sweetly naïve blonde bit of shrapnel permanently on the losing side in the game of life. This particular day Seymour is bumbling through his re-potting when Audrey checks in with a black eye. She has this boyfriend who beats her up, but when a girl lives 'Downtown' on Skid Row she doesn't deserve anything better. How lovely it would be to get out of this place.

It seems they may have the chance sooner than they think for Mr Mushnik is terminally depressed and is going to shut down the shop. But Seymour has a suggestion. Rather than shut down, why not try a new direction. He has been experimenting with this weird and exotic plant which he picked up from an old Chinese man during a total eclipse of the sun ('Da Doo'). He calls it the Audrey Two after his colleague, and perhaps if they put it in the window it might attract some interest. Mushnik pooh-poohs the idea but, sure enough, no sooner has Seymour put Audrey Two in the window than a curious customer comes in and buys a hundred dollars' worth of roses. Mushnik's Flower Shop is back in business.

There is no doubt, however, that Audrey Two (rather like Audrey One) is a girl in a poor condition. In spite of all the attention Seymour lavishes on her, she wilts (rather like Audrey One) and will not blossom. Seymour cannot imagine how to save his plant ('Grow for Me'). As he works, however, the young man pricks his finger on a rose thorn and, to his amazement and horror, he sees a reaction from the plant. It is soon clear to him what the plant's favourite diet is—it is blood! A few drops from Seymour's finger and Audrey Two is back in the bloom of health and beginning to grow beautifully.

The new plant brings success to Mushnik's shop and to Seymour Krelbourn. The orphan raised as a Skid Row skivvy is suddenly famous. It just shows, 'Ya Never Know'. Audrey One is ever so pleased for him, but she goes right on dating her sadistic boyfriend. She suffers from severely low self-esteem and believes that Seymour is far too sweet and nice for a bad girl like her. She just knows that she could never deserve such a sweet little man and the wonderful world of lower middle class suburbia of which she dreams ('Somewhere That's Green').

Mushnik's shop undergoes a transformation ('Closed for Renovation') as both business and Audrey Two grow and grow, and the increasing number of Band-Aids on Seymour's fingers doesn't provoke too much comment. Audrey One still has her ration of bruises and one evening the cause of them puts in an appearance on Skid Row. Orin Scrivello is a black-leather-jacketed professional pain inflicter, a 'Dentist'. Before he whisks a trembling Audrey away on his motor cycle he plants an idea in Seymour's mind. The boy doesn't have to be bullied by Mushnik any more: Audrey Two is a star, and she's his. Other florists would give Seymour a partnership if he took the plant to them. Orin's rebellious words are overheard by Mushnik and the old man takes instant fright and action. Rather than lose his newly found source of prosperity, he offers to adopt Seymour and take him into the business as his son ('Mushnik and Son').

One night a new development occurs in the botanical history of Skid Row. Seymour is becoming a little anaemic with the repeated feeding of the plant, and this night he just can't squeeze out the drop of blood required to keep Audrey Two happy. So he pops his Band-Aids back on and takes a raincheck on the plant food, but what is his amazement when a deep voice growls out, 'Feed Me'. The plant can talk! And when it talks it wants blood, and it wants it now. It doesn't care whose it is, but Seymour has got to get nice fresh blood for it and get it quickly. In return Audrey Two will give him his heart's desire ('Get It').

The idea of killing to provide the plant with food horrifies Seymour. No one deserves to be chopped up and fed to man-eating plant. Well, almost no one. At that moment the brutal Orin brings Audrey back to the shop to pick up a forgotten sweater and everything clicks into place in Seymour's brain. The next day he goes to Orin's surgery with intent and a gun, but Orin bundles him into the dentist's chair with horrifying descriptions of a diseased mouth and delightedly prepares to go to work on him with an antique drill.

While Seymour agitatedly tries to steel himself to his deadly deed ('Now'/ 'It's Just the Gas'), the dentist decides to take a little whiff of his own gas, to increase his enjoyment of the operation on his patient's molars. Unfortunately for him, the gas mask gets stuck and, under Seymour's unhelpful gaze, Orin Scrivello laughs himself to death. The deed has been done without Seymour having to commit anything but a crime of neglect, and Audrey Two has its blood. Gobbling up the minced dentist, the insatiable plant calls for more and more as the sickened Seymour hides the dentist's white coat—all that remains of what was a biker and a brute—in a Skid Row bin.

ACT 2

Business at Mushnik's Flower Shop is still growing ('Call Back in the Morning') and the hungry Audrey Two is now six feet tall and showing no signs of reaching maximum size. Audrey One's bruises are disappearing now that Orin is no longer in evidence and Seymour, all dressed up in a brand new leather jacket, finally steels himself to offer himself to her ('Suddenly Seymour'). The sun begins at last to rise in the life of the battered belle of Skid Row.

But Mr Mushnik is having suspicions. A Mushnik's plastic bag was discovered in the surgery of the vanished dentist, the police have been around, and the florist has discovered the discarded overall in his dustbin. It looks as if Seymour's secret may be discovered. The plant sees its opportunity for its first decent 'Suppertime' since the day of the dentist and urges Seymour to take action against this man who may inform against him. Seymour finally gives in. He tells Mushnik that, having forgotten the combination of the safe, he has hidden the day's receipts in the plant for safety. The florist climbs into the gaping mouth of Audrey Two and, before he can realise what is happening, the giant jaws of the plant close around him.

Still Seymour's celebrity grows ('The Meek Shall Inherit') as television, *Life* magazine, the William Morris Agency and all the other rewards of a successful public life gather round him. It's all due to the plant. To keep all this and, above all, to keep Audrey, he has to ensure that the plant stays healthy and that means blood. But where shall he find it? He cannot. When Audrey admits that she would love him with or without his plant, he comes to a momentous decision. He will kill the plant, just as soon as he and it have been photographed for the cover of *Life* magazine.

That night a sleepless Audrey comes down to the shop, brought there by some urgent call in her head that Seymour needs her ('Sominex') but what

My Fair Lady. Smut-faced Eliza Doolittle (Julie Andrews) has her Lisson Grove vowels jotted down by Professor Henry Higgins (Rex Harrison). Mark Hellinger Theatre, 1956.

The Music Man. Wide boy Harold Hill (Robert Preston) makes up for past faults with the joy he brings to the children of River City. Majestic Theatre, 1957.

How to Succeed in Business Without Really Trying. J. Pierrepoint Finch (Robert Morse) explains his way out of problems with the pneumatic Hedy la Rue (Virginia Martin). 46th Street Theatre, 1961.

A Funny Thing Happened on the Way to the Forum. John Carradine (Marcus Lycus), Jack Gilford (Hysterium), David Burns (Senex) and a bouncing Zero Mostel (Pseudolus) take the Marcus out of classical Rome. Alvin Theatre, 1962.

Sweet Charity. 'I'm a Brass Band'. Charity (Juliet Prowse) in an eternally optimistic mood. Prince of Wales Theatre, 1967.

Mame. Patrick Dennis's Auntie Mame (Ginger Rogers) is no little grey-haired lady – she's a brash and brassy broad with a trumpet. Theatre Royal, Drury Lane, 1969.

Godspell. Julie Covington, Marti Webb, David Essex and Jeremy Irons. Wyndham's Theatre, London, 1971.

Barnum. P.T. Barnum (Michael Crawford) leads a cast of singing, dancing and feat-performing actors at the Opera House, Manchester, 1985.

she meets is the rampaging Audrey Two who sees in her a much needed 'Suppertime'. As the screaming girl is enfolded in the plant's tendrils, Seymour returns and forces Audrey Two to release its prey, but Audrey One is broken and dying. Seymour tells her the truth of what he has done, and of how Mushnik and Orin are already inside the plant, and Audrey comes to a great resolve. If that is what has made the plant so big and strong and brought such great success to Seymour, then she wants him to give her poor dying body to the plant too. In that way she can at last do something positive for her beloved Seymour, and in that way they can kind of be together still, for she will be a part of the plant and he can tend her truly 'Somewhere That's Green'. Thus Audrey dies and the brokenhearted Seymour gives her to the plant.

The next day Seymour has a visit and a proposition from the Licensing and Marketing Division of World Botanical Enterprises. They wish to propagate Audrey Two as a house plant throughout the country. Now Seymour understands. Audrey Two is not just after food for itself. There is a wider and deeper plan afoot: lots of little Audrey Twos eating up the whole country. Why, it is nothing less than a plan for World Conquest! Deliriously Seymour attacks the plant which has killed and eaten the only thing he ever loved, but bullets, poison and blades have no effect on the chortling chunk of horticulture and, finally, Seymour leaps inside the gaping maw to attack Audrey Two from its softer inner portions. The plant closes, and this is the last the world will see of Seymour Krelbourn. World Botanical Services returns and sets to taking cuttings. Audrey Two's plan is on its way (Finale/ 'Don't Feed the Plants').

LA CAGE AUX FOLLES

a musical in two acts by Harvey Fierstein based on the play by Jean Poiret. Lyrics and music by Jerry Herman. Produced at the Palace Theatre, New York, 21 August 1983 with Gene Barry (Georges) and George Hearn (Albin).

Produced at the London Palladium 7 May 1986 with Denis Quilley and Hearn.

Produced at the Theater des Westens, Berlin, in a version by Erika Gesell and Christian Severin 23 October 1985 with Gunter König and Helmut Baumann.

CHARACTERS

Georges
Jean-Michel, *his son*
Albin
Jacob
Francis
Edouard Dindon
Madame Dindon
Anne, *their daughter*

Jacqueline
Monsieur Renaud
Chantal, Monique, Dermah, Nicole, Hanna, Mercedes, Bitelle, Lo Singh, Odette, Angélique, Phaedra, Clo-Clo, *Les Cagelles*
Madame Renaud, Paulette, Hercule, Etienne, Babette, Colette, Tabarro, Pepé, etc.

ACT 1

At the famous St Tropez nightclub, La Cage aux Folles, Georges, our host for the evening, introduces the 'girls' of the revue ('We Are What We Are')—Chantal the carolling songstress, Hanna from Hamburg with her whip, and the enigmatic Phaedra whose talent lies in her tongue. The girls in this club are, however, boys, for La Cage aux Folles is the Riviera's mecca of drag.

Tonight, when the girls finish their number and crowd off in the wings to take off their high heels, they are shoved back on to the stage. The show's star, Zaza, isn't ready and they have to do their number again. There are grumbles: Zaza is clearly not being temperamental for the first time.

Zaza—otherwise Albin, Georges' lover, helpmate and star of twenty years—is having a monumental sulk, and not without cause. Having slaved lovingly over a complicated lunch for Georges, he waited and waited and waited. No Georges, no explanation, so no show. Zaza is still in her bathrobe with not a sequin in sight and five hundred people are waiting in a packed nightclub for the star to appear. A little scene is played, Albin gets his moment of genuine remorse and love from Georges, and Zaza is in business again. Albin sits down at his dressing table and, with the addition of makeup, wig and gown transforms himself into Zaza ('A Little More Mascara').

The evening which has begun so dramatically still has another surprise in store. Jacob, the black 'maid' of the household, unveils a dashing young lad. He is Jean-Michel, the son of the family. Biologically, of course, he is only Georges' son, but Albin has been his mother for twenty years. Jean-Michel is back home and he has some wonderful news. He's getting married. Her name is Anne and her father is Edouard Dindon, the deputy general of the Tradition, Family and Morality Party who has pledged as part of his platform to close down the drag clubs of the coast.

The second bit of good news is that Dindon and his wife are coming here to meet Jean-Michel's family. Jean-Michel has not exactly told the truth about his family: Georges has been described as a retired diplomat and Albin hasn't been described at all. Jean-Michel simply asks that he isn't around.

Georges is mortified. How can the boy treat the mother who has loved him so dearly in such an ungrateful and cavalier fashion? But Jean-Michel is truly in love ('With Anne on My Arm'), with all the selfishness of youth, and he is unaware of the hurt he offers elsewhere. There is worse to come, however. When Anne's parents come he wants them to meet his real mother. It's not that he wants to see her himself—she hasn't put in an appearance since he was a baby—but the Dindons expect a mother, so a mother there must be. Weakly, Georges agrees to try, but who is to tell Albin?

News travels fast and an outraged Albin flies on to the scene, awash with horror at the thought of wedding bells for his son. Georges lovingly encourages him to a little walk in the evening air ('With You on My Arm'). It will be easier to break the rest of the news away from home. On 'The Promenade' Jean-Michel has met Anne who is all aglow at the thought of meeting her beloved's family, but he forces her into a hurried exit when Georges and Albin appear on the horizon.

Georges gradually starts to get down to details. Sybil first. The mother. Albin merely threatens murder if she is allowed in the house. But that's the easy bit. The rest is almost impossible. There is a moon out and love is in Georges' heart ('Song on the Sand') as Albin softens. He withdraws the murder threat. Sybil can come. But just as Georges has braced himself for the hard bit the clock chimes and they have to flee back to the club for the second show.

While they have been away, Jean-Michel has taken Georges' courage and Albin's acquiescence for granted and he has started shifting out the more extravagant furniture and homophile *objets d'art* from the apartment. Georges has to cover up but, to make sure the boy realises the enormity of what he is asking his father to do, he makes him stand and watch Albin, the one person solely responsible for his upbringing and comfort, as he performs 'La Cage aux Folles' to a packed house. But as Albin comes to change his costume in the wings, Jean-Michel passes too blatantly close with an armful of gowns taken from Albin's cupboard and Albin demands to know what is going on.

While Albin changes costume behind the screen, Georges, more able to do the deed now he doesn't have to look him in the eye, attempts jokily to put forward the plan. When Albin emerges his face shows his devastation. He walks whitely to the stage to perform 'We Are What We Are' but, after a few lines, he sends the other girls scurrying from the stage and delivers his ultimatum to Georges and the world ('I Am What I Am'). When he has finished, he tears his wig from his head, flings it to the floor and walks out of the club.

ACT 2

It is morning when Georges tracks Albin down in the town. He explains that Jean-Michel has acted with the foolishness of love and, as for himself, he too acted foolishly, but is none the less equally in love ('Song on the Sand'). Albin cannot stay too angry very long, especially as Georges has devised a plan for bringing him back into the ménage. If he can just butch his act up a bit he can pass off as Uncle Al. It is a hideously distasteful charade for a lady and a star but, since he is quite sure they will mess the whole thing up of he is not there, Albin agrees and is made to suffer a crash course in 'Masculinity'.

Jean-Michel has stripped the apartment and decorated it in a style reminiscent of a medieval chapel. It is deeply and religiously camp and Jacob's effort to be a butler, instead of a maid, under a powdered wig is nothing short of desperately unconvincing. Albin's Uncle Al at least has the merit of genuine effort behind it. While the nervous preparations go on, it is Albin who takes delivery of a telegram and, when he reads it, he goes quiet.

There is no quiet in the rest of the room: Jean-Michel's nervousness has surfaced in a great resentment that Georges has allowed Albin to be present and to threaten the exercise. This time Georges will not give way: the boy has no right to such ingratitude ('Look Over There'). Jean-Michel knows he is in the wrong, but the conflict of feelings in him is too much and he rushes out. Then Albin shows Georges the telegram: it is from Sybil and she isn't coming. There will be no mother for the Dindons. Then the doorbell rings. While Jacob rushes to the door and Jean-Michel tries to organise his failing spirits, Albin rushes, petrified, into his room.

The introduction of the Dindons gets off to a shaky start when the Cage aux Folles creeps dangerously into the conversation in the first seconds, again when Georges forgets his allotted identity and poses as a legionnaire instead of a diplomat and, worst of all, when Jacob serves the hors d'oeuvres on plates decorated with erotic classical Greek motifs (Cocktail Counterpoint). Things are going extremely stickily and, of course, there is no mother. Until, that is, the bedroom door opens and a buxom fortyish mother emerges. It is Albin in a smart two-piece and all a-twitter with joyful conversation.

Before the Dindons can gather their thoughts, mother is quick to score a point. Jacob has burned the dinner, so they must all go to a restaurant. They must go to Chez Jacqueline. Madame Dindon is thrilled, for Chez Jacqueline is the most exclusive place in town and you have to book months ahead. Dindon is sceptical, but Albin picks up the phone, calls his dear friend Jacqueline and *voilà, c'est fait*. In a twinkling they are Chez Jacqueline, being greeted by the hostess herself, happy to return a favour to Zaza who paid such delicious attentions to her special customers at La Cage the previous night.

Unfortunately, no one has warned Jacqueline of the occasion and, when she introduces Zaza as a celebrity and begs for a song, Jean-Michel collapses inside. Goodbye, wedding! Pushed by a delighted Madame Dindon, Zaza obliges and soon the whole restaurant is joining in 'The Best of Times'. But, carried away on the élan of her song, Zaza forgets she is not at La Cage aux Folles and, reaching the final chord she ritually pulls her wig from her head. Pandemonium breaks loose.

Back at the apartment, Dindon is indulging in a feast of moral outrage prior to staging an effective exit, but his exit is spoiled when Anne refuses to go with him. She loves Jean-Michel and, whatever her parents may say, she also likes Georges and Albin. After the events of the evening, Jean-Michel has also been restored to his senses. He has an apology to make, not to Dindon but to Albin and to Georges ('Look Over There') who are very much more real people than the Dindons will ever be.

When Dindon goes to sweep out on a puff of moral indignation he is greeted at the door by Jacqueline, and Jacqueline has brought a Press cameraman or two. How remiss of her to have had the famous Deputy

Dindon at her restaurant and to have let him escape without even a photo-graph. Now he, the most famous anti-homosexual of the coast, simply must have his photo taken dining with the most famous homosexuals of St Tropez. Dindon is cooked. Bravo Jacqueline! Then Albin and Georges intervene. They have a plan. First of all, the children must be allowed to wed and Anne must, of course, have her dowry. When that is agreed, then they will help Dindon to escape the Press.

The finale of the first show is playing at the adjacent Cage aux Folles. As Georges announces the artists, they descend the staircase one by one—the girls of the show followed by Anne, dapper in tails, Jacob glittering in sequins and making the entrance he has dreamed of all his life only to trip on his train and tumble all the way down, Madame Dindon looking sensational and moving every portion just as it should be moved and, finally, Dindon himself, the ugliest woman imaginable. As they parade down the stage of La Cage aux Folles, Jacqueline takes revenge on behalf of mankind. She brings in the Press, their cameras flashing ravenously. While Georges hurries the Dindons out, Jean-Michel and Anne escape in a different direction and soon the whole singing, dancing company vanish into the distance.

Alone, under the Mediterranean night sky, Albin and Georges walk towards each other and meet ('Song on the Sand') as the curtain falls.

Part 4

AUSTRIA, GERMANY AND HUNGARY

It was the spreading success of Offenbach's operettas in the major German-language theatrical centres during the late 1850s and the 1860s that first persuaded theatre managers in Vienna and Berlin that they must produce comparable works of their own, in order to compete with the wave of French importations. The principal German capitals already had a thriving popular musical theatre tradition of their own, with a range of productions that varied from full-scale comic opera down to cosy local farces with interpolated humorous songs, but there was nothing amongst this variety of entertainment which was quite like the satirical Offenbach works which were attracting such ferocious popular acclaim and such large and lucrative audiences.

Vienna had a promising candidate for the position of 'the German Offenbach' to hand in Franz von Suppé. Suppé already had a vast output of comic operas and incidental theatrical scores to his credit, and some of their rousing overtures, such as those to the topical local piece *Ein Morgen, ein Mittag, ein Abend in Wien* ('Morning, Noon and Night in Vienna', 1844) and the comedy *Dichter und Bauer* ('Poet and Peasant', 1846) are still well-known. It was Suppé who produced the first significant Viennese response to Offenbach with the one-act *Das Pensionat* ('The Boarding School', 1860) and, during the 1860s, he followed this with a further series of similar comic works, many of which are also remembered today largely through their overtures: *Pique Dame* ('The Queen of Spades', 1862), *Leichte Kavallerie* ('Light Cavalry', 1866) and *Banditenstreiche* ('Bandits' Tricks' 1867). The one enduring stage success amongst them is, as it happens, the one that followed most closely Offenbach's model of mythological satire—*Die schöne Galathee* ('Beautiful Galatea', 1865), a work that is frequently revived to this day.

Although Suppé stood out above the other Viennese writers of his period, he was still not quite of sufficient international stature to see off the Offenbach challenge. That was left to another, to a composer already in his forties who until then had no experience whatsoever of writing for the theatre and was hitherto known exclusively for the composition of dance music: Johann Strauss.

Strauss never did become a sure-handed composer of music for the theatre. However, his exceptional inventive gifts were such that he was able to fashion a tradition of an essentially Viennese style of operetta after his own inclinations and strengths, namely one based upon his unequalled gift for swaying waltzes and affecting lyrical writing. He was especially fortunate in having the collaboration of Richard Genée—not merely his lyricist but also a conductor and operetta composer in his own right—who was able to provide the theatrical experience that Strauss himself lacked and, given the further added ingredient of a book based on a tried French success, the result was a sparkling and enduring masterpiece in *Die Fledermaus* ('The Bat', 1874), which Strauss subsequently supplemented with his descriptive evocation of Venice in *Eine Nacht in Venedig* ('A Night in Venice', 1883) and the more sturdy drama of *Der Zigeunerbaron* ('The Gipsy Baron', 1885).

889

French comedies long remained an invaluable source material for Viennese operettas, and the leading team of Viennese operetta librettists, 'F Zell' (really the theatre director Camillo Walzel) and his lyricist Genée became past masters of the art of adaptation. A contemporary Viennese cartoon depicting them stealing out of a French theatrical library at dead of night with the material for the book of *Eine Nacht in Venedig* was very much to the point. Without the discipline of such sources, Viennese operetta books were often ill-shaped affairs which—due also, of course, to radical changes in theatrical conventions—have failed to sustain the delightful music composed for them. As a result, many of the successful stage works with which Johann Strauss's music is nowadays associated are actually works put together by later hands using his melodies, beginning with *Wiener Blut* (compiled by Adolf Müller junior, 1899) and *1001 Nacht* (Ernst Reiterer, 1906) and extending to *Casanova* (Ralph Benatzky, 1928) and *Walzer aus Wien* (Julius Bittner and Erich Wolfgang Korngold, 1930).

While Johann Strauss gave the Viennese operetta its identity, Franz von Suppé continued to produce works that demonstrated his superb command of musico-dramatic flow, amongst which *Boccaccio* (again with a Zell and Genée libretto, 1879) is his undoubted masterpiece. Much in the same essentially theatrical vein were the works of Carl Millöcker, a composer whose effective command of dramatic structure was seen to best effect in *Der Bettelstudent* ('The Beggar Student', 1882) and *Gasparone* (1884).

Suppé, Strauss and Millöcker were the three undoubted masters of the classical nineteenth-century age of Viennese operetta. By the 1890s their powers were fading, though still sufficient to keep the Viennese operetta tradition very much alive alongside the works of newcomers such as Carl Zeller and Richard Heuberger. The former, a civil servant by profession and composer by inclination, added the important ingredient of charm to the standard constituent of a good waltz, and his *Der Vogelhändler* ('The Bird Seller', 1891) remains a classic of the genre, its lasting success obscuring (apart from a single number) his *Der Obersteiger* ('The Mine Foreman', 1894)—a lesser work undoubtedly, but one that possesses many of the same charms.

Although a few of the lasting successes of nineteenth century Viennese operetta were first produced at the Carltheater, the vast bulk of them first saw the light of day at the Theater an der Wien and a crucial constituent in its sequence of successes was the team of artists who created roles in one Viennese success after another, in the same way that the performers of Offenbach at the Théâtre des Variétés and those of Gilbert and Sullivan at the Savoy did. Outstanding amongst these performers was Alexander Girardi, who stepped into the role of Falke in *Die Fledermaus* in 1874, when the role's creator was killed in a stage accident, and who was still creating major operetta roles some forty years later.

Girardi's popularity and influence were such that he was able to get composers to write songs specially for him which, if they often had little or nothing to do with the plot, were undoubtedly enjoyable. The sequence of songs that Girardi introduced is an astonishing one, amongst them (to take solely the works included in this volume) 'Nur für Natur' (*Der lustige Krieg*), 'Ich knüpfte manche zarte Bande' (*Der Bettelstudent*), 'Ach wie so herrlich zu schau'n' (*Eine Nacht in Venedig*), 'Er soll dein Herr sein' (*Gasparone*), 'Ja das Schreiben und das Leben' (*Der Zigeunerbaron*), 'Ich bin der arme Jonathan' (*Der arme Jonathan*), 'Wie mein Ahnl zwanzig Jahr' (*Der Vogelhändler*), 'Sei nicht bös' (*Der Obersteiger*—a number only subsequently appropriated by sopranos), 'Ja, beim Militär' (*Der Fremdenführer*) and 'Mein alte Stradivari' (*Der Zigeunerprimás*).

Though most of the classic Viennese operettas still performed today achieved international currency from their first production, C M Ziehrer's *Der Fremdenführer* ('The Tourist Guide', 1902) is a good example of a work that, at the time of its original production, aroused no particular interest but which has since come to be regarded affectionately as a portrayal of turn-of-the-century Vienna in the way that *La Vie Parisienne* epitomises Second Empire Paris. The work was revived successfully on the occasion of Ziehrer's centenary and more recently has achieved huge success at the Vienna Volksoper, the modern home of the Viennese operetta.

Despite the output of composers such as Zeller, Ziehrer and Richard Heuberger (with his *Der Opernball*—'The Opera Ball', 1898), the Viennese operetta was losing its way by the end of the 1890s in favour of works such as Sidney Jones's all-conquering *The Geisha*. Berlin, too, came to the fore through the works of Paul Lincke, a composer who was a superb melodist in the more forthright turn-of-century style. He put his training as musical director at the Folies Bergère to good use in works such as *Frau Luna* ('Mistress Moon', 1899) which, following the style of the works from the Gaiety Theatre in London, were more in the manner of spectacular burlesque than traditional comic opera-based operetta.

Another increasingly significant source of turn-of-the-century operetta was Hungary—then still part of the Austro-Hungarian Empire, but maintaining its own cultural heritage. *János Vitéz* ('John the Hero', 1904) remains the classic Hungarian folk operetta but is in a tradition far removed from that of the international operetta. More in the prevailing international style—though unusual in its subject matter—was Jenö Huszka's *Bob herceg* ('Prince Bob', 1902), a work that reached Vienna and is still revived in Hungary. It treated Britain as the same kind of Ruritania that English writers established around Hungary and the story features the Queen of England and her son, Prince George, who chooses to roam the streets of London under the name of 'Bob' and ends up triumphing over the barber Plumpudding for the hand of a student named Annie.

Hungary continued to play an increasingly crucial role in the development of central-European operetta. Viktor Jacobi's *Leányvásár* ('The Marriage Market', 1911) and *Szibill* ('Sybil', 1914) are delightful examples—still prized in Hungary—of the work of a composer who died all too young and whose work would surely be much better known if written to German libretti. Other Hungarians, moreover, moved to Vienna, and it was they who provided the real shot in the arm for German-language operetta.

The brilliant new era for Viennese operetta opened with *Die lustige Witwe*

('The Merry Widow', 1905)—yet another work that owes much to a tried and tested French book, but one that also derives its lasting power over its listeners not only from the spontaneity and freshness of its melodic riches but also to the orchestral mastery of its composer, Franz Lehár. From that time the power of muted strings was a crucial factor in weaving a seductive spell over listeners as Lehár followed his first great triumph with other successes—none quite as great—including *Der Graf von Luxemburg* ('The Count of Luxembourg', 1909) and, ever the innovator, the fantasy of *Zigeunerliebe* ('Gipsy Love', 1910). His lead was followed conspicuously by Oscar Straus in *Ein Walzertraum* ('A Waltz Dream', 1907) and *Der tapfere Soldat* ('The Chocolate Soldier', 1908—an adaptation of George Bernard Shaw's *Arms and the Man*). On the back of Lehár's successes, these helped the Viennese operetta conquer musical theatres of the world as never before or after.

The third member of the triumvirate of composers that dominated the Viennese operetta of the time was Leo Fall, composer of *Der fidele Bauer* ('The Merry Peasant', 1907), *Die Dollarprinzessin* ('The Dollar Princess', 1907), *Die geschiedene Frau* ('The Girl in the Train', 1908) and others. Fall never cultivated the big audience-grabbing melodies in the way that Lehár was readily able to. Rather, he was a musician's musician whose scores contain delightful rhythmic twists and a distinctly conversational style of word-setting. At a time when the specialist theatre orchestrator was coming increasingly into his own he was, with Lehár, a rarity in attending to his own orchestration, and his scores contain many endearing orchestral effects, such as the sound of typewriters in the opening scene of *Die Dollarprinzessin*.

Least of all the major Viennese operetta composers can Leo Fall be said to have written to a formula. One who, by contrast, perfected an extremely successful formula was the other major exponent of the Viennese operetta to appear in the years up to the First World War—Emmerich Kálmán. He was another Hungarian, and Hungarian subjects and Hungarian rhythms dominated such works as *Der Zigeunerprimás* ('The Gipsy Violinist', 1912), *Die Csárdásfürstin* ('The Gipsy Princess', 1915) and *Gräfin Mariza* ('Countess Maritza', 1924). His rhythmic patterns provide a distinctive tinge to his scores, but revivals have shown how superbly effective his works are on the stage.

Vienna continued to produce new works after the First World War, above all at the Theater an der Wien under the direction of Hubert Marischka. However, the Austro-Hungarian Empire was now a thing of the past, and with it went Vienna's domination of the German-language operetta stage. From now on the centre of German operetta activity was Berlin, which since the days of Paul Lincke had increasingly produced its own eminent exponents in composers such as Jean Gilbert (*Die keusche Susanne*, 1911), Walter Kollo (*Wie einst im Mai*, 1913) and Léon Jessel, who created in his *Schwarzwaldmädel* ('Black Forest Girl', 1916) one of the most richly melodic and most charming works in the German operetta repertory. Another Berlin-based composer, Eduard Künneke, won international acclaim during the 1920s and continuing popularity in Germany with *Der Vetter aus Dingsda*

('The Cousin from Nowhere', 1921).

Previously, Viennese-based composers such as Oscar Straus, Fall and Lehár moved to Berlin for the premières of their later works such as the Straus's *Der letzte Walzer* ('The Last Waltz', 1920), Fall's *Madame Pompadour* (1922) and Lehár's *Der Zarewitsch* ('The Tsarevitch', 1927). The first two of these works were able to boast the participation of Fritzi Massary, Berlin's leading lady of the 1920s, while the last of the three had a title role created for the operatic tenor Richard Tauber, a factor which was an indication of the way in which Lehár was now attempting to extend the emotional and dramatic range of the operetta to counter the forces that were tending to make traditional operetta an anachronism in the jazz age. Lehár's more ambitious style perhaps found its ideal expression in *Giuditta*, produced at the Vienna State Opera in 1934 with Richard Tauber in the tenor lead.

Increasingly now the operetta seemed to belong to an age of princesses, barons and dukes that no longer existed, whilst its formula of romantic intrigue, disguise and misunderstanding was becoming repetitive. The operetta score had come a long way from its comic opera origins and Suppé, and the standard formula now provided little more than a sequence of songs and duets for the romantic soprano and tenor leads, comic dance numbers for the buffo and soubrette secondary pair, a few choruses, and dramatic dénouements in the musical finales involving spoken contributions from the supporting cast of actors.

The Brecht-Weill *Die Dreigroschenoper* ('The Threepenny Opera', 1928) was an example of how the musical theatre was responding to a vastly different social and political environment in a form very different from operetta. For operetta itself new ideas had to be found. One solution was to evoke nostalgia for earlier days by raiding the melodies of the classical operetta masters for 'new' works such as Johann Strauss for *Casanova* (1928) and *Walzer aus Wien* ('Waltzes from Vienna', 1930) and Carl Millöcker for *Die Dubarry* ('The Dubarry', 1931). Associated with the search for a new solution was the 'spectacular revue' approach of producer Erik Charell, who followed *Casanova* with Benatzky's *Im weissen Rössl* ('White Horse Inn', 1930), whilst Paul Abrahám's *Viktoria und ihr Husar* ('Victoria and Her Hussar', 1930) and *Die Blume von Hawaii* ('The Flower of Hawaii', 1931) showed how the new dance rhythms could be reconciled with traditional subjects.

The German operetta of the 1930s thus provided a refreshing variety of approaches to the problem of reviving afresh the operetta tradition. Robert Stolz's *Zwei Herzen im Dreivierteltakt* ('Two Hearts in Waltz-Time', 1933) showed how a stage operetta could be derived from a successful sound-film, while Nico Dostal showed how the film world and South American political rebellion could be used as a new background for traditional romantic intrigue in *Clivia* (1933). While the same composers were also associated with unashamed evocations of the traditional operetta world of princesses, dukes, bandits and mistaken identity in *Venus in Seide* ('Venus in Silk', 1934) and *Die ungarische Hochzeit* ('The Hungarian Wedding', 1939) respectively, others of their works featured modern characters and situations.

893

Prominent in this movement was the director Heinz Hentschke, under whose direction Fred Raymond's *Maske in Blau* ('Mask in Blue', 1937) and Friedrich Schröder's *Hochzeitsnacht im Paradies* ('Wedding Night in Paradise', 1942) appeared. Stage techniques now permitted and encouraged more frequent changes of scene than the one-scene-per-act of the traditional operetta, though this could also be used to somewhat artificial effect. Rudolf Kattnigg's *Balkanliebe* ('Balkan Love', 1938) somehow brought both a Venetian element and the currently smart subjects of tennis and horoscopes into what was basically a traditional story of Balkan bandits and political and romantic intrigue.

Highly successful though these works were, and popular though they remain in German-speaking countries, they have had little international exposure. By the Second World War the traditional operetta had become essentially a thing of the past, and new native works contained more of the features of the musical. Though Paul Burkhardt's *Feuerwerk* ('Fireworks', 1950) achieved an international currency through the success of the song 'Oh, my Papa!', the German musical theatre has since made little impact on the international stage.

By the 1960s the fate of the German-language operetta was crystallised. Major opera companies were increasingly accepting the outstanding classics into their repertory while the Volksoper in Vienna and specialist operetta festivals such as those at Bad Ischl and on the lake stages at Bregenz and Mörbisch were recognised as homes for what was essentially a form of the past. Efforts to revive the operetta movement were made with commissions for 'new' works from the last surviving exponent of pre-First World War operetta, Robert Stolz. Bregenz staged his *Trauminsel* ('Dream Island', 1962) and *Hochzeit am Bodensee* ('Wedding on Lake Constance', 1969) and the Volksoper his *Frühjahrsparade* ('Spring Parade', 1964), but all three were in reality adaptations of earlier material.

At the same time Stolz was one of the conductors on hand to preserve on LP record some of the scores of the earlier age, and these recordings have in many cases been transferred with great success to compact disc. The availability of such recordings, whether of complete scores, substantial excerpts or isolated gems, has been an important factor in determining the continued popularity of certain works and also, along with accessibility of works on stage, the selection of works for inclusion here.

DIE SCHÖNE GALATHEE

(Beautiful Galatea)

a comic mythological opera in one act by 'Poly Henrion' (L Kohl von Kohlenegg). Music by Franz von Suppé. Produced at Meysel's Theatre, Berlin, 30 June 1865(?).

Produced at the Carltheater, Vienna, 9 September 1865 with Herr Telek (Pygmalion), Amalie Kraft (Galatea), Carl Treumann (Midas) and Anna Grobecker (Ganymede). Produced at the Neue Welt 7 July 1868, at the Theater an der Wien 25 December 1872, at the Colosseum-Theater 18 June 1893, at the Theater in der Josefstadt 30 April 1896, at Ronachers Operetten-Theater 13 July 1896, at Venedig in Wien 16 June 1898, at the Volksoper 26 January 1909 and 24 October 1981, and at the Rex-Theater (Stadt-Theater) 8 March 1946. Frequently revived throughout German-speaking countries.

Played at the Opera Comique, London, 6 November 1871 with Collin, Frln Paliska, Pfeiffer and Frln Paliska II. Produced at the Gaiety Theatre in an English version as *Ganymede and Galatea* 20 January 1872 with Frank Wood, Constance Loseby, Nellie Farren and Fred Sullivan.

Produced at the Stadt Theater, New York, 6 September 1867 with Friedrich Hermann, Hedwig L'Arronge-Sury, Theodore L'Arronge and Laura Haffner. Produced at Tony Pastor's Music Hall, New York, in an English version as *The Beautiful Galatea* 14 September 1882 with Pauline Hall and Pauline Canissa.

CHARACTERS

Pygmalion, *a young sculptor*
Ganymede, *his servant*
Midas, *an art collector*
Galatea, *a statue*
Worshippers at the temple of Venus

The scene is the studio of the sculptor Pygmalion on the isle of Cyprus in ancient times. Dawn is breaking, and worshippers can be heard outside making offerings at the temple of Venus ('Aurora ist erwacht'). Pygmalion is amongst them, but his servant Ganymede prefers to take advantage of his master's absence by catching up with some rest on a couch in the studio ('Zieht in Frieden'). However, Ganymede's slumbers are disturbed by the arrival of the art collector Midas, who explains that he has come in search of Pygmalion, having heard of his latest creation—the statue of a beautiful woman, Galatea.

Ganymede is adamant that he is not permitted to show the creation to anyone, even in the face of Midas's insistence that he is a man of substance, who has inherited the finest of virtues from his father and mother ('Meinem Vater Gordios'). Midas persists in his requests to see the statue and eventually, in Pygmalion's continuing absence, Ganymede finds Midas's offers of backhanders irresistible. Midas looks at the statue and is enchanted. Just then Pygmalion returns and, in an angry exchange, he orders Midas out ('Hinaus!' 'Auweh!'). Midas protests in vain at a man of his standing being treated in this way, while Ganymede cowers in the background.

When Midas has gone, Pygmalion looks admiringly at the statue of Galatea and laments that such a beautiful creature is not alive. Ganymede points out that only the gods can bring her to life, at which Pygmalion begins to offer up prayers to Venus ('Zum Altar zieht die Schaar'). Gradually, as Pygmalion looks on entranced, Galatea starts to move ('Sie regt sich, sie erwacht'), finally stepping off her pedestal into the room. Far from reciprocating Pygmalion's affection for her, she merely says how hungry she is. Pygmalion obligingly departs in search of an ancient Greek schnitzel with pickles, leaving Galatea singing a tender romance to a lyre she has found lying around ('Was sagst du? Ich lausche').

Ganymede muses that there are none as dissolute as the Greeks where women are concerned, and yet at the same time none as classical ('Wir Griechen sind sicherlich'). His musings attract Galatea's interest, and she finds the young man altogether quite to her liking. She begins to flirt with him, only for them to be interrupted by the reappearance of Midas. He stands astonished at seeing Galatea alive. Ever resourceful, however, he produces from his purse an enormous jewel with which he starts to tempt Galatea ('Seht den Schmuck den ich für Euch gebracht'). She takes it and craftily extracts from Midas ever more pieces of jewellery, but remains cold towards him, still preferring the youth of Ganymede.

When Pygmalion returns, Midas hides while Pygmalion, Galatea and Ganymede sit down to eat. Galatea now discovers a distinct liking for the wine ('Hell im Glas da schäumt das duft'ge Nass'). She becomes increasingly out of control and, in the ensuing commotion, Midas is revealed in his hiding-place. Pygmalion throws him into the street and races after him. Left alone again with Ganymede, Galatea is able to continue her flirtation, and together they explore the art of kissing ('Ach, mich zieht's zu dir').

Pygmalion returns, followed soon afterwards by Midas who has come back in pursuit of his jewels. Pygmalion's patience is near exhaustion. He begs Venus to turn Galatea back to stone and, after a crash of thunder, they find her duly back on her plinth. Pygmalion has it in mind to smash the statue to pieces, but Midas is dismayed that his jewellery has also been turned into stone. He manages to rescue something from the whole incident by buying the sculpture from Pygmalion, who for his part is cured for ever of the desire to see his works of art come to life (Finale: 'Meinem Vater Gordios').

The above synopsis follows the original version of the operetta. There have been many twentieth-century adaptations, some in three acts, from one of which derives the song 'Einmal möcht' ich', set to the big waltz melody of the overture.

896

DIE FLEDERMAUS

(The Bat)

a comic operetta in three acts by Carl Haffner and Richard Genée, after *Le Réveillon* by Henri Meilhac and Ludovic Halévy. Lyrics by Richard Genée. Music by Johann Strauss. Produced at the Theater an der Wien, Vienna, 5 April 1874 with Jani Szika (Eisenstein), Marie Geistinger (Rosalinde), Ferdinand Lebrecht (Falke), Karoline Charles-Hirsch (Adele) and Irma Nittinger (Orlofsky). Produced at the Court Opera 28 October 1894 and in 1920 with Maria Jeritza (Rosalinde), conducted by Richard Strauss. Produced at the State Opera 31 December 1960 with Eberhard Wächter (Eisenstein), Hilde Güden (Rosalinde), Rita Streich (Adele) and Walter Berry (Orlofsky). Produced at the Stadt-Theater, Salzburg, 1926 with Willi Domgraf-Fassbaender (Falke), conducted by Felix Weingartner. Produced on the lake stage, Bregenz, 1954 and 1970. Produced at the Volksoper 18 May with Peter Minich, Mirjana Irosch, Ilonka Szep and Karl Dönch (Frank).

Produced at the Friedrich-Wilhelmstädtisches Theater, Berlin, 8 July 1874. Produced at the Stadt-Theater, Hamburg, 1880 and revived there 1894 with Ernestine Schumann-Heink (Orlofsky), conducted by Gustav Mahler. Produced at the Deutsches Theater, Berlin, 8 June 1928 in a version by Max Reinhardt and Erich Wolfgang Korngold with Hermann Thimig (Eisenstein), Maria Rajdl (Rosalinde), Adele Kern (Adele) and Oscar Karlweis (Orlofsky).

Produced at the Alhambra Theatre, London, in a version by Hamilton Clarke 18 December 1876 with Mlle Cabella, Emma Chambers, Kate Munroe, Adelaide Newton, G Loredan, Edmund Rosenthal and J H Jarvis. Produced at His Majesty's Theatre in a version by Armand Kalisch 4 August 1910 with Carrie Tubb, Joseph O'Mara, Frederick Ranalow, Beatrice de la Palme, John Bardesley and Muriel Terry. Produced at the Lyric Theatre in a version by Gladys Unger and Arthur Anderson as *Nightbirds* 30 December 1911 with C H Workman, Constance Drever, Claude Flemming, Muriel George and John Deverell. Produced at Sadler's Wells Theatre 1934 with Joan Cross, Tudor Davies, Percy Heming, Redvers Llewellyn, Gladys Parr and Arthur Cox. Produced at the Palace Theatre in the Reinhardt/Korngold version adapted by Austin Melford, Rudolf Bernauer and Sam Heppner as *Gay Rosalinda* 8 March 1945 with Cyril Ritchard, Ruth Naylor, Bernard Clifton, Irene Ambrus and Peter Graves, conducted by Richard Tauber. Produced at the Royal Opera House, Covent Garden, 14 May 1930 with Willi Wörle, Lotte Lehmann, Gerhard Hüsch, Elisabeth Schumann and Maria Olczewska, conducted by Bruno Walter, and 31 December 1977 with Hermann Prey, Kiri Te Kanawa, Benjamin Luxon, Hildegard Heichele and Robert Tear. Produced at the London Coliseum in a version by Christopher Hassall 16 April 1959 with Alexander Young/Peter Grant, Victoria Elliott/Joan Smart, John Heddle Nash/Raimund Herincx, Marion Studholme/June Bronhill and Anna Pollack/Patricia Johnson. Produced at Sadler's Wells Theatre in a version by Christopher Hassall and Edmund Tracey 28 March 1966 with Emile Belcourt, Ava June, David Bowman, Eric Shilling and Jennifer Eddy.

Produced at Stadt Theater, New York, 21 November 1874 with Schütz, Lina Mayr, Schönwolff, Antonie Heynold and Louise Beckmann. Produced at the Casino Theatre 16 March 1885 with Mark Smith, Rosalba Beecher, De Wolf Hopper and Mathilde Cottrelly, and played at Wallacks Theatre 14 September 1885. Produced at the Metropolitan Opera, New York, 16 February 1905 with Andreas Dippel, Marcella Sembrich, Emil Greder, Bella Alten and Edyth Walker. Revived there *inter alia* in a version by Howard Dietz 22 February 1951 with Set Svanholm, Maria Jeritza, John Brownlee, Patrice Munsel and Jarmila Novotna. Produced at the Casino Theatre in the Unger/Anderson version as *The Merry Countess* 20 August 1912 with José Collins, Maurice Farkoa and Claude Flemming. Produced at the Majestic Theatre in a version by F Todd Mitchell as *A Wonderful Night* 31 October 1929, at the Morosco Theatre in a version by A Child and R A Simon as *Champagne Sec* 14 October 1933 with Peggy Wood (Rosalinde), and at the Forty-Fourth Street Theatre 28 October 1942 as *Rosalinde* with Dorothy Sarnoff (Rosalinde), Virginia MacWatters (Adele) and Oscar Karlweis (Orlofsky). Produced at the New York City Opera in a version by Ruth and Thomas Martin 8 April 1953 with Jack Russell, Laurel Hurley, William Shriner and Elaine Malbin. Produced at the Opera House, San Francisco, 1973 with Joan Sutherland (Rosalinde) and Walter Slezak (Frosch).

Produced at the Théâtre de la Renaissance, Paris, with a new libretto by Alfred Delacour and Victor Wilder as *La Tzigane* 30 October 1877 with Zulma Bouffar (Princesse Arabelle), Ismael (Mathias), Berthelier, Mlle d'Asco (Lena) and Urbain (Prince). Produced at the Théâtre des Variétés in a version by Paul Ferrier as *La Chauve-Souris* 22 April 1904 with Cécile Thévenet (Caroline), Jane Saulier (Arlette), Albert Brasseur (Gaillardin), Max Dearly (Tourillon) and Eve Lavallière (Orlofsky). Produced at the Théâtre Pigalle in a version by Nino of the Reinhardt-Korngold adaptation 5 October 1929 with Lotte Schoene, Jarmila Novotna, Dorville and Roger Tréville. Played at the Théâtre de l'Alhambra September 1961. Produced at the Théâtre National de l'Opéra-Comique 20 February 1969 with Andrée Esposito, Anne-Marie Sanial, Rémy Corazza and Michel Roux. Played at the Paris Opéra February 1983 and at the Théâtre du Châtelet 24 November 1984 with André Jobin, Christiane Eda-Pierre, and Danielle Chlostawa.

Performed frequently in opera houses and operetta theatres throughout the world.

Film versions were produced by Carl Lamac in 1931 with Anny Ondra, Georg Alexander, Ivan Petrovitch and Hans Junkermann; by Paul Verhoven in 1937 with Lidia Baarova, Hans Söhnker, Friedl Szepa, Harald Paulsen, Georg Alexander, Hans Moser, Robert Dorsay and Karl Stepanek; and by Geza von Bolvary in 1945 with Marte Harell, Willy Fritsch, Johannes Heesters, Siegfried Breuer, Dorit Kreysler and Hans Brauswetter. An English film version under the title *Oh, Rosalinda!* was produced by Pressberger and Powell in 1955 with Michael Redgrave, Anneliese Rothenberger, Ludmilla Tcherina (sung by Sári Bárabás), Anton Wallbrook (sung by Walter Berry) and Dennis Price (sung by Denis Dowling).

CHARACTERS

Gabriel von Eisenstein, *a man of private means*
Rosalinde, *his wife*
Frank, *a prison governor*
Prince Orlofsky
Alfred, *his singing teacher*
Dr Falke, *a notary*
Dr Blind, *a lawyer*
Adele, *Rosalinde's maid*
Frosch, *a court usher*
Ali-Bey, *an Egyptian*, Ramusin, *an embassy attaché*, Murray, *an American*, Carikoni, *a Marquis*, Lord Middleton, Baron Oskar, Ida, Melanie, Felicita, Sidi, Minni, Faustine, Silvia, Sabine, Bertha, Lori, Paula, *guests of Prince Orlofsky*

898

Yvan, *the Prince's valet*
Servants of the Prince, a beadle

ACT I

The curtain rises on a room in Gabriel von Eisenstein's house, a well-appointed home in a spa town, near to a large city. A voice is heard off-stage serenading Rosalinde, the lady of the house ('Täubchen, das entflattert ist'), and she instantly recognises the voice of her lover, the singing teacher Alfred, whose ringing tenor tones she finds irresistible.

Adele, Rosalinde's maid, has received a letter from her sister Ida, with an invitation to a ball that evening at the villa of the young Russian Prince Orlofsky but when she asks her mistress for the evening off, giving the excuse that she wishes to visit a sick aunt, Rosalinde refuses, as her husband is due to start a short prison sentence that evening for assault. When the discontented Adele has left the room, Alfred puts in an eager appearance, and he can only be persuaded to leave on condition that he can return that evening when Eisenstein has gone safely to jail.

Eisenstein enters, arguing angrily with his stuttering lawyer Blind ('Nein, mit solchen Advokaten') who has conducted his case so clumsily that his sentence has been increased on appeal. After Blind has left, Eisenstein's friend Falke arrives and tries to persuade Eisenstein to delay starting his prison sentence in order to go with him to Orlofsky's party. If Eisenstein turns up at the prison the following morning at six instead of this evening, Falke says, no harm will have been done. At the prospect of an evening in the company of all the attractive young ladies who are promised to be at the party, Eisenstein is soon persuaded ('Komm mit mir zum Souper').

When Adele reappears, Rosalinde, now looking forward to an evening alone with Alfred, tells her that she may have the evening off after all. At the prospect of poor, bereft Rosalinde being left alone for the evening, Rosalinde, Eisenstein and Adele each feigns a sadness that none of them feels ('So muss allein ich bleiben?'). Eisenstein and Adele leave for their supposed evening commitments, whereupon Alfred reappears and quickly makes himself at home as he settles down for an intimate supper with Rosalinde, decked out in Eisenstein's smoking cap and dressing gown (Finale I: 'Trinke, Liebchen, trinke schnell').

The pair are interrupted by the arrival of the prison governor, Frank, who has come to collect Eisenstein to start his prison sentence. Found alone in the company of a man wearing her husband's smoking cap and dressing gown, Rosalinde has, for propriety's sake, to deny vehemently the notion that he could be anyone but her husband ('Mein Herr, was dächten Sie von mir?'), and Alfred is forced to go along with the pretence. Frank paints a tempting picture of the house he keeps for his jailbirds ('Mein schönes grosses Vogelhaus') and Alfred reluctantly allows himself to be led off, fortified by a lingering farewell kiss from Rosalinde.

ACT 2

At Prince Orlofsky's villa the guests are all thoroughly enjoying the party

('Ein Souper heut' uns winkt'). Adele, posing as an actress named Olga, is there with her sister Ida, while Falke is in conversation with the Prince and, from their conversation, it soon emerges that an elaborate charade is in progress, set up by Falke to amuse Orlofsky. 'The bat's revenge' he calls it, as he picks out for the Prince the characters. Adele is apparently one of them, but the leading character—why, here he is arriving now. It is none other than Eisenstein, who is introduced as the 'Marquis Renard'. Orlofsky commands his guests to drink. His wealth has left him permanently bored, but he insists that his guests enjoy themselves ('Ich lade gern mir Gäste ein').

Eisenstein soon spots Adele in her mistress's dress but, when he comments on her likeness to his maid, she laughs it off. 'My dear Marquis, a man like you should know better than that,' she says. 'Fancy mistaking a lady for a lady's maid!' ('Mein Herr Marquis'). Next Falke introduces Eisenstein to a guest who has arrived somewhat late. It is Frank, the prison governor, posing as the 'Chevalier Chagrin', and the two phoney Gallic gentlemen struggle to hold a conversation in schoolboy French.

The guests are getting hungry, but Falke announces that they must wait before they sup for the arrival of a special guest—a Hungarian countess who must remain masked. When eventually Falke shows the lady in, it turns out to be none other than Rosalinde. Eisenstein has meanwhile been flirting outrageously with a whole gaggle of young ladies at the party, demonstrating his unusual repeater watch as a conversation piece. When he tries the same technique on the supposed Hungarian countess ('Dieser Anstand, so manierlich'), to his dismay, the lady ends up pocketing it.

The guests press the Hungarian countess to remove her mask, but Orlofsky defends her and she proceeds to convince everyone of her Magyar credentials by singing a fiery Hungarian csárdás ('Klänge der Heimat'). The guests are enchanted by her performance, and they then turn to Falke to urge him to tell them his story of the bat. However, it is Eisenstein who triumphantly relates the story of how some years ago, after a fancy-dress ball, he had left Falke to walk home in broad daylight dressed as a bat.

The guests sit down to supper, and Orlofsky proposes a toast to champagne, the king of all wines (Finale II: 'Im Feuerstrom der Reben'). As the wine flows, Falke leads the guests in a declaration of everlasting brotherhood ('Brüderlein und Schwesterlein'), after which they sit back to enjoy a ballet display consisting of a series of national dances—Spanish, Scottish, Russian, Bohemian and Hungarian. When it is over, all embark on a swirling waltz ('Ha, welch' ein Fest!'), but, as the clock strikes six in the morning, Eisenstein and Frank both seize their hats and cloaks and rush off.

ACT 3

Back in the prison governor's office all is quiet, except for the sound of the imprisoned Alfred singing irrepressibly. Frosch, the jailer, much the worse for slibowitz, enters with a lantern and seeks to quieten the vocalising occupant of cell number 12 as Frank enters unsteadily, recalling the delights of Orlofsky's party, dancing and whistling to himself and holding imaginary conversations with the other guests. Adele and Ida arrive in pursuit of the Chevalier Chagrin. Adele confesses that she is not really an actress, but she believes that the Chevalier, as a man of obvious influence, will be able to help her to get on the stage, and she proceeds to give him a demonstration of her acting talent, showing him her ability to take the roles of a simple country girl or a queen ('Spiel' ich die Unschuld vom Lande').

Eisenstein arrives to start his prison sentence and is surprised to find the Chevalier Chagrin at the jail but, when Eisenstein gives his real identity, Frank points out that it cannot be so. He personally arrested Gabriel von Eisenstein the previous evening and has him safely under lock and key in cell number 12. Frosch goes to get the mysterious prisoner as Dr Blind arrives, claiming that Eisenstein had summoned him.

Anxious to discover who it might be who was been found in his smoking cap and dressing gown supping at his table in his wife's company, Eisenstein borrows Blind's wig, gown and spectacles in order to be able to see and not be seen. Frosch returns with Alfred and, when they are joined shortly afterwards by Rosalinde, Eisenstein, affecting Blind's stutter, proceeds to question them about the events of the previous evening. He finds it difficult to remain impassive as the details emerge ('Ich stehe voll Zagen') and eventually, unable to control his husbandly indignation any longer, reveals his identity.

Rosalinde shows herself equal to the challenge by producing the repeater-watch with which the Marquis Renard had the previous evening sought to seduce the Hungarian countess. Now all the other principal characters arrive, and Falke reveals to Eisenstein that the whole affair had been set up by him as a revenge for the affair of the fancy-dress ball. It is the bat's revenge. Eisenstein can do nothing but take his discomfort in good heart, and the whole company agree that the blame for any misdemeanours can be laid firmly at the door of King Champagne (Finale III: 'O Fledermaus, o Fledermaus').

FATINITZA

an operetta in three acts by F Zell and Richard Genée, after Scribe's *La Circassienne*. Music by Franz von Suppé. Produced at the Carltheater, Vienna, 5 January 1876 with Antonie Link (Wladimir/Fatinitza), Hermine Meyerhoff (Lydia), Wilhelm Knaak (General Kantschukoff), Karl Blasel (Julian von Golz) and Josef Matras (Izzet Pasha). Produced at the Raimundtheater 24 January 1900.

Produced at the Friedrich-Wilhelmstäditsches Theater, Berlin, 16 September 1876. Produced at the Theater am Gärtnerplatz, Munich, in new version by Eduard Rogati, Herbert Witt and Bruno Uher 1950.

Produced at the Théâtre des Nouveautés, Paris, in a version by Alfred Delacour and Victor Wilder 15 March 1879 with Mlle Preciosi, Mlle Nadaud, Pradeau, Paul Ginet, Ernest Vois and Edouard Georges and revived there 6 April 1882 with Marguerite Ugalde, Berthelier and Juliette Darcourt.

Produced at the Alhambra Theatre, London, in a version by Henry S Leigh 20 June 1878 with Miss Greville, Mlle Marcus, Thomas Aynsley Cook, Fred Mervin and W H Leigh.

Produced at the Germania Theatre, New York, 14 April 1879 with Helene Kuhse, Emma Kuster, Adolf Franosch, Bernhard Rank and Oscar Will. Produced at the Fifth Avenue Theatre in a version by Josiah B Polk 22 April 1879 with Jeannie Winston, Sallie Reber, W H Hamilton, W A Morgan and Vincent Hogan. Played at the Olympic Theatre 10 November 1879 with Reca Murelli, Frederika Rokohl, Franosch, George S Weeks and A van Houten, and at the Standard Theatre from 17 November with Verona Jarbeau as Wladimir. Played at the Thalia Theater 3 January 1880 with Mathilde Cottrelly, Frln Meta, Gustave Adolfi, Fritz Schnelle and Max Lube. Played at Booth's Theatre 1880 by the Boston Ideal Company with Adelaide Phillips (Wladimir) and performed by them in repertoire over the following seasons. Played at Wallack's Theatre 1887. Produced at the Broadway Theatre 26 December 1904 with Fritzi Scheff.

CHARACTERS

Count Timofey Kantschukoff, *a Russian general*
Princess Lydia Iwanowna, *his niece*
Basil Starawieff, *a captain*
Olipp Safonoff, *a lieutenant*
Iwan, Fedor, Osip, Dimitri, *cadets*
Steipann, *a sergeant*
Wladimir Samoiloff, *a lieutenant*
Julian von Golz, *a German newspaper reporter*
Wuika, *a Bulgarian*
Hanna, *his wife*
Izzet Pascha, *governor of the Turkish fortress of Isaktscha*
Nursida, Zuleika, Diana, Besida, *his wives*
Mustapha, *keeper of the harem*
Hassan Bey, *leader of the Baschi-Bozuks*
Soldiers, cossacks, cadets, slaves

ACT I

The curtain rises on a Russian military outpost outside the Turkish fortress of Isaktscha, on the lower Danube, during the Crimean War of 1854-55. It is early morning in the depths of winter, and snow lies heavily on the ground. To one side of the stage is a sentry hut, in front of which a fire is burning. At the sound of approaching footsteps the sentry emerges from the hut to issue a challenge ('Halt, wer da?') but it is only Sergeant Steipann, coming to sound the reveille and to get the sleeping soldiers on parade.

Steipann shivers profusely in the cold, but the colder it is, the wilder the wind, and the more crackly the ice, the more he loves it, because it reminds him of his native Russia ('Liegt der Schnee so weiss'). To help the soldiers start their day, a Bulgarian peasant named Wuika appears, offering glasses of vodka ('Wutki, Wutki, Wutki wenn die Flaschen leer'). What the soldiers in the camp do not know is that Wuika is actually a Turkish spy, sent to infiltrate behind Russian lines.

902

The cadets and soldiers prepare themselves for duty ('Erwache frei von allem Kummer'). Wladimir, a young lieutenant, is not too happy at being roused from his sleep because it has disturbed his dream about a young woman named Lydia with whom he once fell in love in Odessa ('Sie, die ich darf nie nennen'). Suddenly the camp springs to life as a bunch of cossacks bring in a captive whom they suspect of being a spy ('Was gibt's da?' 'Ein Spion!'). The prisoner is, in fact, Julian von Golz, war correspondent of a German newspaper and, to convince his captors of his identity, he has to tell them all about his work as a reporter ('Ein Reporter ist ein Mann, dem man nichts verbergen kann').

As it happens, Lieutenant Wladimir knows Julian of old and is readily able to testify on his behalf. Moreover, Julian knows the full story of Wladimir's Odessa infatuation with Lydia. In order to get past her uncle, a Russian general named Kantschukoff, Wladimir had dressed in female clothes and passed himself off as a young lady called Fatinitza. What he had not counted on was that General Kantschukoff himself would then fall madly in love with Fatinitza.

Julian's arrival in the Russian camp proves something of a godsend. Morale has for quite a time been low, with little activity on the battle-front, and Julian comes up with the idea of staging some camp theatricals. The soldiers are delighted with the idea, and Julian leads them off to prepare their parts ('Aber deswegen niemals verlegen'). Julian is to be the director of the play and Steipann the prompter, while Wladimir finds himself cast as the female lead and is given some Bulgarian woman's clothing that has been found in an outbuilding in the camp as a costume.

While the soldiers are busy making themselves up, General Kantschukoff himself appears on a visit of inspection. 'Heaven, fire and water!' he exclaims when he finds nobody at his post ('Himmel, Bomben, Element!'). He is even more outraged when the soldiers eventually appear dressed, ready for the play, in a variety of civilian clothes and he is just about to dish out punishments to the whole of the company when Wladimir appears in his costume as a peasant girl. Kantschukoff at once recognises Fatinitza. All thought of punishing the soldiers is forgotten as Kantschukoff renews his wooing of Fatinitza, who responds suitably coyly ('Woll'n sie mich lieben').

Relieved to have escaped punishment, the soldiers troop off happily ('Liegt der Schnee so weiss'). Fatinitza finds it increasingly difficult to keep the general at bay, but salvation is just around the corner. The sound of approaching sleigh-bells heralds the arrival of a visitor, who turns out to be none other than the General's niece Lydia, who has come to visit her uncle ('Teurer Oheim, länger konnt ich diesem Drang nicht widersteh'n'). When he sees her, Wladimir's feelings for Lydia come flooding back.

Kantschukoff's concern is now to find suitable accommodation for the two girls. He seeks to find it in a nearby convent ('Eine Influcht winket dir'), and Lydia and Fatinitza are left in the care of Julian while Kantschukoff pursues his military inspection. The spy Wuika chooses this moment to let into the camp a band of Baschi-Bozzuks led by the villainous Hassan (Finale I: 'Nur kein Geschrei'). They take the two girls captive for the harem of Izzet

Pascha, while Julian is left to institute efforts for their rescue. He is enough of a newspaperman to realise also that he has a story on his hands.

ACT 2

In Izzet Pascha's harem in Isaktscha his four existing wives are busy preparing themselves for the Pascha ('Den Gebieter zu entzücken'). The Pascha is a man with distinct political views, and he has a long list of reforms that he believes the nation needs if the Turkish half-moon is not to decline to a mere crescent ('Reformen tun Not'). Now he has decided to add two Christian wives to his existing collection. When Hassan brings in Lydia and Fatinitza, Izzet Pascha takes a very distinct liking to Lydia. He decides that she shall be his favourite wife, and he deputes Fatinitza to dress her in suitable clothes ready for his attention. With his wives and slaves, Izzet departs ('Ein bissel auffrischen, ein bissel aufmischen').

Left behind with Lydia, Fatinitza finds his heart trembling as he does his inexpert best to dress Lydia in her diamonds and prepare her hair ('Mein Herz, es zagt'). Decorum finally decrees that the line be drawn at helping Lydia to undress. At first Fatinitza excuses this curious reticence as being due to 'brother' Wladimir's love for Lydia, but then Wladimir admits who he really is. Lydia counters with her own declaration of love, after which the two get down to planning how they are to escape the Pascha's clutches.

They decide that they should first make a clean breast of the situation to the four wives, who respond with understandable shock at the news of the real identity of Fatinitza ('Ha! Ein Mann, ein Mann, ist's wahr?') but, jealous of the attention the Pascha is giving Lydia, they readily enough agree to help. Then Julian arrives with Steipann, seeking to negotiate the release of the 'girls'. The Pascha is, understandably, not prepared to give Lydia up, but Julian contrives to send Steipann away with a message for Kantschukoff, making sure that, before Steipann departs, he leaves a uniform for Wladimir.

Julian and Izzet Pascha get deeply into conversation, with alcoholic refreshment liberally dispensed ('Jeder Trinker ist anfangs nüchtern'). Indeed the Pascha relaxes to the point where he agrees to take Julian on a tour of his harem ('Silberglöckchen rufen helle'). It is all for journalistic reasons, of course, though Julian can scarcely restrain his delight. To follow, the Pascha puts on a shadow-play. Suddenly the shadows of Kantschukoff and Steipann appear in the display (Finale II: 'Zwei Russen, der Spass ist gar nicht schlecht'). However, Izzet's joy at the apparent joke proves short-lived. The Russians have arrived, and Isaktscha is captured. Lydia is freed, while Fatinitza simply vanishes—back into the person of Lieutenant Wladimir.

ACT 3

In General Kantschukoff's palace in Odessa, Lydia is listening to the bells ringing out celebrating the declaration of peace ('Glockenklänge künden Frieden'). She wonders also whether those bells of freedom might lead to her heart being freed from the ache of her love for Wladimir. Kantschukoff has agreed that this very day she shall marry the old, deaf and blind Prince Swertikoff, while he himself has never lost any of his passion for Fatinitza. He is determined to track her down, and Julian, who is staying at the palace, vividly describes his own supposed efforts to trace Fatinitza ('Um Fatinitza's Spur zu finden'). He has followed her movements over three continents, through the slave markets of Istanbul, to a succession of owners.

Wladimir arrives from the battlefield to seek Lydia's hand, and Julian manages to arrange some time together for the two young lovers. They are overjoyed to see each other again ('Dich wieder zu seh'n, o welch' ein himmlisch süsses Glück'), and Wladimir tells Lydia how, at the height of battle, his love for her helped him to march on with renewed courage ('Vorwärts mit frischem Mut'). Kantschukoff is outraged at the idea of a mere lieutenant marrying Lydia but, recognising Wladimir as the brother of Fatinitza, he is persuaded to agree to a bargain. If Wladimir will produce Fatinitza for him to marry, Wladimir shall marry Lydia.

Fatinitza duly appears once more and, amidst general jubilation, Wladimir is allowed to take his place in the wedding ceremony previously arranged for Prince Swertikoff (Finale III: 'Jubelsang ertönt der Fremden zum Empfang'). Julian has meanwhile arranged for the General to receive a letter from Fatinitza explaining that she no longer exists and asking his blessing on Wladimir and Lydia. When Kantschukoff reads it, he happily takes a charitable view of matters and vows to resign himself to his military duties, while Wladimir and Lydia are left to march on through life with renewed courage ('Vorwärts mit frischem Mut').

BOCCACCIO

a comic opera in three acts by F Zell and Richard Genée based on a play by Bayard, de Leuven and Beauplan. Music by Franz von Suppé. Produced at the Carltheater, Vienna, 1 February 1879 with Antonie Link (Boccaccio), Rosa Streitmann (Fiametta), Franz Tewele (Pietro) and Karl Blasel (Lambertuccio). Produced at the Theater an der Wien 16 September 1882, at Venedig in Wien 5 July 1899, at the Volksoper 10 November 1908 and 9 June 1977 with Peter Minich, Anita Ammersfeld, Heinz Ehrenfreund and Erich Kuchar, and at the State Opera in an operatic version by Artur Bodanzky 2 May 1932. Produced on the lake stage, Bregenz, 1953.

Produced at Frankfurt 13 March 1879. Produced at the Friedrich-Wilhelm-städitsches Theater, Berlin, 20 September 1879.

Produced at the Thalia Theater, New York, 23 April 1880 with Mathilde Cottrelly, Frln Ahl, Fritz Schnelle and Max Lube. Produced at the Union Square Theatre 15 May 1880 in an English version with Jeannie Winston, Alice Hosmer, W A Morgan and A H Bell and played at Niblo's Garden 17 November 1881. Played at Wallack's Theatre 11 March 1888 with Marion Manola, Laura Joyce Bell, Digby Bell, DeWolf Hopper, Jefferson De Angelis, Annie Myers, C W Dungan and Laura Moore. Produced at the Broadway Theatre in a version by Harry B Smith 27

February 1905 with Fritzi Scheff. Produced at the Metropolitan Opera House, 2 January 1931 in the operatic version by Artur Bodanzky with Maria Jeritza (Boccaccio).

Produced at the Comedy Theatre, London, in a version by H B Farnie and Robert Reece 22 April 1882 with Violet Cameron, Alice Burville, J G Taylor and Lionel Brough, and revived there 30 May 1885 with Miss Cameron, Marie Tempest, Arthur Roberts and Victor Stevens.

Produced at the Galeries Saint-Hubert, Brussels, in a version by Henri Chivot and Alfred Duru 3 February 1882 and at the Théâtre des Folies-Dramatiques, Paris, 29 March 1882 with Mlle Montbazon (Jean Boccace), Berthe Thibault (Béatrice), Maugé (Pandolfo), Désiré (Prince Orlando), Luco (Quiquibio), and Noémie Vernon (Frisca). Produced at the Nouveau Théâtre 1896 with Anna Tariol-Baugé. Played at the Théâtre de la Gaîté-Lyrique 1914 with Jane Alstein and revived there in 1921 with Marthe Chenal.

A film version was produced by Herbert Maisch in 1936 with Willy Fritsch, Heli Finkzeller, Albrecht Schoenhals, Fita Benkoff, Paul Kemp and Gina Falckenberg.

CHARACTERS

Giovanni Boccaccio
Pietro, *Prince of Palermo*
Scalza, *a barber*
Beatrice, *his wife*
Lotteringhi, *a cooper*
Isabella, *his wife*
Lambertuccio, *a grocer*
Peronella, *his wife*
Fiametta, *their foster daughter*
Leonetto, Tofano, Chichibio, Guido, Cisti, Federico, Giotto, Rinieri, Lanto, *student friends of Boccaccio*
Checco, *a beggar*
An unknown
Fresco, *Lotteringhi's apprentice*
Major-domo *of the Duke of Tuscany*
A travelling bookseller, beggars, maids, servants, people of Florence

ACT I

In front of the church of Santa Maria Novella in 14th century Florence a crowd is gathering. It is a sunny June 24, the feast day of John the Baptist, patron saint of Florence, and Checco and his fellow beggars are wondering how well they will profit from the crowds who will soon be appearing for the church service ('Heut' am Tag des Patrons von Florenz'). The crowd includes a group of students whose leader, Leonetto, is on his way to keep an amorous appointment with Beatrice, wife of the barber Scalza, while her husband is away on business. A travelling bookseller enters the square, selling the latest novels ('Neueste Novellen'). The women are eager to buy the writings of the author Boccaccio, with their tales of amorous intrigue, but their husbands are scandalised by the way Boccaccio's novels portray them as cuckolds.

906

When Scalza returns early from his trip to Pisa, he tells the menfolk of an encounter with the retinue of the Prince of Palermo, who is travelling to Florence to marry the daughter of the Duke of Tuscany. 'But our Duke only has sons!' replies the grocer Lambertuccio. It seems, Scalza tells them, that he also has an illegitimate daughter. Scalza knocks on his door of his house, only to find it locked. Romantically he holds his umbrella as if it were a guitar and sings a serenade outside his wife's window ('Holde Schöne').

He is interrupted by the sound of his wife screaming for help. When she opens the door, she claims that a masked man has entered the house pursued by another ('Ha, sie sind's, sie kommen schon heran'). To bear out the story, Leonetto and his friend Boccaccio emerge from the house masked and fighting a mock duel, as Beatrice screams for mercy and Scalza looks on helplessly. When Beatrice and Scalza finally lock themselves inside their home the students gather around Leonetto and Boccaccio. It turns out that Leonetto had gone to meet Beatrice, but Boccaccio had got there first. Boccaccio is especially pleased with this latest episode, since he takes all his story plots from real life ('Ich sehe einen jungen Mann dort stehn'/'Das ist doch jedem klar').

Boccaccio, however, has a more serious love in his life—a young lady whom he has only recently met. She is Fiametta, foster daughter of the grocer Lambertuccio, and she now arrives with her foster mother for the church service ('Die Glocken läuten hell und rein'). Word has been received with the latest quarterly maintenance payment from Fiametta's unknown real father that a marriage has been arranged for her, but her mind is on the mysterious young man she has recently encountered. She sings to herself an old song about true love ('Hab' ich nur deine Liebe') and, as she does so, she recognises the voice of Boccaccio. He briefly emerges from the crowd, takes up the song, and blesses her and her mother with holy water from the church.

While the church service is in progress, Pietro, Prince of Palermo, arrives on the scene. He is passing himself off as a Sicilian student named Alessandro Chiarmontesi and is dressed in simple clothes and a cloak. He is a fervent admirer of Boccaccio's work and keen to become an author himself, and he eagerly seizes the opportunity to make the famous author's acquaintance. The church service is over and the congregation emerges ('Die Glocken läuten hell und rein'). For Pietro's benefit the students size up the various ladies as potential conquests. Women become available for conquest, Leonetto reckons, as soon as they get married. The women, for their part, are discussing their respective husbands. Isabella, it seems, has brutal scenes every day with her husband, the cooper Lotteringhi. 'Does he beat you?' asks Beatrice. 'No, I beat him,' she replies.

The sight of Checco begging gives Boccaccio another idea for getting past the protective care of Fiametta's mother. Disguising himself as a beggar, he is able to approach Fiametta, begging for alms but recognisable to her by his voice ('Ein armer Blinder'). However, the men of the town are determined to rid themselves of the trouble-making Boccaccio (Finale I: 'Ehrsame Bürger der Stadt'). They set off after his blood, Scalza leaving his customers getting increasingly impatient in his barber shop.

When the men come upon Pietro, he is flattered at their suggestion that he is a novelist but, thinking that he is therefore Boccaccio, they set upon him. Fortunately Scalza, who had met him in Pisa, is able to confirm Pietro's assurances as to his real identity ('Ein Prinz bin ich'). When the travelling bookseller reappears, the men of the town decide to settle for the next best thing—burning all the books of Boccaccio they can lay their hands on.

ACT 2

Later on, Boccaccio, Leonetto, Pietro and the other students gather in front of the premises of Lambertuccio and Lotteringhi ('Beim Liebchen, beim Liebchen'). They have come to put to the test their ideas about the fidelity of women and provide Pietro with material for a novel. Accompanying themselves on lutes, they sing a serenade, Boccaccio outside Fiametta's window, Pietro outside Isabella's, and Leonetto in front of Peronella's ('Ein Stern zu sein'). They retreat into hiding when voices are heard and Lotteringhi appears, bombarded by abuse from his wife for drinking when he should be working. He promptly sets to work with his workmen, making a barrel, a noisy job that serves admirably to drown the sound of his wife's nagging ('Tagtäglich zankt mein Weib').

The barrel finished, the men retire for further liquid refreshment, at which Isabella and Peronella emerge from their homes. From his hiding place Boccaccio lobs stones, with letters attached, to land at their feet and, when Fiametta appears, the same happens to her. Their hearts beating in anticipation of the romantic messages they bear, each reads her letter and then joyfully kisses it ('Wie pocht mein Herz so ungestüm'/'Wonnevolle Kunde, neu belebend'). While Fiametta runs into her garden, Isabella and Peronella impatiently await their mysterious suitors. Soon Leonetto appears and approaches Peronella, while Pietro in false beard and officer's uniform comes up to Isabella.

Pietro is destined to get rich material for his projected novel for, when Lotteringhi returns, Isabella has to hide Pietro in the newly completed barrel. Lotteringhi starts to roll the barrel away for a customer to whom he has sold it for two cecchini and Isabella has to counter by saying that she has sold it for five cecchini, which Pietro hands to her from inside the barrel. When Lotteringhi discovers Pietro inside the barrel, the latter has to pretend that he is the purchaser checking that it is watertight. Lotteringhi promises to fetch some more pitch to make sure, leaving Pietro taking off his false beard and summing up the material he already has for the first three chapters of his novel ('Um die Spannung zu erhöh'n').

Next door Boccaccio arrives, pretending to be a simple peasant sent by his master to collect some fruit from Lambertuccio's olive tree ('So oft man mich nach Neuem fragt'). Fiametta again recognises his voice beneath the disguise. Boccaccio climbs up the tree, but quickly comes down again to ask Lambertuccio why he has been kissing his foster-daughter so ardently. When Lambertuccio denies doing so, Boccaccio claims that from the tree he could see him doing so. If Lambertuccio really were not kissing Fiametta, then the tree must be a magic one, from which everything appears romanticised. Lambertuccio climbs up to see for himself, while Boccaccio moves towards to Fiametta (Finale II: 'Benützen wir den Augenblick'). When Lambertuccio looks down from the tree, there indeed is Fiametta embracing the stranger. Moreover, when he looks next door, there is Isabella in the arms of the disguised Pietro, while Lotteringhi can be heard scrabbling around inside the barrel unable to find any hole. And when Lambertuccio looks into his own garden, he even sees his own wife Peronella with Leonetto. A magic tree indeed!

The men of the town gather round, led by Scalza, calling to Lotteringhi and Lambertuccio with the news that Boccaccio has been reported on Lotteringhi's premises ('Lotteringhi, Lambertuccio, macht doch auf!'). The men surround the house and pounce upon the first stranger, only to find that they have got the wrong man. This time the unfortunate person is a messenger sent by Fiametta's real father to take her in a sedan chair to her marriage ('Ich bin nicht hier von ungefähr'). At first Fiametta is reluctant to leave, but Boccaccio, hiding behind a tree, reassures her. As she is taken away, he emerges dressed in a devil's mask and, as the superstitious locals cower in fear, Boccaccio and his companions make their getaway unmolested.

ACT 3

In the garden of the palace of the Duke of Tuscany, Boccaccio sits telling one of his stories to a rapt audience comprising Pietro and various court attendants ('Erfrische Quellen sind seine Novellen'). Pietro is due to marry the Duke's daughter, who turns out to be none other than Fiametta, and Boccaccio is asked to prepare an entertainment for the reception to be given that evening to celebrate the event.

The citizens of Florence are there for the occasion, including, of course, Lambertuccio and Peronella who naturally express a desire to meet the Duke whose daughter they have fostered. The major-domo tells them that they have done so already. He it was who called at their home to collect Fiametta three days before. Lambertuccio quakes at the memory of the unfriendly way he had greeted the unknown visitor, and thinks it advisable to send in his wife to make peace with the Duke ('Um des Fürsten Zorn zu meiden').

Boccaccio is saddened at the prospect of his beloved Fiametta marrying Pietro. For her part, Fiametta has discovered only here at the palace that the man who had won her affections is none other than Boccaccio, the author of the scandalous novels. She is unperturbed, though, and together they recall their happy days in Florence and the traditional Tuscan song that the students sang ('Mia Bella Fiorentina').

The men of Florence who have gathered for the reception are appalled to find Boccaccio there, especially when Lambertuccio realises that he was the peasant who came to pick olives, while Beatrice recognises him as the student who entered her house. In this more relaxed confrontation Boccaccio is able to use his rhetoric to persuade them of the wit and humour of his novels ('Ihr Toren, ihr wollt hassen mich'). Moreover, when Boccaccio's *commedia dell' arte* entertainment is staged, it is very obvious to Pietro that it carries a strong moral. He takes it readily to heart, agrees to forego the marriage that has been arranged for him, and allows Fiametta to marry the man she really loves—Giovanni Boccaccio (Finale III: 'Der Witz, die Laune').

DAS SPITZENTUCH DER KÖNIGIN

(The Queen's Lace Handkerchief)

an operetta in three acts by Heinrich Bohrmann-Riegen and Richard Genée. Music by Johann Strauss. Produced at the Theater an der Wien, Vienna, 1 October 1880 with Eugenie Erdösy (the King), Karoline Tellheim (the Queen), Hermine Meyerhoff (Donna Irene), Alexander Girardi (Don Sancho), Felix Schweighofer (Count Villalobos) and Ferdinand Schütz (Cervantes). Produced at the Johann Strauss Theater in a completely new version by Rudolf Oesterreicher and Julius Wilhelm with music arranged by Karl Pauspertl 1931.

Produced at the Friedrich Wilhlemstädtisches Theater, Berlin, 24 November 1880. Produced at the Deutsches Opernhaus in a revised version 22 May 1931. Produced in East Germany in a completely new version by Wilhelm Neef during 1950s.

Produced at the Casino Theatre, New York, 21 October 1882 with Signor Perugini (Cervantes), Lilly Post (the Queen) and Mathilde Cottrelly (Donna Irene), and revived there 30 December 1882 with Francis Wilson (Don Sancho).

CHARACTERS

The King
The Queen
Donna Irene, *a lady in waiting*
The Marquise of Villareul
Miguel de Cervantes
Count Villalobos, *Prime Minister and Regent*
Don Sancho d'Avallanreda y Villapinquedones, *the King's tutor*
Marquis de la Mancha
The Brazilian envoy
Ministers, ladies in waiting, chamberlains, courtiers, students, watchmen, pages, peasants

ACT 1

At the court of Portugal in Lisbon, in 1580, the young King's tutor and confidant, Don Sancho d'Avallanreda, is standing watch while the King keeps an early morning assignation with a lady ('Stundenlang nun harr ich auf die Majestät') when the poet Miguel Cervantes arrives in the garden of the royal palace with a group of his student friends ('Heran, heran! Ich führ' Euch') to sing a mocking serenade beneath the window of the detested Prime Minister, Count Villalobos ('Welch holdes Bild des Haupt umhüllt').

The Prime Minister, angered by the jeering singing, appears at his window and calls for his watchmen, but the guards have all been dismissed temporarily by Don Sancho to allow the young King to keep his tryst in secret. What Villalobos does not know is that the King is in that very house visiting his wife and, indeed, the King almost runs into the Prime Minister as he is leaving the house. The royal visitor is nearly exposed, but Cervantes provides him with cover and Villalobos jumps to the conclusion that the poet is the man who has been paying court to his wife and swears vengeance. As soon as the King has made his getaway the watchmen return and Cervantes and his mocking serenaders are arrested as disturbers of the peace, but the King orders his release and, in gratitude, appoints him to the post of reader to the Queen.

In addition to being Prime Minister, Count Villalobos is also Regent, for the King is still a minor. As Regent, the Count makes it his business to keep the young monarch as far away as possible from any effective state business, and he has manipulated affairs so that the King is virtually his pawn. He also keeps the King away from his young Queen. She sees through the ambitious Premier's machinations and anxiously awaits the King's attainment of his majority, sadly reflecting how much things have changed for the worse since the magic of her wedding night, even though the King did fall asleep after his wedding supper (''s war eine zaubrisch wundervolle Nacht'). The King, meanwhile, allows his roving eye to turn in the direction of the Queen's lady-in-waiting, Irene, but she, feeling sorry for the Queen, rejects all his attentions ('Sie lacht mich aus—glaubt wohl an seine Liebe").

The King's particular memory of his wedding night is of the magnificent aroma of the delicious truffle pie the Queen set before him ('Stets kommt mir wieder in den Sinn'). He is devoted to good food and, besides his amorous adventures, he obtains ready relief from the restrictions that surround him in the enjoyment of exuberant feasts. Villalobos has capitalised on this, and setting tasty dishes before the King has become a major part of the Premier's efforts to exercise influence over him ('Die Austern wie fein'/ 'Jetzt will ich trinken').

Villalobos is planning a coup, to be put into action at the psychological moment, which will depose the King and unite Portugal with Spain. The royal favour shown towards Cervantes does not suit him at all, for in Cervantes he recognises an enemy and he determines to engineer his downfall. Cervantes, for his part, has arranged with the connivance of his sweetheart, Donna Irene, that, at the forthcoming opening of the Court, a declaration of the King's majority that Cervantes has prepared will be substituted for the speech from the throne.

The famous poet soon enjoys the full confidence of the Queen, who is well aware of the King's infidelities and who seeks, through Cervantes, to arouse the King's jealousy. While the King is enjoying his dancing hour, and Cervantes is busy reading to the Queen (Finale I: 'Einst sass ein Jüngling blöd und traurig'), she writes on one of her lace handkerchiefs the words 'A Queen loves you, but you are not a King.' She conceals the handkerchief in Cervantes' book and awaits his answer. When the dancing and reading are over ('Da, die Lektüre jetzt zu End'), Cervantes takes the handkerchief from his book but he misunderstands its message, believing it is intended for the King, and that the words simply refer to the King not behaving as a king should. The Prime Minister, however, uses this pretext to have Cervantes arrested and plans to have him brought before the inquisition.

ACT 2

In the throne-room of the royal palace, awaiting trial, Cervantes works on the composition of a new ode ('Wo die wilde Rosen erblüht'). The Regent, anxious to have Cervantes got out of the way as quickly as possible, has the council summoned ('Weil so äusserst wichtig diese Sitzung'/'Wenn ich leite ein Verhör'), but Cervantes' student friends from Salamanca appear and speak in his defence ('Professoren und Doktoren rief aus Salamanca'). Irene also lends him her support ('Hier in der Mitte ein Hügel'), with the result that the council finally declares Cervantes nothing worse than a harmless fool and lets him go free.

Cervantes has meanwhile broached with the Queen the subject of the lace handkerchief and its message and, told the truth, he has promised to use such influence as he possesses to persuade the King to mend his ways. As a special favour, he begs the Queen to allow him to retain the lace handkerchief, as he turns his efforts to setting up a meeting between the King and the Queen. Villalobos continues to try to confound matters by creating confusion on the culinary front ('An hoher Tafel speisen, wenn das Menu misslang'), but the royal meeting finally takes place.

Cervantes appears disguised as an English envoy ('Sei'n Sie willkommen, Excellenz!'/'In England gibt's ein Spiel') and tries to persuade the King to take over the reins of his country's government and to dismiss the Prime Minister. He uses the example of his romantic serenades to persuade the King to adopt a much more endearing approach towards the Queen ('Lichter Glanz erfüllt sein Gemüth'). Villalobos is now more determined than ever to defeat Cervantes and, as ill luck would have it, the poet loses the Queen's lace handkerchief, which comes into the possession of the Prime Minister.

The Court assembles for the speech from the throne (Finale II: 'Heil, unser'm Land dem Könige Heil!') but, instead of the expected speech, the King reads the declaration of his majority prepared by Cervantes. The consequent ending of the Regency is warmly greeted by the whole court and the Prime Minister is sneered at and mocked ('Hell wie ein Strahl aus den himmlischen Höhen') but, to Cervantes' dismay, he turns defeat to victory by producing the lace handkerchief with its incriminating inscription. The King, assuming on this evidence that there has been something between the Queen and Cervantes and that he has been cuckolded, banishes Cervantes from the country and condemns the Queen to a distant convent, as the Regent celebrates his triumph.

ACT 3

In defiance of his banishment, Cervantes has rented a country inn in the countryside of the Sierra de Suazzo, near to the convent where the Queen has been imprisoned, and is posing as an innkeeper. He is visited there by Don Sancho ('In der Nacht mit seinem Zither') who brings news that, ever since the Queen's departure, the King has been plunged in melancholia and has virtually handed the control of government back to the Prime Minister. Cervantes' ambition is still to bring the royal pair together again and, when he hears that the King is to come hunting in the region, he collects together a party of friends and, disguised as brigands, they hold up the carriage in which the Queen and her ladies-in-waiting are taking the air. Cervantes tells her the situation, and the Queen, reflecting that she can never regain the years which have been lost ('Siebzehn Jahre war ich eben und mein Spiegel sagt galant'), agrees to fall in with his plan to win her husband back.

When the hunt arrives ('Singt dem König Heil!'), the King decides to take some refreshment at the inn and settles down for a hearty meal and entertainment presented by the Queen and her ladies-in-waiting who have disguised themselves as waitresses ('Gibt's ein Stiergefecht'). In her disguise the Queen serves the King that same type of truffle pie that he had so much enjoyed on their wedding night. Since only she knows the recipe, the King recognises his wife, and there is a grand rapprochement between them. Cervantes tells the King his interpretation of the words on the lace handkerchief, and His Majesty accepts the implied rebuke of his behaviour with good humour. As all ends happily, Cervantes is rewarded for his troubles with the hand of his beloved Donna Irene (Finale III: 'Eine Königin liebt dich').

The music of *Das Spitzentuch der Königin* is best known through the waltz 'Rosen aus dem Süden' ('Roses from the South'), based on the operetta's themes and prominently featuring the melodies of 'Stets kommt mir wieder in den Sinn' and 'Wo die wilde Rosen erblüht'.

DER LUSTIGE KRIEG

(The Merry War)

an operetta in three acts by F Zell and Richard Genée based on the opéra-comique *Dames Capitaines* by Mélesville and Reber. Music by Johann Strauss. Produced at the Theater an der Wien, Vienna, 25 November 1881 with Alexander Girardi (Marchese Sebastiani), Felix Schweighofer (Balthasar Groot), Ferdinand Schütz (Umberto), Therese Schäfer (Artemisia), Caroline Finaly (Violetta) and Rosa Streitmann (Else). Produced at the Carltheater 25 November 1883. Produced at the Volksoper 29 June 1924. Produced at the Johann Strauss-Theater in a new version by Wilhelm Sterk and Felix Günther 23 December 1929 with Ernst Tautenhayn (Sebastiani), Richard Waldemar (Groot), Anny Ahlers (Violetta) and Hans Heinz Bollmann (Umberto).

Produced at the Friedrich-Wilhelmstädtisches Theater, Berlin, 19 January 1882.

Produced at the Alcazar Royale, Brussels, in a version by Alfred and Maurice Hennequin and Maurice Kufferath as *La Guerre Joyeuse* 21 November 1885 with Minne (Ugon Ganaceti), Thierry (Poot), Lamy (Uberto Petrezzano), Marie Lyonnel (Renée de Montecuculli), Claire Cordier (Violetta) and Mlle Buire (Jeanne).

Produced at the Alhambra Theatre, London, in a version by Robert Reece as *The Merry War* 16 October 1882 with Albert Lefèvre (Marquis di Malespina), Allen Thomas (Balthazar), Henry Walsham (Umberto), Mme Amadi (Artemisia), Constance Loseby (Violetta) and Lory Stubel (Elsie).

Produced at the Thalia Theater, New York, 15 March 1882 with Adolf Link, Gustave Adolfi, Mlle Jules, Jenny Stubel and Marie Seebold. Produced at the Germania Theatre in a version by L C Elson 27 June 1882 with Richard Golden, Gustave Adolfi, Dora Wiley, Belle Cole, Louise Paullin and W T Carleton. Played at Haverley's Theatre 2 October 1882 with W H Fitzgerald, Max Freeman, Jennie Reiffarth and Amy Gordon. Produced at the Casino Theatre 4 February 1884 with Perugini, Fred Leslie, Gertrude Orme, Lilly Post, Mathilde Cottrelly and W T Carleton.

CHARACTERS

Artemisia, *Princess Malaspina, wife of the ruling Prince of Massa-Carrara*
Violetta, *widowed Countess of Lomellini, her cousin*
Marchese Filippo Sebastiani, *the Princess's nephew*
Umberto Spinola, Ricardo Durazzo, Carlo Spinzi, Fortunato Franchetti,
 young noblemen in the service of the Genoese republic
Colonel van Scheelen, *a colonel in the service of the Duke of Limburg*
Balthasar Groot, *a tulip grower from Haarlem*
Else, *his wife*
Panfilio Podestà
Men and women officers, soldiers, people of Society, peasants

ACT 1
It is the beginning of the eighteenth century, and war has broken out between Massa-Carrara and Genoa. It has been a very uneventful war so far ('Keinen Kampf, keinen Sieg bracht' bisher dieser Krieg') and the Genoese commander-in-chief, Umberto Spinola, finds the lack of action distinctly off-putting ('Wie schlüg' ich mich gern ein wenig herum'). The monotony is relieved when soldiers bring in the Marchese Filippo Sebastiani, the nephew of the Princess Malaspina, wife of the ruling prince of Massa-Carrara, as a prisoner. However, the Marchese apparently reckons it a clever move on his part to allow himself to be captured and thus infiltrate behind enemy lines ('Weil den Skandal ich gern vermiede'/'Der klügere gibt nach').

This war is over nothing more serious than a dancer who was apparently engaged simultaneously by the Doge of Genoa and the Prince of Carrara, neither of whom will give way to the other. It is a war completely without bloodshed—a merry war, as Umberto reckons it ('Noch kam man ohne Blutvergiessen in diesem lustigen Krieg'/'Ein Blitz, ein Knall'). The Massa-Carrara army is currently composed entirely of women, commanded by Princess Artemisia, who occupies herself teaching the ladies military matters

914

whilst awaiting the arrival of her niece Violetta, the widowed Princess Lomellini.

The Genoese learn from the talkative Marchese Sebastiano that Violetta has been making arrangements to become the wife of the Duke of Limburg in order to gain access to his money and enlist his 4,000 troops to join the fight against Genoa. The Duke's authorised wedding proxy is already on his way to finalise the marriage details. They also learn that a plot is being hatched to enable Violetta to sneak through the camp of the Genoese army to the fortress of the Massa-Carrara forces in disguise, and Umberto makes preparations to capture her. He also lies in wait for Colonel van Scheelen, the Duke of Limburg's representative and, when he appears, waylays him and confiscates his papers.

At the same time the Dutch tulip grower Balthasar Groot is brought in in a state of considerable anxiety. He has made the journey from Haarlem in Holland with his young wife, Else, to bring some valuable tulip bulbs to Florence ('Herr General, Herr General'/'Wir machten zusammen aus Holland die Reise'). Now he is lamenting both the loss of his wife, who has become separated from him in the confusion of their capture, and also of his precious tulip bulbs which the soldiers have confiscated and eaten for breakfast. Balthasar is temporarily retained in custody.

Disguised as a peasant girl, Violetta appears in the Genoese camp, looking around anxiously, her way seemingly blocked on every side ('Umsonst! Ich kann nicht fort'). She is by no means happy about the many sacrifices she is having to make on account of the war, most particularly that of entering into marriage again ('Für diese Kriegszugs Wohl und Wehe bring' ich die schwersten Opfer doch'). When she comes upon Umberto she asks him for a pass. Her pleas are initially in vain ('Bitte! Bitte!' ''s ist ganz unmöglich') but she manages to use her charms to such effect that ultimately Umberto agrees to give way and trade a pass for a kiss ('Von einem Mann liess ich mich küssen').

In the circumstances of the war so far the only casualties may be said to be those Genoese officers who have fallen for the charms of their opposite numbers in the Massa-Carrara camp. Violetta, the Marchese, Umberto and his fellow officers agree that turning a blind eye to such romantic situations is the easy way to avoid any suggestion of treason ('Kommen und gehen'). Umberto himself is so taken with Violetta that he decides to use the papers of the Limburg envoy, Colonel von Scheelen, in order to pass himself off as the wedding proxy. With his fellow soldiers he prepares a warm reception for the Princess (Finale I: 'Was lange währt, wird gut'), before presenting himself as the Duke's proxy. Astonished, but with undoubted interest, the Countess accepts his assurances but insists that the ceremony must take place straight away as she has to be in Massa in the morning. So, with trumpeters taking the place of an organ and soldiers as witnesses, Violetta follows the substitute Duke to the altar ('Schlagt ein, Herr Substitut! Schnell geht es zum Altar!').

ACT 2

In a hall of the besieged Castle Malaspina, the militarily drilled ladies are gathering for a council of war that has all the atmosphere of a coffee morning ('Die Fürstin lud zum Café und Kriegsrath heute uns ein'). Artemisia expresses her satisfaction with them ('Mit Ihrer Haltung bin ich zufrieden') and proceeds to issue instructions ('Commandirt, instruirt hab' ich manche Compagnie exercirt!'/'Den Feind, den möcht' ich seh'n der da kann widersteh'n!'). The Princess is impatiently awaiting the arrival of her cousin Violetta, but instead she has to receive the Marchese whom the Genoese have discharged as harmless. He brings with him Else Groot, the despondent wife of the tulip grower, whom he has met on the way wandering around lost ('Durch Wald und Feld bin ich geirrt').

Trumpet fanfares announce the arrival of Violetta ('Heil! Heil der Gräfin Lomellini. Hoch! Hoch!'), who proceeds to recount the details of her journey through the enemy camp and her proxy marriage ('Es war ein lustig' Abenteuer'). The Marchese Sebastiani is left to hold his peace on the full extent of all that went on in the Genoese camp behind his thoughts about a nature-loving countess ('Nur für Natur').

Violetta is soon followed by Umberto, accompanied by his Genoese officers in disguise ('Der Langersehnte, den fern man wähnte traf ein'). His love for the Countess Violetta is persuading him to try everything he can to end up winning her as his own. To this end he persuades the plump Balthasar at pistol-point to present himself as the newly arrived Duke of Limburg, and Balthasar has little option but to obey ('Me frown, ick wensch u gooden dag'). Else is taken aback by her husband's reappearance and, when Umberto won't let him return to her, she misunderstands the situation and simply assumes that Balthasar is being unfaithful to her ('Schöne Geschichten muss ich erleben?'/'Was ist an einen Kuss gelegen').

Umberto's heart still beats for Violetta (Finale II: 'Schon dunkelt rings die Nacht'), and eventually he finds the opportunity to speak to her of his love. She protests to him her honour, but he persists. However, the trembling Marchese has recognised the Genoese officers under their disguises, and he succeeds in leading troops from Massa into the castle and overpowering Umberto and his colleagues. Violetta promptly releases them and declares that she considers them her guests at the party she has arranged to celebrate her wedding. Balthasar suffers agonies of embarrassment when Princess Artemisia seeks to lead him on her arm into the bridal apartment, under both Umberto's warning pistol and Else's threatening eyes ('Herr Herzog, reichen Sie mir den Arm'). Whether at the dance or in politics, life all seems very much of a merry-go-round ('Sei's bei Tanz, bei Politik').

ACT 3

In a hall of the castle in Massa, the court salutes Violetta's arrival ('Die Commandantin kam an'). She is very conscious of the fact that, though her hand may officially be in Massa, her heart is unofficially in Genoa ('Was ich erstrebt durch lange Zeit'). Else, meanwhile, presses her husband to confess his real identity and bring their ordeal to an end, and the pair reflect on the children they have not seen for two months ('Zwei Monat sind es schon, dass wir die Kinder nicht mehr sah'n').

Their conversation is overheard by the Marchese, who realises the deception which has been practised and runs off to break the news. Else wins Balthasar over and summons Violetta to tell her what she knows of affair. When the Marchese leads in Umberto, the Countess realises that, since the Genoese Commander-in-chief is not the representative of the Duke of Limburg, she is in fact his legally married wife. As Umberto has already won her love, she raises no objection, and determines that Massa-Carrara shall make peace with Genoa. The bells of peace serve also as wedding bells for her and Umberto ('Mein ist das Commando noch für heut''/'Süsse Friedensglocken').

Thus the merry war is over, as news arrives that the dancer who caused the whole affair will come neither to Genoa nor to Massa, since she has eloped with a male dancer. For their part, Violetta and Umberto can give hearty thanks for the war that brought them together (Finale III: 'Mag um Ruhm und um Ehr').

DER BETTELSTUDENT

(The Beggar Student)

an operetta in three acts by F Zell and Richard Genée based on *Fernande* by Victorien Sardou and *The Lady of Lyons* by Edward Bulwer-Lytton. Music by Carl Millöcker. Produced at the Theater an der Wien, Vienna, 6 December 1882 with Alexander Girardi (Symon), Josef Joseffy (Jan), Caroline Finaly (Laura), Frln Jona (Bronislawa), Therese Schäfer (Palmatica) and Felix Schweighofer (Ollendorf). Produced at the Carltheater 18 November 1883. Produced at the Raimundtheater 8 May 1901. Produced at the Jantsch-Theater 17 October 1902. Produced at the Volksoper in a version by Eugen Otto 24 March 1909 and 29 October 1983 with Adolf Dallapozza, Kurt Schreibmayer, Milena Rudiferia, Elisabeth Kales, Sonja Mottl and Peter Minich. Produced at the Staatsoper 17 June 1936 with Margit Bokor, Dora Komarek, Richard Sallaba, Alfred Jerger and Frederick Gynrod.

Produced at the Friedrich-Wilhelmstädtisches Theater, Berlin, 24 January 1883.

Produced at the Thalia Theater, New York, 19 October 1883 with Marie Geistinger, Schütz, Emma Seebold, Dora Friese and Carl Adolf Friese. Produced at the Casino Theatre in a version by Emil Schwab as *The Beggar Student* 29 October 1883 with William T Carleton, W S Rising, Bertha Ricci, Mathilde Cottrelly and Fred Leslie. Revived there 6 October 1884 with Mark Smith, Charles H Clark, Lilly Post, Laura Joyce Bell, Cottrelly and Digby Bell; and again 22 March 1913 with George Macfarlane, Arthur Aldridge, Blanche Duffield, Anna Wheaton and De Wolf Hopper. Played at the Heckscher Theatre 17 November 1930 with Robert Betts.

Produced at the Alhambra Theatre, London, in a four-act version by W Beatty-Kingston 12 April 1884 with Fannie Leslie, Henry Hallam, Marion Hood, Madge

Stavart, Irene Verona and Fred Mervin. Produced at the Comedy Theatre 13 December 1886 with Henry Bracy, John Child, Ada Lincoln, Lucy Franklein, Elinor Loveday and Mervin. Played at the Royalty Theatre 12 January 1895 with Ilona Cservary, Amanda Borges, Georg Schulhof and Emil Katzorke.

Produced at the Théâtre des Menus-Plaisirs, Paris, in a version by E Hermil and A J Numès as *L'Étudiant Pauvre* 18 January, 1889 with Marcellin, Clara Lardinois and Mlle Freder. Played at the Théâtre du Vaudeville 30 June 1911.

Film versions were produced in 1922; by Jacob and Luise Fleck in 1927 with Harry Liedtke; by Victor Janson in 1931 with Hans Heinz Bollmann, Jarmila Novotna, Fritz Schulz, Truus van Alten and Hans Jaray; by Georg Jacoby in 1936 with Johannes Heesters, Marika Rökk, Carola Höhn, Ida Wüst and Fritz Kampers; and in 1956.

CHARACTERS

Palmatica, *Countess Nowalska*
Laura }
Bronislawa, } *her daughters*
Colonel Ollendorf, *Governor of Crakow*
Major von Wangenheim, Captain von Henrici, Lieutenant von Schweinitz, Cornettist von Richthofen, *in the service of Saxony*
Bogumil Malachowsky, *Palmatica's cousin*
Eva, *his daughter*
Jan Janicki, Symon Rymanovicz, *students at Cracow University*
The Mayor of Cracow
Onuphrie, *Palmatica's womanservant*
Enterich, *a disabled Saxon soldier and jail superintendent*
Piffke, Puffke, *jailers of the Citadel in Cracow*
Rej, a *landlord*
A courier, students, noblemen, noblewomen, citizens of Cracow, traders, country folk, Polish jews, a group of musicians, Saxon soldiers, colour-bearers, pages, servants, children, prisoners

ACT 1

It is the year 1704 and Poland is ruled by Friedrich August II, known as August the Strong, who has become King of Poland as well as Elector of his native Saxony. A group of women are gathered in the courtyard of the jail in Cracow where their menfolk are held as political prisoners from the troubles between Poland and Saxony ('Ach, unsre Lieben sperrte man ein'). The women have come with provisions for their loved ones and, when the jail superintendent Enterich comes to warn them to stop making disturbance, they manage to persuade him to let the prisoners out for a while ('Ach guter Meister Enterich'). As his reward, the jailer helps himself to a good deal of the food, which provides a hearty breakfast for himself and for his assistants Piffke and Puffke ('Beim Trinken, Essen fliehet der Verdruss').

Suddenly the admissions bell rings and a troop of royal officers appears. They have been ordered there by the governor, Colonel Ollendorf. The young soldier von Richthofen starts to tells of how Ollendorf had taken a fancy to the Polish Countess Laura Nowalska at a ball the previous day but, before the whole tale can be told, Ollendorf storms in. He promptly proceeds to give his own version of how he gave the proud Countess a kiss on her shoulder, only to receive a slap across the face from her fan as his reward ('Und da soll man noch galant sein'/'Ach ich hab' sie ja nur auf die Schulter geküsst').

Ollendorf is furious over the insult and his anger is all the greater for a letter he has received from Laura's mother calling him a braggart and dismissing the entire Saxon army as stable-boys. The old Countess goes on to write that her daughter will only marry a Polish prince, and this boast has given Ollendorf the idea for a plan of revenge. He tells Enterich to bring out his most handsome young prisoner and the jailer offers a choice of two—a couple of Polish rebel students called Jan Janicki and Symon Rymanowicz who have befriended each other in jail. The two men have lost their belongings and their freedom, but certainly not their high spirits ('Die Welt hat das genialste Streben'/'Aus solchem Chaos bricht der Humor').

Ollendorf's proposition that one of them should get married inclines the two to feel that they would merely be changing one form of imprisonment for another, but the Colonel's offer of 10,000 thalers is sufficient to win them over. It is agreed that Symon should pose as the wealthy Prince Wybicki with the aim of winning the Countess Laura Nowalska in marriage. Jan will pose as the Prince's secretary. The two young Poles do not know the reason for the deception, but they are happy enough to be free again to serve their beloved Poland. Both swear never to reveal details of their agreement, and they bid farewell to their cramped cell with enthusiasm ('So leb' denn wohl, du enge Zelle').

In the Ringplatz in Cracow, the spring holiday is beginning with the celebration of mass ('Juchheissa! die Messe beginnt') when Countess Palmatica comes by with her daughters, Laura and Bronislawa, out to do their shopping ('Einkäufe machen'). Their reduced circumstances mean that they haven't any money at the moment, but Palmatica's pride will not allow her to admit this and so the family press on with mere window-shopping. It becomes evident that Laura has inherited the pride of her mother, but Bronislawa has retained more of her natural modesty.

Ollendorf and his officers meet the Countess and her daughters, and find them most receptive to an invitation to dinner. During the meal, Ollendorf tells them of the young Polish prince and millionaire who is seeking to marry a young and pretty Cracow girl within the week. Soon Symon and Jan Janicki arrive and are presented as Prince Wybicki and his secretary ('Das ist der Fürst Wybicki mit seinem Sekretär!'). To the officers' great delight, Symon makes an excellent job of playing the role of the Prince and he cleverly courts Countess Laura, glorifying Polish women at the expense of other nationalities he has known ('Ich knüpfte manche zarte Bande').

Laura is instantly taken by the Prince and is soon happy to agree to becoming his wife (Finale I: 'Du bist die Seine? Er ist die Deine?'). Ollendorf and his men join in the congratulations, but the colonel is taken aback at the pleasure Symon takes in inviting all the soldiers to the sumptuous wedding reception—all, Ollendorf reflects, at his expense. Laura persuades the soldiers that they should all learn a Polish national song, which she and Symon proceed to teach them ('Höchste Lust und tiefstes Leid') and, as the town band marches on, everyone joins in the celebrations of the national holiday ('Bei solchem Feste').

ACT 2

In a elegant room in Countess Nowalska's palace, the Countess, Laura and Bronislawa are dressing for the wedding ceremony ('Einen Mann hat sie gefunden'). Palmatica gives Laura a few words of pre-marital advice ('Die Eh' macht dann erst Spass der Frau'), before she and Laura go off, leaving Bronislawa alone. When Jan comes to find her, it becomes evident that they are now deeply in love and ready to tread the same path as her sister and Symon ('Durch diesen Kuss'/'Nur das Eine bitt' ich dich, liebe mich'). They depart arm in arm.

All is not, however, going as well as it seems for Symon. The 10,000 thalers placed at his disposal by Ollendorf have all gone and, to his horror, he believes that he really loves Laura. He decides that he must reveal the truth to her at once and, when Jan comes to him and tells him that he and Bronislawa are in love, Symon reflects wryly that Jan seems to be intoxicated, while he is the one with the hangover. Now Jan reveals to his friend that he is not a student at all, but a Polish officer and a supporter of the exiled Polish King Stanislaus Leszczynski whose nephew, Duke Adam Casimir, is currently in Cracow maturing plans to overthrow the regime of the Saxon Elector. Jan begs Symon to keep silent for the sake of the fatherland.

When Symon is left alone with Laura, who has by now quite definitely come to love her bridegroom-to-be, he debates whether he dare make his confession to her but, in the end, he does no more than test what her reaction would be ('Soll ich reden? Darf ich schweigen?'/'Ich setz' den Fall'). Their hearts are by now beating too strongly for serious discussion.

Laura departs, and Symon decides that the best he can do is to set down the truth in a letter. When Palmatica comes to fetch her prospective son-in-law for the wedding ceremony, Symon gives her the letter but Ollendorf and his followers arrive in the nick of time, having been warned by Jan of Symon's state of mind, and Ollendorf cunningly manages to extract the paper from the old Countess as the bridal procession approaches ('Glückliche Braut').

Assured by Ollendorf that Laura has received his letter, Symon assumes that she has read the confession and wishes to be married to him nonetheless. Ollendorf and his officers are anticipating the success of their plot with amusement but, during the ceremony, Ollendorf receives a message telling him that Jan Janicki is really Count Opalinski and a Captain of the expelled Polish king's army. He calls the supposed student to account and demands that he reveal the whereabouts of Adam Casimir. Jan pretends to allow himself to be bribed with the sum of 200,000 gulden, money which he intends to employ in the fight for Poland's freedom, and departs, leaving

Ollendorf delighting over the apparent success of yet another scheme ('Schwamm drüber!').

The wedding procession now returns (Finale II: 'Klinget, Feierglocken, klinget!'). The officers congratulate the couple, and the champagne is uncorked ('Trinkt uns zu, trinkt uns zu') but, as the dancing begins, the sound of voices is heard outside and Ollendorf sarcastically announces the arrival of the bridegroom's especial friends. In come Enterich, Piffke and Puffke, at the head of the whole company of political prisoners ('Heidahi, heidaha! Sind wir auch nicht invitiert?'). As the jailers reveal that Symon is nothing but a beggar student, Symon discovers to his dismay that Laura had never received his letter, and Ollendorf is able to rejoice in the apparent success of his revenge.

ACT 3

Symon stumbles out into the garden of the Countess Nowalska's palace, his clothes in disarray, as the wedding guests chase him from the house in disgust ('Lumpen, Bagage, Bettelstudent!'). As he contemplates his unhappy situation, Bronislawa passes by, no less depressed at the ending of her own dream ('Der Fürst soll nur ein Bettler sein').

Symon is in despair, but Jan points out that the situation can still be retrieved. He suggests a way in which Symon can play a part for his country such that, if the Polish King is returned from exile to power, Symon will most certainly be well rewarded. Symon must once more play a role, this time pretending to be Duke Adam Casimir, whom Jan has promised to render up to Ollendorf. It is a masquerade which could turn out badly for Symon, but he is glad to give his life's blood for his beloved Poland ('Ich hab' kein Geld, bin vogelfrei').

Jan presents Symon to Ollendorf as the Polish Duke ('Still man kommt!' 'Dort steht der Patron!'). Ollendorf pronounces him under arrest but, in the meantime, the insurgent Poles have begun storming the fortress. The sound of cannon-fire is heard, and in no time at all the Saxon forces are overwhelmed. The Polish King is reinstated, and Symon is made a Count as a reward for his loyal and dangerous impersonation. He is reunited with Laura, who knows that she truly loves him, and Jan and Bronislawa likewise announce that their future lies together. There is great rejoicing amongst the Nowalska family and amongst the entire Polish nation (Finale III: 'Befreit das Land! Geknüpft das Band!').

EINE NACHT IN VENEDIG

(A Night in Venice)

an operetta in three acts by F Zell and Richard Genée after *Le Château Trompette* by

Jules Cormon and Michel Carré. Music by Johann Strauss. Produced at the Friedrich-Wilhelmstädtisches Theater, Berlin, 3 October 1883 with Jani Szika (Caramello), Ottilie Collin (Annina), Sigmund Steiner (Duke) and Reinhold Wellhof (Pappacoda). Produced at Baden-Baden in a revised version by Carl Hagemann August 1918. Produced at the Opernhaus, Berlin, in the Korngold/Marischka version 20 February 1931. Produced at the Komische Oper, Berlin, in a revised version by Walter Felsenstein, 1954.

Produced at the Theater an der Wien, Vienna, 9 October 1883 with Alexander Girardi, Caroline Finaly, Josef Joseffy, Felix Schweighofer and Rosa Streitmann (Ciboletta). Produced there in a revised version by Ernst Marischka and Erich Wolfgang Korngold 1923 with Richard Tauber (Duke). Produced at the Carltheater 16 November 1883. Produced at the Staatsoper 23 June 1929. Produced at the Raimundtheater in a revised version by Gustav Quedtenfeld 31 December 1944. Produced at the Volksoper in a revised version by Anton Paulik 1948 with Esther Réthy and Helge Roswaenge, and revived there 25 October 1975 with Adolf Dallapozza, Mirjana Irosch, Alois Aichorn, Kurt Huemer and Julia Migenes. Produced on the lake stage at Bregenz in a further revised version by Anton Paulik 1955, 1965 and 1975.

Produced at the Cambridge Theatre, London, in a version by Lesley Storm and Dudley Glass as *A Night in Venice* 25 May 1944 with Dennis Noble, Daria Bayan, Henry Wendon and Jerry Verno. Produced at the London Coliseum (English National Opera) in a revised version by Murray Dickie, Anton Paulik and László Imre 8 December 1976 with Ramon Remedios, Valerie Masterson, Emile Belcourt and Alan Opie.

Produced at Daly's Theatre, New York, in an English version 26 April 1884 with W H Fitzgerald, Louise Lester, Wallace Macreery, E L Connell and Marie Hunter. Produced at the Jones Beach Marine Theatre 1952.

Produced at the Théâtre de Monte-Carlo, Monaco, 19 March 1930.

CHARACTERS

Guido, *Duke of Urbino*
Bartolomeo Delacqua, Stefano Barbaruccio, Giorgio Testaccio, *senators of Venice*
Barbara Delacqua, Agricola Barbaruccio, Constantia Testaccio, *their wives*
Annina, *a fisher-girl, Barbara's foster-sister*
Caramello, *the Duke's personal barber*
Pappacoda, *a macaroni cook*
Ciboletta, *a cook in Delacqua's service*
Enrico Piselli, *a naval officer, Delacqua's nephew*
Centurio, *the Duke's page*
Senators' wives, musicians, servants, gondoliers, people of Venice

ACT 1

It is an evening in eighteenth-century Venice. In a square on the Grand Canal, with a view across to the Ducal Palace and the Isle of San Giorgio, the people are are strolling around as the sun goes down ('Wenn vom Lido sacht wieder Kühlung weht'), while the tradeswomen call their wares ('Peschi, peschi freschi!'). The young Neapolitan macaroni cook Pappacoda pipes up with the observation that, for all the splendours of Venice, they do not

922

have everything without their macaroni cook ('Ihr Venetianer, hört, was Pappacoda wert!'/'Ihr habet euren Markusplatz'). 'Macaroni as long as the Grand Canal, with as much cheese as there is sand in the Lido'—that is what Pappacoda offers. The young man is approached by Enrico, a naval officer, enquiring whether the Senator Delacqua is at home. When he is told that he is at a sitting of the Senate, Enrico sees it as an opportunity for a few private minutes with the Senator's young wife Barbara. However, she too is out, so Enrico slips Pappacoda a coin to give Barbara a letter, with the message that Enrico will be ready for her at nine o'clock that evening.

As the people watch, a boat arrives carrying Annina, a fisher-girl, calling her wares ('Seht, o seht! Seht, o seht!' 'Frutti di mare!'). Pappacoda greets her, hinting that what has really brought her hither is the imminent arrival of the Duke of Urbino, and more particularly his barber Caramello, Annina's sweetheart. 'Caramello is a monster, a ne'er-do-well, and a conceited block-head into the bargain,' she pouts. 'Stupidity is no hindrance to love,' Pappa-coda retorts, sampling an oyster. 'After all, I'm passionately in love with Ciboletta, Signora Delacqua's pretty cook—a girl as stupid as this oyster, and yet just as appetising, just as worthy of catching!'

When Barbara Delacqua returns home, Pappacoda gives her the message from Enrico and receives another tip for his troubles. Annina departs with Barbara, leaving Pappacoda to greet his own girlfriend, Ciboletta. She is wondering when they are going to get married, and he promises that they will do so just as soon as he gets a position in service ('Heiraten, ja, das wird mich freu'n'/''s ist wahr, ich bin nicht allzu klug').

The senators return from a stormy session, discussing the banquet that the Duke of Urbino is to give today when he arrives for his annual Carnival-time visit to Venice. The Duke is a notorious womaniser and has already cast his avid eyes on Barbara, so Delacqua has taken the precaution of arranging for his wife to be taken by gondola to Murano to stay with an old abbess aunt in the convent there.

The Duke's arrival is signalled by the appearance of a gondola carrying his personal barber, Caramello, who is warmly greeted by the crowd ('Eviva Caramello, des Herzogs Barbier!'). He proceeds to show off his close acquaintance with the Duke ('Der Herzog von Urbino') and rounds things off with an agile tarantella for good measure ('Eine neue Tarantelle zeig' ich'). He quickly spots Annina ('Annina!' 'Caramello!'), but she is not too pleased that he has practically ignored her for the past year. She becomes interested enough when the subject of their talk turns to marriage, but Caramello explains that he is anxious to obtain the position as the Duke's steward before committing himself to matrimony.

In pursuit of amorous adventures on his master's behalf, Caramello has learned with interest from Pappacoda that a gondolier is due to take Barbara Delacqua to Murano at 9 p.m. What he does not know is that his own girlfriend, Annina, has been persuaded by Barbara to take her place in the gondola, so that Barbara may spend her time with Enrico Piselli. Annina is determined to be back within the hour so that she may join in the Carnival dancing with Caramello, Pappacoda and Ciboletta in masks borrowed from

923

their masters ('Alle maskiert').

The Duke arrives and greets Venice and its people. He loves them all, he tells them, though it is noticed that he seems to love the pretty girls rather more than the rest. To the Duke's great delight, Caramello reveals to him his plan to take the place of the gondolier in the gondola calling for Barbara. Instead of taking her to Murano, he will then deliver her to the Duke's palace. Pulling on a gondolier's cloak and hood, he sets off on his adventure.

The scene is set and the evening still, as the Duke looks up to Delacqua's balcony and sings a serenade (Finale I: 'Hier ward es still'/'Der Mond hat schwere Klag' erhob'n'). Inside the Delacqua house Barbara and Annina are making their final preparations, putting on the dominoes that will disguise them, as they await the sound of the gondolier's song that is to be the agreed signal. Down below Ciboletta brings Pappacoda a carnival costume ('Hast du mir ein Kostüm gebracht für uns're heut'ge Faschingsnacht?').

Finally the voice of Caramello is heard from the gondola singing the gondolier's song ('Ho-aho! Ho-aho! Komm in die Gondel!'). Delacqua helps into the gondola the masked figure he believes to be his wife ('Komm nur, liebes Kind!'), and he bids her farewell as the Duke looks on with keen anticipation. A group of sailors appear and, with Enrico at their head, they sing a serenade to Delacqua for his birthday the following day ('Zur Serenade!'/'Mit der Würde die dir eigen'). While Delacqua is on the balcony thanking the singers, Barbara slips out below to join Enrico. The birthday serenade merges with the sound of Caramello's gondola song as night falls on Venice and the disguised Caramello glides away with his masked sweetheart Annina, neither knowing the true identity of the other.

ACT 2

Watching from a room in his palace, the Duke is eagerly awaiting the arrival of the gondola in which Caramello is due to bring Barbara, as Agricola, Constantia and the other senators' wives arrive in their carnival costumes, ignoring their husbands' fears for their moral safety ('Nur ungeniert hereinspaziert!'/'Venedigs Frauen herzuführen'/'So ängstlich sind wir nicht'). Finally the gondola in seen approaching, and the Duke ushers his guests into the ballroom while he prepares to greet his special lady guest. When Caramello and Annina arrive and masks are removed, Caramello is dismayed to discover who it is he has brought for the Duke's pleasure, but Annina fancies making the most of the opportunity with the Duke that fate has given her ('Was mir der Zufall gab'').

Caramello does his best to warn the Duke off Annina. 'Don't trust her. She scratches and bites!' he warns. Finally Annina and the Duke are left alone ('So sind wir endlich denn allein'), and the disguised Annina is shocked and thrown on the defensive when the Duke rhapsodises over the receptive response that his advances to Barbara had previously aroused ('Sie sagten meinem Liebesfleh'n Gewährung zu'). As the orchestra in the ballroom strikes up a waltz, the Duke takes the reluctant Annina into his arms ('Ach, was ist das?'/'Im Saale tanzen meine Gäste').

Caramello finds an excuse to interrupt the amorous scene and Annina persuades the Duke to take her into the ballroom. While they are away, Caramello opens the doors to the Duke's apartments and a crowd enters, including Pappacoda, prominent in a faded, shabby senator's costume with false, misshapen nose and spectacles and with his pockets stuffed with sausages, meat and pastries. Pappacoda has brought with him all his tradesmen friends, to whom he has distributed invitations given to him by Caramello. They are wide-eyed at the scale of the Duke's hospitality ('Solch ein Wirtshaus lob' ich mir') and, having introduced his friends to Caramello, Pappacoda invites them to help themselves ('Man steckt ein').

As the Duke seeks somewhere to be alone with Annina, a group of senators and their wives detain him. Among them are Senator Delacqua and his supposed wife, and the Duke is taken aback at being introduced to a second Barbara. However, Annina identifies this 'wife' for the Duke as the masked Ciboletta. The Duke goes along with Ciboletta's pretence, as he recalls the serenade he had sung to Barbara at previous carnival times ('Ninana, Ninana, Dir will ich singen').

Delacqua pushes the supposed Barbara forward to put his own case for the position of the Duke's steward, but Ciboletta instead asks for a place for Pappacoda as the Duke's personal cook and the Duke is only too ready to oblige her. Delacqua departs to join Barbara in Murano, leaving the Duke to take supper with Annina and Ciboletta (Finale II: 'Lasset die ander'n nur tanzen da'). Caramello has sent away the servants, and he and Pappacoda wait on the trio personally in order to keep their eyes open for any unwelcome developments.

As the Duke courts the two ladies, Caramello and Pappacoda repeatedly interrupt. The cook gives a timely discourse on his culinary arts ('Takke, takke, tack, erst hack' ich fein') before the senators' wives arrive seeking the Duke's attention ('Nur ungeniert hereinspaziert'). By now midnight is approaching—the time when the Duke must go to lead the revels in Saint Mark's Square ('Jetzt ist's Zeit zur Lustbarkeit'). When the bells of Saint Mark's sound out ('Horch! Von San Marco der Glocken Geläut''), Annina joins in the revelry ('Jetzt gebietet nur Humor') and all go off in masks to enjoy themselves ('Alle maskiert')

ACT 3

In Saint Mark's Square, before the moonlit cathedral, the revellers are celebrating ('Karneval ruft uns zum Ball') but Caramello stands alone, reflecting upon Annina's flirtation with the Duke and lamenting the fickleness of women ('Ach, wie so herrlich zu schau'n').

Ciboletta, meanwhile, is looking for Pappacoda to tell him of his appointment as the Duke's personal cook, a piece of news that dispels Pappacoda's wrath at Ciboletta's adventures with the Duke. Now they can marry. When Pappacoda goes to pay his respects to the Duke, Ciboletta reveals to the Duke that the young lady on whom he had been lavishing his attention was not Barbara but Caramello's sweetheart Annina. When the Duke finally

925

catches up with Annina, he finds her telling the senators' wives all about her escapade with him ('Ein Herzog reich und mächtig'). Fanfares announce the start of the grand Carnival procession, in which all sections of Venetian life are represented and, when it is over, the pigeons of Saint Mark's flutter down into the square (Finale III: 'Die Tauben von San Marco').

Delacqua has returned, distressed by the discovery that Barbara is not in Murano and, when she appears with Enrico, the young man reassures Delacqua with a story of how he has rescued his aunt Barbara from an impostor gondolier. The Duke is decidedly less interested in Barbara when he discovers that she has a nephew as big as Enrico, and he rewards Caramello for delivering him from a potentially awkward situation by making him his steward. Caramello and Annina can therefore join Pappacoda and Ciboletta in marrying, and the revelries are set fair to go on long into the night ('Wie sich's gebührt, hat er's gespürt').

The above synopsis follows the original text as finalised during the first Viennese run. The work is commonly performed in the 1923 revision by Ernst Marischka and Erich Wolfgang Korngold which, in the interests of smoothing the action, makes cuts and revisions to both dialogue and music. In particular, two numbers are added to build up the part of the Duke—'Sei mir gegrüsst, du holdes Venezia!' (to music from *Simplicius*) in Act 1 and 'Treu sein—das liegt mir nicht' in Act 2 to the music originally given to Annina for 'Was mir der Zufall gab'.

GASPARONE

an operetta in three acts by F Zell and Richard Genée. Music by Carl Millöcker. Produced at the Theater an der Wien, Vienna, 26 January 1884 with Maria Therese Massa (Carlotta), Rosa Streitmann (Sora), Alexander Girardi (Benozzo), Josef Joseffy (Erminio) and Felix Schweighofer (Nasoni). Produced at the Jantsch-Theater 24 October 1901. Produced at the Volksoper 21 April 1915, and again in a revised version by Paul Knepler and Ernst Steffan 10 February 1933. Revived there 3 March 1980 with Marjon Lambriks, Helga Papouschek, Erich Kuchar, Franz Wächter and Karl Dönch. Produced on the lake stage, Bregenz, 1950 in a further revised version by Rudolf Kattnigg and Anton Paulik.

Produced at Dresden 13 April 1884. Produced at the Friedrich-Wilhelmstädt-isches Theater, Berlin, 26 September 1884.

Produced at the Thalia Theater, New York, 21 February 1885 with Max Lube (Nasoni), Eduard Elsbach (Erminio), Bertha Kierschner (Carlotta), Emmy Meffert (Cora) and Ernst Gschmeidler (Sindulfo), and at the Standard Theatre in an English version on the same date with Richard Mansfield, Harry Hilliard, Emma Seebold, Mae St John and W H Fitzgerald. Played at the Thalia Theater in a new version as *Die Banditen* January 1887 with Carl Adolf Friese, R Sinnhold, Sophie Offeney, Meffert and Conrad Junker.

A film version with music by Peter Kreuder and Friedrich Schröder was produced by Georg Jacoby in 1937 with Marika Rökk, Leo Slezak and Johann Heesters.

CHARACTERS

Carlotta, *widowed Countess of Santa Croce*
Baboleno Nasoni, *Mayor of Syracuse*
Sindulfo, *his son*
Count Erminio
Luigi, *his friend*
Benozzo, *a landlord*
Sora, *his wife*
Zenobia, *duenna of the Countess*
Marietta, *the Countess's maid*
Massaccio, *a smuggler, Benozzo's uncle*
Colonel Ruperto Corticelli
Lieutenant Guarini
Pamfilio, Pietro, Giuseppe, Dominico, *smugglers*
Bianca, Marguerita, Isabella, *Sora's friends*
Lucia, Fiametta, Sybilla, Giugliana, *milkmaids*
Beata, Eleonora, Emilia, Renata, *peasant-girls*
People of Syracuse, policemen, customs officers, smugglers, boatmen, peasants

ACT 1

The year is 1820 and the scene the Mediterranean coast near the town of Syracuse in Sicily. A band of smugglers approach a seaside inn and begin concealing a ship's cargo of sugar and coffee in the cellar ('Hört nur, hört den wohlbekannten Ton'). The landlord of the inn, Benozzo, is the nephew of the leader of the smugglers, Massaccio, and he has circulated the rumour that the notorious bandit, Gasparone, is again active in Sicily in order to set the customs officers off on a false trail and keep them occupied away from the activities at the inn. As a result of Benozzo's well laid stories, the mayor of Syracuse, Nasoni, is even now on the bandit's trail together with a posse of customs officers.

The conversation between Massaccio and Benozzo is overheard by a young nobleman, Erminio, and his friend Luigi, but the price of their silence is soon enough agreed. Count Erminio happens to have acquired an admiration for a widowed countess, Carlotta, and it is arranged that Massaccio and Benozzo will waylay the coach carrying the Countess Carlotta and carry off her old dragon of a duenna, Zenobia. Erminio will then appear on the scene as Carlotta's saviour. The customs officers arrive, despairing of their unavailing search for Gasparone ('Erscheinen wir als Rächer'/'Der verdammte Gasparone') and Nasoni is discussing with Benozzo whether the bandit has actually been seen in Sicily, when the landlord's wife, Sora, arrives crying for assistance for the Countess Carlotta, who has been attacked by bandits ('Da ist sie—sprich, was ist geschehen?'). However, before Nasoni can go to her assistance, the Countess arrives on the scene with a description

927

of how she was rescued from her attackers by a gallant gentleman ('Ein höchst romantisch Abenteuer').

When Count Erminio appears following his gallant 'rescue' of Carlotta, Nasoni notices that his glances and hers are already meeting with a disturbing frequency. Since he is himself hoping to marry his son Sindulfo to the rich Countess in order to improve his family's finances, he insinuates that Count Erminio is the bandit Gasparone, but Erminio laughs off the suggestion. 'If only I were the robber!' he says, imagining what he would do with the proceeds of some profitable banditry ('O, dass ich doch der Räuber wär").

The Countess's old duenna, Zenobia, sweeps in, reporting that the bandits have not only freed her but given her two ducats to help her on her way. She and Nasoni watch with concern and interest the seeming decline in the Countess's interest in Nasoni's son ('Nun denn, so geh'n auch wir hinein'/'Ja, so sind die jungen Leute von heute!'). As mayor, Nasoni happens to know that a lawsuit the widowed Countess has been conducting to secure a considerable inheritance will shortly end in her favour and he intends that, before she learns of her resultant millions, she should become engaged to Sindulfo. Sindulfo, however, is a good-for-nothing fellow who spends much of his time chasing after Benozzo's young wife. This fact does not go unnoticed by Erminio and, when he and Countess Carlotta find themselves alone, he warns her about the unscrupulous pair ('Wie freu' ich mich, dass Sie noch hier!'/'Hüten Sie sich vor dem Räuberpaar').

Nasoni manages to persuade Carlotta that he can help sway the outcome of her legal case and, although Carlotta knows she does not love Sindulfo, she finally gives Nasoni her word that she will marry his son in return for his assistance. Conveniently, news now comes of the result of the judgement (Finale I: 'Hört von ferne das Geschrei') and the mayor unfolds a scroll and proceeds to read the verdict, detailing the extent of Carlotta's wealth ('So hört, was mein Mund euch jetzt verkündert!'). With the exception of Erminio, everyone is very happy for the Countess, and Sora, her former servant, leads them all in a lively tarantella ('Anzoletto sang Komm, mia bella!'). Suddenly Benozzo rushes in with the news that the prospective bridegroom, Sindulfo, has been kidnapped. It is the work of Gasparone, who has left a note demanding a ransom of 10,000 zechinen. Nasoni does not have the money to pay, but Carlotta at once agrees to find it and the wily Benozzo agrees to act as go-between in taking the ransom to Gasparone.

ACT 2

In the ballroom of the castle of Santa Croce much merrymaking and dancing is taking place to celebrate the engagement of the Countess and Sindulfo ('Hör doch die Töne, Estrella') while, in an adjoining room containing a safe holding Carlotta's newly acquired millions, Marietta, Sora and Zenobia are deep in conversation. Sora and Marietta are surprised that the Countess should go through with her engagement to Sindulfo in view of her evident attraction to Erminio, while the old duenna is still sulking over the fact that her encounter with the supposed Gasparone ended with her not even being deemed worthy of a ransom ('Der Blick von diesem Ungeheuer'/'Ach, es gibt keine Männer mehr!').

Nasoni is in a fearful rage, since his son has still not been released by Gasparone, but Countess Carlotta is perfectly happy in the company of Erminio as they go off to the ballroom together ('Durch dieses Schlosses weite Hallen'). Meanwhile Benozzo, with a fresh cargo of contraband to attend to, is wondering how he can get away from his unsuspecting wife Sora, but he ends up admitting his smuggling activities to her (''s ist gar nicht schön, mit solchen Fragen'/'Stockfinster war die Nacht').

Despite everything, Carlotta persists in honouring her word to Nasoni that she will marry Sindulfo, but she is dismayed when Erminio suddenly finds it necessary to leave the party. She is alone in the ante-room when a violent thunderstorm breaks out ('Dunkel breitet sich über das Meer'). Suddenly a window opens and Erminio climbs into the ante-room dressed as a robber. He demands from Carlotta the key to the safe, takes the millions of her inheritance that have been deposited there, and leaves, thanking the Countess courteously as he goes.

When Zenobia and Marietta come to call Carlotta for supper, they see what has happened and raise the alarm (Finale II: 'Herein! Herein! Nur alles herein!'). Although Carlotta has recognised the thief as Erminio, her feelings for him persuade her to say that it was the dreaded Gasparone who robbed her ('Weh! Kein Zweifel waltet nunmehr'). Suddenly Sindulfo appears with a tale of having been kept blindfold in a cellar full of sugar and coffee but, learning that the Countess's millions have been stolen, Nasoni is not anxious to confirm his son's engagement until the bandit has been captured and the money recovered.

ACT 3

Martial law is in force across Syracuse and the guards are assembled in front of the town hall ('Die Carabinieri marschieren ein'), preparing to flush out the elusive Gasparone. A judicial hearing has been arranged, much to the concern of Benozzo and Massaccio who, although they know that they are the kidnapping arm of Gasparone, have no idea who stole the Countess's millions. What if they were convicted of the whole lot? Benozzo determines to devote more attention to his loving wife in the future and less to the smuggling side of Syracuse ('Er soll dein Herr sein!').

Nasoni opens the judicial hearing and Sora and Zenobia give colourfully conflicting evidence to which Carlotta adds a deliberately confusing and false picture of the man who robbed her. But still, despite such efforts to protect Erminio, she continues to honour her word regarding her engagement to Sindulfo.

Erminio, who has noted with joy the protection that Carlotta continues to give him, seizes the opportunity to explain to her that he is really no robber and that his actions have been designed solely to show Nasoni in his true light. Benozzo and Massaccio, anxious to extricate themselves from the seemingly dangerous situation, arrive with a letter for Nasoni ('Herr Podestà, Herr Podestà!') which announces that, weary of tormenting Nasoni, Gasparone has decided to return to the mainland. He will even be returning the 10,000 zechinen ransom he obtained for Sindulfo. Although pleased by the bandit's strange change of heart, Nasoni's main interest still centres on the whereabouts of the very much larger sum which he is apparently not offering to return.

Erminio gives Nasoni a packet which he says contains a wedding present, but Nasoni returns it. He wants to hear no more about the wedding now that Carlotta has no fortune left. Now that she is formally released from her engagement, Carlotta falls into Erminio's arms. Then Erminio hands the packet to Carlotta. It contains the millions he had stolen earlier. Too late does Nasoni now protest that he would like the marriage between Sindulfo and the Countess to take place after all, as universal rejoicing breaks out that the affair of Gasparone is finally at an end (Finale III: 'Gasparone scheint Bess'rung zu zeigen!').

The synopsis follows the original version. The 1932 version by Ernst Steffan, which is most frequently heard and which introduces the song 'Dunkelrote Rosen', offers a substantial rewriting of both book and score.

DER ZIGEUNERBARON

(The Gipsy Baron)

a comic opera in three acts by Ignaz Schnitzer after the story *Sáffi* by Mór Jókai. Music by Johann Strauss. Produced at the Theater an der Wien, Vienna, 24 October 1885 with Carl Streitmann (Barinkay), Ottilie Colin (Sáffi), Alexander Girardi (Zsupán), Carl Adolf Friese (Carnero), Antonie Hartmann (Czipra) and Josef Joseffy (Homonay). Produced at the Staatsoper 26 December 1910. Produced at the Volksoper 23 March 1910, in 1948 with Esther Réthy and 16 October 1977 with Osvaldo di Pianduni, Mirjana Irosch, Erich Kunz, Hans Kraemmer, Gertrude Jahn and Heinz Holecek. Produced at the Schönbrunner Schloss-Theater 31 March 1946. Produced at the Rex-Theater 28 February 1949. Produced on the lake stage, Bregenz, 1951, 1961 and 1982.

Produced at the Friedrich-Wilhelmstädtisches Theater, Berlin, 5 February 1886.

Produced at Sadler's Wells Theatre, London, in a version by Geoffrey Dunn as *The Gipsy Baron* 9 June 1964 with Nigel Douglas, June Bronhill, Derek Hammond Stroud, Lawrence Folley, Ann Howard and James Hawthorne.

Produced at the Théâtre des Folies-Dramatiques, Paris, in a version by Armand Lafrique as *Le Baron Tzigane* 20 December 1895 with Monteux, Jane Pernyn, Paul Hittemans, Cave, Mlle Maya and Joubert. Played at the Théâtre du Vaudeville 1910.

Produced at the Casino Theatre, New York, in a version by Sydney Rosenfeld 15 February 1886 with William Castle, Pauline Hall, Francis Wilson, W H Fitzgerald and Mae St John. Produced at the Thalia Theater 1 April 1886 with Schütz, Franziska Kaberg, Bernhard Rank, Johanna Schatz and Eduard Elsbach. Produced at the New York City Opera 14 November 1944 with William Horne and Polyna Stoska. Produced at the Metropolitan Opera 1957 with Lisa Della Casa, Nicolai Gedda and Walter Slezak.

Film versions were produced by Karl Hartl in 1931; in 1935; and by Arthur Maria Rabenalt in 1954 in French and German versions with Georges Guétary, Gerhard Riedmann, Maria Sebalt, Oskar Sima, Harald Paulsen, Karl Schönböck and Margit Saad.

CHARACTERS

Count Peter Homonay, *Governor of Temesvar Province*
Conte Carnero, *Royal Comissioner*
Sándor Barinkay, *a young exile*
Kálmán Zsupán, *a wealthy pig-farmer of the Banat district*
Arsena, *his daughter*
Mirabella, *governess to Zsupán's daughter*
Ottokar, *her son*
Czipra, *a gipsy woman*
Sáffi, *a gipsy girl*
Pali, Józsi, Ferko, Mihály, Jancsi, *gipsies*
The Mayor of Vienna
Seppl, *a link boy*
Miksa, *a boatman,*
Irma, Tercsi, Aranka, Katicza, Juleska, Etelka, Jolan, Ilka, *Arsena's friends*
István, *Zsupán's servant*
A herald, boatmen, gipsies, gipsy children, gentlemen-at-arms, soldiers, pages, nobles, people

ACT I

The scene is a riverside swamp in the Banat district of the Hungarian province of Temesvar towards the middle of the eighteenth century. In the background is a ruined castle. The sound of oars and the voices of boatmen are heard in the distance, heralding the approach of two boats ('Das wär kein rechter Schiffersknecht'). Ottokar, son of the governess to the daughter of the wealthy pig farmer Zsupán, appears carrying an axe and spade, and starts to dig ('Jeden Tag, Müh und Plag'). He comes here every day to dig for the gold that is reputedly hidden on the land, but he never finds anything. The gipsy woman Czipra, peering out of her hut, mocks his efforts. Why, she asks him, is he not satisfied with the prospect of the dowry that would come with the hand of Arsena, the pig farmer's daughter, whom she has seen him courting?

The two boats reach the shore, and from them step the smartly dressed Royal Commissioner, Conte Carnero, and the somewhat down-at-heel young Sándor Barinkay. As the son of a landowner who was disgraced for having too close contacts with the former Turkish rulers of the province, Barinkay has been in exile for twenty years, but now he has been brought back to his estate by Carnero. The Commissioner asks him how he has been earning his living over the years, and Barinkay answers with a remarkable catalogue of occupations, including working in a zoo, sword-swallowing and other branches of entertainment ('Als flotter Geist'). Impressed though Carnero is by the young man's versatility, he wonders, as a member of the Morality Commission, whether such occupations are quite appropriate for someone who is now being restored to his position as a member of the landed gentry.

Carnero requires witnesses to the handing over of the title deeds to Barinkay's estate, so he enlists the services of Czipra and goes in search of Zsupán. Czipra's predictive powers have already told her that one day the owner of the estate would return ('So täuchte mich die Ahnung nicht') and now, as she goes on to read Barinkay's hand, she tells him that one day he will acquire not only an untold treasure but also a wife. When Carnero asks for his fortune to be told as well, she replies, to his disbelief, that he will recover a precious jewel that he had lost ('Verloren hast du einen Schatz').

Zsupán points out that he is not much use as a witness as he has never learned to read or write. He has always been too engrossed in pig-breeding ('Ja, das Schreiben und das Lesen'). He dutifully draws the shape of a pig on the land document as his mark, though he is none too pleased at the implications that Barinkay's return has for him. In the absence of his over-lord, Zsupán has made free use of his lands for his farming. However, when he hears that Barinkay is in search of a wife and notices the young man's undisguised interest in the fact that he has a beautiful daughter, Zsupán sees his chance of getting his hands on the treasure that is reputedly hidden on the estate. He is more than amenable to the idea of a match between Barinkay and his daughter.

He sends for Arsena, but it is the governess Mirabella and her son Ottokar who arrive first on the scene. Mirabella looks with considerable curiosity at Carnero and slowly realises that he is her long-lost husband and Ottokar's father. The second part of Czipra's prophecy, about the discovery of a lost jewel, has come true. Mirabella has not seen Carnero since the battle of Belgrade twenty-four years before. She had followed him there, disguised as his adjutant but, during the battles, she became separated from him and was eventually given up for dead ('Just sind es vierundzwanzig Jahre').

The veiled Arsena arrives, accompanied by her maids, to meet the man her father wants to urge as her husband ('Dem Freier naht die Braut'). Carnero, anxious in his offical position to maintain traditional moral standards, is concerned that Barinkay should not see his bride before the bridal cake is brought but, when a group of girls duly arrive with the cake ('Hochzeitskuchen, bitte zu versuchen') and the veil is lifted, Barinkay is suitably enchanted with what he sees. Arsena, however, with her heart set on Ottokar, swears that she will never marry Barinkay, and she issues a dark warning to her suitor to beware the moth that went too near the flame ('Ein Falter schwirt ums Licht'). She tells him that she has noble blood in her veins and that she could never consent to marry him unless he were at least a baron.

Barinkay is disappointed, but not defeated and, since he has no roof on his castle, he asks Zsupán for shelter for the night. However Carnero steps in again with the warning that a bridegroom should not enter the bride's home before a wedding and, as the company troop off ('Hochzeitskuchen, bitte zu versuchen'), Barinkay is left to fend for himself. Then he hears the voice of Sáffi, Czipra's daughter, singing a gipsy song ('So elend und so treu') and, watching and listening with growing interest, he recognises the song as one that his mother used to sing. Barinkay asks Czipra and Sáffi for help to find his way across the marshland to his castle but, when voices are heard, Czipra takes him into their hut.

The voices turn out to be those of Ottokar and Arsena on a lovers' meeting (Finale I: 'Arsena! Arsena!') and Barinkay reacts angrily when he hears his intended bride swear to Ottokar that she will never marry Barinkay. A band of gipsies arrive and greet Barinkay as their long-awaited lord and master and, seeing himself ennobled by the gipsies at least, he gets them to knock on Zsupán's door. 'Your son-in-law must be a baron?' he enquires. 'Well, now I am one.' He introduces himself as the baron of the gipsies, and Sáffi leads a declaration of allegiance ('Hier in diesem Land'), before he again asks Arsena for her hand. When she rejects him, he turns instead to Sáffi and asks her to be his wife, but his jibes at Arsena leave her, Zsupán and Ottokar vowing vengeance. Carnero, ever anxious to protect public morals, seeks to prevent Sáffi leaving with Barinkay but the gipsies swear to protect their 'baron' and, as Sáffi marvels at her good fortune, they raise him shoulder-high and carry him off in triumph.

ACT 2

Barinkay is asleep in the ruined castle's tower, while outside Sáffi lies cradled in Czipra's lap alongside the smithy buildings of the gipsy village. As dawn breaks, Czipra awakes ('Mein Aug' bewacht'), and Barinkay rises to describe the beautiful dream of his new beloved that he has just enjoyed, joining Sáffi in the mutual declaration of their new-found love. Czipra points out that a further part of her prophecy has come true, since Barinkay has now found a bride—and a treasure. Yet there is another treasure awaiting him. Czipra, too, has had a dream, in which the ghost of Barinkay's father appeared to her and told her the location of the treasure he had hidden on the estate ('Ein Greis ist mir im Traum erschienen'). It is hidden, she tells them, in a hollow stone in the tower. After Barinkay has spent some time tapping away, he duly finds a hollow stone which he wrenches free to reveal a hoard of gold and precious stones ('Ha, seht es winkt').

The gipsy Pali appears amongst the gipsy homes, beating a drum and summoning the gipsies to their day's duties ('Auf, auf, vorbei ist die Nacht'). They set to work in the smithy, singing as they work, and, when Barinkay arrives amongst them, they salute him as their master. Zsupán appears on the scene, his carriage having become stuck in the mud, bringing with him Arsena, Mirabella, Ottokar and Carnero. The President of the Morality Commission is fussing over Barinkay's elopement with Sáffi, but Barinkay presents Sáffi to him as his wife according to gipsy law. 'Who married you?' Carnero asks. 'Who married us?' Barinkay replies. 'The bullfinch—he married us.' And he proceeds to tell of their marriage under the stars, with the nightingale singing and two storks as witnesses ('Wer uns getraut?').

Carnero is not impressed by this lyrical version of marriage, and he proclaims in detail the duty of the Morality Commission to ensure decency and propriety ('Nur keusch und rein'). Barinkay reacts with contempt but, just then, Ottokar and Arsena spot the gold the Barinkay has found in the tower. Barinkay bars their way, claiming the treasure as his, but Carnero counter-claims that it is the spoils of an old war stolen by Barinkay's father.

Suddenly the sound of trumpets heralds the arrival of the governor of the province, Count Homonay, at the head of a troop of hussars. He has come to enrol Barinkay and the other men of the district in the war against Spain. Anyone who drinks a glass of recruiting wine pledges himself to fight for the fatherland ('Her die Hand, es muss ja sein'). A number of the men testify to their allegiance, but Zsupán and Ottokar, coming late onto the scene, drink the wine and only then realise that they have unwittingly enrolled.

Carnero takes the opportunity to seek the support of the governor in his case against Barinkay but Barinkay resolves the problem of the supposed theft of the treasure by freely giving it to the state. As for the morality charge, Homonay looks at Sáffi, and proclaims it scarcely surprising that Barinkay should wish to elope with such an attractive young woman. And now he has much more important matters to attend to than those of the Morality Commission.

All prepare to depart for Vienna (Finale II: 'Nach Wien!') but, as Zsupán and his household continue to fling insults at the gipsies, Czipra reveals that Sáffi is in reality not her daughter. She is, in fact, of princely birth, her father having been the last Pasha in Hungary. Now it is Barinkay who sees himself as unworthy of her. He declares that he will join the Hussars, takes the oath of allegiance, and marches off with the enlisted Hungarian soldiers into battle.

ACT 3

Two years later the war in Spain is over, and the crowds are gathered in front of the Kärntnertor in Vienna to welcome the victorious troops ('Freuet Euch!'). Arsena is there with Mirabella and Carnero, confessing to them that she has had little success in love since the war started and Ottokar was taken from her ('Ein Mädchen hat es gar nicht gut'). As they wait, Count Homonay arrives with a document addressed to Carnero, telling him of the dissolution of the Morality Commission. Then Zsupán enters to the cheers of the crowd, his Hussar's uniform covered with medals and with a rousing tale to tell of his exploits, which seem to have consisted largely of keeping away from the action and pillaging the victims of war ('Von des Tajos Strand').

Following this hero comes the main crowd of soldiers ('Hurrah die Schlacht mitgebracht') and at their head is the real hero of the war, Sándor Barinkay. Homonay hands him the certificate of his elevation to the nobility as a real baron and returns his treasure to him. At once, Zsupán changes his attitude to the gipsy baron. Barinkay, he decides, would now be a highly suitable son-in-law. But Barinkay points to Ottokar. He and only he must be Zsupán's future son-in-law ('Heiraten, Vivat!'). Then, to Barinkay's delight, he hears the voice of Sáffi pledging her loyalty to him. She is the real queen of his heart, from whom nothing can now keep him apart.

DER ARME JONATHAN

(Poor Jonathan)

an operetta in three acts by Hugo Wittmann and Julius Bauer. Music by Carl Millöcker. Produced at the Theater an der Wien, Vienna, 4 January 1890 with Alexander Girardi (Jonathan) and Ottilie Collin (Harriet). Produced at the Colosseumtheater 4 March 1897. Produced at the Volksoper 21 December 1952.

Produced at the Friedrich-Wilhelmstädtisches Theater, Berlin, 16 January 1890. Produced in East Berlin in a revised version by Walter Felsenstein in 1959. Produced at the Theater am Gärtnerplatz, Munich, 22 October 1959 with Ferry Gruber (Jonathan), Ingeborg Hallstein (Harriet), John van Kesteren (Vandergold) and E M Görgen (Molly).

Produced at the Casino Theatre, New York, in a version by J P Jackson and R A Weill as *Poor Jonathan* 6 October 1890 with Jefferson de Angelis (Jonathan), Lillian Russell (Harriet), Fanny Rice (Molly), Edwin Stevens (Tobias) and Harry Mac-Donough (Rubygold). Produced at the Amberg Theatre 2 January 1891 with J Brackl, Emma Seebold, Paula Loewe, Bernhard Rank and Adolf Philipp.

Produced at the Prince of Wales Theatre, London, in a version by C H E Brookfield and Harry Greenbank with additional music by Isaac Albéniz as *Poor Jonathan* 15 June 1893 with Harry Monkhouse, Annie Schuberth, Jessie Bond and Sidney Tower.

CHARACTERS

Vandergold, *a rich American*
Tobias Quickly, *an impresario*
Catalucci, *a composer*
Brostolone, *a bass singer*
Professor Dryander
Harriet, *his niece*
Count Nowalsky
Arabella, *his sister*
Holmes, *a lawyer*
Jonathan Tripp, Billy (*a Negro*), Molly, *servants of Vandergold*
François, *a police inspector*
Miss Big, Miss Hunt, Miss Grant *and other girl students*
A sheriff
Guests in Vandergold's house, visitors to Monaco, overseers, Negroes, Chinese, servants.

ACT 1

In the splendidly appointed dining hall of the Bostonian millionaire, Vandergold, his guests are seated at table celebrating their host's birthday ('Uns'rem edlen Wirthe, dieses Hauses Zirde'). They are thoroughly enjoying themselves, but having their work cut out to raise the spirits of their wealthy host. Nothing seems to cheer him, not even the performance by the composer Catalucci of a song he has written in his honour ('Wer ist der glücklichste Mensch auf der Welt?'). Vandergold has so much of everything that nothing means anything to him any more and he just sits there ill-humouredly, tired of his immense wealth and of the whole world.

The star attraction of the dinner is a lemon ice cream made in the shape of the sensation of the 1889 Paris Exhibition, the Eiffel tower. When this magnificent piece is carried in, it is greeted by the guests with great excitement and wonderment, but when they try it, they find it tastes abominable. Billy, the Negro servant, is summoned, and it becomes apparent that the cook has accidentally used soap as an ingredient instead of lemon. This incident does nothing to improve the mood of the glowering host, and he orders Billy to sack the careless cook at once.

This little upset does not disturb the guests' pleasure for too long, and the impresario, Tobias Quickly, tries to cheer Vandergold up with an account of some of the livelier incidents of his life ('Ja nur ein Impresario wird immer seines Lebens froh'). Then Vandergold's lawyer, Doctor Holmes, is announced. He has brought his wealthy client a deed of assignment, prepared on Vandergold's instructions, which gives away all the multimillionaire's possessions. Only the name of the intended recipient and Vandergold's own signature are missing. Everyone is astounded at this latest whim, but they are unable to dissuade Vandergold from his scheme. He intends to give away his entire fortune.

Harriet, the beautiful niece of Professor Dryander, has recently passed her medical examinations and she has been invited to the party with some of her fellow students. They come dressed in all their academic trappings ('Studentinnen in voller Wichs, das ist der neueste!') and the last to appear is Harriet, hailed by her friends with great acclaim on account of her newly won doctor's qualifications ('Vor alter Zeit wir hiessen das schwächere Geschlecht').

Vandergold is enchanted with Harriet, but the impresario Quickly is more taken by her glorious voice. She is asked to sing another song, and Vandergold offers her money to do so, but he is rebuffed by Harriet and her friends, who point out that he cannot acquire everything with money. However, anxious to dissuade Harriet from embarking on her career as a doctor, the impresario offers her a contract as singer in his opera company ('Wohlan, so unterschrieb' ich den Contract') and only then does she oblige with another song ('Willst du mein Liebster sein?').

When the guests have left the room, Jonathan, the sacked cook, appears, wondering what to do with himself now that he is out of a job ('O Gott, o Gott, was soll ich jetzt?'/'Ich bin der arme Jonathan') and his sweetheart, Molly, Vandergold's kitchen-maid, comes to join him in a tearful farewell.

Billy moves the sorrowful pair aside as Professor Dryander and Harriet enter. The Professor reproaches his niece over her rebuff of Vandergold. Does she not realise that she could have been the lucky recipient of the millionaire's largesse? When Harriet is left alone, Vandergold appears. He asks Harriet whether she loves him, but he receives only an evasive reply from the girl ('Mir ist es noch als ob es gestern wär') before she rushes off, leaving Vandergold with even this latest wish—to earn her love—unfulfilled.

Birthday or not, Vandergold decides that he will kill himself and, seating himself at his writing-table, he pulls a gun out of a drawer. First, though, he must make his will, and he unfolds the deed of settlement. The name of the beneficiary is still missing. While he is pondering as to whose name should go on the document, Jonathan enters the room with his bundle of belongings. He has no idea where he can lay his unemployed head, and he too has decided to kill himself. With his last few pfennigs he has bought himself a revolver and intends to end it all here and now.

And so, at one end of the room sits the wealthy man with a surfeit of everything, while at the other is the poor fellow who cannot make ends meet ('Nun ist es genug!' 'Nun bin ich entschlossen!'), and both are about to shoot themselves. They each move to the window and suddenly stand facing each other, revolvers in their hands. Vandergold assumes that the cook who mixed the dreadful desert now wants to kill him, but the misunderstanding is soon cleared up when he discovers that Jonathan only lacks money to be able to marry and be happy. The wealthy man has found what he has been seeking—a suitable recipient for his millions.

As the guests return, praising the impresario for brightening up the party (Finale I: 'Brillant, brillant, bei Gott, brillant!'), Vandergold brings in Jonathan and Molly. He asks Molly to tell him her heart's desire, at which she pours out her unhappiness at Jonathan's dismissal. Nothing good can come to Vandergold from it. Then Vandergold formally signs away his whole fortune to Jonathan, and all the millionaire's false friends and flatterers immediately begin to busy themselves courting the favour of the new master and mistress of the castle.

Jonathan and Molly want to set out immediately upon their wedding journey but, before bidding them farewell, Vandergold imposes one condition. If either Jonathan or Vandergold should again become tired of life, he should communicate it to the other through the song that Harriet had sung at the party, 'Willst du mein Liebster sein?'. Then they will pick up where they left off earlier and take their lives together.

ACT 2

In a gaming salon in Monaco, Molly, dressed in all her finery and telling stories of her travels, is thoroughly enjoying herself playing the part of the *grande dame* ('Zu gütig, oui, messieurs, c'est sûr'/'Wir reisen im ganzen Italien'). Jonathan is winning money from all his fellow-players, among them Count Nowalsky, his sister Arabella, and Quickly. While Jonathan is breaking the bank, Count Nowalsky takes the opportunity to make approaches to

Molly, but he is interrupted by the arrival of Jonathan. Already the two newlyweds are discovering that being rich is not all fun ('Als einst wir noch arm und dürftig waren').

Harriet, now a celebrated singer, appears complaining about the perils of the journey to Monte Carlo ('Unter tausend Fährlichkeiten'). Like Jonathan and Molly, she is not wholly happy. One way and another she is not finding the life of a prima donna as glamorous as she had imagined it would be ('Ach wir armen Primadonnen'). She says that she will not sing if Vandergold is not in the audience and, when she discovers that he is not there, she cancels her engagement. Quickly sees financial ruin staring him in the face ('Heuchler, Verleunder, Bruder Franz').

Vandergold is in town, but he, for some reason, has got the idea that Harriet has turned her attentions to Jonathan. Once more he believes he has lost the dearest thing left to him on earth and he decides once again to bring his life to an end (Finale II: 'Auf, auf, auf! Und lass' den Muth nicht sinken!') but, when he tries to sing the agreed song, despite a wholesale search among melodies from the operatic repertory, he finds cannot remember the tune. Jonathan, for his part, would be happy enough to hand back the entire fortune at once but, when it is discovered that Harriet has flown, Vandergold hurries despairingly after her.

ACT 3

In the gardens of Vandergold's former mansion in New York, the servants are up in arms. They consider that they are being subjected to all manner of drudgery and inconvenience and are threatening to walk out if they do not receive more pay ('Länger sind sie nicht zu tragen diese Qualen, diese Plagen').

This situation has been engineered by Harriet, who has decided to help Vandergold get back his belongings and she has enlisted Count Nowalsky and Arabella to assist her. They have determined to make life really difficult for Jonathan and Molly who are, indeed, finding their position a little too hot for comfort ('Die erste Fächerdame'). Things reach their nadir when Jonathan is arrested on suspicion of causing the mysterious disappearance of Vandergold.

Harriet arrives on the scene, hailed by her old student friends ('Sie kommt, sie kommt, schon ist sie da!') and greeting a crowd of reporters with a detailed account of her life story ('Geboren bin ich'). She is soon followed by the missing Vandergold in the uniform of a simple sailor. He has been round the world, and life at sea has enabled him to regain his zest for living ('Kreuz und quer bin ich gezogen auf dem weiten Erdenrund'). Harriet is overjoyed to see him and gladly accepts his proposal of marriage, while Jonathan is only too happy to give Vandergold back his property and resume service as his paid employee (Finale III: 'Willst du mein Liebster sein?').

DER VOGELHÄNDLER

(The Bird Seller)

an operetta in three acts by Moritz West and Ludwig Held after the comedy *Ce Qui Deviennent les Roses* by Varin and Biéville. Music by Carl Zeller. Produced at the Theater an der Wien, Vienna, 10 January 1891 with Alexander Girardi (Adam), Ilka Palmay (Christel) and Ottilie Collin (Princess Marie). Produced at the Landstrasser Theater 15 November 1900. Produced at the Volksoper 21 October 1974 with Adolf Dallapozza, Julia Migenes and Eva Serning. Produced on the lake stage, Bregenz, 1952 and 1984.

Produced at the Friedrich-Wilhelmstädtisches Theater, Berlin, 20 February 1891.

Produced at the Casino Theatre, New York, in a version by H F Tretbar as *The Tyrolean* in a double-bill with *Cavalleria Rusticana* 5 October 1891 with Marie Tempest, Annie Myers, Anna Mantell, Fred Solomon (Weps) and Jefferson De Angelis (Tipple). Produced at the Amberg Theatre 26 December 1892 with Carl Schulz, Lucie Berdier, Charlotte Tischler and Leopold Deutsch.

Played at the Theatre Royal, Drury Lane, London, 17 June 1895 with Mahling, Ilka Palmay, Frln Farkas, Reer and Bernhardt. Produced at the Palace Theatre in a version by Austin Melford, Rudolf Bernauer and Harry S Pepper as *The Bird-seller* 29 May 1947 with James Hetherington, Irene Ambrus and Adele Dixon, conducted by Richard Tauber.

Film versions were produced by E W Emo in 1935 with Wolf-Albach Retty, Maria Andergast, Lil Dagover, Georg Alexander and Hans Zesch-Ballott and in 1953 with Gerhard Riedmann and Ilse Werner.

CHARACTERS

Princess Marie
Baroness Adelaide, Countess Mimi, *ladies at Court*
Baron Weps, *Master of the Hunt*
Count Stanislaus, *his nephew, a Guards officer*
Süffle, Würmchen, *professors*
Adam, *a bird seller from the Tyrol*
Christel, *the post mistress*
Schneck, *the village mayor*
Frau Nebel, *the inn landlady*
Jette, *a waitress*
Tyroleans, people of the Pfalz, country folk, society people

ACT 1

In a village in the Rhineland Pfalz at the beginning of the eighteenth century, the country folk have gathered for a spot of illegal hunting on the estate of the elected prince ('Hurrah, hurrah! Her die Gewehr'!'). They feel safe from detection, for the Prince himself never comes that way and his wardens are too stupid to catch them. However, Schneck, the village mayor, suddenly appears, white-faced, and warns the poachers to hide their weapons. His Highness is coming in person, and Schneck's consternation is all the greater for the knowledge that the villagers have already shot all the wild boar on the estate.

939

Before the guilty crowd have had time to make their escape, Baron Weps, the Master of the Prince's Hunt, arrives on the scene. He is concerned as much as anything over what will happen to him if the Prince finds there are no wild boar for him to shoot ('Ihr habt gestohlen niederträchtig'). Schneck's offer of some tame pigs in replacement does not mollify the Baron until a handsome bribe comes into the reckoning. His Highness has also commanded that a pretty village girl should present him with a bouquet as a birthday gift. She has to be a virgin, though, and there aren't many more of those left in the village than there are wild pigs. 'How would a widow do?' they ask. Finally the matter is tactfully resolved, and Weps accepts the villagers' promise of a suitably respectful reception for the Prince.

When Weps has departed, a group of Tyroleans arrives ('Grüss enk Gott, alle miteinander'). Their leader is a young man named Adam, a bird seller who is besotted with the village postmistress Christel. She is the little dove he cares for above all else. Unfortunately for him Christel is busy on her post-round, and Jette, the waitress as the inn, suggests that perhaps Christel would give up her job and accept Adam's offer of marriage if he could win the vacant post of Menagerie Inspector in the Prince's employ.

Baron Weps has a Guards officer nephew called Stanislaus who has been running up some rash gambling debts. Up to now, Weps has dug into his purse to help the boy out, but he has no intention of doing so any more. He delivers some harsh words to the unreliable Stanislaus and suggests that he should seriously consider marrying the Princess's lady-in-waiting, Baroness Adelaide, who has a tidy sum of money at her disposal.

When a letter arrives for Weps with the news that the Prince has been called away on urgent business and will not be coming to hunt after all, the Baron is dismayed. No visit, no bribe! And what about the maid-of-honour who is being lined up for presentation to the Prince? It is Stanislaus who comes up with the suggestion that, for the sake of the money, he should himself impersonate the Prince, and Weps joins eagerly in a discussion of how they should greet the maid-of honour ('Als dir die Welt voll Rosen hing').

Baroness Adelaide happens to be amongst a group of ladies who now appear on the scene in the retinue of the Princess ('Schnell, kommt nur alle! Sind in der Falle'). The Princess has a particular love of this part of the Rhineland ('Fröhlich Pfalz'), but the purpose of the ladies' visit is not just pleasure. They have all come in disguise as village girls in the hope of being able to catch their men *in flagrante delicto*. Their disguise seems to work well enough. Very soon Adam is indulging in a spot of flirtation with a supposed peasant girl called Marie, who is actually none other than the Princess herself, and he even offers her a sprig of edelweiss in exchange for a kiss.

He is distracted when his sweetheart Christel arrives on the scene ('Ich bin die Christel von der Post'). Apparently Christel finds that some of her customers expect a kiss as a receipt for the postage payment, but she gets over it by retorting that the post doesn't move that quickly. She is genuinely fond of Adam, but their finances will not allow them to settle down to raise a family. So she, too, has in mind the thought of proposing Adam for the lucrative post of Menagerie Inspector.

When Weps and Stanislaus appear, Christel approaches the supposed Prince timidly ('Ach, Ihre Reputation ist just die beste nicht—Pardon!'). The two men are happy to give her a private audience in the pavilion nearby, and they assure her that the chances of someone as pretty as she is getting her wishes granted are distinctly good. Meanwhile the people are gathering to welcome the Prince (Finale I: 'Vivat! Hoch! Hurra! Nun gilt's loyal zu sein'). Schneck has some village girls ready lined up for the presentation, and he is most surprised to be told that the Prince already has a girl with him in the pavilion. Marie, determined to find out what her husband is up to, insists that she wishes to present the Prince with a bunch of roses all the same.

Weps prevaricates, but Christel is finally discovered inside the pavilion with Stanislaus. Adam is furious when he sees that the bouquet he has just given his sweetheart has now apparently been passed on to another man but Marie offers Adam her bouquet instead. Adam reacts with astonishment. After all, when people give each other roses in the Tyrol, it means that they are giving their hearts as well ('Schenkt man sich Rosen in Tirol').

Christel rushes out of the pavilion to tell Adam that he has been granted the appointment as Menagerie Inspector. Now they can get married. 'Man and wife? You and I?' he retorts. 'Never!' 'What do you mean, treasure?' she replies. 'Where is my bouquet?' Adam asks, and Christel has to admit that she has given it to 'the Prince'. Marie says that she will sort matters out, but she is too late for Stanislaus has flown. Pledging himself to take Marie as his wife instead of Christel, Adam bids farewell to the village.

ACT 2

The Prince's summer residence is buzzing with rumours of dreadful scenes between the Princess and her husband ('Haben Sie gehört? Alles ist verstört!'). When Weps returns, everyone crowds round him for news, and he does his best to give a convincing account without giving away his own rather suspect part in events. Meanwhile, Adam's recommendation for the post of Menagerie Inspector has involved him in coming before a selection panel consisting of two eccentric professors, Süffle and Würmchen, who pride themselves on their abilities as examiners ('Ich bin der Prodekan'). The Princess impresses upon the pair that Adam must win the selection, but Adam does not make things easy for them by refusing to take any examination. Nonetheless his deliberately obstructive answers to the professors' questions about his way with animals are greeted with warm approbation and he gets the job.

Christel bursts in, anxious to prove to Adam that her encounter in the pavilion was perfectly innocent. The Princess listens carefully to her tale ('Bescheiden, mit verschämten Wangen'), and she promises to do her best to restore Adam to Christel. When Christel has been left alone, Stanislaus enters. He tries to follow up the amorous approaches which he had begun in the pavilion, but Christel, still believing him to be the Prince, tells him that he is merely making a fool of himself and hotly denies that she was the girl in the pavilion ('Mir scheint, ich kenn' dich Spröde Fee!'/'Schau mir nur recht ins Gesicht').

Amidst the comings and goings, Adam finally discovers Marie's true identity when he hears Christel address the Princess as 'Your Highness'. Then Stanislaus's imposture starts to crumble. Christel tells the Princess that she has been speaking with her husband, but Marie knows that this cannot be so and, when she shows Christel a photograph of the real Prince, the postmistress confirms that her interview in the pavilion was with an impostor. Princess Marie, relieved that her doubts about her husband's fidelity have proved unfounded, is determined that the culprit will be exposed. A court entertainment is just about to start, and she arranges that Christel will ring a bell when the guilty man clinks glasses with the Princess.

To Adam's delight, he and his Tyrolean friends are invited to join the celebrations (Finale II: 'Wir spiel'n bei Hof gar heut") and, when the Tyroleans demand a song from Adam, he responds with a piece about an ancestor's escapades with the girls at the age of twenty and how, at the age of seventy, he wished for such an experience just once more ('Wie mein Ahnl zwanzig Jahr'). A toast to the fatherland is declared, and glasses clink, but the little bell stays silent. Weps, meanwhile, has succeeded in tying up matters for his nephew to marry the wealthy Baroness Adelaide, and he happily brings in the engaged pair. Glasses are raised afresh but, when the Princess clinks glasses with the bridegroom-to-be, Christel's bell rings out. The impostor is unmasked.

Weps and Stanislaus protest that their crime was not too serious but, since Adam is the one most upset by the episode, he is permitted to decide the culprit's punishment. Still bitter, he decides that, having accepted Christel's bouquet, Stanislaus should marry her or else be dishonourably cashiered from the Guards. Christel makes one last desperate plea to Adam that she is innocent of any wrong-doing, but he is adamant. Stanislaus decides that poverty and a pretty young wife are better than disgrace, and he therefore renounces Adelaide in favour of Christel.

ACT 3

In the Prince's residence, preparations for the wedding are taking place, but Christel is in no mood to submit passively to being married off to Stanislaus. Her refusal to co-operate drives her maids to leave her to her own devices and, outside in the grounds, Weps is unable to placate them ('Nein, nein, nein, nein, nein, das ist uns zu gemein'). Meanwhile, the Princess, now reassured of her own husband's fidelity, recalls with pleasure the day when she herself was married with the cherry trees in blossom ('Als geblüht der Kirschenbaum') and she reassures Christel, who is still worried over the mysterious girl, Marie, who turned Adam's head, that she need fear nothing from that quarter.

Adelaide is equally unhappy at the idea of Stanislaus's marriage to Christel, but Weps has now changed his plan and decided that the only way to make sure that the Baroness's money comes into the family is for him to marry her himself. As for Adam, he is merely longing to go home and forget everything about this series of unhappy events ('Kom' ih iazt wieder ham'). Fortunately, he overhears Christel telling Stanislaus that she neither wishes nor intends to marry him, and that she loves Adam. Finally convinced that her meeting with Stanisalus in the pavilion was truly well-intentioned, the bird-seller needs little more to reassure him that Christel is the girl for him. Christel, for her part, is able to lecture both men on the perils of taking on a fight with a woman ('Kämpfe nie mit Frau'n'). All that now remains is for Adelaide to be united with Stanislaus, and for Adam to renounce his new position as Menagerie Inspector and return to settle down with Christel in the Tyrol (Finale III: 'B'hüt enk Gott, alle mit einander').

DER OBERSTEIGER

(The Mine Foreman)

an operetta in three acts by Moritz West and Ludwig Herzer. Music by Carl Zeller. Produced at the Theater an der Wien, Vienna, 6 January 1894 with Alexander Girardi (Martin). Produced at the Carltheater 15 November 1901, and at the Raimundtheater 18 December 1953.

CHARACTERS

Prince Roderich, *an estate owner*
Countess Fichtenau
Zwack, *a mine manager*
Elfriede, *his wife*
Tschida, Dusel, *mine officials*
Martin, *a mine foreman*
Nelly, *a lacemaker*
Strobl, *a landlord*
Miners, villagers, festival guests, lacemakers

ACT 1

In a mountain village on the border of Germany and Austria is situated the entrance to the Marienzeche mine. Some of the local people are playing cards outside the village inn, opposite the mine, when a whistle announces the approach of the little train which twice daily provides, together with the telegraph, their main contact with the outside world ('Hört endlich auf und sputet euch 's ist sieben gleich'). Suddenly Strobl, the landlord, rushes out from the inn in excitement. An almost unprecedented event has occurred. Someone has telegraphed to book a room! Whoever it is has failed to telegraph any name but he will be arriving by the next train. The villagers are

943

sceptical and dismiss it as no more than a joke by the fun-loving mine foreman. Then, suddenly, the mystery guest appears.

The visitor is Zwack, the director of the region's mining operation, who has come to investigate the current state of the Marienzeche pit. For the present he prefers to keep his identity secret from the villagers as he prises information from them about the mine and the miners. He is concerned, for one thing, at the drinking that he has seen going on amongst the miners during his train ride—particularly by one man who drank enough for three ('Als mich dieser Bummelzug'). 'Ah, that would be the foreman,' Strobl explains. Then there are the young ladies who wait at every station to receive kisses from the miners—especially from one man who kissed enough for three. 'Ah, that would be the foreman,' Strobl again explains.

While the menfolk of the village are occupied in the mine, the girls are busy at the village's other main industry of lace-making. A group of them come by, singing their wares ('Spitzen kaufen, bitte sehr') on their way to meet their friend Nelly. 'Designs as lovely and elegant as mine can only be had from me,' Nelly declares prettily ('Muster, wie meine, so hübsche, so feine').

Zwack is much taken by Nelly, especially as she reminds him of a young lady named Julie Fahnenschwinger with whom he had an affair in the village some twenty years before. He asks Strobl what became of Julie, but all the landlord can tell him is that she gave birth to a daughter—father unknown—before leaving the village with her child. Zwack has his own idea of who the father might be, but scarcely has he recovered from this shock than his wife Elfriede arrives on the scene.

The villagers are a merry bunch who believe that life is to be lived as if every day may be one's last ('So sollt' man leb'n'), and the merriest of them all is the mine foreman, Martin, who soon appears with his fellow miners. Although he is engaged to Nelly, he has a lacemaker on each arm. Martin's immediate interest is in a display of brotherly solidarity in a call for strike action. 'Less work, more pay!' is his battle-cry, and the miners enthusiastically support him ('Wenn der Bergmann, der von Leder'). Martin believes that the miners' chances of obtaining their demands are good, and he is counting on the support of a mystery man of independent means who is known to be interested in working in the mine as a volunteer.

The men vote for strike action, and set off for a game of skittles as a young lady appears clad in climbing garb, complete with a knapsack and a green hat with feather. She turns out to be the Countess Fichtenau who, under pressure to marry against her will, has fled her home under cover of darkness ('Dort in den Bergen drin'). She means to make her own choice of husband and take him back to her castle ('Als Comtesse hab' ich ein Schloss') and, in the meanwhile, she has come to find shelter with Nelly, an old friend. Since the Countess wishes to keep her identity secret, Nelly suggests that she should adopt the name of her cousin, Julie Fahnenschwinger. Martin, having lost all his money at skittles, comes knocking on Nelly's door in the hope of borrowing five gulden and, when he encounters the supposed Julie Fahnenschwinger, he at once takes a considerable fancy to her.

The volunteer appears, all decked out in his mining gear, and is surprised to discover that the miners are on strike. Chancing to meet Zwack, he reveals that he is, in fact, Prince Roderich, the local estate owner and demands that Zwack brings the strike to an end. The helpless Zwack gets even more annoyed when Martin demands a payment of 3,000 gulden for the discovery of a new seam of silver in the mine and, for this ultimate piece of cheek, Zwack ends up dismissing him.

Still unaware of the identity of the amateur miner, Martin confides in him his wish to use the 3,000 gulden to set up a miners' wind band. He also confides his interest in the new young lady visitor and, to avoid arousing Nelly's suspicions, he persuades the stranger to sound out the young lady as to her feelings about him. Roderich approaches the supposed Julie Fahnenschwinger on Martin's behalf, but finds that the Countess and he are immediately attracted to each other ('Er ist just so im Schwunge').

Martin is furious at the way things have turned out and he decides to declare the strike at an end and call the miners back to work ('Halloh, halloh! ihr Knappen all!'). The strikers are dismayed at having to give way so soon, but no more than Zwack is when Martin makes it clear that he too should enter the mine to further his inspection in person. Zwack is persuaded to go under ground only when Nelly promises him a midnight rendezvous if he goes. Then, when Roderich appears on the scene, Martin demands that he should lead the miners into the mine, but Roderich in turn needs the bribe of a midnight rendezvous with the Countess before he can summon up the courage. For safety reasons, the Prince demands that Martin must be present, but Martin merely shrugs his shoulders and points out that he has been dismissed and is thus no longer foreman. Roderich promptly gives him the 3,000 gulden that Martin demanded to lead them to the seam of silver, and everyone promptly returns to the mine ('Glück auf! Glück auf!').

ACT 2

In the chief town of the region Miners' Day is being celebrated in the festival hall. The delegates are greeting each other and animatedly discussing the candidates for the post of president, but it is clear that Zwack's is the name on everyone's lips ('Ergeb'nster Diener, ergeb'nster Diener, hab' die Ehr!'). The choice of a man they consider a mere ignoramus as their leader is not at all to the liking of two mine officials called Tschida and Dusel, the more so when they prise from him his views of how matters will run when he becomes president ('Der Forstrath fährt auf Commission und sein Kanzlist als Zweiter!'), and they determine to prevent his election at all costs.

Martin has founded his miners' band but he has found that, with the cost of new outfits, instruments and wages, his 3,000 gulden have soon gone and he is anxious to recoup some of his expenditure by having the band engaged to play at the Miners' Day celebrations. Only the gala organiser is able to arrange that, and she happens to be Zwack's wife Elfriede. Martin proves equal to the situation by making amorous advances to the lady. 'If one day you should be a widow—which I hope you never will—perhaps I could be

945

your second husband?' he says to her ('Schöne Frau, nie wollt' ich's wagen, mich persönlich anzufragen'). Elfriede is soon prepared to grant him permission for his band to play, and anything else he may wish.

Meanwhile the Prince has discovered the Countess's real identity, and their relationship blossoms as they begin telling each other what they seek in a partner. 'I want my husband to be young and dashing—but not too much!' she tells him. 'I want my wife to be of slim build—but not too much!' he replies ('Ich wollte, dass mein Gatte wär'/'Mag mein Schatz wie immer sein'). The Prince is sufficiently encouraged at her response to telegraph the Countess's father to announce their engagement at the Miners' Day gala ball, and he arranges with Frau Zwack for the Countess and Nelly to be invited to the ball. Nelly borrows a gown from the Countess, who laughingly tells her that a ball is no more than a big game hunt, where girls hunt men ('Ein Ball ist, so zu sagen, nur eine Art von Jagd'/'Mädel, gehst du auf die Pirsch').

As the festivities begin, Martin engages Zwack in conversation and, to the delight of Tschida and Dusel, he eventually succeeds in stealing from him the notes he has prepared for his speech of candidacy for the presidency. The ball guests flood into the hall admiring the decorations (Finale II: 'O, wie herrlich, o, wie schön!'), and Nelly and Martin soon meet each other. Seeing her wearing the Countess's finery, Martin believes that she must have become the Prince's lover. 'Do you really believe, then, that I am as fickle as you?' she retorts as Martin, declaring he will have no more to do with her, leaves her to lead in his miners' band.

The Countess enters with Elfriede to occupy a position of honour and, seeing her there, Martin is astonished. She tells him that really she is a Countess, but Martin refuses to believe her any more than he will believe that his friend Roderich is really the Prince. Turning to Roderich, he tells a fable that he feels sure the supposed Julie Fahnenschwinger will understand. It is a story of a mill girl who rejects a fisherman's love because she wishes to do better for herself. 'Don't be cross,' she tells him, and off she goes into the wide world ('Wo sie war die Müllerin'/'Sei nicht bös'). Eventually she returns—no longer so proud, and now begging for his love. But this time it is his turn to say to her, 'Don't be cross.' Martin tells the Prince that the young lady who claims to be a Countess is only Julie Fahnenschwinger, and now it is Zwack's turn to be shocked. To his wife's even greater discomfort, he proclaims the Countess as his daughter, and Prince Roderich tactfully decides that the best thing to do is to declare the ball open.

ACT 3

The Countess and Prince Roderich are preparing for their marriage and, in the park of the Countess's castle, they meet and listen to the romantic sounds of nature issuing from the woods ('Mädchen, erwach, erwach!'). Tschida and Dusel appear, rejoicing over the success of their plan to discredit Zwack at the Miners' Day gala. The whole affair ended up with Zwack looking a complete fool and being sent on enforced leave. Moreover, his marriage is now on the rocks.

Although Martin has been forced by financial considerations to disband his band and has now to make do with a barrel organ, he still dreams that he might some day find his Aladdin's lamp ('Es war einmal in Asien drin ein g'wisser Herr von Aladdin'). Elfriede, her head full of his blandishments at the gala, still follows him about while Zwack renews his courtship of Nelly but all come to their senses soon enough for the Zwacks to be reconciled and for Martin, finally persuaded that Nelly's 'cousin' really is a Countess, to return to his old love. The Prince even decides that Zwack should return to his post. After all, anybody else might be even worse. Everything is thereby neatly resolved in time for all to accompany the Prince and his bride to the altar (Finale III: 'Glück auf, Glück auf!').

DER OPERNBALL

(The Opera Ball)

an operetta in three acts by Victor Léon and Heinrich von Waldberg after the comedy *Les Dominos Roses* by Alfred Hennequin and Alfred Delacour. Music by Richard Heuberger. Produced at the Theater an der Wien, Vienna, 5 January 1898 with Anna Dirkens (Hortense), Mme Ottmann, Mme Reichsberg, Mme Frey, Mme Biedermann, Carl Streitmann, Josef Joseffy and Karl Blasel (Beaubuisson). Produced at the Raimundtheater 14 April 1901. Produced at the Volksoper 12 February 1908, 29 February 1952 and 27 October 1985 with Karl Dönch (Beaubuisson), Adolf Dallapozza (Duménil), Sigrid Martikke (Marguerite), Elisabeth Kales (Angèle), Helga Papouschek (Hortense), Gertrud Ottenthal (Henri) and Peter Minich (Aubier). Produced at the Staatsoper 24 January 1931. Produced on the lake stage, Bregenz, 1957.

Produced at the Theater unter den Linden, Berlin, 11 March 1898.

First produced in New York, 24 May 1909. Produced at the Liberty Theatre in a version by Sydney Rosenfeld and Clare Kummer 12 February 1912 with Marie Cahill and Harry Conor.

A film version was produced by Geza von Bolvary in 1939 with Marte Harell, Heli Finkenzeller, Hans Moser and Paul Hörbiger.

CHARACTERS

Beaubuisson, *a man of independent means*
Madame Beaubuisson, *his wife*
Henri, *their nephew, a naval cadet*
Paul Aubier
Angèle, *his wife, niece of Madame Beaubuisson*
Georges Duménil
Marguerite, *his wife*
Germain, *the Duménils' servant*
Hortense, *the Duménils' maid*
Féodora, *a cabaret singer*
Philippe, *head waiter*
Waiters, ball guests

ACT 1

In his elegant Parisian home, Georges Duménil is telling his friend Paul Aubier of the lunch he has just enjoyed enriched with good food, good wine and excellent female company. Whilst he recognises that such behaviour is hardly appropriate for a married man, he adheres keenly to the philosophy that 'you only live once' ('Man lebt nur einmal in der Welt'). Tired of the pressures of business life, Paul feels like practising a little of the same philosophy himself while he and his wife Angèle are up from Orléans for a few days staying with Duménil and his wife Marguerite. Paul confesses that he has never had much luck with amorous adventures and would particularly like to indulge in one now with a genuine Parisienne. Georges promises to take him in hand and tells him how easy it is to arrange an evening away from one's wife with the help of a suitably arranged telegram to oneself.

Anxious to see the Aubiers while they are in Paris, Angèle's uncle and aunt, M and Mme Beaubuisson, call at the Duménils' house. Mme Beaubuisson is a very straight-laced woman, who happens to consider the Duménils a rather fast couple. Nor does she approve when she catches her husband flirting somewhat ridiculously with the Duménils' maid Hortense, and she delivers him a very stern lecture. When Angèle appears and greets her aunt and uncle ('Lieber Onkel! Gute Tante!'), she goes on to tell them how very much she is enjoying Paris, with its theatres, concerts, sights and fashions. She considers it 'the most beautiful rose in the world's bouquet' ('Überall, überall ist es schön in Paris').

Marguerite Duménil invites all her guests for drinks in an adjoining room and thus, when Henri, the Beaubuissons' young nephew, appears, he finds the coast clear to indulge in a little of his own, less practised attempts to flirt with Hortense. The latter feigns to keep him at bay, at which he assures her that as a naval cadet he has travelled the world unable to get her out of his mind ('Ich habe die Fahrt um die Welt gemacht'). Needless to say, when Madame Beaubuisson chances upon them together, she is highly disapproving. She orders Henri off on an errand to have her bracelet altered. Her husband suggests that, if the bracelet is too big for her wrist, she should try wearing it around her ankle. Henri has been assured by a lady he came across in the Boulevard des Capucines that such a fashion is all the rage ('Es war am Boulevard des Capucines').

When the Duménils and Aubiers re-enter the room, Paul pleads that he has work to do, and both men depart. Left alone the wives inevitably get to comparing notes about their husbands. With provincial naïvety, Angèle has complete trust in her husband's fidelity; but the worldly-wise Marguerite expresses doubts born of experience and wagers Angèle that she is mistaken. Despite Angèle's grave misgivings ('Mir ist, als wär's nicht recht'), they hatch a plot to test out the two husbands. Taking from the bureau two pieces of imposing notepaper headed with a coat-of-arms, Marguerite gets Hortense to write two identical letters at her dictation. They are designed for Georges and Paul, each ostensibly from a society lady, inviting one and the other to a midnight date by the clock in the foyer of the Opéra at that night's Carnival ball ('Heute Abend'). Each is told that he will recognise the anonymous sender by her pink domino.

The wives leave Hortense to deliver the notes to their husbands, whilst they go about getting themselves pink dominoes. Marguerite already has an old one, but they decide that it is too shabby for the Opéra ball. This gives an idea to Hortense who decides to use the discarded garment herself. Taking another sheet of notepaper from the bureau, she writes a third identical note. To whom should she send it? She does not yet know.

She has no sooner finished than Paul returns (Finale I: 'Ach,... Herr Aubier'). She hands him the note which is addressed to him, saying that it has just been delivered by a liveried servant. Striving to hide his excitement from Hortense, he recalls the advice that Georges has given him about a suitably arranged telegram. He rushes out to the post office, passing Georges coming in. The latter, in turn, is given his letter by Hortense and he likewise hurries out. Then M Beaubuisson and Henri appear and Hortense hands the third letter to Henri, who excitedly asks his uncle for the loan of the twenty francs to pay his admission to the ball.

Paul returns, making a great play of having set business matters aside so that he can be at his wife's disposal, but then Hortense announces the arrival of a telegram, which tells Paul of urgent business to attend to in Orléans ('So eine Depesche ist oft fatal'). With mock dismay, Paul prepares to leave, as Hortense notes, for the wives' benefit, that his travelling needs apparently include full evening dress. Georges knowingly sees his colleague off, at the same time confiding in Beaubuisson, who decides that he too would like to sample the excitement of an Opéra ball.

ACT 2

In the foyer of the Paris Opéra that night, the masked revellers are making merry to the accompaniment of a dance orchestra playing a mazurka ('Im Carnevale'). As the crowds disappear into the ballroom, Beaubuisson enters with a young cabaret singer named Féodora. As is customary on these occasions, the boxes of the Opéra have been set aside for the night as *chambres séparées* or private rooms. Beaubuisson books box number 4, and settles down in it with Féodora, who has ordered herself a sumptuous meal. Then Henri appears. This is the first time he has had a blind date with a lady, and he stands nervously checking the details of his meeting in front of the clock ('Hier ist die Uhr'). 'Where is my pink domino?' he asks impatiently, but then she appears. It is, of course, Hortense, unrecognisable to him under her mask, and she is scarcely less nervous than Henri but, when finally the introductions are done, she takes the boy by the arm and leads him into box number 3 ('Geh'n wir in's Chambre séparée').

Next Georges appears in the company of his lady in a pink domino who, unknown to him, is none other than Angèle. They go into box number 2, Angèle taking the precaution of arranging with the head waiter that, if she should ring the service bell three times, he should enter with the message that someone wishes to speak with M Georges. Finally Paul enters with Marguerite. He is concerned to ensure that his mysterious partner is indeed

949

a genuine Parisienne ('Mein Herr, es ist eine Beleidigung') and, reassured, he disappears with her into box number 1, Marguerite having also given instructions to the head waiter that, if she rings three times, he should enter with a message for M Paul.

Meanwhile Féodora, having consumed her dinner, has grown tired of Beaubuisson. She emerges from box number 4 with the old man in pursuit, telling him that she fancies a dance—perhaps the Slovak peasant dance that is her particular favourite at the moment ('Babuschka, o Babuschka'). He returns to finish his meal alone. Suddenly the bells of boxes 1 and 2 ring out, and Georges and Paul are called away. Moreover, Henri and Beaubuisson, looking out from their respective boxes, catch a glimpse of each other and decide that they would be better disguising themselves behind masks.

While Henri is away finding himself a mask, Hortense wanders out into the foyer. She is now wearing Madame Beaubuisson's bracelet, which has been given to her by Henri. At that very moment Georges returns, having failed to find out who wanted him. Seeing Hortense, he mistakes her for his own pink domino (Finale II: 'Verzeihung, schöne Unbekannte'). Accidentally he scorches the costume with his cigarette, but, having suitably apologised, proceeds to make ardent advances to her. Marguerite sees it all, but imagines that it is Angèle he is with. At Hortense's suggestion, Georges rushes off to book a cab.

When Paul returns, he thinks that Hortense is *his* pink domino. Watched by Angèle, he gets involved in a similar scene with Hortense, during which he accidentally tears her costume. Finally Paul, in his turn, is also sent to order a cab. The ladies are thus all left behind, as a crowd of masked revellers dancing the cotillion threaten to submerge them. When Georges and Paul return, they look in vain for their partners, while Henri and Beaubuisson, in ridiculous masks, enter upon the confusion. Buffeted by the dancers, they eventually come face to face as their masks are ripped off in the crush.

ACT 3

Back in the Duménils' house the following morning, Hortense is attempting to get on with the housework. She is understandably tired, and sinks into a chair, only recovering as she re-lives little by little all the delights of the previous night ('Zum ach, zu dem süssen *Tête-à-tête*'). The others reappear in their turn. First come Henri and Beaubuisson, the former convinced that he is now sufficiently experienced in encounters with women to give his uncle a lesson in the art ('Lieber Onkel, du hast keine Ahnung').

Marguerite, of course, has proved her point to Angèle about her husband only too well, and the two settle down to await Paul's return. When eventually he arrives, to ironic welcomes from the ladies, he is full of the supposed rigours of the train journey ('Jetzt bin ich wieder da!'). Georges, however, has discovered in the bureau writing paper identical to that on which their *billets-doux* of the previous day were written. Quickly adding two and two together, he apprises Paul of how they have been set up. Paul decides that the best method of defence is attack, and the two of them confront their wives with the knowledge that they were at the Opéra ball. As far as the men are concerned, no harm can have been done since they were, so they believe, with their own wives. In the eyes of the wives, however, it was to each other's wives that each husband had been making love—a quite different situation, and one that almost leads the two men into a duel. But, when reference is made to the burn and the tear in the dominoes, the wives produce their costumes unblemished. Great is the consternation that all four feel.

Now the head waiter from the Opéra arrives, bringing Madame Beaubuisson's bracelet which had been found after the previous night's confusion and she begins to wonder what was going on at the Opéra Ball. Only when Henri brings up the matter of the letter that he, too, had received, written in the same handwriting on the same notepaper, is Hortense's whole part in the episode finally uncovered. Her costume duly reveals the burn and the tear. Paul discovers that even she is a provincial, from Orléans, and not a Parisienne. Happily all finally agree that no harm has been done and, amidst general reconciliation, they confirm that all is well with the world and, above all, with Paris ('Üuberall, überall, ist es schön in der Welt').

The sole choral contribution in the original score, 'Im Carnevale, auf diesem Balle', was subsequently dropped, leaving the music as an orchestral mazurka. The two numbers 'Es war am Boulevard des Capucines' and 'Babuschka, o Babuschka' were added at the same time.

FRAU LUNA

(Mistress Moon)

an operetta in two acts by Heinz (Heinrich) Bolten-Bäckers. Music by Paul Lincke. Originally produced as a spectacular burlesque-fantastic operetta in one act and four scenes at the Apollo-Theater, Berlin, 2 May 1899 with Robert Steidl (Hans Steppke), Emmy Krochert (Frau Pusebach), Henry Bender (Theophil) and Willy Walden (Frau Luna). Produced at the Stadt-Theater, Döbeln, 1929, in an extended two-act (eleven scene) version.

Produced at L'Olympia, Paris, in a version by Fabrice Lémon and Maurice de Marsan as *Madame la Lune* 1904.

Produced at the Scala Theatre, London, in a version by Mrs Cayley Robinson and Adrian Ross as *Castles in the Air* 11 April 1911 with Ivy Moore (Letty Lane), Sybil Lonsdale (Mrs Bloggins), Frank Wood (Theophilus), St John Hamund (Montmorency) and Sybil Tancredi (Lady Moon).

A film version was produced by Theo Lingen in 1941 with Lizzi Waldmüller, Fita Benkhoff, Irene von Meyendorff, Karl Schönböck, Theo Lingen, Georg Alexander and Paul Kemp.

CHARACTERS

Frau Luna, *the lady in the moon*
Prince Sternschnuppe (*Prince Shooting Star*)
Stella, *Frau Luna's maid*
Theophil, *steward on the moon*
Frau Pusebach, *a widow*
Marie, *her niece*
Fritz Steppke, *a mechanic*
Lämmermeier, *a tailor*
Pannecke, *a tax official*
Venus
Mars
Moon groom
Moon elves and moon guards

SCENE 1

In the attic room of Frau Pusebach's lodging-house in Berlin, the engineer Fritz Steppke and his tailor friend Lämmermeier are busy at their different occupations. Steppke is sitting out on the roof, holding the strings of a number of colourful balloons with which he is testing the wind direction, trying to decide whether the conditions are right for a trial of the balloon he has designed for a trip to the moon. Inside the room, Lämmermeier is ironing a newly tailored uniform in blue cloth with grey collar ('Es ist was Wunderbares ums Genie') but when he goes to check how Steppke is faring, he leaves the iron to burn through the table.

The landlady has decided that she has had enough of the two of them, and she instructs them to leave. When Steppke was a hard-working engineer she was happy to have him as her niece's fiancé, but her attitude has changed since he came into an inheritance and began devoting himself to this non-sensical balloon project. Frau Pusebach herself is engaged to Pannecke, a tax collector, though she can't help reminiscing about a lost love named Theophil ('O Theophil, o Theophil').

Lämmermeier leaves, followed soon afterwards by Frau Pusebach, who is threatening to call the police, and her niece, Marie, then comes in with Steppke's supper. He is delighted to see her, but she breaks the news to him that she feels unable to go against the will of her aunt who took her in as a child. He must give up his mad scheme, or she and Steppke will have to go their separate ways. He must stop building castles in the air that merely bring trouble ('Schlösser, die im Monde liegen'). Steppke is shattered, but he agrees to sleep on it and bids her goodnight.

Steppke settles down on the sofa to sleep but he is soon disturbed by the sound of whistles from outside. He steps out onto the balcony and looks up at the full moon. 'Ah, the man in the moon!' he says. 'Now you will never have the honour of making my acquaintance.' At this, the moon becomes visibly sad, and tears come from his eyes. Then the whistles are heard again. It is Lämmermeier and Pannecke and they are dressed ready for a journey.

They are intent on accompanying him to the moon, and Pannecke has even arranged for the members of his skittles club to assist the launch. Hastily they prepare to depart and set off quietly over the rooftops ('Leise nur, leise nur!').

SCENE 2
Frau Pusebach enters the room, looking for Pannecke, and she is just in time to catch sight of the fleeing figures. She calls Marie and, together, they chase across the rooftops after the three men.

SCENE 3
At the airstrip, a policemen is holding back a crowd of curious spectators, as the members of the skittles club prepare the balloon for take-off. Steppke climbs into the pilot's seat, with Lämmermeier and Pannecke behind him as Frau Pusebach and Marie come panting up, calling after their loved ones. As the balloon departs, the landlady just manages to catch hold of the ladder leading to the balloon and haul herself in.

SCENE 4
The balloon climbs ever higher towards the moon (Orchestral waltz: 'Ach Frühling, wie bist du so schön').

SCENE 5
On the moon, elves dressed as window-cleaners are busy cleaning glittering banks of rock ('Schnell, putzet fein rings das Gestein'). The steward, Theophil, urges them on, bemoaning all the while his thankless task of looking after the moon ('Auf unsrer Reise nächtlicherweise'). Theophil knows all about the romantic connotations that moonlight has for people on earth, since he himself once went there. He tells the elves how he landed in the zoo at Berlin, only to find that there was a lunar eclipse. Nonetheless, though unable to see his hand in front of his face, he soon found himself with his arms round a comfortably rounded female.

On the moon the amorous Theophil has the affections of Stella, maid to Frau Luna, the woman in the moon. 'Old blitherer!' she declares, as she hears him telling the elves of his earthly adventures, but he hastily assures her that now he has eyes only for her. 'Then give me a little bit of love,' they urge each other ('Schenk mir doch ein kleines bisschen Liebe').

Just then a sound is heard at the cloud doorway of the moon ('Ich höre lautes Läuten'). It is the four intrepid visitors from Berlin, who describe their journey in the balloon across the sea of cloud ('Im Expressballon'). Theophil is not inclined to welcome them. 'The Berliners stick their noses into everything,' he declares, and goes on to tell them that the moon is already full up. 'What? Full up?' Steppke retorts, 'With a full moon? There must be a real

953

crush when there's a half moon!' 'Then we raise the rent,' Theophil replies. During the ensuing exchanges Theophil grabs Frau Pusebach by the arm. 'That's Theophil's grip,' she declares delightedly, recognising the touch of the man who had charmed her in the dark in the Berlin zoo.

Theophil, anxious to avoid any jealousy on Stella's part, is less pleased about this reunion. He summons the moon guards, who catch and tie up the three men from Berlin (Guards' March) but Frau Pusebach manages to hide and, when the guards have left, she springs out on Theophil. The two soon become affectionate to each other again, but Frau Pusebach tells him that, to overcome her grief at his departure, she has become engaged. 'Pannecke is not up to much,' she says, 'but a husband in the registry office is much better than a fiancé on the moon.' With a threat to compromise him in front of everyone if he will not help, she demands that Theophil get her and Pannecke back to earth and he promises to try to get them a lift with Prince Sternschnuppe in his space automobile.

Just then the bell at the cloud door rings, and it is opened to reveal Prince Sternschnuppe himself. He's a lighthearted fellow, who has come to try for a third time to win the hand of Frau Luna ('Lose, muntre Lieder'). Theophil begs for the use of his space automobile and the three Berliners are brought on in handcuffs. Steppke is demanding to see the man in the moon, though already all the Berliners are longing to taste the air of their native city again ('Das macht die Berliner Luft').

SCENE 6

In a splendid room of Frau Luna's palace, pages and constellations of stars are in attendance for Frau Luna's welcome to her guests, Mars and Venus ('Wenn der Abend niedersinkt'). Frau Luna herself steps forward to correct the popular illusion of there being a man in the moon. She is a lively widow and, at her court, all is fun and cheerfulness ('Lasst den Kopf nicht hängen'). She welcomes Mars and Venus but is surprised when the latter ventures to congratulate her on the rumour that she has become engaged to Prince Sternschnuppe. 'I have no intention of giving up my freedom,' she insists. Left alone with the Prince, she maintains her position despite his efforts to change her mind ('Wenn die Sonne schlafen geht').

Informed of the arrival of the people from Berlin, Frau Luna arranges for them to be brought before her in the presence of Mars and Venus ('Wer kam zu Gast im Mondpalast?'). The four travellers are introduced to Venus and Mars, but Steppke persists in insisting on meeting the man in the moon. Finally Frau Luna steps forward and introduces herself as goddess of the moon ('Von Sternen umgeben'). Steppke can scarcely believe his ears or his eyes. He is overcome with her attractions, as she is with his. 'What a lovely young man,' she says. 'My type at last!' and, telling her guests to make themselves at home, she goes off with Steppke to discuss a 'building project'.

SCENE 7

Prince Sternschnuppe remains with Theophil, bemoaning the way in which

Steppke has snatched Frau Luna from under his nose, but he resolves to have one more go.

SCENE 8
In Frau Luna's boudoir, Stella and a pair of stars dress their sovereign in a gleaming white dress. Reclining on a divan, she rings for Steppke and tries to seduce him, but his thoughts are of Berlin and his sweetheart Marie. Finally she fixes him with her eyes and leads him, as though hypnotised, into her garden of stars (Melodrama).

SCENE 9
In the garden of stars the rose elves and spirits of the air weave their spell on Steppke (Ballet).

SCENE 10
Hiding behind a cloud, Theophil and Prince Sternschnuppe spy upon Steppke and Frau Luna. When Frau Luna takes Fritz by the arm, the Prince realises that his own hopes of winning the lady in the moon have gone and he decides to leave at once. When Frau Pusebach appears, deep in conversation with Stella, Theophil attempts to slink away but, when the conversation turns to Marie, Theophil has an idea. The Prince should go down to Berlin and bring Marie back to the moon in order to tempt Steppke away from Frau Luna. When Pannecke and Lämmermeier turn up with a star maiden on each arm, it is Frau Pusebach's turn to become jealous, while Theophil is similarly affected by the information that Lämmermeier has been writing affectionate messages in Stella's autograph album. However, they all soon decide that life is too precious to waste on petty flirtations and jealousies ('Ist die Welt auch noch so schön').

SCENE 11
On a terrace on the moon a party is under way, and Frau Luna and Steppke drink each other's health in champagne ('Auf euer Wohl!'). Steppke moves to kiss Frau Luna, but just then Prince Sternschnuppe steps forward with Marie, whom he has transported up from earth in his space automobile. When he sees his fiancée, Steppke stops in his tracks, then rushes to take Marie in his arms. Frau Pusebach indicates her approval and declares her own commitment to Pannecke.

Frau Luna now realises that Steppke's heart lies with Marie, and she bids farewell to the visitors from earth ('So lebt denn wohl, zur Erde kehrt zurück'). Suddenly the sound of a large explosion is heard. Steppke's balloon has burst. Having by now reconsidered her attitude towards Prince Sternschnuppe, Frau Luna turns to them and declares that her fiancé will take them all back in his space automobile, and Theophil decides that he will go with them to enjoy once more the Berlin air ('Das macht die Berliner Luft').

The synopsis follows the expanded and updated version of 1929, into which Lincke incorporated some of his earlier successes including 'Schenk mir doch ein kleines bisschen Liebe' and 'Das macht die Berliner Luft' from his 1904 burlesque *Berliner Luft* and the orchestral waltz 'Ach Frühling, wie bist du so schön' ('Beautiful Spring').

WIENER BLUT

(Viennese Blood)

an operetta in three acts by Victor Léon and Leo Stein. Music from the works of Johann Strauss selected and arranged by Adolf Müller jr. Produced at the Carltheater, Vienna, 26 October 1899 with Julius Spielmann (Count Zedlau), Ilona Szoyer (Franziska), Louis Treumann (Josef), Valerie Stefan (Pepi) and Eduard Steinberger (Prince). Produced at the Raimundtheater 17 January 1900. Produced at the Theater an der Wien in a revised version 23 April 1905. Produced at the Volksoper 13 June 1928. Produced at the Theater im Redoutensaal 3 June 1945. Produced on the lake stage, Bregenz, 1960.

Produced at the Broadway Theatre, New York, in a version by Glen MacDonough as *Vienna Life* 23 January 1901 with Ethel Jackson, Raymond Hitchcock, Amelia Stone, Charles H Drew and Thomas L Persse. Played at the Lunt-Fontanne Theatre 11 September 1964.

Played at the Théâtre du Vaudeville, Paris, 1911. Produced at the Trianon-Lyrique in a version by André Mauprey as *Les Jolies Viennoises* 22 December 1934 with Jeanne Guyla, Janine Dellile, Coecilia Navarre and Max Moutia.

A film version was produced in 1942 with Willy Fritsch and Maria Holst.

CHARACTERS

Prince Ypsheim-Gindelbach, *Prime Minister of Reuss-Schleiz-Greiz*
Balduin, Count Zedlau, *envoy of Reuss-Schleiz-Greiz in Vienna*
Gabriele, *his wife*
Count Bitowski
Demoiselle Franziska (Franzi) Cagliari, *a dancer at the Kärntnertor-Theater in Vienna*
Kagler, *her father, proprietor of a merry-go-round*
Pepi Pleininger, *a mannequin*
Josef, *Count Zedlau's valet*
Anna, *Demoiselle Cagliari's maid*
The proprietor of the Hietzing Casino
Lisl vom Himmelpfortgrund, Lori vom Thurybrückerl, *washerwomen*
A coachman, soldiers, musicians, waiters, diplomats, party guests, dancing girls

956

ACT 1

It is the time of the Vienna Congress of 1815. We are in the Viennese suburb of Döbling, inside the villa of Count Zedlau, envoy of the state of Reuss-Schleiz-Greiz to Vienna, where he lives with his mistress, the dancer Franziska Caligliari. Josef, the Count's valet, enters calling for Anna, Demoiselle Cagliari's maid ('Anna! Anna! Anna! Ich such jetzt da, ich such jetzt dort'). There is important diplomatic business to be attended to and Josef has come to seek out his master. However, he finds neither Anna nor his master, only Demoiselle Cagliari herself ('Pepi! Er?' 'Ach Demoiselle') who has no more idea than Josef of where the Count may be. She has not seen him for five days, and is suspicious that he may have found himself another woman. Josef attempts to put her mind at rest by suggesting that the Count is probably busy with his wife. The Countess is a Viennese who, shortly after her marriage, found herself ill-suited to her husband's provincial mentality and went back to live with her parents in their country home.

The impressively styled Demoiselle Cagliari is actually a Viennese girl called Franzi Kagler, daughter of the proprietor of a merry-go-round. Herr Kagler, Franzi's father, has no idea that the Count is married and is fully expecting his daughter to become a Countess. He arrives to see Franzi and what he believes to be his prospective son-in-law, and he is concerned at never managing to find the Count in. No sooner has he left, however, than the Count turns up. He greets Franzi cheerily ('Grüss Gott mein liebes Kind') and, when Franzi receives him coldly, he attempts to set her mind at rest by assuring her that he has merely been with his wife. Finally she accepts his assurances and goes off to make his supper. Left alone with Josef, the Count confesses that he has indeed a new lady friend. He decides to invite her to have supper with him at the fête in Hietzing that evening, and he proceeds to dictate a letter ('Na, also schreib' und tu nicht schmieren!'), affectionately addressing her as his 'sweet little sugar dove' ('Du süsses Zuckertäuberl mein'). As Josef writes, he little realises that the letter is intended for his own sweetheart, Pepi Pleininger.

Explaining that his wife is in Vienna and that he must at all costs prevent her from visiting the villa in Döbling, the Count goes off with the letter. He has only just left, when Pepi herself arrives with a costume Franzi has ordered for the dancing display at a ball being given that evening by Count Bitowski. Josef and Pepi greet each other warmly ('Wünsch' gut'n Morgen, Herr von Pepi!'), and they look forward to meeting that evening at a public fête at the casino in Hietzing while the Count is busy at the ball ('Drausst in Hietzing, gibt's a Remasuri'). When Franzi comes to try on the dress that Pepi has brought, she finds that it doesn't fit. However, coincidentally it fits Pepi perfectly and, since Pepi has been present at all the rehearsals, Franzi decides that Pepi should take her place as the principal dancer of the troupe for the evening.

After Pepi has left, Franzi, Josef, and Franzi's father are joined by a completely unexpected visitor, Prince Ypsheim-Gindelbach, Prime Minister of Reuss-Schleiz-Greiz. Kagler has great fun mimicking the name of Reuss-Schleiz-Greiz, while the Prince Ypsheim, for his part, has great difficulty

957

with Kagler's Viennese dialect (Finale I: 'Das ist sie ja!' 'Das ist sie? Ah!'). Prince Ypsheim mistakenly assumes that the lady he has just met is the Count's wife and, when Kagler and Josef have left the room, he tells her that the Count is having an affair with the dancer Franziska Cagliari. Indeed Prince Ypsheim has seen the Count riding in an open carriage with this other woman. Franzi is much upset and leaves the room, with Prince Ypsheim following to comfort her.

Now Gabriele, the Count's wife, appears, having decided to check up on her husband. She had found him a dull diplomat, and she does not know that he has developed into a dashing man-about-town. Looking around her old home, she finds things much as she knew them, but she is surprised to find the adventures of Casanova on the bookshelves alongside the writings of Homer, Wieland and Voltaire ('Grüss Dich Gott, du liebes Nesterl'). When Prince Ypsheim returns, he recognises Gabriele as the supposed mistress he had seen in the open carriage with the Count, and he takes her severely to task for daring to come to the house. To confuse matters further, the Count arrives back and finds himself confronted by his wife and mistress. To save his face, he asks Prince Ypsheim to introduce Franzi to Gabriele as his own wife. Ever the diplomat, Prince Ypsheim seeks to oblige but, of course, it is Gabriele whom he proceeds to introduce as his wife, before taking her by the arm and ushering her out to his waiting carriage. Now the confusion is absolute.

ACT 2
Count Bitowski's ball that evening is a glittering affair. Everyone who is anybody has come from north and south, east and west ('Ach, wer zählt die vielen Namen'). Count Zedlau is there, as are both his wife and mistress, and he is desperately endeavouring to keep the two of them happy and simultaneously explain the goings-on at his villa. The Countess, especially, is deeply suspicious of what her husband has been up to and the two of them seek to attribute blame to each other for what has come about ('Das Eine kann ich nicht verzeih'n').

The Countess points out that she was a real full-blooded young Viennese girl, and he an unsophisticated provincial from Reuss-Schleiz-Greiz ('Ich war ein echtes Wiener Blut'), while the Count claims that, if Viennese blood was what he was lacking, he has now acquired it with a vengeance ('Wiener Blut'). As they launch into a dance together, the Count makes a resolution that the rendezvous he is lining up with Pepi will be his last before he settles down to lead a solid, blameless existence with his wife ('Als ich ward ihr Mann')

For the moment, this proposed meeting with Pepi, who is, of course, present at the ball as one of the dancing girls, is uppermost in his mind. He gives his letter to her ('So nimm, mein süsser Schatz'), but she tells him that she cannot meet him in Hietzing, as she has other arrangements. Just then Josef comes hurrying up, having been allowed into the hall with a message for his master. Pepi is delighted to see him but, when he tells her that he will

958

not be able to take her to Hietzing that evening as promised, they quarrel and she determines to take up the Count's invitation after all. Then she goes to take part with the dancing troupe, 'The Countesses', in the evening's floor show ('Bei dem Wiener Kongresse').

Meanwhile, matters have begun to get even more complicated. To the Count's considerable dismay, both Gabriele and Franzi have separately asked him to take them to the festivities in Hietzing. The Count has excused himself by telling his wife that he has a meeting with the Prime Minister, Prince Ypsheim, and by telling his mistress that he is going with his wife. Countess Gabriele checks out with Prince Ypsheim himself whether her husband really has an appointment with him (Finale II: 'Durchlaucht!' 'Ah! Jetzt heisst es operieren') but poor, confused Ypsheim, still imagining that the Countess is Franzi, assures Gabriele that the Count has no such meeting and himself arranges to take her to Hietzing.

When Prince Ypsheim then encounters the real Franzi, whom he imagines to be the Countess, he tells her of his date ('Ich habe gewonnen, ich habe gesiegt'). Franzi asks who the lady is and, when Gabriele comes up, Prince Ypsheim apologises for his confusion at the Count's villa and introduces the two—getting their names the wrong way round, of course. Prince Ypsheim imagines that he has managed things splendidly, and is astonished when the two ladies burst out laughing. When he asks for an explanation, the complications merely increase. Having seen Pepi performing in the dancing troupe, Gabriele imagines that she is Franzi and, when she opportunely appears, identifies her as such to Prince Ypsheim.

When Josef turns up, still looking for his master, Prince Ypsheim asks him to tell him which of the three ladies really is Franziska Cagliari, and the ladies themselves await his answer with great interest. Josef resolves his dilemma by denying that any of the three is Demoiselle Cagliari. The problem then passes to the Count who finds himself faced with his three women together. The Count hesitates, but the matter is resolved when Count Bitowski makes a particular point of welcoming the Countess Zedlau back into Viennese society. Franzi and Prince Ypsheim are left standing amazed, as Count Zedlau leads the assembled company into a grand waltz ('Die Wienerstadt, sie hat ein Symbol').

ACT 3

At the public fête at the Casino in Hietzing, two Viennese washerwomen, Lisl and Lori, are performing a Viennese folk number ('Geht's und verkauft's mei G'wand'). Pepi is there with the Count, who is anxious to make the most of his last amorous intrigue. Gabriele arrives escorted by Prince Ypsheim, who is surprised to find himself in Hietzing. He had thought he was merely escorting the Countess home, but now she persuades him to go with her into a summerhouse ('O kommen Sie und zögern Sie nicht länger'). Then Franzi appears, escorted by Josef, and they take a second summerhouse. Finally the Count and Pepi take a third, and champagne corks are heard popping in all three ('Stoss' an!').

Like Gabriele, Franzi has come to Hietzing with the intention of catching the Count with his new girlfriend, while Josef is anxious to warn his master of the imminent threat from his wife and mistress. When he finds the Count closeted with his own sweetheart, however, he begins to see matters very differently. The events of the past few hours have been sufficient to convince Franzi that she has had enough of the Count so, when she bumps into Gabriele and the two discover that the Count is with neither of them, they decide to work together to find the other woman and bring the Count to book ('So wollen wir uns denn verbünden!').

While Prince Ypsheim is fast asleep, Gabriele changes places with Franzi and manages to arouse the Count's jealousy by having him find her in the summerhouse apparently in the pursuit of her own amorous liaison. This discovery persuades the Count to renounce his amorous ways and concentrate his attentions upon his wife. Moreover, since he can honestly say that he has not so much as kissed Pepi in the summerhouse, she and Joseph are soon reconciled. Even Prince Ypsheim, awakened from his slumbers, is found kneeling at Franzi's feet, kissing her hand. All agree to put everything down to the power and ardour provided by Viennese blood (Finale III: 'Wiener Blut').

The operetta was arranged by Adolf Müller junior from published dances of Johann Strauss, who gave his approval for the project shortly before his death.

DER FREMDENFÜHRER

(The Tourist Guide)

an operetta in a prologue and three acts by Leopold Krenn and Carl Lindau. Music by C M Ziehrer. Produced at the Theater an der Wien, Vienna, 11 October 1902 with Adalbert Minnich (Niki), Alexander Girardi (Ratz), Lina Abarbanell (Bianca), Mila Theren (Gabriele), Karl Meister (Hanns) and Sigmund Natzler (Weisskopf). Produced at the Raimundtheater in a new version by W Hauttmann and E Jaksch 30 April 1943 with Alfred Hülgert, Toni Niessner, Maja Mayska, Magda Steiner, Franz Lagrange and Fritz Imhoff. Produced at the Volksoper in a further new version 22 October 1978 with Alois Aichhorn, Erich Kuchar, Gisela Ehrensperger, Helga Papouschek, John Dickie and Rudolf Wasserlof.

CHARACTERS

Baron Niki Schlipp
Baron Stöber
Prince Toni Hohenthal
Baron Sándor Veresz
Baron Lerchenfeld
Count Germain

Prince Tagala of Indopur
Bianca Testa, *a soubrette*
Gabriele, *her maid*
Ratz, *a corporal in a military band*
Elise, *a nursemaid*
Weisskopf
Hedwig, *his daughter*
Hanns Stauber, *a forest worker*
Blöcher, *a landlord*
Nowak, *a corporal*
A servant, a sentry, a porter, a flower girl, a lady, two pickpockets, a builder

PROLOGUE

It is early evening at the Gentry Club in Vienna, where the titled members—all men of independent means—are doing their best to keep themselves amused with a musical evening. Count Lerchenfeld has composed a song for everyone to sing ('Holdestes, lieblichstes, reizendes Kind'), and Prince Toni Hohenthal and Baron Sándor Veresz indulge in a spot of yodelling ('Springt der Hirsch frisch und froh'). It is nonetheless difficult to avoid a general atmosphere of idleness and indolence, though young Baron Niki Schlipp has his own recipe for countering boredom by recalling the sights and pleasures of his beloved Vienna in summer ('O Wien, mein liebes Wien').

By way of a further attempt at amusement the club members offer Niki a wager, challenging him to go out and earn his living for a fortnight. A condition of the bet is that it must be kept secret and that a commission of club members should be in attendance watching him. Niki cannot resist the challenge (Finaletto: 'Einverstanden! Akzeptiert!') and, though his fellow members have little faith in his ability to succeed, Niki tells them not to celebrate too soon. Even if he fails, he will at least have enjoyed himself.

ACT 1

The Ringstrasse in the early evening is, as usual, a hive of activity, with the public promenading up and down, strolling in the Stadtpark, buying from the flower sellers, and watching the sentries on parade ('Buntes Leben und Gedränge'). Amongst the people to be seen there is a military bandsman named Ratz, who is looking forward to seeing his sweetheart Gabriele, maid of Vienna's current reigning prima donna, Bianca Testa. Unfortunately for Ratz, he has arranged to meet not one young lady but two. One way and another he finds life in the army hard, what with the heavy duties, the tight uniform, the meagre pay and the strict discipline, but the hardest part of all appears to be keeping track of all the young ladies who demand his attention throughout the day. He takes Fanny to the morning market, meets Hanni when the shops open, takes Lori for lunch, has afternoon tea with Dori, takes evening strolls with Klementine and Serafine, and ends up having supper with Dorothee. Military life is indeed hard ('Ja, beim Militär').

A crowd of Bianca Testa's admirers gather to greet the prima donna after her matinée performance ('Hurra! Vivat! Sie lebe Hoch!'). As she is finishing her guest season at the Court Opera, the crowd demand a farewell speech from her and, for good measure, she treats them to a song of hers that is a special favourite with her public, and which offers an ample demonstration of her coloratura talents ('Töne Liedchen, töne durch die Nacht').

On her way back to her hotel, Bianca comes across Niki, who happens to have been a former suitor of hers when she was still known by her real name of Anna Weisskopf. The relationship foundered when Niki's wealthy aunt forbade his liaison with the mere chorus singer that she then was. She is shocked at the apparent reversal of their fortunes since then, she being now a highly successful singer and Niki, so it seems, reduced to working for his living. She tells him that her father is coming to Vienna, from the provinces, for her sister's marriage, and suggests that he should offer his services as their guide. Niki is happy to take up the idea, especially as he is keen to resume his courtship of Bianca, but this is not as easy as it might be, for she has another ardent suitor in the Indian prince, Tagala of Indopur. Bianca makes clear to both of them the virtues that she considers are needed to win a woman—discretion, tenderness, and above all patience ('Gescheit muss man sein').

Weisskopf, Bianca's father, is also the manager of her estates, though he does not know that it is his own daughter for whom he is working. He was completely opposed to her going on the stage and, when she persisted, he disinherited her. He does not know that she Italianised her name and became the celebrated prima donna, Bianca Testa. With his younger daughter Hedwig and her husband-to-be, the forestry worker Hanns Stauber, Weisskopf is trying to take in all the sights around the Ringstrasse when Niki offers his services to them as a guide ('Nein, das Leben und das Treiben überall').

The offer is accepted, and Weisskopf and his entourage prepare to retire to their hotel to change (Finale I: 'Ja, Kinder, kommt's ins Hotel'). Gabriele reappears with Ratz, still furious with him over the affair of the double date and denouncing him as a veritable Don Juan, but he pleads with her that he will forever be faithful to her ('Gabriele, süsser Schatz').

The crowds assembled for the changing of the guard part to allow Prince Tagala through. He is contemptuous of the way that the people stand and gaze at him, and remarks loftily that in his own country they know how to keep the lower orders in their place ('Im Heimatslande Tagalas'). As Tagala passes near Niki, two pickpockets snatch his watch but, seeing the police approaching, they drop it into an umbrella which Niki is carrying. Prince Tagala accuses his rival in love of stealing the watch, and Niki is arrested but, when Niki points out that the umbrella belongs to Weisskopf, he too is taken into custody. Niki calls upon the members of his club watch committee standing nearby to vouch for him, but, anxious to win their bet, they laughingly deny all knowledge of him and Niki is marched away.

962

ACT 2

At the restaurant in the Prater, where Hedwig and Hanns are to have their wedding reception, some soldiers and their girls are enjoying themselves dancing a Czech polka ('Hesky Holka! Hesky Holka!'). Niki has been freed, but Weisskopf is still fuming over the scandal that has so upset his daughter's wedding day. For Hanns and Hedwig, though, their love for each other is of most importance. 'Who needs velvet and silk and precious stones? Can't one be happy in simple clothes?' they ask each other ('Braucht es denn Samt und Seide').

Weisskopf has invited his prima donna employer and her maid to the wedding reception but, when they arrive, they are dressed in each other's clothes ('Gott sei Dank, hier sind wir endlich'). Bianca has realised that her proud and stubborn father would rather believe her a maid than admit he was wrong in forbidding her to go on stage. In their unaccustomed garb, they present themselves to the wedding party and, for the present, Bianca is not recognised by her family.

Gabriele is much taken by the feel of silk, and Ratz is equally taken by the sight of his sweetheart dressed in her mistress's gorgeous clothes. 'Are they all real?' he asks of the jewels. 'Yes,' he realises, 'they're all real.' And he decides that now is the time for him and Gabriele to be married before they get too old ('Mädel, wirst schon zwanzig alt!').

Looking at her family, Bianca cannot help thinking back to all that has happened since she was little Anna Weisskopf in the family home they all shared ('O liebes Vaterhaus, der eitle Traum ist aus!') but, for the present, she keeps her incognito while the wedding guests enjoy a splendid meal and, one way and another, the celebrations turn out to be a great success ('Die Hochzeitstafel war auf Ehre wunderbar'). Eventually Bianca reveals her identity to Hedwig, who declares to the guests that there is one thing that mars her wedding day, and that is the absence of her sister. When her father agrees, Bianca holds back no longer. She presents herself to them, and her father throws his arms around her long-lost neck.

As the dancing gets under way, Niki tries to further his courtship of Bianca, but Weisskopf is not enthusiastic at the thought of his daughter associating with a tourist guide (Finale II: 'Gibt's ein grösseres Vergnügen'). The celebrations come to a premature end when the storm that has been threatening all evening breaks. Weisskopf and the family return to their hotel, but Gabriele and Ratz decide to stick it out and dance on.

ACT 3

Ratz and Gabriele arrive back at the Hotel Bristol fully reconciled to each other and hoping to make the most of their time there together, while Gabriele's mistress is not around. When the cat's away, the mice will play ('Ist die Katze aus dem Haus'). Weisskopf, meanwhile, has mounted watch on the entrance to the hotel to prevent Niki seeing his daughter, but Niki solves the problem by climbing in through a window. Unfortunately he is spotted by Tagala, who comes running to the scene with a gun. In his rage and jealousy he threatens everyone in sight, and at one point he believes that he has killed Ratz, whom he has mistaken for the seducer of his beloved. When Ratz seemingly comes back to life, Prince Tagala bolts—never to be seen in Vienna again.

Hanns and Hedwig, meanwhile, are behaving like any two lovebirds on their honeymoon, and Hanns reflects in sentimental fashion on the home in the green meadows where he first saw his beloved ('Mitten in der grünen Wiesen'). Finally Weisskopf is persuaded to accept the fact that his daughter's suitor is actually a wealthy baron and, further, that Anna-Bianca is not a maid at all but a famous prima donna. By this time the period of Niki's bet is coming to an end, and his fellow club members arrive and greet him with friendly laughter. He has not only won his bet and had a great deal of fun, but has won the hand of the beautiful Bianca too (Finale III: 'Ist die Katze aus dem Haus').

JÁNOS VITÉZ

(John the Hero)

a play with songs in three acts by Károly Bakonyi after the dramatic poem by Sándor Petöfi. Lyrics by János Heltai. Music by Pongrác Kacsóh. Produced at the Király Szinház (King's Theatre), Budapest, 18 November 1904 with Sári Fedák (János), Vilma Medgyasszay (Iluska), Mihály Papp (Bagó) and Elza Szamosi (the French princess).

CHARACTERS

Jancsi Kukorica
Iluska
Bagó
The French King
The French Princess
The wicked stepmother
The commander of the hussars
A field watchman
Bartoló
Farmers, Hungarian villagers, hussars, French courtiers, fairies

ACT 1

A regiment of hussars arrive in a small Hungarian village, warmly greeted by the local village girls ('Megjöttek a szép huszárok'). Prominent amongst the villagers is a young man named Bagó ('A fuszulyka szára'). The soldiers have come to seek recruits for the French army in the war against the Turks ('Melletem csatázó pajtásom adj kezet') and the girls of the village prepare to say farewell to their loved ones ('A haja szinarany'). The most beautiful girl in the village, Iluska, ceremoniously beribbons the regiment's three-coloured banner with a red bow before the hussars march off.

Bagó is deeply in love with Iluska, but he knows his love is hopeless. Iluska is in love with the shepherd boy János, known as Kukorica Jancsi, who appears driving his flock ('Én a pásztorok királya') and, at his beckoning, she steals out of the house where she lives with her stepmother. Poor Iluska is an orphan ('Van egy szegény kis árva lány'), and she is brutally treated by her wicked stepmother. Kukorica Jancsi represents the whole happiness of her life, and she listens enthralled as he plays to her on his shepherd's pipe ('Én vagyok a bojtár gyerek').

Their idyllic moment is soon over. While they have been together, Iluska's stepmother has hired the drunken field watchman of the village to drive János's flock into a prohibited area. When the lovers notice what has happened it is already too late, and János has to suffer the rage of all the farmers as they fall upon the errant young shepherd (Finale I: 'Mily casapás mi szörnyü kár'). János feels that he has no choice but to join the regiment, become a hussar and see the world. He takes his leave of Iluska but promises never to forget her. When he comes back victorious, he will take her away from her stepmother and marry her. As he leaves, Bagó seeks to console the disconsolate girl.

ACT 2

From the French camp, the courtiers are watching the battle between the French and the Turks through telescopes. Amongst them is the French crown princess ('Oh csak ne volnék gyönge leányka'). There is great gloom in the camp, for the French appear to be losing the battle. The French king's crown and lands are at risk as he is forced to flee from the battlefield ('Vivtam életemben sok nehéz csatát').

Suddenly, the Hungarian hussars arrive under the leadership of János ('Szép huszárok') who declares himself ready to come to the aid of the beleaguered French. Under the admiring eyes of the French princess, he leads the men into battle. The course of the battle is completely changed, the Turks are set to flight and conquered.

János is proclaimed as a hero, above all by the Princess ('Szép a huszár, ha lóra pattan') and, to demonstrate his gratitude, the French king ennobles the heroic young hussar and offers him his daughter and half his kingdom ('Ha egy király világra jö'). János thanks the king but, to everyone's surprise, refuses to accept either the king's daughter or the half of his kingdom (Finale II: 'Gyözelem diadal szállj feléjök'). He remembers his Iluska back home, and his heart and soul crave only for her. The princess is greatly saddened, since she has lost her heart to János.

Just then the sound of a pipe is heard approaching. It is played by Bagó, who arrives, dusty and tired from his wandering, bringing the saddest of news from home. Iluska's wicked stepmother has tortured the girl to death. Bagó has brought with him a rose that had grown on Iluska's grave, and he gives it to János for remembrance ('Egy rózsaszál szebben beszél'). János is heartbroken. His soul racked with pain, he determines to find his sweetheart, even if he has to go to the afterworld to do so and, taking his leave of the French king, he sets out with Bagó to pursue his quest.

ACT 3

János and Bagó arrive in a dreary, deserted mountain region and sit down for a while to rest ('A furulyám jaj be búsan szól'). Their hearts are full of sorrow, and they cannot help but think of their native village and Iluska. Iluska's stepmother appears in the guise of an old woman carrying brushwood, and she spares no effort to frighten the two young men away from the Lake of Life, where they are resting. János hurls the old woman into the abyss but, being a witch, she escapes on her broomstick.

János gazes into the lake ('Kék tó, tiszta tó'), and fairy voices are heard, telling him that he will find his beloved Iluska at this very spot ('A nap leszáll nyugodni tér'). He throws his rose onto the lake and, suddenly, miraculous things begin to happen (Finale III: ballet). Fairies with flowers emerge from the waves, and Fairyland stands before him. The fairies then introduce Iluska as their fairy queen ('Uj királyunk hös királyunk'). The lovers embrace each other warmly, and Iluska persuades János to stay with her as king of Fairyland. However, they cannot detain Bagó, who prefers to return to his village.

As Bagó departs, his simple, heartfelt playing is heard retreating into the distance and, hearing the music, János realises that he really belongs not in Fairyland but in his tiny, native village. Despite the fairies' pleading, Iluska decides that she must go too. She rushes after János, and the two lovers set off homeward in the steps of Bagó. Fairyland disappears, and János and Iluska arrive back at her small house on the outskirts of their village in the Hungarian countryside. They are united in everlasting love, whilst Bagó is left reclining on the bank of the village brook, weeping over his unfulfilled love.

DIE LUSTIGE WITWE

(The Merry Widow)

an operetta in three acts by Victor Léon and Leo Stein after *L'Attaché d'Amabassade* by Henri Meilhac. Music by Franz Lehár. Produced at the Theater an der Wien, Vienna, 30 December 1905 with Mizzi Günther (Hanna), Louis Treumann (Danilo), Siegmund Natzler (Zeta), Annie Wünsch (Valencienne) and Karl Meister (Camille), played at the Raimundtheater from 29 April 1906 and subsequently at the Theater an der Wien again. Played frequently thereafter to the present day.

Produced at Hamburg 3 March 1906 and at the Berliner Theater, Berlin, 1 May 1906.

Produced at Daly's Theatre, London, in a version by Basil Hood and Adrian Ross

8 June 1907 with Lily Elsie (Sonia), Joseph Coyne (Danilo), George Graves (Popoff), Elizabeth Firth (Natalie) and Robert Evett (Camille). Revived there 19 May 1923 with Evelyn Laye, Carl Brisson, Graves, Nancie Lovat and Derek Oldham and played at the Lyceum 28 May 1924 with Nancie Lovat and Brisson. Played at the London Hippodrome 29 September 1932 with Helen Gilliland and Brisson. Produced at His Majesty's Theatre 4 March 1943 with Madge Elliott, Cyril Ritchard, Graves, Nancy Evans and Charles Dorning and played at the London Coliseum 19 September 1944 with Miss Elliott and Ritchard. Produced at Sadler's Wells Theatre in a version by Christopher Hassall 1958 with June Bronhill and Thomas Round. Produced at the Cambridge Theatre 19 February 1969 with Lizabeth Webb and John Rhys Evans. Produced at the London Coliseum (English National Opera) 7 December 1972. Produced at Sadler's Wells Theatre 1985 with Eiddwen Harrhy.

Produced at the New Amsterdam Theatre, New York, 21 October 1907 with Ethel Jackson, Donald Brian, R E Graham, Lois Ewell and William Weedon. Produced at the Knickerbocker Theatre 5 September 1921 with Lydia Lipkowska, Reginald Pasch, Raymond Crane, Dorothy Francis and Frank Webster; at Jolson's Theatre 2 December 1929 with Beppi de Vries, Evan Thomas, Richard Powell, Dene Dickens and Roy Cropper; and at Erlanger's Theatre 7 September 1931. Produced at the Majestic Theatre 4 August 1943 with Martha Eggerth, Jan Kiepura, Melville Cooper, Ruth Matteson and Robert Rounseville. Produced at the New York City Opera 27 October 1957 with Beverly Sills and Robert Rounseville.

Produced at the Théâtre Apollo, Paris, in a version by Robert de Flers and Gaston de Caillavet as *La Veuve Joyeuse* 28 April 1909 with Constance Drever (Missia), Henri Defreyn (Danilo), Félix Galipaux (Popoff), Thérèse Cerny (Nadia) and Soudieux (Camille), revived there 1910 with Alice O'Brien, Defreyn, Guyon fils, Mlle Cébron-Norbens and Georges Foix, and played there regularly over the next four years. Revived there 17 April 1925 with Mary Lewis, Defreyn, Félix Oudart, Léone Pascale and Max Bussy. Produced at the Théâtre de la Gaîté-Lyrique 1932 with Nini Roussel, Gilbert Nabos, Duvaleix, Ninon Guéral and Rozani and revived there 1 September 1934 with Corinne Harris, André Gaudoin, André Balbon and André Noël. Produced at the Théâtre Mogador 13 March 1942 with Jeanne Aubert and Jacques Jansen and revived there 17 November 1951 with Marina Hotine and Marcel Merkès, 8 June 1957 with Jenny Marlaine, Jansen, Perchik, Jacqueline de Bourges and Roger Darvic, 1 December 1962 with Géori Boué, Jacques Luccioni, Jean-Marie Proslier, Jacqueline Valois and Darvic. Produced at the Théâtre du Châtelet 16 November 1982.

Revived repeatedly in theatres and opera houses throughout the world.

Film versions were produced by MGM in 1925 (silent) with Mae Murray and John Gilbert, in 1934 with Jeanette Macdonald and Maurice Chevalier and in 1952 with Lana Turner and Fernando Lamas.

CHARACTERS

Baron Mirko Zeta, *Pontevedrin envoy in Paris*
Valencienne, *his wife*
Count Danilo Danilowitsch, *secretary to the legation, a cavalry lieutenant*
Hanna Glawari
Camille de Rosillon
Vicomte Cascada
Raoul de St Brioche
Bogdanowitsch, *Pontevedrin consul*

967

Sylviane, *his wife*
Kromow, *counsellor to the Pontevedrin legation*
Olga, *his wife*
Pritschitsch, *a retired Pontevedrin colonel*
Praskowia, *his wife*
Njegus, *clerk at the Pontevedrin legation*
Lolo, Dodo, Jou-Jou, Frou-Frou, Clo-Clo, Margot, *grisettes*
Parisian and Pontevedrin society, musicians, servants

ACT 1

In a salon of the Parisian legation of the Balkan state of Pontevedro, a party to mark the birthday of the ruling prince is in progress. Vicomte Cascada, a French aristocratic guest, proposes a vote of thanks and a toast ('Verehrteste Damen und Herren'), to which the envoy, Baron Mirko Zeta, replies before conversation turns to the expected arrival in Paris of a rich, young Pontevedrin widow, Hanna Glawari. Hanna's husband, a wealthy old court banker, obligingly died only a week after their wedding, leaving her his considerable fortune. She is now anxious to marry again, and the state faces the embarrassing prospect that, if she should choose to marry a Frenchman, her millions would be lost to impoverished Pontevedro.

During the celebrations, the envoy's wife, Valencienne, is left alone in the salon with another French aristocrat, Camille de Rosillon. He makes no secret of his love for her, but she firmly rebuffs him with the assurance that she is a highly respectable married woman ('So kommen Sie!'/'Ich bin eine anständige Frau'). Since she forbids him to talk to her of love, Camille expresses his passion by writing on her fan the words 'I love you'.

Totally oblivious to what is going on, gullible old Zeta compliments his wife on her hospitality towards their guests. He is more concerned with politics and with the plan he has conceived to save the rich widow's twenty millions for the fatherland. He will find a Pontevedrin husband for Hanna Glawari. He believes that he has found this potential saviour of the national economy in the person of the secretary to the legation, an eligible bachelor named Danilo Danilowitsch, and he has sent Njegus, the clerk of the legation, to seek Danilo out.

Excited voices announce Hanna's arrival, and she has all the men swooning over her as she sweeps glamorously in ('Bitte meine Herr'n!'/'Hab' in Paris mich noch nicht ganz so acclimatisiert'). Dismissing their advances, Hanna leaves them professing their dignity hurt at her suggestion that it is her money rather than herself that they are interested in, but she invites them all to a real Pontevedrin party at her home the following day.

As she moves into the ballroom on the arm of Baron Zeta, Count Danilo enters. Njegus has succeeded in tracking him down at his favourite nightspot, Maxim's, and Danilo has been dragged back protesting that he does enough for the fatherland by day without having to give up his nocturnal pleasures with the girls ('O Vaterland'/'Da geh' ich zu Maxim'). He has had four consecutive nights with a lot of activity and little sleep and, seeing a curtained-off alcove, he pops inside to lie down and sleep off the effects of the champagne.

Hanna, meanwhile, is still fighting off the attentions of her suitors and, while escaping from the ballroom, she hears snoring and, looking behind the curtain, discovers Danilo. Touching him on the face, she wakes him, whereupon it at once becomes apparent that the two are well acquainted. Indeed they are former lovers whom circumstances had caused to drift apart. Looking at his raffish and rumpled state, she smilingly reminds him that she always said she never could see him settling down, but he counters with the reminder that it was her uncle's opposition that prevented him from marrying her. But that was then. Things have changed and he swears that she will never hear him utter the words 'I love you' now, since it would class him with all the other men chasing after her money. It is, they agree, an amicable war between them.

Valencienne is still working hard at holding off the insistent attentions of Camille. Fond of him though she is, she insists that he remember that she is already married, although she allows him to join her in imagining the domestic bliss that they might enjoy if circumstances were different ('Ja was?' 'Ein trautes Zimmerlein') and they resolve to spend one last hour in each other's company before saying farewell for ever.

Baron Zeta catches up with Danilo and explains to him why he has been summoned from Maxim's. It is a delicate mission. He must marry Hanna Glawari and save her twenty millions for their country. At the sound of Hanna's name, Danilo recoils. 'Never!' he exclaims. The most he will agree to do is to waylay any other man who approaches her in a suspicious way.

Just then a ladies' choice is announced in the ballroom (Finale I: 'Damenwahl!'). With Cascada and St Brioche at their head, the men clamour to be Hanna's chosen partner, but she finds it impossible to choose among them. To divert the suitors, Danilo enters the ballroom with a bevy of girls on his arms ('O kommet doch, o kommt, Ihr Ballsirenen'), and Hanna's choice of partner is complicated further when Valencienne enters, promoting the candidacy of Camille. Hanna resolves her problem by choosing the one man who ignores her, namely Danilo. He perversely declines, and he adds that, if the dance belongs to him, he will offer it for sale at the price of ten thousand francs for charity. All the other men immediately lose interest, leaving Hanna and Danilo alone with each other. Now that his point has been made, he is prepared to dance with her and she, at first unwilling, finally lets herself be taken into his arms as the two sweep into the dance.

ACT 2

The following day the company are gathered anew in the grounds of Hanna's Parisian residence, and Hanna urges her guests to enjoy themselves ('Ich bitte, hier jetzt zu verweilen'). A company of singers and dancers in Pontevedrin costume dance a kolo, a typical national dance, and Hanna herself sings a traditional national folk tale of a maid of the woods and a huntsman's unrequited love for her ('Es lebt eine Vilja, ein Waldmägdelein').

Rumour is rife that Hanna intends to marry Camille, and Baron Zeta is busy seeking a way of dissuading him. Njegus points out that Camille is known to be in love with a married woman, at which the Baron, unaware that he is the man in question, insists that the lady's husband must give her up to the Frenchman for the sake of the fatherland. Hanna, meanwhile, accuses Danilo of avoiding her, but he explains that he is merely reconnoitring like the true cavalry officer he is ('Heia, Mädel, aufgeschaut'/'Dummer, dummer Reitersmann').

Cascada and St Brioche continue to run clamorously after Hanna, but Danilo mischievously stirs up matters for them by telling them that their affairs with the wives of Bogdanowitsch and Kromow have been discovered by the wronged husbands. These two last named, along with Zeta and the retired colonel Pritschitsch, appear on the scene and join in an animated discussion on how to handle women ('Wie die Weiber man behandelt?'/'Ja, das Studium der Weiber ist schwer') at the end of which Cascada and St Brioche beat a hasty retreat.

It is not lost on Hanna that Danilo appears to be driving all her guests away and she asks him whether, since *he* does not love her, he could advise her on the choice of a husband and she does not fail to notice the reaction of anger and jealousy that the remark provokes. Provocatively she goes on to ask how she might enjoy herself in Paris before she marries, and he demonstrates with some kolo steps that she might enjoy a Pontevedrin legation ball. But supposing she fancied something a little livelier, she suggests? His answer is 'Maxim's'. There, he says, the most reluctant ladies dance, and forget their virtue in three-four time. And he takes Hanna in his arms and demonstrates the point, before they remember themselves and return to the party (Dance scene).

Valencienne enters with Camille, who is still reluctant to take 'no' for an answer. She gives him as a souvenir the fan on which she has written 'I am a respectable wife!' alongside his own inscription 'I love you' and tells him that he must be sensible ('Mein Freund, Vernunft!'). She urges him to turn his attentions to Hanna, but he reiterates his passion for Valencienne, flamboyantly describing how it blossoms in his heart like a rosebud in May ('Wie eine Rosenknospe'), and finally persuades her to join him for yet another farewell kiss—this time in the privacy of the summerhouse ('Sieh dort den kleinen Pavillon').

As they disappear inside, they are spotted by Njegus and, when Baron Zeta approaches the summerhouse, Njegus hurriedly tells him that it is already occupied by Camille and a lady. Anxious to further his plans for getting Camille married off to anyone but Hanna, Zeta is keen to discover the lady's identity, and he sends Njegus for a key but, getting impatient, he finally resorts to looking through the keyhole, and to his horror he spies his wife. In the ensuing confusion Njegus returns and manages to enter the summerhouse by the back door, quickly substituting the helpful Hanna for the flustered Valencienne. Thus, when the front door is finally opened, Camille and Hanna step out, asking what the fuss is all about (Finale II: 'Ha! Ha! Ha!' 'Wir fragen was man von uns will'). Zeta is persuaded that he was mistaken over the identity of the lady in the summerhouse, and Camille, playing his part, repeats his passionate declaration of love—this time to Hanna ('Wie eine Rosenknospe').

Playing the game to the hilt, Hanna now announces her engagement to Camille, promising to live in the liveliest Parisian style ('Ein flotter Ehestand muss sein'). Her announcement elicits a very mixed reception from the other guests, and Danilo is furious at the thought that he has failed in his mission to keep Hanna away from the Frenchman. Finally he bursts out with a parable about a prince who kept silent about his love for a princess, only for her to repay him by giving her hand to another ('Es waren zwei Königskinder'). Then he turns on his heel and storms off to the place where he really feels at home—Maxim's. The delighted Hanna is now absolutely sure that he loves her.

ACT 3

Somewhat later, Hanna's residence has been decked out as a cabaret spot, complete with stage and orchestra. Zeta and Njegus put the finishing touches to the arrangements, and the band strikes up a cakewalk as Danilo comes in, astonished and delighted. His amazement increases when Valencienne appears on stage as a grisette, accompanied by Lolo, Dodo, Jou-Jou, Frou-Frou, Clo-Clo and Margot—the genuine grisettes from Maxim's ('Ja, wir sind es die Grisetten'). Danilo is amazed to hear that Hanna has put on this whole entertainment for his benefit.

At the bidding of Baron Zeta he insists that Hanna should not marry Camille and he is taken aback when she readily agrees. She tells him that she never had a rendezvous with Camille in the summerhouse and became involved only to protect another lady. At last Danilo admits that he had been green with jealousy—but only, of course, for the sake of the fatherland. Actions, though, speak volumes, even if their love remains unspoken ('Lippen schweigen').

Njegus announces that a fan has been found in the summerhouse and Zeta, still suspicious, recognises it as his wife's. He denounces her, declares that he considers himself divorced and asks Hanna to marry him for the sake of the fatherland. She refuses and surprises everyone by explaining that, if she remarries, she loses all her fortune. Danilo, seeing that he can no longer be suspected of wanting her for her money, now happily offers her his hand and heart at which Hanna, equally happily, explains that she would lose her fortune only because it would pass to her new husband. Danilo, his bluff called, declares that he would marry her for twice her fortune. Now Valencienne pacifies her husband by pointing to the words she has written on the fan—'I am a respectable wife'. Zeta asks her forgiveness for doubting her, and the whole company reflects afresh on the difficulty of understanding women ('Ja, das Studium der Weiber ist schwer!').

In the first London production the final act was set in the real Maxim's and included two additional numbers composed by Lehár.

971

1001 NACHT

(1001 Nights)

a fantastic operetta in a prologue and two acts by Leo Stein and Carl Lindau. Music by Johann Strauss, arranged by Ernst Reiterer. Produced at Venedig in Wien, Vienna, June 1906. Produced at the Volksoper, Vienna, 27 October 1907, and revived there as recently as the 1960s and 1970s. Produced on the lake stage, Bregenz, 1949 with Esther Réthy, Helge Roswaenge, Tony Niessner, Franz Bierbach and Kurt Preger, 1959 with Hanny Steffek, Eta Köhrer, Anton Dermota, Friedrich Nidetzky, Peter Klein, Alfred Pfeifle and Franz Böheim, and 1978 with Hildegard Uhrmacher, Celia Jeffreys, Anton de Ridder, Herbert Prikopa, Peter Lindner, Helmut Berger-Tuna and Hans Kraemmer.

CHARACTERS

Prince Suleiman Ben Akbar
Mossu, *a fisherman*
Eddin Abu Hassarak, *private secretary of the prince*
Mahmud Nerin, *grand vizier*
The Kaimakan, Babbuk, Zuleima, Nahare, Sammat, *dignitaries of the regime*
Ormuz, *a magician*
Leila, *his niece*
Wally, *Eddin's wife*
Neruda, Zaire, Zoraide, Fatme, Zuleima, Annahar, *ladies of the harem*
Fioly, *an oriental dandy*
Dumin, *guardian of the harem*
Kiossim, *servant of Ormuz*
Princes, dignitaries, odalisks, slaves, water-sprites

PROLOGUE

On board a barque, with a view across a watery seascape, the women of the harem of Prince Suleiman Ben Akbar are rejoicing at their master's return from a journey abroad ('Wenn nach des Tages drückender Schwüle'). The Prince has been to the west where, as his personal secretary Eddin Abu Hassarak reveals, he has found many ideas for reforms at home ('Ja, die Civili-, die Civili-, die Civilisation'). Eddin has even brought back with him a Viennese girl, Wally, and, deeply in love though they are, they still find some difficulty in coming to terms with the differences between east and west ('O du sanfte, gute, süsse Zuckerschnute').

Suleiman enters to due acclaim ('Hoch leb' der Herrscher, der mächt'ge Sohn der Sonne'), and he proceeds to list the ideas for reforms that he feels worth introducing—parliament, tramways, taxes, and even monogamy. This last is the most contentious issue of all, and Eddin is one of the first to oppose it in spite of his love for Wally. Timidly he asks whether the Prince himself would be prepared to observe such a law, and Suleiman thinks back dreamily to the one girl—Leila—to whom he would certainly have been happy to devote his whole self.

It seems that Suleiman is not alone in his longing for this lost love, for

972

Leila herself appears on the boat with her uncle, the magician Ormuz. Ormuz warns her that they are taking great risks being there, but Leila cannot help her longing ('Niemals kann man die vergessen'). Suleiman appears, but he is so lost in his dream that he does not recognise Leila behind her veil and Ormuz introduces her as Scheherazade, a poor girl who, like her famous namesake, can tell fairy tales and drive away the listener's cares. Suleiman agrees to let her begin (Finale I: 'Beginne, Mädchen, nun'). At Leila's beckoning, Ormuz puts a dose of hashish in the tobacco pipe of the calif, and fantastic dreams flutter around Suleiman's mind as Leila begins to tell her story: 'There was once a fisherman, who looked so much like the king of the country that nobody could tell the two apart! And it happened one day....' (Intermezzo)

ACT 1
In a splendidly decorated room in the Prince's palace, the wives of Suleiman and Eddin are following the lead of Zoraide in swearing opposition to the proposed western reforms ('Den Frieden unsres Hauses will man durch Reformen stören'/'Wir sind nicht nur Zeitvertreiber, wir sind Weiber, schöne Weiber'). Though Wally attempts to win the ladies of the harem over to the principle of monogamy, they will not have it, and the grand vizier comes out strongly in their support, declaring that, if the Prince does not back down from the reform at the day's council meeting, he risks being overthrown.

The grand vizier complains to the Prince that Eddin has given admittance to the palace to two men posing as magicians. He believes them to be spies and swindlers and has had them arrested. The two are Ormuz and his servant, Kiossim, and, having viewed their tricks, Suleiman agrees that they should be thrown into jail, to the great approval of the Kaimakan and the other leaders of the regime ('Wer ins Serail gedrungen frech ein').

Leila appears, unveiled, to ask for mercy for her uncle and Suleiman is dismayed but, at the same time, delighted to see his beloved again. He orders the prisoners released and asks Leila to remain with him but, when he tries to embrace her, she tells him that she is now married to a fisherman, Mossu. She wed him only because he looked so astonishingly like the Prince that she could thereby picture herself in the arms of her beloved. Suleiman asks if she still loves him ('Sag', bist du mir gut?') and she answers that she does but, now that she is a married woman, she must leave.

Eddin brings news of a general revolt at the proposed reforms, but the Prince is preoccupied with the return of Leila. However, the mention of Leila's husband who looks so much like the Prince gives Eddin an idea. Why not let Mossu take the Prince's place for a day? The fisherman can forswear the reforms in public, and the real Suleiman will be bound to nothing. At the same time, the Prince could go off and take the fisherman's place for the day. For Suleiman that last suggestion is a truly electrifying one ('Nun lachst du mir wieder').

Eddin goes off and returns with the fisherman, who really is the spitting image of the calif. He is terrified at the idea of having to rule the city for a day and even the money offered him seems little enough attraction. Finally he is persuaded and goes off to change clothes with the Prince, leaving Eddin to fill in some time by teaching Wally a typical oriental dance ('Hier unter Euren Sternen'/'Alle Männer, alle Weiber tanzen wie die Eseltreiber').

Officials, courtiers and wives arrive for the grand council (Finale II: 'Gerufen wurden wir vom Grossvezier'). Mossu takes the Prince's place and, prompted by Eddin, begins the discussion. He readily agrees to reinstate polygamy, and suddenly begins to take an uncommonly keen interest in the ladies of the harem. Much to the anger of Eddin, Wally particularly excites his fancy, and in no time the supposed Prince is swaying with the Viennese girl to the lilt of a waltz from her homeland ('Ja, so singt man').

ACT 2

On the bank of the magic lake, in front of Mossu's hut, Leila is rapturously reliving the thrill of having seen her beloved Suleiman again ('Heut' hab' ich ihn wieder geseh'n') when Wally appears with Fioly and a group of oriental dandies, smothering her with kisses. As orientals, they are so used to having their ladies veiled that they have had little opportunity to get close to a woman, and Wally generously gives them some hints on how courting proceeds in Vienna ('Na, was wünschen denn die Herren?').

Suleiman appears dressed in Mossu's clothes and is led by Leila into the hut while, outside, Eddin encounters Zoraide, who has been to Ormuz for a rejuvenation brew that seems to have been a complete waste of time. Eddin suggests that she should go to Ormuz and adopt the rough methods he does to deal with trouble ('Fort mit Schaden ist mein Motto').

Now the real Mossu returns, still wearing the Prince's clothes, having escaped from the palace under cover of darkness. Leila is astonished to see the man she genuinely believes is the Prince, and Mossu in turn is outraged to be told that Leila already has her husband with her in the hut. As the grand vizier arrives in pursuit of the missing prince, with his band of state dignitaries in support, Leila blocks the way to Mossu (Finale III: 'Weib! Ich vergreif' mich an dir'). Nobody believes his story that he is merely a fisherman, but when Leila is asked to adjudicate she recognises her husband by a tattoo on his arm. However, she fears for Suleiman, whom she still loves, and she therefore declares that Mossu is indeed the Prince and that it is her husband who is in the hut. The state dignitaries drag Mossu away as Suleiman, who has watched everything from the hut, comes forth and enfolds Leila in his arms.

EPILOGUE

On the Prince's barque, Leila is just completing her story: 'The Prince recognised the true, deep, honest love of a woman who would unhesitatingly

974

sacrifice anything, and he took this woman as his one and only, beloved wife.' The Prince awakes, sees Leila on his bed and declares to his ministers: 'Monogamy will be introduced.' The grand vizier accepts it unreservedly, and everyone salutes Suleiman and Leila with the words 'Long live the Prince and his lady!'

The music of the operetta is largely a reworking, to a totally new book, of the score of Strauss's 1871 operetta *Indigo und die vierzig Räuber*, on themes from which Strauss arranged his waltz '1001 Nacht.'

EIN WALZERTRAUM

(A Waltz Dream)

an operetta in three acts by Felix Dörmann and Leopold Jacobson after a short story from Hans Müller's *Buch der Abenteuer*. Music by Oscar Straus. Produced at the Carltheater, Vienna, 2 March 1907 with Mizzi Zwerenz (Franzi), Fritz Werner (Niki) and Artur Guttmann (Lothar). Produced at the Volksoper in a revised version 9 February 1974 with Helga Papouschck, Peter Minich, Heinz Reincke and Hilda de Groote (Helene) and 4 February 1987 with Ulrike Steinsky, Benedikt Kobel, Siegfried Walther and Gertrud Ottenthal.

Produced at the Theater des Westens, Berlin, 21 December 1907.

Produced at the Broadway Theatre, New York, in a version by Joseph Herbert as *A Waltz Dream* 27 January 1908 with Sophie Brandt, Edward Johnson and Joseph Herbert.

Produced at the Hicks Theatre, London, in a version by Basil Hood and Adrian Ross as *A Waltz Dream* 28 March 1908 with Gertie Millar, Robert Evett, George Grossmith jr and Arthur Williams (Joachim). Produced at Daly's Theatre 7 January 1911 with Lily Elsie, Robert Michaelis and W H Berry. Produced at the Winter Garden Theatre 20 December 1934 with Lea Seidl, Carl Esmond, W H Berry and Bertram Wallis.

Produced at Théâtre Apollo, Paris, in a version by Léon Xanrof and Jules Chancel as *Rêve de Valse* 3 March 1910 with Alice Bonheur, Henri Defreyn and Paul Ardot. Revived there 16 June 1913. Produced at the Théâtre des Folies-Dramatiques 8 December 1922. Produced at the Théâtre de la Porte-Saint-Martin 11 June 1934. Produced at the Théâtre Mogador 22 March 1947 with Paulette Merval, Marcel Merkès and Robert Allard and revived there 24 February 1962 with Merval, Merkès and Perchik and 31 July 1976 with Odette Romagnoni, Michel Philippe and Philippe Andrey.

A film version was produced by Ludwig Berger in 1927 with Mady Christians, Xenia Desni, Willy Fritsch, Lydia Potechina, Hermann Picha and Julius Falkenstein.

CHARACTERS

Joachim XIII, *Prince of Flausenthurm*
Princess Helene, *his daughter*
Count Lothar, *cousin of the Prince*
Lieutenant Niki

Lieutenant Montschi
Friederike von Insterburg, *chief lady-in-waiting*
Wendolin, *major-domo*
Sigismund, *a valet*
Franzi Steingruber, *conductor of a ladies' orchestra*
Tschinellenfifi, *a member of the ladies' orchestra*
Annerl, *a violinist in the ladies' orchestra*
Members of the princely household, servants, Austrian officers, members of
the ladies' orchestra

ACT 1

There is a great bustle in the halls of the castle of Prince Joachim III of
Flausenthurm as the courtiers assemble to welcome the Prince's daughter,
Princess Helene, following her wedding ceremony ('Wir sind so aufgeregt').
Niki, the bridegroom, is a foreigner, a Viennese Lieutenant of the Hussars,
with whom the Princess fell in love when he was appointed to guard her and
her father while they were on a visit to Vienna ('Ein Mädchen, das so lieb
und brav').

The courtiers do not have long to wait before the wedding procession
arrives ('O Jubel sondergleichen'). The ruling prince makes a speech of
welcome, after which Niki is invited to say a few words but, when he does so,
he is unable to hide the impatience that, as a lively young officer, he feels at
the strictures of the court etiquette he has recently had to endure ('Ich hab'
mit Freuden angehört'/'Alles was keck und fesch').

Princess Helene is blissfully happy at the love match, as she readily
confides to her lady-in-waiting, Friederike ('Vorüber ist die Feier'/'Ich hab'
einen Mann'), but Niki is not so sure that he has made the right decision. He
has been unable to get as much as five minutes alone with the Princess since
he arrived at the castle and he feels that, as an outsider, he is treated as
nothing but an operetta figure. Not the least of his worries is the obvious
antipathy of the Prince's cousin, Count Lothar, who stands to inherit the
throne if Helene has no children.

Scarcely is the ceremony over than Niki tells his new father-in-law that he
feels he will be unable to uphold the role assigned to him. The marriage is
doomed even before it has properly begun. In desperation the husband and
the father consult with Friederike, who so actively promoted the marriage,
over their fears for the dynasty and how the news of Niki's unwillingness to
further the marriage should be broken to the Princess ('Ah, was vernehm'
ich!'/'Und die arme Dynastie').

Suddenly Niki hears the enticing sounds of Viennese music floating
through the air like a veritable waltz dream ('Da draussen im duftigen
Garten'/'Leise, ganz leise klingt's durch den Raum'). His brother officer
and close friend, Lieutenant Montschi, tells him that it comes from a Viennese ladies' orchestra which is giving open-air concerts in the castle gardens
and Niki determines to sneak out to listen to them play that evening, wedding night or no wedding night.

976

For now, Niki has Princess Helene to face. She stands before him, her wedding bouquet in her hand, complaining that he is ignoring her and asking him whether he really loves her (Finale I: 'Mein lieber Freund, du lässt mich lang allein!'). 'Of course, of course,' he replies, and pleads shyness towards someone of her rank, suggesting that for now they should say 'Good Night' and then talk afresh in the morning. Helene confesses that she did not think married bliss was quite like this but she dutifully retires to her room, while he goes to his.

Before long Montschi appears, calling outside Niki's door. The bridegroom emerges softly from his room, dressed in his hussars' uniform, and the two of them steal joyfully away, unaware that their departure has been spotted by Lothar.

ACT 2

On the bandstand at the restaurant in the nearby park the Viennese ladies' orchestra is playing a march with vocal and whistled refrain ('Mädel, sei net dumm!') and, in the interval, their conductor Franzi Steingruber reflects with her lady players on how they make their audiences happy—the gentlemen especially—with their Viennese music ('G'stellte Mädl'n, resch und fesch').

Franzi is looking forward to the supper she has arranged with one of the lieutenants of the hussars who are in Flausenthurm for the court wedding. This lucky man is Montschi who arrives shortly after with Niki in tow but, very soon, Niki is dominating the conversation with Franzi, who is evidently as taken with him as he with her, and Montschi eventually feels it best to leave them alone together. Niki sees his meeting with the charming young Franzi as a sign from heaven ('Komm' her, du mein reizendes Mäderl!'/'O du lieber, o du g'scheiter') and, as the two of them go happily off to sup together, the girl has no idea that she is in the company of the royal consort.

Scarcely have they gone than Prince Joachim and Lothar arrive in pursuit of the fugitive bridegroom. With his own aspirations to the throne of the principality foremost in his thoughts, Lothar is keen that Niki should be caught *in flagrante delicto* and banished from the country, but Prince Joachim is more concerned for his daughter's happiness. The attention of both men, however, is distracted from their detective work by the ladies of the orchestra. Joachim soon gets talking to Tschinellenfifi, the bass drummer, and the two men seek to find out with whom the orchestra leader is taking supper.

Helene, full of anxiety about her husband and her marriage, is also out and about. The Princess and Friederike meet Franzi and, when they discover that she is a member of the ladies' orchestra and a Viennese, they seek to tap her experience of Viennese men. Are they really always merely courteous, sleepy and cool, without enthusiasm, excitement or feeling as Niki is? Franzi assures them that the truth is quite the opposite ('Das Geheimnis sollst du verraten'/'Temperament! Temperament!') and tells them that she has lost her heart to a Viennese lieutenant that very day.

When Lothar returns he seizes the opportunity to make advances towards

Franzi, but she is by no means eager to begin a flirtation with an 'older man' although she is more than willing, when he happens to mention that he is able to play the flute a little, to collect a piccolo from her orchestra's instruments and accompany him on the violin ('Lehn' deine Wang an meine Wang'/'Piccolo! Piccolo! Tsin-tsin-tsin').

Franzi and Niki express their deep new feelings for each other—,it seems like a dream that each of them has often dreamed ('Wenn zwei Menschen sich anschau'n'/'Du bist der Traum, den oft ich geträumt')—but, when Franzi goes back to restart the concert, the Prince and Lothar, Niki and Montschi, and Helene and Friederike all converge upon each other (Finale II: 'Ist es möglich?' 'O fatal!'). Helene asks her husband how he can have been so tired earlier and yet is now able to enjoy the night life and Niki tells her that it is merely the inexplicable, magnetic qualities of the Viennese waltz. As Franzi's orchestra strikes up its waltz music, Montschi takes the floor with Friederike and Niki with Helene, leaving the Prince and Lothar to do the best they can with each other.

As she leads with her violin, Franzi suddenly turns round, spots what is going on, and rushes towards Niki and Helene. 'He belongs to me!' she cries out, and the assembled courtiers who have by now joined the group by the bandstand express their astonishment and outrage. Suddenly the realisation strikes Franzi that her Niki is the Princess's husband, and she recoils. Then, turning away hurriedly, she resumes her place at the head of the orchestra while Niki returns with Helene to the castle.

ACT 3

Back in the castle the gossip amongst the courtiers is all about what the Prince Consort might have got up to on his wedding night ('Es geht von Mund zu Mund') and Sigismund, the personal lackey, fuels their speculation with news of a veiled lady who comes to the castle daily.

It is clear, at all events, that Niki is still thoroughly miserable in the castle. He feels himself a nobody, he feels tied, and he has nothing to do. Helene sadly suggests that, things being as they are, they would be better off apart. He may return to his Viennese girl. Niki regrets that Helene was not herself Viennese, and she regrets that it is something she can do nothing about but, at least, they can part friends and write a few lines to each other on birthdays and at the New Year ('Ja, was ist denn nur los mit dir, Niki?'). And so the two bid each other farewell.

The mysterious veiled lady then appears and turns out to be none other than Franzi. Sigismund believes that she has come for assignations with Niki, but, when she and Niki meet, she tells him that their fairy-tale romance must be at an end ('Mann muss manches im Leben vergessen'). Soon the reason for Franzi's mysterious visits to the castle becomes clear. Under her guidance, the place has been transformed, with furniture, dress, cooking and service all now in the Viennese fashion, and a Viennese entertainment specially laid on ('Macht's auf die Tür'n, macht's auf die Fenster'). As he witnesses it all, Niki not only feels at home but realises how much his wife must love him to have gone to such trouble. As for Franzi, she leaves to universal thanks to take up an engagement with her orchestra in Vienna (Finale III: 'Einmal noch beben, eh' es vorbei').

DER FIDELE BAUER

(The Merry Peasant)

an operetta in a prologue and two acts by Victor Léon. Music by Leo Fall. Produced at the Hoftheater, Mannheim, 27 July 1907. Produced at the Theater an der Wien, Vienna, 1 June 1908 with Louis Treumann (Mathaeus). Produced at the Raimundtheater 15 May 1945.

Produced at the Theater des Westens, Berlin, 23 October 1908.

Produced at the Strand Theatre, London, in a version by Cosmo Hamilton with additional songs by Theodore Holland as *The Merry Peasant* 23 October 1909 with Courtice Pounds (Mathaeus), Arthur Williams (Zopf), Julius Walther (Stefan), Marie West (Frieda) and Florence St John (Lisi)

Produced at the Théâtre Molière, Brussels, in a version by Gustave Jonghbeys as *Le Joyeux Paysan* 20 October 1910 with Michel Dufour and Germaine Huber.

CHARACTERS

Lindoberer, *a peasant, of the Lindoberer farm*
Vincenz, *his son*
Mathaeus Scheichrelroither
Stefan, Annamirl, *his children*
Raudaschl, Endletzhofer, *peasants*
Zopf, *a policeman*
Red Lisi, *a cowherd*
Heinerle, *her little boy*
Privy Councillor von Grunow, *a health official*
Victoria, *his wife*
Horst, *their son, lieutenant of the hussars*
Friederike, *their daughter*
Postilion, maids, servants, peasants, a juggler, tradesmen, students, members of the public

PROLOGUE (The Student)

It is the autumn of 1896 in the village of Oberwang in Upper Austria where stands the Lindoberer farm, and the owner of the farm is urging his servant girls not to allow themselves to be diverted from their work by the sound of the accordion that is coming from the next-door home of Mathaeus Scheichelroither ('Horcht's nit auf die Harmonika'). Mathaeus is an old-fashioned peasant, known by everyone as the peasant with the pointed cap, who has lived in the village all his life and has no wish to leave it. His son Stefan, on the other hand, is an ambitious young man, eagerly studying to improve himself. He has been at school in Linz for eight years and is now moving on to university and, at this very moment, he is awaiting the arrival of the stage coach which will take him to Vienna. He is saying farewell to his younger sister Annamirl, admitting that, if he could, he would much rather stay at home than venture to the capital where, as a peasant boy, he will feel very much out of place ('Ja, mei' liebe Annamirl').

Mathaeus worries little about the way in which the young villagers laugh at him and his curious pointed cap ('Lacht's mich nur aus'). After all, he is only a peasant and has no wish to be anything else ('Ich bin nix wie a Bauer'/'Und i trag' a Zipfelhaub'n'). His son Stefan is his pride and joy, and he spares no expense on his behalf—though he often has to borrow ready cash from his neighbour Lindoberer, Stefan's godfather. Mathaeus takes up his squeeze-box to bid his son a musical farewell (Finaletto: 'Juchhu, jetzt sitz'n m'r da'). He tells the boy to cheer up, but Stefan is sad at leaving home.

A group of peasant children come out to add their farewells, forming a ring around Stefan and shaking his hand ('Stefan, Stefan, pfi Di Gott'). Then the posthorn is heard, and Annamirl collects together her brother's luggage. She gives him a snack for the journey ('Dass D' uns nit verhungern tust') to which Lindoberer adds a jug of wine as Stefan climbs into the post coach and waves a sad farewell to his home and family.

ACT 1 (The Doctor)

Eleven years have passed and, on a spring day in 1907, Oberwang is merrily celebrating its parish fair, complete with town band and a roundabout for the children. Vincenz, the son of Lindoberer is leading the fun and games as he prepares to leave the following day for three years' military service in Salzburg ('Hollodrioh, rekruten sind wir vier'). He much prefers wearing peasant clothes to military uniform.

A young woman known as Red Lisi arrives with her small son, Heinerle, protesting that she hasn't the money to meet his request to buy him something at the fair ('Mutterl, Du musst mir was schön's jetzt kaufen'). Lisi is anxious to find someone to adopt the fatherless boy, but she meets with no takers amongst the people of the village.

Annamirl is at the fair, dancing with some peasant girl friends ('Lasst's mich! So lasst's mich!'), but she is fussy whom she dances with now that her brother is a graduate. Even Vincenz, with whom she was once especially friendly, now hardly seems good enough for her. When he comes to bid her farewell before he departs for his military service, she treats him callously ('Morgen muss ich fort von hier'). The sound of laughter and the mocking cry 'pointed cap!' announces the arrival of Mathaeus ('Ja, ich trag' a Zipfelhaub'n'). Stefan has not become a priest, as had been expected, but a doctor of medicine and Mathaeus is immensely proud, but he does not omit to give thanks to God ('Jeder tragt sein Pinkerl').

Mathaeus has not seen Stefan since that day eleven years ago when he took the mail-coach to Vienna but now, at last, he is expected home this very day. While they await him, Mathaeus, Lindoberer and Annamirl amuse themselves by singing an old army song ('Wir waren unser drei!' 'Ein Infant'rist!' 'Ein Artill'rist!'). Then Stefan arrives, warmly greeted by his family and friends (Finale: 'Grüss Dich Gott, Vater—Schwesterl, grüss Gott'). He excuses his long absence on all his many tasks, which include the writing of a medical book ('Mein lieber, guter Alter').

Even though he has only just arrived, Stefan proposes to leave again almost straight away for Berlin. He tells his father that he is engaged, and he produces his fiancée's photograph. Mathaeus is saddened that they have not been told before ('Na, na, mein guter Sohn, von dem is kei' Red"), but he looks forward to the wedding, which is due to take place in Berlin in a week's time. Stefan tells his father that the journey would be too difficult for him, but finally he admits the truth. His in-laws are too high-class for him to present his peasant family. Embarrassed, he bids Oberwang farewell, leaving his father and sister deeply saddened.

ACT 2 (The Professor)

Six months later, in an elegant room of his home in Vienna, Stefan and his wife Friederike are awaiting the arrival of her parents and brother from Berlin for celebrations marking Stefan's appointment to a professorship. Friederike observes how sad it is that Stefan's father takes no interest in them. Stefan feels that she is becoming obsessed with the idea of meeting his family, and he protests that his father would not even understand what his appointment to the professorship meant. Left alone, he observes to himself that one cannot confide all one's secrets to small children or sweet young ladies ('Kleinen Kindern und auch süssen kleinen Frauen'/'O, frag' mich nicht').

Then a servant announces a visitor. It is his godfather, Lindoberer, who happens to be in Vienna with a consignment of wood from the country. Stefan greets him somewhat formally and awkwardly, and Lindoberer tells him how much his father and sister miss hearing from him. Then he springs his surprise. He has brought them both with him. Friederike overhears this news and is appalled to hear that her husband's family have put up at a lodging house. She immediately arranges to give up her own room and prepare couches so that they, as well as her own parents, can stay with them.

Stefan and Friederike have only just left for the station to meet her parents, when Mathaeus enters. He is not really happy to learn from Lindoberer that his son is a professor. 'That's only a sort of schoolmaster,' he observes. They do their best to reason it out, and have similar difficulty figuring out some of the unfamiliar aspects of the well-appointed house— not least the feather mattresses and silk trappings.

Vincenz Lindoberer also appears on the scene, in the uniform of a lance-corporal. He has been transferred from the infantry in Salzburg to the cavalry in Vienna and Annamirl is much more impressed with him now that he has got on so well ('Als Lackenpatscher bin ich zuerst zum Militär'). By the time Vincenz has to rush off back to the barracks, they have already decided to become man and wife. There is, Lindoberer, Mathaeus and

Annamirl decide, a lot to be said for peasant stock ('Was, ich bin ein g'hauter Kerl'/'Is man auch ein Bauer').

The party return from the railway station, with Friederike's parents waxing lyrical over their fine son-in-law and Stefan endeavours to prepare them for meeting his family. 'They are really quite simple country-dwellers,' he tells them. 'Half peasant folk.' 'I know the agricultural sort,' exclaims Friederike's father. 'We have them in Prussia, too.' The first members of the respective families to meet each other are Annamirl and Friederike's brother, Horst. Her Upper Austrian dialect and his Berlin accent make communication difficult but they are rescued by the arrival of the carriages bringing guests for the professorial ceremony.

A group of elegantly dressed ladies and gentlemen enter, together with students in academic robes, to be greeted proudly by Friederike (Finale: 'Mein gelehrtester Herr Professor'). Champagne is served and the new professor's health drunk, but the appearance of Stefan's father generates universal astonishment. Mathaeus greets his daughter-in-law ('Bist von mein Sohn das Weib'), but he is so ill-at-ease that he readily provokes laughter amongst the guests as they set about the food and drink. Their behaviour so upsets Friederike's parents that her father and brother protest to Stefan who demands that his guests apologise to his father for their attitude. The society folk are about to walk out, but Mathaeus speaks so highly of his daughter-in-law that they are shamed into apologising. Truly there is nothing wrong with being of peasant stock, everyone agrees ('Is man auch ein Bauer').

DIE DOLLARPRINZESSIN

(The Dollar Princess)

an operetta in three acts by A M Willner and Fritz Grünbaum after a comedy by Gatti-Trotha. Music by Leo Fall. Produced at the Carltheater, Vienna, 2 November 1907 with Mizzi Günther (Alice), Louis Treumann (Fredy) and Louise Kartousch (Daisy).

Produced at the Neue Schauspielhaus, Berlin, 6 June 1908.

Produced at the Prince's Theatre, Manchester, in a version by Basil Hood and Adrian Ross with additional numbers by Richard Fall as *The Dollar Princess* 24 December 1908 with Hilda Moody, Robert Michaelis and Kitty Gordon (Olga). Produced at Daly's Theatre, London, in a revised version with additional numbers by Richard and Leo Fall 25 September 1909 with Lily Elsie, Michaelis, Gabrielle Ray (Daisy), Emmy Wehlen (Olga), W H Berry (Bulger) and Joseph Coyne (Harry Q Conder). Revived there 4 February 1925 with Evelyn Laye, Paul England, Mary Leigh, Mai Bacon, Edward d'Arcy and Carl Brisson.

Produced at the Knickerbocker Theatre, New York, in a version by George Grossmith with additional numbers by Jerome Kern 6 September 1909 with Valli Valli, Donald Brian, Adrienne Augarde, Louie Pounds and F Pope Stamper (Marquis de Jolifontaine).

Played at the Théâtre du Vaudeville, Paris, 16 June 1911. Produced at the Olympia Casino, Nice, in a version by Henri Gauthier-Villars (Willy), Antony Mars and Maurice Desvallières as *Princesse Dollar* 11 March 1911 and at the Théâtre Scala, Paris, 6 December 1911 with Alice O'Brien, Dutilloy and Edmée Favart.

A film version was produced by Felix Basch in 1927.

CHARACTERS

John Couder, *president of a coal combine*
Alice, *his daughter*
Dick, *his nephew*
Daisy Gray, *his niece*
Fredy Wehrburg
Hans Freiherr von Schlick
Olga Labinska, *a cabaret singer*
Tom, *Couder's brother*
Miss Thompson, *a housekeeper*
James, *Couder's valet*
Bill, *a chauffeur*
Typists, cabaret singers, guests, servants, porters

ACT 1

In the New York offices of the millionaire businessman John Couder, the typists are hard at work ('Schreibmaschinenmädel muss schnell die Hände rühren') but Couder's daughter, Alice, complains about the way the girls dally with their young men at the expense of good time-keeping in the office. 'Every girl should serve just one master, and yours is the typewriter,' she tells them. Alice takes pride in being a real self-made Yankee girl and she considers men as mere playthings ('Ein echtes Selfmademädel'/'Wigl wagl wigl wak my monkey').

Alice's father has a curious taste for employing impoverished titled Europeans and teaching them how to earn their living by daily work and among these unfortunates is Baron Hans von Schlick, whom Couder has taken on as his head groom. Hans has had to rebuild his life after falling on hard times at his castle on the Rhine ('Hans Heinrich Baron von, zu und auf Schlick'/'Bin jetzt ja in Amerika') but he makes it clear that he does not think too highly of Couder, the coal king, who treats his formerly aristocratic employees as ordinary lackeys. When Couder takes Hans to task for failing to turn up for Couder's morning horse ride, Hans boldly asserts that he will not turn up the next day either.

Hans has been teaching Couder's niece, Daisy, to ride, and the two of them have found it a most enjoyable experience ('Will meine Schülerin gerüh'n'). Hans, indeed, has developed amorous feelings towards Daisy, but she is only interested in their remaining just good friends. Their discussions are disturbed by the arrival of Fredy Wehrburg, an old friend of Hans. He has left Europe because his father, a wealthy coal-mine owner, wanted him to marry a local girl whom Fredy considered a silly goose and now he has come to take a job with Couder and, he admits to Daisy and Hans, to try to

983

marry Alice, even though he knows her only by sight. Hans and Daisy warn him that Alice is a hard nut, but Fredy is not easily put off. He has never been a wayside rose, and he has always had a fancy for blonde plaits and blue eyes ('Ein Röslein auf der Heide war ja nie recht mein Geschmack'/'Will sie dann lieben treu und heiss').

Alice gives Fredy the once over to see whether his background and character make him a suitable employee, and to test his attitude to having a young lady as his boss ('Ich mag im Hause nie Visagen'). She tests him further by flirting with him but, when she ends by asking him whether she appeals to him, Fredy replies, 'Absolutely not!'

Couder, a widower, has sent his nephew, Dick, to Europe to find a titled lady to act as hostess for him and Dick now returns with his father Tom, Couder's brother, and a young lady—all three of them full of enthusiasm for their trip ('Hipp, hipp, hurrah'). The young lady is in reality a cabaret singer named Olga Labinska but, to impress Couder, the three of them prefer to pass her off as Countess Olga Przibiczewska, a field-marshal's widow who has lost all her property through political disorder.

Couder summons the staff to meet this new lady of the house (Finale I: 'Und nun befehle ich als Principal') and the girls are suitably impressed but, when Hans and Fredy are introduced, they and Olga recognise each other immediately, for she is a former girlfriend of Fredy. Olga attempts to cover up by telling Couder that she met the two of them at a Court Ball in Berlin, but Fredy and Hans know it was more likely the Jardin de Paris or Maxim's. Olga backs up her assertion with some dance steps with Hans, and then she calls for champagne. Couder is dubious about allowing anything of this sort in his office until he is assured that it is the custom in Europe, but Alice and Daisy are rather put out by this lady who now has annexed the attention of Fredy and Hans. 'You can have your countess,' Daisy tells Hans, while Fredy, likewise taunted by Alice, detects what he hopefully sees as a sign of jealousy.

ACT 2
Olga is thoroughly enjoying her new-found status, and she expresses her happiness by performing a cossack dance with some of her friends in the grounds of Couder's home ('Als Kosaken kommen heut' wir'/'Olga von der Wolga'). Alice, meanwhile, has appointed Fredy as her private secretary. They emerge from the mansion for a game of tennis, but the game seems more one of verbal banter and one-upmanship than anything else. Alice summons her servants to bring out a typewriter, and she tests Fredy's feelings towards her by dictating a letter to an imaginary lover ('Man hat vor seinem Sekretär'). Neither of them is as yet prepared to admit the growing feelings they have for each other.

Couder has decided to call a family conference to announce his plan to marry Olga. He has been completely taken in by her, and Dick cannot bring himself to tell him the truth. With the future of his business concerns in mind, Couder is also anxious for Alice to marry and he is happy enough with

Alice's preference for Fredy. The sole problem is that Fredy himself knows nothing about it.

Daisy, too, feels that she would like to marry, but her uncle considers her still too young, and Hans doesn't quite share Daisy's view that they should elope and yet maintain a pure, platonic, brother-and-sister relationship. Daisy proceeds to draw up her proposed marriage contract, which includes separate rooms, polite address of each other, and all the other ingredients of what seems like a Hänsel and Gretel type of relationship ('Paragraph Eins'/ 'Wir tanzen Ringelreih'n').

Alice, convinced that absolutely anything is possible for dollar princesses for whom money is no object, changes into an elegant evening dress in readiness for the announcement of her engagement ('Kennt ihr die Mädchen?'). First Couder announces to the assembled company his engagement to Olga (Finale II: 'How do you do?') but, when Alice steps forward to announce her own engagement and, to everyone's astonishment, identifies her fiancé as Fredy, the young man bids her farewell. Even fifty million dollars will not persuade him to marry someone who considers that a man should be her slave. 'You can never forget all your money,' he accuses the family, as Alice comes to the sad realisation that dollar princesses are really the poorest beauties in the world.

ACT 3

In the year since he walked out on the Couders, Fredy has set up home in the backwoods of Aliceville, Canada. He has acquired valuable oil properties and, amongst his assets, there is one bankrupt company called Smith & Co whose rights have been offered to Couder. Fredy is awaiting a visit from Couder, who knows nothing of Fredy's involvement with this company, to close a deal. Fredy sees this meeting also as an occasion to get Couder's forgiveness for Hans and Daisy. The pair finally eloped and they are at this very moment staying with Fredy in his log cabin.

The sound of a motor-horn signals the arrival of Couder, Olga and Alice, who take great pleasure in making hens, geese, horses, children and dogs flee as their car approaches ('Reizend ist es, so dahinzufliegen'/'Drum fahr meinetwegen Automobil'). Couder is astonished to see Hans, but delighted to learn that his niece is safe and in seventh heaven over her marriage. Delighted in turn with this reception, Daisy make it clear that their relationship is no longer just a Hänsel and Gretel one ('Möchte gerne euch was fragen'/'Die tanzen Ringelreih'n einmal hin und her'). By contrast, Couder's marriage to Olga has not been a success, and he readily offers Hans half a million dollars to be rid of her. Hans is absolutely sure that, for half a million dollars, Olga would travel to the other end of the earth. It will be a problem easily solved.

When Couder meets the proprietor of Smith & Co, he is astonished to find it is Fredy and amazed to learn the extent of his wealth. Alice is equally astonished at seeing Fredy again (Finale III: 'Sie? Hier? Er!'). She attempts to hold aloof from him but, finally, she can no longer hide her feelings. Now

985

that Fredy has shown he is in every way Alice's financial equal, there is no longer any bar to their love and everything can come to a tidy happy ending.

DER TAPFERE SOLDAT

(The Brave Soldier)

an operetta in three acts by Rudolf Bernauer and Leopold Jacobson after George Bernard Shaw's *Arms and the Man*. Music by Oscar Straus. Produced at the Theater an der Wien, Vienna, 14 November 1908 with Max Pallenberg (Colonel Popoff), Grete Holm (Nadina) and Gustav Werner (Bumerli).

Produced at the Theater des Westens, Berlin, 23 December 1908.

Produced at the Lyric Theatre, New York, in a version by Stanislaus Stange as *The Chocolate Soldier* 13 September 1909 with William Pruette (Popoff), Ida Brooks Hunt (Nadina) and Jack E Gardener (Bumerli). Produced at the Century Theatre 12 December 1921 with Detmar Poppen, Tessa Kosta and Donald Brian. Produced at Jolson's Theatre 27 January 1930 with Alice McKenzie and Charles Purcell. Produced at Erlanger's Theatre 21 September 1931 with Poppen, Vivienne Segal and Purcell and 2 May 1934 with Purcell, Berenice Claire and Brian. Produced at Carnegie Hall 23 June 1942 with Poppen, Helen Gleason and Allan Jones. Produced at the Century Theatre in a revised version by Guy Bolton and Bernard Hanighen 12 March 1947 with Billy Gilbert, Frances McCann and Keith Andes.

Produced at the Lyric Theatre, London, 10 September 1910 with John Dunsmure, Constance Drever and C H Workman and revived there 5 September 1914. Produced at the Shaftesbury Theatre 31 March 1932 and revived there 20 August 1940 with Leo Sheffield, Doris Francis and Bruce Carfax.

Produced at the Théâtre des Célestins, Lyon, in a version by Pierre Véber as *Le Soldat de Chocolat* 1911 with Raoul Villot, Alice Gillet and Descombes and at the Théâtre Apollo, Paris, 7 November 1912 with Villot, Brigitte Régent and Henri Defreyn. Played at the Trianon-Lyrique 1 March 1935 with Marcelle Ragon and Paul Francil.

A film version with a different story was produced by MGM in 1941 with Nelson Eddy and Risë Stevens.

CHARACTERS

Colonel Kasimir Popoff
Aurelia, *his wife*
Nadina, *their daughter*
Mascha, *a relative in Popoff's house*
Major Alexius Spiridoff
Bumerli
Captain Massakroff
Stephan, *a servant*
Soldiers, townspeople

ACT 1

It is the mid-1880s, and the Serbo-Bulgarian War is in full swing. From her bedroom in the home of Colonel Popoff in a small town in Bulgaria, his daughter Nadina can hear the soldiers marching past ('Wir marschieren durch die Nacht'). If the soldiers are feeling lonely without their sweethearts, that feeling is reciprocated by Nadina, her mother Aurelia, and their relative Mascha, as they watch the soldiers go by. They have now been a whole year without their loved ones, and they are feeling bored and neglected. At the sound of cannon-fire in the distance they start with fright, and they decide that the time has come to close the shutters tightly as they think afresh of their menfolk in the midst of the fighting—Popoff himself and Major Alexius Spiridoff, who is engaged to Nadina but who is no less a hero for Mascha ('Mein Held!').

The three ladies retire to bed and, in the privacy of her room, Nadina takes up the photograph of Alexius that sits by her bed. She gazes admiringly at his features—so bold and severe, and yet so gentle, the forehead firm, the cheeks full-blooded, the eyes glowing with fire and courage ('Wie schön ist dieses Männerbild') and, clasping the photograph to her bosom, she calls the hero of her dreams to her ('Komm', komm'! Held meiner Träume').

As she puts the photograph down, she hears a sound from the window and in steps a soldier. He is a very ordinary looking soldier, far from the brave ideal that Nadina has just been worshipping. Though in Serbian uniform, he is a Swiss named Bumerli and he is almost entirely without menace. He has escaped from the fighting, and has found his way via the drainpipe to the balcony of Nadina's bedroom. He has not eaten for forty-eight hours and he begs Nadina to give him some food, but she refuses dramatically. He searches in his cartridge box, but he has not a single chocolate drop left. Apparently it is these, rather than cartridges, that he prefers to carry with him. In spite of herself, Nadina cannot help being taken by this strange person. She tells him that she has never come across a soldier like him ('In meinem Leben sah ich nie einen Helden, so wie Sie!'), and she mockingly christens him her 'little chocolate soldier' ('Ach, du kleiner Praliné-Soldat').

Their conversation turns to the subject of a recent cavalry charge of Bulgarian troops, led by Nadina's fiancé Alexius, from which he emerged acclaimed as a hero. Unfortunately Bumerli was there, and he cannot restrain his mirth when he recalls the Bulgarian officer whose horse ran away with him against his will, and who then called upon his colleagues to help him in his headlong dash. The Serbians were overcome with laughter, but then they found that they were unable to fire on the Bulgarians as they had the wrong ammunition with them. Nadina is furious at his making fun of Alexius and destroying the wonderful picture she had in her heart of his heroic actions. She declares that he is hateful and tells him to go, but Bumerli has no wish to go outside and get shot at, least of all while Nadina is still angry with him ('Es ist ein Schicksal, schwer zu tragen'/'Weil's Leben süss und herzlich ist').

When Nadina continues her imperious pouting, Bumerli finally makes as if to leave. He will climb out through the window and commit himself to his fate. But Nadina cannot let him go and, as he was sure she would, she cries to him to come back. When trumpets are heard outside, she hides him behind a curtain. There is a knock on the door, and Mascha enters with Captain Massakroff and a group of Bulgarian soldiers. They are searching for a Serbian spy who they suspect is hidden in the house ('Suchet, suchet, suchet alle Mann, der Serbe nicht entwischen kann!'). Nadina assures them that there is nobody there but, while they continue to search the house, Aurelia and Mascha find Bumerli's revolver and, anxious to protect Nadina, they join in the deception.

By the time the soldiers have left, Bumerli is sound asleep behind the curtain. The three women wake him up, but they are so taken by his handsome features and engaging patter that they cannot bring themselves to do other than let him enjoy the sleep he so desperately needs. They bring him clothes in which to make his escape when he awakes, each taking care also to ensure that her photograph is in a pocket, and they watch over him tenderly as he sleeps (Finale I: 'Drei Frauen sassen am Feuerherd'/'Tiralala!').

ACT 2

Six months later the war is over and, in the courtyard and gardens outside Colonel Popoff's home, the household is joining in welcoming home the conquering heroes ('Ein Hoch, ein Hoch der Heldenschar!'). Popoff and Alexius are delighted to be home, but Nadina finds her fiancé scarcely matches up to the idealised image that she cherished in his absence. She finds him stuffy and undemonstrative towards her, and seemingly concerned mainly that she should acknowledge how fortunate she is to have such a hero as he for her future husband ('Ich bin gewöhnt stets nur zu siegen'/'Mein Mädchenherz, das schlägt'). The family thank the Lord that the war is over, but Alexius becomes increasingly insufferable as he goes on and on boasting of his bravery in battle ('Ich habe die Feinde geschlagen auf's Haupt').

When Alexius tells the story of his celebrated cavalry charge, he is much put out to discover that Nadina apparently knows it was not all that it seemed. However, the ladies are embarrassed in their turn when Popoff tells them of a Swiss soldier serving with the Serbian army, whom they had met after hostilities were over, and who told them of how he had avoided capture by the Bulgarians by being sheltered by three women who all fell in love with him. The three ladies are even more concerned at the thought that Bumerli went off wearing the house coat for which Popoff is now searching high and low.

The women's embarrassment increases when Bumerli turns up, having come back to return the clothes in which he escaped. The men are surprised and puzzled to see him, but Popoff hospitably invites him to stay for his daughter's marriage to Alexius. When Bumerli finds himself alone with Nadina, it transpires that it is the attraction he feels towards her that has really drawn him back to the house ('Ein Jeder hat es schon erfahren'/'Wenn man so dürfte, wie man wollte').

988

Since he cannot bear to witness Nadina's marriage to someone else, Bumerli declares that he will not stay. Nadina asks for the return of her photograph, but it appears that he never felt in the pockets of the coat and thus had never found it. Nor had he found those which, unknown to each other, Mascha and Aurelia had also placed there. Now the coat is back in Popoff's possession and the three ladies are each in fear and trepidation at what will happen when he feels in his pockets ('Ach, es ist doch ein schönes Vergnügen'). Matches and handkerchief are promptly produced for Popoff to prevent him putting his hands in his pockets, and every argument is produced to urge him not to wear the coat. Eventually, to their immense relief, each of the three manages to slip a hand into a pocket of the coat and extract a photograph—never imagining that it might not be her own.

Bumerli prepares to leave, regretting that Nadina should persevere in marrying another, while she tries to dismiss from her mind what life might be like with Bumerli instead of Alexius ('Es war einmal ein Fräulein'). Nadina offers to return her photograph to him, but when she pulls from her pocket the photograph she had rescued from her father's coat she discovers that it is a photograph of Mascha. What is more, it bears a distinctly compromising message. Bumerli seeks to explain, but Nadina is adamant that there is no longer anything to explain.

The guests gather for the wedding ceremony (Finale II: 'Leute, Leute, kommt herbei') and all congratulate the happy pair. However, Captain Massakroff is amongst the guests and, when he sees Bumerli, he expresses his surprise at seeing the man who climbed Nadina's balcony and avoided their search. Moreover, Mascha chooses to stir things up further by triumphantly producing Nadina's photograph inscribed to her 'chocolate soldier' and the penny begins to drop in the minds of Popoff and Alexius. The bridegroom turns on Nadina and denounces her. 'I was the hero of your dreams, but now you have betrayed me,' he cries ('Ich war der Held deiner Träume'). When Bumerli offers to step in and take his place as bridegroom, Nadina tells Alexius that she no longer loves him.

ACT 3

Nadina is sitting in her room writing a letter to Bumerli ('Mein lieber Herr von Bumerli'). She is telling him that she despises him. He is indiscreet, too late with his remorse, and arrogant—as well as being totally unamusing, a rake and a Don Juan. But who should appear just then, but Bumerli? When she reminds him that she had instructed him never to come through her door again, he merely replies that he climbed in via the balcony ('Pardon, Pardon, Pardon! Ich steig' ja nur auf den Balcon!'). When Nadina gives him her letter, Bumerli shows not the slightest sign of taking it as a rebuff. So far as he is concerned, her anger merely proves how much she loves him.

Bumerli has come to tell Nadina that her jealousy over Mascha was entirely misplaced but, before he can do so, Massakroff arrives, announcing that Alexius has challenged Bumerli to a duel. Bumerli accepts, much to the alarm of Nadina who is all of a twitter at the prospect of his getting hurt, but also to the horror of Alexius, who had confidently calculated that Bumerli was such a coward that he was bound to decline. Alexius discusses this unexpected turn of events with Mascha, with whom he is finding himself more in tune ('Du magst dein Köpfchen noch so heftig schütteln'/'Freundchen, Freundchen nur nicht toben').

Matters are finally sorted out by Popoff, who is anxious for a peaceful solution. He points out that, having compromised his daughter and made a fool of her, Bumerli's duty is to marry her, and Bumerli is not inclined to object ('Wenn ein Mann ein Mädchen kompromittiert'/'Lieber Schwiegerpapa, liebe Schwiegermama'). To prove the satisfactory nature of arrangements beyond any argument, Bumerli reveals that he is the son of a well-to-do Swiss businessman, and Nadina finally settles for the happy life that her 'chocolate soldier' offers her (Finale III: 'Ich geb' Dir morgens einen Kuss').

DIE GESCHIEDENE FRAU

(The Divorcée)

an operetta in three acts by Victor Léon. Music by Leo Fall. Produced at the Carltheater, Vienna, 23 December 1908 with Anny Dirkens (Gonda), Mizzi Zwerenz (Jana), Hubert Marischka (Karel) and Richard Waldemar (Lucas).

Produced at the Vaudeville Theatre, London, in a version by Adrian Ross as *The Girl on the Train* 4 June 1910 with Phyllis Dare, Clara Evelyn, Robert Evett, Huntley Wright and Rutland Barrington (Pieter).

Produced at the Globe Theatre, New York, in a version by Harry B Smith as *The Girl on the Train* 3 October 1910 with Vera Michelena and Melville Stewart.

Produced at the Théâtre Apollo, Paris, in a version by Maurice Vaucaire as *La Divorcée* 18 February 1911 with Jane Marnac, Jane Alba, Henri Defreyn and Tréville. Produced at the Théâtre Ba-ta-Clan 1924 with Odette Darthys, Jane Montange, Tirmont and Félix Oudart.

A film version was produced by Victor Janson in 1926 with Mady Christians.

CHARACTERS

Karel van Lysseweghe, *a civil servant*
Jana, *his wife*
Pieter te Bakkenskijl, *her father, director of the Brussels Wagons Lits company*
Gonda van der Loo
de Leije, *a solicitor*
Lucas van Deesteldonck, *a judge*
Ruitersplat, Dender, *court attendants*
Scrop, *a sleeping car attendant*
Adeline
Willem Krouwevliet, *a fisherman*
Martje, *his wife*

Professor Tjonger, Professor Wiesum, legal experts
Servants, journalists, public, court officials

ACT 1

In an Amsterdam court, final submissions are being made in the petition by Jana van Lysseweghe for divorce from her husband Karel ('Die wen'gen Worte nur'). The case has been brought following a series of events which occurred when the two of them were on holiday together. Karel, suddenly recalled to Amsterdam on business, booked a sleeping car for himself and his wife to return home but then, on hearing of the bitterly cold weather prevailing in Amsterdam, he persuaded his wife to remain behind in Nice.

At the station in Nice he chanced to meet a young actress called Gonda van der Loo, who was vainly attempting to book herself a sleeping compartment on the overcrowded train. What could Karel do but offer the spare berth in his compartment to the helpless young lady? Having helped her into the compartment, he went to leave to find a seat, only to discover that the door had jammed. He had thus been forced to spend the night in the compartment with the extremely attractive Miss van der Loo. Unfortunately for him, the episode came to the attention of his wife, who promptly sued for divorce.

As the defendant is called upon to give his own version of events, the public are ushered out of court—much to their dismay at missing 'all the best bits' ('O jemine, o jemine'). Karel, of course, maintains that absolutely nothing improper occurred between him and Gonda. What else could he do but offer the berth to her? 'Gallantry,' he reminds the judge, 'is an unwritten law, and no gentleman would violate it!' The judge, however, seems eager to put an unfavourable complexion on anything that Karel has to say.

Among those called to give evidence are the sleeping car attendant, Scrop, whose attitude towards people seems to be determined largely by the size of their tips, and the fisherman, Willem Krouwevliet, and his wife Martje, who work for the Lysseweghes. They were married on the very same day as their employers and have come to give evidence of the defendant's good character. However, they are simple people, and their evidence leads to some confusion in court, as well as a good deal of merriment over their broad dialect ('Wir chaben tesammen die Chochzeit gechädt'/'O Echestand, o Echestand, wie schön bist du!').

Amidst great anticipation, the young actress finally enters the witness box. She captures all hearts—not least the judge's—with her account of how poor actresses such as she are forced to make long journeys across country by night, sleeping wherever they can make themselves reasonably comfortable when all the sleeping cars are full ('Bei reisen genügt nicht die Eisenbahn'/ 'O Schlafcoupé, o Schlafcoupé') but unfortunately her declaration in the witness box of her belief in free love does not help Karel's case.

While they await the verdict the Lysseweghes sadly wonder whether this really will be the end of their married life, whilst the fisherman and his wife view the impending break-up with alarm (Finale I: 'Nun, Jana, sprich, was soll es mit uns beiden?'). Gonda makes attempts to smooth matters over, but her support for the concept of free love is hardly to Jana's liking ('Jede Ehe ist ein Zwang'/'Freie Liebe, freie Liebe').

The judge returns to give his verdict and announces that the defendant has been found guilty of adultery and the divorce granted. Karel's pleas that he is innocent and that he still loves his wife are to no avail, and he feels that, under the circumstances, he is obliged to offer his hand to Gonda. 'Only on a basis of free love!' is her retort. 'However you wish!' Karel replies, as the judge indicates quite obviously his own desire for the lady's favours.

ACT 2

In the Lysseweghes' home in Amsterdam a party is under way, and Willem and Martje are leading a Sir Roger de Coverley ('Sir Roger! Sir Roger! Hollahe!'). They are painfully aware that the following day is the anniversary not only of their own marriage but also of that of Karel and Jana. Karel is giving this party in honour of Gonda, whom he still persists in asking to marry him, but Gonda is staunch in her belief that marriage is not for her ('Nicht um Ihre Liebe, noch Ihre Treu' ist mir's zu tun'/'Gonda, liebe, kleine Gonda').

All the main participants in the divorce case have been invited to the party, apart from Karel's ex-wife, and it comes as very much of a surprise to him when she turns up. She has received a telegram from her father, Pieter te Bakkenskijl, telling her that he is returning from abroad and intends calling on his daughter and her husband. Jana dreads her father finding out about the divorce, and she begs Karel to pretend for this one evening only that they are still man and wife. Karel is only too happy to promise to do what he can. It reminds him of a man on the verge of divorce who, at a masked ball, danced with a shapely and exciting lady in a violet silk domino. He told her that she danced just like his wife, but only when eventually she removed her mask did it transpire that it really was his wife ('Ein Mann, ein Wort?'/'Kind, du kannst tanzen wie meine Frau').

The deception is agreed before Jana's father arrives. At first he feels that he detects something wrong between his daughter and her husband but they put on such a demonstration of tenderness towards each other that he is soon reassured ('Kinder, ihr kommt mir so wonderbar vor'/'Welch Muster von Zärtlichkeit'). Meanwhile, Gonda is in great demand with all the men, and she has great fun showing Karel, Jana's father, the judge and the lawyer de Leije the steps of the latest novelty dance ('Also keinen Streit noch Strauss'/'Ich und du und Müllers Kuh').

Another guest at the party is Scrop, the sleeping car attendant, who is taken aback when he hears that Jana's father is there, as Pieter te Bakkenskijl happens to be the managing director of the sleeping car company. Scrop has decided that it is time to reveal the whole truth about the episode of Karel and Gonda, but Pieter's presence sidetracks him. It seems that the voyeuristic Scrop has a custom of taking compromising photographs of couples on his sleeping cars, and he offers Jana's father one of Karel and Gonda. Pieter, however, assumes that the photograph he is being offered is of himself, taken when he himself had a very similar experience in a sleeping car, albeit one which was apparently a good deal less innocent.

When the time comes once more for a Sir Roger de Coverley, Jana tells the party guests the story of how the man after whom the dance was named came to Holland (Finale II: 'Sir Roger, dem zu Ehren man diesen Tanz benannt'). The party is going with a great swing, and Jana's father has just commented once more on how well his daughter and Karel now seem to be getting on, when Scrop unwittingly puts a spoke in things by commenting on how the divorced couple seem to be back together again. 'Divorced?' asks Jana's father. 'But that's the man in the sleeping car,' Scrop protests. 'I gave you his photograph!' 'I thought that was me!' is Pieter's shocked reply.

The judge is still determined to win Gonda for himself, and jealousy is the weapon he proceeds to employ to that end. To Karel's astonishment and pique, the judge asks if Karel will be at the church festival at Makkum the following day as a witness to his wedding to Jana. His mind in a whirl, Karel accepts and, on the rebound, he renews his proposal to Gonda who, irritated into jealousy by the judge's attentions to Jana, decides that this time she will accept.

ACT 3

At Makkum the following day the church festival is in full swing, with clog dancing and singing in which the fisherman Willem and his wife Martje are much in evidence ('Mahndach, Dinsdach, Wunsdach!'). Jana is there with the judge, and the recent sequence of events moves her to ponder on the curious workings of fate that make people seem like puppets on strings, pulled hither and thither ('Wir Menschen sind wie Marionetten'/'Puppenspiel, Puppenspiel').

Scrop is there, too, and he exchanges ideas with Gonda on the procedures that men and women go through in the course of courting ('Denn es nützt doch, nützt doch dann und wann!'/'Man steigt nach'). Scrop's hitherto less than creditable part in the divorce of Jana and Karel becomes rather more understandable when it transpires that it was his own young lady, Adeline, with whom Jana's father had passed the night in his sleeping car.

Thanks to the judge, all is eventually unravelled when Karel finally learns that his appearance at the church festival had been designed right from the start to get him to demonstrate his jealousy and to bring him and Jana together again (Finale III: 'Warum? Warum? Es ist für mich genant'). That it does, and Karel is mightily relieved to learn that Jana never had any intention of marrying the judge. Soon the two of them are once more swearing they will ever be each other's, leaving Gonda to realise the judge's ambition by agreeing to settle down as his wife.

DER GRAF VON LUXEMBURG

(The Count of Luxembourg)

an operetta in three acts by A M Willner and Robert Bodanzky based on Willner's libretto *Die Göttin der Vernunft*. Music by Franz Lehár. Produced at the Theater an der Wien, Vienna, 12 November 1909 with Otto Storm (René), Annie von Ligety (Angèle), Louise Kartousch (Juliette), Bernhard Bötel (Brissard) and Max Pallenberg (Basil). Produced at the Theater am Wallensteinplatz 9 March 1946. Produced at the Volksoper 28 February 1954 and 1924 April 1977 with Adolf Dallapozza, Mirjana Irosch, Guggi Löwinger, Kurt Huemer and Rudolf Wasserlof.

Produced in a revised version at the Theater des Volkes, Berlin, 4 March 1937 with Hans Heinz Bollmann, Elisa Illiard, Mara Jakisch, Hans Hessling and Alfred Haase.

Produced at Daly's Theatre, London, in a version by Basil Hood and Adrian Ross 20 May 1911 with Bertram Wallis, Lily Elsie, May de Sousa, W H Berry and Huntley Wright. Produced at Sadler's Wells Theatre in a version by Nigel Douglas and Eric Maschwitz 24 January 1983 with Neil Jenkins, Marilyn Hill Smith, Vivian Tierney, Harry Nicoll and Lawrence Richard.

Produced at the New Amsterdam Theatre, New York, in a version by Glen MacDonough 16 September 1912 with George L Moore, Ann Swinburne, Frances Cameron, Frank Moulan and Fred Walton. Produced at Jolson's Theatre 17 February 1930 with Roy Cropper, Manila Powers, Trudy Mallina, J Charles Gilbert and Florenz Ames.

Played at the Théâtre du Vaudeville, Paris, 1911. Produced at the Théâtre Apollo in a version by Robert de Flers and Gaston de Caillavet 13 March 1912 with Henri Defreyn, Brigitte Régent, Angèle Gril and Félix Galipaux.

CHARACTERS

René, *Count of Luxembourg*
Prince Basil Basilowitsch
Countess Stasa Kokozow
Armand Brissard, *a painter*
Angèle Didier, *a singer at the Paris Opéra*
Juliette Vermont
Sergei Metschikoff, *a notary*
Pawel von Pawlowitsch, *a Russian Embassy counsellor*
Pélégrin, *a municipal official*
Anatole Saville, Henri Boulanger, Charles Lavigne, *painters*
Sidonie, Caroline, *models*
François, *a servant*
The manager of the Grand Hotel
James, *a lift-boy*
Models, music students, servants

ACT 1

In the streets of Montmartre a festive crowd, celebrating the pleasures of Carnival time ('Karneval, ja, du allerschönste Zeit'), pause to salute the leader of their revelries, René, Count of Luxembourg. A devil-may-care fellow, René may be of distinguished ancestry but he has managed to squander all the fortune he has inherited ('Mein Anherr war der Luxemburg') and has been forced to find lodgings in the humble studio of an artist friend, Armand Brissard.

Back in Armand's studio, we meet the artist and his girlfriend, Juliette Vermont. Armand wants to use her as the model for a painting of Venus, but Juliette's thoughts are rather less on art and more on marriage and the comfortable home in which she hopes they will live ('Ein Stübchen so klein'). Suddenly a crowd of festive folk burst into the studio carrying food and drink, which Juliette accepts graciously ('Denn doppelt schmeckt's dem Bübchen'), and they are soon followed by the Count of Luxembourg himself, bent on revelry ('So liri, liri, lari'). Before long, however, their merry-making is interrupted by the entrance of three extremely sinister-looking men who announce that they have a matter of some delicacy to discuss with René.

The visitors are the municipal official Pélégrin, the Russian notary Sergei Mentschikoff, and the Russian Embassy counsellor Pawel von Pawlowitsch and their delicate situation concerns their Prince, Basil Basilowitsch. Basil is desperately in love with the opera singer Angèle Didier but, given his high position, is unable to marry her because she is a mere commoner. To solve this problem it is necessary that she should somehow come by a title. In other words, she must marry an aristocrat. The marriage will, of course, be a sham and will end in a convenient divorce after three months, allowing the freshly ennobled Angèle to become Princess Basilowitsch. Knowing of the Count of Luxembourg's impecunious situation, the Russians have selected him as the ideal candidate for this role of temporary husband, since there will, of course, be ample payment for such very personal services.

When Basil bursts into the room, obviously deliriously in love ('Ich bin verliebt'), he finds that René is only too pleased to go along with these arrangements—especially the bit about the money ('Ein Scheck auf die englische Bank!'). However, there are conditions. The Prince insists that, as soon as the marriage has been made, René is to leave Paris and live at a tactful distance under an assumed name for the whole three-month period. Above all, he is not to consummate the marriage. As an additional safeguard, it is decreed that René is not even to see his bride's face. Since Basil's eagerness insists that the ceremony should take place right away, René is sent off to make himself presentable, whilst the four visitors set about preparing the room for the nuptials.

Once René is out of the way, Angèle herself comes in. She is understandably apprehensive, not just at the idea of marriage itself, but at the prospect of wedding a complete stranger ('Heut' noch werd' ich Ehefrau'). The studio is divided into two by means of an easel and the bride is placed on one side, while René stands on the other. The ceremony is conducted without mention of the bride's name and the exchange of rings takes place through a hole in the easel.

Once the ceremony is over, the husband and wife exchange pleasantries across the divide (Finale I: 'Frau Gräfin, Sie erlauben wohl!') and marvel at a marriage in which husband and wife are destined to be kept apart in such a way ('Sie geht links, er geht rechts'). It seems that just the sound of each other's voice and the touch of each other's hand has stirred their feelings, and they begin to have some small doubts about throwing their marriage away so lightly ('Bist du's, lachendes Glück'). René wonders at the effect created by this tiny hand thrust through a gap in the easel ('Sah nur die kleine Hand'). 'Can it be love?' he asks himself. His reveries are soon interrupted by the return of the crowd of revellers ('Leichtsinn ist die Parole'), and, all thoughts of marriage forgotten, he sets off with his friends to enjoy squandering his latest fortune.

ACT 2

Three months later, on the eve of her divorce, Angèle has invited all her friends to a party in her Paris home. The guests greet her ('Hoch, evoë, Angèle Didier'), and try to dissuade her from her decision that the performance she has given that night shall be her last appearance in the theatre. Angèle is uneasy over her imminent marriage to Prince Basil, and her unease has been increased by an exchange of looks that took place at the evening's performance between herself and a stranger in a stage box. The stranger was René, who has returned to Paris, still under his assumed name of the Baron von Reval, and who was, by pure chance, present at Angèle's farewell performance at the Opéra.

René has fallen head-over-heels in love with the singer, and he has managed to ease his way into the party at her home in the company of Armand and Juliette. Having learned from them that the singer is very soon to marry a high ranking person, René cannot hold himself back from making his own confession of love to her. 'Are you out of your mind, dear Baron?' she replies with some hauteur, 'One shouldn't reach for the stars.' ('Sind Sie von Sinnen, Herr Baron?'/'Lieber Freund, man greift nicht nach den Sternen'). Then, rather less harshly, she adds that she is already married. Juliette, too, has her mind on marriage and she applies her own little bit of pressure on Armand, who assures her that some day she will be his sweet, little wife ('Mädel klein, Mädel fein').

Prince Basil is shocked to see René at the party. He does his best to get him to leave, telling him how pale he looks and insisting that he must, at least, have a headache ('Ach seh'n Sie doch, er ist ganz blass') but René sees the best remedy to such an illness as being a glass of brandy and, when Angèle brings him one, the sight of her tiny hand as she hands it to him stirs memories. There is, moreover, the scent of that same perfume—*Trèfle incarnat*—that he had noticed at the marriage ceremony three months before ('Der Handschuh, wie pikant' 'Es duftet nach Trèfle incarnat').

As the dance orchestra strikes up a polka-mazurka, Basil describes to Juliette what a terror he used to be in the ballroom ('Ein Löwe war ich im Salon') before going on to announce to the assembled guests in highly poetic language his engagement to Angèle ('Kam ein Falter leicht geflattert'). His oration is interrupted, however, when Armand steps forward to ask how such a marriage can be when, according to the information René has passed on to him, Angèle is already married.

Basil is compelled to tell the whole, true story, going so far as to let slip the name of Angèle's useful husband and, to the laughter of the guests, Angèle adds her own expression of contempt for the man who would thus sell his name for money. At this, René steps forward and reveals his true identity (Finale II: 'Bin jener Graf von Luxemburg'). Basil asks Angèle to tell him that she still loves him, but, with René standing before her, she no longer feels able to and, when René declares himself unworthy of her for having sold his name, and makes to leave, Angèle cannot bring herself to let him. He is her husband, and she now knows that she loves him. To Basil's despair, the two leave the party arm in arm.

ACT 3

In the vestibule of the Grand Hotel that evening we meet a certain Countess Stasa Kokozow, newly arrived from Saint Petersburg with a proclaimed philosophy to take life at a leisurely pace ('Alles mit Ruhe geniessen'). This seems appropriate, for she has been engaged for the past three years to Prince Basil without having stirred herself into sufficient action to find out what he has been up to in Paris.

Also passing through this same foyer comes Juliette with Armand, who has finally decided to give in to her not-so-subtle entreaties and has agreed to get married the following morning ('Mädel klein, Mädel fein'), and they are soon joined by Basil, bemoaning the way that he has been made to look an old fool by Angèle ('Liebe, ach, du Sonnenschein').

When René arrives with Angèle he finds that a telegram is awaiting him with the news that all his seized estates have been returned to him. His financial problems have been solved. However, all is not yet happy. Although Angèle uses all her feminine wiles to convince him ('Es duftet nach Trèfle incarnat'), he feels unable to break his word of honour to Prince Basil.

His scruples are lightened when they encounter Countess Kokozow who tells them of her engagement to Basil and of her journey to Paris to marry him. Basil is forced to accept the inevitable and René is happy to repay from his new-found wealth the 500,000 francs he had received for the mock marriage. The adventure ends with three couples preparing to face the prospect of going through life together—Armand and Juliette, René and Angèle, and Prince Basil and Countess Kokozow (Finale III: 'Wir bummeln durch's Leben').

The above synopsis follows the 1937 revision, with a revised opening scene in a Montmartre street, René's entrance song immediately after the opening chorus, and a spectacular, interpolated ballet sequence. In the original the whole first act was set in Armand's studio, with René's entrance song placed at his entry into the studio.

ZIGEUNERLIEBE

(Gipsy Love)

a romantic operetta in three acts by A M Willner and Robert Bodanzky. Music by Franz Lehár. Produced at the Carltheater, Vienna, 8 January 1910 with Grete Holm (Zorika), Willi Strehl (Józsi), Max Rohr (Jonel) and Hubert Marischka (Kajetan). Produced in Salzburg, 1921 with Richard Tauber (Józsi).

Produced at the Komische Oper, Berlin, 12 February 1911 with Martha Winternitz-Dorda (Zorika), Jean Nadolovitch (Józsi) and Mary Hagen (Ilona).

Produced at the Globe Theatre, New York, in a version by Harry B Smith and Robert B Smith 17 October 1911 with Phyllis Partington (Zorika) and Albert Albro (Józsi).

Produced at Daly's Theatre, London, in a version by Basil Hood and Adrian Ross with additional numbers by Lehár as *Gipsy Love* 1 June 1912 with Sári Petráss (Ilona), Robert Michaelis (Józsi), Webster Millar (Jonel), W H Berry (Dragotin) and Gertie Millar (Lady Babby).

Played at the Théâtre du Vaudeville, Paris, 1911. Produced at the Théâtre Molière, Brussels, in a version by Henri Gauthier-Villars (Willy) and Jean Bénédict as *L'Amour Tzigane* 19 January 1911 with Germaine Huber. Produced at the Théâtre de l'Opéra, Marseille, in a version by Saugey 16 December 1911 with Suzanne Cesbron (Zorika), Fernand Lemaire (Józsi), Jean Marny (Jonel), Boyer (Dragotin) and Louise Mantoue (Ilona) and subsequently at the Trianon-Lyrique, Paris, 1911 with Jane de Poumayrac, Obein, Baillard and José Théry. Revived there 1921.

A revised operatic version with a Hungarian libretto by Ernö Innocent-Vincze was produced as *Garabonciás diák* at the State Opera, Budapest, 20 February 1943 with Tibor Udvardy and Julia Orosz.

The 1930 MGM film *Rogue Song*, allegedly based on *Zigeunerliebe*, used a different story and only a little of the score.

CHARACTERS

Peter Dragotin
Jonel Bolescu
Dimitreanu, *the Mayor*
Kajetán Dimetreanu, *his son*
Józsi, *a gipsy*
Mihály, *an innkeeper*
Moschu, *Dragotin's valet*
Zorika, *Dragotin's daughter*
Jolán, *Dragotin's niece*
Ilona von Körösháza, *a landowner*
Boyars, Hungarian soldiers, Romanian and Hungarian countryfolk, gipsies, gipsy musicians, waitresses, village children

ACT 1

In Siebenbürgen, a town on the river Czerna, near the Romanian border with early nineteenth century Hungary, a storm is breaking as, outside the hunting lodge of the landowner Dragotin, his daughter Zorika appears, dressed in Romanian peasant garb, with wild flowers in her hair, and looking

998

decidedly dishevelled ('Heissa, heissa!'). Then, as the storm dies away, the skies brighten, and the sound of a violin is heard. The player is József, a gipsy fiddler, and he apologises for interrupting Zorika's thoughts, but today is the day of the party to celebrate Zorika's engagement to Jonel Bolescu, József's legitimate half-brother, and József will be providing the music.

The gipsy boy is deferential to the daughter of the local landowner, but Zorika is a democratic girl, and she is happy to let a conversation develop. József talks lyrically to her about the love that she will soon be enjoying with her fiancé, but his words speak of feelings that, in fact, Zorika has never experienced when she is with Jonel ('So sprach noch niemals ein Mann zu mir!'). József talks to her of a fairy-tale garden of flowers and love and suggests that they walk there hand in hand ('Es liegt in blauen Fernen') and Zorika has to pull herself together to remember her duty towards her fiancé.

Jonel arrives for the engagement party, decked out in a splendid Boyar costume and accompanied by army officers and other guests, to be welcomed happily by the elderly widower Dragotin ('So treaska! Liebe Gäste!'). Being an outdoor girl, Zorika has insisted on holding her engagement party out-of-doors and, when she appears with her maids of honour, Jonel offers her a bunch of wild roses ('Trägst den Zweig in deinen Händen rosig zart'). Zorika, her mind in a turmoil, refuses the flowers and insists that Jonel has yet to prove that he is the right man for her. Then, spurred on by the magic tones of József's violin, she throws Jonel's roses in the river. The assembled guests are horrified, but the neighbouring landowner Ilona von Köröshaza backs up Zorika's right to decide for herself. A woman has every right to put men in their place and she herself does it frequently ('Will die Männer ich berücken').

Zorika knows that, when she finally gives Jonel the traditional engagement kiss, it will be purely at her father's bidding and not out of any feeling of affection and, as József wishes the future bride and groom well, he offers them a gipsy warning of ill-luck if that first kiss should take place before nightfall. The guests go in to supper, leaving Dragotin's niece Jolán trying to persuade the Mayor's shy young son Kajetán to admit that he really loves her. Fortunately Ilona von Köröshaza is on hand to give Jolán some practical demonstrations of the art of wooing ('Zuerst sucht man Gelegenheit').

Zorika soon finds herself disgusted with the stuffy company at the party and she quietly slips away from the house and her guests, only to run into József, lingering outside. The gipsy tells Zorika that, now the moon is out, she may safely kiss Jonel ('Finale I: Da habt Ihr nun den Mond in voller Pracht') but Zorika is fed up with Jonel and everything he represents, and longs to be as free as József. She begs him to take her to the enchanted garden he spoke to her of ('Lass' uns nach dem Garten ziehen') and gives him her hand, which József kisses passionately.

As the sounds of merriment from the house build up, Ilona appears to ask József to play his violin for them. He does so, counting his success with Zorika ('Glück hat als Gast—nie lange Rast!') and, when Jonel comes in search of his engagement kiss, Zorika, her mind and heart in a whirl, refuses him. In her confusion, she remembers a superstition told her by her nurse, telling that anyone drinking from the River Czerna on Annunciation Eve will see into the future. She bends down and drinks from the water, and then she falls asleep as the glow-worms and fireflies dance around about and mysterious voices call to her in the darkness.

ACT 2

Zorika's vision takes her into the future and she sees herself a few years hence on a gipsy encampment on Ilona von Körösházy's estate. Józsi enters with Zorika and calls for Mihály, the innkeeper, who cannot believe his eyes at seeing Józsi returning from Hungary after two years' absence ('Kutyaláncos, der Spektakel'). 'We were a long way away, weren't we, Zorika?' Józsi replies. 'I am a gipsy, who never stays long in one place—a gipsy child!' ('Ich bin ein Zigeunerkind'). Weddings and funerals have not been the same without Józsi's violin playing, and he is warmly welcomed back into the encampment.

Zorika clearly feels deeply about Józsi, but his conversations with Mihály make it clear that he regards her purely as a passing fancy. After all, Ilona herself has always shown an interest in him, and there are plenty of other gipsy girls to welcome him back with practical expressions of delight ('Endlich, Józsi, endlich Józsi, bist du hier!').

Ilona is giving a party in the local inn that evening, and Zorika suggests that it might make a memorable night for a gipsy wedding between herself and Józsi. The gipsies move off to prepare for the occasion ('Welche von uns allen, würde Dir gefallen?') as Zorika clings excitedly to Józsi and muses on the twists of fate that have brought her from being a girl dressed magnificently in velvet and silk but knowing nothing about love to this wild and abandoned existence ('War einst ein Mädel'). 'Give me all the stars in the world from out of the heavenly canopy!' she declares ('Gib mir dort vom Himmelszelt!').

Now Ilona appears, in a fetching hunting costume, accompanied by Dragotin, who has come to join the party. Old Dragotin is trying to impress the free-living lady with his potential as a lover and overcome her doubts about his virility, but Ilona reckons that she knows the only recipe for eternal youth ('Ich weiss ein Rezept'). 'Only love makes us young. Only love gives us verve,' she proclaims ('Nur die Liebe macht uns jung').

Jolan and Kajetán arrive, seeking accommodation at the inn. They have been married for more than three years, and Kajetán is pushing a pram in which sit a small boy and girl. He is obviously finding marriage harder work than he had imagined and Jolán has turned out a decidedly bossy little wife ('Liebes Männchen, folge mir').

Ilona and Józsi obviously have eyes very much for each other and Ilona finds the idea of Józsi settling down to married life a humorous one indeed ('Ha, ha, das find' ich köstlich'). Józsi is strongly drawn to her, but she runs off as Zorika appears dressed for the gipsy wedding ceremony and Józsi coolly confirms his readiness for the wedding. His violin begins to play, as the voice of Jonel is heard calling romantically ('Lass Dich bezaubern, ach, durch mein Fleh'n') through the night. Jonel asks Zorika why she has rejected him and begs her to come back to him ('Zorika, Zorika, kehre zurück'), but Józsi's violin playing continues to hold her in its power.

Mihály summons all his serving girls to prepare for the party (Finale II: 'Vorwärts, Mädeln, rührt die Hände') and the gipsy orchestra starts playing, as Ilona tells her guests of the gipsy wedding that is to be part of the evening's entertainment. Seeing her father, Zorika goes to him, but he denies her. He does not have a gipsy daughter. Ilona tells her that she must dance and sing for them, but Zorika makes a poor effort at being a gipsy. Then bells are heard ringing and she declares her intention to get married in church, but Józsi treats the idea with contempt. A gipsy wedding is good enough for him, he says, and he produces a red scarf that he says will bind them together. For Zorika it is not enough, and she asks Józsi to tell her that he really loves her. 'I am a gipsy child,' he replies defiantly ('Ich bin ein Zigeunerkind') and Zorika, knowing that she can never love in gipsy style, turns on her heels and flees.

ACT 3

While Zorika has been looking into the future, the party for her engagement to Jonel has continued at Dragotin's hunting lodge. Jonel looks out and sees the figure of Zorika, lying asleep by the river, and longs for her pledge of love ('Gib mir das Zweiglein').

Helped by the party and by the practical Ilona, Jolán has finally managed to tie up matters for her marriage to Kajetán, and they have been listening to Dragotin recalling the days when he had a reputation as a lady-killer ('Lieber Onkel, hör mich nur an'). His reputation is a little dusty now and Ilona continues to keep him at bay without too much trouble, viewing the whole proceedings with an air of cynicism until the champagne brings out all her wild gipsy instincts ('Hör' ich Cymbalklänge').

The men clamour round her, longing to know if she will reward one of them with her favours. She looks pointedly at Józsi, but he has had enough of this company. These people are not his people and he wants only to return to the gipsy world he knows ('Ich bin ein Zigeunerkind'). As he leaves, Zorika rouses from her sleep, and Jonel hurries to her side. 'Do you still love me despite everything that has happened?' she asks. 'But nothing has happened,' he replies, 'You've been dreaming.' As he opens his arms to her, she declares that she is his and will devote her entire life to him ('Zorika, Zorika, nun bist du mein'). Not for her the vagabond life and vagabond love of the gipsy folk.

In the first London production, for which Lehár wrote some additional numbers, the events of Act 2 were treated as reality rather than a vision of the future. The role of Zorika was renamed Ilona, and the role of Ilona rechristened Lady Babby. The name Zorika was given to a subsidiary role.

The above synopsis includes the song and csárdás 'Hör' ich Cymbalklänge', originally an independent Lehár composition and added to the score of Zigeunerliebe only at a much later date.

DIE KEUSCHE SUSANNE

(Modest Susanne)

an operetta in three acts by Georg Okonkowski after the farce *Fils à Papa* by Antony Mars and Maurice Desvallières. Music by Jean Gilbert. Produced at the Wilhelm Theater, Magdeburg, 26 February 1910.

Produced at the Carltheater, Vienna, 18 March 1911.

Produced at the Liberty Theatre, New York, in a version by Harry B Smith and Robert B Smith as *Modest Suzanne* 1 January 1912 with Sallie Fisher (Suzanne), Lawrence Wheat (Hubert), Arthur Stanford (René) and Harriet Burt (Rose).

Produced at the Lyric Theatre, London, in a version by Frederick Fenn and Arthur Wimperis as *The Girl in the Taxi* 5 September 1912 with Yvonne Arnaud (Susanne), Arthur Playfair (Baron Dauvray), C H Workman (Pomarel), Alec Fraser (René), Margaret Paton (Jacqueline), Robert Averell (Hubert) and Amy Augarde (Baroness) and revived there 1 November 1913. Produced at the Garrick Theatre 23 January 1915 and played at the New Theatre from 1 March and the Criterion Theatre from 15 March 1915.

Produced at the Théâtre des Célestins, Lyon, in a version by Antony Mars and Maurice Desvallières as *La Chaste Suzanne* February 1913 with Mlle Alkins, Tréville, Raoul Villot, Armand Franck, Mlle Forcy, Georges Cahuzac and Sarah Morin and at the Théâtre de l'Apollo, Paris, 29 March 1913 with Mlle Alkins, Tréville, Villot, Edmond Tirmont, Nina Sergy, Henri Defreyn and Mme Marquet (Delphine). Produced at the Théâtre Cluny 1913 with Rachel Damour, Philippe Dolne and Mme Marquet. Produced at the Théâtre de l'Eden 24 December 1921 with Nina Myral, Max Dearly, Félix Oudart, Franck, Mlle Manetty, Defreyn and Mady Berry. Produced at the Théâtre de la Gaîté-Lyrique 20 April 1935 with Nadia Dauty and revived there 1945 and again October 1960 with Germaine Roger, Lestelly, Léo Bardollet, Philippe Andrey, Michèle Raynaud, Jacques Monteuil and Ione Claire.

A film version was produced by Richard Eichberg and Hans Sturm in 1926 with Lillian Harvey, Willy Fritsch, Albert Paulig and Ruth Wyeher. A French film version was produced by André Berthommier as *La Chaste Suzanne* in 1937 with Meg Lemonnier, Henri Garat and Raimu, and a British version also by Berthommier for British Unity in the same year with Frances Day, Garat, Laurence Grossmith, Jean Gillie, Helen Haye and John Deverell.

CHARACTERS

Baron Conrad des Aubrais, *an academic*
Delphine, *his wife*
Jacqueline, *their daughter*
Hubert, *their son*
René Boislurette, *a lieutenant*
Pomarel, *a perfume manufacturer*
Susanne, *his wife*
Charencey
Rose, *his wife*
Alexis, *head waiter at the Moulin Rouge*
Mariette, *chambermaid of the des Aubrais family*

1002

Police commissioner, members of society, members of the Academy, students, guests, policemen

ACT 1

In the hall of the villa of Baron des Aubrais, around the turn of the century, a group of elegant society ladies and gentlemen are gathered ('Liebe Baronin, wie fühlen welch' Glück!'), complimenting Delphine, the baroness, upon the admission of her husband, an eminent scientist and philosopher, to the Academy of Sciences. Proud as she is of her husband and his achievements, Delphine is no less proud of her son Hubert and daughter Jacqueline, who is a young lady brought up on all the right lines, taught never to speak to strangers and generally to do just as her mother says ('Ja solch ein Mädchen in der Jugend').

When the Baron himself arrives, he is warmly greeted by the guests ('Er kommt, er kommt, empfanget in voller Zeremonie') whom he proceeds to tell something of the high moral standards for which he is renowned, and of his theory of heredity that has won him admission to the Academy ('Richelieu war doch ein grosser Mann'). His success is the source of a great deal of envy on the part of his colleague and rival academic, Charencey, who is at the gathering, as usual, without his wife Rose.

Delphine is anxious that Jacqueline and Hubert should take after their father, but they have reached the stage of their lives when they are somewhat fed up of saying 'Yes, Papa! Yes, Mama!' Jacqueline has got herself attached to a notorious womaniser, the young Lieutenant René Boislurette. On account of the lieutenant's reputation, Baron des Aubrais has refused him his daughter's hand, but he has agreed to accept René's bargain that he would reverse his decision if he himself should ever be found in any indiscretion.

René's reputation doesn't seem to worry Jacqueline. 'Is it true, then, what everyone says about you?' she asks him ('Ist es denn wahr, was alle sagen?') and when it seems, indeed, that rumour does not lie, far from being dismayed, Jacqueline expresses a lively wish to join René in painting the town red. René's success with the girls is much envied by Hubert and he is all admiration at the story of how René once got so embroiled with a married woman that, to save her face and reputation in front of a stranger, he had to pose as her husband.

The des Aubrais family get a surprise when the scent manufacturer Pomarel and his wife Susanne arrive from the country to see them. The Pomarels, like their friends, lead an apparently blameless life ('Wir sind ein zärtlicher Ehepaar') and, indeed, Susanne has recently won first prize in a competition for exemplary and modest living. In reality, however, Madame Pomarel is by no means as virtuous as her husband and the world in general believe her to be, and she recalls with particular delight an occasion recently when she had a most agreeable flirtation with a young lieutenant. Imagine her surprise when, after her husband has departed for another engagement, she finds that same young lieutenant standing before her in the des Aubrais drawing-room. René's little adventure has come home to roost.

1003

To make matters worse, it turns out the person from whom René had sought to protect Susanne by his pretence was none other than the Baron's academic rival, Charencey. Fortunately René and Susanne are quick-witted enough to be able to save appearances when, while they are chatting earnestly together, Charencey greets them as Monsieur and Madame Pomarel. When Hubert joins the couple, he proves an instant victim to Susanne's charms, and he is agog when the conversation turns to the pleasures of Paris and especially of nights at the Moulin Rouge ('Am Tag hörst du die Riesenstadt'/'Das ist Paris, dein Parfüm und dein Duft'). Susanne would like to enjoy another evening on the town with René but he suggests that Hubert should take his place for a trip to the Moulin Rouge. Poor, quivering Hubert wonders how his meagre allowance will stretch to cover the expenses of such a thrilling but costly evening.

Before his guests depart, the Baron des Aubrais introduces Susanne to them as the winner of the prize for virtue (Finale I: 'Welch' hohe Ehr' uns heute wiederfährt'), and she gives them an account of her modest way of life ('Das ist Madame Tugendpreis'). When all are gone, the Baron declares that it is time for bed. René and Hubert, looking pointedly at their watches as well as at each other, make a great show of their intentions to retire as well. The lights are switched off and everyone goes to his or her separate bedroom.

After a short while René emerges stealthily, dressed for a night on the town. A minute later he is joined by Jacqueline. Next Hubert comes out of his room, takes a Corot painting from the wall and creeps out of the house. The painting must be pawned to finance his night out. Then the Baron comes out quietly from his room. Unfortunately he knocks over a vase, which brings the Baroness out and forces her husband to hide but, when the she eventually retires with a final 'Good Night!' at the door of each of the family's now empty bedrooms, the Baron dances off for his own night of fun.

ACT 2
At the Moulin Rouge everyone is dancing the night away with gay abandon ('Es lebe der Tanz, das Glutelixir'). One of the liveliest of the dancers is a middle-aged gentleman who is apparently an habitué of the place and whom everyone there knows as M Boboche—though his friends, if by any unfortunate chance they could see him, would recognise him as the Baron des Aubrais. Having rushed out of the family home, he hailed a taxi, only to find it being claimed also by a lady. Since it turned out that she, too, was off to the Moulin Rouge, what could be more natural than that they should share a cab and then have supper together in a private box? The two are now getting on famously.

The only person who does not seem to be enjoying himself is the head waiter, Alexis. Such, indeed, is his disenchantment with the gay life that only that day he has obtained a new post as butler in a fashionable private house where life is lived with more dignity. Little does he guess that his new master—the Baron des Aubrais—is one of his regular customers at the Moulin Rouge.

1004

Hubert is also there with Susanne Pomarel. He is understandably shy on this, his first evening alone with a lady in a private box ('Zum erstenmal im Séparé'), and his efforts to play the gallant Romeo all too readily expose him as the novice he really is, but Susanne is not slow to let him have the benefit of her own experience ('Der Kleine, der gefällt mir sehr'/'Doch immer musst Du artig sein'). René has chosen the same venue for his night out, paying eloquent courtship to Jacqueline but thoroughly enjoying himself dancing the waltz with a group of other young ladies and their partners ('Mädels, Ihr süssen, mit Eurem Leichtsinn, dem holden'/'Wenn die Füsschen sie heben').

The first complication arises when Hubert bumps into his father, but the Baron can do little in the way of reprimanding his son without justifying his own presence. Matters begin to get more out of hand when the Baron and Hubert come across Jacqueline ('Ha, Jacqueline, wo kommst du her?'). The Baron is outraged to find his daughter in such a place, but Jacqueline is quite unabashed and delighted at catching her father with another woman. The Baron is reluctantly forced to abide by the terms of his agreement with René and accept their engagement as the price of their silence. Susanne observes that it is a fine family indeed that has three members each out on the spree together, and the Baron agrees that it is indeed a remarkable proof of his theory of heredity ('Wenn der Vater mit dem Sohne').

The guests join in celebrating the engagement of Jacqueline and René (Finale I: 'Eine Verlobung wird hier gefeiert'), and Susanne proposes a toast to the happy young couple ('Trink, wenn du allein bist'). However, real trouble now comes along in the person of Monsieur Pomarel and Charencey. Earlier in the evening Charencey had gone to the Moulin Rouge as part of one of his moral crusades against licentiousness and there he spotted the couple he knew as the Pomarels each with a different partner. He had then bumped into the real M Pomarel, who had decided to go to the Moulin Rouge after missing the train to his business appointment. One thing led to another, and now Pomarel has arrived bringing the police with him.

Hubert attempts to spirit Susanne out of the place unseen, while Charencey avidly expresses his disgust at the debauchery of the two-faced des Aubrais family. It will look well in the press the next day. However, it is Charencey's turn to be discomforted when Pomarel pulls aside the veil that covers the face of the Baron des Aubrais's partner and reveals her to be none other than Charencey's wife, Rose. The others reflect on the fact that someone who sets a trap should be careful lest he get caught in it himself as Charencey calls furiously for the arrest of Hubert and his father, and the two are unceremoniously marched off to the police station.

ACT 3

Back into the des Aubrais family drawing-room the following morning creep the Baron and his son, released from custody just in time to get home before Delphine has begun her day's activity. One by one the members of the family sleepily appear from the rooms to which they have only shortly before retired. Jacqueline and Hubert are still under the influence of the amorous atmosphere of the previous evening and are full of ideas of love nests by the sea ('Ich weiss ein gar reizendes Plätzchen'/Singe, mein Schatz, wie die Lerche, juchhe!').

Then Susanne appears, in a state of great alarm lest her husband, who has spent the whole night searching for her, should find out the truth. The new butler is summoned to assist with some trumped-up evidence, but who should walk in in reply to the bell but Alexis, the erstwhile head waiter of the Moulin Rouge? Everyone except Delphine does his or her best to keep out of his sight, until the offer of an immediate pay rise ensures his silence. One way and another Susanne and des Aubrais are beginning to realise that nights on the town can be risky affairs, and that there is much to be said for the safety of home ('Auf einem Hühnerhofe da lebt ein stolzer Mann'/ 'Komm, du mein kleines Hahnemännchen').

Fortunately, to protect himself and his wife, Charencey has managed to persuade Pomarel that the ladies were at the Moulin Rouge only as part of his crusade on behalf of the virtue of fallen young women. Pomarel, of course, believes implicitly in the virtue of his Susanne, and the others are scarcely inclined to disabuse him—least of all Hubert. Like father, like son indeed (Finale III: 'Wenn der Vater mit dem Sohne')!

LEÁNYVÁSÁR

(The Girls' Market)

an operetta in three acts by Miksa Bródy and Ferenc Martos. Music by Viktor Jacobi. Produced at the Királyszinház (King's Theatre), Budapest, 14 November 1911 with Sári Petráss (Lucy), Sári Fedák (Bessy), Ernö Király (Tom Fleetwood) and Arpád Latabár (Fritz Rottenberg).

Produced at the Carltheater, Vienna, as *Der Mädchenmarkt* 7 May 1913. Produced at the Stadttheater 1 March 1915.

Produced at Daly's Theatre, London, in a version by Gladys Unger, Arthur Anderson and Adrian Ross with additional numbers by Paul Rubens and others as *The Marriage Market* 17 May 1913 with Sári Petráss (Mariposa), Gertie Millar (Kitty), Robert Michaelis (Slippery Jack), W H Berry (Blinker) and G P Huntley (Lord Hurlingham).

Produced at the Knickerbocker Theatre, New York, with additional numbers by M E Rourke, Edwin Burch and Jerome Kern 22 September 1913 with Venita Fitzhugh (Mariposa), Moya Mannering (Emma), Donald Brian (Edward) and Percival Knight (Hurlingham).

Produced at the Théâtre des Célestins, Lyon, in a version by Charles Quinel and Pierre d'Aumier with additional numbers by Alfred Haakman, Eugène Cools, H Tichaner and Pierre Letorey as *Le Beau Voyage* 15 March 1923 with Cécile Dessaud, Gabrielle Ristori, Géo Bury, Armand Franck and Morton.

CHARACTERS

Jack Fleetwood (*known as 'Slippery Jack'*)
Lord Hurlingham
Blinker, *his valet*
Senator Abe K Gilroy
Bald-Faced Sandy, *Sheriff of Mendocino Bluff and proprietor of the Palace Hotel*
Mexican Bill, Shorty, Tabasco Ted, Cheyne Harry, *cowboys*
Hi-Ti, *a Chinese bar-keeper*
Padre Pedro, a *Spanish priest*
Captain *of the 'Mariposa'*
Cabin-boy *on the 'Mariposa'*
Kitty Kent
Mariposa Gilroy
Emma, *her maid*
Pansy, Peach, Dora, *guests on the yacht*
Spanish and American cowboys, Spanish and American girls, miners, sailors, guests, middies, footmen.

ACT 1

In Mendocino Bluff, in a clearing high in the mountains of Southern California, a group of gold miners are sitting playing poker ('Then Pay and Shuffle the Pack') as the Chinese bar-keeper Hi-Ti comes by calling out 'Dlinks!', and a Mexican sings a rousing native song ('Little Chiquita'). On one of the huge redwood trees is a sign proclaiming 'Marriage Market Here Today'. It seems that this is an old Spanish custom, whereby girls are rounded up each spring and auctioned to the men for the privilege of courting them. Usually a cowboy dresses up as a priest and conducts a mock marriage ceremony, but this year the Sheriff, Bald-Faced Sandy, has arranged for a genuine priest to attend and marry the couples for real.

Three young ladies have come to this unlikely place from San Francisco. They are Mariposa Gilroy, daughter of the millionaire owner of the Mariposa gold mine, her friend Kitty Kent, and her English maid Emma. Mariposa's father believes that they are in San Diego, but the girls have decided instead to come for a bit of fun at the marriage market. Their clothes mark them out unmistakeably as townsfolk, and Mariposa suggests that they rearrange their dress to make themselves look like farmers' girls. Of course, the girls have no idea that this year the marriages will be for real. All they are out for is a lively time and Mariposa is looking forward to a change from the cityfied courting of such gentlemen as persistent Lord Hurlingham.

In their country disguises, the girls meet up with a cowboy known as Slippery Jack, son of the late John Fleetwood, former joint owner of the Mariposa mine. Fleetwood senior was frozen out by his partner, Abe K Gilroy, and was thereby denied the chance of becoming the millionaire that Gilroy himself now is. Mariposa and Kitty are keen to hear all about the marriage market from him but Jack has only chanced to be in the area that day and has no intention of taking part—though if he did, he tells them, he wouldn't want to win anyone but them ('Can You Tell Us when the Festival Begins?'/'Compliments Are Rare').

This remote part of the country is a popular place today. Blinker, Lord Hurlingham's valet, apprised of the girls' escapade by his sweetheart Emma, now turns up to book a suite at the Palace Hotel for his master. Bald-Faced Sandy greets him in his other role of landlord of the hotel and tells him about the marriage market and how this year the marriages will be for real. Blinker sees this as an excellent chance to get his master married off to Mariposa and an exchange of bank notes soon persuades Sandy to let Blinker take his place and act as auctioneer. When Emma appears, she is astonished to see Blinker and she chides him roundly for breaking her confidence, warning him that her mistress isn't going to accept just anyone as a husband simply because he's a peer ('Never Count Your Chickens Before They're Hatched!').

Lord Hurlingham duly arrives and is delighted to hear that Blinker has had himself made auctioneer so that he can knock Mariposa down to his lordship. Blinker keeps quiet about the fact that this year the marriage will be for real. When Lord Hurlingham meets Kitty, he mistakenly takes her to be Emma, Mariposa's maid, and Kitty decides to go along with the pretence. Lord Hurlingham tells Kitty that Blinker has suggested he should bid for Kitty at the auction, but Kitty isn't sure that she would welcome it. After all, American girls expect to be wooed, and Lord Hurlingham has to admit that he doesn't know anything about courting American-style. Kitty proceeds to tell him all about it ('American Courtship').

Lord Hurlingham has a rival, for Slippery Jack has decided that he must bid for Mariposa—though he stresses to Bald-Faced Sandy that she must not know it was his father who was ruined by hers. Sandy points out that he has fixed it for Mariposa to be knocked down to Lord Hurlingham, at which Jack gives him money and tells him to un-fix it. Then he gets down to the business of wooing Mariposa ('If I Could But Find My Unknown Girl'/'The One I Love').

The cowboys gather for the start of the market, the girls reacting coyly as the men eye them up ('Come On Boys, For This Is Market Day'). Sandy announces Blinker's engagement as auctioneer, and the first girl is knocked down for two cows and a mustang. When Emma is put up as lot six, Blinker makes sure that she is bought in for twenty-five cents, and then Mariposa is put up as lot seven. Unfortunately for him, Lord Hurlingham hasn't even arrived at the sale, and Blinker has no option but to knock Mariposa down to Slippery Jack, who has bid his life for her. Lord Hurlingham decides to make the best of a bad job and, to Blinker's dismay, proceeds to bid for, and get, Kitty.

Blinker has only just reached the end of the sale when Slippery Jack and Mariposa, and Lord Hurlingham and Kitty return from the marriage ceremony. Other than Slippery Jack, none of them is aware that they are really married, as they enjoy some fun together ('Hand in Hand'). Now it is all over, the girls make to leave. 'It's been great fun pretending to be married,' Mariposa declares, but Slippery Jack stops them. 'Pretending? Didn't you know it was to be a real wedding?' he asks in astonishment.

1008

As Blinker bemoans the way in which everything has gone wrong, Lord Hurlingham and the girls take in the enormity of the situation (Finale I: 'Really, Truly, Isn't it Awful?'). The crowd support the idea that Jack cannot really hold Mariposa to the marriage against her will, but he is adamant. Mariposa attempts to reason with him, but Jack assures her that he will make her love him and will build her a home finer than any she has now ('My Home Is Fair'). Finally he tells Mariposa that she can go on condition that, if the ring he places on her finger is still there in six months' time, he will know that she wants him. If not, she will never see him again.

ACT 2
Six months later, a group of people are to be seen taking life easy on the deck of Senator Gilroy's yacht *Mariposa*, anchored in San Francisco Bay ('Half a Mile Away From 'Frisco Town'). The yacht's captain is very much enjoying being the idol of all the young ladies—something that he finds wherever he may be sailing ('All the Little Girls Love a Sailor Man').

Senator Gilroy is throwing a party to help rouse his daughter from the languor she has sunk into ever since the day in the mountains when she was unwittingly married to Slippery Jack. He has sent off to the Sheriff of Mendocino Bluff to establish whether his daughter really is married, and meanwhile he wants her to enjoy the gayest party in the harbour. He is adamant that Slippery Jack shall be kept at a distance but, little does he realise, Jack is already on board as a member of the crew. Even Mariposa does not recognise him and, close though they are to each other on deck, they have to keep their loving thoughts of each other very much to themselves ('Oh, How Near and Yet How Far'/'Love of Mine').

The girls on the boat have some extra excitement when a British man o' war, the *Invincible*, is spotted in the harbour with lots of handsome midshipmen on board. Kitty invites them all to tea and, after six months cruising, they are only too glad to accept the offer of some female company. Kitty knows that a British middy never fails a lady in distress ('I Love to Meet the Sailors of the Fleet'/'Yes, I'm in Love With the Middy Boy').

Blinker also arrives on board, having been instructed by Lord Hurlingham to take a bouquet to Miss Gilroy's maid, which is still what he believes his marriage-market wife to be. Emma denies Blinker's suggestion that she and his lordship have been 'carrying on' and she is more concerned that, in six months, she has received no more than a single postcard from Blinker, in spite of the fact they are supposed to be engaged. He explains that he has been in Europe whilst his lordship sorted out family problems consequent upon his accession to the title of Marquis of Mudchester but, for the present, Blinker finds that he has plenty of success with some of the other girls on board. He is, he tells them, very near to the peerage ('Just A.1').

Shortly afterwards Lord Hurlingham approaches in a boat, but he has trouble getting on board past the sailors watching out for Slippery Jack—especially in view of his change of title. He calls for Miss Gilroy's maid and is nonplussed when Emma appears. Blinker, however, takes their conversation

1009

as confirmation that his sweetheart has indeed been 'carrying on' with his lordship and persists in interrupting them. It is only when Kitty walks past that Lord Hurlingham sorts out who really is the new Marchioness of Mudchester, leaving Blinker and Emma to enjoy renewed thoughts of marriage and the honeymoon to follow ('On Their Honeymoon').

It is Kitty who recognises 'that cowboy' amongst the sailors. Jack persuades her not to give him away and to bring Mariposa to him, and he is furious when she tells him that Mariposa's father believes that Jack wants her as his wife only for her money. He swears that Senator Gilroy will never get the better of Slippery Jack, and that he truly loves Mariposa. Moreover, from watching her, he is sure that she really loves him, and the ring is still on her finger to prove it. Senator Gilroy is furious to discover that Slippery Jack has got aboard, but he is content to grant Mariposa's request that he should be allowed to stay for the evening's dance, since he feels sure that it will show him up as the cowboy he is. Now Mariposa feels able to respond more enthusiastically to Jack's advances ('June Is in the Air'/'Come, Nestle in My Arms at Last').

In response to Senator Gilroy's query, Bald-Faced Sandy turns up and confirms that the marriages at Mendocino Bluff six months earlier were indeed legal. This is reassurance of a kind for Lord Hurlingham, who now only has to decide whether to go on honeymoon or to law. He'd much rather do the former, but Kitty has the age-old difficulty of girls of any nationality in deciding whether the answer should be 'yes' or 'no' ('When a Girl of Any Nation'/'Answers'). In the end Lord Hurlingham's seeming lack of real concern as to what her answer should be makes her decide that it should be 'no', and his lordship is forced to seek comfort in the platitudes of the ever resourceful Blinker ('I Like a Girl'/'It's Extraordinary How Things Happen').

It is now dark, the ship's lights are on, and the captain makes ready to receive the guests for the dance (Finale II: 'Belay, my Men!'). Mariposa's heart is all a-flutter as she waits for her Slippery Jack, but when he appears he is elegantly attired in full evening dress. They waltz together, expressing their ever deepening feelings for each other ('And Once I Used to Fear You'/'Do Not Fear').

Suddenly Senator Gilroy calls out to Mariposa to come away from Jack. He has just discovered that he is the son of his late partner, and Gilroy is convinced that he has married Mariposa simply to be revenged for what Gilroy had done to his father. Jack admits that, when he married her, he knew that she was Mariposa Gilroy, and she realises now what he meant when he said that Slippery Jack wasn't going to be beaten by Senator Gilroy. She tells him that she never wants to see him again and, true to his promise, Slippery Jack sets off back on the trail.

ACT 3

In Senator Gilroy's San Francisco mansion two days later, Blinker and Emma are having their health toasted at their wedding breakfast ('We Drink

Success to Both of You'). Blinker isn't sure that it wouldn't simply have been better just to be best man, but of course it's too late to change things now ('I'm the Bridegroom Just at Present'/'It's Too Late Now'). Having been refused by Kitty, Lord Hurlingham is decidedly envious of Blinker but he refuses to give up his quest for Kitty, even though she remains hard to convince of his earnestness ('When I'm Up a Tree'/'Jilolo'). Finally, fortified by some well-chosen advice from Blinker, he manages to state simply that he wishes to remain her husband because he loves her, and not simply because he is a gentleman.

Senator Gilroy, meanwhile, has summoned Slippery Jack to his presence, and he offers him $200,000 if he will release his daughter from her marriage. Jack agrees to do so if it should be Mariposa's wish and, when she confirms that it is, he simply signs the relevant papers and declines the cheque. As he walks away, Mariposa finally realises that she cannot bear to see him go and admits that she loves him (Finale III: 'Now the Clouds Have Passed Away').

The synopsis follows the English version by Gladys Unger, with lyrics by Arthur Anderson and Adrian Ross. Mariposa Gilroy and Jack Fleetwood are Lucy Harrison and Tom Fleetwood in the original Hungarian, whilst Lord Hurlingham/Blinker and Kitty/Emma are single characters, Count Fritz Rottenberg and Bessy.

EVA (Das Fabriksmädel)

(Eva, or The Factory Girl)

an operetta in three acts by A M Willner and Robert Bodanzky. Music by Franz Lehár. Produced at the Theater an der Wien, Vienna, 24 November 1911 with Mizzi Günther (Eva), Louis Treumann (Octave), Louise Kartousch (Pipsi) and Ernst Tautenhayn (Dagobert).

Produced at the New Amsterdam Theatre, New York, 30 December 1912 with Sallie Fisher (Eva).

Produced at the Alhambra, Brussels, in a version by Maurice Ordonneau 1912 with Germaine Huber, Charles Casella, Hélène Gerard and Camus. Produced at the Théâtre Ba-ta-Clan, Paris, in a version by Lucien Meyrargue 1924 with Maguy Warna, Fernand Francell and Robert Hasti.

CHARACTERS

Octave Flaubert, *a factory owner*
Dagobert Millefleurs
Pepita Désirée Paquerette, *known as* Pipsi
Bernard Larousse, *head foreman in Flaubert's factory*
Eva
Mathieu, *a servant in Flaubert's house*

Voisin, *head bookkeeper in Flaubert's factory*
Prunelles, *assistant bookkeeper in Flaubert's factory*
George, Teddy, Fredy, Elli, Schischi, Gustave, Henri, Gaston, Ferry
Factory workers, a chauffeur, servants

ACT 1

In Flaubert's glass factory in Brussels, the workers are dressed up in their party clothes and gathering with presents to celebrate the birthday of one of their number ('Heissa, jucheia, jetzt gibt's was zu seh'n'). The birthday girl is Eva, a golden-headed lass of twenty who is brought in by the head foreman, Larousse. He reminds the older workers of the grey, foggy winter morning fifteen years earlier when he first brought Eva to them, a little girl of five who had come into his care and who he had suggested should be cared for by the factory folk. Since then she has been loved by them as a daughter, and now he presents her with a bank book showing the sum of 1,200 francs, which has been collected for the time when, before too long, she will wish to marry.

Eva feels that, despite all the kindness shown to her, she doesn't really belong at the factory. She feels that she belongs to the bright lights of the city and the world of the elegant dresses that she sees on the boulevards. She is anxious, too, to know how she came to be left in Larousse's care and she is unconvinced by the good man's story of how, ill and needy and going off with a new lover, her mother had brought little Eva to be looked after by one she knew would love her. Eva has rather different memories. She can still see her mother, a beautiful woman dressed in silk and wearing pearl earrings, standing before a large mirror in a room with elegant drapes and plush carpets. That is how she would like to be some day, even if only for a moment ('Im heimlichen Dämmer der silbernen Ampel'/'Wär' es auch nichts als ein Augenblick').

It is an important day for the workers, for today the factory has a new boss. He is Octave Flaubert, nephew of the previous owner, and there is a great deal of speculation as to how he will turn out. 'Is he young? Old? Married? Single?' is what the female workers are especially anxious to know. He proves to be an elegant, bearded and monocled man, but fond of good living and obviously with little idea of how to run a factory. His major concern seems to be the proximity of good restaurants, and he appears utterly bemused by the idea that he should have become a factory boss ('Bestimmung—Fatum—das ist alles!'). His knowledge of the glass business seems to have been gained exclusively through a song sung by the popular singer Lavallière at the Moulin Rouge, a song which he is delighted to discover that the bookkeeper Prunelles is also familiar with ('Glück und Glas, klingeling').

Octave receives a visit from an old school chum named Dagobert, who enters in great excitement, having left a taxi outside with the meter running. Dagobert tells Octave that he was dining alone in a restaurant in Paris when a lady rushed in, apparently fleeing from her husband, and begged Dagobert to save her. The gallant Dagobert has reckoned that the best place to hide

1012

her is Octave's factory. The young lady is Pepita Paquerette, known to her friends as Pipsi, and it is obvious that Dagobert has fallen head over heels in love with her ('Nur keine Angst—hier kann uns nichts passieren'/'Pipsi, holdes Pipsi').

While Dagobert goes off with Octave to arrange to make his apartment ready to receive the lady in distress, Prunelles comes face to face with Pipsi. He recognises her immediately as Pipsi Paquerette of the Printemps store—men's underwear department—and it seems that he himself was once a victim of her standard trick. Apparently Pipsi uses the same ploy every year, around holiday-time, to find herself a protector who will take her on a fortnight's holiday. She manages to persuade Prunelles not to give her away and, while Dagobert is outside paying his taxi, she and Octave quickly find that they share a taste for the night life of Montmartre ('Um zwölf in der Nacht'/'Die Geister von Montmartre').

By the time the mid-day bell brings Octave's first morning at the factory to an end, he has made the acquaintance of Eva, and become immediately attracted, and he has also received a message from fourteen of his Parisian friends, saying that, since he won't go to Paris to see them, they are coming to Brussels to see him. Prunelles is charged with arrangements for the party.

As the workers return for their next working session, Prunelles introduces their new boss, who favours them with a few well-chosen words (Finale I: 'Halt! Ein Augenblick, ihr Leute'). When the others have gone, Octave tries to bring Eva out with tempting talk of the elegant life in the world outside, but he finds Larousse decidedly possessive. He insists that Larousse leave Eva alone with him but, when Larousse has gone, Eva reacts angrily. 'What am I to you?' she asks. Octave assures her that it is simply gentlemanly concern. He tries to fan the flames of her passion for elegant clothes, but merely receives the response that 'workers remain workers'. Octave offers her a job as his secretary, but she rebuffs him as the workers outside his office embark upon a further round of cheers for their new boss.

ACT 2

In Octave's apartment at the factory his guests from Paris are enjoying the party he has laid on for them, and a quadrille is under way. Pipsi is among those present, still availing herself of Dagobert's willing protection from the attentions of other men ('Retten Sie mich, Dagobert, die Herren sind zu keck!').

Octave's friends make fun of his transition from Parisian man-about-town to Belgian manufacturer. What is more, they laugh, he shows signs of being in love. Octave finds he cannot simply throw away his years of good life in Paris, and soon he is joining his friends in a gay celebration of its pavements, its atmosphere and its vices ('Hat man das erste Stiefelpaar vertreten in Paris'/'O du Pariser Pflaster') but, when Prunelles comes to ask how Octave finds the arrangements, the old bon viveur confides his concern that he has not seen Eva for a couple of days.

Prunelles, meanwhile, has decided to apprise Dagobert of Pipsi's real situation, but Pipsi defends herself by claiming that Prunelles is the brutal husband from whom she is escaping. Dagobert, willingly believing, insists that Prunelles give Pipsi a divorce, as she manages to play the one off against the other quite brilliantly ('Rechts das Männchen meiner Wahl'/'Geschieden muss sein, so heisst es im Lied').

In spite of the festivities, Octave is still unable to get Eva out of his thoughts. Then, suddenly, she appears at the doorway, modestly dressed and marvelling at the brilliance of the decor and dresses she sees around her. If only she herself could experience the rustling of silk just once! Suddenly she sees Octave ('Erschrecken Sie nicht—ich bin's!') and, afraid of being seen with her boss, she apologises profusely for intruding and explains that she simply couldn't resists the music and the bright lights. Octave brushes away her apologies and assures her that she would pass for a queen in any company. He makes passionate advances to her, and this time she is unable to resist ('Nur das eine Wort—sprich es aus!'/'Schwül aus tiefen Kelchen lockt dich ein Duft').

Concerned at what might happen if Larousse knew she was with Octave, she soon rushes off, but this time not without a fond farewell. Octave decides to get Larousse out of the way, and he arranges for Prunelles to send him on the night train to Antwerp to deliver an order. Then Prunelles is to take the finest ball-gown from Pipsi's wardrobe and bring Eva along in it. Octave reflects on how he is, for the very first time, deeply in love, and how he has for once found a woman who is not merely a source of passing amusement ('Octave, gesteh' dir's ein—du bist verliebt!').

Meanwhile Pipsi has lost heavily at cards, and Dagobert is ruefully counting the cost. Pipsi tells him he will have to write to his father for some more money, but Dagobert has already done so. His father's reply is that Dagobert is a fool, that he can have no more money, and that he should come home at once. Pipsi seeks to build up his courage to go and face the music ('Ziehe hin zu deinem Vater'/'Sei nicht bös'—nicht nervös').

Now Eva reappears at the door, dressed in supreme elegance ('Eva, Sie sehen reizend aus!') and Octave takes her on his arm and leads her into the world of high society. To her it is just a dream, a case of Cinderella in the royal palace, the more so when Octave places a string of pearls around her neck. It is a dream, moreover, that recalls that fleeting memory of her mother ('Mädel! Mein süsses Aschenbrödel du'/'Wär' es auch nichts als ein Augenblick') as she and Octave dance together around the room.

Their joy is interrupted when Larousse appears, demanding Eva. Octave manages to send him away, and as the dancing gains momentum Dagobert proposes a toast to Octave and his new-found happiness (Finale II: 'Silentium! Silentium! Ich bringe einen Toast!'), but the clinking of champagne glasses is interrupted by the sound of Larousse and his fellow factory workers demanding to be let in. After ushering everyone into another room, Octave agrees to receive Larousse, who tells him that there are two hundred workers outside demanding their Eva back. Octave reassures them by telling them that Eva is his fiancée, and they finally leave quietly. Back with Eva, Octave congratulates himself on the little white lie with which he has staved off the attack, and he urges Eva to leave the factory and go with him to Paris but Eva reflects on the full implications of his admission that his description of her as his fiancée was merely a white lie. 'No! A thousand times no!' she says. 'I shall go my own way!' Octave is left calling out helplessly after her, 'Eva! What have I done?'

ACT 3

Pipsi is sitting relaxing in a rented villa in Paris's Bois de Boulogne with Octave's friend Fredy. Eva is staying there with Pipsi, and it seems that she has acquired a taste for the high life for, under Pipsi's tutelage, she has become a lady of fashion in Paris. She has even aroused the interest of the Duc de Morny but Pipsi and Fredy are agreed that, before this new relationship can be allowed to blossom, Octave should be warned of her whereabouts. Meanwhile Pipsi encourages Eva with a description of how they have all Paris at their pretty feet ('Wenn die Pariserin spazieren fährt'/ 'Manches diskret man zeigt') for the girls have been invited, along with all their Parisian friends, to a soirée given by the Duc de Morny, and they are preparing themselves for the merry social whirl ('Gib acht, gib acht, mein schönes Kind'/'Herrgott, lass mir doch meinen Leichtsinn nur').

Prunelles and Dagobert arrive at the villa, having arranged to lure Octave there on the pretext of looking over the quarterly accounts whilst he is in Paris for the Duke de Morny's reception. Prunelles is surprised to find Pipsi in residence. 'On holiday again?' he asks her. It seems, though, that Dagobert is really the one man for her. It is at her invitation that he has come, but he is all the more welcome for the fact that he has taken up a book-keeping position with a salary of 15,000 francs. It should be enough for two to live on—perhaps even three ('Pipsi, holdes Pipsi').

Octave arrives in evening dress and is astonished when Eva appears in an elegant *robe de soir*. She affects coldness towards him, even contempt, as she recalls his fatal words (Finale III: 'Ein Mädel wie Sie, so nett und so fein'). Octave draws her to him, but she tells him to forget her. Then, catching sight of herself in the mirror, in her elegant dress, she recalls once more the vision of her mother and realises that Octave can save her from a similar fate. As he makes a final plea, she finally acknowledges that she has forgiven him and lets him take her in his arms.

DER LIEBE AUGUSTIN

(Dear Augustin)

an operetta in three acts by Rudolf Bernauer and Ernst Welisch, a revised version of *Der Rebell* (Theater an der Wien 29 November 1905). Music by Leo Fall. Produced at the Neues Theater, Berlin, 3 February 1912 with Fritzi Massary (Princess

Helene).

Produced at the Raimundtheater, Vienna, 12 October 1912 with Mizzi Zwerenz and Hubert Marischka.

Produced at the Shaftesbury Theatre, London, in a version by Alexander M Thompson, A Scott Craven, Harry Beswick and Percy Greenbank as *Princess Caprice* 11 May 1912 with Harry Welchman (Augustin), Courtice Pounds (Jasomirgott), George Graves (Bogumil), Clara Evelyn (Princess Helene) and Cicely Courtneidge (Clementine).

Produced at the Casino Theatre, New York, in a version by Edwin Smith as *Lieber Augustin* 3 September 1913 with George Macfarlane (Augustin), Viola Gilette (Captain Pip), De Wolf Hopper (Bogumil), May de Sousa (Helen), Rozsika Dolly (Clementine) and Fred Leslie (Prince Nikola).

CHARACTERS

Bogumil, *Regent of Thessaly*
Helene, *his niece*
Gjuro, *Prime Minister*
Nicola, *Prince of Mikolics*
Colonel Burko
Captain Mirko
Cadet Pips
Pasperdu, *a lawyer*
Augustin Hofer, *a piano teacher*
Jasomirgott, *Princess Helene's valet*
Anna, *his daughter*
Sigiloff, *a bailiff*
Mattaeus, *a lay brother and gate-keeper in a monastery*
Servants, courtiers, members of parliament, officers, officials, musicians, soldiers, servants, maids, bridesmaids.

ACT 1

Bogumil, Regent of Thessaly until his niece Helene comes of age, has fallen upon hard times. At this very moment the bailiff Sigiloff and other unpleasant officials are knocking on the door of the palace and demanding to be let in ('Macht auf, macht auf, sonst sprengen wir'). In the capriciously furnished boudoir of Princess Helene, menservants and maids are fluttering around in alarm, as Jasomirgott, Princess Helene's valet, resists the bailiff's demands, but eventually he has to give in. Despite the protests of Jasomirgott and his daughter Anna, the bailiff and his men seize clocks, sculptures, porcelain and anything else that they can lay hands upon—even a piano.

Anna is a somewhat haughty young lady, ever conscious of the fact that she and Princess Helene were born together and weaned together. All that she lacks, she feels, is a father of noble birth. She is not too impressed with the fiancé her father has found for her, for he is Augustin, a humble Viennese whom Bogumil has brought to Thessaly as Court piano teacher. 'A musician!' exclaims Anna contemptuously. 'Not a musician, but a real artist,' retorts her father. 'A man who plays the piano beautifully. With both hands. And something different with each hand!'

Bogumil seems not the slightest bit put out by his financial situation nor by the creditors who, he declares, must wait while he takes things easy and drinks his champagne ('Ich bin im Land der Herr Regent'/'Will wer von uns bezahlet sein'). Nonetheless the financial position cannot be ignored for ever and, having tried everything else, his Prime Minister finally suggests a rich marriage for Princess Helene. Prince Nicola of Mikolics is clearly the man, even though he is Bogumil's deadly enemy. It was Nicola who locked up Bogumil's brother, the late Prince, around the time of Helene's birth, so that Bogumil himself had to help deliver the baby.

Augustin, the piano teacher, arrives to give Princess Helene her piano lesson. He is a simple soul, and he can't help thinking how much better a wife the musicianly Princess would make him than the unmusical Anna. While he is waiting he looks around the empty room, noticing the various items that are missing and, on the desk, the bailiff's seizure order, signed by a lawyer named Pasperdu. Suddenly he realises that the piano has gone. What should he do now? 'Take your time. Wait and see,' he tells himself ('Lass' dir Zeit').

When eventually the door opens, it is Anna. She tells him to wait just a moment longer and the conversation between the engaged pair, while they wait together, only emphasises the difference in their aspirations. When the Princess arrives, she immediately sees something is wrong between the couple and, when Anna has left, she extracts from Augustin his worries that Anna is too grand for him, the son of a mere cobbler. Their conversation becomes increasingly more intimate and, when finally they get round to the piano lesson, they make light of the fact that there is no piano. 'We'll play on the silent piano,' suggests Augustin. 'That will keep the neighbours happy.' And the lesson duly proceeds on an imaginary piano ('Es war einmal ein Musikus').

Bogumil's latest disastrous news is that the army is in revolt. A deputation of rebel soldiers comprising Colonel Mirko, Captain Burko and Cadet Pips arrives. They demand to be paid, or they will down arms ('Wir wollen uns're Gage'). Bogumil does not know what he can do, but then the Prime Minister arrives with a telegram. It is from Prince Nicola, expressing his interest in the offer of the Princess's hand and saying that he is coming to Thessaly at once. Everyone's hopes and hearts are raised except for poor Princess Helene who is horrified at becoming engaged, so to speak, behind her back. Her uncle can only point out that the alternative is for Thessaly to be wiped off the map.

Helene is desolate. She can think of only one person who can console her in her misery and, late as it is, she asks her valet to bring Augustin to her. While she waits alone she picks up a book and begins to read almost in a trance (Finale I: 'Es war ein alter König'). The arrival of Augustin rouses her from her daze, and she tells him the whole awful story of what is in store for her. Not least of the horrors is the fact that their music-making must be over. 'Be my companion,' she says to him 'and think of the lovely hours that we have shared together' ('Sei mein Kamerad'). Jasomirgott returns with a candle and persuades the Princess that it is her bedtime and, as she goes into her room, she drops a rose. Augustin picks it up and puts in in his button-hole, as Jasomirgott shows him out.

ACT 2

In a hall of the castle the servants are preparing a banquet to welcome Prince Nicola ('Der Freier ist erschienen'). The procession of diners appears, headed by a group of Thessalian hussars followed by Prince Nicola himself. The Prime Minister bangs his ceremonial rod three times on the ground, and Princess Helene enters to the sound of the Thessalian national anthem. She attempts to persuade Prince Nicola that her moods, her caprices and her temper would make her a quite unsuitable bride, but Nicola seems quite determined on the match and he slips an engagement ring on her finger. Clearly, though, all he is interested in is the Thessalian throne. 'The Princess may have the title,' he says, 'but the power is mine. Everything is set down in the marriage contract. Paragraphs 1 to 199 set out my rights, paragraph 200 the Princess's.' Princess Helene is furious. 'I am young,' she says, 'I want to live, I want happiness—and you come to me with paragraphs!'

Augustin is still carrying around Helene's rose but Jasomirgott warns him that there can be no truck between a poor musician and a princess, and he encourages Augustin to go with Anna to Vienna and take over an inn where he can provide music with his own instrumental group. Anna, however, has no intention of leaving her affluent surroundings in the castle ('Anna, was ist denn mit dir?'), particularly as she and Nicola have become quite taken with each other. She tells the Prince the full story of how she and the Princess were born together at the ruling family's ancestral castle home while their mothers were in flight, and how they were baptised and brought up together, and Nicola soon decides that he wants Anna as a lady-in-waiting at his Court—as a 'friend' in the manner of Madame Lavallière at the Court of Louis XIV ('Louis Quatorze, so hiess der König').

Augustin tells Princess Helene that he plans to leave. Helene would gladly swap places with Anna and go with him to the inn, that joyful inn where everyone enjoys the wine and where heaven seems full of violins ('Ich weiss ein kleines Wirtshaus'/'Und der Himmel hängt voller Geigen'). 'That would indeed be lovely,' says Augustin.

As Augustin leaves, he catches part of a conversation between Nicola and a man he addresses as Pasperdu. The name rings a bell in his brain. Surely it is the name of the mysterious lawyer behind the seizure of Bogumil's posses-sions. Augustin lingers, unseen, and overhears Nicola congratulating Pasperdu on the seizure of Thessaly's assets, discussing how to prevent Bogumil getting his hands on any money, and planning to set up a mistress in the castle. Augustin hurries to tell Jasomirgott what he has heard and the valet promises to warn Helene.

Bogumil has already made plans on how to use the latest intake of money, and he intends to start with a riotous party with his officers that evening ('Heut' Nacht nach acht'). His plans receive a setback when Helene arrives declaring that the marriage is off because Nicola has a lover in the castle, but Bogumil pooh-poohs the idea, and the courtiers all assemble for the signing of the wedding contract (Finale II: 'Die Damen sind erschienen'). The appearance of Anna amongst the royal ladies-in-waiting is greeted with some shock, but Helene is equal to the situation. She points out that, since Anna is engaged in the royal household, her fiancé should have similar status and so Augustin is summoned and promptly made a gentleman-in-waiting.

ACT 3

In the outer court of the ancestral castle of the Kings of Thessaly, Nicola is getting ready for his wedding. It is his express wish that he and Helene be married in this historic place, and he does not realise that Bogumil sold it to a brotherhood of monks some twenty-one years ago. Now the monks brew a liqueur here, and the amazed Nicola finds that he has actually ordered his wedding to take place in a distillery.

The castle is the place where Helene and Anna were born when their mothers were on the run with Bogumil and Jasomirgott. Old Brother Mattheus remembers that occasion well. He even remembers the birthmark like a champagne cork that the Princess inherited from her father. Jasomirgott interrupts to point out that there must be some mistake, since it is *his* daughter who has such a birthmark, but Mattheus is adamant, and Bogumil and Jasomirgott realise with horror that they must have mixed the children up. Yet now it seems obvious—Jasomirgott's supposed daughter with the lofty airs, and the supposed Princess with the temperament that causes her to be known as 'Princess Caprice'. They resolve to tell nobody and ensure Mattheus's silence by declaring that he was to blame because of the effect his liqueur had on their faculties that fateful night ('Was hilft in bösen Tagen?').

As the time for the marriage grows nearer, Helene feels more strongly than ever her wish that she were not a Princess and could go away with Augustin, but the Bishop has arrived to solemnise the wedding, and she can see no way out. Unless! Could she, perhaps, enter a nunnery? A nice nunnery where, perhaps, Augustin might be needed to play the harmonium ('Wenn die Sonne schlafen geht'). It is clear that this is the only way out. She breaks the news to Anna and Jasomirgott that she is going into a convent. Anna believes that it is because Helene has found out about Anna's fondness for Nicola, but Helene disabuses her. It is because of her own love for Augustin. Jasomirgott realises that he can help both the girls with a few simple words, and knows he can keep silent no longer. The two young ladies are delighted to find that they are, in effect, each other and they beg Jasomirgott to speak out right away ('Hast du lieber mich?').

Nicola enters just in time to see his intended bride being kissed by Jasomirgott, but all is rapidly sorted out. Helene insists that Augustin go through with his promise to marry Jasomirgott's daughter—herself—while Nicola is assured that, if he marries Anna, he will be able to see for himself the family's champagne cork birthmark (Finale III: 'Er kommt, er kommt').

And so it is Anna who walks to the altar as Nicola's bride while the bells ring and the organ plays.

DER LILA DOMINO

(The Lilac Domino)

an operetta in three acts by Emmerich von Gatti and Béla Jenbach. Music by Charles Cuvillier. Produced at the Stadttheater, Leipzig, 3 February 1912.

Produced at the 44th Street Theatre, New York, in a version by Harry B Smith and Robert B Smith as *The Lilac Domino* 28 October 1914 with Eleanor Painter (Georgine) and John E Hazzard.

Produced at the Empire Theatre, London, in a version with additional dialogue by S J Adair Fitzgerald and additional numbers by Howard Carr and Donovan Parsons 21 February 1918 with Clara Butterworth (Georgine), Jamieson Dodds (André), Josephine Earle (Leonie) and Vincent Sullivan (Elliston Deyn). Produced at the Palace Theatre 23 October 1919 with the same stars. Produced at His Majesty's Theatre in a revised version by H C Sargent 5 April 1944 with Pat Taylor, Bernard Clifton, Elizabeth French and Graham Payn and revived there 14 September 1944.

A film version was produced by Grafton-Capitol-Cecil in 1937 with June Knight, Michael Bartlett, Richard Dolman, Athene Seyler and Fred Emney.

CHARACTERS

Gaston Le Sage, *a wealthy Lyon silk merchant*
Paul Dorien, *his nephew*
Léonie Lemonnier, *a merry widow*
Major Montague Drake, Bertie Raymond, Jack Allison, *expatriate remittance men*
Krovani, *leader of a gipsy orchestra*
Georgine, *Le Sage's daughter*
Madame Delcasse, *principal of a finishing school for young ladies*
Marcel, *Le Sage's butler*
Waiters, dominoes, maskers, dancers, guests

ACT 1

It is gala night at the Hôtel Parnasse in Nice, and a masquerade is in progress. Guests are gathered in a lounge leading to the ballroom, when a girl runs in excitedly with the news that the wealthy old Lyon silk merchant Gaston Le Sage has found himself a young widow as his third wife ('No Fools Like Old Fools').

Le Sage enters with his young bride-to-be, Léonie, but, although he fusses around her attentively, she seems to be more interested in his nephew, Paul Dorien. Gaston promised Paul's mother, Gaston's late step-sister, that Paul would eventually be married to Gaston's own daughter, Georgine. The two are due to be reunited the following day after some years apart, but Paul seems to have no great interest either in women in general or Georgine in particular. Léonie, however, attempts to bring the boy out a little, offering him advice from her own experience ('We Girls Don't Like Them Shy').

Elsewhere in the lounge are to be found a couple of expatriate Englishmen—Major Montague Drake, a dapper, regimental type, and a young man named Bertie Raymond. Both of them are somewhat down on their luck and they have to struggle from day to day to finance their gambling interests. They are hoping that their friend Jack Allison may have succeeded in raising more cash, but he is currently putting his gambling interests to one side in favour of the pursuit of romance ('Let the Gypsies Play'). Jack is, in reality, the Duke of Everset, but he has chosen to hide his aristocratic identity since he settled on the Riviera because of the way prices are put up when a titled gentleman approaches.

Georgine, Gaston's eighteen-year-old daughter, appears accompanied by Madame Delcasse, the principal of her finishing school. Madame Delcasse is evidently concerned to keep Georgine on the straight and narrow and she has only agreed to attend the masquerade under pressure from Georgine herself. Georgine is determined to enjoy the champagne that is flowing freely, and to see what fate may produce for her in the form of a mate ('My Fate'). She promises Madame Delcasse that she will not remove her mask and she is unrecognisable under her domino when Gaston and Paul come upon her and begin chatting. She conjures up an air of mystique as she introduces herself to them merely as the Lilac Domino ('The Lilac Domino').

Drake, Bertie Raymond and Jack Allison reappear. Jack has now lost all his remaining money, but a possible remedy for their troubles is at hand. When they seek solace in music from the gipsy orchestra, the leader Krovani reveals himself as a representative of a matrimonial agency and produces a list of wealthy ladies seeking husbands. The three friends reckon that they are on to a winner when they find on the list a young lady of eighteen, the daughter of a Lyon silk merchant and fresh from finishing school. The only question is which of them should be forced into matrimony for the good of the others. The problem is resolved by a throw of the dice, which Jack wins (Finale I: 'This Seems to Me a Tricky Business').

Meanwhile, the men come upon the figure of the Lilac Domino, who has passed out under the influence of too much unaccustomed champagne. Jack kisses her and wakes her up and, after a brief display of reluctance, the two of them waltz away together.

ACT 2

In the garden of Le Sage's villa near Monte Carlo, a cocktail party and informal dance are being held to celebrate Georgine's coming out and her engagement to Paul. Léonie is still looking for some real sign of tender recognition from Gaston ('For Your Love I Am Waiting') and, when he appears with a young lady on each arm, she challenges his devotion to her. She proposes that he should give her a million francs if he should be discovered flirting with a young lady within the next forty-eight hours, and Gaston agrees to write out the cheque there and then. Léonie can retain it as a hostage.

When Gaston has gone, Léonie turns her attentions to Paul and tests him on the training that she has been giving him in readiness for wooing Georgine. However, Paul's parting shot is an admission that he is in love with Léonie. Major Drake and Bertie Raymond arrive, having followed up the details of Georgine issued by Krovani's matrimonial agency, and they press upon Gaston the claims of the Duke of Everset as a suitor for Georgine, undeterred by Gaston's insistence that she is already promised. The Major reckons that Jack will never be persuaded to come to the house to meet Georgine, but Bertie explains that he has sought to trick Jack there by claiming that he will find there the mysterious Lilac Domino over whom he has so completely lost his head. They both feel pretty pleased with themselves as they mature their little plot ('A Pretty Pair!').

The arrival of the Duke of Everset is duly announced, and Jack immediately greets Georgine as his Lilac Domino ('Hello! Lilac Domino!'). Georgine naturally rejects the suggestion that she could have been at a masquerade, and Madame Delcasse adds forcefully that she would never have allowed Georgine to visit such an event. Jack's two friends try to persuade him to forget the Lilac Domino nonsense and concentrate on the heiress. They tell him that the invitation was just their trick to get him there, but Jack is not to be put off. He insists that the voice of the Lilac Domino remains in his mind as clear as a bell ('The Bells of Bon Secour'), and he knows that that voice was Georgine's.

Drake and Raymond are delighted to see how well Jack and Georgine are getting on—so much so that they indulge in some impromptu dancing with Léonie, Gaston and Paul ('Dancing, Dancing')—while Paul has now quite definitely decided that he is in love with Léonie. Whenever he and Georgine get together they squabble like the children they were when they last met, and they are quite resolved not to marry each other. So, while Paul returns to Léonie, Georgine now welcomes Jack's expressions of love ('What Has Gone').

The radiantly happy Georgine bumps into Krovani, who has arrived to provide the music for the occasion. He has been instructed to remove Georgine's name from his list of matrimonial prospects, as her engagement to her cousin is to be announced that evening. Seeing her looking so happy, he comments on the joy of true love. It is a far cry from the situation at the masquerade he recently attended where three gentlemen threw dice to decide which one should find a wife purely for her money. Somewhat the worse for wine, Krovani carelessly adds the name of the winner of the gamble—the Duke of Everset! Georgine is horrified.

Now Jack is brought in blindfolded to test whether he really can recognise his Lilac Domino (Finale II: 'Seek, Find, Love's Blind') but Georgine bitterly renounces him and declares that her hand is Paul's. She will have nothing to do with Jack's assurance that, though he did indeed throw the dice, his love for Georgine is real.

1022

ACT 3

It is carnival night at the Café de Paris, Monte Carlo, and the guests are all in fancy dress ('Carnival Night'). Jack has arranged a private supper, and Drake and Raymond are surprised and concerned to learn that he intends it as a farewell, even though he seems to have little idea of where he is going to go. They attempt to reassure him with the news that they have selected another likely candidate from the matrimonial list to restore their fortunes, and this time they will take on the challenge. Krovani provides more realistic reassurance with the news that he has told Georgine, Léonie and Madame Delcasse the full story of what had happened and they are on their way to the Café de Paris.

As the evening progresses, Drake becomes involved in a party game with a bunch of girls ('All Line Up in a Queue') and the revels continue unabated ('Ah! Ah! Ah!' / Tarantella). Georgine, Léonie and Madame Delcasse have appeared, with Georgine obviously much distressed, and Gaston and Paul arrive separately. Gaston is much taken by the sight of Madame Delcasse and, indeed, he is soon alone with her, flirting madly until Léonie catches them about to embrace. Léonie has won her million francs from Gaston, and, no longer in need of him for his money, she turns to Paul ('We Girls Don't Like Them Shy').

Gaston is furious at this turn of events, but only for as long as it takes Madame Delcasse to offer a few words of comfort and affection. She also points out to Gaston how well it would sound to have the Duchess of Everset as a daughter and, by the time that the guests are enjoying supper ('Carte de jour'), almost all the romantic pairings are resolved. Then Georgine comes to bid Jack a fond farewell and, before long, his little Lilac Domino has accepted his offer of marriage. The news that one of his estates has been sold for a large sum of money is merely the icing on their future wedding cake (Finale III: 'The Domino! The Lilac Domino!').

The synopsis follows the revised (1953) English version by H F Maltby, which retains the songs 'For your love I am waiting', 'Carnival Night' and 'All Line Up in a Queue', with lyrics by Donovan Parsons and music by Howard Carr, interpolated in the first British production. The names of the characters and the settings have varied between the various productions as follows:-

Leipzig	*New York and London*	*Revised version*
Vicomte de Sorize	Cornelius Clevedon	Gaston Le Sage
Georgine	Georgine	Georgine
Marquis d'Elledon	Elliston Deyn	Paul Dorien
Lony d'Andorcet	Leonie Forde	Leonie Lemonnier
Count Anatol de Saint-Vallé	André d'Aubigny	Jack Allison
Prosper Buzot	Prosper Woodhouse	Montague Drake
Raimond de Constard	Norman J Calmain	Bertie Raymond
Baroness Alary	Baroness de Villiers	Madame Delcasse
István	Carabana	Krovani

1023

Jean   Parker   Marcel
Setting: Paris   Palm Beach, Florida   Nice and Monte Carlo

DER ZIGEUNERPRIMÁS

(The Gipsy Violinist)

an operetta in three acts by Julius Wilhelm and Fritz Grünbaum. Music by Emmerich Kálmán. Produced at the Johann Strauss Theater, Vienna, 11 October 1912 with Alexander Girardi (Pali Rácz), Grete Holm (Sári), Willy Strehl and Max Brod.

Produced at the Liberty Theatre, New York, in a version by Catherine Chisholm Cushing and E P Heath as *Sári* 13 January 1914, with Mitzi Hajos (Sári), Van Rensslaer Wheeler (Pali Rácz), Blanche Duffield (Juliska), Charles Meakins (Gaston) and J Humbird Duffy (Laczi). Played at the Liberty Theatre 29 January 1930 with Mitzi Hajos, Boyd Marshall, Marybeth Conoley and Duffy.

CHARACTERS

Pali Rácz
Laczi, Sári, Pista, Ferko, Gyuri, Boldizár, Andris, Jóska, Marci, Erzsi, Ilonka, Etelka, Kata, Piroska, Rozsika, Klári, *his children*
Juliska Rácz, *his niece*
Gaston, Count Irini
The Countess Irini
King Heribert VII, *incognito as* Count Estragon
Mustari
Monsieur Cadeau
Jóska Fekete, Sándor Babári, Lajcsi Banda, Ferkó Vörös, Károly Balog, Kálmán Dombovári, Imre Pongracz, *gipsies*
Pierre, *a servant*
Gipsies, countryfolk, musicians, servants, ladies and gentlemen of society

ACT 1

Pali Rácz is an internationally renowned gipsy orchestra leader. When first we meet him, in the music room of his country house in Lörinczfalva, he is despairing over the efforts of his sixteen children to reach his standards with their music lessons ('Aufhör'n, aufhör'n, kutya lánczos, wos ist dos für Kratzerei!'). Finally he takes the violin from one of them to demonstrate his point, only to find that he himself now has difficulty achieving the musical effect he wants. 'It's all over!' he cries out. 'I can't do it. This damned gout! Go out to play, if you want.'

The children rush into the garden, leaving Rácz despondent, until his daughter Sári appears carrying a tray with a large dish of soup. Rácz asks for his niece Juliska, whom he is hoping to make his fourth wife, but Sári refers him to his doctor's orders that he should not get excited. 'I get excited if she comes, and I get excited if she doesn't,' he replies irritably. 'But, when she is here,' he adds more calmly, 'I feel so well and so young.' His daughter points out that he has already been married three times which, in her opinion, is quite enough and Rácz is left to think back over the days when he was the world's leading virtuoso gipsy violinist and the object of all the young ladies' adulation ('Vor paar Jahren noch ein König').

Rácz is pleased when Juliska at last arrives, bringing him a bundle of letters that demonstrates the extent of his international fame—letters from as far afield as London, Paris, Manchester, Florence and Odessa. Rácz sees it as natural enough. Heidsieck exports champagne, Krupp cannons, and Rácz gipsy musicians. Even now Stockholm is ordering a double-bass player and the Trocadero in Paris a clarinettist. Among the letters is one marked 'Private', which turns out to be from his friend Count Irini, announcing that he intends to pay a visit. Rácz is delighted, though he takes care to warn Juliska not to flirt with the young Count.

Rácz's eldest son and musical heir, Laczi, enters just in time to interrupt his father and Juliska in a farewell embrace, and Rácz scolds Laczi for failing to knock. A more constant source of discord between Rácz and his son is the younger man's discovery of the music of Wagner, Bach and Händel, which he finds more stimulating than the old gipsy songs and, when Sári returns, she senses a distinct atmosphere between the two. She suggests they behave more sensibly and turns to attending to the children who are asking for food, though not before they have got her to sing a fairy-tale song with them ('Auf dem gold'nen Throne'/'Ein Soldat, ein Magnat, und ein Jäger mit Gewehr').

Gaston, Count Irini, arrives with Cadeau, the representative of the Count's guardians and, seeing Sári bending over Klari, Rácz's youngest child, he cannot resist giving her a kiss. The visitors are greeted by Rácz with a bottle of Tokay wine, and Gaston chides Rácz for never having let on that he has such an attractive daughter. Gaston reveals that he has come to ask Rácz to play at a concert he is giving in Paris for the King of Massilia. Rácz is attracted by the idea, as he once received a decoration from the King, but he is inhibited by an even older memory. Once, when he was eighteen and playing for a ball in London, he met a young French lady who invited him to her home in Paris. Alas, her father forbade it, and he has avoided Paris ever since. In that French lady and in Paris, he feels, resides his youth. Gaston pleads with him to change his mind, but Rácz is adamant in his refusal.

When Juliska comes to set the table, Gaston is astonished to discover that Rácz is hoping to marry her but, as Rácz comments, marrying is like smoking—it's difficult to give it up. While Rácz takes his guests to show them around his property, Laczi joins Juliska in the room, but she pretends not to notice him. 'I never notice people who don't take their hats off indoors,' she tells him. 'And I don't take my hat off to young ladies who let themselves be kissed by old men,' Laczi replies, sitting himself at the piano and playing increasingly ambitious modern strains ('Laut dringt der fromme Chor'). Juliska mockingly dances and trills, ever more piqued at being ignored by Laczi ('Und mit der Zunge schnalzen'/'Du, du, du, lieber Gott schaust zu').

1025

Gaston comes in looking for ink for Rácz to sign the contract to play in Paris and finds Sári. 'Ink?' she comments. 'You've come all the way from Paris for that?' She suggests that Gaston leave her father in peace, but the Count is determined not only to take her father back with him but to win another kiss from Sári. She is not unimpressed when he reels off his pedigree, particularly when he mentions that his years as a ward are over and he is looking for a bride, and she playfully suggests that she has a bride for him. Gaston plays along, convinced that she is referring to herself ('Sie wüssten eine Braut für mich?'/'Du reizendes Täubchen, Gukuruku').

In spite of Gaston's forceful pleading, Rácz remains adamant that he will not go to Paris, and Gaston tries to enlist Juliska to help change his mind. Laczi suggests that he should go instead, but old Rácz, who has little opinion of his son's talents, is scathing. He points out all the assets that a genuine gipsy violinist must have—the fire, the ability to laugh and cry, to play and lead at the same time, to flirt with attractive women, to be in command and yet a heart-breaker. Laczi rejects the criticism (Finale I: 'Vater, du beleidigst mich'), but Rácz persists. 'You're a fine fellow, but a rotten musician!' he maintains. Laczi determines to go and to prove himself, though Juliska pleads with him to stay ('Geh' nicht fort, heute brummt er'). As a last throw, Gaston brings some members of Rácz's orchestra who beg him to agree to go to Paris. Finally, in spite of Sári's pleas with him to stay home, he leaps up and, to the delight of Gaston and the gipsies, tells them he is prepared to go.

ACT 2

In a room of Count Irini's castle in Paris a dance is under way. Mustari, the master of ceremonies, announces the King of Massilia, and everyone joins in the Massilian national anthem ('Stolz wie ein Held zwingst du die Welt'). The King, who is on vacation in Paris under the pseudonym of Count Estragon, offers his thanks for the reception ('Meinen Verehrten, besten Dank') and declares himself ready for whatever Gaston has to offer—so long as it is not boring. Gaston retorts that his life has been one long struggle against boredom. He has already got through eight million francs in his battle against boredom, and now his allowance has been turned off until he marries. There are, however, prospects in that area, for he admits to being hopelessly in love with a Hungarian village beauty.

Then, to Gaston's astonishment, Cadeau enters, followed by Juliska and Sári. He is delighted to see them—for his own sake for Sári, and for Rácz's sake for Juliska—but the attention that Gaston pays to Juliska disappoints Sári and, though she soon becomes the centre of attention for the Parisian young ladies, she feels uncomfortable in her Hungarian costume amid the fashions of France ('Ich armes Mädel aus dem Ungarland'/'So ein armes, dummes, kleines Ding vom Land').

When Rácz puts in an appearance, he has undergone a complete transformation. He no longer looks an old gipsy, but a elegant man of the world. His hair has been dyed black, his beard has gone in favour of a neat moustache, he is wearing evening dress, and carrying a top hat in one hand

and his violin in the other. The King is introduced to him as Count Estragon but, keen to get in a mention of his decoration from the King, he is reluctant to observe the monarch's incognito, and Gaston finally has to step in to save the King from embarrassment.

At the sound of dance music, Rácz begins to make some comparisons between modern music and gipsy violin playing. 'For a gipsy a violin is not just a dead piece of wood, but his treasure, his loved one. He drinks with it, he eats with it—a real love affair.' For him, the choice between his violin and a woman has often been difficult ('Manchmal fällt die Wahl mir schwer'/ 'Mein alter Stradivari').

Sári and Juliska greet the old man warmly. They are surprised to see him looking so young, but he gives the credit to three weeks treatment at the spa of Pistyán. He introduces his daughter and niece to the disguised King, who takes something of a fancy to Sári and, when Juliska laughs at the idea of Sári marrying a King, Sári retorts that it is no funnier than the idea of the young Juliska marrying old Rácz. Juliska answers that she has agreed to do so purely out of gratitude and, when Sári suggests that she would be better off with Laczi, Juliska tells her that the problem is to get her cousin to speak to her of love.

Who should then turn up, but Laczi himself? It seems that it is he who has been engaged as director of the music during dinner. Away from home, he seems to have much more to say to Juliska, and the two are soon making up for lost time until she feels obliged to tell him that she is already engaged to someone else. It is all his fault for being so backward in showing interest in her ('Bist plötzlich durchgegangen'/'Lang, lang währt der Sommer nicht'). Laczi leaves, and Juliska is joined by the King, arm in arm with Sári, and finally by old Rácz, and the four make merry as Rácz enjoys his familiarity with the King ('Wie charmant, wie charmant'/'Vive le roi!').

Laczi is now determined to find out whether Juliska is engaged to his father or, perhaps, to the Count. He asks the servant, Pierre, to tell his father that a man from Lörinczfalva wishes to speak to him, and Rácz, surprised to see Laczi in Paris and here at the ball, greets his son warmly. But what is he doing here? Whatever it is, he can't be doing too badly to be mixing in this company. Didn't he always say the boy should give up music? When he discovers that Laczi is there in charge of the music, he is horrified and begs him to give it all up and return home.

Now Gaston is showing more interest in Sári and goes as far as to suggest that he should go with her to Hungary and become a shepherd on the puszta. They indulge in a prolonged kiss and Sári's heart beats faster as at last he speaks to her of love ('Endlich, endlich hab' ich dich'/'O komm mit mir, ich tanz mit dir ins Himmelreich hinein!'). Juliska and Laczi oversee Sári and Gaston embrace and decide to take a leaf out of their book (Finale II: 'O, komm mit mir, ich tanz mit dir') but their enjoyment is interrupted when the news comes that old Rácz has gone missing just as it is time for him to play.

Gaston begs Laczi to step into the breach and fill his father's place and, borrowing a violin from one of his musicians, the young man takes the stand and begins to play. Rácz, returning, stands and listens motionless, watching,

1027

as Laczi's performance is greeted with a storm of applause and the King steps forward to shake the young man warmly by the hand. Rácz cannot believe that such music should attract such acclaim, but paternal pride is stronger than personal pride, and he hurries forward to embrace his son. When Rácz is asked to play in his turn, the result is anti-climax. The King thinks little of his 'outdated gipsy scraping' and everyone goes off to dance, leaving Rácz alone, realising that it is the end for him. The world has moved on and he has been left behind.

ACT 3

In her boudoir, Countess Irini, the Count's grandmother, is playing cards with three friends. She is concerned that, for the past three weeks, her grandson has been depressed. Indeed, when he joins the group, he can manage nothing more than 'So so' in response to their questions. His whole life, he says, is monotonous and the Countess is shrewd enough to recognise the symptons of lovesickness.

To Gaston's delight, Sári arrives, looking for her father. Gaston wants her to talk of marriage, but she refers to a letter she has already sent him telling him she cannot marry him. He has thrown it in the waste basket. He presses his suit ardently and tells her that she protests too much ('Ich tu' das Meinige, tu' du das Deinige'/'Aug' an Aug', Mund an Mund'). He introduces her to his grandmother, who thoroughly approves and, when Juliska appears, the old Countess promises also to speak to Rácz to persuade him to give way to his son as Juliska's husband. Cadeau, meanwhile, has got it into his head that he will marry either Sári and Juliska and he is looking forward to the trip to Lörinczfalva—compared with which he reckons London, Paris, Berlin and Vienna have little to offer ('Tief in unserm lieben Heimatland'/ 'Du bleibt doch meine Residenz').

Rácz has desperately been giving concerts to ever dwindling audiences and now, knowing that his playing days are over, he is ready to accept Gaston's offer to buy his Stradivarius violin. The old man is presented to the Countess Irini, and is most taken by her faded but still evident beauty, and he tells her that he will return to Lörinczfalva the following morning to marry Juliska. The Countess declares that it has been her life's mission to mend broken hearts, and she recalls the day, thirty-eight years before, when she flirted with a young gipsy violinist at a ball in London. 'Through marriage and love affairs I have never forgotten him,' she adds. 'And he has never forgotten you, Countess,' Rácz replies. 'I have never been able to forget how you kissed me.' Only then does the Countess realise who it was she befriended all those years ago. She takes him by the hand and says, 'Rácz, old friend, look at me, whose first love you were, and then fancy that I am about to marry again....' 'Impossible!' cries Rácz. 'Then say the same of yourself,' she tells him. Rácz departs, shaking his head.

A servant shows in Laczi, who is overjoyed to see Juliska. The Countess instructs them to kiss each other, and they dutifully but happily embrace. 'Do you really love me then?' she asks. 'More then words can say,' he replies.

Rácz, left alone with only his Stradivarius for comfort, is interrupted by Cadeau, who has now made up his mind to marry Juliska. 'Half a minute too late,' he is told. Then Gaston presents his grandmother with his intended bride—Sári ('Erstens juckt's mich in den Beinen') and Rácz is sagely reflecting that love and energy belong to the young, when Cadeau reappears, having now decided to marry Sári. 'Three-quarters of a minute too late,' is the reply this time. 'Come back in twelve years. I shall reserve my little Klári for you.'

'There is your youth,' the Countess observes to Rácz, pointing to Laczi, Juliska, Sári and Gaston, and Rácz finally accepts the truth of the matter. To Laczi he hands his Stradivarius, to Gaston the scarf-pin he received from the King of England, to Sári the ring he was given by the Tsar of Russia, and to Juliska the ring he received from the Queen of Spain. 'Rácz, you deserve a kiss,' declares the Countess (Finale III: 'Das alte Lied').

Pali Rácz (1830-86) and his son Laczi were real-life gipsy musicians of international repute. The above synopsis includes the third act in its final, revised version.

WIE EINST IM MAI

(As Once in May)

a farce with songs in four scenes by Rudolf Bernauer and Rudolph Schanzer. Music by Walter Kollo and Willy Bredschneider. Produced at the Berliner Theater, Berlin, 4 October 1913 with Lisa Weise (Ottilie) and Oscar Sabo (Fritz Jüterbog). Produced at the Grosses Schauspielhaus, Berlin, 1927 with Camilla Spira (Ottilie) and Alfred Braun (Fritz Jüterbog). Produced in a revised version as an operetta in eight scenes by Willi Kollo and Walter Lieck with music by Walter and Willi Kollo at the Theater des Volkes, Berlin, 1943 with Edith Schollwer and Hubert von Meyerinck. Produced at the Staatstheater, Braunschweig, 1966 with René Kollo, and subsequently at the Theater des Westens, Berlin, with Angela Müthel and Wolfgang Ziffer.

Produced at the Shubert Theatre, New York, in a version by Rida Johnson Young with a new score by Sigmund Romberg as *Maytime* 16 August 1917.

CHARACTERS

von Henkeshoven, *a colonel*
Ottilie, *his daughter*
Vera, *her daughter*
Tilla, *Vera's daughter*
Stanislaus von Methusalem, Ernst Cicero von Henkeshoven, *the colonel's nephews*
Mechthildis von Kieferspeck, *Ottilie's governess*
Angostura, *Methusalem's second wife, later* Countess of Bornholm
Mizzi, *his third wife*

1029

Pergamenter senior, Pergamenter junior, *counsellors of justice*
Fritz Jüterbog, *later* Commerzienrat Friedrich Jüterbog
Heinrich, *his son, later* Heinz Freiherr von Jüterbog
Fritzchen, *later* Fred, *Heinrich's son*
Arthur Müller, *a chief engineer*
Countess Hohenberg-Tiefenthal
Clothilde, Belinde, Lucinde, Agathe, Bettina, Annette, Babette *and other relations of the colonel*
Frida, Ida *and other dancers at Kroll's*
Kitty, *manager of Vera Müller's fashion house*
Guests of the colonel, ball guests, ladies of society, servants, mannequins and milliners.

SCENE 1

In 1838, in the small community of Schöneberg just outside Berlin, at the country home of the retired Colonel von Henkeshoven, members of the family have gathered to celebrate the sixteenth birthday of the colonel's daughter, Ottilie ('Lasst uns das Geburtstagstischen schmükken'). Ottilie's governess lights the candles on the birthday cake, and the members of the family hand over their birthday presents to the happy girl who, in thanking everyone, makes it clear that she knows just how fortunate she is to belong to such a fine and well-to-do family ('Ist man ein Kind aus noblem Hause'/'So aber stört mich früh und spät die Etepetetität').

Amongst those offering their congratulations is the colonel's nephew, Stanislaus von Methusalem. He is a young man-about-town, a favourite with all the young ladies, whose extravagant life-style keeps him permanently in financial difficulties ('Mein Stammbaum hat viel Ästchen'/'Das ist Herr von Methusalem') and who is constantly on the lookout for ways of enabling himself to live from day to day in the manner to which he likes to be accustomed. He even grits his teeth and proposes marriage to Ottilie's ageing, spinster governess, Mechthildis von Kieferspeck, when he hears that she has inherited her late uncle's entire fortune, and together they dance a stately gavotte ('Heissgeliebtes Firlefänzchen'—first verse).

Ottilie is secretly in love with a journeyman locksmith, Fritz Jüterbog, who peeps in at the party to offer Ottilie his congratulations and a modest bunch of flowers. The colonel asks Fritz to open the lock of a casket, and this provides the boy with the opportunity to speak to Ottilie of the love they have felt for each other since they were at school together and shared a first, never-to-be-forgotten kiss. Now Fritz is a young man and Ottilie is as good as grown up, and they determine to ask her father's approval for them to become engaged, but, when he stands before the colonel, holding Ottilie's hand, to make his request, he merely arouses laughter. A journeyman locksmith marrying an aristocrat? Impossible! The colonel bans him from the house, and Fritz has to part from his Ottilie. He will somehow try to make his fortune, perhaps in industry, perhaps on the young and blossoming railway system and, while they wait, they will never forget that first kiss one day in Schöneberg in the month of May ('War es denn nicht wunderschön'/ 'Es war in Schöneberg im Monat Mai').

SCENE 2

It is twenty years on, and Ottilie has long been married to her cousin Cicero von Henkeshoven who, like other husbands in the upper classes, spends many of his evenings in Kroll's, Berlin's most fashionable pleasure resort, dancing with the ladies who frequent the place ('In ganz Berlin tanzt man nie so toll wie bei Kroll'). Methusalem also frequents Kroll's but he brings his wife with him: his second wife, for Mechthildis has been succeeded by Angostura, an exotic dancer. Methusalem is still full of his old charm as he invites Angostura to step out in a polka ('Heissgeliebtes Firlefänzchen'—second verse). Yet another person amusing himself in this same venue on this same evening is Fritz Jüterbog. Fritz has become a successful and well-to-do businessman and he is delighted to be back in Berlin after several years in London and Paris ('Nu bin ich wieder in Berlin'/'Der hat recht').

Ottilie has had enough of the excuses she gets from her husband about his nights out. She knows full well that he is at Kroll's, and she is determined to catch him *in flagrante delicto*. She turns up at the night spot with a group of her lady friends, moving in stealthily on their prey and disguised behind masks ('Leise, leise, aufgepasst') for the ladies have not the slightest doubt about what drives their menfolk to such a place, and they know that all men are rogues ('Ein Jüngling trifft dich irgendwo'/'Die Männer sind alle Verbrecher').

Things are not going too well between Methusalem and the temperamental Angostura, and she finds solace with Fritz Jüterbog with whom she reminisces about her Caribbean homeland of Haiti ('Es war auf einem Dampfgeschiffe') while Ottilie and her lady friends, still on the rampage, seek out Cicero. In the hunt, Ottilie also discovers her childhood sweetheart. Fritz is still unattached, but since Ottilie is tied to Cicero the two must once again take their leave of each other. At the end of the evening, Ottilie and her friends are even more convinced that all men are rotters, and Angostura has decided to leave Methusalem and return to Haiti (Finale II: 'Seht Ihr, seht Ihr, falsche Brut'/'Die Männer sind alle Verbrecher').

SCENE 3

Since that meeting at Kroll's a further thirty years have passed. It is 1888, the era of Bismarck, and Fritz has been rewarded for his achievements in industry by his appointment as a *Commercienrath*—a counsellor of commerce—and by ennoblement which permits him to use the word 'von' before his surname. He has, some time before, bought the former country home of the von Henkeshofen family in Schöneberg, and there he is receiving the congratulations of his family and friends on his rise to the top of society ('Det halt ick nich für wahrscheinlich'). Among those who bring their congratulations is Methusalem, well advanced in years but still as fun-loving as ever.

1031

He is now married to his third wife, Mizzi, with whom he risks a few turns of a mazurka ('Heissgeliebtes Firlefänzchen'—third verse).

Fritz has long since married and has a son Heinrich and a young grandson, who is also named Fritz. Heinrich is pursuing a lady book-keeper in his father's factory, a Fräulein Vera Schmidt but, since Vera Schmidt is in love with Arthur Müller, a chief engineer in Jüterbog's works, she has told her mother of the attentions of the junior boss. Vera's mother determines to sort matters out with the old *Commercienrath*. Thus does Ottilie, Frau Schmidt by her second marriage, find herself back in her old home. Ottilie sees the young grandson, Fritz, playing and she reflects on his resemblance to the boy she herself once knew. Had things been otherwise, she might well have been the youngster's grandmother ('Grossmama, Grossmama').

Vera talks to Methusalem and Mizzi about the pleasures of working for the Jüterbog firm and of her colleagues ('Komm ich frühmorgens auf das Comptoir'/'So eine kleine, süsse') while the two old folk, Ottilie and Fritz, sit with each other reflecting on their old love and their memories of Schöneberg in the month of May ('Das war in Schöneberg im Monat Mai'). And then the two of them part again—this time for ever.

SCENE 4

By the year 1913 Ottilie and Fritz are both long dead. Ottilie's daughter Vera runs a fashion house where she is at the head of a small army of milliners and mannequins ('Noch ein letztes buntes Schleifchen'). Vera also has a daughter, Tilla, who resembles her grandmother Ottilie to a quite astonishing extent.

A customer of the fashion house is the late *Commercienrath*'s son and heir, Herr Heinrich von Jüterbog, who brings his son, Fred, to the shop ('Wenn Siegestaten, führe ich Ihnen vor'). Fred resembles his grandfather, when the latter was still a journeyman locksmith, to a no less amazing extent than Tilla does her grandmother. The two young people are very soon getting on famously, and Fred urges Tilla to go away with him ('Kind, schliess die Ladentüre zu'/'Liebling, komm auf Sommerwohnung').

The only survivor of the generation of Fritz and Ottilie is Ottilie's cousin, Methusalem who, at the age of 100, is still as fond of life and the ladies as in his youth. Also amongst the customers in the salon this day is Angostura, Countess of Bornholm, formerly Methusalem's second wife, and she, even at the age of eighty or so, still possesses her aptitude for dancing, as she demonstrates in her ability to tackle the currently fashionable Argentine tango ('El Sabo'). Methusalem, for his part, is not unmoved by the charms of the manager of the fashion salon, Kitty, and he is just as ready to shake a leg with her to the latest ragtime dance ('Heissgeliebtes Firlefänzchen'—fourth verse) as he was to try a gavotte all those years ago.

By now Fred and Tilla have agreed to do what their grandparents, from considerations of rank and other restrictions, never did. They will be married and fulfil the relationship that was so hopefully begun by Fritz and Ottilie in Schöneberg one month in May (Finale IV: 'Die ganze Possenspiel ist jetzt vorbei, das war in Schöneberg im Monat Mai').

The synopsis follows the original version of the work. The revised 1943 version follows the action of the four scenes closely, but with further scenes added and additional music by Walter and Willi Kollo in place of Bredschneider's and some of Kollo's original numbers.

POLENBLUT

(Polish Blood)

an operetta in three scenes by Leo Stein. Music by Oskar Nedbal. Produced at the Carltheater, Vienna, 25 October 1913. Revived at the Volksoper in a revised version 10 October 1954 and 1 February 1986 with Kurt Schreibmayer (Bolo), Mirjana Irosch (Helena), Jack Poppell (Popiel), Ernst Gutstein (Jan) and Melanie Holliday (Wanda).

A film version was produced by Carl Lamac in 1934.

CHARACTERS

Pan Jan Zarémba, *a landowner in Russian-occupied Poland*
Heléna, *his daughter*
Count Boléslaw Baránski
Bronio von Popiel, *his friend*
Wanda Kwasinskaja, *a dancer at the Warsaw Opera*
Jadwiga Páwlówa, *her mother*
Mirski, Górski, Wolénski, Senówicz, *noblemen friends of Count Baránski*
Frau von Dragálska
Countess Jozia Napólska
Wlastek, *Baránski's servant*
Ball guests, noblemen, country folk, maids, musicians, bailiff's men, lackeys

SCENE 1

It is carnival time in Warsaw, and the guests at the Polish national ball are all greatly enjoying themselves. All, that is, except for the noble Bronio von Popiel, who is not dancing and is looking decidedly downhearted. It does not take Count Boléslaw Baránski—known to his friends as Bolo—long to realise that Popiel is head over heels in love ('Na, Freundchen, du tanzt nicht?'). Bolo has heard all his lovesick chatter many times before, and he is enough of an old hand at the game himself to be able to describe without difficulty the sort of girl with whom Popiel will be in love ('Ein goldiges Mädel').

Popiel's current flame is a dancer at the Warsaw Opera, by the name of Wanda Kwasinskaja. She is late for the ball and, when in due course she puts in an appearance, it is in the company of her mother, Jadwiga Páwlówa. Popiel is full of compliments for Wanda, but the mother makes sure that she herself does not miss out on a share of Popiel's flattery ('Wie schön Sie heute wieder sind!'). But poor Popiel has to contend not only with Wanda's mother but also with the competition of his friend Bolo who is soon inviting the delicious Wanda to dance with him to the orchestra's lilting waltz measures ('Hören Sie, wie es singt und klingt') and to the strains of a fiery Krakowiak, leaving Popiel to look sadly on.

For all his lively appearance, Bolo is a man with a problem. Krasnowola, his estate in Galicia, has become so run down that he faces ruin, and his friends see his only chance of salvation in a marriage to some wealthy young lady. A highly suitable candidate is at hand in the person of Heléna, the daughter of a rich but unaristocratic landowner, Pan Jan Zarémba. Zarémba has brought his daughter along to the ball in the hope of urging the relationship, but Bolo wants to hear nothing of the chains of marriage—he is enjoying himself hugely with Wanda and he will not even look at Heléna.

Heléna has little sympathy with her father's idea. She is a country girl with little interest in society functions and she has come to the ball very much under protest ('Nein, dass ich hieher jetzt kommen soll'). She wants a real man as a husband, not some over-bred fool forced to live on credit, and yet, as she watches Bolo dance, something about what she sees begins to fascinate her and Bolo's refusal even to meet her stirs her Polish blood and makes her determined to have revenge on him.

With Popiel's help, a plan is conceived to win Bolo round. Bolo has declared that, sooner than marry, he would have Popiel's housekeeper, Marynia, move in to help him bring his estate back into good order. Popiel plans that he will recommend Bolo to take Marynia on but, since Bolo has never seen the woman, Heléna will take her place and proceed to bring Bolo to heel. As the plotters plot, the ball continues with its Polish vigour unabated (Finale I: 'Hej, hej, hej, hej, zgozy').

SCENE 2
A few days later Bolo is back on his country estate where, despite his financial problems, he is entertaining some of his well-to-do noble friends: Mirski, Gorski, Wolenski and Senowicz. They are playing cards and thoroughly enjoying themselves ('Ich kaufe!' 'Ich laufe') and they are all so engrossed in their game that they continue even when Bolo's servant, Wlastek, comes in to announce the arrival of some visitors. These are no ordinary visitors, but bailiffs who have come to seize his assets and they have been brought by Zarémba, who has purposely been buying up Bolo's debts. The card party carries on as Bolo's property is carried off piece by piece and, when the table and chairs go, they continue playing on the floor.

The friends are in no way downhearted. 'Lucky at cards, lucky in love,' they cry ('Glück im Spiel, Glück in der Liebe') and the subject leads naturally to talk of Bolo's blossoming friendship with the ballet girl, Wanda, about whom he is still waxing enthusiastic ('Ich kenn' ein süsses Frauchen'). 'Brothers, I'm up to my ears in love,' he declares. However, the plan to win him over to Heléna is already under way.

While Bolo and his friends are out of the way, Zarémba returns with

Heléna and Popiel and, looking round with satisfaction at the empty room, prepares to leave his daughter to take up her new position. Heléna is looking forward to turning the tables on Bolo and, to help her keep her cover, her father will continue to deal with the irresponsible Count as if nothing has happened and with all the diplomacy for which he is noted—seeing all, hearing all, and yet remaining silent ('Ich bin ein Diplomate').

Popiel primes Heléna for the role he has planned for her. He tells her of Bolo's weakness for women and how the relationship between them will certainly develop ('Verzeihen Sie, ich lüge nie!'). With practical demonstrations that gain some edge from his own affection for her, Popiel takes Heléna graphically through the prospective stages of Bolo's increasing affection— the winks and glances, the peck on the cheek, the embrace and the stolen kiss. Heléna in turn indicates how she will take him in hand and control him—albeit always in as thoroughly reasonable a way as things are always done in the countryside ('Immer nur ländlich und sittlich').

Under Popiel's recommendation, Bolo is easily persuaded to take on Heléna as his new housekeeper, 'Marynia', and the two get their relative positions firmly established—he the master and gentleman, and she the maid ('Nur Geduld'/'Ihr seid ein Kavalier')—before 'Marynia' sets to work. It is not long before she skilfully persuades Bolo that only with hard work from himself will the estate be put completely in order.

Bolo agrees to put his shoulder to the wheel (Finale II: 'Ach, wie weit ist's noch zum Ziel!') and, when his worthless friends reappear, 'Marynia' shocks them with the information that Bolo will start work on the estate the following day, before ushering them firmly out of the house. Bolo takes surprisingly readily to the idea of being alone in the house with this young lady looking after him ('Mädel, dich hat mir die Glücksfee gebracht') but, when Wanda puts in an appearance, she is surprised and not very pleased to find another woman there. Bolo assures her that Marynia is only his maid. 'But what a maid!' he adds.

SCENE 3

The summer brings the rewards of Bolo's labours in the form of a rich harvest crop and, in the gardens of his castle, the celebration of the completion of the harvest takes place in a more joyful mood than in previous years. The workers bring the harvest wreath to honour Bolo, but he insists that it rightly belongs to 'Marynia' ('Freut euch, Bursche, freut euch Mädels').

Bolo's society friends are at the party, among them Wanda and Popiel, and Popiel eagerly takes Heléna on one side to prepare her for the revelation to Bolo of how she has gained her revenge on his indifference. Moreover, now that her mission with Bolo is about to be completed, Popiel feels able to declare the passionate feelings he himself has for Heléna ('Heléna! Heléna! Mir wird so schwül, und Sie sind kühl!'), but she knows only that she feels unhappy at the idea of leaving Bolo and warns Popiel against getting too keen on her.

To an accompaniment provided by four local musicians, dancing begins

('Spielt auf, ihr Musikanten') and, when it comes to finding a dancing partner, Bolo is torn between the attentions and attractions of Wanda and 'Marynia'. He soon realises, however, which way his heart is guiding him. As the local country folk warm to the celebrations (Finale III: 'Freut euch, Bursche, freut euch Mädel'), Bolo declares that the country men should dance with the titled ladies and the noblemen with the peasant girls. He will set an example by dancing with 'Marynia'. Indeed, he declares, he will dance through life with her.

At this outspoken declaration of his love, Wanda's jealousy is aroused, and she takes her revenge by telling Bolo who his housekeeper really is. For a moment he is angry, especially when Heléna reveals that the whole thing had been set up as an elaborate plan of revenge on him, but when Popiel tells Heléna to laugh in Bolo's face and complete her revenge, she will not. Bolo and Heléna know that they suit each other down to the ground and, when he asks Zarémba for his daughter's hand, the request is readily granted. As for Popiel, well, at least he is finally able to get his Wanda.

SZIBILL

(Sybil)

an operetta in three acts by Miksa Bródy and Ferenc Martos. Music by Viktor Jacobi. Produced at Királyszinház (King's Theatre), Budapest, 27 February 1914 with Sári Fedák (Sybil), Ernö Király (Grand Duke) and Márton Rátkay (Poire).

Produced at the Stadttheater, Vienna, as *Sybill* 12 February 1919 and at the Theater an der Wien 6 November 1919 with Fritzi Massary

Produced at the Metropol-Theater, Berlin, October 1919 with Fritzi Massary and Guido Thielscher.

Produced at the Liberty Theatre, New York, in a version by Harry B Smith with additional numbers by Jacobi as *Sybil* 10 January 1916 with Julia Sanderson (Sybil), Donald Brian (Grand Duke) and Joseph Cawthorn (Otto Spreckles).

Produced at the Prince's Theatre, Manchester, in a version by Harry Graham as *Sybil* 26 December 1920 and at Daly's Theatre, London, 19 February 1921 with José Collins, Harry Welchman (Grand Duke) and Huntley Wright (Poire).

CHARACTERS

The Grand Duke Constantine
The Grand Duchess Anna Pavlovna
The Governor of Bomsk
Captain Dologov, Lieutenant Koyander, *his aides-de-camp*
Count Milovski, *a court courier*
Lieutenant Zelenoy
Sybil Renaud, *an opera singer*
Charles Poire, *an impresario*
Margot, *his wife*

Lieutenant Paul Petrov, *a guards officer*
Bortschakov, *an hotel manager*
The Governor's Major-domo
Ladies of society, officers, cossacks, hotel guests, hotel servants, orphans

ACT 1

The entrance hall of the Grand Hotel in the Russian provincial town of Bomsk is packed with tourist guests and hotel staff eagerly awaiting the arrival of the Grand Duchess Anna Pavlovna ('All Hearts With a Keen Curiosity Burn'). Great confusion reigns as to the precise hour of her arrival, and the hotel manager is anxiously awaiting information as he briefs the staff on their duties for the distinguished guest ('The Staff Must Try'/'Politeness Pays').

Among the other guests at this busy hotel is the celebrated opera singer Sybil Renaud, who recently arrived on the express from St Petersburg and who has been allocated a suite of rooms opposite the Grand Duchess's apartment. Amongst Sybil's retinue is her manager, the impresario Charles Poire, who has been ringing in vain for a maid to help him fasten the hooks and eyes of his wife Margot's dress. After a fortnight's marriage he has still not mastered the art. One way and another, he and Margot are finding it somewhat trying spending their honeymoon amidst the bustle of busy hotels ('Life in a Large Hotel').

Poire, of course, is not the impresario's real name, and sometimes the French accent slips. It just happens to be necessary for an impresario to have a foreign name. He's an eccentric individual who, when he spots a small flag in the reception lobby, feels compelled to touch it. The manager barely manages to stop him, warning him of the dire consequences if he should do so—a warning which merely makes the little flag even more intriguing to Poire.

Up in her room, Sybil has been crying her eyes out. In St Petersburg she fell in love with a Lieutenant Petrov, an infatuation that almost ruined her concert season. In the end Petrov's father threatened her and her entourage with jail if they didn't get out of town in twenty-four hours. When Sybil finally comes down the stairs, her eyes are dry but her demeanour is downcast as she sits down and writes a letter to her beloved Petrov, apologising for leaving him without a word and bidding him a last farewell ('My Dearest Paul, I Beg to Be Forgiven').

She has no sooner finished it and folded it up than Petrov himself appears in the hotel foyer ('Ah, Dear, I've Sought You Far and Near!'). He has deserted from his regiment to follow Sybil from St Petersburg, and he faces imprisonment, perhaps even death, if he is caught. He urges Sybil to run away with him that night to Paris, and she agrees, leaving Poire faced with the disastrous financial consequences of cancelling the concert fixed for the following day. Poire's advice to Sybil is that marriage is definitely not to be recommended. For him, and he speaks through experience, it is an end, though Sybil naturally sees it as a beginning ('Now, My Child, I'm Your Truest Friend'/'Good Advice').

A group of hussars in their crimson uniforms arrive, led by the Governor of Bomsk, who has come to inspect a special contrivance set up by the hotel manager for the reception of the Grand Duchess. It is the little flag. The turning down of the flag, it seems, will signal to the whole town the Grand Duchess's departure for the reception. Church bells will ring out, trumpets sound, bands play, and the whole town will be brightly illuminated.

On a less festive note, the Governor also has a warrant for the arrest of a deserter named Petrov and, when he sees the tall, dark officer conversing with Poire, he instantly arrests both of them. 'Stop!' says Sybil, and such is her air of authority that the Governor mistakenly assumes her to be the Grand Duchess who, according to his information, has arrived on the mid-day train. After a moment's hesitation, Sybil takes up the pretence, identifying the officer as her equerry, Lieutenant Sarov, and securing the release of both prisoners.

Flapping aside the hotel manager's attempts to interject, the Governor insists on presenting to Sybil the crimson-uniformed 55th Regiment of Hussars—the Grand Duchess's own regiment. The regiment has taken the liberty of having a uniform made especially for its colonel-in-chief, and Sybil soon reappears clad in the magnificent crimson costume. The soldiers greet her with loud acclaim, and Sybil assumes her unusual role with increasingly evident relish ('Hip Hooray! We Proudly Greet Today'/'The Colonel of the Crimson Hussars').

Arrangements are being made for the state coach to collect Sybil for the reception being given for the Grand Duchess, when Margot comes in calling to Sybil by name. The only way out of this particular fix is to pretend that Margot is herself the opera singer, demanding to be presented to the Grand Duchess, though it has an embarrassing consequence when the Governor demands that she should sing at the Grand Duchess's reception that evening. The Governor marches the hussars off, but he returns to pay court to Margot, for whose singing engagement that evening the embarrassed Poire at least manages to negotiate ample terms.

Petrov endeavours to arrange with the manager for a cab to be ordered to transport the party away from a side entrance, and he and Sybil ponder on how they may get safely away together (Finale I: 'Sybil! Sybil!' 'Your Highness, You Should Say'). Dressed as if they were going to the reception, the four of them appear in the entrance hall. Sybil, Petrov and Margot move to slip out by the side entrance, but Poire, who all day long has scarcely managed to resist the temptation of turning down the flag, can hold himself back no longer. The moment he touches the flag, the bells ring out, bands play and the whole town is illuminated as men and women in evening dress, together with a Cossack guard, rush in and surround Sybil and her friends. Escape is no longer feasible, and the four realise that they must go through with the pretence.

No sooner has the party departed for the reception than the Grand Duke Constantine arrives, having finished his military duties unexpectedly early and intending to accompany his wife, the Grand Duchess, to the reception. He is told that she has just left, but is asked to take with him a shawl that she has left behind. Puzzled that he recognises neither the shawl nor the scent it carries, he leaves for the reception.

ACT 2

That evening, in his palace, the Governor is with Margot amidst a large group of ladies and gentlemen, nervously awaiting the arrival of the Grand Duchess ('We're Feeling Overcome With Shyness'). Margot, who has claimed to know the great lady very well, supports her assertions with a tale of how Her Royal Highness once invited her for a cup of tea ('She Took a Cup of Tea'). The Grand Duchess is announced, and Sybil enters, preceded by a footman carrying an incense burner and followed by two more carrying her train. Petrov and Poire are with her.

Sybil is introduced to all the local notables, after which she agrees to open the dancing. While she is away, the Governor confides in Poire how desperately he has fallen in love with the supposed opera singer. Poire, who can see his new wife's virtue more threatened every minute, tries to discourage the Governor by telling him that she loves someone else, but he backs down when the Governor threatens to break every bone in this rival's body. Their little chat is interrupted by the arrival of the Grand Duke Constantine who, warmly welcomed by the assembled crowd, finds himself face to face with Sybil. The Grand Duke greets his supposed wife with a distinct note of sarcasm, but then warms to the pretence and, brushing aside her whispered attempts to apologise, urges her not to make a scene ('Ah See, 'Tis She, the Wife Whom I Adore').

The Grand Duke invites Sybil to dance and, when Sybil persists in begging his pardon, the Grand Duke pretends not to understand. He becomes increasingly affectionate, ignoring Sybil's pleas to him not to tease her and, only when Sybil begs to be excused in order to dance with Petrov, does the Grand Duke once more adopt a sarcastic tone. Poire, meanwhile, is ready to explain everything, but the Grand Duke, who now has a very bright twinkle in his eye, refuses to accept that Sybil could be anyone but his wife. Poire is dismissed as demented and has to be warned by Margot to keep his cool ('Do Be Sprightly!'/'Keep Cool!').

To Sybil's increasing embarrassment, the Duke continues his pretence of failing to understand her wish to clear the air but, finally, he weakens. 'What would you say if I really *was* in love with you?' he asks, and together they act out a romantic scene, with the snow falling outside and their love glowing as warmly as the embers inside ('The Firelight Flickers Warm and Bright'/'Though Love May Be a Mystery').

When Sybil again manages to get away and return to Petrov, he is highly jealous, furious at the thought of how he has risked his life to be with her, only to watch her flirting with another man. Sybil assures him that she is doing all this only for his benefit, and she points out that they are both increasingly in the Grand Duke's power. Only the arrival of the Grand Duchess can now save them, and Sybil sends Petrov to seek her out. Soon, accompanied by Petrov, the Grand Duchess Anna sweeps in, announced by the footmen as Madame Sybil Renaud of the Opéra-Comique, Paris.

The Grand Duke and Sybil are completely taken aback (Finale II: 'My Wife! Good Heavens! What Shall I Do?'). The Grand Duke seeks to take a dance with this new Sybil, but the Grand Duchess regrets that all her dances have been booked by Petrov, and the two of them join in the dance in each other's arms. Now it is the Grand Duke's turn to suffer pangs of jealousy as, in whispered asides, the Grand Duchess persuades Petrov to pay her romantic compliments. Then the Grand Duke plays his only remaining card. He bids goodbye to the Governor and instructs Sybil to accompany him back to his hotel. Anna promptly does likewise with Petrov, and the two couples march off to the sound of the public wishing them sweet dreams.

ACT 3
At the Grand Hotel the guests are arriving back from the reception ('Good Night! Or We Might Say Rather Good Morning'). The hotel staff and the Cossacks on guard outside the Grand Duchess's suite are hurriedly brought to attention as first the Grand Duke returns with Sybil, and then the Grand Duchess, looking immensely jealous, with Petrov. The Grand Duchess tells Petrov how hurt she has been by the evening's events, thanks him for his help, and wishes him well with Sybil, while, at the same time the Grand Duke has begun to apologise to Sybil for forcing himself upon her. He assures her that there is nothing he would not do for her if she will help him win back his wife's love, before bidding her goodnight.

Poire returns after what, for him, has been a disastrous evening which ended with the Governor going off with his wife. But then Margot, too, appears. She is concerned for Sybil, but Poire manages to win her round to the idea of bed and the calls of Cupid ('You Often Say You're Through'/ 'When Cupid Calls').

Mindful of the Grand Duke's plea, Sybil emerges from her room and knocks on the Grand Duchess's door. The Grand Duchess is angry, and scornful of her husband for dallying with a woman of Sybil's class but Sybil persists, telling the Grand Duchess how Petrov deserted for her, how she was quite innocently mistaken for the Grand Duchess, and how the Grand Duke just as innocently kept up the charade. The Grand Duchess cannot fail to be touched. Now that Sybil has reassured the Grand Duchess of her husband's love, she can ask the Grand Duke to keep his promise to do anything he can for her. She begs pardon for Petrov's desertion, which is readily granted, and the opera singer and her lover are able to look forward to a future unclouded by their past (Finale III: 'Though Love May Be a Mystery').

The synopsis follows the English version by Harry Graham, with additional lyrics by Harry B Smith and a revised score by Jacobi including the added song 'The Colonel of the Crimson Hussars'. In the original Hungarian version Margot is known as Charlotte.

DIE CSÁRDÁSFÜRSTIN

(The Csardas Princess)

an operetta in three acts by Leo Stein and Béla Jenbach. Music by Emmerich Kálmán. Produced at the Johann Strauss Theater, Vienna, 17 November 1915 with Mizzi Günther (Sylva), Susanne Bachrich (Stasi), Karl Bachmann, Josef König and Max Brod. Produced at the Volksoper 23 October 1982 with Milena Rudiferia, Elisabeth Kales, Franz Wächter, Jack Poppell and Sandor Németh.

Produced at the New Amsterdam Theatre, New York, in a version by Guy Bolton and P G Wodehouse as *The Riviera Girl* 24 September 1917 with Wilda Bennett, Carl Gantvoort and Eugene Lockhart.

Produced at the Prince of Wales Theatre, London, in a version by Arthur Miller and Arthur Stanley as *The Gipsy Princess* 20 May 1921 with Sári Petráss (Sylva), M de Jari (Ronald), Billy Leonard (Boniface), Mark Lester (Feri) and Phyllis Titmuss (Stasi) and subsequently played at the Strand Theatre with Ena Towler replacing Miss Petráss. Produced at the Saville Theatre in a revised version 14 June 1944 with Tessa Deane and James Etherington. Produced at Sadler's Wells Theatre in a version by Nigel Douglas 1 August 1981 with Marilyn Hill Smith, Nigel Douglas, Tudor Davies and Ann Mackay.

Produced at the Théâtre du Trianon-Lyrique, Paris, in a version by René Peter, André Mauprey and Henri Falk as *Princesse Czardas* 12 March 1930 with Louise Balazy, Léon Marcel, Paul Darnois, Charles Darthez and Reine Prévost. Produced at the Théâtre de la Gaîté 7 August 1931 with Maya Silva, Gilbert Nabos and Marcel Lamy. Produced at the Théâtre de Paris 27 January 1950 with Marta Eggerth, Jan Kiepura, Pasquali and Alice Tissot.

Film versions were produced by Hans Schwarz in 1927; by Georg Jacoby in 1934 with Marta Eggerth, Hans Söhnker, Paul Hörbiger, Paul Kemp and Inde List; and again in 1950 with Marika Rökk, Johannes Heesters, Hubert Marischka and Jeannette Schultze.

CHARACTERS

Leopold Maria, Prince von und zu Lippert-Weylersheim
Anhilte, *his wife*
Edwin Ronald, *their son*
Countess Stasi, *the Prince's niece*
Count Boni Káncsiánu
Sylva Varescu
General von Rohnsdorff
Eugen, *his son, a lieutenant*
Feri von Kerekes, *known as* Feri bácsi
Mac Grave, *an ambassador*
von Billing, *section head*
von Vihar, von Szerényi, von Endrey, von Merö, *gentlemen*
Juliska, Aranka, Cleo, Rizzi, Selma, Mia, Daisy, Vally, *chorus girls*
Miksa, *head waiter*
Gentlemen, society people, gipsy band, lackeys, waiters

ACT 1

In an intimate Budapest café-cabaret, the singer Sylva Varescu is performing one of her most popular numbers, a passionate song about the mountains ('Heia, heia! In den Bergen ist mein Heimatland!'). She is about to leave Hungary to go on an American tour, and the applause is tumultuous as, with a short speech, she bids *Viszontlatásra* to her faithful public.

After the show is over, the tables and chairs around the small stage are prepared for a farewell party being thrown for Sylva by one of her greatest admirers, Count Boni Káncsiánu. He and his friend Feri von Kerekes are real old-fashioned men-about-town, who live for the night life and the girls of the *café chantant* ('Alle sind wir Sünder!'/'Die Mädis, die Mädis, die Mädis vom *Chantant*'). Fond of Boni and Feri as Sylva is, her heart belongs to another admirer, Prince Edwin von und zu Lippert-Weylersheim. When Edwin arrives, he greets Sylva warmly, declaring his love and his admiration for her ('Sich verlieben kann man öfters'/'Mädchen gibt es wunderfeine'), but this love and admiration are not shared by his family. Even now, Boni has a telegram for him, the latest of many from Edwin's father in Vienna, attempting to get him to return home. His family can never countenance his liaison with a mere cabaret singer.

Boni is accompanying Sylva to America. Somewhat tongue-in-cheek, he declares that he is getting too old to enjoy the night life of Budapest. He finds that girls aren't interested in him so much these days, and things are definitely not the same without them ('Aus ist's mit der Liebe bei mir ein für allemal'/'Ganz ohne Weiber geht die Chose nicht').

As the party gets under way, Sylva drinks a toast with Boni, Feri and Edwin to friendship, love and happiness ('O jag dem Glück nicht nach auf meilenfernen Wegen'/'Ja, so ein Teufelsweib') but their festivities are interrupted by the arrival of Edwin's cousin, Lieutenant Eugen von Rohnsdorff, who comes with news that Edwin must return to Vienna to report for military duty. Edwin sees this merely as another device concocted by his father to get him away from Sylva, but Rohnsdorff tells Boni that Edwin's father considers him betrothed to his cousin, Countess Anastasia, and he shows Boni one of the cards that have already been printed to announce the engagement.

When his cousin has left, Edwin decides upon action. He tells Sylva that she shall not go to America. He does so, he says, with the right of a husband. He summons a notary and has a marriage contract drawn up (Finale I: 'Ich, Edwin Ronald Karl Maria, Fürst Lippert-Weylersheim') in which he commits himself to marry Sylva within two months. In view of the difference in their social situation and his family's attitude, Sylva is reluctant to sign, and Feri warns them to be sure of what they are doing but, finally, declaring their love ('O jag dem Glück nicht nach auf meilenfernen Wegen'), they sign the contract, and a celebratory dance breaks out to a decidely fiery, Hungarian version of Mendelssohn's Wedding March.

Edwin and Sylva bid each other a fond farewell ('Mädchen gibt es wunderfeine'), as he sets out for Vienna. Boni, meanwhile, has been away packing and, when he returns and discovers what has happened, he points out that this marriage cannot possibly take place and produces the card that

Rohnsdorff has given him announcing the engagement of Edwin to Anastasia. Sylva sadly believes the evidence and resigns herself to overcoming her sorrow on her trip to America. As the night club empties, Feri is left behind, reflecting on the girls of the variety theatre ('Die Mädis, die Mädis, die Mädis vom *Chantant*').

ACT 2
Eight weeks later a ball is being given in the palace of Prince Lippert-Weylersheim in Vienna ('Erstrahlen die Lichter im heller Glanz'). Edwin is dancing with Stasi, and his parents are delighted to see how well they appear to be getting on together, but Edwin constantly rejects the suggestion that their engagement should be announced, and Stasi is well aware that his obsession with Sylva is coming between them. Stasi is, herself, less than overjoyed at the prospect of marriage to Edwin and the two of them agree that life, as arranged for them by other people, is less than ideal. Perhaps they should just make their nest together and then each fly around a little as the swallows do ('Ich warte auf das grosse Wunder, tralala'/'Machen wir's den Schwalben nach').

Boni and Sylva arrive, and Sylva insists that she be introduced as Boni's wife. As such they are warmly welcomed by the Prince and Princess, to whom Boni is an old friend, and when one of the guests remarks on Sylva's similarity to the Budapest cabaret singer who, since the signing of the wedding contract with Edwin, has been known as the 'Csárdás Princess', Sylva comments that it is not the first time this similarity has been noticed. When Edwin and Sylva meet, he demands furiously to know the reason behind her rejection of the marriage contract and her supposed marriage to Boni. She refers bitterly to Edwin's betrothal to Stasi, and they try with no great success to laugh off the unfulfilled promise of their relationship ('Weisst du es noch?'/'So ein lustiger Roman').

The first bitter exchanges past, Edwin and Sylva soon begin to enjoy each other's company again and since, at the same time, Boni finds himself getting on exceedingly well with Stasi, the four of them end up celebrating together the joys of life ('Liebchen, mich reisst es'/'Hurra! Hurra! Man lebt nur einmal!'). Boni's advances towards Stasi reach the point where she has to warn him about the responsibilities of a married man but Boni, still having to keep up the pretence for Sylva's sake, retorts that it takes all sorts—some finding themselves a woman who is a mouse, others taking on a dragon. That's love! ('Mädel, guck!'/'Das ist die Liebe.')

As Edwin and Sylva continue to repair their estrangement, and Edwin assures her that he never had any intention of marrying Stasi, Boni comes to tell Sylva that he is fed up with their arrangement. He finds it too restrictive and, in any case, she is spending most of her time with someone else. He considers their 'marriage' at an end and hands her over to Edwin. The two lovers want to sing and dance to express their joy and feel as though a thousand angels are singing ('Tanzen möcht ich, jauchzen möcht ich!'/ 'Tausend kleine Engel singen'). Sylva is concerned as to what the reaction of

Edwin's parents will be when they discover who she is, but Edwin tells her that they need never know. They will be content enough for him to marry the woman they know as Countess Káncsiánu.

The old Prince Lippert-Weylersheim chooses this moment to announce to the guests the engagement of Edwin and Stasi (Finale II: 'Verehrte, liebe Gäste!') but Edwin stops him and declares that he is in love with the Countess Káncsiánu. Sylva, however, is not prepared to go along with any such deception. She produces her marriage contract and reveals herself as the 'Csárdás Princess'. Edwin declares that he is happy to keep to the contract, but Sylva tears it up and, telling him that she will not hold him to it, she sweeps out of the palace.

ACT 3

In a Viennese hotel Boni and Sylva are collecting themselves after the recent society-shaking events and discussing the whole sad affair, when they hear the voice of their friend Feri. As he attempts to cheer them up and to persuade Sylva not to leave the stage, a gipsy orchestra in the hotel helps to buoy their spirits ('Nimm Zigeuner, deine Geige'/'Jaj, mamám, Bruderherz, ich kauf' mir die Welt').

Edwin appears, looking for Sylva, followed by his father, seeking Edwin. The Prince is furious at the dreadful happenings that have upset his proposed alliance between Edwin and Stasi, and he is concerned at the way Stasi has been compromised. Boni, however, steps in to insist that Stasi is in no way compromised. He wants to marry her, and he promptly puts a through a telephone call to allow her to confirm her acceptance of his proposal.

When it comes to the question of the Prince's refusal to allow Edwin to marry a cabaret singer, Feri comments that he, too, had once wished to marry a singing girl and he produces his loved one's photograph. At the sight of the photograph the old Prince goes distinctly pink and, when Princess Lippert-Weylersheim arrives, the cause of his discomfort is only too clear. Feri greets the Princess fondly as his former cabaret-singer lover. The old Prince may have married her when she was a widowed countess but, under the circumstances, he can no longer object to Edwin marrying a singer.

Stasi hurries on, and Boni greets her joyously ('Das ist die Liebe') before going to work on Sylva. She readily admits that she still loves Edwin and, when he reveals that there is no longer any family objection to their marriage, the two finally come together in a happy ending ('Tausend kleine Engel singen').

DAS DREIMÄDERLHAUS

(The House of the Three Little Girls)

a play with songs in three acts by A M Willner and Heinz Reichert adapted from the novel *Schwammerl* by Rainer H Bartsch. Music from the works of Franz Schubert selected and arranged by Heinrich Berté. Produced at the Raimundtheater, Vienna, 15 January 1916 with Fritz Schrödter (Schubert) and Anny Rainer (Hannerl).

Produced at the Lyric Theatre, London, in a version by Adrian Ross with music arranged by G H Clutsam as *Lilac Time* 22 December 1922 with Courtice Pounds (Schubert), Clara Butterworth (Lili) and Percy Heming (Schober). Revived there 26 May 1930 with Frederick Blamey, Gertrude Wolfle and Thorpe Bates. Produced at Daly's Theatre 23 December 1927 with Blamey, Evelyn Laye and Heming. Revived there 24 December 1928 with the same leading players. Produced at the Globe Theatre 26 December 1932 with Maurice d'Oisly, Rose Hignell and Heming. Played at the Aldwych Theatre in a version by Richard Tauber 22 September 1933 with Tauber, Kathe Slijn and Willy Vos-Mendes. Produced at the Alhambra Theatre 23 December 1933 with d'Oisly, Helen Gilliland and Derek Oldham. Produced at the London Coliseum 29 July 1936 with d'Oisly, Miss Gilliland and Charles Mayhew. Produced at the Stoll Theatre 13 October 1942 with Frank Titterton, Irene Eisinger and Oldham. Produced at His Majesty's Theatre 24 Februay 1949 with John Lewis, Celia Lipton and Bruce Trent. A version by Rodney Ackland entitled *Blossom Time* was produced at the Lyric Theatre 17 March 1942 with Richard Tauber and Leueen McGrath (Vicki).

Produced at the Ambassador Theatre, New York, in a version by Dorothy Donnelly with music arranged by Sigmund Romberg as *Blossom Time* 29 September 1921 with Bertram Peacock, Olga Cook (Mitzi) and Howard Marsh (Schober). Revived there 1931. Produced at the Jolson Theatre 19 May 1924 and 8 March 1926. Played at the 46th Street Theatre 26 December 1938 with Everett Marshall. Played at the Ambassador Theatre 4 September 1943.

Produced at the Théâtre Marigny, Paris, in a version by Hugues Delorme and Léon Alric as *Chanson d'Amour* 7 May 1921 with Henri Fabert (Schubert), Marcelle Ragon (Annette) and Louis Marie (Baron Franz). Played at the Théâtre de la Gaîté-Lyrique 1928 with Gilbert Moryn, Renée Camia and André Noël, and produced there 1931 with Fabert, Renée Camia and Louis Arnoult. Played at the Théâtre de la Porte Saint-Martin 20 June 1933 in the original version with Richard Tauber, Irene Eisinger and May.

Film versions were produced by Richard Oswald in 1917, by E W Emo in 1936 (*Drei Mäderl um Schubert*) and by Ernst Marischka in 1958 with Karlheinz Böhm, Johanna Matz, Magda Schneider, Rudolf Schock and Ewald Balser. An English film version was produced by Paul Ludwig Stein in 1934 as *Blossom Time* with Richard Tauber, Paul Graetz and June Baxter.

CHARACTERS

Franz Schubert
Baron Schober, *a poet*
Moriz von Schwind, *a painter*
Kupelwieser, *a draughtsman*
Johann Michael Vogl, *a singer at the Court Opera*
Count Scharntorff, *Danish envoy in Vienna*
Christian Tschöll, *the court glazier*

1045

Frau Marie Tschöll, *his wife*
Hederl, Haiderl, Hannerl, *their daughters*
Demoiselle Lucia Grisi, *a court singer*
Andreas Bruneder, *a master saddler*
Ferdinand Binder, *a postmaster*
Nowotny, *a private detective*
Frau Brametzberger, *a landlady*
Frau Weber, *a lodger*
Musicians, children, maids, society men and women, policemen

ACT 1

It is the spring of 1826. Outside the Viennese apartments where the com-poser Franz Schubert lives, a couple of street musicians are performing some typical Austrian folk music ('Fesch und schneidig, allweil g'mütlich') which does not altogether please the landlady, Frau Brametzberger, who reckons she already has enough music to put up with from her composer-lodger playing his piano late into the night.

Into the courtyard come three young girls—Haiderl, Hederl and Hannerl, daughters of the Court glazier Christian Tschöll ('Haiderl und Hederl und Hannerl Tschöll'). They have come to rendezvous with the master saddler Andreas Bruneder and the postmaster Ferdinand Binder, to whom Hederl and Haiderl are secretly engaged. Hannerl, the youngest of the three, has come along as chaperone.

At the same time, four of Schubert's artistic friends call on him—the poet Schober, the painter Schwind, the opera singer Vogl, and the draughtsman Kupelwieser. They have brought food and wine to share with the ever impecunious composer, and they anounce their arrival with his setting of Shakespeare's 'Hark, hark, the lark' from *Cymbeline* ('Horch, horch, die Lerch' im Ätherblau').

The friends take a tub to use as a table and, rolling it underneath a lilac tree, they set about their meal. Full of the joys of spring, they discuss their personal ambitions. Vogl wants a Rhine wine as old as the world, Schwind a pair of wings and Kupelwieser good friends for life, while Schubert longs for the spring to bring him a fair maiden all his own, with lilac blossom on her swelling breast ('Unter einem Fliederbaum'/'Es soll der Frühling mir künden'). As the wine flows, the conversation centres particularly on the singer, Lucia Grisi. Grisi has been conducting a long-standing affair with the Danish envoy, Count Scharntorff, but recently she has begun an amorous relationship with Schober, the jolly man-about-town of Schubert's circle of friends.

While her two sisters are dallying with their fiancés, Hannerl seeks advice from Schober about the problem of keeping these visits to Schubert's home secret from her father, and Schober suggests she should tell him that her sisters have been bringing her for singing lessons with Schubert. She is certainly a warm admirer of Schubert's music. After all, as she tells Schubert, 'what could be more beautiful than a Viennese song?' ('Bin so glücklich, augenblicklich'/'Was Schön'res könnt's sein als ein Wiener Lied?').

As it happens, the girls' father is already on their trail and, when he arrives, the suitors have to make a sudden disappearance. The friends invite Tschöll to join them in some refreshment and, a few glasses of wine and some sweet-talking later, he is ready to give his blessing to the marriages of Haiderl and Hederl.

Everyone drinks to the betrothal underneath the lilac tree (Finale I: 'Unter einem Fliederbaum'), and Tschöll contemplates the prospect of having only one daughter left in the house by the ramparts known by everyone as the 'house of the three little girls' (''s steht in Wien wo auf der Bastei ein Haus'/''s Kleeblatt vom Wienerwald gibt's nur amal'). Schubert's four artistic friends accompany Tschöll, Haiderl, Hederl and their fiancés back to the family home, leaving Schubert to assure Hannerl that he will be only too delighted to give her singing lessons ('Was Schön'res kann's sein als ein Wiener Lied?').

ACT 2

At the double wedding feast for Haiderl and Hederl, Vogl has a great success with Schubert's song 'Der Erlkönig'. He deflects the applause onto the composer, who tells the story of how he employs his musical gifts ('Licht senkt es sich vom Himmel nieder'). As spirits rise ever higher, the two brides and bridegrooms tease Hannerl as to when it will be her turn to get married and Schober joins them in song in praise of the pleasures of love ('Wer's Mädel freit'). When Schober's current lover, Demoiselle Grisi, turns up at the celebrations, she becomes suspicious of Schober's apparent interest in the unmarried sister and reacts jealously ('Sei g'scheit, wer wird denn schmollen?'). As it happens, Grisi has herself been followed by Nowotny, a private detective employed by her official fiancé, Count Scharntorff.

Over three months of taking singing lessons from Schubert, Hannerl and the composer have built up a deep feeling for each other but, when the two are alone together, the desperately shy Schubert can never bring himself to tell her of his love, and Hannerl feels that she may learn more from the petals of a flower as to what he really feels for her ('Was uns dies Blümlein verschafft'/'Liebes Schicksalsblümlein, sprich!').

Now, in her jealousy over Schober, Grisi warns Hannerl against the philandering 'Franz'. Her reference is to the poet, in whom Grisi believes Hannerl to be interested, but the only Franz in Hannerl's thoughts is Franz Schubert and, as a result of Grisi's careless jealousy, she is turned violently away from Schubert. She pours out her feelings angrily to Schober, who cannot understand why she has suddenly turned against the idea of marriage ('Was ist übers Leberl krochen'/'Mädel, sei nicht dumm!').

As the guests and the young married couples leave the reception, Tschöll comforts his wife at having two of her daughters leave home ('Wenn uns Gott Kinder schickt'/'Geh, Alte, schau'). Schubert stays behind with Schober to keep them company, and the shy composer asks the poet to try a passionate love song that he has composed expressing his love for Hannerl. With the composer at the piano, Schober obliges (Finale II: 'Ich schnitt es gern in alle Rinden ein') but Hannerl takes the song as an expression of Schober's own love for her, and responds with an eager expression of her reciprocal feelings for him. Schober reacts with joy at this unexpected good fortune, and Schubert is left to reflect alone on his fate.

ACT 3

In the village square of Hietzing, all the friends are again gathered together. Schober has a meeting arranged with Grisi but he asks Schubert to break the news to the singer that their romance is over. Schubert, ever amenable, and selflessly wanting for Hannerl what she wants for herself, agrees to do so, reflecting on how his shyness has turned fate against him ('Kam der Tag'/ 'Vorüber, vorbei!').

Schober and Hannerl decide to marry ('Tritt ein Jüngling in die Ehe'/'Da gehst her und rührst dich nicht') and, only now, when it is too late, does Schubert discover how Grisi's gossip turned Hannerl against him. There is nothing for him to do but reconcile himself to finding comfort in his music (Finale III: 'Es soll der Frühling mir künden').

DIE ROSE VON STAMBUL

(The Rose of Stamboul)

an operetta in three acts by Julius Brammer and Alfred Grünwald. Music by Leo Fall. Produced at the Theater an der Wien, Vienna, 2 December 1916 with Hubert Marischka (Achmed Bey), Betty Fischer (Kondja), Louise Kartousch (Midili) and Ernst Tautenhayn (Fridolin).

Produced in Berlin with Fritzi Massary (Kondja).

Produced at the Century Theatre, New York, in a version by Harold Atteridge with additional music by Sigmund Romberg 7 March 1922 with Marion Green, Tessa Kosta, Mabel Withe, Henry Warwick and Jack McGowan.

Film versions were produced in 1919 with Fritzi Massary, and in 1953.

CHARACTERS

His Excellence Kamek Pascha
Kondja Gül, *his daughter*
Midili Hanum, Güzela, Fatme, Durlane, Emine, Sobeide, *Kondja's friends*
Achmed Bey
Müller senior, *from Hamburg*
Fridolin, *his son*
Desirée, *Kondja's European companion*
Lydia Kooks, *Midili's European companion*
Black, *an American journalist*

Sadi, *Kamek Pascha's steward*
The manager, porter, musical director *and* lift-boy *of the Honeymoon Hotel*
A foreigner
Bül-Bül, Djamileh, *Kondja's Circassian servants*
Ladies and gentlemen of society, hotel guests

ACT 1

The early morning sun is streaming into the harem of Kamek Pascha in Stamboul as Bül-Bül and the palace's other Circassian servants await the appearance of their mistress, Kondja Gül, beautiful daughter of the Pascha ('Wonnig mögen deine Träume sein').

Although this is a Turkish harem, the Pascha is very much in sympathy with European customs, not to mention European ladies. He has given his daughter a thoroughly European education and also a European companion, Desirée, but now he has taken a turn towards tradition and she is to be married in five days' time to Achmed Bey, the son of the Pascha's Prime Minister. Kondja Gül has thoroughly enjoyed her exposure to European culture. She has taken a particular musical interest in the works of Wagner, Strauss and Lehár and an especial literary interest in the poet André Lery, and she regrets vivaciously that she must now revert to Eastern customs and the wearing of the traditional veil ('Rosig strahle heut' dein Angesicht').

A gong announces the arrival of Midili Hanum and Kondja's other friends ('Guten Morgen, Kondja') who, like Kondja, dream of the day when European reform crosses the Bosporus ('Die Mädchen aus dem Abend-land'/'Von Reformen ganz enormen träumen wir am Bosporus'). Midili has a letter for her friend addressed simply to 'The Rose of Stamboul, Poste restante, Constantinople' and, to Kondja's joy, it turns out to be from her favourite author, André Lery, to whom she had written of her admiration. The letter reciprocates to a considerable degree the admiration expressed by Kondja, and includes the surprising information that the writer is currently in Stamboul.

Midili, also, has a European admirer, Herr Fridolin Müller, son of a German millionaire from Hamburg, whom she met at afternoon tea at the ambassador's residence. He has asked to see a genuine Turkish harem and has arrived at the palace hoping to have his wish granted. He and Midili exchange information on European and Turkish customs, and Fridolin goes on to explain that he has come to Stamboul in search of a wife as none of the senators' daughters in Hamburg has suited him. He is anxious to lift Midili's veil, but she insists that, much as she is in favour of reforms, she is forbidden to allow him to do so ('Als fromme Tochter des Propheten'/''s ist alles im Leben Bestimmung'). Finally Fridolin tricks her. 'Is it true what they say, then, that you have two ugly freckles on your left cheek?' Midili instinctively lifts her veil to prove him wrong and Fridolin is delighted with what he sees.

Kondja is over the moon with her letter from André Lery and with the prospect of going, veiled, to see him the following morning, but her father has other plans for her. Desirée brings her a casket containing a beautiful diadem—a present from her intended husband, Achmed Bey. Kondja dreads the idea of becoming some unknown man's plaything, and Desirée's assurances that he must surely be a real gentleman fail to convince her. 'I hate him and will never love him!' Kondja declares.

A gong announces the appearance of Achmed Bey, an elegant man smartly dressed in modern Turkish uniform and obviously deeply impressed by the thought of being in the home and the presence of the beautiful 'Rose of Stamboul' who is destined to be his Scheherazade ('Man sagt uns nach'/ 'O Rose von Stambul'). Kamek Pascha greets him, and Achmed Bey speaks of the reports of Kondja's beauty but he also brings up the subject of the man he knows to be his rival for Konja's attention: André Lery, the author who in his writings fights for the freedom of the Turkish woman. But Achmed Bey has a surprise in store. André Lery is none other than himself. He agrees with the Pascha that he will go on writing love letters to Kondja under his pseudonym whilst wooing her in his real name, and Kamek Pascha declares that there is the making of a good romantic novel in all this.

The Pascha then introduces his daughter who, in spite of her determined antipathy, finds the first sight of her intended husband not altogether unappealing. He pays her extravagant compliments, but Kondja declares that such Eastern customs are outdated. 'Ah, you want European conversation!' he declares. 'As you wish! I was several years at the embassies in Berlin and Vienna, and I love and treasure the cultures of those countries.' Kondja continues to put up a resistance to him (Finale I: 'Kennen Sie das alte schöne wundersame Keramlied?'), but Achmed Bey is in no way put out at having to win her over. 'I may belong to you,' she declares, 'but my heart and my soul never!' He leaves her still resisting but, when he has gone, she has to admit to herself that his elegance, his stature, his looks, and above all his eyes have undoubted appeal.

ACT 2

A few days later, in Achmed Bey's villa in Stamboul, guests in full evening dress are assembled for the ceremony of his marriage to Kondja Gül and the moment when tradition dictates she shall remove her veil ('Bald naht die Stunde der holdesten Feier'). Midili and Fridolin are amongst the guests, discussing the peculiar European taste for nicotine ('Ihr süssen Zigaretten'/ 'Sie glühen wie Sternlein in der Nacht').

Achmed confesses to his prospective father-in-law the stage-fright he feels at having to challenge André Lery for his wife's love. Now that the marriage is to take place, he has written her a farewell letter in the poet's name telling her of Lery's departure for Switzerland. He greets his bride's ladies-in-waiting and suggests that he ought to see them all without their veils and he is delighted when they oblige ('Ihr stillen süssen Frau'n').

The friendship of Midili and Fridolin progresses apace. 'What a fitting Christmas present you would be for my father's only son,' he declares. Her dimples seem to be especially pleasing to him and his anxiety to progress matters with her is strengthened by the news from home that his father has found a wife for him—a wife who will help Müller to resolve a business lawsuit. He gives Midili an engagement kiss—the first kiss she has ever received—and how she likes it, prickly moustache and all! ('Kind du hast mich nie geküsst'/'Fridolin, ach wie dein Schnurrbart sticht')

The servants prepare for Kondja's arrival and the signing of the wedding contract ('Sie kommt, schon naht die Bangen sich die holde Braut'), and soon Achmed welcomes his 'Rose of Stamboul'. As they prepare to sign the paper, Kondja lays down her terms for what he must do to win her. He must pay her court every day for a month, sending flowers as one would to a woman in Vienna ('Sie glauben mein Herr'/'Das ist der Glück nach der Mode'). Only when that month has passed will she be his.

When everyone else has left, Fridolin, who cannot bear the thought of leaving Midili, appears disguised in female dress. It is the only way he can think of to stay behind when all the men are thrown out, but he inevitably feels uneasy in such unfamiliar garb ('Ich bin noch etwas schüchtern'). He declares himself to be Lili from the ballet ('Ich bin die Lili vom Ballett'), but Midili soon recognises his prickly moustache.

The servants prepare to leave the newly married couple together ('Nachtigallen zärtlich singen') but, even though he can now see how temptingly beautiful Kondja is, Achmed considers himself bound by his promise to woo her for a month ('Süsse Kondja, mein Wort bleibt ungebrochen'). For three weeks there will not be even so much as a kiss. They must start slowly, European style. For now, Kondja decides, they will take supper together and start to learn about each other. Achmed agrees, but declares that, if his wedding night is to be no such thing, he must be permitted to behave as though he were unmarried. He will attend a ball and dance the waltz with the lovely ladies. Kondja is shocked, but curious, all the same, to know what it feels like to dance with a man. 'One cannot describe it—one must experience it,' is Achmed's reply, and he takes her in his arms and gently waltzes her around the room ('Willst du an die Welt vergessen'/'Ein Walzer muss es sein').

The waltz brings forth irresistible temptations, but Kondja resists Achmed's advances, and he begins to lose his temper (Finale II: 'Dem Glücklichen schlägt keine Stunde'). 'You are breaking your word,' Kondja tells him, and declares that she is leaving him to join her idol, André Lery, in Switzerland. Achmed laughs. 'Then I am the victor,' he declares, 'because I am André Lery.' She laughs back at him, declaring the idea to be ridiculous and, as she disappears into the night, he reaffirms his love for the 'Rose of Stamboul'.

ACT 3

A few days later, in the Honeymoon Hotel in a Swiss spa, the hotel manager is finalising with the musical director the programme for music during the meal, including the bridal chorus from *Lohengrin* for the hors d'oeuvre and Mendelssohn's wedding march for the joint. Fridolin and Midili are there on their honeymoon, smothering each other with terms of endearment and kisses. There are limits, though. Midili will go so far as to call him 'Bussi', but not 'Schnucki' ('Ach es macht mir wirklich Angst'/'Geh' sag doch Schnucki zu mir').

Kondja arrives and asks for Fridolin and Midili, who are astonished to see her. She tells them how she had gone searching for André Lery, but could not find his name on the steamer's passenger list for the sailing he had quoted. She tries to book a first floor room in the hotel but, to her horror, she is told that the whole floor has been booked by André Lery and his young wife. 'André Lery married! And he wrote me such letters!' She and Midili rush off, set on vengeance.

The hotel manager announces the arrival of André Lery's car, and Achmed enters. He is well known to the hotel staff, whom he tells that he is alone and that he has changed his mind about the booking. Should they let a room to the lady who asked for one on the first floor, then? At the moment Achmed is in no mood for anything to do with women ('Zwei Augen, die wollen mir nicht aus dem Sinn'/'Heut' wär ich so in der gewissen').

Achmed bumps into Fridolin, and it is clear that their experiences of marriage are so far diametrically opposed insofar as rapture and fulfilment are concerned. Fridolin is more concerned when he bumps into his father who still knows nothing of his marriage. His father is full of the arrangements he has been making for Fridolin's wedding to the bride he has selected back in Hamburg, but finally Fridolin and Midili manage to pacify him with assurances of what a fine grandfather he will make for their offspring ('Papachen, Papachen').

Achmed is sitting down to dinner alone, when he is approached by Kondja, whom the manager has promised to introduce to André Lery. Achmed and Kondja are astonished to find each other in the hotel, but now, at least, she knows that he spoke the truth. Achmed and Lery are one and the same. Moreover, after three days without him, she realises what her feelings for Achmed truly are. To her it seems as though they have been married for weeks, and thus she is ready for the first kiss. As they kiss, she starts to tear the dates off a calendar that is conveniently to hand and in no time at all the courting period Kondja demanded is over—according to their calendar, at least (Finale III: 'Ich bin verliebt').

SCHWARZWALDMÄDEL

(Black Forest Girl)

an operetta in three acts by August Neidhart. Music by Léon Jessel. Produced at the Komische Oper, Berlin, 25 August 1917, with Gustav Charlé (Blasius Römer).

Produced at Haslingers Volksbühne, Vienna, 1946.

Film versions were produced by Victor Jansson in 1929 with Lina Haid, Fred Louis Lerch, Walter Janssen, Georg Alexander and Olga Limburg; and by Georg Zoch in 1933.

CHARACTERS

Blasius Römer, *the cathedral music master*
Hannele, *his daughter*
Bärbele, *his maidservant*
Jürgen, *landlord of the 'Blue Ox'*
Lorle, *his daughter*
Malwine von Hainau
Hans
Richard
Old Woman Traudel
Schmussheim, *a Berliner*
Theobald
Musicians and country folk

ACT 1

In the heart of the Black Forest stands the cathedral town of St Christoph, and there in his music room, Blasius Römer, the cathedral music master, is seated at the harmonium practising for the following day's festival of St Cecilia ('O sancta Cäcilia'). Though grey-haired and widowed, he still considers himself young at heart and, as he contemplates the festivities of the following day, he moves over to the piano and turns his music into the strains of a merry waltz. His young housemaid Bärbele joins in the merriment as she brings in Römer's coffee.

Römer's daughter Hannele comes in, announcing that she has brought with her two young men who have arrived in the village for the festival celebrations and have had difficulty finding accommodation. They announce themselves as itinerant musicians named Hans and Richard ('Wir sind auf der Walz") and Römer, greeting them warmly as members of his own profession, has Bärbele prepare food and drink for them ('Das ist der richt'ge Musikus, den niemals Sorgen drücken').

In fact the two are not musicians at all. Hans is on the run from the enthusiastic attentions of a young lady named Malwine von Hainau, and Richard has joined him in an escape from the city life of Berlin. Their opinion of women seems indeed to have struck rock-bottom ('Ach die Weiber sind ein übel') but, drawing on his somewhat longer experience, Römer assures them that women are not all that bad ('Die Weibsleut, die sind eine Brut—aber gut!').

The resourceful Malwine, meanwhile, has managed to trail Hans to St Christoph. She has put up at the local inn, the 'Blue Ox', and has been brought by the landlord to the home of the church organist. Besides his musical interests, Römer has a fine collection of traditional peasant dresses, and Malwine is keen to borrow one for the festivities the following day. Inevitably, she runs into Richard and, amused at his pretence of being a musician, she begins to tease him and set her cap at him, despite his warning that she is playing with fire ('Mein Fräulein, ach, ich warne Sie'/'Lockende Augen holder Sirenen leuchten euch tief ins Herz hinein').

1053

Romance seems to be rife in the village just at the moment. The landlord himself has a daughter, Lorle, who has for some time been walking out with a lad called Theobald but, when she comes to Römer to practise her solo for the following day, she confesses her disappointment that Theobald seems more inclined to devote himself to writing poetry than to settling down to married bliss ('Wenn der Mensch immer wüsst"/'Das Glück kehrt niemals bei mir ein').

Finally Hans and Malwine come face to face (Finale I: 'Malwine!' 'Ja, lieber Freund! Malwine!'). She reminds him of all the happy times they have had together, but he merely reproaches her for toying with him. 'Must love always end in tragedy?' she asks him ('Muss denn die Lieb' stets Tragödie sein?'). Hans tells her that he is in love with someone else, but Malwine refuses to believe him and tells him that at the following day's festivities he will dance with no one but her.

Meanwhile, at Malwine's instigation, young Bärbele has also been loaned one of Römer's folk costumes for the following day. As a poor servant girl she has never before been to a dance and, in the moonlight, she tries out a few steps with her own shadow ('Schöner Tänzer, du entschwindest'). She is highly excited and she seeks to share her excitement with Römer, the only person in the village who ever pays any real attention to her ('O Bli-bla-blibla-Blasius'). She puts her arms around his neck and kisses him. She does it in all innocence, but Römer mistakes it for a sign that she returns the amorous feelings he cannot help himself feeling towards her.

ACT 2

In the courtyard of the 'Blue Ox' the following day everything is ready for the festival of St Cecilia. The children of the village are having some fun mocking the village recluse, an impoverished old woman called Traudel, whom they accuse childishly of being a witch ('Ei sehet doch die Hex') until Römer comes along and breaks up their cruel game.

Old Traudel is Bärbele's aunt, and Römer tells her of his feelings for the young girl. Her kiss the previous evening has made him feel years younger, but Traudel laughs at the idea of a man of his age considering marriage with a young woman. Römer refuses to be put off, even when Bärbele herself comes along and apologises for her over-exuberance.

When the revellers gather for the festivities, Richard is enchanted at the sight of Hannele, Lorle and Malwine in their peasant costumes ('Hallo!' 'Hallo?' 'Hallo?'). He likens the sight to the joys of Paris and waxes enthusiastic over the delights of the black forest girl ('Flink durchs kleine Städtele'/'Mädel aus dem schwarzen Wald'). When Bärbele comes to join the group, shining with pride in her pretty costume, the other girls merely taunt her for being a jumped-up servant girl.

Richard partners off with Malwine and begins to tell her the story of his amorous conquests ('Ich liebte manche Frau schon'), whilst stressing that he has never found a girl quite like her ('Malwine, ach Malwine'), and Bärbele, fearing that she is destined to spend the festival on her own ('Alle werden sie sich drehen'), again turns to Römer. As the violins are being tuned for the dancing, she asks him to dance with her ('Erklingen zum Tanze die Geigen'), but the musician feels inhibited by the status of his position and will risk only a few surreptitious steps.

Jürgen, the landlord of the inn, starts the village's traditional 'ladies' choice' (Finale II: 'Haltet! Haltet! Ordnung muss sei!'). The girls are lined up on one side and the boys on the other and the girls go light-heartedly to make their choice. Malwine chooses Hans, who at first refuses but, when the landlord tells him that custom decrees he must accept, he does so. Then it is Malwine's turn to play hard to get and she finally ends up dancing with Richard.

Bärbele has gone to choose Römer, but she has once more been driven away by the other girls, who are now calling her, too, a witch. When Hans declares that he will dance with her, he unleashes an almighty tumult. As the town takes sides, lamps are smashed and, in the moonlight, a general scuffle takes place. Blood is spilled, much of it that of a belligerent visitor from Berlin named Schmussheim, and Richard sinks, black and blue and battered, into Malwine's arms. As the clock strikes midnight, Jürgen finally restores order and declares the festivities at an end.

ACT 3

Inside the village inn, Lorle is sitting at her window, with the sun streaming down on her ('Scheint die Sonn' herein in mein Kämmerlein'). She is longing for Theobald to show her some interest, but suddenly a bunch of roses flies through her window and she rushes happily out to join her lover.

The loutish Schmussheim appears sporting both a considerable hangover and a bodyful of physical injuries and announces that he intends to return to Berlin at once. By now Richard and Malwine have decided that they are meant for each other and, with Hans's blessing, they too intend to return to Berlin, together. Schmussheim volunteers to go with them, and they invite him to be a witness at their wedding, declaring that any longer-term addition to their twosome should come from starting a family. Whether it be a boy or a girl, they don't mind ('Wenn der Mann schon dreissig ist'/'Es kann ein Bub' sein.').

Meanwhile, after a sleepless night, Römer has finally made up his mind to marry Bärbele. However, he has received a letter telling him that her father has died and left her a fortune and he fears that this might make people think that he is marrying her for her money. He does not dream that Bärbele has no interest in marrying him anyway. Her heart lies with Hans, and Römer finally has to accept that his case is hopeless and that his dreams of regained youth were misguided, as he generously gives Bärbele and Hans his blessing (Finale III: 'Erklingen zum Tanze die Geigen').

DER LETZTE WALZER

(The Last Waltz)

an operetta in three acts by Julius Brammer and Alfred Grünwald. Music by Oscar Straus. Produced at the Berliner Theater, Berlin, 12 February 1920 with Fritzi Massary (Vera Lisaweta).

Produced at the Theater an der Wien, Vienna, 27 October 1921.

Produced at the Century Theatre, New York, in a version by Harold Atteridge and Edward Delaney Dunn as *The Last Waltz* 10 May 1921 with Eleanor Painter (Vera), Walter Woolf (Jack Merrington) and Harrison Brockbank (Prince Paul).

Produced at the Gaiety Theatre, London, in a version by Reginald Arkell and Robert Evett 7 December 1922 with José Collins (Vera), Bertram Wallis (Paul), Kingsley Lark (Jack), Amy Augarde (Alexandrowna), Alfred Wellesley (General Krasian) and Billy Leonard (Baron Ippolith Mekowitch).

Produced at the Trianon-Lyrique, Paris, and subsequently at Théâtre de la Gaîte-Lyrique in a version by Léon Uhl and Jean Marietti 21 May 1936 with Suzanne Laplace, Raymond Chanel, André Balbon, Robert Allard (Hippolyte) and Monette Dinay (Babouchka).

A film version was produced by Georg Jacoby in 1934 with Camille Horn, Ivan Petrovitch and Susi Lanner, and another by Arthur Maria Rabenalt in 1953 with Eva Bartok, Curt Jürgens, O E Hasse, Christl Mardayn, Rudolf Schundler and Siegfried Breuer.

CHARACTERS

General Miecu Krasinski
Baron Ippolith Mrkowitsch Baschmátschkin, *his nephew*
Countess Alexandrowna Nastasja Opalinski, *a general's widow*
Vera Lisaweta, Annuschka, Hannuschka, Petruschka, Babuschka, *her daughters*
Prince Paul
Count Dimitry Wladimir Sarrasow
Count Kaminski, Lieutenant Swietzinski, Lieutenant Labinski, Cadet Orsinski, *Guards officers*
Uncle Jaroschkin
Chochotte, Lolo, Sylvette, *dancers of the Warsaw Opera ballet*
Wladek
Adjutant to the Prince, guests, society ladies and gentlemen, dancers, servants

ACT 1

On a winter night in 1910 a masked ball is under way in General Krasinski's castle near Warsaw. The assembled company, including many officers and their guests, drink a champagne toast to their host ('Es lebe der Herr General!') and another to a brother officer who is due to be executed the following day. The unfortunate man is Count Wladimir Dimitry Sarrasow, who is being kept under custody in the castle before being taken to Warsaw for his execution. His exact crime is not fully understood, but it is known that he was committed for trial at the instigation of Prince Paul and the mystery

1056

surrounding his crime has merely served to heighten the widespread sympathy felt for him.

General Krasinski has done everything possible to make Dimitry's stay at his castle as pleasant as possible, and Dimitry is in high spirits as he is brought in, his hands tied behind his back, to enjoy his last supper. His hands are untied and, as he takes a glass of champagne with his fellow officers, he reflects that his death will mean the end of the Sarrasow family ('Bei Lied und Wein') before going on to tell them the story of how he came to find himself in his current situation. It all came about because he rescued a young lady from the unwelcome attentions of Prince Paul at the last Court Ball at the Winter Palace of the Tsars.

For the General, the following day is to be memorable also for the fact that he is due to be married for the third time and it is to celebrate this that he is holding tonight's ball. Since Dimitry has no close relatives, he decides to present the General with his prized family ring for his bride-to-be to wear at her wedding, as an appreciation of the hospitality he has received. When the lovely Vera Lisaweta receives the ring, she recognises it at once. It was she whom Dimitry rescued from Prince Paul's clutches, and she realises that the officer who rescued her must be the very one who is detained by the General. Her memories of the handsome young man and a feeling of help-lessness at his fate make her heart flutter and conjure up all manner of images ('Rosen, die wir nicht erreichten'). She realises, too, that Prince Paul must have commanded General Krasinski to marry her, and she vows to have vengeance on the Prince.

Vera has three younger sisters—Annuschka, Hannuschka and Petruschka. They have each had all the right education for a young lady and they are now looking to find themselves a man ('Mama, Mama! Wir wollen einen Mann!'). They have all been especially taken by the charms of the young nobleman Ippolith Mrkowitsch Baschmátschkin, and their mother Alexandrowna is highly content as Ippolith is on her list of elegible young men with a three-star rating. Ippolith is as enamoured of the three sisters as they of him, and his only problem is to know which one of them to marry. As the dance orchestra plays a polka, the three girls parade their respective claims for his perusal ('O kommt, o kommt und tanzt mit mir').

Disguised behind her mask, Vera encounters Dimitry. She expresses concern for his destiny as together they listen to what Dimitry considers must be his last waltz ('Das ist der letzte Walzer'). Even with death approaching fast, Dimitry is not one to waste an opportunity for pleasure and he begs to be allowed to join in the merriment on this, the last night of his life. Captain Kaminski tells him that he is going too far (Finale I: 'Graf Sarrasow, Sie geh'n zu weit'), but Dimitry gives Kaminski his word of honour that he will not attempt to escape, and the General accedes to his request. Dimitry goes to dress for the occasion and, with only an hour to spare before his departure for Warsaw, he enters the ballroom in his elegant white dress suit.

ACT 2

As Dimitry enters the ballroom, a waltz is about to get under way. It is time, too, for the ladies to take off their masks and, when the General asks his fiancée to unmask, Dimitry is astounded to discover that the lady who has so taken his fancy is the one whose rescue from Prince Paul's clutches had brought about his death sentence. For the time being, he covers his shock by bidding the company to embark on a swirling waltz ('Hört ihr die liebliche, zwingende, singende, werbende Walzermusik') but, under cover of the dancing, Dimitry and Vera engage in conversation. She urges him to flee, but he insists that he is bound not to by his word of honour. All she can do for him, he says, is to join him in the dance, his last waltz.

Ippolith is still trying to resolve his dilemma over which sister to marry. When the ladies' choice is called, he imagines that all he has to do is to wait and see which of the sisters is most eager to dance with him, but they prefer *him* to be the one to make up his mind and they go off to dance with three other officers ('Dann weiss der Jüngling, dass es Zeit ist'). Vera, meanwhile, has had an idea of how she might help Dimitry and she sends the cadet Orsinski with a message to the stationmaster. Trembling at the thought of how she must enchant Dimitry to persuade him to follow her plan, she picks up a hand-mirror and gazes at her reflection, seeking desperately for reassurance. 'Dance, Vera Lisaweta,' it tells her ('Tanze, Vera Lisaweta').

Besides Annuschka, Hannuschka and Petruschka, Vera has yet another sister, Babuschka, who is considered too young to attend the ball. However, Babuschka has decided that it is time she broke out from her Cinderella-like role, and she arrives at the ball under the guardianship of her Uncle Jaroschka. Ippolith is still trying to resolve his three-cornered predicament when he comes upon Babuschka and invites her to dance. Her uncle has forbidden her to speak to any young man, but they dispose of that problem by singing to each other—he not least of the dimples in her cheeks ('Du hast zwei Grübchen').

Orsinski returns with the news that the stationmaster has agreed to Vera's request and, meeting up again with Dimitry, Vera tells him that a troika waits below the window to take him to the station. 'At forty minutes after midnight the Nice express passes through the station. The stationmaster has promised me that he will stop the train. You will board the train as a courier for the Emperor. A pass with the necessary official stamps will take you over the border unhindered, and you will be safe.' 'Why are you concerned with the destiny of a man you have seen fleetingly only twice?' Dimitry asks. 'Because I love you,' she replies ('Hast du es nicht erraten?'). 'But my word of honour!' Dimitry replies. 'There is something higher than a man's honour,' she replies, 'and that is a woman's honour. If you don't listen to me and flee, the General and the whole company will find you in my arms.' Dimitry holds Vera for a moment in his arms and then disappears through a secret door.

The evening's entertainment comes to a height with a display of national dancing accompanied by a balalaika (Finale II: 'Der Klang des Guslizither') before the soldiers come to collect Dimitry for his journey. He is nowhere to be found. Vera throws open the window, looks out at the starry winter night and points to the thread of light that is the Nice express. To everyone's surprise the train stops at the local station before setting off again. Vera tells the soldiers that Dimitry has gone, and she explains that she was the lady over whose honour Dimitry was sentenced to death by Prince Paul. 'He broke his word and forgot his duty,' Captain Kaminski declares, but at that very moment Dimitry reappears in the room. 'You are wrong,' he cries. 'That he didn't do!' He explains to Vera that he could not break his promise to his friends and, as he looks into her eyes, they reflect that it really was Dimitry's last waltz after all.

ACT 3

In a salon of Prince Paul's palace, a company of dancing girls are performing for the Prince's pleasure ('Wir sind die Balletteusen'). For them, too, the story of the condemned Count Dimitry has a romantic interest, and they dare to ask the Prince what is to become of him. 'I will show him what it means to get in my way!' he retorts and he offers to show Dimitry to them. The condemned soldier has been brought to the palace as a further twist in Prince Paul's elaborate revenge. Dimitry is brought in blindfolded in front of the Prince and the dancing girls and, asked where he imagines he is, he admits that his nose tells him he is not in the citadel, but in an elegant salon with pretty women. His blindfold is removed and, gallant and cheerful to the end, he bids the ladies a merry farewell ('Bei Lied und Wein').

The Prince has arranged yet one further twist. He has had the sledges carrying the General's wedding party to Warsaw waylaid and Vera brought to him with the promise that Dimitry may yet be saved. He seeks to continue the dialogue that Dimitry had interrupted at the Court Ball, but Vera adopts a haughty stance, puts him onto the defensive, and taunts him with an enigmatic 'O-la-la' ('O du pikantes, kleines O-la-la'). Sadistically Prince Paul extracts from Vera an acknowledgement of her concern for Dimitry, before finally telling her that Dimitry will not, after all, suffer the ultimate penalty.

He is not to die, but he is to be humiliated. Firstly he will be made to suffer by being forced to serve supper to Vera and himself. Using her wiles to the full, Vera points out to Prince Paul how, since the incident, Dimitry has become a source of fascination to every woman at court. 'And now you want to make him even more interesting!' she says. 'Wouldn't it be better if you were the hero in this story?'

As this thought gives him pause, Vera asks that, for once in his life, the Prince should not give the orders. For just ten minutes he should allow her to do so. Paul agrees, whereupon Vera orders Dimitry to be brought before her. Then she orders the Prince to invite Dimitry to take supper with them and, finally, she orders that, just as previously Prince Paul had commanded the General to marry her, he should now order Dimitry to do so. Paul does, and Dimitry accepts without hesitation. 'Now you are the hero of the story,' Vera tells Prince Paul (Finale III: 'Du lieber letzter Walzer').

DER VETTER AUS DINGSDA

(The Cousin From Nowhere)

an operetta in three acts by Herman Haller and 'Rideamus' after a comedy by Max Kempner-Hochstädt. Music by Eduard Künneke. Produced at the Theater am Nollendorfplatz, Berlin, 15 April 1921 with Lori Leux (Julia), Johannes Müller (Stranger) and Ilse Marvenga (Hannchen).

Produced at the Johann Strauss Theater, Vienna, 13 October 1922. Produced at the Philadelphiatheater in a revised version 18 March 1944.

Produced at the Ambassador Theatre, New York, in a version by Harry B Smith and Al Goodman as *Caroline* 31 January 1923 with Tessa Kosta (Caroline), Harrison Brockbank (Calhoun) and J Harold Murray (Robert).

Produced at the Prince's Theatre, London, in a version by Fred Thompson, Adrian Ross and Douglas Furber as *The Cousin From Nowhere* 24 February 1923 with Helen Gilliland (Julia), Walter Williams (Stranger) and Cicely Debenham (Hannchen).

Film versions were produced by Georg Zoch in 1934, and in 1953.

CHARACTERS

Julia de Weert
Hannchen, *her friend*
Josef Kuhbrot, *known as* Josse, *Julia's uncle*
Wilhelmine, *known as* Wimpel, *his wife*
Egon von Wildenhagen
A stranger
A second stranger
Karl *and* Hans, *servants*

ACT 1

In the garden of a villa in southern Holland, on a warm summer's evening, Josef Kuhbrot and his wife are taking their supper with Hannchen, a friend of their niece and ward Julia, and discussing the attempt by Julia's co-guardian, a district official, to marry Julia off to his son, Egon von Wildenhagen ('Noch ein Gläschen Bordeaux?'/'Onkel und Tante'). Julia seems little inclined to come for her meal. 'Does she live on air?' asks her Aunt Wimpel. 'No, on love' replies Hannchen.

The object of Julia's affections is her cousin, Roderich, who left home seven years ago. Julia's aunt and uncle have not heard of him since, but Hannchen insists that Julia hears from Roderich every day. 'What do I hear?' exclaims Uncle Josse. 'My ward has been having a secret correspondence behind my back?' Hannchen tells them that the correspondence is carried out via the moon. When Roderich left, the two young people promised to look up at the moon every evening and thereby keep in touch with each other and, indeed, when Julia appears, she looks up and asks the radiant moon to convey her thoughts and kisses to her beloved ('Strahlender Mond').

Uncle Josse would like to marry Julia to his brother's son, August. That way the de Weert wealth would at least be kept within the family. Josse has already arranged to meet August at the village inn, where he will give him the once over, but when he decides to test the proposal with Julia, she gives it an immediate thumbs down.

Egon von Wildenhagen brings news that the guardianship court has declared that Julia has now come of age. Since this means that she can make her own decision on a marriage partner, Julia is overjoyed. Egon knows that her heart lies with Roderich, but he finds the romance rather curious. 'Believe me, gracious lady,' he says to her, 'if your famous cousin from nowhere suddenly turned up, I bet you wouldn't even recognise him!' 'I would recognise him merely by his voice,' Julia replies as she joins Hannchen in teasing Egon over his naive ideas of marriage ('O werter Verehrter'/ 'Überleg dir's, überleg dir's vorher').

Now that she has come of age, Julia is resolved that she will live life as she pleases (Finale I: 'Rein wird gemacht, aus wird gekehrt!'), and she decides to celebrate her first day of freedom in some appropriate way. Should she and Hannchen go into town for a dance? Or should they call Egon back to stay the night? 'Imagine uncle's face in the morning!' they giggle. They call after the departing Egon to come back, but the voice that replies is not his.

Eager for a bit of fun, Julia prepares a banner to welcome whoever it is, and finally a stranger approaches from across the fields. He is a somewhat unkempt fellow in a green hiking suit with a rucksack and he is astonished by the welcome given to him by the girls. He asks how far it is to the local inn, but Julia tells him it is a three-quarters of an hour's walk and invites him to take a rest in her magic fairy palace. When he tells her how hungry he is, he is immediately offered food, and when he mentions his thirst he is at once brought a glass of wine ('Nicht wahr, hier ist's im Zauberreich?'/'Doch die Märchen, die Märchen sind leider nicht wahr').

The stranger protests that it is time for him to be going but, as his good fairy, Julia says that she still has a third wish to grant him. What is it to be? 'I'd like to sleep in a real four-poster bed with thick silk curtains!' he replies and, once again, Julia tells him that his wish is granted. 'How shall I thank you, my child?' he asks and Julia requests only that, before he goes to bed, he tells her who he is. 'That is quickly told,' he replies, 'but it is no recompense for you. I'm only a poor, wandering fellow. So good night, pretty maiden, good night' ('Ich bin nur ein armer Wandergesell'). Hannchen thinks that Julia must be mad letting a vagrant spend the night in her home, but Julia laughs off her madness—'It is just the summer night, the moonlight, and the memory of another!'—as the three bid each other good night.

ACT 2

Next morning, out on the terrace of the villa, Hannchen and Julia laugh over the memory of the previous evening's fun ('Ja, was ist denn das bloss?'). Julia is especially happy. 'I could hug the whole world,' she says. ('Ach, ich halt's nicht mehr aus'/'Weisst du, warum die Sonne heut'). The stranger, meanwhile, has been having a splendid time, ringing for slippers, for a bath and shower, for warm water to shave in, and for breakfast in bed brought by the pretty maid who had been so kind to him the previous evening. When he finally appears on the terrace, he tells the girls that, at this rate, he would be happy to stay there a week, but he is told that after breakfast he must go. Julia tells him how her uncle's nephew, August Kuhbrot, is expected and, before she can stop herself, launches into the tale of her other cousin Roderich and his departure to Batavia, capital of the south seas island of Java.

Left alone to finish his breakfast, the stranger muses on how fate can make things happen when least expected ('Ganz unverhofft kommt oft das Glück'). When Uncle Josse comes down he is astonished to see a stranger at his table and, introducing himself and Aunt Wimpel, he asks the stranger who he is. The young man tells them to think back seven years to when he last sat here on this same terrace with short trousers and long hair. He is, he tells them, their nephew Roderich. Julia is overjoyed to discover that the stranger is apparently her long-lost cousin—though her uncle can't help wishing he were August instead.

Julia and the stranger are left alone to make up for seven lost years. They say how much they have missed each other, although it is clear that the stranger really does not understand Julia's references to their correspondence via the moon. Neither does he have the ring that Julia gave him on their parting. But he has no difficulty joining in Julia's reminiscences of the games they played as children ('Weisst du noch, wie wir als Kinder gespielt?'/'Kindchen, du musst nicht so schrecklich viel denken').

Egon reappears with a bouquet in his hand, determined to have more success with Julia than the previous day, and he reports importantly that a telegram has arrived in response to one his father cabled to the German consulate in Batavia. He is surprised at Julia's lack of interest and deeply taken aback when she introduces the stranger to him as Roderich. In desperation at her rejection of his love, Egon turns to Hannchen, but she merely mocks his ideas of how to woo a woman ('Ich hab' an sie nur stets gedacht').

At the request of Uncle Josse and Aunt Wimpel, the visitor tells them all about his seven years in Batavia, painting a colourful picture of an exotic tropical existence ('Sieben Jahre lebt' ich in Batavia'/'Mägdelein! Zart und fein!'). 'When a man loves a girl in Batavia,' he tells them, 'he kisses her in the jungle while kangaroos and gnus look on,' diplomatically adding that, of all the beautiful girls he saw there, none was as delightful as Julia, to whom he now declares his love (Finale II: 'Unendlich! Unendlich liebe ich dich!'). It is, they agree, just like a fairy tale.

Just then Egon rushes in with a telegram. 'But the fairy tale is unfortunately not true,' he cries. According to the latest communication from the German consul in Batavia, Roderich was still in Batavia six weeks ago, and not until today will the next boat from Java have docked in Germany. Everyone turns on the stranger. 'Do you love me only if I am Roderich?' he asks Julia, and she admits that it is indeed Roderich she loves. The stranger has to confess that he is not Roderich. 'Tell us who you are then!' everyone cries. The stranger has the perfect answer. 'I'm only a poor, wandering fellow,' he replies ('Ich bin nur ein armer Wandergesell').

ACT 3

As the stranger leaves the Kuhbrot family home, a storm breaks and he reflects that one has to take cover from heaven as much as from women ('Ob Sturm, ob Graus'/'Vor dem Himmel und den Weibern'). He picks up an umbrella that is lying around and departs, as a servant calls in vain after him that he is still wearing a borrowed suit instead of his own green hiking suit.

Julia, meanwhile, has locked herself in her room. 'If only August were here,' her uncle wishes. Then a letter arrives from the station master, reporting August Kuhbrot's arrival. He is wearing a green suit, with a green hat and carrying a green rucksack. Just then the servant Karl brings out the clothes that the departed stranger has left behind—green suit, green hat, green rucksack. Uncle Josse reckons that their strange visitor must have met August on his way through the woods and robbed him, and Egon determines to call out the constabulary to find August, dead or alive.

Hannchen is left alone, reflecting that the stranger was really such a nice man. 'If only Father Christmas would bring *me* a man!' she muses. 'One with his own car and chauffeur!' At that very moment the sound of a motor horn is heard, and another stranger steps out of a car. 'Oh, Father Christmas, I beg your pardon!' she stammers, before hurrying to greet the new visitor. He seems no less pleased at seeing her ('Ach, heil'ger Nikolaus, verzeih'!'/'Na, nu sagen Sie bloss. Na, das ist doch zu toll') and, without wasting time, makes her an immediate proposal of marriage. 'But with whom do I have the pleasure?' asks the breathless Hannchen. 'I am Roderich de Weert,' is the reply.

Just then the first stranger returns, bringing back the clothes which he had taken away in his haste. The two men face each other and, when Roderich introduces himself, he hears the tale of how Julia has waited for him all these years. 'In God's name!' he replies, 'I never thought of that as anything but a crush, a childish folly.' Suddenly Hannchen remembers Egon and the police, and she warns the first stranger of Uncle Josse's theory that he may have murdered his nephew August. 'That would have been suicide!' the young man exclaims, 'for I am August Kuhbrot.'

Hannchen decides the best way to resolve these complications is to have Roderich dress himself up in August's green hiking outfit and present himself to Julia (Finale III: 'Ganz unverhofft kommt oft das Glück'). Uncle Josse and Aunt Wimpel are horrified to see the first stranger back again, but equally relieved to see the other one, now dressed in green, whom they take for August. When the real Roderich presents himself to Julia as August, she tells him that she has no interest in him. She is engaged to another. Her heart is given to Roderich.

He tells her that Roderich is a worthless fellow who has forgotten his promises to her and become engaged to someone else and, having totally antagonised Julia, he finally shows her the ring she gave him seven years before and admits his true identity. Julia is wholly disillusioned. 'And for his sake I turned the other one away!' she reflects bitterly. At these words the first stranger steps out and introduces himself to Julia as August, but she will not have it. 'For me you are Roderich, my Roderich!' she exclaims. 'And you will be my August,' Hannchen declares to Roderich. As for Egon, he can go to Batavia!

DIE BAJADERE

(The Bayadere)

an operetta in three acts by Julius Brammer and Alfred Grünwald. Music by Emmerich Kálmán. Produced at the Carltheater, Vienna, 23 December 1921 with Louis Treumann (Prince Radjami), Christl Mardayn (Odette), Louise Kartousch (Marietta) and Ernst Tautenhayn (Napoléon).

Produced at the Knickerbocker Theatre, New York, in a version by William Baron and B G deSylva as *The Yankee Princess* 2 October 1922 with Thorpe Bates (Radjami), Vivienne Segal (Odette) and John T Murray (Napoleon).

Produced at the Théâtre des Célestins, Lyon, in a version by Pierre Véber, Bertal and Mauban as *La Bayadère* 4 March 1925 with Léonard and Tirmont sharing the role of Radjami, Maguy Warna, Gabrielle Ristori and Urban. Produced at the Théâtre Mogador, Paris, 1926 with Maria Kousnezoff replacing Mlle Warna.

CHARACTERS

Prince Radjami of Lahore
Odette Darimonde
Napoléon St Cloche
Louis-Philippe La Tourette
Marietta, *his wife*
Count Armand
Colonel Parker,*the English Resident in Lahore*
Fefé
Odys, Gattana Rao, Attha, Lydana, Ranja, Sika, *servant girls at Radjami's*
Dewa Singh, *a minister from Lahore*
Dewa, *the Prince's adjutant*
Pimprinette, *leader of the claque of the Châtelet Theatre*
Dr Cohen, *a journalist*
Jonny, *barman*
Mary, *barmaid*
The manager of the bar
Theatre audience, guests of the Prince, theatre boxkeepers

ACT 1

In the dress circle bar of the Châtelet Theatre in Paris, the elegantly dressed members of the audience are discussing in enthusiastic tones the first act of the operetta *La Bayadère* ('Reizend war der erste Akt'). Count Armand, his lady friend Fefé, and another two ladies emerge from their *loge*, with Armand maintaining that the song 'Lotus Blossom' will soon be the rage of Paris. He evidently has inside knowledge of how the plot of the operetta will develop, and Fefé tries to prevent him spoiling the show for the rest of them with his eager gossip. She is spared further embarrassment by the ringing of the bell for the start of the second act.

When the audience have left to take their seats, the exotically dressed Marietta La Tourette and the Marquis Napoléon St Cloche, a lively Parisian man-about-town, appear. They seem to be at the theatre as much for the opportunities it offers for socialising as for the performance. Apparently Marietta has been rejecting the Marquis's advances for three years, but he still persists in his pursuit. He has even changed his name from Casimir to Napoléon because of her insistence that she is interested only in heroes, and he once pretended to have gone on an expedition to India because of her declaration that she was interested only in a globe-trotter. Do as he may, Marietta is adamant that she will not be unfaithful to her husband ('Treu zu sein'/'Muss es denn grad der Eine sein?').

Napoléon takes the pretence over his Indian expedition to great lengths, illustrating his tales with plenty of corroborative detail. One of these details is, unfortunately, the claim that, during his trip, he became friendly with Prince Radjami of Lahore. Because of the Indian setting of the Châtelet's new production, the Prince is, unknown to Napoléon, expected at the theatre that very evening and Marietta is mad to meet him. Radjami arrives to a warm reception, specially orchestrated by Pimprinette, leader of the theatre's claque, and he immediately demonstrates a particular fascination with Odette Darimonde, the actress who is playing the star rôle of the bayadère. She interests him all the more because, of all the women in Paris, she alone shows absolutely no interest in him. Here, he declares, he sees his destiny.

Opening the door of one of the boxes, the Prince hears Odette singing her principal aria ('Ah, Dein will auf ewig ich sein!') and, enraptured, he gives vent to his passion for this Parisian vision of an Indian dancing girl ('Wenn die bleiche Nacht herniedersinkt'/'O Bajadere, wie dein Bild mich berauscht') and begs the theatre manager to arrange an immediate introduction.

Napoléon comes out of his box and spots Radjami and, conscious of the need to keep up his image in Marietta's eyes, he plucks up the courage to approach the Prince and begin a decidedly strained conversation. He is interrupted by the applause as the second act ends and the audience swirl out of their boxes for the second interval ('Reizend war der zweite Akt!') and, almost immediately, Pimprinette comes by, clearing the way for Odette. She is dressed in a cloak, flung over her bayadère costume, and displaying something of the apprehension and nerves she feels before she goes on stage ('Wenn Sie eine Ahnung hätten'/'Sterne der Bühne') at being summoned by this royal command.

Reluctantly she goes forward to meet the Prince who enthuses over her performance and presents her with a bunch of red roses he tells her are from the garden of the Taj Mahal. 'They are called love roses,' he says, 'and anyone who smells their scent will fall in love.' He tells her of his fascination for her, but she replies that in real life she is not like the bayadère she plays on stage, selflessly following her prince. Undeterred, Radjami invites her to a party after the show. She refuses, but the Prince declares that he will not take 'no' for an answer. His will is at least as strong as hers, and he turns to the words that the hero of the operetta spoke to the bayadère—'Lotus blossom, I love you' ('Lotusblume, ich liebe Dich'/'Liebesrosen hüllen mich so schmeichelnd ein').

Meanwhile Marietta and her husband Louis-Philippe are having something of a row. She complains that he always insists on leaving before the end of the show, while he retorts that she always manages to be late. He is concerned that, if they wait for the end, they won't manage to get a good table at the Café de Paris, but Marietta is looking forward to the introduction to Prince Radjami that Napoléon has promised her after the show. Louis-Philippe sees that there might be useful possibilities in such a meeting; it might assist the export to India of the chocolates his company manufactures. Napoléon has no care for chocolates; he has his mind set only on enjoying Paris nightlife at Maxim's, preferably with Marietta ('Reizend ist's, nach Müh' und Plag'/'Wenn die Sterne am Himmel leuchten').

Colonel Parker, British Resident in Lahore, appears at the theatre, anxious to see the prince. The Colonel has been chasing Radjami for a week to point out that in three days time he will be thirty years old, the age at which the law of his country says he must be married or lose the right to the throne of Lahore. Moreover, Parker has a letter from the ruling Prince, Radjami's father, telling him that, in his absence, six Indian beauties have been chosen from whom Radjami may choose his chief wife. He must catch the 10.30 p.m. train to Bordeaux, where a ship is ready to take him to Bombay. Radjami refuses, and Parker is shrewd enough to detect that behind his refusal lies a woman (Finale I: 'O Bajadere, seit dich hab' erschaut').

Radjami insists that he will hold an impromptu party in his villa in the Rue Honoré, off the Champs-Elysées, that night. He will invite Odette, but he also urgently needs other guests. As the audience emerges after the last act of the show, he sees Napoléon approaching with Marietta and, to Napoléon's surprise and delight, greets him as an old friend, invites him to his party, and tells him to bring all his friends. Then Odette appears, Radjami's roses in her hand, and leaves for the Rue Honoré on the Prince's arm.

ACT 2

The guests arriving at Prince Radjami's luxurious villa are greeted by his adjutant ('Champagner, sperrst uns auf das Himmelreich'). Indian custom dictates that the host appears last and, while the guests await the Prince, they are entertained by a group of Indian dancers. In response Marietta demonstrates the latest Parisian dance craze—the foxtrot ('Tanz mit mir!'/ 'Der kleine Tanzkavalier').

Radjami enters with Odette, the two gazing adoringly at each other ('Du, du, du, nur du sollst das Glück meiner Seele nun sein!'). As if waking from a trance, Odette tells him how she was standing in front of the mirror in her dressing room and felt a sudden urge to take up the invitation to his party, and Radjami knows that the love roses have cast their spell. He tells her that his will has begun to work its way and that, before the night is over, she will not only say that she loves him but will put it into writing. Odette declares that, if he really does get her to do that, then she will accept it as her heart's will. They have made a pact ('Jawohl ein Pakt'). Odette asks for a waltz to be played, but Radjami does not understand. In Benares dances have no name: one merely dances grief or happiness, delight or joy. Odette proceeds to teach him the steps of the waltz ('Rechts herum und links herum'/'Mann küsst auch in Benares').

Marietta and Louis-Philippe are enjoying themselves, but in different ways. 'This palace, and the exotic charm of all these rooms,' enthuses Marietta. 'Yes, the buffet is tremendous,' responds her husband. 'If only I knew what is in the sandwiches—the ones with the little red dots.' 'Don't you get the impression of opium and hashish?' she asks dreamily. 'I thought it was caviar with anchovy purée,' is all he can add. If her husband is away on a different wave-length, Marietta has the arrival of Napoléon to look forward to. He has promised to wear the tropical uniform he used for his Indian expedition and, when finally he arrives, Marietta persuades him to tell her all about his tiger-shoot with the Prince in India, an episode which he performs in graphic detail. But what Napoléon really wants is to take Marietta away from all this Eastern glamour to a warm and quiet little boulevard bar ('Bogenlampen glitzern durch den Winternachmittag'/'Die kleine Bar dort am Boulevard').

When Colonel Parker arrives, Radjami tells him that he intends to get married to Odette that very night, even though he has to admit that his bride-to-be doesn't yet know about it. Parker warns him to pay attention to European customs. 'Ah, yes, your customs!' Radjami replies. 'In my country one marries quickly and never separates. In your country one marries slowly and quickly separates.' Parker points out that by law Radjami needs two witnesses who knew him in India. Parker himself could be one. But who would be the other? Well, of course Napoléon claims to have been to India. Surely he could be persuaded to say that he had known the Prince there. And, to Napoléon's astonishment, he finds the Prince co-operating on the story of their tiger-shooting and elephant-hunting in Hindustan. This is the last straw in his pursuit of Marietta. She is sufficiently impressed finally to give in to Napoléon's wooing, and Louis-Philippe seems not the least bit reluctant to give her up ('Na, ist sie nicht ein süsser Schatz'/'Schatzi, ich möchte einen Zobel von dir!').

Radjami reappears in his royal finery, ready for his wedding. Odette still knows nothing about it, but Radjami sets to work to convince her. Once more he lays love roses before her and, as she takes in their scent, she falls quickly under his spell. She agrees that she is wearing the costume of a bayadère under her cloak to please him, and that she fell in love with him the first time she saw him at the Opéra a month previously. Why, then, was she initially so cool towards him? 'Because we often torment the man we love, and love the man we torment,' she replies ('Weil wir oft lieben den Mann, den wir quälen'). Radjami commands Odette to write the words 'I love you' and, as she takes a pen and writes, he tells her that now she will no longer be Odette Darimonde but Leilo Rahl, the bayadère, and he takes off her cloak to reveal her bayadère costume. 'Come and dance,' he tells her, as the two pledge their hearts to each other ('Komm', folg' mir ins Wunderland'/ 'Deine dunklen Augen').

In the centre of the ballroom, Parker announces that everyone present is to be a witness at the wedding of Prince Radjami (Finale II: 'Heut' wird der Prinz noch getraut') and, to general wonderment, Radjami leads Odette in for the ceremony before the minister Dewa Singh. Suddenly Odette arouses herself from her trance. She dismisses the idea that she had ever pledged herself to the Prince and reminds him that she had said that she would be his only when she wrote the words 'I love you'. Radjami brings out the piece of paper on which she had so recently written but, when he opens it he finds this message: 'I told you in our first conversation that here one doesn't win a woman this way. Odette Darimonde won't allow herself to be taken like this. You must submit yourself to waiting a while.' Radjami is furious at being tricked in such a fashion but, as Odette takes her cloak and leaves, Radjami pulls himself together and swears that she will indeed love and wed him.

ACT 3
Three months later Napoléon and Marietta are to be found in the bar of a large Parisian hotel ('Die kleine Bar dort am Boulevard'). They are married now, but already things are going badly. Marietta no longer finds in Napoléon any traits of the heroic adventurer she thought she had married. Already he is virtually a carbon copy of boring old Louis-Philippe. He has acquired her ex-husband's passion for eating and, worse, Marietta knows now that he never was in India. To make her disappointment all the greater, Louis-Philippe appears on the scene, smartly dressed and with a young lady on each arm. Prince Radjami has appointed him Consul in Lahore, where he is due to take up his post the following week, and, as a gay divorcé, he has even taken up dancing and knows all the modern steps—including the shimmy ('Will man heutzutage schick und modern sein'/'Fräulein, bitte, woll'n Sie Shimmy tanzen?')

For weeks Paris has been abuzz with speculation as to whether Odette will or will not marry Radjami. The hotel is preparing a special jubilee supper for the Châtelet Theatre that evening, and Armand, who has taken a large bet on Radjami winning his bride, offers Pimprinette 25,000 francs for the claqueur's undertaking that by midnight the third act of La Bayadère will be enacted with Odette Darimonde in the title role but with Prince Radjami as her partner.

Pimprinette begins by approaching Odette, and he ascertains without difficulty that she is still bewitched by Radjami. 'Tell me, Pimprinette,' she says, 'is it his big, dark eyes or his roses?' 'It is something much deeper,' Pimprinette replies, 'he is in love with you.' 'I hate him,' she says, and she offers Pimprinette 50,000 francs to ensure that she never sees his dark eyes in the theatre again.

Radjami has been at the theatre every evening since the party and he is still wholly enraptured by the Parisian Indian dancing girl ('Lotosblume, ich liebe dich'). Pimprinette, now with 75,000 francs at stake, goes to work. He knows enough about the theatre and its people to know that the way for Radjami to win Odette is to let her think that Radjami is no longer interested in her, and he asks Radjami if he will take part in a short piece of play acting. 'Leave it all to me!' he says, and the Prince is only too glad to offer to pay him 100,000 francs if the plan should succeed.

Napoléon is no more happy with the new situation with Marietta than she is ('Als ich unlängst stand'/'Ach hätt' ich doch nicht 'Ja' gesagt'). He feels like Napoléon after the battle of Waterloo, and somehow he has to become 'the other man' again. With Pimprinette's help, he changes places with Jonny the barman just as Marietta arrives with Louis-Philippe. Napoléon mixes them a decidedly original cocktail while they reminisce over their honeymoon in Nice and, when Marietta admits the trick by which she has got rid of Napoléon for a while, the latter whips aside his disguise and tells Louis-Philippe that he can have Marietta back ('Schatzi, ich möchte einen Zobel von dir').

The stage is set for the final dénouement. Pimprinette tells Odette that he has fulfilled her wish and persuaded the Prince to depart. He produces a letter, reflecting to himself that, in the theatre, a useful letter is always the simplest solution. If things seem to be going wrong, one simply writes a letter. Sardou always did that! Odette reads the letter and is overcome with grief as she reads that Radjami has returned to India to marry. At once Pimprinette admits that the letter was a trick—'une requisite à la Sardou'. Radjami steps forward, and Odette rushes to his arms. 'The role suits him very well!' comments Pimprinette. 'Voilà, ladies and gentlemen, the third act ending of *La Bayadère*' (Finale III: 'O Bajadere, komm—sei mein').

FRASQUITA

an operetta in three acts by A M Willner and Heinz Reichert, based on Pierre Louys's *La Femme et le Pantin*. Music by Franz Lehár. Produced at the Theater an der Wien, Vienna, 12 May 1922 with Betty Fischer (Frasquita), Hubert Marischka and later Richard Tauber (Armand), Henny Hilmar (Dolly) and Hans Thimig (Hippolyt).

Produced at the Lyceum Theatre, Edinburgh, in a version by Fred de Gresac and Reginald Arkell 24 December 1924 with José Collins, Robert Michaelis, Ethel Baird and Edmund Gwenn and at the Prince's Theatre, London, 23 April 1925 with Thorpe Bates succeeding Michaelis.

Produced in a concert version at Town Hall, New York, 1953 with Ilona Massey (Frasquita).

Produced at the Théâtre du Havre, Le Havre, October 1931 with Fanély Revoil, Nuzat, Demonty and Levalois. Produced at the Opéra-Comique, Paris, in an extended comic opera version 5 May 1933 with Conchita Supervia, Louis Arnoult,

Annie Gueldy and René Hérent.

A film version was produced by Carl Lamac in 1935 with Jarmila Novotna, Hans Heinz Bollmann, Hans Moser and Heinz Rühmann.

CHARACTERS

Aristide Girot, *an industrialist*
Dolly, *his daughter*
Armand Mirbeau, *his nephew*
Hippolyt Gallipot, *a scholar*
Frasquita
Sebastiano, *a young gipsy*
Fernandez, *an old gipsy*
Palanka, *an old gipsy woman*
Juan, *the landlord*
Franconi, *head waiter*
Ines, Lola, *singers at the Alhambra night club*
Philippe, *a servant*
Louisa
Diaz, *a peasant*
Sancho, Pedro, *sailors*
Don Diego Cortez
José Alvarez
Hector Goucourt
Gendarmes, dancers, public, sailors, countryfolk, customers of the Alhambra night club, flower girls, waiters

ACT 1

It is a sunny summer morning in Barcelona, and in front of a small hotel a couple of sailors, Pedro and Sancho, are playing cards to decide who pays for the drinks ('Neun gegen acht—das nenn ich Glück'/'Gib mit dem Fächer ein Zeichen mir'). Juan, the landlord, has his hands full dealing with the morning rush of customers, and he keeps his eye particularly on a band of gipsies ('Weit war uns're Wand'rung heut"). Juan refers to them disparagingly as 'thieving riff-raff', which prompts an angry response from one of their number, a comely young woman named Frasquita ('Wer hat das gesagt?').

The industrialist Aristide Girot is staying at the hotel with his daughter Dolly, awaiting a visit that evening from her Parisian cousin Armand. They last saw Armand eighteen years ago when he was ten and Dolly three, but now Girot intends that the two should marry. Armand arrives early, wondering what awaits him in his promised wife ('Wie wird sie wohl sein?'/'Sag' mir, sag' mir') and he brings with him a friend, Hippolyt Gallipot, who is collecting material for a book on Spain.

While Armand waits downstairs for Hippolyt, Girot goes up to find Dolly, but Armand's luggage cart has got stuck in a ditch and, by the time Dolly comes down, her cousin has gone off to see to the luggage and Hippolyt is waiting there in his place. Dolly gives the young man a welcoming kiss, before she learns his true identity but, when Armand returns, he and Dolly are introduced rather more formally ('Einem Kavalier, der so wie dieser'/ 'Wenn ganz sacht über Nacht').

The gipsies and sailors return, Pedro by now arm-in-arm with Frasquita. They ask her for a song and, to great acclaim, Frasquita obliges ('Fragst mich, was Liebe ist?'). Girot suggests to Hippolyt that a display of gipsy dancing might provide him with useful material for his researches and asks Frasquita to perform, but she refuses obstinately, even when he offers to pay. 'I don't need your money. I dance only when it amuses me,' she replies.

Girot manages to persuade another girl, Louisa, to dance instead, and Frasquita sits by, smoking a cigarette and mocking them ('Meine Mutter hat eine Gans'). The atmosphere soon boils up between the gipsy girls, and the two trade insults before coming to blows and having to be forcibly separated. Armand is not unaffected by Frasquita's attractions and offers her a cigarette, only to discover that his gold cigarette case has been stolen. He insists that the police search Frasquita, but it turns out she is completely blameless and an old gipsy woman is the culprit. Frasquita feels insulted by Armand's treatment. 'I shall show what Frasquita can do!' she cries and, despite the pleas of the gipsy Sebastiano, she vows to stay behind and have her revenge on Armand by making him fall in love with her.

Hippolyt reckons that he has gained a useful insight into the Spanish character from the morning's activities. He is especially impressed by the way in which Spanish legs speak as they dance, and he wonders whether Dolly's can do the same. 'And how!' she replies, though her preference is for the fashionable social dances of the time ('Tanzen, das ist jetzt die grosse Mode'/'Darum Mädel suchst du einen Mann').

Spotting Frasquita waiting outside the hotel, Armand apologises to her for his earlier hastiness. He asks her about herself, and she tells him that she is a singer and dancer, living on twenty sous a day. He offers her a bank-note as compensation for his earlier rudeness, but she tells him to give his money to a beggar. She has everything she wants—her youth, her freedom, the scent of oranges, the sea, and her cigarettes (Finale I: 'Ich hab' meine Jugend im Sonnenlicht'). Coquettishly she throws him a rose, telling him that with her rose goes her heart ('Wenn eine Rose ich schenke'/'Du siehst auf jedem kleinen Blatt'). Then, taking his face in her hands, she kisses him and leaves, knowing that she now has him in her power.

ACT 2

In the Moorish-style Alhambra night club, the singers Ines and Lola perform a cabaret number ('Schwärmerisch sprach Don Rodrigo'/'Geh' mit mir in die Alhambra') before the customers are treated to the entertainment's final attraction, a sensuous song and dance from Frasquita ('War in einem Städtchen einst ein armes Mädchen'/'Wüsst' ich, wer morgen mein Liebster ist'). The applause is tumultuous, and flowers are thrown on to the stage as Frasquita takes her bow.

During the entertainment Armand and Dolly have joined Girot and Hippolyt at a table. They are all surprised to see Frasquita there but, when Hippolyt has taken Dolly off to dance, Frasquita approaches with the well-to-do Don Diego Cortez on her arm and makes her way towards Armand. After an initial show of indifference, Armand admits that he has been looking for her ever since that first encounter. He tells her that her kiss still burns on his lips and, before he leaves to rejoin his companions, they have exchanged further passionate words ('So weit sind wir noch lange nicht'/'Weisst du nicht was ein Herz voller Sehnsucht begehrt?').

Hippolyt and Dolly emerge from the ballroom, where a rumba, three foxtrots and five waltzes have proved more than enough for him. Dolly can see that all is not well with Armand. She wonders what her fiancé has been getting up to and feels that perhaps she needs to make him jealous if she wishes him to concentrate on her. Hippolyt suggests that she should do so with him, though he evidently needs some lessons in how to handle women ('Amelie, die gute Tante gab den Rat mir immer'/'Ich gäb' was drum').

Frasquita has dressed in her most colourful gipsy finery for the benefit of Don Diego but, when she returns, she finds Sebastiano waiting, pleading with her to forget her strange revenge on Armand and return to her people. She sends him away and goes off to join Don Diego, as Armand reappears with a huge bunch of red roses. He is now completely infatuated by the gipsy girl and filled with dreams of happiness ('Schatz, ich bitt' dich, komm heut' Nacht'/'Hab' ein blaues Himmelbett').

Girot, meanwhile, has been making something of a fool of himself with some of the young dancers who, he reckons, make him feel twenty years old again ('Kinder, heute fühl' ich mich wie zwanzig Jahr"/'Jung ist jeder, der jung sich noch fühlt'). When Dolly finds Armand with his arms full of roses, she assumes that the flowers are for her. She asks Armand to hold them whilst she goes to find her father, whereupon Frasquita returns and likewise assumes—quite rightly—that the roses are for her. Heated words are exchanged and Dolly soon decides that she can take no more and will go home.

Armand tells Frasquita that he cannot bear the thought of her being with other men, but she scoffs at him and tells him that, if he really loves her, he must not follow Dolly but stay with her (Finale II: 'Sehr viel verlangen Sie, mein Freund!'). When Girot finds Armand on his knees to Frasquita, the situation becomes critical and Armand is forced to make a decision. He decides that he will abandon the Girot family and stay with the gipsy girl, and he pleads with Frasquita to go away with him. Now that he has committed himself fully to her, Frasquita completes her revenge by telling him triumphantly that he bores her ('Lasst dem Tage seine Sonne').

By now the men of the club are clamouring for Frasquita to fulfil her promise to dance for them but, as she does, Armand jealously pushes them to one side. Frasquita orders everyone away and tackles Armand scornfully. 'You're out of your mind,' she tells him. 'What do you want here?' 'I want you!' he replies. 'Come with me, even if you love me only a little!' 'If I love you...? I hate you!' she cries. Armand throws her to the ground and rushes to the door, calling back at her, 'Whore!' Frasquita picks herself up and makes to go after him, and when Sebastiano comes to help her she tells him to go away. 'What does this mean?' the gipsy boy asks. 'That I love him!' she hesitantly admits.

ACT 3
Armand and some of his men friends have gathered in his Paris apartment, ready to go to the big carnival ball that evening ('Durch die schwarze Maske'). Armand is thoroughly despondent and, when his friends leave for the festivities, he stays behind alone. Then Frasquita enters. She is on a visit to Paris and elegantly dressed. She tells him that she loves him, but now it is Armand who plays hard to get. She woos him, first tenderly ('Oh, glaub' mir, mein Freund'), then more seductively ('Wo du weilst, was du immer tust'), but Armand remains unmoved. He tells her to go and, as she leaves, the sound of carnival celebrations is heard outside ('Kinder! Kinder! Heut' ist Karneval!'). When she has gone, Armand spots a glove she has dropped. He picks it up and kisses it tenderly.

Girot arrives to see his nephew and tells the manservant that, after his visit, he will give him a key and a letter which are to be given to the lady in the green car in the street below. He tells Armand that he wishes to borrow his flat for an hour for an assignation with a lady and to put the champagne on ice. He then asks Armand for some coloured notepaper on which to write a billet-doux, and cunningly persuades Armand to write it for him. He, Girot, will address the envelope later, he says. Finally he asks for a key to the flat. As he leaves, he slips the key into the envelope and gives them to Philippe to deliver.

Next Hippolyt and Dolly come by. They are now married, and are showering kisses on each other ('Wenn zwei sich immer küssen'/'Da küss mich immerzu') and Armand congratulates them heartily. 'Lucky people!' he sighs as he opens his writing bureau and takes from it a withered rose which, with the glove, is all that he has left from his unfulfilled romance with Frasquita.

Armand takes up a book and begins to read, but he soon puts it down. He cannot stop thinking of Frasquita (Finaletto III: 'Träumen möcht' ich für mich hin'). Suddenly he hears her voice beside him. 'How did you get in?' he asks. 'You invited me!' she replies, and she shows him the letter she has received. Armand realises how his uncle has set him up, but he is no longer inclined to resist the inevitable. He and Frasquita fall into each other's arms.

The synopsis follows the 1933 comic opera version.

MADAME POMPADOUR

an operetta in three acts by Rudolf Schanzer and Ernst Welisch. Music by Leo Fall. Produced at the Berliner Theater, Berlin, 9 September 1922 with Fritzi Massary (Madame Pompadour), Ralph Arthur Roberts (Calicot) and Claire Waldoff (Belotte). Produced at the Grosses Schauspielhaus 1926 with Massary and Max Pallenberg.

Produced at the Carltheater, Vienna, 2 March 1923 with Massary and Ernst Tautenhayn. Produced at the Volksoper 2 October 1976 with Sylvia Holzmayer and Per Grunden and 7 June 1986 with Elisabeth Kales, Sándor Németh and Helga Papouschek.

Produced at Daly's Theatre, London, in a version by Frederick Lonsdale and Harry Graham 20 December 1923 with Evelyn Laye (Pompadour), Bertram Wallis (King Louis), Huntley Wright (Calicot), Elsie Randolph (Belotte) and Derek Oldham (René).

Produced at the Martin Beck Theatre, New York, in a version by Clare Kummer 11 November 1924 with Wilda Bennett (Pompadour), Frederick Lewis (King Louis) and John Quinlan (René).

Produced at the Théâtre Marigny, Paris, in a version by Albert Willemetz 16 May 1930 with Raymonde Vécart (Pompadour), Robert Burnier (René) and René Hérent (Calicot).

CHARACTERS

The Marquise de Pompadour
King Louis XV
René, Comte d'Estrades
Madeleine
Belotte, *the Marquise's maid*
Joseph Calicot
Maurepas, *the chief of police*
Poulard, *a police informer*
Prunier, *a landlord*
Collin, *the Marquise's chamberlain*
Boucher
Tourelle
The Austrian envoy
The lieutenant
Grisettes, Bohemians, courtiers, soldiers

ACT 1

In a tavern of mid-eighteenth century Paris, a Bohemian audience is being entertained by the revolutionary poet Joseph Calicot. Standing on a stool, amongst an enthusiastic crowd, he is performing a satirical song about the Marquise de Pompadour, the latest mistress of King Louis XV ('Die Pom-, Pom-, Pompadour'), a song which everyone is well aware would put him in danger of his neck if it were overheard by the wrong ears.

Amongst the visitors to the inn that evening is René, Comte d'Estrades, a lively fellow who is celebrating carnival time incognito, with a grisette on each arm ('Laridi, laridon, 's ist Karneval'/'Der brave Bürger lebt in

Frieden'). He and Calicot greet each other as old friends, but René asks that Calicot should keep his real identity secret. He is, after all, a married man who has left his wife, Madeleine, at home in the country and has come to Paris for a bit of fun which it is better she should not know about.

Another visitor to the inn is the Marquise de Pompadour herself who is taking advantage of the King's absence from Versailles on a hunting trip to have a little unsuspected fun of her own. She has replaced her court finery with more ordinary clothes and now she is out on the town, in the mood to enjoy a romantic adventure with someone for an evening ('Ich fühl' heut' in mir einen Überschuss'/'Heut' könnt einer sein Glück bei mir machen').

It is not long before René and Calicot come upon the Marquise and her maid, Belotte, and, while Calicot engages Belotte in conversation, René makes great progress with Pompadour and ends up inviting her to take an intimate supper with him ('Mein Prinzesschen'/'Ein intimes Souper'). When he presses her to tell him her name, she says simply that she is called Jeanne.

To her surprise, Pompadour comes upon the chief of police, Maurepas, in the crowd, watching her movements closely. She suggests that, if he is looking for something to do, he should be arresting singers such as Calicot who circulate satirical songs about her, and Maurepas agrees to bring his guards to the inn to carry out her orders. Meanwhile, Calicot's discussions with Belotte have gone some way beyond the confines of the poet's art towards more tender subjects ('Liebe lehrt die Esel tanzen') but, realising the danger that will threaten Belotte when Maurepas comes to arrest Calicot, Pompadour persuades her maid to have nothing more to do with the poet. As the carnival revelry reaches its climax, she also urges René to leave the place (Finale I: 'Laridi, laridon, laridallallera') although he cannot understand why she insists on them leaving separately. Finally she persuades him to go, just as Maurepas appears with his armed guards.

The crowd are amazed when Pompadour reveals her identity, but she in turn is dismayed when the guards bring René back. He denounces her for her deception, but she protests that she had nothing to do with his arrest. The guards prepare to march René and Calicot off to the Bastille, but Pompadour steps in and announces that she will pronounce her own sentences on them. Calicot will write a play for her, and René will join her personal regiment as one of her bodyguards. René has no hesitation in swearing his undying loyalty.

ACT 2

At Pompadour's palace the courtiers are standing around impatiently waiting for the Marquise to finish dressing ('Bemeisternd unsere Ungeduld') but she quickly loses interest in the court when the soldiers of her personal regiment approach. René is amongst them, and she commands that he should be her personal bodyguard for the night. Left alone with him, she goes through the motions of acting as his commanding officer and instilling into him his duties as a soldier and her loyal servant ('Stillgestanden!

Kerzengerade!'/'Ich bin dein Untertan') and flirtatiously insists that he keep his distance—until midnight.

During the evening, Pompadour receives a visit from a young lady from the country, who announces herself as Madeleine, Countess d'Estrades. Her husband has been missing for a week and, in her desperation, she has turned to a casket given to her by her father on his deathbed. 'If you should ever feel really unhappy and defenceless,' her father had told her, 'take the letter in the casket to the addressee and there you will find protection, advice and help.' The letter is addressed to the Marquise, who discovers that it is from her own father and that she and Madeleine are half-sisters. Pompadour pledges her help in finding the missing Count, never realising that her own René and Madeleine's husband are one and the same. The Marquise calls Belotte, and they deck Madeleine out with the finest clothes, make-up and jewels from the Pompadour's wardrobe, coaching her in every art so that she will in future be able to retain her husband's full attentions ('Wozu hast du denn die Augen?').

The Marquise summons Calicot to see how he is proceeding with the play for her entertainment, but he confesses that inspiration does not come easily in something so different from his usual vein. When it is time for the changing of the guard, René's lieutenant attempts to impress on him what an honour it is to be on watch outside the Marquise's apartments. 'Oh, no! It is much, much more!' he declares ('Madame Pompadour').

Maurepas, meanwhile, has been continuing to keep an eye on the Marquise's movements and contacts in the King's absence. From the frequent summonses Calicot has been receiving to her presence, Maurepas has begun to suspect that the poet must be her lover and, when Calicot learns of these suspicions, he is anxious to get Pompadour to set matters straight. He finds her trying on a costume for an appearance as Potiphar's wife in a play and not at all willing to co-operate. Pompadour is only too happy for people to assume that it is Calicot who is her lover and, when she discovers that his name is Joseph, she cannot help relishing the parallel of his pleading with her not to demand his love just as an earlier Joseph did with the original Potiphar's wife ('Wie's der Potiphar zu Mut war'/'Josef, ach Josef').

The Marquise orders René to change out of his soldier's uniform and wait for her in her boudoir ('Madame Pompadour') but, before she can join him, Madeleine returns and Pompadour spots a medallion around the young woman's neck. It carries a portrait of Madeleine's husband, and Pompadour realises that he and René are the same. Hurriedly dismissing Madeleine, the Marquise promises that her husband will return to her the following day.

Determined not to be guilty of stealing her half-sister's husband, Pompadour orders her horse to be saddled, telling her chamberlain that she is going riding and is not to be expected back before the morning. As she goes to put on her riding garb, Calicot arrives with some verses for her but, suddenly, the King is announced, and Calicot dives into hiding in a trunk containing state papers that the Marquise has been looking after in the King's absence.

The King, summoned by Maurepas to catch Pompadour *in flagrante delicto* with Calicot, demands to see his mistress (Finale II: 'Wo ist Madame?'). The Marquise comes to greet him, and explains that she has state papers to work on, but the King insists on entering her boudoir, and there he discovers René. He orders his arrest and demands that Pompadour discuss the matter with him in the morning. Piqued, and anxious for René's safety, she insists that the King can attend to his own state papers, and the chest containing them—and Calicot—is removed to the King's apartments.

ACT 3

In his study the following morning the King discusses the matter of the Marquise's lover with Maurepas. The police chief still believes the man in the case is Calicot, and a death warrant is signed bearing his name. The King confronts Pompadour with the accusation of her affair with Calicot but, at that moment, the mysterious knocking that has been heard throughout is traced to the chest containing the state papers. When the chest is opened, poor Calicot is revealed. This is Calicot? But this is not the Pompadour's paramour! The King is left to vent his anger on Maurepas as he demands to know who it was that he arrested the previous night.

When they have gone, Calicot is left alone with Belotte. Trembling, he goes to the King's writing desk to look at his undeserved death warrant, only to find that the King has mixed up his documents. Calicot has been awarded a pension of 10,000 francs, whilst Voltaire's request for a pension has been inscribed with the words 'death by shooting'. Armed with the manna of this unexpected document, Calicot and Belotte look forward to setting up house together ('Wenn du meine Wohnung siehst'/'Wenn die Kirschen wieder reifen').

Pompadour is reflecting on how foolish the King makes himself over her ('Dem König geht's in meinem Schachspiel meistens kläglich') when her royal lover returns with Maurepas. They have failed to discover the identity of the young man under arrest, but the Marquise sets the King's mind at rest by informing him that the prisoner is her sister's husband. Then, having explained the situation to the astonished René, she bids him treat his wife more fairly in future and keeps her promise to hand him back to the over-joyed Madeleine. The King delegates a young lieutenant to accompany the Marquise to her Château Bellevue and, from the look she bestows on the young man, it is clear that René's company will readily be replaced.

GRÄFIN MARIZA

(Countess Mariza)

an operetta in three acts by Julius Brammer and Alfred Grünwald. Music by

Emmerich Kálmán. Produced at the Theater an der Wien, Vienna, 28 February 1924 with Betty Fischer (Mariza), Hubert Marischka (Tassilo), Elsie Altmann (Lisa), Max Hansen (Zsupán) and Hans Moser.

Produced at the Shubert Theatre, New York, in a version by Harry B Smith with additional numbers by Sigmund Romberg and Al Goodman as *Countess Maritza* 18 September 1926 with Yvonne d'Arle, Walter Woolf, Vivian Hart, Carl Randall and George Hassell.

Produced at the Palace Theatre, London, in a version by Robert Layer-Parker, Eddie Garr and Arthur Stanley as *Maritza* 6 July 1938 with Mara Lossef, John Garrick, Patricia Leonard, Douglas Byng and Shaun Glenville. Produced at Sadler's Wells Theatre in a version by Nigel Douglas 17 February 1983 with Marilyn Hill Smith, Ramon Remedios, Laureen Livingstone, Tudor Davies and Julian Moyle.

Produced at Mulhouse 27 February 1930 in a version by Max Eddy and Jean Marietti as *Comtesse Maritza* with Anna Martens, Louis Collet, Fanély Revoil, Alphonse Massart and Henri Buck. Produced at the Théâtre des Champs-Elysées, Paris, May 7 1931 with Mary Lewis, Roger Bourdin, Janie Marèse, Paul Clerget and Robert Allard.

Film versions were produced by Hans Steindorff in 1925 with Vivian Gibson and Harry Liedtke; by Richard Oswald in 1932 with Dorothea Wieck, Hubert Marischka and Charlotte Ander; and in 1958.

CHARACTERS

Countess Mariza
Prince Moritz Dragomir Popolescu
Baron Koloman Zsupán, *a landowner from Varasdin*
Count Tassilo Endrödy-Wittenburg
Lisa, *his sister*
Karl Stephan Liebenberg
Princess Bozena Cuddenstein zu Chlumetz
Penizek, *her valet*
Ilka von Dambössy
Grasuvesko, *a cavalry captain*
Tschekko, *an old servant of Mariza*
Berko, *a gipsy*
Manja, *a young gipsy girl*
Sari, Mariska, Ersika, *village children*
Guests, society people, dancers, gipsies, country folk

ACT 1

On the Hungarian border with a Balkan state is one of the many estates of Countess Mariza. She has so many estates that, standing on the terrace of her castle-like mansion, her old servant Tschekko and the gipsy Berko wonder whether they will ever see her there again. From across the fields comes a pretty young gipsy girl, Manja. She is singing ('War einmal ein reicher Prasser') to attract the attention of the new estate manager, Béla Török, undeterred by the fact that he pays her little attention. Török is surrounded by a group of small gipsy girls, all clamouring to give him gifts of thanks for the share of the recent harvest that has been given to their parents ('Wir singen dir, wir bringen dir').

In spite of his position, Béla Török is no man of the people, but the aristocratic Count Tassilo Endrödy-Wittenburg. He was once party to a bet with a friend at the Jockey Club that each could really manage to work for a living, but little did he realise that his father's debts would soon force him to sell all his belongings and go out to do just that. He intends to remain here until he has earned enough money to provide a dowry for his younger sister, Lisa. Tassilo enjoys his work on the estate, being very much his own boss in the Countess's absence, and yet there are times in the evening when he sits alone with a glass of wine, longing for all the joys of Vienna ('Wenn es Abend wird'/'Grüss mir mein Wien').

Tassilo's peace is disturbed when Prince Populescu turns up bringing news of the imminent arrival of Countess Mariza, and instructions to prepare a meal for thirty people, complete with gipsy music. The mistress of the estate is coming to celebrate her engagement to Baron Koloman Zsupán. She has a castle for every occasion, and this is her castle for engagements.

Mariza is indeed on her way, and she soon arrives with a mass of fine guests to be greeted by the local people and the gipsy musicians ('Lustige Zigeunerweisen'), happily returning their greeting with a declaration of her feelings for the gipsy people ('Höre ich Zigeunergeigen'). When she meets her new estate manager, she finds his somewhat refined manner strange, and Tassilo has to restrain himself from answering back in the face of her gentle mocking at what seems like his pretentiousness. When he tells her that he learned his business on the estate of Count Endrödy-Wittenburg, she surprises him by telling him that the Countess Lisa Endrödy-Wittenburg is coming to join the party. When his sister appears, Tassilo has to do some hasty talking to convince her that he truly is Mariza's estate manager and that she must not betray his real identity. She tenderly agrees ('Schwesterlein, Schwesterlein!').

Mariza's engagement party is due to be celebrated without her fiancé, who she says is detained on family business. 'Typical Mariza!' Prince Popolescu declares. She is such an independently minded young lady. In fact, as Mariza confides to her friend Ilka, there is no fiancé at all. She has invented the Baron Zsupán to ward off the perpetual string of suitors that pusues her and has given him the name of a character from the operetta *Der Zigeuner-baron*. Imagine her surprise, then, when Tschekko announces the arrival of Baron Zsupán, a young man in Hungarian costume speaking in the same Hungarian dialect as his *Gipsy Baron* namesake. He has come from his home town of Varasdin, he says, having read in the paper of his engagement to Countess Mariza. Mariza tries to tell him that she is no longer available, but Zsupán is not to be put off. It is a good idea, this marriage. If they put Mariza's 20,000 pigs with his 18,000, they'll have the largest piggery in Europe. She must come back with him to Varasdin ('Komm mit nach Varasdin').

In the hall of the castle the party is well under way, and the gipsy band is playing, but Tassilo is left outside on the terrace, and he feels his position all the more when Mariza condescendingly sends a flask of wine out to him. He sinks into reminiscing about better times and, as the wine takes hold, he sings vigorously, urging the gipsy violinist to play for him ('Auch ich war einst ein feiner Csárdáskavalier'/'Komm, Zigan!').

At the end of the song he dances a fiery *csárdás*, unaware that the guests have come onto the balcony and are watching him. When he has finished, Mariza leads the expressions of admiration and she asks him to sing for her guests (Finale I: 'Ei bravo, Herr Verwalter!'). Tassilo declines, and Mariza, unused to being refused, promptly dismisses him. Now the carriages are ready, and Populescu prepares everyone for a trip to a night club in town ('Geigen schallen, Lichter blitzen') but their departure is delayed by the appearance of Manja, who offers to tell Mariza's fortune. Manja prophesies that within a month Mariza will fall in love with a man of noble origin—a nobleman and gentleman ('Eh ein kurzer Mond ins Land mag entfliehn') and Mariza, who has no intention of falling in love with anyone, decides that she will remain behind at the castle. That way she will avoid any possible contact with men of noble birth and any temptation to fall in love.

She quickly regrets her hasty treatment of Tassilo and asks him to remain and to be friends. Tassilo, too, can be magnanimous and, agreeing to stay, he kisses her hand. Left alone on the terrace, he now feels the urge to sing the gipsy song that Mariza had previously asked him to repeat ('Komm, Zigan') and, from the castle, Mariza joins in the song, throwing down to him a few roses, which he joyfully picks up and presses to his lips.

ACT 2

Mariza and her girl friends, Lisa among them, are dressed for tennis, and Tassilo's help is required to ensure that they have all the equipment they need for the game ('Herr Verwalter, bitte sehr'). The estate manager's multifarious talents as sporting man and dancer are much appreciated, and the girls are reluctant to let him out of their sight. Prince Popolescu telephones to say that the four weeks of Mariza's self-imposed social exile are over and that he has arranged a dance to celebrate her return to the real world, and Baron Zsupán appears, still in pursuit of Mariza. He finds only Lisa, who has become much taken by him, and he admits to himself that, if he were not so much in love with Mariza, he might dream all night of Lisa ('Wenn ich abends schlafen geh"'/'Ich möchte träumen').

Tassilo needs to go over the past quarter's accounts with Mariza. She has no head for figures, and Tassilo's knowledge of the world of work fascinates her. She is also ready enough for him to entertain her in other ways ('Genug, ich will mit Geschäften mich nicht ennuiren'). 'Suppose,' she says, 'that this were a ballroom and you a gentleman.' 'And you were the belle of the ball,' Tassilo adds. They don't need much encouragement to lose themselves fully in their fantasies ('Herrgott, was ist denn heut los?'/'Einmal möcht' ich wieder tanzen').

When Popolescu arrives, he announces that, if Mariza won't go out to a night club, he will bring a night club to her, and he promptly sets about arranging the place for a party ('Geigen schallen, Lichter blitzen'). Mariza is in no hurry to join in the gaieties which she once so enjoyed, for she prefers to spend her time with Tassilo. She asks him about himself, and they even discuss the frivolities and pleasantries that passed between him and the girls he used to court ('Mein lieber Schatz, zieh' an dein schönstes Kleid'/'Sag' ja, mein Lieb, sag' ja').

Zsupán has by now decided that his pursuit of Mariza is hopeless, but he is slow to comprehend Lisa's interest in him. When he does, he is reminded of a very sad story of unrequited love ('Junger Mann ein Mädchen liebt'/ 'Behüt' dich Gott! Komm gut nach Haus!'), but thereafter the progress of their romance is destined to be more straightforward than that of Mariza and Tassilo. Populescu happens to mention to Mariza how friendly her estate manager appears to be with Lisa, and he voices his suspicions that Béla Török is not who he appears to be. He has discovered a letter from Tassilo to a society friend, telling of his determination to remain in his post until he has gained enough money for a dowry and hinting at the hope of a better future, and Popolescu and Mariza take this to mean that Tassilo is posing as an estate manager purely to achieve a financially rewarding marriage for himself.

The arrival of the gipsy orchestra signals the start of Mariza's soirée. Burning with rage at Popolescu's discovery, she urges them to play (Finale II: 'Hei, Mariza! Hei, Mariza!'). She turns her anger on Tassilo and, producing his letter, tells the guests of what she believes to be his duplicity. As a final humiliation she pulls sheafs of banknotes from her safe and pushes them on him, telling him never again to speak to her of love. Tassilo holds on to the money and declares that he will honour her conditions. Then, urging the gipsy orchestra to play, he promises to reward them in princely fashion and throws the notes to the musicians. Mariza realises that she has misjudged him and recalls the gipsy prediction ('Eh' ein kurzer Mond'). 'That is how a man of noble origin—a nobleman and gentleman—pays,' he declares. As he turns to leave, Lisa appears and they greet each other as brother and sister ('Schwesterlein! Schwesterlein!'). Mariza is astonished and delighted and, watching Tassilo storm out, she knows that her heart is his.

ACT 3

The following morning guests and gipsy musicians are still around, sleeping on sofas and chairs and Zsupán, in the middle of them, is singing in his sleep ('Ich möchte träumen'). As the sun wakes them, Mariza appears from her room and reminds them that, as she now has no estate manager, she and they have work to do. Afterwards they will go to a little country inn and enjoy themselves with some native gipsy music, far away from the shimmy, java, blues, boston, foxtrot and all the other modern dances ('Braunes Mädel von der Puszta').

Tassilo returns to hand the estate accounts over to his successor. Mariza offers to write him a reference, and Tassilo dictates to her words that indicate how much she has depended upon him for the efficient management of her estate, but neither is able to get through the new atmosphere of formality between them, and Tassilo is left to reflect upon the complexities of women ('Fein könnt' es auf der Welt sein'/'Wer hat euch gedacht, Ihr süssen Frau'n').

While he is lost in these thoughts, Tschekko shows in the elderly Princess Bozena Cuddenstein. The lady is Tassilo's aunt and she has just heard of the circumstances that have pressed him to take a paid post. If only he had come to her. 'You were too proud,' she adds, 'just like your papa. To sell your heritage—how could you? To sell your horses, your palace—how could you?' She goes on to speak of the porcelain factories she owns and tells him how she and Lisa have bought back all Tassilo's possessions. What is more, she has a prospective bride for him, and she produces a photograph of the young lady. 'Dies Bildnis ist bezaubernd schön! Richard Wagner, *Zauberflöte*!' her valet Penizek comments unhelpfully. He has a habit of making such quotes, having once been prompter at the Municipal Theatre in Chrudim. Tassilo is unimpressed. When Penizek, seeing Mariza in country costume, mistakes her for a servant and mentions Tassilo's wealth, Mariza realises how grievously she has wronged him in believing that he was only after her fortune.

Lisa is preparing to depart with her brother but, when Zsupán asks her to be his wife and settle down with him in Varasdin, she accepts immediately ('Komm mit nach Varasdin'). Tassilo and Mariza have maintained their reserve, since he has promised never to speak to her of his love, but he can, without perjury, write a letter of farewell. 'I would have preferred to say it rather than write it,' Mariza reads. 'I love you.' Mariza in return tells him to read the reference she has given him. 'As estate manager I must dismiss you,' it reads, 'but as husband you would suit me.' The barrier between them is finally broken down (Finale III: 'Sag' ja, mein Lieb, sag' ja!').

PAGANINI

an operetta in three acts by Paul Knepler and Béla Jenbach. Music by Franz Lehár. Produced at the Johann Strauss Theater, Vienna, 30 October 1925 with Carl Clewing (Paganini), Emma Kosáry (Anna Elisa), Fritz Imhoff (Pimpinelli) and Gisela Kolbe (Bella).

Produced at the Deutsches Künstlertheater, Berlin, 30 January 1926 with Richard Tauber, Vera Schwarz, Eugen Rex and Edith Schollwer.

Produced at the Théâtre de la Gaîté-Lyrique, Paris, in a version by André Rivoire 1928 with André Baugé and Louise Dhamarys.

Produced at the Lyceum Theatre, London, in a version by A P Herbert and Reginald Arkell 20 May 1937 with Richard Tauber, Evelyn Laye, Charles Heslop and Joan Panter.

Film versions were produced by Bruno Rahr in 1926 as *Gern hab' ich den Frau'n geküsst* and by E W Emo in 1934.

CHARACTERS

Maria Anna Elisa, *Princess of Lucca and Piombino and sister of the Emperor Napoléon*
Prince Felice Bacchiocchi, *her husband*
Nicolo Paganini
Bartucci, *his impresario*
Count Hédouville, *a general in the service of Napoléon*
Marchese Giacomo Pimpinelli, *the Princess's chamberlain*
Countess de Laplace
Bella Giretti, *prima donna at the Opera in Lucca*
Marco, Philippo, Emanuele, Julia, *residents of Capannari*
A landlord
Anitta, *a dancer*
Foletto, Tofolo, Beppo, *smugglers*
Corallina, *a landlady*
Ladies and gentlemen at Court, dancers of the Court Theatre, soldiers, servants, countryfolk, smugglers, prostitutes

ACT 1

At an inn in the village of Capannari near Lucca, in 1806, the customers are enjoying a mid-day glass of wine and a game of cards when they hear the ravishing sound of virtuoso violin playing coming from a nearby pavilion (Violin solo). The player is Paganini, the greatest violinist of all time, who is due to play in Lucca the following morning.

The Prince and Princess of Lucca are in the vicinity, each out hunting separately with their retinue, and the Prince takes time off from the hunt to spend a furtive hour at the inn with the prima donna of the Court Opera in Lucca, Bella Giretti. What is the point of a Prince having an opera house if he can't have a pretty prima donna sink onto his breast from time to time? ('O Madonna, o Madonna, lass dein kleines Herzchen rühren!'/'Geh' sei lieb zu mir')

Soon after, Pimpinelli, Chamberlain to the Prince's wife, Princess Maria Anna Elisa, also arrives at the inn. The Princess wishes to have a meal prepared for herself and her ladies in waiting and, although Pimpinelli, mindful of the Prince's proximity, endeavours to persuade her that eating in such a place is not etiquette for the sister of Napoléon, the Princess is adamant. Sometimes she likes to escape from the grandeur of Court surroundings and this inn seems to be just the place ('Mein lieber Freund, ich halte viel auf Etikette'/'L'Empereur Napoléon').

As she waits for her food, the Princess hears the devilish violin playing. Fascinated, she sends Pimpinelli to fetch the player, and Paganini enters acknowledging the acclaim of the people and lauding his beautiful Italian fatherland ('Schönes Italien'). If the Princess was enchanted by his violin playing, she is scarcely less charmed by his manner ('So jung noch und schon ein grosser Meister!'/'Was ich denke, was ich fühle'). Just then Paganini's manager, Bartucci, arrives with news that the virtuoso's concert the following day, already sold out, has been banned, but the Princess, fully under Paganini's spell, insists that he play for her ('Feuersglut lodert heiss in meinem Blut'/'So ein Mann ist eine Sünde wert').

Fresh from her rendezvous with the Prince, Bella Giretti emerges from the inn and encounters Pimpinelli, a man whom she knows well as one who loses his heart to every woman he comes across ('Niemals habe ich mich int'ressiert'/'Mit den Frau'n auf du und du'). At the same time, the Princess and her husband come face to face at the inn. As they listen to the cheers of their people (Finale I: 'Des Fürstin Anna Elisa'), the Princess introduces her companion to her husband as the great violinist who is to give a concert in Lucca the following day, but the Prince declares that no adventurer will play at his Court. Paganini insists that he will not play where he is not welcome and that he will leave at once for Florence. 'Will you not play even for me?' asks the Princess. 'For you...anything!' he replies. 'The maestro will stay and give his concert in Lucca,' she declares firmly. She is under no illusions about her husband's affair with Bella, and she gives him a knowing look that carries the threat to disclose it. Faced with this, the Prince has no option but to accede to his wife's demand.

ACT 2

Six months later Paganini is still in Lucca, detained there by the charms of Anna Elisa and elevated to the position of director of Court Music and of the Opera House. In the Prince's castle, Bella, Paganini and Pimpinelli are playing cards, watched by the ladies and gentlemen of Court ('Wenn keine Liebe wär"), and Paganini becomes so carried away that, despite Bella's protests, he pledges his Stradivarius violin as his stake. Pimpinelli duly wins it from him, but he promises to return the instrument if Paganini will teach him the secret of conquering women. Paganini obliges, telling him, 'I have enjoyed kissing women. I have never asked whether it was allowed. I have merely thought to myself, take her and kiss her—that's what you're here for!' ('Gern hab' ich die Frau'n geküsst').

Paganini is not slow to practise on Anna Elisa all that he preaches and, indeed, he has composed a love song for her ('Deiner süssen Rosenmund'). As for Pimpinelli, his lesson from Paganini encourages him to try his hand afresh with Bella, who admits that all women have their moods and that some day she'd like to do something silly ('Launisch sind alle Frau'n'/'Einmal möcht' ich was Närrisches tun').

The Princess's infatuation with Paganini has grown to such an extent that she claims nobody has loved him as much as she has ('Sag' mir, wieviel süsse rote Lippen hast du schon geküsst?'/'Niemand liebt dich so wie ich'), but rumours of the affair have reached as far as Paris and Anna Elisa's royal brother sends one of his generals, Count Hédouville, to Lucca with orders that Paganini should leave town immediately. The Princess reacts angrily. She cannot allow her dream of love to be destroyed and her lover forced from her in such a manner ('Ich kann es nicht fassen, nicht glauben'/'Liebe, du Himmel auf Erden').

Paganini's refusal to move on from Lucca over the last six months has been a source of considerable frustration to his manager, Bartucci. He despairs of the susceptibility of youth for a pretty female, though he admits that—grey hairs or not—he would not be altogether immune to a pretty blonde himself ('Jugend denkt von heute nicht auf morgen'). Now, however, Paganini's inability to resist a woman begins to work against him. Bella has set her cap at him and, in a weak moment, he gives her the manuscript of the love song, 'Deiner süssen Rosenmund', that he had composed originally for Anna Elisa. When the Princess goes to order the prima donna from Court, Bella produces the song. The Princess is stunned at what seems to her like unforgiveable duplicity and she swears vengeance on the man she loves, ordering Hédouville to arrest him during a Court concert that is about to start.

The Courtiers assemble for the concert, clamouring to know from Pimpinelli what is going on (Finale II: 'Was ist's, das unsern Sinn erregt?'). The concert opens with a song from Bella ('Spiel', kleine Silberflöte, die Melodei'), after which Paganini proceeds with his solo, despite Bella's warnings that he is in danger. However, Paganini's playing once again proves sufficient to bring Anna Elisa under his irresistible spell and, as Hédouville moves to arrest him, she steps forward to escort him out of Lucca to safety.

ACT 3

In a sleazy tavern, 'The Rusty Horseshoe', on the outskirts of the province of Lucca, assorted smugglers, prostitutes, thieves and the like are enjoying themselves drinking and gambling ('Liegen um Mitternacht alle Bürger scharchend im Schlaf'/'Oh, wie schön ist es, nichts zu tun'). Paganini arrives there, in preparation for being smuggled over the border by night. He must wait until the patrol has passed, and the hunchback Beppo, Foletto and their companions insist that the violinist should join them in a glass of schnapps ('Hat man den Kopf von Sorgen voll'/'Wenn man das letzte Geld verlumpt').

One by one, Pimpinelli, Bella and Bartucci also appear at the inn. Bella wants to flee at Paganini's side, but Paganini will not allow her to make such a sacrifice. His real love, he tells her, is directed not to any woman but to his violin ('Ja, meine Geige lieb' ich immerdar') and Bella, understanding that she has no chance of winning the man from his music, decides to settle down with Pimpinelli and begin life anew in the theatre ('Jetzt beginnt ein neues Leben'/'Wir gehen ins Theater').

A street singer arrives on the scene, singing a plaintive song and tarantella ('Wo meine Wiege stand?'/'Wer will heut' nacht mein Liebster sein?') and Paganini recognises the voice as that of Princess Anna Elisa. She has been unable to let him go. He persuades her that he must leave and leave alone. It is no other woman who stands between them, he assures her, simply his art. The Princess finally understands, and bids him a sad farewell, promising that she will never forget him ('Du darfst keiner Frau gehören'), as Paganini sets off to conquer the world with his playing.

The musical numbers 'Geh' sei lieb zu mir' and 'Jugend denkt von heute nicht auf morgen', included in the above synopsis, were dropped from Lehár's definitive version of 1936.

DIE ZIRKUSPRINZESSIN

(The Circus Princess)

an operetta in three acts by Julius Brammer and Alfred Grünwald. Music by Emmerich Kálmán. Produced at the Theater an der Wien, Vienna, 26 March 1926 with Hubert Marischka (Mister X), Betty Fischer (Princess Fedora), Fritz Steiner (Toni), Elsie Altmann (Mabel) and Richard Waldemar (Prince Sergius). Produced at the Volksoper, Vienna, 15 February 1988.

Produced at the Winter Garden Theatre, New York, in a version by Harry B Smith as *The Circus Princess* 25 April 1927 with Guy Robertson, Desiree Tabor, Ted Doner, Gloria Foy and George Hassell.

A film version was produced by Adolf Gärtner in 1925 and another by Victor Janson in 1928 with Harry Liedtke, Vera Schmitterlöw, Hilde Rosch and Ernst Verebes.

CHARACTERS

Princess Fedora Palinska
Prince Sergius Wladimir
Captain Count Saskusin, Lieutenant von Petrowitsch, *Russian hussars*
Baron Peter Brusowsky, *the Prince's adjutant*
Director Stanislawski
Mister X
Luigi Pinelli, *stage manager and clown*
Miss Mabel Gibson, *a bareback rider*
Olly, Sonja, Betty, Lilly, Susanne, Daisy, *dancers in the Stanislawski Circus*
Baron Rasumowsky
Samuel Friedländer
Carla Schlumberger, *proprietress of the Archduke Karl hotel*
Toni, *her son*
Pelikan, *head waiter at the Archduke Karl*
Michael, *the Prince's chamberlain*
Society ladies and gentlemen, guests, officers, artists, Cossacks, pages, dancers, clowns, circus musicians, servants, waiters, hotel staff.

ACT 1

In the foyer of the Stanislawski Circus in St Petersburg, during the interval of a performance in the late winter of 1912, the director, Stanislawski, is receiving the plaudits of members of his audience for the brilliance of the show ('Bravo, bravo, Herr Direktor!'). In the Stanislawski Circus, they reckon, one really sees something for one's money. The major attraction of the evening is the world-famous but mysterious Mister X from London. Never in his thirty years as circus director has Stanislawski seen anything better than this performer who, masked and thirty metres above the heads of the audience, plays a romance on the violin before jumping through the air onto a chute from which he is propelled onto the back of a galloping horse.

The second half of the show starts with the clowns and, while they are performing, a group of hussars gathers outside the auditorium with bouquets of roses to greet Princess Fedora Palinska. They have, with difficulty, managed to secure a box for her, for she has expressed a strong desire to see the circus, and above all to see the mysterious Mister X. Princess Fedora is a wealthy widow, so wealthy, in fact, that she comes to the circus direct from an audience with the Tsar, who has expressed his strong wish that she should marry again and thereby save the Palinska properties for the nation. She knows, though, that one really finds true love only when one isn't looking for it, and none of her hussar admirers quite seems to fit the bill ('Was in der Welt geschieht'/'Ja, ist denn die Liebe wirklich gar so schön?')

One who is determined to win Princess Fedora is Prince Sergius Wladimir, nephew of the Tsar. Peeping into the circus ring, he spots Fedora in her box and sends an usherette to bring the man who is sitting next to her to him. As a troupe of girls in Cossack uniform enter the ring for their act, Toni Schlumberger, the son of a wealthy Viennese hotel owner, appears in response to the Prince's summons. Like a little penguin in his evening dress and carrying a large pair of binoculars, he is puzzled to know who should wish to speak to him, since he knows nobody in St Petersburg. He has never before managed to get such a good seat for the circus, and now he finds that the Prince expects him to give it up, but the Prince assures him that even ten minutes in that seat will be enough for him, and assures Toni that he can be back in his seat in time to watch his favourite performer, Miss Mabel Gibson, the bareback rider and singer.

Toni agrees to sit out a while and, as he enjoys a vodka at the bar, he gets his reward. Who should come by but Miss Mabel Gibson herself, trim and tight in her ballet costume and warming up for her act with a few dance steps and a refrain of 'Yes, Sir, that's My Baby'. Toni's heart does cartwheels at the sight of her. If only he could speak English! Unfortunately the only English words he knows are 'waterproof', 'beefsteak' and 'ham and eggs'. Still, he does his best. 'Excuse me!' he ventures. 'I like to make your acquaintance. Have you understand?'

He makes little progress until, in frustration, he lapses into his native Viennese dialect and gets an immediate response. Miss Mabel Gibson is, in reality, Fräulein Liese Burstaller from Vienna. It is fashionable to be a foreigner in show business, she confides, and the audience seems to understand the English-language songs she sings, even though she herself hasn't a clue to their meaning. Toni suggests supper after the show, but Mabel's mother has warned her daughter against casual relationships and, for the meantime, she and Toni limit themselves to reminiscing about the delights of Vienna ('Wenn ein einsames Wienerkind'/'Wo ist der Himmel so blau wie in Wien?').

Now Mister X appears, dressed in a black silk pierrot costume and black velvet mask ('Es ist noch Zeit!'), and calls for a glass of champagne—the habitual prelude to his act. When one views life through a champagne glass, he reckons, one has a vision of two white arms, a red mouth and two fairy-tale eyes ('Zwei Märchenaugen'). Fedora appears with her officer friends, to offer the mysterious Mister X a glass of champagne. She is determined to discover his true identity, but Mister X prefers to keep himself to himself, although he pricks up his ears at mention of the name of Princess Fedora Palinska.

The Princess insists on being left alone with the circus artists, but she is taken aback when Mister X immediately declares his love for her. 'But you have just seen me for the first time in your life,' she protests. 'Perhaps our paths have crossed before,' he replies. 'Perhaps I have seen you in the Paris Opéra, or in the gaming rooms of Monte Carlo.' Fedora is undeniably fascinated by the romance and mystery of the man ('Ich liebe Sie!'/'Leise schwebt das Glück vorüber').

When Mister X goes off to do his act, Toni reappears in the foyer in the company of six ballet girls. There is no doubt why he goes to the circus. For him the girls in frilly skirts with legs like marzipan are the highlight of the programme and they are also the reason why he brings his binoculars with him ('Wenn ich in den Zirkus gehe'/'Die kleinen Mäderln im Trikot').

Prince Wladimir's plan has not worked. He has been snubbed by Princess Fedora and told that she would rather marry this circus performer than him. He is set on revenge and, as the sound of Mister X's violin solo wafts from the ring, the Prince watches and prepares his plan. A loud drum-roll heralds Mister X's death-defying leap, greeted by deafening applause and, when he leaves the ring triumphant, the Prince invites the star of the show to have a drink with him.

Mister X tells the Prince how, once the show is over, he takes off his mask and puts on evening dress. Then, under the name of Baron Korrossow, he is every bit as much a gentleman as those in the boxes at the circus. That, he says, is the revenge of the jester on society. All this is ideal for the Prince. Would Mister X, asks the Prince, attend a party he is giving that evening at the circus in honour of Princess Fedora Palinska? More than that, would he try to woo her? Mister X readily agrees and says that he will turn up at midnight as Baron Korrossow.

Mabel emerges from the ring to distinctly muted applause. Her act has not gone well and the stage manager tells her that she is fired, but Mister X promises to speak to the circus director on her behalf. Mabel tells Mister X that she was not born and bred a circus girl but took it up only to make ends meet when her father lost his position as an officer, and Mister X responds with a story of a dashing young officer of the hussars, the nephew and heir of one of the wealthiest princes in Russia, who lost his position for taking a fancy to his uncle's fiancée. His career destroyed, he used his riding skill to take up a circus career. He tells Mabel to hold her head high in the face of all adversity ('Manchmal treibt das Schicksal Sachen wirklich zu gemein'/'Wer

1088

wird denn gleich weinen, mein Kind').

The Prince begins to round up guests for his impromptu party. The hussars are invited and so is Toni, whom the Prince mistakenly believes to be the son of the Archduke Karl rather than from the hotel of that name. Toni delightedly tells Mabel about his social triumph (Finale I: 'Hoheit hat uns eingeladen heute zum Souper!') as, to his delight, all the circus girls are invited to join the party too.

The Prince's guests excitedly discuss the superb show they have just witnessed and Fedora arrives to join the throng, while the Prince waits expectantly for Mister X. As midnight strikes, a masked figure who looks for all the world like Mister X arrives. 'Has he duped me?' the Prince asks himself but, just then, the usherette announces the elegantly dressed Baron Korrossow. The Baron reassures the startled prince that the masked rider is his valet, and the Prince introduces the newcomer to Fedora. Now she shows none of the reticence she displayed previously towards him as a circus performer, and soon they are deep in conversation as the party gets under way with a swing, and everyone joins in the dance ('Heissa, die Nacht erwacht'/'Juppla, Josefinchen').

ACT 2

Six weeks later, Prince Wladimir is giving an elegant society ball at his palace in St Petersburg ('Freut euch des Lebens'). Tonight, he promises his guests, will be something different, something special. Tonight they will witness a sensational comic drama. The circus party six weeks before was the first act, and this is to be the second.

When Princess Fedora Palinska arrives, the Prince takes the first opportunity to ask her if she is any nearer obeying the Tsar's request that she should marry, and she tells him she is not. The Prince asks her to dance, but she declines. All her dances, she claims, are reserved. The Prince is sure that this means that she is in love with the man he knows as Mister X and she as Baron Korrossow. Then, to everyone's surprise, the Baron arrives in hussar uniform. Saskusin, a captain of the hussars, wagers one of his officers ten bottles of champagne that he has seen the Baron's face somewhere before, but the conversation turns lightly to the reaction of a lady when faced by a hussar ('Der Husar'/'Mädel, gib acht! Schliess' dein Fenster heute Nacht').

When Mister X, alias Baron Korrossow, joins Fedora it is evident that they have seen a great deal of each other since the last party. She is mystified by the way that, every evening at nine o'clock, he regularly disappears for an hour but she does not wish to upset their relationship by breaking her promise never to ask about this mysterious hour. She has also been receiving a bunch of roses daily from Mister X at the circus, but the Baron assures her that he is not jealous of a circus performer, and they pursue their romance with fond words ('Wollen sie mir nicht gestehen, wie sie die Liebe sehen?'/'My Darling, my Darling, muss so sein wie Du!').

Toni, whom the Prince still believes to be the son of the Archduke Karl, is also at the ball with Mabel, to whom such affluent surroundings are like a dream. She still insists that there will be no kissing until after marriage, and Toni finds this most unromantic. He feels that his Mabel—his Liese—needs a touch of the poetry of spring—of primroses, butterflies and roses ('Wieder blüht die Primel'/'Liese, Liese, komm mit mir auf die Wiese').

Now the Prince is ready for his moment of triumph. He takes a letter from his pocket and instructs his chamberlain to take it to Fedora with the explanation that a courier has brought it from the Tsar's palace. Fedora opens the letter and discovers that it is a handwritten message, purporting to come from the Tsar, telling her to report to him tomorrow when he will present to her the man chosen to be her husband. It would seem that there is no way out. But Prince Wladimir has a suggestion. His own palace was built for the Empress Catherine II and has a chapel. In no time at all Fedora could be married and she could then tell the Tsar that his letter came too late. Fedora hurries to show the letter to the Baron, and finally he understands what she is suggesting ('Süsseste von allen Frauen'/'Ich und Du—Du und ich!').

Mister X, however, is suspicious of the Prince and he suspects that there is, in all this, some kind of revenge being taken on Fedora. He also suspects that the supposed letter from the Tsar is a forgery, and he insists that the Prince must tell Fedora the truth . The Prince agrees to do so, but he has no intention of carrying out that promise just yet, as he checks to make sure that the circus folk are all at hand for the denouement. Toni feels that if there is to be a marriage service, he might as well get in on the act with Mabel. By now a little tipsy, she is not inclined to refuse, though the idea of a Russian wedding worries her when she recalls the story of Iwan Peter Petrowitsch who married Sonja Wonjuschka and six months later dreamed of better things ('Iwan Peter Petrowitsch'/'Mein heissgeliebter, süsser Iwan').

The guests make their way to the chapel for the ceremony (Finale II: 'Ein Hochzeitsfest, welche Pracht!') and, no sooner is the marriage concluded than, at a signal from the Prince, the sound of circus music is heard, and the entire company of the Stanislawski Circus enter in their circus costumes. The Prince reveals to Fedora that the man she has married is nothing more than a circus artist. It is, the Prince declares, all a trick, and she is nothing but a circus princess. Fedora turns on her new husband in horror, but he swears his love for her and announces that, although he is indeed Mister X, he is also Fedja Palinski. It was his elderly uncle she had previously married and, on her account, he had been disinherited. Now, though, he declares that he will go back where he came from. Fedora is overwhelmed. 'Fedja, can you ever forgive me?' But Mister X walks slowly off.

ACT 3

Eight weeks later the Stanislawski Circus is in Vienna and Mister X is staying at the Archduke Karl hotel on the Ringstrasse. The circus is due to leave for Budapest the following day, and Mister X is sad to be leaving the delights of Vienna ('Nimmt man Abschied von dieser Stadt'/'Wo ist der Himmel so blau wie in Wien?').

Toni is also staying at his family's hotel with Mabel. Unfortunately he has still not plucked up the courage to tell his parents of his marriage, and so Mabel is merely 'the lady in room 16' to whom Toni keeps having pieces of cake sent up as special treats. Only Pelikan, the head waiter, is in the know. But Mabel has had enough cake by now and she can no longer stand being merely 'the lady in room 16'. Toni doesn't dare to tell his mother than he is married to a circus artist, but Mabel threatens that if he doesn't she will leave him and go on with the Stanislawski Circus to Budapest ('Glaubst Du denn, ich werd' mich kränken?'/'Wenn Du mich sitzen lässt').

Toni endeavours to pluck up courage, but it is Mabel who finally has to complete the deed and tell his mother that they are in love. Fortunately Mabel also mentions that she is the daughter of Baron Burgstaller, with whom it turns out that Toni's mother was once in love, and Frau Schlumberger sensibly reckons that, if God has said 'yes' to their relationship, all that mere humans can say is 'amen' ('Der alte Herrgott, der weiss was er tut').

Toni wants to see Mister X's farewell appearance at the circus but his mother insists that he help with the serving, since Princess Palinska is due to dine at the hotel that evening with a Russian gentleman. Fedora arrives with Prince Wladimir and is seated at table number 1 for what the Prince intends to be their engagement supper. The Prince is surprised to see Toni serving there, but finally the penny drops that he is the son not of the Archduke Karl but of the Archduke Karl hotel. Soon Mister X takes his place at table number 2, and it is clear that Fedora still feels a deep longing for him.

During the course of the meal the Prince finds himself increasingly annoyed by the draught from the ventilator. He goes off for his scarf and, while he is away, Mister X rushes across to speak to Fedora. He asks if she really intends to marry the Prince, and she in turn asks if he will give up the circus. 'Why?' he asks, 'because it doesn't suit your Serene Highness to read your name on all the posters?' 'No,' she insists. 'Because I cannot bear you risking your life every day. I am, after all, your wife!' By the time the Prince returns, Fedora has decided that it will be Fedja—Mister X—and not the Prince with whom she will go on her honeymoon (Finale III: 'Mein Darling muss lieb sein').

DER ZAREWITSCH

(The Tsarevitch)

an operetta in three acts by Béla Jenbach and Heinz Reichert, after the play by Gabryela Zapolska. Music by Franz Lehár. Produced at the Deutsches Künstler-Theater, Berlin, 21 February 1927, with Richard Tauber (the Tsarevitch), Rita Georg (Sonja), Paul Heidemann (Iwan) and Charlotte Ander (Mascha).

Produced at the Johann Strauss-Theater, Vienna, 18 May 1928. Produced at the Raimundtheater 5 November 1954. Produced at the Volksoper 11 December 1978 with Adolf Dallapozza, Bettina Schoeller, Christian Boesch and Guggi Löwinger.

Produced at the Théâtre des Céléstins, Lyon, as *Le Tzarévitch* 16 April 1929 with Goavec, Artus and Lili Grandval and at the Théâtre de la Porte St Martin, Paris, as *Rêve d'un Soir* 30 January 1935, with Roger Bourdin (Sacha), Fanély Revoil (Sonia), Boucot (Ivan) and Simone Lencret (Mascha).

A film version was produced in 1929 with Ivan Petrovitch, Mariette Millner, Paul Otto, Albert Steinrück and John Hamilton, another by Victor Janson in 1933 with Martha Eggerth, Hans Söhnker, Ery Bos, Ida Wüst and Georg Alexander, and another by Arthur Maria Rabenalt in 1954 with Luis Mariano, Sonja Ziemann, Ivan Petrovitch, Paul Henkels, Ernst Wadlow and Maria Sebalt.

CHARACTERS

The Tsarevitch, Aljoscha
The Grand Duke, *his uncle*
The Prime Minister
The Lord Chamberlain
Sonja
Iwan, *a valet*
Mascha, *his wife*
A princess
A countess
Olga
Vera
Ladies of society, officers, dancers, guards, footmen

ACT 1

Outside the Tsar's palace in St Petersburg, the palace guard is on duty ('Es steht ein Soldat am Wolgastrand') while inside an entertainment featuring Cossack dancers, singers and a balalaika orchestra is taking place ('Hell erklingt ein liebliches, frohes Heimatlied'). During the interval of the concert, while the Tsarevitch Aljoscha is out of his apartment, his uncle, the Grand Duke, takes the opportunity to show some society ladies around it. They are the first females to cross the threshold of these rooms, because the Tsarevitch has grown up with a hate of women, and they discover that his apartment is furnished in the most austere fashion, but with a complete range of keep-fit equipment.

When the Grand Duke and the ladies have returned to the concert, the Tsarevitch's valet, Iwan, finds a handbag that one of the ladies has left behind. While he is having a look at it, he is surprised by the arrival of his wife, Mascha, who has slipped past the guards to get inside the palace. Iwan is alarmed. Not only is she not supposed to be there, but Ivan is not even supposed to be married because of the Tsarevitch's dislike of women. Knowing the Tsarevitch's attitude, Mascha can only suspect her own husband has been up to something when she finds him with a lady's handbag. Iwan has to produce some rapid reassurances of his fidelity and some soothing words of love ('Schaukle, Liebchen, schaukle').

Not surprisingly, the Tsarevitch's views on women are of real concern to his father, the Tsar, and the Prime Minister has been deputed to ensure that Aljoscha gets some experience with women in readiness for his marriage. It seems that an entire dancing group at the day's musical entertainment was made up of girls in male costume and, when the Tsarevitch singled out the athletic prowess of one of these 'boys' for particular mention, it was arranged that 'he' should be brought along to the Tsarevitch's apartments—ostensibly for a gymnastic work-out.

Sonja, the dancer chosen, arrives at the Tsarevitch's apartment dressed in a white Cossack uniform, with a long coat and high, patent leather boots. The Prime Minister warns her to respond to the Tsarevitch with complete obedience and to be prepared for some rough treatment when he discovers that she is a woman. Left alone, Sonja looks round the room and apprehensively sits down to await Aljoscha's arrival ('Einer wird kommen').

While Sonja waits in an adjoining room, the Tsarevitch returns and contemplates his lonely existence ('Allein! Wieder allein!'). He likens his isolation to that of a soldier keeping watch on the vast expanses of the River Volga and begs the Lord above to send him an angel before he dies ('Es steht ein Soldat am Wolgastrand'). A groom enters and tells the Tsarevitch that the Cossack boy is here. Sonja is shown into his presence, and the two are soon chatting freely but, when Aljoscha suggests a work-out, Sonja is reluctantly persuaded to take off her coat, revealing her true sex.

Furious, the Tsarevitch makes as if to strike her (Finale I: 'Ein Weib! Du ein Weib!') but Sonja stops him and pleads with him to let her stay. Openly admitting that she had been planted by the Prime Minister, she begins with her honesty to win his confidence and, finally, she suggests that together they might defeat his uncle. She will visit him every evening, making it look as though she were his lover. The Grand Duke would be satisfied by the appearances and cease to push women on him, while they would simply remain good friends.

The Tsarevitch is tempted and agrees. Then, discovering Sonja is hungry, he orders a fine meal to be brought to them. Sonja, seeking to make their situation look more realistic, adds a request for champagne and is astonished to learn that the Tsarevitch has never touched a drop in his life. She tells him of the wonders it can perform, as they clink glasses and drink together ('Trinkt man auf du und du'). As Aljoscha mellows, Sonja continues her counselling, but suddenly he tells her she must go...but she may come back the following day. Left alone, his melancholy returns ('Es steht ein Soldat am Wolgastrand'), but he thanks the Lord for having finally sent him one of His angels.

ACT 2

In the Tsarevitch's palace, Aljoscha is sitting at the dinner table with some of his officers. By contrast with the austere surroundings of his apartments in his father's palace, everything here is bright and friendly and a woman's touch is much in evidence. The atmosphere is distinctly merry, with a balalaika orchestra playing on the terrace, but the Tsarevitch is lost in thought, contemplating his beating heart ('Herz, warum schlägst du so bang'). Is it love at last? Gradually he brightens up and urges his officers to drink up. 'Don't give a thought to what the morrow brings!' he declares, as the party draws to a close.

The Grand Duke finds the Tsarevitch's altered demeanour most encouraging, though Aljoscha is still embarrassed by his uncle's references to the traces of feminine influence he sees around him. The Tsarevitch has a speech to learn for the officers' parade later in the day, but this is forgotten when Sonja arrives. It soon transpires that all the signs of feminine presence about the place have been carefully arranged and that the relationship between the two is still purely platonic but now Aljoscha is anxious for Sonja to give up her dancing career and move into the palace with him. Not only has he fallen for a woman's attractions, but he is convinced that Sonja is the only one for him ('Hab' nur dich allein'). He tells her that she may bring her friends to see her at the palace, and when she has gone he reaffirms to himself the passion that he now feels. He is determined to make the most of the spring of his life ('O komm, es hat der Frühling ach nur einen Mai').

When Aljoscha has left for the parade, Sonia returns with her dancing friends. Iwan comes upon two of them, Olga and Vera, and cannot resist a little mild flirtation but, once again, he has the misfortune for Mascha to turn up and catch him. She complains that ever since the novelty of his balalaika playing wore off he has had little to offer her, and he has to do some swift sweet talking to retrieve the situation ('Heute Abend komm ich zu dir'). Sonja, meanwhile, is revelling in telling her dancing friends of her happiness at her new life ('Das Leben ruft').

Now the dark clouds begin to gather over the relationship between the Tsarevitch and Sonja. As far as the Tsar and his Prime Minister are concerned, Sonja has served her usefulness by breaking down the barriers between the Tsarevitch and womankind. Now a royal wife has been found for him and she is to arrive that evening. The Grand Duke takes it upon himself to dispose of Sonja and, separating her from her friends, he tells her that she will have to leave. He will arrange the break-up by telling Aljoscha of all the previous lovers she has had. Sonja obediently goes along with the plan but, when the Tsarevitch returns, she cannot bring herself to say 'goodbye'. All the two can do is reaffirm their love for each other ('Liebe mich, küsse mich').

The Lord Chamberlain arrives to conduct the Tsarevitch to meet his future wife and Aljoscha instructs the Lord Chamberlain to tell his father that he refuses. He remains at his palace with Sonja, who has arranged a 'Thousand and One Nights' dancing display by all her friends (Finale II: 'Setz' dich her! Denke du bist ein Märchenprinz!'). Aljoscha is delighted with the dancing and, when the girls crowd round him, he tells them of all that Sonja means to him ('Ich bin verliebt'). Suddenly the Grand Duke appears with four officers in full uniform but, once again, Aljoscha refuses to obey his father's command. The Grand Duke then tells him of Sonja's admission to a string of previous lovers, and the Tsarevitch is shattered. 'Whore!' he cries. 'How many hands have you been through?' In such a situation Sonja can no longer hold to the story she had agreed. She swears to Aljoscha that she has belonged to no other man and that she had gone along with the deception only under duress and, the Grand Duke's plan in ruins, they fall into each other's arms.

ACT 3

In a garden in Naples, Sonja and the Tsarevitch are relaxing in front of a villa overlooking the gently lapping sea ('Kosende Wellen'). Why, they ask, is there only one May to each spring? Why does love pass by so quickly? ('Warum hat jeder Frühling, ach, nur einen Mai?') Since they fled to Naples they have thought of nothing but each other, and their days consist of nothing but thoughts of love ('Küss mich!').

Iwan and Mascha have accompanied them to Naples, and Iwan has been finding great delight in the local girls while Mascha has been enjoying the attentions of the Italian men. This time it is Iwan who has to do the pleading, reassuring her that he, no matter what, will always be there when Mascha needs someone ('Ich bin bereit zu jeder Zeit').

One day the Grand Duke appears in Naples with a group of army officers. Once more he has come to plead with the Tsarevitch: the Tsar is ill and may die at any time. He must return. Aljoscha declares that he would renounce the throne rather than give up Sonja, but then a telegram is handed to the Tsarevitch: his father has died, and he is already Tsar. The officers swear their allegiance ('Wir wollen dir dienen'), and Aljoscha realises that duty calls him. He kneels before Sonja, kisses her hand and abruptly departs as the broken-hearted Sonja is left helplessly lamenting the workings of fate ('Warum hat jeder Frühling, ach, nur einen Mai?').

DIE GOLD'NE MEISTERIN

(The Lady Goldsmith)

an operetta in three acts by Julius Brammer and Alfred Grünwald, after the comedy *Die goldene Eva* by Franz von Schönthan and Franz Koppel-Ellfeld. Music by Edmund Eysler. Produced at the Theater an der Wien, Vienna, 13 September 1927 with Betty Fischer (Margarete), Mizzi Zwerenz, Gretl Natzler, Hubert Marischka (Christian), Franz Glawatsch, Richard Waldemar (Ignatius) and Fritz Steiner. Produced at the Raimundtheater, 30 November 1945 with Richard Waldemar (Ignatius) and revived there 29 April 1955. Produced at the Wiener Volksbühne, May 1946.

CHARACTERS

Margarete, *a rich goldsmith's widow*
Countess Giulietta
Christian, *a journeyman goldsmith*
Fridolin von Gumpendorf, *a nobleman*

Count Jaromir von Greifenstein
Portschunkula, *the lady goldsmith's housekeeper*
Friedl, *an apprentice goldsmith*
Sebaldius Paradeiser, *a postal official from Nuremberg*
Brother Ignatius, Brother Severinus, Brother Peregrini
Ladies and gentlemen of society, guests, citizens, soldiers, a sedan-bearer, journeymen goldsmiths, apprentice goldsmiths, musicians, a cooper, wine-servers, pages, lamp boys, troubadours, maids

ACT 1

In a goldsmith's shop in sixteenth-century Vienna, Friedl and his fellow apprentices are feasting their imaginations on the dancing, drinking, fireworks and other celebrations at the banquet the Emperor is giving today for the trade guilds ('Alles ist heut auf den Beinen'). Their mistress, Margarete, is actually attending the banquet, and the housekeeper, Portschunkula, has her work cut out to keep the young men under control and ensure that their work gets done while Margarete is away.

The shop has a visitor in the person of the noble but impoverished Fridolin von Gumpendorf, a plump and hungry fellow who has not come to buy any gold but rather to lavish his attentions on the portly Portschunkula and the cakes and wine he hopes she will serve him ('Schon als ich noch ein Jüngling war'). While he is eating, an old acquaintance of his, Count Jaromir von Greifenstein, arrives on horseback, asking to speak to him. Gumpendorf imagines that the Count will only be trying to borrow money but, when Friedl tells him that Greifenstein is covered with gold and silver, velvet and silk, Gumpendorf decides that he might try touching the Count for some money instead. However, it seems that all Greifenstein's finery is borrowed, and very soon each of the penniless pair is pumping the other for a loan of ten thalers. Greifenstein needs to find a rich wife to fund his programme of debt repayments, and Gumpendorf reckons the ideal solution is right here in this shop—the goldsmith's young widow ('Zwölf Körbe hab ich schon bekommen'/'Jaromir von Greifenstein').

Margarete returns from the guild lunch in a sedan chair to lively greetings from the goldsmiths and apprentices ('Hurra—hurra! Frau Meisterin'). She presented the Emperor with a bouquet on behalf of the goldsmiths and, to her delight, the Emperor rewarded her with a kiss. Margarete can only regret that she is merely a wealthy commoner, rather than a titled countess or princess ('Gräfin sein, Fürstin sein'), but she declares that in celebration of her happy experience there will be double pay, free beer and dancing into the early hours of the morning.

Giulietta, Countess of Caraffi, arrives at the shop, warm with the news of the lady goldsmith's success with the Emperor, and Margarete confides in her that the previous day she had also been at the nobility's masked ball at the 'Blue Paradise' in the Michaelplatz. There the men had clamoured to dance with her, above all one particular person—a real gentleman—who she is sure was a prince.

The Countess has come to order a golden plate as a present for her father. She wants one like those the artists in Rome make, and it occurs to Margarete that this is just the job for the new journeyman goldsmith, Christian, who has come to her employ with warm recommendations from the master goldsmiths in Rome. The head goldsmith warns her that the newcomer is a somewhat difficult fellow and, when he summons him to attend the lady goldsmith, Christian makes it clear that he is determined to show her that he is the master ('Also das hier ist die Stelle'/'Du liebe, gold'ne Meisterin')

When Christian comes to deal with the Countess's order, it transpires that the two know each other. Christian had been a noted sculptor in Rome before turning to the potentially more profitable trade of goldsmith which he had learned from his father in Nuremberg. It also becomes clear that, not only had Christian gone as a joke to the nobility's ball the previous day, but that he was the person with whom the lady goldsmith had so enjoyed herself. Margarete, red with disappointment, is ready to sack him on the spot, but the Countess reminds her of the present she needs for her father's birthday and, in any case, Margarete cannot forget the very real pleasure that Christian's company gave her. She swears him to secrecy over the previous day's events, but both of them clearly retain the happiest memories of the moments when he held her close in the dance ('So tanzt man nur in Wien!').

While Portschunkula calls Friedl to help prepare for the evening's celebrations (Finale I: 'Friedl, Friedl, schnell!'), Gumpendorf arrives with Count von Greifenstein and introduces him to Margarete, who is most taken with his impressive title. However, when Christian returns, finely dressed and bringing a bunch of white roses for Margarete, he at once recognises Greifenstein from his Nuremberg days. He denounces the Count as the scrounger he is and begs Margarete to have nothing to do with him, but Margarete, dazzled by the title, warns Christian that the matter has nothing to do with him, and chooses to dance with the Count rather than with him.

ACT 2

The following day, in the courtyard of Margarete's home, the goldsmiths are busily at work ('Auf unser'm Amboss schmieden wir'). Since the previous evening, when the wine-worn Gumpendorf proposed to her, Portschunkula has been emulating her mistress in the attitude that nothing much less than being a countess or princess will do for her. The gentleman in question prefers to forget yesterday's events and promises now that he has sobered up somewhat, but Portschunkula does all she can to remind him ('Du sagtest: 'Holde, werde mein!''/'Portschunkula! Portschunkula! Wie schön bist du bei Nacht!').

Gumpendorf seizes the opportunity to sound Margarete out as to whether she might be interested in marrying Greifenstein. 'But why hasn't he asked me himself?' she says. 'Because, whenever the Count wants to speak with you, Christian comes and interrupts!' is the reply. 'He has something against us.' Margarete summons Christian to her and seeks to arouse his jealousy by telling him she intends to marry and she asks him to make the ring for her ('Gebt mir die Hand, Frau Meisterin'). Christian retorts by telling her that he, too, intends to marry. He will name no names, but his intended bride has a castle by the sea close to Mount Vesuvius ('Sei mein, o bella Lucia!'). Margarete suggests that he would be better off with a more modest marriage to a Viennese girl ('In Grinzing is' a Gasserl'/'So ein' Wein—so ein' Wein').

The time comes for the afternoon break, and the workers discuss the Count's interest in their mistress and Christian's apparent jealousy. Christian merely produces a letter he has just received from an old friend in Nuremberg, the postal official Sebaldius Paradeiser. It tells him that, in response to Christian's request, he is coming at once to Vienna. Christian sees this as a reason for a celebratory drink ('Lustig ist das G'sellenleben') but he begins to get concerned when Greifenstein arrives with a bouquet of flowers and proposes to Margarete. She tells him that she will give him her formal decision that evening when all the neighbours are present. The Count admits that he may be a shade unromantic and that a little dance would help give him courage ('Ich traute mich bedeutend sehr'/'So ein kleines Tänzerl').

The goldsmiths set out the lanterns and prepare for the evening celebrations (Finale II: 'Wir grüssen dich, Frau Meisterin!') as, with Gumpendorf in support, Greifenstein prepares to serenade his intended ('O hör', du holde Traute'/'O Margarete, Stern meiner Träume'). When Margarete arrives, he repeats his proposal but, before Margarete can accept, Christian appears disguised as Sebaldius Paradeiser. He declares that he is the grandfather of Emerentia Bretzelberger, to whom the Count is already married and by whom he has four children, and Greifenstein and Gumpendorf beat a hasty retreat.

While everyone's attention is diverted, Christian throws off his disguise and reappears in his own person. Margarete is full of thanks and recognition for his earlier warnings and she offers him promotion, but he declares that he wishes to move on. He pauses only to sing a farewell song, a cautionary tale about a nightingale who spurned the attentions of a young siskin ('War einst eine Nachtigall'), before he rushes off, leaving Margarete almost in tears.

ACT 3

In the garden of an inn adjoining the monastery at Klosterneuburg, near Vienna, Margarete's goldsmiths and apprentices ('So ein' Wein!') are celebrating Friedl's promotion from apprentice to journeyman, but they are all sad that Christian is not among them. They are served refreshment by three monks, one of whom is Brother Ignatius, a cleric who is full of worldly wisdom and who tells a tale about the little silver bell in everyone's chest that rings to tell them whether they are doing right or wrong ('Jeder Mensch hat in der Brust'/'Das Glöcklein macht bim bim').

Christian appears, pausing for a rest on his journey out of town, and still absorbed by his feelings for Margarete. He confides to Brother Ignatius that, before he would speak to her again, the Danube would have to flow in the reverse direction and wine turn to water. 'The bit about the Danube is difficult,' Ignatius admits, 'but the bit about the water is as good as done. Leave it to me, and remember—a woeful engagement means a joyful marriage.' Christian admits that he could be right as he gazes pensively down over Vienna for the last time ('Du stolzer Bau in schlanker Pracht'/'Du lieber Stephansturm').

It is a busy monastery, for Margarete and Portschunkula also end up confiding their problems in Brother Ignatius, as do Gumpendorf and Greifenstein who are now without a penny between them. When he encounters Portschunkula, Gumpendorf decides that he would perhaps be better off, after all, to settle for the home comforts she offers, while Greifenstein, hearing from Nuremberg that his young wife has inherited a fortune, decides that it might be in his best interests to return home.

Brother Ignatius sits Margarete in the stool of St Benifacius, which induces absolute honesty from all its occupants, and there she admits that she has loved Christian all along. Finally the good monk arranges everything. Margarete may not be a countess or a princess, but she will be a happy wife, and her journeymen and apprentices will have a fine master (Finale III: 'Du liebe gold'ne Meisterin').

DIE DREIGROSCHENOPER

(The Threepenny Opera)

a piece with music in a prelude and eight scenes by Bertolt Brecht after John Gay's *The Beggar's Opera*. Music by Kurt Weill. Produced at the Theater am Schiffbauerdamm, Berlin, 31 August 1928 with Harald Paulsen (Macheath), Erich Ponto (Peachum), Roma Bahn (Polly), Lotte Lenja (Jenny), Kurt Gerron (Tiger Brown and the Streetsinger) and Kate Kühl (Lucy). Produced at the Theater des Westens 23 May 1987 with Martin Reinke (Macheath), Hans Falar (Peachum) and Ingrid Caven (Jenny).

Produced at the Empire Theatre, New York in a version by Clifford Cochran and Jerrold Krimsky as *The Threepenny Opera* 13 April 1933 with Robert Chisholm (Macheath), Rex Weber (Peachum) and Steffi Duna (Polly). Produced at the Theatre de Lys in a version by Marc Blitzstein 10 May 1954 with Scott Merrill (Macheath), Leon Lishner (Peachum), Jo Sullivan (Polly) and Lotte Lenya (Jenny). Produced at the Vivien Beaumont Theatre, New York, in a version by Ralph Manheim and John Willett 1 May 1976 with Raul Julia, C K Alexander, Caroline Kava and Ellen Greene.

Produced at the Royal Court Theatre, London, in the Blitzstein version 9 February 1956 with Bill Owen, Eric Pohlman, Daphne Anderson and Maria Remusat. Produced at the Prince of Wales Theatre in a version by Hugh MacDiarmid 10 February 1972 with Joe Melia, Ronald Radd, Vanessa Redgrave and Annie Ross. Produced at the National Theatre 13 March 1986 in a version by Robert David MacDonald, with Tim Curry, Stephen Moore, Sally Dexter and Eve Adam.

1099

Produced at the Théâtre Montparnasse, Paris, as *L'Opéra de Quat' Sous* in a version by Jean-Claude Hémery October 1930. Produced at the Théâtre Mogador, 1979 with Louis Grenville (Macheath) and Lise Granvel. Produced at the Théâtre Musical de Paris (Châtelet) in a version by Giorgio Strehler and Myriam Tannant 31 October 1986 with Michael Heltau (Macheath), Yves Robert (Peachum), Barbara Sukowa (Polly), Denise Gence (Mrs Peachum) and Milva (Jenny).

A German film version was produced by Nero Films (Berlin) in 1930 with Rudolf Forster (Macheath), Carola Neher (Polly) and Lotte Lenja (Jenny) and simultaneously a French version (as *L'Opéra de Quat' Sous*) with Albert Préjean, Florelle and Margo Lion. A further German version was produced by Karl Ulrich Film (Berlin) in 1962 with Curt Jürgens, June Ritchie (partly sung by Maria Körber) and Hildegard Neff.

CHARACTERS

Jonathan Jeremiah Peachum, *head of a beggar ring*
Mrs Peachum
Polly Peachum, *their daughter*
Macheath, *head of a ring of street robbers*
'Tiger' Brown, *chief of police in London*
Lucy, *his daughter*
'Weeping-Willow' Walter, 'Hook-Finger' Jake, 'Money' Matthew, Robert 'the Saw', Eddie, Jimmy, *Macheath's street robbers*
Filch, *one of Peachum's beggars*
'Low Dive' Jenny, *a whore*
Smith, *a first constable*
A streetsinger
Beggars, whores, constables

PRELUDE
It is market day in Soho in 1838, and beggars, thieves and whores are going about their business as, to the accompaniment of a barrel organ, a street singer proclaims the story of the bloody deeds of the gangster-murderer Macheath, known as 'Mack the Knife' ('Und der Haifisch, der hat Zähne'). When a man steps out from amongst the whores he is immediately recognised by one of their number as Macheath himself.

SCENE 1
From his headquarters in low London, Jonathan Jeremiah Peachum runs his proud business, providing beggars with clothes and pitches in return for a percentage of their takings, as he exhorts mankind to go about their vicarious deeds (Peachum's Morning Hymn: 'Wach' auf, du verrotteter Christ'). The beggar Filch comes in, having been beaten up while he was at his trade. He had committed the crime of not obtaining a licence from Peachum, the protector of London's beggars. Now, in return for a fifty percent share of Filch's takings, Peachum allots him a permission to operate the top half of Baker Street.

1100

When Mrs Peachum appears, her husband asks her anxiously for the latest news about their daughter Polly and the man who has recently been calling on her with such regularity. Mrs Peachum tells him not to worry over such a smart, well-dressed man as 'the Captain' but, when she describes the scar on the man's neck, Peachum realises that this 'Captain' is none other than Macheath. Peachum runs upstairs, only to discover that Polly's bed has not been slept in, and he and his wife comment sarcastically on the irresponsibility of young girls in love ('Instead of That' Song: 'Anstatt Dass').

SCENE 2

In a dark stable, 'Money' Matthew is peering round by lantern-light to ensure there is nobody there. Macheath enters, followed by Polly, who is wearing a wedding-dress and protesting at the idea of being married in a stable. Macheath silences her, as wagons are heard arriving and Macheath's men bring in fine furniture, carpets and crockery that they have stolen in order to deck the place out for the wedding breakfast. Then the men return, decked out in smart evening dress that is totally out of keeping with their behaviour, and carrying wedding presents.

They have started the wedding breakfast when a parson arrives. Macheath's men welcome him with a wedding song (Wedding Song for Poor Folk: 'Bill Lawgen und Mary Syer'), but Polly thinks that she can do better, and she sings a song that she once heard sung by a washer-up in a Soho bar. In it the singer imagines herself in charge of a pirate ship with eight sails and fifty cannon (Pirate Jenny: 'Meine Herrn heut sehn Sie mich Gläser aufwaschen').

One of the gang rushes in with the news that the chief of police himself, 'Tiger' Brown, is approaching but, when Brown arrives, it transpires that he and Macheath are old friends. The bridegroom invites Brown to join in the wedding breakfast, as they recall their days serving together in India (Cannon Song: 'John war darunter and Jim war dabei'). Because of preparations for the coming Coronation, Brown can stay only a short time and, when he has left, the gang tear down a hanging carpet and reveal a bed. Then they diplomatically depart, leaving Polly and Macheath alone (Love Song: 'Siehst du den Mond über Soho?').

SCENE 3

Polly arrives back at Peachum's establishment with the news of her marriage. She tells her parents of her girlhood expectations for courtship and the way that Macheath's direct methods swept her off her feet (Barbara Song: 'Einst glaubte ich') but her parents are appalled to find their daughter attached to a notorious gangster and womaniser. Peachum determines that Macheath will hang, but Polly points to his friendship with the police chief and the three reflect on the uncertainty of human circumstances (Finale I: 'Was ich möchte, ist es viel?').

SCENE 4

Back in the stable, Macheath is disturbed in his bed by the return of Polly, warning him that her father is about to visit Tiger Brown. Peachum has been so persistent in his efforts to get Macheath sent to the gallows that Brown has told Polly to warn Macheath to lie low for a while. She reads him a list of charges which are sufficiently impressive to make Macheath decide to heed the advice and he instructs Polly how to run the business in his absence. Polly is apprehensive about their parting and begs Macheath to remain faithful to her (Polly's Song: 'Er kommt nicht wieder') and Macheath departs with an assurance of his enduring love ('Die Liebe dauert oder dauert nicht').

SCENE 5

Mrs Peachum goes to find 'Low Dive' Jenny at a brothel in Turnbridge and she tempts the girl with the offer of a reward if she should turn Macheath in to the police. Mrs Peachum has little doubt that Macheath's sexual needs will not allow him to stay away from the brothel for long (Ballad of Sexual Dependence: 'Da ist nun einer schon der Satan selber') and she is right. Macheath duly arrives. He throws his charge sheet on the floor, and Jenny picks it up and reads the damning list. Macheath recalls the happy times he has spent with Jenny, but Jenny's recollections are rather less favourable (Ballad of the Fancy Man: 'In einer Zeit') and before Macheath can escape she brings Constable Smith to the brothel. As the constable attempts to make an arrest, Macheath jumps out of the window only to be apprehended by a bunch of policemen brought by Mrs Peachum.

SCENE 6

Brown comes to find Macheath in his Old Bailey cell. He is sorry that he could do nothing to avoid having his old friend arrested. Macheath comes to a financial arrangement with his jailer, Constable Smith, to be freed of handcuffs, though he reflects that in his present situation being well-to-do hardly makes for a comfortable life (Ballad of the Agreeable Life: 'Da preist man uns das Leben grosser Geister').

Macheath's worries are heightened by contemplation of the fact that, unknown to Brown, he has seduced and married Brown's daughter, Lucy. She, having heard about Macheath's relationship with Polly, has now come down to the jail to find him and, when Polly arrives, the two jealous women begin to violently harangue each other, whilst each proclaims her devotion to Macheath (Jealousy Duet: 'Komm heraus, du Schönheit von Soho'). Macheath sees it as in his interest to take Lucy's side and deny Polly, who eventually is dragged away by her mother. Macheath persuades Lucy to help create a diversion and, when Constable Smith is off his guard, Macheath seizes the opportunity to escape. Peachum arrives to claim a reward for the arrest of Macheath, but finds that the bird has flown and threatens Brown with dire consequences for allowing the criminal's escape.

In an aside to the audience, Macheath and Mrs Peachum point up the moral that man lives only for his own interests and by taking advantage of others (Finale II: 'Ihr Herrn, die ihr uns lehrt').

SCENE 7

Back at his store, Peachum is preparing his band of beggars for the forthcoming Coronation. Jenny arrives to collect the money promised for 'shopping' Macheath, but Mrs Peachum refuses to pay her on the grounds that Macheath is no longer in custody. Jenny reveals that Macheath has visited her since his escape, but has now gone on to another old flame, Suky Tawdry. Peachum immediately sends Filch to direct the police there, but his actions are pre-empted by the arrival of Brown and his men.

Brown attempts to arrest Peachum's band of men for begging, but Peachum defends them as harmless cripples and expounds upon the inadequacy of human endeavour (Song of the Inadequacy of Human Endeavour: 'Der Mensch lebt durch den Kopf'). Peachum warns Brown that his beggars might interrupt the Coronation ceremony and, using this threat, he persuades Brown to go round to Suky Tawdry's house to arrest Macheath once more. Jenny is left to reflect on the downfall of various historic people, from Solomon, Cleopatra and Julius Caesar down to Macheath (Solomon Song: 'Ihr saht den weisen Salomon').

SCENE 8

Macheath is brought back to the Old Bailey and lodged in the death cell. The crowds gather outside for his execution, prior to going on to the Coronation, as Macheath offers Smith a bribe to free him and reinforces it with a plea for pity (Call from the Tomb: 'Nun hört die Stimme, die um Mitleid ruft'). As Macheath counts the minutes to his execution, his men call to wish him farewell and are sent to obtain all the money they can lay their hands on. Polly can bring no cash, but she hurries away to see if she can obtain the Queen's pardon.

Macheath's men come back with the news that they have been unable to get through the Coronation crowds and, as six o'clock sounds, Macheath is led away to the gallows, asking for forgiveness (Epitaph: 'Ihr Menschenbrüder, die ihr nach uns lebt'). As the criminal stands at the gallows, Peachum declares to the audience that mercy and not justice shall prevail. The crowd acclaim the arrival of Brown as a mounted messenger (Finale III: 'Horch! Horch! Horch!') and Brown declares that, on the occasion of her coronation, the Queen has granted the prisoner a pardon and, indeed, raised Macheath to the peerage with an annual pension of £10,000.

CASANOVA

a grand operetta in seven scenes by Rudolph Schanzer and Ernst Welisch. Music by Johann Strauss, arranged by Ralph Benatzky. Produced at the Grosses Schauspielhaus, Berlin, 1 September 1928 with Michael Bohnen (Casanova), Anni Frind (Laura), Anni Ahlers (Barberina), Emmy Sturm, Siegfried Arno and Wilhelm

Bendow.

Produced at the Volksoper, Vienna, 10 October 1935.

Produced at the London Coliseum in a version by Hans Muller and Harry Graham 24 May 1932 with Arthur Fear/Fernando Autori (Casanova), Soffi Schonning (Laura), Grete Natzler/Margaret Carlisle (Barbarina), Dorothy Dickson (Princess Potomska) and Marie Löhr (Maria Theresa).

CHARACTERS

Giacomo Casanova
Costa, *his servant*
Laura Bonasede, *a Venetian senator's daughter*
Barberina, *a dancer*
Count Waldstein, *an Austrian attaché*
Lieutenant von Hohenfels, *his adjutant*
Menuzzi, Titto, Matteo, *conspirators*
Count Dohna, *a Prussian envoy*
Helene, *his wife*
Trude, *her maid*
A theatre manager
Dolores
Ignacia
An abbess
Perez
Empress Maria Theresia
Voltaire, *a playwright*
Pleschke, *a sergeant*
von Knobelsdorff, von Wedepohl, *cadets*
Pschihoda, *a castle owner*
Tonina, *a flower girl*
Conspirators, gamblers, theatre audience, nuns, ball-guests, masked revellers, citizens of Venice

SCENE 1

A clock is striking eleven as a group of conspirators crowds around their leader, Menuzzi, on the Rio di San Lorenzo in Venice ('Schwarz das Herz und schwarz das Gesicht'). They have been commissioned to murder Giacomo Casanova by a senator from whom the celebrated philanderer has plundered the attentions of a dancer named Barberina ('Dolch im Gewand, degen zur Hand').

They have dispersed by the time a gondola glides up carrying a young Austrian officer, Lieutenant von Hohenfels. While the gondolier waits, Hohenfels approaches the house of his beloved Laura, the daughter of Senator Bonasede and, muffled in a cloak and hood, she slips out from the doorway, and they kiss passionately. Laura is greatly upset, for her father, having unsuccessfully tried to force her into a hated marriage, has now decided that she should enter a convent in Tarragona, where his sister is the abbess. The ship that is to take her there is already anchored in the harbour.

1104

Die schöne Galathee. Midas (Franz Suhrada) and Pygmalion (Reinhard Brussmann) haggle over the statue of Galatea (Nadya Zvetkova) while Ganymede (Joseph-René Rumpold) gets friendly with Elizabeth Lombardini-Smith. Wiener Kammeroper, 1988.

Die Fledermaus. Light musical theatre makes a rare appearance at the Royal Opera House, Covent Garden. Rosalinde (Kiri Te Kanawa) enjoys the attentions of Alfred (Ryszard Karczykowski), 1977.

Der Bettelstudent. Symon (Adolf Dallapozza) sets out, dressed in fine clothes, to wreak General Ollendorf's revenge on the lovely Laura. Volksoper, Vienna, 1983.

Gasparone. Soldiers, smugglers and skirts. Angelika Luz (Sora), Kristina Michel (Carlotta), Karl Lobensommer (Erminio) and Peter Branoff (Benozzo) at the Salzburg Landestheater, 1987.

Der Zigeunerbaron. Sandor Barinkay gets himself proclaimed a gipsy baron to woo the pretty daughter of the pig farmer Zsupan (Derek Hammond-Stroud). Sadler's Wells Opera, 1965.

Der Opernball. Karl Donch (Beaubuisson) with a couple of armfuls of masked femininity at the opera ball. Volksoper, 1985.

Die lustige Witwe. Mizzi Günther (Hanna Glawari) and Louis Treumann (Danilo) introduced Lehár's musical at the Theater an der Wien in 1905.

Der Fremdenführer. The prima donna Maria di Cassarolli (Gisela Ehrensperger) gives a free concert to the people of Vienna. Volksoper 1978.

There is no escaping, and Hohenfels tells her that she must follow her father's will. Later, he will rescue her from the convent and, once they have fled far away from Venice, nothing will be able to keep them apart. For the moment, they can only take one last gondola ride together and say their farewells ('Ich steh' zu Dir').

Casanova comes across a bridge, carrying a lute and, stopping in front of Barberina's house, begins to serenade her ('Dort ist das Haus'/'Du schönste aller Frau'n'). When he has finished, Menuzzi steps out from the shadows, clad as a beggar, and begs for alms (Finaletto: 'Ein Almosen um der Madonna willen'). As Casanova reaches for a coin, the conspirators rush to attack him but, at that moment, the gondola carrying Hohenfels and Laura returns and the lieutenant helps Casanova to fight off his attackers. Casanova expresses his deep gratitude to his rescuer and, when Barberina appears on her balcony, he shrugs aside his wound and climbs up to her.

SCENE 2
A group of singers with mandolins and dancers with fans celebrate the sublime attractions of Venice ('Sul mare luccica') while, in the gaming room of the Teatro San Samuele, Casanova is enjoying the gaming tables with Barberina ('Banco!' 'Gagné'). By the time she goes off for her evening's appearance in the theatre, Casanova has managed to lose not only her entire pay but the advance salary for her next engagement in Pisa, an engagement which she has accepted despite a conflicting commitment to appear in Berlin for the King of Prussia.

While Casanova is at the theatre, his servant, Costa, makes the acquaintance of Trude, maid of Countess Dohna, wife of the Prussian envoy. Trude's mistress has a roving eye which is currently roving towards Casanova and Costa points out that, when his master begins an affair with a lady, he himself is duty bound to enter into a similar arrangement with her maid. Trude seems to have no objection, and they are soon finding out about each other—he a Spaniard by birth, she a Berliner ('Für Mädels aus Berlin'/ 'Heut' morgen, da hab' ich an nichts noch gedacht').

At the theatre, Count Waldstein introduces Casanova to Count Dohna as 'the famous darling of the ladies'. Waldstein is anxious to know Casanova's recipe for success, but the only response he gets is, 'If you don't chase women, you won't catch them.' Casanova's next capture will be Helene, Countess Dohna. With the connivance of their servants, they meet, and the Countess is a little surprised. She had formed an impression of the celebrated lover that she confesses is far from reality. She had imagined a handsome man with a sweet smile—a type she hates. She tells Casanova that she is due to leave Venice for Berlin the following day, and he assures her that he would follow her there or to the end of the world, were it necessary. Helene tells him that her husband has been ordered by the Prussian King to find an Italian gentleman to teach the Prussian cadet corps some polish and, as he presses his passion for Helene, Casanova assures her that he is just the man for the job ('Als ich zum ersten Mal Dich sah').

Meanwhile, Lieutenant von Hohenfels has brought a dispatch for Count Waldstein, ordering him to leave for Vienna the following day. Hohenfels had arranged with Waldstein to have some leave so that he could travel to Tarragona to see Laura, but now that is out of the question. Hohenfels is utterly despondent and, when he comes upon Casanova, he tells him that he intends to desert. Casanova persuades him not to. He, Casanova, will repay Hohenfels's kindness of the previous day by travelling to Tarragona and bringing Laura back to him. Hohenfels is delighted, but no more than Costa, who is filled with excitement at the prospect of accompanying his master back to his native country.

Garlanded with flowers, Barberina emerges from the theatre at the end of her performance ('Wenn im hellen Rampenschein'/'Das ist mein südliches Temprament'). Waldstein meets her (Finaletto: 'Brava, Brava, Bravissima!'), and tells her that she will not be travelling to Pisa. He produces a decree from the senate of Venice handing the contract-breaking ballerina over to the King of Prussia. Count Waldstein will himself escort her via Vienna to Berlin. Barberina reacts furiously and, when the love-sick Waldstein kneels in front of her, she kicks his hat off his head ('Ich servier' dem roi de Prusse'/'Das ist mein südliches Temp'rament').

SCENE 3
Beneath the balcony of a house in Zaragoza a group of Spaniards are singing a serenade ('O ametus labios rojor colór ma belamor'). A lady appears on the balcony and throws their leader a red rose, whilst from another door the dancer Dolores emerges and performs a seductive dance. Casanova is sitting in front of an inn close to the door of the convent where Laura is immured. He throws Dolores a gold coin and pays her extravagant compliments and, in exchange for both the tip and the compliment, Dolores offers to read his fortune. She sees women accompanying him wherever he goes, but she also sees him sitting between grey walls, in a gloomy castle somewhere in the cold north.

Meanwhile, disguised as a pilgrim, Costa has been inside the convent attempting to locate Laura. He reports that she is sitting in her cell, clad in white, due to take holy orders as soon as the nuns have returned from their atonement on Mount Calvary. The news that a bullfight is to take place gives Casanova an idea. He instructs Dolores that, when the nuns go to Mount Calvary, she should give a slip of paper to the one clad in white. Dolores assures Casanova that she would do anything for him. 'Send me to hell, and I'd go,' she declares. 'I wouldn't send any woman to hell. I'd rather be in seventh heaven with her,' Casanova replies ('In Hispaniens heissem Sonnenland'/'Stunden der Liebe').

Led by the abbess, the nuns emerge from the convent, each with a burning candle and a lace handkerchief in her hands ('O Madonna auf uns sieh!'). They kneel, and Laura lifts her hands and her gaze in supplication but, while the other nuns ask the Virgin Mary to accept her into holy orders, she is asking how she may escape the convent and the veil ('O Marie—wie entflieh' ich dem Kloster und dem Schleier?').

1106

Dolores kneels before Laura and asks to kiss her hand (Finaletto: 'Madonna! Himmelsbraut!'/'O Madonna, auf uns sieh'') and, as she does so, she hands her the piece of paper. The nuns depart in procession, as the bullfighters arrive. Then Casanova's voice is heard calling out that a bull has broken loose and, as the terrified nuns flee back into the convent, Casanova grabs Laura and carries her off.

SCENE 4

In the assembly hall of the Vienna Opera a masked ball is taking place ('Opernball ist heute'/'Man maskiert sich'). Count Dohna is there, looking for Barberina, who has been leading him a merry dance ever since Venice. Laura enters and rushes to join Hohenfels, overjoyed to be with him again ('Ich hab' Dich lieb').

Waldstein is also there, in his new capacity as chairman of the Morality Commission. Extra vigilance is dictated tonight as the Empress Maria Theresia is expected to attend the ball, and also because Casanova is known to be around. The Empress appears, masked, and Casanova, intrigued by this unknown lady, approaches her and begins paying her extravagant compliments. The Empress plays along with him and, when he sees that she is about to leave, Casanova presses her for an assurance that they will meet again.

As the Empress is leaving, she sees Laura bestowing a gratefully affectionate kiss on Casanova. Barberina also greets Casanova with a kiss, taking care to explain to Helene that it is a sisterly kiss of greeting. Under all these expressions of affection, Casanova feels an ecstasy of pleasure ('Im Rausch der Genüsse'), but they have not gone unnoticed by officialdom. Waldstein informs Casanova that the Morality Commission has instructions to arrest the woman who was seen kissing a gentleman in full view of the Empress and, astonished to learn that the lady he had been so fulsomely addressing was the Empress, Casanova determines to find a way to protect Laura. While Waldstein rallies the police of the Morality Commission ('Fürs Volk ist Schmutz und Schund'/'Die Keuschheitskommission'), Casanova arranges for Laura and Trude to exchange costumes. He tells Laura that Costa is waiting to take her to the Prussian border. She will have male clothes and will travel as his friend Count Baldazzi.

Trude, meanwhile, must provide a diversion to allow them to escape. Her heart is beating fast as Hohenfels approaches the one he assumes to be Laura (Finale: 'Warum so stumm?') until, with a trumpet signal, Waldstein stops the music. 'I am sorry that I must disturb the good humour of this occasion, but there are women here who don't belong,' he declares, pointing to Trude. Hohenfels steps forward to protect her. 'She is my fiancée,' he declares. 'No, Lieutenant,' replies the Empress, removing her mask. 'A woman who kisses another man is no fit bride for a serving officer—especially when the other man is Herr von Casanova.' Four men of the Morality Commission step forward, grab Trude and lead her off, while Casanova is ordered to leave the country the next day. Ever the gentleman, he first

1107

persuades the Empress to taste the experience of a waltz with him ('Im Rausch der Genüsse').

SCENE 5
In the Park of Sanssouci in Berlin, a group of soldiers are being drilled by their sergeant before being presented to their new instructor, Casanova. The Count and Countess Dohna introduce him to the soldiers as the man who will give them their final polish, and Dohna is anxious that Casanova should put on a uniform to be presented before the King that evening. Helene is more interested that he should instruct her in the tactics of love. 'I am at your command, instructor,' she declares ('Kein Weg ist zu weit').

Casanova tells Laura, who is still dressed as a young nobleman, that he has sent Costa back to Vienna with a message for Hohenfels which will clear up the misunderstanding at the ball but, when Costa returns, he explains that he was unable to deliver it. Hohenfels had first been held under house-arrest, and then went immediately on manoeuvres. Meanwhile, Barberina is to dance that evening to music composed by the King himself—a ballet *en pointe* ('Ich spreche mit den Beinen zu').

Trude has also been freed from arrest in Vienna and made her way to Berlin. She is decked with rings, bracelets and necklaces, which she explains she has obtained by honest barter. Costa is unconvinced and declares that their engagement is off ('Da lachen ja die Hühner'/'Du kannst von mir noch lernen').

Dohna has been posted back to Venice by the King and he imagines that Helene, who made such a fuss about leaving, will be pleased. Strangely, she now declares that she is crazy for Berlin. 'The Potsdam climate suits me better than the heat, the smell and the mosquitoes in Venice,' she declares. But then Casanova announces he has decided to give up his post in Prussia to return to Venice. 'You did it for me?' she asks. 'I could do nothing else,' he replies (Finale: 'Das hast Du für mich getan?'). 'Giacomo, I love you!' she declares, as Casanova goes off to give his final class to the soldiers of Prussia.

SCENE 6
Waldstein is sitting in the library of Castle Dux in Bohemia when, to his surprise, Casanova arrives with Laura, Costa and Trude. Casanova presents Laura as Count Baldazzi, but the canny Waldstein realises that she is a woman and wins from Casanova the full story of how he rescued her for Hohenfels. Waldstein promises to arrange immediate leave for Hohenfels so that he may return to Venice and Casanova says that he will himself take Laura back to Venice. Waldstein, however, warns him that he is unwelcome there. Although Laura is reluctant to leave without him, Casanova must stay in Bohemia while Waldstein takes Laura to Italy (Finale: 'Mich hat mit einem Mal'/'Ein Kuss, den man nur träumt').

SCENE 7
Venice is in the midst of carnival revelry ('Karneval, du bunter, toller

1108

Karneval') when the participants in the drama return. Despite the exile imposed on him by the senate, Casanova is there, dressed as a street-singer, masked and carrying a lute, and singing of his deep love for his homeland ('Stadt der Liebe, Stadt der Freuden'). He meets Hohenfels and assures him that, for all his reputation with the women, Casanova has never broken his word as a gentleman. Laura's attachment to him is purely an affectionate one and he has been nothing more than a protector to her. Waldstein comes from the Doges' palace, leading Laura, to assure Hohenfels that he has wronged Casanova and the young man, deeply ashamed, is soon reconciled with Laura ('Ich hab' Dich lieb'), whilst Casanova showers flowers on them and wishes them well. As the celebrations reach their height ('Karneval, du bunter, toller Karneval'), Casanova is recognised by the people and, far from being hounded as an exile, is welcomed joyously back to his beloved Venice (Finale: 'Im Rausch der Genüsse').

FRIEDERIKE

a play with music in three acts by Ludwig Herzer and Fritz Löhner. Music by Franz Lehár. Produced at the Metropol-Theater, Berlin, 4 October 1928, with Richard Tauber (Goethe), Käthe Dorsch (Friederike), Curt Wespermann (Lenz) and Hilde Wörner (Salomea).

Produced at the Johann Strauss Theater, Vienna, 15 February 1929 with Richard Tauber (Goethe) and Lea Seidl (Friederike). Produced at the Rex-Theater (Stadt-Theater) 11 December 1945.

Produced at the Théâtre de la Gaîté-Lyrique, Paris, in a version by André Rivoire as *Frédérique* 17 January 1930 with René Gerbert, Louise Dhamarys, Robert Allard and Janie Marèse.

Produced at the Palace Theatre, London, in a version by Adrian Ross and Harry S Pepper as *Frederica* 9 September 1930 with Joseph Hislop, Lea Seidl, Roddy Hughes and Vera Lennox.

Produced at the Imperial Theatre, New York, in a version by Edward Eliscu 4 February 1937 with Dennis King, Helen Gleason, Ernest Truex and Doris Patston.

A film version was produced by Fritz Friedman-Frederich in 1932 with Hans Heinz Bollmann and Mady Christians.

CHARACTERS

Karl August, *Grand Duke of Saxe-Weimar*
Johann Jakob Brion, *rector of Sesenheim*
Magdalena, *his wife*
Salomea, Friederike, *their daughters*
Johann Wolfgang Goethe, *a law student*
Friedrich Leopold Weyland, *a medical student*
Jakob Michael Reinhold Lenz, *a theological student*
Franz Lerse, Georg Engelbach, *law students*
Johann Heinrich Jung-Stilling, John Meyer, *medical students*

1109

Captain Karl Ludwig von Knebel, *tutor to the princes of the Court of Weimar*
Madame Schöll
Hortense, *her daughter*
Madame Hahn
Liselotte, *her daughter*
Dorothée, Ännchen, Babette, *her friends*
Country folk, boys and girls, gentlemen and ladies of society, Madame Schöll's servants

ACT 1

From the church of the village of Sesenheim in Alsace-Lorraine, on Whit Sunday, 1771, comes the sound of the organ playing for the morning service. The rector, Johann Jakob Brion, and his wife emerge from the church and head towards the rectory, where they sit down in a garden shade for some morning coffee. They call their two daughters to join them, but Friederike, the younger, is far too engrossed in reading a book by her sweetheart Johann Wolfgang Goethe. Goethe is due to complete his medical studies shortly, and Salomea, the elder daughter, speculates that a marriage between him and Friederike might soon follow.

Friederike finally comes out of the house full of the joys of the beautiful spring day ('Gott gab einen schönen Tag') and, as she sits down with her parents, a postilion arrives with a package for her. It is from Goethe, and it contains a binding painted with roses, inside which is a poem full of romantic sentiments, which Friederike reads rapturously ('Kleine Blumen, kleine Blätter').

Salomea excitedly brings news of the arrival of some students from Strasbourg University who march in to a rousing students' song ('Mit Mädchen sich vertragen'). Salomea, the livelier of the two sisters, joins in their merriment and soon has them kneeling before her ('Mädchen sind nur zum Küssen da!'). Salomea's accepted admirer, Friedrich Weyland, is amongst the group, but she seems more interested in the whereabouts of another student, Jakob Lenz. It seems that he is merely delayed, looking for a painted binding after the manner of the one sent to Friederike by Goethe.

Salomea runs off with the students to meet Lenz, just as Goethe arrives. He has a bouquet in his hand, and he stands gazing up at the rectory, admiring it for its idyllic setting and for housing the girl he loves ('O, wie schön, wie wunderschön!'). When Friederike sees him, she rushes from the house to meet him. He gives her the bunch of flowers and they excitedly exchange expressions of love ('Blicke ich auf deine Hände').

Lenz arrives, carrying a basket and several large parcels and leading a lamb by a rope tied around his waist ('Lämmchen brav'). He failed to find a painted binding for Salomea and missed the students as he made a detour to pick up some flowers. While Friederike helps him take the gifts into the house, Goethe sits outside, writing in his notebook a new lyric about a boy who plucked a meadow rose ('Sah ein Knab' ein Röslein stehn'). The idyll must soon be over, for Goethe has work to do for his medical studies in

Strasbourg, but Friederike is planning to visit her lawyer uncle Schöll there, and they will be able to meet.

The students return (Finale I: 'Zu allen guten Stunden'), and dancing begins on the lawn. Goethe finds himself surrounded by a crowd of girls, and Lenz seizes the opportunity to warn Friederike of the dangers of loving Goethe too much. He is known to flit from girl to girl like a butterfly from one bud to another. Friederike thanks him for his concern, but declares that all she knows is that she loves him ('Ich weiss nur, dass ich ihn liebe').

ACT 2

In Madame Schöll's home in Strasbourg, on 6 August of the same year, a small company of young people are dancing a minuet. Friederike and Salomea are there, along with Goethe and his fellow students. Salomea is now engaged to Weyland, but when the ever-sociable Lenz finds himself alone with her he does his best to persuade her that he would gladly marry his 'sweet Alsace child' ('Elsässer Kind'). Goethe and Friederike are anxious to have some time together, but the poet finds himself surrounded by girls clamouring for him to write a verse in each of their albums ('Lieber Doktor, lieber Doktor!').

At last Friederike and Goethe find themselves alone and Goethe reassures her that, for all the attention he gets from the other young ladies, it is to her that his heart is truly given ('All mein Fühlen, all mein Sehnen'). They are interrupted by Weyland asking for a word with Goethe. As Friederike's future brother-in-law, he feels it is his place to tell Goethe not to trifle with her affections. He points out that Goethe is in no financial position to support a wife and Goethe responds by pulling out of his pocket a letter offering him a post as poet at the Court of Weimar. He could scarcely want more than such an appointment, together with the love of a girl such as Friederike ('O Mädchen, mein Mädchen!').

Captain Knebel arrives from Weimar to accompany Goethe to his new position at Court and, in the course of the conversation between the two, it comes out that Goethe's predecessor in the position had lost his post because the pressures of marriage and a family had restricted his creativity. The Duke of Weimar is determined this time to have a bachelor in the post. Goethe at once tells him that he is no longer interested, but Knebel takes him into the garden to talk it over. Friederike asks Weyland what is happening and is told that she will be unable to accompany her lover to Weimar. If she were to stand in his way, it would mean misery for both of them. Broken-hearted, she reflects on the way her feelings of love were awoken by his kisses, only to be dashed by this blow ('Warum hast du mich wachgeküsst?').

Lenz comes up and asks Friederike to dance, but she tells him she is waiting for Goethe and will dance with him later. Goethe comes to tell Friederike that he has turned down the position at Weimar, but in her heart she knows that she cannot allow him to make such a sacrifice and, when Lenz comes by, she pointedly takes up his earlier offer of a dance. Goethe is shocked by her seeming indifference to him (Finale II: 'Liebe, seliger

Traum') and he tells Knebel that he will, after all, accept the Weimar appointment. He bids Friederike a cold farewell and leaves her feeling like the meadow rose plucked by the boy in Goethe's lyric.

ACT 3

Back in Sesenheim, on 25 September 1779, the organ is again playing. Eight years have passed since Friederike's friendship with Goethe was so abruptly ended, and Salomea is married to Weyland, but Friederike has remained single despite the attentions of the faithful Lenz. As Friederike comes out of the house, some of the village girls call to her to dance with them in the meadow ('Riekchen, komm mit uns zum Tanz') but Friederike answers lifelessly, warning the girls against following the urging of one's heart.

Lenz comes to try to cheer her, but she brushes him aside, telling him that nobody who has loved Goethe can love anyone else. Then Salomea enters, announcing that her husband's behaviour has become intolerable and that she is leaving him. Lenz, as usual, is ready to offer himself as a substitute, and together he and Salomea lightheartedly dance a country dance ('Heute tanzen wir den Pfälzertanz'). Once again, however, Lenz's attentions go for nothing, since Weyland himself appears and quickly proceeds to make things up with his wife.

Then Goethe returns. The poet has not seen Friederike in the intervening eight years, but now he is passing through Sesenheim on his way to Switzerland with the Grand Duke Karl-August. He tells the Duke that this was the place where he spent the happiest hours of his life. Here his youth passed and a heart as pure as gold was his ('Ein Herz, wie Gold so rein'). The rector, his wife and Friederike come from the house to meet him. This is the moment for which Friederike has waited eight years and she is overjoyed to see him again. Now Goethe finally realises the truth and the extent of the sacrifice that Friederike made for him all those years ago, but his duties mean that he must move on once again—this time for good. At least, through his writings, Goethe now belongs to the whole world, and thus also to Friederike.

The synopsis follows Lehár's final version of the work, with the placings of 'Elsässer Kind' and 'Heute tanzen wir den Pfälzertanz' reversed from their original positions.

DAS LAND DES LÄCHELNS

(The Land of Smiles)

a romantic operetta in three acts by Ludwig Herzer and Fritz Löhner, based on the libretto *Die gelbe Jacke* by Victor Léon (9 February 1923, Theater an der Wien).

Music by Franz Lehár. Produced at the Metropol-Theater, Berlin, 10 October 1929 with Richard Tauber as Sou-Chong.

Produced at the Theater an der Wien, Vienna, 26 September 1930 with Richard Tauber as Sou-Chong and Vera Schwarz as Lisa. Produced at the Vienna State Opera 30 January 1938. Produced at the Raimundtheater 26 May 1945. Produced at the Volksoper 17 February 1985 with Siegfried Jerusalem and Mirjana Irosch.

Produced at the Theatre Royal, Drury Lane, London, in a version by Harry Graham as *The Land of Smiles* 8 May 1931, with Richard Tauber (Sou-Chong), Renée Bullard (Lisa), Hella Kürty (Mi) and George Vollaire (Gustl). Played at the Dominion Theatre 31 May 1932 with Tauber, Josie Fearon, Kürty and Patrick Waddington and at the Lyric Theatre 18 June 1942 with Tauber, Fearon, Kürty and Charles Gillespie. Produced at Sadler's Wells Theatre in a version by Christopher Hassall 1959 with Charles Craig, Elizabeth Fretwell, June Bronhill and Peter Grant.

Produced at the Shubert Theatre, New York, in a version by Harry Graham, Ira Cobb, Karl Farkas and Felix Guenther as *Yours Is My Heart* 5 September 1946 with Richard Tauber, Stella Andreva and Lillian Held.

Produced at the Théâtre Royal, Ghent, in a version by André Mauprey and Jean Marietti as *Le Pays de Sourire* 1 April 1932 with Louis Izar (Sou-Chong), Germaine Roumans (Lisa), Mlle Berthot (Mi) and Goris de Ville (Gustl). Produced at the Théâtre de la Gaité-Lyrique, Paris, 15 November 1932 with Willy Theunis, Georgette Simon, Coecilia Navarre and Paul Darnois and revived there 24 November 1937, 1940, 1949 with Rudi Hirigoyen and Madeleine Vernon, 1951 with Michel Dens and Jacqueline de Bourges, and 15 September 1957 with Dens. Produced at the Théâtre du Châtelet 20 December 1975 with Hito Hayashi/Aldo Filisted and Monique de Pondeau/Odette Romagnoni. Produced at the Théâtre Mogador 4 November 1978 with Hayashi/François Garcia and Marion Sylvestre/Janine Furno.

A film version was produced by Max Reichmann in 1931 with Tauber and another in 1952 with Jan Kiepura.

CHARACTERS

Count Ferdinand Lichtenfels, *an army lieutenant*
Lisa, *his daughter*
Lora, *his niece*
Count Gustav (Gustl) von Pottenstein, *a lieutenant of the dragoons*
An old lady, *his aunt*
Fini, Franzi, Vally, Toni, *young ladies*
Prince Sou-Chong
Mi, *his sister*
Tschang, *his uncle*
Fu-Li, *First Secretary to the Chinese Embassy*
Officers of various units and their ladies, ladies and gentlemen of society, mandarins, servants

ACT 1

It is 1912, and in a room of Count Lichtenfels's elegant Viennese mansion a soirée is in progress. Amid the dancing, one of the guests offers a special toast to the host's daughter, Lisa, as a congratulation on her success at a horse show. The guests energetically take up the call ('Hoch soll sie leben!'), and Lisa responds with gratitude ('Ich danke für die Huldigung'). She can find little enthusiasm in her heart for the occasion, however, for she is disenchanted with the empty flirting that is a feature of society balls and is anxious for something more lasting and more meaningful to come into her life ('Gern, gern wär' ich verliebt').

Her most particular admirer is Count Gustav von Pottenstein of the dragoons, and Lisa turns most of the credit for her equestrian triumph back to him, as her trainer. Gustl is pinkly pleased, but he is shy at making his feelings for Lisa known to her and, when he presents her with a bouquet, he does so in the name of his regiment. His bouquet is made to look very insignificant, however, by another gift, a very fine Chinese statuette sent by another admirer, the Chinese Prince Sou-Chong.

Tonight, at last, Gustl manages to pluck up courage to tell Lisa of his feelings and to ask for her hand in marriage. He has, he tells her, already saved the twenty thousand crowns required of an officer for permission to marry. Lisa is taken completely by surprise. Fond of him as she is, she cannot think of marriage. Before his disappointed face, she tells him gently that it is neither the first nor the last time that two friends have had to go their separate ways, and he should not make too much of it ('Freunderl, mach' dir nix draus').

Shortly after this, Prince Sou-Chong is announced. He asks for Lisa and, as he stands awaiting her, he gazes in wonder at the place where his beloved lives, but, true to the tradition of Chinese inscrutability, he keeps his feelings hidden behind an expressionless mask ('Immer nur lächeln'). When Lisa comes to meet him, the conversation progresses formally and somewhat uneasily. He thanks her for the invitation and she expresses her gratitude to him for the magnificent gift. It is, he tells her, an heirloom which has been in the family for generations. The difference in their social customs makes it difficult for Lisa to entertain the Prince. Sou-Chong is not accustomed to eat at such an hour and he will not touch alcohol, but Lisa manages to find common ground with the offer of a cup of tea ('Bei einem Tee à deux').

The Prince proves a great attraction for the girls at the party, who ask him to tell them how courting takes place in China. 'On a moonlit night in April I lay a bouquet of apple-blossom by the window of my loved one,' he begins ('Von Apfelblüten einen Kranz'). The girls are enchanted, but further lessons on Chinese love are cut short by the arrival of a messenger from the Chinese Legation. Sou-Chong has been appointed Prime Minister of his country and must return to China immediately.

Lisa is truly upset and seeks a moment alone with the Prince to say farewell (Finale I: 'Wir sind allein'). She tells him that to her he is like someone from another world, and Sou-Chong agrees, telling her how difficult it is for him to fit into Viennese life. She asks if there is nothing that he is sad to be leaving behind, and he replies that he is leaving behind the dearest thing of all. 'Take it with you, then,' she says, adding that she would go with him to the end of the world—if she were that dearest thing. 'Don't you see my strange face and eyes?' he asks. 'I see only you,' she replies, and they declare their love for each other in ways that both of them understand ('Von Apfelblüten einen Kranz').

ACT 2

In Sou-Chong's palace in Peking the ceremony installing him in his new office has begun ('Dschinthien wuomen ju chon ma goa can'). After a ceremonial procession, the Prince's uncle Tschang summons him in the name of Wen Sway Jeh and proudly invests him with the ceremonial yellow jacket. When the investiture is complete, a servant appears with the information that Madame Lotus Blossom wishes to speak to Sou-Chong. This is Lisa, who is now living in China with Sou-Chong as his wife. She has ruffled Tschang's feathers with her western customs, and only Sou-Chong and his sister Mi have made her at all welcome. She is upset at having been excluded from Sou-Chong's installation, but Sou-Chong reassures her that in his eyes there is nobody else who matters in the world, and Lisa gives him a medallion with her portrait as a souvenir of his special day. Their deep affection for each other is instantly reaffirmed ('Wer hat die Liebe uns ins Herz gesenkt').

Mi enters, sighing over the ways in which Chinese customs keep women repressed compared with the western freedom that she sees Lisa enjoying ('Im Salon zur blau'n Pagode'). Then Gustl arrives. He has managed to get himself posted to Peking as a military attaché and today he has been making up numbers for tennis, a sport that Mi has also happily taken up, to the disgust of Uncle Tschang who cannot cope with the sight of Mi in tennis shorts. Gustl and Mi have become quite fond of each other and they muse together over the difference that exists between western and eastern customs despite the fact that God made everyone equal with the same feelings in their heart ('Meine Liebe, deine Liebe').

Sou-Chong and Tschang inevitably come to hard words over his western wife. Tschang reminds Sou-Chong that, according to Chinese custom, Lisa is not his wife but his slave. To satisfy Chinese conventions he must marry four native girls and the date for the ceremony has already been fixed. Sou-Chong insists that, if he were to go through with the ritual, it would be a mere façade. He passionately declares that his whole heart is devoted to Lisa ('Dein ist mein ganzes Herz').

Gustl is about to go and pay his respects to Sou-Chong, when Lisa appears. She is overjoyed to see him and asks about Vienna, but she denies any suggestion that she is unhappy in Peking and she laughs off his suggestion that Sou-Chong would follow the ancient Chinese custom to the extent of taking on his four wives. When Sou-Chong arrives with his uncle, however, he tells her that he must go through with the ceremony, even though it will be an empty ritual, but Uncle Tschang will hear nothing of empty ritual and is emphatic that, as far as he is concerned, following the weddings, Lisa will no longer be allowed in the palace.

Lisa is distraught. She begs Gustl to advise her what to do and suddenly she is overcome by a longing for home ('Ich möcht wieder einmal die Heimat seh'n'). She tells Sou-Chong that she is leaving, but the Prince forbids it. 'By what right?' she retorts (Finale II: 'Mit welchem Recht?'). 'I am your master,' he answers. 'Here you must blindly obey my word.' Lisa sees her dream of love being dashed. 'You have turned love to hate,' she tells him, as she rushes out. Sou-Chong calls to his guards to prevent her leaving, but he too sees his one true love at an end. Taking from his tunic the medallion with Lisa's portrait, he sadly contemplates the love that was his ('Dein war mein ganzes Herz').

ACT 3

A week later, in a room in the women's quarters of the house, Lisa is being consoled by her servants ('Märchen vom Glück'). Mi tells her how much Sou-Chong is suffering without her, but Lisa can no longer love him. A knock at the door announces the arrival of Gustl, who has come to find her despite the danger he runs of being found in the women's quarters. He tells Lisa that he has a plan for her escape.

Overjoyed though Mi is for them, she cannot avoid pangs of sadness at the prospect of losing both Lisa and Gustl, but she covers her feelings with a Chinese expression of joy—Zig, zig, zig, zig, ih! Gustl promises that he will always remember the lovely, sweet, tender, little Chinese girl and the chrysanthemums blooming by the Pa-i-ho river ('Zig, zig, zig, zig, ih! Wenn die Chrysanthemen blüh'n') as Mi bids them farewell and, left alone, gives in to her true feelings of profound unhappiness at the departure of 'the foreign white man' ('Wie rasch verwelkte doch!'). As she bursts into tears, a violent knocking is heard. Lisa and Gustl have returned. They have found their escape barred, and Mi sees nothing for it but to commit the sacrilege of letting them escape through the sacred temple of Buddha. But there too their way is blocked. Sou-Chong is waiting for them. Lisa pleads with him that to let her go is the only solution (Finale III: 'Diesselbe Sonne') and, at last, the Prince relents. He commits Lisa to Gustl's care and, when Lisa has bid her fond farewell to Mi, they slowly depart. Sou-Chong tenderly puts his arm around his weeping sister ('Liebes Schwesterlein') and seeks to hide his own sorrow behind the enigmatic Chinese smile ('Immer nur lächeln').

Das Land des Lächelns is a dramatically and musically much strengthened version of *Die gelbe Jacke*. Several numbers, among them 'Immer nur lächeln' and 'Von Apfelblüten einen Kranz', were taken over virtually unchanged, while new ones (including 'Dein ist mein ganzes Herz') replaced less durable numbers such as a comedy shimmy duet with the refrain 'Wir woll'n in's Kino geh'n und den Charlie Chaplin seh'n'.

VIKTORIA UND IHR HUSAR

(Viktoria and Her Hussar)

an operetta in a prologue and three acts by Alfred Grünwald and Fritz Löhner-Beda from the Hungarian of Emmerich Földes. Music by Paul Abrahám. Produced at the Stadttheater, Leipzig, 7 July 1930 and in Berlin, 1930 with Lizzi Waldmüller (Lia San) and Oscar Dénes (Ferry). Produced at the Theater an der Wien, Vienna, 23 December 1930.

Produced at the Palace Theatre, London, in a version by Harry Graham 17 September 1931 with Roy Russell (Stefan), Margaret Carlisle (Viktoria), Harry Welchman (John Cunlight), Reginald Purdell (Janczi) and Oscar Dénes (Ferry).

Produced at the Théâtre du Moulin-Rouge, Paris, in a version by André Mauprey and René Coens as *Viktoria et son Hussard* 16 December 1933 with Grazia del Rio, Mercier, Péraldi, Marcel Lamy and Lilli Palmer.

A film version was produced by Richard Oswald in 1931 with Michael Bohnen, Friedl Schuster, Ivan Petrovitch, Gretl Theimer, Ernst Verebes and Julius von Szöreghy.

CHARACTERS

John Cunlight, *American Ambassador*
Countess Viktoria, *his wife*
Count Ferry Hegedüs *from Doroszma, Viktoria's brother*
O Lia San, *Ferry's bride*
Riquette, *Viktoria's maid*
Tokeramo Yagami, *Japanese attaché*
Stefan Koltay, *a Captain of the Hussars*
Janczi, *his batman*
Béla Pörkölty, *the mayor of Doroszma*
A Russian officer
A Japanese bonze
Kamaruki o Miki, *a Japanese lackey*
James, *butler at the American Embassy*
Japanese gentlemen, Hungarian peasant girls, servants, maids, a coolie, Cossacks, officers of the Hussars, dignitaries

PROLOGUE

In the wilds of Siberia, in the aftermath of the First World War, a group of prisoners are longing for home ('An des Baikals Strand'). Amongst them are two Hungarians—Stefan Koltay, a Captain of the Hussars, and his batman Janczi. Having unsuccessfully fought in the Russian counter-revolution, Koltay is under sentence of death and is due to be sent before the firing squad in a quarter of an hour. He is enjoying a final reminiscence with Janczi of their home town of Doroszma, and how they enjoyed themselves there in the days of their youth, Koltay the expert dancer of the *csárdás*, and Janczi the gipsy violinist. Stefan tells Janczi to take up his violin, and he sings and dances the *csárdás* one last time ('Nur ein Mädel gibt es auf der Welt').

As he finishes, a Cossack comes up and, looking at Janczi's violin, rasps

1117

out 'Your violin—I want it!' At first Janczi refuses, but then the Cossack reveals that he was once a musician in the imperial orchestra in St Petersburg under Rimsky-Korsakoff and, more to the point, he tells them that, if Janczi will give him his violin, he will let them escape. While the guards are watching elsewhere, the Cossack opens the gate of the camp and hurries them through. When the sergeant of the guard arrives to take Stefan to his execution, the Cossack points to the fleeing figures and the guards set off in pursuit.

ACT 1

In the Japanese garden of the American Embassy in Tokyo, servants and flower-girls are busily preparing a wedding feast ('Glück und Freude heut' im Haus'). The marriage is that of the Ambassadress's brother to a Japanese girl, Lia San, but it is by no means a completely happy occasion for it also marks the departure of their beloved mistress, Viktoria, on the posting of her husband, Ambassador John Cunlight, to St Petersburg.

Viktoria elegantly pays thanks to the staff for the welcome they have given her and reflects sadly that she must bid farewell to them all, as well as to the red orchids and chrysanthemums of the Japanese garden ('Rote Orchideen'). She declares that of all cities Tokyo comes second only to New York in her affections, though there is one small town that almost means more to her than anything—Doroszma, her home town. Viktoria is in a singularly reflective mood this evening and, alone with her husband, she recalls the occasion when he first proposed to her at a Court Ball in Vienna. 'I must have proposed to you twenty times before you would have me,' he laughs. 'Thirty,' she corrects him. 'But that was the first!' ('Pardon, Madame')

After the two have left the garden, Koltay and Janczi appear, and the latter soon becomes engaged in conversation with Riquette, the Ambassadress's French maid. Spotting a statuette, Janczi asks who the bronzed gentleman might be. 'That's Buddha!' is her surprised reply. 'Oh, is he the one who discovered Budapest?' Janczi asks. The two men have come to the Embassy because the previous day Koltay had seen Viktoria in the Ambassador's car. He wonders how she comes to be in Tokyo, and he recalls how, as he went off to war, she swore a vow of everlasting fidelity to him.

When the Ambassador appears, Koltay introduces himself as Captain Czaky, an Hungarian citizen, and tells him that he and Janczi have escaped from imprisonment in Siberia. Cunlight declares himself happy to give them protection, particularly in view of the fact that his wife is herself Hungarian. The Ambassador offers to take Koltay with him to St Petersburg under his diplomatic protection, but Koltay has no wish to go back to Russia. For the present he gladly accepts the Ambassador's offer of a change of clothes.

As the time for the wedding approaches, the bride appears with her four Japanese ladies-in-waiting. Lia San is understandably excited as the bells ring and she reflects that soon her loved one will be hers ('Heut wird er mein!'). To her husband-to-be she confides her joy that the wedding is to take place at this season. How much better it is to marry during winter. 'Why

1118

is that?' he asks. 'Because the nights are much longer,' she replies. 'Ah, this Japan!' Ferry replies. He will never quite come to terms with his wife's international personality—she has a Japanese mother but a Parisian father ('Meine Mama war aus Yokohama'). Meanwhile Janczi, now elegantly decked out in evening dress, is developing his friendship with Riquette. He believes that in her he has at last found the right girl for him, and she offers him eternal love—with a one-year guarantee! She begs him to take her with him when he returns to Hungary the next day ('Ungarland! Donaustrand! Heimatland!').

The assembled guests greet the bride in her white silk wedding dress (Finale I: 'Haho! Haho! Schöne Braut!') and, as the head bonze performs the marriage ceremony, the bells ring out, and Japanese girls perform a wedding dance. 'All very nice,' proclaims Janczi, 'but Hungarian music is something else!' Cunlight invites him to play something and borrows a violin from the dance band. 'You're Hungarian?' Viktoria asks in surprise and, when Janczi starts playing, she joins in the song of her native Doroszma ('Nur ein Mädel gibt es auf der Welt!'). 'And now, Viktoria,' her husband tells her, 'I have a big surprise for you!' He calls forward the supposed Captain Czaky. Viktoria and Koltay gaze in astonishment at each other, both remembering their last sad farewell and Viktoria's pledge to Koltay when he went off to the war.

ACT 2

Koltay and Janczi have accompanied the Ambassador to St Petersburg, where Koltay is now an attaché in the splendidly appointed American Embassy. Janczi is still longing to see Doroszma again, but Koltay tells him that they will go home only when Viktoria goes with him. So far, since their reunion, Viktoria has avoided his further glances. At least Janczi has Riquette with him, though she is hardly less impatient than he is to set off on the promised journey to matrimony. She seeks comfort from Ferry, who promises to try to speed matters up by getting Koltay a meeting with Viktoria. First, though, he confides to Riquette that she reminds him of a variety performer in London, who with her partner sang a very crazy song ('Wir singen beide: Do do do Dodo!').

This evening, during a reception at the Embassy, Viktoria at last brings herself to speak nervously to Koltay. She tells him that he must not linger in St Petersburg where he runs the risk of being retaken by the Russians, but Koltay cannot be satisfied with that. He tells her that only his thoughts of her kept him going through war and imprisonment, and yet now he finds her the wife of another. She assures him that she waited faithfully for him until she received word that his regiment had been wiped out. His name was on the list of casualties, and the War Ministry confirmed the news. Cunlight had helped her get over the shock and, such was his kindness and patience, at length she agreed to marry him. Koltay tells her what she meant to him, and she assures him that he was everything to her, but now she loves another and can do nothing to change it ('Du warst der Stern meiner Nacht').

They are interrupted when Cunlight comes in and takes his wife to dance to the waltz that the orchestra has struck up in the adjoining salon. Janczi rushes to tell Koltay that Viktoria has arranged travel visas for them, but Koltay repeats that Viktoria must come with him or he will not go. Ferry anxiously tells Lia San of the soldiers who can be seen gathering outside in the square and Lia San is frightened, but Ferry tells her to have courage. Together they laugh at the fun they have been having together on their honeymoon, and their laughter soon becomes unrestrained ('Mausi, süss warst du heute Nacht').

Viktoria returns and rejoins Koltay. He tells her that she belongs to him, and to him alone, but she only repeats her warnings of the risks he takes by staying in St Petersburg, and reminds him of the promises that she made to her husband before God. It was a beautiful fairy tale, but now it must be 'good night' ('Reich mir zum Abschied noch einmal die Hände!'). Suddenly Koltay rouses himself from his gloom and tells Janczi that they are going home to Doroszma. Overjoyed, Janczi tells Riquette, who chooses this moment to reveal that she is not really French, but a Budapest girl called Marika which gives him the opportunity to describe to her the trumpets and drums of a military band—the Honved-Banda—that played when he was last in Budapest ('Honved-Banda').

Ferry brings news that the palace is surrounded. Nobody can leave. The Russian soldiers have had word that a Hungarian soldier—a condemned man—is being sheltered there. His name is Koltay. Cunlight realises who Captain Czaky really is, and realises at the same time that his wife's lover is still alive. Viktoria assures him that her husband is the one she now loves, and Cunlight sends word to the waiting soldiers that they must have made a mistake. Koltay, however, asks the Embassy secretary for writing paper.

Russian dancers have been hired for the evening's entertainment (Finale II: 'Hei! Hei! Wolgamädel tanz' mit mir?'), and after their display the Ambassador persuades his reluctant wife to sing a Russian song ('Schöne Petrowna, Fedorowna'). The ball resumes, but then a Russian officer enters the Embassy. 'On what authority do you force your way in?' Cunlight asks him angrily, and the soldier produces a letter in the Ambassador's name. When the Ambassador points out that the signature is not his, Koltay steps forward and admits that he wrote the letter. He tells Viktoria that he cannot accept his life from one who has taken her from him and, from Viktoria's desperate reactions, Cunlight realises that his wife still loves Koltay. Now it is Cunlight who prepares to bid Viktoria 'good night'. He will fulfil the promise he made when she gratefully gave herself to him as his wife, to go away without any ill-will or reproach when she was no longer happy at his side.

ACT 3
A year later, in the town of Doroszma the local people are celebrating the gathering of the grape harvest ('Winzerfest, Weinlesefest!'), and the mayor, Pörkelty, urges on Janczi's gipsy fiddling, before making a speech. He

reminds them of the old custom whereby every year, on the day of the wine festival, three marriages must be celebrated. Janczi and Riquette will form one couple. Ferry and Lia San will be the second, since Japanese marriages are not recognised in Doroszma. As yet, they haven't got a third couple.

Viktoria appears, dressed in the clothes she wore as a young woman in Doroszma ('Nur ein Ungarn, gibt es auf der Welt'). She has been travelling round the world alone, trying to find peace within herself, ever since the dramatic events in St Petersburg, and she is delighted to be back amongst the simple pleasures of her little home town. She finds that not much has changed. Janczi observes to Riquette that Viktoria's marriage to an American was a geographical error. A Hungarian should marry a Hungarian, as Riquette and Janczi have done ('Ja, so ein Mädel, ungarisches Mädel').

Meanwhile Ferry has in mind that Viktoria should form one half of the third couple to be married. Though she has been separated from Cunlight for a year now, Ferry has heard that her husband is in Budapest and he has telegraphed him to come to Doroszma. Their reunion will thus provide the third marriage. A chauffeur-driven car pulls up, and out steps Cunlight. Viktoria is happy to pledge herself anew to him.

Pörkelty reminds everyone of the 'wine test', whereby it is determined whether a bride has made the right choice. If, when a bride has drunk from a flask of Saint Imre wine, she throws her arms around her fiancé's neck, she has made the correct choice. The tests on the three couples begin (Finale III: 'Winzerfest! Weinlesefest!'). Riquette and Lia San pass the test but, as Viktoria raises her glass to Cunlight, there comes the sound of military music and marching hussars. It is Koltay, at the head of his regiment, announcing that he has come to join in the celebrations. Viktoria reaffirms her dedication to Cunlight but, when she has drunk the wine, she turns first to Cunlight, then to Koltay, and finally rushes into Koltay's arms. Cunlight reveals that it is he who has arranged for Koltay to be there. He, himself, would come only to make Viktoria happy, and now he has done that. As the lovers embrace, his chauffeur drives him off into the sunset.

IM WEISSEN RÖSSL

(At the White Horse Inn)

a play with songs in three acts by Hans Müller and Eric Charell, after the comedy of the same name by Oskar Blumenthal and Gustav Kadelburg. Lyrics by Robert Gilbert. Music by Ralph Benatzky, with additional songs by Robert Stolz, Bruno Granichstädten and Robert Gilbert. Produced at the Grosses Schauspielhaus, Berlin, 8 November 1930 with Camilla Spira (Josepha), Max Hansen (Leopold), Otto Wallburger (Giesecke), Trude Lieske (Ottilie), Sig Arno (Sigismund) and Paul Hörbiger (Emperor Franz Joseph).

Produced at the Wiener Stadttheater, Vienna, 25 September 1931, and at the Theater an der Wien, 7 December 1933. Produced at the Wiener Arbeiterbühne, 18

July 1945. Produced at the Volksoper 1 March 1976 with Christiane Hörbiger, Peter Minich, Heinz Reincke, Eva Serning, Ossy Kolmann and Fred Liewehr.

Produced at the London Coliseum in a version by Harry Graham with further interpolated numbers by Robert Stolz as *White Horse Inn* 8 April 1931 with Lea Seidl, Clifford Mollison, Jack Barty, Rita Page, Bruce Carfax, George Gee and Friedrich Leisteg. Revived there 20 March 1940 with Nita Croft, Derek Oldham, Hal Bryan, Nancy Burne, Gordon Little and Eddie Childs.

Produced at the Center Theatre, New York, 1 October 1936 with Kitty Carlisle, William Gaxton and Robert Halliday.

Produced at the Théâtre Mogador, Paris, in a version by Lucien Besnard and René Dorin with further interpolated numbers by Robert Stolz and others by Anton Profès as *L'Auberge du Cheval Blanc* 1 October 1932 with Gabrielle Ristori, Georges Milton, Charpin, Rose Carday, Goavec and Robert Allard, and revived there 31 August 1935 and 9 November 1979 with Arta Verlen, Francis Joffo, Paul Mercey, Maria Baroni, Jean-Paul Caffi and Philippe Andrey. Produced at the Théâtre du Châtelet 30 October 1948 with Yvonne Darries, Luc Barney, Carpentier, Janine Delille, Guy Fontagnères and Luc Frébert, and revived there 19 December 1953 with Colette Riedinger, Barney, Fernand Sardou, Lina Dachary, Bernard Plantey and Jack Claret, 29 October 1960 with Janine Ribot, Bernard Lavalette, Marcel Rozet, Michèle Sylva, Michel Caron and Serge Clin and 29 September 1968 in a revised version with Eliane Varon, Robert Piquet, André Jobin, Jean Louis Simon and Danielle Castaing. Produced at the Théâtre Mogador 1977. Produced at the El Dorado 26 November 1987 with Françoise Peyrol/Sophie Norton, Dozier and Barney (Bistagne).

A film version was produced by Carl Lamac in 1934 with Christl Mardayn, Hermann Thimig and Theo Lingen.

CHARACTERS

Josepha Vogelhuber, *landlady of the White Horse inn*
Leopold Brandmeyer, *head waiter*
Wilhelm Giesecke, *a manufacturer*
Ottilie, *his daughter*
Dr Otto Siedler, *a solicitor*
Sigismund Sülzheimer
Professor Dr Hinzelmann
Klärchen, *his daughter*
Emperor Franz Joseph II
Waiters, guides, guests, servants, children, hunters, villagers and others.

ACT 1

In the picturesque Austrian village of St Wolfgang, on Lake Wolfgang, stands the White Horse inn. Now that the tourist season is under way there is great activity at the inn as another batch of visitors, shepherded by their guide, clamour for their breakfast ('Hallo! Wirtschaft! Frühstück! Frühstück!'). The head waiter, Leopold, is fully master of the situation as he goes calmly from table to table dealing with orders before the tourists settle their bills and move on again, leaving their places free for the next crowd ('Aber, meine Herrschaften! Nur hübsch gemütlich!').

However efficiently Leopold may deal with his customers, he has less control over his heart. His heart draws him most particularly towards his boss, the inn's landlady Josepha, but she gives him little enough encouragement. Indeed, in the three years since her husband's death she has already sacked five head waiters for becoming too familiar with her. Leopold is not to be put off by statistics. 'It would be wonderful to be loved by you, because my love is yours as long as I live on this earth,' he assures her ('Es muss was Wunderbares sein!'). Josepha is much more concerned with the running of the inn than with affairs of the heart, though truth to tell she does pay rather more than usual attention to preparing room number 4 for a certain Dr Siedler, a solicitor from Berlin.

The sound of a ship's siren announces the approach of the next batch of holidaymakers, and chambermaids, mountain guides, porters and children selling sprigs of violets prepare themselves for the onslaught ('Das ist der Zauber der Saison'). Among the new guests brought by the steamer are a honeymoon couple. They care not at all whether they have a room in the main building or the annexe, with or without a lake view, or with a double or single bed. Such is not the case with Herr Giesecke, a manufacturer of ladies' underwear, who has arrived with his daughter Ottilie from Berlin. He very definitely wants a room with a balcony and lake view, and he is not at all pleased to be told by Leopold that the only one left is the one that Josepha has set aside for Dr Siedler. Giesecke knows the name of Siedler well, since the lawyer once acted for a business rival of his named Sülzheimer in a lawsuit over the patenting of a design of cami-knickers, and this makes him even more determined to have room number 4. Since Leopold sees Siedler as his rival in love for Josepha, he is only too glad to spite the lawyer by giving the balcony room to Giesecke.

When Siedler arrives, looking forward to the pleasures of the White Horse inn, he is greeted warmly by Josepha ('Im Weissen Rössl am Wolfgangsee'), but when he discovers Giesecke occupying the room which has been his for the past seven years, sparks begin to fly. Josepha turns the Gieseckes out, and Siedler's anger is mollified further when he discovers that Ottilie Giesecke is a decidedly attractive young woman. She, in her turn, is so taken by Siedler that, when Giesecke decides that they should move on to another hotel, Ottilie refuses. 'Out of the question! I like it here. I'm staying,' she tells her father.

This unforeseen, but highly satisfactory situation gives the ever-resourceful Leopold the opportunity to offer some further services. Anxious to promote the romance between Siedler and Ottilie, he arranges a rendezvous for them by the cow-shed, where the cow-hands are busy ('Eine Kuh, so wie du, ist das Schönste auf der Welt!'), and Siedler loses no time telling Ottilie how much more splendid he has found it in St Wolfgang since she arrived. 'Everything has become so much more beautiful—the mountains, the lake, the sky.' ('Die ganze Welt ist himmelblau')

When Josepha comes looking for Leopold, he asks her if her heart really feels nothing for him. 'Never mind my heart,' she replies. 'Keep your mind on the liver, the kidneys and the veal chops!' When he attempts to kiss her,

1123

she slaps his face and Leopold is left to bewail his lack of success as a lover (Finale I: 'Es muss was Wunderbares sein'). Still, love must take a back seat when there are clamouring guests to be looked after ('Im Weissen Rössl am Wolfgangsee'), especially when their immediate enjoyment is dampened by a sudden downpour which forces everyone to reach for umbrellas ('Wenn es hier mal richtig regnet').

ACT 2

At the market that takes place every week in the square in front of the inn, the stallholders are crying their wares ('Alle schönen guten Gaben'). Josepha is buying flowers to decorate Dr Siedler's room, much to the disgust of Leopold, who refuses to take them up to number 4. By now he has offended so much that Josepha has no choice but to make him the sixth head waiter dismissed in three years. Leopold pleads with her in vain. He would have stolen horses for her and leapt into water for her, but he can hardly be expected to watch impassively her advances to another man ('Zuschau'n kann i net').

From his balcony, Siedler wishes Josepha 'good morning' and, while the good woman is preparing his breakfast, he sidles off to meet up with Ottilie. The two of them have discovered that love at first sight is not merely a fiction of the film industry, though they are concerned that, given recent events, for them it may not be allowed to last ('Es ist wohl nicht das letzte Mal'). Siedler, however, has dreamed up a plan to get Ottilie's father on their side. Giesecke, who has spent the night uncomfortably lodged in the billiard-room and has not slept a wink, is little inclined to appreciate the beauties of the Salzkammergut. He compares it unfavourably with Berlin resorts such as Ahlbeck and Grünewald, but Josepha gets him more into the holiday mood with a spot of thigh slapping and a clog-dance ('Im Salzkammergut, da kann man gut lustig sein!').

In this more receptive frame of mind Giesecke is approached by Siedler with an interesting proposal. The differences between Giesecke and Sülzheimer, his adversary in the cami-knickers dispute, might be settled by a dynastic marriage between Sülzheimer's son, Sigismund, and Ottilie. Giesecke's businessman's soul is most receptive to this idea and he is delighted to hear that Siedler has already made the first steps towards this happy conclusion. Sigismund Sülzheimer is on his way to St Wolfgang at this very moment. Giesecke charges Siedler with the task of keeping a close eye on developments, an uneccessary charge since Siedler has every intention of watching Ottilie closely, though not exactly with Sigismund's interests in mind.

Sigismund arrives wearing a hat, which he removes to reveal that he is completely bald. He nonetheless believes that he has a kind of natural beauty. 'How can Sigismund help it that he's so handsome?' he asks ('Was kann der Sigismund dafür, dass er so schön ist?'). Sigismund's attentions, however, are directed not at Ottilie, but at another guest, Klärchen, daughter of Professor Hinzelmann. Sigismund invites Klärchen to accompany him to the swimming pool, where the bathers are thoroughly enjoying themselves ('Wir tauchen dann zusammen munter'). With Sigismund's baldness matched by Klärchen's stutter, the two make a fine match for each other and they are soon exchanging romantic thoughts ('Und als der Herrgott Mai gemacht').

News arrives that the Emperor Franz Joseph intends to visit St Wolfgang for the shooting festival. There is nowhere better for him to stay than at the White Horse inn. Surely Josepha's hostelry will be honoured with the royal presence. But how can she manage without her head waiter? Leopold is prepared to come back, but on one condition—that it is Dr Siedler's room which is given over to the Emperor. As the band plays, people march and flags are waved in welcome to their Emperor (Finale II: 'Rechtes Bein und linkes Bein'). Leopold nervously makes a speech of welcome but, as he does so, he catches sight of Josepha with Dr Siedler on the balcony of room number 4. Josepha has a bouquet for the Emperor, but Leopold sees her take a single flower from it and place it in Siedler's buttonhole. He instinctively tries to persuade the Emperor against staying at the White Horse inn, and Josepha retrieves the situation only just in time as she presents the Emperor with the remainder of the bouquet. Poor Leopold cannot help his eyes welling up with tears.

ACT 3

As dawn breaks, the people of St Wolfgang and the town band perform a morning serenade to their Emperor ('Leise, leise, leise, leise') and Franz Josef appears on the balcony to give his thanks for the greeting. As Josepha serves him his breakfast, she allows the story of her relationship with Leopold to come out, and the Emperor offers her the benefit of his long experience. One should temper one's ideals with reality and accept one's once-in-a-lifetime opportunities (''s ist einmal im Leben so').

Leopold has by now decided to give up waitering and become a local government officer. He is preparing to say good-bye to the White Horse inn, but when Josepha sees Siedler with Ottilie she realises what the true position between them is and, remembering the Emperor's advice, she looks seriously into her heart. When Leopold comes to get a reference from her he finds that she has written 'Dismissed as head waiter for interference in my private affairs, but engaged for life as my husband.'

In the garden restaurant of the inn, Giesecke and Hinzelmann are sitting chatting together over a glass of wine when Siedler arrives with a telegram from Sülzheimer, giving his consent to his son's marriage and offering heartfelt greetings to the bride. Giesecke is delighted, only to discover to his astonishment that it is Klärchen to whom Sigismund is so attached. 'But I commissioned you to get my daughter engaged!' Giesecke shouts at Seidler. 'I've done that too, Herr Giesecke!' is Seidler's reply. Giesecke has no words left to refuse his consent to his daughter's engagement to Seidler, and the happy couple rapturously celebrate in waltz time ('Mein Liebeslied muss ein Walzer sein').

1125

There remains, of course, the matter of Giesecke's legal action against Sülzheimer, but Sigismund reveals that his father has withdrawn his case, having registered a patent for a new nightdress. Without a doubt happiness waits for everyone at the door of the White Horse inn (Finale III: 'Mein Liebeslied muss ein Walzer sein').

The above follows the original basic plot and score, with the songs 'Die ganze Welt ist Himmelblau' and 'Mein Liebeslied muss ein Walzer sein' with music by Robert Stolz, 'Zuschau'n kann ich nicht' with music by Bruno Granichstaedten and 'Was kann der Sigismund dafür' with lyric and music by Robert Gilbert. Subsequent versions have much amplified the work, including in the final scene of Act 3 the Heurige song 'Erst wann's aus wird sein' with music by Hans Frankowski.

SCHÖN IST DIE WELT

(The World is Beautiful)

an operetta in three acts, a revised version of *Endlich Allein* by A M Willner and Robert Bodanzky (10 February 1914, Theater an der Wien) by Fritz Löhner and Ludwig Herzer. Music by Franz Lehár. Produced at the Metropol-Theater, Berlin, 3 December 1930 with Richard Tauber (Georg), Gitta Alpar (Elisabeth), Lizzi Waldmüller (Mercedes), Kurt Vespermann (Sascha) and Leo Schützendorf (the King).

Produced at the Theater an der Wien, Vienna, 21 December 1931 with Hans Heinz Bollmann (Georg), Adele Kern (Elisabeth), Irene Zilahy (Mercedes), Kalma Latabar (Sascha) and Gustav Charlé (the King).

CHARACTERS

The King
Crown Prince Georg, *his son*
Duchess Maria Branckenhorst
Elisabeth, Princess von und zu Lichtenberg, *her niece*
Count Sascha Karlowitz, *the King's adjutant*
Mercedes del Rossa, *a prima ballerina*
The manager *of the Hôtel des Alpes*
The major-domo *to the Duchess Maria*
The head waiter
A jazz singer
Mercedes' Negro groom
Hotel guests and staff, ladies and gentlemen of society, boys and girls.

ACT 1

In the lounge of the Hôtel des Alpes, in a Swiss mountain resort, an orchestra is playing and guests are dancing, but the hotel manager and the major-domo to the Duchess Maria Branckenhorst are not interested in the music. They are looking out of the windows with anxious faces ('Nichts zu seh'n, gar nichts zu seh'n'). They are expecting a visit from the King of a small but significant European country and his son, Crown Prince Georg, and the major-domo is impressing upon the manager the importance of the King remaining incognito during his stay.

The reason for the meeting and its attendant secrecy is that a marriage has been arranged between the Crown Prince and the Princess Elisabeth von und zu Lichtenberg, the Duchess's niece. It is a marriage of convenience and its object is to relieve Prince Georg's country's dire financial situation through the dowry that the Princess will bring, but Elisabeth, with no thoughts for the mercenary side of marriage, is contemplating the love that lies before her with a mixture of excitement and trepidation ('Wie süss muss die Liebe sein'/'Sag', armes Herzchen, sag'').

When the King arrives, it transpires that he and the Duchess Marie had once been lovers and they still retain great affection for each other ('Herzogin Marie'). Travelling with the King is his adjutant, Count Sascha Karlowitz. Sascha has been married secretly to a fiery South American dancer, Mercedes del Rossa, but he has not been able to inform his King of this detail because he has several times asked the King for permission to marry and been refused. Hence Sascha and Mercedes are compelled to meet furtively and to save their ardour for a nocturnal rendezvous a quarter of an hour before bedtime ('Nur ein Viertelstündchen').

When the Crown Prince arrives, he shatters his father by announcing that he has changed his mind about marrying. He is a fun-loving young man, and he wants for a little longer to make the most of the world that he finds so beautiful and enjoyable ('Bruder Leichtsinn, so werd' ich genannt'/'Schön ist die Welt').

By chance, the Prince and Princess Elisabeth meet and, though they are unaware of each other's true identity, it happens that they are by no means strangers to each other. They met once when the Prince stopped to help Elisabeth mend a puncture on a mountain road. They are delighted to see each other again, and their mutual interest in mountaineering leads them happily to plan an alpine climb together the following day ('Ein Ausflug mit Ihnen'/'Frei und jung dabei').

Mercedes, meanwhile, has decided to take matters into her own hands over gaining the King's approval for her marriage to Sascha. She determines to see what a little sex appeal can do and, since the King is undoubtedly a man with an eye for a pretty face and figure, he is perceptibly taken by her dusky charms when the dance orchestra strikes up and she performs a tempestuous tango ('Tropfenglut hat ihr Blut'/'Rio de Janeiro'). So taken is he, in fact, that he decides she is far too good for a mere officer, and would probably do better with a King.

One way and another, everyone has been diverted from the original purpose of the gathering, but Crown Prince Georg and Princess Elisabeth—both still unaware of each other's identity—are looking forward eagerly to their mountain excursion on the morrow (Finale I: 'Ja, was ist mit mir?').

ACT 2

The following day, high on the mountain, the two mountaineers are pressing on upwards, stimulated by the superb view and by each other's company ('Jetzt mit der rechten Hand'). It is clear that they already have budding feelings of love for each other ('Es steht vom Lieben so oft geschrieben'). They are feeling in need of a rest when they come upon a mountain hut. It is remarkably well equipped, with such comforts as a cooker, food and radio, and Princess Elisabeth volunteers to cook a meal. While she is doing so, Georg stands outside the hut, pondering his situation. No matter what his father may say or wish, there is no doubt in his mind that his companion is the only girl for him ('Liebste, glaub' an mich').

Elisabeth produces a delicious meal of scrambled eggs, ham, bread and fruit, washed down with ice-cold water from a mountain stream. Then, when they have eaten, they switch on the radio and, when they find that it is broadcasting dance music, they dance together. However, the music is interrupted by the broadcast of an S.O.S. reporting that the Princess von und zu Lichtenberg has been missing since daybreak. According to the radio, the Princess is wearing a brown skirt and green blouse and has been seen in the company of a young man in climbing kit. Prince Georg looks at her in disbelief as it dawns on him who his companion is.

Suddenly they realise that they have paused too long at the hut and that it is getting late. What is more, there are signs of a storm coming up and Georg, as an experienced mountaineer, tells Elisabeth that in such conditions it would be dangerous to try to return to the foot of the mountain that night. Elisabeth threatens to make the journey alone, but just then a thunderous noise is heard. 'What was that?' she cries, throwing herself into his arms. 'An avalanche!' he replies (Finale II: 'Was ist geschehen?' 'Eine Lawine!'). He calms her down but assures her that there can be no question of making their way down the mountain. They must spend the night in the hut. Elisabeth realises that the avalanche is not the only thing that has fallen. She has fallen in love. The young people declare their love for each other, and, as the weather eases and night comes, they settle down to pass the night—she inside and he on a bench in front of the hut.

ACT 3

Back at the Hôtel des Alpes, the guests are clamouring around the manager seeking news and wondering whether they themselves may be in danger from avalanches ('Herr Direktor, bitte sehr!'). Fortunately the manager is able to reassure them over both their own safety and that of the Princess. An airman has seen her and her companion together on the mountain. Now speculation redirects itself towards the identity of the stranger who is with Elisabeth, and Mercedes stirs matters up by pointing to the scandal of the Princess spending a night alone with this unknown man. 'Whether rich or poor, love makes all humans the same,' she declares ('Ja, die Liebe ist brutal').

Suddenly, when everyone is occupied elsewhere, the Crown Prince and the Princess arrive quickly and quietly back in the hotel ('Frei, mit frohen Seelen'). They are so thirsty after their climb that the Prince slips into the bar and mixes them a swift drink ('Dort in der kleinen Tanzbar'/'In der kleinen Bar') before Elisabeth goes to find her aunt. The Duchess is understandably relieved at her niece's safe return but she is less happy about Elisabeth's insistence that she will not marry the Crown Prince. She is in love with her mountain companion. 'Listen to me, Elisabeth!' the Duchess declares. 'To be in love—fine! To go climbing mountains alone with a man—fine! To spend a whole night with him—very good! But to marry him—that is decidedly indecent!' But even in front of such practical advice, Elisabeth can only revel in her new found love ('Ich bin verliebt').

The King is still wondering how he is to break to the Duchess the news that Georg is refusing to marry her niece when Sascha tells him who it was who passed the night on the mountain with the Princess. The King is so pleased with Sascha for this excellent piece of news that he immediately gives his approval to his adjutant's marriage to Mercedes, and the lady expresses her delight in typical style ('Heimlich wie in der Nacht die Diebe'/'Schön sind lachende Frau'n').

The Duchess now comes to inform the King of Elisabeth's decision not to marry his son, and the King retorts with some aspersions on a woman who would spend a night alone on a mountain with a man. Finally, however, the real identity of the lovers is revealed, and Georg muses that he went up the mountain to get away from the Princess Elisabeth and merely succeeded in finding her, as the two affirm the strength of their love for each other (Finale III: 'Liebste, glaub' an mich').

The synopsis follows the revised version as performed at the Theater an der Wien in 1931. The basic plot, broad structure and some of the music of *Schön ist die Welt* were taken over from *Endlich allein* but the characters were new, the libretto rewritten, and several new musical numbers added.

WALZER AUS WIEN

(Waltzes From Vienna)

a play with songs in three acts by A M Willner, Heinz Reichert and Ernst Marischka. Music from the works of Johann Strauss I and II selected and arranged by Erich Wolfgang Korngold and Julius Bittner. Produced at the Stadttheater, Vienna, 30 October 1930 with Willy Thaler (Johann Strauss I), Hubert Marischka (Johann Strauss II), Fritz Imhoff (Ebeseder), Paula Brosig (Therese), Betty Fischer (Countess Olga) and Mizzi Zwerenz (Frau Kratochwill). Produced at the Theater an der Wien 18 May 1931.

Produced at the Alhambra Theatre, London, in a version by Desmond Carter, Caswell Garth, G H Clutsam and Hubert Griffiths as *Waltzes From Vienna* 17 August 1931 with C V France (Strauss I), Evelyn Herbert/Adrienne Brune (Resi), Robert

Halliday/Esmond Knight (Schani) and Marie Burke (Olga). Produced at the Theatre Royal, Drury Lane, in a version by Jerome Chodorov, Robert Wright and George Forrest as *The Great Waltz* 9 July 1970 with Walter Cassel, Diane Todd, David Watson and Sári Bárabás.

Produced at the Théâtre de la Porte Saint-Martin, Paris, in a version by André Mouëzy-Eon, Jean Marietti, Max Eddy and Eugène Cools as *Valses de Vienne* 21 December 1933 with Pierre Magnier, André Baugé, Lucienne Tragin and Fanély Revoil. Produced at the Théâtre du Châtelet 30 August 1941 with Maurice Vidal, Lili Grandval and Suzanne Baugé, and revived there 18 April 1947 with Vidal and Madeleine Vernon, May 1957 with Gaston Rey, Henri Gui, Colette Riedinger and Janine Ervil, 31 May 1958 with André Baugé, Gui, Mlle Riedinger and Huguette Boulangeot, 19 December 1964 with Paul Cambo, Gui, Line May and Ervil, 21 December 1974 with Margaret Latour, Jean-Claude Darcey and Nicky Nancel, 20 December 1975 with the same stars, and 17 December 1977 with Brigitte Krafft, Darcey and Nadine Capri. Produced at the Théâtre Mogador 1976.

Produced at the Center Theatre, New York, in a revised version by Moss Hart, Frank Tours and Robert Russell Bennett as *The Great Waltz* 22 September 1934 with H Reeves-Smith, Guy Robertson, Marion Claire and Marie Burke.

A film version was produced by Gaumont in 1934 as *Waltzes from Vienna* with Edmund Gwenn, Esmond Knight, Fay Compton and Jessie Matthews, and another by MGM as *The Great Waltz* in 1938 with Fernand Gravet, Miliza Korjus and Luise Rainer.

CHARACTERS

Johann Strauss I
Johann Strauss II ('Schani')
Hieronymus Ebeseder, *a confectioner*
Therese, *his daughter*
Kathi Pollinger, *his sister*
Franzi, Tini *and* Mali Pollinger, *her daughters*
Ferdinand Wessely, *a master tailor*
Leopold Wessely, *his son*
Countess Olga Barranskaja
Prince Sascha Gogol, *an embassy official*
Captain von Hohenau
Lieutenant Sternau
Gottfried Amadäus Drechsler, *leader of the orchestra of Johann Strauss I*
Dr Sebastian Brandl, *critic of Bäuerles Theaterzeitung*
Karl Friedrich Hirsch, *known as 'Lampel Hirsch'*
Florian Dommayer, *a landlord*
Stefan Kreider, *a cashier at Dommayer's*
Cyrill, *the Countess's footman*
Georg Homolka, *a sergeant*
Fanny Wiesinger
Frau Kratochwill, *landlady of an apartment block*
Pepi, *Ebeseder's apprentice*
A student, a stagecoachman, a gentleman, a guest, members of the public

ACT 1

In Hieronymus Ebeseder's cake shop custom is good. Indeed, sometimes all Vienna seems to be in the shop, demanding service at the same time. Today Ebeseder's job of dealing with the customers is made the more difficult by the presence of the master tailor Ferdinand Wessely, who has come to discuss the proposal that his son Leopold should marry Ebeseder's daughter Resi. The two young people are certainly fond enough of each other, but Resi is not sure that she is yet ready to settle down ('Ob ja, ob nein, das will überdacht sein'/'Wenn die Rosen wieder blühn').

Amongst the customers at Ebeseder's is the young Johann Strauss, and there is general excitement as people catch word of his presence, not least from the young ladies. The young man hastens to explain that he is not the famous Johann Strauss, composer of the 'Radetzky March' that the municipal band has just been playing outside the shop, but his son. Still, he is himself a composer and, as he makes clear, he is not short of inspiration when so many pretty young ladies are around ('Frühlingsgleicher, Mädchenflor'/'Ihr holden Frau'n, in eurem Blick').

It is, in fact, young Schani Strauss who is Resi's reason for hesitation over her father's wish for her to marry Leopold. Resi is much keener on the young musician than she is on Leopold, and Strauss is himself equally taken by the charms of the pastrycook's daughter ('Jeden Abend so nach zehn'/'Ja, ja, die Mäderln, die wissen').

The Countess Olga Baranskaja also calls at Ebeseder's to order confectionery for a soirée she is giving the following evening, and it is soon evident that she is interested not just in Ebeseder's cakes but in the young musician. Learning of his aspirations to be a composer and conductor of his own orchestra, despite his father's objections, she suggests that perhaps some day he will find a good fairy to bring his wishes true ('Hat ein Englein in Himmel'). 'You will certainly hear from me again,' she declares, as she leaves ('Eh' du's denkst').

Resi is understandably jealous to see how Johann has got on so well with Countess Olga, but to young Strauss music means everything, and Resi has to be reassured by his assertion that what is good for his music is good for her too. He wins her smiles back by offering to play a waltz that he has written for her during the night (Finale I: 'Können Sie lesen, was da steht?') but they are interrupted at their music by the arrival of Schani's father. The elder Strauss pours scorn on his son's efforts as a composer but his opinion is not shared by the others present, and Schani's determination to attempt to launch himself upon the musical world is unabated.

ACT 2

It is evening and Dommayer's garden restaurant in Hietzing is brightly lit by fairy-lamps. On the orchestral stage, the elder Strauss is directing his waltz 'Loreley-Rheinklänge', bringing to a close the first part of the concert. During the interval the orchestra's leader, Drechsler, asks his conductor if he won't, for once, play one of his son's waltzes, but the elder Strauss is adamant.

A lackey arrives with a request for Strauss to come to conduct the dance music for the Russian envoy, Prince Yurishkin. He is required to depart immediately, and his manager, Hirsch, helps persuade him that it is money and acclaim he cannot afford to turn down. Drechsler can readily enough conduct the orchestra at Dommayer's in his absence.

Countess Olga enters with her fiancé, the embassy official Prince Gogol, the two of them brought by Captain von Hohenau to hear the famous Strauss orchestra play. Seats are almost impossible to find and, when Prince Gogol offers to clear a couple of spectators away forcibly so that Olga may have a seat, the captain has to remind him, 'We're not in Russia now, you know.' The Countess remarks that words are not always necessary. The language of the eyes is international ('Worte können viel und können nichts besagen'/'Frauenaugen sind gefährlich'). Eventually a place is found for the Prince's party, and the Countess settles down to enjoy the Viennese music that so meets with the public's approval ('Banda! Seid's alle beinander?'/ 'Kinder, heut' muss i mei' Räuscherl hab'n!').

Dommayer's is so packed that the gates have had to be closed, and when Schani turns up he gets in only when Drechsler puts in a word for him at the gate. Resi is there and, when she spots Schani, she rushes up to join him. Schani has come to Dommayer's in response to a letter. He assumed that it must be from Resi, but she knows nothing of it, and he is puzzled. Resi is hoping that there will soon be some positive step in their romance, but Strauss is depressed that he is unable to make a name for himself and he wonders if he should not, perhaps, follow his father's wishes, give up music, and take the job he has been offered in Resi's father's confectionery business. Without music, perhaps he could give his whole heart to her ('So nimm denn mein Wort, hier ist mein Hand'/'Ich hab' dich Lieb und muss an dich immer denken') but, when Resi runs off to arrange for him to speak to her father, Strauss again finds a new waltz melody occupying his mind ('Frühlingsstimmen! Frühlingsklingen').

Resi brings her father and Strauss together, but Ebeseder warns him that he must not think that it is easy to be a pastrycook. 'A waltz is soon composed, but a real Gugelhupf with almonds and raisins is a matter for the greatest concentration and excitement,' he declares, as he invites Schani to sit down with them and enjoy a bottle of wine ('Wo der Wienerwald zur Donau sich neigt'/'A Weinderl und a Musi').

By now the audience is getting impatient, and a cry of 'Music!' spreads around the concert hall, accompanied by the stamping of feet and the banging of glasses, but the elder Strauss is not back from his engagement and the audience make it clear that Drechsler won't do as a replacement. They want Strauss! The Countess persuades Dommayer that the only way to avoid a riot is to allow the young Strauss to stand in for his father. After all, the audience asked for Strauss. Dommayer decides that he has no alternative and Schani is hurried to the stage.

Resi now realises that the letter Schani received was from the Countess. Dreadful thoughts of a liaison between them rush into her head and on the spur of the anguished moment she decides that she will forget Schani and marry dear, safe Leopold. Unaware of all this, Schani mounts the podium, raises his baton, and the orchestra begins to play. When the elder Strauss returns, he is just in time to witness the huge acclaim his son's performance receives. When the music is over, Schani is claimed by the Countess. 'I hope you are not cross with me for encroaching on your destiny,' she says, and only then do father and son realise that they have both, in different ways, been victims of a conspiracy. It is a conspiracy which has had its effect. Schani's reputation is made. 'Good night, father Strauss! Good morning, young Strauss!' declares Dommayer as Ebeseder rushes to join in the congratulations and declares that young Strauss will always be welcome in his house—but as witness to his daughter's wedding to Leopold and not as her husband. 'Schani, you have another bride...music!' declares Drechsler (Finale II: 'Und jetzt soll ich spielen').

ACT 3

Crowds have gathered outside Schani's apartment to hail him on his tremendous success. With a final 'thank you', he closes the window and goes to his piano, relieved to be able to work in peace on his newly composed song ('Frag' mich oft, woran's denn wohl liegt'/'So lang's noch Mäderln gibt in Wien').

His landlady, Frau Kratochwill, brings him a letter which Schani excitedly discovers is from the Countess announcing that she is to visit him but, when she appears it is to tell him that her fiancé, Prince Gogol, has misunderstood her interest in the young composer and that she must leave Vienna. Resi, too, comes by to apologise for her hasty treatment of him, but points out that he has changed and that she must marry Leopold. Her arrival, hard on the heels of the Countess, causes consternation to their respective fiancés when they in turn arrive in Strauss's room, but matters are sorted out in time for Leopold to be reconciled with Resi, and they look forward to their life together ('Reserl, schau' her!'/'Heissgeliebte Therese').

Finally Strauss senior arrives, by now resigned to his son's success and to the fact that there is room in Vienna for them both. Young Schani receives his change of heart with relief and gratitude, not forgetting the debt he owes to his father. After all, as he says to him, 'who have I got it from but you?'

The original production opened with a prologue in which, in old age, Johann Strauss II reminisced with a young composer about the events that surrounded his own début. The various subsequent versions have varied considerably in their content, although the basic story and musical selection have remained largely the same.

DIE BLUME VON HAWAII

(The Flower of Hawaii)

an operetta in three acts by Alfred Grünwald, Fritz Löhner-Beda and Emmerich Földes. Music by Paul Abraham. Produced at the Neues Theater, Leipzig, 24 July 1931. Produced at the Metropoltheater, Berlin, 29 August 1931.

Produced at the Theater an der Wien, Vienna, 19 August 1932.

Produced at the Théâtre de l'Alhambra, Paris, in a version by Georges Delance 1933 with Aimée Mortimer and Max Moutier.

Film versions were produced by Richard Oswald in 1933 with Marta Eggerth, Hans Fidesser, Ivan Petrovitch, Hans Junkermann, Carl Auer, Georg John, Ernst Verebes and Eugen Rex; and in 1953

CHARACTERS

Laya, *Princess of Hawaii*
Prince Lilo-Taro
Kanako Hilo, *an eminent Hawaiian*
Admiral Mackintosh, Captain Reginald Harald Stone, *of the American Marines*
Lloyd Harrison, *American Governor of Hawaii*
John Buffy, *his secretary*
Bessie Worthington, *the Governor's niece*
Raka, *a young Hawaiian girl*
Jim Boy, *a famous American jazz singer*
Susanne Provence, *his partner*
Perroquet, *a head waiter*
Kaluna, *an old Hawaiian*
Chun-Chun, *a Chinese servant*
Lieutenant Sunny Hill, *an American Marine officer*
Cadet Bobbie Flipps
Lilian
Oolea, Kililia, *Hawaiian dancers*
Nahala, Malahini, *Hawaiian singers*
Young Laya, young Taro *(in flashback)*
Cadets, Marine officers, society men and women, Hawaiian singers and dancers

ACT 1

It is early morning on a January day in 1895. The sun is rising over the Honolulu villa of the American governor of Hawaii, and Hawaiian maidens can be heard singing to the accompaniment of twanging guitars ('Ein Paradies an Meeresstrand'). John Buffy, secretary to the governor, is inviting a group of American Marines to a garden party that the governor has arranged in their honour.

Buffy has long been in love with the governor's niece, Bessie Worthington. She is a young lady who reckons that the man she marries should be like a cocktail—a little bit sweet, a little bit bitter, tender and yet brutal. Buffy, a man with a taste for the 'Buffy Flipp'—gin mixed with Worcester sauce—seems to be just her man ('My Little Boy'). However, the Governor has other plans for his niece. The Americans have been governing Hawaii ever since the monarchy on the island was overthrown by republican elements and the Governor now sees it as politically desirable to strengthen the American position by marrying his niece to the native Prince Lilo-Taro, a man thoroughly soaked in the beauties and traditions of his native island ('Ein Paradies am Meeresstrand').

At the same time, Kanako Hilo, a prominent Hawaiian, is plotting with royalist factions in the island for the return from exile in Paris of the pretender to the Hawaiian throne, Princess Laya and, in doing so, he is counting on the support of Prince Lilo-Taro, who considers himself to have been betrothed to Laya ever since she was his childhood sweetheart—his 'flower of Hawaii' ('Blume von Hawaii').

To the enthusiasm of the American cadets, a ship arrives from America, on board which is a famous jazz singer, Jim Boy, travelling with a dusky young lady whom he presents as his partner, Susanne Provence ('Wir singen zur Jazzband im Folies Bergère'). With such entertainments to attract visitors, Hawaii is becoming quite a cosmopolitan social locale ('Was hat der Gentleman im Dschungel zu tun?'). Also on the ship is Captain Reginald Harald Stone, the new Commander of the local Marine Corps. He and Jim Boy's partner have become rather attached to each other during the voyage, and he now tells her he has fallen in love with her ('Will dir die Welt zu Füssen legen?'). What Stone cannot know is that the supposed Susanne Provence is in fact Princess Laya. She has been brought back in secret by Kanako Hilo to restore the Hawaiian dynasty, although she herself is interested only in seeing her beloved home country again.

Jim Boy, meanwhile, is already getting on famously with Bessie and the local girls, as he tells them how he enjoys night life and more particularly being surrounded by pretty faces ('Ich muss Mädeln seh'n'). While Hawaiian guitars twang and lightly clad girls dance the hula (Finale I: 'Haleokalo. Heute ist ganz Hawaii froh'), Kanako Hilo is using the cover of the garden party to enlist the help of Prince Lilo-Taro for his proposed coup. When Taro meets Laya, the two recall the song of their childhood ('Ein Paradies am Meeresstrand'), and Taro declares his undying love for her but, when Stone appears on the scene, Laya affects not to know Taro, and accepts his invitation to dance. Consumed with jealousy, Taro discloses her real identity and calls to the people of Hawaii to salute their queen ('Volk von Hawaii! Jetzt bist du frei'). The governor summons Captain Stone and his Marines and orders a report to be sent to Washington, but Laya is allowed to go freely with Lilo-Taro to the palace.

ACT 2

In the royal palace in Honolulu, Hawaiian girls are busily engaged making garlands of flowers in preparation for the annual flower festival ('Blume von Hawaii'). Jim Boy is thoroughly enjoying himself amongst the local beauties, most particularly with his 'chocolate bonbon', Raka, who has taken it upon herself to provide him with all the comforts that Hawaiian custom dictates should be accorded to visitors ('Rechts Hawaii').

Taro, meanwhile, has been continuing to press his love for Laya, but she responds uncertainly ('Kann nicht küssen ohne Liebe'). She still harbours strong feelings for Stone who, as it happens, is just now marching into the palace for the flower festival along with his corps of cadets ('Wo es Mädels gibt'). John Buffy is still pressing his suit with Bessie, painting a tempting picture of his boudoir complete with table for two and a gramophone playing the latest hits of Dajos Béla, Jack Hylton and Richard Tauber ('Ich hab' ein Diwanpüppchen').

Laya confides in Stone how happy she is to be back enjoying the magical beauty of her homeland ('Traumschöne Perle der Südsee') while, to add to the general atmosphere of good will and enjoyment, Jim Boy entertains Bessie with tales of his life as a public entertainer, surrounded by his fans and with his name in lights ('My golden Baby').

All this time Kanako Hilo is maturing his plan. Under the pretext of crowning the flower queen, Laya will be crowned Queen of Hawaii in the very presence of the Americans. The locals congregate for the ceremony (Finale II: 'Heut' wird die Schöne gekrönt') and Kanako Hilo duly appears, a throne is produced, and the crowning ceremony is performed but, when Kanako Hilo seeks to get Laya to confirm her betrothal to Prince Taro, Stone steps forward and he and Taro compete with their pleas for Laya's hand ('Frage dein Herz').

At that moment, the Governor arrives with Admiral Mackintosh of the Marines, only to be told by Kanako Hilo that Laya has been crowned Queen of Hawaii. The governor insists that Laya should sign a document renouncing her throne for ever, but Hilo and the Hawaiians reject the idea outright. Stone is ordered to arrest Laya, but his love for her leads him to refuse, even though he knows that it means the end of his career. At this, Laya takes matters into her own hands and signs the document.

Taro, seeing this action as an indication of Laya's love for Stone, bids her a bitter farewell and declares that he will sail away from Hawaii for ever and Laya watches helplessly, faced with two men prepared to make such sacrifices for her, as Taro makes off to sea. It is Raka who persuades her that, though Stone may be sacrificing his career, Taro is effectively sacrificing his whole life in leaving Hawaii, and Laya realises that it is Taro who most deserves her love.

ACT 3

In a Chinese bar in Monte Carlo a floor show is under way with singers and dancers performing a lively chorus number ('Wir singen zur Jazzband') until the master of ceremonies announces the appearance, as the star attraction of the evening, 'direct from an engagement in Hawaii', of Jim Boy who performs a Negro number ('Bin nur ein Jonny'). During the ensuing dancing, Jim Boy's partner, the real Susanne Provence, enters somewhat the worse

Ein Walzertraum. Franzi (Mizzi Zwerenz) and Lothar (Arthur Guttman) try out a violin and a piccolo duet in 'Piccolo, Piccolo, Tzin, Tzin, Tzin' during a pause in the plot. Carltheater 1907.

Der Graf von Luxemburg. René (Nigel Douglas) and Angèle Didier (Adele Leigh) go blindly through a marriage of convenience, separated by an artist's easel. BBC-TV.

Polenblut. Bolo (Kurt Schreibmayer) prefers the card-playing, beer-drinking company of his friends (Kurt Ruzicka, Peter Baillie, Volker Vogel, Hanz Kraemmer) to a wife. Volksoper, 1986.

Die Csárdásfürstin. Milena Rudiferia as Sylva Varescu at the Volksoper, 1982.

Madame Pompadour. Calicot (Sándor Nemeth) with a chorus line of soldiers.
Volksoper, 1986.

Das Land Des Lächelns. Nicolai Gedda as Prince Sou Chong. Volksoper, 1988.

Feuerwerk. The folk from the circus represent freedom and excitement to the young people of a bourgeois household, who do not see the unglamorous underside of such a life. Iduna (Helga Papouschek) sings about her little pony (Iris Klauser). Volksoper, 1983.

for drink ('Heut' hab' ich ein Schwipserl!'). Her resemblance to the disguised Laya, who enchanted Stone, is so uncanny that the Marine is happy to settle for Susanne instead of Laya ('Will dir die Welt zu Füssen legen?').

Jim Boy, utterly spoilt by the comforts lavished upon him in Honolulu, decides to settle down with his dusky Hawaiian Raka ('My golden Baby') while Lilo-Taro is now happily tied to Laya, who has been in Monte Carlo, dissipating the settlement that the Americans had made to her at the roulette tables ('Du traumschöne Perle der Südsee'). Since the pairing off is working out so tidily, it is only fair that Bessie and Buffy should also get together before the evening ends (Finale III: 'My golden Baby').

DIE DUBARRY

an operetta in nine scenes by Paul Knepler and J M Welleminsky. Music by Carl Millöcker adapted by Theo Mackeben. Produced at the Admiralspalast, Berlin, 14 August 1931 with Gitta Alpar (Dubarry) and revived there 1938.

Produced at the Theater an der Wien, Vienna, 30 August 1935. Produced at the Stadttheater in a revised version by H M Cramer 30 March 1951.

Produced at His Majesty's Theatre, London, in a version by Desmond Carter and Rowland Leigh 14 April 1932 with Anny Ahlers (Jeanne), Heddle Nash (René), Clarice Hardwicke (Margot) and Charles Heslop (de la Marche).

Produced at the George M Cohan Theatre, New York, November 1932 with Grace Moore.

Produced at the Théâtre de la Porte Saint-Martin in a version by André Mouëzy-Eon 21 October 1933 with Fanély Revoil, Simone Lencret, Boucot and Jacques Varennes.

An English film version was produced in 1935 as *I Give My Heart* with Gitta Alpar and Owen Nares. A German film version was produced in 1951.

CHARACTERS

Louis XV, *King of France*
Duc de Choiseul, *his Prime Minister*
Prince de Soubise
Duc de Lauzun
Radix de Saint-Foix
Comte Chamard
Lebell, *the King's chamberlain*
Princesse de Luxembourg
Marquis de Brissac
Comte Dubarry
Marie-Jeanne Beçu
Margot, Lucille, *her friends*
René Lavallery, *a painter*
Pierre, *his friend*
Madame Labille, *proprietor of a millinery salon*

Marianne *and* Claude Verrières
An abbé, maids, a Negro boy, servants, a woman neighbour, society men and women, milliners, Parisian people

SCENE 1

It is a late Saturday afternoon in spring and the girls in Madame Labille's Parisian millinery establishment are looking forward to the weekend, when they can have a rest from making hats ('Immer nähen, immer nähen'). They are overjoyed when the Marquis de Brissac, the wealthy protector of one of their number, Margot, arrives to invite them all out for the evening.

Margot's success with the Marquis has always been particularly envied by another little milliner, Marie-Jeanne Beçu, but today Jeanne comes back, breathless, from an errand, with a tale to tell. While she was making her delivery, she was picked up in the street by a handsome young painter named René Lavallery ('Heut' hab ich Glück'). Margot boasts that a painter can hardly match her marquis, but Jeanne declares that she is happy enough. 'Today I am in love with my René,' she declares. 'What the future brings, who can know?' Just at that moment the sound of music is heard outside (The King's March), and the girls rush to the window to watch as King Louis XV passes by in a carriage with his mistress, Madame Pompadour. Jeanne throws a rose from the window, and it lands at the King's feet.

So absorbed was Jeanne in René when she met him that she failed to notice the theft of the two hats she was supposed to be delivering to customers' homes and, as a punishment, Madame Labille insists on her staying late at the shop and missing the Marquis's outing. The girls put on their hats to depart ('Aber wenn es Feierabend'), leaving Jeanne behind, but she is not dismayed. Tonight she has a date with René. When Madame Labille has left, she pulls a face in the direction of the departing proprietress, and climbs out of the window.

SCENE 2

In a park just outside Paris the public are enjoying some outdoor dancing ('Seht, wie sich alles schön'). The Comte Dubarry and the Duc de Lauzun are strolling together discussing a very important question—the question of a successor to the ageing Pompadour as the King's mistress. Dubarry is emphatic that, for political reasons, the Prime Minister's sister, the Duchesse de Gramont, should not be chosen, despite her brother's wishes.

René Lavallery is also in the park, with his friend Pierre, waiting for Jeanne and happily recalling their meeting earlier in the day ('Heut' hab' ich Glück'), and the Marquis de Brissac is there too, with Margot and the girls, all thrilled to be freed for a little while from the daily grind and ready for a lively evening ('Stets verliebt, stets verliebt'). When Jeanne turns up for her date, she and René have eyes only for each other ('Der Frühling zieht ins Land'/'Es lockt die Nacht') but, unknown to them, Dubarry has been watching and, while Margot, Brissac and the girls continue their frolicking ('Stets

1138

verliebt, stets verliebt') he makes a mental note of Jeanne's considerable personality and charm.

SCENE 3

René and Jeanne are soon living together in his attic home, and he is deliriously happy with the arrangement ('Wie schön ist alles!') but his work brings in little money, and Jeanne suggests that what he needs is a wealthy patron. She is jealous of all the pretty things that her friend Margot enjoys thanks to the Marquis de Brissac, and her inability to resist buying new clothes is already straining her relationship with René. While René is out looking for food, Margot herself arrives. She is now having some success as an actress, and Jeanne cannot resist trying on some of her fine clothes, looking at herself admiringly in the mirror ('Liebe, kleine Jeanne').

When Margot has gone, Jeanne receives a surprise visit from the Comte Dubarry. He pretends that he wishes to buy a painting, but he takes every chance to refer pointedly to all the material things she is missing in sharing her life with her penniless lover. She swears her faithfulness to René but, when he returns, she conceals Dubarry's visit. When René learns of the aristocratic visitor from a neighbour, and discovers a purse left by the Count to tempt Jeanne, he leaps to the conclusion that she is deceiving him, and unceremoniously throws her out of the studio.

SCENE 4

At a stag party at the Comte Dubarry's palace, the Marquis de Brissac is gossiping about the appearance of a new cabaret artist called Manon Rançon at the night club of the Verrières sisters. 'Cherchez la femme!' the Count declares, and they promptly decide to give the place a visit, agreeing that there is nothing more enchanting than the sight of a lady's feet, her smiles and her eyes ('Blicken dich zwei Augen an').

SCENE 5

At the night club all is gaiety and revelry ('Der Geige Klang lockt zur Nacht von Paris'). The new cabaret artist, who has made such a hit with her dancing and songs, then appears to do her turn ('In dunkler Nacht zog mich Gesang') and Brissac and Dubarry recognise her immediately as Jeanne. The men clamour for her attention, but she remains cool towards them. Brissac is somewhat embarrassed when Margot appears, but he quickly recovers his composure and agrees to go for a stroll with her ('Ja, es ist ein alter Vorgang'/'Wenn verliebte bummeln gehn').

Meanwhile Jeanne has been gambling with money borrowed from a gentleman called Radix de Saint-Foix and has managed to lose it all. Saint-Foix demands repayment in one form or another, but Jeanne is adamant. 'I give my heart only to the one man to whom I can mean everything,' she declares ('Ich habe Liebe schon genossen'/'Ich schenk mein Herz'). Suddenly Dubarry appears on the scene and, claiming that Jeanne is his wife, agrees to pay her debts. The stunned Jeanne leaves the club on the arm of the Count, as he makes his first declarations of love ('Arme kleine Jeanne').

SCENE 6

Jeanne is now living in the house of the Comte Dubarry, who has arranged for her to go through a marriage ceremony with his brother so that he may pass her off in society as the Comtesse Dubarry. An opportunity to launch her society career comes with an invitation to a soirée at the palace of the Princesse de Luxembourg.

SCENE 7

At the salon of the Princesse de Luxembourg, Choiseul, Soubize and Lauzun discuss once more the burning question of a successor to Madame Pompadour. Choiseul continues to press his sister's claims, but he is aware that efforts have been made in favour of Jeanne. The King has been shown a portrait of her, painted by René. Jeanne enters apprehensively, aware that all eyes are on her ('Ob man gefällt oder nicht gefällt'), but it is soon clear that she is a great success.

Brissac and Margot are also at the party, continuing their dizzy romance ('Überglücklich macht die Liebe'/'Reisen wir durchs Liebesland'), but Jeanne is thoroughly taken aback when she meets René and they recall with nostalgic happiness their days together ('Denk' an die Tage'/'Ich denk zurück an jene Zeit'). Jeanne is concerned at the way she is becoming a pawn in political intrigue, and she and René soon decide to get back together again. René tells her that he will have a carriage waiting for her outside as soon as he can but, before she can depart, the Comte Dubarry takes her aside to tell her that the King has approved of her portrait. While René waits with his carriage ('Der uns führen soll ins grosse Glück!'), Jeanne is faced with the biggest choice of her life. Finally, she steps not into René's carriage but, aided by the King's chamberlain Lebell, into one taking her to the King at Versailles.

SCENE 8

In a salon of the Palace of Versailles the King's chamberlain prepares Jeanne for her meeting with the King and gives her some tips on Court etiquette. When finally she meets the King, and he asks her what she thinks about love, she simply repeats her philosophy of giving herself only to the man to whom she can be the most important thing in his life ('Ich habe Liebe schon genossen'/'Ich schenk mein Herz'). The King is well satisfied with her answer, and the Duc de Choiseul is deputed to have the new mistress installed in her splendid residence in the Petit Trianon ('Ich schenke mich nur einem Mann').

SCENE 9

In the park of the Trianon the people are gathering for a party for the King's birthday ('Im Park von Trianon'). When Jeanne is congratulated upon her new found success, she responds with the assurance that whatever she begins in life she completes ('Was ich im Leben beginne'/'Ja, so ist sie, die Dubarry!'). Margot and Brissac, who get everywhere, are there too and, since Brissac has finally asked her to marry him, Margot is contemplating nostalgically the military uniform that she wore in the acting career that she will now have to give up ('Die Uniform freut mich enorm'/'Ich nehm' die Trommel an').

René is also there, anxious to see Jeanne yet again ('Mein Weg führt immer mich zu Dir zurück') and, anxious to discredit Jeanne and further his sister's claims to the royal bed, the Duc de Choiseul tells the King that a meeting has been arranged by the two former lovers. In fact Jeanne has called René to the rendezvous only to bid him a final farewell, and the upshot of Choiseul's attempt to compromise her is his own banishment. Jeanne's position as the King's new favourite is confirmed. 'Long live the King!' cry the people, to which the King replies, 'Long live the Comtesse Dubarry, henceforth the one next to the throne!' ('Ja, so ist sie, die Dubarry'.)

The synopsis follows a revised version by Hans Martin Cremer, which makes considerable changes to detail from the 1931 original and introduces several new songs. Millöcker's 1879 operetta *Gräfin Dubarry* has a completely different book (albeit on the same subject) and only some of the melodic themes of the 1931 work are taken from that original score.

WENN DIE KLEINEN VEILCHEN BLÜHEN

(When the Little Violets Bloom)

a play with music in six scenes by Bruno Hardt-Warden based on *Als ich noch in Flügelkleide* by Albert Kehm and Martin Frehsee. Music by Robert Stolz. Produced at the Princess Theatre, The Hague, 1 April 1932 with Paul Harden (Paul), Friedel Dotza (Liesel), Fritz Hirsch (Katzensteg) and Elly Krasser (Auguste).

Produced at the Stadt-Theater, Zürich, 8 September 1934 with Heinz Rhöden, Elfi König, Carl Goldner and Paula Brosig.

Produced at the Theatre Royal, Drury Lane, in a version by Hassard Short, Desmond Carter and Reginald Purdell as *Wild Violets* 31 October 1932 with John Garrick, Adele Dixon, Jerry Verno, Charlotte Greenwood and Esmond Knight (Otto).

CHARACTERS: SCENES 1 AND 6

Katzensteg
Auguste Katzensteg, *his wife*
Gustl Katzensteg, *their daughter, a philosophy student*
His Excellency Paul Gutbier, *Minister of Justice*
Fritz Gutbier, *a law student, his son*

1141

Horst Südstedt, *a university professor*
Erwin Münster, *a court councillor*
Elisabeth, Trude, Helma
Students

SCENES 2 TO 4

Isolde Gutbier, *head of a girls' boarding school*
Mademoiselle Faure, *a teacher*
Dr Frank, *a professor*
Liesel, Trude, Helma, Steffi, Mary, Lulu, Jettchen, Katharina, *pupils of the finishing school*
Auguste, *Isolde's maid of all work*
His Worship Peter Kühl von Fehérvary, *a cavalry captain*
Paul Gutbier, Horst Südstedt, Erwin Münster, *members of the 'Rhenania' association*
Katzensteg, *steward of the 'Rhenania' association*
Heini, *a small boy*
University students, school girls

SCENE 1

It is a late spring afternoon in the garden of the Katzenstegs' inn at Bacharach on the Rhine ('In Bacharach, in Bacharach, in Bacharach am Rhein') and Gustl Katzensteg, a sporty young lady, is exercising energetically with a punch-bag. Her mother is concerned over her daughter's preoccupation with such an exhausting occupation, but it seems that Gustl is using the bag for more than mere exercise. She imagines that her punches are directed at His Excellency Paul Gutbier, the Justice Minister, who is opposing her friendship with his son Fritz on the grounds that he prefers young ladies to be rather more genteel than this 'boxing, riding, fencing Amazon'.

Her parents are preparing for a visit from the Justice Minister, and Father Katzensteg has got out an old guitar on which the Minister used to play thirty years before. It helps to remind the Katzenstegs of their youthful days and their courtship ('Im Garten war's vom Töchterheim'/'Servus, du gute alte Zeit'). Seeing their daughter and Fritz so happy together and so much in love, the Katzenstegs are all the more strongly in favour of the young couple's marriage, and they reflect that parents such as Fritz's sometimes forget that they too were young once (Finaletto: 'Im Garten war's vom Töchterheim'/'Servus, du gute alte Zeit').

SCENE 2

Thirty years earlier, at the beginning of the twentieth century, a group of young men are singing a serenade outside the walls of the girls' boarding school run by Isolde Gutbier ('Ich hab' ein Mädel gern!'). The young men are all members of the 'Rhenania' students' association, and among them are

1142

Paul Gutbier, Horst Südstedt and Erwin Münster. Paul, the nephew of the school's proprietress, is playing the guitar which ended up with Katzensteg thirty years later.

The girls emerge from the school under the care of their French mistress, Mademoiselle Faure, and the young men follow them. Liesel allows her French book to fall to the ground, and Horst picks it up, but Paul knows that she has dropped it deliberately. He pulls a letter out of his pocket and slips it inside the book. Then he calls little Heini and gives him a groschen to deliver the book back to the school ('Ich hab' ein Mädel gern').

SCENE 3

In the hall of the school the girls are busy at their exercises. Helma is writing poetry and doing her best to ignore the mocking of the other girls ('O Pegasus, du edles Ross'). It will be time shortly for the opening assembly of the new term, and the chairs are rearranged for the event. Mademoiselle Faure enters with Liesel's book in her hand, and has some harsh words for the careless girl before handing the book back. Liesel, who has been anything but careless, waits till she is gone before extracting Paul's letter from between the book's pages, then joyfully reads the message which tells her that he and his friends will be coming to the school at 4 o'clock to see his aunt.

The girls rush off to brush their hair, and Paul, Horst and Erwin march in boisterously ('Drei Korpsstudenten'/'Es lebe die Liebe'). While they are waiting, Auguste, the school maidservant, enters with a telegram. It is addressed simply to 'Gutbier', and so she doesn't know whether it is intended for Paul or his aunt. When Paul sees that it is from Osnabrück he decides that it must be from his Uncle Emil, to whom he has recently written to ask for some money. Only when Auguste has gone does he discover that it is not from his uncle at all, but from Dr Hermann Frank, the new teacher engaged by his aunt. It is to say that he has missed the midday train, and will not arrive until night.

Paul hurriedly hides the telegram, as Liesel, Mary and Helma return. The boys tell them that they have come on a diplomatic errand, about a party their students' singing association is holding that evening to celebrate the start of the new term. The young men and the girls indulge in much good-humoured teasing which ends with Paul betting Liesel a kiss that, before the evening is out, she will have expressed the wish to have him as her husband ('So ein Student ist verwöhnt'/'Der Herrgott schrieb').

Isolde Gutbier is most put out to discover young men on her premises, but Paul explains that he has come to tell her about their party in the hope that she will not complain too much about the noise. The headmistress is unimpressed and makes it clear that the sort of songs she knows they are likely to be singing are not the sort of songs she would ever listen to, as she ushers the girls away into the hall to greet their new teacher.

Now Auguste brings in an officer in Hungarian hussar uniform. He is Captain Kühl von Fehérvary, and he has brought with him his daughter

Trude, a new pupil for the school. He is not looking forward to leaving her, and he wonders how he will manage the horses and pigs at home without her, but Trude assures him that she'll be back home by the time the wild violets blossom and the swallows fly home ('Trudelchen, Pudelchen'/'Wenn die kleinen Veilchen blühen').

While the headmistress introduces Trude to her new teachers and school friends, Auguste is busy with another visitor, her own sweetheart Katzensteg, the steward of the 'Rhenania' association, who has slipped in secretly for a few moments with her. He is planning to buy an inn for the two of them in Bacharach ('Ich wünsche mir ein Häuschen'/'In Bacharach, in Bacharach, in Bacharach am Rhein').

Then Auguste announces the arrival of the new teacher, Dr Frank, but the man who enters is none other than Paul wearing a false, professorial beard which makes an immediate impression on the girls (Finale I: 'Das ist ein Mann voll elan'). Indeed the girls are each so eager for his attentions that, when he has left, Trude announces a lottery to decide which one of them may claim the delicious new teacher. Tickets bearing the name of various items of his clothing are put into a hat, together with the name of the professor himself as the jackpot. Helma draws his overcoat, Steffi his right glove, and Liesel draws the winning ticket.

The girls are surprised at their game by the return of the supposed Dr Frank, who asks what is going on. They tell him that he has been the main prize in a lottery and that Liesel has won him and, to their astonishment, he takes off the false beard and reveals who he is. He points out to Liesel that she has lost her bet and that he has therefore won a kiss from her. Before he can claim it, however, Frau Gutbier is heard returning. She has come to tell the girls that she will be away for the evening with friends—an announcement that is greeted with such hilarity by Liesel that she is given extra homework to do on the subject of Joan of Arc. Paul, meanwhile, has beat a hasty retreat out of the window.

SCENE 4

In the garden of the school that evening, the girls are doing gymnastics under the direction of Mademoiselle Faure ('Un, deux, un, deux, die Arme empor!') when Captain Kühl arrives to speak to Trude. Trude asks him to bring her her diary, which she has left in their hotel, insisting that he must promise not to look inside but, when the Captain returns and meets Auguste, the maidservant offers to deliver the book for him. She and Katzensteg cannot resist peeping inside and they are surprised at some of the amorous messages the diary contains ('Die schönsten Nelken'/'Kleine Fee, süsse Fee').

Liesel and Trude come out of the house with a dish full of apples. Liesel is thinking of the events of the afternoon and of Paul's appearance as Dr Frank but, most particularly, she is thinking of the kiss she owes him—her very first kiss. Trude, it seems, has already had her own first kiss with one of the young men of the 'Rhenania', and she generously gives Liesel the benefit of her experience ('Wenn du einen hast'/'Zu dir, zu dir, zu dir zieht es mich so magisch hin!').

Paul comes upon them sitting together, just as Trude is telling Liesel how glorious a kiss can be. Trude diplomatically decides to go and pick violets and leave the two together, so that Paul can claim the kiss his bet has won. 'Paul, tell me, please, am I the first girl you have kissed?' she asks timidly. 'No, the twenty-fifth,' he replies proudly. 'I'm celebrating my silver jubilee today.' Finally he persuades her to close both eyes, and her historic moment arrives ('Noch schwebt dein süsser Duft um mich'/'Du, du, du, schliess' deine Augen zu').

Trude returns with her bunch of violets, only to find Horst there. He, it seems, is the mysterious young man who claimed her first kiss, for they embrace each other warmly. Horst had no idea that Trude was coming to the school, but he feels that she will get her real education in rather livelier establishments than Frau Gutbier's school—beginning with the Moulin Rouge and moving on from there ('Was die Stadt an Bildungsstätten hat'/'Im Casino da steht ein Pianino').

Erwin and Helma also appear together, and Paul has the pleasure on behalf of the students of inviting all the girls to their party that evening. His aunt has already gone out, and once Mademoiselle Faure is asleep nothing wakes her. Auguste is invited to come with Katzensteg, and Trude's father, the cavalry captain, who is ever anxious to seek to recapture his lost youth, also receives an invitation. They are all prepared for a merry night ('Macht Euch auf die Reise'/'Das wird heut lustig sein').

Liesel is preparing to do her punishment exercise on the subject of Joan of Arc, but Paul arrives with a bottle of champagne and two glasses and, although they try to do the homework together, their minds all too readily ramble to other things. Indeed, before very long Paul is asking Liesel to marry him and, after a lingering kiss, she breaks into sobs of happiness. Paul tells her to dry her tears and assures her that he loves her ('Kind, weine nicht').

When the other students arrive with bottles and glasses to begin their party, the two joyfully announce their engagement (Finale: 'Das wird heut lustig sein!'). Tables are set, and the evening's celebrations proceed merrily on their way until suddenly they are disturbed by the sound of Isolde's voice. She has returned unexpectedly early from her evening out. Paul sums up the situation immediately. 'Everything in trousers under the table!' he calls, and the young men disappear with the bottles and glasses.

When the headmistress appears, Paul, complete with false beard, is leading the girls in a nocturne. Frau Gutbier is shocked to see the girls still up, sends them to bed immediately, and informs the supposed new master that she will deal with him in the morning. Suddenly a new voice is heard, and a stranger appears, announcing himself as Dr Frank, the new teacher. The real teacher and the impostor face each other, and the indignant Dr Frank pulls Paul's beard off. Frau Gutbier is horrified, but, to make matters worse, Captain Kühl is unable to hold his position under the table any longer. The men under the table are revealed and flee in all directions, and Dr Frank decides that this is no place for him. 'This is no educational establishment. It's a pleasure garden!'

SCENE 5

Thirty years, later Katzensteg's voice is heard finishing off the story of that spring day (Ballet of Violets).

SCENE 6

Katzensteg, Auguste, Gustl and Fritz are enjoying the story of those events thirty years before ('Servus, du gute alte Zeit') when Paul, Horst and Erwin appear for their reunion ('In Bacharach, in Bacharach, in Bacharach am Rhein'). They greet the Katzenstegs warmly but, when the conversation turns to the subject of Gustl and Fritz, Paul Gutbier repeats his objection to the Amazon type represented by Gustl.

They settle down to a drinking session, which soon takes them back to reminiscences of their student days ('Und hab' ich weisse Haare'). The wine flows freely, helped on its way by the fact that Gustl has dosed it with rum, as the men drink to the old times and to poor old Dr Frank. 'And I drink to his false beard,' Gustl interjects. 'What!' the men cry. Gustl now puts the Justice Minister himself on trial, and very soon she is challenging him to a duel, with Horst and Erwin as seconds (Finaletto: 'Auf die Mensur!'). Paul is quickly forced to give in, and his distaste for the 'Amazon' is changed to admiration. 'The girl is fabulous,' he admits. 'Then if she is fabulous, father, let me marry her!' chips in Fritz. Paul is forced to give way and acknowledge that another young man has found his partner (Er hat ein Mädel gern').

VENUS IN SEIDE

(Venus in Silk)

an operetta in three acts by Alfred Grünwald and Ludwig Herzer. Music by Robert Stolz. Produced at the Stadttheater, Zürich, 10 December 1932.

Produced at the Volksoper, Vienna, 4 March 1970.

Produced in Britain 1937 with Carl Brisson and Helen Gilliland.

CHARACTERS

Princess Jadja Milewska-Palotay
The stranger
Baron Vilmos Oroszy, *a head-palatine*
Jozsy, *his son*
Countess Mizzi Pottenstein-Oroszy, *the Baron's niece and ward*
A second stranger

A parson
Ladislaus von Köröshazy, *a lieutenant in a Hungarian dragoon regiment*
Giovanni Bambuscheck
Countess Piroska
Vörös-Bacsi
Mihaly, *Jadja's servant*
Zingra, *a gipsy girl*
An innkeeper
Pali, *leader of a gipsy orchestra*
Jani, *a gipsy boy*
Gentlemen and ladies of society, gipsies, countryfolk, guests

ACT 1

The Princess Jadja Milewska-Palotay is holding a party at her Hungarian home, Castle Szegedvar, to celebrate her wedding the following day. The head-palatine, Baron Vilmos Oroszy, who is enjoying himself playing cards with the parson and singing along to the dance music ('Tralala! Tralala! Ein Spielchen, ein kleines'), is looking forward to his son's wedding to the Princess, but he is worried that the boy has so far failed to turn up. He is particularly concerned for his son's safety because of the recent exploits of Sándor Rózsa, a bandit famous for his great audacity, who robs the rich to give to the poor.

The Princess is of Polish origin, and widely known both for her wealth and beauty and as being a fine, warm-hearted woman. As she emerges from the ballroom to the sound of a csárdás, she is warmly greeted by Oroszy and her other guests ('Hoch die schöne Polin') and, as the gipsy violinist plays, she reflects on her progress from her native Poland to the land of Tokay wine and gipsy music ('Fern im schönen Polenland'/'Spiel auf deiner Geige das Lied von Leid und Lust').

The Princess is even more anxious over the delay to her bridegroom in that he is bringing with him the result of a lawsuit she has been contesting. Upon the outcome of that suit depends whether or not the Princess will have to give up her castle. The castle once belonged to a Prince Johannes Teleky, who was exiled from Hungary for political reasons. Before he left, he entrusted the castle to his friend Palotay for safe-keeping. Now Prince Teleky has been granted a political amnesty, and his son Stephan is taking steps to recover the property from Palotay's widow.

Jadja cannot help but feel a deep hate for this man Teleky and, in her last submission to the tribunal, she even went so far as to call him a thief. Her hatred has been compounded by his behaviour over the famous portrait 'Venus in Silk', which the Viennese painter, Hans Makart, painted of her. Now it hangs in the castle but, before the court case, it was being exhibited at the Vienna Exhibition. Because Jadja refused to appear in person at the court during the trial of Teleky's petition, Teleky had the painting taken from the exhibition to court and addressed the judges with the words, 'See, your lordships, there she is, the 'Venus in Silk' who with her beauty persuaded

Prince Palotay to give her everything—even what didn't belong to him.' That mockery, Jadja swears, is something she will never forgive Teleky.

Jadja's friend Mizzi, Oroszy's niece and ward, is disappointed that she has come all the way from Vienna, only to find a distinct shortage of eligible young men in this out-of-the-way castle, but she is deeply concerned for Jadja and worries with her over the outcome of the court case. Jadja and Mizzi use the playing cards to see if they can conjure up any vision of the outcome ('Lasst uns die wissenden Karten befragen'/'Eine wie Du, war immer mein Traum') and the cards tell them some very inexplicit things. Jadja will receive a visit from a stranger, Mizzi will receive one from her sweetheart and, most mysterious of all, the case 'will be lost and yet won'.

The first of these predictions is soon fulfilled when Mizzi's sweetheart, the young lieutenant Ladislaus von Köröshazy, whom she believed to be in Hungary, suddenly appears at the party. Mizzi wonders if his commander has sent him along because there are so few good dancers at the party, but Ladislaus confesses that he has no idea why he is there. The day before, the general had asked for volunteers to go on a mission to Szegedvar. With Mizzi in mind, Ladislaus wasted no time in volunteering, and set off at once with a squadron of men. He has with him an envelope containing details of his assignment, but he was forbidden to open it until reaching Szegedvar. Now he feels that he might as well wait a little longer and enjoy the party. Mizzi is only too happy that, despite the general dearth of men, she now has one of her own ('Männer sind spärlich'/'Fräulein, ach Fräulein').

Oroszy is still worrying about his son's safety when a servant announces the arrival of a sledge. Oroszy is overjoyed. He commands the gipsy orchestra to strike up a greeting, and the guests all join to welcome Jozsy ('Eljen! Baron Jozsy'). However, the person who enters is not Jozsy, but a complete stranger who brings appalling news. Jozsy has been waylaid by Sándor Rózsa. The stranger tells how he met Jozsy in Köröfsalva, and how Sándor Rózsa then appeared and kidnapped Jozsy. Now the bandit is demanding a ransom of 10,000 gulden.

Having delivered his news, the stranger finds himself surrounded by young ladies all eager to know something of the bandit who has captured their imaginations. They are especially keen to hear the stranger's impressions of the bandit's legendary courtesies towards women ('Wir sind gespannt'/'Wie herrlich, wie herrlich, ein Räuber zu sein').

Jadja is horrified at the turn of events. Jozsy was carrying with him all her family jewels from the court jeweller in Budapest. She and Oroszy are curious to know the identity of the mysterious stranger, but he diverts their questions with compliments to Jadja. He is especially enchanted, he says, to see the original of the famous 'Venus in Silk'. 'The painting is a masterpiece of the artist,' he declares, 'but the original is a masterpiece of nature.' Jadja is finally persuaded to respect his anonymity and to observe the Polish saying: 'Look the guest in the eye, but don't ask who he is' ('Schau dem Gast in die Augen'). The stranger certainly cannot help looking straight into the eyes of the 'Venus in Silk' ('Strahlend stehst Du vor mir'/'Venus in Seide'), and in no time at all he is expressing his love for her.

Mizzi is proud that Ladislaus should have been entrusted with a special mission, but she is apprehensive when it turns out that he has been assigned the task of catching Sándor Rózsa. Still, when he succeeds, her uncle will not be able to raise any objections to her marrying Ladislaus. Then they will go and live in Budapest under a sky full of gipsy violins. Looking ahead, Ladislaus wastes no time in giving Mizzi lessons in Hungarian ('Sind wir erst ein bisserl verheirat'/Jonapot—grüss Dich Gott').

Jadja has arranged for the stranger to be accommodated overnight in the guest room which had been reserved for Joszy and, while he is away changing his clothes, the conversation turns to Sándor Rózsa and his predilection for disguise. Only the other week he appeared at a party of the Countess Palffy, with a group of friends, elegantly dressed in a red velvet Hungarian costume, stayed the night, and by the morning had cleared the place out. When the stranger reappears, Oroszy is horrified to see that he is wearing the very same outfit. Timidly he raises the subject of Sándor Rózsa and Ladislaus's commission to apprehend him, but the stranger expresses only a polite interest. 'How will you recognise this bandit?' he asks. 'By the red scar on his left wrist,' Oroszy explains. 'There is nothing special about that!' the stranger replies. 'I have one myself.'

The tension is relieved when Jadja calls everyone to dance (Finale I: 'Wie herrlich, wie herrlich, gelandet zu sein') until a servant arrives with news that sledges are arriving with a crowd of men, and the stranger introduces them as his friends. 'Heavens! Just as at Countess Palffy's!' exclaims Oroszy in horror, and he sends Ladislaus to alert his squadron of dragoons to storm the castle on the stroke of midnight.

Meanwhile a letter has mysteriously arrived from Sándor Rózsa, spelling out the ransom demand: 'I demand just one dukat for your son. He is not worth more. For the horse and carriage in which your son is travelling, however, I demand 9,999 dukats, and I shall not release your son without the horse and carriage.' 'Just as I said!' remarks the stranger. 'Yes, you seem to know a great deal about the brigand,' observes Oroszy. 'I know everything about him!' retorts the stranger, entering on a vigorous defence of the robber's actions that soon has the ladies singing the robber's praises ('Eljen! Erklingt es überall'/'Rózsa Sándor, Traum aller Frauen').

ACT 2

Supper over, the guests stream back into the dance hall ('Wie herrlich, wie herrlich war dieses Souper') and Oroszy discovers the appearance of another mysterious message from the bandit. This one tells him that the Jadja has lost her case and that Prince Teleky is on his way to take over Castle Szegedvar. 'How can that be?' asks Mizzi. 'In the cards it said 'Lost, and yet won'. Jadja at first determines to turn her dogs on the intrusive Teleky when he arrives, but then she rouses herself and, declaring that she is still mistress in the castle, announces that she and her guests will drink the wine-cellar dry ('Jonapot—grüss Dich Gott!').

When the stranger is left alone with the old parson, he is surprised to hear

1149

the old man address him as 'Your Grace'. 'You know?' he asks. 'That you are Prince Stephan Teleky,' the parson replies. 'You resemble your good father so closely. If ever you need anything from me, I would do everything in my power to help.' The Prince admits that he has never met Sándor Rózsa and that the bandit is in no way involved in Jozsy's disappearance. It seems that Teleky fell in love with Jadja the very first time he saw her painting and he has intercepted young Oroszy to stop his wedding, and locked him up overnight with a friend, while he made his way to the castle. The old parson promises to keep the secret, as Teleky reflects on the progress of his wooing of Jadja to date ('Erst hab' ich Komplimente gemacht'/'Augen, ihr rätselhaften Augen').

Jadja is reluctant to accept Oroszy's assertions that the stranger is really the bandit, but she agrees to sound him out while she dances with him. He persuades her to keep her promise to respect his incognito until midnight. He may be Sándor Rózsa, or he may be someone else. He could even be Prince Teleky. 'I would rather become the wife of Sándor Rózsa before I would allow this Teleky to kiss so much as a finger of my hand!' she declares, and the stranger muses on how he would approach her if he were either of the two men ('Gold, Juwelen, schenk' ich Dir'/'Nur für Dich, nur für Dich').

The confusion of the night increases when a second stranger, as elegantly dressed as the first, arrives claiming to be Prince Stephan Teleky. Jadja treats him contemptuously, but he assures her that he does not intend to evict her. All he asks for is the key to the silver room. Jadja walks away, leaving the two strangers face to face with each other. When the first stranger explains that *he* is Prince Teleky, the other retorts that, if Prince Teleky may pass himself off as Sándor Rózsa, then Sándor Rózsa may pass himself off as the Prince.

The new arrival is indeed the bandit. It seems his programme for the day included Castle Hatvany, and there he found the imprisoned Jozsy from whom he learned the full story of the court case. He has taken the documents and the Princess's family jewels which the boy had with him and he is now after the Princess's twelfth-century silver. The two men get down to some hasty haggling, the outcome of which is that Teleky agrees to pay the bandit a substantial sum to hand over the Princess's jewels. In the process the two acquire a firm respect for each other, and the bandit tells Teleky that, if ever he needs his help, he should visit the inn at Körösfalva which is his headquarters and ask for him with the password 'Paprika'. The two men are, they declare, brothers in the cause of love ('Wenn es sich um Liebe handelt'/'Solang es Frauen gibt').

Oroszy invites the second stranger to take a glass of wine with him and, anxious to find a source of finance for freeing his son, he tries to interest the man he believes to be Prince Teleky in the possibility of marrying his niece Mizzi. He tells him that he has identified the first stranger as the bandit. It is the only way that he could have known all about the ransom. 'Of course,' Oroszy adds, 'if I wanted I could pay three times that much.' Shortly afterwards he is puzzled to find a further letter from the bandit announcing that,

1150

since he can afford to pay three times as much, the ransom has duly been trebled.

Mizzi has decided that the time is right to get her uncle's approval to her marriage to Ladislaus, but her uncle has other things on his mind at the moment, and Ladislaus imagines that he may end up reduced to serenading Mizzi on his mandolin ('Was nützt mir eine schöne Maid'/'Spiel' mit mir, immer nur mit mir').

Teleky is now ready to make his crucial play ('Nun naht die Stunde der Entscheidung'). He throws a banknote to the leader of the gipsy orchestra and instructs him to play as beautifully as he can. If he succeeds in enrapturing the Princess, the violinist will receive a further payment. He plays what is, it transpires, Jadja's favourite melody, a tune which she declares would drag her to the end of the world. Believing Teleky to be the bandit, and knowing of Ladislaus's midnight plan of attack, she is concerned for his safety but he declares that he will leave only if she will go with him. Perhaps they might be able to forget everything together somewhere in Italy—in Naples to be precise ('Es steht am blauen Meer'/'O mia bella Napoli').

A messenger arrives from Rózsa bringing the Princess's jewels, and Teleky hands over the agreed price, but the messenger brings also a piece of information: the dragoons will not be coming. Apparently their horses have mysteriously disappeared while they tarried at a tavern to take refreshment. 'Everything is going to plan!' declares Teleky. 'Now comes my triump card'.

The dancing and merrymaking are at their height (Finale II: 'Walzerklang, Champagnerwein!') when midnight sounds and, in accord with his promise, the stranger reveals himself as Prince Stephan Teleky. Jadja is shocked, but the Prince assures her that everything he has done has been from his love for her and through his determination to prevent her marriage the following day. Jadja declares again that she would rather give herself to Sándor Rózsa than suffer familiarity from the man who has so hatefully wronged her and, since Oroszy is still adamant that he is really the bandit, Teleky decides to continue the deception.

To support his claims, he produces the casket containing Jadja's jewels and presents them as his wedding gift to his wife, declaring that nobody may leave the building until they have witnessed his marriage to Jadja. He calls upon the parson to marry them, and the latter, declaring that both parties are well known to him, proceeds to do so. When the wedding is well and truly made, Teleky lets the guests go, leaving him and Jadja in each other's arms.

ACT 3

The following day, in the tavern at Körösfalva where the bandit has his headquarters, a band of gipsies are enjoying a stirring dance ('Tanz in Kleidern'/'Wenn der Zigeuner spielt'). A group of Sándor Rózsa's robbers are awaiting their leader when news comes that they are to expect the arrival of Prince Teleky and his new wife, and that they are not, as they might imagine, to be robbed. On the contrary, their chief is helping the Prince whose wife still believes that her husband is Sándor Rózsa. When Teleky arrives, they dutifully maintain the pretence ('Er ist's, der Held, der Meister') and Jadja is delighted with the brigands' lair ('Kannst Du mir verzeihn, mein Lieb?'/'Ich frag' nicht, wer Du bist').

Oroszy arrives at the inn, still seeking his son and, feeling hungry, he asks the innkeeper for paprika. Since this is the bandit's password, he soon has the real Sándor Rózsa standing before him. Oroszy, of course, believes him to be Teleky and gives him the ransom money he has brought for safekeeping. Ladislaus is also on the bandit's trail, eager to be able to take Oroszy up on the offer of Mizzi's hand if he succeeds in making a capture. Mizzi is so confident of his success that she is already looking beyond marriage to starting a family ('Schon als kleines Mädelchen'/'Ich möcht' so gern ein Baby haben').

Jadja has changed into the costume of a gipsy princess and the beautiful, blonde Venus in Silk with whom Teleky had fallen in love seems even more beautiful to him as a dark and dazzling Romany ('In den Tiefen der Seele'/ 'Nimm Dich in Acht, vor meiner Liebe!'). But now Oroszy is led in and, pointing to Teleky, he calls on Ladislaus to arrest the bandit (Finale III: 'Ein Spion, ein Fremder ist es'). He is made to look very foolish when Jadja steps forward and announces that her husband is no bandit but His Grace Prince Stephan Teleky. As she lay in his arms, she saw a medallion around his neck with the portrait of his father. She may have lost her castle, but she has won it back again, just as the cards predicted.

Oroszy realises to his horror that he has let the real Sándor Rózsa escape with his money but, to the great delight of Mizzi, the bandit now appears and invites Ladislaus to arrest him. When he does, however, there is disappointment in store. Rózsa produces a document declaring him pardoned by the Emperor Franz Josef through the intercession of Prince Teleky. The bandit orders all his captured goods to be returned—including Jozsy who, having shared his captivity with one Countess Piroska, has conveniently found himself a wife.

GLÜCKLICHE REISE

(Bon Voyage)

an operetta in three acts and seven scenes by Max Bertuch. Lyrics by Kurt Schwabach. Music by Eduard Künneke. Produced at the Kurfürstendamm-Theater, Berlin, 23 November 1932, with Walter Jahnkuhn (Robert), Ernst Verebes (Stefan), Hilde Woerner (Lona) and Lizzi Waldmüller (Monika).

A film version was produced by Alfred Abel in 1933.

CHARACTERS

Robert von Hartenau
Stefan Schwarzenberg
Peter Brangersen

Lona Vonderhoff
Monika Brink
Homann, *a travel agent*
Councillor Walter Hübner
Bielefeld, *manager of a dance troupe*
Frau Maschke
Sarah
Käthe Hinz, Ludmila Meyer, Paul Lehrling, *employees of Homann*
Barman, mestizos, crowds, dancing girls

SCENE 1

On his lonely farm in Brazil, a young German, Robert von Hartenau, is
having a hard time with the mestizo farmworkers. He is finding it especially
difficult to get any sense out of the old servant, Sarah, and altogether he is
feeling thoroughly sick of things in Brazil. The sound of a ship's siren
heralds the arrival of the mailboat, and Sarah rushes off to see what letters it
brings for Robert and his colleague Stefan Schwarzenberg. Robert is especially excited at the prospect of news from his pen friend in Germany. Her
letters provide the only relief for his homesickness, and he longs to be able to
meet her in person ('Meine Sehnsucht nach der Einen').

This exchange of letters began when Robert and Stefan inserted an
advertisement in a Berlin newspaper: 'Two friends, farmers in Brazil, seek
exchange of letters with two nice German girls.' It resulted in replies from
two girls in Berlin—Lona Vonderhoff and Monika Brink—with whom they
have been carrying on a romantic correspondence ever since. Stefan gathers
from his letters from Monika that she is a well-to-do and much travelled
young lady. If only they could get to meet them!

To Robert's delight, Brangersen, the captain of the mailboat, proves to
have been a fellow officer of his in the war but, pleased as the young men are
to see him, his descriptions of life back home merely serve to heighten their
longing. Their thoughts centre on the flowers, the happiness and the girls of
Berlin ('Drüben in der Heimat, da blüht ein Rosengarten'). They tell
Brangersen how they long to get back home but cannot afford the fares, and
the captain promptly comes up with the answer. Why don't they work their
passages as stewards on his ship? The two friends accept without hesitation
and gleefully wish each other bon voyage!' ('Auf nach drüben'/'Glückliche
Reise').

SCENE 2

In the office of the South American Line in Berlin. the assistants are
chatting among themselves as they go through their daily work under the eye
of their manager, Homann. Amongst the employees is Lona Vanderhoff, a
somewhat serious young lady who is engaged to the middle-aged Councillor
Hübner—not because she loves him, but simply to satisfy her mother's
wishes for her to settle down. This rather sedate arrangement contrasts

sharply with that of her colleague, Monika Brink, who keeps up a correspondence with an unknown young man in South America. This is something about which Monika keeps very quiet, however, and Lona knows nothing of the details.

A troupe of dancing girls come pirouetting into the office with their manager, Bielefeld. They are about to embark on a voyage and excitedly discuss the joys and drawbacks of a long trip at sea ('Ach, das Wasser ist so nass'). They are still there when Stefan enters. He has come in search of Monika and the travel office is the address which she has used for letters. He chats with Homann and Bielefeld about life on the Amazon and his encounters with man's ancestors, the apes ('Am Amazonas, da wohnen unsere Ahnen'), but when he enquires about Monika, he is surprised to find her there in the office.

Monika is far from the wealthy socialite she pretended to be. She is just one of Homann's secretarial staff but, although she is startled at the unexpected arrival of her pen-friend, she rapidly pulls herself together and plays to the full the part of a society lady visiting the office making travel arrangements. 'Dear friend,' she says to Stefan, 'if you only knew the hectic life a lady of today leads—a new summer hat, a new manor, and in between a quick flight to Monte.' Stefan is enchanted, and they soon agree to spend the evening together at the casino on the Wannsee ('Lieber Freund, ach, wenn Sie wüsten'/'Der erste Blick, der entscheidet so viel').

Robert, whose own pen-friend used a poste restante address, arrives at the shipping office looking for Stefan, and he is received by Lona, who wonders whether, after his voyage from South America, he might wish to book a trip to Switzerland or the Riviera, Tunis or Samarkand ('Oh, helfen Sie mir, meine sehr Geschätzte'/'Liebe kennt keine Grenze'). Robert has not even got as far as asking the young lady's name when Stefan comes by and suggests that they join himself and Monika on their evening trip to the casino on the Wannsee.

SCENE 3
At the casino a singing group is providing an intimate cabaret ('Das Leben ist ein Karusell') while, in the bar, Stefan and Robert are passing the evening with their new girl friends. Monika is still playing the part of the society lady, talking of *thés dansants* and the problems of choosing clothes and having one's hair styled ('Mein liebes Kind'/'Jede Frau geht so gerne mal zum Tanztee') but the conversation between Robert and Lona is of a much more serious tone, as he attempts to draw her out a little ('Wenn man verliebt ist').

Monika is embarrassed to find her boss, Homann, in the casino, and she has to work hard to prevent conversation between him and Stefan taking an embarrassing turn ('Aber, aber, meine Herr'n'/'Schatz, der erste Satz zum grossen Glück') while Lona is dismayed to see that Homann's companion is her fiancé, Hübner. Fortunately Hübner does not seem upset at seeing her with another man, and Lona confesses to Robert that the relationship is no deep affair of the heart ('Die grosse Liebe ist heute nur möglich'/'Nacht muss es sein, wenn sein Herz verschenkt!').

1154

Stefan and Monika are, by now, getting on like a house on fire ('Endlich bist du mein, mein Liebling'/'Warum?—Weshalb?—Wieso, bin ich nach dir verrückt?'), but trouble is just around the corner. The conversation between Robert and his girl friend inevitably gets round to the subject of his pen-friendship and, when he mentions that the name of his correspondent is Lona Vonderhoff, Lona tells him in amazement that that is her name and swears that she knows nothing of the letters.

Knowing that Stefan's correspondent was Monika, Lona manages to add two and two together and, when she gets Monika alone, she tackles her about it. Proudly, Monika admits that she had written all the letters, using her own name to write to Stefan and Lona's name for the letters to Robert ('Ja, ja, auf mich kann man sich verlassen!'). Lona feels deeply embarrassed and angry with Monika for not confiding the truth to her. She declares that she can never face Robert again ('Das hab' ich gemerkt') and she rushes out of the casino leaving Monika to explain to Robert.

Robert assumes that she has run away because she really had written the letters and is now ashamed to admit it. Monika is about to confess the truth, when Homann passes by. 'Monika dear,' he calls. 'Lovely evening, what? Enjoyed yourself? See you in the morning at nine sharp!' Then, to Robert and Stefan, he adds, 'Terrible, fellows, when one is so dependent on a secretary!' The cat is now really out of the bag, and Monika confesses to being not a society lady but a typist. While Stefan recoils in shock, Robert takes things more philosophically, but then Monika admits to Robert that she had written the letters to him as well as those to Stefan. The men depart, deflated, leaving Monika to reflect sadly on the swings and roundabouts of life ('Das Leben ist ein Karussell').

SCENE 4
In a quiet Berlin side street, Stefan and Robert are pacing up and down, blaming each other for what has happened ('Deine ist schuld!'). The street is the one on which Monika and Lona share lodgings, and the men look up at their windows knowing full well that, for all that has happened, they are really deeply fond of the two girls ('Deine nur schuld!').

SCENE 5
The girls are just as miserable about what has happened, and certainly no less in love but, unable to make the first move, they can do no more than watch with beating hearts the two figures in the street below.

SCENE 6
The following morning the two young men are still out in the street and, when the girls leave their lodgings to set off for work, they have to try to slip past Stefan and Robert unrecognised. Lona gets by, but Stefan manages to stop Monika. In no time at all she is in Stefan's arms, agreeing to marry him

and accompany him back to Brazil as a farmer's wife ('Komm, mein kleines Farmerbräutchen'/'Bitte, bitte, sei so nett, schenk mir doch ein Freibillett').

SCENE 7
Robert finally catches up with Lona at the shipping office, and she, in turn, offers no more than token resistance to his overtures. Poor Homann is destined to lose two secretaries, and the shipping office does not even get the compensation of their bookings to South America, since all four will have to work their passage back to Brazil. However, their journey gets under way with the best wishes of all for a 'bon voyage' ('Glückliche Reise').

DER VERLORENE WALZER
(ZWEI HERZEN IM DREIVIERTELTAKT)

(The Lost Waltz/Two Hearts in Waltz Time)

an operetta in three acts and eight scenes by Paul Knepler and J M Welleminsky based on the film *Zwei Herzen im Dreivierteltakt* by Walter Reisch and Franz Schulz. Produced as *Der verlorene Walzer* at the Opera House, Zurich, 30 September 1933.

Produced as *Zwei Herzen im Dreivierteltakt* at the Titania-Theater, Vienna, 15 May 1948. Produced at the Volksoper 29 March 1975 with Peter Minich (Anton), Sylvia Holzmayer (Anny) and Helga Papouschek (Hedi).

Produced at the Greek Theatre, Hollywood, 8 July 1946 in a version by Dailey Paskman and William A Drake with Kenny Baker, Pamela Caveness and Irene Manning.

The original film was produced by Geza von Bolvary in 1930 with Gretl Theimer, Walter Janssen, Oscar Karlweis, Willi Forst, Szöke Szakall, Paul Morgan and Paul Hörbiger.

CHARACTERS

Anton Hofer, *a composer*
Anny Lohmayer, *an operetta leading lady*
Mizzi Reitmayer, *a soubrette*
Nicki Mahler, Vicki Mahler, *librettists*
Hedi
Baron Hartenberg
Fredy Pachinger
Dr Mitislav Isakiewicz, *a notary*
Theatre director
Blaustingl, *the theatre administrator*
Weigl, *a theatre servant*
Franz Gschwendter, *a Heurige singer*
Brigitte, *the Mahlers' housekeeper*
Landlord of the Heurige

1156

Fekete, *a composer*
Blinder, *a Kammersänger*
Heurigen guests, actors, actresses

SCENE 1 (ACT 1)

It is afternoon in the Viennese home of the librettists and twin brothers, Nicki and Vicki Mahler, and the clock is already striking three when their old housekeeper, Brigitte, appears with a breakfast tray and knocks first on Nicki's door ('Herr Nicki! Herr Nicki!') and then on Vicki's. The brothers emerge in pyjamas, their minds on their work. Vicki evidently finds the business of writing lyrics rather easier than Nicki does ('Das muss doch wirken'). The best tonic to their inspiration seems to be a dose of mutual insults and, this completed, they settle down at their desks to work at their new operetta.

They are interrupted by the return of Brigitte with a letter from the brothers' younger sister, Hedi. Nicki and Vicki have not seen Hedi for five years, but now she is coming to Vienna to celebrate her eighteenth birthday. When last they saw her she was still a little girl, and the sight of her photograph, in ski clothes, increases their anticipation of her arrival the following day ('Meine kleine Schwester heisst Hedi').

Their work is further interrupted by a visit from their leading lady, Anny Lohmayer, bringing the news that she has decided not to appear in their next operetta. She has been invited to play the role of the Countess in the new operetta by Fekete at the Residenztheater, and she intends to accept. It soon becomes apparent that this move has something to do with an argument with her lover, the brothers' composer-collaborator, Toni Hofer. Toni now appears on the doorstep and is seemingly oblivious to the fact that Anny completely ignores him. He is more interested in the song he has just composed and he believes it will be the hit of his new show. He has actually written the lyric to it himself, and he sits down at the brothers' piano to demonstrate ('Das ist der Schmerz beim ersten Kuss').

Anny sees the song's theme of heartache as representing the state of her relationship with Toni. When she tells him of her plan to appear in Fekete's operetta, their bickering starts anew and the team have just reached the stage of agreeing that they will all go their separate artistic ways, when the telephone rings. It is the manager of the Zentraltheater, asking whether the new operetta is ready and when they can come round to play it to him. Each in turn seizes the telephone to assure the manager of their utter availability and the excellence of the operetta, and Nicki and Vicki hurry to change out of their pyjamas, while Toni goes over the new song with Anny ('Also hör ein bisserl her').

SCENE 2

In the theatre office, the administrator Blaustingl and the theatre factotum Weigl are trying to keep their spirits up in the face of the present discouraging takings ('Wer ist im Theater der wichtigste Herr?'). Weigl has not always been in the theatre. He was previously employed as an echo in an alpine resort. He had to sit behind a rock and echo the calls of the tourists. This job came to a sudden end when a French tourist shouted out 'Au revoir!' and he called back 'Auf Wiedersehen!'.

Anny, Toni, Nicki and Vicki arrive to see the director about the new operetta. Toni announces that it is to be called *Zwei Herzen im Dreivierteltakt*, and Nicki and Vicki begin to tell the story of a pretty blonde and a young lieutenant. When they play 'Das ist der Schmerz der ersten Kuss', the director is delighted and he is even more taken with the next big number, a song-and-dance comedy routine in which Nicki and Vicki act out the part of the buffo and soubrette ('Grüss dein Fräulein Braut von mir'). The director has heard enough. He can already see the full houses with ticket prices raised 30%, though he is naturally reluctant to discuss authors' percentages. The four friends have seen and heard it all before and have little faith in a fabulous future ('Auch du wirst mich einmal betrügen').

The manager decides that rehearsals are to start at once, but there is one problem. Where is the big waltz? Nicki recites the text for the song, but Toni has to confess that he has not yet composed it. The manager offers to place his whole stock of operetta scores at Toni's disposal, but the composer is indignant. 'You don't believe that I take my ideas from other people's scores, do you?' he asks. 'Better people than you have done it!' is the reply. Toni is instructed to have the waltz by the morning. Then they shall have the contract. Blaustingl and the manager are left congratulating themselves on a good piece of business as they confidently sing one of the new songs to themselves ('Grüss dein Fräulein Braut von mir').

SCENE 3

In a wine bar, a Heurige singer is singing a Viennese song ('Das ist kein Zufall, dass das Glück in Wien wohnt'). Anny and Toni are sitting together, but they have nothing to say to each other. When Anny is recognised by the landlord, she is persuaded to sing and obliges with Toni's new song ('Das ist der Schmerz beim ersten Kuss'). Baron Hartenberg, a Viennese man-about-town, asks Anny for a dance, and, while she is dancing, the singer introduces himself to Toni as an old chum from music college, Franz Gschwendter. The love of wine and women have reduced him from composer of symphonies to Heurige singer.

Toni tells Franz about his new operetta and of how he needs to find a big waltz melody before the morrow, and Franz reminds him of the recipe used by Poletti, another fellow music student who, when he needed inspiration, found it in a new love affair. Anny overhears this piece of advice and tells Toni that Franz is right. She goes to join Hartenberg at his table, and now it is Toni's turn to feel heartbreak ('Das ist der Schmerz der ersten Kuss'), while Anny leads the assembled revellers in another chorus of the Viennese song ('Das ist kein Zufall, dass das Glück in Wien wohnt').

SCENE 4 (ACT 2)

Back at the Mahlers' home, Nicki and Vicki are waiting for Hedi to emerge from her room ('Meine kleine Schwester heisst Hedi'). Brigitte is delighted at seeing her beloved little girl again but Nicki decides that he should be the one to take care of Hedi. He is, after all, the elder. 'The elder!' retorts Vicki. 'By half an hour! Our birth was like a variety programme—first the supporting artist, and then the star turn!' Hedi emerges to find herself deluged with presents and is delighted. 'If only one could live twice!' she exclaims, as Nicki and Vicki both clamour for her attention ('Wenn man zweimal leben könnte!').

The best of the presents is a new dress, which Hedi intends to save for her birthday, which is also the day of the brothers' première. Hedi is anxious to meet Toni, as she knows all his songs and waltzes by heart, but the brothers are more concerned that the composer has still not come up with the much needed waltz.

Their deliberations are interrupted by the arrival of Mizzi Reitmeyer, a soubrette, chasing a role in the new operetta. She is still there when Weigl arrives, seeking a copy of the script for the new show. He happens to mention that Toni has engaged him to invite a dozen people to supper that evening, but Nicki tells him that he will do the task for him, takes the list, and gives Weigl a note for his pains. When Weigl has gone, Nicki tears the list into pieces and announces that instead he will send a good fairy—Mizzi—to inspire Toni to compose his waltz. Mizzi leaves with the hint that her part in the operetta will depend on her success with Toni.

Unseen, on the landing, Hedi has heard everything and has ideas of her own. When the twins have gone out, she takes out her new dress, searches in the telephone book for Mizzi's number, and telephones her to say on behalf of Nicki and Vicki that Mizzi will not, after all, be required at Toni's that evening. Mizzi swallows the story, and Hedi contemplates what her fate may be, as she prepares herself to take the soubrette's place ('Heute besuch' ich mein Glück').

SCENE 5

At Toni's home the table is set for twelve visitors, and Weigl is helping with final preparations when, to their surprise, Anny appears. She has heard that she no longer has a part in the forthcoming operetta and bitterly chides Toni for this display of ingratitude after all that she has done for him. Toni assures her that he has nothing to do with it. He pours out two glasses of cognac and they pass in review the times they have spent together ('Es war so schön—man hat geweint, man hat gelacht!'). Finally Toni agrees to speak to the director the following morning.

When Anny has left, Toni sits at the piano and attempts once more to find the melody for his waltz. Again all is in vain. Now Hedi arrives. Toni is taken aback—the more so when Hedi announces that his expected guests will not be coming. He asks her name, but she tells him that it is unimportant. She is simply his good fairy, Florabella. Toni dismisses Weigl and settles down to a supper for two with Hedi ('Holde Fee, darf ich bitten Ihren Arm zum Souper?'). He is clearly enchanted with the mysterious young woman, and she no less with him ('Du bist meine schönste Träumerei') and it is not long before he takes her tenderly in his arms and kisses her.

Hedi persuades Toni to play her something from his new operetta, something that neither she nor anyone else has yet heard. He plays her 'Das ist der Schmerz beim ersten Kuss' but she insists on a waltz. She picks up the text that is lying on the piano, and Toni immediately produces the waltz tune that he has been seeking ('Zwei Herzen im Dreivierteltakt'). As he joyfully plays it over, Hedi steals away, leaving Toni to contemplate the power and enchantment of his good fairy.

SCENE 6 (ACT 3)

It is late at night when Hedi gets back to her brothers' home, reflecting on her adventure ('Heute besuch' ich mein Glück!'). She tiptoes past the brothers' doors and into her room but, before long, the doorbell rings, and Brigitte goes to answer. It is Toni, come to tell Nicki and Vicki that he has come up with his big waltz ('Ein Walzer, ein Walzer'). He begins to play it for them, only to stop suddenly. He cannot remember it. He tells the twins of the visit of his good fairy ('Du bist meine schönste Träumerei'), before dejectedly taking his leave.

Late though it is, the twins phone Mizzi. She will have remembered the melody. When she tells them that, on their instructions, she had not gone to Toni's, they are flabbergasted, and helpless to work out who Toni's good fairy can have been. They retire to bed, but Hedi, unable to sleep, emerges from her room and sings over the waltz that Toni had composed for her ('Zwei Herzen im Dreivierteltakt').

SCENE 7

The Mahler twins are sitting in their living room attending to their manicure ('Er sagt Ja, sie sagt Nein') and waiting for Hedi to appear on her birthday, before dashing off to the theatre. When they have gone, Hedi stands behind the table, on which is a cake with eighteen candles, and contemplates the joy of being eighteen years old.

Weigl arrives from the theatre for some papers that the brothers have forgotten and he is astonished to see Toni's 'good fairy' at their house. Hedi swears him to secrecy, but Weigl tells her the dramatic news that Toni has forgotten his waltz. And it is not just the waltz he is looking for, but her too. Hedi is ecstatic ('Wenn man zweimal leben könnte').

SCENE 8

In the theatre a rehearsal is under way, and Anny and a chorus of girls in military uniform sing a march medley ('Meine kleine Schwester'/'Wenn man zweimal leben könnte'/'Grüss dein Fräulein Braut von mir'). Toni still hasn't remembered his waltz and offers to use one of his old ones instead, but the director prefers to use the 'Radetzky March'. The rehearsal ends with Toni left alone at the piano, still struggling to recall his lost waltz until Hedi's voice is heard off-stage singing the melody ('Zwei Herzen im Dreivierteltakt'). Toni rapturously takes it up and flings his arms around Hedi, as Nicki and Vicki enter from the wings with astonishment to witness this unexpected dénouement.

The stage operetta was designed to capitalise on the success of the 1930 film musical *Zwei Herzen im Dreivierteltakt*, but the stage score uses only the refrains of the film's two big song hits—the title waltz song and 'Auch du wirst mich einmal betrügen'. The latter song was also interpolated into the French and English versions of *Im weissen Rössl*.

CLIVIA

an operetta in three acts by Charles Amberg. Music by Nico Dostal. Produced at the Theater am Nollendorfplatz, Berlin, 23 December 1933 with Lillie Claus (Clivia). Produced at Liège 1965 and at Bordeaux 1966.

CHARACTERS

E W Potterton, *a financier from Chicago*
Clivia Gray, *a film actress*
Juan Damigo, *known as* Olivero
Yola, *his cousin*
Lelio Down, *a reporter from the Chicago Times*
Caudillo, *an inn landlord*
Diaz, *a police chief*
Valdivo, *a police inspector*
Gustav Kasulke
Members of a film company, girls, gauchos, citizens of Boliguay, officers

ACT 1
In the courtyard of an inn on the border of the South American state of Boliguay, amongst a colourful group of local herdsmen and their women ('Wo die Kordilleren ragen, sind wir stolz in Ehrenfragen'), a white man and a half-caste woman are making sensuous advances to each other, when suddenly an American Indian springs out upon them. With an accusing cry, the Indian stabs the white man, who sinks into the arms of the woman and falls lifeless to the ground.

It transpires that these are merely actors in a film scene. The film's leading lady, Clivia Gray, as usual, exercises her privilege of being late on the set, but eventually she turns up dressed in riding costume and carrying a whip, obviously relishing the fame that she is currently enjoying ('Man spricht heut nur noch von Clivia'). The innkeeper, Caudillo, brings a letter for Clivia, which turns out to be from a fellow actor named Banks. Banks explains that he will not be turning up to play his part in the film, adding, 'I was engaged as an actor, and not to grapple with revolutionary desperados. Something is not right about this film...' 'The fellow is crazy,' responds the film's financier, Potterton, but under Clivia's further questioning he is obliged to explain that Banks has obviously discovered that Potterton is currently insolvent. However, he is a financier and in Boliguay he has oil and mining rights which will provide the finance for the film. As for Banks, he can be replaced locally.

A further problem presents itself when Caudillo points out that an American film company will not get permission to film in Boliguay unless the leading actors are Boliguayans. Since Caudillo, besides being district prefect and chief of police, is also able to perform marriages, he suggests that Clivia should go through a marriage of convenience with a Boliguayan citizen. Once they are inside Boliguay the marriage can easily be terminated.

Clivia contemplates the idea with dismay ('Mir ist nicht ganz geheuer'), but her thoughts are interrupted by the sound of a male voice singing the hit song from her previous film ('Zum Glücklichsein gehört nicht viel'). The voice is that of a gaucho, and Clivia retires into the inn rather than engage in prolonged conversation with him. The stranger tries to extract information from Caudillo about his guests, but the innkeeper will not consider any indiscretion—not, at least, until a large enough bribe is forthcoming.

Caudillo takes the stranger into the inn, as a group of girls in smart uniforms march in with their lieutenant, Jola, at their head. This is the local army of Amazons, soldier girls who act as guards on the border of Boliguay ('Wir sind Mädchen von heute'/'Wenn die Trommeln und Trompete klingen durch die Stadt'), and they bring with them Lelio Down, a Chicago reporter, whom they have just expelled from their country. Never one to miss a chance, Down now busies himself writing a report on the film company's project and the missing Jimmy Banks. When he produces a photograph that he has just taken of a handsome Boliguayan, Potterton, instantly seeing this man as a suitable replacement for Banks, instructs Lelio to bring him to the inn.

Potterton has no sooner left the scene than the stranger who had earlier interrupted Clivia's soliloquising reappears. Lelio recognises him as the man in his photograph and tries to interest him in becoming a film actor. When Clivia returns the stranger introduces himself as Juan Damigo, telling her how greatly he admired her previous film *Spring Night Rendezvous*. Clivia describes the plot of the new film to him, but Juan is more interested in whether real life has always brought her the happy end she enjoys in her films. 'I take life as it comes,' she replies. The two are very soon becoming much better acquainted ('Ich weiss, Sie gehen unbeschwert durchs Leben'/ 'Mit Dir möcht ich durchs Leben wandern') but, for all their strong mutual attraction, Juan regrets that he cannot join her in her film. He has neither the talent nor the time for acting.

Now an 'old banger' of a motor car appears, inscribed with the words

'Around the world—without money', and out of it steps Kasulke, a tourist from Berlin. He is about to drive off again when the Amazons return and begin questioning him on the business that brings him to Boliguay. He tells them that he is an inventor travelling the world to obtain backing for his patents. He was also once a ballet master, and he reckons that if he'd had a ballet troupe like the Boliguayan Amnazons he'd have indulged his passion for travelling by taking them on a world tour ('Reisen und wandern, und möglichst immer weit'/'Man muss mal ab und zu verreisen').

The Amazons agree to escort Kasulke over the border but, as they are departing, Jola catches sight of the mysterious Juan. From their conversation, it becomes evident not only that Jola is Juan's cousin but that he is none other than President Olivero of Boliguay in disguise. It seems that the President is doing some personal undercover investigation into Potterton's plans to take up the options granted to him by a previous régime on Boliguay's oil and mining resources. These options have been declared worthless by the current administration, but he suspects that Potterton is now using the film company as a front to gain entry to Boliguay. Juan tells Jola of the plan to marry him off to Clivia and, since Jola sees this as a means of getting Potterton into Boliguay and legally under arrest, it is agreed that Juan should fall in with the plan.

While those directly involved make preparations for the marriage ceremony, Lelio engages in some mild flirtations with his former captor, Jola ('Fällt der Blick auf soviel Charme und Chic'/'So was Schönes'). As the evening draws in, a group of gauchos sit down at the tables of the inn to enjoy the performance of a pair of Latin dancers dancing a tango (Finale I: 'Wenn die süsse Carinjosa laut in allen Kneipen tönt'). At last Clivia and Juan appear for their wedding. In front of Caudillo they swear allegiance to each other and, while Lelio sends off to his newspaper a cable reporting the marriage of Clivia Gray to a gaucho, the gauchos cheer the newlyweds and wish them and Potterton well. Under cover of the coach taking the film company into Boliguay, Lelio also slips back across the border.

ACT 2
In a large room of the Colon Hotel in Boliguay, looking out over the sea, a party is under way and the guests, in evening dress and masks, are enjoying a ballet and choral performance ('Traumschön ist die Nacht'). Potterton invites the guests into the garden for a buffet and dancing before everyone returns at midnight to take off their masks and enjoy the big surprise he has in store.

Juan has sent Clivia a bunch of roses every day since they arrived in Boliguay and, when he turns up at the party, Clivia expresses herself surprised and flattered by his dedication to their marriage. He explains that in southern America they take matters of the heart seriously ('Liebe ist kein Spiel'/'Das ich mein armes Herz an Dich verlor'). Three masked men now furtively enter the room and seat themselves in a corner ('Wir tragen eine Maske zwar') and, when Potterton joins them, it becomes apparent from

1163

their conversation that they are plotting the overthrow of Olivero and the return of Potterton's friend, the deposed President.

As Potterton shows the three men out, Kasulke enters with Lelio. Kasulke is hoping Potterton will finance one of his inventions, and he offers Lelio a 50-50 share for his help in publicising it, but Lelio is more interested in the Amazon lieutenant, to whom he has taken a considerable fancy. She conveniently appears and is surprised to see the man whom she thought she had deported. Lelio declares that she can deport him her whole life long, but he will be no less enchanted by her ('Fräulein, Sie gefallen mir!'/'Sie sind mir so sympathisch').

The next visitors are Captain Diaz and Inspector Valdivio of the Boliguay Secret Police. Valdivio has been watching Potterton, and he has arranged for the three masked men to be followed. Diaz compliments Juan on tempting Potterton to Boliguay in order to root out his contacts, but Juan is dismayed at Diaz's suggestion that Clivia is mixed up in the plot. When Juan and Clivia are alone together, he asks her what she knows of Olivero, but she tells him that she knows nothing about politics. She is more concerned with her growing affection for Juan, and soon she is telling him how much she loves him. Juan is deeply affected ('Bin ich wirklich die Liebe?'/'Wunderbar, wie nie ein Wunder war'), especially when she declares that, if necessary, she will give up her film career to be with him. While they talk, however, a search of Clivia's room has revealed the letter from Banks, and from this Diaz deduces that Clivia is a party to the planned coup.

When Lelio returns with Jola he is dressed in a bolero and Mexican hat and, to demonstrate how fully he is in the Latin-American mood, he dances a fiery tarantella for the benefit of Jola and Potterton ('Kleines, sag mir eines'/'Am Manzanares'). Clivia, for her part, is simply enjoying the sweet sensations of newly found love ('Ich bin verliebt'). Then midnight sounds, and the guests unmask and crowd around Potterton to hear him announce his big surprise (Finale II: 'Meine Damen und Herr'n, Sie haben sich hier, so hoffe ich, gut amüsiert!'). 'At this very moment,' he begins, 'President Olivero, that talentless upstart, is being held in his headquarters by his—that is to say by *my*—officers.' To the astounded guests he announces that the exiled President is to be recalled and Lelio, who knows a scoop when he hears one, rushes out to cable his newspaper.

Then Diaz appears on the scene and announces the President. When Juan appears, Clivia and Potterton are astounded. 'Are you really Olivero?' she asks, as Juan tells the shrivelling Potterton that his agents were professional swindlers who have run off with their pay-off. Turning to Clivia, he tells her too that the game is up, and refuses to believe her plea that she had nothing to do with the attempted coup. She and Potterton are taken into custody and the guests sent to their rooms. 'We have won, President Olivero,' declares Diaz. 'You may call it a victory,' Juan replies sadly, 'but for me it was a defeat'.

ACT 3
Back in his headquarters Olivero discusses the situation with his officers.

1164

Diaz believes that Potterton and Clivia should stand trial, but Juan thinks otherwise. 'Potterton is played out,' he says. Valdivio brings in Lelio, whom he has succeeded in re-recapturing, and Jola, who is never far behind the newspaperman, follows. She believes that Clivia knew nothing about the plot engineered by Potterton and Banks, and Lelio suggests that Clivia should be given the opportunity to escape. If she takes it, he suggests, her guilt is proven. If she chooses to remain, it will prove her innocence. Juan agrees to turn a blind eye while the scheme is attempted.

Left in Jola's good hands, Lelio resumes his flirtation. As a believer in newspaper horoscopes, he notes the fact that he, born in July, makes the perfect partner for her, born under Taurus ('Schon die alten Chinesen'/'In den Sternen steht geschrieben'). Kasulke is brought in and comes face to face with Potterton, who is demanding to see a lawyer. Kasulke tries to interest the financier in his patents, but Potterton is more interested in the fact that Kasulke knows a local lawyer and he writes out a cheque, demanding that Kasulke bring the lawyer to him. Potterton and Clivia are told that they are to be allowed out of the country and are prepared for departure as, alone in his office, Juan reflects on his love for Clivia ('Dich hab' ich von ganzem Herzen geliebt').

At the Boliguay airfield, Potterton, pursued by Lelio and his camera, is preparing to board a plane. Kasulke, too, is there, his cheque from Potterton having bounced. Clivia arrives accompanied by Jola, who asks Potterton whether Clivia really knew the true meaning of Banks's letter. 'Of course not!' he replies impatiently, as he urges Clivia to get into the plane. Her innocence further affirmed, she realises that she cannot leave Boliguay and Juan. Potterton climbs alone into the plane, urging Lelio to let him know if Clivia is accepted as the President's wife so that he can sell Clivia's old films at an inflated price.

As the plane takes off, Diaz appears with Juan, who begs Clivia's pardon for having doubted her. Lelio gets a photograph of them embracing and, when the Amazon girls appear on the scene, Kasulke declares that he will turn them into a dance troupe to make the Tiller Girls look like lame ducks. The crowd that has gathered joyously salute their President ('Hoch Olivero! Hoch Olivero!') as Boliguay and Clivia arrive at a happy ending.

The synopsis incorporates the ending of the revised book by F Maregg. In the original the final scene is in the square outside Olivero's office.

GIUDITTA

a musical comedy in five scenes by Paul Knepler and Fritz Löhner. Music by Franz Lehár. Produced at the State Opera House, Vienna, 20 January 1934 with Jarmila Novotna (Giuditta), Richard Tauber (Octavio), Margit Bokor (Anita) and Erich Zimmermann (Pierrino). Produced at the Volksoper, 18 October 1951.

Produced at the Théâtre de la Monnaie, Brussels, 1935 with Kate Walter-Lippert, José Janson and Suzanne de Gavre.

CHARACTERS

Manuele Biffi
Giuditta, *his wife*
Octavio, *a Captain*
Antonio, *a Lieutenant*
Eduard Barrymore
A duke
The duke's adjutant
Ibrahim, *proprietor of the Alcazar night club*
Professor Martini
Pierrino, *a fruit seller*
Anita, *a fisher girl*
Lolitta, *a dancer*
Sebastiano, *a landlord*
Officers, soldiers, villagers, dancers, guests, musicians, waiters.

SCENE 1

In the market-place of a Mediterranean town two street singers are performing to the accompaniment of mandolins and a hurdy-gurdy ('Du meine schwarze Donna Antonia'). Pierrino, a fruit seller, enters calling his wares and leading a small donkey pulling a barrow full of produce ('Halli! Hallo! Ihr Leute!'). He has decided to give up his business and, after disposing of all his stock, he auctions off his barrow. Finally, he turns to his faithful donkey, Aristotle, bids him a fond, tearful farewell, and sells him also to the purchaser of the barrow. Then he calls to his girlfriend Anita, a fisher girl, and checks with her that all is prepared for the ship they are to catch that evening. Their plan is to earn their living as touring performers in North Africa. Pierrino asks whether her parents know that she's leaving, but Anita explains that, as one of thirteen children, her departure will scarcely be noticed. They are in high spirits and free of cares at the prospect of their adventure ('Uns ist alles einerlei').

Manuele emerges from his house with a bird in a wooden cage that he has just made for a local dignitary. He plans to spend the money he receives for it on his young wife, Giuditta, on whom he dotes and for whose benefit he keeps up his hard work ('Alle Tag' nichts als Müh' und Plag'!'). It is clear that Giuditta's beauty is widely admired. 'Isn't she too beautiful for you?' the innkeeper Sebastiano asks undiplomatically. Just then a group of officers arrives led by Captain Octavio and Lieutenant Antonio. Their ship has put into port for the evening prior to sailing for manoeuvres in Africa, and they have come to sample the inn's well-known wines. Octavio is a man full of the joys of life, and most particularly partial to the pleasures of a beautiful woman ('Freunde, das Leben ist lebenswert!').

As the officers go to leave, Giuditta's voice is heard singing plaintively. Octavio is enchanted, and he watches as she comes out onto her balcony, sighing for the true love she has never enjoyed ('Liebestraum, du ewiger Liebestraum'). Suddenly Giuditta spots Octavio gazing at her and, when he asks her why there are tears in her eyes, she sadly tells him how she yearns to leave her dreary life and sink into a sea of love ('In einem Meer von Liebe'). Octavio cannot restrain himself from passionately telling her of her beauty ('Schönste der Frauen'). He begs her to spend with him the short time before his ship sails but, when she insists that her husband will return at any moment, he impulsively urges her to come away with him. It is an invitation that she is unable to resist.

When Manuele returns, Octavio treats him to a glass of wine and chats with him about his voyage to Africa, but Manuele is disturbed when he hears Octavio enthusiastically breathing Giuditta's name. He jealously questions his wife and she reacts angrily, accusing him of treating her like a captive bird, locked in one of the cages that he makes. As Manuele hurries into the house, Giuditta symbolically goes to the birdcage hanging on their wall, lets the bird loose and, watching it fly off, she looks heavenwards and expresses her own longing to fly away ('Weit übers Meer'). Giuditta has departed in the direction of the harbour, when Manuele appears on the balcony calling for her. He is already regretting his harsh words and is determined to make it up to her by buying her a present.

A contingent of soldiers passes through, marching to the harbour ('Herr Kapitän, der Weg ist weit von hier bis Navarra'), followed by Anita and Pierrino, knapsacks in their hands. Manuele returns with a present of a coral necklace for Giuditta, but he becomes anxious when he discovers that she is nowhere to be found. A ship's siren is heard in the distance, as the *Aurora* prepares to sail for Africa. Then Manuele spots the empty birdcage, just as a fisherman runs up to report that he has seen Giuditta on board the ship with Octavio. Manuele takes a few helpless steps in the direction of the harbour, calling his wife's name and holding the coral necklace helplessly in his hand.

SCENE 2

Anita and Pierrino arrive at Octavio's villa in a small garrison town on the north coast of Africa. Their happy plans all went awry and now they are broke and have come to see if Octavio and Giuditta can give them work. They are a little hesitant about ringing the bell, but when eventually they do they get no answer. Love seems to have made Giuditta and Octavio deaf to the world ('Zwei die sich lieben vergessen die Welt'). Finally Giuditta appears at the door and, when the pair relate their unhappy story, she offers to give Anita a job while Pierrino returns home to set up his old trade again. Then he will come back to marry her.

Octavio's voice is heard in the background ('Schönste der Frauen') and Giuditta confesses to Anita how much she is in love. For them, at least, the rash decision was the right one. Octavio is disturbed, however, by a report from his lieutenant that the regiment may have to move on. He determines to keep this news from Giuditta and hurries the man away. When Giuditta reappears, they swear their love for each other. He declares that she is as

1167

beautiful as the blue summer night, while she responds that she finds every day as beautiful as a lovely fairytale dream ('Schön wie die blaue Sommernacht!').

Giuditta has promised to put Pierrino up for the night and has offered him and Anita an attic room. However, since Anita insists that nothing improper should take place before they are married, Pierrino has to take alternative accommodation in the servants' quarters. When Giuditta and Octavio are out of the way, he looks enquiringly up at Anita in her attic, puts a ladder up to her window and scrambles up into her waiting arms ('Zwei, die sich lieben vergessen die Welt').

SCENE 3

It is late evening and the military encampment is lit by moonlight and lamps as the soldiers sing of their eternal lot—marching through the barren, hot desert by day, finding female company at an oasis by night ('Uns're Heimat ist die Wüste'). Octavio has still not told Giuditta that they are due to move off, and he thinks of their parting with despair, convinced that she will not remain faithful to him. 'Her father a Spaniard, her mother a Moroccan dancer. African blood flows in her veins—southern, hot blood. You should see her dance! In her dancing you can see the whole wild, sensual heat of the south.'

Despite all Antonio's efforts to reassure him, Octavio declares that he cannot bring himself to leave Giuditta, and the soldiers' singing echoes his thoughts on the fickleness of womankind ('Wirst du aber scheiden müssen') as Octavio wonders at the way two people who were strangers yesterday can today be helplessly bound up together ('Du bist meine Sonne').

He grabs his cloak and képi and is about to move off when Giuditta appears in the lamplight ('Giuditta! Was machst du hier?'). She has been waiting for him at the villa, becoming more and more worried. Now he tells her that he must leave her. The regiment is moving on. She accuses him of having tired of her and will not listen when he tries to make her understand that he must do his duty. She tells him that he must prove his love by coming away with her and, as she speaks, her pleading begins to have its effect on him. He presses her to him ('Du bist meine Sonne') and, when the trumpet sounds, he pretends not to hear it. Antonio comes to tell him that it is time to go, but Octavio declares that he cannot. Finally his sense of duty reasserts itself and, with death in his heart, he marches off. Left alone, Giuditta, in a frenzy of frustrated passion ('In die Stirne fällt die Locke'), breaks down in dreadful weeping.

SCENE 4

Parted from Octavio, Giuditta has decided to become a night club dancer and she appears in the Alcazar night club of a large North African city, winning tremendous applause with her sensuous dance routine ('In einem Meer von Liebe'). In the middle of it all, she lapses for a moment into a trance, remembering her parting from Octavio ('Wirst du aber scheiden müssen'), but she recovers to acknowledge the audience's ecstatic acclaim. She is the greatest success the night club has had in years. Backstage, Anita helps her change, as Ibrahim, the proprietor, comes up with a large bouquet of flowers. They are from Lord Barrymore, an extremely wealthy Englishman and one of Ibrahim's best customers, who is anxious to take Giuditta out to supper.

The floor-show continues with a comedy number by the night club's eccentric master of ceremonies, 'Professor' Martini. He has written it himself, and it is about the ups and downs of love, with the refrain 'Yes, love is just like a see-saw!' ('Ja, die Liebe ist so wie ein Schaukelbrett!'). The cabaret over, the audience are left to enjoy themselves at the bar or in the private rooms.

Pierrino enters the club, somewhat abashed at surroundings that are so unfamiliar to him, and one of the club's dancers, Lolitta, approaches him and suggests that he buy a bottle of wine for the two of them. They have little time to get to know each other before Anita arrives. She is thrilled to see her beloved, especially when Pierrino tells her that he has bought back Aristotle, resumed his trade, and is now ready to get married. Excitedly they contemplate their future together ('Schaut der Mond').

The arrival of Lord Barrymore has the night club personnel falling over themselves to make him at home. Ibrahim has even purchased for his lordship a pearl necklace with which to reward Giuditta's favours. Lord Barrymore kisses Giuditta's hand, and Professor Martini encourages her to tell them the secret of her magical effect on men. She explains that she hardly knows, but she does her best to describe the chemistry that seems to occur within her whenever men are close to her ('Meine Lippen, sie küssen so heiss'). Lord Barrymore assures her that she is the most beautiful woman he has ever seen and that he is wildly in love with her and, giving an order for supper and champagne to be served, he leads Giuditta away into a *chambre séparée*.

During the evening, a new customer arrives. It is Octavio. He has deserted, is in civilian clothes, and asks just to be left alone. Lolitta's attentions have no interest for him, but he shares his wine and cigarettes with Martini and, apparently oblivious to the unrestrained goings-on of the night club, asks him about Giuditta. Can Martini find her and tell her that there is someone here to see her? He reflects on the way that Guiditta has filled his thoughts ever since they parted ('So wie um den Sonnenball'), but he is shaken from his reverie by the sound of laughter and of Giuditta's voice as she and Lord Barrymore emerge from their private room. As Lord Barrymore hangs the pearl necklace around her neck and escorts her to his car, Octavio watches, unseen and wholly wretched.

SCENE 5
Four years later, in a private room of a fine hotel, two waiters are laying the table for a private supper for a Duke and Giuditta, now a famous dancer.

The Duke's adjutant arrives to see that all is in order, and he summons the pianist to tip him off as to the Duke's musical tastes. The pianist is Octavio. As he awaits the guests' arrival, he lingers again over the torment of his broken love for Giuditta ('Schönste der Frau'n') and, when their arrival is announced, he disappears into the alcove and begins playing melodies from Giuditta's past. She looks behind the curtain and springs back at the sight of Octavio ('Octavio! Octavio! Du?').

Octavio tells Giuditta how he has seen her dancing and singing, and how he saw her being escorted by Lord Barrymore, but when Giuditta assures him that he is still the one she really loves, he tells her that love no longer means anything to him. Giuditta entreats him ('Ewige Glut, verflucht ist mein Blut'), but Octavio is a broken man. When the Duke comes to join the dancer, he goes back to the piano and plays. Giuditta responds mechanically to the Duke's advances, and soon she asks to be taken home. Octavio carries on playing until the waiter, arriving to put out the lights, tells him that the guests have gone. Then he closes the piano, takes his hat and slowly leaves.

In a later edition of the score Lehár replaced the song 'Schaut der Mond' for Anita and Pierrino in Scene 4 with an alternative, 'Komm, komm, wir wollen fort von hier!'.

DREI WÄLZER

(Three Waltzes)

an operetta in three parts and twelve scenes by Paul Knepler and Armin Robinson. Music by Oscar Straus (that of part one arranged from Johann Strauss I and that of part two from Johann Strauss II). Produced at the Stadttheater, Zürich, 5 October 1935.

Produced at Brussels in a version by Léopold Marchand and Albert Willemetz as *Trois Valses*. Produced at the Théâtre des Bouffes-Parisiens, Paris, 22 April 1937 with Yvonne Printemps, Pierre Fresnay and René Dary. Produced at the Théâtre de la Michodière 31 January 1939 with Mlle Printemps and Fresnay. Produced at the Théâtre de la Gaîté-Lyrique 1952 with Germaine Roger and Pierre Jourdan and revived there 12 December 1959 with Mlle Roger and Jean Weber.

Produced at the Majestic Theatre, New York, in a version by Rowland Leigh and Clare Kummer 25 December 1937 with Kitty Carlisle and Michael Bartlett.

Produced at the Princes Theatre, London, in a version by Robert MacDermot and Diana Morgan 1 March 1945 with Evelyn Laye and Esmond Knight.

A French film version was produced by Ludwig Berger in 1938 with Mlle Printemps and Fresnay.

1170

PART 1: VIENNA, 1865

CHARACTERS

Fanny Pichler, *a dancer at the Kärntnertor-Theater*
Beltramini, *ballet master at the Kärntnertor-Theater*
Kaliwoda, *ballet stage manager at the Kärntnertor-Theater*
Josef Brunner, *a theatrical agent*
Johann Brunner, *his son*
Countess Katharina Anastasia Schwarzenegg
Count Franz Schwarzenegg, *a field marshal*
Count Egon Carl Maria Schwarzenegg, *leader of an army division*
Count Felix Schwarzenegg, *a colonel*
Count Herbert Schwarzenegg, *a major*
Count Leopold Schwarzenegg
Count Rudolf Schwarzenegg, *a lieutenant*
Frau Zorngrüber
Difflinger, *a painter*
A rehearsal pianist, ballerinas, the Schwarzeneggs' servant

SCENE 1

In the rehearsal room of the Kärntnertor-Theater in Vienna the ballerinas
are being coached by the ballet master Beltramini ('Mehr im Takt, meine
Damen'). Beltramini is most perturbed that his leading dancer, Fanny
Pichler, has so far failed to turn up for this important rehearsal. What can
one expect, a lesser ballerina suggests timidly, when one has a count as an
admirer? The gentleman in question is Count Rudi Schwarzenegg, a
lieutenant in the lancers. When Fanny finally arrives, Beltramini greets her
with a touch of sarcasm, but Fanny is far too full of the joys of the Viennese
life to care ('Aber gehn S'—sein S' net so grantig'/'Wien ist ein Liebeslied').

The theatrical agent Josef Brunner arrives at the theatre with his son
Johann ('Sie gestatten, aber hatten wir nicht längst die Ehre schon'/'Was der
Gärtner für die Rosen'). They are making arrangements for the ballet company to visit Paris, but the stage-manager, Kaliwoda, suggests that there is
little chance of persuading Fanny Pichler to leave Vienna and her admirer.
Brunner junior suggests that he has enough influence with the girl to win her
over to the journey, but his father believes that the eighteen-year-old is
allowing his eye for a pretty girl to carry him away. The best they can manage
is to get her promise that it will be decided one way or the other by the
morrow, and the ballet rehearsal continues (Finaletto: 'Gerne suchen wir
Talent').

SCENE 2

In a salon of the elegant palace of the Countess Katharina Anastasia
Schwarzenegg, the family has been assembled to discuss Rudi's association
with his ballerina ('Hast du was g'hört?'). Even Uncle Leopold has been
summoned from his home in Pottenstein and he is highly irritated at having

to forego his hunting for such a foolishness. Rudi is shown in, and his interrogation begins (Finaletto: 'So ein Eklat war noch nicht da'). His field marshal uncle Franz tells him that he must think of the family name but, to the old Countess's secret admiration, Rudi vigorously defends his right to choose his own wife.

SCENE 3

At her lodgings, Fanny is having her portrait painted whilst awaiting her lover. Her landlady, Frau Zörngruber, expresses her concern over Fanny's predicament and warns her of the dangers of marrying above one's station, but Fanny will not listen to her and when Johann Brunner comes to try to persuade Fanny to sign the contract for Paris, she refuses roundly.

Finally Rudi arrives, fresh from the family council, and Fanny presses him to tell her what happened, but he merely renews his ardent wooing ('Du bist der Tag, du bist die Welt'/'Wien ist ein Liebeslied'). Soon after, Fanny receives a less expected guest, Rudi's Aunt Katharina. She reassures the lovers that she has not come to separate them but only to meet the object of Rudi's love and the cause of his family's concern. She tells Rudi that he has her support, and she assures Fanny that she fully approves of her, but she also wants them to be quite clear about the sacrifices that Rudi will have to make if they are married. He will be obliged to give up his commission.

The sound of a band playing the 'Radetzky March' is heard outside (Finaletto). The procession includes Rudi's own regiment of lancers, and Fanny notices how anxious Rudi is that he should not be seen by his commanding officer. When the soldiers have passed, Rudi prepares to hurry back to the barracks and, as Fanny bids him farewell, she hands him the portrait of herself that she has had painted. As she looks after him, she knows that she may never see him again. She has realised she cannot allow him to sacrifice his social position for her, and she has already signed the contract for the appearance in Paris.

PART 2: VIENNA, 1900
CHARACTERS

Charlotte Pichler, *an operetta singer, Fanny's daughter*
Alexander Jensen, *an actor*
Steffi Castelli, *a soubrette*
Johann Brunner (*now in his fifties*), *an impresario*
Count Otto Schwarzenegg
Fritz von Bodenheim, *his friend*
Baron Liebinger
Helene, *his wife*
The theatre director, the author, a journalist, theatre personnel, singers, dancers, servants of Baron Liebinger, party guests, head waiter at the Hotel Sacher

SCENE 4

In the Theater an der Wien, the première of the operetta *The Marquis of Rivoli* is just reaching its conclusion ('Champagner her! Champagner her!'). The curtain falls to loud applause, with the leading performers, Charlotte Pichler and Alexander Jensen, in each other's arms. It is the first big success in Vienna for Charlotte, who is the daughter of the former dancer Fanny Pichler, and the impresario Johann Brunner is on hand to liken the success of her singing to that of her mother's dancing.

Charlotte is elated after her success, but tired by her exertions and by the attentions of the well-wishers and journalists. When Baron Liebinger invites her to a party at his house, she declines graciously but her interest is aroused by the compliments of a young man who introduces himself as Count Otto Schwarzenegg. The young Count tells her that his father always kept her mother's portrait on his desk, and Charlotte recognises him as the son of the Count Rudolf Schwarzenegg of whom her mother had so often spoken. He asks if she will meet him at Baron Liebinger's party, and Charlotte agrees. Brushing aside Brunner's protests that she must be tired, she asks the impresario to see her to the Count's home.

SCENE 5

Over the past four months Otto has been conducting an affair with the Baroness Liebinger. Now it must be ended, for his family are anxious that he should marry. In his time he has had more than his share of flirtations ('Lieber Freund, wir mir scheint'/'Nur Liebelei und keine wahre Liebe!'), but now there will be no more.

SCENE 6

At Baron Liebinger's house a large group of guests has assembled for the party and the success of the new operetta and its new star, Charlotte Pichler, is the major topic of conversation. Only Baroness Liebinger seems not to have seen the show, but she is planning to go the following day. Meanwhile, she is trying to speak to Otto, but he avoids her with excuses. The party springs to life with the announcement of Charlotte's arrival ('Hoch! Hoch die Diva! Bravo Pichler! Hoch!'). Baron Liebinger welcomes her, and she responds gracefully, but before long she is deep into conversation with Count Otto. 'If the likeness of the portrait in your father's room were not so striking, would you have come on stage to introduce yourself to me?' she asks. He doesn't know, but he has a question in return: 'Would you have changed your mind about coming to Baron Liebinger's this evening if I had not been called Schwarzenegg?' She knows no more than he does.

The operetta's soubrette, Steffi Castelli, is feeling much put out by Charlotte's success. Why can't she achieve the same sort of success? Brunner does his best to help her by allowing her to sing for the guests her comic number from the new operetta ('Wir haben heut die Leute bloss'/'Tschin, tschin, bum—das ist die Militärmusik').

The relationship between Charlotte and Otto develops rapidly. Brunner is anxious to see her home safely, but she has already accepted an invitation from the Count to accompany him to Sacher's. Brunner may come and collect her there in an hour or so's time. They depart, leaving Baroness Liebinger, who has still not managed to speak with Otto, to learn second-hand the bitter news that the Count and Charlotte have left together.

SCENE 7

In a private room in the fashionable Hotel Sacher, Otto and Charlotte sit together, talking once again of the feelings that their parents obviously had for each other. Otto by now has his own expressions of love for Charlotte ('Wie hat denn nur der Walzer angefangen'/'Ich liebe das Leben'). A knock at the door announces the arrival of Johann Brunner who has come to take Charlotte home, leaving Otto to pour out to the waiter his belief that he has at last found 'the only woman' for him. The head waiter observes stonily that he has heard the Count say that many times before.

SCENE 8

The following day the newspapers are full of the operetta's success. In her dressing room during the second interval of the operetta's second perform-ance, Charlotte receives a bunch of red roses from Otto, but her co-star, Jensen, and Brunner are worried about the relationship, especially given the unhappy precedent of her mother. Baroness Liebinger comes to the theatre to see Charlotte and after some fulsome praise for the performance she turns to her with some bitter advice about the Count. 'In an article I once read that every Don Juan, every womaniser has his own distinguishing mark,' she says. 'With Schwarzenegg it is the phrase about 'the only woman''.

Her words strike Charlotte with a cold fear but, as the Baroness leaves, the Count himself appears. He admits that he has made love to lots of women, but he assures her that all that is over since he met Charlotte and that he wishes to marry her. It is now time for Charlotte to take the stage and, when Jensen comes to collect her, she introduces the actor to the Count as her fiancé.

SCENE 9

On stage the chorus are singing prior to Charlotte's entrance ('Finaletto: 'Tralalalala! Tralalalala!'). Charlotte comes to her solo, but suddenly she breaks off and collapses into Jensen's arms. The stage manager calls for the curtain to be lowered and apologises to the public for the interruption of the performance due to Fräulein Pichler's indisposition.

PART 3: VIENNA, 1935
CHARACTERS

Franzi Jensen-Pichler
Count Ferdinand Schwarzenegg

Lindtheim, *a director for Vienna Film A.G.*
Johann Brunner (*now in his eighties*)
Waldner, *an actor*
Film technicians of the Vienna Film A.G., actors, an innkeeper, workmen

SCENE 10

In the production room of the Vienna Film Company, a group of dancers are being put through their paces ('So ist's recht, ich bin wirklich ganz entzückt!'). A film is being made under the title *Fanny Pichler's First Love*, with Franzi Jensen-Pichler playing the part of her grandmother in the story of Fanny's love for Rudi Schwarzenegg. The book of the film has been written by Johann Brunner, now in his eighties and a man with first-hand knowledge of the real-life romance.

Advance publicity for the film has brought a letter from a present-day Count Schwarzenegg protesting about the subject but the director is little concerned. After all, as he points out, the more the protests the better the publicity! Of more concern is the news that the film's intended leading man, Willy Förster, has had to drop out of the film for contractual reasons. Other names are bandied around, but in vain.

Just then a visitor is announced. It is the same Count Ferdinand Schwarzenegg who has been protesting about the film. The director assures him that they have already made films about Esterhazy, Metternich and Napoleon without any complaints from descendants, but the Count assures them that his concern is purely with historical accuracy and he asks to see the script. The director has been watching his visitor closely and suddenly he comes up with the answer to all his concerns: 'Count, *you* will play the role of Count Rudi Schwarzenegg in our film!' Ferdinand is hesitant but is finally flattered into acceptance.

The Count is sent off with Franzi and the musical director to practise their big waltz song, and the two are each astonished to find that the other is also the grandchild of one of the film's leading characters. Seated at the piano, the musical director rehearses them in their big duet ('Man sagt sich beim Walzer Adieu').

SCENE 11

In the garden of a suburban hotel, Johann Brunner is enjoying a few glasses of wine to the sound of a Schrammel quartet. He tells the landlord that, though he manages to keep up with all the changes in dance styles, there is nothing to beat a Viennese waltz ('Was macht an echter Weaner, wenn ihm wohl ist?'/'Wann im Himmel a Musik is').

The film director comes to find Brunner with news of the cast change. The old man is horrified to hear the name of Schwarzenegg and, when Franzi appears, he expresses his concern to her. However, when Count Ferdinand follows, Brunner is bowled over by the young man's resemblance to his grandfather and insists that he must indeed play the role. Franzi and

Ferdinand sit together and the Count touches lightly on the first words of love, but Franzi, remembering the past relationships between her family and his, shies away (Finaletto: 'Man sagt Sich beim Walzer Adieu').

SCENE 12
Back in the studio, the filming has reached its final day and the farewell scene between Fanny and Rudi into which has been built a grand ballet has been arranged around the 'Radetzky March' (ballet). Franzi and Ferdinand play the scene of their grandparents' parting as the band marched past, and they sing their song of farewell ('Man sagt sich beim Walzer Adieu'). The film is complete.

Brunner worries over all the little departures from reality as he remembers it, and he relives his own recollections of the lovers' farewell ('Wien ist ein Liebeslied'). Suddenly, he sees Franzi and Ferdinand locked in each other's arms. The past and present mix in his mind. This time he will not do anything to part his Fanny and her Rudi.

MASKE IN BLAU

(Mask in Blue)

a revue-operetta in six scenes by Heinz Hentschke. Lyrics by Günther Schwenn. Music by Fred Raymond. Produced at the Metropol-Theater, Berlin, 27 September 1937 with Rosita Serrano.

Produced at the Sophiensaal, Vienna, 15 June 1946.

A film version was produced by Georg Jacoby in 1953 with Marika Rökk, Paul Hubschmidt, Walter Müller and Wilfried Seyferth.

CHARACTERS

Marchese Cavalotti
Armando Cellini, Franz Kilian, Josef Fraunhofer (*known as* Seppl), Juliska Varady, *painters*
Evelyne Valera, *a plantation owner*
Sebastiano Rodrigo Diego Bonifacio Gonzala, *her steward*
Pedro dal Vegas
José, *a gaucho*
Landlord *of an inn in Viedma*
Receptionist *at the Grand Hotel in San Remo*
Newspaper-seller, courier, gauchos, painters, servants, hotel guests, society ladies and gentlemen

SCENE 1
In the square in front of the Grand Hotel in San Remo a newspaper-seller is announcing the news that the painter Armando Cellini has won first prize in

an art competition with his painting 'Mask in Blue' ('Gazetta San Remo!') and, when Armando himself appears, he receives a rapturous reception from the people.

His own thoughts are less on his prize than on the model who sat for his winning painting, the never-to-be-forgotten young lady whom he met at a masked ball a year before ('Maske in Blau'). After the ball he had painted her portrait, still behind her mask, but then she left. She never allowed him to see her face, promising only to return to San Remo the following year. Especially delighted with Armando's success are his friends and fellow artists, Seppl Fraunhofer, Franz Kilian and Juliska Varady. Juliska is Seppl's girl-friend, and the two make a happy-go-lucky couple, determined optimists eager to make the most of what they have ('Was nicht ist, kann noch werden').

In fact, the young lady who modelled for Armando is at this very moment arriving back in town. She is an Argentinian plantation owner called Evelyne Valera, who is in San Remo with her steward, Gonzala. She has with her a ring that Armando gave her as a souvenir of their brief acquaintance and as a means by which he might recognise her when she returned to San Remo ('Ich muss dir etwas sagen') but she intends to keep the ring hidden until she has made up her mind as to whether Armando really is the man with whom she would wish to spend the rest of her life. Before she moves on to such serious things as love and matrimony, however, she needs time to soak up the magic of spring in San Remo ('Frühling in San Remo').

The crowds are gathering for San Remo's spring flower festival, and Juliska is in especially ebullient mood. It is, of course, her Hungarian temperament ('Ja das Temp'rament!'). During the festivities Gonzala gets into conversation with Kilian, who tells the steward about Armando's success and of the torch the artist is carrying for the mysterious woman in his painting. Evelyne is delighted to hear this, but she wants to know more of the painter and his world, so a visit to Armando's studio is arranged. For tonight, however, everyone enjoys to the full the colour and excitement of the flower festival (Finale I: 'Narzissen! Narzissen! Wer kauft Narzissen?') and only Armando is a little sad at the apparent non-appearance of his 'Mask in Blue'.

SCENE 2
Juliska contemplates the scene of utter confusion in Armando's studio with growing fury ('Wenn ich hier im Atelier'). How hopeless men are! She wonders why Seppl and Kilian seem to be against marriage but both, in turn, proclaim 'On the contrary, I'm all for marriage!' ('Im Gegenteil!')

While Armando is excitedly awaiting Evelyne's promised visit a stranger arrives. His name is Pedro dal Vegas, and he is apparently interested in buying Armando's prize-winning painting. Armando tells him that it is not for sale, and Pedro asks him instead to paint for him the portrait of a lady he is due to meet the following day at the party to be given in Armando's honour by the Marchese Cavalotti. This time Armand agrees.

Shortly afterwards Evelyne arrives and, as they drink coffee together

(Finale II: 'Ein Tässchen Kaffee'), Evelyne probes to find out how he feels about the lady whom he had painted in his 'Mask in Blue'. They drink a toast to the painting, and Armando can no longer refrain from telling Evelyne how much she reminds him of the lady he painted. Finally she admits her identity and tells him what a long year it has seemed away from him in Argentina as they declare their love for each other ('In dir hab ich mein Glück gefunden').

SCENE 3

The following evening the Marchese Cavalotti is holding his party in honour of Armando, his protégé. Juliska, as usual, is much in evidence, demonstrating her Hungarian passion—this time to Gonzala and the Marchese, as well as to Kilian and Seppl ('Die Juliska aus Budapest').

Gonzala tells Armando of the efforts that Pedro dal Vegas is making to impress Evelyne, though it seems to be her money more than herself that interests him. When Evelyne loses her handbag, Pedro seizes the opportunity to try to alienate her from Armando by making false accusations about the latter, but to no avail. He nonetheless tells Armando that he is going to marry Evelyne, and he gives Armando back his ring, pretending that Evelyne had given it up voluntarily.

At this piece of evidence, Armando believes that his love is at an end. 'Never look too deeply into a beautiful woman's eyes!' he tells himself ('Schau einer schönen Frau nie so tief in die Augen!'). What he cannot know is that Pedro has stolen the ring from the missing handbag. Evelyne, on the contrary, continues to hold the same strong feelings for Armando (Finale III: 'In dir hab' ich mein Glück gefunden!'). At the height of the party, Gonzala and Kilian, knowing nothing of the developments engineered by Pedro, take it upon themselves to announce the engagement of Armando and Evelyne, but the dazed Armando will have nothing of it, and the evening ends in recriminations.

SCENE 4

After such a disappointment, there was nothing left for Evelyne to do but to return to her estate on the the Rio Negro in Argentina where she consoles herself for her lost love with the wild beauty of her homeland and the work that is to be done ('Wenn hell in unserm Land die Sterne glühn') amongst the wild South American dances and music ('Sassa! Sassa!'). She would gladly believe Gonzala's assurance that Armando's deadful rejection of her at the ball in San Remo was due to a misunderstanding, but she knows only that he is gone and her love has gone with him.

Pedro dal Vegas turns up, hoping that events in Europe might have turned Evelyne at last towards him but, although he is again met with indifference, he once more manages to stir up mischief when he intercepts a telegram announcing that the four artists from San Remo have arrived in the nearby town of Vielma. But Pedro has reckoned without Evelyne's faithful gauchos. One of them has seen Pedro intercept the telegram and informed Gonzala.

Since he has been waiting for just such a communication from Kilian, Gonzala is able to deduce that the young people have arrived in Argentina and he duly sets out for Vielma.

SCENE 5

In front of a *taberna* in Vielma, Armando, Kilian, Seppl and Juliska are sitting drinking wine, wondering why they have not had a reply to their telegram ('Im Gegenteil!'). From the landlord they hear talk of the proposed marriage of Evelyne and Pedro, but from the locals they discover that Pedro is deeply in debt and little respected in the neighbourhood. He has one partisan, however, a gaucho named José, and a quarrel threatens to break out, until Juliska drags Seppl from the fray and Armando manages to smooth matters out. Alarmed at the way events are going, he sets out alone for Evelyne's estate, leaving the others to keep their spirits up as best they can ('Die Juliska, die Juliska, aus Buda-Budapest').

SCENE 6

The following morning, Evelyne and Armando finally manage to sort matters out and are once more able to enjoy the romance of being together, this time on the opposite side of the world ('Am Rio Negro'). Gonzala arrives with the three other members of the group, all anxious to know how matters have worked out and, as soon as Armando has settled his scores with Pedro, they are able to announce that there will be a wedding. And not just a single one but a double one, since Seppl Fraunhofer has also finally decided to throw in his lot with Juliska. The gauchos enter into the spirit of the celebrations ('Sassa! Sassa!'), and all pay tribute to the virtues of true temperament (Finale: 'Ja, das Temp'rament').

BALKANLIEBE

(Balkan Love)

an operetta in two acts and four scenes by E Kahr and Bruno Hardt-Warden. Music by Rudolf Kattnigg. Produced in Leipzig, 1937.

CHARACTERS

Marko Franjopan, *exiled Prince of Illyria*
Count Jorgowan Schenoa, Baron Nikola Bakschitsch, *landowners in Illyria*
Branko Juranitsch, *a bandit leader*
Zlata, *his daughter*
Gorin, *a corsair leader*
Daniela von Durazzo, *Countess of Dardinia*

Alfonso, Prince Boccini Montrealt, *Prefect of Venice*
Count Bobby *from Vienna*
Flosshilde, *his wife, born Princess of Chlochowetz-on-Prihan*
Lotte, *a Viennese suburban cabaret singer*
The manager of the Excelsior Palace Hotel *at the Lido*
The manager of the Arlberg Hotel
The Prefect's valet and servant, the head waiter, a boy, a gentleman in the
Excelsior, four companions of the corsair, bandits, hotel guests and staff,
servants, sporting girls, dancers, gondoliers

SCENE 1 (ACT 1)

In the wild, romantic countryside of the Karst in Illyria the bandit leader
Branko Juranitsch is rallying his men as he welcomes the corsair leader
Gorin ('Sei willkommen uns, du mächtiger Korsar'). Unrest has ruled in
Illyria since the Countess Durazzo seized power and sent the rightful ruler,
Prince Marko Franjopan, into exile, and the corsair and his supporters have
come to join a revolutionary group which is taking up arms to attempt to
restore Marko to power. Zlata, the daughter of Branko Juranitsch, holds a
great position in the eyes of all these men, for she is engaged to the exiled
Prince Marko.

The rebel group's aim to restore Prince Marko also has the support of
some of the major landowners of the country, amongst them Count
Jorgowan Schenoa and Baron Nikola Bakschitsch. Bakschitsch is a
somewhat ridiculous fellow, known as Niko, who goes about brandishing a
toy gun and has an all-consuming interest in astrology. It is currently June,
and his horoscope tells him that by April he will have got a kiss out of Zlata
('Im Monat April weiss kein Herz'/'Fix-Stern- und Planetarium').

The rebels are waiting for a signal from Prince Marko to begin their
offensive, but his return comes sooner than they expect. Approaching footsteps are heard and, to the bandits' suprise, Marko appears in their camp in
person, greeted ravenously by his partisans ('Marko Franjopan'), to take his
beloved Zlata in his arms and renew his vow of true love ('Einmal leuchtet
die Sonne').

The conspirators' plans for a shock attack are confounded when the news
is brought by Count Schenoa that a list containing the names of all their
band has fallen into the hands of the Countess Durazzo. The Countess is
just about to embark on a journey to Venice, and Marko decides that he too
will travel to Venice in the company of Count Schenoa and Baron Niko in
order to retrieve the incriminating document. There, on neutral territory, he
will be able to confront his enemy personally.

Marko's plan appeals especially to Count Schenoa, since he has his own
scheme for the future peace and happiness of the fatherland, a scheme
which lies not simply in the prevention of war, but in a dynastic marriage
between Prince Marko and the Countess Durazzo. He discusses this plan
with Zlata and attempts to persuade her to give up her own aspirations for
marriage to the Prince for the greater good but, although Zlata pretends to

go along with the idea, after his departure she enlists the help of Gorin and his fellow corsairs and rallies them to a very different plan of action (Finale I: 'Alle Mann, nur heran, denn es ruft der Trommelschlag').

SCENE 2

In the fashionable Hotel Excelsior on the Lido in Venice, an elegant crowd of people are going about their business and pleasure. Amongst them is a group of young ladies, all dressed up for a game of tennis ('Girls in weissen Röckchen'/'Lass dein Herz heut' Tennis spielen'), and a Viennese cabaret singer named Lotte, accompanied by her ageing but well-to-do fiancé, the Viennese Count Bobby. The Count very soon finds that he has a rival for Lotte's favours when Niko arrives on the scene.

Of the political aims of Marko and his companions nobody in Venice has any idea, and Marko swans about the more obvious social spots in sleek black riding garb surrounded by a group of adoring females attracted by his sporting prowess ('Hurrah! Unser Sieger und Held ist da'/'Ohne Frauen gibt es keinen Sonnenschein'). Whilst the three conspirators await the arrival of the Countess in Venice, Schenoa happens on an alarming newspaper story. It reports that the Countess Daniela von Durazzo's private yacht has been attacked on the way to Venice by a band of corsairs, though apparently the Countess herself escaped unharmed.

Niko has been concentrating mostly on more frivolous matters, and is already teaching Lotte something of the geography of Illyria, with the idea that she might some day return there with him ('Wenn du fahrst in den Karst'/'Glück und Wein blüh'n allein') but all such pastimes have to be put aside when the hotel manager announces the long-awaited arrival of the Countess Durazzo ('Die Gräfin von Durazzo'). What Marko, Niko and Schenoa do not know, though, is that the woman who receives the gushing greetings of her host is none other than Zlata in disguise ('Wenn ich mich wo blicken lass'/'Das macht nur jener gewisse und zärtliche Zauber einer Frau'). Having had the Countess's yacht intercepted by her corsairs, Zlata has taken the Countess's place, and her current retinue comprises Gorin and his men disguised as Illyrian courtiers.

While the supposed Countess settles in, Niko sets off for a bathe with Prince Bobby and a shoal of female companions in the most fashionable bathing costumes ('Denn schon der alte Zarathustra'/'Alle die Blonden, Schwarzen und Braunen'). When Zlata reappears, Marko begins his negotiations with the supposed Countess (Finale II: 'Der Banus selbst!') but their discussions are interrupted by the arrival of the Prefect of Venice, Prince Boccini Montrealt who, having heard of the Countess's unfortunate accident at sea, has put his palace at her disposal for the duration of her visit.

As an old friend of the Countess, Prince Montrealt cannot be hoodwinked by Zlata's impersonation, but he chooses to go along with the deception. Having surmounted this difficulty, however, she finds another and even greater one before her. Marko has fallen in love with the supposed Countess at first sight and, to her great grief, Zlata has to listen to her lover protesting his love to what he believes to be another woman and his sworn enemy.

SCENE 3 (ACT 2)

It is evening, and a ball is under way in the palace of Prince Montrealt on the Grand Canal as Zlata looks out from the window onto the glory of Venice and listens to the bells of the campanile ('Leise erklingen Glocken vom Campanile'). When the Prince engages her in conversation, he makes it clear that he knew from the first moment that she was not the real Countess Durazzo and Zlata explains to him that the real Countess has merely been temporarily waylaid. Of more immediate concern to Zlata is a love-letter she has received from Marko and which she reads with a heavy heart ('Hast du mich schon ganz vergessen?'). She feels that, through his behaviour, not only she herself but also the cause of the fatherland has been betrayed.

Niko continues to worry but little about affairs of the fatherland, as he continues his wooing of Lotte ('Du wirst täglich immer netter'/'Liebe Lotte, kleine Lotte'). Zlata's more weighty matters of the heart come to a head when Marko approaches her with renewed protestations of his love ('Eins nur glaub' mir'/'Wenn sich zwei Menschenherzen zueinander neigen') but, just as he is about to pull her to him and kiss her, the corsair suddenly appears before him.

Gorin warns Marko to return to Illyria, where the struggle has now begun in earnest (Finale III: 'Wie, Bruder, jetzt?') and, when Marko hesitates and continues his protestations of love for the supposed Countess, Zlata reveals her identity. Scornfully, she disassociates herself from him and warns him of his duty to his country and, lost for words, he finally agrees to return with the corsairs. Zlata is left to seek to overcome the pain of the whole unhappy affair in the excitement of the Venetian carnival atmosphere and the fiery music of a tarantella, whilst Marko prepares for his return to Illyria ('Heimat, mit der Seele grüss' ich dich!').

SCENE 4

Weeks later, in the foyer of a winter sports hotel in the Austrian Tirol, Zlata and Lotte find a newspaper announcing that the struggle in Illyria has finally ended in triumph for Prince Marko. Zlata receives the news with patriotic satisfaction, but she still finds herself unable to answer the letters that Marko continues to send her. Despite the luxurious life the two women are living at the hotel, they have little money between them. Lotte is expecting that Baron Bobby will, as usual, bail her out but, in the event, it is Niko who arrives first on Lotte's trail ('Ob aus Wien, aus Venedig'/'Unsre Buam fressen Knödln'). Niko, however, has come to the Tirol not only on his own account but as Marko's travelling companion. Zlata refuses to see the Prince until Lotte leads her to believe he is about to give up and leave. Then her true feelings take over and, when she chances to encounter Marko, she succumbs to his admission of how wretchedly he has treated her and his assurances that it is she alone whom he loves (Finale IV: 'Glück und Wein blüh'n allein nur am Balkan').

SAISON IN SALZBURG (SALZBURGER NOCKERLN)

(Season in Salzburg)

an operetta in two acts and five scenes by Max Wallner and Kurt Feltz. Music by Fred Raymond. Produced in Kiel, 31 December 1938.

Produced at the Raimundtheater, Vienna, as *Salzburger Nockerln* 20 December 1940.

Produced at Verviers in a version by André Mouëzy-Eon and Henri Wernert as *Vacances au Tyrol* 1 April 1967.

CHARACTERS

Alois Oberfellner, *landlord of the inn 'Zum Salzburger Nockerl'*
Stephanie, *known as* Steffi, *his niece*
Vroni Staudinger, *cook at the Hotel Mirabell*
Toni Haberl, *owner of the inn 'Zum blauen Enzian'*
Christian Dahlmann, *head of a tyre manufacturing firm*
Erika, his *daughter*
Olga Rex, *owner of the Rex car works*
Frank, *her nephew*
Friedrich Wilhelm Knopp, *his chief mechanic*
Max Liebling, a *perfume manufacturer from Mödling*
Stasi, a *waitress at the 'Salzburger Nockerl'*
Porter *of the Hotel Mirabell*
A mountain guide, an auctioneer, manager of the Hotel Mirabell, a tourist guide, a zither player, hotel guests, residents, local people, waiters, a barman

SCENE 1 (ACT 1)

The summer season in Salzburg is well under way ('Saison in Salzburg!'). Toni Haberl, owner of the 'Blaue Enzian' inn, is sitting on the terrace of the Hotel Mirabell drinking a glass of beer but, when a tourist guide offers his services to show the guests the sights of the city, Toni jumps up and offers to show them around for nothing. The visitors naturally all follow him, leaving the guide to bewail the fact that a wealthy hotelier should do him out of business. 'He does it for love,' explains the hotel porter, adding that the love is for Vroni, the cook of the Hotel Mirabell, famous for her delicious Salzburger Nockerln—the local vanilla-flavoured fluffy pastry delicacy.

Max Liebling, a perfume manufacturer from the Viennese suburb of Mödling, arrives at the hotel looking for Erika, daughter of the tyre manufacturer Christian Dahlmann. He asks her to marry him, not for the first time, but she, as always, refuses him ('Darf ich fragen, schöne Frau?'). Erika is crazy about Frank Rex, the heir to the Rex car firm, and she reckons her family's tyres would go well with his family's cars. When she spots an advertisement in the local paper for an educated young lady to act as companion to an elderly lady which concludes 'Apply F.R.—Hotel Mirabell, Salzburg,' she realises that the elderly lady must be Frank Rex's Aunt Olga. Perhaps by taking the position she can get closer to Frank. Erika instructs

1183

the hotel porter to tell any further applicants that the post is filled and sets to work.

Scarcely has she departed than Frank arrives by car with Knopp, his chief mechanic and chauffeur ('Am schönsten ist's, inkognito zu reisen'). He imagines that, travelling in dust-coat, cap and gloves, he will not be identifiable, but the porter of the Mirabell recognises him immediately. Frank insists, however, that as far as the other guests are concerned, he should be known as Franz Rieger.

Toni Haberl returns, looking for Vroni. He has sent all the tourists off to Hohensalzburg, so that he can have Vroni to himself for a while and he tells her proudly that the following morning he will be not merely landlord of the 'Blaue Enzian' but also owner of the 'Salzburger Nockerl'. The old inn is to be auctioned, and Toni will be the only bidder. Since he reckons that nobody can make Salzburger Nockerln as Vroni can, he is determined that she should become landlady of his new inn—and his wife. But, in theory, Vroni has to work out a fortnight's notice at the Mirabell, and so it seems to Toni that she will somehow have to get herself sacked. Vroni proceeds to smash a plate, is promptly dismissed by the manager and goes off happily with Toni ('Wenn der Toni mit der Vroni').

Now Steffi, the niece of the current landlord of the 'Salzburger Nockerl', arrives back in town. She has spent three years in Vienna, but finally homesickness has brought her back to Salzburg ('Mein Herz war auf Reisen in der grossen Welt'). She has come to the Mirabell in response to the advertisement and is told by the porter that the position is filled, but she is spotted by Frank Rex, who is by now dressed up in the garb of a mountain guide, complete with ice-pick and rope. Frank introduces himself as Franz Rieger, and in the course of their conversation Steffi points out the 'Salzburger Nockerl' inn, where she was brought up. She tells him that it is to be auctioned the following day, and Frank suggests that together they can still do something to keep Steffi at the inn ('Ich glaub', er treibt mit uns Beiden').

When the tourists return from Hohensalzburg ('Saison in Salzburg!'), the waiters come to take their orders for the evening meal and, encouraged by Toni, they order Nockerln. The manager has to apologise that, because of 'technical difficulties', they cannot serve any Salzburger Nockerln, and Toni happily tells all the guests that Vroni is the 'technical difficulty' and that they are all welcome to come and sample her Nockerln at the 'Salzburger Nockerl' inn the following evening, as he bursts out in praise of his favourite food—'sweet as love and tender as a kiss' ('Salzburger Nockerln').

SCENE 2
The following day, in the landlord's apartments of the 'Salzburger Nockerl', Toni, Vroni and some locals are sitting drinking with the landlord Alois Oberfellner, singing together a song about the blue gentian, the most beautiful flower of the region and the one from which Toni's inn takes its name ('Das ist der wunderschöne blaue Enzian'). The landlord drinks a toast to

Toni as the man who will be his successor and help him to pay off his debts, but the waitress, Stasi, is in tears at the prospect of losing her home. The auctioneer begins the sale and announces Toni's bid of 20,000 Marks, and is about to knock the business down to him when Knopp appears and begins bidding. Toni is shocked, but he continues bidding up to his top limit of 30,000 Marks, only for Knopp to top him with a bid of 31,000 Marks. Toni is heartbroken, and Vroni, who sees her marriage prospects disappearing as well, is distraught.

Stasi hands the keys over to Knopp and, coquettishly describing herself as part of the current assets of the place, pulls the inventory of stocks from her bosom. Stasi is duly taken on, and when Steffi presents herself to the supposed new owner she too is employed. She tells Knopp that she has a good friend outside who would make an excellent head waiter, and she calls Frank in. He, too, is engaged, though he is a little put out at being set to work by his own chauffeur. Left alone, Frank tells Steffi that he loved her at first sight, and she responds that she is of a similar mind ('Warum denn nur bin ich dich verliebt?').

SCENE 3
In the square where the 'Salzburger Nockerl' and 'Blaue Enzian' face each other some of the locals are listening to a zither player ('Sagt der Hintermoser'). As Steffi attends to the tables of the 'Salzburger Nockerl', Toni moves closer to her. It has turned out that Steffi makes even more superlative Nockerln than Vroni, and Toni is desperate to buy her away from his rival. Steffi will have none of it, even when Toni asks her to marry him. 'I have always had a weakness for you,' he says. 'Yes! for my Salzburger Nockerln!' she replies.

Vroni assures Toni that she can do anything Steffi can, and Toni agrees that he will consider marrying her if she manages to entice guests away from the 'Salzburger Nockerln'. Vroni sets to work immediately, waylaying Max Liebling and persuading him to take rooms at the 'Blaue Enzian' instead. She even offers him two rooms with an inter-connecting door, but Max confides his failure with Erika. 'Have you tried making her jealous?' Vroni asks, and she makes a bargain that, if he will take rooms in the 'Blaue Enzian', she will let him flirt with her for that very purpose. First, though, she has to give him lessons in flirting ('Ich bitte dich, ich bitte dich').

In the event, Vroni's glances at Max and the smell of the perfume he has given her merely cause a row with Toni who throws her out, so that she finds herself offering her services to Knopp at the 'Nockerl'. Meanwhile, Frank has found himself repeatedly at a loss with the menial tasks of the position of head barman but at least he has Steffi's sympathy, especially when he assures her that he loves her ('Weisst du denn, wie schwer es ist, ohne dich zu sein?'). However, Steffi's attitude changes when Dahlmann tells her that her Franzl is, in reality, the famous car manufacturer and racing driver, Frank Rex and that he is as good as engaged to Erika. She decides to go away, and thinks of returning to Vienna, but Toni sees her leaving and persuades her to stay at the 'Enzian' ('Reich mir die Hände!').

The guests from the Hotel Mirabell arrive at the 'Nockerl' for the treat that Toni had promised them the previous day (Finale II: 'Salzburger Nockerln') and this time it is Knopp's turn to tell them that 'for technical reasons' they cannot serve Nockerln, but Toni invites them over to the 'Enzian' where Steffi is on hand to meet their orders. Frank appears on the scene and is highly jealous when he sees Steffi with Toni, and so, when Dahlmann announces his daughter's engagement to Frank Rex, Frank retorts by announcing Steffi's engagement to Toni. To complete the confusion, Toni in turn announces Vroni's engagement to Max. With another round of Salzburger Nockerln they all celebrate the engagement of the three ill-matched couples

SCENE 4 (ACT 2)
Inside the Hotel Mirabell guests are dancing to music from a gramophone (Orchestral waltz). Frank dances with anyone but Erika, and finally Erika's fury with him gets the better of her. Grabbing one metal tray after another from the bar, she hurls them to the ground and her father is left to explain that she inherited her temperament from her Russian great-great-grandmother on her mother's side ('Der Grosspapa von Grossmama war Donkosak am Don').

Steffi and Toni are also finding their relationship more of a strain than it ought to be for an engaged couple and, when Vroni turns up, she and Toni cannot help reflecting ruefully on their rashness and the misunderstandings that led up to the present state of affairs. Not least, they find themselves decidedly out of tune with the rather grand people in the hotel ('Und die Musik spielt dazu!'). Steffi remains cold with Frank when he seeks to win her back (Finale IV: 'Weisst du denn, wie schwer es ist ohne dich zu sein?'), and she leaves him to drown his sorrows in champagne.

SCENE 5
In the mountain village of Maria Plein, a few days later, a church fair is under way and Toni has a stall from which he is selling wine and beer, while groups of people in local costume dance round the May garland (March and Costume Parade). Vroni is at the back of the procession, pushing a small cart displaying gingerbread hearts inscribed with girls' names. The tradition is that these are hung on the May garland during the dancing and then the names called in turn. The young man who takes a heart to the young lady whose name is on the gingerbread is then considered engaged to her.

In front of Toni's stall Vroni meets Steffi, and the two of them affect indifference over Toni, but Steffi realises that Vroni genuinely loves the little innkeeper, and, knowing his passion for the best Nockerln, she writes out her special recipe and gives it to Vroni. With her at his side, Toni will be able to offer indisputably the best Nockerln in Salzburg. Toni soon swears that Vroni shall be his cook, his landlady, the mother of his children, and the head of a whole dynasty ('Wenn der Toni mit der Vroni').

1186

Erika's father is there, too, with Frank's Aunt Olga, whom he has long hoped to marry, but she is much more concerned to ensure that her Frank should marry his Steffi. Aware that Steffi does not want to seem to be marrying Frank for his money, she tells Frank that, if Erika is not happily engaged within an hour, he is disinherited. Knopp, meanwhile, seeks to help Frank make up his mind by buying from Vroni two gingerbread hearts inscribed with the names 'Erika' and 'Steffi'. Vroni also asks Knopp to hang up a 'Vroni' for her, and soft-hearted Knopp decides that he had better hang up an 'Olga' too. Appropriately enough, the only 'Olga' that Vroni has is from the previous year and thus not as fresh as it might have been.

As the dance gets under way, Knopp takes down the gingerbread hearts from the May garland one by one. When he calls out 'Vroni', Toni tears the gingerbread heart from his hand and gives it to his sweetheart. Then, when he calls out 'Erika', it is Max who, to Erika's disappointment, steps forward. Only when the name 'Steffi' is called out, does Frank rush forward and take the cake to give it to his beloved. 'See, Aunt, disinheritance hasn't done you much good!' he cries. 'But my condition was merely that Erika should be a happily engaged within an hour,' his aunt replies. 'And isn't she?' 'I am indeed very happy!' Erika sighs. Then, when Knopp calls out the name 'Olga', Dahlmann runs forward and claims it. The happy pairing off is complete and everyone can get on with enjoying what remains of the season in Salzburg (Finale: 'Ja, da staunt halt der Ochs').

DIE UNGARISCHE HOCHZEIT

(The Hungarian Wedding)

an operetta in a prologue and three acts by Hermann Hermecke, after a novel by Koloman Mikszáth. Music by Nico Dostal. Produced at the Staatstheater, Stuttgart, 4 February 1939.

Produced at the Volksoper, Vienna, 6 March 1981 with Kurt Schreibmayer (Stefan), Kurt Huemer (Arpád), Mirjana Irosch (Janka), Rudolf Wasserlof (Kismárty) and Elisabeth Kales (Etelka).

CHARACTERS

Empress Maria Theresia
Baron von Linggen, *her chamberlain*
Count Stefan Bárdossy, *head palatine of Hermannstadt*
His Excellency Desider von Pötök, *his uncle*
Anton von Halmay, *a friend of Count Stefan*
Josef von Kismárty, *president of local jurisdiction in Popláka*
Frusina, *his wife*
Janka, *their daughter*
The commandant of Pressburg castle
Captain Baron von Kiessling, *courier of the Empress*

Lieutenant von Werth, *his companion*
Arpád Erdödy, *Count Stefan's valet*
Michael, Anna, *Kismarty's servants*
The minute-taker, the verger of Popláka, the woman publican, attendants of the Empress, officers, ladies and gentlemen of court, lackeys, servants, peasant girls, villagers, foreign colonists, gipsy musicians, soldiers.

PROLOGUE

It is the year 1750 and, in an ante-room in the castle of Count Stefan Bárdossy, the head palatine of the Transylvanian town of Hermannstadt, his valet Arpád is busily directing his fellow servants in attending to one of the suppers that the Count is accustomed to give for his lady friends ('Nun die Früchte! Das Konfekt!'/'Voll Noblesse und Diskretion!').

Arrangements are interrupted when a courier from the Empress Maria Theresia arrives with an message that is to be conveyed to the Count immediately, commanding that he must at once deal with problems that have arisen in the village of Popláka. A new group of settlers has arrived there who were, it appears, promised not only arable land on which to work but also beautiful young girls as wives. They are rebelling because the president of local jurisdiction, Kismárty, has offered them only old hags.

Although the Count's orders state that he must set out for Popláka immediately, he cannot forget the beautiful young lady awaiting him in the adjoining room and he resolves the problem by charging his valet, Arpád, to travel to the irritating little village in his place and to act there as his substitute. His uncle, His Excellency Desider von Pötök, and a friend, Baron von Halmay, will accompany Arpád, who is quite delighted to have the opportunity to act the role of master for once in his life (Finaletto: 'Ist alles in Ordnung?').

ACT 1

The home of Kismárty, the president of local jurisdiction in Popláka, is set in extensive grounds on the Hungarian plains, where the shepherds can be heard singing as they look after their sheep ('Kann von Sehnsucht mich nicht fassen'). Kismárty is alarmed to hear about the official visit ordered by the Empress, since he fears it may now come out that he has been trying to force upon the settlers the excess widows there have been in the district since the last war. Fortunately Frusina, his wife, has had an idea. She has invited all the prettiest girls of the surrounding district to pose as marriage candidates for the time of the Count's visit and she has not neglected to consider the possibility that she might interest the Count himself in her own beautiful daughter Janka, a young lady fresh from a convent education and ripe for marriage ('Niemals darf man lachen'/'Heimat, deine Lieder'). Janka herself is not at all of a like mind. She wants nothing to do with a man who is known far and wide as a Don Juan.

Cries of welcome greet the arrival of the head palatine ('Éljen! Hoch Graf

1188

Stefan!') but it is, of course, the disguised Arpád who appears and proceeds to open the investigation. The president of local jurisdiction puts his case, after which the spokesman for the settlers steps forward and, to the considerable surprise of Arpád and Desider, turns out to be none other than the real Count Stefan. He has travelled to Popláka in secret and is posing as an immigrant in order to establish the truth about the recent happenings in the village.

The confused settlers now see a whole group of pretty maidens put before them as potential brides. Even Janka has joined them. They soon pair up, with Janka choosing Stefan as her partner ('Wir sitzen beisammen'/'Frag nur dein Herz, was Liebe ist') while Arpád takes advantage of his new-found status and promises himself a bit of fun with a peasant girl named Etelka ('Du bist so schön und tugendreich'/'Kleine Etelka'). Etelka feels immensely flattered at arousing the affections of the supposed Count and, one way and another, everyone is in jolly mood as they are called to join in preparations for the mass wedding the following morning (Finale I: 'Wo ist Graf Stefan?').

ACT 2

In the square in front of the village church of Popláka, Frau Frusina von Kismárty is discussing the preparations for the forthcoming weddings with the verger while taking care to assure all the girls that all marriages today will be for appearances only ('Hochzeitsschleier, zart und fein!'). It would, of course, be terrible if her daughter Janka were to be married to a mere settler. Kismárty is convinced that, after his imbibing the previous evening, the supposed Count Stefan will sleep soundly through the whole charade. When Arpád duly arrives, looking distinctly ill, Etelka is anxious that he should go through with his marriage to her, even though Arpád is not sure that he promised anything so definite ('Man kann sich lieben jederzeit'/'Weil die Trompete bläst').

The real Stefan is by now consumed with a genuine passion for Janka and she, in turn, reciprocates his affections. However, because her feelings are real, she feels compelled to inform him who she really is and that, as a girl of noble birth, she cannot be his ('Niemals kann ich dir entsagen'/'Du bist meines Lebens Seligkeit'). Uncle Desider is horribly concerned when he hears that Stefan wishes to marry what he believes to be a mere peasant girl and, turning to Frusina for advice, he enlightens her as to Stefan's true status. Frusina is naturally highly delighted and gives Uncle Desider the assurance that Count Stefan will quite definitely not be marrying any peasant's daughter.

Kismárty arrives, perturbed that, now that the supposed Count has arrived on the scene, the marriages must go ahead to preserve his position and he instructs the girls on how a true Hungarian bride should behave ('Wollt Ihr meinen Wunsch erfüllen'/'Ungarmädel lieben, dass Atem dir vergeht'). Janka has by now decided that she really loves the man she still believes to be a mere peasant, but her mother tells her the true situation. Frusina, delighted that her daughter is to become a Countess, goes to find her a suitable veil, but Janka reflects bitterly on Stefan's deceit, believing that she is no more than another of the man's little adventures ('Lasst die Glocke läuten, so ist es schrecklich'/'Spiel mir das Lied von Glück und Treu').

Etelka is still excitedly contemplating the prospect of becoming, as she believes, a Countess, and since Arpád finally agrees to marry her they join the other couples on their way to church (Finale II: 'Den Grafen zu erfreuen'). The mass wedding goes ahead but, after the ceremony, when Stefan asks his bride to lift her veil, he sees before him not Janka but her maid Anna. Janka tells the angry and desperate Stefan that she could not forgive his deceit and, in the acrimonious exchanges that follow, Etelka discovers that she has become not a Countess but the wife of a valet.

ACT 3

The Empress has come to the castle at Bratislava for a court ball and has taken the occasion to bring together all those concerned with the occurrences in Popláka so that the confused situation may be cleared up as quickly and as satisfactorily as possible. Stefan hopes that Maria Theresia will dissolve his unwitting marriage with the maid Anna so that he may woo and eventually wed the girl to whom he continues to express his love ('Nun ging sie von mir, zu meinem Schmerz'/'Märchentraum der Liebe').

The Empress looks with considerable disfavour on the events in Popláka and gives Kismárty a serious warning about his future conduct. As for the marriages, she declares all those entered into by the settlers as invalid. Only the marriages of Stefan and Arpád require further consideration. Despite Etelka's protests that she had expected something more, she is soon persuaded that a valet makes a more suitable husband than a nobleman and that the marriage should stand. As for Stefan, she warns that she can dissolve the marriage only if another woman is ready to take him. Now Janka follows the true urgings of her heart, asks forgiveness of him, and gives him her love afresh (Finale III: 'Dass mich so viele Frauen lieben').

HOCHZEITSNACHT IM PARADIES

(Wedding Night in Paradise)

an operetta in six scenes by Heinz Hentschke. Lyrics by Günther Schwenn. Music by Friedrich Schröder. Produced at the Metropol-Theater, Berlin, 24 September 1942 with Johannes Heesters (Ulrich), Hilde Seipp (Regine), Paul Westermeier (Felix), Ingeborg von Kusserow (Veronika), Walter Müller (Poldi) and Gretl Schörg (Dodo). Produced at the Bürgtheater, Vienna, 8 December 1950.

CHARACTERS

Dr Ulrich Hansen
Regine, *his wife*
Felix Wächtel, *a sweet manufacturer*
Poldi Oberländer, *a sports reporter*
Veronika, *Regine's friend*
Doña Dolores, *known as* Dodo
Dajos Lajos Földesy, *her manager*
Professor Fisch
Bastian, *a porter at the Paradise Hotel*
President of the Venice Tennis Club
Romano Pico, *a gondolier*
Egon, *a servant*
Kätchen, *a maid*
A locksmith, wedding guests, waiters, servants, Spanish dancers, hotel guests, tennis players, gondoliers, people of Venice

SCENE 1

In the lobby of Regine's home a group of wedding guests are waiting anxiously for her bridegroom, the celebrated tennis player Ulrich Hansen ('Was ist denn nur, was ist denn nur, was ist denn nur geschehn?'). The sweet manufacturer Felix Wächtel tries to reassure them. 'He'll be here soon,' he says. 'Perhaps he is looking for his collar-stud, or his car won't start.' However, his niece Veronika, a friend of the bride, is not so charitable. All the papers have published a photograph of the bridegroom in a ringside seat at a boxing match the previous day in the company of a Spanish dancer named Doña Dolores, popularly known as Dodo.

Whilst at the boxing match with Ulrich, Felix had befriended Dodo's manager, Dajos Lajos Földesy, and Lajos now rushes up with the news that Dodo is on her way to the house. Soon she bursts in with her dancers in tow, and proves to be a lady with a fiery Latin temperament ('Dodo ist eine Frau, die jeder kennt'). 'Where is my Ulli?' she cries. 'I want to speak with him immediately. I love my Ulli and I won't let him go!' To avoid a scene, Felix ushers Dajos, Dodo and her dance troupe into the wine-cellar, where he says Ulrich is to be found, and shuts them in.

Veronika is determined that, when her time comes to marry her fiancé Poldi, he should put in an appearance five hours before the wedding. 'And after the wedding can I come and go as I please?' he asks. 'Once we are married, you will know full well when you can come and go!' she replies ('Ich hab mir einen Stundenplan'). Meanwhile, the bride herself remains remarkably calm. 'Either one believes in a man, or one doesn't. And I believe in him,' she insists ('Ich glaube an dich und deine Liebe').

As five o'clock approaches, the wedding carriages begin to arrive ('Was ist denn nur, was ist denn nur, was ist denn nur geschehn?'). Then, on the dot of five o'clock, Ulrich steps in, complete with top hat and tails and wondering what all the fuss is about. 'Split-second timing is all important with a beautiful woman,' he declares ('Es kommt an die Sekunde an'). Regine takes him to task over his attendance at the boxing match, but he reassures her. 'That was yesterday. That's a long time ago! Now I'm all yours—yours for ever!' As the two reaffirm their love a commotion is heard from the cellar. Felix emerges, explaining that he must have knocked a bottle over, but then a female voice is heard creating loud and quite distinct mayhem. There is just time to get the bride and groom out the front door before Dodo emerges with her troupe of Spanish dancers.

SCENE 2

During the post-wedding celebrations Felix and Dajos sneak away into Regine's boudoir for a boys' chat, and Felix admits to having taken quite a fancy to Dodo. Together they smoke some of Dodo's own personalised cigarettes but, when they hear a farewell toast being drunk to the newlyweds, they stub out their cigarettes and hurry to see the bride and groom leave.

The toasts over, Regine comes up to her room with Veronika, contemplating the joys of the life with Ulrich that lies ahead ('So stell ich mir die Liebe vor'). When Ulrich follows, Veronika leaves the pair alone to express their feelings for each other ('Alle Wege führen mich zu dir') and Ulrich goes to order some champagne so that he and his new wife may drink to their future (Finale 2: 'Regine, lass auf die Zukunft uns trinken').

While he is away Regine discovers Dodo's cigarette case on the table, together with the two stubs in the ash-tray and, when Ulrich returns, Regine accuses him of having been alone in her boudoir with Dodo. Ulrich vigorously denies such a charge, but Regine is unimpressed and, unable to persuade her that he is telling the truth, Ulrich ends up taking his hat and coat and leaving to stay the night with the wedding guests at the Paradise Hotel. When he has gone, Regine begins to have doubts. She calls for her maid, who confirms that Uncle Felix and a foreign gentleman had been alone smoking in her boudoir and, throwing her coast and shawl over her negligé, Regine in turn leaves for the Paradise Hotel, to make amends.

SCENE 3

In the hall of the Paradise Hotel, the wedding guests are gathered, looking forward to a lively night of fun (Paradise March: 'Willst du heut nacht ins Paradies hinein?'). Felix is anxious to pursue his passion for Dodo, but she says that she will love him only until she sees Ulrich again. 'You won't see him again,' he assures her, pointing out that Ulrich will soon be on his way to Venice for his honeymoon. Felix, Dajos and Dodo go into the hotel bar, while Veronika and Poldi retire to their respective rooms—numbers 49 and 51.

Ulrich arrives seeking a room, and he is given the last remaining one— room 151. The porter greets him as an old friend and recalls all the young ladies he has entertained there. 'That's over now,' Ulrich assures him. 'Now I love only my wife. What a happiness it is that one can be so much in love!'

('Ein Glück, dass man so verlieben kann'). Already a trifle tipsy, he is persuaded to go into the porter's office for yet another drink, while Dodo, Felix and Dajos come out of the bar and retire to their rooms.

SCENE 4

In room 51 Veronika is unpacking her nightdress and toiletries, when Poldi creeps in to say 'good night'. As their conversation becomes more animated they are interrupted from time to time by knocks on the wall from the elderly Professor Fisch who is trying to get to sleep in room 50. Poldi tells a somewhat frightening tale of an occasion when he found a thief under his bed in a hotel room, but Veronika feels safe enough to send him to his room while she undresses. When she is in bed he can come and say 'good night' again, and then in their separate beds they will think of each other ('Was ich dir noch sagen wollte').

When Poldi finally leaves, Veronika goes into her bathroom to get ready for bed and, while she is there, the door of the room opens to reveal Ulrich. He is now very much the worse for drink and has mistaken room 51 for his own room number 151. He bolts the door, takes off his collar and evening dress, and is astonished when Veronika returns. She points out that his room 151 is on the floor above, but she is naturally puzzled as to what he is doing in the hotel. He has just finished telling her of his row with Regine, when Regine's voice is heard outside calling him. He persuades Veronika that he must, at all events, not be found with her and, remembering Poldi's tale, she decides to hide under the bed. Ulrich hides her clothes in the cupboard and opens the door to Regine.

Regine, it seems, had caught sight of Ulrich as he went into room 51. Now the two quickly make up, and Ulrich says that he will dress and return home. Regine, however, will have none of it. 'No, Ulrich,' she says. 'Now I am in Paradise, and in Paradise I want to stay.' And she throws off her coat and stands before Ulrich in her negligé. Then she spots a woman's stocking on a table. To Regine's challenge he quickly replies that the hotel must have left it lying around. 'And did they leave the leg it belongs to as well?' she asks, spotting Veronika's leg under the bed. Ulrich seeks to explain, but Regine is convinced that the leg belongs to Dodo and she rushes off again, oblivious of Ulrich's calls after her.

Veronika climbs out, and she and Ulrich sit together on the bed. Now Poldi enters and is likewise outraged to see the two together. By this time Professor Fisch can stand the commotion no more, and in no time the whole hotel is aroused and guests press into the room. Ulrich determines to go on alone on the honeymoon journey to Venice, but Veronika decides that, given the circumstances, she might as well use the spare ticket and go with him (Finale IV: 'Und wenn auch alles gegen mich spricht').

SCENE 5

While in Venice, Ulrich has entered and won the men's singles of the Venice

1193

tennis tournament. The newspapers carry news of his victory, with the information that he is in Venice on honeymoon, but it is Veronika who stands by his side as the club president congratulates him on his victory. The president invites the two of them to partake of the loving cup at the traditional gondoliers' festival that evening, telling them that the couple who drink from it together are indissolubly bound for their earthly life. The two know that they don't love each other but decide that there is nothing for it but to act as man and wife ('Ich spiel mit dir').

As they depart together, a gondola appears carrying Poldi and Felix. The gondolier is Romano Pico, eighty-two years old and the oldest gondolier in Venice. As such, he tells them, it is he who will pass round the loving cup at the evening's festival. From the conversation of Poldi and Felix, it transpires that they have been summoned by a telegram from Veronika telling Poldi where she is. Poldi has, for his part, reassured Regine that it was Veronika, and not Dodo, that Ulrich was with in the bedroom of the Paradise Hotel.

SCENE 6

Regine has now come to terms with Dodo, and the pair of them have also come to Venice. As the gondoliers begin their festival ('Es grüsst dich, Venedig'), Regine determines that it will be she who drinks from the loving cup with Ulrich. She meets up with Veronika, who is delighted to hear of Poldi's presence in town but she is less pleased to hear that Poldi is lodged under the same roof as Dodo. She is readily reassured, however, by the news that her Uncle Felix is taking care of Dodo. Indeed, that unlikely couple are getting on famously.

The sound of a wind band announces the procession of gondoliers bearing the loving cup (Finale VI: 'Die Stunde ist da, die wir lange ersehnt'). At their head is the costumed, masked and bearded figure of Romano Pico, and the crowd gathers around the podium where the old gondolier stands with the cup. Felix and Dodo come forward and drink from it, thereby declaring themselves joined for life. The cup is passed back to the old gondolier, and Poldi steps forward declaring that he will drink with Frau Doktor Hansen— meaning, of course, Veronika. 'With a married woman?' the old gondolier exclaims in surprise. Poldi begins to explain, but Regine, hearing her name as she appears on the scene, rushes forward declaring that she is the only woman with that name.

Regine drinks from the cup and declares that she will drink a second time as proxy for the one to whom her heart belongs. Suddenly, however, the old bearded gondolier snatches the cup and declares that he will drink with her. Having done so, he pulls off his mask and beard and reveals himself as Ulrich. Once again Ulrich has shown the importance of split second timing. The real Romano Pico mounts the podium and declares Ulrich and Regine united for life. Poldi now begs for the cup, and he and Veronika drink from it, leaving the crowd to salute three happy couples.

FEUERWERK

(Fireworks)

a musical comedy in three acts by Eric Charell and Jürg Amstein, after the comedy
De sächzigscht Giburtstag (*The Sixtieth Birthday*) by Emil Sautter. Lyrics by Jürg
Amstein and Robert Gilbert. Music by Paul Burkhard. Originally produced in a one
act version as *Der schwarze Hecht* (*The Black Pike*) at the Schauspielhaus, Zürich,
1939. Revived there in a revised version 1948.

Produced at the Theater am Gärtnerplatz, Munich, 16 May 1950 with Gustav
Knuth (Obolski) and Rita Wottawa (Iduna).

Produced at the Bristol Old Vic in a version by Eizabeth Montagu as *Oh, My Papa*
2 April 1957 and subsequently at the Garrick Theatre, London, 17 July 1957 with
Laurie Payne (Obolski) and Rachel Roberts (Iduna).

Produced at the Volksoper, Vienna, 19 February 1983 with Kurt Huemer
(Obolski), Helga Papouschek (Iduna) Elisabeth Kales (Anna) and Jack Poppell
(Robert).

Produced at the Théâtre Marigny, Paris, as *Feux d'Artifices* 1952 with Jacqueline
Cadet, Suzy Delair and Jean Bretonnière.

CHARACTERS

Albert Oberholzer, *a manufacturer*
Karline, *his wife*
Anna, *their daughter*
Kati, *the Oberholzers' cook*
Josef, *the butler*
Fritz Oberholzer, *a farmer*
Berta, *his wife*
Gustav Oberholzer, *a government official*
Paula, *his wife*
Heinrich Oberholzer, *a professor*
Klara, *his wife*
Herbert Klusmann, *a ship owner*
Lisa, *his wife*
Alexander Oberholzer, *known as Obolski, director of a circus*
Iduna, *his wife*
Robert Fischer, *a young gardener*
An equerry, servant, circus people, children

ACT 1

In a Swiss town, during the early 1900s, the manufacturer Albert
Oberholzer is celebrating his sixtieth birthday and his wife and his nineteen-
year-old daughter Anna are busy setting the table for the guests who are
coming to join the birthday party ('Mutti! Wer sitzt denn auf Ehren-
plätzen?'). All Albert's brothers are going to be there with their wives, except
for the youngest brother, Alex, who left the family as a child and whom
young Anna has never met.

The birthday cake is a work of art. It has been made by the cook, Kati, a

1195

happy soul, forever singing at her work ('Ich koche gern, ich koche gut'). All that is missing to complete the picture is some flowers, and Anna gladly offers to gather them, snatching at an excuse to go outside to meet the young gardener, Robert. Anna's father has forbidden her to associate with a gardener but, when Robert comes in with baskets full of flowers ('Ich sag' es gern durch die Blume'), he seizes the opportunity to snatch a kiss. Naturally Robert has not been invited to the party. 'What can I do,' he asks, 'if I have been born with a rose in my hand rather than a silver spoon in my mouth?' Before he leaves, he gets Anna to promise to meet him that evening by the garden wall.

Anna calls upon the cook to join her, with her mother at the piano, in a birthday duet composed specially for her father ('O Jubilar, hör gnädig unser Singen'), but they have scarcely started their song when the door bell rings. It is Uncle Fritz the farmer, with his wife Aunt Berta. Everyone greets everyone else warmly and the newcomers are pressed to listen to Anna's composition. 'Perhaps you're raising a female Beethoven,' says Uncle Fritz, but Aunt Berta is not impressed. 'He's the one with the Erotica. The girl's much too young for that!'

The birthday duet is started again, but just as soon interrupted again by the door bell. This time it is Uncle Gustav and Aunt Paula. Gustav suffers from a chronic cough whose history he and Paula proceed to narrate at length ('In seiner Jugend schon wär er'). 'His Latin is poor,' his teacher used to say at school, 'but he coughs well.' The story over, the duet is started once again, but yet again the door bell rings. This time it's Uncle Heinrich, the banker, and his wife Lisa.

Now that everyone is present, they call the birthday celebrant. He tells them all how happy he is at seeing his family reunited, even if his joy is a little tempered by apprehension about his mounting age ('Wie bald wird man alt und steht schon am End'). Kati brings in the soup, and the meal begins, but Anna and her mother keep on whispering about the birthday surprise they have in store and, finally, they decide that, before the fish course, they will sing Anna's birthday duet.

Incredibly, the door bell rings yet again at just the same point as before. The cook goes to answer it and returns excitedly. 'It is Alex, the runaway!' she cries. Everyone jumps up in astonishment as the long-lost brother enters the room and greets his eldest brother joyously. He has brought with him his French-born wife, Iduna, whom he introduces as 'famed on the trapeze and as a bare-back rider—the pride of my life,' before bustling round to greet his brothers, whom he has not seen since he left home at the age of eighteen.

Uncle Alex launches into an account of how, in the thirty years since then, he has worked his way up to be director of a circus ('Man hat's nicht leicht bis man's erreicht!'). He has three lions, two anthropomorphic apes, six full-blooded Arabian steeds and a thousand other sensations. His elephant, he tells them, smokes a cigar, plays the guitar, and tells the time! He goes on to pull a coil of paper from Gustav's mouth, a large bunch of flowers from Mother's skirt pocket, and a live rabbit from Paula's bosom. 'Obolski!' he declares. 'The name means something in the world!' His brothers and sisters-in-law are quite taken aback, but Anna is delighted—no more, though, than Obolski and his wife are with their niece. Iduna is all agog to show Anna all the delights of the circus, especially the most wonderful thing in the world—her little pony ('Ich hab' ein kleines süsses Pony').

Anna can scarcely wait, and Iduna asks why she doesn't go back with them. Her mother is appalled but Anna wants to see the world, and Obolski encourages her ('Die Welt ist gross und weit'). The cook is getting rather anxious about her fish course, but the aunts want to see Albert's birthday presents. The uncles gather round Iduna, who tells them that Gustav's serious face reminds her of her father, as does Heinrich's proud bearing and Fritz's ruddy complexion, and she tells them all about her father—a unique artist, a clown like no other ('O mein Papa war eine wunderbare Clown').

Iduna pretends that she is walking the high wire, and by now Anna is completely hooked with the idea of the circus (Finale I: 'Eh là hopp, eh là hopp! Zirkus!'). This time she will let nobody stop her. The general uproar gets a surprise reinforcement as the cook blows her top. Her wonderful cooking is being totally ignored. Suddenly, a loud explosion is heard and everyone rushes outside,

ACT 2
Out in the garden, watching the fireworks going off, Anna is in especially high spirits, particularly when she finds Robert there ('Heut' hab' ich Flügel'). Her mother calls her back to be sociable to the guests, but she refuses to come. When she tells Robert her plan to go off to join the circus, he asks her to go away with him instead, but she wishes to stand on her own feet and tells him that only when she is rich and famous will she return to marry him. 'When you have gone, for whom shall I pick the most beautiful flowers of the century?' he asks. 'Forget the wandering circus!' And he conjures up for her a vision of the life they can lead together ('Ein Leben lang verliebt').

Now the grown-ups all come out of the house, and Anna's father threatens to disown her if she perseveres with her plan to join the circus ('Zum Zirkus will sie geh'n'), but Uncle Obolski lends her his shoulder to lean on and describes the excitement of the circus life ('Dort, wo man gestern gar nichts sah'). Anna seems to see the pleasures of circus life appear before her. There are three clowns who look distinctly like Uncles Gustav, Fritz and Heinrich ('Ich spring' wie ein Pfeil hinauf auf das Seil'). Then Obolski calls forward the tigers—though Anna can see only her three aunts growling ('Da sagt man: Ah!'). Next, as ringmaster, he introduces Iduna with her little pony, and watches them go through their act ('Ein jeder Kinstler ist empfindlich wie ein Kind').

The vision of the circus fades, and Robert comes through the garden gate in a jealous rage ('Hirngespinste! Larifari! Humbug!').'You confouded Svengali!' he cries at Obolski. Anna attempts to come between them, and tells Robert to go away, and finally he does, vowing never to have any more to do with her. Obolski, convinced that Anna has an artist's blood in her veins, urges her on and all the circus artists march around saluting the circus life ('Hokuspokus-Fidibus!').

ACT 3

Back in the living-room, Heinrich is seated at the piano playing a waltz. Iduna is dancing with Fritz, but Gustav taps his brother on the shoulder to take over. 'When is it my turn?' asks Heinrich. One way and another the brothers are feeling very young at heart in Iduna's company, and she in turn is relishing the effect she has on them ('So jung wie heut"). Paula appears from the next room with Bertha. 'For God's sake, you will be ill again!' she says, seeing the exhausted Gustav.

Then Robert comes in asking for Anna and swearing dire vengeance on her circus uncle. 'He has stolen my love,' he shouts. 'He has juggled himself into my girl's heart.' Iduna steps forward. 'I didn't know that Anna had such a charming fiancé,' she says tenderly. 'What do you do for a living?' Iduna soon pacifies and charms Robert, and then she brings Anna in from the garden and, sitting her down, begins to tell her of the less glamorous side of circus life—the bustle, the loneliness, the travelling—and also the jealousy she feels when her husband has glamorous women around him. 'I have gone through a lot with my dear Alexander,' she says ('Er ist mein Mann und ihm gehöre ich').

Anna goes up to her room deep in thought, just as the cook comes in with her hat, coat and basket, ready to leave. She is pacified only by Mother assuring her that everyone will at last sit down for the meal. All the men try to have Iduna sit next to them, but by now their wives have had enough ('Um Gottes willen, was ist denn passiert?'). Turning on Obolski, they protest that he has brought nothing but discontent and conflict into the house. Obolski turns on them, in turn, telling them how narrow their lives are ('Potz Hagel, Blitz und Peitschenknall!'). 'You don't know the sky, the rustling of the woods, the rushing of the seas, the stillness of the fields!' he tells them. 'We don't understand each other. Two worlds that never meet.

Albert goes to him and bids him farewell. 'I wanted to see you again, to be with you on my sixtieth birthday,' he says. 'Don't worry. Our paths will not cross again.' And he holds his hand out to his youngest brother as he prepares to leave. Obolski asks Anna if she is going with them. Sadly she says not, but she asks Iduna to look after the little pony ('Grüss mir dein kleines, süsses Pony'). 'Tell him everything that happened to you and me today,' she says. Iduna promises that she will, and she and Obolski leave.

The cook comes in again with a tray, but Paula has decided that it is time she and Gustav were leaving. Gustav, however, appears from the kitchen holding a wine-glass and decidedly tipsy. 'I'm going to the circus,' he says. 'Better to be a clown in a circus than a mountebank's assistant at home. I'm going to my brother Obolski and to my beautiful sister-in-law Iduna!' The others try to bring him to his senses (Finale III: 'Aber Gustav, sei doch vernünftig!'), but he departs with the other adults in pursuit.

Anna remains, seated at the piano, but she jumps up when Robert comes in. She runs to him, and the two embrace as Kati comes in with the cooked goose. 'Now we just want to be happy again,' she says. Anna's mother and father return and, delighted that Anna is not going away to join the circus, they give their blessing to her union with Robert. True love, they all agree, is still the finest circus in the world, as a vision of Obolski and Iduna appears to give their approval to the fact that all has ended well ('So endet der kleine Familienbericht').

FRÜHJAHRSPARADE

(Spring Parade)

an operetta in two acts and nine scenes by Hugo Wiener, after the screenplay by Ernst Marischka. Music by Robert Stolz. Produced at the Volksoper, Vienna, 25 March 1964 with Guggi Löwinger (Marika), Erich Kuchar (Willi), Mimi Coertse (Hansi), Peter Minich (Gustl) and Fred Liewehr (the Emperor).

The original film was produced by Geza von Bolvary in 1935 with Paul Hörbiger, Franziska Gaal, Wolf Albach-Retty, Theo Lingen, Annie Rosar and Adele Sandrock. A film version in English was produced by Universal in 1940 as *Spring Parade* with Deanna Durbin, and a further German language version as *Ein Deutschmeister* in 1955 with Romy Schneider, Paul Hörbiger, Hans Moser and Gretl Schörg.

CHARACTERS

Marika Szápári
Willi Sedlmeier, *a corporal*
Hansi Gruber, *a soprano*
Gustl von Laudegg, *a first lieutenant*
Therese Hübner, *a baker*
Fritz, *a baker's apprentice*
Neuwirth, *a court councillor*
Swoboda, *a hairdresser*
von Laudegg, *Court Chamberlain*
Klothilde von Laudegg, *his wife*
Mittermeier, *a sergeant*
The Emperor
The Emperor's adjutant
Ketterl, *a manservant*
A governess, an Archduchess, landlord, secret policemen, ladies, gentlemen, officers, soldiers, Heurige visitors, sideshow owners, servants, children

SCENE 1 (ACT 1)
Around the big wheel in the Prater in Vienna in the spring of 1905 the funfair is in full swing ('Riesenrad und Grottenbahn'). A young Hungarian girl named Marika Szápári passes by in her donkey cart on her way from Balatonfüred to Vienna to visit her aunt, the baker Therese Hübner ('Wiener Klänge, Wiener Luft'/'Selbst die Vöglein musizieren'). She stops to have her fortune read, and is told: 'In the imperial city of Vienna you will fulfil your destiny. You will suffer a loss but it will be made good again. Two men cross your path: an artist and a nobleman. You will set a stone rolling

1199

and bring good luck to a near relation. A high gentleman will come decisively into the spokes of your lucky wheel. Take care over the first man you encounter. He will be your husband for life. Your lucky numbers are 4, 12 and 75.'

Turning round, she discovers that her donkey and cart have disappeared, and in her confusion promptly bumps into an army corporal. He is taken aback by the way in which the young girl looks at him, but she introduces herself, and he offers to show her to her aunt's place. Alas, the address is in her purse, which is in the missing cart. All she knows is that her aunt is a baker. The corporal tells her that his name is Willi, and that he is a drummer in a military band and a composer. He is just on the way to the Jantsch-Theater to see the soprano, Hansi Gruber, who is going to sing one of his waltz songs.

Willi takes Marika to one of the Prater refreshment places, a Hungarian *csárdá*, where a csárdás is being danced. Marika readily joins in ('Jój mámán! Ich glaub' mein Herz zerspringt') and, by the time she has finished, Willi has disappeared, but there are her cart and donkey waiting for her.

SCENE 2

At the Jantsch-Theater, Hansi Gruber is preparing for her stage appearance, while the young Lieutenant Gustl von Laudegg idly plays on the piano. 'Shouldn't you be going?' she asks. 'Your train is leaving.' 'Without me,' he replies firmly. 'I am staying in Vienna. For good.' Gustl has obtained a posting as a lieutenant in the crack Austro-Hungarian Deutschmeister Regiment, and he wants Hansi to give up the theatre and marry him, but his aunt, wife of the Court Chamberlain, will not hear of him marrying an actress. Together, Hansi and Gustl recall their meeting at an Embassy ball, when he offered her a glass of champagne ('Oft genügt ein Gläschen sekt').

Gustl takes Hansi in his arms, only to be disturbed by a knock at the door. It is Willi with his latest composition for Hansi. 'Don't you have anything better to do in the army than to compose?' asks Gustl but, unperturbed, Willi proceeds to accompany Hansi in his waltz song ('Frühjahrsparad' ist heut"). Hansi is delighted with the song and agrees to sing it at her benefit concert at the barracks in a week's time and Willi is equally delighted, as it will be the first time he has had a song performed publicly. 'You're on, Fräulein Gruber!' calls the stage-manager, and Hansi goes on stage to perform a song about the delights of Vienna by night ('Wien wird bei Nacht erst schön').

SCENE 3

A week later, at Therese Hübner's bakery, the proprietress is despairing of the progress of her apprentice, Fritz. The main problem seems to be that he is from Berlin where baking terminology is different ('Mohnzöpfe heissen Stritzerl') but there is another problem, too. Ever since Marika arrived, Fritz has been utterly besotted with her, and has great difficulty concentrating on his work. On the whole, though, Marika's aunt considers her a joy to have around the house, dancing through the days and always finding something in life to be happy about ('Ich freu' mich, wenn die Sonne lacht').

Marika is intrigued to know why her aunt has not remarried in the eight years since her husband died and, remembering her fortune, she wonders whether she shouldn't set a stone rolling somewhere. Frau Hübner doesn't seem to be short of admirers. When the court councillor Neuwirt looks in at the bakery to collect the Emperor's daily supply of Salzstangeln, his favourite baked rolls, he brings her a bunch of flowers and an invitation to accompany him to a Heurige wine tavern in Grinzing the next day. The sight of Neuwirt going into the bakery is enough to bring the hairdresser, Swoboda, running from his barber shop to make sure that Therese doesn't forget him either.

One thing Marika's aunt cannot understand is the way that, every time a military band marches past, Marika runs to the door, waits until the drummer comes past, and then returns disappointed. Now a band can again be heard outside, though this time the drummer is not playing. There he is marching at the side, and when he sees Marika he rushes up to her. It is Willi. 'Marika,' he calls, 'I've looked in every bakery.' 'And I've looked at every bass drummer,' she replies. 'Willi Sedlmeier, corporal in the Imperial Infantry Regiment number 4,' he tells her. 'Four?' she replies delightedly, remembering her fortune.

Willi tells Marika that Hansi is to perform his song at the concert in the barracks that afternoon, and that its success will be the second best thing that has ever happened in his life. 'And the best?' she asks. 'That I have found you again,' he replies, and he asks her if she will accompany him to the Heurige the next day ('Wenn sich zwei wie wir gegenübersteh'n'). When Marika's aunt appears, Willi hurriedly buys some rolls, and Marika adds up the cost. 'That is twelve kreuzer,' she tells him, reflecting again on the fortune-teller's words.

SCENE 4

That afternoon Hansi arrives at the barracks with Gustl, as much concerned with her threatened meeting with Gustl's Aunt Klothilde as with her performance. Gustl promises to speak with his aunt as soon as possible and then, when the performance is over, he will take Hansi to a little place he knows where violins play sweet music ('Ich sing' mein Lied heut' nur für dich!'). Gustl duly briefly introduces Hansi to his aunt, but his aunt makes it clear at once that his liaison with Hansi is no secret and that she doesn't approve. She has a more suitable bride in mind for him in the person of the Countess Traunstein, lady-in-waiting to the Empress. Gustl protests that he finds the Countess Traunstein too old and too ugly, but his aunt insists that the most important thing for an officer is a suitable marriage. 'If your uncle hadn't married me,' she tells him, 'he wouldn't be Court Chamberlain now, he'd be a major in Podwolisziska. That's what you could be, too.'

By now Hansi has changed into her costume and has returned and she is shocked to hear talk of Gustl marrying someone else. 'I'm not going on!' she declares. Willi's disappointment at her forfeit is all the greater because

Marika and Fritz had come to hear his song sung, but he sees a silver lining to the cancellation. He knows that there is something not quite right about the song. 'I don't believe it!' cries Marika, beating the table in time to each syllable of the music. 'That's it!' Willi cries, listening to the rhythm that Marika is banging out, 'It's not a waltz, it's a march!' Willi rushes up to the rostrum and urges the musicians to play the piece for him in march tempo before the bandmaster arrives.

He has barely started, when the arrival of the Archduchess Annunziata forces him to bring the playing to a halt. What is more, the furious Aunt Klothilde reports Willi to the bandmaster and insists that his march shall never be played again, adding as an afterthought 'unless the Emperor commands it!' In despair Willi throws the music away, but Marika turns to Fritz. 'You know you said that you would do anything for me?' she says. 'Would you bake this in one of the Salzstangeln the court councellor Neuwirth collects in the morning?' Meanwhile, Marika can do no more than look forward to the Heurige the next day ('Ich freu' mich, wenn die Sonne lacht'), while a sergeant and contingent of soldiers march on and Willi and Gustl compare notes about a soldier's life ('Ja, wir armen Soldaten'/'Jung san ma, fesch san ma!').

SCENE 5

Therese and Neuwirth are sitting together in a Grinzing wine garden when Marika enters with Willi. Then Hansi puts in an appearance. Therese is all agog and, when Neuwirth promptly introduces the two ladies, the baker begs Hansi to sing for her the pretty piece she remembers her performing in the operetta *Love in Uniform*. Hansi needs little more encouragement ('Im Frühling, im Mondschein, in Grinzing, in Wien'). By now Marika and Willi are getting onto more intimate terms ('Wir trinken einfach Bruderschaft'), and ultimately Willi gets round to giving her a kiss. Marika feels happier than she ever has before.

Gustl has come to find Hansi who is still feeling very upset over her treatment at the hands of Aunt Klothilde but, when Gustl assures her that there is no chance of his marrying the hated Countess, she soon begins to feel happier once again ('Singend, klingend ruft dich das Glück'). Things don't look so good for Willi, though. The sergeant arrives with the news that he is to be arrested. The Emperor has found a music manuscript bearing Willi's name in one of his Salzstangeln. There is a chemical in the ink, and it is thought that it could be an attempt on the Emperor's life. In the face of this frightening news, Marika is no longer sure that quite everything in the world makes her so happy ('Ich freu mich, wenn die Sonne lacht').

SCENE 6 (ACT 2)

Marika's determination to do all she can to help Willi in his hour of need has led her to the palace of Schönbrunn, and there she meets Fritz and Swoboda, both of whom have received an invitation from the Court

Chamberlain. Then Willi appears. He has been held at the barracks, freed and, like Fritz and Swoboda, summoned to appear before the Court Chamberlain. So have Therese and Neuwirth. What is worse, the Emperor has decided to get his Salzstangeln from a different baker in future. Neuwirth, however, has been been named district captain of Ostrau in Moravia and wonders if Therese would care to go with him. Therese tells him that she needs to sleep on it ('Wir Frauen sind kompliziert').

Gustl arrives with Hansi, who cannot imagine what his uncle wants with her. Gustl knows that his aunt will do everything to keep the two of them apart, but he remains firm in his devotion ('Du hast mich bezaubert'). Marika is in tears at the thought of the chain of disasters for which she has been responsible, and she is determined to see the Emperor herself and sort matters out. 'You?' asks Willi. 'How will you manage to get to the Emperor in his palace? Just go back home with your aunt. Tomorrow is the spring parade, and after the parade I'll come to see you and we'll talk together.' ('Wenn sich zwei wie wir gegenübersteh'n') Just then a party of school girls enters the palace on an educational visit, all dressed like Marika ('Selbst die Vöglein musizieren'). Marika rushes to take the hands of two of the girls and marches on with them into the palace.

SCENE 7

The Court Chamberlain returns from a trip to Budapest to find that his wife has arranged what she calls a trial of her nephew for his proposed marriage to his actress friend. Gustl, Hansi, Willi, Therese, Neuwirth, Swoboda and Fritz are all shown in, and Klothilde begins by referring to the previous day's 'plot' against the Emperor. She demands to know who put the manuscript in the Salzstangel, and Fritz immediately confesses, but Willi then goes on to tell the full story. By now tired of asking what he is doing there, Swoboda speaks up in favour of Hansi and Gustl, and the Court Chamberlain, weary from years of being put down by his wife, joins in. 'For thirty years I haven't dared to contradict you, because you got me the position of Court Chamberlain through your connections. I'd have had more freedom as a major in Podwolisziska!' 'Stop! Stop!' is all Klothilde can reply. 'Don't say 'stop' to me,' retorts her husband. 'I'm not a telegram!' Klothilde is finally squashed, and everyone present is delighted. Therese is in such a good mood she even agrees to go with Neuwirth to Ostrau.

SCENE 8

The Emperor Franz Josef's adjutant is updating him on affairs of State, but the Emperor has other, graver matters to concern him. He is not pleased with his breakfast. 'What sort of Salzstangeln do you call these?' he asks his manservant. 'They don't taste at all good.'

It is time for the Emperor's daily audience, and Marika steps forward to tell him timidly about her bandmaster friend, Willi. 'I have lots of members of the Deutschmeister Band called Willi,' he replies. Even more timidly

1203

Marika mentions the name Sedlmeier, at which the Emperor pricks up his ears. Marika explains all about the manuscript in the Salzstangel, at which the Emperor calls his adjutant and commands that the march should be played at the spring parade the following morning. Almost everything in her fortune has come true—except one thing. 'How old is your majesty?' she asks. The Emperor consults his manservant, before coming back with the answer. '64,' he tells her. 'Shame! It says 75 here,' she says, looking at her fortune. The Emperor winks at her with a smile of self-satisfaction. 'Yes, indeed, I'm 75. Ketterl always wants to make me younger.' 'Then everything fits!' Marika cries in delight, as the Emperor promises to do his utmost to sort everything out ('... ich werde mein Möglichstes tun!').

SCENE 9

The following morning the parade ground is a colourful scene with the soldiers marching with their full colours ('Heut geht's los! Es marschiert das Militär!'). The Emperor steps onto the saluting base and commands Corporal Sedlmeier to step forward. He appoints him drum-major of the Fourth Deutschmeister Regiment and announces that he has commanded that the march 'Spring Parade' be taken up as an official Austrian military march to be played at every parade at which he is present. 'Marika, I have you to thank!' Willi cries. 'Not at all!' she replies. 'Thank my aunt's Salzstangeln!' ('Frühjahrsparad' ist heut"/'Singend, klingend ruft uns das Glück!')

Part 5
SPAIN

Compared with the other schools of light musical theatre represented in this volume, the Spanish school of the *zarzuela* remains virtually unknown on an international basis.

The reasons for this are not difficult to find. In the first place, for some reason the international public prefers the foreigner's impression of Spain as epitomised by Bizet's *Carmen* or Chabrier's *España* to the genuine Spanish article. Then again Spanish scores and parts have never been readily available, and non-Spanish musicians faced with an unfamiliar Spanish score can find the Spanish rhythms extremely difficult.

There are further reasons that relate specifically to the *zarzuela*. The works often refuse to conform to the accepted operetta or comic opera convention of a plot framed by musical numbers and with dialogue serving as much as anything to lead up to the next musical number. In the *zarzuela* the musical numbers often seem almost incidental, the songs being perhaps no more important than the folk dances or the detail of the setting and costumes or the sometimes long stretches of dialogue which may, moreover, be in verse. The traditional *zarzuela* is an intensely nationalistic creation, capturing the Spanish character as much as telling a story, portraying Spanish everyday life rather than indulging in the escapism of romantic operetta, and concentrating on the religious festivals and colourful traditions of Spain in a way that can make the works largely incomprehensible to foreign audiences. Yet none of this detracts from the quality of the *zarzuela* music, which is as rich as that of any other national school of light musical theatre.

The Spanish tradition in musical theatre may readily be traced back over several centuries but, as in other countries, it enjoyed a major new lease of life in the second half of the nineteenth century. During the 1850s a small group of composers, led by Francisco Asenjo Barbieri, began producing three-act stage works, amongst which Barbieri's own *Jugar con fuego* ('Playing with Fire', 1851), *Los diamantes de la corona* ('The Crown Diamonds', after Scribe, 1854) and *Pan y toros* ('Bread and Bulls') were outstanding examples. The extent of the success of their writing can be judged from the opening of the Teatro de la Zarzuela, devoted to the genre, in Madrid in 1857.

Other successful *zarzuela* practitioners of the time were the composers Gaztambide, Oudrid and Arrieta. The Italian-trained Arrieta's *Marina* (1855) typified a tendency for Italian comic opera traditions to pervade the *zarzuela*, a tendency that Barbieri attacked most particularly in the classic *El barberillo de Lavapiés* ('The Little Barber of Lavapiés', 1874). Barbieri made his assault not only musically in a score full of intensely Spanish rhythms but specifically in a plot that deals with unrest against the Italian dominated regime of Carlos III and the replacement of a prime minister with the Italian name of Garibaldi by the Spanish-named Floridablanca, and features characters smashing street lamps designed by the Italian architect Sabatini.

It was during the 1880s and 1890s that the *zarzuela* enjoyed its greatest years as a personification of the Spanish life and spirit. There were pieces in the three-act *zarzuela grande* mould such as Ruperto Chapí's *La Bruja* ('The Old Hag', 1887) and Tomas Bretón's *La Dolores* (1891), but the popular success of the *zarzuela* during those eventful decades came most particularly through the one-act works of the *genero chico*. Crucial in establishing this tradition was the essentially revue-like *La Gran Vía* ('The Great Road', 1886) of Federico Chueca, who provided the irresistible melodies, and Joaquin Valverde, who provided the music with its technical finish.

During the 1890s the *genero chico* tradition saw the production at Madrid's Teatro Apolo of Bretón's *La verbena de la Paloma* ('The Festival of the Dove', 1894), Chueca's *Agua, azucarillos y aguardiente* ('Water, Sweets and Liquor', 1897) and Ruperto Chapí's *La Revoltosa* ('The Mischief Maker', 1897) while, alongside them, the Teatro de la Zarzuela staged Manuel Fernández Caballero's *La Viejecita* ('The Little Old Lady', 1897—a work with elements of *Charley's Aunt*) and *Gigantes y cabezudos* ('Carnival Giants and Bigheads', 1898), and Gerónimo Giménez's *La Boda de Luis Alonso* ('Luis Alonso's Wedding', 1897) and *La Tempraníca* ('The Precocious One', 1900).

The efforts, begun by Barbieri some half a century earlier, to establish a Spanish tradition in light musical theatre had been fully consumated by the time the twentieth century saw the *zarzuela* branching out in its settings and its styles. Amadeo Vives's beautiful *Bohemios* ('Bohemians', 1904) was set in Paris, Vicente Lleó's *La corte de Faraón* ('Pharaoh's Court', 1910) in biblical Egypt, Pablo Luna's *Molinos de viento* ('Windmills', 1910) in Holland, José Serrano's *La canción del olvido* ('The Song of Oblivion', 1916) in Naples and Jacinto Guerrero's *La monteria* ('The Hunt', 1922) in Britain and *Los gavilanes* ('The Sparrowhawks, 1923) in Provence, but the same composers continued to do their duty towards native Spanish subjects, as in Luna's *El niño judío* ('The Jewish Boy', 1918), Vives's classic *Doña Francisquita* (1923), Guerrero's *El huésped del Sevillano* ('The Sevillan's Guest', 1926—with a seventeenth-century setting) and Serrano's *Los de Aragón* ('The People of Aragón', 1927). This urge to capture the soul of Spain in musical theatre terms was personified not least by the composer Francisco Alonso, who made a feature of devoting successive works to different regions of Spain. His *La Calesera* (1925), its title referring to the heroine's nickname but also the name of an Andalusian bolero-jacket or vest, typifies not only his own work but the immensely rich vein of melody that is to be found every bit as much in these works as in any other contemporary form of light musical theatre.

Like other schools of operetta, the *zarzuela* scarcely outlived the Second World War as a source of new products. The 1930s were the last decade to produce any significant number of major successes, among them Serrano's *La Dolorosa* ('Our Lady of Sorrows', 1930), Alonso's *La picarona* ('The Jade', 1930), Guerrero's *La rosa del azafrán* ('The Saffron Rose', 1931), Manuel Penella's *Don Gil de Alcalá* ('Don Gil of Alcalá', 1932), Federico Moreno Torroba's classic *Luisa Fernanda* (1932) and Pablo Sorozábal's *La tabernera del puerto* ('The Port Innkeeper's Wife', 1936). Moreno Torroba and Sorozábal both survived into the 1980s to conduct many of the classic works for modern recordings.

It is impossible here to do more than scratch the surface of an exciting and inexhaustibly rewarding school of works largely awaiting discovery. The selection here concentrates on the works of the *genero chico*, framed by an early and a late classic of the three-act genre, to present a microcosm of the *zarzuela* over the sixty years that saw the production of its greatest successes.

EL BARBERILLO DE LAVAPIÉS

(The Little Barber of Lavapiés)

a zarzuela in three acts by Luis Mariano de Larra. Music by Francisco Asenjo Barbieri. Produced at the Teatro de la Zarzuela, Madrid, 18 December 1874 with Franco de Salas (Paloma).

An English version by Geoffrey Dunn, re-orchestrated by Roberto Gerhard, was broadcast by the BBC in 1954 with Maria Perilli (Paloma), Bruce Boyce (Lamparilla), Thomas Round (Don Luis), Ian Wallace (Don Juan) and Marjorie Westbury (the Marquesita) and again c1970.

Produced in Germany as *Lamparilla*.

CHARACTERS

Lamparilla, *a barber*
Lope, *his apprentice*
Paloma
The Marquesita Estrella, *lady-in-waiting to the Infanta*
Don Juan
Don Luis
Don Pedro, *chief of police*
A sergeant
Students, young women about town, apprentice barbers, dressmakers, tradespeople.

ACT 1
The year is 1770 and, in the gardens of the royal estate of El Pardo to the north of Madrid, a crowd has gathered for the festival of the pilgrimage of San Eugenio ('Oh, the Pardo is the park'). Students from Alcalá and fashionable young men and women from Madrid are there in force, all thoroughly enjoying their picnic but also freely expressing their dissatisfaction with current social conditions under the rule of King Carlos III.

Amongst the crowd is Lamparilla, a barber, tooth-extractor and general factotum from Lavapiés, a district in the south of Madrid. He is something of a poor man's version of his rather grander counterpart in Seville and fond of relating the varied experiences that have led him to being, in his opinion, the best barber in Madrid ('I was page-boy to a bishop').

Also in the crowd is Lamparilla's sweetheart, Paloma, a dressmaker in Lavapiés, ever ready to flirt with the barber but equally firm in rebuffing his slightest advances. Born in the Street of the Dove, fluttering around like a dove, and singing like a dove, it is only natural that she should have aquired the nickname of 'the dove' ('Why am I called the Paloma the turtle dove?').

The public's discontent with conditions in Spain has prompted the Infanta Maria Luisa to encourage a plot to replace the Prime Minister, Garibaldi, a man with strong Italian connections, with his bitter political rival, the Count of Floridablanca, and the Infanta has come to El Pardo in person with her lady-in-waiting, the Marquesita Estrella, to make contact with the chief conspirator, Don Juan. Timidly the Marquesita and Juan approach each other and give the password ('This is the right place') but, as the Marquesita is handing over the key to a nearby hideout, they are interrupted by the appearance of Don Luis, a nephew of the Prime Minister and Estrella's lover. Seeing her in such earnest discussion with another man, he denounces her as being unfaithful to him ('When a man has won a woman').

Although Luis seems concerned only with Estrella's fidelity, she and Juan are concerned lest their plot be discovered. They must move into action without delay. The Marquesita prepares to set out across Madrid, but the way is prickling with dangers and it is clear that she must not go alone. Paloma suggests her sweetheart, Lamparilla, as a protector and the two women try to persuade the barber that all he would be doing is taking the young lady back to her convent ('Lamparilla' 'Here I am'). Flattery and, most of all, the promise of Paloma's affections finally persuade Lamparilla to undertake the mission.

As the crowds swell around, continuing their festival celebrations with the dancing of a *jota* (Finale I: 'Here again from Alcalá'), Don Pedro, the police chief, arrives on the scene with his men. The plot against Garibaldi has been uncovered. Lamparilla, who had been about to set off with the Marquesita, is hurriedly given the key to the hideout and persuaded to go there and tell the occupants to flee.

Anxious to protect Estrella, Don Luis insists that, when the guards raid the conspirators' hideout, anyone they find should be brought out hidden in a sedan chair. The raid takes place, and a prisoner is duly brought out in the sedan chair. However, when the curtains are flicked aside, the prisoner is only poor, unsuspecting Lamparilla.

ACT 2

The police are out in force in Lavapiés, guarding against disturbances. They are especially concerned to protect the street lamps that have been introduced by Carlos III but which, being designed by the Italian Sabatini, are frequently being smashed by the rebels ('A party of policemen').

With Lamparilla in jail, the customers in his barber shop have had to suffer his apprentices' less expert efforts with the razor and, after five days, they have become decidedly unhappy at this potentially lethal treatment ('Now when we want our hair cut'/'Lamparilla would whip up a lather'). Suddenly, to their huge relief, Lamparilla appears, explaining that he knows no more why he has been released than why he was imprisoned in the first place ('I was brave—I don't know how, though').

The plot against Garibaldi has reached its climax. That very evening Floridablanca is to be taken by Don Juan and other conspirators through a secret passage to the royal palace to meet the King. The conspirators will first assemble in the Marquesita's palace, which stands just next to Lamparilla's barber shop in the square of Lavapiés. Don Luis, regretting the effect the affair at El Pardo has had on his relationship with Estrella, arrives at her home and the pair reaffirm their affections ('An old and stately mansion rises') but the Marquesita's continuing secretiveness reactivates Don Luis's mistrust ('Though I am dying for love of him').

Paloma arrives to see Lamparilla to make up for the time they have lost while he has been in jail ('Call for the barber, someone's asking to see him') and she listens with interest to his tale of his amazing experiences ('It's never light there') but, when he begins to make advances towards her, she holds him off with her usual coyness (Tirana: 'Never remove all the tacking').

When the plotters begin to assemble in the Marquesita's palace, Lamparilla is charged by Paloma with the task of providing cover for their movements by getting a crowd together to smash all the street lamps. When the police get inquisitive, Lamparilla justifies the crowds assembling in the square by taking up his guitar and singing to them (Seguidillas Manchegas: 'In the temple of Mars') and, under cover of his diversion, the lamps in the square are smashed one by one. Don Luis and the chief of police, Don Pedro, arrive with a squadron of guards and, preparing to open fire, demand that the doors of Estrella's palace be opened (Finale II: 'Unlock the doors within there') but, fortunately, Lamparilla's diversion has enabled the conspirators to break through into the cellar of the barbershop and get clean away.

ACT 3

In Paloma's workshop the dressmakers sing as they work at their sewing ('We are the dressmakers' federation') and, while Paloma feeds her pet bird ('Little linnet, you see us poor lasses'), the girls express their envy of the shirts they are making, for the proximity they will enjoy to the handsome young men who will wear them ('Cotton Shirt, when you're worn').

The Marquesita's part in the plot against Garibaldi has put her life in danger, and Paloma is hiding her in her attic while, in preparation for her escape, she gives her help and advice about how to disguise herself as an ordinary working class girl without makeup, with a shawl and speaking a local dialect ('Does this shawl and mantilla indeed disguise me?'). Don Luis has decided that his love for Estrella is more important than his political position and that he will join her in her flight. A plan is evolved whereby they may leave the city in a carriage with Paloma and Lamparilla, disguised as ordinary townsfolk, ostensibly on the way for a picnic at San Lorenzo ('The sombrero on your eyebrow') but, before they can get away, the guards arrive once more, this time to raid Paloma's attic and to arrest the Marquesita, Paloma and Lamparilla ('They must all be hiding here').

Before the police can break into their hiding place, Lamparilla manages to escape over the roof and, as the police close in on Paloma and Marquesita, he returns with the news that Garibaldi has been overthrown and Floridablanca appointed Prime Minister in his place. Now it is Don Luis, as Garibaldi's nephew, who must go into exile, but the Marquesita is only too willing to go with him, while Paloma decides that the time has finally come to accept Lamparilla's proposal of marriage (Finale III: 'When a girl has an outing')

The excerpts are quoted from the English version by Geoffrey Dunn.

1213

LA GRAN VÍA

(The Great Road)

a comic-lyric-fantastic-street revue of Madrid in one act and five scenes by Felipe Pérez y González. Music by Federico Chueca and Joaquín Valverde. Produced at the Teatro Felipe, Madrid, 2 July 1886 with Joaquín Manini (Caballero de Gracia), Lucía Pastor (Menegilda/Madrid Lyceum) and José and Emilio Mesejo (Rats). Produced subsequently throughout the Spanish-speaking world.

Produced at the Carltheater, Vienna, 7 September 1894. Produced at Danzers Orpheum, 13 April 1902.

Produced at L'Olympia, Paris in a version by Maurice Ordonneau, 1896.

The music of *La Gran Via* was used as part of the score of the comic opera *Castles in Spain* produced at the Royalty Theatre, London in 1906.

CHARACTERS

The accoucheur
A passer-by
The Caballero de Gracia
Menegilda
Three rats
Lidia
Uncle Jindama
The Madrid Lyceum
Streets, squares and districts of Madrid, men and women, soldiers, guards, sea cadets

SCENE 1
(Streets and Squares)

More than thirty streets, squares and alleyways of central Madrid have gathering together to air their concern about the great road—the Gran Vía—that the Municipality of Madrid is planning to construct right across the centre of the city (Polka: 'Somos las calles, somos las plazas, y callejones de Madrid'). The road will affect them all, and many of them will be demolished altogether.

They are joined by a passer-by on his daily stroll through the old quarter, and then by the Caballero de Gracia who doesn't seem at all put out by the proposals. This may be because he is the only street who will have an exit onto the new road. All the other streets scoff and jibe at him as as a bully and show-off (Waltz: 'Caballero de Gracia me llaman').

Their argument is prolonged by a discussion of many of the other current problems of Madrid, after which the streets return to their places and the Caballero de Gracia and the passer-by decide to go together on a tour of inspection of Madrid.

SCENE 2
(On the Outskirts)

On their tour of the city the Caballero de Gracia and the passer-by come to the suburbs and meet a serving girl called Menegilda. She tells them her brief history—a tale of poverty relieved only by petty thieving and easy virtue (Tango: 'Pobre—chica, la que tiene que servir').

There now appear the somewhat perversely named districts of La Prosperidad—a picture of anything but prosperity—and of El Pacifico—which likewise is all but peaceful. They bring with them three rats who also expound their concerns. It seems that they are frequently pursued by the authorities, but seldom caught (Jota: 'Soy el Rata primero' 'Y yo, el segundo').

SCENE 3
(At the Puerta del Sol)

From the Calle de Alcalá can be seen the Puerta del Sol, the major square of the city. A good deal of criticism has been aroused by the thought that the municipal authorities will remove the central feature of the Puerta del Sol, the celebrated Mariblanca fountain. The criticisms extend to other contemporary problems, which prompts the appearance of a group of sea cadets. They are in Madrid on leave but are longing to get back to the sea (Mazurka: 'Somos los marineritos que venimos a Madrid').

SCENE 4
(The Crossing)

On the hoardings is a placard advertising a bullfight at the Madrid Bullring, alongside which is a sign that announces 'Madrid Lyceum: *Bal champêtre*'. In front of them, *Lidia* and *Uncle Jindama*, two sporting magazines of the time, are in animated discussion. The Caballero de Gracia notes critically that the Spanish theatres of the time are announcing only foreign titles such as *Le Fiacre* and *Il Guitarrero*. Finally the Madrid Lyceum herself describes the lively dances that take place within her walls (Schottisch: 'Yo soy el Elisedo, un baile de misto').

Left alone with the accoucheur who is to bring the Gran Vía into the world, the Caballero de Gracia and the passer-by learn that the Madrid municipality has decided to begin construction of the Gran Vía on 30 February.

SCENE 5
(The Great Road)

There appears a vision of the great, broad new road, with sumptuous buildings on either side, adorned with illuminated signs, and decorated for a festival. In reality the new road represents a great advance.

The above follows the standard text of the work. In the original version the fourth scene had three extra numbers—a brief and unimportant duet for a couple of young people going roller-skating, which was dropped, to avoid the introduction of two further singers, and a satirical 'Pasodoble of Sergeants' and 'Waltz of the Chief of Police', which were cut for political reasons during the dictatorships of Primo de Rivera and Franco, though still printed in the vocal score.

LA VERBENA DE LA PALOMA

(The Festival of the Dove)

a lyric farce in one act and three scenes by Ricardo de la Vega. Music by Tomás Bretón. Produced at the Teatro Apolo, Madrid, 17 February 1894 with Emilio Mesejo (Julián), Leocadia Alba (Rita), Manuel Rodriguez (Don Hilarion), José Mesejo (the innkeeper), Luisa Campos (Susana), Irene Alba (Casta) and Pilar Vidal (Aunt Antonia).

CHARACTERS

Don Hilarión, *an elderly chemist*
Don Sebastián, *his friend*
Doña Mariquita, *Don Sebastián's wife*
Teresa, *their niece*
Doña Mariquita, *a friend of Don Sebastián and his family*
Candeleria, *her daughter*
Julián, *a compositor*
The innkeeper
Rita, *his wife*
A janitor and his wife
Susana
Casta, *her sister*
Antonia, *their aunt*
A flamenco singer
Nightwatchman
Police Inspector
Young men and women, shop-boys, policemen, people of Madrid

SCENE 1

It is 14 August, the day of Madrid's annual festival of the Virgin of the Dove, in a year during the last decade of the nineteenth century. In a residential district of the city the old chemist Don Hilarión is sitting outside his shop with his friend Don Sebastián, explaining to him the advances of medical science in the various potions that he sells ('El aceite de ricino'/'Hoy las ciencias adelantan').

Further along the street, in the tavern, the landlord and two of his young friends are sitting at a table playing cards. The landlord's wife, Rita, is serving the customers, but she stops to offer comfort to an unhappy looking young man called Julián. The cause of Julián's woe is his unrequited love for a brunette called Susana ('También la gente del pueblo'). Rita does her best to comfort him and encourage him to forget all about her.

In between the chemist's shop and the tavern is the entrance to an apartment block, outside which the janitor is sitting with his wife with a baby on her lap. As the wife goes to put the baby to bed ('El niño está dormido'), a crowd of noisy young people enter the waffle shop next door (Seguidillas: '¿Cuántos buñuelos nos vais a dar?'). They are getting in the mood for their evening's enjoyment at the celebrations of the festival of the Virgin of the Dove.

Their high spirits are much envied by Julián who confesses to Rita that his depression stems particularly from having seen his Susana and her sister, Casta, that very morning in an open carriage with a man he didn't recognise. And now she has told him that she will not be able to see him that evening. Rita suggests that Julián should go along with her to the house that Susana and Casta share with their aunt, Antonia.

Old Don Hilarión confesses to Don Sebastián that he is greatly looking forward to the evening. Although he is pretending that he will be away looking after a sick friend, he is actually going to the festival in the company of a pair of beautiful young ladies—a brunette and a blonde ('Tiene razón Don Sebastián'/'Una morena y una rubia'). The various residents move off to get ready for the festivities, and Don Hilárión pops back inside his chemist's shop for a final dose of calomel before leaving for his appointment.

SCENE 2

Susana, Casta and their aunt Antonia are seated outside their home in the Latin quarter with some neighbours. Next door, in the 'Café de Melilla', a flamenco singer is performing to the accompaniment of a piano (Soleares: 'En Chiclana me crié') while a pair of policemen stroll up and down the street, and a nightwatchman who is reclining against a wall under a gas-lamp, reading *La Correspondencia*, engages them in conversation about events of the day (Nocturno: 'Buena está la política!').

The ladies' wait ends when Don Hilarión appears, full of high spirits and, after joining wholeheartedly in the dancing in the café (Mazurka), he goes with them into their house. Rita and Julián appear on the scene and Julián is timidly debating what his next step should be ('Ya estás frente a la casa'/'Y escucha, que hablo yo'), when from inside Susana's house they hear the voice of a man raised in merriment.

To Julián's astonishment, Don Hilarión emerges with Susana and Casta, one on each arm. Julián seizes Susana's hand and asks her where she is going in her fancy shawl (Habañera: '¿Donde vas con mantón de Manila?'), and the disturbance brings the landlord and his customers streaming out of the café. Trouble is only prevented when the police step in and separate the squabbling parties, leaving Rita to lead Julián away, looking menacingly after Susana and Don Hilarión.

SCENE 3

Inside a gaily decorated district ballroom the festivities are well under way, with couples dancing to music from a mechanical piano. Prominent among those present is Don Sebastián, with his wife, their niece Teresa and some family friends.

The events of the evening have somewhat cooled Don Hilarión's ardour, but Aunt Antonia has warmed to the fight and, when a disturbance brings festivities in the dance-hall to a halt, we see a police inspector accompanying Susana, Casta, Antonia and Julián away, the last named with his trousers torn by the teeth of Antonia's dogs. Antonia is put under arrest, and it looks as if Julián will accompany her to jail until Susana, repenting of her careless treatment of him, takes his part. The two are reconciled and, when Don Sebastián also speaks up on Julián's behalf, the police inspector releases him and, suggesting that the night would go better free of further trouble, leaves them enjoying the festivities of the Festival of the Dove (Seguidillas: 'Por ser la Virgen').

LA REVOLTOSA

(The Mischief Maker)

a lyric farce in one act and three scenes by Guillermo Fernández Shaw and José Lopez Silva. Music by Ruperto Chapí. Produced at the Teatro Apolo, Madrid, 25 November 1897 with Isabel Brú (Mari-Pepa), Emilio Mesejo (Felipe) and José Mesejo (Señor Candelas).

CHARACTERS

Mari-Pepa
Felipe
Atenedoro
Soledad, *his fiancée*
Cándido
Gorgonia, *his wife*
Their small son
Tiberio
Encarna, *his wife*
Chupitos, *an apprentice tailor with Cándido*
Señor Candelas
Neighbours, young women

SCENE 1

In the courtyard of a two-story apartment block in old Madrid, the inhabitants are passing the time in their various ways. Cándido, Felipe and Tiberio are playing cards, while Atenedoro, seated outside the door of his apartment, is tuning his guitar. Of their ladies, Encarna and Soledad are hanging up lanterns, while Gorgonia is attending to her small son ('¡Vamos, arza!'). Another of the residents of the building is Mari-Pepa, a young woman of great beauty, but one who uses her charms to cause mischief among the men, much to the anger of their womenfolk. Having tuned his guitar, Atenedoro sings some verses directed at Mari-Pepa (Seguidillas: 'Al pie de tu ventana'), which bring her out of her apartment, causing further indignation amongst the women.

Señor Candelas, an inspector in the city's police force, comes out of his apartment to try to restore peace and order and he tells Felipe and the other young men that they should set a better example than to turn the courtyard into a gaming and drinking establishment. Undeterred by the scowls of the women, Mari-Pepa continues to flirt with the men and, with the sole exception of Felipe, all of them are much taken by her. Felipe remains aloof from her and leaves Cándido, Tiberio and Atenedoro to enjoy themselves with the young woman. Mari-Pepa gladly enters into their fun ('¿Qué?' '¿Eh?' '¡Olé!').

The high jinks come to an end when the womenfolk reappear and give the three men the sharp end of their tongues. Señor Candelas reckons that he can settle the troublesome young woman, since nobody gets the better of him, but a brief encounter with Mari-Pepa soon turns his tone from firmness to sweetness. The three women mock Señor Candelas's efforts and the situation is close to coming to blows when Felipe appears. Gorgonia tells Mari-Pepa sourly that he is the sort of man she should expend her charms on, but Mari-Pepa merely flounces off into her apartment and slams the door.

By now the women have had enough of this mischief-maker in their midst, and Gorgonia details to her friends a plan of revenge she has concocted for that evening. The young apprentice Chupitos will deliver to each of their menfolk an invitation bidding him to an assignment with Mari-Pepa that night.

SCENE 2

Later that day, Mari-Pepa is passing by a waffle shop in a side-street of Madrid when she hears the voice of Felipe inside, in happily animated conversation with a pair of young women. Felipe bids the two girls farewell, promising to see them at the festival that night but, as he emerges from the shop, Mari-Pepa engages him in conversation, trying to get him to warm towards her. Felipe seems genuinely well disposed towards her, but neither of them is prepared to make an expression of affection and the conversation ends up with them going their separate ways. Cándido and Gorgonia follow them from the waffle-shop and, as they turn towards the apartment block, the voice of Soledad can be heard getting the evening's festival celebrations under way ('Eso les pasa a las hembras').

SCENE 3

It is night time and, in the courtyard of the apartment block, the lamps are lit and the celebrations of the day's festival are well under way ('¡Olé los niños con esbeltez!'). Under the watchful eye of Gorgonia, Chupitos delivers to Señor Candelas, Atenedoro, Tiberio and Cándido the invitations to meet Mari-Pepa at midnight, as Soledad sings a guajira—a song with much clapping of hands ('Cuando clava mi moreno'). Then, the home-made merrymaking over, the women pretend to go out to enjoy the festival celebrations, while secretly preparing to be on watch at midnight. Each of the men is delighted to see his wife or girlfriend depart and sneaks off to prepare himself for the pleasure he imagines lies in store for him.

Felipe is alone in the courtyard when Mari-Pepa comes in from the street. Once more they start upon their game of cat-and-mouse, with Mari-Pepa attempting to get some reaction from the young man by making him jealous. Now, for the first time, Felipe is unable to hide the fact that he really desires her intensely ('¿Por qué de mis ojos los tuyos retiras?'/'La de los claveles dobles'). Yet pride and jealousy again keep them apart and they return each to their own apartment.

As midnight arrives, the apartment block becomes a scene of deep intrigue, with the three women and Chupitos hiding in Soledad's apartment ('No hay nadie. Adendro') watching as, one by one, the men creep out of their apartments, only to come across each other, have to make an excuse for their actions, and return home. Then Felipe appears, wondering what is going on, and catches Señor Candelas knocking on Mari-Pepa's door and calling her name. Uproar breaks out as the three women rush from their hiding place and confront their menfolk, while Mari-Pepa finds refuge in the protecting arms of Felipe. Now, at last, Mari-Pepa accepts that the woman who is honoured is the one who respects herself.

GIGANTES Y CABEZUDOS

(Carnival Giants and Bigheads)

a zarzuela in one act and four scenes by Miguel Echegaray. Music by Manuel Fernández Caballero. Produced at the Teatro de la Zarzuela, Madrid, 28 November 1898 with Lucrecia Arana (Pilar).

CHARACTERS

Pilar
Antonia
Pepa
Juana
A buyer
The sergeant
Timoteo
Pascual

Jesús
Uncle Isidro
Vicente
Policemen, people of Calatorao, shoppers, traders, carnival giants and big-heads, children, musicians

SCENE 1
It is market day in Zaragoza, and in the hurly burly of the occasion a quarrel develops between two of the tradespeople, Juana and Antonia ('Hay que separarlas') until the butcher, Uncle Isidro, intervenes and takes Antonia to task for her aggressiveness.

The town policeman Timoteo, Antonia's husband, arrives with bad news. There is to be a sharp increase in the municipal rates. This news provokes outrage amongst the traders who are determined not to pay the higher charges (Jota: '¿Pagar nosotras? ¡Nunca, jamás!') and Timoteo is placed in the impossible position of having to reconcile his obligation to collect the charges with that of defending the interests of his wife.

Uncle Isidro has a ward, Pilar, an orphan who, like so many girls in Zaragoza, takes her name from the legend of the marble pillar on which the Virgin Mary is believed to have appeared. Pilar lives, above everything else, for the letters that come from her lover Jesús, who is away at the war in Cuba and today she has a letter ('Esta es su carta'). Unfortunately Pilar cannot read, and she is faced with her perpetual dilemma. Who can she trust to read something so intimate to her? All manner of thoughts go through her mind as to what the letter may contain, until finally she gets young Pascual to read it to her and give her the assurance that all is well.

Pilar is also the target of the amorous attentions of the area sergeant and, as part of his plan to win over her affections, he tells her that he has received another letter from Jesús confirming that the young man has married. Pilar does not take any heed of the Sergeant's lies, and merely tells him that, in that case, she hopes Jesús becomes a widower.

By now the traders' reaction to the municipal rate increase has reached the stage of becoming a major revolt ('No nos asusta nada en la tierra'/'Si las mujeres mandaran'). Antonia is arrested for refusing to pay, and Timoteo, exasperated beyond endurance, resigns from the police force as the militant traders determine to take their protest to higher authorities ('A decir voy al alcalde').

SCENE 2
Repatriated soldiers, returning from the war, are arriving in Zaragoza ('Por fin te miro') and amongst them is Jesús who, at the sight of the River Ebro and the Basilica of Our Lady of Pilar, dreams of seeing his mother and his sweetheart Pilar again ('Por la patria te dejé'). Meanwhile Timoteo, out of work, is obliged to go fishing to get food to eat.

SCENE 3
It is the saint's day of Our Lady of the Pillar. The sergeant is determined to

1221

prevent Pilar and Jesús meeting and, when he bumps into the soldier, he tries to deceive him, telling him that Pilar is married. Jesús takes little heed of him and determines to discover the facts of the matter for himself.

Meanwhile the city is preparing for the carnival ('Zaragoza de gala vestida está') and country-folk are arriving from all parts to celebrate the festival. In the midst of the boisterous crowd of people is Pilar. She is wondering with a heavy heart over the fate of Jesús ('Cuando era niña y jugaba') but she joins in the welcome for the traditional carnival figures (Jota: 'Luchando tercos y rudos').

Pilar runs into the sergeant, who produces yet another letter from which he declares that Jesús is dead but, finally, in a passionate outburst he admits that what he has told her is untrue. Pilar compassionately forgives him, and the sergeant goes off in search of Jesús.

As the procession of the rosary passes by, Pilar's anxiety heightens ('Se marchó, de seguro') but, at the end of the procession, the sergeant appears bringing Jesús to be joyfully reconciled with his Pilar. Carnival day is a day of joy, even for Timoteo who has got his old job back.

LA TEMPRANICA

(The Precocious One)

a zarzuela in one act and three scenes by Julián Romea. Music by Gerónimo Giménez. Produced at the Teatro de la Zarzuela, Madrid, 19 September 1900 with Concha Segura (La Tempranica) and Pepe Sigler (Don Luis).

CHARACTERS

María, 'la Tempranica'
Grabié
Salú
La Moronda
Pastora
The Countess
Don Luis, Count of Santa Fe
Miguel
Don Mariano
Mister James
Señor Chano
Don Ramón
Curro
Zalea
Pilín
Juan

A gipsy
Huntsmen, beaters, gipsies, ladies and gentlemen, mountain guards

SCENE 1

A hunting party is returning from a day's sport towards a farmhouse in the mountains of the province of Granada ('La caza ya se esconde'), all looking forward to another successful foray the following day. Amongst the party are Don Luis, a young Andalucian, and an Englishman, Mister James. Like most foreigners, James knows nothing of the local culture and is anxious to hear some typical Spanish songs and, to satisfy his curiosity, one of the party goes in search of Grabié, a young lad who lives nearby and who has a fondness for singing.

Grabié tells the party of the deep affection that his family feel for Don Luis, affection that, in the case of his sister María, is something greater, but when Don Luis stops Grabié from saying more, his guests' interest is piqued. Don Luis manages to change the subject by getting Grabié to sing something for them, and the boy obliges with a lively song and tap-dance about the tarantula (Zapateado: 'La tarantula é un bicho mu malo').

Don Luis tells Grabié that he should not tell his sister that he has been to the farmhouse again. That way the memory of their previous meeting will not be recalled. When Grabié has left, Don Luis tells his guests the full story of his original meeting with María and her family. Once, while crossing a ravine in the mountains, he fell from his horse. He lost consciousness and, when he came to, he found himself in a modest cottage, being attended to by poor but kindly people. María, a young gipsy girl of about eighteen known as 'La Tempranica'—'the precocious one'—was particularly fervent in her concern for him. At the end of the several days it took for Don Luis to recover his fitness, María had fallen deeply in love with him and, when finally the young nobleman left the cottage, the girl was distraught.

Unfortunately, Grabié does not heed Don Luis's instructions and María soon discovers that he is back in the area. With time, María's love has settled somewhat, but the news of Don Luis's return stirs her feelings once more. She cannot resist going to the farmhouse to see him again, and their passions are aroused afresh ('Yo no zé al verte'/'Te quiero..., porque eres güeno') but Don Luis persuades her that her attentions are hopeless.

SCENE 2

In a gipsy encampment on top of the Granada mountain range María and her family follow the course of their daily life, the men attending to their work, the women looking after the needs of the family ('A trabajá con fatigas'/'Zuzpiros de mi pecho'). In the same encampment lives a hard-working young gipsy named Miguel, who is in love with María. She has finally agreed to marry him, and a great celebration is being prepared.

Don Luis arrives with his friends to show Mister James the beauty of the countryside and let him sample for himself the fascination that the gipsy

1223

world holds for the English. Meeting Miguel, they learn of the impending celebration and turn up to watch the colourful spectacle ('¡Ea! ¡Ea! Vayan peniya afuera'). María appears at the celebration, saluting the beauties of her homeland and the honest gipsy lad who has given her his heart ('Sierras de Granada'), but she suddenly catches sight of Don Luis and once again her heart is stirred to heights of passion and she thinks wildly of abandoning Miguel.

Then Grabié rushes in to tell María that, from a hiding place behind a rock, he has overheard Don Luis talking of his wife. He will be returning to her in Granada the following day. María declares that Grabié must join her on a journey to Granada.

SCENE 3

At the home of Don Luis in Granada a dance is in progress. María and Grabié arrive outside the house but, as she watches the events going on inside, she sees Don Luis with his wife and small son, and her feelings of love for him wither. Now, finally, she appreciates the reality of the situation and remembers her worthy, hard-working fiancé back home—a young man of the same gipsy race and background as herself. She realises that her place is with her people and with him and, filled with emotion, she returns home (Finale: 'Tempranica me yaman').

LUISA FERNANDA

a lyric comedy in three acts by Federico Romero and Guillermo Fernández Shaw. Music by Federico Moreno Torroba. Produced at the Teatro Calderón, Madrid, 26 March 1932.

CHARACTERS

The Duchess Carolina, *lady-in-waiting to Queen Isabel II*
Jeromo, *her valet*
Don Florito, *a former employee of the royal household*
Luisa Fernanda, *his daughter*
Vidal Hernando, *a landowner from Extremadura*
Javier Moreno, *a colonel*
Rosita, *a dressmaker*
Mariana, *proprietress of the San Javier inn*
Aníbal, *a waiter*
Luis Nogales, *a revolutionary*
'Cross-eyed' Porras
Padre Lucas, *priest of San Antonio*
An organ grinder

A captain, salesmen, musicians, dressmakers, soldiers, fruit-pickers, vendors, people of Madrid

ACT 1

In the little square of San Javier in old Madrid, the hotelière Mariana sits outside her inn in a small chair, watching Rosita and her fellow dress-makers hurrying to their work across the square in cheerful fashion ('Mi madre me criaba'). The Duchess Carolina, lady-in-waiting to Her Majesty Queen Isabel II, comes out from the elegant eighteenth-century house next door to the inn, attended by her valet, Jeromo, and, as they pass Mariana, they exchange greetings and expressions of loyalty to the Queen. Then an organ-grinder comes into the square, playing and singing a song in habañera rhythm about a soldier and his beloved ('Marchaba a ser soldado').

In another house in this same square, Don Florito, a former employee of the royal household, lives with his daughter, Luisa Fernanda. Luisa is in love with Javier Moreno, a young man of the town who went away to become a soldier, but he has risen to the rank of colonel and now apparently has little time for his old sweetheart, who has to make do with the less welcome attentions of Vidal Hernando, a wealthy landowner from Extremadura in Western Spain.

Jeromo returns to ask Mariana to put up a certain Luis Nogales at her inn. Nogales is involved in a plot to overthrow the Queen, and Aníbal, a young waiter in Mariana's inn, reports how, the previous evening, a group of self-styled patriots had made the declaration of a republic.

Javier appears in his colonel's uniform, and Mariana takes him to task for his long absence, but he hastens to stress that it is in this particular corner of Madrid that his heart lies ('De este apacible rincón de Madrid'). Mariana goes on to rebuke him for the way in which he has abandoned Luisa Fernanda, but Javier assures her that his old sweetheart is still his only true love. Javier is approached by Aníbal and Luis Nogales who attempt to win him over to their republican cause, and they go off to pursue their discussions in the privacy of the inn.

Luisa Fernanda confides to Mariana her disappointment that Javier never comes to see her, but Vidal declares his own real love for her, describing as temptation the beauties of his estates in Extremadura ('En mi tierra extremeña'). His efforts are in vain, for Luisa Fernanda leaves him in no doubt that her affections go elsewhere.

Javier emerges from the inn to go to Luisa Fernanda's house but, as he passes Carolina's home, he hears a voice calling to him from her balcony. 'Young man with the high-plumed helmet, where are you off to looking so proud?' she asks him ('Caballero del alto plumero'), throwing down a rose to him from the hanging-basket on her balcony.

When Javier goes to join her inside the house, his action does not go unnoticed. Aníbal sees Javier's commitment to Carolina as a commitment to the interests of the royalist faction and declares him an enemy, while Luisa

Fernanda is distraught at the thought that he has forgotten all his words of affection for her under the heat of one casual glance from Carolina. Vidal, encouraged to believe that there might now be hope in his affection for Luisa Fernanda, remains alone in the square, watching Luisa Fernanda retire sadly to her house, as the voices of Carolina and Javier are heard coming from the Duchess's palace.

ACT 2

It is late evening in the Paseo de la Florida, where the pilgrimage of San Antonio is being celebrated. Around the church are various stalls, and Mariana and Rosita are looking after the petitionary table. A small band of street musicians is playing, and everyone is enjoying the fair to the full. Javier is there in civilian clothes with a group of smartly dressed young men, enjoying themselves with a group of equally smartly dressed young ladies among whom is Carolina, all carrying colourful parasols (Mazurka of the sunshades: 'A San Antonio como es un santo'). The extent to which Carolina now seems to have won Javier over is not lost on Mariana and Nogales.

Luisa Fernanda and her father come to the Paseo de la Florida in search of Javier but, when she learns that he has been seen again with Carolina, she attacks his shamelessness and affects indifference over him. When Vidal appears on the scene, still in pursuit of Luisa Fernanda, he is detained by Carolina. However, she is not after another conquest but merely seeking to find in him another recruit to the royalist cause ('Para comprar a un hombre'). Vidal firmly declares that he does not support any party.

Now Luisa Fernanda, out of spite towards Javier, finally accepts Vidal's offer of marriage. Javier passes by on his way to the petitionary table, failing to notice Luisa Fernanda, Don Florito and Vidal. He is looking for Carolina ('¿Dónde estará Carolina?') and, when he turns round and comes face to face with Luisa Fernanda, she takes perverse pleasure in introducing Vidal to him as her fiancé. Javier urges Luisa Fernanda to come aside with him, but Vidal interposes himself politely but firmly between them, and the colonel ends up departing in a rage.

Carolina comes out of the rectory, accompanied by Don Lucas, the priest of San Antonio and, as the itinerant musicians pass by, the Duchess seeks to swell the funds raised by the fair by initiating a charity auction in which the prize will be to be her partner in the dancing ('Señora duquesa...'). Javier bids a Spanish doubloon, but Vidal uses his wealth to embarrass Javier by offering fifty. Then, having won the bidding, he simply gives the prize to Javier, who with great ceremony throws a glove at Vidal's feet in challenge.

A few days later, dawn is breaking over the tavern of 'cross-eyed' Porras by the fountain in the Calle de Toledo. The proprietor complains that barricades have been set up in the streets and the royal troops mobilised, which indicates that the republicans' revolt has been forestalled and, with the help of Aníbal and some other youths, he sets to work dismantling the barricades as Luis Nogales appears, urging everyone on in the cause of the revolution.

Mariana and Luisa Fernanda are praying in front of the effigy of the Virgin of the Dove when Aníbal is brought into the tavern, wounded, but praising the fighting qualities of Don Vidal, who has responded to Javier's challenge by joining the liberals to fight against him. Vidal appears in shirt sleeves, with a gun in his belt and carrying a rifle, and Porras joins in to commend his contribution to the revolutionaries' fight, but Vidal insists that for him this is merely a love struggle ('Luche la fe por el triunfo'/'Por el amor da una mujer').

News comes that the royal mounted hussars are approaching, with Javier at their head. The revolutionaries have shown their hand, and battle has been joined. The Duchess Carolina hurries in with Jeromo to take shelter in the inn and Luisa Fernanda is left alone with Mariana as battle wages outside. Soon Javier is brought in, under armed guard, and the crowd call for him to be put to death ('¡Muera el prisoniero!'), but Luisa Fernanda pleads for his life. When Vidal enters and coldly returns Javier's glove, it is revealed that it was he who knocked Javier from his horse. Suddenly a squadron of hussars arrives. The tables are turned as Javier is freed and the rebels arrested. Javier takes the Duchess's arm, while Luisa Fernanda, seeing him go, agrees to settle down with Vidal on his country estate.

ACT 3

'La Frondosa', the green and wooded estate of Vidal Hernando, stands near to Piedras Albas and the Portugese border. Don Florito is seated outside the door of Vidal's house, reading a newspaper and relaying to Mariana the news that Queen Isabel has been dethroned. The Duchess Carolina, it seems, has sought refuge in Portugal. Mariana is less interested than she might be in the news, for her main concern is with Luisa Fernanda who appears to grow sadder every day. Luisa Fernanda knows she does not love Vidal, but she persists in preparing for the marriage she has promised. Vidal is in love and, as he goes about his work with his fruit-pickers he thinks happily about his beautiful brown-haired bride ('Si por el rido'/'¡Ay, mi morena, morena clara!').

Aníbal arrives at 'La Frondosa' to deliver the wedding dress that has been made for Luisa Fernanda in Portugal and bringing her news of Javier who, he declares, is deeply anxious to see her. Left alone, Luisa Fernanda feels her heart being pulled this way and that ('¡Callate corazón!') but, suddenly, Javier appears before her, expressing his feelings of love anew ('Dichoso el que en su camino'/'¡Subir, subir, y luego caer...!'). Luisa Fernanda tells him not to torment her and sends him away but, when Vidal finds her in tears, and she tries to deny that her heart lies elsewhere, he no longer has any illusions as to her true feelings.

Luisa Fernanda rouses herself sufficiently to enjoy some traditional Extremaduran festivities ('El Cerandero se ha muerto'). During the dancing Javier reappears ('Aunque me cuesta la vida') but, although Luisa Fernanda

1227

tells him to go away and never return, Vidal realises that it is useless for him to fight against true love. In the end Luisa Fernanda departs with Javier, leaving Vidal to overcome his despair as best he can ('Si por el rido, si por la vera').

DISCOGRAPHY

This selective discography of long-playing records has been compiled as a listening aid and not as an exhaustive and scholarly catalogue of the many thousands of cast and studio recordings produced throughout the world of the shows covered in this book. Original cast recordings and soundtracks, both in the original language and in translation, are given preference but often such recordings do not exist on long-playing record, and so the most interesting and accessible of other recordings are listed.

Many of the records listed here have been issued and reissued countless times on various labels both in their country of origin and abroad. We have given the original or current serial numbers where possible but, particularly with such groups as the early French Pathé and Decca LPs and many of the German labels, we have relied upon the numbers on the discs in our own collections or in that of that mighty collector, Bradley Bennett.

GREAT BRITAIN

The Beggar's Opera
Complete with dialogue with John Cameron and Elsie Morison (HMV Greensleeve ESDW 704) (2 records)
Complete with dialogue with Dennis Noble and Carmen Prietto (Argo DPA 591-2) (2 records)
Lyric, Hammersmith cast recordings with Frederick Ranalow and Sylvia Nelis assembled on EMI RTRM 501
1968 revival cast recording with Peter Gilmore and Jan Waters (CBS70046)

Cox and Box
D'Oyly Carte Opera Company 1961 complete with Thomas Round and Alan Styler (LK4404/SKL4140) with *The Gondoliers*
D'Oyly Carte Opera Company 1978 complete with Geoffrey Shovelton and Gareth Jones (Decca TXS128) with *The Zoo*

Trial By Jury
D'Oyly Carte Opera Company 1928 with Leo Sheffield and Winifred Lawson (Decca ALP 1294)

D'Oyly Carte Opera Company 1949 with Richard Watson and Muriel Harding (Decca LK 4001)

Sir Malcolm Sargent recording 1958 with George Baker and Elsie Morison (HMV DW/SXDW3034) with *HMS Pinafore*

D'Oyly Carte Opera Company 1964 with John Reed and Ann Hood (Decca LK/SKL4579) with *Utopia (Ltd)*

D'Oyly Carte Opera Company 1975 (Decca TXS113)

The Sorcerer

D'Oyly Carte Opera Company 1953 complete with Muriel Harding and Peter Pratt (Decca LK4070-1) (2 records)

D'Oyly Carte Opera Company 1966 complete with Valerie Masterson and John Reed (Decca LK/SKL4825/6) (2 records)

HMS Pinafore

D'Oyly Carte Opera Company 1930 with Henry Lytton (ALP 1293-4) (2 records)

D'Oyly Carte Opera Company 1949 complete with Martyn Green and Muriel Harding (Decca LK4002-3) (2 records)

D'Oyly Carte Opera Company 1960 complete with John Reed and Jean Hindmarsh (Decca 4334-5 and SKL 4081-2) (2 records)

D'Oyly Carte Opera Company 1971 complete (Decca OPFS1/2) (2 records)

Sir Malcolm Sargent recording 1958 with George Baker and Elsie Morison (HMV DW/SXDW3034) with *Trial by Jury* (2 records)

New Sadler's Wells Opera revival cast recording 1987 (TER 1150)

The Pirates of Penzance

D'Oyly Carte Opera Company 1950 complete with Muriel Harding and Leonard Osborn (Decca LK4004-5) (2 records)

D'Oyly Carte Opera Company 1958 complete with Jean Hindmarsh and Thomas Round (Decca LK4249-50 and SKL4038/9)

Sir Malcolm Sargent recording 1961 with Elsie Morison and Richard Lewis (HMV DW/SXDW3041) (2 records)

D'Oyly Carte Opera Company 1968 complete (Decca LK/SKL4925-6) (2 records)

Broadway cast recording 1981 with Kevin Kline and Linda Ronstadt (Elektra VE-601)

New Zealand cast recording (Stetson SREP 22)

Patience

D'Oyly Carte Opera Company 1952 complete with Margaret Mitchell (Decca LK4047/8) (2 records)

D'Oyly Carte Opera Company 1961 complete (Decca LK4414/5 and SKL4146/7) (2 records)

Sir Malcolm Sargent recording 1958 with Elsie Morison (HMV DW/SXDW3031) (2 records)

Rip van Winkle

Selection in French as *Rip* with Michel Dens (EMI-Pathé 2C 057.12899)

Iolanthe

D'Oyly Carte Opera Company 1952 with Martyn Green (Decca LK4044-5) (2 records)

D'Oyly Carte Opera Company 1960 with John Reed (Decca LK4378-9 and SKL4119-20) (2 records)

Sir Malcolm Sargent recording 1959 with George Baker (HMV DW/SXDW3047 and SXLP30112-3) (2 records)

Sadler's Wells Opera cast recording 1962 (HMV CLP1564 and CSD1440)

Princess Ida

D'Oyly Carte Opera Company 1955 complete with Victoria Sladen (Decca LK4092/3)

D'Oyly Carte Opera Company 1965 complete (Decca LK/SKL 4708/9)

The Mikado

D'Oyly Carte Opera Company 1936 complete with Henry Lytton (Decca ALP1255-96) (2 records)

D'Oyly Carte Opera Company 1950 complete with Martyn Green (Decca LK4010-1) (2 records)

Sir Malcolm Sargent recording 1956 complete with Geraint Evans (HMV ALP1485/6) (2 records)

D'Oyly Carte Opera Company 1958 complete with Peter Pratt (Decca LK4251/2) (2 records)

Sadler's Wells Opera cast recording 1962 (HMV CSD 1458/9) (2 records)

D'Oyly Carte Opera Company 1973 complete with John Reed (SKL5158/9) (2 records)

English National Opera revival cast recording 1986 with Eric Idle (TER1121)

Spanish cast recording as *El Mikado* (Charot L1314)

American television soundtrack with Groucho Marx (Columbia DS-2022)

Film soundtrack *The Cool Mikado* (Paramount PMC-1194)

Radio soundtrack *The Hot Mikado* (Star-Tone 214) (USA)

London cast recording *The Black Mikado* (Transatlantic TRA 300)

South African cast recording *The Black Mikado* (RPM 1111)

Ruddigore

D'Oyly Carte Opera Company 1950 complete with Margaret Mitchell (Decca LK4027/8) (2 records)

D'Oyly Carte Opera Company 1962 complete (Decca LK/SKL4504/5) (2 records)

Sir Malcolm Sargent recording 1958 with Elsie Morison (HMV DW/SXDW3029) (2 records)

Sadlers Wells revival cast recording 1987 with Marilyn Hill Smith (TER1128) (2 records)

The Yeomen of the Guard

D'Oyly Carte Opera Company 1950 complete with Martyn Green and Muriel Harding (Decca LK2029/30) (2 records)

D'Oyly Carte Opera Company 1964 complete (Decca LK/SKL 4624/5) (2 records)

Sir Malcolm Sargent recording 1958 complete with Geraint Evans and Elsie Morison (HMV DW/SXDW3033) (2 records)

The Gondoliers

D'Oyly Carte Opera Company 1950 complete with Martyn Green (Decca LK4015/6) (2 records)

D'Oyly Carte Opera Company 1961 complete with John Reed (Decca LK4402/4) (3 records) with *Cox and Box*

Sir Malcolm Sargent recording 1957 with Geraint Evans (HMV ALP1504/5) (2 records)

The Geisha
Selection in Italian as *La Geisha* (Fonit-Cetra LPS27)
Selection in Italian as *La Geisha* (EDM4020)
Selection in German as *Die Geisha* (Decca LW5049) (10 inch)
'The Jewel of Asia' sung by Marie Tempest (OC) appears on *Singing Actresses* (WRC SH433) and *Forty Years of Musical Comedy* (Rococo 4007)

Florodora
Original cast recordings assembled on Pearl/Opal 835
'The Queen of the Philippine Islands' sung by Ada Reeve appears on *Singing Actresses* (WRC SH433)

The Rose of Persia
St Albans Operatic Society 1963 complete (Rare Recorded Editions SRRE 152/3)
'The Small Street Arab' sung by C H Workman appears on *The Art of the Savoyard* (Pearl GEMM 120) and on Pearl GEMM 135

A Country Girl
'Try again Johnnie' and 'Not the Little Boy She Knew' sung by Evie Greene appear on *Singing Actresses* (WRC SH433) and 'Peace, Peace' sung by Henry Lytton, and 'Quarrelling' and 'Two Little Chicks' (Lytton and Louie Henri) appear on *The Art of Henry Lytton* (Pearl GEMM 197)

Merrie England
Sadler's Wells Opera Company 1960 complete (revised version) (HMV CLP 1376/7) (2 records)

Tom Jones
Selection with June Bronhill (EMI-Odeon CSD 3628)
The Waltz Song sung by Florence Smithson appears on *Singing Actresses* (WRC SH433)

The Arcadians
Selection with June Bronhill (Columbia TWO 233)
Selection with Cynthia Glover (Music for Pleasure 1323)
'My Motter' sung by Alfred Lester appears on *Forty Years of English Musical Comedy* (Rococo 4007)

The Quaker Girl
'Tony From America', 'The Little Grey Bonnet' and 'A Quaker Girl' sung by Gertie Millar appear on WRC SH185

Chu Chin Chow
Selection with Ian Wallace (MFP 1012)
Selection with Inia te Wiata (HMV CLP1269)

The Maid of the Mountains
Original cast recordings with José Collins assembled on WRC SH169
Revival cast recording with Lynn Kennington 1972 (Columbia SCX6504)
Selection (Australia) (WRC ST794) with *Balalaika*
'Love Will Find a Way' and 'Farewell' sung by Gladys Moncrieff appear on Drum
    8179, and 'A Paradise for Two' (Moncrieff, Colin Crane) and 'My Life Is Love'
    on Columbia MSC7600

Monsieur Beaucaire
Original cast recordings with Maggie Teyte and Marion Green assembled on Opal/
    Pearl 817
French version selection with Michel Dens and Martha Angelici (EMI-Pathé 2C
    151-53336)

Mr Cinders
Revival cast recording King's Head Theatre Club 1982 (TER 1037)
Revival cast recording Fortune Theatre 1983 (TER 1069)
'One-man Girl', 'Spread a Little Happiness', 'Every Little Moment' and 'On the
    Amazon' sung by Bobby Howes and Binnie Hale appear on WRC SH136

Bitter-Sweet
Selection with Adele Leigh (WRC TP80)
Selection with Vanessa Lee (HMV CLP1242)
Selection with Rosalind Elias (Readers Digest 46–N3)
Selection with June Bronhill (Columbia TWO273)
Film soundtrack with Jeanette Macdonald and Nelson Eddy (Bright Tight Discs
    BIS1377)

Balalaika
Selection (Australia) (WRC ST794) with *Maid of the Mountains*
French 1983 touring version selection (TLP 91004)
Film soundtrack with Nelson Eddy (Caliban 600)

Conversation Piece
Complete recording with dialogue with Noël Coward and Lily Pons (US Columbia
    SL163) (2 records)
Original cast recordings with Coward and Yvonne Printemps assembled on HMV
    album 206
'I'll Follow My Secret Heart', 'Nevermore', Melanie's Aria and 'Charming, Charm-
    ing' sung by Joan Sutherland appear on Decca LXT/SXL6255

Glamorous Night
Original cast recordings with Mary Ellis, Trefor Jones and Elisabeth Welch assem-
    bled on WRC SHB23 and partially on HMV DLP 1095
Selection with Vanessa Lee (HMV CSD1263)
Selection with Patricia Johnson (WRC T214)
Selection with Rae Woodland (Columbia TWO 243)

Me and My Girl
Revival cast recording with Robert Lindsay 1985 (EMI-Col EJ24, 0301, 1)
Broadway cast recording with Lindsay (MCA 6196)

Japanese cast recording (all female cast) complete with dialogue (TMP 1133-34) (2 records)

'The Lambeth Walk' sung by Lupino Lane appears on MFP1236 and EMI-Col SXSP655

The Dancing Years
Original cast recordings with Mary Ellis assembled on HMV DLP1028 (10 inch) and WRC SHB23
Selection with Anne Rogers (Columbia TWO188)

Perchance to Dream
Original cast recordings with Muriel Barron and Roma Beaumont assembled on Decca LF1309
Selection with Elisabeth Robinson (Columbia TWO 250)

Bless the Bride
Original cast recordings assembled on EP Columbia SEG7551 (45) and WRC SH228
Selection with Mary Millar and Roberto Cardinali (MFP 1263)

King's Rhapsody
Original cast recordings with Vanessa Lee assembled on HMV DLP1010 and WRC SHB23
Selection with Cynthia Glover (Columbia TWO 270)

The Boy Friend
Original cast recording with Ann Rogers (HMV DLP 1078) (10 inch)
Original Broadway cast recording with Julie Andrews (RCA LOC 1018)
Australian revival cast recording (Spin EL33016)
London revival cast recording 1968 (Par PMC/PCS 7044)
Broadway revival cast recording 1970 (Decca DL79177)
London revival cast recording with Jane Wellman 1984 (TER 1095)
Film soundtrack with Twiggy (EMI-Col SCXA0251)
Excerpts played and sung by Sandy Wilson (author) Overtures OVER1001

Salad Days
Original cast recording (Oriole MG20004)
Original Australian cast recording (Planet P2-030) (45)
Six titles played and sung by Julian Slade (composer) (Overtures OVER1003)
'Let's Take a Stroll Through London' added to the USA production is recorded by Slade on Oriole MG20005

Chrysanthemum
Original cast recording with Pat Kirkwood and Hubert Gregg (Nixa NPL18026)
Selection played by Robb Stewart (composer) Fon TFE17098

Expresso Bongo
Original cast recording with Paul Scofield and Hy Hazell (Nixa NPL18016)
Film version selection sung by Cliff Richard (EP Col SEG7971) (45)

1234

Valmouth
Original cast recording with Cleo Laine (Pye N(S)PL 18029)
Revival cast recording 1982 with Bertice Reading (TER 1019)
'Only a Passing Phase' and 'I Will Miss You' are performed by Sandy Wilson (author) on Overtures OVER1001

Lock Up Your Daughters
Original cast recording with Richard Wordsworth and Hy Hazell (Decca LK4320/SKL4070)
'Lock Up Your Daughters' and 'When Does the Ravishing Begin' are performed by Lionel Bart (lyricist) on Decca LF1324 (10 inch)

Make Me an Offer
Original cast recording with Daniel Massey (HMV CLP1298/CSF1284)

Oliver!
Original cast recording with Ron Moody and Georgia Brown (Decca LK4359/SKL4105)
Original Broadway cast recording with Clive Revill and Brown (RCA LOCD1/LSOD2004)
Original Israeli cast recording (CBS 70018)
Original Dutch cast recording (Philips 840. 332PY)
Hungarian radio cast recording (Qualiton SLPM 16700)
Film soundtrack with Moody and Shani Wallis (RCA SB6777)

Stop the World – I Want to Get Off
Original cast recording with Anthony Newley (Decca LK4408/SKL4142)
Original Broadway cast recording with Newley (AM58001/AMS88001)
Original Swedish cast recording as *Stoppa Varlden – Jag Vill Stiga Av* with *West Side Story* (RCA CL40118)
Original German cast recording as *Halt die Welt an – ich mochte aussteigen* (Philips 838. 904. SY)
Original Netherlands cast recording (Philips P12944L/840 356PY)
Broadway revival cast recording 1978 with Sammy Davis jr (Warner Bros HS3214)
Film soundtrack with Tony Tanner (Warner Brothers W/BS1643)

Half a Sixpence
Original cast recording with Tommy Steele (Decca LK/SKL4521)
Original Broadway cast recording with Steele (TCA LOC/SA0110)
Film soundtrack with Steele (RCA RB/SB6735)

Maggie May
Original cast recording with Rachel Roberts (Decca LK/SKL4643)
Original cast recording additional songs (Decca DFE8602) (45)
These two recordings were combined on TER 1046

Robert and Elizabeth
Original cast recording with June Bronhill and Keith Michell (HMV CLP1820/CSD1575)
Chichester Festival revival cast recording 1987 with Gaynor Miles and Mark Wynter (First Night Cast 8)

1235

Charlie Girl
Original Australian cast recording with Johnny Farnham (HMV OCSD7687)
Revival cast recording 1986 with Paul Nicholas (First Night Cast 3)
The additional song 'Liverpool' was recorded by take-over star Gerry Marsden on CBS 3575 (45)
Revival cast recording 1986 with Paul Nicholas (First Night Cast 3)

Canterbury Tales
Original cast recording with Jessie Evans (Decca LK/SKL4956)
Original Broadway cast recording with Hermione Baddeley (Capitol SW229)

Joseph and the Amazing Technicolor Dreamcoat
Original cast recording with Gary Bond (RSO 2394, 103)
London cast recording, extended version (MCA MCF 2544)
Original Irish cast recording (RAM RMLP 1010)
Original South African cast recording (EMI-Brigadiers EMCJ11506)
Original Israeli cast recording (Hed-Arzi AN14816)
Original Mexican cast recording
Original Broadway cast recording (Chrysalis CHR1387)
Revival cast selection with Jess Conrad (Kerrysmile KSR001) (45)
Canadian concert cast as *Joseph – a rock oratorio* (Kerygama GRT9230, 1004)
A recording including Tim Rice (lyricist) appears on MFP50455

Jesus Christ Superstar
Original Concept Album with Murray Head and Ian Gillan (MCA MKP2011/2) (2 records)
Original Broadway cast recording (MCA DL7-1503)
Original Danish cast recording (Philips 6675. 001)
Original Swedish cast recording (Philips 6675. 002)
Original West German cast recording (Telefunken DD3402/1-2) (2 records)
Original French cast recording (Philips 6325. 007)
Original Australian cast recording (MCA MAPS6244)
Original London cast recording with Stephen Tate and Paul Nicholas (MCA MCF2503)
Original Spanish cast recording as *Jesucristo Superstar* (Ariola 89772-XD)
Original Japanese cast recording (Express ETP(S)60115/6) (2 records)
Original Brazilian cast recording (Sinter 1903)
Original Mexican cast recording (Orfeon JM150)
Spanish revival cast recording 1984 (CBS S26191)
Swedish revival cast recording 1985 (Sonet SLP 2774)
Film soundtrack with Ted Neely (MCA 11000)

The Rocky Horror Show
Original cast recording with Tim Curry (UA UKAL1006)
Original Australian cast recording (Festival L35231)
Original American cast recording (Los Angeles) (ODE SP77026)
Original Norwegian cast recording
Original West German cast recording (Ariola 202. 146. 315)
Original Mexican cast recording as *El Show de Terror de Rocky* (Orfeon 13. 2277)
Australian revival cast recording (Festival L20009)
Film soundtrack *The Rocky Horror Picture Show* (ODE78332)

1236

Billy
Original cast recording with Michael Crawford (CBS 70133)

Evita
Original concept album with Julie Covington (MCA MCX503)
Original cast recording with Elaine Paige (MCA MCG3527)
Original Broadway cast recording with Patti LuPone (MCA 2-11007)
Original Australian cast recording (MCA EV1)
Original Spanish cast recording (Epic EPC88524)
Original Austrian cast recording (Jupiter 6. 25. 307)
Original Mexican cast recording (Peerless M/S2233/4)
Original South African cast recording (Gallo ML4540)
Original Japanese cast recording (Trio 3B-20001) (2 records)
Original New Zealand cast recording (Stetson SRLP 18/19)
Original Brazilian cast recording (Somlivree 403. 6273)
Original Hungarian cast recording (Favorit SLPM 17903)
Argentinian recording of six numbers by Valeria Lynch (Philips 3093)

Cats
Original cast recording (Polydor CATX0001) (2 records)
Original Broadway cast recording (Geffen 2GHS, 2031) (2 records)
Original Austrian cast recording (Polydor 817. 365-1)
Original Japanese cast recording (Canyon C40H0032) (2 records)
Original Hungarian cast recording (Favorit SLPM17837)
Original Australian cast recording (EMI EME24022/3) (2 records)
Original German cast recording (Hamburg) (Polydor 831 092-1) (2 records)
Original Netherlands cast recording (Mercury 832 695-6. 1)

Blood Brothers
Original cast recording with Barbara Dickson (Legacy LLP101)

Starlight Express
Original cast recording (Polydor LNER 1)
Selection with El de Barge, Peter Hewlett, etc. (MCAS5972) (USA)

Chess
Original concept album with Elaine Paige, Tommy Korberg and Murray Head (RCA
  PL70500) (2 records)

The Phantom of the Opera
Original cast recording with Michael Crawford (PODV9) (2 records)

FRANCE

Les Noces de Jeannette
Complete with Liliane Berton and Michel Dens (EMI-Pathé 057-12126)
Complete with Claude Calès and Michèle Claverie (RCA 430. 055)
Complete with Renée Doria and Lucien Huberty (Pléiade P3074)
Complete with Ninon Vallin (1921) (Bourg 4004-5) (2 records)

Les Deux Aveugles
Complete with dialogue with Régis Ducrocq and Gilles Butin (Bourg BG2003)

Ba-ta-clan
Complete with dialogue with Huguette Boulangeot, Raymond Amade, Rémy Corazza and René Terrasson (Erato STU 70 366 and STU 70 351) also on Erato DUE20240 with *Les Bavards* (2 records)
Cast recording Paris 1980 with Anne-Marie Sanial and Jean Kriff (Milan SLP89)

Le Mariage aux Lanternes
Complete in English with Lawrence Chelsi and Evelyn McGarrity (Magic Tone MLP 1005)
Production by Les Petits Chanteurs de Monaco (children's group) (MM090586)

Orphée aux Enfers
Complete with dialogue (1858 version) with Claudine Collart and Jean Mollien (Musidisc Festival 261) (2 records)
Complete with dialogue (1874 version) with Mady Mesplé and Michel Sénéchal (EMI-Pathé C167-16341/3) (3 records)
Selection with Claudine Collart and Aimé Doniat (EMI-Pathé 057–12108)
Sadler's Wells Opera revival cast recording in English as *Orpheus in the Underworld* with June Bronhill and Jon Weaving (HMV CSD 1316/CLP 1385)
English National Opera revival cast as *Orpheus in the Underworld* 1987 (TER 1134)

Geneviève de Brabant
Complete with dialogue with Annick Simon and Monique Stiot (Bourg BG2012/3) (2 records)

La Belle Hélène
Complete with dialogue with Janine Lindenfelder and André Dran (Musidisc Festival 253) (2 records)
Complete with dialogue with Danièle Millet and Charles Burles (EMI-Pathé C193-11194/5) (2 records)
Complete with Jessye Norman, Gabriel Bacquier and Colette Alliot-Lugaz (EMI EX27071-3) (2 records)
Revival cast recording with dialogue, Bouffes-Parisiens 1976 (Vega 8. 054/55) (2 records)
Revival cast recording 1977 with Jane Rhodes and Rémy Corazza (Barclay 90201/2) (2 records)
Selection with Deva Dassy and Claude Devos (EMI-Pathé 057-10852)
Selection with Jane Rhodes and Bernard Plantey (Philips 837. 498, GY)
Sadler's Wells Opera revival cast recording in English with Joyce Blackham (HMV CSD 1505/CLP 1665)

Barbe-Bleue
Complete with dialogue with Henri Legay and Lina Dachary (Bourg BG2005/6) (2 records)

La Vie Parisienne
Complete 4-act version with dialogue with Régine Crespin and Mady Mesplé (EMI C 165 14123/4) (2 records)

Revival cast recording 1974 with Nicole Broissin and Danièle Millet (Carrere CA231. 67. 769) (2 records)
Revival cast recording Barrault/Renaud Company (Paris 313002)
Selection with Deva Dassy and Liliane Berton (EMI-Pathé 057. 10851)
Selection with Renée Doria (Philips P77. 107L)
Sadler's Wells Opera revival cast recording with June Bronhill (HMV CSD1378/CLP1468)

La Grande-Duchesse de Gérolstein
Complete with dialogue with Eugenia Zareska and André Dran (Urania 115-2) (2 records)
Complete with dialogue with Régine Crespin, Mady Mesplé and Alain Vanzo (CBS Masterworks 79207) (2 records)
Revival cast recording with Suzanne Lafaye 1966 (Decca SKL 30. 176/7) (2 records)
Selection with Eliane Lublin and Raymond Amade (EMI-Pathé 057. 11659)

La Périchole
Complete with Suzanne Lafaye and Raymond Amade (EMI Pathé CO53/10669/70) (2 records)
Complete with Régine Crespin (Erato STU 70994/5) (2 records)
Complete with Teresa Berganza, José Carreras and Gabriel Bacquier (EMI SLS 5276) (2 records)
American revival cast (Metropolitan Opera) with Patrice Munsel 1957 (Metropolitan Opera Club issue) (RCA RB 16033)

Le Petit Faust
Complete with Michel Hamel, Lina Dachary and Agnès Disney (Clio 004/005) (2 records)
Complete with Lina Dachary, Aimé Doniat and Liliane Berton (Rare Recorded Editions RRE176-7) (2 records)

Les Brigands
Selection with Robert Manuel and Danièle Perriers (Milan SLP 84)
Selection TV film soundtrack 1970 with Dominique Tirmont and Eliane Manchet (Decca SSL 40. 231)

Les Cent Vièrges
'O Paris, Gai Séjour' recorded by Mathé Altéry on *Airs d'Operette* (Pathé STX 120), by Mady Mesplé on EMI-Pathé CO69 73036 and by Jany Sylvaire on *Les Opérettes de la Belle Époque* (Vega 30LT13. 020)

La Fille de Madame Angot
Complete with dialogue with Mady Mesplé and Christiane Stutzmann (EMI-Pathé C163 12775-6) (2 records)
Complete with dialogue with Colette Riedinger and Suzanne Lafaye (Decca SSL 40. 234/5) (2 records)
Selection with Lina Dachary and Solange Michel (EMI-Pathé 057. 12085)
Selection with Marcel Merkès and Paulette Merval (CBS 88313)
Selection with Lyne Cumia and Claudine Collart (Philips P77. 113L)

Giroflé-Girofla
Selection in German with E Senff-Thies, I Borsow and K Prantsch-Kaufmann (Urania 7054)

Le Grand Mogol
One number recorded by Jany Sylvaire on *Festival d'Opérettes Françaises* (Vega 13002)

Les Cloches de Corneville
Complete with dialogue with Mady Mesplé and Bernard Sinclair (EMI-Pathé C163-12775-6) (2 records)
Complete with dialogue with Huguette Boulangeot and Colette Riedinger (Decca 115. 182/83) (2 records)
Selection with Lyne Cumia and Janine Ribot (Philips P77. 117L)
Selection with Martha Angelici and Nadine Renaux (EMI-Pathé 057. 12107)
Selection with Marcel Merkès and Paulette Merval (CBS S62748)
Selection with Nicole Broissin, Janine Micheau and Michel Dens (EMI-Pathé 051. 10848)
Selection with Suzanne Deilhes, Lina Dachary and Robert Massard (Vega 30LT13043)

L'Étoile
Complete with dialogue with Colette Alliot-Lugaz and Georges Gautier (EMI 270086/7) (2 records)
Complete with Anne-Marie Blanzat and Michel Senechal (MRF records) (3 records) with *Fisch-ton-khan* (1981)

Le Petit Duc
Complete with dialogue with André Jobin and Eliane Thibault (Decca SSL 40219-20 (2 records)
Selection with Nadine Renaux and Liliane Berton (EMI-Pathé 057. 12107)

Madame Favart
Complete with dialogue with Suzanne Lafaye and Lina Dachary (Discoreale 10010/11) (2 records)
Complete with dialogue with Linda Felder and Lina Dachary (Rare Recorded Editions SRRE 159-60) (2 records)

La Fille du Tambour-Major
Complete with dialogue with Christiane Harbell, Étienne Arnaud and André Mallabrera (Decca 115. 184-5) (2 records)
Selection with Michel Dens and Liliane Chatel (EMI-Pathé 057. 12192)

Les Mousquetaires au Couvent
Complete with Mady Mesplé and Michel Trempont (EMI 2C 167 16361-2) (2 records)
Complete with Colette Riedinger and Gabriel Bacquier (Decca SSL 40240-1) (2 records)
Selection with Gabriel Bacquier and Pierre Blanc (Carrere 67/761)
Selection with Liliane Berton, Lina Dachary, Michel Dens and Raymond Amade (EMI-Pathé 057. 10850)
Selection with Lyne Cumia and Rosine Brédy (Philips P77. 130L)

La Mascotte
Complete with dialogue with Robert Massard and Geneviève Moïzan (Decca SSL 40. 223-4) (2 records)
Complete with dialogue with Willy Clement and Freda Betti (Clio 002-3) (2 records)
Selection with Michel Dens and Nadine Renaux (EMI-Pathé 057. 10843)

Le Coeur et la Main
'Un Soir, Perez le Capitaine' performed by Joan Sutherland on Decca 417 337 4DA and elsewhere, and by Mathé Altéry on *Airs d'Opérette* (Pathé STX 120)

Mam'zelle Nitouche
Complete with dialogue with Fernandel and Eliane Thibault (Decca 115. 063/4) (2 records)
Selection with Germaine Roger and Duvaleix (EMI-Pathé 057. 10844)

Les P'tites Michu
Selection with Liliane Berton and Nadine Renaux (Pathé DTX149) included in *André Messager: 5 Opérettes* box set

Véronique
Complete with dialogue with Michel Dens and Mady Mesplé (EMI-Pathé 2C 061-10175/6) (2 records)
Complete with Géori Boué and Roger Bourdin (Decca 458. 559-60) (2 records)
Complete with Colette Riedinger and Bernard Alvi (Decca 115. 194–5) (2 records)
Selection with Camille Maurane and Martha Angelici (EMI-Pathé 057. 10841) included in *André Messager; 5 Opérettes* box set
Selection with Marcel Merkès and Paulette Merval (CBS 63646)

Les Saltimbanques
Complete with Mady Mesplé and Claude Calès (EMI 2C 161 12142-3) (2 records)
Complete with dialogue with Robert Massard and Geneviève Moizan (Decca 115. 071/2 and RCA 530. 008-9) (2 records)
Selection with Liliane Berton and Claude Devos (EMI-Pathé 057. 10842)

Hans le Joueur de Flûte
Selection with Liliane Berton, André Mallabrera and Michel Dens (EMI-Pathé 057. 12194)

Phi-Phi
Complete with Max de Rieux, Mireille and Bernard Alvi (Decca 100. 110/CEP 500. 012) &c (2 records)
Selection with Bourvil and Gise Mey (EMI-Pathé 057. 10840)
Selection with Henri Gènes and Marina Hotine (Westminster WL5413)
Selection with Jean Laffont and Marina Florence (TLP 91. 001)

Déde
Complete with dialogue with Maurice Chevalier (OC), Marina Hotine and Andrée Grandjean (Decca 115. 057/8) (2 records)
Revival cast recording with Antoine (RCA 440. 760)

Ta Bouche
Selection with Fanély Revoil, Jacques Jansen and Suzanne Lafaye (Decca 215. 922)

1241

Ciboulette
Complete with dialogue with Mady Mesplé, Nicolai Gedda and José van Dam (EMI-Pathé 2C167-73105/6) (2 records)
Selection with Géori Boué, Raymond Amade and Roger Bourdin (EMI-Pathé 057. 12089)
Selection by Colette Riedinger (Decca CEP 500. 014)

Pas Sur la Bouche
Selection with Fanély Revoil and Janine Ervil (Decca 215. 925)

La Belle de Cadix
Original cast recordings with Luis Mariano assembled on EMI-Pathé 2C-162-72. 075
Selection with Rudi Hirigoyen (CBS 88 254)
Selection with Rudi Hirigoyen (Odéon XOC 163)

Andalousie
Original cast recordings with Luis Mariano assembled on EMI-Pathé 2C-062-11994. Extracts also reissued on EMI-Pathé 2C-162. 72. 075M
Selection with Rudi Hirigoyen (Odéon XOC168)
Selection with Aldo Filistad, Liliane Berton and Michèle Raynaud (Philips 837. 484. DSY)

Violettes Impériales
Selection with André Dassary and Nicole Broissin (Vega 16. 044A)
Selection with Marcel Merkès and Paulette Merval (Odéon XOC 151) and Odéon 1164 (10 inch) and again on CBS 63457
Selection from film version with Luis Mariano (HMV LDLP 1012)

Quatre Jours à Paris
Selection with Georges Guétary (Festival-Musidisc 315)

La Route Fleurie
Original cast recording with Annie Cordy, Georges Guétary and Bourvil (EMI-Pathé 057. 10532)
Revival cast recording 1980 with José Villamor (Vogue 508658)
Selection with Rudi Hirigoyen and Henri Gènes (TLP 91016)

La Toison d'Or
Selection with Michel Dens and Liliane Berton (EMI-Pathé 057. 12109)
Selection with André Dassary (OC) and Lina Dachary (HMV FCLP 108)
Selection with Colette Riedinger (Decca 458. 532)

Méditerranée
Original cast recording with Tino Rossi (Pathé FSX 119)
Selection with André Dassary (Vega V30 P0941)
Selection with Rudi Hirigoyen (Odéon XOC 186)
Selection with Rudi Hirigoyen (CBS 88. 254)
Selection by Aglaë (OC) (Philips 42. 3. 093) (EP)

1242

Irma la Douce

Colette Renard (OC) recorded four songs on Vogue LD 395 (1956)

Revival cast recording 1967 with dialogue with Colette Renard (Vega 16. 089/90) (2 records)

Selection with Zizi Jeanmaire (Philips B76. 093R) (10 inch) (842. 178 PY) (12 inch)

Original London cast recording with Elizabeth Seal and Keith Michell (Philips BBL 7274)

Original Broadway cast recording with Seal and Michell (Columbia OL5560/OS2029)

Israeli cast recording (CBS S5-0092)

Les Misérables

Original cast recording (Trema 310086/7) (2 records) with excerpts on First Night Scene 2

Original London cast recording with Colm Wilkinson (First Night Encore 1)

Original Broadway cast recording with Wilkinson (Geffen GHS 24151)

UNITED STATES OF AMERICA

Robin Hood

Selection radio cast (AEI 1179)

The Belle of New York

Selection (six songs) with Mary Thomas and Barry Kent HMV 7EG 8442 (UK)(EP) also included on Encore 178 (UK)

'The Purity Brigade' and 'They All Follow Me' sung by Edna May (OC) appear on *Forty Years of English Musical Comedy* (Rococo 4007) (Canada), 'The Purity Brigade' also appears on *Singing Actresses* (WRC SH433) (UK)

Little Johnny Jones

'Give My Regards to Broadway' and 'Yankee Doodle Boy' appear on *George M* (Columbia KOS 3200)

The Prince of Pilsen

Selection radio cast with Jessica Dragonette and Charles Kuhlman (AEI 1172) with *The Pink Lady*

Mlle Modiste

Selection with Doretta Morrow (RCA LPM 3153) (10 inch) with *Naughty Marietta*

Selection with Jeannette Scovotti (Readers Digest RD40–N1) with *Die Fledermaus*

Early recordings assembled on *The Music of Victor Herbert* (Smithsonian R017)

The Red Mill

Selection with Gordon MacRae and Lucille Norman (Capitol L530) (10 inch)

Selection based on 1945 revival with Wilbur Evans and Eileen Farrell (RCA LK1016)

Selection with Rosalind Rees, William Powell and Mukund Marathe (Turnabout TV 34766)

Early recordings 1906 assembled on *The Music of Victor Herbert* (Smithsonian R017)

Naughty Marietta
Washington revival cast 1980 with Judith Blazer and Leslie Harrington (Smithsonian N 026) (2 records)
Selection with Jeanette MacDonald and Nelson Eddy (Sounds Rare SR5006)
Selection with Jeanette MacDonald and Nelson Eddy (JN 115)

The Firefly
Selection with Allan Jones and Elaine Malbin (RCA LM-121) (10 inch)
Selection with Laurie Payne and Stephanie Voss (WRC T210) with *The Chocolate Soldiers*

Sweethearts
Selection based on the 1947 production (RCA LK 1015)
Selection with Rosalind Rees (MMG 1129)
Early recordings assembled on *The Music of Victor Herbert* (Smithsonian R017)

Oh Boy!
Original London cast recordings with Beatrice Lillie assembled as *Oh, Joy!* on *Jerome Kern in London 1914–1923* (WRC SHB 34)

Leave It To Jane
Off-Broadway revival cast recording 1959 (Strand SL 1002)

Irene
Original London cast recordings with Edith Day assembled on Monmouth-Evergreen MES-7057 (USA)
Broadway revival cast recording 1973 with Debbie Reynolds (Columbia KS 32266)
London revival cast recording 1976 with Julie Anthony (EMI EMC 3139)

Sally
Original London cast recordings with Dorothy Dickson assembled on *Jerome Kern in London 1914–1923* (WRC SHB 34) and Monmouth-Evergreen MES 7053 (USA), on Stanyan SR10035 (USA) with *No, No, Nanette* and on EMI SH240 with *Show Boat*

The Student Prince
Selection of early recordings including some by original London cast members assembled on WRC SH279 with *Wildflower* and on Monmouth-Evergreen MES 7054 (USA) with *The Desert Song*
Selection with Dorothy Kirsten and Robert Rounseville (Columbia ML4592)
Film soundtrack with the voice of Mario Lanza (RCA LM 1837)
German cast recording in English based on Heidelberg Castle Summer Festival production (Kanon KOI 132)

Rose Marie
Original London cast recordings with Edith Day and Derek Oldham assembled on *Rudolf Friml in London* (WRC SHB 37 and Monmouth-Evergreen MES 7058 (USA)
Selection with Julie Andrews and Giorgio Tozzi (RCA LOP/LSO 1001)
Selection with Nelson Eddy and Dorothy Kirsten (Columbia 33S 1005 10 inch) and Columbia Special Products P13878 with *The New Moon*
Russian version (Melodiya 033551-54) (2 records)

Selection in French with Marcel Merkès and Paulette Merval (CBS 62346)
Selection in French with Lina Dachary and Guy Fontagnère (Pathè-Marconi DTX 30146) with *No, No, Nanette*
Selection in French with André Dassary and Michèle Claverie (Decca 115 015) with *Le Chant du Désert*
Film soundtrack 1954 with Howard Keel and Ann Blyth (MGM E3769ST)

Lady, Be Good
Original London cast recordings with Fred and Adele Astaire assembled with others on Smithsonian R008 (Columbia Special Products P14271)
Original London cast recordings assembled on WRC SH124 and on *George Gershwin in London* (WRC SH 185)

The Vagabond King
Original London cast recordings assembled on *Rudolf Friml in London* (WRC SHB 37)
Selection with Mario Lanza (RCA LM/LSC 2509)
Selection with Alfred Drake (Decca DL 7014) (10 inch)
Selection with John Hanson (Pye PKL 5568) with *The Student Prince*
Film score with Oreste and Jean Fenn (HMV ALP 1378)

No, No, Nanette
Original London cast recordings with Binnie Hale assembled on WRC SH176 with *Hit the Deck* and on Stanyan SR 10035 (USA) with *Sunny*
Broadway revival cast recording 1971 with Ruby Keeler (Columbia S30563)
London revival cast recording 1973 with Anna Neagle (CBS 70126)
Selection in French with Marcel Merkès and Paulette Merval (CBS 62638)
Selection in French with Liliane Berton, Lina Dachary and Duvaleix (Pathé-Marconi DTX 30146) with *Rose-Marie*

Oh, Kay!
Original London cast recordings with Gertrude Lawrence assembled on Smithsonian R-011 (USA)
Selection with Jack Cassidy and Barbara Ruick (Columbia CL1050)
Off-Broadway revival cast recording 1960 (20th Fox 4003)

The Desert Song
Original London cast recordings with Edith Day and Harry Welchman assembled on WRC SH254 with *The New Moon* and on Monmouth-Evergreen 7054 (USA) with *The Student Prince*
Selection with Nelson Eddy and Doretta Morrow (Columbia ACL 831)
Selection with Edmund Hockridge and June Bronhill (HMV CLP 1274) (UK)
Selection with Judith Raskin and Mario Lanza (RCA LPM/LSC 2240)
Selection in French as *Le Chant du Desert* with André Dassary and Mathé Altéry (Decca 115 015) with *Rose Marie*
Selection in French as *Le Chant du Desert* with Claudine Granger and Jean-Marie Joye (TLP 91014)

Hit the Deck
Original London cast recordings with Stanley Holloway and Ivy Tresmand assembled on WRC SH176 with *No, No, Nanette*

1245

Selection with Denis Quilley and Doreen Hume (UK) (Epic LN3569) with *The Cat and the Fiddle*

Film soundtrack (MGM 2-SES-43-ST)

The New Moon

Original London cast recordings with Evelyn Laye and Howett Worster assembled on WRC SH254 with *The Desert Song* and on Monmouth-Evergreen MES7051 (USA)

Selection with Nelson Eddy and Eleanor Steber (Columbia ML2164) (10 inch) (Columbia SP P13878) with *Rose Marie*

Film soundtrack with Jeanette MacDonald and Nelson Eddy (Pelican LP103) with *I Married an Angel*

Film soundtrack with Grace Moore and Lawrence Tibbett (Pelican LP2020)

Show Boat

Original London cast recordings with Edith Day, Howett Worster and Paul Robeson assembled on WRC SH240 and Monmouth-Evergreen MES 7058 (USA) with *Sunny*

Revival cast recording 1946 with Jan Clayton (Columbia ML/OL4058)

Lincoln Center revival cast recording 1966 with Barbara Cook, Constance Towers and Stephen Douglass (RCA LOC/LSO 1126)

London revival cast 1971 with André Jobin (Columbia SCX6480). An extended version by this cast, including songs previously used in *Show Boat* but not played in this production, was issued on Stanyan 25R-10048

Film soundtrack 1936 with Irene Dunne (Xeno 251)

Film soundtrack 1951 with Kathryn Grayson and Howard Keel (MGM E559) 10 inch

Radio broadcast with Irene Dunn, Allan Jones and Charles Winninger (Sunbeam P501)

Selection with Paul Robeson (OLC) and Helen Morgan (OC) assembled on Columbia Special Products AC55

Selection with Robert Merrill, Patrice Munsel and Risë Stevens (RCA LM 2008 SLP9)

Early recordings assembled on *A Collector's Show Boat* (RCA Victrola AVM1-1741)

Selection in Swedish as *Teaterbåten* (Telestar TRS 11129) with *Viktorias Husar*

The Cat and the Fiddle

Selection with Doreen Hume and Denis Quilley (UK) (Fontana TLP5028/Epic LN3569) with *Hit the Deck*

'Try to Forget', 'She Didn't Say Yes', 'The Night Was Made for Love' and 'A New Love Is Old' sung by Peggy Wood appear on *Jerome Kern in London* (WRC SH171)

Of Thee I Sing

Broadway revival cast recording 1952 (Capitol S350)

Television cast recording 1972 (Columbia S31763)

Concert cast recording 1987 (Columbia S2M 42522) with *Let 'Em Eat Cake*

Music in the Air

Selection with Jane Pickens (RCA LK1025)

Selection with Marion Grimaldi and Andy Cole (WRC T121) (UK) with *Roberta*

Anything Goes
Original Broadway and London cast recordings assembled on Smithsonian R007
Original London cast recordings assembled on *Cole Porter in London* (WRC SHB 26)
Off-Broadway revival cast recording 1962 (Epic FLS/FLM 15100)
London revival cast recording 1969 (Decca SKL 5031 and TER 1080)
New York revival cast recording 1987 (RCA 7769-1-RC)
Film soundtrack 1956 (Decca DL 8318)

On Your Toes
Broadway revival cast recording 1954 with Vera Zorina and Bobby Van (Decca DL9015)
Broadway revival cast recording 1983 with Natalia Makarova and Lara Teeter (Polydor 8813 667-1)

Pal Joey
Selection with Vivienne Segal (OC) and Harold Lang (Columbia ML54364)
Selection with Jane Frohman (Capitol S-310)
London revival cast recording 1980 with Sian Phillips and Denis Lawson (TERX1005)
Film soundtrack (Capitol W/DW 912)

Lady in the Dark
Selection with Gertrude Lawrence (OC) (RCA LPV503) with *Down in the Valley*
Selection with Danny Kaye (OC) (Columbia CL-6249) and re-recorded on several Kaye compilation albums
Television cast recording 1954 with Ann Sothern (RCA LM-1882)
Selection with Risë Stevens (Columbia OL-5990/2390)

Carmen Jones
Original cast recording (Decca DL 8014)
Selection with Grace Bumbry, George Webb and Elisabeth Welch (Heliodor HS 25046)
Film soundtrack with the voice of Marilyn Horne (RCA LM1881)

Oklahoma
Original cast recording with Alfred Drake and Joan Roberts (Decca DL8000)
Original London cast recordings with Howard Keel and Betty Jane Watson issued on WRC SH393 with *Annie Get Your Gun* and *Carousel*, and on Stanyan 10069 (USA) with *Annie Get Your Gun*
Broadway revival cast recording 1979 (RCA CBLI, 3572)
London revival cast recording 1980 (Stiff OAK-1)
Australian revival cast recording 1982 (RCA VPLI-0376)
Selection in German with Christine Görner and Benno Kusche (Ariola S70627IU)
Six songs in French appear on *Comédies Musicales Americaines* (TLP 91008)
Film soundtrack (Capitol WAO/SWAO 595)

One Touch of Venus
Original cast recording with Mary Martin (Decca DL 9122/79122)

Song of Norway
Original cast recording (with Kitty Carlisle substituting for Irra Petina) (Decca DL8002)

Jones Beach revival cast recording 1958 (Columbia CL 1328)
Film soundtrack (ABC Records ABCS. OC. 14)

On the Town
Original cast members with John Reardon (Columbia OL5440/OS 2028)
Original London cast recording (CBS APG/SAPG 60005)
Film soundtrack (Show Biz 5063)

Carousel
Original cast recording with John Raitt and Jan Clayton (Decca DL8003)
Original London cast recording (Columbia DX8345/6)
Broadway revival cast recording 1965 (RCA LOC/LSO 1114)
Selection with Alfred Drake and Roberta Peters (Command RS 843SD)
Selection with Robert Merrill and Patrice Munsel (RCA LPM/LSP 1048)
Selection with Samuel Ramey and Barbara Cook (MCA 6209)
Three songs in French appear on *Comédies Musicales Americaines* (TLP91008)
Film soundtrack with Gordon Macrae and Shirley Jones (Capitol W/SW 694)

Annie Get Your Gun
Original cast recording with Ethel Merman and Ray Middleton (Decca DL-8001)
Original London cast recordings with Dolores Gray and Bill Johnson assembled on
    WRC SH-393 with *Oklahoma!* and *Carousel* and on Stanyan SR-10069 with
    Oklahoma!
Television cast recording 1957 with Mary Martin and John Raitt (Capitol W-913)
Broadway revival cast recording 1966 with Merman (RCA LOC/LSO 1124)
West German revival cast recording 1963 as *Annie Schiess Los* with Heidi Bruhl
    (Philips 838 900PY)
London revival cast recording 1986 with Suzi Quatro and Eric Flynn (First Night
    Cast 4)
Original Mexican cast recording (Orfeon LP13-2282)
Film soundtrack (MGM E-509) &c

Brigadoon
Original cast recording (RCA LOC/LSO 1001)
Original Japanese cast recording (Toho AX8022)
Original Mexican cast recording (RCA MKL 1300)
Television cast recording 1954 with Sally Ann Howes and Robert Goulet (Columbia
    Special Products CSM-385)
Film soundtrack (MGM E-3135)

Kiss Me, Kate
Original cast recording with Alfred Drake and Patricia Morison (Columbia DL
    4140/OS2300)
Original London cast recordings assembled on *Cole Porter in London* (WRC SHB 26)
Selection in German (Ariola S74343 IE)
Original Netherlands cast recording (CNR LCT-8010)
London revival cast recording 1987 (First Night Cast 10)
Selection with Frank Sinatra, Dean Martin and Dinah Shore (Reprise FS2017)
Film soundtrack (MGM 2-SES-44-ST)

1248

South Pacific

Original cast recording with Ezio Pinza and Mary Martin (Columbia ML/OL 4180)
Original London cast recordings with Wilbur Evans and Martin assembled on Columbia 7EG-7668 and 7677 (EPs)
Broadway revival cast recording 1967 with Giorgio Tozzi and Florence Henderson (Columbia OL6700/OS3100)
London revival cast 1988 with Emile Belcourt and Gemma Craven (First Night Cast 11)
Selection with Frank Sinatra, Debbie Reynolds and Bing Crosby (Reprise FS 2018)
Selection with Kiri te Kanawa and Jose Carreras (CBS SM 42205)
Film soundtrack with Mitzi Gaynor and the voice of Tozzi (RCA LOCD2000)

Gentlemen Prefer Blondes

Original cast recording with Carol Channing (Columbia OL4290)
Original London cast recording with Dora Bryan (HMV CLP 1602 CSD 1464)
Film soundtrack with Marilyn Monro (MGM E208) (10 inch)
The revised version entitled *Lorelei* was recorded by its touring cast (MGM Verve MV5097) and by its 1974 Broadway cast (MGM M3G-55)

Call Me Madam

Original cast recording with Dinah Shore replacing Ethel Merman (RCA LOC-1000)
Selection with Ethel Merman (OC) (Decca DL-5304) (10 inch)
Original London cast recording (Columbia 33SX-1002)
Film soundtrack with Merman (Decca DL-5465)

Guys and Dolls

Original cast recording (Decca DL 8036)
Broadway revival cast recording 1976 (Motown M6-876S1)
London revival cast recording 1982 (Chrysalis CDL 1388)
Selection with Frank Sinatra, Bing Crosby, Dean Martin, Dinah Shore and Debbie Reynolds (Reprise F/FS-2016)
Film soundtrack with Frank Sinatra, Marlon Brando, Vivian Blaine and Jean Simmons (Decca ED-2332) (EP)

The King and I

Original cast recording with Gertrude Lawrence and Yul Brynner (Decca DL-9008)
Original London cast recording with Valerie Hobson and Herbert Lom (Philips BBL 7002)
New York revival cast 1964 with Risë Stevens (RCA LOC/LSO 1092)
Broadway revival cast 1977 with Constance Towers and Brynner (RCA ABLI-2610)
Original Israeli cast recording (Embassy 31571)
Original West German cast recording as *Der König und Ich* (Philips 838 908 SY)
Selection with Inia te Wiata and June Bronhill (MFP 1064)
Film soundtrack with Deborah Kerr and Brynner (Capitol W/SW 740)

Paint Your Wagon

Original cast recording with James Barton and Olga San Juan (RCA LOC/LSO 1006)
Film soundtrack with Clint Eastwood, Harve Presnell, Lee Marvin and the voice of Anita Gordon (Paramount PMS 1001)

Can-Can
Original cast recording with Lilo (Capitol S452)
Original London cast recording with Irene Hilda (Parlophone PMD 1017)
Original Austrian cast recording (Philips 844 313 PY)
Original Swedish cast recording (Amigo AMLP 812)
Film soundtrack with Shirley Maclaine (Capitol W/SW 1301)

Kismet
Original cast recording with Alfred Drake (Columbia OL4850/OS2060)
Broadway revival cast recording 1965 with Drake (RCA LOC/LSO 1112)
Selection with Robert Merrill, Adele Leigh and Regina Resnik. (London SP44043)
Film soundtrack with Howard Keel (MGM E-3281)

Wonderful Town
Original cast recording with Rosalind Russell (Decca DL9010)
Television cast recording 1958 with Russell (Columbia OL5360)
London revival cast recording with Maureen Lipman (First Night Cast 6)

The Pajama Game
Original cast recording with John Raitt and Janis Paige (Columbia OL4840)
Original London cast recording with Edmund Hockridge and Joy Nichols (HMV CLP1062)
Film soundtrack with Raitt and Doris Day (Columbia OL5210)

Damn Yankees
Original cast recording (RCA LOC 1021)
Film soundtrack (RCA LOC 1047)

My Fair Lady
Original cast recording with Rex Harrison and Julie Andrews (Columbia OL 5090)
Original London cast recording with Harrison and Andrews (CBS SEPG 68001)
Original Austrian cast recording (Preiser SPR 3210)
Original Danish cast recording (Philips Polyphon PP8000)
Original Israeli cast recording (Columbia OL8050)
Israeli revival cast recording 1986 (Acum 8024)
Original Italian cast recording (CBS 62. 222)
Original Mexican cast recording as *Mi Bella Dama* (Columbia WL 155/WS 305)
Original Netherlands cast recording (Philips PO8051L/840318PY)
Original Swedish cast recording (Sonet BFB LP101)
West German cast recording (Theater des Westens) (Philips 840 411 SY)
West German cast recording (Hamburg) (Metronome HLP 10. 055/10, 010)
Original Japanese cast recording (King SKJ 1044)
Hungarian cast recording (Qualiton LPX6556)
Two songs in French appear on *Comédies Musicales Americaines* (TLP91008)
Film soundtrack with Harrison and Audrey Hepburn (Columbia KOL8000)
Film soundtrack dubbed in French (CBS70001)
Film soundtrack dubbed in German (CBS70002)
Film soundtrack dubbed in Italian (CBS70003)

The Most Happy Fella
Original cast recording with Robert Weede (Columbia 03L-240) (3 records) with excerpts on Columbia OL 5118
Original London cast recording with Inia te Wiata (HMV CLP 1365/CSD 1306)

Bells Are Ringing
Original cast recording with Judy Holliday (Columbia OL5170)
Film soundtrack with Holliday (Capitol W/SW 1435)

Candide
Original cast recording with Max Adrian, Barbara Cook and Robert Rounseville (Columbia OL5180/OS2350)
Broadway revival cast recording 1973 with Lewis J Stadlen, Maureen Brennan and Mark Baker (Columbia S2X 32923)
New York City Opera revival cast recording 1986 (New World NW340/1)
Scottish Opera cast 1988 (TER 1156)

The Music Man
Original cast recording with Robert Preston (Capitol W/SW 990)
Original London cast recording with Van Johnson (HMV CLP 1444)
Selection with Meredith Willson (author) Capitol ST 1320
Film soundtrack with Preston (Warner Brothers B/BS 1459)

West Side Story
Original cast recording (Columbia OL5230/OS2001)
Original Austrian cast recording (CBS S70040)
Original Japanese cast recording (Toshiba EMI Express ETP 60262/3) (2 records)
Original Australian cast recording (K-Tel NA642)
Selection with Kiri Te Kanawa and Jose Carreras (Deutsche Gramaphon 415253-1)
Selection in Swedish (RCA LPM 9928) with *Stoppa Varlden*
Selection in German (Polydor 249 157) with *Mary Poppins*
Two songs in French appear on *Comédies Musicales Americaines* (TLP91008)
Film soundtrack (Columbia OL 5670/OS2070)

The Sound of Music
Original cast recording with Mary Martin (Columbia KOL5450/KOS2020)
Original London cast recording with Jean Bayless (HMV CLP1453/CSD1365)
Original Australian cast recording with June Bronhill (HMV OCLP/OCSD7580)
Original Mexican cast recording (Orfeon LP13. 2226)
Original Netherlands cast recording (Philips 625821)
Original Mexican cast recording as *La Novicia Rebelde* (Orfeon LP13-2226)
Original Israeli cast recording (Disneyland HD30210)
London revival cast recording 1981 with Petula Clark (Epic EPC 70212)
Australian revival cast recording 1983 with Julie Anthony (EMI EMX123)
Film soundtrack with Julie Andrews (RCA LOCD/LSOD 2005)
Film soundtrack dubbed in French as *La Melodie du Bonheur* (RCA 440 6965)
Film soundtrack dubbed in Spanish as *Sonrisas y Lagrimas* (RCA LSP 10309)

Once Upon a Mattress
Original cast recording with Carol Burnett (Kapp KDL/KDS 7004)
Original London cast recording with Jane Connell (HMV CLP1410)

1251

Gypsy
Original cast recording with Ethel Merman (Columbia OL5420/OS2017)
Original London cast recording with Angela Lansbury (RCA SER 5686)
Original South African cast recording (Philips STO 774)
Film soundtrack with Rosalind Russell (Warner Brothers B/BS 1480)

Bye Bye, Birdie
Original cast recording with Dick van Dyke (Columbia KOL5510/KOS2025)
Original London cast recording with Peter Marshall (Philips ABL/FBL3383)
Film soundtrack with van Dyke (RCA LOC/LSO 1081)

The Fantasticks
Original cast recording with Jerry Orbach (MGM E/SE 3872)
Original Mexican cast recording (Columbia DCA 178)
Original French cast recording (Polydor 27, 344) (EP)
Original Japanese cast recording (RCA JRS 7301)

Camelot
Original cast recording with Richard Burton and Julie Andrews (Columbia
 KOL5620/KOS 2031)
Original London cast recording with Lawrence Harvey and Elizabeth Larner (HMV
 CLP1756/CSD1559)
London revival cast recording 1982 with Richard Harris (TER 1030)
Film soundtrack with Harris and Vanessa Redgrave (Warner Brothers B/BS 1712)
Film soundtrack dubbed in German (Warner Brothers BSG 1712)

How to Succeed in Business Without Really Trying
Original cast recording (RCA LOC/LSO 1066)
Original London cast recording (RCA RO/SF 7564)
Original French cast recording as *Comment Réussir Dans les Affaires Sans Vraiment Se
 Fatiguer* (Philips B77988)
Original German cast recording as *Wie man was wird im Leben ohne sich anzustrengen*
 (Ariola Eurodisc 74007)
Film soundtrack (United Artists (UAL4151)

Little Me
Original cast recording with Sid Caesar (RCA LOC/LSO 1078)
Original London cast recording with Bruce Forsyth (Pye NPL 18107)

A Funny Thing Happened on the Way to The Forum
Original cast recording with Zero Mostel (Capitol WAS/SWAO 1717)
Original London cast recording with Frankie Howerd (HMV CLP 1685/CSD 1518)
Israeli cast recording (Hed-Arzi 14009)
Film soundtrack with Mostel (United Artists VAL4144/UAS5144)

Funny Girl
Original cast recording with Barbara Streisand (Capitol VAS/SVAS 2059)
Film soundtrack with Streisand (Columbia BOS 3220)

Hello Dolly!
Original cast recording with Carol Channing (RCA LOCD/LSOD 1087)
Original London cast recording with Mary Martin (RCA RD/SF 7768)
London replacement cast recording with Dora Bryan (HMV CLP/CSD 3545)
Broadway black replacement cast recording with Pearl Bailey (RCA LOC/LSO 1147)
Original West German cast recording (Columbia OL6710/053110)
Original French cast recording with Annie Cordy (CBS 65115)
Original Mexican cast recording (RCA AVL 3745)
Original Israeli cast recording (CBS S70047)
Original Austrian cast recording with Marika Rökk (Metronome KMLP332)
Original East German cast recording (Amiga 8 45 097)
Original Russian cast recording (Melodiya 16601/6) (3 records)
Original Brazilian cast recording (CBS 60139)
Film soundtrack with Barbra Streisand (20th Century Fox DTCS 5103)

Fiddler on the Roof
Original cast recording with Zero Mostel (RCA LOC/LSO 1093)
Original London cast recording with Topol (CBS 70030)
Original West German cast recording as *Anatevka* (Decca 621409)
Original Austrian cast recording as *Anatevka* (Preiser SPR 3200)
Original French cast recording as *Un Violon Sur le Toit* (CBS 70065)
Original South African cast recording (RCA 38149)
Original Israeli cast recording (in Yiddish) (Columbia OL 6650)
Original Israeli cast recording (in Hebrew) Columbia OL 6490)
Original Japanese cast recording (Toho AX6044/6) (2 records)
Original Mexican cast recording as *Violinista en el Tejado* (Capitol SLEM 221)
Original Hungarian cast recording as *Hegedüs a Häztetön* (Qualiton SPLM 16719)
Original Argentine cast recording as *Violinista en el Tejado* (PAR 5001)
Original Norwegian cast recording as *Spelemann Pa Taket* (Nordisc NOR LP 1000) (10 inch)
Original Danish cast recording as *Spillemand pa en tagryg* (Decca EP F44452) EP)
Original Icelandic cast recording (SG 560) (EP) with *Zorba*
Swiss recording as *Anatevka* (J188) (Charity recording)
Film soundtrack with Topol (United Artists UAS 29301)

Do I Hear a Waltz
Original cast recording (Columbia KOL/KOS 2770)

Man of La Mancha
Original cast recording with Richard Kiley (Kapp KL4505/KS5505)
Original London cast recording with Keith Michell (MUPS-334) and double-album (MUCS-123)
Original Mexican cast recording as *El Hombre de La Mancha* (Decca DL 79171)
Original French cast recording as *L'Homme de la Mancha* (Barclay 83, 381)
Original Norwegian cast recording as *Mannen fra La Mancha* (Triola TNLP S29)
Original Israeli cast recording (CBS S 70033)
Original West German cast recording as *Mann von La Mancha* (Polydor 249 297)
Original Austrian cast recording as *Mann von La Mancha* (Polydor 249 219)
Original Spanish cast recording with Luis Sagi-Vela (Philips 436 853 PE) (45)

Original Netherlands cast recording (Philips PY844-085)
Film soundtrack with the voice of Simon Gilbert (United Artists UAS 9906)

Sweet Charity
Original cast recording with Gwen Verdon (Columbia KOL6500/KOS2900)
Original London cast recording with Juliet Prowse (CBS 70035)
Original West German cast recording with Dagmar Koller (Decca SLK 16 643-P)
Original French cast recording with Magali Noël (CBS S-70084)
Original Netherlands cast recording with Jasperina de Jong (Philips 844 089 PY)
Broadway revival cast recording 1986 with Debbie Allen (EMI SV 17196)

Cabaret
Original cast recording with Jill Haworth and Joel Grey (Columbia KOL 6640/KOS 3040)
Original London cast recording with Judi Dench and Barry Dennen (CBS (S) 70039)
Original Austrian cast recording with Violetta Ferrari and Blanche Aubry (Preiser SPR 3220)
London revival cast recording 1986 with Kelly Hunter and Wayne Sleep (First Night Cast 5)
Film soundtrack with Liza Minelli and Grey (ABC ABCD752)

Mame
Original cast recording with Angela Lansbury (Columbia KOL 6600/KOS 3000)
Original Mexican cast recording with Silvia Pinal (Orfeon LP/12/837)
Film soundtrack with Rosalind Russell (Warner Brothers W2773)

Hair
Original off-Broadway cast recording (RCA LOC/LSO 1143)
Original Broadway cast recording (RCA LOC/LSO 1150)
Original London cast recording (Polydor 583 043)
Original Australian cast recording (Spin SEL 933544)
Original Finnish cast recording (Scandia SLP 534)
Original Brazilian cast recording (PDU PldA 5014)
Original French cast recording (Philips 844, 987, BY)
Original Israeli cast recording (CBS S70074)
Original Argentine cast recording (RCA AVL 4031)
Original Danish cast recording (Polydor 2380 010)
Original Norwegian cast recording (Polydor 2382 006)
Original Swedish cast recording (Sonnet SLP 70)
Original Japanese cast recording (RCA LSO 1170)
Original Netherlands cast recording (Polydor 2441 002)
Original West German cast recording (Polydor 249 266)
Original Hamburg cast recording as *Haare* (Polydor 2459 188)
Original Munich cast recording as *Das Ganze Hair* (Polydor 2630 025)
Original Italian cast recording (RCA PSL 10479)
Original Mexican cast recording (Orfeon LP-JM-53)
Film Soundtrack (RCA CBL 2, 3274/1-2) (2 records)

Promises, Promises
Original cast recording with Jerry Orbach (United Artists UAS 9902)

1254

Original London cast recording with Tony Roberts (United Artists UAS 29075)
Original Italian cast recording as *Promesse, Promesse* with Johnny Dorelli (CGD FGS 5063)

1776
Original cast recording (Columbia BOS 3310)
Original London cast recording (EMI Columbia SCX 6424)
Film soundtrack (Columbia 31741)

Applause
Original cast recording with Lauren Bacall (ABC-OCS-11)

Company
Original cast recording with Dean Jones (Columbia OS 3550)

Follies
Original cast recording (Capitol SO 761)
Original London cast recording (First Night Encore 3)
New York concert recording 1985 with Barbara Cook, Lee Remick, Mandy Patinkin and George Hearn (RCA HBC2-7128)

Godspell
Original cast recording (Bell 1102)
Original London cast recording (Bells 203)
Original Australian cast recording (Melbourne) SFL 934486)
Original Australian cast recording (Sydney) EMI HMV SOELP 9939)
Original French cast recording (Philips 6332 037)
Original West German cast recording (Reprise 44 176)
Original Nairobi cast recording (ACP 701)
Original South African cast recording (CAL 16000)
Original Swedish cast recording (Aksent 130)
Original Netherlands cast recording (Polydor 2925 011)
Original Spanish cast recording (Noviola NLX 1048)
South African revival cast recording 1985 (CAT KVL 5010)
West German revival cast recording 1986 (Backstage BS1-986G)
Film soundtrack (Bell 1119)

Grease
Original cast recording (MGM 1SE-340C)
Original Mexican cast recording as *Vaselina* (Orfeon LP-16H-5148)
Film soundtrack (RSO RS2-4002)

A Little Night Music
Original cast recording with Glynis Johns and Len Cariou (Columbia KS32265)
Original London cast recording with Jean Simmons and Joss Ackland (RCA LRL1 5090)
Film soundtrack with Elizabeth Taylor and Cariou (JS 35333)

Chicago
Original cast recording with Gwen Verdon, Chita Rivera and Jerry Orbach (Arista AL9005)
Original Australian cast recording (Polydor 2907 068)

A Chorus Line
Original cast recording with Donna McKechnie (Columbia PS 33581)
Original Norwegian cast recording (Polygram NORLP 422)
Film soundtrack (Casablanca 826 306. IM 1)

Annie
Original cast recording with Dorothy Loudon, Reid Shelton and Andrea McArdle
    (Columbia PS 34712)
Original London cast recording with Sheila Hancock, Stratford Johns and McArdle
    (CBS 70160)
Original Australian cast recording with Jill Perryman (Festival L36861)
Original Spanish cast recording (Bocacio BS-32137)
Original Danish cast recording (Polydor 2444 089)
Film soundtrack (Columbia JS 38000)
Film soundtrack dubbed in French (CBS 25193)

On the Twentieth Century
Original cast recording with John Cullum and Madeleine Kahn (Columbia JS 35330)

The Best Little Whorehouse in Texas
Original cast recording with Carlin Glynn and Henderson Forsythe (MCA-3049)
Film soundtrack with Burt Reynolds and Dolly Parton (MCA-6112)

They're Playing Our Song
Original cast recording with Robert Klein and Lucie Arnaz (Casablanca NBLP7141)
Original London cast recording with Tom Conti and Gemma Craven (Chopper
    CHOP E-6)
Original Australian cast recording with John Waters and Jackie Weaver (Festival
    L37356)
Original Italian cast recording as *Stanno Suonando La Nostra Canzone* (Polydor 2448
    129)
Original Mexican cast recording as *Están Tocando Nuestra Cancion* (Polydor
    LP16394)
Original Austrian cast recording as *Sie Spielen Unser Lied* (Casablanca LB 27 133
    509)

Sweeney Todd
Original cast recording with Len Cariou and Angela Lansbury (RCA CBL2-3379)

Barnum
Original cast recording with Jim Dale (Columbia JS 36576)
Original London cast recording with Michael Crawford (Air CDL 1348)
Original French cast recording with Jean-Luc Moreau (JMB ZL 37467)
Original Australian cast recording with Reg Livermore (RCA VPLI 0366)
Original Italian cast recording with Massimo Ranieri (CGD 20392)
Original Spanish cast recording with Emilio Aragon (BAT BM-001)

42nd Street
Original cast recording with Tammy Grimes and Jerry Orbach (RCA CBLI-3891)

Little Shop of Horrors
Original cast recording with Ellen Greene (Geffen GHSP 2020)
Original French cast recording as *La Petite Boutique des Horreurs* with Fabienne Guyon (HI 1740 121)
Original Icelandic cast recording as *Litla Hryillingsbúdin* with Edda Heidrún Backman (Steinar STLP 082)
Film Soundtrack (Geffen GHS 24125)

La Cage aux Folles
Original cast recording with George Hearn and Gene Barry (RCA HBCI-4824)
Original Australian cast recording with Jon Ewing and Keith Michell (RCA VPLI 0520)
Original West German cast recording (Polydor 829 646-1)

GERMANY/AUSTRIA/HUNGARY

Die schöne Galathee
Complete with Elisabeth Roon, Kurt Preger and Otto Wiener (Saga 5418)
Complete with Anna Moffo and René Kollo (RCA RL 25108)
Complete with Renate Holm and Reinhold Bartel (RCA VL 30352)

Die Fledermaus
Complete with Julius Patzak and Hilde Güden (Decca DPA 585-6) (2 records)
Complete with Nicolai Gedda and Elisabeth Schwarzkopf (EMI SLS 823) (2 records)
Complete with Karl Terkal and Gerda Scheyrer (EMI CFPD 4072) (2 records)
Complete with Waldemar Kmentt and Hilde Güden with gala concert (Decca SET 201-3) (3 records)
Complete with Eberhard Wächter and Adele Leigh (RCA SER 5514-5) (2 records)
Complete with Rudolf Schock and Wilma Lipp (Eurodisc 88610 XDE) (2 records)
Complete with Nicolai Gedda and Anneliese Rothenberger (HMV SLS 964) (2 records
Complete with Eberhard Wächter and Gundula Janowitz (Decca SET 540-1) (2 records)
Complete with Hermann Prey and Julia Varady (Deutsche Grammophon 2707 088) (2 records)
Complete with with Mirjana Irosch and Waldemar Kmentt (2 records)
Vienna Volksoper cast recording (Teletheater 120757/8) (2 records)
Complete with Peter Seiffert and Lucia Popp (EMI EX 2704723) (2 records)
Complete in English with Charles Kuhlman and Ljuba Welitch (CBS SL 108) (2 records)
Complete in Russian with Neverov and Sakharova (MK DO 1774-7) (2 records)
Complete in Hungarian with Tibor Udvardy and Karola Agay (Qualiton 16658-9) (2 records)
Complete in French as *La Chauve-Souris* with André Mallabrera and Nicole Broissin (Polydor 237905-6) (2 records)
Selection with Hugo Meyer-Welfing and Rosette Anday (Saga 5363)
Selection with Peter Anders and Elfriede Trötschel (Polydor 478108)
Selection with A Kunz and Uta Graf (Concert Hall CM 2022)

Selection with Rudolf Schock and Sári Barabas (EMI Electrola SME 73464) with
Eine Nacht in Venedig
Selection with Sándor Kónya (Polydor 237 160 SLPHM) with *Der Zigeunerbaron*
Selection with Peter Anders and Rita Streich (Polydor 21432) (EP)
Selection with Hilde Güden and Kurt Equiluz (EMI CFP 40251)
Selection with Hilde Güden and Eberhard Wächter (live from Vienna State Opera) (I
Gioielli della Lirica GML 25)
Selection with Donald Grobe and Sonja Schöner (Pye MAL 561)
Selection with Heinz Hoppe and Sári Barabas (Eurodisc Z 72333 E)
Selection with Peter Alexander and Ingeborg Hallstein (Polydor 2430 264)
Selection with Lutze and Janz (Philips 6592 001)
Selection in English with James Melton and Regina Resnik (RCA RB 16109)
Selection in English from soundtrack of *Oh, Rosalinda!* with Michael Redgrave and
Sári Barabas (Mercury MG 20145)
Sadler's Wells Opera cast recording in English with Alexander Young and Victoria
Elliott (CSD1266)
Selection in English with Nagy and Scovotti (RCA RDS 9331)
Selection in English with Richard Lewis and Anna Moffo (RCA LSC 2728)
Selection in French as *La Chauve-Souris* with Jacqueline Brumaire and Liliane
Berton (EMI-Pathé 57. 12195)
Selection in French as *La Chauve-Souris* with C Collins and Darclée (Bellaphon CV
1013)
Selection in Hungarian with Julia Orosz and Tibor Udvardy (Qualiton HLP 6509)
(10 inch) with *Der Zigeunerbaron* and *Eine Nacht in Venedig*

Fatinitza
Selection with Ruth Müller-Inden (Amiga 5 40 145) (EP)

Boccaccio
Complete with Hermann Prey and Anneliese Rothenberger (EMI Electrola 1C 157-
30216/17) (2 records)
Selection with Waldemar Kmentt and Elisabeth Roon (Philips NBL 5026)
Selection with Rudolf Schock and Renate Holm (Eurodisc 89 898 1E)
Selection with Hans Löffler and Elisabeth Roon (Symphony Tone GLK 613) (10
inch) with *Der Opernball*
Selection with Heinz Hoppe and Anneliese Rothenberger (EMI Electrola SME
73940) with *Gasparone*
Selection with Heinz Hoppe and Sonja Schöner (Telefunken SUX 4833) (EP)
Selection in Hungarian with Zsuzsa Petress (Qualiton HLP 6526) (10 inch) with *Der
Bettelstudent*

Das Spitzentuch der Königin
The principal melodies may be heard in recordings of the overture and the walt
'Rosen aus dem Suden'

Der lustige Krieg
Selection with Elisabeth Roon and Waldemar Kmentt (Vox PL 20600), also dis-
guised as Operette Ensemble of the City Theater, Salzburg (Summit SUM5003)
Selection with Dorothea Siebert and Waldemar Kmentt (Philips 02216 AL) with
Cagliostro in Wien

Der Bettelstudent

Complete with Wilma Lipp and Rudolf Christ (Amadeo AVRS 6026/27) (2 records)
Complete with Hilde Güden and Rudolf Schock (Eurodisc 27 187 XDE) (2 records)
Complete with Rita Streich and Hermann Prey (EMI 1C 30162-3) (2 records)
Selection with Erika Köth and Reinhold Bartel (Telefunken 6, 21287)
Selection with Richard Tauber and Vera Schwarz (Asco A104) with *Casanova*
Selection with Sándor Kónya and Ingeborg Hallstein (Polydor 46661) with *Gasparone*
Selection with Donald Grobe and Sonja Schöner (Telefunken 6, 21241) with *Der Vogelhändler*
Selection with Melitta Muszely and Horst Wilhelm (Somerset 599) with *Der Vogelhandler*
Selection with Erika Köth and Gerhard Unger (Eurodisc 71 255 IE)
Selection (Philips P 08180L) with *Die Dollarprinzessin*
Selection with Rita Streich and Peter Anders (Polydor 21433) (EP)
Selection with Herta Talmar and Sándor Kónya (Polydor 237 161) with *Gasparone*
Selection with Erika Köth, Rudolf Schock and Fritz Wunderlich (EMI Electrola 1C 037-28 127)
Selection in Hungarian with Zsuzsa Petress (Qualiton LP 6526) with *Boccaccio*

Eine Nacht in Venedig

Complete with Esther Rethy, Karl Friedrich and Kurt Preger (CBS SL 119) (2 records)
Complete with Elisabeth Schwarzkopf, Nicolai Gedda and Erich Kunz (HMV SXDWS 3043) (2 records)
Complete with Rita Streich, Nicolai Gedda and Cesare Curzi (EMI TC 157-29 095-6) (2 records)
Complete with Jeanette Scovotti and Wolfgang Grendel (Acanta EB 225275)
Selection with Dorothea Siebert and Rudolf Christ (Philips S 04026 L)
Selection with Rita Streich and Peter Anders (Polydor 21436) (EP)
Selection with Lisa Otto, Fritz Wunderlich and Rudolf Schock (EMI Electrola 1C 037 28127)
Selection with Erika Köth, Rudolf Schock and Cesare Curzi (Eurodisc 89 894 IE)
Selection with Sonja Schöner and Donald Grobe (Europa 564)
Selection with Ingeborg Hallstein and Reinhold Bartel (Polydor 237162) with *Wiener Blut*
Selection with Elisabeth Ebert and Harald Neukirch (Philips 6530 047)
Selection with Janet Perry (Telefunken 6. 22916)
Selection with Anton de Ridder and Sylvia Geszty (Philips 420 659-2)
Selection with Sonja Schöner and Heinz Hoppe (Telefunken 6. 21244) with *Wiener Blut*
Jones Beach cast recording 1952 in English with Laurel Hurley (Everest SBDR 3028)
Selection in English with Anna Moffo and William Lewis (RCA RDS 9332)

Gasparone

Complete with Anneliese Rothenberger and Hermann Prey (2 records) EMI 157 46571-2)
Selection with Sári Barabas and Wilfried Barorek (Telefunken 6, 21288)
Selection with Else Liebesberg and Rudolf Christ (Amadeo AVRS EP 15099) (EP)

Selection with Else Liebesberg and Karl Terkal (Fontana 701 514 WPY) with *Die Dubarry*

Selection with Annaliese Rothenberger and Heinz Hoppe (Electrola SME 73940) with *Boccaccio*

Selection with Lotte Rysanek and Hans Strohbauer (Philips 421 085 PE) (EP)

Selection with Sonja Schöner and Donald Grobe (Telefunken SUX 5068) (EP)

Selection with Sándor Kónya and Herta Talmar (Polydor 46661) with *Der Bettelstudent*

Selection with Rosemarie Moogk and Rudolf Scherfling (Vienna Disc TR 6214) with *Im weissen Rössl, Der Vogelhändler* and *Der arme Jonathan*

Der Zigeunerbaron

Complete with Julius Patzak and Hilde Zadek (Decca ECM 2148-9) (2 records)

Complete with Waldemar Kmentt and Gerda Scheyrer (Vanguard VRS 486–7) (2 records)

Complete with Nicolai Gedda and Elisabeth Schwarzkopf (EMI SXDW 3046) (2 records)

Complete with Karl Terkal and Hilde Güden (EMI ASD 394-5 (2 records)

Complete with with Rudolf Schock and Erzsébet Házy (Eurodisc 88 613 XDE) (2 records)

Complete with Nicolai Gedda and Grace Bumbry (EMI 1C 163-28354-5X) (2 records)

Complete with Martin Ritzmann and Elisabeth Ebert (Fontana 701 522-3) (2 records)

Complete with Josef Protschka and Julia Varady (EMI 157-270 651/3) (2 records)

Complete in Russian (Melodiya SM 03129-34) (3 records)

Selection with Peter Anders and Sena Jurinac (RCA VL 30310)

Selection with Walter Ludwig and Maud Cunitz (Mercury MG 15005)

Selection with Hugo Meyer-Welfing and Lea Seidl (Saga EROS 8004)

Selection with Elfriede Trötschel and Peter Anders (Polydor 21435) (EP)

Selection with A Kunz and Uta Graf (Concert Hall SMS 2025)

Selection with Rudolf Christ and Sári Barabas (Epic LC 3041)

Selection with Rudolf Schock and Erika Köth (EMI Electrola SMA 72443)

Selection with Donald Grobe and Melitta Muszely (Pye MAL 560)

Selection with Reinhold Bartel and Erika Köth (Telefunken 6, 21286)

Selection in English as *The Gipsy Baron* with William Lewis and Jeannette Scovotti (RCA RDS 5041)

Sadler's Wells cast recording in English as *The Gipsy Baron* with Nigel Douglas and June Bronhill (HMV CSD 1629)

Selection in French as *Le Baron Tzigane* with Georges Guétary (EMI-Pathé 051. 10531) with *Pour Don Carlos*

Selection in French as *Le Baron Tzigane* with Guy Chauvet and Janine Micheau (Véga 130. 516)

Selection in Hungarian with Tibor Udvardy and Julia Orosz (Qualiton HLP 6509) with *Die Fledermaus* and *Eine Nacht in Venedig*

Selection in Hungarian with Tibor Udvardy and Erzsébet Házy (Qualiton SPLX 16557)

Der arme Jonathan

Selection with Rosemarie Moogk and Rudolf Scherfling (Vienna Disc TR 6214) with *Im weissen Rössl, Der Vogelhändler* and *Gasparone*

Der Vogelhändler

Complete with Julius Patzak, Wilma Lipp and Hilde Zadek (Philips SBL 5215) (2 records)

Complete with Renate Holm, Anneliese Rothenberger and Adolf Dallapozza (EMI 1C 157 30194-5) (2 records)

Selection with Karl Terkal and Maud Cunitz (Telefunken BLE 14126-P) with *Die lustige Witwe* and *Im weissen Rössl*

Selection with Franz Fehringer and Ingeborg Hallstein (Polydor 237163) with *Schwarzwaldmädel*

Selection with Heinz Hoppe and Sonja Schöner (EMI Columbia SMC 73456) with *Der fidele Bauer*

Selection with Erika Köth and Ferry Gruber (Telefunken SUX 5290) (EP)

Selection with Rudolf Schock, Erika Köth and Renate Holm (Eurodisc 89 899 IE)

Selection with Horst Wilhelm and Melitta Muszely (Somerset 599) with *Der Bettelstudent*

Selection with Josef Traxel and Anneliese Rothenberger (Electrola E 73452) with *Schön ist die Welt*

Selection with Peter Anders and Anny Schlemm (Polydor 21434) (EP)

Selection with Peter Minich and Hilde Güden (Telefunken 6, 21256)

Selection with with Donald Grobe and Sonja Schöner (Telefunken 6, 21241) with *Der Bettelstudent*

Selection with Rosemarie Moogk and Rudolf Scherfling (Vienna Disc TR 6214) with *Im seissen Rössl, Gasparone* and *Der arme Jonathan*

Selection with Adolf Dallapozza and Lucia Popp (Philips 420 665-2) with *Die Dollarprinzessin*

Selection in Hungarian with Erzsébet Házy and Sandor Kónya (Qualiton SPLX 16583) with *Die Dubarry*

Der Obersteiger

Selection with Jola Koziel and Walter Schmidt (Amiga 5 40 184) (EP)

Selection with Rosemaria Moogk and Rudolf Scherfling with *Der Vogelhändler* and *Die Dubarry*

Der Opernball

Selection with Karl Terkal and Else Liebesberg (Philips P 08183 L) with *Die Dubarry*

Selection with Elisabeth Roon and Hans Löffler (Symphony Tone GLK 613)

Selection with Margit Schramm, Erika Köth and Ferry Gruber (Eurodisc 41 183 CE) (EP)

Frau Luna

Selection with Ingeborg Hallstein (RCA VL 30316)

Selection with Erika Köth and Heinz Hoppe (EMI Electrola SME 73982) with *Lysistrata* and *Im Reiche des Indra*

Selection with Margit Schramm and Brigitte Mira (Eurodisc 42 185 CE) M(EP)

Selection with Sonja Knittel and Heinz Hoppe (Telefunken 6, 21245) with *Die Csardasfürsting*

Selection with Herta Talmar and Franz Fehringer (Polydor 237158) with *Die Csárdásfürstin*

Wiener Blut
Complete with Rita Streich (Urania UR 209) (2 records)
Complete with Elisabeth Schwarzkopf and Nicolai Gedda (EMI SXDWS 3042) (2 records)
Complete with Rudolf Schock, Wilma Lipp and Hilde Güden (Eurodisc 89 616 XDE) (2 records)
Complete with Nicolai Gedda and Anneliese Rothenberger (EMI 157. 30 688–70) (2 records)
Complete with Adolf Dallapozza and Sigrid Martikke (Wiener Volksoper) (2 records)
Selection with Karl Terkal and Else Liesbesberg (Fontana 701517 WPY)
Selection with Nicolai Gedda and Anneliese Rothenberger (EMI Electrola SME 73941) with *Giuditta*
Selection with René Kollo and Ingeborg Hallstein (Philips 420. 661-2)
Selection with Sonja Schöner and Donald Grobe (Telefunken 6. 21244) with *Eine Nacht in Vendig*
Selection with Herta Talmar and Sándor Kónya (Polydor 237162) with *Eine Nacht in Venedig*

Der Fremdenführer
Selection with Mirjana Irosch and Harald Serafin (Philips 9105 054) with other Ziehrer operetta items and *Die lustige Witwe*

János Vitéz
Complete in Hungarian with Róbert Ilosfalvy and Anna Zentay (Qualiton LPX 6529-31) (3 records)
Complete in Hungarian with József Kovács and Marika Oszvald (Qualiton SLPX 16618-20) (3 records)
Selection in Hungarian with Julia Drosz and I Palló (Qualiton LP 6505) (10 inch)

Die lustige Witwe
Complete with Elisabeth Schwarzkopf and Erich Kunz (EMI SXDW 3045) (2 records)
Complete with Hilde Güden and Per Grundén (Decca DPA 573–4) (2 records)
Complete with Elisabeth Schwarzkopf and Eberhard Wächter (EMI SLS 823) (2 records)
Complete with Margit Schramm and Rudolf Schock (Eurodisc 27 184 XDE) (2 records)
Complete with Elizabeth Harwood and René Kollo (Deutsche Grammophon 2725 102 (2 records)
Complete with Edda Moser and Hermann Prey (EMI SLS 5202) (2 records)
Complete with Mirjana Irosch and Peter Minich (Wiener Volksoper) (Denon C37-7384/5) (2 records)
Complete in Italian as *La Vedova Allegra* with Lia Origoni and Paolo Civil (2 records)
Complete in Russian (Melodiya 021629-32) (2 records)
Selection with Mizzi Günther and Louis Treumann (original cast) (Rococo 4012) with *Der Graf von Luxemburg, Das Fürstenkind*, and *Eva*
Selection with Nora Jungwirth and Max Lichtegg (Decca ACL 185)
Selection with Gerda Scheyrer (Philips 6593 012)
Selection with Mimi Coertse and Karl Terkal (Saga 5365)
Selection with Wilma Lipp and Per Grundén (Eurodisc Z 72021 E)
Selection with Melitta Muszely and Rudolf Schock (EMI Eurodisc STE 41161)

Selection with Herta Talmar and Franz Fehringer (Polydor 224422) (EP)

Selection with Jutta Vulpius and Martin Ritzmann (Philips 6593 004)

Selection with Anneliese Rothenberger and Nicolai Gedda (EMI IC 061 28194)

Selection with Ingeborg Hallstein and Peter Alexander (Polydor 249 280)

Selection in English as *The Merry Widow* with Risë Stevens (CBS ML 2064)

Selection in English as *The Merry Widow* with Elaine Malbin and Donald Richards (RCA CDN 106)

Selection in English as *The Merry Widow* with Kitty Carlisle and Wilbur Evans (Brunswick LAT 8003)

Selection in English as *The Merry Widow* with Dorothy Kirsten and Robert Rounseville (CBS CL 838)

Selection in English as *The Merry Widow* with Gordon MacRae (Capitol LC 6564)

Selection in English as *The Merry Widow* from soundtrack of 1952 film with Fernand Lamas and voice of Trudy Erwin (MGM E 157) (10 inch)

Selection in English as *The Merry Widow* with John Hanson (Embassy WLP 6016)

Sadler's Wells cast recording 1958 in English as *The Merry Widow* with June Bronhill and Thomas Round (CSD1259)

Selection in English as *The Merry Widow* with Anna Moffo and William Lewis (RCA RDS 9331)

Selection in English as *The Merry Widow* with Jacqueline Delman and John Larsen (World Records ST 60)

Selection in English as *The Merry Widow* with Lisa Della Casa and John Reardon (CBS 61833)

Music Theater of Lincoln Center cast recording in English as *The Merry Widow* with Patrice Munsel and Bob Wright (RCA LSO 1094)

Selection in English as *The Merry Widow* with Thomas and Philips (Fontana SFL 13026)

Selection in English as *The Merry Widow* with June Bronhill and Jeremy Brett (Columbia TWO 234)

Scottish Opera cast recording 1976 in English as *The Merry Widow* with Catherine Wilson and Jonny Blanc (EMI CFP 40276)

Selection in English as *The Merry Widow* with Joan Sutherland and Werner Krenn (Decca SET 629)

New York City Opera cast recording 1978 in English as *The Merry Widow* with Beverly Sills and Alan Titus (EMI ASD 3500)

New Sadler's Wells Opera cast recording 1985 in English with Eiddwen Harrhy (TER 1111)

Selection in French as *La Veuve Joyeuse* with Colette Riedinger and Reda Caire (Decca ACL 910)

Selection in French as *La Veuve Joyeuse* with Marcel Merkès and Paulette Merval (Odeon XOC139)

Selection in French as *La Veuve Joyeuse* with Lina Dachary (Guild International de Disque M2346)

Selection in French as *La Veuve Joyeuse* with Jacques Jansen and Denise Duval (EMI-Pathé 051. 12072)

Selection in French as *La Veuve Joyeuse* with Janette Vivalda and Michel Dens (Pathé-EMI 057. 10849)

Selection in French as *La Veuve Joyeuse* with Renée Doria (Philips P77, 106L)

Selection in Hungarian with Erzsébet Házy and Tibor Udvardy (Qualiton HLP 6516) (10 inch)

Selection in Italian as *La Vedova Allegra* (Fonit-Cetra EDM 4008) with *Paganini*

1263

Selection in Swedish as *Glada Änken* with Sonja Sternquist and Per Grundén (London TW 91099)
Selection in Swedish as *Glada Änken* with Ake Ljungholm and Gunnel Eklund (Philips 6378 523)
Selection in Spanish (Zafiro)

1001 Nacht
Complete with Herbert Ernst Groh and Rosl Seegers (Urania UR 203) (2 records)

Ein Walzertraum
Complete with Anneliese Rothenberger and Nicolai Gedda (EMI IC 157 29041-2) (2 records)
Complete in Italian as *Sogno di Valzer* (RAI) (2 records)
Selection with Rudolf Christ (Period RL 1903)
Selection with Else Liesesberg and Karl Terkal (Fontana 701518 WPY)
Selection with Else Liebesberg and Peter Minich (Telefunken 6, 21310)
Selection with Rudolf Schock, Margit Schramm and Wilma Lipp (Eurodisc 25 288 OE) with Straus items from *Der tapfere Soldat, Rund um die Liebe, Der letzte Walzer* et al
Selection with Renate Holm and Rudolf Christ (Concert Hall SMS 2591) with *Hochzeitsnacht in Paradies*
Selection with Herta Talmar and Sándor Kónya (Polydor 287157 LPHM with *Der Vetter aus Dingsda*
Selection with Melitta Muszely and Rudolf Schock (EMI Electrola 1C 037-28 134)
Selection in English as *A Waltz Dream* with June Bronhill and David Hughes (HMV CSD 1321)
Selection in Italian as *Sogno di Valzer* (Fonit-Cetra EDM 4018) with *Cin-ci-la*
Selection in French as *Rêve de Valse* with Marcel Merkès and Paulette Merval (CBS 63 155)
Selection in French as *Rêve de Valse* with Colette Riedinger and Reda Caire (Decca 215, 828)
Selection in French as *Rêve de Valse* with Mado Robin and Michel Dens (EMI-Pathé 057, 10351)
Selection in French as *Rêve de Valse* with Lina Dachary and André Dassary (Vega 30 LT 13039)
Selection in French as *Rêve de Valse* with Renée Doria and André Mallabrera (Opérama OPE 1003)
Selection in French as *Rêve de Valse* with Marie Darclée and Charles Collins (Musidisc CV 1004)
Selection in French as *Rêve de Valse* with Marina Hotine and Henri Gui (Philips P 77 121 L)

Der fidele Bauer
Selection with Else Liebesberg and Karl Terkal (Philips 6593 010) with *Die Dollarprinzessin*
Selection with Sonja Knittel, Heinz Hoppe and Fritz Wunderlich (EMI Columbia SMC 73456) with *Der Vogelhändler*
Selection (Amadeo AVRS EP 17510) (EP)
Selection (Polydor 249148) with *Die Rose von Stambul*
Selection with Sonja Schöner and Heinz Hoppe (Telefunken BLE 14310-P) with *Der Vogelhändler, Der Bettelstudent* and *Der Graf von Luxemburg*

Die Dollarprinzessin

Selection with Else Liebesberg and Karl Terkal (Philips 6593 010) with *Der fidele Bauer*

Selection with Sári Barabas and Heinz Hoppe (EMI Columbia SMC 41 582) (EP)

Selection with Herta Talmar and Reinhold Bartel (Polydor 249 054) with *Die Zirkusprinzessin*

Selection with Gabriele Jacoby and Gerhart Lippert (Philips 420, 665-2) with *Der Vogelhändler*

Selection in Italian as *La Principessa dei Dollari* with Lucia Barbero and Carlo Pierangeli (Fonit-Cetra SFC 120) with *La Duchessa del Bal Tabarin*

Der tapfere Soldat

Selection in English as *The Chocolate Soldier* with Nelson Eddy and Risë Stevens (CBS ML 4060) with *The Student Prince*

Selection in English as *The Chocolate Soldier* with Robert Merrill and Risë Stevens (RCA LSO 6005)

Selection in English as *The Chocolate Soldier* with Stephanie Voss and Laurie Payne (WRC T210) with *The Firefly*

Die geschiedene Frau

Selection with Margit Schramm and Rudolf Schock (Eurodisc 41 303 CE) (EP)

Der Graf von Luxemburg

Complete with Nicolai Gedda and Lucia Popp (EMI 157-28 982-3) (2 records)

Selection with Annie von Ligety and Otto Sturm (original cast) (Rococo 4012) with *Die lustige Witwe, Das Fürstenkind* and *Eva*

Selection with Nora Jungwirth and Rupert Glawitsch (Decca ACL 195)

Selection with Hertha Schmidt and Horst Heinrich Braun (Philips P 10132 R)

Selection with Hilde Güden and Waldemar Kmentt (Decca SDD 461) with *Der Zarewitsch*

Selection with Else Liebesberg and Rudolf Christ (Westminster WPS 121) with *Die lustige Witwe*

Selection with Sonja Schöner and Heinz Hoppe (Telefunken 6, 21246) with *Paganini*

Selection with Herta Talmar and Franz Fehringer (Polydor 237 156 SLPHM) with *Die lustige Witwe*

Selection with Erika Köth and Rudolf Schock (EMI Electrola STE 73451) with *Paganini*

Selection with Rudolf Schock and Margit Schramm (Eurodisc 89 880 IE)

Selection with Friedl Loor and Karl Terkal (Intercord 185823)

Selection in English with June Bronhill and Neville Jason (Columbia TWO 246)

Sadler's Wells cast recording in English as *The Count of Luxembourg* with Marilyn Hill Smith and Neil Jenkins (TER 1050)

Selection in Italian as *Il Conte di Lussemburgo* (Fonit-Cetra EDM 4006) with *Vottoria e il suo Ussaro*

Selection in French with Marcel Merkès and Paulette Merval (Odeon XOC182) with *Princess Csardas*

Selection in French with Colette Riedinger and Gabriel Bacquier (Decca 215, 836)

Selection in Spanish as *El Conde de Lusemburgo* with Elsa Marval and Luis Sagi-Vela (Zafiro LM-3, 038)

Zigeunerliebe
Selection with Rosl Seegers and Herbert Ernst Groh (Urania UR 205) (2 records)
Selection with Margit Schramm and Rudolf Schock (Eurodisc 89 886 IE)
Selection with Sári Barabas and Heinz Hoppe (EMI Columbia SMC 73457) with *Die Dollarprinzessin*
Selection in Hungarian with Erzsébet Házy and Róbert Ilosfalvy (Qualiton SLPX 6550) with *Der Zigeunerprimás*

Leányvásár
Selection in Hungarian with Marika Németh and Róbert Rátonyi (Qualiton LPX6527)

Eva
Selection with Mizzi Günther and Louis Treumann (original cast) (Rococo 4012) with *Die lustige Witwe, Der Graf von Lusemburg* and *Das Fürstenkind*
Selection in Spanish with Ana Maria Olaria and Alfredo Kraus (Zafiro LM-3, 029)
Selection in Italian with Romana Righetti and Carlo Pierangeli (Fonit-Cetra EDM 4020) with *Addio Giovinezza*

Der liebe Augustin
Selection with Sári Bárabás and Heinz Hoppe (EMI Electrola SMC 83 454) with *Die Rose von Stambul*
Selection with Rudolf Schock and Margit Schramm (Eurodisc 41 301 CE) (EP)

Der lila Domino
Selection in English with Aileen Cochran and Charles Young (HMV GES 5778) (EP)

Der Zigeunerprimás
Selection in Hungarian as *Cigányprimás* with Zsuzsa Petress and György Radnai (Qualiton SLPX 6550) with *Zigeunerliebe*

Wie einst im Mai
Selection with Angela Müthel and Wolfgang Ziffer (RCA VL 30413)

Polenblut
Selection with Hertha Schmidt and Karl Terkal (Philips P 10133 R)
Selection with Margit Schramm and Rudolf Schock (Eurodisc 89 888 IE)

Szibill
Selection in Hungarian with Marika Németh and Róbert Ilosfalvy (Qualiton SLPX 6543)

Die Csárdásfürstin
Complete with Anneliese Rothenberger and Nicolai Gedda (EMI 157 29066-7) (2 records)
Complete with Dagmar Kollar and René Kollo (Eurodisc 27 190 XDE) (2 records)
Complete with Milena Rudifera and Franz Wächter (Wiener Volksoper) (Denon 70C37-7933-34) (2 records)
Complete in Hungarian with Hanna Honthy, Erzsébet Házy and György Korondy (Qualiton LPX 16564-66) (3 records)

Complete (without dialogue) in French with Michèle Le Bris, Henri Legay and Aimé Doniat (Chant du Monde 2LDX 78800)
Selection with Mimi Coertse and Karl Terkal (Saga 5366)
Selection with Liselott Maikl and Hans Strohbauer (CBS 52 032)
Selection with Margit Schramm and Rudolf Schock (Eurodisc 89 875 IE)
Selection with Sonja Knittel and Heinz Hoppe (Telefunken 6. 21244) with *Frau Luna*
Selection with Sári Barabas and Rudolf Schock (EMI Columbia C 40315) (EP)
Selection with Sári Barabas and Rudolf Schock (EMI Columbia SMC 73449) with *Gräfin Mariza*
Selection (Amadeo SVRS EP 17509) (EP)
Selection with Herta Talmar and Willy Hofmann (Polydor 224419 SLPHM) with *Frau Luna*
Selection with Lotte Rysanek and Rudolf Christ (Westminster WPS 122) with *Gräfin Mariza*
Selection with Erika Köth and Franz Fehringer (RCA VL 30363)
Selection in Hungarian with Hanna Honthy, Marika Németh and Róbert Rátonyi (Qualiton SLPX 6537)˙
Selection in Italian as *La Principessa della Czarda* with Romana Righetti and Carlo Pierangeli (Fonit-Cetra EDM 4004) with *Il Paese dei Campanelli*
Selection in French with Marcel Merkës and Paulette Merval (Odeon XOC143) with *Rêve de Valse*

Das Dreimäderlhaus
Complete in French as *Chanson d'Amour* (Decca 115. 055/56) (2 records)
Selection with Adolf Dallapozza and Margit Schramm (EMI IC 061, 1288211)
Selection with Rudolf Schock and Renate Holm (Eurodisc 87 873 IE)
Selection with Sonja Schöner and Donald Grobe (Telefunken 6, 21240) with *Im weissen Röss*
Selection with Rudolf Schock and Erika Köth (EMI Electrola SME 73453) with *Ein Walzertraum*
Selection with Karl Terkal and Herta Talmar (Polydor 20072 EPH) (EP)
Selection in English as *Lilac Time* with June Bronhill and Thomas Round (EMI Note NTS 124)
Selection in English as *Lilac Time* with John Hanson (Philips SBL 7626) with *The Maid of the Mountains*
Selection in English as *Lilac Time* with Jacqueline Delman and Peter Glossop (WRC SLM 4)
Selection in English as *Blossom Time* with Earl Wrightson (RCA LK 1018)
Selection in Italian as *La Casa delle Tre Ragazze* with Lucia Barbero and Carlo Pierangeli (Fonit-Cetra SFC 121) with *La Mazurka Blu*
Selection in French as *Chanson d'Amour* (EMI-Pathé 057. 12197)
Selection in Hungarian with Róbert Ilosfalvy and Júlia Orosz (Qualiton SLPX 16584) with Brahms waltzes

Die Rose von Stambul
Selection with Erika Köth and Rudolf Schock (Eurodisc 89 892 IE) with *Die Dubarry*
Selection with Fritz Wunderlich (RCA VL 20407) with *Die Kaiserin*
Selection with Melitta Muszely and Fritz Wunderlich (EMI Columbia SMC 73454) with *Der liebe Augustin*
Selection (Polydor 249 148) with *Der fidele Bauer*

Schwarzwaldmädel

Selection with Margit Schramm and Rudolf Schock (Eurodisc 89 874 IE)
Selection with Sári Barabas and Heinz Hoppe (Telefunken 6. 21242) with *Friederike*
Selection with Ingeborg Hallstein and Franz Fehringer (Polydor 237 163) with *Der Vogelhändler*
Selection with Erika Köth and Rudolf Schock (EMI Electrola SME 41173) (EP)
Selection with Erika Köth and Heinz Hoppe (EMI Electrola SME 73939) with *Der Vetter aus Dingsda*
Selection (Amadeo SVRS EP 17508) EP)

Der letzte Walzer

Selection with Rudolf Christ and Margit Opawsky (Period RL 1904)

Der Vetter aus Dingsda

Complete with René Kollo and Grit van Jüten (RCA RL 30867) (2 records)
Selection with Rudolf Schock and Renate Holm (Eurodisc 89 878 IE)
Selection with Rudolf Christ and Ruthilde Boesch (Fontana 701 515 WPY) with *Glückliche Reise*
Selection with Erika Köth and Heinz Hoppe (EMI Electrola SME 73939) with *Schwarzwaldmäde*
Selection with Erika Köth and Rudolf Schock (EMI SME 41174) (EP)
Selection with Herta Talmar and Franz Fehringer (Polydor 237 157 SLPHM) with *Ein Walzertraum*

Die Bajadere

Selection in Hungarian as *Bajadér* with Marika Németh and Tibor Udvardy (Qualiton SLPX 6549)
Selection in Hungarian as *Bajadér* with Hanna Honthy and Árpád Baksay (Qualiton LPX 6535) with *A Primadonna Álma, Fityfiritty* and Lehár melodies
Selection in Italian as *Bajadera* (Fonit-Cetra EDM 4022) with *Federica*

Frasquita

Selection in Italian with Romana Righetti and Carlo Pierangeli (Fonit-Cetra EDM 4021) with *L'Acqua Cheta*
Selection in French with Conchita Supervia and Louis Arnould (Pacific LDP-B 2263)
Selection in French with Maria Murano, André Dassary and Nicole Broissin (Vega 16. 045)
Selection in French with Kleuza de Pennafort and Bernard Alvi (Decca 215. 829)

Madame Pompadour

Selection with Melitta Muzsely and Rudolf Schock (EMI Electrola E60 760) with *Die Dubarry*
Selection with Margit Schramm and Waldemar Kmentt (Eurodisc 41 305 CE) (EP)

Gräfin Mariza

Complete with Rita Zorn and Martin Ritzmann (Bruno BR 501 160/161) (2 records)
Complete with Anneliese Rothenberger and Nicolai Gedda (EMI 157 29068-9) (2 records)
Selection with Lotte Rysanek and Rudolf Christ (Westminster WPS 122) with *Die Csárdásfürstin*

Selection with Friedl Loor and Hans Strohbauer (CBS 52031)

Selection with Sonja Schöner and Donald Grobe (Eurodisc 70 825 IE)

Selection with Herta Talmar and Reinhold Bartel (Polydor 237 173) with *Der Zarewitsch*

Selection with Erzsébet Házy and René Kollo (Philips 420 658-2)

Selection with Rudolf Schock and Margit Schramm (Eurodisc 89 876 IE)

Selection with Peter Minich and Marika Németh (RCA SF 5105)

Selection with Fritz Wunderlich and Christine Görner (RCA VL 30315)

Sadler's Wells cast recording in English as *Countess Maritza* with Marilyn Hill Smith (TER 1051)

Selection in Italian as *La Contessa Maritza* (Fonit-Cetra EDM 4041) with *Il Re di Chez Maxime*

Selection in Hungarian as *Marica Grófnó* with Marika Németh and Róbert Ilosfalvy (Qualiton SLPX 6551)

Paganini

Complete with Anneliese Rothenberger and Nicolai Gedda (EMI SLS 5184) (2 records)

Complete in French with Robert Massard and Colette Riedinger (Decca 115, 190/91) (2 records)

Selection with Karl Terkal and Lotte Rysanek (Westminster WPS 123) with *Im weissen Rössl*

Selection with Peter Anders and Anny Schlemm (RCA VL 30314)

Selection with Herbert Ernst Groh and Melitta Muszely (Eurodisc 70 822 IE)

Selection with Rudolf Schock and Melitta Muszely (EMI Electrola SME 73 450) with *Der Graf von Luxemburg*

Selection with Rudolf Schock and Margit Schramm (Eurodisc 89 883 IE)

Selection with Antonio Theba and Teresa Stratas (Philips 420 664-2) with *Der Zarewitsch*

Selection with Heinz Hoppe and Sonja Schöner (Telefunken 6, 21246) with *Der Graf von Luxemburg*

Selection with Sándor Kónya and Herta Talmar (Polydor 237 151 SLPHM) with *Das Land des Lächelns*

Selection in French with Michel Dens and Andrine Forli (EMI-Pathé 057 12127)

Selection in Italian (Fonit-Cetra EDM 4008) with *La Vedova Allegra*

Die Zirkusprinzessin

Selection with Margit Schramm and Rudolf Schock (Eurodisc 89 877 IE)

Selection with Herta Talmar and Reinhold Bartel (Polydor 249 054) with *Die Dollarprinzessin*

Selection with Maria Croonen and Walter Schmidt (Amiga 5 40 209) (EP)

Selection in Hungarian as *Cirkushercegnö* with Erzsébet Házy and Árpád Kishegyi (Qualiton SLPX 6553)

Der Zarewitsch

Complete with Rita Streich and Nicolai Gedda (EMI IC 157-29020/21) (2 records)

Complete with Lucia Popp and René Kollo (Eurodisc 301291-435) (2 records)

Selection with Rudolf Schock and Margit Schramm (Eurodisc 89 885 IE)

Selection with Waldemar Kmentt and Hilde Güden (Decca SDD 461) with *Der Graf von Luxemburg*

Selection with Giuseppe di Stefano and Dagmar Koller (Telefunken 6. 21273)

Selection with Erika Köth and Rudolf Schock (EMI Electrola SME 73931) with *Das Land des Lächelns*
Selection with Friedl Loor and Hans Strohbauer (Amadeo AVRS EP 15102) (EP)
Selection with Melitta Muszely and Fritz Wunderlich (EMI Columbia SMC 73455) with *Das Land des Lächelns*
Selection with Sonja Schöner and Josef Traxel (Eurodisc 70 799 IE)
Selection with Sonja Schöner and Heinz Hoppe (Telefunken SUX 4787) (EP)
Selection with Herta Talmar and Reinhold Bartel (Polydor 237 173) with *Gräfin Mariza*
Selection with Wieslaw Ochman and Teresa Stratas (Philips 420 664-2)
Selection in Italian with *Clo-Clo*

Die gold'ne Meisterin

Selection (Philips P 10138 R)
Selection with Mirjana Irosch and Peter Minich with other Eysler operetta items

Die Dreigroschenoper

Complete with Kurt Preger and Liane Augustin (Vanguard SRV 2735D)
Complete with Erich Schellow and Lotte Lenya (CBS Odyssey Y2-32977) (2 records)
Complete with Hans Korte and Karin Huebner (Fontana SFL 14077-8) (2 records)
Complete in French (Théâtre de l'Est Parisien) as *L'Opéra de Quat' Sous* (Jacques Canetti 48, 839/42) (4 records)
Selection with Willy Trenk-Trebitsch and Lotte Lenja (original cast) (Telefunken 6. 41911)
Selection on Top Classic-Historia H625 includes two numbers performed by Bertolt Brecht (author)
Film soundtrack with Curt Jürgens (London M 76004)
New York cast recording (Theatre de Lys, 1954) with Scott Merrill (MGM S-31210C)
New York revival cast recording 1976 with Raul Julia (CBS PS 34326)
Selection in English (1964 film version) (RCA LSO 1086)
Selection in English with Mike Sammes (World Records ST 253)

Casanova

Selection with Anny Ahlers and Michael Bohnen (original cast) (EMI Odeon O 41479) (EP)
Selection with Richard Tauber and Vera Schwartz (Acso A104) with *Der Bettelstudent*

Friederike

Complete with Helen Donath and Adolf Dallapozza (EMI/HMV SLS 5230) (2 records)
Selection with Rudolf Schock and Margit Schramm (Eurodisc 89 884 IE) with *Schön ist die Welt*
Selection with Sonja Schöner and Donald Grobe (Telefunken 6, 21242) with *Schwarzwaldmädel*
Selection with Erika Köth and Rudolf Schock (EMI Electrola E 40100) (EP)
Selection with Gerda Scheyrer and Walter Anton Dotzer (Philips 423 156 PE) (EP)
Selection in Italian as *Federica* (Fonit-Cetra EDM 4022) with *Bajadera*

Das Land des Lächelns

Complete with Elisabeth Schwarzkopf and Nicolai Gedda (Columbia 33CX 1114-5) (2 records)

Complete with Rudolf Schock and Margit Schramm (Eurodisc 27 181 XDE) (2 records)

Complete with Anneliese Rothenberger and Nicolai Gedda (EMI 157 128 991-3) (2 records)

Complete with Siegfried Jerusalem and Helen Donath (EMI 157 46624-5) (2 records)

Complete in French as *Le Pays de Sourire* with Michel Dens and Liliane Berton (EMI) (2 records)

Selection with René Kollo and Birgit Pitsch-Sarata (Philips 420 660, 2)

Selection with Giuseppe de Stefano and Dagmar Koller (Preiser SPR 3144)

Selection with Sándor Kónya and Renate Holm (Polydor 237 151 SLPHM) with *Paganini*

Selection with Erika Köth and Rudolf Schock (EMI Electrola SME 73931) with *Der Zarewitsch*

Selection with Melitta Muszely and Fritz Wunderlich (EMI Columbia SMC 73455) with *Der Zarewitsch*

Selection with Anneliese Rothenberger and Heinz Hoppe (Telefunken SUX 4809) (EP)

Selection with Peter Anders and Anneliese Rothenberger (Polydor 21437) (EP)

Selection in Italian as *Il Paese del Sorriso* (Fonit-Cetra EDM 4040) with *La Duchessa della Bal Tabarin*

Selection in Hungarian with Julia Orosz and Tibor Udvardy (Qualiton SLPX 6541)

Selection in Hungarian with József Simándy and Erzsébet Házy (Qualiton SLPX 16612)

Selection in English as *The Land of Smiles* with Elizabeth Fretwell, Charles Craig and June Bronhill (HMV CSD 1267)

Selection in French as *Le Pays de Sourire* with Colette Riedinger and Bernard Alvi (Decca ACL 914)

Selection in French as *Le Pays de Sourire* with Renée Doria (Philips P77. 116L)

Viktoria und ihr Husar

Selection with Margit Schramm and Rudolf Schock (Eurodisc 89 870 1E) with *Die Blume von Hawaii*

Selection with Donald Grobe and Sonja Schöner (Telefunken 6, 21247) with *Die Blume von Hawaii*

Selection with Sári Barabas and Heinz Hoppe (EMI Columbia SMC 41567) (EP)

Selection with Kurt Wehofschitz (Kristall SMGL 14042) with *Die Blume von Hawaii*

Selection with Friedl Loor and Kurt Equiluz (Westminster WPS 124) with *Die Blume von Hawaii*

Selection with Rita Bartos and Sándor Kónya (Polydor 237149 SLPHM) with *Die Blume von Hawaii*

Selection with Rudolf Christ and Sári Barabas (Fontana 701519 WPY) with *Die Blume von Hawaii*

Selection with Anneliese Rothenberger and Rudolf Schock (EMI Electrola E 41177) (EP)

Selection in French with Claudine Granger (TLP 91011)

Selection in Italian as *Vittoria e il suo Ussaro* (EDM 4006) with *Il Conte di Lussemburgo*

Selection in Swedish with Kjerstin Dellert and Sven Erik Wikström (Telestar TRS11129) with *Teaterbåten*

Im weissen Rössl

Complete with Peter Minich and Hedi Klug (Amadeo AVRS 9143)

Complete with Ingeborg Hallstein, Erika Köth and Peter Alexander (Eurodisc 27 178 XDE) (2 records)

Complete with Anneliese Rothenberger and Peter Minich (HMV SLS 5184) (2 records)

Complete in French as *L'Auberge du Cheval Blanc* with Colette Riedinger and Luc Barney (Decca 115. 053/54) (2 records)

Complete in French as *L'Auberge du Cheval Blanc* with Andrine Forli and Michel Dens (EMI IC 161 12087/8) (2 records)

Complete in French as *L'Auberge du Cheval Blanc* with Eliane Varon and Christiane Borel (Festival 251) (2 records)

Selection with Marion Briner and Peter Minich (Telefunken 6. 21255)

Selection with Sonja Schöner and Heinz Hoppe (Telefunken 6. 21240) with *Das Dreimäderlhaus*

Selection with Sonja Knittel and Erich Kuchar (EMI Electrola SHZE 155)

Selection with Per Grundén and Hedi Fassler (Telefunken UX4743)

Selection with Margit Opawsky and Hans Strohbauer (Amadeo AVRS EP 15100) (EP)

Selection with Anneliese Rothenberger and Harry Friedauer (Electrola SME 41182) (EP)

Selection with Herta Talmar and Franz Fehringer (Polydor 2244423) (EP)

Selection with Friedl Loor and Karl Terkal (Westminster WPS 123) with *Paganini*

Selection with Herta Talmar and Peter Alexander (Polydor 237155) with *Maske in Blau*

Cast recording 1985 (Mörbisch Festival) with Dagmar Koller and Harald Serafin

Selection in English as *White Horse Inn* with Marion Grimaldi and David Croft (EMI MFP 1011)

Selection in English as *White Horse Inn* with Mary Thomas and Andy Cole

Selection in French as *L'Auberge du Cheval Blanc* with Marcel Merkès and Paulette Merval (CBS 63457)

Selection in French as *L'Auberge du Cheval Blanc* with Eliane Varon and Luc Barney (Barclay 950 048)

Selection in French as *L'Auberge du Cheval Blanc* with Marina Hotine and Guy Fontagnère (Philips P 77 128 L)

Selection in Italian as *Al Cavallino Blanco* (EDM 4002) with *La Danza della Libellule*

Selection in Italian as *Al Cavallino Blanco* with Romana Righetti and Franco Artioli (RCA NL 33083) with other operetta excerpts

Schön ist die Welt

Selection with Lotte Rysanek and Karl Terkal (Philips P 13511 R)

Selection with Rudolf Schock and Sylvia Geszty (Eurodisc 89 884 IE) with *Friederike*

Selection with Gerda Scheyrer and Walter Anton Dotzer (Philips 423 155 PE) (EP)

Selection with Rudolf Schock and Renate Holm (EMI Electrola E 41411) (EP)

Walzer aus Wien

Complete in French as *Valses de Vienne* with Mady Mesplé and Bernard Sinclair (EMI-Pathé 191 12001-2) (2 records)

Selection in French as *Valses de Vienne* with Mado Robin and Michel Dens (EMI-Pathé 57. 10354)

Selection in French as *Valses de Vienne* with Colette Riedinger, Gabriel Bacquier and Janine Ervil (Decca 215. 758)

Selection in French as *Valses de Vienne* with Margaret Latour and Jean-Claude Darcey (Carrere 67. 030)

Selection in French as *Valses de Vienne* with Henri Guy, Janine Tavernier, Nicole Broissin and Rosine Bredy (Philips P77. 2541)

Cast recording in English as *The Great Waltz* with Sári Barabas and Walter Cassel (Columbia SCX 6429)

Die Blume von Hawaii

Selection with Rita Georg and Harald Paulsen (original cast) (EMI Odeon 0 41477) (EP)

Selection with Sári Barabas and Rudolf Christ (Philips P 08 184L) with *Die ungarische Hochzeit*

Selection with Margit Schramm and Rudolf Schock (Eurodisc 89 870 IE) with *Viktoria und ihr Husar*

Selection with Anneliese Rothenberger and Rudolf Schock (EMI Electrola SME 41176) (EP)

Selection with Heinz Hoppe and Sonja Knittel (Telefunken 6. 21247) with *Viktoria und ihr Husar*

Selection with Heinz Hoppe and Sonja Knittel (EMI Columbia SMC 41568) (EP)

Selection with Elfie Mayerhofer and Kurt Wehofschitz (Kristall SMGL 14042) with *Viktoria und ihr Husar*

Selection with Friedl Loor and Kurt Equiluz (Westminster WPS 124) with *Viktoria und ihr Husar*

Selection with Herta Talmar and Franz Fehringer (Polydor 237149 SLPHM) with *Viktoria und ihr Husar*

Selection with Traute Richter and Jean Löhe (Telefunken TM 68029) with *Clivia* (10 inch)

Selection in Italian as *Fior d'Haway* (EDM 4017) with *Scugnizza*

Die Dubarry

Selection with Erika Köth and Horst Wilhelm (Eurodisc 89 892 IE) with *Die Rose von Stambul*

Selection with Else Liebesberg and Karl Terkal (Philips P 08183L) with *Der Operball*

Selection with Melitta Muszely and Rudolf Schock (HMV E60760) with *Madame Pompadour*

Grace Moore (OBC) sings numbers from the score in English on *The Music of Broadway 1932* (JJA 19779), etc

Selection in Hungarian with Erzsébet Házy and Sándor Kónya (Qualiton SLPX 16583) with *Der Vogelhändler*

Wenn die kleinen Veilchen blühen

Selection with Melitta Muszely and Rudolf Schock (Eurodisc 89 893 IE) with *Zwei Herzen in Dreivierteltakt*

Selection in French as *Quand Fleurissent les Violettes* (TLP91006) with *Parade de Printemps* etc

Venus in Seide
Selection with Rudolf Schock and Margit Schramm (Eurodisc 89 872 IE)

Glückliche Reise
Selection with Ilse Hübener and Karl-Heinz Stracke (Elite Special SOLP 33-233)
  with *Maske in Blau, Saison in Salzburg* and *Perle von Tokay*
Selection with Erika Köth (Da Capo CO47-28 129) with *Das Vetter aud Dingsda*
Selection with Ruthhilde Boesch and Rudolf Christ (Fontana 701 515 WPY) with
  Der Vetter aus Dingsda
Selection with Christine Görner and Kurt Wehofschitz (EMI Columbia STC
  41415) (EP)
Selection with Hedi Klug and Ferry Gruber (Eurodisc 41 181 CE) (EP)

Zwei Herzen in Dreivierteltakt
Selection with Rudolf Christ and Kurt Preger (Period RL 1902)
Selection with Renate Holm, Rudolf Schock and Adolf Dallapozza (Eurodisc 89 893
  IE) with *Wenn die kleinen Veilchen blühen*

Clivia
Selection with Rudolf Schock and Margit Schramm (Eurodisc 80 585 XDE) with
  Monika, Manina and *Die ungarische Hochzeit*
Selection with Renate Holm and Peter Minich (RCA VL 30364)
Selection with Traute Richter and Jean Löhe (Telefunken UX4526) (10 inch) with
  Die Blume von Hawaii
Selection with Sári Barabas and Heinz Hoppe (EMI Electrola SME 73933) with *Die
  ungarische Hochzeit*
Selection with Rosemarie Moogk and Rudolf Scherfling with *Die Vielgeliebte, Monika*
  and *Die ungarische Hochzeit*

Giuditta
Complete with Edda Moser and Nicolai Gedda (EMI EX 27 0257-3) (2 records)
Complete with Hilde Güden, Waldemar Kmentt and Emmy Loose (Decca Ace of
  Diamonds GOS 583/4) (2 records)
Selection with Rudolf Schock and Sylvia Geszty (Eurodisc 89 879 IE)
Selection with Melitta Muszely and Rudolf Schock (EMI Electrola E 41 397) (EP)
Selection with Anneliese Rothenberger and Nicolai Gedda (EMI Electrola SME
  73941) with *Wiener Blut*
Selection in Hungarian (Qualiton SLPM 16664) with other items

Drei Walzer
Complete in French as *Trois Valses* with Suzy Delair and Jean Desailly (Decca 115,
  188/89) (2 records)
Selection in French as *Trois Valses* with Yvonne Printemps and Pierre Fresnay (EMI
  1C 051 12092)
Selection in French as *Trois Valses* with Mathé Altéry (EMI-Pathé CPTPM 130,
  186)
Selection in French as *Trois Valses* with Colette Riedinger (Decca CEP 500, 103)

Balkanliebe
Selection with Rudolf Schock and Margit Schramm (Eurodisc 89 873 IE) with *Die
  Försterchristl*

Selection with Rudolf Schock and Melitta Muszely (EMI Electrola SME 73462) wiuth *Eine Nacht in Venedig, Die Dubarry* and *Giuditta*

Maske in Blau
Selection with Margit Schramm, Marika Rökk and Rudolf Schock (Eurodisc 89 890 IE)
Selection with Sári Barabas and Karl Terkal (EMI Electrola SME 41409) (EP)
Selection with Sári Barabas, Erika Köth and Heinz Hoppe (EMI SME 83465) with *Hochzeitsnacht im Paradies*
Selection with Traute Richter and Jean Löhe (Telefunken UX 4502) with *In weissen Rössl*
Selection with Heinz Hoppe and Emmy Loose (Telefunken 6, 21239) with *Hochzeitsnacht im Paradies*
Selection (Philips P 14 707 L) with *Glückliche Reise*
Selection with Herta Talmar and Herbert Ernst Groh (Polydor 224 420) (EP)
Selection with Ilse Hübener and Karl-Heinz Stracke (Elite Special SOLP 33-233) with *Saison in Salzburg, Perle von Tokay* and *Glückliche Reise*

Die ungarische Hochzeit
Selection with Sylvia Geszty and Rudolf Schock (Eurodisc 80 585 XDE) with *Manina, Clivia* and *Monika* (Eurodisc 80 585 XDE)
Selection with Sári Barabas and Rudolf Christ (Philips P 08 184L) with *Die Blume von Hawaii*
Selection with Sári Barabas and Heinz Hoppe (EMI Electrola SME 73933) with *Clivia*
Selection with Rudolf Schock and Erika Köth (Eurodisc 41 615 CE)
Selection with Rosemarie Moogk and Rudolf Scherfling with *Clivia, Die Vielgeliebte* and *Monika*

Saison in Salzburg
Selection with Herta Talmar, Renate Holm and Peter Alexander (Polydor 237159) with *Hochzeitsnacht im Paradies*
Selection with Ilse Hübener and Karl-Heinz Stracke (Elite Special SOLP 33-233) with *Maske in Blau, Perle von Tokay* and *Glückliche Reise*

Hochzeitsnacht im Paradies
Selection with Anneliese Rothenberger, Christine Görner, Heinz Hoppe and Ernst Schütz (EMI Electrola SME 83465) with *Maske in Blau*
Selection with Renate Holm, Herta Talmar and Peter Alexander (Polydor 237159) with *Saison in Salzburg*
Selection with Friedl Loor and Kurt Equiluz (SMS 2591) with *Ein Walzertraum*
Selection with Sonja Schöner and Donald Grobe (Telefunken 6, 21239) with *Maske in Blau*
Selection with Sári Barabas and Karl Terkal (EMI Electrola SME 41414) (EP)

Feuerwerk
Selection with Liselotte Ebnet and Brigitte Mira (Eurodisc 74 103 IE)
Selection as *Der Schwarze Hecht* with Ines Torelli (Pan 132042)

1275

Frühjahrsparade
Original stage cast recording with Guggi Löwinger and Erich Kuchar (Eurodisc 71 569 IE)
Selection in French with Claudine Granger (TLP91006) with *Quand Fleurissent les Violettes* etc

SPAIN

El Barberillo de Lavapiés
Complete with Teresa Berganza, Gerardo Monreal and Ana Maria Olaria (Alhambra/Columbia C 30030)
Complete with Dolores Pérez, Santiago Ramallé and Isabel Garcisanz (Montilla/Zafiro LM 3005)
Complete with Dolores Pérez, Luis Sagi-Vela and Mari Carmen Ramirez (EMI VUL 210)

La Gran Via
Complete with Ana Maria Triate, Toñy Rosado and Manuel Ausensi (Alhambra/Columbia C30064)
Complete with Inés Rivadeneira and Luis Rodrigo (Montilla/Zafiro ZCL 1010)
Complete with Teresa Tourné and Renato Cesari (Hispavox HH 10-230)
Complete with Pura Maria Martinez and Antonia Blancas (Columbia SCE 951)

La Verbena de la Paloma
Complete with A Rojo Tino Pardo (Philips N 009996 R)
Complete with Ana Maria Iriate and Manuel Ausensi (Alhambra/Columbia C 30000)
Complete with A Aguila and Lolita Torrentó (EMI Regal 040-20255)
Complete with Dolores Pérez and Santiago Ramallé (Montilla/Zafiro FM 168)
Complete with Teresa Tourné and Renato Cesari (Hispavox HH 10-170)
Complete with Francisco Kraus and Angeles Chamorro (Edigsa CAL 19)

La Revoltosa
Complete with Ana Maria Iriate and Manuel Ausensi (Alhambra/Columbia C 30001)
Complete with Isabel Penagos and Vincente Sardinero (Montilla/Zafiro ZOR 216)
Complete with Teresa Tourné and Renato Cesari (Hispavox HH 10-229)
Complete with Isabel Rivas and Luis Sagi-Vela (EMI VUL 200)
Complete with Inés Rivadeneira and Alfredo Kraus (Edigsa CAL 20)

Gigantes y Cabezudos
Complete with Ana Maria Iriate and Carlos Munguia (Alhambra/Columbia C 30009)
Complete with Dolores Pérez (*alias* Lily Berchman) and Francisco Cano (Montilla/Zafiro ZOR 180)
Complete with Maria Espinalt and José Permanyer (EMI Regal LREG 8027)
Complete with Isabel Rivas and Carlo del Monte (EMI VUL 205)

La Tempranica

Complete with Teresa Berganza and Manuel Ausensi (Alhambra/Columbia CS 42043)

Complete with Doroles Pérez and Luis Sagi-Vela (Montilla/Zafiro ZOR 125)

Luisa Fernanda

Complete with Selica Pérez Carpio and Marcos Redondo (Columbia C 7520)

Complete with Maria de los Angeles Morales, Carlos Munguia and Manuel Ausensi (Alhambra/Columbia C 30022)

Complete with Dolores Pérez and Luis Sagi-Vela (Montilla/Zafiro ZOR 102)

Complete with Teresa Tourné, Pedro Lavirgen and Renato Cesari (Hispavox HH 10-156)

Complete with Teresa Berganza and Antonio Blancas (Columbia SCE 936)

Complete with Dolores Pérez, Carlo del Monte and Luis Sagi-Vela (EMI VUL 206)

INDEX OF TITLES, AUTHORS, COMPOSERS
AND LYRICISTS

INDEX OF SONG TITLES

In this index, the titles of the songs and first lines of the ensembles, choruses and finales have been arranged in an order which ignores the definite and indefinite article (The, A, Le, La, Les, Un, Une, Der, Die, Das, El). Where a title begins with such an article, the title can be found under the initial letter of the second word.

1304

1320